Standard Catalog of®

WORLD PAPER MONEY

Modern Issues • 1961-Present

20th Edition

Editor
George S. Cuhaj

Designer
Sandi Carpenter

Special Contributors
Thomas Augustsson, Flemming Lyngbeck Hansen,
Juozas Minikevicius, David Murek,
Herbert Stein, Frank Tesson, James Warmus

Published by

Krause Publications, a division of F+W Media, Inc.
700 East State Street • Iola, WI 54990-0001
715-445-2214 • 888-457-2873
www.krausebooks.com

To order books or other products call toll-free 1-800-258-0929
or visit us online at www.shopnumismaster.com

ISSN 1538-2028

ISBN-13: 978-1-4402-4037-9
ISBN-10: 1-4402-4037-X

Cover Design by Jana Tappa
Designed by Sandi Carpenter
Edited by George Cuhaj

Printed in the United States of America

Introduction

Welcome to this 20th edition of the *Standard Catalog of World Paper Money, Modern Issues.*

For those of you already familiar with this volume, you will be glad to see a continued upgrade in image quality. Expanded text descriptions as well as price increases have been made. Foreign Exchange Certificates, Military use notes and Regional notes are now presented in the *Standard Catalog of World Paper Money, Specialized Issues volume* now in its 12th edition.

In our constant endeavor to provide as much detail as possible, we have expanded our detailed signature variety information. For the ease of identification, notes are listed under their historic country identification (British Honduras is no longer hidden within Belize). North Korea and South Korea are now under N and S respectively, not under K. Northern Ireland is under N. Please consult the country index or bank issuer index if you continue to experience difficulty.

Notes of a particular bank are listed in release date order, and then grouped in ascending denomination order. In the cases of countries where more than one issuing authority is in effect at a single time, follow the bank headings in the listings and it will become apparent if that country's listing are by date or alphabetical by issuing authority. In the cases where a country has changed from a kingdom to a republic all the banknotes of the kingdom's era would be listed before that of the republic.

If you wish to contribute images, please contact us first and follow the guidelines as set forth in the information notice. We can accept them as JPGs, and preferably on a disc, rather than as an email attachment. But please contact us first before you do a lot of work, which could be duplicating items already in progress for Inclusion in future editions.

Table of Contents

Introduction & review of modern paper money collecting . . 3
Acknowledgements 4
Country Index. 5
Issuer and Bank Index 6
How To Use This Catalog 10
IBNS Grading Standards 12
Printer Abbreviations 13
Standard International Grading Terminology & Abbreviations. 14
Foreign Exchange Table 15
Standard International Numeral Systems. 16
International Numerics. 17
Dating. 18
Hejira Chart 19
Bank Identification Guide 20
IBNS Membership Application 22
Specimen Notes. 22
International Months 23
Security Devices. 24
Listings by Country 33

An Invitation

Users of this catalog may find a helpful adjunct to be the *Bank Note Reporter*, the only monthly newspaper devoted exclusively to North American and world paper money. Each issue presents up-to-date news, feature articles and valuable information. All purchasers of this catalog are invited to subscribe to the *Bank Note Reporter*. See www.shopnumismaster.com

A review of modern paper money collecting

Paper money collecting is probably as old as paper money itself. However, this segment of the numismatic hobby did not begin to reach a popularity approaching that of coin collecting until the latter half of the 1970's. While coins and paper money are alike in that both served as legal obligations to facilitate commerce, long-time paper money enthusiasts know the similarity ends there.

Coins were historically guaranteed by the intrinsic value of their metallic content - at least until recent years when virtually all circulating coins have become little more than legal tender tokens, containing little or no precious metal - while paper money possesses a value only when it is accepted for debts or converted into bullion or precious metals. With many note issues, this conversion privilege was limited and ultimately negated by the imposition of redemption cutoff dates.

The development of widespread collector interest in paper money of most nations was inhibited by a near total absence of adequate documentation. No more than four decades ago collectors could refer to only a few catalogs and dealer price lists of limited scope, most of which were difficult to acquire, or they could build their own knowledge through personal collecting pursuits and contact with fellow collectors.

The early catalogs authored by Albert Pick chronicled issues of Europe and the Americas and were assembled as stepping-stones to the ultimate objective, which became reality with publication of the first *Standard Catalog of World Paper Money* in 1975. That work provided collectors with fairly complete listings and up-to-date valuations of all recorded government note issues of the 20th century, incorporating Pick's previously unpublished manuscripts on Africa, Asia and Oceania, plus many earlier issues.

This completely revised and updated 20th Edition of Modern Issues, along with the companion 14th Edition of General Issues, presents a substantial extension of the cataloging effort initiated in 1975. As the most comprehensive world paper money references ever assembled, they fully document the many and varied legal tender paper currencies issued and circulated by over 380 past and current government issuing authorities of the world from 1300's to present.

George S. Cuhaj
Editor

Acknowledgements

Over time contributor enhancements to this catalog have been many and varied, and to recognize them all would be a volume in itself. Accordingly, we wish to acknowledge these invaluable collectors, scholars and dealers in the world paper money field, both past and present, for their specific contributions to this work through the submission of notes for illustration, improved descriptive information and market valuations.

Emmanuel K. Aboagye
Dundar Acikalin
Esko Ahlroth
Jan Alexandersson
Paulo Almeida
Carl A. Anderson
Dr. Jorge E. Arbelaez
Donald Arnone
David B. August
Thomas Augustsson
Keith Austin
Oksana Bandriuska
Cem Barlok
Adriaan C. F. Beck
Dan Bellan
Daniel Bena
Abdullah Beydoun
Milt Blackburn
Ed Bohannon
Joseph E. Boling
Wilfried A. Bracke
Jean Bricaud
Alejandro Brill
Mahdi Bseiso
Christopher J. Budesa
Weldon D. Burson
Lance K. Campbell
Arthur Chadwick
David F. Cieniewicz
Arthur D. Cohen
Scott E. Cordry
Guido Crapanzano
Vincent Craven-Bartl
Ray Czahor
Howard A. Daniel III
Antonio de Albergaria
Jacques Desbordes
Bruce Donahue
Michel Dufour
Arnoldo Efron
Wilhelm R. Eglseer
Esko Ekman
Ricardo Faillace
Edward Feltcorn
Wolfgang A. Frick
Yves Gilles
Flemming Lyngbeck Hansen
Victor S. Holden
Anton Holt
Armen Hovsepian
Yu Jian Hua
Jaya Hari Jha
A. J. Jacobs
Edouard Jean-Pierre
William M. Judd
Reese Kayhani
Alex Kaglyan
Dimitri Kharitonov
Olaf Kiemer
Josef Klaus
Ladislav Klaus
Michael E. Knabe
Tristan Kolm
Lazare Kouami
Michael Kvasnica
Samson K.C. Lai
Michael Lang
Akos Ledai
Dr. Edmund Lee
C. K. Leong
David Leong
Owen Linzmayer
Alan Luedeking
Stu Lumsden
Dr. Dennis Lutz
Martin MacDaeid
Ma Tak Wo
Ranko Mandic
Claudio Marana
Arthur C. Matz
Ali Mehilba
Daniel Meyer
Juozas Minikevicius
Arthur Morowitz
Jon Morowitz
Michael Morris
Rene Muller
Richard Murdoch
Tanju Mutlu
Quoc Nguyen
Fred O'Connell
Frank Passic
Antonio E. Pedraza
Juan Pena
Elena Pop
Laurence Pope
Savo Popovic
Yahya J. Qureshi
Kavan Ratnatunga
Mircea Raicopol
Bob Reis
Ilan Rinetzky
John Rishel
Alistar Robb
Kerry Rodgers
William Rosenblum
Juri Rudich
Alan Sadd
Remy Said
Walter Schmidt
Wolfgang Schuster
Harmut Schoenawa
Robert Schwartz
Christian Selvais
Victor F. Seper Jr.
Joel Shafer
Lee Sing Song
George Slusarczuk
Gary F. Snover
Jimmie C. Steelman
Herbert Stein
Jeremy Steinberg
Tim Steiner
Georg H. Stocker
Alim A. Sumana
Peter Symes
Steven Tan
Frank Tesson
Reinhardt Tetting
Anthony Tumonis
W. J. van der Drift
Norbert von Euw
Michael Vort-Ronald
Ludek Vostal
Evangelos Vyzas
Wakim Wakim
James Warmus
Pam West
Joseph Zaffern
Christof Zellweger

Associations & Publications

International Bank Note Society
L.A.N.S.A.
East Midland Chapter, I.B.N.S.

Le Change des Monnaies Etrangers
by R. L. Martin. 12, rue Poincaré, F 55800 Revigny, France.
(Illustrated guide of current world bank notes.)

MRI Bankers' Guide to Foreign Currency
by Arnoldo Efron, Monetary Research Institute, P.O. Box 3174, Houston, Texas, U.S.A., 77253-3174.
(Quarterly illustrated guide of current world bank notes.)

Country Index

Afghanistan . . . 33
Albania . . . 38
Algeria . . . 44
Angolia . . . 48
Antigua and Barbuda . . . 336
Argentina . . . 56
Armenia . . . 67
Aruba . . . 71
Australia . . . 74
Austria . . . 79
Azerbaijan . . . 81
Bahamas . . . 84
Bahrain . . . 91
Bangladesh . . . 95
Barbados . . . 103
Belarus . . . 109
Belgium . . . 114
Belize . . . 118
Bermuda . . . 124
Bhutan . . . 130
Biafra . . . 135
Bolivia . . . 136
Bosnia-Herzegovina . . . 146
Botswana . . . 158
Brazil . . . 163
British Caribbean Territories . 178
British Honduras . . . 179
British West Africa . . . 180
Brunei . . . 181
Bulgaria . . . 186
Burkina Faso . . . 1111
Burma . . . 191
Burundi . . . 193
Cambodia . . . 199
Cameroun . . . 208, 229
Canada . . . 211
Cape Verde . . . 216
Cayman Islands . . . 219
Central African Republic 225, 230
Central African States . . . 227
Ceylon . . . 233
Chad . . . 232, 236
Chile . . . 239
China, Peoples Republic . . . 245
China, Taiwan . . . 249
Colombia . . . 254
Comoros . . . 265
Congo . . . 228
Congo Democratic Republic . 268
Congo Republic . . . 274
Cook Islands . . . 276
Costa Rica . . . 278
Cote d'Ivoire . . . 1106
Croatia . . . 286
Cuba . . . 290
Cyprus . . . 295
Czech Republic . . . 300
Czechoslovakia . . . 304
Denmark . . . 306
Djibouti . . . 312
Dominican Republic . . . 313
East Africa . . . 326
East Caribbean States . . . 328
East Germany . . . 411
Ecuador . . . 337
Egypt . . . 342
El Salvador . . . 350
Equatorial African States . . . 358
Equatorial Guinea . . . 231, 359
Eritrea . . . 362
Estonia . . . 364
Ethiopia . . . 367
European Union . . . 372
Faeroe Islands . . . 374
Falkland Islands . . . 377
Fiji . . . 379
Finland . . . 388
France . . . 391
French Afars & Issas . . . 395
French Antilles . . . 396
French Guiana . . . 398
French Pacific Territories . . . 398
Gabon . . . 230, 399
Gambia . . . 401
Georgia . . . 406
Germany - Democratic Republic . . . 411
Germany - Federal Republic . . 413
Ghana . . . 417
Gibraltar . . . 424
Great Britain . . . 428
Greece . . . 432
Greenland . . . 435
Guatemala . . . 436
Guernsey . . . 445
Guinea . . . 448
Guinea-Bissau . . . 453, 1119
Guyana . . . 455
Haiti . . . 457
Honduras . . . 467
Hong Kong . . . 474
Hungary . . . 487
Iceland . . . 492
India . . . 495
Indonesia . . . 507
Iran . . . 518
Iraq . . . 532
Ireland . . . 539
Ireland, Northern . . . 760
Isle of Man . . . 542
Israel . . . 545
Italy . . . 551
Ivory Coast . . . 1106
Jamaica . . . 555
Japan . . . 562
Jersey . . . 564
Jordan . . . 569
Katanga . . . 575
Kazakhstan . . . 577
Kenya . . . 582
Korea, North . . . 754
Korea, South . . . 943
Kuwait . . . 591
Kyrgyzstan . . . 596
Lao . . . 600
Latvia . . . 606
Lebanon . . . 608
Lesotho . . . 613
Liberia . . . 617
Libya . . . 619
Lithuania . . . 626
Luxembourg . . . 630
Macau . . . 633
Macedonia . . . 641
Madagascar . . . 645
Malawi . . . 650
Malaya & British Borneo . . . 659
Malaysia . . . 659
Maldives . . . 666
Mali . . . 668, 1112
Malta . . . 671
Mauritania . . . 675
Mauritius . . . 679
Mexico . . . 684
Moldova . . . 694
Mongolia . . . 697
Morocco . . . 702
Mozambique . . . 706
Muscat & Oman . . . 776
Myanmar . . . 711
Namibia . . . 714
Nepal . . . 717
Netherlands . . . 723
Netherlands Antilles . . . 726
New Caledonia . . . 730
New Hebrides . . . 731
New Zealand . . . 732
Nicaragua . . . 738
Niger . . . 1114
Nigeria . . . 749
North Korea . . . 754
North Viet Nam . . . 1098
Northern Ireland . . . 760
Norway . . . 772
Oman . . . 777
Pakistan . . . 783
Papua New Guinea . . . 789
Paraguay . . . 795
Peru . . . 801
Philippines . . . 813
Poland . . . 826
Portugal . . . 832
Portuguese Guinea . . . 836
Qatar . . . 838
Qatar & Dubai . . . 842
Reunion . . . 843
Rhodesia . . . 845
Rhodesia & Nyasaland . . . 847
Romania . . . 848
Russia . . . 853
Rwanda . . . 860
Rwanda-Burundi . . . 865
Saint Helena . . . 866
Saint Pierre & Miquelon . . . 868
Saint Thomas & Prince . . . 869
Salvador . . . 350
Samoa . . . 872
Saudi Arabia . . . 874
Scotland . . . 879
Senegal . . . 1115
Serbia . . . 895
Seychelles . . . 899
Sierra Leone . . . 905
Singapore . . . 910
Slovakia . . . 917
Slovenia . . . 921
Solomon Islands . . . 926
Somalia . . . 930
Somaliland . . . 934
South Africa . . . 937
South Korea . . . 943
South Sudan . . . 947
South Viet Nam . . . 948
Spain . . . 952
Sri Lanka . . . 955
Sudan . . . 953
Suriname . . . 971
Swaziland . . . 978
Sweden . . . 984
Switzerland . . . 988
Syria . . . 995
Tahiti . . . 998
Taiwan . . . 249
Tajikistan . . . 1000
Tanzania . . . 1003
Tatarstan . . . 1009
Thailand . . . 1011
Timor . . . 1020
Togo . . . 1117
Tonga . . . 1021
Transnistria . . . 1026
Trinidad & Tobago . . . 1030
Tunisia . . . 1034
Turkey . . . 1038
Turkmenistan . . . 1045
Uganda . . . 1049
Ukraine . . . 1057
United Arab Emirates . . . 1064
United States of America . . . 1069
Upper Volta . . . 1111
Uruguay . . . 1077
Uzbeekistan . . . 1085
Vanuatu . . . 1088
Venezuela . . . 1090
Viet Nam . . . 1098
Viet Nam, North . . . 1098
Viet Nam, South . . . 948
West African States . . . 1105
West Germany . . . 413
Western Samoa . . . 1120
Yemen Arab Republic . . . 1122
Yemen Democratic Republic 1127
Yugoslavia . . . 1129
Zaïre . . . 1139
Zambia . . . 1147
Zimbabwe . . . 1154

Issuer and Bank Index

Allied Irish Banks Ltd. . . . 760
Allied Irish Banks Public Limited Company . . . 760
Arab Republic of Egypt . . . 349
Armenian Republic Bank . . . 67
Australia, Reserve Bank . . . 75
Austrian National Bank . . . 79
Azerbaycan Merkezi Banki . . . 83
Azerbaycan Milli Banki . . . 81
Azerbaycan Republic State Loan Bonds . . . 82
Baanka Somaliland . . . 934
Bahamas Government . . . 84, 90
Bahamas Monetary Authority . . . 85, 90
Bahrain Currency Board . . . 91
Bahrain Monetary Agency . . . 91, 94
Banc Ceannais na hÉireann . . . 539
Banca d'Italia . . . 552
Banca Nationala a Moldovei . . . 695
Banca Nationala a Republicii Socialiste România . . . 848
Banca Nationala a României . . . 849
Banca Nazionale Somala . . . 930
Banco Central . . . 359
Banco Central de Bolivia . . . 136
Banco Central de Chile . . . 239
Banco Central de Costa Rica . . . 278
Banco Central de Cuba . . . 293
Banco Central de Honduras . . . 467
Banco Central de la Republica Argentina . . . 56
Banco Central de la República Dominicana . . . 313
Banco Central de Nicaragua . . . 738
Banco Central de Reserva de el Salvador . . . 350
Banco Central de Reserva del Peru . . . 801
Banco Central de S. Tomé e Príncipe . . . 871
Banco Central de Venezuela . . . 1090
Banco Central del Ecuador . . . 337
Banco Central del Paraguay . . . 795
Banco Central del Uruguay . . . 1077
Banco Central di Aruba . . . 71
Banco Central do Brasil . . . 166
Banco da China, Macau . . . 638, 641
Banco de Angola . . . 49
Banco de Cabo Verde . . . 216
Banco de Credito del Peru . . . 812
Banco de España . . . 952
Banco de Guatemala . . . 436
Banco de Guinea Ecuatorial . . . 361
Banco de la Nacion . . . 813
Banco de la Republica, Colombia . . . 254
Banco de México . . . 684
Banco de Moçambique . . . 707, 710
Banco de Portugal . . . 832
Banco Nacional da Guiné-Bissau . . . 453
Banco Nacional de Angola . . . 50
Banco Nacional de Cuba . . . 290, 295
Banco Nacional de S. Tomé e Príncipe . . . 869
Banco Nacional Ultramarino, Cabo Verde . . . 216
Banco Nacional Ultramarino, Guiné . . . 836
Banco Nacional Ultramarino, Macau . . . 633, 641
Banco Nacional Ultramarino, Moçambique . . . 706
Banco Nacional Ultramarino, S. Tomé e Príncipe . . . 869
Banco Nacional Ultramarino, Timor . . . 1020
Banco Popular . . . 360
Bangko Sentral ng Pilipinas . . . 816
Bangladesh Bank . . . 96
Bank al-Maghrib . . . 703
Bank Centrali ta'Malta . . . 672
Bank Indonesia . . . 508
Bank Markazi Iran . . . 519
Bank Negara Malaysia . . . 659
Bank Nistriana . . . 1027
Bank of Afghanistan . . . 33
Bank of Biafra . . . 135
Bank of Botswana . . . 158
Bank of Canada . . . 211
Bank of China Limited, Hong Kong . . . 485
Bank of England . . . 428
Bank of Eritrea . . . 362
Bank of Estonia . . . 361
Bank of Ghana . . . 417
Bank of Greece . . . 432
Bank of Guyana . . . 455
Bank of Ireland . . . 761
Bank of Ireland . . . 771
Bank of Israel . . . 545
Bank of Italy . . . 552
Bank of Jamaica . . . 555
Bank of Japan . . . 562
Bank of Korea . . . 943
Bank of Libya . . . 619
Bank of Lithuania . . . 626
Bank of Mauritius . . . 679
Bank of Namibia . . . 715
Bank of Papua New Guinea . . . 790
Bank of Rhodesia and Nyasaland . . . 847
Bank of Russia . . . 857
Bank of Scotland . . . 879
Bank of Sierra Leone . . . 905
Bank of South Sudan . . . 947
Bank of Sudan . . . 963
Bank of Taiwan . . . 249
Bank of Tanzania . . . 1003
Bank of Thailand . . . 1013
Bank of the Lao PDR . . . 603
Bank of Uganda . . . 1049
Bank of Uzbekistan . . . 1086
Bank of West Samoa . . . 1120
Bank of Yemen . . . 1128
Bank of Zambia . . . 1147
Banka e Shqiperise . . . 41
Banka e Shtetit Shqiptar . . . 38
Banka Slovenije . . . 921
Banki Kuu Ya Kenya . . . 583
Banki Nasiyonali Y'u Rwanda . . . 860

Banki Nkuru Y'u Rwanda 864
Bankiga Dhexe ee Soomaaliya 932
Bankiga Qaranka Soomaaliyeed 931
Banky Foiben'I Madagasikara....646
Banky Foiben'ny Repoblika Malagasy....646
Banque Central des Etats de l'Afrique Equatoriale et du Cameroun....358
Banque Central du Congo....270
Banque Central Etats de l'Afrique Equatoriale....358
Banque Centrale d'Algérie 45
Banque Centrale de Djibouti 313
Banque Centrale de la République de Guinée 448
Banque Centrale de la République Malgache 646
Banque Centrale de Mauritanie....675
Banque Centrale de Syrie 995
Banque Centrale de Tunisie 1034
Banque Centrale de Vanuatu....1088
Banque Centrale des Comores 266
Banque Centrale des Etats de l'Afrique de l'Ouest 1106
Banque Centrale du Mali....670
Banque Centrale, Cameroun....208
Banque Centrale, Chad 236
Banque Centrale, Congo Republic 274
Banque Centrale, Gabon....399
Banque de France....391
Banque de la République d'Haiti....460
Banque de la Republique du Burundi 195
Banque de la République du Mali 669
Banque de l'Algérie....44, 47
Banque de l'Indochine, Papeete 998
Banque de Madagascar et des Comores....265
Banque de Reserve de Vanuatu 1089
Banque de Syrie et du Liban....608
Banque d'Emission du Rwanda et du Burundi 865
Banque des Etats de l'Afrique Central, Central African Republic 225
Banque des Etats de l'Afrique Central, Chad....236
Banque des Etats de l'Afrique Centrale....362, 399
Banque des Etats de l'Afrique Centrale, Cameroun....209
Banque des Etats de l'Afrique Centrale, Central African States 228
Banque des Etats de l'Afrique Centrale, Congo Republic 274
Banque du Canada 211
Banque du Liban....609
Banque du Maroc....702
Banque du Royaume du Burundi 193
Banque du Zaïre 1139
Banque Internationale a Luxembourg....630
Banque National du Congo 268
Banque Nationale de Belgique 115
Banque Nationale de Djibouti 312
Banque Nationale de la République d'Haiti....457
Banque Nationale du Cambodge....200
Banque Nationale du Katanga....575
Banque Nationale du Laos 600
Banque Nationale du Rwanda....860
Banque of Kampuchea 202
Belarus National Bank....110
Belarus Republic.... 109
Belfast Banking Company Limited.... 763
Benki Kuu Ya Tanzania 1004
Bermuda Government.... 124
Bermuda Monetary Authority 125
Biglietto di Stato 551
Board of Commissioners of Currency, Malaysia and British Borneo 659
Board of Commissioners of Currency, Singapore 910
British Caribbean Territories, Eastern Group.... 178
British Linen Bank.... 883
Bulgarian National Bank 186
Bundeskassenschein.... 414
Caisse Centrale de la France d'Outre-Mer 398
Caisse Centrale de la France d'Outre-Mer, Saint Pierre et Miquelon 868
Cayman Islands Currency Board.... 219, 224
Cayman Islands Monetary Authority 222
Central Bank Blong Vanuatu 1088
Central Bank of Bahrain.... 93
Central Bank of Barbados 103
Central Bank of Belize 119
Central Bank of Ceylon 233, 955
Central Bank of Cyprus 296
Central Bank of Egypt 343
Central Bank of Iceland 492
Central Bank of Iraq 532
Central Bank of Ireland 539
Central Bank of Jordan 569
Central Bank of Kenya.... 583
Central Bank of Kuwait 592
Central Bank of Lesotho 614
Central Bank of Liberia 617
Central Bank of Libya 620
Central Bank of Malta 672
Central Bank of Myanmar 711
Central Bank of Nepal 717
Central Bank of Nigeria 749
Central Bank of Oman 778
Central Bank of Samoa 872
Central Bank of Seychelles 902
Central Bank of Somalia 932
Central Bank of Sri Lanka 957
Central Bank of Sudan.... 970
Central Bank of Swaziland.... 979
Central Bank of Syria.... 995
Central Bank of the Bahamas 85
Central Bank of the Gambia.... 402
Central Bank of the Islamic Republic of Iran 529
Central Bank of the Philippines 814
Central Bank of the Republic of Armenia.... 68
Central Bank of Trinidad and Tobago 1030
Central Bank of Turkey 1038
Central Bank of Turkmenistan.... 1045
Central Bank of Uzbekistan Republic.... 1087
Central Bank of Vanuatu 1088
Central Bank of Yemen 1124
Central Monetary Authority.... 381

Centrale Bank van Aruba . . . 71
Centrale Bank van Suriname . . . 972
Centralna Banka Bosne I Hercegovine . . . 152
Certificat de Liberation Economique . . . 466
Ceská Narodní Banka . . . 300
Ceskoslovenská Socialistická Republika . . . 304
Chartered Bank . . . 474
Clydesdale and North of Scotland Bank Ltd. . . . 883
Clydesdale Bank Limited . . . 884
Clydesdale Bank PLC . . . 885, 895
Commonwealth of Australia Reserve Bank . . . 74
Cook Islands . . . 276
Cook Islands, Aitutaki . . . 277
Cook Islands, Ngaputoru & Mangaia . . . 277
Cook Islands, Northern Group . . . 277
Cook Islands, Rarotonga . . . 277
Czech National Bank . . . 300
Da Afghanistan Bank . . . 35
Danmarks Nationalbank . . . 306
De Bederkabdsche Bank . . . 723
Den Kongelige Grønlandske Handel . . . 435
Deutsche Bundesbank . . . 413
Deutsche Notenbank . . . 411
East African Currency Board, Nairobi . . . 326
East Caribbean Central Bank . . . 329
East Caribbean Currency Authority . . . 328
Eesti Pank . . . 361
European Central Bank . . . 372
Fale Tupe o Samoa I Sisifo . . . 1121
Faletupe Tutotonu o Samoa . . . 872
Federal Reserve Note . . . 1070
Finlands Bank . . . 388
First Trust Bank . . . 764
Føroyar . . . 374
Gambia Currency Board . . . 401
Georgian National Bank . . . 406
Gouvernment Katanga . . . 575
Government of Antigua and Barbuda . . . 336
Government of Belize . . . 118
Government of British Honduras . . . 179
Government of Brunei . . . 181
Government of Fiji . . . 379
Government of Gibraltar . . . 424
Government of Hong Kong . . . 484, 487
Government of India . . . 500
Government of Malta . . . 671
Government of Pakistan . . . 783
Government of Seychelles . . . 899
Government of St. Helena . . . 866
Government of Thailand . . . 1013
Government of the Cook Islands . . . 276
Government of the Falkland Islands . . . 377
Government of Tonga . . . 1021, 1025
Government Treasurer, Maldivian State . . . 666
Government, Tatarstan . . . 1010
Government, Transnistria . . . 1026
Government, Uzbekistan . . . 1085
Grand Duché de Luxembourg . . . 631
Hong Kong & Shanghai Banking Corporation Ltd. . . . 479
Hong Kong & Shanghai Banking Corporation, Hong Kong . . . 476
Hrvatska Narodna Banka . . . 288
Hungarian National Bank . . . 487
Institut d'Emission des Comores . . . 265
Institut d'Emission des Départements d'Outre-Mer, Réunion . . . 843
Institut d'Emission des Departments d'Outre-Mer . . . 396
Institut d'Emission des Departments d'Outre-Mer, Republique Francaise . . . 396
Institut d'Emission d'Outre-Mer . . . 398
Institut d'Emission d'Outre-Mer, Nouméa . . . 730
Institut d'Emission d'Outre-Mer, Nouvelles Hébrides . . . 731
Institut d'Emission d'Outre-Mer, Papeete . . . 999
Institut d'Emission Malgache . . . 645
Institut Monetaire Luxembourgeois . . . 632
International Bank in Luxembourg . . . 630
Isle of Man Government . . . 542
Kazakhstan National Bank . . . 577
Kerajaan Brunei . . . 181
Kibris Cumhuriyeti . . . 295
Kibris Merkez Bankasi . . . 296
Kingdom of Tonga . . . 1023
Komiti Faatino o Tupe a Samoa I Sisifo . . . 1122
Koninkrijk Belgie . . . 115
Korean Central Bank . . . 754
Kuwait Currency Board . . . 591
Kyrgyz Bank . . . 597
Kyrgyz Republic . . . 596
Kyrgyzstan Bank . . . 597
Labank Santral Sesel . . . 902
Lao Peoples Democratic Republic . . . 603
Latvia Government . . . 606
Latvijas Bankas Naudas Zime . . . 606
Lesotho Monetary Authority . . . 613
Lieuvos Bankas . . . 626
Lloyds Bank Limited . . . 542
Magyar Nemzeti Bank . . . 487
Maldives Monetary Authority . . . 666
Mercantile Bank Limited . . . 481
Minister of Finance, Moldova . . . 694
Monetary Authority of Belize . . . 118
Monetary Authority of Singapore . . . 916
Monetary Authority of Swaziland . . . 978
Monetary Board of Western Samoa . . . 1122
Mongol Bank . . . 698
Muntbiljet . . . 971
Namibia Reserve Bank . . . 714
Narodna Banka Bosne I Hercegovine . . . 146
Narodna Banka Hrvatske . . . 287
Narodna Banka Jugoslavije . . . 1129
Narodna Banka Republike Srpske . . . 156
Národná Banka Slovenska . . . 917
Narodna Banka Srbija . . . 895
Narodna Banka Srpske Republike Bosne I Hercegovine . . . 155

Narodowy Bank Polski .826
National Bank of Cambodia .204
National Bank of Cuba .290
National Bank of Ethiopia .368
National Bank of Liberia .617
National Bank of Macedonia .641
National Bank of Serbia .895
National Bank of Tajikistan .1001
National Bank of the Republic of Macedonia .642
National Bank of the Republic of Tajikistan .1000
National Bank of Viet Nam .948
National Bank of Yugoslavia .1129
National Bank van Belgie .115
National Commercial Bank of Scotland Limited .888
National Reserve Bank of Tonga .1023
Nederlandse Antillen .726
Negara Brunei Darussalam .182
Netherlands Bank .723
Ngan Hang Nhua Nu'o'c Viet Nam .1098
Ngan Hang Viet Nam .951
Ngan-Hang Quo'c-Gia Viet-Nam .948
Norges Bank .772
Northern Bank Limited .765
Novcani Bon .151
Oesterreichische Nationalbank .79
Oman Currency Board .777
Pathet Lao Government .602
Peoples Bank of Burma .191
Peoples Bank of China .246
Peoples National Bank of Cambodia .204
Peoples Republic of Bangladesh .95
Polish National Bank .826
Provincial Bank of Ireland Limited .768, 771
Pule' Anga 'o Tonga .1022
Qatar and Dubai Currency Board .842
Qatar Central Bank .839
Qatar Monetary Agency .838
Repubblica Italiana .551
Republic of Croatia .286
Republic of Cyprus .295
Republic of Seychelles .900
Republic of Slovakia .917
Republica dos Estados Unido do Brasil .164
República Popular de Moçambique .708
Republik Indonesia .507
Republika Hrvatska .286
Republika Slovenija .921
Republique du Congo Conseil Monetaire de la Republique du Congo .268
Reserve Bank Blong Vanuatu .1089
Reserve Bank of Fiji .383
Reserve Bank of India .496
Reserve Bank of Malawi .650
Reserve Bank of New Zealand .732
Reserve Bank of Rhodesia .845
Reserve Bank of Vanuatu .1089
Reserve Bank of Zimbabwe .1154
Reserve Bank, Australia 75
Reserve Bank, Commonwealth of Australia 74
Royal Bank of Scotland 889
Royal Bank of Scotland Limited 890
Royal Bank of Scotland PLC 891
Royal Government of Bhutan 130
Royal Monetary Authority of Bhutan 131
Royaume de Belgique 115
Russian Federation 856
Saudi Arabian Monetary Agency 874
Schweizerische Nationalbank 990
Sedlabanki Islands 492
Severiges Riksbank 984
Seychelles Monetary Authority 901
Slovak National Bank 917
Slovenska Republika 917
Solomon Islands Monetary Authority 926
Somali National Bank 931
South African Reserve Bank 937
South Arabian Currency Authority 1127
Special Argo-Cheque 1158
Srí Lanká Maha Bänkuva 957
Staatsbank der DDR 411
Standard Chartered Bank 482, 1156
State Bank Note, U.S.S.R. 854
State Bank of Democratic Kampuchea 203
State Bank of Ethiopia 367
State Bank of Pakistan 784
State Bank of Viet Nam 1098
State Bank, Mongolia 697
State of Lao 602
State Treasury Note, U.S.S.R. 854
States of Guernsey 445
States of Jersey 564
Státní Banka Ceskoslovensk 304
Suid-Afrikaanse Reserwebank 937
Sultimate of Muscat and Oman 776
Suomen Pankki 388
Swiss National Bank 990
Taiwan Bank 250
Territory of Western Samoa 1120
Treasury, Tatarstan 1009
Treasury, Ukraine 1057
Trésor Public, Territorie Français des Afars et des Issas 395
Türkiye Cümhuriyet Merkez Bankasi 1038
Türkmenistanyn Merkezi Döwlet Banky 1045
Ukrainian National Bank 1058
Ulster Bank Limited 769
Union of Burma Bank 191
United Arab Emirates Central Bank 1065
United Arab Emirates Currency Board 1064
United Arab Republic 348
United States Note 1069
West African Currency Board 180
Westminister Bank Limited 542
Yemen Currency Board 1122

How To Use This Catalog

Catalog listings consist of all regular and provisional notes attaining wide circulation in their respective countries for the period covered. Notes have been listed under the historical country name. Thus Dahomey is not under Benin, as had been the case in some past catalogs. The listings continue to be grouped by issue range rather than by denomination, andthe listing format should make the bank name, issue dates as well as catalog numbers and denominations easier to locate. These improvements have been made to make the catalog as easy to use as possible for you.

The editors and publisher make no claim to absolute completeness, just as they acknowledge that some errors and pricing inequities will appear. Correspondence is invited with interested persons who have notes previously unlisted or who have information to enhance the presentation of existing listings in succeeding editions of this catalog.

Catalog Format

Listings proceed generally according to the following sequence: country, geographic or political, chronology, bank name and sometimes alphabetically or by date of first note issue. Release within the bank, most often in date order, but sometimes by printer first.

Catalog number — The basic reference number at the beginning of each listing for each note. For this Modern Issues volume the regular listings require no prefix letters except when 'a' or 'b' appear within the catalog number as a suffix or variety letter. (Military and Regional prefixes are explained later in this section.)

Denomination — the value as shown on the note, in western numerals. When denominations are only spelled out, consult the numerics chart.

Date — the actual issue date as printed on the note in day-month-year order. Where more than one date appears on a note, only the latest is used. Where the note has no date, the designation ND is used, followed by a year date in parentheses when it is known. If a note is dated by the law or decree of authorization, the date appears with an L or D.

Descriptions of the note are broken up into one or more items as follows:

Color — the main color(s) of the face, and the underprint are given first. If the colors of the back are different, then they follow the face design description.

Design — The identification and location of the main design elements if known. Back design elements identified if known.

Printer — often a local printer has the name shown in full. Abbreviations are used for the most prolific printers. Refer to the list of printer abbreviations elsewhere in this introduction.

Valuations — are generally given under the grade headings of Good, Fine and Extremely Fine for early notes; and Very Good, Very Fine and Uncirculated for the later issues. Listings that do not follow these two patterns are clearly indicated. UNC followed by a value is used usually for specimens and proofs when lower grade headings are used for a particular series of issued notes.

Catalog suffix letters

A catalog number followed by a capital 'A', 'B' or 'C' indicated the incorporation of a listing as required by type or date it may indicate newly discovered lower or higher denominations to a series which needed to be fit into long standing listings. Listings of notes for regional circulation are distinguished from regular national issues with the prefix letter 'R'; military issues use a 'M' prefix; foreign exchange certificates are assigned a 'FX' prefix. These are now presented in the *Standard Catalog of World Paper Money, Specialized Issues Volume, 12th Edition.* Varieties, specific date or signature listings are shown with small letters 'a' following a number within their respective entries. Some standard variety letters include: 'ct' for color trials, 'p' for proof notes, 'r' for remainder notes, 's' for specimen notes and 'x' for counterfeits or errors.

Denominations

The denomination as indicated on many notes issued by a string of countries stretching from eastern Asia, through western Asia and on across northern Africa, often appears only in unfamiliar non-Western numeral styles. With the listings that follow, denominations are always indicated in Western numerals.

A comprehensive chart keying Western numerals to their non-Western counterparts is included elsewhere in this introduction as an aid to the identification of note types. This compilation features not only the basic numeral systems such as Arabic, Japanese and Indian, but also the more restricted systems such as Burmese, Ethiopian, Siamese, Tibetan, Hebrew, Mongolian and Korean. Additionally, the list includes other localized variations that have been applied to some paper money issues.

In consulting the numeral systems chart to determine the denomination of a note, one should remember that the actual numerals styles employed in any given area, or at a particular time, may vary significantly from these basic representations. Such variations can be deceptive to the untrained eye, just as variations from Western numeral styles can prove deceptive to individuals not acquainted with the particular style employed.

Dates and Date Listing Policy

In previous editions of this work it was the goal to provide a sampling of the many date varieties that were believed to exist. In recent times, as particular dates (and usually signature combinations) were known to be scarcer, that particular series was expanded to include listings of individual dates. At times this idea has been fully incorporated, but with some series it is not practicable, especially when just about every day in a given month could have been an issue date for the notes.

Accordingly, where it seems justifiable that date spans can be realistically filled with individual dates, this has been done. In order to accommodate the many new dates, the idea of providing variety letters to break them up into narrower spans of years has been used. If it appears that there are too many dates for a series, with no major differences in value, then a general inclusive date span is used (beginning and ending) and individual dates within this span are not shown.

For those notes showing only a general date span, the only important dates become those that expand the range of years, months or days earlier or later. But even they would have no impact on the values shown.

Because a specific date is not listed does not necessarily mean it is rare. It may be just that it has not been reported. Those date varieties known to be scarcer are cataloged separately. Newly reported dates in a wide variety of listings are constantly being reported. This indicates that research into the whole area is very active, and a steady flow of new dates is fully expected upon publication of this edition.

Valuations

Valuations are given for most notes in three grades. Earlier issues are usually valued in the grade headings of Good, Fine and Extremely Fine; later issues take the grade headings of Very Good, Very Fine and Uncirculated. While it is true that some early notes cannot be valued in Extremely Fine and some later notes have no premium value in Very Good, it is felt that this coverage provides the best uniformity of value data to the collecting community. There are exceptional cases where headings are adjusted for either single notes or a series that really needs special treatment.

Valuations are determined generally from a consensus of individuals submitting prices for evaluation. Some notes have NO values; this does not necessarily mean they are expensive or even rare, but it shows that no pricing information was forthcoming. A number of notes have a 'Rare' designation, and no values. Such notes are generally not available on the market, and when they do appear the price is a matter between buyer and seller. No book can provide guidance in these instances except to indicate rarity.

Valuations used in this book are based on the IBNS grading standards and are stated in U.S. dollars. They serve only as aids in evaluating paper money since actual market conditions throughout the worldwide collector community are constantly changing. In addition, particularly choice examples of many issues listed often bring higher premiums than values listed. Users should remember that a catalog such as this is only a guide to values.

FV (for Face Value) is used as a value designation on new issues as well as older but still redeemable legal tender notes in lower conditions. FV may appear in one or both condition columns before Uncirculated, depending on the relative age and availability of the note in question. Some non-current notes which are still exchangeable carry FV designations.

Collection care

The proper preservation of a collection should be of paramount importance to all in the hobby - dealers, collectors and scholars. Only a person who has housed notes in a manner giving pleasure to him or herself and others will keep alive the pleasure of collecting for future generations. The same applies to the way of housing as to the choice of the collecting specialty: it is chiefly a question of what most pleases the individual collector.

Arrangement and sorting of a collection is most certainly a basic requirement. Storing the notes in safe paper envelopes and filing boxes should, perhaps, be considered only when building a new section of a collection, for accommodating varieties or for reasons of saving space when the collection has grown quickly.

Many paper money collections are probably housed in some form of plastic-pocketed album, which are today manufactured in many different sizes and styles to accommodate many types of world paper money. Because the number of bank note collectors has grown continually over the past thirty-five years, some specialty manufacturers of albums have developed a paper money selection. The notes, housed in clear plastic pockets, individually or in groups, can be viewed and exchanged without difficulty. These albums are not cheap, but the notes displayed in this manner do make a lasting impression on the viewer.

A word of concern: certain types of plastic and all vinyl used for housing notes may cause notes to become brittle over time, or cause an irreversible and harmful transfer of oils from the vinyl onto the bank notes.

The high demand for quality that stamp collectors make on their products cannot be transferred to the paper money collecting fraternity. A postage stamp is intended for a single use, then is relegated to a collection. With paper money, it is nearly impossible to acquire uncirculated specimens from a number of countries because of export laws or internal bank procedures. Bends from excessive counting, or even staple holes, are commonplace. Once acquiring a circulated note, the collector must endeavor to maintain its state of preservation.

The fact that there is a classification and value difference between notes with greater use or even damage is a matter of course. It is part of the opinion and personal taste of the individual collector to decide what is considered worthy of collecting and what to pay for such items.

For the purposed of strengthening and mending torn paper money, under no circumstances should one use plain cellophane tape or a similar material. These tapes warp easily, with sealing marks forming at the edges, and the tape frequently discolors. Only with the greatest of difficulty (and often not at all) can these tapes be removed, and damage to the note or the printing is almost unavoidable. The best material for mending tears is an archival tape recommended for the treatment and repair of documents.

There are collectors who, with great skill, remove unsightly spots, repair badly damaged notes, replace missing pieces and otherwise restore or clean a note. There is a question of morality by tampering with a note to improve its condition, either by repairing, starching, ironing, pressing or other methods to possibly deceive a potential future buyer. Such a question must, in the final analysis, be left to the individual collector.

IBNS GRADING STANDARDS FOR WORLD PAPER MONEY

The following introduction and Grading Guide is the result of work prepared under the guidance of the Grading Committee of the International Bank Note Society (IBNS). It has been adopted as the official grading standards of that society.

Introduction

Grading is the most controversial component of paper money collecting today. Small differences in grade can mean significant Vdifferences in value. The process of grading is so subjective and dependent on external influences such as lighting, that even a very experienced individual may well grade the same note differently on separate occasions.

To facilitate communication between sellers and buyers, it is essential that grading terms and their meanings be as standardized and as widely used as possible. This standardization should reflect common usage as much as practicable. One difficulty with grading is that even the actual grades themselves are not used everywhere by everyone. For example, in Europe the grade 'About Uncirculated' (AU) is not in general use, yet in North America it is widespread. The European term 'Good VF' may roughly correspond to what individuals in North America call 'Extremely Fine' (EF).

The grades and definitions as set forth below cannot reconcile all the various systems and grading terminology variants. Rather, the attempt is made here to try and diminish the controversy with some common-sense grades and definitions that aim to give more precise meaning to the grading language of paper money.

How to look at a banknote

In order to ascertain the grade of a note, it is essential to examine it out of a holder and under a good light. Move the note around so that light bounces off of it at different angles. Try holding the note obliquely, so the note is even with your eye as you look up at the light. Hard-to-see folds or slight creases will show up under such examination. Some individuals also lightly feel along the surface of the note to detect creasing.

Cleaning, Washing, Pressing of Banknotes

a) Cleaning, washing or pressing paper money is generally harmful and reduces both the grade and the value of a note. At the very least, a washed or pressed note may lose its original sheen and its surface may become lifeless and dull. The defects a note had, such as folds and creases, may not necessarily be completely eliminated and their telltale marks can be detected under a good light. Carelessly washed notes may also have white streaks where the folds or creases were (or still are).

b) Processing of a note which started out as Extremely Fine will automatically reduce it at least one full grade.

Unnatural Defects

Glue, tape or pencil marks may sometimes be successfuly removed. While such removal will leave a cleaned surface, it will improve the overall appearance of the note without concealing any of its defects. Under such circumstances, the grade of that note may also be improved.

The words "pinholes", "staple holes", "trimmed", "graffiti", "writing on face", "tape marks" etc. should always be added to the description of a note. It is realized that certain countries routinely staple their notes together in groups before issue. In such cases, the description can include a comment such as "usual staple holes" or something similar. After all, not everyone knows that certain notes cannot be found otherwise.

The major point of this section is that one cannot lower the overall grade of a note with defects simply because of the defects. The value will reflect the lowered worth of a defective note, but the description must always include the specific defects.

GRADING

Definitions of Terms

UNCIRCULATED: A perfectly preserved note, never mishandled by the issuing authority, a bank teller, the public or a collector.

Paper is clean and firm, without discoloration. Corners are sharp and square without any evidence of rounding. (Rounded corners are often a tell-tale sign of a cleaned or "doctored" note.)

NOTE: Some note issues are most often available with slight evidence of very light counting folds which do not "break" the paper. Also, French-printed notes usually have a slight ripple in the paper. Many collectors and dealers refer to such notes as AU-UNC.

ABOUT UNCIRCULATED: A virtually perfect note, with some minor handling. May show very slight evidence of bank counting folds at a corner or one light fold through the center, but not both. An AU note canot be creased, a crease being a hard fold which has usually "broken" the surface of the note.

Paper is clean and bright with original sheen. Corners are not rounded.

NOTE: Europeans will refer to an About Uncirculated or AU note as "EF-Unc" or as just "EF". The Extremely Fine note described below will often be referred to as "GVF" or "Good Very Fine".

EXTREMELY FINE: A very attractive note, with light handling. May have a maximum of three light folds or one strong crease.

Paper is clean and firm, without discoloration. Corners are sharp and square without any evidence of rounding. (Rounded corners are often a tell-tale sign of a cleaned or "doctored" note.)

VERY FINE: An attractive note, but with more evidence of handling and wear. May have several folds both vertically and horizontally.

Paper may have minimal dirt, or possible color smudging. Paper itself is still relatively crisp and not floppy.

There are no tears into the border area, although the edges do show slight wear. Corners also show wear but not full rounding.

FINE: A note that shows consideralble circulation, with many folds, creases and wrinkling.

Paper is not excessively dirty but may have some softness.

Edges may show much handling, with minor tears in the border area. Tears may not extend into the design. There will be no center hole because of excessive folding.

Colors are clear but not very bright. A staple hole or two would would not be considered unusual wear in a Fine note. Overall appearance is still on the desirable side.

VERY GOOD: A well used note, abused but still intact.

Corners may have much wear and rounding, tiny nicks, tears may extend into the design, some discoloration may be prsent, staining may have occurred, and a small hole may sometimes be seen at center from excessive folding.

Staple and pinholes are usually present, and the note itself is quite limp but NO pieces of the note can be missing. A note in VG condition may still have an overall not unattractive appearance.

GOOD: A well worn and heavily used note. Normal damage from prolonged circulation will include strong multiple folds and creases, stains, pinholes and/or staple holes, dirt, discoloration, edge tears, center hole, rounded corners and an overall unattractive appearance. No large pieces of the note may be missing. Graffiti is commonly seen on notes in G condition.

FAIR: A totally limp, dirty and very well used note. Larger pieces may be half torn off or missing besides the defects mentioned under the Good category. Tears will be larger, obscured portions of the note will be bigger.

POOR: A "rag" with severe damage because of wear, staining, pieces missing, graffiti, larger holes. May have tape holding pieces of the note together. Trimming may have taken place to remove rough edges. A Poor note is desiralble only as a "filler" or when such a note is the only one known of that particular issue.

A word on crimps to otherwise uncirculated notes.

Due to inclusion of wide security foils, crimps appear at the top and bottom edge during production or counting. Thus notes which are uncirculated have a crimp. Examples without these crimps are beginning to command a premium.

Bank Note Printers

Printers' names, abbreviations or monograms will usually appear as part of the frame design or below it on face and/or back. In some instances the engraver's name may also appear in a similar location on a note. The following abbreviations identify printers for many of the notes listed in this volume:

ABNC . . . . American Bank Note Company (USA)
BABN(C) . . . . British American Bank Note Co., Ltd. (Canada)
B&S . . . . Bouligny & Schmidt (Mexico)
BDDK . . . . Bunddesdruckerei (Germany)
BEPP . . . . Bureau of Engraving & Printing, Peking (China)
BF . . . . Banque de France (France)
BFL . . . . Barclay & Fry, Ltd. (England)
BWC . . . . Bradbury, Wilkinson & Co. (England)
CABB . . . . Compania Americana de Billetes de Banco (ANBC)
CBC . . . . Columbian Banknote Co. (US)
CBNC . . . . Canadian Bank Note Company (Canada)
CC . . . . Ciccone Calcografica S.A. (Italy)
CCBB . . . . Compania Columbiana de Billetes de Banco (CBC)
CdM- . . . . Casa de Moeda (Brazil)
CdM- . . . . Casa de Moeda (Argentina, Chile, etc.)
CHB . . . . Chung Hua Book Co. (China)
CMN . . . . Casa de Moneda de la Nacion (Argentina)
CMPA . . . . Commercial Press (China)
CNBB . . . . Compania Nacional de billetes de Banco (NBNC)
CONB . . . . Continental Bank Note Company (US)
CPF . . . . Central Printing Factory (China)
CSABB . . . . . Compania Sud/Americana de billetes de Banco (Argentina)
CS&E . . . . Charles Skipper & East (England)
DLR or (T)DLR . . . . De La Rue (England)
DTB . . . . Dah Tung Book Co., and Ta Tung Printing (China)
E&C . . . . Evans & Cogswell (CSA)
EAW . . . . E.A. Wright (US)
FLBN . . . . Franklin-Lee Bank Note Company (US)
FNMT . . . . Fabrica Nacional de Moneda y Timbre (Spain)
G&D . . . . Giesecke & Devrient (Germany)
HBNC . . . . Hamilton Bank Note Company (USA)
HKB . . . . Hong Kong Banknote (Hong Kong)
HKP . . . . Hong Kong Printing Press (Hong Kong)
H&L . . . . Hoyer & Ludwig, Richmond, Virginia (CSA)
HLBNC . . . . Homer Lee Bank Note Co. (US)
H&S . . . . Harrison & Sons, Ltd. (England)
IBB . . . . Imprenta de Billetes-Bogota (Colombia)
IBSFB . . . . Imprenta de Billetes-Santa Fe de Bogota (Colombia)
IBNC . . . . International Bank Note Company (US)
JBNC . . . . Jeffries Bank Note Company (US)
JEZ . . . . Joh, Enschede en Zonen (Netherlands)
K&B . . . . Keatinge & Ball (CSA)
KBNC . . . . Kendall Bank Note Company, New York (USA)
LN . . . . Litographia Nacional (Colombia)
NAL . . . . Nissen & Arnold (England)
NBNC . . . . National Bank Note Company (US)
OCV . . . . Officina Carte-Valori (Italy)
OBDI . . . . Officina Della Banca D'Italia (Italy)
OFZ . . . . Orell Füssli, Zurich (Switzerland)
P&B . . . . Perkins & Bacon (England)
PBC . . . . Perkins, Bacon & Co. (England)
PB&P . . . . Perkins, Bacon & Petch (England)
SBNC . . . . Security Banknote Company (US)
TDLR or (T)DLR . . . . Thomas De La Rue (England)
UPC . . . . Union Printing Co., Ltd. (China)
UPP . . . . Union Publishers & Printers Fed. Inc. (China)
USBNC . . . . United States Banknote Corp. (US)
WDBN . . . . Western District Banknote Fed. Inc.
W&S . . . . Waterlow & Sons Ltd. (England)
WPCo . . . . Watson Printing Co. (China)
WWS . . . . W.W. Sprague & Co. Ltd. (England)

Standard International Grading Terminology and Abbreviations

U.S. and ENGLISH SPEAKING LANDS	UNCIRCULATED	EXTREMELY FINE	VERY FINE	FINE	VERY GOOD	GOOD	POOR
Abbreviation	UNC	EF or XF	VF	FF	VG	G	PR
BRAZIL	(1) DW	(3) S	(5) MBC	(7) BC	(8)	(9) R	UTGeG
DENMARK	O	O1	1+	1	1÷	2	3
FINLAND	0	01	1+	1	1?	2	3
FRANCE	NEUF	SUP	TTB or TB	TB or TB	B	TBC	BC
GERMANY	KFR	II / VZGL	III / SS	IV / S	V / S.g.E.	VI / G.e.	G.e.s.
ITALY	FdS	SPL	BB	MB	B	M	—
JAPAN	未使用	極美品	美品	並品	—	—	—
NETHERLANDS	FDC	Pr.	Z.F.	Fr.	Z.g.	G	—
NORWAY	0	01	1+	1	1÷	2	3
PORTUGAL	Novo	Soberbo	Muito bo	—	—	—	—
SPAIN	Lujo	SC, IC or EBC	MBC	BC	—	RC	MC
SWEDEN	0	01	1+	1	1?	2	—

BRAZIL

FE — Flor de Estampa
S — Soberba
MBC — Muito Bem Conservada
BC — Bem Conservada
R — Regular
UTGeG — Um Tanto Gasto e Gasto

DENMARK

O — Uncirkuleret
01 — Meget Paent Eksemplar
1+ — Paent Eksemplar
1 — Acceptabelt Eksemplar
1 —Noget Slidt Eksemplar
2 — Darlight Eksemplar
3 — Meget Darlight Eskemplar

FINLAND

00 — Kiiltolyönti
0 — Lyöntiveres
01 — Erittäin Hyvä
1+ — Hyvä
1? — Heikko
2 — Huono

FRANCE

NEUF — New
FDC — Fleur De Coin
SPL — Splendide
SUP — Superbe
TTB — Très Très Beau
TB — Très Beau
B — Beau
TBC — Tres Bien Conserve
BC — Bien Conserve

GERMANY

VZGL — Vorzüglich
SS — Sehr schön
S — Schön
S.g.E. — Sehr gut erhalten
G.e. — Gut erhalten
G.e.S. — Gering erhalten Schlecht

ITALY

Fds — Fior di Stampa
SPL — Splendid
BB — Bellissimo
MB — Molto Bello
B — Bello
M — Mediocre

JAPAN

未使用 — Mishiyo
極美品 — Goku Bihin
美品 — Bihin
並品 — Futuhin

NETHERLANDS

Pr. — Prachtig
Z.F. — Zeer Fraai
Fr. — Fraai
Z.g. — Zeer Goed
G — Goed

NORWAY

0 — Usirkuleret eks
01 — Meget pent eks
1+ — Pent eks
1 — Fullgodt eks
1- — Ikke Fullgodt eks
2 — Darlig eks

ROMANIA

NC — Necirculata (UNC)
FF — Foarte Frumoasa (VF)
F — Frumoasa (F)
FBC — Foarte Bine Conservata (VG)
BC — Bine Conservata (G)
M — Mediocru Conservata (POOR)

SPAIN

EBC — Extraordinariamente Bien Conservada
SC — Sin Circular
IC — Incirculante
MBC — Muy Bien Conservada
BC — Bien Conservada
RC — Regular Conservada
MC — Mala Conservada

SWEDEN

0 — Ocirkulerat
01 — Mycket Vackert
1+ — Vackert
1 — Fullgott
1? — Ej Fullgott
2 — Dalight

Foreign Exchange Table as of December 2013

The latest foreign exchange rates below apply to trade with banks in the country of origin. The left column shows the number of units per U.S. dollar at the official rate. The right column shows the number of units per dollar at the free market rate. Rates recorded Nov. 12, 2013.

Country	#/$	#/$
Afghanistan (New Afghani)	58	–
Albania (Lek)	104	–
Algeria (Dinar)	80	–
Andorra uses Euro	.745	–
Angola (Readjust Kwanza)	98	–
Anguilla uses E.C. Dollar	2.70	–
Antigua uses E.C. Dollar	2.70	–
Argentina (Peso)	5.97	–
Armenia (Dram)	406	–
Aruba (Florin)	1.79	–
Australia (Dollar)	1.08	–
Austria (Euro)	.745	–
Azerbaijan (New Manat)	.784	–
Bahamas (Dollar)	1.00	–
Bahrain Is. (Dinar)	.377	–
Bangladesh (Taka)	78	–
Barbados (Dollar)	2.00	–
Belarus (Ruble)	9,295	–
Belgium (Euro)	.745	–
Belize (Dollar)	2.01	–
Benin uses CFA Franc West	488	–
Bermuda (Dollar)	1.00	–
Bhutan (Ngultrum)	64	–
Bolivia (Boliviano)	6.91	–
Bosnia-Herzegovina (Conv. marka)	1.46	–
Botswana (Pula)	8.75	–
British Virgin Islands uses U.S. Dollar	1.00	–
Brazil (Real)	2.33	–
Brunei (Dollar)	1.25	–
Bulgaria (Lev)	1.46	–
Burkina Faso uses CFA Franc West	488	–
Burma (Kyat)	975	–
Burundi (Franc)	1,546	–
Cambodia (Riel)	4,010	–
Cameroon uses CFA Franc Central	490	–
Canada (Dollar)	1.05	–
Cape Verde (Escudo)	82	–
Cayman Islands (Dollar)	.820	–
Central African Rep.	490	–
CFA Franc Central	490	–
CFA Franc West	488	–
CFP Franc	89	–
Chad uses CFA Franc Central	490	–
Chile (Peso)	520	–
China, P.R. (Renminbi Yuan)	6.09	–
Colombia (Peso)	1,935	–
Comoros (Franc)	366	–
Congo uses CFA Franc Central	490	–
Congo-Dem.Rep. (Congolese Franc)	916	–
Cook Islands (Dollar)	1.22	–
Costa Rica (Colon)	500	–
Croatia (Kuna)	5.68	–
Cuba (Peso)	1.00	27.00
Cyprus (Euro)	.745	–
Czech Republic (Koruna)	20.1	–
Denmark (Danish Krone)	5.55	–
Djibouti (Franc)	178	–
Dominica uses E.C. Dollar	2.70	–
Dominican Republic (Peso)	43	–
East Caribbean (Dollar)	2.70	–
East Timor (U.S. Dollar)	1.00	–
Ecuador (U.S. Dollar)	1.00	–
Egypt (Pound)	6.89	–
El Salvador (U.S. Dollar)	1.00	–
Equatorial Guinea uses CFA Franc Central	490	–
Eritrea (Nafka)	15.3	–
Estonia (Euro)	.745	–
Ethiopia (Birr)	19.0	–
Euro	.745	–
Falkland Is. (Pound)	.629	–

Country	#/$	#/$
Faroe Islands (Krona)	5.55	–
Fiji Islands (Dollar)	1.87	–
Finland (Euro)	.745	–
France (Euro)	.745	–
French Polynesia uses CFP Franc	89	–
Gabon (CFA Franc)	490	–
Gambia (Dalasi)	38	–
Georgia (Lari)	1.68	–
Germany (Euro)	.745	–
Ghana (New Cedi)	2.25	–
Gibraltar (Pound)	.629	–
Greece (Euro)	.745	–
Greenland uses Danish Krone	5.55	–
Grenada uses E.C. Dollar	2.70	–
Guatemala (Quetzal)	7.87	–
Guernsey uses Sterling Pound	.629	–
Guinea Bissau uses CFA Franc West	488	–
Guinea Conakry (Franc)	7,005	–
Guyana (Dollar)	212	–
Haiti (Gourde)	42	–
Honduras (Lempira)	20.4	–
Hong Kong (Dollar)	7.75	–
Hungary (Forint)	222	–
Iceland (Krona)	123	–
India (Rupee)	64	–
Indonesia (Rupiah)	11,605	–
Iran (Rial)	24,880	–
Iraq (Dinar)	1,171	–
Ireland (Euro)	.745	–
Isle of Man uses Sterling Pound	.629	–
Israel (New Sheqel)	3.53	–
Italy (Euro)	.745	–
Ivory Coast uses CFA Franc West	488	–
Jamaica (Dollar)	104	–
Japan (Yen)	100	–
Jersey uses Sterling Pound	.629	–
Jordan (Dinar)	.707	–
Kazakhstan (Tenge)	153	–
Kenya (Shilling)	86	–
Kiribati uses Australian Dollar	1.08	–
Korea-PDR (Won)	135	–
Korea-Rep. (Won)	1,071	–
Kuwait (Dinar)	.284	–
Kyrgyzstan (Som)	49	–
Laos (Kip)	7,932	–
Latvia (Lats)	.523	–
Lebanon (Pound)	1,508	–
Lesotho (Maloti)	10.4	–
Liberia (Dollar)	73	–
Libya (Dinar)	1.25	–
Liechtenstein uses Swiss Franc	.918	–
Lithuania (Litas)	2.57	–
Luxembourg (Euro)	.745	–
Macao (Pataca)	7.99	–
Macedonia (New Denar)	46	–
Madagascar (Ariary)	2,256	–
Malawi (Kwacha)	400	–
Malaysia (Ringgit)	3.21	–
Maldives (Rufiya)	15.4	–
Mali uses CFA Franc West	488	–
Malta (Euro)	.745	–
Marshall Islands uses U.S.Dollar	1.00	–
Mauritania (Ouguiya)	298	–
Mauritius (Rupee)	31	–
Mexico (Peso)	13.2	–
Moldova (Leu)	12.9	–
Monaco uses Euro	.745	–
Mongolia (Tugrik)	1,718	–
Montenegro uses Euro	.745	–
Montserrat uses E.C. Dollar	2.70	–
Morocco (Dirham)	8.34	–
Mozambique (New Metical)	30	–
Namibia (Rand)	10.4	–
Nauru uses Australian Dollar	1.08	–
Nepal (Rupee)	98	–
Netherlands (Euro)	.745	–

Country	#/$	#/$
Netherlands Antilles (Gulden)	1.64	–
New Caledonia uses CFP Franc	89	–
New Zealand (Dollar)	1.22	–
Nicaragua (Cordoba Oro)	25	–
Niger uses CFA Franc West	488	–
Nigeria (Naira)	159	–
Northern Ireland uses Sterling Pound	.629	–
Norway (Krone)	6.20	–
Oman (Rial)	.385	–
Pakistan (Rupee)	108	–
Palau uses U.S.Dollar	1.00	–
Panama (Balboa) uses U.S.Dollar	1.00	–
Papua New Guinea (Kina)	2.45	–
Paraguay (Guarani)	4,427	–
Peru (Nuevo Sol)	2.80	–
Philippines (Peso)	43.8	–
Poland (Zloty)	3.13	–
Portugal (Euro)	.745	–
Qatar (Riyal)	3.64	–
Romania (New Leu)	3.32	–
Russia (Ruble)	32.9	–
Rwanda (Franc)	671	–
St. Helena (Pound)	.629	–
St. Kitts uses E.C. Dollar	2.70	–
St. Lucia uses E.C. Dollar	2.70	–
St. Vincent uses E.C. Dollar	2.70	–
Samoa (Tala)	2.32	–
San Marino uses Euro	.745	–
Sao Tome e Principe (Dobra)	18,347	–
Saudi Arabia (Riyal)	3.75	–
Scotland uses Sterling Pound	.629	–
Senegal uses CFA Franc West	488	–
Serbia (Dinar)	85	
Seychelles (Rupee)	12.0	–
Sierra Leone (Leone)	4,312	–
Singapore (Dollar)	1.25	–
Slovakia (Euro)	.745	–
Slovenia (Euro)	.745	–
Solomon Islands (Dollar)	7.17	–
Somalia (Shilling)	1,225	–
Somaliland (Somali Shilling)	1,225	4,000
South Africa (Rand)	10.4	–
Spain (Euro)	.745	–
Sri Lanka (Rupee)	131	–
Sudan (Pound)	4.40	–
Surinam (Dollar)	3.30	–
Swaziland (Lilangeni)	10.4	–
Sweden (Krona)	6.65	–
Switzerland (Franc)	.918	–
Syria (Pound)	140	–
Taiwan (NT Dollar)	30	–
Tajikistan (Somoni)	4.77	–
Tanzania (Shilling)	1,605	–
Thailand (Baht)	32	–
Togo uses CFA Franc West	488	–
Tonga (Pa'anga)	1.82	–
Transdniestra (Ruble)	33	–
Trinidad & Tobago (Dollar)	6.41	–
Tunisia (Dinar)	1.66	–
Turkey (New Lira)	2.05	–
Turkmenistan (Manat)	2.85	–
Turks & Caicos uses U.S. Dollar	1.00	–
Tuvalu uses Australian Dollar	1.08	–
Uganda (Shilling)	2,520	–
Ukraine (Hryvnia)	8.22	–
United Arab Emirates (Dirham)	3.67	–
United Kingdom (Sterling Pound)	.629	–
Uruguay (Peso Uruguayo)	21.5	–
Uzbekistan (Sum)	2,179	–
Vanuatu (Vatu)	96	–
Vatican City uses Euro	.745	–
Venezuela (New Bolivar)	6.29	35
Vietnam (Dong)	21,098	–
Yemen (Rial)	215	–
Zambia (Kwacha)	5.51	–
Zimbabwe (Dollar)	–	–

Standard International Numeral Systems

Prepared especially for the ***Standard Catalog of World Paper Money***© 2013 by Krause Publications

Western	0	½	1	2	3	4	5	6	7	8	9	10	50	100	500	1000
Roman			I	II	III	IV	V	VI	VII	VIII	IX	X	L	C	D	M
Arabic-Turkish	٠	١/٢	١	٢	٣	٤	٥	٦	٧	٨	٩	١٠	٥٠	١٠٠	٥٠٠	١٠٠٠
Malay-Persian	٠	١/٢	۱	۲	۳	۴	۵	۶ or ٦	۷	۸	۹	۱۰	۵۰	۱۰۰	۵۰۰	۱۰۰۰
Eastern Arabic	۰	۱/۲	۱	۲	۳	۴	۵	۶	۷	۸	۹	۱۰	۵۰	۱۰۰	۵۰۰	۱۰۰۰
Hyderabad Arabic	۰	۱/۲	۱	۲	۳	۴	۵	۶	۷	۸	۹	۱۰	۵۰	۱۰۰	۵۰۰	۱۰۰۰
Indian (Sanskrit)	०	१/२	१	२	३	४	५	६	७	८	९	१०	५०	१००	५००	१०००
Assamese	০	১/২	১	২	৩	৪	৫	৬	৭	৮	৯	১০	৫০	১০০	৫০০	১০০০
Bengali	০	১/২	১	২	৩	৪	৫	৬	৭	৮	৯	১০	৫০	১০০	৫০০	১০০০
Gujarati	૦	૧/૨	૧	૨	૩	૪	૫	૬	૭	૮	૯	૧૦	૫૦	૧૦૦	૫૦૦	૧૦૦૦
Kutch	०	१/२	१	२	३	४	५	६	७	८	९	१०	५०	१००	५००	१०००
Devavnagri	०	१/२	१	२	३	४	५	६ or ६	७	८	९ or ९	१०	५०	१००	५००	१०००
Nepalese	०	१/२	१	२	३	४	५	६	७	८	९	१०	५०	१००	५००	१०००
Tibetan	༠	༡/༢	༡	༢	༣	༤	༥	༦	༧	༨	༩	༡༠	༥༠	༡༠༠	༥༠༠	༡༠༠༠
Mongolian	᠐	᠑/᠒	᠑	᠒	᠓	᠔	᠕	᠖	᠗	᠘	᠙	᠑᠐	᠕᠐	᠑᠐᠐	᠕᠐᠐	᠑᠐᠐᠐
Burmese	၀	၁/၂	၁	၂	၃	၄	၅	၆	၇	၈	၉	၁၀	၅၀	၁၀၀	၅၀၀	၁၀၀၀
Thai-Lao	๐	๑/๒	๑	๒	๓	๔	๕	๖	๗	๘	๙	๑๐	๕๐	๑๐๐	๕๐๐	๑๐๐๐
Lao-Laotian	໐		໑	໒	໓	໔	໕	໖	໗	໘	໙	໑໐				
Javanese	꧐		꧑	꧒	꧓	꧔	꧕	꧖	꧗	꧘	꧙	꧑꧐	꧕꧐	꧑꧐꧐	꧕꧐꧐	꧑꧐꧐꧐
Ordinary Chinese Japanese-Korean	零	半	一	二	三	四	五	六	七	八	九	十	十五	百	百五	千
Official Chinese			壹	貳	叁	肆	伍	陸	柒	捌	玖	拾	拾伍	佰	佰伍	仟
Commercial Chinese			〡	〢	〣	〤	〥	〦	〧	〨	〩	十	〥十	〡百	〥百	〡千
Korean		반	일	이	삼	사	오	육	칠	팔	구	십	오십	백	오백	천
Georgian			ა	ბ	გ	დ	ე	ვ	ზ	ჱ	თ	ი	ნ	რ	ფ	ჩ
Georgian			11 ია	20 კ	30 ლ	40 მ	60 ჲ	70 ო	80 პ	90 ჟ	200 ს	300 ტ	400 უ	600 ქ	700 ღ	800 ყ
Ethiopian	◆		፩	፪	፫	፬	፭	፮	፯	፰	፱	፲	፶	፻	፭፻	፲፻
Ethiopian				20 ፳	30 ፴	40 ፵	60 ፷	70 ፸	80 ፹	90 ፺						
Hebrew			א	ב	ג	ד	ה	ו	ז	ח	ט	י	נ	ק	תק	
Hebrew				20 כ	30 ל	40 מ	60 ס	70 ע	80 פ	90 צ	200 ר	300 ש	400 ת	600 תר	700 תש	800 תת
Greek			Α	Β	Γ	Δ	Ε	Τ	Ζ	Η	Θ	Ι	Ν	Ρ	Φ	Α
Greek				20 Κ	30 Λ	40 Μ	60 Ξ	70 Ο	80 Π		200 Σ	300 Τ	400 Υ	600 Χ	700 Ψ	800 Ω

SELECTED PORTRAITS OF ELIZABETH II

Australia, Pound, #34

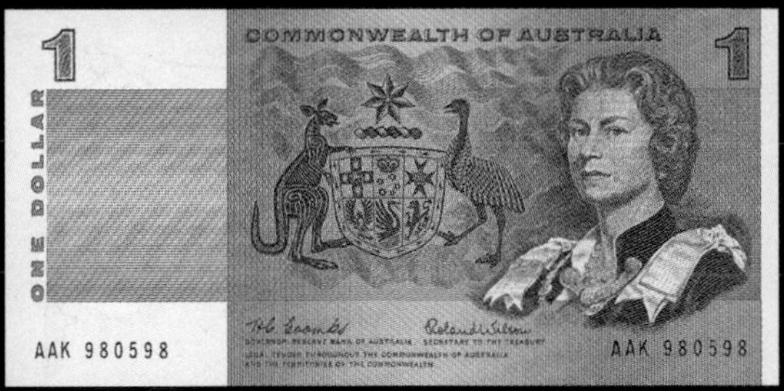

Australia, Pound, #37

Bahamas, 4 Shillings, #13

Bahamas, 3 Dollars, #19

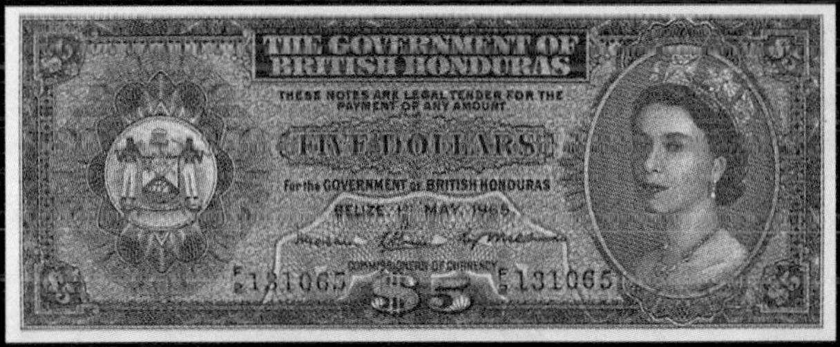

British Honduras, 5 Dollars, #30

Bermuda, 5 Shillings, #18

Bermuda, Dollar, #23

British Caribbean Territories, Dollar, #7

Canada, 2 Dollars, #67

Canada, 5 Dollars, #77

Canada, Dollar, #85

Falkland Islands, Pound, #8

Fiji, Dollar, #53

Fiji, Dollar, #59

Gibraltar, 5 Pounds, #21

Gibraltar, 10 Pounds, #30

Great Britain, 5 Pounds, #375

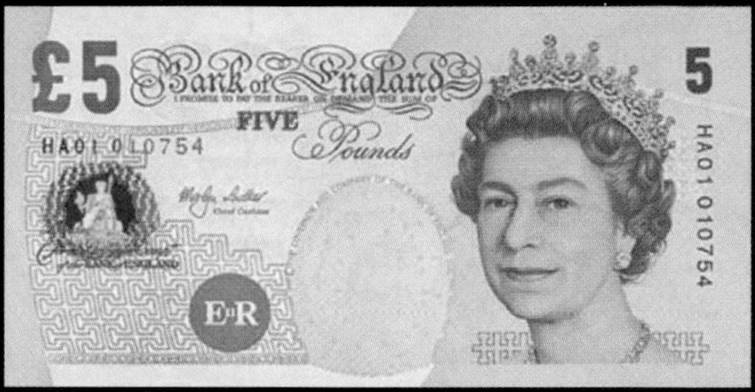

Great Britain, 5 Pounds, #391

Hong Kong, Cent, #325

Isle of Man, Pound, #25

Jamaica, Pound, #51C

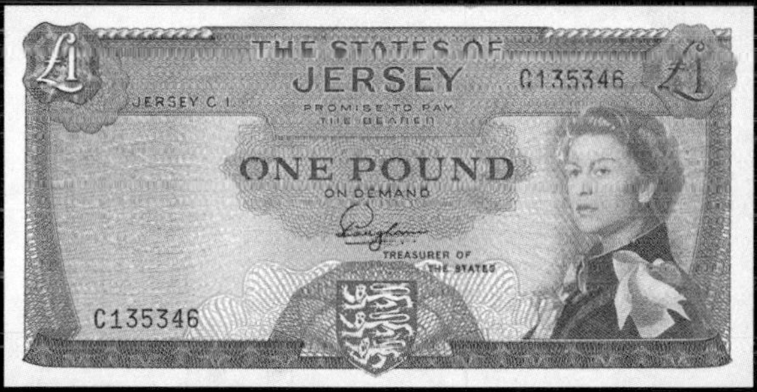

Jersey, Pound, #8

Jersey, 100 Pounds, #37

Malaya and British Borneo, 5 Dollars, #2

Malta, Pound, #26

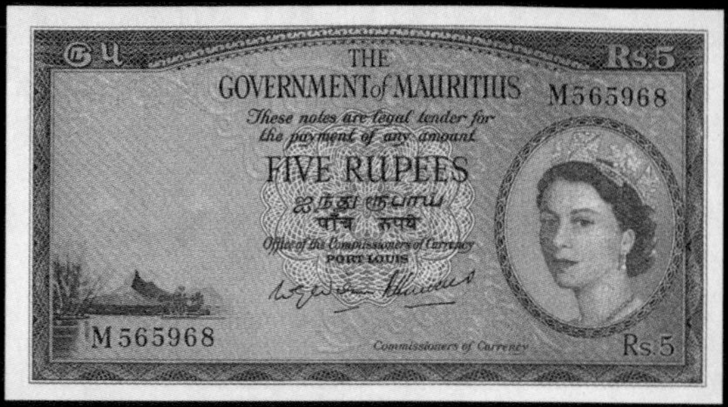

Mauritius, 5 Rupees, #27

New Zealand, Dollar, #163

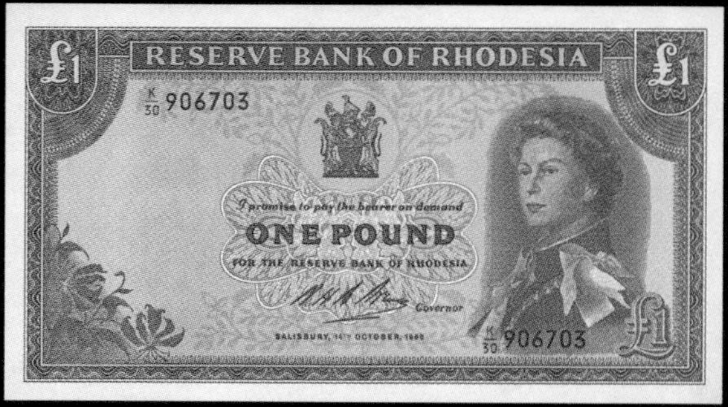

Rhodesia, Pound, #28

St Helena, Pound, #6

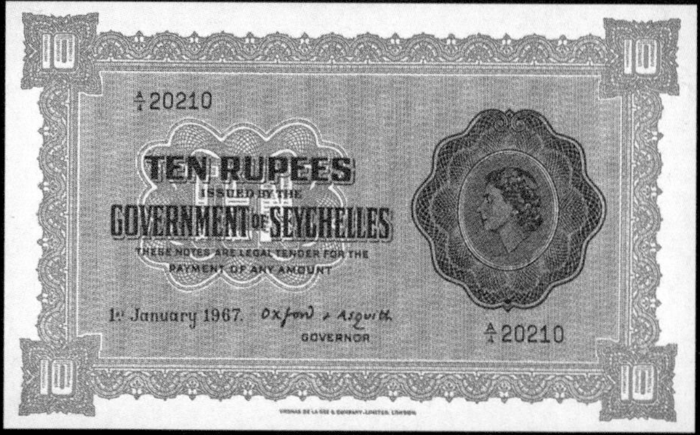

Seychelles, 10 Rupees, #12

Seychelles, 10 Rupees, #15

Trinidad and Tobago, Dollar, #26

SELECTED WORLD BANK NOTES

Australia, 10 Dollars, #49

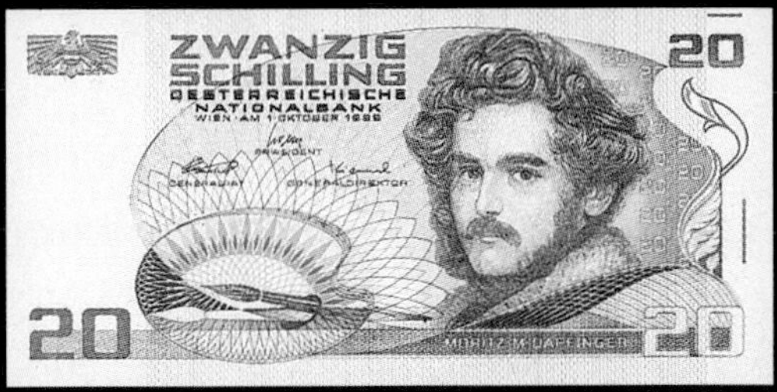

Austria, 20 Schilling, #148

Belgium, 1000 Francs, #144

Brunei, 10 Ringgit, #24

Canada, 100 Dollars, #105

Chad, 5000 Francs, #8

China, 5 Yuan, #886

Cook Islands, 50 Dollars, #10

Comoros, 5000 Francs, #9

Comoros, 1000 Francs, #16

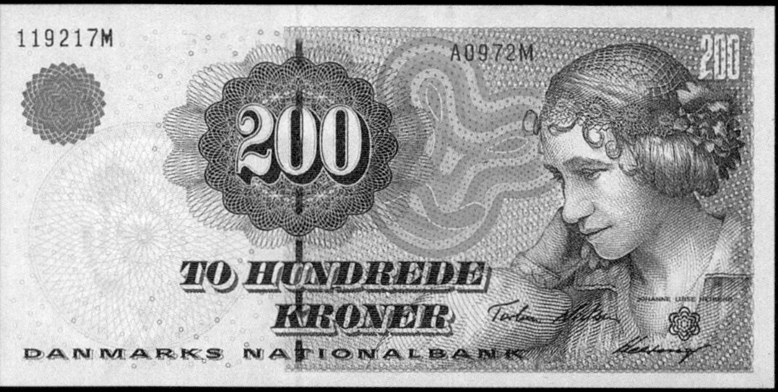

Denmark, 200 Kroner, #57

Dominican Republic, 5 Pesos Oro, #152

European Union, 500 Euro, #7

France, 5 Nouveaux Francs, #141a

Germany – Federal Republic,
1000 Mark, #24s

Ghana, 2000 Cedis, #33

Hong Kong, 20 Dollars, #279b

Hungary, 500 Forint, #194

India, 50 Rupees, #90

Italy, 10,000 Lire, #112d

Japan, 5000 Yen, #101

Lebanon, 100 Livres, #60b

Malaya & British Borneo, 10 Dollars, #9

Netherlands, 100 Gulden, #101

Norway, 1000 Kroner, #35

Papua New Guinea, 20 Kina, #23

Samoa, 1 Pound, #14

Slovakia, 500 Korun, #38

St. Pierre & Miquelon, 1 Nouveau Franc, #30

Sweden, 10 Kronor, #56

Switzerland, 1000 Francs, #52

West African States, 5000 Francs, #104A

A GUIDE TO INTERNATIONAL NUMERICS

	ENGLISH	CZECH	DANISH	DUTCH	ESPERANTO	FRENCH
1/4	quarter	jedna ctvrina	én kvart	een-kwart	unu-kvar'ono	quart
1/2	half	jedna polovinal	én halv	halve	unu-du'one	demi
1	one	jedna	én	een	unu	un
2	two	dve	to	twee	du	deux
3	three	tri	tre	drie	tri	trois
4	four	ctyri	fire	vier	kvar	quatre
5	five	pet	fem	vijf	kvin	cinq
6	six	sest	seks	zes	ses	six
7	seven	sedm	syv	zeven	sep	sept
8	eight	osm	otte	acht	ok	huit
9	nine	devet	ni	negen	nau	neuf
10	ten	deset	ti	tien	dek	dix
12	twelve	dvanáct	tolv	twaalf	dek du	douze
15	fifteen	patnáct	femten	vijftien	dek kvin	quinze
20	twenty	dvacet	tyve	twintig	du'dek	vingt
24	twenty-four	dvacetctyri	fireogtyve	viertentwintig	du'dek kvar	vingt-quatre
25	twenty-five	dvacetpet	femogtyve	vijfentwintig	du'dek kvin	vingt-cinq
30	thirty	tricet	tredive	dertig	tri'dek	trente
40	forty	ctyricet	fyrre	veertig	kvar'dek	quarante
50	fifty	padesát	halvtreds	vijftig	kvin'dek	cinquante
60	sixty	sedesát	tres	zestig	ses'dek	soixante
70	seventy	sedmdesát	halvfjerds	zeventig	sep'dek	soixante-dix
80	eighty	osemdesát	firs	tachtig	ok'dek	quatre-vingt
90	ninety	devadesát	halvfems	negentig	nau'dek	quatre-vingt-dix
100	one hundred	sto	hundrede	honderd	unu-cento	cent
1000	thousand	tisíc	tusind	duizend	mil	mille

	GERMAN	HUNGARIAN	INDONESIAN	ITALIAN	NORWEGIAN	POLISH
1/4	viertel	egy-negyed	satu per empat	quarto	en-fjeerdedel	jedna czwarta
1/2	halb	fél	satu per dua	mezzo	halv	podowa
1	ein	egy	satu	uno	en	jeden
2	zwei	kettö	dua	due	to	dwa
3	drei	három	tiga	tre	tre	trzy
4	vier	négy	empat	quattro	fire	cztery
5	fünf	öt	lima	cinque	fem	piec'
6	sechs	hat	enam	sei	seks	szes'c'
7	sieben	hét	tujuh	sette	sju	siedem
8	acht	nyolc	delapan	otto	atte	osiem
9	neun	kilenc	sembilan	nove	ni	dziewiec'
10	zehn	tíz	sepuluh	dieci	ti	dziesiec'
12	zwölf	tizenketto	dua belas	dodici	tolv	dwanas' cie
15	fünfzehn	tizenöt	lima belas	quindici	femten	pietnas'cie
20	zwanzig	húsz	dua puluh	venti	tjue or tyve	dwadzies'cia
24	vierundzwanzig	húszonégy	dua puluh empat	ventiquattro	tjue-fire or tyve-fire	dwadzies'cia-cztery
25	fünfundzwanzig	huszoöt	dua puluh lima	venticinque	tjue-fem or tyve-fem	dwadzies'cia-piec
30	dreissig	harminc	tiga puluh	trenta	tredve	trydzies'ci
40	vierzig	negyven	empat puluh	quaranta	forti	czterdzies'ci
50	fünfzig	ötven	lima puluh	cinquanta	femti	piec'dziesiat
60	sechzig	hatvan	enam puluh	sessanta	seksti	szes'c'dziesiat
70	siebzig	hetven	tujuh pulu	settanta	sytti	siedemdziesiat
80	achtzig	nyolcyan	delapan puluh	ottonta	åttio	osiemdziesiat
90	neunzig	kilencven	sembilan puluh	novanta	nitti	dziewiec'dziesiat
100	hundert	száz	seratus	cento	hundre	jeden-sto
1000	tausend	ezer	seribu	mille	tusen	tysiac

	PORTUGUESE	ROMANIAN	SERBO-CROATIAN	SPANISH	SWEDISH	TURKISH
1/4	quarto	un-sfert	jedna ceturlina	carto	en-fjärdedel	bir ceyrek
1/2	meio	o-jumatate	jedna polovina	medio	hälft	bir yarim
1	um	un	jedan	uno	en	bir
2	dois	doi	dva	dos	tva	iki
3	trés	trei	tri	tres	tre	üc
4	quatro	patru	cetiri	cuatro	fyra	dört
5	cinco	cinci	pet	cinco	fem	bes
6	seis	sase	sest	seis	sex	alti
7	sete	sapte	sedam	siete	sju	yedi
8	oito	opt	osam	ocho	åtta	sekiz
9	nove	noua	devet	nueve	nio	dokuz
10	dez	zece	deset	diez	tio	on
12	doze	doisprezece	dvanaest	doce	tolv	oniki
15	quinze	cincisprezece	petnaest	quince	femton	onbes
20	vinte	douazeci	dvadeset	veinte	tugu	yirmi
24	vinte-quatro	douacei si patru	dvadeset cetiri	veinticuatro	tjugu fyra	jirmidört
25	vinte-cinco	douacei si cinci	dvadeset pet	veinticinco	tjugu fem	yirmibes
30	trinta	treizeci	trideset	treinta	trettio	otuz
40	quarenta	patruzeci	cetrdeset	cuarenta	fyrtio	kirk
50	cinquenta	cincizeci	padeset	cincuenta	femtio	elli
60	sessenta	saizeci	sezdeset	sesenta	sextio	altmis
70	setenta	saptezeci	sedamdeset	setenta	sjuttio	yetmis
80	oitenta	optzeci	osamdeset	ochenta	åttio	seksen
90	noventa	nouazeci	devedeset	noventa	nittio	doksan
100	cem	suta	sto	cien	hundra	yüz
1000	mil	mie	Serbo hiljada	mil	tusen	bin

Dating

Determining the date of issue of a note is a basic consideration of attribution. As the reading of dates is subject not only to the vagaries of numeric styling, but to variations in dating roots caused by the observation of differing religious eras or regal periods from country to country, making this determination can sometimes be quite difficult. Most countries outside the North African and Oriental spheres rely on Western date numerals and the Christian (AD) reckoning, although in a few instances note dating has been tied to the year of a reign or government.

Countries of the Arabic sphere generally date their issues to the Muslim calendar that commenced on July 16, 622 AD when the prophet Mohammed fled from Mecca to Medina. As this calendar is reckoned by the lunar year of 354, its is about three percent (precisely 3.3 percent) shorter than the Christian year. A conversion formula requires you to subtract that percent from the AH date, and then add 621 to gain the AD date.

A degree of confusion arises here because the Muslim calendar is not always based on the lunar year (AH). Afghanistan and Iran (Persia) used a calendar based on a solar year (SH) introduced around 1920. These dates can be converted to AD by simply adding 621. In 1976, Iran implemented a solar calendar based on the founding of the Iranian monarchy in 559 BC. The first year observed on this new system was 2535(MS) which commenced on March 20, 1976.

Several different eras of reckoning, including the Christian (AD) and Muslim (AH), have been used to date paper money of the Indian subcontinent. The two basic systems are the Vikrama Samvat (VS) era that dates from October 18, 58 BC,. and the Saka (SE) era, the origin of which is reckoned from March 3, 78 AD.

Dating according to both eras appears on notes of several native states and countries of the area.

Thailand (Siam) has observed three different eras for dating. The most predominant is the Buddhist (BE) era originating in 543 BC. Next is the Bangkok or Ratanakosind-sok (RS) era dating from 1781 AD (and consisting of only 3 numerals), followed by the Chula-Sakarat (CS) era dating from 638 AD, with the latter also observed in Burma.

Other calendars include that of the Ethiopian (EE) era that commenced 7 years, 8 months after AD dating, and that of the Hebrew nation beginning on October 7, 3761 BC. Korea claims a dating from 2333 BC which is acknowledged on some note issues.

The following table indicates the years dating from the various eras that correspond to 2012 by Christian (AD) calendar reckoning. It must be remembered that there are overlaps between the eras in some instances:

Christian Era (AD)	—	2012
Mohammedan era (AH)	—	AH1433
Solar year (SH)	—	SH1391
Monarchic Solar era (MS)	—	MS2571
Vikrama Samvat era (VS)	—	SE2068
Saka era (SE)	—	Saka 1933
Buddhist era (BE)	—	BE2555
Bangkok era (RS)	—	RS301
Chula-Sakarat era (CS)	—	CS1374
Ethiopian era (EE)	—	EE2004
Jewish era	—	5772
Korean era	—	4345

Paper money of Oriental origin - principally Japan, Korea, China, Turkestan and Tibet - generally date to the year of the government, dynastic, regnal or cyclical eras, with the dates indicated in Oriental characters usually reading from right to left. In recent years some dating has been according to the Christian calendar and in Western numerals reading from left to right.

More detailed guides to the application of the less prevalent dating systems than those described, and others of strictly local nature, along with the numeral designations employed, are presented in conjunction with the appropriate listings.

Some notes carry dating according to both the locally observed and Christian eras. This is particularly true in the Arabic sphere, where the Muslim date may be indicated in Arabic numerals and the Christian date in Western numerals.

In general the date actually shown on a given paper money issue is indicated in some manner. Notes issued by special Law or Decree will have L or D preceding the date. Dates listed within parentheses may differ from the date appearing on the note; they have been documented by other means. Undated notes are listed with ND, followed by a year only when the year of actual issue is known.

Timing differentials between the 354-day Muslim and the 365-day Christian year cause situations whereby notes bearing dates of both eras have two date combinations that may overlap from one or the other calendar system.

China - Republic 9th year, 1st month, 15th day (15.1.1920), read r. to l.

Russia-1 October 1920

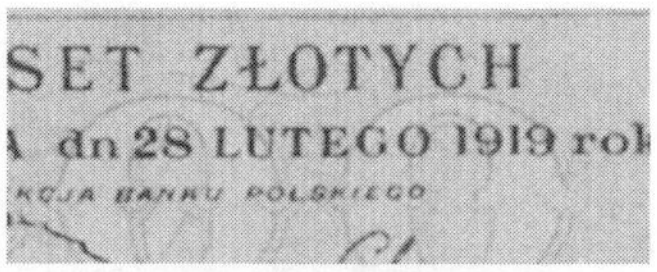

Poland - 28 February 1919

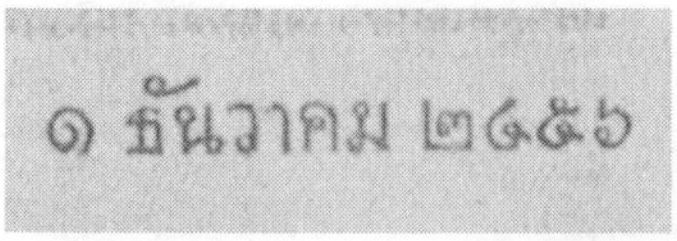

Thailand (Siam) - 1 December 2456

Israel - 1973, 5733

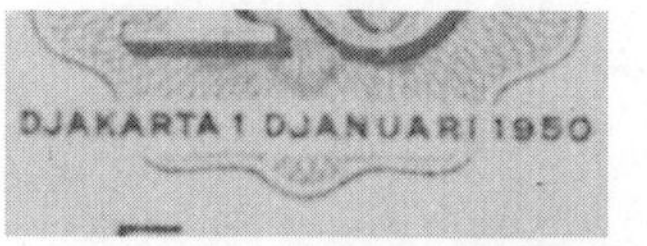

Indonesia - 1 January 1950

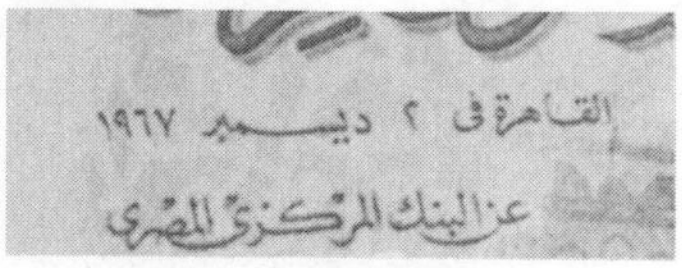
Egypt - 1967 December 2

Korea - 4288 (1955)

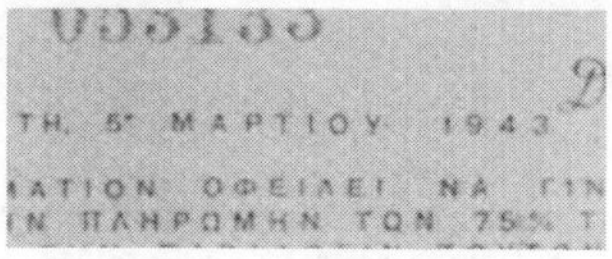
Greece - 5 March 1943

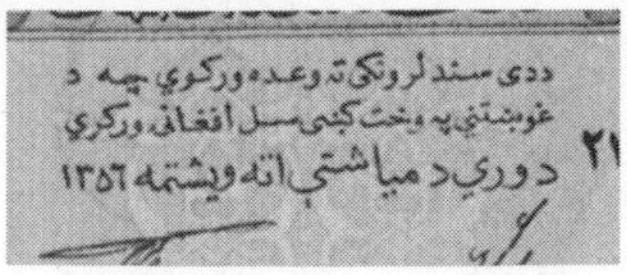
Afghanistan - Solar Year 1356

HEJIRA DATE CONVERSION CHART

HEJIRA (Hijira, Hegira), the name of the Muslim era (A.H. = Anno Hegirae) dates back to the Christian year 622 when Mohammed "fled" from Mecca, escaping to Medina to avoid persecution from the Koreish tribemen. Based on a lunar year the Muslim year is 11 days shorter.

*=Leap Year (Christian Calendar)

AH Hejira	AD Christian Date
1010	1601, July 2
1011	1602, June 21
1012	1603, June 11
1013	1604, May 30
1014	1605, May 19
1015	1606, May 19
1016	1607, May 9
1017	1608, April 28
1018	1609, April 6
1017	1608, April 28
1018	1609, April 6
1019	1610, March 26
1020	1611, March 16
1021	1612, March 4
1022	1613, February 21
1023	1614, February 11
1024	1615, January 31
1025	1616, January 20
1026	1617, January 9
1027	1617, December 29
1028	1618, December 19
1029	1619, December 8
1030	1620, November 26
1031	1621, November 16
1032	1622, November 5
1033	1623, October 25
1034	1624, October 14
1035	1625, October 3
1036	1626, September 22
1037	1627, Septembe 12
1038	1628, August 31
1039	1629, August 21
1040	1630, July 10
1041	1631, July 30
1042	1632, July 19
1043	1633, July 8
1044	1634, June 27
1045	1635, June 17
1046	1636, June 5
1047	1637, May 26
1048	1638, May 15
1049	1639, May 4
1050	1640, April 23
1051	1641, April 12
1052	1642, April 1
1053	1643, March 22
1054	1644, March 10
1055	1645, February 27
1056	1646, February 17
1057	1647, February 6
1058	1648, January 27
1059	1649, January 15
1060	1650, January 4
1061	1650, December 25
1062	1651, December 14
1063	1652, December 2
1064	1653, November 22
1065	1654, November 11
1066	1655, October 31
1067	1656, October 20
1068	1657, October 9
1069	1658, September 29
1070	1659, September 18
1071	1660, September 6
1072	1661, August 27
1073	1662, August 16
1074	1663, August 5
1075	1664, July 25
1076	1665, July 14
1077	1666, July 4
1078	1667, June 23
1079	1668, June 11
1080	1669, June 1
1081	1670, May 21
1082	1671, may 10
1083	1672, April 29
1084	1673, April 18
1085	1674, April 7

AH Hejira	AD Christian Date
1086	1675, March 28
1087	1676, March 16*
1088	1677, March 6
1089	1678, February 23
1090	1679, February 12
1091	1680, February 2*
1092	1681, January 21
1093	1682, January 10
1094	1682, December 31
1095	1683, December 20
1096	1684, December 8*
1097	1685, November 28
1098	1686, November 17
1099	1687, November 7
1100	1688, October 26*
1101	1689, October 15
1102	1690, October 5
1103	1691, September 24
1104	1692, September 12*
1105	1693, September 2
1106	1694, August 22
1107	1695, August 12
1108	1696, July 31*
1109	1697, July 20
1110	1698, July 10
1111	1699, June 29
1112	1700, June 18
1113	1701, June 8
1114	1702, May 28
1115	1703, May 17
1116	1704, May 6*
1117	1705, April 25
1118	1706, April 15
1119	1707, April 4
1120	1708, March 23*
1121	1709, March 13
1122	1710, March 2
1123	1711, February 19
1124	1712, Feburary 9*
1125	1713, January 28
1126	1714, January 17
1127	1715, January 7
1128	1715, December 27
1129	1716, December 16*
1130	1717, December 5
1131	1718, November 24
1132	1719, November 14
1133	1720, November 2*
1134	1721, October 22
1135	1722, October 12
1136	1723, October 1
1137	1724, September 19
1138	1725, September 9
1139	1726, August 29
1140	1727, August 19
1141	1728, August 7*
1142	1729, July 27
1143	1730, July 17
1144	1731, July 6
1145	1732, June 24*
1146	1733, June 14
1147	1734, June 3
1148	1735, May 24
1149	1736, May 12*
1150	1737, May 1
1151	1738, April 21
1152	1739, April 10
1153	1740, March 29*
1154	1741, March 19
1155	1742, March 8
1156	1743, Febuary 25
1157	1744, February 15*
1158	1745, February 3
1159	1746, January 24
1160	1747, January 13
1161	1748, January 2
1162	1748, December 22*
1163	1749, December 11
1164	1750, November 30
1165	1751, November 20
1166	1752, November 8*
1167	1753, October 29
1168	1754, October 18
1169	1755, October 7
1170	1756, September 26*
1171	1757, September 15
1172	1758, September 4
1173	1759, August 25
1174	1760, August 13*
1175	1761, August 2
1176	1762, July 23

AH Hejira	AD Christian Date
1177	1763, July 12
1178	1764, July 1*
1179	1765, June 20
1180	1766, June 9
1181	1767, May 30
1182	1768, May 18*
1183	1769, May 7
1184	1770, April 27
1185	1771, April 16
1186	1772, April 4*
1187	1773, March 25
1188	1774, March 14
1189	1775, March 4
1190	1776, February 21*
1191	1777, February 91
1192	1778, January 30
1193	1779, January 19
1194	1780, January 8*
1195	1780, December 28*
1196	1781, December 17
1197	1782, December 7
1198	1783, November 26
1199	1784, November 14*
1200	1785, November 4
1201	1786, October 24
1202	1787, October 13
1203	1788, October 2*
1204	1789, September 21
1205	1790, September 10
1206	1791, August 31
1207	1792, August 19*
1208	1793, August 9
1209	1794, July 29
1210	1795, July 18
1211	1796, July 7*
1212	1797, June 26
1213	1798, June 15
1214	1799, June 5
1215	1800, May 25
1216	1801, May 14
1217	1802, May 4
1218	1803, April 23
1219	1804, April 12*
1220	1805, April 1
1221	1806, March 21
1222	1807, March 11
1223	1808, February 20*
1224	1809, February 16
1225	1810, Febauary 6
1226	1811, January 26
1227	1812, January 16*
1228	1813, Janaury 26
1229	1813, December 24
1230	1814, December 14
1231	1815, December 3
1232	1816, November 21*
1233	1817, November 11
1234	1818, October 31
1235	1819, October 20
1236	1820, October 9*
1237	1821, September 28
1238	1822, September 18
1239	1823, September 18
1240	1824, August 26*
1241	1825, August 16
1242	1826, August 5
1243	1827, July 25
1244	1828, July 14*
1245	1829, July 3
1246	1830, June 22
1247	1831, June 12
1248	1832, May 31*
1249	1833, May 21
1250	1834, May 10
1251	1835, April 29
1252	1836, April 18*
1253	1837, April 7
1254	1838, March 27
1255	1839, March 17
1256	1840, March 5*
1257	1841, February 23
1258	1842, February 12
1259	1843, February 1
1260	1844, January 22*
1261	1845, January 10
1262	1845, December 30
1263	1846, December 20
1264	1847, December 9
1265	1848, November 27*
1266	1849, November 17
1267	1850, November 6

AH Hejira	AD Christian Date
1268	1851, October 27
1269	1852, October 15*
1270	1853, October 4
1271	1854, September 24
1272	1855, September 13
1273	1856, September 1*
1274	1857, August 22
1275	1858, August 11
1276	1859, July 31
1277	1860, July 20*
1278	1861, July 9
1279	1862, June 29
1280	1863, June 18
1281	1864, June 6*
1282	1865, May 27
1283	1866, May 16
1284	1867, May 5
1285	1868, April 24*
1286	1869, April 13
1287	1870, April 3
1288	1871, March 23
1289	1872, March 11*
1290	1873, March 1
1291	1874, February 18
1292	1875, Febuary 7
1293	1876, January 28*
1294	1877, January 16
1295	1878, January 5
1296	1878, December 26
1297	1879, December 15
1298	1880, December 4*
1299	1881, November 23
1300	1882, November 12
1301	1883, November 2
1302	1884, October 21*
1303	1885, October 10
1304	1886, September 30
1305	1887, September 19
1306	1888, September 7*
1307	1889, August 28
1308	1890, August 17
1309	1891, August 7
1310	1892, July 26*
1311	1893, July 15
1312	1894, July 5
1313	1895, June 24
1314	1896, June 12*
1315	1897, June 2
1316	1898, May 22
1317	1899, May 12
1318	1900, May 1
1319	1901, April 20
1320	1902, april 10
1321	1903, March 30
1322	1904, March 18*
1323	1905, March 8
1324	1906, February 25
1325	1907, February 14
1326	1908, February 4*
1327	1909, January 23
1328	1910, January 13
1329	1911, January 2
1330	1911, December 22
1332	1913, November 30
1333	1914, November 19
1334	1915, November 9
1335	1916, October 28*
1336	1917, October 17
1337	1918, October 7
1338	1919, September 26
1339	1920, September 15*
1340	1921, September 4
1341	1922, August 24
1342	1923, August 14
1343	1924, August 2*
1344	1925, July 22
1345	1926, July 12
1346	1927, July 1
1347	1928, June 20*
1348	1929, June 9
1349	1930, May 29
1350	1931, May 19
1351	1932, May 7*
1352	1933, April 26
1353	1934, April 16
1354	1935, April 5
1355	1936, March 24*
1356	1937, March 14
1357	1938, March 3
1358	1939, February 21
1359	1940, February 10*

AH Hejira	AD Christian Date
1360	1941, January 29
1361	1942, January 19
1362	1943, January 8
1363	1943, December 28
1364	1944, December 17*
1365	1945, December 6
1366	1946, November 25
1367	1947, November 15
1368	1948, November 3*
1369	1949, October 24
1370	1950, October 13
1371	1951, October 2
1372	1952, September 21*
1373	1953, September 10
1374	1954, August 30
1375	1955, August 20
1376	1956, August 8*
1377	1957, July 29
1378	1958, July 18
1379	1959, July 7
1380	1960, June 25*
1381	1961, June 14
1382	1962, June 4
1383	1963, May 25
1384	1964, May 13*
1385	1965, May 2
1386	1966, April 22
1387	1967, April 11
1388	1968, March 31*
1389	1969, march 20
1390	1970, March 9
1391	1971, February 27
1392	1972, February 16*
1393	1973, February 4
1394	1974, January 25
1395	1975, January 14
1396	1976, January 3*
1397	1976, December 23*
1398	1977, December 12
1399	1978, December 2
1400	1979, November 21
1401	1980, November 9*
1402	1981, October 30
1403	1982, October 19
1404	1984, October 8
1405	1984, September 27*
1406	1985, September 16
1407	1986, September 6
1409	1987, August 26
1408	1988, August 14*
1410	1989, August 3
1411	1990, July 24
1412	1991, July 13
1413	1992, July 2*
1414	1993, June 21
1415	1994, June 10
1416	1995, May 31
1417	1996, May 19*
1418	1997, May 9
1419	1998, April 28
1420	1999, April 17
1421	2000, April 6*
1422	2001, March 26
1423	2002, March 15
1424	2003, March 5
1425	2004, February 22*
1426	2005, February 10
1427	2006, January 31
1428	2007, January 20
1429	2008, January 10*
1430	2008, December 29
1431	2009, December 18
1432	2010, December 8
1433	2011, November 27*
1434	2012, November 15
1435	2013, November 5
1436	2014, October 25
1437	2015, October 15*
1438	2016, October 3
1439	2017, September 22
1440	2018, September 12
1441	2019, September 11*
1442	2020, August 20
1443	2021, August 10
1444	2022, July 30
1445	2023, July 19*
1446	2024, July 8
1447	2025, June 27
1448	2026, June 17
1449	2027, June 6*
1450	2028, May25

Country / Bank Identification Guide

Afghanistan / Bank of Afghanistan

Belarus / Belarus National Bank

Algeria / Banque Centrale D' Algerie

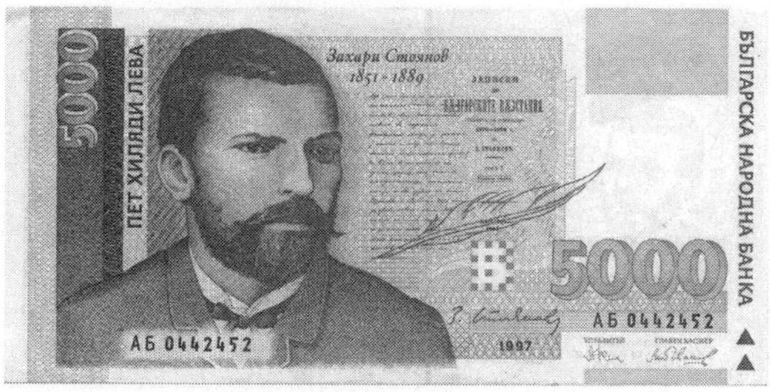

Bulgaria / Bulgarian National Bank

Armenia / Armenia Republic Bank

Cambodia / National Bank of Cambodia

Armenia / Armenia Republic Bank

Georgia / Georgian National Bank

Belarus / Belarus National Bank

Greece / Bank of Greece

Kazakhstan / Kazakhsta National Bank

Mongolia / Mongol Bank

North Korea / Korean Central Bank

Nepal / State Bank

Kyrgystan / Kyrgyz Bank

Thailand / Bank of Thailand

Lao / Bank of the Lao PDR

Transnistria / Banka Nistriana

Libya / Bank of Libya

Uzbekistan / Central Bank of Uzbekistan Republic

Macedonia / National Bank of the Republic of Macedonia

Ukraine / Ukrainian National Bank

International Bank Note Society

The International Bank note Society (IBNS) was formed in 1961 to promote the study and collecting of world paper money. A membership of almost 2,000 in over 90 nations draws on the services of the Society for advancing their knowledge and their collections.

The benefits of the society include the quarterly IBNS Journal, a full color, 80-page magazine featuring learned writings on the notes of the world, their history, artistry and technical background. Additionally each member receives a directory, which lists members by name—with their contact details and collecting interests—as well as by geographic location. The Society conducts auctions in which all members may participate.

One of the greatest strengths of IBNS membership is the facility for correspondence with other members around the world for purposes of exchanging notes, and for obtaining information and assistance with research projects or the identification of notes. Information about the Society can be found at www.theIBNS.org

Application for Membership in the International Bank Note Society

Name: ______________________________

Address: ______________________________

City: ______________________________

Province/State: ______________________________

Postal/Zip Code: ______________________________

Country: ______________________________

Telephone: ______________________________

E-mail: ______________________________

Website: ______________________________

Collecting Interest: ______________________________

Do you want your postal address and web site published in the printed Membership Directory? ❑ Yes ❑ No

Do you want your e-mail address published in the printed Membership Directory? ❑ Yes ❑ No

Do you want your postal address and web site published in the PDF version of the Membership Directory? ❑ Yes ❑ No

Do you want your email address published in the PDF version of the Membership Directory? ❑ Yes ❑ No

Do you want your e-mail address to appear on the IBNS web site? ❑ Yes ❑ No

Are you a banknote dealer? ❑ Yes ❑ No

Type of Membership:

Individual	❑ $US33.00	❑ £20.00	❑ €25
Group	❑ $US33.00	❑ £20.00	❑ €25
Junior (Under 18)	❑ $US16.50	❑ £10.00	❑ €12.50
Family	❑ $US33.00	❑ £20.00	❑ €25

Application for membership must be completed on line at:
www.theIBNS.org

For further information please contact **us-secretary@ibns.biz** or **uk-secretary@ibns.biz**

Specimen notes

To familiarize private banks, central banks, law enforcement agencies and treasuries around the world with newly issued currency, many nations provide special "Specimen" examples of their notes. Specimens are actual bank notes, complete with dummy or all zero serial numbers and signatures bearing the overprinted and/or perforated word "SPECIMEN" in the language of the country of origin itself or where the notes were printed.

Some countries have made specimen notes available for sale to collectors. These include Cuba, Czechoslovakia, Poland and Slovakia after World War II and a special set of four denominations of Jamaica notes bearing red matched star serial numbers. Also, in 1978, the Franklin Mint made available to collectors specimen notes from 15 nations, bearing matching serial numbers and a Maltese cross device used as a prefix. Several other countries have also participated in making specimen notes available to collectors at times.

Aside from these collectors issues, specimen notes may sometimes comand higher prices than regular issue notes of the same type, even though there are far fewer collectors of specimens. In some cases, notably older issues in high denominations, specimens may be the only form of such notes available to collectors today. Specimen notes are not legal tender or redeemable, thus have no real "face value".

The most unusual forms of specimens were produced by Waterlow and Sons. They printed special off colored notes for salesman's sample books adding the word SPECIMEN and their seal.

Some examples of how the word "SPECIMEN" is represented in other languages or on notes of other countries follow:

AMOSTRA: Brazil
CAMPIONE: Italy
CONTOH: Malaysia
EKSEMPLAAR: South Africa
ESPÉCIME: Portugal and Colonies
ESPECIMEN: Various Spanish-speaking nations
GIAY MAU: Vietnam
MINTA: Hungary
MODELO: Brazil
MODEL: Albania
MUSTER: Austria, Germany
MUESTRA: Various Spanish-speaking nations
NUMUNDEDIR GECMEZ: Turkey
ORNEKTIR GECMEZ: Turkey
ОБРАЗЕЦ or **ОБРАЗЕЦЪ:** Bulgaria, Russia, U.S.S.R.
PARAUGS: Latvia
PROFTRYK: Sweden
UZORAK: Croatia
WZOR: Poland
ЗАГВАР: Mongolia

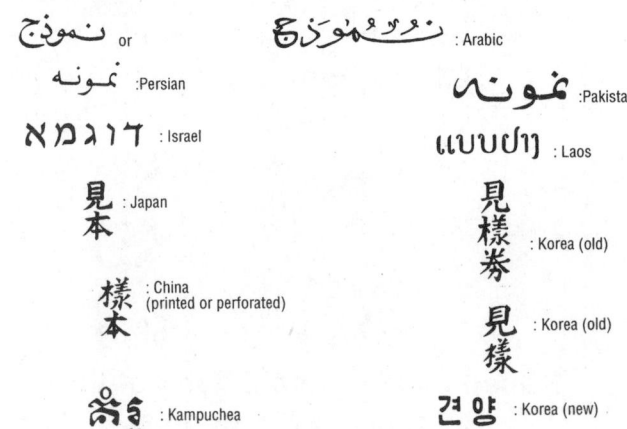

نموذج or نموذج : Arabic
نمونه :Persian
نمونہ :Pakistan
דוגמא : Israel
ແບບຢ່າງ : Laos
見本 : Japan
見樣券 : Korea (old)
樣本 : China (printed or perforated)
見樣 : Korea (old)
គំរូ : Kampuchea
견양 : Korea (new)

English	January	February	March	April	May	June	July	August	September	October	November	December
Albanian	Kallnuer	Fruer	Mars	Prill	Maj	Qershuer	Korrik	Gusht	Shtatuer	Tetuer	Nanduer	Dhetuer
Czech	Leden	Únor	Brezen	Duben	Kveten	Cerven	Cervenec	Srpen	Zári	Ríjen	Listopad	Prosinec
Danish	Januar	Februari	Maart	April	Maj	Juni	Juli	August	September	Oktober	November	December
Dutch	Januari	Februari	Maart	April	Mei	Juni	Juli	Augustus	September	Oktober	November	December
Estonian	Jaanuar	Veebruar	Marts	Aprill	Mai	Juuni	Juuli	August	September	Oktoober	November	Detsember
French	Janvier	Fevrier	Mars	Avril	Mai	Juin	Jillet	Août	Septembre	Octobre	Novembre	Decembre
Finnish	Tammikuu	Helmikuu	Maaliskuu	Huhtikuu	Toukokuu	Kesakuu	Heinakuu	Elokuu	Syyskuu	Lokakuu	Marraskuu	Joulukuu
German	Januar	Februar	Marz	April	Mai	Juni	Juli	August	September	Oktober	November	Dezember
Hungarian	Januar	Februar	Marcius	Aprilis	Majus	Junius	Julius	Augusztus	Szeptember	Oktober	November	December
Indonesian	Djanuari	Februari	Maret	April	Mai	Djuni	Djuli	Augustus	September	Oktober	Nopember	Desember
Italian	Gennaio	Fabbraio	Marzo	Aprile	Maggio	Giugno	Luglio	Agosto	Settembre	Ottobre	Novembre	Dicembre
Lithuanian	Sausis	Vasaris	Kovas	Balandis	Geguzis	Birzelis	Liepos	Rugpiutis	Rugsejis	Spalis	Lapkritis	Gruodis
Norwegian	Januar	Februar	Mars	April	Mai	Juni	Juli	August	September	Oktober	November	Desember
Polish	Styczen	Luty	Marzec	Kwiecien	Maj	Cerwiec	Lipiec	Sierpien	Wrzesien	Pazdziernik	Listopad	Grudzien
Portuguese	Janerio	Fevereiro	Marco	Abril	Maio	Junho	Julho	Agosto	Setembro	Outubro	Novembro	Dezembro
Romanian	Ianuarie	Februarie	Martie	Aprilie	Mai	Iunie	Iulie	August	Septembrie	Octombrie	Noiembrie	Decembrie
Croatian	Sijecanj	Veljaca	Ozujak	Travanj	Svibanj	Lipanj	Srpanj	Kolovoz	Rujan	Listopad	Studeni	Prosinac
Spanish	Enero	Febrero	Marzo	Abril	Mayo	Junio	Julio	Agosto	Septiembre	Octubre	Noviembre	Diciembre
Swedish	Januari	Februari	Mars	April	Maj	Juni	Juli	Augusti	September	Oktober	November	December
Turkish	Ocak	Subat	Mart	Nisan	Mayis	Haziran	Temmuz	Agusto	Eylul	Ekim	Kasim	Aralik
Arabic-New (condensed)	يناير	فبراير	مارس	ابريل	مايو	يونيو	يوليو	أغسطس	سبتمبر	أكتوبر	نوفمبر	ديسمبر
(extended)	يناير	فبراير	مارس	ابريل	مايو	يونيه	يوليه	اغسطس	سبتمبر	اكتوبر	نوفمبر	ديسمبر
Persian (Solar)	فروردين	ارديبهشت	خرداد	تير	مرداد	شهريور	مهر	آبان	آذر	دی	بهمن	اسفند
(Lunar)	محرم	صفر	ربيع الاول	ربيع الثانى	جمادى الاول	جمادى الثانى	رجب	شعبان	رمضان	شوال	ذيقعد	ذوالحجه
Chinese	正月	二月	三月	四月	五月	六月	七月	八月	九月	十月	十一月	十二月
Japanese	月 一	月 二	月 三	月 四	月 五	月 六	月 七	月 八	月 九	月 十	月 十一	月 十二
Greek	Ιανοναριοδ	Φεβροναριοδ	Μαρτιοδ	Απιλιοδ	Μαιοδ	Ιουνιοδ	Ιουλιοδ	Αυγουατοδ	Εεπτεμβπιοδ	Οκτωβπιοδ	Νοεμπιοσ	Δεκεμβριος
Russian	ЯНВАРЬ	ФЕВРАЛЬ	МАРТ	АПРЕЛЬ	МАИ	ИЮНЬ	ИЮЛЕ	АВГУСТ	СЕПТЯБРЬ	ОКТЯБРЬ	НОЯБРЬ	ДЕКАБРЬ
Serbian	Јануар	Фебруар	Марг	Април	Мај	Јун	Јул	Август	Септембар	Октобар	Новембар	Децембар
Ukranian	Січень	Лютий	Березень	Квітень	Травень	Червень	Липень	Серпень	Вересень	Жовтень	Листопад	Грудень
Yiddish	יאַנואַר	פֿעברואַר	מערץ	אַפּריל	מײַ	יוני	יולי	אויגוסט	סעפּטעמבער	אָקטאָבער	נאָװעמבער	דעצעמבער
Hebrew (Israeli)	ינואר	פברואר	מרץ	אפריל	מאי	יוני	יולי	אוגוסט	ספטמבר	אוקטובר	נובמבר	דצמבר

Note: Word spellings and configurations as represented on actual notes may vary significantly from those shown on this chart.

Security Devices

ASCENDING SIZE SERIAL NUMBER - A serial number with each digit slightly increasing in height and width. Both horizontal and vertical formats have been used. Czech Republic and Slovakia are among the countries where this may be found.

BAR CODE AND NUMERALS - Used mainly by banks for checks. Some countries have used these on banknotes. Scotland has a bar code, and Canada has used it with serial numbers. Sometimes magnetic.

COLORED FIBERS - Fibers usually red, blue or green, that are added either into the pulp mix to be randomly flowed onto the paper as it is made, or distributed onto the drying paper in particular areas of the page forming 'bars' of colored fibers, quite visible to the naked eye.

EMBEDDED SECURITY THREAD - A high strength thread, sometimes magnetic, embedded into the paper at the beginning of the drying stage. Looks to the eye as a solid dark strip within the paper.

FACE-BACK OPTICAL REGISTRATION DESIGN (TRANSPARENT REGISTER) - A design technique where half of an image in a framed area is printed on the face, and the other half is printed on the back, in exact register, so when held to a light, the two half images form one full image.

FOIL IMPRINTS - Shaped metal foil applied to the printed note, usually with an adhesive. Sometimes the foil is embossed with an image.

HOLOGRAM - Shiny application to the note containing an image that changes in design and color depending upon the viewing angle.

INVISIBLE PRINTING - Designs printed with inks detectable only when viewed under bright sunlight or ultraviolet light. Sometimes used to replace the more expensive watermark on low value notes.

LATENT IMPRESSIONS -Portions of the note containing sculptured engraving, making some legends or designs visible only when held to the light at certain angles.

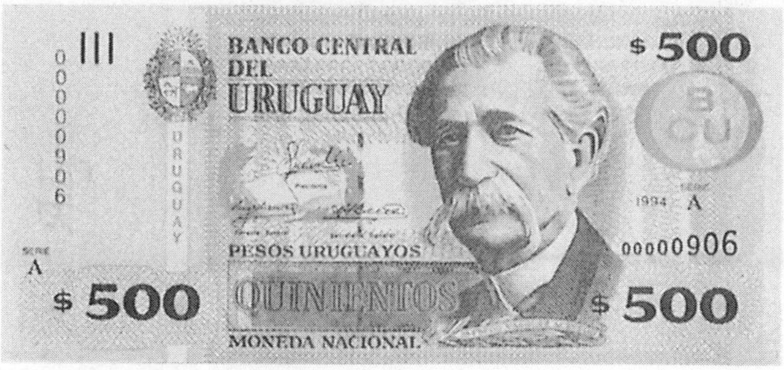

KINEGRAM(r) - Similar to a foil imprint, the design and color changes at different viewing angles.

METALLIC INK - An ink with very fine granules of metal, thus giving the ink a metallic sheen.

MICRO PRINTING - Very small letters added to an intaglio printing plate, sometimes as single lines, or in multiple repeating lines forming a larger block in the underprint design. Intaglio printing keeps the design sharp and clear, but if the note is counterfeit the microprinted area usually becomes muddy and unclear.

OPTICAL VARIABLE DEVICE (OVD) - A foil that displays a three-dimensional image when viewed under proper lighting conditions. Similar to foil imprints.

OPTICALLY VARIABLE INK - An ink when printed in a special pattern changes shades when viewed and then tilted slightly.

PLANCHETTES - Tiny multicolored discs of paper embedded into the pulp mix or randomly sprinkled throughout the paper as it is drying.

RAISED MARKS - A type of braille design in notes, enabling blind people to identify note values.

SEGMENTED SECURITY THREAD -A continuous security thread, usually wide and with lettering, that is added into the paper during the drying process. Once added, a special tool is used to scrape the wet paper off only above the thread, and usually in a particular pattern, thus exposing alternate areas of the embedded thread.

UV-ULTRAVIOLET (FLOURESCENT) - When viewed in a darkened area, and exposed to a special low or high frequency UV light, a design, value, or paper fibers will glow.

WATERMARK - Extensively used as a security measure, the watermark is created by a raised design on a drying cylinder applied towards the end of the paper manufacturing process. The raised design causes a thin area in the paper which when held to the light reveals an image. This image can be words, design, or a portrait. Recent developments have made graduations available. Thus, rather than a light/dark watermark, a gradual light to dark fade can be achieved.

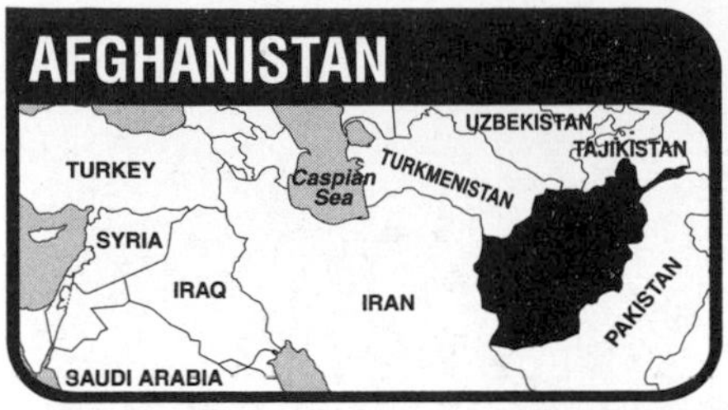

The Islamic Republic of Afghanistan, which occupies a mountainous region of Southwest Asia, has an area of 647,500 sq. km. and a population of 32.74 million. Capital: Kabul. It is bordered by Iran, Pakistan, Tajikistan, Turkmenistan, Uzbekistan and Peoples Republic of China's Sinkiang Province. Agriculture and herding are the principal industries; textile mills and cement factories are recent additions to the industrial sector. Cotton, wool, fruits, nuts, sheepskin coats and hand-woven carpets are exported but foreign trade has been sporadic since 1979.

Ahmad Shah Durrani unified the Pashtun tribes and founded Afghanistan in 1747. The country served as a buffer between the British and Russian empires until it won independence from national British control in 1919. A brief experiment in democracy ended in a 1973 coup and a 1978 Communist counter-coup. The Soviet Union invaded in 1979 to support the tottering Afghan Communist regime, touching off a long and destructive war. The USSR withdrew in 1989 under relentless pressure by internationally supported anti-Communist mujahedin rebels. A series of subsequent civil wars saw Kabul finally fall in 1996 to the Taliban, a hardline Pakistani-sponsored movement that emerged in 1994 to end the country's civil war and anarchy. Following the 11 September 2001 terrorist attacks in New York City, a US, Allied, and anti-Taliban Northern Alliance military action toppled the Taliban for sheltering Osama Bin Ladin. The UN-sponsored Bonn Conference in 2001 established a process for political reconstruction that included the adoption of a new constitution, a presidential election in 2004, and National Assembly elections in 2005. In December 2004, Hamid Karzai became the first democratically elected president of Afghanistan and the National Assembly was inaugurated the following December. Despite gains toward building a stable central government, a resurgent Taliban and continuing provincial instability - particularly in the south and the east - remain serious challenges for the Afghan Government.

RULERS:

Amanullah, SH1298-1307/1919-1929AD
Habibullah Ghazi (rebel, known as Baccha-i-Saqao) SH1347-1348/1929AD
Muhammad Nadir Shah, SH1310-1312/1929-1933AD
Muhammad Zahir Shah, SH1312-1352/1933-1973AD

MONETARY SYSTEM:

1 Rupee = 100 Paise to 1925
1 Rupees = 10 Afghani, 1925-
1 Afghani = 100 Pul
1 Amani = 20 Afghani

Kingdom - Post Rebellion

Bank of Afghanistan

1961-63 Issues

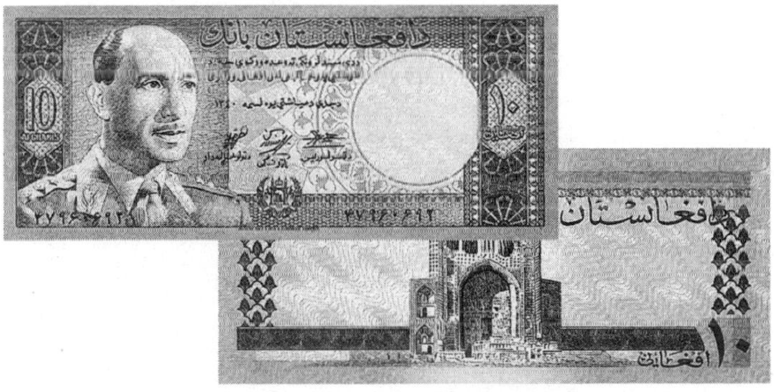

		VF	UNC
37	**10 Afghanis** SH1340 (1961). Brown on multicolor underprint. King Muhammad Zahir(third portrait) at left. Back: Mosque of Khwajeh Mohammad Abu-Nasr Parsa in Balkh at center. Watermark: Muhammad Zahir. Printer: TDLR.		
	a. Issued note.	1.00	6.00
	s. Specimen.	—	75.00

		VF	UNC
38	**20 Afghanis** SH 1340 (1961). Blue on multicolor underprint. King Muhammad Zahir(third portrait) at left. Back: Independence monument in Kabul at center. Watermark: Muhammad Zahir. Printer: TDLR.	1.00	9.00

		VF	UNC
39	**50 Afghanis** SH1340 (1961). Green on multicolor underprint. King Muhammad Zahir(third portrait) at left. Back: Mausoleum of King Nadir Shah in Kabul at center. Watermark: Muhammad Zahir. Printer: TDLR.		
	a. Issued note.	1.50	15.00
	s. Specimen.	—	75.00

		VF	UNC
40	**100 Afghanis** SH1340 (1961). Red on multicolor underprint. King Muhammad Zahir(third portrait) at left. Watermark: Muhammad Zahir. Printer: TDLR.	7.50	32.50

		VF	UNC
40A	**500 Afghanis** SH1340 (1961). Orange on multicolor underprint. King Muhammad Zahir(third portrait) at left. Watermark: Muhammad Zahir. Printer: TDLR.		
	a. Issued note.	50.00	200.
	s. Specimen.	—	125.

		VF	UNC
41	**500 Afghanis** SH1340 (1961); SH1342 (1963). Olive-brown on multicolor underprint. King Muhammad Zahir(third portrait) at left. Watermark: Muhammad Zahir. Printer: TDLR.		
	a. 8 digit serial #. SH1340.	25.00	100.
	b. Serial # with prefix. SH1342.	30.00	150.
	s. Specimen.	—	125.

42	1000 Afghanis	VF	UNC
	SH1340 (1961); SH1342 (1963), Blue-gray on multicolor underprint. King Muhammad Zahir(third portrait) at left. Back: Arch of Qila'-e Bost in Lashkargah at right. Watermark: Muhammad Zahir. Printer: TDLR.		
	a. 8 digit serial #. SH1340.	35.00	200.
	b. Prefix serial #. SH1342.	20.00	150.

1967 Issue

43	50 Afghanis	VF	UNC
	SH1346 (1967). Green on multicolor underprint. King Muhammad Zahir at left. Back: Arg-e Shahi, King's palace at center right. Watermark: Muhammad Zahir. Printer: TDLR without imprint.		
	a. Issued note.	1.50	6.00
	s. Specimen.	—	75.00

44	100 Afghanis	VF	UNC
	SH 1346 (1967). Lilac on multicolor underprint. King Muhammad Zahir at left. Back: Mosque in Kabul at center right. Watermark: Muhammad Zahir. Printer: TDLR without imprint.		
	a. Issued note.	2.50	9.00
	s. Specimen.	—	75.00

45	500 Afghanis	VF	UNC
	SH1346 (1967). Black and dark blue on multicolor underprint. King Muhammad Zahir at left. Back: Qandahar Airport at right. Watermark: Muhammad Zahir. Printer: TDLR without imprint.		
	a. Issued note.	12.50	50.00
	s. Specimen.	—	75.00

46	1000 Afghanis	VF	UNC
	SH1346 (1967). Brown on multicolor underprint. King Muhammad Zahir at left. Watermark: Muhammad Zahir. Printer: TDLR without imprint.		
	a. Issued note.	15.00	80.00
	s. Specimen.	—	75.00

Republic

Bank of Afghanistan

1973-78 Issue

47	10 Afghanis	VF	UNC
	SH1352 (1973); SH1354 (1975); SH1356 (1977). Green on multicolor underprint. President Muhammad Daud at left. Back: Arch of Qila'-e Bost in Lashkargah at center. Watermark: Muhammad Daud.		
	a. SH1352 (1973).	.50	2.25
	b. SH1354 (1975).	.50	2.25
	c. SH1356 (1977).	.50	2.25
	s. Specimen.	—	50.00

48	20 Afghanis	VF	UNC
	SH1352 (1973); SH1354 (1975); SH1356 (1977). Purple on multicolor underprint. President Muhammad Daud at left. Back: Canal at right. Watermark: Muhammad Daud.		
	a. SH1352 (1973).	.50	3.00
	b. SH1354 (1975).	.50	3.00
	c. SH1356 (1977).	.50	3.00
	s. Specimen.	—	50.00

49	50 Afghanis	VF	UNC
	SH1352 (1973); SH1354 (1975); SH1356 (1977). Green on multicolor underprint. President Muhammad Daud at left. Back: Men riding yaks at center. Watermark: Muhammad Daud.		
	a. SH1352 (1973).	1.00	5.00
	b. SH1354 (1975).	1.00	5.00
	c. SH1356 (1977).	1.00	5.00
	s. Specimen.	—	50.00

50	100 Afghanis	VF	UNC
	SH1352 (1973); SH1354 (1975); SH1356 (1977). Brown-lilac on multicolor underprint. President Muhammad Daud at left. Back: Friday Mosque in Herât at center right. Watermark: Muhammad Daud.		
	a. SH1352 (1973).	2.00	14.00
	b. SH1354 (1975).	2.00	14.00
	c. SH1356 (1977).	2.00	14.00
	s. Specimen.	—	50.00

51	500 Afghanis	VF	UNC
	SH1352 (1973), SH1354 (1975). Blue on multicolor underprint. President Muhammad Daud at left. Back: Fortified tribal village at center right. Watermark: Muhammad Daud.		
	a. SH1352 (1973).	3.00	30.00
	b. SH1354 (1975).	3.00	30.00
	s. Specimen.	—	50.00

52	500 Afghanis	VF	UNC
	SH1356 (1977). Brown on multicolor underprint. President Muhammad Daud at left. Back: Fortified tribal village at center right. Watermark: Muhammad Daud.		
	a. Issued note.	5.00	25.00
	s. Specimen.	—	50.00

53	1000 Afghanis	VF	UNC
	SH1352 (1973); SH1354 (1975); SH1356 (1977). Brown on multicolor underprint. President Muhammad Daud at left. Back: Mosque of Mazâr-e Sharîf, the Noble Shrine at center right. Watermark: Muhammad Daud.		
	a. SH1352 (1973).	3.50	25.00
	b. SH1354 (1975).	3.50	25.00
	c. SH1356 (1977).	3.50	25.00

Khalq Democratic Republic

Da Afghanistan Bank

1978 Issue

53A	20 Afghanis	VF	UNC
	AH1357 (1978). Purple on multicolor underprint. With Khalq Government emblem from flag at top left. Back: Fortress at center. Specimen, punched hole cancelled.	—	175.

54	50 Afghanis	VF	UNC
	SH1357 (1978). Blue-green on multicolor underprint. With Khalq Government emblem from flag at top right center. Back: Dar-al-Aman Palace in Kabul.	3.00	20.00

Democratic Republic

Da Afghanistan Bank

1979 Issue

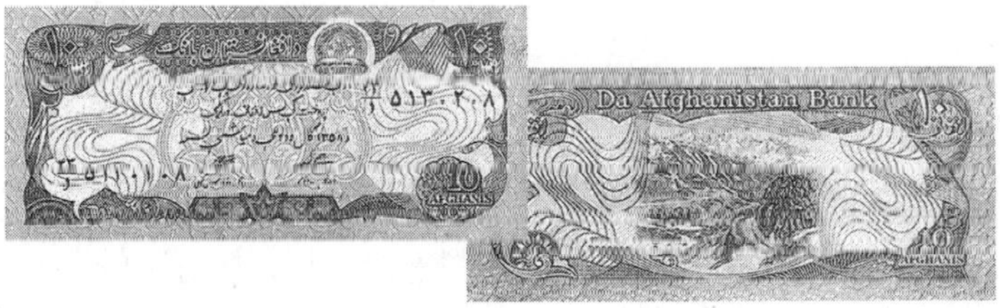

55	10 Afghanis	VF	UNC
	SH1358 (1979). Green and blue on multicolor underprint. Bank arms with horseman at top center right. Back: Mountain road scene at center.		
	a. Issued note.	.20	.75
	s. Specimen. Punch hole cancelled, overprint: *SPECIMEN.*	—	8.00

56	20 Afghanis	VF	UNC
	SH 1358 (1979). Purple on multicolor underprint. Bank arms with horseman at top center right. Signature varieties. Back: Building and mountains at center.		
	a. Issued note.	.25	1.25
	s. Specimen. Punch hole cancelled, overprint *SPECIMEN.*	—	20.00

		VF	UNC
57	**50 Afghanis** SH 1358-70 (1979-91). Greenish black with black text on multicolor underprint. Bank arms with horseman at top center left. Back: Dar-al-Aman Palace in Kabul.		
	a. SH1358 (1979). 2 signature varieties.	.20	1.00
	b. SH1370 (1991).	.25	1.25
	s. Specimen. As a. Punch hole cancelled, overprint: *SPECIMEN.*	—	40.00

		VF	UNC
58	**100 Afghanis** SH1358-70 (1979-91). Deep red-violet on multicolor underprint. Bank arms with horseman at top center. Farm worker in wheat field at right. Back: Hydroelectric dam in mountains at center. UV: threads fluoresce blue, values yellow.		
	a. SH1358 (1979). 2 signature varieties.	.50	2.00
	b. SH1369 (1990).	.50	1.50
	c. SH1370 (1991).	.25	1.25

		VF	UNC
59	**500 Afghanis** SH1358 (1979). Biolet and dark blue on multicolor underprint. Bank arms with horseman at top center; horsemen competing in Buzkashi at right. Back: Fortress at Kabul at left center.	2.00	12.00

		VF	UNC
60	**500 Afghanis** SH1358-70 (1979-91). Reddish-brown, deep green and deep brown on multicolor underprint. Bank arms with horseman at top center; horsemen competing in Buzkashi at right. Back: Deep green on multicolor underprint. Fortress at Kabul at left center. UV: threads fluoresce blue.		
	a. SH1358 (1979).	.75	2.00
	b. SH1369 (1990).	1.00	4.00
	c. SH1370 (1991).	.25	1.00

		VF	UNC
61	**1000 Afghanis** SH1358-70 (1979-91). Dark brown and deep red-violet on multicolor underprint. Bank arms with horseman at top center; Mosque at Mazar-e-Sharif at right. Back: Victory Arch near Kabul at left center.		
	a. SH1358 (1979).	2.50	5.00
	b. SH1369 (1990).	.50	2.50
	c. SH1370 (1991). UV: Face value fluoresce orange. One or two letter characters in series denominator.	.25	1.25

1993 Issue

		VF	UNC
62	**5000 Afghanis** SH1372 (1993). Violet and blue-black on multicolor underprint. Mosque with minaret at right. Bank arms with horseman at top center. Back: Tomb of King Habibullah, Jalalabad at center. Watermark: Bank arms. UV: Fibers fluoresce green, red; face: value yellow, serial #s red, security thread red.	.50	3.00
63	**10,000 Afghanis** SH1372 (1993). Black, deep olive-green and deep blue-green on multicolor underprint. Bank arms with horseman at top left center; gateway between minarets at right. Back: Arched gateway at Bost in center. Watermark: Bank arms. UV: Fibers fluoresce green, red; face: value green, serial #s red.		
	a. Without small space between *Da* and *Afghanistan* on back.	.75	4.00
	b. With small space between *Da* and *Afghanistan* on back.	.50	2.00

Republic (2001)

Da Afghanistan Bank

2002 Issue

1000 'old' afghani = 1 'new' afghani.

		VF	UNC
64	**1 Afghani** SH1381 (2002); SH1383 (2004). Purple on multicolor underprint. Bank arms with horseman at top left center; bank name around ancient coin, cornucopia pair below. Back: Mosque at Mazar-i Sharif at center. Watermark: Bank arms. 131x55mm.		
	a. SH1381 (2002).	FV	.50
	b. SH1383 (2004).	FV	.50

		VF	UNC
65	**2 Afghanis** SH1381 (2002); SH1383 (2004). Slate blue on multicolor underprint. Bank name around ancient coin, cornucopia pair below. Back: Victory Arch in Paghman Gardens near Kabul. 131x55mm.		
	a. SH1381 (2002).	FV	.50
	b. SH1383 (2004).	FV	.50
	s. Specimen.	—	10.00

66 **5 Afghanis** — VF UNC

SH1381 (2002); SH1383 (2004). Olive on multicolor underprint. Bank name around ancient coin, cornucopia pair below. Back: Bala Hissar Fortress in Kabul at center. 131x55mm.

	VF	UNC
a. SH1381 (2002).	FV	.75
b. SH1383 (2004).	FV	.75

67 **10 Afghanis** — VF UNC

SH1381 (2002); SH1383 (2004). Green and brown on multicolor underprint. Ahmed Shah Durrashi Mausoleum in Kandahar at right. Back: Victory Arch in Paghman Gardens near Kabul at center. Segmented security thread. 106x56mm.

	VF	UNC
a. SH1381 (2002).	FV	1.25
b. SH1383 (2004).	FV	1.25
c. SH1383 (2004). Signature Noorullah Delawari and Anwar ul-Haq Ahady).	FV	1.00

68 **20 Afghanis** — VF UNC

SH1381 (2002); SH1383 (2004). Green and purple on multicolor underprint. Rowza Sultan Mahmud of Ishazni's Tomb at right. Back: Arg-e Shahi, King's Palace at center. 140x58mm.

	VF	UNC
a. SH1381 (2002).	FV	1.50
b. SH1383 (2004).	FV	1.50
c. SH1383 (2004). Signature Noorullah Delawari and Anwar ul-Haq Ahady.	FV	1.25

69 **50 Afghanis** — VF UNC

SH1381 (2002); SH1383 (2004); SH1387 (2008). Green and brown on multicolor underprint. Shah Do Shamira Mosque at right. Back: Salang Pass at center. 144x60mm.

	VF	UNC
a. SH1381 (2002).	FV	3.00
b. SH1383 (2004).	FV	3.00
c. SH1387 (2008). Cornerstone watermarks. Slight color change in center.	FV	2.00
d. SH1389 (2010).	FV	2.00

70 **100 Afghanis** — VF UNC

SH1381 (2002); SH1383 (2004). Pule Khighti Mosque at right. Back: Arch at Qila'-e Bost. 148x62mm.

	VF	UNC
a. SH1381 (2002).	FV	5.00
b. SH1383 (2004).	FV	5.00

71 **500 Afghanis** — VF UNC

SH 1381; SH1383. Violet and blue on multicolor underprint. Khwaja Abdullah Ansari in Herat at right, bank seal above. Back: Kandahar Airport control tower at center. Printer: G&D. 152x64mm.

	VF	UNC
a. SH 1381 (2002).	FV	17.50
b. SH 1383 (2004).	FV	17.50

72 **1000 Afghanis** — VF UNC

SH 1381; SH 1383. Orange and brown on yellow and multicolor underprint. Mazaz e-Sharif Shrine of Hazrat Ali at right, bank seal above. Back: Mausoleum of Ahmad Shah Durani in Kandahar at center. Printer: G&D. 156x66mm.

	VF	UNC
a. SH 1381 (2002).	FV	35.00
b. SH 1383 (2004).	FV	35.00

2004 Issue

No.	Denomination	VF	UNC
73	**500 Afghanis** SH1383 (2004). Violet and blue on multicolor underprint. Masjid-i Jami' (Friday Mosque) in Herat at right, bank seal above. Left end value at top. Back: Kandahar Airport control tower at center. Printer: G&D. 152x64mm.	FV	17.50
74	**1000 Afghanis** SH1383 (2004). Orange and brown on yellow and multicolor underprint. Blue Mosque in Mazari Sharif at right, bank seal above. Left end value at top. Signatrue varieties. Back: Mausoleum ofr Ahmad Shah Durrani in Kandahar at center. Printer: G&D. 158x66mm.	FV	35.00

2004; 2008 Issue

75 **100 Afghanis** — VF — UNC

SH 1387 (2008); SH 1389 (2010). Purple and multicolor. Pul-e Khishti Mosque in Kabul at right, bank seal above. Segmented security thread. Back: Arch at Qila'-e Bost at center. Printer: TDLR. 148x62mm.

	VF	UNC
a. SH 1387 (2008).	FV	5.00
b. SH 1389 (2010).	FV	5.00

76 **500 Afghanis** — VF — UNC

SH 1383 (2004). Blue and multicolor. Masjid-i Jami' (Friday Mosque) in Herat at right, bank seal above. Holographic strip at left center. Back: Kandahr Airport control tower at center. Windowed security thread. Printer: TDLR.

	VF	UNC
a. SH1383 (2004).	FV	17.50
b. SH1389 (2010).	FV	17.50

77 **1000 Afghanis**

SH 1387 (2008); SH 1389 (2010). Orange and multicolor. Blue Mosque in Mazari Sharif at right, bank seal above. Holographic strip at left center. Back: Mausoleum of Ahmad Shah Durrani in Kandahar at center. Windowed security thread. Printer: TDLR. 158x66mm.

	VF	UNC
a. SH 1387 (2008).	FV	50.00
b. SH 1389 (2010).	FV	45.00

The Republic of Albania, a Balkan republic bounded by the rump Yugoslav state of Montenegro and Serbia, Macedonia, Greece and the Adriatic Sea, has an area of 11,100 sq. mi. (28,748 sq. km.) and a population of 3.5 million. Capital: Tirana. The country is mostly agricultural, although recent progress has been made in the manufacturing and mining sectors. Petroleum, chrome, iron, copper, cotton textiles, tobacco and wood products are exported.

Since it had been part of the Greek and Roman Empires, little is known of the early history of Albania. After the disintegration of the Roman Empire, Albania was overrun by Goths, Byzantines, Venetians and Turks. Skanderbeg, the national hero, resisted the Turks and established an independent Albania in 1443, but in 1468 the country again fell to the Turks and remained part of the Ottoman Empire for more than 400 years.

Independence was re-established by revolt in 1912, and the present borders established in 1913 by a conference of European powers which, in 1914, placed Prince William of Wied on the throne; popular discontent forced his abdication within months. In 1920, following World War I occupancy by several nations, a republic was set up. Ahmet Zogu seized the presidency in 1925, and in 1928 proclaimed himself king with the title of Zog I. King Zog fled when Italy occupied Albania in 1939 and enthroned King Victor Emanuel of Italy. Upon the surrender of Italy to the Allies in 1943, German troops occupied the country. They withdrew in 1944, and communist partisans seized power, naming Gen. Enver Hoxha provisional president. In 1946, following a victory by the communist front in the 1945 elections, a new constitution modeled on that of the USSR was adopted. In accordance with the constitution of Dec. 28, 1976, the official name of Albania was changed from the People's Republic of Albania to the People's Socialist Republic of Albania. A general strike by trade unions in 1991 forced the communist government to resign. A new government was elected in March 1992. In 1997 Albania had a major financial crisis which caused civil disturbances and the fall of the administration.

Peoples Republic

Banka e Shtetit Shqiptar

1964 Issue

33 **1 Lek** — VF — UNC

1964. Green and deep blue on multicolor underprint. Peasant couple at center. Back: Shkoder fortress at left center; arms at upper right. Watermark: Curved BSHSH repeated.

	VF	UNC
a. Issued note.	1.00	4.00
s. Specimen overprint: *MODEL* or *SPECIMEN.*	—	3.00

34 **3 Lekë** — VF — UNC

1964. Brown and lilac on multicolor underprint. Woman with basket of grapes at left. Back: Vlora view at left center; arms at upper right. Watermark: Curved BSHSH repeated.

	VF	UNC
a. Issued note.	1.00	6.00
s. Specimen overprint: *MODEL* or *SPECIMEN.*	—	4.00

35 **5 Lekë** — VF — UNC

1964. Purple and dark blue on multicolor underprint. Truck and steam passenger train crossing viaduct at left center. Back: Ship at left; arms at upper right. Watermark: Curved BSHSH repeated.

	VF	UNC
a. Issued note.	2.00	8.00
s. Specimen overprint: *MODEL* or *SPECIMEN.*	—	5.00

36 10 Lekë VF UNC

1964. Dark green on multicolor underprint. Woman working with cotton spinning frame. Back: People outside the palace of culture at left center, Naim Frashëre portrait and arms at upper right. Watermark: Curved BSHSH repeated.

	VF	UNC
a. Issued note.	3.00	10.00
s. Specimen overprint: *MODEL* or *SPECIMEN*.	—	6.00

37 25 Lekë

1964. Blue-black on multicolor underprint. Peasant woman with sheaf at left, combine and truck at center. Back: Farm tractor at left center. Watermark: Curved BSHSH repeated.

	VF	UNC
a. Issued note.	4.00	15.00
s. Specimen overprint: *MODEL* or *SPECIMEN*.	—	7.50

38 50 Lekë VF UNC

1964. Red-brown on multicolor underprint. Soldiers on parade at left center, bust of Skanderbeg at upper right. Back: Rifle and pick axe at left, modern apartment building under construction at left center; arms at upper right. Watermark: Curved BSHSH repeated.

	VF	UNC
a. Issued note.	8.00	25.00
s. Specimen overprint: *MODEL* or *SPECIMEN*.	—	8.50

39 100 Lekë VF UNC

1964. Brown-lilac. Worker and boy at hydroelectric dam at left center. Back: Steel worker and well rigger at center; arms at upper right. Watermark: Curved BSHSH repeated.

	VF	UNC
a. Issued note.	15.00	40.00
s. Specimen overprint: *MODEL* or *SPECIMEN*.	—	10.00

Peoples Socialist Republic

Banka e Shtetit Shqiptar

1976 Issue

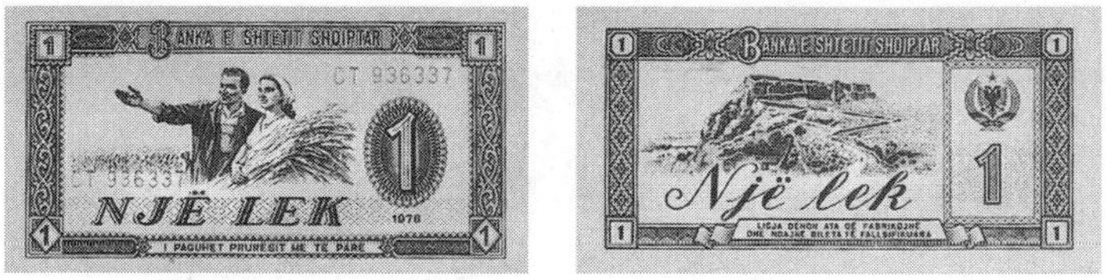

40 1 Lek VF UNC

1976. Green and deep blue on multicolor underprint. Peasant couple at center. Back: Shkoder fortress at left center. Arms at upper right. Watermark: Bank name around radiant star, repeated.

	VF	UNC
a. Issued note.	.50	2.00
s1. Red overprint: *SPECIMEN* with all zeros serial #.	—	3.50
s2. Red overprint: *SPECIMEN* with normal serial #.	—	.50
s3. Large blue overprint: *SPECIMEN* on face. Black overprint: *E PRANUESHME* on back.	—	—

41 3 Lekë VF UNC

1976. Brown and lilac on multicolor underprint. Woman with basket of grapes at left. Back: Saranda view at left center. Arms at upper right. Watermark: Bank name around radiant star, repeated.

	VF	UNC
a. Issued note.	.50	3.00
s1. Red overprint: *SPECIMEN* with all zeros serial #.	—	4.00
s2. Red overprint: *SPECIMEN* with normal serial #.	—	.75

42 5 Lekë VF UNC

1976. Lilac and blue on multicolor underprint. Truck and steam passenger train crossing viaduct at left center. Back: Ship at left; arms at upper right. Watermark: Bank name around radiant star, repeated.

	VF	UNC
a. Issued note.	1.00	5.00
s1. Red overprint: *SPECIMEN* with all zeros serial #.	—	4.50
s2. Red overprint: *SPECIMEN* with normal serial #.	—	1.00
s3. Large blue overprint: *SPECIMEN* on face. Black overprint: *E PRANUESHME* on back.	—	—

43 10 Lekë VF UNC

1976. Dark green on multicolor underprint. Woman working with cotton spinning frame. Back: People at left center, male portrait at upper right. Arms at upper right. Watermark: Bank name around radiant star, repeated.

	VF	UNC
a. Issued note.	1.00	8.00
s1. Red overprint: *SPECIMEN* with all zeros serial #.	—	5.50
s2. Red overprint: *SPECIMEN* with normal serial #.	—	1.25

44 25 Lekë VF UNC

1976. Blue-black on multicolor underprint. Peasant woman with sheaf at left. Combine and truck at center. Back: Farm tractor at left center. Arms at upper right. Watermark: Bank name around radiant star, repeated.

	VF	UNC
a. Issued note.	2.00	10.00
s1. Red overprint: *SPECIMEN* with all zeros serial #.	—	6.50
s2. Red overprint: *SPECIMEN* with normal serial #.	—	1.75

45 50 Lekë VF UNC

1976. Red-brown on multicolor underprint. Soldiers on parade at left center, bust of Skanderbeg at upper right. Back: Rifle and pick axe at left, modern building under construction at left center. Arms at upper right. Watermark: Bank name around radiant star, repeated.

	VF	UNC
a. Serial # prefix without serifs. Chinese printing.	2.00	15.00
b. Serial # prefix with serifs. Crossbar of 4 is thicker than bottom serif. (1st European printing).	2.50	20.00
c. Serial # prefix with serifs. Crossbar of 4 is same thickness as bottom serif. (2nd European printing).	2.00	15.00
s1. Red overprint: *SPECIMEN* with all zeros serial #.	—	7.50
s2. Red overprint: *SPECIMEN* with normal serial #.	—	2.50
s3. Large blue overprint: *SPECIMEN* on face. Black overprint: *E PRANUESNHME* on back.	—	—

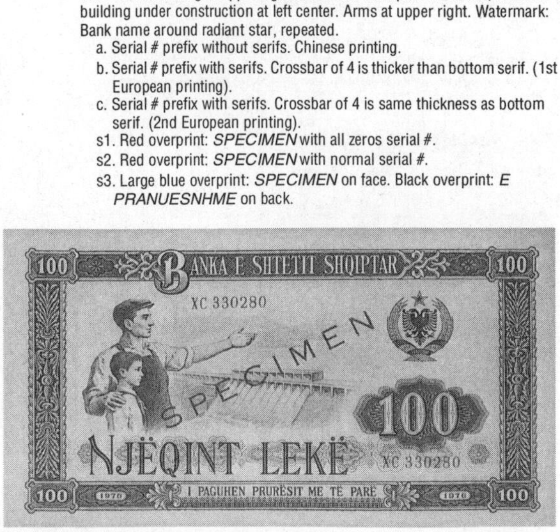

46 100 Lekë VF UNC

1976. Brown-lilac on multicolor underprint. Worker and boy at hydroelectric dam at left center. Back: Steel worker and well rigger at center. Arms at upper right. Watermark: Bank name around radiant star, repeated.

	VF	UNC
a. Issued note.	3.00	20.00
s1. Red overprint: *SPECIMEN* with all zeros serial #.	—	8.50
s2. Red overprint: *SPECIMEN* with normal serial #.	—	3.00

ND Issue

46A 100 Lekë VF UNC

ND. Steel workers at left, steel mill at center. Back: Oil well derricks at left center, arms at upper right.

	VF	UNC
a. Blue and dull red on light green and light yellow underprint. Specimen only.	—	250.
b. Brown and dull red on light green and light yellow underprint. Specimen only.	—	250.

1991 Issue

47 100 Lekë VF UNC

1991. Deep brown and deep purple on pale orange and multicolor underprint. Steel workers at left, steel mill at right. Back: Refinery at left center; arms at upper right. Watermark: Bank name around radiant star, repeated.

	VF	UNC
a. Issued note.	3.00	15.00
s. Specimen.	—	5.00

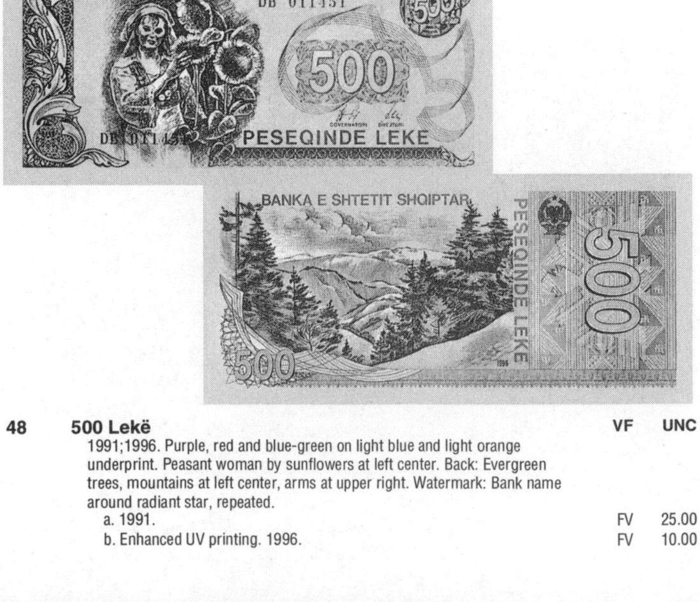

48 500 Lekë VF UNC

1991;1996. Purple, red and blue-green on light blue and light orange underprint. Peasant woman by sunflowers at left center. Back: Evergreen trees, mountains at left center, arms at upper right. Watermark: Bank name around radiant star, repeated.

	VF	UNC
a. 1991.	FV	25.00
b. Enhanced UV printing. 1996.	FV	10.00

1992 ND Issue

48A **1 Lek Valutë (= 50 Lekë)** VF UNC
ND (1992). Purple and gray-green on multicolor underprint. Steelworker at center. Back: Electrical transmission towers at left, arms at upper center, hydroelectric generator at right. Watermark: B.SH.SH. below star, repeated. (Not issued). FV 40.00

49 **10 Lek Valutë (= 500 Lekë)**
ND (1992). Deep green and purple on multicolor underprint. Steelworker at center. Back: Electrical transmission towers at left, arms at upper center, hydroelectric generator at right. Watermark: B.SH.SH. below star, repeated.

	VF	UNC
a. With serial #.	5.00	20.00
b. Without serial #.	5.00	20.00
s. Specimen.	—	—

50 **50 Lek Valutë (= 2500 Lekë)**
ND (1992). Deep brown-violet and gray-green on multicolor underprint. Steelworker at center. Back: Electrical transmission towers at left, arms at upper center, hydroelectric generator at right. Watermark: B.SH.SH. below star, repeated.

	VF	UNC
a. With serial #.	20.00	60.00
b. Without serial #.	6.00	25.00
s. Specimen.	—	25.00

Republic

Banka e Shqiperise

1992 Issue

52 **200 Lekë**
1992. Deep reddish-brown on multicolor underprint. Ismail Qemali at left. Back: Citizens portrayed in double-headed eagle outline. Watermark: Repeated ring of letters B.SH.SH. 162x78mm.

	VF	UNC
a. Issued note.	4.00	15.00
s. Specimen.	—	—

53 **500 Lekë**
1992. Deep blue on blue and multicolor underprint. Naim Frashëri at left. Back: Poetry of Frashëri: Rural mountains at left, candle at center. Watermark: Repeated ring of letters B.SH.SH. 170x78mm.

	VF	UNC
a. Issued note.	8.00	25.00
s. Specimen.	—	—

54 **1000 Lekë**
1992. Deep green and green on multicolor underprint. Skanderbeg at left. Back: Kruja Castle at left, crowned arms at center. Watermark: Repeated ring of letters B.SH.SH. 178x78mm.

	VF	UNC
a. Issued note.	18.00	40.00
s. Specimen.	—	12.00

1993-94 Issue

55	100 Lekë	VF	UNC
	1993-96. Purple on multicolor underprint. L. Kombetar at left. Back: Mountain peaks at left center, Lanner Falcon at center. 154x72mm.		
	a. 1993.	7.50	30.00
	b. 1994.	4.00	8.00
	c. Enhanced U-V printing. 1996.	3.50	5.00
	s. Specimen.	—	2.50

56	200 Lekë	VF	UNC
	1994. Deep reddish brown on multicolor underprint. Ismail Qemali at left. Back: Citizens portrayed in double-headed eagle outline. 162x78mm.		
	a. Issued note.	3.00	10.00
	s. Specimen.	—	6.00

57	500 Lekë	VF	UNC
	1994. Deep blue on blue and multicolor underprint. Naim Frashëri at left. Back: Frashëri poetry: Rural mountains at left, candle at center. 170x78mm.		
	a. Issued note.	8.00	20.00
	s. Specimen.	—	10.00
58	1000 Lekë		
	1994. Deep green on green and multicolor underprint. Skanderbeg at left. Back: Kruja Castle at left, crowned arms at center. 178x78mm.		
	a. Issued note.	18.00	40.00
	s. Specimen.	—	12.50

1995-96 Issue

59	200 Lekë	VF	UNC
	1996. Deep reddish brown on multicolor underprint. Ismail Qemali at left. Segmented foil over security thread. Back: Citizens portrayed in double-headed eagle outline. 162x78mm.		
	a. Issued note.	3.00	10.00
	s. Specimen. Red overprint: *SPECIMEN*.	—	40.00
60	500 Lekë		
	1996. Deep blue on blue and multicolor underprint. Naim Frashëri at left. Segmented foil over security thread. Back: Frashëri poetry: Rural mountains at left, candle at center. 170x78mm.		
	a. Issued note.	8.00	15.00
	s. Specimen. Red overprint: *SPECIMEN*.	—	50.00

61	1000 Lekë	VF	UNC
	1995-96. Deep green and green on multicolor underprint. Skanderbeg at left. Segmented foil over security thread. Back: Kruja Castle at left, crowned arms at center. 178x78mm.		
	a. 1995. Olive-green signature	18.00	30.00
	b. 1995. Black signature	18.00	20.00
	c. 1996. Black signature	18.00	20.00
	s. Specimen. As c. Red overprint: *SPECIMEN*.	—	90.00

1996 Issue

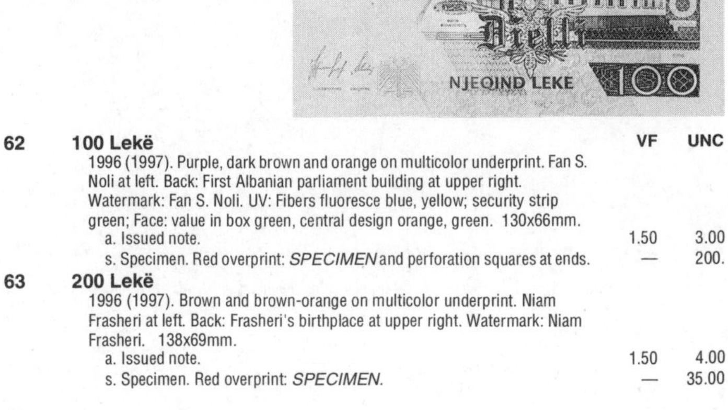

62	100 Lekë	VF	UNC
	1996 (1997). Purple, dark brown and orange on multicolor underprint. Fan S. Noli at left. Back: First Albanian parliament building at upper right. Watermark: Fan S. Noli. UV: Fibers fluoresce blue, yellow; security strip green; Face: value in box green, central design orange, green. 130x66mm.		
	a. Issued note.	1.50	3.00
	s. Specimen. Red overprint: *SPECIMEN* and perforation squares at ends.	—	200.
63	200 Lekë		
	1996 (1997). Brown and brown-orange on multicolor underprint. Niam Frasheri at left. Back: Frasheri's birthplace at upper right. Watermark: Niam Frasheri. 138x69mm.		
	a. Issued note.	1.50	4.00
	s. Specimen. Red overprint: *SPECIMEN*.	—	35.00

64 **500 Lekë** — VF | UNC

1996 (1997). Dark blue, purple and brown on multicolor underprint. Ismail Qemali at left. Back: Conference table and movie projector at center, Independence house in Vlora at upper right. Watermark: Ismail Qemali. 146x69mm.

	VF	UNC
a. Issued note.	5.00	10.00
s. Specimen. Red overprint: *SPECIMEN.*	—	60.00

65 **1000 Lekë**

1996 (1997); 1999. Green and dark green on multicolor. Pjeter Bogdani at left. Back: Church of Vau i Dejes at upper right. Watermark: Pjeter Bogdani. 153x72mm. — 12.50 | 20.00

66 **5000 Lekë**

1996 (1999). Olive green and multicolor. Skanderbeg at left. Back: Kruja castle, equestrian statue, and crown. Watermark: Skanderbeg. 160x72mm.

	VF	UNC
a. Issued note.	40.00	120.
s. Specimen. Red overprint: *SPECIMEN*	—	225

2001 Issue

67 **200 Lekë** — VF | UNC

2001. Brown and brown-orange on multicolor underprint. N. Frasheri at left. Back: Frasheri's birthplace at upper right. Watermark: N. Frasheri. 138x69mm. — FV | 3.00

68 **500 Lekë** — VF | UNC

2001. Dark blue, purple and brown on multicolor underprint. I. Qemali at left. Back: Independence House at upper right, conference table and movie projector at center. Watermark: I. Qemali. 146x69mm. — FV | 8.00

69 **1000 Lekë** — VF | UNC

2001. Green and dark green on multicolor underprint. P. Bogadani at left. Back: Sun at center, Church of Vau i Dejes at upper right . Watermark: P. Bogadani. 153x72mm. — FV | 18.00

70 **5000 Lekë** — VF | UNC

2001 (2004). Olive green and multicolor. Skanderbeg at left. Back: Kruja castle, equestrian statue, and crown. Watermark: Skanderbeg. 160x72mm. — FV | 110.

2007 Issue

71 **200 Lekë** — VF | UNC

2007. Brown on multicolor underprint. Naim Frasheri at left. Back: Poem manuscript and Frasheri's birthplace. Watermark: N. Frasheri. Printer: TDLR. 138x69mm. — FV | 4.00

72 **500 Lekë**

2007. Blue on multicolor underprint. Ismail Qemali at left. Back: House were Independence was declared. Watermark: I. Qemali. Printer: TDLR. 145x68mm. — FV | 7.00

73 **1000 Lekë**

2007, 2011. Green on multicolor underprint. Pjeter Bogdani at left, sunburst at center. Back: Bogdani's heliocentric system, church in Vau i Dejës. Watermark: P. Bogdani. Printer: TDLR. 151x72mm.

	VF	UNC
a. 2007.	FV	20.00
b. 2011.	FV	25.00

74 **2000 Lekë**

2007. Violet and brown on multicolor underprint. Mbreti Gent at left. Back: Butrint amphitheater near Sarandë at right. Watermark: M. Gent. Printer: TDLR. 160x72mm. — FV | 30.00

75 **5000 Lekë**

2007. Brown and yellow on multicolor underprint. Gjergi Kastrioti at left. Back: Kruja Castle at right. Watermark: Skanderbeg. Printer: TDLR. 160x72mm. — FV | 80.00

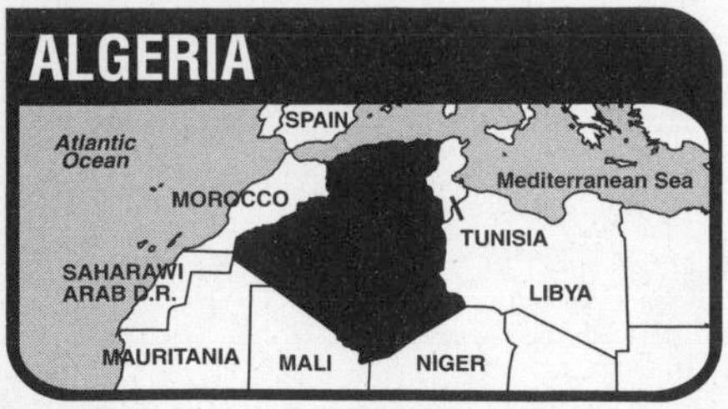

The Republic of Albania, a Balkan republic bounded by the rump Yugoslav state of Montenegro and Serbia, Macedonia, Greece and the Adriatic Sea, has an area of 11,100 sq. mi. (28,748 sq. km.) and a population of 3.5 million. Capital: Tirana. The country is mostly agricultural, although recent progress has been made in the manufacturing and mining sectors. Petroleum, chrome, iron, copper, cotton textiles, tobacco and wood products are exported.

Since it had been part of the Greek and Roman Empires, little is known of the early history of Albania. After the disintegration of the Roman Empire, Albania was overrun by Goths, Byzantines, Venetians and Turks. Skanderbeg, the national hero, resisted the Turks and established an independent Albania in 1443, but in 1468 the country again fell to the Turks and remained part of the Ottoman Empire for more than 400 years.

Independence was re-established by revolt in 1912, and the present borders established in 1913 by a conference of European powers which, in 1914, placed Prince William of Wied on the throne; popular discontent forced his abdication within months. In 1920, following World War I occupancy by several nations, a republic was set up. Ahmet Zogu seized the presidency in 1925, and in 1928 proclaimed himself king with the title of Zog I. King Zog fled when Italy occupied Albania in 1939 and enthroned King Victor Emanuel of Italy. Upon the surrender of Italy to the Allies in 1943, German troops occupied the country. They withdrew in 1944, and communist partisans seized power, naming Gen. Enver Hoxha provisional president. In 1946, following a victory by the communist front in the 1945 elections, a new constitution modeled on that of the USSR was adopted. In accordance with the constitution of Dec. 28, 1976, the official name of Albania was changed from the People's Republic of Albania to the People's Socialist Republic of Albania. A general strike by trade unions in 1991 forced the communist government to resign. A new government was elected in March 1992. In 1997 Albania had a major financial crisis which caused civil disturbances and the fall of the administration.

RULERS:

French to 1962

MONETARY SYSTEM:

1 Franc = 100 Centimes to 1960
1 Nouveau Franc = 100 Old Francs, 1959-64
1 Dinar = 100 Centimes, 1964-

FRENCH ADMINISTRATION

BANQUE DE L'ALGÉRIE

1959 ISSUE

		VF	UNC
118	**5 Nouveaux Francs** 1959. Green and multicolor. Ram at bottom center, Bacchus at right. Back: Like #106.		
	a. 31.7.1959; 18.12.1959.	85.00	340.
	s. Specimen. 31.7.1959.	—	175.

		VF	UNC
119	**10 Nouveaux Francs** 1959-61. Brown and yellow. Isis at right. Back: Like #104.		
	a. 31.7.1959-2.6.1961.	100.	350.
	s. Specimen. 31.7.1959.	—	185.

		VF	UNC
120	**50 Nouveaux Francs** 1959. Multicolor. Pythian Apollo at left, penal code shows at bottom center. Back: Like #109.		
	a. 31.7.1959; 18.12.1959.	175.	550.
	s. Specimen. 31.7.1959.	—	400.

		VF	UNC
121	**100 Nouveaux Francs** 1959-61. Blue and multicolor. Seagulls with city of Algiers in background. Back: Like #110.		
	a. 31.7.1959; 18.12.1959.	225.	600.
	b. 3.6.1960; 25.11.1960; 10.2.1961; 2.6.1961; 29.9.1961.	115.	425.
	s. Specimen. 31.7.1959.	—	200.

Republic

Banque Centrale d'Algérie

1964 Issue

		VF	UNC
122	**5 Dinars** 1.1.1964. Purple and lilac. Griffon vulture, tawny eagle perched on rocks at left center. Back: Sheep herder and native objects. Watermark: Amir Abd el-Kader. Two styles of numerals in date and serial number.		
	a. Issued note.	50.00	250.
	s. Specimen.	—	100.

		VF	UNC
123	**10 Dinars** 1.1.1964. Lilac and multicolor. Pair of storks and minaret. Back: Carpert weavers. Watermark: Amir Abd el-Kader. 2 styles of numerals in date and serial #.		
	a. Issued note.	20.00	100.
	s. Specimen.	—	100.

		VF	UNC
124	**50 Dinars** 1.1.1964. Light brown and multicolor. 2 mountain sheep. Back: Camel caravan. Watermark: Amir Abd el-Kader.		
	a. Issued note.	25.00	100.
	s. Specimen.	—	150.

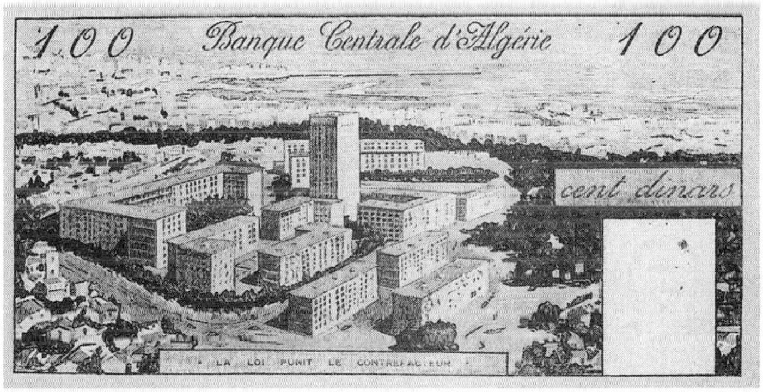

		VF	UNC
125	**100 Dinars** 1.1.1964. Multicolor. Port of d'Algers harbor scene. Back: Modern building complex at left center on back. Watermark: Amir Abd el-Kader. 2 styles of numerals in date and serial #.		
	a. Issued note.	20.00	80.00
	s. Specimen.	—	200.

1970 Issue

		VF	UNC
126	**5 Dinars** 1.11.1970. Blue and multicolor. Warrior with shield and sword at center right. Back: Ruppel's sand fox at left center, village in background at center right. Watermark: Amir Abd el-Kader. Signature varieties.		
	a. Issued note.	6.00	20.00
	s. Specimen.	—	30.00

127	10 Dinars	VF	UNC
	1.11.1970. Red-brown and multicolor. Sheep at left, peacock at right. Back: Seated elderly man at left, ornate building at right. Minor plate varieties in French text. Watermark: Amir Abd el-Kader.		
	a. Issued note.	6.00	25.00
	s. Specimen.	—	30.00

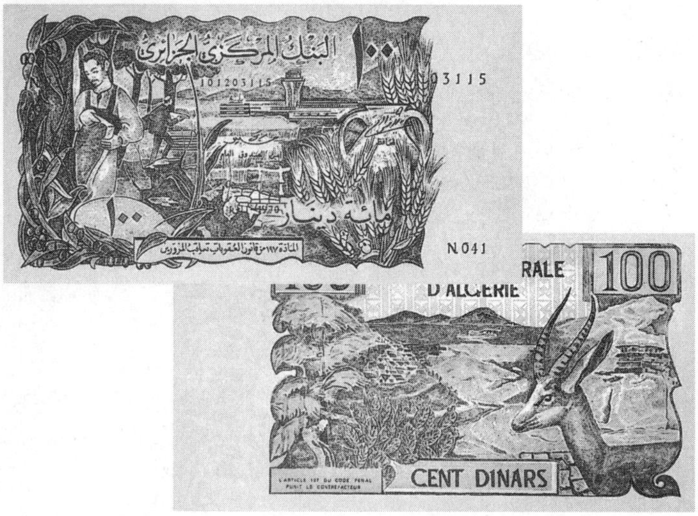

128	100 Dinars	VF	UNC
	1.11.1970. Brown, brown-orange, blue-gray and pale yellow-orange. Two men at at left, airport at center, wheat ears at right. Back: Scenery with edmi gazelle at right.		
	a. Deep brown.	12.50	55.00
	b. light brown.	10.00	45.00
	s. Specimen.	—	50.00

129	500 Dinars	VF	UNC
	1.11.1970. Purple. View of city. Back: Galleon and fortress.		
	a. Issued note.	20.00	75.00
	s. Specimen.	—	50.00

1977; 1981 Issue

130	50 Dinars	VF	UNC
	1.11.1977. Dark green on multicolor underprint. Shepherd with flock at lower left center. 3 Signature varieties. Back: Farm tractor. Watermark: Amir Abd el-Kader.		
	a. Issued note.	2.50	10.00
	s. Specimen.	—	25.00

131	100 Dinars	VF	UNC
	1.11.1981. Dark blue and aqua on light blue underprint. Village with minarets at left. 3 Signature varieties. Back: Man working with plants at center. Watermark: Amir Abd el-Kader.		
	a. Issued note.	4.00	12.50
	s. Specimen.	—	50.00

1982-83 Issue

132	10 Dinars	VF	UNC
	2.12.1983. Black on brown and blue-green underprint. Diesel passenger train at center. Back: Blue, Blue-green and brown. Mountain village at center. Watermark: Amir Abd el-Kader. UV: security strip fluoresce blue.		
	a. Issued note.	.75	3.50
	s. Specimen.	—	25.00

133	20 Dinars	VF	UNC
	2.1.1983. Red-brown on ochre underprint. Vase at left center, handcrafts at right. Back: Tower at center. Watermark: Amir Abd el-Kader.		
	a. Issued note.	1.00	5.00
	s. Specimen.	—	40.00

134 100 Dinars VF UNC

8.6.1982. Pale blue and gray. Similar to #131 but without bird at upper right. Back: Man working with plants at center. Watermark: Amir Abd el-Kader.

	VF	UNC
a. Issued note.	17.50	50.00
s. Specimen.	—	75.00

135 200 Dinars VF UNC

23.3.1983. Brown and dark green on multicolor underprint. Back: Monument to the Algerian martyrs at left, bridge over canyon at center, amphora at right. Watermark: Amir Abd el-Kader.

	VF	UNC
a. Issued note.	5.00	20.00
s. Specimen.	—	100.

Banque d'Algérie

1992 Dated (1995; 1996) Issue

137 100 Dinars VF UNC

21.5.1992 (1996). Dark blue with black text on pale blue and multicolor underprint. Battle of El Harrach, army charging at right. Back: Seal with horsemen charging at left, ancient galley at center. Watermark: Horse's head. 131x72mm. FV 7.50

138 200 Dinars VF UNC

21.5.19921996). Dark brown and red-brown on multicolor underprint. Back: Koranic school at center right, building at center. Watermark: Horse's head. UV: security strip fluoresce blue; back: design elements green. 141x72mm. FV 12.50

139 500 Dinars VF UNC

21.5.1992 (1996). Deep purple, violet and red-violet on multicolor underprint. Hannibal's troops and elephants engaging the Romans at center right. Back: Waterfalls at left, tomb ruins of Numid King Massinissa at left center, elephant mounted troops at center right. Watermark: Elephant heads. 151x72mm. FV 30.00

140 1000 Dinars VF UNC

21.5.1992 (1995). Red-brown and orange on multicolor underprint. Tassili cave carvings of animals at lower center, water buffalo's head at right. Back: Hoggar cave painting of antelope at left, ruins at center. Watermark: Water buffalo head. 160x72mm. FV 50.00

1998 Dated (2000) Issue

		VF	UNC
141	**500 Dinars** 10.6.1998. Deep purple, violet and red-violet on multicolor underprint. Hannibal's troops and elephants engaging the Romans at center right, waterfalls at left, tomb ruins of Numid King Massinissa at left center. Holographic band at left center. 2 Signature varieties. Back: Elephant mounted troops at center right. UV: security strip fluoresce blue; face: either side of foil yellow, design elements pink. 151x72mm.	FV	20.00

		VF	UNC
142	**1000 Dinars** 1992; 1998. Red-brown, grey-green and orange on multicolor underprint. Tassili cave carvings of animals at lower center, water buffalo's head at right. Holographic band at left center. Back: Hoggar cave painting of antelope at left, ruins at center. 160x72mm.		
	a. 21.5.1992.	15.00	60.00
	b. 6.10.1998. 2 Signature varieties.	FV	35.00

2005 Commemorative Issue

		VF	UNC
143	**1000 Dinars** 22.3.2005. Red-brown and orange on multicolor underprint. Arab League's 60th Anniversary seal and holographic band added. 160x72mm.	FV	45.00

2011 Issue

		VF	UNC
144	**2000 Dinars** 24.3.2011. Blue-green and multicolor.	FV	65.00

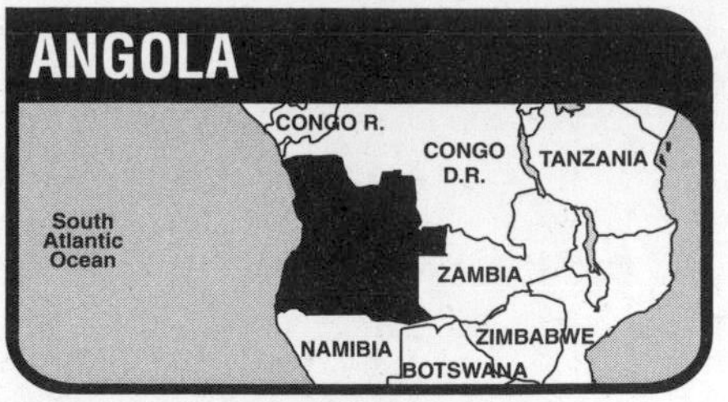

The Peoples Republic of Angola, a country on the west coast of southern Africa bounded by Zaïre, Zambia and Namibia (South-West Africa), has an area of 1.25 million sq. km. and a population of 12.53 million, predominantly Bantu in origin. Capital: Luanda. Most of the people are engaged in subsistence agriculture. However, important oil and mineral deposits make Angola potentially one of the richest countries in Africa. Iron and diamonds are exported.

Angola is rebuilding its country after the end of a 27-year civil war in 2002. Fighting between the Popular Movement for the Liberation of Angola (MPLA), led by Jose Eduardo Dos Santos, and the National Union for the Total Independence of Angola (UNITA), led by Jonas Savimbi, followed independence from Portugal in 1975. Peace seemed imminent in 1992 when Angola held national elections, but UNITA renewed fighting after being beaten by the MPLA at the polls. Up to 1.5 million lives may have been lost - and 4 million people displaced - in the quarter century of fighting. Savimbi's death in 2002 ended UNITA's insurgency and strengthened the MPLA's hold on power. President Dos Santos has announced legislative elections will be held in September 2008, with presidential elections planned for sometime in 2009.

RULERS:

Portuguese to 1975

MONETARY SYSTEM:

1 Milreis = 1000 Reis = 20 Macutas to 1911
100 Centavos - 1 Escudo, 1911
1 Escudo = 1 Milreis
1 Escudo = 100 Centavos, 1954-77
1 Kwanza = 100 Lwei, 1977-95
1 Kwanza Reajustado = 1,000 "old" Kwanzas, 1995-

SIGNATURE VARIETIES

1	Governor	Administrator
2	Governor	Administrator
3	Governor	Administrator
4	Governor	Vice-Governor
5	Governor	Vice-Governor
6	Governor	Vice-Governor
7	Governor	Administrator
8	Governor	Administrator
9	Governor	Administrator
10	Governor	Administrator

SIGNATURE VARIETIES

11	Governor	Vice-Governor
12	Governor	Administrator
13	Governor	Administrator
14	Governor	Vice-Governor
15	Governor	Vice-Governor
16	Governor	Vice-Governor
17	Governor	Vice-Governor
18	Governor	Vice-Governor
19	Governor	Vice-Governor
20	Governor	Administrator

STEAMSHIP SEALS

Type I
LOANDA

Type II
LISBOA

Type III
C,C,A

C,C,A = Colonias, Commercio, Agricultura.

Portuguese Administration

Banco de Angola

1962 Issue

		VF	UNC
92	**20 Escudos** 10.6.1962. Black on multicolor underprint. Portrait of Americo Tomas at right, dock at left. Signature 1. Back: Gazelles running. Printer: TDLR.	10.00	40.00

		VF	UNC
93	**50 Escudos** 10.6.1962. Light blue on multicolor underprint. Portrait of Americo Tomas at right, airport at left. Signature 2. Back: Various animals at water hole. Printer: TDLR.	12.50	50.00
94	**100 Escudos** 10.6.1962. Lilac on multi color underprint. Portrait of Americo Tomas at right, Salazar bridge at left. Signature 3. Back: Elephants at watering hole.	30.00	125.
95	**500 Escudos** 10.6.1962. Red on multicolor underprint. Portrait of Americo Tomas at left or right, Port of LUanda at center. Signature 4. Back: 2 Black rhinoceros. Printer: TDLR.	50.00	325.
96	**1000 Escudos** 10.6.1962. Blue on multicolor underprint. Portrait of Americo Tomas at left or right, dam at center. Signature 4. Back: Herd. Printer: TDLR.	45.00	260.

1970 Issue

		VF	UNC
97	**500 Escudos** 10.6.1970. Red on multicolor underprint. Portrait of Americo Tomas at left, Port of Luanda at center. Signature 5. Back: 2 Rhinoceros. Printer: TDLR.	40.00	215.
98	**1000 Escudos** 10.6.1970. Blue on multicolor underprint. Portrait of Americo Tomas at left or right, dam at center. Signature 5. Back: Herd. Printer: TDLR.	45.00	225.

1972 Issue

		VF	UNC
99	**20 Escudos** 24.11.1972. Red and brown on multicolor underprint. Arms at left, M. Carmona at center right. Signature 7. Back: Flowers. Watermark: M. Carmona. Printer: TDLR.	1.25	6.50

No.	Description	VF	UNC
100	**50 Escudos** 24.11.1972. Green and brown on multicolor underprint. Arms at left, M. Carmona at center right. Signature 8. Back: Plants. Watermark: M. Carmona. Printer: TDLR.	1.25	6.50

No.	Description	VF	UNC
101	**100 Escudos** 24.11.1972. Light and dark brown on multicolor underprint. Arms at left, M. Carmona at center right. Signature 7. Back: Tree and plants. Watermark: M. Carmona. Printer: TDLR.	1.50	6.50

No.	Description	VF	UNC
102	**500 Escudos** 24.11.1972. Blue on multicolor underprint. Arms at left, M. Carmona at center right. Signature 6. Back: Rock formation at Pungo Andongo at center right. Watermark: M. Carmona. Printer: TDLR.	5.00	20.00

No.	Description	VF	UNC
103	**1000 Escudos** 24.11.1972. Purple on multicolor underprint. Arms at left, M. Carmona at center right. Signature 5. Back: Waterfall. Watermark: M. Carmona. Printer: TDLR.	6.00	37.50

1973 Issue

No.	Description	VF	UNC
104	**20 Escudos** 10.6.1973. Blue, purple and green on multicolor underprint. Luiz de Camoes at right. Signature 10. Back: Cotton plant. Watermark: Luiz de Camoes.		
	a. Issued note.	5.00	32.50
	s. Specimen.	—	75.00
	ct. Color trial.	—	225.

No.	Description	VF	UNC
105	**50 Escudos** 10.6.1973. Blue and brown on multicolor underprint. Luiz de Camoes at right. Signature 9. Back: Plant. Watermark: Luiz de Camoes.		
	a. Issued note.	1.00	5.00
	s. Specimen.	—	75.00
	ct. Color trial. Blue, purple and green on multicolor underprint.	—	225.

No.	Description	VF	UNC
106	**100 Escudos** 10.6.1973. Brown, black and maroon on multicolor underprint. Luiz de Camoes at right. Signature 10. Back: Dark green and maroon on multicolor underprint. Tree at left. Watermark: Luiz de Camoes.	1.50	7.50

No.	Description	VF	UNC
107	**500 Escudos** 10.6.1973. Dark brown, violet and purple on multicolor underprint. Luiz de Camoes at right. Signature 11. Back: High rock formation. Watermark: Luiz de Camoes.	4.50	20.00

No.	Description	VF	UNC
108	**1000 Escudos** 10.6.1973. Olive and blue on multicolor underprint. Luiz de Camoes at right. Signature 11. Back: Waterfall. Watermark: Luiz de Camoes.	9.00	35.00

Peoples Republic

Banco Nacional de Angola

1976 Issue

109 20 Kwanzas VF UNC

11.11.1976. Brown, green and orange. Antonio Agostinho Neto at right. Signature 12. Back: Arms at lower left, soldiers in field.

	VF	UNC
a. Issued note.	3.50	12.75
s. Specimen.	—	20.00

110 50 Kwanzas VF UNC

11.11.1976. Purple, brown and black. Antonio Agostinho Neto at right. Signature 12. Back: Field workers, arms at lower left.

	VF	UNC
a. Issued note.	2.00	9.50
s. Specimen.	—	30.00

111 100 Kwanzas VF UNC

11.11.1976. Green on multicolor underprint. Antonio Agostinho Neto at right. Signature 12. Back: Textile factory workers, arms at lower left.

	VF	UNC
a. Issued note.	1.50	15.00
s. Specimen.	—	40.00

112 500 Kwanzas VF UNC

11.11.1976. Blue on multicolor underprint. Antonio Agostinho Neto at right. Signature 12. Back: Cargo ships dockside, arms at lower left.

	VF	UNC
a. Issued note.	6.00	30.00
s. Specimen.	—	50.00

113 1000 Kwanzas VF UNC

11.11.1976. Red on multicolor underprint. Antonio Agostinho Neto at right. Signature 12. Back: School class, arms at lower left.

	VF	UNC
a. Issued note.	9.50	40.00
s. Specimen.	—	50.00

1979 Issue

114 50 Kwanzas VF UNC

14.8.1979. Purple, brown and black. Antonio Agostinho Neto at right, 2 serial numbers, signature titles, date of independence added under bank name. Signature 13. Back: Field workers, arms at lower left. 2.50 10.00

115 100 Kwanzas VF UNC

14.8.1979. Green on multicolor underprint. Antonio Agostinho Neto at right, 2 serial numbers, signature titles, date of independence added under bank name. Signature 13. Back: Textile factory workers, arms at lower left.

	VF	UNC
a. Issued note.	1.75	7.50
s. Specimen.	—	75.00

116 500 Kwanzas

14.8.1979. Blue on multicolor underprint. Antonio Agostinho Neto at right, 2 serial numbers, signature titles, date of independence added under bank name. Signature 13. Back: Cargo ships dockside, arms at lower left. 17.50 75.00

117 1000 Kwanzas VF UNC

14.8.1979. Red on multicolor underprint. Antonio Agostinho Neto at right, 2 serial numbers, signature titles, date of independence added under bank name. Signature 13. Back: School class, arms at lower left.

	VF	UNC
a. Issued note.	10.00	47.50
s. Specimen.	—	75.00

1984-87 Issue

Replacement notes: Serial # prefixes ZA, ZD, ZO, etc.

118 50 Kwanzas VF UNC

7.1.1984. Deep brown and green on light green and tan underprint. Conjoined busts of José Eduardo dos Santos and Antonio Agostinho Neto at right. Signature 14. Back: Classroom and teacher, arms at lower left. Watermark: Bird, (weak). 1.25 5.00

119 100 Kwanzas VF UNC

7.1.1984;11.11.1987. Deep blue, violet and brown on light blue and multicolor underprint. Conjoined busts of José Eduardo dos Santos and Antonio Agostinho Neto at right. Signature 14. Back: Picking cotton, arms at lower left. Watermark: Bird, (weak). 10.00 35.00

120 500 Kwanzas — VF UNC

Brown, red-brown and red on lilac and multicolor underprint. Conjoined busts of José Eduardo dos Santos and Antonio Agostinho Neto at right. Back: Offshore oil platform at left, worker at right, arms at lower left. Overprint: 1984; 1987. Watermark: Bird (weak).

	VF	UNC
a. Signature 14. 7.1.1984.	11.00	50.00
b. Signature 15. 11.11.1987.	10.00	60.00

121 1000 Kwanzas — VF UNC

Purple, blue-black and blue on light blue and multicolor underprint. Conjoined busts of José Eduardo dos Santos and Antonio Agostinho Neto at right. Back: Soldiers embarking dockside at left center and soldier at right, arms at lower left. Overprint: 1984; 1987. Watermark: Bird (weak).

	VF	UNC
a. Signature 14. 7.1.1984.	12.50	65.00
b. Signature 15. 11.11.1987.	11.00	45.00

1991 Provisional Issue

122 50 Novo Kwanza on 50 Kwanzas — VF 10.00, UNC 50.00

ND (-old date 11.11.1987). Conjoined busts of José Eduardo dos Santos and Antonio Agostinho Neto at right. Signature 15. Back: Arms at lower left. Overprint: *NOVO KWANZA* on unissued date of #118. Watermark: Conjoined busts of José Eduardo dos Santos and Antonio Agostinho Neto.

123 500 Novo Kwanza on 500 Kwanzas — VF 13.00, UNC 65.00

ND (-old date 11.11.1987). Conjoined busts of José Eduardo dos Santos and Antonio Agostinho Neto at right. Back: Arms at lower left. Overprint: *NOVO KWANZA* IN LIGHT GREEN ON #120b. Watermark: Conjoined busts of José Eduardo dos Santos and Antonio Agostinho Neto.

124 1000 Novo Kwanza on 1000 Kwanzas — VF 13.00, UNC 65.00

ND (-old date 11.11.1987). Conjoined busts of José Eduardo dos Santos and Antonio Agostinho Neto at right. Back: Arms at lower left. Overprint: *NOVO DWANZA* in red on #121b. Watermark: Conjoined busts of José Eduardo dos Santos and Antonio Agostinho Neto.

125 5000 Novo Kwanza on 100 Kwanzas — VF 100., UNC 285.

ND (-old date 11.11.1987). Conjoined busts of José Eduardo dos Santos and Antonio Agostinho Neto at right. Signature 15. Back: Arms at lower left. Overprint: *NOVO KWANZA 5000* in brown on unissued date of #119. Watermark: Conjoined busts of José Eduardo dos Santos and Antonio Agostinho Neto.

1991 Issue

126 100 Kwanzas — VF 1.25, UNC 5.75

4.2.1991. Purple, green and brown. Conjoined busts of José Eduardo dos Santos and Antonio Agostinho Neto at right. Signature 16. Back: Rock formation at Pungo Andongo at left center, tribal mask at right, arms at lower left. Watermark: Conjoined busts of José Eduardo dos Santos and Antonio Agostinho Neto.

127 500 Kwanzas — VF —, UNC —

4.2.1991. Blue and violet. Conjoined busts of José Eduardo dos Santos and Antonio Agostinho Neto at right. Back: Blue, violet, green and brown. Rock formation at Pungo Andongo at left center, tribal mask at right, arms at lower left. Watermark: Conjoined busts of José Eduardo dos Santos and Antonio Agostinho Neto. Specimen.

128 500 Kwanzas — VF UNC

4.2.1991. Purple and deep blue-green on multicolor underprint. Conjoined busts of José Eduardo dos Santos and Antonio Agostinho Neto at right. Back: Serra da Leba at left center, native pot at right, arms at lower left. Watermark: Conjoined busts of José Eduardo dos Santos and Antonio Agostinho Neto.

	VF	UNC
a. Signature 16.	5.00	25.00
b. Signature 17.	2.50	10.00
c. Signature 18.	3.25	12.50

129 1000 Kwanzas — VF UNC

4.2.1991. Brown, orange, purple and red-violet on multicolor underprint. Conjoined busts of José Eduardo dos Santos and Antonio Agostinho Neto at right. Back: Banco Nacional at left center, native doll at right, arms at lower left. Watermark: Conjoined busts of José Eduardo dos Santos and Antonio Agostinho Neto.

	VF	UNC
a. Signature 16.	7.50	37.50
b. Signature 17.	2.75	12.75
c. Signature 18.	5.00	16.00

130 5000 Kwanzas VF UNC

4.2.1991. Dark green, blue-green and dark brown on multicolor underprint. Conjoined busts of José Eduardo dos Santos and Antonio Agostinho Neto at right. Back: Waterfall and stylized statue of "The Thinker", arms at lower left. Watermark: Conjoined busts of José Eduardo dos Santos and Antonio Agostinho Neto.

	VF	UNC
a. Signature 16.	15.00	50.00
b. Signature 17.	5.00	20.00
c. Signature 18.	7.50	22.50

131 10,000 Kwanzas VF UNC

4.2.1991. Red, olive-green and purple on multicolor underprint. Conjoined busts of José Eduardo dos Santos and Antonio Agostinho Neto at right. Back: Sable antelope herd and shell, arms at lower left. Watermark: Conjoined busts of José Eduardo dos Santos and Antonio Agostinho Neto.

	VF	UNC
a. Signature 17.	15.00	80.00
b. Signature 18.	3.25	12.50

132 50,000 Kwanzas VF 5.00 UNC 20.00

4.2.1991. Bright green, yellow-green and dark brown on multicolor underprint. Conjoined busts of José Eduardo dos Santos and Antonio Agostinho Neto. Signature 18. Back: Waterfall and stylized statue of "The Thinker", arms at lower left. Watermark: Conjoined busts of José Eduardo dos Santos and Antonio Agostinho Neto.

133 100,000 Kwanzas VF UNC

4.2.1991 (1993). Orange and aqua on emerald green and multicolor underprint. Conjoined busts of José Eduardo dos Santos and Antonio Agostinho Neto at right. Signature 18. Back: Sable antelope herd and shell, arms at lower left. Watermark: Conjoined busts of José Eduardo dos Santos and Antonio Agostinho Neto.

	VF	UNC
a. Microprint around watermark area reads: *100000 BNA*, latent print: *100000 CEM MIL*. watermark: *100000*.	5.00	9.50
x. Microprint around watermark. area reads: *10000 BNA*, latent print: *10000 DEZ MIL*. watermark: *10,000*. (error).	15.00	57.50

134 500,000 Kwanzas VF 2.00 UNC 6.50

4.2.1991 (1994). Red, brown and violet on multicolor underprint. Conjoined busts of José Eduardo dos Santos and Antonio Agostinho Neto at right. Signature 19. Back: Rhinoceros at left, arms at lower left. Watermark: Conjoined busts of José Eduardo dos Santos and Antonio Agostinho Neto.

134A 1,000,000 Kwanzas — —

4.2.1991. Requires confirmation.

1995 Issue

135 1000 Kwanzas Reajustados VF 1.50 UNC 3.75

1.5.1995. Black and blue on multicolor underprint. Conjoined busts of José Eduardo dos Santos and Antonio Agostinho Neto at right. Signature 20. Back: Sable antelope at left, arms at lower left, mask at upper right. Watermark: Sculpture.

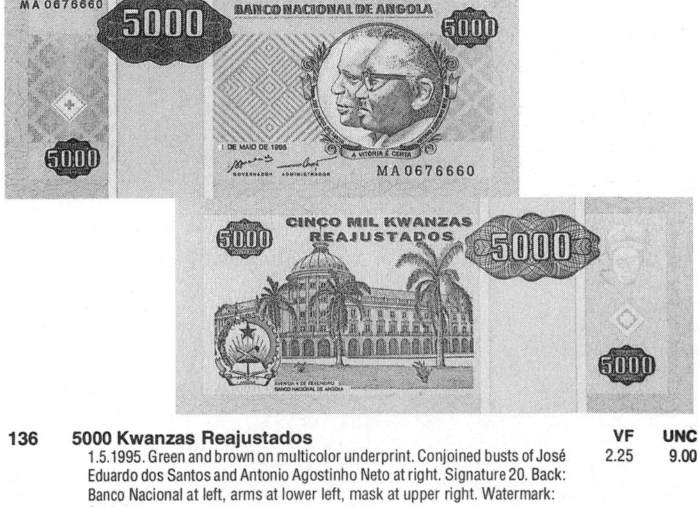

136 5000 Kwanzas Reajustados VF 2.25 UNC 9.00

1.5.1995. Green and brown on multicolor underprint. Conjoined busts of José Eduardo dos Santos and Antonio Agostinho Neto at right. Signature 20. Back: Banco Nacional at left, arms at lower left, mask at upper right. Watermark: Sculpture.

137 **10,000 Kwanzas Reajustados** — VF / UNC
1.5.1995. Red and purple on multicolor underprint. Conjoined busts of José Eduardo dos Santos and Antonio Agostinho Neto at right. Signature 20. Back: Off shore oil platform at left, arms at lower left, mask at upper right. Watermark: Sculpture. — 2.25 / 9.50

138 **50,000 Kwanzas Reajustados**
1.5.1995. Orange and green on multicolor underprint. Conjoined busts of José Eduardo dos Santos and Antonio Agostinho Neto at right. Signature 20. Back: Telecommunications station in Luanda at left center, arms at lower left, mask at upper right. Watermark: Sculpture. — 1.75 / 9.00

139 **100,000 Kwanzas Reajustados** — VF / UNC
1.5.1995 Dark blue and brown-violet on multicolor underprint. Conjoined busts of José Eduardo dos Santos and Antonio Agostinho Neto at right. Signature 20. Back: Mask and pottery at left center, arms at lower left, mask at upper right. Watermark: Sculpture. UV: Fibers fluoresce green; face: logo and value yellow. — 1.75 / 6.50

140 **500,000 Kwanzas Reajustados** — VF / UNC
1.5.1995. Dark brown and red-brown on multicolor underprint. Conjoined busts of José Eduardo dos Santos and Antonio Agostinho Neto at right. Signature 20. Back: Matala dam at left center, arms at lower left, mask at upper right. Watermark: Sculpture. — 3.00 / 4.50

141 **1,000,000 Kwanzas Reajustados** — VF / UNC
1.5.1995. Bright blue and red-brown on multicolor underprint. Conjoined busts of José Eduardo dos Santos and Antonio Agostinho Neto at right. Signature 20. Back: School girl at left center, arms at lower left, mask at upper right. Watermark: Sculpture. — 3.50 / 8.50

142 **5,000,000 Kwanzas Reajustados** — VF / UNC
1.5.1995. Violet and red-brown on multicolor underprint. Conjoined busts of José Eduardo dos Santos and Antonio Agostinho Neto at right. Signature 20. Back: Serra da Leba at left center, arms at lower left, mask at upper right. Watermark: Sculpture. — 7.50 / 35.00

1999; 2003 Issue

143 **1 Kwanza** — VF / UNC
Dark brown, pink and light blue on multicolor underprint. Conjoined busts of José Eduardo dos Santos and Antonio Agnostinho Neto at right Signature 21. Back: Women picking cotton, arms at lower left, mask at upper right. Overprint: 10.1999. Watermark: Sculpture. Printer: FCO. — FV / 1.00

144 **5 Kwanzas** — VF / UNC
10.1999; 5.2010. Purple, light-blue and dark blue on multicolor underprint. Conjoined busts of José Eduardo dos Santos and Antonio Agnostinho Neto at right. Signature 21. Back: Mountain pass, arms at lower left, mask at upper right. Watermark: Sculpture. Printer: FCO. 138x66mm.

	VF	UNC
a. 10.1999.	FV	3.00
b. 5.2010.	FV	2.00

145 10 Kwanzas VF UNC

10.1999; 5.2010. Brown, orange and purple on multicolor underprint. Conjoined busts of José Eduardo dos Santos and Antonio Agnostinho Neto at right. Signature 21. Back: Two antelope, arms at lower left, mask at upper right. Watermark: Sculpture. Printer: FCO. 144x66mm.

		VF	UNC
	a. 10.1999.	FV	4.00
	b. 5.2010.	FV	3.00

146 50 Kwanzas VF UNC

10.1999; 5.2010. Conjoined busts of José Eduardo dos Santos and Antonio Agnostinho Neto at right. Back: Off-shore oil rig. Watermark: Sculpture. Printer: FCO. UV: Fibers fluoresce green; face: logo, value and legend green; lower serial # orange. 160x66mm.

		VF	UNC
	a. 10.1999.	FV	5.00
	b. 5.2010.	FV	4.00

147 100 Kwanzas VF UNC

10.1999; 5.2010; 1.2011. Olive and multicolor underprint. Back: Banco Nacional building. 160x66mm.

		VF	UNC
	a. 10.1999.	FV	10.00
	b. 5.2010.	FV	7.00
	c. 1.2011.	FV	3.00

148 200 Kwanzas VF UNC

11.2003; 1.2011. Mauve, aqua, pink and orange on multicolor underprint. Signature 22. Back: Aerial view of Luanda's coastline boulevard. 160x66mm.

		VF	UNC
	a. 11.2004.	FV	10.00
	b. 1.2011.	FV	6.00

149 500 Kwanzas VF UNC

11.2003; 1.2011. Mauve, yellow and green on multicolor underprint. Signature 22. Back: Cotton harvesting scene. 160x66mm.

		VF	UNC
	a. 11.2003.	FV	20.00
	b. 1.2011.	FV	15.00

150 1000 Kwanzas VF UNC

11.2003; 1.2011. Red, orange, blue and purple on multicolor underprint. Signature 22. Back: Coffee plantation. 163x66mm.

		VF	UNC
	a. 11.2003.	FV	60.00
	b. 1.2011.	FV	30.00

151 2000 Kwanzas VF UNC

11.2003; 1.2011. Light and dark green on multicolor underprint. Back: Seashore. 165x66mm.

		VF	UNC
	a. 11.2003.	FV	110.
	b. 1.2011.	FV	60.00

2012 Issue

152 **50 Kwanzas** | VF FV | UNC 2.50

10.2012. Ochre and brown. Conjoined busts of José Eduardo dos Santos and Antonio Agnostinho Neto at right center. Back: Ochre and blue. Cuemba waterfall.

153 **100 Kwanzas** | VF FV | UNC 5.00

10.2012. Ochre and brown. Conjoined busts of José Eduardo dos Santos and Antonio Agnostinho Neto at right center. Back: Ochre and blue. Binga waterfall.

154 **200 Kwanzas** | VF FV | UNC 7.50

10.2012. Blue and brown. Conjoined busts of José Eduardo dos Santos and Antonio Agnostinho Neto at right center. Back: Blue and green. Tchimbue waterfall.

155 **500 Kwanzas** | VF FV | UNC 10.00

10.2012. Brown and tan. Conjoined busts of José Eduardo dos Santos and Antonio Agnostinho Neto at right center. Back: Tan, blue and green. Andulo waterfall.

The Argentine Republic, located in South America, has an area of 2.76 million sq. km. and a population of 40.48 million. Capital: Buenos Aires. Its varied topography ranges from the subtropical lowlands of the north to the towering Andean Mountains in the west and the windswept Patagonian steppe in the south. The rolling, fertile pampas of central Argentina are ideal for agriculture and grazing, and support most of the republic's population. Meat packing, flour milling, textiles, sugar refining and dairy products are the principal industries. Oil is found in Patagonia, but most of the mineral requirements must be imported.

In 1816, the United Provinces of the Rio Plata declared their independence from Spain. After Bolivia, Paraguay, and Uruguay went their separate ways, the area that remained became Argentina. The country's population and culture were heavily shaped by immigrants from throughout Europe, but most particularly Italy and Spain, which provided the largest percentage of newcomers from 1860 to 1930. Up until about the mid-20th century, much of Argentina's history was dominated by periods of internal political conflict between Federalists and Unitarians and between civilian and military factions. After World War II, an era of Peronist authoritarian rule and interference in subsequent governments was followed by a military junta that took power in 1976. Democracy returned in 1983, and has persisted despite numerous challenges, the most formidable of which was a severe economic crisis in 2001-02 that led to violent public protests and the resignation of several interim presidents. The economy has recovered strongly since bottoming out in 2002.

MONETARY SYSTEM:

1 Peso (m/n) = 100 Centavos to 1970
1 'New' Peso (Ley 18.188) = 100 'Old' Pesos (m/n), 1970-83
1 Peso Argentino = 10,000 Pesos, (Ley 18.188) 1983-85
1 Austral = 100 Centavos = 1000 Pesos Argentinos, 1985-92
1 Peso = 10,000 Australes, 1992-
1 Peso = 8 Reales = 100 Centavos

REPLACEMENT NOTES:

#260d onward: R prefix before serial #.

SIGNATURE TITLES:

A - GERENTE GENERAL
B - SUBGERENTE GENERAL
C - GERENTE GENERAL and PRESIDENTE
D - SUBGERENTE GENERAL and VICE-PRESIDENTE
E - SUBGERENTE GENERAL and PRESIDENTE
F - VICE PRESIDENTE and PRESIDENTE
G - PRESIDENT B.R.C.A. and PRESIDENT H.C. SENADORES
H - PRESIDENT B.C.R.A. and PRESIDENT H.C. DIPUTADOS
I - VICE PRESIDENTE and GERENTE GENERAL

REPUBLIC

BANCO CENTRAL DE LA REPUBLICA ARGENTINA

1960-69 ND ISSUE

276 **50 Pesos** | VF 1.25 | UNC 5.00

ND (1968-69). Green. General José de San Martin in uniform at right, *SERIE D*. 2 signature varieties. Signature titles: C. Back: Army in mountain pass.

277 **100 Pesos**

	VF	UNC
ND (1967-69). Red-brown. General José de San Martin in uniform at right. 2 signature varieties. *SERIES E, F, G.* Signature titles: C. Back: Spanish and Indians.	1.25	4.00

278 **500 Pesos**

	VF	UNC
ND (1964-69). Blue on blue and gold underprint. Portrait of elderly General José de San Martin not in uniform at right. 4 signature varieties. Serie A. Back: Grand Bourg House in France.		
a. Signature titles: E.	10.00	17.50
b. Signature titles: C.	4.00	10.00

279 **1000 Pesos**

	VF	UNC
ND (1966-69). Purple. Portrait young General José de San Martín in uniform at right. 3 signature varieties. Serie C, D. Back: Sailing ship.		
a. Signature titles: E.	3.75	15.00
b. Signature titles: C.	3.25	10.00

280 **5000 Pesos**

	VF	UNC
ND (1962-69). Brown on yellow-green underprint. Portrait young General José de San Martín in uniform. 6 signature varieties. Serie A. Back: Capitol.		
a. Signature titles: E.	15.00	50.00
b. Signature titles: C.	12.50	37.50
s. As a. Specimen.	—	200.

281 **10,000 Pesos**

	VF	UNC
ND (1961-69). Deep red on blue and yellow underprint. Portrait elderly General José de San Martin not in uniform at right. 5 signature varieties. Serie A, B. Back: Armies in the field.		
a. Signature titles: E. Serie A, B.	15.00	50.00
b. Signature titles: C. Serie B.	12.50	35.00
s. As a. Specimen.	—	200.

1969 ND Provisional Issue

283 **5 Pesos on 500 Pesos**

	VF	UNC
ND (1969-71). Blue on blue and gold underprint. Overprint of new denomination on #278 in watermark area. 2 signature varieties. Signature titles. C. *Series A.*	7.50	22.50

284 **10 Pesos on 1000 Pesos**

	VF	UNC
ND (1969-71). Purple. Overprint of new denomination on #279 in watermark area. Signature titles:C. *SERIES D, E.*	7.50	22.50

285 **50 Pesos on 5000 Pesos**

	VF	UNC
ND (1969-71). Brown on yellow green underprint. Overprint of new denomination on #280 in watermark area. *SERIES A.*	12.50	37.50

286 **100 Pesos on 10,000 Pesos**

	VF	UNC
ND (1969-71). Deep red on blue and yellow underprint. Overprint of new denomination on #281 in watermark area. *SERIES B.* 2 signature varieties. Signature titles: C.	22.50	75.00

Ley 18.188; 1970-73 ND Issue

#287-292 Replacement notes: Serial # suffix *R*.

287 **1 Peso**

	VF	UNC
ND (1970-73). Orange on multicolor underprint. General Manuel Belgrano at right. *SERIES A-E.* 5 signature varieties. Back: Scene of Bariloche-Llao-Llao at center. Watermark: Varieties. Printer: CMN. Without colored threads in white or grayish tint paper. UV: face: background details fluoresce pink.	.40	1.50

288 **5 Pesos**

	VF	UNC
ND (1971-73). Multicolor underprint. General Manuel Belgrano at right. 2 signature varieties. Back: Monument to the Flag at Rosario at center. Watermark: Varieties. Printer: CMN. Without colored threads in white or grayish tint paper.	1.00	4.50

289 **10 Pesos**

	VF	UNC
ND (1970-73). Purple on multicolor underprint. General Manuel Belgrano at right. *SERIES A, B.* 6 signature varieties. Back: Waterfalls at Iguazu at center. Purple on multicolor underprint. Watermark: Varieties. Printer: CMN. Without colored threads in white or grayish tint paper.	.30	2.00

290 **50 Pesos**

	VF	UNC
ND (1972-73). Black and brown on multicolor underprint. General José de San Martin at right. 3 signature varieties. Back: Hot springs at Jujuy at center. Watermark: Arms. Colored threads in paper.	3.00	15.00

291 **100 Pesos**

	VF	UNC
ND (1971-73). Red on multicolor underprint. General José de San Martin at right. *SERIE A, B.* 4 signature varieties. Back: Coastline at Ushuaia at center. Watermark: Arms. Colored threads in paper.	5.00	20.00

292 **500 Pesos**

	VF	UNC
ND (1972-73). Green on multicolor underprint. José de San Martin at right. 2 signature varieties. Back: Army monument at Mendoza at center. Watermark: Arms. Colored threads in paper.	10.00	30.00

Decreto-Ley 18.188/69; 1973-76 ND Issue

#293-299 Replacement notes: Serial # suffix: *R*.

293 **1 Peso**

	VF	UNC
ND (1974). Orange on multicolor underprint. General Manuel Belgrano at right. *SERIE E,F.* Signature varieties. Back: Scene of Bariloche-Llao-Llao at center. Watermark: Arms. Without colored threads in paper (varieties).	.50	1.50

294 **5 Pesos** | VF | UNC
ND (1974-76). Blue on multicolor underprint. General Manuel Belgrano at right. *SERIE A,B.* 2 signature varieties. Back: Monument to the Flag at Rosario at center. Watermark: Arms. Without colored threads in paper (varieties). | .40 | 1.25

295 **10 Pesos** | VF | UNC
ND (1973-76). Purple on multicolor underprint. General Manuel Belgrano at right. *SERIE C,D.* 4 signature varieties. Back: Waterfall at Iguazu at center. Watermark: Arms. Without colored threads in paper (varieties). | .50 | 2.50

296 **50 Pesos** | VF | UNC
ND (1974-75). Black and brown on multicolor underprint. General José San Martin at right. *SERIE A, B.* 2 signature varieties. Back: Hot springs at Jujuy at center. Watermark: Arms. Colored threads in paper. | .50 | 1.50

297 **100 Pesos** | VF | UNC
ND (1973-76). Red on multicolor underprint. General José de San Martin at right. *SERIE B, C.* 3 signature varieties. Back: Ushuaia Harbor scene at center. Watermark: Arms. Colored threads in paper. | 1.00 | 3.50

298 **500 Pesos** | VF | UNC
ND (1974-75). Green on multicolor underprint. General José de San Martin at right. 2 signature varieties. Back: Army monument at Mendoza at center. Watermark: Arms. Colored threads in paper.

	VF	UNC
a. Signature titles: C.	3.00	10.00
b. Signature titles: F.	2.00	7.50
c. Signature titles : I.	3.00	10.00

299 **1000 Pesos** | VF | UNC
ND (1973-76). Brown on multicolor underprint. General José de San Martin at right. *SERIE A-C.* 3 signature varieties. Back: *Plaza de Mayo* in Buenos Aires at center. Watermark: Arms. Colored threads in paper. | 5.00 | 12.50

1976-83 ND Issue

W/o Decreto or Ley

#301-310 Replacement notes: Serial # suffix: *H.*

300 **10 Pesos** | VF | UNC
ND (1976). Purple on multicolor underprint. General Manuel Belgrano at right. *SERIES D, E.* Back: Waterfall at Iguazu at center. Watermark: Arms. | .20 | 1.00

301 **50 Pesos** | VF | UNC
ND (1976-78). Black on multicolor underprint. General José de San Martin at right. *SERIE B, C.* 2 signature varieties. Back: Hot springs at Jujuy at center. Watermark: Arms. Engraved or lithographed back.

	VF	UNC
a. Without colored threads in paper.	5.00	10.00
b. Colored threads in paper.	.20	.75

302 100 Pesos VF UNC

ND (1976-78). Red on multicolor on underprint. General José de San Martin at right *SERIE C-E.* Signature varieties. Back: Coastline at Ushuaia at center. Watermark: Arms.

	VF	UNC
a. Without colored threads in paper. 2 signature varieties.	.50	2.50
b. Colored threads in paper. 2 signature varieties.	.30	1.00

303 500 Pesos VF UNC

ND (1977-82). Green on multicolor underprint. General José de San Martin at right. *SERIE A-D.* 4 signature varieties.. Back: Army monument at Mendoza at center. UV: face: design elements fluoresce orange.

	VF	UNC
a. Watermark: Arms. without colored threads in paper.	.20	1.50
b. Watermark: Arms. Colored threads in paper.	.50	2.50
c. Watermark: Multiple sunbursts. Colored threads. Back lithographed. *SERIE C, D.* UV: threads fluoresce blue.	.20	.75

304 1000 Pesos VF UNC

ND (1976-83). Brown on multicolor underprint. General José de San Martin at right *SERIE C-I.* 5 signature varieties. Back: *Plaza de Mayo* in Buenos Aires at center. Color varieties in underprint: yellow or green, maroon or ochre.

	VF	UNC
a. Watermark: Arms. without colored threads in paper.	.30	2.00
b. Watermark: Arms. Colored threads in paper. 2 signature varieties.	.20	1.50
c. Watermark: Multiple sunbursts. Back engraved.	.20	1.00
d. Watermark: Multiple sunbursts. Back lithographed. *SERIE I.*	.15	.75

305 5000 Pesos VF UNC

ND (1977-83). Blue and olive-green on multicolor underprint. General José de San Martin at right. Back: Coastline of Mar del Plata. Color varieties in underprint: yellow or green, maroon or ochre.

	VF	UNC
a. Watermark: Arms. 2 signature varieties. *SERIE A, B.*	.40	2.00
b. Watermark: Multiple sunbursts. 2 signature varieties. *SERIE B.*	.20	1.00

306 10,000 Pesos VF UNC

ND (1976-83). Orange and red on multicolor underprint. General José de San Martin at right. 4 signature varieties. Back: National park on back. Watermark: Varieties. With colored threads.

	VF	UNC
a. Watermark: Arms. 3 signature varieties. *SERIE A-G.*	.75	3.00
b. Watermark: Multiple sunbursts. *SERIE G.*	.50	1.50

307 50,000 Pesos VF UNC

ND (1979-83). Brown on multicolor underprint. General José de San Martin at right. 2 signature varieties. Back: Banco Central building at left center. Watermark: Arms. With colored threads. 1.00 3.00

308 100,000 Pesos VF UNC

ND (1979-83). Gray and red on multicolor underprint. General José de San Martin at right. Signature varieties. Back: Mint building at left center. Watermark: Varieties. With colored threads.

	VF	UNC
a. Watermark: Arms. *SERIE A, B.*	2.00	10.00
b. Watermark: Multiple sunbursts. *SERIE B.*	1.00	3.00

309 500,000 Pesos VF UNC

ND (1980-83). Green, brown and blue on multicolor underprint. General José de San Martin at right. 2 signature varieties. Back: Founding of Buenos Aires at left center. Watermark: Multiple sunbursts. With colored threads. 1.00 5.00

310 **1,000,000 Pesos** — VF 7.50 — UNC 17.50
ND (1981-83). Blue and pink on multicolor underprint. General José de San Martin at right. *SERIE A, B.* 3 signature varieties. Back: Independence Declaration with *25 de Mayo* at left center. Watermark: Multiple sunbursts.

1983-85 ND Issue

#311-319 Replacement notes: Serial # suffix: *R.*

311 **1 Peso Argentino**

		VF	UNC
ND (1983-84). Red-orange and purple on blue and multicolor underprint. General José de San Martin at right. *SERIE A, B.* 2 signature varieties. Colored threads. Back: Scene of Bariloche-Llao-Llao at center. Watermark: Multiple sunbursts. Printer: CdM. UV: fibers fluoresce green.			
	a. Issued note.	.15	.75
	s. Specimen. Overprint: *MUESTRA* twice on both sides.	—	25.00

312 **5 Pesos Argentinos**

		VF	UNC
ND (1983-84). Brown-violet and black on multicolor underprint. General José de San Martin at right. 2 signature varieties. Back: Monument to the Flag at Rosario at center. White or grayish tint. Watermark: Multiple sunbursts. Printer: CdM. With colored threads.			
	a. Issued note.	.15	.75
	s. Specimen. Overprint: *MUESTRA* twice on both sides.	—	25.00

313 **10 Pesos Argentinos**

		VF	UNC
ND (1983-84). Black and red on green and multicolor underprint. General José de San Martin at right. *SERIE A, B.* 2 signature varieties. Back: Waterfall at Iguazu at center. White or grayish tint. Watermark: Multiple sunbursts. Printer: CdM. With colored fibers. UV: Fibers fluoresce green.			
	a. Issued note.	.15	.75
	s. Specimen. Overprint: *MUESTRA* twice on both sides.	—	25.00

314 **50 Pesos Argentinos**

		VF	UNC
ND (1983-85). Brown on green and multicolor underprint. General José de San Martin at right. 2 signature varieties. Back: Hot springs at Jujuy at center. Watermark: Multiple sunbursts. Printer: CdM. With colored fibers. UV: Fibers fluoresce blue.			
	a. Issued note.	.15	.75
	s. Specimen. Overprint: *MUESTRA* twice on both sides.	—	25.00

315 **100 Pesos Argentinos**

		VF	UNC
ND (1983-85). Blue on multicolor underprint. General José de San Martin at right. *SERIE A, B.* 2 signature varieties. Back: Coastline at Ushuaia at center. Watermark: Multiple sunbursts. Printer: CdM. With colored threads.			
	a. Issued note.	.50	1.50
	s. Specimen. Overprint: *MUESTRA* twice on both sides.	—	25.00

316 **500 Pesos Argentinos**

		VF	UNC
ND (1984). Purple on multicolor underprint. General José de San Martin at right. Back: Town meeting of May 22, 1810. White or grayish tint. Watermark: Multiple sunbursts. Printer: CdM. With colored threads.			
	a. Issued note.	.50	1.50
	s. Specimen. Overprint: *MUESTRA* on each side.	—	25.00

317 1000 Pesos Argentinos | VF | UNC

ND (1983-85). Blue-green and brown on multicolor underprint. General José de San Martin at right. Back: *El Paso de los Andes* battle scene. Watermark: Varieties. With colored threads.

		VF	UNC
a.	*SERIE A, B.* 2 signature varieties.	1.50	7.00
b.	Watermark: Multiple sunbursts (1984). *SERIE C, D.*	.50	1.50
s1.	As a. Specimen. Overprint: *MUESTRA* on each side.	—	25.00
s2.	As b. Specimen. Overprint.: *MUESTRA* on each side.	—	25.00

318 5000 Pesos Argentinos | VF | UNC

ND (1984-85). Red-brown on multicolor underprint. J. B. Alberdi at right. *SERIES A, B.* Back: Constitutional meeting of 1853. Watermark: Young San Martín. With colored threads.

		VF	UNC
a.	Issued note.	2.00	10.00
s.	Specimen. Overprint: MUESTRA on each side.	—	25.00

319 10,000 Pesos Argentinos | VF | UNC

ND (1985). Blue-violet on multicolor underprint. M. Belgrano at right. Back: Creation of Argentine flag. Watermark: Young San Martín. With colored threads.

		VF	UNC
a.	Issued note.	3.50	15.00
s.	Specimen. Overprint: *MUESTRA* on each side.	—	25.00

1985 ND Provisional Issue

#320-322 Rectangle overprint in watermark area on face of Peso Argentino notes.

320 1 Austral | VF .50 | UNC 2.50

ND (1985). New denomination overprint in numeral and wording in box, green on face and blue on back of #317b. Series D. Rectangle on watermark area. Overprint: Peso Argentino notes. Watermark: Sunburst.

321 5 Australes | VF 2.00 | UNC 5.00

ND (1985). New denomination overprint as #320, purple on face and brown on back of #318, Series B. Rectangle on watermark area. Overprint: Peso Argentino notes. Watermark: San Martin.

322 10 Australes | VF | UNC

ND (1985). New denomination overprint as #320 on #319. Rectangle in watermark area. Overprint: Peso Argentino notes.

		VF	UNC
a.	Blue overprint on face and back. Watermark: San Martín. Series A; B.	4.00	9.00
b.	Blue overprint on face and back. Watermark: Multiple sunbursts. Series A-C.	1.75	6.00
c.	Blue overprint on face, light olive-green overprint on back. Series B; C. Watermark Multiple sunbursts.	1.75	5.00
d.	Series B without overprint. Watermark: Multiple sunbursts.	30.00	60.00
s.	As b. Specimen.	—	25.00

1985-91 ND Issue

323 1 Austral | VF | UNC

ND (1985-89). Blue-green and purple on multicolor underprint. B. Rivadavia at center, latent image "BCRA". Signature varieties. Back: Liberty (Progreso) with torch and shield seated at left center. Watermark: Multiple sunbursts. Printer: CdM. UV: threads fluoresce green; back: design elements pink.

		VF	UNC
a.	Signature titles E. Series A.	.75	3.00
b.	Signature titles C. Series B; C. 2 Signature varieties.	.15	.40
s.	Signature titles C. Series A. Specimen.	—	25.00

324 5 Australes | VF | UNC

Brown and deep olive-green on multicolor underprint. J. J. de Urquiza at center, latent image "BCRA". Signature varieties. Back: Liberty (Progreso) with torch and shield seated at left center. Watermark: Multiple sunbursts. Printer: CdM. UV: threads fluoresce green; black design elements orange.

		VF	UNC
a.	Signature titles E. Series A.	.25	2.00
b.	Signature titles C. Series A.	.15	.40

325 10 Australes

ND (1985-89). Dark blue and purple on multicolor underprint. S. Derqui at center, latent image "BCRA". Signature varieties. Back: Liberty (Progreso) with torch and shield seated at left center. Watermark: Multiple sunbursts. Printer: CdM. UV: threads fluoresce green; back: design elements pink, orange.

	VF	UNC
a. Coarse portrait in heavy horizontal wavy lines. Signature titles E. Series A.	.75	3.50
b. Modified portrait in finer horizontal wavy lines. Signature titles C. Series A; B; C.	.15	.40

326 50 Australes

ND (1986-89). Purple and deep brown on multicolor underprint. B. Mitre at center, latent image "BCRA". Signature varieties. Back: Liberty (Progreso) with torch and shield seated at left center. Watermark: Multiple sunbursts. Printer: CdM. UV: threads fluoresce green; back: design elements orange.

	VF	UNC
a. Signature titles E. Series A.	6.00	20.00
b. Signature titles C. Series A. 3 Signature varieties.	.15	.50
s. As b. Specimen.	—	25.00

327 100 Australes

ND (1985-90). Dark red and purple on multicolor underprint. D. F. Sarmiento at center, latent image "BCRA". Signature varieties. Back: Liberty (Progreso) with torch and shield seated at left center. Watermark: Multiple sunbursts. Printer: CdM. UV: threads fluoresce green.

	VF	UNC
a. Signature titles E. Series A.	4.00	15.00
b. Signature titles C. Engraved back. Series A; B. 3 signature varieties.	.20	.75
c. Signature titles C. Back pink and lithographed; without purple and blue. Series C; D.	.15	.50
s. As b. Specimen.	—	25.00

328 500 Australes

ND (1988-90). Pale olive-green on multicolor underprint. N. Avellaneda at center, latent image "BCRA". Signature titles: C. 2 signature varieties. Back: Liberty (Progreso) with torch and shield seated at left center. Printer: CdM.

	VF	UNC
a. Metallic green guilloche by *500*. Back olive-green, black and multicolor. Watermark: Liberty. Series A. (1988).	.50	2.00
b. Dark olive-green guilloche by *500*. Back pale olive-green and multicolor; lithographed (without black). Watermark: Multiple sunbursts. Series A. (1990).	.25	.85
s. As a. Specimen.	—	25.00

329 1000 Australes

ND (1988-90). Violet-brown and purple on multicolor underprint. J. A. Roca at center, latent image"BCRA". Signature titles: *GERENTE GENERAL* and *PRESIDENTE*. Signature varieties. Back: Liberty (Progreso) with torch and shield seated at left center. Printer: CdM.

	VF	UNC
a. Vertical green guilloche near *1000*. Watermark: Liberty. Series A.	.20	.75
b. Vertical brown-violet guilloche near *1000*. Watermark: Liberty. Series B.	.25	1.00
c. Like b. but watermark: Multiple sunbursts.	.25	1.00
d. Like c. but signature titles: F. Series C.	.50	2.00
s. As a. Specimen.	—	25.00

330 5000 Australes

ND (1989-91). Dark brown and red-brown on multicolor underprint. M. Juarez at center, latent image "BCRA". Signature varieties. Back: Liberty (Progreso) with torch and shield seated at left center. Printer: CdM.

	VF	UNC
a. Green shield design at upper center r. Sign titles: E. Watermark: Liberty. Series A.	3.00	12.50
b. Green shield design at upper center r. Sign titles: C. Watermark: Liberty. Series A.	5.00	17.50
c. Dark brown shield design at upper center r. signature titles: E. Watermark: Liberty. Series B.	2.50	8.00
d. Dark brown shield designature signature titles: C. Watermark: Liberty. Series B.	2.00	7.00
e. Dark brown shield designature signature titles: F. Lithographed back. Watermark: Multiple sunbursts. Series C.	1.00	4.00
f. Series D (1991).	60.00	125.

1989; 1991 ND Provisional Issue

331 10,000 Australes

	VF	UNC
ND (1989). Black-blue, deep blue-green and brown on multicolor underprint. San Martin at right, overprint value in olive-green in box at left, word "PESOS" at center blocked out. Signature titles: C. Back: Denomination repeated in lines of text and overprint value at right. Watermark: Multiple sunbursts. Printer: CdM-A.	7.50	25.00

332 **50,000 Australes** — VF 8.00 — UNC 27.50
ND (1989). Deep olive-green and blue on multicolor underprint. San Martin at right, overprint value in violet in box at left, word "PESOS" at center blocked out. Series M. Signature titles: E. Back: Denomination repeated in lines of text and overprint value at right, value in light brown at right. Watermark: Multiple sunbursts. Printer: CdM-A.

333 **500,000 Australes** — VF 30.00 — UNC 75.00
ND (1990). Black, purple and red on multicolor underprint. San Martin at right, overprint value in box at left, word "PESOS" at bottom right blocked out. Signature titles: F. Signature varieties. Series M. Back: Denomination repeated in lines of text and overprint value at right. Watermark: Multiple sunbursts. Printer: CdM-A.

1989-91 ND Issue

334 **10,000 Australes** — VF — UNC
ND (1989-91). Black on deep blue, brown and multicolor underprint with brown diamond design at upper center right. C. Pellegrini at center. Back: Liberty (Progreso) with torch and shield seated at left center. Watermark: Liberty head. Printer: CdM-A.

	VF	UNC
a. Signature titles: C. Series A; B.	1.25	3.50
b. Signature titles: F. Series C. Watermark: sunbursts.	1.50	6.00

335 **50,000 Australes** — VF 6.00 — UNC 25.00
ND (1989-91). Black on ochre, olive-green and multicolor underprint with black flower design at upper center right Saenz Peña at center, signature titles: C. Series A; B. Back: Liberty (Progreso) with torch and shield seated at left center. Watermark: Liberty head. Printer: CdM-A.

336 **100,000 Australes** — VF 10.00 — UNC 45.00
ND (1990-91). Dark brown and reddish brown on pale brown and multicolor underprint. Coarsely engraved portrait of J. Evaristo Uriburu at center. Black signature titles: F. Series A; B. Back: Liberty (Progreso) with torch and shield seated at left center. Watermark: Liberty head. Printer: CdM-A.

337 **100,000 Australes** — VF 8.00 — UNC 50.00
ND (1991). Dark brown and reddish brown on brown and multicolor underprint. Finely engraved portrait of J. Evaristo Uriburu at center. Brown signature titles. Series B. Back: Liberty (Progreso) with torch and shield seated at left center. Watermark: Liberty head. Printer: CdM-A.

338 **500,000 Australes** — VF 25.00 — UNC 75.00
ND (1991). Black-violet, red and blue on multicolor underprint. M. Quintana at center. Series A, B. 2 signature varieties. Back: Liberty (Progreso) with torch and shield seated at left center. Watermark: Liberty head. Printer: CdM-A.

1991-92 ND Issue

#339-345 replacement notes: Serial # prefix *R*.

339 **1 Peso** — VF — UNC
ND (1992-94). Dark blue and violet-brown on multicolor underprint. C. Pelligrini at right. Back: Gray on multicolor underprint. National Congress building at left center. Watermark: Multiple sunbursts. Printer: CdM-A. 155x65mm.

	VF	UNC
a. Signature titles: F. (1992). Series A, B.	FV	3.00
b. Signature titles: G. (1993). Series B, C, D.	FV	2.50
c. Signature titles as a. Serial # prefix L. (1994).	FV	5.00

340 2 Pesos VF UNC

ND (1992-97). Deep blue and red-violet on multicolor underprint. B. Mitre at right. Back: Light blue on multicolort underprint. Mitre Museum at left center. Watermark: Multiple sunbursts. Printer: CdM-A.

	VF	UNC
a. Signature titles: F. (1992). Series A.	FV	5.00
b. Signature titles: H. (1993). Series A-C.	FV	4.00

341 5 Pesos VF UNC

ND (1992-97). Deep olive-green and red-orange on multicolor underprint. General José de San Martín at right. Back: Light olive-gray on multicolor underprint. Monument to the Glory of Mendoza at left center. Watermark: Multiple sunbursts. Printer: CdM-A.

	VF	UNC
a. Signature titles: F. (1992). Series A.	FV	8.00
b. Signature titles: G. (1993). Series A-C.	FV	9.00
c. Signature titles as a. Serial # prefix L. (1994).	FV	10.00

342 10 Pesos VF UNC

ND (1992-97). Deep brown and dark green on multicolor underprint. M. Belgrano at right. Back: M. Belgrano at right. Monument to the Flag at Rosario with city in background at left center. Watermark: Liberty head. Printer: CdM-A.

	VF	UNC
a. Signature titles: F. (1992). Series A-B.	FV	20.00
b. Signature titles: H. (1993). Series C-E.	FV	17.50

343 20 Pesos VF UNC

ND (1992-97). Carmine and deep blue on multicolor underprint. J. Manuel de Rosas at right. Back: *Vuelta de Obligado* battle scene at left center. Watermark: Liberty head. Printer: CdM-A.

	VF	UNC
a. Signature titles: F. (1992). Series A.	FV	30.00
b. Signature titles: G. (1993). Series A-B.	FV	25.00

344 50 Pesos VF UNC

ND (1992-97). Black and red on multicolor underprint. D. Faustino Sarmiento at right. Back: Plaza de Mayo in Buenos Aires at left center. Watermark: D. Faustino Sarmiento.

	VF	UNC
a. Signature titles: F. (1992). Series A.	FV	65.00
b. Signature titles: H. (1993). Series A-B.	FV	60.00

345 100 Pesos

ND (1992-97). Violet, lilac and green on multicolor underprint. J. A. Roca at right. Back: Violet and multicolor. *La Conquista del Desierto* scene at left center. Watermark: J. A. Roca.

	VF	UNC
a. Signature titles: F. (1992). Series A.	FV	125.
b. Signature titles: G. (1993). Series A-D.	FV	110.

1997-2000 ND Issue

#346-351 Replacement notes: Serial # prefix *R*.

346 2 Pesos VF UNC

ND (1997-2002). Deep blue and brown-violet on multicolor underprint. B. Mitre at right, ornate gate at center. Ascending size serial number at upper right. Signature titles: H. 2 signature varieties. Series A-D. Back: Mitre Museum at left center. Printer: CdM-A. Uncut sheets and partial sheets exist. 155x65mm. — FV 3.00

347 5 Pesos VF UNC

ND (1998-2003). Deep olive-green and purple on multicolor underprint. General José de San Martín at right and on horseback with troops at center. Signature titles: G. 4 signature varieties. Series A-C. Ascending size serial number at upper right. Back: Monument to the Glory at Mendoza at left center. Printer: CdM-A. Uncut sheets and partial sheets exist. 155x65mm. — FV 7.00

348 **10 Pesos**
ND (1998-2003). Deep brown and dark green on multicolor underprint. M. Belgrano at right, Liberty with flag at center, ascending size serial number at upper right. Signature titles: H. 3 signature varieties. Series A-E. Back: Monument to the Flag at Rosario with city in background at left center. Watermark: M. Belgrano. Printer: CdM-A. Uncut sheets and partial sheets exist. 155x65mm.

VF	UNC
FV	15.00

349 **20 Pesos**
ND (1999-2003). Red-brown and purple on multicolor underprint. J. Manuel de Rosas at right, ascending size serial number at upper right. Signature titles: G. 4 signature varieties. Series A, B. Back: *Vuelta de Obligado* battle scene at left center. Watermark: J. Manuel de Rosas. Printer: CdM-A. 155x65mm.

VF	UNC
FV	30.00

350 **50 Pesos**
ND (1999-2003). Multicolor. D. Faustino Sarmiento at right , ascending size serial number at upper right. Signature titles: H. 3 signature varieties. Series A. Back: Government office with monuments, palm trees in foreground at left center. Watermark: D. Faustino Sarmiento. Printer: CdM-A. 155x65mm.

VF	UNC
FV	65.00

351 **100 Pesos**
ND (1999-2002). Multicolor. J. A. Roca at right, ascending size serial number at upper right Signature titles: G. 4 signature varieties. Series A, B.. Back: *La Conquista del Desierto* scene at left center. Watermark: J. A. Roca. Printer: CdM-A. Uncut sheets and partial sheets exist. 155x65mm.

VF	UNC
FV	120.

2002-03 ND Issue

352 **2 Pesos**
ND (2002). B. Mitre at right, ascending size serial number at upper right, ornate gate at center. Series D-L. 5 signature varieties. Back: Mitre Museum at left center. No clause: *CONVERTIBLES DE CURSO LEGAL.* 155x65mm.

VF	UNC
FV	3.00

353 **5 Pesos**
ND (2003). Gen. J. de San Martin at right and on horseback with troops at center. Ascending size serial numbers at upper right. Series C-G. 3 signature varieties. Back: Monument to the Glory at Mendoza at left center. No clause: *CONVERTIBLES DE CURSO LEGAL.* 155x65mm.

VF	UNC
FV	7.00

354 **10 Pesos**
ND (2003). M. Belgrano at right, Liberty with flag at center, ascending size serial number at upper right.Series E-N. 3 signature varieties. Back: Monument to the Flag at Rosario with city in background at left center. Watermark: M. Belgrano. No clause: *CONVERTIBLES DE CURSO LEGAL.* 155x65mm.

VF	UNC
FV	7.00

355 **20 Pesos**
ND (2003). J. Manuel de Rosas at right, ascending size serial numbers at upper right. Series B-D. 3 signature varieties. Back: Vuelta de Obligado battle scene at left center. Watermark: J. Manuel de Rosas. No clause: *CONVERTIBLES DE CURSO LEGAL.* 155x65mm.

VF	UNC
FV	20.00

356 **50 Pesos**
ND (2003). D. Faustino Sarmiento at right, ascending size serial numbers at upper right. Series A-C. 3 signature varieties. Back: Government office with monuments, palm trees in foreground at left center. Watermark: D. Faustino Sarmiento. No clause: *CONVERTIBLES DE CURSO LEGAL.* 155x65mm.

VF	UNC
FV	55.00

357 100 Pesos | VF | UNC
ND (2003). J. A. Roca at right, ascending size serial numbers at upper right. Series B-J. 3 signature varieties. Back: La Conquista del Desierto scene at left center. Watermark: J. A. Roca. No clause: *CONVERTIBLES DE CURSO LEGAL.* 155x65mm. | FV | 100.

2012 Commemorative Issue

358 100 Pesos | VF | UNC
ND (2012). Violet and multicolor. Eva PerÛn profile at right. Back: Allegorical woman and two children. Watermark: Eva PerÛn and signature.
a. 100 at left edge in center. Serial # prefix A. | FV | 40.00
b. 100 at left edge in center. Serial # prefix B. | FV | 30.00

The Republic of Armenia is bounded to the north by Georgia, to the east by Azerbaijan and to the south and west by Turkey and Iran. It has an area of 29,743 sq. km and a population of 2.97 million. Capital: Yerevan. Agriculture including cotton, vineyards and orchards, hydroelectricity, chemicals - primarily synthetic rubber and fertilizers, and vast mineral deposits of copper, zinc and aluminum and production of steel and paper are major industries.

Armenia prides itself on being the first nation to formally adopt Christianity (early 4th century). Despite periods of autonomy, over the centuries Armenia came under the sway of various empires including the Roman, Byzantine, Arab, Persian, and Ottoman. During World War I in the western portion of Armenia, Ottoman Turkey instituted a policy of forced resettlement coupled with other harsh practices that resulted in an estimated 1 million Armenian deaths. The eastern area of Armenia was ceded by the Ottomans to Russia in 1828; this portion declared its independence in 1918, but was conquered by the Soviet Red Army in 1920. Armenian leaders remain preoccupied by the long conflict with Muslim Azerbaijan over Nagorno-Karabakh, a primarily Armenian-populated region, assigned to Soviet Azerbaijan in the 1920s by Moscow. Armenia and Azerbaijan began fighting over the area in 1988; the struggle escalated after both countries attained independence from the Soviet Union in 1991. By May 1994, when a cease-fire took hold, Armenian forces held not only Nagorno-Karabakh but also a significant portion of Azerbaijan proper. The economies of both sides have been hurt by their inability to make substantial progress toward a peaceful resolution. Turkey imposed an economic blockade on Armenia and closed the common border because of the Armenian separatists' control of Nagorno-Karabakh and surrounding areas.

MONETARY SYSTEM:
1 Ruble = 100 Kopeks
1 Dram = 100 Lumma

Republic

Armenian Republic Bank

1993 Bond - Coupon Issue

32A 500 Dram | VF | UNC
1993. Multicolor. | — | —

1993-95 Issue

33 10 Dram | VF | UNC
1993. Dark brown, light blue and pale orange on multicolor underprint. Statue of David from Sasoun at upper center right, main railway station in Yerevan at upper left center. Back: Mount Ararat at upper center right. Watermark: Crude outlined arms, or refined arms. Printer: G&D (without imprint). | .50 | 2.00

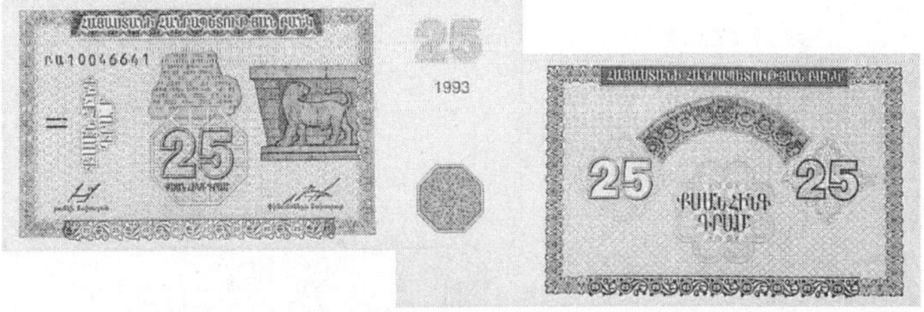

34 25 Dram | VF | UNC
1993. Brown and light red on multicolor underprint. Frieze with lion from Erebuni Castle at center right, cuneiform tablet at upper left center. Back: Arched ornament at upper center right. Watermark: Crude outlined arms, or refined arms. Printer: G&D (without imprint). | 1.00 | 3.00

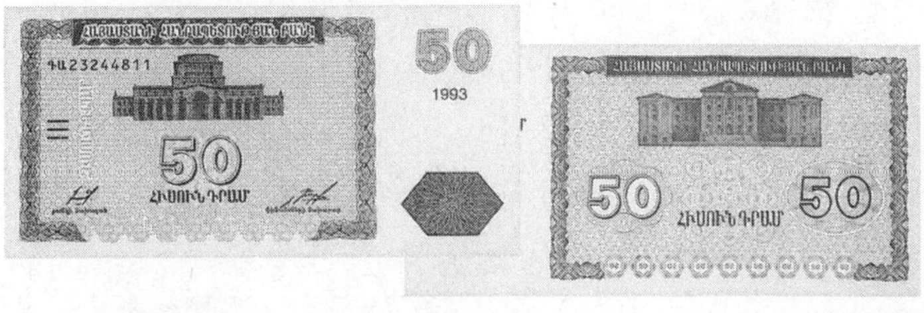

35 50 Dram | VF | UNC
1993. Dark blue on pink and multicolor underprint. State Museum of History and National Gallery at upper left center. Back: Parliament building at upper center right . Watermark: Crude outlined arms, or refined arms. Printer: G&D (without imprint). | 2.00 | 4.00

36 100 Dram VF UNC
1993. Purple, light blue and light red on multicolor underprint. Mt. Ararat at upper left center, Church of Zvarnots at center right. Back: Opera and ballet theater in Yerevan at upper center right. Printer: G&D (without imprint).

	VF	UNC
a. Watermark: Crude outline arms.	3.00	6.00
b. Watermark: Refined arms.	3.00	6.00

37 200 Dram VF UNC
1993. Brown, green and red on multicolor underprint. Church of St. Hripsime in Echmiadzin at center right. Back: Circular design at upper center right. Printer: G&D (without imprint).

	VF	UNC
a. Watermark: Crude outline arms.	4.00	9.00
b. Watermark: Refined arms.	4.00	9.00

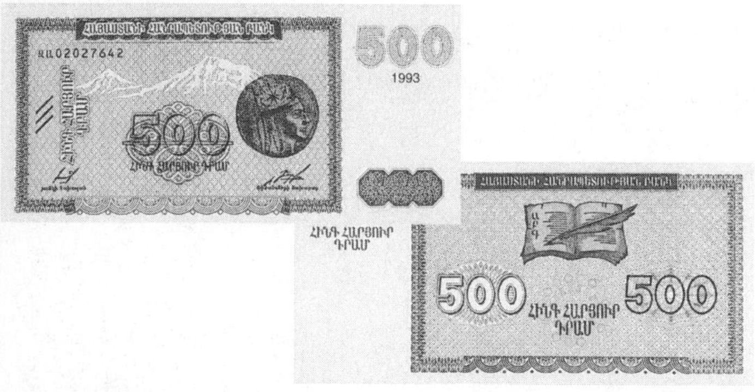

38 500 Dram VF UNC
1993. Dark green and red-brown on multicolor underprint. Tetradrachm of King Tigran II the Great aat center right, Mt. Ararat at upper left. Back: Center Open book and quill pen at upper center right. Printer: G&D (without imprint).

	VF	UNC
a. Watermark: Crude outline arms.	7.00	16.00
b. Watermark: Refined arms.	7.00	16.00

39 1000 Dram VF UNC
1994. Dark brown and brown on multicolor underprint. Statue of Mesrop Mashtotz at left. Back: Matenadaran façade at right. Watermark: Arms. FV 20.00

40 5000 Dram VF UNC
1995. Temple of Garni at center. Back: Goddess Anahit. Brown-violet on multicolor underprint. FV 50.00

Central Bank of the Republic of Armenia

1998-99 Issue

#41, 42, 44 replacement notes serial # first digit is 9.

41 50 Dram VF UNC
1998. Brownish pink and slate blue on multicolor underprint. Aram Khachaturian at left, opera house at right. Back: Scene from *Gayaneh* Ballet and Mt. Ararat. Printer: TDLR (without imprint). .50 2.00

42 100 Dram VF UNC
1998. Light and dark blue on multicolor underprint. Victor Hambartsumyan at left, solar system map at right. Back: Byurakan Observatory on Mt. Arakadz. Watermark: Victor Hambartsumyan. Printer: TDLR (without imprint). UV: threads fluoresce blue and yellow; value at left yellow; vertical serial # red. .50 3.00

44 500 Dram VF UNC
1999 (2000). Black on red and multicolor underprint. Alexander Tamanyan and city plan. Back: House of the Government in Yerevan at left center. Watermark: A. Tamanyan. Printer: TDLR (without imprint). 129x72mm. 2.00 5.00

45 **1000 Dram** | VF | UNC
1999. Aqua and green on multicolor underprint. Yeghishe Charents at left, lines of poetry at right. Back: Old Yerevan city scene. Watermark: Y. Charents. Printer: TDLR (without imprint). 136x72mm. | 3.50 | 12.00

46 **5000 Dram** | VF | UNC
1999 (2000). Dark and light brown on green, gold and multicolor underprint H. Tumanyan at left. Back: Saryan's picture of Lory mountains. Watermark: H. Tumanyan. Printer: JEZ. 143x72mm. | FV | 40.00

47 **20,000 Dram** | VF | UNC
1999. Brown and yellow on multicolor underprint. Martiros Saryan, painter at left, abstract painting in center. Hologram at right. Back: Saryan painting *Armenia* . Watermark: M. Saryan. 150x72mm. | FV | 100.

2001 Commemorative Issue

#48, 1700 years of Christianity in Armenia

48 **50,000 Dram** | VF | UNC
2001. Brown and multicolor. Cathedral of Holy Echmiatzin at center, holographic strip at left with commemorative text vertically. Back: St Gregory and King Tiridat holding church. Akhachkar at right. Watermark: Portrait. Printer: TDLR (without imprint). 1700 years of Christianity in Armenia. 160x79mm. | FV | 200.

2001; 2003 Issue

50 **1000 Dram** | VF | UNC
2001 (2002). Aqua and green on multicolor underprint. Yeghishe Charents at left, lines of poetry at right, additional security features. Back: Old Yerevan city scene. Watermark: Y. Charents. 136x72mm. | FV | 7.50

51 **5000 Dram** | VF | UNC
2003. H. Tumanyuan at left. Back: Saryan's picture of Lory Mountains. Watermark: H. Tumanyuan. 143x72mm. | FV | 35.00

52 **10,000 Dram** | VF | UNC
2003; 2006; 2008. Purple and light violet on multicolor unpt. Avetik Isahakyan (poet) at left, Mt. Aragats at center. Back: Gyumri city view. Watermark: A. Isahakyan. 151x72mm.

	VF	UNC
a. 2003.	FV	55.00
b. 2006.	FV	50.00
c. 2008.	FV	50.00

		VF	UNC
53	**20,000 Dram** 2007. Brown and yellow on multicolor underprint. Martiros Saryan, painter, at left, abstract painting at center. Holographic foil at left. Back: Saryan painting *Armenia*. Watermark: M. Saryan. 150x72mm.	FV	125.

		VF	UNC
54	**100,000 Dram** 2009 Slate blue, brown and multicolor. King Abgar V standing at left, 1st century map at center. Back: St. Thaddeus transfers the painting of Jesus Christ to Abgar V of Edessa. Watermark: Abgar V. Printer: TDLR. 160x72mm.		
	a. Issued note.	FV	350.
	s. Specimen.	—	450.

2011-12 Issue

		VF	UNC
55	**1000 Dram** 2011. Aqua and green on multicolor underprint. Yeghishe Charents at left, lines of poetry at right. Foil strip at left. Back: Old Yerevan city scene.	FV	7.50

		VF	UNC
56	**5000 Dram** 2011. Green and brown on multicolor underprint. H. Tumanyuan at left. Back: Saryan's pictre of Lory Mountains. Watermark: H. Tumanyuan.	FV	35.00

		VF	UNC
57	**10,000 Dram** 2012. Lilac and black on multicolor underprint. Avetik Isahakyan at left, foil strip at left. Back: Gyumri city view. Watermark: A. Isahakyan	FV	55.00

		VF	UNC
58	**20,000 Dram** 2012. Brown and multicolor. Martiros Saryan at left, foil strip at left. Back: Saryan painting *Armenia*. Watermark: M. Saryan.	FV	125.

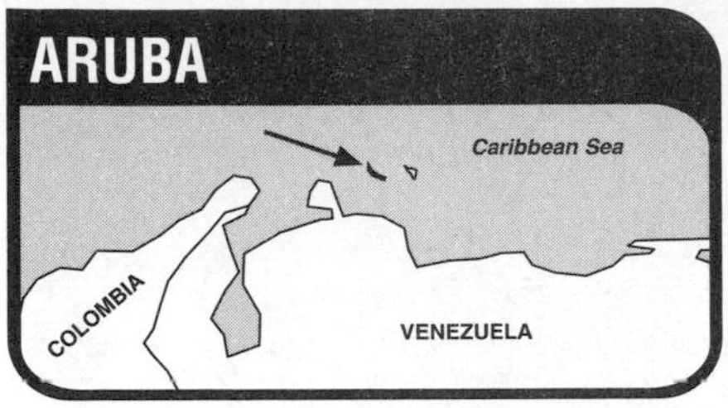

Aruba was the second-largest island of the Netherlands Antilles and is situated near the Venezuelan coast. The island has an area of 193 sq. km. and a population of 101,500. Capital: Oranjestad, named after the Dutch royal family.

Discovered and claimed for Spain in 1499, Aruba was acquired by the Dutch in 1636. The island's economy has been dominated by three main industries. A 19th century gold rush was followed by prosperity brought on by the opening in 1924 of an oil refinery. The last decades of the 20th century saw a boom in the tourism industry. Aruba seceded from the Netherlands Antilles in 1986 and became a separate, autonomous member of the Kingdom of the Netherlands. Movement toward full independence was halted at Aruba's request in 1990.

MONETARY SYSTEM:

1 Florin = 100 Cents

Dutch Administration

Banco Central di Aruba

1986 Issue

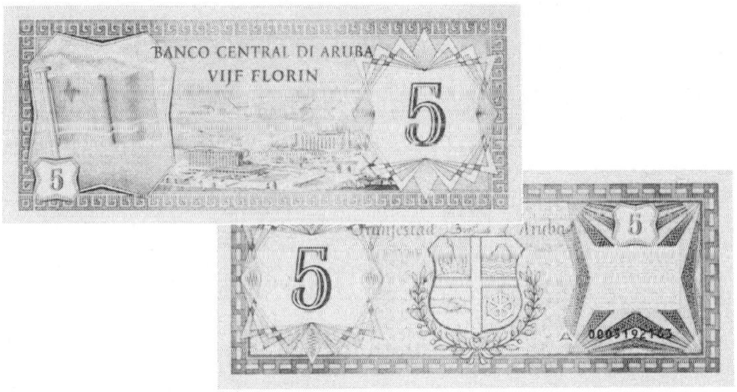

1 **5 Florin** — VF: FV — UNC: 50.00

1.1.1986. Green. Flag at left, coastal hotels at center. Back: Arms of Aruba at center. Printer: JEZ. 146x66mm.

2 **10 Florin** — VF: FV — UNC: 65.00

1.1.1986. Green. Flag at left, coastal hotels at center. Back: Arms of Aruba at center. Printer: JEZ. 147x66mm.

3 **25 Florin** — VF: FV — UNC: 110.

1.1.1986. Green. Flag at left, coastal hotels at center. Back: Arms of Aruba at center. Printer: JEZ. 147x66mm.

4 **50 Florin** — VF: FV — UNC: 160.

1.1.1986. Green. Flag at left, coastal hotels at center. Back: Arms of Aruba at center. Printer: JEZ. 147x66mm.

5 **100 Florin** — VF: FV — UNC: 340.

1.1.1986. Green. Flag at left, coastal hotels at center. Back: Arms of Aruba at center. Printer: JEZ. 147x66mm.

Centrale Bank van Aruba

1990 Issue

6 **5 Florin** — VF: FV — UNC: 37.50

1.1.1990. Purple and multicolor. Tortuga Blanco (sea turtle) at center right. Back: Geometric forms with pre-Columbian Aruban art. Watermark: Stylized tree. Printer: JEZ. 147x66mm.

7 **10 Florin** — VF: FV — UNC: 40.00

1.1.1990. Blue and multicolor. Calco Indian conch *(Melongena melongena)* at center right. Back: Geometric forms with pre-Columbian Aruban art. Watermark: Stylized tree. Printer: JEZ. 147x66mm.

8 **25 Florin** | VF FV | UNC 55.00

1.1.1990. Brown and multicolor. Rattlesnake *(Crotalus durissus unicolor)* at right. Back: Geometric forms with pre-Columbian Aruban art. Watermark: Stylized tree. Printer: JEZ. 147x66mm.

9 **50 Florin** | VF FV | UNC 80.00

1.1.1990. Red-brown and multicolor. Burrowing owl *(Speotyto cunicularia arubensis)* at center right. Back: Geometric forms with pre-Columbian Aruban art. Watermark: Stylized tree. Printer: JEZ. 147x66mm.

10 **100 Florin** | VF FV | UNC 325.

1.1.1990. Olive-green and multicolor. Frog *(Pleurodema brachyops)* at center right. Back: Geometric forms with pre-Columbian Aruban art. Watermark: Stylized tree. Printer: JEZ. 147x66mm.

1993 Issue

11 **10 Florin** | VF FV | UNC 40.00

16.7.1993. Blue and multicolor. Calco Indian conch *(Melongona melongena)* at center right, with text: *Wettig Betaalmiddel* (legal tender). Back: Geometric forms with pre-Colombian Aruban art. Watermark: Stylized tree. Printer: JEZ. With additional security features and new signatures. 147x66mm.

12 **25 Florin** | VF FV | UNC 37.50

16.7.1993. Brown and multicolor. Rattlesnake *(Speotyto cunicularia arubensis)* at right, with text: *Wettig Betaalmiddel* (legal tender). Back: Geometric forms with pre-Colombian Aruban art. Watermark: Stylized tree. Printer: JEZ. With additional security features and new signatures. 147x66mm.

13 **50 Florin** | VF FV | UNC 67.50

16.7.1993. Red-brown and multicolor. Burrowing owl *(Speotyto cunicularia arubensis)* at center right, with text: *Wettig Betaalmiddel* (legal tender). Back: Geometric forms with pre-Colombian Aruban art. Watermark: Stylized tree. Printer: JEZ. With additional security features and new signatures. 147x66mm.

14 **100 Florin** | VF FV | UNC 130.

16.7.1993. Olive-green and multicolor. Frog at center right, with text: *Wettig Betaalmiddel* (legal tender). Back: Geometric forms with pre-Colombian Aruban art. Watermark: Stylized tree. Printer: JEZ. With additional security features and new signatures. 147x66mm.

15 **500 Florin** | VF FV | UNC 515.

16.7.1993. Blue and multicolor. Grouper fish *(Epinephelus morio)*at center right, with text: *Wettig Betaalmiddel* (legal tender). Back: Geometric forms with pre-Colombian Aruban art. Watermark: Stylized tree. Printer: JEZ. With additional security features and new signatures. 147x66mm.

2003 Issue

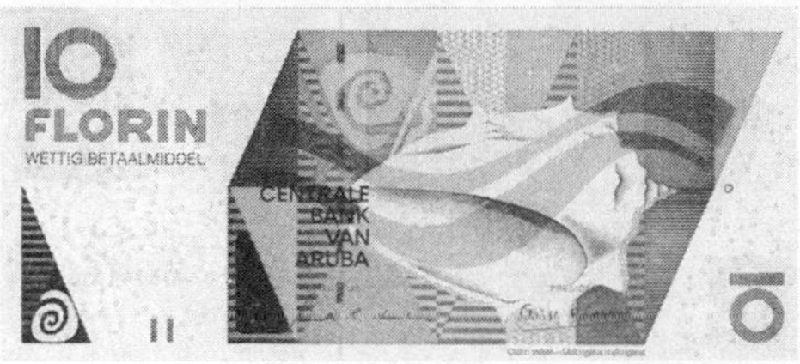

16 **10 Florin** — VF | UNC

1.12.2003; 1.7.2008. Blue and multicolor. Calco Indian conch *(Melongena melongena)* at center right with text: *Wettig Betaalmiddel* (legal tender). Back: Geometric forms with pre-Colombian Aruban art. Printer: JEZ. With additional security features. 147x66mm.

	VF	UNC
a. 1.12.2003.	FV	17.50
b. 1.7.2008. New right hand signature.	FV	15.00

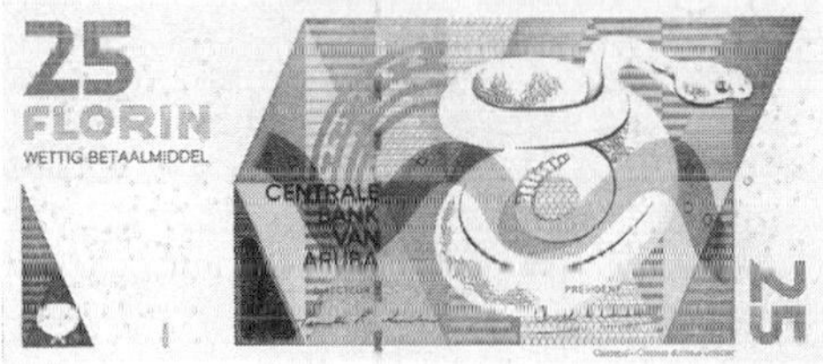

17 **25 Florin** — VF | UNC

1.12.2003; 1.7.2008. Brown and multicolor. Rattlesnake *(Crotalus durissus unicolor)* at right, with text: *Wettig Betaalmiddel* (legal tender). Back: Geometric forms with pre-Colombian Aruban art. Watermark: Stylized tree. Printer: JEZ. With additional security features. 147x66mm.

	VF	UNC
a. 1.12.2003.	FV	32.50
b. 1.7.2008. New right hand signature.	FV	30.00

18 **50 Florin** — VF | UNC

1.12.2003; 1.7.2008. Red-brown and multicolor. Burrowing owl (Speotyto cunicularia arubensis) at center right, with text: *Wettig Betaalmiddel* (legal tender). Back: Geometric forms with pre-Colombian Aruban art. Watermark: Stylized tree. Printer: JEZ. With additional security features. 147x66mm.

	VF	UNC
a. 1.12.2003.	FV	60.00
b. 1.7.2008. New right hand signature.	FV	55.00

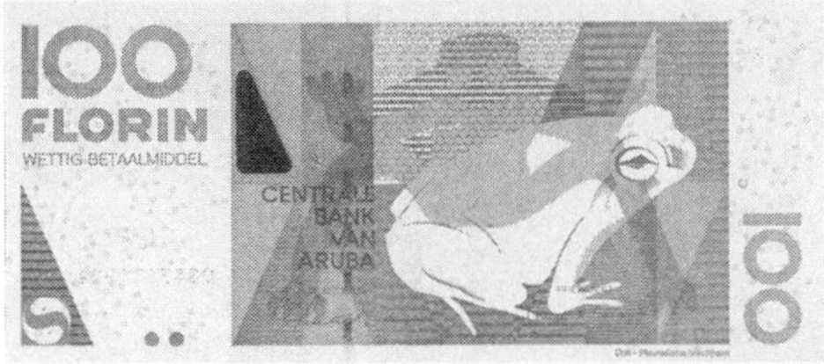

19 **100 Florin** — VF | UNC

1.12.2003; 1.7.2008. Olive-green and multicolor. Frog *(Pleurodema brachyops)* at center right, with text: *Wettig Betaalmiddel* (legal tender). Back: Geometric forms with pre-Colombian Aruban art. Watermark: Stylized tree. Printer: JEZ. With additional security features. 147x66mm.

	VF	UNC
a. 1.12.2003.	FV	250.
b. 1.7.2008. New right hand signature.	FV	115.

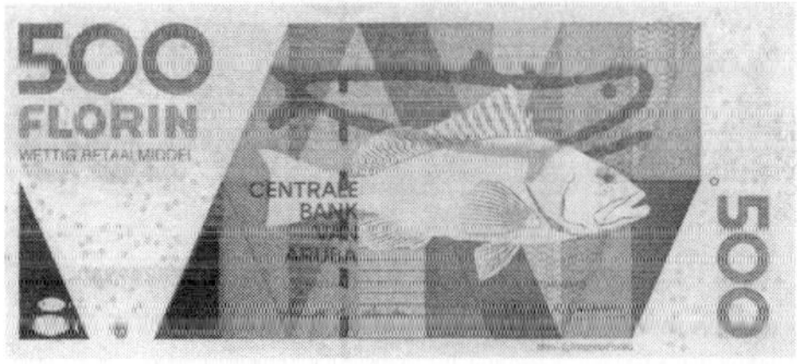

20	500 Florin	VF	UNC
	1.12.2003. Blue and multicolor. Grouper fish *(Epinephelus morio)* at center right, with text: *Wettig Betaalmiddel* (legal tender). Back: Geometric forms with pre-Colombian Aruban art. Watermark: Stylized tree. Printer: JEZ. With additional security features. 147x66mm.	FV	455.

Collector Series

Centrale Bank van Aruba

1990 Issue

CS1	1990 5-100 Florin	Mkt. Value
	#6-10 with low matched serial numbers housed in a six-page special presentation folder. 200 sets produced.	710.

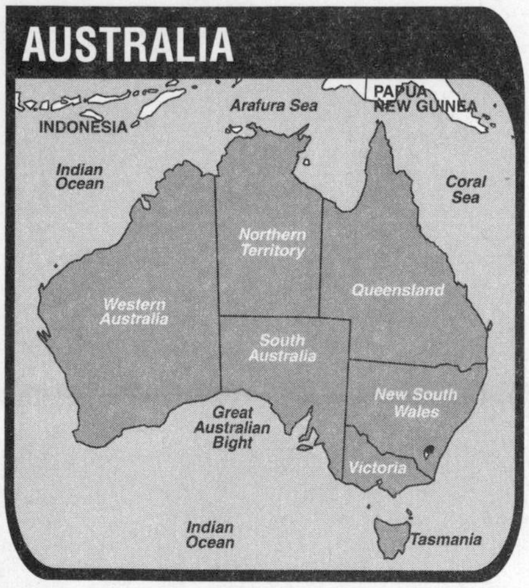

The Commonwealth of Australia, the smallest continent and largest island in the world, is located south of Indonesia between the Indian and Pacific oceans. It has an area of 7.68 million sq. km. and a population of 21 million. Capital: Canberra. Due to its early and sustained isolation, Australia is the habitat of such curious and unique fauna as the kangaroo, koala, platypus, wombat and barking lizard. The continent possesses extensive mineral deposits, the most important of which are gold, coal, silver, nickel, uranium, lead and zinc. Livestock raising, mining and manufacturing are the principal industries. Chief exports are wool, meat, wheat, iron ore, coal and nonferrous metals.

Aboriginal settlers arrived on the continent from Southeast Asia about 40,000 years before the first Europeans began exploration in the 17th century. No formal territorial claims were made until 1770, when Capt. James Cook took possession in the name of Great Britain. Six colonies were created in the late 18th and 19th centuries; they federated and became the Commonwealth of Australia in 1901. The new country took advantage of its natural resources to rapidly develop agricultural and manufacturing industries and to make a major contribution to the British effort in World Wars I and II. In recent decades, Australia has transformed itself into an internationally competitive, advanced market economy. It boasted one of the OECD's fastest growing economies during the 1990s, a performance due in large part to economic reforms adopted in the 1980s. Long-term concerns include climate-change issues such as the depletion of the ozone layer and more frequent droughts, and management and conservation of coastal areas, especially the Great Barrier Reef.

RULERS:

British

MONETARY SYSTEM:

1 Shilling = 12 Pence
1 Pound = 20 Shillings = 2 Dollars
1 Pound = 20 Shillings; to 1966
1 Dollar = 100 Cents, 1966-

COMMONWEALTH OF AUSTRALIA

RESERVE BANK

1960-61 ND ISSUE

		VF	UNC
33	**10 Shillings** ND (1961-65). Dark brown on orange and green underprint. Arms at lower left, portrait Matthew Flinders at right. Signature H. C. Coombs with title: *GOVERNOR / RESERVE BANK of AUSTRALIA* below lower left, signature R. Wilson. Back: Old Parliament House in Canberra. Watermark: Capt. James Cook.		
	a. Issued note.	100.	400.
	r. Serial # suffix *, replacement.	2500.	25,000.
	s. Specimen.	20,000.	60,000.

		VF	UNC
34	**1 Pound** ND (1961-65). Black on green and yellow underprint. Arms at upper center, cameo portrait Queen Elizabeth II at right. Signature H. C. Coombs with title: *GOVERNOR / RESERVE BANK of AUSTRALIA* below lower left, signature R. Wilson. Back: Green. Facing portrait Charles Sturt and Hamilton Hume. Watermark: Capt. James Cook.		
	a. Issued note.	60.00	300.
	r. Serial # suffix *, replacement.	3000.	30,000.
	s. Specimen.	17,500.	45,000.

1966-67 ND ISSUE

		VF	UNC
37	**1 Dollar** ND (1966-72). Dark brown on orange and multicolor underprint. Arms at center, Queen Elizabeth II at right, with text: *COMMONWEALTH OF* in heading. Back: Stylized aboriginal figures and animals. Watermark: Capt. James Cook. 140x70mm.		
	a. Signature H. C. Coombs and R. Wilson. (1966).	20.00	80.00
	b. Signature H. C. Coombs and R. J. Randall. (1968).	170.	850.
	c. Signature J. G. Phillips and R. J. Randall. (1969).	15.00	65.00
	d. Signature J. G. Phillips and F. H. Wheeler. (1972).	16.00	70.00
	s1. Specimen in oval on each side.	3000.	10,000.
	s2. Specimen eight times each side.	6000.	25,000.
	s3. Specimen twice diagonally each side.	8000.	35,000.
	ar. As a, serial # suffix *, replacement.	600.	3000.
	br. As b, serial # suffix *, replacement.	2000.	8500.
	cr. As c, serial # suffix *, replacement.	650.	3500.

		VF	UNC
38	**2 Dollars** ND (1966-72). Black on green, blue and yellow multicolor underprint. John MacArthur at right, sheep at center, with text: *COMMONWEALTH OF* in heading. Back: William Farrer at left, wheat at center. Watermark: Capt. James Cook. 145x71mm.		
	a. Signature H. C. Coombs and R. Wilson. (1966).	20.00	80.00
	b. Signature H. C. Coombs and R. J. Randall. (1967).	50.00	200.
	c. Signature J. G. Phillips and R. J. Randall. (1968).	20.00	80.00
	d. Signature J. G. Phillips and F. H. Wheeler. (1972).	20.00	80.00
	s1. As a. Specimen.	3000.	10,000.
	ar. As a, serial # suffix *, replacement.	750.	3500.
	br. As b, serial # suffix *, replacement.	2000.	8500.
	cr. As c, serial # suffix *, replacement.	100.	400.

39 5 Dollars VF UNC

ND (1967-72). Deep purple on multicolor underprint. Sir Joseph Banks at right, plants at center, with text: *COMMONWEALTH OF* in heading. Back: Caroline Chisholm, ship, buildings, and women. Watermark: Capt. James Cook. 152x76mm.

	VF	UNC
a. Signature H. C. Coombs and R. J. Randall. (1967).	50.00	275.
b. Signature J. G. Phillips and R. J. Randall. (1969).	50.00	265.
c. Signature J. G. Phillips and F. H. Wheeler. (1972).	45.00	240.
s1. As a. Specimen in oval each side.	3000.	10,000.
s2. As b. Specimen eight time each side.	6500.	26,500.
s3. As c. Specimen twice diagonally each side.	9000.	36,500.
ar. As a, serial # suffix *, replacement.	2000.	9000.
br. As b, serial # suffix *, replacement.	2500.	11,000.

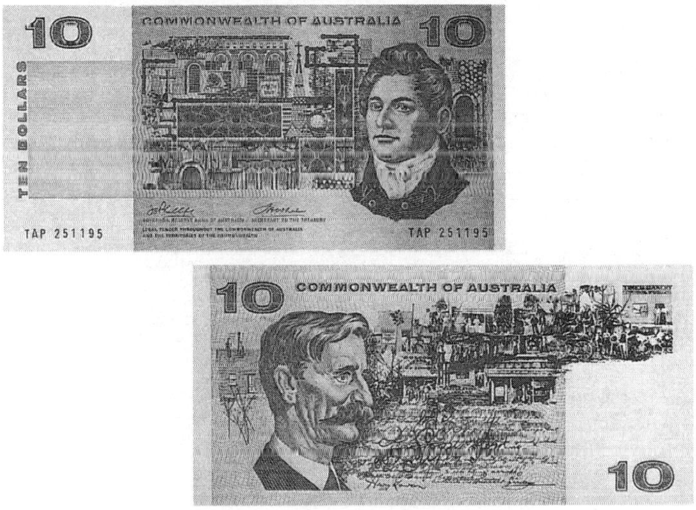

40 10 Dollars VF UNC

ND (1966-72). Black on blue, orange and multicolor underprint. Francis Greenway at right, village scene at center, with text: *COMMONWEALTH OF* in heading. Back: Henry Lawson and buildings. Watermark: Capt. James Cook. 155x76mm.

	VF	UNC
a. Signature H. C. Coombs and R. Wilson. (1966).	20.00	80.00
b. Signature H. G. Coombs and R. J. Randall. (1967).	150.	700.
c. Signature J. G. Phillips and R. J. Randall. (1968).	30.00	130.
d. Signature J. G. Phillips and F. H. Wheeler. (1972).	25.00	90.00
s1. As a. Specimen in oval each side.	3000.	10,000.
s2. As b. Specimen eight time each side.	6750.	28,000.
s3. As c. Specimen twice diagonally each side.	10,000.	38,000.
ar. As a, serial # suffix *, replacement.	1000.	4500.
br. As b, serial # suffix *, replacement.	2000.	8000.
cr. As c, serial # suffix *, replacement.	1250.	5500.

41 20 Dollars VF UNC

ND (1966-72). Black on red, yellow and multicolor underprint. Sir Charles Kingsford-Smith at right, with text: *COMMONWEALTH OF* in heading. Back: Lawrence Hargrave at left, aeronautical devices. Watermark: Capt. James Cook. 160x81mm.

	VF	UNC
a. Signature H. C. Coombs and R. Wilson. (1966).	30.00	90.00
b. Signature H. G. Coombs and R. J. Randall. (1968).	1000.	7500.
c. Signature J. G. Phillips and R. J. Randall. (1968).	50.00	300.
d. Signature J. G. Phillips and F. H. Wheeler. (1972).	50.00	325.
s1. As a. Specimen in oval each side.	3000.	12,000.
s2. As b. Specimen eight times each side.	6750.	10,000.
s3. As c. Specimen twice diagonally each side.	1400.	28,000.
cr. As c, serial # suffix *, replacement.	4000.	12,000.

Australia, Reserve Bank

1973; 1984 ND Issue

42 1 Dollar VF UNC

ND (1974-83). Dark brown on orange and multicolor underprint. Arms at center, Queen Elizabeth II at right, without text: *COMMONWEALTH OF* in heading. Back: Stylized aboriginal figures and animals. Watermark: Capt. James Cook. 140x70mm.

	VF	UNC
a. Signature J. G. Phillips and F. H. Wheeler. (1974).	15.00	60.00
b1. Signature H. M. Knight and F. H. Wheeler. (1976). Center security thread.	8.00	35.00
b2. As b1. Side security thread.	8.00	25.00
b3. KW test note DBP.	40.00	190.
c. Signature H. M. Knight and J. Stone. (1979).	5.00	15.00
d. Signature R. A. Johnston and J. Stone. (1983).	2.00	7.00
s1. As a. Specimen twice diagonally each side.		12,600.
s2. As b1. Specimen twice diagonally each side.	—	25,000.

43 2 Dollars VF UNC

ND (1974-85). Black on green, blue and yellow underprint. John MacArthur at right, sheep at center, without text: *COMMONWEALTH OF* in heading. Back: William Farrer at left, wheat at center. Watermark: Capt. James Cook. 145x71mm.

	VF	UNC
a. Signature J. G. Phillips and F. H. Wheeler. (1974).	15.00	70.00
b1. Signature H. M. Knight and F. H. Wheeler. (1976). Gothic serial #.	40.00	170.
b2. Signature H. M. Knight and F. H. Wheeler. (1976). Ocrb serial #. Center thread.	30.00	100.
b3. Signature H. M. Knight and F. H. Wheeler. (1976). Ocrb serial #. Side thread.	8.00	40.00
c. Signature H. M. Knight and J. Stone. (1979).	5.00	17.00
d. Signature R. A. Johnston and J. Stone. (1983).	5.00	17.00
e. Signature R. A. Johnston and B. W. Fraser. (1985).	2.00	8.00
s1. As a. Specimen twice diagonally each side.	5000.	10,000.
s2. As b. Specimen twice diagonally each side.	—	15,000.

44 5 Dollars VF UNC

ND (1974-91). Deep purple on multicolor underprint. Sir Joseph Banks at right, plants at center, without text: *COMMONWEALTH OF* in heading. Back: Caroline Chisholm, ship, buildings and women. Watermark: Capt. James Cook. 152x76mm.

	VF	UNC
a. Signature J. G. Phillips and F. H. Wheeler. (1974).	40.00	220.
b1. H.M. Knight and F.H. Wheeler. Centre metal thread.	20.00	80.00
b2. H.M. Knight and F.H. Wheeler. Side metal thread.	15.00	70.00
b3. H.M. Knight and F.H. Wheeler. Ocrb (last type) serials.	15.00	60.00
c. Signature H. M. Knight and J. Stone. (1979).	12.00	35.00
d. Signature R. A. Johnston and J. Stone. (1983).	12.00	35.00
e. Signature R. A. Johnston and B. W. Fraser. (1985). 2 serial # varieties.	10.00	30.00
f. Signature B. W. Fraser and C. I. Higgins. (1990).	10.00	30.00
g. Signature B. W. Fraser and A. S. Cole. (1991).	8.00	25.00
s1. As a. Specimen twice diagonally each side.	5000.	10,000.
s2. As b1. Specimen twice diagonally each side.	—	15,000.

45 10 Dollars VF UNC

ND (1974-91). Black on blue and orange underprint. Francis Greenway at right, village scene at center, without text: *COMMONWEALTH OF* in heading. Back: Henry Lawson and buildings. Watermark: Capt. James Cook. 155x76mm.

	VF	UNC
a. Signature J. G. Phillips and F. H. Wheeler. (1974).	55.00	220.
b. Signature H. M. Knight and F. H. Wheeler. (1976).	50.00	200.
c. Signature H. M. Knight and J. Stone. (1979). 2 serial # varieties.	30.00	100.
d. Signature R. A. Johnston and J. Stone. (1983).	25.00	95.00
e. Signature R. A. Johnston and B. W. Fraser. (1985).	15.00	40.00
f. Signature B. W. Fraser and C. I. Higgins. (1990).	18.00	45.00
g. Signature B. W. Fraser and A. S. Cole. (1991).	15.00	40.00
s1. As a. Specimen.	5500.	11,000.

46 20 Dollars VF UNC

ND (1974-94). Black on red, yellow and multicolor underprint. Sir Charles Kingsford-Smith at right, without text: *COMMONWEALTH OF* in heading. Back: Lawrence Hargrave at left, aeronautical devices. Watermark: Capt. James Cook. 160x81mm.

	VF	UNC
a. Signature J. G. Phillips and F. H. Wheeler. (1974).	75.00	375.
b. Signature H. M. Knight and F. H. Wheeler. (1975).	50.00	300.
c. Signature H. M. Knight and J. Stone. (1979). 2 serial # varieties.	65.00	220.
d. Signature R. A. Johnston and J. Stone. (1983).	40.00	180.
e. Signature R. A. Johnston and B. W. Fraser. (1985) 2 serial # varieties.	30.00	90.00
f. Signature M. J. Phillips and B. W. Fraser. (1989).	35.00	125.
g. Signature B. W. Fraser and C. I. Higgins. (1989).	30.00	105.
h. Signature B. W. Fraser and A. S. Cole. (1991).	28.00	90.00
i. Signature B. W. Fraser and E. A. Evans. (1994).	28.00	90.00
s1. As a. Specimen.	5000.	10,000.

47 50 Dollars VF UNC

ND (1973-94). Dark brown and black on multicolor underprint. Teaching implements at center, Lord Howard Walker Florey at right, without text: *COMMONWEALTH OF* in heading. Back: Ian Clunies-Ross at left, space research at center. Watermark: Capt. James Cook. 165x82mm.

	VF	UNC
a. Signature J. G. Phillips and F. H. Wheeler. (1973).	120.	300.
b. Signature H. M. Knight and F. H. Wheeler. (1975).	120.	325.
c. Signature H. M. Knight and J. Stone. (1979).	100.	250.
d. Signature R. A. Johnston and J. Stone. (1983).	90.00	230.
e. Signature R. A. Johnston and B. W. Fraser. (1985). 2 serial # varieties.	100.	250.
f. Signature M. J. Phillips and B. W. Fraser. (1989).	80.00	200.
g. Signature B. W. Fraser and C. I. Higgins. (1989).	100.	250.
h. Signature B. W. Fraser and A. S. Cole. (1991).	65.00	140.
i. Signature B. W. Fraser and E. A. Evans. (1994).	70.00	150.

48 100 Dollars VF UNC

ND (1984-92). Blue and gray on multicolor underprint. Sir Douglas Mawson at center, without text: *COMMONWEALTH OF* in heading. Back: J. Tebbutt at left center. Watermark: Capt. James Cook. 172x82.5mm.

	VF	UNC
a. Signature R. A. Johnston and J. Stone. (1984).	125.	250.
b. Signature R. A. Johnston and B. W. Fraser. (1985).	125.	250.
c. Signature B. W. Fraser and C. I. Higgins. (1990).	125.	250.
d. Signature B. W. Fraser and A. S. Cole. (1992).	125.	250.

1988 ND Commemorative Issue

49 **10 Dollars** VF UNC

1988; ND. Brown and green on multicolor underprint. Captain James Cook OVD at upper left, colonists across background; Cook's ship *Supply* at lower right shoreline. Signature R. A. Johnston and B. W. Fraser. Back: Aboriginal youth, rock painting and ceremonial *Morning Star* pole at center. Printer: NPA. Polymer plastic.

a. Serial # prefix AA. 26.1.1988. Issued in folder.	15.00	40.00
b. Issued note. Serial # prefix AB. ND.	15.00	45.00

1992-2001 Issues

50 **5 Dollars** VF UNC

ND (1992); (19)93. Black, red and blue on multicolor underprint. Branch at left, Queen Elizabeth II at center right, issue dates are indicated by the first two digits of the serial number. Back: Black on lilac and umlticolor underprint. Old and new Parliament Houses in Canberra at center, gum flower OVD at lower right. Printer: NPA. UV: serial # fluoresce yellow; Face: blue. 130x65mm.

a. Signature B. W. Fraser and A. S. Cole. (1992).	10.00	35.00
b. Signature B. W. Fraser and E. A. Evans. (1993).	10.00	40.00

51 **5 Dollars** VF UNC

(19)95-(20)01. Black, red and bright purple. Branch at left, Queen Elizabeth II at center right. Orientation bands in upper and lower margins, gum flower OVD at lower right, issue dates are indicated by the first two digits of the serial number. Back: Black on lilac with darker multicolor underprint. Old and new Parliament Houses in Canberra at center. Printer: NPA. 130x65mm.

a. With 4 diagonal white lines in orientation band at lower left signature B. W. Fraser and E. A. Evans. (1995-96).	15.00	35.00
b. As a, but with 11 diagonal white lines in orientation band at lower left Plate error. (1995).	25.00	50.00
c. Signature I. Macfarlane and E. A. Evans. (1996-98) 2002-03.	15.00	35.00

52 **10 Dollars** VF UNC

(19)93-(20)01. Dark blue and purple on multicolor underprint. Man on horseback at left, A. B. "Banjo" Paterson at center, windmill OVD in transparent window at lower right, issue dates are indicated by the first two digits of the serial number. Back: Dame Mary Gilmore at center right. Dark blue and purple on multicolor underprint. Printer: NPA. 137x65mm.

a. Signature B. W. Fraser and E. A. Evans. (1993-94).	30.00	35.00
b. Signature I. Macfarlane and E. A. Evans. (1996-98).	28.00	35.00

53 **20 Dollars** VF UNC

(19)94-(20)01. Blaack and red on orange and pale green underprint. Mary Reiby at center, sailing ship at left, compass OVD in treanspareint window at lower right, issue dates are indicated by the first two digits of the serial number. Back: Biplane at left, Rev. John Flynn at center right, camel at right. Printer: NPA. 144x65mm.

a. Signature B. W. Fraser and E. A. Evans. (1994-96).	40.00	75.00
b. Signature I. Macfarlane and E. A. Evans. (1997-98).	30.00	55.00

54 **50 Dollars** VF UNC

(19)95-(20)01. Black and deep purple on yellow-brown, green and multicolor underprint. David Unaipon at left center, Mission Church at Point McLeay at lower left, patent drawings at upper center right, Southern Cross constellation OVD in transparent window at lower right, issue dates ar Back: Edith Cowan, foster mother with children at center, W. Australia's Parliament House at upper left, Cowan at lectern at right. Printer: NPA. 151x65mm.

a. Signature B. W. Fraser and E. A. Evans. (1995-96).	75.00	150.
b. Signature I. Macfarlane and E. A. Evans. (1997-98).	70.00	120.

55 **100 Dollars** VF UNC

(19)96-(20)01. Black and green on orange and multicolor underprint. Opera stage at left, Dame Nellie Melba at center, stylized peacock OVD in transparent window at lower right, issue dates are indicated by the first two digits of the serial number. Back: Sir John Monash and WWI battle scenes and insignia. Printer: NPA. 158x65mm.

a. Signature B. W. Fraser and E. A. Evans. (1996).	135.	200.
b. Signature I. Macfarlane and E. A. Evans. (1998-2001).	120.	175.

2001 Commemorative Issue

#56, Centennial of the Commonwealth

56 **5 Dollars** VF UNC

1.1.2001. Black, violet and blue on multicolor underprint. Sir Henry Parkes at center, issue date is the first two digits of the serial number. Back: Catherine Helen Spence at center. Printer: NPA. UV: back branch of leaves and 5 fluoresce yellow. 130x65mm.	10.00	20.00

2002-09 Issue

57 5 Dollars

(20)03-(20)12. Black, red and blue on multicolor un derprint. Branch at left, Queen Elizabeth II at center right with name under portrait. Issue dates are first two digits of serial number. Back: Black on lilac with darker multicolor underprint. Old and new Parliament Houses in Canberra at center. Printer: NPA. 130x65mm.

	VF	UNC
a. (20)02. Signature I. Macfarlane and K. Henry.	7.50	12.50
b. (20)03. Signature I. Macfarlane and K. Henry.	7.50	12.50
c. (20)05. Signature I. Macfarlane and K. Henry.	6.00	10.00
d. (20)06. Signature I. Macfarlane and K. Henry.	FV	9.00
e. (20)07. Signature Glenn R. Stevens and K. Henry.	FV	9.00
f. (20)08. Signature Glenn R. Stevens and K. Henry.	FV	8.00
g. (20)12. Signature Glenn R, Stevens and Martin Parkinson.	FV	8.00

58 10 Dollars

(20)02-03; (20)06-07. Dark blue and purple on multicolor underprint. Man on horseback at left, A. B. "Banjo" Paterson at center with name below, windmill OVD in transparent window at lower right, issue date is first two digits of the serial number. Back: Dame Mary Gilmore at center right. Printer: NPA. Polymer plastic. 137x65mm.

	VF	UNC
a. (20)02. Signature I. Macfarlane and K. Henry.	15.00	25.00
b. (20)03. Signature I. Macfarlane and K. Henry.	15.00	25.00
c. (20)06. Signature I. Macfarlane and K. Henry.	15.00	25.00
d. (20)07. Signature Glenn R. Stevens and K. Henry.	FV	20.00
e. (20)08. Signature Glenn R. Stevens and K. Henry.	FV	20.00
f. (20)12. Signature Glenn R. Stevens and Martin Parkinson.	FV	17.50

59 20 Dollars

(20)02-03; (20)05-10. Black and red on orange and pale green underprint. Mary Reiby at center, name below, sailing ship at left, compass OVD in transparent window at lower right, issue date is first two digits of the serial number. Back: Biplane at left, Rev. John Flynn at center right, camel at right. Printer: NPA. Polymer plastic. 144x65mm.

	VF	UNC
a. (20)02. Signature I. Macfarlane and K. Henry.	25.00	35.00
b. (20)03. Signature I. Macfarlane and K. Henry.	25.00	35.00
c. (20)05. Signature I. Macfarlane and K. Henry.	25.00	35.00
d. (20)06. Signature I. Macfarlane and K. Henry.	25.00	35.00
e. (20)07. Signature Glenn R. Stevens and K. Henry	25.00	35.00
f. (20)08. Signature Glenn R. Stevens and K. Henry.	25.00	35.00
g. (20)10.	25.00	35.00

60 50 Dollars

(20)03-(20)12. Black and deep purple on yellow-brown, green and multicolor. David Unaipon at left center, name below. Mission church at Point McLeay at lower left, patent drawings at upper center. Southern Cross OVD in transpoarent window at lower right. Back: Edith Cowan, foster mother with children at center. W. Australia's Parliament House at upper left. Printer: NPA. 151x65mm.

	VF	UNC
a. (20)03. Signature I. Macfarlane and K. Henry.	65.00	75.00
b. (20)04. Signature I. Macfarlane and K. Henry.	65.00	75.00
c. (20)05. Signature I. Macfarlane and K. Henry.	65.00	75.00
d. (20)06. Signature I. Macfarlane and K. Henry.	65.00	75.00
e. (20)07. Signatures Glenn R. Stevens and K. Henry.	65.00	75.00
f. (20)08. Signatures Glenn R. Stevens and K. Henry.	FV	75.00
g. (20)09. Signatures Glenn R. Stevens and K. Henry.	FV	75.00
h. (20)10.	FV	75.00
i. (20)12. Signatures Glenn R. Stevens and Martin Parkinson.	FV	75.00

61 100 Dollars

(20)08; (20)10. Black and green on orange and multicolor underprint. Opera stage at left, Dame Nellie Melba at center, name below. Stylized peacock OVD in transparent window at lower right. Back: Sir John Monash with WWI battle scenes and insignia. 158x65mm.

	VF	UNC
a. (20)08. Signatures Glenn R. Stevens and Ken Henry.	FV	115.
b. (20)10.	FV	15.00

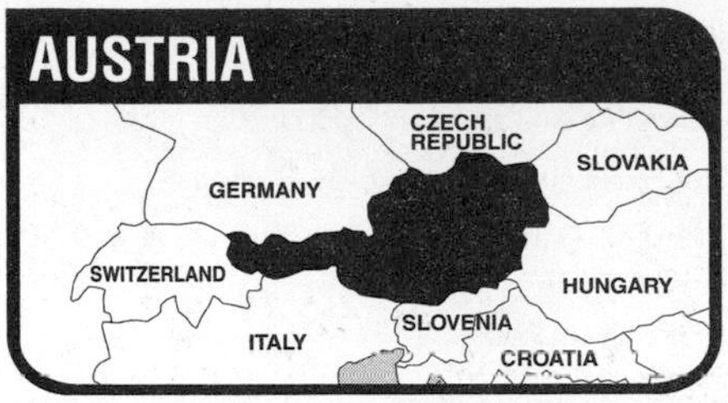

The Republic of Austria (Oesterreich), a parliamentary democracy located in mountainous central Europe, has an area of 83,870 sq. km. and a population of 8.2 million. Capital: Vienna. Austria is primarily an industrial country. Machinery, iron and steel, textiles, yarns and timber are exported.

Once the center of power for the large Austro-Hungarian Empire, Austria was reduced to a small republic after its defeat in World War I. Following annexation by Nazi Germany in 1938 and subsequent occupation by the victorious Allies in 1945, Austria's status remained unclear for a decade. A State Treaty signed in 1955 ended the occupation, recognized Austria's independence, and forbade unification with Germany. A constitutional law that same year declared the country's "perpetual neutrality" as a condition for Soviet military withdrawal. The Soviet Union's collapse in 1991 and Austria's entry into the European Union in 1995 have altered the meaning of this neutrality. A prosperous, democratic country, Austria entered the EU Economic and Monetary Union in 1999.

MONETARY SYSTEM:

1 Gulden = 60 Kreuzer, 1754-1857
1 Gulden = (Florin) = 100 Kreuzer, 1857-1892
1 Krone = 100 Heller, 1892-1924
1 Schilling = 100 Groschen, 1924-1938, 1945-2002
1 Euro = 100 Cents, 2002-

Republic

Oesterreichische Nationalbank

Austrian National Bank

1956-65 Issues

		VF	UNC
137	**50 Schilling** 2.7.1962 (1963). Purple on multicolor underprint. Richard Wettstein at right, arms at bottom center. Back: Mauterndorf castle in Salzburg.		
	a. Issued note.	12.50	25.00
	s. Specimen.	—	50.00

		VF	UNC
139	**500 Schilling** 1.7.1965 (1966). Red-brown on multicolor underprint. Josef Ressel at right. Back: Steam powered screw propeller ship *Civetta* at left, arms at lower right. 155x80mm.		
	a. Issued note.	75.00	150.
	s. Specimen. Red overprint: *MUSTER* on face and *SPECIMEN* on back.	—	500.

1966-70 Issues

		VF	UNC
142	**20 Schilling** 2.7.1967 (1968). Brown on olive and lilac underprint. Carl Ritter von Ghega at right, arms at lower center. Back: Semmering Railway bridge over the Semmering Pass (986 meters). 132x65mm.		
	a. Issued note.	2.50	4.50
	s. Specimen.	—	250.

		VF	UNC
143	**50 Schilling** 2.1.1970 (1972). Purple on multicolor underprint. Ferdinand Raimund at right, arms at left. Back: Burg Theater in Vienna at left center.		
	a. Issued note.	6.00	12.00
	s. Specimen. Overprint: *Muster.*	—	500.

		VF	UNC
144	**50 Schilling** 2.1.1970 (1983). Ferdinand Raimund at right, arms at left, with overprint *2. AUFLAGE* (2nd issue) at lower left center. Back: Burg Theater in Vienna at left center.	6.00	12.00

145 100 Schilling VF UNC
2.1.1969 (1970). Dark green on multicolor underpritn. Angelika Kauffmann at right. Back: Large house.

	VF	UNC
a. Issued note.	10.00	22.50
s. Specimen. Overprint: *Muster*.	—	750.

146 100 Schilling VF UNC
2.1.1969 (1981). Angelika Kauffmann at right, with overprint; *2 AUFLAGE* (2nd issue) at upper left. Back: Large house.

	VF	UNC
a. Issued note.	12.00	22.50
s. Specimen.	—	250.

147 1000 Schilling
1.7.1966 (1970). Blue-violet on multicolor underprint. Bertha von Suttner at center right, arms at right. Back: Leopoldskron Castle and Hohensalzburg Fortress.

	VF	UNC
a. Issued note.	90.00	275.
s. Specimen. Overprint: *Muster*.	—	1250.

1983-88 Issue

148 20 Schilling VF UNC
1.10.1986 (1988). Dark brown and brown on multicolor underprint. Federal arms at upper left, Moritz Daffinger at right. Back: Vienna's *Albertina* Museum at left center. Watermark: Federal arms and parallel vertical lines. UV: Fibers fluoresce blue; security strip yellow; back: bottom serial # orange. 123x62mm. FV 3.25

149 50 Schilling VF UNC
2.1.1986 (1987). Purple and violet on multicolor underprint. Federal arms at upper left, Sigmund Freud at right. Back: Vienna's *Josephinum* Medical School at left center. Watermark: Federal arms and parallel vertical lines. 130x65mm. FV 7.00

150 100 Schilling VF UNC
2.1.1984 (1985). Dark green, gray and dark brown on multicolor underprint. Federal arms at upper left, Eugen Böhm v. Bawerk at right. 3 serial number varieties. Back: Wissenschaften Academy in Vienna at left center. Watermark: Federal arms and parallel vertical lines. 137x69mm. FV 17.50

151 500 Schilling VF UNC
1.7.1985 (1986). Dark brown, deep violet and orange-brown on multicolor underprint Federal arms at upper left, Architect Otto Wagner at right. Back: Vienna's Post Office Savings Bank at left center. Watermark: Federal arms and parallel vertical lines. 144x72mm. FV 75.00

152 1000 Schilling VF UNC
3.1.1983. Dark blue and purple on multicolor underprint. Federal arms at upper left, Erwin Schrödinger at right. Back: Vienna University at left center. Watermark: Federal arms and parallel vertical lines. 152x72mm. FV 150.

153 **5000 Schilling** — VF / UNC

4.1.1988 (1989). Light brown and purple on multicolor underprint. Federal arms at upper left, Woflgang Amadeus Mozart at right, kinegram of Mozart's head at lower left. Back: Vienna Opera House at center. Watermark: Federal arms and parallel vertical lines. 160x80mm.

	VF	UNC
a. Issued note.	FV	675.
s. Specimen. Overprint *MUSTER.* in red.	—	850.

1997 Issue

154 **500 Schilling** — VF / UNC

1.1.1997. Brown on multicolor underprint. Rosa Mayreder at left. Back: Rosa and Karl Mayreder with group at right. 147x72mm. — FV / 70.00

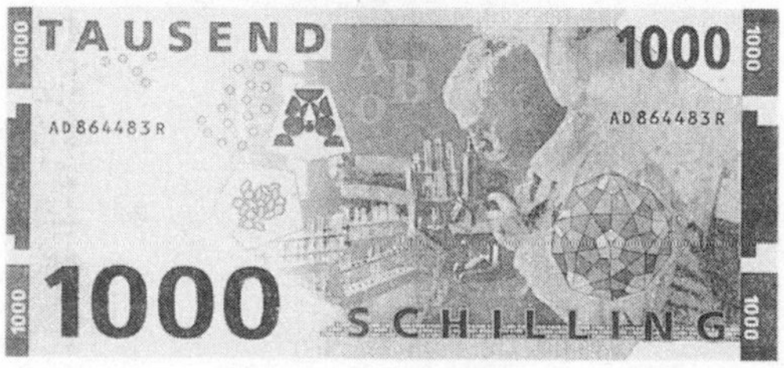

155 **1000 Schilling** — VF / UNC

1.1.1997. Blue on multicolor underprint. Karl Landsteiner at left. Back: Landsteiner working in his laboratory in Licenter at right. 154x72mm. — FV / 135.

The Republic of Azerbaijan includes the Nakhichevan Autonomous Republic and Nagorno-Karabakh Autonomous Region (which was abolished in 1991). Situated in the eastern area of Transcaucasia, it is bordered in the west by Armenia, in the north by Georgia and the Russian Federation of Dagestan, to the east by the Caspian Sea and to the south by Iran. It has an area of 86,600 sq. km. and a population of 8.18 million. Capital: Baku. The area is rich in mineral deposits of aluminum, copper, iron, lead, salt and zinc, with oil as its leading industry. Agriculture and livestock follow in importance.

Azerbaijan - a nation with a majority-Turkic and majority-Muslim population - was briefly independent from 1918 to 1920; it regained its independence after the collapse of the Soviet Union in 1991. Despite a 1994 cease-fire, Azerbaijan has yet to resolve its conflict with Armenia over the Azerbaijani Nagorno-Karabakh enclave (largely Armenian populated). Azerbaijan has lost 16% of its territory and must support some 600,000 internally displaced persons as a result of the conflict. Corruption is ubiquitous, and the government has been accused of authoritarianism. Although the poverty rate has been reduced in recent years, the promise of widespread wealth from development of Azerbaijan's energy sector remains largely unfulfilled.

Republic

Azerbaycan Milli Banki

1992 ND Issue

In 1993, due to a cash crisis, bonds of the State Loan of Azerbaijan Republic were officially used as currency; however, they were not freely accepted in the local bazaars. The acceptance term of these bonds in the branches of the State Savings Bank was until 1 June 2000.

11 **1 Manat** — VF / UNC

ND (1992). Deep olive-green on multicolor underprint. Baku's Maiden Tower at center. — 3.00 / 7.50

12 **10 Manat** — VF / UNC

ND (1992). Deep brown-violet on multicolor underprint. Baku's Maiden Tower at center. — 7.50 / 15.00

13 **250 Manat** — VF / UNC

ND (1992). Deep blue-gray on multicolor underprint. Baku's Maiden Tower at center. UV: threads fluoresce blue. AMB yellow, 250 green; back design elements green.

	VF	UNC
a. First issue with fraction prefix.	25.00	75.00
b. Second issue with 2 prefix letters.	2.50	5.00

Azerbaycan Republic State Loan Bonds

1993 Issue

No.	Denomination	VF	UNC
13A	**250 Manat** 1993. Olive-green on multicolor underprint. Printer: Goznak.	—	—
13B	**500 Manat** 1993. Pinkish-red on multicolor underprint. Printer: Goznak.	—	—
13C	**1000 Manat** 1993. Steel-blue on multicolor underprint. Printer: Goznak.	—	—

Azerbaycan Milli Banki

1993 ND; 1994-95 Issue

No.	Denomination	VF	UNC
14	**1 Manat** ND (1993). Deep blue on tan, dull orange and green underprint. Baku's Maiden Tower ruins at center. Back: Ornate "value". Watermark: 3 flames. UV: AMB fluoresce yellow; back: design elements yellow.	FV	5.00

No.	Denomination	VF	UNC
15	**5 Manat** ND (1993). Deep brown on lilac and multicolor underprint. Baku's Maiden Tower ruins at center. Back: Ornate "value". Watermark: 3 flames.	FV	7.00

No.	Denomination	VF	UNC
16	**10 Manat** ND (1993). Deep grayish blue-green on pale blue and multicolor underprint. Baku's Maiden Tower ruins at center. Back: Ornate "value". Watermark: 3 flames.	FV	10.00

No.	Denomination	VF	UNC
17	**50 Manat** ND (1993). Red on ochre and multicolor underprint. Baku's Maiden Tower ruins at center. Back: Ornate "value". Watermark: 3 flames.		
	a. First issue with fraction prefix.	5.00	15.00
	b. Second issue with 2 prefix letters.	1.00	2.00

No.	Denomination	VF	UNC
18	**100 Manat** ND (1993). Red-violet on pale blue and multicolor underprint. Baku's Maiden Tower ruins at center. Back: Ornate "value". Watermark: 3 flames.		
	a. First issue with fraction prefix.	5.00	20.00
	b. Second issue with 2 prefix letters.	1.00	3.00

No.	Denomination	VF	UNC
19	**500 Manat** ND (1993). Deep brown on pale blue, pink and multicolor underprint. Portrait N. Gencevi at right. Back: Ornate "value". Watermark: 3 flames.		
	a. First issue with fraction prefix.	7.00	25.00
	b. Second issue with 2 prefix letters.	1.00	5.00

No.	Denomination	VF	UNC
20	**1000 Manat** ND (1993). Dark brown and blue on pink and multicolor underprint. M. E. Resulzado at right. Back: Ornate "value". Watermark: 3 flames.		
	a. First issue with fraction prefix.	5.00	20.00
	b. Second issue with 2 prefix letters.	1.00	5.00

No.	Denomination	VF	UNC
21	**10,000 Manat** 1994. Dull dark brown and pale violet on multicolor underprint. Shirvansha's Palace at center right. Watermark: AMB repeated.		
	a. Security thread.	20.00	60.00
	b. Segmented foil over security thread.	2.00	15.00

22 **50,000 Manat** — VF: FV — UNC: 50.00
1995. Blue-green and light brown on multicolor underprint. Mausoleum in Nachziban at center right. Back: Carpet design at left. Segmented foil over security thread.

2001 Issue

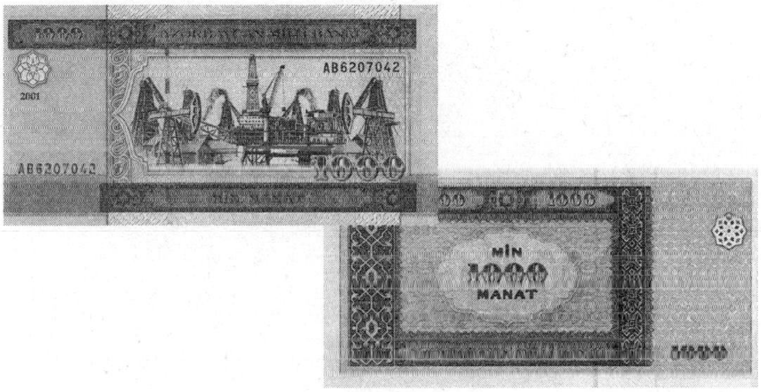

23 **1000 Manat** — VF: FV — UNC: 6.00
2001. Slate blue on light blue and multicolor underprint. Oil rigs and pumps at center right. Back: Value. UV: fibers fluoresce yellow, blue; Face: value in box green, lower serial # orange, background elements yellow.

2005 Issue

24 **1 Manat** — VF: FV — UNC: 3.00
2005. Olive gray on yellow. Azerbaijani folk musical instruments. Back: Map and carpets 119x70mm.

26 **5 Manat** — VF: FV — UNC: 12.00
2005. Yellowish-brown. Writers, poets and books. Back: Map. 127x70mm.

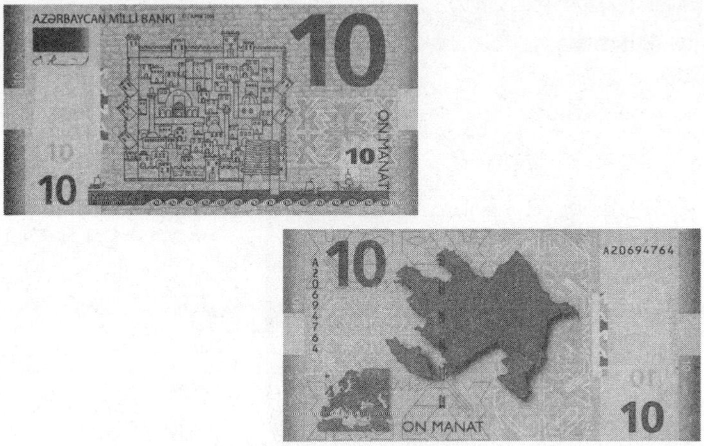

27 **10 Manat** — VF: FV — UNC: 24.00
2005. Slate blue and blue. Old Baku City view, Sharvanshah's Palace, Maiden Tower. Back: Map. 130x70mm.

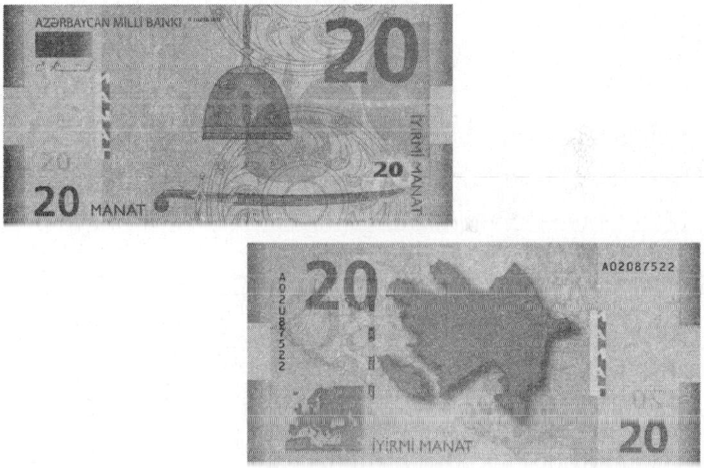

No.	Denomination	VF	UNC
28	**20 Manat** 2005. Green on light orange. Sword, helmet and shield. Back: Map. 141x70mm.	FV	45.00
29	**50 Manat** 2005. Olive green, blue and multicolor. Stairs. Back: Map. 148x70mm.	FV	100.
30	**100 Manat** 2005. Lilac, brown on blue and multicolor. 155x70mm.	FV	200.

Azerbaycan Merkezi Banki

2009 Issue

No.	Denomination	VF	UNC
31	**1 Manat** 2009.	FV	3.00
32	**5 Manat** 2009.	FV	12.00

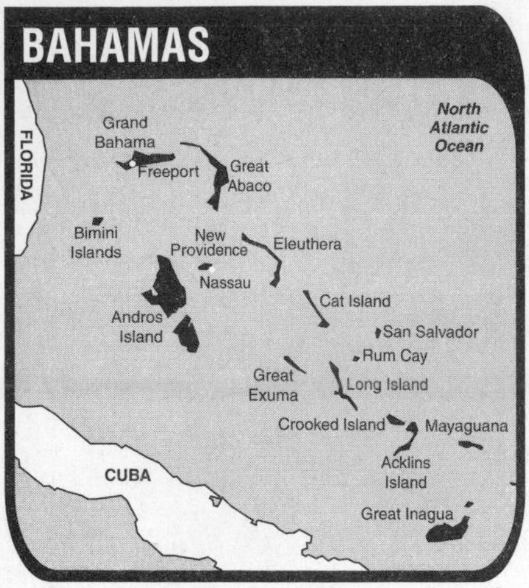

The Commonwealth of The Bahamas is an archipelago of about 3,000 islands, cays and rocks located in the Atlantic Ocean east of Florida and north of Cuba. The total land area of the chain of islands is 10,070 sq. km. They have a population of 307,400. Capital: Nassau. The Bahamas imports most of their food and manufactured products and exports cement, refined oil, pulpwood and lobsters.

Lucayan Indians inhabited the islands when Christopher Columbus first set foot in the New World on San Salvador in 1492. British settlement of the islands began in 1647; the islands became a colony in 1783. Since attaining independence from the UK in 1973, The Bahamas have prospered through tourism and international banking and investment management.

RULERS:
British

MONETARY SYSTEM:
1 Shilling = 12 Pence
1 Pound = 20 Shillings to 1966
1 Dollar = 100 Cents 1966-

Commonwealth

Bahamas Government

1965 Currency Note Act

Replacement notes: Serial # prefix *Z.*

		VF	UNC
17	**1/2 Dollar** *L.1965.* Purple on multicolor underprint. Queen Elizabeth II at left. Back: Straw market, arms at right. Watermark: Shellfish. Printer: TDLR. 156x67mm.		
	a. 2 signatures.	15.00	80.00
	b. 3 signatures.	13.00	70.00
	s. Specimen.	—	280.

		VF	UNC
18	**1 Dollar** *L.1965.* Green on multicolor underprint. Queen Elizabeth II at left. Back: Sea garden, arms at right. Watermark: Shellfish. Printer: TDLR. 156x67mm.		
	a. 2 signatures.	40.00	180.
	b. 3 signatures.	55.00	200.
	s. As b. Specimen.	—	370.

		VF	UNC
19	**3 Dollars** *L.1965.* Red on multicolor underprint. Queen Elizabeth II at left. Back: Paradise Beach, arms at right. Watermark: Shellfish. Printer: TDLR. 156x67mm.		
	a. 2 signatures, Sands and Higgs.	45.00	200.
	b. 3 signatures.	55.00	200.
	s. Signature Francis and Higgs. Specimen.	—	470.

		VF	UNC
20	**5 Dollars** *L.1965.* Green on multicolor underprint. Queen Elizabeth II at left. Back: Government House, arms at right. Watermark: Shellfish. Printer: TDLR. 156x67mm.		
	a. 2 signatures.	80.00	380.
	b. 3 signatures.	100.	450.
	s. Specimen.	—	360.
21	**5 Dollars** *L.1965.* Orange on multicolor underprint. Queen Elizabeth II at left. Back: Government House, arms at right. Watermark: Shellfish. Printer: TDLR. 156x67mm.		
	a. 2 signatures.	175.	700.
	b. 3 signatures.	450.	1300.
	s. Specimen.	—	600.

		VF	UNC
22	**10 Dollars** *L.1965.* Dark blue on multicolor underprint. Queen Elizabeth II at left. Back: Flamingos, arms at right. Watermark: Shellfish. Printer: TDLR. 156x67mm.		
	a. 2 signatures.	300.	1350.
	b. 3 signatures.	500.	2400.
	s. Specimen.	—	820.
23	**20 Dollars** *L.1965.* Dark brown on multicolor underprint. Queen Elizabeth II at left. Back: Surrey, arms at right. Watermark: Shellfish. Printer: TDLR. 156x67mm.		
	a. 2 signatures.	680.	3300.
	b. 3 signatures.	800.	4200.
	s. Specimen. 3 signatures.	—	800.
24	**50 Dollars** *L.1965.* Brown on multicolor underprint. Queen Elizabeth II at left. Back: Produce market, arms at right. Watermark: Shellfish. Printer: TDLR. 156x67mm.		
	a. Issued note.	1650.	8400.
	s. Specimen. 3 signatures.	—	850.
25	**100 Dollars** *L.1965.* Blue on multicolor underprint. Queen Elizabeth II at left. Signature varieties. Back: Deep sea fishing, arms at right. Watermark: Shellfish. Printer: TDLR. 156x67mm.		
	a. 2 signatures.	2900.	14,000.
	b. 3 signatures.	5200.	—
	s. Specimen. 3 signatures.	—	1200.

Bahamas Monetary Authority

1968 Monetary Authority Act

#26-33 Replacement notes: Serial # prefix *Z*.

26 **1/2 Dollar**

L.1968. Purple on multicolor underprint. Queen Elizabeth II at left. Back: Straw market, arms at right. Watermark: Shellfish. Printer: TDLR. 156x67mm.

	VF	UNC
a. Issued note.	9.00	40.00
s. Specimen.	—	120.

27 **1 Dollar**

L.1968. Green on multicolor underprint. Queen Elizabeth II at left. Back: Sea garden, arms at right. Watermark: Shellfish. Printer: TDLR. 156x67mm.

	VF	UNC
a. Issued note.	20.00	95.00
s. Specimen.	—	120.

28 **3 Dollars**

L.1968. Red on multicolor underprint. Queen Elizabeth II at left. Back: Paradise Beach, arms at right. Watermark: Shellfish. Printer: TDLR. 156x67mm.

	VF	UNC
a. Issued note.	50.00	140.
s. Specimen.	—	120.

29 **5 Dollars**

L.1968. Orange on multicolor underprint. Queen Elizabeth II at left. Back: Government House, arms at right. Watermark: Shellfish. Printer: TDLR. 156x67mm.

	VF	UNC
a. Issued note.	80.00	360.
s. Specimen. Overprint: *SPECIMEN* on each side.	—	160.

30 **10 Dollars**

L.1968. Dark blue on multicolor underprint. Queen Elizabeth II at left. Back: Flamingos, arms at right. Watermark: Shellfish. Printer: TDLR. 156x67mm.

	VF	UNC
a. Issued note.	500.	3000.
s. Specimen. Overprint: *SPECIMEN* on each side.	—	210.

31 **20 Dollars**

L.1968. Dark brown on multicolor underprint. Queen Elizabeth II at left. Back: Surrey, arms at right. Watermark: Shellfish. Printer: TDLR. 136x67mm.

	VF	UNC
a. Issued note.	1000.	8750.
s. Specimen. Overprint: *SPECIMEN* on each side.	—	300.

32 **50 Dollars**

L.1968. Brown on multicolor underprint. Queen Elizabeth II at left. Back: Produce market, arms at right. Watermark: Shellfish. Printer: TDLR. 156x37mm.

	VF	UNC
a. Issued note.	1500.	6000.
s. Specimen. Overprint: *SPECIMEN* on each side.	—	570.

33 **100 Dollars**

L.1968. Blue on multicolor underprint. Queen Elizabeth II at left. Back: Deep sea fishing, arms at right. Watermark: Shellfish. Printer: TDLR. 156x67mm.

	VF	UNC
a. Issued note.	3000.	15,000.
s. Specimen. Overprint: *SPECIMEN* on each side.	—	500.

Central Bank of the Bahamas

1974 Central Bank Act

#35-41 Replacement notes: Serial # prefix *Z*.

35 1 Dollar
L.1974. Dark blue-green on multicolor underprint. Queen Elizabeth II at left. Back: Sea garden, arms at right. Watermark: Shellfish. Printer: TDLR. 156x67mm.

	VF	UNC
a. Signature T. B. Donaldson.	18.00	85.00
b. Signature W. C. Allen.	20.00	130.
r. Replacement note. Serial # prefix *Z*.	100.	200.
s. Specimen.	—	—

37 5 Dollars
L.1974. Orange on multicolor underprint. Queen Elizabeth II at left. Back: Government House, arms at right. Watermark: Shellfish. Printer: TDLR. 156x67mm.

	VF	UNC
a. Signature T. B. Donaldson.	80.00	350.
b. Signature W. C. Allen.	130.	570.
r. Replacement note. Serial # prefix *Z*.	—	—
s. Specimen.	—	—

38 10 Dollars
L.1974. Dark blue on multicolor underprint. Queen Elizabeth II at left. Back: Flamingos, arms at right. Watermark: Shellfish. Printer: TDLR. 156x37mm.

	VF	UNC
a. Signature T. B. Donaldson.	215.	930.
b. Signature W. C. Allen.	350.	1600.
r. Replacement note. Serial # prefix *Z*.	300.	640.
s. Specimen.	—	—

39 20 Dollars
L.1974. Dark brown on multicolor underprint. Queen Elizabeth II at left. Back: Surrey, arms at right. Watermark: Shellfish. Printer: TDLR. 156x67mm.

	VF	UNC
a. Signature T. B. Donaldson.	310.	1300.
b. Signature W. C. Allen.	450.	2000.
r. Replacement note. Serial # prefix *Z*.	—	—
s. Specimen.	—	—

40 50 Dollars
L.1974. Brown on multicolor underprint. Queen Elizabeth II at left. Back: Produce market, arms at right. Watermark: Shellfish. Printer: TDLR. 156x67mm.

	VF	UNC
a. Signature T. B. Donaldson.	850.	3900.
b. Signature W. C. Allen.	1300.	5700.
r. Replacement note. Serial # prefix *Z*.	—	—
s. Specimen.	—	—

41 100 Dollars
L.1974. Blue on multicolor underprint. Queen Elizabeth II at left. Back: Deep sea fishing, arms at right. Watermark: Shellfish. Printer: TDLR. 156x67mm.

	VF	UNC
a. Signature T. B. Donaldson.	1200.	5400.
b. Signature W. C. Allen.	1550.	7000.
s. Specimen.	—	—

1974 Central Bank Act; 1984 ND Issue

#42-49 Replacement notes: Serial # prefix *Z*.

42 1/2 Dollar
L.1974 (1984). Green on multicolor underprint. Baskets at left, map at center left, mature portrait of Queen Elizabeth II at center right. Signature W. C. Allen. Back: Sister Sarah in Nassau market, arms at right. Watermark: Sailing ship. Printer: TDLR. UV: 1/2 in box fluoresce orange. 156x67mm.

	VF	UNC
a. Issued note.	4.00	20.00
r. Replacement note. Serial # prefix *Z*.	19.00	90.00
s. Specimen.	—	220.

43 1 Dollar
L.1974 (1984). Deep green on multicolor underprint. Fish at left, map at center left, mature portrait of Queen Elizabeth II at center right. Back: Royal Bahamas Police band at center, arms at right. Watermark: Sailing ship. Printer: TDLR. UV: value in box fluoresce orange. 156x67mm.

	VF	UNC
a. Signature W. C. Allen.	7.00	32.50
b. Signature James H. Smith. 2 horizontal serial #.	12.00	50.00
r. Replacement note. Serial # prefix: *Z*.	40.00	100.

44 3 Dollars
L.1974 (1984). Red-violet on multicolor underprint. Paradise Beach at left, map at center left, mature portrait of Queen Elizabeth II at center right. Signature James H. Smith. Back: Family Island sailing regatta, arms at right. Watermark: Sailing ship. Printer: TDLR. UV: value in box fluoresce orange. 156x67mm.

	VF	UNC
a. Issued note.	15.00	60.00
r. Replacement note. Serial # prefix *Z*.	50.00	180.
s. Specimen.	—	—

45 5 Dollars
L.1974 (1984). Orange on multicolor underprint. Statue at left. map at center left, mature portrait of Queen Elizabeth II at center right. Back: Local dancers *Junkanoo* at center, arms at right. Watermark: Sailing ship. Printer: TDLR. 156x67mm.

	VF	UNC
a. Signature W. C. Allen.	50.00	215.
b. Signature James H. Smith. 2 horizontal serial #.	37.50	135.
r. Replacement note. Serial # prefix *Z*.	67.50	295.
s. Specimen.	—	—

46 10 Dollars VF UNC

L.1974 (1984). Pale blue on multicolor underprint. Two flamingos at left, map at center left, mature portrait of Queen Elizabeth II at center right. Back: Lighthouse and Abaco Settlement, arms at right. Watermark: Sailing ship. Printer: TDLR. 156x67mm.

	VF	UNC
a. Signature W. C. Allen.	75.00	340.
b. Signature James H. Smith. 2 horizontal serial #.	125.	540.
r. Replacement note. Serial # prefix *Z*.	—	—

47 20 Dollars VF UNC

L.1974 (1984). Red and black on multicolor underprint. Horse and carriage at left, map at center left, mature portrait of Queen Elizabeth II at center right. Back: Nassau harbor, arms at right. Watermark: Sailing ship. Printer: TDLR. 156x67mm.

	VF	UNC
a. Signature W. C. Allen.	120.	520.
b. Signature James H. Smith. 2 horizontal serial #.	85.00	380.
s. Specimen.	—	—

48 50 Dollars VF UNC

L.1974 (1984). Purple, orange and green on multicolor underprint. Lighthouse at left, map at center left, mature portrait of Queen Elizabeth II at center right. Back: Central Bank, arms at right. Watermark: Sailing ship. Printer: TDLR. 156x67mm.

	VF	UNC
a. Signature W. C. Allen.	500.	1400.
b. Signature James H. Smith. 2 horizontal serial #.	930.	4300.
s. Specimen.	—	—

49 100 Dollars VF UNC

L.1974 (1984). Purple, deep blue and red-violet on multicolor underprint. Sailboat at left, map at center left, mature portrait of Queen Elizabeth II at center right. Signature W. C. Allen. Back: Blue marlin, arms at right. Watermark: Sailing ship. Printer: TDLR. 156x67mm.

	VF	UNC
a. Issued note.	480.	2100.
s. Specimen.	—	—

1992 Commemorative Issue

#50, Quincentennial of First Landfall by Christopher Columbus

50 1 Dollar VF UNC

ND (1992). Dark blue and deep violet on multicolor underprint. Commercial seal at left, bust of Christopher Columbus right with compass face behind. Signature James H. Smith. Back: Flamingos, rose-throated parrots, lizard, islands, ships across back with arms at lower right. Printer: CBNC. UV: fibers fluoresce red and yellow. $1 at right and design elements yellow. 156x67mm.

	VF	UNC
a. Issued note.	FV	27.50
s. Specimen.	—	250.

1974 Central Bank Act; 1992-95 ND Issue

51 1 Dollar VF UNC

L.1974 (1992). Deep green on multicolor underprint. Map at left center, mature portrait Queen Elizabeth II at center. Signature James H. Smith. Fish at left. Vertical and horizontal serial #. Back: Police band at center. Watermark: Caravel sailing ship. Printer: BABN 156x67mm. FV 30.00

52 5 Dollars VF UNC

L.1974 (1995). Dark brown, brown and orange on multicolor underprint Statue of Columbus at left, Wallace-Whitfield at right. Signature James H. Smith. Back: Local dancers *Junkanoo* at center, arms at right. Watermark: Caravel sailing ship. Printer: TDLR. 156x67mm.

	VF	UNC
a. Issued note.	FV	105.
s. Specimen.	—	—

53 10 Dollars VF UNC

L.1974 (1992). Pale blue on multicolor underprint. Two flamingos at left, map at center left, mature portrait of Queen Elizabeth II at center right. Signature James H. Smith. 1 serial number vertical and horizontal. Back: Lighthouse and Abaco Settlement, arms at right. Watermark: Caravel sailing ship. Printer: BABN. 156x67mm. 50.00 230.

54 20 Dollars VF UNC

L.1974 (1993). Black and red on multicolor underprint. Sir Milo B. Butler at right, horse drawn surrey at left. Signature James H. Smith. Back: Aerial view of ships in Nassau's harbor at center, arms at right. Watermark: Caravel sailing ship. Printer: TDLR. 156x67mm.

	VF	UNC
a. Issued note.	60.00	280.
r. Replacement note. Serial # prefix *Z*.	150.	300.
s. Specimen.	—	—

55 **50 Dollars** — VF — UNC

L.1974 (1992). Brown, blue-green and orange on multicolor underprint. Lighthouse at left, map at center left, mature portrait of Queen Elizabeth II at center right. Signature James H. Smith, 1 vertical and horizontal serial number. Back: Central Bank, arms at right. Watermark: Caravel sailing ship. Printer: TDLR. 156x67mm.

	VF	UNC
a. Issued note.	130.	550.
s. Specimen.	—	—

56 **100 Dollars**

L.1974 (1992). Purple, deep blue and red-violet on multicolor underprint. Sailboat at left, map at center left, mature portrait of Queen Elizabeth II at center right. Signature James H. Smith. 1 vertical and horizontal serial number. Back: Blue marlin, arms at right. Watermark: Caravel sailing ship. Printer: TDLR. 156x67mm.

	VF	UNC
a. Issued note.	320.	1400.
s. Specimen.	—	—

1974 Central Bank Act; 1996 Series

57 **1 Dollar** — VF — UNC

1996. Deep green on multicolor underprint. Fish at left, map at center left, mature bust of Queen Elizabeth II at center right. Vertical and ascending size horizontal serial number at lower left. Signature James H. Smith. Back: Royal Bahamas Police band aat center, arm at right. Watermark: Caravel sailing ship. Printer: BABN. 156x67mm.

	VF	UNC
a. Issued note.	FV	30.00
s. Specimen.	—	—

59 **10 Dollars** — VF — UNC

1996. Deep blue-green, green and violet on multicolor underprint. Two flamingos at left, map at center left, mature bust of Queen Elizabeth II at center right. Vertical and ascending size horizontal serial number at lower left. Signature James H. Smith Back: Lighthouse and Abaco Settlement, arms at right. Watermark: Caravel sailing ship. Printer: TDLR. 156x67mm.

	VF	UNC
a. Issued note.	FV	150.
s. Specimen.	—	—

61 **50 Dollars** — VF — UNC

1996. Red-brown and deep green on multicolor underprint. Lighthouse at left, map at center left, mature bust of Queen Elizabeth II at center right. Vertical and ascending size horizontal serial number at lower left. Signature James H. Smith. Back: Central Bank, arms at right. Watermark: Caravel sailing ship. Printer: TDLR. 156x67mm.

	VF	UNC
a. Issued note.	FV	425.
s. Specimen.	—	—

62 **100 Dollars** — VF — UNC

1996. Purple, deep blue and violet on multicolor underprint. Sailboat at left, map at center left, mature bust of Queen Elizabeth II at center right. Vertical and ascending size horizontal serial number. Signature James H. Smith. Back: Blue marlin, arms at right. Watermark: Caravel sailing ship. Printer: BABN. 156x67mm.

	VF	UNC
a. Issued note.	400.	1000.
s. Specimen.	—	—

1974 Central Bank Act; 1997; 2000-01 Series

63 **5 Dollars** — VF — UNC

1997; 2001. Dark brown, brown and orange on multicolor underprint. Statue of Columbus at left, Wallace-Whitfield at right. Vertical and ascending size horizontal serial numbers. Signature J. W. Francis. Back: Local dancers *Junkanoo* at center, arms at right. Watermark: Caravel sailing ship. Printer: TDLR. UV: threads fluoresce green. 5 in box green. Back: center design and flowers yellow. 156x67mm.

	VF	UNC
a. 1997. *GOVERNOR* title in orange.	FV	105.
b. 2001. *GOVERNOR* in black.	FV	70.00

64 **10 Dollars** — VF 35.00 — UNC 115.

2000. Deep blue-green, green and violet on multicolor underprint. Sir Stafford Sands and OVD at right, pair of flamingos at left. Vertical and ascending size horizontal serial numbers. Signature J. W. Francis. Printer: TDLR. 156x67mm.

65 **20 Dollars**

1997. Multicolor. Sir Milo B. Butler at right. Vertical and ascending size horizontal serial numbers. Back: Aerial view of ships in Nassau's Harbor at center. Printer: TDLR. 156x67mm.

	VF	UNC
a. 1997. 2 signature varieties.	FV	210.
r. Replacement note.	FV	340.

65A **20 Dollars** | VF | UNC
2000. Multicolor. Sir Milo B. Butler at right. Vertical and ascending size serial #. Signature J.W. Francis. Back: Aerial view of ships in Nassau's harbor at center. Printer: TDLR 156x67mm. | FV | 190.

66 **50 Dollars** | VF | UNC
2000. Sir Roland Symonette and OVD at right, lighthouse at left. Vertical and ascending size horizontal serial numbers. Signature J. W. Francis. Printer: TDLR. 156x67mm. | 100. | 300.

67 **100 Dollars** | VF | UNC
2000. Multicolor. Queen Elizabeth II, OVD at right. Vertical and ascending size horizontal serial numbers. Signature J. W. Francis. Back: Blue marlin, arms at lower right. Printer: TDLR. 167x67mm. | 200. | 600.

2000 Central Bank Act; 2001 Series

68 **1/2 Dollar** | VF | UNC
2001. Slate blue and green on tan and multicolor underprint. Queen Elizabeth II at right, baskets at left. Vertical and sscending size horizontal serial numbers. Signature J. W. Francis. Back: Sister Sarah in Nassau market. Printer: TDLR. UV: value in box fluoresce green, background elements orange; back: background elements green. 156x67mm. | FV | 8.50

69 **1 Dollar** | VF | UNC
2001. Green, brown and multicolor. Sir Lynden O. Pindling at right. Vertical and ascending size horizontal serial numbers. Signature J. W. Francis. Back: Royal Bahamas Police band at center, arms at right. Printer: TDLR. 156x67mm. | FV | 12.50

2000 Central Bank Act; 2002 Series

70 **1 Dollar** | VF | UNC
2002. Deep green on multicolor underprint. Fish at left, map at center left, mature portrait of Queen Elizabeth II at center right. Signature J. W. Francis. Back: Royal Bahamas Police band at center, arms at right. Watermark: Sailing ship. Printer: TDLR. Segmented foil security strip. Emergency issue of 6 million notes. Reuse of P#43 design. 156x67mm. | FV | 30.00

2000 Central Bank Act; 2005-2010 CRISP Series

71 **1 Dollar** | VF | UNC
2008. Green on multicolor underprint. Sir Lynden O. Pindling at right. Signature W. Craigg. Back: Royal Bahamas Police band at center. Printer: FC-O. 156x67mm. | FV | 7.50

72 **5 Dollars** — VF / UNC
2007. Multicolor. Wallace-Whitfield at right. Signature W. Craigg. Back: Local dancers *Junkanoo* at center. Printer: TDLR. 156x67mm. — FV / 27.50

73 **10 Dollars** — VF / UNC
2005. Blue on multicolor underprint. Queen Elizabeth II at right. Signature J. W. Francis. Printer: TDLR. 156x67mm.

	VF	UNC
a. Issued note	FV	85.00
r. Replacement note. Serial # prefix *Z*.	60.00	130.

73A **10 Dollars** — VF / UNC
2009. Dark blue, dark green and maroon on multicolor underprint. Sir Stafford Sands at right. Signature W. Craigg. Back: Hope town, lighthouse at left. Watermark: S. Sands. Printer: (T)DLR. 156x67mm. — FV / 50.00

74 **20 Dollars** — VF / UNC
2006. Multicolor. Sir Milo B. Butler at right. Signature W. Craigg. Printer: FC-O. 156x67mm. — FV / 95.00

74A **20 Dollars**
2010. Sir Milo B. Butler at right. Signature W. Craigg. Printer: G&D.

	VF	UNC
a. Issued note.	FV	85.00
r. Replacement note. Serial # prefix: *Z*.	—	150.

75 **50 Dollars** — VF / UNC
2006. Multicolor. Sir Roland T. Symonette at right. Signature W. Craigg. Printer: FC-O. 156x67mm. — FV / 145.

75A **50 Dollars**
2006. Multicolor. Sir Roland T. Symonette at right. Signature W. Craigg. Printer: G+D. 156x67mm. — FV / 145.

76 **100 Dollars** — VF / UNC
2009. Multicolor. Queen Elizabeth II at right. Signature W. Craigg. Back: Blue marlin at center. Printer: TDLR. 156x67mm.

	VF	UNC
a. Issued note.	FV	250.
r. Replacement note. *Z* serial # prefix.	150.	375.

Collector Series

Bahamas Government

1965 Issue

		Mkt. Value
CS1	**1/2-100 Dollars** *L.1965.* #17-25 overprint: *SPECIMEN.* (100 sets).	7100.

Bahamas Monetary Authority

1968 Issues

		Mkt. Value
CS2	**1/2-100 Dollars** *L.1968.* #26-33 overprint: *SPECIMEN*, punch hole cancelled.	1600.
CS3	**1/2-100 Dollars** *L.1968.* #26-33 overprint: *SPECIMEN*, punched hole cancelled. In blue presentation book.	2600.

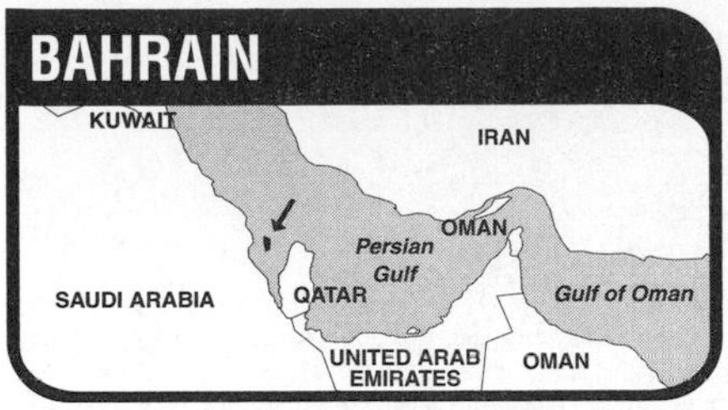

The State of Bahrain, a group of islands in the Persian Gulf off Saudi Arabia, has an area of 665 sq. km. and a population of 718,300. Capital: Manama. Prior to the depression of the 1930s, the economy was d on pearl fishing. Petroleum and aluminum industries and transit trade are the vital factors in the economy today.

In 1783, the al-Khalifa family captured Bahrain from the Persians. In order to secure these holdings, it entered into a series of treaties with the UK during the 19th century that made Bahrain a British protectorate. The archipelago attained its independence in 1971. Bahrain's small size and central location among Persian Gulf countries require it to play a delicate balancing act in foreign affairs among its larger neighbors. Facing declining oil reserves, Bahrain has turned to petroleum processing and refining and has transformed itself into an international banking center. King Hamad bin Isa al-Khalifa, after coming to power in 1999, pushed economic and political reforms to improve relations with the Shia community. Shia political societies participated in 2006 parliamentary and municipal elections. Al Wifaq, the largest Shia political society, won the largest number of seats in the elected chamber of the legislature. However, Shi'a discontent has resurfaced in recent years with street demonstrations and occasional low-level violence.

RULERS:

Isa Bin Sulman al-Khalifa, 1961-

MONETARY SYSTEM:

1 Dinar = 1000 Fils

KINGDOM

BAHRAIN CURRENCY BOARD

AUTHORIZATION 6/1964

#1-6 For specimen notes with a maltese cross serial # prefix, see #CS1 at the end of the country listing.

		VF	UNC
1	**100 Fils** *L.1964.* Ochre on multicolor underprint. Dhow at left, arms at right. Back: Green and orange. Palm trees at center. Watermark: Falcon's head.		
	a. Issued note.	4.00	22.00
	s. Specimen.	—	50.00

		VF	UNC
2	**1/4 Dinar** *L.1964.* Brown on multicolor underprint. Dhow at left, arms at right. Back: Oil derricks. Watermark: Falcon's head.		
	a. Issued note.	6.00	30.00
	s. Specimen.	—	60.00

		VF	UNC
3	**1/2 Dinar** *L.1964.* Purple on multicolor underprint. Dhow at left, arms at right. Back: Ships at the Mina Sulman Jetty. Watermark: Falcon's head.		
	a. Issued note.	9.00	40.00
	s. Specimen.	—	80.00

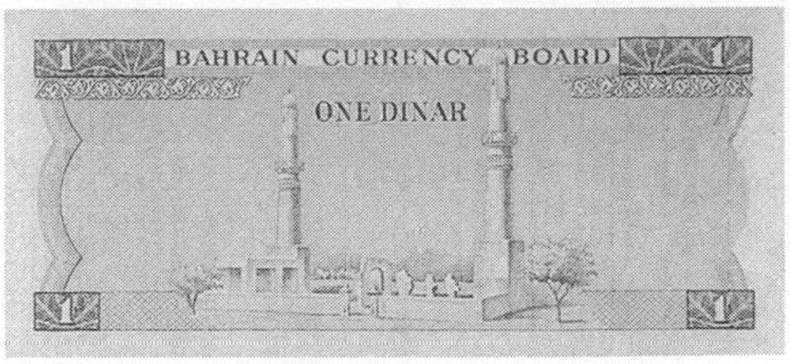

		VF	UNC
4	**1 Dinar** *L.1964.* Brownish red on multicolor underprint. Dhow at left, arms at right. Back: Ruins of the Suq al-Khamis mosque, dominated by two minarets. Watermark: Falcon's head.		
	a. Issued note.	13.00	50.00
	s. Specimen.	—	100.

		VF	UNC
5	**5 Dinars** *L.1964.* Blue-black on multicolor underprint. Dhow at left, arms at right. Back: Two pearling dhows. Watermark: Falcon's head.		
	a. Issued note.	100.	650.
	s. Specimen.	—	275.

		VF	UNC
6	**10 Dinars** *L.1964.* Green on multicolor underprint. Dhow at left, arms at right. Back: Aerial view of the town of Isa. Watermark: Falcon's head.		
	a. Issued note.	80.00	550.
	s. Specimen.	—	225.

BAHRAIN MONETARY AGENCY

AUTHORIZATION 23/1973

		VF	UNC
7	**1/2 Dinar** *L.1973.* Brown on multicolor underprint. Cast copper head of bull at lower left. Map at left, dhow at center, arms at right. Back: Smelting works of Aluminium Bahrain at left. Watermark: Falcon's head. UV: Arabic value twice fluoresces orange.	6.00	12.00

8 **1 Dinar** | VF | UNC
L.1973. Red on multicolor underprint. Minaret of the Manama Mosque at left, map at left, dhow at center, arms at right. Back: Headquarters of Bahrain Monetary Agency at left. Watermark: Falcon's head. UV: Arabic value twice fluoresces orange. | 6.00 | 14.00

8A **5 Dinars** | VF | UNC
L.1973. Dark blue on multicolor underprint. Minaret of the Suq al-Khamis mosque at left, map at left, dhow at center, arms at right. Back: Pearling dhows at left. Watermark: Falcon's head. UV: Arabic value twice fluoresces orange. | 28.00 | 75.00

9 **10 Dinars** | VF | UNC
L.1973. Green on multicolor underprint. Wind tower and map at left, dhow at center, arms at right. Back: Dry dock at left. Watermark: Falcon's head.
a. 2 horizontal serial #. | 55.00 | 100.
b. Serial # vertical and horizontal. | 60.00 | 110.

10 **20 Dinars** | VF | UNC
L.1973. Reddish-brown on multicolor underprint. Minaret of the al-Fadhel mosque and map at left, dhow at center, arms at right. Back: Government House at left. Watermark: Falcon's head.
a. Issued note. | 100. | 275.
s. Specimen. | — | —

11 **20 Dinars** | VF | UNC
L.1973. Map at left, dhow at center, arms at right, symbol changed at right of map. Silvering added at lower left denomination. Back: Open frame and symbol around watermark area. Watermark: Falcon's head. Also various color differences.
a. 2 horizontal serial #. | 100. | 220.
b. Serial # vertical and horizontal. | 110. | 250.

Authorization 23/1973; 1993 ND Issue

12 **1/2 Dinar** | VF | UNC
L.1973 (1986). Dark brown and violet on violet on multicolor underprint. Red shield of arms at center, man weaving at right, outline map at left. Back: Brown and violet on multicolor underprint. "Aluminum Bahrain" facility at left center. Watermark: Antelope's head. | 3.50 | 8.00

13 **1 Dinar** | VF | UNC
L.1973 (1993). Violet and red-orange on multicolor underprint. Ancient Dilmun seal at right, arms at center, outline map at left. Back: Bahrain Monetary Agency building at left center. Watermark: Antelope's head. | 6.00 | 15.00

14 **5 Dinars** | VF | UNC
L.1973 (1993). Dark blue and deep blue-green on multicolor underprint. Riffa Fortress at right, arms at center, outline map at left. Back: Bahrain International Airport at left center. Watermark: Antelope's head. | 24.00 | 95.00

15 **10 Dinars** | VF | UNC
L.1973 (1993). Deep olive-green and green on multicolor underprint. Dhow at right, arms at center, outline map at left. Back: Aerial view of King Fahad Causeway at left center. Watermark: Antelope's head. | 65.00 | 120.

		VF	UNC
16	**20 Dinars** *L.1973* (1993). Purple and violet multicolor underprint. Bab al-Bahrain gate at right, arms at center, outline map at left. Back: Ahmed al-Fateh Islamic Center at left center. Watermark: Antelope's head.	95.00	250.

Authorization 23/1973; 1996 ND Issue

		VF	UNC
17	**1/2 Dinar** *L.1973* (1996). Deep brown, violet and brown with deep brown shield at center. Arms at center, outline map at left, man weaving at right. Back: "Aluminum Bahrain" facility at left center. Watermark: Antelope's head. Narrow security thread. 142x72mm.	FV	9.00

Authorization 23/1973; 1998 ND Issue

		VF	UNC
18	**1/2 Dinar** *L.1973* (1998). Deep brown, violet and brown. Deep brown shield of arms at lower center, man weaving at right, outline map at left. Back: "Aluminum Bahrain" facility at left center. Watermark: Antelope's head. Wide security thread. No microprinting. 142x72mm.	FV	8.00
19	**1 Dinar** *L.1973* 1998. Violet and red-orange on multicolor underprint. Ancient Dilmun seal at right, arms at lower center, outline map at left. Back: Bahrain Monetary Agency building at left center. Watermark: Antelope's head. Wide security thread. 142x72mm.		
	a. With *BMA* microprinting on security thread.	FV	15.00
	b. Without microprinting on security thread.	FV	12.00

		VF	UNC
20	**5 Dinars** *L.1973* (1998). Blue on multicolor underprint. Arms at lower center, outline map at left, Riffa Fortress at right. Back: Bahrain International Airport at left center. Watermark: Antelope's head. Wide security thread. Hologram at lower left. 142x72mm.		
	a. With *BMA* microprinting on security thread.	55.00	90.00
	b. Without microprinting on security thread.	50.00	65.00

		VF	UNC
21	**10 Dinars** *L.1973* (1998). Green on multicolor underprint. Arms at center, outline map at left, dhow at right. Back: Aerial view of King Fahad Causeway at left center. Watermark: Antelope's head. Hologram at lower left. 142x72mm.		
	a. With *BMA* microprinting on security thread.	85.00	150.
	b. Without microprinting on security thread.	FV	90.00

		VF	UNC
22	**20 Dinars** *L.1973* (1998). Purple on multicolor underprint. Bab al-Bahrain gate at right, arms at center, outline map at left. Back: Ahmed al-Fateh Islamic Center at left center. Watermark: Antelope's head. With hologram and wide micro-printed security thread. 142x72mm.	280.	600.
23	**20 Dinars** *L. 1973* (1998). Orange and black on multicolor underprint. Bab al-Bahrain gate at right, arms at center, outline map at left. Back: Ahmed al-Fateh Islamic Center at left center. Watermark: Antelope's head. Hologram at lower left. 142x72mm.	95.00	220.

Authorization 23/1973; 2001 ND Issue

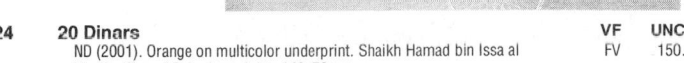

		VF	UNC
24	**20 Dinars** ND (2001). Orange on multicolor underprint. Shaikh Hamad bin Issa al Khalifa, King of Bahrain at right. 142x72mm.	FV	150.

Central Bank of Bahrain

2007 ND First Issue

25 1/2 Dinar VF UNC

ND (2008). Orange and brown on multicolor underprint. Old Bahrain Court building at left. Back: Bahrain International Circuit Court building. UV: bottom corner device and box at lower center yellow, vertical serial # orange; back: background elements blue, orange. 155x74mm. FV 4.00

26 1 Dinar VF UNC

ND (2008). Red and rose on multicolor underprint. Al Hedaya al Khaliflya School at left. Back: Arabian horses and the Sail and Pearl Monument. 155x74mm. FV 7.00

27 5 Dinars VF UNC

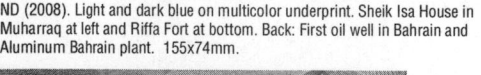

ND (2008). Light and dark blue on multicolor underprint. Sheik Isa House in Muharraq at left and Riffa Fort at bottom. Back: First oil well in Bahrain and Aluminum Bahrain plant. 155x74mm. FV 35.00

28 10 Dinars VF UNC

ND (2008). Brown, green and tan on multicolor underprint. King Hamad bin isa al Khalifa at left. Back: Sheik isa bin al Khalifa causeway. 155x74mm. FV 45.00

29 20 Dinars VF UNC

ND (2008). Brown and dark green on multicolor underprint. King Hamad bin isa al Khalifa at left. Back: Al Fateh Islamic Center. 155x74mm. FV 85.00

Collector Series

Bahrain Monetary Agency

Authorization 23/1973

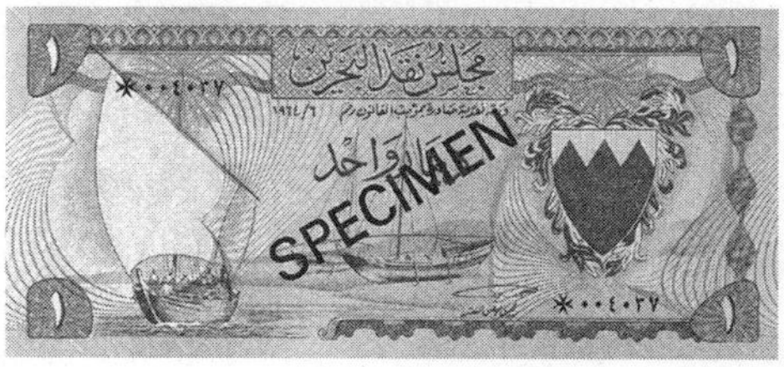

CS1 100 Fils - 20 Dinars Mkt. Value

ND (1978). #1-6 and 10 with overprint: *SPECIMEN* and Maltese cross serial # prefix. 80.00

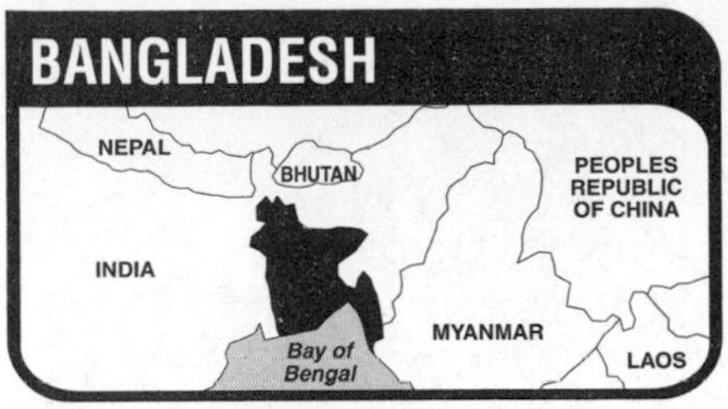

The Peoples Republic of Bangladesh (formerly East Pakistan), a parliamentary democracy located on the Bay of Bengal bordered by India and Burma, has an area of 144,000 sq. km. and a population of 153.55 million. Capital: Dhaka (Dacca). The economy is predominantly agricultural. Jute products and tea are exported.

Europeans began to set up trading posts in the area of Bangladesh in the 16th century; eventually the British came to dominate the region and it became part of British India. In 1947, West Pakistan and East Bengal (both primarily Muslim) separated from India (largely Hindu) and jointly became the new country of Pakistan. East Bengal became East Pakistan in 1955, but the awkward arrangement of a two-part country with its territorial units separated by 1,600 km left the Bengalis marginalized and dissatisfied. East Pakistan seceded from its union with West Pakistan in 1971 and was renamed Bangladesh. A military-backed caretaker regime suspended planned parliamentary elections in January 2007 in an effort to reform the political system and root out corruption; the regime has pledged new democratic elections by the end of 2008. About a third of this extremely poor country floods annually during the monsoon rainy season, hampering economic development.

MONETARY SYSTEM:

1 Rupee = 100 Paise to 1972
1 Taka = 100 Paisas 1972-

REPUBLIC

PEOPLES REPUBLIC OF BANGLADESH

1971 ND PROVISIONAL ISSUE

#1-3 The Bangladesh Bank never officially issued any Pakistan notes with overprints. These are considered locally issued by some authorities.

			VF	UNC
1	**1 Rupee**	ND (1971). Blue. Purple overprint *BANGLADESH* on Pakistan #9. Four different overprints are documented.	30.00	90.00

			VF	UNC
1A	**1 Rupee**	ND (1971). Blue. Purple Bengali overprint on Pakistan #9. Two different overprints are documented.	30.00	90.00

			VF	UNC
2	**5 Rupees**	ND (1971). Brown-violet. Purple Bengali overprint on Pakistan #15.	32.50	100.
2A	**5 Rupees**	ND (1971). Purple Bengali overprint on Pakistan #9.	32.50	100.

			VF	UNC
3	**10 Rupees**	ND (1971). Brown. Purple Bengali overprint on Pakistan #13.	35.00	120.
3A	**5 Rupees**	ND (1971). English overprint on Pakistan #18.	75.00	175.

			VF	UNC
3B	**10 Rupees**	ND (1971). English overprint on Pakistan #19.	125.	225.

1972-89 ND ISSUES

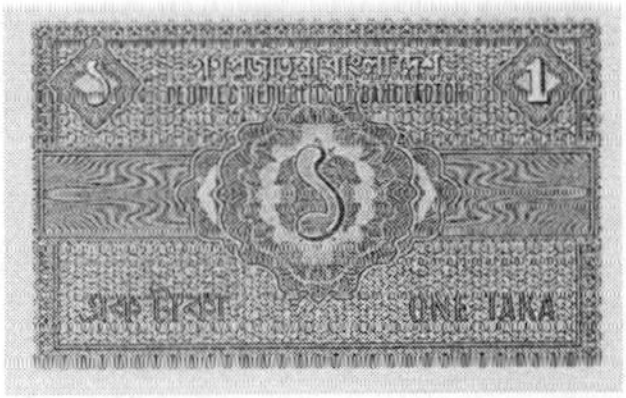

			VF	UNC
4	**1 Taka**	ND (1972). Brown on orange and blue underprint. Map of Bangladesh at left.	7.00	25.00

			VF	UNC
5	**1 Taka**	ND (1973). Purple and ochre. Hand holding rice plants at left. Back: Arms at right.		
		a. With watermark: Tiger's head.	1.00	9.00
		b. Without watermark. (2 signature varieties).	1.00	8.00

			VF	UNC
6	**1 Taka**	ND (1973). Purple on ochre and blue underprint. Woman preparing grain at left. Back: Hand holding rice plants at center, arms at right. Watermark: Tiger's head.		
		a. Issued note.	.60	7.00
		s. Specimen.	—	100.

6A	1 Taka	VF	UNC
	ND (1979). Purple on multicolor underprint. Arms at right. Back: Deer at left center. Watermark: Tiger's head.	.50	4.50

6B	1 Taka	VF	UNC
	ND (1982). Purple on multicolor underprint. Arms at right, no printing on watermark area at left. Back: Deer at left center. Watermark: Modified tiger.		
	a. Signature title in Bengali: *FINANCE SECRETARY.* Solid security thread. Six signature varieties.	.10	2.00
	b. Signature title in Bengali: *PRINCIPAL FINANCE SECRETARY.* Solid security thread.	.10	1.00
	c. Signature title in Bengali: *FINANCE SECRETARY.* Micro-printed security thread.	.10	1.00

6C	2 Taka	VF	UNC
	ND (1988-). Gray-green on orange and green underprint. Shahid Minar, Martyr's Monument at right. Back: Dhyal or Magpie-robin at left. Watermark: Tiger's head. 100x60mm.		
	a. Solid security thread. 4 signature varieties.	.50	4.00
	b. Security thread reads: *BANGLADESH BANK* in Bengali.	.50	2.50
	c. Security thread reads: *GOVERNMENT OF BANGLADESH* in Bengali. One signature variety.	.50	2.50
	d. As c. but smaller watermark.	.50	2.50
	e. 2002 date on back. Security thread reads: Government of Bangladesh.	.50	2.00
	f. 2003 date on back. Signature in brown ink.	.50	2.00
	g. 2003. Signature in black ink.	.50	2.00
	h. 2004 date on back.	.50	2.00
	i. 2006 date on back.	.25	1.00
	j. 2007. 3mm wide segmented security thread.	.25	1.00
	k. 2007. Embedded microprinted security thread.	.25	1.00
	l. 2008.	.25	1.00
	m. 2009.	.25	1.00
	n. 2010.	.25	1.00

Bangladesh Bank

1972 ND Issue

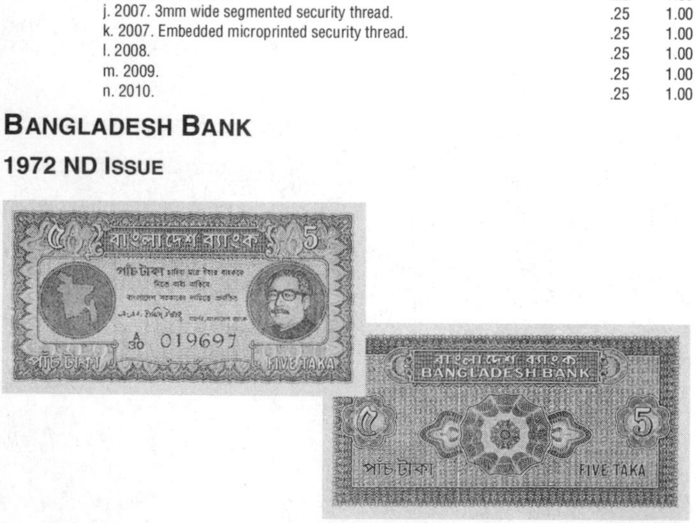

7	5 Taka	VF	UNC
	ND (1972). Purple on multicolor underprint. Map of Bangladesh at left, portrait of Mujibur Rahman at right.	3.00	17.50

8	10 Taka	VF	UNC
	ND (1972). Blue on multicolor underprint. Map of Bangladesh at left, portrait of Mujibur Rahman at right.	6.00	32.50

9	100 Taka	VF	UNC
	ND (1972). Green on multicolor underprint. Map of Bangladesh at left, portrait of Mujibur Rahman at right.		
	a. Serial # panel at upper right with a blue backgorund.	8.00	75.00
	b. Serial # panel at upper right with a brown tint backgorund.	8.00	75.00

1973 ND Issue

10	5 Taka	VF	UNC
	ND (1972). Red on multicolor underprint. Mujibur Rahman at left. Back: Lotus plants at center right. Watermark: Tiger's head.		
	a. Issued note.	1.50	10.00
	s. Specimen.	—	—

11	10 Taka	VF	UNC
	ND (1972). Green on multicolor underprint. Mujibur Rahman at left. Back: River scene. Watermark: Tiger's head.		
	a. Serial # in Western numerals.	4.00	17.50
	b. Serial # in Bengali numerals.	7.50	25.00
	s. Specimen.	—	—

12	100 Taka	VF	UNC
	ND (1972). Brown on multicolor underprint. Mujibur Rahman at left. Back: River scene. Watermark: Tiger's head.		
	a. Serial # in western numerals.	5.00	25.00
	b. Serial # in Bengali numerals.	50.00	100.

1974 ND Issue

			VF	UNC
13	**5 Taka**	ND (1973). Red on multicolor underprint. Mujibur Rahman at right. 2 signature varieties. Back: Aerial view of factory. Watermark: Tiger's head.		
		a. Issued note.	1.50	12.50
		s. Specimen.	—	110.

			VF	UNC
14	**10 Taka**	ND (1973). Green on multicolor underprint. Mujibur Rahman at right. 2 signature varieties. Back: Rice harvesting scene at left center.		
		a. Issued note.	1.00	10.00
		s. Specimen.	—	110.

1976; 1977 ND Issue

			VF	UNC
15	**5 Taka**	ND (1977). Light brown on multicolor underprint. Star mosque in Dhaka at right. Back: Aerial view of factory. Watermark: Tiger's head.		
		a. Issued note.	1.50	7.50
		s. Specimen.	—	100.

			VF	UNC
16	**10 Taka**	ND (1977). Violet on multicolor underprint. Star mosque in Dhaka at right. Back: Rice harvesting scene at left center. Watermark: Tiger's head.		
		a. Issued note.	2.00	17.50
		s. Specimen.	—	110.

			VF	UNC
17	**50 Taka**	ND (1976). Orange on multicolor underprint. Star mosque in Dhaka at right. Back: Harvesting scene. Watermark: Tiger's head.		
		a. Issued note.	5.00	25.00
		s. Specimen.	—	100.

			VF	UNC
18	**100 Taka**	ND (1976). Blue-violet on multicolor underprint. Star mosque in Dhaka at left. Back: River scene. Watermark: Tiger's head.	10.00	50.00

			VF	UNC
19	**500 Taka**	ND (1976). Blue and lilac on multicolor underprint. Star mosque in Dhaka at right. Back: High Court in Dhaka. Watermark: Tiger's head.	90.00	250.

1978-82 ND Issue

			VF	UNC
20	**5 Taka**	ND (1978). Brown on multicolor underprint. Mihrab in *Kushumba* mosque at right. Back: Aerial view of factory. Watermark: Tiger's head. 119x64mm.		
		a. Issued note.	1.00	5.50
		s. Specimen.	—	100.

			VF	UNC
21	**10 Taka**	ND (1978). Violet on multicolor underprint. *Atiya Jam-e* mosque in Tangali at right. Back: Rice harvesting scene at left center. Watermark: Tiger's head.		
		a. Issued note.	2.00	9.00
		s. Specimen.	—	110.

#		VF	UNC
22	**20 Taka**	VF	UNC
	ND (1979). Dark blue-green on multicolor underprint. *Chote Sona* mosque at right. Underprint over watermark area at left. Back: Harvesting scene. Watermark: Tiger's head. Micro-printed security thread.	4.00	20.00

#		VF	UNC
23	**50 Taka**	VF	UNC
	ND (1979). Orange on multicolor underprint. Sat Gamnbuj Mosque in Dhaka at right. Back: Women harvesting tea. Watermark: Tiger's head.	2.50	20.00

#		VF	UNC
24	**100 Taka**	VF	UNC
	ND (1977). Blue-violet, deep brown and orange on multicolor underprint. Star mosque in Dhaka at right, underprint throughout watermark area at left. Back: Ruins of Lalbagh Fort at left center. Watermark: Tiger's head.	6.00	30.00

1982-88 ND Issue

#		VF	UNC
25	**5 Taka**	VF	UNC
	ND (1981). Mihrab in *Kushumba* mosque at right, without printing on watermark area at left. Back: Industrial landscape scene at left center. Watermark: Modified tiger's head. 119x64mm.		
	a. Solid security thread. Black signature Large serial #.	2.00	7.50
	b. Micro-printed security thread. Black signature Small serial #. 2 signature varieties.	1.00	6.00
	c. Micro-printed security thread. Brown signature Small serial #. 3 signature varieties.	.75	3.50
	d. 2006. Wide segmented security thread added right.	—	2.50
	s. Specimen.	—	50.00

#		VF	UNC
26	**10 Taka**	VF	UNC
	ND (1982). Violet and red-violet on multicolor underprint. *Atiya Jam-e* mosque in Tangali at right, without printing in watermark area. Back: Spillway of Kaptai Dam at left center. Watermark: Modified tiger's head.		
	a. With curved line of text above and below mosque. Solid security thread.	2.50	12.50
	b. Without curved line of text above mosque. Solid security thread. 2 signature varieties.	2.50	10.00
	c. Micro-printed security thread. 3 signature varieties.	2.00	7.50

#		VF	UNC
27	**20 Taka**	VF	UNC
	ND (1988); 2002. Blue-green on multicolor underprint. *Chote Sona* mosque at right, without printing on watermark area. Signature varieties. Back: Harvesting scene. Watermark: Modified tiger's head.		
	a. Black signature Large serial #. 2 signature varieties.	2.50	9.00
	b. Green signature Small serial #. 2 signature varieties.	2.00	7.50
	c. Foil security thread. Green signature small serial #.	1.00	5.00

#		VF	UNC
28	**50 Taka**	VF	UNC
	ND (1987). Black, red and deep green on multicolor underprint. National Monument at Savar at center. Back: National Assembly building at center. Watermark: Modified tiger's head.		
	a. 7-digit serial #.	2.75	12.50
	b. 8-digit serial #.	2.75	12.50
	c. Different tiger in watermark. Clouds on back have been re-engraved. Underprint colors changed.	2.75	12.50

29 **100 Taka** | VF 3.50 | UNC 17.50

ND (1981). Blue-violet, deep brown and orange on multicolor underprint. Star mosque in Dhaka at right, without printing on watermark area at left. Signature varieties. Back: Ruins of Lalbagh Fort at left center. Watermark: Modified tiger's head.

30 **500 Taka**

ND (1982). Gray, blue and violet on multicolor underprint. Star mosque in dhaka at right, without printing on watermark area at left. Signature varieties. Back: High Court in Dhaka. Watermark: Modified tiger's head.

	VF	UNC
a. Without segmented foil. 2 signature varieties.	FV	55.00
b. With segmented foil over security thread. 2 signature varieties.	FV	30.00
c. Eight numerals in serial #.	FV	30.00

31 **100 Taka**

ND (1983). Star mosque in Dhaka at right, without printing on watermark area at left. Circular toothed border added around watermark area. Back: Ruins of Lalbagh Fort at left center. Circular toothed order added around watermark area. Watermark: Modified tiger's head.

	VF	UNC
a. Solid security thread. 2 signature varieties.	FV	6.50
b. Micro printed security thread. 2 signature varieties.	FV	6.00
c. Segmented foil security thread. 2 signature varieties.	FV	6.00
d. Segmented foil thread with micro-printing.	FV	6.00
e. Solid foil thread with micro-printing.	FV	6.00

1996 ND Commemorative Issue

#35, Victory Day. Ovpt: ***VICTORY DAY SILVER JUBILEE '96*** **in lower l. wmk. area.**

32 **10 Taka** | VF FV | UNC 2.50

ND (1996). Violet on multicolor underprint. Commemorative overprint on #26b in lower left watermark area. 2 signature varieties. Overprint: *VICTORY DAY SILVER JUBILEE '96.*

1997 ND Issue

33 **10 Taka** | VF FV | UNC 3.00

ND (1997). Dark brown and deep blue-green on multicolor underprint. Mujibur Rahman at right. 2 signature varieties. Back: Arms at left, Lalbagh fort mosque at left center. Watermark: Mujibur Rahman.

1998 ND Issue

34 **500 Taka** | VF FV | UNC 30.00

ND (1998). Brown, blue, purple and red on multicolor underprint. National Monument in Savar at center right. Back: Slate blue. High Court building in Dhaka.

2000-01 Issue

35 **10 Taka** | VF FV | UNC 2.00

2000. Brown, red and multicolor. Mujibur Rahman at left. Back: National Assembly building. Polymer plastic. 152x64mm.

36 **50 Taka** | VF FV | UNC 3.00

ND (2000). Brown and blue on multicolor underprint. National Assembly building at left. Back: Bagha Mosque of Rajshahi at right.

37 **100 Taka** | VF FV | UNC 5.00

2001. Dark blue on light red-brown underprint. Mujibur Rahman at left, Sixty Dome Mosque at right. Back: Bangabandhu Bridge.

38 **500 Taka** — VF | UNC

2000. Brownish purple on multicolor underprint. Mujibur Rahman at right, *Sat Gambuj* mosque in center. Back: High Court building in Dhaka. 152x65mm. — FV | 22.50

2002 Issue

39 **10 Taka** — VF | UNC

2002-2005. Brown, red and multicolor. National emblem at left; Baitul Mukarram at lower right. Back: National Assembly building, Jatiyo Sangshad Bhaban. 130x60mm.

		VF	UNC
	a. 2002.	FV	2.00
	b. 2003.	FV	2.00
	c. 2004.	FV	2.00
	d. 2005.	FV	2.00

39A **10 Taka**

2006-08. Brown, red and multicolor. National emblem at left, building at lower right. Only blue signature surrounded in white. Back: National Assembly building. 123x60mm.

		VF	UNC
	a. 2006.	FV	2.00
	b. 2007.	FV	2.00
	c. 2008.	FV	2.00

40 **20 Taka** — VF | UNC

2002-08. Blue-green on multicolor underprint. *Chote Sona* mosque at right. Underprint in watermark area at left. Back: Washing jute scene. Reduced size. Enhanced security features. 130x60mm.

		VF	UNC
	a. 2002.	FV	3.50
	b. 2003.	FV	3.50
	c. 2004.	FV	3.50
	d. 2005.	FV	3.50
	e. 2006.	FV	3.50
	f. 2008.	FV	3.50

41 **50 Taka** — VF | UNC

2003-10. Brown and blue on multicolor underprint. National Assembly building at left. Back: Bagha Mosque of Rajshahi at right. Reduced size. Iridescent security thread, sight impaired features. 130x60mm.

		VF	UNC
	a. 2003.	FV	4.00
	b. 2004.	FV	4.00
	c. 2005. Signature 8.	FV	4.00
	d. 2005. Signature 9.	FV	4.00
	e. 2008.	FV	4.00
	f. 2010. Signature 10.	FV	4.00

42 **100 Taka** — VF | UNC

2002-04. Dark blue on light red-brown underprint. National monument at Savar at center. Back: Bangabandhu Bridge. 152x65mm.

		VF	UNC
	a. 2002.	FV	5.00
	b. 2003.	FV	5.00
	c. 2004.	FV	5.00

43 **500 Taka** — VF | UNC

2002; 2003. Brownish purple on multicolor underprint. National Monument at Savar at right, *Sat Gambuj* mosque in center. Back: High Court building in Dhaka. Value line in solid ink. 152x65mm.

		VF	UNC
	a. 2002.	FV	22.50
	b. 2003.	FV	22.50

2004-05 Issue

44 **100 Taka** — VF | UNC

2005. Multicolor. National monument at Savar at center, value in upper left is a solid color. Back: Jamuna Bridge. 2005. 152x65mm. — FV | 5.00

45 **500 Taka**

2003-08. National monument at Savar at right, *Sat Gambuj* Mosque in center. Back: High Court building in Dhaka. Value at upper left is in solid color. Value in text is in color shifting ink. 152x65mm.

		VF	UNC
	a. 2003.	FV	22.50
	b. 2004.	FV	22.50
	c. 2005. Signature 8.	FV	22.50
	d. 2005. Signature 9.	FV	22.50
	e. 2006.	FV	22.50
	f. 2007.	FV	22.50
	g. 2008.	FV	22.50

2006-07 Issue

46 5 Taka

2006. Brown on orange and tan underprint. Kusumbag mosque in Rajshahi at right. Back: Riverfront industria scene. 119x62mm.

	VF	UNC
a. 2006. Segmented security thread.	FV	1.50

46A 5 Taka

2007; 2009; 2010. Brown on orange and tan underprint. Kusumbag masque in Rajshahi at right. Back: Riverfont industria scene.

	VF	UNC
a. 2007. Segmented security thread.	FV	1.50
b. 2009.	FV	1.50
c. 2010.	FV	1.50

47 10 Taka

2008; 2009; 2010. Brown, red and multicolor. National emblem at left; building at lower right. Text in center and signature surrounded in white. Back: National Assembly building. 120x60mm.

	VF	UNC
a. 2008.	FV	2.00
b. 2009.	FV	2.00
c. 2010.	FV	2.00

48 20 Taka

2006; 2008; 2009; 2011. Blue-green on multicolor underprint. *Chote Sona* mosque at right. Segmented security thread. Back: Harvesting scene. Like #40 but reduced size. 127x60mm.

	VF	UNC
a. 2006. Signature 9.	FV	3.50
b. 2008.	FV	3.50
c. 2009. Signature 10.	FV	3.50
d. 2011.	FV	3.50

49 100 Taka

2006-10. Multicolor. National monument at Savar at right, *Sat Gambuj* mosque in center. Back: High court building in Dhaka. Like #44 but reduced size. 140x62mm.

	VF	UNC
a. 2006. Signature 9. Bengali digits in serial #.	FV	3.50
b. 2007.	FV	3.50
c. 2008.	FV	3.50
d. 2009.	FV	3.50
e. 2009. Signature 10.	FV	4.00
f. 2009. Signature 10. New name of bridge on back.	FV	5.00
g. 2010.	FV	3.50

50 500 Taka

2009; 2010. Purple and brown on multicolor underprint. Mujibur Rahman at right. Back: Supreme Court. 153x66mm.

	VF	UNC
a. 2009.	FV	17.50
b. 2010.	FV	17.50

51 1000 Taka

2008-10. Rose on light blue underprint. Shahid Minar Monument. Serial # font varieties. Back: Curzon Hall, Dhaka University 160x72mm.

	VF	UNC
a. 2008. Signature 9.	FV	25.00
b. 2009. Signature 10.	FV	25.00
c. 2010.	FV	25.00

2011 Issue

52 2 Taka

	VF	UNC
2011. Green and tan.	FV	.25

53 5 Taka

2011. Brown and tan on multicolor underprint. Muhibur Rahman at left, National Martyr's Monument in Savar at center. Back: Naogaon Kusumba mosque at center. 117x60mm.

	VF	UNC
a. Dark portrait. (2011).	FV	.30
b. Light portrait. (2012).	FV	.30

54 10 Taka

	VF	UNC
2012. Brown on light purple underprint. Muhibur Rahman at left, National Martyr's Monument in Savar at center. Back: National Mosque at center. 122x60mm.	FV	1.00

55 20 Taka

2012. Dark green on light green andmulticolor underprint. Muhibur Rahman at left, National Martyr's Monument in Savar at center. Back: Sixty Dome Mosque at center. 127x60mm.

	VF	UNC
a. Black vertical lathework on face at right end.	FV	2.50
b. Green vertical lathework on face at right end.	FV	1.50

55A 20 Taka

	VF	UNC
2012. Dark green on light green andmulticolor underprint. Muhibur Rahman at left, National Martyr's Monument in Savar at center. Orange vertical lathework at right. Back: Sixty Dome Mosque at center. 2012. 127x60mm.	FV	1.00

56 50 Taka

2011-. Brown on multicolor underprint. Muhibur Rahman at left, National Martyr's Monument in Savar at center. Back: Ploughing scene. 130x60mm.

	VF	UNC
a. 2011. Spelling error in artist's name on back (eight blocks of letters).	FV	3.00
b. 2012. Corrected artist's name on back (six blocks of letters).	FV	2.50

57 **100 Taka** VF UNC

2011-. Slate black on blue underprint. Muhibur Rahman at left, National Martyr's Monument in Savar at center. Back: Star Mosque in Dhaka on back. 140x62mm.

	VF	UNC
a. 2011.	FV	5.00
b. 2012.	FV	5.00

58 **500 Taka** VF UNC

2011-. Slate black, green and blue on multicolor underprint. Muhibur Rahman at left, National Martyr's Monument in Savar at center. Back: Farmers plowing field at riverbank. 152x65mm.

	VF	UNC
a. 2011.	FV	15.00
b. 2012.	FV	15.00

59 **1000 Taka** VF UNC

2011-. Slate black and violet on multicolor underprint. Muhibur Rahman at left, National Martyr's Monument in Savar at center. Back: National Parliament buildign at center. 160x70mm.

	VF	UNC
a. 2011.	FV	30.00
b. 2012.	FV	30.00

2011 Commemorative Issue

60 **40 Taka** VF UNC

2011. Violet, orange and green on multicolor underprint. Mujibur Rahman with hand raised at right, National Martyr's Monument in Savar at right. Back: Six men holding rifles aloft. 122x60mm. FV 2.50

61 **60 Taka** VF UNC

2012. Multicolor. Martyrs' Monument of the Language Movement in Dhaka at center. Back: Five portraits and obelisk monument at center. 130x60mm. FV 2.50

2013 Commemorative Issues

62 **25 Taka** VF UNC

26.1.2013. Purple and blue on multicolor underprint. National monument at Savar at left, montage of banknotes at center. Back: Purple and multicolor. Security Printing Company building. 123x60mm. FV 2.00

63 **100 Taka** VF UNC

2013. Red-brown and multicolor. 18th century terra-cotta fragment depicting a horse rider. Signature Atiur Rahman. Back: Bangladesh National Museum building. Watermark: Sheikh Mujibur Rahman. 140x62mm.

	VF	UNC
a. Issued note. 100,000 pieces.	FV	4.50
b. Commemorative folder. 11,000 pieces.	—	6.00

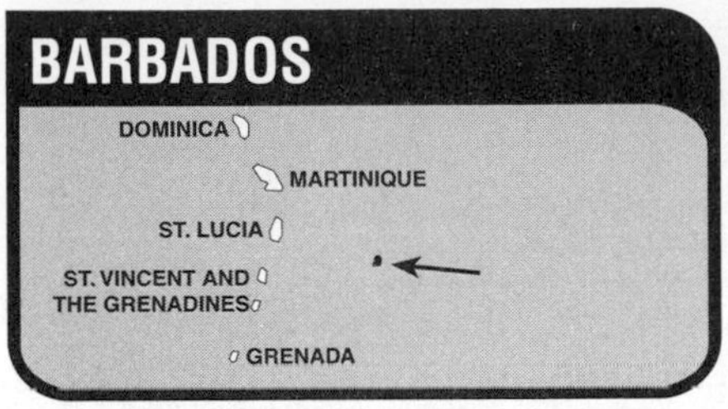

Barbados, an independent state within the British Commonwealth, is located in the Windward Islands of the West Indies east of St. Vincent. The coral island has an area of 431 sq. km and a population of 281,900. Capital: Bridgetown.

The island was uninhabited when first settled by the British in 1627. Slaves worked the sugar plantations established on the island until 1834 when slavery was abolished. The economy remained heavily dependent on sugar, rum, and molasses production through most of the 20th century. The gradual introduction of social and political reforms in the 1940s and 1950s led to complete independence from the UK in 1966. In the 1990s, tourism and manufacturing surpassed the sugar industry in economic importance.

RULERS:

British to 1966

MONETARY SYSTEM:

1 British West Indies Dollar = 4 Shillings - 2 Pence
5 British West Indies Dollars = 1 Pound - 10 Pence
1 Dollar = 100 Cents, 1950-

STATE

CENTRAL BANK OF BARBADOS

1973 ND ISSUE

#29-35 Replacement notes: serial # prefix Z1.

#	Description	VF	UNC
29	**1 Dollar** ND (1973). Red on multicolor underprint. Portrait S. J. Prescod at right, arms at left center. Signature C. Blackman. Back: Trafalgar Square in Bridgetown. Watermark: Map of Barbados. Printer: (T)DLR. 150x65mm.		
	a. Issued note.	5.00	27.50
	s. Specimen.	—	90.00

#	Description	VF	UNC
30	**2 Dollars** ND (1980). Blue on multicolor underprint. Portrait J. R. Bovell at right, arms at left center. Signature C. Blackman. Back: Trafalgar Square in Bridgetown. Watermark: Map of Barbados. Printer: (T)DLR. 150x65mm.		
	a. Issued note.	6.00	37.50
	s. Specimen.	—	90.00

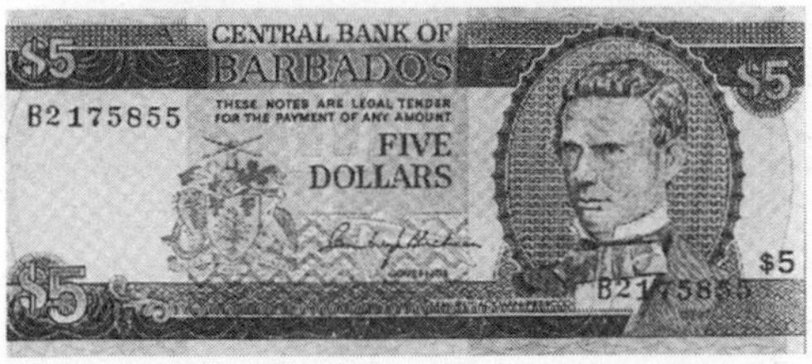

#	Description	VF	UNC
31	**5 Dollars** ND (1973). Green on multicolor underprint. Portrait S. J. Prescod at right, arms at left center. Signature C. Blackman. Back: Trafalgar Square in Bridgetown. Watermark: Map of Barbados. Printer: (T)DLR. 150x65mm.		
	a. Issued note.	15.00	70.00
	s. Specimen.	—	90.00

#	Description	VF	UNC
32	**5 Dollars** ND (1975). Dark green on multicolor underprint. Portrait Sir. F. Worrell at right, arms at left center. Signature C. Blackman. Back: Trafalgar Square. Watermark: Map of Barbados. Printer: (T)DLR. 150x65mm.		
	a. Issued note.	14.00	60.00
	s. Specimen.	—	120.

#	Description	VF	UNC
33	**10 Dollars** ND (1973). Dark brown on multicolor underprint. Portrait C. D. O'Neal at right, arms at left center. Signature C. Blackman. Back: Trafalgar Square. Watermark: Map of Barbados. Printer: (T)DLR. 150x65mm.		
	a. Issued note.	19.00	85.00
	s. Specimen. Overprint: *SPECIMEN* on each side.	—	180.

#	Description	VF	UNC
34	**20 Dollars** ND (1973). Purple on multicolor underprint. Portrait S. J. Prescod at right, arms at left center. Signature C. Blackman. Back: Trafalgar Square. Watermark: Map of Barbados. Printer: (T)DLR. 150x65mm.		
	a. Issued note.	30.00	110.
	s. Specimen. Overprint: *SPECIMEN* on each side.	—	225.

35 **100 Dollars** | VF | UNC

ND (1973). Gray and blue on multicolor underprint. Portrait Sir. G. H. Adams at right, arms at left center. Signature C. Blackman. Serial number to E3 200000. Back: Trafalgar Square, treetops are grayish blue. 150x65mm.

	VF	UNC
a. Issued note.	95.00	320.
s. Specimen. Overprint: *SPECIMEN* on each side.	—	480.

1986 ND Issue

35A **10 Dollars** | VF 17.50 | UNC 75.00

ND. Dark brown and green on multicolor underprint. Portrait C. D. O'Neal at right, arms at left center, without seahorse at left. Signature K. King. Back: Trafalgar Square in Bridgetown, seahorse at right. Watermark: Map of Barbados. Printer: (T)DLR.

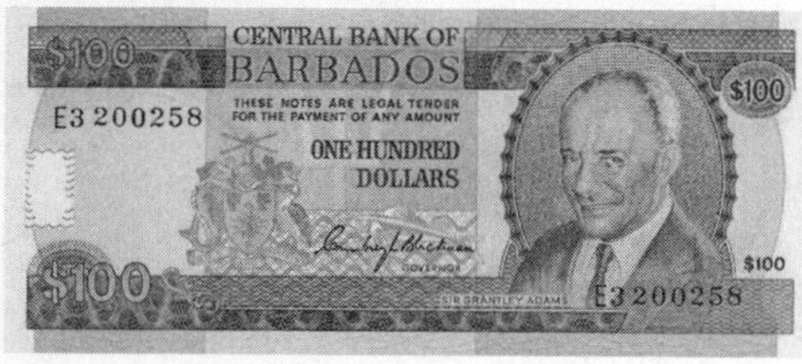

35B **100 Dollars** | VF 95.00 | UNC 285.

ND. Brown, purple and gray-blue on multicolor underprint. Portrait Sir. G. H. Adams at right, arms at left center, seahorse emblem at right. Signature C. Blackman. Serial number above E3 200000. Back: Trafalgar Square in Bridgetown, seahorse emblem at left, treetops are green. Watermark: Map of Barbados. Printer: (T)DLR.

1986-89 ND Issue

#36-41 Replacement notes: serial # prefix *Z1*.

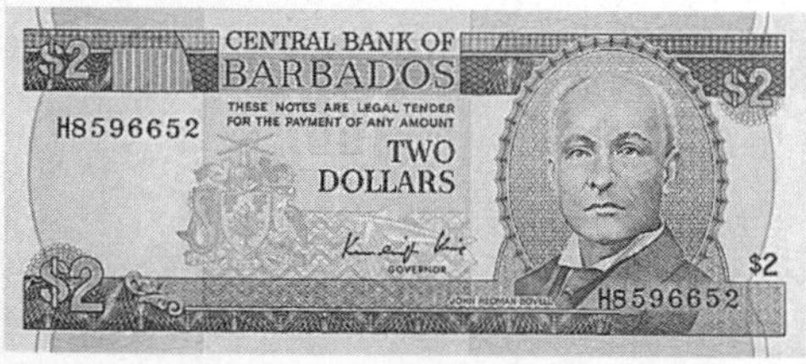

36 **2 Dollars** | VF 7.00 | UNC 37.50

ND (1986). Blue on multicolor underprint. Portrait J. R. Bovell at right. Signature K. King. Printer: (T)DLR. 150x65mm.

37 **5 Dollars** | VF 12.00 | UNC 52.50

ND (1986). Dark green on multicolor underprint. Portrait Sir. F. Worrell at right. Signature K. KIng. Printer: (T)DLR. 150x65mm.

38 **10 Dollars** | VF 14.00 | UNC 70.00

ND (1988). Dark Brown and green on multicolor underprint. Portrait C. D. O'Neal at right, arms at left center, seahorse in rectangle at left. Signature K. King. Back: Trafalgar Square in Bridgetown. Watermark: Map of Barbados. Printer: (T)DLR. 150x65mm.

39 **20 Dollars** | VF 23.00 | UNC 105.

ND (1988). Purple on multicolor underprint. Portrait of S. J. Prescod at right, arms at left center, bird emblem in rectangle at left. Signature K. King. Back: Trafalgar Square in Bridgetown. Watermark: Map of Barbados. Printer: (T)DLR. 150x65mm.

40 **50 Dollars** | VF | UNC

ND (1989). Orange, blue and gray on multicolor underprint. Portrait Prime Minister E. W. Barrow at right, trident emblem at left. Signature K. King. Printer: (T)DLR. 150x65mm.

	VF	UNC
a. Issued note.	52.50	170.
r. Replacement note. Serial # prefix: Z/1.	85.00	255.

41 **100 Dollars** | VF 87.50 | UNC 295.

ND (1989). Brown, purple and gray-blue on multicolor underprint. Portrait of Sir. G. H. Adams at right, arms at left center, seahorse emblem at right. Signature K. King. Back: Trafalgar Square at Bridgetown, treetops are green. Watermark: Map of Barbados. Printer: (T)DLR. 150x65mm.

1993-94 ND Issue

#42-45 Replacement notes: serial # prefix *Z1*.

No.	Denomination / Description	VF	UNC
42	**2 Dollars** ND (1993). Blue on multicolor underprint. Portrait J. R. Bovell at right, arms at left center. Signature C. M. Springer. Back: Trafalgar Square in Bridgetown. Watermark: Map of Barbados. Printer: (T)DLR. 150x65mm.	FV	35.00
43	**5 Dollars** ND (1993). Dark green on multicolor underprint. Portrait Sir. F. Worrell at right, arms at left center. Signature C. M. Springer. Back: Trafalgar Square in Bridgetown. Purple on multicolor underprint. Watermark: Map of Barbados. Printer: (T)DLR. 150x65mm.	FV	45.00
44	**20 Dollars** ND (1993). Portrait S. J. Prescod at right, arms at left center. Signature C. M. Springer. Back: Trafalgar Square in Bridgetown. Purple on multicolor underprint. Watermark: Map of Barbados. Printer: (T)DLR. 150x65mm.	FV	100.

		VF	UNC
45	**100 Dollars** ND (1994). Brown, purple and gray-blue multicolor underprint. Portrait Sir. G. H. Adams at left, arms at left center. Signature C. M. Springer. Back: Trafalgar Square in Bridgetown. Watermark: Map of Barbados. Printer: (T)DLR. 150x65mm.	FV	320.

1995-96 ND Issue

#46-49 Replacement notes: serial # prefix *Z1*.

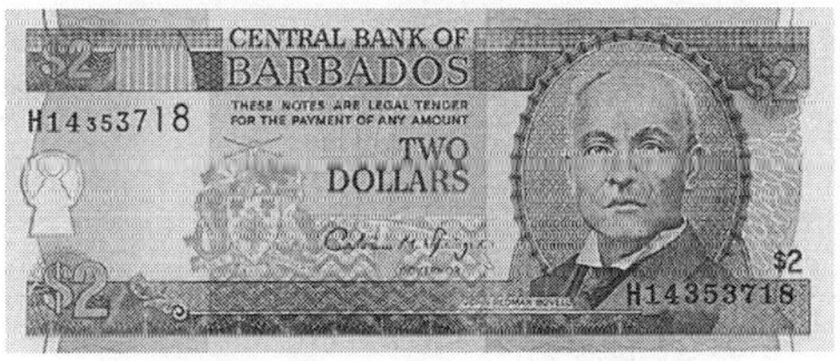

		VF	UNC
46	**2 Dollars** ND (1995). Blue on multicolor underprint. Portrait J. R. Bovell at right, arms at left center, ascending size serial number at upper left. Signature C. M. Springer. Back: Trafalgar Square in Bridgetown. Watermark: Map of Barbados. Printer: (T)DLR. Enhanced security features. 150x65mm.	FV	32.50

		VF	UNC
47	**5 Dollars** ND (1996). Dark green on multicolor underprint. Portrait Sir. F. Worrell at right, arms at left center, ascending size serial number at upper left. Signature C. M. Springer. Back: Trafalgar Square in Bridgetown. Watermark: Map of Barbados. Printer: (T)DLR. Enhanced security features. 150x65mm.	FV	37.50

		VF	UNC
48	**10 Dollars** ND (1995). Dark brown and green on multicolor underprint. Portrait C. D. O'Neal at right, arms at left center, seahorse in rectangle at left, asceding size serial number at upper left. Signature C. M. Springer. Back: Trafalgar Square in Bridgetown. Watermark: Map of Barbados. Printer: (T)DLR. Enhanced security features. 150x65mm.	FV	57.50

		VF	UNC
49	**20 Dollars** ND (1996). Red-violet and purple on multicolor underprint. Portrait of S. J. Prescod at right, arms at left center, bird emblem in rectangle at left, ascending size serial number at upper left. Signature C. M. Springer. Back: Trafalgar Square in Bridgetown. Watermark: Map of Barbados. Printer: (T)DLR. Enhanced security features. 150x65mm.	FV	90.00

1996-97 ND Issue

#50-52 Replacement notes: serial # prefix *Z1*.

		VF	UNC
50	**20 Dollars** ND (1997). Red-violet and purple on multicolor underprint. Portrait of S. J. Prescod at right, arms at left center, bird emblem in rectangle at left, ascending size serial number and enlarged denomination numerals at upper left. Signature C. M. Springer. Back: Trafalgar Square in Bridgetown. Watermark: Map of Barbados. Printer: (T)DLR. 150x65mm.	FV	80.00

		VF	UNC
51	**50 Dollars** ND (1997). Orange, blue and gray on multicolor underprint. Portrait Prime Minister E. W. Barrow at right, trident emblem at left, enlarged denomination numerals at upper left. Signature C. M. Springer. Watermark: Map of Barbados. Printer: (T)DLR. 150x65mm.	FV	155.
52	**100 Dollars** ND (1996). Brown, purple and blue-gray on multicolor underprint. Portrait Sir. G. H. Adams at left, arms at left center, enlarged denomination numerals at upper left. Signature C. M. Springer. Back: Trafalgar Square in Bridgetown. Watermark: Map of Barbados. Printer: (T)DLR. 150x65mm.	FV	285.

1997 ND Commemorative Issue

#53, 25th Anniversary Central Bank.

53 100 Dollars — VF | UNC

ND (1997). Brown, purple and blue-gray on multicolor underprint. Portrait Sir G. H. Adams at left, arms at left center, enlarged denomination numerals at upper left. Signature C. M. Springer. Back: Trafalgar Square in Bridgetown. Overprint: At left watermark area. Watermark: Map of Barbados. Printer: (T)DLR. 150x65mm.

	VF	UNC
a. Issued note.	FV	290.
r. Replacement note.	FV	395.
s. Specimen.	—	525.

1998 ND Issue

#54-59 Replacement notes: serial # prefix *Z1*.

54 2 Dollars — VF | UNC

ND (1998). Blue on multicolor underprint. Portrait J. R. Bovell at right, arms at left center, ascending size serial number at upper left. Signature W. Cox. Back: Trafalgar Square in Bridgetown. Watermark: Map of Barbados. Printer: (T)DLR. Enhanced security features. 150x65mm.

	VF	UNC
a. ND (1998). Face-to-back register device of surveyors target with quadrants all white.	FV	30.00
b. ND (1999). Face-to-back register device of surveyors target with two quadrants filled in.	FV	25.00

55 5 Dollars — VF: FV | UNC: 30.00

ND (1999). Dark green on multicolor underprint. Portrait Sir. F. Worrell at right, arms at left center, ascending size serial number at upper left. Signature W. Cox. Back: Trafalgar Square in Bridgetown. Watermark: Map of Barbados. Printer: (T)DLR. Enhanced security features. 150x65mm.

56 10 Dollars — VF: FV | UNC: 40.00

ND (1999). Dark brown and green on multicolor underprint. Portrait C. D. O'Neal at right, arms at left center, seahorse in rectangle at left, asceding size serial number at upper left. Signature W. Cox. Back: Trafalgar Square in Bridgetown. Watermark: Map of Barbados. Printer: (T)DLR. Enhanced security features. 150x65mm.

57 20 Dollars — VF: FV | UNC: 70.00

ND (1999). Red-violet and purple on multicolor underprint. Portrait of S. J. Prescod at right, arms at left center, bird emblem in rectangle at left, ascending size serial number and enlarged denomination numerals at upper left. Signature W. Cox. Back: Trafalgar Square in Bridgetown. Watermark: Map of Barbados. Printer: (T)DLR. Enhanced security features. 150x65mm.

58 50 Dollars — VF: FV | UNC: 140.

ND (1999). Orange, blue and gray on multicolor underprint. Portrait Prime Minister E. W. Barrow at right, trident emblem at left, enlarged denomination numerals at upper left. Signature W. Cox. Back: Trafalgar Square in Bridgetown. Watermark: Map of Barbados. Printer: (T)DLR. Enhanced security features. 150x65mm.

59 100 Dollars — VF: FV | UNC: 230.

ND (1999). Brown, purple and blue-gray on multicolor underprint. Portrait Sir. G. H. Adams at left, arms at left center, enlarged denomination numerals at upper left. Signature W. Cox. Back: Trafalgar Square in Bridgetown. Watermark: Map of Barbados. Printer: (T)DLR. Enhanced security features. 150x65mm.

2000 ND Issue

#60-65 Replacement notes: Serial # prefix *Z1*.

60 2 Dollars — VF: FV | UNC: 20.00

ND (2000). Blue on multicolor underprint. Portrait J. R. Bovell at right, arms at left center, ascending size serial number at upper left. Signature M. Williams. Back: Trafalgar Square in Bridgetown. Watermark: Map of Barbados. Printer: (T)DLR. Enhanced security features. UV: value in box fluoresce green, arms in multicolor, background elements and serial #s green. 150x65mm.

61 5 Dollars — VF: FV | UNC: 25.00

ND (2000). Dark on multicolor underprint. Portrait Sir. Frank Worrell at right, arms at left center, ascending size serial number at upper left. Signature M. Williams. Back: Trafalgar Square in Bridgetown. Printer: (T)DLR. Enhanced security features. 150x65mm.

62 10 Dollars — VF | UNC
ND (2000). Dark brown and green on multicolor underprint. Portrait C. D. O'Neal at right, arms at left center, seahorse in rectangle at left, asceding size serial number at upper left. Signature M. Williams. Back: Trafalgar Square in Bridgetown. Watermark: Map of Barbados. Printer: (T)DLR. Enhanced security features. 150x65mm. — FV | 35.00

63A 20 Dollars — VF | UNC
ND (2000). Red-violet and purple on multicolor underprint. Portrait of S. J. Prescod at right, arms at left center, bird emblem in rectangle at left, ascending size serial number and enlarged denomination numerals at upper left. Signature M. Williams. Back: Trafalgar Square in Bridgetown. Watermark: Map of Barbados. Printer: (T)DLR. Enhanced security features. 150x65mm. — FV | 60.00

63B 20 Dollars
ND (2006). Red-violet and purple on multicolor underprint. Portrait of J.S. Prescod at right, arms at left center, bird emblem in rectangle at left, ascending size serial number and enlarged denomination numerals at upper left. Signature M. Williams Back: Trafalgar Square in Bridgetown. Watermark: Map of Barbados. Printer: (T)DLR. Enhanced security features, narrow segmented security foil. 150x65mm. — FV | 115.

64 50 Dollars — VF | UNC
ND (2000). Orange, blue and gray on multicolor underprint. Portrait Prime Minister E. W. Barrow at right, trident emblem at left, enlarged denomination numerals at upper left. Signature M. Williams. Back: Trafalgar Square in Bridgetown. Watermark: Map of Barbados. Printer: (T)DLR. Enhanced security features. 150x65mm. — FV | 115.

65 100 Dollars — VF | UNC
ND (2000). Brown, purple and blue-gray on multicolor underprint. Portrait Sir. G. H. Adams at left, arms at left center, enlarged denomination numerals at upper left. Signature M. Williams. Back: Trafalgar Square in Bridgetown. Watermark: Map of Barbados. Printer: (T)DLR. Enhanced security features. 150x65mm. — FV | 185.

2002 Commemorative Issue

65A 5 Dollars — VF | UNC
ND (2002). Dark green on multicolor underprint. Portrait Sir Frank Worell at right, arms at left center. Signature M. Williams. Back: Trafalgar Square in Bridgetown. Overprint: Large 30 in gold foil and commemorative legend at left. Printer: (T)DLR. Note was issued glued on the back into a 4-page folder. 1000 presented to Central Bank employees. Not sold to the public. 150x65mm. — — | 190.

2007; 2012 Issue

66 2 Dollars — VF | UNC
1.5.2007; 2.5.2012. Blue on multicolor underprint. Portrait J. R. Bovell at right, arms at left center, ascending size serial number at upper left. Back: Trafalgar Square in Bridgetown. Watermark: Map of Barbados. Printer: (T)DLR. Wide segmented security foil. 150x65mm.
- a. Signature M. Williams (2007). — FV | 12.00
- b. Signature Delisle Worrell (2009). — FV | 10.00
- c. 2.5.2012. — FV | 13.00

67 5 Dollars
1.5.2007; 2.5.2012. Dark green on multicolor underprint. Portrait Sir F. Worrell at right, arms at left center, ascending size serial number at upper left. Back: Trafalgar Square in Bridgetown. Watermark: Map of Barbados. Printer: (T)DLR. Wide segmented security foil. 150x65mm.
- a. Signature M. Williams. — FV | 20.00
- b. Signature Delisle Worrell (2009). — FV | 14.00
- c. 2.5.2012. — FV | 18.00

68 10 Dollars — VF | UNC
1.5.2007; 2.5.2012. Dark brown and green on multicolor underprint. Portrait C. D. O'Neal at right, arms at left center, seahorse in rectangle at left, ascending size serial number at upper left. Back: Trafalgar Square in Bridgetown. Watermark: Map of Barbados. Printer: (T)DLR. Wide segmented security foil. 150x65mm.
- a. Signature M. Williams. — FV | 25.00
- b. Signature Delisle Worrell (2009). — FV | 20.00
- c. 2.5.2012. — FV | 23.00

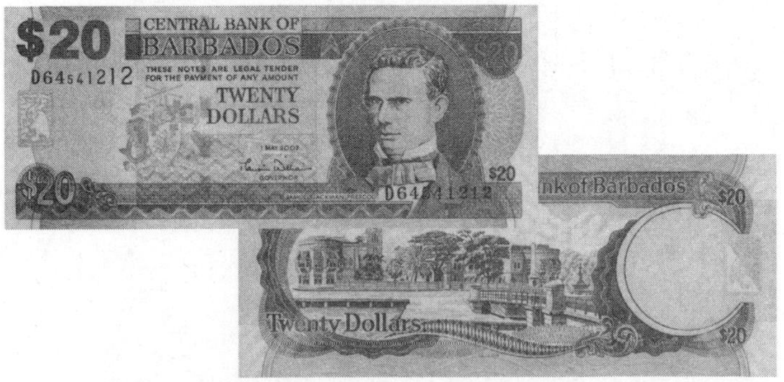

69 20 Dollars — VF | UNC
1.5.2007. Red-violet and purple on multicolor underprint. Portrait S. J. Prescod at right, arms at left center, bird emblem in rectangle at left, ascending size serial number and enlarged denomination numerals at upper left. Back: Trafalgar Square in Bridgetown. Watermark: Map of Barbados. Printer: (T)DLR. Wide segmented security foil. 150x65mm.
- a. Signature M. Williams. — FV | 42.50
- b. Signature Delisle Worrell (2009). — FV | 35.00

		VF	UNC
70	**50 Dollars**		
	1.5.2007. Orange, blue and gray on multicolor underprint. Portrait Prime Minister E. W. Barrow at right, trident emblem at left, enlarged denomination numerals at upper left. Back: Trafalgar Square in bridgetown. Watermark: Map of Barbados. Printer: (T)DLR. Wide segmented security foil. 150x65mm.		
	a. Signature M. Williams.	FV	90.00
	b. Signature Delisle Worrell (2009).	FV	80.00
71	**100 Dollars**		
	1.5.2007. Brown, purple and blue-gray on multicolor underprint. Portrait Sir G. H. Adams at left, arms at left center. Signature M. Williams. Back: Trafalgar Square in Bridgetown. Watermark: Map of Barbados Printer: (T)DLR. 150x65mm.		
	a. Signaturre M. Williams.	FV	140.
	b. Signature Delisle Worrell (2009).	FV	130.

2012 Commemorative Issue

		VF	UNC
72	**20 Dollars**		
	2.5.2012. Red-violet and purple on multicolor underprint. Portrait S. J. Prescod at right, arms at center. Back: Trafalgar Square in Bridgetown. Overprint: 40 YEARS at left. Watermark: Map of Barbados. Printer: (T)DLR. 150x65mm.	FV	45.00

2013 Issue

		VF	UNC
73	**2 Dollars**		
	2.5.2013. Light and dark blue on multicolor underprint. John R. Bovell at right. Back: Morgan Lewis windmill, St. Andrew, at left. Watermark: John Bovell and 2. 150x65mm.	FV	4.00
74	**5 Dollars**		
	2.5.2013. Printer: DLR.	—	9.00
75	**10 Dollars**		
	2.5.2013. Brown on multicolor underprint. Charles D. O'Neal. Back: O'Neil bridge over the Careenage in Bridgetown. Watermark: Charles O'Neal and 10. Printer: DLR. 150x65mm.	—	15.00

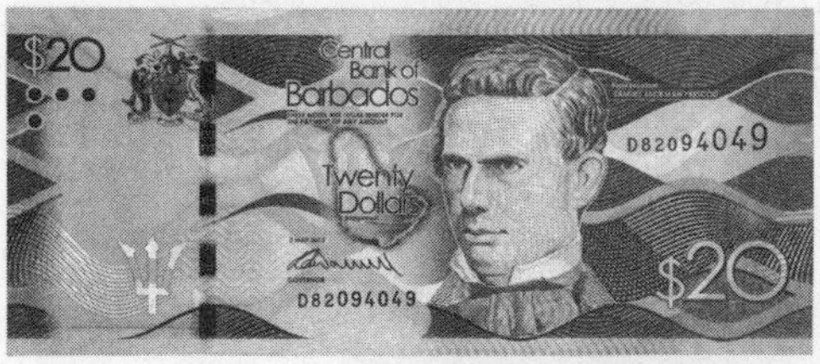

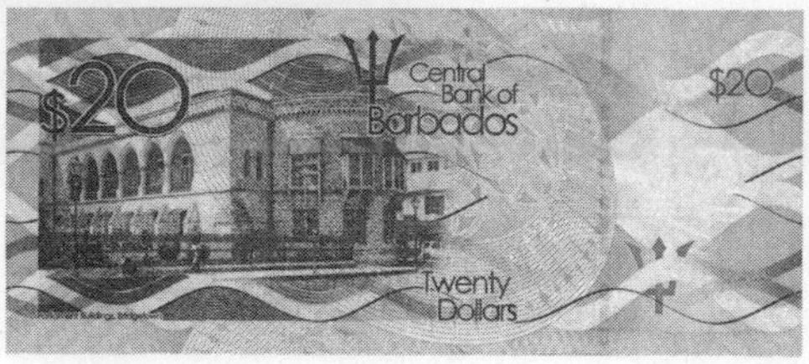

		VF	UNC
76	**20 Dollars**		
	2.5.2013. Light and dark pruple on multicolor underprint. Samuel J. Prescod at right. Back: Parliament buildings, Bridgetown. Watermark: Samuel Prescod and 20. Printer: DLR. 150x65mm.	FV	30.00

		VF	UNC
77	**50 Dollars**		
	2.5.2013. Blue and tan on multicolor underprint. Prime Minister Errol W. Barrow at right. Back: Independence Squire, Bridgetown. Watermark: Errol Barrow and 50. Printer: DLR. 150x65mm.	FV	60.00
78	**100 Dollars**		
	2.5.2013. Brown, purple and gray on multicolor underprint. Grantley Adams and Pride of Barbados flowers Back: Grantley Adams International Airport. Watermark: Grantley Adams and 100. 150x65mm.	FV	125.

Belarus is bounded in the west by Poland, to the north by Latvia and Lithuania, to the east by Russia and the south by the Ukraine. It has an area of 207,600 sq. km. and a population of 9.68 million. Capital: Minsk. Peat, salt, agriculture including flax, fodder and grasses for cattle breeding and dairy products, along with general manufacturing industries comprise the economy.

After seven decades as a constituent republic of the USSR, Belarus attained its independence in 1991. It has retained closer political and economic ties to Russia than any of the other former Soviet republics. Belarus and Russia signed a treaty on a two-state union on 8 December 1999 envisioning greater political and economic integration. Although Belarus agreed to a framework to carry out the accord, serious implementation has yet to take place. Since his election in July 1994 as the country's first president, Alexandr Lukashenko has steadily consolidated his power through authoritarian means. Government restrictions on freedom of speech and the press, peaceful assembly, and religion continue.

MONETARY SYSTEM:

1 Ruble = 100 Kapeek

Republic

КУПОН РЭСПУБЛІКА БЕЛАРУСЬ

Belarus Republic

1991 First Ruble Control Coupon Issue

		VF	UNC
A1	**20 Rublei** ND (1991). Blue. Uniface.		
	a. Full sheet of 12 coupons and registry.	2.00	6.00
	b. Single coupon.	.10	.15
A2	**50 Rublei** ND (1991). Light blue.		
	a. Full sheet of 28 coupons and registry.	2.00	6.00
	b. Single coupon.	.10	.15
A3	**75 Rublei** ND (1991). Blue.		
	a. Full sheet of 28 coupons and registry.	2.00	6.00
	b. Single coupon.	.10	.15

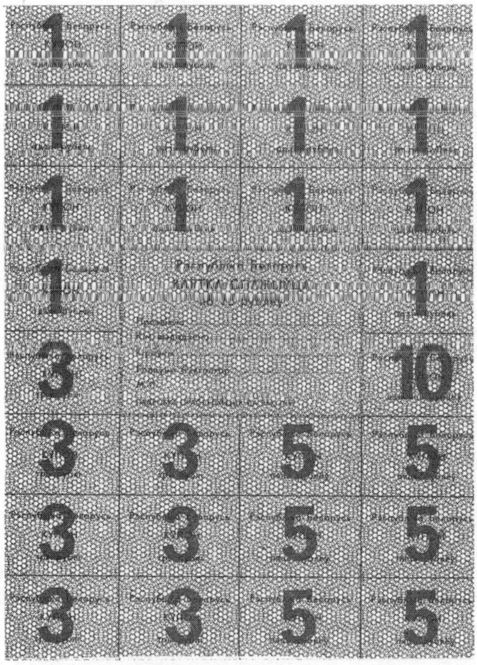

		VF	UNC
A4	**75 Rublei** ND (1991). Light green-blue.		
	a. Full sheet of 28 coupons and registry.	2.00	6.00
	b. Single coupon.	.10	.15

		VF	UNC
A5	**100 Rublei** ND (1991). Red.		
	a. Full sheet of 28 coupons and registry.	2.00	6.00
	b. Single coupon.	.10	.15
A6	**100 Rublei** ND (1991). Pink.		
	a. Full sheet of 28 coupons and registry.	2.00	6.00
	b. Single coupon.	.10	.15
A7	**200 Rublei** ND (1991). Light pink.		
	a. Full sheet of 28 coupons and registry.	2.00	6.00
	b. Single coupon.	.10	.15
A8	**300 Rublei** ND (1991). Pink.		
	a. Full sheet of 28 coupons and registry.	2.00	6.00
	b. Single coupon.	.10	.15
A9	**300 Rublei** ND (1991). Red.		
	a. Full sheet of 28 coupons and registry.	2.00	6.00
	b. Single coupon.	.10	.15

1992 Second Ruble Control Coupon Issue

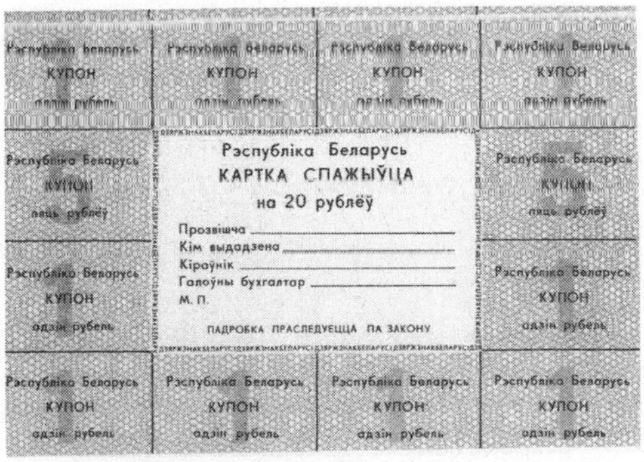

		VF	UNC
A10	**20 Rublei** ND (1992). Dark yellow.		
	a. Full sheet of 12 coupons and registry.	2.00	6.00
	b. Single coupon.	.10	.15
A11	**50 Rublei** ND (1992). Light blue without corner markings.		
	a. Full sheet of 28 coupons and registry.	2.00	6.00
	b. Single coupon.	.10	.15
A12	**50 Rublei** ND (1992). Dark blue without corner markings.		
	a. Full sheet of 28 coupons and registry.	2.00	6.00
	b. Single coupon.	.10	.15
A13	**50 Rublei** ND (1992). Violet without corner markings.		
	a. Full sheet of 28 coupons and registry.	2.00	6.00
	b. Single coupon.	.10	.15
A14	**50 Rublei** ND (1992). Blue without corner markings.		
	a. Full sheet of 28 coupons and registry.	2.00	6.00
	b. Single coupon.	.10	.15

No.	Denomination / Description	VF	UNC
A15	**75 Rublei**		
	ND (1992). Violet with black text.		
	a. Full sheet of 28 coupons and registry.	2.00	6.00
	b. Single coupon.	.10	.15
A16	**75 Rublei**		
	ND (1992). Light violet with black text.		
	a. Full sheet of 28 coupons and registry.	2.00	6.00
	b. Single coupon.	.10	.15
A17	**75 Rublei**		
	ND (1992). Dark violet with black text.		
	a. Full sheet of 28 coupons and registry.	2.00	6.00
	b. Single coupon.	.10	.15
A18	**75 Rublei**		
	ND (1992). Light violet with brown text.		
	a. Full sheet of 28 coupons and registry.	2.00	6.00
	b. Single coupon.	.10	.15
A19	**100 Rublei**		
	ND (1992). Light pink without corner markings.		
	a. Full sheet of 28 coupons and registry.	2.00	6.00
	b. Single coupon.	.10	.15
A20	**100 Rublei**		
	ND (1992). Pink without corner markings.		
	a. Full sheet of 28 coupons and registry.	2.00	6.00
	b. Single coupon.	.10	.15
A21	**100 Rublei**		
	ND (1992). Orange.		
	a. Full sheet of 28 coupons and registry.	2.00	6.00
	b. Single coupon.	.10	.15
A22	**200 Rublei**		
	ND (1992). Pink.		
	a. Full sheet of 28 coupons and registry.	2.00	6.00
	b. Single coupon.	.10	.15
A23	**200 Rublei**		
	ND (1992). Light pink.		
	a. Full sheet of 28 coupons and registry.	2.00	6.00
	b. Single coupon.	.10	.15
A24	**300 Rublei**		
	ND (1992). Orange.		
	a. Full sheet of 28 coupons and registry.	2.00	6.00
	b. Single coupon.	.10	.15
A25	**300 Rublei**		
	ND (1992). Red.		
	a. Full sheet of 28 coupons and registry.	2.00	6.00
	b. Single coupon.	.10	.15
A26	**500 Rublei**		
	ND (1992). Violet-yellow.		
	a. Full sheet of 28 coupons and registry.	2.00	6.00
	b. Single coupon.	.10	.15

1992 Third Ruble Control Coupon Issue

No.	Denomination / Description	VF	UNC
A27	**20 Rublei**		
	ND (1992). Blue.		
	a. Full sheet of 28 coupons and registry.	2.00	6.00
	b. Single coupon.	.10	.15

1992-94 Privatisation Checks

No.	Denomination / Description	VF	UNC
A28	**100 Rublei**		
	ND (1992).	—	—
A29	**500 Rublei**		
	ND (1992).	—	—
A30	**1000 Rublei**		
	ND (1992).	—	—
A31	**5000 Rublei**		
	ND (1992).	—	—

НАЦЫЯНАЛЬНАГА БАНКА БЕЛАРУСІ

Belarus National Bank

1992-96 РАЗЛІКОВЫ БІЛЕТ - Exchange Note Issue

1 **50 Kapeek** VF UNC
1992. red and brown-orange on pink underprint. *"Pagonya"* warrior on horseback at center. Back: Squirrel at center right. Watermark: Interlocked S's. 105x53mm. .10 2.00

2 **1 Ruble** VF UNC
1992. Blue-green and blue. *"Pagonya"* warrior on horseback at center. Back: Brown on multicolor underprint. Rabbit at center. Watermark: Interlocked S's. 105x53mm. 1.00 4.00

3 **3 Rublei** VF UNC
1992. Green, red-orange and pale olive-green on multicolor underprint. *"Pagonya"* warrior on horseback at center. Back: Two beavers at center right. Watermark: Interlocked S's. UV: fibers fluoresce red; back: serial #s orange. 105x53mm. 1.00 5.00

4 **5 Rublei** VF UNC
1992. Deep blue on light blue, lilac, violet and multicolor underprint. *"Pagonya"* warrior on horseback at center. Back: Two wolves at center right. Watermark: Interlocked S's. UV: fibers fluoresce red; back: serial #s orange. 105x53mm. .50 2.00

5 **10 Rublei** VF UNC
1992. Deep green on light green, orange and multicolor underprint. *"Pagonya"* warrior on horseback at center. Back: Lynx with kitten at center right. Watermark: Interlocked S's. UV: fibers fluoresce red; back: serial #s orange. 105x53mm. .30 1.00

6 **25 Rublei** VF UNC
1992. Violet on red, green and multicolor underprint. *"Pagonya"* warrior on horseback at center. Back: Moose at center right. Watermark: Interlocked S's. UV: fibers fluoresce red; back: serial #s orange. 105x52mm.
a. Horizontal watermark. .10 1.00
b. Horizontal watermark. .10 1.00

7 **50 Rublei** VF UNC
1992. Deep purple on red and green underprint. *"Pagonya"* warrior on horseback at center. Back: Bear at center right. Watermark: Interlocked S's. 105x53mm. .20 1.00

8 **100 Rublei** VF UNC
1992. Brown, gray and tan on multicolor underprint. *"Pagonya"* warrior on horseback at center. Back: Wisent (European Bison) at center. Watermark: Interlocked S's. UV: fibers fluoresce red; back: serial #s orange. 105x53mm. .20 1.00

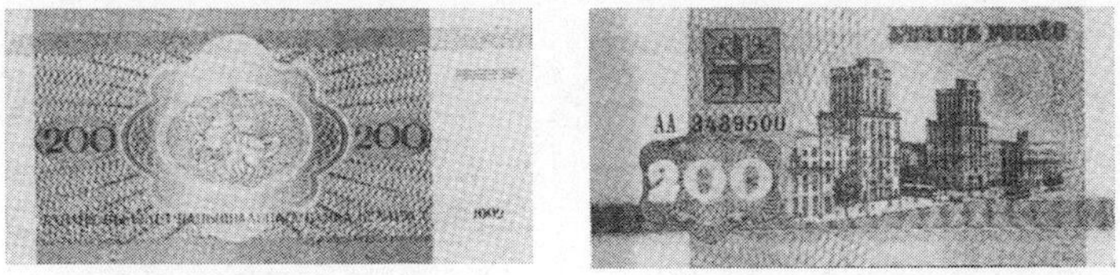

9 **200 Rublei** — VF | UNC
1992. Deep brown-violet, orange, green and ochre on multicolor underprint. *"Pagonya"* warrior on horseback at center. Back: City view at center right. Watermark: Interlocked S's. 105x53mm. — 1.00 | 6.00

10 **500 Rublei** — VF | UNC
1992. Violet, tan, light blue and orange on multicolor underprint. *"Pagonya"* warrior on horseback at center. Back: Victory Plaza in Minsk at center right. Watermark: Interlocked S's. 105x53mm. — 1.50 | 8.00

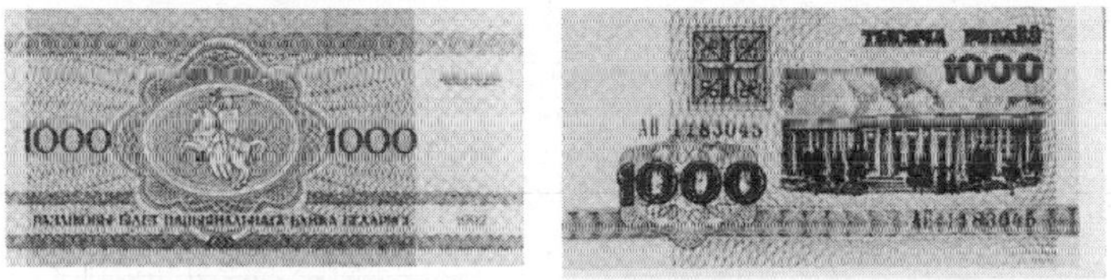

11 **1000 Rublei** — VF | UNC
1992 (1993). Light blue, pale olive-green and pink. *"Pagonya"* warrior on horseback at center. Back: Dark blue and dark green on multicolor underprint. Academy of Sciences building at center right. 105x53mm. — 1.00 | 3.00

12 **5000 Rublei** — VF | UNC
1992 (1993). Purple and red-violet on multicolor underprint. *"Pagonya"* warrior on horseback at center. Back: Brown-violet and olive-green on multicolor underprint. Buildings in Minsk lower city at center right. 105x53mm. — 1.00 | 4.00

1994-96 Issue

13 **20,000 Rublei** — VF | UNC
1994. Dark brown on multicolor underprint. National Bank building at left center. Back: *"Pagonya"* warrior on horseback. Watermark: Tower and tree. 150x69mm. — 1.00 | 6.00

14 **50,000 Rublei** — VF | UNC
1995. Dark brown on multicolor underprint. Brest's tower, Holmsky Gate at left, tapestry at center right. Back: Star shaped war memorial gateway at center right. Yellow 150x69mm.
- a. Security thread with bank initials. — 3.00 | 10.00
- b. Security thread with bank initials and value. — 3.00 | 10.00

15 **100,000 Rublei** — VF | UNC
1996. Deep blue and violet on multicolor underprint. Bolshoi Opera and Ballet Theatre at center, tapestry at left. Back: Scene from Glebov's ballet *Vibrannitsa* at center. 150x69mm.
- a. Security thread with bank initials. — 4.00 | 15.00
- b. Security thread with bank initials and value. — 4.00 | 15.00

1998 Issue

16 **1000 Rublei** — VF | UNC
1998. Light blue, pale olive-green and pink. Single value moved to oval replacing *Pagonya*, warrior on horseback at left center. Back: Academy of Sciences building at center right. Watermark: Paper. 110x60mm. — .50 | 2.00

1998-99 Issue

17 **5000 Rublei** — VF | UNC
1998. Multicolor. Back: Buildings in Minsk lower city at center right. 110x60mm. — .50 | 2.00

18 **500,000 Rublei**

1998. Light red and green on yellow underprint. Palace of Culture building at center. Back: Façade fragment. 150x69mm.

	VF	UNC
18	5.00	18.00

19 **1,000,000 Rublei**

1999. Green on multicolor underprint. National Museum of Art at center. Back: Artwork: *Wife's Portrait with Flowers and Fruits.* 150x69mm.

	VF	UNC
19	5.00	20.00

20 **5,000,000 Rublei**

1999. Purple and green on multicolor underprint. Minsk sports complex at center. Back: Winter sports complex. 150x69mm.

	VF	UNC
20	10.00	25.00

2000 Issue

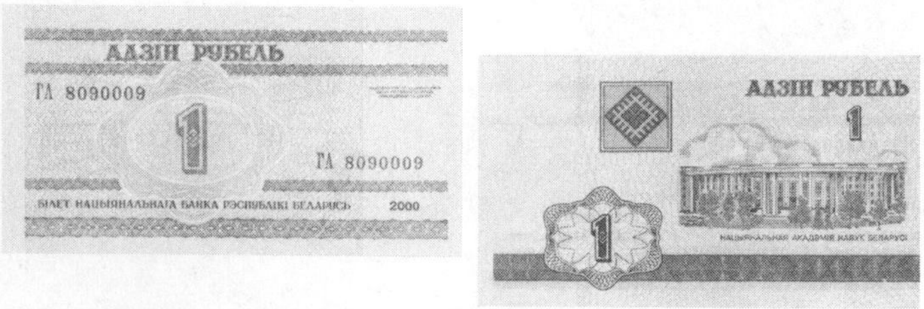

21 **1 Ruble**

2000. Green on multicolor underprint. Back: Academy of Sciences building at center right. 110x60mm.

	VF	UNC
21	.25	1.00

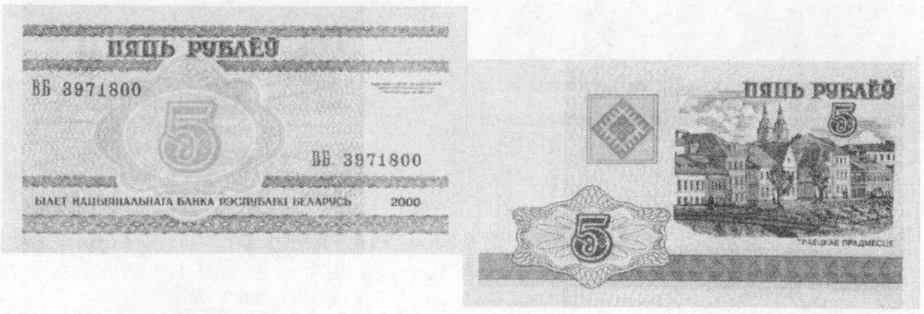

22 **5 Rublei**

2000. Pale red and violet on multicolor underprint. Back: Buildings in Minsk lower city at center right. 110x60mm.

	VF	UNC
22	.25	1.00

23 **10 Rublei**

2000. Lilac on multicolor underprint. Back: National Library at right. 110x60mm.

	VF	UNC
23	.25	1.00

24 **20 Rublei**

2000. Brown on multicolor underprint. National Bank building at left center. Back: Interior view. 150x69mm.

	VF	UNC
24	.25	1.50

25 **50 Rublei**

2000. Red-borwn on multicolor underprint. Brest's tower, Holmsky Gate at left, tapestry at center right. Back: Star shaped war memorial gateway at center right. UV: fibers fluoresce red, blue security thread yellow; back: upper serial # red, "50" yellow in watermark area. 150x69mm.

	VF	UNC
a. Solid security thread with bank initials. Old spelling of 50 with a 3E (2000).	.50	2.00
b. Without security thread. New spelling of 50 (2010).	.50	2.00

26 **100 Rublei** VF UNC

2000. Green on multicolor underprint. Bolshoi Opera and Ballet Theater at center, tapestry at left. Back: Scene from ballet *Vibrannitsa*. Watermark: Ballerina. UV: fibers fluoresce red, blue; security thread yellow, value yellow; back: upper serial # red. 150x69mm.

	VF	UNC
a. Solid security thread (2000).	.25	3.00
b. Without security thread (2011).	.25	3.00

27 **500 Rublei** VF UNC

2000. Brown and green on tan underprint. Palace of Culture. Back: Façade fragment. 150x74mm.

	VF	UNC
a. Solid security thread with bank initials (2000).	1.50	6.00
b. Segmented security thread with bank initials (2011).	1.50	6.00

28 **1000 Rublei** VF UNC

2000. Blue on yellow underprint. National Museum of Art at left center. Back: Flowers and fruits still-life. UV: fibers fluoresce red, blue security thread yellow; back: upper serial # red, value yellow. 150x74mm.

	VF	UNC
a. Solid secuity thread with bank initials (2000).	2.50	8.00
b. Segmented security thread with bank initials (2011).	2.50	8.00

29 **5000 Rublei** VF UNC

2000. Purple and slate gray on multicolor underprint. Minsk Sports complex at center. Back: Winter sports complex (three ski jump hills). UV: fibers fluoresce red, blue; security thread yellow; vlaue yellow; back: upper serial # red. 150x74mm.

	VF	UNC
a. Solid security thread with bank initials (2000).	FV	12.50
b. Segmented security thread with bank initials (2011).	FV	12.50

30 **10,000 Rublei** VF UNC

2000 (2001). Orange and blue on multicolor underprint. Viciebsk city view. Back: Amphitheater in Viciebsk. 150x74mm.

	VF	UNC
a. Solid security thread with bank initials.	FV	20.00
b. Segmented security thread with bank initials.	FV	20.00

31 **20,000 Rublei** VF UNC

2000 (2001). Olive on multicolor underprint. Palace in Gomel at center. Back: Mountain top palace. 150x74mm.

	VF	UNC
a. Solid security thread with bank initials.	FV	30.00
b. Segmented security thread with bank initials.	FV	30.00

32 **50,000 Rublei** VF UNC

2000 (2002). Blue, gray, lilac on multicolor underprint. Mir castle at left center. Back: Details of Mir castle. Printer: Goznak. 150x74mm.

	VF	UNC
a. Old spelling of 50,000 with 3E. Solid security thread with bank initials.	FV	70.00
b. New spelling of 50,000. Segmented security thread (2010).	FV	70.00

2001 Commemorative Issue

#33, 10th Anniversary National Bank of Belarus

		VF	UNC
33	**20 Rublei** 2001. Brown on multicolor underprint. #24 with OVD denomination at upper center right and gold-stamped dates *1991-2001* with bank initials at right. Issued in a special folder. 150x74mm.	1.50	6.00

2005 Issue

		VF	UNC
34	**100,000 Rublei** ND (2005). Brown on rose and multicolor underprint. Radziwill Castle in Neswizh at center. Back: Castle. 150x74mm.	FV	80.00

2011 Commemorative Issue

		VF	UNC
35	**20,000 Rublei** 2011. Olive on multicolor underprint. Palace in Gomel at center. Back: Mountain top palace. Overprint: Logo and 1981-2011 at right. Printer: Goznak.	FV	35.00

2012 Issue

		VF	UNC
36	**200,000 Rublei** 2000 (2012). Green, orange, blue and yellow. Mogilev regional Art Museum at left center. Back: Architectural elements from the museum. Watermark: Architectural elemetns 150x74mm.	FV	60.00

Collector Series

Belarus National Bank

2000 Commemorative

		Mkt.	Value
CS1	**Rublei - Various Amounts** Back: The 20 Rublei and higher include an overprint: *MILLENNIUM* at the lower left. 10-piece set of notes in blue folder. Set consists of #21-30 dated 2000 and with matching serial #.		25.00

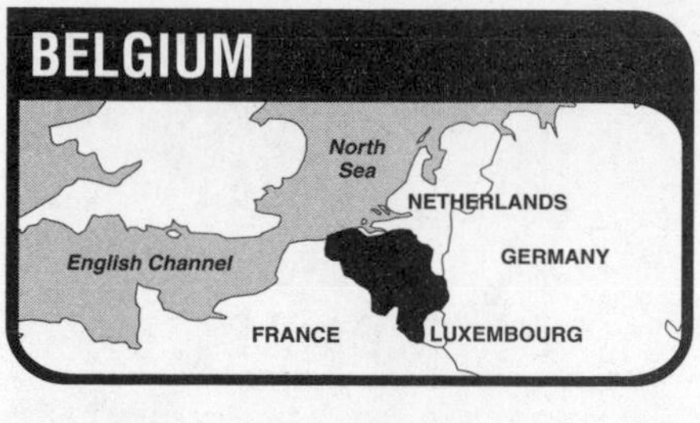

The Kingdom of Belgium, a constitutional monarchy in northwest Europe, has an area of 30,528 sq. km. and a population of 10.40 million, chiefly Dutch-speaking Flemish and French-speaking Walloons. Capital: Brussels. Agriculture, dairy farming, and the processing of raw materials for re-export are the principal industries. "Beurs voor Diamant" in Antwerp is the world's largest diamond trading center. Iron and steel, machinery, motor vehicles, chemicals, textile yarns and fabrics comprise the principal exports.

Belgium became independent from the Netherlands in 1830; it was occupied by Germany during World Wars I and II. The country prospered in the past half century as a modern, technologically advanced European state and member of NATO and the EU. Tensions between the Dutch-speaking Flemings of the north and the French-speaking Walloons of the south have led in recent years to constitutional amendments granting these regions formal recognition and autonomy.

RULERS:

Baudouin I, 1952-93
Albert II, 1993-

MONETARY SYSTEM:

1 Franc = 100 Centimes to 2001
1 Belga = 5 Francs
1 Euro = 100 Cents, 2002-

	GOUVERNEURS de la BANQUE NATIONALE de BELGIQUE		DIRECTEURS GÉNÉRAUX de la TRÉSORERIE
1	Hubert Ansiaux 08.08.1957 - 17.02.1971	17	Maurice Williot 02.04.1956 - 31.01.1963
2	Robert Vandeputte 01.03.1971 - 25.02.1975	18	Marcel d'Haeze 01.02.1963 - 31.05.1975
3	Cecil de Strijcker 26.02.1975 - 28.02.1982	19	Maurice Esselens 01.06.1975 - 30.09.1976
4	Jean Godeaux 01.03.1982 - 02.07.1989	20	Emiel Kestens 01.10.1976 - 31.11.1984
5	Alfons Verplaetse 03.07.1989 -	21	René Lauwerijns 01.12.1984 - 31.03.1988
		22	Edgard Van De Pontseele 01.04.1988 - 31.10.1990
		23	Gregoire Brouhns 01.11.1990 -

	TREASURERS		
6	Jean Jacques Vincent 01.07.1953 - 19.02.1960	11	Maurice Demanet 17.11.1982 - 30.09.1984
7	René Magdonelle 19.02.1960 - 30.10.1968	12	Georges Lakière 01.10.1984 - 21.12.1986
8	Maurice Jordens 30.10.1968 - 02.06.1977	13	Paul Génie 25.12.1986 - 02.08.1989

9	Raymond Simonis 03.06.1977 - 03.10.1979	14	Jacques Van Droogenbroeck 03.08.1989 - 28.02.1992
10	Pol Dasin 04.10.1979 - 17.11.1982	15	Bertholomé 01.03.1992 -

KINGDOM

BANQUE NATIONALE DE BELGIQUE

NATIONALE BANK VAN BELGIE

1961-71 ISSUE

134 100 Francs VF UNC

1.2.1962-2.6.1977. Violet on multicolor underprint. Lambert Lombard at left. 4 signature varieties. Back: Allegorical figure at center. Watermark: King Baudouin I. 138x60mm.

	VF	UNC
a. Serial # 00001 A 001 to 10000 Z 999. Signature (1 and 7), (1 and 8).	4.00	13.00
b. Serial # 1001 A 0001 to 2350 Z 999. Signature (1 and 8), (2 and 8) and (3 and 8).	4.00	13.00
c. Series 3000. Coated with plastic. Signature (2 and 8).	25.00	75.00

135 500 Francs VF UNC

2.5.1961-28.4.1975. Blue-gray and multicolor. Bernard Van Orley at center. 4 signature varieties. Back: Margaret of Austria and Malines Palace façade at right. Watermark: King Baudouin I. 147x74mm.

	VF	UNC
a. Serial # 0001 A 001 to 2500 Z 999. signature (1 and 7) and (1 and 8).	30.00	80.00
b. Serial # 251 A 0001 to 556 Z 9999. signature (1 and 8), (2 and 8) and (3 and 8).	30.00	80.00
s. Specimen.	—	600.

136 1000 Francs VF UNC

2.1.1961-8.12.1975. Brown and blue. Gérard Kremer (called Mercator) at left. 4 signature varieties. Back: Atlas holding globe. Watermark: King Baudouin I. 157x79mm.

	VF	UNC
a. Serial # 0001 A 001 to 10400 Z 999. signature (1 and 7).	50.00	100.
b. Serial # 1041 A 0001 to 1877 Z 999. signature (1 and 8), (2 and 8) and (3 and 8).	50.00	100.
s. Specimen.	—	600.

137 5000 Francs VF UNC

6.1.1971-15.9.1977. Green. André Vesalius at center. Signature (1 and 8), (2 and 8), (3 and 8) and (3 and 9). Back: Escapelus statue and temple of Epidaure. Watermark: King Baudouin I. 167x84mm.

	VF	UNC
a. Issued note.	275.	400.
s. Specimen.	—	600

KINGDOM

ROYAUME DE BELGIQUE - KONINKRIJK BELGIE

TRÉSORERIE - THESAURIE (TREASURY NOTES)

1964-66 ISSUE

#138 and 139 replacement notes: Serial # prefix *Z/1*.

138 20 Francs VF UNC

15.6.1964. Black on blue, orange and multicolor underprint. King Baudouin I at left, arms at lower right. Signature 18, 19, 20. Back: Atomium complex in Brussels at right. Watermark: King Baudouin I. .50 3.00

139 50 Francs VF UNC

16.5.1966. Brown-violet and orange-brown on multicolor underprint. Arms at lower left center, King Baudouin I and Queen Fabiola at right. Signature 18, 19, 20, 21. Back: Parliament building in Brussels. Watermark: King Baudouin I. 2.00 4.00

Banque Nationale de Belgique - Continued

1978; 1980 ND Issue

140	**100 Francs**	VF	UNC
	ND (1978-81). Maroon, blue and olive-green on multicolor underprint. Hendrik Beyaert at center right. Architectural view and plan at left. Signature (3 and9), (3 and 10) only on face. Back: Geometric design. Watermark: King Baudouin I. UV: Back, central design fluoresces yellow. 142x76mm.		
	a. Issued note.	10.00	30.00
	s. Specimen.	—	—

141	**500 Francs**	VF	UNC
	ND (1980-81). Deep blue-violet and deep green on blue and multicolor underprint. Constantin Meunier at left center underprint of two coal miners and mine conveyor tower at center right. Signature (3 and 8). Back: Five circular designs. Watermark: King Baudouin I. Signature on face only. 147x76mm.		
	a. Issued note.	50.00	90.00
	s. Specimen.	—	—

1981-82 ND Issue

142	**100 Francs**	VF	UNC
	ND (1982-94). Hendrik Beyaert at center right. Architectural view and plan at left. Signature (3 and 10), (4 and 10), (4 and 11), (4 and 12), (4 and 13), (5 and 14), (5 and 15). Back: Geometric design. Watermark: King Baudouin I. Signature on face and back. 142x76mm.		
	a. Issued note.	6.00	10.00
	s. Specimen.	—	—

143	**500 Francs**	VF	UNC
	ND (1982-98). Deep blue-violet and deep green on blue and multicolor underprint. Constantine Meunier at left center, underprint of two coal miners and mine conveyor tower at center right. Signature (3 and 10), (4 and 10), (4 and 11), (4 and 12), (4 and 13), (5 and 14), (5 and 15). Back: Five circular designs. Watermark: King Baudouin I. Signature on face and back. 147x76mm.		
	a. Issued note.	25.00	60.00
	s. Specimen.	—	—

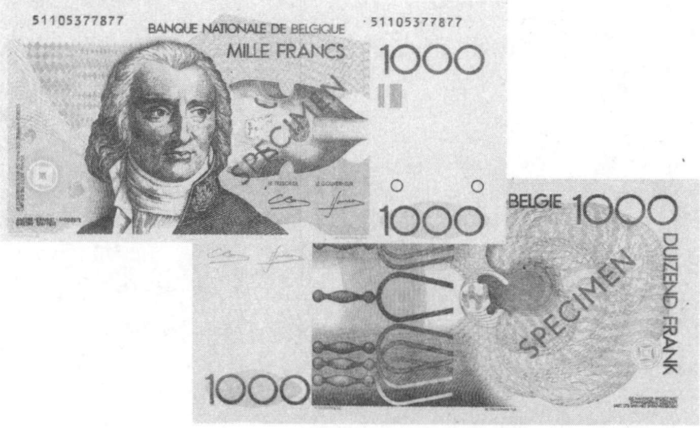

144	**1000 Francs**	VF	UNC
	ND (1980-96). Brown and green on multicolor underprint. André Gretry at left center, bass violin center right in background. Signature (3 and 10), (4 and 10), (4 and 11), (4 and 12), (4 and 13), (5 and 14), (5 and 15). Back: Tuning forks and view of inner ear. Watermark: King Baudouin I. 154x76mm.		
	a. Name as: *ANDRÉ ERNEST MODESTE GRETRY. 1741-1813.*	50.00	90.00
	s. Specimen.	—	300.
	x1. Name as: *• ERNEST • MODESTE.*	120.	300.
	x2. Name as: *ANDRÉ ERNEST MODESTE TRY.*	75.00	180.

145	**5000 Francs**	VF	UNC
	ND (1982-92). Green on multicolor underprint. Guido Gezelle at left center, tree and stained glass window behind. Signature (4 and 10), (4 and 11), (4 and 12), (4 and 13), (5 and 14). Back: Green, red and brown. Dragonfly and leaf at center. Watermark: King Baudouin I. 160x76mm.		
	a. Issued note.	225.	400.
	s. Specimen.	—	400.

1992 ND Issue

146 10,000 Francs — VF 475. UNC 900.

ND (1992-97). Grayish purple on multicolor underprint. King Baudouin I and Queen Fabiola at left , aerial map as underprint. Signature (5 and 15). Back: Flora and greenhouses at Laeken (royal residence) at center. Watermark: King Baudouin I and Queen Fabiola. 166x76mm.

1994-97 ND Issue

147 100 Francs — VF 5.00 UNC 7.50

ND (1995-2001). Red-violet and black on multicolor underprint. James Ensor at left and as watermark, masks at lower center and at right. Signature (5 and 15), (6 and 16). Back: Beach scene at left. 139x76mm.

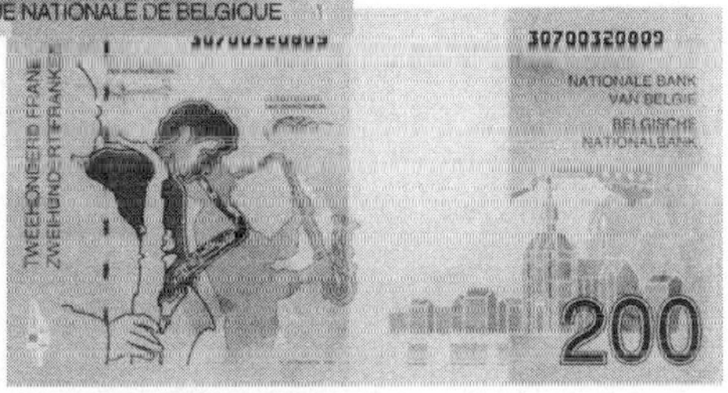

148 200 Francs — VF 10.00 UNC 25.00

ND (1995). Black and brown on yellow and orange underprint. Adolphe Sax at left, saxophone at right. Signature (5 and 15). Back: Saxophone players outlined at left, church, houses in Dinant outlined at lower right. Watermark: Adolphe Sax. 144x76mm.

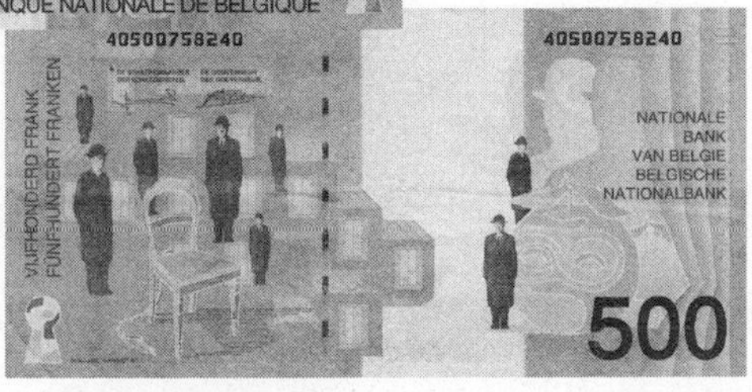

149 500 Francs — VF 25.00 UNC 50.00

ND (1998). Blue-black, purple and blue-green on multicolor underprint. René Magritte at left, birds in plants at lower center, tree at right. Signature (5 and 15). Back: Six men, chair at left, men at center right. Watermark: René Magritte. 150x76mm.

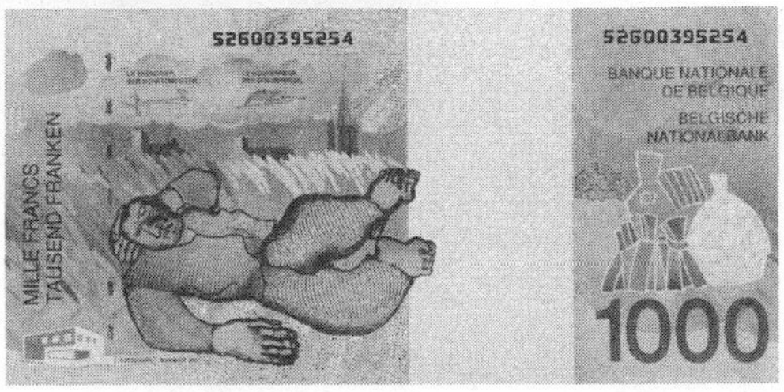

150 1000 Francs — VF 40.00 UNC 80.00

ND (1997). Dark brown on multicolor underprint. Constant Permeke at left, sailboat at center. Signature (5 and 15). Back: *Sleeping Farmer* painting at left. Watermark: Constant Permeke. 154x76mm.

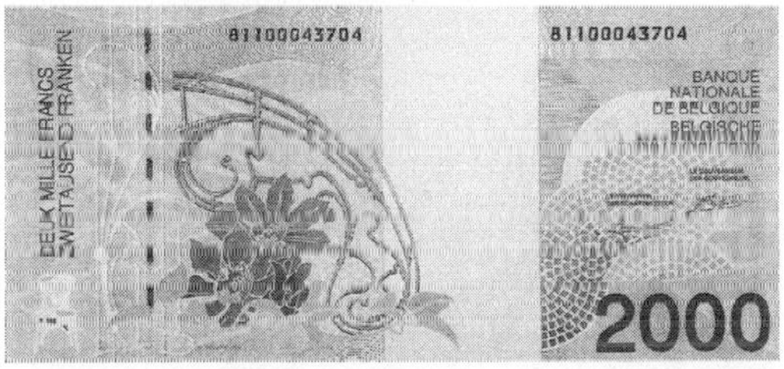

151 2000 Francs — VF 80.00 UNC 110.

ND (1994-2001). Purple and blue-green on multicolor underprint. Baron Victor Horta at left. Signature (5 and 15). Back: Flora and *Art Nouveau* design at left. Watermark: Baron Victor Horta. 159x76mm.

152 10,000 Francs — VF 375. UNC 600.

ND (1997). Deep purple on multicolor underprint. King Albert II and Queen Paola at left, aerial view of Parliamentary chamber at right. Signature (5 and 15). Back: Greenhouses at Laeken (royal residence). Watermark: King Albert II. 169x76mm.

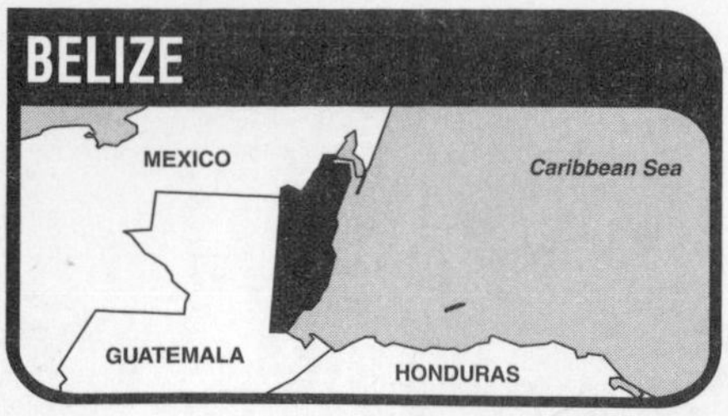

Belize (formerly British Honduras) is situated in Central America south of Mexico and east and north of Guatemala. It has an area of 22,965 sq. km. and a population of 301,300. Capital: Belmopan. Sugar, citrus fruits, chicle and hard woods are exported.

Belize was the site of several Mayan city states until their decline at the end of the first millennium A.D. The British and Spanish disputed the region in the 17th and 18th centuries; it formally became the colony of British Honduras in 1854. Territorial disputes between the UK and Guatemala delayed the independence of Belize until 1981. Guatemala refused to recognize the new nation until 1992. Tourism has become the mainstay of the economy.

MONETARY SYSTEM:

1 Dollar = 100 Cents

BELIZE

GOVERNMENT OF BELIZE

1974-75 ISSUE

33	**1 Dollar**	VF	UNC
	1974-76. Green on multicolor underprint. Portrait of Queen Elizabeth II at right, arms at left.		
	a. 1.1.1974.	20.00	100.
	b. 1.6.1975.	15.00	85.00
	c. 1.1.1976.	15.00	80.00
	s. Specimen, punch hole cancelled.	—	150.
	ct. Color trial. Blue, green and pale orange.	—	225.

34	**2 Dollars**	VF	UNC
	1974-76. Violet on lilac and multicolor underprint. Portrait of Queen Elizabeth II at right, arms at left.		
	a. 1.1.1974.	35.00	175.
	b. 1.6.1975.	25.00	125.
	c. 1.1.1976.	20.00	110.
	s. Specimen, punch hole cancelled.	—	250.
	ct. Color trial. Brown, orange and red.	—	325.

35	**5 Dollars**	VF	UNC
	1975; 1976. Red on multicolor underprint. Portrait of Queen Elizabeth II at right, arms at left.		
	a. 1.6.1975.	60.00	300.
	b. 1.1.1976.	50.00	250.
	s. Specimen, punch hole cancelled.	—	350.
	ct. Color trial. Red on multicolor underprint.	—	425.

36	**10 Dollars**	VF	UNC
	1974-76. Black on multicolor underprint. Portrait of Queen Elizabeth II at right, arms at left.		
	a. 1.1.1974.	600.	3300.
	b. 1.6.1975.	200.	950.
	c. 1.1.1976.	250.	1000.
	s. Specimen, punch hole cancelled.	—	950.
	ct. Color trial. Green and orange.	—	725.

37	**20 Dollars**	VF	UNC
	1974-76. Brown on multicolor underprint. Portrait of Queen Elizabeth II at right, arms at left.		
	a. 1.1.1974.	375.	1650.
	b. 1.6.1975.	250.	1100.
	c. 1.1.1976.	250.	1000.
	s. Specimen, punch hole cancelled.	—	900.
	ct. Color trial. Blue, green and pale yellow.	—	1250.

MONETARY AUTHORITY OF BELIZE

ORDINANCE NO. 9 OF 1976; 1980 ISSUE

38	**1 Dollar**	VF	UNC
	1.6.1980. Green on multicolor underprint. Linear border on arms in upper left corner, Queen Elizabeth II at center right 3/4 looking left, underwater scene with reef and fish in center background. Back: House of Representatives at center. Jabiu stork at right. Watermark: Carved head of the "sleeping giant".		
	a. Issued note.	15.00	60.00
	r. Replacement note. Serial # prefix: *Z/1.*	35.00	100.
	s. Specimen.	—	—

39 5 Dollars — VF / UNC

1.6.1980. Red on multicolor underprint. Linear border on arms in upper left corner, Queen Elizabeth II at center right 3/4 looking left, underwater scene with reef and fish in center background. Back: House of Representatives at center. Jabiu stork at right. Watermark: Carved head of the "sleeping giant".

	VF	UNC
a. Issued note.	35.00	125.
r. Replacement note. Serial # prefix: *Z/1.*	65.00	200.
s. Specimen.	—	—

40 10 Dollars — VF / UNC

1.6.1980. Violet on multicolor underprint. Linear border on arms in upper left corner, Queen Elizabeth II at center right 3/4 looking left, underwater scene with reef and fish in center background. Back: House of Representatives at center. Jabiu stork at right. Watermark: Carved head of the "sleeping giant".

	VF	UNC
a. Issued note.	75.00	275.
s. Specimen.	—	—

41 20 Dollars — VF 150. — UNC 650.

1.6.1980. Brown on multicolor underprint. Linear border on arms in upper left corner, Queen Elizabeth II at center right 3/4 looking left, underwater scene with reef and fish in center background. Back: House of Representatives at center. Jabiu stork at right. Watermark: Carved head of the "sleeping giant".

42 100 Dollars — VF 500. — UNC 2000.

1.6.1980. Blue on multicolor underprint. Linear border on arms in upper left corner, Queen Elizabeth II at center right 3/4 looking left, underwater scene with reef and fish in center background. Back: House of Representatives at center. Jabiu stork at right. Watermark: Carved head of the "sleeping giant".

Central Bank of Belize

Act 1982; 1983 Issue

43 1 Dollar — VF 10.00 — UNC 50.00

1.7.1983. Green on multicolor underprint. Wreath border on arms in upper left corner, Queen Elizabeth II at center right 3/4 looking left, underwater scene with reef and fish in center background. Back: House of Representatives at center. Jabiu stork at right. Watermark: Carved head of the "sleeping giant".

44 10 Dollars — VF / UNC

1.7.1983. Black on red and multicolor underprint. Wreath border on arms in upper left corner, Queen Elizabeth II at center right 3/4 looking left, underwater scene with reef and fish in center background. Back: House of Representatives at center. Jabiu stork at right. Watermark: Carved head of the "sleeping giant".

	VF	UNC
a. Issued note.	50.00	175.
s. Specimen.	—	125.

45 20 Dollars — VF 140. — UNC 550.

1.7.1983. Brown on multicolor underprint. Wreath border on arms in upper left corner, Queen Elizabeth II at center right 3/4 looking left, underwater scene with reef and fish in center background. Back: House of Representatives at center. Jabiu stork at right. Watermark: Carved head of the "sleeping giant".

Act 1982; 1983-87 Issue

46 1 Dollar — VF / UNC

1983-87. Green on multicolor underprint. Wreath border on arms with large tree behind in upper left corner, Queen Elizabeth II at center right 3/4 looking left, underwater scene with reef and fish in center background. Signature varieties. Back: House of Representatives at center. Jabiu stork at right. Watermark: Carved head of the "sleeping giant".

	VF	UNC
a. 1.11.1983.	8.00	35.00
b. 1.1.1986.	7.00	30.00
c. 1.1.1987.	6.00	25.00
s. Specimen.	—	75.00

47 5 Dollars

1987; 1989. Red on multicolor underprint. Wreath border on arms with large tree behind in upper left corner, Queen Elizabeth II at center right 3/4 looking left, underwater scene with reef and fish in center background. Signature varieties. Back: House of Representatives at center. Jabiu stork at right. Watermark: Carved head of the "sleeping giant".

	VF	UNC
a. 1.1.1987.	100.	350.
b. 1.1.1989.	25.00	85.00

48 10 Dollars

1987; 1989. Black on red and multicolor underprint. Wreath border on arms with large tree behind in upper left corner, Queen Elizabeth II at center right 3/4 looking left, underwater scene with reef and fish in center background. Signature varieties. Back: House of Representatives at center. Jabiu stork at right. Watermark: Carved head of the "sleeping giant".

	VF	UNC
a. 1.1.1987.	50.00	200.
b. 1.1.1989.	150.	550.

49 20 Dollars

1986; 1987. Brown on multicolor underprint. Wreath border on arms with large tree behind in upper left corner, Queen Elizabeth II at center right 3/4 looking left, underwater scene with reef and fish in center background. Signature varieties. Back: House of Representatives at center. Jabiu stork at right. Watermark: Carved head of the "sleeping giant".

	VF	UNC
a. 1.1.1986.	110.	350.
b. 1.1.1987.	50.00	150.

50 100 Dollars

1983; 1989. Blue on multicolor underprint. Wreath border on arms with large tree behind in upper left corner, Queen Elizabeth II at center right 3/4 looking left, underwater scene with reef and fish in center background. Signature varieties. Back: House of Representatives at center. Jabiu stork at right. Watermark: Carved head of the "sleeping giant".

	VF	UNC
a. 1.11.1983.	225.	850.
b. 1.1.1989.	250.	950.
r. Replacement note. Serial # prefix: Z/1.	FV	1250.

Act 1982; 1990 Issue

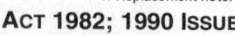

51 1 Dollar

1.5.1990. Green on light brown, blue and multicolor underprint. Mature facing portrait of Queen Elizabeth II at right, lobster at left. Back: Green and red. Marine life of Belize across center. Watermark: Carved head of the "sleeping giant". Printer: TDLR. 158x69mm.

	VF	UNC
	5.00	27.50

52 2 Dollars

1990; 1991. Purple on light green, blue and multicolor underprint. Mature facing portrait of Queen Elizabeth II at right, carved stone pillar at left. Back: Mayan ruins of Belize. Watermark: Carved head of the "sleeping giant". Printer: TDLR. UV: fish and stork fluoresce yellow, reial #s and right design orange. Back: value green. 158x69mm.

	VF	UNC
a. 1.5.1990.	6.00	37.50
b. 1.6.1991.	5.00	37.50

53 5 Dollars

1990; 1991. Red-orange, orange and violet on multicolor underprint. Mature facing portrait of Queen Elizabeth II at right, C. Columbus medallion at left, silver tiger fish below. Back: St. George's Caye, coffin, outline map and building. Watermark: Carved head of the "sleeping giant". Printer: TDLR. 158x69mm.

	VF	UNC
a. 1.5.1990.	12.50	60.00
b. 1.6.1991.	10.00	52.50

54 10 Dollars VF UNC

1990; 1991. Black, olive-brown and deep blue-green on multicolor underprint. Court House clock tower at left, mature facing portrait of Queen Elizabeth II at right. Back: Government House, Court House and St. John's Cathedral. Watermark: Carved head of the "sleeping giant". Printer: TDLR. 158x69mm.

	VF	UNC
a. 1.5.1990.	20.00	90.00
b. 1.6.1991.	17.00	75.00

55 20 Dollars VF UNC

1.5.1990. Dark brown on multicolor underprint. Jaguar at left, mature portrait of Queen Elizabeth II at right. Back: Fauna of Belize. Watermark: Carved head of the "sleeping giant". Printer: TDLR. Upper left dog-like bat; lower left Kinkajou; upper center Black Howler Monkey; lower center left Collared Peccary; upper center right Northern Tamandua; lower center right Red Brocket; upper right Ringtail; lower right Jaguar. 158x69mm. 30.00 125.

56 50 Dollars VF UNC

1990; 1991. Purple, brown and red on multicolor underprint. Mature facing portrait of Queen Elizabeth II at right, boats at left. Back: Bridges of Belize. Watermark: Carved head of the "sleeping giant". Printer: TDLR. 158x69mm.

	VF	UNC
a. 1.5.1990.	65.00	240.
b. 1.6.1991.	60.00	215.

57 100 Dollars VF UNC

1990-94. Blue-violet, orange and red on multicolor underprint. Keel-billed toucan at left, mature portrait of Queen Elizabeth II at right. Back: Birds of Belize. Watermark: Carved head of the "sleeping giant". Printer: TDLR. The birds on the back include: jabiru stork, brown pelican, red-footed booby, magnificent frigate bird, yellow-heded parrot and king vulture. 158x69mm.

	VF	UNC
a. 1.5.1990.	150.	475.
b. 1.6.1991.	150.	500.
c. 1.5.1994.	140.	410.

Act 1982; 1996 Issue

58 5 Dollars VF UNC

1.3.1996. Red-orange, orange and violet on multicolor underprint. Mature facing portrait of Queen Elizabeth II at right, C. Columbus medallion at left, silver tiger fish below. Segmented foil over security strip and ascending size serial number at upper right. Back: St. George's Caye, coffin, outline map and building. Watermark: Carved head of the "sleeping giant". Printer: TDLR. 158x69mm. 11.00 52.50

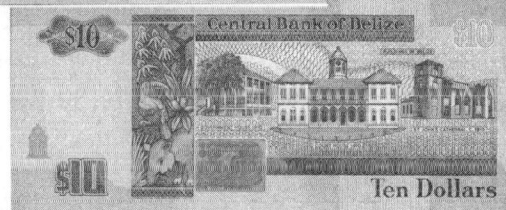

59 10 Dollars VF UNC

1.3.1996. Black, olive brown and deep blue-green on multicolor underprint. Court House clock tower at left, mature facing portrait of Queen Elizabeth II at right. Segmented foil over security strip and ascending size serial number at upper right. Back: Government House, Court House and St. John's Cathedral. Watermark: Carved head of the "sleeping giant". Printer: TDLR. 158x69mm. 15.00 85.00

1997-2002 Issues

#60-65 reduced size. Replacement notes: Serial # prefix: *CZ, DZ.*

60 2 Dollars VF UNC

1999; 2002. Purple on light green, blue and multicolor underprint. Mature facing portrait of Queen Elizabeth II at right, carved stone pillar at left. Back: Mayan ruins of Belize. Watermark: Carved head of the "sleeping giant". Printer: TDLR. Reduced size. 140x70mm.

	VF	UNC
a. 1.1.1999.	FV	35.00
b. 1.1.2002.	FV	32.50
r. Replacement note. 1.1.1999. Serial # prefix: *CZ.*	25.00	110.

61	5 Dollars	VF	UNC
	1999; 2002. Red-orange, orange and violet on multicolor underprint. Mature facing portrait of Queen Elizabeth II at right, C. Columbus medallion at left, silver tiger fish below. Back: St. George's Caye, coffin, outline map and building. Watermark: Carved head of the "sleeping giant". Printer: TDLR. Reduced size. 140x70mm.		
	a. 1.1.1999.	FV	50.00
	b. 1.1.2002.	FV	42.50

62	10 Dollars	VF	UNC
	1997; 2001. Black, olive-brown and deep blue-green on multicolor underprint. Court House clock tower at left, mature facing portrait of Queen Elizabeth II at right. Segmented foil over security strip and ascending size serial number at upper right. Back: Government House, Court House and St. John's Cathedral. Watermark: Carved head of the "sleeping giant". Printer: TDLR. Reduced size. 140x70mm.		
	a. 1.6.1997.	FV	82.50
	b. 1.2001. (no day)	FV	70.00

63	20 Dollars	VF	UNC
	1997; 2000. Dark Brown on multicolor underprint. Jaguar at left, mature portrait of Queen Elizabeth II at right. Back: Fauna of Belize. Watermark: Carved head of the "sleeping giant". Printer: TDLR. Upper left dog-like bat; lower left Kinkajou; upper center Black Howler Monkey; lower center left Collared Peccary; upper center right Northern Tamandua; lower center right Red Brocket; upper right Ringtail; lower right Jaguar. Reduced size. 140x70mm.		
	a. 1.6.1997.	FV	125.
	b. 1.10.2000.	FV	100.

64	50 Dollars	VF	UNC
	1997; 2000. Purple, brown and red on multicolor underprint. Mature facing portrait of Queen Elizabeth Ii at right, boats at left. Back: Bridges of Belize. Watermark: Carved head of the "sleeping giant". Printer: TDLR. Reduced size. 150x75mm.		
	a. 1.6.1997.	FV	220.
	b. 1.9.2000.	FV	195.

65	100 Dollars	VF	UNC
	1.6.1997. Blue-violet, orange and red on multicolor underprint. Keel-billed toucan at left, mature portrait of Queen Elizabeth II at right. Back: Birds of Belize. Watermark: Carved head of the "sleeping giant". Printer: TDLR. The birds on the back include: jabiru stork, brown pelican, red-footed booby, magnificent frigate bird, yellow-headed parrot and king vulture. Reduced size. 150x75mm.	FV	380.

2003-10 Issues

66	2 Dollars	VF	UNC
	2003; 2005; 2007; 2011. Multicolor. Mature facing portrait of Queen Elizabeth II at right, carved stone pillar at left. Back: Mayan ruins of Belize. Watermark: Carved head of the "sleeping giant". Printer: TDLR. With additional security features. 140x70mm.		
	a. 1.6.2003.	FV	25.00
	b. 1.1.2005.	FV	18.00
	c. 1.9.2007.	FV	12.00
	d. 1.11.2011.	FV	12.00

67 5 Dollars

2003-11. Mature facing portrait of Queen Elizabeth II at right, C. Columbus medallion at left, silver tiger fish below. Back: St. George's Caye, Columbus's tomb, outline map and building. Watermark: Carved head of the "sleeping giant". Printer: TDLR. With additional security features. 140x70mm.

	VF	UNC
a. 1.6.2003.	FV	40.00
b. 1.1.2005.	FV	32.50
c. 1.9.2007.	FV	25.00
d. 1.7.2009.	FV	20.00
e. 11.1.2011.	FV	15.00
r. 1.1.2005. Replacement. Serial # prefix: *Z*.	FV	105.

68 10 Dollars

2003; 2005; 2007; 2011. Court House clock tower at left, mature facing portrait of Queen Elizabeth II at right. Segmented foil over security strip and ascending size serial number at upper right. Back: Government House, Court House and St. John's Cathedral. Watermark: Carved head of the "sleeping giant". Printer: TDLR. With additional security features. 140x70mm.

	VF	UNC
a. 1.3.2003.	FV	60.00
b. 1.1.2005.	FV	40.00
c. 1.9.2007.	FV	35.00
d. 11.1.2011.	FV	25.00

69 20 Dollars

2003; 2005; 2007; 2010. Jaguar at left, mature portrait of Queen Elizabeth II at right. Back: Fauna of Belize. Watermark: Carved head of the "sleeping giant". Printer: TDLR. With additional security features. Upper left dog-like bat; lower left Kinkajou; upper center Black Howler Monkey; lower center left Collared Peccary; upper center right Northern Tamandua; lower center right Red Brocket; upper right Ringtail; lower right Jaguar. 140x70mm.

	VF	UNC
a. 1.3.2003.	FV	90.00
b. 1.1.2005.	FV	75.00
c. 1.9.2007.	FV	65.00
d. 1.8.2010.	FV	55.00

70 50 Dollars

2003; 2006; 2009; 2010. Mature facing portrait of Queen Elizabeth Ii at right, boats at left. Back: Bridges of Belize. Watermark: Carved head of the "sleeping giant". Printer: TDLR. With additional security features. 150x75mm.

	VF	UNC
a. 1.3.2003.	FV	175.
b. 1.11.2006	FV	145.
c. 1.2.2009.	FV	125.
d. 1.8.2010.	FV	115.

71 100 Dollars

2003; 2006. Multicolor. Keel-billed toucan at left, mature portrait of Queen Elizabeth II at right. With additional security features. Back: Birds of Belize. Watermark: Carved head of the "sleeping giant". Printer: TDLR. The birds on the back include: jabiru stork, brown pelican, red-footed booby, magnificent frigate bird, yellow-headed parrot and king vulture. 150x75mm.

	VF	UNC
a. 1.1.2003.	FV	255.
b. 1.11.2006.	FV	210.

2012 Commemorative Issue

72 20 Dollars

1.1.2012. Brown and orange on multicolor underprint. Jaguar at left, mature portrait of Elizabeth II at right. Back: Central Bank building at right center. Printer: DLR

	VF	UNC
	FV	75.00

Collector Series

Central Bank of Belize

1984 ND Issue

Note: The Central Bank of Belize will no longer exchange these notes for regular currency. (It is illegal to export the currency afterwards). Value is thus speculative.

CS1 ND (1984) Collection

Queen Elizabeth II and building. Back: Diffrerent animals, ships, fish, birds etc. Stamped from paper bonded within gold foil. Denominations: $1 (1 pc.), $2 (2 pcs.) $5 (3 pcs.), $10 (4 pcs.), $20 (2 pcs.), $25 (6 pcs.), $50 (7 pcs.), $75 (5 pcs.), $100 (6 pcs.). Total 36 pcs.

	Mkt.	Value
		375.

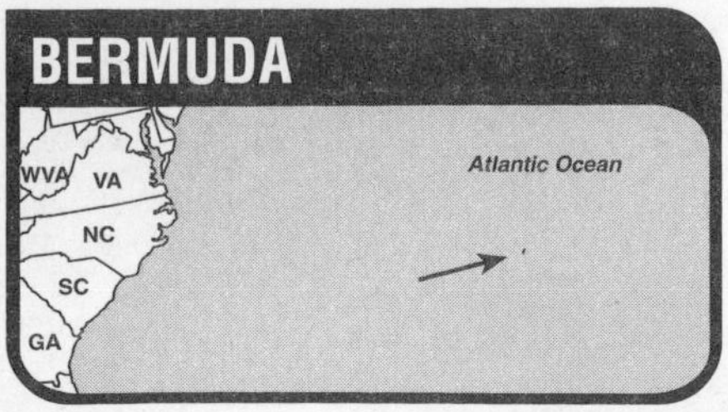

The Parliamentary British Colony of Bermuda, situated in the western Atlantic Ocean 1,062 km. east of North Carolina, has an area of 53.3 sq. km. and a population of 66,500. Capital: Hamilton. Concentrated essences, beauty preparations, and cut flowers are exported.

Bermuda was first settled in 1609 by shipwrecked English colonists headed for Virginia. Tourism to the island to escape North American winters first developed in Victorian times. Tourism continues to be important to the island's economy, although international business has overtaken it in recent years. Bermuda has developed into a highly successful offshore financial center. Although a referendum on independence from the UK was soundly defeated in 1995, the present government has reopened debate on the issue.

RULERS:

British

MONETARY SYSTEM:

1 Shilling = 12 Pence
1 Pound = 20 Shillings, to 1970
1 Dollar = 100 Cents, 1970-

British Administration

Bermuda Government

1952 Issue

		VF	UNC
18	**5 Shillings** 1952; 1957. Brown on multicolor underprint. Portrait Queen Elizabeth II at upper center, Hamilton Harbor in frame at bottom center. Back: Royal crest. Printer: BWC.		
	a. 20.10.1952.	65.00	225.
	b. 1.5.1957.	50.00	150.
	s. As b. Specimen.	—	—

1952-66 Issue

		VF	UNC
19	**10 Shillings** 1952-66. Red on multicolor underprint. Portrait Queen Elizabeth II at upper center, Gate's Fort in St. George in frame at bottom center. Back: Arms at center. Printer: BWC.		
	a. 20.10.1952.	75.00	425.
	b. 1.5.1957.	40.00	200.
	c. 1.10.1966.	60.00	250.
	s. As b. Specimen.	—	—

		VF	UNC
20	**1 Pound** 1952-66. Blue on multicolor underprint. Queen Elizabeth II at right. Bridge at left. Back: Arms at center. Printer: BWC.		
	a. 20.10.1952.	100.	550.
	b. 1.5.1957. Without security strip.	75.00	400.
	c. 1.5.1957. With security strip.	70.00	350.
	d. 1.10.1966.	60.00	275.
	s. As d. Specimen.	—	—
	ct. Green on multicolored underprint.	—	1000.

		VF	UNC
21	**5 Pounds** 1952-66. Orange on multicolor underprint. Portrait Queen Elizabeth II at right, large value at left, ship entering Hamilton Harbor at left. Back: Orange and green. Arms at center. Printer: BWC.		
	a. 20.10.1952.	1250.	2500.
	b. 1.5.1957. Without security strip.	1000.	2000.
	c. 1.5.1957. With security strip.	1125.	2250.
	d. 1.10.1966.	1250.	2500.
22	**10 Pounds** 28.7.1964. Purple on multicolor underprint. Portrait Queen Elizabeth II at right. Back: Arms at center. Printer: BWC.	600.	2750.

1970 Issue

		VF	UNC
23	**1 Dollar** 6.2.1970. Dark blue on tan and aqua underprint. Queen Elizabeth II at right looking 3/4 to left, arms at left center, bermuda petrel or cahow at center. Back: Sailboats at left center, buildings at upper right. Watermark: Tuna fish.		
	a. Issued note.	4.00	27.50
	s. Specimen.	—	25.00

		VF	UNC
24	**5 Dollars** 6.2.1970. Red-violet on aqua and multicolor underprint. Queen Elizabeth II at right looking 3/4 to left, arms at left center. Back: Lighthouse at left, buildings at center right. Watermark: Tuna fish.		
	a. Issued note.	10.00	45.00
	s. Specimen.	—	25.00

		VF	UNC
25	**10 Dollars**		
	6.2.1970. Purple on brown and multicolor underprint. Queen Elizabeth II at right looking 3/4 to left, arms at left center. Back: Bermuda petrel and seashell at center, beach at left. Watermark: Tuna fish.		
	a. Issued note.	15.00	95.00
	s. Specimen.	—	25.00

		VF	UNC
26	**20 Dollars**		
	6.2.1970. Green on multicolor underprint. Queen Elizabeth II at right looking 3/4 to left, arms at left center. Back: Building, sailboat and bridge at left center. Watermark: Tuna fish.		
	a. Issued note.	30.00	150.
	s. Specimen. Overprint: *SPECIMEN* on each side. Punch hole cancelled in each corner.	—	35.00

		VF	UNC
27	**50 Dollars**		
	6.2.1970. Brown on multicolor underprint. Queen Elizabeth II at right looking 3/4 to left, arms at left center. Back: Lighthouse at left, map at upper right. Watermark: Tuna fish.		
	a. Issued note.	80.00	300.
	s. Specimen. Overprint: *SPECIMEN* on each side. Punch hole cancelled in each corner.		60.00

Bermuda Monetary Authority

1974-82 Issue

		VF	UNC
28	**1 Dollar**		
	1975-88. Dark blue on tan and aqua underprint. Queen Elizabeth II at right looking 3/4 to left, arms at left center, bermuda petrel or cahow at center. Back: Sailboats at left center, buildings at upper right. Watermark: Tuna fish.		
	a. Signature titles: *CHAIRMAN* and *MANAGING DIRECTOR.* 1.7.1975; 1.12.1976.	5.00	35.00
	b. 1.4.1978; 1.9.1979; 2.1.1982; 1.5.1984.	3.00	17.50
	c. Signature titles: *CHAIRMAN* and *GENERAL MANAGER.* 1.1.1986.	3.50	20.00
	d. Signature titles: *CHAIRMAN* and *DIRECTOR.* 1.1.1988.	3.00	17.50
	s. Specimen, punch hole cancelled.	—	30.00

		VF	UNC
29	**5 Dollars**		
	1978-88. Red-violet on aqua and multicolor underprint. Queen Elizabeth II at right looking 3/4 to left. Back: Lighthouse at left, buildings at center right. Watermark: Tuna fish.		
	a. Signature titles: *CHAIRMAN* and *MANAGING DIRECTOR.* 1.4.1978.	8.00	45.00
	b. 2.1.1981.	7.50	40.00
	c. Signature titles: *CHAIRMAN* and *GENERAL MANAGER.* 1.1.1986.	7.50	37.50
	d. Signature titles: *CHAIRMAN* and *DIRECTOR.* 1.1.1988.	7.50	35.00
	s. Specimen, punch hole cancelled.	—	—

		VF	UNC
30	**10 Dollars**		
	1978; 1982. Purple on brown and multicolor underprint. Queen Elizabeth II at right looking 3/4 to left, arms at left center. Back: Bermuda petrel and seashell at center, beach at left. Watermark: Tuna fish.		
	a. 1.4.1978.	45.00	200.
	b. 2.1.1982.	40.00	165.
	s. Specimen, punch hole cancelled.	—	—

		VF	UNC
31	**20 Dollars**		
	1974-86. Green on multicolor underprint. Queen Elizabeth II at right looking 3/4 to left, arms at left center. Back: Building, sailboat and bridge at left center.		
	a. 1.4.1974.	125.	550.
	b. 1.3.1976.	50.00	200.
	c. 2.1.1981; 1.5.1984.	25.00	100.
	d. Signature title: *GENERAL MANAGER* at right. 1.1.1986.	25.00	100.
	s. Specimen, punch hole cancelled.	—	—

		VF	UNC
32	**50 Dollars**		
	1974-82. Brown on multicolor underprint. Queen Elizabeth II at right looking 3/4 left., arms at left center. Back: Lighthouse at left, map at upper right.		
	a. 1.5.1974.	350.	1950.
	b. 1.4.1978; 2.1.1982.	100.	450.
	s. Specimen, punch hole cancelled.		—

		VF	UNC
33	**100 Dollars**		
	1982-86. Orange and brown on multicolor underprint. Queen Elizabeth II at right looking 3/4 left. Back: House of Assembly at left, Camden building at upper center right. Watermark: Tuna fish.		
	a. 2.1.1982.	FV	900.
	b. Signature title: *GENERAL MANAGER* overprint at right. 14.11.1984.	FV	875.
	c. Signature title: *GENERAL MANAGER* at right. 1.1.1986.	FV	800.
	s. Specimen, punch hole cancelled.	—	—

1988-89 Issue

		VF	UNC
34	**2 Dollars**		
	1988; 1989. Blue-green on green and multicolor underprint. Mature bust of Queen Elizabeth II at right. Signature titles: *CHAIRMAN* and *DIRECTOR*. Back: Dockyards clock tower building at upper left, map at center, arms at center right. Stylistic changes Watermark: Tuna fish. UV: sea gull fluoresces orange.		
	a. Serial # prefix: *B/1*. 1.10.1988.	FV	10.00
	b. Serial # prefix: *B/2*. 1.8.1989.	FV	9.50

		VF	UNC
35	**5 Dollars**		
	20.2.1989. Red-violet and purple on multicolor underprint. Mature bust of Queen Elizabeth II at right. Signature titles: *CHAIRMAN* and *DIRECTOR*. Back: Lighthouse at left, buildings at center right, arms at upper left. Watermark: Tuna fish. Stylistic changes on back.		
	a. Signature title: *DIRECTOR* on silver background at bottom center Serial # prefix: *B/1*.	7.00	27.50
	b. Signature title: *DIRECTOR* without silver background. Serial # prefix: *B/1, B/2*.	FV	12.50
	r. Replacement.	15.00	50.00

		VF	UNC
36	**10 Dollars**		
	20.2.1989. Purple, blue and ochre on multicolor underprint. Mature bust of Queen Elizabeth II at right. signature titles: *CHAIRMAN* and *DIRECTOR*. Back: Bermuda petrel and seashell at center, beach at left, arms at upper left. Watermark: Tuna fish.	FV	25.00

		VF	UNC
37	**20 Dollars**		
	20.2.1989. Green and red on multicolor underprint. Mature bust of Queen Elizabeth II at right. Signature titles: *CHAIRMAN* and *DIRECTOR*. Back: Building, sailboat and bridge at left center, arms at upper left. Watermark: Tuna fish. Stylistic changes on back.		
	a. Serial # prefix: *B/1*.	FV	42.50
	b. Serial # prefix: *B/2*.	FV	40.00

		VF	UNC
38	**50 Dollars**		
	20.2.1989. Brown and olive on multicolor underprint. Mature bust of Queen Elizabeth II at right. Signature titles: *CHAIRMAN* and *DIRECTOR*. Back: Lighthouse at left, map at upper right, arms at upper left. Watermark: Tuna fish. Stylistic changes on back.	FV	100.

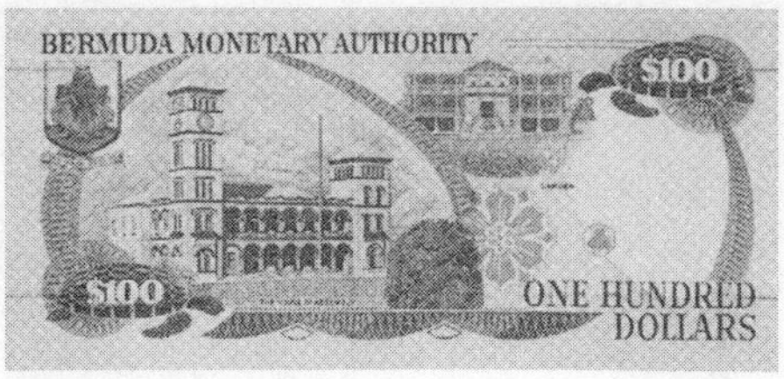

		VF	UNC
39	**100 Dollars**		
	20.2.1989. Orange, brown and violet on multicolor underprint. Mature bust of Queen Elizabeth II at right. Signature titles: *CHAIRMAN* and *DIRECTOR*. Back: House of Assembly at left, Camden building at upper center right, arms at upper left. Watermark: Tuna fish. Stylistic changes on back.	FV	185.

1992 Commemorative Issue; Act 1969

#40, Quincentenary of Christopher Columbus

		VF	UNC
40	**50 Dollars**		
	12.10.1992. Dark blue, brown and red on multicolor underprint. Mature bust of Queen Elizabeth II at right, commemorative details. Maltese cross as serial number prifix at upper left, c/c fractional prefix at right, and overprint: *Christopher Columbus / Quincen* Back: Scuba divers, shipwreck at left, island outline at upper center right above arms. 140x68mm.		
	a. Issued note.	FV	120.
	s. Specimen. Overprint: *SPECIMEN*, punch hole cancelled.	—	125.

Act 1969; 1992-96 Issue

		VF	UNC
40A	**2 Dollars**		
	1996-97. Blue and green on multicolor underprint. Mature bust of Queen Elizabeth II at right, Authorization text in 3 lines at center. Signature titles: *CHAIRMAN* and *DIRECTOR*. Back: Dockyards clock tower building at upper left, map at center, arms at center right. Watermark: Tuna fish. 140x68mm.		
	a. 29.2.1996.	FV	10.00
	b. 6.6.1997.	FV	5.00

		VF	UNC
41	**5 Dollars**		
	1992-97. Red-violet and purple on multicolor underprint. Mature bust of Queen Elizabeth II at right. Authorization text in 3 lines at center. Signature titles: *CHAIRMAN* and *DIRECTOR*. Back: Lighthouse at left, buildings at center right, arms at upper left. Watermark: Tuna fish. 140x68mm.		
	a. 12.11.1992.	FV	12.50
	b. 25.3.1995.	FV	11.00
	c. 20.2.1996.	FV	10.00
	d. 10.6.1997.	FV	10.00

42 **10 Dollars** — VF | UNC

1993-99. Purple, deep blue and orange on multicolor underprint. Mature bust of Queen Elizabeth II at right. Authorization text in 3 lines at center. Signature titles: *CHAIRMAN* and *DIRECTOR*. Back: Bermuda petrel and seashell at center, beach at left, arms at upper left. Watermark: Tuna fish. 140x68mm.

	VF	UNC
a. 4.1.1993.	FV	22.50
b. 15.3.1996.	FV	20.00
c. 17.6.1997.	FV	20.00
d. 31.5.1999. With security strip.	FV	20.00

43 **20 Dollars** — VF | UNC

1996; 1999. Green and red on multicolor underprint. Mature bust of Queen Elizabeth II at right. Authorization text in 3 lines at center. Signature titles: *CHAIRMAN* and *DIRECTOR*. Back: Building, sailboat and bridge at left center, arms at upper left. Watermark: Tuna fish. 140x68mm.

	VF	UNC
a. 27.2.1996.	FV	40.00
b. 13.5.1999. With security strip.	FV	37.50

44 **50 Dollars** — VF | UNC

1992-96. Dark blue, brown and red on multicolor underprint. Mature bust of Queen Elizabeth II at right. Authorization text in 3 lines at center. Signature titles: *CHAIRMAN* and *DIRECTOR*. Back: Scuba divers, shipwreck at left, island outline at upper center right above arms. Watermark: Tuna fish. 140x68mm.

	VF	UNC
a. 12.10.1992.	FV	100.
b. 25.3.1995.	FV	90.00
c. 23.2.1996.	FV	85.00

45 **100 Dollars** — VF | UNC

14.2.1996. Orange, brown and violet on multicolor underprint. Mature bust of Queen Elizabeth II at right. Authorization text in 3 lines at center. Signature titles: *CHAIRMAN* and *DIRECTOR*. Back: House of Assembly at left, Camden building at upper center right, arms at upper left. Watermark: Tuna fish. 140x68mm. — FV | 175.

1994 Commemorative Issue

#46, 25th Anniversary Bermuda Monetary Authority

46 **100 Dollars** — VF | UNC

20.2.1994. Orange, brown and violet on multicolor underprint. Mature bust of Queen Elizabeth II at right. Authorization text in 3 lines at center, overprint: *25th Anniversary....* Signature titles: *CHAIRMAN* and *DIRECTOR*. Back: Arms at upper left, House of Assembly at left, Camden building at upper center right. Watermark: Tuna fish. 140x68mm.

	VF	UNC
a. Issued note.	FV	170.
s. Specimen. Overprint: *SPECIMEN*, punch hole cancelled.	—	150.

1997 Commemorative Issue

#47, Opening of Burnaby House

47 **20 Dollars** — VF | UNC

17.1.1997. Green and red on multicolor underprint. Mature bust of Queen Elizabeth II at right. Overprint on #43. *To commemorate the opening of Burnaby House...* in watermark area at left. Authorization text in 3 lines at center. Signature titles Back: Building, sailboat and bridge at left center. Watermark: Tuna fish. 140x68mm. — FV | 37.50

1997 Regular Issue

48 **50 Dollars** — VF | UNC

6.6.1997. Dark blue, brown and red on multicolor underprint. Mature bust of Queen Elizabeth II at right. Authorization text in 3 lines at center. Signature titles: *CHAIRMAN* and *DIRECTOR*. Back: Scuba divers, shipwreck at left, island outline at upper right above arms. Watermark: Tuna fish. Segmented foil over security thread. 140x68mm. — FV | 87.50

49 **100 Dollars** — VF | UNC

30.6.1997. Orange and brown on multicolor underprint. Mature bust of Queen Elizabeth II at right. Authorization text in 3 lines at center. Signature titles: *CHAIRMAN* and *DIRECTOR*. Back: Arms at upper left, House of Assembly at left, Camden building at upper center right. Watermark: Tuna fish. Segmented foil over security thread. 140x68mm. — FV | 165.

2000 Issue

50 2 Dollars

24.5.2000; 7.5.2007. Blue and green on multicolor underprint. Mature portrait of Queen Elizabeth II at right. Sea horse at center. Back: Boats and building at left, island map at center. Watermark: Tuna fish. 140x68mm.

	VF	UNC
a. 24.5.2000.	FV	4.00
b. 7.5.2007.	FV	4.00
s. As a. Specimen. Overprint: *SPECIMEN* on each side. Punch hole cancelled in each corner.	—	—

51 5 Dollars

25.5.2000. Purple and burgundy on multicolor underprint. Mature portrait of Queen Elizabeth II at right. Shell and fish at center. Back: Lighthouse at left, bay view at center. Watermark: Tuna fish. 140x68mm.

	VF	UNC
a. Issued note.	FV	8.50
s. As a. Specimen. Overprint: *SPECIMEN* on each side. Punch hole cancelled in each corner.	—	—

52 10 Dollars

24.5.2000; 7.5.2007. Dark blue and mauve on multicolor underprint. Mature portrait of Queen Elizabeth II at right. Flower and Bermuda Petrel at center. Back: Bay scene, Bermuda Petrel and shell. Watermark: Tuna fish. 140x68mm.

	VF	UNC
a. 24.5.2000.	FV	17.00
b. 7.5.2007.	FV	17.00
s. As a. Specimen. As a. Overprint: *SPECIMEN* on each side. Punch hole cancelled in each corner.	—	35.00

53 20 Dollars

24.5.2000. Green and red on multicolor underprint. Mature portrait of Queen Elizabeth II at right, building at center. Back: Bridge and harbor scene. Watermark: Tuna fish. 140x68mm.

	VF	UNC
a. Issued note.	FV	37.50
s. As a. Specimen. Overprint: *SPECIMEN* on each side. Punch hole cancelled in each corner.	—	—

53A 20 Dollars

24.5.2000 (2008). Green and red on multicolor underprint. Mature portrait of Queen Elizabeth II at right. Flower and foil patch. Serial # prefix: *D/2.* Back: Bridge and harbor scene. Printer: (T)DLR. 140x68mm. — FV 37.50

54 50 Dollars

24.5.2000; 7.5.2007. Bluish black, red and brown on multicolor underprint. Mature portrait of Queen Elizabeth II at right, building at center. Back: Scuba divers and wreck at left, map at upper center. Watermark: Tuna fish. 140x68mm.

	VF	UNC
a. 24.5.2000.	FV	85.00
b. 7.5.2007.	FV	85.00
r. Replacement note: Serial # prefix *Z.*	FV	150.
s. As a. Specimen. Overprint: *SPECIMEN* on each side. Punch hole cancelled in each corner.	—	—

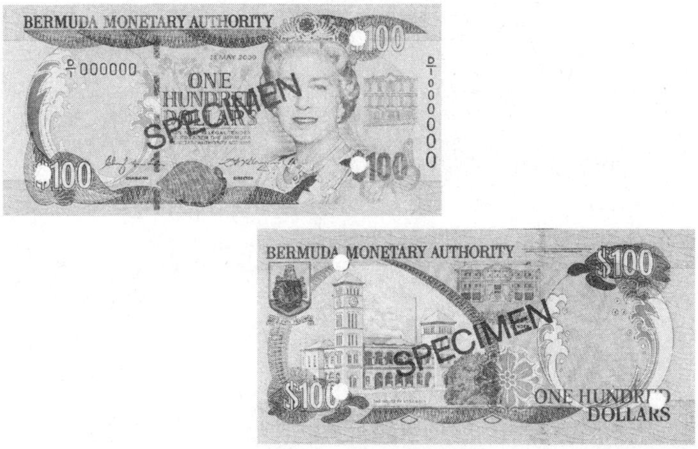

55 100 Dollars

24.5.2000. Red-orange and brown on multicolor underprint. Mature portrait of Queen Elizabeth II at right, flowers and shell at center. Back: House of Assembly at left, Camden building at upper center right, arms at upper left. Watermark: Tuna fish. 140x68mm.

	VF	UNC
a. Issued note.	FV	165.
r. Replacement note: Serial # prefix: *Z.*	FV	250.
s. As a. Specimen. Overprint: *SPECIMEN* on each side. Punch hole cancelled in each corner.	—	—

2003 Commemorative Issue

56 50 Dollars

2.6.2003. Mature portrait of Queen Elizabeth II at right, golden crown at right with overprint: *TO COMMEMORATE THE CORONATION OF QUEEN ELIZABETH II 1953-2003."* 140x68mm.

	VF	UNC
	FV	95.00

2009 Issue

		VF	UNC
57	**2 Dollars**		
	1.1.2009. Blue and multicolor. Bluebird and flowers. Back: Dockyard clocktower, statue of Nepture. Watermark: Hibiscus flower and sail boat. Printer: TDLR. 69x136mm.		
	a. Issued note.	FV	9.00
	s. Specimen. Overprint *SPECIMEN* and punch hole cancelled.	—	50.00
58	**5 Dollars**		
	1.1.2009. Rose and multicolor. Blue marlin and flowers. Back: Horshoe Bay Beach, Somerset Bridge with boat passing below. Watermark: Hibiscus flower and sail boat. Printer: TDLR. Vertical format. 69x136mm.		
	a. Issued note.	FV	20.00
	s. Specimen. Overprint *SPECIMEN* and punch hole cancelled.	—	50.00
59	**10 Dollars**		
	1.1.2009. Violet and multicolor. Blue angel fish and flowers. Back: Commissioner's House in Somerset Parish and the H.M.S. Deliverance. Watermark: Hibiscus flower and sail boat. Printer: TDLR. Vertical format. 69x136mm.		
	a. Issued note.	FV	35.00
	s. Specimen. Overprint *SPECIMEN* and punch hole cancelled.	—	75.00

		VF	UNC
60	**20 Dollars**		
	1.1.2009. Green and multicolor. Whistling frog and flowers. Back: St. Mark's Chruch steeple, Gibbs Hill lighthouse in Southampton Parish. Watermark: Hibiscus flower and sail boat. Printer: TDLR. Vertical format. 69x136mm.		
	a. Issued note.	FV	55.00
	s. Specimen. Overprint *SPECIMEN* and punch hole cancelled.	—	75.00
61	**50 Dollars**		
	1.1.2009. Light orange and multicolor. Red-billed longtail tropic bird and flowers. Back: St. Peter's church in St. George. Watermark: Hibiscus flower and sail boat. Printer: TDLR. Vertical format. 136x69mm.		
	a. Issued note.	FV	65.00
	s. Specimen. Overprint *SPECIMEN* and punch hole cancelled.	—	100.

		VF	UNC
61A	**50 Dollars**		
	1.1.2009 (2012). Yellow and multicolor White longtail tropic bird. Back: St. Peter's Church in Saint George. 69x136mm.	FV	100.
62	**100 Dollars**		
	1.1.2009. Rose and multicolor. Cardinal on branch, flowers. Back: House of Assembly in Hamilton. Watermark: Hibiscus flower and sail boat. Printer: TDLR. Vertical format. 136x69mm.		
	a. Issued note.	FV	175.
	s. Specimen. Overprint *SPECIMEN* and punch hole cancelled.	—	125.

Collector Series

Bermuda Monetary Authority

1978-84 Dated Issue (1985)

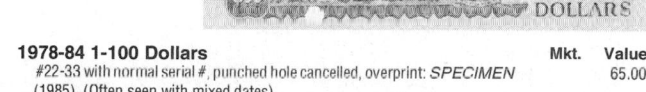

		Mkt.	Value
CS1	**1978-84 1-100 Dollars**		
	#22-33 with normal serial #, punched hole cancelled, overprint: *SPECIMEN* (1985). (Often seen with mixed dates).		65.00

1981-82 Issue (1985)

		Mkt.	Value
CS2	**1981-82 1-100 Dollars**		
	#28-33 with all zero serial #, punched hole cancelled in all 4 corners, overprint: *SPECIMEN* (1985).		65.00

2000 Issue

		Mkt.	Value
CS3	**2000 2-100 Dollars**		
	2000. #50-55 with all zerio serial #, punched hole cancelled in three corners.		75.00

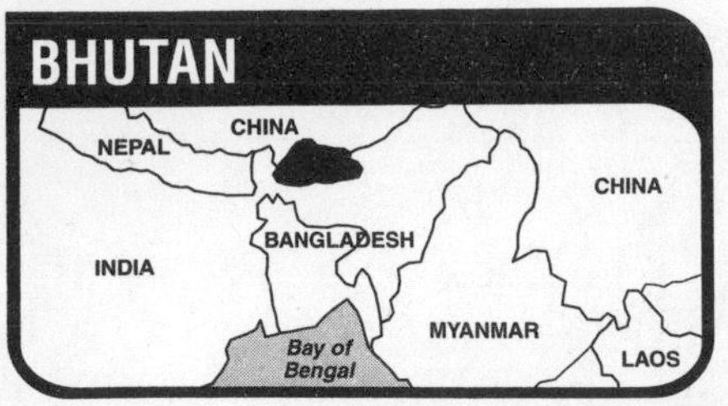

The Kingdom of Bhutan, a landlocked Himalayan country bordered by Tibet, India, and Sikkim, has an area of 47,000 sq. km. and a population of 682,300. Capital: Thimphu. Virtually the entire population is engaged in agricultural and pastoral activities. Rice, wheat, barley, and yak butter are produced in sufficient quantity to make the country self-sufficient in food.

In 1865, Britain and Bhutan signed the Treaty of Sinchulu, under which Bhutan would receive an annual subsidy in exchange for ceding some border land to British India. Under British influence, a monarchy was set up in 1907; three years later, a treaty was signed whereby the British agreed not to interfere in Bhutanese internal affairs and Bhutan allowed Britain to direct its foreign affairs. This role was assumed by independent India after 1947. Two years later, a formal Indo-Bhutanese accord returned the areas of Bhutan annexed by the British, formalized the annual subsidies the country received, and defined India's responsibilities in defense and foreign relations. A refugee issue of over 100,000 Bhutanese in Nepal remains unresolved; 90% of the refugees are housed in seven United Nations Office of the High Commissioner for Refugees (UNHCR) camps. In March 2005, King Jigme Singye Wangchuck unveiled the government's draft constitution - which would introduce major democratic reforms - and pledged to hold a national referendum for its approval. In December 2006, the King abdicated the throne to his son, Jigme Khesar Namgyel Wangchuck, in order to give him experience as head of state before the democratic transition. In early 2007, India and Bhutan renegotiated their treaty to allow Bhutan greater autonomy in conducting its foreign policy, although Thimphu continues to coordinate policy decisions in this area with New Delhi. In July 2007, seven ministers of Bhutan's ten-member cabinet resigned to join the political process, and the cabinet acted as a caretaker regime until democratic elections for seats to the country's first parliament were completed in March 2008. The king ratified the country's first constitution in July 2008.

RULERS:

Jigme Singye Wangchuk, 1972-

MONETARY SYSTEM:

1 Ngultrum (= 1 Indian Rupee) = 100 Chetrums, 1974-

SIGNATURE CHART

1	Chairman Ashi Sonam Wangchuck	2	Bank of Bhutan Yeshe Dorji
3	Chairman Dorji Tsering		

KINGDOM

ROYAL GOVERNMENT OF BHUTAN

1974-78 ND ISSUE

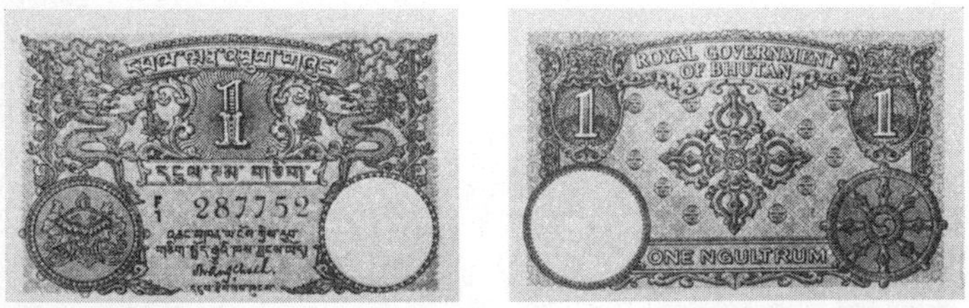

1 **1 Ngultrum** — VF 2.50, UNC 6.00
ND (1974). Blue on multicolor underprint. Dragon design at left and right. Watermark: 4-petaled symbol, called a *dorje,* the Buddhist of a thunderbolt.

2 **5 Ngultrum** — VF 15.00, UNC 50.00
ND (1974). Red-brown on multicolor underprint. Portrait J. Singye Wangchuk at center. Back: Simtokha Dzong palace center right. Watermark: 4-petaled symbol, called a *dorje,* the Buddhist of a thunderbolt.

3 **10 Ngultrum** — VF 30.00, UNC 200.
ND (1974). Blue-violet on multicolor underprint. Portrait J. Dorji Wangchuk at top center. Back: Paro Dzong palace center right. Watermark: 4-petaled symbol, called a *dorje,* the Buddhist of a thunderbolt.

4 **100 Ngultrum** — VF 2000., UNC —
ND (1978). Green and brown on multicolor underprint. Portrait J. Singye Wangchuk at center, circle with 8 good luck symbols at right. Back: Tashichho Dzong palace at left center. Watermark: 4-petaled symbol, called a *dorje,* the Buddhist of a thunderbolt.

1981 ND ISSUE

5 **1 Ngultrum** — VF .25, UNC 3.00
ND (1981). Blue on multicolor underprint. Royal emblem between facing dragons at center, serial number at upper left and right. Back: Simtokha Dzong palace at center.

6 **2 Ngultrum** — VF .50, UNC 4.50
ND (1981). Brown and green on multicolor underprint. Royal emblem between facing dragons at center, serial number at upper left and right. Back: Simtokha Dzong palace at center.

7 **5 Ngultrum** VF UNC
ND (1981). Brown on multicolor underprint. Royal emblem between facing birds at center, serial number at upper left and right. Back: Paro Dzong palace at center. 2.50 10.00

8 **10 Ngultrum** VF UNC
ND (1981). Purple on multicolor underprint. Royal emblem at left, portrait J. Singye Wangchuk at right, serial number at left and right. Back: Paro Dzong palace at center. 5.00 17.50

9 **20 Ngultrum** VF UNC
ND (1981). Olive on multicolor underprint. Facing portrait Jigme Dorji Wangchuk at right, royal emblem at left, serial number at left and right. Back: Punakha Dzong palace at center. 7.50 30.00

10 **50 Ngultrum** VF UNC
ND (1981). Purple, violet and brown on multicolor underprint. Facing portrait Jigme Dorji Wangchuk at right, royal emblem at left, serial number at left and right. Back: Tongsa Dzong palace at center. 15.00 75.00

11 **100 Ngultrum** VF UNC
ND (1981). Dark green, olive-green and brown-violet on multicolor underprint. Bird at center, portrait J. Singye Wangchuk at right, royal emblem at left, serial number at left and right. Back: Tashichho Dzong palace at center. 27.50 150.

Royal Monetary Authority of Bhutan

1985-92 ND Issue

12 **1 Ngultrum** VF UNC
ND (1986). Blue on multicolor underprint. Royal emblem between facing dragons at center. 2 signature varieties. Serial number at lower left and upper right. Back: Simtokha Dzong palace at center. Reduced size. FV .50

13 **2 Ngultrum** VF UNC
ND (1986). Brown and green on multicolor underprint. Royal emblem between facing dragons at center, serial number at lower left and upper right. Back: Simtokhan Dzong palace at center. Reduced size. FV .75

14 **5 Ngultrum** VF UNC
ND (1985; 1990). Brown on multicolor underprint. Royal emblem between facing birds at center, serial number at lower left and upper right. Back: Paro Dzong palace at center. Reduced size. 130x62mm.

a. ND (1985). Signature 1. FV 1.50

b. ND (1990). Signature 3. FV 1.50

15 **10 Ngultrum** VF UNC
ND (1986; 1992). Purple on multicolor underprint. Royal emblem at left, portrait of J. Singye Wangchuk at right, serial number at lower left and upper right. Back: Paro Dzong palace at center. Reduced size. 139x69mm.

	VF	UNC
a. Fractional serial # prefix. (1986).	FV	1.75
b. 2 letter serial # prefix (Chinese printer.) (1992).	FV	2.00

16 **20 Ngultrum** VF UNC
ND (1986; 1992). Olive on multicolor underprint. Facing portrait Jihme Dorji Wangchuk at right, royal emblem at left, serial number at lower left and upper right. Back: Punakha Dzong palace at center. 152x69mm.

	VF	UNC
a. Serial # prefix fractional style. (1986).	FV	4.00
b. Serial # prefix 2 large letters (Chinese printer.) (1992).	FV	3.50

17 **50 Ngultrum** VF UNC
ND (1985; 1992). Violet and brown on multicolor underprint. Facing portrait Jihme Dorji Wangchuk at right, royal emblem at left, serial number at lower left and upper right. Back: Tongsa Dzong palace at center. 154x70mm.

	VF	UNC
a. Serial # prefix fractional style. (1986)	3.00	15.00
b. Serial # prefix letters 2 large letters (Chinese printer.) (1992).	2.00	6.50

18 **100 Ngultrum** VF UNC
ND (1986; 1992). Green and brown on multicolor underprint. Bird at center, royal emblem left, portrait of J. Singye Wangchuk at right, serial number at lower left and right. Back: Tashichho Dzong palace at center. 160x70mm.

	VF	UNC
a. Serial # prefix fractional style. (1986).	5.00	25.00
b. Serial # prefix 2 large letters (Chinese printer.) (1992).	4.00	17.50

1994 ND Issue

19 **50 Ngultrum** VF UNC
ND (1994). Purple, violet and brown on multicolor underprint. Facing portrait Jihme Dorji Wangchuk at right, royal emblem at left, serial number at lower left and upper right. Modified underprint including floral diamond shaped registry design at upper center. Back: Tongsa Dzong palace at center. Watermark: Wavy *ROYAL MONETARY AUTHORITY* repeated. 154x70mm. FV 6.00

20 **100 Ngultrum** VF UNC
ND (1994). Green and brown on multicolor underprint. Bird at center, royal emblem left, portrait of J. Singye Wangchuk at right, serial number at lower left and right. Modified underprint including floral diamond shaped registry design at upper center. Back: Tashichho Dzong palace at center. Watermark: Wavy *ROYAL MONETARY AUTHORITY* repeated. 160x70mm. FV 9.00

1994 ND Commemorative Issue

#21, National Day

21 **500 Ngultrum** VF UNC
ND (1994). Red-orange on multicolor underprint. Portrait King Jigme Singye Wangchuk in headdress at right. Both serial numbers ascending size. Back: Punakha Dzong palace. Watermark: 4-petaled symbol. 160x70mm. FV 40.00

2000-01 ND Issue

22 **10 Ngultrum** — VF | UNC

ND (2000). Purple and blue on multicolor underprint. Royal emblem at left, portrait King Jigme Singye Wangchuk at right. Back: Paro Dzong palace at center. 140x70mm. — FV | 1.75

23 **20 Ngultrum** — VF | UNC

ND (2000). Olive on multicolor underprint. Facing portrait Jigme Dorji Wangchuk at right, royal emblem at left. Signature 3. Back: Punakha Dzong palace at center. 152x69mm. — FV | 4.00

24 **50 Ngultrum** — VF | UNC

ND (2000). Violet and brown on multicolor underprint. Facing portrait Jihme Dorji Wangchuk at right, royal emblem at left, serial number at lower left and upper right. Modified underprint including floral diamond shaped registry design at upper center. Back: Tongsa Dzong palace at center. Watermark: Wavy *ROYAL MONETARY AUTHORITY* repeated. 154x70mm. — FV | 6.50

25 **100 Ngultrum** — VF | UNC

ND (2000). Green and brown on multicolor underprint. Portrait King Jigme Singye Wangchuk at right, vertical serial # at right, both ascending size. Back: Tashichho Dzong palace at center. Watermark: 4-petaled symbol. 160x70mm. — FV | 17.50

26 **500 Ngultrum** — VF | UNC

ND (2000). Red-orange on multicolor underprint. Portrait King Jigme Singye Wangchuk in headdress at right. Back: Punakha Dzong palace. 160x70mm. — FV | 32.50

2006 Series

27 **1 Ngultrum** — VF | UNC

2006; 2013. Dark blue and orange on multicolor underprint. Circle flanked by two dragons. Back: Simtokha Dzong palace.

	VF	UNC
a. 2000.	FV	.50
b. 2013.	FV	.50

28 **5 Ngultrum** — VF | UNC

2006; 2011; 2013. Brown and orange on yellow and multicolor underprint. Circle flanked by two mythylogical birds. Back: Taktsang palace. 125x60mm.

	VF	UNC
a. 2006.	FV	1.00
b. 2011.	FV	1.00
c. 2013.	FV	1.00

29 **10 Ngultrum** — VF | UNC

2006; 2013. Blue-violet on tan and green underprint. King Jigme Dorji Wangchick at right. Back: Paro Dzong palace at center. 125x65mm.

	VF	UNC
a. 2006.	FV	2.50
b. 2013.	FV	2.50

		VF	UNC
30	**20 Ngultrum**	VF	UNC
	2006; 2013. Green on yellow and multicolor underprint. King Jigme Dorij Wangchuk at right. Back: Punakha Dzong palace. 132x66mm.		
	a. 2006.	FV	4.00
	b. 2013.	FV	4.00

		VF	UNC
31	**50 Ngultrum**	VF	UNC
	2006; 2013. King Jihme Doriji Wangchuk at right. Back: Tongsa Dzong palace at left center. 146x70mm.		
	a. 2006.	FV	6.50
	b. 2013.	FV	6.50

		VF	UNC
32	**100 Ngultrum**	VF	UNC
	2006; 2011; 2013. Black and green on multicolor underprint. King Jigme Doriji Wangchuk at right. Back: Paru Rirpung Dzong palace. 146x70mm.		
	a. 2006.	FV	17.50
	b. 2011.	FV	17.50
	c. 2013.	FV	17.50

		VF	UNC
33	**500 Ngultrum**	VF	UNC
	2006; 2011; 2013. Orange on multicolor underprint. King Jigme Singye Wangchuk at right. Back: Prinakha Dzong palace. 154x70mm.		
	a. 2006.	FV	32.50
	b. 2011.	FV	32.50
	c. 2013.	FV	32.50

		VF	UNC
34	**1000 Ngultrum**	VF	UNC
	2008; 2013. Dark green on yellow and tan underprint. King Jigme Khesar Namgyel Wangchuck at right. Signature 6. Back: Tashchho Dzong at center. Watermark: Jigme Khesar Namgyel Wangchuck. Printer: G&D. 165x70mm.		
	a. 2008.	FV	55.00
	b. 2013.	FV	55.00
	s. Specimen.	—	150.

2012 Royal Wedding Commemorative

		VF	UNC
35	**100 Ngultrum**	VF	UNC
	2011. Black and green on multicolor underprint Portraits at right, design at center. Back: Punakha Dzong palace at center. 145x70mm.	FV	25.00

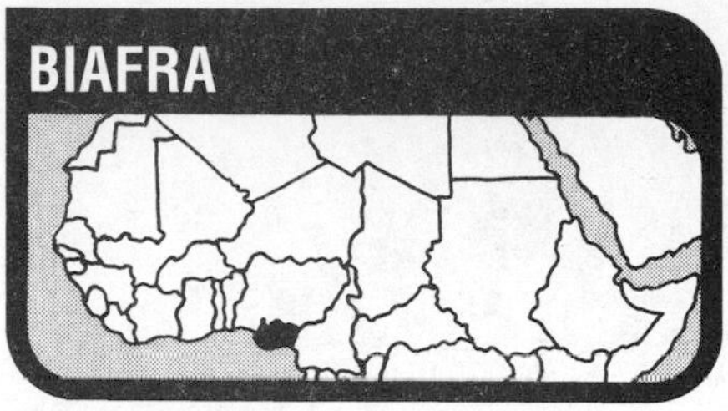

On May 27, 1967, Gen. Yakubu Gowon, head of the Federal Military Government of Nigeria, created three states from the Eastern Region of the country. Separation of the region, undertaken to achieve better regional and ethnic balance, caused Lt. Col. E. O. Ojukwu, Military Governor of the Eastern Region, to proclaim on May 30, 1967, the independence of the Eastern Region as the "Republic of Biafra." Fighting broke out between the Federal Military Government and the forces of Lt. Col. Ojukwu and continued until Biafra surrendered on Jan. 15, 1970. Biafra was then reintegrated into the Republic of Nigeria as three states: East-Central, Rivers, and South-Eastern.

For additional history, see Nigeria.

MONETARY SYSTEM:

1 Shilling = 12 Pence
1 Pound = 20 Shillings

Republic

Bank of Biafra

1967 ND Issue

#	Denomination	VF	UNC
1	**5 Shillings** ND (1967). Blue on lilac underprint. (Rising sun color varies from orange to yellow.) Palm tree, large rising sun at left. Back: Brown on light blue underprint. Four girls at right.	3.00	15.00

#	Denomination	VF	UNC
2	**1 Pound** ND (1967). Blue and orange. Palm tree, large rising sun at left. Back: Brown on light blue underprint. Arms at right.	25.00	100.

1968 ND Issue

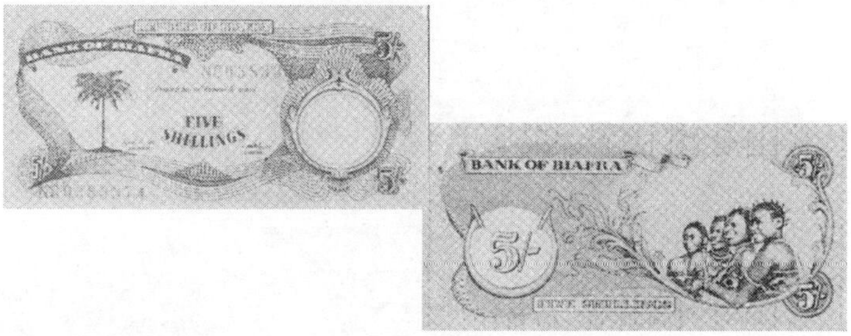

#	Denomination	VF	UNC
3	**5 Shillings** ND (1968-69). Blue on green and orange underprint. Palm tree and small rising sun at top left center. Back: Four girls at right.		
	a. Issued note.	5.00	17.50
	b. Without serial #.	12.50	40.00

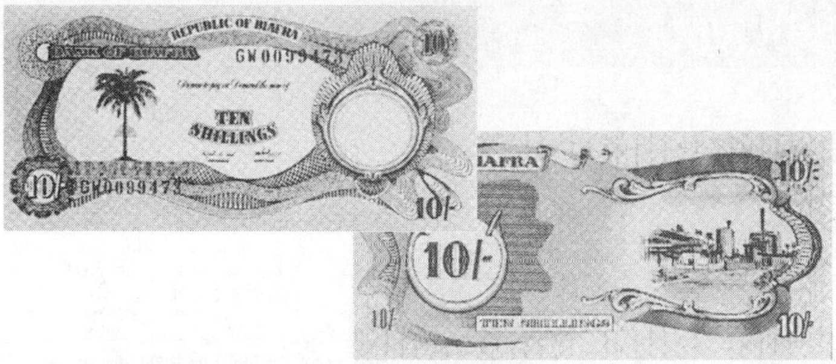

#	Denomination	VF	UNC
4	**10 Shillings** ND (1968-69). Dark green on blue and and orange underprint. Palm tree and small rising sun at top left center. Back: Buildings at rightl.	1.50	4.50

#	Denomination	VF	UNC
5	**1 Pound** ND (1968-69). Dark brown on green, brown and orange underprint. Palm tree and small rising sun at top left center. Back: Arms at right.		
	a. Issued note.	.25	1.50
	b. Without serial #.	5.00	20.00

#	Denomination	VF	UNC
6	**5 Pounds** ND (1968-69). Purple on green and orange underprint. Palm tree and small rising sun at top left center. Back: Arms at left, weaving at left center.		
	a. Issued note.	17.50	70.00
	b. Without serial #.	7.00	30.00

#	Denomination	VF	UNC
7	**10 Pounds** ND (1968-69). Black on blue, brown and orange underprint. Palm tree and small rising sun at top left center. Back: Arms at left, carver at left center.		
	a. Issued note.	15.00	85.00
	b. Without serial #.	7.50	40.00

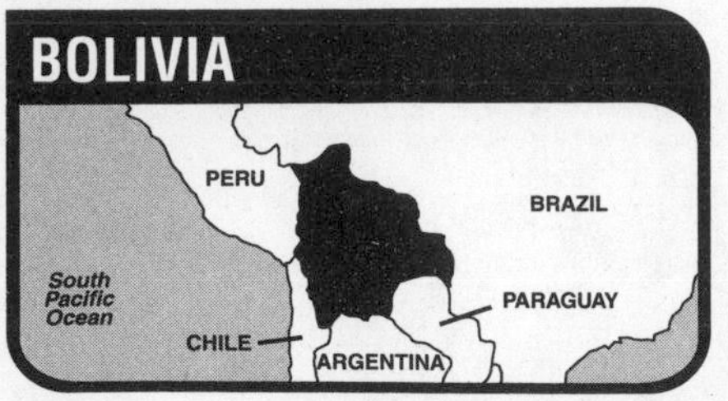

The Republic of Bolivia, a landlocked country in west central South America, has an area of 1,098,580 sq. km. and a population of 9.25 million. Capitals: La Paz (administrative); Sucre (constitutional). Mining is the principal industry and tin the most important metal. Minerals, petroleum, natural gas, cotton and coffee are exported.

Bolivia, named after independence fighter Simon Bolivar, broke away from Spanish rule in 1825; much of its subsequent history has consisted of a series of nearly 200 coups and countercoups. Democratic civilian rule was established in 1982, but leaders have faced difficult problems of deep-seated poverty, social unrest, and illegal drug production. In December 2005, Bolivians elected Movement Toward Socialism leader Evo Morales president - by the widest margin of any leader since the restoration of civilian rule in 1982 - after he ran on a promise to change the country's traditional political class and empower the nation's poor majority. However, since taking office, his controversial strategies have exacerbated racial and economic tensions between the Amerindian populations of the Andean west and the non-indigenous communities of the eastern lowlands.

MONETARY SYSTEM:

1 Boliviano = 100 (Centavos) to 1965
1 Bolivar = 100 Centavos, 1945-1962
1 Peso Boliviano = 100 Centavos, 1962-1987
1 Boliviano = 100 Centavos, 1987-

SPECIMEN NOTES:

All *SPECIMEN, MUESTRA, MUESTRA SIN VALOR* and *ESPECIMEN* notes always have serial #'s of zero.

REPUBLIC

BANCO CENTRAL DE BOLIVIA

LEY DE 13 DE JULIO DE 1962 - FIRST ISSUE

152 1 Peso Boliviano

L.1962. Black on multicolor underprint. Portrait Campesino at right, arms at left. Signature varieties. Series A-E. Back: Agricultural scene at center right, old and new denomination at botom. Printer: TDLR.

	VF	UNC
a. Issued note.	7.50	20.00
p. Proof.	—	750.
s. Specimen with red overprint: *SPECIMEN.* Series A.	—	20.00

153 5 Pesos Bolivianos

L.1962. Blue on multicolor underprint. Portrait Mayor Gualberto Villarroel Lopez at right, arms at left. Signature varieties. Series A-B1. Back: Petroleum refinery, old and new denomination at bottom. Printer: TDLR.

	VF	UNC
a. Issued note.	3.00	12.00
b. Uncut sheet of 4 signed notes.	—	100.
s. Specimen with red overprint: *SPECIMEN.* Series A; T; Z.	—	40.00

154 10 Pesos Bolivianos

L.1962. Olive-green on multicolor underprint. Portrait Colonel Germán Busch Becerra at right, arms at left. Series A-U3. 18 signature varieties. Back: Mountain of Potosí, old and new denomination at bottom. Printer: TDLR.

	VF	UNC
a. Issued note.	.20	.75
b. Uncut sheet of 4 signed notes. Series U2.	—	30.00
s1. Specimen with red overprint: *SPECIMEN.* Series A.	—	35.00
s2. As s1 but with punched hole cancellation and TDLR oval stamp. Series A.	—	50.00
s3. Specimen overprint: *SPECIMEN.* Series U2.	—	35.00
s4. Uncut sheet of 4 specimen notes. Series U2.	—	35.00

155 20 Pesos Bolivianos

L.1962. Purple on multicolor underprint. Portrait Pedro Domingo Murillo at right, arms at left. Series A. Signature varieties. Back: La Paz mountain, old and new denomination at bottom. Printer: TDLR.

	VF	UNC
a. Issued note.	15.00	50.00
s. Specimen with red overprint: *SPECIMEN.* Series A.	—	20.00

156 50 Pesos Bolivianos

L.1962. Orange on multicolor underprint. Portrait Antonio Jose de Sucre at right, arms at left. Series A. Signature varieties. Back: Puerta del Sol, old and new denomination at bottom. Printer: TDLR.

	VF	UNC
a. Issued note.	85.00	225.
s. Specimen with red overprint: *SPECIMEN.* Series A.	—	20.00

		VF	UNC
157	**100 Pesos Bolivianos** *L.1962.* Red on multicolor underprint with green at left, blue at right. Portrait Simón Bolívar at right. Red serial #, and security thread at left center, arms at left. Series A. Signature varieties. Back: Darker red. Engraved, scene of the declaration of the Bolivian Republic. Old and new denomination at bottom. Printer: TDLR.		
	a. Issued note. Large, wide, dark signatures.	85.00	225.
	b. Issued note. Small, thin, light signatures.	75.00	185.
	s. Specimen with red overprint: *SPECIMEN.* Series A.	—	20.00

Ley de 13 de Julio de 1962 - Second Issue

		VF	UNC
158	**1 Peso Boliviano** *L.1962.* Black on multicolor underprint. Portrait Campesino at right, arms at left. Series F-F1. 7 signature varieties. Back: Agricultural scene, new denomination only. Printer: TDLR.		
	a. Issued note.	.75	8.00
	s. Specimen with red overprint: *SPECIMEN.* Series Y.	—	25.00
161	**20 Pesos Bolivianos** *L.1962.* Purple on multicolor underprint. Portrait Pedro Domingo Murillo at right, arms at left. Series B-H. 4 signature varieties. Back: La Paz mountain, new denomination only. Printer: TDLR.		
	a. Issued note.	1.00	10.00
	s. Specimen with red overprint: *SPECIMEN.* Series E.	—	25.00

		VF	UNC
162	**50 Pesos Bolivianos** *L.1962.* Orange on multicolor underprint. Portrait Antonio Jose de Sucre at right, arms at left. Series A-W7. 22 signature varieties. Back: Puerta del Sol, new denomination only. Printer: TDLR.		
	a. Issued note.	.25	1.00
	b. Uncut sheet of 4 signed notes. Series L2, Y2.	—	10.00
	r. Uncut sheet of 4 unsigned notes. Series AZ.	—	20.00
	s1. Specimen with red overprint: *SPECIMEN.* Series F; X; D1.	—	50.00
	s2. As s1 but with punched hole cancellation (in left signature area) and TDLR oval stamp. Series C.	—	125.
	bx. Uncut sheet of 4 notes with signature at top of notes. Series L2; Y2. (error).	—	10.00

		VF	UNC
163	**100 Pesos Bolivianos** *L.1962.* Red on multicolor underprint. Portrait Simón Bolívar at right, arms at left, red serial number and security thread at left center. Lower number prefixes (from B to T9). 19 signature varieties. Back: Brighter red. Engraved, scene of the declaration of the Bolivian Republic, new denomination only. Printer: TDLR.		
	a. Issued note. Prefix Z2.	.25	1.00
	b. Uncut sheet of 4 signed notes. Series X4; D5; U5.	—	12.50
	r. Uncut sheet of 4 unsigned notes. Series AZ.	—	—
	s. Specimen with red overprint: *SPECIMEN.* Series G.	—	50.00

		VF	UNC
164	**100 Pesos Bolivianos** *L.1962* (1983). Red on multicolor underprint. Portrait Simón Bolívar at right, arms at left, red serial number and security thread at left center. Lower number prefixes (from B to T9). 19 signature varieties. Back: Brighter red. Engraved, scene of the declaration of the Bolivian Republic, new denomination only.		
	a. Back dull red, lithographed with poor detail. Black serial #. without security thread. Prefixes #10E-13D. 2 signature varieties.	.75	4.00
	b. As a. but with solid black security thread.	.75	5.00
	c. As a. but with segmented security thread.	2.00	8.00
	r. Unsigned remainder. Prefix #12H.	—	17.50
	s. Specimen with red overprint: *SPECIMEN.* Prefix #10E.	—	75.00
164A	**100 Pesos Bolivianos** *L.1962.* Red on multicolor underprint. Portrait Simón Bolívar at right, arms at left, red serial number and security thread at left center. Higher number prefixes (13E-19T). 2 signature varieties. Back: Engraved, scene of the declaration of the Bolivian Republic, new denomination only. Printer: TDLR.	.25	2.00

1981-84 Various Decrees ND Issue

#165-171 replacement notes. Serial # prefixes: Z, ZY, ZZ.

		VF	UNC
165	**500 Pesos Bolivianos** *D. 1.6.1981.* Deep blue, blue-green and black on multicolor underprint. Arms at center, portrait Eduardo Avaroa at right. Series A. Back: Blue on multicolor underprint. View of Puerto de Antofagasta, ca. 1879 at center. Watermark: Eduardo Avaroa Printer: ABNC.		
	a. Issued note. 2 signature varieties.	.25	2.00
	r. Remainder without series, decreto or signature printing.	45.00	75.00
	s. Specimen with red overprint: *MUESTRA.*	—	75.00

		VF	UNC
166	**500 Pesos Bolivianos**		
	D. 1.6.1981. Deep blue, blue-green and black on multicolor underprint. Arms at center, portrait Eduardo Avaroa at right. Series B; C. Back: View of Puerto de Antofagasta, ca. 1879 at center. Watermark: Eduardo Avaroa. Printer: TDLR.		
	a. Issued note.	.30	1.25
	b. Specimen with red overprint: *SPECIMEN.* Series B.	—	50.00

		VF	UNC
167	**1000 Pesos Bolivianos**		
	D. 25.6.1982. Black on multicolor underprint. Arms at center, portrait Juana Azurday de Padilla at right. Series A1-Z9; (6 digits) A-L; (8 digits) each only to 49,999,999. 3 signature varieties. Back: House of Liberty. Watermark: Juana Azurday de Padilla. Printer: TDLR. UV: fibers fluoresce red, serial #s and value orange, left design gren. Back security thread blue.		
	a. Issued note.	.30	1.00
	s. Specimen with red overprint: *SPECIMEN.* Series A1.	—	25.00

		VF	UNC
168	**5000 Pesos Bolivianos**		
	D. 10.2.1984. Deep brown on multicolor underprint. Arms at center, Marshal J. Ballivian y Segurola at right . Series A. Back: Stylized condor and leopard. Watermark: Marshal J. Ballivian y Segurola. Printer: BDDK. UV: threads fluoresce blue and yellow. Value blue and orange. Back: security thread and value blue.		
	a. Issued note. signature varieties.	1.00	2.00
	s1. Specimen with red overprint: *MUESTRA SIN VALOR.* Series A.	—	25.00
	s2. Specimen pin-holed cancelled: *SPECIMEN.*	—	25.00

		VF	UNC
169	**10,000 Pesos Bolivianos**		
	D. 10.2.1984. Blackish purple and purple with dark green arms on multicolor underprint. Arms at center portrait Marshal Andres de Santa Cruz at right. Series A. Back: Brown, bluish purple and green. Legislative palace at center. Watermark: Marshal Andres de Santa Cruz. Printer: BDDK. UV: threads fluoresce blue, red and yellow. Security strip blue; Value blue, BCB blue. Back: central design wavy stripes yellow.		
	a. Issued note.	.20	.75
	s. Specimen with red overprint: *MUESTRA SIN VALOR.* Series A.	—	25.00

		VF	UNC
170	**50,000 Pesos Bolivianos**		
	D. 5.6.1984. Deep green on multicolor underprint. Arms at left, portrait Gualberto Villarroel Lopez at center. Series A; B. Back: Petroleum refinery. Printer: TDLR. UV: central design fluoresces green.		
	a. Issued note. 2 signature varieties.	.25	1.00
	s. Specimen with red overprint: *MUESTRA SIN VALOR.* Series A.	—	50.00

		VF	UNC
171	**100,000 Pesos Bolivianos**		
	D. 5.6.1984. Brown-violet on multicolor underprint. Arms at left, portrait Campesino at right. Series A; B. Back: Agricultural scene at center right. Printer: TDLR. UV: planchettes fluoresce orange, fibers blue and yellow.		
	a. Issued note. 2 signature varieties.	.50	2.00
	s. Specimen with red overprint: *MUESTRA SIN VALOR.* Series A.	—	50.00

1982-86 Monetary Emergency

Banco Central de Bolivia

W/o Branch

Decreto Supremo No. 19078, 28 Julio 1982

Cheque de Gerencia Issue

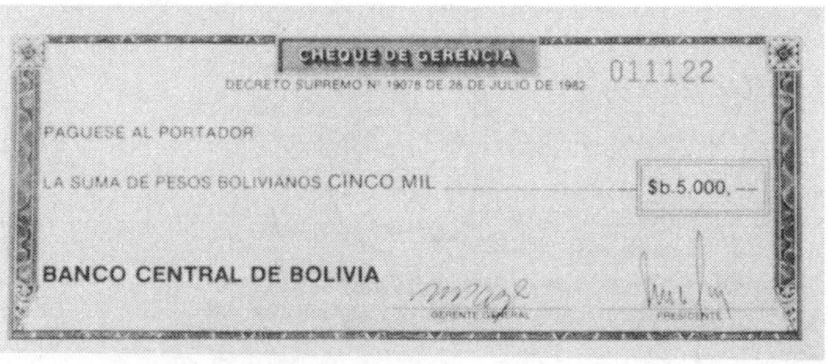

		VF	UNC
172	**5000 Pesos Bolivianos**		
	D.1982.		
	a. Stub with text attached at right.	—	8.00
	b. Without stub at right.	—	7.00

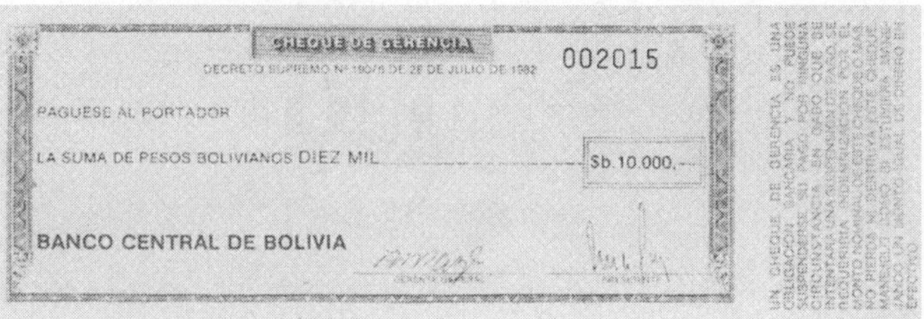

		VF	UNC
173	**10,000 Pesos Bolivianos**		
	D.1982.		
	a. Stub with text attached at right.	—	10.00
	b. Without stub at right.	—	9.00

Decreto Supremo No. 20272, de 5 de Junio de 1984

189 500,000 Pesos Bolivianos — VF .75, UNC 3.50

D.1984. Deep green on green and peach underprint. Back: Without 90-day clause. Printer: CdMB without imprint.

Decreto Supremo No. 20732, 8 Marzo 1985; First Issue

190 1 Million Pesos Bolivianos

D.1985. Blue on yellow and pale blue underprint. Similar to previous issue. Series A. Back: Without 90-day restriction clause at lower right. Printer: CdMB without imprint.

	VF	UNC
a. Issued note.	1.00	5.50
s. Specimen perforated: *SPECIMEN.*	—	—

191 5 Million Pesos Bolivianos

D.1985. Brown-orange and red-brown on multicolor underprint. Similar to previous issues but higher quality printing and appearance. Series A. Back: Multicolor. Bank initials in ornate guilloche at center, without 90-day restriction clause. Printer: G&D.

	VF	UNC
a. Issued note.	1.50	8.00
s. Specimen overprint: *SPECIMEN.*	—	25.00

192 10 Million Pesos Bolivianos

D.1985. Rose, violet and purple on multicolor underprint. Similar to previous issues but higher quality printing and appearance. Series A. Back: Bank initials in ornate guilloche at center, without 90-day restriction clause. Printer: G&D.

	VF	UNC
a. Issued note.	8.00	20.00
s. Specimen overprint: *SPECIMEN.*	—	35.00

Decreto Supremo No. 20732, 8 Marzo 1985; Second Issue

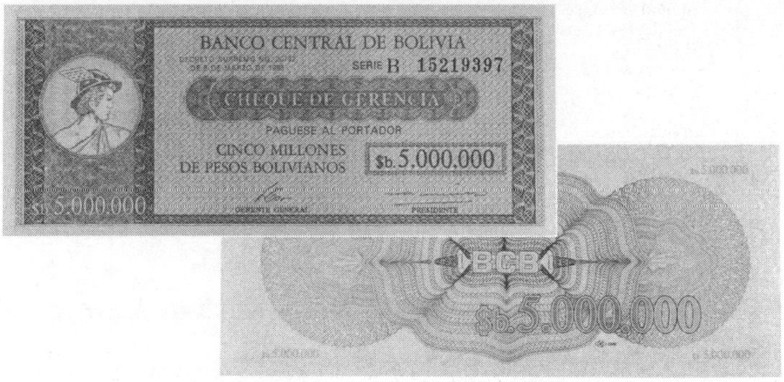

192A 5 Million Pesos Bolivianos — VF 2.00, UNC 7.50

D.1985. Brown-orange and red-brown on multicolor underprint. Similar to previous issues but higher quality printing and appearance. Series B. Back: Multicolor. Bank initials in ornate guilloche at center, without 90-day restriction clause. Printer: CdM-Brazil.

192B 10 Million Pesos Bolivianos — VF 3.50, UNC 10.00

D.1985. Rose, violet and purple on multicolor underprint. Similar to previous issues but higher quality printing and appearance. Series B. Back: Multicolor. Bank initials in ornate guilloche at center, without 90-day restriction clause. Printer: CdM-Brazil.

Decreto Supremo No. 20732, 8 Marzo 1985; Third Issue

192C 1 Million Pesos Bolivianos

D.1985. Blue and multicolor. Large guilloche at left, Mercury head in underprint at right. Series left. Printer: CdM-Argentina.

	VF	UNC
a. Issued note.	.75	3.25
s. Specimen with black overprint: *MUESTRA.*	—	15.00

193 5 Million Pesos Bolivianos

D.1985. Brown with reddish brown text on multicolor underprint. Large guilloche at left, Mercury head in underprint at right. Series N. Printer: CdM-Argentina.

	VF	UNC
a. Issued note.	3.25	7.50
s. Specimen with black overprint: *MUESTRA.*	—	30.00

194	10 Million Pesos Bolivianos	VF	UNC
	D.1985. Violet with lilac text on multicolor underprint. large guilloche at left, Mercury head in underprint at right. Series M. Printer: CdM-Argentina.		
	a. Issued note.	4.00	20.00
	s. Specimen with black overprint: *MUESTRA*.	—	40.00

Santa Cruz

1984 Cheque de Gerencia Issue

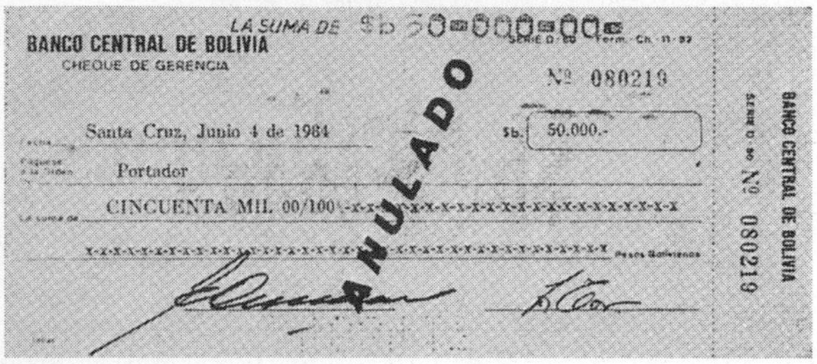

176	50,000 Pesos Bolivianos	Fine	XF
	4.6.1984; 7.6.1984. Black. Mercury in green circular underprint at center.		
	a. Issued note.	—	—
	b. Overprint: *ANULADO* (cancelled) across face.	90.00	200.
178	**1,000,000 Pesos Bolivianos**		
	4.6.1984; 7.6.1984. Black. Mercury in green circular underprint at center.		
	a. Issued note.	—	—
	b. Overprint: *ANULADO* (cancelled) across face.	100.	250.

La Paz

1984 Cheque de Gerencia Issue

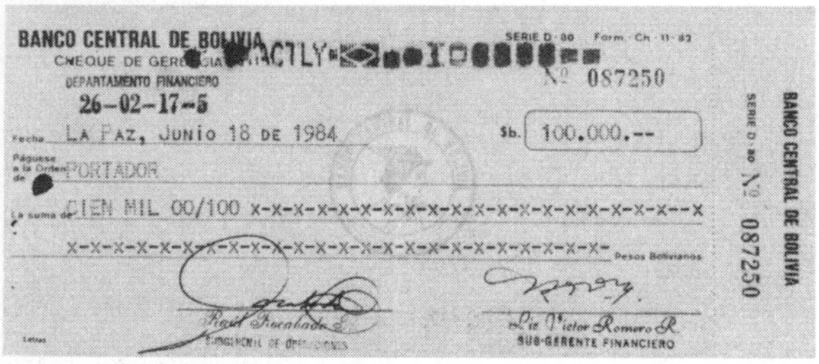

180	100,000 Pesos Bolivianos	Fine	XF
	18.6.1984. Olive-green text on pale green underprint. Mercury in green circular underprint at center. Back: Black text.		
	a. Issued note.	—	—
	b. Overprint: *ANULADO* across face.	100.	210.
	c. Paid. Punched hole cancelled.	150.	275.

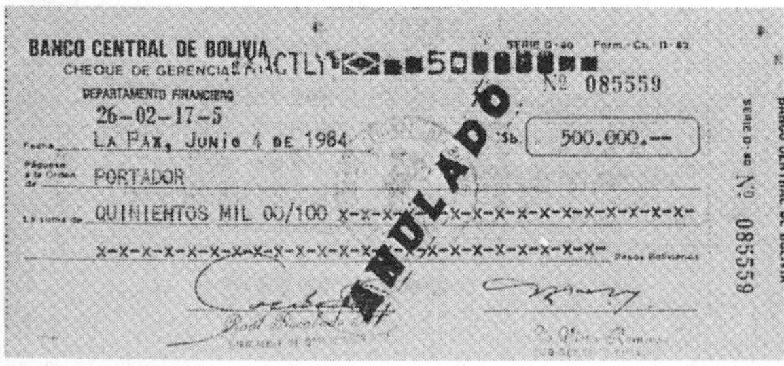

181	500,000 Pesos Bolivianos	Fine	XF
	4.6.1984; 18.6.1984. Black. Mercury in green circular underprint at center.		
	a. Issued note.	—	—
	b. Overprint: *ANULADO* across face.	110.	225.
	c. Paid. Punched hole cancelled.	175.	300.

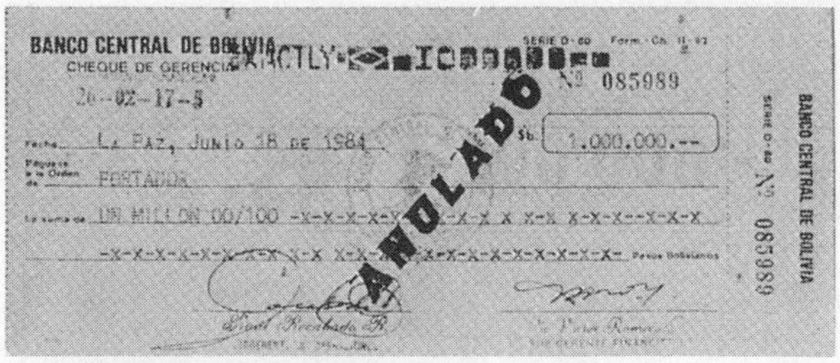

182	1,000,000 Pesos Bolivianos	Fine	XF
	18.6.1984. Black. Mercury in green circular underprint at center.		
	a. Issued note.	—	—
	b. Overprint: *ANULADO* across face.	120.	240.
	c. Paid. Punched hole cancelled.	210.	425.

Decreto Supremo No. 20272, 5 Junio 1984, First Issue

#183-185 Underprint of "B.C.B." and denomination boxes easily fade from pink to light tan to pale yellow.

183	10,000 Pesos Bolivianos	VF	UNC
	D.1984. Brown on pink underprint. Mercury at upper left. Series A. Back: Usable for 90 days after date of issue (Spanish text at lower right). Printer: JBNC.	7.00	20.00

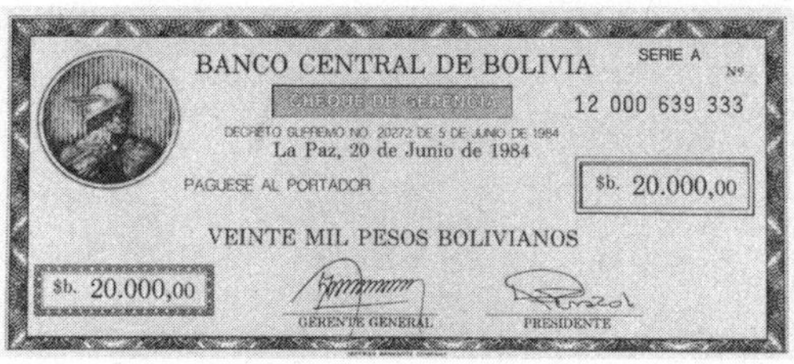

184	20,000 Pesos Bolivianos	VF	UNC
	D.1984. Brown on pink underprint. Mercury at upper left. Series A. Back: Usable for 90 days after date of issue (Spanish text at lower right). Printer: JBNC.	50.00	125.

185	50,000 Pesos Bolivianos	VF	UNC
	D.1984. Brown on pink underprint. Mercury at upper left. Series A. Back: Usable for 90 days after date of issue (Spanish text at lower right). Printer: JBNC.	5.00	17.50

Decreto Supremo No. 20272, 5 Junio 1984, Second Issue

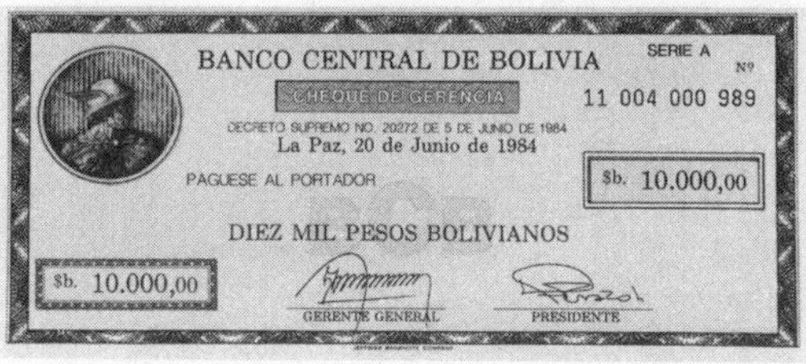

		VF	UNC
186	**10,000 Pesos Bolivianos** *D.1984.* Light blue on pink underprint. Mercury at upper left. Series A. Back: Without 90-day use restriction text. Printer: JBNC.	2.50	8.00
187	**20,000 Pesos Bolivianos** *D.1984.* Green on pink underprint. Mercury at upper left. Series A. Back: Without 90-day use restriction text. Printer: JBNC.	2.50	8.50

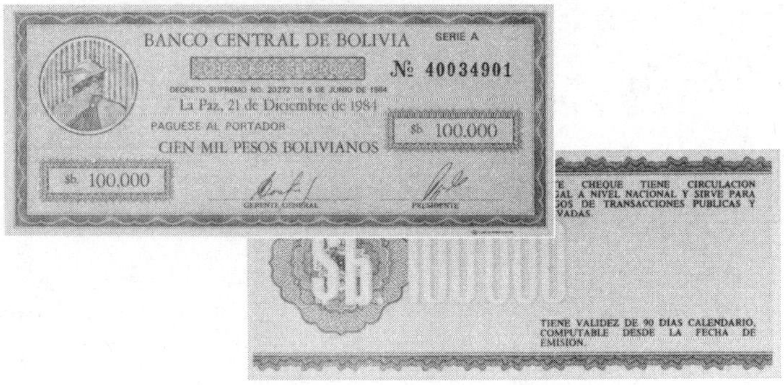

		VF	UNC
188	**100,000 Pesos Bolivianos** 21.12.1984. Reddish brown on light blue and light reddish brown underprint. Series A. Imprint: CdMB. Back: 90 day usage clause at lower right. Watermark: CdMB. UV: threads fluoresce blue.	.75	3.00

Republic, 1986-

Banco Central de Bolivia

1987 ND Provisional Issue

		VF	UNC
195	**1 Centavo on 10,000 Pesos Bolivianos** ND (1987). Back: Overprint at right on back of #169. UV: threads fluoresce blue, red and yellow. Security strip blue; Value blue, BCB blue. Back: central design wavy stripes yellow.	.25	1.00

		VF	UNC
196	**5 Centavos on 50,000 Pesos Bolivianos** ND (1987). Back: Overprint at right on back of #170.	.50	2.25
196A	**10 Centavos on 100,000 Pesos Bolivianos** ND (1987). Back: Overprint at right on back of #171.	1.50	7.00

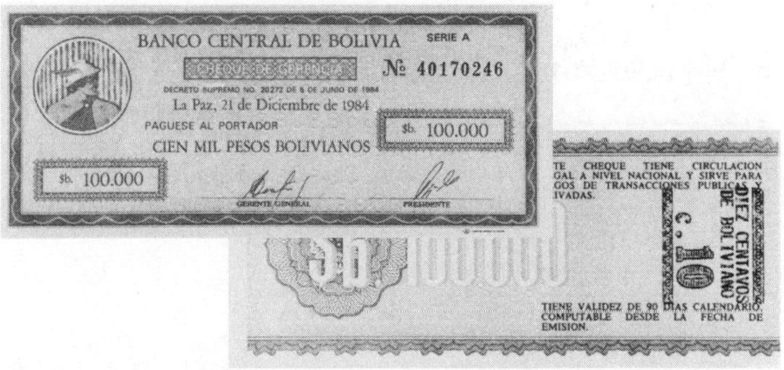

		VF	UNC
197	**10 Centavos on 100,000 Pesos Bolivianos** ND (1987). Back: Overprint at right on back of #188.	.50	3.00

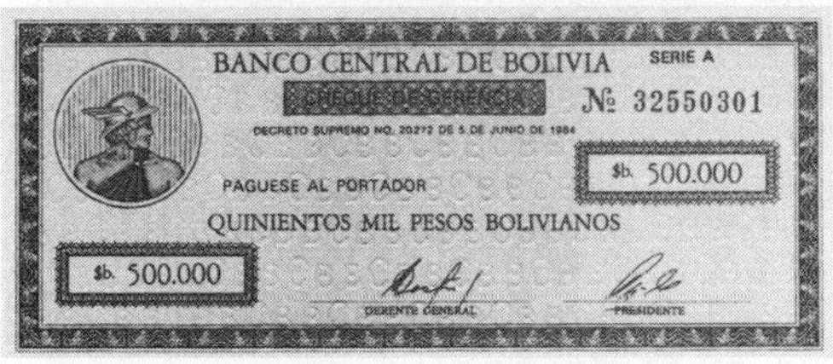

		VF	UNC
198	**50 Centavos on 500,000 Pesos Bolivianos** ND (1987). Back: Overprint at right on back of #189.	.75	3.25

		VF	UNC
199	**1 Boliviano on 1,000,000 Pesos Bolivianos** ND (1987). Back: Overprint at right on back of #192C.	.60	2.60

		VF	UNC
200	**5 Bolivianos on 5,000,000 Pesos Bolivianos** ND (1987). Back: Overprint at left on back of #192A.		
	a. Issued note.	1.25	6.00
	x1. Error. Inverted overprint on left end.	6.00	15.00
	x2. Error. Overprint on right end.	—	—

		VF	UNC
201	**10 Bolivianos on 10,000,000 Pesos Bolivianos** ND (1987), Back: Overprint at left on back of #192B.	4.00	20.00

Ley 901 de 28.11.1986;1987-2001 ND Issues

#202-208 Series A signature titles: *PRESIDENTE BCB* **and** *MINISTRO DE FINANZAS.* **Serial # suffix** *A.*

Series B signature titles: *PRESIDENTE DEL B.C.B.* **and** *GERENTE GENERAL B.C.B.* **Serial # suffix** *B.*

Series E signature titles: *PRESIDENTE BCB* **and** *GERENTE GENERAL BCB.* **Serial # suffix** *E.*

202 2 Bolivianos VF UNC

L.1986. (1987; 1990). Black on multicolor underprint. Antonio Vaca Diez at right, arms at lower center. Back: Trees and buildings at center. Watermark: Simón Bolívar. Printer: F-CO.

	VF	UNC
a. Series A (1987). With control #.	FV	3.50
b. Series B. (1990). With control #.	FV	4.00
s. As a. Specimen with red overprint: *ESPECIMEN.*	—	25.00

203 5 Bolivianos VF UNC

L.1986. (1987; 1990; 1998). Olive-green on multicolor underprint. Adela Zamudio at right, arms at lower left. Back: Religious shrine at left center. Watermark: Simón Bolívar. Printer: F-CO.

	VF	UNC
a. Series A (1987). With control #.	FV	6.00
b. Series B (1990). With control #.	FV	6.50
c. Series E (1998). Without control #.	FV	4.00
s. As a. Specimen with red overprint: *ESPECIMEN.*	—	25.00

204 10 Bolivianos VF UNC

L.1986. (1987-97). Blue-black on multicolor underprint. Cecilio Guzman de Rojas at right, arms at lower left. Back: Figures overlooking city view. Watermark: Simón Bolívar. Printer: F-CO.

	VF	UNC
a. Series A (1987). With control #.	FV	9.50
b. Series B (1990). With control #.	FV	12.50
c. Series E (1997). Without control #.	FV	5.00
s. As a. Specimen with red overprint: *ESPECIMEN.*	—	50.00

205 20 Bolivianos VF UNC

L.1986. (1987; 1990). Orange on multicolor underprint. Pantaleon Dalence at right, arms at lower center. Back: Building at center. Watermark: Simón Bolívar. Printer: F-CO.

	VF	UNC
a. Series A (1987). With control #.	FV	20.00
b. Series B (1990). With control #.	FV	25.00
c. Series E (1997). Without control #.	FV	8.50
s. As a. Specimen with red overprint: *ESPECIMEN.*	—	75.00

206 50 Bolivianos VF UNC

L.1986 (1987; 1997). Purple on multicolor underprint. Melchor Perez de Holguin at right, arms at lower center. Back: Tall building at center. Watermark: Simón Bolívar. Printer: F-CO.

	VF	UNC
a. Series A (1987). With control #.	FV	50.00
b. Series E (1997). Without control #.	FV	17.50
s. As a. Specimen with red overprint: *ESPECIMEN.*	—	100.

207 100 Bolivianos VF UNC

L.1986 (1987; 1997). Red-violet and orange on multicolor underprint. Gabriel Rene Moreno at right, arms at lower right. Back: University building at center. Watermark: Simón Bolívar. Printer: F-CO.

	VF	UNC
a. Watermark: Simon Bolívar.	FV	110.
b. Series E (1997). Without control #. Watermark: Gabriel Rene Moreno.	FV	35.00
s. As a. Specimen with red overprint: *ESPECIMEN.*	—	150.

208 200 Bolivianos VF UNC

L.1986 (1987; 1997). Brown and dark brown on multicolor underprint. Franz Tamayo at right, arms at lower center. Back: Ancient statuary. Watermark: Simón Bolívar. Printer: F-CO.

	VF	UNC
a. Series A (1987). With control #.	FV	225.
b. Series E (1997). Without control #. Watermark: F. Tamayo.	FV	60.00
s. As a. Specimen with red overprint: *ESPECIMEN.*	—	200.

Ley 901 de 28.11.1986; 1993 ND Issue

209 5 Bolivianos VF UNC

L.1986 (1993). Olive-green on multicolor underprint. Adela Zamudio at right, arms at lower left. Series C. Signature titles: *PRESIDENTE BCB* and *GERENTE GENERAL BCB*. Serial number suffix C. Back: Religious shrine at left center. Watermark: Simón Bolívar. Printer: FNMT. FV 17.50

210 10 Bolivianos VF UNC

l.1986(1993). Blue-black on multicolor underprint. Cecilio Guzman de Rojas at right, arms at lower left.Series C. Serial number suffix C.Signature titles: *PRESIDENTE BCB* and *GERENTE GENERAL BCB*. Back: Figures overlooking city view. Watermark: Simón Bolívar. Printer: FNMT. FV 6.50

211 20 Bolivianos VF UNC

L.1986(1993). Orange on multicolor underprint. Pantaleon Dalence at right, arms at lower center. Series C. Serial number suffix C. Signature titles: *PRESIDENTE BCB* and *GERENTE GENERAL BCB*. Back: Building at center. Watermark: Simón Bolívar. Printer: FNMT. FV 10.00

212 50 Bolivianos VF UNC

L.1986(1993). Purple on multicolor underprint. Melchor Perez de Holguin at right, arms at lower center. Series C. Serial number suffix C. Signature titles: *PRESIDENTE BCB* and *GERENTE GENERAL BCB*. Back: Tall buiding at center. Watermark: Simón Bolívar. Printer: FNMT. FV 22.50

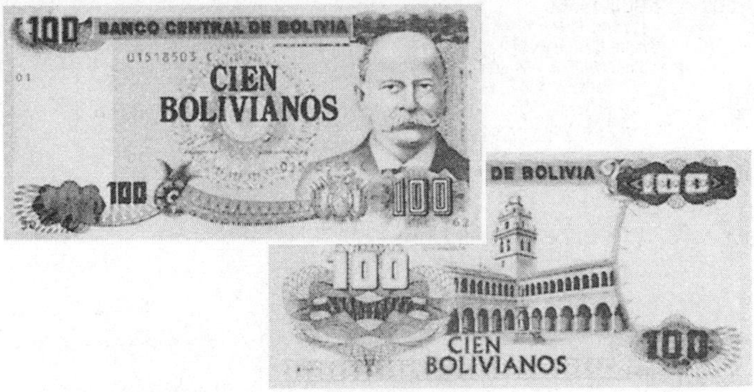

213 100 Bolivianos VF UNC

L.1986(1993). Red and ornage on multicolor underprint. Gabriel Rene Moreno at right, arms at lower right. Series C. Serial number suffix C. Signature titles: *PRESIDENTE BCB* and *GERENTE GENERAL BCB*. Back: University building at center. Printer: FNMT. FV 45.00

214 200 Bolivianos VF UNC

L.1986(1993). Brown and dark brown on multicolor underprint. Franz Tamayo at right, arms at lower center. Series C. Serial number suffix C. Signature titles: *PRESIDENTE BCB* and *GERENTE GENERAL BCB*. Back: Ancient statuary. Printer: FNMT. FV 90.00

Ley 901 de 28.11.1980, 1995 ND Interim Issue

215 5 Bolivianos VF UNC

L.1986 (1995). Olive-green on multicolor underprint. Adela Zamudio at right, arms at lower left. Series C. Signature titles: *PRESIDENTE BCB* and *GERENTE GENERAL BCB*. Serial number suffix C. Back: Religious shrine at left center. Watermark: Simón Bolívar. Printer: TDLR.

a. Issued note.	FV	6.00
s. Specimen with red overprint: *MUESTRA SIN VALOR*.	—	25.00

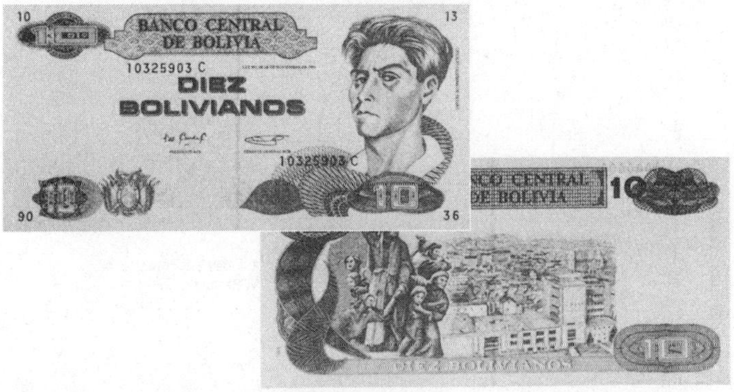

216 10 Bolivianos — VF | UNC

L.1986 (1995). Blue-black on multicolor underprint. Cecilio Guzman de Rojas at right, arms at lower left.Series C. Serial number suffix C.Signature titles: *PRESIDENTE BCB* and *GERENTE GENERAL BCB.* Back: Figures overlooking city view. Watermark: Simón Bolívar. Printer: TDLR. 140x69mm.

	VF	UNC
a. Issued note.	FV	12.00
s. Specimen with red overprint: *MUESTRA SIN VALOR.*	—	25.00

Ley 901 de 28.11.1986; 1995-96 ND Issue

217 5 Bolivianos — VF | UNC

L.1986(1995). Olive-green on multicolor underprint. Adela Zamudio at right, arms at lower left. Series D. Signature titles: *PRESIDENTE BCB* and *GERENTE GENERAL BCB.* Back: Religious shrine at left center. Watermark: Simón Bolívar. Printer: TDLR. 140x69mm. — FV | 3.50

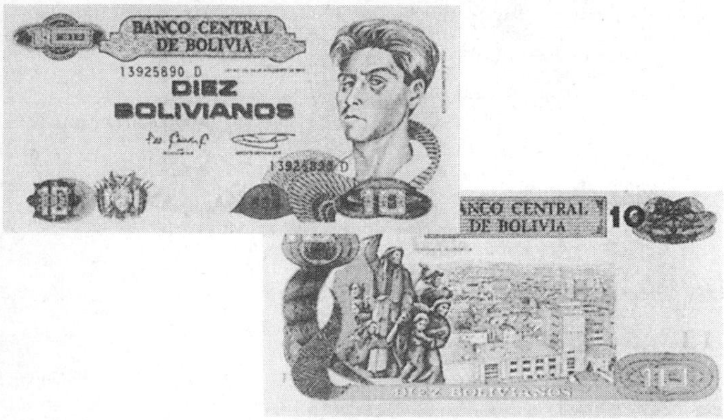

218 10 Bolivianos — VF | UNC

L.1986(1995). Blue-black on multicolor underprint. Cecilio Guzman de Rojas at right, arms at lower left. Series D. Signature titles: *PRESIDENTE BCB* and *GERENTE GENERAL BCB.* Back: Figures overlooking city view. Watermark: Simón Bolívar. Printer: TDLR. 140x69mm. — FV | 5.00

219 20 Bolivianos — VF | UNC

L.1986(1995). Orange on multicolor underprint. Pantaleon Dalence at right, arms at lower left. Series D. Signature titles: *PRESIDENTE BCB* and *GERENTE GENERAL BCB.* Back: Building at center. Watermark: Simón Bolívar. Printer: TDLR. 140x69mm. — FV | 9.00

220 50 Bolivianos — VF | UNC

L.1986(1995). Purple on multicolor underprint. Melchor Perez de Holguin at right, arms at lower left. Series D. Signature titles: *PRESIDENTE BCB* and *GERENTE GENERAL BCB.* Back: Tall building at center. Watermark: Simón Bolívar. Printer: TDLR. 140x69mm.

	VF	UNC
a. Issued note.	FV	20.00
s. Specimen with red overprint: *MUESTRA SIN VALOR.*	—	50.00

221 100 Bolivianos

L.1986(1996). Red and orange on multicolor underprint. Gabriel Rene Moreno at right, arms at lower left. Series D. Signature titles: *PRESIDENTE BCB*and *GERENTE GENERAL BCB.* Back: University building at center. Watermark: Gabriel Rene Moreno. Printer: TDLR. — FV | 35.00

222 200 Bolivianos

L.1986(1996). Brown and dark brown on multicolor underprint. Franz Tamayo at right, arms at lower lef. Series D. Signature titles: *PRESIDENTE BCB* and *GERENTE GENERAL BCB.* Back: Ancient statuary. Watermark: Franz Tamayo. — FV | 65.00

Ley 901 de 28.11.1986; 2001 ND Issue

223 10 Bolivianos — VF | UNC

L.1986 (2001). Blue-black on multicolor underprint. Cecilio Guzman de Rojas at right, arms at lower left. Series F. Signature titles: *PRESIDENTE BCB* and *GERENTE GENERAL BCB.* Raised marks for the blind and narrow clear text security thread Back: Figures overlooking city view. Watermark: Simón Bolívar. Printer: F-CO. 140x69mm. — FV | 4.00

224 20 Bolivianos

L.1986 (2001). Orange and brown-orange on multicolor underprint. Pantaleon Dalence at right, arms at lower left. Series F. Signature titles: *PRESIDENTE BCB* and *GERENTE GENERAL BCB.* Raised marks for the blind and narrow clear text security thread. Back: Building at center. Watermark: Simón Bolívar. Printer: F-CO. — FV | 7.00

225 50 Bolivianos

L.1986 (2001). Purple on multicolor underprint. Melchor Perez de Holguin at right, arms at lower left. Series F. Signature titles: *PRESIDENTE BCB* and *GERENTE GENERAL BCB.* Raised marks for the blind and narrow clear text security threa Back: Tall building at center. Watermark: Simón Bolívar. Printer: F-CO. — FV | 15.00

226 100 Bolivianos

L.1986 (2001). Red-violet and orange on multicolor underprint. Gabriel Rene Moreno at right, arms at lower left. Series F. Signature titles: *PRESIDENTE BCB* and *GERENTE GENERAL BCB.* Raised marks for the blind and narrow clear text security thread. Back: University building at center. Watermark: Gabriel Rene Moreno. Printer: F-CO. Like 207b; Series E (1997). — FV | 30.00

227 200 Bolivianos

L.1986 (2001). Brown and dark brown on multicolor underprint. Franz Tamayo at right, arms at lower left. Series F. Signature titles: *PRESIDENTE BCB* and *GERENTE GENERAL BCB.* Raised marks for the blind and narrow clear text security thre Back: Ancient statuary. Watermark: Franz Tamayo. Printer: F-CO. Like 208b; Series E (1997). — FV | 60.00

Ley 901 de 28.11.1986; 2005 ND Issue

		VF	UNC
228	**10 Bolivianos** *L.1986* (2005). Blue-black on multicolor underprint. Cecilio Guzman de Rojas at right, arms at lower left. Series G. Signature titles: *PRESIDENTE BCB* and *GERENTE GENERAL BCB*. Raised marks for the blind. Back: Figures overlooking city view. Watermark: Cecilio Guzman de Rojas. Printer: F-CO. With value in numerals vertically.	FV	4.00

		VF	UNC
229	**20 Bolivianos** *L.1986* (2005). Orange and brown-orange on multicolor underprint. Pantaleon Dalence at right, arms at lower left. Series G. Signature titles: *PRESIDENTE BCB* and *GERENTE GENERAL BCB*. Raised marks for the blind and narrow clear text security thread. Back: Building at center. Watermark: Pantaleon Dalence. Printer: F-CO. With value in numerals vertically.	FV	7.00

		VF	UNC
230	**50 Bolivianos** *L.1986*(2005). Purple on multicolor underprint. Melchor Perez de Holguin at right, arms at lower left. Series G. Signature titles: *PRESIDENTE BCB* and *GERENTE GENERAL BCB*. Raised marks for the blind and wide clear text security thread. Back: Tall building at center. Watermark: Melchor Perez de Holguin. Printer: F-CO. With value in numerals vertically.	FV	15.00

		VF	UNC
231	**100 Bolivianos** *L.1986(2005)*. Red-violet and orange on multicolor underprint. Gabriel Rene Moreno at right, arms at lower left. Series G. Signature titles: *PRESIDENTE BCB* and *GERENTE GENERAL BCB*. Raised marks for the blind and wide clear text security thread. Back: University building at center. Watermark: Gabriel Rene Moreno. Printer: F-CO. With value in numerals vertically.	FV	30.00
232	**200 Bolivianos** *L.1986* (2005). Brown and dark brown on multicolor underprint. Franz Tomayo at right, arms at lower left. Series G. Signature titles: *PRESIDENTE BCB* and *GERENTE GENERAL BCB*. Raised marks for the blind and wide clear text security thread. Back: Ancient statuary. Watermark: Franz Tomayo. Printer: F-CO. With value in numerals vertically.	FV	60.00

Ley 901 de 28.11.1986; 2007 ND Issue

		VF	UNC
233	**10 Bolivianos** ND (2007). Blue-black on multicolor underprint. Cecilio Guzman de Rojas at right, arms at lower left. Series H. Back: Figures overlooking city view. Watermark: Cecilio Guzman de Rojas. Printer: F-CO.	FV	4.00
234	**20 Bolivianos** ND (2007). Orange and brown-orange on multicolor underprint. Pantaleon Dalence at right, arms a lower left. Series H. Back: Building at center. Watermark: Pantaleon Dalence. Printer: F-CO.	FV	7.00
235	**50 Bolivianos** ND (2007). Purple on multicolor underprint. Melchor Perez de Holguin at right, arms at lower left. Series H. Back: Tall building at center. Watermark: Melchor Perez de Holguin. Printer: F-CO.	FV	15.00
236	**100 Bolivianos** ND (2007). Red-violet and orange on multicolor underprint. Gabriel Rene Moreno at right, arms at lower left. Series H. Back: University building at center. Watermark: Gabriel Rene Moreno. Printer: F-CO.	FV	30.00
237	**200 Bolivianos** ND (2007). Brown and dark brown on multicolor underprint. Franz Tomayo at right, arms at lower left. Series H. Back: Ancient statuary. Watermark: Franz Tomayo. Printer: F-CO.	FV	60.00

The Republic of Bosnia-Herzegovina borders Croatia to the north and west, Serbia to the east and Montenegro in the southeast with only 12.4 miles of coastline. The total land area is 51,209 sq. km. It has a population of 4.59 million. Capital: Sarajevo. Electricity, mining and agriculture are leading industries.

Bosnia and Herzegovina's declaration of sovereignty in October 1991 was followed by a declaration of independence from the former Yugoslavia on 3 March 1992 after a referendum boycotted by ethnic Serbs. The Bosnian Serbs - supported by neighboring Serbia and Montenegro - responded with armed resistance aimed at partitioning the republic along ethnic lines and joining Serb-held areas to form a "Greater Serbia." In March 1994, Bosniaks and Croats reduced the number of warring factions from three to two by signing an agreement creating a joint Bosniak/Croat Federation of Bosnia and Herzegovina. On 21 November 1995, in Dayton, Ohio, the warring parties initialed a peace agreement that brought to a halt three years of interethnic civil strife (the final agreement was signed in Paris on 14 December 1995). The Dayton Peace Accords retained Bosnia and Herzegovina's international boundaries and created a joint multi-ethnic and democratic government charged with conducting foreign, diplomatic, and fiscal policy. Also recognized was a second tier of government comprised of two entities roughly equal in size: the Bosniak/Croat Federation of Bosnia and Herzegovina and the Bosnian Serb-led Republika Srpska (RS). The Federation and RS governments were charged with overseeing most government functions. The Office of the High Representative (OHR) was established to oversee the implementation of the civilian aspects of the agreement. In 1995-96, a NATO-led international peacekeeping force (IFOR) of 60,000 troops served in Bosnia to implement and monitor the military aspects of the agreement. IFOR was succeeded by a smaller, NATO-led Stabilization Force (SFOR) whose mission was to deter renewed hostilities. European Union peacekeeping troops (EUFOR) replaced SFOR in December 2004; their mission is to maintain peace and stability throughout the country. EUFOR's mission changed from peacekeeping to civil policing in October 2007, with its presence reduced from nearly 7,000 to 2,500 troops.

MONETARY SYSTEM:

1 Dinar = 100 Para 1992-1998
1 Convertible Marka = 1 Deutschemark
1 Convertible Marka = 100 Convertible Pfeniga, 1998-

REPUBLIKA BOSNA I HERCEGOVINA

MOSLEM REPUBLIC

НАРОДНА БАНКА БОСНЕ И ХЕРЦЕГОВИНЕ

NARODNA BANKA BOSNE I HERCEGOVINE

W/O BRANCH

1992 FIRST PROVISIONAL ISSUE

		Fine	XF
1	**500 Dinara** ND (1992). Violet handstamp: NARODNA BANKA BOLNE I HERCEGOVINE, also in Cyrillic around Yugoslav arms, on Yugoslav regular issues. Handstamp varieties exist. 27mm or 31mm handstamp on Yugoslavia #109.		
	a. Handstamp without numeral.	30.00	100.
	b. Handstamp with numeral: *1.*	30.00	100.
	c. Handstamp with numeral: *2.*	30.00	100.
	d. Handstamp: Tuzla.	30.00	100.

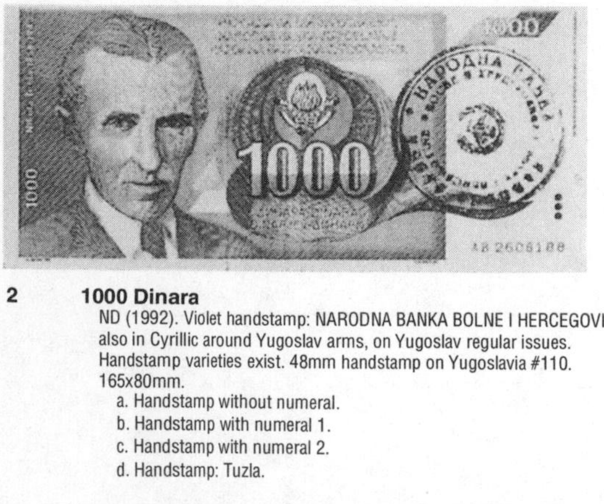

		Fine	XF
2	**1000 Dinara** ND (1992). Violet handstamp: NARODNA BANKA BOLNE I HERCEGOVINE, also in Cyrillic around Yugoslav arms, on Yugoslav regular issues. Handstamp varieties exist. 48mm handstamp on Yugoslavia #110. 165x80mm.		
	a. Handstamp without numeral.	25.00	125.
	b. Handstamp with numeral 1.	25.00	125.
	c. Handstamp with numeral 2.	25.00	125.
	d. Handstamp: Tuzla.	25.00	125.

W/O BRANCH

1992 SECOND PROVISIONAL NOVCANI BON ISSUE

#6-9 issued in various Central Bosnian cities. Example without indication of city of issue are remainders.

		Fine	XF
6	**100 Dinara** 1992. Deep pink on gray and yellow underprint. Peace dove at upper left center.		
	a. Handstamped: *BREZA* on back.	25.00	100.
	b. Circular red handstamp: *FOJNICA* on back.	10.00	50.00
	c. Rectangular purple handstamp on face, circular purple hand-stamp: *KRESEVO* on back.	20.00	80.00
	d. Handstamped: *TESANJ* on back.	20.00	80.00
	e. Handstamped: *VARES* on back.	35.00	110.
	f1. Handstamped: *VISOKO* 31mm on back.	6.00	30.00
	f2. Handstamped: *VISOKO* 20mm on back.	10.00	55.00
	g. Circular red overprint: *ZENICA*, 11.5.1992. on back right with printed signature at either side.	3.00	9.00
	h. Rectangular handstamp: *OSNOVA ZAJEDNICA* on face. Circular handstamp: *BOS. PETROVAC* on back.	3.00	10.00
	i. Large circular purple handstamp: *SARAJEVO* and 16.6.1993 on back.	3.00	10.00
	r. Remainder, without handstamp or overprint.	3.00	10.00

		Fine	XF
7	**500 Dinara** 1992. Pale greenish-gray and yellow underprint. Peace dove at upper left center.		
	a. Handstamped: *BREZA* on back.	17.50	70.00
	b. Circular red handstamp: *FOJNICA* on back.	17.50	70.00
	c. ZRectangular purple handstamp on face. Handstamped: *KRESEVO* on back.	45.00	120.
	d. Handstamped: *TESANJ* on back.	7.50	35.00
	e. Handstamped: *VARES* on back.	17.50	70.00
	f1. Circular 31mm red handstamp: *VISOKO* on back.	12.50	40.00
	f2. Circular 20mm red handstamp: *VISOKO* on back.	12.50	40.00
	g. Circular red handstamp on back: *ZENICA* (small or large), 11.5.1992. Printed signature at either side.	2.00	7.00
	h. Rectangular handstamp: *OSNOVA ZAJEDNICA* on face. Circular handstamp: *BOS. PETROVAC* on back.	12.50	40.00
	i. Circular large purple handstamp: *SARAJEVO* and 16.6.1993 on back.	12.50	40.00
	r. Remainder without handstamp or overprint.	2.00	7.00
8	**1000 Dinara** 1992. Blue on gray underprint. Peace dove at upper left center.		
	a. Handstamped: *BREZA* on back.	15.00	65.00
	b. Handstamped: *FOJNICA* on back.	15.00	65.00
	c. Rectangular purple handstamp on face. Circular purple handstamp: *KRESEVO* on back.	30.00	90.00
	d. Handstamped: *TESANJ* on back.	20.00	75.00
	e. Handstamped: *VARES* on back.	20.00	75.00
	f1. Handstamped: *VISOKO* 31mm on back.	9.00	35.00
	f2. Handstamped: *VISOKO* 20mm on back.	30.00	100.
	g. Circular handstamp: *ZENICA* on face, no date on stamping.	25.00	75.00
	h. Circular red overprint on back: *ZENICA*, 11.5.1992. Pinted signature at either side.	2.00	10.00
	i. Rectangular handstamp: *OSNOVA ZAJEDNICA* on front. Circular handstamp: *BOS. PETROVAC* on back.	20.00	75.00
	j. Circular large purple handstamp: *SARAJEVO* and 16.6.1993 on back.	20.00	75.00
	r. Remainder without handstamp or overprint.	2.00	10.00

9 5000 Dinara

	Fine	XF
1992. Dull brown on gray and yellow underprint. Peace dove at upper left center.		
a. Handstamped: *BREZA* on back.	10.00	35.00
b. Circular red handstamp: *FOJNICA* on back.	8.00	30.00
c. Handstamped: *KRESEVO* on back.	50.00	125.
d. Handstamped: *TESANJ* on back.	85.00	350.
e. Handstamped: *VARES* on back.	20.00	75.00
f1. Handstamped: *VISOKO* 31mm on back.	30.00	90.00
f2. Handstamped: *VISOKO* 20mm on back.	10.00	35.00
g. Circular red handstamp: *ZENICA* and 11.5.1992 with printed signature at each side on back.	22.50	65.00
h. Rectangular handstamp: *OSNOVA ZAJEDNICA* on front. Circular handstamp *BOS. PETROVAC* on back.	2.00	7.50
i. Circular large purple handstamp: *SARAJEVO* and 16.6.1993 on back.	10.00	35.00
r. Remainder, without handstamp or overprint	5.00	20.00

W/O BRANCH

1992-93 ISSUES

10 10 Dinara

	VF	UNC
1.7.1992. Purple on pink underprint. Guilloche at left center, serial number varieties. Back: Mostar stone arch bridge at right. Watermark: Repeated diamonds. Printer: Cetis (Celje, Slovenia). 145x73mm.		
a. Issued note.	.25	1.00
s. Specimen.	—	30.00

11 25 Dinara

	VF	UNC
1.7.1992. Blue-black on light blue underprint. Guilloche at left center, serial number varieties. Back: Crowned arms at center right. Watermark: Repeated diamonds. Printer: Cetis (Celje, Slovenia). 145x73mm.		
a. Issued note.	.20	1.25
s. Specimen.	—	30.00

12 50 Dinara

	VF	UNC
1.7.1992. Blue-black on red-violet underprint. Guilloche at left center, serial number varieties. Back: Mostar stone arch bridge at right. Watermark: Repeated diamonds. Printer: Cetis (Celje, Slovenia). 145x73mm.		
a. Issued note.	.50	1.50
s. Specimen.	—	30.00

13 100 Dinara

	VF	UNC
1.7.1992. Dull black on olive-green underprint. Guilloche at left center, serial number varieties. Back: Crowned arms at center right. Watermark: Repeated diamonds. Printer: Cetis (Celje, Slovenia). 145x73mm.		
a. Issued note.	.50	1.75
s. Specimen.	—	30.00

14 500 Dinara

	VF	UNC
1.7.1992. Dull violet-brown on pink and ochre underprint. Guilloche at left center, serial number varieties. Back: Crowned arms at center right. Watermark: Repeated diamonds. Printer: Cetis (Celje, Slovenia). 145x73mm.		
a. Issued note.	.75	3.50
s. Specimen.	—	30.00

15 1000 Dinara

	VF	UNC
1.7.1992. Deep purple on light green and lilac underprint. Guilloche at left center, serial number varieties. Back: Mostar stone arch bridge at right. Watermark: Repeated diamonds. Printer: Cetis (Celje, Slovenia). 145x73mm.		
a. Issued note.	1.00	4.50
s. Specimen.	—	30.00

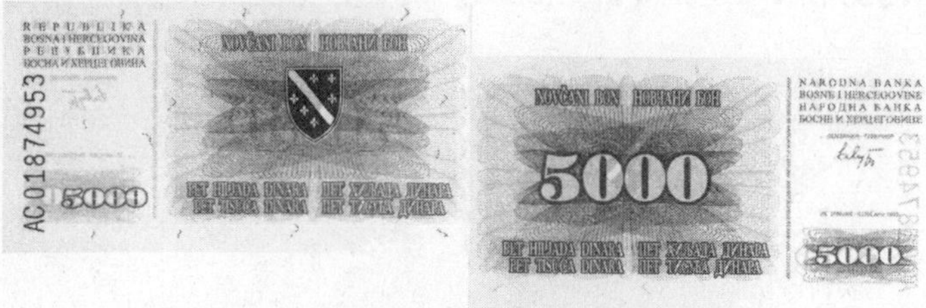

16 5000 Dinara — VF | UNC

25.1.1993. Pale olive-green on yellow-orange underprint. Guilloche at left center, serial number varieties. Back: Grayish blue shield with fleur-de-lis at center right. Printer: Printed in Zenica. 110x61mm.

	VF	UNC
a. Issued note.	3.00	7.50
b. With overprint: *SDK..ZENICA* on back as a handstamp or machine printing.	5.00	15.00
s. Specimen.	—	10.00

17 10,000 Dinara — VF | UNC

25.1.1993. Brown on pink underprint. Guilloche at left center, serial number varieties. Back: Grayish blue shield with fleur-de-lis at center right. Printer: Printed in Zenica. 110x61mm.

	VF	UNC
a. Issued note.	3.50	8.50
b. With overprint: *SDK..ZENICA* on back as a handstamp or machine printing.	5.00	15.00
s. Specimen.	—	10.00

1992-94 Bon Issue

#21-33 Issued during the seige of Sarajevo. Grayish green or yellow unpt. on back.

21 10 Dinara — VF | UNC

1.8.1992. Violet. Back: Grayish green or yellow underprint. Shield at left.

	VF	UNC
a. Issued note.	6.00	35.00
s. Specimen.	—	30.00

22 20 Dinara — VF | UNC

1.8.1992. Blue-violet. Back: Grayish green or yellow underprint. Shield at left.

	VF	UNC
a. Issued note.	5.00	30.00
s. Specimen.	—	30.00

23 50 Dinara — VF | UNC

1.8.1992. Pink. Back: Grayish green or yellow underprint. Shield at left.

	VF	UNC
a. Issued note.	6.00	35.00
s. Specimen.	—	30.00

24 100 Dinara — VF | UNC

1.8.1992. Green. Back: Grayish green or yellow underprint. Shield at left.

	VF	UNC
a. Issued note.	25.00	125.
s. Specimen.	—	30.00

25 500 Dinara — VF | UNC

1.8.1992. Orange. Back: Red-orange on pale purple and grayish green underprint. Shied at left.

	VF	UNC
a. Issued note.	8.00	40.00
s. Specimen.	—	30.00

26 1000 Dinara — VF | UNC

1.8.1992. Brown. Back: Grayish green or yellow underprint. Shield at left.

	VF	UNC
a. Issued note.	6.00	35.00
s. Specimen.	—	30.00

27 5000 Dinara — VF | UNC

1.8.1992. Violet. Back: Grayish green or yellow underprint. Shield at left.

	VF	UNC
a. Issued note.	6.00	35.00
s. Specimen.	—	30.00

28 10,000 Dinara — VF | UNC

6.4.1993. Light blue. Back: Grayish green or yellow underprint. Shield at left.

	VF	UNC
a. Issued note.	6.00	35.00
s. Specimen.	—	30.00

29 **50,000 Dinara** VF UNC

1.5.1993. Pink. Back: Grayish green or yellow underprint. Shield at left.

	VF	UNC
a. Issued note.	10.00	40.00
s. Specimen.	—	30.00

30 **100,000 Dinara** VF UNC

1.8.1993. Green on multicolor underprint. Back: Green on gray underprint. Shield at left text below.

	VF	UNC
a. Issued note.	5.00	30.00
s. Specimen.	—	25.00

31 **100,000 Dinara** VF UNC

1.8.1993. Green. Back: Green on yellow underprint. Shield at left, value below.

	VF	UNC
a. Issued note.	5.00	30.00
s. Specimen.	—	30.00

32 **500,000 Dinara** VF UNC

1.1.1994. Brown. Back: Brown on pale yellow-green underprint. Shield at left.

	VF	UNC
a. Issued note.	5.00	25.00
s. Specimen.	—	30.00

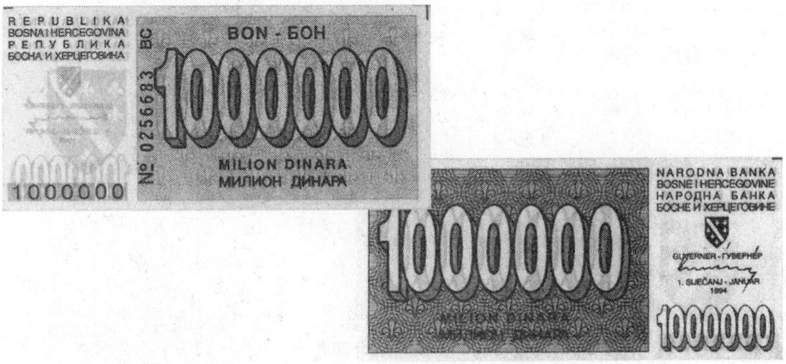

33 **1,000,000 Dinara** VF UNC

1.1.1994. Red. Back: Grayish green or yellow underprint. Shield at left.

	VF	UNC
a. Issued note.	5.00	25.00
s. Specimen.	—	30.00

1993 Novcani Bon Emergency Issue

34 **100,000 Dinara** VF UNC

1993 (-old date 1.7.1992). Rectangular crenalated framed overprint: *NOVCANI BON 100,000...* Back: Mostar stone arch bridge at right.

	VF	UNC
a. Purple overprint. 1.9.1993.	7.50	17.50
b. Blue overprint and signature overprint. 10.11.1993.	7.50	17.50

35 **1,000,000 Dinara** VF UNC

10.11.1993 (old date-1.7.1992).

	VF	UNC
a. Purple overprint. 1.9.1993.	8.00	20.00
b. Blue overprint and signature overprint. 10.11.1993.	3.50	9.00
c. Blue-violet overprint (not issued.	—	—

36 **10,000,000 Dinara** VF UNC

	VF	UNC
10.11.1993 (old date-1.7.1992). Blue-violet overprint on #12. (Not issued)	4.00	12.50

37 **100,000,000 Dinara** VF UNC

10.11.1993 (old date-1.7.1992).

	VF	UNC
a. Blue-violet overprint on #13. (Not issued)	4.00	12.50
b1. As a. but without overprint 100000000 at lower right on front.	—	—

1994 Issue

Currency Reform, 1994

1 New Dinar = 10,000 Old Dinara

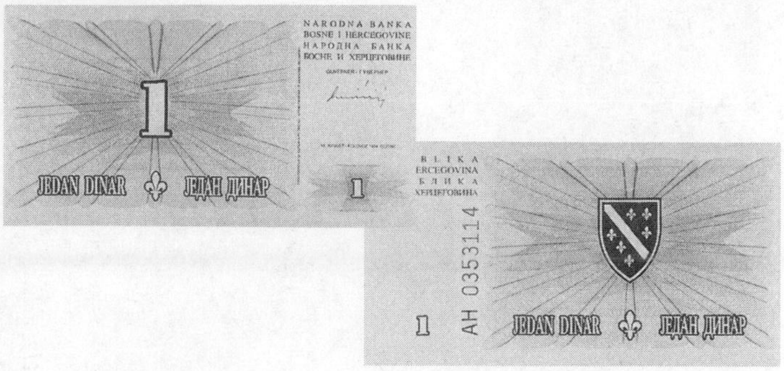

39 1 Dinar VF UNC

15.8.1994. Purplish gray on red-violet and pale green underprint. Back: Shield at center right. Watermark: Block design. Printer: DD "Dom Stampe" Zenica.

	VF	UNC
a. Issued note.	.15	.75
s. Specimen.	—	—

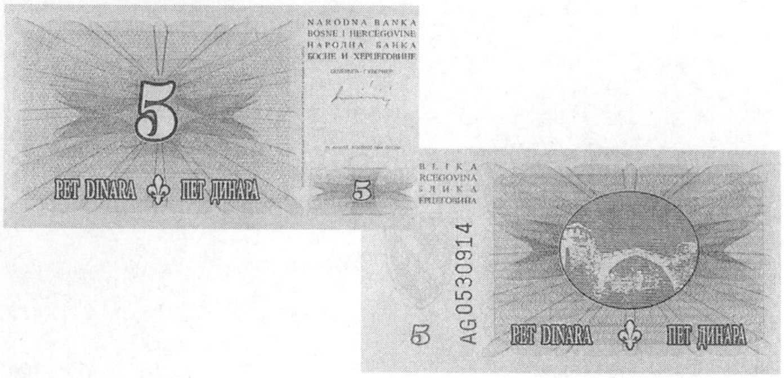

40 5 Dinara VF UNC

15.8.1994. Purplish gray on lilac, red and orange underprint. Back: Mostar stone bridge at center rightl Watermark: Block design. Printer: DD "Dom Stampe" Zenica.

	VF	UNC
a. Issued note.	.15	.75
s. Specimen.	—	—

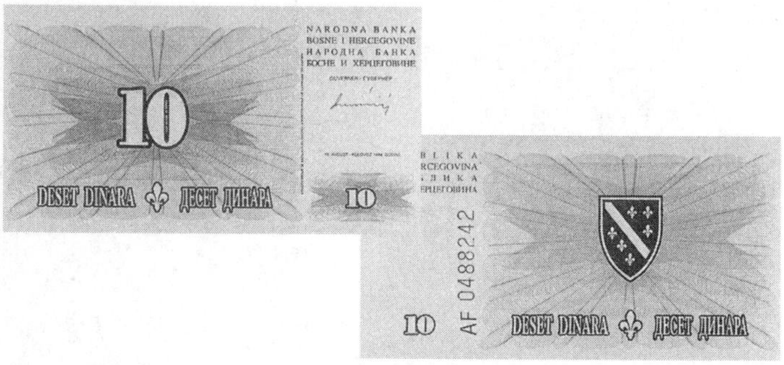

41 10 Dinara VF UNC

15.8.1994. Pruple on red, orange and red-violet underprint. Back: Shield at center right. Watermark: Block design. Printer: DD "Dom Stampe" Zenica.

	VF	UNC
a. Issued note.	.25	1.00
s. Specimen.	—	—

42 20 Dinara VF UNC

15.8.1994. Brown on violet, red and yellow underprint. Back: Mostar stone bridge at center right. Watermark: Block design. Printer: DD "Dom Stampe" Zenica.

	VF	UNC
a. Issued note.	.50	1.50
s. Specimen.	—	—

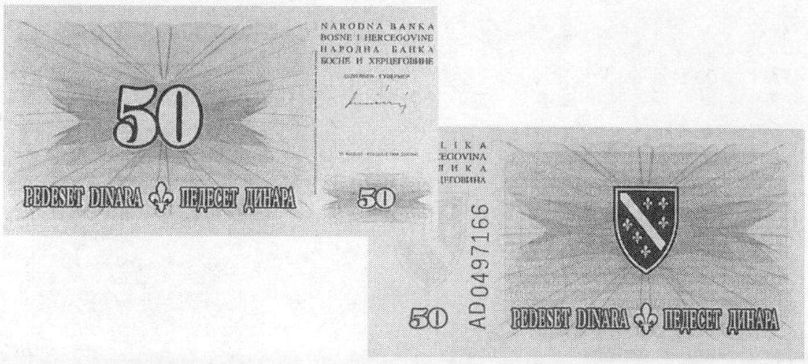

43 50 Dinara VF UNC

15.8.1994. Purplish gray on red-violet and pale purple underprint. Back: Shield at center right. Watermark: Block design. Printer: DD "Dom Stampe" Zenica.

	VF	UNC
a. Issued note.	.50	2.00
s. Specimen.	—	—

44 100 Dinara VF UNC

15.8.1994. Dull black on aqua, yellow and olive-green underprint. Back: Mostar stone bridge at center right. Watermark: Block design. Printer: DD "Dom Stampe" Zenica.

	VF	UNC
a. Issued note.	.50	2.25
s. Specimen.	—	—

45 500 Dinara

15.8.1994. Dull brown on lilac and yellow underprint. Back: Shield at center right. Watermark: Block design. Printer: DD "Dom Stampe" Zenica.

	VF	UNC
a. Large #'s.	1.50	6.00
b. Small #'s.	1.50	6.00
s. Specimen.	—	—

46 1000 Dinara VF UNC

15.8.1994. Blue-gray on gray-green, red-violet and light green underprint. Back: Mostar stone bridge at center right. Watermark: Block design. Printer: DD "Dom Stampe" Zenica.

	VF	UNC
a. Large #'s.	4.50	12.50
b. Small #'s.	4.50	12.50
s. Specimen.	—	—

1995 ND Issue

#47-47C Printed in London but unable to be delivered.

		VF	UNC
47	**50 Dinara** ND (1995). Purple on pink and ochre underprint. Back: Bridge at right. Watermark: Lis.	6.00	20.00
47A	**100 Dinara** ND (1995). Back: Bridge at right. (Not issued).	—	—
47B	**500 Dinara** ND (1995). Back: Bridge at right. (Not issued).	—	—

		VF	UNC
47C	**1000 Dinara** ND (1995). Back: Bridge at right. (Not issued).	—	—

Travnik, Novi Travnik and Vitez

1992 ND Novcani Bon Issue

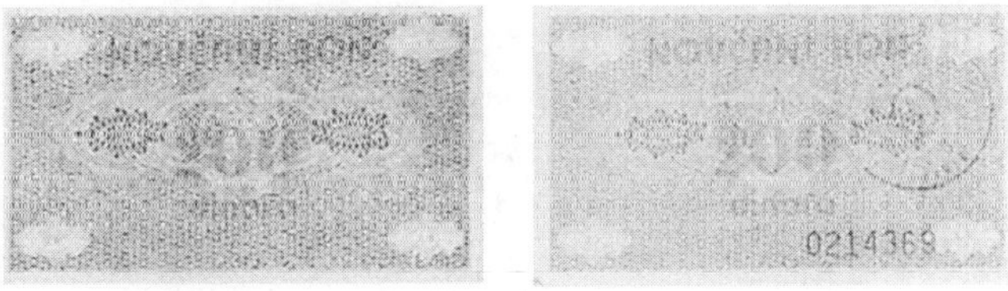

		VF	UNC
48	**200 Dinara** ND (1992). Orange. Plain design with value at center. Back: Plain design with value at center, handstamp at right.		
	a. Handstamped: *TRAVNIK.*	10.00	40.00
	b. Handstamped: *NOVI TRAVNIK.*	20.00	80.00
	c. Handstamped: *VITEZ.*	35.00	110.
	r. Remainder without handstamp.	10.00	40.00

		VF	UNC
49	**500 Dinara** ND (1992). Brown. Plain design with value at center. Back: Plain design with value at center, handstamp at right.		
	a. Handstamped: *TRAVNIK.*	15.00	55.00
	b. Handstamped: *NOVI TRAVNIK.*	30.00	95.00
	c. Handstamped: *VITEZ.*	45.00	120.
	r. Remainder without handstamp.	15.00	55.00

		VF	UNC
50	**1000 Dinara** ND (1992). Lilac. Plain design with value at center. Back: Plain design with value at center, handstamp at right.		
	a. Handstamped: *TRAVNIK.*	8.00	30.00
	b. Handstamped: *NOVI TRAVNIK.*	18.00	70.00
	c. Handstamped: *VITEZ.*	25.00	95.00
	r. Remainder without handstamp.	8.00	30.00

		VF	UNC
51	**5000 Dinara** ND (1992). Light blue. Plain design with value at center. Back: Plain design with value at center.		
	a. Handstamped: *TRAVNIK.*	70.00	500.
	b. Handstamped: *NOVI TRAVNIK.* Rare.	—	—
	c. Handstamped: *VITEZ.* Rare.	—	—
	r. Remainder without handstamp.	30.00	80.00

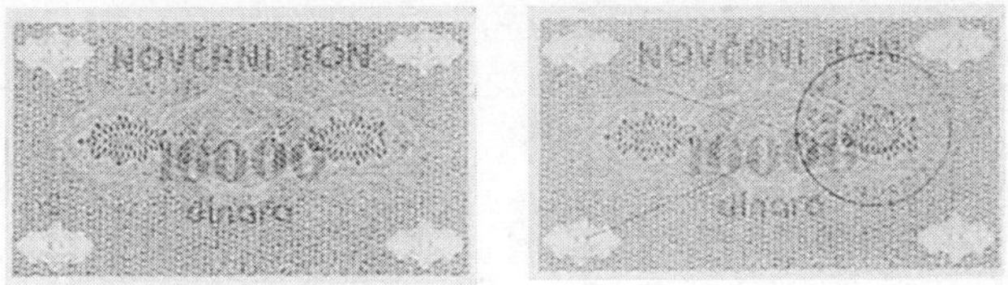

		VF	UNC
52	**10,000 Dinara** ND (1992). Red on blue underprint. Plain design with value at center. Back: Plain design with value at center, handstamp at right.		
	a. Handstamped: *TRAVNIK.*	15.00	45.00
	b. Handstamped: *NOVI TRAVNIK.*	25.00	95.00
	c. Handstamped: *VITEZ.*	35.00	110.
	r. Remainder without handstamp.	15.00	45.00
52A	**20,000 Dinara** ND (1992). Red on underprint.		
	a. Handstamped: *TRAVNIK.*	70.00	300.
	b. Handstamped: *NOVI TRAVINK.*	100.	600.
	c. Handstamped: *VITEZ.*	120.	700.
	r. Remainder wihtout handstamp.	35.00	70.00

Travnik, Novi Travnik and Vitez

1993 Emergency Issue

#53-56 like #10-13 w/additional 3 solid zeroes printed after large value on face w/Travnik Branch dated handstamp.

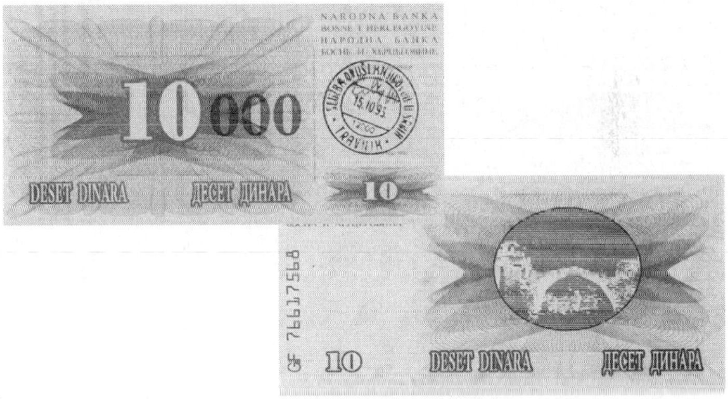

		VF	UNC
53	**10,000 Dinara** 1993. Red on yellow underprint. Guilloche at left center 145x73mm., 3 additional solid zeroes printed after large value. Handstamp. Back: Mostar stone arch bridge at right. Watermark: Repeated diamonds. Printer: Cetis (Celje, Slovenia).		
	a. 15.10.1993. Short green zeroes. Travnik.	2.50	7.50
	b. 15.10.1993. Short red zeroes. Travnik.	2.50	7.50
	c. 24.12.1993. Tall green zeroes. Travnik.	2.50	7.50
	d. 24.12.1993. Tall red zeroes. Travnik.	2.50	7.50
	e. 15.10.1993. Short green zeros. Sarajevo.	2.50	7.50
	f. 15.10.1993. Short red zeros. Sarajevo.	2.50	7.50
	g. 24.12.1993. Tall green zeroes. Sarajevo.	2.50	7.50
	h. 24.12.1993. Tall red zeroes. Sarajevo.	2.50	7.50

		VF	UNC
54	**25,000 Dinara** 1993. Green on blue underprint. Guilloche at left center 145x73mm., 3 additional solid zeroes printed after large value. Handstamp. Back: Crowned arms at center right. Watermark: Repeated diamonds. Printer: Cetis (Celje, Slovenia).		
	a. 15.10.1993. Short green zeroes. Travnik.	2.50	7.50
	b. 15.10.1993. Short red zeroes. Travnik.	2.50	7.50
	c. 24.12.1993. Tall green zeroes. Travnik.	2.50	7.50
	d. 24.12.1993. Tall red zeroes. Travnik.	2.50	7.50
	e. 15.10.1993. Short green zeroes. Sarajevo.	2.50	7.50
	f. 15.10.1993. Short red zeroes. Sarajevo.	2.50	7.50
	g. 24.12.1993. Tall green zeroes. Sarajevo.	2.50	7.50
	h. 24.12.1993. Tall red zeroes. Sarajevo.	2.50	7.50

55	50,000 Dinara	VF	UNC
	1993. Red. Guilloche at left center 145x73mm., 3 additional solid zeroes printed after large value. Handstamp. Back: Mostar stone arch bridge at right. Watermark: Repeated diamonds. Printer: Cetis (Celje, Slovenia).		
	a. 15.10.1993. Short green zeroes. Travnik.	2.50	7.50
	b. 15.10.1993. Short red zeroes. Travnik.	2.50	7.50
	c. 24.12.1993. Tall green zeroes. Travnik.	2.50	7.50
	d. 24.12.1993. Tall red zeroes. Travnik.	2.50	7.50
	e. 15.10.1993. Short green zeroes. Sarajevo.	2.50	7.50
	f. 15.10.1993. Short red zeroes. Sarajevo.	2.50	7.50
	g. 24.12.1993. Tall green zeroes. Sarajevo.	2.50	7.50
	h. 24.12.1993. Tall red zeroes. Sarajevo.	2.50	7.50

56	100,000 Dinara	VF	UNC
	1993. Green. Guilloche at left center 145x73mm., 3 additional solid zeroes printed after large value. Handstamp. Back: Crowned arms at center right. Watermark: Repeated diamonds. Printer: Cetis (Celje, Slovenia).		
	a. 15.10.1993. Short green zeroes. Travnik.	2.50	7.50
	b. 15.10.1993. Short red zeroes. Travnik.	2.50	7.50
	c. 24.12.1993. Tall green zeroes. Travnik.	2.50	7.50
	d. 24.12.1993. Tall red zeroes. Travnik.	2.50	7.50
	e. 15.10.1993. Short green zeroes. Sarajevo.	2.50	7.50
	f. 15.10.1993. Short red zeroes. Sarajevo.	2.50	7.50
	g. 21.10.1993. Tall green zeroes. Sarajevo.	2.50	7.50
	h. 21.10.1993. Tall red zeroes. Sarajevo.	2.50	7.50
	i. 24.12.1993. Tall green zeroes. Sarajevo.	2.50	7.50
	j. 24.12.1993. Tall red zeroes. Sarajevo.	2.50	7.50
	k. 24.8.1993. Short green zeroes. Donji Vakuf.	2.50	7.50
	l. 15.10.1993. Short red zeroes. Donji Vakuf.	2.50	7.50

ЦЕНТРАЛНА БАНКА БОСНЕ И ХЕРЦЕГОВИНЕ

Centralna Banka Bosne I Hercegovine

1998 ND Issue

57	50 Convertible Pfeniga	VF	UNC
	ND (1998). Dark blue on blue and lilac underprint. Portrait S. Kulenovic at right. Back: *Stecak Zgosca* fragment at left center. Watermark: Central Bank monogram repeated vertically. Printer: F-CO (without imprint). Alternating texts of bank name and denominations.		
	a. Issued note.	FV	.75
	s. Specimen.	—	—

58	50 Convertible Pfeniga	VF	UNC
	ND (1998). Dark blue on blue and lilac underprint. Portrait B. Copic at right. Back: Open book, cabin at left center. Watermark: Central Bank monogram repeated vertically. Printer: F-CO (without imprint). Alternating texts of bank name and denominations.		
	a. Issued note.	FV	.75
	s. Specimen.	—	—

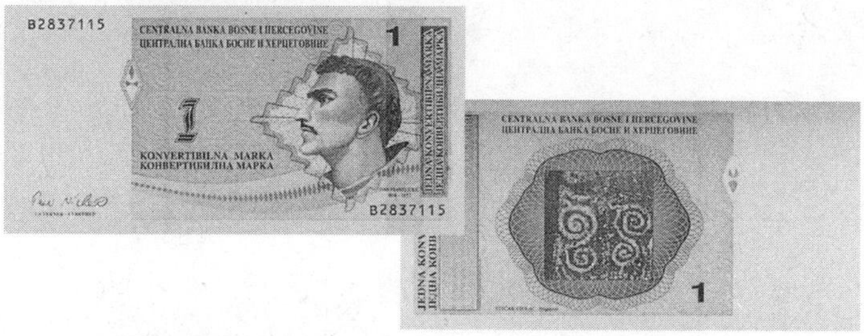

59	1 Convertible Marka	VF	UNC
	ND (1998). Dark green on green and yellow-green underprint. I. F. Jukic at right. Back: *Stecak Stolac* fragment at left center. Watermark: Central Bank monogram repeated vertically. Printer: F-CO (without imprint). Alternating texts of bank name and denominations.		
	a. Issued note.	FV	1.50
	s. Specimen.	—	—

60	1 Convertible Marka	VF	UNC
	ND (1998). Dark green on green and yellow-green underprint. I. Andric at right. Back: Bridge at left center. Watermark: Central Bank monogram repeated vertically. Printer: F-CO (without imprint). Alternating texts of bank name and denominations.		
	a. As prepared. Not issued. Some examples were stolen from stock and have been offered at about 80-100 dollars.	—	—
	s. Specimen.	—	—

61	5 Convertible Maraka	VF	UNC
	ND (1998). Violet on multicolor underprint. M. Selimovic at right. Back: Trees at left center. English letters in bank name as top line Watermark: Central Bank monogram repeated vertically. Printer: F-CO (without imprint). Alternating texts of bank name and denominations. 123x62mm.		
	a. Issued note.	FV	7.50
	s. Specimen.	—	—

62	5 Convertible Maraka	VF	UNC
	ND (1998). Violet on multicolor underprint. M. Selimovic at right. Back: Trees at left center. Cyrillic bank name and denomination as top line. Watermark: Central Bank monogram repeated vertically. Printer: F-CO (without imprint). Alternating texts of bank name and denominations. 123x62mm.		
	a. Issued note.	FV	7.50
	s. Specimen.	—	—

63	10 Convertible Maraka	VF	UNC
	ND (1998). Orange-brown on dull purple and orange-brown underprint. M. M. Dizdar at right. Back: *Stecak Radimlja* fragment at left center. Watermark: Central Bank monogram repeated vertically. Printer: F-CO (without imprint). Alternating texts of bank name and denominations. 130x65mm.		
	a. Issued note.	FV	12.50
	s. Specimen.	—	—

64	10 Convertible Maraka	VF	UNC
	ND (1998). Orange-brown on dull purple and orange-brown underprint. A. Santic at right. Back: Loaf of bread at left center. Watermark: Central Bank monogram repeated vertically. Printer: F-CO (without imprint). Alternating texts of bank name and denominations. 130x65mm.		
	a. Issued note.	FV	12.50
	s. Specimen.	—	—

65	20 Convertible Maraka	VF	UNC
	ND (1998). Dark brown on multicolor underprint. A. B. Simic at right. Back: *Stecak Radimlja* fragment at left center, variable optical device at upper left center. Watermark: Central Bank monogram repeated vertically. Printer: F-CO (without imprint). Alternating texts of bank name and denominations. 138x68mm.		
	a. Issued note.	FV	20.00
	s. Specimen. All zero serial #.	—	75.00

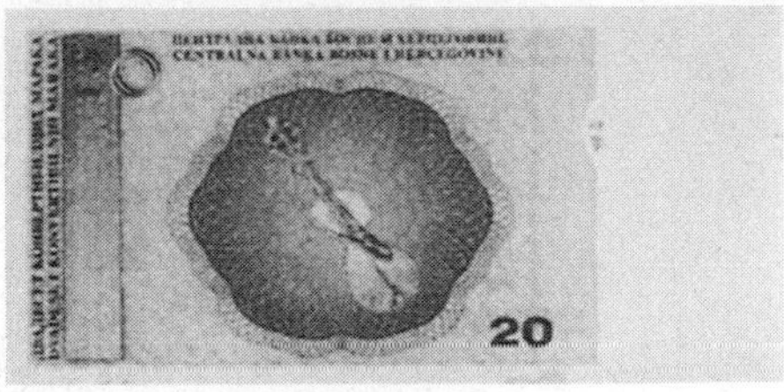

66	20 Convertible Maraka	VF	UNC
	ND (1998). Dark brown on multicolor underprint. F. Visjic at right. Back: "Gusle" musical instrument at left center, variable optical device at upper left center. Watermark: Central Bank monogram repeated vertically. Printer: F-CO (without imprint). Alternating texts of bank name and denominations. 138x68mm.		
	a. Issued note.	FV	20.00
	s. Specimen. All zero serial #.	—	75.00

67	50 Convertible Maraka	VF	UNC
	ND (1998); 2002. Purple on lilac and multicolor underprint. M. C. Catic at right. Back: Stone relief at left center, variable optical device at upper left center. Watermark: Central Bank monogram repeated vertically. Printer: F-CO (without imprint). Alternating texts of bank name and denominations. 146x71mm.		
	a. ND (1998).	FV	60.00
	b. 2002. Windowed security thread.	FV	55.00
	s1. Specimen. All zero serial #.	—	75.00
	s2. Specimen. As a. Regular serial #, overprint *SPECIMEN.*	—	—
	s3. Specimen. As b. Regular serial #, overprint *SPECIMEN.*	—	—

68	50 Convertible Maraka	VF	UNC
	ND (1998); 2002. Purple on lilac and multicolor underprint. I. Ducic at right. Back: Pen, glasses and book at left center, variable optical device at upper left center. Watermark: Central Bank monogram repeated vertically. Printer: F-CO (without imprint). Alternating texts of bank name and denominations. 146x71mm.		
	a. ND (1998).	FV	120.
	b. 2002.	FV	100.
	s1. Specimen. As a. Zero serial #.	—	—
	s2. Specimen. As a. Regular serial #, overprint *SPECIMEN.*	—	—
	s3. Specimen. As b. Regular serial #, overprint *SPECIMEN.*	—	—

69 100 Convertible Maraka VF UNC

ND (1998); 2002. Dark brown on yellow and multicolor underprint. N. Sop at right. Back: "Stecak Sgosca" fragment at left center, variable optical device at upper left center. Watermark: Central Bank monogram repeated vertically. Printer: F-CO (without imprint). Alternating texts of bank name and denominations. 154x74mm.

	VF	UNC
a. NS (1998).	FV	100.
b. 2002.	FV	100.
s1. Specimen. All zero serial #.	—	75.00
s2. Specimen. As a. Regular serial #, overprint *SPECIMEN*.	—	—
s3. Specimen. As b. Regular serial #, overprint *SPECIMEN*.	—	—

70 100 Convertible Maraka VF UNC

ND (1998); 2002. Dark brown on yellow and multicolor underprint. P. Kocic at right. Back: Pen, glasses and book at left center, variable optical device at upper left center. Watermark: Central Bank monogram repeated vertically. Printer: F-CO (without imprint). Alternating texts of bank name and denominations. 154x74mm.

	VF	UNC
a. ND (1998).	FV	100.
b. 2002.	FV	85.00
s1. Specimen. Zero serpial #.	—	—
s2. Specimen. As a. Regular serial #, overprint *SPECIMEN*.	—	—
s3. Specimen. As b. Regular serial #, overprint *SPECIMEN*.	—	—

71 200 Convertible Maraka VF UNC

ND (2002). Blue. 156x76mm.

	VF	UNC
a. Issued note.	FV	165.
s. Specimen.	—	—

2008 ND Issue

72 10 Convertible Maraka VF UNC

2008.

	VF	UNC
a. Issued note.	FV	12.50
s. Specimen.	—	—

73 10 Convertible Maraka

2008.

	VF	UNC
a. Issued note.	FV	12.50
s. Specimen.	—	—

74 20 Convertible Maraka

2008.

	VF	UNC
a. Issued note.	FV	20.00
s. Specimen.	FV	75.00

75 20 Convertible Maraka

2008.

	VF	UNC
a. Issued note.	FV	20.00
s. Specimen.	—	75.00

76 50 Dinara VF UNC

2007; 2008, 2009. Purple on Lilac and multicolor underprint. M. C. Catic at right. Windowed security thread. Back: Stone relief at left center. 146x71mm.

	VF	UNC
a. 2007.	FV	75.00
b. 2008.	FV	55.00
c. 2009.	FV	55.00
s. Specimen.	—	—

77 50 Convertible Maraka

2007; 2008; 2009.

	VF	UNC
a. 2007.	FV	75.00
b. 2008.	FV	55.00
c. 2009.	FV	55.00
s. Specimen.	—	—

78 100 Dinara VF UNC

2007; 2008. Dark brown on yellow and multicolor underprint. P. Kocic at right. Window security thread. Back: Pen, glass and book at left center. 154x74mm.

	VF	UNC
a. 2007.	FV	150.
b. 2008.	FV	100.
s. Specimen.	—	—

79 100 Convertible Maraka

2007; 2008.

	VF	UNC
a. 2007.	FV	150.
b. 2008.	FV	100.
s. Specimen.	—	—

2012 Issue

80 10 Convertible Maraka VF UNC

2012. M.M. Dizar at right.

	VF	UNC
a. Issued note.	FV	12.50
s. Specimen.	—	50.00

81 10 Convertible Maraka

2012. A. Santic at right.

	VF	UNC
a. Issued note.	FV	12.50
s. Specimen.	—	50.00

82 20 Convertible Maraka

2012. A.B. Simic at right.

	VF	UNC
a. Issued note.	FV	20.00
s. Specimen.	—	50.00

83 20 Convertible Maraka

2012. F. Visjic at right.

	VF	UNC
a. Issued note.	FV	20.00
s. Specimen.	—	50.00

84 50 Convertible Maraka

2012. M.C. Catric at right. Wide segmented security thread.

	VF	UNC
a1. Issued note.	FV	50.00
s. Specimen.	—	50.00

85 50 Convertible Maraka

2012. I. Ducic at right. Wide segmented security thread.

	VF	UNC
a. Issued note.	FV	50.00
s. Specimen.	—	50.00

86 100 Convertible Maraka

2012. N. Sop at right. Wide segmented security thread.

	VF	UNC
a. Issued note.	FV	100.
s. Specimen.	—	50.00

87 100 Convertible Maraka

2012. P. Kocic at right. Wide segmented security thread.

	VF	UNC
a. Issued note.	FV	130.
s. Specimen.	FV	50.00

Srpska (Serbian) Republic

1,000,000 old dinars = 1 new Dinar.

НАРОДНА БАНКА СРПСКЕРЕПУБЛИКЕБОСНЕ И ХЕРЦЕГОВИНЕ

Narodna Banka Srpske Republike Bosne I Hercegovine

National Bank of the Serbian Republic of Bosnia-Herzegovina

1992-93 Banja Luka Issue

133 10 Dinara | VF | UNC

1992. Deep brown or orange and silver underprint. Arms at left, numerals in heart-shaped design below guilloche at center right. Back: Ochre underprint. Curved artistic design at left center, arms at right. Watermark: Portrait of a young girl. 139x66mm.

	VF	UNC
a. Issued note.	.50	1.50
s. Specimen.	—	5.00

134 50 Dinara

1992. Deep olive-gray on ochre and multicolor underprint. Arms at left, numerals in heart-shaped design below guilloche at center right. Back: Curved artistic design at left center, arms at right. Watermark: Portrait of a young girl. 139x66mm.

	VF	UNC
a. Issued note.	.50	1.50
s. Specimen.	—	5.00

135 100 Dinara

1992. Dark blue on lilac and silver underprint. Arms at left, numerals in heart-shaped design below guilloche at center right. Back: Curved artistic design at left center, arms at right. Watermark: Portrait of a young girl. 139x66mm.

	VF	UNC
a. Issued note.	1.00	3.00
s. Specimen.	—	5.00

136 500 Dinara

1992. Dark blue on pink and multicolor underprint. Arms at left, numerals in heart-shaped design below guilloche at center right. Back: Curved artistic design at left center, arms at right. Watermark: Portrait of a young boy. 147x70mm.

	VF	UNC
a. Issued note.	1.50	4.50
s. Specimen.	—	5.00

137 1000 Dinara

1992. Slate gray on peach and tan underprint. Arms at left, numerals in heart-shaped design below guilloche at center right. Back: Orange underprint. Curved artistic design at left center, arms at right. Watermark: Portrait of a young boy. 147x70mm.

	VF	UNC
a. Issued note.	1.25	3.75
s. Specimen.	—	5.00

138 5000 Dinara

1992. Violet on lilac and light blue underprint. Arms at left, numerals in heart-shaped design below guilloche at center right. Back: Curved artistic design at left center, arms at right. Watermark: Portrait of a young boy. 147x70mm.

	VF	UNC
a. Issued note.	2.50	10.00
s. Specimen.	—	5.00

139 10,000 Dinara

1992. Gray on tan and light blue underprint. Arms at left, numerals in heart-shaped design below guilloche at center right. Back: Curved artistic design at left center, arms at right. Watermark: Portrait of a young boy. 147x70mm.

	VF	UNC
a. Issued note.	2.50	10.00
s. Specimen.	—	5.00

140 50,000 Dinara

1993. Brown on olive-green and multicolor underprint. Arms at left, numerals in heart-shaped design below guilloches at center right. Back: Curved artistic design at left center, arms at right. Watermark: Portrait of a young boy. 147x70mm.

	VF	UNC
a. Issued note.	8.00	30.00
s. Specimen.	—	7.50

141 100,000 Dinara

1993. Purple on brown and multicolor underprint. Arms at left, numerals in heart shaped design below guilloche at center right. Back: Curved artistic design at left center, arms at right. Watermark: Portrait of a young woman with head covering. 151x73mm.

	VF	UNC
a. Issued note.	1.50	4.00
s. Specimen.	—	7.50

142 **1 Million Dinara** **VF** **UNC**
1993. Deep purple on pink, yellow and multicolor underprint. Arms at left, numerals in heart-shaped design below guilloche at center right. Watermark: Portrait of a young girl. 139x66mm.

	VF	UNC
a. Issued note.	8.00	40.00
s. Specimen.	—	7.50

143 **5 Million Dinara**
1993. Dark brown on light blue and yellow-orange underprint. Arms at left, numerals in heart-shaped design below guilloche at center right. Back: Curved artistic design at left center, arms at right. Watermark: Portrait of a young girl. 139x66mm.

	VF	UNC
a. Issued note.	1.00	3.00
s. Specimen.	—	7.50

144 **10 Million Dinara** **VF** **UNC**
1993. Dark blue-violet on loive-green and yellow-orange underprint. Arms at left, numerals in heart-shaped design below guilloche at center right. Back: Curved artistic design at left center, arms at right. Watermark: Portrait of a young girl. 139x66mm.

	VF	UNC
a. Issued note.	1.50	4.50
s. Specimen.	—	7.50

НАРОДНА БАНКА РЕПУБЛИКЕСРПСКЕ

Narodna Banka Republike Srpske

National Bank of the Serbian Republic

1993 Banja Luka First Issue

145 **50 Million Dinara** **VF** **UNC**
1993. Dark brown on pink and gray underprint. Arms at left, numerals in heart-shaped design below guilloche at center right. Back: Curved artistic desing at left center, arms at right. 139x66mm.

	VF	UNC
a. Issued note.	2.50	7.50
s. Specimen.	—	5.00

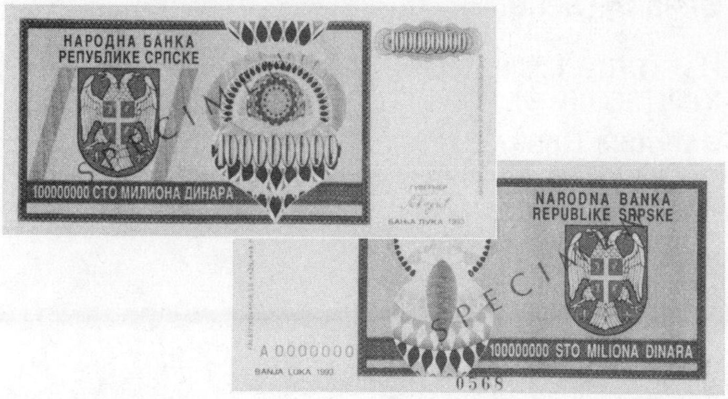

146 **100 Million Dinara** **VF** **UNC**
1993. Pale blue-gray on light blue and gray underprint. Arms at left, numerals in heart-shaped design below guilloche at center right. Back: Curved artistic design at left center, arms at right. 139x66mm.

	VF	UNC
a. Issued note.	1.50	4.00
s. Specimen.	—	5.00

147 **1 Milliard Dinara** **VF** **UNC**
1993. Orange on pale blue and light orange underprint. Arms at left, numerals in heart-shaped design below guilloche at center right. Back: Curved artistic design at left center, arms at right. 139x66mm.

	VF	UNC
a. Issued note.	1.50	5.00
s. Specimen.	—	5.00

148 **10 Milliard Dinara** **VF** **UNC**
1993. Black on pink and pale orange underprint. Arms at left, numerals in heart-shaped design below guilloche at center right. Back: Curved artisitc design at left center, arms at right. 139x66mm.

	VF	UNC
a. Issued note.	1.50	5.00
s. Specimen.	—	5.00

1993 Banja Luka Second Issue

1,000,000 old dinars = 1 new Dinar.

149	**5000 Dinara**	VF	UNC
	1993. Red-violet and purple on pale blue-gray underprint. Petar Kocic, novelist, at left. Back: Serbian arms at center right. Watermark: Greek design repeated. 139x66mm.		
	a. Issued note.	1.00	3.00
	s. Specimen.	—	7.50

150	**50,000 Dinara**	VF	UNC
	1993. Brown and dull red on ochre underprint. Petar Kocic, novelist, at left. Back: Serbian arms at center right. Watermark: Greek design repeated. 139x66mm.		
	a. Issued note.	1.00	3.00
	s. Specimen.	—	7.50

151	**100,000 Dinara**	VF	UNC
	1993. Violet and blue-gray on pink underprint. Petar Kocic, novelist, at left. Back: Serbian arms at center right. Watermark: Greek design repeated. 139x66mm.		
	a. Issued note.	1.00	3.00
	s. Specimen.	—	7.50

152	**1,000,000 Dinara**	VF	UNC
	1993. Black and blue-gray on pale purple underprint. P. Kocic at left. Back: Serbian arms at center right. Watermark: Greek design repeated.		
	a. Issued note.	1.50	5.00
	s. Specimen.	—	7.50

153	**5,000,000 Dinara**	VF	UNC
	1993. Orange and gray-blue on pale orange underprint. P. Kocic at left. Back: Serbian arms at center right. Watermark: Greek design repeated.		
	a. Issued note.	1.50	5.00
	s. Specimen.	—	7.50

154	**100,000,000 Dinara**	VF	UNC
	1993. Dull grayish green and pale olive-brown on light blue underprint. P. Kocic at left. Back: Serbian arms at center right. Watermark: Greek design repeated.		
	a. Issued note.	1.50	5.00
	s. Specimen.	—	7.50

155	**500,000,000 Dinara**	VF	UNC
	1993. Brown-violet and grayish green on pale olive-brown underprint. P. Kocic at left. Back: Serbian arms at center right. Watermark: Greek design repeated.		
	a. Issued note.	1.50	5.00
	s. Specimen.	—	7.50

156	**10,000,000,000 Dinara**	VF	UNC
	1993. Blue and red.		
	a. As prepared. Not issued.	—	100.
	s. Specimen.	Unc	50.00

157	**50,000,000,000 Dinara**	VF	UNC
	1993. Brown.		
	a. As prepared. Not issued.	—	100.
	s. Specimen.	—	50.00
158	**10,000,000 Dinara**		
	1993. Overprint on #133.		
	a. As prepared. Black overprint. Not issued.	—	100.
159	**50,000,000 Dinara**		
	1993. Overprint on #134.		
	a. As prepared. Dark purple overprint. Not issued.	—	100.
	b. As prepared. Dark green overprint. Not issued.	—	100.
160	**100,000,000 Dinara**		
	1993. Overprint on #135.		
	a. As prepared. Black overprint. Not issued.	—	100.

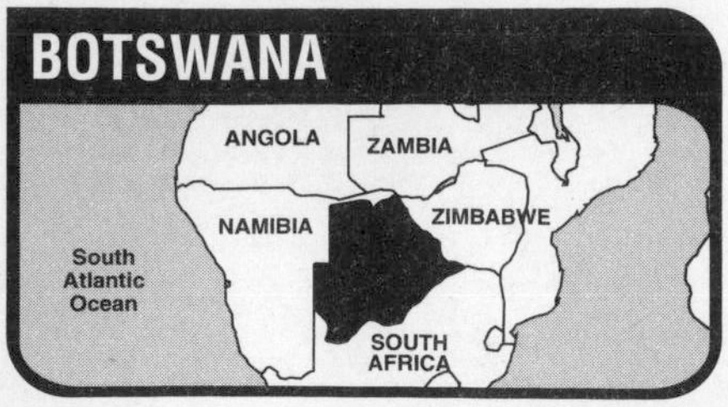

The Republic of Botswana, located in south central Africa between Namibia and Zimbabwe has an area of 600,370 sq. km. and a population of 1.84 million. Capital: Gaborone. The economy is primarily pastoral with a rapidly developing mining industry, of which diamonds, copper and nickel are the chief elements. Meat products and diamonds comprise 85 percent of the exports.

Formerly the British protectorate of Bechuanaland, Botswana adopted its new name upon independence in 1966. Four decades of uninterrupted civilian leadership, progressive social policies, and significant capital investment have created one of the most dynamic economies in Africa. Mineral extraction, principally diamond mining, dominates economic activity, though tourism is a growing sector due to the country's conservation practices and extensive nature preserves.

MONETARY SYSTEM:

1 Pula (Rand) = 100 Thebe (Cents)

	MINISTER OF FINANCE	GOVERNOR
1	Sir Q.K.J. Masire	Q. Hermans
2	Sir Q.K.J. Masire	B.C. Leavitt
3	P.S. Mmusi	F.G. Mogae
4	P.S. Mmusi	C. Kilonyogo
5	P.S. Mmusi	Q. Hermans
6a	F.G. Mogae	Q. Hermans
6b	F.G. Mogae	Q. Hermans
7a	P.H.K. Kedikilwe	B. Gaolatlhe
7b	P.H.K. Kedikilwe	B. Gaolatlhe
8a	B. Gaolatlhe	Mrs. L.K. Mohohlo
8b	B. Gaolatlhe	Mrs. L.K. Mohohlo

REPUBLIC

BANK OF BOTSWANA

1976-79 ND ISSUE

#1-5 For specimen notes with a maltese cross serial # prefix see the CS1 listing at the end of the country.

		VF	UNC
1	**1 Pula**		
	ND (1976). Brown on multicolor underprint. Sir Seretse Khana at left, bird at center, arms at upper right. Back: Farmer milking cow at center right. Watermark: Rearing Zebra. Printer: TDLR.		
	a. Issued note.	1.75	6.00
	s. Specimen. Serial # prefix: *A/1*.	—	95.00

		VF	UNC
2	**2 Pula**		
	ND (1976). Blue on multicolor underprint. Sir Seretse Khana at left, bird at center, arms at upper right. Back: Various workers at center right. Watermark: Rearing Zebra. Printer: TDLR.		
	a. Issued note.	3.00	14.00
	s. Specimen. Serial # prefix: *B/1*.	—	95.00

		VF	UNC
3	**5 Pula**		
	ND (1976). Purple on multicolor underprint. Sir Seretse Khana at left, bird at center, arms at upper right. Back: Gemsbok antelope at center right. Watermark: Rearing Zebra. Printer: TDLR.		
	a. Issued note.	6.00	35.00
	s. Specimen. Serial # prefix: *C/1*.	—	90.00
4	**10 Pula**		
	ND (1976). Green on multicolor underprint. Sir Seretse Khana at left, bird at center, arms at upper right. Back: Large building at center right. Watermark: Rearing Zebra. Printer: TDLR.		
	a. Signature 1.	30.00	150.
	b. Signature 2.	45.00	300.
	s1. As a. Specimen. Serial # prefix: *D/1*.	—	95.00
	s2. As b. Specimen. Serial # prefix: *D/4*.	—	95.00

5	**20 Pula**	VF	UNC
	ND (1979). Red, pruple and brown on multicolor underprint. Sir Seretse Khana at left, bird at center, arms at upper right. Back: Mining conveyors at center right. Watermark: Rearing Zebra. Printer: TDLR.		
	a. Signature 1.	50.00	300.
	b. Signature 2.	55.00	400.
	s1. As a. Specimen. Serial # prefix: *E/1.*	—	95.00
	s2. As b. Specimen. Serial # prefix: *E/2.*	—	95.00

1982-83 ND Issue

6	**1 Pula**	VF	UNC
	ND (1983). Dark brown. President Q. K. J. Masire at left wearing coarsely striped pinstripe suit. Signature 4. Back: Cattle, arms and plants. Printer: TDLR.		
	a. Issued note.	.75	4.00
	s. Specimen. Serial # prefix: *A/1.*	—	70.00

7	**2 Pula**	VF	UNC
	ND (1982). Blue on multicolor. President Q. K. J. Masire at left wearing coarsely striped pinstripe suit, Grey Lourie at center, arms at upper right. Back: Various workers at center right. Watermark: Rearing Zebra. Printer: TDLR.		
	a. Signature 3.	2.50	16.00
	b. Signature 4.	1.00	8.50
	c. Signature 5.	1.50	13.00
	d. Signature 6a.	1.00	7.00
	s1. As a. Specimen. Serial # prefix *B/6.*	—	70.00
	s2. As b. Specimen. Serial # prefix *B/7.*	—	70.00
	s3. As c. Specimen. Serial # prefix *B/16.*	—	70.00
	s4. As d. Specimen. Serial # prefix *B/21.*	—	70.00

8	**5 Pula**	VF	UNC
	ND (1982). Deep violet on multicolor underprint. President Q. K. J. Masire at left wearing coarsely striped pinstripe suit, Helmeted guinea fowl at center, arms at upper right. Back: Gemsbok antelope at center right. Watermark: Rearing Zebra. Printer: TDLR.		
	a. Signature 3.	5.00	35.00
	b. Signature 4.	2.00	19.00
	c. Signature 5.	1.50	15.00
	s1. As a. Specimen. Serial # prefix *C/5.*	—	70.00
	s2. As b. Specimen. Serial # prefix *C/6.*	—	70.00
	s3. As c. Specimen. Serial # prefix *C/10.*	—	70.00

9	**10 Pula**	VF	UNC
	ND (1982). Green on multicolor underprint. President Q. K. J. Masire at left wearing coarsely striped pinstripe suit, crowned hornbill at center, arms at upper right. Back: Large building at center right. Watermark: Rearing Zebra. Printer: TDLR.		
	a. Signature 3.	10.00	50.00
	b. Signature 4.	3.50	28.50
	c. Signature 5.	4.00	35.00
	d. Signature 6a.	3.00	22.50
	s1. As a. Specimen. Serial # prefix: *D/7.*	—	70.00
	s2. As b. Specimen. Serial # prefix: *D/12.*	—	70.00
	s3. As c. Specimen. Serial # prefix: *D/21.*	—	70.00
	s4. As d. Specimen. Serial #	—	70.00

10	**20 Pula**	VF	UNC
	ND (1982). Red, purple and brown on multicolor underprint. President Q. K. J. Masire at left wearing coarsely striped pinstripe suit, Ostrich at center, arms at upper right. Back: Mining conveyors at center right. Watermark: Rearing Zebra. Printer: TDLR.		
	a. Signature 3.	17.50	70.00
	b. Signature 4.	7.50	58.00
	c. Signature 5.	8.50	60.00
	d. Signature 6a.	5.00	37.50
	s1. As a. Specimen. Serial # prefix: *E/2.*	—	70.00
	s2. As b. Specimen. Serial # prefix: *E/5.*	—	70.00
	s3. As c. Specimen. Serial # prefix: *E/9.*	—	70.00
	s4. As d. Specimen. Serial # prefix: *E/13.*	—	70.00

1992-95 ND Issue

11	**5 Pula**	VF	UNC
	ND (1992). Deep violet on multicolor underprint. President Q. K. J. Masire at left wearing pinstripe suit, helmeted guinea fowl at center, arms at upper right. Signature 6a. Back: Gemsbok antelope at center right. Watermark: Rearing Zebra. Printer: Harrison.		
	a. Issued note.	1.50	6.00
	s. *C/18, C/19, C/27.*	—	125.

12 **10 Pula** — VF | UNC

ND (1992). Green on multicolor underprint. President Q. K. J. Masire at left wearing pinstripe suit, crowned hornbill at center, arms at upper right. Signature 6a. Back: Large building at center right. Watermark: Rearing Zebra. Printer: Harrison.

	VF	UNC
a. Issued note.	2.50	10.00
s. Specimen. Serial # prefix: *D/45, D/46.*	—	135.

13 **20 Pula** — VF | UNC

ND (1993). Red, purple and brown on multicolor underprint. President Q. K. J. Masire at left wearing pinstripe suit, Ostrich at center, arms at upper right. Signature 6a. Watermark: Rearing Zebra. Printer: Harrison.

	VF	UNC
a. Issued note.	6.00	20.00
s. Specimen. Serial # prefix: *E/21, E/29.*	—	150.

14 **50 Pula** — VF | UNC

ND (ca. 1992). Dark brown and dark green on multicolor underprint. President Q. K. J. Masire at left wearing pinstripe suit, Malachite Kingfisher at center, arms at upper right. Signature 6b. Back: Man in canoe and African fish eagle at center right. Watermark: Rearing Zebra. Printer: Fidelity Printers (Zimbabwe - Harare), without imp .

	VF	UNC
a. Issued note.	15.00	65.00
s1. Specimen. Serial # *F000000A.*	—	60.00
s2. Specimen. Serial # *F000000A.* Punch-hole cancelled.	—	60.00

15 **50 Pula**

ND (1995). Dark brown and dark green on multicolor underprint. President Q. K. J. Masire at left wearing pinstripe suit, Malachite Kingfisher at center, arms at upper right. Signature 6b. Back: African fish eagle at center right. Watermark: Rearing Zebra. Printer: TDLR.

	VF	UNC
a. Issued note.	12.50	52.50
s. Specimen. Serial # prefix: *F...C.* (suffix)	—	60.00

16 **100 Pula** — VF | UNC

ND (1993). Blue-violet and ochre on multicolor underprint. President Q. K. J. Masire at left wearing pinstripe suit, diamond and fish eagle at center, arms at upper right Back: Worker sorting rough diamonds at center right. Watermark: Rearing Zebra. Printer: TDLR.

	VF	UNC
a. Issued note.	FV	75.00
b. Specimen. Serial # prefix: *G/1, G/6.*	—	60.00

1997 ND Issue

17 **10 Pula** — VF | UNC

ND (1997). Green on multicolor underprint. President Q. K. J. Masire at left wearing finer striped pinstripe suit, crowned hornbill at center, arms at upper right. Signature 6a. Back: Large building at center right. Watermark: Rearing Zebra. Printer: TDLR, LIMITED.

	VF	UNC
a. Issued note. signature 6a.	3.00	17.50
s. Specimen. Serial # prefix: *D/54.*	—	60.00

18 **20 Pula**

ND (1997). Red, purple and brown on multicolor underprint. President Q. K. J. Masire at left wearing finer striped pinstripe suit, Ostrich at center, arms at upper right. Signature 6a. Back: Mining conveyors at center right. Watermark: Rearing Zebra. Printer: TDLR, LIMITED.

	VF	UNC
a. Issued note. signature 6a.	5.00	22.50
s. Specimen. Serial # prefix: *E/33.*	—	60.00

19 **50 Pula**

ND (1997). Dark brown and dark green on multicolor underprint. President Q. K. J. Masire at left wearing finer striped pinstripe suit, Malachite Kingfisher at center, arms at upper right. Signature 6b. Back: Man in canoe and African fish eagle at center right. Watermark: Rearing Zebra. Printer: TDLR, LIMITED.

	VF	UNC
a. Issued note. signature 6b.	12.50	42.50
s. Specimen. Serial # prefix: *F/13.*	—	60.00

1999-2000 ND Issue

20 **10 Pula** — VF | UNC

ND (1999). Green on multicolor underprint. President F. Mogae at left, Hornbill at center, arms at upper right. Back: Parliament building. Watermark: Rearing Zebra. Printer: F-CO. 138x69mm.

	VF	UNC
a. Signature 7a.	FV	11.00
b. Sign 8a.	FV	6.50
s1. As a. Specimen. Serial # prefix *D/62.*	—	60.00
s2. As b. Specimen. Serial # prefix *D/72.*	—	60.00

21 **20 Pula** — VF | UNC

ND (1999). Red, purple and brown on multicolor underprint. K. Motsete at left, Ostrich at center, arms at upper right. Back: Mining conveyors at center right. Watermark: Rearing Zebra. Printer: SABN. 144x72mm.

	VF	UNC
a. Sign 7b.	FV	16.00
s1. As a. Specimen. Serial # prefix *E/42.*	—	60.00

No.	Denomination	VF	UNC
22	**50 Pula**	VF	UNC
	ND (2000). Dark brown and dark green on multicolor underprint. Sir Seretse Khama at left, Malachite Kingfisher at center, arms at upper right. Optical variable ink star at right. Back: Man in canoe and fish eagle at center right. Watermark: Rearing Zebra. Printer: F-CO. 150x75mm.		
	a. Signature 8a.	FV	22.50
	s. As a. Specimen. Serial # prefix *F/18.*	—	60.00

No.	Denomination	VF	UNC
23	**100 Pula**	VF	UNC
	ND (2000). Blue-violet and ochre on multicolor underprint. Three chiefs: Sebeli I, Bathoen I and Khama III at left, fisheagle at center, arms and optical variable ink diamond at right. Back: Worker sorting rough diamonds at center. Watermark: Rearing Zebra. Printer: F-CO. 156x78mm.		
	a. Signature 8a.	FV	52.50
	s. As a. Specimen. Serial # prefix *G/11.*		60.00

2002 ND Issue

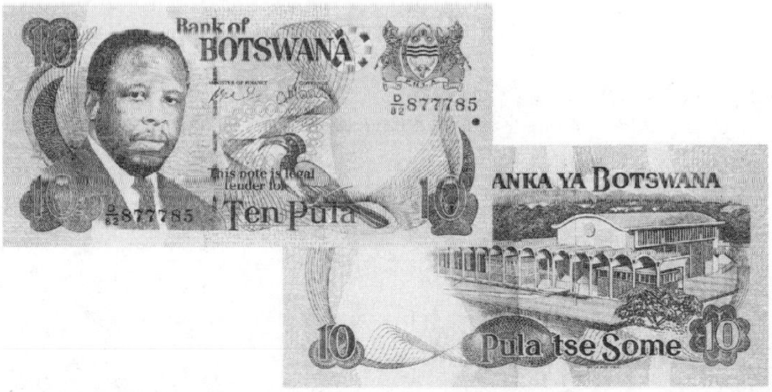

No.	Denomination	VF	UNC
24	**10 Pula**	VF	UNC
	2002; 2007. Green on multicolor underprint. President F. Mogae at left, hornbill at center, arms at upper right. Back: Parliament building. Watermark: Rearing Zebra. Printer: DLR. Wide security thread. 138x69mm.		
	a. 2002. Signature 8b.	FV	6.50
	b. 2007.	FV	6.50
	s. As a. Specimen. Serial # prefix *D/82.*	—	60.00

No.	Denomination	VF	UNC
25	**20 Pula**	VF	UNC
	2002; 2008. Red, purple and brown on multicolor underprint. K. Motsete at left, ostrich at center, arms at upper right. Back: Mining conveyors at center right. Watermark: Rearing Zebra. Wide security thread. 144x72mm.		
	a. 2002. Signature 8b.	FV	9.50
	b. 2008.	FV	9.50
	s. As a. Specimen. Serial # prefix *E/52.*	—	60.00

2004-07 Issue

No.	Denomination	VF	UNC
26	**10 Pula**	VF	UNC
	2007. Green on multicolor underprint. President F. Mogae at left, hornbill at center, arms at upper right. Back: Parliament building. Watermark: Rearing Zebra. Printer: (T)DLR. 138x69mm.	FV	6.50
27	**20 Pula**		
	2004; 2006. Red, purple and brown on multicolor underprint. K. Motsete at left, ostrich at center, arms at upper right. Wide segmented security foil. Back: Mining conveyors at center right. Printer: F-CO. 144x72mm.		
	a. 2004.	FV	16.00
	b. 2006.	FV	16.00

No.	Denomination	VF	UNC
28	**50 Pula**	VF	UNC
	2005. Dark brown and dark green on multicolor underprint. Sir Seretse Khama at left, Malachite Kingfisher at center. Hologram. Back: Man in canoe, fish-eagle and Ikavango Delta. Watermark: Rearing Aebra. Printer: DLR. 150x75mm.		
	a. Issued note.	FV	15.00
	b. Specimen.	—	50.00

No.	Denomination	VF	UNC
29	**100 Pula**	VF	UNC
	2004; 2005. Blue-violet and ochre on multicolor underprint. Three chiefs: Sebeli I, Bathoen I and Khama III at left, fish eagle at center, arms and variable ink diamond at right, circular Kinegram at lower right. Signature 8a. Back: Worker sorting rough diamonds at center. Printer: TDLR. 156x78mm.		
	a. 2004.	FV	52.50
	b. 2005.	FV	50.00

2009 ND Issue

30	**10 Pula**	VF	UNC
	ND (2009); 2010. Light green, dark green and tan. President Seretse Khama Ian Khama at left center. Back: National Assembly building in Gaborone. Watermark: Rearing zebra and 10. Printer: DLR. 132x66mm.		
	a. ND (2009).	FV	2.50
	b. 2010.	FV	2.50

31	**20 Pula**	VF	UNC
	ND (2009); 2010. Purple and rose on multicolor underprint. Dr. Kgalemang Motsete at left center. Back: Mining conveyors at center right. Watermark: Rearing zebra and 20. 138x69mm.		
	a. ND (2009).	FV	4.00
	b. 2010.	FV	4.00

32	**50 Pula**	VF	UNC
	ND (2009). Brown and tan on multicolor underprint. Sir Seretse Khama at left center. Back: Brown and green. Okawango Delta wetlands. Watermark: Rearing zebra and 50. Printer: DLR. 144x72mm.	FV	10.00

33	**100 Pula**	VF	UNC
	ND (2009); 2010. Slate black, blue-violet and ochre on multicolor underprint. Three chiefs: Sebeli I, Bathoen I and Khama III at left, arms at upper right. Back: Worker sorting rough diamonds at center. Watermark: Rearing zebra and 100. 150x75mm.		
	a. ND (2009).	FV	20.00
	b. 2010.	FV	20.00

34	**200 Pula**	VF	UNC
	ND (2009). Purple, brown and violet on green and multicolor underprint. Female teaching children to read at left center, arms at upper center. Back: Herd of zebras at waterhole. Watermark: Rearing zebra and 200. 156x78mm.		
	a. ND (2009).	FV	40.00
	b. 2010.	FV	40.00
35	**200 Pula**		
	ND (2009). Brown and purple on multicolor underprint. Female teaching children to read at left center, arms at upper right. Back: Herd of zebras at waterhole. Watermark: Rearing zebra and 200. 156x78mm.	FV	50.00

Collector Series

Bank of Botswana

1979 ND Issue

CS1	**ND (1979) 1-20 Pula**	Mkt.	Value
	#1-3, 4a, 5a. overprint: *SPECIMEN* and Maltese cross serial # prefix.		40.00

The Federative Republic of Brazil, which comprises half the continent of South America, is the only Latin American country deriving its culture and language from Portugal. It has an area of 8,511,965 sq. km. and a population of 196.34 million. Capital: Brasília.

Following three centuries under the rule of Portugal, Brazil became an independent nation in 1822 and a republic in 1889. By far the largest and most populous country in South America, Brazil overcame more than half a century of military intervention in the governance of the country when in 1985 the military regime peacefully ceded power to civilian rulers. Brazil continues to pursue industrial and agricultural growth and development of its interior. Exploiting vast natural resources and a large labor pool, it is today South America's leading economic power and a regional leader. Highly unequal income distribution and crime remain pressing problems.

SIGNATURE VARIETIES

8	Sebastião P. Almeida	
9	Clemente Mariani	Carlos A. Carrílho
10	Walter M. Salles	Reginaldo F. Nunes
11	Reginaldo F. Nunes, 1962	Walter M. Salles
12	Reginaldo F. Nunes, 1963	Miguel Calmon
13	Reginaldo F. Nunes, 1964	Otávio Gouvex Bulhões
14	Sérgio A. Ribeiro, 1964-66	Otávio Gouvex Bulhões
15	Dénio Nogueira, 1966-67	Otávio Gouvex Bulhões
16	Ruy Leme, 1967	Antônio Delfim Netto
17	Ername Galveas, 1967-72	Antônio Delfim Netto
18	Mário Henrique Simonsen, 1974-79	Paulo H.P. Lira

SIGNATURE VARIETIES

19	Karlos Rischbieter, 1979-80	Ernane Galvêas
20	Ernane Galvêas, 1980-81	Carlos P. Langoni
21	Ernane Galvêas, 1983-85	Alfonso C. Pastore
22	Francisco Dornélles, 1985	Antonio Lengruber
23	Dilson Funaro, 1985-86	Fernao C.B. Bracher
24	Dilson Funaro, 1987	Francisco Gross
25	Luiz Carlos Bresser Pereira, 1987	Fernando M. Oliveira
26	Maílson Ferreira Da Nóbrega, 1988-89	Elmo Camões
27	Maílson Ferreira Da Nóbrega, 1989-90	Wadico Bucchi
28	Zélia Cardoso De Mello, 1990	Ibrahim Éris
29	Marcílio M. Moreira, 1991-92	Francisco Gross
30	Paulo R. Haddad, 1993	Gustavo Loyola
31	Elizeu Resende, 1993	Paulo Ximenes
32	Fernando H. Cardoso, 1993	Paulo Ximenes
33	Fernando H. Cardoso, 1993-94	Pedro Malan
34	Rubens Ricúpero, 1994	Pedro Malan
35	Ciro Gomes, 1994	Pedro Malan

SIGNATURE VARIETIES

36	Pedro Malan, 1995	Pérsio Arida
37	Pedro Malan, 1995-97	Gustavo Loyola
38	Pedro Malan, 1998	Gustavo Franco
39	Pedro Malan, 1999-	Arminia Fraganeto
40	Antonio Palocci Filho, 2003-	Henrique De Campos Meirelles

SIGNATURE VARIETIES

Affonso Almino	Afonso Celso Pastore	Antonio Delfin Netto
Carlos Augusto Carrilho	Carlos Geraldo Langoni	Claudionor de Souza Lemos
Clemente Mariani	Dênio Nogueira	Dilson Funaro
Eliseu Resende	Elmo Camões	Ernane Galveas
Eugenio Gudin	Fernando Henrique Cardoso	Fernando Milliet de Oliveira
Fernão Bracher	Francisco Dornelles	Francisco Gross
Gustavo J.L. Loyola	Horácio Lafer	Ibrahim Éris
José Maria Alkimin	José Maria Whytaker	Karlos Rischbieter
Lucas Lopes	Luiz Carlos Bresser Pereira	Mailson Ferreira da Nóbrega
Marcílio Marques Moreira	Mário Henrique Simonsen	Miguel Calmon
Oswaldo Aranha	Octávio Gouvêa de Bulhões	Paulo Henrique Pereira Lira
Paulo R. Haddad	Paulo Ximenes	Pedro Malan
Reginaldo Fernandes Nunes	Ruy Leme	Sebastião Paes de Almeida

SIGNATURE VARIETIES

Sérgio Augusto Ribeiro	Wadico Bucchi	Walter Moreira Salles
Zélia Cardoso de Mello		

REPUBLIC

TESOURO NACIONAL

ESTAMPA 3; 1961 ND ISSUE

		VF	UNC
166	**5 Cruzeiros** ND (1961-62). Dark brown and brown. Raft with sail at left, male Indian at right. Back: Flower. Printer: CdM-B.		
	a. Signature 8. Series #1-75.	.50	2.00
	b. Signature 10. Series #76-111.	.25	1.25

ESTAMPA 1A; 1961 ND ISSUE

		VF	UNC
167	**10 Cruzeiros** ND (1961-63). Dark blue on microcolor underprint. Portrait G. Vargas at center. 2 printed signatures. Back: Green. Allegory of "Industry" at center. Printer: ABNC.		
	a. Signature 9. Series #331-630. (1961).	.50	2.00
	b. Signature 12. Series #631-930. (1963).	.50	1.75
	s. As a or b. Specimen.	—	125.

		VF	UNC
168	**20 Cruzeiros** ND (1961-63). Dark blue on microcolor underprint. Portrait D. da Fonseca at center. 2 printed signatures. Back: Red. Allegory of "the Republic" at center. Printer: ABNC.		
	a. Signature 9. Series #461-960. (1961).	.50	2.25
	b. Signature 12. Series #961-1260. (1963).	.50	2.00
	s. As a or b. Specimen.	—	135.

169	50 Cruzeiros	VF	UNC
	ND (1961). Dark blue on microcolor underprint. Portrait Princess Isabel at center. 2 printed signatures. Signature 9. Series # 721-1220. Back: Purple. Allegory of "Law" at center. Printer: ABNC.		
	a. Issued note.	1.50	7.50
	s. Specimen.	—	135.

170	100 Cruzeiros	VF	UNC
	ND (1961-64). Dark blue on microcolor underprint. Portrait D. Pedro at center. 2 printed signatures. Back: Red-brown. Allegory of "National Culture" at center. Printer: ABNC.		
	a. Signature 9. Series #761-1160. (1961).	2.25	9.00
	b. Signature 13. Series #1161-1360. (1964).	1.00	4.50
	c. Signature 14. Series #1361-1560. (1964).	2.00	8.00
	s. As a, b or c. Specimen.	—	150.

171	200 Cruzeiros	VF	UNC
	ND (1961-64). Dark blue on microcolor underprint. Portrait D. Pedro at center. 2 printed signatures. Back: Olive-green. Battle scene at center. Printer: ABNC.		
	a. Signature 9. Series #671-1070. (1961).	3.50	15.00
	b. Signature 13. Series #1071-1370. (1964).	3.00	12.00
	c. Signature 14. Series #1371-1570. (1964).	3.00	12.00
	s. As a, b or c. Specimen.	—	150.

172	500 Cruzeiros	VF	UNC
	ND (1961-62). Dark blue on microcolor underprint. Portrait D. Joao VI at center. 2 printed signatures. Back: Blue-black. Allegory of "Maritime Industry" at center. Printer: ABNC.		
	a. Signature 9. Series #261-660. (1961).	5.00	25.00
	b. Signature 11. Series #661-1460. (1962).	4.00	20.00
	s. As a, b. Specimen.	—	125.

173	1000 Cruzeiros		
	ND (1961-63). Dark blue on microcolor underprint. Portrait P. Alvares Cabral at center. 2 printed signatures. Back: Orange. Scene of the "First Mass" at center. Printer: ABNC.		
	a. Signature 9. Series #1331-1730. (1961).	8.00	50.00
	b. Signature 11. Series #1731-3030. (1962).	6.00	40.00
	c. Signature 12. Series #3031-3830. (1963).	7.00	45.00
	s. As a, b or c. Specimen.	—	135.

174	5000 Cruzeiros	VF	UNC
	ND (1963-64). Blue-gray on multicolor underprint. Portrait Tiradentes at right. Back: Red. Tiradentes in historical scene at center. Printer: ABNC.		
	a. Signature 12. Series #1-400. (1963).	5.00	35.00
	b. Signature 13. Series #401-1400. (1964).	4.50	30.00
	c. Signature 14. Series #1401-1650. (1965).	8.00	50.00
	s. As a, b or c. Specimen.	—	150.

Estampa 2A; 1962-63 ND Issue

#175 *Deleted,* **see #182B.**

176	5 Cruzeiros	VF	UNC
	ND (1962-64). Brown on multicolor underprint. Portrait Barao do Rio Branco at center. 2 printed signatures. Printer: TDLR.		
	a. Signature 11. Series #2301-3500. (1962).	.25	1.00
	b. Signature 12. Series #3501-3700. (1963).	.25	2.50
	c. Signature 13. Series #3701-3748; 4149-4180; 4201-4232. (1964).	.25	5.00
	d. Signature 14. Series #3749-4148; 4181-4200; 4233-4700. (1964).	.25	.75

177	10 Cruzeiros		
	ND (1962). Green on multicolor underprint. Portrait G. Vargas at center. 2 printed signatures Back: Green. Allegory of "Industry" at center Printer: TDLR.		
	a. Signature 10. Series # 2365-3055.	.25	1.50
	b. Signature 11. Series # 2394A.	.25	1.50

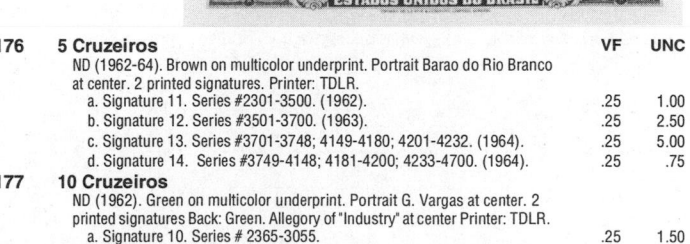

178	20 Cruzeiros	VF	UNC
	Red-brown on multicolor underprint. Portrait D. da Fonseca at center. 2 printed signatures. Signature 11. Series # 1576-2275. Back: Red. Allegory of "the Republic" at center. Printer: TDLR. UV: planchettes fluorese yellow.	.50	2.25

179 50 Cruzeiros | VF | UNC
ND (1963). Purple on multicolor underprint. Portrait Princess Isabel at center. 2 printed signatures. Signature 12. Series # 586-785. Back: Purple. Allegory of "Law" at center. Printer: TDLR. | 1.00 | 4.00

180 100 Cruzeiros
ND (1963). Red on multicolor underprint. Portrait D. Pedro at center. 2 printed signatures. Signature 12. Series # 216-415. Back: Red-brown. Allegory of "National Culture" at center. Printer: TDLR. | 2.00 | 9.00

181 1000 Cruzeiros | VF | UNC
ND (1963). Orange on multicolor underprint. Portrait P. Alvares Cabral at center. 2 printed signatures. Signature 12. Series # 791-1590. Back: Orange. Scene of the "First Mass" at center. Printer: TDLR. | 3.00 | 15.00

182 5000 Cruzeiros | VF | UNC
ND (1963-64(. Red on multicolor underprint. Portrait Tiradentes at right. 2 printed signatures. Signature at left with title: *Director Caixa de Amortizacao*. Back: Red. Tiradentes in historical scene at center. Printer: TDLR.
a. Signature 12. Series #1-400. (1963). | 4.50 | 30.00
b. Signature 13. Series #401-1400. (1964). | 4.00 | 25.00
c. Signature 14. Series #1401-1700. (1964). | 6.00 | 40.00

Banco Central do Brasil

1965; 1966 ND Issue

182A 5000 Cruzeiros | VF | UNC
ND (1965). Red on multicolor underprint. Portrait Tiradentes at right. 2 printed signatures. Signature D. Nogueira with title: *Presidente do Banco Central* and O. Gouvea de Bulhões. Signature 15. Series # 1701-2200. Back: Red. Tiradentes in historical scene at center. Printer: ABNC. | 5.00 | 35.00

182B 10,000 Cruzeiros | VF | UNC
ND (1966). Gray on multicolor underprint. Portrait S. Dumont at right. Signature 15. Back: Blue. Early airplane at right. Printer: ABNC.
a. Series #1-493. | 17.50 | 70.00
b. Series #561-590. | 175. | 350.
s. As a. Specimen. | — | 375.

1966; 1967 ND Provisional Issue

Feb. 1967 Monetary Reform: 1 Cruzeiro Novo = 1,000 Cruzeiros

183 1 Centavo on 10 Cruzeiros | VF | UNC
ND (1966-67). Green on multicolor underprint. Black circular overprint: *BANCO CENTRAL* and new currency unit in black circle. Signature 15. Overprint on #177. UV: planchettes fluoresce yellow.
a. Error: *Minstro* below right signature (2 types of 1 in overprint.) (1966). Series #3056-3151. | .20 | 1.00
b. *Ministro* below right signature (1967). Series # 3152-4055. | .20 | 1.00
s. As b. Specimen overprint: *MODELO.* | — | —

184 5 Centavos on 50 Cruzeiros | VF | UNC
ND (1966-67). Purple on multicolor underprint. Black circular overprint: *BANCO CENTRAL* and new currency unit in black circle. Signature 15. Overprint on #179.
a. Type of #183a. Series #786-1313. | .25 | 1.50
b. Type of #183b. Series #1314-1885. | .25 | 1.50

185 10 Centavos on 100 Cruzeiros | VF | UNC
ND (1966-67). Red on multicolor underprint. Black circular overprint: *BANCO CENTRAL* and new currency unit in black circle. Signature 15. Overprint on #180. UV: planchettes fluoresce yellow.
a. Type of #183a. Series #416-911. | .25 | 2.00
b. Type of #183b. Series #912-1515. | .25 | 1.75

186 50 Centavos on 500 Cruzeiros

ND (1967). Blue on multicolor underprint. Black circular overprint: *BANCO CENTRAL* and new currency unit in black circle. Signature 15. Series # 1461-2360. Overprint on #172.

	VF	UNC
a. Issued note.	2.00	4.50
s. Specimen.	—	150.

187 1 Cruzeiro Novo on 1000 Cruzeiros

ND (1966-67). Blue on multicolor underprint. Black circular overprint: *BANCO CENTRAL* and new currency unit in black circle. Overprint on #173.

	VF	UNC
a. Signature 14. Series #3831-3930.	7.50	22.50
b. Signature 15. Series #3931-4830.	2.50	7.50
s. As b. Specimen.	—	150.

188 5 Cruzeiros Novos on 5000 Cruzeiros

ND (1966-67). Blue-green on multicolor underprint. Black circular overprint: *BANCO CENTRAL* and new currency unit in black circle. Overprint on #174.

	VF	UNC
a. Signature 14. Series #1651-1700.	30.00	60.00
b. Signature 15. Series #1701-2900.	8.00	22.50
s. As b. Specimen.	—	150.

189 10 Cruzeiros Novos on 10,000 Cruzeiros

ND (1966-67). Gray on multicolor underprint. Black circular overprint: *BANCO CENTRAL* and new currency unit in black circle. Printer: ABNC. Bold or semi-bold overprint on #182B.

	VF	UNC
a. Signature 15. Series #404-560 and 561-700. (1966).	25.00	85.00
b. Signature 16. Series #701-1700. (1967).	6.00	25.00
c. Signature 17. Series #1701-2700. (1967).	5.00	20.00
s. As b. Specimen.	—	175.

190 10 Cruzeiros Novos on 10,000 Cruzeiros

ND (1967). Brown on pink and multicolor underprint. Black circular overprint: *BANCO CENTRAL* and new currency unit in black circle. Portrait S. Dumont at right. Signature 15. Back: Blue. Early airplane at right. Printer: TDLR.

	VF	UNC
a. Signature 16. Series #1-1000.	3.50	15.00
b. Signature 17. Series #1001-2100.	2.25	10.00

1970 ND Issues

191 1 Cruzeiro

ND (1970-72). Dark green and blue on ochre and green underprint with medallic. Liberty head at right in brown. Series number prefix A. 5 digit series number above serial number. Signature 17. Back: Banco Central building at left. Watermark: Liberty head. Printer: CdM-B.

	VF	UNC
a. Series #1-3000.	.50	2.00
s1. Specimen. Overprint: *MODELO*.	—	25.00
s2. Specimen. Overprint: *SEM VALOR* and perforated *MODELO*.	—	60.00

191A 1 Cruzeiro

ND (1972-80). Dark green and blue with medallic. Liberty head in green. Series number prefix B. 5 digit series number above serial number. Back: Banco Central building at left. Watermark: Liberty head. Printer: CdM-B.

	VF	UNC
a. Signature 17. Series #1-3781 (1972).	.25	1.00
b. Signature 18. Series #3782-13194 (1975).	.15	.75
c. Signature 20. Series #13195-18094 (1980).	.10	.50
s. As a. Specimen overprint and perforated: *MODELO*.	—	25.00

192 5 Cruzeiros

ND (1970-80). Blue on orange and green underprint. Portrait D. Pedro I at right. 5 digit series number above serial number. Back: Maroon. Parade square at left. Watermark: D. Pedro I. Printer: CdM-B.

	VF	UNC
a. Back darkly printed. Signature 17. Series # prefix A. Series #1-107 (1970-71).	5.00	20.00
b. Back lightly printed. Signature 17. Series # prefix B. Series #1-2467 (1973).	.25	1.25
c. Signature 18. Series #2468-6050 (1974).	.25	1.50
d. Signature 19. Series #6051-6841 (1979).	.25	2.00
s. As a. Specimen overprint: *SEM VALOR*, perforated: *MODELO*.	—	25.00

193 10 Cruzeiros

ND (1970-80). Grayish purple and dark brown on orange-brown, blue-green and multicolor underprint. Portrait D. Pedro II at right. 5 digit series number above serial number. Back: Green, violet and brown. Statue of the Prophet Daniel. Watermark: D. Pedro II. Printer: CdM-B.

	VF	UNC
a. Back darkly printed. Signature 17. Series # prefix A. Series #1-1429 (1970).	2.50	15.00
b. As a. signature 18. Series #1430-7745 (1974).	.50	1.75
c. Back lightly printed. Signature 18. Series # prefix B. Series #1-2394 (1979).	1.00	5.00
d. As c. Signature 19. Series #2395-2870 (1980).	.50	2.50
e. As d. Signature 20. Series #2871-5131 (1980).	.50	2.00
s. Specimen. Overprint: *MODELO* and pin hole cancelled.	—	80.00

194 50 Cruzeiros

ND (1970-81). Black, purple, blue-black and violet on lilac and multicolor underprint. Portrait D. da Fonseca at right. 5 digit series number above serial number. Back: Brown, lilac and blue. Coffee loading. Watermark: D. da Fonseca. Printer: CdM-B. 161x76mm.

	VF	UNC
a. Signature 17. Series #1-1250 (1970).	3.00	20.00
b. Signature 18. Series #1251-3841 (1974).	.50	3.00
c. Signature 20. Series #3842-5233 (1980).	.50	2.50
s. Specimen. As a. Overprint: *SEM VALOR* and perforated: *MODELO.*	—	125.

195 100 Cruzeiros

ND (1970-81). Purple and violet on pink and multicolor underprint. Portrait Marshal F. Peixoto at right. Signature 17 (with imprint CdM-B). Series number 1-01358. 5 digit series number above serial number. Back: Blue, brown and violet. National Congress at left. Watermark: Marshal F. Peixoto. Printer: TDLR.

	VF	UNC
a. Issued note.	6.00	35.00
s. Specimen. Overprint: *SEM VALOR* on both sides.	—	75.00

195A 100 Cruzeiros

ND (1974-81). Purple and violet on pink and multicolor underprint. Portrait Marshal F. Peixoto at right. Signature 17 (with imprint CdM-B). Series number 1-01358. 5 digit series number above serial number. Back: Blue, brown and violet. National Congress at left. Printer: CdM-B.

	VF	UNC
a. Signature 18. Series #01359-10455 (1974).	.75	6.00
b. Signature 20. Series #10456-12681 (1981).	.75	6.00
s. Specimen.	—	25.00

1972 Commemorative Issue

#196, 196A, 150th Anniversary of Brazilian Independence

196 500 Cruzeiros

1972 (1972-74). Dark olive-green and brown on violet and multicolor underprint. Portrait of five men of differing racial groups. Back: 5 different maps of Brazil. Watermark: Dates *1822 1972* in clear area at left. Printer: CdM-B.

	VF	UNC
a. Signature 17. Series # prefix A. #1-90 (1972).	100.	300.
b. As a. Signature 18. Series #91-2636 (1974).	5.00	35.00
s1. Specimen. Signature 17. Overprint: *MODELO.*	—	175.
s2. Specimen. Signature 18. Overprint: *MODELO.*	—	50.00

196A 500 Cruzeiros

1972 (1979-80). Dark olive-green and brown on violet and multicolor underprint. Portrait of five men of differing racial groups, watermark area has vertical lines. Back: 5 different maps of Brazil, watermark area has vertical lines. Watermark: Dates *1822 1972* in clear area at left. Printer: CdM-B.

	VF	UNC
a. Signature 18. Series # prefix B. #1-1401 (1979).	4.00	25.00
b. As a. Signature 19. Series #1402-1959 (1979).	4.00	25.00
c. As a. Signature 20. Series #1960-2763 (1980).	4.00	25.00
s. Specimen.	—	50.00

1978 ND Issue

197 1000 Cruzeiros

ND (1978-80). Green and brown. Double portrait B. do Rio Branco, *BANCO CENTRAL DO BRASIL* in two lines. The first 4 digits of the serial number represent the series number. Back: Double view of machinery. Watermark: B. do Rio Branco.

	VF	UNC
a. Signature 18. Series #1-665 (1978).	8.00	50.00
b. Signature 19. Series #666-2072 (1979).	6.00	32.50
c. Signature 20. Series #2073-3297 (1980).	6.00	35.00

1981-85 ND Issue

198 **100 Cruzeiros** — VF / UNC

ND (1981-84). Red and purple on multicolor underprint. Double portrait D. de Caxias at center. The first 4 digits of the serial number represent the series number. Back: Gray-blue and red. Double view of a battle scene and sword at center. Watermark: D. de Caxias. Printer: CdM-B.

	VF	UNC
a. Signature 20. Series #1-4081 (1981).	.15	.50
b. Signature 21. Series #4082-8176 (1984).	.15	.50

199 **200 Cruzeiros** — VF / UNC

ND (1981-84). Green and violet on multicolor underprint. Double portrait of Princess Isabel at center. The first 4 digits of the serial number represent the series number. Back: Brown and green. Double view of two women cooking outdoors. Watermark: Princess Isabel. Printer: CdM-B.

	VF	UNC
a. Signature 20. Series #1-2996 (1981).	.15	.50
b. Signature 21. Series #2997-4960 (1984).	.15	.50

200 **500 Cruzeiros** — VF / UNC

ND (1981-85). Blue and brown on multicolor underprint. Double portrait of D. da Fonseca at center. The first 4 digits of the serial number represent the series number. Back: Pink, brown and purple. Double view of a group of legislators Watermark: D. da Fonseca. Printer: CdM-B.

	VF	UNC
a. Signature 20. Series #1-3510 (1981).	.20	1.00
b. Signature 21. Series #3511-4238 (1985).	.15	.75

201 **1000 Cruzeiros** — VF / UNC

ND (1981-86). Brown and dark olive on multicolor underprint. Double portrait B. do Rio Branco, *BANCO CENTRAL DO BRASIL* in two lines. The first 4 digits of the serial number represent the series number. Back: Tan and blue. Double view of machinery. Watermark: B. do Rio Branco. Printer: CdM-B.

	VF	UNC
a. Signature 20. Series # prefix A, #1-5733 (1981).	.50	2.50
b. As a. Signature 21. Series #5734-7019 (1984).	.15	.75
c. As b. Signature 22. Series #7020-9999 (1985).	.15	.75
d. Signature 22. Series # prefix B, #1-788 (1986).	.15	.75

202 **5000 Cruzeiros** — VF / UNC

ND (1981-85). Purple and brown on multicolor underprint. Double portrait of C. Branco at center. The first 4 digits of the serial number represent the series number. Back: Brown, purple and blue. Double view of antennas. Watermark: C. Branco. Printer: CdM-B.

	VF	UNC
a. Signature 20. Series # prefix A, #1-9205 (1981).	.75	6.50
b. As a. Signature 21. Series #9206-9999 (1983).	.25	1.50
c. Signature 21. Series # prefix B, #1-2118 (1984).	.25	1.00
d. As c. Signature 22. Series #2119-2342 (1985).	.50	2.00

203 **10,000 Cruzeiros** — VF / UNC

ND (1984-85). Brown on multicolor underprint. Desk top at center, double portrait of Rui Barbosa at center. The first 4 digits of the serial number represent the series number. Back: Double view of a conference scene. Watermark: Rui Barbosa. Printer: CdM-B.

	VF	UNC
a. Signature 21. Series #1-3619 (1984).	1.25	4.50
b. Signature 22. Series #3620-3696 (1985).	4.00	22.50

204	50,000 Cruzeiros	VF	UNC
	ND (1984-86). Purple on multicolor underprint. Microscope at center, double portrait of O. Cruz at right. The first 4 digits of the serial number represent the series number. Back: Double view of the O. Cruz Institute at center. Watermark: O. Cruz. Printer: CdM-B.		
	a. Signature 21. Series #1-1673 (1984).	3.75	20.00
	b. Signature 22 (reversed). Series #1674-2170 (1985).	5.00	15.00
	c. Signature 22 (corrected). Series #2171-3248 (1985).	1.75	7.00
	d. Signature 23. Series #3249-3290 (1986).	2.00	12.50

205	100,000 Cruzeiros	VF	UNC
	ND (1985). Black on blue, gold and multicolor underprint. Electric power station at center, double portrait Pres. J. Kubitschek at right. Signature 23. Series number 1-4347. The first 4 digits of the serial number represent the series number. Back: Double view of old and modern buildings at center. Watermark: Pres. J. Kubitschek. Printer: CdM-B.		
	a. Issued note.	2.50	5.50
	s. Specimen.	—	150.

1986 ND Provisional Issue

Feb. 1986 Monetary Reform: 1 Cruzado = 1,000 Cruzeiros

206	10 Cruzados on 10,000 Cruzeiros	VF	UNC
	ND (1986). Black circular overprint: *Banco Central Do Brasil* and new currency unit on #203. Signature 23. Series number 3697-5124.	.20	1.50

207	50 Cruzados on 50,000 Cruzeiros	VF	UNC
	ND (1986). Black circular overprint: *Banco Central Do Brasil* and new currency unit on #204. Signature 23. Series number 3291-4592.	.75	2.50

208	100 Cruzados on 100,000 Cruzeiros	VF	UNC
	ND (1986). Black circular overprint: *Banco Central Do Brasil* and new currency unit on #205. Signature 23. Series number 4348-6209.		
	a. Issued note.	.75	5.00
	s. Specimen. Overprint: *MODELO* and pin hole cancelled.	—	150.

1986 ND Issue

209	10 Cruzados	VF	UNC
	ND (1986-87). Brown on multicolor underprint. Desk top at center, portrait of Rui Barbosa at center right. Back: Conference scene. Watermark: Rui Barbosa. Printer: CdM-B.		
	a. Signature 23. Series #1-1155 (1986).	.20	1.00
	b. Signature 25. Series #1156-1505 (1987).	.15	.50

210	50 Cruzados	VF	UNC
	ND (1986-88). Purple on multicolor underprint. Microscope at center, O. Cruz at right. Back: Cruz Institute at center. Watermark: O. Cruz. Printer: CdM-B.		
	a. Signature 23. Series #1-1617 (1986).	.20	.75
	b. Signature 25. Series #1618-2044 (1987).	.20	.75
	c. Signature 26. Series #2045-2051 (1988).	15.00	100.

211	100 Cruzados	VF	UNC
	ND (1986-88). Black on blue, gold and multicolor underprint. Electric power station at center, Pres. J. Kubitschek at right. Back: Old and modern buildings at center. Watermark: President J. Kubitschek. Printer: CdM-B.		
	a. Signature 23. Series #1-1176 (1986).	.40	2.00
	b. Signature 24. Series #1177-1582 (1987).	.40	2.00
	c. Signature 25. Series #1583-3045 (1987).	.15	.50
	d. Signature 26. Series #3046-3059 (1988).	3.00	17.50
	s. Specimen. As a. Overprint: *MODELO* and pin hole cancelled.	—	100.

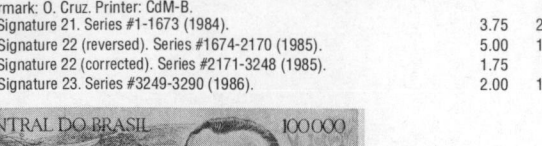

1986 ND Commemorative Issue

#212, Birth Centennial of H. Villa-Lobos

212	**500 Cruzados**	VF	UNC
	ND (1986). Blue-green on green and multicolor underprint. H. Villa-Lobos at center. Back: Villa-Lobos conducting at left center. Watermark: H. Villa-Lobos. Printer: CdM-B.		
	a. Signature 23. Series #1-2352 (1986).	.50	3.00
	b. Signature 24. Series #2353-2842 (1987).	.50	2.50
	c. Signature 25. Series #2843-7504 (1987).	.15	.50
	d. Signature 26. Series #7505-8309 (1988).	.20	1.00
	s. Specimen. As a. Overprint: *MODELO* and pin hole cancelled.	—	100.

1987 ND Regular Issue

213	**1000 Cruzados**	VF	UNC
	ND (1987-88). Purple and brown-violet on multicolor underprint. J. Machado at right. Series numbers are first 4 digits of serial number. Back: Street scene from old Rio de Janeiro. Watermark: J. Machado. Printer: CdM-B.		
	a. Signature 25. Series #1-2744 (1987).	1.00	6.00
	b. Signature 26. Series #2745-9919 (1988)	.15	.75
	s. Specimen. As a. Overprint: *MODELO* and pin hole cancelled.	—	100.

214	**5000 Cruzados**	VF	UNC
	ND (1988). Blue on multicolor underprint. Portion of mural at left center, C. Portinari at right. Series numbers are first 4 digits of serial number.Signature 26. Series # 1-1757. Back: Portinari painting at center. Watermark: C. Portinari. Printer: CdM-B.		
	a. Issued note.	1.00	4.00
	s. Specimen. Overprint: *MODELO* and pin hole cancelled.	—	125.

215	**10,000 Cruzados**	VF	UNC
	ND (1989). Red and brown on multicolor underprint. C. Chagas at right. Signature 26. Series # 1-1841. Series numbers are first 4 digits of serial number. Back: Chagas with lab instruments. Watermark: C. Chagas. Printer: CdM-B.		
	a. Issued note.	1.00	7.00
	s. Specimen. Overprint: *MODELO* and pin hole cancelled.	—	175.

1989 ND Provisional Issue

Jan. 1989 Monetary Reform: 1 Cruzado Novo = 1,000 Cruzados

216	**1 Cruzado Novo on 1000 Cruzados**	VF	UNC
	ND (1989). Purple and brown-violet on multicolor underprint. J. Machado at right. Series numbers are first 4 digits of serial number. Back: Street scene from old Rio de Janeiro. Overprint: Black triangular overprint of new currency unit. Watermark: J. Machado. Printer: CdM-B.		
	a. Signature 26. Series # prefix A, #9920-9999 (1989).	.50	2.00
	b. Signature 26. Series # prefix B, #1-1617 (1989).	.15	.50
	c. As b. signature 27. Series #1618-1792 (1989).	.25	1.25

217	**5 Cruzados Novos on 5000 Cruzados**	VF	UNC
	ND (1989). Blue on multicolor underprint. Portion of mural at left center, C. Portinari at right. Signature 26. Series number 1-1757. Series numbers are first 4 digits of serial number. Back: Portinari painting at center. Overprint: Black triangular overprint of new currency unit. Printer: CdM-B.		
	a. Signature 26. Series #1758-3531 (1989).	.50	1.75
	b. Signature 27. Series #3532-3818 (1989).	.50	1.75

218	**10 Cruzados Novos on 10,000 Cruzados**	VF	UNC
	ND (1989-90). Red and brown on multicolor underprint. C. Chagas at right. Signature 26. Series number 1-1841. Series numbers are first 4 digits of serial number. Back: Chagas with lab instruments. Overprint: Black triangular overprint of new currency unit. Watermark: C. Chagas. Printer: CdM-B.		
	a. Signature 26. Series #1842-4171 (1989).	.25	1.50
	b. Signature 27. Series #4172-4502 (1990).	.50	2.50

1989 ND Issue

219 50 Cruzados Novos

ND (1989-90). Brown and black on multicolor underprint. C. Drummond de Andrade at right. Back: Black, red-brown and blue. de Andrade writing poetry. Watermark: Liberty head. Printer: CdM-B.

	VF	UNC
a. Signature 26. Series #1-3340 (1989).	.25	1.50
b. Signature 27. Series #3341-3358 (1990).	2.00	15.00

220 100 Cruzados Novos

ND (1989). Orange, purple and green on multicolor underprint. C. Meireles at right. Back: Brown, black and multicolor. Child reading and people dancing. Watermark: Liberty head. Printer: CdM-B.

	VF	UNC
a. Signature 26. Series #1-6772.	.75	1.50
b. Signature 27. Series #6773-8794.	1.00	5.00
s. Specimen. As a. Overprint: *MODELO* and pin hole cancelled.	—	125.

1989 ND Commemorative Issue

#221, Republic Centennial

221 200 Cruzados Novos

ND (1989). Blue and black on multicolor underprint. Political leaders at center, sculpture of the Republic at center right, arms at right. Signature 27. Series # 1-1964. Back: Oil painting *Patria* by P. Bruno with flag being embroidered by a family. Watermark: Liberty head. Printer: CdM-B.

	VF	UNC
a. Issued note.	1.00	5.00
s. Specimen. Overprint: *MODELO* and pin hole cancelled.	—	175.

1990 ND Issue

222 500 Cruzados Novos

ND (1990). Green and purple on multicolor underprint. Orchids at center, A. Ruschi at right. Signature 27. Series # 1-3700. Back: Light orange, purple and blue. Swallow-tailed hummingbird, orchids and Ruschi at center. Watermark: Liberty head.

	VF	UNC
a. Issued note.	2.00	7.50
s. Specimen. Overprint: *MODELO* and pin hole cancelled.	—	200.

1990 ND Provisional Issue

March 1990 Monetary Reform: 1 Cruzeiro = 1 Cruzado Novo

223 50 Cruzeiros on 50 Cruzados Novos

	VF	UNC
ND (1990). Brown and black on multicolor underprint. C. Drummond de Andrade at right. Series number 3359-5338. Signature 27. Back: Black, red-brown and blue. C. Drummond de Andrade writing poetry. Overprint: Black rectangular overprint of new currency unit. Watermark: Liberty head. Printer: CdM-B. UV: fibers fluoresce blue.	.15	.50

224 100 Cruzeiros on 100 Cruzados Novos

ND (1990). Orange, purple and green on multicolor underprint. C. Meireles at right. Signature 27. Back: Brown, black and multicolor. Child reading and people dancing. Overprint: Black rectangular overprint of new currency unit. Watermark: Liberty head. Printer: CdM-B.

	VF	UNC
a. Series #8601.	50.00	140.
b. Series #8795-9447.	.40	1.50

225 200 Cruzeiros on 200 Cruzados Novos

ND (1990). Blue and black on multicolor underprint. Political leaders at center, sculpture of the Republic at center right, arms at right. Signature 27. Back: Oil painting *Patria* by P. Bruno with flag being embroidered by a family. Overprint: Black rectangular overprint of new currency unit. Watermark: Liberty head. Printer: CdM-B. UV: fibers fluoresce blue.

	VF	UNC
a. Series #1725.	75.00	175.
b. Series #1965-2668.	.50	1.00

226 500 Cruzeiros on 500 Cruzados Novos

ND (1990). Green and pruple on multicolor underprint. Orchids at center, A. Ruschi at right. Signature 27. Back: Light orange, purple and blue. Swallow-tailed hummingbird, orchids and Ruschi at center. Overprint: Black rectangular overprint of new currency unit. Watermark: Liberty head.

	VF	UNC
a. Series #3111.	35.00	100.
b. Series #3701-7700.	.25	.75

1992 ND Emergency Issue

227 5000 Cruzeiros — VF | UNC

ND (1990). Deep olive-green and deep brown on multicolor underprint. Liberty head in green at right. Signature 28. Series # 1-1520. Back: Arms at left. Watermark: Liberty head. Printer: CdM-B. — .75 | 2.00

1990-93 ND Regular Issue

228 100 Cruzeiros — VF | UNC

ND (1990). Orange, purple and green on multicolor underprint. C. Meireles at right. Signature 28. Series # 1-1045. Back: Brown, black and multicolor. Child reading and people dancing. Watermark: Liberty head. Printer: CdM-B. UV: fibers fluoresce blue. — .20 | .50

229 200 Cruzeiros — VF | UNC

ND (1990). Blue and black on multicolor underprint. Political leaders at center, sculpture of the Republic at center right, arms at right. Signature 28. Series # 1-1646. Back: Oil painting "Patria" by P. Bruno with flag being embroidered by a family. Watermark: Liberty head. Printer: CdM-B. UV: fibers fluoresce blue. — .15 | .50

230 500 Cruzeiros — VF | UNC

ND (1990). Green and purple on multicolor underprint. Orchids at center, A. Ruschi at right. Signature 28. Series # 1-0210. Back: Light orange, purple and blue. Swallow-tailed hummingbird, orchids and Ruschi at center. Watermark: Liberty head. Printer: CdM-B.

	VF	UNC
a. Issued note.	.75	3.00
s. Specimen. Overprint: *MODELO* and pin hole cancelled.	—	125.

231 1000 Cruzeiros — VF | UNC

ND (1990-91). Dark brown, brown, violet and black on multicolor underprint. C. Rondon at right, native hut at center, map of Brazil in background. Back: Two Indian children and local food from Amazonia. Watermark: Liberty head. Printer: CdM-B. UV: fibers fluoresce blue.

	VF	UNC
a. Signature 28. Upper Signature title: *MINISTRO DA ECONOMIA,...* Series #1-4268 (1990).	.40	2.50
b. Upper signature title: *MINISTRA DA ECONOMIA,...* Series #4269-6796 (1990).	.30	2.00
c. Signature 29. Series #6797-8453 (1991).	.15	.50
s. Specimen. As b. Overprint: MODELO and pin hole cancelled.	—	150.

232 5000 Cruzeiros — VF | UNC

ND (1990-93). Blue-black, black and deep brown on light blue and multicolor underprint. C. Gomes at center right, Brazilian youths at center. Back: Statue of Gomes seated, grand piano in background at center. Printer: CdM-B. UV: fibers fluoresce blue.

	VF	UNC
a. Signature 28. Series #1-4489 (1990).	.50	2.00
b. Signature 29. Series #4490-5501 (1992).	.25	1.50
c. Signature 30. Series #5502-6041 (1993).	.20	1.00
s. Specimen. As a. Overprint: *MODELO* and pin hole cancelled.		150.

233 10,000 Cruzeiros — VF | UNC

ND (1991-93). Black and brown-violet on multicolor underprint. Extracting poisonous venom at center, V. Brazil at right. Back: One snake swallowing another at center. Watermark: V. Brazil. Printer: CdM-B. UV: fibers fluoresce blue.

	VF	UNC
a. Signature 28. Series #1-3136 (1991).	.50	3.00
b. Signature 29. Series #3137-6937 (1992).	.25	1.25
c. Signature 30. Series #6938-7365 (1993).	.15	1.00

234 50,000 Cruzeiros

ND (1992). Dark brown and red-orange on multicolor underprint. C. Cascudo at center right, two men on raft in background at left center. Signature 29. Series # 1-6289. Back: Folklore dancers at left center. Printer: CdM-B. UV: fibers fluoresce blue.

	VF	UNC
a. Issued note.	.25	1.25
s. Specimen. Overprint: *MODELO* and pin hole cancelled.	—	125.

235 100,000 Cruzeiros

ND (1992-93). Brown, green and purple on multicolor underprint. Hummingbird feeding nestlings at center, butterfly at right. Back: Butterfly at left, Iguacú cataract at center. Watermark: Sculptured head of Brasilia. Printer: CdM-B.

	VF	UNC
a. Signature 29. Series #1-6052 (1992).	.50	6.00
b. Signature 30. Series #6053-6226 (1993).	.50	5.00
c. Signature 31. Series #6227-6290 (1993).	.50	5.00
d. Signature 32. Series #6291-6733 (1993).	.25	1.25
s. Specimen. As a. Overprint: *MODELO* and pin hole cancelled.	—	150.

236 500,000 Cruzeiros

ND (1993). Red-violet, brown and deep purple on multicolor underprint. M. de Andrade at right, native Indian art in underprint. Back: Building; de Andrade teaching children at center. Watermark: Sculptured head of Brasilia. Printer: CdM-B.

	VF	UNC
a. Signature 30. Series #1-3410 (1993).	2.50	12.00
b. Signature 31. Series #3411-4404 (1993).	2.00	10.00
c. Signature 32. Series #4405-8291 (1993).	.50	4.00

1993 ND Provisional Issue

August 1993 Monetary Reform: 1 Cruzeiro Real = 1,000 Cruzeiros

237 50 Cruzeiros Reais on 50,000 Cruzeiros — VF .20, UNC 1.00

ND (1993). Dark brown and red-orange on multicolor underprint. C. Cascudo at center right, two men on raft in background at left center. Signature 32. Series # 6290-6591. Back: Folklore dancers at left center. Overprint: Black circle overprint of new value on face of #234. Printer: CdM-B.

238 100 Cruzeiros Reais on 100,000 Cruzeiros — VF .20, UNC 1.00

ND (1993). Brown, green and purple on multicolor underprint. Hummingbird feeding nestlings at center, butterfly at right. Signature 32. Series # 6291-6733. Back: Butterfly at left, Iguacú cataract at center. Overprint: Black circle of new value on face of #235d. Series #6734-7144. Watermark: Sculptured head of *Brasilia*.

239 500 Cruzeiros Reais on 500,000 Cruzeiros

ND (1993). Red-violet, brown and deep purple on multicolor underprint. M. de Andrade at right, native Indian art in underprint. Signature 32. Series # 4405-8291. Back: Building; de Andrade teaching children a center. Overprint: Black circle overprint of new value on face of #236c. Watermark: Sculpture head of *Brasilia*. UV: fibers fluoresce blue.

	VF	UNC
a. Series prefix A, #8292-9999.	.50	3.00
b. Series prefix B, #1-717.	.25	2.25

1993-94 ND Issue

240 1000 Cruzeiros Reais — VF .50, UNC 2.00

ND (1993). Black, dark blue and brown on multicolor underprint. A. Teixeira at center right. "Parque" school at left center. Signature 33. Series numbers 1-2515. Back: Children and workers. Watermark: Sculptured head of *Brasilia*. Printer: CdM-B.

241	**5000 Cruzeiros Reais**	VF	UNC
	ND (1993). Black, red-brown and dark olive-green on multicolor underprint. Gaucho at acenter right, urins of São Miguel das Missões at left center. Signature 33. Series numbers 1-9999. Back: Vertical format; gaucho on horseback roping steer at center. Watermark: Sculptured head of *Brasilia*. Printer: CdM-B.	2.50	12.50

242	**50,000 Cruzeiros Reais**	VF	UNC
	ND (1994). Deep purple and brown-violet on multicolor underprint. Dancer at left center, Baiana at center right. Signature 33. Series numbers 1-1200. Back: Vertical format; Baina do Acarajé priparing food at center. Watermark: Sculptured head of *Brasilia*. Printer: CdM-B.	25.00	50.00

1994 ND Issue

July 1994 Monetary Reform: 1 Real = 2750 Cruzeiros Reals

243	**1 Real**	VF	UNC
	ND (1994-97). Black, olive-green and blue-green on aqua and pale green underprint. Sculpture of the Republic at center right. Series # is the first 4 digits of serial #. Back: Vertical format; white-necked jacobin hummingbirds at center. Printer: CdM-B or with additional imprint. 140x65mm.		
	a. Signature 33. without text *DEUS SEJA LOUVADO*, Series #1-2409 (1994). Serial #A-A.	1.00	6.00
	b. Signature 34. Series 2410-3833 (1994).	1.00	6.00
	c. Signature 34. with text: *DEUS SEJA LOUVADO* at lower left Series #3834-6568.	1.00	6.00
	d. Signature 35. Series 6569-7019.	1.00	9.00
	e. Signature 37. Series 7020-9999.	1.00	5.00
	f. Signature 37. Series 0001-0072, serial #A-B.	2.00	17.50

243A	**1 Real**	VF	UNC
	ND (1997-). Black,olive-green on aqua and pale green underprint. Sculpture of the Republic at center right. Series # is the first 4 digits of serial #. Serial # A-B, B-B or C-B. Back: Vertical format. White-necked jacobin hummingbirds at center. Watermark: Flag. Printer: CdM-B or with additional imprint. UV: fibers fluoresce blue.		
	a. Signature 37. Series #0001-3247.	1.00	4.00
	b. Signature 38. Series #3248-7561.	1.00	4.00
	c. Signature 39. Series #7562-8948.	1.00	6.00
	d. Signature 39. Series #8949-9999.	1.00	4.00
	e. Signature 39. Series #0001-9999, series B-B.	FV	3.00
	f. Signature 39. Serial C-B. Series #0001-3382.	FV	2.00
	g. Signature 40. Series 3383-4505.	FV	2.00

244	**5 Reais**	VF	UNC
	ND(1994-97). Violet, dark brown and blue on lilac underprint. Sculpture of the Republic at center right. Series # is the first 4 digits of serial #. Serial # A-A. Back: Vertical format: great egret at center. Watermark: Republic. Printer: CdM-B or with additional imprint. 140x65mm.		
	a. Signature 33. without text: *DEUS SEJA LOUVADO*. Series #0001-1411.	5.00	22.50
	b. Signature 33. without text. Printer: G & D. Series A-B,#1-1000.	20.00	55.00
	c. Signature 34. without text. Series A-A: #1412-1609.	50.00	130.
	d. Signature 34. with text: *DEUS SEJA LOUVADO. Series #1610-4093.*	5.00	17.50
	e. Signature 35. with text. Series 4094-5378.	5.00	17.50
	f. Signature 36. with text. Series 5379-5798.	5.00	22.50
	g. Signature 37. with text. Series #5799-8232.	5.00	17.50

244A	**5 Reais**		
	ND (1997-). Violet, dark brown and blue on lilac underprint. Sculpture of the Republic at center right. Series # is the first 4 digits of serial #. Back: Vertical format. Great egret at center. Watermark: Flag. Printer: CdM-B or with additional imprint. 140x65mm.		
	a. Signature 37. Series #0001-1504.	5.00	17.50
	b. Signature 38. Series #1505-3034.	5.00	17.50
	c. Signature 39. Series #3035-3196.	7.50	22.50
	d. Signature 39. Series #3197-8817.	2.00	6.00
	e. Signature 40. Series #8818-9999.	FV	5.00
	f. Signature 40. Series #B0001-5158.	FV	5.00
	g. Signature 41. 1st signature variety. Series #B5159-B7387.	FV	5.00
	h. Signatrue 41. 2nd signature variety. Series #B7388-.	FV	5.00

245 10 Reais VF UNC

ND (1994). Dark brown, brown-violet and brown-orange on lilac and pale orange underprint. Sculpture of the Republic at center right. Series # is the first 4 digits of serial #. Back: Vertical format. Macaw at center. Watermark: Republic. Printer: CdM-B or with additional imprint. 140x65mm.

	VF	UNC
a. Signature 33. without text: *DEUS SEJA LOUVADO*. Series A-A: #1-0713.	10.00	45.00
b. Signature 33. Printer: TDLR. Series #A-B: #0001-1200.	15.00	55.00
c. Signature 34. without text: *DEUS SEJA LOUVADO* at lower left Series #0714-1817.	10.00	30.00
d. Signature 34. with text at lower left Series #1818-3403.	10.00	30.00
e. Signature 35. Series #3404-6102.	10.00	30.00
f. Signature 36. Series #6103-6714.	15.00	55.00
g. Signature 37. Series #6715-9999.	10.00	30.00
h. Signature 37. Series #0001-4844. Serial A-B.	15.00	55.00

245A 10 Reais VF UNC

ND (1997-). Dark brown, brown-violet and brown-orange on lilac and pale orange underprint. Sculpture of the Republic at center right. Series # is the first 4 digits of serial #. Back: Vertical format. Macaw at center. Watermark: Flag. Printer: CdM-B or with additional imprint. UV: fibers fluoresce blue. 140x65mm.

	VF	UNC
a. Signature 37. Series #0001-4571. Serial A-C.	7.00	22.50
b. Signature 38. Series #4572-9179.	7.00	22.50
c. Signature 39. Series #9180-9999.	7.00	22.50
d. Signature 39. Series #0001-0075. Serial B-C.	10.00	27.50
e. Signature 39. Series #0076-9999.	5.00	12.50
f. Signature 39. Serial C-C. Series #0001-1136.	FV	8.00
g. Signature 40. Series #1137-9999.	FV	8.00
h. Signature 40. Series #D0001-D3438.	FV	8.00
i. Signature 41. 1st signature variety. Series #D3439-D9100.	FV	8.00
j. Signature 41. 2nd signature variety. Series #D9101-D9999.	FV	8.00
k. Signature 41. 2nd signature variety. Series #E0001-.	FV	8.00

246 50 Reais VF UNC

ND (1994-). Dark brown and red-brown on multicolor underprint. Sculpture of the Republic at center right. Series # is the first 4 digits of serial #. Back: Vertical format, Jaguar. Printer: CdM-B or with additional imprint. 140x65mm.

	VF	UNC
a. Signature 33. Without text: *DEUS SEJA LOUVADO*. Series A-A: #0001-1249.	50.00	115.
b. Signature 33. Without text. Printer: F-CO. Series A-B: #0001-0400.	50.00	165.
c. Signature 34. Without text. Series #1250-1338.	40.00	135.
d. Signature 34. With text. Series #1339-1438.	50.00	165.
e. Signature 36. Series #1439-1636.	100.	550.
f. Signature 37. Series #1637-8405.	50.00	120.
g. Signature 38. Series #8406-9999.	40.00	135.
h. Signature 38. Series #0001-1004. Serial #B-A.	40.00	135.
i. Signature 39. Series #1005-1483. Serial #B-A.	40.00	135.
j. Signature 39. Series #1484-9057.	25.00	60.00
k. Signature 40. Series #9058-9999.	FV	30.00
l. Signature 40. Series #C0001-C8342.	FV	30.00
m. Signature 41. 1st signature variety. Series #C8343-C9999.	FV	30.00
n. Signature 41. 1st signature variety. Series #D0001-D2492.	FV	30.00
o. Signature 41. 2nd signature variety. Series #D2493-.	FV	30.00

247 100 Reais VF UNC

ND(1994-). Blue-green and purple on multicolor underprint. Sculpture of the Republic at center right. Series # is the first 4 digits of serial #. Back: Vertical format. Garoupa fish. Printer: CdM-B or with additional imprint. 140x65mm.

	VF	UNC
a. Signature 33. Without text: *DEIS SEJA LOUVADO*. Series #0001-1198.	100.	175.
b. Signature 34. Series #1199-1201.	150.	325.
c. Signature 34. Series #1202-1301. With text: *DEUS SEJA LOUVADO* at lower left.	125.	225.
d. Signature 37. Series #A1302-A1310.	125.	225.
e. Signature 41. 1st signature variety. Series #A1311-A2818.	125.	225.
f. Signature 41. 2nd signature variety. Series #A2819-.	125.	225.

2000 Commemorative Issue

#248, 500th Anniversary of the Discovery of Brazil

		VF	UNC
248	**10 Reais**		
	ND (2000). Dark Blue, blue and orange. Pedro Alvares Cabral at center, compass to left. Back: Map and many portraits. Polymer plastic. 140x65mm.		
	a. Name as: *PEDRO A. CABRAL.* Series #0001-0586.	FV	15.00
	b. Name as: *PEDRO ALVARES CABRAL.* Series #0587-2536.	FV	10.00

2001-02 Issue

		VF	UNC
249	**2 Reais**		
	ND (2001-). Blue-green and black on multicolor underprint. Back: Tartaruga Marinha turtles. UV: fibers fluoresce blue. 140x65mm.		
	a. Signature 39. Series #0001-2798.	FV	2.50
	b. Signature 40. Series #2799-7980.	FV	2.50
	c. Signature 41. 1st signature variety. Series #A7981-A9999.	FV	2.50
	d. Signature 41. 1st signature variety. Series #B0001-B2036.	FV	2.50
	e. Signature 41. 2nd signature variety. Series #B2037-.	FV	2.50

		VF	UNC
250	**20 Reais**		
	ND (2002-). Yellow and rose on multicolor underprint. Back: Lion monkey. 140x65mm.		
	a. Signature 39. Series #0001-2125.	FV	12.50
	b. Signature 40. Series #2126-7521.	FV	10.00
	c. Signature 41. 1st signature variety. Series #A7522-A9398.	FV	10.00
	d. Signature 41. 2nd signature variety. Series #A9399-A9999.	FV	10.00
	e. Signature 41. 2nd signature variety. Series #B0001-.	FV	10.00

Republica Federativa do Brazil

Banco Central do Brazil

2003 Issue

		VF	UNC
251	**1 Real**		
	ND (2003-). Black, olive-green and blue-green on aqua and pale green underprint. Sculpture of the Republic at center right. Series # is first 4 digits of serial #. Serial # A-C. Back: Vertical format. White-necked jacobin hummingbirds at center. Watermark: Flag. Printer: CdM-B. 140x65mm.		
	a. Signature 40. Series 0001-3995.	FV	2.00
252	**2 Reais**		
	2010. Sculpture of the Republic. Back: Turtles. Watermark: Turtles and 2. 121x65mm.	FV	2.50
253	**5 Reais**		
	ND; 2010. Violet. Sculpture of the Republic. Back: Heron. Watermark: Heron and 5. 128x65mm.		
	a. ND (2005).	FV	5.00
	b. 2010.	FV	5.00

		VF	UNC
254	**10 Reais**		
	2010. Brown and rose on multicolor underprint Republica head at right. Back: Macaw at left, two in flight at right. 135x65mm.	FV	8.00

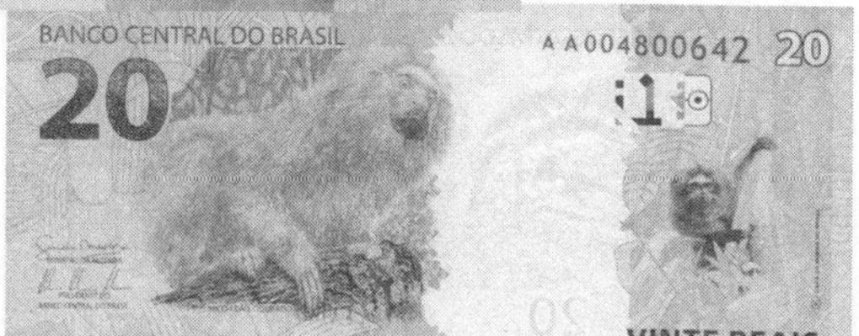

		VF	UNC
255	**20 Reais**		
	ND. Orange on yellow and multicolor underprint Republica head at right. Back: Lion Monkey at left and right. 156x70mm.	FV	10.00

		VF	UNC
256	**50 Reais** 2010. Dark brown. 149x70mm.	FV	25.00

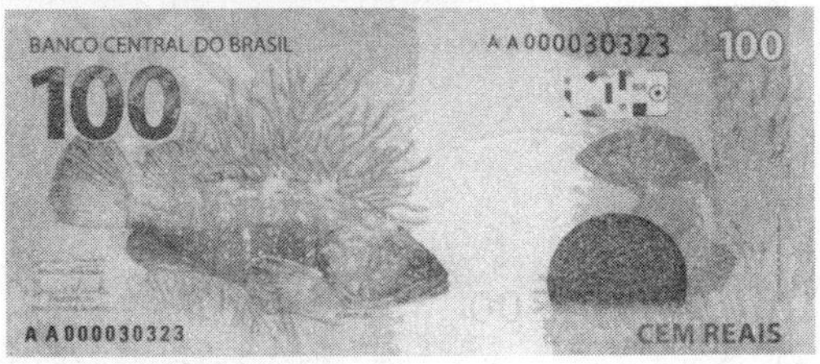

		VF	UNC
257	**100 Reais** 2010. Blue on multicolor underprint. 156x70mm.	FV	50.00

The British Caribbean Territories (Eastern Group), a currency board formed in 1950, comprised the British West Indies territories of Trinidad and Tobago; Barbados; the Leeward Islands of Anguilla, St. Christopher, Nevis and Antigua; the Windward Islands of St. Lucia, Dominica, St. Vincent and Grenada; British Guiana and the British Virgin Islands.

As time progressed, the members of this Eastern Group varied.

For later issues see East Caribbean States listings in Volume 3, Modern issues.

RULERS:
British

MONETARY SYSTEM:
1 Dollar = 100 Cents

British Administration

British Caribbean Territories, Eastern Group

1953 Issue

		VF	UNC
7	**1 Dollar** 1953-64. Red on multicolor underprint. Map at lower left, portrait of Queen Elizabeth II at right. Back: Arms in all four corners. Printer: BWC.		
	a. Watermark: Sailing ship. 5.1.1953.	100.	400.
	b. Watermark: Queen Elizabeth II. 1.3.1954-2.1.1957.	40.00	275.
	c. 2.1.1958-2.1.1964.	40.00	275.

		VF	UNC
8	**2 Dollars** 1953-64. Blue on multicolor underprint. Map at lower left, portrait of Queen Elizabeth II at right. Back: Arms in all four corners. Printer: BWC.		
	a. Watermark: Sailing ship. 5.1.1953.	550.	1750.
	b. Watermark: Queen Elizabeth II. 1.3.1954-1.7.1960.	100.	700.
	c. 2.1.1961-2.1.1964.	100.	700.

9 **5 Dollars** — VF / UNC

1953-64. Green on multicolor underprint. Map at lower left, portrait of Queen Elizabeth II at right. Back: Arms in all four corners. Printer: BWC.

	VF	UNC
a. Watermark: Sailing ship. 5.1.1953.	300.	1250.
b. Watermark: Queen Elizabeth II. 3.1.1955-2.1.1959.	125.	1000.
c. 2.1.1961-2.1.1964.	100.	900.
s. As b. Specimen. Perforated: *SPECIMEN.*	—	750.

10 **10 Dollars** — VF / UNC

1953-64. Brown on multicolor underprint. Map at lower left, portrait of Queen Elizabeth II at right. Back: Arms in all four corners. Printer: BWC.

	VF	UNC
a. Watermark: Sailing ship. 5.1.1953.	400.	—
b. Watermark: Queen Elizabeth II. 3.1.1955-2.1.1959.	250.	2000.
c. 2.1.1961; 2.1.1962; 2.1.1964.	200.	1800.

11 **20 Dollars**

1953-64. Purple on multicolor underprint. Map at lower left, portrait of Queen Elizabeth II at right. Back: Arms in all four corners. Printer: BWC.

	VF	UNC
a. Watermark: Sailing ship. 5.1.1953.	600.	—
b. Watermark: Queen Elizabeth II. 2.1.1957-2.1.1964.	300.	—

12 **100 Dollars**

1953-63. Black on multicolor underprint. Map at lower left, portrait of Queen Elizabeth II at right. Back: Arms in all four corners. Printer: BWC.

	VF	UNC
a. Watermark: Sailing ship. 5.1.1953.	6000.	—
b. Watermark: Queen Elizabeth II. 1.3.1954.	4000.	—
c. 2.1.1957.	8800.	—
d. 2.1.1963.	4000.	—
s. As b. Specimen.	—	2500.

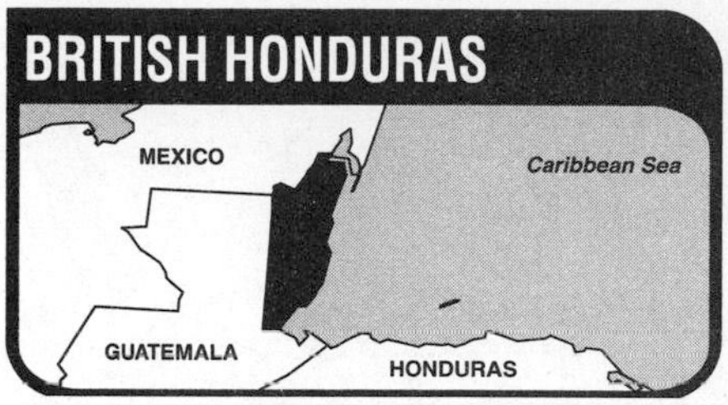

The former British colony of British Honduras is now Belize, a self-governing dependency of the United Kingdom situated in Central America south of Mexico and east and north of Guatemala, has an area of 8,867 sq. mi. (22,965 sq. km.) and a population of 209,000. Capital: Belmopan. Sugar, citrus fruits, chicle and hard woods are exported.

The area, site of the ancient Mayan civilization, was sighted by Columbus in 1502, and settled by shipwrecked English seamen in 1638. British buccaneers settled the former capital of Belize in the 17th century. Britain claimed administrative right over the area after the emancipation of Central America from Spain, and declared it a colony subordinate to Jamaica in 1862. It established as the separate Crown Colony of British Honduras in 1884. The anti-British People's United Party, which attained power in 1954, won a constitution, effective in 1964 which established self-government under a British appointed governor. British Honduras became Belize on June 1, 1973, following the passage of a surprise bill by the Peoples United Party, but the constitutional relationship with Britain remained unchanged.

In Dec. 1975, the U.N. General Assembly adopted a resolution supporting the right of the people of Belize to self-determination, and asking Britain and Guatemala to renew their negotiations on the future of Belize. Belize obtained independence on Sept. 21, 1981.

RULERS:

British

MONETARY SYSTEM:

1 Dollar = 100 Cents

British Honduras

Government of British Honduras

1952-53 Issue

28 **1 Dollar** — VF / UNC

1953-73. Green on multicolor underprint. Arms at left, portrait of Queen Elizabeth II at right.

	VF	UNC
a. 15.4.1953-1.10.1958.	125.	500.
b. 1.1.1961-1.5.1969.	75.00	400.
c. 1.6.1970-1.1.1973.	75.00	300.
s. As a, b, c. Specimen. Overprint: *SPECIMEN,* Punch hole cancelled.	—	100.

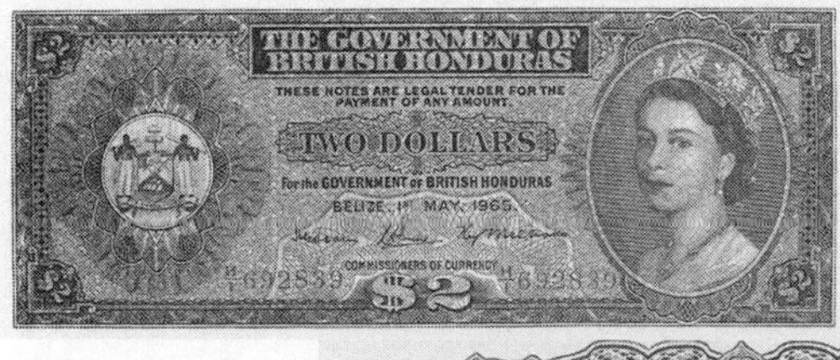

29 **2 Dollars** — VF / UNC

1953-73. Purple on multicolor underprint. Arms at left, portrait of Queen Elizabeth II at right.

	VF	UNC
a. 15.4.1953-1.10.1958.	100.	750.
b. 1.10.1960-1.5.1965.	50.00	400.
c. 1.1.1971-1.1.1973.	40.00	300.
s. As a, b, c. Specimen. Overprint: *SPECIMEN,* Punch hole cancelled.	—	125.

30	**5 Dollars**	VF	UNC
	1953-73. Red on multicolor underprint. Arms at left, portrait of Queen Elizabeth II at right.		
	a. 15.4.1953-1.10.1958.	125.	1000.
	b. 1.3.1960-1.5.1965.	75.00	650.
	c. 1.1.1970-1.1.1973.	75.00	500.
	s. As a, c. Specimen. Overprint: *SPECIMEN,* Punch hole cancelled.	—	150.

31	**10 Dollars**	VF	UNC
	1958-73. Black on multicolor underprint. Arms at left, portrait of Queen Elizabeth II at right.		
	a. 1.1.1958-1.11.1961.	250.	—
	b. 1.4.1964-1.5.1969.	150.	1250.
	c. 1.1.1971-1.1.1973.	125.	1000.
	s. As a, c. Specimen. Overprint: *SPECIMEN,* Punch hole cancelled.	—	200.

32	**20 Dollars**	VF	UNC
	1952-73. Brown on multicolor underprint. Arms at left, portrait of Queen Elizabeth II at right.		
	a. 1.12.1952-1.10.1958.	500.	—
	b. 1.3.1960-1.5.1969.	350.	2500.
	c. 1.1.1970-1.1.1973.	300.	2250.
	s. As a, c. Specimen. Overprint: *SPECIMEN,* Punch hole cancelled.	—	400.

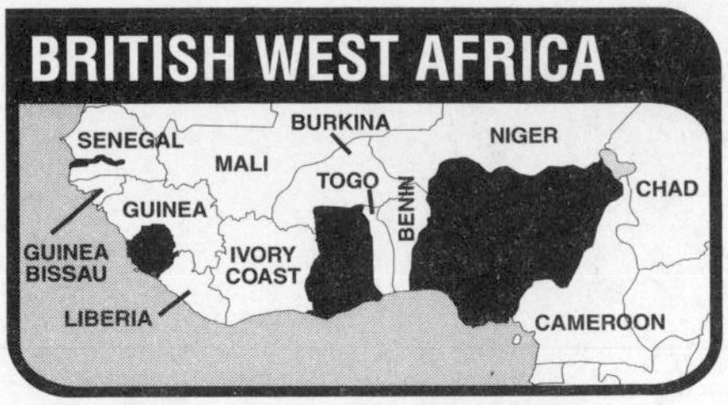

British West Africa was an administrative grouping of the four former British colonies of Gambia, Sierra Leone, Nigeria and Gold Coast (now Ghana). All are now independent republics and members of the British Commonwealth of Nations. These four colonies were supplied with a common currency by the West African Currency Board from 1907 through 1962.

Also see Gambia, Ghana, Nigeria and Sierra Leone for related currency and for individual statistics and history.

MONETARY SYSTEM:

1 Shilling = 12 Pence
1 Pound = 20 Shillings

British Administration

West African Currency Board

1962 Issue

12	**20 Shillings**	VF	UNC
	17.4.1962. Black and red. River scene with palm trees at left. Back: Harvesting scene. Printer: TDLR.	75.00	400.

BRUNEI

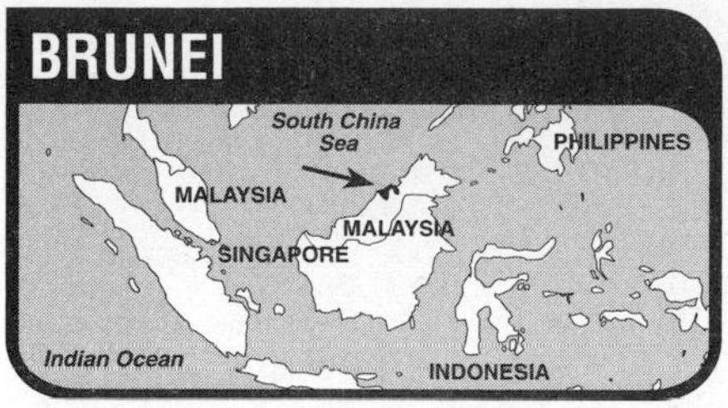

Negara Brunei Darussalam (The State of Brunei), a member of the British Commonwealth is located on the northwest coast of the island of Borneo, has an area of 5,770 sq. km. and a population of 381,370. Capital: Bandar Seri Begawan.

The Sultanate of Brunei's influence peaked between the 15th and 17th centuries when its control extended over coastal areas of northwest Borneo and the southern Philippines. Brunei subsequently entered a period of decline brought on by internal strife over royal succession, colonial expansion of European powers, and piracy. In 1888, Brunei became a British protectorate; independence was achieved in 1984. The same family has ruled Brunei for over six centuries. Brunei benefits from extensive petroleum and natural gas fields, the source of one of the highest per capita GDPs in Asia.

RULERS:

Sultan Sir Omar Ali Saifuddin III, 1950-1967
Sultan Hassanal Bolkiah I, 1967-

MONETARY SYSTEM:

1 Dollar = 100 Sen to 1967
1 Ringgit (Dollar) = 100 Sen, 1967-

STATE

KERAJAAN BRUNEI

GOVERNMENT OF BRUNEI

1967 ISSUE

		VF	UNC
1	**1 Ringgit** 1967. Dark blue on multicolor underprint. Sultan Omar Ali Saifuddin III with military cap at right. Back: Gray and lavender on pink underprint. Mosque. Watermark: Sultan Omar Ali Saifuddin III. Printer: BWC.		
	a. Issued note.	35.00	70.00
	s. Specimen.	—	—

		VF	UNC
2	**5 Ringgit** 1967. Dark green on multicolor underprint. Sultan Omar Ali Saifuddin III with military cap at right. Back: Green on pink underprint. Mosque. Watermark: Sultan Omar Ali Saifuddin III. Printer: BWC.		
	a. Issued note.	50.00	175.
	s. Specimen.	—	—

		VF	UNC
3	**10 Ringgit** 1967. Red on multicolor underprint. Sultan Omar Ali Saifuddin III with military cap at right. Back: Red. Mosque. Watermark: Sultan Omar Ali Saifuddin III. Printer: BWC.		
	a. Issued note.	125.	250.
	s. Specimen.	—	—

		VF	UNC
4	**50 Ringgit** 1967. Dark brown on multicolor underprint. Sultan Omar Ali Saifuddin III with military cap at right. Back: Olive. Mosque. Watermark: Sultan Omar Ali Saifuddin III. Printer: BWC.	200.	400.

		VF	UNC
5	**100 Ringgit** 1967. Blue on multicolor underprint. Sultan Omar Ali Saifuddin III with military cap at right. Back: Purple. Mosque. Watermark: Sultan Omar Ali Saifuddin III. Printer: BWC.	350.	700.

1972-79 ISSUE

		VF	UNC
6	**1 Ringgit** 1972-88. Blue on multicolor underprint. Sultan Hassanal Bolkiah I in military uniform at right. Back: Mosque. Watermark: Sultan Hassanal Bolkiah I. Printer: BWC.		
	a. 1972; 1976; 1978.	6.00	30.00
	b. 1980; 1982.	6.00	22.50
	c. 1983-1986.	5.00	20.00
	d. 1988.	4.00	15.00
	s. Specimen.	—	130.

		VF	UNC
7	**5 Ringgit** 1979-86. Green on multicolor underprint. Sultan Hassanal Bolkiah I in military uniform at right. Back: Mosque. Watermark: Sultan Hassanal Bolkiah I. Printer: BWC.		
	a. 1979; 1981.	15.00	90.00
	b. 1983; 1984; 1986.	12.50	75.00
	s. Specimen.	—	150.

8 **10 Ringgit**

1976-86. Red on multicolor underprint. Sultan Hassanal Bolkiah I in military uniform at right. Back: Mosque. Watermark: Sultan Hassanal Bolkiah I. Printer: BWC.

	VF	UNC
a. 1976; 1981.	30.00	175.
b. 1983; 1986.	27.50	100.
s. Specimen.	—	225.
x. Issued note, double printed.	175.	—

9 **50 Ringgit**

1973-86. Dark brown on multicolor underprint. Sultan Hassanal Bolkiah I in military uniform at right. Back: Mosque. Watermark: Sultan Hassanal Bolkiah I. Printer: BWC.

	VF	UNC
a. 1973.	100.	200.
b. 1977; 1982.	90.00	175.
c. 1981.	110.	150.
d. 1986.	70.00	225.
s. Specimen.	—	400.

10 **100 Ringgit**

1972-88. Blue on multicolor underprint. Sultan Hassanal Bolkiah I in military uniform at right. Back: Mosque. Watermark: Sultan Hassanal Bolkiah I. Printer: BWC.

	VF	UNC
a. 1972; 1976.	100.	400.
b. 1978; 1980.	90.00	375.
c. 1982; 1983; 1988.	80.00	350.
s. Specimen.	—	400.

1979; 1987 Issue

11 **500 Ringgit**

1979; 1987. Orange on multicolor underprint. Sultan Hassanal Bolkiah I in royal uniform at right. Back: Mosque at center. Watermark: Sultan Hassanal Bolkiah I. Printer: BWC.

	VF	UNC
a. 1979.	450.	1500.
b. 1987.	425.	1200.
s. Specimen.	—	1100.

12 **1000 Ringgit**

1979; 1986; 1987. Gray, brown and greenish blue. Sultan Hassanal Bolkiah I in royal uniform at right. Back: Brunei Museum. Watermark: Sultan Hassanal Bolkiah I. Printer: BWC.

	VF	UNC
a. 1979.	900.	2000.
b. 1986-87.	850.	1800.
s. Specimen.	—	1750.

Negara Brunei Darussalam

1989 Issue

13 **1 Ringgit**

1989-95. Purple on multicolor underprint. Sultan Hassanal Bolkiah I at right. Back: Aerial view of Bandar Seri. Watermark: Sultan Hassanal Bolkiah I.

	VF	UNC
a. 1989; 1991; 1992.	2.00	10.00
b. 1994-95.	FV	9.00

14 5 Ringgit — VF | UNC

1989-91; 1993; 1995. Blue-gray and deep green on multicolor underprint. Sultan Hassanal Bolkiah I at right. Back: Houses and boats. Watermark: Sultan Hassanal Bolkiah I. — FV | 20.00

15 10 Ringgit — VF | UNC

1989-92; 1995. Purple and red-orange on multicolor underprint. Sultan Hassanal Bolkiah I at right. Back: Waterfront village with mosque. Watermark: Sultan Hassanal Bolkiah I. — FV | 35.00

16 50 Ringgit — VF | UNC

1989-91;1994; 1995. Brown, olive-green and orange on multicolor underprint. Sultan Hassanal Bolkiah I at right. Back: People in power launch. Watermark: Sultan Hassanal Bolkiah I. Printer: TDLR.

a. Issued note. — FV | 110.

s. 1989. Specimen. Punch hole cancelled. Red oval DLR stamps. — — | 500.

17 100 Ringgit — VF | UNC

1989-92; 1994. Blue and violet on ulticolor underprint. Sultan Hassanal Bolkiah I at right. Back: River scene. Watermark: Sultan Hassanal Bolkiah I. — FV | 200.

18 500 Ringgit — VF | UNC

1989-92. Red-orange, purple olive and black on multicolor underprint. Sultan Hassanal Bolkiah I at right, houses at left center. Back: Padian woman paddling her boat in Kampong Ayer. Watermark: Sultan Hassanal Bolkiah I. — FV | 900.

19 1000 Ringgit — VF | UNC

1989-91. Red-violet, purple, olive and blue-green on multicolor underprint. Sultan Hassanal Bolkiah I at right. Back: Waterfront village of Kampong Ayer and Istana Nurul Iman. Watermark: Sultan Hassanal Bolkiah I. — FV | 1500.

20 10,000 Ringgit — VF | UNC

1989. Dark brown and dark green on multicolor underprint. Sultan Hassanal Bolkiah I at right. Back: Aerial view of Bandar Seri Begawan harbor. Watermark: Sultan Hassanal Bolkiah I.

a. Issued note. — FV | 13,000.

s. Specimen. Overprint: *CONTOH SPECIMEN* in two lines. — — | 4500.

1992 Commemorative Issue

#21, 25th Anniversary of Accession

21	**25 Ringgit**	VF	UNC
	1992. Brown, lilac, green and multicolor. Royal procession at center, Sultan Hassanal Bolkiah I at right. Back: Crown at left, coronation at center. Dates *1967* and *1992* with text at top. Watermark: Sultan Hassanal Bolkiah I.	FV	75.00

1996 Issue

22	**1 Ringgit**	VF	UNC
	1996; 2007; 2008. Blue-black and deep green on multicolor underprint. Sultan Jam'Asr Hassan Bolkiah I at right. Riverside simpur plant at left center. Back: Blue and multicolored. Rain forest waterfall at left center, arms at upper left. Printer: NPA (without imprint). Polymer plastic. 141x69mm.		
	a. 1996.	FV	4.00
	b. 2007.	FV	3.75
	c. 2008.	FV	3.00

23	**5 Ringgit**	VF	UNC
	1996; 2002. Black on green and multicolor underprint. Sultan Jam'Asr Hassan Bolkiah I at right, pitcher plant at left center. Back: Rain forest floor, arms at upper left. Printer: NPA (without imprint). Polymer plastic. 141x69mm.	FV	10.00

24	**10 Ringgit**	VF	UNC
	1996; 1998; 2008. Dark brown and brown on red and multicolor underprint. Sultan Jam'Asr Hassan Bolkiah I at right, purple-leafed forest yam at left center. Back: Rain forest canopy, arms at upper left. Printer: NPA (without imprint). Polymer plastic. 141x69mm.		
	a. 1996.	FV	20.00
	b. 1998.	FV	17.50
	c. 2008.	FV	15.00

25	**50 Ringgit**	VF	UNC
	1996. Brown,blue and purple on multicolor underprint. Sultan Jam'Asr Hassan Bolkiah I at right. Back: Offshore oil rig.	FV	75.00

26	**100 Ringgit**	VF	UNC
	1996. Brown and orange on multicolor underprint. Sultan Jam'Asr Hassan Bolkiah I at right. Back: Brunei International Airport.	FV	125.

27	**500 Ringgit**	VF	UNC
	2000. Deep orange and brown on multicolor underprint. Sultan Jam'Asr Hassan Bolkiah I at right. Back: Bolkiah Mosque.	FV	650.

2004 Commemorative Issue

28 50 Ringgit VF UNC

15.7.2004. Brown, green and blue on multicolor underprint. Kantan medicinal flower at center. Polymer plastic. 158x75mm. FV 100.

29 100 Ringgit VF UNC

15.7.2004; 2008. Brown, orange and yellow on multicolor underprint. Kjojk medicinial flower at center. Polymer plastic. 158x75mm.

	VF	UNC
a. 15.7.2004.	FV	125.
b. 2008. (Date at lower right on back.)	FV	120.

2006-7 Issue

30 1 Ringgit VF UNC

2007. Blue and rose on multicolor underprint. Sultan Jam'Asr Hassan Bolkiah I at right in military uniform. Back: Ariel view of Mosque and buildings. Polymer plastic. FV 3.00

31 500 Ringgit

2006. Brown on green and rose underprint. Sultan Omar Ali Saifuddin III at right, java tea flowers at center. Back: Omar Ali Saifuddin mosque in Bandar Seri Begawan. Watermark: Sultan Omar Ali Saifuddin III Printer: NPA. Polymer plastic. 175x80mm.

a. Issued note.	FV	500.
s. Specimen.	—	650.

32 1000 Ringgit VF UNC

2006. Black and tan on multicolor underprint. Sultan Hassanal Bolkiah at right, akar bilaran flower at center. Back: Ministry of Finance building in Bandar Seri Begawan. Watermark: Sultan Hassanal Bolkiah. Printer: NPA. Polymer plastic. 175x80mm.

a. Issued note.	FV	1000.
s. Specimen.	FV	1250.

33 10,000 Ringgit

2006. Green and brown. Sultan Haji Hassanal Bolkiah at right, pangarus timun dendang flower at center. Back: Legslative Council building in Bandar Seri Begawan at center. Watermark: Sultan Haji Hassanal Bolkiah. Printer: NPA. Polymer plastic. 180x90mm.

a. Issued note.	—	9500.
s. Specimen.	—	10,000.

2007 Commemorative Issue

34 20 Ringgit VF UNC

2007. Orange. Sultan Hassanal Bolkiah at right, Ipomoea pes-capre plant at center. Back: Singapore skyline and Sultan Ali Saifuddien mosque. Watermark: Sultan Hassanal Bolkiah and HB. Polymer plastic. 149x72mm.

a. Serial # prefix A.	FV	30.00
b. Serial # prefix BND.	FV	35.00
s. Specimen.	—	125.

2011 Polymer Issue

35 1 Ringgit VF UNC

2011. Dark and light blue on multicolor underprint. Sultan Hassanal Bolkiah at right. Back: Bandar Seri Begawan at center Polymer plastic. 141x69mm. FV 3.00

36 5 Ringgit — VF | UNC

2011. Olive and green on multicolor underprint. Sultan Hassanal Bolkiah at right, pitcher plant at center. Back: Lapau - Royal Ceremonial Hall at center Polymer plastic. 141x69mm. — FV | 10.00

37 10 Ringgit — VF | UNC

2011. Brown and rose on multicolor underprint. Sultan Hassanal Bolkiah at right, leafed forest yam at center. Back: Jame Asr Hassanii Bolkiah Mosque at center Polymer plastic. 141x69mm. — FV | 18.00

The Republic of Bulgaria (formerly the Peoples Republic of Bulgaria), a Balkan country on the Black Sea in southeastern Europe, has an area of 110,910 sq. km. and a population of 7.26 million. Capital: Sofia. Agriculture remains a key component of the economy but industrialization, particularly heavy industry, has been emphasized since the late 1940's. Machinery, tobacco and cigarettes, wines and spirits, clothing and metals are the chief exports.

The Bulgars, a Central Asian Turkic tribe, merged with the local Slavic inhabitants in the late 7th century to form the first Bulgarian state. In succeeding centuries, Bulgaria struggled with the Byzantine Empire to assert its place in the Balkans, but by the end of the 14th century the country was overrun by the Ottoman Turks. Northern Bulgaria attained autonomy in 1878 and all of Bulgaria became independent from the Ottoman Empire in 1908. Having fought on the losing side in both World Wars, Bulgaria fell within the Soviet sphere of influence and became a People's Republic in 1946. Communist domination ended in 1990, when Bulgaria held its first multiparty election since World War II and began the contentious process of moving toward political democracy and a market economy while combating inflation, unemployment, corruption, and crime. The country joined NATO in 2004 and the EU in 2007.

MONETARY SYSTEM:

1 Lev = 100 Stotinki until 1999
1 Lev = 1,000 "Old" Lev, 1999
Silver Lev = Lev Srebro
Gold Lev = Lev Zlato

PEOPLES REPUBLIC

БЪЛГАРСКА НАРОДНА БАНКА

BULGARIAN NATIONAL BANK

1962 ISSUE

88 1 Lev

1962. Brown-lilac on multicolor underprint. Arms at left. Back: Monument for the Battle of Shipka Pass (1877) at left center. Printer: Gosnak.

	VF	UNC
a. Issued note.	.25	2.00
s1. Specimen. Serial # as 000000.	—	60.00
s2. Specimen. Serial # as 240xxx.	—	50.00

89 2 Leva

1962. Black and blue on green underprint. Arms at left. Back: Woman picking grapes in vineyard at right. Printer: Gosnak.

	VF	UNC
a. Issued note.	.40	3.00
s1. Specimen. Serial # as 000000.	—	60.00
s2. Specimen. Serial # as 040xxx.	—	50.00

90 5 Leva

1962. Red on blue and multicolor underprint. Arms at left. Back: Coastline village. Printer: Gosnak.

	VF	UNC
a. Issued note.	.50	6.00
s1. Specimen. Serial # as 000000.	—	60.00
s2. Specimen. Serial # as 600xxx.	—	50.00

91	10 Leva	VF	UNC
	1962. Black on blue and multicolor underprint. G. Dimitrov at left, arms at upper center. Back: Factory. Printer: Gosnak.		
	a. Issued note.	.50	9.00
	s1. Specimen. Serial # as 000000.	—	80.00
	s2. Specimen. Serial # as 225xxx.	—	70.00

92	20 Leva	VF	UNC
	1962. Brown-lilac on multicolor underprint. G. Dimitrov at left, arms at upper right center. Back: Factory. Printer: Gosnak.		
	a. Issued note.	.50	14.00
	s1. Specimen. Serial # as 000000.	—	90.00

1974 Issue

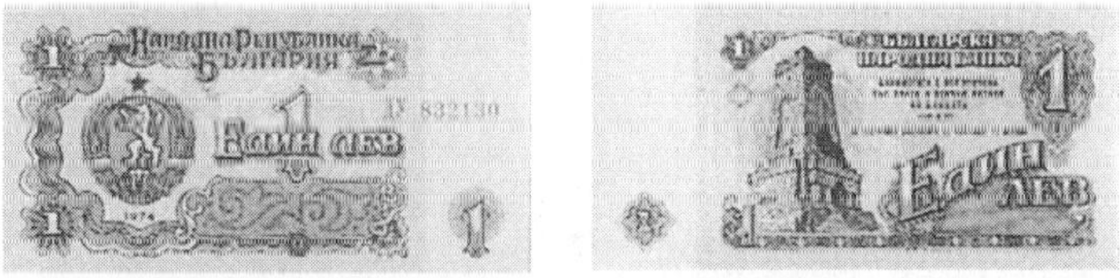

93	1 Lev	VF	UNC
	1974. Brown on multicolor underprint. Modified arms with dates at left. Back: Monument for the battle of Shipka Pass (1877) at keft center. Watermark: Decorative design.		
	a. Issued note.	.20	1.00
	s1. Specimen. 6-digit serial #. 000000.	—	50.00
	s2. Specimen. 7-digit serial #. 0000000.	—	50.00

94	2 Leva	VF	UNC
	1974. Black and blue on green underprint. Modified arms with dates at left. Back: Woman picking grapes in vineyard at right. Watermark: Decorative design.		
	a. Issued note.	.25	2.00
	s1. Specimen. 6-digit serial #. 000000.	—	50.00
	s2. Specimen. 7-digit serial #. 0000000.	—	50.00

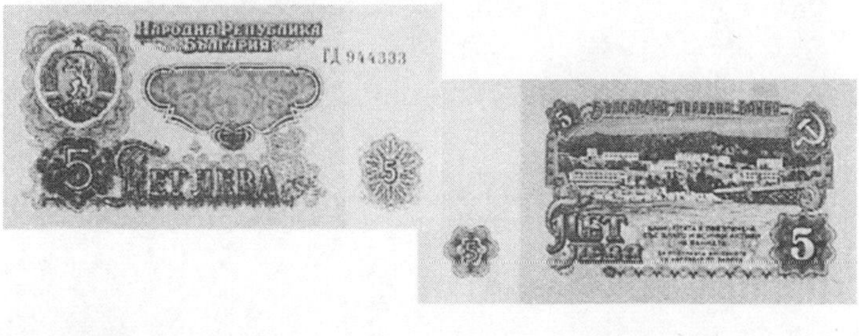

95	5 Leva	VF	UNC
	1974. Red on blue and multicolor underprint. Modified arms with dates at left. Back: Coastline village. Watermark: Decorative design.		
	a. Issued note.	.50	3.00
	s1. Specimen. 6-digit serial #. 000000.	—	50.00
	s2. Specimen. 7-digit serial #. 0000000.	—	50.00

96	10 Leva	VF	UNC
	1974. Black on blue and multicolor underprint. G. Dimitrov at left, modified arms at upper center. Back: Factory. Watermark: Hands holding hammer and sickle.		
	a. Issued note.	.50	6.00
	s1. Specimen. 6-digit serial #. 000000	—	70.00
	s2. Specimen. 7-digit serial #. 0000000.	—	70.00

97	20 Leva	VF	UNC
	1974. Brown-lilac on multicolor underprint. G. Dimitrov at left, modified arms at upper center. Back: Factory. Watermark: Hands holding hammer and sickle.		
	a. Issued note.	1.00	10.00
	s1. Specimen. 6-digit serial #. 000000.	—	80.00
	s2. Specimen. 7-digit serial #. 0000000.	—	80.00

1989; 1990 Issues

98	50 Leva	VF	UNC
	1990. Brown and daark blue on multicolor underprint. Arms at left. center. Back: Brown and dark green. Castle ruins at center right. Watermark: Hands holding hammer and sickle.		
	a. Issued note.	3.00	12.00
	s. Specimen.	—	120.

99	100 Leva	VF	UNC
	1989. Purple on lilac underprint. Arms at left center. Back: Horseman with two dogs at center right. Watermark: Rampant lion. (Not issued).	—	150.

Republic

БЪЛГАРСКА НАРОДНА БАНКА

Bulgarian National Bank

1991-94 Issue

100 20 Leva VF UNC

1991. Blue-black and blue-green on multicolor underprint. Dutchess Sevastokratoritza Desislava at left center. Back: Boyana Church at right. Watermark: Arms (lion). Printer: Wertpapierdruckerei-Germany. UV: fibers fluoresce blue.

	VF	UNC
a. Issued note	.50	1.00
s1. Specimen.	FV	150.

101 50 Leva VF UNC

1992. Purple and violet on multicolor underprint. Khristo G. Danov at left. Back: Platen printing press at right. Watermark: Arms (lion). UV: fibers fluoresce blue.

	VF	UNC
a. Issued note.	.50	1.00
s. Specimen.	FV	150.

102 100 Leva VF UNC

1991; 1993. Dark brown and maroon on multicolor underprint. Zhary Zograf (artist) at left center. Back: Wheel of Life at right. Watermark: Arms (lion). UV: fibers fluoresce yellow and blue.

	VF	UNC
a. 1991.	1.00	5.00
b. 1993.	.50	1.00
s1. As a. Specimen.	—	150.
s2. As b. Specimen.	—	200.

103 200 Leva VF UNC

1992. Deep violet and brown-orange on multicolor underprint. Ivan Vazov at left, village in underprint. Back: Lyre with laurel wreath at right. Watermark: Arms (lion). UV: fibers fluoresce blue

	VF	UNC
a. Issued note.	FV	1.00
s. Specimen.	—	150.

104 500 Leva VF UNC

1993. Dark green and black on multicolor underprint. D. Christov at left. Back: Opera house in Varna at center right, herring gulls at lower right. Watermark: D. Christov.

	VF	UNC
a. Issued note.	FV	1.50
s. Specimen.	—	200.

105 1000 Leva VF UNC

1994; 1997. Dark green and olive-brown on multicolor underprint. V. Levski at left, Liberty with flag, sword and lion at upper center right. Back: Monument and writings of Levski at center right. Watermark: V. Levski. Printer: G&D.

	VF	UNC
a. Issued note.	FV	2.00
s. Specimen.	—	150.

1994-96 Issue

106 1000 Leva VF UNC

1996. Dark green and olive-brown on multicolor underprint. V. Levski at left, Liberty with flag, sword and lion at upper center right. Wide hologram foil strip at left. Back: Monument and writings of Levski at center right. Watermark: V. Levski.

	VF	UNC
a. Issued note.	FV	12.00
s. Specimen.	—	150.

107	2000 Leva	VF	UNC
	1994; 1996. Black and dark blue on multicolor underprint. N. Ficev at left, building outlines at center, wide hologram foil strip at left. Back: Steeple, building plans at center right. Watermark: N. Ficev.		
	a. 1994.	2.00	15.00
	b. 1996.	2.00	15.00
	s1. As a. Specimen.	—	150.
	s2. As b. Specimen.	—	150.

108	5000 Leva	VF	UNC
	1996. Violet on multicolor underprint. Z. Stoyanov at left, quill pen at center right. Back: Monument (two views) at center, and *1885 Proclamation to the Bulgarian People* at right. Watermark: Z. Stoyanov.		
	a. Issued note.	4.00	9.00
	s. Specimen.	—	150.

109	10,000 Leva	VF	UNC
	1996. Brown and purple on multicolor underprint. V. Dimitrov at left, palette, brushes, Academy of the Arts at center, wide hologram foil strip at left. Back: Sketches at center, *Bulgarian Madonna* at right. Watermark: V. Dimitrov.		
	a. Issued note.	8.00	20.00
	s. Specimen.	—	200.

1997 Issue

111	5000 Leva	VF	UNC
	1997. Violet on multicolor underprint. Z. Stoyanov at left, quill pen at center, without wide hologram foil strip. Back: Monument (two views) at center, and *1885 Proclamation to the Bulgarian People* at right. Watermark: Z. Stoyanov. Printer: G&D.		
	a. Issued note.	4.00	9.00
	s. Specimen.	—	200.

112	10,000 Leva	VF	UNC
	1997. Multicolor. Dr. P. Beron at left, wide hologram foil strip at left. Back: Telescope at right. Reduced size.		
	a. Issued note.	7.00	12.00
	s. Specimen.	—	200.

113	50,000 Leva	VF	UNC
	1997. Purple on multicolor underprint. St. Cyril at left, St. Methodius at center right, with wide hologram foil strip at left. Back: Architectural monuments of the ancient Bulgarian capitals of Pliska and Preslav.		
	a. Issued note.	35.00	60.00
	s. Specimen.	—	250.

1999-2003 Issue

Monetary Reform: 1 Lev = 1000 "Old" Leva.

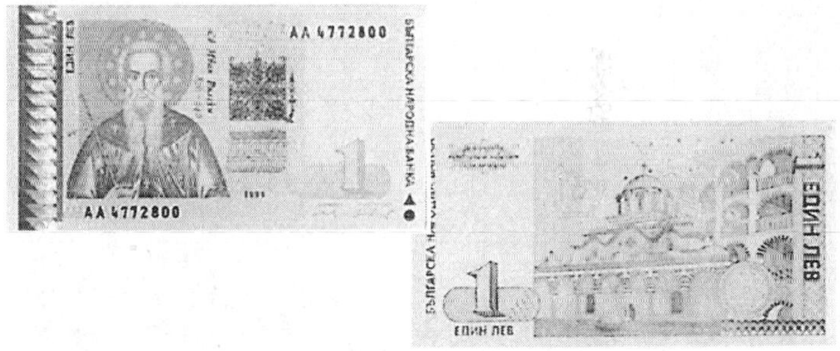

114	1 Lev	VF	UNC
	1999. Red and blue on yellow underprint. Icon of St. John of Rila at left, holographic strip at left. Back: Rila Monastery. 112x60mm.	FV	1.00

115	2 Leva	VF	UNC
	1999; 2005. Violet and pink on light blue underprint. Paisii Hilendarski at left, holographic strip at left. Back: Heraldic lion. 116x64mm.		
	a. 1999.	FV	1.75
	b. 2005.	FV	1.75

116	5 Leva	VF	UNC
	1999; 2009. Red, brown and green on multicolor undeerprint. Ivan Milev at left, holographic strip at left. Back: Parts of paintings. 121x67mm.		
	a. 1999.	FV	4.50
	b. 2009.	FV	4.50

117 10 Leva VF UNC

1999; 2008. Dark green on ochre underprint. Dr. Peter Beron at left, holographic strip at left. Back: Astronomy sketches and telescope. UV: fibers fluoresce yellow and blue, series of 10 fluoresce yellow at left end. 126x70mm.

	VF	UNC
a. 1999.	FV	10.00
b. 2008. Improved security devices.	FV	9.00

118 20 Leva VF UNC

1999; 2007. Blue on multicolor underprint. S. Stambolov at left, holographic strip at left. Back: National Assembly building and Eagles' and Lions' Bridges in Sofia. 131x72mm.

	VF	UNC
a. 1999.	FV	17.50
b. 2007. Bank initials added to watermark.	FV	17.50

119 50 Leva VF UNC

1999; 2006. Brown and yellow on multicolor underprint. Pencho Slaveykov at left, holographic strip at left. Back: Illustrations from his poetry works. 136x76mm.

	VF	UNC
a. 1999. Building in circle at lower center. Serial number prefix *A*.	FV	45.00
b. 2006. Solid device at lower center. Serian number prefix *B*.	FV	45.00

120 100 Leva VF UNC

2003. Green on multicolor underprint. Aleka Konstantinov at right. Back: His character "Uncle Ganyo". FV 85.00

2005 Commemorative Issue

121 20 Leva VF UNC

2005. Purple and yellow on multicolor underprint. Architectural renderings, three shields at bottom. Back: Bank building and bank notes. 134x74mm. FV 25.00

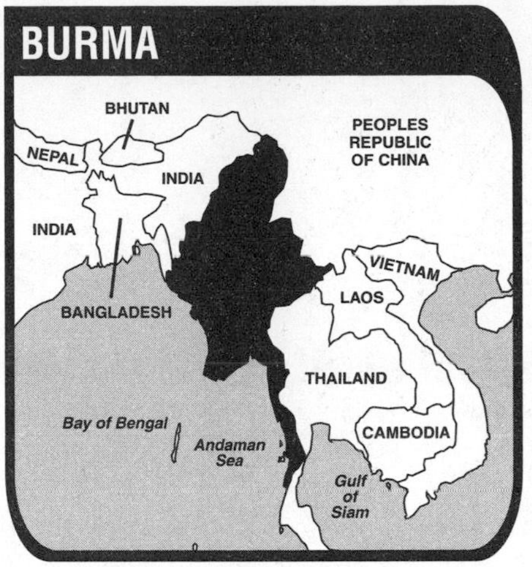

The Socialist Republic of the Union of Burma (now called Myanmar), is a country of Southeast Asia fronting on the Bay of Bengal and the Andaman Sea, has an area of 261,228 sq. mi. (676,577 sq. km.) and a population of 49.34 million. Capital: Rangoon. The first European to reach Burma, about 1435, was Nicolo Di Conti, a merchant of Venice. During the beginning of the reign of Bodawpaya (1782-1819AD) the kingdom comprised most of the same area as it does today including Arakan which was taken over in 1784-85. The British East India Company, while unsuccessful in its 1612 effort to establish posts along the Bay of Bengal, was enabled by the Anglo-Burmese Wars of 1824-86 to expand to the whole of Burma and to secure its annexation to British India. In 1937, Burma was separated from India, becoming a separate British colony with limited self-government. The Japanese occupied Burma in 1942, and on Aug. 1, 1943 Burma became an "independent and sovereign state" under Dr. Ba Maw who was appointed the Adipadi (head of state). This puppet state later collapsed with the surrender of Japanese forces. Burma became an independent nation outside the British Commonwealth on Jan. 4, 1948, the constitution of 1948 providing for a parliamentary democracy and the nationalization of certain industries. However, political and economic problems persisted, and on March 2, 1962, Gen. Ne Win took over the government, suspended the constitution, installed himself as chief of state, and pursued a socialistic program with nationalization of nearly all industry and trade. On Jan. 4, 1974, a new constitution adopted by referendum established Burma as a "socialist republic" under one-party rule. The country name was changed formally to the Union of Myanmar in 1989.

For later issues refer to Myanmar.

MONETARY SYSTEM:

1 Kyat = 100 Pya, 1943-45, 1952-89

Republic

Peoples Bank of Burma

1965 ND Issue

#52-55 Replacement notes have special Burmese characters with serial #.

52 **1 Kyat** — VF .30 — UNC 1.00
ND(1965). Purple and blue-gray on multicolor underprint. Portrait of General Aung San at center. Serial # varieties. Back: Fisherman at center, arms at upper left. Watermark: Pattern throughout paper. Printer: East Berlin.

53 **5 Kyats** — VF 1.00 — UNC 2.50
ND (1965). Green and light blue. Portrait of General Aung San at center. Back: Green. Man with ox, arms at upper left. Watermark: Pattern throughout paper. Printer: East Berlin.

54 **10 Kyats** — VF 1.50 — UNC 5.00
ND (1965). Red-brown and violet. Portrait of General Aung San at center. Back: Red-brown. Woman picking cotton at right, arms at upper left. Watermark: Pattern throughout paper. Printer: East Berlin.

55 **20 Kyats** — VF 2.50 — UNC 8.00
ND (1965). Brown and tan. Portrait of General Aung San at center. Back: Farmer on tractor at center right, arms at upper left. Watermark: Pattern throughout paper. Printer: East Berlin.

Union of Burma Bank

1972-79 ND Issue

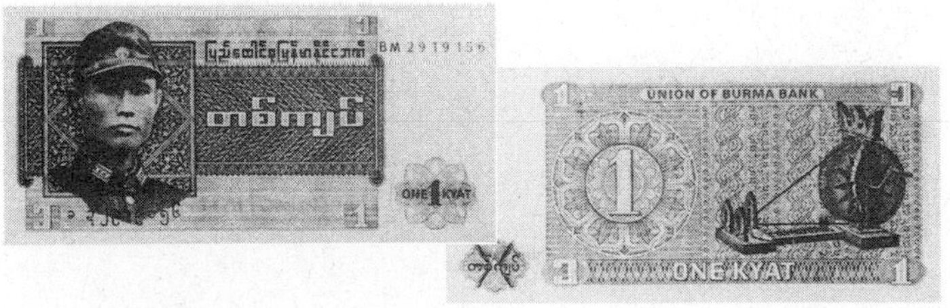

56 **1 Kyat** — VF .15 — UNC .40
ND (1972). Green and blue on multicolor underprint. Military portrait of General Aung San at left. Back: Ornate native wheel assembly at right. Watermark: General Aung San. UV: fibers fluoresce blue.

57	**5 Kyats** ND (1973). Blue and purple on multicolor underprint. Military portrait of General Aung San at left. Back: Palm tree at left center. Watermark: General Aung San.	VF .25	UNC 1.00

58	**10 Kyats** ND (1973). Red and violet on multicolor underprint. Military portrait of General Aung San at left. Back: Native ornaments at left center. Watermark: General Aung San.	VF .50	UNC 1.00

59	**25 Kyats** ND (1972). Brown and tan on multicolor underprintl Military portrait of General Aung San at left. Back: Mythical winged creature at center. Watermark: General Aung San.	VF .75	UNC 1.50

60	**50 Kyats** ND (1979). Brown and violet on multicolor underprintl Military portrait of General Aung San at left. Back: Mythical dancer at left center. Watermark: General Aung San.	VF 10.00	UNC 25.00

61	**100 Kyats** ND (1976). Blue and green on multicolor underprint. Military portrait of General Aung San at left. Back: Native wheel and musical string instrument at left center. Watermark: General Aung San.	VF	UNC
	a. Issued note.	4.00	15.00
	s. Specimen. Overprint and rubber stamped: *SPECIMEN.*	—	—

1985-87 ND Issue

62	**15 Kyats** ND (1986). Blue-gray and green on multicolor underprint. Portrait of General Aung San at left center. Back: Mythical dancer at left. Watermark: General Aung San. Reduced size.	VF FV	UNC 2.00

63	**35 Kyats** ND (1986). Brown-violet and purple on multicolor underprint. General Aung San in military hat at left center. Back: Mythical dancer at left. Watermark: General Aung San. Reduced size.	VF .50	UNC 1.50

64 **45 Kyats**

	VF	UNC
ND (1987). Blue-gray and blue on multicolor underprint. Po Hla Gyi at right. Back: Two workers with rope and bucket at left center, oil field at center. Watermark: General Aung San. Reduced size.	FV	4.00

65 **75 Kyats**

	VF	UNC
ND (1985). Brown on multicolor underprint. General Aung San at left center. Back: Dancer at left. Watermark: General Aung San. Reduced size.	.75	2.75

66 **90 Kyats**

	VF	UNC
ND (1987). Brown, green and blue on multicolor underprint. Seya San at right. Back: Farmer plowing with oxen at left center, rice planting at upper right. Watermark: General Aung San. Reduced size.	FV	6.00

FOR LATER ISSUES SEE MYANMAR.

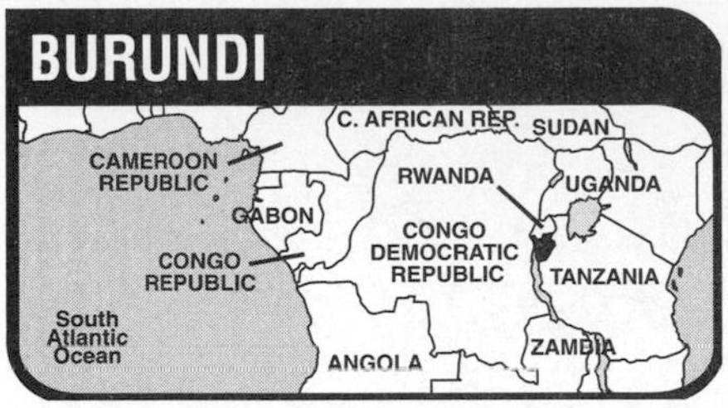

The Republic of Burundi, a landlocked country in central Africa, east of Lake Taganyila has an area of 27,830 sq. km. and a population of 8.69 million. Capital: Bujumbura. Burundi has a predominantly agricultural economy. Coffee, tea and cotton are exported.

Burundi's first democratically elected president was assassinated in October 1993 after only 100 days in office, triggering widespread ethnic violence between Hutu and Tutsi factions. More than 200,000 Burundians perished during the conflict that spanned almost a dozen years. Hundreds of thousands of Burundians were internally displaced or became refugees in neighboring countries. An internationally brokered power-sharing agreement between the Tutsi-dominated government and the Hutu rebels in 2003 paved the way for a transition process that led to an integrated defense force, established a new constitution in 2005, and elected a majority Hutu government in 2005. The new government, led by President Pierre Nkurunziza, signed a South African brokered ceasefire with the country's last rebel group in September of 2006 but still faces many challenges.

RULERS:

Mwambutsa IV, 1962-1966
Ntare V, 1966

MONETARY SYSTEM:

1 Franc = 100 Centimes

KINGDOM

BANQUE DU ROYAUME DU BURUNDI

1964 ND PROVISIONAL ISSUE

1 **5 Francs**

	Fine	XF
ND (1964 - old dates 15.5.1961; 15.4.1963). Light brown. Large black overprint on Rwanda Burundi #1. Overprint: *BURUNDI*.	45.00	200.

2 **10 Francs**

	Fine	XF
ND (1964 - old date 5.10.1960). Gray. Large red overprint on Rwanda-Burundi #2. Overprint: *BURUNDI*.	75.00	250.

3 **20 Francs**

	Fine	XF
ND (1964 - old date 5.10.1960). Green. Large black overprint on Rwanda-Burundi #3. Overprint: *BURUNDI*.	75.00	250.

4 **50 Francs** — Fine | XF

ND (1964 - old dates 15.9.1960-1.10.1960). Red. Large black overprint on Rwanda-Burundi #4. Overprint: *BURUNDI*. — 75.00 | 250.

5 **100 Francs** — Fine | XF

ND (1964 - old dates 1.10.1960; 31.7.1962). Blue. Large red overprint on Rwanda-Burundi #5. Overprint: *BURUNDI*. — 65.00 | 235.

6 **500 Francs**

ND (1964 - old dates 15.9.1960-15.5.1961). Lilac brown. Large black overprint on Rwanda-Burundi #6. Overprint: *BURUNDI*. — 650. | 1150.

7 **1000 Francs** — Fine | XF

ND (1964 - old date 31.7.1962). Green. Large black overprint on Rwanda-Burundi #7. Overprint: *BURUNDI*. — 400. | 1250.

1964; 1965 Regular Issue

8 **5 Francs** — VF | UNC

1.10.1964; 1.12.1964; 1.5.1965. Light brown on gray-green underprint. Two young men picking coffee beans at left. Back: Arms at center. — 10.00 | 30.00

9 **10 Francs** — VF | UNC

20.11.1964; 25.2.1965; 20.3.1965; 31.12.1965. Dark brown on lilac-brown underprint. Cattle at center. Back: Arms at center. — 10.00 | 35.00

10 **20 Francs** — VF | UNC

20.11.1964; 25.2.1965; 20.3.1965. Blue-green. Dancer. Back: Arms at center. — 35.00 | 125.

11 **50 Francs** — VF | UNC

1964-66. Red-orange. View of Bujumbura. Back: Arms at center.

a. Signature titles: *LE VICE-PRESIDENT* and *LE PRESIDENT*. 1.10.1964-31.12.1965. — 65.00 | 200.

b. Signature titles: *L'ADMINISTRATEUR* and *LE PRESIDENT*. 1.7.1966. — — | —

ct. Color trial. Purple on light blue underprint. Punch hole cancelled. 1.10.1964. — — | 750.

12 **100 Francs** — VF | UNC

1964-66. Bluish pruple. Prince Rwagasore at center. Back: Arms at center.

a. Signature titles: *LE VICE-PRESIDENT* and *LE PRESIDENT*. 1.10.1964; 1.12.1964; 1.5.1965. — 65.00 | 200.

b. Signature titles: *L'ADMINISTRATEUR* and *LE PRESIDENT*. 1.7.1966. — — | —

ct. Color trial. Rose. Punch hole cancelled. 1.10.1964. — — | 750.

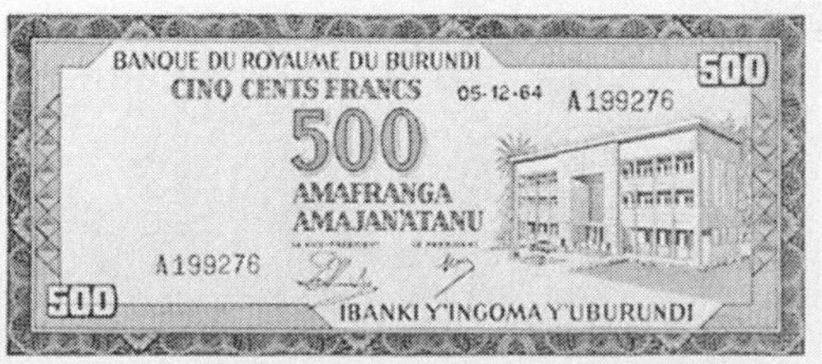

13 **500 Francs** — VF | UNC

5.12.1964; 1.8.1966. Brown on yellow underprint. Bank at right. Back: Arms at center. — 175. | —

14 **1000 Francs** — VF | UNC

1.2.1965. Green on multicolor underprint. King Mwami Mwambutsa IV at right. Back: Arms at center. — 625. | —

REPUBLIC

BANQUE DE LA RÉPUBLIQUE DU BURUNDI

1966 ND PROVISIONAL ISSUE

		VF	UNC
15	**20 Francs** ND (1966 - old date 20.3.1965). Dancer at center, black overprint. Back: Arms at center. Overprint: *DE LA REPUBLIQUE and YA REPUBLIKA.*	55.00	200.
16	**50 Francs** ND (1966 - old dates 1.5.1965; 31.12.1965; 1.7.1966). Black overprint. Overprint: *DE LA REPUBLIQUE and YA REPUBLIKA.*		
	a. Overprint on #11a.	75.00	250.
	b. Overprint on #11b.	85.00	275.

		VF	UNC
17	**100 Francs** ND (1966). Black overprint. Overprint: *DE LA REPUBLIQUE and YA REPUBLIKA.*		
	a. Overprint on #12a. (- old date 1.5.1965).	55.00	200.
	b. Overprint on #12b. (- old date 1.7.1966).	55.00	200.

		VF	UNC
18	**500 Francs** ND (1966 - old dates 5.12.1964; 1.8.1966). Bank at right, black overprint. Back: Arms at center. Overprint: *DE LA REPUBLIQUE and YA REPUBLIKA.*	250.	—

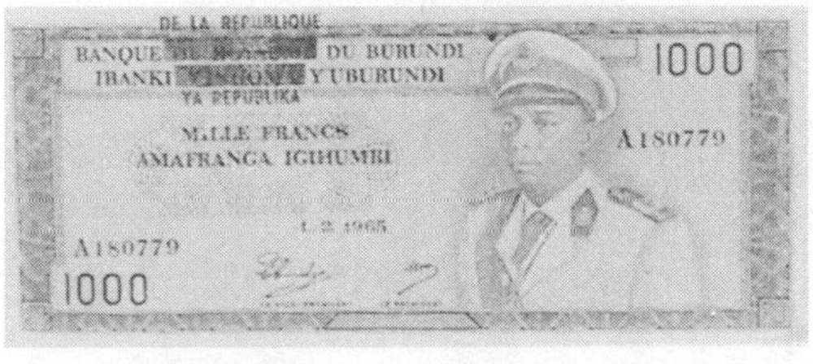

		VF	UNC
19	**1000 Francs** ND (1966 - old date 1.2.1965). King Mwami Mwambutsa IV at right, black overprint. Back: Arms at center. Overprint: *DE LA REPUBLIQUE and YA REPUBLIKA.*	725.	—

1968-75 ISSUES

		VF	UNC
20	**10 Francs** 1968; 1970. Red on green and blue underprint. *Place de la Revolution* monument at right. Signature titles: *L'ADMINISTRATEUR* and *LE PRESIDENT.*		
	a. 1.11.1968.	5.00	15.00
	b. 1.4.1970.	1.50	7.50

		VF	UNC
21	**20 Francs** 1968-73. Blue on green and violet underprint. Dancer at center, signature variation. Back: Text.		
	a. Signature titles: *LE PRESIDENT* and *LE VICE PRESIDENT.* 1.11.1968.	10.00	40.00
	b. Signature titles:*LE PRESIDENT* and *L'ADMINISTRATEUR.* 1.4.1970; 1.11.1971; 1.7.1973.	7.00	30.00

		VF	UNC
22	**50 Francs** 1968-73. Pale red on multicolor underprint. Watermark: Drummer at left center. Signature varieties. UV: $1 and central emblem fluoresces green.		
	a. Signature titles: *LE VICE-PRESIDENT* and *LE PRESIDENT.* 15.5.1968; 1.10.1968.	25.00	100.
	b. Signature titles: *ADMINISTRATEUR* and *PRESIDENT.* 1.2.1970; 1.8.1971; 1.7.1973.	15.00	40.00
	s. Specimen.	—	200.

		VF	UNC
22A	**50 Francs** 1.6.1975. Brown on multicolor underprint. Drummer at left center, signature titles: *ADMINISTRATEUR and PRESIDENT.*		
	a. Issued note.	35.00	115.
	s. Specimen.	—	—

23 100 Francs

1968-85. Brown on pale orange, lilac and blue underprint. Prince Rwagasore at right.

	VF	UNC
a. Signature titles: *LE VICE-PRESIDENT* and *LE PRESIDENT.* 15.5.1968; 1.10.1968.	50.00	150.
b. Signature titles: *ADMINISTRATEUR* and *LE PRESIDENT.* 1.2.1970; 1.8.1971; 1.7.1973; 1.6. 1975.	30.00	100.
s. Specimen.	—	200.

24 500 Francs

1968-75. Brown. Bank building at right.

	VF	UNC
a. Signature titles: *LE PRESIDENT* and *LE VICE-PRESIDENT.*1.8.1968.	250.	900.
b. Signature titles: *LE PRESIDENT* and *L'ADMINISTRATEUR.* 1.4.1970; 1.8.1971.	200.	750.
c. Signature titles: *LE PRESIDENT* and *LE VICE-PRESIDENT.* 1.7.1973; 1.6.1975.	200.	750.
s. Specimen.	—	—

25 1000 Francs

1968-75. Blue and multicolor. Paradise whydah and flowers. Back: Blue and light brown. Cattle at center.

	VF	UNC
a. Signature titles: *L'ADMINISTRATEUR* and *LE PRESIDENT.* 1.4.1968; 1.5.1971; 1.2.1973.	175.	550.
b. Signature title: *LE VICE-PRESIDENT* 1.6.1975; 1.9.1976.	150.	500.
s. Specimen.	—	850.

26 5000 Francs

1968; 1971; 1973. Blue. President Micombero in military uniform at right. Back: Loading at dockside.

	VF	UNC
a. Signature titles: *LE VICE-PRESIDENT* and *LE PRESIDENT.* 1.4.1968; 1.7.1973.	500.	1500.
b. Signature title: *L'ADMINISTRATEUR.* 1.5.1971.	500.	1750.
ct. As a. Color trial in purple. Punch hole cancelled.	—	1000.

1975-78 Issue

27 20 Francs

1977-2007. Red on multicolor underprint. Dancer at center. Signature titles: *LE GOUVERNEUR* and *L'ADMINISTRATEUR.* Back: Arms at center.

	VF	UNC
a. 1.7.1977; 1.6.1979; 1.12.1981.	1.00	5.00
b. 1.12.1983; 1.12.1986; 1.5.1988; 1.10.1989.	.50	2.00
c. 1.10.1991; 25.5.1995.	FV	1.25
d. Signature titles: *LE GOUVERNEUR* and *LE 2e VICE-GOUVERNEUR.* 5.2.1997; 1.8.2001; 1.7.2003; 5.2.2005; 1.11.2007	FV	.75
s. Specimen.	—	100.

28 50 Francs

1977-93. Brown on multicolor underprint. Drummer at left center. Back: Arms at center.

	VF	UNC
a. 1.7.1977; 1.5.1979.	1.50	7.50
b. 1.12.1981; 1.12.1983.	1.00	5.00
c. 1.5.1988; 1.10.1989; 1.10.1991; 1.5.1993.	.75	4.00
s. Specimen.	—	100.

29 100 Francs

1977-93. Purple on multicolor underprint. Prince Rwagasore at right. Signature titles: *L'ADMINISTRATEUR* and *LE GOUVERNEUR.* Back: Arms at center.

	VF	UNC
a. 1.7.1977; 1.5.1979.	1.00	3.50
b. 1.1.1981; 1.7.1982; 1.11.1984; 1.11.1986.	.75	3.00
c. 1.5.1988; 1.7.1990; 1.5.1993.	FV	2.00
s. Specimen.	—	100.

30 500 Francs

1977-88. Dark blue on multicolor underprint. Bank building at right, numeral and date style varieties. Signature titles: *LE GOUVERNEUR* and *LE VICE-GOUVERNEUR*. Back: Arms at center.

	VF	UNC
a. 1.7.1977; 1.9.1981.	10.00	40.00
b. 1.7.1985; 1.9.1986.	7.00	20.00
c. 1.5.1988.	5.00	12.50
s. Specimen. 1.1.1980; 1.7.1985.	—	175.

31 1000 Francs

1977-91. Dark green on multicolor underprint. Paradise whydah and flowers. Back: Cattle at center.

	VF	UNC
a. Signature titles: *LE VICE-GOUVERNEUR* and *LE GOUVERNEUR*.1.7.1977; 1.1.1978; 1.5.1979; 1.1.1980.	15.00	50.00
b. 1.1.1981; 1.5.1982; 1.1.1984; 1.12.1986.	12.50	35.00
c. Signature titles: *L'ADMINISTRATEUR* and *LE VICE-GOUVERNEUR*. 1.6.1987.	20.00	65.00
d. Signature titles: *LE VICE-GOUVERNEUR* and *LE GOUVERNEUR*. 1.5.1988; 1.10.1989; 1.10.1991.	7.50	12.50
s. Specimen.	—	175

32 5000 Francs

1978-95. Dark brown and grayish purple on multicolor underprint. Arms at upper center; building at lower right. Back: Ship dockside. 179x79mm.

	VF	UNC
a. 1.7.1978; 1.10.1981.	60.00	200.
b. 1.1.1984; 1.9.1986.	30.00	100.
c. 1.10.1989; 1.10.1991.	20.00	80.00
d. Sign titles: *LE 1ER VICE-GOUVERNEUR* and *LE GOUVERNEUR*. 19.5.1994; 25.5.1995.	FV	62.50

1979-81 Issues

#33 and 34 replacement notes: Serial # prefix *Z*.

33 10 Francs

1981-2007. Blue-green on tan underprint. Map of Burundi with arms superimposed at center. Back: Text.

	VF	UNC
a. Signature titles: *LE GOUVERNEUR* and *ADMINISTRATEUR*. 1.6.1981; 1.12.1983.	FV	2.50
b. 1.12.1986; 1.5.1988; 1.10.1989; 1.10.1991.	FV	1.25
c. 25.5.1995.	FV	.75
d. Signature titles: *LE GOUVERNEUR* and *LE 2eme VICE-GOUVERNEUR*. 5.2.1997; 1.8.2001; 1.7.2003.	FV	.50
e. Signature titles: *LE GOUVERNEUR* and *LE 2E VICE GOUVERNEUR*. 5.2.2005; 1.11.2007.	FV	.50

34 500 Francs

1.6.1979; 1.1.1980. Tan, blue-black, purple and green on multicolor underprint. Bank building at right. Signature titles: *LE GOUVERNEUR*and *LE VICE-GOUVERNEUR.* Back: Purple on multicolor underprint.

	VF	UNC
a. 1.6.1979.	12.50	50.00
b. 1.1.1980.	12.50	50.00

1993-97 Issue

#35 not assigned.

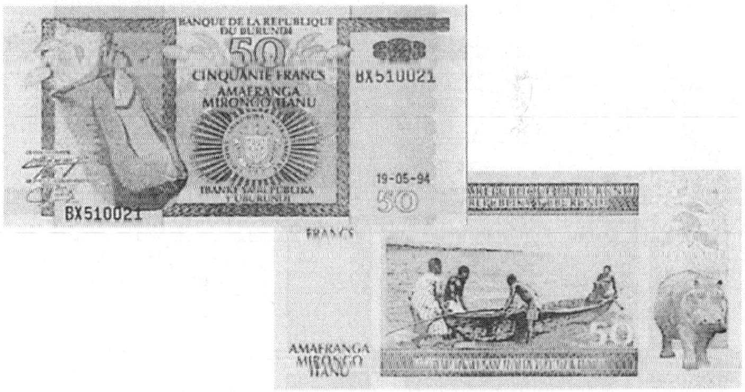

36 50 Francs

1994-. Dull brown-violet on multicolor underprint. Man in dugout canoe at left, arms at lower center. Back: Four men with canoe at center, hippopotamus at lower right.

	VF	UNC
a. 19.5.1994.	FV	2.00
b. 5.2.1999.	FV	2.00
c. 1.8.2001.	FV	2.00
d. 1.7.2003.	FV	2.00
e. 5.2.2005.	FV	2.00
f. 1.5.2006.	FV	2.00
g. 1.11.2007.	FV	2.00

37 100 Francs

1993-. Dull purple on multicolor underprint. Archway at left center, Prince Rwagasore at right. Signature titles: *LE 2eme VICE-GOUVERNEUR* and *LE GOUVERNEUR.*. Back: Arms at lower left, home construction at center.

	VF	UNC
a. 1.10.1993.	FV	3.00
b. 1.12.1997.	FV	3.00
c. 1.8.2001.	FV	3.00
d. 1.5.2004.	FV	3.00
e. 1.5.2006.	FV	3.00
f. 1.10.2007.	FV	3.00
s. Specimen.	—	125.

37A 500 Francs

5.2.1995 (2005). Blue and lilac on multicolor underprint. President facing at left. Back: Bank building at center. — Unc 7.50

38 500 Francs — VF UNC

1995-. Gray and violet on multicolor underprint. Native painting at left. Back: Blue on multicolor underprint. Bank building at center, arms at right. Watermark: Ox. 160x73mm.

	VF	UNC
a. 1.5.1997.	FV	7.50
b. 5.2.1999.	FV	7.50
c. 1.7.2003.	FV	6.00
d. 1.10.2007.	FV	6.00
e. 1.5.2009.	FV	6.00

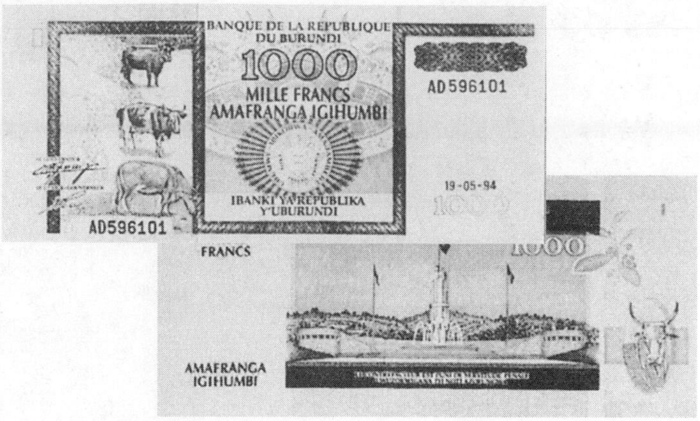

39 1000 Francs — VF UNC

1994-. Greenish black and brown-violet on multicolor underprint. Cattle at left, arms at lower center. Signature titles: *LE GOUVERNEUR* and *LE 1ER VICE-GOUVERNEUR*. Back: Monument at center. Watermark: President Micombero. 170x76mm.

	VF	UNC
a. 19.5.1994.	FV	17.50
b. 1.12.1997.	FV	9.00
c. 1.7.2000.	FV	9.00
d. 1.5.2006.	FV	9.00
e. 1.5.2009.	FV	9.00

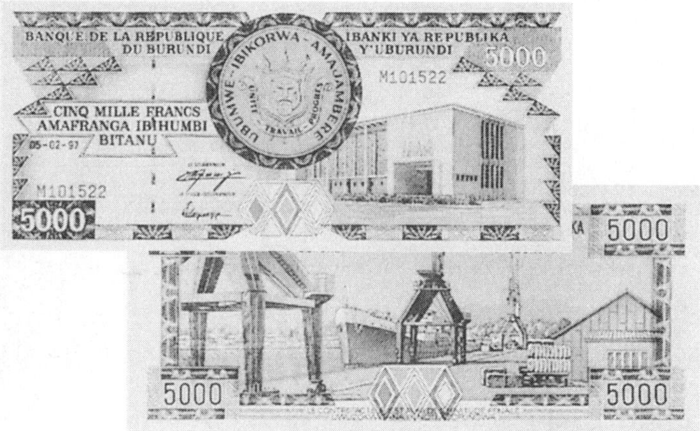

40 5000 Francs — VF UNC

5.2.1997. Olive-green and dark green on multicolor underprint. Arms at upper center, building at lower right, date at left, segmented foil over security thread. Back: Ship dockside. 179x79mm. — FV 55.00

1999-2001 Issue

41 2000 Francs — VF UNC

2001; 2008. Blue and green on multicolor underprint. Harvest scene at right. Back: Lake and dam. 176x77mm.

	VF	UNC
a. 25.6.2001.	FV	15.00

42 5000 Francs — VF UNC

1999; 2003; 2005. Green, olive and light red on multicolor underprint. Arms at upper center, building at lower right, date at left, printed bull's head with OVD ink at lower left center. Segmented foil over security thread. Back: Ship dockside. 179x79mm.

	VF	UNC
a. 5.2.1999.	FV	40.00
b. 1.7.2003.	FV	25.00
c. 5.2.2005.	FV	25.00

43 10,000 Francs — VF UNC

2004; 2006. Multicolor. Prince Rwagasore and President Ndadaye at lower left. Back: Three students at desks at center. 150x75mm.

	VF	UNC
a. 25.10.2004.	FV	60.00
b. 1.5.2006.	FV	60.00

2008 Issue

44 100 Francs — VF UNC

1.5.2010; 9.11.2011. Purple on multicolor underprint. Prince Ragawasore at right. Back: Home construction 125x65mm.

	VF	UNC
a. 1.5.2010.	FV	.50
b. 9.11.2011.	FV	.50

45 500 Francs

1.5.2009; 1.9.2011. Dark blue and multicolor. Bas relief of natives, trees and couldron. Back: Central Bank of Burundi building at center. 132x67mm.

	VF	UNC
a. 1.5.2009.	FV	2.00
b. 1.9.2011.	FV	1.50

46 1000 Francs

1.5.2009. Multicolor. Three cattle at left. Back: Monument with fountian at center. Watermark: Cattle. 137x69mm. — FV 3.00

47 **2000 Francs** | VF FV | UNC 5.00

1.12.2008. Blue and green on multicolor underprint. Harvest scene at right. Silver foil bull's head at lower center. Back: Lake and dam. Watermark: Cattle. 140x71mm.

48 **5000 Francs** | VF FV | UNC 9.00

1.12.2008. Green, olive and light red on multicolor underprint. Arms at upper center, building at lower right, date a left. Bull's head hologram at lower left. Back: Ship dockside. Watermark: Cattle Printer: TDLR (without imprint). 145x73mm.

49 **10,000 Francs** | VF FV | UNC 60.00

1.7.2009. Multicolor. Prince Rwagasore and President Ndadaye at lower left. Eagle hologram above. Back: Three students at desks at center.

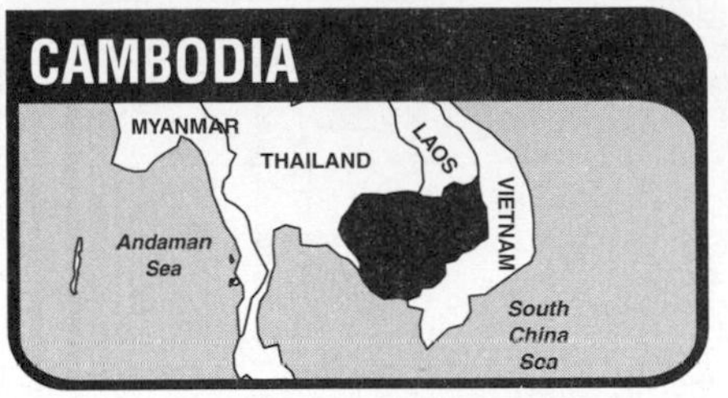

Kingdom of Cambodia, formerly known as Democratic Kampuchea, People's Republic of Kampuchea, and the Khmer Republic, a land of paddy fields and forest-clad hills located on the Indo-Chinese peninsula fronting on the Gulf of Thailand, has an area of 181,040 sq. km. and a population of 14.24 million. Capital: Phnom Penh. Agriculture is the major part of the economy, with rice the chief crop. Native industries include cattle breeding, weaving and rice milling. Rubber, cattle, corn, and timber are exported.

Most Cambodians consider themselves to be Khmers, descendants of the Angkor Empire that extended over much of Southeast Asia and reached its zenith between the 10th and 13th centuries. Attacks by the Thai and Cham (from present-day Viet Nam) weakened the empire, ushering in a long period of decline. The king placed the country under French protection in 1863 and it became part of French Indochina in 1887. Following Japanese occupation in World War II, Cambodia gained full independence from France in 1955

In April 1975, after a five-year struggle, communist Khmer Rouge forces captured Phnom Penh and evacuated all cities and towns. At least 1.5 million Cambodians died from execution, forced hardships, or starvation during the Khmer Rouge regime under Pol Pot. A December 1978 Vietnamese invasion drove the Khmer Rouge into the countryside, began a 10-year Vietnamese occupation, and touched off almost 13 years of civil war.

The 1991 Paris Peace Accords mandated democratic elections and a ceasefire, which was not fully respected by the Khmer Rouge. UN-sponsored elections in 1993 helped restore some semblance of normalcy under a coalition government. Factional fighting in 1997 ended the first coalition government, but a second round of national elections in 1998 led to the formation of another coalition government and renewed political stability. The remaining elements of the Khmer Rouge surrendered in 1998.

The colition governments parliament decided to restore the constitutional monarchy on September 24, 1993 and King Sihanouk became chief of state. He abdicated on October 6, 2004 and one of his sons, Prince Norodom Sihamoni, now sits on the throne.

RULERS:

Norodom Suramarit, 1955-1960
Norodom Sihanouk (as Chief of State), 1960-1970
Lon Nol, 1970-1975
Pol Pot, 1975-1979
Heng Samrin, 1979-1985
Hun Sen, 1985-1991
Norodom Sihanouk (as Chairman, Supreme National Council), 1991-1993
Norodom Sihanouk (as King), 1993-2002
Boromneath Norodom Sihamoni, 2004-

MONETARY SYSTEM:

1 Riel = 100 Sen

REPLACEMENT NOTES:

#4b-c, 5b, 7b use 3 special Cambodian prefix characters (equivalent to 290).

SIGNATURE CHART

	Governor	Chief Inspector	Advisor	Date
1				28.10.1955
2				1956
3				1956
4				Late 1961
5				Mid 1962
6				1963
7				1965
8				1968
9				1968
10				1969
11				1970
12				1972

SIGNATURE CHART		
13	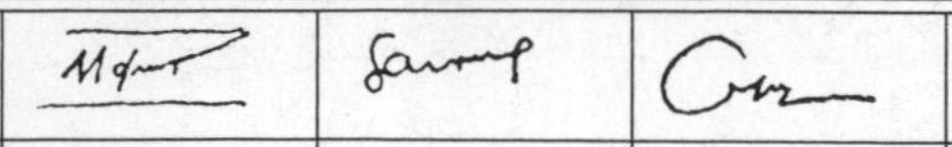	1972
14	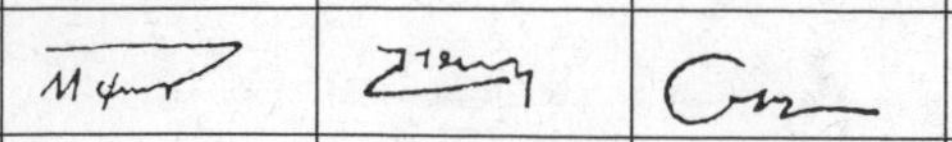	1974
15	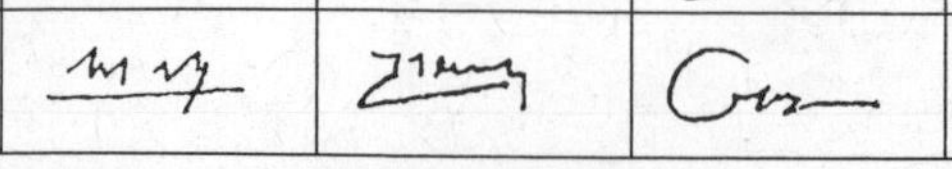	March, 1975 (printed 1974)

Kingdom of Cambodia

Banque Nationale du Cambodge

1956; 1958 ND Second Issue

4 **1 Riel** VF UNC

ND (1956-75). Grayish green on multicolor underprint. Boats dockside in port of Phnom-Penh. Back: Royal palace throne room. Printer: BWC (without imprint).

	VF	UNC
a. Signature 1; 2.	3.00	15.00
b. Signature 6; 7; 8; 10; 11.	.25	3.00
c. Signature 12.	.15	1.00
r. Replacement note.	2.00	5.00
s. Specimen. Signature 1. Perforated and printed: *SPECIMEN*.	—	150.
ct. Color trial. Purple and blue. Specimen.	—	—

5 **20 Riels** VF UNC

ND (1956-75). Brown on multicolor underprint. Combine harvester at right. Back: Phnom Penh pagoda. Watermark: Buddha. Printer: BWC (without imprint).

	VF	UNC
a. Signature 3.	1.00	10.00
b. Signature 6.	.75	4.00
c. Signature 7; 8; 10.	.50	3.00
d. Signature 12.	.25	1.00
r. Replacement note.	2.00	5.00
ct. Color trial. Green. Specimen.	—	—

7 **50 Riels** VF UNC

ND (1956-75). Blue and orange. Fishermen fishing from boats with Large nets in Lake Tonle Sap at left and right. Back: Blue and brown. Angkor Wat complex. Watermark: Buddha. Printer: TDLR (without imprint).

	VF	UNC
a. Western numeral in plate block designator. Signature 3.	3.00	20.00
b. Cambodian numeral in plate block designator. 5-digit serial #. Signature 7; 10.	1.00	4.00
c. As b. Signature 12.	.50	1.00
d. Cambodian serial # 6-digits. Signature 12.	.20	1.00
r. Replacement note.	—	5.00
s1. As a. Specimen.	—	150.
s2. As c. Specimen. (TDLR).	—	150.

8 **100 Riels** VF UNC

ND (1957-75). Brown and green on multicolor underprint. Statue of Lokecvara at left. Back: Long boat. Watermark: Buddha.

	VF	UNC
a. Imprint: *Giesecke & Devrient AG, Munchen.* Signature 3.	3.00	20.00
b. As a. Signature 7; 8; 11.	1.00	4.00
c. Imprint: *Giesecke & Devrient-Munchen.* Signature 12; 13; 15.	.50	2.00
s. Specimen. As a. Signature 3. Perforated *Specimen. Uniface printings.*	—	200.

9 **500 Riels** VF UNC

ND (1958-70). Green and brown on multicolor underprint. Sculpture of two royal women dancers - *Devatas* at left. Back: Two royal dancers in ceremonial costumes. Watermark: Buddha. Printer: G&D.

	VF	UNC
a. Signature 3.	50.00	150.
b. Signature 6.	35.00	100.
c. Signature 9.	3.00	12.50
s. As a. Signature 3. Specimen.		
x. Counterfeit.	2.00	5.00

1962-63 ND Third Issue

10 **5 Riels** VF UNC

ND (1962-75). Red on multicolor underprint. Bayon stone 4 faces of Avalokitesvara at left. Back: Royal Palace Entrance - Chanchhaya at right. Watermark: Buddha. Printer: BWC (without imprint).

	VF	UNC
a. Signature 4; 6.	3.00	20.00
b. Signature 7; 8; 11.	.50	4.00
c. Signature 12.	.25	1.00
s. Specimen. Signature 4, 8. Perforated *SPECIMEN.*	—	200.
ct. Color trial. Green. Specimen.	—	—

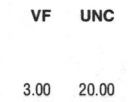

		VF	UNC
11	**10 Riels**		
	ND (1962-75). Red-brown on multicolor underprint. Temple of Banteay Srei at right. Back: Central Market building at Phnom-Penh at left. Watermark: Buddha. Printer: TDLR (without imprint).		
	a. Signature 5; 6.	3.00	20.00
	b. Signature 7; 8; 11.	.50	3.00
	c. Signature 12. 5 digit serial #.	.25	1.00
	d. As c. 6 digit serial #.	.50	2.00
	s. Specimen. Signature 5, 6, 8. TDLR.	—	125.

		VF	UNC
12	**100 Riels**		
	ND (1963-72). Blue-black, dark green and dark brown on multicolor underprint. Sun rising behind Temple of Preah Vihear at left. Back: Blue, green and brown. Aerial view of the Temple of Preah Vihear. Watermark: Buddha. Printer: G&D.		
	a. Signature 6.	3.00	20.00
	b. Signature 13. (Not issued).	.20	1.00
	s. Specimen. Signature 6.	—	200.

		VF	UNC
13	**100 Riels**		
	ND (1956-1972). Blue on light blue underprint. Two oxen at right. Back: Three ceremonial women.		
	a. Printer: ABNC with imprint on lower margins, face and back. Signature 3.	20.00	100.
	b. Without imprint on either side. Signature 12.	.25	2.00
	p. Uniface proofs.	FV	75.00
	s. As a. Specimen. Signature 3.	—	300.

		VF	UNC
14	**500 Riels**		
	ND (1958-1970). Multicolor. Farmer plowing with two water buffalo. Back: Pagoda at right, doorway of Preah Vihear at left. Watermark: Buddha. Printer: BdF (without imprint).		
	a. Signature 3.	4.00	30.00
	b. Signature 5; 7.	2.00	10.00
	c. Signature 9.	1.50	9.00
	d. Signature 12.	1.00	5.00
	x1. Lithograph counterfeit; watermark. barely visible. Signature 3; 5.	70.00	120.
	x2. As x1. Signature 7; 9.	60.00	100.
	x3. As x1. Signature 12.	45.00	80.00

Khmer Republic

Banque Nationale du Cambodge

1973 ND Issue

		VF	UNC
15	**100 Riels**		
	ND. Purple and violet on multicolor underprint. Carpet weaving. Back: Angkor Wat. Watermark: Man's head. Printer: TDLR (without imprint). (Not issued). Replacement notes: Series # 90.		
	a. Signature 13.	.35	2.00
	b. Signature 14.	1.25	7.50
	r. Replacement note.	2.00	5.00

		VF	UNC
16	**500 Riels**		
	ND(1973-75). Green and black on multicolor underprint. Girl with vessel on head at left. Back: Rice paddy scene. Watermark: Man's head. Printer: TDLR (without imprint).		
	a. Signature 13; 14.	2.00	10.00
	b. Signature 15.	.20	1.00
	r. Replacement note.	2.00	5.00
	s. As a. Specimen.	—	—

17 **1000 Riels** | VF | UNC
ND. Green on multicolor underprint. School children. Signature 13. Back: Head of Lokecvara at Ta Som. Watermark: School girl. Printer: BWC. (Not issued). | .20 | 1.00

17A **5000 Riels** | VF | UNC
ND (1974). Brown, tan, yellow and green. Male bust at right. Back: Building. Unissued. Only released starting in 2005. | — | 7.50

Kampuchea

Bank of Kampuchea

1975 Issue

#18-24 Printed bythe People's Republic of China for the Khmer Rouge. They were briefly issued in two locations in 1975 but soon recalled because Pol Pot decided he wanted an "agrarian moneyless society." All notes dated 1975.

18 **0.1 Riel (1 Kak)** | VF | UNC
1975. Purple and green on orange and multicolor underprint. Mortar crew left. Back: Threshing rice.
a. Issued note. | .50 | 3.00
s. Specimen. | — | 200.

19 **0.5 Riel (5 Kak)**
1975. Red on light green and multicolor underprint. Troops marching at left center. Back: Bayon sculpture at left, machine and worker at right.
a. Issued note. | .50 | 3.00
s. Specimen. | — | 200.

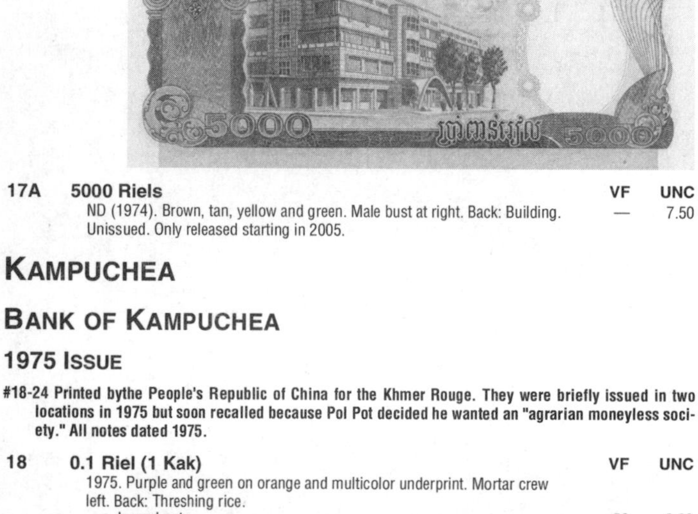

20 **1 Riel** | VF | UNC
1975. Red-violet and red on multicolor underprint. Women farm workers at left center. Back: Woman operating machine. Watermark: Angkor Wat.
a. Issued note. | .50 | 3.00
s. Specimen. | — | 200.

21 **5 Riels** | VF | UNC
1975. Deep green on multicolor underprint. Ancient temples of Angkor Wat at center right. Back: Landscaping crew. Watermark: Angkor Wat.
a. Issued note. | .40 | 3.50
s. Specimen. | — | 200.

22 **10 Riels** | VF | UNC
1975. Brown and red on multicolor underprint. Soldiers (Machine gun crew) at center right. Back: Rice harvesting. Watermark: Angkor Wat.
a. Issued note. | .75 | 6.00
s. Specimen. | — | 200.

23 **50 Riels** | VF | UNC
1975. Purple on multicolor underprint. Planting rice at left, Bayon sculpture at right. Back: Woman's militia at center right. Watermark: Angkor Wat.
a. Issued note. | 2.00 | 12.00
s. Specimen. | — | 200.

24 **100 Riels** | VF | UNC
1975. Deep green on multicolor underprint. Factory workers at left, center. Back: Black. Harvesting rice. Watermark: Angkor Wat.
a. Issued note. | 4.00 | 17.50
s. Specimen. | — | 200.

State Bank of Democratic Kampuchea

1979 Issue

		VF	UNC
25	**0.1 Riel (1 Kak)** 1979. Olive-green on light blue underprint. Arms at center. Back: Water buffalos.		
	a. Issued note.	.15	.50
	s. Specimen. Overprint *SPECIMEN* in red on both sides.	—	15.00
26	**0.2 Riel (2 Kak)** 1979. Grayish green on tan underprint. Arms at center. Back: Rice workers.		
	a. Issued note.	.20	.50
	s. Specimen. Overprint *SPECIMEN* in red on both sides.	—	15.00
27	**0.5 Riel (5 Kak)** 1979. Red-orange on tan and gray underprint. Arms at left, modern passenger train at right. Back: Men fishing from boats with nets.		
	a. Issued note.	.20	1.00
	s. Specimen. Overprint *SPECIMEN* in red on both sides.	—	20.00

		VF	UNC
28	**1 Riel** 1979. Brown on yellow and multicolor underprint. Arms at center. Back: Women harvesting rice. UV: fibers fluoresce blue.		
	a. Issued note.	.20	.50
	s. Specimen. Overprint *SPECIMEN* in red on both sides. 2 serial # var.	—	15.00

		VF	UNC
29	**5 Riels** 1979. Dark brown on light green and multicolor underprint. Four people at left, arms at right. Back: Independence from France (now Victory) monument. UV: fibers fluoresce blue.		
	a. Issued note.	.30	2.00
	s. Specimen. Overprint *SPECIMEN* in red on both sides.	—	15.00
	x. Counterfeit (contemporary).	1.00	3.00

		VF	UNC
30	**10 Riels** 1979. Dark gray on lilac and multicolor underprint. Arms at left, harvesting fruit trees at right. Back: School. UV: fibers fluoresce blue.		
	a. Issued note.	.50	4.00
	s. Specimen. Overprint *SPECIMEN* in red on both sides.	—	15.00

		VF	UNC
31	**20 Riels** 1979. Purple on pink and multicolor underprint. Arms at left. Back: Water buffalos hauling logs. Watermark: Arms.		
	a. Issued note.	.35	5.00
	s. Specimen. Overprint *SPECIMEN* in red on both sides.	—	20.00
	x. Counterfeit (contemporary).	2.00	4.00

		VF	UNC
32	**50 Riels** 1979. Deep red on yellow-green and multicolor underprint. Arms at left, Bayon stone head at center. Back: Angkor Wat. Watermark: Arms.		
	a. Issued note.	.35	7.50
	s. Specimen. Overprint *SPECIMEN* in red on both sides.	—	20.00

1987 Issue

		VF	UNC
33	**5 Riels** 1987. Red and brown on light yellow and light green underprint. Four people at left, arms at right. Back: Red on pale yellow underprint. Independence from France (now Victory) monument. UV: fibers fluoresce blue. Back serial # fluoresce orange.	.35	2.00

		VF	UNC
34	**10 Riels** 1987. Green on light blue and multicolor underprint. Arms at left, harvestinf fruit trees at right. Back: Deep green and lilac on light blue underprint. School.	.35	2.00

State of Cambodia

Peoples National Bank of Cambodia

1990-92 Issue

35 **50 Riels** VF UNC
1992. Dull brown on multicolor underprint. Arms at center, male portrait at right. Back: Ships dockside. Watermark: Stylized lotus flowers. Printer: NBC (without imprint).

	VF	UNC
a. Issued note.	.25	2.00
s. Specimen. Overprint *SPECIMEN* in red on both sides.	—	35.00

36 **100 Riels** VF UNC
1990. Dark green and brown on light blue and lilac underprint. Independence from France (now Victory) monument at left center, male portrait at right. Back: Rubber trees. Watermark: Stylized lotus flowers.

	VF	UNC
a. Issued note.	.50	3.00
s. Specimen. Overprint *SPECIMEN* in red on both sides.	—	75.00

37 **200 Riels** VF UNC
1992. Dull olive-green and tan on multicolor underprint. Floodgates at right. Back: Bayon sculpture in Angkor Wat center. Watermark: Stylized lotus flowers. Printer: NBC.

	VF	UNC
a. Issued note.	.50	2.00
s. Specimen. 1993.	—	125.

38 **500 Riels** VF UNC
1991. Red, purple and brown-violet on multicolor underprint. Arms above Angkor Wat at center. Back: Animal statue at left, cultivating with tractors at center. Watermark: Sculptured heads.

	VF	UNC
a. Issued note.	.50	3.00
s. Specimen. Overprint *SPECIMEN* in red on both sides. (two different serial # varieties.)	—	50.00

39 **1000 Riels** VF UNC
1992. Dark green, brown and black on multicolor underprint. Bayon Temple ruins in Angkor Wat. Back: Fishermen fishing in boats with large nets in Lake Tonle Sap. Watermark: Chinze. (Not released). — 10.00

40 **2000 Riels** VF UNC
1992. Black, deep blue and violet-brown on multicolor underprint. King N. Sihanouk at left. Back: Temple portal at Preah Vihear at right. Watermark: King N. Sihanouk. (Not released). — 10.00

National Bank of Cambodia

1995 Issue

SIGNATURE VARIETIES

	Le Gouverneur	Le Caissier Général
16	Thor Peng Leath,	Tieng Seng, 1999-2005
17	Chea Chanto, 1999-	Tieng Seng, 1999-2005
18	Chea Chanto, 1999-	Tha Yao

41 100 Riels

1995; 1998. Grayish green and brown on multicolor underprint. Chinze, Independence from France (Now Victory) monument at right, arms at upper left. Back: Tapping rubber trees. Watermark: Stylized lotus flowers. Printer: NBC. UV: fibers fluoresce blue. Back 100 in Cambodian fluoresce yellow at right.

	VF	UNC
a. 1995. Signature 16.	.20	2.00
b. 1998. Signature 16; 17.	.20	.50
s. Specimen. Overprint *SPECIMEN* in red either on face or on both sides. 1995; 1998.	—	35.00

42 200 Riels

1995; 1998. Dark olive-green and brown on multicolor underprint. Floodgates at right, but smaller size, arms at upper left. Back: Bayon sculpture in Angkor Wat, center. Watermark: Stylized lotus flowers. Printer: NBC.

	VF	UNC
a. 1995. Signature 16.	FV	2.00
b. 1998. Signature 16; 17.	FV	.35
s. Specimen. Overprint *SPECIMEN* in red on face.1995.	—	40.00

43 500 Riels

1996, 1998. Red and purple on multicolor underprint. Angkor Wot at right, arms at upper left. Back: Mythical animal at left, rice fields at center. Watermark: Stylized lotus flowers. Printer: NBC.

	VF	UNC
a. 1996. Signature 16.	FV	1.00
b. 1998. Signature 16; 17.	FV	1.00
s. Specimen. Overprint *SPECIMEN* in red on face or both sides. 1996, 1998.	—	35.00

44 1000 Riels

ND (1995). Blue-green on gold and multicolor underprint. Bayon stone four faces of Avalokitesvara at left. Back: Prasat Chan Chaya at right. Watermark: Cube design. Printer: F-CO.

	VF	UNC
a. ND (1995).	FV	2.00
r. Replacement note. Zero after prefix letter.	2.00	5.00
s. Specimen. Overprint *SPECIMEN* in rectangle in red on both sides.	—	50.00

45 2000 Riels

ND (1995). Reddish brown on multicolor underprint. Fishermen fishing from boats with nets in Lake Tonle Sap at left and right. Back: Temple ruins at Angkor Wat. Watermark: Cube design. Printer: F-CO.

	VF	UNC
a. Issued note.	FV	3.50
r. Replacement note. Zero after prefix letter.	3.00	7.50
s. Specimen. Overprint *SPECIMEN* in rectangle in red on both sides.	—	40.00

46 5000 Riels

ND (1995); 1998. Deep purple and blue-black with black text on multicolor underprint. King N. Sihanouk at right, Temple of Banteal Srei at lower left center. Back: Central market in Phnom-Penh. Watermark: King N. Sihanouk. Printer: F-CO.

	VF	UNC
a. ND (1995). Signature 16.	FV	10.00
b. 1998. Signature 16, 17.	FV	6.50
r. Replacement note. Zero after prefix letter.	4.00	12.50
s. Specimen. Overprint *SPECIMEN* in red on both sides.. ND (1995) Signature 16; 1998, Signature 17.	—	40.00

47 10,000 Riels

ND (1995); 1998. Blue-black, black and dark green on multicolor underprint. King N. Sihanouk at right, statue of Lokecvara at lower left center. Back: People rowing long boat during the water festival at lower center. Watermark: King N. Sihanouk. Printer: F-CO.

	VF	UNC
a. ND (1995). Signature 16.	FV	12.50
b. 1998. Signature 16, 17.	FV	12.00
r. Replacement note. Zero after prefix letter.	7.00	15.00
s. Specimen. Overprint *SPECIMEN* in red on both sides. ND (1995) Signature 16; 1998, signature 17.	—	50.00

48 20,000 Riels VF UNC

ND (1995). Violet and red on multicolor underprint. King N. Sihanouk at right, boats dockside in Port of Phnom-Penh at center. Signature 16. Back: Throne Room in National Palace. Watermark: King N. Sihanouk. Printer: F-CO.

		VF	UNC
a.	Issued note.	FV	30.00
r.	Replacement note. Zero after prefix letter.	15.00	35.00
s.	Specimen. Overprint *SPECIMEN* in red on both sides.	—	55.00

49 50,000 Riels VF UNC

ND (1995); 1998. Dark brown, brown and deep olive-green on multicolor underprint. Preah Vihear Temple at center. Back: Road to Preah Vihear Temple. Watermark: King N. Sihanouk. Printer: F-CO.

		VF	UNC
a.	ND (1995). Signature 16.	FV	52.50
b.	1998. Signature 16, 17.	FV	50.00
r.	Replacement note. Zero after prefix letter.	25.00	55.00
s.	Specimen. ND (1995); 1998, signature 16, 17.	—	35.00

50 100,000 Riels VF UNC

ND (1995). Green, blue-green and black on multicolor underprint. Chief and First Lady at right. Signature 16. Back: Chief and First Lady receiving homage of people at center right. Watermark: Chief and First Lady. Printer: F-CO.

		VF	UNC
a.	Issued note.	FV	95.00
r.	Replacement note. Zero after prefix letter.	45.00	100.
s.	Specimen. Perforated: *SPECIMEN.*	—	100.

1999 Issue

51 1000 Riels VF UNC

1999. Dark brown and dark olive-green on multicolor underprint. Temples at center right, signature 17. Back: Brown and slate blue. Construction site at center.

		VF	UNC
a.	Issued note.	FV	1.25
s.	Specimen. Overprint *SPECIMEN* in red on both sides.	—	30.00

2001-02 Issue

52 50 Riels VF UNC

2002. Dark brown and tan on multicolor underprint. Preah Vihear temple at center, naga heads sculpture at lower left center. Signature 17. Back: Dam at center. Watermark: Bayon sculpture in Angkor Wat.

		VF	UNC
a.	Issued note.	FV	.35
s.	Specimen. Overprint *SPECIMEN* in red on both sides.	—	25.00

53 100 Riels VF UNC

2001. Purple, brown and green. Independence monument at right, naga heads sculpture at lower left center. Signature 17. Back: Students and school. Watermark: Multiple lines of text. UV: fibers fluoresce blue. Back 100 in Cambodian fluoresce yellow at right.

		VF	UNC
a.	Issued note.	FV	.50
s.	Specimen. Overprint *SPECIMEN* in red on both sides.	—	15.00

54 500 Riels VF UNC

2002; 2004. Red and purple on multicolor underprint. Angkor Wat temple at center, naga heads sculpture at lower left center. Signature 17. Back: Bridge spanning Mekong river at Kampong Cham at center. Watermark: Baylon sculpture in Angkor Wat.

		VF	UNC
a.	2002. Dark sky on back.	FV	1.50
b.	2004. Light sky on back.	FV	1.00
s.	Specimen. Overprint *SPECIMEN* in red on both sides. 2002; 2004.	FV	15.00

#	Denomination	VF	UNC
55	**5000 Riels**	VF	UNC
	2001; 2002; 2004; 2007. Green and gray. King Norodom Sihanouk at right, signature 17. Back: Bridge of Kampong Kdei in Siemreap Province.		
	a. 2001.	FV	5.00
	b. 2002.	FV	5.00
	c. 2004.	FV	4.00
	d. 2007.	FV	3.00
	s. Specimen. As a. Overprint *SPECIMEN* in red on face.	—	50.00

#	Denomination	VF	UNC
56	**10,000 Riels**	VF	UNC
	2001; 2005. Violet, brown and blue. King Norodom Sihanouk at right, signature 17. Back: Water festival before Royal Palace.		
	a. 2001.	FV	6.00
	b. 2005.	FV	5.00
	s. Specimen. As a. Overprint *SPECIMEN* in red on face.	—	50.00

#	Denomination	VF	UNC
57	**50,000 Riels**	VF	UNC
	2001. Violet, brown and blue. King Norodom Sihanouk at right, signature 17. Back: Angkor Wat temple.		
	a. Issued note.	FV	40.00
	s. Specimen.	—	30.00

2005-12 Issue

#	Denomination	VF	UNC
58	**1000 Riels**	VF	UNC
	2005; 2007. Brown and lilac on multicolor underprint. Temple at center. Back: Cargo ships.		
	a. 2005.	FV	2.25
	b. 2007.	FV	2.25
	s. Specimen. Overprint *SPECIMEN* in red on both sides. 2005.	—	40.00

#	Denomination	VF	UNC
59	**2000 Riels**	VF	UNC
	2007. Dark and light green on multicolor underprint. Portal ruins at the Preah Vihear Temple. Back: Female farm worker in rice fields and Angkopr Wat temple complex in distance. Watermark: Bayon sculpture. 146x68mm.		
	a. Issued note.	FV	2.00
	s. Specimen. Perforated *SPECIMEN.*	—	50.00

#	Denomination	VF	UNC
60	**20,000 Riels**	VF	UNC
	2008. Purple and violet on multicolor underprint. King Norodom Sohamoni at right. Back: Aerial view of Angkor Thom Temple complex at center, Four faced Buddah in bayon temple at right. Watermark. Bayon sculpture. 155x72mm.		
	a. Issued note.	FV	9.00
	s. Specimen.	FV	20.00
61	**50,000 Riels**		
	2009.		
	a. Issued note.	FV	18.00
	s. Specimen.	—	—

#	Denomination	VF	UNC
62	**100,000 Riels**	VF	UNC
	2012. Slate grey and green on multicolor underprint. King Norodom Sihanouk and Queen Norodom Monineath Sihanouk at right center. Back: Green and multicolor. King-Father and Queen-Mother and King Norodom Sihamoni. 170x77mm.		
	a. Issued note.	FV	65.00
	s. Specimen. Pin hole cancelled: *SPECIMEN.*	—	150.

2013 Issue

#	Denomination	VF	UNC
63	**1000 Riels**	VF	UNC
	2012. Brown and blue on multicolor underprint. The late King Samdech Preah Norodom Sihanouk at right center. Back: Tan and blue. Royal boat parade float at right center. Watermark: Lotus flower. 146x68mm.		
	a. Issued note.	FV	5.00
	s. Specimen. Pin hole cancelled: *SPECIMEN.*	—	50.00

Collector Series

National Bank of Cambodia

1995 ND Issue

#	Denomination	Mkt.	Value
CS1	**1000 - 100,000 Riels**	Mkt.	Value
	ND (1995). #44-50. Specimen.		250.

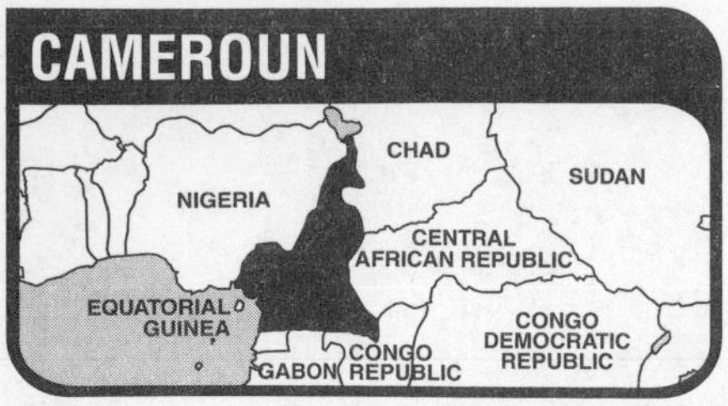

The United Republic of Cameroun, located in west-central Africa on the Gulf of Guinea, has an area of 475,440 sq. km. and a population of 18.46 million. Capital: Yaounde. About 90 percent of the labor force is employed on the land; cash crops account for 80 percent of the country's export revenue. Cocoa, coffee, aluminum, cotton, rubber and timber are exported.

The former French Cameroon and part of British Cameroon merged in 1961 to form the present country. Cameroon has generally enjoyed stability, which has permitted the development of agriculture, roads, and railways, as well as a petroleum industry. Despite a slow movement toward democratic reform, political power remains firmly in the hands of President Paul Biya.

MONETARY SYSTEM:

1 Franc = 100 Centimes

SIGNATURE VARIETIES:

Refer to introduction of Central African States.

RÉPUBLIQUE DU CAMEROUN

BANQUE CENTRALE

1961 ND ISSUE

#7-9 denominations in French only, or French and English.

		Fine	XF
7	**1000 Francs** ND (1961). Multicolor. Man with basket harvesting cocoa. Signature 1A.	750.	1850.
8	**5000 Francs** ND (1961). Multicolor. President A. Ahidjo at right. Signature 1A.	300.	1500.

		Fine	XF
9	**5000 Francs** ND. Multicolor. President A. Ahidjo at right. Signature 1A, denomination in English words at lower left.	600.	2000.

RÉPUBLIQUE FÉDÉRALE DU CAMEROUN

BANQUE CENTRALE

1962 ND ISSUE

		VF	UNC
10	**100 Francs** ND (1962). Multicolor. President of the Republic at left, denomination in French and English. Signature 1A. Back: Ships. Watermark: Antelope's head.		
	a. Issued note.	30.00	125.
	s. Specimen. Overprint: *SPECIMEN* in black and perforated.	—	300.

		VF	UNC
11	**500 Francs** ND (1962). Multicolor. Man with 2 oxen, denomination in French and English. Signature 1A. Back: Man with bananas at left, truck on road at center right, two ships in background at upper right. Engraved (intaglio) and lithographic varieties.	150.	475.

		VF	UNC
12	**1000 Francs** ND (1962). Multicolor. Denominations in French and English.Signature 1A. Back: Like #7 but with title: *RÉPUBLIQUE FÉDÉRALE*.		
	a. Issued note. Engraved.	250.	750.
	b. Issued note. Lithographic.	250.	750.
	s. Specimen. Overprint: *SPECIMEN* in black and perforated.	—	750.
13	**5000 Francs** ND (1962). Multicolor. Denominations in French and English.Signature 1A. Back: Like #9 but with title: *RÉPUBLIQUE FÉDÉRALE*.		
	a. Issued note.	500.	1650.
	s. Specimen. Overprint: *SPECIMEN* in black and perforated.	—	1250.

1972 ND ISSUE

14	10,000 Francs	VF	UNC
	ND (1972). Multicolor. President A. Ahidjo at left, fruit at center, wood carving at right. Signature 2. Back: Statue at left and right, tractor plowing at center.	125.	375.

République Unie Du Cameroun

Banque des États de l'Afrique Centrale

1974 ND Issue

15	500 Francs	VF	UNC
	ND (1974; 1984); 1978-83. Red brown and multicolor. Woman wearing hat at left, aerial view of modern buildings at center. Back: Mask at left, students and chemical testing at center, statue at right.		
	a. Signature titles: *LE DIRECTEUR GÉNÉRAL* and *UN CENSEUR.* Engraved. watermark: Antelope in half profile. Signature 3. ND (1974).	75.00	250.
	b. As a. signature 5.	12.50	45.00
	c. Signature titles: *LE GOUVERNEUR* and *UN CENSEUR.* watermark: Antelope in profile. Signature 10. 1.4.1978.	8.00	35.00
	d. Signature 12. 1.6.1981; 1.1.1983.	6.00	25.00
	e. Signature 12. 1.1.1982.	25.00	75.00

16	1000 Francs	VF	UNC
	ND (1974); 1978-83. Blue and multicolor. Hut at center, girl with plaits at right. Back: Mask at left, trains, planes and bridge at center, statue at right.		
	a. Signature titles: *LE DIRECTEUR GÉNÉRAL* and *UN CENSEUR.* Engraved. watermark: Antelope in half profile. Signature 5. ND (1974).	15.00	60.00
	b. Signature titles like a. Lithographed. watermark. like c. Signature 8. ND (1978).	55.00	175.
	c. Signature titles: *LE GOUVERNEUR* and *UN CENSEUR.* Lithographed. watermark: Antelope in profile. Signature 10. 1.4.1978, 1.7.1980.	10.00	40.00
	d. Signature 12. 1.6.1981; 1.1.1982; 2; 1.1.1983.	8.00	35.00
	s. As a. Specimen.	—	—

17	5000 Francs	VF	UNC
	ND (1974). Brown and multicolor. President A. Ahidjo at left, railway loading equipment at right. Back: Mask at left, industrial college at center, statue at right.		
	a. Signature titles: *LE DIRECTEUR GÉNÉRAL* and *UN CENSEUR.* Engraved. Signature 3. ND (1974).	175.	550.
	b. Like a. signature 5.	100.	350.
	c. Signature titles: *LE GOUVERNEUR* and *UN CENSEUR.* Signature 11; 12.	80.00	250.
	s. As a. Specimen. Overprint: *SPECIMEN* in black and perforated.	—	1000.

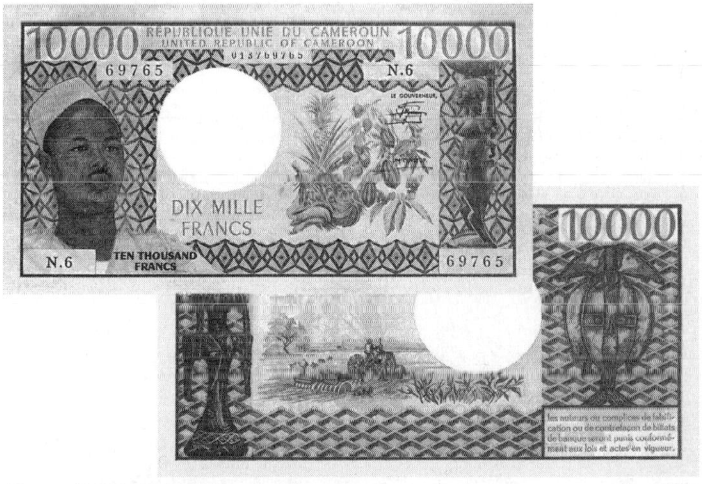

18	10,000 Francs	VF	UNC
	ND (1974; 1978; 1981). Multicolor. President A. Ahidjo at left. Back: Statue at left and right, tractor plowing at center.		
	a. Signature titles: *LE DIRECTEUR GÉNÉRAL* and *UN CENSEUR.* Signature 5. ND (1974).	100.	400.
	b. Signature titles: *LE GOUVERNEUR* and *UN CENSEUR.* Signature 11; 12. ND (1978; 1981).	75.00	300.

1981 ND Issue

19	5000 Francs	VF	UNC
	ND (1981). Brown and multicolor. Mask at left, woman carrying bundle of fronds at right, signature 12. Back: Plowing and mine ore conveyor.		
	a. Issued note.	25.00	100.
	s. Specimen. Overprint: *SPECIMEN* in black and perforated.	—	750.

		VF	UNC
20	**10,000 Francs** ND (1981). Brown, green and multicolor. Stylized antelope heads at left, woman at right, signature 12. Back: Loading of fruit onto truck at left.	50.00	175.

République du Cameroun

Banque des États de l'Afrique Centrale

1984 ND Issue

		VF	UNC
21	**1000 Francs** 1.6.1984. Blue and multicolor. Hut at center, girl with plaits at right, signature 12. Back: Mask at left, trains, planes, and bridge at center, statue at right.	7.50	30.00
22	**5000 Francs** ND (1984; 1990; 1992). Brown and multicolor. Mask at left, woman carrying bundle of fronds at right, signature 12; 13; 15. Back: Plowing and mine ore conveyor.	25.00	100.
23	**10,000 Francs** ND (1984; 1990). Brown, green and multicolor. Stylized antelope heads at left, woman at right, signature 12; 13. Back: Loading of fruit onto truck at left.	50.00	175.

1985-86 Issue

		VF	UNC
24	**500 Francs** 1985-90. Brown on multicolor underprint. Carving and jug at center. Back: Man carving mask at left center. Watermark: Carving.		
	a. Signature 12. 1.1.1985-1.1.1988.	5.00	20.00
	b. Signature 13. 1.1.1990.	4.00	15.00

		VF	UNC
25	**1000 Francs** 1.1.1985. Dark blue on multicolor underprint. Carving at left, small figurines at center, man at right, incomplete map of Chad at top. Back: Elephant at left, carving at right. Watermark: Carving.	10.00	40.00

		VF	UNC
26	**1000 Francs** 1986-92. Dark blue on multicolor underprint. Carving at left, small figurines at center, man at right, completed outline map of Chad at top center. Back: Elephant at left, carving at right. Watermark: Carving.		
	a. Signature 12. 1.1.1986-1.1.1989.	8.00	35.00
	b. Signature 13. 1.1.1990.	7.00	30.00
	c. Signature 15.1.1.1992.	6.00	25.00

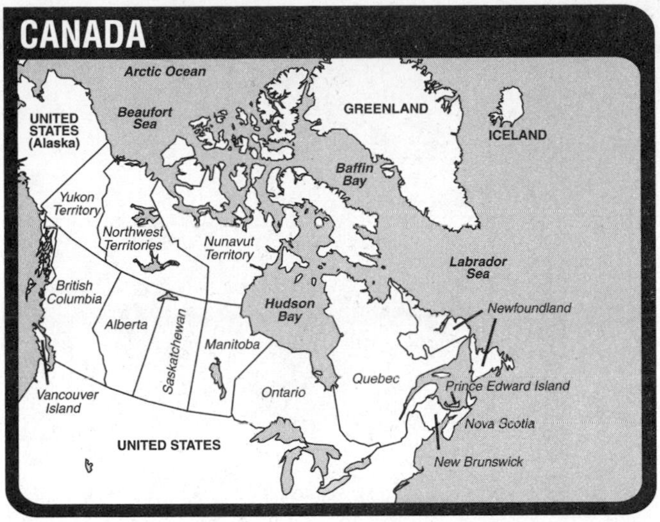

Canada is located to the north of the United States, and spans the full breadth of the northern portion of North America from Atlantic to Pacific oceans, except for the State of Alaska. It has a total area of 9,984,670 sq. km. and a population of 33.21 million. Capital: Ottawa.

A land of vast distances and rich natural resources, Canada became a self-governing dominion in 1867 while retaining ties to the British crown. Economically and technologically the nation has developed in parallel with the US, its neighbor to the south across an unfortified border. Canada faces the political challenges of meeting public demands for quality improvements in health care and education services, as well as responding to separatist concerns in predominantly francophone Quebec. Canada also aims to develop its diverse energy resources while maintaining its commitment to the environment.

RULERS:

French 1534-1763
British 1763-

MONETARY SYSTEM:

French:
12 Deniers = 1 Sou (sols)
20 Sous or Sols = 1 Livre Coloniale
1 Liard = 3 Deniers
1 Ecu = 6 Livres
1 Louis D'or = 4 Ecus
English:
4 Farthings = 1 Penny
12 Pence = 1 Shilling
20 Shillings = 1 Pound
Canadian Decimal Currency
100 Cents = 1 Dollar

REPLACEMENT NOTES:

#66-70A and 74b, asterisk in front of fractional prefix letters. #76, 78-81, triple letter prefix ending in X (AAX, BAX, etc.). Exceptions: #82, no asterisk but serial number starts with 510 or 516; #83, serial number starts with 31 (instead of 30).
#84-90, as #76 and 78-81.

Dominion

Banque du Canada / Bank of Canada

1954 Modified Hair Style Issue

		VF	UNC
74	**1 Dollar**		
	1954 (1955-72). Black on green underprint. Like #66 but Queen's hair in modified style. Back: Green. Western prairie scene. Printer: CBNC.		
	a. Signature Beattie-Coyne. (1955-61).	2.50	15.00
	b. Signature Beattie-Rasminsky. (1961-72).	2.00	12.50

		VF	UNC
75	**1 Dollar**		
	1954 (1955-74). Black on green underprint. Queen's hair in modified style. Like #74. Back: Green. Western prairie scene. Printer: BABNC.		
	a. Signature Beattie-Coyne. (1955-61).	2.50	40.00
	b. Signature Beattie-Rasminsky. (1961-72).	2.00	12.50
	c. Signature Bouey-Rasminsky. (1972-73).	2.00	10.00
	d. Signature Lawson-Bouey. (1973-74).	2.00	10.00

		VF	UNC
76	**2 Dollars**		
	1954 (1955-75). Black on red-brown underprint. Like #67 but Queen's hair in modified style. Back: Red-brown. Quebec scenery. Printer: BABNC. UV: planchettes fluoresce blue.		
	a. Signature Beattie-Coyne. (1955-61).	8.00	55.00
	b. Signature Beattie-Rasminsky. (1961-72).	3.00	12.50
	c. Signature Bouey-Rasminsky. (1972-73).	3.00	15.00
	d. Signature Lawson-Bouey. (1973-75).	3.00	15.00

		VF	UNC
77	**5 Dollars**		
	1954 (1955-72). Black on blue underprint. Like #68 but Queen's hair in modified style. Back: Blue. River in the north country. Printer: CBNC.		
	a. Signature Beattie-Coyne. (1955-61).	15.00	70.00
	b. Signature Beattie-Rasminsky. (1961-72).	10.00	45.00
	c. Signature Bouey-Rasminsky. (1972).	10.00	35.00
78	**5 Dollars**		
	1954 (1955-61). Black on blue underprint. Queen's hair in modified style. Like #77. Signature Beattie-Coyne. Back: Blue. River in the north country. Printer: BABNC.	12.50	70.00

79 **10 Dollars** | VF | UNC

1954 (1955-71). Black on purple underprint. Like #69 but Queen's hair in modified style. Back: Purple. Rocky Mountain scene. Printer: BABNC.

	VF	UNC
a. Signature Beattie-Coyne. (1955-61).	15.00	85.00
b. Signature Beattie-Rasminsky. (1961-71).	13.00	60.00

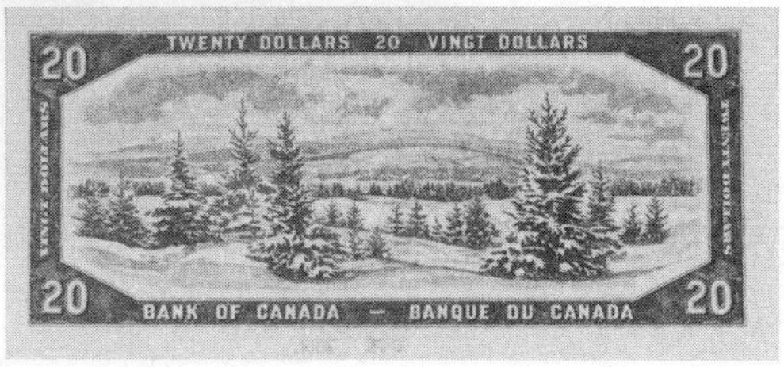

80 **20 Dollars** | VF | UNC

1954 (1955-70) Black on olive olive-green underprint. Like #70 but Queen's hair in modified style. Back: Olive-green. Laurentian hills in winter. Printer: CBNC.

	VF	UNC
a. Signature Beattie-Coyne. (1955-61).	25.00	150.
b. Signature Beattie-Rasminsky. (1961-70).	25.00	100.

81 **50 Dollars** | VF | UNC

1954 (1955-75). Black on orange underprint. Like #71 but Queen's hair in modified style. Back: Orange. Atlantic coastline. Printer: CBNC.

	VF	UNC
a. Signature Beattie-Coyne. (1955-61).	75.00	400.
b. Signature Beattie-Rasminsky. (1961-72).	75.00	300.
c. Signature Lawson-Bouey. (1973-75).	75.00	350.

82 **100 Dollars** | VF | UNC

1954 (1955-76). Black on brown underprint. Queen's hair in modified style. Back: Brown. Mountain lake. Printer: CBNC.

	VF	UNC
a. Signature Beattie-Coyne. (1955-61).	125.	375.
b. Signature Beattie-Rasminsky. (1961-72).	125.	300.
c. Signature Lawson-Bouey. (1973-76).	125.	350.

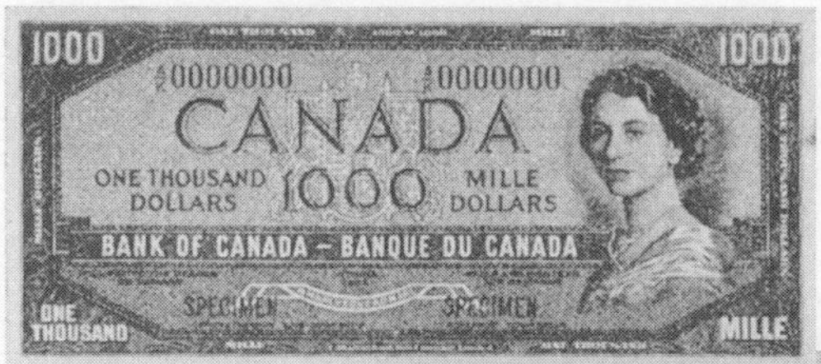

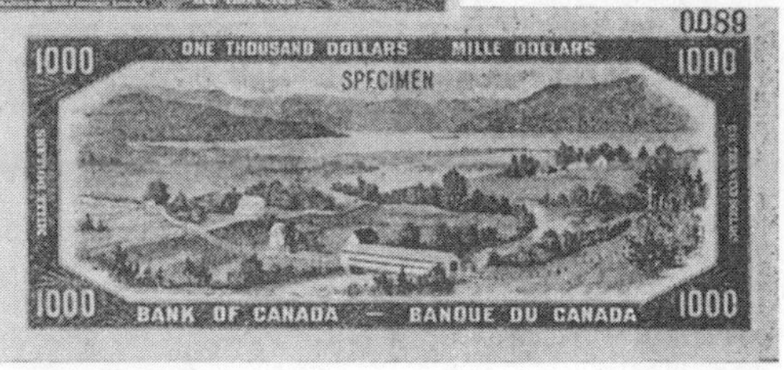

83 **1000 Dollars** | VF | UNC

1954 (1955-87). Black on rose underprint. Like #73 but Queen's hair in modified style. Back: Rose. Central Canadian landscape.

	VF	UNC
a. Signature Beattie-Coyne. (1955-61).	1400.	4500.
b. Signature Beattie-Rasminsky. (1961-72).	1100.	2750.
c. Signature Bouey-Rasminsky. (1972).	1100.	2250.
d. Signature Lawson-Bouey. (1973-84).	1075.	1500.
e. Signature Thiessen-Crow. (1987).	1250.	2250.

1967 Commemorative Issue

#84, Centennial of Canadian Confederation

84 **1 Dollar** | VF | UNC

1967. Black on green underprint. Queen Elizabeth II at right. Signature Beattie-Rasminsky. Back: Green. First Parliament Building. Centennial of Canadian Confederation. UV: planchettes fluoresce blue.

	VF	UNC
a. Centennial dates: *1867-1967* replaces serial #.	1.50	4.00
b. Regular serial #'s.	2.00	7.50

1969-75 Issue

85 **1 Dollar** | VF | UNC

1973. Black on light green and multicolor underprint. Queen Elizabeth II at right, arms at left. Back: Parliament Building as seen from across the Ottawa River. UV: planchettes fluoresce blue.

	VF	UNC
a. Engraved back. signature Lawson-Bouey.	1.00	5.00
b. Lithographed back. signature as a. Serial # prefix: *AFF-*.	1.00	6.00
c. Signature Crow-Bouey.	1.00	3.50

86 **2 Dollars**

1974. Red-brown on multicolor underprint. Queen Elizabeth II at right, arms at left. Back: Inuits preparing for hunt. UV: planchettes fluoresce blue.

	VF	UNC
a. Signature Lawson-Bouey.	2.25	12.50
b. Signature Crow-Bouey.	2.25	12.00

87 **5 Dollars**

1972. Blue on multicolor underprint. Sir Wilfred Laurier at right, serial # on face, arms at left. Back: Salmon fishing boat at Vancouver Island. UV: planchettes and fibers fluoresce blue.

	VF	UNC
a. Signature Bouey-Rasminsky.	6.00	40.00
b. Signature Lawson-Bouey.	6.00	37.50

88 **10 Dollars**

1971. Purple on multicolor underprint. Sir John A. MacDonald at right, arms at left. Back: Oil refinery at Sarnia, Ontario.

	VF	UNC
a. Signature Beattie-Rasminsky.	12.50	70.00
b. Signature Bouey-Rasminsky.	15.00	85.00
c. Signature Lawson-Bouey.	FV	45.00
d. Signature Crow-Bouey.	FV	40.00
e. Signature Thiessen-Crow.	FV	42.50

89 **20 Dollars**

1969. Green on multicolor underprint. Queen Elizabeth II at right, serial # on face, arms at left. Back: Alberta's Lake Moraine and Rocky Mountains.

	VF	UNC
a. Signature Beattie-Rasminsky.	25.00	95.00
b. Signature Lawson-Bouey.	22.50	90.00

90 **50 Dollars**

1975. Red on multicolor underprint. William Lyon MacKenzie King at right, arms at left. Back: Mounted Police in *Dome* formation (from their Musical Ride program).

	VF	UNC
a. Signature Lawson-Bouey.	65.00	220.
b. Signature Crow-Bouey.	55.00	185.

91 **100 Dollars**

1975. Brown on multicolor underprint. Sir Robert Borden at right, arms at left. Back: Lunenburg, Nova Scotia harbor scene.

	VF	UNC
a. Signature Lawson-Bouey.	105.	250.
b. Signature Crow-Bouey.	100.	225.

1979 Issue

92 **5 Dollars**

1979. Blue on multicolor underprint. Sir Wilfred Laurier at right, arms at left, different design element at upper center. Back: Salmon fishing boat at Vancouver Island, serial #.

	VF	UNC
a. Signature Lawson-Bouey.	FV	35.00
b. Signature Crow-Bouey.	FV	40.00

93 **20 Dollars**

1979. Deep olive-green on multicolor underprint. Queen Elizabeth II at right, arms at left, similar to # 89, but different guilloches. Back: Alberta's Lake Moraine and Rocky Mountains, serial number. UV: planchettes fluoresce blue.

	VF	UNC
a. Signature Lawson-Bouey.	FV	75.00
b. Signature Crow-Bouey.	FV	70.00
c. Signature Thiessen-Crow.	FV	50.00

1986-91 Issue

#94-100 Replacement notes: Third letter of serial # prefix is *X*.

94	**2 Dollars**	VF	UNC
	1986. Brown on multicolor underprint. Queen Elizabeth II, Parliament building at right, arms at upper left center. Back: Pair of robins. Replacement notes: Third letter of serial # prefix is X.		
	a. Signature Crow-Bouey.	FV	8.50
	b. Signature Thiessen-Crow.	FV	4.00
	c. Signature Bonin-Thiessen.	FV	4.00

95	**5 Dollars**	VF	UNC
	1986. Blue-gray on multicolor underprint. Sir Wilfrid Laurier, Parliament buildings at right, arms at upper left center. Back: Kingfisher.		
	a1. Signature Crow-Bouey. Yellow plate # on back.	5.50	35.00
	a2. Signature Crow-Bouey. Blue plate # on back.	FV	27.50
	b. Signature Thiessen-Crow.	FV	15.00
	c. Signature Bonin-Thiessen.	FV	12.00
	d. Signature Knight-Thiessen.	FV	11.00
	e. Signature Knight-Dodge.	FV	10.00

96	**10 Dollars**	VF	UNC
	1989. Purple on multicolor underprint. Sir John A. Macdonald, Parliament buildings at right, arms at upper left center. Back: Osprey in flight.		
	a. Signature Thiessen-Crow.	FV	20.00
	b. Signature Bonin-Thiessen.	FV	18.50
	c. Signature Knight-Thiessen.	FV	17.50

97	**20 Dollars**	VF	UNC
	1991. Deep olive-green and olive-green on multicolor underprint. Green foil optical device with denomination at upper left, Queen Elizabeth II, Parliament library at right, arms at upper left center. Back: Common loon. Note: The letter "I" in the serial # prefix exists serif and sans-serif.		
	a. Signature Thiessen-Crow.	FV	35.00
	b. Signature Bonin-Thiessen.	FV	35.00
	c. Signature Knight-Thiessen.	FV	32.50
	d. Signature Knight-Dodge.	FV	32.50

98	**50 Dollars**	VF	UNC
	1988. Red on multicolor underprint. William Lyon MacKenzie King, Parliament building at right, gold optical device with denomination at upper left, arms at upper left center. Back: Snowy owl.		
	a. Signature Thiessen-Crow.	FV	95.00
	b. Signature Bonin-Thiessen.	FV	100.
	c. Signature Knight-Thiessen.	FV	85.00
	d. Signature Knight-Dodge.	FV	80.00

99	**100 Dollars**	VF	UNC
	1988. Dark brown on multicolor underprint. Sir Robert Bordon, Parliament building at right, green optical device with denomination at upper left, arms at upper left center. Back: Canadian geese.		
	a. Signature Thiessen-Crow.	FV	175.
	b. Signature Bonin-Thiessen.	FV	225.
	c. Signature Knight-Thiessen.	FV	150.
	d. Signature Knight-Dodge.	FV	135.

100	**1000 Dollars**	VF	UNC
	1988. Pink on multicolor underprint. Queen Elizabeth II, Parliament library at right, Optical device with denomination at upper left, arms at upper left center. Back: Pine grosbeak pair on branch at right.		
	a. Signature Thiessen-Crow.	FV	1650.
	b. Signature Bonin-Thiessen.	FV	1500.

2001-03 Issue

101 5 Dollars — VF / UNC

2002. Blue and tan-yellow. Sir Wilfrid Laurier at left, west block of Parliament at center. Back: Winter sports - children skating, tobogganing, and playing hockey.

	VF	UNC
a. 2002/2001. Signature Knight-Dodge.	FV	8.50
b. 2002/2003. Signature Knight-Dodge.	FV	8.50
c. 2002/2004. Signature Jenkins-Dodge.	FV	8.50
d. 2002/2005. Signature Jenkins-Dodge.	FV	8.50

101A 5 Dollars — VF / UNC

2006-. Blue and tan-yellow. Sir Wilfrid Lauier at left, west block of Parliament at center, holographic strip at left. Back: Winter sports - children skating, tobogganing, and playing hockey.

	VF	UNC
a. 2006/2006. Signature Jenkins-Dodge.	FV	8.00
b. 2006/2008. Signature Jenkins-Carney.	FV	7.50
c. 2006/2009. Signature Jenkins-Carney.	FV	7.50
d. 2006/2010. Signature Jenkins-Carney.	FV	7.50

102 10 Dollars

2001. Purple and tan on multicolor underprint. Sir John A. Macdonald at left, Parliament Library at center. Back: Veteran and children at memorial at right, peacekeeper with binoculars at center, poppies and doves.

	VF	UNC
a. 2001/2000. Signature Knight-Thiessen.	FV	15.00
b. 2001/2001. Signature Knight-Dodge.	FV	13.50
c. 2001/2002. Signature Knight-Dodge.	FV	13.50
d. 2001/2003. Signature Jenkins-Dodge.	FV	17.50
e. 2001/2004. Signature Jenkins-Dodge.	FV	17.50

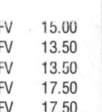

102A 10 Dollars — VF / UNC

2005-. Purple and tan on multicolor underprint. Sir John A. Macdonald at left, Parliament Library at center, holographic strip at left. Back: Veteran and children at memorial at right, peacekeeper with binoculars at center, poppies and doves.

	VF	UNC
a. 2005/2004. Signature Jenkins-Dodge.	FV	14.00
b. 2005/2005. Signature Jenkins-Dodge.	FV	14.00
c. 2005/2007. Signature Jenkins-Dodge.	FV	14.00
d. 2005/2008. Signature Jenkins-Carney.	FV	13.00
e. 2005/2009. Signature Jenkins-Carney.	FV	12.00

103 20 Dollars — VF / UNC

2004-. Green and tan on multicolor underprint. Queen Elizabeth II at left. Back: Westcoast native art theme.

	VF	UNC
a. 2004/2004. Signature Jenkins-Dodge.	FV	30.00
b. 2004/2005. Signature Jenkins-Dodge.	FV	27.50
c. 2004/2006. Signature Jenkins-Dodge.	FV	27.50
d. 2004/2007. Signature Jenkins-Dodge.	FV	27.50
e. 2004/2008. Signature Jenkins-Dodge.	FV	25.00
f. 2004/2009. Signature Jenkins-Carney.	FV	25.00
g. 2004/2010. Signature Jenkins-Carney.	FV	25.00
h. 2004/2011. Signature Maclem-Carney	FV	22.50

104 50 Dollars — VF / UNC

2004-. Red-orange and tan on multicolor underprint. William Lyon MacKenzie King at left. Back: Accomplishments of the Famous Five and Thérèse Casgrain. 152x69mm.

	VF	UNC
a. 2004/2004. Signature Jenkins-Dodge.	FV	80.00
b. 2004/2006. Signature Jenkins-Dodge.	FV	75.00
c. 2004/2008. Signature Jenkins-Carney.	FV	75.00
d. 2004/2011. Signature Maclem and Carney.	FV	70.00

105 100 Dollars — VF / UNC

2004-. Brown and green on multicolor underprint. Sir Robert Borden at right. Back: Historic and satellite maps of Canada.

	VF	UNC
a. 2004/2003. Signature Jenkins-Dodge.	FV	150.
b. 2004/2005. Signature Jenkins-Dodge.	FV	140.
c. 2004/2006. Signature Jenkins-Dodge.	FV	140.
d. 2004/2008. Signature Jenkins-Carney.	FV	135.
e. 2004/2010.	FV	135.

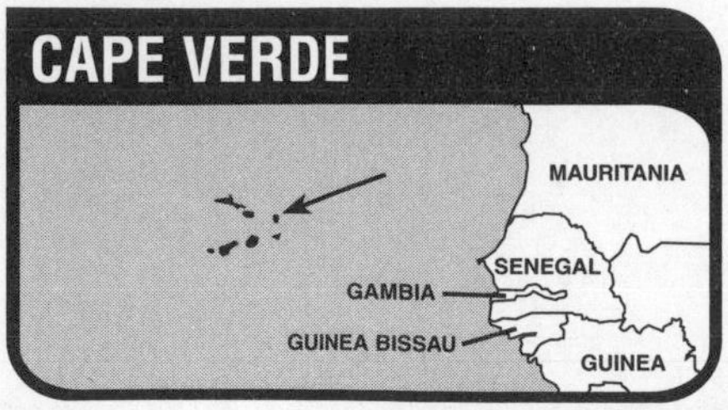

The Republic of Cape Verde, is located in the Atlantic Ocean, about 370 miles (595 km.) west of Dakar, Senegal off the coast of Africa. The 14-island republic has an area of 4,033 sq. km. and a population of 427,000. Capital: Praia. Fishing is important and agriculture is widely practiced, but the Cape Verdes are not self-sufficient in food. Fish products, salt, bananas, coffee, peanuts and shellfish are exported.

The uninhabited islands were discovered and colonized by the Portuguese in the 15th century; Cape Verde subsequently became a trading center for African slaves and later an important coaling and resupply stop for whaling and transatlantic shipping. Following independence in 1975, and a tentative interest in unification with Guinea-Bissau, a one-party system was established and maintained until multi-party elections were held in 1990. Cape Verde continues to exhibit one of Africa's most stable democratic governments. Repeated droughts during the second half of the 20th century caused significant hardship and prompted heavy emigration. As a result, Cape Verde's expatriate population is greater than its domestic one. Most Cape Verdeans have both African and Portuguese antecedents.

RULERS:

Portuguese to 1975

MONETARY SYSTEM:

1 Mil Reis = 1000 Reis
1 Escudo = 100 Centavos, 1911-

STEAMSHIP SEALS

Type I
LOANDA

Type II
LISBOA

Type III
C,C,A

C,C,A = Colonias, Commercio, Agricultura.

Portuguese Administration

Banco Nacional Ultramarino

Cabo Verde

1971; 1972 Issue

		VF	UNC
52	**20 Escudos** 4.4.1972. Green on multicolor underprint. Portrait of S. Pinto at right, bank seal at left, arms at lower center. Two signature varieties. Signature titles: *ADMINISTRATOR* and *VICE-GOVERNADOR.* Back: Allegorical woman with ships. Security thread.		
	a. Issued note.	150.	400.
	s. Specimen.	—	250.

		VF	UNC
53	**50 Escudos** 4.4.1972. Blue on multicolor underprint. Portrait of S. Pinto at right, bank seal at left, arms at lower center. Signature titles: *ADMINISTRATOR* and *VICE-GOVERNADOR.* Back: Allegorical woman with ships. Security thread.		
	a. Issued note.	175.	500.
	s. Specimen.	—	325.

		VF	UNC
53A	**500 Escudos** 16.6.1971; 29.6.1971. Olive-green on multicolor underprint. Infante D. Henrique at right.		
	a. Issued note.	225.	600.
	s. Specimen.	—	500.
	ct. Color trial. Blue on multicolor underprint.	—	650.

Republic

Banco de Cabo Verde

1977 Issue

		VF	UNC
54	**100 Escudos** 20.1.1977. Red and multicolor. Bow and musical instruments at left, A. Cabral with native hat at right. Back: Mountain at left center. Watermark: A. Cabral. Printer: BWC.		
	a. Issued note.	7.50	25.00
	s1. Specimen. Overprint: *ESPECIME* in red on both sides. Punch hole cancelled.	—	95.00
	s2. Specimen. Overprint: *ESPECIME* in black. Punch hole cancelled.	—	95.00
	s3. Specimen. Overprint: *SPECIMEN.* in red. Punch hole cancelled.	—	95.00

55	500 Escudos	VF	UNC
	20.1.1977. Blue and multicolor. Shark at left, A. Cabral with native hat at right. Back: Harbor at Praia. Watermark: A. Cabral. Printer: BWC.		
	a. Issued note.	15.00	40.00
	s1. Specimen. Overprint: *ESPECIMEN* in red on both sides. Punch hole cancelled.	—	95.00
	s2. Specimen. Overprint: *SPECIMEN* on both sides. Punch hole cancelled.	—	95.00

56	1000 Escudos	VF	UNC
	20.1.1977. Brown and multicolor. Electrical appliance at left, A. Cabral with native hat at right. Back: Workers at quarry at left center, banana stalk at right. Watermark: A. Cabral. Printer: BWC.		
	a. Issued note.	27.50	75.00
	s1. Specimen. Overprint: *ESPECIMEN* on both sides. Punch hole cancelled.	—	200.
	s2. Specimen. Overprint: *SPECIMEN* on both sides. Punch hole cancelled.	—	200.

1989 Issue

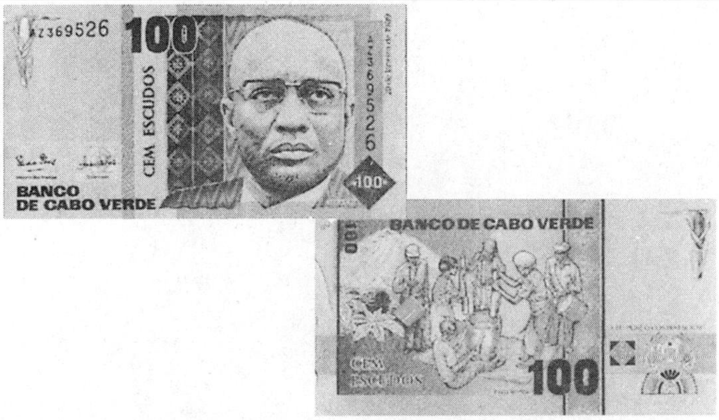

57	100 Escudos	VF	UNC
	20.1.1989. Red and dark purple on multicolor underprint. A. Cabral at right, serial number black at left, red at right. Back: Festival at left center. Watermark: A. Cabral. Printer: TDLR.		
	a. Issued note.	FV	6.00
	s. Specimen. Overprint: *ESPECIMEN* in red on both sides. Punch hole cancelled.	—	25.00

58	200 Escudos	VF	UNC
	20.1.1989. Green and black on multicolor underprint. A. Cabral at right, Serial number black at left, red at right. Back: Modern airport collage in vertical format. Watermark: A. Cabral. Printer: TDLR.		
	a. Issued note.	FV	10.00
	s. Specimen. Overprint: *ESPECIMEN* in red on both sides. Punch hole cancelled.	—	35.00

59	500 Escudos	VF	UNC
	20.1.1989. Blue on multicolor underprint. A. Cabral at right, serial number black at left, red at right. Back: Shipyard. Watermark: A. Cabral. Printer: TDLR.		
	a. Issued note.	FV	20.00
	s. Specimen.	—	40.00

60	1000 Escudos	VF	UNC
	20.1.1989. Brown and red-brown on multicolor underprint. A Cabral at right, serial number black at left, red at right. Back: Insects at left center. Watermark: A. Cabral. Printer: TDLR.		
	a. Issued note.	FV	35.00
	s. Specimen.	—	50.00

61 2500 Escudos — VF | UNC

20.1.1989. Violet on multicolor underprint. A. Cabral at right, serial number black at left, red at right. Back: Palace of National Assembly. Watermark: A. Cabral. Printer: TDLR.

	VF	UNC
a. Issued note.	FV	70.00
s. Specimen. Overprint: *ESPECIMEN* in red on both sides. Punch hole cancelled.	—	75.00

1992 Issue

63 200 Escudos — VF | UNC

8.8.1992. Black and blue-green on multicolor underprint. Sailing ship *Ernestina* at center right. Back: Modern airport collage in vertical format. Watermark: A. Cabral. Printer: TDLR.

	VF	UNC
a. Issued note.	FV	6.00
s. Specimen. Overprint: *ESPECIME* in red on both sides. Punch hole cancelled.	—	35.00

64 500 Escudos — VF | UNC

23.4.1992; 1.7.2002. Purple, blue and dark brown on multicolor underprint. Doctor B. Lopes da Silva at center right. Back: Shipyard. Watermark: A. Cabral. Printer: TDLR

	VF	UNC
a. 23.4.1992.	FV	15.00
b. 1.7.2002.	FV	12.50
s1. Specimen. As a. Overprint: *ESPECIME* on both sides. Punch hole cancelled.	—	100.
s2. Specimen. As b. Overprint: *ESPECIMEN* in red on both sides. Punch hole cancelled.	—	100.

65 1000 Escudos — VF | UNC

5.6.1992; 1.7.2002. Dark brown, red-orange and purple on multicolor underprint. Cape Verde warbler at center right. Back: Insects at left center. 145x68mm.

	VF	UNC
a. 5.6.1992.	FV	25.00
b. 1.7.2002.	FV	22.50
s1. Specimen. As a. Red overprint: *ESPECIME* on both sides. Punch hole cancelled.	—	60.00
s2. Specimen. As b. Red overprint: *ESPECIMEN* on both sides. Punch hole cancelled.	—	60.00

1999-2000 Issue

66 2000 Escudos — VF | UNC

1.7.1999. Brown, green, red and multicolor. Eugenio Tavares at bottom. Back: Cardeal flower and stanza from poem *Morna de Aguada*.

	VF	UNC
a. Issued note.	FV	35.00
s. Specimen. Overprint: *ESPECIME* in red on both sides. Punch hole cancelled.	—	100.

67 5000 Escudos — VF | UNC

5.7.2000. Orange, red and multicolor. Woman carrying stones. Back: Fortress details.

	VF	UNC
a. Issued note.	FV	75.00
s. Specimen. Overprint: *ESPECIME* in red on both sides. Punch hole cancelled.	—	120.

2005 Issue

68 200 Escudos — VF | UNC

20.1.2005. Sailing ship *Ernestina*. Back: Modern airport collage. Printer: DLR Vertical format.

	VF	UNC
a. Issued note.	FV	7.50
s. Specimen. Red overprint: *ESPECIMEN.*	FV	75.00

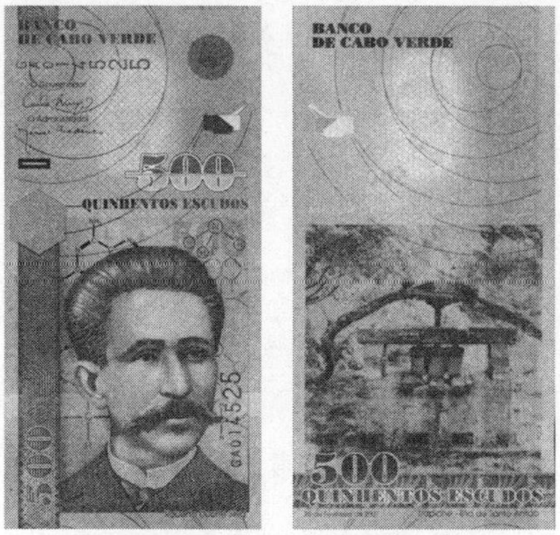

69 **500 Escudos** | VF | UNC
25.2.2007. Green, yellow, red and multicolor. Roberto Duarte Silva at bottom. Back: Brown and multicolor. Sugar cain press on the island of Santa Antáo. Watermark: Roberto Duarte Silva Printer: F-CO. Vertical format. 130x65mm.

		VF	UNC
	a. Issued note.	FV	12.50
	s. Specimen. Red overprint: *ESPECIMEN.*	FV	75.00

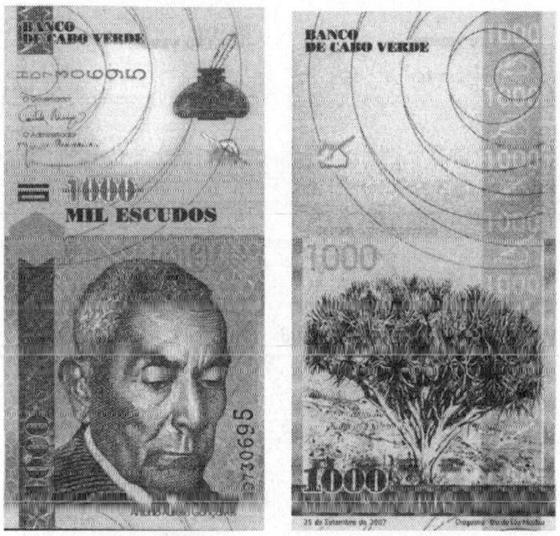

70 **1000 Escudos** | VF | UNC
25.9.2007. Violet, blue and rose on multicolor underprint. Antonio Aurelio Conçalves at bottom. Back: Dragon tree.

		VF	UNC
	a. Issued note.	FV	20.00
	s. Specimen. Overprint: *ESPECIME* in red on both sides.	FV	125.

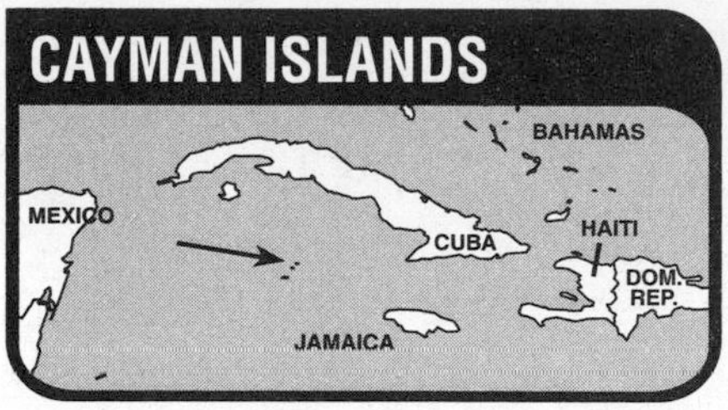

The Cayman Islands, a British Crown Colony situated about 290 km. northwest of Jamaica, consists of three islands: Grand Cayman, Little Cayman and Cayman Brac. The islands have an area of 262 sq. km. and a population of 47,900. Capital: Georgetown. Seafaring, commerce, banking and tourism are the principal industries.

The Cayman Islands were colonized from Jamaica by the British during the 18th and 19th centuries, and were administered by Jamaica after 1863. In 1959, the islands became a territory within the Federation of the West Indies, but when the Federation dissolved in 1962, the Cayman Islands chose to remain a British dependency.

RULERS:
British

MONETARY SYSTEM:
1 Dollar = 100 Cents

British Administration

Cayman Islands Currency Board

1971 Currency Law

1 **1 Dollar** | VF | UNC
L.1971 (1972). Blue on multicolor underprint. Arms at upper center, Queen Elizabeth II at right. Back: Fish, coral at center. Watermark: Tortoise. Printer: TDLR.

		VF	UNC
	a. Serial # Prefix *A/1.*	30.00	140.
	b. Serial # Prefix *A/2.*	25.00	130.
	c. Serial # Prefix *A/3.*	25.00	125.
	r. Replacement. Serial # Prefix *Z/1.*	40.00	175.
	s. Specimen.	—	220.

2 **5 Dollars** | VF | UNC
L.1971 (1972). Green on multicolor underprint. Arms at upper center, Queen Elizabeth II at right. Back: Sailboat at center. Watermark: Tortoise. Printer: TDLR.

		VF	UNC
	a. Issued note.	45.00	225.
	r. Replacement. Serial # prefix *Z/l.*	55.00	290.
	s. Specimen.	—	275.

3 **10 Dollars** | VF | UNC
L.1971 (1972). Red on multicolor underprint. Arms at upper center, Queen Elizabeth II at right. Back: Beach scene at center. Watermark: Tortoise. Printer: TDLR. | 115. | 530.

		VF	UNC
4	**25 Dollars** *L.1971* (1972). Brown on multicolor underprint. Arms at upper center, Queen Elizabeth II at right. Back: Compass and map at center. Watermark: Tortoise. Printer: TDLR.	335.	1625.

1974 Currency Law

		VF	UNC
5	**1 Dollar** *L.1974* (1985). Blue on multicolor underprint. Arms at upper center, Queen Elizabeth II at right. Back: Fish, coral at center. Watermark: Tortoise. Printer: TDLR. UV: back left design fluoresce green.		
	a. Signature as SCWPM #1 illustration. Serial # prefix *A/3*.	25.00	130.
	b. Signature Jefferson. Serial # prefix *A/3*.	23.00	110.
	c. Signature Jefferson. Serial # prefix *A/4*.	12.00	95.00
	d. Signature Jefferson. Serial # prefix *A/5*.	8.00	70.00
	e. Signature Jefferson. Serial # prefix *A/6*.	8.00	65.00
	f. Signature Jefferson. Serial # prefix *A/7*.	8.00	60.00
	r1. Replacement. As a. Serial # prefix *Z/1*.	35.00	190.
	r2. Replacement. As b. Serial # prefix *Z/1*.	35.00	170.
	s. Specimen. As. a.	—	210.

		VF	UNC
6	**5 Dollars** *L.1974.*. Green on multicolor underprint. Arms at upper center, Queen Elizabeth II at right. Back: Sailboat at center. Watermark: Tortoise. Printer: TDLR.		
	a. Issued note.	25.00	125.
	r. Replacement. Serial # prefix *Z/1*.	40.00	180.
	s. Specimen.	—	280.

		VF	UNC
7	**10 Dollars** *L.1974.* Red on multicolor underprint. Arms at upper center, Queen Elizabeth II at right. Back: Beach scene at center. Watermark: Tortoise. Printer: TDLR.		
	a. Issued note.	70.00	285.
	r. Replacement. Serial # prefix *Z/1*.	100.	560.
	s. Specimen.	—	330.

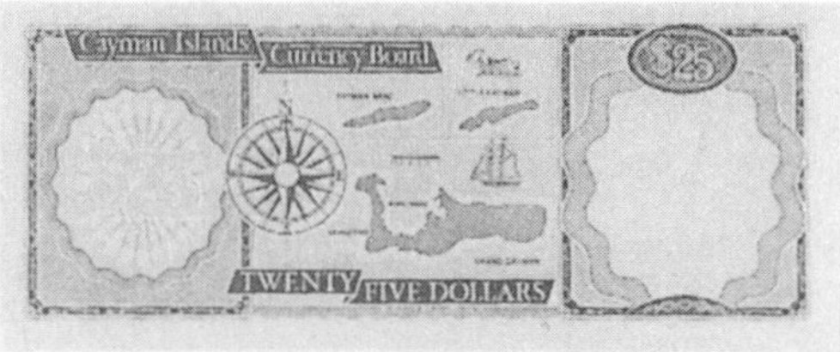

		VF	UNC
8	**25 Dollars** *L.1974.* Brown on multicolor underprint. Arms at upper center, Queen Elizabeth II at right. Back: Compass and map at center. Watermark: Tortoise. Printer: TDLR.		
	a. Issued note.	60.00	325.
	r. Replacement. Serial # prefix *Z/1*.	80.00	435.
	s. Specimen.	—	420.

		VF	UNC
9	**40 Dollars** *L.1974* (1981). Purple on multicolor underprint. Arms at upper center, Queen Elizabeth II at right. Back: Pirates' Week Festival (crowd on beach) at center. Watermark: Tortoise. Printer: TDLR.		
	a. Issued note.	80.00	320.
	r. Replacement. Serial # prefix *Z/1*.	100.	430.

		VF	UNC
10	**50 Dollars** *L.1974* (1987). Blue on multicolor underprint. Arms at upper center, Queen Elizabeth II at right. Back: Government House at center. Watermark: Tortoise. Printer: TDLR.		
	a. Issued note.	120.	480.
	r. Replacement. Serial # prefix *Z/1*.	270.	940.

		VF	UNC
11	**100 Dollars** *L.1974* (1982). Deep orange on multicolor underprint. Arms at upper center, Queen Elizabeth II at right. Back: Seacoast view of George Town at center. Watermark: Tortoise. Printer: TDLR.	235.	1050.

1991 Issue

12 **5 Dollars** VF UNC

1991. Dark green, blue-green and olive-brown on multicolor underprint. Arms at upper center, Queen Elizabeth II at right, treasure chest at lower left center. Back: Sailboat in harbor waters at center, red coral at left. Watermark: Tortoise. Printer: TDLR.

	VF	UNC
a. Issued note.	17.50	75.00
r. Replacement. Serial # prefix *Z/1*.	45.00	150.

13 **10 Dollars** VF UNC

1991. Red and purple on multicolor underprint. Arms at upper center, Queen Elizabeth II at right, treasure chest at lower left center. Back: Open chest, palm tree along coastline at center, red coral at left. Watermark: Tortoise. Printer: TDLR.

	VF	UNC
a. Golden colors around counch shell on back.	FV	155.
b. Orange colors around counch shell on back.	FV	175.

14 **25 Dollars** VF UNC FV 155.

1991. Deep brown, tan and orange on multicolor underprint. Arms at upper center, Queen Elizabeth II at right, Treasure chest at lower left center. Back: Island outlines and compass at center, red coral at left. Watermark: Tortoise. Printer: TDLR.

15 **100 Dollars** VF UNC FV 380.

1991. Orange and dark brown on multicolor underprint. Arms at upper center, Queen Elizabeth II at right, treasure chest at lower left center. Back: Harbor view at center, red coral at left. Watermark: Tortoise. Printer: TDLR.

1996 Issue

16 **1 Dollar** VF UNC

1996. Purple, orange and deep blue on multicolor underprint. Queen Elizabeth II at right. Back: Fish, coral at center. Watermark: Tortoise. Printer: TDLR.

	VF	UNC
a. Serial # prefix: *B/1*.	6.00	37.50
b. Serial # prefix: *B/2*.	5.00	35.00

17 **5 Dollars** VF UNC FV 70.00

1996. Dark green, blue-green and olive-brown on multicolor underprint. Queen Elizabeth II at right. Back: Sailboat in harbor waters at center, red coral at left. Watermark: Tortoise. Printer: TDLR.

18 **10 Dollars** VF UNC

1996. Red and purple on multicolor underprint. Queen Elizabeth II at right. Back: Open chest, palm trees along coastline at center, red coral at left.(Two varieties in color of conch shell at upper center, red coral at left. Watermark: Tortoise. Printer: TDLR.

	VF	UNC
a. Serial # prefix *B/l*.	FV	80.00
b. Serial # prefix *X/l*. Experimental paper. (100,000 pieces issued).	1650.	—

19 **25 Dollars** VF UNC FV 135.

1996. Deep brown, tan and orange on multicolor underprint. Queen Elizabeth II at right. Back: Island outines and compass at center. Watermark: Tortoise. Printer: TDLR.

20	100 Dollars	VF	UNC
	1996. Orange and brown on multicolor underprint. Queen Elizabeth II at right. Back: Harbor view at center. Watermark: Tortoise. Printer: TDLR.	160.	325.

Cayman Islands Monetary Authority

1998 Issue; 1996 Law

21	1 Dollar	VF	UNC
	1998. Purple, orange and deep blue on multicolor underprint. Queen Elizabeth II at right. Back: Fish, coral at center. Watermark: Tortoise. Printer: (T)DLR. Segmented foil over security thread.		
	a. Serial # prefix: *C/1.*	4.00	32.50
	b. Serial # prefix: *C/2.*	4.00	30.00
	r. Replacement. Serial # prefix *Z/1.*	20.00	110.

22	5 Dollars	VF	UNC
	1998. Olive-green and blue-green on multicolor underprint. Queen Elizabeth II at right. Back: Sailboat in harbor waters at center, red coral at left. Watermark: Tortoise. Printer: (T)DLR. Segmented foil over security thread.		
	a. Issued note.	12.00	55.00
	r. Replacement. Serial # prefix *Z/I*	30.00	140.

23	10 Dollars	VF	UNC
	1998. Red and purple on multicolor underprint. Queen Elizabeth II at right. Back: Open chest, palm tree along coastline at center,(two varieties in color of conch shell at upper center, red coral at left. Watermark: Tortoise. Printer: (T)DLR. Segmented foil over security thread.	22.50	80.00

24	25 Dollars	VF	UNC
	1998. Deep brown, tan and orange on multicolor underprint. Queen Elizabeth II at right. Back: Island outlines and compass at center, red coral at left. Watermark: Tortoise. Printer: (T)DLR. Segmented foil over security thread.	FV	150.

25	100 Dollars	VF	UNC
	1998. Orange and brown on multicolor underprint. Queen Elizabeth II at right. Back: Harbor view at center, red coral at left. Watermark: Tortoise. Printer: (T)DLR. Segmented foil over security thread.	FV	265.

2001 Issue; 2001 Law Revision

26	1 Dollar	VF	UNC
	2001. Multicolor. Queen Elizabeth II at right. Back: Fish, coral at center. Watermark: Tortoise and CIMA. Printer: (T)DLR. Segmented foil over security thread.		
	a. Serial # prefix: *C/2.*	FV	29.00
	b. Serial # prefix: *C/3.*	FV	27.50
	c. Serial # prefix: *C/4.*	FV	25.00
	r. Replacement. Serial # prefix *Z/1.*	17.50	110.
	s. Specimen.	—	165.

27 5 Dollars VF UNC

2001. Multicolor. Queen Elizabeth II at right. Back: Sailboat in harbor waters at center, red coral at left. Watermark: Tortoise and CIMA. Printer: (T)DLR. Segmented foil over security thread.

	VF	UNC
a. Issued note.	FV	37.50
s. Specimen.	—	165.

28 10 Dollars VF UNC

2001. Multicolor. Queen Elizabeth II at right. Back: Open chest, palm tree along coastline at center, (two varieties in color of conch shell at upper center, red coral at left. Watermark: Tortoise and CIMA. Printer: (T)DLR. Segmented foil over security thread.

	VF	UNC
a. Issued note.	FV	60.00
s. Specimen.	—	175.

29 50 Dollars VF UNC

2001. Multicolor. Queen Elizabeth II at right. Watermark: Tortoise and CIMA. Printer: (T)DLR. Segmented foil over security thread.

	VF	UNC
a. Issued note.	FV	210.
r. Replacement. Serial # prefix *Z/1*.	105.	375.
s. Specimen.	—	325.

2003 Commemorative Issue; 2002 Law Revision

500th Anniversary of discovery.

30 1 Dollar VF UNC

2003. Multicolor. Signature titles: *FINANCIAL SECRETARY* and MANAGING DIRECTOR. UV: face right crab fluoresces green. Back: Left sea turtle, CIMA, and center design all fluoresce green.

	VF	UNC
a. Issued note.	FV	35.00
b. Issued note in presentation folder (4000 made).	—	75.00
r. Replacement note. Serial # prefix *Z/1*.	15.00	85.00
s. Specimen.	—	225.

2003 Issue; 2002 Law Revision

31 25 Dollars VF UNC

2003. Multicolor. Signature titles: *FINANCIAL SECRETARY* and *MANAGING DIRECTOR*.

	VF	UNC
a. Issued note.	FV	85.00
s. Specimen.	—	240.

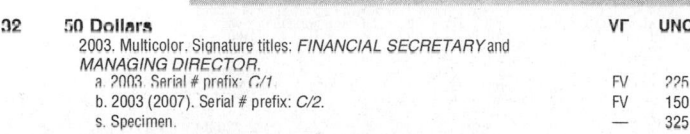

32 50 Dollars VF UNC

2003. Multicolor. Signature titles: *FINANCIAL SECRETARY* and *MANAGING DIRECTOR*.

	VF	UNC
a. 2003. Serial # prefix: *C/1*.	FV	225.
b. 2003 (2007). Serial # prefix: *C/2*.	FV	150.
s. Specimen.	—	325.

2005-2006 Issue; 2004 Law Revision

33 1 Dollar VF UNC

2006. Blue on multicolor underprint. Signature titles: *FINANCIAL SECRETARY* and *MANAGING DIRECTOR*. Watermark: Design in each corner.

	VF	UNC
a. Serial # prefix *C/4*.	3.00	20.00
b. Serial # prefix: *C/5*.	2.50	15.00
c. Serial # prefix *C/6*.	2.50	14.00
d. Serial # prefix *C/7*.	FV	10.00
r. Replacement note. As d.	10.00	65.00
s. Specimen.	—	155.

34 **5 Dollars** — VF — UNC

2005. Green on peach and multicolor underprint. Signatue titles: *FINANCIAL SECRETARY* and *MANAGING DIRECTOR.* Watermark: Design in each corner.

	VF	UNC
a. Serial # prefix *C/1.*	FV	40.00
b. Serial # prefix *C/2.* (2009).	FV	20.00
s. Specimen.	—	170.

35 **10 Dollars** — VF — UNC

2005. Rose on blue and multicolor underprint. Signatue titles: *FINANCIAL SECRETARY* and *MANAGING DIRECTOR.* Watermark: Design in each corner.

	VF	UNC
a. Issued note.	FV	35.00
r. Replacement note. Serial # prefix *Z/1.*	55.00	215.
s. Specimen.	—	240.

36 **25 Dollars** — VF — UNC

2006. Multicolor. Signatue titles: *FINANCIAL SECRETARY* and *MANAGING DIRECTOR.* Watermark: Design in each corner.

	VF	UNC
a. Issued note.	FV	72.50
r. Replacement note.	70.00	280.
s. Specimen.	—	315.

37 **100 Dollars** — VF — UNC

2006. Multicolor. Signatue titles: *FINANCIAL SECRETARY* and *MANAGING DIRECTOR.* Watermark: Design in each corner.

	VF	UNC
a. Issued note.	FV	205.
s. Specimen.	—	380.

2010 Series

38 **1 Dollar** — VF — UNC

2011. Blue and violet on multicolor underprint. Queen Elizabeth II at right. Back: Cliffs. Printer: DLR. 156x66mm.

	VF	UNC
a. Series D/1.	FV	8.00
b. Series D/2.	—	7.50
c. Series D/3.	—	—
s. Specimen.	—	150.

39 **5 Dollars** — VF — UNC

2010. Green and peach on multicolor underprint. Queen Elizabeth II at right. Back: Pair of parrots at center. Printer: DLR. 156x66mm.

	VF	UNC
a. Issued note.	FV	17.50
s. Specimen.	—	180.

40 **10 Dollars**

2010. Rose adn blue on multicolor underprint. Queen Elizabeth II at right. Printer: DLR. 156x66mm.

	VF	UNC
a. Issued note.	FV	30.00
s. Specimen.	—	240.

41 **25 Dollars**

2010. Brown and tan on multicolor underprint. Queen Elizabeth II at right. Printer: DLR. 156x66mm.

	VF	UNC
a. Issued note.	FV	60.00
s. Specimen.	—	275.

42 **50 Dollars**

2010. Multicolor. Queen Elizabeth II at right. Printer: DLR. 156x66mm.

	VF	UNC
a. Issued note.	FV	115.
s. Specimen.	FV	340.

43 **100 Dollars**

2010. Multicolor. Queen Elizabeth II at right. Printer: DLR. 156x66mm.

	VF	UNC
a. Issued note.	FV	175.
s. Specimen.	FV	400.

Collector Series

Cayman Islands Currency Board

1974 Currency Law Issue

		Mkt. Value
CS1	*L.1974.* **1-100 Dollars** #5-11 overprint: *SPECIMEN.* (300 sets.)	3400.

1991 Issue

		Mkt. Value
CS2	**1991 5-100 Dollars** #12-15 overprint: *SPECIMEN.* (300 sets.)	1700.

1996 Issue

		Mkt. Value
CS3	**1996 1-100 Dollars** #16-20 overprint: *SPECIMEN.* (300 sets.)	1600.

1998 Issue

		Mkt. Value
CS4	**1998 1-100 Dollars** #21-25 overprint: *SPECIMEN.* (100 sets.)	2350.

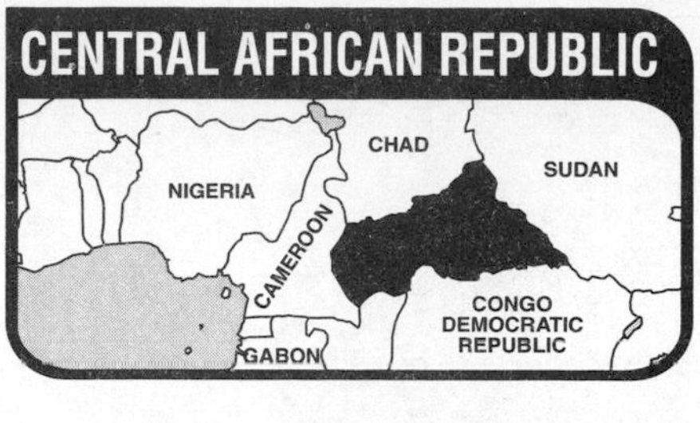

The Central African Republic, a landlocked country in Central Africa, bounded by Chad on the north, Cameroon on the west, Democratic Republic of the Congo and the Republic of the Congo on the south, and The Sudan on the east, has an area of 622,984 sq. km. and a population of 4.44 million. Capital: Bangui. Deposits of uranium, iron ore, manganese and copper remain to be developed. Diamonds, cotton, timber and coffee are exported.

The former French colony of Ubangi-Shari became the Central African Republic upon independence in 1960. After three tumultuous decades of misrule - mostly by military governments - civilian rule was established in 1993 and lasted for one decade. President Ange-Felix Patasse's civilian government was plagued by unrest, and in March 2003 he was deposed in a military coup led by General Francois Bozize, who established a transitional government. Though the government has the tacit support of civil society groups and the main parties, a wide field of candidates contested the municipal, legislative, and presidential elections held in March and May of 2005 in which General Bozize was affirmed as president. The government still does not fully control the countryside, where pockets of lawlessness persist. Unrest in neighboring nations, Chad, Sudan, and the DRC, continues to affect stability in the Central African Republic as well. It is a member of the "Union Monetaire des Etats de l'Afrique Centrale."

See also Central African States, Equatorial African States, and French African States.

RULERS:

Emperor J. B. Bokassa I, 1976-79

MONETARY SYSTEM:

1 Franc = 100 Centimes

SIGNATURE VARIETIES:

Refer to introduction to Central African States.

RÉPUBLIQUE CENTRAFRICAINE

BANQUE DES ÉTATS DE L'AFRIQUE CENTRALE

1974-76 ND ISSUE

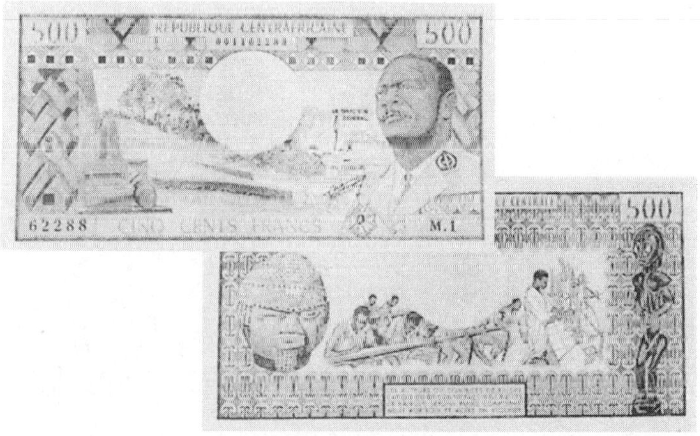

			VF	UNC
1	**500 Francs** ND (1974). Lilac-brown and multicolor. President J.B. Bokassa at right, landscape at center, signature 6. Back: Mask at left, students and chemical testing at center, statue at right. Watermark: Antelope's head.		40.00	175.

			VF	UNC
2	**1000 Francs** ND (1974). Blue and multicolor. President J.B. Bokassa at right, rhinoceros at left, water buffalo at center, signature 6. Back: Mask at left, trains, planes and bridge at center, statue at right. Watermark: Antelope's head.		60.00	250.

		VF	UNC
3	**5000 Francs** ND (1974). Brown and multicolor. President J.B. Bokassa at right, field workers hoeing at left, combine at center. Back: Mask at left, buildings at center, statue at right. Watermark: Antelope's head.		
	a. Signature 4.	150.	600.
	b. Signature 6.	125.	550.

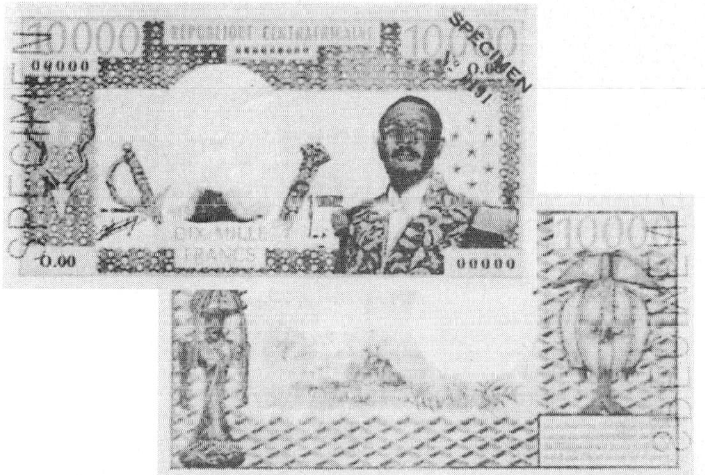

		VF	UNC
4	**10,000 Francs** ND (1976). Multicolor. President J.B. Bokassa at right, sword hilts at left and center, signature 6. Back: Mask at left, tractor cultivating at center, statue at right. Watermark: Antelope's head.	300.	900.

EMPIRE CENTRAFRICAIN

BANQUE DES ÉTATS DE L'AFRIQUE CENTRALE

1978-79 ISSUE

		VF	UNC
5	**500 Francs** 1.4.1978. Lilac-brown and multicolor. Emperor J.B. Bokassa I at right, landscape at center. Back: Mask at left, students and chemical testing at center, statue at right. Watermark: Antelope's head. Specimen.	—	2000.

		VF	UNC
6	**1000 Francs** 1.4.1978. Blue and multicolor. Emperor J.B. Bokassa I at right, rhinoceros at left, water buffalo at center, signature 9. Back: Mask at left, trains, planes and bridge at center, statue at right. Watermark: Antelope's head.	200.	800.

		VF	UNC
7	**5000 Francs** ND (1979). Brown and multicolor. Emperor J.B. Bokassa I at right, field workers hoeing at left, combine at center, signature 9. Back: Mask at left, buildings at center, statue at right. Watermark: Antelope's head.	225.	900.

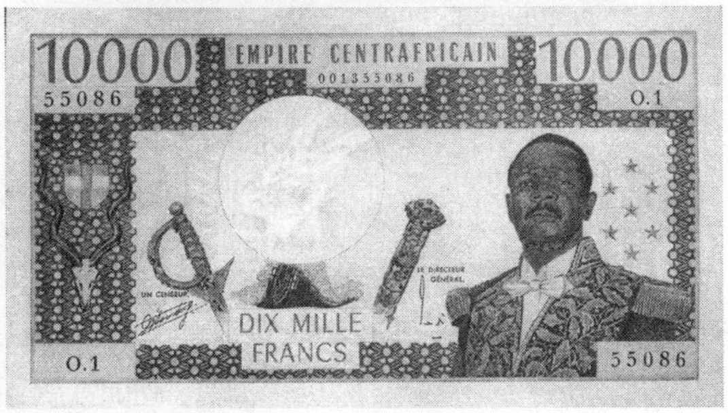

		VF	UNC
8	**10,000 Francs** ND (1978). Multicolor. Emperor J.B. Bokassa I at right, sword hilts at left and center, signature 6. Back: Mask at left, tractor cultivating at center, statue at right. Watermark: Antelope's head.	200.	800.

République Centrafricaine

Banque des États de l'Afrique Centrale

1980 Issue

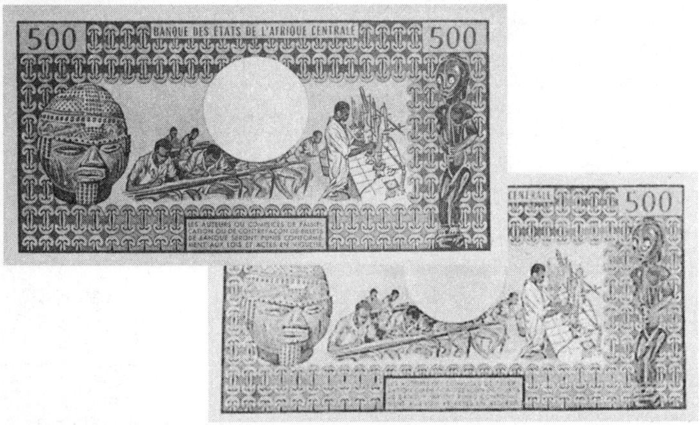

		VF	UNC
9	**500 Francs** 1.1.1980; 1.7.1980; 1.6.1981. Red and multicolor. Woman weaving basket at right, signature 9. Back: Mask at left, students and chemical testing at center, statue at right. Lithographed.	7.50	25.00

		VF	UNC
10	**1000 Francs** 1.1.1980; 1.7.1980; 1.6.1981; 1.1.1982; 1.6.1984. Blue and multicolor. Butterfly at left, waterfall at center, water buffalo at right, signature 9. Back: Mask at left, trains, planes, and bridge at center, statue at right. Lithographed.	10.00	35.00

		VF	UNC
11	**5000 Francs** 1.1.1980. Brown and multicolor. Girl at left, village scene at center, signature 9. Back: Carving at left, airplane, train crossing bridge and tractor hauling logs at center, man with pipe at right. Similar to Equatorial African States #6.	50.00	250.

1983-84 ND Issue

		VF	UNC
12	**5000 Francs** ND (1984). Brown and multicolor. Mask at left, woman with bundle of fronds at right. Back: Plowing and mine ore conveyor.		
	a. Signature 9.	35.00	150.
	b. Signature 14.	25.00	100.
	s. Specimen. Perforated *SPECIMEN*.	—	150.

13 **10,000 Francs** — VF 50.00 — UNC 200.
ND (1983). Brown, green and multicolor. Stylized antelope heads at left, woman at right, signature 9. Back: Loading fruit onto truck at left.

1985 Issue

14 **500 Francs** — VF — UNC
1985-91. Brown on orange and multicolor underprint. Carving and jug at center, signature 9. Back: Man carving mark at left center. Watermark: Carving.

	VF	UNC
a. 1.1.1985.	6.00	25.00
b. 1.1.1986.	5.00	20.00
c. 1.1.1987.	5.00	20.00
d. 1.1.1989; 1.1.1991.	5.00	20.00

15 **1000 Francs** — VF 10.00 — UNC 40.00
1.1.1985. Dull blue-violet on multicolor underprint. Carving at left, map at center, General Kolingba at right, incomplete map of Chad at top center, signature 9. Back: Elephant at left, animals at center, carving at right. Watermark: Carving.

1986 Issue

16 **1000 Francs** — VF 8.00 — UNC 30.00
1.1.1986-1.1.1990. Dull blue-violet on multicolor underprint. Carving at left, map at center, General Kolingba at right, complete outline map of Chad at top center, signature 9. Back: Elephant at left, animals at center, carving at right. Watermark: Carving.

CENTRAL AFRICAN STATES

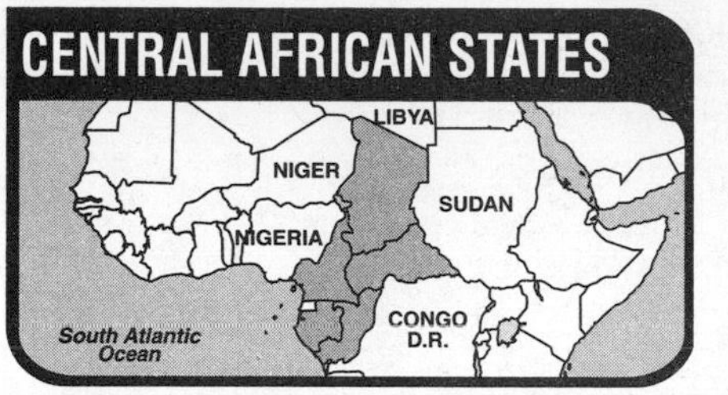

The Bank of the Central African States (BEAC) is a regional central bank for the monetary and customs union formed by Cameroun, Central African Republic, Chad, Congo (Brazzaville), Gabon, and (since 1985) Equatorial Guinea. It succeeded the Equatorial African States Bank in 1972-73 when the latter was reorganized and renamed to provide greater African control over its operations. The seat of the BEAC was transferred from Paris to Yaounde in 1977 and an African governor assumed responsibility for direction of the bank in 1978. The BEAC is a member of the franc zone with its currency denominated in CFA francs and pegged to the French franc at a rate of 50-1.

BEAC notes carry country names on the face and the central bank name on the back. The 1974-84 series had common back designs but were face-different. A new series begun in 1983-85 uses common designs also on the face except for some 1000 franc notes. The notes carry the signatures of *LE GOUVERNEUR (LE DIRECTEUR GENERAL* prior to 1-4-78) and *UN CENSEUR* (since 1972). Cameroun, Gabon, and France each appoint one censeur and one alternate. Cameroon and Congo notes carry the Cameroun censeur signature. Central African Republic, Equatorial Guinea, and Gabon notes carry the Gabon censeur signature. Chad notes have been divided between the two.

Prior to 1978, all BEAC notes were printed by the Bank of France. Since 1978, the 500 and 1000 franc notes have been printed by the private French firm F. C. Oberthur. The Bank of France notes are engraved and usually undated. The F. C. Oberthur notes are lithographed and most carry dates.

See individual member countries for additional note listings. Also see Equatorial African States and French Equatorial Africa.

CONTROL LETTER or CODE

	1993 - 2001	2002 Onward
Cameroun	E	U
Central African Republic	F	M
Chad	P	C
Congo	C	T
Equatorial Guinea	N	F
Gabon	L	A

SIGNATURE VARIETIES

1	Le Directeur-Genera Panouillot	Le President Gautier	
1a	Le Directeur-Genera Panouillot	Un Censeur Duouedi	
2	Le Directeur-Genera Panouillot	Un Censeur Koulla	1955-72
3	Le Directeur-Genera Joudiou	Un Censeur Koulla	1961-72
4	Le Directeur-Genera Joudiou	Un Censeur Renombo	1972-73
5	Le Directeur-Genera Joudiou	Un Censeur Ntang	1974-77
6	Le Directeur-Genera Joudiou	Un Censeur Ntoutoume	1974-78

SIGNATURE VARIETIES

7	Le Directeur-Genera Joudiou	Un Censeur Beke Bihege	1977
8	Le Directeur-Genera Joudiou	Un Censeur Kamgu	1978
9	Le Gouvemeur Oye Mba	Un Censeur Ntoutoume	1979-90
10	Le Gouvemeur Oye Mba	Un Censeur Kamgueu	1978-86
11	Le Gouvemeur Oye Mba	Un Censeur Kamgueu	1978-80
12	Le Gouvemeur Oye Mba	Un Censeur Tchepannou	1981-89
13	Le Gouvemeur Oye Mba	Un Censeur Dang	1990
14	Le Gouvemeur Mamalepot	Un Censeur Ntoutoume	1991
15	Le Gouvemeur Mamalepot	Un Censeur Mebara	1991-93
16	Le Gouvemeur Mamalepot	Un Censeur Ognagna	1994
17	Le Gouvemeur Mamalepot	Un Censeur Kaltjob	1994-
18	Le Gouvemeur Mamalepot		
19	Le Gouvemeur Mamalepot		
20	Le Gouvemeur Mamalepot		

Central African States

Banque des États de l'Afrique Centrale

C for Congo (1993-2001)

1993; 1994 Issue

101C 500 Francs VF UNC

(19)93-(20)00. Dark brown and gray on multicolor underprint. Shepherd at right, zebus at center, map of Central African states at lower left center. Back: Baobab, antelopes and Kota mask. Watermark: Shepherd.

	VF	UNC
a. Signature 15. (19)93.	FV	5.00
b. Signature 16. (19)94.	FV	4.50
c. Signature 16. (19)95.	FV	4.50
d. Signature 16. (19)97.	FV	4.00
e. Signature 16. (19)98.	FV	4.00
f. Signature 16. (19)99.	FV	4.00
g. Signature 19. (20)00.	FV	4.00
h. Signature 19. (20)02.	FV	4.00

102C 1000 Francs VF UNC

(19)93-(20)00. Dark brown and red with black text on multicolor underprint. Young man at right, harvesting coffee beans at center, map of Central African States at lower left center. Back: Forest harvesting, Okoume raft and Bakele wood mask. Watermark: Young man.

	VF	UNC
a. Signature 15. (19)93.	FV	9.00
b. Signature 16. (19)94.	FV	8.00
c. Signature 16. (19)95.	FV	8.00
d. Signature 16. (19)97.	FV	7.50
e. Signature 16. (19)98.	FV	7.50
f. Signature 16. (19)99.	FV	7.50
g. Signature 19. (20)00.	FV	7.00
h. Signature 19. (20)02.	FV	7.50

103C 2000 Francs

(19)93-(19)99. Dark brown and green with black text on orange and multicolor underprint. Woman's head at right, surrounded by tropical fruit, map of Central African States at lower left center. Back: Exchange of passengers and produce with ship at left center. Watermark: Woman's head.

	VF	UNC
a. Signature 15. (19)93.	FV	14.00
b. Signature 16. (19)94.	FV	12.50
c. Signature 16. (19)95.	FV	12.00
d. Signature 16. (19)97.	FV	12.00
e. Signature 16. (19)98.	FV	12.00
f. Signature 16. (19)99.	FV	12.00
g. Signature 19. (20)00.	FV	9.00
h. Signature 19. (20)02.	FV	10.00

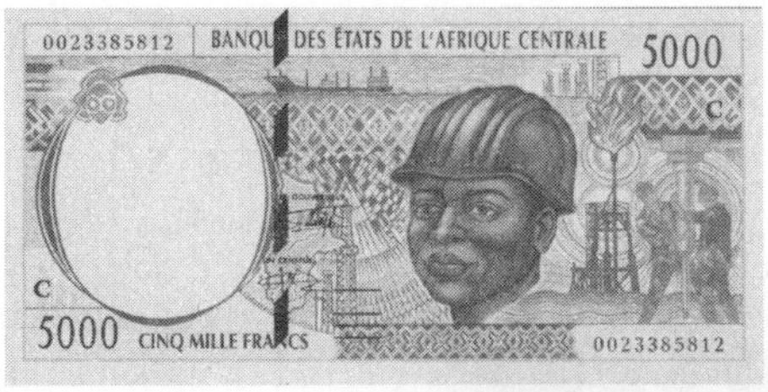

104C 5000 Francs VF UNC

(19)94-(20)00. Dark brown, brown and blue with violet text on multicolor underprint. Laborer wearing hard hat at center right, riggers with well drill at right. Back: Woman with head basket at lower left, gathering cotton at center.

	VF	UNC
a. Signature 16. (19)94.	FV	27.50
b. Signature 16. (19)95.	FV	27.50
c. Signature 16. (19)97.	FV	25.00
d. Signature 16. (19)98.	FV	25.00
e. Signature 16. (19)99.	FV	25.00
f. Signature 19. (20)00.	FV	25.00

105C 10,000 Francs

(19)94-(20)00. Dark brown and blue with blue-black text on multicolor underprint. Modern building at center, young woman at right. Back: Fisherman, boats and villagers along shoreline at left center.

	VF	UNC
a. Signature 16. (19)94.	FV	47.50
b. Signature 16. (19)95.	FV	45.00
c. Signature 16. (19)97.	FV	42.50
d. Signature 16. (19)98.	FV	45.00
e. Signature 16. (19)99.	FV	45.00
f. Signature 19. (20)00.	FV	45.00
g. Signature 19. (20)02.	FV	45.00

T FOR CONGO (2002-)

2002 ISSUE

	VF	UNC
106T 500 Francs 2002. Signature 19.	FV	4.00
107T 1000 Francs 2002. Signature 19.	FV	7.00
108T 2000 Francs 2002. Signature 19.	FV	10.00

	VF	UNC
109T 5000 Francs 2002. Signature 19.	FV	25.00
110T 10,000 Francs 2002. Signature 19.	FV	45.00

E FOR CAMEROUN (1993-2001)

1993; 1994 ISSUE

201E 500 Francs

(19)93-(20)02. Dark brown and gray on multicolor underprint. Shepherd at right, map of Central African States at lower left center. Back: Baobab, antelopes and Kota mask. Watermark: Shepherd.

	VF	UNC
a. Signature 15. (19)93.	FV	5.00
b. Signature 17. (19)94.	FV	4.50
c. Signature 17. (19)95.	FV	4.50
d. Signature 17. (19)97.	FV	4.50
e. Signature 18. (19)98.	FV	4.50
f. Signature 18. (19)99.	FV	4.50
g. Signature 20. (20)00.	FV	4.00
h. Signature 20. (20)02.	FV	4.00

202E 1000 Francs

(19)93-(20)02. Dark brown and red with black text on green and multicolor underprint. Young man at right, harvesting coffee beans at center, map of Central African States at lower left center. Back: Forest harvesting, Okoume raft and Bakele wood mask. Watermark: Young man.

	VF	UNC
a. Signature 15. (19)93.	FV	9.00
b. Signature 17. (19)94.	FV	8.00
c. Signature 17. (19)95.	FV	8.00
d. Signature 17. (19)97.	FV	8.00
e. Signature 18. (19)98.	FV	8.00
f. Signature 18. (19)99.	FV	7.00
g. Signature 20. (20)00.	FV	6.50
h. Signature 20. (20)02.	FV	6.50

203E 2000 Francs

(19)93-(20)02. Dark brown and green with black text on orange and multicolor underprint. Woman's head at right, surrounded by tropical fruit, map of Central African States at lower left center. Back: Exchange of passengers and produce with ship at left center. Watermark: Woman's head.

	VF	UNC
a. Signature 15. (19)93.	FV	15.00
b. Signature 17. (19)94.	FV	12.50
c. Signature 17. (19)95.	FV	12.50
d. Signature 17. (19)97.	FV	12.00
e. Signature 18. (19)98.	FV	11.00
f. Signature 18. (19)99.	FV	12.00
g. Signature 20. (20)00.	FV	12.00
h. Signature 20. (20)02.	FV	12.00

204E 5000 Francs

(19)94-(20)02. Dark brown, brown and blue with violet text on multicolor underprint. Laborer wearing hard hat at center right, riggers with well drill at right. Back: Woman with head basket at lower left, gathering cotton at center.

	VF	UNC
a. Signature 17. (19)94.	FV	27.50
b. Signature 17. (19)95.	FV	27.50
c. Signature 17. (19)97.	FV	25.00
d. Signature 18. (19)98.	FV	25.00
e. Signature 18. (19)99.	FV	25.00
f. Signature 20. (20)00.	FV	22.00
g. Signature 20. (20)02.	FV	22.00

205E 10,000 Francs

(19)94-(20)00. Dark brown and blue with blue-black text on multicolor underprint. Modern building at center, young woman at right. Back: Fisherman, boats and villagers along shoreline at left center.

	VF	UNC
a. Signature 17. (19)94.	FV	45.00
b. Signature 17. (19)95.	FV	45.00
c. Signature 17. (19)97.	FV	45.00
d. Signature 18. (19)98.	FV	46.00
e. Signature 18. (19)99.	FV	45.00
f. Signature 20. (20)00.	FV	45.00
h. Signature 20. (20)02.	FV	45.00

U FOR CAMEROUN (2002-)

2002 ISSUE

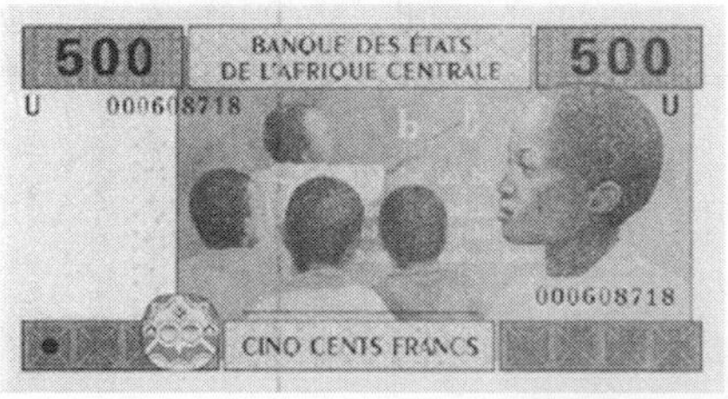

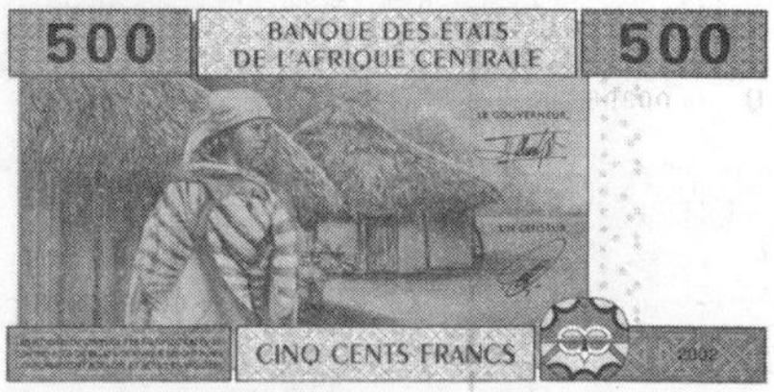

	VF	UNC
206U 500 Francs 2002. Signature 20.	FV	4.00

		VF	UNC
207U	**1000 Francs** 2002. Signature 20.	FV	7.00

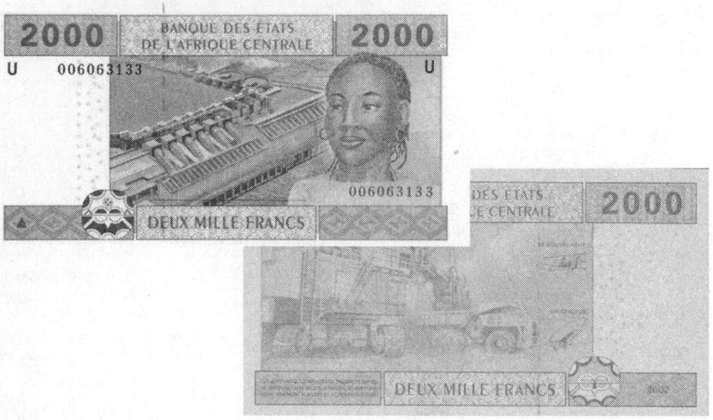

		VF	UNC
208U	**2000 Francs** 2002. Signature 20.	FV	10.00

		VF	UNC
209U	**5000 Francs** 2002. Signature 20.	FV	25.00

		VF	UNC
210U	**10,000 Francs** 2002. Signature 20.	FV	45.00

F for Central African Republic (1993-2001)

1993; 1994 Issue

		VF	UNC
301F	**500 Francs** (19)93-(19)99. Dark brown and gray on multicolor underprint. Shepherd at right, zebus at center, map of Central African States at lower left center. Back: Baobab, antelopes and Kota mask. Watermark: Shepherd.		
	a. Signature 15. (19)93.	FV	6.00
	b. Signature 16. (19)94.	FV	5.00
	c. Signature 16. (19)95.	FV	5.00
	d. Signature 16. (19)97.	FV	4.00
	e. Signature 16. (19)98.	FV	4.00
	f. Signature 16. (19)99.	FV	4.00
	g. Signature 19. (20)00.	FV	4.00
302F	**1000 Francs** (19)93-(19)99. Dark brown and red with black text on green and multicolor underprint. Young man at right, harvesting coffee beans at center, map of Central African States at lower left center. Back: Forest harvesting, Okoume raft and Bakele wood mask. Watermark: Young man.		
	a. Signature 15. (19)93.	FV	9.00
	b. Signature 16. (19)94.	FV	8.50
	c. Signature 16. (19)95.	FV	8.00
	d. Signature 16. (19)97.	FV	7.50
	e. Signature 16. (19)98.	FV	7.00
	f. Signature 16. (19)99.	FV	7.00
303F	**2000 Francs** (19)93-(19)99. Dark brown and green with black text on orange and multicolor underprint. Woman's head at right, surrounded by tropical fruit, map of Central African States at lower left center. Back: Exchange of passengers and produce with ship at left center. Watermark: Woman's head.		
	a. Signature 15. (19)93.	FV	17.50
	b. Signature 16. (19)94.	FV	15.00
	c. Signature 16. (19)95.	FV	13.00
	d. Signature 16. (19)97.	FV	13.00
	e. Signature 16. (19)98.	FV	13.00
	f. Signature 16. (19)99.	FV	12.00
304F	**5000 Francs** (19)94-(19)99. Dark brown, brown and blue with violet text on multicolor underprint. Laborer wearing hard hat at center right, riggers with well drill at right. Back: Woman with head basket at lower left, gathering cotton at center.		
	a. Signature 16. (19)94.	FV	32.50
	b. Signature 16. (19)95.	FV	30.00
	c. Signature 16. (19)97.	FV	25.00
	d. Signature 16. (19)98.	FV	25.00
	e. Signature 16. (19)99.	FV	25.00
305F	**10,000 Francs** (19)94-(19)99. Dark brown and blue with blue-black text on multicolor underprint. Modern building at center, young woman at right. Back: Fisherman, boats and villagers along shoreline at left center.		
	a. Signature 16. (19)94.	FV	55.00
	b. Signature 16. (19)95.	FV	50.00
	c. Signature 16. (19)97.	FV	45.00
	d. Signature 16. (19)98.	FV	45.00
	e. Signature 16. (19)99.	FV	45.00
	f. Signature 19. (20)00.	FV	45.00

M for Central African Republic (2002-)

2002 Issue

		VF	UNC
306M	**500 Francs** 2002. Signature 19.	FV	4.00
307M	**1000 Francs** 2002. Signature 19.	FV	7.00
308M	**2000 Francs** 2002. Signature 19.	FV	10.00
309M	**5000 Francs** 2002. Signature 19.	FV	25.00
310M	**10,000 Francs** 2002. Signature 19.	FV	45.00

L for Gabon (1993-2001)

1993; 1994 Issue

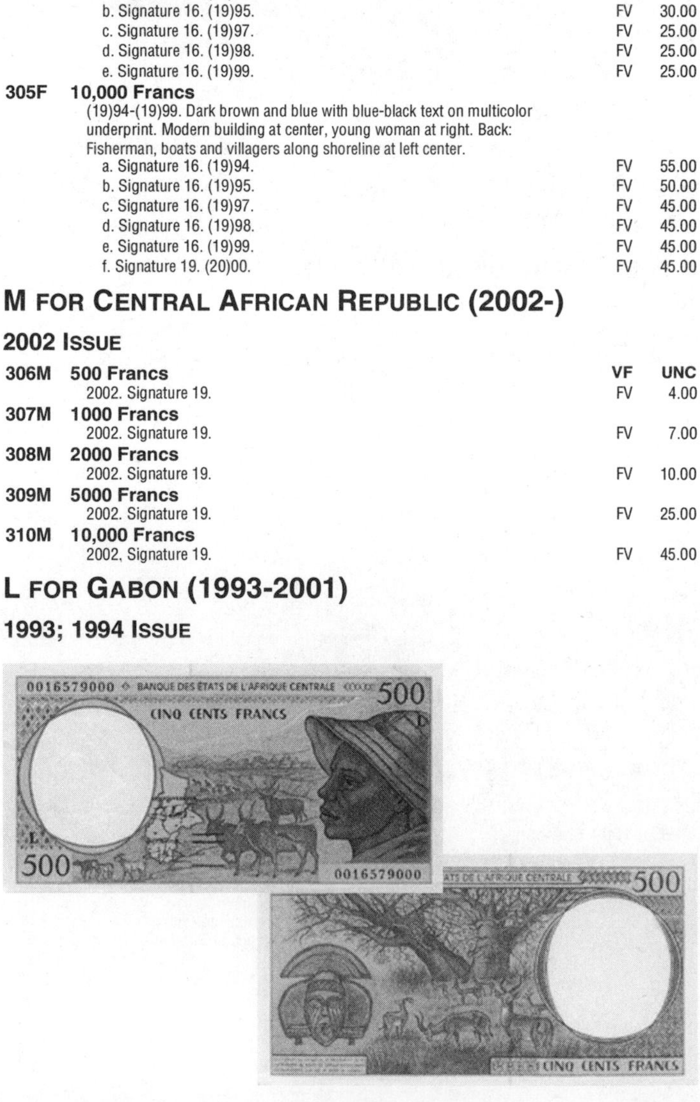

401L 500 Francs VF UNC

(19)93-(20)00. Dark brown and gray on multicolor underprint. Shepherd at right, zebus at center, map of Central African States at lower left center. Back: Baobab antelopes and Kota mask. Watermark: Shepherd.

	VF	UNC
a. Signature 15. (19)93.	FV	5.00
b. Signature 16. (19)94.	FV	4.50
c. Signature 16. (19)95.	FV	4.50
g. Signature 16. (20)00.	FV	4.50

402L 1000 Francs VF UNC

(19)93-(20)00. Dark brown and red with black text on green and multicolor underprint. Young man at right, harvesting coffee beans at center, map of Central African States at lower left center. Back: Forest harvesting, Okoume raft and Bakele wood mask. Watermark: Young man.

	VF	UNC
a. Signature 15. (19)93.	FV	8.50
b. Signature 16. (19)94.	FV	8.00
c. Signature 16. (19)95.	FV	7.50
d. Signature 16. (19)97.	FV	7.50
e. Signature 16. (19)98.	FV	7.50
f. Signature 16. (19)99.	FV	7.50
g. Signature 19. (20)00.	FV	7.50
h. Signature 19. (20)02.	FV	7.50

403L 2000 Francs VF UNC

(19)93-(20)00. Dark brown and green with black text on orange and multicolor underprint. Woman's head at right, surrounded by tropical fruit, map of Central African States at lower left center. Back: Exchange of passengers and produce with ship at left center. Watermark: Woman's head.

	VF	UNC
a. Signature 15. (19)93.	FV	15.00
b. Signature 16. (19)94.	FV	15.00
c. Signature 16. (19)95.	FV	15.00
d. Signature 16. (19)97.	FV	12.50
e. Signature 16. (19)98.	FV	12.50
f. Signature 16. (19)99.	FV	12.50
g. Signature 19. (20)00.	FV	12.50
h. Signature 19. (20)02.	FV	7.50

404L 5000 Francs

(19)94-(20)00. Dark brown, brown and blue with violet text on multicolor underprint. Laborer wearing hard hat at center right, riggers with well drill at right. Back: Woman with head basket at lower left, gathering cotton at center.

	VF	UNC
a. Signature 16. (19)94.	FV	25.00
b. Signature 16. (19)95.	FV	25.00
c. Signature 16. (19)97.	FV	25.00
d. Signature 16. (19)98.	FV	25.00
e. Signature 16. (19)99.	FV	25.00
f. Signature 16. (20)00.	FV	25.00

405L 10,000 Francs VF UNC

(19)94-(20)00. Dark brown and blue with blue-black text on multicolor underprint. Modern building at center, young woman at right. Back: Fisherman, boats and villagers along shoreline at left center.

	VF	UNC
a. Signature 16. (19)94.	FV	52.50
b. Signature 16. (19)95.	FV	47.50
c. Signature 16. (19)97.	FV	45.00
d. Signature 16. (19)98.	FV	45.00
e. Signature 16. (19)99.	FV	45.00
f. Signature 19. (20)00.	FV	45.00
g. Signature 19 (20)02.	FV	45.00

A for Gabon (2002-)

2002 Issue

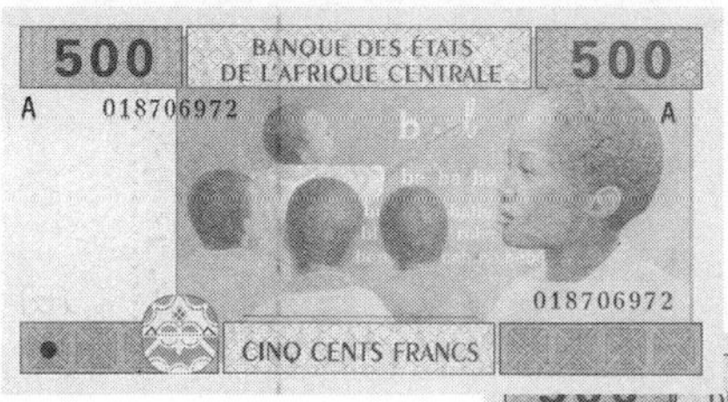

		VF	UNC
406A	**500 Francs** 2002. Signature 19.	FV	4.00
407A	**1000 Francs** 2002. Signature 19.	FV	7.00

		VF	UNC
408A	**2000 Francs** 2002. Signature 19.	FV	10.00
409A	**5000 Francs** 2002. Signature 19.	FV	25.00
410A	**10,000 Francs** 2002. Signature 19.	FV	45.00

N for Equatorial Guinea (1993-2001)

1993; 1994 Issue

501N 500 Francs VF UNC

(19)93-(20)00. Dark brown and gray on multicolor underprint. Shepherd at right, zebus at center, map of Central African States at lower left center. Back: Baobab, antelopes and Kota mask. Watermark: Shepherd.

	VF	UNC
a. Signature 15. (19)93.	FV	6.00
b. Signature 16. (19)94.	FV	6.00
c. Signature 16. (19)95.	FV	6.00
d. Signature 16. (19)97.	FV	4.50
f. Signature 16. (19)99.	FV	4.50
g. Signature 19. (20)00.	FV	4.50

502N 1000 Francs

(19)93-(20)00. Dark brown and red with black text on multicolor underprint. Young man at right, harvesting coffee beans at center, map of Central African States at lower left center. Back: Forest harvesting, Okoume raft and Bakele wood mask. Watermark: Young man.

	VF	UNC
a. Signature 15. (19)93.	FV	9.00
b. Signature 16. (19)94.	FV	8.00
c. Signature 16. (19)95.	FV	7.50
d. Signature 16. (19)97.	FV	7.50
e. Signature 16. (19)98.	FV	7.50
f. Signature 16. (19)99.	FV	7.50
g. Signature 16. (20)00.	FV	7.00
h. Signature 19. (20)00.	FV	7.50

503N **2000 Francs**	VF	UNC
(19)93-(20)00. Dark brown and green with black text on multicolor underprint. Woman's head at right, surrounded by tropical fruit. map of Central African States at lower left center. Back: Exchange of passengers and produce with ship at left center. Watermark: Woman's head.		
a. Signature 15. (19)93.	FV	15.00
b. Signature 16. (19)94.	FV	15.00
c. Signature 16. (19)95.	FV	15.00
d. Signature 16. (19)97.	FV	12.50
g. Signature 19. (20)00.	FV	12.50

504N **5000 Francs**		
(19)94-(20)00. Dark brown, brown and blue with violet text on multicolor underprint. Laborer wearing hard hat at center right, riggers and well drill at right. Back: Woman with head basket at lower left, gathering cotton at center.		
a. Signature 16. (19)94.	FV	25.00
b. Signature 16. (19)95.	FV	25.00
d. Signature 16. (19)98.	FV	25.00
e. Signature 16. (19)99.	FV	25.00
f. Signature 19. (20)00.	FV	25.00

505N **10,000 Francs**		
(19)94-(20)00. Dark brown and blue with blue-black text on multicolor underprint. Modern building at center, young woman at right. Back: Fisherman, boats and villagers along shoreline at left center.		
a. Signature 16. (19)94.	FV	47.50
b. Signature 16. (19)95.	FV	47.50
c. Signature 16. (19)97.	FV	45.00
d. Signature 16. (19)98.	FV	47.50
e. Signature 16. (19)99.	FV	45.00
f. Signature 19. (20)00.	FV	45.00

F for Equatorial Guinea (2002-)

2002 Issue

506F **500 Francs**	VF	UNC
2002. Signature 19.	FV	4.00

507F **1000 Francs**	VF	UNC
2002. Signature 19.	FV	7.00
508F **2000 Francs**		
2002. Signature 19.	FV	10.00

509F **5000 Francs**	VF	UNC
2002. Signature 19.	FV	25.00
510F **10,000 Francs**		
2002. Signature 19.		
a. 2002.	FV	45.00
b. 2003.	FV	45.00

P for Chad (1993-2001)

1993; 1994 Issue

601P **500 Francs**	VF	UNC
(19)93-(20)00. Dark brown and gray on multicolor underprint. Shepherd at right, zebus at center, map of Central African States at lower left center. Back: Baobab, antelopes and Kota mask. Watermark: Shepherd.		
a. Signature 15. (19)93.	FV	6.00
b. Signature 16. (19)94.	FV	5.00
c. Signature 16. (19)95.	FV	5.00
d. Signature 16. (19)97.	FV	5.00
e. Signature 16. (19)98.	FV	4.50
f. Signature 16. (19)99.	FV	4.50
g. Signature 19. (20)00.	FV	4.50

602P **1000 Francs**	VF	UNC
(19)93-(20)00. Dark brown and red with black text on green and multicolor underprint. Young man at right, harvesting coffee beans at center, map of Central African States at lower left center. Back: Forest harvesting, Okoume raft and Bakele wood mask. Watermark: Young man.		
a. Signature 15. (19)93.	FV	8.50
b. Signature 16. (19)94.	FV	7.50
c. Signature 16. (19)95.	FV	7.00
d. Signature 16. (19)97.	FV	7.00
e. Signature 16. (19)98.	FV	7.50
f. Signature 16. (19)99.	FV	7.50
g. Signature 19. (20)00.	FV	7.50

603P **2000 Francs**		
(19)93-(20)00. Dark brown and green with black text on orange and multicolor underprint. Woman's head at right, surrounded by tropical fruit, map of Central African States at lower left center. Back: Exchange of passengers and produce with ship at left center. Watermark: Woman's head.		
a. Signature 15. (19)93.	FV	15.00
b. Signature 16. (19)94.	FV	15.00
c. Signature 16. (19)95.	FV	12.50
d. Signature 16. (19)97.	FV	12.50
e. Signature 16. (19)98.	FV	12.50
f. Signature 16. (19)99.	FV	12.50
g. Signature 16. (20)00.	FV	12.50

604P	**5000 Francs**	**VF**	**UNC**
	(19)94-(20)00. Dark brown, brown and blue with violet text on multicolor underprint. Laborer wearing hard hat at center right, riggers with well drill at right. Back: Woman with head basket at lower left, gathering cotton at center.		
	a. Signature 16. (19)94.	FV	30.00
	b. Signature 16. (19)95.	FV	27.50
	c. Signature 16. (19)97.	FV	27.50
	d. Signature 16. (19)98.	FV	25.00
	e. Signature 16. (19)99.	FV	25.00
	f. Signature 19. (20)00.	FV	25.00

605P	**10,000 Francs**	**VF**	**UNC**
	(19)94-(20)00. Dark brown and blue with blue-black text on multicolor underprint. Modern building at center, young woman at right. Back: Fisherman, boats and villagers along shoreline at left center.		
	a. Signature 16. (19)94.	FV	50.00
	b. Signature 16. (19)95.	FV	50.00
	c. Signature 16. (19)97.	FV	47.50
	d. Signature 16. (19)98.	FV	45.00
	e. Signature 16. (19)99.	FV	45.00
	f. Signature 19. (20)00.	FV	45.00

C for Chad (2002-)

2002 Issue

		VF	**UNC**
606C	**500 Francs**		
	2002. Signature 19.	FV	4.00
607C	**1000 Francs**		
	2002. Signature 19.	FV	7.00
608C	**2000 Francs**		
	2002. Signature 19.	FV	10.00
609C	**5000 Francs**		
	2002. Signature 19.	FV	25.00
610C	**10,000 Francs**		
	2002. Signature 19.	FV	45.00

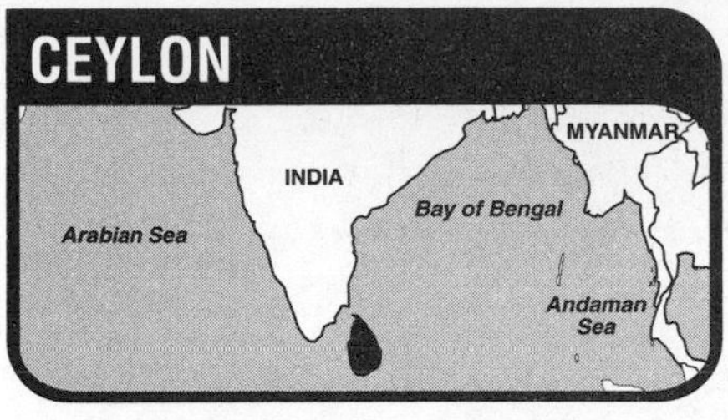

Ceylon (later to become the Democratic Socialist Republic of Sri Lanka), situated in the Indian Ocean 18 miles (29 km.) southeast of India, has an area of 25,332 sq. mi. (65,610 sq. km.) and a population of 18.82 million. Capital: Colombo. The economy is chiefly agricultural. Tea, coconut products and rubber are exported.

The earliest known inhabitants of Ceylon, the Veddahs, were subjugated by the Sinhalese from northern India in the 6th century BC. Sinhalese rule was maintained until 1498, after which the island was controlled by China for 30 years. The Portuguese came to Ceylon in 1505 and maintained control of the coastal area for 150 years. They were supplanted by the Dutch in 1658, who were in turn supplanted by the British who seized the Dutch colonies in 1796, and made them a Crown Colony in 1802. In 1815, the British conquered the independent Kingdom of Kandy in the central part of the island. Constitutional changes in 1931 and 1946 granted the Ceylonese a measure of autonomy and a parliamentary form of government. Ceylon became a self-governing dominion of the British Commonwealth on February 4, 1948. On May 22, 1972, the Ceylonese adopted a new constitution which declared Ceylon to be the Republic of Sri Lanka - "Resplendent Island." Sri Lanka is a member of the Commonwealth of Nations. The president is Chief of State. The prime minister is Head of Government.

For later issues, see Sri Lanka.

RULERS:

Dutch to 1796
British, 1796-1972

MONETARY SYSTEM:

1 Rix Dollar = 48 Stivers
1 Rupee = 100 Cents

State

Central Bank of Ceylon

1956 Issue

56	**1 Rupee**	**VF**	**UNC**
	1956-63. Blue on orange, green and brown underprint. Arms of Ceylon at left. Back: Ornate stairway. Watermark: Chinze. Printer: BWC. 108x60mm.		
	a. 30.7.1956. Signature: Stanley de Soysa and A. G. Ranasingha.	7.00	25.00
	b. 31.5.1957; 9.4.1958; 7.11.1958.	5.00	15.00
	c. With security strip. 11.9.1959.	2.00	7.50
	d. 18.8.1960; 29.1.1962. Signatures: Felix R. Dias Bandaranaike and W. Rajapatirana.	2.00	7.50
	e. 6..5.1963. Signature: T. B. Illangaratne and W. Rajapatirana.	2.00	7.50

57	**2 Rupees**	**VF**	**UNC**
	1956-62. Brown and lilac on blue and green underprint. Arms of Ceylon at left. Back: Pavilion. Watermark: Chinze. Printer: BWC. 121x67mm.		
	a. 30.7.1956; 31.5.1957; 6.10.1958; 7.11.1958. Signature: Stanley de Soysa and A. G. Ranasingha. Without security strip.	12.00	40.00
	b. 11.9.1959; Signature: Stanley de Soysa and W. Rajapatirana. With security strip.	12.00	40.00
	c. 18.8.1960; 29.1.1962. Signature: Felix R. Dias Bandaranaike and W. Rajapatirana.	10.00	30.00

58 5 Rupees VF UNC

1956-62. Orange on aqua, green and brown underprint. Arms of Ceylon at left. Back: Standing figure. Watermark: Chinze. Printer: BWC. 133x73mm.

	VF	UNC
a. 30.7.1956; 31.5.1957; 10.6.1958. Signature: Stanley de Soysa and A. G. Ranasingha. Without security strip.	20.00	120.
b. 1.7.1959; 11.9.1959. Signature: Stanley de Soysa and W. Rajapatirana. With security strip.	20.00	120.
c. 18.8.1960; 29.1.1962. Signarues: Felix R. Dias Bandaranaike and W. Rajapatirana.	15.00	75.00

59 10 Rupees VF UNC

1956-63. Green on violet, brown and blue underprint. Arms of Ceylon at left. Back: Ceremonial figures. Watermark: Chinze. Printer: BWC. 146x76mm.

	VF	UNC
a. 30.7.1956; 7.11.1957; 7.11.1958. Signatures Stanley de Soysa and A. G. Ranasingha. Without security strip.	25.00	100.
b. 11.9.1959. With security strip.	25.00	100.
c. 18.8.1960; 7.4.1961; 5.6.1963. Signatures Felix R. Dias Bandaranaike and W. Rajapatirana.	15.00	75.00

60 50 Rupees VF UNC

30.7.1956; 9,4,1958; 7.11.1958; 11.9.1959. Blue and violet on multicolor underprint. Arms of Ceylon at left. Back: Ornate stairway. Watermark: Chinze. Printer: BWC. 159x89mm.

	VF	UNC
a. 30.7.1956; 9.4.1958; 7.11.1958. Signatures: Stanley de Soysa and A. G. Ranasingha.	90.00	300.
b. 11.9.1959. Signatures: Stanley de Soysa and W. Rajapatirana.	90.00	300.

61 100 Rupees

	VF	UNC
24.10.1956. Brown on multicolor underprint. Arms of Ceylon at left. Signature: Stanley de Soysa and A. G. Ranasingha. Back: Two women in national dress. Watermark: Chinze. Printer: BWC. 171x98mm.	200.	800.

1962-65 Issue

62 2 Rupees VF UNC

1962-65. Light brown on lilac, green and blue underprint. S. W. R. D. Bandaranaike at right. Back: Pavilion at left center. Watermark: Chinze. Printer: BWC. 114x59mm.

	VF	UNC
a. Signature P. B. G. Kalugalla and D. W. Rajapatirana. 8.11.1962.	6.00	20.00
b. Signature T. B. Illangaratue and D. W. Rajapatirana. 11.4.1964; 12.6.1964.	15.00	40.00
c. Signature U. B. Wanninayake and D. W. Rajapatirana. 6.4.1965.	7.00	30.00

63 5 Rupees VF UNC

1962; 1964. Orange and brown on multicolor underprint. S. W. R. D. Bandaranaike at right. Back: Green and orange. Standing figure at center. Watermark: Chinze. Printer: BWC. 125x64mm.

	VF	UNC
a. Signature P. B. G. Kalugalla and D. W. Rajapatirana. 8.11.1962.	9.00	35.00
b. Signature N. M. Perera and D. W. Rajapatirana. 12.6.1964.	20.00	60.00

64 10 Rupees

	VF	UNC
12.6.1964; 28.8.1964; 19.9.1964. Green and purple on orange and blue underprint. S. W. R. D. Bandaranaike at right. Signatures: N. M. Perera and W. Rajapatirana. Back: Ceremonial figures. Watermark: Chinze. Printer: BWC. 140x70mm.	10.00	70.00

65 50 Rupees VF UNC

1961-65. Blue and purple on multicolor underprint. S. W. R. D. Bandaranaike at right. Back: Blue. Ornate stairway. Watermark: Chinze. Printer: BWC. 151x79mm.

	VF	UNC
a. Signature: Felix R. Dias Bandaranaike and W. Rajapatirana. 2.11.1961.	30.00	120.
b. Signature: T. B. Illangaratne and W. Rajapatirana. 5.6.1963.	25.00	90.00
c. Signature: U. B. Wanninayake and W. Rajapatirana. 6.4.1965.	20.00	80.00
d. Signature: N. M. Perera and W. Rajapatirana. 12.6.1964. (Not released and destroyed).	—	—

66 100 Rupees

	VF	UNC
5.6.1963. Brown and blue on multicolor underprint. S W. R. D. Bandaranaike at right. Signatures: T. B. Illangaratne and W. Rajapatirana. Back: Two women in national dress. Watermark: Chinze. Printer: BWC. 171x98mm.	55.00	225.

1965-68 Issue

#	Denomination / Description	VF	UNC
67	**2 Rupees** 1965-68. Light brown on lilac, light green and blue underprint. Statue of King Parakkrama at right. Back: Pavilion. Watermark: Chinze. Printer: BWC. 114x59mm.		
	a. Signature U. B. Wanninayake and D. W. Rajapatirana. 9.9.1965; 15.7.1967.	3.00	9.00
	b. Signature U. B. Wanninayake and W. Tennekoon. 10.1.1968.	2.50	7.00
68	**5 Rupees** 1965-68. Orange and brown on multicolor underprint. Statue of King Parakkrama at right. Back: Back green and orange. Standing figure. Watermark: Chinze. Printer: BWC. 125x64mm.		
	a. Signature U. B. Wanninayake and D. W. Rajapatirana. 9.9.1965; 15.7.1967.	3.00	20.00
	b. Signature U. B. Wanninayake and W. Tennekoon. 1.9.1967; 10.1.1968.	2.00	17.50
69	**10 Rupees** 10.1.1968. Green and purple on orange and blue underprint. Statue of King Parakkrama at right. Signatures: U. B. Wanninayake and William Tennekoon. Back: Ceremonial figures. Watermark: Chinze. Printer: BWC. 140x70mm.	12.00	50.00
70	**50 Rupees** 1967; 1968. Blue and purple on multicolor underprint. Statue of King Parakkrama at right. Back: Ornate stairway. Watermark: Chinze. Printer: BWC. 151x79mm.		
	a. Signature U. W. Wanninayake and D. W. Rajapatirana. 7.3.1967.	70.00	300.
	b. Signature U. B. Wanninayake and W. Tennekoon. 10.1.1968.	60.00	225.
71	**100 Rupees** 1966-68. Brown and blue on multicolor underprint. Statue of King Parakkrama at right. Back: Two women in national dress. Watermark: Chinze. Printer: BWC. 171x98mm.		
	a. Signature U. W. Wanninayake and D. W. Rajapatirana. 20.5.1966; 22.11.1966.	50.00	250.
	b. Signature U. B. Wanninayake and W. Tennekoon. 10.1.1968.	40.00	200.

1969-77 Issue

Central Bank of Ceylon text in English and Tamil.

#	Denomination / Description	VF	UNC
72	**2 Rupees** 1969-77. Light brown on lilac, light green and blue underprint. Statue of King Parakkrama at right. Back: Pavilion. Watermark: Chinze. Printer: BWC. 114x59mm.		
	a. Signature U. B. Wanninayake and W. Tennekoon. 10.5.1969.	2.00	9.00
	b. Signature N. M. Perera and W. Tennekoon. 1.6.1970; 1.2.1971; 7.6.1971.	2.00	6.00
	c. Signature N. M. Perera and W. Tennekoon. 12.5.1972; 21.8.1973; 27.8.1974.	2.00	6.00
	d. Signature R. J. G. de Mel and H. E. Tennekoon. 26.8.1977.	1.50	5.00

#	Denomination / Description	VF	UNC
73	**5 Rupees** 1969-77. Orange and brown on multicolor underprint. Statue of King Parakkrama at right. Back: Green and orange. Standing Figure. Watermark: Chinze. Printer: BWC. 125x64mm.		
	a. Signature U. B. Wanninayake and W. Tennekoon. 10.5.1969.	5.00	15.00
	b. Signature N. M. Perera and W. Tennekoon. 1.6.1970; 1.2.1971; 21.8.1973; 16.7.1974; 27.8.1974.	4.00	10.00
	c. Signature F. R. D. Bandaranaike and H. E. Tennekoon. 26.8.1977.	4.00	10.00
	ct. Color trial.	—	150.

#	Denomination / Description	VF	UNC
74	**10 Rupees** 1969-77. Green and purple on orange and blue underprint. Statue of King Parakkrama at right. Back: Ceremonial figures. Watermark: Chinze. Printer: BWC. 140x70mm.		
	a. Signature U. B. Wanninayake and W. Tennekoon. 20.10.1969.	15.00	50.00
	b. Signature N. M. Perera and W. Tennekoon. 1.6.1970; 1.2.1971; 7.6.1971; 21.8.1973; 16.7.1974.	5.00	15.00
	c. Signature Felix R. Dias Bandaranaike and H. E. Tennekoon. 6.10.1975.	4.00	10.00
	d. Signature R. J. G. de Mel and H. E. Tennekoon. 26.8.1977.	2.00	10.00
	ct. Color trial.	—	175.
75	**50 Rupees** 20.10.1969. Blue and purple on multicolor underprint. Statue of King Parakkrama at right. Back: Ornate stairway. Watermark: Chinze. Printer: BWC. 151x79mm.		
	a. Signature: U. B. Wanninayake and William Tennekoon. 20.10.1969.	90.00	300.
	b. Signature: N. M. Perera and William Tennekoon. 1.6.1970. (Not released and destroyed).	—	—

#	Denomination / Description	VF	UNC
76	**100 Rupees** 10.5.1969. Brown and blue on multicolor underprint. Statue of King parakkrama at right. Back: Two women in national dress. Watermark: Chinze. Printer: BWC. 162x86mm.		
	a. Signature: U. B. Wanninayake and William Tennekoon. 10.5.1969.	40.00	150.
	b. Signature: N. M. Perera and William Tennekoon. 1.6.1970.(Not released and destroyed).	—	—

1970 Issue

#	Denomination / Description	VF	UNC
77	**50 Rupees** 26.10.1970; 29.12.1970. Blue on lilac, yellow and brown underprint. Smiling President S. W. R. D. Bandaranaike with raised hand. Signature: N. M. Perera and William Tennekoon. Serial # prefix *D*. Back: Monument. Watermark: Chinze. Printer: TDLR. 151x79mm.		
	a. 26.10.1970.	20.00	100.
	b. 9.12.1970.	40.00	150.
	r. Replacement note: Serial # Prefix *W/1*.	—	—

78	**100 Rupees**	VF	UNC
	26.10.1970; 9.12.1970. Red-violet on multicolor underprint. Smiling President S. W. R. D. Bandaranaike with raised hand. Signature: N. M. Perera and William Tennekoon. Serial # prefix: *E*. Back: Female dancers. Watermark: Chinze. Printer: TDLR. 162x86mm.		
	a. 26.10.1970.	60.00	250.
	b. 9.12.1970.	70.00	300.
	r. Replacement note. Serial # prefix: *V/1*.	—	—

1971-75 Issue

79	**50 Rupees**	VF	UNC
	28.12.1972; 27.8.1974. Purple and multicolor. Smiling President S. W. R. D. Bandaranaike without raised hand. Signatures: N. M. Perera and Herbert Tennekoon. Back: Landscape. Watermark: Chinze. Printer: BWC. 151x79mm.		
	a. Issued note.	12.50	75.00
	s. Specimen.	—	175.

80	**100 Rupees**	VF	UNC
	1971-75. Brown and purple on multicolor underprint. Smiling President . W. R. D. Bandaranaike without raised hand. Back: Ornate stairway. Watermark: Chinze. Printer: BWC. 162x86mm.		
	a. Signature N. M. Perera and H. E. Tennekoon. 18.12.1971; 16.7.1974; 27.8.1974.	17.50	100.
	b. Signature F. R. D. Bandaranaike and H. E. Tennekoon. 6.10.1975.	15.00	80.00

For later issues refer to Sri Lanka

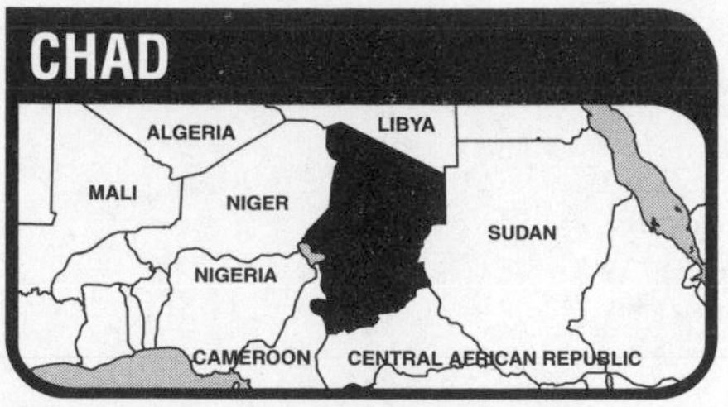

The Republic of Chad, a landlocked country of central Africa, is the largest country of former French Equatorial Africa. It has an area of 1.284 million sq. km. and a population of 10.11 million. Capital. N'Djaména. An expanding livestock industry produces camels, cattle and sheep. Cotton (the chief product), ivory and palm oil are important exports.

Chad, part of France's African holdings until 1960, endured three decades of civil warfare as well as invasions by Libya before a semblance of peace was finally restored in 1990. The government eventually drafted a democratic constitution, and held flawed presidential elections in 1996 and 2001. In 1998, a rebellion broke out in northern Chad, which has sporadically flared up despite several peace agreements between the government and the rebels. In 2005, new rebel groups emerged in western Sudan and made probing attacks into eastern Chad, despite signing peace agreements in December 2006 and October 2007. Power remains in the hands of an ethnic minority. In June 2005, President Idriss Deby held a referendum successfully removing constitutional term limits and won another controversial election in 2006. Sporadic rebel campaigns continued throughout 2006 and 2007, and the capital experienced a significant rebel threat in early 2008.

For later issues, see Central African States.

MONETARY SYSTEM:

1 Franc = 100 Centimes

SIGNATURE VARIETIES:

Refer to introduction to Central African States.

République du Tchad

For notes with similar back designs see Cameroun Republic, Central African Republic, Congo (Brazzaville) and Gabon.

Banque Centrale

1971 Issue

1	**10,000 Francs**	VF	UNC
	ND (1971). Multicolor. President Tombalbaye at left, cattle watering at center right, signature 1. Back: Mask at left, tractor plowing at center, statue at right.	1750.	3750.

Banque des États de l'Afrique Centrale

1974-78; ND Issue

2	**500 Francs**	VF	UNC
	ND (1974); 1978. Brown and red on multicolor underprint. Woman at left, flamingos, crowned cranes, abdim's stork at center and at right. Back: Mask at left, students and chemical testing at center, statue at right.		
	a. Signature titles and watermark like #3a. Signature 6. (1974).	12.50	40.00
	b. Signature titles, watermark and date like #3c. Signature 10. 1.4.1978.	75.00	200.
	s1. As a. Specimen. Overprinted and perforated: *SPECIMEN*.	—	400.
	s2. As b. Specimen. Overprinted and perforated: *SPECIMEN*..	—	750.

3 **1000 Francs** | VF | UNC

ND; 1.4.1978. Blue and brown on multicolor underprint. Woman at right.
Back: Mask at left, trains, planes and bridge at center, statue at right.

	VF	UNC
a. Signature titles: *LE DIRECTEUR GÉNÉRAL* and *UN CENSEUR*. Engraved. Watermark: Antelope in half profile. Signature 5; 7.	85.00	100.
b. Signature titles: *LE DIRECTEUR GÉNÉRAL* and *UN CENSEUR*. Lithographed. Watermark: Antelope in profile. Signature 8.	20.00	75.00
c. Signature titles: *LE GOUVERNEUR* and *UN CENSEUR*. Signature 10. 1.4.1978.	12.50	50.00
s. As a. Specimen. Overprinted and perforated: *SPECIMEN*.	—	250.

4 **5000 Francs** | VF | UNC

ND (1974). Brown-orange on multicolor underprint. President Tombalbaye at left, signature 4. Back: Mask at left, industrial collage at center, statue at right. | 500. | 2000.

5 **5000 Francs** | VF | UNC

ND. Brown on multicolor underprint. Woman at left. Back: Mask at left, industrial collage at center, statue at right.

	VF	UNC
a. Signature 6. (1976).	75.00	275.
b. Signature 9. (1978).	70.00	250.
s. As a. Specimen. Overprinted and perforated: *SPECIMEN*.	—	750.

1980 Issue

6 **500 Francs** | VF | UNC

1.6.1980; 1.6.1984. Red and brown on multicolor underprint. Woman weaving basket at right, signature 10. Back: Mask at left, students and chemical testing at center, statue at right. | 10.00 | 45.00

7 **1000 Francs** | VF | UNC

1.6.1980; 1.6.1984. Blue and dull purple on multicolor underprint. Water buffalo at right, signature 9; 10. Back: Mask at left, trains, planes and bridge at center, statue at right. | 15.00 | 60.00

8 **5000 Francs** | VF | UNC

1.1.1980. Brown and multicolor. Girl at lower left, village scene at center, signature 9. Back: Carving, airplane, train, tractor and man smoking pipe. Similar to Central African Republic #11 and others. | 60.00 | 250.

1984-85; ND Issue

For notes with similar back designs see Cameroun Republic, Central African Republic, Congo (Brazzaville) and Gabon.

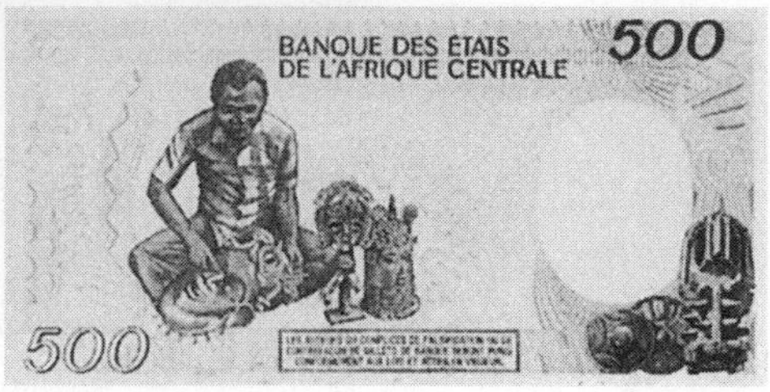

9	500 Francs	VF	UNC
	1985-92. Brown on multicolor underprint. Carved statue and jug at center. Back: Man carving mask at left center. Watermark: Carving.		
	a. Signature 10. 1.1.1985; 1.1.1986.	5.00	25.00
	b. Signature 12. 1.1.1987.	5.00	20.00
	c. Signature 13. 1.1.1990.	5.00	20.00
	d. Signature 15. 1.1.1991.	5.00	20.00
	e. Signature 15. 1.1.1992.	5.00	20.00

10	1000 Francs	VF	UNC
	1.1.1985. Dull blue-violet on multicolor underprint. Animal carving at lower left, map at center, starburst at lower right, incomplete outline map of Chad at top center, signature 9. Back: Elephants at left, statue at right. Watermark: Animal carving.	60.00	125.

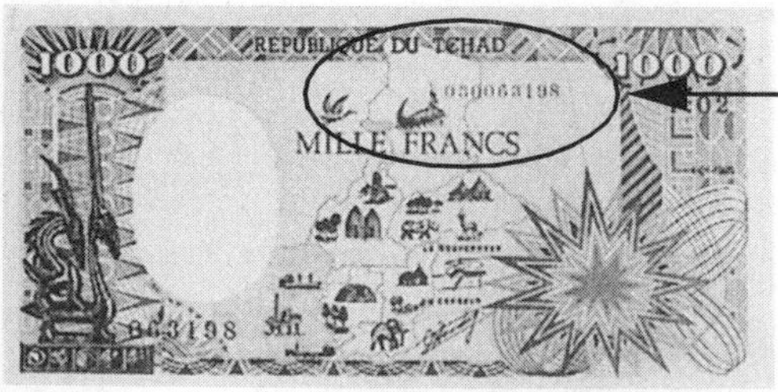

10A	1000 Francs	VF	UNC
	1985-92. Dull violet-blue on multicolor underprint. Animal carving at lower left, map at center, starburst at lower right, complete outine map of Chad at top center. Back: Elephants at left, statue at right. Watermark: Animal carving.		
	a. Signature 9. 1.1.1985; 1.1.1988; 1.1.1989; 1.1.1990.	7.50	30.00
	b. Signature 15. 1.1.1991.	15.00	40.00
	c. Signature 15. 1.1.1992.	7.50	30.00

11	5000 Francs	VF	UNC
	ND (1984-91). Brown on multicolor underprint. Mask at left, woman with bundle of fronds at right, signature 9; 15. Back: Plowing and mine ore conveyor.	35.00	150.

12	10,000 Francs	VF	UNC
	ND (1984-91). Black, brown and dark green on multicolor underprint. Stylized antelope heads at left, woman at right. Back: Loading fruit onto truck at left. Watermark: Woman.		
	a. Signature 9.	50.00	200.
	b. Signature 15.	40.00	175.

The Republic of Chile, a ribbonlike country on the Pacific coast of southern South America, has an area of 756,950 sq. km. and a population of 16.45 million. Capital: Santiago. Copper, of which Chile has about 25 percent of the world's reserves, has accounted for a major portion of Chile's export earnings in recent years. Other important exports are iron ore, iodine, fruit and nitrate of soda.

Prior to the coming of the Spanish in the 16th century, northern Chile was under Inca rule while Araucanian Indians (also known as Mapuches) inhabited central and southern Chile. Although Chile declared its independence in 1810, decisive victory over the Spanish was not achieved until 1818. In the War of the Pacific (1879-83), Chile defeated Peru and Bolivia and won its present northern regions. It was not until the 1880s that the Araucanian Indians were completely subjugated. A three-year-old Marxist government of Salvador Allende was overthrown in 1973 by a military coup led by Augusto Pinochet, who ruled until a freely elected president was installed in 1990. Sound economic policies, maintained consistently since the 1980s, have contributed to steady growth, reduced poverty rates by over half, and have helped secure the country's commitment to democratic and representative government. Chile has increasingly assumed regional and international leadership roles befitting its status as a stable, democratic nation.

MONETARY SYSTEM:

1 Peso = 100 Centavos
1 Condor = 100 Centavos = 10 Pesos to 1960
1 Escudo = 100 Centesimos, 1960-75
1 Peso = 100 "old" Escudos, 1975-

REPLACEMENT NOTES:

#140, 143, 145-148 w/*R* next to serial #.
#149-158 w/*R* near to plate position #.

PROVINCIAL

Province of Valdivia#S101-S102

REPUBLIC

BANCO CENTRAL DE CHILE

1960 ND PROVISIONAL ISSUE

1 Escudo = 1000 Pesos (= 100 Centesimos)

		VF	UNC
124	**1/2 Centesimo on 5 Pesos** ND (1960-61). Blue. Portrait Bernard O'Higgins at left, signature titles: *PRESIDENTE* and *GERENTE GENERAL*. Overprint: Red Escudo denomination on #119. Watermark: D. Diego Portales. Printer: CdM-Chile. Rare.	—	—

		VF	UNC
125	**1 Centesimo on 10 Pesos** ND (1960-61). Red-brown. Portrait Manuel Bulnes at left. Series F. Signature titles: *PRESIDENTE* and *GERENTE GENERAL*. Overprint: Red Escudo denomination on #120. Watermark: D. Diego Portales. Printer: CdM-Chile.	2.50	12.50

		VF	UNC
126	**5 Centesimos on 50 Pesos** ND (1960-61). Green. Portrait Anibal Pinto at left. Series C. 3 signature varieties. Signature titles: *PRESIDENTE* and *GERENTE GENERAL*. Overprint: Red Escudo denomination on #121. Watermark: D. Diego Portales. Printer: CdM-Chile.		
	a. Imprint on face 25mm wide.	1.00	2.50
	b. Imprint on face 22mm wide.	.20	2.00
	s. Specimen.	—	12.50

		VF	UNC
127	**10 Centesimos on 100 Pesos** ND (1960-61). Red. Portrait Arturo Prat at left. 3 signature varieties. Series C-K. Signature titles: *PRESIDENTE* and *GERENTE GENERAL*. Back: Light and dark varietes. Overprint: Red Escudo denomination on #122. Watermark: D. Diego Portales. Printer: CdM-Chile.		
	a. Issued note.	1.00	3.00
	s. Specimen.	—	12.50

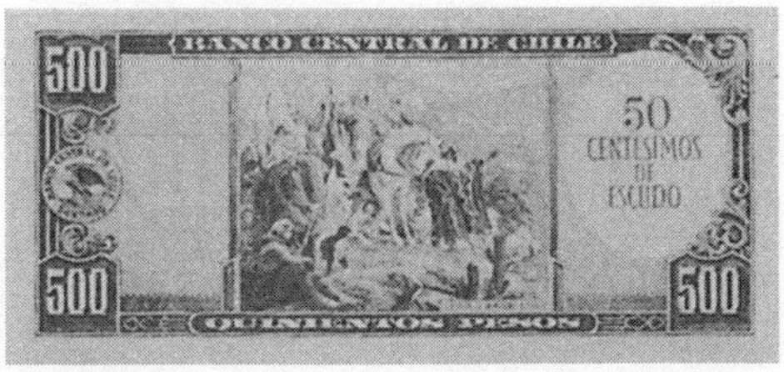

		VF	UNC
128	**50 Centesimos on 500 Pesos** ND (1960-61). Blue. Portrait Manuel Montt at right. Series A. Signature titles: *PRESIDENTE* and *GERENTE GENERAL*. Overprint: Red Escudo denomination on #115. Watermark: D. Diego Portales. Printer: CdM-Chile.	2.50	15.00

		VF	UNC
129	**1 Escudo on 1000 Pesos** ND (1960-61). Dark brown. Portrait Manuel Blanco Encalada at left. Series A. Signature titles: *PRESIDENTE* and *GERENTE GENERAL*. Overprint: Red Escudo denomination on #116. Watermark: D. Diego Portales. Printer: CdM-Chile.	2.00	12.50

130 **5 Escudos on 5000 Pesos** | VF | UNC
ND (1960-61). Brown-violet. Portrait Manuel Antonio Tocornal at left. 2 signature varieties. Series J. Signature titles: *PRESIDENTE* and *GERENTE GENERAL*. Overprint: Red Escudo denomination on #117. Watermark: D. Diego Portales. Printer: CdM-Chile. — 5.00 | 25.00

131 **10 Escudos on 10,000 Pesos**
ND (1960-61). Purple on light blue underprint. Portrait Jose Manuel Balmaceda at left. Series F. Signature titles: *PRESIDENTE* and *GERENTE GENERAL*. Overprint: Red Escudo denomination on #118. Watermark: D. Diego Portales at left, words *DIEZ MIL* at right. Printer: CdM-Chile. — 10.00 | 40.00

132 **10 Escudos on 10,000 Pesos**
ND (1960-61). Red-brown. Portrait Jose Manuel Balmaceda at left. Similar to #131. Series F. Signature titles: *PRESIDENTE* and *GERENTE GENERAL*. Overprint: Red Escudo denomination. Watermark: D. Diego Portales. Printer: CdM-Chile. — 15.00 | 55.00

133 **50 Escudos on 50,000 Pesos**
ND (1960-61). Blue-green and brown on multicolor underprint. Portrait Arturo Alessandri at left. Series A. Signature titles: *PRESIDENTE* and *GERENTE GENERAL*. Overprint: Red Escudo denomination on #123. Watermark: D. Diego Portales. Printer: CdM-Chile. — 25.00 | 75.00

Signatures 1962-1975

Gerente Gral	Presidente
Francisco Ibáñez 1962-70	Louis MacKenna 1962-70
Sergio Molina 1964-67	
Carlos Massad 1967-70	
Alfonso Inostroza 1970-73	Jamie Barrios 1970-73
Carlos Matus 1973	Carlos Trucco 1973
Eduardo Cano 1973-75	Carlos Molina 1973-85
Pablo Baraona 1975-76	

1962-75 ND Issue

134 **1/2 Escudo** | VF | UNC
ND. Dark blue on pale orange and light blue underprint. Portrait General Bernardo O'Higgins at center, signature varieties. Back: Explorer on horseback at left center. Red serial #. Watermark: D. Diego Portales P. Printer: CdM-Chile.
- a. Paper of #122. Series A. 3 signature varieties. — .50 | 3.00
- b. Paper of #121. Series B. 2 signature varieties. — .50 | 3.00
- s. Specimen. — — | 15.00

134A **1/2 Escudo** | VF | UNC
ND. Dark blue on pale orange on tan underprint. Portrait of General Bernardo O'Higgins at center, signature varieties. Back: Explorer on horseback at left center. Black serial #. Watermark: D. Diego Portales P. Printer: CdM-Chile.
- a. Paper of #121. Series B-G. — .25 | 2.00
- s. Specimen. — — | 17.50

135 **1 Escudo** | VF | UNC
ND. Brown-violet with lilac guilloche on tan underprint. Portrait Arturo Prat at center, signature varieties. Back: Red-brown arms with founding of Santiago. Watermark: Balmaceda. Printer: CdM-Chile. Engraved.
- a. Large and small brown serial #. Watermark: *1000* at right. Series A. — 3.00 | 10.00
- b. Large and small black serial #. Watermark: *500* at right. Series A. — 5.00 | 20.00
- c. Without watermark at right. Series A; B. — 1.50 | 5.00
- d. Small black serial #. Without watermark. at right. Arms in red-brown at left on back. — .50 | 2.00
- s. As c. Specimen. — — | 17.50

135A **1 Escudo** | VF | UNC
ND. Brown-violet with lilac guilloche on tan underprint. Portrait Arturo at center, 2 signature varieties. Series A; B. Back: Olive arms at left, founding of Santiago. Printer: CdM-Chile.
- a. Series G-I. Without watermark at right. — .20 | 1.00
- b. With *V* under portrait Paper of #121. Series J-N. — .20 | 1.00

136 **1 Escudo** | VF | UNC
ND (1964). Dull violet on tan underprint. Portrait Arturo Prat, 3 signature varieties. Back: Light olive arms with founding of Santiago. Watermark: D. Diego Portales P. Printer: CdM-Chile. Lithographed. 6 or 7 digit serial #. Series N; P; Q. — .25 | 1.00

137 5 Escudos

ND. Reddish brown on multicolor underprint. Portrait Manuel Bulnes at center, signature varieties. Back: Battle of Rancagua at center, yellow-orange arms at left. Watermark: D. Diego Portales P. Printer: CdM-Chile.

	VF	UNC
a. Series A.	2.00	12.50
s. Specimen.	—	17.50

138 5 Escudos

ND (1964). Red and brown-violet on multicolor underprint. Portrait Manuel Bulnes at center, 4 signature varieties. Back: Red-brown arms at left. Watermark: D. Diego Portales P. Printer: CdM-Chile. 6 or 7 digit serial #. Series A-E.

VF	UNC
.25	2.00

139 10 Escudos

ND. Violet, blue-gray and dull purple on multicolor underprint. Portrait Jose Manuel Balmaceda at center, 3 signature varieties. Back: Dark or light brown arms at left, soldiers meeting at center. Watermark: D. Diego Portales P. Printer: CdM-Chile.

	VF	UNC
a. Series A-G.	.75	5.00
s. Specimen.	—	25.00

140 50 Escudos

ND. Dark green and olive-brown on multicolor underprint. Portrait Arturo Alessandri at center. 5 signature varieties. Back: Back brown and green. Banco Central building. Watermark: D. Diego Portales P. Printer: CdM-Chile.

	VF	UNC
a. Series A-D.	1.75	8.00
b. Series E-F.	.25	3.00
s. Specimen.	—	25.00

141 100 Escudos

ND. Blue-gray and violet-brown on tan underprint. Portrait Manuel Regifo at right. 2 signature varieties. Back: Sailing ships at center, arms at left. Watermark: D. Diego Portales P. Printer: CdM-Chile.

	VF	UNC
a. Series A-G.	.75	4.00
s. Specimen.	—	25.00

1967-76 ND Issues

#142-148 Replacement notes: Serial # suffix *R* or *R* in area of sheet position #.

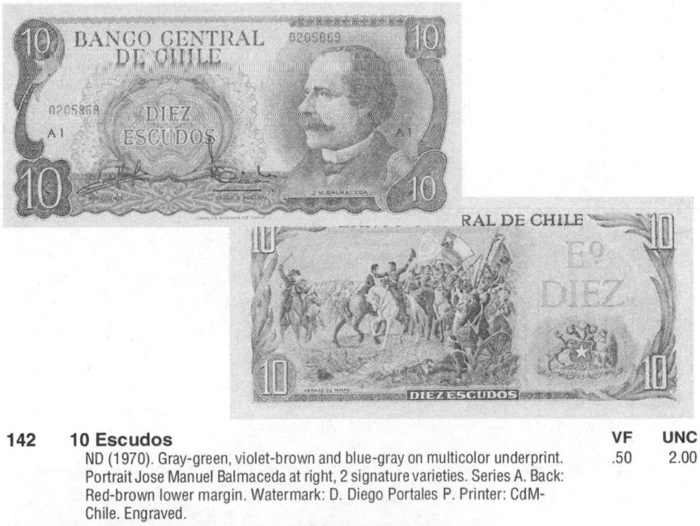

142 10 Escudos

ND (1970). Gray-green, violet-brown and blue-gray on multicolor underprint. Portrait Jose Manuel Balmaceda at right, 2 signature varieties. Series A. Back: Red-brown lower margin. Watermark: D. Diego Portales P. Printer: CdM-Chile. Engraved.

VF	UNC
.50	2.00

142A 10 Escudos | VF | UNC
ND. Gret-green, violet-brown and blue-grey on multicolor underprint. Portrait Jose Manuel Balmaceda at right, signature varieties. Back: Green lower margin. Watermark: D. Diego Portales P. Printer: CdM-Chile. Lithographed.

	VF	UNC
a. Series B.	.50	2.00
s. Specimen.	—	20.00

143 10 Escudos | VF | UNC
ND. Grayish brown on tan underprint. Portrait Jose Manuel Balmaceda at right, 3 signature varieties. Series A. Back: Red-brown lower margin. Watermark: D. Diego Portales P. Printer: CdM-Chile. Lithographed. | .25 | 1.50

144 500 Escudos
1971. Red-brown on multicolor underprint. Copper worker at left. Back: Strip mining at center right. Without 3-line text: *NO DEBEMOS CONSENTIR...* at bottom. Watermark: D. Diego Portales P. Printer: CdM-Chile. Nationalization of iron and copper mines commemorative. Rare. | — | —

145 500 Escudos | VF | UNC
1971. Red-brown on multicolor underprint. Copper worker at left, 2 signature varieties. Series A; B. Back: Strip mining at center right, 3-line text: *NO DEBEMOS CONSENTIR...*at bottom. Watermark: D. Diego Portales P. Printer: CdN-Chile. Nationalization of iron and copper mines commemorative. | .50 | 2.50

146 1000 Escudos | VF | UNC
ND. Purple and violet on multicolor underprint. Jose Miguel Carrera at left. 2 signature varieties. Series A; B. Back: Carrera House at center right. Watermark: D. Diego Portales P. Printer: CdM-Chile. | .50 | 3.00

147 5000 Escudos | VF | UNC
ND. Dark green and brown on multicolor underprint. Jose Miguel Carrera at left, signature varieties. Back: Carrera House at center right. Watermark: D. Diego Portales P. Printer: CdM-Chile.

	VF	UNC
a. Back with deep green vignette. Lithographed. Series A.	1.50	5.00
b. Back with dark olive-green vignette. Partially engraved. Series B. 2 signature varieties.	.75	3.00

148 10,000 Escudos | VF | UNC
ND. Orange-brown on multicolor underprint. General Bernardo O'Higgins at left. Blue serial #. 2 signature varieties. Series A. Back: Battle of Rancagua. Watermark: D.Diego Portales P. Printer: CdM-Chile. | 3.50 | 6.00

Signatures 1975-1999

Gerente Gral	Presidente
Carlos Molina 1973-85	Pablo Barona 1975-76
	Alvaro Bardón 1977-81
	Sergio de La Cuadra 1981-82
	Miguel Kast 1982
	Carlos Cáceres 1982-83
	Hernán Errázuriz 1984-85
	Francisco Ibáñez 1984-85
Jorge Court 1985-86	Enrique Sequel 1985-89
Jorge Correa 1986-89	
Julio Acevedo 1990	Manuel Concha 1989

Signatures 1975-1999	
Juan Rodriguez 1989-90 (Interum)	Andrés Bianchi 1989-91
Enrique Tassara 1990-91 (Interum)	Roberto Zahler 1991-97
Enrique Marshall 1991-94	Carlos Massad 1997-
Camilo Carrasco 1994-	

1975-89 Issues

#149-152 Replacement notes: ***R*** **serial # suffix.**

149	5 Pesos	VF	UNC
	1975-76. Green on olive underprint. Jose Miguel Carrera at right. Signature varieties. Back: Carrera House at center right. Watermark: D. Diego Portales P. Printer: CdM-Chile.		
	a. 1975.	2.00	7.50
	b. 1976.	25.00	55.00
	s. As a. Specimen.	—	25.00

150	10 Pesos	VF	UNC
	1975-76. Red on multicolor underprint. General Bernardo O'Higgins at right. Signature varieties. Back: Battle of Rancagua. Watermark: General Bernardo O'Higgins. Printer: CdM-Chile.		
	a. *B. O'HIGGINS* under portrait 1975.	1.75	8.00
	b. *LIBERTADOR B. O'HIGGINS* under portrait 1975; 1976.	1.00	7.50
	s. As a. Specimen.	—	25.00

151	50 Pesos	VF	UNC
	1975-81. Dark blue and aqua on green and light blue underprint. Portrait Captain Arturo Prat at right. 3 signature varieties. Back: Sailing ships at center. Watermark: D. Diego Portales P. Printer: CdM-Chile.		
	a. 1975; 1976; 1977; 1978.	.50	3.00
	b. 1980; 1981 (2 signature varieties.)	.25	2.00
	s. Specimen. 1975.	—	25.00

152	100 Pesos	VF	UNC
	1976-84. Purple and red-violet on multicolor underprint. Diego Portales at right. 6 signature varieties. Back: 1837 meeting at left center. Watermark: D. Diego Portales P. Printer: CdM-Chile.		
	a. Normal serial # without prefix letter. Series A. 1976.	4.00	10.00
	b. Electronic sorting serial # with prefix letter. 1976-77, 1979-84. 6 signature varieties (2 for 1981).	.50	3.00
	s. Specimen. 1976.	—	25.00

153	500 Pesos	VF	UNC
	1977-2000. Dark brown and brown-violet with black text on multicolor underprint. Pedro de Valdivia at right. 11 signature varieties. Back: Founding of Santiago at center. Watermark: Ignacio Carrera Pinto.		
	a. 1977; 1978.	1.50	7.50
	b. 1980-82; 1985-90.	FV	4.50
	c. Signature titles: *PRESIDENTE* and *GERENTE GENERAL INTERINO*. 1991.	2.00	7.50
	d. 1991-93.	FV	4.00
	e. 1994-2000. (1999 without imprint).	FV	3.00
	s. Specimen. 1977.	—	25.00

154	1000 Pesos	VF	UNC
	1978-. Deep blue-green, dark olive-brown on multicolor underprint. Ignacio Carrera Pinto at right, military arms at center. 12 signature varieties. Back: Monument to Chilean heroes. Watermark: Ignacio Carrera Pinto.		
	a. Signature titles: *PRESIDENTE* and *GERENTE GENERAL*. 1978-80.	4.00	25.00
	b. 1982.	FV	10.00
	c. 1984-90.	FV	9.50
	d. Signature titles: *PRESIDENTE* and *GERENTE GENERAL INTERINO*. 1990.	FV	9.00

	VF	UNC
e. Signature titles as a. 1991-94. (2 Signature varieties in 1994).	FV	7.50
f. Designer's names omitted from lower left and right. 1995-2005. (without imprint 1999; 2001-2002, 2004-6).	FV	5.00
g. One horizontal bar added to assist sight impaired. 2006; 2007; 2008; 2009.	FV	5.00
s. Specimen. 1978. Overprint: *Especimen.*	—	50.00

155 5000 Pesos VF UNC

1981-. Brown and red-violet on multicolor underprint. Allegorical woman with musical instrument, seated male at center. 9 signature varieties. Back: Statue of woman with children at left center, Gabriela Mistral at right. Watermark: Gabriela Mistral.

	VF	UNC
a. Signature titles: *PRESIDENTE* and *GERENTE GENERAL*. 1981. Plain security thread.	FV	70.00
b. 1986-90.	FV	50.00
c. Signature titles: *PRESIDENTE* and *GERENTE GENERAL INTERINO*. 1991.	FV	35.00
d. Signature titles: *PRESIDENTE* and *GERENTE GENERAL*. 1991-94.	FV	27.50
e. As d but with segmented foil security thread. 1994-2005. (without imprint, 2002-2005).	FV	20.00
f. Two horizontal bars added to assist sight impaired. 2006; 2007.	FV	20.00
g. 2008.	FV	17.50
s. Specimen. 1981; 1993.	—	100.

156 10,000 Pesos VF UNC

1989-94. Dark blue and dark olive-green on multicolor underprint. Captain Arturo Prat at right. 5 signature varieties. Back: Statue of Liberty at left, Hacienda San Agustin de Punual Cuna at left center. Watermark: Captain Arturo Prat.

	VF	UNC
a. Plain security thread. 1989-93.	FV	60.00
b. As a. 1994.	FV	50.00
s. Specimen. 1994.	—	100.

1994 Issue

157 10,000 Pesos VF UNC

1995-99; 2001-08. Dark blue and deep olive-green on multicolor underprint. Captain Arturo Prat at right. 2 signature varieties. Back: Statue of Liberty at left, Hacienda San Agustin de Punual Cuna at left center. Watermark: Captain Arturo Prat. Printer: TDLR.

	VF	UNC
a. Plain security thread. TDLR imprint. 1994.	FV	35.00
b. Segmented security thread. TDLR. 1994-2001.	FV	35.00
c. Without imprint. 2001-6; 2008.	FV	35.00
s. 1998. Specimen. Red overprint: *ESPECIMEN.*	—	100.

1997 Issue

158 2000 Pesos VF UNC

1997; 1999 (with imprint); 2001-03 (without imprint). Purple and dark brown on multicolor underprint. Manuel Rodríguez E. at right, statue of Manuel Rodríguez on horseback at center. Back: Iglesia de los Dominicos (church) at center. Watermark: Manuel Rodríguez E. Printer: CdM-C.

	VF	UNC
a. Issued note.	FV	9.00
s. 1998. Specimen. Red overprint: *ESPECIMEN.*	—	50.00

1998 Issue

159 20,000 Pesos VF UNC

1998-. Lilac brown, green and multicolor. Don Andres Bello at right. Back: University building. Printer: CdM-C.

	VF	UNC
a. 1998-2005.	FV	60.00
b. Circle added to assist slight impaired. 2006-.	FV	60.00
s. 1998. Specimen. Red overprint: *ESPECIMEN.*	—	100.

2004 Polymer Issue

160 2000 Pesos VF UNC

2004-. Lilac and brown on multicolor underprint. Manuel Rodríguez E. at right and as statue on horseback. Back: Iglesia de los Dominicos (church) at center. Watermark: Manuel Rodriguez E. Printer: CdM-C. Polymer plastic.

	VF	UNC
a. 2004. Signature V. Corbo and C.A. Carrasco.	FV	7.50
b. 2007. Signature V. Corbo and A.Z. Silva.	FV	7.50
c. 2008. Signature J. de Gregorio Rebeco and A. Z. Silva.	FV	7.50

2009 Polymer Issue

161 1000 Pesos VF UNC

2011. Green. 120x70mm **FV 4.00**

162	**2000 Pesos**	**VF**	**UNC**
	2009. Black on purple and rose underprint. Manuel Rodriguez at left center. Back: Nalcas National Reserve. Expected new issue.	FV	750

163	**5000 Pesos**	**VF**	**UNC**
	2009; 2011. Rose on blue underprint. Gabriela Mistral facing at center. Back: Chilean palm trees in the La Campana National Park; Tucúquere bird. Printer: NPA.		
	a. 2009.	FV	17.50
	b. 2011	FV	17.50

164	**10,000 Pesos**	**VF**	**UNC**
	2009. Blue. Manuel Rodriguez at left center. Back: Alberto de Agostini National Park.	FV	25.00

165	**20,000 Pesos**	**VF**	**UNC**
	2009. Brown and orange. Andres Bello at left center. Back: Salar de Surire Natural Monument.	FV	40.00

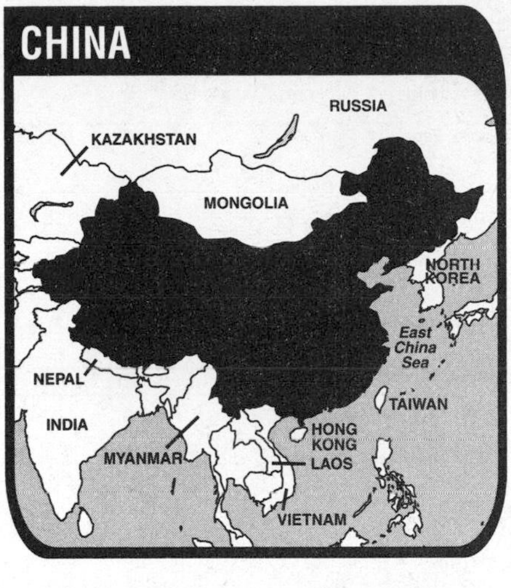

The Republic of China, comprising Taiwan (an island located 90 miles (145 km.) off the southeastern coast of mainland China), the offshore islands of Quemoy and Matsu and nearby islets of the Pescadores chain, has an area of 14,000 sq. mi. (35,981 sq. km.) and a population of 20.2 million. Capital: Taipei. During the past decade, manufacturing has replaced agriculture in importance. Fruits, vegetables, plywood, textile yarns and fabrics and clothing are exported. Chinese migration to Taiwan began as early as the sixth century. The Dutch established a on the island in 1624 and held it until 1661, when they were driven out by supporters of the Ming dynasty who used it as a for their unsuccessful attempt to displace the ruling Manchu dynasty of mainland China. After being occupied by Manchu forces in 1683, Taiwan remained under the suzerainty of China until its cession to Japan in 1895. It was returned to China following World War II. On December 8, 1949, Taiwan became the last remnant of Sun Yatsen's Republic of China when Chiang Kai-shek moved his army and government from mainland China to the island following his defeat by the Communist forces of Mao Tse-tung.

MONETARY SYSTEM: 1 Chiao = 10 Fen (Cents) 1 Yuan (Dollar) = 10 Chiao

MONETARY UNITS	
Yuan	圓 *or* 圜
Pan Yuan	圓 半
5 Jiao	角伍
1 Jiao	角壹
1 Fen	分壹

NUMERICAL CHARACTERS

No.	CONVENTIONAL			FORMAL	
1	一	正	元	壹	弌
2	二			弍	貳
3	三			弎	叁
4	四			肆	
5	五			伍	
6	六			陸	
7	七			柒	
8	八			捌	
9	九			玖	
10	十			拾	什
20	十二	廿		拾貳	念
25	五十二	五廿		伍拾貳	
30	十三	卅		拾叁	

NUMERICAL CHARACTERS

No.	CONVENTIONAL		FORMAL	
100	百一		佰壹	
1,000	千一		仟壹	
10,000	萬一		萬壹	
100,000	萬十	億一	萬拾	億壹
1,000,000	萬百一		萬佰壹	

PEOPLES REPUBLIC OF CHINA

PEOPLES BANK OF CHINA

行銀民人國中

Chung Kuo Jen Min Yin Hang

中國人民銀行

Zhong Guo Ren Min Yin Hang

1953 SECOND ISSUE

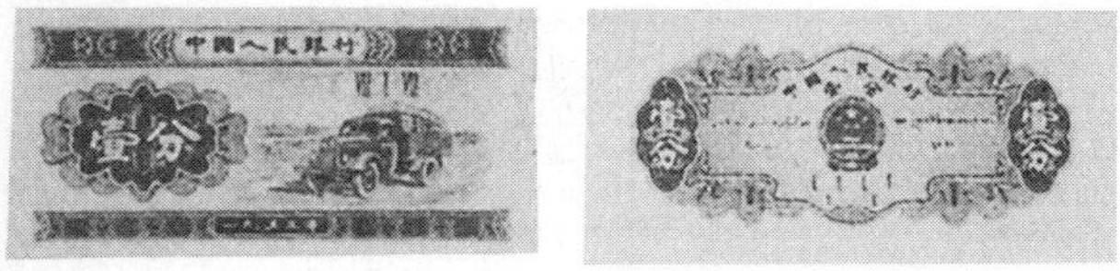

860 1 Fen — VF | UNC

1953. Brown on yellow-orange underprint. Produce truck at right. Back: Arms at center.

	VF	UNC
a. Roman control numerals and serial #.	2.00	10.00
b. 3 Roman control numerals only.	—	.50
c. 2 Roman control numerals.	—	.20

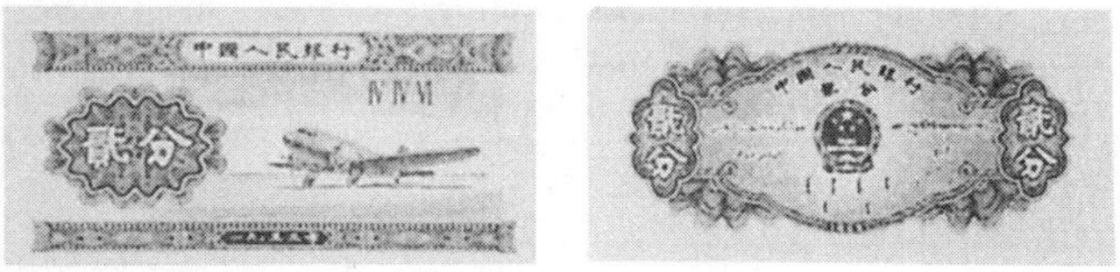

861 2 Fen

1953. Dark blue on light blue underprint. Airplane at right. Back: Arms at center.

	VF	UNC
a. Roman control numerals and serial #.	5.00	30.00
b. Roman control numerals only.	.20	.50

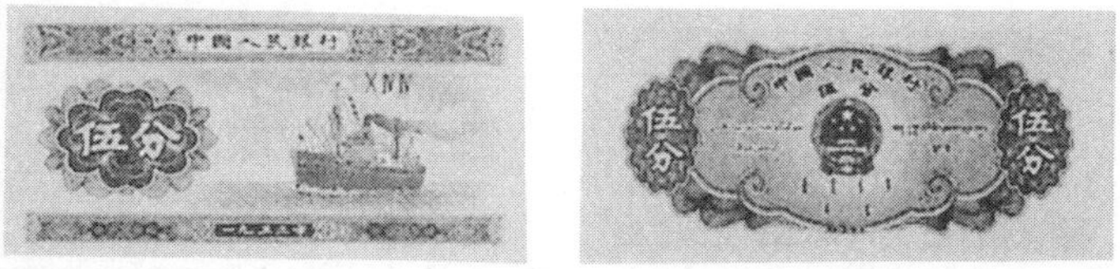

862 5 Fen

1953. Dark green on green underprint. Cargo ship at right. Back: Arms at center.

	VF	UNC
a. Roman control numerals and serial #.	20.00	90.00
b. Roman control numerals only.	.20	.50

1962; 1965 ISSUE

877 1 Jiao

1962. Brown on multicolor underprint. Workers at left. Back: Arms at right.

	VF	UNC
a. Back brown on green and light orange underprint. Without watermark.	100.	300.
b. As a, watermark: stars.	800.	2500.
c. Serial # prefix: 3 blue Roman numerals. Back brown. Without watermark.	.20	1.00
d. Like c, serial # prefix: 2 blue Roman numerals.	.30	1.50
e. Like b, partially engraved. Serial # prefix: 3 red Roman numerals. Watermark: Stars.	.40	1.00
f. Like c but lithographed, serial # prefix: 2 red Roman numerals. Without watermark.	.15	.50

878 2 Jiao

1962. Green. Bridge over Yangtze River at left. Back: Arms at right.

	VF	UNC
a. Engraved face. Serial # prefix: 3 Roman numerals.	5.00	15.00
b. Lithographed face. Serial # prefix: 3 Roman numerals.	.20	.50
c. As b. Serial # prefix: 2 Roman numerals.	.15	.50
x. As b. Red back. Post production chemical alteration.	1.00	3.50

879 10 Yüan

1965. Black on multicolor underprint. Representatives of the National Assembly at center. Back: Arms at right, palace gate at left. Watermark: Great Hall with rays.

	VF	UNC
a. Serial # prefix: 3 Roman numerals.	5.00	25.00
b. Serial # prefix: 2 Roman numerals.	5.00	20.00

1972 ISSUE

880 5 Jiao

1972. Purple and multicolor. Women working in textile factory. Back: Arms at right.

	VF	UNC
a. Engraved bank title and denomination. Serial # prefix: 3 Roman numerals. Watermark: Stars.	1.50	4.00
b. As a, but lithographed face. With watermark.	15.00	60.00
c. Lithographed face. Without watermark.	.20	.75

1980 ISSUE

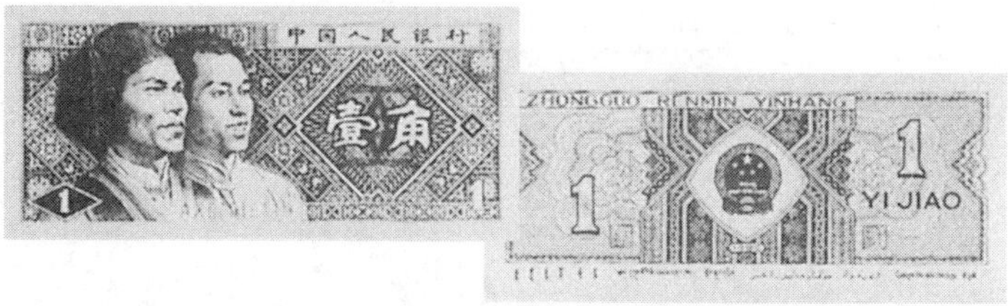

881 1 Jiao

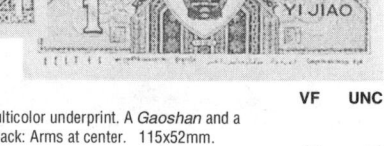

1980. Brown and dark brown on multicolor underprint. A *Gaoshan* and a *Man* ethnic group member at left. Back: Arms at center. 115x52mm.

	VF	UNC
a. Issued note.	FV	.50
s. Specimen.	—	25.00

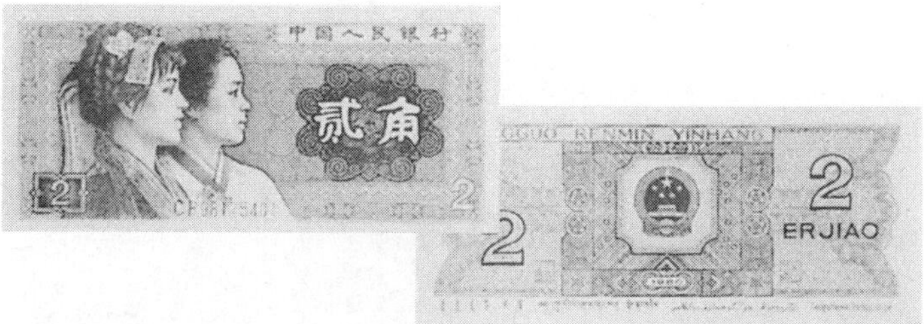

882 2 Jiao

1980. Grayish olive-green on multicolor underprint. Native *Pu Yi* and Korean youth at left. Back: Arms at center. 120x55mm.

	VF	UNC
a. Issued note.	FV	.50
s. Specimen.	—	25.00

883	5 Jiao	VF	UNC
	1980. Purple and red-violet on multicolor underprint. *Miao* and *Zhuang* children at left. Back: Brown-violet on multicolor underprint. Arms at center. 125x58mm.		
	a. Issued note.	FV	.75
	s. Specimen.	—	.25

884	1 Yüan	VF	UNC
	1980; 1990; 1996. Brown-violet on multicolor underprint. *Dong* and *Yao* youths at right. Arms at upper left. Stylized birds in underprint at center, braille dot at lower left for the poor of sight. Back: Great Wall at center. Watermark: Ancient *Pu* (pants) coin repeated. 140x63mm.		
	a. Engraved. dark blue serial #. watermark: Ancient *Pu* (pants) coin repeated. 1980.	FV	2.00
	b. Partially engraved. watermark. as a. Black serial #. 1990.	FV	.75
	c. Litho. watermark: Stars. Black serial #. 1996.	FV	.50
	s. As a. Specimen.	—	50.00

885	2 Yüan	VF	UNC
	1980; 1990. Dark olive-green on multicolor underprint. *Uygur* and *Yi* youths at right. Arms at upper left. Stylized birds in underprint at center. Braille dots at lower left for poor of sight. Back: Pillar of South Heaven in the South China Sea. Watermark: Ancient *Pu* (pants) coin repeated. 145x63mm.		
	a. Engraved back. 1980.	FV	5.00
	b. Litho. back. 1990.	FV	2.50
	s. As a. Specimen.	—	50.00

886	5 Yüan	VF	UNC
	1980. Dark brown on multicolor underprint. Old Tibetan man and young *Hui* woman at right. Arms at upper left. Stylized birds in underprint at center. Braille dots at lower left for poor of sight. Back: Wu Gorge of the Changjiang (Yangtse) River. Watermark: Ancient *Pu* (pants) coin repeated. 150x70mm.		
	a. Issued note.	FV	2.00
	s. Specimen.	—	50.00

887	10 Yüan	VF	UNC
	1980. Black on blue and multicolor underprint. Elder Han and youthful Mongolian man at right. Arms at upper left. Stylized birds in underprint at center. Braille dots at lower left for poor of sight. Back: Mount Qomolangma (Mount Everest) at center. Watermark: Young Mongolian man. 155x70mm.		
	a. Issued note.	FV	4.00
	s. Specimen.	—	50.00

888	50 Yüan	VF	UNC
	1980; 1990. Black on light green and multicolor underprint. Intellectual, farm girl and industrial male worker at center. Stylized birds in underprint at center. Braille dots at lower right for poor of sight. Back: HuKo Waterfall on the Yellow River. Arms at upper left. Watermark: Steel worker. 160x77mm.		
	a. 1980.	FV	200.
	b. Security thread at right. 1990.	FV	25.00
	s. As a. Specimen.	—	150.

889	100 Yüan	VF	UNC
	1980; 1990. Black on multicolor underprint. Four profiles: Mao Zedong, Zhow Enlai, Liu Shaoqi, Zhu De at center. Stylized birds in underprint at center. Braille dots at lower right for poor of sight. Back: Main peak of the Jinggang Mountains (starting point of the "Long March"). Arms at upper left. Watermark: Bust of Mao Zedong. 165x77mm.		
	a. 1980.	FV	150.
	b. 1990. Security thread at right.	FV	25.00
	s. As a. Specimen.	—	150.
890	**500 Yüan**		
	1990. Black on multicolor underprint. Used for inter-bank transfers only.	—	—

1999 Commemorative Issue

891, 50th Anniversary of Revolution

891 **50 Yüan** — VF — UNC
1999. Red on multicolor underprint. Mao Tse-tung delivering speech. Braille dots at lower left for poor of sight. Back: Five pigeons in flight, carvings to left and right. Arms at upper left. — FV — 15.00

1999 Regular Issue

895 **1 Yüan** — VF — UNC
1999. Mao Tse-tung at right, flora at lower center. Watermark: Flora.
a. Serian number prefix format as: Letter, letter, number, number. — FV — 1.00
b. Serial number prefix format as: Letter, number, letter, number — FV — 1.00

897 **5 Yüan** — VF — UNC
1999 (2002). Purple on multicolor underprint. Mao Tse-tung at right, flora at lower center. Back: Mountain valley view. Watermark: Flora. . — FV — 2.00

898 **10 Yüan** — VF — UNC
1999 (2000). Slate blue and multicolor. Mao Tse-tung at right, flora at lower center. Back: Three gorges of Yangtze river. Watermark: Flora. — FV — 4.00

899 **20 Yüan** — VF — UNC
1999. Brown on multicolor underprint. Mao Tse-tung at right, flora at lower center. Back: River scene. Watermark: Flora. — FV — 5.00

900 **50 Yüan** — VF — UNC
1999 (2001). Green and multicolor. Mao Tse-tung at right, flora at lower center. Back: Potala of Tibet. Watermark: Flora. — FV — 20.00

901 **100 Yüan** — VF — UNC
1999. Red and multicolor. Mao Tse-tung at right, flora at lower center. Back: Hall of the People. Watermark: Flora. — FV — 20.00

2000 Commemorative Issue

#902, Year 2000 commemorative

902 **100 Yüan** — VF — UNC
2000. Orange, red and green. Dragon at center, clear window with image at lower left, OVD at upper right. Back: Millenium monument, Beijing. Polymer plastic. The clear window is a lotent hologram, shine a laser pointer through it and view the character "Zhong."
a. Series I — FV — 800.
b. Series J. — FV — 400.

2005 Issue

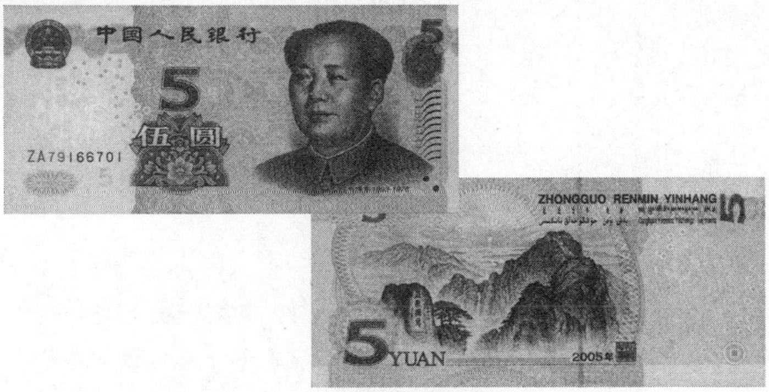

903 **5 Yüan** — VF | UNC
2005. Purple on multicolor underprint. Mao Tse-Tung at right. Back: Mountain valley view. — FV | 1.00

904 **10 Yüan** — VF | UNC
2005. Slate blue on mullticolor underprint. Mao Tse-Tung at right. Back: Three gorges of the Yangtze river. — FV | 2.50

905 **20 Yüan** — VF | UNC
2005. Brown on peach and multicolor underprint. Mao Tse-Tung at right. Back: River scene. — FV | 5.00

906 **50 Yüan** — VF | UNC
2005. Multicolor. Mao Tse-Tung at right. — FV | 10.00

907 **100 Yüan** — VF | UNC
2005. Red on multicolor underprint. Mao Tse-Tung at right. Back: Hall of the People. — FV | 20.00

2008 Commemorative Issue

908 **10 Yüan** — VF | UNC
2008. Light and dark green. The "Bird's Nest" olympic stadium. Back: Discus thrower statue.
a. Issued note. — FV | 20.00

Chinese Administration of Taiwan

Bank of Taiwan

臺灣銀行
T'ai Wan Yin Hang

PORTRAIT ABBREVIATIONS

SYS = Dr. Sun Yat-sen, 1867-1925
President of Canton Government, 1917-25
Taiwan, 1949-1975

CKS = Chiang Kai-shek, 1886-1975
President in Nanking, 1927-31
Head of Formosa Government,

Note: Because of the frequency of the above appearing in the following listings, their initials are used only in reference to their portraits.

PRINTERS

CPF: (Central Printing Factory) 中央印製廠

CPFT: (Central Printing Factory, Taipei) 中央印製廠台北廠

FPFT: (First Printing Factory) 第一印刷廠

PFBT: (Printing Factory of Taiwan Bank) 臺灣銀行印刷所

1961 Issue

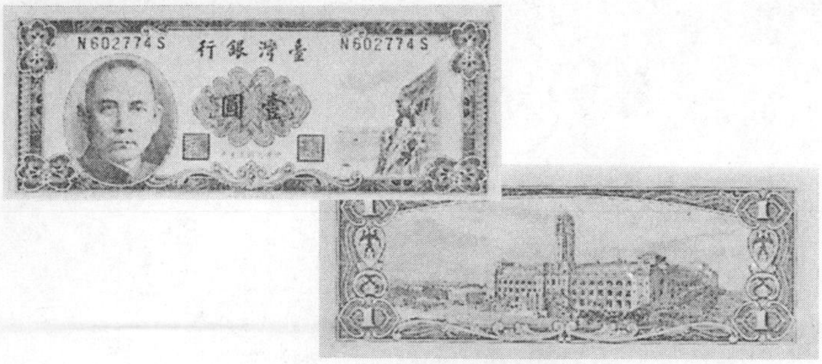

		VF	UNC
1971	**1 Yüan** 1961. Dark blue-green and purple on multicolor underprint. Portrait SYS at left, steep coastline at right. Printer: PFBT.		
	a. Engraved.	.75	5.00
	b. Lithographed. (1972).	1.50	3.00

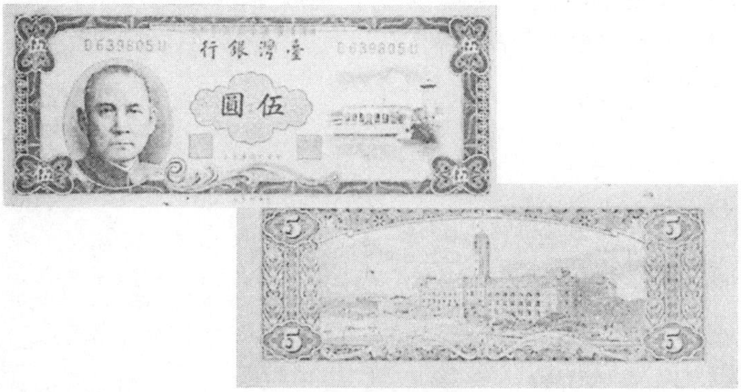

		VF	UNC
1972	**5 Yüan** 1961. Red on multicolor underprint. Portrait SYS at left, house with tower at right. Printer: CPF.	.75	4.00

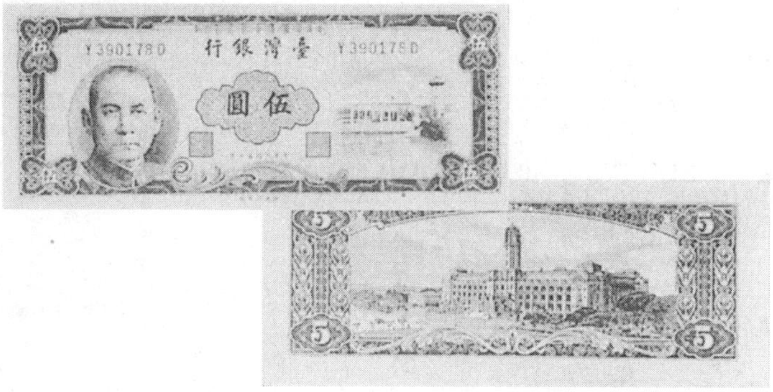

		VF	UNC
1973	**5 Yüan** 1961. Brown on multicolor underprint. Portrait SYS at left, house with tower at right. Printer: CPF.	1.50	10.00
1974	**50 Yüan** 1961. Purple on multicolor underprint. Portrait SYS at left. Printer: CPF.	3.00	20.00
1975	**100 Yüan** 1961. Green on multicolor underprint. Portrait SYS at left. Printer: CPF.	3.25	22.00

1964 Issue

		VF	UNC
1976	**50 Yüan** 1964. Purple on multicolor underprint. Portrait SYS at left. Printer: CPF.	2.00	15.00

		VF	UNC
1977	**100 Yüan** 1964. Green on multicolor underprint. Portrait SYS at left. Printer: CPF.	3.00	20.00

Republic of China-Taiwan Bank

行銀灣臺 國民華

Chung Hua Min Kuo-T'ai Wan Yin Hang

1969 Issue

		VF	UNC
1978	**5 Yüan** 1969. Blue on multicolor underprint. Portrait SYS at left. Printer: CPF.		
	a. Issued note.	.40	3.00
	s. Specimen. Uniface impression of each side.	—	150.

		VF	UNC
1979	**10 Yüan** 1969. Red on multicolor underprint. Portrait SYS at left. Printer: CPF.		
	a. Without plate letter.	.50	3.00
	b. Plate letter A at lower right. on face.	.35	2.50
	s. As a. Specimen. Uniface printing of each side.	—	150.

1970 Issue

		VF	UNC
1980	**50 Yüan** 1970. Purple on multicolor underprint. Portrait SYS at left. Printer: CPF.	2.25	10.00
1981	**100 Yüan** 1970. Green on multicolor underprint. Portrait SYS at left. Printer: CPF.	4.50	15.00

1972 Issue

1982 50 Yüan — VF | UNC

1972. Purple and light blue on multicolor underprint. Portrait SYS at left. Wide margin with guilloche at right. Back: Chungshan building. Printer: CPF.

	VF	UNC
a. Issued note.	2.00	6.00
s. Specimen. Uniface printing of each side.	—	150.

1983 100 Yüan

1972. Dark green, light green and orange on multicolor underprint. Portrait SYS at left. Wide margin with guilloche at right. Back: Palace. Printer: CPF.

	VF	UNC
a. Issued note.	3.50	8.00
s. Specimen. Uniface printing of each side.	—	150.

1976 Issue

1984 10 Yüan

	VF	UNC
1976. Red on multicolor underprint. Portrait SYS at left. Back: Bank. Printer: CPF.	.50	2.00

1985 500 Yüan

	VF	UNC
1976. Olive, purple and multicolor. CKS at left. Back: Chungshan building. Without watermark at right. Printer: CPF.	20.00	45.00

1986 1000 Yüan

1976. Blue-black, olive-brown and violet on multicolor underprint. CKS at left. Back: Presidential Office building. Without watermark at right. Printer: CPF.

	VF	UNC
a. Issued note.	40.00	120.
s. Specimen.	—	600.

1981 Issue

1987 500 Yüan

	VF	UNC
1981. Brown and red-brown on multicolor underprint. CKS at left. Back: Presidential Office. Watermark: CKS. Printer: CPF.	FV	40.00

1988 1000 Yüan

	VF	UNC
1981. Blue-black on multicolor underprint. CKS at left. Back: Presidential Office building. Watermark: CKS. Printer: CPF.	FV	80.00

1987 Issue

1989 100 Yüan

	VF	UNC
1987 (1988). Red, red-brown and brown-violet on multicolor underprint. SYS at left. Back: Chungshan building. Watermark: SYS.	FV	7.00

1999 Commemorative Issue

1990 50 Yüan

	VF	UNC
Red on multicolor underprint. Currency and high-speed train at left. Back: Bank building. Polymer plastic. 50th Anniversary of Taiwan.	FV	4.00

1999; 2001 Issue

1991 100 Yüan	VF	UNC
2001. Red on tan underprint. Sun-Yat Sen at right. Back: Building complex.	FV	7.50

1992 200 Yüan	VF	UNC
2001. Dark green on light green and tan underprint. Chaing Kai-shek at right. Back: Building.	FV	8.50

1993 500 Yüan	VF	UNC
1999; 2001. Brown and rose on multicolor underprint. Boy's baseball team at center, Professional Pitcher at right. Back: Formosan Sika Deer family and Mt. Dabajian.	
a. 1999.	FV	25.00
b. 2001.	FV	25.00

1994 1000 Yüan	VF	UNC
1999. Light and dark blue on light green underprint. School children studying globe at center. Back: Two Mikado Pheasant and mountian vista.	FV	40.00

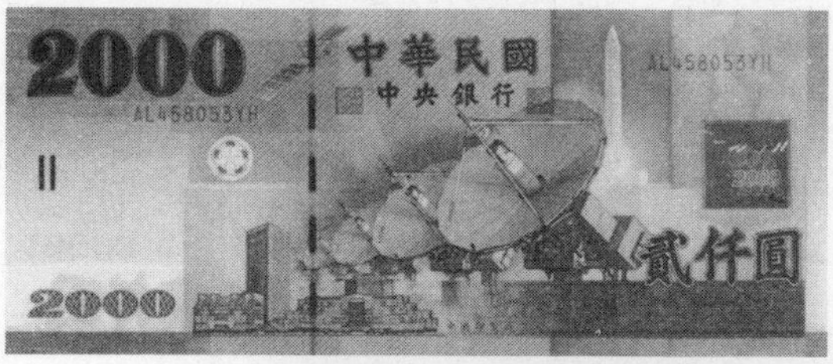

1995 2000 Yüan	VF	UNC
2002. Purple and lilac on multicolor underprint. Satellite Dishes and rocket. Back: Two salmon and Mt. Nanhu.	FV	80.00

2005 Issue

1996 500 Yüan	VF	UNC
2005. Brown and rose on multicolor underprint. Boy's baseball team at center, Professional Pitcher at right. Back: Formosan Sika Deer family. Wide security foil at right.	FV	25.00

1997 1000 Yüan	VF	UNC
2005. Light and dark blue on light green underprint. School children studying globe at center. Back: Two Mikado Pheasant and mountain vista. With wide security foil at right.	FV	40.00

Off-Shore Island Currency

Bank of Taiwan

T'ai Wan Yin Hang

Kinmen (Quemoy) Branch

1949-51 (1963; 1967) Issue

		VF	UNC
R101	**1 Yüan** 1949 (1963). Green on multicolor underprint. Portrait SYS at upper center. Printer: CPF. Vertical format.	2.00	10.00

Matsu Branch

1950-51 Dated (1964; 1967) Issue

		VF	UNC
R117	**10 Yüan** 1950 (1964). Blue on multicolor underprint. Portrait SYS at upper center. Printer: CPF. Vertical format.	3.00	25.00

		VF	UNC
R118	**50 Yüan** 1951 (1967). Green on multicolor underprint. Portrait SYS at upper center. Printer: FPDT. Vertical format.	8.00	80.00

Kinmen (Quemoy) Branch

1950-51 Issues

		VF	UNC
R106	**10 Yüan** 1950 (1963). Blue. Portrait SYS at upper center. Printer: CPF. Vertical format.	1.50	18.00

		VF	UNC
R107	**50 Yüan** 1951 (1967). Green. Portrait SYS at upper center. Printer: FPFT. Vertical format.	20.00	120.

Matsu Branch

1969; 1972 Issue

		VF	UNC
R122	**10 Yüan** 1969 (1975). Red on multicolor underprint. Overprint: On #1979a. Printer: CPF.	1.00	10.00

		VF	UNC
R123	**50 Yüan** 1969 (1970). Violet on multicolor underprint. Printer: CPF.	4.00	30.00
R124	**100 Yüan** 1972 (1975). Dark green, light green and orange on multicolor underprint. Overprint: Green on #1983. Printer: CPF.	10.00	80.00

Kinmen (Quemoy) Branch

1955-72 Issues

		VF	UNC
R109	**5 Yüan** 1966. Violet-brown. Portrait SYS at upper center. Printer: CPF. Vertical format.	3.00	20.00

R110 10 Yüan | VF | UNC
1969 (1975). Red on multicolor underprint. Overprint: Red on #1979a. | 2.00 | 10.00

R111 50 Yüan | VF | UNC
1969 (1970). Dark blue on multicolor underprint. SYS at right. | 3.50 | 25.00

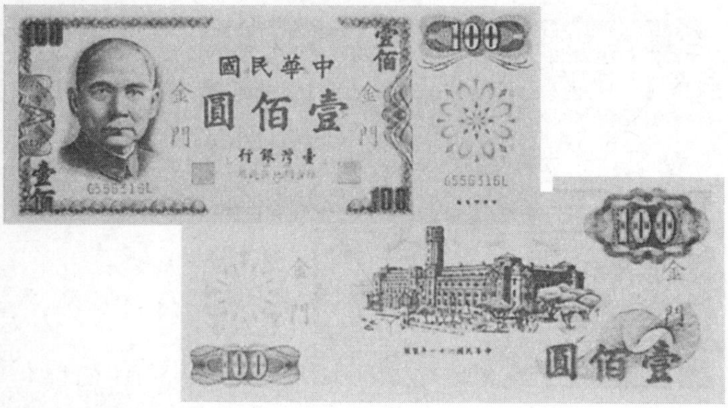

R112 100 Yüan | VF | UNC
1972 (1975). Overprint: Green on #1983. | 7.50 | 40.00

Matsu Branch

1976; 1981 Issue

		VF	UNC
R125	**10 Yüan** 1976. Red on multicolor underprint. Overprint: On #1984.	1.00	8.00
R126	**500 Yüan** 1981. Brown and red-brown on multicolor underprint. Overprint: On #1987.	20.00	80.00
R127	**1000 Yüan** 1981. Blue-black on multicolor underprint. Overprint: On #1988.	37.50	200.

Kinmen (Quemoy) Branch

1976; 1981 Issue

		VF	UNC
R112A	**10 Yüan** 1976. Overprint: On #1984.	.75	10.00
R112B	**100 Yüan** 1981. Overprint: On #1988.	8.00	30.00
R112C	**1000 Yüan** 1981. Overprint: On #1988.	50.00	200.

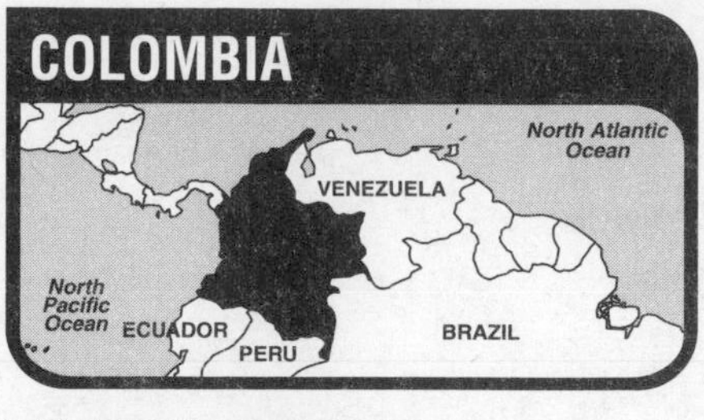

The Republic of Colombia, located in the northwestern corner of South America, has an area of 1.139 million sq. km. and a population of 45.01 million. Capital: Bogotá. The economy is primarily agricultural with a mild, rich coffee the chief crop. Colombia has the world's largest platinum deposits and important reserves of coal, iron ore, petroleum and limestone; precious metals and emeralds are also mined. Coffee, crude oil, bananas, sugar, coal and flowers are exported.

Colombia was one of the three countries that emerged from the collapse of Gran Colombia in 1830 (the others are Ecuador and Venezuela). A 40-year conflict between government forces and anti-government insurgent groups and illegal paramilitary groups - both heavily funded by the drug trade - escalated during the 1990s. The insurgents lack the military or popular support necessary to overthrow the government, and violence has been decreasing since about 2002, but insurgents continue attacks against civilians and large swaths of the countryside are under guerrilla influence. More than 32,000 former paramilitaries had demobilized by the end of 2006 and the United Self Defense Forces of Colombia (AUC) as a formal organization had ceased to function. Still, some renegades continued to engage in criminal activities. The Colombian Government has stepped up efforts to reassert government control throughout the country, and now has a presence in every one of its administrative departments. However, neighboring countries worry about the violence spilling over their borders.

MONETARY SYSTEM:

1 Real = 1 Decimo = 10 Centavos, 1870's
1 Peso = 10 Decimos = 10 Reales, 1880's
1 Peso = 100 Centavos 1993
1 Peso Oro = 100 Centavos to 1993

REPLACEMENT NOTES:

Earlier issues, small *R* just below and between signatures. Larger *R* used later. Some TDLR printings have *R* preceding serial number. Later Colombian-printed notes use circled asterisk usually close to sign. or a star at r. of upper serial #. Known replacements: #389-407, 409, 413-15, 417-19, 421-22, 425-29, 431-433, 436-41, 443, 445-48.

Republic

Banco de la República

1943 Pesos Oro Issue

392 20 Pesos Oro

1943-63. Purple and multicolor. Bust of Francisco José de Caldas at left, bust of Simon Bolívar at right. Back: Liberty at center. Printer: ABNC.

	VF	UNC
a. Series U in red. 20.7.1943.	200.	500.
b. Series U in purple. 20.7.1944; 1.1.1945.	60.00	200.
c. Series U. Prefix A. 7.8.1947.	15.00	80.00
d. Series DD. 1.1.1950; 1.1.1951.	7.50	50.00
e. Series DD. 2.1.1963.	7.50	50.00
s. Specimen.	—	65.00

1953 Pesos Oro Issue

400 10 Pesos Oro

1953-61. Blue on multicolor underprint. Similar to #377, but palm trees at right instead of watermark. Portrait General Antonio Nariño with Mercury alongside at left. Back: Bank building at Cali. Series N. Printer: TDLR.

	VF	UNC
a. 1.1.1953.	7.50	50.00

	VF	UNC
b. 1.1.1958; 1.1.1960.	7.50	50.00
c. 2.1.1961.	7.50	50.00
s1. Specimen. With red TDLR and *SPECIMEN* overprint. Punched hole cancelled.	—	100.
s2. Specimen. Red overprint: *SPECIMEN*.	—	100.

401 20 Pesos Oro

1953-65. Red-brown on multicolor underprint. Similar to #378, but Liberty in circle at right instead of watermark. Portrait Francisco José de Caldas and allegory at left. Series O. Back: Newer bank building at Barranquilla on back. Printer: TDLR.

	VF	UNC
a. 1.1.1953.	7.50	45.00
b. 1.1.1960.	7.50	45.00
c. 2.1.1961; 2.1.1965.	6.00	40.00
s1. Specimen. With red TDLR overprint and *SPECIMEN*. Punched hole cancelled.	—	100.
s2. Specimen. Red overprint: *SPECIMEN*. Punched hole cancelled.	—	65.00

1958 Pesos Oro Issue

402 50 Pesos Oro

1958-67. Light brown on multicolor underprint. Portrait Antonio José de Sucre at lower left. Series Z. Back: Olive-green. Liberty at center. Printer: ABNC.

	VF	UNC
a. 20.7.1958; 7.8.1960.	10.00	100.
b. 1.1.1964; 12.10.1967.	8.00	70.00
s1. Specimen.	—	135.
s2. Specimen. Red overprint: *SPECIMEN*. Punched hole cancelled.	—	150.

403 100 Pesos Oro

1958-67. Gray on multicolor underprint. Portrait General Francisco de Paula Santander at right. Series Y. Back: Green. Liberty at center. Printer: ABNC.

	VF	UNC
a. 7.8.1958.	8.00	70.00
b. 1.1.1960; 1.1.1964.	6.00	90.00
c. 20.7.1965; 20.7.1967.	6.00	90.00
p1. Face proof. Without date, signatures, series or serial #. Punched hole cancelled.	—	150.
s. Specimen.	—	125.

1959-60 Pesos Oro Issue

404 1 Peso Oro

1959-77. Blue on multicolor underprint. Portrait Simón Bolívar at left, portrait General Francisco de Paula Santander at right. Back: Liberty head and condor with waterfall and mountain at center. Printer: Imprenta de Billets-Bogota.

	VF	UNC
a. Security thread. 12.10.1959.	2.50	12.50
b. Security thread. 2.1.1961; 7.8.1962; 2.1.1963; 12.10.1963; 2.1.1964; 12.10.1964.	2.00	9.00
c. As b. 20.7.1966.	10.00	40.00
d. Without security thread. 20.7.1966; 20.7.1967; 1.2.1968; 2.1.1969.	1.25	6.00
e. Without security thread. 1.5.1970; 12.10.1970; 7.8.1971; 20.7.1972; 7.8.1973; 7.8.1974.	.50	4.00
f. As e. 1.1.1977.	5.00	35.00
s1. Specimen.	—	50.00
s2. Specimen. Red overprint: *ESPECIMEN*.	—	50.00

1961-64 Issue

#406-407 replacement notes: Serial # prefix *R* or *.

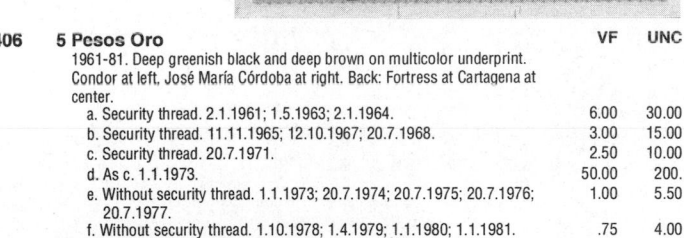

406 5 Pesos Oro

1961-81. Deep greenish black and deep brown on multicolor underprint. Condor at left, José María Córdoba at right. Back: Fortress at Cartagena at center.

	VF	UNC
a. Security thread. 2.1.1961; 1.5.1963; 2.1.1964.	6.00	30.00
b. Security thread. 11.11.1965; 12.10.1967; 20.7.1968.	3.00	15.00
c. Security thread. 20.7.1971.	2.50	10.00
d. As c. 1.1.1973.	50.00	200.
e. Without security thread. 1.1.1973; 20.7.1974; 20.7.1975; 20.7.1976; 20.7.1977.	1.00	5.50
f. Without security thread. 1.10.1978; 1.4.1979; 1.1.1980; 1.1.1981.	.75	4.00
s. Specimen.	—	40.00

407	10 Pesos Oro	VF	UNC
	1963-80. Lilac and slate blue on green and multicolor underprint. General Antonio Nariño at left, condor at right. Back: Back red-brown and slate blue. Archaeological site with monoliths.		
	a. Security thread. 20.7.1963.	10.00	40.00
	b. As a. 20.7.1964.	4.00	25.00
	c. 20.7.1965; 20.7.1967; 2.1.1969.	4.00	17.50
	d. As c. with segmented security thread. 12.10.1970; 1.1.1973.	2.00	10.00
	e. As d. 20.7.1974.	75.00	300.
	f. Without security thread. 20.7.1974; 1.1.1975; 20.7.1976; 1.1.1978.	.75	6.00
	g. As f. 7.8.1979; 7.8.1980.	.35	4.00
	h. Like f., but *SERIE AZ* at left center and upper right. on face. 7.8.1980. *Serie AZ.*	.50	5.00
	s. Specimen.	—	40.00

408	500 Pesos Oro	VF	UNC
	20.7.1964. Olive-green on multicolor underprint. Portrait Simon Bolívar at right. Back: No open space under Liberty head. Printer: ABNC. Series *AA*.		
	a. Six digit serial #.	200.	750.
	b. Seven digit serial #.	50.00	200.
	s. Specimen. Overprint *MUESTRA* and punched hole cancelled.	—	175.

1966-68 Issue

#409 replacement note: Serial # prefix *R* or *.

409	20 Pesos Oro	VF	UNC
	1966-83. Brown, gray and green on multicolor underprint. Francisco José de Caldas with globe at right. Back: Brown and green on multicolor underprint. *Balsa Muisca* from the Gold Museum.		
	a. Security thread. 12.10.1966; 2.1.1969; 1.5.1972; 1.5.1973.	4.00	30.00
	b. As a. 20.7.1974.	150.	400.
	c. Without security thread. 20.7.1974; 20.7.1975; 20.7.1977.	2.50	15.00
	d. As c. 1.4.1979; 1.1.1981; 1.1.1982; 1.1.1983.	2.00	10.00
	s. Specimen.	—	50.00

410	100 Pesos Oro	VF	UNC
	1968-71. Blue on multicolor underprint. General Francisco de Paula Santander at right. Series Y. Back: Capitol at Bogotá. Watermark: Simon Bolívar. Printer: TDLR.		
	a. 1.1.1968.	12.50	50.00
	b. 2.1.1969.	7.50	40.00
	c. 1.5.1970; 20.7.1971.	5.00	30.00
	s. Specimen.	—	75.00

411	500 Pesos Oro	VF	UNC
	1968; 1971. Green on multicolor underprint. Simón Bolívar at right. Series A. Back: Zipaquirá subterranean salt cathedral at center. Watermark: Liberty head. Printer: ABNC.		
	a. 1.1.1968.	30.00	125.
	b. 12.10.1971.	40.00	125.
	s. Specimen. Punch hole cancelled.	—	150.

1969 Issue

412	50 Pesos Oro	VF	UNC
	1969-70. Purple on pale blue, lilac and pink underprint. Blue design without border at left, Camilo Torres at right. Back: Arms and flowers. Watermark: Camilo Torres. Printer: TDLR.		
	a. 2.1.1969.	FV	45.00
	b. 12.10.1970.	FV	30.00
	s. Specimen. Overprint: *SPECIMEN* in red on both sides. Punched hole cancelled.	—	140.

1972-73 Issue

#413-415 replacement notes: Serial # prefix *R* or *.

413	2 Pesos Oro	VF	UNC
	1972-77. Purple on multicolor underprint. Policarpa Salavarietta at left. Back: Brown. *El Dorado* from the Gold Museum.		
	a. Large size serial #, and # at right. near upper border. 1.1.1972; 20.7.1972; 1.1.1973.	FV	5.00
	b. Small size serial #, and # at right. far from upper border. 20.7.1976; 1.1.1977; 20.7.1977.	FV	5.00
	s. Specimen.	—	75.00

414	**50 Pesos Oro**	**VF**	**UNC**
	20.7.1973; 20.7.1974. Purple on pale blue, lilac and pink underprint. Curved dark border added at left and right, Camilo Torres at right. Back: Curved dark border at right, Arms and flowers. Watermark: Camilo Torres. Printer: TDLR.	FV	20.00

415	**100 Pesos Oro**	**VF**	**UNC**
	20.7.1973; 20.7.1974. Blue on multicolor underprint. Curved dark border added at left and right, General Francisco de Paula Santander at right. Series Y. Back: Curved dark border at right, Capital at Bagota. Printer: TDLR.		
	a. Issued note.	FV	30.00
	s. Specimen. Overprint: *SPECIMEN* in red on both sides. Punched hole cancelled.	—	165.

416	**500 Pesos Oro**	**VF**	**UNC**
	7.8.1973. Red on multicolor underprint. Simón Bolívar at right. Series A. Back: Zipaquirá subterranean salt cathedral at center. Watermark: Liberty head. Printer: ABNC.		
	a. Issued note.	FV	100.
	s. Specimen.	—	100.

1974 Issue

#417 replacement note: Serial # prefix *R*.

417	**200 Pesos Oro**	**VF**	**UNC**
	1974; 1975. Green on multicolor underprint. Simón Bolívar at center right, church at right. *BOGOTÁ COLOMBIA* at lower left center. Back: Man picking coffee beans. Watermark: Simón Bolívar. Printer: TDLR.		
	a. 20.7.1974.	FV	50.00
	b. 7.8.1975.	FV	20.00
	s. Specimen. As b. Overprint: *SPECIMEN* in red on both sides. Punched hole cancelled.	—	165.

1977-79 Issue

#418-420 replacement notes: Serial # prefix *R* or *.

418	**100 Pesos Oro**	**VF**	**UNC**
	1977-80. Purple and black on multicolor underprint. General Francisco de Paula Santander at center right. Back: Capitol at Bogota. Watermark: Liberty head. Printer: TDLR.		
	a. 1.1.1977.	FV	10.00
	b. 1.1.1980. Numerals at upper center and upper right are darker, as is the word *CIEN*.	FV	8.00
	c. As b. Serial # prefix *A-C*. 1.1.1980.	FV	6.00
	s1. Specimen.	—	75.00
	s2. Specimen. Red overprint: *SPECIMEN*. Punch hole cancelled.	—	50.00

419	**200 Pesos Oro**	**VF**	**UNC**
	20.7.1978; 1.1.1979; 1.1.1980. Green on multicolor underprint. Simón Bolívar at center right, church at right. *COLUMBIA* at lower left center. Back: Man picking coffee beans. Watermark: Simón Bolívar. Printer: TDLR.	FV	10.00

420	**500 Pesos Oro**	**VF**	**UNC**
	1977; 1979. Olive and multicolor. General Francisco de Paula Santander at left. Back: Gray. Subterranean church and Liberty head. Watermark: General Francisco de Paula Santander in profile. Printer: ABNC.		
	a. 20.7.1977.	FV	40.00
	b. 1.4.1979.	FV	30.00
	s. Specimen. As a. Specimen. Overprint: *MUESTRA* in red on both sides. Punched hole cancelled.	—	100.

421	1000 Pesos Oro	VF	UNC
	1.4.1979. Black and multicolor. José Antonio Galan at right. Back: Nariño Palace. Watermark: José Antonio Galan. Printer: ABNC.		
	a. Issued note.	FV	10.00
	s. Specimen. Specimen. Overprint: *SPECIMEN* in red on both sides. Punched hole cancelled.	—	200.

1980-82 Issues

#422 replacement note: Serial # prefix *.

422	50 Pesos Oro	VF	UNC
	1980-83. Purple on pale blue, lilac and pink underprint. *COLOMBIA* added near border at upper left center. Printer: TDLR (without imprint).		
	a. 1.1.1980; 7.8.1981.	1.00	7.50
	b. 1.1.1983.	.75	5.00
	s. Specimen.	—	50.00

423	500 Pesos Oro	VF	UNC
	1981-86. Brown, dark green and red-brown on multicolor underprint. General Francisco de Paula Santander at left. Back: Bogotá; screw coinage press at lower right. Watermark: General Francisco de Paula Santander in profile. Printer: TDLR.		
	a. 20.7.1981.	FV	30.00
	b. 20.7.1984; 20.7.1985.	FV	15.00
	c. 12.10.1985; 20.7.1986.	FV	10.00
	s1. Specimen. 20.7.1984; 20.7.1986. Overprint: *SPECIMEN* in red on both sides. Punched hole cancelled.	—	90.00
	s2. Specimen. Overprint: *MUESTRA SIN VALOR* in red on both sides. Punched hole cancelled.	—	100.
	s3. Specimen. 20.7.1986. Overprint in black: *MUESTRA SIN VALOR* once on each side.	—	100.

424	1000 Pesos Oro	VF	UNC
	1982-87. Deep blue and olive-brown on multicolor underprint. Simón Bolívar at left. Back: Scene honoring 1819 battle heroes. Watermark: Simón Bolívar. Printer: TDLR.		
	a. 1.1.1982.	FV	20.00
	b. 7.8.1984.	FV	12.50
	c. 1.1.1986; 1.1.1987.	FV	10.00
	s. Specimen. As a, b, c. Overprint: *SPECIMEN* in red on both sides. Punched hole cancelled.	—	150.

1982-84 Issues

#425-430 replacement notes: Serial # prefix circled-*.

425	50 Pesos Oro	VF	UNC
	1984-86. Purple on pale blue, lilac and pink underprint. Camillo Torres at right, curved dark border added at left and right. Back: Curved dark border added at right, Arms and flowers. Printer: IBB.		
	a. 12.10.1984; 1.1.1985.	FV	6.00
	b. 1.1.1986.	FV	5.00
	s. Specimen. 1.1.1985. Overprint: *MUESTRA SIN VALOR* in red on both sides.	—	100.

426	100 Pesos Oro	VF	UNC
	1983-91. Violet, brown, orange and dark red on multicolor underprint. General Antonio Nariño at left. Back: Villa de Leyva; flat bed letterpress at lower right. Watermark: General Antonio Nariño. Printer: IBB.		
	a. 1.1.1983; 12.10.1984.	1.00	7.50
	b. 12.10.1985; 1.1.1986; 12.10.1986.	FV	7.00
	c. Larger stylized serial #. 12.10.1986; 1.1.1987; 12.10.1988.	FV	5.00
	d. Back colors slightly off shade from earlier issues. 7.8.1989.	FV	4.00
	e. Signature titles: *GERENTE* and *SECRETARIO*. 1.1.1990; 1.1.1991.	FV	3.00
	s. Specimen. 12.10.1984; 1.1.1986; 12.10.1986; 1.1.1987. Overprint: *MUESTRA SIN VALOR* in red on both sides.	—	100.
426A	**100 Pesos Oro**		
	7.8.1991. Violet, brown, orange and dark red on multicolor underprint. General Antonio Nariño at left. Back: Red omitted. Villa de Leyva; flat bed letterpress at lower right. Watermark: General Antonio Nariño. Printer: IBSFB.	FV	1.00

427 200 Pesos Oro — VF | UNC

1.1.1982. Green on multicolor underprint. Simón Bolívar at center right, church at right, COLUMBIA at lower left center. Back: Man picking coffee beans. Watermark: Simón Bolívar. Printer: IBB. — FV | 5.00

428 200 Pesos Oro — VF | UNC

1.4.1983. Deep green and black on multicolor underprint. Church and Fr. José Celestino Mutis at left, arms at upper right. Back: Monastery of Nuestra Señora del Rosario at right. Watermark: Church and Fr. José Celestino Mutis. Printer: TDLR.

	VF	UNC
a. Issued note.	FV	10.00
s. Specimen. Overprint: *SPECIMEN* in red on both sides. Punched hole cancelled.	—	150.

429 200 Pesos Oro — VF | UNC

1983-91. Deep green and black on multicolor underprint. Church and Fr. José Celestino Mutis at left, Arms at upper right. Back: Monastery of Nuestra Señora del Rosario at right. Watermark: Church and Fr. José Celestino Mutis. Printer: TDLR.

	VF	UNC
a. Printer: IBB. 1.4.1983; 20.7.1984.	FV	25.00
b. 20.7.1984; 1.11.1984; 1.4.1985.	FV	10.00
c. 1.11.1985.	FV	7.00
d. Larger stylized and bold serial #. 1.4.1987; 1.4.1988; 1.11.1988; 1.4.1989; 1.11.1989; 1.4.1991.	FV	4.00
s. Specimen. 1.4.1987. Red overprint: *MUESTRA SIN VALOR.* Punch hole cancelled.	—	100.

429A 200 Pesos Oro

10.8.1992. Dark brown and brown-orange on multicolor underprint. Simón Bolívar at left, *EL* deleted from title, *ORO* deleted from value. Back: Scene at *Peso del Paramo de Pisba* at center right. Printer: IBSFB. — FV | 4.00

430 2000 Pesos Oro — VF | UNC

1983-86. Dark brown and brown-orange on multicolor underprint. Simón Bolívar at left. Back: Scene at *Paso del Paramo de Pisba* at center right. Watermark: Simón Bolívar. Printer: TDLR.

	VF	UNC
a. 24.7.1983.	FV	35.00
b. 24.7.1984.	FV	20.00
c. 17.12.1985.	FV	15.00
d. 17.12.1986.	FV	10.00
s. Specimen. Some punched hole cancelled.	—	50.00

1986-87 Issue

#431-433 replacement notes: Serial # prefix *.

431 500 Pesos Oro — VF | UNC

20.7.1986; 12.10.1987; 20.7.1989; 12.10.1990. Brown, dark green and red-brown on multicolor underprint. General Francisco de Paula Santander at left. Back: Bogotá scene; screw coinage press at lower right. Watermark: General Francisco de Paula Santander in profile. Printer: IBB. — FV | 5.00

431A 500 Pesos Oro — VF | UNC

2.3.1992; 4.1.1993. Brown, dark green and red-brown on multicolor underprint. General Francisco de Paula Santander at left. Back: Green omitted. Bogotá; screw coinage press at lower right. Watermark: General Francisco de Paula Santander in profile. Printer: IBSFB. — FV | 3.00

432 1000 Pesos Oro — VF | UNC

1.1.1987; 1.1.1990; 1.1.1991. Black, blue-green and deep olive-brown on multicolor underprint. Simón Bolívar at left. Back: Scene honoring 1819 battle heroes. Watermark: Simón Bolívar. Printer: IBB. — FV | 9.00

432A 1000 Pesos Oro | VF | UNC
31.1.1992; 1.4.1992; 4.1.1993. Black, blue-green and deep olive-brown on multicolor underprint. Simón Bolívar at left. Back: Scene honoring 1819 battle heroes. Watermark: Simón Bolívar. Printer: IBSFB. | FV | 5.00

433 2000 Pesos Oro | VF | UNC

17.12.1986; 17.12.1988; 17.12.1990. Dark brown and brown-orange on multicolor underprint. Simón Bolívar at left, redesigned *2's* in denomination. Back: Scene at *Paso del Paramo de Pisba* at center right. Watermark: Simón Bolívar. Printer: IBB.

a. 17.12.1986.	FV	9.00
b. 17.12.1988.	FV	9.00
c. 17.12.1990.	FV	9.00

433A 2000 Pesos Oro | VF | UNC

1992. Dark brown and brown-orange on multicolor underprint. Simón Bolívar at left, redesigned *2's* in denomination. Back: Scene at *Paso del Paramo de Pisba* at center right. Watermark: Simón Bolívar. Printer: IBSFB.

a. 2.3.1992; 1.4.1992.	FV	5.00
b. 3.8.1992.	FV	50.00

1986 Commemorative Issue

#434, Centennial of the Constitution

434 5000 Pesos Oro | VF | UNC

5.8.1986. Deep violet and red-violet on multicolor underprint. Rafael Nuñez at left. Back: Statue of Miguel Antonio Caro at center right. Watermark: Rafael Nuñez. Printer: BDDK.

a. Issued note.	FV	50.00
s. Specimen. Red serial # at upper right. Overprint: *SPECIMEN* in red on both sides. Punched hole cancelled.	—	165.

1987 Issue

435 5000 Pesos Oro | VF | UNC

5.8.1987; 5.8.1988; 1.1.1990. Deep violet and red-violet on multicolor underprint. Rafael Nuñez at left. Back: Statue of Miguel Antonio Caro at center right. Watermark: Rafael Nuñez. Printer: IPS-Roma.

a. 5.8.1987.	FV	40.00
b. 5.8.1988.	FV	40.00
c. 1.1.1990.	FV	35.00
s. Specimen. As b. Overprint: *SPECIMEN* in red on both sides. Punched hole cancelled.	—	140.

1990 Issue

#436 replacement note: Serial # prefix *.

436 5000 Pesos Oro | VF | UNC
1.1.1990. Deep violet and red-violet on multicolor underprint. Rafael Nuñez at left. Back: Statue of Miguel Antonio Caro at center right. Watermark: Rafael Nuñez. Printer: IBB. | FV | 25.00

436A 5000 Pesos Oro | VF | UNC
31.1.1992. 4.1.1993. Deep violet and red-violet on multicolor underprint. Rafael Nuñez at left. Back: Statue of Miguel Antonio Caro at center right. Watermark: Rafael Nuñez. Printer: IBSFB. | FV | 25.00

1992 Commemorative Issue

#437, Quincentennial of Columbus' Voyage, 12.10.1492

437	**10,000 Pesos Oro**	VF	UNC
	1992. Light and dark brown on multicolor underprint. Early sailing ships at center, youthful woman *Mujer Embera* at center right, native gold statue at right. Back: Native birds around antique world map at left center, Santa Maria sailing ship at lower right. Watermark: youthful woman *Mujer Embera*. Printer: BDM. The birds are left to right: greater flamingo, andean condor, green honeycreeper, andean cock of the rock, blue and yellow macaw, hotzin, scarlet ibis, yellow-hooded blackbird, metallic green tanager, white pelican, magnificent frigatebird, keel billed toucan, baltimore oriole, scarlet macaw, yellow crowned parrot, red-capped cardinal.		
	a. Issued note.	FV	60.00
	s. Specimen.	—	100.

1993 Issue

437A	**10,000 Pesos Oro**	VF	UNC
	1993; 1994. Deep brown and black on multicolor underprint. Early sailing ships at center, youthful woman *Mujer Embera* at center right, native gold statue at right. Back: Native birds around antique world map at left center, Santa Maria sailing ship at lower right. Watermark: Youthful woman *Mujer Embera*. Printer: IBSFB. The birds are left to right: greater flamingo, andean condor, green honeycreeper, andean cock of the rock, blue and yellow macaw, hotzin, scarlet ibis, yellow-hooded blackbird, metallic green tanager, white pelican, magnificent frigatebird, keel-billed toucan, baltimore oriole, scarlet macaw, yellow crowned parrot, red-capped cardinal.	FV	40.00

1993-95 Issues

Peso System

438	**1000 Pesos**	VF	UNC
	3.1.1994; 1.11.1994; 1.7.1995; 2.8.1995; 2.10.1995. Black, blue-green and deep olive-brown on multicolor underprint. Simón Bolívar at left. *EL* omitted from title and *ORO* omitted from value. Back: Black omitted. Scene honoring 1819 battle heroes. Watermark: Simón Bolívar. Printer: IBSFB.	FV	5.00

439	**2000 Pesos**	VF	UNC
	1993-94. Dark brown and brown-orange on multicolor underprint. Simón Bolívar at left, *EL* deleted from title, *ORO* deleted from value. Back: Scene at *Peso del Paramo de Pisba* at center right. Watermark: Simón Bolívar. Printer: IBSFB.		
	a. 1.7.1993.	FV	10.00
	b. Orange omitted from back. 1.7.1994; 1.11.1994; 17.12.1994.	FV	8.00

440	**5000 Pesos**	VF	UNC
	3.1.1994; 4.7.1994; 2.1.1995. Deep violet and red-violet on multicolor underprint. Rafael Nuñez at left, *EL* deleted from the title, *ORO* deleted from the value. Back: Statue of Miguel Antonio Caro at center right. Watermark: Rafael Nuñez. Printer: IBSFB.	FV	20.00

441	**5000 Pesos**	VF	UNC
	1.3.1995; 1.3.1996. Dark brown, brown and deep blue-green on multicolor underprint. José Asunción Silva and bug at upper right, trees at left and center. Back: Woman, trees and monument at center. Watermark: Asunción Silva. Printer: IBSFB.		
	a. Issued note.	FV	20.00
	s. Specimen.	—	75.00

442 **5000 Pesos** — VF / UNC
1.7.1995. Dark brown, brown and deep blue-green on multicolor underprint. José Asunción Silva and bug at upper right, trees at left and center. Back: Woman, trees and monument at center. Watermark: Portrait. Printer: TDLR.

a. Issued note.	FV	25.00
s. Specimen.	—	75.00

443 **10,000 Pesos**
1.3.1995; 1.8.1996; 23.7.1997; 6.1.1998; 23.7.1998; 23.7.1999; 17.12.1999; 1.6.2001. Deep brown and black on multicolor underprint. Youthful woman *Mujer Embera* at center right, native gold statue at right. *EL* omitted from title, *ORO* omitted from value, different signature and titles. Back: Native birds around antique world map at left center, Santa Maria sailing ship at lower right. Watermark: Portrait. Printer: IBSFB. The birds are left to right: greater flamingo, andean condor, green honeycreeper, andean cock of the rock, blue and yellow macaw, hotzin, scarlet ibis, yellow-hooded blackbird, metallic green tanager, white pelican, magnificent frigatebird, keel-billed toucan, baltimore oriole, scarlet macaw, yellow crowned parrot, red-capped cardinal.

a. Issued note.	FV	20.00
s. Specimen.	—	75.00

1995 Commemorative Issue

#444, 200th Anniversary of Policarpa Salavarrieta *"La Pola"*

Replacement note: Serial # prefix *.

444 **10,000 Pesos** — VF / UNC
1.7.1995; 1.8.1995. Red-brown and green on multicolor underprint. Policarpa Salavarrieta at right. Back: Village of Guaduas (ca. 1846) at left center. Printer: TDLR.

a. Issued note.	FV	30.00
s. Specimen.	—	75.00

1996-97, 2000 Issue

445 **2000 Pesos** — VF / UNC
1996-99. Dark olive-green, red-brown and dark brown on multicolor underprint. General Francisco de Paula Santander at right. Back: Casa de Moneda building, entrance at left center. Watermark: General Francisco de Paula Santander. Printer: IBSFB.

a. 2.4.1996.	FV	6.00
b. 6.5.1997.	FV	6.00
c. 6.1.1998.	FV	6.00
d. 7.8.1998.	FV	6.00
e. 9.4.1999.	FV	6.00
s. Specimen.	—	50.00

446 **5000 Pesos** — VF / UNC
2.1.1997. Dark brown and deep blue-green on multicolor underprint. José Asunción Silva and bug at upper right, trees at left and center. Back: Woman, trees and monument at center. Watermark: Asunción Silva. Printer: IBSFB.

a. Issued note.	FV	15.00
s. Specimen.	—	75.00

447 **5000 Pesos** — VF / UNC
1997-99. Deep violet and red-violet on multicolor underprint. José Asunción Silva and bug at upper right, trees at left and center, bank seal at bottom right. Back: Woman, trees and monument at center. Watermark: Joeé Asunción Silva. Printer: IBSFB.

a. 12.10.1997.	FV	10.00
b. 2.4.1998.	FV	10.00
c. 23.7.1999.	FV	10.00
d. 12.10.1999.	FV	10.00
s. Specimen.	—	75.00

448 **20,000 Pesos** — VF / UNC
1996-2000. Black, deep green and dark blue on multicolor underprint. Julio Garavito Armero at right. View of the moon at center. Back: Satellite view of earth at center right, moon's surface along bottom, geometric forms in underprint. Watermark: Julio Garavito Armero. Printer: IBSFB.

a. 23.7.1996.	FV	25.00
b. 6.1.1998.	FV	25.00
c. 7.8.1998.	FV	25.00
d. 6.5.1999.	FV	25.00
e. 1.5.2000.	FV	25.00
f. 12.10.2000.	FV	25.00
s. Specimen.	—	60.00

449 50,000 Pesos

7.8.2000. Purple, green and light orange on multicolor underprint. Jorge Isaacs at lower center. Maria, character from book, at center. Back: *Hacienda el Paraiso*. Printer: IBSFB. Vertical format.

	VF	UNC
a. Issued note.	FV	50.00
s. Specimen.	—	100.

2001 Issue

450 1000 Pesos

2001-05. Brown and orange on multicolor underprint. Crowd at center, Jorge Eliécer Gaitán at right. Back: Gaitán with right arm raised, crowd behind at center. Watermark: Jorge Eliécer Gaitán. Printer: IBBR. UV: fibers fluoresce yellow and blue. Car in box yellow, serial #s green. Back: security thread blue, bottom right design green. 140x70mm.

	VF	UNC
a. 7.8.2001.	FV	2.00
b. 27.9.2001.	FV	2.00
c. 17.12.2001.	FV	2.00
d. 7.5.2002.	FV	2.00
e. 30.5.2003.	FV	2.00
f. 16.2.2004.	FV	2.00
g. 17.2.2004.	FV	2.00
h. 2.3.2005.	FV	2.00
i. 3.3.2005.	FV	2.00
s. Specimen.	—	50.00

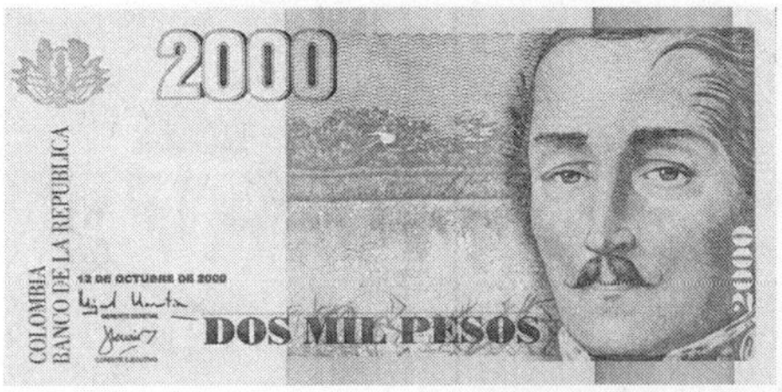

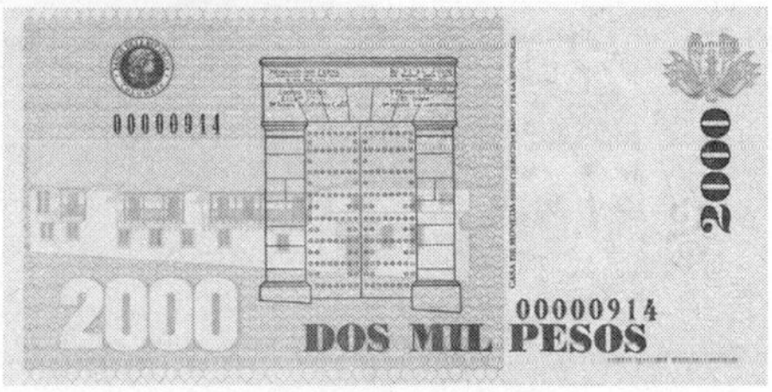

451 2000 Pesos

2000-05. Dark olive-green, red-brown and dark brown on multicolor underprint. General Francisco de Paula Santander at right. Back: Casa de Moneda building, entrance at left center. Watermark: General Francisco de Paula Santander. Printer: IBBR. 140x70mm.

	VF	UNC
a. 12.10.2000.	FV	4.00
b. 23.7.2001.	FV	4.00
c. 12.10.2001.	FV	4.00
d. 11.11.2001.	FV	4.00
e. 8.5.2002.	FV	4.00
f. 13.5.2002.	FV	4.00
g. 2.6.2003.	FV	4.00
h. 18.2.2004.	FV	4.00
i. 19.2.2004. Triangles added at left front for visually impaired.	FV	4.00
j. 4.3.2005.	FV	4.00
s. Specimen.	—	50.00

452 5000 Pesos

2001-10. Deep violet and red-violet on multicolor underprint. José Asunción Silva and bug at upper right, trees at left and center, bank seal at center. Back: Woman, trees and monument at center. Watermark: José Asunción Silva. Printer: IBBR. UV: security strip fluoresces blue. Value, logo, and design elements at left and right yellow.

	VF	UNC
a. 11.11.2001.	FV	7.50
b. 17.12.2001.	FV	7.50
c. 9.5.2002.	FV	6.00
d. 6.6.2003.	FV	6.00
e. 20.2.2004.	FV	5.00
f. 2.11.2005.	FV	5.00
g. 4.2.2006.	FV	5.00
h. 15.11.2006.	FV	5.00
i. 18.8.2007.	FV	5.00
j. 31.8.2008.	FV	5.00
k. 21.8.2009. Braille 5 added at left near frog.	FV	5.00
l. 31.7.2010.	FV	5.00
m. 1.9.2010.	FV	5.00
s. Specimen.	—	50.00

453 10,000 Pesos

2001-10. Deep brown and black on multicolor underprint. Youthful woman *Mujer Embera* at center right, native gold statue at right. *EL* omitted from title, *ORO* omitted from value, different signature and titles. Back: Native birds around antique world map at left center, Santa Maria sailing ship at lower right. Watermark: Portrait.

	VF	UNC
a. 1.6.2001. Printer: IBSFB.	FV	15.00
b. 20.7.2001. Printer: IBBR.	FV	15.00
c. 10.5.2002.	FV	15.00
d. 20.11.2002.	FV	15.00
e. 25.11.2002.	FV	15.00
f. 9.6.2003.	FV	15.00
g. 21.2.2004.	FV	15.00
h. 16.11.2006.	FV	15.00
i. 17.11.2006.	FV	15.00
j. 19.8.2007.	FV	15.00
k. 20.8.2007.	FV	15.00
l. 1.9.2008.	FV	15.00
m. 27.8.2009.	FV	12.00
n. 2.8.2010.	FV	12.00
s. Specimen.	—	75.00

454 20,000 Pesos

2001-09. Black, deep green and dark blue on multicolor underprint. Julio Garavito Armero at right. View of the moon at center. Back: Satellite view of earth at center right, moon's surface along bottom, geometric forms in underprint. Watermark: Julio Garavito Armero. Printer: IBBR.

	VF	UNC
a. 1.6.2001.	FV	25.00
b. 23.7.2001.	FV	25.00
c. 7.8.2001.	FV	25.00
d. 14.5.2002.	FV	25.00
e. 20.11.2002.	FV	25.00
f. 13.6.2003.	FV	25.00
g. 16.6.2003.	FV	25.00
h. 21.9.2004.	FV	25.00
i. 22.9.2004.	FV	25.00
j. 8.3.2005.	FV	25.00
k. 3.11.2005.	FV	25.00
l. 5.2.2006.	FV	25.00
m. 20.11.2006.	FV	20.00
n. 21.11.2006.	FV	20.00
o. 22.11.2006.	FV	20.00
p. 21.8.2007.	FV	20.00
q. 3.9.2008.	FV	20.00
r. 23.8.2009.	FV	20.00
s. Specimen.	—	75.00

455 50,000 Pesos

2001-09. Purple, green and light orange on multicolor underprint. Jorge Isaacs at lower center. Maria, character from book, at center. Back: *Hacienda el Paraiso.* Printer: IBBR. Vertical format.

	VF	UNC
a. 1.5.2001.	FV	40.00
b. 23.7.2001	FV	40.00
c. 15.5.2002.	FV	40.00
d. 20.6.2003.	FV	37.50
e. 9.3.2005.	FV	37.50
f. 20.7.2005.	FV	37.50
g. 6.2.2006.	FV	37.50
h. 23.11.2006.	FV	37.50
i. 24.11.2006.	FV	37.50
j. 22.8.2007.	FV	37.50
k. 4.9.2008.	FV	37.50
l. 6.9.2008.	FV	37.50
m. 25.8.2009.	FV	37.50
n. 26.8.2009.	FV	37.50
s. Specimen.	—	100.

2005 Issue

456 1000 Pesos

2005-. Brown and orange on multicolor underprint. Crown at center. Jorge Elíecer Gaitán at right. Back: Gaitán with right arm raised, crowd behind at center. Watermark: Jorge Elíecer Gaitán. 130x65mm.

	VF	UNC
a. 1.11.2005.	FV	1.50
b. 31.1.2006.	FV	1.50
c. 1.2.2006.	FV	1.50
d. 7.11.2006.	FV	1.50
e. 8.11.2006.	FV	1.00
f. 9.11.2006.	FV	1.00
g. 13.8.2007.	FV	1.00
h. 14.8.2007.	FV	1.00
i. 15.8.2007.	FV	1.00
j. 27.8.2008.	FV	1.00
k. 28.8.2008.	FV	1.00
l. 28.8.2009.	FV	1.00
m. 23.11.2010.	FV	1.00
n. 10.6.2011.	FV	1.00
o. 11.6.2011.	FV	1.00
p. 13.6.2011.	FV	1.00
s. Specimen. Punch hole cancelled.	—	50.00

457 2000 Pesos

2006-. Darf olive-green, red-brown and dark brown on multicolor underprint. General Francisco de Paula Santander at right. Green tint over watermark area. Back: Casa de Moneda building, entrance at left center. Watermark: Francisco de Paula Santander. 130x65mm.

	VF	UNC
a. 2.2.2006.	FV	2.00
b. 3.2.2006.	FV	2.00
c. 10.11.2006.	FV	2.00
d. 14.11.2006.	FV	2.00
e. 20.11.2006.	FV	2.00
f. 16.8.2007.	FV	2.00
g. 17.8.2007.	FV	2.00
h. 29.8.2008.	FV	2.00
i. 30.8.2008.	FV	2.00
j. 19.8.2009.	FV	2.00
k. 20.8.2009.	FV	2.00
l. 22.7.2010.	FV	2.00
m. 28.7.2010.	FV	2.00
n. 29.7.2010.	FV	2.00

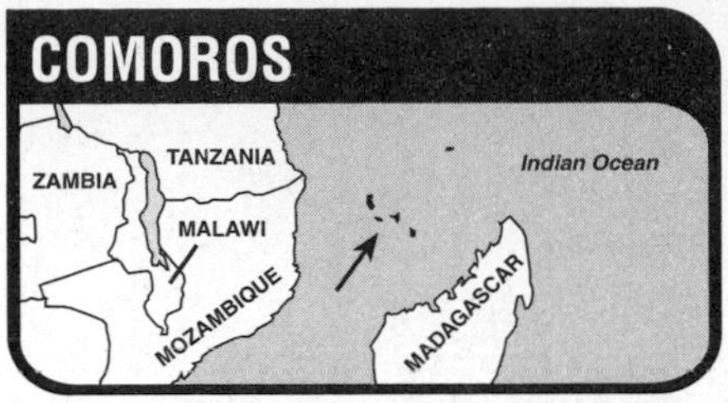

The Union of the Comoros, a volcanic archipelago located in the Mozambique Channel of the Indian Ocean 483 km. northwest of Madagascar, has an area of 2,170 sq. km. and a population of 731,800. Capital: Moroni. The economy of the islands is d on agriculture. There are practically no mineral resources. Vanilla, essence for perfumes, copra and sisal are exported.

Comoros has endured more than 20 coups or attempted coups since gaining independence from France in 1975. In 1997, the islands of Anjouan and Moheli declared independence from Comoros. In 1999, military chief Col. Azali seized power in a bloodless coup, and helped negotiate the 2000 Fomboni Accords power-sharing agreement in which the federal presidency rotates among the three islands, and each island maintains its own local government. Azali won the 2002 Presidential election, and each island in the archipelago elected its own president. Azali stepped down in 2006 and President Sambi took office. Since 2006, Anjouan's President Mohamed Bacar has refused to work effectively with the Union presidency. In 2007, Bacar effected Anjouan's de-facto secession from the Union, refusing to step down in favor of fresh Anjouanais elections when Comoros' other islands held legitimate elections in July. The African Union (AU) initially attempted to resolve the political crisis by applying sanctions and a naval blockade on Anjouan, but in March 2008, AU and Comoran soldiers seized the island. The move was generally welcomed by the island's inhabitants. Its present status is that of a French Territorial Collectivity. Euro coinage and currency circulates there.

RULERS:

French to 1975

MONETARY SYSTEM:

1 Franc = 100 Centimes

REPUBLIC

BANQUE DE MADAGASCAR ET DES COMORES

1960 ND PROVISIONAL ISSUE

		VF	UNC
2	**50 Francs**		
	ND (1960-63). Brown and multicolor. Woman with hat at right. Back: Man. Overprint: Red *COMORES* on Madagascar #45.		
	a. Signature titles: *LE CONTROLEUR GAL.* and *LE DIRECTEUR GAL.* ND (1960).	—	—
	b. Signature titles: *LE DIRECTEUR GAL. ADJOINT* and *LE PRESIDENT DIRECTEUR GAL.* ND (1963). 2 sign varieties.	30.00	110.
	s. Specimen.	—	—

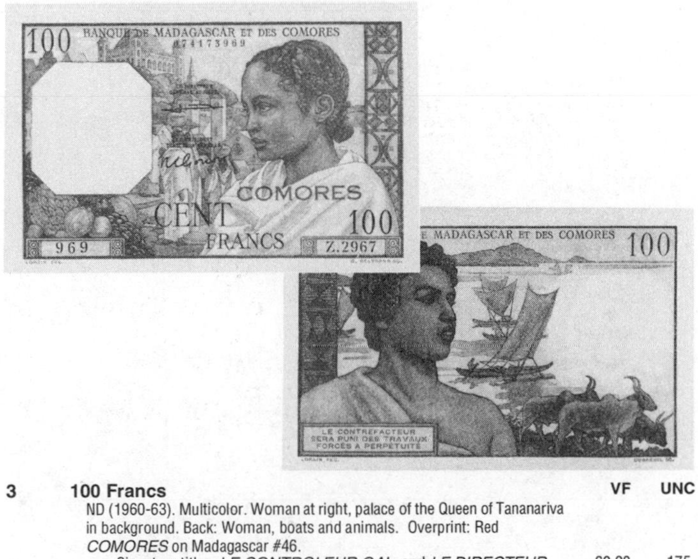

		VF	UNC
3	**100 Francs**		
	ND (1960-63). Multicolor. Woman at right, palace of the Queen of Tananariva in background. Back: Woman, boats and animals. Overprint: Red *COMORES* on Madagascar #46.		
	a. Signature titles: *LE CONTROLEUR GAL.* and *LE DIRECTEUR GAL.* ND (1960).	60.00	175.
	b. Signature titles: *LE DIRECTEUR GAL. ADJOINT* and *LE PRESIDENT DIRECTEUR GAL.* ND (1963).	18.00	70.00
	s. Specimen.	—	—

		VF	UNC
4	**500 Francs**		
	ND (1960-63). Multicolor. Man with fruit at center. Overprint: Red *COMORES* on Madagascar #47.		
	a. Signature titles: *LE CONTROLEUR GAL* and *LE DIRECTEUR GAL.* - old date 30.6.1950; 9.10.1952 (1960).	170.	550.
	b. Signature titles: *LE DIRECTEUR GAL. ADJOINT* and *LE PRESIDENT DIRECTEUR GAL.* ND (1963).	110.	380.
5	**1000 Francs**		
	ND (1960-63). Multicolor. Woman and man at left center. Back: Center Ox cart. Overprint: Red *COMORES* on Madagascar #48.		
	a. Signature titles: *LE CONTROLEUR GAL.* and *LE DIRECTEUR GAL.* - old date 1950-52; 9.10.1952 (1960).	220.	650.
	b. Signature titles: *LE DIRECTEUR GAL. ADJOINT* and *LE PRESIDENT DIRECTEUR GAL.* ND (1963).	130.	425.

		VF	UNC
6	**5000 Francs**		
	ND (1960-63). Multicolor. Portrait Gallieni at upper left, young woman at right. Back: Huts at left, woman with baby at right. Overprint: Red *COMORES* on Madagascar #49.		
	a. Signature titles: *LE CONTROLEUR GAL.* and *LE DIRECTEUR GAL.* - old date 30.6.1950 (1960).	450.	1000.
	b. Signature titles: *LE DIRECTEUR GAL. ADJOINT* and *LE PRESIDENT DIRECTEUR GAL.* ND (1963).	350.	850.
	c. Signature titles: *LE DIRECTEUR GÉNÉRAL* and *LE PRÉSIDENT DIRECTEUR GAL.*	350.	850.

INSTITUT D'ÉMISSION DES COMORES

1976 ND ISSUE

7	500 Francs	VF	UNC
	ND (1976). Blue-gray, brown and red on multicolor underprint. Building at center, young woman wearing a hood at right. Two signature varieties. Back: Two women at left, boat at right. Watermark: Cresent on Maltese cross.		
	a. Issued note.	10.00	40.00
	s. Specimen.	—	50.00

8	1000 Francs	VF	UNC
	ND (1976). Blue-gray, brown and green on multicolor underprint. Woman at right, palm trees at water's edge in background. Back: Women. Watermark: Cresent on Maltese cross.		
	a. Issued note.	20.00	85.00
	s. Specimen.	—	60.00

9	5000 Francs	VF	UNC
	ND (1976). Green on multicolor underprint. Man and woman at center, boats and building in left background. Back: President Djohr at center. Watermark: Cresent on Maltese cross.		
	a. Issued note.	50.00	130.
	s. Specimen.	—	1200.

Banque Centrale des Comores

1984-86 ND Issue

10	500 Francs	VF	UNC
	ND (1986-). Blue-gray, brown and red on multicolor underprint. Building at center, young woman wearing a hood at right. Two signature varieties. Back: Two women at left, boat at right. Watermark: Maltese cross with cresent.		
	a. Partially engraved. signature titles: *LE DIRECTEUR GÉNÉRAL* and *LE PRÉSIDENT DU CONSEIL D'ADMINISTRATION* (1986).	5.00	20.00
	b. Offset. signature titles: *LE GOUVERNEUR* and *PRÉSIDENT DU...* (1994). (2 signature varieties.)	4.00	18.00

11	1000 Francs	VF	UNC
	ND (1984-). Blue-gray, brown and green on multicolor underprint. Woman at right, palm trees at water's edge in background. Back: Women. Watermark: Maltese cross with cresent.		
	a. Partially engraved. signature titles: *LE DIRECTEUR GÉNÉRAL* and *LE PRÉSIDENT DU CONSEIL D'ADMINISTRATION.* (1986).	15.00	60.00
	b. Offset. signature titles: *LE GOUVERNEUR* and *PRÉSIDENT DU...* (1994). (2 signature varieties.)	10.00	30.00

12	5000 Francs	VF	UNC
	ND (1984-). Green on multicolor underprint. Man and woman at center, boats and building in left background. Back: President Djohr at center. Watermark: Maltese cross with cresent. Engraved.		
	a. Signature titles: *LE DIRECTEUR GÉNÉRAL* and *LE PRÉSIDENT DU CONSEIL D'ADMINISTRATION.*	25.00	95.00
	b. Signature titles: *LE GOVERNEUR* and *LE PRESIDENT...*	20.00	90.00

1997 ND Issue

		VF	UNC
13	**2500 Francs** ND (1997). Purple and blue on multicolor underprint. Woman wearing colorful scarf at left. Back: Sea turtle at lower left center. Watermark: Four stars below cresent (arms).	10.00	150.

		VF	UNC
14	**10,000 Francs** ND (1997). Yellow, brown and blue on multicolor underprint. Two seated women weaving baskets at center. Back: Al-Habib Seyyid O. Bin Sumeit at left, mosque at center. Watermark: Four stars below cresent (arms).	35.00	185.

2005-06 Issue

		VF	UNC
15	**500 Francs** 2006. Pink, green and multicolor. Lemur at upper center. Back: Orchard. 120x66mm.	FV	8.00

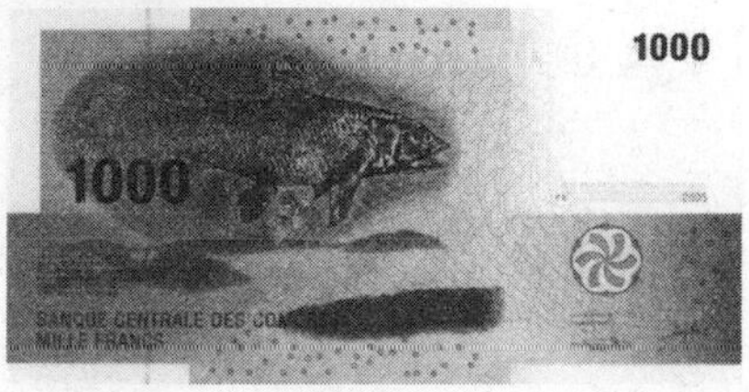

		VF	UNC
16	**1000 Francs** 2005. Blue and multicolor. Fish. Back: Man in outrigger canoe. 126x65mm.	FV	9.00

		VF	UNC
17	**2000 Francs** 2005. Green and multicolor. Mosque and market scene. Back: Village huts. 132x65mm.	FV	11.50

		VF	UNC
18	**5000 Francs** 2006. Purple on lilac and multicolor. Portrait. Back: Tree.	FV	30.50

		VF	UNC
19	**10,000 Francs** 2006. Brown, yellow on multicolor underprint. Friday Mosque in Moroni at left, al-Habib Seyyid O. bin Sumeit at center. Back: Cananga tree, ylang-ylanf flowers and turtle. Watermark: Four stars and crescent. 144x73mm.	FV	66.00

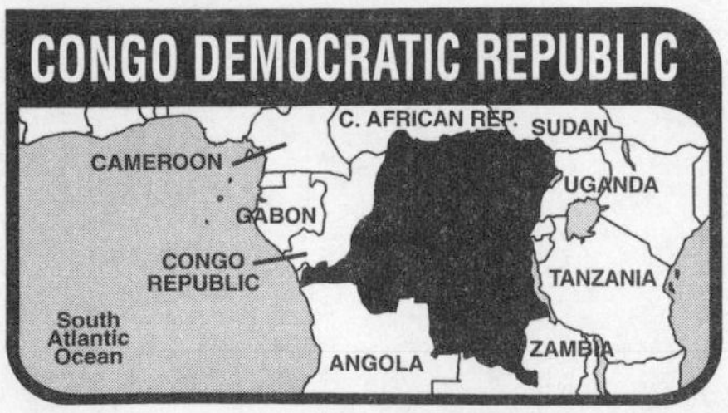

The Congo Democratic Republic (formerly Zaïre), located in the south-central part of Africa, has an area of 2.345 million sq. km. and a population of 66.51 million. Capital: Kinshasa. The mineral-rich country produces copper, tin, diamonds, gold, zinc, cobalt and uranium.

Established as a Belgian colony in 1908, the Republic of the Congo gained its independence in 1960, but its early years were marred by political and social instability. Col. Joseph Mobutu seized power and declared himself president in a November 1965 coup. He subsequently changed his name - to Mobutu Sese Seko - as well as that of the country - to Zaire. Mobutu retained his position for 32 years through several sham elections, as well as through the use of brutal force. Ethnic strife and civil war, touched off by a massive inflow of refugees in 1994 from fighting in Rwanda and Burundi, led in May 1997 to the toppling of the Mobutu regime by a rebellion backed by Rwanda and Uganda and fronted by Laurent Kabila. He renamed the country the Democratic Republic of the Congo (DRC), but in August 1998 his regime was itself challenged by a second insurrection again backed by Rwanda and Uganda. Troops from Angola, Chad, Namibia, Sudan, and Zimbabwe intervened to support Kabila's regime. A cease-fire was signed in July 1999 by the DRC, Congolese armed rebel groups, Angola, Namibia, Rwanda, Uganda, and Zimbabwe but sporadic fighting continued. Laurent Kabila was assassinated in January 2001 and his son, Joseph Kabila, was named head of state. In October 2002, the new president was successful in negotiating the withdrawal of Rwandan forces occupying eastern Congo; two months later, the Pretoria Accord was signed by all remaining warring parties to end the fighting and establish a government of national unity. A transitional government was set up in July 2003. Joseph Kabila as president and four vice presidents represented the former government, former rebel groups, the political opposition, and civil society. The transitional government held a successful constitutional referendum in December 2005 and elections for the presidency, National Assembly, and provincial legislatures in 2006. Kabila was inaugurated president in December 2006. The National Assembly was installed in September 2006. Its president, Vital Kamerhe, was chosen in December. Provincial assemblies were constituted in early 2007, and elected governors and national senators in January 2007. A change to a Francs-Congolese currency has been considered, but meanwhile "hard" currencies such as U.S. dollars circulate freely.

See also Rwanda, Rwanda-Burundi, and Zaïre.

MONETARY SYSTEM:

1 Franc = 100 Centimes to 1967
1 Zaïre = 100 Makuta, 1967-71
1 Franc = 100 Centimes, 1997-

Congo (Kinshasa)

République du Congo Conseil Monétaire de la République du Congo

1962-63 Issue

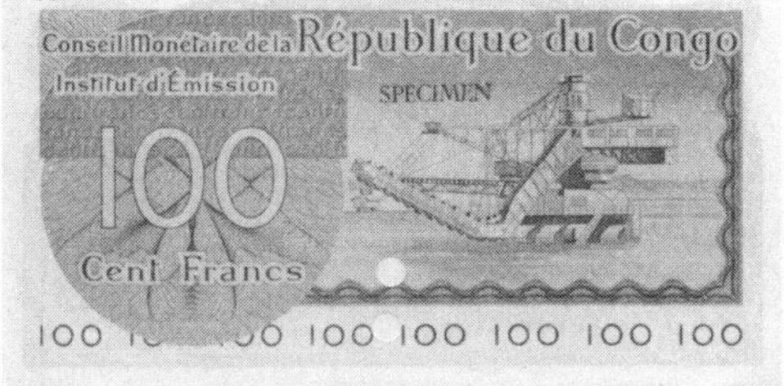

No.	Denomination	VF	UNC
1	**100 Francs** 1.6.1963-8.7.1963. Green and multicolor. Dam at left. Signature varieties. Back: Dredging at right.		
	a. Issued note.	40.00	160.
	s. Specimen. Punch hole cancelled.	85.00	145.
	ct. Color trial. Blue on multicolor underprint.	—	175.

No.	Denomination	VF	UNC
2	**1000 Francs** 15.2.1962. Purple on multicolor underprint. Portrait African man at left. Text: *EMISSION DU CONSEIL MONÉTAIRE DE LA REPUBLIQUE DU CONGO* in place of watermark. Signature varieties. Back: Back deep violet on pink underprint. Waterbuck drinking in stream.		
	a. Issued note.	100.	525.
	s. Specimen.	—	385.

No.	Denomination	VF	UNC
3	**5000 Francs** 1.12.1963. Gray-green. Portrait African woman at left. Signature varieties. Back: Standing oarsmen.		
	a. Issued note.	1800.	—
	s. Specimen. Punch hole cancelled.	—	4000.
	ct. Color trial. Blue on multicolor underprint.	—	4500.

Banque Nationale du Congo

1961 Issue

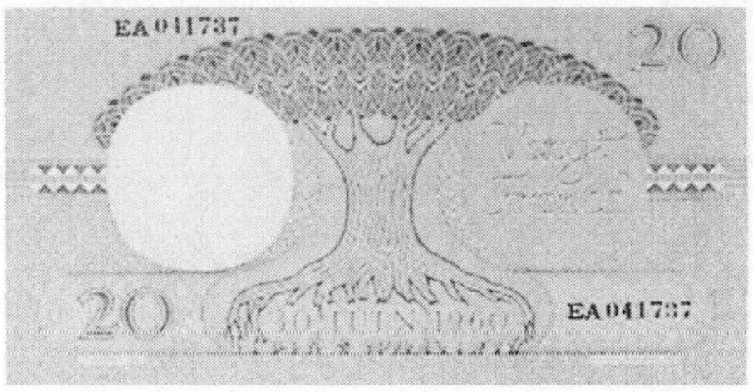

4 20 Francs

15.11.1961-15.9.1962. Green, blue and brown. Girl seated at right. Signature 1. Back: Stylized tree at center. Watermark: Seated girl. Printer: JEZ.

	VF	UNC
a. Issued note.	15.00	80.00
s. Specimen.	—	80.00

5 50 Francs

1.9.1961-1.7.1962. Green. Lion at left, bridge and lake at center right in background. Signature 1. Back: Long building at bottom.

	VF	UNC
a. Issued note.	25.00	145.
s. Specimen. Punch hole cancelled.	—	100.
ct. Color trial. Brown on multicolor underprint.	—	150.

6 100 Francs

1.9.1961-1.8.1964. Dark brown on multicolor underprint. J. Kasavubu at left, two crowned cranes at right. Sinature 1. Back: Long building at bottom. Printer: TDLR.

	VF	UNC
a. Issued note.	15.00	110.
s. Specimen.	—	80.00

7 500 Francs

15.10.1961; 1.12.1961; 1.1.1962; 1.8.1964. Lilac. Mask at left. Signature 1. Back: Long building at bottom. Watermark: Bird.

	VF	UNC
a. Issued note.	40.00	180.
s. Specimen.	—	150.

8 1000 Francs

15.10.1961; 15.12.1961; 1.8.1964. Dark blue on multicolor underprint. J. Kasavubu at left, carving at right. Signature 1. Back: Long building at bottom. Watermark: Antelope's head. Printer: TDLR.

	VF	UNC
a. Issued note.	30.00	150.
s. Specimen.	—	100.

1967 Issue

#9-13 Replacement notes: Serial # prefix ZZ.

9 10 Makuta

2.1.1967, 1.9.1968, 14.1.1970, 21.1.1970. Blue on olive-green and multicolor underprint. Stadium at left, Mobutu at right. Signature 1. Back: Long building. Printer: TDLR.

	VF	UNC
a. Issued note.	12.50	60.00
s. Specimen.	—	40.00

10 20 Makuta

1967-70. Black on green, blue and multicolor underprint. Man with flag at center, P. Lumumba at right. Signature varieties. Back: People in long boat at left center. Watermark: Antelope's head. Printer: TDLR.

	VF	UNC
a. Signature 1. 24.11.1967; 21.1.1970.	32.50	140.
b. Signature 2. 1.10.1970.	00.00	140.
s. Specimen. 21.1.1970.	—	170.

11 50 Makuta

1967-70. Red on olive-green and multicolor underprint. Stadium at center left, Mobutu at right. Signature varieties. Back: Gathering coconuts. Printer: TDLR.

	VF	UNC
a. Signature 1. 2.1.1967; 1.9.1968; 21.1.1970.	30.00	145.
b. Signature 2. 1.10.1970.	30.00	145.
s1. Specimen. 1.9.1968.	—	100.
s2. Specimen. 21.1.1970.		100.

12 1 Zaïre = 100 Makuta

1967-70. Brown and green on multicolor underprint. Stadium at left, Mobutu at right. Signature varieties. Back: Mobutu's "time to work" to gathering of people at left center. Watermark: Antelope's head. Printer: TDLR.

	VF	UNC
a. Signature 1. 2.1.1967; 24.11.1967; 1.9.1968.	25.00	100.
b. Signature 2. 21.1.1970; 1.10.1970.	25.00	100.
s1. Specimen. 24.11.1967.	—	100.
s2. Specimen. 1.9.1968.	—	100.
s3. Specimen. 1.10.1970. Overprint: *SPECIMEN* in red on both sides.	—	165.

13 5 Zaïres = 500 Makuta

1967-70. Green and multicolor. Mobutu at right. Signature varieties. Back: Long building at left center. Watermark: Antelope's head. Printer: TDLR.

	VF	UNC
a. Signature 1 above title: *LE GOUVERNEUR*. Green date. 2.1.1967; 24.6.1967.	95.00	385.
b. Signature 2 below title: *LE GOUVERNEUR*. Black date. 2.1.1967; 24.11.1967; 1.9.1968; 21.1.1970.	75.00	285.
s1. Specimen. 2.1.1967.	—	200.
s2. Specimen. 1.9.1968.	—	200.
s3. Specimen. 21.1.1970.	—	200.

1971 Issue

#14 and 15 Replacement notes: Serial # suffix Z.

14 5 Zaïres VF UNC

24.11.1971. Green, black and multicolor. Portrait Mobuta at left, leopard at lower right facing right. Signature 2. Back: Carving at left center, hydroelectric dam at center right. Watermark: Mobuta. Printer: G&D.

	VF	UNC
a. Issued note.	60.00	300.
s. Specimen.	—	50.00

15 10 Zaïres VF UNC

30.6.1971. Blue, brown and multicolor. Portrait Mobuta at left, leopard at lower right facing right. Signature 2. Back: Arms with yellow star. Watermark: Mobuta. Printer: G&D.

	VF	UNC
a. Issued note.	60.00	300.
s. Specimen.	—	50.00

Democratic Republic

Banque Centrale du Congo

1997 Issue

80 1 Centime VF UNC

1.11.1997. Deep olive-green, violet and dark brown on multicolor underprint. Woman harvesting coffee beans at left. Bank monogram at center. Back: Nyiragongo volcano erupting at right. Watermark: Single Okapi head or multiple heads repeated vertically. Printer: ATB. UV: fibers fluoresce yellow and blue, upper right serial # red.

	VF	UNC
a. Issued note.	FV	1.00
s. Specimen. Overprint: *SPECIMEN* in red on both sides.	—	12.50

81 5 Centimes VF UNC

1.11.1997. Purple on multicolor underprint. Suku mask at left. Bank monogram at center. Back: Zande Harp at center right. Watermark: Single Okapi head or multiple heads repeated vertically. Printer: G&D. UV: fibers fluoresce yellow and blue, upper right serial # red.

	VF	UNC
a. Issued note.	FV	1.00
s. Specimen. Overprint: *SPECIMEN* in red on both sides.	—	15.00

82 10 Centimes VF UNC

1.11.1997. Red-violet and dark brown on multicolor underprint. Pende mask at left. Bank monogram at center. Back: Pende dancers at center right. Watermark: Single Okapi head or multiple heads repeated vertically. Printer: ATB. UV: fibers fluoresce blue, upper right serial # red, security strip interrupted blue.

	VF	UNC
a. Issued note.	FV	1.25
s. Specimen. Overprint: *SPECIMEN* in red on both sides.	—	17.50

83 20 Centimes VF UNC

1.11.1997. Blue-green and black on multicolor underprint. Waterbuck at left. Bank monogram at center. Back: Waterbuck herd by large tree at center right. Watermark: Single Okapi head or multiple heads repeated vertically. Printer: ATB.

	VF	UNC
a. Issued note.	FV	1.25
s. Specimen. Overprint: *SPECIMEN* in red on both sides.	—	20.00

84 50 Centimes VF UNC

1.11.1997. Dark brown and brown on multicolor underprint. Okapi's head at left. Bank monogram at center. Back: Family of Okapis at left center. Watermark: Single Okapi head or multiple heads repeated vertically. Printer: G&D. UV: fibers fluoresce orange, upper right serial # red, security strip interrupted blue.

	VF	UNC
a. Issued note.	FV	1.75
s. Specimen.	—	10.00

84A 50 Centimes FV 1.75

1.11.1997. Dark brown and brown on multicolor underprint. Okapi's head at left. Bank monogram at center. Back: Family of Okapis at left center. Watermark: Single Okapi head or multiple heads repeated vertically. Printer: ATB. Serial # prefix: E; suffix: A-E, T.

85 1 Franc — VF | UNC

1.11.1997 (1998). Deep purple and blue-violet on multicolor underprint. Large mining complex at left. Bank monogram at center. Back: Prisoners Lumumba and two companions at center right. Watermark. Single Okapi head or multiple heads repeated vertically. Printer: G&D.

	VF	UNC
a. Issued note.	35.00	100.
s. Specimen.	—	20.00

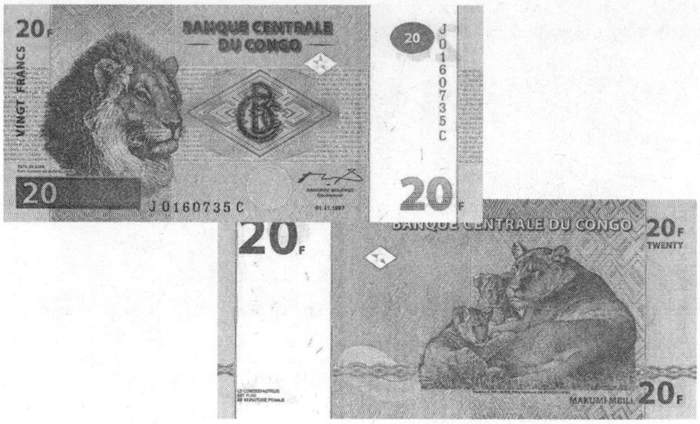

86 5 Francs — VF | UNC

1.11.1997 (1998). Purple and black on multicolor underprint. White rhinoceros at left. Bank monogram at center. Back: Kamwanga Falls at center right. Watermark: Single Okapi head or multiple heads repeated vertically. Printer: NBBPW.

	VF	UNC
a. Issued note.	FV	05.00
s. Specimen.	—	12.50

86A 5 Francs

1.11.1997 (1998). Purple and black on multicolor underprint. White rhinoceros at left. Bank monogram at center. Back: Kamwanga Falls at center right. Watermark: Single Okapi head or multiple heads repeated vertically. Printer: HdM. — FV | 65.00

87 10 Francs — VF | UNC

1.11.1997 (1998). Olive-brown, olive-green and deep blue-green on multicolor underprint. *Apui-tete Chef Luba* carving of a couple at left. Bank monogram at center. Back: *Coupe en Bois Luba* carving at right. Watermark: Single Okapi head or multiple heads repeated vertically. Printer: NBBPW. Serial # prefix: *H*; suffix: *A*.

	VF	UNC
a. Issued note.	4.00	15.00
s. Specimen. Overprint: *SPECIMEN* in red on both sides.	—	22.50

87A 10 Francs

1.11.1997. Olive-brown, olive-green and deep blue-green on multicolor underprint. "Apui-tete Chef Luba" carving of a couple at left. Bank monogram at center. Back: "Coupe en Bois Luba" carving at right. Watermark: Single Okapi head or multiple heads repeated vertically. Printer: G&D. Serial # prefix: H; suffix: B-E. — 5.00 | 17.50

87B 10 Francs

1.11.1997. Olive-brown, olive-green and deep blue-green on multicolor underprint. "Apui-tete Chef Luba" carving of a couple at left. Bank monogram at center. Back: "Coupe en Bois Luba" carving at right. Watermark: Single Okapi head or multiple heads repeated vertically. Printer: HdM. — FV | 15.00

88 20 Francs — VF | UNC

1.11.1997 (1998). Brown-orange and red-orange on multicolor underprint. Male lion's head at left. Bank monogram at center. Back: Lioness lying with two cubs at center right. Watermark: Single Okapi head or multiple heads repeated vertically. Printer: NBBPW.

	VF	UNC
a. Issued note.	5.00	20.00
s. Specimen.	—	17.50

88A 20 Francs

1.11.1997 (1998). Brown-orange and red-orange on multicolor underprint. Male lion's head at left. Bank monogram at center. Back: Lioness lying with two cubs at center right. Watermark: Single Okapi head or multiple heads repeated vertically. Printer: HdM. — 4.00 | 15.00

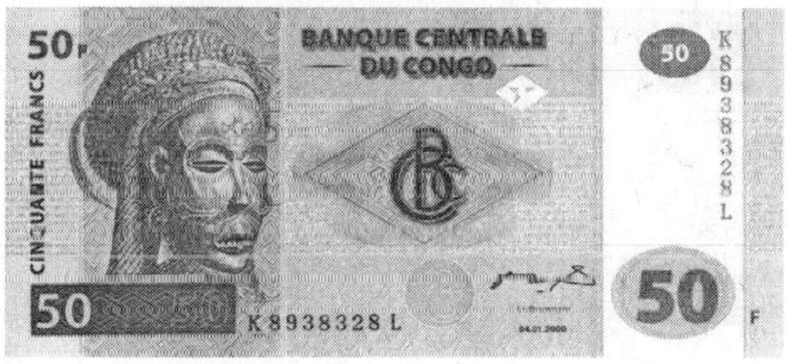

89 50 Francs — VF | UNC

1.11.1997 (1998). Olive-green. Head at left. Bank monogram at center. Back: Village scene. Watermark. Single Okapi head or multiple heads repeated vertically. Printer: NBBPW.

	VF	UNC
a. Issued note.	10.00	50.00
s. Specimen. Overprint: *SPECIMEN* in red on both sides.	—	30.00

90 100 Francs

1.11.1997 (1998). Brown. Elephant at left. Bank monogram at center. Back: Dam. Watermark: Single Okapi head or multiple heads repeated vertically. Printer: NBBPW.

	VF	UNC
a. Issued note.	17.50	90.00
s. Specimen.	—	30.00

90A 100 Francs

1.11.1997. Brown. Elephant at left. Bank monogram at center. Back: Dam. Watermark: Single Okapi head or multiple heads repeated vertically. Printer: HDM. — FV | 90.00

2000 Issue

91 50 Francs — VF | UNC

4.1.2000. Lilac brown. Head at left. Bank monogram at center. Back: Village scene. Watermark: Single Okapi head or multiple heads repeated vertically. Printer: G&D.

	VF	UNC
a. Issued note.	FV	10.00
s. Specimen.	—	15.00

91A 50 Francs

4.1.2000. Lilac brown. Head at left. Bank monogram at center. Back: Village scene. Watermark: Single Okapi head or multiple heads repeated vertically. Printer: HDM. — FV | 10.00

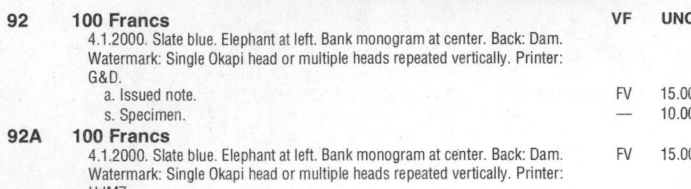

92 100 Francs — VF | UNC

4.1.2000. Slate blue. Elephant at left. Bank monogram at center. Back: Dam. Watermark: Single Okapi head or multiple heads repeated vertically. Printer: G&D.

	VF	UNC
a. Issued note.	FV	15.00
s. Specimen.	—	10.00

92A 100 Francs

4.1.2000. Slate blue. Elephant at left. Bank monogram at center. Back: Dam. Watermark: Single Okapi head or multiple heads repeated vertically. Printer: HdMZ. — FV 15.00

2003 Issue

93 10 Francs — VF | UNC

30.6.2003. Brown and red on orange and blue multicolor underprint. *Apuitete Chef Luba* carving of a couple at left. Bank monogram at center. Back: *Coupe en Bois Luba* carving at right. Watermark: Single Okapi head or multiple heads repeated vertically. Printer: G&D. Serial # prefix: *H*; suffix: *A*.

	VF	UNC
a. Issued note.	FV	3.00
s. Specimen.	—	10.00

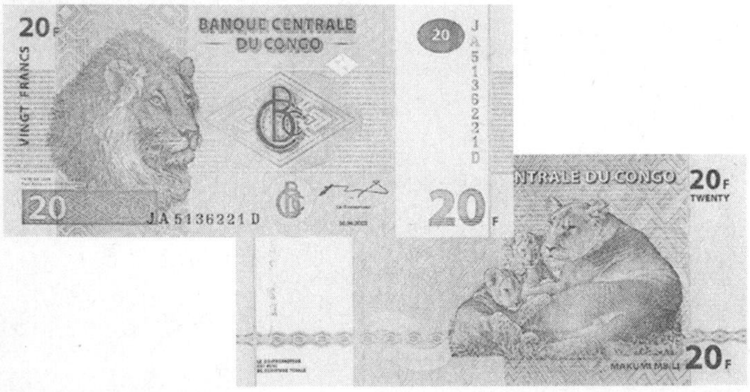

94 20 Francs — VF | UNC

30.6.2003. Blue-green on green multicolor underprint. Male lion's head at left. Back: Lioness lying with two cubs at center right. Printer: HdM-B.O.C.

	VF	UNC
a. Issued note.	FV	5.00
s. Specimen.	—	10.00

94A 20 Francs

30.6.2003. Blue-green on green multicolor underprint. Male lion's head at left. Back: Lioness lying with two cubs at center right. Printer: G&D. — FV 6.00

95 200 Francs — VF | UNC

30.6.2000 (2003). Lilac and olive green on multicolor underprint. Two farmers at left. Back: Four men working on logs. Printer: G&D.

	VF	UNC
a1. Issued note.	FV	6.00
s. Specimen.	—	10.00

95A 200 Francs — VF | UNC

30.6.2000 (2006). Lilac and olive green on multicolor underprint. Two farmers at left. Back: Four men working on logs. Printer: HdM. Like #95. — Unc .75

96 500 Francs — VF | UNC

4.1.2002 (2004). Blue on multicolor underprint. Miners and diamond at left. Printer: G&D.

	VF	UNC
a. Issued note.	FV	12.00
s. Specimen.	—	10.00

2007 Issue

97 50 Francs — VF | UNC

31.7.2007. Serial # prefix KA or KB, suffix A. Printer: G&D.

	VF	UNC
a. Issued note.	FV	5.00
s. Specimen.	—	15.00

		VF	UNC
98	**100 Francs**		
	31.7.2007. Serial # prefix MA, suffix T-X. Printer: HdM.		
	a. Issued note.	FV	5.00
	s. Specimen.	—	15.00

		VF	UNC
99	**200 Francs**		
	31.7.2007. Serial # prefix N, suffix W. Printer: G&D. 162x70mm.		
	a. Issued note.	FV	5.00
	s. Specimen.	—	15.00

2010-2012 Issue

		VF	UNC
100	**500 Francs**		
	30.6.2010. Light and dark green. Port of Matadi at right center. Back: Kinsuka bridge. 50th Anniversary of Independence logo at lower right. Printer: G&D. 151x70mm.		
	a. Issued note.	FV	5.00
	s. Specimen.	—	15.00

		VF	UNC
101	**1000 Francs**		
	2.2.2005 (2012). Green and gray. Ancient pottery. Back: Parrot. 151x70mm.		
	a. Issue note.	FV	5.00
	s. Specimen.	—	15.00

		VF	UNC
102	**5000 Francs**		
	2.2.2005 (2012). Brown and orange-brown. Zebras and statuette. Back: Two birds. 150x70mm.		
	a. Issued note.	FV	8.00
	s. Specimen.	—	15.00

		VF	UNC
103	**10000 Francs**		
	18.2.2006 (2012). Lilac, violet and gray. Two water buffalo and statuette. Back: Bird. 150x70mm.		
	a. Issued note.	FV	15.00
	s. Specimen.	—	15.00

		VF	UNC
104	**20000 Francs**		
	2.18.2006 (2012) Yellow and brown. Two giraffes and vase in shape of a head. Back: Two birds. 150x70mm.		
	a. Issued note.	FV	30.00
	s. Specimen.	—	15.00

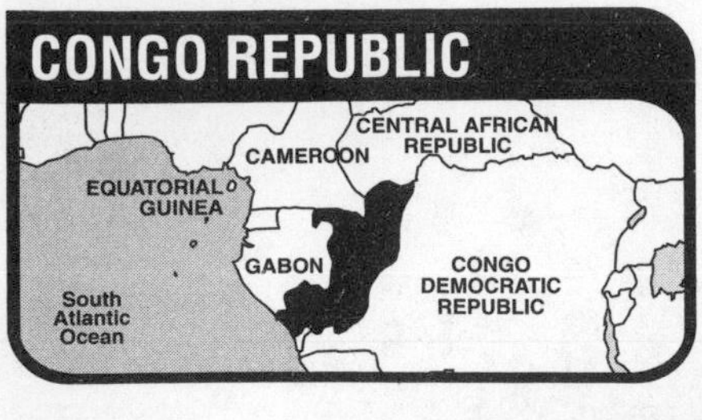

The Republic of the Congo is located on the equator in west-central Africa, has an area of 342,000 sq. km. and a population of 3.90 million. Capital: Brazzaville. Agriculture forestry, mining, and food processing are the principal industries. Timber, industrial diamonds, potash, peanuts, and cocoa beans are exported.

Upon independence in 1960, the former French region of Middle Congo became the Republic of the Congo. A quarter century of experimentation with Marxism was abandoned in 1990 and a democratically elected government took office in 1992. A brief civil war in 1997 restored former Marxist President Denis SASSOU-NGUESSO, and ushered in a period of ethnic and political unrest. Southern-d rebel groups agreed to a final peace accord in March 2003, but the calm is tenuous and refugees continue to present a humanitarian crisis. The Republic of Congo was once one of Africa's largest petroleum producers, but with declining production it will need new offshore oil finds to sustain its oil earnings over the long term.

RULERS:

French to 1960

MONETARY SYSTEM:

1 Franc = 100 Centimes

SIGNATURE VARIETIES:

Refer to introduction of Central African States.

République Populaire du Congo

Banque Centrale

1971 Issue

		VF	UNC
1	**10,000 Francs** ND (1971). Multicolor. Young Congolese woman at left, people marching with sign at center. Signature 1. Back: Statue at left and right, tractor plowing at center.	1000.	2750.

Banque des États de l'Afrique Centrale

1974 ND Issue

		VF	UNC
2	**500 Francs** ND (1974)-1983. Lilac-brown and multicolor. Woman at left, river scene at center. Back: Mask at left, students and chemical testing at center, statue at right.		
	a. Signature titles: *LE DIRECTEUR GENERAL* and *UN CENSEUR.* Engraved. Signature 5. ND (1974).	15.00	50.00
	b. Signature titles: *LE GOUVERNEUR* and *UN CENSEUR.* Lithographed. Signature 10. 1.4.1978.	25.00	90.00
	c. Titles as b. signature 10; 1.7.1980.	7.50	25.00
	d. Titles as b. signature 12. 1.6.1981; 1.1.1982; 1.1.1983; 1.6.1984.	6.00	25.00

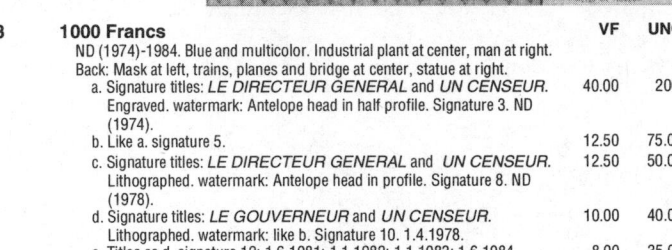

		VF	UNC
3	**1000 Francs** ND (1974)-1984. Blue and multicolor. Industrial plant at center, man at right. Back: Mask at left, trains, planes and bridge at center, statue at right.		
	a. Signature titles: *LE DIRECTEUR GENERAL* and *UN CENSEUR.* Engraved. watermark: Antelope head in half profile. Signature 3. ND (1974).	40.00	200.
	b. Like a. signature 5.	12.50	75.00
	c. Signature titles: *LE DIRECTEUR GENERAL* and *UN CENSEUR.* Lithographed. watermark: Antelope head in profile. Signature 8. ND (1978).	12.50	50.00
	d. Signature titles: *LE GOUVERNEUR* and *UN CENSEUR.* Lithographed. watermark: like b. Signature 10. 1.4.1978.	10.00	40.00
	e. Titles as d. signature 12; 1.6.1981; 1.1.1982; 1.1.1983; 1.6.1984.	8.00	35.00

		VF	UNC
4	**5000 Francs** ND (1974; 1978). Brown. Man at left. Back: Mask at left, buildings at center, statue at right.		
	a. Signature titles: *LE DIRECTEUR GENERAL* and *UN CENSEUR.* Signature 3. ND (1974).	100.	450.
	b. Like a. signature 5.	75.00	300.
	c. Signature titles: *LE GOUVERNEUR* and *UN CENSEUR.* Signature 11; 12. ND (1978).	50.00	250.

		VF	UNC
5	**10,000 Francs** ND (1974-81). Multicolor. Young Congolese women at left, people marching with sign at center. Signature 1. Back: Statue at left and right, tractor plowing at center, new bank name.		
	a. Signature titles: *LE DIRECTEUR GENERAL* and *UN CENSEUR*. Signature 5; 7. ND (1974; 1977).	125.	500.
	b. Signature titles: *LE GOUVERNEUR* and *UN CENSEUR*. Signature 11; 12. ND (1978; 1981).	100.	400.

1983-84 ND Issue

		VF	UNC
6	**5000 Francs** ND (1984; 1991). Brown and multicolor. Mask at left, woman with bundle of fronds at right. Back: Plowing and mine ore conveyor.		
	a. Signature 12. (1984).	50.00	200.
	b. Signature 15. (1991).	40.00	150.

		VF	UNC
7	**10,000 Francs** ND (1983). Brown, green and multicolor. Stylized antelope heads at left, woman at right. Signature 12. Back: Loading fruit onto truck at left.	50.00	200.

1985-87 Issues

Note: For issues w/similar back designs see Cameroun Republic, Central African Republic, Chad and Gabon.

		VF	UNC
8	**500 Francs** 1985-91. Brown on multicolor underprint. Statue at left center, jug at center. Signature titles: *LE GOUVERNEUR* and *UN CENSEUR*. Back: Man carving mask at left center. Watermark: Statue.		
	a. Signature 12. 1.1.1985; 1.1.1987; 1.1.1989.	4.00	15.00
	b. Signature 12. 1.1.1988.	—	—
	c. Signature 13. 1.1.1990.	4.00	12.50
	d. Signature 15. 1.1.1991.	4.00	12.50

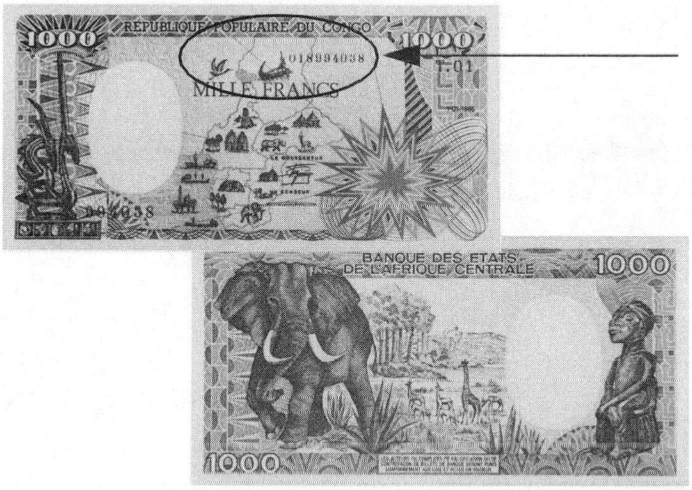

		VF	UNC
9	**1000 Francs** 1.1.1985. Dull blue-violet on multicolor underprint. Animal carving at lower left, map of 6 member states at center. Unfinished map of Chad at upper center. Signature Titles: *LE GOUVERNEUR* and *UN CENSEUR*. Signature 12. Back: Elephant at left, animals at center, carving at right. Watermark: Animal carving.	10.00	35.00

		VF	UNC
10	**1000 Francs** 1987-91. Dull blue-violet on multicolor underprint. Animal carving at lower left, map of 6 member states at center. Completed map of Chad at upper center. Signature Titles: *LE GOUVERNEUR* and *UN CENSEUR*. Signature 12. Back: Elephant at left, animals at center, carving at right. Watermark: Animal carving.		
	a. Signature 12. 1.1.1987; 1.1.1988; 1.1.1989.	6.00	25.00
	b. Signature 13. 1.1.1990.	5.00	20.00
	c. Signature 15. 1.1.1991.	5.00	20.00

République du Congo

Banque des États de l'Afrique Centrale

1992 Issue

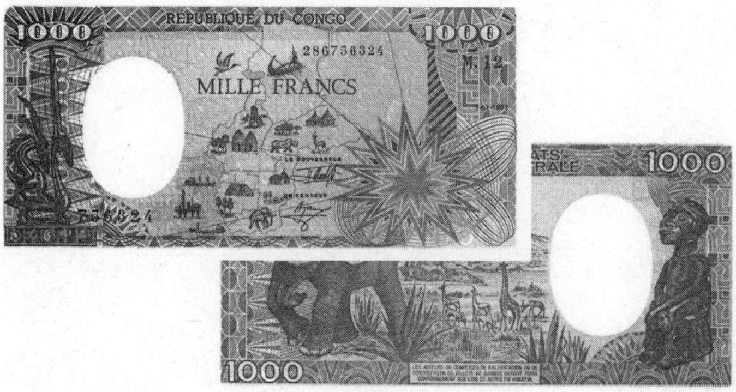

		VF	UNC
11	**1000 Francs** 1.1.1992. Dull blue-violet on multicolor underprint. Animal carving at lower left, map of 6 member states at center. Unfinished map of Chad at upper center. Signature Titles: *LE GOUVERNEUR* and *UN CENSEUR.* Signature 15. Back: Elephant at left, animals at center, carving at right, new country name.	5.00	17.50

1992 ND Issue

		VF	UNC
12	**5000 Francs** ND (1992). Black text and brown on pale yellow and multicolor underprint. African mask at left, woman carrying bundle of cane at right. Signature 15. Back: African string instrument at far left, farm tractor plowing at left center, mineshaft cable ore bucket lift at right. Watermark: African mask.	25.00	100.

		VF	UNC
13	**10,000 Francs** ND (1992). Greenish-black text, brown on pale green and multicolor underprint. Artistic antelope masks at left, woman's head at right. Signature 15. Back: Loading produce truck with bananas at left. Watermark: Woman's head.	40.00	150.

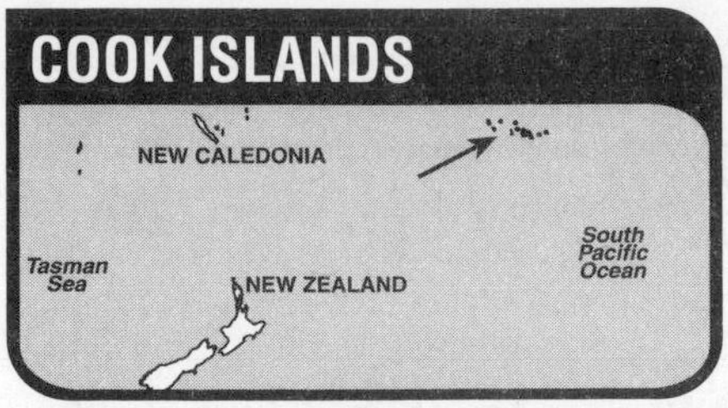

Cook Islands, a political dependency of New Zealand consisting of 15 islands located in the South Pacific Ocean about 3,218 km. northeast of New Zealand, has an area of 236.7 sq. km. and a population of 12,270. Capital: Avarua. The United States claims the islands of Danger, Manahiki, Penrhyn and Rakahanga atolls. Citrus, canned fruits and juices, copra, clothing, jewelry and mother-of-pearl shell are exported.

Named after Captain Cook, who sighted them in 1770, the islands became a British protectorate in 1888. By 1900, administrative control was transferred to New Zealand; in 1965, residents chose self-government in free association with New Zealand. The emigration of skilled workers to New Zealand and government deficits are continuing problems.

Note: In June 1995 the Government of the Cook Islands began redeeming all 10, 20 and 50 dollar notes in exchange for New Zealand currency while most coins originally intended for circulation along with their 3 dollar notes will remain in use.

RULERS:

New Zealand, 1901-

MONETARY SYSTEM:

1 Shilling = 12 Pence
1 Pound = 20 Shillings, to 1967
1 Dollar = 100 Cents, 1967-

New Zealand Administration

Government of the Cook Islands

1987 ND Issue

		VF	UNC
3	**3 Dollars** ND (1987). Deep green, blue and black on multicolor underprint. Ina and the shark at left. Back: Fishing canoe and statue of the god of Te-Rongo.		
	a. Issued note.	3.00	6.50
	s. Specimen.	—	25.00

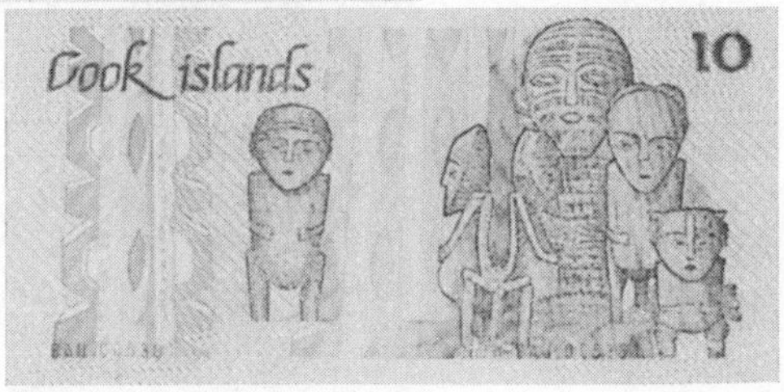

		VF	UNC
4	**10 Dollars** ND (1987). Violet-brown, blue and black on multicolor underprint. Ina and the shark at left. Back: Pantheon of gods.		
	a. Issued note.	8.50	17.50
	s. Specimen.	—	17.50

5 **20 Dollars** | VF | UNC

ND (1987). Blue, black and purple on multicolor underprint. Ina and the shark at left. Back: Conch shell, turtle shell and drum.

	VF	UNC
a. Signature T. Davis.	17.50	37.50
b. Signature M. J. Fleming.	17.50	35.00
s. Specimen.	—	20.00

1992 Commemorative Issue

#6, 6th Festival of Pacific Arts, Rarotonga, Oct. 16-27, 1992

		VF	UNC
6	**3 Dollars** Oct. 1992. Black commemorative text overprint at left on back of #3.	3.00	6.00

1992 ND Issue

7 **3 Dollars** | VF | UNC

ND (1992). Lilac and green on multicolor underprint. Worshipers at church with cemetery at center. Back: Purple, orange and multicolor. *AITUTAKI* at upper center, local drummers at left, dancers at center, blue lorikeet and fish a Watermark: Sea turtle. UV: center design fluoresces yellow. Back: value and rectangles yellow, serial #s orange.

	VF	UNC
a. Issued note.	FV	6.00
s. Specimen.	—	20.00

8 **10 Dollars** | VF | UNC

ND (1992). Green and olive on multicolor underprint. Worshippers at church with cemetery at center. Back: Cook Islands Fruit Dove. *RAROTONGA* above hillside gathering. Watermark: Sea turtle.

	VF	UNC
a. Issued note.	FV	12.50
s. Specimen.	—	25.00

9 **20 Dollars** | VF | UNC

ND (1992). Brown-orange and olive on multicolor underprint. Worshippers at church with cemetery at center. Back: *NGAPUTORU & MANGAIA* above two islanders with canoe at center. Mangaia kingfisher at right. Watermark: Sea turtle.

	VF	UNC
a. Issued note.	FV	22.50
s. Specimen.	—	20.00

10 **50 Dollars** | VF | UNC

ND (1992). Blue and green on multicolor underprint. Worshippers at church with cemetery at center. Back: Three islanders in canoe at left, *NORTHERN GROUP* above two seated women weaving at center, s Watermark: Sea turtle.

	VF	UNC
a. Issued note.	FV	55.00
s. Specimen.	—	25.00

Collector Series

Government of the Cook Islands

1987 ND Issue

		Mkt. Value
CS1	**ND (1987) 3-20 Dollars** #3-5 with matched serial # in special pack.	60.00

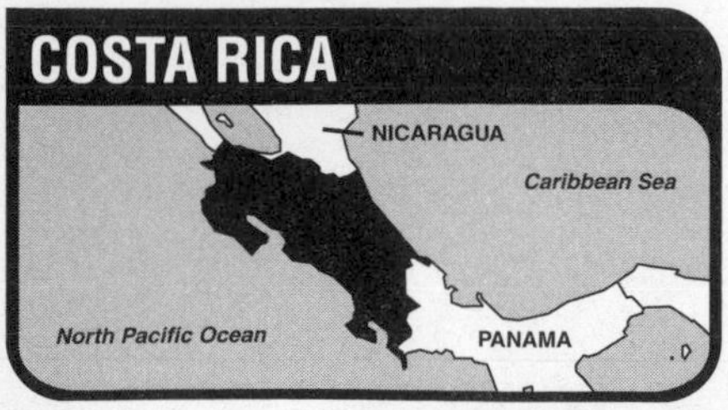

The Republic of Costa Rica, located in southern Central America between Nicaragua and Panama, has an area of 51,100 sq. km. and a population of 4.19 million. Capital: San Jose. Agriculture predominates; coffee, bananas, beef and sugar contribute heavily to the country's export earnings.

Although explored by the Spanish early in the 16th century, initial attempts at colonizing Costa Rica proved unsuccessful due to a combination of factors, including: disease from mosquito-infested swamps, brutal heat, resistance by natives, and pirate raids. It was not until 1563 that a permanent settlement of Cartago was established in the cooler, fertile central highlands. The area remained a colony for some two and a half centuries. In 1821, Costa Rica became one of several Central American provinces that jointly declared their independence from Spain. Two years later it joined the United Provinces of Central America, but this federation disintegrated in 1838, at which time Costa Rica proclaimed its sovereignty and independence. Since the late 19th century, only two brief periods of violence have marred the country's democratic development. Although it still maintains a large agricultural sector, Costa Rica has expanded its economy to include strong technology and tourism industries. The standard of living is relatively high. Land ownership is widespread.

MONETARY SYSTEM:

1 Peso = 100 Centavos to 1896
1 Colon = 100 Centimos

REPUBLIC

BANCO CENTRAL DE COSTA RICA

1951; 1952 ISSUE - SERIES A

220	**5 Colones**	VF	UNC
	1951-58. Green on multicolor underprint. Portrait B. Carillo at right. Back: Green. Coffee worker. Printer: ABNC.		
	a. *POR* (for) added to left of signature title at right. 20.11.1952.	15.00	55.00
	b. Without signature title changes. 2.7.1952-6.8.1958.	15.00	50.00
	c. Signature title: *SUB-GERENTE* overprint at right. 11.7.1956.	15.00	50.00
	d. *POR* added to left of signature title at left. 12.9.1951; 26.5.1954.	15.00	50.00
	s. Specimen. Punch hole cancelled.	—	150.

221	**10 Colones**	VF	UNC
	1951-62. Blue on multicolor underprint. Portrait A. Echeverria at center. Back: Blue. Ox-cart at center. Printer: W&S.		
	a. *POR* added to left of sign title at left. 24.10.1951; 8.11.1951; 19.11.1951; 5.12.1951; 29.10.1952.	25.00	100.
	b. *POR* added to both signature titles. 28.11.1951.	25.00	100.
	c. Without *POR* title changes. 2.7.1952; 28.10.1953-27.6.1962.	25.00	100.
	d. *POR* added to left of signature title at right. 20.11.1952.	25.00	100.

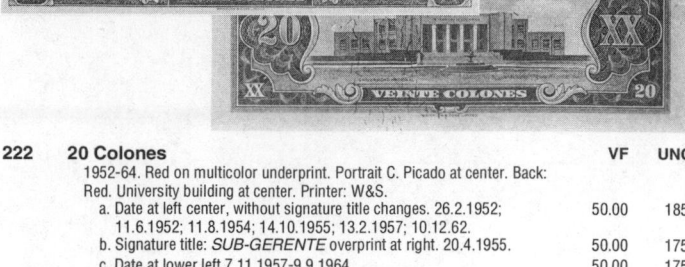

222	**20 Colones**	VF	UNC
	1952-64. Red on multicolor underprint. Portrait C. Picado at center. Back: Red. University building at center. Printer: W&S.		
	a. Date at left center, without signature title changes. 26.2.1952; 11.6.1952; 11.8.1954; 14.10.1955; 13.2.1957; 10.12.62.	50.00	185.
	b. Signature title: *SUB-GERENTE* overprint at right. 20.4.1955.	50.00	175.
	c. Date at lower left 7.11.1957-9.9.1964.	50.00	175.
	d. *POR* added at left of signature title at left. 25.3.1953; 25.2.1954.	50.00	175.

223	**50 Colones**	VF	UNC
	1952-64. Olive on multicolor underprint. Portrait right. F. Guardia at center. Back: Olive. National Library at center. Printer: W&S.		
	a. 10.6.1952-25.11.1959.	50.00	225.
	b. 14.9.1960-9.9.1964.	45.00	200.

224	**100 Colones**	VF	UNC
	1952-60. Black on multicolor underprint. Portrait J. R. Mora at center. Back: Black. Statue of J. Santamaría at center.		
	a. Without signature title changes: 11.6.1952-29.4.1960.	35.00	200.
	b. Signature title: *SUB-GERENTE* overprint at right. 27.3.1957.	35.00	200.

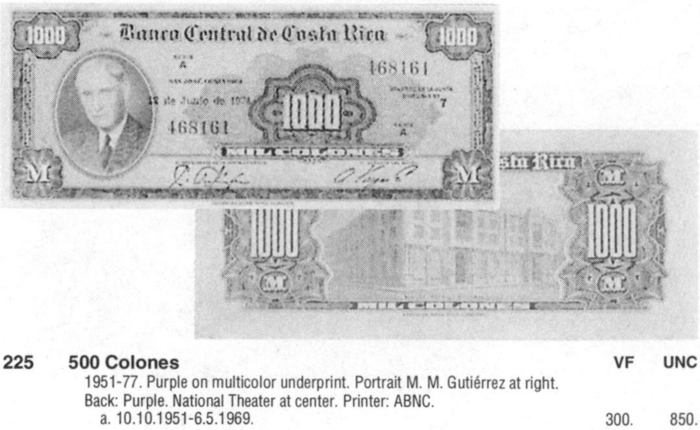

225	**500 Colones**	VF	UNC
	1951-77. Purple on multicolor underprint. Portrait M. M. Gutiérrez at right. Back: Purple. National Theater at center. Printer: ABNC.		
	a. 10.10.1951-6.5.1969.	300.	850.
	b. 7.4.1970-26.4.1977.	250.	650.
	s. Specimen. Punch hole cancelled.	—	1000.

226 1000 Colones — VF | UNC

1952-74. Red on multicolor underprint. Portrait J. Pena at left. Back: Red. Central and National Bank at center. Printer: ABNC.

	VF	UNC
a. 11.6.1952-6.10.1959.	500.	1350.
b. 25.4.1962-6.5.1969.	350.	850.
c. 7.4.1970-12.6.1974.	150.	400.
s. Specimen. Punch hole cancelled.	—	600.

1958 Issue

227 5 Colones — VF 15.00 | UNC 50.00

29.10.1958-8.11.1962. Green on multicolor underprint. Portrait B. Carrillo at center. Series B. Back: Green. Coffee worker at center. Printer: W&S.

1963-70 Issues

228 5 Colones — VF | UNC

3.10.1963-29.5.1967. Green on multicolor underprint. Portrait B. Carrillo at center. Series C. Back: Green. Coffee worker at center. Printer: TDLR.

	VF	UNC
a. Issued note.	10.00	45.00
s. Specimen. Overprint: *MUESTRA* twice.	—	—

229 10 Colones — VF 20.00 | UNC 80.00

19.9.1962-9.10.1967. Blue on multicolor underprint. Portrait Echeverría at center. Series B. Back: Blue. Ox-cart at center. Printer: TDLR.

230 10 Colones — VF | UNC

1969-70; ND. Blue on multicolor underprint. Portrait right. Facio Brenes at right. Series C. Back: Blue. Banco Central building at center. Printer: ABNC.

	VF	UNC
a. 4.3.1969; 17.6.1969.	8.50	40.00
b. 30.6.1970.	6.00	30.00
s. Specimen. overprint *MUESTRA*. Punch hole cancelled.	—	—
x. Without date or signature	—	—

231 20 Colones — VF | UNC

11.11.1964-30.6.1970. Brown on multicolor underprint. Portrait Picado at center. Series B. Back: Brown. University building at center. Printer: TDLR.

	VF	UNC
a. Issued note.	15.00	60.00
s. Specimen.	—	—

232 50 Colones — VF 30.00 | UNC 125.

9.6.1965-30.6.1970. Greenish-brown on multicolor underprint. Portrait Guardia at center. Series B. Back: Greenish-brown. National Library at center. Printer: TDLR.

233 100 Colones — VF | UNC

1961-66. Black on multicolor underprint. Portrait J. R. Mora at center. Series B. Back: Statue of J. Santamaría at center. Printer: TDLR.

	VF	UNC
a. Brown underprint. 18.10.1961-3.12.1964.	40.00	150.
b. Olive underprint. and with security thread. 9.6.1965; 14.12.1965; 27.4.1966.	30.00	150.

234 100 Colones VF UNC

29.8.1966-27.8.1968. Black on multicolor underprint. Portrait Mora at center, without *C* in corners or at right. Series C. Back: Black. Statue of J. Santamaría at center. Printer: TDLR.

	VF	UNC
a. Issued note.	30.00	135.
s. Specimen. Overprint: *MUESTRA.*	125.	500.

1967 Provisional Issue

#235 ovpt: ***BANCO CENTRAL DE COSTA RICA/SERIE PROVISIONAL*** **on Banco Nacional notes.**

235 2 Colones VF UNC

	VF	UNC
5.12.1967. Black overprint on #203 (Vol. 2). Series F. Overprint: *BANCO CENTRAL DE COSTA RICA/SERIE PROVISIONAL* on Banco Nacional notes.	15.00	75.00

1968-72 Issues

236 5 Colones VF UNC

1968-92. Deep green and lilac on multicolor underprint. Rafael Yglesias Castro at left, flowers at right. Series D. Back: Green on multicolor underprint. National Theater scene. Printer: TDLR. UV: fibers fluoresce orange.

	VF	UNC
a. Date at center. Watermark: *BCCR CINCO.* Security thread. Error name *T. VILLA* on back. 20.8.1968; 11.12.1968.	5.00	25.00
b. Date at right center. With watermark and security thread. Error name *T. VILLA* on back. 1.4.1969; 30.6.1970; 24.5.1971; 8.5.1972.	1.25	10.00
c. Date at right center. Watermark and security thread. Corrected name *J. VILLA* on back. 4.5.1973-4.5.1976.	.75	7.00
d. Without watermark or security thread. Changed signature titles. 28.6.1977-4.10.1989.	FV	5.00
e. As d. 24.1.1990-15.1.1992.	FV	3.50
s. As d. Specimen. Overprint: *MUESTRA.*	—	50.00
x. As d. but with error date: 7.4.1933 (instead of 1983).	10.00	30.00

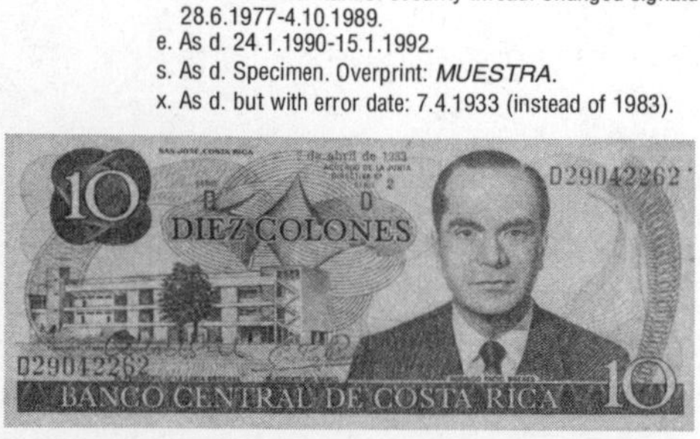

237 10 Colones VF UNC

1972-87. Dark blue on multicolor underprint. University building at left, Rodrigo Facio Brenes at right. Series D. Back: Central Bank. Watermark: *BCCR 10.* Printer: ABNC (without imprint).

	VF	UNC
a. Security thread. 6.9.1972-1977.	3.00	10.00
b. Without security thread. 26.4.1977-18.2.1987.	1.00	6.50
s. As a. Specimen. Overprint: *MUESTRA.*	—	60.00

238 20 Colones VF UNC

1972-83. Dark brown on multicolor underprint. President Cleto González Viquez at left, buildings and trees at right. Series C. Back: Allegorical scene of Justice. Printer: ABNC (without imprint).

	VF	UNC
a. Watermark: *BCCR 20.* (error). *BARBA* - etc. text under buildings at center. Signature titles: *EL PRESIDENTE DE LA JUNTA DIRECTIVA* and *EL GERENTE DEL BANCO.* Date at upper right, with security strip. 10.7.1972; 6.9.1972.	7.50	25.00
b. Watermark as a. Text and signature as a, date position at upper center, with security strip. 13.11.1972-26.4.1977.	3.00	12.00
c. Without watermark. Light brown. Signature titles: *PRESIDENTE EJECUTIVO* and *GERENTE.* Without security thread. (corrected). *BARVA...* etc. text under buildings at center. Date at upper right center or upper center. 1.6.1978-7.4.1983.	1.50	10.00
s1. Specimen. Overprint: *MUESTRA.* 1.6.1978.	—	80.00
s2. Specimen. ND.	—	80.00

239 50 Colones VF UNC

	VF	UNC
6.9.1972-26.4.1977. Olive-green multicolor underprint. Meeting scene at left, M. M. de Peralta y Alfaro at right. Series C. Back: Casa *Amarilla* (Yellow House). Printer: TDLR (without imprint).	7.50	30.00

240 100 Colones VF UNC

26.8.1969-26.4.1977. Black on multicolor underprint. Ricardo Jimenez O. at left, cows and mountains at center. Series D. Back: Supreme Court at left center, figures at right. Printer: TDLR.

	VF	UNC
a. Issued note.	12.50	45.00
s. Specimen. Overprint: *MUESTRA.*	—	—

1971 Commemorative Issue

#241-246 circular ovpt: 150 ***AÑOS DE INDEPENDENCIA*** **1821-1971**

241 5 Colones — VF | UNC
24.5.1971. Series D. Overprint: Circular; *150 ANOS DE INDEPENDENCIA* 1821-1971 on #236b. — 10.00 | 50.00

242 10 Colones — VF | UNC
24.5.1971. Series C. Overprint: Circular; *150 ANOS DE INDEPENDENCIA* 1821-1971 on #230. — 25.00 | 125.

243 50 Colones — VF | UNC
24.5.1971. Series B. Overprint: Circular; *150 ANOS DE INDEPENDENCIA* 1821-1971 on #232. — 75.00 | 325.

244 100 Colones — VF | UNC
24.5.1971; 13.12.1971. Series D. Overprint: Circular; *150 ANOS DE INDEPENDENCIA* 1821-1971 on #240 — 100. | 500.

245 500 Colones — VF | UNC
24.5.1971. Series A. Overprint: Circular; *150 ANOS DE INDEPENDENCIA* 1821-1971 on #225. — 500. | 1000.

246 1000 Colones — VF | UNC
24.5.1971. Series A. Overprint: Circular; *150 ANOS DE INDEPENDENCIA* 1821-1971 on #226. — 650. | 1500.

1975 Commemorative Issue

247 5 Colones — VF | UNC
20.3.1975. Series D. Overprint: Circular; *XXV ANIVERSARIO BANCO CENTRAL DE COSTA RICA* on #236. — 12.50 | 50.00

1975-79 Issue

248 100 Colones — VF | UNC
1977-88. Black on multicolor underprint. Ricardo Jimenez O. at left. Series E. Printer: TDLR.
- a. 26.4.1977-24.12.1981. — 4.00 | 20.00
- b. 18.5.1982-9.11.1988. — 3.00 | 15.00

249 500 Colones — VF | UNC
1979-85. Purple on multicolor underprint. M. M. Gutiérrez at right. Series B. Back: National Theatre at center right. Printer: TDLR.
- a. Red serial #. 4.6.1979-12.3.1981. — 15.00 | 75.00
- b. Black serial #. 17.9.1981; 24.12.1981; 18.5.1982; 7.8.1984; 20.3.1985. — 12.50 | 40.00

250	1000 Colones	VF	UNC
	9.6.1975; 13.11.1978; 24.12.1981; 8.7.1982; 4.11.1982; 7.4.1983; 2.10.1984; 20.3.1985. Red on multicolor underprint. T. Soley Guell at left. Series B. Back: National Insurance Institute at center right. Printer: ABNC.	10.00	50.00

1978 Commemorative Issue

#251, Centennial - Bank of Costa Rica 1877-1977

251	50 Colones	VF	UNC
	1978-86. Olive-green and multicolor. Obverse of 1866-dated 50 Centimos coin at left, Gaspar Ortunoy Ors at right. Series D. Back: Old bank, reverse of 50 Centimos coin and commemorative text: *1877-CENTENARIO...* Printer: TDLR.		
	a. 30.10.1978; 30.4.1979; 18.3.1980; 2.4.1981.	7.50	27.50
	b. 18.5.1982; 28.8.1984; 22.11.1984; 20.3.1985; 2.4.1986.	5.00	25.00

1983-88 Issue

252	20 Colones	VF	UNC
	28.6.1983. Without watermark. Light brown. Signature titles: *PRESIDENTE EJECUTIVO* and *GERENTE.* Without security thread. (corrected). *BARVA...* etc. text under buildings at center. Date at up Printed on Tyvek.		
	a. Issued note.	5.00	20.00
	s. Specimen. Punch hole cancelled.	—	350.

253	50 Colones	VF	UNC
	15.7.1987; 26.4.1988. Olive-green on multicolor underprint. Obverse of 1866-dated 50 Centimos coin at left, Gaspar Ortunoy Ors at right. Series E. Back: Old bank, reverse of 50 Centimos coin and commemorative text: *ANTIGUO EDIFICIO...* Watermark: *BCCR 50* with security thread. Printer: CdM-Brazil.	2.00	10.00

1986; 1987 Issue

254	100 Colones	VF	UNC
	30.11.1988; 4.10.1989; 5.10.1990. Black on multicolor underprint. Ricardo Jimenez O. at left. Series F. Printer: ABNC.		
	a. Issued note.	2.50	15.00
	s. Specimen.	—	350.

255	500 Colones	VF	UNC
	21.1.1987; 14.6.1989. Brown-orange, brown and olive-brown on multicolor underprint. M. M. Gutiérrez at right. Series C. Clear watermark area at left. Back: National Theatre at center right. Printer: TDLR.	4.00	20.00

256	1000 Colones	VF	UNC
	19.11.1986; 17.6.1987; 6.1.1988; 17.1.1989. Red on multicolor underprint. T. Soley Guell at left. Series C. Back: National Insurance Institute at center right. Printer: ABNC.		
	a. Issued note.	7.50	40.00
	s. Specimen.	—	125.

1990-92 Issue

257 50 Colones | VF | UNC

19.6.1991; 28.8.1991; 29.7.1992; 2.6.1993; 7.7.1993. Olive-green on multicolor underprint. Obverse of 1866-dated 50 Centimos coin at left, Gaspar Ortunoy Ors at right. Series E. Without security thread. Back: Old bank, reverse of 50 Centimos coin and commemorative text: *ANTIGUO EDIFICIO...* Printer: TDLR.

	VF	UNC
a. Issued note.	.75	10.00
s. Specimen. Overprint: *MUESTRA*.	—	120.

258 100 Colones | VF | UNC

	VF	UNC
17.6.1992. Black on multicolor underprint. Ricardo Jimenez O. at left. Series G. Printer: CdM-Brazil.	2.50	12.50

259 1000 Colones | VF | UNC

1990-94. Red on multicolor underprint. T. Soley Guell at left. Series C. Back: National Insurance Institute at center right. Printer: USBN.

	VF	UNC
a. 24.4.1990; 3.10.1990; 23.10.1991.	4.00	22.50
b. 2.2.1994; 20.4.1994; 15.6.1994; 10.10.1994.	FV	17.50

260 5000 Colones | VF | UNC

1991-95. Dark blue, blue and dark brown on multicolor underprint. Local sculpture at left center. Series A. Back: Toucan, leopard, local carving, foliage and sphere. Printer: TDLR.

	VF	UNC
a. 28.8.1991;11.3.1992; 29.7.1992.	20.00	70.00
b. 4.5.1994; 18.1.1995.	FV	55.00

1993-97 Issue

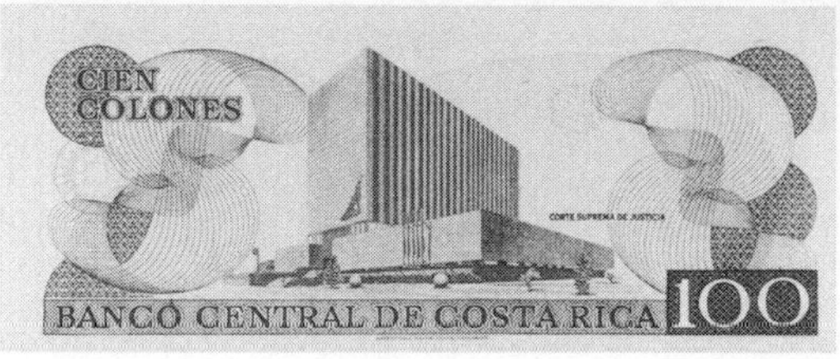

261 100 Colones | VF | UNC

28.9.1993. Black on multicolor underprint. Ricardo Jimenez O. at left. Series H. Watermark: *BCCR-100* (repeated). Printer: ABNC.

	VF	UNC
a. Issued note.	.75	7.00
s. Specimen. Overprint: *MUESTRA*. 28.9.1993.	—	125.

262 500 Colones | VF | UNC

6.7.1994. Brown-orange, brown and olive-brown on multicolor underprint. M. M. Gutiérrez at right, printing in watermark area at left. Series D. Ascending size serial # at lower left. Back: National Theatre at center right. Printer: TDLR.

	VF	UNC
a. Issued note.	FV	10.00
s. Specimen. Overprint: *MUESTRA*. 6.7.1994.	—	150.

264 1000 Colones | VF | UNC

1997-99; 2003-05. Red on multicolor underprint. T. Soley Guell at left. Series D. Ascending size serial # at upper right. Back: National Insurance Institute at center right. Printer: F-CO. 146x67mm.

	VF	UNC
a. 23.7.1997.	FV	15.00
b. 23.9.1998.	FV	15.00
c. 24.2.1999.	FV	15.00
d. 9.4.2003.	FV	15.00
e. 27.9.2004.	FV	15.00
f. 14.9.2005.	FV	15.00
s. Specimen. Overprint: *MUESTRA*. 23.7.1997.	—	200.

265	2000 Colones	VF	UNC
	1997-99; 2003-05. Brown-orange and dark brown on multicolor underprint. C. Picado T. at center right, Coco Island in underprint at center. Series A. Back: Hammerhead shark at left, dolphin at lower center. Watermark: C. Picado T. Printer: F-CO.		
	a. 30.7.1997 (1998).	FV	25.00
	b. 16.9.1998.	FV	25.00
	c. 9.4.1999.	FV	25.00
	d. 9.4.2003.	FV	25.00
	e. 14.9.2005.	FV	25.00
	s. Specimen. Overprint: *MUESTRA* or *MUESTRA SIN VALOR.* 30.7.1997.	—	250.

266	5000 Colones	VF	UNC
	1996; 2004-05. Dark blue and dark brown on multicolor underprint. Local sculpture at left center. Series B, C. Ascending size serial #. Back: Toucan, leopard, local carving, foliage and sphere. Printer: TDLR.		
	a. 27.3.1996 (1997).	FV	45.00
	b. 27.9.2004.	FV	45.00
	c. 14.9.2005.	FV	45.00
	s. Specimen. Overprint: *MUESTRA* or *MUESTRA SIN VALOR.* 27.3.1996.	—	300.

267	10,000 Colones	VF	UNC
	1997; 2004-05; 2007. Dark blue and deep blue-green on multicolor underprint. E. Gamboa A. at center right, volcanoes in underprint at center. Series A. Back: Puma at upper center. Watermark: E. Gamboa A. Printer: F-CO. 146x67mm.		
	a. 30.7.1997 (1998).	FV	85.00
	b. 20.3.2002.	FV	85.00
	c. 27.9.2004.	FV	85.00
	d. 14.9.2005.	FV	85.00
	e. 26.9.2007.	FV	85.00
	s. Specimen. Overprint: *MUESTRA* or *MUESTRA SIN VALOR.* 30.7.1997.	—	500.

1999 Issue

267A	1000 Colones	VF	UNC
	1999. Multicolor.	FV	10.00

268	5000 Colones	VF	UNC
	24.2.1999. Dark blue and dark brown on multicolor underprint. Local sculpture at left center. Series C. Ascending size serial #. Microprinting and security thread added. Back: Toucan, leopard, local carving, foliage and sphere. Printer: TDLR. 146x67mm.		
	a. Issued note.	FV	45.00
	s. Specimen. Overprint: *MUESTRA* or *MUESTRA SIN VALOR.*	—	400.

268A	5000 Colones	VF	UNC
	24.2.1999; 14.9.2005. Dark blue and dark brown on multicolor underprint. Local sculpture at left center. Back: Toucan, leopard, locar carving, foliage and sphere. Printer: FC-O. 146x67mm.		
	a. 24.2.1999.	FV	55.00
	b. 14.9.2005.	FV	55.00

2000 Commemorative Issue

50th Anniversary Banco Central

#269-273 as #262-267 but w/commemorative ovpt. ***50 BCCR ANIVERSARIO*** **added at lower r. 10,000 notes of each denomination were overprinted, but not all on uncirculated notes. All of #269-271 were sold as collectors' items; however, approximately 1/3 of #272-73 were put into general circulation.**

269	500 Colones	VF	UNC
	6.7.1994. Brown-orange, brown on multicolor underprint. M. M. Gutiérrez at right, printing in watermark area at left. Series D. Ascending size serial # at lower left. Commemorative overprint added at lower right. Back: National Theatre at center right. Overprint: *50 BCCR ANIVERSARIO.* Printer: TDLR.	FV	12.50

270	1000 Colones	VF	UNC
	23.9.1998. Red on multicolor underprint. T. Soley Guell at left. Series D. Ascending size serial number at upper right. Commemorative overprint added at lower right. Back: National Insurance Institute at center right. Overprint: *50 BCCR ANIVERSARIO.* Printer: F-CO.	FV	17.50

271 2000 Colones VF UNC
30.7.1997. Brown-orange and dark brown on multicolor underprint. C. Picado T. at center right, Coco Island in underprint at center. Series A. Commemorative overprint added at lower right. Back: Hammerhead shark at left, dolphin at lower center. Overprint: *50 BCCR ANIVERSARIO.* Printer: F-CO. FV 35.00

272 5000 Colones VF UNC
24.2.1999. Dark blue and dark brown on multicolor underprint. Local sculpture at left center. Series B. Ascending size serial number. Commemorative overprint added at lower right. Back: Toucan, leopard, local carving, foliage and sphere. Overprint: *50 BCCR ANIVERSARIO.* Printer: TDLR. FV 75.00

273 10,000 Colones
30.7.1997. Dark blue and deep blue-green on multicolor underprint. E. Gamboa A. at center right, volcanoes in underprint at center. Series A. Commemorative overprint added at lower right. Back: Puma at upper center. Overprint: *50 BCCR ANIVERSARIO.* Printer: F-CO.
a. Issued note. FV 150.
s. Specimen. — —

2010 Issue

274 1000 Colones VF UNC
2.9.2009. Red and multicolor. Braulio Carrillo Colina at left. Back: Tree, cactus and white-tailed deer. Printer: OT. Polymer plastic. 125x67mm. FV 9.00

275 2000 Colones VF UNC
2.9.2009. Blue and multicolor. Mauro Ferandez Acuna at left. Back: Bull shark, fish, coral reef star fish, turtles at right center. Printer: OT. 132x67mm. FV 16.00

276 5000 Colones VF UNC
9.2.2009. Yellow and multicolor. Alfredo Gonzalez Flores Back: Mangrove swamp, monkey, crab at right center. Printer: OT. 139x67mm. FV 30.00

277 10,000 Colones VF UNC
2.9.2009. Green and multicolor. Jose Figueres Ferrer at left. Back: Rainforest, orchid, three-toed sloth at right center. 146x67mm. FV 50.00

278 20,000 Colones VF UNC
2.9.2009. Orange and multicolor. Maria I. Carvajal "Carmen Lyra" at left. Back: Chispita hummingburg at right center. Printer: OT 153x67mm. FV 150.

279 50,000 Colones VF UNC
2.9.2009. Purple and multicolor. Ricardo Jimenez Oremuno at left. Back: Cloud forest, mushroom flowers and Morpho butterfly at right center. Printer: OT. 160x67mm. FV 250.

The Republic of Croatia (Hrvatska), has an area of 56,542 sq. km. and a population of 4.49 million. Capital: Zagreb.

The lands that today comprise Croatia were part of the Austro-Hungarian Empire until the close of World War I. In 1918, the Croats, Serbs, and Slovenes formed a kingdom known after 1929 as Yugoslavia. Following World War II, Yugoslavia became a federal independent Communist state under the strong hand of Marshal Tito. Although Croatia declared its independence from Yugoslavia in 1991, it took four years of sporadic, but often bitter, fighting before occupying Serb armies were mostly cleared from Croatian lands. Under UN supervision, the last Serb-held enclave in eastern Slavonia was returned to Croatia in 1998.

Local Serbian forces supported by the Yugoslav Federal Army had developed a military stronghold and proclaimed an independent "SRPSKE KRAJINA" state in the area around Knin, located in southern Croatia. In August 1995 Croat forces overran this political-military enclave.

MONETARY SYSTEM:

1 Dinar = 100 Para 1918-1941, 1945-
1 Kuna = 100 Banica 1941-1945
1 Kuna = 100 Lipa, 1994-
1 Dinar = 100 Para

Republic

Republika Hrvatska

Republic of Croatia

1991-93 Issue

16 1 Dinar VF UNC

8.10.1991. Dull orange-brown on multicolor underprint. R. Boskovic at center, geometric calculations at upper right. 4.5mm serial number. Back: Vertical back with Zagreb cathedral and artistic rendition of city buildings behind. Watermark: Lozenges. Printer: Swedish. UV: fibers fluoresce yellow.

	VF	UNC
a. Issued note.	.50	1.00
s. Specimen.	—	15.00

17 5 Dinara VF UNC

8.10.1991. Pale purple on multicolor underprint. R. Boskovic at center, geometric calculations at upper right. 4mm serial number. Back: Vertical back with Zagreb cathedral and artistic rendition of city buildings behind. Watermark: Lozenges. Printer: Swedish. UV: fibers fluoresce yellow.

	VF	UNC
a. Issued note.	.50	1.00
s. Specimen.	—	15.00

18 10 Dinara VF UNC

8.10.1991. Pale red-brown on multicolor underprint. R. Boskovic at center, geometric calculations at upper right. 4.5mm serial number. Back: Vertical back with Zagreb cathedral and artistic rendition of city buildings behind. Watermark: Lozenges. Printer: Swedish.

	VF	UNC
a. Issued note.	1.00	1.50
s. Specimen.	—	20.00

19 25 Dinara VF UNC

8.10.1991. Dull purple on multicolor underprint. R. Boskovic at center, geometric calculations at upper right. Buff paper with 2.8mm serial #. (Printed in Sweden). Back: Vertical back with Zagreb cathedral and artistic rendition of city buildings behind. Watermark: 5's in crossed wavy lines. Printer: Swedish.

	VF	UNC
a. Issued note.	1.50	2.00
b. Inverted watermark.	15.00	35.00
s. Specimen.	—	20.00

20 100 Dinara VF UNC

8.10.1991. Pale green on multicolor underprint. R. Boskovic at center, geometric calculations at upper right. Back: Vertical back with Zagreb cathedral and artistic rendition of city buildings behind. Printer: Swedish.

	VF	UNC
a. Issued note.	2.50	4.00
s. Specimen.	—	35.00

21 500 Dinara VF UNC

8.10.1991. Lilac on multicolor underprint. R. Boskovic at center, geometric calculations at upper right. Back: Vertical back with Zagreb cathedral and artistic rendition of city buildings behind. Watermark: Baptismal font. Printer: Swedish.

	VF	UNC
a. Issued note.	3.50	12.00
s. Specimen.	—	35.00

22 1000 Dinara VF UNC

8.10.1991. Pale blue-violet on multicolor underprint. R. Boskovic at center, geometric calculations at upper right. Back: Vertical back with Zagreb cathedral and artistic rendition of city buildings behind. Watermark: Baptismal font. Printer: Swedish.

	VF	UNC
a. Issued note.	4.50	15.00
s. Specimen.	—	35.00

23 2000 Dinara VF UNC

15.1.1992. Deep brown on multicolor underprint. R. Boskovic at center, geometric calculations at upper right. Back: Statue of seated Glagolica *Mother Croatia* at center. Watermark: Baptismal font. Printer: Swedish.

	VF	UNC
a. Issued note.	2.50	8.00
s. Specimen.	—	40.00

24 5000 Dinara

15.1.1992. Dark gray on multicolor underprint. R. Boskovic at center, geometric calculations at upper right. Back: Statue of seated Glagolica *Mother Croatia* at center. Watermark: Baptismal font. Printer: Swedish.

	VF	UNC
a. Issued note.	2.50	10.00
s. Specimen.	—	40.00

25 10,000 Dinara

15.1.1992. Olive-green on multicolor underprint. R. Boskovic at center, geometric calculations at upper right. Back: Statue of seated Glagolica *Mother Croatia* at center. Watermark: Baptismal font. Printer: Swedish.

	VF	UNC
a. Issued note.	4.00	15.00
s. Specimen.	—	40.00

26 50,000 Dinara

30.5.1993. Deep red on multicolor underprint. R. Boskovic at center, geometric calculations at upper right. Back: Statue of seated Glagolica *Mother Croatia* at center. Watermark: Baptismal font. Printer: Swedish.

	VF	UNC
a. Issued note.	1.00	3.50
s. Specimen.	—	25.00

27 100,000 Dinara

30.5.1993. Dark blue-green on multicolor underprint. R. Boskovic at center, geometric calculations at upper right. Back: Statue of seated Glagolica *Mother Croatia* at center. Printer: Swedish. UV: left shield fluoresces yellow. Back, right design yellow and orange.

	VF	UNC
a. Issued note.	1.50	6.50
s. Specimen.	—	25.00

Narodna Banka Hrvatske

1993 Issue

28 5 Kuna

31.10.1993 (1994). Dark green and green on multicolor underprint. F. K. Frankopan and P. Zrinski at right, shield at upper left center. Back: Fortress in Varazdin at left center. Watermark: F. K. Frankopan and P. Zrinski. Printer: G&D.

	VF	UNC
a. Issued note.	3.00	5.00
s. Specimen.	—	20.00
x. Error without date or signature	30.00	60.00

29 10 Kuna

31.10.1993 (1994). Purple and violet on multicolor underprint. J. Dobrila at right, shield at upper left center. Back: Pula arena at left center. Watermark: J. Dobrila. Printer: G&D.

	VF	UNC
a. Issued note.	4.00	7.00
s. Specimen.	—	20.00

30 20 Kuna

31.10.1993 (1994). Brown, red and violet on multicolor underprint. J. Jelacic at right, shield at upper left center. Back: Pottery dove and castle of Count Eltz in Vukovar at left center. Watermark: J. Jelacic. Printer: G&D.

	VF	UNC
a. Issued note.	5.00	10.00
s. Specimen.	—	25.00

31 50 Kuna

31.10.1993 (1994). Dark blue and blue-green on multicolor underprint. I. Gundulic at right, shield at upper left center. Back: Aerial view of old Dubrovnik at left center. Watermark: I. Gundulic. Printer: G&D.

	VF	UNC
a. Issued note.	8.00	20.00
s. Specimen.	—	25.00

32 100 Kuna

31.10.1993 (1994). Red-brown and brown-orange on multicolor underprint. I. Mazuranic at right, shield at upper left center. Back: Plan of and church of St. Vitus in Rijeka at left center. Watermark: I. Mazuranic. Printer: G&D.

	VF	UNC
a. Issued note.	10.00	25.00
s. Specimen.	—	30.00
x. Error without serial #.	25.00	50.00

33 200 Kuna

31.10.1993 (1994). Dark brown and brown on multicolor underprint. S. Radic at right, shield at upper left center. Back: Town command in Osijek at left center. Watermark: S. Radic. Printer: G&D.

	VF	UNC
a. Issued note.	15.00	30.00
s. Specimen.	—	30.00

34 500 Kuna

31.10.1993 (1994). Dark brown and olive-brown on multicolor underprint. M. Marulic at right, shield at upper left center. Back: Palace of Diocletian in Spit at left center. Watermark: M. Marulic. Printer: G&D.

	VF	UNC
a. Issued note.	35.00	80.00
s. Specimen.	—	35.00

35 1000 Kuna

31.10.1993 (1994). Dark brown and purple on multicolor underprint. Ante Starcevic at right, shield at upper left center. Back: Equestrian statue of King Tomislav at left center, Zagreb Cathedral at center right. Watermark: Ante Starcevic. Printer: G&D.

	VF	UNC
a. Issued note.	60.00	120.
s. Specimen.	—	40.00

1995 Issue

36 10 Kuna

15.1.1995. Black and brown on green and multicolor underprint. J. Dobrilla at right, shield at upper left center. Back: Pula arena at left center. Watermark: J. Dobrilla. Printer: G&D.

	VF	UNC
a. Issued note.	.25	2.00
s. Specimen.	—	40.00

Hrvatska Narodna Banka

2001 Issue

37 5 Kuna

7.3.2001. Multicolor. F. K. Frankopan and P. Zrinski at right, shield at upper left center. Back: Fortress in Varazdin at left center. Watermark: F. K. Frankopan and P. Zrinski. Printer: G&D.

	VF	UNC
a. Issued note.	.25	2.00
s. Specimen.	—	25.00

38 10 Kuna

7.3.2001; 9.7.2012. Multicolor. J. Dobrila at right, shield at upper left center. Back: Pula arena at left center. Watermark: J. Dobrila. Printer: G&D. 126x63mm.

	VF	UNC
a. 7.3.2001.	.50	2.50
b. 9.7.2012.	.50	2.50
s. Specimen.	—	25.00

		VF	UNC
39	**20 Kuna**		
	7.3.2001; 9.7.2012. Multicolor. J. Jelacic at right, shield at upper left center. Back: Pottery dove and castle of Count Eltz in Vukovar at left center. Watermark: J. Jelacic. Printer: G&D. 130x65mm.		
	a. 7.3.2001.	.50	5.00
	b. 9.7.2012.	.50	5.00
	s. Specimen.	—	25.00

		VF	UNC
40	**50 Kuna**		
	7.3.2002. Multicolor. I. Gundulic at right, shield at upper left center. Back: Aerial view of old Dubrovnik at left center. Watermark: I. Gundulic. Printer: OEBS. 134x67mm.		
	a. Issued note.	1.75	10.00
	s. Specimen.	—	25.00

		VF	UNC
41	**100 Kuna**		
	7.3.2002; 9.7.2012. Multicolor. I. Mazuranic at right, shield at upper left center. Back: Plan of and church of St. Vitus in Rijeka at left center. Watermark: I. Mazuranic. Printer: OEBS. 138x69mm.		
	a. 7.3.2002.	2.50	20.00
	b. 9.7.2012.	2.50	20.00
	s. Specimen.	—	50.00

		VF	UNC
42	**200 Kuna**		
	7.3.2002; 9.7.2012. Brown on multicolor underprint. S. Radic at right, shield at upper left center. Back: Town command in Osijek at left center. Watermark: S. Radic. Printer: OEBS. 142x71mm.		
	a. 7.3.2002.	5.00	35.00
	b. 9.7.2012.	5.00	35.00
	s. Specimen.	—	50.00

2004 Commemorative Issue

#45, 10th Anniversary of the National Bank of Croatia.

		VF	UNC
43	**10 Kuna**		
	30.8.2004. Multicolor. J. Dobrilla at right, shield at upper left center. Back: Pula arena at left center. Watermark: J. Dobrilla. Large 10 added. Printer: G&D.	1.00	5.00

Collector Series

Republic of Croatia

1998 Issue

		Mkt. Value
CS1	**1991-93 1-100,000 Dinara** #16-27 with matched serial #. (50,000).	—
CS2	**1993 5-1000 Kuna** #28-36 with matched serial #. (50,000).	—

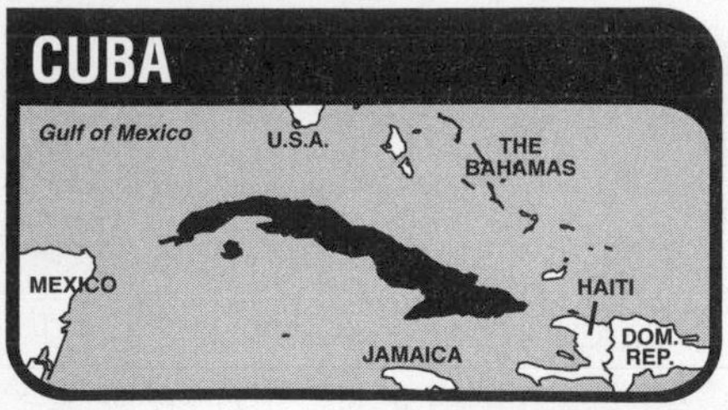

The Republic of Cuba, situated at the northern edge of the Caribbean Sea about 145 km. south of Florida, has an area of 110,860 sq. km. and a population of 11.4 million. Capital: Havana. The Cuban economy is d on the cultivation and refining of sugar, which provides 80 percent of export earnings.

The native Amerindian population of Cuba began to decline after the European discovery of the island by Christopher Columbus in 1492 and following its development as a Spanish colony during the next several centuries. Large numbers of African slaves were imported to work the coffee and sugar plantations, and Havana became the launching point for the annual treasure fleets bound for Spain from Mexico and Peru. Spanish rule, marked initially by neglect, became increasingly repressive, provoking an independence movement and occasional rebellions that were harshly suppressed. It was US intervention during the Spanish-American War in 1898 that finally overthrew Spanish rule. The subsequent Treaty of Paris established Cuban independence, which was granted in 1902 after a three-year transition period. Fidel Castro led a rebel army to victory in 1959; his iron rule held the subsequent regime together for nearly five decades. He stepped down as president in February 2008 in favor of his younger brother Raul Castro. Cuba's Communist revolution, with Soviet support, was exported throughout Latin America and Africa during the 1960s, 1970s, and 1980s. The country is now slowly recovering from a severe economic downturn in 1990, following the withdrawal of former Soviet subsidies. Cuba portrays its difficulties as the result of the US embargo in place since 1961.

RULERS:

Spanish to 1898

MONETARY SYSTEM:

1 Peso = 100 Centavos
1 Peso Convertible = 1 U.S.A. Dollar, 1995-

Republic

Banco Nacional de Cuba

National Bank of Cuba

1961 Issue

94 1 Peso VF UNC

1961-65. Olive-green on ochre underprint. Portrait J. Martí at center, denomination at left and right. Signature titles: *PRESIDENTE DEL BANCO* at left, *MINISTRO DE HACIENDA* at right. Back: F. Castro with rebel soldiers entering Havana in 1959. Printer: STC-P (without imprint).

	VF	UNC
a. 1961.	3.00	17.00
b. 1964.	2.50	10.00
c. 1965.	1.75	8.00
s. As a. Specimen.	—	6.00

95 5 Pesos VF UNC

1961-65. Dull deep green on pink underprint. Portrait A. Maceo at center, denomination at left and right. Signature titles: *PRESIDENTE DEL BANCO* at left, *MINISTRO DE HACIENDA* at right. Back: Invasion of 1958. Printer: STC-P (without imprint).

	VF	UNC
a. 1961.	3.75	19.00
b. 1964.	3.00	12.50
c. 1965.	2.50	10.00
s. As a. Specimen.	—	6.00

96 10 Pesos VF UNC

1961-65. Brown on tan and yellow underprint. Portrait M. Gómez at center, denomination at left and right. Signature titles: *PRESIDENTE DEL BANCO* at left, *MINISTRO DE HACIENDA* at right. Back: Castro addressing crowd in 1960. Printer: STC-P (without imprint).

	VF	UNC
a. 1961.	5.00	23.00
b. 1964.	4.50	17.50
c. 1965.	4.00	15.00
s. As a. Specimen.	—	6.00

97 20 Pesos VF UNC

1961-65. Blue on pink underprint. Portrait C. Cienfuegos at center, denomination at left and right. Signature titles: *PRESIDENTE DEL BANCO* at left, *MINISTRO DE HACIENDA* at right. Back: Soldiers on the beach in 1956. Printer: STC-P (without imprint).

	VF	UNC
a. 1961.	12.50	60.00
b. 1964.	8.00	35.00
c. 1965.	7.50	30.00
s. As a. Specimen.	—	8.00
x. U.S.A. counterfeit. Series F69; F70, 1961.	20.00	100.

98 50 Pesos VF UNC

1961. Purple on green underprint. Portrait C. García Iñiguez at center, denomination at left and right. Signature titles: *PRESIDENTE DEL BANCO* at left, *MINISTRO DE HACIENDA* at right. Back: Nationalization of international industries. Printer: STC-P (without imprint).

	VF	UNC
a. Issued note.	35.00	150.
s. Specimen.	—	10.00

99	100 Pesos	VF	UNC
	1961. Light red on orange underprint. Portrait C. M. de Céspedes at center, denomination at left and right. Signature titles: *PRESIDENTE DEL BANCO* at left, *MINISTRO DE HACIENDA* at right. Back: Attack on Moncada in 1953. Printer: STC-P (without imprint).		
	a. Issued note.	60.00	210.
	s. Specimen. Overprint: *SPECIMEN* in red on face.	—	250.

1966 Issue

100	1 Peso	VF	UNC
	1966. Olive-green on ochre underprint. Portrait J. Martí at center. Denomination at left and right. Signature titles: *PRESIDENTE DEL BANCO* at left and right. Back: F. Castro with rebel soldiers entering Havana in 1959. Printer: STC-P (without imprint).		
	a. Issued note.	1.00	5.00
	s. Specimen.	—	6.00
101	10 Pesos		
	1966. Brown on tan and yellow underprint. Portrait M. Gómez at center, denomination at left and right. Signature titles: *PRESIDENTE DEL BANCO* at left and right. Back: Castro addressing crowd in 1960. Printer: STC-P (without imprint).		
	a. Issued note.	7.50	20.00
	s. Specimen.	—	6.00

1967; 1971 Issue

102	1 Peso	VF	UNC
	1967-88. Olive-green on ochre underprint. Portrait J. Martí at center, denomination at left. Signature title: *PRESIDENTE DEL BANCO* at lower right. Back: F. Castro with rebel soldiers entering Havana in 1959. Printer: STC-P (without imprint).		
	a. 1967-70; 1972.	1.00	5.00
	b. 1978-85.	.50	3.50
	c. 1986.	.50	3.00
	d. 1988.	.50	2.50
	s1. Specimen. As a, b. Overprint: *SPECIMEN* in red on both sides.	—	8.00
	s2. Specimen. As b. Overprint: *MUESTRA* in red on both sides.	—	8.00
	s3. Specimen. As d. Overprint: *MUESTRA* in red twice on both sides.	—	8.00

103	5 Pesos	VF	UNC
	1967-90. Dull deep green on pink underprint. Portrait A. Maceo at center, denomination at left. Signature title: *PRESIDENTE DEL BANCO* at lower right. Back: Invasion of 1958. Printer: STC-P (without imprint).		
	a. 1967-68.	1.00	15.00
	b. 1970; 1972.	.75	12.50
	c. 1984-87.	.75	10.00
	d. 1988; 1990.	.50	4.00
	s. Specimen.	—	6.00

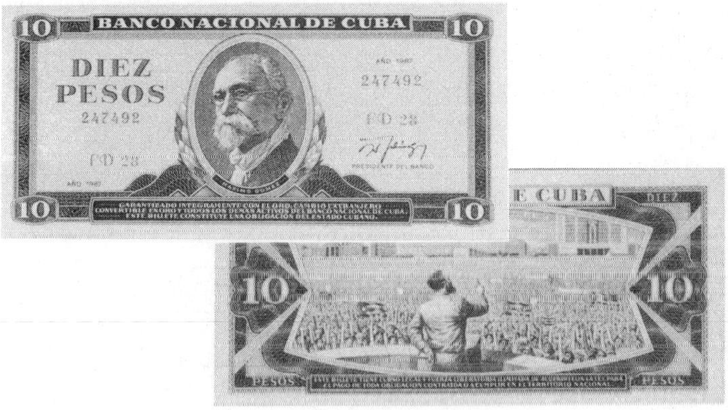

104	10 Pesos	VF	UNC
	1967-89. Brown on tan and yellow underprint. Portrait M. Gómez at center, denomination at left. Signature title: *PRESIDENTE DEL BANCO* at lower right. Back: Castro addressing crowd in 1960. Printer: STC-P (without imprint). 150x70mm.		
	a. 1967-71.	1.00	15.00
	b. 1978.	1.00	15.00
	c. 1983-84; 1986-87.	1.00	10.00
	d. 1988-89.	1.00	10.00
	s. Specimen. Overprint: *MUESTRA* in red on both sides.	—	20.00

105	20 Pesos	VF	UNC
	1971-90. Blue on pink underprint. Portrait C. Cienfuegos at center, denomination at left. Signature title: *PRESIDENTE DEL BANCO* at lower right. Back: Soldiers on the beach in 1956. Printer: STC-P (without imprint).		
	a. 1971.	3.50	20.00
	b. 1978.	3.50	20.00
	c. 1983.	3.50	15.00
	d. 1987-90.	3.50	10.00
	s. Specimen.	—	6.00

1975 Commemorative Issue

#106, 15th Anniversary Nationalization of Banking

106 1 Peso | VF | UNC

1975. Olive on violet underprint. Portrait J. Martí at left, arms at right. Back: Ship dockside.

	VF	UNC
a. Issued note.	1.25	5.00
s. Specimen.	—	5.00

1983 Issue

107 3 Pesos

1983-89. Red on multicolor underprint. Portrait E. "Che" Guevara at center. Back: Red on orange underprint. "Che" cutting sugar cane at center.

	VF	UNC
a. 1983-86.	1.00	5.00
b. 1988-89.	1.00	2.00
s. 1983. Specimen with black overprint: *MUESTRA* once on each side.	—	20.00
s2. 1983. Specimen with black overprint: *MUESTRA* twice on each side.	—	10.00

1990; 1991 Issue

Replacement notes: #108-112: *EX, DX, CX, BX, AX* **series #, by denomination.**

108 5 Pesos

1991. Deep green and blue on multicolor underprint. A. Maceo at right. Back: Conference between A. Maceo and Spanish General A. Martínez Campos at Mangos de Baraguá in 187 Watermark: J. Marti.

	VF	UNC
a. Issued note.	.50	1.25
s. Specimen.	—	5.00

109 10 Pesos

1991. Deep brown and olive-green on multicolor underprint. M. Gómez at right. Back: "Guerra de todo el Pueblo" at left center. Watermark: J. Marti.

	VF	UNC
a. Issued note.	FV	2.50
s. Specimen.	—	5.00

110 20 Pesos

1991. Blue-black and purple on multicolor underprint. Camilio Cienfuegos at right. Back: Agricultural scenes at left center. Watermark: Celia Sánchez Manduley.

	VF	UNC
a. Issued note.	FV	5.00
s. Specimen.	—	5.00

111 50 Pesos

1990. Deep violet and dark green on multicolor underprint. Arms at center. C. García Iñiguez at right center. Back: Genetic Engineering and Biotechnology at left center. Watermark: Celia Sánchez Manduley.

	VF	UNC
a. Issued note.	FV	6.00
s. Specimen.	—	5.00

1995 Issue

112 1 Peso

	VF	UNC
1995. Dull olive-green and orange on light blue and multicolor underprint. J. Martí at left, arms at upper center right. Back: F. Castro with rebel soldiers entering Havana in 1959.	FV	.75

113 3 Pesos — VF | UNC

1995. Red-brown, purple and green on multicolor underprint. E. *Che* Guevara at left. Arms at upper center right. Back: Guevara cutting sugar cane. — FV | 1.50

1995 Dual Commemorative Issue

#114, 45th anniversary of central banking in Cuba and 100th of death of José Martí

114 1 Peso — VF | UNC

1995. Black and olive-green on green and brown underprint. J. Martí at left, arms and commemorative text at center right. Back: Horseback riders at center, commemorative text and dates at left. Specimen. — — | 200.

Banco Central de Cuba

1997-98 Issue

116 5 Pesos — VF | UNC

1997-. Green on multicolor underprint. A. Maceo at right. Back: Conference between A. Maceo and Spanish General A. Martínez Campos at Mangos de Baraguá in 187 Watermark: J. Marti.

	VF	UNC
a. 1997.	FV	1.25
b. 1998.	FV	1.25
c. 2000.	FV	1.25
d. 2001.	FV	1.25
e. 2002.	FV	1.25
f. 2003.	FV	1.25
g. 2004.	FV	1.25
h. 2005.	FV	1.25
i. 2006.	FV	1.25
j. 2009.	FV	1.25

117 10 Pesos — VF | UNC

1997-. Brown on multicolor underprint. M. Gómez at right. Back: *Guerra de todo el Pueblo* at left center. Watermark: J. Marti.

	VF	UNC
a. 1997.	FV	17.50
b. 1998.	FV	17.50
c. 2000.	FV	17.50
d. 2001.	FV	15.00
e. 2002.	FV	15.00
f. 2003.	FV	15.00
g. 2004.	FV	15.00
h. 2005.	FV	15.00
i. 2007.	FV	15.00
j. 2008.	FV	15.00
k. 2009.	FV	13.00
l. 2010.	FV	13.00
m. 2011.	FV	13.00

118 20 Pesos — VF | UNC

1998-2002. Blue-black and light blue on violet and blue underprint. C. Cienfuegos at right. Back: Agricultural scenes at left center. Watermark: Celia Sánchez Manduley.

	VF	UNC
a. 1998.	FV	5.00
b. 2000.	FV	5.00
c. 2001.	FV	5.00
d. 2002.	FV	5.00

119 50 Pesos — VF | UNC

1998; 1999; 2001. Light purple on green underprint. C. Garcia Iñiguez at right center. Back: Genetic Engineering and Biotechnology at left center. Watermark: Celia Sánchez Manduley. — FV | 6.00

2000 Commemorative Issue

#120, 50th anniversary of central banking in Cuba

120 100 Pesos — VF | UNC

2002. Reddish brown on yellow underprint. Carlos Manuel de Cespedes at right, commemorative symbol and text at left. Back: Martí and scene of Havana. Watermark: National heroine. — FV | 8.00

2001-02 Issue

121 1 Peso — VF | UNC

2001-. Black and olive green. J. Martí at right. Back: Fidel Castro and victory parade scene.

	VF	UNC
a. 2001. Series prefix in red.	FV	1.25
b. 2002. Series prefix in red.	FV	1.25
c. 2003. Series prefix in olive green.	FV	1.25
d. 2004. Series prefix in red.	FV	1.25
e. 2005. Series prefix in red.	FV	1.25
f. 2006. Series prefix in red.	FV	1.25
g. 2007. Series prefix in red.	FV	1.25
h. 2008. Series prefix in red.	FV	1.25
i. 2009. Series prefix in red.	FV	1.25

122 20 Pesos — VF | UNC

2004-. Blue-black and light blue on violet and blue underprint. C. Cienfuegos at right. Back: Agricultural scenes at left center. Watermark: Celia Sanchez Manduley

	VF	UNC
a. 2004.	FV	5.00
b. 2005.	FV	5.00
c. 2006.	FV	5.00
d. 2007.	FV	5.00
e. 2009.	FV	5.00
f. 2012.	FV	5.00

123 50 Pesos — VF | UNC

2002-. Light purple on green underprint. C. Garcia Iniguez at right center. Braile added to top right. Back: Genetic Engineering and Biotechnology buildign at left center. Watermark: Celia Canchez Manduley.

	VF	UNC
a. 2002.	FV	7.50
b. 2003.	FV	7.50
c. 2005.	FV	7.50
d. 2007.	FV	7.50
e. 2009.	FV	7.50
f. 2012.	FV	7.50
g. 2013.	FV	10.00

124 100 Pesos — VF | UNC

2001. Reddish brown on yellow underprint. Carlos Manuel de Cespedes at right, without commemorative overprint. Back: Martì and scene of Havana. Watermark: National heroine. — FV | 15.00

2003 First Commemorative Issue

150th Anniversary birth of Jose Martí.

125 1 Peso — VF | UNC

2003. José Martí at right. Back: Martí's birthplace. — FV | 1.50

2003 Second Commemorative Issue

#122A 50th Anniversary of the Moncada Assault.

126 20 Pesos

2003. Violet, blue and rose. Camilo Cienfuegos. — Unc | 8.00

2004 Commemorative Issue

127 3 Pesos — VF | UNC

2004. Brown on tan underprint. E. "Che" Guevara at right. Back: View of Guevara in sugar cane fields. — FV | 2.00

2004 Issue

128 1 Peso — VF | UNC

2004; 2005; 2007. Multicolor. José Martí at right. Back: Martí's birthplace.

	VF	UNC
a. 2004.	FV	1.50
b. 2005.	FV	1.50
c. 2007.	FV	1.50

129 **100 Pesos** — VF | UNC
2004. Multicolor. Carlos Manuel de Cespedes at right. Braile at upper right.
Back: Martí and scene of Havana. 150x70mm.
a. 2004. — FV | 20.00
b. 2005. — FV | 20.00

Collector Series

Banco Nacional de Cuba

1961-1995 Issues

The Banco Nacional de Cuba had been selling specimen notes regularly of the 1961-1989 issues. Specimen notes dated 1961-66 have normal block # and serial # while notes from 1967 to date all have normal block # and all zero serial #.

No.	Description	Mkt. Value
CS1	**1961 1-100 Pesos** Overprint: *SPECIMEN* on #94a-97a, 98, 99.	110.
CS2	**1964 1-20 Pesos** Overprint: *SPECIMEN* on #94b-97b.	20.00
CS3	**1965 1-20 Pesos** Overprint: *SPECIMEN* on #94c-97c.	14.00
CS4	**1966 1, 10 Pesos** Overprint: *SPECIMEN* on #100, 101.	7.00
CS5	**1967 1-10 Pesos** Overprint: *SPECIMEN* on #102a-104a.	10.00
CS6	**1968 1-10 Pesos** Overprint: *SPECIMEN* on #102a-104a.	10.00
CS7	**1969 1, 10 Pesos** Overprint: *SPECIMEN* on #102a, 104a.	7.00
CS8	**1970 1-10 Pesos** Overprint: *SPECIMEN* on #102a, 103b, 104a.	7.00
CS9	**1971 10, 20 Pesos** Overprint: *SPECIMEN* on #104a, 105a.	8.00
CS10	**1972 1, 5 Pesos** Overprint: *SPECIMEN* on #102a, 103b.	7.00
CS11	**1975 1 Peso** Overprint: *SPECIMEN* on #106.	10.00
CS12	**1978 1, 10, 20 Pesos** Overprint: *ESPECIMEN* on #102b, 104b, 105b.	11.00
CS13	**1979 1 Peso** Overprint: *ESPECIMEN* on #102b.	3.00
CS14	**1980 1 Peso** Overprint: *ESPECIMEN* on #102b.	3.00
CS15	**1981 1 Peso** Overprint: *ESPECIMEN* on #102b.	3.00
CS16	**1982 1 Peso** Overprint: *MUESTRA* on #102b.	3.00
CS17	**1983 3, 10, 20 Pesos** Overprint: *MUESTRA* on #104c, 105c, 107a.	12.00
CS18	**1984 3, 5, 10 Pesos** Overprint: *MUESTRA* on #103c, 104c, 107a.	12.00
CS19	**1985 1, 3, 5 Pesos** Overprint: overprint: *MUESTRA* on #102b, 103c, 107a.	12.00
CS20	**1986 1-10 Pesos** Overprint: *MUESTRA* on #102b, 103c, 104c, 107a.	12.50
CS21	**1987 5, 10, 20 Pesos** Overprint: *MUESTRA* on #103c-105c.	12.00
CS22	**1988 1-20 Pesos** Overprint: *MUESTRA* on #102c, 103d-105d, 107b.	12.50
CS23	**1989 3, 20 Pesos** Overprint: *MUESTRA* on #105d, 107b.	7.00
CS24	**1990 5, 20, 50 Pesos** Overprint: *SPECIMEN* on #103d, 105d, 111.	10.00
CS25	**1991 5, 10, 20 Pesos** Overprint: *SPECIMEN* on #108-110.	10.00
CS26	**1994 1-100 Peso Convertibles** Overprint: *MUESTRA* on FX37-FX43.	60.00
CS27	**1995 1, 3 Pesos** Overprint: *MUESTRA* on #112 and 113.	5.00

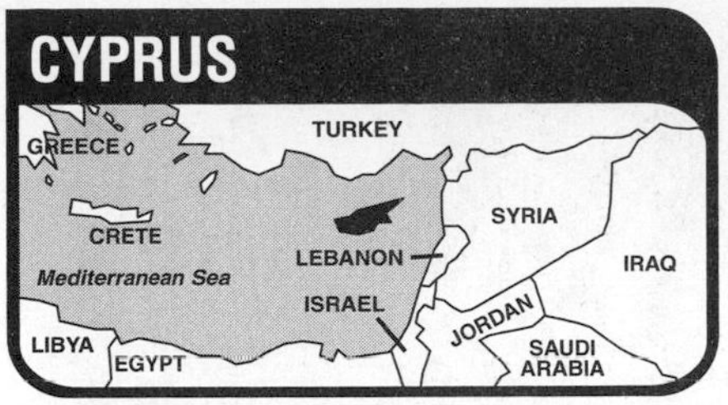

The Republic of Cyprus lies in the eastern Mediterranean Sea 71 km. south of Turkey and 97 km. west of Syria. It is the third largest island in the Mediterranean Sea, having an area of 9,250 sq. km. and a population of 792,600. Capital: Nicosia. Agriculture and mining are the chief industries. Asbestos, copper, citrus fruit, iron pyrites and potatoes are exported.

A former British colony, Cyprus became independent in 1960 following years of resistance to British rule. Tensions between the Greek Cypriot majority and Turkish Cypriot minority came to a head in December 1963, when violence broke out in the capital of Nicosia. Despite the deployment of UN peacekeepers in 1964, sporadic intercommunal violence continued forcing most Turkish Cypriots into enclaves throughout the island. In 1974, a Greek Government-sponsored attempt to seize control of Cyprus was met by military intervention from Turkey, which soon controlled more than a third of the island. In 1983, the Turkish-held area declared itself the "Turkish Republic of Northern Cyprus" (TRNC), but it is recognized only by Turkey. The latest two-year round of UN-brokered talks - between the leaders of the Greek Cypriot and Turkish Cypriot communities to reach an agreement to reunite the divided island - ended when the Greek Cypriots rejected the UN settlement plan in an April 2004 referendum. The entire island entered the EU on 1 May 2004, although the EU acquis - the body of common rights and obligations - applies only to the areas under direct government control, and is suspended in the areas administered by Turkish Cypriots. However, individual Turkish Cypriots able to document their eligibility for Republic of Cyprus citizenship legally enjoy the same rights accorded to other citizens of European Union states. The election of a new Cypriot president in 2008 served as the impetus for the UN to encourage both the Turkish and Cypriot Governments to reopen unification negotiations.

RULERS:
British to 1960

MONETARY SYSTEM:
1 Shilling = 9 Piastres
1 Pound = 20 Shillings to 1963
1 Shilling = 50 Mils
1 Pound = 1000 Mils, 1963-83
1 Pound = 100 Cents, 1983-2007.
1 Euro = 100 cents, 2008 -

Democratic Republic

ΚΥΠΡΙΑΚΗ ΔΗΜΟΚΡΑΤΙΑ

Kibris Cumhuriyeti

Republic of Cyprus

1961 Issue

37 **250 Mils** — VF | UNC
1.12.1961. Blue on multicolor underprint. Fruit at left, arms at right, map at lower right. Back: Mine. Watermark: Eagle's head. Printer: BWC (without imprint).
a. Issued note. — 40.00 | 225.
s. Specimen. — — | 170.

38 **500 Mils**
1.12.1961. Green on multicolor underprint. Arms at right, map at lower right. Back: Mountain road lined with trees. Watermark: Eagle's head. Printer: BWC (without imprint).
a. Issued note. — 95.00 | 440.
s. Specimen. — — | 180.

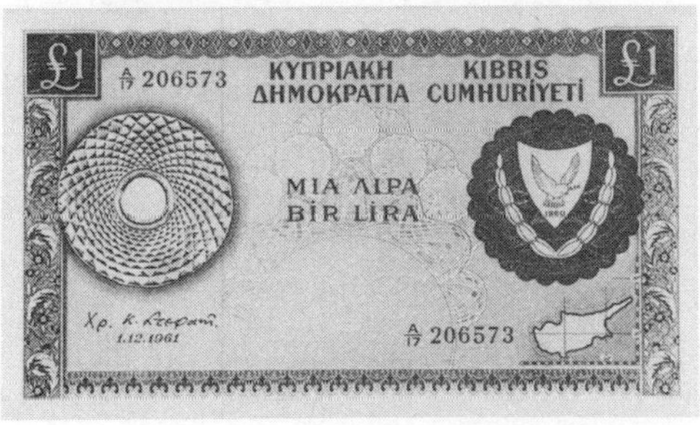

39 **1 Pound**

1.12.1961. Brown on multicolor underprint. Arms at right, map at lower right. Back: Viaduct and pillars. Watermark: Eagle's head. Printer: BWC (without imprint).

	VF	UNC
a. Issued note.	60.00	260.
s. Specimen.	—	190.

40 **5 Pounds**

1.12.1961. Dark green on multicolor underprint. Arms at right, map at lower right. Back: Embroidery and floral design. Watermark: Eagle's head. Printer: BWC (without imprint).

	VF	UNC
a. Issued note.	100.	525.
s. Specimen.	—	195.

ΚΕΝΤΡΙΚΗ ΤΡΑΠΕΖΑ ΤΗΣ ΚΥΠΡΟΥ

Kibris Merkez Bankasi

Central Bank of Cyprus

1964-66 Issue

41 **250 Mils**

1964-82. Blue on multicolor underprint. Fruit at left, arms at right, map at lower right. Signature varieties. Back: Mine. Watermark: Eagle's head. Printer: BWC (without imprint).

	VF	UNC
a. 1.12.1964-1.12.1969; 1.9.1971.	35.00	160.
b. 1.3.1971; 1.6.1972; 1.5.1973; 1.6.1974.	27.50	130.
c. 1.7.1975-1.6.1982.	20.00	115.
s. Specimen. Punch hole cancelled.	—	250.
ct. Color trial. Brown on multicolor underprint.	—	370.

42 **500 Mils**

1964-79. Green on multicolor underprint. Arms at right, map at lower right. Signature varieties. Back: Mountain road lined with trees. Watermark: Eagle's head. Printer: BWC (without imprint).

	VF	UNC
a. 1.12.1964-1.6.1972.	45.00	215.
b. 1.5.1973; 1.6.1974; 1.7.1975; 1.8.1976.	35.00	180.
c. 1.6.1979; 1.9.1979.	30.00	150.
s. Specimen. Punch hole cancelled.	—	250.

43 **1 Pound**

1966-78. Brown on multicolor underprint. Arms at right, map at lower right. Signature varieties. Back: Viaduct and pillars. Watermark: Eagle's head. Printer: BWC (without imprint).

	VF	UNC
a. 1.8.1966-1.6.1972.	60.00	300.
b. 1.11.1972; 1.5.1973; 1.6.1974; 1.7.1975.	37.50	165.
c. 1.8.1976; 1.5.1978.	30.00	150.
s. Specimen. Punch hole cancelled.	—	260.

44 **5 Pounds**

1966-76. Blue on multicolor underprint. Arms at right, map at lower right. Signature varieties. Back: Embroidery and floral design. Watermark: Eagle's head. Printer: BCW (without imprint).

	VF	UNC
a. 1.8.1966; 1.9.1967; 1.12.1969.	80.00	350.
b. 1.6.1972; 1.11.1972; 1.5.1973.	55.00	255.
c. 1.6.1974; 1.7.1975; 1.8.1976.	50.00	230.

1977-82 Issue

45 **500 Mils**

1.6.1982. Light brown on green and multicolor underprint. Woman seated at right, arms at top left center. Back: Yermasoyia Dam. Watermark: Moufflon (ram's) head. Printer: BWC (without imprint).

	VF	UNC
a. Issued note.	27.50	130.
s. Specimen. Punch hole cancelled.	—	215.

46 1 Pound — VF | UNC

1.6.1979. Dark brown and brown on multicolor underprint. Mosaic of nymph Acme at right, arms at top left center. Back: Bellapais Abbey. Watermark: Moufflon (ram's) head. Printer: TDLR (without imprint). — 17.50 | 75.00

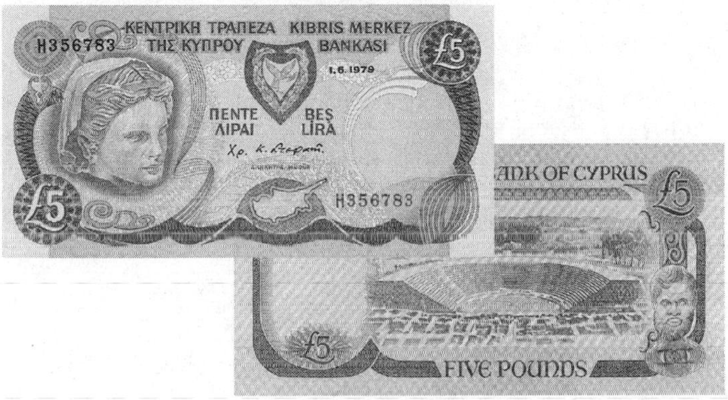

47 5 Pounds — VF | UNC

1.6.1979. Violet on multicolor underprint. Limestone head from Hellenistic period at left, arms at upper center right. Back: Ancient Theater at Salamis. Watermark: Moufflon (ram's) head. Printer: TDLR (without imprint). — 42.50 | 175.

48 10 Pounds — VF | UNC

1977-85. Dark green and blue-black on multicolor underprint. Archaic bust at left, arms at right. Back: Two Cyprus warblers. Watermark: Moufflon (ram's) head. Printer: BWC (without imprint).

		VF	UNC
a.	1.4.1977; 1.5.1978; 1.6.1979.	70.00	300.
b.	1.7.1980; 1.10.1981; 1.6.1982; 1.9.1983; 1.6.1985.	65.00	275.
s.	As a. Specimen.	—	240.

1982-87 Issue

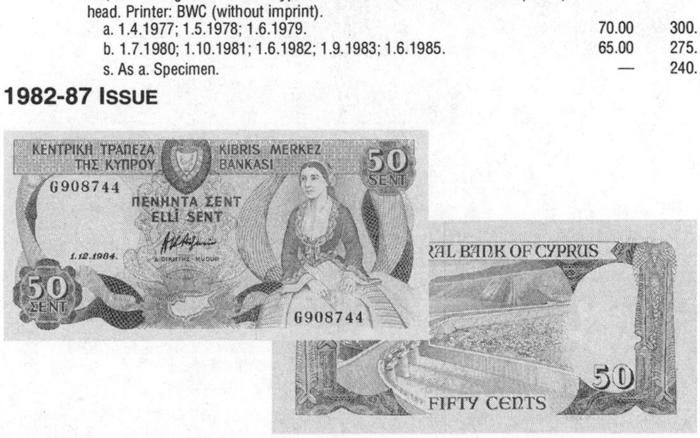

49 50 Cents — VF | UNC

1.10.1983; 1.12.1984. Brown and multicolor. Woman seated at right, arms at top left center. Back: Yermasoyia Dam. Watermark: Moufflon (ram's) head. Printer: BWC (without imprint).

		VF	UNC
a.	Issued note.	9.00	40.00
s.	Specimen.	—	205.

50 1 Pound — VF | UNC

1.2.1982; 1.11.1982; 1.3.1984; 1.11.1985. Dark brown and multicolor. Mosaic of nymph Acme at right, arms at top left center, bank name in outlined (white) letters by dark underprint. Back: Bellapais Abbey. Watermark: Moufflon (ram's) head. Printer: TDLR (without imprint). — 13.50 | 65.00

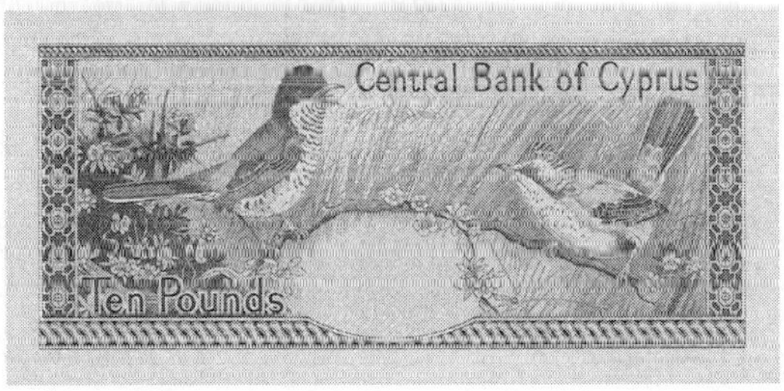

51 10 Pounds — VF | UNC

1.4.1987; 1.10.1988. Dark green and blue-black on multicolor underprint. Archaic bust at left, date above at left of modified arms on right. Back: Two Cyprus warblers. Watermark: Moufflon (ram's) head. Printer: TDLR (without imprint). — 60.00 | 260.

1987-92 Issue

52 50 Cents — VF | UNC

1.4.1987; 1.10.1988; 1.11.1989. Brown and multicolor. Woman seated at right, arms at top left center, bank name in micro-printing alternately in Greek and Turkish just below upper frame. Back: Yermasoyia Dam. Watermark: Moufflon (ram's) head. Printer: BABN (without imprint). — 7.00 | 30.00

53 **1 Pound** — VF — UNC

1987-96. Dark brown and multicolor. Mosaic of nymph Acme at right, arms at top left center, bank name in unbroken line of micro-printing with Greek at left and Turkish at right just below upper frame. Back: Bellapais Abbey. Watermark: Moufflon (ram's) head. Printer: TDLR (without imprint).

	VF	UNC
a. Without light beige underprint color on back. Micro-print line under dark bar at top. Printer: TDLR (Without imprint). 1.4.1987; 1.10.1988; 1.11.1989.	FV	65.00
b. Light beige color added to center underprint on back for security. Printer: F-CO (without imprint). 1.11.1989; 1.2.1992.	FV	40.00
c. Dot added near upper left corner. 1.3.1993; 1.3.1994.	FV	37.50
d. 1.9.1995.	FV	32.50
e. 1.10.1996.	10.00	50.00

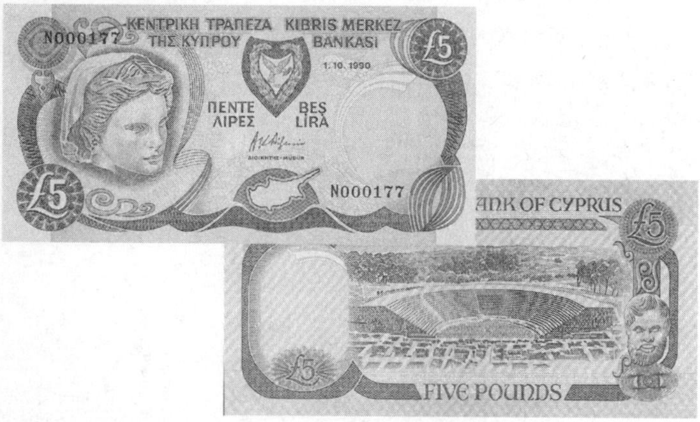

54 **5 Pounds** — VF — UNC

1990; 1995. Violet on multicolor underprint. Limestone head from Hellenistic period at left, arms at upper center right, line of micro-printing added within bank titles. Back: Ancient Theater at Salamis. Watermark: Moufflon (ram's) head. Printer: TDLR (without imprint).

	VF	UNC
a. 1.10.1990.	FV	160.
b. 1.9.1995.	FV	140.

55 **10 Pounds** — VF — UNC

1989-95. Dark green and blue-black on multicolor underprint. Archaic bust at left, arms at right, enhanced security features and micro-printing. Back: Two Cyprus warblers. Watermark: Moufflon (ram's) head. Printer: TDLR (without imprint).

	VF	UNC
a. 1.11.1989; 1.10.1990.	FV	260.
b. 1.2.1992.	FV	225.
c. 1.6.1994.	FV	210.
d. 1.9.1995.	FV	195.

56 **20 Pounds** — VF — UNC

1992; 1993. Deep blue on multicolor underprint. Bust of Aphrodite at left, arms at upper center, ancient bird (pottery art) at right. Enhanced designs with micro-printing. Back: Kyrenia boat at center, ancient pottery jugs at lower right. Watermark: Moufflon (ram's) head. Printer: TDLR (without imprint).

	VF	UNC
a. Error: No dot over 'i' in *YIRMI LIRA*. 1.2.1992.	95.00	390.
b. Corrected: *YiRMi LiRA*. 1.3.1993.	80.00	295.

1997 First Issue

57 **1 Pound** — VF — UNC

1.2.1997. Brown on pink and multicolor underprint. Cypriot girl at left, arms at upper center. Thin security thread. Back: Handcrafts and Kato Drys village scene in background. Watermark: Bust of Aphrodite. Printer: F-CO (without imprint). — FV — 32.50

58 **5 Pounds** — VF — UNC

1.2.1997. Purple and violet on multicolor underprint. Archaic limestone head of young man at left, arms at upper center. Thin security thread. Back: Peristerona church and Turkish mosque. Watermark: Bust of Aphrodite. Printer: F-CO (without imprint). — FV — 80.00

59	**10 Pounds**	VF	UNC
	1.2.1997. Olive-green and blue-green on multicolor underprint. Marble head of Artemis at left, arms at upper center. Thin security thread. Back: Ruppell's warbler green turtle, butterfly, moufflon, tulip and cyclamen plants. Watermark: Bust of Aphrodite. Printer: F-CO (without imprint).	FV	140.

1997-2001 Issue

60	**1 Pound**	VF	UNC
	1.10.1997; 1.12.1998; 1.2.2001; 1.4.2004. Brown on light tan and multicolor underprint. Cypriot girl at left, arms at upper center with slightly modified colors. Back: Handcrafts and Kato Drys village scene in background. Watermark: Bust of Aphrodite. Printer: F-CO (without imprint). Wide security foil.		
	a. 1.10.1997.	FV	27.50
	b. 1.12.1998.	FV	23.00
	c. 1.2.2001.	FV	21.00
	d. 1.4.2004. Signature: Chr. Christodoulou.	FV	12.50

61	**5 Pounds**	VF	UNC
	1.2.2001; 1.9.2003. Purple and violet on multicolor underprint. Archaic limestone head of young man at left, arms at upper center. Back: Peristerona church and Turkish mosque. Watermark: Bust of Aphrodite. Wide security foil.		
	a. 1.2.2001. Printer: F-CO (without imprint).	FV	75.00
	b. 1.9.2003. Printer: TDLR (without imprint). Signature: Chr. Christodoulou.	FV	50.00

62	**10 Pounds**	VF	UNC
	1.10.1997; 1.12.1998; 1.2.2001; 1.9.2003. Olive-green and blue-green on multicolor underprint. Marble head of Artemis at left, arms at upper center. Back: Ruppell's warbler green turtle, butterfly, moufflon, tulip and cyclamen plants Watermark: Bust of Aphrodite. Wide security foil.		
	a. 1.10.1997. Printer: F-CO (without imprint).	FV	155.
	b. 1.12.1998. Printer: F-CO (without imprint).	FV	145.
	c. 1.2.2001. Printer: F-CO (without imprint).	FV	135.
	d. 1.9.2003. Printer: TDLR (without imprint). Signature: Chr. Christodoulou.	FV	100.
	e. 1.4.2005.	FV	85.00

63	**20 Pounds**	VF	UNC
	1.10.1997; 1.10.2001; 1.4.2004. Deep blue on multicolor underprint. Bust of Aphrodite at left, arms at upper center, ancient bird (pottery art) at right. Enhanced designs with micro-printing. Corrected: *YiRMi LiRA*. Back: Kyrenia boat at center, ancient pottery jugs at lower right. Watermark: Bust of Aphrodite. Printer: TDLR (without imprint). Wide security foil.		
	a. 1.10.1997.	FV	255.
	b. 1.10.2001.	FV	235.
	c. 1.4.2004. Signature: Chr. Christodoulou.	FV	150.

The Czech Republic is bordered to the west by Germany, to the north by Poland, to the east by Slovakia and to the south by Austria. It consists of 3 major regions: Bohemia, Moravia and Silesia. It has an area of 78,866 sq. km. and a population of 10.22 million. Capital: Prague (Praha). Industrial production in cities and agriculture and livestock in the rural areas are chief occupations while coal deposits are the main mineral resources.

Following the First World War, the closely related Czechs and Slovaks of the former Austro-Hungarian Empire merged to form Czechoslovakia. During the interwar years, the new country's leaders were frequently preoccupied with meeting the demands of other ethnic minorities within the republic, most notably the Sudeten Germans and the Ruthenians (Ukrainians). After World War II, a truncated Czechoslovakia fell within the Soviet sphere of influence. In 1968, an invasion by Warsaw Pact troops ended the efforts of the country's leaders to liberalize Communist party rule and create "socialism with a human face." Anti-Soviet demonstrations the following year ushered in a period of harsh repression. With the collapse of Soviet authority in 1989, Czechoslovakia regained its freedom through a peaceful "Velvet Revolution." On 1 January 1993, the country underwent a "velvet divorce" into its two national components, the Czech Republic and Slovakia. The Czech Republic joined NATO in 1999 and the European Union in 2004.

MONETARY SYSTEM:

1 Czechoslovak Koruna (Kcs) = 100 Haleru Jan. - Feb. 1993
1 Czech Koruna (Kc) = 100 Haleru since Feb. 1993

REPUBLIC

CESKÁ NÁRODNÍ BANKA

CZECH NATIONAL BANK

1993 ND PROVISIONAL ISSUE

#1-3 were released 8.2.1993 having adhesive revalidation stamps affixed (later a printed *1000* was also circulated). Valid until 31.8.1993 but could be exchanged in deposits until 31.5.1994. Old Czechoslovak notes of 100 Korun and higher denominations became obsolete on 7.2.1993. Smaller denominations remained in circulation until 30.11.1993.

Note: In 1997 the CNB made available uncirculated examples of #1-3a and 3b to collectors. The notes are without cancellation marks and have regular serial #.

1 **100 Korun** — VF / UNC
ND (1993-old date 1961). Dark green. *C-100* adhesive stamp affixed to Czechoslovakia #91a or 91b. .

	VF	UNC
a. Stamp on Czechoslovakia #91a.	50.00	100.
b. Stamp on Czechslovakia #91b.	12.50	30.00
c. Stamp on Czechslovakia #91c.	5.00	27.50

2 **500 Korun**

	VF	UNC
ND (1993-old date 1973). Dark green. *D-500* adhesive stamp affixed to Czechoslovakia #93. Series prefixes: U, W, Z.	15.00	50.00

3 **1000 Korun**
ND (1993-old date 1985). Deep green. *M-1000* revalidation stamp on Czechoslovakia #98.

	VF	UNC
a. Adhesive stamp affixed. Series prefixes: C, U.	40.00	155.
b. Stamp image printed. Series prefix: U.	40.00	155.

1993 REGULAR ISSUE

#4-7 replacement notes: Serial # prefix *Z*.

4 **50 Korun**
1993. Violet and black on pink and gray underprint. St. Agnes of Bohemia at right with crown, arms at center right. Serial number prefix *A*. Back: Large A within gothic window frame at left center. Watermark: St. Agnes of Bohemia with crown. Printer: TDLR. 134x64mm.

	VF	UNC
a. Issued note.	4.00	14.00
r. Serial # prefix *Z*, replacement.	50.00	150.

5 **100 Korun**
1993. Blue-green, green and blue-black on lilac and multicolor underprint. King Karel IV at right, arms at center right. Serial number prefix *A*. Back: Large seal of Charles University at left center. Watermark: King Karel IV. Printer: TDLR. 140x69mm.

	VF	UNC
a. Issued note.	11.00	35.00
r. Serial # prefix *Z*, replacement.	35.00	80.00

		VF	UNC
6	**200 Korun** 1993. Deep brown on light orange and light green underprint. Jan Ámos Komensky at right, arms at center right. Serial number prefix *A*. Back: Hands outreached at left center. Watermark: Jan Ámos Komensky. Printer: STC-P. 146x69mm.		
	a. Security filament with *200 KCS*.	18.00	65.00
	b. Security filament with *200 KC*.	16.00	27.50
	x. Error. Security filament reads: *REPUBLIQUE DU ZAÏRE*.	2000.	3500.

		VF	UNC
7	**500 Korun** 1993. Dark brown, brown & brown-violet on pink and tan underprint. Rose in underprint at upper center, Bozena Nemcová at right, arms at center right. Serial number prefix *A*. Back: Laureate young woman's head at left center. Watermark: Bozena Nemcová. Printer: TDLR. 152x69mm.		
	a. Issued note.	38.00	52.50
	r. Serial # prefix *Z*, replacement.	60.00	150.
	s. Specimen.	—	—

		VF	UNC
8	**1000 Korun** 1993. Purple and lilac on multicolor underprint. Frantisek Palacky, arms at center right. Serial number prefix *A*; *B*. Back: Eagle and Kromeriz Castle. Watermark: Frantisek Palacky. Printer: STC-P. 158x74mm.		
	a. Issued ntoe.	70.00	100.
	s. Specimen.	—	—

		VF	UNC
9	**5000 Korun** 1993. Black, blue-gray and violet on pink and light gray underprint. President Tomas Garrigue Masaryk at right, arms at center right. Serial number prefix *A*. Back: Montage of Prague Gothic and Baroque buildings. Printer: STC-P. 170x74mm.	350.	450.

1994-96 Issue

		VF	UNC
10	**20 Korun** 1994. Blue-black and gray on light blue underprint. King Premysl Otakar I at right. Back: Crown with seal above at center, stylized crown at lower right. Watermark: King Premysl Otakar I. Printer: STC-P. 128x64mm.		
	a. Serial # prefix *A*; *B*. Security filament at center (74mm from left edge). (1994).	FV	6.00
	b. Serial # prefix *B*. Security filament at left center (50mm from left edge). (1995).	FV	3.50

		VF	UNC
11	**50 Korun** 1994. Violet and black on multicolor underprint. St. Agnes of Bohemia with crown at right , arms at center right, without gray in underprint. Serial number prefix *B*. Back: Stylized heart at lower right. Watermark: St. Agnes of Bohemia. Printer: STC-P. 134x64mm.	FV	7.50

		VF	UNC
12	**100 Korun** 1995. Blue-green, green and blue-black on lilac and multicolor underprint. King Karel IV at right. Serial number prefix *B*. Back: Large seal of Charles University at left center with stylized *K* in circle at lower right. Watermark: King Karel IV. Printer: STC-P. 140x69mm.	FV	14.00

13 **200 Korun** | VF FV | UNC 18.00

1996. Deep brown on pale orange and light green underprint. Jan Ámos Komensky at right. Serial number prefix *B*. Back: Hands outreached at left center, stylized open book at lower right. Watermark: Jan Ámos Komensky. Printer: STC-P.

14 **500 Korun** | VF FV | UNC 42.50

1995. Dark brown, brown and brown-violet on pink and tan underprint. Bozena Nemcová at right, arms at center right. Serial number prefix *B*. Back: Laureate young woman's head at left center, stylized rose at lower right. Watermark: Bozena Nemcová. Printer: STC-P. 152x69mm.

15 **1000 Korun** | VF FV | UNC 110.

1996. Purple and lilac on multicolor underprint. Frantisek Palacky with metallic linden leaf at upper center. Serial number prefix *C, D, E, F*. Back: Eagle and Kromeriz Castle, stylized *P* and tree at lower right. Watermark: Frantisek Palacky. Printer: STC-P. 158x74mm.

16 **2000 Korun** | VF FV | UNC 220.

1996. Dark olive-green, gray and violet on tan underprint. Ema Destinová at right, lyre at at upper left in spray. Serial number prefix *A*. Back: Muse of music and lyric poetry Euterpe at left center, violin and cello and a large *D*, stylized lyre at lower right. Printer: STC-P. 164x74mm.

1997-99 Issue

17 **50 Korun** | VF FV | UNC 5.50

1997. Violet and purple on multicolor underprint. St. Agnes of Bohemia with crown at right , arms at center right, without gray in underprint. Serial number prefix *C, D, E*. Back: Stylized heart at lower right. Watermark: St. Agnes of Bohemia. Printer: STC-P. 134x64mm.

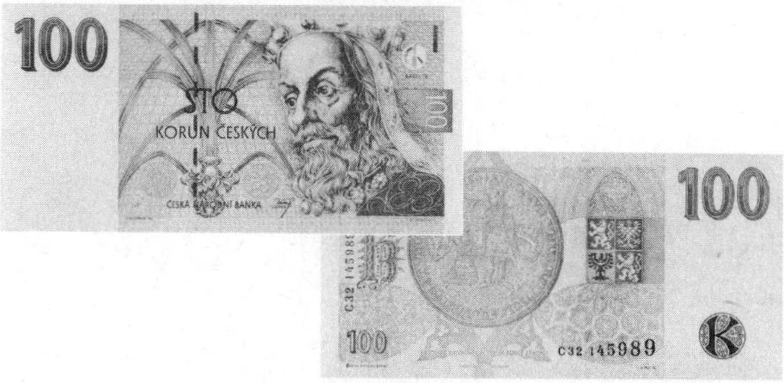

18 **100 Korun** | VF FV | UNC 10.00

1997. Dark green, dark olive-green and black on multicolor underprint. King Karel IV at right. Serial number prefix *C, D, E, F*. Back: Large seal of Charles University at left center with stylized *K* in circle at lower right. Watermark: King Karel IV. Printer: STC-P. 140x69mm.

19 **200 Korun** | VF FV | UNC 20.00

1998. Deep brown on pale orange and light green underprint. Jan Ámos Komensky at right, arms at center right. Stylized open book at lower right. Serial number prefix *C, D, E*. Back: Hands outreached at left center, stylized open book at lower right. Watermark: Jan Ámos Komensky. Printer: STC-P. Fibers added in the paper. 146x69mm.

20 **500 Korun** | VF FV | UNC 42.50

1997. Dark brown, brown and brown-violet on pink and tan underprint. Bozena Nemcová at right, arms at center right. Serial number prefix *C, D*. Back: Laureate young woman's head at left center, stylized rose at lower right. Watermark: Bozena Nemcová. Printer: STC-P. Fibers added in the paper. 152x69mm.

22 2000 Korun VF UNC

1999. Dark olive-green and violet on tan underprint. Ema Destinová at right, lyre at upper left in spray. Three metallic vertical bars in lyre at top center. Serial number prefix *B*. Back: Muse of music and lyric poetry Euterpe at left center, violin, cello, large D, stylized lyre at lower right. Printer: STC-P. Fibers added in the paper. 164x74mm. FV 200.

23 5000 Korun VF UNC

1999. Black, blue-gray and violet on pink and light gray underprint. President Tomas Garrigue Masaryk at right. Metallic hexagon emblem at top center. Serial number prefix *B*. Back: Montage of Prague Gothic and Baroque buildings. Linden leaf in watermark area. Fibers added in the paper. 170x74mm. FV 425.

2007-09 Issue

24 500 Korun VF UNC

2009. Dark brown, brown and brown-violet on pink and tan. Bozena Nemcová at right. Back: Laureate young woman's head at center. Watermark: Bozena Nemcová. Printer: STC-P 152x69mm. FV 40.00

25 1000 Korun VF UNC

2008. Purple and lilac on multicolor underprint. Frantisek Palacky at right. Series G. Wide security thread. Back: Eagle and Kromeriz Castle. Printer: STC-P. 157x74mm.

	VF	UNC
a. 2008.	FV	80.00

26 2000 Korun VF UNC

2007. Dark olive-green and violet on tan underprint. Ema Destinová at right, lyre at upper left in spray. Three metallic vertical bars in lyre at top center. Serial number prefix *C*. Back: Muse of music and lyric poetry Euterpe at left center, violin, cello, large D, stylized lyre at lower right. Printer: STC-P 164x74mm. FV 160.

27 5000 Korun VF UNC

2009. Black, blue-gray and violet on pink and light gray underprint. President Tomas Garrigue Masaryk at right. Back: MOntage of Prague Gothic and Baroque architecture. Printer: STC-P. 170x74mm. FV 425.

The Republic of Czechoslovakia, located in central Europe, had an area of 49,365 sq. mi. (127,859 sq. km.). Capital: Prague (Praha). Industrial production in the cities and agriculture and livestock in the rural areas were the chief occupations.

The Czech lands to the west were united with the Slovak to form the Czechoslovak Republic on October 28, 1918 upon the dissolution of the Austrian-Hungarian Empire. Tomas G. Masaryk was the first president. In the 1930s Hitlet provoked Czechoslovakia's German minority in the Sudetenland to agitate for autonomy. The territory was broken up for the benefit of Germany, Poland and Hungary by the Munich agreement signed by the United Kingdom, France, Germany and Italy on September 29, 1938. On March 15, 1939, Germany invaded Czechoslovakia and incorporated the Czech lands into the Third Reich as the "Protectorate of Bohemia and Moravia." eastern Slovakia, was constituted as a republic under Nazi infulence. A government-in-exile was set up in London in 1940. The Soviet and American forces liberated the area by May 1945. After World War II the physical integrity and independence of Czechoslovakia was re-established, while bringing it within the Russian sphere of influence. On February 23-25, 1948, the Communists seized control of the government in a *coup d'etat,* and adopted a constitution making the country a "people's republic." A new constitution adopted June 11, 1960, converted the country into a "socialist republic." Communist infulence increased steadily while pressure for liberalization culminated in the overthrow of the Stalinist leader Antonçin Novotny and his associates in January, 1968. The Communist Party then introduced far reaching reforms which received warnings from Moscow, followed by occupation of Warsaw Pact forces on August 21, 1968 resulting in stationing of Soviet troops. Student demonstrations for reform began in Prague on November 17, 1989. The Federal Assembly abolished the Communist Party's sole right to govern. In December, 1989, communism was overthrown. In January, 1990 the Czech and Slovak Federal Republic (CSFR) was formed. The movement for a democratic Slovakia was apparent in the June 1992 elections with the Slovak National Council adopting a declaration of sovereignty. The CSFR was disolved on December 31, 1992, and both new republics came into being on January 1, 1993.

See the Czech Republic and Slovakia sections for additional listings.

MONETARY SYSTEM:

1 Koruna = 100 Haleru

SPECIMEN NOTES:

Large quantities of specimens were made available to collectors. Notes issued after 1945 are distinguished by a perforation consisting of three small holes or a letter S (for Solvakia). Since the difference in value between issued notes and specimen notes is frequently very great, both types of notes are valued. Earlier issues recalled from circulation were perforated: *SPECIMEN* or *NEPLATNE* or with a letter *S* for collectors. Caution should be exercised while examining notes as examples of perforated notes having the holes filled in are known.

NOTE AVAILABILITY:

The Czech National Bank in 1997 made available to collectors uncirculated examples of #78-98, as a full set or in issue groups. As the notes were demonetized they had no cancellation holes nor were overprinted. These notes have regular serial #'s and thus can not be distinguished from regular uncirculated notes of the period.

Socialist Republic

Ceskoslovenská Socialistická Republika

Czechoslovak Socialist Republic

1961 Issue

		VF	UNC
81	**3 Koruny** 1961. Blue on blue-green underprint. Large three at center and upper corners. Back: Socialist arms at center. Watermark: Star in circle, repeated. Printer: STC-P. 113x56mm.		
	a. Issued note. Serial # prefix 2.5mm in height.	1.00	3.00
	b. Issued note. Serial # prefix 3mm in height.	1.00	3.00
	s. Perforated with 3 holes or *SPECIMEN.*	.50	3.00

		VF	UNC
82	**5 Korun** 1961. Dull black on pale green underprint. Text in frame. Back: Socialist arms at center. Watermark: Star in circle, repeated. Printer: STC-P. 123x60mm.		
	a. Issued note. Serial # prefix 2.5mm in height.	1.00	3.00
	b. Issued note. Serial # prefix 3mm in height.	1.00	3.00
	s. Perforated with 3 holes or *SPECIMEN.*	.50	3.00

Státní Banka Ceskoslovenská

Czechoslovak State Bank

1960-64 Issue

		VF	UNC
88	**10 Korun** 1960. Brown on multicolor underprint. Two girls with flowers at right. Back: Orava Dam. Watermark: Star and linden leaf. Printer: STC-Prague. 133x65mm.		
	a. Series prefix: H; F (wet photogravure printing). (Smaller image area).	20.00	50.00
	b. Series prefixes: E, J, L, M, S, X (dry photogravure printing).	1.50	6.00
	s. Specimen.	—	3.00

		VF	UNC
89	**25 Korun** 1961 (1962). Blue-black on light blue underprint. Arms at left center. Portrait Jan Zizka at right. Back: Tábor town square. Printer: STC-Prague. 138x70mm.		
	a. Series prefix: E. (wet printing).	50.00	200.
	b. Series prefix: Q. (dry printing)	5.00	20.00
	s. Perforated: *SPECIMEN.*	—	2.00

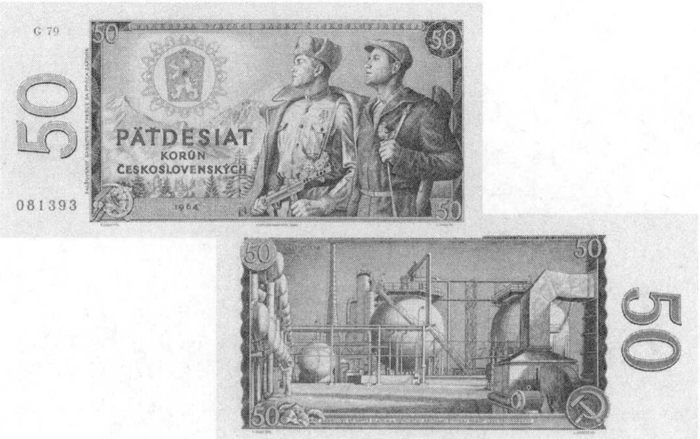

		VF	UNC
90	**50 Korun** 1964 (1965). Red-brown. Arms at left, Russian soldier and partisan at right. Back: Slovnaft refinery in Bratislava. Printer: STC-Prague. 150x74mm.		
	a. Series prefix: K. (wet printing).	100.	500.
	b. Series prefix: A; N; G; J (dry printing).	5.00	15.00

91 **100 Korun** — VF — UNC

1961. Deep green on multicolor underprint. Factory at lower left, farm couple at right. Back: Charles Bridge and Hradcany in Prague. Watermark: Star and linden leaf. Printer: STC-Prague. 164x80mm.

	VF	UNC
a. Watermark: Star within linden leaf, repeated. Series prefix: B01-40; C; D (wet printing).	30.00	60.00
b. As a. Series prefix: B41-99; P; R; T; Z; X01-24 (dry printing).	10.00	20.00
c. Reissue watermark: Multiple stars and linden leaves. Series prefix: X25-96; G; M. (1990-92).	5.00	10.00

1970; 1973 Issue

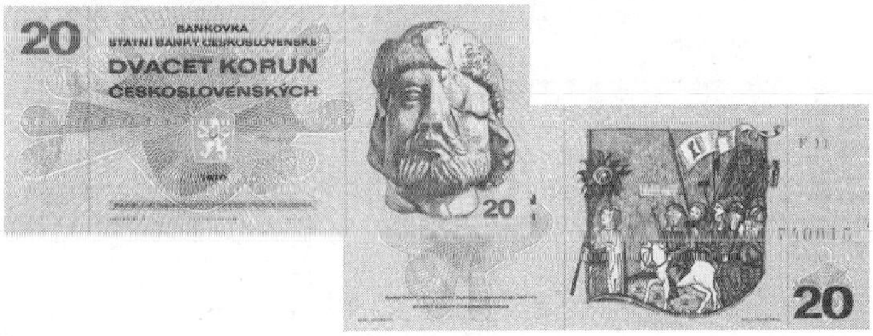

92 **20 Korun** — VF — UNC

1970 (1971). Blue on light blue and multicolor underprint. Arms at center, Jan Zizka at right. Series prefix: F, H, L, M. Back: Husite soldiers. Printer: STC-Prague. 132x58mm. — 1.00 — 2.50

93 **500 Korun** — VF — UNC

1973. Deep brown-violet and multicolor. Soldiers at right. Series prefix: U, W, Z. Back: Medieval shield at lower center, mountain fortress ruins at Devin at right. Printer: STC-Prague. 154x68mm. — 10.00 — 30.00

1985-89 Issue

94 **10 Korun** — VF — UNC

1986. Deep brown on blue and multicolor underprint. Pavol Orszag-Hviezdoslav at right. Series prefix: J, P, V. Back: Bird at lower left, view of Orava mountains. Printer: STC-Prague. 132x67mm. — .50 — 2.00

95 **20 Korun** — VF — UNC

1988. Blue and multicolor. Jan Ámos Komensky at right, circular design with open book at left. Series prefix: E, H. Back: Alphabet at left, Tree of life growing from book at center, young couple at right. Printer: STC-Prague. 137x67mm. — .75 — 2.50

96 **50 Korun** — VF — UNC

1987. Brown-violet and blue on red and orange underprint. Ludovít Stúr at right, shield and spotted eagle at right. Back: Bratislava castle and town view. Printer: STC-Prague. 142x67mm.

	VF	UNC
a. Series prefix: *F.*	1.50	5.00
b. Series prefix: *I.*	2.50	8.00

97 **100 Korun** — VF — UNC

1989. Dark green on green and red underprint. Klement Gottwald at right. Series prefix: A. Back: Hradcany in Prague. Printer: STC-Prague. — 5.00 — 12.00

98 **1000 Korun** — VF — UNC

1985. Blue-black, blue and purple on multicolor underprint. Bedrich Smetana at right. Back: Vysehrad Castle at left. Printer: SCT-Prague. 157x67mm.

	VF	UNC
a. Serial # prefix *C.*	20.00	50.00
b. Serial # prefix *U.*	30.00	100.

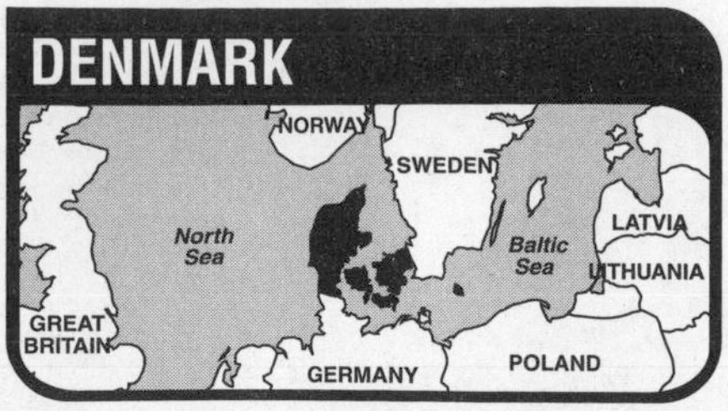

The Kingdom of Denmark, a constitutional monarchy located at the mouth of the Baltic Sea, has an area of 43,094 sq. km. and a population of 5.48 million. Capital: Copenhagen. Most of the country is arable. Agriculture, which used to employ the majority of the people, is now conducted by large farms served by cooperatives. The largest industries are food processing, iron and metal, and shipping. Machinery, meats (chiefly bacon), dairy products and chemicals are exported.

Once the seat of Viking raiders and later a major north European power, Denmark has evolved into a modern, prosperous nation that is participating in the general political and economic integration of Europe. It joined NATO in 1949 and the EEC (now the EU) in 1973. However, the country has opted out of certain elements of the European Union's Maastricht Treaty, including the European Economic and Monetary Union (EMU), European defense cooperation, and issues concerning certain justice and home affairs.

RULERS:

Frederik IX, 1947-1972
Margrethe II, 1972-

MONETARY SYSTEM:

1 Krone (1/2 Rigsdaler) = 100 Øre 1874-

REPLACEMENT NOTES:

#42-45 although dated (19)50, they were issued from 1952 onwards.
#42-47, suffix OJ (for whole sheets) or OK (for single notes).

KINGDOM

DANMARKS NATIONALBANK

1944-46 ISSUE

#35-41 first signatrue: Svendsen for 1944-45. Halberg for 1945-49. Riim for 1948-62.

41 500 Kroner

1944-62. Orange-red. Farmer with horses at center, plowing a field. Back: Arms. 175x108mm.

	VF	UNC
a. 1944. Prefix D. Left signature: Svendsen.	700.	2000.
b. 1945. Prefix D. Left signature: Halberg.	950.	2300.
c. 1948. Prefix D. Left signature: Halberg.	950.	2300.
d. 1948. Prefix D. Left signature: Riim.	950.	2300.
e. 1951. Prefix D. Left signature: Riim.	1200.	2700.
f. 1953. Prefix D. Left signature: Riim.	1200.	2700.
g. 1954. Prefix D. Left signature: Riim.	1400.	3200.
h. 1956. Prefix D. Left signature: Riim.	850.	2300.
i. 1959. Prefix D. Left signature: Riim.	725.	1900.
j. 1961. Prefix D. Left signature: Riim.	1100.	2500.
k. 1962. Prefix D. Left signature: Riim.	850.	2400.
s. Specimen.	—	—

1950 (1952)-63 ISSUE

Law of 7.4.1936

#42-47 first signatrue changes. Usually there are 3 signatrue combinations per prefix A0, A1, A2 etc. Second signature Riim, (19)51-68 for #42, 43, 44a-f, (19)51-68 for #42, 43, 44a-f, 45a-b, 46a-b, 47. Valeur for (19)69 for #44g-h, 45c and 46b. The prefixes mentioned in the listings refer to the first two characters of the left serial #. The middle two digits indicate the year date of issue, and the last two characters indicate the sheet position of the note. Replacement Notes: #42-47, Serial # suffix: *OJ* (for whole sheet replacements) or *OK* (for single note replacements).

42 5 Kroner

(19)50; (19)52; (19)54-60. Blue-green. Portrait Bertil Thorvaldsen at left, three Graces at right. Back: Kalundborg city view with five spire church at center. Watermark: *5* repeated. 125x65mm.

	VF	UNC
a. 5 in the watermark 11mm high. Without dot after *7* in law date. (19)52. Prefix A0; A1.	30.00	120.
b. As a. (19)52. Prefix A2.	60.00	235.
c. As a, but with dot after 7 in law date. (19)52. Prefix A2.	40.00	150.
d. As c. (19)52. Prefix A3.	70.00	250.
e. As c. (19)54. Prefixes A3-A5.	35.00	135.
f. As c. (19)54. Prefix A6.	45.00	180.
g. As c. (19)55. Prefixes A7-A8.	35.00	135.
h. As c. (19)55. Prefix A9.	45.00	180.
i. 5 in the watermark 13mm high. Prefix B0.	20.00	80.00
j. As i. (19)55. Prefix B1.	45.00	180.
k. As i. (19)56. Prefix B1.	40.00	150.
l. As i. (19)56. Prefixes B2-B3.	30.00	120.
m. As i. (19)56. Prefix B4.	60.00	240.
n. As i. (19)57. Prefixes B4-B6.	12.00	35.00
o. As i. (19)58-59. Prefixes B7-B9, C0.	12.00	34.00
p. As i. (19)59. Prefix C1.	8.00	28.00
q. As i. (19)59. Prefix C3.	400.	800.
r. As i. (19)60. Prefixes C3.	8.00	28.00
r1. Replacement note. (19)50. Prefixes as e, g. suffix 0J.	70.00	180.
r2. Replacement note. (19)50. Prefixes as f, h, j, m,q, suffix 0J.	100.	280.
r3. Replacement note. (19)50. Prefixes as i, l, suffix 0J.	60.00	160.
r4. Replacement note. (19)50. Prefixes as n, o, suffix 0J.	45.00	110.
r5. Replacement note. (19)60. Prefixes as p, r, s, suffix 0J.	30.00	80.00
r6. Replacement note. (19)50. Prefixes as a, suffix 0K.	450.	—
r7. Replacement note. (19)50. Prefixes as e, suffix 0K.	450.	—
r8. Replacement note. (19)60. Prefixes as f, suffix 0K.	450.	—
r9. Replacement note (19)50. Prefixes as o, suffix 0K.	450.	900.
r10. Replacement note. (19)60. Prefixes as s, suffix 0K.	450.	—
s. As i. (19)60. Prefix C4.	10.00	32.00
s1. Specimen.	—	350.

43 10 Kroner

(19)50-52. Black and olive-brown. Portrait Hans Christian Andersen at left, white storks in nest at right. Back: Green landscape of Egeskov Mølle Fyn at center. Watermark: *10* repeated. 125x65mm.

	VF	UNC
a. (19)51. Prefix A0.	60.00	220.
b. (19)51. Prefix A3.	125.	400.
c. (19)51. Prefix A4.	90.00	275.
d. (19)52. Prefix A1-A2; A5-A8.	50.00	180.
e. (19)52. Prefix A9.	550.	—
f. (19)52. Prefix B0.	115.	325.
g. (19)52. Prefix B1.	150.	450.
r1. (19)51. Replacement note. Suffix 0K.	650.	—
r2. (19)52. Replacement note. Suffix 0K.	550.	—

44 10 Kroner

(19)50; (19)54-74. Black and brown. Portrait Hans Christian Andersen at left, white storks in nest at right, text line added in upper and lower frame. Portrait Hans Christian Andersen at left. Back: Black landscape at center. 125x71mm.

	VF	UNC
a. Top and bottom line in frame begins with *10*. Watermark: *10* repeated, 11mm high. (19)54. Prefix C0.	30.00	120.
b. As a. Prefix C1.	60.00	200.
c. As a. Watermark 13mm high. (19)54. Prefix C1.	60.00	200.
d. As c. (19)54-55. Prefixes C2-D5.	27.00	110.
e. As c. (19)55. Prefix D6.	100.	275.
f. As c. (19)56. Prefix D6.	80.00	240.
g. As a. (19)56. Prefix D6.	100.	275.
h. As a. (19)56. Prefix D7.	70.00	240.
i. As a. (19)56. Prefix D8.	70.00	220.
j. As c. (19)56. Prefixes D8-E1.	24.00	90.00

	VF	UNC
k. As c. (19)56. Prefix E2.	350.	750.
l. As c. (19)57. Prefixes E2-E4.	22.00	85.00
m. Top and bottom line in frame begins with *Tl.* (19)57. Prefix E4.	350.	750.
n. As m. (19)57. Prefixes E5-E6.	22.00	85.00
o. As m. (19)57. Prefix E7.	180.	450.
o. As m. (19)58. Prefixes E7-F3.	20.00	75.00
q. As m. (19)58. Prefix F4.	22.00	85.00
r. As m. (19)59. Prefix F4.	27.00	110.
s. As m. (19)59. Prefixes F5-F8.	20.00	75.00
t. As m. (19)60. Prefixes F9-G3.	18.00	60.00
u. As m. (19)61-62. Prefixes G4-H1.	16.00	50.00
v. As m. (19)62. Prefix H2.	27.00	110.
w. As m. (19)63-64. Prefixes H2-J3.	14.00	40.00
x. As m. (19)64. Prefix J4.	25.00	75.00
y. As m. (19)65-67. Prefixes J5-K9.	12.00	30.00
z. As m. (19)68. Prefixes A0-A3.	8.00	25.00
aa. As m. (19)68. Second signature: Riim. Prefix A4.	11.00	22.50
ab. As m. (19)69. Second signature: Valear. Prefix A4.	11.00	22.50
ac. As aa. (19)69. Prefixes A5-A8.	9.00	18.00
ad. As aa. (19)69. Prefix A9.	120.	300.
ae. As aa. (19)70-71. Prefixes A9-B9.	5.00	14.00
af. As aa. (19)71. Prefix C0.	120.	300.
ag. As aa. (19)72-73. Prefixes C0-C9.	4.75	12.50
ah. As aa. (19)74. Prefix C9.	120.	300.
ai. As aa. (19)74. Prefixes D0-D5.	4.00	10.00
aj. As aa. (19)74. Prefix D6.	5.00	14.00
r1. Replacement note. (19)50. Prefixes as d. Suffix 0J.	100.	200.
r2. Replacement note. (19)50. Prefixes as e-i, m. Suffix 0J.	150.	400.
r3. Replacement note. (19)50. Prefixes as j, l. Suffix 0J.	95.00	220.
r4. Replacement note. (19)50, (19)60. Prefixes as n, p-s. Suffix 0J.	50.00	135.
r5. Replacement note. (19)60. Prefixes as t. Suffix 0J.	45.00	110.
r6. Replacement note. (19)61-64. Prefixes as u, w. Suffix 0J.	35.00	70.00
r7. Replacement note. (19)62. Prefixes as v. Suffix 0J.	50.00	140.
r8. Replacement note. (19)64. Prefixes as x. Suffix 0J.	40.00	90.00
r9. Replacement note. (19)65-69 Prefixes as y-ac. Suffix 0J.	15.00	40.00
r10. Replacement note. (19)70-71. Prefixes as ae. Suffix 0J.	12.00	30.00
r11. Replacement note. (19)69, (19)71. Prefixes as ad, af. Suffix 0J.	200.	425.
r12. Replacement note. (19)74. Prefixes as ag, ai. Suffix 0J.	9.00	22.00
r13. Replacement note. (19)74. Prefix as aj. Suffix 0J.	11.00	25.00
r14. Replacement note. (19)50. Prefixes as d. Suffix 0K.	650.	—
r15. Replacement note. (19)62-64. Prefixes as u-w. Suffix 0K.	550.	—
r16. Replacement note. (19)65-69. Prefix as y-ac. Suffix 0K.	350.	—
r17. Replacement note. (19)69, (19)71. Prefixes as ad, af. Suffix 0K.	400.	—
r18. Replacement note. (19)70-73. Prefixes as ae, ag. Suffix 0K.	175.	350.
r19. Replacement note. (19)74. Prefixes as ai-aj. Suffix 0K.	250.	450.
s1. Specimen.	—	500.

45 **50 Kroner**

(19)50; (19)56-70. Blue on green underprint. Portrait Ole Rømer at left, Round Tower in Copenhagen at right. Back: Blue. Stone Age burial site Dolmen of Stenvad, Djursland at center. 153x78mm.

	VF	UNC
a. Handmade paper. Watermark: Crowns and *50* (19)56, Prefix A1.	140.	350.
b. As a. (19)57. Prefix A1.	140.	350.
c. As a. (19)57. Prefix A2.	165.	400.
d. As a. (19)58. Prefix A2.	75.00	250.
e. As a. (19)58. Prefix B0.	600.	1250.
f. As a. (19)60. Prefix A2.	1500.	—
g. Machine made paper. Watermark: Rhombuses and 50. (19)61/1962. Prefix A4.	75.00	250.
h. As f. (19)62. Prefix A4.	80.00	260.
i. As f. (19)63. Prefix A4.	75.00	250.
j. As f. (19)63. Prefix A5.	60.00	120.
k. As f. (19)66. Prefix A6-A7.	40.00	85.00
l. As f. (19)66. Prefix A8.	80.00	160.
m. As g. (19)70. Prefix A8-A9.	35.00	80.00
r1. As a. Replacement note. (19)50/1956. Suffix 0J.	120.	300.
r2. As b. Replacement note. (19)50/1957. Suffix 0J.	120.	300.
r3. As c. Replacement note. (19)57 Suffix 0J.	150.	375.
r4. As d. Replacement note. (19)50/1958. Suffix 0J.	90.00	275.
r5. As f. Replacement note. Prefixes A2-A3. (19)60.	75.00	250.
r6. As g-j. Replacement note. (19)61-63. Suffix 0J.	80.00	250.
r7. As k. Replacement note. (19)66. Suffix 0J.	50.00	140.
r8. As l. Replacement note. (19)66. Suffix 0J.	90.00	200.
r9. As m. Replacement note. (19)70. Suffix 0J.	40.00	90.00
r10. As b. Replacement note. (19)50/1957. Suffix 0K.	550.	1500.
r11. As d. Replacement note. (19)50/1958. Suffix 0K.	700.	1750.
r12. As f. Replacement note. (19)60. Suffix 0K.	550.	1500.
r13. As k-l. Replacement note. (19)66. Suffix 0K.	450.	1250.
r14. As m. Replacement note. (19)70 Suffix 0K.	400.	1000.
s. Specimen.	—	600.

46 **100 Kroner**

(19)61-70. Red-brown on red-yellow underprint. Portrait Hans Christian Ørsted at left, compass card at right. Back: Brown. Kronborg castle in Elsinore. 155x84mm.

	VF	UNC
a. Handmade paper. Watermark: Close wavy lines and compass. (19)61. Prefix A0.	400.	1000.
b. Machine made paper. Watermark: *100.* (19)61. Prefix A2- A3.	75.00	265.
c. (19)62. Prefix A4-A5.	90.00	300.
d. (19)65. Prefix A6-B1.	50.00	130.
e. (19)65. Prefix B2.	120.	425.
f. (19)70. Prefix B2-B4.	40.00	100.
r1. As a. Replacement note. (19)61. Suffix 0J.	45.00	400.
r2. As b. Replacement note. (19)62. Suffix 0J.	80.00	300.
r3. As c. Replacement note. (19)62. Suffix 0J.	110.	350.
r4. As d. Replacement note. (19)65. Suffix 0J.	60.00	150.
r5. As e. Replacement note. (19)65. Suffix 0J.	120.	400.
r6. As f. Replacement note. (19)70. Suffix 0J.	40.00	110.
r7. As a. Replacement note. (19)61. Suffix 0K.	650.	1250.
r8. As d. Replacement note. (19)65. Suffix 0K.	650.	1250.
r9. As f. Replacement note. (19)70. Suffix 0K.	650.	1250.
s. Specimen.	—	600.

47 **500 Kroner**

1963-67. Green. Portrait C.D.F. Reventlow at left, farmer plowing at right. Small date at lower right. Back: Roskilde city view. 175x90mm.

	VF	UNC
a. 1963. Prefix A0.	300.	800.
b. 1965. Prefix A0.	300.	900.
c. 1967. Prefix A0.	200.	525.
d. 1967. Prefix A1.	240.	575.
r1. As a. Replacement note. (19)63. Suffix 0J.	325.	900.
r2. As b. Replacement note. (19)65. Suffix 0J.	340.	1050.
r3. As c. Replacement note. (19)67. Suffix 0J.	225.	650.
r4. As d. Replacement note. (19)67. Suffix 0J.	240.	575.
s. Specimen.	—	900.

1972; 1979 Issue

Issued under *L. 1936*. The year of issue is shown by the 2 middle numerals within the alpha-numeric series code at lower left or right. Signature varieties.

48 10 Kroner

(19)72-78. Black on olive and multicolor underprint. Portrait Catherine Sophie Kirchhoff by Jens Juel at right. Back: Eider duck at left, *SERIE* 1972 at lower right. Printer: Nationalbanken, Copenhagen (without imprint). 125x67mm.

	VF	UNC
a. (19)72. Prefix A0-A2.	7.00	20.00
b. (19)72. Prefix A3.	25.00	80.00
c. (19)75. Prefix A4. Blight security thread.	5.00	12.00
d. (19)75. Prefix A4. Light-colored security thread.	35.00	90.00
e. (19)75. Prefixes A5-A7.	4.00	9.00
f. (19)76. Prefixes A8-A9, B10.	3.00	6.00
g. (19)77. Prefixes B1-B7.	FV	4.00
h. (19)78. Prefix B8.	FV	4.00

49 20 Kroner

(19)79-88. Dark blue on brown and multicolor underprint. Portrait PaulineTutein by Jens Juel at right. Back: Male and female House Sparrow at left center, *SERIE* 1972 at lower right. Watermark: Painter's palette, brushes and *20*. Printer: Nationalbanken, Copenhagen (without imprint). 125x72mm.

	VF	UNC
a. (19)79. Prefix A0-A4.	4.50	12.00
b. (19)80. Prefix A5.	5.50	16.00
c. (19)81. Prefix A6, C0-C1.	5.00	14.00
d. (19)83. Prefix C2.	5.00	14.00
e. (19)84. Prefix C3-C4.	FV	12.00
f. (19)85. Prefix C5.	FV	12.00
g. (19)87. Prefix C6.	FV	8.00
h. (19)88. Prefix C7-C8.	FV	7.00

50 50 Kroner

(19)72-98. Dark gray on pale blue, dull purple and pale green underprint. Portrait Mrs. Ryberg by Jens Juel at right. Back: *Carassius-Carassius* fish at left, *SERIE* 1972 at lower right. Printer: Nationalbanken, Copenhagen (without imprint). 139x72mm.

	VF	UNC
a. (19)72. Prefix A0-A1.	50.00	150.
b. (19)76. Prefix A2-A3.	40.00	125.
c. (19)78. Prefix A4-A5.	27.50	75.00
d. (19)79. Prefix A6.	35.00	100.
e. (19)82. Prefix C0-C1.	27.50	75.00
f. (19)84. Prefix C2-C3.	25.00	65.00
g. (19)85. Prefix C4.	20.00	45.00
h. (19)89. Prefix C5.	16.00	30.00
i. (19)90. Prefixes C6-C7.	12.00	23.00
j. (19)92. Prefixes C8-C9.	12.00	23.00
k. (19)94. Prefix D0.	12.50	25.00
l. (19)95. Prefix D1.	27.50	75.00
m. (19)96. Prefixes D2-D3.	11.00	18.00
n. (19)97. Prefix D4.	FV	16.00
o. (19)98. Prefix D5.	FV	16.00
s. Specimen.	—	400.

51 100 Kroner

(19)72-93. Black and red on multicolor underprint. Jens Juel's self-portrait (ca.1773-74) at right. Back: Danish Red Order Ribbon moth at left, *SERIE* 1972 at lower right. Printer: Nationalbanken, Copenhagen (without imprint). 150x78mm.

	VF	UNC
a. (19)72. Prefix A0-A2.	50.00	200.
b. (19)75. Prefix A3-A5.	45.00	150.
c. (19)76. Prefix A6.	37.50	100.
d. (19)77. Prefix A7.	70.00	275.
e. (19)78. Prefixes A8-A9, B0.	35.00	90.00
f. (19)79. Prefixes B1-B3.	32.00	85.00
g. (19)81. Prefix B4.	170.	425.
h. (19)81. Prefixes C0-C1.	25.00	70.00
i. (19)82. Prefix C2.	30.00	80.00
j. (19)83. Prefix C3-C4.	25.00	70.00
k. (19)84. Prefixes C5-C6.	25.00	70.00
l. (19)84. Prefix C7.	30.00	80.00
m. (19)85. Prefixes C8-C9.	22.50	60.00
n. (19)85. Prefix H0.	100.	350.
o. (19)86. Prefix D0-D2.	22.50	60.00
p. (19)86. Prefix R1.	85.00	300.
q. (19)87. Prefixes D3-D4.	20.00	50.00
r. (19)88. Prefixes D5-D6.	FV	45.00
s. (19)89. Prefix D7.	FV	40.00
t. (19)90. Prefixes D8-D9, E0.	FV	37.50
u. (19)91 Prefix E1.	FV	32.50
v. (19)91. Prefix E2.	30.00	80.00
w. (19)93. Prefix E3-E4.	FV	32.50
s1. Specimen.	—	500.

52 **500 Kroner** VF UNC

(19)72-88. Black on green and multicolor underprint. *Unknown Lady* portrait by Jens Juel, possibly von Qualen at right. Back: Lizard, *SERIE* 1972 at lower right. Watermark: Jens Juel and *500* repeated. Printer: Nationalbanken, Copenhagen (without imprint). 164x85mm.

	VF	UNC
a. (19)72. Prefix A0-A1.	160.	300.
b. (19)76. Prefix A2.	140.	275.
c. (19)80. Prefix A3-A5.	125.	235.
d. (19)88. Prefix C0-C1.	FV	220.

53 **1000 Kroner** VF UNC

(19)72-02. Black on gray and multicolor underprint. Portrait Thomasine Heiberg by Jens Juel at right. Back: European or Red squirrel, *SERIE* 1972 at lower right. Watermark: Double portrait Jens Juel and his wife and *1000*. Printer: Nationalbanken, Copenhagen (without imprint). 176x94mm.

	VF	UNC
a. (19)72. Prefixes A0-A1.	300.	600.
b. (19)77. Prefix A2.	275.	500.
c. (19)80. Prefix A3.	250.	400.
d. (19)80. Prefix C0.	230.	350.
e. (19)81. Prefix C1.	250.	400.
f. (19)86. Ptrefixes C2-C3.	FV	290.
g. (19)02. Prefixes C4-C5.	FV	270.

1972A Issue

54 **100 Kroner** VF UNC

(19)94-98. Black and orange on multicolor underprint. Jens Juel's self-portrait (ca.1773-74) at right. Additional security devices. Back: Danish Order Ribbon moth at left, *SERIE* 1972 at lower right. Additional security devices. Watermark: Jens Juul and 100. 150x78mm.

	VF	UNC
a. (19)94. Prefix F0.	20.00	40.00
b. (19)95. Prefix F1.	20.00	40.00
c. (19)95. Prefix F2.	FV	30.00
d. (19)95. Prefix F3.	FV	35.00
e. (19)95. Prefixes F4-F5.	FV	30.00
f. (19)96. Prefix F6.	FV	35.00
g. (19)97. Prefix F7.	FV	30.00
h. (19)97. Prefix F8.	40.00	100.
i. (19)98. Prefixes F9-G0.	FV	27.50

1997-2001 Issue

55 **50 Kroner** VF UNC

(19)99-(20)02. Black and deep purple on multicolor underprint. Green latent image at upper left, Karen Blixen at right. Back: Centaur stone relief from Landet Church, Tåsinge at left center. Watermark: Karen Blixen. 125x72mm.

	VF	UNC
a. (19)99. Prefixes A0-A1.	FV	22.00
b. (20)00. Prefixes A2-A3.	FV	22.00
c. (20)01. Prefixes A4-A6.	FV	16.00
d. (20)01. Prefix A7.	20.00	65.00
e. (20)02. Prefix A8.	FV	16.00
f. (20)02. Prefix A9.	FV	20.00

56 **100 Kroner** VF UNC

(19)99-(20)01. Black and red-brown on orange and multicolor underprint. Blue latent image at upper left, Carl Nielsen at right. Back: Basilisk stone relief from Tømmerby Church in Thy at left center. Watermark: Carl Nielsen. 135x72mm.

	VF	UNC
a. (19)99. Prefixes A0-A2.	FV	32.50
b. (20)00. Prefixes A3-A4.	FV	32.50
c. (20)00. Prefix A5.	30.00	100.
d. (20)01. Prefixes A6-A7.	FV	27.50
e. (20)01. Prefix A8.	30.00	100.

57 200 Kroner

(19)97; (20)00. Black and dark blue on turquoise green and multicolor underprint. Pale red-violet latent image at upper left, J. L. Heiberg at right. Back: Stone lion relief from Viborg Cathedral at left center. Watermark: J. L. Heiberg. 145x72mm.

	VF	UNC
a. (19)97. Prefixes A0-A1.	FV	60.00
b. (20)00. Prefix A2.	FV	65.00

58 500 Kroner

(19)97-(20)03. Black on blue, orange and multicolor underprint. Niels Bohr at right. Back: Knight and dragon relief from Lihme Church at left center. Watermark: Niels Bohr. 155x72mm.

	VF	UNC
a. (19)97. Prefix A0.	FV	160.
b. (19)97. Prefix A1.	100.	200.
c. (19)99. Prefix A2.	100.	200.
d. (20)00. Prefix A3.	FV	140.
e. (20)00. Prefix A4.	100.	200.
f. (20)03. Prefix A5.	95.00	190.

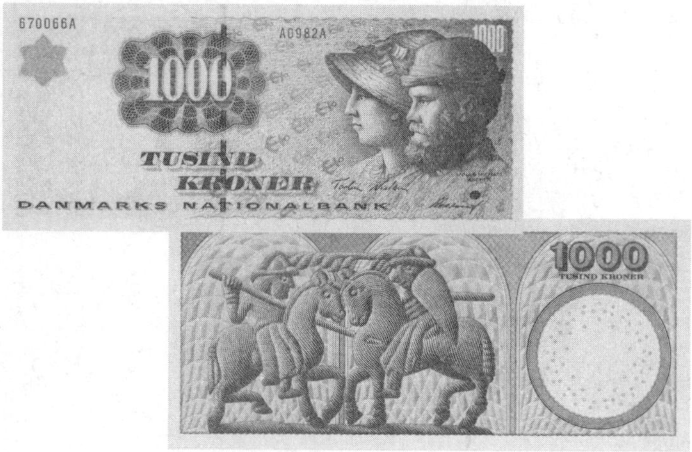

59 1000 Kroner

(19)98. Violet, dark red-brown and green. Green latent image at upper left, Anna and Michael Ancher at right. Serial number prefix A0-A1. Back: Back purple, turquoise, and orange on multicolor underprint. Tournament scene relief from Bislev Church at left center. Watermark: Anna Archer. 165x72mm.

	VF	UNC
a. (19)98. Prefix A0.	FV	250.
b. (19)98. Prefix A1.	FV	250.

2002 Issue

60 50 Kroner

(20)04-(20)07. Black and deep purple on multicolor underprint. Karen Blixen at right. iridescent metallic strip. Hologram at upper left. Back: Centaur stone relief from Landet Church, Tåsinge at left center. Watermark: Karen Blixen. 125x72mm.

	VF	UNC
a. (20)04. Prefixes B0-B1.	FV	18.00
b. (20)05. Prefix B2.	FV	20.00
c. (20)06. Prefix B3.	FV	16.00
d. (20)07. Prefix B4.	FV	16.00
e. (20)07. Preifx B5.	FV	22.50
f. (20)07. Preifx B6.	FV	20.00

61 100 Kroner

(20)02-(20)08. Black and red-brown on orange and multicolor underprint. Carl Nielsen at right. Iridescent metallic strip. Hologram at upper left. Back: Basilisk stone relief from Tømmerby Church in Thy at left center. Watermark: Carl Nielsen. 135x72mm.

	VF	UNC
a. (20)02. Prefixes B0-B6.	FV	25.00
b. (20)03. Prefixes B7-B8.	FV	27.50
c. (20)04. Prefixes B9-C0.	FV	27.50
d. (20)04. Prefix C1.	FV	40.00
e. (20)05. Prefix C2.	FV	30.00
f. (20)06. Prefixes C3-C5.	FV	25.00
g. (20)07. Prefixes C6-C9.	FV	22.50
h. (20)07. Prefix D0.	60.00	200.
i. (20)08. Prefix D2.	FV	40.00
j. (20)08. Prefix D3.	FV	35.00

62 200 Kroner

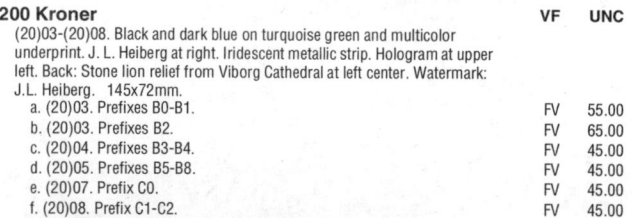

(20)03-(20)08. Black and dark blue on turquoise green and multicolor underprint. J. L. Heiberg at right. Iridescent metallic strip. Hologram at upper left. Back: Stone lion relief from Viborg Cathedral at left center. Watermark: J.L. Heiberg. 145x72mm.

	VF	UNC
a. (20)03. Prefixes B0-B1.	FV	55.00
b. (20)03. Prefixes B2.	FV	65.00
c. (20)04. Prefixes B3-B4.	FV	45.00
d. (20)05. Prefixes B5-B8.	FV	45.00
e. (20)07. Prefix C0.	FV	45.00
f. (20)08. Prefix C1-C2.	FV	45.00
g. (20)08. Prefix C4.	FV	50.00

63 500 Kroner

(20)03-(20)08. Black on blue, orange and multicolor underprint. Niels Bohr at right. Iridescent metallic strip. Hologram at upper left. Back: Knight and dragon relief from Lihme Church at left center. Watermark: Niels Bohr. 155x72mm.

	VF	UNC
a. (20)03. Prefixes B0-B2.	FV	130.
b. (20)03. Prefix B3.	FV	155.
c. (20)06. Prefixes B4-B6.	FV	130.
d. (20)06. Prefix B7.	FV	165.
e. (20)08. Prefix B8.	FV	145.

64 1000 Kroner

(20)04-(20)06. Violet, dark red-brown and green. Anna and Michael Ancher at right. Iridescent metallic strip. Hologram at upper left. Back: Tournament scene relief from Bislev Church at left center. Watermark: Anna Ancher. 165x72mm.

	VF	UNC
a. (20)04. Prefix B0.	FV	235.
b. (20)04. Prefix B1.	FV	250.
c. (20)06. Prefix B2.	FV	235.
d. (20)06. Prefix B3.	FV	235.

2009-2010 Issue

65 50 Kroner

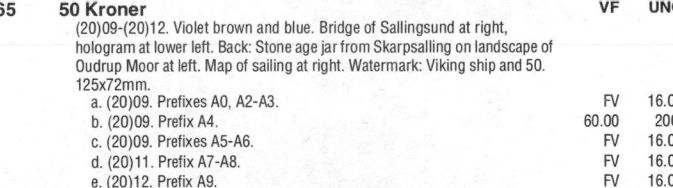

(20)09-(20)12. Violet brown and blue. Bridge of Sallingsund at right, hologram at lower left. Back: Stone age jar from Skarpsalling on landscape of Oudrup Moor at left. Map of sailing at right. Watermark: Viking ship and 50. 125x72mm.

	VF	UNC
a. (20)09. Prefixes A0, A2-A3.	FV	16.00
b. (20)09. Prefix A4.	60.00	200.
c. (20)09. Prefixes A5-A6.	FV	16.00
d. (20)11. Prefix A7-A8.	FV	16.00
e. (20)12. Prefix A9.	FV	16.00

66 100 Kroner

(20)09-(20)13. Orange-yellow on multicolor underprint. Little Belt Bridge at right. Hologram at lower left. Back: Stone age flint dagger - The Hindsgavl dagger from the island of Faenø at left. 135x72mm.

	VF	UNC
a. (20)09. Prefixes A0-A2.	FV	27.00
b. (20)10. Prefixes A3-A6.	FV	27.00
c. (20)13. Prefix A8.	FV	25.00

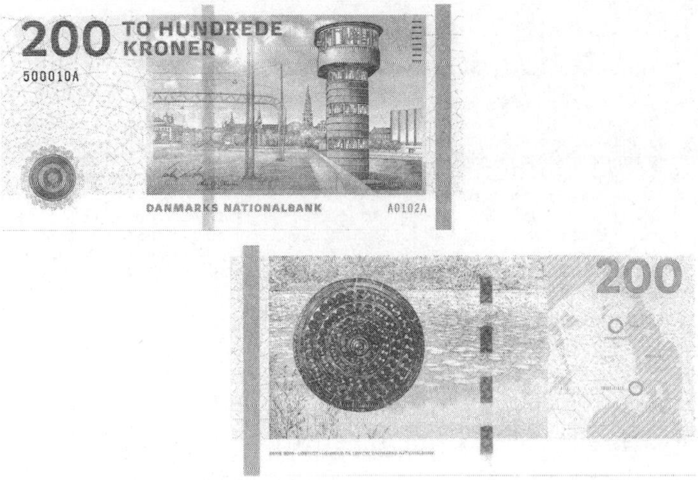

67 200 Kroner

(20)10-(20)12. Black, green and blue. Knippel Bridge in Copenhagen at right center. Hologram at lower left. Back: Bronze-age belt plate from Langstrip in North Zealand at center left. 145x72mm.

	VF	UNC
a. (20)10. Prefixes A0-A3.	FV	45.00
b. (20)11. Prefix A4.	FV	45.00
c. (20)12. Prefix A5.	FV	45.00

68 500 Kroner

(20)10-(20)12. Black, blue and brown. Queen Alexandrine Bridge / Møn Bridge at center right. Hologram at lower left. Back: Bronze age bucket of Greek/Thrician origin found in Keldby. 155x72mm.

	VF	UNC
a. (20)10. Prefix A2.	FV	120.
b. (20)11. Prefixes A0-A1.	FV	120.
c. (20)11. Prefix A3.	FV	140.
d. (20)12. Prefix A4.	FV	120.

69 1000 Kroner

(20)11-(20)12. Black, red and green. Great-Belt Bridge at center right. Back: Sun chariot found at Trundholm in NW Zealand at center left. 165x72mm.

	VF	UNC
a. (20)11. Prefixes A0-A2.	FV	225.
b. (20)12. Prefix A3-A4.	FV	225.

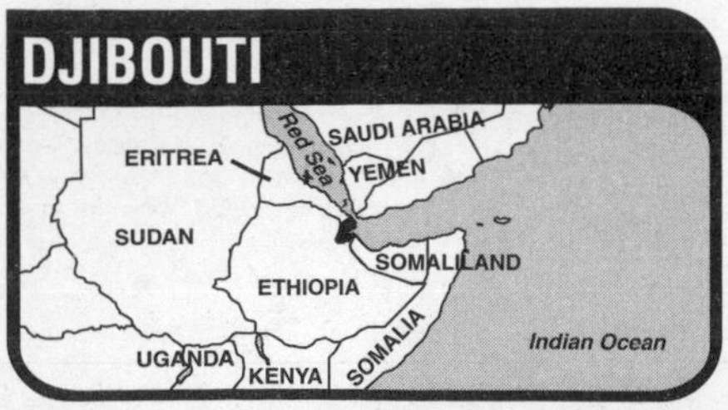

The Republic of Djibouti is located in northeast Africa at the Bab el Mandeb Strait connecting the Suez Canal and the Red Sea with the Gulf of Aden and the Indian Ocean, has an area of 23,000 sq. km. and a population of 506,200. Capital: Djibouti. The nation has very little arable land and few natural resources. The commercial activities of the trans-shipment port of Djibouti and the Addis Ababa-Djibouti railroad are the basis of the economy also French and American military activity. Salt, fish and hides are exported.

The French Territory of the Afars and the Issas became Djibouti in 1977. Hassan Gouled Aptidon installed an authoritarian one-party state and proceeded to serve as president until 1999. Unrest among the Afars minority during the 1990s led to a civil war that ended in 2001 following the conclusion of a peace accord between Afar rebels and the Issa-dominated government. In 1999, Djibouti's first multi-party presidential elections resulted in the election of Ismail Omar Guelleh; he was re-elected to a second and final term in 2005. Djibouti occupies a strategic geographic location at the mouth of the Red Sea and serves as an important transshipment location for goods entering and leaving the east African highlands. The present leadership favors close ties to France, which maintains a significant military presence in the country, but also has strong ties with the US.

MONETARY SYSTEM:

1 Franc = 100 Centimes

Republic of Djibouti

Banque Nationale de Djibouti

1979; 1984 ND Issue

36 500 Francs

ND (1979; 1988). Multicolor. Man at left, rocks in sea, storks at right. Back: Stern of ship at right.

	VF	UNC
a. Blue underprint. Without signature. (1979).	15.00	40.00
b. Pale blue underprint. Signature title: *LE GOUVERNEUR* added. (1988).	12.00	37.50

37 1000 Francs

ND (1979; 1988). Brown and multicolor. Woman at left, people by diesel passenger trains at center. Back: Trader with camels at center.

	VF	UNC
a. Long Arabic text on back. Without signature. Engraved. (1979).	22.00	50.00
b. Signature title: *LE GOUVERNEUR* added above *MILLE*. Short Arabic text at top on back. Lithographed. (1988).	18.00	45.00
c. Long Arabic text on back. (1991).	15.00	42.00
d. As c. but with security thread. 2 signature varieties.	10.00	30.00
e. as d. but bluish microprint frame on both sides.	FV	28.00

38 5000 Francs

ND (1979). Multicolor. Man at right, forest scene at center. Back: Aerial view at center.

	VF	UNC
a. Without signature.	50.00	150.
b. With signature.	45.00	150.
c. As b. but with security thread.	35.00	125.
d. As c. but fluorescent security stripe.	FV	85.00

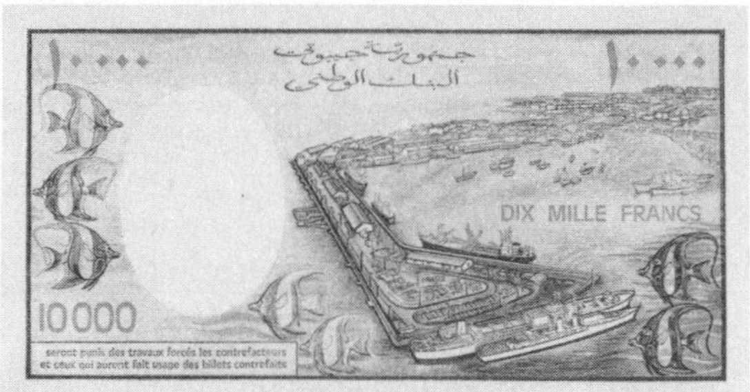

39 10,000 Francs

ND (1984). Brown and red on yellow and green. Woman holding baby at left, goats in tree at right. Back: Fish and harbor scene.

	VF	UNC
a. Signature title: *TRÉSORÍER.*	110.	235.
b. Signature title: *GOUVERNEUR* . with security thread.	FV	160.

1997; 1999 ND Issue

40 2000 Francs

ND (1997). Dark blue, blue-black and black on yellow and multicolor underprint. Young girl at right, camel caravan at center. Wide security overprint at right center. Back: Statue with spear and shield at lower left, government building at center. 170x80mm.

	VF	UNC
	FV	40.00

		VF	UNC
41	**10,000 Francs** ND (1999). Blue and multicolor. President Hassan Gouled Aptidon at right, undersea life at center. Back: Central Bank building at center.	FV	145.

Banque Centrale de Djibouti

2002 ND Issue

		VF	UNC
42	**1000 Francs** ND (2005). Reddish brown and multicolor.		
	a. Issued note.	FV	16.00
	r. Replacement note. Z prefix.	FV	55.00

		VF	UNC
43	**2000 Francs** ND (2005). Dark blue, blue-black and black on yellow and multicolor underprint. Young woman and camel caravan. Back: Statue and palace. 170x80mm.	FV	28.00

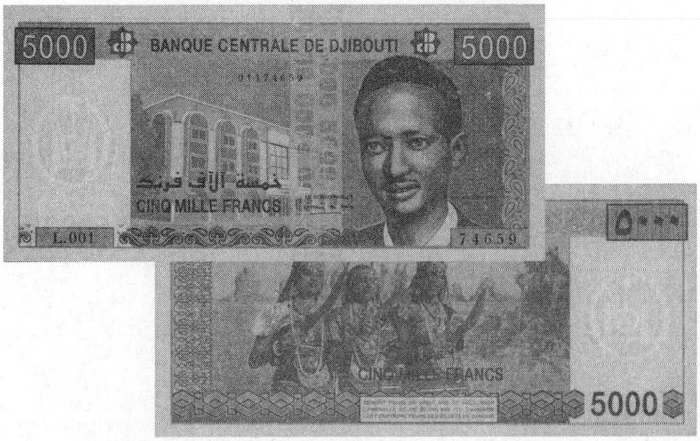

		VF	UNC
44	**5000 Francs** ND (2002). Purple and multicolor. Central bank building and M. Harbi. Back: Three females dancing with swords, rock landscape.	FV	55.00
45	**10,000 Francs** ND (2005). president Hassan Gouled Aptidon at right, undersea wildlife at center. Back: Central Bank building at center.	FV	100.

The Dominican Republic, occupying the eastern two-thirds of the island of Hispañiola, has an area of 48,730 sq. km. and a population of 9.50 million. Capital: Santo Domingo. The agricultural economy produces sugar, coffee, tobacco and cocoa.

Explored and claimed by Christopher Columbus on his first voyage in 1492, the island of Hispaniola became a springboard for Spanish conquest of the Caribbean and the American mainland. In 1697, Spain recognized French dominion over the western third of the island, which in 1804 became Haiti. The remainder of the island, by then known as Santo Domingo, sought to gain its own independence in 1821, but was conquered and ruled by the Haitians for 22 years; it finally attained independence as the Dominican Republic in 1844. In 1861, the Dominicans voluntarily returned to the Spanish Empire, but two years later they launched a war that restored independence in 1865. A legacy of unsettled, mostly non-representative rule followed, capped by the dictatorship of Rafael Leonidas Trujillo from 1930-61. Juan Bosch was elected president in 1962, but was deposed in a military coup in 1963. In 1965, the United States led an intervention in the midst of a civil war sparked by an uprising to restore Bosch. In 1966, Joaquin Balaguer defeated Bosch in an election to become president. Balaguer maintained a tight grip on power for most of the next 30 years when international reaction to flawed elections forced him to curtail his term in 1996. Since then, regular competitive elections have been held in which opposition candidates have won the presidency. Former President (1996-2000) Leonel Fernandez Reyna won election to a second term in 2004 following a constitutional amendment allowing presidents to serve more than one term.

MONETARY SYSTEM:

1 Peso Oro = 100 Centavos Oro

SPECIMEN NOTES:

In 1998 the Banco Central began selling various specimens over the counter to the public.

REPLACEMENT NOTES:

#117-124: Z prefix and suffix (TDLR printings).

Republic

Banco Central de la República Dominicana

1961 ND Issues

		VF	UNC
85	**10 Centavos Oro** ND (1961). Blue and black. Banco de Reservas in round frame at center. Back: Blue. Printer: ABNC.		
	a. Issued note.	3.50	15.00
	s. Specimen.	—	20.00

		VF	UNC
86	**10 Centavos Oro** ND (1961). Black on light blue-green safety paper. Banco de Reservas in oval frame at center. Back: Green. Printer: Banco Central.		
	a. Issued note.	10.00	40.00
	s. Specimen.	—	25.00

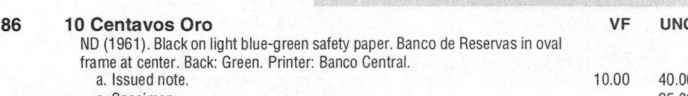

		VF	UNC
87	**25 Centavos Oro** ND (1961). Red and black. Entrance to the Banco Central in rectangular frame at center. Back: Red. Printer: ABNC.		
	a. Issued note.	4.00	12.50
	s. Specimen.	—	20.00

88 25 Centavos Oro

ND (1961). Black. Entrance to the Banco Central in oval frame at center. Back: Green. Printer: Banco Central.

	VF	UNC
a. Pink safety paper.	10.00	50.00
b. Plain cream paper.	10.00	50.00
s. Specimen.	—	30.00

89 50 Centavos Oro

ND (1961). Purple and black. Palacio Nacional in circular frame at center. Back: Purple. Printer: ABNC.

	VF	UNC
a. Issued note.	4.00	15.00
s. Specimen.	—	20.00

90 50 Centavos Oro

ND (1961). Black on yellow safety paper. Palacio Nacional in oval frame at center. Back: Green. Printer: Banco Central.

	VF	UNC
a. Issued note.	25.00	80.00
s. Specimen.	—	30.00

1962 ND Issue

91 1 Peso Oro

ND (1962-63). Red. Portrait J. P. Duarte at center, text over seal: *SANTO DOMINGO / DISTRITO NACIONAL / REPÚBLICA DOMINICANA.* Back: Medallic portrait of Liberty head at left, arms at right. Printer: ABNC.

	VF	UNC
a. Issued note.	25.00	100.
s. Specimen.	—	175.

92 5 Pesos Oro

ND (1962). Red. Portrait J. Sánchez at right center, text over seal: *SANTO DOMINGO / DISTRITO NACIONAL / REPÚBLICA DOMINICANA.* Back: Purple. Medallic portrait of Liberty head at left, arms at right. Printer: ABNC.

	VF	UNC
a. Issued note.	40.00	150.
s. Specimen.	—	250.

93 10 Pesos Oro

ND (1962). Red. Portrait Mella at center, text over seal: *SANTO DOMINGO / DISTRITO NACIONAL / REPÚBLICA DOMINICANA.* Back: Brown. Medallic portrait of Liberty head at left, arms at right. Printer: ABNC.

	VF	UNC
a. Issued note.	65.00	250.
s. Specimen.	—	300.

94 20 Pesos Oro

ND (1962). Red. *Puerta del Conde* at center, text over seal: *SANTO DOMINGO / DISTRITO NACIONAL / REPÚBLICA DOMINICANA.* Back: Olive. Medallic portrait of Liberty head at left, arms at right. Printer: ABNC.

	VF	UNC
a. Issued note.	125.	350.
s. Specimen.	—	400.

95 50 Pesos Oro

ND (1962). Red. Tomb of Columbus at center, text over seal: *SANTO DOMINGO / DISTRITO NACIONAL / REPÚBLICA DOMINICANA.* Back: Blue-gray. Medallic portrait of Liberty head at left, arms at right. Printer: ABNC.

	VF	UNC
a. Issued note.	250.	750.
s. Specimen.	—	400.

96 100 Pesos Oro

ND (1962). Red. Woman with coffee pot and cup at center, text over seal: *SANTO DOMINGO / DISTRITO NACIONAL / REPÚBLICA DOMINICANA.* Back: Blue-gray. Medallic portrait of Liberty head at left, arms at right. Printer: ABNC.

	VF	UNC
a. Issued note.	275.	800.
s. Specimen.	—	400.

97 **500 Pesos Oro**

ND (1962). *Obelisco de Ciudad Trujillo* at center, text over seal: *SANTO DOMINGO / DISTRITO NACIONAL / REPÚBLICA DOMINICANA.* Back: Medallic portrait of Liberty head at left, arms at right. Printer: ABNC.

	VF	UNC
a. Issued note.	1000.	2000.
s. Specimen.	—	500.

98 **1000 Pesos Oro**

ND (1962). Minor Basilica of Santa Maria at center, text over seal: *SANTO DOMINGO / DISTRITO NACIONAL / REPÚBLICA DOMINICANA.* Back: Medallic portrait of Liberty head at left, arms at right. Printer: ABNC.

	VF	UNC
a. Issued note. Unique.	1750.	5000.
s. Specimen.	—	500.

1964 ND Issue

99 **1 Peso Oro**

ND (1964-73). Black on multicolor underprint. Portrait J. P. Duarte at center with eyes looking left, white bow tie. Orange bank seal at right. Signature varieties. Back: Medallic portrait of Liberty head at left, arms at right. Printer: TDLR. 156x67mm.

	VF	UNC
a. Issued note.	7.50	30.00
s1. Specimen. Black overprint: *MUESTRA* twice on face.	—	140.
s2. Specimen. Black overprint: *MUESTRA* once on face.	—	140.
s3. Specimen. Black overprint: *MUESTRA* once on each side.	—	140.

100 **5 Pesos Oro**

ND (1964-74). Brown on multicolor underprint. Portrait J. Sánchez at right center. Orange bank seal at right. Signature varieties. Back: Medallic portrait of Liberty head at left, arms at right. Printer: TDLR. 156x67mm.

	VF	UNC
a. Issued note.	10.00	40.00
s1. Specimen. Black overprint: *MUESTRA* twice on each side. Punch hole cancelled.	—	100.
s2. Specimen. Black overprint: *ESPECIMEN* once on each on each side. Punch hole cancelled.	—	100.
s3. Specimen. Black overprint: *MUESTRA*once on face.	—	100.
s4. Specimen. Black overprint: *MUESTRA* once on each side.	—	100.

101 **10 Pesos Oro**

ND (1964-74). Deep green on multicolor underprint. Portrait Mella at center. Orange bank seal at right. Signature varieties. Back: Medallic portrait of Liberty head at left, arms at right. Printer: TDLR. 156x67mm.

	VF	UNC
a. Issued note.	17.50	60.00
s1. Specimen. Black overprint: *MUESTRA* once on each side.	—	100.
s2. Specimen. Black overprint: *MUESTRA* twice on each side. Punch hole cancelled.	—	100.
s3. Specimen. Black overprint: *ESPECIMEN* once on each side. Punch hole cancelled.	—	100.

102 **20 Pesos Oro**

ND (1964-74). Dark brown on multicolor underprint. *Altar de la Patria* at center. Orange bank seal at right. Signature varieties. Back: Medallic portrait of Liberty head at left, arms at right. Printer: TDLR. 156x67mm.

	VF	UNC
a. Issued note.	30.00	125.
s1. Specimen. Black overprint: *MUESTRA* twice on each side.	—	100.
s2. Specimen. Black overprint: *MUESTRA* once on each side.	—	100.
s3. Specimen. Black overprint: *ESPECIMEN* once on each side. Punch hole cancelled.	—	100.

103 **50 Pesos Oro**

ND (1964-74). Purple on multicolor underprint. Ox cart at center. Orange bank seal at right. Signature varieties. Back: Medallic portrait of Liberty head at left, arms at right. Printer: TDLR. 156x67mm.

	VF	UNC
a. Issued note.	75.00	175.
s1. Specimen. Black overprint: *MUESTRA* once on each side.	—	100.
s2. Specimen. Black overprint: *MUESTRA* twice on each side. Punch hole cancelled.	—	100.
s3. Specimen. Black overprint: *ESPECIMEN* once on each side. Punch hole cancelled.	—	100.

104	100 Pesos Oro	VF	UNC
	ND (1964-74). Orange-brown on multicolor underprint. Banco Central at center. Orange bank seal at right. Signature varieties. Back: Medallic portrait of Liberty head at left, arms at right. Printer: TDLR. 156x67mm.		
	a. Issued note.	125.	300.
	s1. Specimen. Black overprint: *ESPECIMEN* on both sides. Punch hole cancelled.	—	100.
	s2. Specimen. Black overprint: *MUESTRA* twice on both sides. Punch hole cancelled.	—	100.
	s3. Specimen. Black overprint: *MUESTRA* once on both sides.	—	100.
	s4. Specimen. Black overprint: *MUESTRA* once on both sides. Punch hole cancelled.	—	100.

105	500 Pesos Oro	VF	UNC
	ND (1964-74). Dark blue on multicolor underprint. Columbus tomb and cathedral at center. Orange bank seal at right. Signature varieties. Back: Medallic portrait of Liberty head at left, arms at right. Printer: TDLR. 156x67mm.		
	a. Issued note.	450.	1200.
	s1. Specimen with black overprint: *MUESTRA* once on each side.	—	175.
	s2. Specimen with black overprint: *MUESTRA* twice on each side. Punch hole cancelled.	—	190.
106	**1000 Pesos Oro**		
	ND (1964-74). Red and multicolor underprint. National Palace at center. Orange bank seal at right. Signature varieties. Back: Medallic portrait of Liberty head at left center, arms at right center. Printer: TDLR. 156x67mm.		
	a. Issued note.	1250.	3000.
	s1. Specimen. Black overprint: *ESPECIMEN* once on both sides. Punch hole cancelled.	—	250.
	s2. Specimen. Black overprint: *MUESTRA* twice on both sides. Punch hole cancelled.	—	250.
	s3. Specimen. Black overprint: *MUESTRA* once on each sides. Punch hole cancelled.	—	250.

1973 ND Issue

107	1 Peso Oro	VF	UNC
	ND (1973-74). Black on light green and pinkish tan underprint. Portrait J. P. Duarte with eyes looking front, black bow tie. Orange bank seal at right. Signature varieties. Back: Medallic portrait of Liberty head at left, arms at right. Printer: TDLR. 156x67mm.		
	a. Issued note.	2.00	10.00
	s. Specimen with black overprint: *ESPECIMEN* once on each side. Punch hole cancelled.	—	35.00

1975 Issue

108	1 Peso Oro	VF	UNC
	1975-78. Black on light green and pinkish tan underprint. Portrait J. P. Duarte with eyes looking front, black bow tie. Orange bank seal at right. Signature varieties. Back: Medallic portrait of Liberty head at left, arms at right. Dates at center in upper margin. Printer: TDLR. 156x67mm.		
	a. Issued note.	1.50	7.50
	s. Specimen. Black overprint: *ESPECIMEN* on each side. Punch hole cancelled.	—	35.00

109	5 Pesos Oro	VF	UNC
	1975-76. Brown on light green and lilac underprint. Portrait J. Sánchez at right center. Orange bank seal at right. Signature varieties. Back: Medallic portrait of Liberty head at left, arms at right. Dates at center in upper margin. Printer: TDLR. 156x67mm.		
	a. Issued note.	5.00	20.00
	s. Specimen with black overprint: *ESPECIMEN* once on each side. Punch hole cancelled.	—	50.00
110	**10 Pesos Oro**		
	1975-76. Green on light green and lilac underprint. Portrait Mella at center. Orange bank seal at right. Signature varieties. Back: Medallic portrait of Liberty head at left, arms at right. Dates at center in upper margin. Printer: TDLR. 156x67mm.		
	a. Issued note.	10.00	35.00
	s. Specimen.	—	50.00
111	**20 Pesos Oro**		
	1975-76. Brown on light green and blue underprint. *Altar de la Patria* at center. Orange bank seal at right. Signature varieties. Back: Medallic portrait of Liberty head at left, arms at right. Dates at center in upper margin. Printer: TDLR. 156x67mm.		
	a. 1975.	15.00	55.00
	b. 1976.	15.00	55.00
	s. 1975. Specimen. Black overprint: *ESPECIMEN* once on each side. Punch hole cancelled.	—	50.00
	s2. 1976. Specimen. Black overprint: *ESPECIMEN* once on each side. Punch hole cancelled.	—	50.00

112	50 Pesos Oro	VF	UNC
	1975-76. Purple on multicolor underprint. Ox cart at center. Orange bank seal at right. Signature varieties. Back: Medallic portrait of Liberty head at left, arms at right. Dates at center in upper margin. Printer: TDLR. 156x67mm.		
	a. 1975	35.00	110.
	b. 1976.	35.00	110.
	s1. 1975. Specimen. Black overprint: *ESPECIMEN* once on each side. Punch hole cancelled.	—	75.00

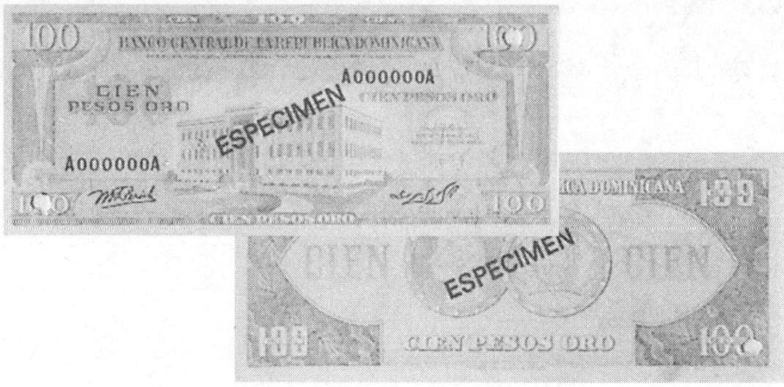

113 100 Pesos Oro

1975-76. Orange-brown on multicolor underprint. Banco Central at center. Orange bank seal at right. Signature varieties. Back: Medallic portrait of Liberty head at left, arms at right. Dates at center in upper margin. Printer: TDLR. 156x67mm.

	VF	UNC
a. 1975.	60.00	190.
b. 1976.	60.00	190.
s1. 1975. Specimen with black overprint: *ESPECIMEN* on both sides. Punch hole cancelled.	—	100.
s2. 1976. Specimen with black overprint: *ESPECIMEN* on both sides. Punch hole cancelled.	—	100.

114 500 Pesos Oro

1975. Dark blue on multicolor underprint. Columbus tomb and cathedral at center. Orange bank seal at right. Signature varieties. Back: Medallic portrait of Liberty head at left, arms at right. Dates at center in upper margin. Printer: TDLR. 156x67mm.

	VF	UNC
a. Issued note.	250.	750.
s. Specimen with black overprint: *ESPECIMEN* once on each side. Punch hole cancelled.	—	100.

115 1000 Pesos Oro

1975-76. Red on multicolor underprint. National Palace at center. Orange bank seal at right. Signature varieties. Back: Medallic portrait of Liberty head at left center, arms at right center. Dates at center in upper margin. Printer: TDLR. 156x67mm.

	VF	UNC
a. 1975.	500.	1500.
b. 1976.	500.	1500.
s1. 1975. Specimen. Black overprint: *ESPECIMEN* once on both sides. Punch hole cancelled.	—	125.
s2. 1976. Specimen. Black overprint: *ESPECIMEN* once on both sides. Punch hole cancelled.	—	125.

1977-80 Issues

#116-124 Replacement notes: Serial # prefix and suffix *Z*.

116 1 Peso Oro

1978-79. Black, dark green and dark brown on multicolor underprint. J. P. Duarte at right, orange seal at left. Back: Sugar refinery, dates in upper margin. Printer: ABNC. 156x67mm.

	VF	UNC
a. Issued note.	1.00	5.00
s. Specimen with red overprint: *MUESTRA / SIN VALOR*. 1978; 1980. Punch hole cancelled.	—	35.00

117 1 Peso Oro

1980-82. Black, dark green and dark brown on multicolor underprint. J. P. Duarte at right, orange bank seal at left. Back: Sugar refinery, dates (lightly printed) in upper margin. Printer: TDLR. 156x67mm.

	VF	UNC
a. 1980.	1.00	4.50
b. 1981.	1.00	4.50
c. 1982.	1.00	4.50
s1. Specimen. Black overprint: *ESPECIMEN* on both sides. 1980. Punch hole cancelled.	—	35.00
s2. Specimen. Black overprint: *ESPECIMEN* on both sides. 1981. Punch hole cancelled.	—	35.00
s3. Specimen. Black overprint: *ESPECIMEN* on both sides. 1982. Punch hole cancelled.	—	35.00

118 5 Pesos Oro

1978-88. Deep brown, red-brown and red on multicolor underprint. J. Sánchez at right, arms at center. Orange bank seal at left. Back: Hydroelectric dam, dates in upper margin. Printer: TDLR. 156x67mm.

	VF	UNC
a. 1978.	3.00	12.50
b. 1980-82.	2.50	9.00
c. 1984; 1985; 1987; 1988.	1.60	8.00
s1. Specimen with black overprint: *ESPECIMEN*. 1978; 1980; 1981. Punch hole cancelled.	—	15.00
s2. Specimen with red overprint: *MUESTRA SIN VALOR* and TDLR oval seals. 1985; 1987.	—	15.00
s3. Specimen with black overprint: *MUESTRA SIN VALOR* and red overprint: TDLR oval seals. 1988.	—	15.00
s4. Specimen with pinhole cancellation: *MUESTRA SIN VALOR*. TDLR oval.	—	15.00

119 10 Pesos Oro

1978-88. Black and green on multicolor underprint. Mella at right, medallic Liberty head at center. Orange bank seal at left. Back: Quarry mining scene, dates in upper margin. Printer: TDLR. 156x67mm.

	VF	UNC
a. 1978.	5.00	25.00
b. 1980-82.	4.00	20.00
c. 1985; 1987; 1988.	3.00	17.50
s1. Specimen with black overprint: *ESPECIMEN* once on each side. 1978; 1980; 1981; 1982.	—	20.00
s2. Specimen with red overprint: *MUESTRA SIN VALOR* and TDLR oval seals. 1985; 1987.	—	25.00
s3. Specimen with black overprint: *MUESTRA SIN VALOR* and red overprint: TDLR oval seals. 1988.	—	25.00

120 20 Pesos Oro

1978-88. Black, dark brown and olive-brown on multicolor underprint. *Altar de la Patria* at center. Orange bank seal at left. Back: *Puerta del Conde* , dates in upper margin. Printer: TDLR. 156x67mm.

	VF	UNC
a. 1978.	8.00	40.00
b. 1980-82.	6.00	30.00
c. 1985; 1987; 1988.	5.00	20.00
s1. Specimen. Black overprint: *ESPECIMEN* once on each side. 1978; 1980; 1981, 1982.	—	20.00
s2. Specimen. Red overprint: *MUESTRA SIN VALOR* and TDLR oval seals. 1985; 1987.	—	22.50
s3. Specimen. Black overprint: *MUESTRA SIN VALOR* and red overprint: TDLR oval seals. 1988.	—	22.50

121 50 Pesos Oro

1978-87. Black and purple on multicolor underprint. Basilica at center, orange bank seal at left. Back: First cathedral in America at center right, dates in upper margin. Printer: TDLR. 156x67mm.

	VF	UNC
a. Watermark: Indian head. 1978; 1980; 1981.	25.00	65.00
b. Watermark: J. P. Duarte. 1985; 1987.	30.00	70.00
s1. As a. Specimen with black overprint: *ESPECIMEN.* 1978; 1980; 1981. Punch hole cancelled.	—	22.50
s2. As b. Specimen with perforated *MUESTRA SIN VALOR* and red overprint: TDLR oval seals. 1985; 1987.	—	25.00
s3. As b. Specimen with red overprint: *MUESTRA SIN VALOR* on both sides. TDLR oval. Punch hole cancelled.	—	25.00

122 100 Pesos Oro

1977-87. Violet, brown-orange and yellow-orange on multicolor underprint. Entrance to 16th century mint at center, orange bank seal at left. Back: Banco Central at center right, dates in upper margin. Printer: TDLR. 156x67mm.

	VF	UNC
a. Watermark: Indian head. 1977; 1978; 1980; 1981.	50.00	145.
b. Watermark: J.P. Duarte. 1984; 1985; 1987.	60.00	175.
s1. As a. Specimen with black overprint: *ESPECIMEN.* 1978; 1980; 1981.	—	30.00
s2. As b. Specimen with perforated: *MUESTRA SIN VALOR* and red TDLR oval seals. 1984; 1985; 1987.	—	25.00
s3. As b. Specimen with black overprint: *MUESTRA SIN VALOR* and red TDLR oval seals. 1987.	—	25.00

123 500 Pesos Oro

1978-87. Deep blue, blue and brown on multicolor underprint. National Theater at center, orange bank seal at left. Back: Fort San Felipe at center right, dates in upper margin. Printer: TDLR. 156x67mm.

	VF	UNC
a. Watermark: Indian head. 1978; 1980; 1981.	225.	450.
b. Watermark: J. P. Duarte. 1985; 1987.	200.	400.
s1. As a. Specimen with black overprint: *ESPECIMEN.* 1978; 1980; 1981.	—	40.00
s2. As b. Specimen with perforated: *MUESTRA SIN VALOR* and red overprint: TDLR oval seals. 1985; 1987.	—	40.00
s3. As b. Specimen with black overprint: *MUESTRA SIN VALOR* and red overprint: TDLR oval seals. Punch hole cancelled. 1987.	—	40.00

124 1000 Pesos Oro

1978-87. Red, purple and violet on multicolor underprint. National Palace at center, orange bank seal at left. Back: Columbus' fortress at center right, dates in upper margin. Printer: TDLR. 156x67mm.

	VF	UNC
a. Watermark: Indian head. 1978; 1980.	275.	550.
b. Watermark: J. P. Duarte. 1984; 1985; 1987.	225.	450.
s1. As a. Specimen with black overprint: *ESPECIMEN.* 1978; 1980; 1981. Punch hole cancelled.	—	50.00
s2. As b. Specimen with perforated: *MUESTRA SIN VALOR* and red overprint: TDLR oval seals. 1984; 1985; 1987.	—	50.00
s3. As b. Specimen with red overprint: *ESPECIMEN / MUESTRA SIN VALOR* once on each side and red TDLR oval in two corners.	—	50.00

1978 Commemorative Issue

#125, Inauguration of new Banco Central building.

125 100 Pesos Oro

	VF	UNC
15.8.1978 (- old date 1977). 1977; 1978; 1980; 1981. Violet, brown-orange and yellow-orange on multicolor underprint. Entrance to 16th century mint at center, orange bank seal at left. Back: Banco Central at center right, dates in upper margin. Overprint: Special commemorative text in black script at left on back. Watermark: Indian head. Printer: TDLR. Specimen in red folder. 156x67mm.	—	200.

1982 Commemorative Issue

#125A, 35th Anniversary Banco Central, 1947-1982

125A 100 Pesos Oro

22.10.1982 (old dates 1978, 1981). 1977; 1978; 1980; 1981. Violet, brown-orange and yellow-orange on multicolor underprint. Entrance to 16th century mint at center, orange bank seal at left. Back: Banco Central at center right, dates in upper margin. Overprint: Special commemorative text overprint in black below bank at right on back of #122a. Watermark: Indian head. Printer: TDLR.

	VF	UNC
s1. Old date 1978. Face without adhesive stamp or handstamp. Specimen.	—	135.
s2. Old date 1981. Banco Central commemorative adhesive stamp affixed at left, handstamp with date 22.10.1982 at center left. Specimen.	—	150.

1984 Issue

126 1 Peso Oro

1984; 1987; 1988. Black and brown on multicolor underprint. New portrait J. P. Duarte at right. Back: Sugar refinery, dates (lightly printed) in upper margin. Printer: TDLR. UV: UNO, five 1s and seal fluoresce orange. 156x67mm.

	VF	UNC
a. 1984.	FV	4.00
b. 1987.	FV	4.00
c. 1988.	FV	4.00
s1. 1984. Specimen. Perforated: *MUESTRA SIN VALOR.* and TDLR oval seal.	—	10.00
s2. 1987. Specimen. Red overprint: *MUESTRA SIN VALOR* and TDLR oval seals.	—	10.00
s3. 1988. Specimen Black overprint: *MUESTRA SIN VALOR* and red overprint: TDLR oval seals. Punch hole cancelled.	—	10.00

1988 Issue

127 50 Pesos Oro — VF / UNC

1988; 1990. Black and purple on multicolor underprint. Basilica at center, orange bank seal at left. Back: First cathedral in America at center right, dates in upper margin. Watermark: Duarte (profile). Printer: USBNC.

	VF	UNC
a. 1988.	FV	17.50
b. 1990.	FV	17.50
s. Specimen with red overprint: *ESPECIMEN / MUESTRA SIN VALOR* once on each side.	—	20.00

128 100 Pesos Oro — VF / UNC

1988; 1990. Violet, brown-orange and brown on multicolor underprint. Entrance to 16th century mint at center, orange bank seal at left. Back: Banco Central at center right, dates in upper margin. Watermark: Duarte (profile). Printer: USBNC. 156x67mm.

	VF	UNC
a. 1988.	FV	25.00
b. 1990.	FV	25.00
s1. 1988. Specimen with red overprint: *ESPECIMEN / MUESTRA SIN VALOR* on both aides.	—	22.50
s2. 1990. Specimen with red overprint: *ESPECIMEN / MUESTRA SIN VALOR* on both aides.	—	22.50

129 500 Pesos Oro — VF / UNC

1988. Deep blue, blue, and brown on multicolor underprint. National Theater at center, orange bank seal at left. Back: Fort San Felipe at center right, dates in upper margin. Watermark: Daurte (profile). Printer: USBNC. 156x67mm.

	VF	UNC
a. Issued note.	FV	75.00
s. Specimen with red overprint: *ESPECIMEN / MUESTRA SIN VALOR* once on each side.	—	35.00

130 1000 Pesos Oro — VF / UNC

1988; 1990. Purple, red-violet and violet on multicolor underprint. National Palace at center, orange bank seal at left. Back: Columbus' fortress at center right, dates in upper margin. Watermark: Duarte (profile). Printer: USBNC. 156x67mm.

	VF	UNC
a. 1988.	FV	135.
b. 1990.	FV	135.
s1. 1988. Specimen with red overprint: *ESPECIMEN / MUESTRA SIN VALOR* once on each side.	—	45.00
s2. 1990. Specimen with red overprint: *ESPECIMEN / MUESTRA SIN VALOR* once on each side.	—	45.00

1990 Issue

131 5 Pesos Oro — VF / UNC

1990. Deep brown, red-brown and red on multicolor underprint. J. Sánchez at right, arms at center. Orange bank seal at left. Silver leaf-like underlays at left and right. Back: Hydroelectric dam, dates in upper margin. Printer: H&S. 156x67mm. — FV 5.00

132 10 Pesos Oro — VF / UNC

1990. Deep green and black on multicolor underprint. Mella at right, medallic Liberty head at center. Orange bank seal at left. Silver leaf-like underlays at left and right. Back: Quarry mining scene, dates in upper margin. Printer: H&S. 156x67mm. — FV 7.50

133 20 Pesos Oro

1990. Deep brown and brown on multicolor underprint. *Altar de la Patria* at center. Orange bank seal at left. Silver leaf-like underlays at left and right. Back: *Puerta del Condo* , dates in upper margin. Printer: H&S. 156x67mm. — FV 12.50

134 500 Pesos Oro

1990. Deep blue-green, black and brown on multicolor underprint. National Theater at center, orange bank seal at left. Silver leaf-like underlays at left and right. Back: Fort San Felipe at center right, dates in upper margin. Printer: H&S. 156x67mm. — FV 75.00

1991 Issue

135 50 Pesos Oro — VF / UNC

1991; 1994. Black and purple on multicolor underprint. Basilica at center, orange bank seal at left. Back: First cathedral in America at center right, dates in upper margin. Watermark: Columbus. Printer: TDLR. 156x67mm.

	VF	UNC
a. 1991.	FV	15.00
b. 1994.	FV	10.00
s1. 1991. Specimen. Overprint: *MUESTRA SIN VALOR* in black and TDLR oval seals in red. Punch hole cancelled.	—	20.00
s2. 1994. Specimen. Overprint: *MUESTRA SIN VALOR* in black and TDLR oval seals in red. Punch hole cancelled.	—	20.00

136 100 Pesos Oro — VF / UNC

1991; 1994. Orange and violet on multicolor underprint. Entrance to 16th century mint at center, orange bank seal at left. Back: Banco Central at center right, dates in upper margin. Printer: TDLR. 156x67mm.

	VF	UNC
a. 1991.	FV	25.00
b. 1994.	FV	20.00
s1. 1991. Specimen with black overprint: *MUESTRA SIN VALOR* and red overprint: TDLR oval seals. Punch hole cancelled.	—	35.00
s2. 1994. Specimen with black overprint: *MUESTRA SIN VALOR* and red overprint: TDLR oval seals. Punch hole cancelled.	—	35.00

137 500 Pesos Oro — VF / UNC

1991; 1994. Deep blue, blue and dark brown on multicolor underprint. National Theater at center, orange bank seal at left. Silver leaf-like underlays at left and right. Back: Fort San Felipe at center right, dates in upper margin. Printer: TDLR. 156x67mm.

	VF	UNC
a. 1991.	FV	65.00
b. 1994.	FV	65.00
s1. 1991. Specimen with black overprint: *MUESTRA SIN VALOR* and red overprint: TDLR oval seals.	—	35.00
s2. 1994. Specimen with black overprint: *MUESTRA SIN VALOR* and red overprint: TDLR oval seals.	—	35.00

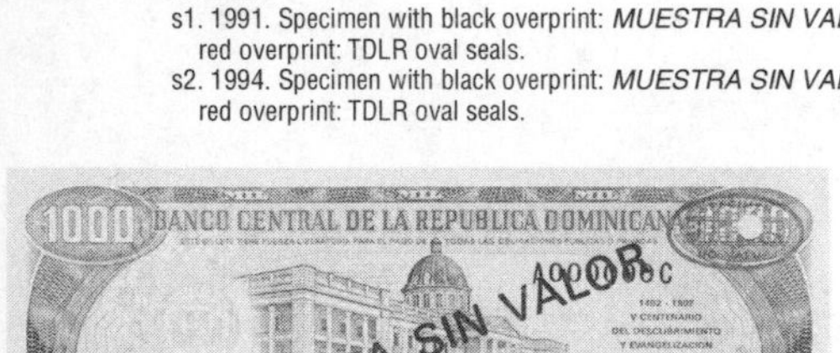

138 1000 Pesos Oro — VF / UNC

1991; 1992; 1994. Purple, red-violet and violet on multicolor underprint. National Palace at center, orange bank seal at left. Back: Columbus' fortress at center right, dates in upper margin. Printer: TDLR. 156x67mm.

	VF	UNC
a. 1991.	FV	125.
b. 1992.	FV	125.
c. 1994.	FV	125.
s1. 1991. Specimen with black overprint: *MUESTRA SIN VALOR* and red overprint: TDLR oval seals. Punch hole cancelled.	—	50.00
s2. 1992. Specimen with black overprint: *MUESTRA SIN VALOR* and red overprint: TDLR oval seals. Punch hole cancelled.	—	50.00
s3. 1994. Specimen with black overprint: *MUESTRA SIN VALOR* and red overprint: TDLR oval seals. Punch hole cancelled.	—	50.00

1992 Commemorative Issue

#139-142, Quincentennial of First Landfall by Christopher Columbus, 1992

139 20 Pesos Oro — VF / UNC

1992. Deep brown and brown on multicolor underprint. *Altar de la Patria* at center. Orange bank seal at left. Silver leaf-like underlays at left and right. Brown commemorative text: *1492-1992 V Centenario...* at left over orange seal. Back: *Puerta del Conde*, dates in upper margin. Printer: BABNC. 156x67mm.

	VF	UNC
a. Issued note.	FV	8.00
s. Specimen with red overprint: *ESPECIMEN* in red in upper corners and black overprint: *ESPECIMEN / MUESTRA SIN VALOR* once on each side.	—	25.00

140 500 Pesos Oro — VF / UNC

1992. Brown and blue-black on multicolor underprint. Sailing ships at center, C. Columbus at center right. Back: Arms at left, Columbus Lighthouse, placement of Cross of Christianity and map outline at center. Watermark: C. Columbus. Printer: CBNC. 156x67mm.

	VF	UNC
a. Issued note.	FV	110.
s1. Specimen with black overprint: *MUESTRA SIN VALOR* and red overprint: TDLR oval seals.	—	110.
s2. Specimen with red overprint: *MUESTRA*.	—	100.

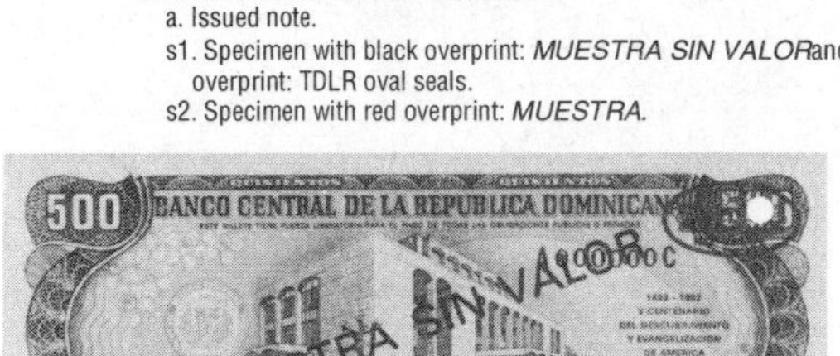

141 500 Pesos Oro — VF / UNC

1992. Deep blue, blue and dark brown on multicolor underprint. National Theater at center, orange bank seal at left. Silver leaf-like underlays at left and right. Back: Fort San Felipe at center right, dates in upper margin. Overprint: Black commemorative text at right. Watermark: C. Columbus. Printer: TDLR. 156x67mm.

	VF	UNC
a. Issued note.	FV	110.
s. Specimen with black overprint: *MUESTRA SIN VALOR* and red overprint: TDLR oval seals. Punch hole cancelled.	—	35.00

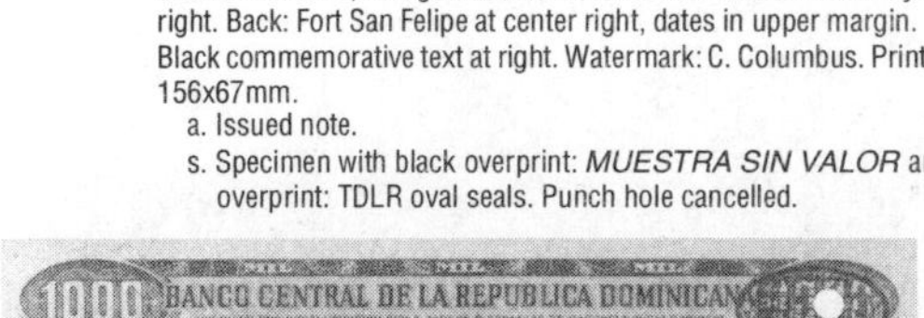

142 1000 Pesos Oro — VF / UNC

1992. Purple, red-violet and violet on multicolor underprint. National Palace at center, orange bank seal at left. Back: Columbus' fortress at center right, dates in upper margin. Overprint: Black commemorative text at right. Watermark: C. Columbus. Printer: TDLR. 156x67mm.

	VF	UNC
a. Issued note.	FV	150.
s. Specimen with black overprint: *MUESTRA SIN VALOR* and red overprint: TDLR oval seals. Punch hole cancelled.	—	40.00

1993 Regular Issue

143 5 Pesos Oro — VF — UNC

1993. Deep brown, red-brown and red on multicolor underprint. J. Sánchez at right, arms at center. Orange bank seal at left. Silver leaf-like underlays at left and right. Back: Hydroelectric dam, dates in upper margin. Printer: USBNC. 156x67mm.

	VF	UNC
a. Issued note.	FV	2.00
s. Specimen. Overprint in black: *ESPECIMEN / MUESTRA SIN VALOR* on each side.	—	75.00

144 100 Pesos Oro

1993. Orange and violet on multicolor underprint. Entrance to 16th century mint at center, orange bank seal at left. Back: Banco Central at center right, dates in upper margin. Printer: FNMT. 156x67mm.

	VF	UNC
a. Issued note.	FV	17.50
s. Specimen. Overprint: *ESPECIMEN / MUESTRA SIN VALOR* in black on each side. Punch hole cancelled.	—	100.

145 1000 Pesos Oro

1993. Red, purple and violet on multicolor underprint. National Palace at center, orange bank seal at left. Back: Columbus' fortress at center right, dates in upper margin. Printer: FNMT. 156x67mm.

	VF	UNC
a. Issued note.	FV	120.
s. Specimen. Overprint in black: *ESPECIMEN / MUESTRA SIN VALOR* once on each side. Punch hole cancelled.	—	150.

1994 Issue

146 5 Pesos Oro — VF — UNC

1994. Deep brown, red-brown and red on multicolor underprint. J. Sánchez at right, arms at center. Orange bank seal at left. Silver leaf-like underlays at left and right. Back: Hydroelectric dam, dates in upper margin. Printer: TDLR.

	VF	UNC
a. Issued note.	FV	1.75
s. Specimen with black overprint: *MUESTRA SIN VALOR* once on each side. Punch hole cancelled. TDLR oval.	—	50.00

1995 Issue

147 5 Pesos Oro — VF — UNC

1995. Deep brown, red-brown and red on multicolor underprint. J. Sánchez at right, bright colored arms at center. Orange bank seal at left. Silver leaf-like underlays at left and right. Back: Hydroelectric dam, dates in upper margin. Printer: F-CO. 156x67mm.

	VF	UNC
a. Issued note.	FV	1.25
s. Specimen with black overprint: *ESPECIMEN / MUESTRA SIN VALOR* once on each side. Punch hole cancelled.	—	25.00

148 10 Pesos Oro — VF — UNC

1995. Deep green and black on multicolor underprint. Mella at right, medallic Liberty head at center. Orange bank seal at left. Silver leaf-like underlays at left and right. Back: Quarry mining scene, dates in upper margin. Printer: F-CO. 156x67mm.

	VF	UNC
a. Issued note.	FV	3.00
s. Specimen with black overprint: *ESPECIMEN / MUESTRA SIN VALOR* once on each side. Punch hole cancelled.	—	20.00

149 50 Pesos Oro — VF — UNC

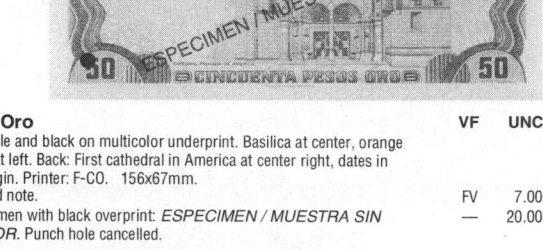

1995. Purple and black on multicolor underprint. Basilica at center, orange bank seal at left. Back: First cathedral in America at center right, dates in upper margin. Printer: F-CO. 156x67mm.

	VF	UNC
a. Issued note.	FV	7.00
s. Specimen with black overprint: *ESPECIMEN / MUESTRA SIN VALOR*. Punch hole cancelled.	—	20.00

150 100 Pesos Oro — VF — UNC

1995. Orange, violet and brown on multicolor underprint. Entrance to 16th century mint at center, orange bank seal at left, silver overlays at left and right, purple design with *RD* also at right. Back: Banco Central at center right, dates in upper margin. Luminescent strip at right with text. Printer: F-CO. 156x67mm.

	VF	UNC
a. Issued note.	FV	12.50
s. Specimen with black overprint: *ESPECIMEN / MUESTRA SIN VALOR* on each side. Punch hole cancelled.	—	30.00

151 500 Pesos Oro — VF — UNC

1995. Deep blue, blue and brown on multicolor underprint. National Theater at center, orange bank seal at left. Silver overlays at left and right, gold design with *RD* also at right. Back: Fort San Felipe at center right, dates in upper margin. Luminescent strip at right with text. Printer: F-CO. 156x67mm.

	VF	UNC
a. Issued note.	FV	70.00
s. Specimen with black overprint: *ESPECIMEN / MUESTRA SIN VALOR* once on each side. Punch hole cancelled.	—	60.00

1996-97 Issue

152 5 Pesos Oro — VF — UNC

1996; 1997. Deep brown, red-brown and red on multicolor underprint. J. Sánchez at right, bright colored arms at center. Date under orange bank seal at left. Silver leaf-like underlays at left and right. Back: Hydroelectric dam, dates in upper margin. Printer: F-CO. 156x67mm.

	VF	UNC
a. 1996.	FV	2.00
b. 1997.	FV	2.00
s1. 1996. Specimen. Black overprint: *ESPECIMEN MUESTRA SIN VALOR* once on each side. Punch hole cancelled.	—	25.00
s2. 1997. Specimen. Black overprint: *ESPECIMEN MUESTRA SIN VALOR* once on each side. Punch hole cancelled.	—	25.00

153 10 Pesos Oro

1996; 1997; 1998. Deep green and black on multicolor underprint. Mella at right, medallic Liberty head at center. Date under orange bank seal at left. Silver leaf-like underlays at left and right. Back: Quarry mining scene, dates in upper margin. Printer: F-CO. 156x67mm.

	VF	UNC
a. Issued note.	FV	3.00
s. Specimen. Black overprint: *ESPECIMEN / MUESTRA SIN VALOR* once on each side. Punch hole cancelled.	—	25.00

154 20 Pesos Oro

1997; 1998. Deep brown and brown on multicolor underprint. *Altar de la Patria* at center. Date under orange bank seal at left. Silver leaf-like underlays at left and right. Back: *Puerta del Conde,* dates in upper margin. Printer: F-CO. 156x67mm.

	VF	UNC
a. 1997.	FV	5.00
b. 1998.	—	5.00
s1. 1997. Specimen. Black overprint: *ESPECIMEN / MUESTRA SIN VALOR* once on each side. Punch hole cancelled.	—	10.00
s2. 1998. Specimen Black overprint: *ESPECIMEN / MUESTRA SIN VALOR* once on each side. Punch hole cancelled.	—	10.00

155 50 Pesos Oro

1997; 1998. Purple and black on multicolor underprint. Basilica at center, date under orange bank seal at left. Back: First cathedral in America at center right, dates in upper margin. Watermark: Daurte. Printer: F-CO. 156x67mm.

	VF	UNC
a. 1997.	FV	10.00
b. 1998.	FV	10.00
s1. 1997. Specimen. Overprint: *ESPECIMEN / MUESTRA SIN VALOR* in black on each side. Punch hole cancelled.	—	15.00
s2. 1998. Specimen. Overprint: *ESPECIMEN / MUESTRA SIN VALOR* in black on each side. Punch hole cancelled.	—	15.00

156 100 Pesos Oro

1997; 1998. Orange and violet on multicolor underprint. Entrance to 16th century mint at center, date under orange bank seal at left, silver overlays at left and right, purple design with *RD* also at right. Back: Banco Central at center right, dates in upper margin. Luminescent strip at right with text. Watermark: Duarte. Printer: F-CO. 156x67mm.

	VF	UNC
a. 1997.	FV	17.50
b. 1998.	FV	17.50
s1. 1997. Specimen with black Overprint: *ESPECIMEN / MUESTRA SIN VALOR* on each side. Punch hole cancelled.	—	20.00
s2. 1998. Specimen with black Overprint: *ESPECIMEN / MUESTRA SIN VALOR* on each side. Punch hole cancelled	—	20.00

157 500 Pesos Oro

1996; 1997; 1998. Deep blue, blue and brown on multicolor underprint. National Theater at center, date under orange bank seal at left. Silver overlays at left and right, gold design with *RD* also at right. Back: Fort San Felipe at center right, dates in upper margin. Luminescent strip at right with text. Watermark: Duarte. Printer: F-CO. 156x67mm.

	VF	UNC
a. 1996.	FV	55.00
b. 1997.	FV	55.00
c. 1998.	FV	55.00
s1. 1996. Specimen with black overprint: *ESPECIMEN / MUESTRA SIN VALOR* on each side. Punch hole cancelled.	—	25.00
s2. 1997. Specimen with black overprint: *ESPECIMEN / MUESTRA SIN VALOR* on each side. Punch hole cancelled.	—	25.00
s3. 1998. Specimen with black overprint: *ESPECIMEN / MUESTRA SIN VALOR* on each side. Punch hole cancelled.	—	25.00

158 1000 Pesos Oro

1996; 1997; 1998. Red, purple, violet on multicolor underprint. National Palace at center, date under orange bank seal at left. Back: Columbus' fortress at center right, dates in upper margin. Watermark: Duarte. Printer: F-CO. 156x67mm.

	VF	UNC
a. 1996.	FV	120.
b. 1997.	FV	120.
c. 1998.	FV	120.
s1. 1996. Specimen. Overprint in black: *ESPECIMEN / MUESTRA SIN VALOR* once on both sides. Punch hole cancelled.	—	30.00
s2. 1997. Specimen. Overprint in black: *ESPECIMEN / MUESTRA SIN VALOR* once on both sides. Punch hole cancelled.	—	30.00
s3. 1998. Specimen. Overprint in black: *ESPECIMEN / MUESTRA SIN VALOR* once on both sides. Punch hole cancelled.	—	30.00

2000 Issue

159 10 Pesos Oro

2000. Dark green on multicolor underprint. Matí as Ramón Mella at right. Back: *Altar de la Patria*. Printer: BABN. 156x67mm.

	VF	UNC
a. Issued note.	FV	3.00
s. Specimen. Black overprint: *ESPECIMEN MUESTRA SIN VALOR* in two lines once on each side. Punch hole cancelled.	—	25.00

160 20 Pesos Oro

2000. Brown on multicolor underprint. Gregorio Luperon at right. Back: *Panteón Nacional* at left. Printer: F-CO. 156x67mm.

	VF	UNC
a. Issued note.	FV	4.00
s. Specimen with black overprint: *ESPECIMEN / MUESTRA SIN VALOR* once on both sides. Punch hole cancelled.	—	10.00

161	**50 Pesos Oro**	**VF**	**UNC**
	2000. Purple and dark brown on multicolor underprint. Santa Maria la Menor Cathedral at right. Back: Basilica de Nuestra Señora de la Altagracia at left. Watermark: Duarte. Printer: F-CO. 156x67mm.		
	a. Issued note.	FV	9.00
	s. Specimen. With black overprint: *ESPECIMEN / MUESTRA SIN VALOR* on both sides. Punch hole cancelled.	—	12.50

162	**500 Pesos Oro**	**VF**	**UNC**
	2000. Dark brown and aqua on multicolor underprint. Salome Ureña de Henriquez and Pedro Henriquez Ureña at right. Back: Banco Central building at left. Watermark: Duarte. Printer: F-CO. 156x67mm.		
	a. Issued note.	FV	45.00
	s. Specimen. With black overprint: *ESPECIMEN / MUESTRA SIN VALOR* on both sides. Punch hole cancelled.	—	35.00

163	**1000 Pesos Oro**	**VF**	**UNC**
	2000. Red and deep lilac on multicolor underprint. *Palacio Nacional* at right. Back: Alcazar de Don Diego Colon at left. Watermark: Duarte. Printer: F-CO. 156x67mm.		
	a. Issued note.	FV	125.
	s. Specimen with black overprint: *ESPECIMEN / MUESTRA SIN VALOR* once on both sides. Punch hole cancelled.	—	75.00

164	**2000 Pesos Oro**	**VF**	**UNC**
	2000. Black and blue on multicolor underprint. Emillo Prud-Homme and José Reyes at right. Back: *Teatro Nacional.* 156x67mm.		
	a. Issued note.	FV	220.
	s. Specimen. Overprint in black: *ESPECIMEN / MUESTRA SIN VALOR* in two lines once on each side. Punch hole cancelled.	—	—

2000-01 Issue

165	**10 Pesos Oro**	**VF**	**UNC**
	2000; 2001. Dark green on multicolor underprint. Matías Ramón Mella at right. Back: *Altar de la Patria.* Printer: F-CO. 156x67mm.		
	a. 2000.	FV	3.00
	b. 2001.	FV	3.00
	s1. 2000. Specimen with black overprint: *ESPECIMEN / MUESTRA SIN VALOR* once on each side. Punch hole cancelled.	—	25.00
	s2. 2001. Specimen with black overprint: *ESPECIMEN / MUESTRA SIN VALOR* once on each side. Punch hole cancelled.	—	25.00

166	**20 Pesos Oro**	**VF**	**UNC**
	2000; 2001. Brown on multicolor underprint. Gregorio Luperon at right. Back: *Panteón Nacional* at left. Watermark: Duarte. Printer: BABN. The 2000 note has a special rendition of the date and a millennium commemorative text. 156x67mm.		
	a. 2000.	FV	4.00
	b. 2001.	FV	4.00
	s. Specimen.	—	10.00
167	**100 Pesos Oro**		
	2000; 2001. Dark brown and orange on multicolor underprint. F. R. Sanches, J. P. Duarte and M. R. Mella at right. Back: *Puerta del Conde* at left. Watermark: Duarte. Printer: BABN. 156x67mm.		
	a. 2000.	FV	20.00
	b. 2001.	FV	20.00
	s1. 2000. Specimen with black overprint: *ESPECIMEN / MUESTRA SIN VALOR* on each side. Punch hole cancelled	—	20.00
	s2. 2001. Specimen with black Overprint: *ESPECIMEN / MUESTRA SIN VALOR* on each side. Punch hole cancelled	—	20.00

2001-02 Issue

168	**10 Pesos Oro**	**VF**	**UNC**
	2001; 2002; 2003. Dark green on multicolor underprint. Matí as Ramón Mella at right. Wide border printing at upper center right. Back: *Altar de la Patria.* Printer: (T)DLR. 156x67mm.		
	a. 2001. Yellow to left on both sides.	FV	2.00
	b. 2002. Green to left on face.	FV	2.00
	c. 2003. Green to left on face.	FV	2.00
	s1. 2001. Specimen. Overprint in black: *ESPECIMEN / MUESTRA SIN VALOR* on both sides. Punch hole cancelled.	—	25.00
	s2. 2002. Specimen. Overprint in black: *ESPECIMEN / MUESTRA SIN VALOR* on both sides. Punch hole cancelled.	—	25.00
	s3. 2003. Specimen. Overprint in black: *ESPECIMEN / MUESTRA SIN VALOR* on both sides. Punch hole cancelled.	—	25.00

169 20 Pesos Oro — VF — UNC

2001-04. Brown on peach, green and multicolor underprint. Gregorio Luperon at right. Wide border printing at upper center right. Back: *Panteón Nacional* at left. Printer: (T)DLR. 156x67mm.

	VF	UNC
a. 2001. Yellow to left on both sides.	FV	3.00
b. 2002. Pink to left on face.	FV	3.00
c. 2003. Pink to left on face.	FV	3.00
d. 2004. Pink to left on face.	FV	3.00
s1. Specimen. 2001. Overprint: *ESPECIMEN / MUESTRA SIN VALOR* in black on both sides. Punch hole cancelled.	—	10.00
s2. Specimen. 2002. Overprint: *ESPECIMEN / MUESTRA SIN VALOR* in black on both sides. Punch hole cancelled.	—	10.00
s3. Specimen. 2003. Overprint: *ESPECIMEN / MUESTRA SIN VALOR* in black on both sides. Punch hole cancelled.	—	10.00
s4. Specimen. 2004. Overprint: *ESPECIMEN / MUESTRA SIN VALOR* in black on both sides. Punch hole cancelled.	—	10.00

170 50 Pesos Oro — VF — UNC

2001; 2002; 2003; 2004. Purple and dark brown on multicolor underprint. Santa Maria la Menor Cathedral at right. Wide border printing at upper center right. Back: Basilica de Nuestra Señora de la Altagracia at left. Watermark: Duarte. Printer: (T)DLR. 156x67mm.

	VF	UNC
a. 2001.	FV	8.00
b. 2002. Violet to left on face.	FV	8.00
c. 2003. Violet to left on face.	FV	8.00
d. 2004. Violet to left on face.	FV	8.00
s1. 2001. Specimen. Overprint: *ESPECIMEN / MUESTRA SIN VALOR* in black on each side. Punch hole cancelled.	—	12.50
s2. 2002. Specimen. Overprint: *ESPECIMEN / MUESTRA SIN VALOR* in black on each side. Punch hole cancelled.	—	12.50
s3. 2003. Specimen. Overprint: *ESPECIMEN / MUESTRA SIN VALOR* in black on each side. Punch hole cancelled.	—	12.50
s4. 2004. Specimen. Overprint: *ESPECIMEN / MUESTRA SIN VALOR* in black on each side. Punch hole cancelled.	—	12.50

171 100 Pesos Oro — VF — UNC

2001; 2002; 2003; 2004. Dark brown and orange on multicolor underprint. F. R. Sanches, J. P. Duarte and M. R. Mella at right. Wide border printing at upper center right. Back: *Puerta del Conde* at left. Watermark: Duarte. Printer: (T)DLR. 156x67mm.

	VF	UNC
a. 2001. Yellow to left on face and back.	FV	17.50
b. 2002. Green to left on face.	FV	17.50
c. 2003. Green to left on face.	FV	17.50
d. 2004. Green to left on face.	FV	17.50
s1. 2001. Specimen. Overprint: *ESPECIMEN / MUESTRA SIN VALOR* in black on both sides. Punch hole cancelled.	—	20.00
s2. 2002. Specimen. Overprint: *ESPECIMEN / MUESTRA SIN VALOR* in black on both sides. Punch hole cancelled.	—	20.00
s3. 2003. Specimen. Overprint: *ESPECIMEN / MUESTRA SIN VALOR* in black on both sides. Punch hole cancelled.	—	20.00
s4. 2004. Specimen. Overprint: *ESPECIMEN / MUESTRA SIN VALOR* in black on both sides. Punch hole cancelled.	—	20.00

172 500 Pesos Oro — VF — UNC

2002; 2003; 2004. Dark brown and aqua on multicolor underprint. Salome Ureña de Henriquez and Pedro Henriquez Ureña at right. Wide border printing at upper center right. Back: Banco Central building at left. Watermark: Duarte. Printer: (T)DLR. Placement of security strip varies slightly. 156x67mm.

	VF	UNC
a. 2002.	FV	40.00
b. 2003.	FV	40.00
c. 2004.	FV	40.00
s1. 2002. Specimen. Overprint in black: *ESPECIMEN / MUESTRA SIN VALOR* on both sides. Punch hole cancelled.	—	20.00
s2. 2003. Specimen. Overprint in black: *ESPECIMEN / MUESTRA SIN VALOR* on both sides. Punch hole cancelled.	—	20.00
s3. 2004. Specimen. Overprint in black: *ESPECIMEN / MUESTRA SIN VALOR* on both sides. Punch hole cancelled.	—	20.00

173 1000 Pesos Oro — VF — UNC

2002; 2003; 2004. Red and deep lilac on multicolor underprint. *Palacio Nacional* at right. Wide border printing at upper center right. Back: Alcazar de Don Diego Colon at left. Watermark: Duarte. Printer: (T)DLR. 156x67mm.

	VF	UNC
a. 2002.	FV	105.
b. 2003.	FV	105.
c. 2004.	FV	105.
s1. 2002. Specimen. Overprint in black: *ESPECIMEN / MUESTRA SIN VALOR* once on each side. Punch hole cancelled.	—	30.00
s2. 2003. Specimen. Overprint in black: *ESPECIMEN / MUESTRA SIN VALOR* once on each side. Punch hole cancelled.	—	30.00
s3. 2004. Specimen. Overprint in black: *ESPECIMEN / MUESTRA SIN VALOR* once on each side. Punch hole cancelled.	—	30.00

174 2000 Pesos Oro — VF — UNC

2002. Black and blue on multicolor underprint. Emillo Prud-Homme and José Reyes at right. Wide border printing at upper center right. Back: *Teatro Nacional*. Watermark: Duarte. Printer: (T)DLR. 156x67mm.

	VF	UNC
a. 2002.	FV	200.
b. 2003.	FV	200.
c. 2004.	FV	200.
s1. 2002. Specimen. Overprint in black: *ESPECIMEN / MUESTRA SIN VALOR* once on each side. Punch hole cancelled.	—	40.00
s2. 2003. Specimen. Overprint in black: *ESPECIMEN / MUESTRA SIN VALOR* once on each side. Punch hole cancelled.	—	40.00
s3. 2004. Specimen. Overprint in black: *ESPECIMEN / MUESTRA SIN VALOR* once on each side. Punch hole cancelled.	—	40.00

2002 Commemorative Issue

#175, 55th Anniversary of the Central Bank.

		VF	UNC
175	**100 Pesos Oro**		
	2002. Dark Brown and orange on multicolor underprint. F. R. Sanches, J. P. Duarte and M. R. Mella at right. Wide border printing at upper center right. Back: *Puerta del Conde* at left. Commemorative overprint. Watermark: Duarte. Printer: (T)DLR. 156x67mm.		
	a. 2002.	FV	17.50
	s1. 2002. Specimen. Overprint: *ESPECIMEN / MUESTRA SIN VALOR* in black on both sides. Punch hole cancelled.	—	50.00

2006 Issue

		VF	UNC
176	**50 Pesos Oro**		
	2006; 2008. Printer: (T)DLR. Clear text security thread. 156x67mm.		
	a. 2006. Upper right background border engraving has flat bottom.	FV	8.00
	b. 2008. Upper right background border engraving has curved bottom.	FV	8.00
	s1. 2006. Specimen. Overprint: *ESPECIMEN / MUESTRA SIN VALOR* in black on both sides. Punch hole cancelled.	—	25.00
	s2. 2008. Specimen. Overprint: *ESPECIMEN / MUESTRA SIN VALOR* in black on both sides. Punch hole cancelled.	—	25.00

		VF	UNC
177	**100 Pesos Oro**		
	2006; 2009; 2010. Dark brown and orange on multicolor underprint. F.R. Sanches, J.P. Duarte and M.R. Mella at right. Clear text security thread. Back: *Puerta del Conde* at left. Watermark: J.P. Duarte and 100. Printer: (T)DLR. 156x67mm.		
	a. 2006.	FV	8.00
	b. 2009.	FV	8.00
	c. 2010.	FV	8.00
	s1. 2006. Specimen. Overprint: *ESPECIMEN / MUESTRA SIN VALOR* in black on both sides. Punch hole cancelled.	—	20.00
	s2. 2009. Specimen. Overprint: *ESPECIMEN / MUESTRA SIN VALOR* in black on both sides. Punch hole cancelled.	—	20.00
	s3. 2010. Specimen. Overprint: *ESPECIMEN / MUESTRA SIN VALOR* in black on both sides. Punch hole cancelled.	—	20.00

		VF	UNC
178	**200 Pesos Oro**		
	2007. Violet on multicolor underprint. Three women at right. Back: Monument at left center. Watermark: Value added to watermark. 156x67mm.	FV	35.00
179	**500 Pesos Oro**		
	2006; 2009; 2010. Watermark: Value added, Printer: (T)DLR. 156x67mm.		
	a. 2006.	FV	17.50
	b. 2009.	FV	17.50
	c. 2010.	FV	17.50
	s1. 2006. Specimen. Overprint in black: *ESPECIMEN/ MUESTRA SIN VALOR* on both sides. Punch hole cancelled.	—	50.00
	s2. 2009. Specimen. Overprint in black: *ESPECIMEN/ MUESTRA SIN VALOR* on both sides. Punch hole cancelled.	—	50.00
	s3. 2010. Specimen. Overprint in black: *ESPECIMEN/ MUESTRA SIN VALOR* on both sides. Punch hole cancelled.	—	50.00

		VF	UNC
180	**1000 Pesos Oro**		
	2006; 2009; 2010. Red and deep lilac on multicolor underprint. *Palacio Nacional* at right. Back: Alcazae de Don Diego Colon at left. Watermark: Duarte and value. 156x67mm.		
	a. 2006.	FV	55.00
	b. 2009.	FV	55.00
	c. 2010.	FV	55.00
	s1. 2006. Specimen. Overprint in black: *ESPECIMEN / MUESTRA SIN VALOR* once on each side. Punch hole cancelled.	—	40.00
	s2. 2009. Specimen. Overprint in black: *ESPECIMEN / MUESTRA SIN VALOR* once on each side. Punch hole cancelled.	—	40.00
	s3. 2010. Specimen. Overprint in black: *ESPECIMEN / MUESTRA SIN VALOR* once on each side. Punch hole cancelled.	—	40.00
181	**2000 Pesos Oro**		
	2006; 2009; 2010. Black and blue on multicolor underprint. Emilo Prud Homme and José Reyes at right. Back: *Teatro Nacional* at left. Watermark: Duarte and value. 156x67mm.		
	a. 2006.	FV	100.
	b. 2009.	FV	100.
	c. 2010.	FV	100.
	s1. 2006. Specimen. Overprint in black: *ESPECIMEN / MUESTRA SIN VALOR* once on each side. Punch hole cancelled.	—	50.00
	s2. 2009. Specimen. Overprint in black: *ESPECIMEN / MUESTRA SIN VALOR* once on each side. Punch hole cancelled.	—	50.00
	s3. 2010. Specimen. Overprint in black: *ESPECIMEN / MUESTRA SIN VALOR* once on each side. Punch hole cancelled.	—	50.00

2010 Polymer Issue

		VF	UNC
182	**20 Pesos Oro**		
	2009. Brown, orange and green on multicolor underprint. Gregorio Luperon at right. Back: Panteon Nacional. Printer: F-CO. Polymer plastic. 156x67mm.		
	a. Issued note.	FV	3.00
	s. Specimen. Overprint: *ESPECIMEN / MUESTRA SIN VALOR* in black on both sides. Punch hole cancelled.	—	50.00

2011 Pesos Dominicanos Issue

		VF	UNC
183	**50 Pesos Dominicanos**		
	2010. Santa Maria la Menor Cathedral at right. Printer: F-CO.		
	a. Issued note.	FV	8.00
	s. Specimen. Overprint in black: *ESPECIMEN / MUESTRA SIN VALOR* once on each side. Punch hole cancelled.	—	30.00
184	**100 Pesos Dominicanos**		
	2010. F.dR. Sanchez, J.P. Duarte and M.R. Mella at right. Printer: F-CO.		
	a. Issued note.	FV	16.00
	s. Specimen. Overprint in black: *ESPECIMEN / MUESTRA SIN VALOR* once on each side. Punch hole cancelled.	—	50.00
185	**500 Pesos Dominicanos**		
	2010. S.U. de Heriquez and P.H. Quziurena at right. Printer: F-CO.		
	a. Issued note.	FV	25.00
	s. Specimen. Overprint in black: *ESPECIMEN / MUESTRA SIN VALOR* once on each side. Punch hole cancelled.	—	50.00
186	**1000 Pesos Dominicanos**		
	2010. Palacio Nacional at right. Printer: F-CO.		
	a. Issued note.	FV	50.00
	s. Specimen. Overprint in black: *ESPECIMEN / MUESTRA SIN VALOR* once on each side. Punch hole cancelled.	—	75.00
187	**2000 Pesos Dominicanos**		
	2011. E.P. Homme and J. Reyes at right.		
	a. Issued note.	FV	100.
	s. Specimen. Overprint in black: *ESPECIMEN / MUESTRA SIN VALOR* once on each side. Punch hole cancelled.	—	75.00

Collector Series

Banco Central de la República Dominicana

1974 Issues

		Mkt. Value
CS1	**1-1000 Pesos Oro** ND(1974). #99-106. Overprint: *MUESTRA* twice on face.	450.
CS2	**1-1000 Pesos Oro** ND(1974). #99-106. Overprint: *MUESTRA* on face and back.	450.

1978 Issues

		Mkt. Value
CS3	**Pesos Oro** 1978. #116, 118-124. Overprint: *MUESTRA / SIN VALOR* on face, *ESPECIMEN* on back.	235.

		Mkt. Value
CS4	**Pesos Oro** 1978. #116, 118a-120a, 121, 122a, 123, 124a. Overprint: *SPECIMEN* with serial # prefix Maltese cross. #122a is dated 1977.	75.00

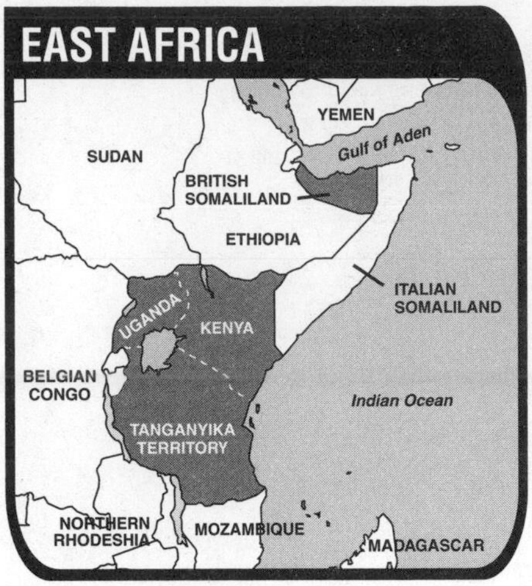

East Africa was an administrative grouping of several neighboring British territories: Kenya, Tanganyika, Uganda and Zanzibar.

The common interest of Kenya, Tanzania and Uganda invited cooperation in economic matters and consideration of political union. The territorial governors, organized as the East Africa High Commission, met periodically to administer such common activities as taxation, industrial development and education. The authority of the Commission did not infringe upon the constitution and internal autonomy of the individual colonies. The common monetary system circulated for the territories by the East African Currency Board and was also used in British Somaliland and the Aden Protectorate subsequent to the independence of India (1947) whose currency had previously circulated in these two territories.

Also see British Somaliland, Zanzibar, Kenya, Uganda and Tanzania. Also see Somaliland Republic, Kenya, Uganda and Tanzania.

RULERS:

British

MONETARY SYSTEM:

1 Rupee = 100 Cents to 1920
1 Florin = 100 Cents, 1920-1921
1 Shilling = 100 Cents

British Administration

East African Currency Board, Nairobi

1961 ND Issue

		VF	UNC
41	**5 Shillings** ND (1961-63). Various. Brown on light red underprint. Portrait Queen Elizabeth II at upper left. Three signatures at left and four at right. Printer: TDLR.		
	a. Top left signature: E. B. David. (1961).	20.00	250.
	b. Top left sign: A. L. Adu. (1962-63).	15.00	200.

		VF	UNC
42	**10 Shillings** ND (1961-63). Various. Green on multicolor underprint. Portrait Queen Elizabeth II at upper left. Three signatures at left and four at right. Printer: TDLR.		
	a. Top left signature: E. B. David. (1961).	25.00	350.
	b. Top left signature: A. L. Adu. (1962-63).	20.00	300.
43	**20 Shillings** ND (1961-63). Various. Blue on light pink underprint. Portrait Queen Elizabeth II at upper left. Three signatures at left and four at right. Printer: TDLR.		
	a. Top left signature: E. B. David. (1961).	75.00	500.
	b. Top left signature: A. L. Adu. (1962-63).	50.00	350.

		VF	UNC
44	**100 Shillings** ND (1961-63). Various. Red on multicolor underprint. Portrait Queen Elizabeth II at upper left. Three signatures at left and four at right. Printer: TDLR.		
	a. Top left signature: E. B. David. (1961).	150.	1000.
	b. Top left signature: A. L. Adu. (1962-63).	100.	750.

1964 ND Issue

45	5 Shillings	VF	UNC
	ND (1964). Brown on multicolor underprint. Sailboat at left center. Back: Various plants. Watermark: Rhinoceros.	15.00	100.

46	10 Shillings	VF	UNC
	ND (1964). Green on multicolor underprint. Sailboat at left center. Back: Various plants. Watermark: Rhinoceros.		
	a. Issued note.	25.00	150.
	s. Specimen, punch hole cancelled.	—	250.

47	20 Shillings	VF	UNC
	ND (1964). Blue on multicolor underprint. Sailboat at left center. Back: Various plants. Watermark: Rhinoceros.		
	a. Issued note.	40.00	400.
	s. Specimen. Punched hole cancelled.	—	600.

48	100 Shillings	VF	UNC
	ND (1964). Deep red on multicolor underprint. Sailboat at left center. Back: Various plants. Watermark: Rhinoceros.		
	a. Issued note.	50.00	250.
	s. Specimen. Punched hole cancelled.	—	400.

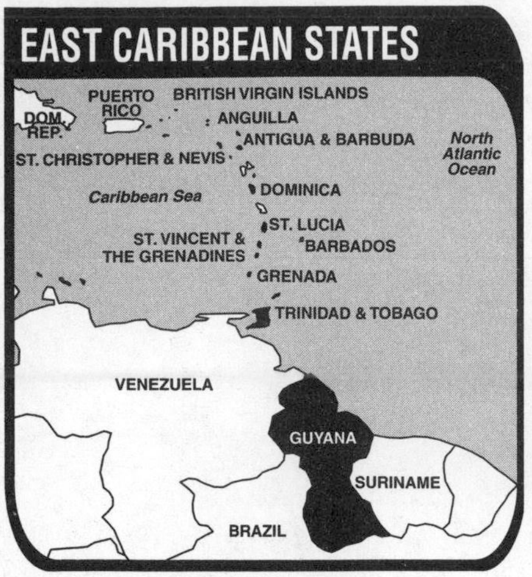

The East Caribbean States, formerly the British Caribbean Territories (Eastern Group), a currency board formed in 1950, comprised the British West Indies territories of Trinidad and Tobago, Barbados, the Leeward Islands of Anguilla, St. Christopher, Nevis and Antigua; the Windward Islands of St. Lucia, Dominica, St. Vincent and Grenada; British Guiana and the British Virgin Islands.

As time progressed, the member countries varied and is reflected on the backs of #13-16. The first issue includes Barbados but not Grenada, while the second issue includes both Barbados and Grenada and the third issue retains Grenada while Barbados is removed. Barbados attained self-government in 1961 and independence on Nov. 30, 1966.

On May 26, 1966 British Guiana became independent as Guyana which later became a cooperative Republic on Feb. 23, 1970.

The British Virgin Islands became a largely self-governing dependent territory of the United Kingdom in 1967. United States currency is the official medium of exchange.

St. Christopher and Nevis became fully independent on Sept. 19, 1983.

Trinidad & Tobago became an independent member state of the Commonwealth on August 31, 1962.

RULERS:

British

MONETARY SYSTEM:

1 Dollar = 100 Cents

ISLAND PARTICIPATION

Variety I

Variety II

Variety III

Variety I: Listing of islands on back includes barbados but not Grenada.

Variety II: Listing included Barbados and Grenada.

Variety III: Listing retains Grenada while Barbados is denied.

British Administration

East Caribbean Currency Authority

1965 ND Issue

#13-16 Replacement notes: Serial # prefix *Z1*.

Beginning in 1983, #13-16 were overprinted with circled letters at left indicating their particular areas of issue within the Eastern Group.

		VF	UNC
13	**1 Dollar**		
	ND (1965). Red on multicolor underprint. Fish at center, map at left, Queen Elizabeth II at right. Signature varieties. Back: Coastline with rocks and trees at left center. Watermark: Queen Elizabeth II. Printer: TDLR. 145x69mm.		
	a. Signature 1; 2. Back variety 1.	25.00	135.
	b. Signature 3. Back variety 2.	14.00	75.00
	c. Signature 4.	36.00	200.
	d. Signature 5; 6; 7.	14.00	75.00
	e. Signature 8. Back variety 3.	12.00	65.00
	f. Signature 9; 10. Darker red on back as previous varieties, to Series B82.	9.00	50.00
	g. Signature 10. Brighter red on back. Series B83-B91.	9.00	50.00
	h. overprint: *A* in circle.	9.00	50.00
	i. overprint: *D* in circle.	10.00	55.00
	j. overprint: *G* in circle.	9.00	50.00
	k. overprint: *K* in circle.	9.00	50.00
	l. overprint: *L* in circle.	10.00	55.00
	m. overprint: *M* in circle.	9.00	50.00
	n. overprint: *U* in circle.	9.00	50.00
	o. overprint: *V* in circle.	9.00	50.00
	s. As a, j-n. Specimen.	—	230.

		VF	UNC
14	**5 Dollars**		
	ND (1965). Green on multicolor underprint. Flying fish at center, map at left, Queen Elizabeth II at right. Signature varieties. Back: Coastline with rocks and trees at left center. Watermark: Queen Elizabeth II. Printer: TDLR. 145x69mm.		
	a. Signature 1. Back variety 1.	60.00	320.
	b. Signature 2.	60.00	320.
	c. Signature 3. Back variety 2. Reported not confirmed.	—	—
	d. Signature 4.	45.00	260.
	e. Signature 5; 6.	28.00	155.
	f. Signature 7.	28.00	155.
	g. Signature 8. Back variety 3.	18.00	100.
	h. Signature 9; 10.	14.00	75.00
	i. overprint: *A* in circle.	14.00	75.00
	j. overprint: *D* in circle.	15.00	85.00
	k. overprint: *G* in circle.	14.00	75.00
	l. overprint: *K* in circle.	14.00	75.00
	m. overprint: *L* in circle.	40.00	220.
	n. overprint: *M* in circle.	15.00	85.00
	o. overprint: *U* in circle.	14.00	80.00
	p. overprint: *V* in circle.	14.00	80.00
	s. As a, b. Specimen.	—	390.

		VF	UNC
15	**20 Dollars**		
	ND (1965). Purple on multicolor underprint. Turtles at center, map at left, Queen Elizabeth II at right. Signature varieties. Back: Coastline with rocks and trees at left center. Watermark: Queen Elizabeth II. Printer: TDLR. 145x69mm.		
	a. Signature 1. Back variety 1.	270.	1500.
	b. Signature 2.	230.	1250.
	c. Signature 3. Back variety 2. Reported not confirmed.	—	—
	d. Signature 4.	125.	690.
	e. Signature 5; 6; 7.	90.00	560.
	f. Signature 8. Back variety 3.	30.00	170.
	g. Signature 9; 10.	26.00	145.
	h. overprint: *A* in circle.	24.00	135.
	i. overprint: *D* in circle.	26.00	145.
	j. overprint: *G* in circle.	26.00	145.
	k. overprint: *K* in circle.	45.00	250.
	l. overprint: *L* in circle.	27.00	150.
	m. overprint: *M* in circle.	27.00	150.
	n. overprint: *U* in circle.	27.00	150.
	o. overprint: *V* in circle.	27.00	150.
	s. As a; e; g. Specimen.	—	800.

16	100 Dollars	VF	UNC
	ND (1965). Black on multicolor underprint. Sea horses at center, map at left, Queen Elizabeth II at right. Signature varieties. Back: Coastline with rocks and trees at left center. Watermark: Queen Elizabeth II. Printer: TDLR. 145x69mm.		
	a. Signature 1. Back variety 1.	650.	3600.
	b. Signature 2. Reported not confirmed.	—	—
	c. Signature 5. Back variety 2.	685.	3800.
	d. Signature 3; 4; 6; 7. Reported not confirmed.	—	—
	e. Signature 8. Back variety 3. Reported not confirmed.	—	—
	f. Signature 9; 10.	160.	1300.
	g. overprint: *A* in circle.	160.	880.
	h. overprint: *D* in circle.	290.	1000.
	i. overprint: *G* in circle.	200.	1100.
	j. overprint: *K* in circle.	260.	1450.
	k. overprint: *L* in circle.	160.	880.
	l. overprint: *M* in circle.	160.	880.
	m. overprint: *U* in circle.	160.	880.
	n. overprint: *V* in circle.	160.	880.
	s. As a. Specimen.	—	1100.

Eastern Caribbean Central Bank

SIGNATURE VARIETIES			
	Governor		Governor
1		2	

1985-87 ND Issue

#17-25 Replacement notes: Serial # prefix *Z1*. #17-20 do not have name Anguilla at island near top of map at right.

17	1 Dollar	VF	UNC
	ND (1985-88). Red on multicolor underprint. Windsurfer at left, Queen Elizabeth II at center right, map at right. Back: Palm tree, swordfish at center right, shoreline in background. Watermark: Queen Elizabeth II. Printer: TDLR. 145x69mm.		
	a. Suffix letter *A*.	7.00	37.50
	d. Suffix letter *D*.	7.00	37.50
	g. Suffix letter *G*.	7.00	37.50
	k. Suffix letter *K*.	7.00	37.50
	l. Suffix letter *L*.	7.00	37.50
	m. Suffix letter *M*.	7.00	37.50
	u. overprint: *U* in circle on suffix letter *V* issue (1988).	7.00	37.50
	v. Suffix letter *V*.	7.00	37.50

18	5 Dollars	VF	UNC
	ND (1986-88). Deep green on multicolor underprint. Windsurfer at left, Queen Elizabeth II at center right, map at right. Back: Palm tree, swordfish at center right, shoreline in background. Watermark: Queen Elizabeth II. Printer: TDLR. 145x69mm.		
	a. Suffix letter *A*.	11.00	60.00
	d. Suffix letter *D*.	11.00	60.00
	g. Suffix letter *G*.	11.00	60.00
	k. Suffix letter *K*.	11.00	60.00
	l. Suffix letter *L*.	11.00	60.00
	m. Suffix letter *M*.	11.00	60.00
	u. overprint: *U* in circle on suffix letter *V* issue (1988).	11.00	60.00
	v. Suffix letter *V*.	11.00	60.00
	ur. Replacement note. Z/1 serial # prefix.	25.00	140.

19	20 Dollars	VF	UNC
	ND (1987-88). Purple and brown on multicolor underprint. Windsurfer at left, Queen Elizabeth II at center right, map at right. Back: Palm tree, swordfish at center right, shoreline in background. Watermark: Queen Elizabeth II. Printer: TDLR. 145x69mm.		
	a. Suffix letter *A*.	37.50	210.
	d. Suffix letter *D*.	37.50	210.
	g. Suffix letter *G*.	37.50	210.
	k. Suffix letter *K*.	37.50	210.
	l. Suffix letter *L*.	37.50	210.
	m. Suffix letter *M*.	37.50	210.
	u. overprint: *U* in circle.	37.50	210.
	v. Suffix letter *V*.	37.50	210.

20	100 Dollars	VF	UNC
	ND (1986-88). Black and orange on multicolor underprint. Windsurfer at left, Queen Elizabeth II at center right, map at right. Back: Palm tree, swordfish at center right, shoreline in background. Watermark: Queen Elizabeth II. Printer: TDLR. 145x69mm.		
	a. Suffix letter *A*.	145.	800.
	d. Suffix letter *D*.	145.	800.
	g. Suffix letter *G*.	145.	800.
	k. Suffix letter *K*.	145.	800.
	l. Suffix letter *L*.	145.	800.
	m. Suffix letter *M*.	145.	800.
	u. overprint: *U* in circle on suffix letter *V* issue (1988).	145.	800.
	v. Suffix letter *V*.	145.	800.

1985-88 ND Issue

21 **1 Dollar** — VF — UNC

ND (1988-89). Red on multicolor underprint. Windsurfer at left, Queen Elizabeth II at center right, map at right. *Anguilla island* named near top of map at right. Signature 1. Back: Harbor at St. Lucia. Watermark: Queen Elizabeth II. Printer: TDLR. 145x69mm.

	VF	UNC
a. Suffic letter *A*.	9.00	50.00
d. Suffix letter *D*.	9.00	50.00
k. Suffix letter *K*.	9.00	50.00
l. Suffix letter *L*.	9.00	50.00
m. Suffix letter *M*.	9.00	50.00
u. Suffix letter *U*.	9.00	50.00
ur. Suffix letter *U*. Replacement note. Serial # prefix *Z*.	20.00	110.

22 **5 Dollars** — VF — UNC

ND (1988-93). Deep green on multicolor underprint. Windsurfer at left, Queen Elizabeth II at center right, map at right. *Anguilla island* named near top of map at right. Back: Harbor at St. Lucia. Watermark: Queen Elizabeth II. Printer: TDLR. 145x69mm.

	VF	UNC
a1. Suffix letter *A*. Signature 1.	10.00	55.00
a2. Like a1. Signature 2.	10.00	55.00
d. Suffix letter *D*. Signature 1.	10.00	55.00
g1. Suffix letter *G*. Signature 1.	10.00	55.00
g2. Like g1. Signature 2.	10.00	55.00
k1. Suffix letter *K*. Signature 1.	10.00	55.00
k2. Like k1. Signature 2.	10.00	55.00
l1. Suffix letter *L*. Signature 1.	10.00	55.00
l2. Like l1. Signature 2.	10.00	55.00
m. Suffix letter *M*. Signature 1.	10.00	55.00
u. Suffix letter *U*. Signature 1.	10.00	55.00
v2. Suffix letter *V*. Signature 2.	10.00	55.00
v1. Suffix letter *V*. Signature 1.	10.00	55.00

23 **10 Dollars** — VF — UNC

ND (1985-93). Blue on multicolor underprint. Windsurfer at left, Queen Elizabeth II at center right, map at right. *Anguilla island* named near top of map at right. Back: Harbor at Grenada, sailboats at left and center. Watermark: Queen Elizabeth II. Printer: TDLR. 145x69mm.

	VF	UNC
a1. Suffix letter *A*. signature 1.	19.00	105.
a2. Like a1. signature 2.	19.00	105.
d1. Suffix letter *D*. signature 1.	19.00	105.
d2. Like d1. signature 2.	19.00	105.
g. Suffix letter *G*. signature 1.	19.00	105.
k1. Suffix letter *K*. signature 1.	19.00	105.
k2. Like k1. signature 2.	19.00	105.
l1. Suffix letter *L*. signature 1.	19.00	105.
l2. Like l1. signature 2.	19.00	105.
m. Suffix letter *M*. signature 1.	19.00	105.
u. Suffix letter *U*. signature 1.	19.00	105.
v1. Suffix letter *V*. signature 1.	19.00	105.
v2. Like v1. signature 2.	19.00	105.
ar. As a2. Replacement note. Serial # prefix: *Z*.	36.00	200.

24 **20 Dollars** — VF — UNC

ND (1988-93). Purple and brown on multicolor underprint. Windsurfer at left, Queen Elizabeth II at center right, map at right. *Anguilla island* named near top of map at right. Back: Harbor at St. Lucia. Watermark: Queen Elizabeth II. Printer: TDLR. 145x69mm.

	VF	UNC
a1. Suffix letter *A*. Signature 1.	32.00	180.
a2. Like a1. Signature 2.	32.00	180.
d1. Suffix letter *D*. Signature 1.	32.00	180.
d2. Like d1. signature 2.	32.00	180.
g1. Suffix letter *G*. Signature 1.	32.00	180.
g2. Like g1. Signature 2.	32.00	180.
k1. Suffix letter *K*. Signature 1.	32.00	180.
k2. Like k1. Signature 2.	32.00	180.
l1. Suffix letter *L*. Signature 1.	32.00	180.
l2. Like l1. Signature 2.	32.00	180.
m1. Suffix letter *M*. Signature 1.	32.00	180.
m2. Like m1. Signature 2.	32.00	180.
u. Suffix letter *U*. Signature 1.	32.00	180.
v. Suffix letter *V*. Signature 1.	32.00	180.

25 **100 Dollars** — VF — UNC

ND (1988-93). Black and orange on multicolor underprint. Windsurfer at left, Queen Elizabeth II at center right, map at right. *Anguilla island* named near top of map at right. Back: Harbor at St. Lucia. Watermark: Queen Elizabeth II. Printer: TDLR. 145x69mm.

	VF	UNC
a1. Suffix letter *A*. signature 1.	200.	1100.
a2. Like a1. signature 2.	200.	1100.
d1. Suffix letter *D*. signature 1.	200.	1100.
d2. Like d1. signature 2.	200.	1100.
g. Suffix letter *G*. signature 1.	200.	1100.
k1. Suffix letter *K*. signature 1.	200.	1100.
k2. Like k1. signature 2.	200.	1100.
l1. Suffix letter *L*. signature 1.	200.	1100.
l2. Like l1. signature 2.	200.	1100.
m1. Suffix letter *M*. signature 1.	200.	1100.
m2. Like m1. signature 2.	200.	1100.
u. Suffix letter *U*. signature 1.	200.	1100.
v. Suffix letter *V*. signature 1.	200.	1100.

Antigua (A)	▮	▮	▮		▮	**St. Lucia (L)**	▮		▮		▮
Dominica (D)	▮	▮			▮	**Montserrat (M)**	▮		▮	▮	▮
Grenada (G)	▮				▮	**Anguilla (U)**	▮	▮	▮	▮	▮
St. Kitts (K)	▮			▮	▮	**St. Vincent (V)**	▮	▮		▮	▮

1993 ND Issue

26 5 Dollars VF UNC

ND (1993). Dark green, black and violet on multicolor underprint. Queen Elizabeth II at center right, turtle at lower center, green-throated carib at top right. Signature 2. Back: Admiral's House in Antigua and Barbuda at left, Trafalgar Falls in Dominica at right, island map at center. Watermark: Queen Elizabeth II. Printer: TDLR. 145x69mm.

	VF	UNC
a. Suffix letter *A* .	FV	60.00
d. Suffix letter *D* .	FV	60.00
g. Suffix letter *G* .	FV	60.00
k. Suffix letter *K* .	FV	60.00
l. Suffix letter *L* .	FV	60.00
m. Suffix letter *M* .	FV	80.00
u. Suffix letter *U* .	FV	60.00
v. Suffix letter *V* .	FV	60.00

27 10 Dollars VF UNC

ND (1993). Dark blue, black and red on multicolor underprint. Queen Elizabeth II at center right, turtle at lower center, green-throated carib at top right. Signature 2. Back: Admiralty Bay in St. Vincent and Grenadines at left, sailing ship *Warspite* and brown pelican at right center, island map at right center. Watermark: Queen Elizabeth II. Printer: TDLR. 145x69mm.

	VF	UNC
a. Suffix letter *A* .	FV	90.00
d. Suffix letter *D* .	FV	90.00
g. Suffix letter *G* .	FV	90.00
k. Suffix letter *K* .	FV	90.00
l. Suffix letter *L* .	FV	90.00
m. Suffix letter *M* .	FV	140.
u. Suffix letter *U* .	FV	90.00
v. Suffix letter *V* .	FV	90.00

28 20 Dollars VF UNC

ND (1993). Brown-violet, blue-gray and orange on multicolor underprint. Queen Elizabeth II at center right, turtle at lower center, green-throated carib at top right. Signature 2. Back: Government House in Montserrat at left, nutmeg in Grenada at right, island map at center. Watermark: Queen Elizabeth II. Printer: TDLR. 145x69mm.

	VF	UNC
a. Suffix letter *A* .	FV	130.
d. Suffix letter *D* .	FV	130.
g. Suffix letter *G* .	FV	130.
k. Suffix letter *K* .	FV	130.
l. Suffix letter *L* .	FV	130.
m. Suffix letter *M* .	FV	200.
u. Suffix letter *U* .	FV	130.
v. Suffix letter *V* .	FV	130.

29 50 Dollars VF UNC

ND (1993). Purple and olive green on multicolor underprint. Queen Elizabeth II at center right, turtle at lower center, green-throated carib at top right. Signature 2. Back: Brimstone Hill in St. Kitts at left, Los Pitons mountains in St. Lucia and sooty tern at right , island map at center. Watermark: Queen Elizabeth II. Printer: TDLR. 145x69mm.

	VF	UNC
a. Suffix letter *A* .	FV	260.
d. Suffix letter *D* .	FV	260.
g. Suffix letter *G* .	FV	260.
k. Suffix letter *K* .	FV	260.
l. Suffix letter *L* .	FV	260.
m. Suffix letter *M* .	65.00	370.
u. Suffix letter *U* .	FV	260.
v. Suffix letter *V* .	FV	260.

30 100 Dollars VF UNC

ND (1993). Dark brown, dark olive-green and tan on multicolor underprint. Queen Elizabeth II at center right, turtle at lower center, green-throated carib at top right. Signature 2. Back: Sir Arthur Lewis at left, E.C.C.B. Central Bank building and Lesser Antillean Swift at right, island map at center. Watermark: Queen Elizabeth II. Printer: TDLR. 145x69mm.

	VF	UNC
a. Suffix letter *A* .	65.00	380.
d. Suffix letter *D* .	65.00	380.
g. Suffix letter *G* .	65.00	380.
k. Suffix letter *K* .	65.00	380.
l. Suffix letter *L* .	65.00	380.
m. Suffix letter *M* .	85.00	470.
u. Suffix letter *U* .	65.00	380.
v. Suffix letter *V* .	65.00	380.

1994 ND Issue

#31-35 like #26-30 but w/clear bold values at upper l. and lower r. Thin security thread. Sign. 2. Replacement notes: Serial # prefix *Z* are scarce and command a premium.

31	**5 Dollars**	VF	UNC
	ND (1994). Dark green, black and violet on multicolor underprint. Queen Elizabeth II at center right, turtle at lower center, green-throated carib at top right. Clear bold values at upper left and lower right. Signature 2. Back: Admiral's House in Antigua and Barbuda at left, Trafalgar Falls in Dominica at right, island map at center. Watermark: Queen Elizabeth II. Printer: TDLR. Thin security thread. 145x69mm.		
	a. Suffix letter *A*.	FV	50.00
	d. Suffix letter *D*.	FV	50.00
	g. Suffix letter *G*.	FV	50.00
	k. Suffix letter *K*.	FV	50.00
	l. Suffix letter *L*.	FV	50.00
	m. Suffix letter *M*.	14.00	80.00
	u. Suffix letter *U*.	FV	50.00
	v. Suffix letter *V*.	FV	50.00

32	**10 Dollars**	VF	UNC
	ND (1994). Dark blue, black and red on multicolor underprint. Queen Elizabeth II at center right, turtle at lower center, green-throated carib at top right. Clear bold values at upper left and lower right. Signature 2. Back: Admiralty Bay in St. Vincent and Grenadines at left, sailing ship *Warspite* and brown pelican at right center, island map at center. Watermark: Queen Elizabeth II. Printer: TDLR. Thin security thread. 145x69mm.		
	a. Suffix letter *A*.	FV	70.00
	d. Suffix letter *D*.	FV	70.00
	g. Suffix letter *G*.	FV	70.00
	k. Suffix letter *K*.	FV	70.00
	l. Suffix letter *L*.	FV	70.00
	m. Suffix letter *M*.	20.00	110.
	u. Suffix letter *U*.	FV	70.00
	v. Suffix letter *V*.	FV	70.00

33	**20 Dollars**	VF	UNC
	ND (1994). Brown-violet, blue-gray and orange on multicolor underprint. Queen Elizabeth II at center right, turtle at lower center, green-throated carib at top right. Clear bold values at upper left and lower right. Signature 2. Back: Government House in Montserrat at left, nutmeg in Grenada at right, island map at center. Watermark: Queen Elizabeth II. Printer: TDLR. Thin security thread. 145x69mm.		
	a. Suffix letter *A*.	FV	110.
	d. Suffix letter *D*.	FV	110.
	g. Suffix letter *G*.	FV	110.
	k. Suffix letter *K*.	FV	110.
	l. Suffix letter *L*.	FV	110.
	m. Suffix letter *M*.	35.00	190.
	u. Suffix letter *U*.	FV	110.
	v. Suffix letter *V*.	FV	110.

34	**50 Dollars**	VF	UNC
	ND (1994). Tan, red-orange and green on multicolor underprint. Queen Elizabeth II at center right, turtle at lower center, green-throated carib at top right. Clear bold values at upper left and lower right. Signature 2. Back: Brimstone Hill in St. Kitts at left, Les Pitons mountains in St. Lucia and sooty tern at right , island map at center. Watermark: Queen Elizabeth II. Printer: TDLR. Thin security thread. 145x69mm.		
	a. Suffix letter *A*.	40.00	220.
	d. Suffix letter *D*.	40.00	220.
	g. Suffix letter *G*.	40.00	220.
	k. Suffix letter *K*.	40.00	220.
	l. Suffix letter *L*.	40.00	220.
	m. Suffix letter *M*.	80.00	450.
	u. Suffix letter *U*.	40.00	220.
	v. Suffix letter *V*.	40.00	220.

35	**100 Dollars**	VF	UNC
	ND (1994). Dark brown and dark green on multicolor underprint. Queen Elizabeth II at center right, turtle at lower center, green-throated carib at top right. Clear bold values at upper left and lower right. Signature 2. Back: Sir Arthur Lewis at left, E.C.C.B. Central Bank building and Lesser Antillean Swift at right, island map at center. Watermark: Queen Elizabeth II. Printer: TDLR. Thin security thread. 145x69mm.		
	a. Suffix letter *A*.	60.00	330.
	d. Suffix letter *D*.	60.00	330.
	g. Suffix letter *G*.	60.00	330.
	k. Suffix letter *K*.	60.00	330.
	l. Suffix letter *L*.	60.00	330.
	m. Suffix letter *M*.	90.00	510.
	u. Suffix letter *U*.	60.00	330.
	v. Suffix letter *V*.	60.00	330.

1998 ND Issue

#36 Building rendering is long, partially covering signature. Printer: (T)DLR.

36 100 Dollars

ND (1998). Dark brown and dark green on multicolor underprint. Queen Elizabeth II at center right, turtle at lower center, green-throated carib at top right. Signature 2. Back: Sir Arthur Lewis at left, Central Bank building and Lesser Antillean Swift at right, island map at center. Watermark: Queen Elizabeth II. Printer: (T)DLR. Gold foil flower enhanced colors and segmented foil over security thread. 145x69mm.

	VF	UNC
a. Suffix letter *A*.	55.00	270.
d. Suffix letter *D*.	55.00	270.
g. Suffix letter *G*.	55.00	270.
k. Suffix letter *K*.	55.00	270.
l. Suffix letter *L*.	55.00	270.
m. Suffix letter *M*.	80.00	360.
u. Suffix letter *U*.	55.00	270.
v. Suffix letter *V*.	55.00	270.

2000 ND Issue

#37-41. Modified security features. Segmented security thread. Gold foil devices in upper r. of face. Shorter building rendering above signature.

37 5 Dollars

ND (2000). Green, dark green, slate blue on multicolor underprint. Queen Elizabeth II at center right, turtle at lower center, green-throated carib at top right. Signature 2. Gold foil fish at right. Back: Admiral's House in Antigua and Barbuda at left, Trafalgar Falls in Dominica at right, island map at center. Watermark: Queen Elizabeth II. Printer: TDLR. 145x69mm.

	VF	UNC
a. Suffix letter *A*.	FV	37.50
d1. Suffix letter *D*.	FV	37.50
d2. Suffix letter *D*. FIVE in burgundy color.	10.00	50.00
g. Suffix letter *G*.	FV	37.50
k1. Suffix letter *K*.	FV	37.50
k2. Suffix letter *K*. FIVE in burgundy color.	10.00	50.00
l. Suffix letter *L*.	FV	37.50
m. Suffix letter *M*.	FV	42.50
u. Suffix letter *U*.	FV	40.00
v. Suffix letter *V*.	FV	37.50

38 10 Dollars

ND (2000). Blue and black on multicolor underprint. Queen Elizabeth II at center right, turtle at lower center, green-throated carib at top right. Signature 2. Gold foil fish at right. Back: Admiralty Bay in St. Vincent and Grenadines at left, sailing ship *Warspite* and brown pelican at right, island map at center. Watermark: Queen Elizabeth II. Printer: TDLR. 145x69mm.

	VF	UNC
a. Suffix letter *A*.	FV	55.00
d. Suffix letter *D*.	FV	55.00
g. Suffix letter *G*.	FV	55.00
k. Suffix letter *K*.	FV	55.00
l. Suffix letter *L*.	FV	55.00
m. Suffix letter *M*.	FV	72.50
u. Suffix letter *U*.	FV	60.00
v. Suffix letter *V*.	FV	55.00

39 20 Dollars

ND (2000). Purple and slate blue on multicolor underprint. Queen Elizabeth II at center right, turtle at lower center, green-throated carib at top right. Signature 2. Gold foil butterfly at right. Back: Government House in Montserrat at left, nutmeg in Grenada at right, island map at center. Watermark: Queen Elizabeth II. Printer: TDLR. 145x69mm.

	VF	UNC
a. Suffix letter *A*.	FV	80.00
d. Suffix letter *D*.	FV	80.00
g. Suffix letter *G*.	FV	80.00
k. Suffix letter *K*.	FV	80.00
l. Suffix letter *L*.	FV	80.00
m. Suffix letter *M*.	FV	120.
u. Suffix letter *U*.	FV	85.00
v. Suffix letter *V*.	FV	80.00

40 50 Dollars

ND (2000). Bronze and orange on multicolor underprint. Queen Elizabeth II at center right, turtle at lower center, green-throated carib at top right. Signature 2. Gold foil flower at right. Back: Brimstone Hill in St. Kitts at left, Les Pitons mountains in St. Lucia and sooty tern at right , island map at center. Watermark: Queen Elizabeth II. Printer: TDLR. 145x69mm.

	VF	UNC
a. Suffix letter *A*.	FV	170.
d. Suffix letter *D*.	FV	170.
g. Suffix letter *G*.	FV	170.
k. Suffix letter *K*.	FV	170.
l. Suffix letter *L*.	FV	170.
m. Suffix letter *M*.	FV	280.
u. Suffix letter *U*.	FV	175.
v. Suffix letter *V*.	FV	170.

41 100 Dollars

ND (2000). Dark brown and dark green on multicolor underprint. Queen Elizabeth II at center right, turtle at lower center, green-throated carib at top right. Gold foil flower at upper right. Signature 2. Back: Sir Arthur Lewis at left, Central Bank building and Lesser Antillean Swift at right, island map at center. Watermark: Queen Elizabeth II. Printer: TDLR. 145x69mm.

	VF	UNC
a. Suffix letter *A*.	FV	235.
d. Suffix letter *D*.	FV	235.
g. Suffix letter *G*.	FV	235.
k. Suffix letter *K*.	FV	235.
l. Suffix letter *L*.	FV	235.
m. Suffix letter *M*.	FV	290.
u. Suffix letter *U*.	FV	240.
v. Suffix letter *V*.	FV	235.

2003 ND Issue

42 5 Dollars

ND (2003). Green, dark green, slate blue on multicolor underprint. Queen Elizabeth II at center right, turtle at lower center, green-throated carib at top right. Signature 2. Gold foil fish at right. Back: Admiral's House in Antigua and Barbuda at left, Trafalgar Falls in Dominica at right, island map at center. Watermark: Queen Elizabeth II. Printer: TDLR. Silver foil devices in the upper right of the face and wide security thread. Fish at lower left has a brown eyeball. 145x69mm.

	VF	UNC
a. Suffix letter *A*.	FV	15.00
d. Suffix letter *D*.	FV	29.00
g. Suffix letter *G*.	FV	29.00
k. Suffix letter *K*.	FV	29.00
l. Suffix letter *L*.	FV	29.00
m. Suffix letter *M*.	FV	37.50
u. Suffix letter *U*.	FV	32.50
v. Suffix letter *V*.	FV	29.00
ur. Suffix letter *U*. Replacement note. Serial # prefix *Z/1*.	20.00	115.

42A 5 Dollars

ND (2003). Green, dark green, slate blue on multicolor underprint. Queen Elizabeth II at center right, turtle at lower center. Signature 2. Back: Admiral's House in Antigua and Barbuda at left, Trafalgar Falls in Dominica at right, island map at center. Printer: TDLR. Fish at lower left has a green eyeball. 145x69mm.

	VF	UNC
a. Suffix letter *A*.	FV	35.00
l. Suffix letter *L*.	FV	35.00
m. Suffix letter *M*.	FV	42.50
v. Suffix letter *V*.	FV	35.00

43 10 Dollars

ND (2003). Blue and black on multicolor underprint. Queen Elizabeth II at center right, turtle at lower center, green-throated carib at top right. Signature 2. Gold foil fish at right. Back: Admiralty Bay in St. Vincent and Grenadines at left, sailing ship *Warspite* and brown pelican at right center, island map at center. Watermark: Queen Elizabeth II. Printer: TDLR. Silver foil devices in the upper right of the face and wide security thread. 145x69mm.

	VF	UNC
a. Suffix letter *A*.	FV	42.50
d. Suffix letter *D*.	FV	42.50
g. Suffix letter *G*.	FV	42.50
k. Suffix letter *K*.	FV	25.00
l. Suffix letter *L*.	FV	42.50
m. Suffix letter *M*.	FV	47.50
u. Suffix letter *U*.	FV	47.50
v. Suffix letter *V*.	FV	25.00

44 20 Dollars

ND (2003). Purple and slate blue on multicolor underprint. Queen Elizabeth II at center right, turtle at lower center, green-throated carib at top right. Signature 2. Gold foil butterfly at right. Back: Government House in Montserrat at left, nutmeg in Grenada at right, island map at center. Watermark: Queen Elizabeth II. Printer: TDLR. Silver foil devices in the upper right of the face and wide security thread. 145x69mm.

	VF	UNC
a. Suffix letter *A*.	FV	62.50
d. Suffix letter *D*.	FV	35.00
g. Suffix letter *G*.	FV	62.50
k. Suffix letter *K*.	FV	62.50
l. Suffix letter *L*.	FV	62.50
m. Suffix letter *M*.	FV	82.50
u. Suffix letter *U*.	FV	70.00
v. Suffix letter *V*.	FV	62.50

45 50 Dollars

ND (2003). Bronze and orange on multicolor underprint. Queen Elizabeth II at center right, turtle at lower center, green-throated carib at top right. Signature 2. Gold foil flower at right. Back: Brimstone Hill in St. Kitts at left, Les Pitons mountains in St. Lucia and sooty tern at right, island map at center. Watermark: Queen Elizabeth II. Printer: TDLR. Silver foil devices in the upper right of the face and wide security thread. 145x69mm.

	VF	UNC
a. Suffix letter *A*.	FV	138.
d. Suffix letter *D*.	FV	138.
g. Suffix letter *G*.	FV	138.
k. Suffix letter *K*.	FV	138.
l. Suffix letter *L*.	FV	138.
m. Suffix Letter *M*.	FV	190.
u. Suffix letter *U*. Not issued.	—	—
v. Suffix letter *V*.	FV	138.

46 **100 Dollars** — VF | UNC

ND (2003). Black Brown and dark green on multicolor underprint. Queen Elizabeth II at center right, turtle at lower center, green-throated carib at top right. Signature 2. Back: Sir Arthur Lewis at left, Central Bank building and Lesser Antillean Swift at right, island map at center. Watermark: Queen Elizabeth II. Printer: TDLR. Silver foil devices in the upper right of the face and wide security thread. 145x69mm.

	VF	UNC
a. Suffix letter *A*.	FV	215.
d. Suffix letter *D*.	FV	215.
g. Suffix letter *G*.	FV	215.
k. Suffix letter *K*.	FV	215.
l. Suffix letter *L*.	FV	215.
m. Suffix letter *M*.	FV	275.
u. Suffix letter *U*. Not issued.	—	—
v. Suffix letter *V*.	FV	215.

2008 ND Issue

47 **5 Dollars** — VF | UNC

ND (2008). Green, dark green and slate blue on multicolor underprint. Queen Elizabeth II at center right, turtle at lower center. Back: Admiral's House in Antigua and Barbuda at left, Trafalgar falls in Dominica at right. Printer: DLR. 145x69mm.

	VF	UNC
a. Issued note.	FV	8.50
r. Replacement note. Serial # prefix *Z1*.	FV	85.00

48 **10 Dollars**

ND (2008). Blue and black on multicolor underprint. Queen Elizabeth II at center right, turtle at lower center, green-throated carib at top right. Back: Admiralty Bay in St. Vincent and Grenadines at left, sailing ship *Warspite*. Printer: DLR. 145x69mm.

VF	UNC
FV	22.50

49 **20 Dollars**

ND (2008). Purple and slate blue on multicolor underprint. Queen Elizabeth II at center right, turtle at lower center, green-throated carib at top right. Back: Government House in Monserrat at left, nutmeg in Grenada at right. Printer: DLR. 145x69mm.

VF	UNC
FV	30.00

50 **50 Dollars**

ND (2008). Bronze and orange on multicolor underprint. Queen Elizabeth II at center right, turtle at lower center, green-throated carib at top right. Back: Brimstone Hill in St. Kitts at left. Les Pitons mountains in St. Lucia and sooty tern at right. Printer: DLR. 145x69mm.

VF	UNC
FV	60.00

51 **100 Dollars**

ND (2008). Black, brown and dark green on multicolor underprint. Queen Elizabeth II at center right, turtle at lower center, green-throated carib at top right. Back: Sir Arthur Lewis at left, Central Bank Building and Lesser Antillean Swift at right center. Printer: DLR. 145x69mm.

VF	UNC
FV	110.

2012 ND Issue, Tactile Markings Added

52 **10 Dollars**

ND (2012). Blue and black on multicolor underprint. Queen Elizabeth II at center right, turtle at lower center. Tactile markings at lower left. Back: Admiralty Bay in St. Vincent and Grenadines at left, sailing ship *Warspite*. Printer: DLR. 145x69mm.

VF	UNC
FV	15.00

53 **20 Dollars**

ND (2012). Purple and slate blue on multicolor underprint. Queen Elizabeth II at center right, turtle at lower center. Tactile markings at lower left. Back: Government House in Monserrat at left, nutmeg in Grenada at right. Printer: DLR. 145x69mm.

VF	UNC
FV	28.00

54	50 Dollars	VF	UNC
	ND (2012). Bronze and orange on multicolor underprint. Queen Elizabeth II at center right, turtle at lower center. Tactile markings at lower left. Back: Brimstone Hill in St. Kitts at left, Les Pitons mountains in St. Lucia and sooty tern at right. Printer: DLR. 145x69mm.	FV	60.00

55	100 Dollars	VF	UNC
	ND (2012). Black, brown and dark green on multicolor underprint. Queen Elizabeth II at center right, turtle at lower center. Tactile markings at lower left. Back: Sir Arthur Lewis at left, Central Bank Building and Lesser Antillean Swift at right center. Printer: DLR. 145x69mm.	FV	110.

Collector Series

Government of Antigua and Barbuda

1983 ND Issue

This set is made with thin gold and silver foil bonded to paper.

CS1 30 Dollars

ND (1983). 12 different notes showing various flowers and animals.

	Mkt. Value
a. Hibiscus / Egret. Beauties of the islands.	25.00
b. Hummingbird / Yellow elder. The search for nectar.	25.00
c. Green Turtle / Yellow Goatfish. Food from the sea.	25.00
d. Queen Angel Fish / Coral. Wonders of the sea garden.	25.00
e. Petrea Butterfly / Caribbean Buckeye. Brilliance in the bushes.	25.00
f. Sea Horse / Shells. Underwater treasures.	25.00
g. Dolphins. Seafearubg symbols.	25.00
h. Iguana. Newcomer to a new nation.	25.00
i. Brown Pelican. Endangered coastal bird.	25.00
j. Clown Fish / Anemone. The prefect relationship.	25.00
k. Zebra Butterfly / Jacaranda. Tropical Beauties.	25.00
l. Spiny Lobster. Delacy of the sea.	25.00
m. Full set of 12 notes.	300.

1984 ND Issue

CS2 30 Dollars

ND (1984). 12 different notes showing various animals and plants.

	Mkt. Value
a. Red-billed Tropic Bird. Beauty over the sea.	25.00
b. White-spotted Octopus. Hermit of the Sea.	25.00
c. Humpback Whale. Playful singer of the deep.	25.00
d. Queen Conch, Helmet Shell, Triton Trumpet shells.	25.00
e. Blue Euphonia Bird / Blue Passion-Flower. Beauties in blue.	25.00
f. Butterfly Fish / Sea Fan, Sea Rod. Colorful sea creatures	25.00
g. Black Skimmer Shore Bird. One of a kind.	25.00
h. Bananaquit Bird / Banana Tree. Tropical treasures.	25.00
i. Queen of the Night Cactus. Startling splendor	25.00
j. Sailfish. Popular sport fish.	25.00
k. Frigatebird. Pirate of the tropical seas.	25.00
l. Stilt Bird. Long-legged wader.	25.00
m. Set of 12 notes.	300.

1985 ND Issue

CS3 30 Dollars

ND (1985). 6 different notes showing various animals and plants.

	Mkt. Value
a. Monarch Butterfly / Lantana Flower. Famous and familiar wanderer	25.00
b. Queen Triggerfish. Vivid underwater beauty.	25.00
c. Mangrove Cuckoo Bird. Elusive bird of the tropics.	25.00
d. Squirrelfish, Soldierfish / Fanworms. Colorful reef fish.	25.00
e. Mountain Dove / Tree of Life. Colorful tropic sights.	25.00
f. Man of War Fish / Portuguese Man of War. Unusual pair.	25.00
g. Set of 6 notes.	225.

cs4 50 Dollars

ND (1985) 30 different notes showing various captains and ships.

a. Captain Howell Davis and the *King James.*	30.00
b. Captain Edward Low and his brigantine.	30.00
c. Jean LaFfite and the *Pride.*	30.00
d. Francois l'Ollonois attacks Puerto Caballos	30.00
e. Captain Charles Gibb's schooner *Maria.*	30.00
f. Admiral Piet Heyn and the *Amsterdam.*	30.00
g. Captain Jean Fleury and the *Dieppe.*	30.00
h. Easton Attacks on the Newfoundland coast.	30.00
i. Captain henry Avery and the *Gang-i-Saway.*	30.00
j. Captain William Dampier and the *St. George.*	30.00
k. Bartolomeo the Portuguese and his barque.	30.00
l. Captain Henry Mainwaring and the *Resistance.*	30.00
m. Pierre Legrand captures the Vice-Admiral's ship.	30.00
n. Captain Thomas Anstis and the *Good Fortune.*	30.00
o. Ann Bonny boards John Halman's sloop.	30.00
p. Captain Thomas Tew and the *Amity.*	30.00
q. Captain WilliamTaylor and the *Victory.*	30.00
r. Captain Samuel Bellamy and the *Whidah.*	30.00
s. Calico Jack Rackam and his *Merchantman.*	30.00
t. Captain Kidd and the *Adventure Galley.*	30.00
u. Sir Henry morgan captures the *Marquesa.*	30.00
v. Captain Thomas Cocklyn and the *Bird Galley.*	30.00
w. Captain Edward England and the *Cassandra.*	30.00
x. Sir Francis Drake and the *Golden Hind.*	30.00
y. Captain George Lowther and the *Happy Delivery.*	30.00
z. Benito de Soto and the *Black Joke.*	30.00
aa. Sede Bonnet's sloop *Royal James.*	30.00
ab. Charles Vane's ship challenges *HMS Buck.*	30.00
ac. Bartholomew Robert's *Royal Fortune.*	30.00
ad. Blackbeard's *Queen Ann's Revenge.*	30.00
ae. Set of 30 ntoes.	1100.

CS5 100 Dollars

11.1981 (1988). 30 different notes showing various pirate and treasure sailing ships. (20,000 sets).

a. Jean LaFfite / The Pride.	40.00
b. Howell Davis / King James.	40.00
c. Captian Kidd / Adventure Galley.	40.00
d. Thomas Cocklyn / Bird Galley.	40.00
e. Sir Francis Drake / Golden Hind.	40.00
f. Stede Bonnetts / Royal James.	40.00
g. Charles Vane / Challenges (HMS Buck).	40.00
h. George Lowther / Happy Delivery.	40.00
i. Edward England / Cassandra.	40.00
j. Henry Avery / Gaing-i-Saway.	40.00
k. Piet Heyn / Amsterdam.	40.00
l. William Taylor / Victory.	40.00
m. Anne Bonny / John Halmans Sloop.	40.00
n. Bartolomeo the Portuguese / Barque.	40.00
o. Bartholomew Robert / Royal Fortune.	40.00
p. Blackbeard / Queen Ann's Revenge.	40.00
q. Benito de Soto / Black Jake.	40.00
r. Calico Jack Rackman / Merchantman.	40.00
s. Charles Gibbs / Maria.	40.00
t. Henry Mainwaring / Resistance.	40.00
u. Edward Low / Brigantine.	40.00
v. Jean Fleury / Dieppe.	40.00
w. Thomas Anstis / Good Fortune.	40.00
x. Thomas Tew / Amity.	40.00
y. Easton Attacks on the Newfoundland Coast.	40.00
z. François l'Ollonois Attacks Puerto Caballos.	40.00
aa. Pierre LeGrand Captures the Vice-Admiral's ship.	40.00
ab. Sir Henry Morgan Captures the Marquesa.	40.00
ac. Samuel Bellamy / Whidah.	40.00
ad. William Dampier / The St. George.	40.00
ae. Set of 30 notes.	1100.

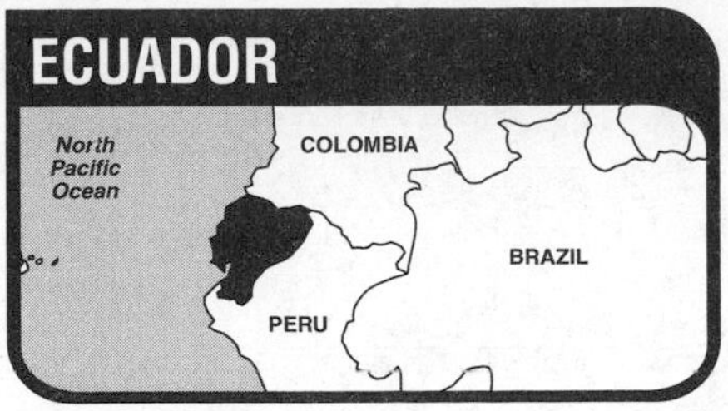

The Republic of Ecuador, located astride the equator on the Pacific coast of South America, has an area of 283,560 sq. km. and a population of 13.93 million. Capital: Quito. Agriculture is the mainstay of the economy but there are appreciable deposits of minerals and petroleum. It is the world's largest exporter of bananas and balsa wood. Coffee, cacao and shrimp are also valuable exports. What is now Ecuador formed part of the northern Inca Empire until the Spanish conquest in 1533. Quito became a seat of Spanish colonial government in 1563 and part of the Viceroyalty of New Granada in 1717. The territories of the Viceroyalty - New Granada (Colombia), Venezuela, and Quito - gained their independence between 1819 and 1822 and formed a federation known as Gran Colombia. When Quito withdrew in 1830, the traditional name was changed in favor of the "Republic of the Equator." Between 1904 and 1942, Ecuador lost territories in a series of conflicts with its neighbors. A border war with Peru that flared in 1995 was resolved in 1999. Although Ecuador marked 25 years of civilian governance in 2004, the period has been marred by political instability. Protests in Quito have contributed to the mid-term ouster of Ecuador's last three democratically elected Presidents. In 2007, a Constituent Assembly was elected to draft a new constitution; Ecuador's twentieth since gaining independence.

MONETARY SYSTEM:

1 Sucre = 10 Decimos = 100 Centavos
1 Condor = 25 Sucres
1 USA Dollar = 25,000 Sucres (March 2001)

REPUBLIC

BANCO CENTRAL DEL ECUADOR

1944-67 ISSUE

		VF	UNC
96	**500 Sucres** 1944-66. Black on multicolor underprint. Mercury seated at center. With text: *CAPITAL AUTORIZADO 20,000,000 SUCRES.* 3 signatures. Back: Deep orange. Printer: ABNC.		
	a. Signature title overprint: *PRESIDENTE* at left. 12.5.1944; 27.6.1944.	400.	—
	b. Signature title overprint: *GERENTE GENERAL* at left, *VOCAL* at right. 31.7.1944; 7.9.1944.	375.	—
	c. Signature title overprint: *GERENTE GENERAL* at right. 12.1.1945-12.7.1947.	300.	—
	d. As c. 21.4.1961-17.11.1966.	300.	—
	s. Specimen. ND.	—	700.

		VF	UNC
97	**1000 Sucres** 1944-67. Black on multicolor underprint. Woman reclining ("Telephone Service") at center. With text: *CAPITAL AUTORIZADO 20,000,000 SUCRES.* 3 signatures. Back: Greenish-gray. Overprint: Various signature titles. Printer: ABNC.		
	a. Signature title overprint: *PRESIDENTE* at left. 12.5.1944; 27.6.1944.	650.	—
	b. Signature title overprint: *GERENTE GENERAL* at left, *VOCAL* at right. 31.7.1944; 7.9.1944.	550.	—
	c. Signature title overprint: *PRESIDENTE* at left, *GERENTE GENERAL* at right. 12.1.1945.	500.	—
	d. Signature title overprint: *GERENTE GENERAL* at right. 16.10.1945; 12.7.1947.	450.	—
	e. As d. 21.4.1961; 27.2.1962; 4.3.1964; 23.7.1964; 17.11.1966; 6.4.1967.	350.	—
	s. Specimen. ND.	—	850.

The following reduced size notes are listed by printer.

1950 Issue (1950-59) #98-99 printer: W&S.
1950-71 Issue (1950-74) #100-107 printer: ABNC.
1975-80 Issue (1975-83) #108-112 printer: ABNC.
1957-71 Issue (1957-82) #113-118 printer: TDLR.

1950 ISSUE - REDUCED SIZE NOTES

		VF	UNC
98	**5 Sucres** 1950-55. Black on green underprint. Portrait Antonio Jose de Sucre at center. Date at left or right. Back: Red. Arms at center. Printer: W&S.		
	a. 11.5.1950-13.7.1953.	15.00	75.00
	b. Signature title overprint: *SUBGERENTE GENERAL* at left. 21.9.1953.	20.00	85.00
	c. 31.5.1954-28.11.1955.	12.50	55.00
99	**50 Sucres** 1950-59. Black on green underprint. National monument at center with buildings in background. Back: Green. Arms at center. Printer: W&S.		
	a. 11.5.1950; 26.7.1950; 13.10.1950; 3.4.1951; 26.9.1951.	50.00	150.
	b. Signature title overprint: *SUBGERENTE GENERAL* at left. 3.9.1952; 8.10.1954; 24.9.1957.	50.00	150.
	c. 10.12.1953; 19.6.1956; 25.11.1957; 25.11.1958; 8.4.1959.	40.00	125.
	s1. Specimen. Black overprint: *ESPÉCIMEN* on both sides. ND, with 0000 serial #, unsigned.	—	175.
	s2. Specimen. Red overprint: *MUESTRA* twice on both sides. ND, without serial # or signs. Punched hole cancelled.	—	175.

1950-71 ISSUE

		VF	UNC
100	**5 Sucres** 1956-73. Black on multicolor underprint. Portrait Antonio Jose de Sucre at center. Back: Red. Arms 31mm. wide, without flagpole stems below. Printer: ABNC. Several varieties in signature title overprints and serial # styles.		
	a. 19.6.1956; 28.8.1956; 2.4.1957; 19.6.1957; 19.7.1957.	5.00	40.00
	b. Signature title overprint: *SUBGERENTE GENERAL*. 24.9.1957; 2.1.1958.	5.00	40.00
	c. 2.2.1958; 1.1.1966.	2.50	20.00
	d. 27.2.1970; 3.9.1973. Serial # varieties.	1.50	3.50
101	**10 Sucres** 1950-1955. Black on multicolor underprint. Portrait Sebastian de Benalcazar at center. Plain background. Back: Blue. Arms 31mm. wide, without flagpole stems below. Printer: ABNC. Several varieties in signature title overprints and serial # styles.		
	a. 14.1.1950-28.11.1955.	8.00	45.00
	b. 21.9.1953; 16.3.1954; 3.10.1955. Overprint: *SUB GERENTE GENERAL*.	10.00	50.00
	s. Specimen.	—	150.

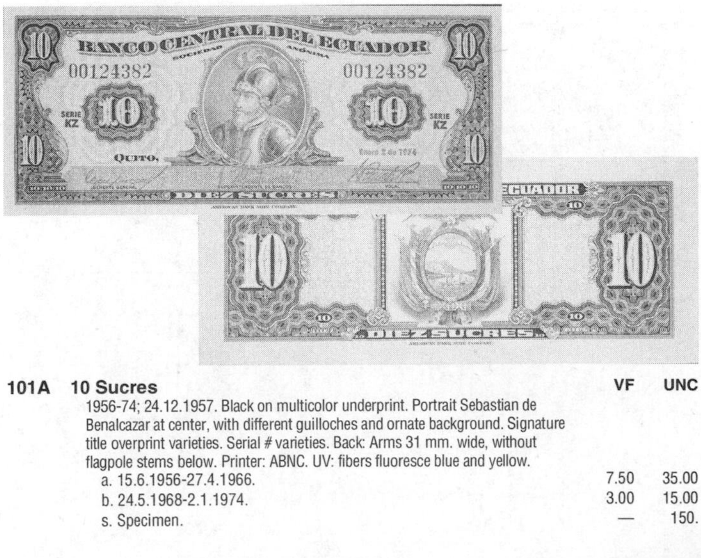

		VF	UNC
101A	**10 Sucres** 1956-74; 24.12.1957. Black on multicolor underprint. Portrait Sebastian de Benalcazar at center, with different guilloches and ornate background. Signature title overprint varieties. Serial # varieties. Back: Arms 31 mm. wide, without flagpole stems below. Printer: ABNC. UV: fibers fluoresce blue and yellow.		
	a. 15.6.1956-27.4.1966.	7.50	35.00
	b. 24.5.1968-2.1.1974.	3.00	15.00
	s. Specimen.	—	150.

102	20 Sucres	VF	UNC
	28.2.1950-28.7.1960. Black on multicolor underprint. Church façade at center. Back: Brown. Arms 31 mm. wide, without flagpole stems below. Printer: ABNC. Several varieties in signature title overprints and serial # styles.		
	a. Issued note.	15.00	50.00
	s. Specimen. Overprint: *SPECIMEN* in red on face.	—	80.00
103	**20 Sucres**		
	1962-73. Black on multicolor underprint. Church façade at center, different guilloches and darker underprint. Back: Arms 31 mm. wide, without flagpole stems below. Printer: ABNC. Several varieties in signature title overprints, and serial # styles.		
	a. 12.12.1962-4.10.1967.	5.00	25.00
	b. 24.5.1968-3.9.1973.	3.00	15.00
	s. Specimen. ND.	—	175.

104	50 Sucres	VF	UNC
	1968-71. Black on multicolor underprint. National monument at center with buildings in background. Signature title overprint varieties. Serial # varieties. Back: Green. Arms 31 mm. wide, without flagpole stems below. Printer: ABNC. UV: planchettes fluoresce pink.		
	a. 24.5.1968; 5.11.1969.	5.00	30.00
	b. 20.5.1971.	4.00	20.00
	s. Specimen. ND.	—	50.00
104A	**100 Sucres**		
	1952-57. Black on multicolor underprint. Portrait Simón Bolívar at center. Back: Purple. Arms 31 mm. wide, without flagpole stems below. Printer: ABNC. Several varieties, signature title overprints, and serial # styles.		
	a. 3.9.1952-19.6.1957.	75.00	220.
	b. Signature title: *SUBGERENTE.* 3.9.1952; 10.12.1953.	75.00	220.
105	**100 Sucres**		
	27.6.1964-7.7.1970. Black on multicolor underprint. Portrait Simón Bolívar at center with different guilloches. Back: Purple. Arms 31 mm. wide, without flagpole stems below. Printer: ABNC. Several varieties, signature title overprints, and serial # styles.		
	a. Issued note.	10.00	50.00
	s. Specimen. Overprint: *SPECIMEN* in red on face.	—	80.00
106	**500 Sucres**		
	ND (ca.1971). Black on multicolor underprint. Mercury seated at center with different guilloches and other changes. Back: Red. Printer: ABNC. Archive example.	Unc	1000.

107	1000 Sucres	VF	UNC
	30.5.1969-20.9.1973. Black on multicolor underprint. Banco Central building at center. Back: Olive-gray. Arms 31 mm. wide, without flagpole stems below. Printer: ABNC. Several varieties, signature title overprints, and serial # styles.		
	a. Issued note.	85.00	250.
	s. Specimen. ND.	—	75.00

1957-71 Issue

113	5 Sucres	VF	UNC
	1958-88. Black on multicolor underprint. Portrait Antonio Jose de Sucre at center. Back: Red. New rendition of arms. Printer: TDLR.		
	a. 2.1.1958-7.11.1962.	4.00	17.50
	b. 23.5.1963-27.2.1970.	1.00	12.50
	c. 25.7.1979-24.5.1980.	.50	7.50
	d. 22.11.1988.	.25	3.00
	s. Specimen. ND; 24.5.1968; 25.7.1979; 24.5.1980. Overprint: *MUESTRA SIN VALOR* in red on both sides.	—	125.

114	10 Sucres	VF	UNC
	1968-83. Black on multicolor underprint. Portrait Sebastian de Benalcazar at center. Back: Blue. New rendition of arms. Printer: TDLR.		
	a. 24.5.1968; 20.5.1971.	3.00	20.00
	b. 24.5.1980; 30.9.1982; 20.4.1983.	1.00	12.50
	s1. Specimen. 24.5.1968. Series KV. Overprint: *MUESTRA SIN VALOR* in red on both sides.	—	100.
	s2. Specimen. 20.5.1971. Series KY.	—	100.
	s3. Specimen. 30.9.1982. Series LI.	—	100.

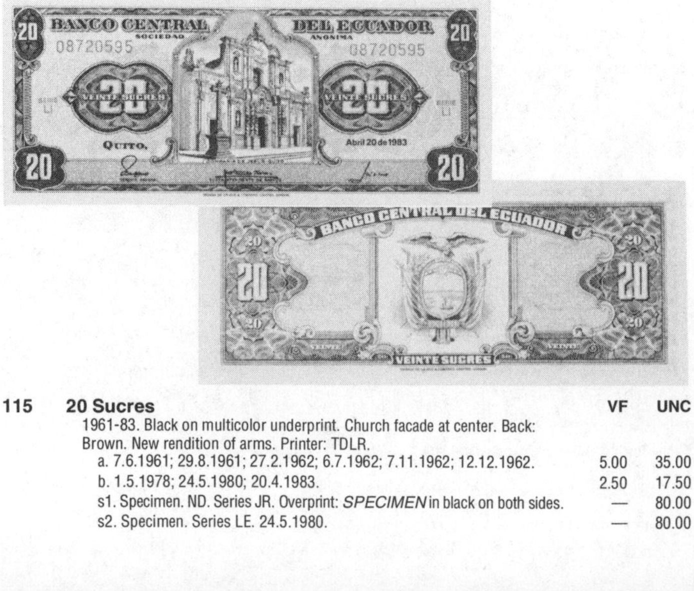

115	20 Sucres	VF	UNC
	1961-83. Black on multicolor underprint. Church facade at center. Back: Brown. New rendition of arms. Printer: TDLR.		
	a. 7.6.1961; 29.8.1961; 27.2.1962; 6.7.1962; 7.11.1962; 12.12.1962.	5.00	35.00
	b. 1.5.1978; 24.5.1980; 20.4.1983.	2.50	17.50
	s1. Specimen. ND. Series JR. Overprint: *SPECIMEN* in black on both sides.	—	80.00
	s2. Specimen. Series LE. 24.5.1980.	—	80.00

116 50 Sucres VF UNC

1957-82. Black on multicolor underprint. National monument at center. Back: Green. New rendition of arms. Printer: TDLR.

		VF	UNC
a.	2.4.1957; 7.7.1959.	15.00	60.00
b.	7.11.1962; 29.10.1963; 27.6.1964; 29.1.1965; 6.8.1965.	8.00	35.00
c.	1.1.1966; 27.4.1966; 17.11.1966.	4.00	25.00
d.	4.10.1967; 30.5.1969; 17.7.1974.	2.00	15.00
e.	24.5.1980; 20.8.1982.	1.25	10.00
s1.	Specimen. ND; 1.1.1966. Overprint: *SPECIMEN* in red on both sides.	—	80.00
s2.	Specimen. 20.8.1982. Overprint: *MUESTRA SIN VALOR* in red on both sides.	—	100.

117 100 Sucres VF UNC

29.8.1961-6.8.1965. Black on multicolor underprint. Crude portrait Simón Bolívar at center with light clouds behind. Back: Purple. New rendition of arms. Printer: TDLR.

		VF	UNC
a.	Issued note.	20.00	50.00
s.	Specimen. Without signature. Series TW.	—	75.00

118 100 Sucres VF UNC

1971-77. Black on multicolor underprint. Finer portrait Simón Bolívar at center with dark clouds behind. Back: Purple. New rendition of arms. Printer: TDLR. UV: planchetts fluoresce yellow.

		VF	UNC
a.	20.5.1971; 17.7.1974.	8.00	40.00
b.	10.8.1976; 10.8.1977.	5.00	25.00
s.	Specimen. 20.5.1971. Overprint: *MUESTRA SIN VALOR* in red on both sides.	—	80.00

1975-80 Issue

108 5 Sucres VF UNC

1975-83. Black on multicolor underprint. Portrait Antonio Jose de Sucre at center. Back: Red. New rendition of arms. 29mm. wide with flag-pole stems below. Printer: ABNC. UV: planchettes fluoresce red, fibers yellow.

		VF	UNC
a.	14.3.1975; 29.4.1977.	1.50	9.00
b.	20.8.1982; 20.4.1983.	1.00	6.00

109 10 Sucres VF UNC

14.3.1975; 10.8.1976; 29.4.1977; 24.5.1978. Black on multicolor underprint. Portrait Sebastian de Benalcazar at center. Back: Blue. New rendition of arms. 29mm. wide with flag-pole stems below. Printer: TDLR. — VF 2.00, UNC 12.50

110 20 Sucres VF UNC

10.8.1976. Black on multicolor underprint. Church facade at center. Back: Brown. New rendition of arms. 29mm. wide with flag-pole stems below. Printer: TDLR. — VF 2.50, UNC 17.50

111 50 Sucres VF UNC

10.8.1976. Black on multicolor underprint. National monument at center with buildings in background. Back: Green. New rendition of arms. 29mm. wide with flag-pole stems below. Printer: ABNC.

		VF	UNC
a.	Issued note.	4.00	27.50
s.	Specimen.	—	100.

		VF	UNC
112	**100 Sucres**		
	24.5.1980. Black on multicolor underprint. Portrait Simón Bolívar at center with different guilloches. Back: Purple. New rendition of arms. 29mm. wide with flag-pole stems below. Printer: ABNC.		
	a. Issued note.	1.50	15.00
	s. Specimen. Overprint: *MUESTRA* in red twice on both sides. Punch hole cancelled.	—	80.00
112A	**100 Sucres**		
	ND (ca. 1980). Black on multicolor undeprint. Printer: ABNC. Printed on tyvek as a test note.	—	500.

1976 Issue

		VF	UNC
119	**500 Sucres**		
	1976-82. Black, violet-brown and dark olive on multicolor underprint. Dr. Eugenio de Santa Cruz y Espejo at left. Back: Blue on multicolor underprint. Arms at center. Watermark: Arms. Printer: TDLR.		
	a. 24.5.1976; 10.8.1977; 9.10.1978; 25.7.1979.	12.50	50.00
	b. 20.7.1982.	7.50	30.00
	s1. Specimen. ND. Series AB. Overprint: *MUESTRA SIN VALOR* in red on both sides.	—	85.00
	s2. Specimen. 20.7.1982.	—	85.00

		VF	UNC
120	**1000 Sucres**		
	1976-82. Dark green and red-brown on multicolor underprint. Ruminahui at right. Back: Dark green on multicolor underprint. Arms at center. Watermark: Arms. Printer: TDLR.		
	a. 24.5.1976-25.7.1979.	7.50	50.00
	b. 24.5.1980; 20.7.1982.	5.00	25.00
	s1. Specimen. ND. Series AB. Overprint: *MUESTRA SIN VALOR* in red on both sides.	—	80.00
	s2. Specimen. Series HP. 24.5.1980. Overprint: *MUESTRA SIN VALOR* in red on both sides.	—	100.

1984-88 Issues

#120A-125 w/o text: *SOCIEDAD ANONIMA* below bank title.

		VF	UNC
120A	**5 Sucres**		
	22.11.1988. Black on multicolor underprint. Portrait A. J. de Sucré at center. Back: Red-violet. Arms, 26mm wide. Printer: TDLR without imprint. UV: planchettes fluoresce yellow and red. Left design green, fibers yellow.	.50	4.00

		VF	UNC
121	**10 Sucres**		
	29.4.1986; 22.11.1988. Black on multicolor underprint. Portrait Sebastian de Benalcazar at center. Back: Blue. New rendition of arms. Printer: TDLR without imprint.	.75	3.50

		VF	UNC
121A	**20 Sucres**		
	1986-88. Black on multicolor underprint. Church façade at center. Back: Brown. New rendition of arms. Printer: TDLR without imprint.		
	a. 29.4.1986; 22.11.1988.	.75	5.00
	s1. Specimen. 29.4.1986. Series LM.	—	20.00
	s2. Specimen. 22.11.1988. Series LP. Overprint: *MUESTRA SIN VALOR* in red on both sides.	—	80.00

		VF	UNC
122	**50 Sucres**		
	5.9.1984; 22.11.1988. Black on multicolor underprint. National monument at center. Back: Green. New rendition of arms. Printer: TDLR without imprint.		
	a. Issued note.	1.00	7.50
	s. Specimen. 5.9.1984. Overprint: *MUESTRA SIN VALOR* in red on both sides.	—	100.

		VF	UNC
123	**100 Sucres**		
	29.4.1986; 20.4.1990. Black on multicolor underprint. Finer portrait Simón Bolívar at center with dark clouds behind. Back: Purple. New rendition of arms. Printer: TDLR without imprint. Black, dark blue or light blue serial number.	2.00	15.00

		VF	UNC
123A	**100 Sucres**		
	1988-97. Black on multicolor underprint. Finer portrait Simón Bolívar at center with dark clouds behind. Back: Purple. New rendition of arms. Printer: TDLR without imprint. Plate differences on face and back. Serial # style varieties.		
	a. Blue serial #. 8.6.1988; 21.6.1991; 11.10.1991.	.50	5.00
	b. 9.3.1992; 4.12.1992; 20.8.1993.	.50	5.00
	c. Black serial #. 21.2.1994.	.50	5.00
	d. As c. 3.4.1997.	.50	5.00
	s1. As a. Specimen. 8.6.1988. Punched hole cancelled.	—	35.00
	s2. As b. Specimen. 21.6.1991; 20.8.1993. Series WF. Overprint: *ESPECIMEN SIN VALOR* in red on both sides.	—	100.

124 500 Sucres

5.9.1984. Black, violet-brown and dark olive on multicolor underprint. Dr. Eugenio de Santa Cruz y Espejo at left. Signature varieties. Back: Arms at center. Watermark: Arms. Printer: TDLR without imprint.

	VF	UNC
a. Issued note.	2.00	15.00
s. Specimen. Overprint: *MUESTRA SIN VALOR* in red on both sides.	—	110.

124A 500 Sucres

8.6.1988. Black, violet-brown and dark olive on multicolor underprint. Dr. Eugenio de Santa Cruz y Espejo at left. Signature varieties. Back: Arms at center. Printer: TDLR. Many minor plate differences from #124.

	VF	UNC
a. Issued note.	1.25	10.00
s. Specimen. Overprint: *SPECIMEN* in red on face.	—	100.

125 1000 Sucres

1984-88. Dark green and red-brown on multicolor underprint. Ruminahui at right. Without *EL* in bank title. Serial # style varieties. Back: Arms at center. Watermark: Arms. Printer: TDLR. UV: planchetts fluoresce red and yellow. Value and central design orange.

	VF	UNC
a. 5.9.1984; 29.9.1986.	2.00	15.00
b. 8.6.1988.	1.50	10.00
s1. Specimen. 5.9.1984. Overprint: *MUESTRA SIN VALOR* in red on both sides.	—	100.
s2. Specimen. Overprint: *ESPECIMEN SIN VALOR* in red on both sides.	—	100.

126 5000 Sucres

1.12.1987. Purple and brown on multicolor underprint. Juan Montalvo at left, arms at center. Back: Flightless cormoran, Galapagos penguin and Galapagos tortoise. Watermark: Juan Montalvo. Printer: BCdE.

	VF	UNC
a. Issued note.	2.00	25.00
s. Specimen. Series AB. Overprint: *MUESTRA SIN VALOR* in red on both sides.	—	100.

127 10,000 Sucres

1988-98. Dark brown and reddish brown on multicolor underprint. Vicente Rocafuerte at left. Back: Arms upper left center, Independence monument in Quito at center right. Watermark: Vicente Rocafuerte. Printer: BCdE. Serial # varieties exist.

	VF	UNC
a. Signature title by itself at left: *VOCAL*. 30.7.1988; 21.2.1994; 13.10.1994.	2.00	15.00
b. Signature title at lleft: *PRESIDENTE JUNTA MONETARIA*. 6.2.1995; 8.3.1995; 8.8.1995; 4.1.1996; 23.9.1996.	2.00	15.00
c. Signature title at lleft: *PRESIDENTE DEL DIRECTORIO*. 14.12.1998.	.75	10.00
d. Signatrue title left; *VOCAL* in black; signature title right in brown. 4.1.1996; 23.9.1996.	.75	10.00
e. Signature title left: *PRESIDENTE DEL DIRECTORIO* in black; signature title right in black. 14.12.1998.	.75	10.00
s1. As a. Specimen. Series AB. Overprint: *ESPECIMEN SIN VALOR* in red on face.	—	100.
s2. As a. Specimen. 13.10.1994 Series AH.	—	100.
s3. As b. Specimen. 8.3.1995. Series AL. Overprint: *ESPECIMEN / MUESTRA SIN VALOR* in red on both sides.	—	100.
s4. As e. Specimen. Overprint: *ESPECIMEN SIN VALOR* in red on both sides.	—	100.

1991-95 Issue

128 5000 Sucres

1991-99. Purple and brown on multicolor underprint. Juan Montalvo at left, arms at center. Repositioned signature and both serial number horizontal. Back: Flightless cormoran, Galapagos penguin and Galapagos tortoise. Watermark: Juan Montalvo. Printer: BCdE. UV: planchetts fluoresce yellow and red. Value and design yellow.

	VF	UNC
a. Signature title by itself at left: *VOCAL*. 21.6.1991; 17.3.1992; 22.6.1992; 20.8.1993.	1.25	10.00
b. Signature title at left: *PRESIDENTE JUNTA MONETARIA*. 31.1.1995; 8.8.1995; 13.1.1996; 31.10.1996.	1.25	7.50
c. Signature title at left: *PRESIDENTE DEL DIRECTORIO*. 26.3.1996; 6.3.1999; 26.3.1999.	1.25	7.50
s1. Specimen. 21.6.1991. Series AG. Overprint: *MUESTRA SIN VALOR* in red on both sides.	—	100.
s2. As a. Specimen. 17.3.1992. Series AJ. Overprint: *MUESTRA SIN VALOR* in red on both sides.	—	100.
s3. As b. Specimen. 31.1.1995.	—	100.

129	20,000 Sucres	VF	UNC
	1995-99. Brown, black and deep blue on multicolor underprint. Dr. Gabriel Garcia Moreno at right . Back: Arms at center. Watermark: Dr. Gabriel Garcia Moreno.		
	a. Signature title at right: *PRESIDENTE JUNTA MONETARIA.* 31.1.1995; 20.11.1995.	2.00	20.00
	b. Signature title at right: *PRESIDENTE JUNTA MONETARIA.* 2.6.1997.	1.50	15.00
	c. Signature title at right: *VOCAL*. 1.6.1998.	7.50	30.00
	e. Without security thread. signature title at right: *PRESIDENTE DEL DIRECTORIO.* 5.10.1999.	1.50	7.50
	f. Two security threads. signature title at right: *PRESIDENTE DEL DIRECTORIO.* 5.10.1998; 26.3.1999.	1.50	10.00
	s1. As a. Specimen. 31.1.1995. Overprint: *ESPECIMEN SIN VALOR* in red on both sides. With or without punch holes.	—	110.
	s2. As b. Specimen. 2.6.1997. Series AD.	—	100.
	s3. As c. 10.3.1999.	—	100.

130	50,000 Sucres	VF	UNC
	1995-99. Gray and red-brown on multicolor underprint. Eloy Alfaro at right. Back: Arms. Watermark: Eloy Alfaro. Segmented foil over security thread.		
	a. Two security threads. signature title at left: *PRESIDENTE JUNTA MONETARIA.* 31.1.1995; 2.6.1997; 20.4.1998; 6.3.1999; 26.3.1999.	2.50	15.00
	b. 2 security threads. 6.3.1999.	2.50	10.00
	c. Decreased security features. withoutne security thread. signature title at left: *GERENTE GENERAL.* 10.3.1999; 26.3.1999.	2.50	10.00
	s1. As a. Specimen. 31.1.1995; 2.6.1997 Series AB. Overprint: *MUESTRA SIN VALOR* in red on both sides.	—	150.
	s2. Specimen. 31.1.1995, without series. Overprint: *SPECIMEN* in red on both sides. Punch hole cancelled.	—	130.
	s3. Specimen. 31.1.1995, Series AB. Overprint: *MUESTRA SIN VALOR* in red on both sides. Punch hole cancelled.	—	130.

EGYPT

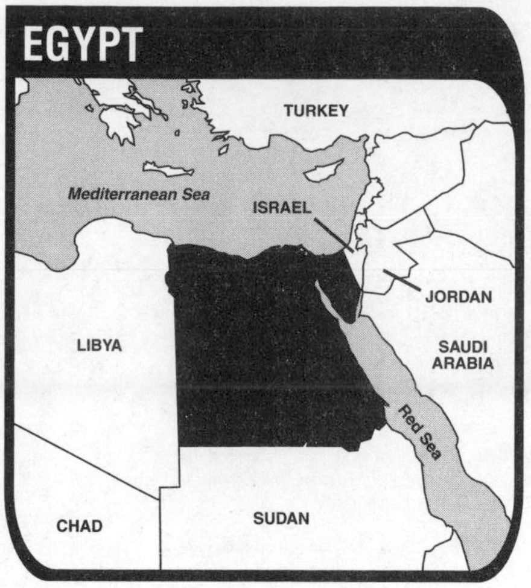

The Arab Republic of Egypt, located on the northeastern corner of Africa, has an area of 1,001,450 sq. km. and a population of 81.71 million. Capital: Cairo. Although Egypt is an almost rainless expanse of desert, its economy is predominantly agricultural. Cotton, rice and petroleum are exported.

The regularity and richness of the annual Nile River flood, coupled with semi-isolation provided by deserts to the east and west, allowed for the development of one of the world's great civilizations. A unified kingdom arose circa 3200 B.C., and a series of dynasties ruled in Egypt for the next three millennia. The last native dynasty fell to the Persians in 341 B.C., who in turn were replaced by the Greeks, Romans, and Byzantines. It was the Arabs who introduced Islam and the Arabic language in the 7th century and who ruled for the next six centuries. A local military caste, the Mamluks took control about 1250 and continued to govern after the conquest of Egypt by the Ottoman Turks in 1517. Following the completion of the Suez Canal in 1869, Egypt became an important world transportation hub, but also fell heavily into debt. Ostensibly to protect its investments, Britain seized control of Egypt's government in 1882, but nominal allegiance to the Ottoman Empire continued until 1914. Partially independent from the UK in 1922, Egypt acquired full sovereignty with the overthrow of the British-backed monarchy in 1952. The completion of the Aswan High Dam in 1971 and the resultant Lake Nasser have altered the time-honored place of the Nile River in the agriculture and ecology of Egypt. A rapidly growing population (the largest in the Arab world), limited arable land, and dependence on the Nile all continue to overtax resources and stress society. The government has struggled to meet the demands of Egypt's growing population through economic reform and massive investment in communications and physical infrastructure.

MONETARY SYSTEM:

1 Pound (Junayh) = 100 Piastres, 1916-

REPLACEMENT NOTES:

Starting in 1969, 2 types exist. Earlier system uses a single Arabic letter as series prefix instead of normal number/letter prefix. Known notes: #38-. Later system has the equivalent of English "200" or "300" in front of a single Arabic series letter. Known notes: #46-.

SIGNATURE VARIETIES			
11	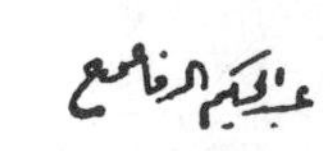 A. El-Refay, 1961-63	12	 A. Zendo, 1962-66
13	 A. Nazmy A. A El Hamed, 1967-70	14	 A. Zendo, 1972-75
15	 M. Ibrahim, 1976-81	16	 M. S. A. Shalaby, 1981-84
17	 A. Negm, 1985	18	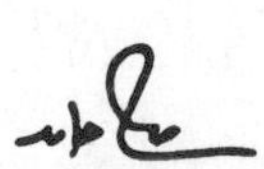 S. Hamed, 1986
19	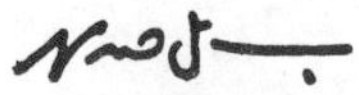 I. H. Mohamed	20	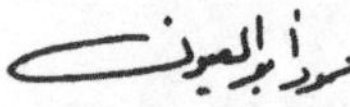 M. Abou El-Oyoun
21	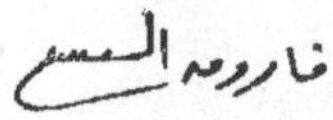 Farouk Abdel Baky El Okda 1st kind	22	 Farouk Abdel Baky El Okda II 2nd kind

Republic

Central Bank of Egypt

1961-64 Issues

		VF	UNC
35	**25 Piastres** 1.11.1961-18.8.1966. Blue on multicolor underprint. U. A. R. arms at right.		
	a. 1.11.1961-24.4.1963. Signature 11. Series #1-18.	2.00	6.00
	b. 3.7.1965-18.8.1966. Signature 12. Series #19-42.	2.00	6.00
	s. Specimen.	—	—

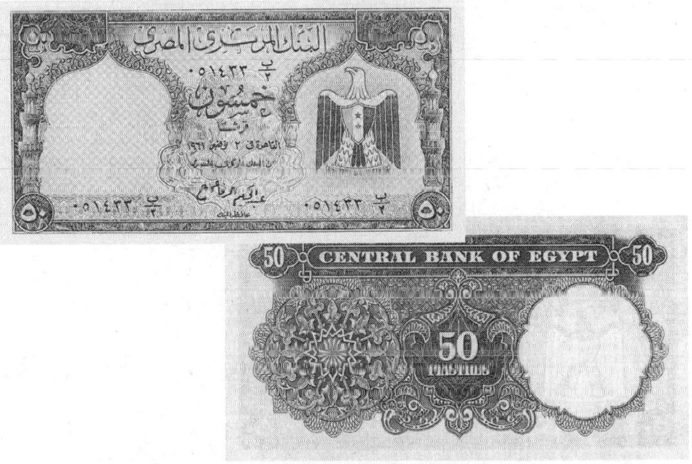

		VF	UNC
36	**50 Piastres** 1.11.1961-14.8.1966. Blackish green multicolor underprint. U. A. R. arms at right. Watermark: U. A. R. arms.		
	a. 1.11.1961-13.4.1963. Signature 11. Series #1-18.	3.00	15.00
	b. 6.2.1965-14.8.1966. Signature 12. Series #19-42.	3.00	15.00
	s. Specimen.	—	—

		VF	UNC
37	**1 Pound** 1.11.1961-23.2.1967. Blue-green on lilac and multicolor underprint. Tutankhamen's mask at right. Signature 11; 12; 13. Back: Green. Watermark: Arms.		
	a. Issued note.	2.50	6.00
	s. Specimen.	—	—

		VF	UNC
38	**5 Pounds** 1.11.1961-12.11.1961. Green and brown on multicolor underprint. Circular guilloche at left, Tutankhamen's mask at right. Signature 11. Back: Value at left and right. Watermark: Flower.	25.00	150.

		VF	UNC
39	**5 Pounds** 13.11.1961-16.6.1964. Green and brown on multicolor underprint. Clear watermark area at left, Tutankhamen's mask at right. Guilloche at bottom center. Signature 11; 12. Back: Value at left, clear watermark area at right. Watermark: Arms.		
	a. Issued note.	7.50	27.50
	s. Specimen.	—	—

		VF	UNC
40	**5 Pounds** 17.6.1964-13.2.1965. Lilac and brown on multicolor underprint. Clear circular area at left, Tutankhamen's mask at right. Guilloche at bottom center. Signature 12. Back: Value at left, clear watermark area at right. Watermark: Arms.	5.00	22.50

41 **10 Pounds** — VF | UNC
1.11.1961-13.2.1965. Dark green and dark brown on multicolor underprint. Tutankhamen's mask at right. Signature 11; 12. Back: Brown. Watermark: Arms. — 7.50 | 30.00

1967-69 Issue

#42-46 Replacement notes: Serial # prefix single Arabic letter.

42 **25 Piastres** — VF | UNC
6.2.1967-4.1.1975. Blue, green and brown on multicolor underprint. Sphinx with statue at left center. Signature 13; 14. Back: U.A.R. arms at center. Watermark: Archaic Egyptian scribe. — .50 | 3.00

43 **50 Piastres** — VF | UNC
2.12.1967-28.1.1978. Red-brown and brown on multicolor underprint. Al Azhar mosque at right. Signature 13; 14; 15. Back: Ramses II at center right. Watermark: Archaic Egyptian scribe.
- a. Issued note. — 1.00 | 3.50
- s. Specimen. — — | —

44 **1 Pound** — VF | UNC
12.5.1967-19.4.1978. Brown and black on multicolor underprint. Sultan Quayet Bey mosque at left center. Signature 12; 13; 14; 15. Back: Archaic statues. Watermark: Archaic Egyptian scribe.
- a. Issued note. — 1.00 | 5.00
- s. Specimen. — — | —

45 **5 Pounds** — VF | UNC
1.1.1969-78. Black on blue and multicolor underprint. Ahmad ibn Tulun mosque at Cairo at center right. Signature 13; 14; 15. Back: Ruins at left, frieze at center right. Watermark: Archaic Egyptian scribe.
- a. Issued note. — 3.50 | 20.00
- s. Specimen. Black overprint: *ANNULE* and *CANCELLED.* — — | 750.

46 **10 Pounds** — VF | UNC
1.9.1969-78. Red-brown and brown on multicolor underprint. Sultan Hassan Mosque at Cairo at left center. Signature 13; 14; 15. Back: Pharaoh and pyramids. Watermark: Archaic Egyptian scribe. — 6.00 | 25.00

1976 Issue

#47 and 48 replacement notes: Serial # prefix single Arabic letter.

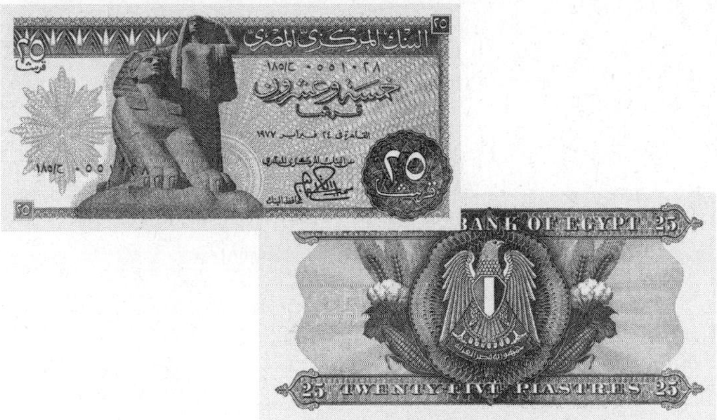

		VF	UNC
47	**25 Piastres** 12.4.1976-9.6.1978; 12.6.1978; 28.8.1978. Blue, green and grayish brown on blue and orange underprint. Sphinx with statue at left center. Signature 15. Back: A. R. E. arms. Watermark: Archaic Egyptian scribe.		
	a. Issued note.	1.00	4.00
	s. Specimen.	—	—

		VF	UNC
48	**20 Pounds** 5.7.1976; 1978. Green and black on multicolor underprint. Mohammed Ali mosque at left, Arabic legends at right. Signature 15. Back: Archaic war chariot at left center, frieze at center right. Watermark: Archaic Egyptian scribe.	10.00	35.00

1978-79 Issue

#49-62 no longer have conventional dates with Arabic day, month and year. In place of this are six Arabic numerals, the first and last making up the year, the second and third the day, the fourth and fifth the month of issue; YDDMMY; i.e. 825029 will be 25 Feb. 1989. Replacement notes: Serial # prefix. Arabic *200* or *300* before single Arabic letter.

		VF	UNC
49	**25 Piastres** 2.1.-11.5.(19)79. Black and brown on gray, pale blue and orange underprint. Al-Sayida Aisha mosque at center. Signature 15. Back: Stylized A. R. E. arms, cotton, wheat and corn plants at center. Watermark: Tutankhamen's mask.	.50	2.00

		VF	UNC
50	**1 Pound** (19)78-2008. Brown, purple and deep olive-green on multicolor underprint. Sultan Qait Bey mosque at left center. Back: Statues from the Abu Simbel Temple. Watermark: Tutankhamen's mask. 140x70mm.		
	a. Back deep brown. Solid security thread. 29.5.1978-15.8.1981. Series #1-129. Signature 15.	FV	1.50
	b. 3.4.1982-6.3.1984. Series #130-150. Signature 16.	FV	1.50
	c. 2.5.1985-2.1.1986. Series #151-165. Signature 17.	FV	1.50
	d. Back pale brown. Solid security thread or segmented security thread with bank name repeated. 16.11.1986-1.6.1992. Series #166-246. Signature 18.	FV	1.50
	e. 17.10.1993-25.1.2001. Series #247-380. Signature 19.	FV	1.50
	f. 22.11.2001-14.8.2003. Series #381-428. Signature 20.	FV	1.50
	g. 23.12.2003. Series #429-432. Signature 21.	FV	1.50
	h. 23.12.2003. Series #432-; 12.4.2005. Signature 22.	FV	1.50
	i. 7.7.(20)04; 4.1.2005; 17.4.2005. Signature 25.	FV	1.50
	j. 5.3.2006. Signature 25.	FV	1.50
	k. 31.1.2007. Signature 25.	FV	1.50
	l. 25.3.2007.	FV	1.50
	m. 15.5.2008.	FV	1.50
	s. Specimen. Red overprint in Arabic script. Punch hole cancelled.	—	500.

		VF	UNC
51	**10 Pounds** 24.6.(19)78-27.9.(20)00. Red-brown and brown-violet on multicolor underprint. Al-Rifai mosque at center. Signature 15; 16; 17; 18; 19. Back: Pharaoh. Watermark: Tutankhamen's mask. 150x70mm.	FV	10.00

		VF	UNC
52	**20 Pounds** 6.9.(19)78-92. Black, gray-violet and deep green on multicolor underprint. Muhammed Ali mosque at center. Back: Archaic sculptures from Chapel of Sesostris I and archaic war chariot. Watermark: Tutankhamen's mask. 175x70mm.		
	a. Date below watermark. Solid security thread. 6.9.(19)78-22.4.(19)82. Signature 15; 16.	5.00	35.00
	b. Date at lower right of watermark. Solid security thread. 9.12.(19)86; 3.3.(19)87; 4.10.(19)87. Signature 18.	FV	20.00
	c. Segmented security thread with bank name repeated. (19)88-(19)92. Signature 19.	FV	17.50

		VF	UNC
53	**100 Pounds**		
	(19)78; (19)92. Blue and green on multicolor underprint. Al-Sayida Zainab mosque at center. Back: Pharaoh's mask above frieze at center of vertical format. Watermark: Tutankhamen's mask.		
	a. Series 1-6.(19)78. Signature 15.	30.00	100.
	b. (19)92. Signature 18.	22.50	90.00

1980-81 Issue

Replacement notes: Serial # prefix Arabic *200* or *300* before single Arabic series letter.

		VF	UNC
54	**25 Piastres**		
	17.1.(19)80-10.1(19)84. Dark green on light green, orange and blue underprint. Al-Sayida Aisha mosque at center. Signature 15; 16. Back: Stylized A. R. E. arms, cotton, wheat and corn plants at center. Watermark: Tutankhamen's mask.	.30	1.50

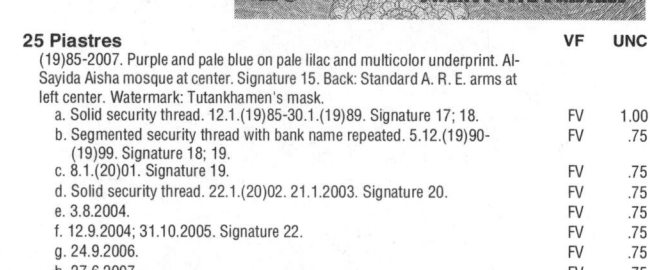

		VF	UNC
55	**50 Piastres**		
	1.1.(19)81-10.6.(19)83. Green and brown on multicolor underprint. Al Azhar mosque at center. Signature 15; 16. Back: Sculptured wall design at left, Ramses II at center, archaic seal at right. Watermark: Tutankhamen's mask.	.50	3.00

		VF	UNC
56	**5 Pounds**		
	(19)81; (19)86; (19)87. Olive-black and blue-black on multicolor underprint. Ibn Toulon mosque at center. Back: Design symbolizing bounty of the Nile River at center. Watermark: Tutankhamen's mask. 145x70mm.		
	a. 1.2.(19)81. Signature 15. Top left serial # above border design and close to top edge of paper. Series 1.	5.00	35.00
	b. 2.2.(19)81. Signature 15. Top left serial # below border design. Series 2.	5.00	35.00
	c. (19)86; 6.1.(19)87. Signature 16; 17; 18.	3.00	15.00

1985 Issue

Replacement notes: Serial # prefix Arabic *200* or *300* before single Arabic series letter.

		VF	UNC
57	**25 Piastres**		
	(19)85-2007. Purple and pale blue on pale lilac and multicolor underprint. Al-Sayida Aisha mosque at center. Signature 15. Back: Standard A. R. E. arms at left center. Watermark: Tutankhamen's mask.		
	a. Solid security thread. 12.1.(19)85-30.1.(19)89. Signature 17; 18.	FV	1.00
	b. Segmented security thread with bank name repeated. 5.12.(19)90-(19)99. Signature 18; 19.	FV	.75
	c. 8.1.(20)01. Signature 19.	FV	.75
	d. Solid security thread. 22.1.(20)02. 21.1.2003. Signature 20.	FV	.75
	e. 3.8.2004.	FV	.75
	f. 12.9.2004; 31.10.2005. Signature 22.	FV	.75
	g. 24.9.2006.	FV	.75
	h. 27.6.2007.	FV	.75
	s. Specimen. Red overprint in Arabic script.	—	500.

		VF	UNC
58	**50 Piastres**		
	(19)85-94. Black on pale orange, pink and multicolor underprint. Al Azhar mosque at center right. Back: Sculptured wall design at left, Ramses II at center, archaic seal at right. Watermark: Tutankhamen's mask. UV: security strip fluoresces orange.		
	a. No text line at lower left on face. Solid security thead. 2.7.(19)85-(19)87. Signature 17; 18.	.25	2.00
	b. Text line added at lower left on face. 1.2.(19)87-17.8.(19)89. Signature 18.	FV	1.25
	c. Segmented security thread with bank name repeated. 5.1.(19)90-15.8.(19)94. Signature 18, 19.	FV	1.00
	s. As a. Specimen. Overprinted in Arabic and English.	—	400.

1989-94 Issue

Replacement notes: Serial # prefix Arabic *200* or *300* before single Arabic series letter.

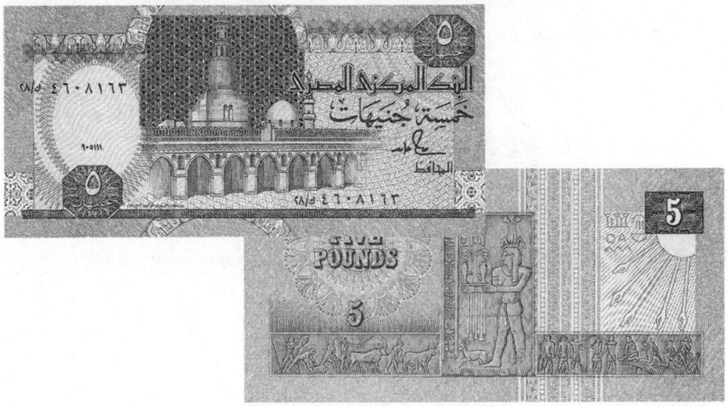

			VF	UNC
59	**5 Pounds**	2.4.(19)89-1.2.(20)01. Black and blue-black on multicolor underprint. Multicolor scrollwork added in underprint. Ibn Toulon mosque at center. Signature 18; 19; 20. Back: Archaic design over watermark area at right. Watermark: Tutankhamen's mask. Multicolor scrollwork added in underprint and into watermark area. 145x70mm.	FV	6.00

			VF	UNC
60	**50 Pounds**	9.2.(19)93-18.11.(19)99. Brown, violet and multicolor. Abu Hariba Mosque at right. Signature 18; 19. Back: Isis above archaic boat, interior view of Edfu temple at left center. Watermark: Tutankhamen's mask. 160x70mm.	12.50	35.00

			VF	UNC
61	**100 Pounds**	14.9.(19)94; (19)97. Dark brown and brown-violet on multicolor underprint. Sultan Hassan Mosque at lower left center. Signature 19. Back: Sphinx at center. Watermark: Tutankhamen's mask. 165x70mm.	25.00	80.00

1995 Issue

			VF	UNC
62	**50 Piastres**	23.8.(19)94-2007. Dull olive-gray on multicolor underprint. Al Azhar mosque at center right. Signature 19; 20; 22. Back: Sculptured wall design at left, Ramses II at center, archaic seal at right. Watermark: Tutankhamen's mask.		
		a. 23.8.(19)94.	FV	.75
		b. 6.7.(19)95.	FV	.75
		c. 9.7.(19)95.	FV	.75
		d. 28.5.1997.	FV	.75
		e. 17.7.2002.	FV	.75
		f. 25.12.2003.	FV	.75
		g. 3.8.2004.	FV	.75
		h. 12.5.2005.	FV	.75
		i. 21.7.2005.	FV	.75
		j. 14.11.2006.	FV	.75

2000-03 Issue

#63-64 w/wide segmented silver security strip and added rosette printed in optical variable ink.

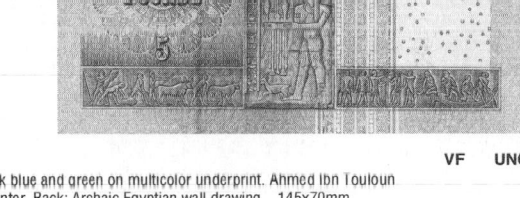

			VF	UNC
63	**5 Pounds**	2001-10. Dark blue and green on multicolor underprint. Ahmed Ibn Touloun Mosque at center. Back: Archaic Egyptian wall drawing. 145x70mm.		
		a. 4.2.2001; 21.2.2002; 16.12.2002. Signature 20.	FV	4.00
		b. 6.1.2004; 11.1.2004; 13.1.2004; 16.2.2005; 5.9.2006; 18.8.2008. Signature 22.	FV	3.00
		c. 2.5.2009.	FV	3.00
		d. 2.8.2010.	FV	3.00

			VF	UNC
64	**10 Pounds**	2003-. Brown and violet on multicolor underprint. Mosque. 150x70mm.		
		a. 28.8.2003. Signature 20.	FV	5.00
		b. 12.8.2003; 31.8.2003. Signature 21.	FV	5.00
		c. 13.6.2004; 28.12.2004; 22.11.2006; 5.12.2009. Signature 22.	FV	4.00

65 20 Pounds

3.10.2001-2009. Black, gray-violet and deep green on multicolor underprint. Muhammed Ali mosque at center. Signature 19, 20, 21, 22. Back: Archaic sculptures from Chapel of Sesostris I and archaic war chariot. Watermark: Tutankhamen's mask. 175x70mm.

	VF	UNC
a. Signature 19.	FV	8.00
b. Signature 20.	FV	8.00
c. 10.12.2003. Signature 21.	FV	7.00
d. 7.11.2004; 11.11.2004; 26.1.2006. Signature 22.	FV	7.00
e. 14.8.2006.	FV	7.00
f. 16.1.2008.	FV	7.00
g. 15.3.2009.	FV	7.00

66 50 Pounds

2001-. Multicolor. Mosque. Signature 20, 21, 22. Back: Temple and Nile boat. 160x70mm.

	VF	UNC
a. 25.11.2001.	FV	17.50
b. 2003.	FV	17.50
c. 28.9.2004. Signature 22.	FV	17.00
d. 2005.	FV	17.00
e. 16.4.2007.	FV	16.00
f. 3.3.2008.	FV	16.00
g. 25.3.2009.	FV	16.00
h. 16.9.2009.	FV	16.00
i. 27.10.2009.	FV	16.00

67 100 Pounds

2000-. Dark brown and brown-violet on multicolor underprint. Sultan Hassan Mosque at lower left center. Signature 19; 20; 21, 22. Back: Sphinx at center. Watermark: Tutankhamen's mask and value. 165x70mm.

	VF	UNC
a. 4.10.2000. Signature 19. Narrow value in watermark.	FV	35.00
b. Signature 19. Wide value in watermark.	FV	35.00
c. Signature 20.	FV	32.50
d. 29.12.2003. Signature 21.	FV	32.50
e. 18.4.2006.	FV	32.50
f. 4.6.2006.	FV	32.50
g. 13.6.2007.	FV	30.00
h. 18.6.2009.	FV	30.00

68 200 Pounds

3.4.2007-. Violet, brown and green on multicolor underprint. Qani-Bay Mosque at right center. Back: Seated scribe. 176x80mm.

	VF	UNC
a. 3.4.2007.	FV	80.00
b. 12.11.2007.	FV	75.00
c. 11.6.2009.	FV	75.00
d. 1.3.2010.	FV	65.00
r. Replacement note. 3.4.2007.	—	85.00

69 200 Pounds

3.4.2007-. Violet, brown and green on multicolor underprint. Qani-Bay Mosque at right center. Back: Seated scribe. Watermark: Seated scribe. 165x74mm.

	VF	UNC
a. Issued note.	FV	75.00
r. Replacement note. 3.4.2007.	FV	85.00

Currency Notes

United Arab Republic

1961 ND Issue

180 5 Piastres

L.1940. Lilac. Queen Nefertiti at right. Watermark: *U A R.*

	VF	UNC
a. Signature Baghdady with titles: *VICE-PRESIDENT AND MINISTER OF TREASURY*. Series 15; 16.	6.00	30.00
b. Signature Kaissouni with titles: *MINISTER OF TREASURY AND PLANNING*. Series 16-18.	3.00	12.00
c. Signature Daif with titles: *MINISTER OF TREASURY*. Color lilac to blue. Watermark 3mm tall. Series 18-22.	2.00	10.00
d. Signature and titles as c. Watermark 5mm tall. Series 22-26.	2.00	10.00
e. Signature Hegazy with titles as d. Series 26-33.	2.00	10.00

180A **5 Piastres** | VF | UNC
L.1940. . Lilac. Queen Nefertiti at right. Back: Signature Kaissouni with title: *MINISTER OF TREASURY* (error). Watermark: *U A R.* Series 16. — 60.00 — 175.

181 **10 Piastres** | VF | UNC
L.1940. Black. Group of militants with flag having only two stars.

	VF	UNC
a. Signature Daghdady with titles: *VICE-PRESIDENT AND MINISTER OF TREASURY.* Series 16.	15.00	45.00
b. Signature Kaissouni with titles: *MINISTER OF TREASURY AND PLANNING.* Series 16-18.	3.00	12.00
c. Signature Kaissouni with titles: *MINISTER OF TREASURY.* Series 16.	50.00	175.
d. Signature Daif with title as c. Series 18-24.	3.00	12.00
e. Signature Hegazy with title as c. Series 24-29.	3.00	10.00

Arab Republic of Egypt

1971 ND Issue

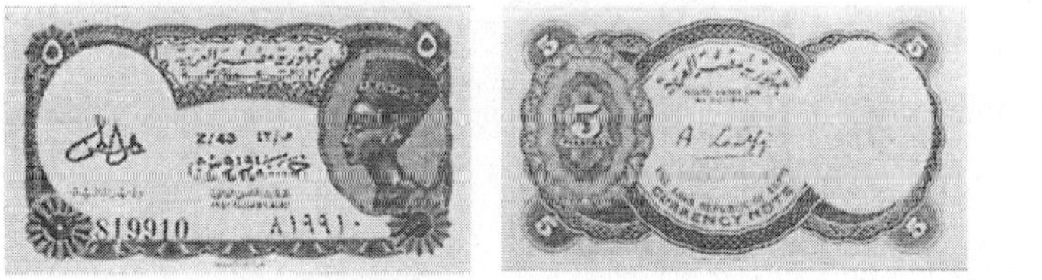

182 **5 Piastres** | VF | UNC
L.1940. Lilac. Queen Nefertiti at right. Watermark: *U A R.* Imprint: Survey of Egypt.

	VF	UNC
a. Signature Hegazy with title: *MINISTER OF TREASURY.* Watermark: *U A R.* Series 33-34.	5.00	20.00
b. Signature Hegazy with title: *MINISTER OF TREASURY.* Watermark: *A R E.* Series 34-36.	4.00	15.00
c. Signature Ibrahim with title: *MINISTER OF FINANCE.* Watermark: *A R E.* Series 36-37.	1.50	6.00
d. Signature El Nashar with title as c. Series 37.	2.50	10.00
e. Signature Ismail. with title as c. Series 37-40.	.75	3.00
f. Signature M. S. Hamed. Series 40-42.	1.00	4.00
g. Signature Loutfy. Series 42-47.	.75	3.00
h. Signature Meguid. Series 47-50.	.60	3.00
i. Signature Hamed. Series. 50.	6.00	25.00
j. Like c. Printer: Postal Printing House. Signature Hamed. Series 50-72.	.50	2.50
k. Signature El Razaz. Series 72.	1.00	5.00

183 **10 Piastres**
L.1940. Black. Group of militants with flag having only two stars. Printer: Survey Authority.

	VF	UNC
a. Signature Hegazy with title: *MINISTER OF TREASURY.* Watermark: *U A R.* Series 29-30.	10.00	45.00
b. Signature Hegazy with title: *MINISTER OF TREASURY.* Watermark: *A R E.* Series 30-31.	5.00	25.00
c. Signature Ibrahim with title: *MINISTER OF FINANCE.* Watermark: *A R E.* Series 31-32.	2.00	9.00
d. Signature El Nashar with titles as c. Series 32-33.	4.00	15.00
e. Signature Ismail with titles as c. Series 33-35.	1.00	4.00
f. Signature M. S. Hamed with titles as c. Series 35-38.	1.75	7.00
g. Signature Loutfy with titles as c. Series 38-43.	1.00	4.00
h. Signature Meguid with titles as c. Series 43-46.	.75	3.00
i. Signature Hamed with titles as c. Series 46.	8.00	30.00

184 **10 Piastres**
L.1940. Black. Group of militants, new flag with eagle. Signature title: *MINISTER OF FINANCE.*

	VF	UNC
a. Signature Hamed. Series 46-69.	.50	2.50
b. Signature El Razaz. Series 69-75.	.75	3.00

1997; 1998 ND Issue

Law 50 of 1940.

185 **5 Piastres** | VF | UNC
L.1940. Green and orange. Queen Nefertiti at right. Signature El-Ghareeb with title: *MINISTER OF FINANCE.* Arabic Series 1-2. Watermark: Tutankhamen's mask. Printer: Postal Printing House. — .25 — 1.25

186 **5 Piastres**
L.1940. Green and orange. Queen Nefertiti at right. Signatrue El-Ghareeb with title: *MINISTER OF FINANCE.* Arabic Series 1-2. Back: Mule issue with signature Salah Hamad with title: *MINISTER OF FINANCE.* Mule issue with signature Salah Hamad with title: *MINISTER OF FINANCE* on back. — 3.00 — 12.50

187 **10 Piastres** | VF | UNC
L.1940. Black and orange. Sphinx, pyramids at right. Signature El Ghareeb with title: *MINISTER OF FINANCE.* Arabic Series 1-2. Back: Mosque of Mohamed Ali at Citadel at left. Watermark: Tutankhamen's mask. — .50 — 1.50

1998; 1999 ND Issue

Law 50 of 1940

188 **5 Piastres** | VF | UNC
L.1940. Blue-gray on blue and lilac underprint. Queen Nefertiti at right. Signature El-Ghareeb with title: *MINISTER OF FINANCE.* Arabic Series 1-6. Watermark: Tutankhamen's mask. Printer: Postal Printing House. — .25 — 1.25

189 **10 Piastres**
L.1940. Dull purple and blue on multicolor underprint. Sphinx, pyramids at right. Signature El Ghareeb with title: *MINISTER OF FINANCE.* Arabic Series 1-2. Back: Mosque of Mohamed Ali at Citadel at left. Watermark: Tutankhamen's mask.

	VF	UNC
a. Signature El Ghareeb.	.25	1.00
b. Signature.	.25	1.00

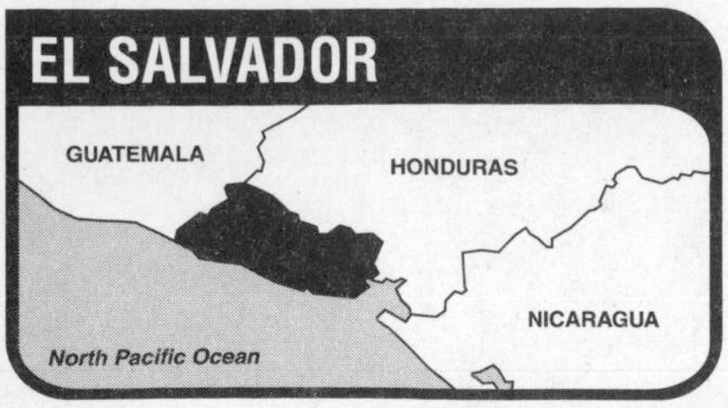

The Republic of El Salvador, a Central American country bordered by Guatemala, Honduras and the Pacific Ocean, has an area of 21,040 sq. km. and a population of 7.07 million. Capital: San Salvador. This most intensely cultivated country of Latin America produces coffee (the major crop), sugar and balsam for export. Gold, silver and other metals are largely unexploited.

El Salvador achieved independence from Spain in 1821 and from the Central American Federation in 1839. A 12-year civil war, which cost about 75,000 lives, was brought to a close in 1992 when the government and leftist rebels signed a treaty that provided for military and political reforms.

On January 1, 2001, a monetary reform established the U.S. dollar as the accounting unit for all financial transactions, and fixed the exchange rate as 8.75 colones per dollar. In addition, the Central Reserve Bank has indicated that it will cease issuing coins and notes.

MONETARY SYSTEM:

1 Peso = 100 Centavos to 1919
1 Colón = 100 Centavos 1919-

SUPERINTENDENCIA DE BANCOS Y OTRAS INSTITUCIONES FINANCIERAS:

Juan S. Quinteros	1962-1975	Marco T. Guandique	1977-Feb. 1981
Jose A. Mendoza	1968-1975	Rafael T. Carbonell	1981
Jorge A. Dowson	1975-1977	Raul Nolasco	1981-

DATING SYSTEM:

Dates listed for notes are those found on the face, regardless of the ovpt. issue dates on back which were applied practically on a daily basis as notes were needed for circulation.

REPUBLIC

BANCO CENTRAL DE RESERVA DE EL SALVADOR

1962; 1963 ISSUE

100 **1 Colón** — VF / UNC
12.3.1963; 25.1.1966; 23.8.1966. Black on multicolor underprint. Central Bank at center. Back: Orange. Portrait of Christopher Columbus at center left. Printer: TDLR.

	VF	UNC
a. Issued note.	10.00	35.00
s. Specimen. 12.3.1963.	—	150.

101 **2 Colones** — VF / UNC
15.2.1962; 9.6.1964. Black on multicolor underprint. Coffee bush at left, workers at left center. Back: Red-brown. Portrait of Christopher Columbus at center left. Printer: TDLR.

	VF	UNC
a. Issued note.	15.00	75.00
s. Specimen. 15.2.1962. Red overprint: *MUESTRA SIN VALOR* on both sides.	—	185.

102 **5 Colones** — VF / UNC
15.2.1962; 12.3.1963. Black on multicolor underprint. Woman with basket of fruit on her head at left. Back: Green. Portrait of Christopher Columbus at center left. Printer: TDLR.

	VF	UNC
a. Issued note.	15.00	80.00
s. Specimen. 15.2.1962.	—	150.

103 **10 Colones** — VF / UNC
15.2.1962; 9.6.1964; 27.12.1966. Black on multicolor underprint. Portrait Manuel José Arce at center, serial number at lower left and upper right. Back: Brown. Portrait of Christopher Columbus at center left. Printer: TDLR.

	VF	UNC
a. Issued note.	20.00	100.
s. Specimen. 15.2.1962; 9.6.1964. Red overprint: *MUESTRA SIN VALOR* on both sides.	—	200.

104 **25 Colones** — VF / UNC
1963; 1966. Black on multicolor underprint. Fifth of November Dam at center. Back: Dark blue. Portrait of Christopher Columbus at center left. Printer: TDLR. .

	VF	UNC
a. 12.3.1963.	25.00	130.
b. 27.12.1966.	25.00	110.
s1. As a. Specimen. Red overprint: *MUESTRA SIN VALOR* on both sides.	—	200.
s2. As b. Specimen.	—	75.00

1964; 1965 ISSUE

105 **1 Colón** — VF / UNC
8.9.1964. Black on pink and green underprint. Farmer plowing at center, *SAN SALVADOR* at upper left. Black serial number and series letters. Back: Orange. Portrait of Christopher Columbus at center left. Printer: ABNC.

	VF	UNC
a. Issued note.	7.50	30.00
s. Specimen.	—	150.

106 5 Colones — VF / UNC

8.9.1964. Black on green and multicolor underprint. José Matías Delgado addressing crowd at center, *SAN SALVADOR* at upper left. Black serial number at lower left and upper right. Back: Deep olive-green. Portrait of Christopher Columbus at center left. Printer: ABNC.

	VF	UNC
a. Issued note.	10.00	50.00
s. Specimen.	—	150.

107 100 Colones — VF / UNC

12.1.1965. Brown and green underprint. Independence monument at center but *SAN SALVADOR* at upper left. Serial number at lower left and upper right. Back: Olive-green. Portrait of Christopher Columbus at center left. Printer: ABNC.

	VF	UNC
a. Issued note.	75.00	250.
s. Specimen. Red overprint: *MUESTRA SIN VALOR* twice on both sides. Punch hole cancelled.	—	325.

1967 Commemorative Issue

#108-109 These notes are reportedly commemoratives for the Bicentennial of the Birth of José Cañas.

108 1 Colón — VF / UNC

20.6.1967. Black on multicolor underprint. Juan José Cañas at right, *UN COLON* at center *SAN SALVADOR* and date at right. Back: Orange. Portrait of Christopher Columbus at center left. Printer: TDLR.

	VF	UNC
a. Issued note.	4.00	25.00
s. Specimen. Punched hole cancelled.	—	40.00

109 5 Colones — VF / UNC

20.6.1967. Black on pink and green underprint. Scene of Juan José Cañas freeing the slaves, *31.12.1823* at center. Back: Green. Portrait of Christopher Columbus at center left. Printer: TDLR.

	VF	UNC
a. Issued note.	125.	325.
s. Specimen.	—	100.

1968-70 Issue

110 1 Colón — VF / UNC

1968; 1970. Black on light orange and pale blue underprint. Juan José Cañas at right, *1 COLON* at center. Back: Orange. Portrait of Christopher Columbus at center left. Printer: USBNC.

	VF	UNC
a. Signature title: *CAJERO* at right. 13.8.1968.	5.00	25.00
b. Signature title: *GERENTE* at right. 12.5.1970.	5.00	22.50
s1. As a. Specimen.	—	35.00
s2. As b. Specimen.	—	35.00

111 5 Colones — VF / UNC

1968-70. Black on green and ochre underprint. José Matías Delgado addressing crowd at center, *5 COLONES* at right. Back: Dark green. Portrait of Christopher Columbus at center left. Printer: USBNC.

	VF	UNC
a. Signature title: *CAJERO* at right. 13.8.1968; 4.2.1969.	7.50	35.00
b. Signature title: *GERENTE* at right. 12.5.1970.	6.00	30.00
s1. As a. Specimen. 13.8.1968; 4.2.1969.	—	35.00
s2. As b. Specimen.	—	35.00

112 10 Colones — VF / UNC

13.8.1968. Black on tan and pale blue underprint. Manuel José Arce at right, *10 COLONES* at center. Back: Black. Portrait of Christopher Columbus at center left. Printer: USBNC.

	VF	UNC
a. Issued note.	15.00	60.00
s. Specimen.	—	40.00

113 25 Colones — VF / UNC

12.5.1970. Black on light orange and pale blue underprint. Fifth of November Dam at right. Back: Dark blue. Portrait of Christopher Columbus at center left. Printer: USBNC.

	VF	UNC
a. Issued note.	25.00	90.00
s. Specimen.	—	50.00

114 100 Colones VF UNC

12.5.1970. Black on pink and pale olive-green underprint. Independence monument at center. Back: Olive-green. Portrait of Christopher Columbus at center left. Printer: USBNC.

	VF	UNC
a. Issued note.	75.00	250.
s. Specimen. Red overprint: *MUESTRA SIN VALOR* twice on both sides.	—	275.

1971; 1972 Issue

115 1 Colón VF UNC

31.8.1971; 24.10.1972. Black on multicolor underprint. *SAN SALVADOR* and date at left, *UN COLON* at center, Juan José Cañas at right. Back: Red. Portrait of Christopher Columbus at center left. Printer: TDLR.

	VF	UNC
a. Issued note.	2.00	12.50
s. Specimen. 31.8.1971; 24.10.1972.	—	30.00

116 2 Colones VF UNC

1972; 1974. Black on multicolor underprint. Colonial church of Panchimalco at center, *DOS COLONES* at right. Back: Red-brown. Portrait of Christopher Columbus at center left. Printer: TDLR.

	VF	UNC
a. 24.10.1972.	3.00	17.50
b. 15.10.1974.	2.50	15.00
s. As a, b. Specimen.	—	30.00

117 5 Colones VF UNC

31.8.1971-24.6.1976. Black on pale blue and multicolor underprint. José Matías Delgado addressing crowd at center. Back: Green. Portrait of Christopher Columbus at center left. Printer: TDLR.

	VF	UNC
a. Issued note.	4.00	25.00
s. Specimen. 31.8.1971; 24.10.1972; 15.10.1974.	—	30.00

118 10 Colones VF UNC

31.8.1971-23.12.1976. Black on multicolor underprint. *DIEZ COLONES* at center, Manuel José Arce at right. Back: Dull black. Portrait of Christopher Columbus at center left. Printer: TDLR.

	VF	UNC
a. Issued note.	7.50	40.00
s. Specimen. 31.8.1971; 24.10.1972; 15.10.1974.	—	35.00

119 25 Colones VF UNC

31.8.1971. Black on multicolor underprint. Fifth of November Dam at center. Back: Blue. Portrait of Christopher Columbus at center left. Printer: TDLR.

	VF	UNC
a. Issued note.	15.00	75.00
s. Specimen.	—	32.50

1974 Issue

120 1 Colón VF UNC

15.10.1974. Black on multicolor underprint. Cerron Grande Dam at center, without *UN COLON* at left. Back: Red. Portrait of Christopher Columbus at center left. Printer: TDLR. 3.00 15.00

121 25 Colones — VF — UNC

15.10.1974; 24.6.1976; 23.12.1976. Black on multicolor underprint. Aerial view of Acajutla port. Back: Blue. Portrait of Christopher Columbus at center left. Printer: TDLR.

	VF	UNC
a. Issued note.	12.50	55.00
s. Specimen. 15.10.1974.	—	150.

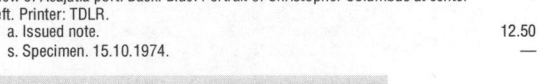

122 100 Colones — VF — UNC

1974-79. Black on multicolor underprint. Indian pyramid at Tazumal at center, arms at lower right. Back: Olive-green on multicolor underprint. Portrait of Christopher Columbus at center left. Printer: TDLR.

	VF	UNC
a. Regular serial #. 15.10.1974-11.5.1978.	20.00	100.
b. Electronic sorting serial #. 3.5.1979.	17.50	80.00
s. As a. Specimen. 15.10.1974.	—	60.00

1976 Issue

123 1 Colón — VF — UNC

28.10.1976. Black on multicolor underprint. Cerron Grande Dam at center, *UN COLON* at left. Back: Portrait of Christopher Columbus at center left. Printer: TDLR.

	VF	UNC
a. Issued note.	2.00	12.50
s. Specimen.	—	30.00

124 2 Colones — VF — UNC

24.6.1976. Black on multicolor underprint. Colonial church of Panchimalco at center, *DOS COLONES* at left and right. Denomination added at left. Back: Brown-violet. Portrait of Christopher Columbus at center left. Printer: TDLR.

	VF	UNC
a. Issued note.	1.75	17.50
s. Specimen.	—	30.00

1977-79 Issues

125 1 Colón — VF — UNC

1977-80. Black on multicolor underprint. Cerron Grande Dam at center, *UN COLON* at left. Underprint in margins. Back: Red. Portrait of Christopher Columbus at center left. Printer: TDLR.

	VF	UNC
a. Regular style serial #. 7.7.1977; 11.5.1978.	1.50	11.00
b. Electronic sorting serial #. 3.5.1979; 19.6.1980.	1.00	8.50
s. As b. Specimen.	—	75.00

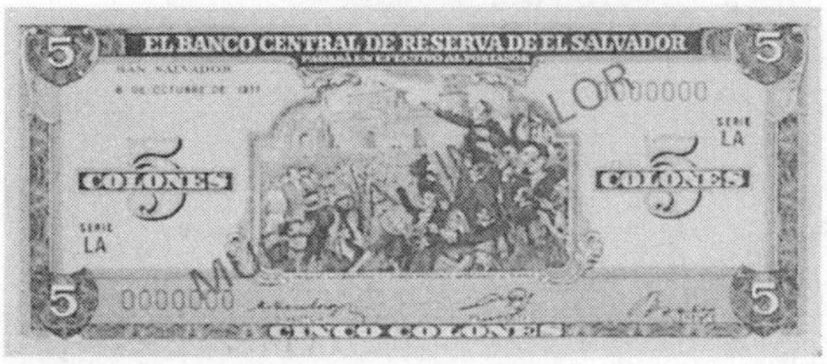

126 5 Colones — VF — UNC

6.10.1977. Black on multicolor underprint. José Matías Delgado addressing crowd at center. *5 COLONES* at left and right. Underprint in margins. Back: Green. Portrait of Christopher Columbus at center left. Printer: TDLR.

	VF	UNC
a. Issued note.	3.50	22.50
s. Specimen.	Unc	32.50

127 10 Colones

7.7.1977. Black on multicolor underprint. *DIEZ COLONES* at center, Manuel José Arce at center right. Back: Black. Portrait of Christopher Columbus at center left. Printer: ABNC.

	VF	UNC
a. Issued note.	5.00	30.00
s. Specimen.	—	125.

128 10 Colones — VF — UNC

13.10.1977. Black on multicolor underprint. *DIEZ COLONES* at center, Manuel José Arce at center right. Blue arms added. Back: Black. Portrait of Christopher Columbus at center left. Blue arms added. Printer: ABNC.

	VF	UNC
a. Issued note.	5.00	25.00
s. Specimen.		125.

129 10 Colones — VF — UNC

1978-80. Black on multicolor underprint. Manuel José Arce at right. Underprint in margins. Back: Black. Portrait of Christopher Columbus at center left. Printer: TDLR.

	VF	UNC
a. Regular serial #. 11.5.1978.	3.00	17.50
b. Electronic sorting serial #. 3.5.1979; 21.7.1980.	2.00	15.00
s. As b. Specimen. 3.5.1979.	—	35.00

130 25 Colones — VF — UNC

1978-80. Black on multicolor underprint. Aerial view of Acajutla port. Underprint in margins. Back: Blue. Portrait of Christopher Columbus at center left. Printer: TDLR.

	VF	UNC
a. Regular serial #. 11.5.1978.	5.00	40.00
b. Electronic sorting serial #. 3.5.1979; 19.6.1980.	3.00	25.00
s. As b. Specimen. 19.6.1980. Red overprint: *MUESTRA SIN VALOR* on both sides.	—	90.00

131	50 Colones	VF	UNC
	1979; 1980. Purple on multicolor underprint. Large building and statue at left, Captain General Gerardo Barrios at right. Back: Ships at left, Christopher Columbus at center. Printer: TDLR.		
	a. 3.5.1979.	8.00	60.00
	b. 19.6.1980.	5.00	30.00
	s. As a. Specimen.	—	30.00

132	100 Colones	VF	UNC
	7.7.1977. Deep olive-green on multicolor underprint. Independence monument at right. Back: Portrait of Christopher Columbus at center left. Printer: ABNC.		
	a. Issued note.	20.00	100.
	s. Specimen.	—	300.

1980 Issue

132A	5 Colones	VF	UNC
	19.6.1980 (1992). Black on multicolor underprint. Back: Portrait of Christopher Columbus at center left. Printer: ABNC. Like #134.	FV	10.00

133	100 Colones	VF	UNC
	17.7.1980. Black on multicolor underprint. Indian pyramid at Tazumal at center, arms at lower right. Flag below, date at upper left. Back: Olive-green on multicolor underprint. Portrait of Christopher Columbus at center left. Printer: TDLR.	17.50	60.00

1982; 1983 Issue

#133A-137 w/o sign. title *GERENTE* at r.

133A	1 Colón	VF	UNC
	3.6.1982. Black on multicolor underprint. Cerron Grande Dam at center, *UN COLON* at left. Back: Red. Portrait of Christopher Columbus at center left. Printer: TDLR.		
	a. Issued note.	FV	10.00
	s. Specimen.	—	30.00

134	5 Colones	VF	UNC
	1983; 1988. Black on multicolor underprint. Back: Green. Portrait of Christopher Columbus at center left. Printer: ABNC. Like #132A.		
	a. 25.8.1983.	FV	12.00
	b. 17.3.1988.	FV	10.00
	s1. As a. Specimen. Red overprint: MUESTRA SIN VALOR on both sides. Punch hole cancelled.	—	125.
	s2. As b. Specimen.	—	100.

135	10 Colones	VF	UNC
	1983; 1988. Black on multicolor underprint. *DIEZ COLONES* at center, Manuel José Arce at center right. Back: Black. Portrait of Christopher Columbus at center left. Printer: ABNC.		
	a. 25.8.1983.	FV	15.00
	b. 17.3.1988.	FV	12.50
	s1. As a. Specimen. Red overprint: *MUESTRA SIN VALOR* twice on face.	—	125.
	s2. As b. Specimen.	—	100.

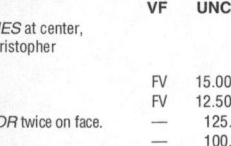

136 25 Colones — VF | UNC

29.9.1983. Black on multicolor underprint. Bridge and reservoir at center. Back: Blue. Portrait of Christopher Columbus at center left. Printer: ABNC.

	VF	UNC
a. Issued note.	FV	35.00
s. Specimen.	—	35.00

137 100 Colones — VF | UNC

1983; 1988. Deep olive-green on multicolor underprint. Independence monument at right. Back: Portrait of Christopher Columbus at center left. Printer: ABNC.

	VF	UNC
a. 29.9.1983.	FV	45.00
b. 17.3.1988.	FV	50.00
s1. As a. Specimen.	—	40.00
s2. As b. Specimen.		27.50

1990-93 Issues

138 5 Colones — VF | UNC

16.5.1990. Black on multicolor underprint. José Matías Delgado addressing crowd at center. *5 COLONES* at left and right. Underprint in margins. Back: Olive-green and dark gray. Portrait of Christopher Columbus at center left. Printer: TDLR. Without signature title: *GERENTE* at right, with electronic sorting serial number.

	VF	UNC
a. Issued note.	FV	10.00
s. Specimen.	—	35.00

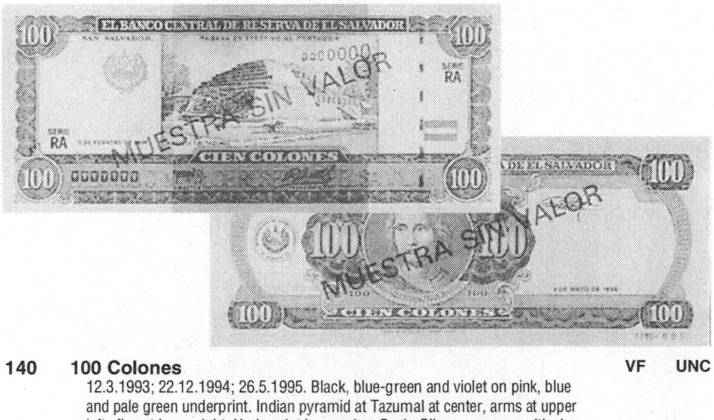

140 100 Colones — VF | UNC

12.3.1993; 22.12.1994; 26.5.1995. Black, blue-green and violet on pink, blue and pale green underprint. Indian pyramid at Tazumal at center, arms at upper left, flag at lower right. Underprint in margins. Back: Olive-green on multicolor underprint. Portrait of Christopher Columbus at center left. Printer: TDLR.

	VF	UNC
a. Issued note.	FV	40.00
s. Specimen.	FV	40.00

1995 Issue

141 10 Colones — VF | UNC

26.5.1995. Black on multicolor underprint. Manuel José Arce at right. Underprint in margins. Ascending size serial number at upper right. Back: Black. Portrait of Christopher Columbus at center left. Watermark: Christopher Columbus wearing hat. Printer: TDLR.

	VF	UNC
a. Issued note.	FV	10.00
s. Specimen.	—	40.00

142 25 Colones — VF | UNC

26.5.1995; 9.2.1996. Black on multicolor underprint. Aerial view of Acajutla port. Underprint in margins. Ascending size serial number at upper right. Back: Blue. Portrait of Christopher Columbus at center left. Watermark: Christopher Columbus wearing hat. Printer: TDLR. Without signature title: *GERENTE* at right.

	VF	UNC
a. Issued note.	FV	20.00
s. Specimen. Red overprint: *MUESTRA SIN VALOR* on both sides.	—	70.00

143 50 Colones

26.5.1995. Purple on multicolor underprint. Large building and statue at left, Captain General Gerardo Barrios at right. Ascending size serial number at upper right. Back: Ships at left, Christopher Columbus at center. Watermark: Christopher Columbus wearing hat. Printer: TDLR. Without signature, title: *GERENTE* at right.

	VF	UNC
a. Issued note.	FV	30.00
s. Specimen.	—	40.00

1996 Issue

144 10 Colones — VF | UNC

9.2.1996. Black on multicolor underprint. Manuel José Arce at right. Underprint in margins. Ascending size serial number at upper right. Back: Black. Portrait of Christopher Columbus at center left. Watermark: Christopher Columbus wearing hat. Printer: CBNC.

	VF	UNC
a. Issued note.	FV	10.00
s. Specimen.	—	40.00

145 50 Colones — VF | UNC

9.2.1996. Purple on multicolor underprint. Large building and statue at left, Captain General Gerardo Barrios at right. Ascending size serial number at upper right. Back: Portrait of Christopher Columbus at center left. Watermark: Christopher Columbus wearing hat. Printer: CBNC. Segmented foil over security thread.

	VF	UNC
a. Issued note.	FV	27.50
s. Specimen.	—	40.00

146 100 Colones VF UNC

9.2.1996. Black, blue-green and violet on pink, blue and pale green underprint. Indian pyramid at Tazumal at center, arms at upper left, flag at lower right. Underprint in margins. Back: Olive-green on multicolor underprint. Portrait of Christopher Columbus at center left. Watermark: Christopher Columbus wearing hat. Printer: CBNC. Segmented foil over security thread.

a. Issued note.	FV	37.50
s. Specimen.	—	50.00

1997 Issue

147 5 Colones VF UNC

18.4.1997; 2.3.1998. Black, dark green and brown on multicolor underprint. National Palace at center right. Special marks for the poor of sight above arms at left center. Signature titles: *PRESIDENTE* and *DIRECTOR*. Back: Christopher Columbus wearing hat at left, continents over his three ships at center. Watermark: Christopher Columbus wearing hat.

a. Issued note. Series D, E, K.	FV	7.50
s. Specimen. Series A.	—	22.50

148 10 Colones VF UNC

18.4.1997; 2.3.1998. Dark blue-violet, brown and deep blue-green on multicolor underprint. Izalco volcano at center right. Special marks for the poor of sight above arms at left center. Signature titles: *PRESIDENTE* and *DIRECTOR*. Back: Christopher Columbus wearing hat at left, continents over his three ships at center. Watermark: Christopher Columbus wearing hat.

a. Issued note. Series A; C.	FV	10.00
s. Specimen. Series A.	—	22.50

149 25 Colones VF UNC

1997; 1998. Black, brown and blue-black on multicolor underprint. San Andres pyramid at center right. Special marks for the poor of sight above arms at left center. Signature titles: *PRESIDENTE* and *DIRECTOR*. Back: Christopher Columbus wearing hat at left, continents over his three ships at center. Watermark: Christopher Columbus wearing hat.

a. Issued note. Series A-D. 18.4.1997.	FV	15.00
b. Issued note. Series F. 2.3.1998.	FV	12.00
s. Specimen. Series A.	—	22.50

150 50 Colones VF UNC

18.4.1997. Purple, brown and blue-black on multicolor underprint. Lake Coatepeque at center right. Special marks for the poor of sight above arms at left center. Signature titles: *PRESIDENTE* and *DIRECTOR*. Back: Christopher Columbus wearing hat at left, continents over his three ships at center. Watermark: Christopher Columbus wearing hat.

a. Issued note. Series A-G.	FV	20.00
s. Specimen. Series A.	—	50.00

151 100 Colones VF UNC

18.4.1997; 4.5.1998. Deep olive-green and dark brown on multicolor underprint. Tazumal pyramid at center right. Special marks for the poor of sight above arms at left center. Signature titles: *PRESIDENTE* and *DIRECTOR*. Back: Christopher Columbus wearing hat at left, continents over his three ships at center. Watermark: Christopher Columbus wearing hat.

a. Issued note. Series A.	FV	27.50
s. Specimen. Series A.	—	27.50

152 200 Colones — VF — UNC

1997-98. Brown, red-violet and purple on multicolor underprint. *EL SALVADOR DEL MUNDO* monument at center right. Special marks for the poor of sight above arms at left center. Signature titles: *PRESIDENTE* and *DIRECTOR*. Back: Christopher Columbus wearing hat at left, continents over his three ships at center. Watermark: Christopher Columbus wearing hat.

	VF	UNC
a. 1997; 1998. Series B.	FV	45.00
s. Specimen. Series A.	—	35.00

1999 Issue

153 5 Colones — VF — UNC

19.4.1999. Green and olive on multicolor underprint. National Palace at center right. Special marks for the poor of sight above arms at left center. Signature titles: *PRESIDENTE* and *DIRECTOR*. Back: Christopher Columbus wearing hat at left, continents over his three ships at center. Watermark: Christopher Columbus wearing hat. Added security features.

	VF	UNC
a. Issued note.	FV	5.00
s. Specimen. Overprint: *MUESTRA SIN VALOR.*	—	—

154 10 Colones — VF — UNC

19.4.1999. Purple and green on multicolor underprint. Izalco volcano at center right. Special marks for the poor of sight above arms at left center. Signature titles: *PRESIDENTE* and *DIRECTOR*. Back: Christopher Columbus wearing hat at left, continents over his three ships at center. Watermark: Christopher Columbus wearing hat. Added security features.

	VF	UNC
a. Issued note.	FV	7.50
s. Specimen. Overprint: *MUESTRA SIN VALOR.*	—	—

155 25 Colones — VF — UNC

19.4.1999. Brown and green on multicolor. San Andres pyramid at center right. Special marks for the poor of sight above arms at left center. Signature titles: *PRESIDENTE* and *DIRECTOR*. Back: Christopher Columbus wearing hat at left, continents over his three ships at center. Watermark: Christopher Columbus wearing hat. Added security features.

	VF	UNC
a. Issued note.	FV	12.50
s. Specimen. Overprint: *MUESTRA SIN VALOR.*	—	—

156 50 Colones — VF — UNC

19.4.1999. Violet and orange on multicolor underprint. Lake Coatepeque at center right. Special marks for the poor of sight above arms at left center. Signature titles: *PRESIDENTE* and *DIRECTOR*. Back: Christopher Columbus wearing hat at left, continents over his three ships at center. Watermark: Christopher Columbus wearing hat. Added security features.

	VF	UNC
a. Issued note.	FV	25.00
s. Specimen. Overprint: *MUESTRA SIN VALOR.*	—	—

157 100 Colones — VF — UNC

19.4.1999. Dark green and light green on multicolor underprint. Tazumal pyramid at center right. Special marks for the poor of sight above arms at left center. Signature titles: *PRESIDENTE* and *DIRECTOR*. Back: Christopher Columbus wearing hat at left, continents over his three ships at center. Watermark: Christopher Columbus wearing hat. Added security features.

	VF	UNC
a. Issued note.	FV	37.50
s. Specimen. Overprint: *MUESTRA SIN VALOR.*	—	—

158 200 Colones — VF — UNC

19.4.1999. Brown, red and multicolor. *EL SALVADOR DEL MUNDO* monument at center right. Special marks for the poor of sight above arms at left center. Signature titles: *PRESIDENTE* and *DIRECTOR*. Back: Christopher Columbus wearing hat at left, continents over his three ships at center. Watermark: Christopher Columbus wearing hat. Added security features.

	VF	UNC
a. Issued note.	FV	60.00
s. Specimen. Overprint: *MUESTRA SIN VALOR.*	—	—

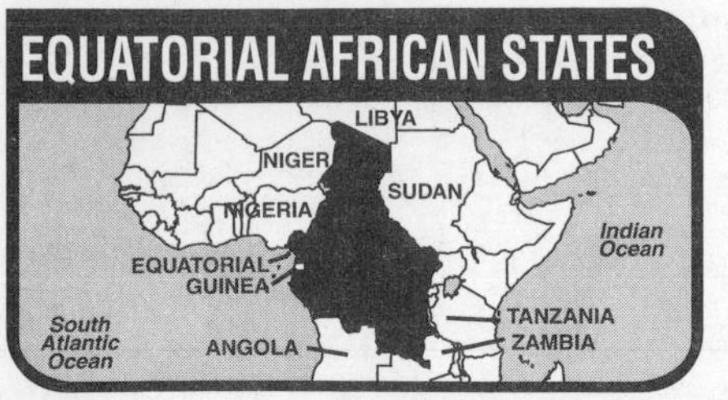

Equatorial African States (Central African States), a monetary union comprising the former French possessions and now independent states of the Republic of Congo (Brazzaville), Gabon, Central African Republic, Chad and Cameroon, issues a common currency for the member states from a common central bank. The monetary unit, the African Financial Community Franc, is tied to and supported by the French franc.

In 1960, an abortive attempt was made to form a union of the newly independent republics of Chad, Congo, Central Africa and Gabon. The proposal was discarded when Chad refused to become a constituent member. The four countries then linked into an Equatorial Customs Unit, to which Cameroon became an associate member in 1961. A more extensive cooperation of the five republics, identified as the Central African Customs and Economic Union, was entered into force at the beginning of 1966.

In 1974 the Central Bank of the Equatorial African States, which had issued coins and paper currency in its own name and with the names of the constituent member nations, changed its name to the Bank of the Central African States.

MONETARY SYSTEM:

1 Franc (C.F.A.) = 100 Centimes

CONTROL LETTER or SYMBOL CODE

Country	1961-72
Cameroun	*
Central African Republic	B
Chad	A
Congo	C
Equatorial Guinea	
Gabon	D

EQUATORIAL AFRICAN STATES

BANQUE CENTRALE DES ÉTATS DE L'AFRIQUE ÉQUATORIALE ET DU CAMEROUN

1961 ND ISSUES

		VF	UNC
1	**100 Francs** ND (1961-62). Blue and multicolor. Portrait of Governor Felix Eboue at center, woman with jug at left, people in canoe at right. Back: Cargo ships at center, man at right.		
	a. Code letter *A*.	125.	450.
	b. Code letter *B*.	150.	500.
	c. Code letter *C*.	125.	450.
	d. Code letter *D*.	125.	450.
	e. * for Cameroun.	200.	750.
	f. Without code letter.	40.00	300.
	s. Specimen. Prefix letter O, serial #0000000s	—	500.
2	**100 Francs** ND (1961-62). Multicolor. Portrait of Governor Felix Eboue at center, woman with jug at left, people in canoe at right. Denomination also in English with * for Cameroun. Back: Cargo ships at center, man at right.	150.	500.

BANQUE CENTRALE ÉTATS DE L'AFRIQUE ÉQUATORIALE

1963 ND ISSUE

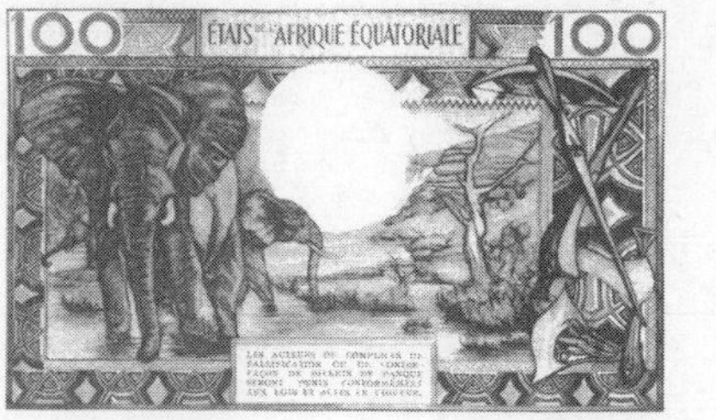

		VF	UNC
3	**100 Francs** ND (1963). Brown and multicolor. Musical instrument at left, hut at left center, man at right. Back: Elephant at left, tools at right.		
	a. Code letter *A*.	40.00	125.
	b. Code letter *B*.	50.00	150.
	c. Code letter *C*.	40.00	125.
	d. Code letter *D*.	40.00	125.

		VF	UNC
4	**500 Francs** ND (1963). Green and multicolor. Girl wearing bandana at right, track mounted crane with ore bucket in background. Back: Radar unit at left, man on camel at right.		
	a. Engraved. Code letter *A*. Block #1-4.	70.00	260.
	b. As a. Code letter *B*.	125.	400.
	c. As a. Code letter *C*.	70.00	260.
	d. As a. Code letter *D*.	70.00	260.
	e. Lithographed. Code letter *A*. Block #5-.	55.00	240.
	f. As e. Code letter *B*.	65.00	260.
	g. As e. Code letter *C*.	55.00	240.
	h. As e. Code letter *D*.	55.00	240.
	s. Specimen. Black overprint: *SPECIMEN* and perforated.	—	750.

		VF	UNC
5	**1000 Francs** ND (1963). Multicolor. People gathering cotton. Back: Young men logging.		
	a. Engraved. Code letter *A*. Block #1-5.	125.	400.
	b. As a. Code letter *B*.	150.	450.
	c. As a. Code letter *C*.	125.	400.
	d. As a. Code letter *D*.	125.	400.
	e. Lithographed. Code letter *A*. Block #7-.	100.	350.
	f. As e. Code letter *B*.	125.	400.
	g. As e. Code letter *C*.	100.	350.
	h. As e. Code letter *D*.	100.	350.

6	5000 Francs	VF	UNC
	ND (1963). Multicolor. Girl at left, village scene at center. Back: Carving at left, airplane, train crossing bridge and tractor hauling logs at center, man smoking a pipe at right.		
	a. Code letter *A.*	375.	1150.
	b. Code letter *B.*	375.	1150.
	c. Code letter *C.*	375.	1150.
	d. Code letter *D.*	375.	1150.
	s. As a. Specimen. Overprinted and perforated: *SPECIMEN.*	—	1000.

7	10,000 Francs	VF	UNC
	ND (1968). Multicolor. President Bokassa at right, Rock Hotel, Bangui, C.A.R. in background, arms of the Central African Republic at lower left.		
	a. Issued note.	3500.	10,000.
	s. Specimen. Serial #00000.	—	8000.

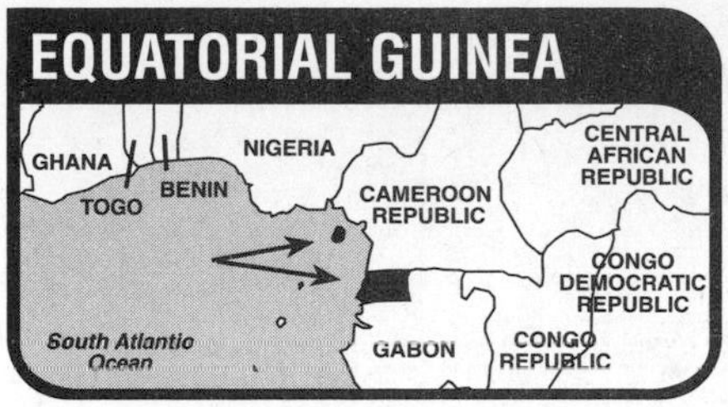

The Republic of Equatorial Guinea consists of Rio Muni, located on the coast of west-central Africa between Cameroon and Gabon, and several offshore islands, principally Isla de Corisco and Isla de Bioko. The country has an area of 28,051 sq. km. and a population of 616,460. Capital: Malabo. The economy is d on agriculture and forestry. Cacao, wood and coffee are exported.

Equatorial Guinea gained independence in 1968 after 190 years of Spanish rule. This tiny country, composed of a mainland portion plus five inhabited islands, is one of the smallest on the African continent. President Teodoro Obiang Nguema Mbasogo has ruled the country since 1979 when he seized power in a coup. Although nominally a constitutional democracy since 1991, the 1996 and 2002 presidential elections - as well as the 1999 and 2004 legislative elections - were widely seen as flawed. The president exerts almost total control over the political system and has discouraged political opposition. Equatorial Guinea has experienced rapid economic growth due to the discovery of large offshore oil reserves, and in the last decade has become Sub-Saharan Africa's third largest oil exporter. Despite the country's economic windfall from oil production resulting in a massive increase in government revenue in recent years, there have been few improvements in the population's living standards.

Additional listings can be found under Central African States.

MONETARY SYSTEM:

1 Peseta Guineana = 100 Centimos to 1975
1 Ekuele = 100 Centimos, 1975-80
1 Epkwele (pl. Bipkwele) = 100 Centimos, 1980-85
1 Franc (C.F.A.) = 100 Centimes, 1985-
1 Franco (C.F.A.) = 4 Bipkwele

Republic

Banco Central

1969 Issue

1	100 Pesetas Guineanas	VF	UNC
	12.10.1969. Red-brown on light tan underprint. Banana tree at left. Back: Shoreline and man with boat. Watermark: Woman's head. Printer: FNMT.	10.00	40.00

2	500 Pesetas Guineanas	VF	UNC
	12.10.1969. Green on multicolor underprint. Derrick loading logs at left, shoreline at center. Back: Woman with bundle on head at right. Watermark: Man's head. Printer: FNMT.	15.00	60.00

3 **1000 Pesetas Guineanas** — **VF** 20.00 — **UNC** 85.00
12.10.1969. Blue on multicolor underprint. President M. Nguema Biyogo at center. Back: Tree at left, arms at center. Watermark: King and queen. Printer: FNMT.

Banco Popular

1975 First Dated Issue

#4-8 Replacement notes: Serial # prefix *Z1*.

4 **25 Ekuele** — **VF** 4.00 — **UNC** 15.00
7.7.1975. Purple on light orange and green underprint. Trees at center. Portrait of President M. N. Biyogo at right. Name underneath: *PUENTE MACIAS NGUEMA BIYOGO.* Back: Arms at left, bridge at center. Watermark: M. N. Biyogo. Printer: TDLR.

5 **50 Ekuele** — **VF** 4.00 — **UNC** 15.00
7.7.1975. Brown on green and pink underprint. Plants at center. Portrait of President M. N. Biyogo at right. Name underneath: *MACIAS NGUEMA BIYOGO.* Back: Arms at left, logging at center. Watermark: M. N. Biyogo. Printer: TDLR.

6 **100 Ekuele** — 4.00 — 15.00
7.7.1975. Green on pink and multicolor underprint. Arms at center. Portrait of President M. N. Biyogo at right. Name underneath: *MACIAS NGUEMA BIYOGO.* Back: Bridge and boats. Watermark: M. N. Biyogo. Printer: TDLR.

7 **500 Ekuele** — **VF** 6.00 — **UNC** 25.00
7.7.1975. Blue on multicolor underprint. Arms at center. Portrait of President M. N. Biyogo at right. Name underneath: *MACIAS NGUEMA BIYOGO.* Back: National Palace. Watermark: M. N. Biyogo. Printer: TDLR.

8 **1000 Ekuele** — **VF** 7.50 — **UNC** 30.00
7.7.1975. Red on multicolor underprint. Arms at center. Portrait of President M. N. Biyogo at right. Name underneath: *MACIAS NGUEMA BIYOGO.* Back: Bank. Watermark: M. N. Biyogo. Printer: TDLR.

1975 Second Dated Issue

#9-13 Replacement notes: Serial # prefix *Z1*.

9 **25 Ekuele** — **VF** 4.00 — **UNC** 15.00
7.7.1975. Purple on light orange and green underprint. Trees at center. Portrait of President M. N. Biyogo at right. Name underneath: *MAISE NGUEMA BIYOGO NEGUE NDONG*. Back: Arms at left, bridge at center. Watermark: M. N. Biyogo. Printer: TDLR.

10 **50 Ekuele** — **VF** 4.00 — **UNC** 15.00
7.7.1975. Brown on green and pink underprint. Plants at center. Portrait of President M. N. Biyogo at right. Name underneath: *MAISE NGUEMA BIYOGO NEGUE NDONG*. Back: Arms at left, logging at center. Watermark: M. N. Biyogo. Printer: TDLR.

11 **100 Ekuele** — VF 4.00 — UNC 15.00
7.7.1975. Green on pink and multicolor underprint. Arms at center. Portrait of President M. N. Biyogo at right. Name underneath: *MAISE NGUEMA BIYOGO NEGUE NDONG* . Back: Bridge and boats. Watermark: M. N. Biyogo. Printer: TDLR.

12 **500 Ekuele** — VF 5.00 — UNC 20.00
7.7.1975. Blue on multicolor underprint. Arms at center. President M. N. Biyogo at right. Back: National Palace. Watermark: M. N. Biyogo. Printer: TDLR.

13 **1000 Ekuele** — VF 5.00 — UNC 20.00
7.7.1975. Red on multicolor underprint. Arms at center. Portrait of President M. N. Biyogo at right. Back: Central Bank building. Watermark: M. N. Biyogo. Printer: TDLR.

Banco de Guinea Ecuatorial

1979 Issue

14 **100 Bipkwele** — VF 6.00 — UNC 25.00
3.8.1979. Dark olive-green and multicolor. Arms at center, T. E. Nkogo at right. Back: Boats along pier of Puerto de Bata. Watermark: T. E. Nkogo. Printer: FNMT.

15 **500 Bipkwele** — VF 25.00 — UNC 100.
3.8.1979. Black on green and pink underprint. Arms at center right. Uganda at right. Back: Brown and black. Sailboat, shoreline and trees at left center. Watermark: T. E. Nkogo. Printer: FNMT.

16 **1000 Bipkwele** — VF 25.00 — UNC 100.
3.8.1979. Brown, black and multicolor. Arms at center right. Bioko at right. Back: Maroon and brown. Men cutting food plants at left center. Watermark: T. E. Nkogo. Printer: FNMT.

17 **5000 Bipkwele** — VF 15.00 — UNC 60.00
3.8.1979. Blue-gray on multicolor underprint. Arms at center, E. N. Okenve at right. Back: Blue-gray and blue. Logging scene at center. Watermark: T. E. Nkogo. Printer: FNMT.

1980 Provisional Issue

18 **1000 Bipkwele on 100 Pesetas** — VF 8.00 — UNC 30.00
21.10.1980 (-old date 12.10.1969). Red-brown on light tan underprint. Banana tree at left. Back: Shoreline and man with boat. Overprint: Black overprint of new denomination and date on number 1. (Not issued). Watermark: Woman's head. Printer: FNMT.

19 **5000 Bipkwele on 500 Pesetas** — VF 12.50 — UNC 45.00
21.10.1980 (-old date 12.10.1969). Green on multicolor underprint. Derrick loading logs at left, shoreline at center. Back: Woman with bundle on head at right. Overprint: Red overprint. (Not issued). Watermark: Man's head. Printer: FNMT.

Banque des États de l'Afrique Centrale

1985 Issue

#20-22 For signature chart see Central African States listings.

		VF	UNC
20	**500 Francos** 1.1.1985. Brown on multicolor underprint. Carving and jug at center. Signature 9. Back: Man carving mask at left center. Watermark: Carving (as printed on notes).	4.00	15.00

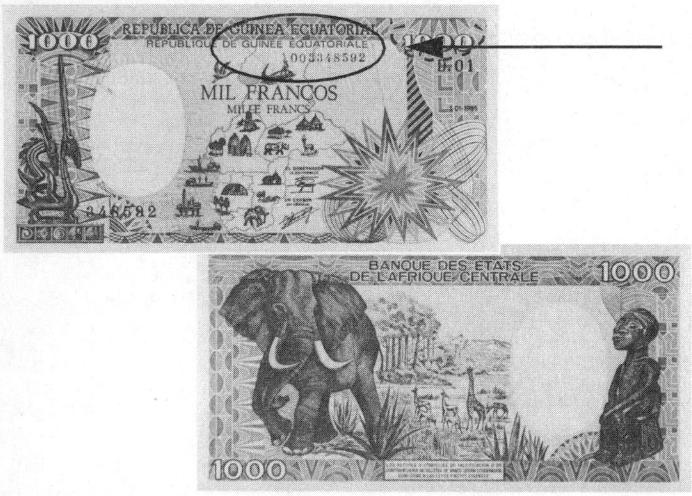

		VF	UNC
21	**1000 Francos** 1.1.1985. Dark blue on multicolor underprint. Animal carving at lower left, map at center, starburst at lower right. Incomplete map of Chad at upper center. Signature 9. Back: Elephant at left, statue at right. Watermark: Carving (as printed on notes).	8.00	30.00

		VF	UNC
22	**5000 Francos** 1.1.1985; 1.1.1986. Brown, yellow and multicolor. Carved mask at left, woman carrying bundle at right. Signature 9. Back: Farmer plowing with tractor at left, ore lift at right. Watermark: Carving (as printed on notes).		
	a. 1.1.1985.	35.00	140.
	b. 1.1.1986.	30.00	125.

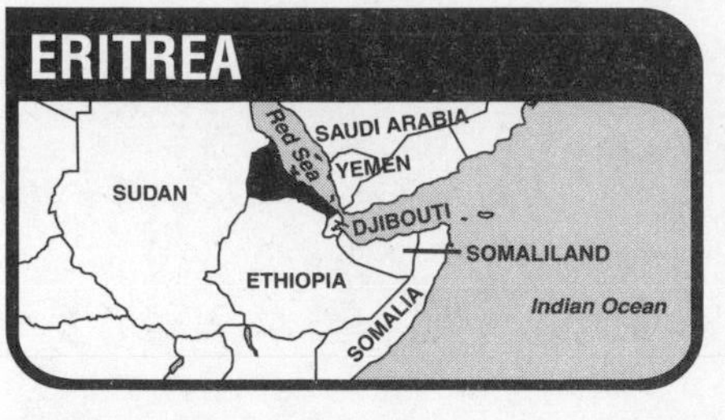

The State of Eritrea, a former Ethiopian province fronting on the Red Sea, has an area of 121,320 sq. km. and a population of 5.50 million. Eritrea was awarded to Ethiopia in 1952 as part of a federation. Ethiopia's annexation of Eritrea as a province 10 years later sparked a 30-year struggle for independence that ended in 1991 with Eritrean rebels defeating governmental forces; independence was overwhelmingly approved in a 1993 referendum. A two-and-a-half-year border war with Ethiopia that erupted in 1998 ended under UN auspices in December 2000. Eritrea currently hosts a UN peacekeeping operation that is monitoring a 25 km-wide Temporary Security Zone (TSZ) on the border with Ethiopia. An international commission, organized to resolve the border dispute, posted its findings in 2002. However, both parties have been unable to reach agreement on implementing the decision. On 30 November 2007, the Eritrea-Ethiopia Boundary Commission remotely demarcated the border by coordinates and dissolved itself, leaving Ethiopia still occupying several tracts of disputed territory, including the town of Badme. Eritrea accepted the EEBC's "virtual demarcation" decision and called on Ethiopia to remove its troops from the TSZ which it states is Eritrean territory. Ethiopia has not accepted the virtual demarcation decision.

MONETARY SYSTEM:

1 Nakfa = 100 Cents

Republic

Bank of Eritrea

1997 Issue

#1-6 Notes designed by Clarence Holbert of the U.S. Bureau of Engraving and Printing.

		VF	UNC
1	**1 Nakfa** 24.5.1997. Dark brown and black on multicolor underprint. Three girls at center. Flag raising at left. Back: Dark green. Children in bush school at center right. Watermark: Camel's head. Printer: G&D (without imprint). UV: fibers fluoresce yellow and blue. 140x70mm.	FV	1.00

		VF	UNC
2	**5 Nakfa** 24.5.1997. Dark brown and black on multicolor underprint. Young boy, young and old man at center. Flag raising at left. Kinnegram vertical foil strip at left. Back: Dark green. Cattle grazing under huge Jacaranda tree at center right. Watermark: Camel's head. Printer: G&D (without imprint). 140x70mm.	FV	3.50

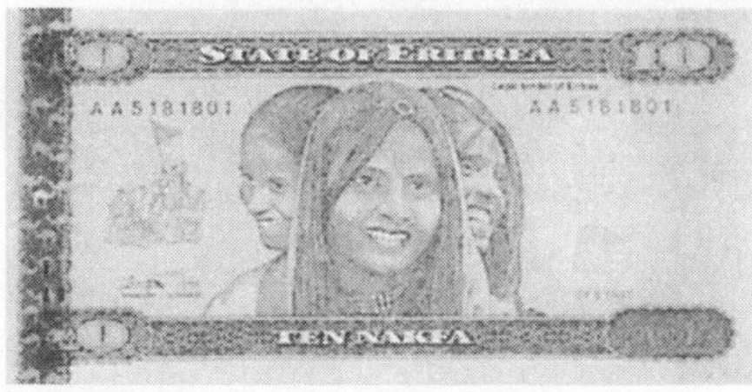

3 **10 Nakfa** VF UNC

24.5.1997. Dark brown and black on multicolor underprint. Three young women at center. Flag raising at left. Kinnegram vertical foil strip at left. Back: Dark green. Truck on rails hauling box cars across viaduct over the Dogali River at center right. Watermark: Camel's head. Printer: G&D (without imprint). 140x70mm. FV 7.50

4 **20 Nakfa** VF UNC

24.5.1997. Dark brown and black on multicolor underprint. Three young girls at center. Flag raising at left. Kinnegram vertical foil strip at left. Back: Dark green. Farmer plowing with camel, woman harvesting, woman on farm tractor at center right. Watermark: Camel's head. Printer: G&D (without imprint). 140x70mm. FV 12.50

5 **50 Nakfa** VF UNC

24.5.1997. Dark brown and black on multicolor underprint. Three young women at center. Flag raising at left. Kinnegram vertical foil strip at left. Back: Dark green. Ships in Port of Masawa at center right. Watermark: Camel's head. Printer: G&D (without imprint). 140x70mm. FV 25.00

6 **100 Nakfa** VF UNC

24.5.1997. Dark brown and black on multicolor underprint. Three young girls at center. Flag raising at left. Kinnegram vertical foil strip at left. Back: Dark green. Farmers plowing with oxen at center right. Watermark: Camel's head. Printer: G&D (without imprint). 140x70mm. FV 45.00

2004 Issue

7 **50 Nakfa** VF UNC

24.5.2004 Brown- red on pale yellow underprint. Three young women at center. Back: Ships in Port of Masawa at right center. 140x70mm. FV 20.00

8 **100 Nakfa** VF UNC

24.5.2004. Slate blue on pale yellow underprint. Three young girls at center. Back: Farmers plowing with oxen at center right. 140x70mm. FV 37.50

2011 Issues

9 **50 Nakfa** VF UNC

24.5.2011. Purple and green on multicolor underprint. Three young women at center. Back: Ships in port of Masawa at right center. FV 20.00

10 **50 Nakfa** VF UNC

24.5.2011. Green and olive on multicolor underprint. Three young women at center. Back: Ships in port of Masawa at right center. FV 20.00

The Republic of Estonia is the northernmost of the three Baltic states in eastern Europe. It has an area of 45,226 sq. km. and a population of 1.31 million. Capital: Tallinn. Agriculture and dairy farming are the principal industries. Butter, eggs, bacon, timber are exported.

After centuries of Danish, Swedish, German, and Russian rule, Estonia attained independence in 1918. Forcibly incorporated into the USSR in 1940 - an action never recognized by the US - it regained its freedom in 1991, with the collapse of the Soviet Union. Since the last Russian troops left in 1994, Estonia has been free to promote economic and political ties with Western Europe. It joined both NATO and the EU in the spring of 2004.

MONETARY SYSTEM

1 Mark = 100 Penni to 1928
1 Kroon = 100 Senti

Republic

Eesti Pank

Bank of Estonia

1991-92 Issue

#69-71 replacement notes: Serial # prefix *.

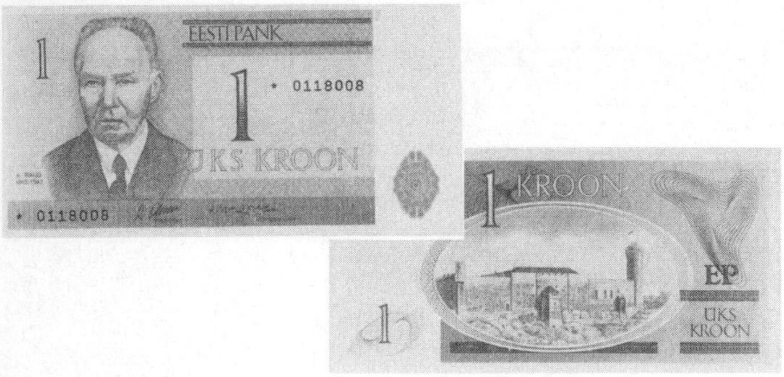

#		VF	UNC
69	**1 Kroon** 1992. Brownish black on yellow-orange and dull violet-brown underprint. K. Raud at left. Back: Toampea castle with Tall Hermann (national landmarks). Watermark: Fortress. UV: fibers fluoresce blue, value orange. 140x70mm.		
	a. Issued note. Serial # prefix A.	1.00	4.00
	r. Replacement note. Serial # prefix *.	5.00	25.00
	s. Specimen.	—	45.00

#		VF	UNC
70	**2 Krooni** 1992. Black on light blue-violet and grayish green underprint. K. E. von Baer at left. Back: Tartu University building at center. Watermark: Fortress. 140x70mm.		
	a. Issued note. Serial # prefix A.	1.00	3.00
	r. Replacement note. Serial # prefix *.	8.00	30.00
	s. Specimen.	—	45.00

#		VF	UNC
71	**5 Krooni** 1991 (92); 1992 (94). Black and tan on multicolor underprint. P. Keres at center, chessboard and arms at upper right. Back: Teutonic fortress along Narva River, church. Watermark: Arms (three lions). 140x70mm.		
	a. 1991. Serial # prefix A.	1.00	5.00
	b. 1992. Serial # prefix B.	1.00	5.00
	s. Specimen.	—	60.00

#		VF	UNC
72	**10 Krooni** 1991 (92); 1992 (94). Purple and red on multicolor underprint. J. Hurt at left center. Back: Tamme-lauri oak tree at Urvaste at right. Watermark: Arms (three lions). 140x70mm.		
	a. 1991. Serial # prefix A.	1.00	6.00
	b. 1992. Serial # prefix B.	1.00	3.00
	s. Specimen.	—	60.00

#		VF	UNC
73	**25 Krooni** 1991 (92); 1992 (94). Deep olive-green on multicolor underprint. A. Hansen-Tammsaare at left center, wilderness in background at right. Back: Early rural log construction farm; view of Vargamãe. Watermark: Arms (three lions). 140x70mm.		
	a. 1991. Serial # prefix A.	2.00	15.00
	b. 1992. Serial # prefix A.	2.00	10.00
	s. Specimen.	—	70.00

#		VF	UNC
74	**100 Krooni** 1991 (92); 1992 (94). Black and deep blue on light blue and multicolor underprint. L. Koidula at left center, cuckoo bird at lower right. Back: Waves breaking against rocky cliffs of north coast at center to right. Watermark: Arms (three lions). 140x70mm.		
	a. 1991. Serial # prefix A.	FV	20.00
	b. 1992. Serial # prefix A.	FV	30.00
	s. Specimen.	—	85.00

75	500 Krooni	VF	UNC
	1991 (92). Blue-black and purple on multicolor underprint. C. R. Jakobson at left center, harvest between two farmers with Sakala above at right. Back: Barn swallow in flight over rural pond at right, value at upper right. Watermark: Arms (three lions). 140x70mm.		
	a. 1991. Serial # prefix A.	FV	100.
	b. 1992. Serial # prefix A.	FV	80.00
	s. Specimen.	—	200.

1994 Issue

76	5 Krooni	VF	UNC
	1994 (97). Black and tan on multicolor underprint. P. Keres at center, chessboard and arms at upper right. Modified design at lower right. Ascending size serial number at right. Back: Teutonic fortress along Narva River, church. Modified design at lower left. Watermark: Arms (three lions). 140x70mm.		
	a. Serial # prefix B, C.	1.00	3.00
	s. Specimen.	—	60.00

77	10 Krooni	VF	UNC
	1994 (97). Purple and red on multicolor underprint. J. Hurt at left center. Modified design at lower right. Ascending size serial number at right. Back: Tamme-lauri oak tree at Urvaste at right. Modified design at lower left. Watermark: Arms (three lions). 140x70mm.		
	a. Serial # prefix B.	1.00	4.00
	s. Specimen.	—	60.00

78	50 Krooni	VF	UNC
	1994; 1995. Green and black on multicolor underprint. R. Tobias at left center, gates at lower center right. Ascending size serial number at right. Back: Opera house in Tallinn at center right. 140x70mm.		
	a. 1994. Serial # prefix A.	FV	12.00
	b. 1995. Serial # prefix A.	FV	10.00
	s. Specimen.	—	60.00

79	100 Krooni	VF	UNC
	1994. Black and dark blue on multicolor underprint. L. Koidula at left center, cuckoo bird at lower right. Gray seal at upper right. Ascending size serial number at right. Back: Waves breaking against rocky cliffs of north coast at center to right. Different rosette at lower left. Watermark: Arms (three lions). 140x70mm.		
	a. 1994. Serial # prefix B.	FV	25.00
	b. 1995. Serial # prefix B, C.	FV	20.00
	s. Specimen.	—	75.00

80	500 Krooni	VF	UNC
	1994; 1995. Blue-black and purple on multicolor underprint. C. R. Jakobson at left center, harvest between two farmers with Sakala above at right. Dark gray bank seal at upper right. Ascending size serial number at right. Back: Barn swallow in flight over rural pond at right, value at upper right. Different rosette at lower left. Watermark: Arms (three lions). 140x70mm.		
	a. 1994. Serial # prefix A.	FV	100.
	b. 1995. Serial # prefix B, C.	FV	90.00
	s. Specimen.	—	200.

1996 Issue

81	500 Krooni	VF	UNC
	1996; 1997. Blue, black and purple on multicolor underprint. C. R. Jakobson at left center, harvest between two farmers with Sakala above at right. Dark gray bank seal at upper right, hologram at upper left. Back: Barn swallow in flight over rural pond at right, value at upper right. Different rosette at lower left. Watermark: Arms (three lions). 140x70mm.		
	a. 1996. Serial # prefix A.	FV	90.00
	b. 1997. Serial # prefix B, C.	FV	85.00
	s. Specimen.	—	200.

1999-2000 Issue

82	100 Krooni	VF	UNC
	1999. Blue on light blue and multicolor underprint. L. Koidula at left center, cuckoo bird at lower center. Holographic band at left. Gray seal at upper right. Back: Blue on light red underprint. Waves breaking against rocky cliffs of north coast at center to right. Watermark: Arms (three lions). 140x70mm.		
	a. 1999. Serial # prefix C.	FV	20.00
	s. Specimen with overprint: *PROOV*.	—	35.00

83	500 Krooni	VF	UNC
	2000. Dark blue and blue on multicolor underprint. C. R. Jakobson at left. Back: Barn swallow. Watermark: C. R. Jakobson. 140x70mm.		
	a. Serial # prefix A.	FV	100.
	s. Specimen.	—	125.

2002 Issue

84	25 Krooni	VF	UNC
	2002. Green, black and lilac on multicolor underprint. Anton Hansen-Tammsaare at left, arms at upper right. Wide holographic band at left. Back: Estonian farm view Vargamae. 140x70mm.		
	a. Serial # prefix B, C.	FV	15.00
	s. Specimen.	—	50.00

2006 Issue

85	2 Krooni	VF	UNC
	2006-. Black on light blue-violet and grayish green underprint. K. E. von Baer at left. Back: Tartu University buildign at center. Watermark: K. E. von Baer. 140x70mm.		
	a. 2006.	FV	2.00
	b. 2007.	FV	2.00

86	10 Krooni	VF	UNC
	2006; 2007. Purple and red on multicolor underprint. Jacob Hurt at left center. Back: Tamme-lauri oak tree at Urvaste at right. Watermark: Jacob Hurt. 140x70mm.		
	a. 2006.	FV	5.00
	b. 2007.	FV	5.00

87 **25 Krooni** — VF / UNC

2006; 2007. Deep olive-green on multicolor underprint. A. Hansen-Tammsaare at left center. Back: Early rural log construction farm. Watermark: A. Jansen-Tammsaare. Printer: G&D. 140x70mm.

	VF	UNC
a. 2006.	FV	8.00
b. 2007.	FV	8.00

88 **100 Krooni** — VF / UNC

2006; 2007. Light and dark blue on multicolor underprint. L. Koidula at left center. Back: Waves breaking against rocky cliff at right. Watermark: L. Koidula. 140x70mm.

	VF	UNC
a. 2006.	FV	20.00
b. 2007.	FV	20.00

89 **500 Krooni**

2006. Blue-black and purple on multicolor underprint. C. R. Jakobson at left center. Back: Barn swallow in flight over rural pond. Watermark: C. R. Jakobson. 140x70mm. — FV 90.00

2008 Commemorative Issue

90 **10 Krooni** — VF / UNC

2008 Blue on tan underprint. Female holding wheat at left. Back: Oak tree. Sold in Bank packet. 140x70mm. — — 50.00

Collector Series

Eesti Pank

Bank of Estonia

1999 Collector's Set

80th Anniversary of Bank

CS1 **100 Krooni** — Mkt. Value

1999. Set includes: 100 Krooni specimen note (#82), 5 Krooni coin, and 4 stamps. 3,000 pcs. — 80.00

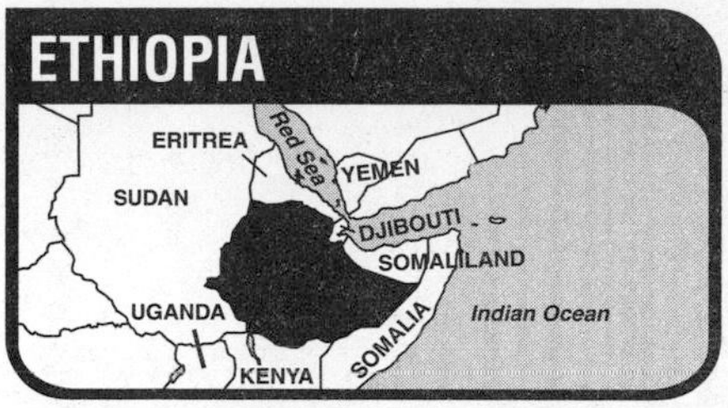

The Federal Republic of Ethiopia is located in east-central Africa. The country has an area of 1.13 million sq. km. and a population of 82.54 million people. Capital: Addis Ababa. The economy is predominantly agricultural and pastoral. Gold and platinum are mined and petroleum fields are being developed. Coffee, oil, seeds, hides and cereals are exported.

Unique among African countries, the ancient Ethiopian monarchy maintained its freedom from colonial rule with the exception of the 1936-41 Italian occupation during World War II. In 1974, a military junta, the Derg, deposed Emperor Haile Selassie (who had ruled since 1930) and established a socialist state. Torn by bloody coups, uprisings, wide-scale drought, and massive refugee problems, the regime was finally toppled in 1991 by a coalition of rebel forces, the Ethiopian People's Revolutionary Democratic Front (EPRDF). A constitution was adopted in 1994, and Ethiopia's first multiparty elections were held in 1995. A border war with Eritrea late in the 1990s ended with a peace treaty in December 2000. The Eritrea-Ethiopia Border Commission in November 2007 remotely demarcated the border by geographical coordinates, but final demarcation of the boundary on the ground is currently on hold because of Ethiopian objections to an international commission's finding requiring it to surrender territory considered sensitive to Ethiopia.

RULERS:

Menelik II, 1889-1913
Lij Yasu, 1913-1916
Zauditu, Empress, 1916-1930
Haile Selassie I, 1930-1936, 1941-1974

MONETARY SYSTEM:

1 Birr = 1 Thaler = 16 Gersh (Piastres) to 1930
1 Birr = 1 Thaler = 100 Matonas, 1931-1935
1 Birr (Dollar) = 100 Santeems (Cents), since 1944

Empire

State Bank of Ethiopia

1961 ND Issue

18 **1 Dollar** — VF / UNC

ND (1961). Green on lilac and light orange underprint. Coffee bushes at left. Emperor Haile Selassie at right. Back: Arms at center. Printer: BWC.

	VF	UNC
a. Issued note.	18.00	60.00
s. Specimen. Punched hole cancelled.	—	50.00

19 **5 Dollars** — VF / UNC

ND (1961). Orange on green and multicolor underprint. Addis Ababa University (old palace) at left. Emperor Haile Selassie at right. Back: Arms at center. Printer: BWC.

	VF	UNC
a. Issued note.	35.00	130.
s. Specimen. Punched hole cancelled.	—	80.00

			VF	UNC
20	**10 Dollars**			
	ND (1961). Red on multicolor underprint. Harbor at Massawa at left. Emperor Haile Selassie at right. Back: Arms at center. Printer: BWC.			
		a. Issued note.	75.00	200.
		s. Specimen. Punched hole cancelled.	—	150.

			VF	UNC
21	**20 Dollars**			
	ND (1961). Brown on multicolor underprint. Ancient stone monument (Axum) at left. Emperor Haile Selassie at right. Back: Arms at center. Printer: BWC.			
		a. Issued note.	110.	325.
		s. Specimen. Punched hole cancelled.	—	140.
22	**50 Dollars**			
	ND (1961). Blue on multicolor underprint. Bridge over Blue Nile at left. Emperor Haile Selassie at right. Back: Arms at center. Printer: BWC.			
		a. Issued note.	150.	500.
		s. Specimen. Punched hole cancelled.	—	200.

			VF	UNC
23	**100 Dollars**			
	ND (1961). Purple on multicolor underprint. Trinity Church at Addis Ababa at left. Emperor Haile Selassie at right. Back: Arms at center. Printer: BWC.			
		a. Signature title: *GOVERNOR.*	175.	600.
		b. Signature title: *ACTING GOVERNOR.*	150.	550.
		s. Specimen.	—	200.
24	**500 Dollars**			
	ND (1961). Dark green on multicolor underprint. Fasilides castle at Gondar at left. Emperor Haile Selassie at right. Back: Arms at center. Printer: BWC.			
		a. Issued note.	450.	1200.
		s. Specimen. Punched hole cancelled.	—	300.

ARMS VARIETIES			
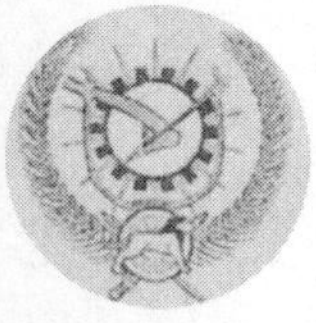			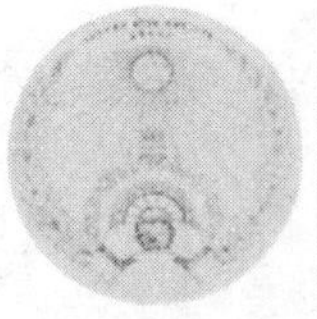
Type A	Type B	Type C	Type D
1975-1987	1987-		

SIGNATURE VARIETIES			
1	Teferra Deguefe, 1974-76 CHAIRMAN OF THE BOARD	2	Tadesse G. Kidan, 1978-87 ADMINISTRATOR

SIGNATURE VARIETIES			
3	Bekele Tamirat, 1987-91 ADMINISTRATOR	4	Leikun Berhanu, 1991-97 GOVERNOR
5	Thbale Tala, 1997-98 GOVERNOR	6	Teklewold Atnafu, 1998- GOVERNOR

National Bank of Ethiopia

1966 ND Issue

			VF	UNC
25	**1 Dollar**			
	ND (1966). Dark green on multicolor underprint. Aerial view of Massawa harbor, city at left. Emperor Haile Selassie at right. Back: Arms at center. Printer: TDLR.			
		a. Issued note.	7.50	20.00
		s. Specimen.	—	50.00

			VF	UNC
26	**5 Dollars**			
	ND (1966). Brown on multicolor underprint. Bole Airport, Addis Ababa at left. Emperor Haile Selassie at right. Back: Orange. Arms at center. Printer: TDLR.			
		a. Issued note.	25.00	80.00
		r. Replacement note. Serial # prefix *X.*	30.00	140.
		s. Specimen.	—	50.00

			VF	UNC
27	**10 Dollars**			
	ND (1966). Dark red on multicolor underprint. National Bank at Addis Ababa at left. Emperor Haile Selassie at right. Back: Arms at center. Printer: TDLR.			
		a. Issued note.	15.00	60.00
		s. Specimen.	—	60.00

28	**50 Dollars**	VF	UNC
	ND (1966). Blue on multicolor underprint. Koka High Dam on the Awash River at left. Emperor Haile Selassie at right. Back: Arms at center. Printer: TDLR.		
	a. Issued note.	40.00	150.
	s. Specimen.	—	165.

29	**100 Dollars**	VF	UNC
	ND (1966). Purple on green and multicolor underprint. Rock church *Bet Giorgis* in Lalibela at left. Emperor Haile Selassie at right. Back: Arms at center. Printer: TDLR.		
	a. Issued note.	40.00	150.
	s. Specimen.	—	125.

PEOPLES DEMOCRATIC REPUBLIC

NATIONAL BANK OF ETHIOPIA

EE 1969 (1987) ISSUE

Law EE Meskerem 1969 (September 1976 AD). EE date in Ethiopian figures only. Replacement notes: Serial # prefix *ZZ*.

30	**1 Birr**	VF	UNC
	L.EE1969 (1976). Black and dark green on light brown and green underprint. Young man at center right, longhorns at right. Map at left, lion's head in underprint at left center. Back: Black on multicolor underprint. White-throated bee-eaters and Tisisat waterfalls of Blue Nile. Arms (Type A) at right. 135x60mm.		
	a. Signature 1.	2.00	7.00
	b. Signature 2.	1.50	4.00

31	**5 Birr**	VF	UNC
	L.EE1969 (1976). Black and brown-orange on multicolor underprint. Man picking coffee beans at center right, plant at right. Map at left, lion's head in underprint at left center. Back: Kudu, caracal and Semien Mountains. Arms (Type A) at right. 140x65mm.		
	a. Signature 1.	3.25	12.50
	b. Signature 2.	2.75	10.00

32	**10 Birr**		
	L.EE1969 (1976). Brown-violet and red on multicolor underprint. Woman weaving basket at center right, wicker work dining table with lid at right. Map at left, lion's head in underprint at left center. Back: Plowing with tractor. Arms (Type A) at right. 142x67mm.		
	a. Signature 1.	6.00	20.00
	b. Signature 2.	4.00	15.00

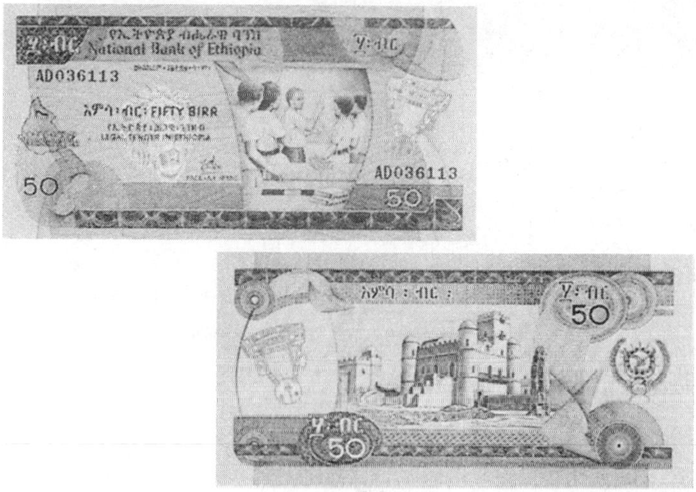

33	**50 Birr**	VF	UNC
	L.EE1969 (1976). Blue-black and dark brown on lilac and multicolor underprint. Science students at center right, musical instrument at right. Map at left, lion's head in underprint at left center. Back: Fasilides Castle at Gondar. Arms (Type A) at right. .		
	a. Signature 1.	30.00	110.
	b. Signature 2.	25.00	90.00

34	**100 Birr**	VF	UNC
	L.EE1969 (1976). Purple, violet and dark brown on multicolor underprint. Warrior standing at center right, flowers at right. Map at left, lion's head in underprint at left center. Back: Young man with microscope. Arms (Type A) at right. 147x72mm.		
	a. Signature 1.	50.00	150.
	b. Signature 2.	40.00	125.

EE 1969 (1987) ISSUE

Law EE Meskerem 1969 (September 1976 AD). EE date in Ethiopian figures only. Replacement notes: Serial # prefix *ZZ*.

		VF	UNC
36	**1 Birr** *L.EE1969* (1987). Black and green on light brown and green underprint. Young man at center right, longhorns at right. Map at left, lion's head in underprint at left center. Signature 3. Back: Black on multicolor underprint. White-throated bee-eaters and Tisisat waterfalls of Blue Nile. Arms (Type A) at right. Ornate design 135x60mm.	1.00	3.00
37	**5 Birr** *L.EE1969* (1987). Black and brown-orange on multicolor underprint. Man picking coffee beans at center right, plant at right. Map at left, lion's head in underprint at left center. Signature 3. Back: Kudu, caracal and Semien Mountains. Arms (Type A) at right. Ornate design at ends. 140x65mm.	3.00	10.00
38	**10 Birr** *L.EE1969* (1987). Brown-violet and red on multicolor underprint. Woman weaving basket at center right, wicker work dining table with lid at right. Map at left, lion's head in underprint at left center. Signature 3. Back: Plowing with tractor. Arms (Type A) at right. Ornate design at ends. 142x67mm.	5.00	15.00
39	**50 Birr** *L.EE1969* (1987). Blue-black and dark brown on lilac and multicolor underprint. Science students at center right, musical instrument at right. Map at left, lion's head in underprint at left center. Signature 3. Back: Fasilides Castle at Gondar. Arms (Type A) at right. Ornate design at ends.	20.00	40.00
40	**100 Birr** *L.EE1969* (1976). Purple, violet and dark brown on multicolor underprint. Warrior standing at center right, flowers and dark silvered shield at right. Map at left, lion's head in underprint at left center. Signature 3. Back: Young man with microscope. Arms (Type A) at right. Ornate design at ends. 147x72mm.	40.00	135.

Federal Democratic Republic

National Bank of Ethiopia

EE 1969 (1991) Issue

Law EE Meskerem 1969 (September 1976 AD). EE date in Ethiopian figures only.

		VF	UNC
41	**1 Birr**		
	L.EE1969 (1991). Dark green on light brown and green underprint. Young man at center right, longhorns at right. Map at left, lion's head in underprint at left center. Signature 3. Back: Black on multicolor underprint. White-throated bee-eaters and Tisisat waterfalls of Blue Nile. Arms (Type D) at right. Ornate design 135x60mm.		
	a. Signature 3 with title in Amharic script. Serial # prefix larger sans-serif letters.	1.00	2.50
	b. Signature 4 with title: *GOVERNOR* and also in Amharic script.	1.00	2.50
	c. As b. but with serial # prefix smaller serif letters.	.75	2.00

		VF	UNC
42	**5 Birr**		
	L.EE1969 (1991). Black and brown-orange on multicolor underprint. Man picking coffee beans at center right, plant at right. Map at left, lion's head in underprint at left center. Signature 3. Back: Kudu, caracal and Semien Mountains. Arms (Type D) at right. Ornate design at ends. 135x60mm.		
	a. Sign 3 with title in Amharic script. Arms Type B.	3.00	6.00
	b. Signature 4 with title *GOVERNOR* and also in Amharic script. Arms Type C.	3.00	6.00
	c. As b. Arms Type D. Reported not confirmed.	—	—

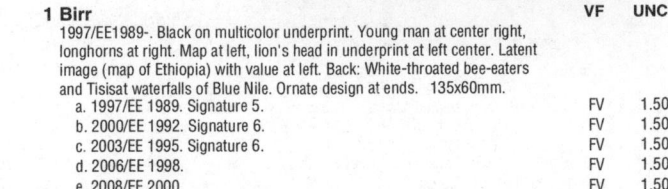

		VF	UNC
43	**10 Birr**		
	L.EE1969 (1991). Brown-violet and red on multicolor underprint. Woman weaving basket at center right, wicker work dining table with lid at right. Map at left, lion's head in underprint at left center. Signature 3. Back: Plowing with tractor. Arms (Type D) at right. Ornate design at ends. 142x67mm.		
	a. Signature 3 with title in Amharic script.	3.75	7.50
	b. Signature 4 with title: *GOVERNOR* and also in Amharic script.	3.00	6.00

		VF	UNC
44	**50 Birr**		
	L.EE1969 (1991). Blue-black and dark brown on lilac and multicolor underprint. Science students at center right, musical instrument at right. Map at left, lion's head in underprint at left center. Signature 3. Back: Fasilides Castle at Gondar. Arms (Type D) at right. Ornate design at ends.		
	a. Signature 3 with title in Amharic script. Arms Type B.	25.00	60.00
	b. Signature 4 with title: *GOVERNOR* and also in Amharic script. Arms Type C.	25.00	50.00
	c. As b. Arms Type D.	25.00	40.00

		VF	UNC
45	**100 Birr**		
	L.EE1969 (1991). Purple, violet and dark brown on multicolor underprint. Warrior standing at center right, flowers and dark silvered shield at right. Map at left, lion's head in underprint at left center. Signature 3. Back: Young man with microscope. Arms (Type D) at right. Ornate design at ends. 147x72mm.		
	a. Signature 3 with title in Amharic script.	30.00	60.00
	b. Signature 4 with title: *GOVERNOR* and also in Amharic script.	25.00	50.00

1997/EE1989 Issue

		VF	UNC
46	**1 Birr**		
	1997/EE1989-. Black on multicolor underprint. Young man at center right, longhorns at right. Map at left, lion's head in underprint at left center. Latent image (map of Ethiopia) with value at left. Back: White-throated bee-eaters and Tisisat waterfalls of Blue Nile. Ornate design at ends. 135x60mm.		
	a. 1997/EE 1989. Signature 5.	FV	1.50
	b. 2000/EE 1992. Signature 6.	FV	1.50
	c. 2003/EE 1995. Signature 6.	FV	1.50
	d. 2006/EE 1998.	FV	1.50
	e. 2008/EE 2000.	FV	1.50

47 5 Birr VF UNC

1997/EE1989-. Dark blue on multicolor underprint. Man picking coffee beans at center right, plant at right. Map at left, lion's head in underprint at left center. Latent image (map of Ethiopia) with value at left. Segmented foil security thread. Back: Kudu, caracal and Semien Mountains. Ornate design at ends. 140x65mm.

		VF	UNC
a.	1997/EE1989. Signature 5.	FV	4.00
b.	2000/EE1992. Signature 6.	FV	3.50
c.	2003/EE 1995. Signature 6.	FV	3.00
d.	2006/EE 1998.	FV	2.50
e.	2008/EE 2000.	FV	2.50

48 10 Birr VF UNC

1997/EE1989-. Deep brown, red and green on multicolor underprint. Woman weaving basket at center right, wicker work dining table with lid at right. Map at left, lion's head in underprint at left center. Latent image (map of Ethiopia) with value at left. Segmented fo Back: Plowing with tractor. Ornate design at ends. 142x67mm.

		VF	UNC
a.	1997/EE 1989. Signature 5.	FV	5.00
b.	2000/EE 1992. Signature 6.	FV	4.50
c.	2003/EE 1995. Signature 6.	FV	4.50
d.	2006/EE 1998.	FV	3.50
e.	2008/EE 2000.	FV	2.00

49 50 Birr VF UNC

1997/EE1989; 2000/EE1992. Tan and orange-brown on multicolor underprint. Farmer plowing with oxen at center. Lion's head in underprint at left center. Latent image (map of Ethiopia) with value at left. Segmented foil security thread. Back: Fasilides Castle at Gondar.

		VF	UNC
a.	1997/EE1989. Signature 5.	FV	25.00
b.	2000/EE1992. Signature 6.	FV	20.00

50 100 Birr VF UNC

1997/EE1989; 2000/EE1992. Deep blue-green, olive-green and dark green on multicolor underprint. Farmer plowing with oxen at center. Lion's head in underprint at left center. Latent image (map of Ethiopia) with value at left. Segmented foil security thread. Back: Young man with microscope. 147x72mm.

		VF	UNC
a.	1997/EE1989. Signature 5.	FV	40.00
b.	2000/EE1992. Signature 6.	FV	33.00

2003/EE1995; 2004/EE1997; 2006/EE1998 Issue

51 50 Birr VF UNC

2003/EE 1996-. Tan and orange-brown on multicolor underprint. Farmer plowing with oxen at center. Increased security features.

		VF	UNC
a.	2003/EE 1996.	FV	15.00
b.	2004/EE 1997.	FV	12.00
c.	2006/EE 1998.	FV	10.00
d.	2008/EE 2000.	FV	8.00
e.	2011/EE 2003.	FV	8.00

52 100 Birr VF UNC

2003/EE1995-. Deep blue-green, olive-green and dark green on multicolor underprint. Increased security features. 147x72mm.

		VF	UNC
a.	2003/EE 1995.	FV	30.00
b.	2004/EE 1997.	FV	25.00
c.	2006/EE 1998.	FV	22.50
d.	2008/EE 2000.	FV	22.50
e.	2011/EE 2003.	FV	22.50
f.	2012/EE 2004.	FV	20.00

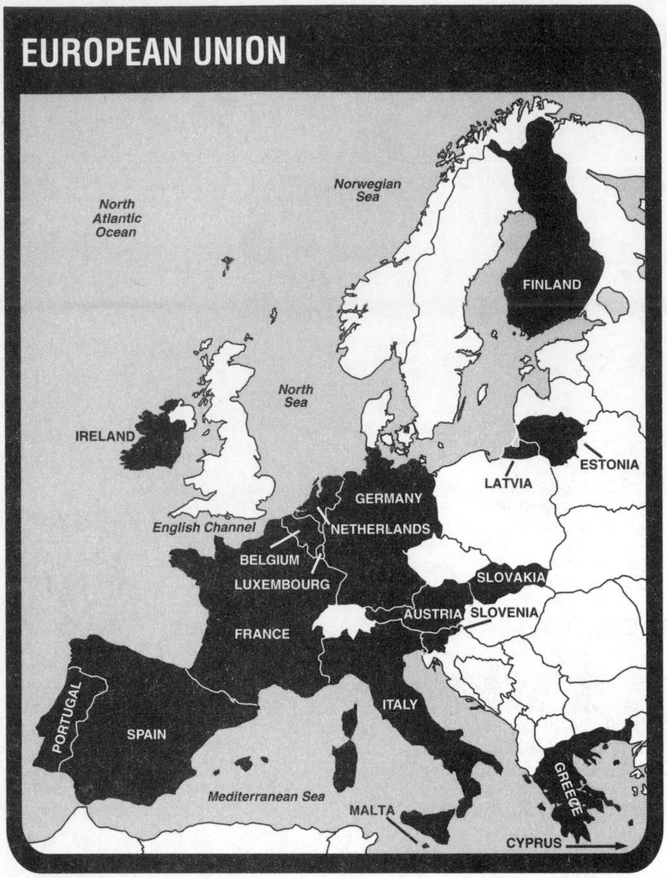

The Treaty of Rome (1958) declared a common European market as a European objective with the aim of increasing economic prosperity and contributing to an ever closer union among the peoples of Europe.

The Single European Act (1986) and the Treaty on European Union (1992) have built on this, introducing the Economic and Monetary Union and laying the foundations for the single currency.

In January 1999 the exchange rate was irrevocably set for the original participating countries. These were: Austria, Belgium, Finland, France, Germany, Ireland, Italy, Luxembourg, Netherlands, Portugal and Spain. Greece became a participating member in January 2001.

Denmark, Sweden and the United Kingdom, although members of the European Union, decided not to participate in the single currency at its inception. The currency was introduced on January 1, 2002. Since the original group, Cyprus, Estonia, Latvia, Malta, Slovakia and Slovenia have introduced Euro notes.

The French overseas departments: French Guiana, Guadeloupe, Martinique; these dependencies: Saint Martin, Saint Barthélemy; and territories: Saint Pierre et Miquelon and Mayotte all use the Euro Currency, and are depicted on the map section on the notes along with Réunion and the Canary Islands.

MONETARY SYSTEM:

1 Euro = 100 Cent

European Union

European Central Bank

2002 Issue, Signature 1, Duisenberg.

1 5 Euro

2002. Gray and multicolor. Classical architecture, arch. Signature Willem F. Duisenberg. Printer code by RO in EURO. Back: Bridges, map of Europe and European Union flag. 120x62mm.

	VF	UNC
l. Serial # prefix *L.*	FV	14.00
m. Serial # prefix *M.*	FV	11.00
n. Serial # prefix *N.*	FV	10.00
p. Serial # prefix *P.*	FV	10.00
s. Serial # prefix *S.*	FV	10.00
t. Serial # prefix *T.*	FV	11.00
u. Serial # prefix *U.*	FV	10.00
v. Serial # prefix *V.*	FV	11.00
x. Serial # prefix *X.*	FV	10.00
y. Serial # prefix *Y.*	FV	10.00
z. Serial # prefix *Z.*	FV	11.00

2 10 Euro

2002. Red and multicolor. Romanesque architecture, arch. Signature Willem F. Duisenberg. Printer code in star at 8 o'clock. Back: Bridges, map of Europe and European Union flag. 127x67mm.

	VF	UNC
l. Serial # prefix *L.*	FV	25.00
m. Serial # prefix *M.*	FV	22.50
n. Serial # prefix *N.*	FV	20.00
p. Serial # prefix *P.*	FV	21.50
s. Serial # prefix *S.*	FV	20.00
t. Serial # prefix *T.*	FV	20.00
u. Serial # prefix *U.*	FV	20.00
v. Serial # prefix *V.*	FV	21.50
x. Serial # prefix *X.*	FV	25.00
y. Serial # prefix *Y.*	FV	20.00
z. Serial # prefix *Z.*	FV	20.00

3 20 Euro

2002. Blue and multicolor. Gothic architecture, window. Signature Willem F. Duisenberg. Printer code in star at 9 o'clock. Back: Bridges, map of Europe and European Union flag. 133x72mm.

	VF	UNC
l. Serial # prefix *L.*	FV	45.00
m. Serial # prefix *M.*	FV	42.50
n. Serial # prefix *N.*	FV	37.50
p. Serial # prefix *P.*	FV	37.50
s. Serial # prefix *S.*	FV	37.50
t. Serial # prefix *T.*	FV	37.50
u. Serial # prefix *U.*	FV	42.50
v. Serial # prefix *V.*	FV	37.50
x. Serial # prefix *X.*	FV	45.00
y. Serial # prefix *Y.*	FV	37.50
z. Serial # prefix *Z.*	FV	37.50

4 50 Euro

2002. Orange and multicolor. Renaissance architecture, arch. Signature Willem F. Duisenberg. Printer code above OVD at right. Back: Bridges, map of Europe and European Union flag. 140x77mm.

	VF	UNC
l. Serial # prefix *L.*	FV	100.
m. Serial # prefix *M.*	FV	95.00
n. Serial # prefix *N.*	FV	90.00
p. Serial # prefix *P.*	FV	90.00

	VF	UNC
s. Serial # prefix *S.*	FV	90.00
t. Serial # prefix *T.*	FV	90.00
u. Serial # prefix *U.*	FV	90.00
v. Serial # prefix *V.*	FV	100.
x. Serial # prefix *X.*	FV	100.
y. Serial # prefix *Y.*	FV	90.00
z. Serial # prefix *Z.*	FV	90.00

5 **100 Euro**

2002. Green and multicolor. Baroque and Rococo architecture, arch. Signature Willem F. Duisenberg. Printer code in star at 10 o'clock. Back: Bridges, map of Europe and European Union flag. 147x82mm.

	VF	UNC
l. Serial # prefix *L.*	FV	185.
m. Serial # prefix *M.*	FV	180.
n. Serial # prefix *N.*	FV	175.
p. Serial # prefix *P.*	FV	175.
s. Serial # prefix *S.*	FV	175.
t. Serial # prefix *T.*	FV	175.
u. Serial # prefix *U.*	FV	175.
v. Serial # prefix *V.*	FV	180.
x. Serial # prefix *X.*	FV	175.
y. Serial # prefix *Y.*	FV	175.
z. Serial # prefix *Z.*	FV	175.

6 **200 Euro**

2002. Yellow-brown and multicolor. Iron and glass architecture, window. Signature Willem F. Duisenberg. Printer code vertically between 7 and 8 o'clock stars. Back: Bridges, map of Europe and European Union flag. 153x82mm.

	VF	UNC
l. Serial # prefix *L.*	FV	360.
n. Serial # prefix *N.*	FV	350.
p. Serial # prefix *P.*	FV	335.
s. Serial # prefix *S.*	FV	335.
u. Serial # prefix *U.*	FV	335.
v. Serial # prefix *V.*	FV	350.
x. Serial # prefix *X.*	FV	350.
y. Serial # prefix *Y.*	FV	335.
z. Serial # prefix *Z.*	FV	335.

7 **500 Euro**

2002. Purple and multicolor. Modern 20th century architecture, window. Signature Willem F. Duisenberg. Printer code in star at 9 o'clock. Back: Bridges, map of Europe and European Union flag. 160x82mm.

	VF	UNC
l. Serial # prefix *L.*	FV	900.
n. Serial # prefix *N.*	FV	875.
p. Serial # prefix *P.*	FV	850.
s. Serial # prefix *S.*	FV	850.
t. Serial # prefix *T.*	FV	850.
u. Serial # prefix *U.*	FV	850.
v. Serial # prefix *V.*	FV	875.
x. Serial # prefix *X.*	FV	850.
y. Serial # prefix *Y.*	FV	850.
z. Serial # prefix *Z.*	FV	850.

2002 Issue, Signature 2, J. C. Trichet.

8 **5 Euro**

2002. Gray and multicolor. Classical architecture, arch. Signature Jean-Claude Trichet. Printer code by RO in EURO. Back: Bridges, map of Europe and European Union flag. 120x62mm.

	VF	UNC
e. Serial # prefix *E.*	FV	14.00
f. Serial # prefix *F.*	FV	14.00
g. Serial # prefix *G.*	FV	14.00
h. Serial # prefix *H.*	FV	11.00
l. Serial # prefix *L.*	FV	14.00
m. Serial # prefix *M.*	FV	11.00
n. Serial # prefix *N.*	FV	10.00
p. Serial # prefix *P.*	FV	10.00
t. Serial # prefix *T.*	FV	11.00
u. Serial # prefix *U.*	FV	10.00
v. Serial # prefix *V.*	FV	11.00
x. Serial # prefix *X.*	FV	10.00

9 **10 Euro**

2002. Red and multicolor. Romanesque architecture, arch. Signature Jean-Claude Trichet. Printer code in star at 8 o'clock. Back: Bridges, map of Europe and European Union flag. 127x67mm.

	VF	UNC
m. Serial # prefix *M.*	FV	22.50
n. Serial # prefix *N.*	FV	20.00
p. Serial # prefix *P.*	FV	21.50
s. Serial # prefix *S.*	FV	20.00
t. Serial # prefix *T.*	FV	20.00
u. Serial # prefix *U.*	FV	20.00
x. Serial # prefix *X.*	FV	20.00
y. Serial # prefix *Y.*	FV	20.00

10 **20 Euro**

2002. Blue and multicolor. Gothic architecture, window. Signature Jean-Claude Trichet. Printer code in star at 9 o'clock. Back: Bridges, map of Europe and European Union flag. 133x72mm.

	VF	UNC
e. Serial # prefix *E.*	FV	45.00
f. Serial # prefix *F.*	FV	45.00
g. Serial # prefix *G.*	FV	45.00
h. Serial # prefix *H.*	FV	42.50
l. Serial # prefix *L.*	FV	45.00
m. Serial # prefix *M.*	FV	42.50
n. Serial # prefix *N.*	FV	37.50
p. Serial # prefix *P.*	FV	37.50
s. Serial # prefix *S.*	FV	37.50
t. Serial # prefix *T.*	FV	37.50
u. Serial # prefix *U.*	FV	37.50
v. Serial # prefix *V.*	FV	37.50
x. Serial # prefix *X.*	FV	37.50
y. Serial # prefix *Y.*	FV	37.50

11 **50 Euro**

2002. Orange and multicolor. Renaissance architecture, arch. Signature Jean-Claude Trichet. Printer code above 50 OVD at right. Back: Bridges, map of Europe and European Union flag. 140x77mm.

	VF	UNC
p. Serial # prefix *P.*	FV	90.00
s. Serial # prefix *S.*	FV	90.00
v. Serial # prefix *V.*	FV	100.
x. Serial # prefix *X.*	FV	90.00
y. Serial # prefix *Y.*	FV	90.00
z. Serial # prefix *Z.*	FV	90.00

12 **100 Euro**

2002. Green and multicolor. Baroque architecture, arch. Signature Jean-Claude Trichet. Printer code in star at 10 o'clock. Back: Bridges, map of Europe and European Union flag. 147x82mm.

	VF	UNC
l. Serial # prefix *L.*	FV	180.
n. Serial # prefix *N.*	FV	175.
p. Serial # prefix *P.*	FV	175.
s. Serial # prefix *S.*	FV	175.
x. Serial # prefix *X.*	FV	175.

		VF	UNC
13	**200 Euro** 2002. Yellow-brown and multicolor. Iron and glass architecture, window. Signature Jean-Claude Trichet. Printer code vertically between 7 and 8 o'clock stars. Back: Bridges, map of Europe and European Union flag. 153x82mm.		
	x. Serial # prefix *X*.	FV	335.
14	**500 Euro** 2002. Purple and multicolor. Modern 20th Century architecture, window. Signature Jean-Claude Trichet. Printer code in star at 9 o'clock. Back: Bridges, map of Europe and European Union flag. 160x82mm.		
	n. Serial # prefix *N*.	FV	850.
	x. Serial # prefix *X*.	FV	850.

2002 Issue, Signatrue 3, M. Draghi

		VF	UNC
15	**10 Euro** 2002. Red and multicolor. Romanesque architecture, arch. Signature M. Draghi. Printer code in star at 8 o'clock. Back: Bridges, map of Europe and European Union flag. 127x67mm.		
	x. Serial # prefix X.	FV	20.00
16	**20 Euro** 2002. Blue and multicolor. Gothic architecture, window. Signature M. Draghi. Printer code in star at 9 o'clock. Back: Bridges, mape of Europe and European Union flag. 133x72mm.		
	d. Serial # prefix D.	FV	40.00
	e. Serial # prefix E.	FV	40.00
	f. Serial # prefix F.	FV	40.00
	g. Serial # prefix G.	FV	40.00
	h. Serial # prefix H.	FV	40.00
	l. Serial # prefix L.	FV	40.00
	p. Serial # prefix P.	FV	40.00
	s. Serial # prefix S.	FV	40.00
	u. Serial # prefix U.	FV	40.00
	x. Serial # prefix X.	FV	40.00
	y. Serial # prefix Y.	FV	40.00
17	**50 Euro** 2002. Orange and multicolor. Renaissance architecutre, arch. Signature M. Draghi. Printer code above 50 OVD at right. Back: Bridges, map of Europe and European Union flag. 140x77mm.		
	p. Serial # prefix P.	FV	90.00
	s. Serial # prefix S.	FV	90.00
	v. Serial # prefix V.	FV	90.00
	x. Serial # prefix X.	FV	90.00
	z. Serial # prefix Z.	FV	90.00
18	**100 Euro** 2002. Green and multicolor. Baroque architecutre, arch. Signature M. Draghi. Printer code in star at 10 o'clock. Back: Bridges, map of Europe and European Union flag. 147x82mm.		
	x. Serial # prefix X.	FV	175.
19	**200 Euro** 2002. Yellow-brown and multicolor. Iron and glass architecture, arch. Signature M. Draghi. Pringter code vertially better 7 and 8 o'clock stars. Back: Bridges, map of Europe and European Union flag. 153x82mm.		
	x. Serial # prefix X.	FV	350.

2013-19 Issue, Signature 3, M. Draghi

		VF	UNC
20	**5 Euro** 2002. Gray and multicolor. Classical architecutre, arch. Signature M. Draghi. Printer code at top right near foil. Back: Viaduct bridge at top left, map of Europe within circle of stars at lower left center. Watermark: Europa. 120x62mm.		
	n. Serial # prefix N.	FV	10.00
	s. Serial # prefix S.	FV	10.00
	u. Serial # prefix U.	FV	10.00
	v. Serial # prefix V.	FV	10.00
	z. Serial # prefix Z.	FV	10.00
21	**10 Euro** Expected new issue.	—	—
22	**20 Euro** Expected new issue.	—	—
23	**50 Euro** Expected new issue.	—	—
24	**100 Euro** Expected new issue.	—	—
25	**200 Euro** Expected new issue.	—	—
26	**500 Euro** Expected new issue.	—	—

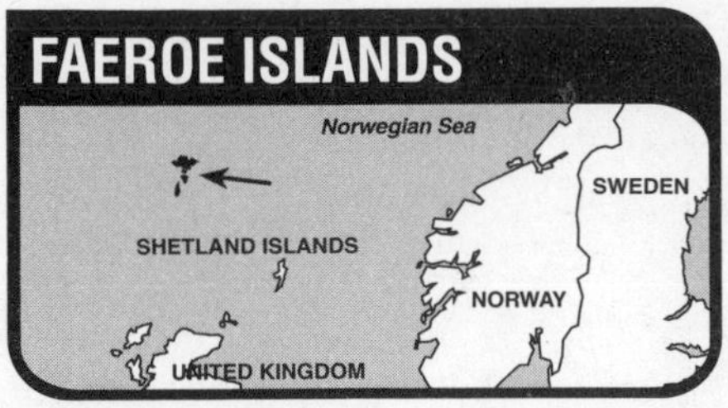

The Faroes, a self-governing community within the kingdom of Denmark, are situated in the North Atlantic between Iceland and the Shetland Islands. The 17 inhabited islets and reefs have an area of 1,399 sq. km. and a population of 46,668. Capital: Thorshavn. The principal industries are fishing and grazing. Fish and fish products are exported.

The population of the Faroe Islands is largely descended from Viking settlers who arrived in the 9th century. The islands have been connected politically to Denmark since the 14th century. A high degree of self government was attained in 1948.

RULERS:
Danish

MONETARY SYSTEM:
1 Króne = 100 Øre

Danish Administration

Føroyar

1978-86 Issue

#19-23 Replacement notes: Serial # suffix *OJ; OK.*

		VF	UNC
16	**10 Krónur** *L.1949* (19)74. Green. Shield with ram at left. Coded year date in the upper right seriel # (the two middle digits). Signature: Leif Groth and Atli P. Dam. Back: Rural scene at center. Watermark: Anchor chain. 125x67mm.		
	a. Issued note.	FV	9.00
	s. Specimen.	—	100.

1964-74 Issue

#16-18 Replacement notes: Serial # suffix *OJ; OK.*

		VF	UNC
17	**50 Krónur** *L.1949* (19)67. Black on light blue and blue-green underprint. Portrait Nölsoyar Pall at left. Coded year dates in the left series number (the two middle digits). Signature: M. Wahl and P. M. Dam. Back: Blue on green underprint. Drawing of homes and church in Nólsoy village across center. Watermark: Anchor chain. 155x79mm.		
	a. (19)67. Issued note.	20.00	90.00
	r1. Replacement note. Suffix OJ.	30.00	105.
	r2. Replacement note. Suffix OK.	500.	—

18 **100 Krónur** — VF — UNC

L.1949 (19)64; 69; 72; 75. Black on pink and gold underprint. Portrait V. U. Hammershaimb at left. Coded year dates in the left series (the two middle digits). Back: Blue on tan underprint. Drawing of house and mountains. Watermark: Anchor chain. 155x84mm.

	VF	UNC
a. (19)75. Signature L. Groth and A.P. Dam.	35.00	90.00
r1. (19)64. Signature M. Wahl and H. Djurhuus. Suffix 0J.	65.00	225.
r2. (19)64. As r1 but suffix 0K.	700.	—
r3. (19)69. Signature M. Wahl and K. Djurhuus. Suffix 0J.	50.00	175.
r4. (19)72. Signature as r3. Suffix 0J.	45.00	175.
r5. (19)75. Signature L. Groth and Atli P. Dam. Suffix 0J.	35.00	90.00
s. Specimen. As a.	—	250.

1978-86 Issue

#19-23 Replacement notes: Serial # suffix *OJ; OK.*

19 **20 Krónur** — VF — UNC

L.1949 (19)86; (19)88. Deep purple on pink and aqua underprint. Shephard at right. Coded year dates in upper right serial # (the two middle digits). Back: Red and black. Drawing of animals at center. Watermark: Anchor chain. 125x72mm.

	VF	UNC
a. Signature N. Bentsen and A. P. Dam. (19)86.	6.00	15.00
b. Signature B. Klinte and A. P. Dam. (19)88.	15.00	30.00
r. Replacement note. As a. Suffix 0J.	30.00	100.

20 **50 Krónur** — VF — UNC

L.1949 (19)78-94. Black on light blue and gray underprint. Portrait Nölsoyar Pall at left. Coded year dates in the left series number (the two middle digits). Back: Drawing of homes and church in Nólsoy village across center. Watermark: Chain links. Reduced size. 140x72mm.

	VF	UNC
a. Signature L. Groth and A. P. Dam. (19)78.	30.00	90.00
b. Signature as a. (19)87.	40.00	130.
c. Signature N. Bentsen and A. P. Dam. (19)87.	25.00	50.00
d. Signature B. Klinte and E. Joensen (19)94.	15.00	30.00
s. Specimen. As a.	—	200.

21 **100 Krónur** — VF — UNC

L.1949 (19)78-94. Black on tan underprint. Portrait V. U. Hammershaimb at left. Coded year dates in the left series (the two middle digits). Back: Black and green on ochre underprint. Drawing of house and mountains. Watermark: Chain links. Reduced size. 150x78mm.

	VF	UNC
a. Signature L. Groth and A. P. Dam. (19)78.	30.00	100.
b. Signature N. Bentsen and P. Ellefsen. (19)83.	25.00	85.00
c. Signature N. Bentsen and A. P. Dam. (19)87.	35.00	120.
d. Signature B. Klinte and A. P. Dam. (19)88.	22.50	60.00
e. Signature B. Klinte and J. Sunstein. (19)90.	24.00	70.00
f. Signature B. Klinte and E. Joensen. (19)94.	FV	37.50
s. Specimen. As a.	—	400.

22 **500 Krónur** — VF — UNC

L.1949 (19)78; (19)94. Black on green and dull purple underprint. Sketch of fisherman at right. Coded year dates in the left series number (the two middle digits). Back: Sketch of fishermen in boat at sea. Watermark: Anchor chain. 164x85mm.

	VF	UNC
a. Signature L. Groth and A. P. Dam. (19)78.	FV	190.
b. Signature B. Klinte and E. Joensen. (19)94.	FV	190.

		VF	UNC
23	**1000 Krónur**		
	L.1949 (19)78; 83; 87; 89; 94. Blue-green, black and green. J. H. O. Djurhuus at left. Coded year dates in the left series number (the two middle digits). Back: Tórshaven street scene sketch. Watermark: Anchor chain. 176x94mm.		
	a. Signature L. Groth and A. P. Dam. (19)78.	300.	750.
	b. Signature N. Bentsen and P. Ellefsen. (19)83.	270.	650.
	c. Signature N. Bentsen and A. P. Dam. (19)87.	260.	575.
	d. Signature B. Klinte and A. P. Dam. (19)89.	FV	350.
	e. Signature B. Klinte and M. Petersen. (19)94.	FV	300.

2001-2005 Issue

		VF	UNC
24	**50 Krónur**		
	(20)01. Black on gray underprint. Ram's horn and lilac segmented security strip at right. Back: Hillside in Sumba. Watermark: Ram's head. 125x72mm.	FV	18.00

		VF	UNC
25	**100 Krónur**		
	(20)02. Dull yellow. Codfish tail at right. Back: View of Klaksvík. Watermark: Ram's head. 135x72mm.	FV	27.00

		VF	UNC
26	**200 Krónur**		
	(20)03. Dull purple. Ghost Moth at right. Back: View of Tindhólmur near Vágur. Watermark: Ram's head. 145x72mm.	FV	50.00

		VF	UNC
27	**500 Krónur**		
	(20)04. Dull green. Beach Crab's claw at right. Back: View of Hvannasundi. Watermark: Ram's head. 155x72mm.	FV	140.

		VF	UNC
28	**1000 Krónur**		
	(20)05. Dull red. Wing of Black-Grey Sandpiper at right. Back: View from the island of Sandoy. Watermark: Ram's head. 165x72mm.	FV	275.

2011 Issue

		VF	UNC
29	**50 Krónur**		
	(20)11. Black on gray underprint. Ram's horn and lilac segmented security strip. Back: Hillside in Sumba. Watermark: Ram's head. 125x72mm.	FV	16.00
30	**100 Krónur**		
	(20)11. Dull yellow. Codfish tail at right. Back: View of Klaksvík. Watermark: Ram's head. 135x72mm.	FV	25.00
31	**200 Krónur**		
	(20)11. Dull purple. Ghost Moth at right. Back: View of Tindhólmur near Vágur. Watermark: Ram's head. 145x72mm.	FV	45.00
32	**500 Krónur**		
	(20)11. Dull green. Beach Crab's claw at right. Back: View of Hvannasundi. Watermark: Ram's head. 155x72mm.	FV	125.
33	**1000 Krónur**		
	(20)11. Dull red. Wing of Black-Grey Sandpiper at right. Back: View of the island of Sandoy. Watermark: Ram's head. 165x72mm.	FV	230.

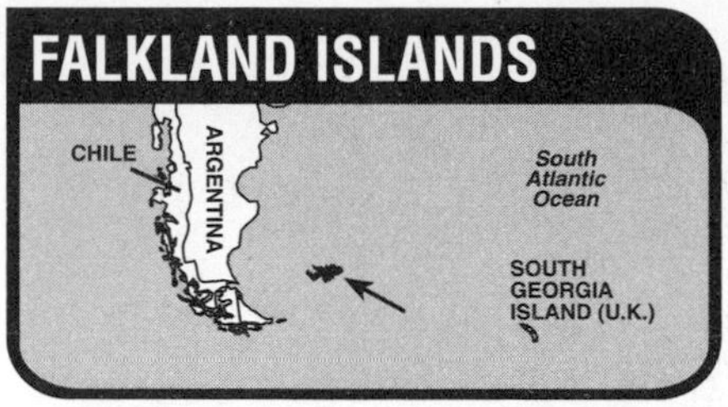

The Colony of the Falkland Islands and Dependencies, a British colony located in the South Atlantic about 500 miles northeast of Cape Horn, has an area of 12,173 sq. km. and a population of 3,140. East Falkland, West Falkland, South Georgia, and South Sandwich are the largest of the 200 islands. Capital: Port Stanley. Fishing and sheep are the industry. Wool, whale oil, and seal oil are exported.

Although first sighted by an English navigator in 1592, the first landing was by the English almost a century later in 1690, and the first settlement was by the French in 1764. The colony was turned over to Spain two years later and the islands have since been the subject of a territorial dispute, first between Britain and Spain, then between Britain and Argentina. The UK asserted its claim to the islands by establishing a naval garrison there in 1833. The Islands were important in the days of sail and steam shipping as a location to re-stock fresh food and fuel, and make repairs after trips around Cape Horn. In April 1982 Argentine forces invaded and after a short military campaign Britain regained control in June 1982. In 1990 the Argentine congress declared the Falklands and Dependencies as the province Tierra del Fuego.

RULERS:

British

MONETARY SYSTEM:

1 Shilling = 12 Pence
1 Pound = 20 Shillings to 1966
1 Pound = 100 Pence, 1966-

British Administration

Government of the Falkland Islands

1960-67 Issue

		VF	UNC
7	**10 Shillings** 10.4.1960. Brown on gray underprint. Portrait of Queen Elizabeth II at right. Printer: TDLR.		
	a. Issued note.	300.	900.
	s. Specimen.	—	850.

		VF	UNC
8	**1 Pound** 1967-82. Blue on gray-green and lilac underprint. Portrait of Queen Elizabeth II at right. Printer: TDLR.		
	a. 2.1.1967. Signature L. Gleadell.	45.00	190.
	b. 20.2.1974. Signature H. T. Rowlands.	27.50	135.
	c. 1.12.1977. Signature H. T. Rowlands.	70.00	310.
	d. 1.1.1982. Signature H. T. Rowlands.	25.00	120.
	e. 15.6.1982. Signature H. T. Rowlands.	25.00	110.
	s. Specimen. As a-e.	—	330.

		VF	UNC
9	**5 Pounds** 1960; 1975. Red on green underprint. Portrait of Queen Elizabeth II at right. Printer: TDLR.		
	a. Signature L. Gleadel. 10.4.1960.	250.	1000.
	b. Signature H. T. Rowlands. 30.1.1975.	200.	900.
	s. Specimen. As a, b.	—	1075.

1969; 1975 Issue

		VF	UNC
10	**50 Pence** 1969; 1974. Brown on gray underprint. Portrait of Queen Elizabeth II at right. Printer: TDLR.		
	a. Signature L. Gleadell. 25.9.1969.	21.00	115.
	b. Signature H. T. Rowlands. 20.2.1974.	18.00	100.
	s. Specimen. As a, b.	—	250.

		VF	UNC
11	**10 Pounds** 1975-82. Green on light orange and yellow-green underprint. Portrait of Queen Elizabeth II at right. Signature H. T. Rowlands. Printer: TDLR.		
	a. 5.6.1975.	300.	900.
	b. 1.1.1982.	350.	1075.
	c. 15.6.1982.	275.	850.
	s. Specimen. As a.	—	850.

1983 Commemorative Issue

#12, 150th Anniversary of English rule, 1833-1983

		VF	UNC
12	**5 Pounds** 14.6.1983. Red on multicolor underprint. Queen Elizabeth II at right, King penguins and shield at left, seals at right. Commemorative legend at lower center. Back: Governor's home and church. 145x75mm.		
	a. Issued note.	FV	90.00
	s. Specimen.	—	210.

1984-90 Regular Issue

		VF	UNC
13	**1 Pound** 1.10.1984. Blue on brown and yellow underprint. Queen Elizabeth II at right, King penguins and shield at left, seals at right. Back: Governor's home and church. 145x75mm.		
	a. Issued note.	15.00	75.00
	s. Specimen.	—	210.

		VF	UNC
14	**10 Pounds** 1.9.1986. Green on blue and multicolor underprint. Queen Elizabeth II at right, King penguins and shield at left, seals at right. Back: Governor's home and church. 145x75mm.		
	a. Issued note.	FV	95.00
	s. Specimen.	—	210.

		VF	UNC
15	**20 Pounds** 1.10.1984. Brown on multicolor underprint. Queen Elizabeth II at right, King penguins and shield at left, seals at right. Back: Governor's home and church. 145x75mm.		
	a. Issued note.	45.00	125.
	s. Specimen.	—	270.

		VF	UNC
16	**50 Pounds** 1.7.1990. Blue on multicolor underprint. Queen Elizabeth II at right, King penguins and shield at left, seals at right. Back: Governor's home and church. 145x75mm.		
	a. Issued note.	FV	250.
	s. Specimen.	—	440.

2005 Issue

		VF	UNC
17	**5 Pounds** 14.6.2005. Red on multicolor underprint. King penguins at left, island map at center, Queen Elizabelth II at right center, seals at right. Three signatures. Back: Government House and Christ Church Cathedral in Stanley. Like #12 but without commemorative legend. 145x75mm.		
	a. Issued note.	FV	40.00
	s. Specimen.	—	290.

2011 Issue

		VF	UNC
18	**10 Pounds** 1.1.2011.	FV	60.00

FIJI

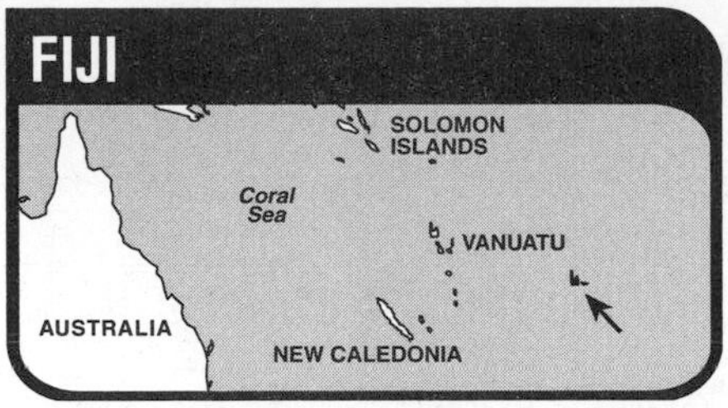

The republic of Fiji consists of about 320 islands located in the southwestern Pacific 1,770 km. north of New Zealand. The islands have a combined area of 18,270 sq. km. and a population of 931,750. Capital: Suva, on the island of Viti Levu. Fiji's economy is d on agriculture, tourism and mining. Sugar, fish, timber, coconut products, and gold are exported.

Fiji became independent in 1970, after nearly a century as a British colony. Democratic rule was interrupted by two military coups in 1987, caused by concern over a government perceived as dominated by the Indian community (descendants of contract laborers brought to the islands by the British in the 19th century). The coups and a 1990 constitution that cemented native Melanesian control of Fiji, led to heavy Indian emigration; the population loss resulted in economic difficulties, but ensured that Melanesians became the majority. A new constitution enacted in 1997 was more equitable. Free and peaceful elections in 1999 resulted in a government led by an Indo-Fijian, but a civilian-led coup in May 2000 ushered in a prolonged period of political turmoil. Parliamentary elections held in August 2001 provided Fiji with a democratically elected government led by Prime Minister Laisenia Qarase. Re-elected in May 2006, Qarase was ousted in a December 2006 military coup led by Commodore Voreqe Bainimarama, who initially appointed himself acting president. In January 2007, Bainimarama was appointed interim prime minister. In Sptember 2009 Fiji was suspended from the British Commonwealth.

RULERS:

Thakombau (Cakobau), until 1874
British, 1874-1970.

MONETARY SYSTEM:

1 Dollar = 100 Cents, 1871-73
1 Shilling = 12 Pence
1 Pound = 20 Shillings to 1969
1 Dollar = 100 Cents, 1969-

REPLACEMENT NOTES:

#64-85: Z/1 prefix; #96-108: Z prefix; #109-114: ZA prefix.

BRITISH ADMINISTRATION

FIJI GOVERNMENT

1953-67 ISSUE

51 5 Shillings

1957-65. Gray-blue on lilac, green and blue underprint. Arms at upper center, portrait of Queen Elizabeth II at right. Watermark: Fijian youth's bust. Printer: BWC.

	VF	UNC
a. 1.6.1957. Signature Davidson, Griffiths, Marais.	75.00	550.
b. 28.4.1961. Signature Bevington, Griffiths, Cruickshank.	75.00	550.
c. 1.12.1962. Signature Ritchie, Griffiths, Cruickshank.	60.00	525.
d. 1.9.1964. Signature Ritchie, Griffiths, Cruickshank.	50.00	475.
e. 1.10.1965. Signature Ritchie, Griffiths, Cruickshank.	40.00	400.
s. Specimen. Various dates.	—	750.
cs. Commercial (false color) specimen.	—	550.

52 10 Shillings

1957-65. Brown on green, pink and yellow underprint. Arms at upper center, portrait of Queen Elizabeth II at right. Watermark: Fijian youth's bust. Printer: BWC.

	VF	UNC
a. 1.6.1957. Signature Davidson, Griffiths, Marais.	100.	750.
b. 28.4.1961. Signature Bevington, Griffiths, Cruickshank.	120.	800.
c. 1.12.1962. Signature Ritchie, Griffiths, Cruickshank.	80.00	750.
d. 1.9.1964. Signature Ritchie, Griffiths, Cruickshank.	125.	500.
e. 1.10.1965. Signature Ritchie, Griffiths, Cruickshank.	75.00	600.
s. Specimen. Various dates.	—	850.
cs. Commercial (false color) specimen.	—	700.

53 1 Pound

1954-67. Green on yellow and blue underprint. Arms at upper center, portrait of Queen Elizabeth II at right. Watermark. Fijian youth's bust. Printer: BWC.

	VF	UNC
a. 1.7.1954. Signature Davidson, Donovan, Davis.	130.	825.
b. 1.6.1957. Signature Davidson, Griffiths, Marais.	145.	875.
c. 1.9.1959. Signature Bevington, Griffiths, Marais.	130.	825.
d. 1.12.1961. Signature Ritchie, Griffiths, Cruickshank.	145.	900.
e. 1.12.1962. Signature Ritchie, Griffiths, Cruickshank.	145.	925.
f. 20.1.1964. Signature Ritchie, Griffiths, Cruickshank.	140.	825.
g. 1.5.1965. Signature Ritchie, Griffiths, Cruickshank.	130.	750.
h. 1.12.1965. Signature Ritchie, Griffiths, Cruickshank.	135.	725.
i. 1.1.1967. Signature Ritchie, Griffiths, Cruickshank.	125.	725.
s. Specimen. Various dates.	—	1050.
cs. Commercial (false color) specimen.	—	900.

54 5 Pounds

1954-67. Purple on orange, green and purple underprint. Arms at upper center, portrait of Queen Elizabeth II at right. Watermark: Fijian youth's bust. Printer: BWC.

	VF	UNC
a. 1.7.1954. Signature Davidson, Donovan, Davis.	850.	1950.
b. 1.9.1959. Signature Bevington, Griffiths, Marais.	[illegible]	2150.
c. 1.10.1960. Signature Bevington, Griffiths, Cruickshank.	850.	1950.
d. 1.12.1962. Signature Ritchie, Griffiths, Cruickshank.	825.	1900.
e. 20.1.1964. Signature Ritchie, Griffiths, Cruickshank.	800.	1950.
f. 1.1.1967. Signature Ritchie, Griffiths, Cruickshank.	800.	1800.
s. Specimen. Various dates.	—	1400.
cs. Commercial (false color) specimen.	—	1050.

55 10 Pounds

1954-65. Blue on blue, orange and green underprint. Arms at upper center, portrait of Queen Elizabeth II at right. Watermark: Fijian youth's bust. Printer: BWC.

	VF	UNC
a. 1.7.1954. Signature Davidson, Donovan, Davis.	1250.	2750.
b. 1.9.1959. Signature Bevington, Griffiths, Marais.	1250.	2500.
c. 1.10.1960. Signature Bevington, Griffiths, Cruickshank.	1100.	3250.
d. 20.1.1964. Signature Ritchie, Griffiths, Cruickshank.	1000.	2250.
e. 11.6.1964. Signature Ritchie, Griffiths, Cruickshank.	900.	2100.
f. 1.5.1965. Not released. Signature Ritchie, Griffiths, Cruickshank.	—	—
s. Specimen. Various dates.	—	2250.
cs. Commercial (false color) specimen.	—	1100.

56 20 Pounds

1953. Black and purple on purple underprint. Arms at upper center, portrait of Queen Elizabeth II at right. Watermark: Fijian youth's bust. Printer: BWC.

	VF	UNC
a. 1.1.1953. Signature Davidson, Donovan, Smith.	1850.	8250.
s. Specimen.	—	4250.
cs. Commercial (false color) specimen.	—	2750.

57 **20 Pounds** VF UNC
1954-58. Red on red and green underprint. Arms at upper center, portrait of Queen Elizabeth II at right. Watermark: Fijian youth's bust. Printer: BWC.

	VF	UNC
a. 1.7.1954. Signature Davidson, Donovan, Davis.	2000.	6500.
b. 1.11.1958. Signature Bevington, Griffiths, Marais.	2000.	5500.
s. Specimen.	—	4000.
cs. Commercial (false color) specimen.	—	2000.

1969 Commissioners of Currency Issue

58 **50 Cents** VF UNC
ND (1969). Blue-green on multicolor underprint. Queen Elizabeth at right, arms and heading: *GOVERNMENT OF FIJI* at upper center. Signature Ritchie and Barnes. Back: Thatched bure (house) and coconut palms on back. Watermark: Profile Fijian head. Printer: TDLR. .

	VF	UNC
a. Issued note.	4.00	25.00
s1. Specimen. Red seals. Signatures punched out.	—	175.
s2. Specimen. No seals. Corners punched out.	—	250.

59 **1 Dollar** VF UNC
ND (1969). Brown on brown, green and pink underprint. Queen Elizabeth at right, arms and heading: *GOVERNMENT OF FIJI* at upper center. Signature Ritchie and Barnes. Back: Yanuca beach scene in Yasewas. Watermark: Profile Fijian head. Printer: TDLR.

	VF	UNC
a. Issued note.	7.50	55.00
s1. Specimen. Red seals. Singatures punched out.	—	200.
s2. Specimen. No seals. Corners punched out.	—	350.

60 **2 Dollars** VF UNC
ND (1969). Green on brown and light blue underprint. Queen Elizabeth at right, arms and heading: *GOVERNMENT OF FIJI* at upper center. Signature Ritchie and Barnes. Back: Geometric lathe pattern. Watermark: Profile Fijian head. Printer: TDLR.

	VF	UNC
a. Issued note.	15.00	110.
s1. Specimen. Red seals. Signatures punched out.	—	350.
s2. Specimen. No seals. Corners punched out.	—	400.

61 **5 Dollars** VF UNC
ND (1970). Orange on purple and gray underprint. Queen Elizabeth at right, arms and heading: *GOVERNMENT OF FIJI* at upper center. Signature Ritchie and Barnes. Back: Geometric lathe pattern. Watermark: Profile Fijian head. Printer: TDLR.

	VF	UNC
a. Issued note.	22.50	250.
s1. Specimen. Red seals. Signatures punched out.	—	500.
s2. Specimen. No seals. Corners punched out.	—	750.

62 **10 Dollars** VF UNC
ND (1969). Purple on orange and purple underprint. Queen Elizabeth at right, arms and heading: *GOVERNMENT OF FIJI* at upper center. Signature Ritchie and Barnes. Back: Geometric lathe pattern. Watermark: Profile Fijian head. Printer: TDLR.

	VF	UNC
a. Issued note.	55.00	800.
s1. Specimen. Red seals. Signatures punched out.	—	800.
s2. Specimen. No seals. Corners punched out.	—	1000.

63 **20 Dollars** VF UNC
ND (1969). Blue on light green, orange and blue underprint. Queen Elizabeth at right, arms and heading: *GOVERNMENT OF FIJI* at upper center. Signature Ritchie and Barnes. Back: Geometric lathe pattern. Watermark: Profile Fijian head. Printer: TDLR.

	VF	UNC
a. Issued note.	125.	1350.
s1. Specimen. Red seals. Signatures punched out.	—	1100.
s2. Specimen. No seals. Corners punched out.	—	1300.

1971-73 Ad-Interim Currency Board Issue

64 50 Cents

ND (1971). Blue-green on multicolor underprint. Queen Elizabeth at right, arms and heading: *GOVERNMENT OF FIJI* at upper center. One signature. Back: Thatched bure (house) and coconut palms. Watermark: Profile Fijian head. Printer: TDLR.

	VF	UNC
a. Signature Wesley Barrett.	4.00	25.00
b. Signature C. A. Stinson.	3.50	22.50
s1. Specimen. As a.	—	200.
s2. Specimen. As b.	—	175.
ar. As a. Replacement *Z/1* prefix.	35.00	125.
br. As b. Replacement *Z/I* prefix.	20.00	90.00

65 1 Dollar

ND (1971). Brown on brown, green and pink underprint. Queen Elizabeth at right, arms and heading: *GOVERNMENT OF FIJI* at upper center. One signature. Back: Yanuca beach scene in Yasewas. Watermark: Profile Fijian head. Printer: TDLR.

	VF	UNC
a. Signature Wesley Barrett.	7.50	75.00
b. Signature C. A. Stinson.	15.00	60.00
s1. Specimen. As a.	—	250.
s2. Specimen. As b.	—	250.
ar. As a. Replacement. *Z/I* prefix.	50.00	350.
br. As b. Replacement. *Z/I* prefix.	35.00	250.

66 2 Dollars

ND (1971). Green on brown and light blue underprint. Queen Elizabeth at right, arms and heading: *GOVERNMENT OF FIJI* at upper center. One signature. Back: Geometric lathe pattern. Watermark: Profile Fijian head. Printer: TDLR.

	VF	UNC
a. Signature Wesley Barrett.	10.00	125.
b. Signature C. A. Stinson. Not issued.	—	—
s1. Specimen. As a.	—	450.
s2. Specimen. As b.	—	400.
ar. As a. Replacement. *Z/I* prefix.	100.	450.
br. As b. Replacement. *Z/I* prefix. Not issued.	—	—

67 5 Dollars

ND (1971). Orange on purple and gray underprint. Queen Elizabeth at right, arms and heading: *GOVERNMENT OF FIJI* at upper center. One signature. Back: Geometric lathe pattern. Watermark: Profile Fijian head. Printer: TDLR.

	VF	UNC
a. Signature Wesley Barrett.	25.00	300.
b. Signature C. A. Stinson.	22.50	250.
s1. Specimen. As a.	—	650.
s2. Specimen. As b.	—	550.
ar. As a. Replacement. *Z/I* prefix.	350.	850.
br. As b. Replacement. *Z/I* prefix.	300.	750.

68 10 Dollars

ND (1971). Purple on orange and purple underprint. Queen Elizabeth at right, arms and heading: *GOVERNMENT OF FIJI* at upper center. One signature. Back: Geometric lathe pattern. Watermark: Profile Fijian head. Printer: TDLR.

	VF	UNC
a. Signature Wesley Barrett.	100.	850.
b. Signature C. A. Stinson.	75.00	750.
s1. Specimen. As a.	—	850.
s2. Specimen. As b.	—	750.
ar. As a. Replacement. *Z/I* prefix.	550.	1250.
br. As b. Replacement. *Z/I* prefix.	400.	1500.

69 20 Dollars

ND (1971). Blue on light green, orange and blue underprint. Queen Elizabeth at right, arms and heading: *GOVERNMENT OF FIJI* at upper center. One signature. Back: Geometric lathe pattern. Watermark: Profile Fijian head. Printer: TDLR.

	VF	UNC
a. Signature Wesley Barrett.	350.	1200.
b. Signature C. A. Stinson.	250.	1050.
s1. Specimen. As a.	—	1000.
s2. Specimen. As b.	—	900.
ar. As a. Replacement. *Z/I* prefix.	1250.	2000.
br. As b. Replacement. *Z/I* prefix.	800.	1750.

Central Monetary Authority

1974 ND Issue

70 50 Cents

ND (1974). Blue-green on multicolor underprint. Queen Elizabeth at right, arms and heading *FIJI* at top center. Issuing authority name across lower center. Back: Thatched bure (house) and coconut palms . Watermark: Profile Fijian head. Printer: TDLR. 156x67mm.

	VF	UNC
a. Signature D. J. Barnes and R. J. Earland. (Not issued.)	—	—
s. Specimen.	—	1000.

71 1 Dollar

ND (1974). Brown on brown, green and pink underprint. Queen Elizabeth at right, arms and heading *FIJI* at top center. Issuing authority name across lower center. Back: Yanuca beach scene in Yasewas. Watermark: Profile Fijian head. Printer: TDLR. 156x67mm.

	VF	UNC
a. Signature D. J. Barnes and R. J. Earland.	3.00	22.50
b. Signature D. J. Barnes and H. J. Tomkins.	3.00	20.00
s1. Specimen. As a.	—	300.
s2. Specimen. As b.	—	200.
ar. As a. Replacement. *Z/I* prefix.	9.00	40.00
br. As b. Replacement. *Z/I* prefix.	7.50	30.00

72 2 Dollars

ND (1974). Green on brown and light blue underprint. Queen Elizabeth at right, arms and heading *FIJI* at top center. Issuing authority name across lower center. Back: Geometric lathe pattern. Watermark: Profile Fijian head. Printer: TDLR. 156x67mm.

	VF	UNC
a. Signature D. J. Barnes and I. A. Craik.	25.00	100.
b. Signature D. J. Barnes and R. J. Earland.	7.00	37.50
c. Signature D. J. Barnes and H. J. Tomkins.	7.00	35.00
s1. Specimen. As a.	—	450.
s2. Specimen. As b.	—	350.
s3. Specimen. As c.	—	300.
ar. As a. Replacement. *Z/I* prefix.	150.	850.
br. As b. Replacement. *Z/I* prefix.	25.00	135.
cr. As c. Replacement. *Z/I* prefix.	15.00	100.

73 5 Dollars

ND (1974). Orange on purple and gray underprint. Queen Elizabeth at right, arms and heading *FIJI* at top center. Issuing authority name across lower center. Back: Geometric lathe pattern. Watermark: Profile Fijian head. Printer: TDLR. 156x67mm.

	VF	UNC
a. Signature D. J. Barnes and I. A. Craik.	85.00	850.
b. Signature D. J. Barnes and R. J. Earland.	45.00	250.
c. Signature D. J. Barnes and H. J. Tomkins.	45.00	225.
s1. Specimen. As a.	—	650.
s2. Specimen. As b.	—	600.
s3. Specimen. As c.	—	550.
ar. As a. Replacement. *Z/I* prefix.	350.	1250.
br. As b. Replacement. *Z/I* prefix.	225.	750.
cr. As c. Replacement. *Z/I* prefix.	95.00	400.

74 10 Dollars

ND (1974). Purple on orange and purple underprint. Queen Elizabeth at right, arms and heading *FIJI* at top center. Issuing authority name across lower center. Back: Geometric lathe pattern. Watermark: Profile Fijian head. Printer: TDLR. 156x67mm.

	VF	UNC
a. Signature D. J. Barnes and I. A. Craik.	275.	1500.
b. Signature D. J. Barnes and R. J. Earland.	35.00	350.
c. Signature D. J. Barnes and H. J. Tomkins.	85.00	300.
s1. Specimen. As a.	—	750.
s2. Specimen. As b.	—	650.
s3. Specimen. As c.	—	600.
ar. As a. Replacement *Z/1* prefix.	450.	2000.
br. As b. Replacement *Z/1* prefix.	225.	800.
cr. As c. Replacement *Z/1* prefix.	125.	650.

75 20 Dollars

ND (1974). Blue on light green, orange and blue underprint. Queen Elizabeth at right, arms and heading *FIJI* at top center. Issuing authority name across lower center. Back: Geometric lathe pattern. Watermark: Profile Fijian head. Printer: TDLR. 156x67mm.

	VF	UNC
a. Signature D. J. Barnes and I. A. Craik.	675.	2000.
b. Signature D. J. Barnes and R. J. Earland.	100.	600.
c. Signature D. J. Barnes and H. J. Tomkins.	100.	600.
s1. Specimen. As a.	—	850.
s2. Specimen. As b.	—	750.
s3. Specimen. As c.	—	700.
ar. As a. Replacement. *Z/I* prefix.	650.	3000.
br. As b. Replacement. *Z/I* prefix.	225.	1000.
cr. As c. Replacement. *Z/I* prefix.	200.	1200.

1980 ND Issue

76 1 Dollar

ND (1980). Brown on multicolor underprint. Queen Elizabeth II at right center, arms at center, artifact at right. Signatures; D. J. Barnes and H. J. Tomkins. Back: Open air Suva markets at center. Watermark: Profile Fijian head. Printer: TDLR. Denomination figures are 8 mm high. 156x67mm.

	VF	UNC
a. Issued note.	3.00	25.00
r. As a. Replacement. *Z/I* prefix.	12.50	75.00
s1. Specimen. Signatures punch hole cancelled.	—	300.
s2. Specimen. Corners punch hole cancelled.	—	225.

77 2 Dollars

ND (1980). Green on multicolor underprint. Queen Elizabeth II at right center, arms at center, artifact at right. Signatures; D. J. Barnes and H. J. Tomkins. Back: Khaki. Train and sugar cane harvest at center. Watermark: Profile Fijian head. Printer: TDLR. Denomination figures are 8 mm high. 156x67mm.

	VF	UNC
a. Issued note.	5.00	45.00
r. As a. Replacement. *Z/I* prefix.	18.50	125.
s1. Specimen. Signatures punched hole cancelled.	—	400.
s2. Specimen. Corners punched hole cancelled.	—	300.

78 5 Dollars

ND (1980). Orange on multicolor underprint. Queen Elizabeth II at right center, arms at center, artifact at right. Signatures; D. J. Barnes and H. J. Tomkins. Back: Fishing group with net at center. Watermark: Profile Fijian head. Printer: TDLR. Denomination figures are 8 mm high. 156x67mm.

	VF	UNC
a. Issued note.	7.50	80.00
r. As a. Replacement. *Z/I* prefix.	35.00	250.
s1. Specimen. Signatures punch hole cancelled.	—	450.
s2. Specimen. Corners punched hole cancelled.	—	350.

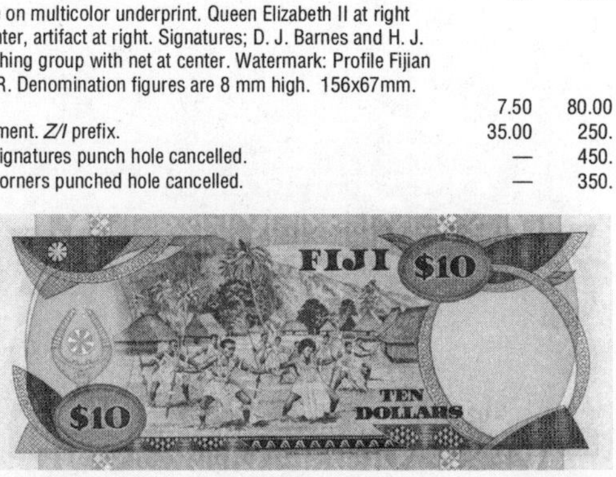

79 10 Dollars

ND (1980). Purple on multicolor underprint. Queen Elizabeth II at right center, arms at center, artifact at right. Signatures; D. J. Barnes and H. J. Tomkins. Back: Ceremonial tribal dance scene at center. Watermark: Profile Fijian head. Printer: TDLR. Denomination figures are 8 mm high. 156x67mm.

	VF	UNC
a. Issued note.	25.00	225.
r. As a. Replacement. *Z/I* prefix.	75.00	400.
s1. Specimen. Signatures punched hole cancelled.	—	550.
s2. Specimen. Corners punched hole cancelled.	—	450.

80 20 Dollars VF UNC

ND (1980). Blue on multicolor underprint. Queen Elizabeth II at right center, arms at center, artifact at right. Signatures; D. J. Barnes and H. J. Tomkins. Back: Fijian bure (house) at center. Watermark: Profile Fijian head. Printer: TDLR. Denomination figures are 8 mm high. 156x67mm.

	VF	UNC
a. Issued note.	50.00	350.
r. As a. Replacement. Z/I prefix.	100.	600.
s. Specimen. Signatures punched hole cancelled.	—	650.
s2. Specimen. Corners punch hole cancelled.	—	550.

1983-86 ND Issue

81 1 Dollar VF UNC

ND (1983). Gray on multicolor underprint. Queen Elizabeth II at right center, arms at center, artifact at right. Signatures; D. J. Bares and S. Siwatibau. Back: Open air Suva markets at center, lithographed. Watermark: Profile Fijian head. Printer: TDLR. Denomination figures 9.5 mm high. 156x67mm.

	VF	UNC
a. Issued note.	2.00	9.00
r. As a. Replacement. Z/I prefix.	10.00	45.00
s1. Specimen. Signatures punched out.	—	200.
s2. Specimen. Corners punched out.	—	125.

82 2 Dollars VF UNC

ND (1983). Green on multicolor underprint. Queen Elizabeth II at right center, arms at center, artifact at right. Signatures; D. J. Bares and S. Siwatibau. Back: Green. Sugar cane harvest at center, lithographed. Watermark: Profile Fijian head. Printer: TDLR. Denominatiion figures 9.5 mm high. 156x67mm.

	VF	UNC
a. Issued note.	4.50	15.00
r. As a. Replacement. Z/I prefix.	22.50	150.
s1. Specimen. Signatures punched out.	—	275.
s2. Specimen. Corners punched out.	—	175.

83 5 Dollars VF UNC

ND (1986). Orange on multicolor underprint. Queen Elizabeth II at right center, arms at center, artifact at right. Signatures; D. J. Bares and S. Siwatibau. Back: Circle of fishermen with net at center, lithographed. Watermark: Profile Fijian head. Printer: TDLR. Denomination figures 9.5 mm high. 156x67mm.

	VF	UNC
a. Issued note.	6.00	55.00
r. As a. Replacement. Z/I prefix.	30.00	185.
s1. Specimen. Signatures punched out.	—	300.
s2. Specimen. Corners punched out.	—	225.

84 10 Dollars VF UNC

ND (1986). Purple on multicolor underprint. Queen Elizabeth II at right center, arms at center, artifact at right. Signatures; D. J. Bares and S. Siwatibau. Back. Ceremonial dance scene at center, lithographed. Watermark: Profile Fijian head. Printer. TDLR. Denomination figures 9.5 mm high. 156x67mm.

	VF	UNC
a. Issued note.	12.50	100.
r. As a. Replacement. Z/I prefix.	50.00	275.
s1. Specimen. Signatures punched out.	—	400.
s2. Specimen. Corners punched out.	—	285.

85 20 Dollars VF UNC

ND (1986). Blue on multicolor underprint. Queen Elizabeth II at right center, arms at center, artifact at right. Signatures; D. J. Bares and S. Siwatibau. Back: Fijian bure (house) at center, lithographed. Watermark: Profile Fijian head. Printer: TDLR. Denomination figures 9.5 mm high. 156x67mm.

	VF	UNC
a. Issued note.	20.00	175.
r. As a. Replacement. Z/I prefix.	85.00	350.
s1. Specimen. Signatures punched out.	—	500.
s2. Specimen. Corners punched out.	—	350.

Reserve Bank of Fiji

1987-88 ND Issue

#86-88 No replacement notes.

86 1 Dollar VF UNC

ND (1987). Gray on multicolor underprint. Modified portrait of Queen Elizabeth II at right, arms at center, artifact at right. Signature S. Siwatibau. Back: Open air Suva markets at center. Watermark: Profile Fijian head. Printer: BWC. 156x67mm.

	VF	UNC
a. Issued note.	FV	8.00
s1. Specimen. Signature punched out.	—	100.
s2. Specimen. No punch cancellation.	—	75.00

87 **2 Dollars** | VF | UNC

ND (1988). Green on multicolor underprint. Modified portrait of Queen Elizabeth II at right, arms at center, artifact at right. Signature S. Siwatibau. Back: Green. Sugar cane harvest at center. Watermark: Profile Fijian head. Printer: BWC. UV: native design and value fluoresce orange. 156x67mm.

	VF	UNC
a. Issued note.	FV	20.00
s1. Specimen. Signature punched out.	—	125.
s2. Specimen. No punch cancellation.	—	100.

88 **20 Dollars** | VF | UNC

ND (1988). Blue on multicolor underprint. Modified portrait of Queen Elizabeth II at right, arms at center, artifact at right. Signature S. Siwatibau. Back: Fijian bure (house) at center. Watermark: Profile Fijian head. Printer: BWC. 156x67mm.

	VF	UNC
a. Issued note.	15.00	110.
s1. Specimen. Signature punched out.	—	200.
s2. Specimen. No punch cancellation.	—	175.

1991 ND Issue

#89-92 No replacement notes.

89 **1 Dollar** | VF | UNC

ND (1993). Gray on multicolor underprint. Modified portrait of Queen Elizabeth II at right, arms at center, artifact at right. Signature J. Kuabuabola. Back: Open air Suva markets at center. Watermark: Profile Fijian head. Printer: TDLR. 156x67mm.

	VF	UNC
a. Issued note.	FV	4.00
s1. Specimen. Signature punched out.	—	125.
s2. Specimen. No punch cancellation.	—	85.00

90 **2 Dollars** | VF | UNC

ND (1995). Green on multicolor underprint. Modified portrait of Queen Elizabeth II at right, arms at center, artifact at right. Signature J. Kuabuabola. Back: Sugar cane harvest at center. Watermark: Profile Fijian head. Printer: TDLR. 156x67mm.

	VF	UNC
a. Issued note.	FV	15.00
s1. Specimen. Signature punched out.	—	150.
s2. Specimen. No punch cancellation.	—	100.

91 **5 Dollars** | VF | UNC

ND (1989). Orange on multicolor underprint. Modified portrait of Queen Elizabeth II at right, arms at center, artifact at right. Signature J. Kuabuabola. Back: Circle of fishermen with net at center. Watermark: Profile Fijian head. Printer: TDLR. 156x67mm.

	VF	UNC
a. Issued note.	7.50	40.00
s1. Specimen. Signature punched out.	—	200.
s2. Specimen. No punch cancellation.	—	175.

92 **10 Dollars** | VF | UNC

ND (1989). Purple on multicolor underprint. Modified portrait of Queen Elizabeth II at right, arms at center, artifact at right. Signature J. Kuabuabola. Back: Ceremonial dance scene at center. Watermark: Profile Fijian head. Printer: TDLR. 156x67mm.

	VF	UNC
a. Issued note.	10.00	55.00
s1. Specimen. Signature punched out.	—	250.
s2. Specimen. No punch cancellation.	—	225.

1992 ND Issue

93 **5 Dollars** | VF | UNC

ND (1992). Orange and violet on multicolor underprint. Modified portrait of Queen Elizabeth II at right, arms at center, artifact at right. Signature J. Kuabuabola. Vertical and horizontal serial number. Back: Circle of fishermen with net at center. Watermark: Profile Fijian head. Printer: TDLR. 146x67mm.

	VF	UNC
a. Issued note.	5.00	40.00
s1. Specimen. Signature punched out.	—	185.
s2. Specimen. No punch cancellation.	—	150.

94 **10 Dollars** | VF | UNC

Purple and brown on multicolor underprint. Modified portrait of Queen Elizabeth II at right, arms at center, artifact at right. Signature J. Kuabuabola. Vertical and horizontal serial number. Back: Ceremonial dance scene at center. Watermark: Profile Fijian head. Printer: TDLR. 146x67mm.

	VF	UNC
a. Issued note.	10.00	60.00
s1. Specimen. Signature punched out.	—	200.
s2. Specimen. No punch cancellation.	—	185.

95 20 Dollars

ND (1992). Blue and black on multicolor underprint. Modified portrait of Queen Elizabeth II at right, arms at center, artifact at right. Signature J. Kuabuabola. Vertical and horizontal serial number. Back: Fijian bure (house) at center. Watermark: Profile Fijian head. Printer: TDLR. 146x67mm.

	VF	UNC
a. Issued note.	15.00	95.00
s1. Specimen. Signature punched out.	—	250.
s2. Specimen. No punch cancellation.	—	200.

1992-95 ND Issue

96 2 Dollars

ND (1996). Green, blue and gold on multicolor underprint. Mature bust of Queen Elizabeth II at right, arms at upper right. Kaka (Masked Shining Parrot) at lower left. Segmented foil security thread. Back: Culturally diverse group of five at left center. Watermark: Profile Fijian head. Printer: TDLR. UV: value in box fluoresces yellow; back design elements at left and right orange. 156x67mm.

	VF	UNC
a. Single letter prefix.	FV	6.00
b. Double letter prefix. Amended security thread.	FV	4.00
s. Specimen.	—	100.
ar. As a. Replacement. *Z* prefix.	3.00	15.00
br. As b. Replacement. *X* prefix.	3.00	10.00

97 5 Dollars

ND (1995). Red, orange and maroon on multicolor underprint. Mature bust of Queen Elizabeth II at right, arms at upper right. Bunedamu (White-throated Pigeon) at lower left. Segmented foil security thread. Back: Aerial view Nadi International Airport at center, ferry boat at lower center right. Watermark: Profile Fijian head. Printer: TDLR. 156x67mm.

	VF	UNC
a. Issued note.	FV	12.50
r. Replacement. *Z* prefix.	12.50	65.00
s. Specimen.	—	250.

98 10 Dollars

ND (1996). Purple, violet and brown onmulticolor underprint. Mature bust of Queen Elizabeth II at right, arms at upper right. Kikau (Orange-breasted Myzomela) at lower left. Segmented foil security thread. Back: Traditional boat with thatched shelter at center. Watermark: Profile Fijian head. Printer: TDLR. 156x67mm.

	VF	UNC
a. Single letter prefix.	—	45.00
b. Double letter prefix.	FV	25.00
r. Replacement. *Z* prefix.	35.00	125.
s. Specimen.	—	300.

99 20 Dollars

ND. Blue, purple and dark blue on multicolor underprint. Mature bust of Queen Elizabeth II at right, arms at upper right. Manusa (Fantail) at lower left. Segmented foil security thread. Back: Parliament House at left, Reserve Bank building at center right. Watermark: Profile Fijian head. Printer: TDLR. 156x67mm.

	VF	UNC
a. Single letter prefix.	FV	55.00
b. Double letter prefix.	FV	40.00
r. Replacement. *Z* prefix.	60.00	185.
s. Specimen.	—	450.

100 50 Dollars

ND (1996). Black, red, orange and violet on multicolor underprint. Mature bust of Queen Elizabeth II at right, arms at upper right. Kaka (Petrel) at lower left. Segmented foil security thread. Novel serial numbers at left only. Back: Flag raising ceremony at left, signing of Deed of Cession, Cession Stone. Watermark: Profile Fijian head. Printer: TDLR. 156x67mm.

	VF	UNC
a. Single letter prefix. Signature J. Kuabuabola.	30.00	185.
b. Signature Savenaca Narube.	50.00	450.
r1. As a. Replacement. *Z* prefix.	300.	750.
r2. As b. Replacement. *Z* prefix.	450.	900.
s1. Specimen as a. Signature J. Kuabuabola.	—	600.
s2. Specimen as b. Signature Savenaca Narube.	—	900.

1998 ND Issue

101 5 Dollars

ND. Brown on multicolor underprint. Mature bust of Queen Elizabeth II at right, arms at upper right. Bunedamu bird (White-throated Pigeon) at lower left. Back: Aerial view Nadi International Airport at left center, ferry boat at lower center right. Watermark: Profile Fijian head. 156x67mm.

	VF	UNC
a. Signature J. Kuabuabola.	FV	12.50
b. Signature Savenaca Narube.	FV	15.00
s1. As a. Specimen.	—	50.00
s2. As b. Specimen.	—	65.00
ar. As a. Replacement. *Z* prefix.	30.00	125.
br. As b. Replacement. *Z* prefix.	50.00	200.

2000 Commemorative Issue

102 2 Dollars VF UNC

2000. Green, blue and brown on multicolor underprint. Kaka (Parrot) at left, Sir Penaia Ganilau at right, arms at upper right, y2k at center. Segmented foil security thread. Back: Culturally diverse group and turtle. Watermark: Profile Fijian head. Printer: TDLR. UV: value in box fluoresces yellow. 156x67mm.

	VF	UNC
a. Issued note.	FV	2.00
b. Uncut pair.	FV	5.00
c. Uncut sheet of 20.	—	75.00
d. Uncut sheet of 32.	—	150.
s. Specimen.	—	100.

103 2000 Dollars VF UNC

2000. Blue and gold on multicolor underprint. Sir Kamisese Mara at right, Kulawaj (Parrot) at lower left, arms at upper right, y2k at center. Segmented foil security thread. Back: Earth, rising sun, island map, shells. Watermark: Profile Fijian head. Printer: TDLR.

	VF	UNC
a. Isused note.	FV	2500.
s. Specimen, individually numbered.	—	800.

2002 ND Issue

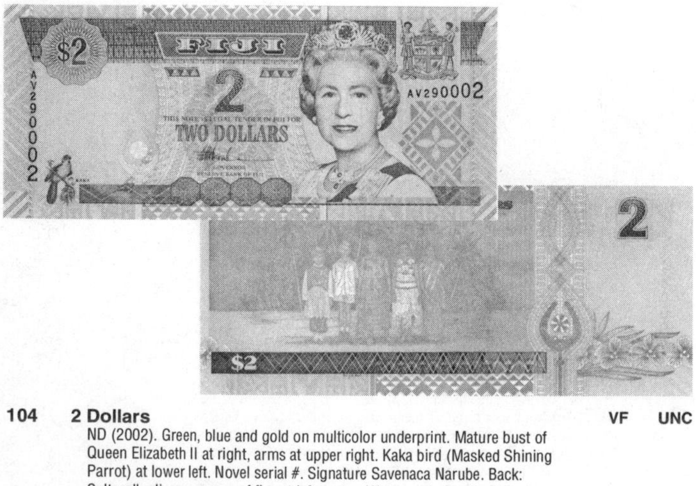

104 2 Dollars VF UNC

ND (2002). Green, blue and gold on multicolor underprint. Mature bust of Queen Elizabeth II at right, arms at upper right. Kaka bird (Masked Shining Parrot) at lower left. Novel serial #. Signature Savenaca Narube. Back: Culturally diverse group of five at left center. Watermark: Profile Fijian head. Printer: TDLR. Additional security features. 156x67mm.

	VF	UNC
a. Double letter prefix.	FV	3.00
r. Replacement. *Z* prefix.	4.00	10.00
s. Specimen.	—	45.00

105 5 Dollars VF UNC

ND (2002). Brown on multicolor underprint. Mature bust of Queen Elizabeth II at right, arms at upper right. Bunedamu bird (White-throated Pigeon) at lower left. Novel serial #. Signature Savenaca Narube. Back: Aerial view Nadi International Airport at left center, ferry boat at lower center right. Watermark: Profile Fijian head. Printer: TDLR. Additional security features. 156x67mm.

	VF	UNC
a. Single letter prefix.	FV	10.00
b. Double letter prefix.	FV	5.00
r. Replacement. *Z* prefix.	7.00	20.00
s. Specimen.	—	85.00

106 10 Dollars VF UNC

ND (2002). Purple, violet and brown onmulticolor underprint. Mature bust of Queen Elizabeth II at right, arms at upper right. Novel serial #. Kikau bird at lower left. Signature Savenaca Narube. Back: Traditional boat with thatched shelter at center. Watermark: Profile Fijian head. Printer: TDLR. Additional security features. 156x67mm.

	VF	UNC
a. Double letter prefix.	FV	17.50
r. Replacement. *Z* prefix.	17.50	30.00
s. Specimen.	—	180.

107 20 Dollars VF UNC

ND (2002). Blue, purple and dark blue on multicolor underprint. Mature bust of Queen Elizabeth II at right, arms at upper right. Novel serial #. Manusa bird at lower left. Signature Savenaca Narube. Back: Parliament House at left, Reserve Bank building at center right. Watermark: Profile Fijian head. Printer: TDLR. Additional security features. 156x67mm.

	VF	UNC
a. Double letter prefix.	FV	35.00
r. Replacement. *Z* prefix.	22.50	85.00
s. Specimen.	—	250.

108 50 Dollars

ND (2002). Black, red, orange and violet on multicolor underprint. Mature bust of Queen Elizabeth II at right, arms at upper right. Novel serial #. Kaka birk at lower left. Additional security features. Signature Savenaca Narube. Back: Flag raising ceremony at left, signing of Deed of Cession, Cession Stone. Watermark: Profile Fijian head. Printer: TDLR. 156x67mm.

	VF	UNC
a. Single letter prefix.	FV	75.00
r. Replacement. *Z* prefix.	30.00	180.
s. Specimen.	—	400.

2007 ND Issue

109 2 Dollars

ND (2007; 2012). Green on multicolor underprint. Mature bust Queen Elizabeth II at right, arms at upper right. Novel numbering on both serial #. Mohar (sovereign locket) at lower left. Signature Savenaca Narube. Back: Faces of diverse group of children during school games. Fiji National Stadium at left; Mount Korobasanasaga at center right. Printer: TDLR. 131x67mm.

	VF	UNC
a. Signature Savenaca Narube. Signature title: Governor.	FV	2.00
b. Signature Barry Whiteside. Signature title: Acting Governor.	FV	2.00
r1. As a. Replacement note. Serial # prefix: *ZA*.	3.00	7.50
r2. As b. Replacement note. Serial # prefix: *ZA*.	2.50	10.00
s. As a. Specimen.	—	45.00
s2. As b. Specimen.	—	45.00

110 5 Dollars

ND (2007; 2012). Brown on multicolor underprint. Mature bust Queen Elizabeth II at right, arms at upper right. Novel numbering on both serial #. Kato ni Masima (salt basket) at lower left. Signature Savenaca Narube. Back: Crested Iguana at left, Balaka palm center, Masiratu flower at right, Mount Valili at far left. Printer: TDLR. 136x67mm.

	VF	UNC
a. Signature Savenaca Narube. Signature title: Governor.	FV	5.00
b. Signature: Barry Whiteside. Signature title: Acting Governor.	FV	5.00
r1. As a. Replacement note. Serial # prefix: *ZA*.	5.00	15.00
r2. As b. Replacement note. Serial # prefix: *ZA*.	4.00	15.00
s1. As a. Specimen.	—	85.00
s2. As b. Specimen.	—	85.00

111 10 Dollars

ND (2007; 2012). Purple on multicolor underprint. Mature bust Queen Elizabeth II at right, arms at upper right. Novel numbering on both serial #. i Buburau ni Bete (dish) at lower left. Foil security insert with motion. Signature Savenaca Narube. Back: Grand Pacific Hotel at right center. Joske's Thumb at left center. Printer: TDLR. 141x67mm.

	VF	UNC
a. Signature Savenaca Narube. Signature title: Governor.	FV	10.00
b. Signature: Barry Whiteside. Signature title: Acting Governor.	FV	10.00
r1. As a. Replacement note. Serial # prefix: *ZA*.	10.00	25.00
r2. As b. Replacement note. Serial # prefix: *ZA*.	8.50	20.00
s1. As a. Specimen.	—	125.
s2. As b. Specimen.	—	125.

112 20 Dollars

ND (2007). Blue on multicolor underprint. Mature bust Queen Elizabeth II at right, arms at upper right. Novel numbering on both serial #. Foa (coconut scraper) at lower left. Fan shaped hologram at right. Signature Savenaca Narube. Back: Sugarcane, fishery, forestry and mining scenes. Mount Uluinabukelevu at right center. Printer: TDLR. 146x67mm.

	VF	UNC
a. Issued note.	FV	22.50
r. Replacement note. Serial # prefix: *ZA*.	20.00	100.
s. Specimen.	—	150.

113 50 Dollars

ND (2007). Orange on multicolor underprint. Mature bust Queen Elizabeth II at right, arms at upper right. Novel numbering on both serial #. Wasekaseka (whale tooth necklace) at lower left. Turtle-shaped hologram at right. Signature Savenaca Nar Back: Ceremonial presentation of tabua and yaqona. Printer: TDLR. 151x67mm.

	VF	UNC
a. Issued note.	FV	55.00
r. Replacement note. Serial # prefix: *ZA*.	50.00	150.
s. Specimen.	—	200.

114 100 Dollars

ND (2007). Yellow. Mature bust Queen Elizabeth II at right, arms at upper right. Novel numbering on both serial #. Buli Kula (Golden Cowry) at lower left. OPTIKS 18mm wide security foil at right. Signature Savenaca Naru Back: Tourism: map, smiling faces, cruise boat, snorkeling. Printer: TDLR. 156x67mm.

	VF	UNC
a. Issued note.	FV	110.
r. Replacement note. Serial # prefix: *ZA*.	100.	250.
s. Specimen.	—	300.

The Republic of Finland, the second most northerly state of the European continent, has an area of 338,145 sq. km. and a population of 5.24 million. Capital: Helsinki. Electrical, optical equipment, shipbuilding, metal and woodworking are the leading industries. Paper, wood pulp, plywood and telecommunication equipment are exported.

Finland was a province and then a grand duchy under Sweden from the 12th to the 19th centuries, and an autonomous grand duchy of Russia after 1809. It won its complete independence in 1917. During World War II, it was able to successfully defend its freedom and resist invasions by the Soviet Union - albeit with some loss of territory. In the subsequent half century, the Finns made a remarkable transformation from a farm/forest economy to a diversified modern industrial economy; per capita income is now among the highest in Western Europe. A member of the European Union since 1995, Finland was the only Nordic state to join the euro system at its initiation in January 1999.

RULERS:

Gustaf III, 1771-1792, of Sweden
Gustaf IV Adolph, 1792-1809
Alexander I, 1809-1825, of Russia
Nicholas I, 1825-1855
Alexander II, 1855-1881
Alexander III, 1881-1894
Nicholas II, 1894-1917

MONETARY SYSTEM:

(With Sweden to 1809)
1 Riksdaler Specie = 48 Skilling Specie
(With Russia 1809-1917)
1 Ruble = 100 Kopeks, 1809-1860
1 Markka = 100 Penniä, 1860-1963
1 Markka = 100 "Old" Markkaa, 1963-2001
1 Euro = 100 Cents, 2002-

REPLACEMENT NOTES: Replacement notes were introduced in 1955. Until 1980, replacement notes have an asterisk after the serial number. Series 1986 show 2nd and 3rd digits of serial # as 99.

REPUBLIC

SUOMEN PANKKI - FINLANDS BANK

1963 DATED ISSUE

		VF	UNC
98	**1 Markka**		
	1963. Lilac-brown on olive underprint. Wheat ears. Back: Arms at center.		
	a. Issued note.	.50	2.00
	r. Replacement note. Serial # suffix *.	8.00	25.00
	s. Specimen.	—	100.

		VF	UNC
99	**5 Markkaa**		
	1963. Blue and blue-green. Conifer branch. Back: Arms at center.		
	a. Issued note.	3.00	12.50
	r. Replacement note. Serial # suffix *.	20.00	40.00
	s. Specimen.	—	125.

		VF	UNC
100	**10 Markkaa**		
	1963. Dark green and blue. Juho Kusti Paasikivi at left. Back: Arms at center right. Watermark: Juho Kusti Paasikivi, (direction varies).		
	a. Issued note.	15.00	30.00
	r. Replacement note. Serial # suffix *.	250.	500.
	s. Specimen.	—	150.

		VF	UNC
101	**50 Markkaa**		
	1963. Brown. Kaarlo Juho Ståhlberg at left. Back: Arms at center right. Watermark: Kaarlo Juho Ståhlberg (direction varies).		
	a. Issued note.	20.00	50.00
	r. Replacement note. Serial # suffix *.	700.	1000.
	s. Specimen.	—	175.

		VF	UNC
102	**100 Markkaa**		
	1963. Violet. Juhana Vilhelm Snellman at left. Back: Arms at center right.		
	a. Issued note.	25.00	60.00
	r. Replacement note. Serial # suffix *.	350.	1000.
	s. Specimen.	—	200.

1963 DATED ISSUE, LITT. A

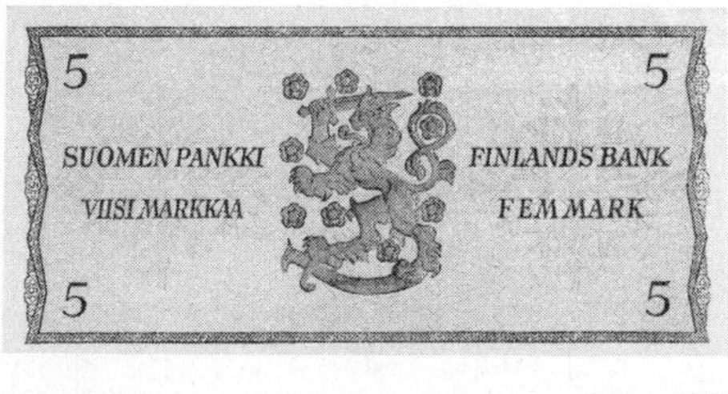

		VF	UNC
103	**5 Markkaa**		
	1963. Blue and blue-green. Conifer branch, border and date designs are more detailed. Back: Arms at center.		
	a. Issued note.	3.00	13.00
	r. Replacement note. Serial # suffix *.	5.00	30.00

		VF	UNC
104	**10 Markkaa**		
	1963. Dark green and blue. Juho Kusti Paasikivi at left. Back: Arms at center right. Watermark: Juho Kusti Paasikivi, (position varies).		
	a. Issued note.	3.00	9.00
	r. Replacement note. Serial # suffix *.	5.00	10.00

105	50 Markkaa	VF	UNC
	1963. Brown. Kaarlo Juho Ståhlberg at left. Back: Arms at center right.		
	a. Issued note.	20.00	50.00
	r. Replacement note. Serial # suffix *.	250.	400.

106	100 Markkaa	VF	UNC
	1963. Violet. Juhana Vilhelm Snellman at left. Back: Arms at center right.		
	a. Issued note.	25.00	40.00
	r. Replacement note. Serial # suffix *.	40.00	75.00

1963 Dated Issue, Litt. B

106A	5 Markkaa	VF	UNC
	1963. Blue and blue-green. Conifer branch. Back: Arms at center.		
	a. Issued note.	1.50	4.00
	r1. Replacement note. Serial # suffix *.	5.00	8.00
	r2. Replacement note. Serial # suffix /.	75.00	150.
107	50 Markkaa		
	1963. Brown. Kaarlo Juho Ståhlberg at left. Back: Arms at center right. Watermark: Kaarlo Juho Ståhlberg (direction varies).		
	a. Issued note.	15.00	35.00
	r. Replacement note. Serial # suffix *.	30.00	60.00

1975-77 Issue

108	50 Markkaa	VF	UNC
	1977. Brown and multicolor. Kaarlo Juho Ståhlberg at left. Watermark: Kaarlo Juho Ståhlberg, (position and direction varies).		
	a. Issued note.	12.50	20.00
	r1. Replacement note. Serial # suffix *.	20.00	40.00
	r2. Replacement note. Serial # suffix /.	300.	600.
	s. Specimen.	—	200.

109	100 Markkaa	VF	UNC
	1976. Violet. Juhana Vilhelm Snellman at left. Watermark: Juhana Vilhelm Snellman, (position and direction varies).		
	a. Issued note.	25.00	35.00
	r1. Replacement note. Serial # suffix *.	25.00	48.00
	r2. Replacement note. Serial # suffix /.	150.	300.

110	500 Markkaa	VF	UNC
	1975. Blue and violet. Urho Kaleva Kekkonen at left. Back: Arms and nine small shields. Watermark: Urho Kaleva Kekkonen at left, (position varies).		
	a. Thin metallic security thread.	150.	200.
	b. Broad yellow plastic security thread.	100.	150.
	r1. As a. Replacement note. Serial # suffix *.	400.	750.
	r2. As b. Replacement note. Serial # suffix *.	250.	350.
	r3. As b. Replacement note. Serial # suffix /.	800.	1200.
	s. Specimen.	—	350.

1980 Issue

111	10 Markkaa	VF	UNC
	1980. Green and brown on orange and multicolor underprint. Juho Kusti Paasikivi at left, four raised discs at right center for denomination identification by the blind. Back: Green and purple. Arms at center right. Watermark: Juho Kusti Paasikivi.		
	a. Issued note.	3.00	8.00
	r1. Replacement note. Serial # suffix *.	5.00	14.00
	r2. Replacement note. Serial # suffix /.	75.00	150.

1980 Issue; Litt. A

112	10 Markkaa	VF	UNC
	1980. Green and brown on orange and multicolor underprint. Juho Kusti Paasikivi at left, date under portrait, five small circles at bottom center. *Litt. A*. Back: Green and purple. Arms at center right. Watermark: Juho Kusti Paasikivi.		
	a. Issued note.	3.00	6.00
	r. Replacement note. *99* as 2nd and 3rd numerial in serial #.	5.00	10.00

1986 Issue

#113-115, and 117 replacement notes: w/*99* as 2nd and 3rd digits in serial #.

113	10 Markkaa	VF	UNC
	1986. Deep blue and green underprint. Paavo Nurmi at left, circles above lower right serial number. Back: Helsinki Olympic Stadium. Watermark: Paavo Nurmi.		
	a. Issued note.	2.50	6.00
	r. Replacement note.	4.00	12.50

114	50 Markkaa	VF	UNC
	1986. Black on red-brown and multicolor underprint. Alvar Aalto at left, four raised circles above lower right serial number. Back: Finlandia Hall. Watermark: Alvar Aalto.		
	a. Issued note.	12.50	25.00
	r. Replacement note.	30.00	50.00

115	100 Markkaa	VF	UNC
	1986. Black on green and multicolor underprint. Jean Sibelius at left, three raised circles above lower right serial number. Back: Whooper Swans. Watermark: Jean Sibelius.		
	a. Issued note.	25.00	40.00
	r. Replacement note.	40.00	60.00

116	500 Markkaa	VF	UNC
	1986. Black on red, brown and yellow underprint. Elias Lönnrot at left, two circles above lower right serial number. Back: Punkaharju. Watermark: Elias Lönnrot.		
	a. Issued note.	125.	175.
	r. Replacement note.	150.	200.

117	1000 Markkaa	VF	UNC
	1986. Blue and purple on multicolor underprint. Anders Chydenius at left, one circle above lower right serial number. Back: King's gate, sea fortress of Suomenlinna in Helsinki harbor, seagulls. Watermark: Anders Chydenius.		
	a. Issued note.	200.	300.
	r. Replacement note.	250.	325.

1986 Dated (1991) Issue, Litt. A

118	50 Markkaa	VF	UNC
	1986 (1991). Black on red-brown and multicolor underprint. Alvar Aalto at left, *Litt. A* above denomination at lower left, 4 raised circles above bank name, optical variable device (OVD) at upper right. Back: Finlandia Hall. Watermark: Alvar Aalto. Latent image at upper right.	10.00	20.00
119	**100 Markkaa**		
	1986 (1991). Black on green and multicolor underprint. Jean Sibelius at left, *Litt. A* above denomination at lower left, 3 raised circles above bank name, optical variable device (OVD) at upper right. Back: Whooper Swans. Watermark: Jean Sibelius. Latent image at upper right.	17.50	27.50

120	500 Markkaa	VF	UNC
	1986 (1991). Black on red, brown and yellow underprint. Elias Lönnrot at left, *Litt. A* above denomination at lower left, 2 raised circles above bank name, optical variable device (OVD) at upper right. Back: Punkaharju. Watermark: Elias Lönnrot.	135.	160.

121 **1000 Markkaa** | **VF** 250. | **UNC** 300.

1986 (1991). Blue and purple on multicolor underprint. Anders Chydenius at left, *Litt. A* above denomination at lower left, 1 raised circle above bank name, optical variable device (OVD) at upper right. Back: King's gate, sea fortress of Suomenlinna in Helsinki harbor, seagulls. Watermark: Anders Chydenius.

1993 Issue

122 **20 Markkaa** | **VF** 7.50 | **UNC** 12.50

1993. Black on blue and gold underprint. Väinö Linna at left, latent image at upper right, four circles above bank name at lower center. Back: Tampere street scene. Watermark: Väinö Linna.

1993 Dated (1997) Issue; Litt. A.

123 **20 Markkaa** | **VF** 5.00 | **UNC** 8.00

1993 (1997). Black on blue and green underprint. Väinö Linna at left, four circles above bank name at lower center, with optical variable device at upper right. *Litt. A.* at lower left. Back: Tampere street scene. Watermark: Väinö Linna.

The French Republic, largest of the West European nations, has an area of 547,026 sq. km. and a population of 64.05 million. Capital: Paris. Agriculture, manufacturing and tourism are the most important elements of France's diversified economy. Textiles and clothing, iron and steel products, machinery and transportation equipment, agricultural products and wine are exported.

Although ultimately a victor in World Wars I and II, France suffered extensive losses in its empire, wealth, manpower, and rank as a dominant nation-state. Nevertheless, France today is one of the most modern countries in the world and is a leader among European nations. Since 1958, it has constructed a hybrid presidential-parliamentary governing system resistant to the instabilities experienced in earlier more purely parliamentary administrations. In recent years, its reconciliation and cooperation with Germany have proved central to the economic integration of Europe, including the introduction of a common exchange currency, the euro, in January 1999. At present, France is at the forefront of efforts to develop the EU's military capabilities to supplement progress toward an EU foreign policy.

MONETARY SYSTEM:

1 Franc = 10 Decimes = 100 Centimes, 1794-1960
1 Nouveau Franc = 100 "old" Francs, 1960-1962
1 Franc = 100 Centimes, 1962-2002
1 Euro = 100 Cents, 2002-

Republic

Banque de France

1959 Issue

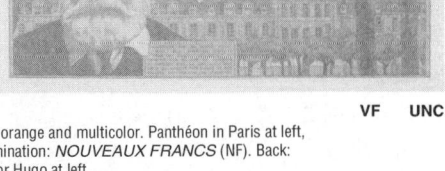

141 **5 Nouveaux Francs** | **VF** | **UNC**

5.3.1959-5.11.1965. Blue, orange and multicolor. Panthéon in Paris at left, Victor Hugo at right,denomination: *NOUVEAUX FRANCS* (NF). Back: Vosges place at right, Victor Hugo at left.

	VF	UNC
a. Issued note.	200.	500.
s. Specimen.	—	1250.

		VF	UNC
142	**10 Nouveaux Francs**		
	5.3.1959-4.1.1963. Multicolor. *Palais Royal* across bottom, Armand du Plessis, Cardinal Richelieu at right,denomination: *NOUVEAUX FRANCS* (NF). Back: Town gate (of Richelieu, in *Indre et Loire*) at right.		
	a. Issued note.	125.	450.
	s. Specimen.	—	1250.
143	**50 Nouveaux Francs**		
	5.3.1959-6.7.1961. Multicolor. Henry IV at center, Paris' *Pont Neuf* bridge in background, denomination: *NOUVEAUX FRANCS* (NF). Back: Henry IV at center, *Château de Pau* at left.		
	a. Issued note.	400.	1750.
	s. Specimen.	—	1750.
144	**100 Nouveaux Francs**		
	5.3.1959-2.4.1964. Multicolor. Arc de Triomphe at left, Napoléon Bonaparte at right, denomination: *NOUVEAUX FRANCS* (NF). Back: Paris' *Church of the Invalides* at right, Bonaparte at left.		
	a. Issued note.	50.00	800.
	s. Specimen.	—	1250.
145	**500 Nouveaux Francs**		
	1959-66. Multicolor. Jean Baptiste Poquelin called Molière at center Paris' *Palais Royal* in background, denomination: *NOUVEAUX FRANCS* (NF). Back: Theater in Versailles.		
	a. Signature G. Gouin D'Ambrières, R. Tondu and P. Gargam. 2.7.1959-8.1.1965.	250.	1200.
	b. Signature H. Morant, R. Tondu and P. Gargam. 6.1.1966.	300.	1500.
	s. Specimen. As b.	—	1500.

1962-66 Issue

		VF	UNC
146	**5 Francs**		
	1966-70. Brown, purple and multicolor. Louis Pasteur at left, Pasteur Institute in Paris at right. Back: Laboratory implements, man fighting a rabid dog, Pasteur at right.		
	a. Signature R. Tondu, P. Gargam and H. Morant. 5.5.1966-4.11.1966.	25.00	250.
	b. Signature R. Tondu, H. Morant and G. Bouchet. 5.5.1967-8.1.1970.	35.00	350.
	s. Specimen. As a. Overprint and perforated: *SPECIMEN.*	—	900.

		VF	UNC
147	**10 Francs**		
	1963-73. Red and multicolor. Paris' *Palais des Tuileries* at center, Voltaire at right. Back: Château de Cirey at right, Voltaire at left. Watermark: Voltaire.		
	a. Signature G. Gouin D'Ambrières, P. Gargam and R. Tondu. 4.1.1963-2.12.1965.	40.00	150.
	b. Signature H. Morant, P. Gargam and R. Tondu. 6.1.1966-6.4.1967.	20.00	150.
	c. Signature G. Bouchet, H. Morant and R. Tondu. 6.7.1967-4.2.1971.	15.00	120.
	d. Signature G. Bouchet, H. Morant and P. Vergnes. 3.6.1971-6.12.1973.	10.00	55.00
	s. Specimen. As a-c. Overprint and perforated: *SPECIMEN.*	—	900.

		VF	UNC
148	**50 Francs**		
	1962-76. Multicolor. Port Royal des Champs Abbey at center, Jean Racine at right. Back: Jean Racine at left, view of La Ferté-Milon.		
	a. Signature G. Gouin d'Ambrieres, R. Tondu and P. Gargam. 7.6.1962-4.3.1965.	65.00	175.
	b. Signature H. Morant, R. Tondu and P. Gargam. 2.2.1967.	85.00	200.
	c. Signature H. Morant, R. Tondu and G. Bouchet. 7.12.1967-5.11.1970.	35.00	150.
	d. Signature G. Bouchet, P. Vergnes and H. Morant. 3.6.1971-3.10.1974.	20.00	125.
	e. Signature G. Bouchet, J. J. Tronche and H. Morant. 6.3.1975-2.10.1975.	20.00	125.
	f. Signature P. A. Strohl, G. Bouchet and J. J. Tronche. 2.1.1976-3.6.1976.	20.00	125.
	s. Specimen. Overprint and perforated: *SPECIMEN.*	—	750.

		VF	UNC
149	**100 Francs**		
	1964-79. Multicolor. Pierre Corneille at center, Theater in Versailles around. Back: Corneille's bust in cartouche at center, View of Rouen.		
	a. Signature R. Tondu. G. Gouin D'Ambrières and P. Gargam. 2.4.1964-2.12.1965.	35.00	200.
	b. Signature R. Tondu, H. Morant and P. Gargam. 3.2.1966-6.4.1967.	30.00	150.
	c. Signature R. Tondu, G. Bouchet and H. Morant. 5.10.1967-1.4.1971.	30.00	150.
	d. Signature P. Vergnes, G. Bouchet and H. Morant. 1.7.1971-3.10.1974.	25.00	100.
	e. Signature J. J. Tronche, G. Bouchet and H. Morant. 6.2.1975-6.11.1975.	25.00	100.
	f. Signature P. A. Strohl, G. Bouchet and J. J. Tronche. 2.1.1976-1.2.1979.	25.00	70.00
	s. Specimen. Overprint and perforated: *SPECIMEN.*	—	800.

1968-81 Issue

		VF	UNC
150	**10 Francs**		
	1972-78. Red, brown and olive. Hector Berlioz at right, conducting in the Chapelle des Invalides. Back: Berlioz at left, musical instrument at right and Rome's Villa Medici in background.		
	a. Signature H. Morant, G. Bouchet and P. Vergnes. 23.11.1972-3.10.1974.	7.50	50.00
	b. Signature H. Morant, G. Bouchet and J. J. Tronche. 6.2.1975-4.12.1975.	6.50	40.00
	c. Signature P. A. Strohl, G. Bouchet and J. J. Tronche. 2.1.1976-6.7.1978.	5.00	30.00
	s. Specimen. As b. Overprint and perforated: *SPECIMEN.*	—	600.

151 20 Francs	VF	UNC
1980-97. Dull violet, brown and multicolor. Claude Debussy at right, sea scene in background *(La Mer)*. Back: Claude Debussy at left, lake scene in background. Watermark: Claude Debussy. 140x75mm.		
a. Without security thread. Signature P. A. Strohl, J. J. Tronche and B. Dentaud. 1980-86.	7.50	75.00
b. Signature P. A. Strohl, D. Ferman and B. Dentaud. 1987.	5.00	45.00
c. Signature D. Ferman, B. Dentaud and A. Charriau. 1988; 1989.	4.00	35.00
d. With security thread. Signature as c. 1990.	FV	30.00
e. Signature D. Bruneel, B. Dentaud and A. Charriau. 1991.	FV	25.00
f. Signature D. Bruneel, J. Bonnardin and A. Charriau. 1992; 1993.	FV	25.00
g. Signature D. Bruneel, J. Bonnardin and C. Vigier. 1993.	FV	25.00
h. Signature as g. New *Ley* (law) on back. 1995.	FV	20.00
i. Signature D. Bruneel, J. Bonnardin and Y. Barroux. 1997.	FV	20.00
s. Specimen. Overprint and perforated: *SPECIMEN*.	—	500.

152 50 Francs	VF	UNC
1976-92. Deep blue-black on multicolor underprint. Maurice Quentin de la Tour at center right, and Palace of Versailles at left center in background. Back: Quentin de la Tour and St.Quentin City Hall at center right in background. Watermark: Maurice Quentin de la Tour.		
a. Signature P. A. Strohl, G. Bouchet and J. J. Tronche. 1976-79.	FV	75.00
b. Signature P. A. Strohl, J. J. Tronche and B. Dentaud. 1979-86.	FV	65.00
c. Signature P. A. Strohl, D. Ferman and B. Dentaud. 1987.	FV	80.00
d. Signature D. Ferman, B. Dentaud and A. Charriau. 1988; 1989.	FV	70.00
e. Signature D. Bruneel, B. Dentaud and A. Charriau. 1990; 1991.	FV	75.00
f. Signature D. Bruneel, J. Bonnardin and A. Charriau. 1992.	FV	80.00
s. Specimen. Overprint and perforated: *SPECIMEN*.	—	550.

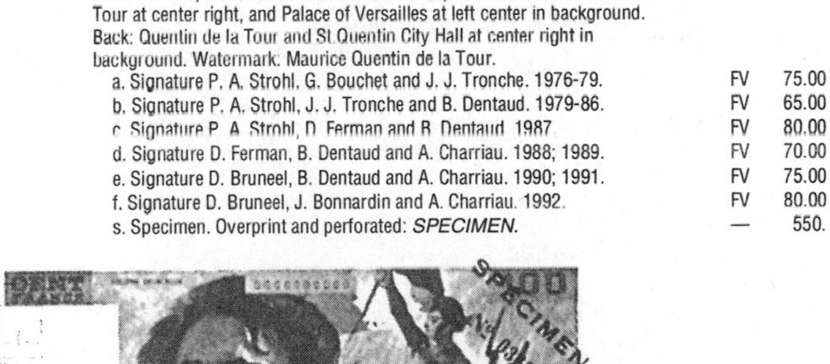

153 100 Francs	VF	UNC
1978. Brown. Eugène Delacroix at left center, Marianne holding tricolor, part of Delacroix's painting *La Liberté Guidant le Peuple* at right. Signature P. A. Strohl, G. Bouchet and J. J. Tronche. Back: Delacroix at right with quill pen. Watermark: Eugène Delacroix.	80.00	250.

154 100 Francs	VF	UNC
1978-95. Brown. Eugène Delacroix at left center. Marianne holding tricolor, park of Delacroix's painting *La Liberté Guident le Peuple at right. Like #153 but 100 CENT FRANCS retouched with heavier di* Back: Delacroix at right holding quill pen.		
a. Signature P. A. Strohl, G. Bouchet and J. J. Tronche. 1978-79.	45.00	175.
b. Signature P. A. Strohl, J. J. Tronche and B. Dentaud. 1979-86.	FV	75.00
c. Signature P. A. Strohl, D. Ferman and B. Dentaud. 1987.	FV	65.00
d. Signature D. Ferman, B. Dentaud and A. Charriau. 1988-90.	FV	65.00
e. Signature D. Bruneel, B. Dentaud and A. Charriau. 1990-91.	FV	125.
f. Signature D. Bruneel, J. Bonnardin and A. Charriau. 1991.	FV	125.
g. Signature D. Bruneel, J. Bonnardin and C. Vigier. 1993.	FV	65.00
h. Signature as g. New Ley (law) on back. 1994; 1995.	FV	65.00
s. Specimen. Overprint and perforated: *SPECIMEN*.	—	600.

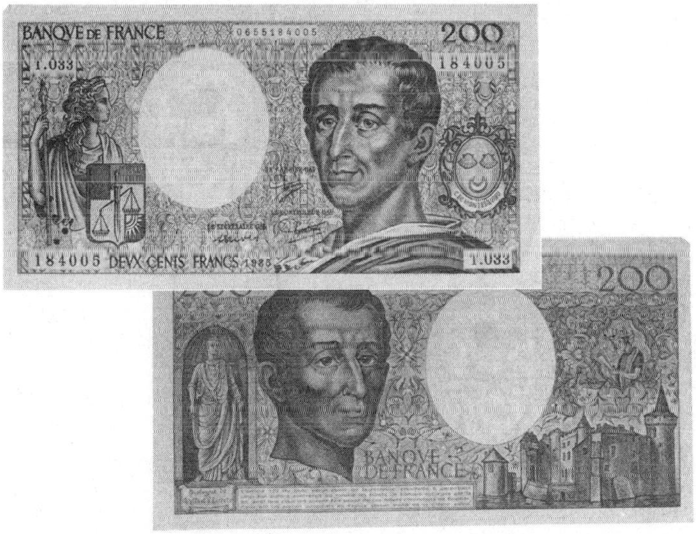

155 200 Francs	VF	UNC
1981-94. Blue-green, yellow and multicolor. Figure with staff at at left, Charles Baron de Montesquieu at right. Back: Montesquieu at left, Castle of Labrède on back (Montesquieu's birthplace). Watermark: Charles Baron de Montesquieu.		
a. Signature P. A. Strohl, J. J. Tronche and B. Dentaud. 1981-86.	FV	200.
b. Signature P. A. Strohl, D. Ferman and B. Dentaud. 1987.	FV	200.
c. Signature D. Ferman, B. Dentaud and A. Charriau. 1988; 1989.	FV	125.
d. Signature D. Bruneel, B. Dentaud and A. Charriau. 1990; 1991.	FV	125.
e. Signature D. Bruneel, J. Bonnardin and A. Charriau. 1992.	FV	90.00
f. Signature D. Bruneel, J. Bonnardin and C. Vigier. New Ley (law) on back. 1994.	FV	300.
s. Specimen. Overprint and perforated: *SPECIMEN*.	—	600.

156	500 Francs	VF	UNC
	1968-93. Yellow-brown and dark brown. Tower of St. Jacques in Paris at left, Blaise Pascal at center. Back: Blaise Pascal at left, abbey of Port Royal.		
	a. Signature G. Bouchet, R. Tondu and H. Morant. 4.1.1968-8.1.1970.	175.	600.
	b. Signature G. Bouchet, P. Vergnes and H. Morant. 5.8.1971-5.9.1974.	175.	600.
	c. Signature G. Bouchet, J. J. Tronche and H. Morant. 5.12.1974-6.11.1975.	125.	400.
	d. Signature P. A. Strohl, G. Bouchet and J. J. Tronche. 1.4.1976-7.6.1979.	110.	300.
	e. Signature P. A. Strohl, J. J. Tronche and B. Dentaud. 7.6.1979-6.2.1986.	FV	240.
	f. Signature P. A. Strohl, D. Ferman and B. Dentaud. 8.1.1987; 22.1.1987; 5.11.1987.	FV	240.
	g. Signature of D. Ferman, B. Dentaud and A. Charriau. 3.3.1988-1.2.1990.	FV	175.
	h. Signature D. Bruneel, B. Dentaud and A. Charriau. 5.7.1990-2.5.1991.	FV	160.
	i. Signature D. Bruneel, J. Bonnardin and A. Charriau. 3.10.1991-7.1.1993.	FV	160.
	j. Signature D. Bruneel, J. Bonnardin and C. Vigier. 2.9.1993.	FV	350.
	s. Specimen. Overprint and perforated: *SPECIMEN.*	—	700.

1993-97 Issue

#157-160 Many technical anti-counterfeiting devices added

157	50 Francs	VF	UNC
	1992-93. Purple and dark blue on blue, green and multicolor underprint. Drawing of *le Petit Prince* at left. Old airplane at top left, topographical map of Africa at center, Antoine de Saint-Exupéry at right. Back: Breguet XIV biplane. Name as Éxupéry, old law clause. Watermark: Antoine de Saint-Exupéry. 123x80mm.		
	a. Signature D. Bruneel, J. Bonnardin and A. Charriau. 1992.	FV	125.
	b. Signature D. Bruneel, J. Bonnardin and C. Vigier. 1993.	FV	75.00

157A	50 Francs	VF	UNC
	1994-99. Drawing of *le Petit Prince* at left. Old airplane at top left, topographical map of Africa at center, Antoine de Saint-Exupéry at right. Back: Breguet XIV biplane. Name as Exupéry, new law clause. 123x80mm.		
	a. Signature D. Bruneel, J. Bonnardin and C. Vigier. 1994. 8 cardinal points in compass solid. Underline *al.* in signature titles.	FV	35.00
	b. Signature D. Bruneel, J. Bonnardin and C. Vigier. 1994. 8 cardinal points in compass striped. without underlined *al.* in signature title.	FV	35.00
	c. Signature D. Bruneel, J. Bonnardin and Y. Barroux. 1996.	FV	45.00
	d. Signature as c. 1997, 1999.	FV	30.00

158	100 Francs	VF	UNC
	1997; 1998. Deep brown on orange, pink and light green underprint. Paul Cézanne at right. Signature D. Bruneel, J. Bonnardin and Y. Barroux. Back: Painting of fruit at left. Watermark: Paul Cézanne. 133x80mm.		
	a. Issued note.	FV	75.00
	s. Specimen.	—	600.

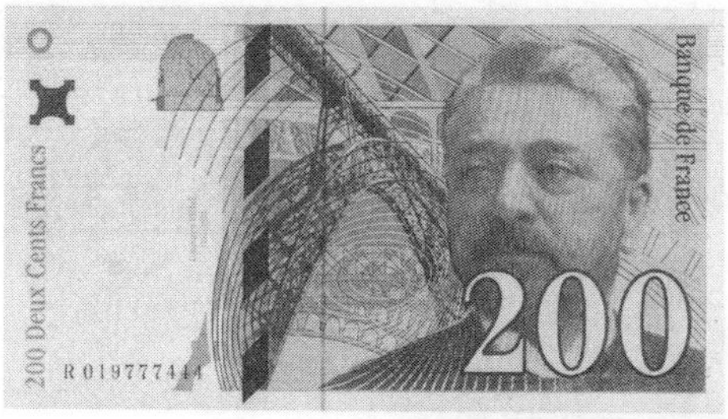

159	200 Francs	VF	UNC
	1995-99. Brown and pink on multicolor underprint. Gustave Eiffel at right, observatory at upper left center, Eiffel tower truss at center. Back: View through tower base across exhibition grounds at left. Watermark: Gustave Eiffel. 145x80mm.		
	a. Signature D. Bruneel, J. Bonnardin and C. Vigier. 1995; 1996.	FV	100.
	b. Signature D. Bruneel, J. Bonnardin and Y. Barroux. 1996; 1997.	FV	80.00
	c. Signature D. Bruneel, J. Bonnardin and Y. Barroux. 1999.	FV	75.00
	s. Specimen.	—	750.

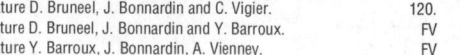

160	500 Francs	VF	UNC
	1994-2000. Dark green and black on multicolor underprint. Marie and Pierre Curie at center right. Segmented foil strip at left. Back: Laboratory utensils at left center. Watermark: Marie Curie. 154x80mm.		
	a. 1994-95. Signature D. Bruneel, J. Bonnardin and C. Vigier.	FV	250.
	b. 1996. Signature D. Bruneel, J. Bonnardin and C. Vigier.	120.	325.
	c. 1998. Signature D. Bruneel, J. Bonnardin and Y. Barroux.	FV	225.
	d. 2000. Signature Y. Barroux, J. Bonnardin, A. Vienney.	FV	200.
	s. Specimen.	—	750.

FRENCH AFARS & ISSAS

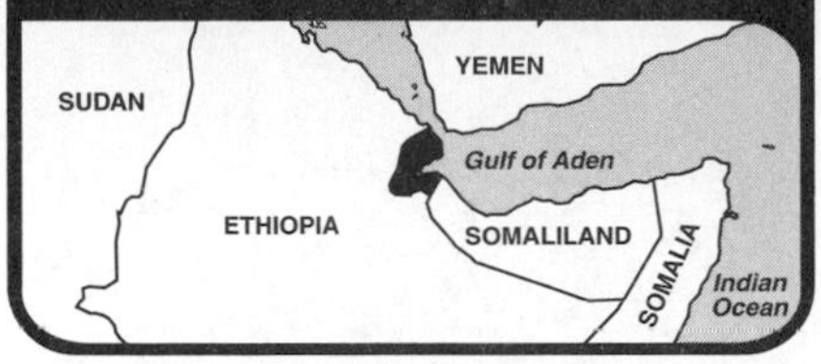

The French Overseas Territory of Afars and Issas (formerly French Somaliland, later to be independent as Djibouti) is located in northeast Africa at the Bab el Mandeb Strait connecting the Suez Canal and the Red Sea with the Gulf of Aden and the Indian Ocean, has an area of 8,494 sq. mi. (22,000 sq. km.) and a population of 542,000. Capital: Djibouti. The tiny nation has less than one sq. mi. of arable land, and no natural resources except salt, sand and camels. The commercial activities of the trans-shipment port of Djibouti and the Addis Ababa-Djibouti railroad are the basis of the economy. Salt, fish and hides are exported.

French interest in former French Somaliland began in 1839 with concessions obtained by a French naval lieutenant from the provincial sultans. French Somaliland was made a protectorate in 1884 and its boundaries were delimited by the Franco-British and Ethiopian accords of 1887 and 1897. It became a colony in 1896 and a territory within the French Union in 1946. In 1958, it voted to join the new French Community as an overseas territory, and reaffirmed that choice by a referendum in March 1967. Its name was changed from French Somaliland to the French Territory of Afars and Issas on July 5, 1967.

The French Tricolor, which had flown over the strategically important territory for 115 years, was lowered for the last time on June 27, 1977, when French Afars and Issas became Djibouti.

Note: For later issues see Djibouti.

RULERS:

French to 1977

MONETARY SYSTEM:

1 Franc = 100 Centimes

French Administration

Trésor Public, Territoire Français des Afars et des Issas

1969 ND Issue

		VF	UNC
30	**5000 Francs** ND (1969.). Multicolor. Aerial view of Djibouti harbor at center. Back: Ruins at center.	275.	750.

1973; 1974 ND Issue

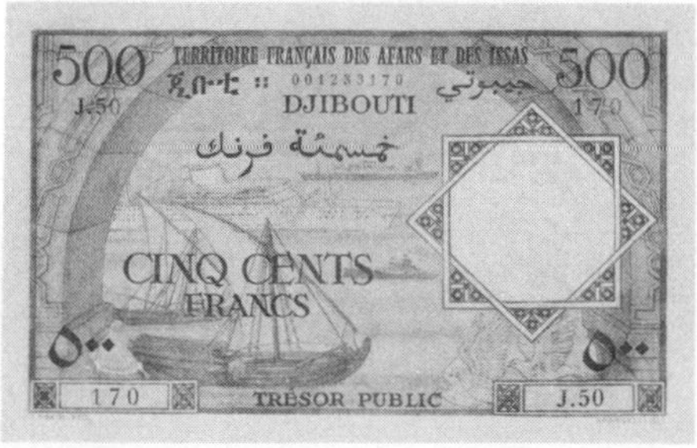

		VF	UNC
31	**500 Francs** ND (1973). Multicolor. Ships at left center. Back: Rearing antelope at center.	50.00	185.

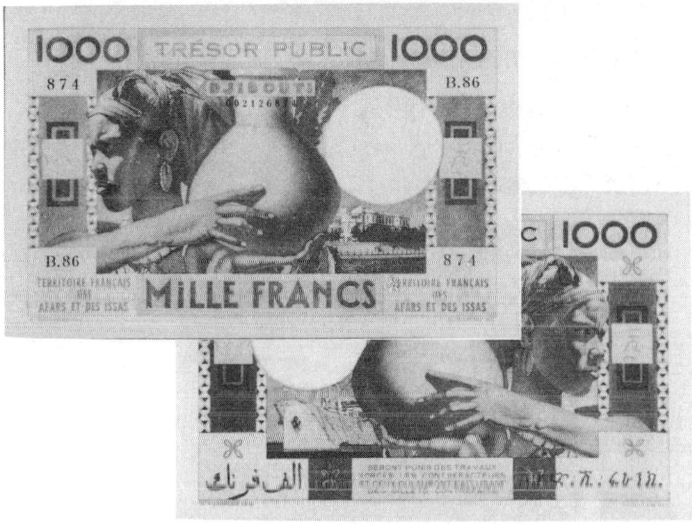

		VF	UNC
32	**1000 Francs** ND (1974). Multicolor. Woman holding jug at left center. Back: Woman holding jug, reversed image of note's face.	80.00	325.

1975 ND Issue

		VF	UNC
33	**500 Francs** ND (1975). Multicolor. Man at left, rocks in sea, storks at right. Back: Stern of ship at right.	20.00	80.00

		VF	UNC
34	**1000 Francs** ND (1975). Multicolor. Woman at left, people by diesel passenger trains at center. Back: Trader with camels.	35.00	150.

		VF	UNC
35	**5000 Francs** ND (1975). Multicolor. Man at right, forest scene at center. Back: Aerial view at center.	85.00	350.

FRENCH ANTILLES

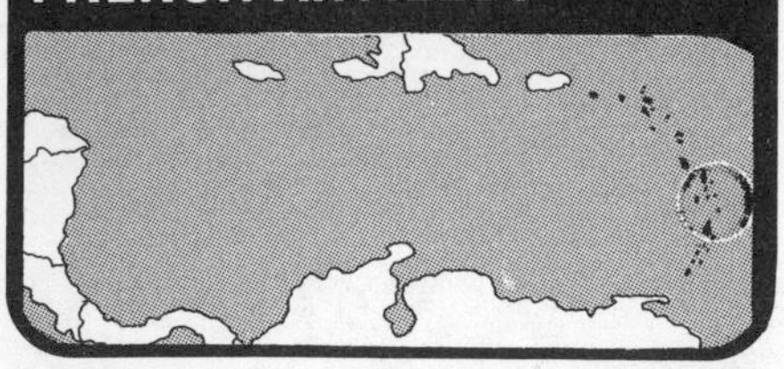

Three French overseas departments, Guiana, Guadeloupe and Martinique which issued a common currency from 1961-1975. Since 1975 Bank of France notes have circulated.

RULERS:
French

MONETARY SYSTEM:
1 Nouveau Franc = 100 "old" Francs
1 Franc = 100 Centimes

French Administration

Institut d'Emission des Départements d'Outre-Mer

1961 ND Provisional Issue

Nouveau Franc System

1 **1 Nouveau Franc on 100 Francs** — VF | UNC
ND (1961). Multicolor. La Bourdonnais at left. Signature 1. Back: Woman at right. Overprint: *GUADELOUPE, GUYANE, MARTINIQUE.*

	VF	UNC
a. Issued note.	250.	750.
s. Specimen.	—	600.

2 **10 Nouveaux Francs on 1000 Francs** — VF 1000. UNC 3000.
ND (1961). Multicolor. Fishermen from the Antilles. Signature 1. Overprint: *GUADELOUPE, GUYANE, MARTINIQUE.*

3 **50 Nouveaux Francs on 5000 Francs** — VF | UNC
ND (1961). Multicolor. Woman with fruit bowl at center right. Signature 1. Overprint: *GUADELOUPE, GUYANE, MARTINIQUE.*

	VF	UNC
a. Issued note.	1250.	3500.
s. Specimen.	—	2000.

Second 1961 ND Provisional Issue

4 **5 Nouveaux Francs on 500 Francs** — VF | UNC
ND (1961). Brown on multicolor underprint. Sailboat at left, two women at right. Signature 1. Back: Men with carts containing plants and wood. Overprint: *DEPARTEMENT DE LA GUADELOUPE - DEPARTEMENT DE LA GUYANE - DEPARTEMENT DE LA MARTINIQUE.*

	VF	UNC
a. Issued note.	650.	2000.
s. Specimen.	—	2500.

Institut d'Emission des Départements d'Outre-Mer République Francaise

1963 ND Issue

5 **10 Nouveaux Francs** — VF | UNC
ND (1963). Brown and green on multicolor underprint. Girl at right, coastal scenery in background. Signature 1. Back: People cutting sugar cane. Overprint: *DEPARTEMENT DE LA GUADELOUPE - DEPARTEMENT DE LA GUYANE - DEPARTEMENT DE LA MARTINIQUE.*

	VF	UNC
a. Issued note.	200.	650.
s. Specimen.	—	550.

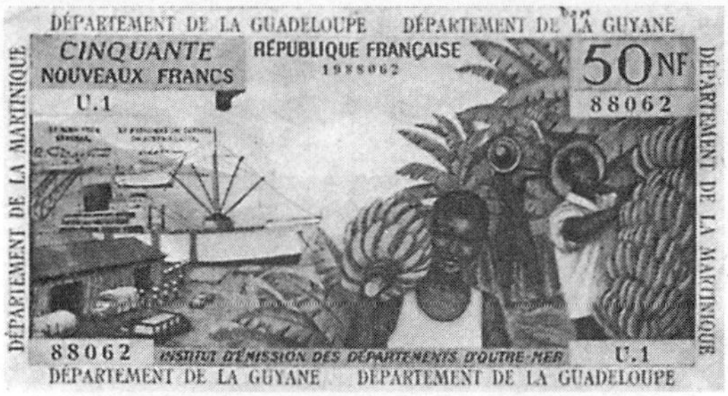

6	50 Nouveaux Francs	VF	UNC
	ND (1963). Green on multicolor underprint. Banana harvest. Signature 1. Back: Shoreline with houses at left, man and woman at right. Overprint: *DEPARTEMENT DE LA GUADELOUPE - DEPARTEMENT DE LA GUYANE - DEPARTEMENT DE LA MARTINIQUE.*		
	a. Issued note.	325.	1100.
	s. Specimen.	—	1000.

1964 ND Issue

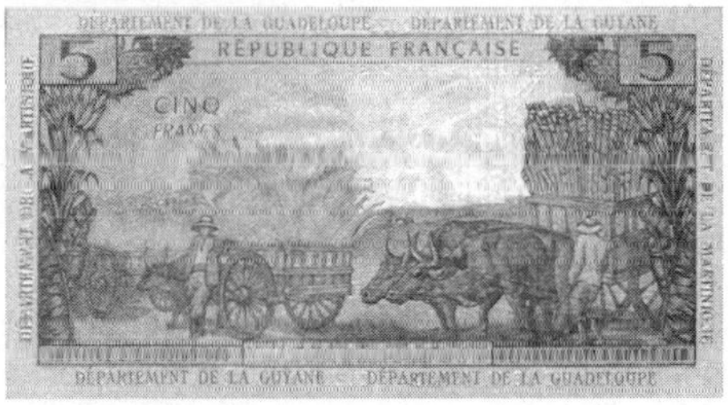

7	5 Francs	VF	UNC
	ND (1964). Brown on multicolor underprint. Sailboat at left, two women at right. Back: Men with carts containing plants and wood. Overprint: *DEPARTEMENT DE LA GUADELOUPE - DEPARTEMENT DE LA GUYANE - DEPARTEMENT DE LA MARTINIQUE.* Like #4, but smaller size.		
	a. Signature 1.	300.	1100.
	b. Signature 2.	250.	950.
	s. As b. Specimen.	—	—

8	10 Francs	VF	UNC
	ND (1964). Green on multicolor underprint. Banana harvest. Back: Shoreline with houses at left, man and woman at right. Overprint: *DEPARTEMENT DE LA GUADELOUPE - DEPARTEMENT DE LA GUYANE - DEPARTEMENT DE LA MARTINIQUE.*		
	a. Signature 1.	185.	600.
	b. Signature 2.	150.	500.

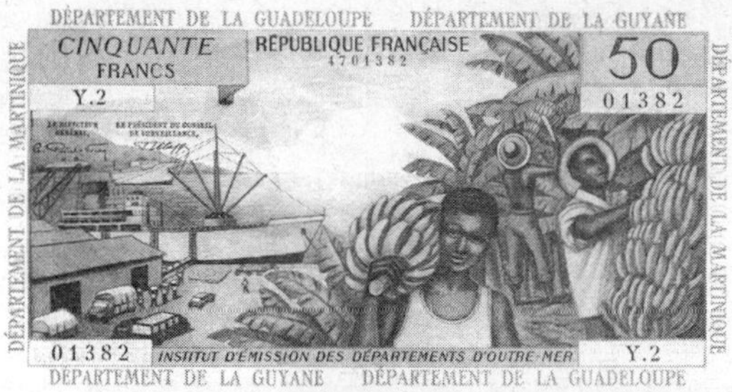

9	50 Francs	VF	UNC
	ND (1964). Banana harvest. Back: Shoreline with houses at left, man and woman at right. Overprint: *DEPARTEMENT DE LA GUADELOUPE - DEPARTEMENT DE LA GUYANE - DEPARTEMENT DE LA MARTINIQUE.*		
	a. Signature 1.	300.	1000.
	b. Signature 2.	275.	900.

10	100 Francs	VF	UNC
	ND (1964). Brown and multicolor. General Schoelcher at center right. Back: Schoelcher at left center, various arms and galleon around. Overprint: *DEPARTEMENT DE LA GUADELOUPE - DEPARTEMENT DE LA GUYANE - DEPARTEMENT DE LA MARTINIQUE.*		
	a. Signature 1.	500.	1500.
	b. Signature 2.	450.	1350.

The French Overseas Department of French Guiana, located on the northeast coast of South America, bordered by Surinam and Brazil, has an area of 32,252 sq. mi. (91,000 sq. km.) and a population of 173,000. Capital: Cayenne. Placer gold mining and shrimp processing are the chief industries. Shrimp, lumber, gold, cocoa and bananas are exported.

The coast of Guiana was sighted by Columbus in 1498 and explored by Amerigo Vespucci in 1499. The French established the first successful trading stations and settlements, and placed the area under direct control of the French Crown in 1674. Portuguese and British forces occupied French Guiana for five years during the Napoleonic Wars. Devil's Island, the notorious penal colony in French Guiana where Capt. Alfred Dreyfus was imprisoned, was established in 1852 - and finally closed in 1947. When France adopted a new constitution in 1946, French Guiana voted to remain within the French Union as an overseas department.

Note: For later issues see French Antilles.

RULERS:

French

MONETARY SYSTEM:

1 Franc = 10 Decimes = 100 Centimes to 1960
1 Nouveau (new) Franc = 100 "old" Francs, 1961-

French Administration

Caisse Centrale de la France d'Outre-Mer

1961 ND Provisional Issue

		VF	UNC
29	**1 Nouveau Franc on 100 Francs** ND (1961). Multicolor. La Bourdonnais at left, women at right. Back: B. d'Esnambuc at left, sailing ship at right. Overprint: *GUYANE*	45.00	325.
30	**5 Nouveaux Francs on 500 Francs** ND (1961). Multicolor. Sailboat at left, two women at right. Overprint: *GUYANE* Overprint on #24.	165.	675.
31	**10 Nouveaux Francs on 1000 Francs** ND (1961). Multicolor. Fishermen. Overprint: *GUYANE*	500.	1300.
32	**10 Nouveaux Francs on 1000 Francs** ND. Multicolor. Two women at right. Back: Woman at right. Overprint: *GUYANE*	350.	900.
33	**50 Nouveaux Francs on 5000 Francs** ND. Multicolor. Woman with fruit bowl. Overprint: *GUYANE*	800.	1800.

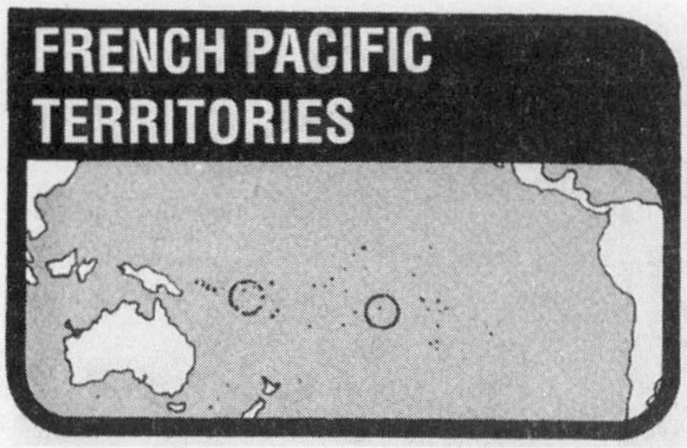

The French Pacific Territories include French Polynesia, New Caledonia and formerly the New Hebrides Condominium. For earlier issues also refer to French Oceania and Tahiti.

French Administration

Institut d'Emission d'Outre-Mer

1985-96 ND Issue

Notes w/o *NOUMEA* **or** *PAPEETE*.

Above notes in CPF francs (change frans Pacifique). Common currency of French Polynesia, New Caledonia, and Wallis & Futuna Islands. Design types of # 1-3 like issues for New Caledonia and New Hebrides but without NOUMEA or PAPEETE. Signature varieties correspond to those used for New Caledonia and New Hebrides issues.

		VF	UNC
1	**500 Francs** ND (1992). Multicolor. Sailboat at center, fisherman at right. Back: Man at left, objects at right. 150x80mm.		
	a. 2 signatures. Without security thread. Signature 2.	FV	25.00
	b. 3 Signatures. With security thread. Signature 3.	FV	20.00

		VF	UNC
2	**1000 Francs** ND (1996). Multicolor. Hut in palm trees at left, girl at right. 160x85mm.		
	a. Signature 3.	FV	32.50
	b. Signature 4.	FV	30.00

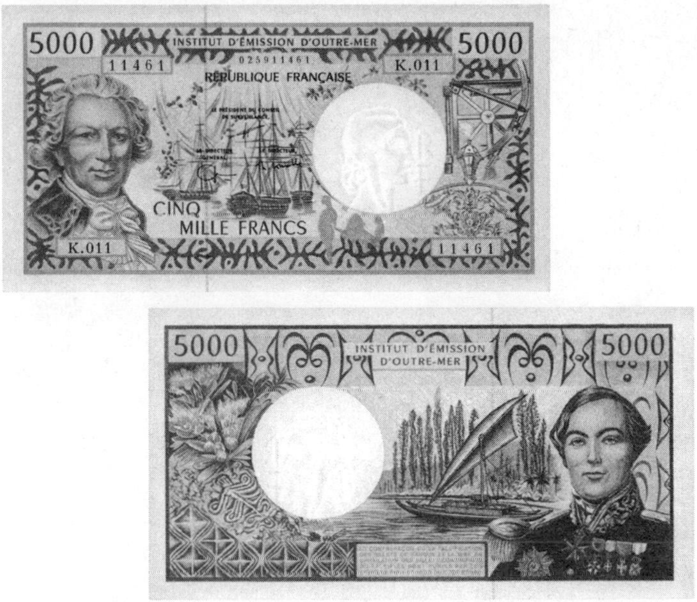

3	5000 Francs	VF	UNC
	ND (1996). Multicolor. Bougainville at left, sailing ships at center. Signature 3. 172x90mm.		
	a. Issued note.	FV	140.
	s. Specimen. Perforated cancelled.	—	750.

4	10,000 Francs	VF	UNC
	ND (1985). Multicolor. Tahitian girl with floral headdress at upper left topuristic bungalows at center. Back: Fish at center, Melanesian girl wearing flower at right on back. Watermark: Two ethnic heads. 172x92mm.		
	a. 2 signatures. Without security thread. Signature 1.	FV	250.
	b. 3 signatures. With security thread. (New Ley on back.) Signature 5.	FV	225.

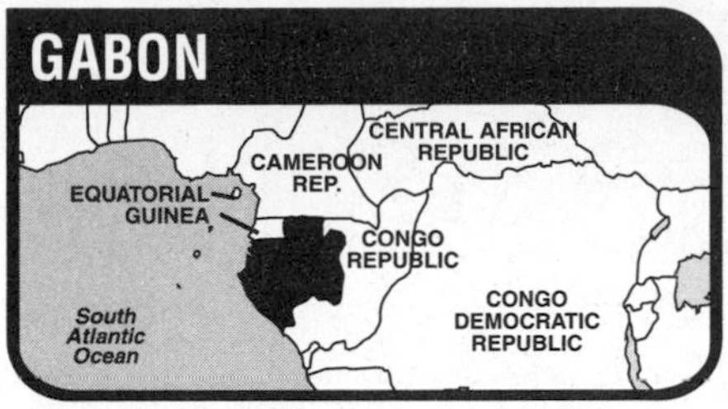

The Gabonese Republic, a member of the French Community, straddles the equator on the west coast of Africa. The hot and humid rain forest country has an area of 267,667 sq. km. and a population of 1.48 million, almost all of Bantu origin. Capital: Libreville. Extravagantly rich in resources, Gabon exports crude oil, manganese ore, gold and timbers.

Only two autocratic presidents have ruled Gabon since independence from France in 1960. The current president of Gabon, El Hadj Omar Bongo Ondimba - one of the longest-serving heads of state in the world - has dominated the country's political scene for four decades. President Bongo introduced a nominal multiparty system and a new constitution in the early 1990s. However, allegations of electoral fraud during local elections in 2002-03 and the presidential elections in 2005 have exposed the weaknesses of formal political structures in Gabon. Gabon's political opposition remains weak, divided, and financially dependent on the current regime. Despite political conditions, a small population, abundant natural resources, and considerable foreign support have helped make Gabon one of the more prosperous and stable African countries.

Note: For related currency, see the Equatorial African States.

RULERS:

French to 1960

MONETARY SYSTEM:

1 Franc = 100 Centimes

SIGNATURE VARIETIES:

Refer to introduction to Central African States.

République Gabonaise

Banque Centrale

1971 ND Issue

1	10,000 Francs	VF	UNC
	ND (1971). Multicolor. President O. Bongo at right, mask at left, mine elevator at center. Signature 1. Back: Statue at left and right, tractor plowing at center.		
	a. Issued note.	200.	750.
	s. Specimen. Overprinted and perforated: *SPECIMEN.*	—	850.

Banque des États de l'Afrique Centrale

1974 ND Issue

2 **500 Francs** VF UNC

ND (1974); 1978. Lilac-brown on multicolor underprint. Woman wearing kerchief at left, logging at center. Back: Mask at left, students and chemical testing at center, statue at right.

	VF	UNC
a. Engraved. Signature 6. ND (1974).	7.00	30.00
b. Lithographed. Signature 9. 1.4.1978.	5.00	20.00

3 **1000 Francs** VF UNC

ND (1974; 1978); 1978-84. Red and blue on multicolor underprint. Ship and oil refinery at center, President O. Bongo at right. Back: Mask at left, trains, planes and bridge at center, statue at right.

	VF	UNC
a. Signature 4 with titles: *LE DIRECTEUR GÉNÉRAL* and *UN CENSEUR*. Engraved. Watermark: Antelope head in half profile. ND (1974).	150.	350.
b. Like a. Signature 6.	25.00	80.00
c. Signature 6 with titles: *LE DIRECTEUR GÉNÉRAL* and *UN CENSEUR*. Lithographed. Watermark: Antelope head in profile. ND (1978).	15.00	50.00
d. Signature 9 with titles: *LE GOUVERNEUR* and *UN CENSEUR*. Lithographed. Watermark: Antelope head in profile. 1.4.1978; 1.1.1983; 1.6.1984.	10.00	35.00

4 **5000 Francs** VF UNC

ND (1974; 1978). Brown. Oil refinery at left, open pit mining and President O. Bongo at right. Back: Mask at left, buildings at center, statue at right.

	VF	UNC
a. Signature 4 with titles: *LE DIRECTEUR GENERAL* and *UN CENSEUR*. ND (1974).	100.	400.
b. Like a. Signature 6.	50.00	200.
c. Signature 9 with titles: *LE GOUVERNEUR* and *UN CENSEUR*. ND (1978).	50.00	200.
x1. Error. As a. Without signature.	60.00	200.
x2. Error. As c. Without signature.	50.00	200.

5 **10,000 Francs** VF UNC

ND (1974; 1978). Multicolor. Prisident O. Bongo at right, mask at left, mine elevator at center. Back: Statue at left and right, tractor polwing at center, new bank name.

	VF	UNC
a. Signature 6 with titles: *LE DIRECTEUR GÉNÉRAL* and *UN CENSEUR*. ND (1974).	75.00	250.
b. Signature 9 with titles: *LE GOUVERNEUR* and *UN CENSEUR*. ND (1978).	50.00	200.
s. Specimen. Perforated and overprint *SPECIMEN*..	—	350.

1983; 1984 ND Issue

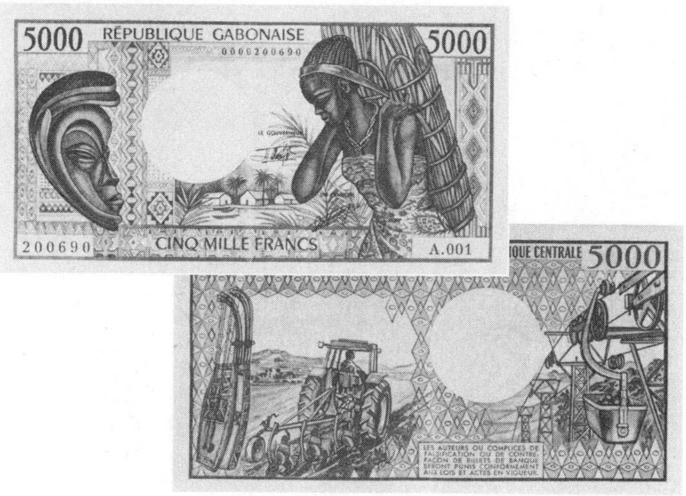

6 **5000 Francs** VF UNC

ND (1984-91). Brown on multicolor underprint. Mask at left, woman with fronds at right. Back: Plowing and mine ore conveyor.

	VF	UNC
a. Signature 9. (1984).	20.00	75.00
b. Signature 14. (1991).	15.00	50.00
s. As a. Specimen. Overprinted and perforated: *SPECIMEN*.	—	250.

		VF	UNC
7	**10,000 Francs** ND (1983-91). Brown and green on multicolor underprint. Stylized antelope heads at left, woman at right. Back: Loading fruit onto truck at left.		
	a. Signature 9. (1984).	35.00	150.
	b. Signature 14. (1991).	25.00	100.
	s. Specimen. Perforated and overprint *SPECIMEN.*	—	150.

1985 Issue

		VF	UNC
8	**500 Francs** 1.1.1985. Brown on orange and multicolor underprint. Carving and jug at center. Signature 9. Back: Man carving mask at left center. Watermark: Carving.	4.00	15.00

		VF	UNC
9	**1000 Francs** 1.1.1985. Deep blue on multicolor underprint. Carving at left, map at center, President O. Bongo at right. Incomplete outline map of Chad at top center. Signature 9. Back: Elephant at left, animals at center, man carving at right. Watermark: Carving.	9.50	35.00

1986 Issue

		VF	UNC
10	**1000 Francs** 1986-91. Deep blue on multicolor underprint. Carving at left, map at center, President O. Bongo at right. Complete outline map of Chad at top center. Back: Elephant at left, animals at center, man carving at right.		
	a. Signature 9. 1.1.1986; 1.1.1987; 1.1.1990.	7.50	30.00
	b. Signature 14. 1.1.1991.	7.00	25.00

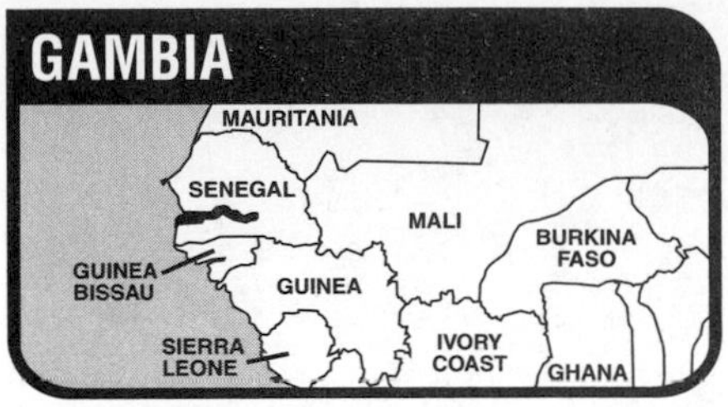

The Republic of The Gambia, an independent member of the British Commonwealth, occupies a long strip of land encompassing both sides of West Africa's Gambia River, and completely surrounded by Senegal. The republic, one of Africa's smallest , has an area of 11,300 sq. km. and a population of 1.76 million. Capital: Banjul. Agriculture and tourism are the principal industries. Peanuts constitute 95 per cent of export earnings.

The Gambia gained its independence from the UK in 1965. Geographically surrounded by Senegal, it formed a short-lived federation of Senegambia between 1982 and 1989. In 1991 the two nations signed a friendship and cooperation treaty, but tensions have flared up intermittently since then. Yahya A. J. J. Jammeh led a military coup in 1994 that overthrew the president and banned political activity. A new constitution and presidential elections in 1996, followed by parliamentary balloting in 1997, completed a nominal return to civilian rule. Jammeh has been elected president in all subsequent elections, including most recently in late 2006.

RULERS:

British to 1970

MONETARY SYSTEM:

1 Shilling = 12 Pence
1 Pound = 20 Shillings to 1970
1 Dalasi = 100 Bututs 1970-

REPLACEMENT NOTES:

#13-16, Z prefix.

SIGNATURE VARIETIES

1	CHAIRMAN / DIRECTOR	10	GENERAL MANAGER / GOVERNOR
2	GENERAL MANAGER / GOVERNOR	11	
3		12	
4		13	
5		14	
6		15	
8		16	
9	GENERAL MANAGER / GOVERNOR		

British Administration

The Gambia Currency Board

1965 ND Issue

Pound System

1 10 Shillings

ND (1965-70). Green and brown on multicolor underprint. Sailboat at left. Signature 1. Back: Workers in field. Watermark: Crocodile's head.

	VF	UNC
a. Issued note.	25.00	150.
s. Specimen.	—	235.
ct. Color trial. Blue and green on multicolor underprint.	—	350.

2 1 Pound

ND (1965-70). Red and brown on multicolor underprint. Sailboat at left. Signature 1. Back: Loading sacks at dockside. Watermark: Crocodile's head.

	VF	UNC
a. Issued note.	40.00	205.
s. Specimen.	—	290.
ct. Color trial. Brown and gray on multicolor underprint.	—	400.

3 5 Pounds

ND (1965-70). Blue and green on multicolor underprint. Sailboat at left. Signature 1. Back: Blue. Man and woman operating agricultural machine at center right. Watermark: Crocodile's head.

	VF	UNC
a. Issued note.	90.00	350.
s. Specimen.	—	525.
ct. Color trial. Gray-brown and green on multicolor underprint.	—	450.

Republic

Central Bank of The Gambia

1971; 1972 ND Issue

Dalasi System

4 1 Dalasi

ND (1971-87). Purple on multicolor underprint. Sailboat at left, Pres. D. Kairaba Jawara at right. Back: Workers in field. Watermark: Crocodile's head.

	VF	UNC
a. Signature 2.	35.00	100.
b. Signature 3.	45.00	105.
c. Signature 4.	15.00	52.50
d. Signature 5.	10.00	31.00
e. Signature 6.	4.75	14.00
f. Signature 7.	4.50	8.75
g. Signature 8.	9.00	14.50
p. Proof.	—	500.
s. Specimen. Overprint: *SPECIMEN* and Punch hole cancelled.	—	170.

5 5 Dalasis

ND (1972-86). Red on multicolor underprint. Sailboat at left, Pres. D. Kairaba Jawara at right. Back: Loading sacks at dockside. Watermark: Crocodile's head.

	VF	UNC
a. Signature 2.	75.00	185.
b. Signature 4.	15.00	90.00
c. Signature 6.	10.00	48.00
d. Signature 7.	9.00	30.00
s. Specimen. Overprint: *SPECIMEN* and Punch hole cancelled.	—	145.

6 10 Dalasis

ND (1972-86). Green on multicolor underprint. Sailboat at left, Pres. D. Kairaba Jawara at right. Back: Fishermen in boat with net. Watermark: Crocodile's head.

	VF	UNC
a. Signature 3.	30.00	145.
b. Signature 6.	15.00	65.00
c. Signature 7.	15.00	60.00
s. Specimen. Overprint: *SPECIMEN* and Punch hole cancelled.	—	300.
ct. Color trial. Purple-brown on multicolor underprint.	—	400.

7 25 Dalasis

ND (1972-83). Blue on multicolor underprint. Sailboat at left, Pres. D. Kairaba Jawara at right. Back: Man and woman operating agricultural machine at left center. Watermark: Crocodile's head.

	VF	UNC
a. Signature 2.	150.	700.
b. Signature 6.	40.00	150.
s. As a, b. Specimen. Overprint: *SPECIMEN* and Punch hole cancelled.	—	550.
ct. Color trial. Slate on multicolor underprint.	—	750.

1978 ND Commemorative Issue

#8, Opening of Central Bank on 18.2.1978

8 **1 Dalasi**

ND (1978). Purple on multicolor underprint. Sailboat at left, Pres. D. Kairaba Jawara at right. Signature 5. Back: Central Bank building on back; commemorative legend beneath. Watermark: Crocodile's head.

	VF	UNC
a. Issued note.	30.00	120.
s. Specimen. Overprint: *SPECIMEN* and Punch hole cancelled.	—	200.

1987 ND Issue

9 **5 Dalasis**

ND (1987-90). Red and orange on multicolor underprint. Sailboat at left, President D. Kairaba Jawara at right, line of microprint under text: *PROMISE TO PAY*. Back: Fishermen in boat with net. Watermark: Crocodile's head.

	VF	UNC
a. Signature 8.	8.00	41.00
b. Signature 10.	7.00	20.00

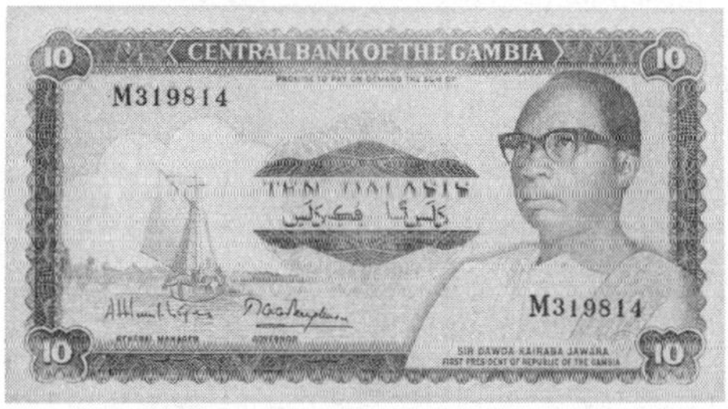

10 **10 Dalasis**

ND 91987-90). Green on multicolor underprint. Sailboat at left, Pres. D. Kairaba Jawara at right, line of microprint under text: *PROMISE TO PAY*. Back: Green and light olive. Fishermen in boat with net. Watermark: Crocodile's head.

	VF	UNC
a. Signature 8 with title: *GOVERNOR* at right.	10.00	35.00
b. Signature 9 with title: *ACTING GOVERNOR* at right.	10.00	26.00

11 **25 Dalasis**

ND (1987-90). Blue on multicolor underprint. Sailboat at left, Pres. D. Kairaba Jawara at right, line of microprint under text: *PROMISE TO PAY*. Back: Blue, black and aqua. Man and woman operating agricultural machine at left center. Watermark: Crocodile's head.

	VF	UNC
a. Signature 8 with title: *GOVERNOR* at right.	30.00	220.
b. Signature 9 with title: *ACTING GOVERNOR* at right.	22.50	115.
c. Signature 10.	17.00	90.00
s. Specimen.	—	300.

1989-91 ND Issue

#12-15 Replacement notes: serial # prefix *Z/1*.

12 **5 Dalasis**

ND (1991-95). Red and orange on multicolor underprint. Giant Kingfisher at center, Pres. D Kairaba Jawara at right. Microprinting of bank name above and below title. Back: Herding cattle. Watermark: Crocodile's head. 132x69mm.

	VF	UNC
a. Signature 10.	4.00	22.00
b. Signature 11.	5.50	8.00
s. Specimen.	—	90.00

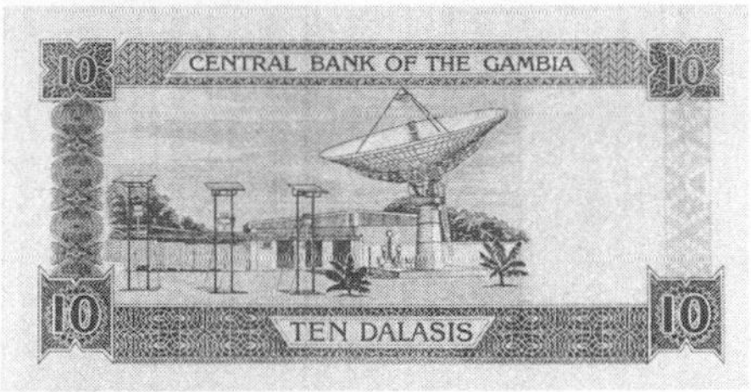

13 **10 Dalasis**

ND (1991-95). Dark green, green and olive-green on multicolor underprint. Sacred Ibis at center, Pres. D Kairaba Jawara at right. Microprinting of bank name above and below title. Back: Abuko Earth satellite station at left center. Watermark: Crocodile's head. 138x72mm.

	VF	UNC
a. Signature 10.	7.00	12.00
b. Signature 11.	6.00	10.75
s. Specimen.	—	90.00

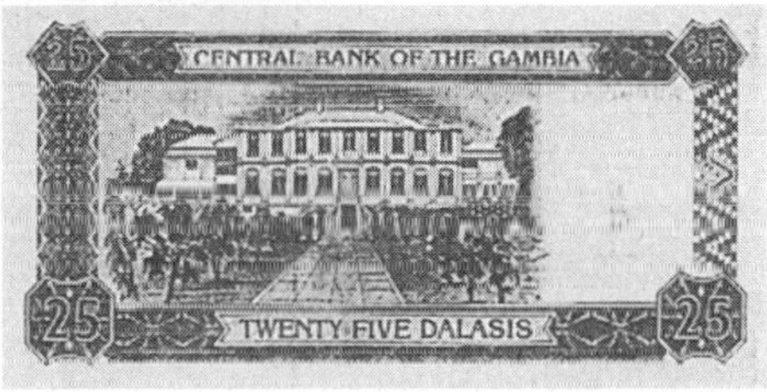

14 **25 Dalasis**

ND (1991-95). Dark blue-violet, black and blue on multicolor underprint. Carmine Bee Eater at center, Pres. D Kairaba Jawara at right. Microprinting of bank name above and below title. Signature 10. Back: Government house at left center. Watermark: Crocodile's head. 144x75mm.

	VF	UNC
a. Issued note.	9.00	23.00
s. Specimen.	—	200.

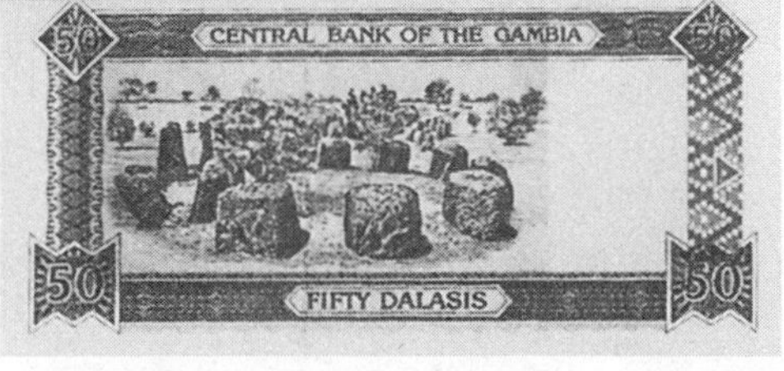

15 **50 Dalasis**

ND (1989-95). Purple and violet on multicolor underprint. Hoopoe birds at center, Pres. D. Kairaba Jawara at right. Microprinting of bank name above and below title. Signature 10. Back: Stone circles at Wassu. Watermark: Crocodile's head. 154x78mm.

	VF	UNC
a. Issued note.	25.00	50.00
s. Specimen.	—	145.

1996 ND Issue

#16-19 Replacement notes: Serial # prefix *Z*.

16 5 Dalasis VF UNC

ND (1996). Red, orange and dark brown on multicolor underprint. Giant Kingfisher at center, young girl a right. Signature 12. Back: Herding cattle. Watermark: Crocodile's head, without imprint. 132x69mm.

	VF	UNC
a. Issued note.	3.50	5.00
s. Specimen.	—	90.00

17 10 Dalasis VF UNC

ND (1996). Dark green, bright green and olive-green on multicolor underprint. Sacred Ibis at center, young boy at right. Signature 12. Back: Abuko Earth satellite station at left center. Watermark: Crocodile's head, without imprint. 138x72mm.

	VF	UNC
a. Issued note.	4.25	8.00
s. Specimen.	—	90.00

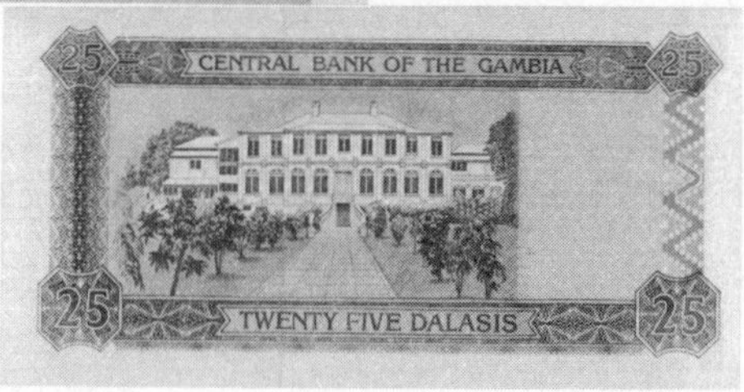

18 25 Dalasis VF UNC

ND (1996). Deep blue-violet, black and blue on multicolor underprint. Carmine Bee Eater at center, man at right. Signature 12. Back: Government house at left center. Watermark: Crocodile's head, without imprint. 144x75mm.

	VF	UNC
a. Issued note.	9.00	16.00
s. Specimen.	—	90.00

19 50 Dalasis VF UNC

ND (1996). Purple and violet on multicolor underprint. Hoopoe birds at center, woman at right. Signature 12. Back: Stone circles a Wassu. Watermark: Crocodile's head, without imprint. 154x78mm.

	VF	UNC
a. Issued note.	17.50	35.00
s. Specimen.	—	95.00

2001 ND Issue

20 5 Dalasis VF UNC

ND (2001). Multicolor. Giant Kingfisher at center, young girl at right. Signature 12. Ascending size vertical serial number. Back: Herding cattle. Watermark: Crocodile's head, without imprint. 132x69mm.

	VF	UNC
a. Signature 13.	FV	4.00
b. Signature 14.	FV	3.50
c. Signature 15.	FV	2.50

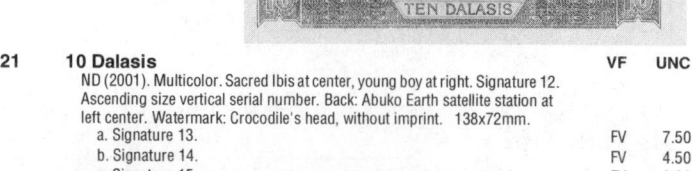

21 10 Dalasis VF UNC

ND (2001). Multicolor. Sacred Ibis at center, young boy at right. Signature 12. Ascending size vertical serial number. Back: Abuko Earth satellite station at left center. Watermark: Crocodile's head, without imprint. 138x72mm.

	VF	UNC
a. Signature 13.	FV	7.50
b. Signature 14.	FV	4.50
c. Signature 15.	FV	3.00

22	25 Dalasis	VF	UNC
	ND (2001). Multicolor. Carmine Bee Eater at center, man at right. Ascending size vertical serial number. Signature 12. Back: Government house at left center. Watermark: Crocodile's head, without imprint. 144x75mm.		
	a. Signature 13.	FV	15.00
	b. Signature 14.	FV	8.00
	c. Signatrure 15.	FV	5.00

23	50 Dalasis	VF	UNC
	ND (2001). Multicolor. Hoopoe birds at center, woman at right. Ascending size vertical serial number. Signature 12. Back: Stone circles at Wassu. Watermark: Crocodile's head, without imprint. 154x78mm.		
	a. Signature 13.	10.00	14.00
	b. Signature 14.	7.50	10.00
	c. Signature 15.	FV	6.00

24	100 Dalasis	VF	UNC
	ND (2001). Multicolor. Senegal Parrot at center, male bust facing at right. Watermark: Crocodile's head, without imprint. 157x81mm.		
	a. Signature 13.	12.50	20.00
	b. Signature 14.	15.00	40.00
	c. Signature 15.	FV	8.50

2006 ND Issue

25	5 Dalasis	VF	UNC
	2006. Multicolor. Giant Kingfisher at center, young girl at right. Signature 15. Back: Hearding cattle. 132x69mm.	FV	2.00

26	10 Dalasis	VF	UNC
	2006. Multicolor. Sacred Ibis at center, young boy at right. Signature 15. Back: Abuko Earth satellite station at left center. 138x72mm.	FV	3.00

27	25 Dalasis	VF	UNC
	2006. Multicolor. Carmine Bee Eater at cetner, man at right. Signature 15. Back: Government house at left center. 144x75mm.	FV	4.00

28	50 Dalasis	VF	UNC
	2006. Multicolor. Hoopoe birds at center, woman at right. Back: Stone circles at Wassu. 154x78mm.		
	a. Signature 15.	FV	6.00
	b. Signature 16.	FV	6.00

29	100 Dalasis	VF	UNC
	2006; 2010. Multicolor. Back: Arch 22 Monument. 157x81mm.		
	a. Signature 15. Hologram with value on left center.	FV	11.00
	b. Signature 16. Hologram with man's head.	FV	11.00

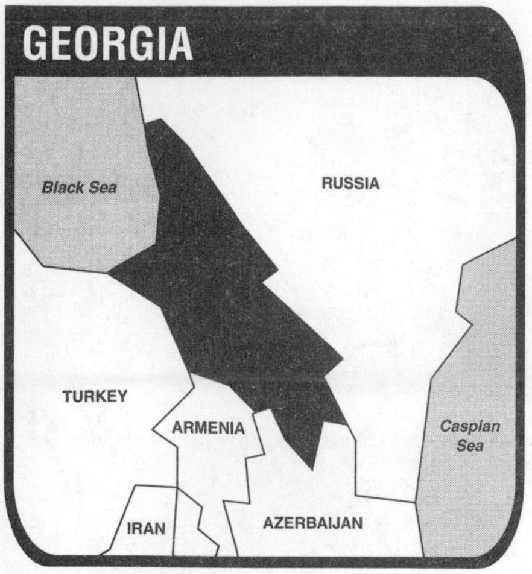

MONETARY SYSTEM:

1 Lari = 100 Thetri to 1995
1 Lari = 1,000,000 'old' Laris, 1995-

REPUBLIC OF GEORGIA

GEORGIAN NATIONAL BANK

FIRST 1993 *KUPONI* ND ISSUE

#25-32 Fractional serial # prefix w/1 as denominator.

			VF	UNC
25	**5 (Laris)**	ND (1993). Dull brown on lilac underprint. View of Tbilisi at center right with equestrian statue of King V. Gorgosal in foreground, Mount Tatzminda in background. Rosettes at sides of value. Back: Cave dwellings at left center. Rosettes at sides of value. Watermark: Hexagonal design repeated.	1.00	4.00

			VF	UNC
26	**10 (Laris)**	ND (1993). Yellow-brown on lilac underprint. View of Tbilisi at center right with equestrian statue of King V. Gorgosal in foreground, Mount Tatzminda in background. Back: Cave dwellings at left center. Watermark: Hexagonal design repeated.	1.00	6.00

			VF	UNC
27	**50 (Laris)**	ND (1993). Light blue on lilac underprint. View of Tbilisi at center right with equestrian statue of King V. Gorgosal in foreground, Mount Tatzminda in background. Back: Cave dwellings at left center. Watermark: Hexagonal design repeated.	1.00	8.00
28	**100 (Laris)**	ND (1993). Greenish gray and light brown on lilac underprint. View of Tbilisi at center right with equestrian statue of King V. Gorgosal in foreground, Mount Tatzminda in background. Back: Cave dwellings at left center. Watermark: Hexagonal design repeated.	1.00	10.00

			VF	UNC
29	**500 (Laris)**	ND (1993). Purple on lilac underprint. View of Tbilisi at center right with equestrian statue of King V. Gorgosal in foreground, Mount Tatzminda in background. Back: Cave dwellings at left center. Watermark: Hexagonal design repeated.	2.00	12.00

			VF	UNC
30	**1000 (Laris)**	ND (1993). Blue-gray and brown on lilac underprint. View of Tbilisi at center right with equestrian statue of King V. Gorgosal in foreground, Mount Tatzminda in background. Back: Cave dwellings at left center. Watermark: Hexagonal design repeated.	3.00	15.00

			VF	UNC
31	**5000 (Laris)**	ND (1993). Green and brown on lilac underprint. View of Tbilisi at center right with equestrian statue of King V. Gorgosal in foreground, Mount Tatzminda in background. Back: Green on pale brown-orange. Cave dwellings at left center. Watermark: Hexagonal design repeated.	3.00	10.00

			VF	UNC
32	**10,000 (Laris)**	ND (1993). Violet on lilac and brown underprint. View of Tbilisi at center right with equestrian statue of King V. Gorgosal in foreground, Mount Tatzminda in background. Back: Cave dwellings at left center. Watermark: Hexagonal design repeated.	5.00	20.00

SECOND 1993 *KUPONI* ND ISSUE

#33-38 Fractional serial # prefix w/2 as denominator.

			VF	UNC
33	**1 (Laris)**	ND (1993). Red-orange and light brown on lilac underprint. View of Tbilisi at center right with equestrian statue of King V. Gorgosal in foreground, Mount Tatzminda in background. Ornate triangular design at left of large value in box at left center. Back: Cave dwellings at left center. Ornate triangular design at sides of value at right. Watermark: Hexagonal design repeated.	.50	2.00

			VF	UNC
34	**3 (Laris)**	ND (1993). Purple and light brown on lilac underprint. View of Tbilisi at center right with equestrian statue of King V. Gorgosal in foreground, Mount Tatzminda in background. Ornate triangular design at left of large value in box at left center. Back: Cave dwellings at left center. Ornate triangular design at sides of value at right. Watermark: Hexagonal design repeated.	.50	2.00

35	5 (Laris)	VF	UNC
	ND (1993). Dull brown on lilac underprint. View of Tbilisi at center right with equestrian statue of King V. Gorgosal in foreground, Mount Tatzmlnda In background. Ornate triangular designat left of large value in box at left center. Back: Cave dwellings at left center. Ornate triangular design at sides of value at right. Watermark: Hexagonal design repeated.	.50	3.00

36	10 (Laris)	VF	UNC
	ND (1993). Yellow-brown on lilac underprint. View of Tbilisi at center right with equestrian statue of King V. Gorgosal in foreground, Mount Tatzminda in background. Ornate triangular design at left of large value in box at left center. Back: Cave dwellings at left center. Ornate triangular design at sides of value at right. Watermark: Hexagonal design repeated.	.50	2.00

37	50 (Laris)	VF	UNC
	ND (1993). Light blue on lilac underprint. View of Tbilisi at center right with equestrian statue of King V. Gorgosal in foreground, Mount Tatzminda in background. Ornate triangular design at left of large value in box at left center. Back: Cave dwellings at left center. Ornate triangular design at sides of value at right. Watermark: Hexagonal design repeated.	.50	2.00

38	100 (Laris)	VF	UNC
	ND (1993). Greenish gray and light brown on lilac underprint. View of Tbilisi at center right with equestrian statue of King V. Gorgosal in foreground, Mount Tatzminda in background. Ornate triangular design at left of large value in box at left center. Back: Cave dwellings at left center. Ornate triangular design at sides of value at right. Watermark: Hexagonal design repeated.	1.00	4.00

Third 1993 Dated Issue

#39-42 Fractional serial # prefix w/3 as denominator.

39	10,000 (Laris)	VF	UNC
	1993. Violet on lilac and brown underprint. View of Tbilisi at center right with equestrian statue of King V. Gorgosal in foreground, Mount Tatzminda in background. Back: Cave dwellings at left center. Watermark: Hexagonal design repeated.	1.00	8.00

40	25,000 (Laris)	VF	UNC
	1993. Orange and dull brown on lilac underprint. View of Tbilisi at center right with equestrian statue of King V. Gorgosal in foreground, Mount Tatzminda in background. Back: Cave dwellings at left center. Watermark: Hexagonal design repeated.	3.00	10.00

41	50,000 (Laris)	VF	UNC
	1993. Pale red-brown and tan on lilac underprint. View of Tbilisi at center right with equestrian statue of King V. Gorgosal in foreground, Mount Tatzminda in background. Back: Dull red-brown on pale brown-orange underprint. Cave dwellings at left center. Watermark: Hexagonal design repeated.	2.00	6.00

42	100,000 (Laris)	VF	UNC
	1993. Olive-green and brown on lilac underprint. View of Tbilisi at center right with equestrian statue of King V. Gorgosal in foreground, Mount Tatzminda in background. Back: Pale olive-green on dull brown-orange underprint. Cave dwellings at left center. Watermark: Hexagonal design repeated.	2.00	8.00

Fourth 1993 Dated Issue

43	250 (Laris)	VF	UNC
	1993. Dark blue on green, lilac and light blue underprint. Griffin at left and right of ornate round design at center. Back: Two bunches of grapes with vine above and below value on vertical format. Watermark: Isometric rectangular design.		
	a. With security thread.	.50	2.00
	b. Without security thread.	—	—

44	2000 (Laris)	VF	UNC
	1993. Green and blue on gold and green underprint. Griffin at left and right of ornate round design at center. Back: Two bunches of grapes with vine above and below value on vertical format. Watermark: Isometric rectangular design.	1.00	4.00

45 3000 (Laris)

1993. Brown and yellow on light brown underprint. Griffin at left and right of ornate round design at center. Back: Two bunches of grapes with vine above and below value on vertical format. Watermark: Isometric rectangular design.

	VF	UNC
	1.00	4.00

46 20,000 (Laris)

1993; 1994. Purple on light red and blue underprint. Griffin at left and right of ornate round design at center. Back: Two bunches of grapes with vine above and below value on vertical format. Watermark: Isometric rectangular design.

	VF	UNC
a. Large watermark. 1993.	2.00	6.00
b. With security foil printing at left edge of signature. Small watermark. 1994.	1.00	3.00

1994 Issue

47 30,000 (Laris)

1994. Dull red-brown on pale orange and light gray underprint. Griffin at left and right of ornate round design at center. Security foil at left. Back: Two bunches of grapes with vine above and below value on vertical format. Watermark: Isometric rectangular design repeated.

	VF	UNC
	2.00	6.00

48 50,000 (Laris)

1994. Dark olive-green and dull black on pale olive-green and tan underprint. Griffin at left and right of ornate round design at center. Security foil at left. Back: Two bunches of grapes with vine above and below value on vertical format. Watermark: Isometric rectangular design repeated.

	VF	UNC
	2.00	6.00

48A 100,000 (Laris)

1994. Dark gray on light blue and light gray underprint. Griffin at left and right of ornate round design at center. Security foil at left. Back: Two bunches of grapes with vine above and below value on vertical format.

	VF	UNC
a. With security thread. Large watermark.	2.00	6.00
b. Without security thread. Small watermark.	2.00	6.00

49 150,000 (Laris)

1994. Dark blue-green on pale blue, light gray and lilac underprint. Griffin at left and right of ornate round design at center. Security foil at left. Back: Two bunches of grapes with vine above and below value on vertical format. Watermark: Isometric rectangular design repeated.

	VF	UNC
	2.00	7.00

50 250,000 (Laris)

1994. Brown-orange on pale orange and light green underprint. Griffin at left and right of ornate round design at center. Security foil at left. Back: Two bunches of grapes with vine above and below value on vertical format. Watermark: Isometric rectangular design repeated.

	VF	UNC
	2.00	7.00

51 500,000 (Laris)

1994. Deep violet on pale purple and pink underprint. Griffin at left and right of ornate round design at center. Security foil at left. Back: Two bunches of grapes with vine above and below value on vertical format. Watermark: Isometric rectangular design repeated.

	VF	UNC
	2.00	7.00

52 1 Million (Laris)

1994. Red on pink and pale yellow-brown underprint. Griffin at left and right of ornate round design at center. Security foil at left. Back: Two bunches of grapes with vine above and below value on vertical format. Watermark: Isometric rectangular design repeated.

	VF	UNC
	2.00	7.00

1994 Privatization Check Voucher Issue

52A Various Denominations

1994. Orange, black and multicolor.

	VF	UNC
	10.00	30.00

1995 Issue

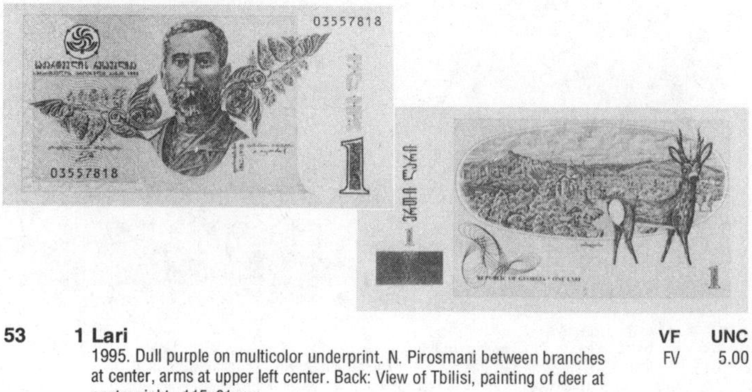

53 1 Lari

1995. Dull purple on multicolor underprint. N. Pirosmani between branches at center, arms at upper left center. Back: View of Tbilisi, painting of deer at center right. 115x61mm.

	VF	UNC
	FV	5.00

54 **2 Lari**

	VF	UNC
1995. Deep olive-green on multicolor underprint. Arms above bars of music at left, Z. Paliashvili at center right. Back: Opera House in Tbilisi at center right. 115x61mm.	FV	8.00

55 **5 Lari**

	VF	UNC
1995. Brown on multicolor underprint. Arms at upper left, I. Javakhishvili at center. Back: Map above ornate lion statue at left center, Tbilisi State University above open book at right. 115x61mm.	FV	15.00

56 **10 Lari**

	VF	UNC
1995. Blue-black on multicolor underprint. Flowers at left, arms at upper center, A. tsereteli and barn swallow at center right. Back: Woman seated on stump while spinning yarn with a crop spindle between ornamental branches at center Watermark: Arms repeated vertically. 125x63mm.	FV	25.00

57 **20 Lari**

	VF	UNC
1995. Dark brown on multicolor underprint. Open book and newspaper at upper left, arms at lower left, I. Chavchavadze at center. Back: Statue of King V. Gorgosal between views of Tbilisi at center right. Watermark: Griffin. 130x65mm.	FV	40.00

58 **50 Lari**

	VF	UNC
1995. Dark brown and deep blue-green on multicolor underprint. Griffin at left, arms at upper left, Princess Tamara at center right. Back: Mythical figure at center right. Watermark: Griffin. 135x66mm.	FV	90.00

		VF	UNC
59	**100 Lari** 1995. Dark brown, purple and black on multicolor underprint. Carved bust of S. Rustaveli at center right, arms at upper left center. Back: Frieze at upper center right. Watermark: Griffin. 140x67mm.	FV	150.
60	**500 Lari** 1995. Deep purple on multicolor underprint. King David *the Builder* with building at center. Back: Early Georgian inscriptions, cross on back. (Not issued).	—	800.

1999 Issue

		VF	UNC
61	**1 Lari** 1999. Deep purple on multicolor underprint. N. Pirosmani between branches at center, arms at upper left center. Country name in English; *GEORGIA*. Back: View of Tbilisi, painting of deer at center right. 115x61mm.	FV	2.00
62	**2 Lari** 1999. Deep olive-green on multicolor underprint. Arms above bars of music at left, Z. Paliashvili at center right. Country name in English; *GEORGIA*. Back: Opera House in Tbilisi at center right. 115x61mm.	FV	5.00
63	**5 Lari** 1999. Brown on multicolor underprint. Arms at upper left, I. Javakhishvili at center. Country name in English; *GEORGIA*. Back: Map above ornate lion statue at left center, Tbilisi State University above open book at right. 115x61mm.	FV	12.50
64	**10 Lari** 1999. Blue-black on multicolor underprint. Flowers at left, arms at upper center, A. tseriteli and barn swallow at center right. Country name in English; *GEORGIA*. Back: Woman seated on stump while spinning yarn with a crop spindle between ornamental branches at center Similar to #56. 125x63mm.	FV	25.00
65	**20 Lari** 1999. Dark brown on multicolor underprint. Open book and newspaper at upper left, arms at lower left, I. Chavchavadze at center. Country name in English; *GEORGIA*. Back: Statue of King V. Gorgosal between views of Tbilisi at center right. Watermark: Griffin. 130x65mm.	FV	35.00

66 **50 Lari**

	VF	UNC
1999. Dark brown and deep blue-green on multicolor underprint. Griffin at left, arms at upper left, Princess Tamara at center right. Back: Mythical figure at center right. Watermark: Griffin. 135x66mm.	FV	65.00

67 **100 Lari** VF UNC
1999. Dark brown, purple and black on multicolor underprint. Carved bust of S. Rustaveli at center right, arms at upper left center. Country name in English; *GEORGIA*. Back: Frieze at upper center right. 140x67mm. FV 125.

2002; 2004 Issue

68 **1 Lari** VF UNC
2002; 2007. Deep purple on multicolor underprint. Niko Pirosmani at center. Back: Deer and view of Tbilisi. 115x61mm.

	VF	UNC
a. 2002.	FV	2.00
b. 2007.	FV	2.00

69 **2 Lari** VF UNC
2002. Deep olive-green on multicolor underprint. Zakaria Paliashvili at right center. Back: Opera House in Tbilisi. 115x61mm. FV 5.00

70 **5 Lari** VF UNC
2002; 2008; 2011. Brown on multicolor underprint. Ivane Javakhishvili at center. Back: Tibilisi State University Building at right, map at upper left. 115x61mm.

	VF	UNC
a. 2002.	FV	10.00
b. 2008.	FV	10.00
c. 2011.	FV	10.00

71 **10 Lari** VF UNC
2002; 2007; 2008; 2012. Blue-black on multicolor underprint. Akaki Tsereteli at left center. Back: Woman weaving. 125x63mm.

	VF	UNC
a. 2002.	FV	20.00
b. 2007.	FV	20.00
c. 2008.	FV	20.00
d. 2012.	FV	20.00

72 **20 Lari** VF UNC
2002; 2008; 2011. Dark brown on multicolor underprint. Ila Chavchavadze. Back: King Vakhtang Gorasale, founder of Tbilisi. 130x65mm.

	VF	UNC
a. 2002.	FV	30.00
b. 2008.	FV	30.00
c. 2011.	FV	30.00

73 **50 Lari** VF UNC
2004; 2008; 2011. Brown and multicolor underprint. Statue of Queen at left center. Back: Ancient mythical drawing. 135x66mm.

	VF	UNC
a. 2004.	FV	60.00
b. 2008.	FV	55.00
c. 2011.	FV	50.00

74 **100 Lari** VF UNC
2004; 2008; 2012. Green on multicolor underprint. Ancient statue Back: Medevial carving. 140x67mm.

	VF	UNC
a. 2004.	FV	110.
b. 2008.	FV	110.
c. 2012. Signatures; Giorgi Kadagidze adn Dmitri Gvindadze.	FV	110.

75 **200 Lari** VF UNC
2006. Brown and yellow on multicolor underprint. Kakutsa Choloashvili at left center. Back: Seaside town view. 146x72mm. FV 200.

The German Democratic Republic (East Germany), located on the great north European plain, ceased to exist in 1990. During the closing days of World War II in Europe, Soviet troops advancing into Germany from the east occupied the German provinces of Mecklenburg, Brandenburg, Saxony-Anhalt, Saxony and Thuringia. These five provinces comprised the occupation zone administered by the Soviet Union after the cessation of hostilities. The other three zones were administered by the United States, Great Britain and France. Under the Potsdam agreement, questions affecting Germany as a whole were to be settled by the commanders in chief of the occupation zones acting jointly and by unanimous decision. When Soviet intransigence rendered the quadripartite commission inoperable, the three western zones were united to form the Federal Republic of Germany, May 23, 1949. Thereupon the Soviet Union dissolved its occupation zone and established it as the Democratic Republic of Germany, Oct. 7, 1949. East and West Germany became reunited as one country on Oct. 3, 1990.

MONETARY SYSTEM:

1 Mark = 100 Pfennig

Democratic Republic

Deutsche Notenbank

1964 Issue

#22-26 replacement notes: Serial # prefix *YA-YZ; ZA-ZZ.*

		VF	UNC
22	**5 Mark** 1964. Brown on multicolor underprint. Alexander von Humboldt at right. Back: Humboldt University in Berlin at left center, arms at left. Watermark: Hammer and compass.		
	a. Issued note.	5.00	10.00
	s. Specimen.	—	150.

		VF	UNC
23	**10 Mark** 1964. Green on multicolor underprint. Friedrich von Schiller at right. Back: Zeiss factory in Jena at left center, arms at upper center right. Watermark: Hammer and compass.		
	a. Issued note.	9.00	20.00
	s. Specimen.	—	200.

		VF	UNC
24	**20 Mark** 1964. Red-brown on multicolor underprint. Johann Wolfgang von Goethe at right. Back: National Theater in Weimar at left center, arms at upper center right. Watermark: Johann Wolfgang von Goethe.		
	a. Issued note.	10.00	25.00
	s. Specimen.	—	150.

		VF	UNC
25	**50 Mark** 1964. Deep green on multicolor underprint. Friedrich Engels at right. Back: Wheat threshing at left center, arms at left. Watermark: Friedrich Engels.		
	a. Issued note.	10.00	25.00
	r. Replacement note. Serial # prefix ZA-ZE.	20.00	35.00
	s. Specimen.	—	225.

		VF	UNC
26	**100 Mark** 1964. Blue on multicolor underprint. Karl Marx at right. Back: Brandenburg Gate in Berlin at left center, arms at upper center right. Watermark: Karl Marx.		
	a. Issued note.	15.00	30.00
	r. Replacement note. Serial # prefix ZA, ZB.	20.00	35.00
	s. Specimen.	—	225.

Staatsbank der DDR

1971-85 Issue

#27-31 Replacement notes: Serial # prefix *YA-YI, YZ, ZA-ZQ.*

27	5 Mark	VF	UNC
	1975. Purple on multicolor underprint. Thomas Müntzer at right, arms at upper left. Back: Harvesting scene, arms at left. Watermark: Thomas Müntzer.		
	a. 6 digit wide serial #.	2.00	7.00
	b. 6 digit narrow serial #. (1987).	2.00	7.00
	s. As b. Specimen.	—	50.00
	x. Mismatched serial number.	60.00	—

28	10 Mark	VF	UNC
	1971. Brown on multicolor underprint. Clara Zetkin at right, arms at upper left. Back: Woman at radio station, arms at left. Watermark: Clara Zetkin.		
	a. 6 digit wide serial #.	4.00	6.00
	b. 7 digit narrow serial #. (1985).	2.00	4.00
	s. As a. Specimen.	—	125.

29	20 Mark	VF	UNC
	1975. Green on multicolor underprint. Johann Wolfgang von Goethe at right, arms at upper left. Back: Children leaving school, arms at left. Watermark: Johann Wolfgang von Goethe.		
	a. 6 digit wide serial #.	4.00	7.00
	b. 7 digit narrow serial #. (1986).	6.00	9.00
	s. As b. Specimen.	—	175.

30	50 Mark	VF	UNC
	1971. Dark red on multicolor underprint. Friedrich Engels at right, arms at upper left. Back: Oil refinery, arms at left. Watermark: Friedrich Engels.		
	a. 7 digit wide serial #.	5.00	10.00
	b. 7 digit narrow serial #. (1986).	5.00	10.00
	s. Specimen.	—	225.

31	100 Mark	VF	UNC
	1975. Blue on multicolor underprint. Karl Marx at right, arms at upper left. Back: Street scene in East Berlin, arms at left. Watermark: Karl Marx.		
	a. 7 digit wide serial #.	7.00	10.00
	b. 7 digit narrow serial #. (1986).	10.00	17.50
	s. Specimen.	—	175.

32	200 Mark	VF	UNC
	1985. Dark olive-green and dark brown on multicolor underprint. Family at right. Back: Teacher dancing with children in front of modern school building at center. Watermark: Dove. (Not issued.)	—	25.00

33	500 Mark	VF	UNC
	1985. Dark brown on multicolor underprint. Arms at right. Back: Government Building Staatsrat (in Berlin) at center. Watermark: Arms. (Not issued.)	—	25.00

Collector Series

Staatsbank der DDR

1989 Commemorative Issue

#CS1, Opening of Brandenburg Gate, 1989. Not legal tender.

CS1	20 Mark 22.12.1989	Mkt. Value
	Black and purple on multicolor underprint. Brandenburg Gate in Berlin at center.	500.

The Federal Republic of Germany (formerly West Germany), located in north-central Europe, since 1990 with the unification of East Germany, has an area of 137,782 sq. mi. (356,854 sq. km.) and a population of 82.69 million. Capital: Berlin. The economy centers about one of the world's foremost industrial establishments. Machinery, motor vehicles, iron, steel, chemicals, yarns and fabrics are exported.

During the post-Normandy phase of World War II, Allied troops occupied the western German provinces of Schleswig-Holstein, Hamburg, Lower Saxony, Bremen, North Rhine-Westphalia, Hesse, Rhineland-Palatinate, Baden-Wurttemberg, Bavaria and Saarland. The conquered provinces were divided into American, British and French occupation zones. Five eastern German provinces were occupied and administered by the forces of the Soviet Union.

The western occupation forces restored the civil status of their zones on Sept. 21, 1949, and resumed diplomatic relations with the provinces on July 2, 1951. On May 5, 1955, nine of the ten western provinces, organized as the Federal Republic of Germany, became fully independent. The tenth province, Saarland, was restored to the republic on Jan. 1, 1957.

The post-WW II division of Germany ended on Oct. 3, 1990, when the German Democratic Republic (East Germany) ceased to exist and its five constituent provinces were formally admitted to the Federal Republic of Germany. An election Dec. 2, 1990, chose representatives to the united federal parliament (Bundestag), which then conducted its opening session in Berlin in the old Reichstag building.

MONETARY SYSTEM:

1 Deutsche Mark (DM) = 100 Pfennig, 1948-2001
1 Euro = 100 Cents, 2002-

FEDERAL REPUBLIC

DEUTSCHE BUNDESBANK

1960 ISSUE

#18-24 Replacement notes: Serial # prefix *Y, Z*.

#18-22 with or without ultraviolet sensitive features.

			VF	UNC
18	**5 Deutsche Mark**	2.1.1960. Green on multicolor underprint. *Young Venetian Woman* by Albrecht Dürer (1505) at right. Back: Oak sprig at left center. Watermark: Young Venetian woman. 120x60mm.		
		a. Issued note.	8.50	17.50
		s. Specimen.	—	150.

			VF	UNC
19	**10 Deutsche Mark**	2.1.1960. Blue on multicolor underprint. *Young Man* by Albrecht Dürer at right. Back: Sail training ship *Gorch Fock*. Watermark: Young man. 130x65mm.		
		a. Issued note.	15.00	50.00
		s. Specimen.	—	150.

			VF	UNC
20	**20 Deutsche Mark**	2.1.1960. Black and green on multicolor underprint. *Elsbeth Tucher* by Albrecht Dürer (1499) at right. Back: Violin, bow and clarinet. Watermark: Elsbeth Tucher. 140x70mm.		
		a. Issued note.	65.00	100.
		s. Specimen.	—	150.

			VF	UNC
21	**50 Deutsche Mark**	2.1.1960. Brown and olive-green on multicolor underprint. *Hans Urmiller* by Barthel Beham (about 1525) at right. Back: Holsten-Tor gate in Lübeck. Watermark: Hans Urmiller. 150x75mm.		
		a. Issued note.	55.00	135.
		s. Specimen.	—	150.

			VF	UNC
22	**100 Deutsche Mark**	2.1.1960. Blue on multicolor underprint. *Master Sebastian Münster* by Christoph Amberger (1552) at right. Back: Eagle. Watermark: Sebastian Münster. 160x80mm.		
		a. Issued note.	125.	250.
		s. Specimen.	—	250.

		VF	UNC
23	**500 Deutsche Mark**		
	2.1.1960. Brown-lilac on multicolor underprint. Male portrait by Hans Maler zu Schwaz. Back: Eltz Castle. Watermark: Male portrait. 170x85mm.		
	a. Issued note.	750.	1500.
	s. Specimen.	—	800.

		VF	UNC
24	**1000 Deutsche Mark**		
	2.1.1960. Dark brown on multicolor underprint. Astronomer Johann Schöner by Lucas Cranach the Elder (1529) at right. Back: Cathedral of Limburg on the Lahn. Watermark: Johan Schöner. 180x90mm.		
	a. Issued note.	1250.	2000.
	s. Specimen.	—	1200.

Bundeskassenschein

1967 ND Issue

#25-29A small change notes. Printed for use in a coin shortage which never developed. Not issued. Replacement notes: Serial # prefix 4 petals (+).

		VF	UNC
25	**5 Pfennig**		
	ND. Black and dark green on lilac underprint. Value at center and in underprint. Printer: BDDK, without imprint. (Not issued).	—	110.

		VF	UNC
26	**10 Pfennig**		
	ND. Dark brown on tan underprint. Value at center and in underprint. Printer: BDDK, without imprint. (Not issued).	—	15.00
27	**50 Pfennig**		
	ND. Dark brown. Value at center and in underprint. Printer: BDDK, without imprint. (Not issued).	—	4200.

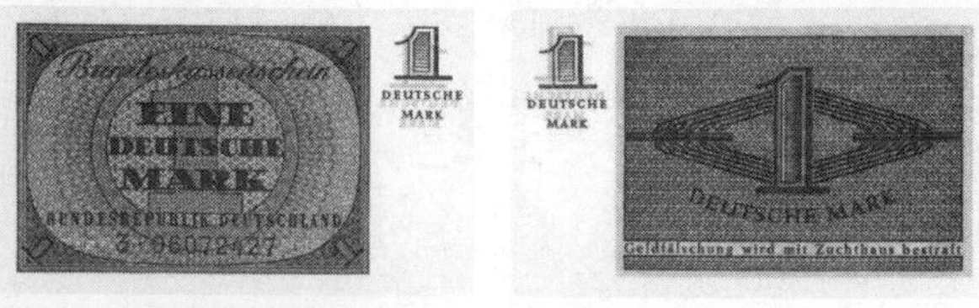

		VF	UNC
28	**1 Deutsche Mark**		
	ND. Brown and blue on multicolor underprint. Value at center and in underprint. Printer: BDDK, without imprint. (Not issued).	—	150.

		VF	UNC
29	**2 Deutsche Mark**		
	ND. Purple and tan on multicolor underprint. Value at center and in underprint. Printer: BDDK, without imprint. (Not issued).	—	35.00
29A	**5 Deutsche Mark**		
	1.7. 1963. Brown. Young Venetian woman by Albrecht Dürer. Back: Oak sprig at left center. Printer: BDDK, without imprint. (Not issued).	—	—

Deutsche Bundesbank

1970-80 Issue

#30-36 Replacement notes: Serial # prefix *Y, Z, YA-, ZA-*. Values are significantly higher.

		VF	UNC
30	**5 Deutsche Mark**		
	1970; 1980. Green on multicolor underprint. Young Venetian woman by Albrecht Dürer. Back: Oak sprig at left center. Watermark: Portrait. 120x60mm.		
	a. 2.1.1970.	25.00	70.00
	b. With © *DEUTSCHE BUNDESBANK 1963* on back. 2.1.1980.	7.00	12.00
	s. Specimen. As a.	—	100.

		VF	UNC
31	**10 Deutsche Mark**		
	1970-80. Blue on multicolor underprint. Young man by Albrecht Dürer at right. Back: Sail training ship *GORCH FOCK*. Watermark: Portrait. 130x65mm.		
	a. 2.1.1970. Letters of serial # either 2.8 or 3.3mm in height.	15.00	30.00
	b. 1.6.1977.	10.00	15.00
	c. Without © notice. 2.1.1980.	25.00	45.00
	d. With © *DEUTSCHE BUNDESBANK 1963* on back. 2.1.1980.	7.50	15.00
	s. Specimen.	—	100.

		VF	UNC
32	**20 Deutsche Mark**		
	1970-80. Black and green on multicolor underprint. *Elsbeth Tucher* by Albrecht Dürer (1499) at right. Back: Violin, bow and clarinet. Watermark: Portrait. 140x70mm.		
	a. 2.1.1970. Letters of serial # either 2.8 or 3.3mm in height.	30.00	70.00
	b. 1.6.1977.	25.00	60.00
	c. Without © notice. 2.1.1980.	45.00	100.
	d. With © *DEUTSCHE BUNDESBANK 1961* on back. 2.1.1980.	20.00	40.00
	s. Specimen.	—	100.

33 **50 Deutsche Mark** VF UNC

1970-80. Brown and olive-green on multicolor underprint. Portrait of *Hand Urmiller* by Barthel Beham (about 1525) at right. Back: Holsten-Tor gate in Lübeck. Watermark: Portrait. 150x75mm.

	VF	UNC
a. 2.1.1970. Letters of serial # either 2.8 or 3.3mm in height.	40.00	90.00
b. 1.6.1977.	40.00	90.00
c. Without © notice. 2.1.1980.	55.00	210.
d. With © *DEUTSCHE BUNDESBANK 1962* on back. 2.1.1980.	55.00	125.
s. Specimen.	—	100.

34 **100 Deutsche Mark** VF UNC

1970-80. Blue on multicolor underprint. *Master Sebastian Münster* by Christoph Amberger (1552) at right. Back: Eagle. Watermark: Portrait. 160x80mm.

	VF	UNC
a. 2.1.1970. Letters of serial # either 2.8 or 3.3mm in height.	75.00	170.
b. 1.6.1977.	85.00	170.
c. Without © notice. 2.1.1980.	180.	275.
d. With © *DEUTSCHE BUNDESBANK 1962* on back. 2.1.1980.	100.	160.
s. Specimen.	—	100.

35 **500 Deutsche Mark**

1970-80. Brown-lilac on multicolor underprint. Male portrait by Hans Maler zu Schwaz. Back: Eltz Castle. Watermark: Portrait. 170x85mm.

a. 2.1.1970.	775.	110.
b. 1.6.1977.	700.	950.
c. 2.1.1980.	900.	1250.
s. Specimen.	—	700.

36 **1000 Deutsche Mark** VF UNC

1977-80. Dark brown on multicolor underprint. Astronomer Johannes Schöner by Lucas Cranach the elder (1529) at right. Back: Cathedral of Limburg on the Lahn. Watermark: Portrait. 180x90mm.

	VF	UNC
a. 1.6.1977.	1300.	1800.
b. 2.1.1980.	1450.	1900.
s. Specimen.	—	1000.

1989-91 Issue

#37-44 replacement notes: Serial # prefix *ZA; YA.*

37 **5 Deutsche Mark** VF UNC

1.8.1991. Green and olive-green on multicolor underprint. Bettina von Arnim (1785-1859) at right, Signature Schlesinger-Tietmeyer. Back: Bank seal and Brandenburg Gate in Berlin at left center, script on open envelope at lower right. 122x62mm. 7.50 10.00

38 **10 Deutsche Mark** VF UNC

1989-99. Purple, violet and blue on multicolor underprint. Carl Friedrich Gauss (1777-1855) at right. Back: Sextant at left center, mapping at lower right. 130x65mm.

	VF	UNC
a. Signature Pöhl-Schlesinger. 2.1.1989.	8.00	25.00
b. Signature Schlesinger-Tietmeyer. 1.8.1991.	7.00	20.00
c. Signature Tietmeyer-Gaddum. 1.10.1993.	5.00	15.00
d. Signature Welteke-Stark. 1.9.1999.	6.00	20.00
e. Uncut sheet of 54 notes, signature as c or d.	—	500.

39 **20 Deutsche Mark** VF UNC

1991; 1993. Green and red-violet on multicolor underprint. Annette von Droste-Hülshoff (1797-1848) at right. Back: Quill pen and beech-tree at left center, open book at lower right. 138x68mm.

	VF	UNC
a. Signature Schlesinger-Tietmeyer. 1.8.1991.	15.00	35.00
b. Signature Tietmeyer-Gaddum. 1.10.1993.	15.00	30.00

40 **50 Deutsche Mark** VF UNC

1989-93. Dark brown and red-brown on multicolor underprint. Balthasar Neuman (1687-1753) at right. Back: Architectural drawing of Bishop's residence in Würzburg at left center, blueprint at lower right in watermark area. 146x71mm.

	VF	UNC
a. Signature Pöhl-Schlesinger. 2.1.1989.	70.00	125.
b. Signature Schlesinger-Tietmeyer. 1.8.1991.	55.00	85.00
c. Signature Tietmeyer-Gaddum. 1.10.1993.	45.00	70.00

41 **100 Deutsche Mark** VF UNC

1989-93. Deep blue and violet on multicolor underprint. Clara Schumann (1819-1896) at center right. Back: Building at left in background, grand piano at center, multiple tuning forks at lower right in watermark area. 154x74mm.

	VF	UNC
a. Signature Pöhl-Schlesinger. 2.1.1989.	125.	170.
b. Signature Schlesinger-Tietmeyer. 1.8.1991.	110.	170.
c. Signature Tietmeyer-Gaddum. 1.10.1993.	100.	145.

42 **200 Deutsche Mark** VF UNC

2.1.1989. Red-orange and blue on multicolor underprint. Paul Ehrlich (1854-1915) at right. Signature Pöhl-Schlesinger. Back: Microscope at left center, medical science symbol at lower right. 162x77mm. 300. 400.

43 **500 Deutsche Mark** VF UNC

1991; 1993. Red-violet and blue on multicolor underprint. Maria Sibylla Merian (1647-1717) at right. Back: Dandelion with butterfly and caterpillar at center, flower at lower right. 170x80mm.

	VF	UNC
a. Signature Schlesinger-Tietmeyer. 1.8.1991.	450.	650.
b. Signature Tietmeyer-Gaddum. 1.10.1993.	500.	725.

44 **1000 Deutsche Mark** VF UNC

1.8.1991; 1.10.1993. Deep brown-violet and blue-green on multicolor underprint. City drawing at center, Wilhelm and Jakob Grimm (1786-1859 and 1785-1863) at center right. Back: Bank seal at left, book frontispiece of *Deutches Würterbuch* over entry for freedom at left center, child collecting falling stars at lower right in watermark area. 178x83mm.

	VF	UNC
a. Signature Schlesinger-Tietmeyer. 1.8.1991.	825.	1100.
b. Signature Tietmeyer-Gaddum. 1.10.1993.	825.	1100.

1996 Issue

45 **50 Deutsche Mark** VF UNC

2.1.1996. Dark brown and red-brown on multicolor underprint. Balthasar Neuman (1687-1753) at right. Square-shaped Kinegram foil at left center. Signature Tietmeyer-Gaddum. Back: Architectural drawing of Bishop's residence in Würzburg at left center, blueprint at lower right. 146x71mm. 35.00 65.00

46 **100 Deutsche Mark** VF UNC

2.1.1996. Deep blue and violet on multicolor underprint. Clara Schumann (1819-1896) at center right. Lyre-shaped Kinegram foil at left center. Signature: Tietmeyer-Gaddum. Back: Building at left in background, grand piano at center, multiple tuning forks at lower right. 154x74mm. 60.00 120.

47 **200 Deutsche Mark** VF UNC

2.1.1996. Red-orange and blue on multicolor underprint. Paul Ehrlich (1854-1915) at right. Double hexagon-shaped Kinegram foil. Signature; Tietmeyer-Gaddum. Back: Microscope at left center, medical science symbol at lower right. 162x77mm. 150. 350.

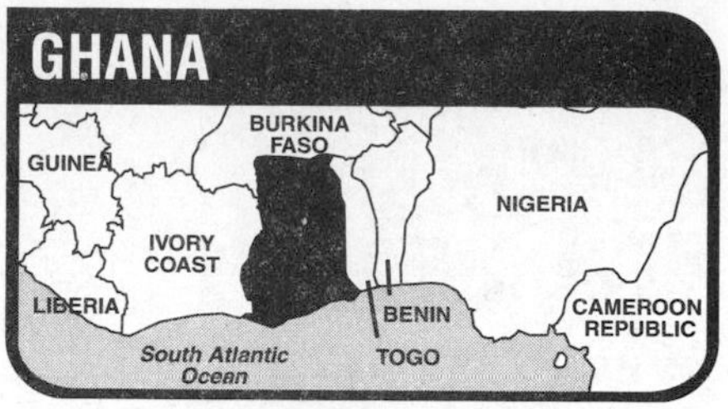

The Republic of Ghana, a member of the British Commonwealth situated on the West Coast of Africa between the Ivory Coast and Togo, has an area of 239,460 sq. km. and a population of 23,38 million, almost entirely African. Capital: Accra. Traditional exports include cocoa, coffee, timber, gold, industrial diamonds, maganese and bauxite. Additional exports include pineapples, bananas, yams, tuna, cola and salt.

Formed from the merger of the British colony of the Gold Coast and the Togoland trust territory, Ghana in 1957 became the first sub-Saharan country in colonial Africa to gain its independence. Ghana endured a long series of coups before Lt. Jerry Rawlings took power in 1981 and banned political parties. After approving a new constitution and restoring multiparty politics in 1992, Rawlings won presidential elections in 1992 and 1996, but was constitutionally prevented from running for a third term in 2000. John Kufuor succeeded him and was reelected in 2004. Kufuor is constitutionally barred from running for a third term in upcoming Presidential elections, which are scheduled for December 2008.

Ghana's monetary denomination of "cedi" is derived from the word "sedie" meaning cowrie, a shell money commonly employed by coastal tribes.

MONETARY SYSTEM:

1 Shilling = 12 Pence
1 Pound = 20 Shillings to 1965
1 Cedi = 100 Pesewas, 1965-

REPUBLIC

BANK OF GHANA

1958-63 ISSUE

1	**10 Shillings**	VF	UNC
	1958-63. Green and brown on multicolor underprint. Bank of Ghana building in Accra at center right. Back: Star. Watermark: *GHANA* in star.		
	a. 1.7.1958. 2 signatures. Printer: TDLR.	30.00	90.00
	b. 1.7.1961. Without imprint.	22.50	70.00
	c. 1.7.1962. Without imprint.	35.00	100.
	d. 1.7.1963. 1 signature.	15.00	50.00
	s. As a. Specimen.	—	200.

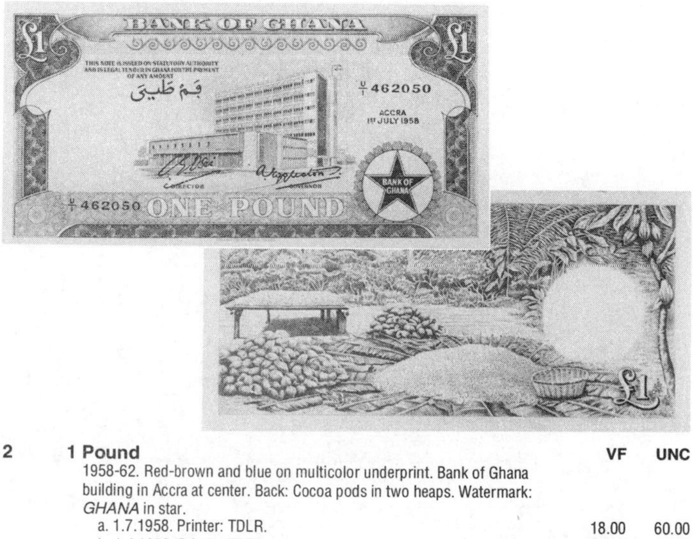

2	**1 Pound**	VF	UNC
	1958-62. Red-brown and blue on multicolor underprint. Bank of Ghana building in Accra at center. Back: Cocoa pods in two heaps. Watermark: *GHANA* in star.		
	a. 1.7.1958. Printer: TDLR.	18.00	60.00
	b. 1.4.1959. Printer: TDLR.	15.00	45.00
	c. 1.7.1961. Without imprint.	12.50	45.00
	d. 1.7.1962. Without imprint.	8.00	25.00
	s. As a. Specimen.	—	75.00

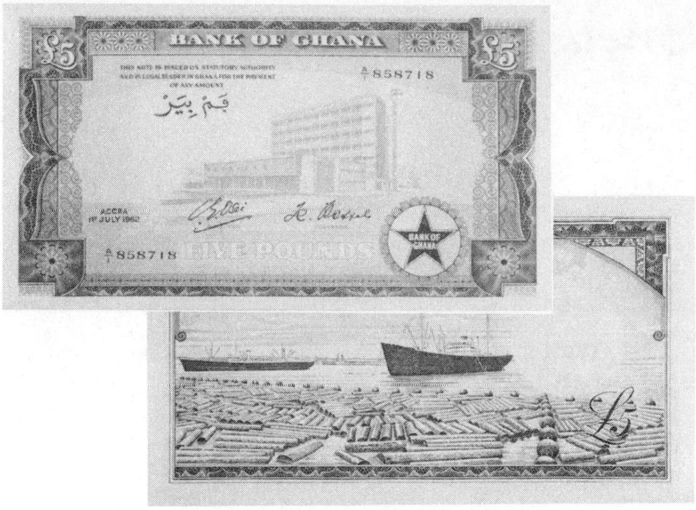

3	**5 Pounds**	VF	UNC
	1.7.1958-1.7.1962. Purple and orange on multicolor underprint. Bank of Ghana building in Accra at center. Back: Cargo ships, logs in water. Watermark: *GHANA* in star.		
	a. 1.7.1958.	75.00	250.
	b. 1.4.1959.	60.00	225.
	c. 1.7.1961.	50.00	200.
	d. 1.7.1962.	20.00	70.00
	s1. Specimen. 1.7.1958.	—	225.
	s2. Specimen. Perforated: *CANCELLED.*	—	350.

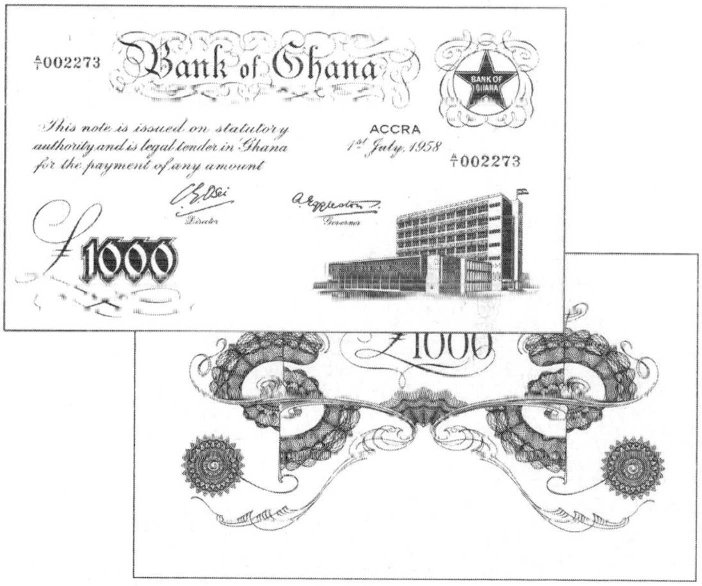

4	**1000 Pounds**	VF	UNC
	1.7.1958. Blackish brown. Bank of Ghana building in Accra at lower right. Back: Ornate design. Watermark: *GHANA* in star. Used in interbank transactions only.	150.	500.

1965 ISSUE

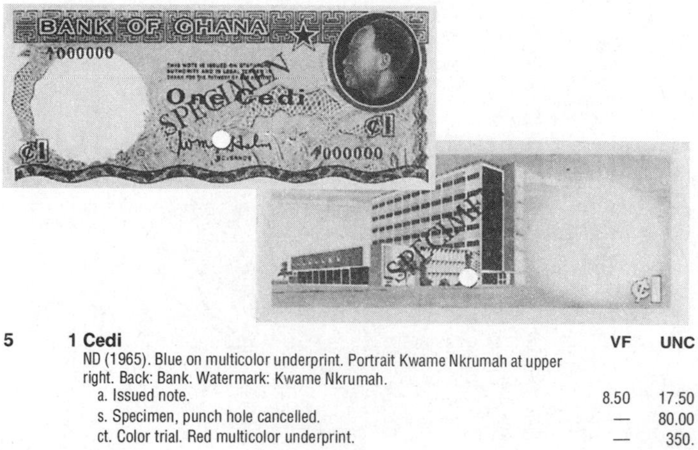

5	**1 Cedi**	VF	UNC
	ND (1965). Blue on multicolor underprint. Portrait Kwame Nkrumah at upper right. Back: Bank. Watermark: Kwame Nkrumah.		
	a. Issued note.	8.50	17.50
	s. Specimen, punch hole cancelled.	—	80.00
	ct. Color trial. Red multicolor underprint.	—	350.

6 **5 Cedis**

ND (1965). Dark brown on multicolor underprint. Portrait Kwame Nkrumah at upper right. Signature 3. Back: Parliament House at left center. Watermark: Kwame Nkrumah.

	VF	UNC
a. Issued note.	9.00	27.50
s. Specimen, punch hole cancelled.	—	80.00
ct. Color trial. Green multicolor underprint.	—	350.

7 **10 Cedis**

ND (1965). Green on multicolor underprint. Portrait Kwame Nkrumah at upper left. Signature 3. Back: Independence Square at center. Watermark: Kwame Nkrumah.

	VF	UNC
a. Issued note.	15.00	45.00
s. Specimen, punch hole cancelled.	—	80.00
ct. Color trial. Dark blue multicolor underprint.	—	375.

8 **50 Cedis**

ND (1965). Red on multicolor underprint. Portrait Kwame Nkrumah at upper left. Signature 3. Back: Island and coconut trees. Watermark: Kwame Nkrumah.

	VF	UNC
a. Issued note.	32.50	90.00
s. Specimen, punch hole cancelled.	—	85.00
ct. Color trial. Light blue on multicolor underprint.	—	400.

9 **100 Cedis**

ND (1965). Purple on multicolor underprint. Portrait Kwame Nkrumah at upper right. Signature 3. Back: Hospital. Watermark: Kwame Nkrumah.

	VF	UNC
a. Issued note.	65.00	130.
s. Specimen.	—	150.
ct. Color trial. Brown multicolor underprint.	—	500.

9A **1000 Cedis**

ND(1965). Black. Large star at upper left. Signature 3. Back: Bank of Ghana building in Accra at right.

	VF	UNC
a. Issued note.	275.	700.
s. Specimen.	—	700.
ct. Color trial. Purple.	—	1250.

1967 Issue

Replacement notes: Serial # prefix *Z/99*.

10 **1 Cedi**

23.2.1967; 8.1.1969; 1.10.1970; 1.10.1971. Blue on multicolor underprint. Cacao tree with pods at right. Signature 4, 5. Back: Shield and ceremonial sword. Watermark: Arms-Eagle's head above star. UV: fibers fluoresce blue, value 10 orange.

	VF	UNC
a. 23.2.1967.	5.00	10.00
b. 8.1.1969.	8.00	17.50
c. 1.10.1970.	4.00	9.00
d. 1.10.1971.	3.50	9.00
s. Specimen.	—	80.00

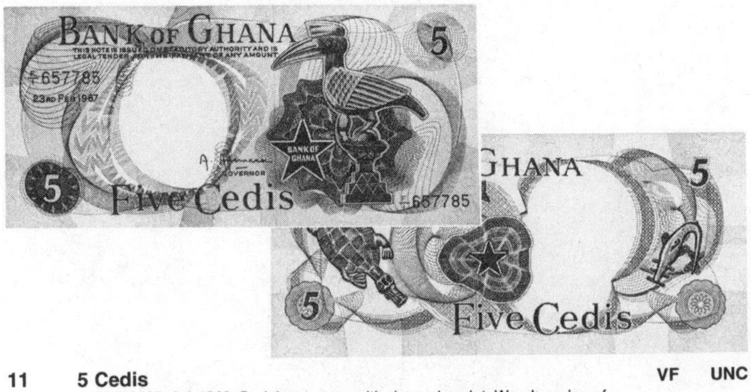

11 **5 Cedis**

23.2.1967; 8.1.1969. Dark brown on multicolor underprint. Wood carving of a bird at right. Signature 4, 5. Back: Animal carvings. Watermark: Arms-Eagle's head above star.

	VF	UNC
a. 23.2.1967.	17.50	60.00
b. 8.1.1969.	17.50	55.00
s. Specimen.	—	80.00

12 10 Cedis

23.2.1967; 8.1.1969; 1.10.1970. Red on multicolor underprint. Art products at right. Signature 4, 5. Back: Small statuettes. Watermark: Arms-Eagle's head above star.

	VF	UNC
a. 23.2.1967.	17.50	60.00
b. 8.1.1969.	20.00	65.00
c. 1.10.1970.	6.50	27.50
s. Specimen.	—	45.00

1972-73 Issue

13 1 Cedi

1973-76. Dark blue, deep green and purple on multicolor underprint. Young boy with slingshot at right. Signature 5, 6, 7. Back: Man cutting Cacao pods from tree at left center. Watermark: Arms-Eagle's head above star. UV: value 1 fluoresces orange.

	VF	UNC
a. 2.1.1973.	3.00	9.00
b. 2.1.1975.	2.50	7.50
c. 2.1.1976. Two minor varieties in length of *"2nd"* as part of date.	2.00	6.00
d. 2.1.1978.	1.00	5.00
s. As a. Specimen. Red overprint: *SPECIMEN* on both sides.	—	55.00

14 2 Cedis

1972-78. Green on multicolor underprint. Young man with hoe at right. Signature 5, 6, 7. Back: Workers in field at left center. Watermark: Arms-Eagle's head above star.

	VF	UNC
a. 21.6.1972. Signature J. J. Ansah.	5.00	18.00
b. 21.6.1972. Signature G. Nikoi.	4.00	13.00
c. 2.1.1977; 2.1.1978.	1.25	6.00
s. As a. Specimen.	—	65.00

15 5 Cedis

1973-78. Brown on multicolor underprint. Woman wearing large hat at right. Signature 5, 6, 7. Back: Huts. Watermark: Arms-Eagle's head above star. UV: value 5 fluoresces orange.

	VF	UNC
a. 2.1.1973; 2.1.1975; 2.1.1976.	1.50	9.00
b. 2.1.1977; 4.7.1977; 2.1.1978.	1.25	7.50
s. As a. Specimen.	—	65.00

16 10 Cedis

1973-78. Red, violet and dark brown on multicolor underprint. Elderly man smoking a pipe a right. Signature 5, 6, 7. Back: Dam. Watermark: Arms-Eagle's head above star. UV: value 10 fluoresces orange.

	VF	UNC
a. 2.1.1973. Serial # prefix *A/1*.	5.50	10.00
b. 2.1.1973. Serial # prefix *B/1-*.	5.00	10.00
c. 2.1.1975.	6.50	12.00
d. 2.1.1976.	2.50	7.50
e. 2.1.1977.	2.50	7.50
f. 2.1.1978.	1.50	6.00
s. As a. Specimen.	—	65.00

1979 Issue

#17-22 Replacement notes: Serial # prefix *XX*; *ZZ*.

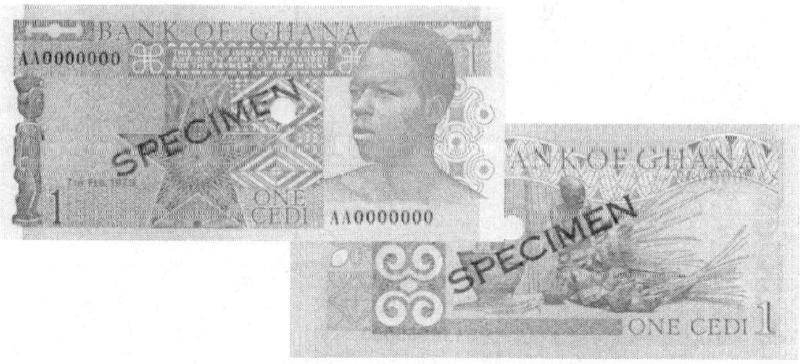

17 1 Cedi

7.2.1979; 6.3.1982. Green and multicolor. Young man at right. Signature 7. 2 serial number varieties. Back: Man weaving at center right. Watermark: Arms-Eagle's head above star.

	VF	UNC
a. 7.2.1979.	2.00	7.50
b. 6.3.1982.	1.50	4.25
s. As b. Specimen. Red overprint: *SPECIMEN* on both sides.	—	90.00

18 2 Cedis VF UNC

7.2.1979; 2.1.1980; 2.7.1980; 6.3.1982. Blue and multicolor. School girl at right. Signature 7. 2 serial number varieties. Back: Workers tending plants in field at center right. Watermark: Arms-Eagle's head above star. UV: country name and value 2 fluoresces orange.

	VF	UNC
a. 7.2.1979.	1.25	7.50
b. 2.1.1980.	2.00	8.00
c. 2.7.1980.	1.00	6.00
d. 6.3.1982.	1.50	7.50
s. Specimen.	—	70.00

19 5 Cedis VF UNC

7.2.1979; 2.1.1980; 6.3.1982 Elderly man at right, Signature 7. 2 serial number varieties. Back: Man cutting log at left center. Watermark: Arms-Eagle's head above star.

	VF	UNC
a. 7.2.1979.	3.00	11.00
b. 2.1.1980.	2.75	10.00
c. 6.3.1982.	2.50	8.00
s. Specimen.	—	75.00

20 10 Cedis VF UNC

7.2.1979; 2.1.1980; 2.7.1980; 6.3.1982. Purple, green and multicolor. Young woman at right. Signature 7. 2 serial number varieties. Back: Fishermen with long net at left center. Watermark: Arms-Eagle's head above star.

	VF	UNC
a. 7.2.1979.	7.50	25.00
b. 2.1.1980.	5.75	17.00
c. 2.7.1980.	6.00	20.00
d. 6.3.1982.	6.50	22.00
s. Specimen.	—	100.

21 20 Cedis VF UNC

7.2.1979; 2.7.1980; 6.3.1982. Green and multicolor. Miner at right. Signature 7. 2 serial number varieties. Back: Man weaving at center right. Watermark: Arms-Eagle's head above star.

	VF	UNC
a. 7.2.1979.	9.50	35.00
b. 2.7.1980.	8.50	27.50
c. 6.3.1982.	8.00	25.00
s. Specimen.	—	100.

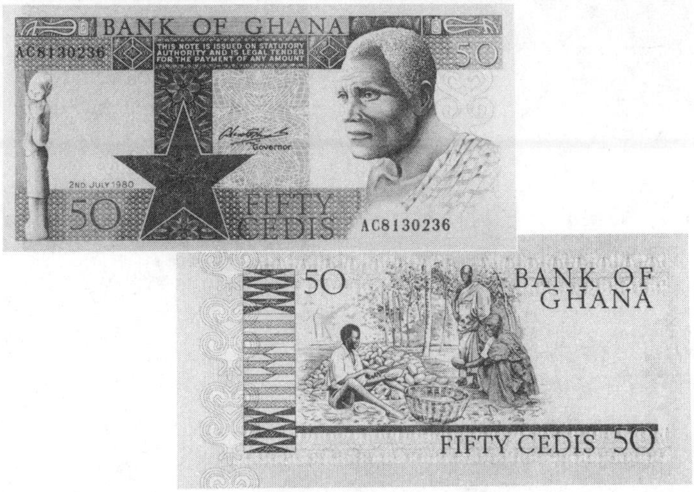

22 50 Cedis VF UNC

7.2.1979; 2.7.1980. Brown and multicolor. Oil man at right. Signature 7. 2 serial number varieties. Back: Men splitting cacao pods. Watermark: Arms-Eagle's head above star.

	VF	UNC
a. 7.2.1979.	5.50	16.00
b. 2.7.1980.	5.00	14.00
s. Specimen.	—	120.

1983-91 Issue

#23-31 Replacement notes: Serial # prefix *Z/1*.

23 10 Cedis VF UNC

15.5.1984. Purple and multicolor. W. Larbi, F. Otoo, E. Nukpor at left, arms at top center right. Signature 8. Without security thread. Back: People going to rural bank at center.

	VF	UNC
a. Issued note.	1.75	6.50
s. Specimen.	—	40.00

24 20 Cedis VF UNC

15.5.1984; 15.7.1986. Shades of green and aqua. Queen Mother Yaa Asantewa at left, arms at top center right. Signature 8. Back: Workers and flag procession. Watermark: Arms-Eagle's head above star.

	VF	UNC
a. Issued note.	2.00	9.00
s. Specimen. Red overprint: *SPECIMEN* on each side.	—	45.00

25 **50 Cedis** | VF | UNC
1.4.1983; 15.5.1984; 15.7.1986. Brown, violet and multicolor. Boy with hat at left center, arms at top center right. Signature 8. Back: Drying grain at center. Watermark: Arms-Eagle's head above star. | 2.00 | 10.00

26 **100 Cedis** | VF | UNC

1983-91. Purple, blue and multicolor. Woman at left center, arms at top center right. Signature 8, 9. Back: Loading produce onto truck at center. Watermark: Arms-Eagle's head above star.

	VF	UNC
a. Signature J. S. Addo. 1.4.1983; 15.5.1984; 15.7.1986.	4.25	18.00
b. Signature G. K. Agama. 19.7.1990; 19.9.1991.	2.25	10.00
s. As a. 1983. Specimen. Red overprint SPECIMEN on each side.	—	70.00

27 **200 Cedis** | VF | UNC

1983-93. Light brown, orange and multicolor. Old man at left center, arms at top center right. Signature 8, 9. Back: Children in classroom at center. Watermark: Arms-Eagle's head above star.

	VF	UNC
a. Signature J. S. Addo. 1.4.1983; 15.5.1984; 15.7.1986.	3.50	14.00
b. Signature G. K. Agama. 20.4.1989; 19.7.1990; 19.9.1991; 14.10.1992; 10.8.1993.	2.00	7.00
s. Specimen. 1.4.1983.	—	100.

28 **500 Cedis** | VF | UNC

1986-94. Purple and blue-green on multicolor underprint. Arms at right. Signature 8, 9. Back: Cacao trees with cacao pods and miner at center. Watermark: Arms-Eagle's head above star.

	VF	UNC
a. Signature J. S. Addo. 31.12.1986.	5.00	30.00
b. Signature G. K. Agama. 20.4.1989; 19.7.1990.	3.50	10.00
c. Signature G. K. Agama. 19.9.1991; 14.10.1992; 10.8.1993; 10.6.1994.	3.50	8.00
s. Specimen.	—	100.

29 **1000 Cedis** | VF | UNC

1991-96. Dark brown, dark blue and dark green on multicolor underprint. Jewels at right, arms at lower left. Signature 9, G. K. Agama. Back: Harvesting, splitting cacao pods at left center. Watermark: Arms-Eagle's head above star.

	VF	UNC
a. 22.2.1991.	4.00	18.00
b. Segmented foil security thread. 22.7.1993, 6.1.1995, 23.2.1996.	2.25	10.00

30 **2000 Cedis** | VF | UNC

1994-96. Red-brown, green and multicolor. Suspension bridge at right, arms at lower right. Signature 9, G. K. Agama. Back: Fisherman loading nets into boat at left center. Watermark: Arms-Eagle's head above star.

	VF	UNC
a. 15.6.1994.	5.00	20.00
b. 6.1.1995.	5.00	20.00
c. 23.1.1996.	5.00	20.00

31 5000 Cedis

1994-96. Green and red-orange on multicolor underprint. Large stars in underprint at center, supported shield of arms at upper right, arms at lower left. Signature 9, G. K. Agama. Back: Map at left center, freighter in harbor at center, log flow in foreground. Watermark: Arms-Eagle's head above star.

	VF	UNC
a. 26.6.1994.	12.00	50.00
b. 6.1.1995.	9.00	35.00
c. 23.2.1996.	9.00	30.00

1996 Issue

32 1000 Cedis

1996-2003. Dark brown, dark blue and dark green on multicolor underprint. Jewels at right, arms at lower left. Signature 9, 10, 11. Back: Harvesting, splitting cacao pods at left center. Watermark: Arms-Eagle's head above star. Reduced size.

	VF	UNC
a. 5.12.1996.	3.00	7.50
b. 1.12.1997.	2.50	6.50
c. 2.5.1998.	2.50	6.50
d. 1.7.1999.	2.50	6.50
e. 1.7.2000.	2.50	6.50
f. 3.9.2001.	4.50	18.00
g. 22.10.2001.	FV	4.50
h. 2.9.2002.	FV	4.50
i. 4.8.2003.	FV	4.50
s. Specimen. 1.7.2000.	—	55.00

33 2000 Cedis

1996-. Red-brown, green and multicolor. Suspension bridge at right, arms at lower left. Signature 9, 10, 11. Back: Fisherman loading nets into boat at left center. Watermark: Arms-Eagle's head above star. Reduced size.

	VF	UNC
a. 5.12.1996.	FV	8.00
b. 1.12.1997.	FV	7.00
c. 2.5.1998.	FV	6.00
d. 1.7.1999.	FV	5.00
e. 1.7.2000.	FV	5.00
f. 3.9.2001.	FV	5.00
f. 22.10.2001.	FV	5.00
g. 2.9.2002.	FV	5.00
h. 4.8.2003.	FV	5.00
i. 4.8.2006.	FV	5.00
s. Specimen. 2.5.1998.	—	55.00

34 5000 Cedis

1996-. Green and red-orange on multicolor underprint. Large stars in underprint at center, supported shield of arms at upper right, arms at lower left. Signature 9, 10, 11. Back: Map at left ceneter, freighter in harbor at center, log flow in foreground. Watermark: Arms-Eagle's head above star. Reduced size.

	VF	UNC
a. 5.12.1996.	FV	11.00
b. 1.12.1997.	FV	11.00
c. 2.5.1998.	FV	11.00
d. 1.7.1999.	FV	11.00
e. 1.7.2000.	FV	10.00
f. 3.9.2001.	FV	10.00
g. 22.10.2001.	FV	9.00
h. 2.9.2002.	FV	9.00
i. 4.8.2003.	FV	9.00
j. 4.8.2006.	FV	9.00

2002 Issue

35 10,000 Cedis

2002-03; 2006. Purple and red-yellow on multicolor underprint. Kwame Nkrumah and five other leaders at right. Signature 11.

	VF	UNC
a. 2.9.2002.	FV	14.00
b. 4.8.2003.	FV	10.00
c. 4.8.2006.	FV	10.00

36 20,000 Cedis

2002-03; 4.8.2006. Red-orange and pink-yellow on multicolor underprint. Ephraim Amu, musician, at right. Signature 11.

	VF	UNC
a. 2.9.2002.	FV	22.50
b. 4.8.2003.	FV	19.00
c. 4.8.2006.	FV	13.50

2007 Issue

37 1 Cedi VF UNC
1.7.2007; 6.3.2010. Red and rose on multicolor underprint. Kwame Nkrumah and five other leaders at right. Back: Dam and water spillway. 137x65mm.

	VF	UNC
a. 1.7.2007.	FV	4.00
b. 6.3.2010.	FV	4.00

37A 2 Cedis VF UNC
6.3.2010. Olive brown on yellow and orange underprint. Kwame Nkrumah at right. Back: Old and new Parliament buildings. 140x67mm. FV 4.50

38 5 Cedis VF UNC
1.7.2007; 6.3.2010. Light and dark blue and tan on multicolor underprint. Kwame Nkrumah and five other leaders at right. Back: Buildings and monuments. 141x68mm.

	VF	UNC
a. 1.7.2007.	FV	5.00
b. 6.3.2010.	FV	5.00

39 10 Cedis VF UNC
1.7.2007; 6.3.2010; 1.7.2011. Light and dark green and peach on multicolor underprint. Kwame Nkrumah and five other leaders at right. Back: Bank of Ghana building. 145x71mm.

	VF	UNC
a. 1.7.2007.	FV	10.00
b. 6.3.2010.	FV	10.00
c. 1.7.2011.	FV	10.00

40 20 Cedis VF UNC
1.7.2007. Violet on multicolor underprint. Kwame Nkrumah and five other leaders at right. Back: Government Building. 149x65mm. FV 17.50

41 50 Cedis VF UNC
1.7.2007; 6.3.2010. Brown and tan on multicolor underprint. Kwame Nkrumah and five other leaders at right. Back: Buildings. 153x77mm.

	VF	UNC
a. 1.7.2007.	FV	45.00
b. 6.3.2010.	FV	45.00

Collector Series

Bank of Ghana

1977 Issue

CS1 1977 1-10 Cedis Mkt. Value
#13b, 14c, 15b, 16d. with overprint: *SPECIMEN* and Maltese cross prefix serial #. 50.00

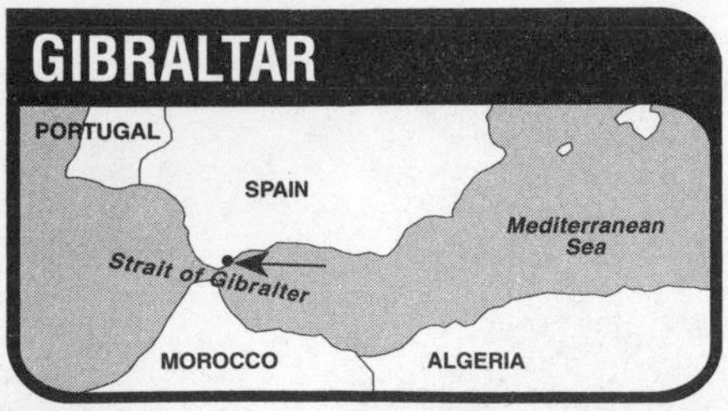

The British Colony of Gibraltar, located at the southernmost point of the Iberian Peninsula, has an area of 6.5 sq. km. and a population of 28,000. Capital (and only town): Gibraltar. Strategically important, Gibraltar was reluctantly ceded to Great Britain by Spain in the 1713 Treaty of Utrecht; the British garrison was formally declared a colony in 1830. In a referendum held in 1967, Gibraltarians voted overwhelmingly to remain a British dependency. The subsequent granting of autonomy in 1969 by the UK led to Spain closing the border and severing all communication links. A series of talks were held by the UK and Spain between 1997 and 2002 on establishing temporary joint sovereignty over Gibraltar. In response to these talks, the Gibraltar Government called a referendum in late 2002 in which the majority of citizens voted overwhelmingly against any sharing of sovereignty with Spain. Since the referendum, tripartite talks on other issues have been held with Spain, the UK, and Gibraltar, and in September 2006 a three-way agreement was signed. Spain agreed to remove restrictions on air movements, to speed up customs procedures, to implement international telephone dialing, and to allow mobile roaming agreements. Britain agreed to pay increased pensions to Spaniards who had been employed in Gibraltar before the border closed. Spain will be allowed to open a cultural institute from which the Spanish flag will fly. A new noncolonial constitution came into effect in 2007, but the UK retains responsibility for defense, foreign relations, internal security, and financial stability.

RULERS:

British

MONETARY SYSTEM:

1 Shilling = 12 Pence
1 Pound = 20 Shillings to 1971
1 Pound = 100 New Pence, 1971-

British Administration

Government of Gibraltar

1934 Ordinance; 1958 Issue

		VF	UNC
17	**10 Shillings** 3.10.1958; 1.5.1965. Blue on yellow-brown underprint. Rock of Gilbraltar at left. Back: Arms at center. Printer: TDLR.	100.	380.

		VF	UNC
18	**1 Pound** 1958-75. Green on yellow-brown underprint. Rock of Gibraltar at bottom center. Back: Arms at center. Printer: TDLR.		
	a. Signature title: *FINANCIAL SECRETARY.* 3.10.1958; 1.5.1965.	27.50	150.
	b. Signature title: *FINANCIAL AND DEVELOPMENT SECRETARY.* 20.11.1971.	22.50	115.
	c. 20.11.1975.	45.00	230.
	s. Specimen. As a-c.	—	—

		VF	UNC
19	**5 Pounds** 1958-75. Brown. Rock of Gibraltar at bottom center. Back: Arms at center. Printer: TDLR.		
	a. Signature title: *FINANCIAL SECRETARY.* 3.10.1958; 1.5.1965.	155.	800.
	b. Signature title: *FINANCIAL AND DEVELOPMENT SECRETARY.* 1.5.1965; 20.11.1971; 20.11.1975.	120.	640.
	s. Specimen. As a-b.	—	—

1975; 1986 Issue; Ordinance Cap 39

		VF	UNC
20	**1 Pound** 1975-88. Brown and red on multicolor underprint. Queen Elizabeth II at center right. Three signatue varieties. Back: The Covenant of Gibraltar at left center. Watermark: Queen Elizabeth II. Printer: TDLR.		
	a. 20.11.1975 (1978).	20.00	120.
	b. 15.9.1979.	19.00	110.
	c. 10.11.1983.	18.00	105.
	d. 21.10.1986.	11.00	85.00
	e. 4.8.1988.	FV	30.00
	s. Specimen. As a; b; d.	—	260.

		VF	UNC
21	**5 Pounds** 1975; 1988. Green on multicolor underprint. Queen Elizabeth II at right. Signature varieties. Back: The Covenant of Gibraltar at left center. Watermark: Queen Elizabeth II. Printer: TDLR.		
	a. 20.11.1975.	35.00	185.
	b. 4.8.1988.	16.00	80.00

		VF	UNC
22	**10 Pounds** 1975; 1986. Deep violet, dark brown and deep blue-green on multicolor underprint. Queen Elizabeth II at right. Signature varieties. Back: Governor's house. Watermark: Queen Elizabeth II. Printer: TDLR.		
	a. 20.11.1975 (1977).	55.00	260.
	b. 21.10.1986.	FV	130.

23 **20 Pounds** VF UNC
1975-86. Light brown on multicolor underprint. Queen Elizabeth II at right. Signature varieties. Back: Governor's house. Watermark: Queen Elizabeth II. Printer: TDLR.

	VF	UNC
a. 20.11.1975 (1978).	185.	630.
b. 15.9.1979.	175.	570.
c. 1.7.1986.	110.	330.

24 **50 Pounds** VF UNC
27.11.1986. Purple on multicolor underprint. Queen Elizabeth II at right. Signature varieties. Back: Rock of Gibraltar. Watermark: Queen Elizabeth II. Printer: TDLR. 125. 380.

1995 Issue

25 **5 Pounds** VF UNC
1.7.1995. Green and purple on multicolor underprint. Mature image of Queen Elizabeth II at right, shield of arms at left. Urn above gateway at left center. Back: Tavik ibn Zeyad with sword at right, Moorish castle at upper left. Watermark: Queen Elizabeth II. 135x70mm.

	VF	UNC
a. Issued note.	FV	65.00
s. Specimen.	—	140.

26 **10 Pounds** VF UNC
1.7.1995. Orange-brown and violet on multicolor underprint. Mature image of Queen Elizabeth II at right, shield of arms at left. Lighthouse above cannon at left center. Back: Portrait General Eliott at right, scene of *The Great Siege, 1779-85* at upper left center. Watermark: Queen Elizabeth II. 142x75mm.

	VF	UNC
a. Issued note.	FV	115.
s. Specimen.	—	250.

27 **20 Pounds** VF UNC
1.7.1995. Purple and violet on multicolor underprint. Mature image of Queen Elizabeth II at right, shield of arms at left, bird above cannon at left center. Back: Portrait Admiral Nelson at right, H.M.S. Victory at upper left center. Watermark: Queen Elizabeth II. 150x80mm.

	VF	UNC
a. Issued note.	FV	185.
s. Specimen.	—	330.

28 **50 Pounds** VF UNC
1.7.1995. Red and violet on multicolor underprint. Mature image of Queen Elizabeth II at right, shield of arms at left. Gibraltar monkey above horse and carriage at left center. Back: Portrait W. Churchill at upper right, Spitfire airplanes at the North Front, 1942 at upper left center. Watermark: Queen Elizabeth II. 157x85mm.

	VF	UNC
a. Issued note.	150.	480.
s. Specimen.	—	580.

2000 Issue

#29, Millennium Commemorative

29 5 Pounds — VF | UNC

2000. Green on multicolor underprint. Mature image of Queen Elizabeth at right, shield of arms at lower left, urn above gateway at left center. Enhanced security devices. Back: Gibraltar monkey at left, city & harbor view at center, gondola on right. 135x70mm. — FV | 57.50

30 10 Pounds — VF | UNC

10.9.2002. Orange-brown and violet on multicolor underprint. Mature image of Queen Elizabeth II at right. Back: Large square with butterflies and grouse within. 142x72mm. — FV | 110.

2004 Commemorative Issue

31 20 Pounds — VF | UNC

4.8.2004. Mauve, tan and black on multicolor underprint. Mature image of Queen Elizabeth II at right. Back: Blue, tan and brown. John Mackintosh Square at center, 19th century townfolk at right edge. 150x80mm.

a. Issued note. — FV | 175.

s. Specimen. — — | 300.

2006 Issue

32 10 Pounds — VF | UNC

1.12.2006. Orange-brown and violet on multicolor underprint. Mature image of Queen Elizabeth II at right. Back: Large square. Reprint of #26a with new date and signature. 142x75mm.

a. Issued note. — FV | 50.00

s. Specimen. — — | 240.

33 20 Pounds — VF | UNC

1.12.2006. Purple and violet on multicolor underprint. Mature image of Queen Elizabeth II at right. Back: Portrait Admiral Nelson at right, H.M.S. Victory at upper left center. Reprint of #27a with new date and signature. 150x80mm.

a. Issued note. — FV | 160.

s. Specimen. — — | 285.

34 50 Pounds — VF | UNC

1.12.2006. Red and violet on multicolor underprint. Mature image of Queen Elizabeth II at right. Back: Winston Churchill at right, Spitfire airplanes at the North Front. Reprint of #28a with new date and signature. 157x85mm.

a. Issued note. — FV | 230.

s. Specimen. — — | 525.

2010 Issue

35 5 Pounds — VF | UNC

1.1.2011. Green on multicolor underprint. Queen Elizabeth II at left center. Back: Upper Ward and Tower of Homage of the Moorish Castle. Printer: TDLR (without imprint). 133x70mm. — FV | 30.00

36 **10 Pounds** | VF | UNC
1.1.2010. Blue on multicolor underprint. Queen Elizabeth II at left center. Back: John Trumbull's painting "Sortie made by the Garrison of Gibraltar." Printer: TDLR (without imprint.) 142x75mm. | FV | 55.00

37 **20 Pounds** | VF | UNC
1.1.2011. Orange and purple on multicolor underprint. Queen Elizabeth II at left center. Back: H.M.S. Victory returning to Gibraltar being towed by H.M.S. Neptune after Battle of Trafalgar. Printer: TDLR (without imprint.) 150x80mm. | FV | 100.

38 **50 Pounds** | VF | UNC
1.1.2010. Red and brown on multicolor underprint. Queen Elizabeth II at left center. Back: Casemates Square buildings. 157x85mm. | FV | 225.

39 **100 Pounds** | VF | UNC
1.1.2011. Purple on multicolor underprint. Queen Elizabeth II at left center. Back: King's Bastion. Printer: TDLR (without imprint). 164x90mm. | FV | 350.

Collector Series

Government of Gibraltar

1975 Issue

CS1 **1975 1-20 Pounds** | Mkt. Value
#20a, 21a, 22, 23a. with overprint: *SPECIMEN* and serial # prefix: Maltese cross. | 350.

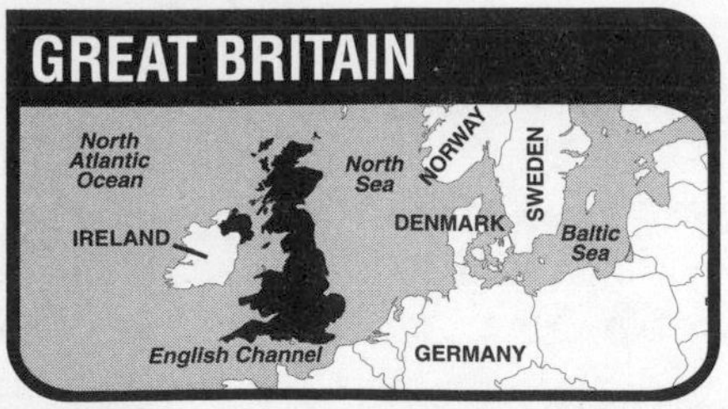

The United Kingdom of Great Britain and Northern Ireland, (including England, Scotland, Wales and Norhtern Ireland) is located off the northwest coast of the European continent, has an area of 94,227 sq. mi. (244,046 sq. km.), and a population of 59.45 million. Capital: London.

The economy is d on industrial activity, trading and financial services. Machinery, motor vehicles, chemicals and textile yarns and fabrics are exported.

After the departure of the Romans, who brought Britain into an active relationship with Europe, Britain fell prey to invaders from Scandinavia and the Low Countries who drove the original Britons into Scotland and Wales, and established a profusion of kingdoms that finally united in the 11th century under the Danish King Canute. Norman rule, following the conquest of 1066, stimulated the development of those institutions which have since distinguished British life. Henry VIII (1509-47) turned Britain from continental adventuring and faced it to the sea - a decision that made Britain a world power during the reign of Elizabeth I (1558-1603). Strengthened by the Industrial Revolution and the defeat of Napoleon, 19th century Britain turned to the remote parts of the world and established a colonial empire of such extent and prosperity that the world has never seen its like. World Wars I and II sealed the fate of the Empire and relegated Britain to a lesser role in world affairs by draining her resources and inaugurating a worldwide movement toward national self-determination in her former colonies.

By the mid-20th century, most of the former British Empire had gained independence and had evolved into the Commonwealth of Nations. This association of equal and and autonomous states, set out to agree views and special relationships with one another (appointing High Commissioners rather than Ambassadors) for mutual benefit, trade interests, etc. The Commonwealth is presently (1999) composed of 54 member nations, including the United Kingdom. All recognize the monarch as Head of the Commonwealth; 16 continue to recognize Queen Elizabeth II as Head of State. In addition to the United Kingdom, they are: Antigua & Barbuda, Australia, The Bahamas, Barbados Belize, Canada, Grenada, Paupa New Guinea, St. Christopher & Nevis, St. Lucia, St. Vincent & the Grenadines, Solomon Islands.

RULERS:

William III, 1694-1702
Anne, 1702-1714
George I, 1714-1727
George II, 1727-1760
George III, 1760-1820
George IV, 1820-1830
William IV, 1830-1837
Victoria, 1837-1901
Edward VII, 1901-1910
George V, 1910-1936
Edward VIII, 1936
George VI, 1936-1952
Elizabeth II, 1952-

MONETARY SYSTEM:

1 Shilling = 12 Pence
1 Pound = 20 Shillings to 1971
1 Pound = 100 (New) Pence, 1971-
<RNR>REPLACEMENT NOTES: <P>#368, ##A series prefix. #369, S-S or S-T, #373-376, letter M as one of the letters in series prefix. #377-380, Page sign. only, M## or ##M series prefix.

KINGDOM

BANK OF ENGLAND

1957-61 ND ISSUE

			VF	UNC
371	**5 Pounds**	ND (1957-61). Blue and multicolor. Helmeted Britannia head at left, St. George and dragon at lower center. Signature L.K. O'Brien. Back: Lion standing left. Denomination *£5* in blue print on back. 159x88mm.		
		a. Issued note.	65.00	150.
		s. Specimen.	—	1500.
372	**5 Pounds**	ND (1961-63). Blue and multicolor. Helmeted Britannia head at left, St. George and dragon at lower center. Signature L. K. O'Brien at left. Back: Denomination *£5* in white on back. 159x88mm.		
		a. Issued note.	65.00	150.
		s. Specimen.	—	1500.

1960-64 ND ISSUE

			VF	UNC
373	**10 Shillings**	ND (1961-70). Brown on multicolor underprint. Portrait Queen Elizabeth II at right. Back: Britannia seated with shield in circle at center right. Watermark: Laureate heads in continuous vertical row at left. 140x67mm.		
		a. Signature L. K. O'Brien. (1961-62).	5.00	16.00
		b. Signature J. Q. Hollom. (1962-66).	4.50	14.00
		c. Signature J. S. Fforde. (1966-70).	4.00	12.50
		s. Specimen. As a-c.	—	1000.

			VF	UNC
374	**1 Pound**	ND (1960-78). Deep green on multicolor underprint. Portrait Queen Elizabeth II at right. Watermark: Laureate heads in continuous vertical row at left. Back: Britannia seated with shield in circle at center right. Watermark: Laureate heads in continuous vertical row at left. 150x72mm.		
		a. Signature L. K. O'Brien. (1960-61).	5.00	14.00
		b. Signature as a. Small letter *R* (for Research) at lower left center on back. (Notes printed on web press.) Serial # prefixes A01N; A05N; A06N.	400.	1250.
		c. Signature J. Q. Hollom. (1962-66).	4.00	12.00
		d. Signature as c. Letter *G* at lower left center on back. (Printed on the experimental German Goebel Press.)	12.50	27.50
		e. Signature J. S. Fforde. (1966-70).	4.00	12.00
		f. Signature as e. Letter *G* at lower center on back.	14.00	32.50
		g. Signature J. B. Page. (1970-77).	4.00	10.00
		s. Specimen. As a, e, g.	—	1100.

			VF	UNC
375	**5 Pounds**	ND (1963-71). Deep blue on multicolor underprint. Portrait of Queen Elizabeth II at right. Back: Britannia seated with shield in 8-petalled pattern at center. Watermark: Laureate heads in continuous vertical row. 140x85mm.		
		a. Signature J. Q. Hollom. (1963-66).	27.50	80.00
		b. Signature J. S. Fforde. (1966-70).	25.00	70.00
		c. Signature J. B. Page. (1970-71).	27.50	80.00
		s. Specimen. As a, b.	—	1500.

376 10 Pounds

ND (1964-75). Deep brown on multicolor underprint. Portrait of Queen Elizabeth II at right. Back: Lion facing left at center. Watermark: Queen Elizabeth II. 151x93mm.

	VF	UNC
a. Signature J. Q. Hollom. (1964-66).	45.00	110.
b. Signature J. S. Fforde. (1966-70).	45.00	110.
c. Signature J. B. Page. (1970-75).	40.00	100.
r. As c. Replacement note. Serial # prefix *M*.	60.00	135.
s. Specimen. As a; b; c.	—	1800.

1971-82 ND Issue

377 1 Pound

ND (1978-84). Deep green on multicolor underprint. Queen Elizabeth II in court robes at right. Back: Sir Isaac Newton at center right, guilloches gray at lower left and right corners. Watermark: Sir Isaac Newton. 135x67mm.

	VF	UNC
a. Green signature J. B. Page. (1978-80).	4.00	10.00
b. Black signature D. H. F. Somerset. Back guilloches are light green at lower left and right. (1981-84).	4.00	10.00
s. Specimen. As a; b.	—	1500.

378 5 Pounds

ND (1971-91). Blue-black and blue on multicolor underprint. Queen Elizabeth II in court robes at right. Back: Arthur Wellesley, Duke of Wellington at center right, battle scene in Spain at left center. Watermark: Wellington's head. 145x77mm.

	VF	UNC
a. Blue-gray signature. J. B. Page. (1971-72).	17.50	50.00
b. Black signature. J. B. Page. Litho back with small *L* at lower left (1973-80).	17.50	50.00
c. Black signature. D. H. F. Somerset. (1980-87). Thin security thread.	15.00	40.00
d. As c. Without signature.	120.	350.
e. Signature D. H. F. Somerset. Wide security thread. (1987-88).	18.00	55.00
f. Signature G. M. Gill (1988-91).	15.00	40.00
s. Specimen. As a; e.	—	1400.

379 10 Pounds

ND (1975-92). Deep brown on multicolor underprint. Queen Elizabeth II in court robes at right. Back: Florence Nightingale at center right, hospital scene with Florence Nightingale as the *Lady with* / Watermark: Florence Nightingale. 150x85mm.

	VF	UNC
a. Signature J. B. Page. (1975-80).	35.00	90.00
b. Signature D. H. F. Somerset (1980-84).	40.00	110.
c. Signature D. H. F. Somerset. Litho printing with *L* at lower left on back. (1984-86).	25.00	75.00
d. Signature D. H. F. Somerset. Segmented security thread. (1987-88).	30.00	85.00
e. Signature G. M. Gill (1988-91).	25.00	75.00
f. Signature G. E. A. Kentfield (1991-92).	40.00	115.
r. As a. Replacement note. Serial # prefix *M*.	110.	325.
s. Specimen. As a; d.	—	1700.

380 20 Pounds

ND (1970-91). Purple on multicolor underprint. Queen Elizabeth II in court robes at right. Back: William Shakespeare statue at center right. Watermark: William Shakespeare. 160x90mm.

	VF	UNC
a. Watermark: Queen Elizabeth II. Signature J. S. Fforde. (1970).	190.	600.
b. Watermark as a. Signature J. B. Page. (1970-80).	60.00	185.
c. Watermark as a. Signature D. H. F. Somerset. (1981-84).	70.00	225.
d. Watermark: Shakespeare. Modified background colors. Segmented security thread. D. H. F. Somerset. (1984-88).	55.00	175.
e. Signature G. M. Gill (1988-91).	55.00	165.
s1. Specimen. As a.	—	2000.
s2. Specimen. As d.	—	1800.

381 50 Pounds — VF — UNC

ND (1981-93). Olive-green and brown on multicolor underprint. Queen Elizabeth II in court robes at right. Back: View and plan of St. Paul's Cathedral at left, Sir C. Wren at center right. Watermark: Queen Elizabeth II. 169x95mm.

	VF	UNC
a. Black signature. D. H .F. Somerset (1981-88).	140.	350.
b. Modified background and guilloche colors. Segmented foil on security thread on surface. Signature G. M. Gill (1988-91).	160.	425.
c. Signature G. E. A. Kentfield (1991-93).	150.	375.
s. Specimen. As a; b.	—	1900.

1990-92 Issue

382 5 Pounds — VF — UNC

©1990 (1990-2002). Dark brown and deep blue-green on multicolor underprint. Queen Elizabeth II at right, crown at upper right corner, Britannia seated at upper left center. Back: Rocket locomotive at left, George Stephenson at right. Watermark: Queen Elizabeth II. 135x70mm.

	VF	UNC
a. Signature G. M. Gill (1990-91). Light and dark signature varieties.	FV	40.00
b. Signature G. E. Kentfield (1991-98).	FV	25.00
c. Signature M. Lowther (1999-2002).	FV	25.00
s1. Specimen. As a.	—	1750.
s2. Specimen. As b.	—	1600.

383 10 Pounds

©1992 (1992-93). Black, brown and red on multicolor underprint. Queen Elizabeth II at right, crown at upper right corner, Britannia at left. Signature G. E. A. Kentfield (1992). Back: Cricket match at left, Charles Dickens at right. Watermark: Queen Elizabeth II. 142x75mm.

	VF	UNC
a. Issued note.	FV	60.00
s. Specimen.	—	1600.

384 20 Pounds — VF — UNC

©1991 (1991-93). Queen Elizabeth II, crown at upper right corner, Britannia at left. Segmented vertical foil strip and purple optical device at left center.Serial # olive-green to maroon at upper left and dark blue at Back: M. Faraday with students at left, portrait at right. Watermark: Queen Elizabeth II. 150x80mm.

	VF	UNC
a. Signature G. M. Gill (1990-91).	FV	115.
b. Signature G. E. A. Kentfield (1991-93).	FV	125.
s. Specimen. As a.	—	1800.

1993 Modified Issue

386 10 Pounds — VF — UNC

©1993 (1993-2000). Black, brown and red on multicolor underprint. Queen Elizabeth II at right, Britannia at left, enhanced symbols for value £10 at upper right. Back: Cricket match at left, Charles Dickens at right, value symbol at top right. Watermark: Queen Elizabeth II. 142x75mm.

	VF	UNC
a. Signature G. E. A. Kentfield (1993-98).	FV	60.00
b. Signature M. Lowther (1999-2000).	FV	55.00

387 20 Pounds — VF — UNC

©1993 (1993-2006). Black, teal-violet and purple on multicolor underprint. Queen Elizabeth II at right, Britannia at left, dark £ 20 value symbol at upper left corner and at upper right corner. Segmented vertical foil strip at left. Back: M. Faraday with students at left, portrait at right, £ 20 value symbol at top right. Watermark: Queen Elizabeth II. 150x80mm.

	VF	UNC
a. Signature G. E. A. Kentfield (1993-98).	FV	100.
b. Signature M. Lowther (1999).	FV	155.

388 50 Pounds — VF — UNC

©1994 (1993-). Brownish-black, red and violet on multicolor underprint. Queen Elizabeth II at right, Allegory in oval in underprint at left, £ 50 value at upper right corner. Back: Bank gatekeeper at lower left, his house at left and Sir J. Houblon at right. Watermark: Queen Elizabeth II. 156x85mm.

	VF	UNC
a. Signature G. E. A. Kentfield (1993-98).	FV	240.
b. Signature M. Lowther (1999-2003).	FV	225.
c. Signature A. Bailey (2006-).	FV	190.

1999-2000 Issue

389 10 Pounds — VF | UNC

© 2000. (2000-12). Brown, orange and multicolor. Queen Elizabeth II at right. Back: Brown and multicolor. Charles Darwin at right, Hummingbird magnifying glass and flora to left. 142x75mm.

	VF	UNC
a. Copyright notice reads: *THE GOVERNOR AND THE COMPANY...* signature M. Lowther (2000).	FV	50.00
b. Copyright notice reads: *THE GOVERNOR AND COMPANY...* signature M. Lowther (2000-03).	FV	42.50
c. Signature A. Bailey (2004).	FV	35.00
d. Signature Chris Salmon (2012).	FV	35.00

390 20 Pounds — VF | UNC

© 1999 (1999-2004). Brown and purple on red and green underprint. Queen Elizabeth II at right, 20 and Britannia in OVD, modified top left and right value numerals. Back: Worchester Cathedral at left, Sir Edward Elgar at right. 150x80mm.

	VF	UNC
a. Signature M. Lowther (1999-2003).	FV	75.00
b. Signature A. Bailey (2004).	FV	70.00

2002 Issue

391 5 Pounds — VF | UNC

© 2002. Brown and green on multicolor underprint. Queen Elizabeth II at right. Back: Light blue and multicolor. Elizabeth Fry at right, scene of women and children in workhouse at left. 135x70mm.

	VF	UNC
a. Serial # on varnished paper, easily rubbed off. Withdrawn. From serial # prefix: HA 01. Signature M. Lowther (2002).	FV	40.00
b. Serial # prefix on paper, varnished. From serial # prefix: HC 01. Signature M. Lowther (2002-03).	FV	20.00
c. Signature A. Bailey (2004).	FV	17.50
d. Signature Chris Salmon (2012).	FV	17.50

2006 Issue

392 20 Pounds — VF | UNC

© 2006 (2007-12). Deep violet, purple and black on multicolor underprint. Queen Elizabeth II at right, façade of Buckingham Palace at lower center. Britannia at lower left. Back: Adam Smith at left and pin factory at center. Watermark: Adam Smith. 150x80mm.

	VF	UNC
a. Sign. A. Bailey. (2006).	FV	65.00
b. Signature Chris Salmon (2012).	FV	65.00

393 50 Pounds — VF | UNC

(2011). Queen Elizabeth II at right. Back: Matthew Boulton and James Watt.; staem engine and the Soho (Birmingham) Factory. 156x85mm.

	VF	UNC
a. Signature Chris Salmon.	FV	175.

Collector Series

Bank of England

1995 Issue

#CS1 and CS2, 200th Anniversary of the First 5 Pound Note

		Mkt. Value
CS1	**5 Pounds** Uncut sheet of three notes #385 in folder. Serial #AB16-AB18. Last sheet printing.	170.
CS2	**5 Pounds** Uncut sheet of three notes #385 in folder. Serial #AC01-AC03. First web printing.	170.
CS3	**10 Pounds** As #386 with serial #HM70. 70th Birthday of Queen Elizabeth II. Issued in a case with £5 Proof coin. 2,000 sets.	140.
CS4	**20 Pounds** Uncut pair of #384b. Kentfield first issue. 1000 pair in folder.	460.

1996 Issue

		Mkt. Value
CS5	**5 Pounds** As #386 with serial # prefix *HM70* for the 70th Birthday of Queen Elizabeth II. Limited to 5000.	80.00
CS6	**5 Pounds** Uncut sheet of 8 of #383c. Limited to 5000 sheets.	220.

1997 Issue

CS7 5 Pounds — Mkt. Value

As #385a with serial # prefix HK issued commemorating the Return of Hong Kong to the People's Republic of China.

	Mkt. Value
a. Single note in a special card.	25.00
b. Uncut sheet of 12.	440.
c. Uncut sheet of 35.	700.

CS8 5, 10, 20 Pounds

As #385b, 386b, 387b with serial # prefix BE98 with matching numbers. Limited to 1888. — 160.

1999 Issue

CS9 5, 10, 20, 50 Pounds — Mkt. Value

New Lowther issue. In folder: #385b, 386b, 387b and 388b. — 600.

2000 Issue

CS10 5 Pounds — Mkt. Value

As 385b but with serial # prefix *YR20.* Millenium. Limited to 1500. — 40.00

CS11 10 Pounds

As #386b with serial # prefix *YR20.*Millenium. Limited to 1500. — 65.00

CS12 5 Pounds

As #385b with serial # prefix *QM10. With CN crown in folder.* Queen Mother's 100th birthday. Limited to 10,000. — 60.00

CS13 5 Pounds

As #CS12 with 5 pound stamp in folder. Limited to 1000. — 80.00

GREECE

The Hellenic Republic of Greece is situated in southeastern Europe on the southern tip of the Balkan Peninsula. The republic includes many islands, the most important of which are Crete and the Ionian Islands. Greece (including islands) has an area of 131,940 sq. km. and a population of 10.72 million. Capital: Athens. Greece is still largely agricultural. Tobacco, cotton, fruit and wool are exported.

Greece achieved independence from the Ottoman Empire in 1829. During the second half of the 19th century and the first half of the 20th century, it gradually added neighboring islands and territories, most with Greek-speaking populations. In World War II, Greece was first invaded by Italy (1940) and subsequently occupied by Germany (1941-44); fighting endured in a protracted civil war between supporters of the king and Communist rebels. Following the latter's defeat in 1949, Greece joined NATO in 1952. A military dictatorship, which in 1967 suspended many political liberties and forced the king to flee the country, lasted seven years. The 1974 democratic elections and a referendum created a parliamentary republic and abolished the monarchy. In 1981, Greece joined the EC (now the EU); it became the 12th member of the European Economic and Monetary Union in 2001.

RULERS:

Paul I, 1947-1964
Constantine II, 1964-1973

MONETARY SYSTEM:

1 Drachma = 100 Lepta, 1841-2001
1 Euro = 100 Cents, 2002-

REPLACEMENT NOTES:

#195-: OOA prefix.

GREEK ALPHABET

Α	α	Alpha	(ä)	Ι	ι	Iota	(ē)	Ρ	ρ	Rho	(r)
Β	β	Beta	(b)	Κ	κ	Kappa	(k)	Σ	σ	Sigma	(s)6
Γ	γ	Gamma	(g)	Λ	λ	Lambda	(l)	Τ	τ	Tau	(t)
Δ	δ	Delta	(d)	Μ	μ	Mu	(m)	Υ	υ	Upsilon	(o͞o)
Ε	ε	Epsilon	(e)	Ν	ν	Nu	(n)	Φ	φ	Phi	(f)
Ζ	ζ	Zeta	(z)	Ξ	ξ	Xi	(ks)	Χ	χ	Chi	(H)
Η	η	Eta	(ā)	Ο	ο	Omicron	(o)	Ψ	ψ	Psi	(ps)
Θ	θ	Theta	(th)	Π	π	Pi	(p)	Ω	ω	Omega	(ō)

Kingdom

ΤΡΑΠΕΖΑ ΤΗΣ ΕΛΛΑΔΟΣ

Bank of Greece

1964-70 Issue

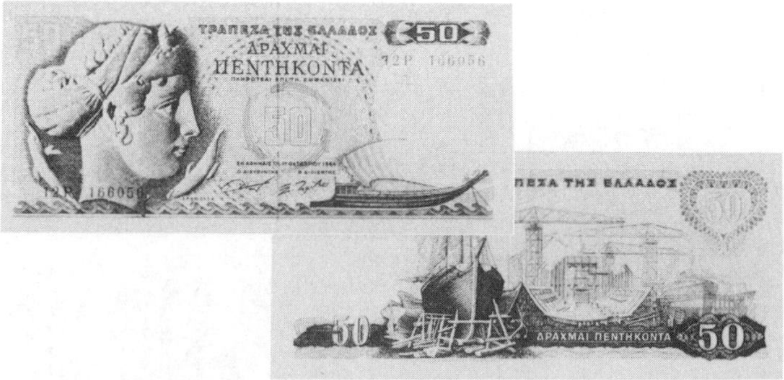

195 50 Drachmai

1.10.1964. Blue on multicolor underprint. Arethusa at left, galley at bottom right. Back: Shipyard. Watermark: Ephebus.

	VF	UNC
a. Issued note.	1.00	1.50
s. Specimen.	—	100.

196 100 Drachmai VF UNC

1966-67. Red-brown on multicolor underprint. Demokritos at left, building and atomic symbol at right. Back: University at center. Watermark: Ephebus.

		VF	UNC
a.	Signature Zolotas as Bank President. 1.7.1966.	10.00	32.50
b.	Signature Galanis as Bank President. 1.10.1967.	1.00	2.00
s.	Specimen. As b.	—	100.

197 500 Drachmai VF UNC

1.11.1968. Olive on multicolor underprint. Relief of Elusis at center. Back: Relief of animals at bottom left, fruit at bottom center. Watermark: Ephebus.

		VF	UNC
a.	Issued note.	5.00	20.00
s.	Specimen.	—	100.

198 1000 Drachmai VF UNC

1.11.1970. Brown on multicolor underprint. Zeus at left, stadium at bottom center. Back: Brown and green. Woman at left and view of city Hydra on the Isle of Hydra.

		VF	UNC
a.	Watermark: Aphrodite of Knidus (hair in knot at top of head) profile (1970).	30.00	100.
b.	Watermark: Ephebus of Anticythera in 3/4 profile (1972).	1.50	5.00
s.	As b. Specimen.	—	100.

Republic

ΤΡΑΠΕΖΑ ΤΗΣ ΕΛΛΑΔΟΣ

Bank of Greece

1978 Issue

199 50 Drachmai VF UNC

8.12.1978. Blue on multicolor underprint. Poseidon at left. Back: Sailing ship at left center, man and woman at right. Watermark: Charioteer Polyzalos of Delphi.

		VF	UNC
a.	Issued note.	FV	1.50
r.	Replacement note. Series *00A*.	FV	30.00
s.	Specimen.	—	100.

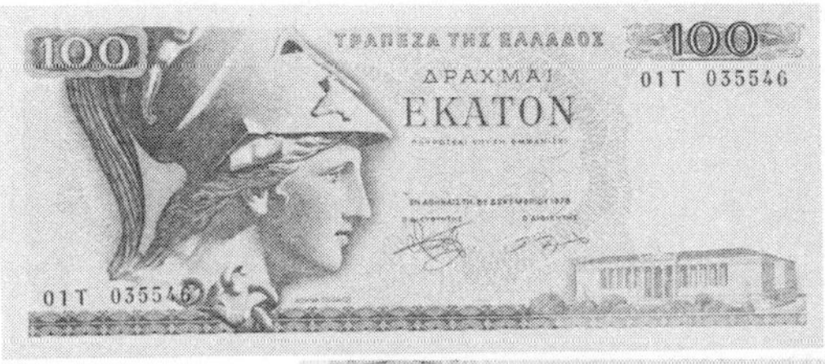

200 100 Drachmai VF UNC

8.12.1978. Brown and violet on multicolor underprint. Athena Peiraios at left. Back: Maroon, green and orange. A. Koraes at left, Church of Arkadi Monastery in Crete at bottom right. Watermark: Charioteer Polyzalos of Delphi. 158x67mm.

		VF	UNC
a.	Original issue. Without *L* at lower left on back.	FV	1.50
b.	Second issue. With *L* at lower left on back.	FV	1.25
r.	As b. Replacement note. Series *00A*.	FV	30.00
s.	Specimen.	—	125.

1983-87 Issue

201 500 Drachmaes VF UNC

1.2.1983. Deep green on multicolor underprint. I. Capodistrias at left center, his birthplace at lower right. Back: Fortress overlooking Corfu. Watermark: Charioteer Polyzalos of Delphi. 158x72mm.

		VF	UNC
a.	Issued note.	FV	3.50
r.	Replacement note. Series *00A*.	FV	125.
s.	Specimen.	—	125.

202	1000 Drachmaes	VF	UNC
	1.7.1987. Brown on multicolor underprint. Apollo at center right, ancient coin at bottom left center. Back: Discus thrower and Hera Temple ruins at Olympia. Watermark: Charioteer Polyzalos of Delphi. 158x77mm.		
	a. Issued note.	FV	5.00
	r. Replacement note. Series *00A* .	FV	80.00
	s. Specimen.	—	125.

203	5000 Drachmaes	VF	UNC
	23.3.1984. Deep blue on multicolor underprint. T. Kolokotronis at left, Church of the Holy Apostles at Calamata at bottom center right. Back: Landscape and view of town of Karytaina at center right. Watermark: Charioteer Polyzalos of Delphi. 163x81mm.		
	a. Issued note.	FV	40.00
	r. Replacement note. Series *00A* .	FV	150.
	s. Specimen.	—	175.

1995-98 Issue

204	200 Drachmaes	VF	UNC
	2.9.1996. Deep orange on multicolor underprint. R. Velestinlis-Feraios at left. Velestinlis-Feraios singing his patriotic song at lower right. Back: Secret school run by Greek priests (during the Ottoman occupation) at center right. Watermark: Philip of Macedonia. 129x65mm.		
	a. Issued note.	FV	3.25
	s. Specimen.	—	125.

205	5000 Drachmaes	VF	UNC
	1.6.1997. Purple and yellow-green on multicolor underprint. T. Kolokotronis at left, Church of the Holy Apostles at Calamata at bottom center right. Back: Landscape and view of town of Karytaina at center right. Watermark: Philip of Macedonia. Reduced size. 147x74mm.		
	a. Issued note.	FV	27.50
	r. Replacement note. Serie *00A* .	FV	175.
	s. Specimen.	—	175.

206	10,000 Drachmaes	VF	UNC
	16.1.1995. Deep purple on multicolor underprint. Dr. Georgios Papanikolaou at left center, microscope at lower center right. Back: Medical care frieze at bottom center, statue of Asklepios at center right. 153x77mm.		
	a. Issued note.	FV	55.00
	r. Replacement note. Series *00A* .	FV	250.
	s. Specimen.	—	250.

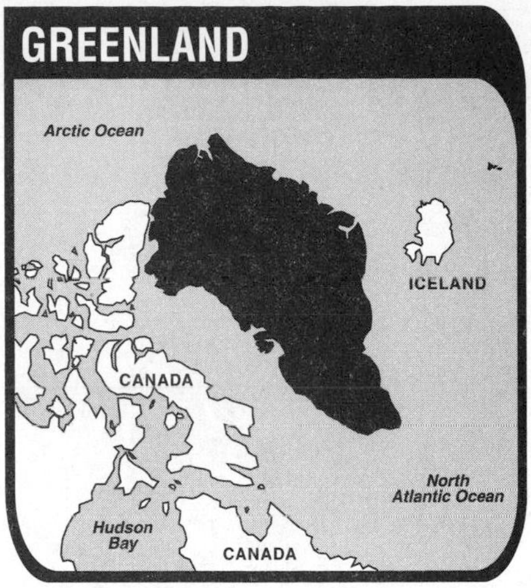

Greenland, an integral part of the Danish realm, is a huge island situated between the North Atlantic Ocean and the Polar Sea, almost entirely within the Artic Circle. It has an area of 2.166 million sq. km. and a population of 57,564. Capital: Nuuk (Godthab). Greenland is the world's only source of natural cryolite, a fluoride of sodium and aluminum important in making aluminum. Fish products and minerals are exported.

Greenland, the world's largest island, is about 81% ice-capped. Vikings reached the island in the 10th century from Iceland; Danish colonization began in the 18th century, and Greenland was made an integral part of Denmark in 1953. It joined the European Community (now the EU) with Denmark in 1973, but withdrew in 1985 over a dispute centered on stringent fishing quotas. Greenland was granted self-government in 1979 by the Danish parliament; the law went into effect the following year. Denmark continues to exercise control of Greenland's foreign affairs in consultation with Greenland's Home Rule Government.

RULERS:

Danish

MONETARY SYSTEM:

1 Rigsbankdaler = 96 Skilling to 1874
1 Krone = 48 Skilling
1 Krone = 100 Øre, 1874-

DANISH ADMINISTRATION

DEN KONGELIGE GRØNLANDSKE HANDEL

1953 ISSUE

18 **5 Kroner**

ND (1953-67). Green. Polar bear on ice at center. *DEN KONGELIGE GRØNLANDSKE HANDEL* at left and right margin, across bottom. Back: *DEN KONGELIGE GRØNLANDSKE HANDEL* around map at center.

	VF	UNC
a. Signature: Hans C. Christensen. Size: 84x125mm.	90.00	200.
b. Signature: Hans C. Christensen. Size: 84x130mm.	90.00	200.
s. Specimen.	—	200.

19 **10 Kroner**

ND (1953-67). Brown. Hump-back whale at center. *DEN KONGELIGE GRØNLANDSKE HANDEL* at left and right margin, across bottom. Back: *DEN KONGELIGE GRØNLANDSKE HANDEL* around map at center.

	VF	UNC
a. Serial number type as #16A. Signature: Hans C. Christensen.	180.	400.
b. Serial number type as #20. Signature: Hans C. Christensen.	100.	250.
s1. Specimen. As a.	200.	—
s2. Specimen. As b.	—	200.

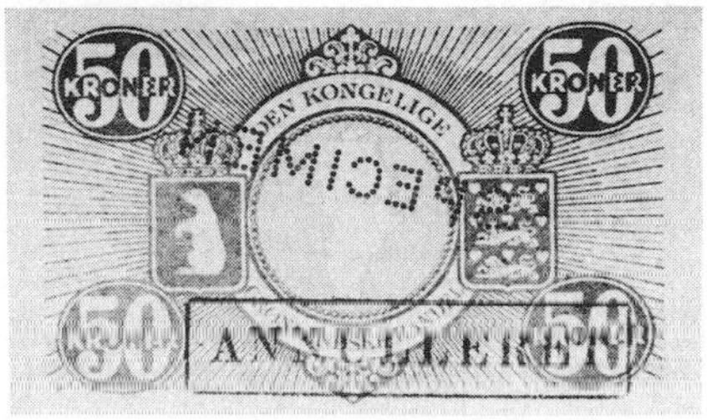

20 **50 Kroner**

ND (1953-67). Lilac. Clipper ship at center. *DEN KONGELIGE GRØNLANDSKE HANDEL* at left and right margin, across bottom. Back: *DEN KONGELIGE GRØNLANDSKE HANDEL* around map at center.

	VF	UNC
a. Signature: Hans C. Christensen.	375.	700.
s. Specimen.	—	475.

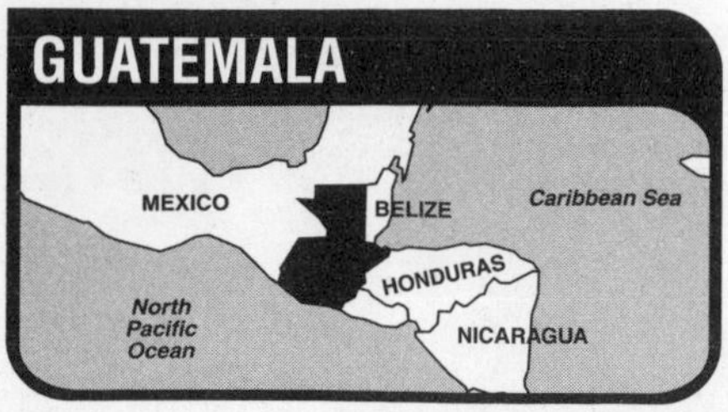

The Republic of Guatemala, the northernmost of the five Central American republics, has an area of 108,890 sq. km. and a population of 13 million. Capital: Guatemala City. The economy of Guatemala is heavily dependent on resources which are being developed. Coffee, cotton and bananas are exported.

The Mayan civilization flourished in Guatemala and surrounding regions during the first millennium A.D. After almost three centuries as a Spanish colony, Guatemala won its independence in 1821. During the second half of the 20th century, it experienced a variety of military and civilian governments, as well as a 36-year guerrilla war. In 1996, the government signed a peace agreement formally ending the conflict, which had left more than 100,000 people dead and had created, by some estimates, some 1 million refugees.

MONETARY SYSTEM:

1 Peso = 100 Centavos to 1924
1 Quetzal = 100 Centavos, 1924-

Republic

Banco de Guatemala

1957-63 Issue

		VF	UNC
35	**1/2 Quetzal** 22.1.1958. Brown on multicolor underprint. Hermitage of Cerro del Carmen at left. Signature title: *JEFE DE...* Back: Two Guatemalans. Printer: ABNC.	20.00	100.
36	**1 Quetzal** 1957-58. Green on multicolor underprint. Palace of the Captains General at left. Signature title: *JEFE DE...* Back: Lake Atitlan. Printer: ABNC.		
	a. 16.1.1957.	15.00	90.00
	b. 22.1.1958.	15.00	90.00

		VF	UNC
37	**5 Quetzales** 22.1.1958. Purple. Vase *Vasija de Uaxactum* at left. Signature title: *JEFE DE...* Back: Mayan-Spanish battle scene. Printer: ABNC.		
	a. Issued note.	35.00	175.
	s. Specimen.	—	50.00
38	**10 Quetzales** 1958; 1962-64. Red. Round stone carving *Ara de Tikal* at left. Signature title: *JEFE DE...* Back: Founding of old Guatemala. Printer: ABNC.		
	a. 22.1.1958.	65.00	225.
	b. 12.1.1962.	65.00	225.
	c. 9.1.1963.	65.00	225.
	d. 8.1.1964.	65.00	225.

		VF	UNC
39	**20 Quetzales** 1963-65. Blue. Landivar at left. Signature title: *JEFE DE...* Back: Meeting of Independence. Printer: ABNC.		
	a. 9.1.1963.	75.00	275.
	b. 8.1.1964.	75.00	275.
	c. 15.1.1965.	75.00	275.

1959-60 Issues

		VF	UNC
40	**1/2 Quetzal** 18.2.1959. Signature title: *JEFE DE...* at right. Lighter brown shadings around value guilloche at left. 6-digit serial #. Signature varieties. Printer: W&S. Printed area 2mm smaller than #41.	15.00	100.

		VF	UNC
41	**1/2 Quetzal** 1959-1961. Signature title: *JEFE DE...* at right. Darker brown shadings around value guilloche at left. 7-digit serial #. Signature varieties. Printer: W&S.		
	a. 18.2.1959.	10.00	45.00
	b. 13.1.1960.	10.00	45.00
	c. 18.1.1961.	10.00	45.00
	s. Specimen.	—	30.00
42	**1 Quetzal** 18.2.1959. Signature title: *JEFE DE...* at right. Building at center right. Green palace. 6-digit serial #. Signature varieties. Back: Dull green. Printer: W&S.		
	a. Issued note.	10.00	75.00
	s. Specimen.	—	80.00
43	**1 Quetzal** 1959-1964. Signature title: *JEFE DE...* at right. Black palace. 7-digit serial #. Signature varieties. Back: Bright green. Printer: W&S.		
	a. 18.2.1959.	7.50	45.00
	b. 13.1.1960.	7.50	45.00
	c. 18.1.1961.	7.50	45.00
	d. 12.1.1962.	7.50	45.00
	e. 9.1.1963.	7.50	45.00
	f. 8.1.1964.	7.50	45.00
	s. Specimen.	—	80.00

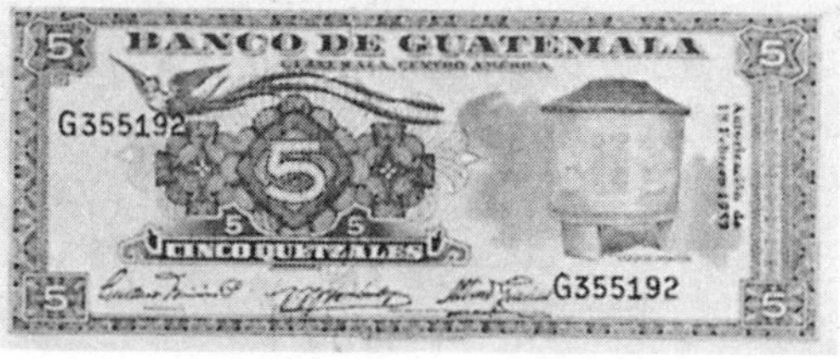

		VF	UNC
44	**5 Quetzales** 18.2.1959. Value at left center. Vase in purple. Signature title: *JEFE DE...* at right. Signature varieties. Printer: W&S.	50.00	200.

		VF	UNC
45	**5 Quetzales** 1959-1964. Redesigned guilloche. Value at center. Vase in brown. Signature title: *JEFE DE...* at right. Signature varieties. Printer: W&S.		
	a. 18.2.1959.	25.00	100.
	b. 12.1.1962.	25.00	100.
	c. 18.1.1961.	25.00	100.
	d. 12.1.1962.	25.00	100.
	e. 9.1.1963.	25.00	100.
	f. 8.1.1964.	25.00	100.
	s. Specimen.	—	—
46	**10 Quetzales** 18.2.1959. Signature title: *JEFE DE...* at right. Round red stone at right. Signature varieties. Printer: W&S.		
	a. Issued note.	70.00	250.
	s. Specimen.	—	135.

47	**10 Quetzales**	VF	UNC
	1959-1961. Similar to #46 but redesigned guilloche. Round stone in brown. Signature title: *JEFE DE...* at right. Signature varieties. Printer: W&S.		
	a. 18.2.1959.	35.00	175.
	b. 13.1.1960	35.00	175.
	c. 18.1.1961.	35.00	175.
	s. Specimen.	—	—

48	**20 Quetzales**	VF	UNC
	1960-65. Blue. Signature title: *JEFE DE...* at right. Portrait at right Landivar at right. Signature varieties. Printer: W&S.		
	a. 13.1.1960.	65.00	200.
	b. 18.1.1961.	65.00	200.
	c. 12.1.1962.	65.00	200.
	d. 9.1.1963.	65.00	200.
	e. 8.1.1964.	65.00	200.
	f. 15.1.1965.	65.00	200.
	s. Specimen.	—	—
49	**100 Quetzales**		
	18.2.1959. Dark blue. Signature title: *JEFE DE...* at right. *Indio de Nahuala* in blue at center. Signature varieties. Printer: W&S.	250.	650.

50	**100 Quetzales**	VF	UNC
	1960-65. Dark blue. Signature title: *JEFE DE...* at right. Portrait *Indio de Nahuala* in brown at right. Signature varieties. Printer: W&S.		
	a. 13.1.1960.	250.	500.
	b. 18.1.1961.	250.	500.
	c. 12.1.1962.	250.	500.
	d. 9.1.1963.	250.	500.
	e. 8.1.1964.	250.	500.
	f. 15.1.1965.	250.	500.
	s. Specimen.	—	—

1964-67 Issue

51	**1/2 Quetzal**	VF	UNC
	1964-1972. Brown on multicolor underprint. Signature title: *JEFE DE...* at right. Darker brown shadings around value guilloche at left. 7-digit serial #. Hermitage of Cerro del Carmen at left. Back: Two Guatemalans at center. Printer: TDLR. Signature varieties.		
	a. 8.1.1964.	10.00	40.00
	b. 15.1.1965.	15.00	40.00
	c. 21.1.1966.	15.00	40.00
	d. 13.1.1967.	15.00	40.00
	e. 3.1.1968.	15.00	40.00
	f. 3.1.1969.	15.00	40.00
	g. 7.1.1970.	15.00	40.00
	h. 6.1.1971.	15.00	40.00
	i. 5.1.1972.	15.00	40.00

52	**1 Quetzal**	VF	UNC
	1964-1972. Black and green on multicolor underprint. Palace of the Captains General at center right. Signature varieties. Back: Lake Atitlan Printer: TDLR.		
	a. 8.1.1964.	7.50	37.50
	b. 15.1.1965.	7.50	37.50
	c. 21.1.1966.	7.50	37.50
	d. 13.1.1967.	7.50	37.50
	e. 3.1.1968.	7.50	37.50
	f. 3.1.1969.	7.50	37.50
	g. 7.1.1970.	7.50	37.50
	h. 6.1.1971.	7.50	37.50
	i. 5.1.1972.	7.50	37.50
53	**5 Quetzales**		
	1964-1971. Purple on multicolor underprint. Vase *Vasija de Uaxactum* at right. Signature varieties. Watermark: 2 varieties. Printer: TDLR.		
	a. 8.1.1964.	10.00	60.00
	b. 15.1.1965.	10.00	60.00
	c. 21.1.1966.	10.00	60.00
	d. 13.1.1967.	10.00	60.00
	e. 3.1.1968.	10.00	60.00
	f. 3.1.1969.	10.00	60.00
	g. 7.1.1970.	10.00	60.00
	h. 6.1.1971.	10.00	60.00
54	**10 Quetzales**		
	1965-1970. Red on multicolor underprint. Round carved stone *Arade Tikal* at right. Signature varieties. Back: Mayan-Spanish battle scene. Watermark: 2 varieties. Printer: TDLR.		
	a. 15.1.1965.	25.00	120.
	b. 21.1.1966.	25.00	120.
	c. 13.1.1967.	25.00	120.
	d. 3.1.1968.	25.00	120.
	e. 3.1.1969.	25.00	120.
	f. 7.1.1970.	25.00	120.
55	**20 Quetzales**		
	1965-1971. Blue on multicolor underprint. R. Landivar at right. Signature varieties. Back: Founding of Guatemala. Watermark: 2 varieties. Printer: TDLR.		
	a. 15.1.1965.	45.00	200.
	b. 21.1.1966.	45.00	200.
	c. 13.1.1967.	45.00	200.
	d. 3.1.1968.	45.00	200.
	e. 3.1.1969.	45.00	200.
	f. 7.1.1970.	45.00	200.
	g. 6.1.1971.	45.00	200.

56	**50 Quetzales**	VF	UNC
	1967-1973. Orange and blue on multicolor underprint. General J. M. Orellana at right. Signature varieties. Back: Orange. Bank at center. Watermark: 2 varieties. Printer: TDLR.		
	a. 13.1.1967.	175.	450.
	b. 3.1.1968.	175.	450.
	c. 3.1.1969.	175.	450.
	d. 7.1.1970.	175.	450.
	e. 6.1.1971.	175.	450.
	f. 5.1.1972.	175.	450.
	g. 5.1.1973.	175.	450.

57 100 Quetzales

1966-1970. Blue-black and brown on pale green and multicolor underprint. *Indio de Nahuala* at right. Signature varieties. Back: City and mountain in valley Antihua. Watermark: 2 varieties.

	VF	UNC
a. 21.1.1966.	150.	400.
b. 13.1.1967.	150.	400.
c. 3.1.1968.	150.	400.
d. 3.1.1969.	150.	400.
e. 7.1.1970.	150.	400.

1969-75 Issue

58 1/2 Quetzal

1972-83. Brown on multicolor underprint. Tecun Uman (national hero) at right. Quetzal bird at upper center. Signature varieties. Back: Tikal temple. Printer: TDLR. 156x68mm.

	VF	UNC
a. Without security (flourescent) imprint. 5.1.1972; 5.1.1973.	1.75	20.00
b. Security (flourescent) imprint on back. 2.1.1974; 3.1.1975; 7.1.1976; 20.4.1977.	1.50	17.00
c. 4.1.1978; 3.1.1979; 2.1.1980; 7.1.1981; 6.1.1982; 6.1.1983.	1.50	14.00
s. Specimen. As c.	—	10.00

59 1 Quetzal

1972-83. Green on multicolor underprint. General J. M. Orellana at right, Quetzal bird at upper center. Signature varieties. Back: Banco de Guatemala building. Printer: TDLR. 156x68mm.

	VF	UNC
a. Security (flourescent) imprint on face. Date at lower right. 5.1.1972; 5.1.1973.	2.50	25.00
b. Security imprint as a. on face and back. 2.1.1974; 3.1.1975; 7.1.1976.	2.00	17.00
c. Date at center r. 5.1.1977; 20.4.1977; 4.1.1978; 3.1.1979; 2.1.1980; 7.1.1981; 6.1.1982; 6.1.1983; 30.12.1983.	1.25	15.00
s. Specimen. As c.	—	10.00

60 5 Quetzales

1969-83. Purple on multicolor underprint. General (later President) J. R. Barrios at right, Quetzal bird at upper center. Signature varieties. Back: Classroom scene. Watermark: Tecun Uman. Printer: TDLR. 156x68mm.

	VF	UNC
a. 3.1.1969; 6.1.1971; 5.1.1972; 5.1.1973.	6.00	35.00
b. 2.1.1974; 3.1.1975; 7.1.1976; 5.1.1977; 20.4.1977.	4.00	25.00
c. 4.1.1978; 3.1.1979; 2.1.1980; 7.1.1981; 6.1.1982; 6.1.1983.	3.00	20.00
s. Specimen. As c. ND.	—	10.00

61 10 Quetzales

1971-83. Red on multicolor underprint. General M. G. Granados at right, Quetzal bird at upper center. Signature varieties. Back: National Assembly session of 1872. Watermark: Tecun Uman. Printer: TDLR. 156x68mm.

	VF	UNC
a. 6.1.1971; 5.1.1972; 3.1.1973.	10.00	60.00
b. 2.1.1974; 3.1.1975; 7.1.1976; 5.1.1977; 20.4.1977.	7.50	45.00
c. 4.1.1978; 3.1.1979; 2.1.1980; 7.1.1981; 6.1.1982; 6.1.1983.	5.00	35.00
s. Specimen. As c. ND.	—	10.00

62 20 Quetzales

1972-83; 1988. Blue on multicolor underprint. Dr. M. Galvez at right, Quetzal bird at upper center. Signature varieties. Back: Granting of Independence to Central America. Watermark: Tecun Uman. Printer: TDLR. 156x68mm.

	VF	UNC
a. 5.1.1972; 5.1.1973.	15.00	100.
b. 2.1.1974; 3.1.1975; 7.1.1976; 5.1.1977; 20.4.1977.	10.00	75.00
c. 4.1.1978; 2.1.1979; 2.1.1980; 7.1.1981; 6.1.1982; 6.1.1983.	10.00	55.00
d. 6.1.1988.	7.00	40.00

63 50 Quetzales | VF | UNC

1974; 1981-83. Orange on multicolor underprint. C. O. Zachrisson at right, Quetzal bird at upper center. Signature varieties. Back: Crop workers. Watermark: Tecun Uman. Printer: TDLR. 156x68mm.

	VF	UNC
a. 2.1.1974.	45.00	275.
b. 7.1.1981; 6.1.1982; 6.1.1983.	35.00	200.

64 100 Quetzales | VF | UNC

1972-83. Brown on multicolor underprint. F. Marroquin at right, Quetzal bird at upper center. Signature varieties. Back: University of San Carlos de Borromeo. Watermark: Tecun Uman. Printer: TDLR. 156x68mm.

	VF	UNC
a. 5.1.1972.	75.00	350.
b. 3.1.1975; 7.1.1976; 3.1.1979.	60.00	275.
c. 6.1.1982; 6.1.1983.	45.00	200.

1983 Issue

65 1/2 Quetzal | VF | UNC

6.1.1983-4.1.1989. Brown on multicolor underprint. Tecun Uman at right, Quetzal bird at upper center. Back: Tikal temple. Watermark: Tecun Uman. Printer: G&D. 156x68mm. | FV | 14.00

66 1 Quetzal | VF | UNC

30.12.1983-4.1.1989. Blue-green and green on multicolor underprint. General J. Orellana at right, Quetzal bird at upper center. Back: Banco de Guatemala building. Watermark: Tecun Uman. Printer: G&D. UV: fibers fluoresce yellow, design on left green. Back: left and right ends orange. 156x68mm. | FV | 14.00

67 5 Quetzales

6.1.1983-6.1.1988. Purple on multicolor underprint. J. R. Barrios at right, Quetzal bird at upper center. Back: Classroom scene. Watermark: Tecun Uman. Printer: G&D. 156x68mm. | 2.50 | 20.00

68 10 Quetzales | VF | UNC

30.12.1983-6.1.1988. Red and red-brown on multicolor underprint. General M. G. Granados at right, Quetzal bird at upper center. Back: National Assembly session of 1872. Watermark: Tecun Uman. Printer: G&D. 156x68mm. | 5.00 | 30.00

69 20 Quetzales | VF | UNC

6.1.1983-7.1.1987. Blue on multicolor underprint. Dr. M. Galvez at right, Quetzal bird at upper center. Back: Granting of Independence to Central America. Watermark: Tecun Uman. Printer: G&D. 156x68mm. | 10.00 | 45.00

70 50 Quetzales | VF | UNC

30.12.1983-7.1.1987. Orange and yellow-orange on multicolor underprint. C. O. Zachrisson at right, Quetzal bird at upper center. Back: Crop workers. Watermark: Tecun Uman. Printer: G&D. 156x68mm. | 24.00 | 125.

71 100 Quetzales

30.12.1983-7.1.1987. Brown on multicolor underprint. F. Marroquin at right, Quetzal bird at upper center. Back. University of San Carlos de Borromeo. Watermark. Tecun Uman. Printer. G&D. 156x68mm. | 35.00 | 175.

1989; 1990 Issue

72 1/2 Quetzal | VF | UNC

1989; 1992. Brown on multicolor underprint. Tecun Uman at right, Quetzal bird at upper center. Signature varieties. Back: Tikal temple. Printer: CBN. 156x68mm.

	VF	UNC
a. 4.1.1989.	FV	6.00
b. 14.2.1992.	FV	5.00

73 1 Quetzal

1990-92. Blue-green on multicolor underprint. General J. Orellana at right, Quetzal bird at upper center. Signature varieties. Back: Banco de Guatemala building. Printer: CBN. UV: fibers fluoresce blue and green. Back, value 1 yellow. 156x68mm.

	VF	UNC
a. 3.1.1990.	FV	6.00
b. 6.3.1991.	FV	6.00
c. 22.1.1992.	FV	6.00
d. 14.2.1992.	FV	6.00

74 **5 Quetzales** — VF — UNC

1990-92. Purple on multicolor underprint. J. R. Barrios at right, Quetzal bird at upper center. Signature varieties. Back: Classroom scene. Printer: CBN. 156x68mm.

	VF	UNC
a. 3.1.1990.	FV	12.00
b. 6.3.1991.	FV	12.00
c. 22.1.1992.	FV	12.00

75 **10 Quetzales** — VF — UNC

1989; 1990; 1992. Brown-violet and red on multicolor underprint. General M. G. Granados at right, Quetzal bird at upper center. Signature varieties. Vertical serial number at left. Back: National Assembly session of 1872. Watermark: Tecun Uman. Printer: TDLR. 156x68mm.

	VF	UNC
a. 4.1.1989.	FV	17.00
b. 3.1.1990.	FV	17.00
c. 22.1.1992.	FV	17.00

76 **20 Quetzales** — VF — UNC

1989; 1990; 1992. Blue-black, purple and blue on multicolor underprint. Dr. M. Galvez at right, Quetzal bird at upper center. Signature varieteis. Vertical serial number at left. Back: Granting of Independence to Central America. Watermark: Tecun Uman. Printer: TDLR. 156x68mm.

	VF	UNC
a. 4.1.1989.	FV	24.00
b. 3.1.1990.	FV	24.00
c. 22.1.1992.	FV	24.00

77 **50 Quetzales** — VF — UNC

1989-90. Orange and green on multicolor underprint. C. O. Zachrisson at right, Quetzal bird at upper center. Signature varieties. Vertical serial number at left. Back: Crop workers. Watermark: Tecun Uman. Printer: TDLR. 156x68mm.

	VF	UNC
a. 4.1.1989.	7.50	55.00
b. 3.1.1990.	7.50	55.00

78 **100 Quetzales** — VF — UNC

1989; 1990; 1992. Brown and red-brown on multicolor underprint. F. Marroquin at right, Quetzal bird at upper center. Signature varieties. Vertical serial number at left. Back: Lilac and multicolor. University of San Carlos de Borromeo. Watermark: Tecun Uman. Printer: TDLR. 156x68mm.

	VF	UNC
a. 4.1.1989.	20.00	90.00
b. 3.1.1990.	20.00	90.00
c. 22.1.1992.	20.00	90.00

1992 Issue

No.	Denomination	VF	UNC
79	**1/2 Quetzal** 16.7.1992. Brown on multicolor underprint. Tecun Uman at right, Quetzal bird at upper center. Signature varieties. Back: Tikal temple. Printer: F-CO. 156x68mm.	FV	4.00
80	**1 Quetzal** 16.7.1992. Blue-green on multicolor underprint. General J. Orellana at right, Quetzal bird at upper center. Signature varieties. Back: Banco de Guatemala building. Printer: F-CO. 156x68mm.	FV	5.00

No.	Denomination	VF	UNC
81	**5 Quetzales** 16.7.1992. Purple on multicolor underprint. J. R. Barrios at right, Quetzal bird at upper center. Signature varieties. Back: Classroom scene. Printer: F-CO. 156x68mm.	FV	10.00
82	**10 Quetzales** 16.7.1992. Brown-violet and red on multicolor underprint. General M. G. Granados at right, Quetzal bird at upper center. Signature varieties. Back: National Assembly session of 1872. Watermark: Tecun Uman. 156x68mm.	FV	14.00
83	**20 Quetzales** 12.8.1992. Blue-black, purple and blue on multicolor underprint. Dr. M. Galvez at right, Quetzal bird at upper center. Signature varieties. Back: Granting of Independence to Central America. Watermark: Tecun Uman. Printer: BABN. 156x68mm.	FV	20.00
84	**50 Quetzales** 12.8.1992. Orange and green on multicolor underprint. C. O. Zachrisson at right, Quetzal bird at upper center. Signature varieties. Back: Crop workers. Watermark: Tecun Uman. Printer: BABN. 156x68mm.	6.00	40.00

No.	Denomination	VF	UNC
85	**100 Quetzales** 27.5.1992. Brown on multicolor underprint. F. Marroquin at right, Quetzal bird at upper center., date at lower left, gold colored device at right. Signature varieties. Back: Light brown and multicolor. University of San Carlos de Borromeo. Watermark: Tecun Uman. Printer: BABN. 156x68mm.	10.00	60.00

1993; 1995 Issue

86 **1/2 Quetzal** VF UNC

1993-95. Brown on multicolor underprint. Tecun Uman at right, Quetzal bird at upper center. Signature varieties. Back: Multicolor. Tikal temple. Printer: CBNC. 156x68mm.

	VF	UNC
a. 27.10.1993.	FV	3.00
b. 27.9.1994.	FV	2.50
c. 6.9.1995.	FV	2.50

87 **1 Quetzal** VF UNC

1993-95. Dark green on green and multicolor underprint. General J. Orellana at right, Quetzal bird at upper center. Signature varieties. Back: Multicolor. Banco de Guatemala building. Printer: CBNC. 156x68mm.

	VF	UNC
a. 27.10.1993	FV	4.00
b. 6.9.1994.	FV	3.50
c. 6.9.1995.	FV	3.50

88 **5 Quetzales** VF UNC

1993; 1995. Purple on multicolor underprint. J. R. Barrios at right, Quetzal bird at upper center. Signature varieties. Back: Multicolor. Classroom scene. Printer: CBNC. UV: fibers fluoresce blue, quetzal green. Back value 5 orange. 156x68mm.

	VF	UNC
a. 27.10.1993.	1.50	7.50
b. 16.6.1995.	1.50	7.50
c. Without imprint. 16.6.1995.	FV	5.00

89 **10 Quetzales** VF UNC

16.6.1995. Brown-violet and red on multicolor underprint. General M. G. Granados at right, Quetzal bird at upper center. Signature varieties. Back: Multicolor. National Assembly session of 1872. Printer: CNBC. Large and small printer imprint on back. 156x68mm. FV 12.50

1994; 1995 Issue

90 **1 Quetzal** VF UNC

27.9.1994. Dark green on green and multicolor underprint. General J. Orellana at right, Quetzal bird at upper center. Signature varieties. Back: Multicolor. Banco de Guatemala building. Printer: F-CO. 156x68mm. FV 2.50

91 **10 Quetzales**

29.6.1994. Brown-violet and red on multicolor underprint. General M. G. Granados at right, Quetzal bird at upper center. Signature varieties. Vertical serial number at left. Back: Multicolor. National Assembly session of 1872. Printer: F-CO. 156x68mm. FV 10.00

92 **5 Quetzales** VF UNC

29.6.1994. Orange and green on multicolor underprint. J. R. Barrios at right, Quetzal bird at upper center. Signature varieties. Back: Multicolor. Classroom scene. Printer: TDLR. 156x68mm. FV 5.00

93 **20 Quetzales**

16.6.1995. Blue-black, purple and blue on multicolor underprint. Dr. M. Galvez at right, Quetzal bird at upper center. Back: Granting of Independence to Central America. Printer: G&D. 156x68mm. FV 14.00

94 **50 Quetzales** VF UNC

16.6.1995. Orange and green on multicolor underprint. Similar to #77. Back: Multicolor. 156x68mm. FV 30.00

95 **100 Quetzales** VF UNC

1994-95. Brown on multicolor underprint. F. Marroquin at right, Quetzal bird at upper center. Signature varieties. Vertical serial number at left. Back: Multicolor. University of San Carlos de Borromeo. Printer: TDLR. 156x68mm.

	VF	UNC
a. 29.6.1994.	FV	50.00
b. 16.6.1995.	FV	50.00

1996 Issue

96 **1/2 Quetzal** VF UNC

28.8.1996. Brown on multicolor underprint. Tecun Uman at right, Quetzal bird at upper center. Signature varieties. Back: Tikal temple. Printer: H&S. 156x68mm.

	VF	UNC
a. Issued note.	FV	1.50
s. Specimen.	—	75.00

97 **1 Quetzal** | VF | UNC
28.1.1996. Dark green on green and multicolor underprint. General J. Orellana at right, Quetzal bird at upper center. Signature varieties. Back: Banco de Guatemala building. Printer: H&S. 156x68mm.

	VF	UNC
a. Issued note.	FV	2.50
s. Specimen.	—	75.00

1998-99 Issue

		VF	UNC
98	**1/2 Quetzal** 9.1.1998. Brown on multicolor underprint. Tecun Uman at right, Quetzal bird at upper center. Signature varieties. Back: Tikal temple. Printer: (T)DLR. 156x68mm.	FV	1.00
99	**1 Quetzal** 9.1.1998. Dark green and green on multicolor underprint. General J. Orellana at right, Quetzal bird at upper center. Signature varieties. Back: Banco de Guatemala building. Printer: (T)DLR 156x68mm.	FV	1.50

		VF	UNC
100	**5 Quetzales** 29.7.1998. Purple on multicolor underprint. J. R. Barrios at right, Quetzal bird at upper center. Signature varieties. Back: Classroom scene. 156x68mm.	FV	3.00

		VF	UNC
101	**10 Quetzales** 29.7.1998. Brown-violet and red on multicolor underprint. General M. G. Granados at right, Quetzal bird at upper center. Signature varieties. Vertical serial number at left. Back: National Assembly session of 1872. Printer: BABN. 156x68mm.	FV	6.50

		VF	UNC
102	**20 Quetzales** 17.6.1999. Blue-black, purple and blue on multicolor underprint. Dr. M. Galvez at right, Quetzal bird at upper center. Signature varieties. Back: Granting of Independence to Central America. Printer: TDLR. 156x68mm.	FV	15.00
103	**100 Quetzales** 29.7.1998. Multicolor. F. Marroquin at right. Back: University of San Carlos de Borromeo. Printer: BABN. 156x68mm.	FV	40.00

2001 Issue

104 **100 Quetzales** | VF | UNC
2001; 2006-07. Multicolor. F. Marroquin at right. Back: University of San Carlos de Borromeo. Printer: G&D. 156x68mm.

	VF	UNC
a. 9.4.2001.	FV	30.00
b. 25.8.2006.	FV	30.00
c. 24.1.2007.	FV	30.00

2001 Second Issue

		VF	UNC
105	**50 Quetzales** 9.4.2001. Orange and green on multicolor underprint. C. O. Zachrisson at right. Back: Crop workers. Watermark: Mayan head. Printer: G&D. 156x68mm.	FV	20.00

2003 Issue

106 **5 Quetzales** | VF | UNC
2003; 2006; 2007. Purple on multicolor underprint. J. R. Barrios at right. Back: Classroom scene. Printer: F-CO. 156x68mm.

	VF	UNC
a. 12.2.2003.	FV	3.50
b. 22.11.2006.	FV	3.50
c. 17.1.2007.	FV	3.50

		VF	UNC
107	**10 Quetzales** 12.2.2003. Brown-violet and red on multicolor underprint. General M. G. Granados at right. Back: National Assembly session of 1872. Printer: F-CO. 156x68mm.	FV	6.00

		VF	UNC
108	**20 Quetzales** 12.2.2003. Blue-black, purple and blue on multicolor underprint. Dr. M. Galves at right. Back: Granting of Independence to Central America. Printer: FC-O. 156x68mm.	FV	10.00

2006 Issue

		VF	UNC
109	**1 Quetzal** 20.12.2006. Green on multicolor underprint. General J. Orellana at right. Back: Banco de Guatemala building. Printer: CBNC. Polymer plastic. 156x68mm.	FV	1.00

		VF	UNC
111	**10 Quetzales** 2006-07. Brown-violet and red on multicolor underprint. General M. G. Granados at right. Back: National Assembly session of 1872. Watermark: Denomination added. Printer: CBNC. 156x68mm.		
	a. 25.8.2006.	FV	4.50
	b. 17.1.2007.	FV	4.50

		VF	UNC
112	**20 Quetzales** 25.8.2006; 24.1.2007. Blue-black, purple and blue on multicolor underprint. Dr. M. Galvez at right. Back: Granting of Independence to Central America. Watermark: Denomination added. Printer: DLR. 156x68mm.		
	a. 25.8.2006.	FV	6.50
	b. 24.1.2007.	FV	5.00

		VF	UNC
113	**50 Quetzales** 15.11.2006. Orange and green on multicolor underprint. C. O. Zachrisson ar right. Back: Crop workers. Watermark: Denomination added. Printer: DLR. 156x68mm.	FV	25.00

		VF	UNC
114	**100 Quetzales** 2006-07. Brown on multicolor underprint. F. Marroquin at right. Back: University of San Carlos de Borromeo. Watermark: Denomination added. Printer: G&D. 156x68mm.		
	a. 25.8.2006.	FV	40.00
	b. 24.1.2007.	FV	36.00

2008 Issue

		VF	UNC
115	**1 Quetzal** 12.3.2008. Green on multicolor undeprint. General J. Orellana at right. Back: Banco de Guatemala building. Printer: FC-O. 156x68mm.	FV	1.00

		VF	UNC
116	**5 Quetzales** 12.3.2008. Purple and tan on multicolor underprint. General J. Rufino Barrios at right. Back: Classroom. Printer: FC-O. 156x68mm.	FV	1.50

		VF	UNC
117	**10 Quetzales** 12.3.2008. Red and tan on multicolor underprint. General M. Garcis Granados at right. Back: National Assembly of 1872. Printer: FC-O. 156x68mm.	FV	2.50
118	**20 Quetzales** 12.3.2008. Blue and rose on multicolor underprint. Dr. M. Galvez at right. Back: Granting of Independence to Central America.	FV	10.00

		VF	UNC
119	**100 Quetzales** 12.3.2008. Brown and tan on multicolor underprint. Bishop Francisco Marroquin at right. Back: Universidad de San Carlos. Printer: Enschede. 156x68mm.	FV	30.00

		VF	UNC
120	**200 Quetzales** 18.2.2009. Blue and brown on multicolor underprint. Sebastian Hurtado, Mariano Valverde and German Alcantara at right. Back: Score of "La Flor del Cafe", Marimba cromatica and "Noche de luna entre ruinas." Printer: FC-O. 156x68mm.	FV	40.00

2010-11 Issue

		VF	UNC
122	**5 Quetzales** 19.5.2010. Violet and purple on multicolor underprint. Back: Classroom.	FV	1.50

		VF	UNC
123	**10 Quetzales** 19.5.2010. Red on multicolor underprint. Back: National Assembly of 1872.	FV	2.50

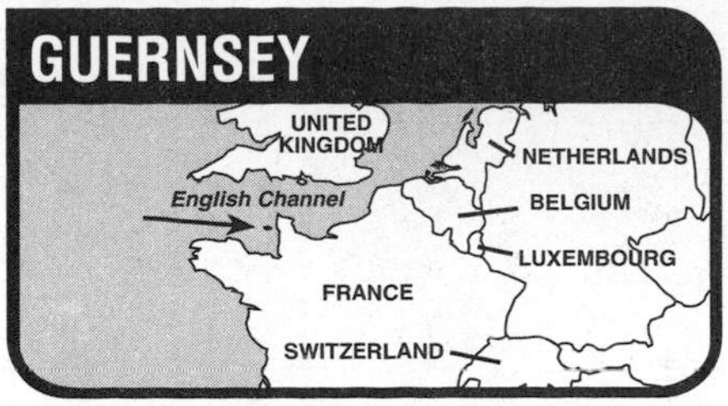

The Bailiwick of Guernsey, a British crown dependency located in the English Channel 48 km. west of Normandy, France, has an area of 78 sq. km., including the Isles of Alderney, Jethou, Herm, Brechou and Sark, and a population of 58,681. Capital: St. Peter Port. Agriculture and cattle breeding are the main occupations.

Guernsey and the other Channel Islands represent the last remnants of the medieval Dukedom of Normandy, which held sway in both France and England. The islands were the only British soil occupied by German troops in World War II. Guernsey is a British crown dependency, but is not part of the UK. However, the UK Government is constitutionally responsible for its defense and international representation.

United Kingdom bank notes and coinage circulate concurrently with Guernsey money as legal tender.

RULERS:

British to 1940, 1944-
German Occupation, June 1940-June 1944

MONETARY SYSTEM:

1 Pound = 20 Shillings to 1971
1 Pound = 100 New Pence 1971-

British Administration

States of Guernsey

1945; 1956 Issue

42	10 Shillings	VF	UNC
	1945-66. Lilac on light green underprint. Value at center and in underprint. Back: Purple. Printer: PBC.		
	a. 1.8.1945-1.9.1957.	225.	600.
	b. 1.7.1958-1.3.1965.	100.	325.
	c. 1.7.1966.	45.00	125.
	s. As c. Specimen.	—	—

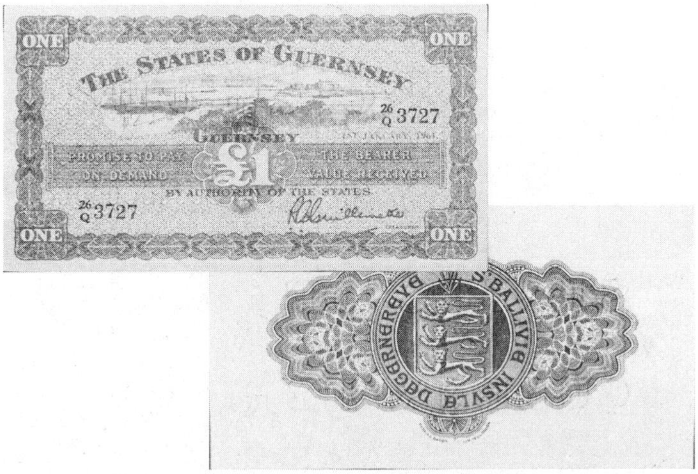

43	1 Pound	VF	UNC
	1945-66. Purple on green underprint. Harbor entrance across top center. Back: Green. Printer: PBC.		
	a. 1.8.1945-1.3.1957.	650.	1250.
	b. 1.9.1957-1.3.1962; 1.6.1963; 1.3.1965.	120.	375.
	c. 1.7.1966.	90.00	300.
	s. As c. Specimen.	—	—

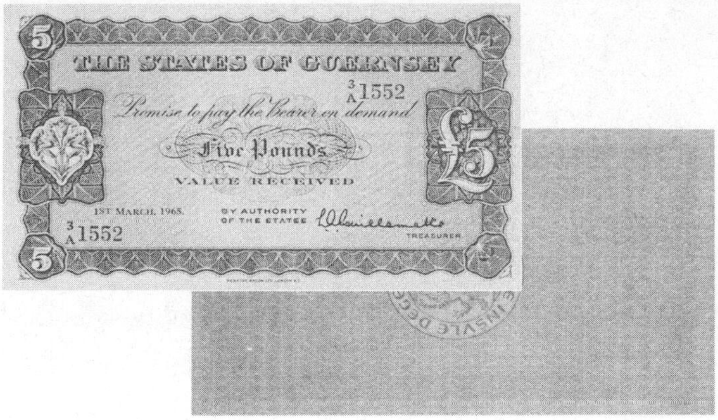

44	5 Pounds	VF	UNC
	1956; 1965-66. Green and blue. Flowers at left. Printer: PBC.		
	a. 1.12.1956.	650.	1500.
	b. 1.3.1965.	650.	1500.
	c. 1.7.1966.	650.	1500.

1969; 1975 ND Issue

#45-47 Replacement notes: Serial # prefix *Z*.

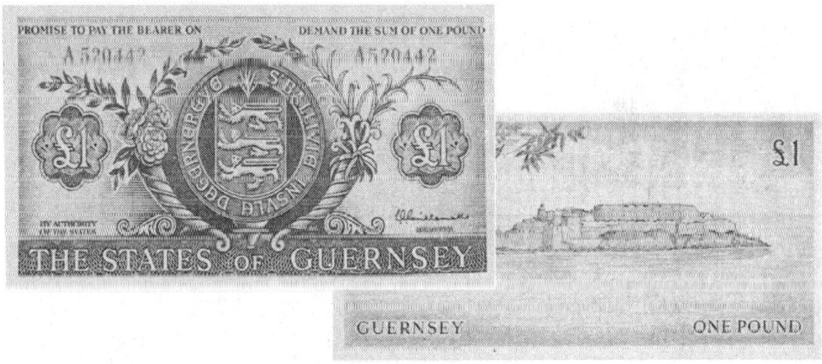

45	1 Pound	VF	UNC
	ND (1969-75). Olive on pink and yellow underprint. Arms at center. Back: Castle Cornet. Printer: BWC.		
	a. Signature Guillemette.	25.00	110.
	b. Signature Hodder.	12.00	50.00
	c. Signature Bull.	12.00	45.00

46	5 Pounds	VF	UNC
	ND (1969-75). Purple on light brown underprint. Arms at right. Back: City view and harbor wall. Printer: BWC.		
	a. Signature Guillemette.	85.00	325.
	b. Signature Hodder.	60.00	200.
	c. Signature Bull.	40.00	150.
	s. As a. Specimen.	—	900.

47	10 Pounds	VF	UNC
	ND (1975-80). Blue, green and multicolor. Britannia with lion and shield at left. Signature; Hodder. Back: Blue. Sir I. Brock and Battle of Queenston Heights. Printer: BWC.	150.	575.

1980 ND Issue

48 **1 Pound**

ND (1980-89). Dark green and black on multicolor underprint. Market square scene of 1822 at lower center in underprint. Guernsey States seal at lower left. Back: D. De Lisle Brock and Royal Court of St. Peter Port. Watermark: Guernsey States seal. Printer: TDLR. 135x67mm.

	VF	UNC
a. Signature W. C. Bull.	FV	23.00
b. Black signature M. J. Brown.	FV	25.00
r. As a. Replacement note.	—	30.00
s. Specimen.	—	—
ct. Color trial.	—	—

49 **5 Pounds**

ND (1980-89). Purple, dark brown and olive-brown on multicolor underprint. Guernsey States seal at lower left. Fort Grey at lower center in underprint. signature W. C. Bull. Back: Thomas de la Rue and Fountain Street at center, workers at envelope making machine at lower right. Watermark: Guernsey States seal. Printer: TDLR. 146x78mm.

	VF	UNC
a. Issued note.	15.00	55.00
r. Replacement note.	—	110.
s. Specimen.	—	—
ct. Color trial.	—	—

50 **10 Pounds**

ND (1980-89). Purple, blue and blue-black on multicolor underprint. Guernsey States seal. Castle Cornet at lower center. Back: Major Sir Isaac Brock and battle of Queenston Heights. Watermark: Guernsey States seal. Printer: TDLR. 151x85mm.

	VF	UNC
a. Signature W. C. Bull.	30.00	110.
b. Black signature M. J. Brown.	27.50	95.00
r. As a. Replacement note.	—	130.
s. Specimen.	—	—
ct. Color trial.	—	—

51 **20 Pounds**

ND (1980-89). Red, red-violet, brown and orange on multicolor underprint. Guernsey States seal, 1815 scene of Saumarez Park at lower center in underprint. Back: Adm. Lord de Saumarez and ships on back. Watermark: Guernsey States seal. Printer: TDLR. 161x90mm.

	VF	UNC
a. Signature W. C. Bull.	75.00	210.
b. Black signature M. J. Brown.	75.00	190.
r. As a. Replacement note.	—	—
s. Specimen.	—	—
ct. Color trial.	—	—

1990; 1991 ND Issue

#52-55 similar to #48-51 but reduced size. Replacement notes: Serial # prefix *Z*.

52 **1 Pound**

ND (ca.1991-). Dark green and black on multicolor underprint. Market square scene of 1822 at lower center in underprint. Guernsey States seal at lower left. Back: D. De Lisle Brock and Royal Court of St. Peter Port. Watermark: Guernsey States seal. Printer: (T)DLR. 128x65mm.

	VF	UNC
a. Green signature M. J. Brown.	FV	9.00
b. Signature D. P. Trestain.	FV	8.00
c. Signature D. M. Clark.	FV	7.00
r. As b. Replacement note.	FV	12.00

53 **5 Pounds**

ND (1990-95). Purple, dark brown and olive-brown on multicolor underprint. Guernsey States seal at lower left. Fort Grey at lower center in underprint. signature W. C. Bull. Back: Thomas de la Rue and Fountain Street at center, workers at envelope making machine at lower right. Watermark: Guernsey States seal. Printer: DLR. 136x70mm.

	VF	UNC
a. Brown signature M. J. Brown.	15.00	50.00
b. Signature D. P. Trestain.	12.50	40.00

54 **10 Pounds**

ND (ca.1991-95). Purple, blue and blue-black on multicolor underprint. Guernsey States seal. Castle Cornet at lower center. Back: Major Sir Isaac Brock and battle of Queenston Heights. Watermark: Guernsey States seal. Printer: DLR. 142x75mm.

	VF	UNC
a. Blue signature M. J. Brown.	25.00	85.00
r. Replacement note.	—	—

55	20 Pounds	VF	UNC
	ND (ca.1991-95). Red, red-violet, brown and orange on multicolor underprint. Guernsey States seal, 1815 scene of Saumarez Park at lower center in underprint. Back: Adm. Lord de Saumarez and ships on back. Watermark: Guernsey States seal. Printer: DLR. 149x80mm.		
	a. Red-orange signature M. J. Brown.	60.00	150.
	b. Signature D. P. Trestain.	60.00	130.
	r. As a. Replacement note.	65.00	165.

1994-96 ND Issue

56	5 Pounds	VF	UNC
	ND (1996). Dark brown and purple on multicolor underprint. Queen Elizabeth II at right, Brown Guernsey States seal at bottom center right. St. Peter Port Town Church at lower left. Back: Fort Grey at upper left center, Hanois Lighthouse at center right. Watermark: Queen Elizabeth II. Printer: TDLR. 135x70mm.		
	a. Signature D. P. Trestain.	FV	30.00
	b. Signature D. M. Clark.	FV	30.00
	r. As a. Replacement note.	FV	40.00

57	10 Pounds	VF	UNC
	ND (1995). Violet, blue and dark blue on multicolor underprint. Queen Elizabeth II at right, Guernsey States seal at bottom center right. Elizabeth College at lower left. Back: Saumarez Park above Le Niaux Watermill and Le Trepid Dolmen at left center. Watermark: Queen Elizabeth II. Printer: TDLR. 142x75mm.		
	a. Signature D. P. Trestain.	FV	60.00
	b. Signature D. M. Clark.	FV	55.00
	c. As b. Stardust thread above serial #D900001.	FV	45.00
	r. As a, b. Replacement note.	FV	70.00

58	20 Pounds	VF	UNC
	ND (1996). Pink, dark brown and orange on multicolor underprint. Queen Elizabeth II at right, Guernsey States seal at bottom center right. St. James Concert Hall at lower left. Back: Flowers at lower left, St. Sampson's Church at left center, sailboats below Vale Castle at center right, ship at upper right. Watermark: Queen Elizabeth II. Printer: TDLR. 142x79mm.		
	a. Signature D. P. Trestain.	FV	90.00
	b. Signature D. M. Clark.	FV	80.00
	c. Signature Bethan Haines. Signature title: *CHIEF ACCOUNTANT*. Segmented security thread, foil device added top center.	FV	80.00
	r. As a,b . Replacement note.	FV	110.

59	50 Pounds	VF	UNC
	ND (1994). Dark brown, dark green and blue-black on multicolor underprint. Queen Elizabeth II at right, Guernsey States seal at bottom center right. Royal Court House at lower left. Back: Stone carving, letter of Marque at lower left, St. Andrew's Church at center right. Watermark: Queen Elizabeth II. Printer: TDLR. 156x85mm.	FV	220.

2000 Issue

#60, Millennium Commemorative

60	5 Pounds	VF	UNC
	2000. Dark brown and purple on multicolor underprint. Queen Elizabeth II at right, Blue Guernsey States seal at bottom center. St. Peter Port Town Church at lower left, commemorative text at left. Back: Fort Grey at upper left center, Hanois Lighthouse at center right. Printer: DLR. 135x70mm.	FV	30.00

2012 Commemorative Issue

61	20 Pounds	VF	UNC
	2012. Rose and orange on multicolor underprint. Queen Elizabeth II bust at right, St. James Concert Hall at lower left. Anniversary seal at bottom center. Back: Multicolor. Vale Castle at top center, St. Sampson's Church at center, small sailing boats, flower at lower left. Printer: DLR. 149x80mm.	FV	90.00

2013 Commemorative Issue

62	1 Pound	VF	UNC
	2013. Dark green and black on multicolor underprint. Market square scene of 1822 at lower center in underprint. Guernsey States seal at lower left. Signature Bethan Haines. Back: Thomas de la Rue. Printer: TDLR. 300,000 notes printed.	FV	12.00

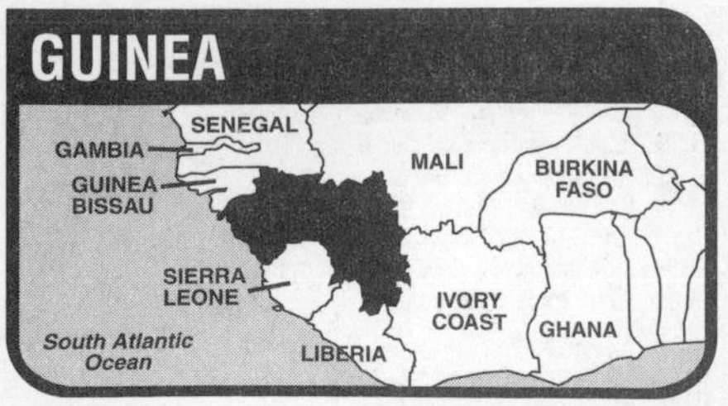

The Republic of Guinea (formerly French Guinea), situated on the Atlantic coast of Africa between Sierra Leone and Guinea-Bissau, has an area of 245,857 sq. km. and a population of 9.8 million. Capital: Conakry. Although Guinea contains one-third of the world's reserves of bauxite and significant deposits of iron ore, gold and diamonds, the economy is still dependent on agriculture. Aluminum, bananas, copra and coffee are exported.

Guinea has had only two presidents since gaining its independence from France in 1958. Lansana Conte came to power in 1984 when the military seized the government after the death of the first president, Sekou Toure. Guinea did not hold democratic elections until 1993 when Gen. Conte (head of the military government) was elected president of the civilian government. He was reelected in 1998 and again in 2003, though all the polls have been marred by irregularities. Guinea has maintained its internal stability despite spillover effects from conflict in Sierra Leone and Liberia. As those countries have rebuilt, Guinea's own vulnerability to political and economic crisis has increased. Declining economic conditions and popular dissatisfaction with corruption and bad governance prompted two massive strikes in 2006; a third nationwide strike in early 2007 sparked violent protests in many Guinean cities and prompted two weeks of martial law. To appease the unions and end the unrest, Conte named a new prime minister in March 2007.

RULERS:

French to 1958

MONETARY SYSTEM:

1 Franc = 100 Centimes to 1971
1 Syli = 10 Francs, 1971-1980
Franc System, 1985-

REPUBLIC

BANQUE CENTRALE DE LA RÉPUBLIQUE DE GUINÉE

1960 ISSUE

12 — 50 Francs	VF	UNC
1.3.1960. Brown on multicolor underprint. President Sekou Toure at left. Back: Heavy machinery. Watermark: Dove.	
a. Issued note.	4.00	20.00
s. Specimen.	—	25.00

13 — 100 Francs	VF	UNC
1.3.1960. Dark brown on pale olive-green, pale orange, pink and lilac underprint. President Sekou Toure at left. Back: Dark brown on orange and pink underprint. Pineapple field workers. Watermark: Dove.	
a. Issued note.	6.00	35.00
s. As a. Specimen.	—	25.00
x. (Error). dark brown and pale olive-green, light blue and pale yellow-orange underprint. Back dark brown on yellow underprint.	—	—

14 — 500 Francs	VF	UNC
1.3.1960. Blue on multicolor underprint. President Sekou Toure at left. Back: Men pulling long boats ashore. Watermark: Dove.	
a. Issued note.	20.00	150.
s. Specimen.	—	35.00

15 — 1000 Francs	VF	UNC
1.3.1960. Green on multicolor underprint. President Sekou Toure at left. Back: Banana harvesting. Watermark: Dove.	
a. Issued note.	15.00	75.00
s. Specimen.	—	35.00

15A — 5000 Francs	VF	UNC
1.3.1960. Purple on green and multicolor underprint. Pres. Sekou Toure at left. Back: Woman in headdress at left, huts at right. Watermark: Dove. (Not issued). Specimen.	—	400.

1971 Issue

#16-19 issued under Law of 1960.

16	10 Sylis	VF	UNC
	1971. Brown on multicolor underprint. Patrice Lumumba at right. Back: People with bananas.	1.50	3.00

17	25 Sylis	VF	UNC
	1971. Dark brown on multicolor underprint. Man smoking a pipe at right. Back: Man and cows.	2.00	5.00

18	50 Sylis	VF	UNC
	1971. Green on multicolor underprint. Bearded man at left. Back: Landscape with large dam and reservoir.	2.00	10.00

19	100 Sylis	VF	UNC
	1971. Purple on multicolor underprint. A. S. Toure at left. Back: Steam shovel and two dump trucks.	2.00	9.00

1980; 1981 Issue

#20-27 issued under Law of 1960.

20	1 Syli	VF	UNC
	1981. Olive on green underprint. Mafori Bangoura at right.		
	a. Issued note.	.15	.50
	s. Specimen.	—	6.00

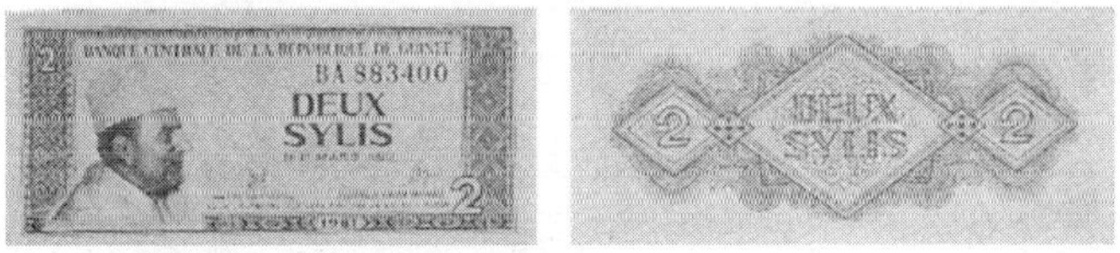

21	2 Sylis	VF	UNC
	1981. Black and brown on orange underprint. Green guilloche at center, King Mohammed V of Morocco at left.		
	a. Issued note.	.25	.75
	s. Specimen.	—	7.00

22	5 Sylis	VF	UNC
	1980. Blue on pink underprint. Kwame Nkrumah at right. Back: People with bananas.		
	a. Issued note.	.50	2.00
	s. Specimen.	—	8.00

23	10 Sylis	VF	UNC
	1980. Red and red-orange on multicolor underprint. Patrice Lumumba at right. Back: People with bananas.		
	a. Issued note.	.50	2.50
	s. Specimen.	—	9.00

24 **25 Sylis**

1980. Dark green on multicolor underprint. Man smoking a pipe at right. Back: Man and cows.

	VF	UNC
a. Issued note.	.50	4.00
s. Specimen.	—	10.00

25 **50 Sylis**

1980. Dark red and brown on multicolor underprint. Bearded man at left. Back: Landscape with large dam and reservoir.

	VF	UNC
a. Issued note.	1.50	7.00
s. Specimen.	—	10.00

26 **100 Sylis**

1980. Blue on multicolor underprint. A. S. Toure at left. Back: Steam shovel and two dump trucks.

	VF	UNC
a. Issued note.	4.00	17.50
s. Specimen.	—	15.00

27 **500 Sylis**

1980. Dark brown on multicolor underprint. J. Broz Tito at left. Back: Modern building.

	VF	UNC
a. Issued note.	2.00	12.50
s. Specimen.	—	20.00

1985 Issue

#28-33 Issued under Law of 1960.

28 **25 Francs**

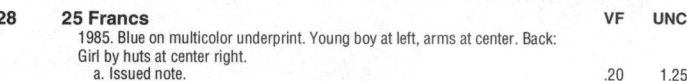

1985. Blue on multicolor underprint. Young boy at left, arms at center. Back: Girl by huts at center right.

	VF	UNC
a. Issued note.	.20	1.25
s. Specimen.	—	3.00

29 **50 Francs**

1985. Red-violet on multicolor underprint. Bearded man at left, arms at center. Back: Plowing with water buffalo at center.

	VF	UNC
a. Issued note.	.25	1.50
s. Specimen.	—	50.00

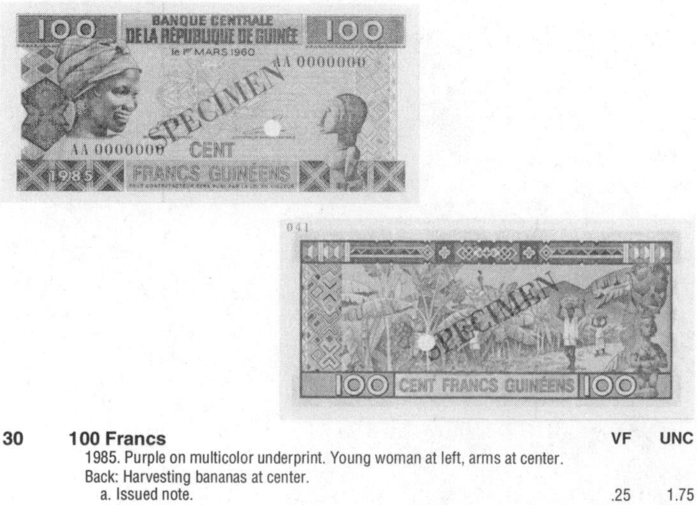

30 **100 Francs**

1985. Purple on multicolor underprint. Young woman at left, arms at center. Back: Harvesting bananas at center.

	VF	UNC
a. Issued note.	.25	1.75
s. Specimen.	—	50.00

31 **500 Francs** VF UNC

1985. Green on multicolor underprint. Woman at left, arms at center. Back: Minehead at center.

	VF	UNC
a. Issued note.	1.00	4.50
s. Specimen.	—	65.00

32 **1000 Francs** VF UNC

1985. Brown and blue on multicolor underprint. Girl at left, arms at center. Back: Shovel loading ore into open end dump trucks at center, mask at right. 150x80mm.

	VF	UNC
a. Issued note.	1.50	6.50
s. Specimen.	—	65.00

33 **5000 Francs** VF UNC

1985. Blue and brown on multicolor underprint. Woman at left, arms at center. Back: Dam at center, mask at right. 156x86mm.

	VF	UNC
a. Issued note.	4.50	20.00
s. Specimen.	—	100.

1998 Issue

35 **100 Francs** VF UNC

1998; 2012. Multicolor. Young woman at left, arms at center. Back: Harvesting bananas at center.

	VF	UNC
a. 1998.	FV	1.50
b. 2012.	FV	1.50

36 **500 Francs** VF UNC

1998. Multicolor. Woman at left, arms at center. Back: Minehead at center. 132x62mm. FV 3.50

37 **1000 Francs** VF UNC

1998. Brown and red-brown on multicolor underprint. Female head at left, arms at center. Back: Mining scene. 146x73mm. FV 5.00

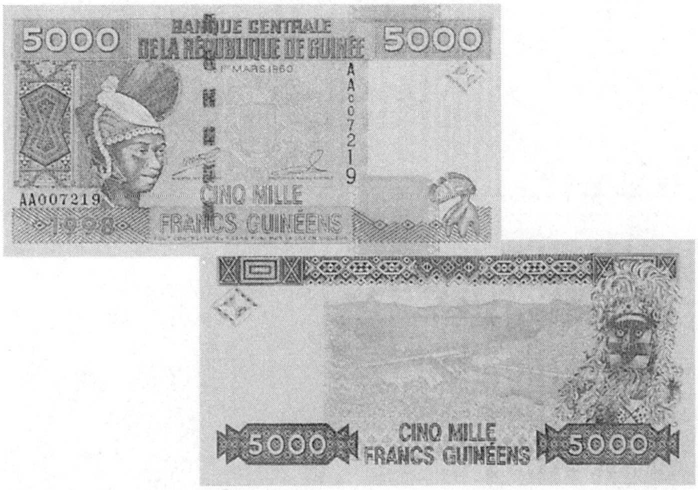

38 **5000 Francs** VF UNC

1998. Multicolor. Female at left, arms at center; thick security thread. Back: Dam at center, mask at right. 158x79mm. FV 17.50

2006-07 Issue

39 500 Francs — VF | UNC

2006; 2012. Green on multicolor underprint. Female at left. Back: Industrial scene. 132x63mm.

	VF	UNC
a. 2006.	FV	3.50
b. 2012.	FV	1.50

40 1000 Francs — VF | UNC

2006. Brown, orange and red on multicolor underprint. Girls at left, drum at lower right. Back: Ore loading. 138x67mm. — FV | 5.00

41 5000 Francs — VF | UNC

2006; 2012. Violet, blue and brown on multicolor underprint. Female at left, sculpture at lower right. Back: Dam at center, mask at right. 150x75mm.

	VF	UNC
a. 2006.	FV	10.00
b. 2012.	FV	7.50

42 10,000 Francs

2007; 2008. Blue-green on multicolor underprint. Young male head at left, pineapple at lower right. Back: Cultivated field.

	VF	UNC
a. 2007.	FV	35.00
b. 2008.	FV	35.00

2010 Commemorative Issue

43 1000 Francs — VF | UNC

1.3.2010. Brown, orange and red on multicolor underprint. Girls at left, drum at lower right. Back: Ore loading. Overprint: 50th Anniversary logo at right. 139x68mm. — FV | 6.00

44 5000 Francs — VF | UNC

1.3.2010. Violet, blue and brown on multicolor underprint. Female at left, sculpture at lower right. Back: Dam at center, mask at right. Overprint: 50th Anniversary logo at right. 151x76mm. — FV | 10.00

45 10,000 Francs — VF | UNC

1.3.2010. Blue-green on multicolor underprint. Young male head at left, pineapple at lower right. Back: Cultivated field. Overprint: 50th Anniversary logo at right. — FV | 17.50

2012 Issue

46 10,000 Francs — VF | UNC

2012. Purple, green and multicolor Young male head at left, hologram nearby. Pineapple at lower right. Back: Cultivated field. — FV | 35.00

The Republic of Guinea-Bissau, a former Portuguese overseas province on the west coast of Africa between Senegal and Guinea, has an area of 36,120 sq. km. and a population of 1.5 million. Capital: Bissau. The country has undeveloped deposits of oil and bauxite. Peanuts, oil-palm kernels and hides are exported.

Since independence from Portugal in 1974, Guinea-Bissau has experienced considerable political and military upheaval. In 1980, a military coup established authoritarian dictator Joao Bernardo 'Nino' Vieira as president. Despite setting a path to a market economy and multiparty system, Vieira's regime was characterized by the suppression of political opposition and the purging of political rivals. Several coup attempts through the 1980s and early 1990s failed to unseat him. In 1994 Vieira was elected president in the country's first free elections. A military mutiny and resulting civil war in 1998 eventually led to Vieira's ouster in May 1999. In February 2000, a transitional government turned over power to opposition leader Kumba Yala, after he was elected president in transparent polling. In September 2003, after only three years in office, Yala was ousted by the military in a bloodless coup, and businessman Henrique Rosa was sworn in as interim president. In 2005, former President Vieira was re-elected president pledging to pursue economic development and national reconciliation.

RULERS:

Portuguese until 1974

MONETARY SYSTEM:

1 Peso = 100 Centavos, 1975-1997
1 Franc = 65 Pesos, 1997-

Republic

Banco Nacional da Guiné-Bissau

1975 Issue

1 — 50 Pesos — VF — UNC

24.9.1975. Blue and brown on multicolor underprint. P. Nalsna at left, group at center. Back: Field workers at center, woman at right. Watermark: A. Cabral. Printer: Algerian.

		VF	UNC
a.	Issued note.	6.00	40.00
s.	Specimen. Red overprint: *SPECIMEN*.	—	100.

2 — 100 Pesos — VF — UNC

24.9.1975. Brown (shades) on multicolor underprint. D. Ramos at left, group in open hut at lower left center. Back: Objects and woman. Watermark: A. Cabral. Printer: Algerian.

		VF	UNC
a.	Issued note.	5.00	30.00
s.	Specimen. Red overprint: *SPECIMEN*.	—	200.

3 — 500 Pesos — VF — UNC

24.9.1975. Green, black and brown on multicolor underprint. Pres. A. Cabral at left, arms at center, soldier at right. Back: Carving and two youths. Watermark: A. Cabral. Printer: Algerian.

		VF	UNC
a.	Issued note.	30.00	150.
s.	Specimen. Red overprint: *SPECIMEN*.	—	250.

1978-84 Issue

#5-9 Replacement notes: Serial # prefix *Z*.

5 — 50 Pesos — VF — UNC

28.2.1983. Orange on blue and multicolor underprint. Artifact at left center, P. Nalsna at right, arms at lower right. Back: Local scene. Watermark: A. Cabral. Printer: BWC.

		VF	UNC
a.	Issued note.	2.50	12.00
s.	Specimen. Red overprint: *ESPECIMEN* on each side.	—	55.00

6 — 100 Pesos — VF — UNC

28.2.1983. Red on multicolor underprint. Carving at left, D. Ramos at right, arms at lower right. Back: Building at left center. Watermark: A. Cabral. — 1.25 — 4.50

7 **500 Pesos** VF UNC

28.2.1983. Deep blue on multicolor underprint. Carving at left, F. Mendes at right, arms at lower right. Back: Slave trade scene. Watermark: A. Cabral. 154x65mm.

	VF	UNC
a. Issued note.	2.00	6.00
s. Specimen. Overprint: *SPECIMEN* in back on both sides.	—	35.00

8 **1000 Pesos**

24.9.1978. Green on brown and multicolor underprint. Weaver and loom at lower left center, Pres. A. Cabral at right, arms at lower right. Back: Allegory with title: *Apoteose ao Triunfo* Watermark: A. Cabral. Printer: BWC.

	VF	UNC
a. Signature titles: *COMISSARIO PRINCIPAL, COMISSARIO DE ESTADO DAS FINANCAS* and *GOVERNADOR.*	20.00	85.00
b. Signature titles: *PRIMEIRO MINISTRO, MINISTRO DE ECONOMIA E FINANCAS* and *GOVERNADOR.*	3.00	8.00
s. As a. Specimen.	—	185.

9 **5000 Pesos**

12.9.1984. Brown and black on multicolor underprint. Map at left center, Pres. A. Cabral at right, arms at lower right. Back: Harvesting grain at center. Watermark: A. Cabral.

	VF	UNC
	4.00	15.00

1990 Issue

#10-15 Replacement notes: Serial # prefixes *AZ; BZ; CZ; DZ; ZA* **or** *ZZ.*

10 **50 Pesos**

1.3.1990. Pale red on multicolor underprint. Artifact at left center, P. Nalsna at right, arms at lower right. Signature titles: *MINISTRO-GOVERNADOR and VICE-GOVERNADOR.* Back: Local scene. Watermark: BCG. Printer: TDLR. Reduced size. UV: security strip fluoresces orange.

	VF	UNC
	.25	1.00

11 **100 Pesos**

1.3.1990. Olive-gray on multicolor underprint. Carving at left, D. Ramos at right, arms at lower right. Signature titles: *MINISTRO-GOVERNADOR and VICE-GOVERNADOR.* Back: Building at left center. Watermark: BCG. Printer: TDLR. Reduced size.

	VF	UNC
	.25	1.00

12 **500 Pesos**

1.3.1990. Deep blue on multicolor underprint. Carving at left, F. Mendes at right, arms at lower right. Signature titles: *MINISTRO-GOVERNADOR and VICE-GOVERNADOR.* Back: Slave trade scene. Watermark: BCG. Printer: TDLR. Reduced size.

	VF	UNC
	.50	2.50

13 **1000 Pesos**

1990; 1993. Dark brown, brown-violet and orange on multicolor underprint. Weaver and loom at lower left center, Pres. A. Cabral at right, arms at lower right. Back: Allegory with title: *Apoteose ao Triunfo.* Watermark: A. Cabral. Printer: TDLR.

	VF	UNC
a. Signature titles: *MINISTRO-GOVERNADOR* and *VICE-GOVERNADOR.* 1.3.1990.	.50	3.50
b. Signature titles: *GOVERNADOR* and *VICE-GOVERNADOR.* 1.3.1993.	.50	2.50

14 **5000 Pesos**

1990; 1993. Purple, violet and brown on multicolor underprint. Map at left center, Pres. A. Cabral at right, arms at lower right. Back: Harvesting grain at center. Watermark: A. Cabral. Printer: TDLR.

	VF	UNC
a. Signature titles: *MINISTRO-GOVERNADOR* and *VICE-GOVERNADOR.*	1.00	8.00
b. Signature titles: *GOVERNADOR* and *VICE-GOVERNADOR.* 1.3.1993.	1.00	5.00

15 **10,000 Pesos**

1990; 1993. Green, olive-brown and blue on multicolor underprint. Statue at lower left center, outline map at center, A. Cabral at right. Back: Local people fishing with nets in river at center. Watermark: A. Cabral. Printer: TDLR.

	VF	UNC
a. Signature titles: *MINISTRO-GOVERNADOR* and *VICE-GOVERNADOR.* 1.3.1990.	2.00	15.00
b. Signature titles: *GOVERNADOR* and *VICE-GOVERNADOR.* 1.3.1993.	1.00	12.50

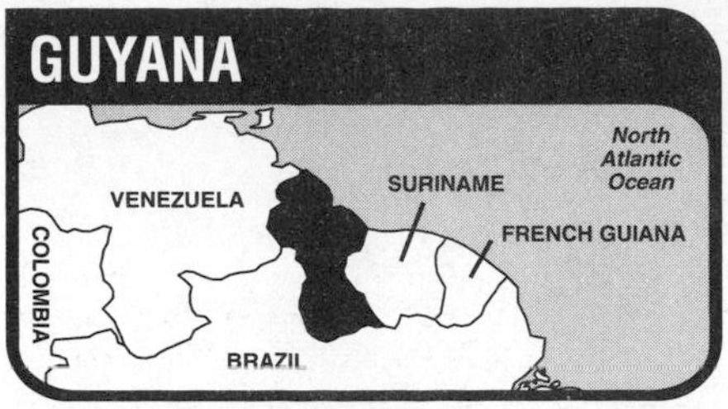

The Cooperative Republic of Guyana, an independent member of the British Commonwealth situated on the northeast coast of South America, has an area of 214,970 sq. km. and a population of 770,800. Capital: Georgetown. The economy is basically agrarian. Sugar, rice and bauxite are exported.

Originally a Dutch colony in the 17th century, by 1815 Guyana had become a British possession. The abolition of slavery led to black settlement of urban areas and the importation of indentured servants from India to work the sugar plantations. This ethnocultural divide has persisted and has led to turbulent politics. Guyana achieved independence from the UK in 1966, and since then it has been ruled mostly by socialist-oriented governments. In 1992, Cheddi Jagan was elected president in what is considered the country's first free and fair election since independence. After his death five years later, his wife, Janet JAGAN, became president but resigned in 1999 due to poor health. Her successor, Bharrat Jagdeo, was reelected in 2001 and again in 2006.

Notes of the British Caribbean Currency Board circulated from 1950-1965.

RULERS:

British to 1966

MONETARY SYSTEM:

1 Joe = 22 Guilders to 1836
1 Dollar = 4 Shillings 2 Pence, 1837-1965
1 Dollar = 100 Cents, 1966-

SIGNATURE VARIETIES

1	GOVERNOR	MINISTER OF FINANCE	2	GOVERNOR / MINISTER OF FINANCE
3	GOVERNOR	MINISTER OF FINANCE	4	GOVERNOR / MINISTER OF FINANCE
4A	GOVERNOR	MINISTER OF FINANCE	5	GOVERNOR / MINISTER OF FINANCE
6	GOVERNOR	VICE PRESIDENT ECONOMIC MINISTER OF FINANCE	7	GOVERNOR / MINISTER OF FINANCE
8	GOVERNOR	MINISTER OF FINANCE	9	GOVERNOR / MINISTER OF FINANCE
10	GOVERNOR	MINISTER OF FINANCE	11	GOVERNOR / MINISTER OF FINANCE
12	GOVERNOR	MINISTER OF FINANCE	13	
14				

REPUBLIC

BANK OF GUYANA

1966 ND ISSUE

#21-27 Color shading variations.

		VF	UNC
21	**1 Dollar** ND (1966-92). Red on multicolor underprint. Arms at center, Kaieteur Falls at right. Back: Black bush polder at left, rice harvesting at right. Watermark: Macaw's (parrot) head. Printer: TDLR. 156x65mm.		
	a. Signature 1; 2.	3.00	15.00
	b. Signature 3; 4.	6.00	30.00
	c. Signature 4A.	.25	1.50
	d. Signature 5.	1.00	4.00
	e. Signature 6 (1983).	.25	1.50
	f. Serial # prefix *B/1* or higher. Signature 7 (1989).	FV	1.00
	g. Signature 8 (1992); 9. Back darker red.	FV	.75
	s. As a. Specimen.	—	25.00

		VF	UNC
22	**5 Dollars** ND (1966-92). Dark green on multicolor underprint. Arms at center, Kaieteur Falls at right. Back: Cane sugar harvesting at left, conveyor at right. Watermark: Macaw's (parrot) head. Printer: TDLR. 156x65mm.		
	a. Signature 1; 2.	9.00	45.00
	b. Signature 3.	10.00	55.00
	c. Signature 5.	1.00	7.50
	d. Signature 6 (1983).	.50	5.00
	e. Serial # prefix *A/27* or higher. Signature 7 (1989).	FV	3.00
	f. Signature 8 (1992); 9.	FV	.75
	s. As a. Specimen.	—	25.00

		VF	UNC
23	**10 Dollars** ND (1966-92). Dark brown on multicolor underprint. Arms at center, Kaieteur Falls at right. Back: Bauxite mining at left, aluminum plant at right. Watermark: Macaw's (parrot) head. Printer: TDLR. UV: shiled fluoresces yellow and blue. 156x65mm.		
	a. Signature 1; 2; 3.	10.00	75.00
	b. Signature 4; 5.	2.50	15.00
	c. Signature 6 (1983).	1.25	7.50
	d. Serial # prefix *A/16* or higher. Signature 7 (1989).	FV	1.00
	e. Signature 8 (1992).	FV	1.50
	f. Signature 9.	FV	1.00
	s. As a. Specimen.	—	25.00

		VF	UNC
24	**20 Dollars**		
	ND (1966-89). Brown and purple on multicolor underprint. Arms at center, Kaieteur Falls at right. Back: Shipbuilding at left, ferry *Malali* at right. Watermark: Macaw's (parrot) head. Printer: TDLR. 156x65mm.		
	a. Signature 1; 2; 4; 4A.	10.00	50.00
	b. Signature 5.	3.00	15.00
	c. Signature 6 (1983).	2.50	12.50
	d. Serial # prefix *A/42* or higher. Signature 7 (1989).	FV	1.50
	s. As a. Specimen.	—	25.00

1989; 1992 ND Issue

		VF	UNC
27	**20 Dollars**		
	ND (1989). Brown and purple on multicolor underprint. Arms at center, Kaieteur Falls at right. Signature 7; 9. Back: Shipbuilding at left, ferry *Malali* at right. Design element in colored border at ends. Watermark: Macaw's (parrot) head. Printer: TDLR. 156x65mm.	FV	2.50

		VF	UNC
28	**100 Dollars**		
	ND (1989). Blue on multicolor underprint. Map of Guyana at right, bank arms at center. Signature 7; 8. Back: Cathedral at center. Watermark: Macaw's (parrot) head. Printer: TDLR. 156x65mm.	FV	6.00

		VF	UNC
29	**500 Dollars**		
	ND (ca. 1992). Lilac-brown and purple on multicolor underprint. Map of Guyana at right, bank arms at center. Back: Public buildings in Georgetown. Watermark: Macaw's (parrot) head. Printer: TDLR. 156x65mm.		
	a. Signature 8.	FV	35.00
	b. Signature 9.	FV	10.00

1996; 1999 ND Issue

		VF	UNC
30	**20 Dollars**		
	ND (1996). Brown and purple on multicolor underprint. Map of Guyana at right, bank arms at center. Ascending size serial number at upper right. Back: Shipbuilding at left, ferry *Malali* at right. Design element in colored border at ends. Watermark: Macaw's (parrot) head. 156x65mm.		
	a. Signature 10.	FV	1.00
	b. Signature 11.	FV	1.00
	b. Signature 12.	FV	1.00
	c. Signature 13. Signature title as Acting Governor.	FV	1.00
	d. Signature 13. Signature title as Governor.	FV	1.00
	e. Signature 14.	FV	1.00

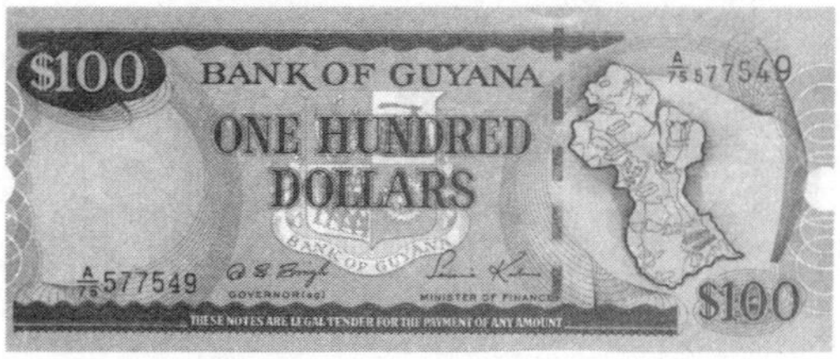

		VF	UNC
31	**100 Dollars**		
	ND (1999). Blue on multicolor underprint. Map of Guyana at right, bank arms at center. Ascending size serial number at upper right. Signature 10; 11; 12. Back: Cathedral at center. Watermark: Macaw's (parrot) head. 156x65mm.	FV	4.00

		VF	UNC
32	**500 Dollars**		
	ND (1996). Lilac-brown and purple on multicolor underprint. Map of Guyana at right, bank arms at center. Ascending size serial number at upper right. Silver OVD map at right. Segmented foil over security thread. Signature 10. Back: Public buildings in Georgetown. Watermark: Macaw's (parrot) head. 156x65mm.	FV	10.00

		VF	UNC
33	**1000 Dollars**		
	ND (1996). Dark green, deep red and brown on multicolor underprint. Map of Guyana at right, bank arms at center. Ascending size serial number at upper right. Gold OVD map at right. Segmented foil over security thread. Signature 10. Back: Bank building at center. Watermark: Macaw's (parrot) head. 156x65mm.	FV	15.00

2000 ND Issue

34 500 Dollars VF UNC

ND (2002). Lilac-brown and purple on multicolor underprint. Map of Guyana at right, bank arms at center. Ascending size serial number at upper right. OVD in watermark area at right. Segmented joil over security thread. Back: Public buildings in Georgetown. Watermark: Macaw's (parrot) head. 156x65mm.

	VF	UNC
a. Signature 11.	FV	8.50
b. Signature 12.	FV	8.50

35 1000 Dollars VF UNC

ND (2000). Dark green, deep red and brown on multicolor underprint. Map of Guyana at right, bank arms at center. Ascending size serial number at upper right. Gold OVD shield at right. Signature 11, 12. Back: Bank building at center. Watermark: Macaw's (parrot) head. 156x65mm. FV 15.00

2006 ND Issue

36 100 Dollars VF UNC

ND (2006) Green-blue on green, tan and multicolor underprint. Island map at right. Back: St. George's Cathedral at center. Printer: DLR. 156x65mm.

	VF	UNC
a. Signature 13.	FV	2.00
b. Signature 14.	FV	1.75
s. Specimen.	—	50.00

37 500 Dollars VF UNC

ND (2011). Lilac-brown and purple on multicolor underprint. Map of Guyana at right. Wide security foil with Macaw bird. Back: Public buildings in Georgetown at center. Segmented security foil. 156x65mm. FV 8.50

38 1000 Dollars VF UNC

ND (2006). Olive green on orange and rose multicolor underprint. Arms at center, island map at right. Wide security strip with Macaw bird. Back: Bank of Guyana building at center. Segmented security strip at center left. Printer: DLR. 156x65mm.

	VF	UNC
a. Signature 13.	FV	15.00
b. Signature 14.	FV	15.00

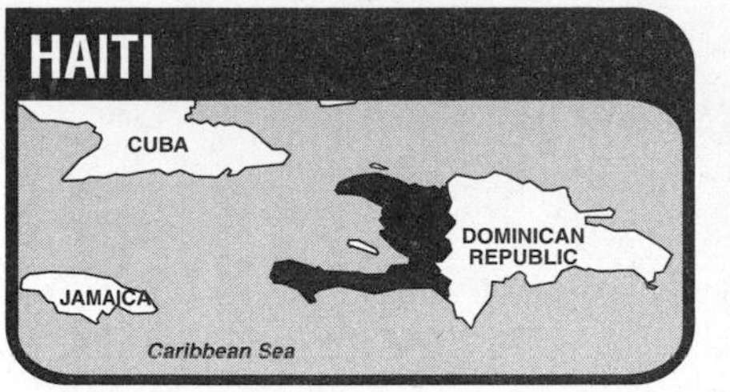

The Republic of Haiti, occupying the western one third of the island of Hispañola in the Caribbean Sea between Puerto Rico and Cuba, has an area of 27,750 sq. km. and a population of 8.92 million. Capital: Port-au-Prince. The economy is d on agriculture, light manufacturing and tourism which is becoming increasingly important. Coffee, bauxite, sugar, essential oils and handicrafts are exported.

The native Taino Amerindians - who inhabited the island of Hispañiola when it was discovered by Columbus in 1492 - were virtually annihilated by Spanish settlers within 25 years. In the early 17th century, the French established a presence on Hispaniola, and in 1697, Spain ceded to the French the western third of the island, which later became Haiti. The French colony, d on forestry and sugar-related industries, became one of the wealthiest in the Caribbean, but only through the heavy importation of African slaves and considerable environmental degradation. In the late 18th century, Haiti's nearly half million slaves revolted under Toussaint L'Ouverture. After a prolonged struggle, Haiti became the first black republic to declare its independence in 1804. The poorest country in the Western Hemisphere, Haiti has been plagued by political violence for most of its history. After an armed rebellion led to the forced resignation and exile of President Jean-Bertrand Aristide in February 2004, an interim government took office to organize new elections under the auspices of the United Nations Stabilization Mission in Haiti (Minustah). Continued violence and technical delays prompted repeated postponements, but Haiti finally did inaugurate a democratically elected president and parliament in May of 2006.

MONETARY SYSTEM:

5 Gourdes = 1 U.S. Dollar, 1919-89

Republic

Banque Nationale de la République d'Haiti

Convention du 12 Avril 1919 - Sixth Issue (ca.1951-64)

178 1 Gourde VF UNC

L.1919. Dark brown on light blue and multicolor underprint. Closeup view of Citadel Rampart at center. Prefix letters AS-BM. 5 signature varieties. First signature title: *Le Président.* Back: Arms at center. Printer: ABNC.

	VF	UNC
a. Issued note.	2.00	17.50
s. Specimen. Punch hole cancelled.	—	35.00

179 2 Gourdes VF UNC

L.1919. Blue and multicolor. Light green in underprint. Citadel rampart at center. Prefix letters Y-AF. 6 signature varieties. First signature title: *Le President.* Back: Arms at center. Printer: ABNC.

	VF	UNC
a. Issued note.	4.00	25.00
s. Specimen. Punch hole cancelled.	—	60.00

180 5 Gourdes

L.1919. Orange and multicolor. Green in underprint. Woman harvesting coffee at left. Prefix letters G-M. 3 signature varieties. First signature title:*Le President.* Back: Arms at center. Printer: ABNC.

	VF	UNC
a. Issued note.	6.00	35.00
s. Specimen. Punch hole cancelled.	—	50.00

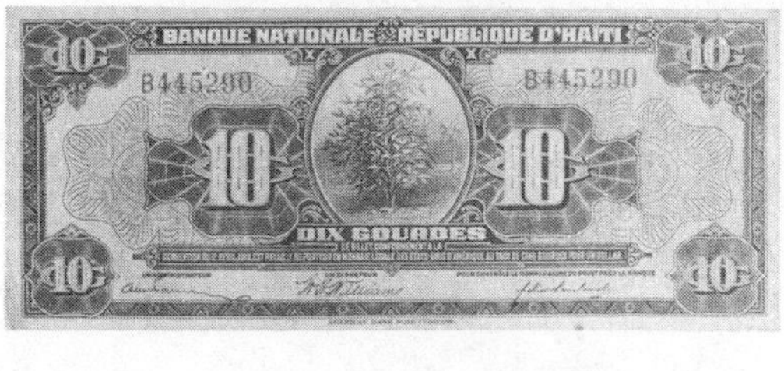

181 10 Gourdes VF UNC

L.1919. Green on multicolor underprint. Coffee plant at center. Prefix letters B-D. 2 signature varieties. First signature title: *Le President.* Back: Arms at center. Printer: ABNC.

a. Issued note.	12.50	55.00
s. Specimen, punch hole cancelled.	—	70.00

183 50 Gourdes VF UNC

L.1919. Olive-green on multicolor underprint. Cotton bolls at center. First signature title: *Le President.* Back: Arms at center. Printer: ABNC. Specimen. — 225.

184 100 Gourdes VF UNC

L.1919. Purple on multicolor underprint. Field workers at left. Prefix letter A. First signature title: *Le President.* Back: Arms at center. Printer: ABNC.

a. Issued note.	125.	350.
s. Specimen, punch hole cancelled.	—	175.

Convention du 12 Avril 1919 - Seventh Issue (ca.1964)

#185-189 like #178-180 but incorporating new guilloche patterns without green in underprint.

185 1 Gourde VF UNC

L.1919. Dark brown on light blue and multicolor underprint. Citadel rampart at center. Like #178. Serial # prefix letters: *BK-BT.*

a. Issued note.	1.50	7.50
s. Specimen. Red overprint: *SPECIMEN* twice on face.	—	40.00

186 2 Gourdes

L.1919. Blue on light blue and multicolor underprint. Citadel rampart at center. Like #179. Serial # prefix letters: *AE-AJ.*

a. Issued note.	1.50	7.50
s. Specimen. Red overprint: *SPECIMEN* twice on face.	Unc	45.00

187 5 Gourdes VF UNC

L.1919. Orange on light blue and multicolor underprint. Woman harvesting corree beans at left. Like #180. Serial # prefix letter: *N.*

a. Issued note.	1.00	7.00
s. Specimen.	Unc	25.00

188 50 Gourdes

L.1919. Olive-green on blue and magenta underprint. Like #183. Back: Cotton bolls at center. Not issued. Archive example. — —

189 100 Gourdes

L.1919. Purple on multicolor underprint. Like #184. Back: Field workers at left. Not issued. Archive example. — —

Convention du 12 Avril 1919 - Eighth Issue (ca.1967)

190 1 Gourde VF UNC

L.1919. Brown on multicolor underprint. Citadel rampart at center, new guilloche patterns, without green in underprint. Prefix letters DA-DL. Second signature title: *LE DIRECTEUR.* Back: Arms at center. Printer: TDLR.

a. Issued note.	1.00	7.50
s. Specimen.	—	27.50

191 2 Gourdes VF UNC

L.1919. Grayish blue on multicolor underprint. Citadel rampart at center. New guilloche patterns, without green in underprint. Prefix letters DA-DF. 6 signature varieties. Second signature title: *LE DIRECTEUR.* Back: Arms at center. Printer: TDLR.

a. Issued note.	1.50	10.00
s. Specimen.	—	27.50

192 5 Gourdes VF UNC

L.1919. Orange on light blue and multicolor underprint. Woman harvesting coffee at left, new guilloche patterns, without green in underprint. Prefix letters DA-DK. 3 signature varieties. Second signature title: *LE DIRECTEUR.* Back: Arms at center. Printer: TDLR.

a. Issued note.	4.00	12.50
s. Specimen.	—	27.50

193 10 Gourdes VF UNC

L.1919. Green on multicolor underprint. Coffee plant at center. Prefix letters DA. 2 signature varieties. Second signature title: *LE DIRECTEUR.* Back: Arms at center. Printer: TDLR.

a. Issued note.	8.00	30.00
s. Specimen.	—	35.00

194 50 Gourdes VF UNC

L.1919. Olive-green on multicolor underprint. Cotton bolls at center. Prefix letters DA. Second signature title: *UN DIRECTEUR.* Back: Arms at center. Printer: TDLR.

	VF	UNC
a. Issued note.	17.50	80.00
s. Specimen.	—	170.

195 100 Gourdes VF UNC

L.1919. Purple on multicolor underprint. Field workers at left, with new guilloche patterns, without green in underprint. Prefix letters DA. Second signature title: *LE DIRECTEUR.* Back: Arms at center. Printer: TDLR.

	VF	UNC
a. Issued note.	35.00	150.
s. Specimen.	—	—

Convention du 12 Avril 1919 - Ninth Issue

196 1 Gourde VF UNC

L.1919. Dark brown on multicolor underprint. Pres. Dr. François Duvalier at center. Prefix letters DK-DT. Back: Arms at center. Printer: TDLR.

	VF	UNC
a. Issued note.	.75	3.50
s. Specimen.	—	20.00

197 2 Gourdes VF UNC

L.1919. Grayish blue on multicolor underprint. Pres. Dr. François Duvalier at center. Prefix letters DG-DK. Back: Arms at center. Printer: TDLR.

	VF	UNC
a. Issued note.	1.25	4.50
s. Specimen.	—	25.00

198 5 Gourdes VF UNC

L.1919. Orange on multicolor underprint. Pres. Dr. François Duvalier at left. Prefix letters DG-DK. Back: Arms at center. Printer: TDLR.

	VF	UNC
a. Issued note.	2.50	7.50
s. Specimen.	—	25.00

Convention du 12 Avril 1919 - Tenth Issue

200 1 Gourde VF UNC

L.1919. Dark brown on multicolor underprint. Portrait President Dr. François Duvalier at center. Prefix letters A-Z; AA-CR. Three signature varieties. Back: Arms at center. Printer: ABNC.

	VF	UNC
a. Issued note.	.75	3.00
s. Specimen.	—	20.00

201 2 Gourdes

L.1919. Blue on multicolor underprint. Portrait of Dr. François Duvalier at center. Three signature varieties. First issued without prefix, then letters A-Q. Back: Arms at center, with 4 lines of text on back. Printer: ABNC. 1.50 5.00

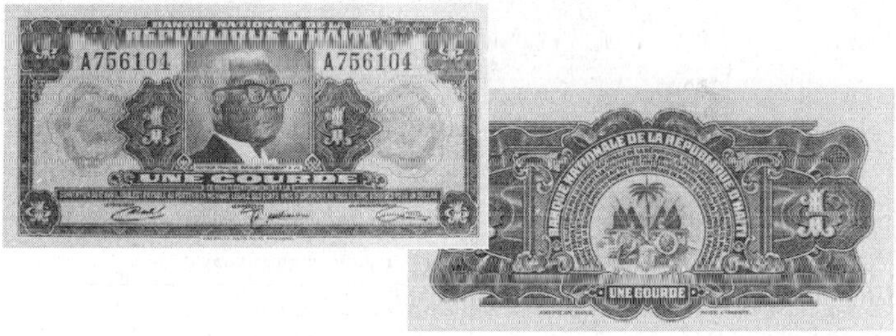

202 5 Gourdes VF UNC

L.1919. Orange on multicolor underprint. Portrait President Dr. François Duvalier at left. First issued without prefix, then letters A-Z; AA-AP. Three signature varieties. Back: Arms at center, with 4 lines of text on back. Printer: ABNC.

	VF	UNC
a. Issued note.	3.00	12.50
s. Specimen.	—	25.00

203 10 Gourdes

L.1919. Dark green on multicolor underprint. Portrait President Dr. François Duvalier at center. First issued without prefix, then letter A. Back: Arms at center, with 4 lines of text on back. Printer: ABNC.

	VF	UNC
a. Issued note.	5.00	15.00
s. Specimen.	—	30.00

204 50 Gourdes VF UNC

L.1919. Dark gray on multicolor underprint. Portrait President Lysius Félicité Salomon Jeune at center. First issued without prefix, then letters A-C. Two signature varieties. Back: Arms at center, with 4 lines of text on back. 162x70mm.

	VF	UNC
a. Issued note.	17.50	30.00
s. Specimen. Overprint: *SPECIMEN* twice in red. Punch hole cancelled.	—	40.00

205 **100 Gourdes** VF UNC

L.1919. Purple on multicolor underprint. Portrait Henri Christophe (Pres., later King) at left. Without prefix letter. Two signature varieties. Back: Arms at center, with 4 lines of text on back.

	VF	UNC
a. Issued note.	40.00	75.00
s. Speicmen. Red overprint: *SPECIMEN* on face. Punch hole cancelled. With or without serial #.	—	100.

206 **250 Gourdes** VF UNC

L.1919. Dark yellow-green on multicolor underprint. Jean-Jacques Dessalines at right. Without prefix letter. Back: Arms at center, with 4 lines of text on back.

	VF	UNC
a. Issued note.	110.	225.
s. Specimen. Red overprint: *SPECIMEN* on face. Punch hole cancelled.	—	200.

207 **500 Gourdes** VF UNC

L.1919. Red on multicolor underprint. Portrait President Dr. François Duvalier at center. Issued without prefix Back: Arms at center, with 4 lines of text on back.

	VF	UNC
a. Issued note.	165.	350.
s. Specimen.	—	350.

Eleventh Issue (ca.1973)

Lois des 21 Mai 1935 et 15 Mai 1953 et au Décret du 22 Novembre 1973 (issued 1979).

210 **1 Gourde** VF UNC

L.1973, etc. Dark brown on multicolor underprint. Portrait of President Dr. François Duvalier at center. Prefix letters A-Z; AA-AC. Back: Arms at center. Printer: ABNC. UV: Duvalier and 1G fluoresce orange. .60 4.00

211 **2 Gourdes**

L.1973, etc. Blue on multicolor underprint. Portrait of Dr. François Duvalier at center. Prefix letters A-J. Three signature varieties Back: Arms at center with 3 lines of text. Printer: ABNC. 1.25 7.50

212 **5 Gourdes** VF UNC

L.1973, etc. Orange on multicolor underprint. Portrait Pres. Dr. François Duvalier at left. First issued without prefix, then letters A-AA. Three signature varieties. Back: Arms at center with 3 lines of text. Printer: ABNC. 3.00 12.50

213 **50 Gourdes** VF UNC

L.1973, etc. Dark gray on multicolor underprint. Portrait Pres. Lysius Félicité Salomon Jeune at center. Prefix letter A. Two signature varieties. Two serial number varieties. Back: Arms at center with 3 lines of text. Printer: ABNC. 17.50 35.00

214 **100 Gourdes**

L.1973, etc. Purple on multicolor underprint. Portrait Henri Christophe (Pres., later King) at left. Without prefix letter. Two signature varieties. Two serial number varieties. Back: Arms at center with 3 lines of text. Printer: ABNC.

	VF	UNC
a. Issued note.	35.00	70.00
s. Specimen. Black overprint: *SPECIMEN* on face. Punch hole cancelled.	—	70.00

Twelfth Issue

Lois des 21 Mai 1935 et 15 Mai 1953 et au Décret du 22 Novembre 1973

218 **25 Gourdes** VF UNC

L.1973, etc. Dark blue and brown-violet on multicolor underprint. President Jean-Claude Duvalier at left, antenna at right. Prefix letters DA-DD. Back: National Palace. Printer: TDLR.

	VF	UNC
a. Issued note.	7.50	22.50
s. Specimen.	—	30.00

Banque de la République d'Haiti

Loi du 17 Aout 1979 (1980-82)

230 **1 Gourde** VF UNC

L.1979. Dark brown on multicolor underprint. Portrait of President Dr. François Duvalier at center. Without prefix letter. Signature titles: *LE GOUVERNEUR, LE GOUVERNEUR ADJOINT* and *LE DIRECTEUR.* Small size numerals in serial #. Back: Arms at center. Printer: ABNC. UV: planchettes fluoresce yellow, red and blue. Duvalier and 1G green, design elements yellow and green. .50 2.75

230A **1 Gourde**

L.1979. Dark brown on multicolor underprint. Portrait of Pres. Dr. FranÁois Duvalier at center. Without prefix letter. Larger size numerals in serial number. Signature titles: *LE GOUVERNEUR, LE GOUVERNEUR ADJOINT* and *LE DIRECTEUR.* Back: Arms at center. Printer: ABNC. Printed on Tyvek. UV: Duvalier and IG and central design fluourese orange.

	VF	UNC
a. Issued note.	.50	4.00
s. Specimen. Overprinted: *SPECIMEN* and punch hole cancelled.	—	250.

231 2 Gourdes — VF | UNC

L.1979. Blue on multicolor underprint. Portrait of President Dr. François Duvalier at center. Without prefix letter. Signature titles: *LE GOUVERNEUR, LE GOUVERNEUR ADJOINT* and *LE DIRECTEUR.* Small size serial #. Back: Arms at center. Printer: ABNC. Printed on paper with planchettes. — .50 | 4.00

231A 2 Gourdes

L.1979. Blue on multicolor underprint. Portrait of Pres. Dr. François Duvalier at center. Without prefix letter. Signature titles: *LE GOUVERNEUR, LE GOUVERNEUR ADJOINT* and *LE DIRECTEUR.* Larger size serial #. Back: Arms at center. Printer: ABNC. Printed on Tyvek.

- a. Issued note. — 1.00 | 7.50
- s. Specimen. Overprinted: *SPECIMEN* and punch hole cancelled. — — | 300.

232 5 Gourdes

L.1979. Orange on multicolor underprint. Portrait President Dr. François Duvalier at left. Prefix letters A-T, AA-. Signature titles: *LE GOUVERNEUR, LE GOUVERNEUR ADJOINT* and *LE DIRECTEUR.* Back: Arms at center. Printer: ABNC. — 1.25 | 10.00

235 50 Gourdes

L.1979. Dark brown on green and multicolor underprint. Portrait President Lysius Félicité Salomon Jeune at center. Two serial number varieties. Without prefix letter or with *A, B, E, G.* Signature titles: *LE GOUVERNEUR, LE GOUVERNEUR ADJOINT* Back: Arms at center. Dull white with planchettes. Printer: ABNC.

- a. Issued note. — 12.50 | 30.00
- s. Specimen. Black overprint: *SPECIMEN* twice on face. Punch hole cancelled. — — | 35.00

235A 50 Gourdes — VF | UNC

L.1979. Dark brown on green and multicolor underprint. Portrait Pres. Lysius Félicité Salomon Jeune at center. Two serial number varieties. Without prefix letter or with *A, B, G.* Signature titles: *LE GOUVERNEUR, LE GOUVERNEUR ADJOINT* and Back: Arms at center. Dull white with planchettes. Printer: ABNC. Printed on Tyvek.

- a. Prefix letter C. Watermark: American bald eagle symbol of ABNC. — 12.50 | 45.00
- b. Without watermark. Prefix letter D; E; F. — 12.50 | 40.00
- s. Specimen. Red overprint: *SPECIMEN.* Punch hole cancelled. — — | 450.

236 100 Gourdes — VF | UNC

L.1979. Purple on multicolor underprint. Portrait Henri Christophe (Pres., later King) at left. Prefix letters A; B. Signature titles: *LE GOUVERNEUR, LE GOUVERNEUR ADJOINT* and *LE DIRECTEUR.* Back: Arms at center. Printer: ABNC. Printed on paper with planchettes.

- a. Issued note. — 20.00 | 55.00
- s. Specimen. Black overprint: *SPECIMEN* on face. Punch hole cancelled. — — | 35.00

236A 100 Gourdes — VF | UNC

L.1979. Purple on multicolor underprint. Portrait Henri Christophe (Pres., later King) at left. Prefix letters C, D, E. Signature titles: *LE GOUVERNEUR, LE GOUVERNEUR ADJOINT* and *LE DIRECTEUR.* Back: Arms at center. Printer: ABNC. Printed on Tyvek. — 20.00 | 55.00

237 250 Gourdes

L.1979. Dark yellow-green on multicolor underprint. Jean-Jacques Dessalines at right. Without prefix letter. Signature titles: *LE GOUVERNEUR, LE GOUVERNEUR ADJOINT* and *LE DIRECTEUR.* Back: Arms at center. Printer: ABNC. Printed on Tyvek.

- a. Issued note. — 45.00 | 125.
- p. Proof. Without serial numbers, date, signatures. — — | 300.
- s. Specimen. — — | 100.

238 500 Gourdes

L.1979. Red on multicolor underprint. Portrait Pres. Dr. François Duvalier at center. Issued without prefix. Signature titles: *LE GOUVERNEUR, LE GOUVERNEUR ADJOINT* and *LE DIRECTEUR.* Back: Arms at center. Printer: ABNC. Printed on Tyvek.

- a. Issued note. — 90.00 | 250.
- p. Proof. Without serial #, date, signatues. — — | 300.
- s. Specimen. — — | 300.

1984; 1985 ND Issue

#239-240 Replacement notes: Serial # prefix *ZZ*.

239 1 Gourde — VF | UNC

L.1979 (1984). Dark brown on multicolor underprint. President Dr. François Duvalier at center. Double prefix letters. Signature titles: *LE GOUVERNEUR, LE GOUVERNEUR ADJOINT* and *LE DIRECTEUR.* Back: Arms at center. Printer: TDLR. — .25 | 2.75

240 2 Gourdes

L.1979 (1985). Grayish blue on multicolor underprint. Citadel rampart at center. New guilloche patterns, without green in underprint. Prefix letters DA-DF. 6 signature varieties. Second signature title:*LE DIRECTEUR.* Back: Arms at center. Printer: TDLR. — .50 | 4.75

241 5 Gourdes — VF | UNC

L.1979 (1985). Orange on multicolor underprint. Jean-Claude Duvalier at left. Signature title at right: *LE DIRECTEUR GENERAL.* Back: Arms at center. Watermark: Jean-Claude Duvalier. Printer: G&D.

- a. Issued note. — 1.00 | 7.50
- s. Specimen. — — | 35.00

242 10 Gourdes — VF | UNC

L.1979 (1984). Green on multicolor underprint. Portrait President Dr. François Duvalier at center. Signature title at right: *LE DIRECTEUR GENERAL.* Back: Arms at center. Printer: ABNC.

- a. Issued note. — 2.00 | 12.50
- s. Specimen. — — | 27.50

243 25 Gourdes VF UNC

L.1979 (1985). Blue on pink and multicolor underprint. Jean-Claude Duvalier at left. Signature title at right: *LE DIRECTEUR GENERAL*. Back: Arms at center. Printer: G&D.

	VF	UNC
a. Issued note.	4.50	20.00
s. Specimen.	—	30.00

1986-88 Issue

245 1 Gourde VF UNC

1987. Dark brown and brown-black on multicolor underprint. Toussaint L'Ouverture with long hair at center. Signature title at right: *LE DIRECTEUR GENERAL*. Back: Arms at center. Printer: G&D. UV: back 1G arms legends fluoresce yellow.

	VF	UNC
a. Issued note.	FV	2.00
s. Specimen.	—	22.50

245A 2 Gourdes VF UNC

L.1979. Grayish blue on multicolor underprint. Citadel rampart at center. Two prefix letters. Signature title at right: *LE DIRECTEUR GENERAL*. Back: Arms at center. Printer: TDLR. UV: serial # fluoresce orange. .25 3.00

246 5 Gourdes VF UNC

1987. Orange and brown on multicolor underprint. Statue of Combat de Vertiéres at upper center. Signature title at right: *LE DIRECTEUR GENERAL*. Back: Arms at center. Watermark: Palm tree. Printer: G&D. UV: bank name, left, right and center elements and 5 fluoresce orange. Back shield and 5 orange, fibers orange.

	VF	UNC
a. Issued note.	FV	5.00
s. Specimen.	—	25.00

247 10 Gourdes VF UNC

1988. Green, red and blue on multicolor underprint. Catherine Flon Arcahaie seated sewing the first flag of the Republic at right. Signature title at right: *LE DIRECTEUR GENERAL*. Back: Green. Arms at center. Printer: ABNC.

	VF	UNC
a. Issued note.	FV	9.00
s. Specimen.	—	27.50

248 25 Gourdes VF UNC

1988. Dark blue and purple on multicolor underprint. Palace of Justice at center. Signature title at right: *LE DIRECTEUR GENERAL*. Back: Arms at center. Watermark: Palm tree. Printer: G&D.

	VF	UNC
a. Issued note.	FV	15.00
s. Specimen.	—	28.50

249 50 Gourdes VF UNC

1986. Dark brown on green and multicolor underprint. Portrait President Lysius Félicité Salomon Jeune at center. Signature titles: *LE GOUVERNEUR, LE DIRECTEUR GENERAL* and *LE Arms at center.* Back: Arms at center. Printer: ABNC.

	VF	UNC
a. Issued note.	FV	30.00
s. Specimen.	—	25.00

250 100 Gourdes

1986. Purple on multicolor underprint. Portrait Henri Christophe (Pres., later King) at left. Signature title at right: *LE DIRECTEUR GENERAL*. Back: Arms at center. Printer: TDLR. Similar to #236 (but more colorful).

	VF	UNC
a. Issued note.	FV	45.00
s. Specimen.	—	35.00

251 250 Gourdes

1988. Tan on multicolor. Jean-Jacques Dessalines at right. Signature title at right: *LE DIRECTEUR GENERAL*. Back: Arms at center. Printer: ABNC.

	VF	UNC
a. Issued note.	FV	80.00
s. Specimen.	—	70.00

252 500 Gourdes

1988. Red on multicolor underprint. President Alexandre Pétion at right. Signature title at right: *LE DIRECTEUR GENERAL*. Back: Arms at center. Printer: ABNC.

	VF	UNC
a. Issued note.	FV	150.
s. Specimen.	—	85.00

1989-91 Issue

253 1 Gourde

1989. Dark brown and brown-black on multicolor underprint. Toussaint L'Ouverture with short hair at center. Back: Arms at center. Printer: USBC. Legal clause includes reference to the United States.

	VF	UNC
a. Issued note.	FV	1.50
s. Specimen.	—	22.50

254 2 Gourdes

1990. Blue-black on multicolor underprint. Citadel rampart at center. Back: Arms at center. Printer: USBC. Legal clause without reference to the United States.

	VF	UNC
a. Issued note.	.50	3.50
s. Specimen.	—	25.00

255 5 Gourdes

1989. Orange and brown on multicolor underprint. Statue of Combat de Vertiéres at upper center. Back: Arms at center. Watermark: Palm tree. Printer: USBC. Legal clause includes reference to the United States.

	VF	UNC
a. Issued note.	FV	5.00
s. Specimen.	—	25.00

256 10 Gourdes

1991; 1998; 1999. Dark green, red and blue on multicolor underprint. Catherine Flon Arcahaie seated sewing the first flag of the Republic at center. Back: Arms at center. Watermark: Palm tree. Printer: G&D. Legal clause on face and back without reference to the United States. 162x70mm.

	VF	UNC
a. Issued note.	FV	4.00
s. Specimen.	—	25.00

257 50 Gourdes

1991; 1999. Dark olive-green on multicolor underprint. Portrait President L. F. Salomon Jeune at center. Back: Arms at center. Watermark: Palm tree. Printer: G&D. Legal clause on face and back without reference to the United States. 162x70mm.

	VF	UNC
a. Issued note.	FV	10.00
s. Specimen.	—	50.00

258 100 Gourdes

1991. Purple on multicolor underprint. Portrait H. Christophe at left. Back: Arms at center. Watermark: Palm tree. Printer: G&D. Legal clause on face and back without reference to the United States. 162x70mm.

	VF	UNC
a. Issued note.	FV	20.00
s. Specimen.	—	25.00

1992-94 Issue

#259-261 Replacement notes: Serial # prefix *ZZ*.

259 1 Gourde

1992; 1993. Dark brown and brown-black on multicolor underprint. Toussaint L'Ouverture with long hair at center, without laws. Back: Arms at center. Printer: TDLR. Shortened clause on face and back: *CE BILLET EST EMIS CONFORMEMENT...*

	VF	UNC
a. Issued note.	FV	1.00
s. Specimen.	FV	25.00

260 2 Gourdes

1992. Blue-black on multicolor underprint. Citadel rampart at center, without laws. Back: Arms at center. Printer: TDLR. Shortened clause on face and back: *CE BILLET EST EMIS CONFORMEMENT...*

	VF	UNC
a. Issued note.	FV	1.75
s. Specimen. Red overprint:SPECIMEN. and perforated *SPECIMEN* twice.	—	25.00

261	**5 Gourdes**	VF	UNC
	1992. Orange and brown on multicolor underprint. Statue of Combat de Vertiéres at upper center, without laws. Back: Arms at center. Printer: TDLR. Shortened clause on face and back: *CE BILLET EST EMIS CONFORMEMENT...* 162x70mm.		
	a. Issued note.	FV	3.00
	s. Specimen.	—	22.50

262	**25 Gourdes**	VF	UNC
	1993. Dark blue and purple on multicolor underprint. Palace of Justice at center, without laws. Back: Arms at center. Printer: G&D. Shortened clause on face and back: *CE BILLET EST EMIS CONFORMEMENT...* 162x70mm.		
	a. Issued note.	FV	4.50
	s. Specimen.	—	25.00

263	**250 Gourdes**	VF	UNC
	1994. Olive-brown and dark brown on multicolor underprint. Portrait J. J. Dessalines at left, without laws. Back: Arms at center. Printer: G&D. Shortened clause on face and back: *CE BILLET EST EMIS CONFORMEMENT...* 162x70mm.		
	a. Issued note.	FV	35.00
	s. Specimen.	—	100.

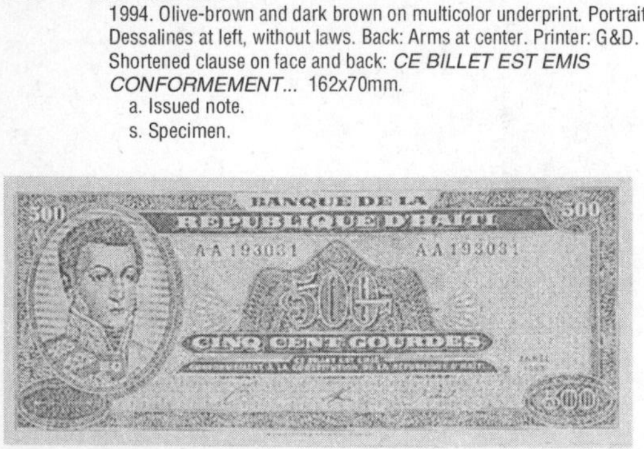

264	**500 Gourdes**	VF	UNC
	1993. Red-violet on multicolor underprint. Portrait President A. Pétion at left, without laws. Back: Arms at center. Printer: G&D. Shortened clause on face and back: *CE BILLET EST EMIS CONFORMEMENT...* 162x70mm.		
	a. Issued note.	FV	60.00
	s. Specimen.	—	200.

2000 Issue

265	**10 Gourdes**	VF	UNC
	2000; 2004; 2006. Dark green and multicolor. Catherine Flon Arcahaie seated sewing the first flag of the Republic at center. Ascending size serial number. Letters BRH at right in various color combinations. Back: Arms at center. Watermark: Palm tree. Printer: (T)DLR. Colorful, especially on borders. 162x70mm.		
	a. 2000.	FV	1.25
	b. 2004.	FV	1.25
	c. 2006.	FV	1.25
	s. Specimen. Red overprint: *SPECIMEN.*	—	50.00

266	**25 Gourdes**	VF	UNC
	2000; 2004; 2006; 2009. Dark blue and black on multicolor underprint. Palace of Justice at center. Ascending size serial number. Letters BRH at right in various color combinations. Back: Arms at center. Watermark: Palm tree. Printer: G&D. 162x70mm.		
	a. 2000.	FV	3.50
	b. 2004.	FV	3.50
	c. 2006.	FV	3.50
	d. 2009.	FV	3.00
	s. Specimen. Red overprint: *SPECIMEN.*	—	100.

267	**50 Gourdes**	VF	UNC
	2000; 2003. Dark olive-green and black on multicolor underprint. Portrait Pres. L. F. Salomon Jeune at center. Ascending size serial number. Letters BRH at right in various color combinations. Back: Arms at center. Printer: (T)DLR. Colorful, especially on borders. 162x70mm.		
	a. 2000.	FV	8.00
	b. 2003.	FV	8.00

268 **100 Gourdes**

2000. Purple on multicolor underprint. Portrait H. Christophe at left. Ascending size serial number. Letters BRH at right in various color combinations. Back: Arms at center. Printer: G&D. Colorful, especially on borders. 162x70mm.

	VF	UNC
	FV	18.00

269 **250 Gourdes**

2000; 2003; 2005. Olive-brown and dark brown on multicolor underprint. Portrait J. J. Dessalines at left. Ascending size serial number. Letters BRH at right in various color combinations. Back: Arms at center. Printer: (T)DLR. Colorful, especially on borders. 162x70mm.

	VF	UNC
a. 2000.	FV	30.00
b. 2003.	FV	30.00
c. 2005.	FV	30.00
s. Specimen. Red overprint: *SPECIMEN*.	—	100.

270 **500 Gourdes**

2000; 2003; 2005. Red and violet on multicolor underprint. Portrait Pres. A. Pétion at left. Ascending size serial number. Letters BRH at right in various color combinations. Back: Arms at center. Printer: (T)DLR. Colorful, especially on borders. 162x70mm.

	VF	UNC
a. 2000.	FV	45.00
b. 2003.	FV	45.00
c. 2005.	FV	45.00
s. Speciemn. Red overprint: *SPECIMEN*.	—	100.

2001 Commemorative Issue

Bicentennial of the Constitution, 1801-2001

271 **20 Gourdes**

2001. Brown, orange and yellow. Bust at left. Foil impressions flank center wreath. Back: Open Constitution book. 162x70mm.

	VF	UNC
	FV	4.00

271A **20 Gourdes**

2001. Brown, orange and yellow. Bust at left. Foil impressions flank center wreath. Without commemorative legent at right. Back: Open Constitution book at center.

	VF	UNC
a. Issued note.	FV	4.00
s. Specimen.	—	—

2004 Commemorative Issue

#272-277 Bicentennial of Haiti. Signature titles in France French and Haitian Creole.

272 **10 Gourdes**

2004; 2006; 2008; 2010. Blue. Sanite Belair at left. Back: Fort Cap-Rouge (Jacmel). Printer: DLR (without imprint). UV: fibers fluoresce red, blue and yellow. 10s in a box yellow. 130x65mm.

	VF	UNC
a. 2004.	FV	2.00
b. 2006.	FV	1.50
c. 2008.	FV	1.25
d. 2010.	FV	1.25
s. Specimen.	—	—

273 **25 Gourdes**

2004. Purple on tan and green underprint. Nicolas Gieffrard at left. Back: Fortress des Plantons (Dussio). 155x65mm.

	VF	UNC
a. Issued note.	FV	3.00
s. Specimen.	—	—

274 50 Gourdes VF UNC

2004; 2008; 2010. Purple. Francois Cappoix at left. Back: Fort Jalousiere (Marmelade). Printer: DLR (without imprint). 155x65mm.

	VF	UNC
a. 2004.	FV	9.00
b. 2008. Reinforced corners.	FV	9.00
c. 2010.	FV	8.00
s. Specimen.	—	—

275 100 Gourdes VF UNC

2004; 2008. Blue and gray. Henry Christophé at left. Back: Citadelle Henry (Milot). 155x65mm.

	VF	UNC
a. 2004.	FV	18.00
b. 2008. Reinforced corners.	FV	18.00
s. Specimen.	—	—

276 250 Gourdes VF UNC

2004; 2007; 2008. Blue on tan and brown underprint. Jean-Jacques Dessalines at left. Back: Fort Decidé (Marchand). Printer: DLR (without imprint). 155x65mm.

	VF	UNC
a. 2004.	FV	17.50
b. 2007. Reinforced corners.	FV	15.00
c. 2008.	FV	12.50
s. Specimen.	—	—

277 500 Gourdes VF UNC

2004; 2007; 2008. Purple on tan underprint. Alexandre Petion at left. Back: Fort Jacques (Fermathe). 155x65mm.

	VF	UNC
a. 2004.	FV	45.00
b. 2007. Reinforced corners.	FV	45.00
c. 2008.	FV	45.00
s. Specimen.	—	—

2006 Issue

278 1000 Gourdes VF UNC

ND (2000); 2004; 2007; 2009. Violet, blue adn lilac on multicolor underprint. Florvil Hyppolite at left. Back: *Marche Valliere* at right.

	VF	UNC
a. ND (2000). Series AA.	FV	85.00
b. 2004. Series AB.	FV	85.00
c. 2007. Series AF. Reinforced corners.	FV	85.00
d. 2009.	FV	85.00
s1. Specimen. Series AA.	—	—
s2. Specimen. Series AB.	—	—
s3. Specimen. Series AF.	—	—

Certificat de Liberation Economique

Loi du 17 Septembre 1962

		VF	UNC
501	**1 Gourde**		
	1.10.1962. Green with black text.	25.00	65.00
502	**5 Gourdes**		
	1.10.1962. Red with black text.		
	a. Series A.	25.00	65.00
	b. Series B.	25.00	65.00
	c. Series C.	25.00	65.00
503	**25 Gourdes**		
	1.10.1962. Yellow-orange with black text.	30.00	80.00

		VF	UNC
504	**100 Gourdes**		
	1.10.1962. Blue with black text.	100.	250.

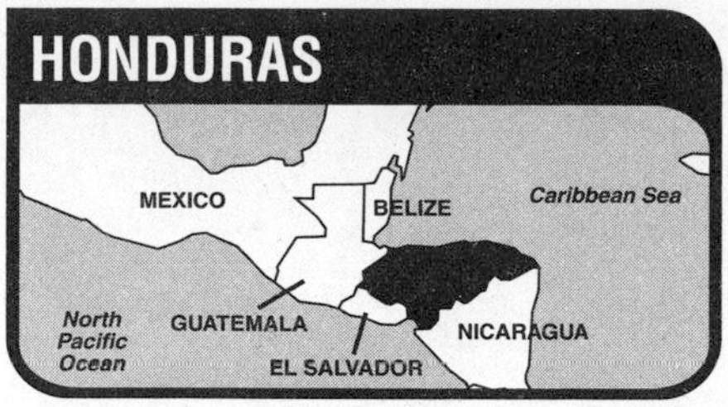

The Republic of Honduras, situated in Central America between El Salvador, Nicaragua and Guatemala, has an area of 43,277 sq. mi. (112,088 sq. km.) and a population of 6.48 million. Capital: Tegucigalpa. Tourism, agriculture, mining (gold and silver), and logging are the chief industries. Bananas, timber and coffee are exported.

Once part of Spain's vast empire in the New World, Honduras became an independent nation in 1821. After two and a half decades of mostly military rule, a freely elected civilian government came to power in 1982. During the 1980s, Honduras proved a haven for anti-Sandinista contras fighting the Marxist Nicaraguan Government and an ally to Salvadoran Government forces fighting leftist guerrillas. The country was devastated by Hurricane Mitch in 1998.

MONETARY SYSTEM:

1 Lempira = 100 Centavos, 1926-

República de Honduras

Banco Central de Honduras

1950-51 Issue

		VF	UNC
49	**100 Lempiras** 1951-73. Yellow on multicolor underprint. Valle at left, arms at right. Back: Village and bridge.		
	a. Without security thread, lilac-pink underprint. Printer: W&S. 16.3.1951; 8.3.1957.	300.	1500.
	b. Without security thread, With fibers at right center, light green and light orange underprint. Printer: W&S. 5.2.1964; 5.11.1965; 22.3.1968; 10.12.1969.	300.	1500.
	c. With security thread, yellow underprint. 13.10.1972. Reported not confirmed.	—	—
	d. As c. but without security thread. 13.10.1972; 23.3.1973.	175.	500.
	s. Specimen, punch hole cancelled.	—	250.

1953-56 Issue

		VF	UNC
51	**5 Lempiras** 1953-68. Gray on multicolor underprint. Morazán at left, arms at right. Serial # at upper left and upper right. Back: Battle of Trinidad. Printer: ABNC. 156x67mm.		
	a. Date horizontal. 17.3.1953; 19.3.1954; 26.3.1954; 7.5.1954.	50.00	300.
	b. Date horizontal. 22.11.1957-7.1.1966.	35.00	225.
	c. Date vertical. 15.4.1966; 29.9.1967; 22.3.1968.	20.00	150.
	s. Specimen.	—	300.

		VF	UNC
52	**10 Lempiras** 1954-69. Brown on multicolor underprint. Cabañas at left, arms at right. Back: Old bank building. Printer: TDLR. Date and signature style varieties. 156x67mm.		
	a. Right signature title: *MINISTRO DE HACIENDA*... 19.11.1954.	75.00	550.
	b. Right signature title: *MINISTRO DE ECONOMIA*... 19.2.1960-10.1.1969.	50.00	400.

		VF	UNC
53	**20 Lempiras** 1954-72. Green. D. de Herrera at left, arms at right. Back: Waterfalls. Printer: TDLR. 156x67mm.		
	a. 4.6.1954; 26.11.1954; 5.4.1957; 6.3.1959; 8.5.1959.	90.00	600.
	b. 19.2.1960; 27.4.1962; 19.4.1963; 6.3.1964.	60.00	450.
	c. 7.1.1966; 3.3.1967; 8.3.1968; 5.4.1968; 10.1.1969; 11.4.1969; 13.1.1970; 2.4.1971; 18.2.1972.	60.00	400.

1961 Issue

		VF	UNC
54A	**1 Lempira** 1961; 1965. Red on multicolor underprint. Lempira at left, modified design of #45 with black serial #. Two signature varieties. Back: Dios del Maiz/Idolo Maya and Mayan artifacts. Printer: TDLR.		
	a. 10.2.1961.	4.00	25.00
	b. 30.7.1965.	4.00	25.00
	s. Specimen. Punched hole cancelled. 10.2.1961.	—	50.00

1968; 1970 Issue

		VF	UNC
55	**1 Lempira** 1968; 1972. Red-orange on green and pink underprint. Lempira at left, design different from #45 and 54A. Back: *Ruinas de Copan Juego de Pelota.* Printer: TDLR. 156x67mm.		
	a. Right signature title: *MINISTRO DE ECONOMIA*... 25.10.1968.	3.00	17.50
	b. Right signature title: *MINISTRO DE HACIENDA*... 21.1.1972.	1.00	12.50

56	5 Lempiras	VF	UNC
	1968-74. Black on multicolor underprint. Morazan at left, arms at right. Serial number at lower left and upper right. Back: Battle scene of Trinidad at center. Printer: ABNC. 156x67mm.		
	a. Date horizontal. 29.11.1968; 11.4.1969; 10.3.1970.	20.00	65.00
	b. Date vertical. 20.11.1970-24.8.1974.	10.00	60.00

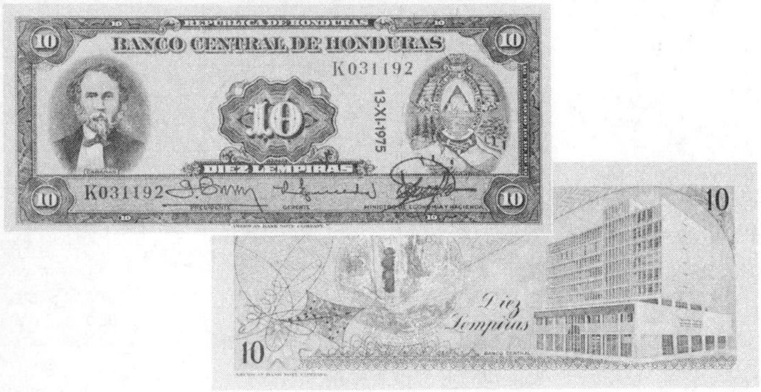

57	10 Lempiras	VF	UNC
	27.8.1970-13.11.1975. Brown on multicolor underprint. Cabañas at left, arms at right. Back: Ruins and new bank. Printer: ABNC. 156x67mm.	20.00	100.

1973; 1974 Issue

58	1 Lempira	VF	UNC
	11.3.1974. Red on green and lilac underprint. Lempira without feather at left, arms at right. Back: Different view of Ruinas de Copan. Printer: TDLR. 156x67mm.	2.00	10.00

59	5 Lempiras	VF	UNC
	1974-78. Black on multicolor underprint. Morazán at left, arms at right. Back: Battle of Trinidad at left. Printer: ABNC. 156x67mm.		
	a. Date vertical. 24.10.1974.	10.00	50.00
	b. Date horizontal. 12.12.1975; 26.2.1976; 16.9.1976; 9.12.1976; 13.1.1977; 3.6.1977; 25.11.1977; 13.2.1978.	5.00	30.00

60	20 Lempiras	VF	UNC
	1973-77. Green on multicolor underprint. D. de Herrera at left, arms at right. Back: Presidential residence. Printer: (T)DLR. Date placement varieties. 156x67mm.		
	a. 2.3.1973.	40.00	150.
	b. 13.8.1973.	40.00	150.
	c. 30.11.1973.	40.00	150.
	d. 1.3.1974.	40.00	150.
	e. 22.4.1974.	40.00	150.
	f. 5.6.1975.	40.00	150.
	g. 15.1.1976.	40.00	150.
	h. 18.3.1976.	40.00	150.
	i. 13.1.1977.	40.00	150.
	j. 3.6.1977.	40.00	150.

1976 Commemorative Issue

#61, Centennial of the Marco Aurelio Soto Government

61	2 Lempiras	VF	UNC
	23.9.1976. Purple on multicolor underprint. Arms at left, M. A. Soto at right. Back: Island and Port of Amapala. Printer: TDLR. 156x67mm.	1.50	9.00

1975-78 Regular Issue

62	1 Lempira	VF	UNC
	30.6.1978. Red. Lempira without feather at left, arms at right. Back: View of Ruinas de Copan. Indian symbols below bank name. Printer: TDLR. 156x67mm.	.75	7.00

63 5 Lempiras VF UNC

1978-94. Black, dark blue, and deep olive-green on multicolor underprint. Arms at left, Morazán at right. Back: Battle of Trinidad scene (Nov. 11, 1827). Printer: TDLR. UV: fibers fluoresce orange and blue, serial #s orange, central design elements and 5s yellow. 156x67mm.

		VF	UNC
a.	4.10.1978; 8.5.1980.	4.00	15.00
b.	8.12.1985; 30.3.1989.	1.50	12.50
c.	Red serial # at upper left in ascending size. 14.1.1993; 25.2.1993.	FV	7.50
d.	Brown serial # as c. 12.5.1994.	FV	5.00
s.	As d. Specimen. *MUESTRA SIN VALOR.*	—	—

64 10 Lempiras VF UNC

1976-89. Brown on multicolor underprint. Cabañas at left. Back: City University. Printer: ABNC. 156x67mm.

		VF	UNC
a.	18.3.1976-10.5.1979.	5.00	30.00
b.	23.6.1982-10.11.1989.	3.00	17.50

65 20 Lempiras

1978-93. Green on multicolor underprint. D. de Herrera at right. Back: Port of Puerto Cortes. Watermark: D. de Herrera. Printer: ABNC. Date placement varieties. 156x67mm.

		VF	UNC
a.	2.11.1978; 10.9.1979.	8.00	40.00
b.	Vertical date at right. 8.1.1981-10.2.1989.	4.00	25.00
c.	Horizontal date at upper left. 22.6.1989-2.10.1992.	3.50	15.00
d.	10.12.1992; 18.3.1993; 1.7.1993.	FV	10.00

66 50 Lempiras VF UNC

1976-93. Deep blue on multicolor underprint. J. M. Galvez D. at left. Back: National Agricultural Development Bank. Watermark: Tree. Printer: ABNC. 156x67mm.

		VF	UNC
a.	Vertical date at right. 29.1.1976; 13.1.1977; 3.6.1977; 13.2.1978; 10.9.1979.	15.00	55.00
b.	5.1.1984; 3.7.1986; 24.9.1987; 10.2.1989.	10.00	40.00
c.	Horizontal date at upper left. 1.3.1990; 13.12.1990; 29.8.1991.	7.00	30.00
d.	18.3.1993; 1.7.1993.	FV	25.00

67 100 Lempiras VF UNC

1975-79. Brown-orange on multicolor underprint. Valle at left. Back: Signatepeque school of forestry. Printer: TDLR. 156x67mm.

		VF	UNC
a.	16.1.1975.	25.00	150.
b.	29.1.1976.	25.00	150.
c.	18.3.1976.	25.00	150.
d.	13.1.1977.	25.00	150.
e.	12.1.1978.	25.00	150.
f.	10.9.1979.	25.00	150.

1980-81 Issue

68 1 Lempira VF UNC

1980; 1984; 1989. Red on multicolor underprint. Arms at left, Lempira at right. Back: Ruins of Copan. Printer: TDLR. UV: security strip fluoresces blue. 156x67mm.

		VF	UNC
a.	Without security thread. 29.5.1980.	.75	6.00
b.	As a. 18.10.1984.	.75	5.00
c.	With security thread. 30.3.1989.	FV	4.00

69 100 Lempiras VF UNC

1981-94. Brown-orange, dark olive-green, and deep purple on multicolor underprint. J. C. del Valle at right. Back: Forestry school. Watermark: J. C. del Valle. Printer: TDLR. 156x67mm.

		VF	UNC
a.	Regular serial #. 8.1.1981; 23.6.1982; 8.9.1983.	15.00	75.00
b.	5.1.1984-13.12.1989.	12.50	50.00
c.	21.12.1989-1.7.1993.	FV	40.00

1989 Issue

70 10 Lempiras VF UNC

21.9.1989. Dark brown and red on multicolor underprint (of vertical stripes). Arms at left, Cabañas at right. Back: City University. Printer: TDLR. UV: fibers and serial #s fluoresce orange, central design yellow. Back, elements orange. 156x67mm.

		VF	UNC
a.	Issued note.	2.50	12.50
s.	Specimen. *MUESTRA SIN VALOR.*	—	—

1992-93 Issue

		VF	UNC
71	**1 Lempira** 10.9.1992. Dark red on multicolor underprint. Arms at left, Lempira at right. Back: Paler colors. Ruins of Copan. Printer: CNBC. 156x67mm.	FV	2.50

		VF	UNC
72	**2 Lempiras** 1993-94. Purple on multicolor underprint. Arms at left, M. A. Soto at right. Ascending size serial number at upper left. Back: Island and Port of Amapala. Printer: TDLR. Like #61 but with light blue underprint at left. UV: fibers fluoresce orange and blue, serial #s orange. 156x67mm.		
	a. 14.1.1993. Red serial #.	FV	4.50
	b. 25.2.1993. As a.	FV	4.50
	c. 12.5.1994. Brown serial #.	FV	4.50
	s. Specimen. *MUESTRA SIN VALOR.*	—	—

		VF	UNC
73	**20 Lempiras** 1993-97. Deep green and dark brown on multicolor underprint. D. de Herrera at right. Back: Vertical; Presidential House at center. Watermark: D. de Herrera. Printer: TDLR. 156x67mm.		
	a. 14.1.1993. Red serial #.	FV	7.50
	b. 25.2.1993.	FV	7.50
	c. 12.5.1994. Brown Serial #.	FV	7.50
	d. 12.12.1996.	FV	7.50
	e. 18.9.1997.	FV	7.50
	s. Specimen. *MUESTRA SIN VALOR.* 12.5.1994.	—	—
73A	**20 Lempiras** 3.9.1998. Deep green and dark brown on multicolor underprint. D. de Herrera at right. Back: Vertical; Presidential House at center. Watermark: D. de Herrera. Printer: FC-O.	FV	7.50

		VF	UNC
74	**50 Lempiras** 1993-98. Blue-black and dark brown on multicolor underprint. J. M. Galvez D. at right. Back: Vertical; Central Bank Annex at center. Watermark: J. M. Galvez D. Printer: TDLR. 156x67mm.		
	a. 14.1.1993. Red serial #.	FV	17.50
	b. 25.2.1993.	FV	17.50
	c. 12.5.1994.	FV	17.50
	d. 12.12.1996.	FV	17.50
	e. 18.9.1997.	FV	17.50
	f. 3.9.1998.	FV	17.50
	s. Specimen. *MUESTRA SIN VALOR.* 12.5.1994.	—	—

		VF	UNC
75	**100 Lempiras** 1993-94. Brown-orange, dark olive-green and dark brown on multicolor underprint. J. C. del Valle at right. Red serial number at upper left in ascending size. Black signature. Back: Forestry school. Enhanced underprint in watermark area. Watermark: J. C. del Valle. Printer: (T)DLR. 156x67mm.		
	a. 14.1.1993.	FV	30.00
	b. 25.2.1993.	FV	30.00
	c. 12.5.1994.	FV	30.00
	s. Specimen. *MUESTRA SIN VALOR.* 12.5.1994.	—	—

1994; 1995 Issue

		VF	UNC
76	**1 Lempira** 12.5.1994. Red on multicolor underprint. Arms at left, Lempira at right. Brown ascending size serial number at upper left Printer: TDLR. UV: serial #s and 1 in box fluoresce yellow, fibers orange and green. 156x67mm.		
	a. Issued note.	FV	1.50
	s. Specimen. *MUESTRA SIN VALOR.*	—	—

77 100 Lempiras — VF | UNC

1994-2004. Brown-orange, black and olive-green on multicolor underprint. J. C. del Valle at center right, bridge over the Choluteca River at right. Brown serial number. Back: Valle's house at left. Watermark: J. C. del Valle. Printer: TDLR (without imprint). 156x67mm.

	VF	UNC
a. Signature titles: *MINISTRO DE HACIENDA Y CREDITO PUBLICO*. 12.5.1994.	FV	25.00
b. Signature titles: *SECRETARIO DE FINANZAS*. 18.9.1997.	FV	20.00
c. 3.9.1998.	FV	20.00
d. 14.12.2000.	FV	20.00
e. 30.8.2001.	FV	15.00
f. 23.1.2003.	FV	15.00
g. 26.8.2004	FV	15.00
h. 17.4.2008.	FV	12.50

78 500 Lempiras — VF | UNC

1995-2010. Violet and purple on multicolor underprint. Dr. R. Rosa at right, National Gallery of Art in background. Back: View of Rosario de San Juancito at left center. Watermark: Dr. R. Rosa. 156x67mm.

	VF	UNC
a. Signature titles: *MINISTRO DE HACIENDA Y CREDITO PUBLICO*. 16.11.1995.	FV	95.00
b. Signature titles: *SECRETARIO DE FINANZAS*. 3.9.1998.	FV	90.00
c. 14.12.2000.	FV	90.00
d. 30.8.2001	FV	90.00
e. 23.1.2003.	FV	90.00
f. 26.8.2004.	FV	90.00
g. 6.5.2010.	FV	90.00

1996-98 Issue

79 1 Lempira — VF | UNC

1996; 1998. Dark red on multicolor underprint. Arms at left, Lempira at right, brown serial number with ascending size serial number at upper left. Back: Ruins of Copan. Printer: F-CO. UV: fibers fluoresce blue and yellow, 1 in box yellow. 156x67mm.

	VF	UNC
a. 12.12.1996.	FV	1.00
b. 3.9.1998.	FV	1.00

79A 1 Lempira

18.9.1997. Dark red on multicolor underprint. Arms at left, Limpira at right, brown serial number with ascending size serial number at upper left. Back: Ruins of Copan. Printer: TDLR (without imprint). — FV | 1.00

80 2 Lempiras — VF | UNC

18.9.1997. Purple on multicolor underprint. Arms at left, M. A. Soto at right, brown serial number with ascending size serial number at upper left. Back: Port of Amapala. Printer: TDLR. 156x67mm. — FV | 1.50

80A 2 Lempiras — VF | UNC

1998-2008. Purple on multicolor underprint. Arms at left, M. A. Soto at right, brown serial number with ascending size serial number at upper left. Back: Port of Amapala. Printer: F-CO.

	VF	UNC
a. 3.9.1998.	FV	1.50
b. 14.12.2000.	FV	1.50
c. 30.8.2001.	FV	1.50
d. 23.1.2003.	FV	1.50
e. 26.8.2004.	FV	1.50
e. 13.7.2006.	FV	1.50
f. 17.4.2008.	FV	1.50

81 5 Lempiras — VF | UNC

1996-98. Black, dark blue and deep olive-green on multicolor underprint. Arms at left, Morazán at right, brown serial number with ascending size serial number at upper left. Back: Battle of Trinidad scene (Nov. 11. 1827). Printer: TDLR. 156x67mm.

	VF	UNC
a. 12.12.1996.	FV	2.00
b. 18.9.1997.	FV	2.00
c. 3.9.1998.	FV	2.00

82 10 Lempiras — VF | UNC

1996-2000. Dark brown and red on multicolor underprint. Arms at left, Cabañas at right. Back: City University. Printer: TDLR. 156x67mm.

	VF	UNC
a. 12.12.1996.	FV	3.50
b. 18.9.1997.	FV	3.50
c. 3.9.1998.	FV	3.50
d. 14.12.2000.	FV	3.50

2000 Commemorative Issue

#83, 50th Anniversary of the Central Bank and Year 2000

83 20 Lempiras — VF | UNC

30.3.2000. Dark green and brown on multicolor underprint. D. Herrera and Government House at right. Back: Work, effort and unity sculpture. 156x67mm. — FV | 5.00

2000-03 Issue

		VF	UNC
84	**1 Lempira** 2000-06. Dark red on multicolor underprint. Arms at left, Lempira at right. Back: Ruins of Copán. Printer: CBNC. 156x67mm.		
	a. 14.12.2000.	FV	1.00
	b. 30.8.2001.	FV	1.00
	c. 23.1.2003.	FV	1.00
	d. 26.8.2004.	FV	1.00
	e. 13.7.2006.	FV	1.00

		VF	UNC
85	**5 Lempiras** 2000-04. Multicolor. Arms at left, Morazán at right. Back: Battle of Trinidad scene (Nov. 11. 1827). Printer: CBNC. 156x67mm.		
	a. 14.12.2000.	FV	1.75
	b. 30.8.2001.	FV	1.75
	c. 23.1.2003.	FV	1.75
	d. 26.8.2004.	FV	1.75

		VF	UNC
86	**10 Lempiras** 2001-10. Multicolor. Arms at left, Cabañas at right. Back: City University. Printer: FC-O. 156x67mm.		
	a. 30.8.2001.	FV	2.75
	b. 23.1.2003.	FV	2.75
	c. 26.8.2004.	FV	2.75
	d. 13.7.2006.	FV	2.75
	e. 6.5.2010.	FV	2.75
87	**20 Lempiras** 2001; 2003. Green and violet on multicolor underprint. Printer: G&D. 156x67mm.		
	a. 30.8.2001.	FV	4.50
	b. 23.1.2003.	FV	4.50

		VF	UNC
88	**50 Lempiras** 2001; 2003; 2006. Multicolor. J. M. Galvez D. at right, vertical serial number at left. Back: Central Bank Annex at center. Printer: TDLR. 156x67mm.		
	a. 30.8.2001.	FV	9.50
	b. 23.1.2003.	FV	9.50
	c. 13.7.2006.	FV	9.50

2004-06 Issue

		VF	UNC
89	**1 Lempira** 17.4.2008; 6.5.2010. Dark red on multicolor underprint. Arms at left, Lempira at right. Back: Ruins of Copán. Printer: FC-O. 156x67mm.		
	a. 17.4.2008.	FV	1.00
	b. 6.5.2010.	FV	1.00

		VF	UNC
90	**2 Lempiras** 17.4.2008. Purple on multicolor underprint. Marco Aurello Soto at right. 156x67mm.	FV	1.50

91 5 Lempiras VF UNC

2006; 2008; 2010. Printer: FC-O. 156x67mm.

	VF	UNC
a. 13.7.2006.	FV	1.75
b. 17.4.2008.	FV	1.75
c. 6.5.2010.	FV	1.75

92 20 Lempiras VF UNC

26.8.2004. Green and tan on multicolor underprint. Bust at right, arms at left. Back: Presidential palace at center. Printer: G&D. Similar to #87 but redesigned. 156x67mm. FV 4.50

93 20 Lempiras VF UNC

2006; 2008. Green on multicolor underprint. Bust at right, arms at left Back: Presidential manision. Printer: (T)DLR. 156x67mm.

	VF	UNC
a. 13.7.2006.	FV	4.50
b. 31.7.2008.	FV	4.50

94 50 Lempiras VF UNC

2004; 2008; 2010. Blue on multicolor underprint. Juan Manuel Galvez D. at right with building. Back: Central Bank building at left. Printer: G&D. 156x67mm.

	VF	UNC
a. 26.8.2004.	FV	9.50
b. 17.4.2008.	FV	7.50
c. 6.5.2010.	FV	6.00

94A 50 Lempiras VF UNC

2006; 2008. Blue on multicolor underprint. Printer: TDLR. 156x67mm.

	VF	UNC
a. 13.7.2006.	FV	9.50
b. 17.4.2008.	FV	9.50

2008 Polymer Issue

95 20 Lempiras VF UNC

31.7.2008. Green on multicolor underprint Dionisio de Herrera at right. Signature varieties. Back: Presidential mansion. Polymer plastic. 156x67mm. FV 4.50

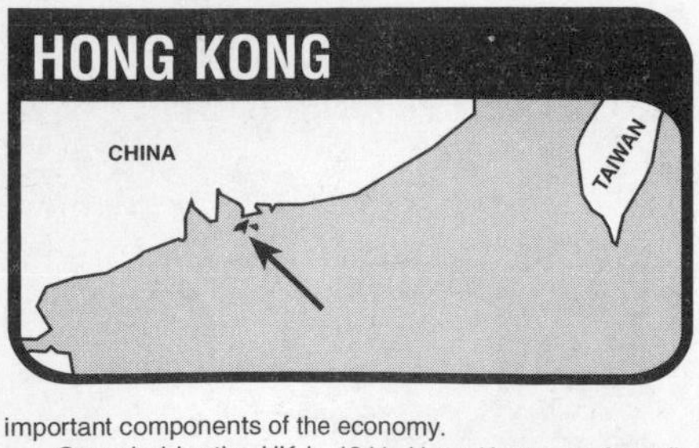

Hong Kong S.A.R., a former British Colony, is situated at the mouth of the Canton or Pearl River 90 miles (145 km.) southeast of Canton, has an area of 1,092 sq. km. and a population of 7.01 million. Capital: Central (formerly Victoria). The port of Hong Kong had developed as the commercial center of the Far East, a transshipment point for goods destined for China and the countries of the Pacific rim. Light manufacturing and tourism are important components of the economy.

Occupied by the UK in 1841, Hong Kong was formally ceded by China the following year; various adjacent lands were added later in the 19th century. Pursuant to an agreement signed by China and the UK on 19 December 1984, Hong Kong became the Hong Kong Special Administrative Region (SAR) of China on 1 July 1997. In this agreement, China promised that, under its "one country, two systems" formula, China's socialist economic system would not be imposed on Hong Kong and that Hong Kong would enjoy a high degree of autonomy in all matters except foreign and defense affairs for the next 50 years.

RULERS:

British (1842-1997)

MONETARY SYSTEM:

1 Dollar = 100 Cents

British Administration

Chartered Bank

行銀打渣[1]

Cha Ta Yin Hang

1961; 1967 ND Issues

		VF	UNC
68	**5 Dollars** 1961-62; ND. Black and green on multicolor underprint. Arms at lower left. Back: Chinese junk and sampan at center. Watermark: Helmeted warrior's head. Printer: TDLR.		
	a. 1.7.1961.	80.00	250.
	b. 3.3.1962.	125.	400.
	c. ND (1962-70).	40.00	120.
	s. Specimen. As a.	—	—

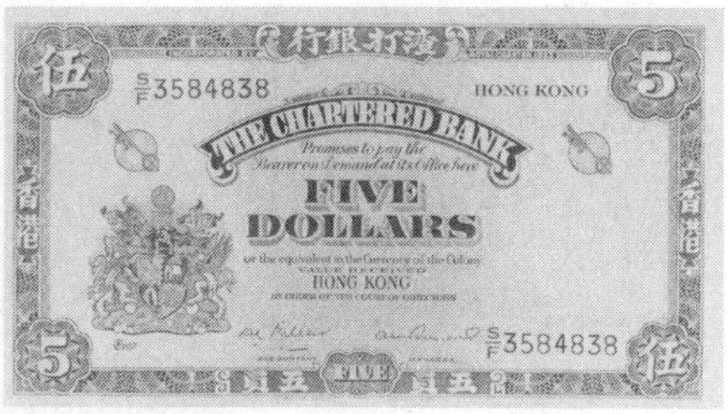

		VF	UNC
69	**5 Dollars** ND (1967). Black and yellow-brown on multicolor underprint. Arms at lower left. Back: Chinese junk and sampan at center. Watermark: Helmeted warrior's head. Printer: TDLR.	30.00	120.

		VF	UNC
70	**10 Dollars** 1961-62; ND. Black and red-violet on red underprint. Arms at left. Back: Chartered Bank building at center. Watermark: Helmeted warrior's head. Printer: TDLR.		
	a. 1.7.1961.	125.	400.
	b. 3.3.1962.	60.00	250.
	c. ND (1962-70).	25.00	80.00
	s. Specimen. As a, c.	—	—

		VF	UNC
71	**100 Dollars** 1961; ND. Dark green and brown on multicolor underprint. Arms at center. Back: Harbor view. Watermark: Helmeted warrior's head. Printer: TDLR.		
	a. 1.7.1961.	750.	1400.
	b. ND (1961-70).	425.	750.

		VF	UNC
72	**500 Dollars** 1961-77. Black and dark brown on multicolor underprint. Male portrait at left. Back: Ship, harbor view at center. Watermark: Helmeted warrior's head. Printer: TDLR.		
	a. Signature titles: *ACCOUNTANT* and *MANAGER*. 1.7.1961.	1500.	2250.
	b. Signature titles as a. ND (1962-?).	650.	1500.
	c. Signature titles: *ACCOUNTANT* and *CHIEF MANAGER IN HONG KONG*. ND (?-1975).	600.	1300.
	d. Signature titles as c. 1.1.1977.	350.	1000.
	s. Specimen. As a, d.	—	600.

1970 ND; 1975-77 Issue

		VF	UNC
73	**5 Dollars** ND (1970-75); 1975. Dark brown on multicolor underprint. Bank building at left, bank crest at center. Back: City Hall at center right. Watermark: Helmeted warrior's head. Printer: TDLR.		
	a. Signature titles: *ACCOUNTANT* and *MANAGER*. ND (1970-75).	4.00	15.00
	b. Signature titles: *ACCOUNTANT* and *CHIEF MANAGER IN HONG KONG* at right. ND; 1.6.1975.	15.00	45.00
	s. Specimen. As b.	—	—

74 **10 Dollars** VF UNC

ND; 1975; 1977. Dark green on multicolor underprint. Bank building at left, bank crest at center. Back: Ocean terminal at center. Watermark: Helmeted warrior's head. Printer: TDLR.

	VF	UNC
a. Signature titles: *ACCOUNTANT* and *MANAGER*. ND (1970-75).	10.00	45.00
b. Signature titles: *ACCOUNTANT* and *CHIEF MANAGER IN HONG KONG*. ND; 1.6.1975.	20.00	60.00
c. Signature titles as b. 1.1.1977.	6.00	26.00
s. Specimen. As b.	—	350.

75 **50 Dollars** VF UNC

ND (1970-75). Blue on multicolor underprint. Bank building at left, bank crest at center. Back: City Hall at center right. Watermark: Helmeted warrior's head. Printer: TDLR.

	VF	UNC
a. Issued note.	200.	550.
s. Specimen.	—	500.

76 **100 Dollars** VF UNC

ND; 1977. Red on multicolor underprint. Bank building at left, bank crest at center. Watermark: Helmeted warrior's head. Printer: TDLR.

	VF	UNC
a. ND (1970-75).	125.	350.
b. 1.1.1977.	60.00	215.
s. Specimen. As a.	—	350.

1979; 1980 Issue

77 **10 Dollars** VF UNC

1980-81. Green on multicolor underprint. Stylistic carp at right. Back: Bank building at left, arms at center. Watermark: Helmeted warrior's head. Printer: TDLR (without imprint).

	VF	UNC
a. 1.1.1980.	4.00	12.00
b. 1.1.1981.	4.00	12.00

78 **50 Dollars** VF UNC

1979-82 Blue on multicolor underprint. Chinze at right. Back: Bank building at left, arms at center. Watermark: Helmeted warrior's head. Printer: TDLR (without imprint).

	VF	UNC
a. 1.1.1979.	25.00	90.00
b. 1.1.1981.	FV	60.00
c. 1.1.1982.	FV	60.00
s. Specimen.	—	300.

79 **100 Dollars** VF UNC

1979-82. Red on multicolor underprint. Mythical horse *Qilin* at right. Back: Bank building at left, arms at center. Watermark: Helmeted warrior's head. Printer: TDLR (without imprint).

	VF	UNC
a. 1.1.1979.	40.00	160.
b. 1.1.1980.	35.00	90.00
c. 1.1.1982.	30.00	75.00
s. Specimen.	—	175.

80 **500 Dollars** VF UNC

1979; 1982. Brown on multicolor underprint. Mythical phoenix at right. Back: Bank building at left, arms at center. Watermark: Helmeted warrior's head. Printer: TDLR (without imprint).

	VF	UNC
a. 1.1.1979.	FV	450.
b. 1.1.1982.	FV	400.
s. Specimen.	—	500.

81 1000 Dollars

1979; 1982. Yellow-orange on multicolor underprint. Dragon at right. Back: Bank building at left, arms at center. Watermark: Helmeted warrior's head. Printer: TDLR (without imprint).

	VF	UNC
a. 1.1.1979.	250.	800.
b. 1.1.1982.	160.	600.
s. Specimen.	—	500.

Hong Kong & Shanghai Banking Corporation

行銀理滙海上港香

Hsiang K'ang Shang Hai Hui Li Yin Hang

Hong Kong

1932-35 Issue

179 500 Dollars

1935-69. Brown and blue. Arms at top center, Sir T. Jackson at right. Back: Blue. Allegorical female head at left, bank building at center. Printer: BWC. 201x123mm.

	VF	UNC
a. Handsigned. 1.6.1935-1.7.1937.	2250.	5250.
b. Printed signature. 1.4.1941-1.8.1952.	700.	1800.
c. 11.7.1960-1.8.1966.	700.	1800.
d. 31.7.1967.	300.	600.
e. 11.2.1968.	180.	600.
f. 27.3.1969.	180.	700.

1959 Issue

181 5 Dollars

1959-75. Brown on multicolor underprint. Woman seated at right. Back: New bank building at center. Watermark: Helmeted warrior's head. Printer: BWC. 142x79mm.

	VF	UNC
a. Signature titles: *CHIEF ACCOUNTANT* and *CHIEF MANAGER.* 2.5.1959-29.6.1960.	15.00	45.00
b. 1.5.1963.	175.	750.
c. 1.5.1964-27.3.1969.	5.00	25.00
d. Signature titles: *CHIEF ACCOUNTANT* and *GENERAL MANAGER.* 1.4.1970-18.3.1971.	5.00	18.00
e. 13.3.1972; 31.10.1972.	2.00	13.00
f. Small serial #. 31.10.1973; 31.3.1975.	1.25	11.00
s. Specimen.	—	—

182 10 Dollars

1959-83. Dark green on multicolor underprint. Dark green on multicolor underprint. Back: New bank building at left center. Watermark: Helmeted warrior's head. Printer: BWC. 152x85mm.

	VF	UNC
a. Signature titles: *CHIEF ACCOUNTANT* and *CHIEF MANAGER.* 21.5.1959-1.9.1962.	15.00	45.00
b. 1.5.1963; 1.9.1963.	20.00	60.00
c. 1.5.1964; 1.9.1964.	15.00	55.00
d. 1.10.1964.	200.	800.
e. 1.2.1965; 1.8.1966; 31.7.1967.	6.00	25.00
f. 20.3.1968; 23.11.1968; 27.3.1969.	6.00	25.00
g. Signature titles: *CHIEF ACCOUNTANT* and *GENERAL MANAGER.* 1.4.1970-31.3.1976.	3.75	15.00
h. Signature titles: *CHIEF ACCOUNTANT* and *EXECUTIVE DIRECTOR.* 31.3.1977; 31.3.1978; 31.3.1979.	3.00	15.00
i. Signature titles: *CHIEF ACCOUNTANT* and *GENERAL MANAGER.* 31.3.1980; 31.3.1981.	3.00	12.50
j. Signature titles: *MANAGER* and *GENERAL MANAGER.* 31.3.1982; 31.3.1983.	3.00	12.50
s. Specimen.	—	—

183	100 Dollars	VF	UNC
	1959-72. Red on multicolor underprint. Woman seated at left with open book, arms at upper center. Watermark: Helmeted warrior's head and denomination. Printer: BWC. 160x89mm.		
	a. Signature titles: *CHIEF ACCOUNTANT* and *CHIEF MANAGER.* 12.8.1959-1.10.1964.	100.	350.
	b. 1.2.1965-27.3.1969.	50.00	250.
	c. Signature titles: *CHIEF ACCOUNTANT* and *GENERAL MANAGER.* 1.4.1970; 18.3.1971; 13.3.1972.	40.00	175.

1968-73 Issue

184	50 Dollars	VF	UNC
	1968-83. Dark blue on light blue and multicolor underprint. Arms at right. Back: New bank building at left center. Watermark: Helmeted warrior's head and denomination. Printer: BWC.		
	a. Signature titles: *CHIEF ACCOUNTANT* and *CHIEF MANAGER.* 31.5.1968; 27.3.1969.	45.00	120.
	b. Signature titles: *CHIEF ACCOUNTANT* and *GENERAL MANAGER.* 31.10.1973; 31.3.1975; 31.3.1978.	35.00	90.00
	c. Signature titles as b. 31.3.1977.	35.00	90.00
	d. Signature titles: *CHIEF ACCOUNTANT* and *EXECUTIVE DIRECTOR.* 31.3.1977.	35.00	90.00
	e. 31.3.1979.	175.	450.
	f. Signature titles: *CHIEF ACCOUNTANT* and *GENERAL MANAGER.* 31.3.1980.	12.50	65.00
	g. 31.3.1981.	15.00	65.00
	h. Signature titles: *MANAGER* and *GENERAL MANAGER.* 31.3.1982; 31.3.1983.	12.50	50.00
	s. Specimen.	—	—

185	100 Dollars	VF	UNC
	1972-76. Red on multicolor underprint. Arms at left. Back: Facing lions at lower left and right, bank building at center, dragon in medallion at right. Printer: BWC.		
	a. With 4 Large serial # on back. 13.3.1972; 31.10.1972.	50.00	125.
	b. Smaller electronic sorting serial # on face. without serial # on back. 31.10.1972.	60.00	185.
	c. 31.10.1973.	35.00	125.
	d. 31.3.1975; 31.3.1976.	35.00	100.

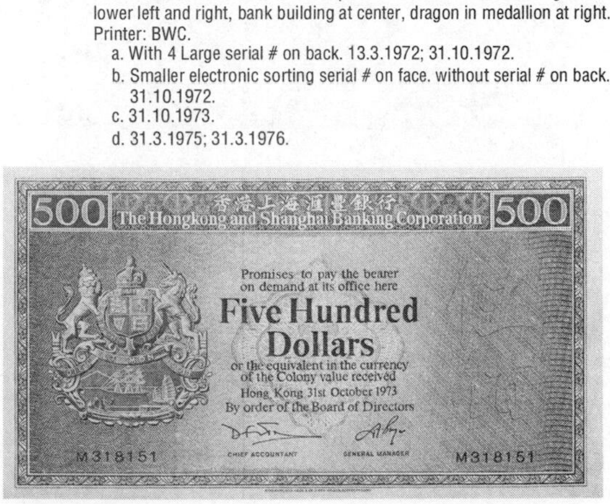

186	500 Dollars	VF	UNC
	1973-76. Brown on multicolor underprint. Arms at left. Back: Bank building at left, lion's head at right. Printer: BWC.		
	a. 31.10.1973.	225.	600.
	b. 31.3.1975.	300.	700.
	c. 31.3.1976.	250.	550.

1977; 1978 Issue

187	100 Dollars	VF	UNC
	1977-83. Red on lighter multicolor underprint. Arms at left. Back: Facing lions at lower left and right, bank building at center, dragon in medallion at right. Watermark: Lion's head. Printer: BWC.		
	a. Signature titles: *CHIEF ACCOUNTANT* and *EXECUTIVE DIRECTOR.* 31.3.1977; 31.3.1978.	25.00	75.00
	b. Signature titles as a. 31.3.1979.	25.00	125.
	c. 31.3.1980; 31.3.1981.	FV	60.00
	d. Signature titles: *MANAGER* and *GENERAL MANAGER.* 31.3.1982; 31.3.1983.	FV	45.00

189	500 Dollars	VF	UNC
	1978-83. Brown and black on multicolor underprint. Arms at left. Back: Bank building at left, lion's head at right. Watermark: Lion's head. Printer: BWC. Modified frame designs.		
	a. 31.3.1978.	FV	300.
	b. 31.3.1980.	FV	300.
	c. 31.3.1981.	FV	300.
	d. 31.3.1983.	FV	250.

190	1000 Dollars	VF	UNC
	1977-83. Gold and black on multicolor underprint. Arms at right. Back: Lion at left, bank building at center right. Watermark: Lion's head. Printer: BWC.		
	a. 31.3.1977.	FV	725.
	b. 31.3.1979.	FV	600.
	c. 31.3.1980.	FV	550.
	d. 31.3.1981.	FV	500.
	e. 31.3.1983.	FV	450.

1985-87 Issue

#191-196 Replacement notes: Serial # prefix *ZZ*.

191	10 Dollars	VF	UNC
	1985-92. Deep green on multicolor underprint. Arms at left. Back: Sampan and ship at right. Facing lions at lower left and right with new bank building at center. Watermark: Lion's head. Printer: TDLR. 138x69mm.		
	a. Signature title: *GENERAL MANAGER.* 1.1.1985; 1.1.1986; 1.1.1987.	1.50	7.50
	b. Signature title: *EXECUTIVE DIRECTOR.* 1.1.1988.	.75	6.00
	c. Signature title: *GENERAL MANAGER.* 1.1.1989; 1.1.1990; 1.1.1991; 1.1.1992.	.50	5.00
	s. Specimen. As a.	—	250.

192	20 Dollars	VF	UNC
	1986-89. Deep gray-green and brown on purple and multicolor underprint. Arms at left. Back: Clock tower, ferry in harbor view at right. Facing lions at lower left and right with new bank building at center. Watermark: Lion's head. Printer: TDLR. 131x95mm.		
	a. Signature title: *GENERAL MANAGER.* 1.1.1986; 1.1.1987.	2.50	12.50
	b. Signature title: *EXECUTIVE DIRECTOR.* 1.1.1988.	1.50	10.00
	c. Signature title: *GENERAL MANAGER.* 1.1.1989.	FV	7.50
	s. Specimen. As a.	—	300.

193	50 Dollars	VF	UNC
	1985-92. Purple on multicolor underprint. Arms at left. Back: Men in boats at right. Facing lions at lower left and right with new bank building at center. Watermark: Lion's head. Printer: TDLR. 148x74mm.		
	a. Signature title: *GENERAL MANAGER.* 1.1.1985; 1.1.1986; 1.1.1987.	FV	25.00
	b. Signature title: *EXECUTIVE DIRECTOR.* 1.1.1988.	FV	20.00
	c. Signature title: *GENERAL MANAGER.* 1.1.1989; 1.1.1990; 1.1.1991; 1.1.1992.	FV	15.00
	s. Specimen.	—	400.

194	100 Dollars	VF	UNC
	1985-88. Red on multicolor underprint. Arms at left. Back: Tiger Balm Garden pagoda at right. Facing lions at lower left and right with new bank building at center. Watermark: Lion's head. Printer: TDLR. 154x77mm.		
	a. Signature title: *GENERAL MANAGER.* 1.1.1985; 1.1.1986; 1.1.1987.	FV	30.00
	b. Signature title: *EXECUTIVE DIRECTOR.* 1.1.1988.	FV	25.00
	s. Specimen.	—	450.

195	500 Dollars	VF	UNC
	1987-92. Brown on multicolor underprint. Arms at left. Back: Old tower at right. Facing lions at lower left and right with new bank building at center. Watermark: Lion's head. Printer: TDLR. 158x79mm.		
	a. Signature title: *GENERAL MANAGER.* 1.1.1987.	FV	120.
	b. Signature title: *EXECUTIVE DIRECTOR.* 1.1.1988.	FV	110.
	c. Signature title: *GENERAL MANAGER.* 1.1.1989; 1.1.1990; 1.1.1991; 1.1.1992.	FV	110.

196	1000 Dollars		
	1985-87. Red, brown and orange on multicolor underprint. Arms at left. Back: Old Supreme Court building at right. Facing lions at lower left and right with new bank building at center. Watermark: Lion's head. Printer: TDLR. 164x82mm.		
	a. 1.1.1985.	FV	800.
	b. 1.1.1986.	FV	450.
	c. 1.1.1987.	FV	450.

1988-90 Issue

#197-199 Replacement notes: Serial # prefix *ZZ*.

197 20 Dollars — VF | UNC

1990-92. Gray and black on orange, pink and multicolor underprint. Arms at left. Signature title: *GENERAL MANAGER.* Back: Clock tower, ferry in harbor view at right. Facing lions at lower left and right with new bank building at center. Watermark: Lion's head. Printer: TDLR. 144x72mm.

	VF	UNC
a. 1.1.1990.	FV	6.00
b. 1.1.1991.	FV	6.00
c. 1.1.1992.	FV	6.00

198 100 Dollars — VF | UNC

1989-92. Red on multicolor underprint. Arms at left. Signature title: *GENERAL MANAGER.* Back: Red and black on multicolor underprint. Tiger Balm Garden pagoda at right. Facing lions at lower left and right with new bank building at center. Watermark: Lion's head. Printer: TDLR. 154x77mm.

	VF	UNC
a. 1.1.1989.	FV	25.00
b. 1.1.1990.	FV	25.00
c. 1.1.1991.	FV	25.00
d. 1.1.1992.	FV	25.00

199 1000 Dollars — VF | UNC

1988-91. Red, brown and orange on multicolor underprint. Arms at left. Back: Orange, brown and loive-brown on multicolor underprint. Old Supreme Court building at right. Facing lions at lower left and right with new bank building at center. Printer: TDLR. 164x82mm.

	VF	UNC
a. Signature title: *EXECUTIVE DIRECTOR.* 1.1.1988.	FV	325.
b. Sign title: *GENERAL MANAGER.* 1.1.1989.	FV	750.
c. 1.1.1990.	FV	300.
d. 1.1.1991.	FV	300.

Hong Kong & Shanghai Banking Corporation Limited

1993; 1995 Issue

#201-205 Replacement notes: Serial # prefix *ZZ*.

#200 not assigned.

201 20 Dollars — VF | UNC

1993-99. Gray on brown on multicolor underprint. Lion's head at left, city view in underprint at center. Back: Latent image of value in box at lower right, new bank building at center between facing lions. Watermark: Lion's head. Printer: TDLR. 144x72mm.

	VF	UNC
a. Signature title: *EXECUTIVE DIRECTOR.* 1.1.1993; 1.1.1994.	FV	10.00
b. Signature titles as a. Copyright clause on both sides. 1.1.1995; 1.1.1996.	FV	7.50
c. Signature title: *GENERAL MANAGER.* 1.1.1997; 1.7.1997.	FV	6.00
d. Signature title as c. 1.1.1998; 1.1.1999; 1.1.2000; 1.1.2001; 1.1.2002.	FV	6.00

202 50 Dollars — VF | UNC

1993-99. Purple, violet and black on multicolor underprint. Lion's head at left, city view in underprint at center. Back: New bank building at center between facing lions, latent image of value in box at lower right. Watermark: Lion's head. Printer: TDLR. 148x74mm.

	VF	UNC
a. Signature title: *EXECUTIVE DIRECTOR.* 1.1.1993; 1.1.1994.	FV	19.00
b. Signature title as a. Copyright clause on both sides. 1.1.1995; 1.1.1996.	FV	15.00
c. Signature title: *GENERAL MANAGER.* 1.1.1997; 1.7.1997.	FV	12.00
d. Signature title as a. 1.1.1998; 1.1.2000; 1.1.2001.	FV	12.00
e. Signature title as c. 1.1.2002.	FV	12.00

203 100 Dollars — VF | UNC

1993-99. Red, orange and black on multicolor underprint. Lion's head at left, city view in underprint at center. Back: New bank building at center between facing lions, latent image of value in box at lower right. Ten t Watermark: Lion's head. Printer: TDLR. 154x77mm.

	VF	UNC
a. Signature title: *EXECUTIVE DIRECTOR.* 1.1.1993; 1.1.1994; 1.1.1996.	FV	30.00
b. Signature title: *GENERAL MANAGER.* 1.1.1997; 1.7.1997; 1.1.1998.	FV	30.00
c. Signature title as a. 1.1.1999; 1.1.2000.	FV	25.00
d. Signature title as b. 1.1.2001; 1.1.2002.	FV	25.00

204 500 Dollars

1993-99. Brown and red-orange on multicolor underprint. Lion's head at left, city view in underprint at center. Back: New bank building at center between facing lions, latent image of value in box at lower right. Gover Watermark: Lion's head. Printer: TDLR. 158x79mm.

	VF	UNC
a. Signature title: *EXECUTIVE DIRECTOR*. 1.1.1993; 1.1.1994.	FV	155.
b. Signature title as a. Copyright clause on both sides. 1.1.1995; 1.1.1996.	FV	150.
c. Signature title: *GENERAL MANAGER*. 1.1.1997; 1.7.1997.	FV	140.
d. Signature title as a. 1.1.1999.	FV	140.
e. Signature title as c. 1.1.2002.	FV	140.

205 1000 Dollars

1993-99. Orange, red-brown and loive-green on pink and multicolor underprint. Lion's head at left, city view in underprint at center. Back: New bank building at center between facing lions, latent image of value in box at lower right. Legis Watermark: Lion's head. Printer: TDLR. 164x82mm.

	VF	UNC
a. Signature title: *EXECUTIVE DIRECTOR*. 1.1.1993; 1.1.1994.	FV	250.
b. Signature title: *GENERAL MANAGER*. 1.1.1997; 1.7.1997.	FV	220.
c. Signature titles as a. 1.1.1998; 1.1.1999.	FV	220.

2000 Issue

206 1000 Dollars

2000; 2002. Orange, red-brown and olive-green on pink and multicolor underprint. Signature title: *GENERAL MANAGER*. Wide security thread added. 164x82mm.

	VF	UNC
a. 1.9.2000.	FV	215.
b. 1.1.2002.	FV	215.

2003 Issue

207 20 Dollars

2003-09. Dark blue on light blue and multicolor underprint. Back: The Peak Tram. 144x72mm.

	VF	UNC
a. 1.7.2003. Signature title: *GENERAL MANAGER*.	FV	6.00
b. 1.1.2005. As a.	FV	6.00
c. 1.1.2006. As a.	FV	6.00
d. 1.1.2007. Signature title: *EXECUTIVE DIRECTOR*.	FV	6.00
e. 1.1.2008.	FV	5.00
f. 1.1.2009. As d.	FV	5.00

208 50 Dollars

2003-09. Green on multicolor underprint. Back: Po Lin Temple. 148x74mm.

	VF	UNC
a. 1.7.2003. Signature title: *GENERAL MANAGER*.	FV	15.00
b. 1.1.2005. As a.	FV	15.00
c. 1.1.2006. As a.	FV	15.00
d. 1.1.2007. Signature title: *EXECUTIVE DIRECTOR*.	FV	15.00
e. 1.1.2008.	FV	12.50
f. 1.1.2009.	FV	12.50

209 100 Dollars

2003-08. Red on multicolor underprint. Back: Tsing-Ma Bridge. 154x77mm.

	VF	UNC
a. 1.7.2003. Signature title: *GENERAL MANAGER*.	FV	25.00
b. 1.1.2005. As. a.	FV	25.00
c. 1.1.2006. As a.	FV	25.00
d. 1.1.2007. Signature title: *EXECUTIVE DIRECTOR*.	FV	22.50
e. 1.1.2008. As d.	FV	20.00

		VF	UNC
210	**500 Dollars**		
	2003-09. Brown on multicolor underprint. Back: Hong Kong Airport. 158x79mm.		
	a. 1.7.2003. Signature title: *GENERAL MANAGER.*	FV	125.
	b. 1.1.2005. As a.	FV	125.
	c. 1.1.2006. As a.	FV	100.
	d. 1.1.2007. Signature title: *EXECUTIVE DIRECTOR.*	FV	95.00
	e. 1.1.2009.	FV	85.00

		VF	UNC
211	**1000 Dollars**		
	2003; 2005. Orange, red-brown and olive-green on multicolor underprint. Back: Hong Kong Convention and Exhibition Center. 164x82mm.		
	a. 1.7.2003. Signature title: *GENERAL MANAGER.*	FV	215.
	b. 1.1.2005.	FV	215.
	c. 1.1.2006. Signature title: *EXECUTIVE DIRECTOR.*	FV	200.
	d. 1.1.2007.	FV	190.
	e. 1.1.2008.	FV	180.
	f. 1.1.2009.	FV	150.

2010 Issue

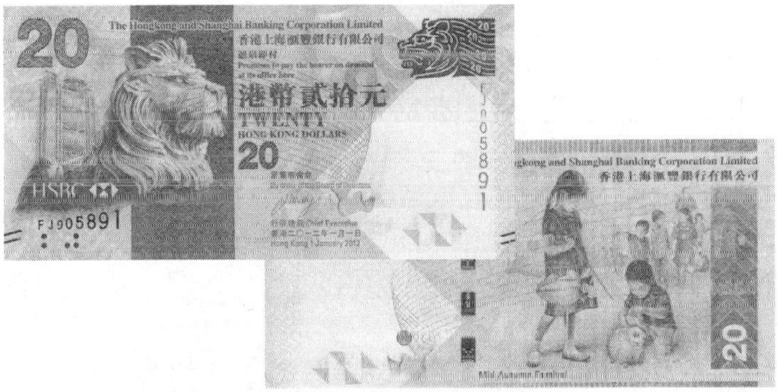

		VF	UNC
212	**20 Dollars**		
	2010-. Dark blue and blue on multicolor underprint. Lion and Bank headquarters at right. Back: Mid-Autumn festival at right. 144x72mm.		
	a. 1.1.2010.	FV	6.00
	b. 1.1.2012.	FV	6.00

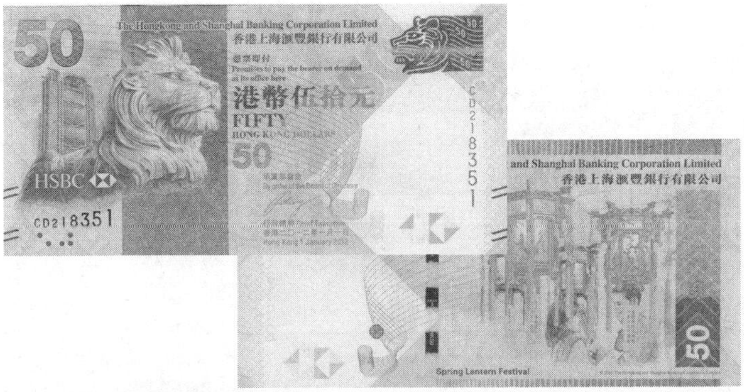

		VF	UNC
213	**50 Dollars**		
	2010-. Green on multicolor underprint. Lion and Bank headquarters at right. Back: Spring Lantern Festival. 148x74mm.		
	a. 1.1.2010.	FV	15.00
	b. 1.1.2012.	FV	15.00
214	**100 Dollars**		
	1.1.2010. Red on multicolor underprint. Lion and Bank headquarters at right. 154x77mm.	FV	25.00
215	**500 Dollars**		
	1.1.2010. Brown on multicolor underprint. Lion and Bank headquarters at right. 158x79mm.	FV	125.

		VF	UNC
216	**1000 Dollars**		
	1.1.2010. Orange on multicolor underprint. Lion and Bank headquarters at right. 164x82mm.	FV	215.

Mercantile Bank Limited

行銀利有 港香

Hsiang K'ang Yu Li Yin Hang

1964 Issue

		VF	UNC
244	**100 Dollars**		
	1964-73. Red-brown on multicolor underprint. Aerial view of coastline. Back: Woman standing with pennant and shield at center. Watermark: Dragon. Printer: TDLR.		
	a. 28.7.1964.	900.	2600.
	b. 5.10.1965.	600.	1350.
	c. 27.7.1968.	750.	1750.
	d. 16.4.1970.	400.	1100.
	e. 1.11.1973.	350.	950.

1974 Issue

245 **100 Dollars** | VF | UNC
4.11.1974. Red, purple and brown on multicolor underprint. Woman standing with pennant and shield. Back: Red on multicolor underprint. City view at center. Watermark: Dragon. Printer: TDLR. | 65.00 | 220.

STANDARD CHARTERED BANK

府政港香

Hong Kong Cha Ta Yin Hang

1985-89 ISSUES

278 **10 Dollars** | VF | UNC
1985-91. Dark green on yellow-green and multicolor underprint. Mythological carp at right. Back: Bank building at left, bank arms at center. Watermark: Helmeted warrior's head. 138x69mm.

a. Signature titles: *FINANCIAL CONTROLLER* and *AREA GENERAL MANAGER*. 1.1.1985.	FV	10.00
b. Signature titles: *AREA FINANCIAL CONTROLLER* and *AREA GENERAL MANAGER*. 1.1.1986; 1.1.1987; 1.1.1988; 1.1.1989.	FV	7.00
c. Signature titles: *AREA FINANCIAL CONTROLLER* and *GENERAL MANAGER*. 1.1.1990.	FV	6.00
d. Signature titles: *CHIEF FINANCIAL OFFICER* and *GENERAL MANAGER*. 1.1.1991.	FV	6.00

279 **20 Dollars** | VF | UNC
1985; 1992. Dark gray, orange and brown on multicolor underprint. Mythological tortoise at right. Back: Bank building at left, bank arms at center. Watermark: Helmeted warrior's head. 144x72mm.

a. Signature titles: *FINANCIAL CONTROLLER* and *AREA GENERAL MANAGER*. 1.1.1985.	FV	10.00
b. Signature titles: *CHIEF FINANCIAL OFFICER* and *AREA GENERAL MANAGER*. 1.1.1992.	FV	7.00

280 **50 Dollars** | VF | UNC
1985-91. Purple, violet and dark gray on multicolor underprint. Mythological lion at right. Back: Bank building at left, bank arms at center. Watermark: Helmeted warrior's head. 148x74mm.

a. Signature titles: *FINANCIAL CONTROLLER* and *AREA GENERAL MANAGER*. 1.1.1985.	FV	35.00
b. Signature titles: *AREA FINANCIAL CONTROLLER* and *AREA GENERAL MANAGER*. 1.1.1987; 1.1.1988.	FV	30.00
c. Signature titles: *AREA FINANCIAL CONTROLLER* and *GENERAL MANAGER*. 1.1.1990.	FV	25.00
d. Signature titles: *CHIEF FINANCIAL OFFICER* and *GENERAL MANAGER*. 1.1.1991.	FV	25.00

281 **100 Dollars** | VF | UNC
1985-92. Red on multicolor underprint. Mythological horse (unicorn) at right. Back: Bank building at left, bank arms at center. Watermark: Helmeted warrior's head. 154x77mm.

a. Signature titles: *FINANCIAL CONTROLLER* and *AREA GENERAL MANAGER*. 1.1.1985.	FV	48.00
b. Signature titles: *AREA FINANCIAL CONTROLLER* and *AREA GENERAL MANAGER*. 1.1.1986-1.1.1989.	FV	37.50
c. Signature titles: *FINANCIAL CONTROLLER* and *AREA GENERAL MANAGER*. 1.1.1990.	FV	35.00
d. Signature titles: *FINANCIAL CONTROLLER* and *AREA GENERAL MANAGER*. 1.1.1991; 1.1.1992.	FV	30.00

282 **500 Dollars**
1988-92. Maroon, gray and green on multicolor underprint. Mythological phoenix at right. Back: Bank building at left, bank arms at center. Watermark: Helmeted warrior's head. 158x79mm.

a. Signature titles: *FINANCIAL CONTROLLER* and *AREA GENERAL MANAGER*. 1.1.1988; 1.1.1989; 1.10.1989.	FV	180.
b. Signature titles: *FINANCIAL CONTROLLER* and *AREA GENERAL MANAGER*. 1.1.1990.	FV	170.
c. Signature titles: *FINANCIAL CONTROLLER* and *AREA GENERAL MANAGER*. 1.1.1991; 1.1.1992.	FV	160.

283 **1000 Dollars** | VF | UNC
1985-92. Yellow-orange on multicolor underprint. Mythological dragon at right. Back: Bank building at left, bank arms at center. Watermark: Helmeted warrior's head. 164x82mm.

a. Signature titles: *FINANCIAL CONTROLLER* and *AREA GENERAL MANAGER*. 1.1.1985.	FV	300.
b. Signature titles: *AREA FINANCIAL CONTROLLER* and *AREA GENERAL MANAGER*. 1.1.1987.	FV	320.
c. Signature titles as b. 1.1.1988.	FV	270.
d. Signature titles: *FINANCIAL CONTROLLER* and *AREA GENERAL MANAGER*. 1.1.1992.	FV	240.

1993 ISSUE

284 **10 Dollars** | VF | UNC
1993-95. Dark green on yellow-green underprint. Mythological carp at right. Back: Bank building at left, Bauhinia flower at center. Watermark: SCB above helmeted warrior's head. 138x69mm.

a. Signature titles: *CHIEF FINANCIAL OFFICER* and *AREA GENERAL MANAGER*. 1.1.1993.	FV	6.00
b. Signature titles: *HEAD OF FINANCE* and *GENERAL MANAGER*. 1.1.1994; 1.1.1995.	FV	5.00

285 20 Dollars — VF | UNC

1993-2002. Dark gray, orange and brown on multicolor underprint. Mythological tortoise at right. Back: Bank building at left, Bauhinia flower at center. Watermark: SCB above helmeted warrior's head. . 144x72mm.

- a. Signature titles: *CHIEF FINANCIAL OFFICER* and *AREA GENERAL MANAGER*. 1.1.1993. — FV 10.00
- b. Signature titles: *HEAD OF FINANCE* and *GENERAL MANAGER*. 1.1.1994; 1.1.1995; 1.1.1996; 1.1.1997; 1.7.1997. — FV 7.50
- c. Signature titles: *HEAD OF FINANCE* and *CHIEF EXECUTIVE*. 1.1.1998; 1.1.1999, 1.1.2000, 1.1.2001. — FV 6.00
- d. Signature titles: *CHIEF FINANCIAL OFFICER* and CHIEF EXECUTIVE & GENERAL MANAGER. 1.1.2002. — FV 5.00

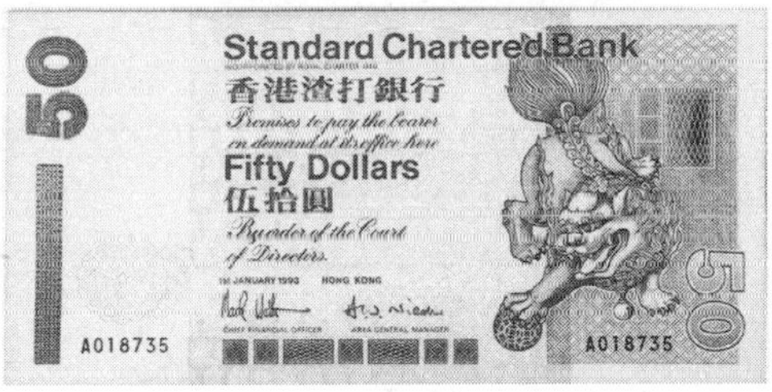

286 50 Dollars — VF | UNC

1993-2002. Purple, violet and dark gray on multicolor underprint. Mythological lion at right. Back: Bank building at left, Bauhinia flower at center. Watermark: SCB above helmeted warrior's head. 148x74mm.

- a. Signature titles: *CHIEF FINANCIAL OFFICER* and *AREA GENERAL MANAGER*. 1.1.1993. — FV 17.50
- b. Signature titles: *HEAD OF FINANCE* and *GENERAL MANAGER*. 1.1.1994; 1.1.1995; 1.1.1996; 1.1.1997; 1.7.1997. — FV 15.00
- c. Signature titles: *HEAD OF FINANCE* and *CHIEF EXECUTIVE*. 1.1.1998; 1.1.1999; 1.1.2000; 1.1.2001; 1.1.2002. — FV 15.00

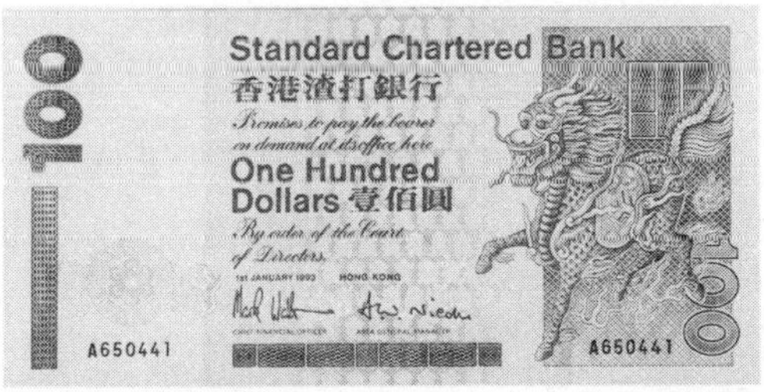

287 100 Dollars — VF | UNC

1993-2002. Red and purple on multicolor underprint. Mythological horse (unicorn) at right. Back: Bank building at left, Bauhinia flower at center. Watermark: SCB above helmeted warrior's head. 154x77mm.

- a. Signature titles: *CHIEF FINANCIAL OFFICER* and *AREA GENERAL MANAGER*. 1.1.1993. — FV 33.00
- b. Signature titles: *HEAD OF FINANCE* and *GENERAL MANAGER*. 1.1.1994; 1.1.1995; 1.1.1996; 1.1.1997; 1.7.1997. — FV 27.50
- c. Signature titles: *HEAD OF FINANCE* and *CHIEF EXECUTIVE*. 1.1.1998; 1.1.1999; 1.1.2000; 1.1.2001. — FV 27.50
- d. Signature titles: *CHIEF FINANCIAL OFFICER* and *CHIEF EXECUTIVE & GENERAL MANAGER*. 1.1.2001; 1.1.2002. — FV 25.00

288 500 Dollars — VF | UNC

1993-2002. Brown and blue-green on multicolor underprint. Mythological phoenix at right. Back: Bank building at left, Bauhinia flower at center. Watermark: SCB above helmeted warrior's head. 158x79mm.

- a. Signature titles: *CHIEF FINANCIAL OFFICER* and *AREA GENERAL MANAGER*. 1.1.1993. — FV 150.
- b. Signature titles: *HEAD OF FINANCE* and *GENERAL MANAGER*. 1.1.1994; 1.1.1995; 1.1.1996; 1.1.1997; 1.7.1997; 1.1.1998; 1.1.1999; 1.1.2000. — FV 135.
- c. Signature titles: *CHIEF FINANCIAL OFFICER* and CHIEF EXECUTIVE & GENERAL MANAGER. 1.1.2001; 1.1.2002. — FV 130.

289 1000 Dollars

1993-2002. Yellow-orange on multicolor underprint. Mythological dragon at right. Back: Bank building at left, Bauhinia flower at center. Watermark: SCB above helmeted warrior's head. 164x82mm.

- a. Signature titles: *CHIEF FINANCIAL OFFICER* and *AREA GENERAL MANAGER*. 1.1.1993. — FV 250.
- b. Signature titles: *HEAD OF FINANCE* and *GENERAL MANAGER*. 1.1.1994; 1.1.1995; 1.1.1997; 1.7.1997; 1.1.1998. — FV 225.
- c. Signature titles: *HEAD OF FINANCE and CHIEF EXECUTIVE. 1.1.1999; 1.1.2000.* — FV 200.
- d. Signature titles: *CHIEF FINANCIAL OFFICER and CHIEF EXECUTIVE & GENERAL MANAGER. 1.1.2001; 1.1.2002.* — FV 200.

2002 Issue

290 1000 Dollars — VF | UNC

1.1.2002. Yellow-orange and blue-green on multicolor underprint. Mythological dragon at right. Signature title: *CHIEF FINANCIAL OFFICER* and CHIEF EXECUTIVE & GENERAL MANAGER. Back: Bank building at left. Bauhinia flower at center. Watermark: SCB above helmeted warrior's head. Enhanced security features. 164x82mm. — FV 215.

2003 Issue

291 20 Dollars — VF | UNC

1.7.2003. Dark Blue on multicolor underprint. Signature titles: *CHIEF FINANCIAL OFFICER* and *DIRECTOR*. Back: Victoria Harbor view ca. 1850. 144x72mm. — FV 6.00

292 50 Dollars — VF | UNC

1.7.2003. Dark green and brown on multicolor underprint. Back: Victoria Harbor view ca. 1890. 148x74mm. — FV 15.00

293 **100 Dollars** — VF | UNC
1.7.2003. Red and brown on multicolor underprint. Back: Victoria Harbor view ca. 1930. 154x77mm. — FV | 25.00

294 **500 Dollars** — VF | UNC
1.7.2003. Dark brown and dark blue on multicolor underprint. Back: Harbor view ca. 1970. 158x79mm. — FV | 135.

295 **1000 Dollars** — VF | UNC
1.7.2003. Red-brown, orange and olive on multicolor underprint. Back: Victoria Harbor view ca. 2003. 164x82mm. — FV | 215.

2009 Commemorative Issue

296 **150 Dollars** — VF | UNC
9.9.2009. Bank Building at left, satelite image of Victoria Harbor Back: Historical views of Hong Kong.

	VF	UNC
a. Issued note.	FV	45.00
b. 4-note sheet.	—	200.
c. 35-note sheet.	—	1800.

2010 Issue

297 **20 Dollars** — VF | UNC
2010-. Blue on multicolor underprint. Back: History and Technology - Abicus and Binary code. 144x72mm.

	VF	UNC
a. 1.1.2010.	FV	6.00
b. 1.1.2012.	FV	6.00

298 **50 Dollars**
1.1.2010. — FV | 15.00

299 **100 Dollars**
1.1.2010. — FV | 25.00

300 **500 Dollars**
1.1.2010. — FV | 135.

301 **1000 Dollars** — VF | UNC
1.1.2010. 164x82mm. — FV | 175.

Government of Hong Kong

府政港香

Hsiang K'ang Cheng Fu

1961 ND Issue

SIGNATURE VARIETIES			
1	J.J. Cowperthwaite, 1961-71	4	Sir Piers Jacobs, 1986-92
2	C.P. Haddon-Cave, 1971-81	5	Sir Hamish Macleod, 1992-95
3	Sir J.H. Bremridge, 1981-86		

325 **1 Cent** — VF | UNC
ND (1961-95). Brown on light blue underprint. Queen Elizabeth at right. Uniface.

	VF	UNC
a. Signature 1. (1961-71).	.10	.25
b. Signature 2. (1971-81).	.25	.50
c. Signature 3. (1981-86).	.75	2.00
d. Signature 4. (1986-92).	.10	.25
e. Signature 5. (1992-95).	.25	.50

326 **5 Cents** — VF | UNC
ND (1961-65). Green on lilac underprint. Queen Elizabeth at right. Uniface. — 1.75 | 8.00

327	10 Cents	VF	UNC
	ND (1961-65). Red on grayish underprint. Queen Elizabeth at right. Uniface.	1.00	5.00

Hong Kong Special Administration Region

Bank of China (Hong Kong) Limited

中國銀行

Chung Kuo Yin Hang

1994 Issue

329	20 Dollars	VF	UNC
	1994-2000. Blue black, blue and purple on multicolor underprint. Bank of China Tower at left. Narcissus flowers at lower center right. Back: Aerial view of Wanchai and Central Hong Kong at center right. Watermark: Chinze. Printer: TDLR (HK) Ltd. (Without imprint). 144x72mm.		
	a. 1.5.1994.	FV	6.00
	b. 1.1.1996.	FV	6.00
	c. 1.7.1997.	FV	6.00
	d. 1.1.1998.	FV	6.00
	e. 1.1.1999.	FV	6.00
	f. 1.1.2000.	FV	6.00

330	50 Dollars	VF	UNC
	1994-2000. Purple and blue on violet and multicolor underprint. Bank of China Tower at left. Chrysanthemum flowers at lower center right. Back: Aerial view of cross-harbor tunnel at center right. Watermark: Chinze. Printer: TDLR (HK) Ltd. (Without imprint). 148x74mm.		
	a. 1.5.1994.	FV	18.00
	b. 1.1.1996.	FV	18.00
	c. 1.7.1997.	FV	18.00
	d. 1.1.1998.	FV	18.00
	e. 1.1.1999.	FV	18.00
	f. 1.1.2000.	FV	18.00

331	100 Dollars	VF	UNC
	1994-2000. Red-violet, orange and red on multicolor underprint. Bank of China Tower at left. Lotus flowers at lower center right. Back: Aerial view of Tsimshatsui, Kowloon Peninsula at center right. Watermark: Chinze. Printer: TDLR (HK) Ltd. (Without imprint). 154x77mm.		
	a. 1.5.1994.	FV	30.00
	b. 1.1.1996.	FV	30.00
	c. 1.7.1997.	FV	30.00
	d. 1.1.1998.	FV	30.00
	e. 1.1.1999.	FV	30.00
	f. 1.1.2000.	FV	30.00

332	500 Dollars	VF	UNC
	1994-2000. Dark brown and blue on multicolor underprint. Bank of China Tower at left. Peony flowers at lower center right. Back: Hong Kong Container Terminal in Kwai Chung at center right. Watermark: Chinze. Printer: TDLR (HK) Ltd. (Without imprint). 158x79mm.		
	a. 1.5.1994.	FV	160.
	b. 1.1.1995.	FV	160.
	c. 1.1.1996.	FV	160.
	d. 1.7.1997.	FV	160.
	e. 1.1.1998.	FV	160.
	f. 1.1.1999.	FV	160.
	g. 1.1.2000.	FV	160.

333	1000 Dollars	VF	UNC
	1994-2000. Reddish brown, orange and pale olive-green on multicolor underprint. Bank of China Tower at left. Bauhinia flowers at lower center right. Back: Aerial view overlooking the Central district at center right. Watermark: Chinze. Printer: TDLR (HK) Ltd. (Without imprint). 164x82mm.		
	a. 1.5.1994.	FV	270.
	b. 1.1.1995.	FV	270.
	c. 1.1.1996.	FV	270.
	d. 1.7.1997.	FV	270.
	e. 1.1.1998.	FV	270.
	f. 1.1.1999.	FV	270.
	g. 1.1.2000.	FV	270.

2001 Issue

		VF	UNC
334	**1000 Dollars** 1.1.2001. Reddish brown, orange and pale olive-green on multicolor underprint. Bank of China Tower at left. Bauhinia flowers at lower center right. Back: Aerial view overlooking the Central district at center right. Watermark: Chinze. Printer: TDLR (HK) Ltd. (Without imprint). Enhanced security features. 164x82mm.	FV	270.

2003 Issue

		VF	UNC
335	**20 Dollars** 2003-07. Dark blue on multicolor underprint. Signature title: *CHIEF EXECUTIVE*. Back: The Peak. 144x72mm.		
	a. 1.7.2003.	FV	6.00
	b. 1.1.2005.	FV	6.00
	c. 1.1.2006.	FV	6.00
	d. 1.1.2007.	FV	6.00

		VF	UNC
336	**50 Dollars** 2003-07. Dark green on multicolor underprint. Back: Aerial view of Tsimshatsui, Kowloon Peninsula. 148x74mm.		
	a. 1.7.2003.	FV	15.00
	b. 1.1.2005.	FV	15.00
	c. 1.1.2006.	FV	15.00
	d. 1.1.2007.	FV	15.00

		VF	UNC
337	**100 Dollars** 2003; 2005-06. Red on pink and multicolor underprint. Back: Tsing-Ma Bridge. 154x77mm.		
	a. 1.7.2003.	FV	25.00
	b. 1.1.2005.	FV	25.00
	c. 1.1.2006.	FV	25.00
	d. 1.1.2007.	FV	25.00

		VF	UNC
338	**500 Dollars** 2003; 2005-07. Dark brown on multicolor underprint. Back: Hong Kong Airport. 158x79mm.		
	a. 1.7.2003.	FV	135.
	b. 1.1.2005.	FV	135.
	c. 1.1.2006.	FV	135.
	d. 1.1.2007.	FV	135.

		VF	UNC
339	**1000 Dollars** 1.7.2003; 1.1.2006. Reddish-brown, orange and olive-green on multicolor underprint. Back: Hong Kong Convention and Exhibition Center. 164x82mm.		
	a. 1.7.2003.	FV	220.
	b. 1.1.2006.	FV	220.

2008 Commemorative Issue

		VF	UNC
340	**20 Dollars** 1.1.2008. Light blue on multicolor underprint. Bank of China building, classical Greek column, Bejing Olympic logo. Back: Bejing Olympic Stadium, *the Bird's Nest*, at left. Watermark: Stadium and value. 144x72mm.		
	a. Two letter serial # prefix.	FV	40.00
	b. Serial number without prefix letters.	FV	40.00
	c. In folder of issue with matching serical # note from Macau.	—	140.

2010 Issue

		VF	UNC
341	**20 Dollars** 1.1.2010.	FV	6.00
342	**50 Dollars** 1.1.2010.	FV	15.00
343	**100 Dollars** 1.1.2010.	FV	25.00
344	**500 Dollars** 1.1.2010.	FV	135.

		VF	UNC
345	**1000 Dollars** 1.1.2010. 164x82mm.	FV	215.

Government of Hong Kong

2002 Issue

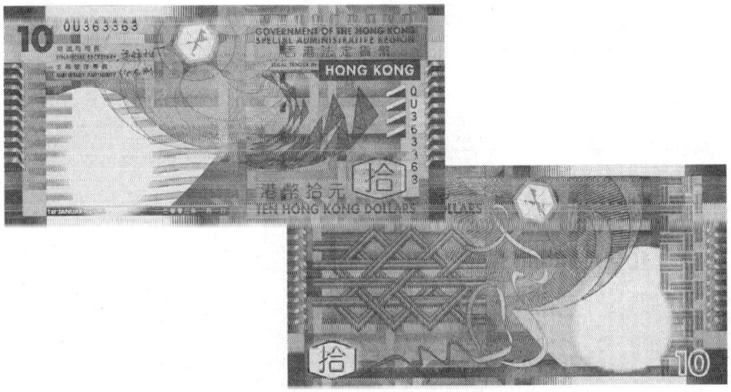

		VF	UNC
400	**10 Dollars** 2002-03; 2005. Purple, blue and multicolor. Geometric patterns. 138x69mm.		
	a. 1.7.2002.	FV	3.00
	b. 1.1.2003.	FV	3.00
	c. 1.1.2005.	FV	3.00

2007 Issue

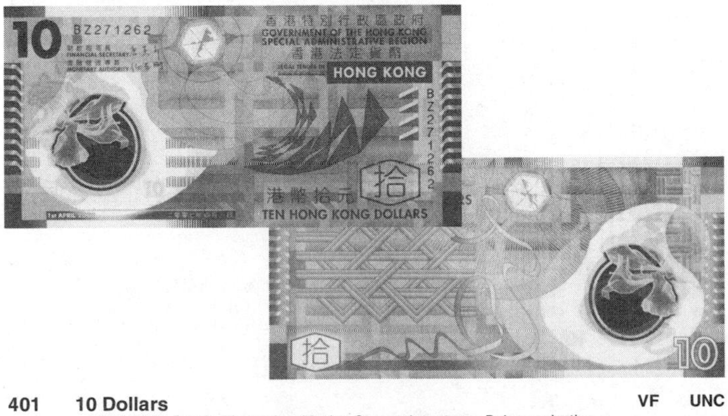

		VF	UNC
401	**10 Dollars** 2007; 2012. Purple, blue and multicolor. Geometric patterns. Polymer plastic. UV: square with 10 fluoresces green. 138x69mm.		
	a. 1.4.2007. Signatures: of Henry Tang Ying-yen and Joseph Yam Chi-kwong.	FV	3.00
	b. 1.10.2007. Signatures: John Tsang Chun-wah and Joseph Yam Chi-kwong.	FV	3.00
	c. 1.1.2012.	FV	3.00

The Hungarian Republic, located in central Europe, has an area of 93,030 sq. km. and a population of 9.93 million. Capital: Budapest. The economy is d on agriculture and a rapidly expanding industrial sector. Machinery, chemicals, iron and steel, and fruits and vegetables are exported.

Hungary became a Christian kingdom in A.D. 1000 and for many centuries served as a bulwark against Ottoman Turkish expansion in Europe. The kingdom eventually became part of the polyglot Austro-Hungarian Empire, which collapsed during World War I. The country fell under Communist rule following World War II. In 1956, a revolt and an announced withdrawal from the Warsaw Pact were met with a massive military intervention by Moscow. Under the leadership of Janos Kadar in 1968, Hungary began liberalizing its economy, introducing so-called *Goulash Communism.* Hungary held its first multiparty elections in 1990 and initiated a free market economy. It joined NATO in 1999 and the EU in 2004.

RULERS:

Austrian to 1918

MONETARY SYSTEM:

1 Forint = 100 Fillér 1946-

Peoples Republic

Magyar Nemzeti Bank

Hungarian National Bank

1957-83 Issue

#168-171 The variety in the serial # occurs in 1975 when the letter and numbers are narrower and larger.

		VF	UNC
168	**10 Forint** 1957-75. Green and slate black on orange and lilac underprint. Portrait Sándar Petőfi at right. Value at left. Arms of 3-bar shield. Back: Trees and river, *Birth of the Song* by János Jankó at center. 174x80mm.		
	a. 23.5.1957.	4.00	10.00
	b. 24.8.1960.	2.00	12.00
	c. 12.10.1962.	2.00	8.00
	d. 30.6.1969. Blue-green center on back.	2.00	8.00
	e. 26.10.1978. Serial # varieties.	2.00	8.00
	s1. As a, b, c. Specimen with red overprint and perforated: *MINTA.*	—	45.00
	s2. As d, e. Specimen.	—	27.50

169	20 Forint	VF	UNC
	1957-80. Blue and green on light green and pink underprint. Arms of 3-bar shield. Portrait György Dózsa at right. Value at left. Back: Penthathlete Csaba Hegedüs with hammer and wheat at center. 174x80mm.		
	a. 23.5.1957.	5.00	15.00
	b. 24.8.1960.	10.00	50.00
	c. 12.10.1962.	2.00	15.00
	d. 3.9.1965.	2.00	15.00
	e. 30.6.1969.	2.00	15.00
	f. 28.10.1975. Serial # varieties.	2.00	15.00
	g. 30.9.1980.	2.00	15.00
	s1. As a; c; d. Specimen with red overprint and perforated: *MINTA*.	—	27.50
	s2. As b. Specimen.	—	35.00
	s3. As e; f; g. Specimen.	—	25.00

170	50 Forint	VF	UNC
	1965-89. Brown on blue and orange underprint. Value at left. Arms of 3-bar shield with star. Portrait Prince Ferencz Rákóczi II at right. Back: Battle of the Hungarian insurrectionists (Kuruc) against pro-Austrian soldiers (Labanc) scene at center. 174x80mm.		
	a. 3.9.1965.	3.00	30.00
	b. 30.6.1969.	3.00	30.00
	c. 28.10.1975. Serial # varieties.	5.00	15.00
	d. Serial # prefix D. 30.9.1980.	3.00	12.50
	e. Serial # prefix H. 30.9.1980.	4.00	20.00
	f. 10.11.1983.	1.00	12.00
	g. 4.11.1986.	1.00	30.00
	h. 10.1.1989.	1.00	20.00
	s1. As a. Specimen. Overprint *MINTA*.	—	50.00
	s2. As b-h. Specimen. Overprint: MINTA.	—	25.00

171	100 Forint	VF	UNC
	1957-89. Red-violet on blue and orange underprint. Arms of 3-bar shield with star. Value at left, portrait Lajos Kossuth at right. Back: Horse-drawn wagon from *Took Refuge from the Storm* by Károly Lotz at center. 174x80mm.		
	a. 23.5.1957.	5.00	18.00
	b. 24.8.1960.	5.00	18.00
	c. 12.10.1962.	5.00	15.00
	d. 24.10.1968.	2.00	15.00
	e. 28.10.1975. Serial # varieties.	3.00	12.00
	f. 30.9.1980.	2.00	12.00
	g. 30.10.1984.	2.00	12.00
	h. 10.1.1989.	2.00	12.00
	s1. As a. Specimen with red overprint and perforted: *MINTA*.	—	65.00
	s2. As b; c. Specimen.	—	—
	s3. As d; e. Specimen.	—	35.00
	s4. As f; g. Specimen.	—	30.00
	s5. As h. Specimen.	—	30.00

172	500 Forint	VF	UNC
	1969-80. Purple on multicolor underprint. Portrait Endre Ady at right, arms of 3-bar shield with star. Back: Aerial view of Budapest and Danube river. 174x80mm.		
	a. 30.6.1969.	FV	12.50
	b. Serial # varieties. 28.10.1975.	FV	12.50
	c. 30.9.1980.	FV	10.00
	s. As a-c. Specimen.	—	30.00

173	1000 Forint	VF	UNC
	1983. Deep green and olive-green on multicolor underprint. Béla Bartók at right, arms of 3-bar shield with star. Back: Green on multicolor underprint. *Anya* sculpture, mother nursing child by F. Medgyessy at center. 172x80mm.		
	a. Serial # prefix: *A; B*. 25.3.1983.	FV	17.50
	b. Serial # prefix: *B; C; D;*. 10.11.1983.	FV	17.50
	s. As a, b. Specimen with red overprint and perforated: *MINTA*.	—	45.00

Republic

Magyar Nemzeti Bank

Hungarian National Bank

1990; 1992 Issue

#174-177 numerous photocopy counterfeits began appearing in mid-1999.

174	100 Forint	VF	UNC
	1992-95. Red-violet on multicolor underprint. Value at left, portrait of L. Kossuth at right, St. Stephan's Crown over Hungarian Arms at top center. Back: Horse-drawn wagon from *Took Refuge from the Storm* by Károly Lotz at center. 174x80mm.		
	a. 15.1.1992.	FV	3.00
	b. 16.12.1993.	FV	3.00
	c. 20.12.1995.	FV	12.50
	s1. As a, b. Specimen with red. overprint and perforated *MINTA*.	—	25.00
	s2. As c. Specimen.	—	65.00

175 500 Forint

31.7.1990. Purple on multicolor underprint. Portrait of E. Ady at right, St. Stephan's Crown over Hungarian Arms. Back: Aerial view of Budapest and Danube river. 174x80mm.

	VF	UNC
a. Issued note.	FV	10.00
s. Specimen.	—	30.00

176 1000 Forint

1992-96. Deep green and olive-green on multicolor underprint. Béla Bartók at right, St. Stephan's Crown over Hungarian Arms. Back: *Anya* sculpture, mother nursing child by F. Medgyessy at center. 174x80mm.

	VF	UNC
a. Serial # prefix: *D*. 30.10.1992.	FV	17.50
b. Serial # prefix: *D; E*. 16.12.1993.	FV	17.50
c. Serial # prefix: *E; F*. 15.1.1996.	FV	17.50
s. Specimen. Serial # prefix: *A-F*.	—	30.00

177 5000 Forint

1990-95. Deep brown and brown on orange and multicolor underprint. Portrait Count Istvan Széchenyi at right, St. Stephan's Crown over Hungarian Arms Back: Academy of Science at center. 174x80mm.

	VF	UNC
a. Serial # prefix: *H; J*. 31.7.1990.	7.50	60.00
b. Serial # prefix: *J*. 30.10.1992.	7.50	60.00
c. Serial # prefix: *J*. 16.12.1993.	7.50	60.00
d. Serial # prefix: *J; K*. 31.8.1995.	7.50	60.00
s. As a-d. Specimen with red overprint and perforated: *MINTA*.	—	75.00

1997-99 Issue

178 200 Forint

1998. Dark green and grayish purple on multicolor underprint. King Robert Károly, crowned arms at left center, latent image in cartouche at upper left. Serial number prefix *FA-FH*. Back: Diósgyóri Castle ruins at left. Watermark: King Robert Károly. 154x70mm.

	VF	UNC
a. Issued note.	FV	5.00
s. Specimen.	—	25.00

179 500 Forint

1998. Brown-violet and brown on multicolor underprint. Ferenc Rákóczi II, crowned arms at left center, latent image in cartouche at upper left. Serial # prefix *EA-EF*. Back: Sárospatak Castle. Watermark: Ferenc Rákóczi II. 154x70mm.

	VF	UNC
a. Issued note.	FV	10.00
s. Specimen.	—	30.00

180 1000 Forint

1998; 1999. Blue and blue-green on multicolor underprint. King Mátyás, crowned arms at left center, latent image in cartouche at upper left. Back: Fountain in the palace at Visegrad. Watermark: King Matyas. 154x70mm.

	VF	UNC
a. 1998. Serial # prefix: *DA-DJ*.	FV	17.50
b. 1999. Serial # prefix: *DA-DD*.	FV	17.50
s. As a, b. Specimen.	—	30.00

181 2000 Forint

1998. Dark brown and brown on multicolor underprint. Prince Gabor Bethlen at right with hologram, crowned arms at left center, latent image in cartouche at upper left. Serial # prefix: *CA-CG*. Back: Bethlen amongst scientists at left center. Watermark: Gabor Bethlen. 154x70mm.

	VF	UNC
a. Issued note.	FV	30.00
s. Specimen.	—	50.00

182 5000 Forint

1999. Deep violet and purple on multicolor underprint. István Széchenyi at right, crowned arms at left center, latent image in cartouche at upper left with hologram. Serial # prefixes: *BA-BJ.* Back: Széchenyi's home at Nagycenk. Watermark: István Széchenyi. 154x70mm.

	VF	UNC
a. Issued note.	FV	60.00
s. Specimen.	—	75.00

183 10,000 Forint

1997-1999. Violet, dull purple and blue-black on multicolor underprint. King St. Stephan at right, crowned arms at left center, latent image in cartouche at upper left with hologram. Back: View of Esztergom at left center. Watermark: King St. Stephan. 154x70mm.

	VF	UNC
a. Serial # prefixes: *AA-AK.* 1997.	FV	120.
b. Serial # prefixes: *AA-AC* with additional security devices. 1998.	FV	120.
c. Serial # prefix: *AA-AE.* 1999.	FV	120.
s. As a-c. Specimen.	—	120.

184 20,000 Forint

1999. Slate gray on red and multicolor underprint. Ferenc Deák at right. Serial number prefix: *GA-GE.* Back: Old House of Commons in Budapest. Watermark: Ferenc Deák. 154x70mm.

	VF	UNC
a. Issued note.	FV	200.
s. Specimen.	—	225.

2000 Commemorative Issues

185 1000 Forint

2000. Blue, light yellow brown on multicolor underprint. King Mátyás at right, MNB in seal at upper left and *MILLENNIUM* at lower left. Serial number prefix: *DA-DE.* Back: Fountain in the palace at Visegrád. Large letter illustration from illuminated manuscript. Millenium Celebration. 154x70mm.

	VF	UNC
a. Issued note.	FV	17.50
s. Specimen.	—	30.00

186 2000 Forint

20.8.2000. Brown on tan and multicolor underprint. Crown of St. Stephan at right. Serial # prefix: *MM.* Back: St. Stephan as bishop baptizing. 1000 Years of the Hungarian State. 154x70mm.

	VF	UNC
a. Issued note.	FV	45.00
s. Specimen.	—	50.00

2001-02 Issue

187 200 Forint

2001-05. Green and multicolor. King Robert Károly, crowned arms at left center, latent image in cartouche at upper left. Back: Diósgyóri Castle ruins at left. Watermark: Robert Károly. Enhanced security features. 154x70mm.

	VF	UNC
a. 2001. Serial # prefix: *FA-FE.*	FV	5.00
b. 2002. Serial # prefix: *FA-FC.*	FV	5.00
c. 2003. Serial # prefix: *FA-FC.*	FV	9.00
d. 2004. Serial # prefix: *FA-FC.*	FV	9.00
e. 2005. Serial # prefix: *FA-FD.*	FV	9.00
f. 2006. Serial # prefix: *FA-FC.*	FV	9.00
g. 2007. Serial # prefix: *FA-FD.*	FV	9.00
s. Specimen.	—	25.00

188 500 Forint

2001-10. Brown-violet and brown on multicolor underprint. Ferenc Rákóczi II, crowned arms at left center, latent image in cartouche at upper left. Back: Sárospatak Castle. Watermark: Ferenc Rákóczi II. Enhanced security features. 154x70mm.

	VF	UNC
a. 2001. Serial # prefix: *EA-EC.*	FV	7.50
b. 2002. Serial # prefix: *EA-EB.*	FV	7.50
c. 2003. Serial # prefix: *EA-EC.*	FV	6.00
d. 2005. Serial # prefix: *EA-EC.*	FV	6.00
e. 2007.	FV	5.00
f. 2008.	FV	5.00
g. 2010.	FV	5.00
s. Specimen.	—	30.00

189 1000 Forint — VF — UNC

2002-04; 2008. Blue and light yellow brown on multicolor underprint. King Mátyás, crowned arms at left center, latent image in cartouche at upper left. Back: Fountain in the palace at Visegrád. Watermark: King Mátyás. Enhanced security features. 154x70mm.

	VF	UNC
a. 2002. Serial # prefix: *DA, DB.*	FV	12.50
b. 2003. Serial # prefix: *DA-DC.*	FV	10.00
c. 2004. Serial # prefix: *DA-DC.*	FV	10.00
d. 2008.	FV	7.50
s. Specimen.	—	30.00

190 2000 Forint — VF — UNC

2002-05. Dark brown and brown on multicolor underprint. Prince Gabor Bethlen at right, crowned arms at left center, latent image in cartouche at upper left. Back: Bethlen amongst scientists at left center. Watermark: Gabor Bethlen. Enhanced security features. 154x70mm.

	VF	UNC
a. 2002. Serial # prefix: *CA, CB.*	FV	25.00
b. 2003. Serial # prefix: *CA.*	FV	25.00
c. 2004. Serial # prefix: *CA-CC.*	FV	25.00
d. 2005. Serial # prefix: *CA-CB.*	FV	25.00
s. Specimen.	—	50.00

191 5000 Forint

2005-06. Multicolor. István Széchenyi at right. Back: Széchenyi's home at Nagycenk. Enhanced security features. 154x70mm.

	VF	UNC
a. 2005. Serial # prefix: *BA-BC.*	FV	60.00
b. 2006. Serial # prefix: *BA-BC.*	FV	60.00
s. Specimen.	—	75.00

192 10,000 Forint

2001-07. Multicolor. King St. Stephan at right. Back: View of Esztergom at left center. Enhanced security features. 154x70mm.

	VF	UNC
a. 2001. Serial # prefix: *AA-AC.*	FV	120.
b. 2003. Serial # prefix: *AA-AC.*	FV	120.
c. 2004. Serial # prefix: *AA-AD.*	FV	120.
d. 2005. Serial # prefix: *AA-AC.*	FV	120.
e. 2006. Serial # prefix: *AA-AC.*		
f. 2007. Serial # prefix: *AA-AC.*	FV	120.
s. Specimen.	—	120.

193 20,000 Forint — VF — UNC

2004-07. Multicolor. Ferenc Deák at right. Back: Old house of Commons in Budapest. 154x70mm.

	VF	UNC
a. 2004. Serial # prefix: *GA-GB.*	FV	200.
b. 2005. Serial # prefix: *GA-GC.*	FV	200.
c. 2006. Serial # prefix: *GA.*	FV	200.
d. 2007. Serial # prefix: *GA-GD.*	FV	200.
s. Specimen.	—	225.

2006 Commemorative Issue

194 500 Forint — VF — UNC

2006 (23.10.1956). Brown-violet and brown on multicolor underprint. Ferenc Rákóczi at right. Serial # prefix EB-EC. Back: Parliament building and tri-color national flag, with a hole thru it. 50th Anniversary of uprising. 154x70mm. — FV — 10.00

2005 Issue

195 1000 Forint — VF — UNC

2005-. Blue on light blue and multicolor underprint. King Mátyás at right, crowned arms at left center. Holographic foil strip. Back: Fountain in the palace at Visegrád. 154x70mm.

	VF	UNC
a. 2005. Serial # prefix: *DA-DD.*	FV	15.00
b. 2006. Serial # prefix: *DA-DF.*	FV	15.00
c. 2007. Serial # prefix: *DA-DC.*	FV	15.00

2008-2010 Issue

196 500 Forint — VF — UNC

2008; 2010-11. Omron rings added. 154x70mm.

	VF	UNC
a. 2008.	FV	5.00
b. 2010.	FV	5.00
c. 2011.	FV	5.00

197 1000 Forint

2009-11. Omron rings added. 154x70mm.

	VF	UNC
a. 2009.	FV	7.50
b. 2010.	FV	7.50
c. 2011.	FV	7.50

198 2000 Forint

2007-08; 2010. Omron rings added. 154x70mm.

	VF	UNC
a. 2007.	FV	17.50
b. 2008.	FV	17.50
c. 2010.	FV	15.00

199 5000 Forint

2008; 2010. Omron rings added. 154x70mm.

	VF	UNC
a. 2008.	FV	35.00
b. 2010.	FV	35.00

200 10,000 Forint

2008; 2009; 2012. Omron rings added. 154x70mm.

	VF	UNC
a. 2008.	FV	80.00
b. 2009.	FV	75.00
c. 2012.	FV	60.00

201 20,000 Forint

2008; 2009. Omron rings added. 154x70mm.

	VF	UNC
a. 2008.	FV	145.
b. 2009.	FV	145.

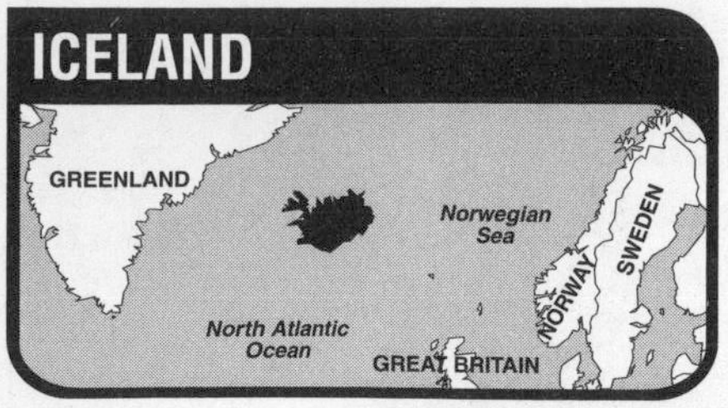

The Republic of Iceland, an island of recent volcanic origin in the North Atlantic east of Greenland and immediately south of the Arctic Circle, has an area of 103,000 sq. km. and a population of 304,367. Capital: Reykjavík. Fishing is the chief industry and accounts for more than 60 percent of the exports.

Settled by Norwegian and Celtic (Scottish and Irish) immigrants during the late 9th and 10th centuries A.D., Iceland boasts the world's oldest functioning legislative assembly, the Althing, established in 930. Independent for over 300 years, Iceland was subsequently ruled by Norway and Denmark. Fallout from the Askja volcano of 1875 devastated the Icelandic economy and caused widespread famine. Over the next quarter century, 20% of the island's population emigrated, mostly to Canada and the US. Limited home rule from Denmark was granted in 1874 and complete independence attained in 1944. Literacy, longevity, income, and social cohesion are first-rate by world standards.

RULERS:

Danish until 1873
Christian IX, 1863-1906
Frederik VIII, 1906-1912
Christian X, 1912-1944

MONETARY SYSTEM:

1 Krona = 100 Aurar, 1874-

SIGNATURE VARIETIES

31	V. Thor - J.G. Mariasson, 1961-64	32	J. Nordal - V. Thor, 1961-64
33	J.G. Mariasson - J. Nordal, 1961-67	34	J. Nordal - J.G. Mariasson, 1961-67
35	S. Klemenzson - J.G. Mariasson, 1966-67	36	J. Nordal - S. Klemenzson, 1966-67
37	J. Nordal - D. Olafsson, 1967-86	38	D. Olafsson - J. Nordal, 1967-86
39	S. Klemenzson - D. Olafsson, 1967-71	40	S. Frimannsson - D. Olafsson, 1971-73
41	J. Nordal - S. Frimannsson, 1971-73	42	G. Hjartarson - D. Olafsson, 1974-84
43	J. Nordal - G. Hjartarson, 1974-84	44	G. Hjartarson - T. Arnason, 1984
45	T. Arnason - J. Nordal, 1984-93	46	T. Arnason - D. Olafsson, 1984-93
47	J. Nordal - T. Arnason, 1984-93	48	G. Hallgrimsson - T. Arnason, 1986-90
49	J. Nordal - G. Hallgrimsson, 1986-90	50	B. I. Gunnarsson - T. Arnason, 1991-93
51	J. Nordal - B. I. Gunnarsson, 1991-93	52	J. Sigurthsson - B. I. Gunnarsson, 1994
53	B. I. Gunnarsson - J. Sigurthsson, 1994	54	E. Guthnason - S. Hermansson, 1994

SIGNATURE VARIETIES

55	S. Hermansson - E. Guthnason, 1994	56	E. Guthnason - S. Hermansson, 1994

Republic

Sedlabanki Íslands

Central Bank of Iceland

Law of 29.3.1961

			VF	UNC
42	**10 Krónur**	*L.1961.* Brown-violet on green and orange underprint. Jón Eriksson at left, ships in Port of Reykjavík at lower center. Signature 33; 34. Back: Green. Ships moored at pier. Printer: BWC (without imprint).	10.00	20.00

			VF	UNC
43	**25 Krónur**	*L.1961.* Purple on multicolor underprint. Magnús Stephensen at left, Fjord at center. Signature 34. Back: Fishing boats near Westmen Islands. Watermark: S. Bjornsson. Printer: BWC (without imprint).	6.00	14.00

			VF	UNC
44	**100 Krónur**	*L.1961.* Dark blue-green on multicolor underprint. Tryggvi Gunnarsson at left. Signature 31-36; 38-44. Back: Tryggvi Gunnarsson at left. Sheepherders on horseback, sheep in foreground, Mt. Hekla in background. Watermark: S. Bjornsson. Printer: BWC (without imprint).		
		a. Issued note.	10.00	20.00
		s. Specimen.	—	165.

45 **500 Krónur** VF UNC

L.1961. Green on lilac and multicolor underprint. Hannes Hafstein at left. Signature 36; 38-43. Back: Sailors. Watermark: S. Bjornsson. Printer: BWC (without imprint).

	VF	UNC
a. Issued note.	10.00	20.00
s. Specimen.	—	235.

46 **1000 Krónur** VF UNC

L.1961. Blue on multicolor underprint. Jón Sigurthsson at right, building at lower center. Signature 31-34; 36; 38-43. Back: Rock formations. Watermark: S. Bjornsson. Printer: BWC (without imprint).

	VF	UNC
a. Issued note.	15.00	30.00
s. Specimen.	—	325.

47 **5000 Krónur** VF UNC

L.1961. Brown on multicolor underprint. Einer Benediktsson at left, dam at lower center.Signature 36; 38-43. Back: Man overlooking waterfall. Watermark: S. Bjornsson. Printer: BWC (without imprint).

	VF	UNC
a. Issued note.	30.00	60.00
s. Specimen.	—	375.

Law 29 March 1961 (1981-86) Issue

48 **10 Krónur** VF UNC

L.1961 (1981). Blue on multicolor underprint. Arngrimúr Jónsson at right. Signature 37; 38; 42; 43. Back: Old Icelandic household scene. Watermark: J. Sigurthsson. Printer: BWC, then later by TDLR (both without imprint).

	VF	UNC
a. Issued note.	1.00	3.00
s. Specimen.	—	105.

49 **50 Krónur** VF UNC

L.1961 (1981). Brown on multicolor underprint. Bishop Guthbranthur Thorláksson at left. Signature 37; 38; 42; 43. Back: Two printers. Watermark: J. Sigurthsson. Printer: BWC, then later by TDLR (both without imprint).

	VF	UNC
a. Issued note.	2.00	6.00
s. Specimen.	—	105.

50 **100 Krónur** VF UNC

L.1961 (1981). Dark green on multicolor underprint. Proffessor Arni Magnússon at right. Signature 37; 38; 42; 43; 45-53. Back: Monk with illuminated manuscript. Watermark: J. Sigurthsson. Printer: BWC, then later by TDLR (both without imprint).

	VF	UNC
a. Issued note.	3.00	8.00
s. Specimen.	—	105.

51 **500 Krónur** VF UNC

L.1961 (1981). Red on multicolor underprint. Jón Sigurthsson at left center. Signature 37; 38; 42; 43; 45; 48-53. Back: Sigurthsson working at his desk. Watermark: J. Sigurthsson. Printer: BWC, then later by TDLR (both without imprint). 145x70mm.

	VF	UNC
a. Issued note.	FV	22.00
s. Specimen.	—	160.

52 **1000 Krónur** — VF — UNC

L.1961 (1984-91). Purple on multicolor underprint. Bishop Byrnijólfur Sveinsson with book at right. Signature 38; 42; 43; 45; 48-51. Back: Church at center. Watermark: J. Sigurthsson. Printer: BWC, then later by TDLR (both without imprint). 150x70mm.

	VF	UNC
a. Issued note.	FV	35.50
s. Specimen.	—	160.

53 **5000 Krónur** — VF — UNC

L.1961 (1986-95). Blue on multicolor underprint. Ragnheithur Jónsdóttir at center. Bishop G. Thorláksson with two previous wives at right. Back: Jónsdóttir teaching two girls embroidery. Watermark: J. Sigurthsson. Printer: BWC, then later by TDLR (both without imprint). 155x70mm.

	VF	UNC
a. Signature 38; 46; 47.	FV	215.
b. Signature 54-56. (1995).	FV	160.
s. Specimen.	—	260.

Law 5 Mai 1986 (1994-00) Issue

54 **100 Krónur** — VF — UNC

L.1986 (1994). Dark green on multicolor underprint. Proffessor Arni Magnússon at right. Signature 52; 53. Back: Monk with illuminated manuscript. Watermark: J. Sigurthsson.

	VF	UNC
a. Issued note.	FV	5.50
s. Specimen.	—	120.

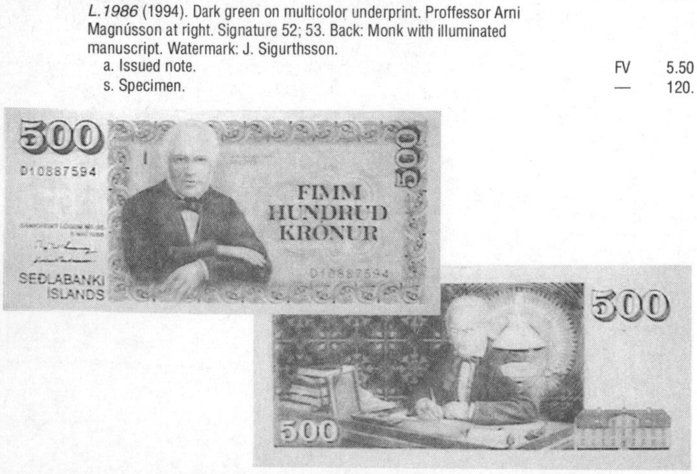

55 **500 Krónur** — VF — UNC

L.1986 (1994). Red on multicolor underprint. Jón Sigurthsson at left center. Signature 45; 50-53. Back: Sigurthsson working at his desk. Watermark: J. Sigurthsson. 145x70mm.

	VF	UNC
a. Issued note.	FV	15.50
s. Specimen.	—	110.

56 **1000 Krónur** — VF — UNC

L.1986 (1994). Purple on multicolor underprint. Bishop Byrnijólfur Sveinsson with book at right. Signature 45; 50; 51; 54-56. Serial # prefix *E*. Back: Church at center. Watermark: J. Sigurthsson. 150x70mm.

	VF	UNC
a. Issued note.	FV	28.00
s. Specimen.	—	160.

57 **2000 Krónur** — VF — UNC

L.1986 (1995). Brown and blue-violet on multicolor underprint. Painting *Inside, Outside* at center, Johannes S. Kjarval at right. Signature 54-56. Serial # prefix *G*. Back: Painting *Yearning for Flight* (Leda and the Swan) and *Woman with Flower*. 150x70mm.

	VF	UNC
a. Issued note.	FV	55.00
s. Specimen.	—	265.

Law 22 Mai 2001 (2001-05) Issue

58 **500 Krónur** — VF — UNC

L. 1986. (2004); 22.5.2001. Red on multicolor underprint. Jón Sigurthsson at left center. Signature 45; 50-53. Back: Sigurthsson working at his desk. Watermark: J. Sigurthsson. Designs to edge of paper. 145x70mm.

	VF	UNC
a. L.1986.	FV	13.00
b. 22.5.2001.	FV	13.00

59 **1000 Krónur** | **VF** | **UNC**

L. 1986. (2005). Red on multicolor underprint. Jón Sigurthsson at left center. Signature 45; 50-53. Back: Sigurthsson working at his desk. Watermark: J. Sigurthsson. Designs to edge of paper. 150x70mm. | FV | 20.50

60 **5000 Krónur** | **VF** | **UNC**

22.5.2001. Blue on multicolor underprint. Ragnheithur Jónsdóttir at center. Bishop G. Thorláksson with two previous wives at right. Serial # prefix: *F.* Back: Jónsdóttir teaching two girls embroidery. Watermark: J. Sigurthsson. Enhanced security decives. 155x70mm. | FV | 120.

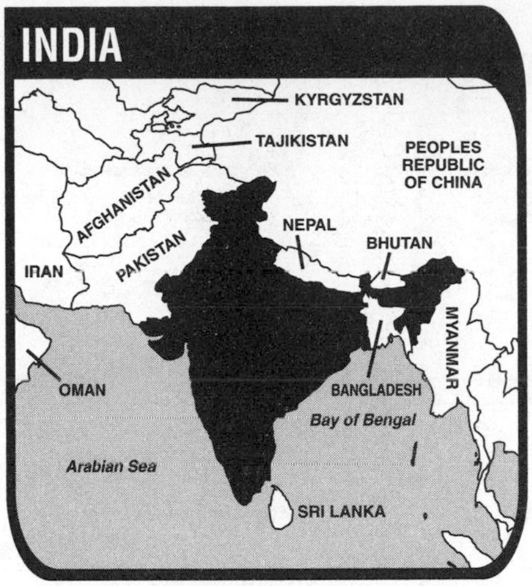

The Republic of India, a subcontinent jutting southward from the mainland of Asia, has an area of 3,287,590 sq. km. and a population of 1,147.9 million, second only to that of the Peoples Republic of China. Capital: New Delhi. India's economy is d on agriculture and industrial activity. Engineering goods, cotton apparel and fabrics, handicrafts, tea, iron and steel are exported.

Aryan tribes from the northwest infiltrated onto the Indian subcontinent about 1500 B.C.; their merger with the earlier Dravidian inhabitants created the classical Indian culture. The Maurya Empire of the 4th and 3rd centuries B.C. - which reached its zenith under Ashoka - united much of South Asia. The Golden Age ushered in by the Gupta dynasty (4th to 6th centuries A.D.) saw a flowering of Indian science, art, and culture. Arab incursions starting in the 8th century and Turkic in the 12th were followed by those of European traders, beginning in the late 15th century. By the 19th century, Britain had assumed political control of virtually all Indian lands. Indian armed forces in the British army played a vital role in both World Wars. Nonviolent resistance to British colonialism led by Mohandas Gandhi and Jawaharlal Nehru brought independence in 1947. The subcontinent was divided into the secular state of India and the smaller Muslim state of Pakistan. A third war between the two countries in 1971 resulted in East Pakistan becoming the separate nation of Bangladesh. India's nuclear weapons testing in 1998 caused Pakistan to conduct its own tests that same year. The dispute between the countries over the state of Kashmir is ongoing, but discussions and confidence-building measures have led to decreased tensions since 2002. Despite impressive gains in economic investment and output, India faces pressing problems such as significant overpopulation, environmental degradation, extensive poverty, and ethnic and religious strife.

NOTE: Staple holes and condition:

Perfect uncirculated notes are rarely encountered without having at least two tiny holes made by staples, stick pins or stitching having been done during age old accounting practices before and after a note is released to circulation. Staples were officially discontinued in 1998.

COLONIAL OFFICES

	Allahabad	K	Karachi
B	Bombay	L	Lahore
C	Calcutta	M	Madras
	Calicut	R	Rangoon, refer to Myanmar listings
A	Cawnpore		

DENOMINATION LANGUAGE PANELS

 Bengali	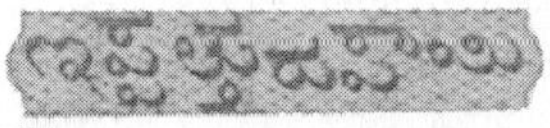 Marathi
 Burmese	 Tamil
 Gujarati	 Telugu
 Gujarati (var.)	 Persian (Farsi)
 Hindi	 Urdu
 Kannada	

SIGNATURE VARIETIES
Governors Of The Reserve Bank Of India

71	Sir C.D. Deshmukh February 1943 - June 1949	72	Sir B. Rama Rue July 1949 - 1957
73	K. G. Ambegoankar January 1957 - February 1957	74	H. V. R. Iengar March 1957 - February 1962
75	P. C. Bhattacharyya March 1962 - June 1967	76	L. K. Jha MJuly 1967 - May 1970
77	B. N. Adarkar May 1970 - June 1970	78	S. Jaganathan May 1970 - June 1970
79	N. C. Sengupta May 1975 - August 1975	80	K. R. Puri August 1975 - May 1975
81	M. Narasimham May 1977-November 1977	82	I. G. Patel December 1977-September 1982
83	Manmohan Singh September 198 January 1984 - February 1985	84	Abhitam Ghosh January 1985 - February 1985
85	R. N. Malhotra February 1985 - December 1990	86	S. Venkitaramanan November 1997 -
87	C. Rangarajan December 1992 - 97 November 1987 - 88	88	Bimal Jalan November 1997 -

Republic of India

Reserve Bank of India

First Series

First Series

Error singular Hindi = *RUPAYA*

Corrected plural Hindi = *RUPAYE*

VARIETIES: #27-28, 33, 38, 42, 46, 48 and 50 have large headings in Hindi expressing the value incorrectly in the singular form as: *Rupaya.*

Note: For similar notes but in different colors, please see the Haj Pilgrim or the Persian Gulf listings at the end of this country listing.

		VF	UNC
27	**2 Rupees** ND. Red-brown on violet and green underprint. Hindi numeral *2* at upper right. Signature 72. Asoka column at right. Large letters in underprint beneath serial number. Back: Tiger head at left. 8 value text lines. Watermark: Asoka column.	75.00	150.
28	**2 Rupees** ND. Red-brown on violet and green underprint. English *2* at upper left and right. Redesigned panels. Asoka column at right. Large letters in underprint beneath serial number. Signature 72. Back: 7 value text lines; third line 18mm long. Watermark: Asoka column.	6.00	16.00

		VF	UNC
29	**2 Rupees** ND. Red-brown on violet and green underprint. Value in English and corrected Hindi on both sides. Asoka column at right. Large letters in underprint beneath serial number. Back: Tiger head at left looking to left, third value text line 24mm long. Watermark: Asoka column.		
	a. Signature 72.	12.00	40.00
	b. Signature 74.	5.00	18.00

		VF	UNC
30	**2 Rupees** ND. Red-brown on green underprint. Value in English and corrected Hindi. Signature 75. Back: Tiger head at left looking to right, with 13 value text lines at center.	9.00	30.00

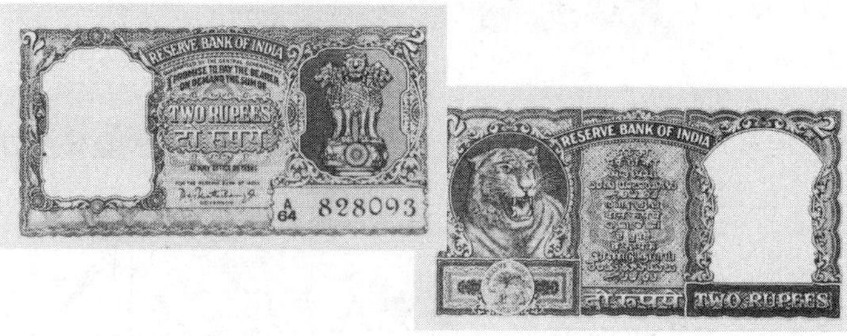

		VF	UNC
31	**2 Rupees** ND. Olive on tan underprint. Value in English and corrected Hindi. Signature 75. Back: Tiger head at left looking to right, with 13 value text lines at center. Watermark: Asoka column.	8.00	25.00

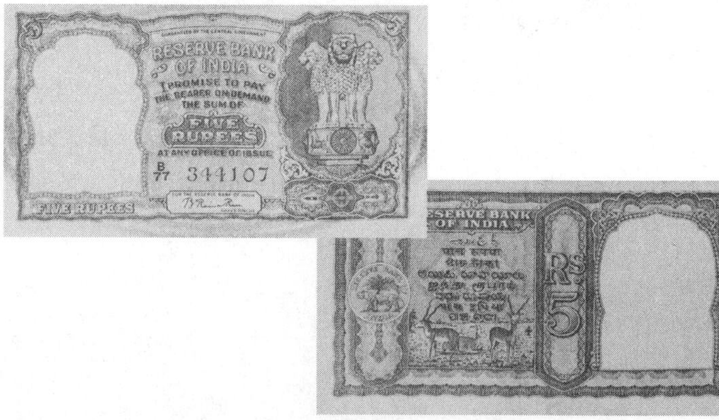

		VF	UNC
32	**5 Rupees** ND. Green on brown underprint. English value only on face, serial number at center. Signature 72. Back: *Rs. 5* and antelope. Watermark: Asoka column.	30.00	125.

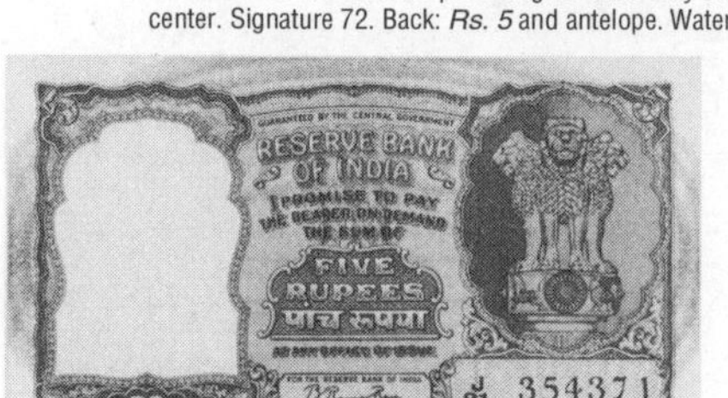

		VF	UNC
33	**5 Rupees** ND. Value in English and error Hindi , serial number at right. Signature 72. Back: 8 value lines; fourth line 21mm long. Watermark: Asoka column.	10.00	35.00

34 5 Rupees — VF / UNC

ND. Hindi corrected. Signature 72. Back: Fourth value text line 26mm long. Watermark: Asoka column. — 35.00 / 150.

35 5 Rupees — VF / UNC

ND. Green on brown underprint. Hindi corrected, redesigned panels at left and right. Asoka columns at right. Large letters in underprint beneath serial number. Watermark: Asoka column.

	VF	UNC
a. Without letter. Signature 74.	10.00	35.00
b. Letter A. Signature 74.	6.00	20.00
c. Letter A. Signature 75.	6.00	20.00
d. Letter B. Signature 75.	6.00	20.00

36 5 Rupees

ND (1962-67). Green on brown underprint. Hindi corrected, redesigned panels at left and right. Asoka column at right. Large letters in underprint beneath serial number. Signature title: *GOVERNOR* centered. Back: Thirteen value text lines. Watermark: Asoka column.

	VF	UNC
a. Letter A. Signature 75.	6.00	20.00
b. Letter B. Signature 75.	7.00	25.00

37 10 Rupees — VF / UNC

ND. Purple on multicolor underprint. English value. Asoka column at right. Large letters in underprint beneath serial number. Back: *Rs. 10* at lower center, 1 serial number. English in both lower corners, dhow at center. Watermark: Asoka column.

	VF	UNC
a. Signature 71.	225.	750.
b. Signature 72.	30.00	125.

38 10 Rupees — VF / UNC

ND. Value in English and error Hindi. Asoka column at right. Large letters in underprint beneath serial number. 2 serial numbers. Signature 72. Back: Third value text line 24mm long. Watermark: Asoka column. — 6.00 / 20.00

39 10 Rupees — VF / UNC

ND. Purple on multicolor underprint. Hindi corrected. Asoka column at right. Large letters in underprint beneath serial number. Back: Third value text line 29mm long. Watermark: Asoka column.

	VF	UNC
a. Without letter. Signature 72.	9.00	30.00
b. Without letter. Signature 74.	9.00	30.00
c. Letter A. Signature 74.	5.00	18.00

40 10 Rupees

ND. Green on brown underprint. Hindi corrected. Asoka column at right. Large letters in underprint beneath serial number. Title: *GOVERNOR* centered. Back: Thirteen value text lines. Watermark: Asoka column.

	VF	UNC
a. Letter A. Signature 75.	7.00	25.00
b. Letter B. Signature 75.	4.50	15.00

41 100 Rupees — VF / UNC

ND. Blue on multicolor underprint. English value. Asoka column at right. Large letters in overprint beneath serial number. Back: Two elephants at center, 8 value text lines below and bank emblem at left. Watermark: Asoka column.

	VF	UNC
a. Dark blue. Signature 72.	140.	375.
b. Light blue. Signature 72.	140.	375.

42 100 Rupees

ND. Purplish-blue on multicolor underprint. Value in English and error Hindi. Asoka column at right. Large letters in underprint beneath serial number. Back: Value in English and error Hindi. 7 value text lines; third 27mm long. Watermark: Asoka column.

	VF	UNC
a. Black serial #. Signature 72.	120.	325.
b. Red serial #. Signature 72.	120.	325.

43 100 Rupees — VF / UNC

ND. Purplish blue on multicolor underprint. Hindi corrected. Asoka column at right. Large letters in underprint beneath serial number. Back: Third value text line 40mm long. Watermark: Asoka column.

	VF	UNC
a. Without letter, thin paper. Signature 72.	120.	325.
b. Without letter, thin paper. Signature 74.	100.	275.
c. Without letter, thick paper. Signature 74.	140.	375.

44 **100 Rupees** — VF | UNC

ND. Purple and multicolor. Heading in rectangle at top, serial numberat upper left and lower right. Asoka column at right. Large letters in underprint beneath serial number. Signature 74. Title: *GOVERNOR* at center right Back: Dam at center with 13 value text lines at left. Watermark: Asoka column. — 90.00 | 250.

45 **100 Rupees**

ND. Violet and multicolor. Heading in rectangle at top, serial numberat upper left and lower right. Asoka column at right. Large letters in underprint beneath serial number. Signature 75. Title: *GOVERNOR* centered. Back: Dam at center with 13 value text lines at left. Watermark: Asoka column. — 90.00 | 250.

46 **1000 Rupees**

ND. Brown on green and blue underprint. Value in English and error Hindi. Asoka column at right. Large letters in underprint beneath serial number. Back: Value in English and error Hindi. Tanjore Temple at center with 7 value text lines at left. Watermark: Asoka column.

	VF	UNC
a. *BOMBAY*. signature 72.	1000.	—
b. *CALCUTTA*. signature 72.	1000.	—
c. *DELHI*. signature 72.	2500.	—
d. *KANPUR*. signature 72.	2000.	—
e. *MADRAS*. signature 72.	2000.	—
s. Like a. Specimen.	—	7000.

47 **1000 Rupees**

ND. Brown on green and blue underprint. Value in English and Hindi corrected. Asoka column at right. Large letters in underprint beneath serial number. Back: Value in English and Hindi corrected. Tanjore Temple at center. Thirteen value text lines. Watermark: Asoka column.

a. *BOMBAY*. Signature 72.	2000.	—
b. *CALCUTTA*. Signature 72.	2000.	—
c. *DELHI*. Signature 72.	4000.	
d. *MADRAS*. Signature 72.	3000.	
e. *BOMBAY*. Signature 74.	4000.	—
f. *BOMBAY*. Signature 75.	3000.	—

48 **5000 Rupees**

ND. Green, violet and brown. Asoka column at left. Value in English and error Hindi. Back: Gateway of India. Value in English and error Hindi.

	VF	UNC
a. *BOMBAY*. Signature 72. Rare.	30,000.	50,000.
b. *CALCUTTA*. Signature 72. Rare.	30,000.	50,000.
c. *DELHI*. Signature 72. Rare.	30,000.	50,000.

49 **5000 Rupees**

ND. Green, violet and brown. Value in English. Hindi corrected. Back: Gateway of India.

a. *BOMBAY*. Signature 74.	30,000.	50,000.
b. *MADRAS*. Signature 74.	30,000.	50,000.
s. As a. Specimen. Red overprint:*SPECIMEN*.	—	17,500.

50 **10,000 Rupees**

ND. Blue, violet and brown. Asoka column at center. Value in English and error Hindi. Back: Value in English and error Hindi.

	VF	UNC
a. *BOMBAY*. Signature 72.	35,000.	60,000.
b. *CALCUTTA*. Signature 72.	35,000.	60,000.
s. As B. Specimen. Signature 72.	—	—

50A **10,000 Rupees**

ND. Asoka column at center. Value in English. Hindi corrected. Back: Value in English. Hindi corrected.

	Fine	XF
a. *BOMBAY*. Signature 74.	45,000.	60,000.
b. *MADRAS*. Signature 74.	45,000.	60,000.
c. *NEW DELHI*. Signature 74.	45,000.	60,000.
d. *BOMBAY*. Signature 76.	45,000.	60,000.

Second Series

Most notes are of reduced size. Large letters found in underprint beneath serial #.

Urd Incorrect

Corrected Urdu (actually Farsi)

51 **2 Rupees** — VF | UNC

ND. Brown and multicolor. Numeral *2* at center 7mm high. Large letters found in underprint beneath serial number. Asoka column at right. Back: Incorrect Urdu inscription at bottom left, tiger at center.

a. Signature 75 with title: *GOVERNOR* centered at bottom.	4.00	14.00
b. Signature 76 with title: *GOVERNOR* at center right	4.00	14.00

52 2 Rupees

	VF	UNC
ND. Deep pink and multicolor. Numeral *2* at center 15mm high. Large letters found in underprint beneath serial number. Asoka column at right. Signature 78. Back: Incorrect Urdu inscription at bottom left, tiger at center.	2.00	8.00

53 2 Rupees

ND. Deep pink and multicolor. English text at left. Large letters found in underprint beneath serial number. Asoka column at right. Back: Corrected Urdu inscription at bottom left, tiger at center.

	VF	UNC
a. Without letter. Signature 78.	1.75	7.00
b. Without letter. Signature 80.	2.00	8.00
c. Letter A. Signature 80.	1.75	7.00
d. Letter A. Signature 82.	1.50	5.00
e. Letter B. Signature 82.	1.50	5.00
f. Letter C. Signature 82.	1.50	5.00
g. Letter C. Signature 83.	1.50	5.00
s. Specimen.	—	300.

53A 2 Rupees

ND. Deep pink and multicolor. English text at right. Large letters found in underprint beneath serial number. Asoka column at right. Smaller size seial number. Back: Corrected Urdu inscription at bottom left, tiger at center.

	VF	UNC
a. Without letter. Signature 83.	1.25	4.50
b. Without letter. Signature 84.	4.00	12.50
c. Letter A. Signature 85.	1.25	4.50
d. Letter B. Signature 85.	1.25	4.50
e. Letter B. Signature 86.	1.25	4.50

54 5 Rupees

ND. Green and multicolor. Numeral *5* at center 11mm high. Large letters found in underprint beneath serial number. Asoka column at right. Back: Incorrect Urdu inscription at bottom left, antelope at center.

	VF	UNC
a. Signature 75 with title: *GOVERNOR* centered at bottom.	9.00	30.00
b. Signature 76 with title: *GOVERNOR* at center right.	9.00	30.00

55 5 Rupees

	VF	UNC
ND. Dark green on multicolor underprint. Numeral *5* at center 17mm high. Large letters found in underprint beneath serial number. Asoka column at right. Signature 78. Back: Incorrect Urdu inscription at bottom left, antelope at center.	7.00	25.00

56 5 Rupees

ND. Dark green on multicolor underprint. Numeral *5* at center 17mm high. Large letters found in underprint beneath serial number. Asoka column at right. Back: Corrected Urdu inscription at bottom left, antelope at center.

	VF	UNC
a. Without letter. Signature 78.	6.00	20.00
b. Letter A. Signature 78.	6.00	20.00

57 10 Rupees

ND. Purple and multicolor. Numeral *10* at center 30mm broad. Large letters found in underprint beneath serial number. Asoka column at right. Back: Dhow at center, incorrect Urdu inscription at bottom left.

	VF	UNC
a. Signature 75 with title: *GOVERNOR* centered at bottom.	6.00	20.00
b. Signature 76 with title: *GOVERNOR* at center right.	6.00	20.00

58 10 Rupees

	VF	UNC
ND. Black on brown and pale green underprint. Numeral *10* at center 18mm broad. Large letters found in underprint beneath serial number. Asoka column at right. Signature 76. Back: Heading in English and Hindi. Incorrect Urdu inscription at bottom left.	8.00	27.50

59 10 Rupees

ND. Dark brown on multicolor underprint. Numeral *10* at center 18mm broad. Large letters found in underprint beneath serial number. Asoka column at right. Back: Dhow at center. Heading in Hindi. Incorrect Urdu inscription at bottom left.

	VF	UNC
a. Without letter. Signature 78.	3.00	10.00
b. Letter A. Signature 78.	3.00	10.00

60 10 Rupees

ND. Dark brown on multicolor underprint. Numeral *10* at center 18mm broad. Large letters found in underprint beneath serial number. Asoka column at right. Back: Heading in Hindi. Corrected Urdu inscription at bottom left.

	VF	UNC
a. Letter A. Signature 78.	4.00	14.00
b. Letter B. Signature 78.	20.00	70.00
c. Letter B. Signature 80.	4.00	14.00
d. Letter B. Signature 81.	1.75	7.00
e. Letter C. Signature 81.	1.75	7.00
f. Letter C. Signature 82.	1.75	7.00
g. Letter D. Signature 82.	1.75	7.00
h. Letter D. Signature 83.	1.75	7.00
i. Letter E. Signature 83.	1.75	7.00
j. Letter E. Signature 84.	1.75	7.00
k. Letter F. Signature 85.	1.75	7.00
l. Letter G. Signature 85.	1.75	7.00

60A 10 Rupees VF UNC

ND. Dark brown on multicolor underprint. Hindi title above *RESERVE BANK OF INDIA* and Hindi text at left of *10* and *I PROMISE...* at right. Sanskrit title added under Asoka column at right. Back: Dhow at center.

	VF	UNC
a. Signature 85.	1.75	7.00
b. Signature 86. Large serial #.	1.75	7.00
c. Signature 86. Small serial #.	1.75	7.00

Incorrect Kashmiri

Corrected Kashmiri (actually Farsi)

61 20 Rupees VF UNC

ND. Orange and multicolor. Large letters found in underprint beneath serial number, Asoka column at right. Signature 78. Back: Parliament House at center.

	VF	UNC
a. Dark colors under signature, error in Kashmiri in fifth line on back.	7.00	25.00
b. Light colors under signature, error in Kashmiri in fifth line on back.	4.00	14.00

61A 20 Rupees VF UNC

ND. Orange and multicolor. Large letters found in underprint beneath serial number, Asoka column at right. Signature 78. Back: Like #61b but corrected Kashmiri in fifth line. 4.00 14.00

62 100 Rupees VF UNC

ND. Blue and multicolor. Numeral *100* at center 43mm broad. Large letters found in underprint beneath serial number. Asoka column at right. Back: Dam at center with only English heading.

	VF	UNC
a. Signature 75.	20.00	70.00
b. Signature 76.	20.00	70.00

63 100 Rupees

ND. Blue and multicolor. Numeral *100* at center 28mm broad. Large letters found in underprint beneath serial number. Asoka column at right. Signature 78. Back: Dam at center with only Hindi heading. 12.50 45.00

64 100 Rupees VF UNC

ND. Blue and multicolor. Numeral *100* at center 28mm broad. Large letters found in underprint beneath serial number. Asoka column at right. Back: Like #63 but corrected Urdu value line.

	VF	UNC
a. Without letter. Signature 78.	12.50	45.00
b. Without letter. Signature 80.	12.50	45.00
c. Without letter. Signature 81.	12.50	45.00
d. Letter A. Signature 82.	12.50	45.00

65 1000 Rupees VF UNC

ND. Brown on multicolor underprint. Text in English and Hindi. Large letters found in underprint beneath serial number. Asoka column at right. *BOMBAY*. at lower right. Back: Temple at center.

	VF	UNC
a. Signature 79.	250.	800.
b. Signature 80.	250.	800.

Government of India

SIGNATURE VARIETIES	
SECRETARIES, MINISTRY OF FINANCE (1 Rupee notes only)	
 K. R. K. Menon, 1944	 A. K. Roy, 1957

SIGNATURE VARIETIES	
SECRETARIES, MINISTRY OF FINANCE (1 Rupee notes only)	
K. G. Ambegaonkar, 1949-1951	L. K. Jha, 1957-1963
H. M. Patel, 1951-1957	

1969 ND Commemorative Issue

#66, Centennial - Birth of M. K. Gandhi

#	Denomination	VF	UNC
66	**1 Rupee** ND (1969-70). Violet and multicolor. Coin with Gandhi and *1869-1948* at right. Signature 82. Back: Reverse of Gandhi coin at left.	2.00	7.00

Reserve Bank of India

1969 ND Commemorative Issue

#67-70, Centennial - Birth of M. K. Gandhi

#	Denomination	VF	UNC
67	**2 Rupees** ND (1969-70). Red-violet and multicolor. Numeral *2* at center 15mm high. Large letters found in underprint beneath serial number. Asoka column at right. Back: Gandhi seated at center.		
	a. Signature 76.	3.00	10.00
	b. Signature 77.	4.00	14.00

#	Denomination	VF	UNC
68	**5 Rupees** ND (1969-70). Dark green on multicolor underprint. Numeral *5* at center 17mm high. Large letters found in underprint beneath serial number. Asoka column at right. Back: Gandhi seated at center.		
	a. Signature 76.	4.50	15.00
	b. Signature 77.	6.00	20.00

#	Denomination	VF	UNC
69	**10 Rupees** ND (1969-70). Brown and multicolor. Numeral *10* at center 18mm broad. Large letters found in underprint beneath serial number. Asoka column at right. Back: Gandhi seated at center.		
	a. Signature 76.	6.00	20.00
	b. Signature 77.	7.00	25.00
	s. Specimen.	—	—

#	Denomination	VF	UNC
70	**100 Rupees** ND (1969-70). Blue and multicolor. Numeral *100* at center 28mm broad. Large letters found in underprint beneath serial number. Asoka column at right. Back: Gandhi seated at center.		
	a. Signature 76.	40.00	140.
	b. Signature 77.	40.00	140.
	s. Specimen.	—	—

Government of India

1957; 1963 Issue

#	Denomination	VF	UNC
75	**1 Rupee** 1957. Violet on multicolor underprint. Redesigned coin with Asoka column at right. Back: Coin dated 1957 and *100 Naye Paise* in Hindi, 7 value text lines. Watermark: Asoka column.		
	a. Letter A. Signature H. M. Patel with signature title: *SECRETARY...* (1957).	2.00	10.00
	b. Letter A. Signature H. M. Patel with signature title: *PRINCIPAL SECRETARY...* 1957.	3.00	12.00
	c. Letter B. Signature A. K. Roy. 1957.	1.00	4.00
	d. Letter B. Signature L. K. Jha. 1957.	50.00	125.
	e. Letter C. Signature L. K. Jha. 1957.	.60	3.00
	f. Letter D. Signature L. K. Jha. 1957.	.60	3.00

#	Denomination	VF	UNC
76	**1 Rupee** 1963-65. Violet on multicolor underprint. Redesigned note. Back: Coin with various dates and *1 Rupee* in Hindi, thirteen value text lines.		
	a. Letter A. Signature 35. 1963.	2.50	9.00
	b. Letter B. Signature 36. 1964.	35.00	120.
	c. Letter B. Signature 36. 1965.	2.50	9.00

#	Denomination	VF	UNC
77	**1 Rupee** 1966-80. Violet on multicolor underprint. Redesigned note, serial number at left. Back: Coin with various dates.		
	a. Without letter. Signature 36. 1966.	2.50	9.00
	b. Letter A. Signature 37. 1967.	4.00	14.00
	c. Letter A. Signature 37. 1968.	3.50	12.00
	d. Letter B. Signature 38 with signature title: *SPECIAL SECRETARY...* 1968.	1.75	7.00
	e. Letter B. Signature 38 with signature title: *SPECIAL SECRETARY...* 1969.	1.75	7.00
	f. Letter C. Signature 38 with title: *SPECIAL SECRETARY...* 1969.	1.75	7.00
	g. Letter C. Signature 38. 1970.	1.75	7.00
	h. Letter C. Signature 38. 1971.	1.75	7.00
	i. Letter D. Signature 38. 1971.	1.75	7.00

	VF	UNC
j. Letter D. Signature 38. 1972.	1.75	7.00
k. Letter E. Signature 38. 1972.	1.75	7.00
l. Letter E. Signature 39. 1973.	1.75	7.00
m. Letter F. Signature 39. 1973.	1.75	7.00
n. Letter F. Signature 39. 1974.	1.75	7.00
o. Letter G. Signature 39. 1974.	1.25	5.00
p. Letter G. Signature 39. 1975.	1.25	5.00
q. Letter H. Signature 39. 1975.	1.25	5.00
r. Letter H. Signature 39. 1976.	1.25	5.00
s. Letter I. Signature 39. 1976.	1.25	5.00
t. Without letter. Small serial #. Signature 40. 1976.	1.25	5.00
u. Small serial #. Signature 40. 1977.	1.25	5.00
v. Letter A. Signature 40. 1978.	1.25	5.00
w. Letter A. Signature 40. 1979.	1.25	5.00
x. Letter A. Signature 40. 1980.	1.25	5.00
y. Letter A. Signature 41. 1980.	1.25	5.00
z. Letter B. Signature 41. 1980.	1.25	5.00

78 1 Rupee

1981. Purple and violet on light blue, brown and multicolor underprint. Coin with Asoka column at upper right. Back: Offshore oil drilling platform and reverse of coin with date.

	VF	UNC
a. Signature 41. 1981.	1.00	4.00
b. Signature 42. 1981.	1.50	6.00

78A 1 Rupee

1983-1994. Coin with Asoka column at upper right. New coin design. Back: Offshore oil drilling platform and reverse of coin with date. New coin design.

	VF	UNC
a. Signature 43 with title: *SECRETARY...* 1983-85.	1.00	4.00
b. Signature 44 with title: *FINANCE SECRETARY...* 1985.	1.00	4.00
c. Letter A. Signature 44. 1986-89.	1.00	4.00
d. Letter B. Signature 45. 1989.	1.25	5.00
e. Letter B. Signature 46. 1990.	1.25	5.00
f. Letter B. Signature 47. 1991.	1.25	5.00
g. Letter B. Signature 48 with title: *SECRETARY...* 1991.	1.25	5.00
h. Letter B. Signature 48. 1992.	1.25	5.00
i. Letter B. Signature 48 with title: *FINANCE SECRETARY...* 1993.	1.25	5.00
j. Letter B. Signature 48. 1994.	1.50	6.00

Reserve Bank of India

Third Series

Large letters in underprint beneath serial #.

79 2 Rupees

ND(1976). Orange on multicolor underprint. Large letters in underprint beneath serial number. Asoka column at right. Back: Space craft at center. Watermark: Asoka column.

	VF	UNC
a. Signature 80.	.75	3.00
b. Signature 81.	.75	3.00
c. Without letter. Without watermark. Signature 82.	.75	3.00
d. Without letter. With watermark: 6 wheels surrounding Asoka column. signature 82.	.75	3.00
e. Letter A. Signature 82.	.75	3.00
f. Letter A. Signature 83.	.75	3.00
g. Letter A. Signature 84.	.75	3.00
h. Letter A. Signature 85.	.75	3.00
i. Letter B. Signature 85.	.75	3.00
j. Without letter. Signature 85 With *Satyameva Jayate* added below the Ashoka Pillar.	.75	3.00
k. Letter A. Signature 85 with *Satyameva Jayate* added below the Ashoka Pillar.	.75	3.00
l. Letter B. Signature 86.	.75	3.00
m. Letter B. Signature 87.	.75	3.00

80 5 Rupees

ND(1975). Grayish green on light blue and orange underprint. Large letters in underprint beneath serial number. Asoka column at right. Back: Farmer plowing with tractor at center. Watermark: Asoka column.

	VF	UNC
a. Without letter. Signature 78.	2.00	8.00
b. Without letter. Signature 80.	1.50	6.00
c. Letter A. Signature 80.	1.00	4.00
d. Letter A. Signature 81.	1.00	4.00
e. Letter A. Signature 82.	1.00	4.00
f. Letter B. Signature 82.	1.00	4.00
g. Letter C. Signature 82.	1.00	4.00
h. Letter C. Signature 83.	1.00	4.00
i. Letter D. Signature 83.	1.00	4.00
j. Letter D. Signature 84.	1.00	4.00
k. Letter D. Signature 85.	1.00	4.00
l. Letter E. Signature 85.	1.00	4.00
m. Letter F. Signature 85.	1.00	4.00
n. Letter G. Signature 85.	1.00	4.00
o. Without letter. New Seal in Hindi & English. Signature 85.	1.00	4.00
p. Letter A. New Seal - do - Signature 85.	1.00	4.00
q. Letter B. Signature 86.	1.00	4.00
r. Letter B. Signature 87.	1.00	4.00
s. Without letter. Signature 88.	.75	3.00

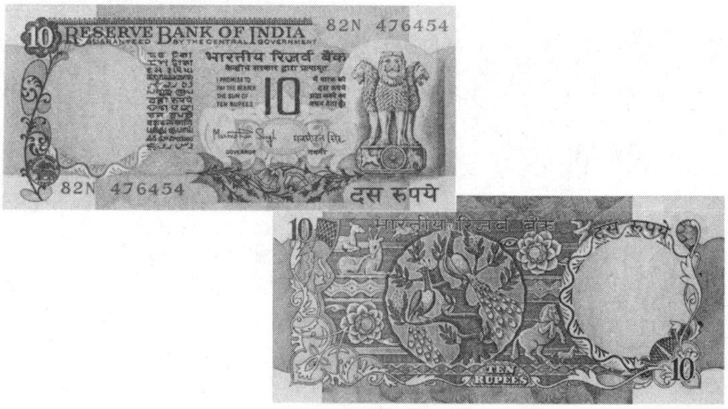

81 10 Rupees

ND. Brown on multicolor underprint. Large letters in inprint beneath serial number. Asoka column at right. Back: Tree with peacocks at center. Watermark: Asoka column. 137x63mm.

	VF	UNC
a. Without letter. Signature 78.	3.50	12.50
b. Without letter. Signature 80.	3.50	12.50
c. Without letter. Signature 81.	6.00	20.00
d. Letter A. Signature 82.	2.50	8.00
e. Without letter. Signature 82.	2.50	8.00
f. Letter A. Signature 83.	2.50	8.00
g. Letter B. Signature 85.	2.50	8.00
h. Letter C. Signature 85.	2.50	8.00

82 20 Rupees

ND. Red and purple on multicolor underprint. Large letters in inprint beneath serial number. Asoka column at right. Back: Orange on multicolor underprint. Hindu Wheel of Time at lower center. Watermark: Asoka column. 147x63mm.

	VF	UNC
a. Signature 78.	10.00	35.00
b. Signature 80.	2.75	9.00
c. Signature 81.	20.00	70.00
d. Without letter. Signature 82.	7.00	25.00

	VF	UNC
e. Letter A. Signature 82.	2.75	9.00
f. Letter A. Signature 83.	2.75	9.00
g. Letter A. Signature 85.	2.75	9.00
h. Letter B. Signature 85.	2.75	9.00
i. Letter B. Signature 87.	2.50	8.00
j. Letter C. Signature 87.	2.50	8.00
k. Letter C. Signature 88.	2.50	8.00
l. Letter C. Signature 89.	2.50	8.00

83 50 Rupees

ND(1975). Black and purple on lilac and multicolor underprint. Large letters in inprint beneath serial number. Asoka column at right. Back: Parliament House at center without flag at top of flagpole. Watermark: Asoka column. 147x73mm

	VF	UNC
a. Signature 78.	6.00	20.00
b. Signature 80.	4.50	15.00
c. Signature 81.	10.00	35.00
d. Signature 82.	4.00	14.00

84 50 Rupees

ND(1978). Black and purple on orange, lilac and multicolor underprint. Large letters in inprint beneath serial number. Asoka column at right. Back: Parliament House at center with flag at top of flagpole. Watermark: Asoka column. 147x73mm.

	VF	UNC
a. Signature 82.	3.50	12.50
b. Signature 83.	3.50	12.50
c. Signature 85.	3.50	12.50
d. Letter A. Signature 85.	3.50	12.50
e. Letter B. Signature 85.	3.50	12.50
f. Letter A. Signature 86.	3.00	10.00
g. Letter B. Signature 86.	3.00	10.00
h. Letter A. Signature 87.	2.75	9.00
i. Letter B. Signature 87.	2.75	9.00
j. Letter C. Signature 87.	2.75	9.00
k. Without letter. Signature 87. Requires confirmation.	—	—
l. Letter B. Signature 88.	2.75	9.00

85 100 Rupees

ND(1975). Black and blue-violet on brown and multicolor underprint (tan at center). Large letters in inprint beneath serial number. Asoka column at right. Denomination above bar at lower right. Black signature. Back: Dam, agricultural work at center. Watermark: Asoka column. 157x73mm.

	VF	UNC
a. Signature 78.	45.00	150.
b. Signature 80.	12.00	40.00
c. Signature 81.	20.00	65.00
d. Signature 82.	12.00	30.00

85A 100 Rupees — VF 12.00, UNC 30.00

ND. Black and blue-violet on brown and multicolor underprint (tan at center). Like #85 but without bar under denomination at lower right. Signature 85. Back: Dam, agricultural work at center. Watermark: Asoka column. 157x73mm.

86 100 Rupees

ND(1979). Black, deep red and purple on multicolor underprint, (pink at center). Like #85 but without bar under denomination at lower right. Signature 85. Deep red signature. Back. Dam, agricultural work at center. Watermark: Asoka column. 157x73mm.

	VF	UNC
a. Signature 82.	12.00	30.00
b. Signature 83.	12.00	30.00
c. Signature 85.	10.00	27.50
d. Signature 86.	7.00	20.00
e. Letter A. Signature 86.	7.00	20.00
f. Without letter. Signature 87.	7.00	20.00
g. Letter A. Signature 87.	7.00	20.00
h. Letter B. Signature 87.	9.00	25.00

87 **500 Rupees**

ND (1987). Brown, deep blue-green and deep blue on multicolor underprint. M. K. Gandhi at center right. Electronic sorting marks at lower left. Large letters in underprint beneath serial number. Asoka column at right. Back: Gandhi leading followers across. Watermark: Asoka column. 167x73mm.

	VF	UNC
a. Signature 85.	30.00	75.00
b. Signature 86.	27.50	70.00
c. Signature 87.	25.00	65.00

1992 Issue

88 **10 Rupees**

ND (1992). Dull brown-violet on orange, green and multicolor underprint. Large letters in underprint beneath serial number. Asoka column at right. Back: Red-violet. Rural temple at left center. Watermark: Asoka column. 137x63mm.

	VF	UNC
a. Signature 86.	1.25	4.00
b. Letter A. Signature 86.	1.25	4.00
c. Letter A. Signature 87.	1.25	4.00
d. Letter B. Signature 87.	1.25	4.00
e. Letter C. Signature 87.	1.25	4.00
f. Letter D. Signature 87.	1.25	3.00
g. Letter E. Signature 87.	1.25	3.00

1996-2002 ND Issue

#89-93 Starting in 1999 the name was spelled out as Mahatma Gandhi.

88A **5 Rupees**

ND(2002)-2011. Green-orange on multicolor underprint. Mahatma Gandhi at right, Reserve Bank seal at lower right. Back: Farmer plowing with tractor at center. Watermark: Mahatma Gandhi.

	VF	UNC
a. Without letter. Signature 88.	FV	2.50
b. Letter L. Signature 88.	FV	2.50
c. Letter R. Signature 88.	FV	2.50
d. Without letter. Signature 89.	FV	2.50
e. Letter L. Signature 89.	FV	2.50
f. Letter R. Signature 89.	FV	2.50
g. 2010.	FV	2.50
h. 2011. Letter R.	FV	2.50

89 **10 Rupees**

ND (1996). Pale brown-violet on multicolor underprint. Mahatma Gandhi at right, Reserve Bank seal at lower right. Back: Ornamented rhinoceros and elephant heads behind tiger at left center. Watermark: Mahatma Gandhi. 137x63mm.

	VF	UNC
a. Without letter. Signature 87.	1.25	3.00
b. Letter L; M; R. Signature 87.	1.25	3.00
c. Letter R; N; A; P; Q; S; T; L; B; M. Signature 88.	1.25	3.00
d. Without letter. Signature 89.	1.25	3.00
e. Letter A, R. Signature 89.	1.25	3.00

89A **20 Rupees**

ND(2002). Red-orange on multicolor underprint. Mahatma Gandhi at right, Reserve Bank seal at lower right. Back: Coconut trees. Watermark: Mahatma Gandhi. 147x63mm.

	VF	UNC
a. Without letter. Signature 88.	FV	4.00
b. Letter A; R. Signature 88.	FV	4.00
c. Without letter. Signature 89.	FV	4.00
d. Letter A; R. Signature 89.	FV	4.00

90 **50 Rupees**

ND (1997). Black and purple on multicolor underprint. Mahatma Gandhi at right, Reserve Bank seal at lower right. Back: Parliament house at left center. Watermark: Mahatma Gandhi. 147x73mm.

	VF	UNC
a. Without letter. Signature 87.	FV	6.00
b. Without letter. Signature 88.	FV	5.00
c. Letter A. Signature 88.	FV	5.00
d. Letter R. Signature 88.	FV	5.00
e. Letter A. Signature 88.	FV	5.00
f. Letter E. Signature 88.	FV	5.00
g. Letter L. Signature 88.	FV	5.00
h. Without letter. Signature 89.	FV	5.00
i. Letter A. Signature 89.	FV	5.00
j. Letter E. Signature 89.	FV	5.00
k. Letter R. Signature 89.	FV	5.00

91 **100 Rupees**

ND (1996). Black, purple and dark olive-green on pale blue-green and multicolor underprint. Mahatma Gandhi at right, Reserve Banl seal at lower right. Back: Himalaya mountains at left center. Watermark: Mahatma Gandhi. Segmented foil over security thread. 157x73mm.

	VF	UNC
a. Without letter. Signature 87.	2.50	9.00
b. Letter E. Signature 87.	2.50	9.00
c. Letter L. Signature 87.	2.50	9.00
d. Letter A. Signature 87.	FV	8.00
e. Letter L. Signature 88.	FV	8.00
f. Letter E. Signature 88.	FV	8.00
g. Without letter. Signature 88.	FV	8.00
h. Letter R. Signature 88.	FV	8.00
i. Letter F. Signature 88.	FV	8.00
j. Letter B. Signature 88.	FV	8.00
k. Without letter. Signature 89.	FV	8.00
l. Letter L. Signature 89.	FV	8.00
m. Letter R. Signature 89.	FV	8.00

92	500 Rupees	VF	UNC
	ND (1997). Dark brown, olive-green and purple on multicolor underprint. Mahatma Gandhi at right, Reserve Bank seal at lower right. Back: Gandhi leading followers across. Watermark: Mahatma Gandhi. Segmented foil over security thread. 167x73mm.		
	a. Without letter. Signature 87.	FV	50.00
	b. Without letter. Signature 88.	FV	50.00
	c. Letter A. Signature 88.	FV	50.00
	d. Letter C. Signature 88.	FV	50.00

2000-02 ND Issue

93	500 Rupees	VF	UNC
	ND (2000-02). Pale yellow, mauve and brown. Mahatma Gandhi at right, Reserve Bank seal at lower right. Value at center in optical variable ink. Back: Gandhi leading followers. Watermark: Mahatma Gandhi. 167x73mm.		
	a. Without letter. Signature 88.	FV	40.00
	b. Letter A. Signature 88.	FV	40.00
	c. Letter B. Signature 88.	FV	40.00
	d. Letter C. Signature 88.	FV	40.00
	e. Without letter. Signature 89.	FV	37.50
	f. Letter A. Signature 89.	FV	37.50
	g. Letter B. Signature 89.	FV	37.50
	h. Letter C. Signature 89.	FV	37.50

94	1000 Rupees	VF	UNC
	ND (2000). Pink and gray. Mahatma Gandhi at right, Reserve Bank seal at lower right. Back: Brown, red and black. Allegory of Indian economy. 177x73mm.		
	a. Without letter. Signature 88.	FV	75.00
	b. Letter A. Signature 88.	FV	75.00
	c. Without letter. Signature 89.	FV	75.00
	d. Letter A. Signature 89.	FV	75.00

2005; 2006 Issue

94A	5 Rupees	VF	UNC
	2009-. Green on orange underprint. Mahatma Gandi at right. Back: Farmer plowing with tractor at center. Watermark: Mahatma Gandhi	FV	2.50

95	10 Rupees	VF	UNC
	2006-. Pale brown-violet on multicolor underprint. Mahatma Gandhi at right. Back: Tiger, rhino and elephant. 137x63mm.		
	a. 2006. Signature Y. V. Reddy.	FV	1.00
	b. 2006. Letter L.	FV	1.00
	c. 2007.	FV	1.00
	d. 2007. Letter M.	FV	1.00
	e. 2008.	FV	1.00
	f. 2008. Letter M.	FV	1.00
	g. 2008. Letter N.	FV	1.00
	h. 2008. Signature D. Subarao.	FV	.75
	i. 2008. Letter R.	FV	.75
	j. 2009.	FV	.75
	k. 2009. Letter L.	FV	.75
	l. 2009. Letter P.	FV	.75
	m. 2009. Letter R.	FV	.75
	n. 2010.	FV	.75
	o. 2010. Letter M.	FV	.75
	p. 2010. Letter R.	FV	.75
	q. 2010. Letter S.	FV	.75
	r. 2011. Letter A.	FV	.75
	s. 2011. Letter B.	FV	.75
	t. 2011. Letter N.	FV	.75
	u. 2011. Letter P.	FV	.75
	v. 2011. Letter S.	FV	.75

96	20 Rupees	VF	UNC
	2006-. Red-orange on multicolor underprint. Mahatma Gandhi at right. Back: Coconut trees. 147x63mm.		
	a. 2006. Signature Y. V. Reddy.	FV	1.50
	b. 2007.	FV	1.50
	c. 2008.	FV	1.50
	d. 2009. Signature D. Subarao.	FV	1.00
	e. 2009. Letter E.	FV	1.00
	f. 2009. Letter R.	FV	1.00
	g. 2010	FV	1.00
	h. 2010. Letter E.	FV	1.00
	i. 2010. Letter R.	FV	1.00
	j. 2011.	FV	1.00
	k. 2011. Letter E.	FV	1.00
	l. 2011. Letter F.	FV	1.00
	m. 2011. Letter R.	FV	1.00
	n. 2012.	FV	1.00
	o. 2012. Letter E.	FV	1.00
	p. 2012. Letter F.	FV	1.00
	q. 2012. Letter R.	FV	1.00

97	50 Rupees	VF	UNC
	2005-2011. Black and purple on multicolor underprint. Mahatma Gandhi at right. Back: Parliament house at left center. 147x73mm.		
	a. 2005. Signature Y. V. Reddy.	FV	2.50
	b. 2006.	FV	2.00
	c. 2007.	FV	2.00
	d. 2008.	FV	1.50
	e. 2008. Letter E.	FV	1.50
	f. 2009. Signature D. Subarao.	FV	1.50
	g. 2009. Letter E.	FV	1.50
	h. 2009. Letter R.	FV	1.50
	i. 2010.	FV	1.50
	j. 2010. Letter E.	FV	1.50

	VF	UNC
k. 2010. Letter L.	FV	1.50
l. 2010. Letter R.	FV	1.50
m. 2011.	FV	1.50
n. 2011. Letter L.	FV	1.50
o. 2011. Letter R.	FV	1.50
p. 2012.	FV	1.50
q. 2012. Letter L.	FV	1.50
r. 2012. Letter R.	FV	1.50

98 100 Rupees

2005-. Black, purple and dark olive-green on pale blue-green and multicolor underprint. Mahatma Gandhi at right. Back: Himalaya mountains at left center. 157x73mm.

	VF	UNC
a. 2005. Signature Y. V. Reddy.	FV	5.00
b. 2006.	FV	5.00
c. 2007.	FV	3.50
d. 2008.	FV	3.50
e. 2009. Signature D. Subarao.	FV	3.00
f. 2009. Letter F.	FV	3.00
g. 2009. Letter R.	FV	2.75
h. 2010.	FV	2.75
i. 2010. Leter F.	FV	2.75
j. 2010. Letter R.	FV	2.75
k. 2011.	FV	2.75
l. 2011. Letter F.	FV	2.75
m. 2011. Letter L.	FV	2.75
n. 2011. Letter R.	FV	2.75

99 500 Rupees

2006-. Multicolor. Mahatma Gandhi at right. Back: Gandhi leading followers. 167x73mm.

	VF	UNC
a. 2006.	FV	20.00
b. 2007.	FV	20.00
c. 2008. Letter R.	FV	17.50
d. 2009.	FV	17.50
e. 2010. Letter R.	FV	17.50

100 1000 Rupees

2006-10. Pink and grey. Mahatma Gandhi at right. Back: Allegory of Indian economy. 177x73mm.

	VF	UNC
a. 2006.	FV	40.00
b. 2007.	FV	35.00
c. 2008.	FV	30.00
d. 2009. Letter L.	FV	30.00
e. 2009. Letter R.	FV	30.00
f. 2010.	FV	30.00
g. 2010. Letter L.	FV	30.00

2011 Issue, New Rupee Symbol

101 5 Rupees

	VF	UNC
2011. Green-orange on multicolor underprint. Mahatma Gandhi at right. Back: Farmer plowing with tractor at center.	FV	2.50

102 10 Rupees

2011-. Pale brown-violet on multicolor underprint. Mahatma Gandhi at right. Back: Tiger, rhino and elephant. 137x63mm.

	VF	UNC
a. 2011.	FV	.75
b. 2011. Letter R.	FV	.75
c. 2012.	FV	.75
d. 2012. Letter L.	FV	.75
e. 2012. Letter P.	FV	.75

103 20 Rupees

2012-. Orange and red brown on multicolor underprint. Mahatma Gandhi at right. Back: Landscape with coconut trees. 147x63mm.

	VF	UNC
a. 2012.	FV	1.25
b. 2012. Letter R.	FV	1.25

104 50 Rupees

Lilac and purple on yellow and multicolor udnerprint. Mahatma Gandhi at right. Back: Parliament house. 147x73mm.

	VF	UNC
a. 2012.	FV	2.00

105 **100 Rupees** VF UNC

2011-. Black, purple and dark olive-green on pale blue-green and multicolor underprint. Mahatma Gandhi at right. Back: Himalaya mountains at left center. Watermark: Mahatma Gandhi. 157x73mm.

a. 2011.	FV	3.50
b. 2011. Letter R.	FV	3.50
c. 2012.	FV	3.50
d. 2012. Letter L.	FV	3.50
e. 2012. Letter R.	FV	3.50

106 **500 Rupees** VF UNC

2011-. Brown on multicolor underprint. Mahatma Gandhi at right. Back: Gandhi leading folowers. Watermark: Mahatma Gandhi. 167x73mm.

a. 2012.	FV	17.50
b. 2012. Letter R.	FV	17.50

107 **1000 Rupees** VF UNC

2011-. Slate black on multicolor underprint. Mahatma Gandhi at right. Back: Allegory of the development of the Indian economy. Watermark: Mahatma Gandhi 177x73mm.

a. 2011.	FV	30.00

The Republic of Indonesia, the world's largest archipelago, extends for more than 4,827 km. along the equator from the mainland of southeast Asia to Australia. The 13,667 islands comprising the archipelago have a combined area of 1,919,440 sq. km. and a population of 237.5 million, including East Timor. Capital: Jakarta. Petroleum, timber, rubber and coffee are exported.

The Dutch began to colonize Indonesia in the early 17th century; the islands were occupied by Japan from 1942 to 1945. Indonesia declared its independence after Japan's surrender, but it required four years of intermittent negotiations, recurring hostilities, and UN mediation before the Netherlands agreed to relinquish its colony. Indonesia is the world's largest archipelagic state and home to the world's largest Muslim population. Current issues include: alleviating poverty, preventing terrorism, consolidating democracy after four decades of authoritarianism, implementing financial sector reforms, stemming corruption, holding the military and police accountable for human rights violations, and controlling avian influenza. In 2005, Indonesia reached a historic peace agreement with armed separatists in Aceh, which led to democratic elections in December 2006. Indonesia continues to face a low intensity separatist movement in Papua.

MONETARY SYSTEM:

1 Rupiah = 100 Sen, 1945-

Republic

Republik Indonesia

1961 Issue

78 **1 Rupiah** VF UNC

1961. Dark green on orange underprint. Rice field workers at left. Back: Farm produce. .25 .75

79 **2 1/2 Rupiah** VF UNC

1961. Black, dark blue and brown on blue-green underprint. Corn field work at left. .25 .75

1961 Borneo Issue

79A **1 Rupiah** VF UNC

1961. Green on orange underprint. President Sukarno at left. Back: Javanese dancers at right. 4.00 10.00

79B **2 1/2 Rupiah** — VF 4.00 — UNC 10.00
1961. Blue on gray-brown underprint. President Sukarno at left. Back: Javanese dancers at right.

1964 Issue (1960 Dated)

No.	Denomination	VF	UNC
80	**1 Rupiah**		
	1964. Black, red and brown. President Sukarno at left. Back: Javanese dancer at right. Watermark: Arms at center.		
	a. Imprint: *Pertjetakan Kebajoran* at bottom center on face.	1.00	3.00
	b. Without imprint.	2.00	6.00
	c. Imprint: *PN Pertjetakan Kebahjoran.*	4.00	10.00
81	**2 1/2 Rupiah**		
	1964. Black, blue and brown. President Sukarno at left. Watermark: Arms at center.		
	a. Imprint like #80a.	2.50	7.50
	b. Without imprint.	3.00	8.00
82	**5 Rupiah**		
	1960. Lilac on yellow underprint. President Sukarno at left. Back: Female dancer at right.		
	a. Watermark: Sukarno.	1.50	5.00
	b. Watermark: Water buffalo.	.60	6.00

Bank Indonesia

1960 Dated (1964) Issue

No.	Denomination	VF	UNC
83	**10 Rupiah**		
	1960. Green on light blue underprint. President Sukarno at left. Back: Two female dancers. Watermark: Sukarno.	2.00	6.50

No.	Denomination	VF	UNC
84	**25 Rupiah**		
	1960. Green on yellow underprint. President Sukarno at left. Back: Female dancer. Watermark: Sukarno.		
	a. Printer: TDLR. Watermark: Sukarno. 3 Letter varieties.	4.00	10.00
	b. Printer: Pertjetakan. Watermark: Water buffalo.	4.00	10.00

No.	Denomination	VF	UNC
85	**50 Rupiah**		
	1960. Dark blue on light blue underprint. President Sukarno at left. Back: Female dancer and two men.		
	a. Printer: TDLR. Watermark: Sukarno. 3 Letter varieties.	8.00	20.00
	b. Printer: Pertjetakan. Watermark: Water buffalo.	4.50	12.50

No.	Denomination	VF	UNC
86	**100 Rupiah**		
	1960. Red-brown. President Sukarno at left. Back: Batak Man and woman dancer.		
	a. Printer: Pertjetakan. Watermark: Sukarno.	10.00	22.50
	b. Watermark: Water buffalo. Requires confirmation.	—	—

No.	Denomination	VF	UNC
87	**500 Rupiah**		
	1960. Black on green underprint. President Sukarno at left. Back: Two Javanese dancers.		
	a. Printer: TDLR. Watermark: Sukarno. 3 Letter varieties.	15.00	75.00
	b. Printer: Pertjetakan. Watermark: Sukarno.	15.00	75.00
	c. Printer like b. Watermark: Water buffalo.	15.00	75.00
	d. Printer like b. Watermark: Arms.	20.00	80.00
	s. Specimen. As a.	—	—

88 1000 Rupiah — VF / UNC

1960. Dark green on yellow. President Sukarno at left. Back: Two Javanese dancers.

	VF	UNC
a. Printer: TDLR. Watermark: Sukarno. 3 Letter varieties.	60.00	175.
b. Printer: Pertjetakan. Watermark: Water buffalo.	40.00	125.

88A 5000 Rupiah — VF / UNC

1960. Back: Grey and pink on multicolor underprint. Female dancer at right. Printer: TDLR.

	VF	UNC
p. Uniface back proof.	—	—

1963 Issue

89 10 Rupiah — VF .50 / UNC 1.50

1963. Pale blue and brown on multicolor underprint. Balinese wood carver at left. Back: Balinese houses at center, mythical figure at right. Watermark: Water buffalo.

1964 Issue

90 1 Sen — VF / UNC

1964. Green-blue and brown. Peasant with straw hat at right.

	VF	UNC
a. Issued note.	.05	.10
s. Specimen. Serial # prefix *X*.	—	15.00

91 5 Sen — VF / UNC

1964. Lilac-brown. Female volunteer in uniform at right.

	VF	UNC
a. Issued note.	.05	.10
s. Specimen. Serial # prefix *X*.	—	15.00

92 10 Sen — VF / UNC

1964. Dark blue on yellow-green underprint. Female volunteer in uniform at right.

	VF	UNC
a. Issued note.	.05	.10
s. Specimen. Serial # prefix *X*.	—	15.00

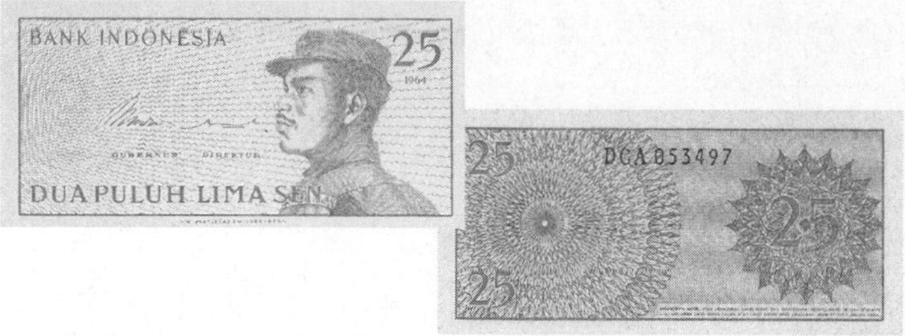

93 25 Sen — VF / UNC

1964. Red on yellow-green underprint. A volunteer man in uniform at right.

	VF	UNC
a. Issued note.	.05	.15
s. Specimen. Serial # prefix *X*.	—	15.00

94 50 Sen — VF / UNC

1964. Purple and red. A volunteer man in uniform at right.

	VF	UNC
a. Issued note.	.10	.25
s. Specimen. Serial # prefix *X*.	—	15.00

95 25 Rupiah — VF / UNC

1964. Green on light brown underprint. Batak woman weaver at left, printed arms in brown at right. Back: Batak house at center.

	VF	UNC
a. Issued note.	.50	2.00
s. Specimen. Serial # prefix *X*.	—	15.00

96 50 Rupiah — VF .50 / UNC 1.50

1964. Black-green on aqua underprint. Timor woman spinner at left, printed arms in pale green at right. Back: Rice barns at center.

97 **100 Rupiah** VF UNC

1964. Red on light tan underprint. Rubber tapper at left. Back: Kalimantan house at center. Watermark: Water buffalo.

		VF	UNC
a.	Printer's name: *P. T. Pertjetakan Kebajoran Imp.* 16mm. long at right on back. 2 Serial # prefix letter type varieties.	2.00	6.00
b.	Printer's name: *PN Pertjetakan Kebajoran Imp.* 22mm. long at right on back.	1.25	4.00

98 **100 Rupiah** VF UNC

1964. Blue on light tan underprint. Rubber tapper at left. Back: Kalimantan house at center. Printer's name: *PN Pertjetakan Kebajoran Imp.* 22mm long at right. Watermark: Water buffalo. 1.50 5.00

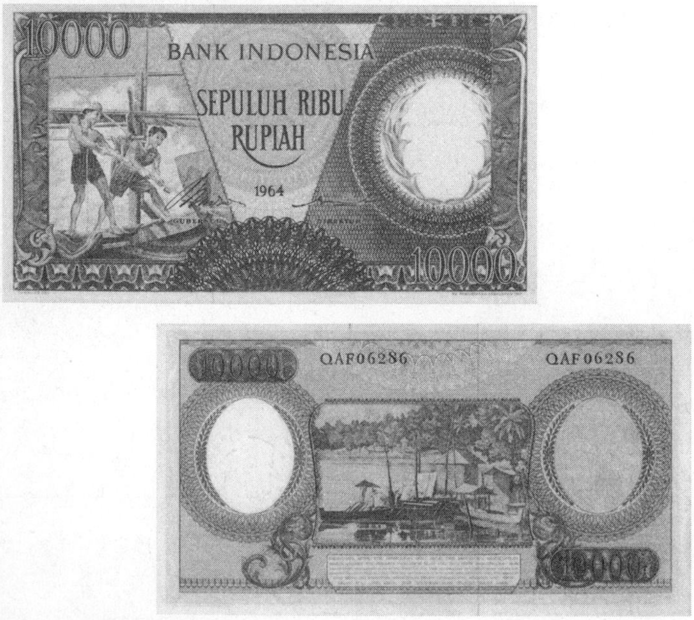

99 **10,000 Rupiah** VF UNC

1964. Red and dark brown on multicolor underprint. Two fishermen at left. Back: Floating houses on Barito river at center. Watermark: Water buffalo. 5.00 20.00

100 **10,000 Rupiah** VF UNC

1964. Green. Two fishermen at left. Back: Floating houses at center. Watermark: Water buffalo. 3.00 10.00

101 **10,000 Rupiah** VF UNC

1964. Green. Two fishermen at left. Back: Floating houses at center, with printed arms in pale green at right. Watermark: Row of arms.

		VF	UNC
a.	Watermark in paper at center.	10.00	25.00
b.	Watermark in paper at left and right.	10.00	25.00

1968 Issue

102 **1 Rupiah** VF UNC

1968. Light red on light blue and purple underprint. General Sudirman at left. Arms at right. Back: Woman collecting copra at left. Watermark: Arms at center.

		VF	UNC
a.	Issued note.	.75	2.25
s.	Specimen. Serial # prefix *X*.	—	15.00

103 2 1/2 Rupiah VF UNC

1968. Dark blue on light green underprint. General Sudirman at left. Arms at right. Back: Woman gathering paddy rice stalks at left. Watermark: Arms at center.

	VF	UNC
a. Issued note.	.75	2.25
s. Specimen. Serial # prefix *X*.	—	15.00

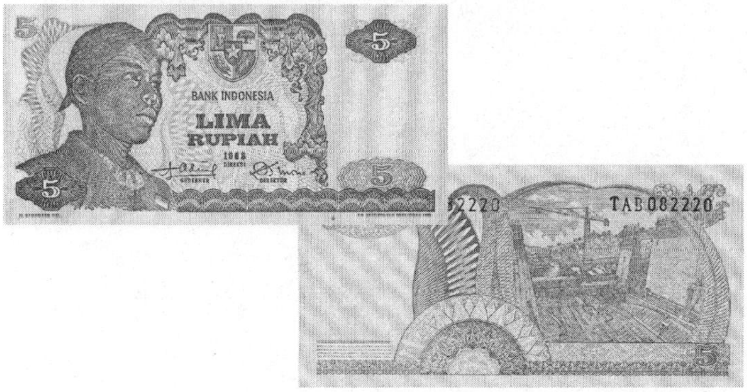

104 5 Rupiah VF UNC

1968. Pale purple on multicolor underprint. General Sudirman at left. Back: Jatiluhur Dam under construction. Watermark: Arms at right upper center.

	VF	UNC
a. Issued note.	1.50	4.50
s. Specimen. Serial # prefix *X*.	—	15.00

105 10 Rupiah VF UNC

1968. Green on multicolor underprint. General Sudirman at left. Back: Oil refinery. Watermark: Arms at upper right center.

	VF	UNC
a. Issued note.	1.00	3.00
s. Specimen. Serial # prefix *X*.	—	15.00

106 25 Rupiah

1968. Dark green on light brown and multicolor underprint. General Sudirman at left. Back: Green. Ampera lift bridge over Musi River at center right. Watermark: Arms at right upper center.

	VF	UNC
a. Issued note.	1.50	4.50
s. Specimen. Serial # prefix *X*.	—	15.00

107 50 Rupiah VF UNC

1968. Purple and dark blue on multicolor underprint. General Sudirman at left. Back: Airplanes in repair hangar at center right. Watermark: Arms at right upper center.

	VF	UNC
a. Issued note.	2.50	7.50
s. Specimen.	—	15.00

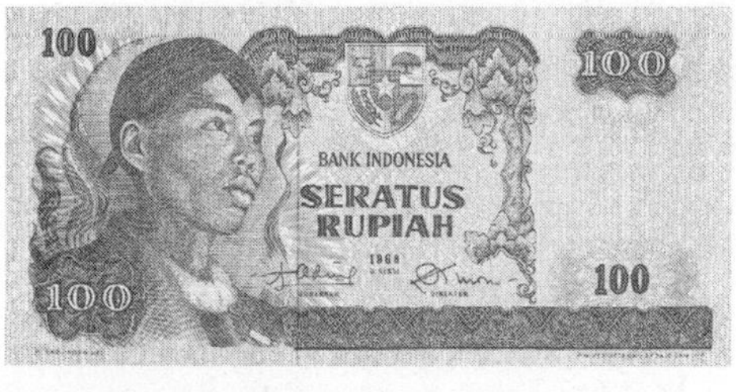

108 100 Rupiah VF UNC

1968. Deep red on multicolor underprint. General Sudirman at left. Back: Coal mining transport facility at the port of Tanjung Priok at center right. Watermark: Arms at right upper center.

	VF	UNC
a. Issued note.	1.50	5.00
s. Specimen. Serial # prefix *X*.	—	15.00

109 500 Rupiah VF UNC

1968. Black and dark green on multicolor underprint. General Sudirman at left. Back: Yarn spinning in cotton mill. Watermark: Arms at right upper center.

	VF	UNC
a. Issued note.	2.50	7.50
s. Specimen.	—	15.00

110 1000 Rupiah VF UNC

1968. Dark orange and black on multicolor underprint. General Sudirman at left. Back: P.T. Pusri fertilizer plant at center right. Watermark: Arms at right upper center.

	VF	UNC
a. Issued note.	3.00	12.00
s. Specimen. Serial # prefix *X*.	—	15.00

		VF	UNC
111	**5000 Rupiah**		
	1968. Blue-green on multicolor underprint. General Sudirman at left. Two serial # varieties. Back: Tonasa cememt plant at center right. Watermark: Prince Diponegoro.		
	a. Issued note.	22.50	70.00
	s1. Specimen. Serial # prefix *X*.	—	80.00
	s2. Specimen. Serial # prefix *DA*.	—	150.

		VF	UNC
112	**10,000 Rupiah**		
	1968. Red-brown and dark brown on multicolor underprint. General Sudirman at left. Two serial # varieties. Back: Purple. Tin mininig facility in Bangla at center right. Watermark: Prince Diponegoro.		
	a. Issued note.	20.00	60.00
	s1. Specimen. Serial # prefix *X*.	—	70.00
	s2. Specimen. Serial # prefix *DA*.	—	150.

1975; ND Issue

		VF	UNC
112A	**100 Rupiah**		
	ND. Red on multicolor underprint. Prince Diponegoro at left. Back: Mountain scene at left center. Watermark: Prince Diponegoro. (Not issued.)		
	a. Normal serial #.	—	—
	s. Specimen.	—	—

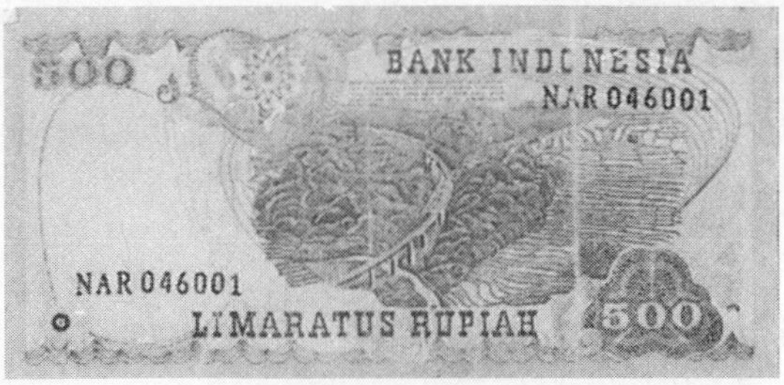

		VF	UNC
112B	**500 Rupiah**		
	ND. Green on multicolor underprint. Prince Diponegoro at left. Back: Terraced rice fields in Sianok Gorge. Watermark: Prince Diponegoro. (Not issued.)		
	a. Normal serial #.	—	—
	s. Specimen.	—	—

		VF	UNC
113	**1000 Rupiah**		
	ND; 1975. Blue-green and blue on multicolor underprint. Prince Diponegoro at left. Back: Farmer plowing in terraced rice fields. .		
	a. 1975. watermark: Majapahit statue.	2.00	7.50
	s1. ND. Specimen. (Not issued.)	—	—
	s2. 1975. Specimen. Serial # prefix *X*.	—	9.00

		VF	UNC
113A	**5000 Rupiah**		
	ND. Brown on multicolor underprint. Prince Diponegoro at right. Back: Three sailing ships. Watermark: Prince Diponegoro. (Not issued.)		
	a. Normal serial #.	—	—
	s. Specimen.	—	—

114 5000 Rupiah VF UNC

1975. Brown and red-brown on multicolor underprint. Fisherman with net at right. Back: Three sailing ships. Watermark: Tjut Njak Din.

	VF	UNC
a. Issued note.	7.50	25.00
s. Specimen. Serial # prefix *X*.	—	—

114A 10,000 Rupiah VF UNC

ND. Green and red on multicolor underprint. Prince Diponegoro at right. Back: Peasants at center. Watermark: Prince Diponegoro. (Not issued.)

	VF	UNC
a. Normal serial #.	—	—
s. Specimen.	—	—

115 10,000 Rupiah VF UNC

1975. Brown, red and multicolor. Stone relief at BorobudurTemple. Back: Large mask from Bali at left. Watermark: General Soedirman. 25.00 75.00

1977 Issue

116 100 Rupiah VF UNC

1977. Red on multicolor underprint. Javanese Rhinoceros at left. Back: Javanese Rhinoceros in jungle scene at center. Watermark: Arms. .50 2.00

117 500 Rupiah VF UNC

1977. Green on pink and multicolor underprint. Woman with orchids at left. Back: Bank of Indonesia at center. Watermark: Bank of Indonesia. 1.00 4.00

1979 Issue

118 10,000 Rupiah VF UNC

1979. Purple on multicolor underprint. Javanese Gamelan Orchestra at center. Back: Prambanan Temple. Watermark: Dr. Soetomo. 9.00 25.00

1980 Issue

119 1000 Rupiah VF UNC

1980. Dark blue on multicolor underprint. Dr. Soetomo at center right. Back: Mountain scene in Sianok Valley. Watermark: Sultan Hasanudin. 1.00 3.50

120 5000 Rupiah VF UNC

1980. Brown on multicolor underprint. Diamond cutter at center. Back: Brown, green and multicolor. Three Torajan houses from Celebes at center.

	VF	UNC
a. Watermark: D. Sartika.	6.00	20.00
p. Proof. Watermark: Prince Diponegoro.	—	—

1982 Issue

121 500 Rupiah

	VF	UNC
1982. Dark green on multicolor underprint. Man standing by Amorphophallus. Titanum giant flower at left. Back: Bank of Indonesia. Watermark: General A. Yani.	.75	2.50

1984-88 Issue

122 100 Rupiah

1984. Red on multicolor underprint. Goura Victoria (Crowned pigeon) at left. Back: Asahan Dam. Watermark: Arms.

	VF	UNC
a. Engraved.	.30	1.25
b. Litho.	.25	.75
s. As a. Specimen. Serial # prefix *X*.	—	15.00

123 500 Rupiah

1988. Brown and dark green on multicolor underprint. Timorese stag at left. Back: Bank of Indonesia Cirebon branch at right. Watermark: General A. Yani.

	VF	UNC
a. Issued note.	.50	1.50
s. Specimen.	—	15.00

124 1000 Rupiah

1987. Blue-black on multicolor underprint. Raja Sisingamangaraja XII at center, arms at left. Back: Yogyakarta Court at center. Watermark: Sultan Hasanuddin.

	VF	UNC
a. Issued note.	1.00	2.00
s. Specimen.	—	15.00

125 5000 Rupiah

1986. Dark brown on multicolor underprint. Teuku Umar at center. Back: Minaret of Kudus mosque at right. Watermark: C. Martha Tijahahu.

	VF	UNC
a. Issued note.	3.50	10.00
s. Specimen.	—	15.00

126 10,000 Rupiah

1985. Purple on multicolor underprint. R. A. Kartini at left. Prambanan Temple in background. Back: Female graduate at center right. Watermark: Dr. T. Mangoenkoesoemo.

	VF	UNC
a. Issued note.	6.00	15.00
s. Specimen.	—	15.00

1992 Issue

#127-129 second date appears after imprint.

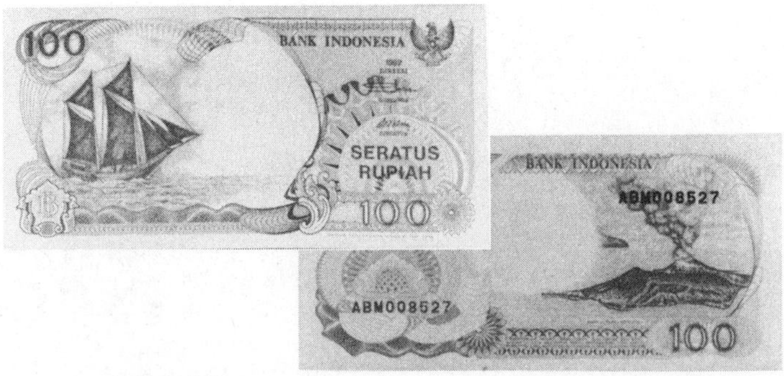

127 100 Rupiah

1992-2000. Pale red on orange and multicolor underprint. Sailboat *Pinisi* at left. Arms at upper right area. Back: Volcano *Anak Krakatau* at right. Watermark: Ki Hajar Dewantara. Printer: Perum Percetakan Uang. UV: fibers fluoresce yellow and red.

	VF	UNC
a. 1992.	FV	.75
b. 1992/1993.	FV	.50
c. 1992/1994.	FV	.50
d. 1992/1995.	FV	.45
e. 1992/1996.	FV	.25
f. 1992/1997.	FV	.25
g. 1992/1999.	FV	.25
h. 1992/2000.	FV	.20

128 **500 Rupiah**

1992-99. Brown and green on multicolor underprint. Orangutan resting on limb at left. Arms at upper right area. Back: Native huts at E. Kalimantan at right. Watermark: H. O. S. Tjokroaminoto. Printer: Perum Percetakan Uang. UV: fibers fluoresce yellow and red.

	VF	UNC
a. 1992.	FV	1.25
b. 1992/1993.	FV	1.00
c. 1992/1994.	FV	1.00
d. 1992/1995.	FV	1.00
e. 1992/1996.	FV	.50
f. 1992/1997.	FV	.40
g. 1992/1998.	FV	.30
h. 1992/1999.	FV	.20

129 **1000 Rupiah**

1992-2000. Deep blue on light blue and multicolor underprint. Aerial view of Lake Toba at left center. Arms at upper right area. Back: Stone jumping attraction on Nias Island at center. Watermark: Tjut Njak Meutia. Printer: Perum Percetakan Uang. UV: fibers fluoresce yellow and red. Back lower left serial # orange.

	VF	UNC
a. 1992.	FV	2.00
b. 1992/1993.	FV	1.75
c. 1992/1994.	FV	1.75
d. 1992/1995.	FV	1.50
e. 1992/1996.	FV	1.00
f. 1992/1997.	FV	.75
g. 1992/1998.	FV	.75
h. 1992/1999.	FV	.50
i. 1992/2000.	FV	.50

130 **5000 Rupiah**

1992-2001. Black, brown and dark brown on multicolor underprint. Sasando musical instrument and Rote Island tapestry at center. Arms at upper right area. Back: Volcano with three-color Lake Kelimutu at center. Watermark: Tjut Njak Din. Printer: Perum Percetakan Uang.

	VF	UNC
a. 1992.	FV	7.50
b. 1992/1993.	FV	7.00
c. 1992/1994.	FV	7.00
d. 1992/1995.	FV	6.50
e. 1992/1996.	FV	3.50
f. 1992/1997.	FV	2.50
g. 1992/1998.	FV	1.50
h. 1992/1999.	FV	1.25
i. 1992/2000.	FV	1.25
j. 1999/2001.	FV	1.25
s. Specimen.	—	—

131 **10,000 Rupiah**

1992-98. Purple and red on multicolor underprint. Sri Sultan Hamengku Buwono IX at left, girl scouts camping at center right. Arms at upper right area. Back: Borobudur Temple on hillside. Watermark: W. R. Soepratman. Printer: Perum Percetakan Uang.

	VF	UNC
a. 1992.	6.00	12.50
b. 1992/1993.	6.00	12.00
c. 1992/1994.	5.00	12.00
d. 1992/1995.	5.00	10.00
e. 1992/1996.	3.00	6.00
f. 1992/1997.	2.00	4.00
g. 1992/1998 & letter prefix.	7.50	15.00
s. Specimen.	—	—

132 **20,000 Rupiah**

1992-95. Black, dark grayish green and red on multicolor underprint. Red bird of paradise at center. Arms at upper right area. Back: Cloves flower at center, map of Indonesian Archipelago at right. Watermark: K. H. Dewantara. Printer: Perum Percetakan Uang.

	VF	UNC
a. 1992.	10.00	22.50
b. 1992/1993.	10.00	20.00
c. 1992/1994.	8.00	17.50
d. 1992/1995.	12.50	25.00
s. Specimen.	—	—

1993 Commemorative Issues

#133 and 134, 25 Years of Development

133 **50,000 Rupiah**

1993-94. Greenish blue, tan and gray on multicolor underprint. President Soeharto at left center surrounded by various scenes of development activities. Anti-counterfeiting design at right. Back: Jet plane over Soekarno-Hatta International Airport at center. Watermark: W. R. Soepratman.

	VF	UNC
a. 1993.	20.00	40.00
b. 1993/1994.	17.50	35.00

134	50,000 Rupiah	VF	UNC
	1993. Pale gray. President Soeharto at left center, surrounded by various scenes of development activities. President Soeharto in OVD at right. Back: Jet plane over Soekarno-Hatta International Airport at center. Polymer plastic.		
	a. Note alone.	20.00	40.00
	b. Included in souvenir folder.	—	50.00

1995 Issue

135	20,000 Rupiah	VF	UNC
	1995-98. Black, dark grayish green and red on multicolor underprint. Red bird of paradise at center, arms at upper right area. Segmented foil over security thread. Back: Cloves flower at center, map of Indonesian Archipelago at right. Watermark: K. H. Dewantara.		
	a. 1995.	5.00	15.00
	b. 1995/1996.	4.00	9.00
	c. 1995/1997.	3.00	8.00
	d. 1995/1998.	3.00	8.00
136	50,000 Rupiah		
	1995-98. Greenish blue, tan and gray on multicolor underprint. President Soeharto at left center, surrounded by various scenes of development activities. Segmented foil over security thread. Back: Jet plane over Soekarno-Hatta International Airport at center. Watermark: W. R. Soepratman.		
	a. 1995.	7.00	42.50
	b. 1995/1996.	5.00	25.00
	c. 1995/1997.	5.00	15.00
	d. 1995/1998.	5.00	15.00

1998-99 Issue

137	10,000 Rupiah	VF	UNC
	1998-2005. Deep brownish purple and black on multicolor underprint. Tjut Njak Dhien at right, arms at upper right, bank monogram at lower right. Back: Segara Anak Volcanic Lake at center right. Watermark: W. R. Soepratman. Printer: Perum Peruri.		
	a. 1998.	FV	3.25
	b. 1998/1999.	FV	3.25
	c. 1998/2000.	FV	3.25
	d. 1998/2001.	FV	3.25
	e. 1998/2002.	FV	3.25
	f. 1998/2003.	FV	3.25
	g. 1998/2004.	FV	3.25
	h. 1998/2005.	FV	3.25

138	20,000 Rupiah	VF	UNC
	1998-2005. Deep green and dark brown on multicolor underprint. Ki Hadjar Dewantara at center, arms at upper left, Ganesha at left, bank monogram at right. Back: Classroom at center right. Watermark: Ki Hadjar Dewantara. Printer: Perum Peruri.		
	a. 1998.	FV	6.00
	b. 1998/1999.	FV	5.00
	c. 1998/2000.	FV	5.00
	d. 1998/2001.	FV	5.00
	e. 1998/2002.	FV	5.00
	f. 1998/2003.	FV	5.00
	g. 1998/2004.	FV	5.00

139	50,000 Rupiah	VF	UNC
	1999-2007. Grayish brown on multicolor underprint. W. R. Soepratman at center. Back: Students guarded by two soldiers, hoisting flag on Independence Day.		
	a. 1999.	FV	22.50
	b. 1999/2000.	FV	20.00
	c. 1999/2001.	FV	20.00
	d. 1999/2002.	FV	20.00
	e. 1999/2003.	FV	20.00
	f. 1999/2004.	FV	20.00
	g. 1999/2005.	FV	20.00
	h. 1999/2007.	FV	20.00

140	100,000 Rupiah	VF	UNC
	1999. Lilac brown, green and orange. Soekarno and Hatta at center. Back: Peoples Consultative Assembly and Parliament building. Printer: Note Printing, Australia and Thailand. Polymer plastic.	FV	30.00

2000 Issue

141	1000 Rupiah	VF	UNC
	2000-. Blue-green and red on multicolor underprint. Kapitan Pattimura at center. Back: Fishing boat and volcano. Watermark: Tjut Njak Dien. UV: upper right serial # fluoresces orange. 141x65mm.		
	a. 2000.	FV	.60
	b. 2000/2001.	FV	.50
	c. 2000/2002.	FV	.50
	d. 2000/2003.	FV	.50
	e. 2000/2004.	FV	2.50
	f. 2000/2005.	FV	.50
	g. 2000/2006.	FV	.50
	h. 2000/2007.	FV	.50
	i. 2000/2008.	FV	.50
	j. 2000/2009.	FV	.50
	k. 2000/2011.	FV	.50
	l. 2000/2012.	FV	.50

2001 Issue

142 5000 Rupiah

2001-. Brown and green on multicolor underprint. Tuanku Imam Bonjol at center. Back: Purple and green on multicolor underprint. Western Sumartran female at hand loom at center. Watermark: Tjut Njak Meutia. 143x65mm.

	VF	UNC
a. 2001.	FV	2.50
b. 2001/2002.	FV	2.50
c. 2001/2003.	FV	2.50
d. 2001/2004.	FV	2.00
e. 2001/2005.	FV	2.00
f. 2001/2006.	FV	2.00
g. 2001/2007.	FV	1.50
h. 2001/2008.	FV	1.50
i. 2001/2009.	FV	1.50
j. 2001/2010.	FV	1.50
k. 2001/2011.	FV	1.50
l. 2001/2012.	FV	1.50
m. 2001/2013.	FV	1.50

143 10,000 Rupiah

2005-. Violet on multicolor underprint. Sultan Mahmud Badaruddin II Back: Rumah Limab, Palembang. 143x65mm.

	VF	UNC
a. 2005.	FV	2.50
b. 2005/2006.	FV	2.50
c. 2005/2007.	FV	2.25
d. 2005/2008.	FV	2.25

144 20,000 Rupiah

2004-. Blue-green on multicolor underprint. Oto Iskandar Dinata at center. Back: Tea pickers, West Java. 149x65mm.

	VF	UNC
a. 2004.	FV	8.00
b. 2004/2005.	FV	5.50
c. 2004/2006.	FV	5.50
d. 2004/2007.	FV	5.00
e. 2004/2008.	FV	5.00
f. 2004/2009.	FV	4.00
g. 2004/2011.	FV	4.00
h. 2004/2012.	FV	

145 50,000 Rupiah

2005-. Dark blue on multicolor underprint. I Gusti Ngurah Rai at center. Back: Beratan Lake, Bali. 149x65mm.

	VF	UNC
a. 2005.	FV	15.00
b. 2005/2007.	FV	15.00

146 100,000 Rupiah

2004-. Red-brown on multicolor underprint. Soekarno and Hatta at center. Back: Parliament building. Similar to #140 but paper. 151x65mm.

	VF	UNC
a. 2004.	FV	20.00
b. 2004/2005.	FV	20.00
c. 2004/2007.	FV	17.50
d. 2004/2008.	FV	17.50
e. 2004/2009.	FV	17.50
f. 2004/2010.	FV	17.50
g. 2004/2011.	FV	17.50

2009-2011 Issue

148 2000 Rupiah

2009-. Gray-brown on multicolor underprint. Prince Antasari at center. Back: Traditional Dayak dance at center. 140x65mm.

	VF	UNC
a. 2009/2009.	FV	1.00
b. 2009/2011.	FV	1.00
c. 2009/2012.	FV	1.00
d. 2010/2013.	FV	1.00

149 5000 Rupiah

	VF	UNC
Expected new issue.	—	—

150	10,000 Rupiah	VF	UNC
	2010-. Purple on multicolor underprint. Sultan Mahmud Badaruddin II at center. Tactile marks added at left edge. Back: Limas House in Palembang. 143x65mm.		
	a. 2005/2010.	FV	3.00
	b. 2005/2012.	FV	2.00
	c. 2005/2013.	FV	2.00

151	20,000 Rupiah	VF	UNC
	2011-. Light and dark green on blue and multicolor underprint. Oto Iskandar Di Nata at center. Tactile squares at left end, omcron dots at right. Back: Tea picker, West Java. 149x65mm.		
	a. 2004/2011.	FV	5.50
	b. 2004/2012.	FV	5.50

152	50,000 Rupiah	VF	UNC
	2011-. Light and dark blue on multicolor underprint. I Gusti Ngurah Ral at center. Tactile triangles added at left edge, omcron dots at right. Back: Beratan Lake, Bali. 149x65mm.		
	a. 2004/2011.	FV	15.00

153	100,000 Rupiah	VF	UNC
	2011-. Red on multicolor underprint. Soekarno and M. Hatta at center. Tactile circles at left edge, omcron dots at right. Back: Parliament building. 151x65mm.		
	a. 2004/2011.	FV	17.50

IRAN

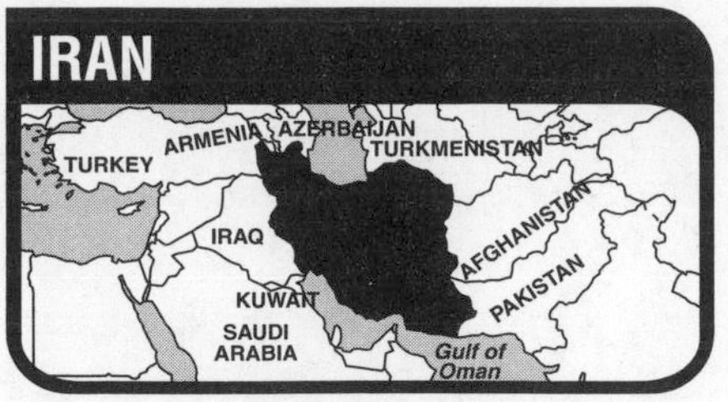

The Islamic Republic of Iran, located between the Caspian Sea and the Persian Gulf in southwestern Asia, has an area of 1,648,000 sq. km. and a population of 65.87 million. Capital: Tehran. Although predominantly an agricultural state, Iran depends heavily on oil for foreign exchange. Crude oil, carpets and agricultural products are exported.

Known as Persia until 1935, Iran became an Islamic republic in 1979 after the ruling monarchy was overthrown and the shah was forced into exile. Conservative clerical forces established a theocratic system of government with ultimate political authority vested in a learned religious scholar referred to commonly as the Supreme Leader who, according to the constitution, is accountable only to the Assembly of Experts. US-Iranian relations have been strained since a group of Iranian students seized the US Embassy in Tehran on 4 November 1979 and held it until 20 January 1981. During 1980-88, Iran fought a bloody, indecisive war with Iraq that eventually expanded into the Persian Gulf and led to clashes between US Navy and Iranian military forces between 1987 and 1988. Iran has been designated a state sponsor of terrorism for its activities in Lebanon and elsewhere in the world and remains subject to US and UN economic sanctions and export controls because of its continued involvement in terrorism and conventional weapons proliferation. Following the election of reformer Hojjat ol-Eslam Mohammad Khatami as president in 1997 and similarly a reformer Majles (parliament) in 2000, a campaign to foster political reform in response to popular dissatisfaction was initiated. The movement floundered as conservative politicians, through the control of unelected institutions, prevented reform measures from being enacted and increased repressive measures. Starting with nationwide municipal elections in 2003 and continuing through Majles elections in 2004, conservatives reestablished control over Iran's elected government institutions, which culminated with the August 2005 inauguration of hardliner Mahmud Ahmadi-Nejad as president.

RULERS: QAJAR DYNASTY

Mohammad Reza Pahlavi, SH1320-58/1941-79AD

MONETARY SYSTEM:

1 Toman = 10 Rials SH1310- (1932-)

SIGNATURE AND TITLE VARIETIES

Kingdom: Mohammad Reza Pahlavi

	GENERAL DIRECTOR	MINISTER OF FINANCE
7	Ebrahim Kashani	Abholbagi Shoaii
8	Dr. Ali Asghar Pouhomayoun	Abdul Hossein Behnia
9	Mehdi Samii	Abdul Hossein Behnia
10	Mehdi Samii	Amir Abbas Hoveyda
11	Mehdi Samii	Dr. Jamshid Amouzegar
12	Khodadad Famanfarmaian	Dr. Jamshid Amouzegar
13	Abdul Ali Jahanshahi	Dr. Jamshid Amouzegar
14	Mohammad Yeganeh	Dr. Jamshid Amouzegar

	GENERAL DIRECTOR	MINISTER OF ECONOMIC AND FINANCIAL AFFAIR
15	Mohammad Yeganeh	Hushang Ansary
16	Hassan Ali Mehran	Hushang Ansary
17	Hassan Ali Mehran	Mohammad Yeganeh

Shah Mohammad Reza Pahlavi, SH1323-58/1944-79 AD

Type V. Imperial Iranian Army (IIA) uniform. Full face. SH1337-40.

Type VI. Imperial Iranian Air Force (IIAF) uniform. Three quarter face. SH1341-44.

Type VII. Imperial Iranian Army (IIA) uniform. Full face. SH1347-48.

Type VIII. Commander in Chief of Iran's Armed Forces. Three quarter face. Large portrait. MS2535 to SH1358.

Type IX. Shah Pahlavi in CinC uniform and his father Shah Reza in Imperial Iranian Army (IIA) uniform. MS2535.

Kingdom of Iran

Bank Markazi Iran

1961; 1962 Issue

		VF	UNC
71	**10 Rials** SH1340 (1961). Blue on green and orange underprint. Geometric design at center. Type V portrait of Shah Pahlavi in army uniform at right. Signature 7. Back: Amir Kabir Dam near Karaj. Watermark: Young Shah Pahlavi. Printer: H&S (without imprint). Yellow security thread runs vertically.	5.00	12.00

		VF	UNC
72	**20 Rials** SH1340 (1961). Dark brown on green and pink underprint. Geometric design at center. Type V portrait of Shah Pahlavi in army uniform at right. Signature 7. Back: Statue of Shah and Ramsar Hotel. Watermark: Young Shah Pahlavi. Printer: H&S (without imprint). Yellow security thread runs vertically.	7.00	16.00

		VF	UNC
73	**50 Rials** SH1341 (1962). Green on orange and blue underprint. Type VI portrait of Shah Pahlavi in air force uniform at right. Signature 8. Back: Koohrang Dam and tunnel. Watermark: Young Shah Pahlavi. Printer: H&S (without imprint). Yellow security thread runs vertically.		
	a. Small date 2.5mm high.	7.00	16.00
	b. Large date 4.0mm high.	9.00	18.00

		VF	UNC
74	**500 Rials** SH1341 (1962). Black on pink and multicolor underprint. Type VI portrait of Shah Pahlavi in air force uniform at center. Signature 8. Back: Winged horses. Watermark: Young Shah Pahlavi. Printer: H&S (without imprint). Yellow security thread runs vertically.	110.	275.

		VF	UNC
75	**1000 Rials** SH1341 (1962). Brown on red and blue underprint. Type VI portrait of Shah Pahlavi in air force uniform at center. Signature 8. Back: Tomb of Hafez in Shiraz. Watermark: Young Shah Pahlavi. Printer: H&S (without imprint). Yellow security thread runs vertically.	135.	375.

1963; 1964 Issue

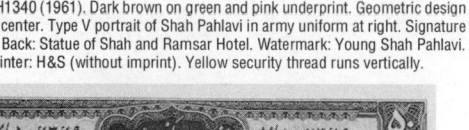

76 **50 Rials**

SH1343 (1964). Dark green on orange and blue underprint. Ornate design at center. Type VI portrait of Shah Pahlavi in armed forces uniform at right. Signature 9. Back: Koohrang Dam and tunnel. Watermark: Young Shah Pahlavi. Printer: H&S (without imprint). Yellow security thread.

	VF	UNC
76	12.00	22.00

77 **100 Rials**

SH1342 (1963). Maroon on light green and multicolor underprint. Ornate design at center. Type VI portrait of Shah Pahlavi in armed forces uniform at right. Signature 9. Back: Oil refinery at Abadan. Watermark: Young Shah Pahlavi. Printer: H&S (without imprint). Yellow security thread.

	VF	UNC
77	12.00	25.00

1965 ND Issue

78 **20 Rials**

ND (1965). Dark brown on pink and green underprint. Ornate design at center. Type VI portrait of Shah Pahlavi in armed forces uniform at right. Back: Oriental hunters on horseback. Watermark: Young Shah Pahlavi. Printer: H&S (without imprint). Yellow security thread.

	VF	UNC
a. Signature 9.	3.00	7.00
b. Signature 10.	3.00	7.00

79 **50 Rials**

ND (1965). Dark green on orange and blue underprint. Ornate design at center. Type VI portrait of Shah Pahlavi in armed forces uniform at right. Back: Koohrang Dam and tunnel. Watermark: Young Shah Pahlavi. Printer: H&S (without imprint). Yellow security thread.

	VF	UNC
a. Signature 9.	8.00	20.00
b. Signature 10.	8.00	20.00

80 **100 Rials**

ND (1965). Maroon on olive-green and multicolor underprint. Ornate design at center. Type VI portrait of Shah Pahlavi in armed forces uniform at right. Signature 10. Back: Oil refinery at Abadan. Watermark: Young Shah Pahlavi. Printer: H&S (without imprint). Yellow security thread.

	VF	UNC
80	9.00	22.00

81 **200 Rials**

ND (1965). Dark blue on orange and lavender underprint. Multicolor ornate design at center. Type VI portrait of Shah Pahlavi in armed forces uniform at right. Signature 9. Back: Railroad bridge. Watermark: Young Shah Pahlavi. Printer: H&S (without imprint). Yellow security thread.

	VF	UNC
81	25.00	55.00

82 **500 Rials**

ND (1965). Black on pink and purple underprint. Type VI portrait of Shah Pahlavi in armed forces uniform at center. Signature 9. Back: Winged horses. Watermark: Young Shah Pahlvi. Printer: H&S (without imprint. Yellow security thread.

	VF	UNC
82	110.	260.

83 **1000 Rials**

ND (1965). Brown on red and blue underprint. Type VI portrait of Shah Pahlavi in armed forces uniform at center. Signature 9. Back: Tomb of Hafez at Shiraz. Watermark: Young Shah Pahlavi. Printer: H&S (without imprint). Yellow security thread.

	VF	UNC
83	125.	350.

1969 ND Issue

#84-89A are called *Dark Panel* notes. The bank name is located on a contrasting dark ornamental panel at the top center.

84 **20 Rials** VF UNC
ND (1969). Dark brown on pink and green underprint. Ornate design at center. Type VII portrait of Shah Pahlavi in army uniform at right. Signature 11. Back: Oriental hunters on horseback. Watermark: Young Shah Pahlavi. Printer: H&S (without imprint). Yellow security thread runs vertically. 4.00 10.00

85 **50 Rials** VF UNC
ND (1969-71). Green on orange and blue underprint. Ornate design at center. Type VII portrait of Shah Pahlavi in army uniform at right. Back: Koohrang Dam and tunnel. Watermark: Young Shah Pahlavi. Printer: Harrison (without imprint). Yellow security thread runs vertically.
a. Signature 11. 5.00 10.00
b. Signature 12. 5.00 10.00

86 **100 Rials** VF UNC
ND (1969-71). Maroon on light green and multicolor underprint. Ornate design at center. Type VII portrait of Shah Pahlavi in army uniform at right. Back: Oil refinery at Abadan. Watermark: Young Shah Pahlavi. Printer: H&S (without imprint). Yellow security thread runs vertically.
a. Signature 11. 7.00 15.00
b. Signature 12. 7.00 15.00

87 **200 Rials** VF UNC
ND (1969-71). Dark blue on orange and purple underprint. Multicolor ornate design at center. Type VII portrait of Shah Pahlavi in army uniform at right. Back: Railroad bridge. Watermark: Young Shah Pahlavi. Printer: H&S (without imprint). Yellow security thread runs vertically.
a. Signature 11. 15.00 35.00
b. Signature 12. 20.00 50.00

88 **500 Rials**
ND (1969). Black on pink and purple underprint. Ornate frame at center. Type VII portrait of Shah Pahlavi in army uniform at center. Signature 11. Back: Winged horses. 25.00 80.00

89 **1000 Rials** VF UNC
ND (1969). Brown on red and blue underprint. Ornate frame at center. Type VII portrait of Shah Pahlavi in army uniform at center. Signature 11. Back: Tomb of Hafez at Shiraz. 44.00 160.

89A **5000 Rials**
ND (1969). Purple on red and multicolor underprint. Ornate frame at center. Type VII portrait of Shah Pahlavi in army uniform at center. Signature 11. Back: Golestan Palace in Tehran. Printer: Printed in Pakistan. 1000. 2000.

1971 ND Issue

#90-96 are called *Light Panel* notes. The bank name is located on a contrasting light ornamental background panel at the top center.

90 **50 Rials** VF UNC
ND (1971). Dark green on orange and blue underprint. Type VII portrait of Shah Pahlavi in army uniform at right. Signature 13. Back: Koohrang Dam and tunnel. Light panel. Watermark: Young Shah Pahlavi. Printer: H&S (without imprint). Yellow security thread runs vertically. 4.00 10.00

91 **100 Rials** VF UNC
ND (1971-73). Maroon on olive-green and multicolor underprint. Ornate design at center. Type VII portrait of Shah Pahlavi in army uniform at right. Light panel. Back: Oil refinery at Abadan. Watermark: Young Shah Pahlavi. Printer: H&S (without imprint). Yellow security thread runs vertically.
a. Signature 11. 5.00 15.00
b. Signature 12. 8.00 10.00
c. Signature 13. 5.00 15.00

92 **200 Rials** VF UNC
ND (1971-73). Dark blue on orange and lavender underprint. Multicolor ornate design at center. Type VII portrait of Shah Pahlavi in army uniform at right. Light panel. Back: Railroad bridge. Watermark: Young Shah Pahlavi. Printer: H&S (without imprint). Yellow security thread runs vertically.
a. Signature 11. 16.00 50.00
b. Signature 12. 20.00 60.00
c. Signature 13. 10.00 22.50

93 500 Rials VF UNC

ND (1971-73). Black on orange, green and multicolor underprint. Ornate frame at center. Type VII portrait of Shah Pahlavi in army uniform at center. Light panel. Back: Winged horses. Watermark: Young Shah Pahlavi.

	VF	UNC
a. Signature 11.	20.00	50.00
b. Signature 12.	40.00	150.
c. Signature 13.	30.00	100.

94 1000 Rials VF UNC

ND (1971-73). Brown on red, blue and multicolor underprint. Ornate frame at center. Type VII portrait of Shah Pahlavi in army uniform at center. Light panel. Back: Tomb of Hafez at Shiraz. Watermark: Young Shah Pahlavi.

	VF	UNC
a. Signature 11.	60.00	200.
b. Signature 12.	50.00	150.
c. Signature 13.	40.00	125.

95 5000 Rials VF UNC

ND (1971-72). Purple on red and multicolor underprint. Ornate frame at center. Type VII portrait of Shah Pahlavi in army uniform at center. Light panel. Back: Golestan Palace in Tehran. Watermark: Young Shah Pahlavi.

	VF	UNC
a. Signature 12.	300.	900.
b. Signature 13.	200.	600.

96 10,000 Rials VF UNC

ND (1972-73). Dark green and brown. Ornate frame at center. Type VII portrait of Shah Pahlavi in army uniform at center. Back: National Council of Ministries in Tehran. Watermark: Young Shah Pahlavi.

	VF	UNC
a. Signature 11.	600.	2000.
b. Signature 13.	400.	1250.

1971 ND Commemorative Issue

#97 and 98, 2,500th Anniversary of the Persian Empire.

97 50 Rials VF UNC

SH1350 (1971). Green on blue, brown and multicolor underprint. Floral design at center. Type VIII portrait of Shah Pahlavi in the "Commander in Chief" of Iranian armed forces uniform at right. Back: Shah Pahlavi giving land deeds to villager. Watermark: Young Shah Pahlavi. Printer: TDLR. Yellow security thread runs vertically.

	VF	UNC
a. Signature 11.	7.00	15.00
b. Signature 13.	10.00	20.00

98 100 Rials VF UNC

SH1350 (1971). Maroon on orange and multicolor underprint. Floral and multicolor geometric design . Type VIII portrait of Shah Pahlavi in the "Commander in Chief" of Iranian armed forces uniform at right. Signature 11. Back: Three vignettes labeled: *HEALTH, AGRICULTURE* and *EDUCATION*. Watermark: Young Shah Pahlavi. Printer: TDLR. Yellow security thread runs vertically.

	VF	UNC
	10.00	22.50

1974 ND Issue

#100-107 Replacement notes: For signatures 14, 15, 16 where the prefix for regular notes is a whole number such as 1, 2, 3 or 4, the replacemnt is 01, 02, 03 or 04. For signatures 17 and 18 where the prefix for regular notes is a fraction, the replacement is 99/9, 98/9 or 97/9.

100 20 Rials VF UNC

ND (1974-79). Brown on orange, lilac and multicolor underprint. Persian carpet design, shepherd and ram. Type VIII portrait of Shah Pahlavi at right. Back: Amir Kabir Dam near Karaj. Watermark: Young Shah Pahlavi. Printer: TDLR. Yellow security thread runs vertically.

	VF	UNC
a1. Signature 16. Farsi denomination short.	3.00	7.00
a2. Signature 16. Farsi denomination long.	3.00	7.00
b. Signature 17.	5.00	10.00
c. Signature 18.	6.00	12.00

101 50 Rials

ND (1974-79). Green on brown, blue and multicolor underprint. Persian carpet design. Type VIII portrait of Shah Pahlavi at right. Back: Tomb of Cyrus the Great at Pasargarde at left center. Watermark: Young Shah Pahlavi. Printer: TDLR. Yellow security thread runs vertically.

	VF	UNC
a. Yellow security thread. Signature 14.	5.00	12.00
b. Yellow security thread. Signature 15.	5.00	10.00
c. Yellow security thread. Signature 16.	5.00	10.00
d. Black security thread. Signature 17.	5.00	10.00
e. Black security thread. Signature 18.	5.00	12.00

102 100 Rials

ND (1974-79). Maroon on orange, green and multicolor underprint. Persian carpet design. Type VIII portrait of Shah Pahlavi at right. Back: Pahlavi Museum at left center. Watermark: Young Shah Pahlavi. Printer: TDLR. Yellow security thread runs vertically.

	VF	UNC
a. Yellow security thread. Signature 15.	6.00	15.00
b. Yellow security thread. Signature 16.	7.00	18.00
c. Black security thread. Signature 17.	7.50	20.00
d. Black security thread. Signature 18.	7.00	18.00

103 200 Rials

ND (1974-79). Blue on green and multicolor underprint. Persian carpet design. Type VIII portrait of Shah Pahlavi at right. Back: Shahyad Square in Tehran. Watermark: Young Shah Pahlavi. Printer: TDLR.

	VF	UNC
a. 6 point star in design on back. Yellow security thread. Monument name as Maidane Shahyad at lower left on back. Signature 15.	20.00	55.00
b. 12 point star in design on back. Yellow security thread. Monument name as Maidane Shahyad. Signature 16.	10.00	35.00
c. 12 point star in design on back. Yelow security thread. Monument name changed to Shahyard Aryamed. Signature 16.	8.00	30.00
d. 12 point star in design on back. Black security thread and Shahyad Aryamer monument. Signature 17.	8.00	30.00
e. 12 point star in design on back. Black security thread and Shahyad Aryamer monument. Signature 18.	8.00	30.00
h. 12 point star in design on back. Yellow security thread. Monument name changed to Shahyad Aryamer. Signature 16.	8.00	30.00

104 500 Rials

ND (1974-79). Black, dark brown and green on orange and multicolor underprint. Persian carpet design. Type VIII portrait of Shah Pahlavi at right. Back: Winged horses. Watermark: Young Shah Pahlavi. Printer: TDLR. Yellow security thread runs vertically.

	VF	UNC
a. 6 point star in design below Shah Pahlavi. Yellow security thread. Signature 15.	20.00	45.00
b. 6 point star in design below Shah Pahlavi. Yellow security thread. Signature 16.	12.00	30.00
c. Diamond design below Shah Pahlavi. Black security thread. Signature 17.	18.00	40.00
d. Diamond design below Shah Pahlavi. Black security thread. Signature 18.	12.50	35.00

105 1000 Rials

ND (1974-79). Brown on green, red, yellow and multicolor underprint. Persian carpet design. Type VIII portrait of Shah Pahlavi at right. Back: Tomb of Hafez in Shiraz. Watermark: Young Shah Pahlavi. Printer: TDLR. Yellow security thread runs vertically.

	VF	UNC
a. Yellow security thread. Signature 15.	35.00	110.
b. Yellow security thread. Signature 16.	12.50	35.00
c. Black security thread. Signature 17.	12.50	35.00
d. Black security thread. Signature 18.	12.50	35.00

106 5000 Rials

ND (1974-79). Purple on pink, green and multicolor underprint. Persian carpet design. Type VIII portrait of Shah Pahlavi at right. Back: Golestan Palace in Tehran. Watermark: Young Shah Pahlavi. Printer: TDLR. Yellow security thread runs vertically.

	VF	UNC
a. Yellow security thread. Signature 15.	100.	300.
b. Yellow security thread. Signature 16.	10.00	50.00
c. Black security thread. Signature 17.	75.00	200.
d. Black security thread. Signature 18.	100.	250.

107 10,000 Rials

ND (1974-79). Dark brown and green on multicolor underprint. Persian carpet design. Type VIII portrait of Shah Pahlavi at right. Back: National Council of Ministries in Tehran. Watermark: Young Shah Pahlavi. Printer: TDLR. Yellow security thread runs vertically.

	VF	UNC
a. Yellow security thread. Signature 15.	200.	550.
b. Yellow security thread. Signature 16.	30.00	100.
c. Black security thread. Signature 17.	100.	300.
d. Black security thread. Signature 18.	125.	350.
s. As a. Specimen.	—	750.

1976 ND Commemorative Issue

#108, 50th Anniversary of the Founding of the Pahlavi Dynasty.

		VF	UNC
108	**100 Rials** ND (1976). Maroon on orange, green and multicolor underprint. Persian carpet design with old Bank Melli at bottom center. Type IX portrait of Shah Pahlavi with Shah Reza at right. Signature 16. Back: 50th anniversary design in purple and lavender consisting of fifty suns surrounding Pahlavi Crown. Watermark: Young Shah Pahlavi. Printer: TDLR. Yellow security thread runs vertically.	10.00	25.00

Islamic Republic

Government

Type 1 ND Provisional Issue

#110-116 Type I overprint: Arabesque design over Shah at right. Watermark area at left without overprint. Replacement notes: Refer to #100-107.

REVOLUTIONARY OVERPRINTS

After the Islamic Revolution of 1978-79, the Iranian government used numerous overprints on existing stocks of unissued paper money to obliterate Shah Pahlavi's portrait. There were many unauthorized and illegal crude stampings such as a large "X" and hand obliterations used by zealous citizens which circulated freely, but only three major types types of official overprints were used by the government.

PROVISIONAL ISSUES

All provisional government ovpt. were placed on existing notes of Shah Pahlavi already printed. Overprinting was an interim action meant to discredit and disgrace the deposed Shah as well as to publicize and give credence to the new Islamic Republic. The overprints themselves gave way to more appropriate seals and emblems, changes of watermarks and finally to a complete redesigning of all denominations of notes.

In all cases the Shah's portr. was covered by an arabesque design. Eight different styles and varieties of this ovpt. were used. Watermark ovpt., when used, are either the former Iranian national emblem of Lion and Sun or the calligraphic Persian text of *JUMHURI-YE-ISLAMI-YE-IRAN* (Islamic Republic of Iran) taken from the obverse of the country's new emblem. All ovpt. colors are very dark and require careful scrutiny to distinguish colors other than black.

PORTRAIT OVERPRINT

Overprint A

Overprint B

Overprint C

Overprint D

Overprint E

Overprint F

Overprint G

Overprint H

Obverse 1

Reverse 1

Obverse 2

Obverse 3

		VF	UNC
110	**20 Rials** ND. Brown on orange, lilac and multicolor underprint. Persian carpet design, shepherd and ram. Type VIII portrait of Shah Pahlavi at right. Watermark area at left without overprint. Back: Amir Kabir Dam near Karaj. Overprint: Type 1 overprint; Arabesque design over Shah at right. Watermark: Young Shah Pahlavi. Printer: TDLR.		
	a. Black type A overprint on #100a1 (short Farsi).	8.00	15.00
	b. Black type A overprint on #100a2 (long Farsi).	8.00	30.00
	c. Black type C overprint on #100a2.	400.	800.
	d. Black type A overprint on #100c.	500.	1000.
	e. Black type A overprint on #100b.	500.	1000.

		VF	UNC
111	**50 Rials** ND. Green on brown, blue and multicolor underprint. Persian carpet design. Type VIII portrait of Shah Pahlavi at right. Yellow security thread. Signature 15. Watermark area at left without overprint. Back: Tomb of Cyrus the Great at Pasargarde at left center. Overprint: Type 1 overprint; Arabesque design over Shah at right. Watermark: Young Shah Pahlavi. Printer: TDLR.		
	a. Black type B overprint.	5.00	12.00
	b. Green type B overprint.	6.00	20.00

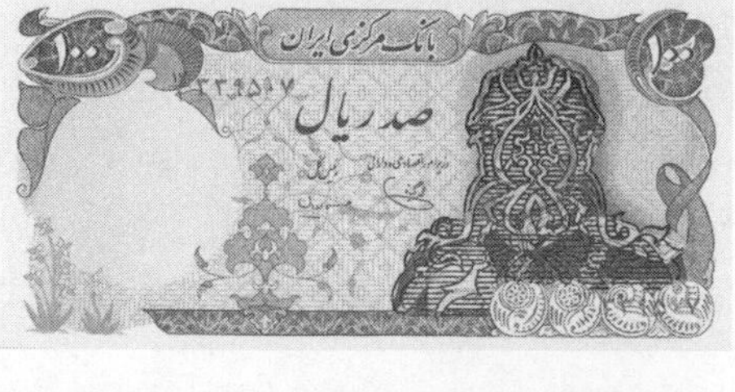

		VF	UNC
112	**100 Rials**		
	ND. Maroon on orange, green and multicolor underprint. Persian carpet design. Type VIII portrait of Shah Pahlavi at right. Black security thread. Signature 17. Watermark area at left without overprint. Back: Pahlavi Museum at left center. Overprint: Type 1 overprint; Arabesque design over Shah at right. Watermark: Young Shah Pahlavi. Printer: TDLR.		
	a. Black type C overprint.	10.00	25.00
	b. Maroon type C overprint.	10.00	25.00
	c. Black type G overprint.	150.	300.

		VF	UNC
113	**200 Rials**		
	ND. Blue on green and multicolor underprint. Persian carpet design. Type VIII portrait of Shah Pahlavi at right. Watermark area at left without overprint. Back: Shahyad Square in Tehran. Overprint: Type 1 overprint; Arabesque design over Shah at right. Watermark: Young Shah Pahlavi. Printer: TDLR.		
	a. Black type E overprint on #103a.	400.	1200.
	b. Black type E overprint on #103b.	500.	1400.
	c. Black type E overprint on #103d.	12.00	30.00
	d. Black type G overprint on #103d.	150.	300.

		VF	UNC
114	**500 Rials**		
	ND. Black, dark brown and green on orange and multicolor underprint. Persian carpet design. Type VIII portrait of Shah Pahlavi at right. Watermark area at left without overprint. Back: Winged horses. Overprint: Type 1 overprint; Arabesque design over Shah at right. Watermark: Young Shah Pahlavi. Printer: TDLR.		
	a. Black type F overprint on #104b.	15.00	50.00
	b. Black type F overprint on #104c.	400.	900.
	c. Black type F overprint on #104d.	16.00	60.00

		VF	UNC
115	**1000 Rials**		
	ND. Brown on green, red, yellow and multicolor underprint. Persian carpet design. Type VIII portrait of Shah Pahlavi at right. Watermark area at left without overprint. Back: Tomb of Hafez in Shiraz. Overprint: Type 1 overprint; Arabesque design over Shah at right. Watermark: Young Shah Pahlavi. Printer: TDLR.		
	a. Black type G overprint on #105b.	15.00	50.00
	b. Black type G overprint on #105d.	20.00	65.00
	c. Brown type G overprint on #105d.	20.00	100.

		VF	UNC
116	**5000 Rials**		
	ND. Purple on pink, green and multicolor underprint. Persian carpet design. Type VIII portrait of Shah Pahlavi at right. Black security thread. Signature 18. Black type H overprint. Watermark area at left without overprint. Back: Golestan Palace in Tehran. Overprint: Type 1 overprint; Arabesque design over Shah at right. Watermark: Young Shah Pahlavi. Printer: TDLR.	1000.	2000.

Type 2 ND Provisional Issue

#117-122 Type II overprint: Arabesque design over Shah at right. Lion and sun national emblem over watermark area at left.

		VF	UNC
117	**50 Rials**		
	ND. Green on brown, blue and multicolor underprint. Persian carpet design. Type VIII portrait of Shah Pahlavi at right. Lion and sun national emblem over watermark area. Back: Cyrus the Great at Pasargarde at left center. Overprint: Type 2 overprint; Arabesque design over Shah at right. Watermark: Young Shah Pahlavi. Printer: TDLR.		
	a. Black type B overprint on #101c.	12.00	30.00
	b. Black type B overprint on #101d.	400.	1000.
	c. Black type B overprint on #101e.	200.	600.

		VF	UNC
118	**100 Rials**		
	ND. Maroon on orange, green and multicolor underprint. Persian carpet design. Type VIII portrait of Shah Pahlavi at right. Lion and sun national emblem over watermark area. Back: Pahlavi Museum at left center. Overprint: Type 2 overprint; Arabesque design over Shah at right. Watermark: Young Shah Pahlavi. Printer: TDLR.		
	a. Black type C overprint on #102c.	150.	400.
	b. Black type D overprint on #102d.	4.00	10.00

		VF	UNC
119	**200 Rials**		
	ND. Blue on green and multicolor underprint. Persian carpet design. Type VIII portrait of Shah Pahlavi at right. Lion and sun national emblem over watermark area. Back: Shahyad Square in Tehran. Overprint: Type 2 overprint; Arabesque design over Shah at right. Watermark: Young Shah Pahlavi. Printer: TDLR.		
	a. Black Type E overprint on #103d.	25.00	60.00

		VF	UNC
120	**500 Rials**		
	ND. Black, dark brown and green on orange and multicolor underprint. Persian carpet design. Type VIII portrait of Shah Pahlavi at right. Lion and sun national emblem over watermark area. Back: Winged horses. Overprint: Type 2 overprint; Arabesque design over Shah at right. Watermark: Young Shah Pahlavi. Printer: TDLR.		
	a. Black type F overprint on #104b.	700.	2000.
	b. Black type F overprint on #104d.	30.00	80.00

121 1000 Rials VF UNC

ND. Brown on green, red, yellow and multicolor underprint. Persian carpet design. Type VIII portrait of Shah Pahlavi at right. Lion and sun national emblem over watermark area. Back: Tomb of Hafez in Shiraz. Overprint: Type 2 overprint; Arabesque design over Shah at right. Watermark: Young Shah Pahlavi. Printer: TDLR.

	VF	UNC
a. Black type G overprint on #105b.	800.	3000.
b. Brown type G overprint on #105b.	20.00	75.00
c. Black type G overprint on #105d.	20.00	75.00

122 5000 Rials VF UNC

ND. Purple on pink, green and multicolor underprint. Persian carpet design. Type VIII portrait of Shah Pahlavi at right. Lion and sun national emblem over watermark area. Back: Golestan Palace in Tehran. Overprint: Type 2 overprint; Arabesque design over Shah at right. Watermark: Young Shah Pahlavi. Printer: TDLR.

	VF	UNC
a. Black type H overprint on #106b.	1000.	2750.
b. Black type H overprint on #106c.	1500.	3000.
c. Black type H overprint on #106d.	800.	1750.

Type 3 ND Provisional Issue

#123-126 Type III overprint: Arabesque design over Shah at right. Calligraphic Persian text *JUMHURI-YE ISLAMI-YE-IRAN* (Islamic Republic of Iran) over watermark area at left.

123 50 Rials VF UNC

ND. Green on brown, blue and multicolor underprint. Persian carpet design. Type VIII portrait of Shah Pahlavi at right. calligraphic Persian text*JUMHURI-YE ISL-AMI YE-IRAN* over watermark area at left. Back: Tomb of Cyrus the Great at Pasargarde at left center. Overprint: Type 3 overprint; Arabesque design over Shah at right. Watermark: Young Shah Pahlavi. Printer: TDLR.

	VF	UNC
a. Black type B overprint, dark green script on #101c.	6.00	20.00
b. Black type D overprint, black script on #101e.	4.00	10.00

124 500 Rials VF UNC

ND. Black, dark brown and green on orange and multicolor underprint. Persian carpet design. Type VIII portrait of Shah Pahlavi at right. Calligraphic Persian text*JUMHURI-YE ISL-AMI YE-IRAN* over watermark area at left. Back: Winged horses. Overprint: Type 3 overprint; Arabesque design over Shah at right. Watermark: Young Shah Pahlavi. Printer: TDLR.

	VF	UNC
a. Black type F overprint, black script on #104b.	15.00	50.00
b. Black type D overprint, black script on #104d.	10.00	30.00

125 1000 Rials VF UNC

ND. Brown on green, red, yellow and multicolor underprint. Persian carpet design. Type VIII portrait of Shah Pahlavi at right. Calligraphic Persian text*JUMHURI-YE ISL-AMI YE-IRAN* over watermark area at left. Back: Tomb of Hafez in Shiraz. Overprint: Type 3 overprint; Arabesque design over Shah at right. Watermark: Young Shah Pahlavi. Printer: TDLR.

	VF	UNC
a. Black type G overprint, black script on #105b.	15.00	50.00
b. Black type G overprint, black script on #105d.	15.00	50.00
c. Brown type G overprint, violet script on #105b.	20.00	75.00
d. Brown type G overprint, brown script on #105b.	20.00	75.00

126 5000 Rials VF UNC

ND. Purple on pink, green and multicolor underprint. Persian carpet design. Type VIII portrait of Shah Pahlavi at right. Calligraphic Persian text*JUMHURI-YE ISL-AMI YE-IRAN* over watermark area at left. Back: Golestan Palace in Tehran. Overprint: Type 3 overprint; Arabesque design over Shah at right. Watermark: Young Shah Pahlavi. Printer: TDLR.

	VF	UNC
a. Purple type H overprint, purple script on #106b.	1000.	2500.
b. Black type H overprint, purple script on #106d.	150.	350.

1980 Emergency Circulating Check Issue

The emergency checks were issed by Bank Melli, the National Bank and not Bank Markazi, the Central Bank, which is only authorized to issue currency. The checks were valid in the country only, not abroad. No English text on the checks.

126A 10,000 Rials VF UNC

	VF	UNC
ND (1980). Dark blue with black text on green underprint. Bank Melli building at left and center. Watermark: Bank name repeated. Uniface.	250.	600.

Bank Markazi Iran

Notes of the Islamic Republic of Iran		
18	Yousef Khoshkish (on ovpt.)	Mohammad Yeganeh (on ovpt.)
19	Mohammad Ali Mowiavi	Ali Ardalan
20	Ali Reza Nobari	Abol Hassan Bani-Sadr
21	Dr. Mohsen Nourbakhsh	Hossein Nemazi
22	Dr. Mohsen Nourbakhsh	Iravani
23	Ghasemi	Iravani
24	Ghasemi	Dr. Mohsen Nourbakhsh
25	Mohammad Hosein Adeli	Dr. Mohsen Nourbakhsh

Notes of the Islamic Republic of Iran		
26	Mohammad Hosein Adeli	Mohammad Khan
27	Dr. Mohsen Nourbakhsh	Mohammad Khan
28	Dr. Mohsen Nourbakhsh	Hossein Nemazi
29	Dr. Mohsen Nourbakhsh	
30		
31		
32		
33		
34		
35		
36		

1981 ND First Issue

#127 and #130 have calligraphic seal printed in the same color as the note (blue and lavender, respectively) and with no variation. #128, 129 and 131 had the calligraphic seal applied locally after notes were printed. Numerous color varieties, misplacement or total omission can be seen on face or back, or both.

127 200 Rials — VF / UNC

ND (1981). Blue and green on multicolor underprint. Calligraphic Persian (Farsi) text from circular republic seal at left, Imam Reza mosque at right without watermark. Signature 19. Back: Circular shield with stars and points at right. Tomb of Ibn-E-Sina in Hamadan at left. Overprint: Dark blue calligraphic seal at right. Printer: TDLR (without imprint). Yellow security thread with *BANK MARKAZI IRAN* in black runs vertically.

	VF	UNC
a. Overprint on watermark: Shah profile.	2.00	6.00
b. Overprint on watermark: Lion & Sun.	4.00	10.00

127A 200 Rials — VF 5000. UNC 12,000.

ND (1981). Blue, blue-violet and deep green on multicolor underprint. Calligraphic Persian (Farsi) text from circular republic seal at left with overprint. Imam Reza mosque at right without watermark. Signature 19. Back: Victory Monument renamed *Banaye Azadi* at left. Overprint: Lion and sun. Printer: TDLR (without imprint). Yellow security thread with *BANK MARKAZI IRAN* in black runs vertically.

128 500 Rials — VF 5.00 UNC 15.00

ND (1981). Dark brown on orange, green and multicolor underprint. Calligraphic Persian (Farsi) text from circular republic seal at left, Imam Reza mosque at right without watermark. Signature 19. Back: Winged horses. Printer: TDLR (without imprint). Yellow security thread with *BANK MARKAZI IRAN* in black runs vertically.

129 1000 Rials — VF 8.00 UNC 25.00

ND (1981). Rust and brown on green and multicolor underprint. Calligraphic Persian (Farsi) text from circular republic seal at left, Imam Reza mosque at right without watermark. Signature 19. Back: Tomb of Hafez in Shiraz. Printer: TDLR (without imprint). Yellow security thread with *BANK MARKAZI IRAN* in black runs vertically.

130 **5000 Rials** VF UNC

ND (1981). Lavender on green and multicolor underprint. Calligraphic Persian (Farsi) text from circular republic seal at left, Imam Reza mosque at right without watermark. Signature 19. Back: Oil refinery at Tehran. Printer: TDLR (without imprint). Yellow security thread with *BANK MARKAZI IRAN* in black runs vertically.

	VF	UNC
a. Security thread.	30.00	80.00
b. Without security thread.	50.00	100.

131 **10,000 Rials** VF UNC

ND (1981). Deep green, olive-brown and dark brown on multicolor underprint. Calligraphic Persian (Farsi) text from circular republic seal at left, Imam Reza mosque at right without watermark. Signature 19. Back: National Council of Ministries in Tehran. Printer: TDLR (without imprint). Yellow security thread with *BANK MARKAZI IRAN* in black runs vertically.

	VF	UNC
a. dark brown circular seal at left. dark brown circular shield seal at right on back.	50.00	200.

1981 ND Second Issue

#132-134 Replacement notes: Serial # prefix *99/99; 98/99; 97/99;* **etc.**

132 **100 Rials** VF UNC

ND (1981). Maroon and light brown on multicolor underprint. Ima Reza shrine at Mashad at right. Signature 20. Back: Madressa Chahr-Bagh in Isfahan. Watermark: Republic seal. Printer: TDLR (without imprint). White security thread with *BANK MARKAZI IRAN* in black Persian script runs vertically. 2.00 5.00

133 **5000 Rials** VF UNC

ND (1981). Violet, red-orange and brown on multicolor underprint. Mullahs leading marchers carrying posters of Ayatollah Khomeini at center. Signature 20. Back: Hazrat Masoumeh shrine at left center. Watermark: Arms. Printer: TDLR (without imprint). White security thread with *BANK MARKAZI IRAN* in black Persian script runs vertically. 25.00 80.00

134 **10,000 Rials** VF UNC

ND (1981). Dark blue and green on yellow and multicolor underprint. Mullahs leading marchers carrying posters of Ayatollah Khomeini at center. Signature 20. Back: Imam Reza shrine in Mashad at center. Printer: TDLR (without imprint). White security thread with *BANK MARKAZI IRAN* in black Persian script runs vertically.

	VF	UNC
a. Signature 20. Watermark: Republic seal.	30.00	125.
b. Signature 21. Watermark: Arms.	30.00	125.
c. Signature 22. Watermark: Arms.	30.00	125.

1982; 1983 ND Issue

135 **100 Rials** VF UNC

ND (1982). Maroon on light brown and multicolor underprint. Ima Reza shrine at Mashad at right. Signature 21. White security thread with *BANK MARKAZI IRAN* in black Persian letters repeatedly runs vertically. Back: Madressa Chahr-Bagh in Isfahan. Printer: TDLR (without imprint). 2.00 4.00

136 **200 Rials** VF UNC

ND (1982-). Aqua and blue-black on multicolor underprint. Mosque at center. White security thread with *BANK MARKAZI IRAN* in black Persian letters repeatedly runs vertically. Back: Farmers and farm tractor at left center. Printer: TDLR (without imprint). UV: security strip fluoresces blue, serial #s orange.

	VF	UNC
a. Signature 21. Watermark: Arms.	3.00	6.00
b. Signature 23. Watermark: Arms.	FV	4.00
c. Signatrue 28. Watermark: Arms.	FV	4.00
d. Signature 28. Watermark: Khomeini.	FV	3.00
e. Signature 31. Watermark: Khomeini.	FV	3.00

137 500 Rials

ND (1982-2002). Gray and olive. Feyzieh Madressa Seminary at lower left, large prayer gathering at center. White security thread with *BANK MARKAZI IRAN* in black Persian letters repeatedly runs vertically. Back: Tehran University. Printer: TDLR (without imprint). UV: fibers fluoresce yellow and blue, security strip rainbow, serial #s orange.

	VF	UNC
a. Signature 21. Watermark: Arms.	FV	12.00
b. Signature 22.	15.00	40.00
c. Signature 23.	FV	10.00
d. Signature 23. Watermark: Mohd. H. Fahmideh (youth).	FV	8.00
e. Signature 24.	FV	6.00
f. Signature 25.	FV	4.00
g. Signature 25. Watermark: Arms. Known as a replacement prefix only.	FV	20.00
h. Signature 27. Watermark: Arms.	FV	3.00
i. Signature 27. Watermark: Mohd. H. Fahmideh (youth).	FV	3.00
j. Signature 28. Watermark: Khomeini.	FV	3.00
k. Signature 30. Watermark: Khomeini.	FV	3.00
l. Signatrue 31. Watermark: Khomeini.	FV	3.00
s. As a. Specimen. Red Arabic overprint.	—	500.

137A 500 Rials

ND (2003-). Gray and olive. Feyzieh Madressa Seminary at lower left, prayer gathering at center. Architectural image at lower left in different position than number 137. White security thread with *BANK MARKAZI IRAN* in bla Back: Tehran University. Watermark: Khomeini Printer: TDLR (without imprint).

	VF	UNC
a. Signature 30.	FV	3.00
b. Signature 31.	FV	3.00
c. Signature 28.	FV	3.00
d. Signature 33.	FV	3.00

138 1000 Rials

ND (1982-2002). Dark olive-green, red-brown and brown on multicolor underprint. Feyzieh Madressa Seminary at center. White security thread with *BANK MARKAZI IRAN* in black Persian letters repeatedly runs vertically. Back: Dome of the Rock in Jerusalem. Printer: TDLR (without imprint). UV: fibers fluoresce yellow, blue and red. Serial #s orange.

	VF	UNC
a. Signature 21. With short line of text under mosque (Error name "Masjed al-Aqsa" on back. Watermark: Arms.	FV	20.00
b. Signature 21. Without line of text under mosque on back. Watermark: Arms.	FV	50.00
c. Signature 22. Watermark: Arms.	FV	25.00
d. Signature 23. Watermark: Arms.	FV	15.00
e. Signature 23. Watermark: Mohd. H. Fahmideh (youth).	FV	7.00
f. Signature 25. Watermark: Mohd. H. Fahmideh (youth).	FV	4.00
g. Signature 25. Watermark: Arms.	FV	4.00
h. Signature 26. Watermark: Mohd. H. Fahmideh (youth).	FV	4.00
i. Signature 27. Watermark: Mohd. H. Fahmideh (youth).	FV	4.00
j. Signature 28. Watermark: Mohd. H. Fahmideh (youth).	FV	4.00
k. Signature 28. Watermark: Arms.	FV	4.00

139 5000 Rials

ND (1983-93). Violet, red-orange and brown on multicolor underprint. Mullahs leading marchers carrying posters of Ayatollah Khomeini at center. Reduced crowd, radiant sun removed from upper left, two playcards of Khomeini added to crowd. Two different signatures. Back: Hazrat Masoumeh shrine at left center. Watermark: Arms. Printer: TDLR (without imprint). White security thread with *BANK MARKAZI IRAN* in black Persian letters repeatedly runs vertically.

	VF	UNC
a. Signature 21. Two signature style varieties.	FV	75.00
b. Signature 22.	FV	75.00

Central Bank of the Islamic Republic of Iran

1985; 1986 ND Issue

140 100 Rials

ND (1985-). Purple on multicolor underprint. Ayatollah Moddaress at right. Back: Parliament at left. Printer: TDLR (without imprint).

	VF	UNC
a. Signature 21. Watermark. Arms.	FV	3.00
b. Signature 22. Watermark: Arms.	FV	2.50
c. Signature 23. Watermark: Arms.	FV	1.50
d. Signature 25. Watermark: Arms.	FV	1.25
e. Signature 26. Watermark: Arms.	FV	1.25
f. Signature 28. Watermark: Khomeini.	FV	1.25
g. Signature 31. Watermark: Khomeini.	FV	1.25
h. Signature 31. Watermark: Arms.	FV	1.25

141 2000 Rials

ND(1986-2005). Purple, olive-green and dark brown on multicolor underprint. Revolutionists before mosque at center right. Back: Kaaba in Mecca. UV: serial #s fluoresce orange, fibers yellow, blue and red, security thread blue, yellow, red. 148x73mm.

	VF	UNC
a. Signature 21. Watermark: Arms.	FV	10.00
b. Signature 22. Watermark: Arms.	FV	10.00
c. Signature 23. Watermark: Arms.	FV	10.00
d. Signature 23. Watermark: Mohd. H. Fahmideh (youth).	FV	6.00
e. Signature 24. Watermark: Mohd. H. Fahmideh (youth).	FV	4.00
f. Signature 25. Watermark: Mohd. H. Fahmideh (youth).	FV	4.00
g. Signature 25. Watermark: Arms.	25.00	125.
h. Signature 26. Watermark: Moh. H. Fahmideh (youth).	FV	3.00
i. Signature 27. Watermark: Arms.	FV	3.00
j. Signature 27. Watermark: Mohd. H. Fahmideh (youth).	FV	3.00
k. Signature 28. Watermark: Khomeini.	FV	3.00
l. Signature 28. Watermark: Mohd. H. Fahmideh (youth).	FV	3.00

1992; 1993 ND Issue

#142 not assigned.

143 1000 Rials

ND (1992-). Brown and dark green on multicolor underprint. Khomeini at right. Back: Dome of the Rock in Jerusalem at center. UV: fibers fluoresce yellow and blue, serial #s orange. 148x73mm.

	VF	UNC
a. Signature 25. Watermark: Mohd. Fahmideh (youth).	FV	12.50
b. Signature 27. Watermark: Mohd. Fahmideh (youth).	FV	5.00
c. Signature 28. Watermark: Mohd. Fahmideh (youth).	FV	3.00
d. Signature 31. Watermark: Khomeini.	FV	3.00
e. Signature 34.	FV	3.00

144 2000 Rials

ND (2005-). Lilac and green on multicolor underprint. Khomeini at right. Back: Mosque interior in Mecca. Watermark: Khomeini. 148x73mm.

	VF	UNC
a. Signature 33.	FV	4.50
b. Signature 34.	FV	4.50
c. Signature 35.	FV	4.50
d. Signature 36.	FV	4.50

145 5000 Rials

ND (1993-). Dark brown, brown and olive-green on multicolor underprint. Khomeini at right. Back: Red-violet and pale olive-green on multicolor underprint. Flowers and birds at center right. Watermark: Khomeini. 154x75mm.

	VF	UNC
a. Signature 25.	FV	10.00
b. Signature 27.	FV	9.00
c. Signature 28.	FV	6.00
d. Signature 29.	FV	6.00
e. Signature 30.	FV	6.00

146 10,000 Rials

ND (1992-). Deep blue-green, blue and olive-green on multicolor underprint. Khomeini at right. Back: Mount Damavand at center right. Watermark: Khomeini. 160x77mm.

	VF	UNC
a. Signature 25.	FV	20.00
b. Signature 26.	FV	20.00
c. Signature 27.	FV	12.50
d. Signature 28.	FV	12.50
e. Signature 29.	FV	9.00
f. Signature 30.	FV	9.00
g. Signature 33.	FV	9.00

147 20,000 Rials

ND (2004-5). Blue and green on multicolor underprint. Large Imam Khomeini bust at right. Back: Khomeini square in Isfahan. Watermark: Khomeini. 164x77mm.

	VF	UNC
a. Signature 30.	FV	20.00
b. Signature 31.	FV	20.00
c. Signature 32.	FV	20.00

148 20,000 Rials VF UNC
2005. Blue and green on multicolor underprint. Smaller Iman Khomeini bust at right. Signature 31. Back: Khomeini square in Isfahan. Watermark: Khomeini. 164x77mm.

	VF	UNC
a. Signature 32.	FV	15.00
b. Signature 33.	FV	15.00

149 50,000 Rials VF UNC
2006-. Purple on brown, green, orange and multicolor underprint. Iman Khomeini at right. Back: Map and atomic emblems. Watermark: Khomeini. 166x70mm.

	VF	UNC
a. Signature 33.	FV	45.00
b. Signature 34.	FV	45.00
c. Signature 36 (2011).	FV	45.00

2009-2010 Issue

150 5000 Rials VF UNC
2009. Lilac and green on multicolor underprint. Iman Khomeini bust at right. Back: Omid Satellite. Watermark: Khomeni. 154x75mm.

	VF	UNC
a. Signature 36.	FV	6.00

151 100,000 Rials VF UNC
2010. Olive green and green on multicolor underprint. Iman Khomeini at right. Back: Tomb of poet Muslih al-din Sa'di. 166x79mm. FV 75.00

2013 Issue

152 5000 Rials VF UNC
2013. Brown and green on multicolor underprint. Iman Khomeini bust at right. Back: Ancient painted bowl and plate. Watermark: Khomeini. FV 4.00

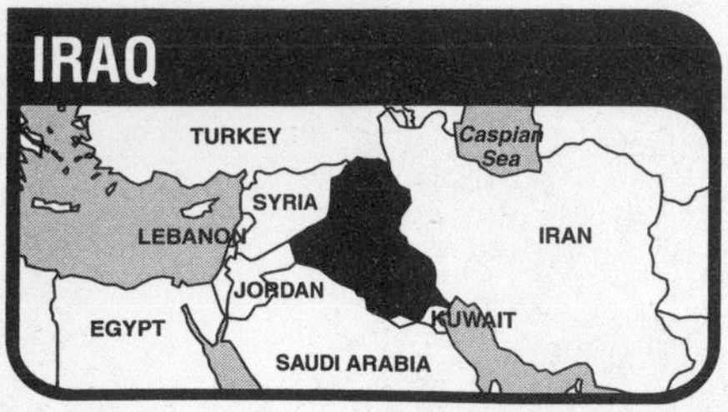

The Republic of Iraq, historically known as Mesopotamia, is located in the Near East and is bordered by Kuwait, Iran, Turkey, Syria, Jordan and Saudi Arabia. It has an area of 437,072 sq. km. and a population of 28.22 million. Capital: Baghdad. The economy of Iraq is d on agriculture and petroleum. Crude oil accounts for 94 percent of the exports before the war with Iran began in 1980.

Formerly part of the Ottoman Empire, Iraq was occupied by Britain during the course of World War I; in 1920, it was declared a League of Nations mandate under UK administration. In stages over the next dozen years, Iraq attained its independence as a kingdom in 1932. A "republic" was proclaimed in 1958, but in actuality a series of military strongmen ruled the country until 2003. The last was Saddam Husayn. Territorial disputes with Iran led to an inconclusive and costly eight-year war (1980-88). In August 1990, Iraq seized Kuwait but was expelled by US-led, UN coalition forces during the Gulf War of January-February 1991. Following Kuwait's liberation, the UN Security Council (UNSC) required Iraq to scrap all weapons of mass destruction and long-range missiles and to allow UN verification inspections. Continued Iraqi noncompliance with UNSC resolutions over a period of 12 years led to the US-led invasion of Iraq in March 2003 and the ouster of the Saddam Husayn regime. Coalition forces remain in Iraq under a UNSC mandate, helping to provide security and to support the freely elected government. The Coalition Provisional Authority, which temporarily administered Iraq after the invasion, transferred full governmental authority on 28 June 2004 to the Iraqi Interim Government, which governed under the Transitional Administrative Law for Iraq (TAL). Under the TAL, elections for a 275-member Transitional National Assembly (TNA) were held in Iraq on 30 January 2005. Following these elections, the Iraqi Transitional Government (ITG) assumed office. The TNA was charged with drafting Iraq's permanent constitution, which was approved in a 15 October 2005 constitutional referendum. An election under the constitution for a 275-member Council of Representatives (CoR) was held on 15 December 2005. The CoR approval in the selection of most of the cabinet ministers on 20 May 2006 marked the transition from the ITG to Iraq's first constitutional government in nearly a half-century.

RULERS:

Faisal I, 1921-1933
Ghazi I, 1933-1939
Faisal II, 1939-1958

MONETARY SYSTEM:

1 Dirham = 50 Fils
1 Riyal = 200 Fils
1 Dinar = 1000 Fils

SIGNATURE AND GOVERNOR VARIETIES

	GENERAL DIRECTOR		
12		13	
14		15	
16		17	
18		19	
20		21	
22		23	
24		25	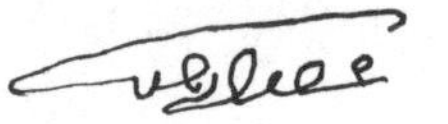

SIGNATURE AND GOVERNOR VARIETIES

	GENERAL DIRECTOR		
26		27	

REPUBLIC

CENTRAL BANK OF IRAQ

1959 ISSUE

51	1/4 Dinar	VF	UNC
	ND (1959). Green on multicolor underprint. Republic arms with 1958 at right. Back: Palm trees at center. Watermark: Republic arms with 1958.		
	a. Without security thread. Signature 13.	5.00	15.00
	b. With security thread. Signature 14, 16.	5.00	10.00
	s. Specimen. Punched hole cancelled.	—	30.00

52	1/2 Dinar	VF	UNC
	ND (1959). Brown on multicolor underprint. Republic arms with 1958 at right. Back: Ruins of the mosque and spiral minaret at Samarra. Watermark: Republic arms.		
	a. Without security thread. Signature 13.	7.50	30.00
	b. With security thread. Signature 14, 16.	7.50	30.00
	s. Specimen. Punched hole cancelled.	—	30.00

53	1 Dinar	VF	UNC
	ND (1959). Blue on multicolor underprint. Republic arms with 1958 at right. Back: The *Harp of Ur* at center. Watermark: Republic arms.		
	a. Without security thread. Signature 13.	8.00	30.00
	b. With security thread. Blue lines over watermark area. Signature 14, 15.	8.00	30.00
	s. Specimen. Punched hole cancelled.	—	30.00

54 5 Dinars VF UNC

ND (1959). Light purple on multicolor underprint. Republic arms with 1958 at right. Back: Ancient carving of Hammurabi receiving the laws. Watermark: Symbol of the Immortal Revolution.

	VF	UNC
a. Without security thread. 1 signature variety.	15.00	45.00
b. With security thread.	15.00	45.00
s. Specimen. Punched hole cancelled.	—	30.00

55 10 Dinars VF UNC

ND (1959). Purple on multicolor underprint. Republic arms with 1958 at right. Signature 10, 11 and 12. Back: Carvings of a winged Assyrian ox and an Assyrian priest. Watermark: Symbol of the Immortal Revolution.

	VF	UNC
a. Without security thread. 1 signature variety.	12.00	65.00
b. With security thread. 2 signature varieties.	12.00	65.00
s. Specimen. Punched hole cancelled.	—	30.00

1971 ND Issue

56 1/4 Dinar VF UNC

ND (1971). Green and brown on multicolor underprint. Harbor at center. Signature 16. Back: *1/4 Dinar* at left, palm trees at center. Watermark: Falcon's head. 3.00 9.00

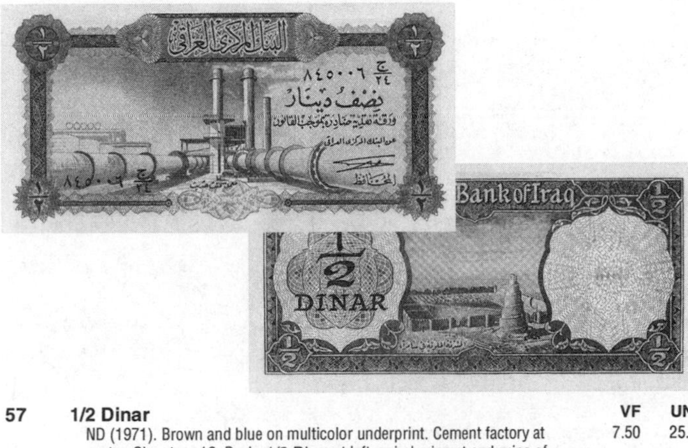

57 1/2 Dinar VF UNC

ND (1971). Brown and blue on multicolor underprint. Cement factory at center. Signature 16. Back: *1/2 Dinar* at left, spiral minaret and ruins of mosque at Samarra at center. Watermark: Falcon's head. 7.50 25.00

58 1 Dinar VF UNC

ND (1971). Blue and brown on multicolor underprint. Oil refinery at center. Signature 16, 17. Back: Entry to the al-Mustansiriyah School at center, *1 Dinar* at left. Watermark: Falcon's head. 6.00 17.50

59 5 Dinars VF UNC

ND (1971). Lilac on brown and multicolor underprint. Parliament building. Signature 16, 17. Back: Hammurabi (left) in conversation with sun god Shamash at center *5 Dinars* at left. Watermark: Falcon's head. 15.00 45.00

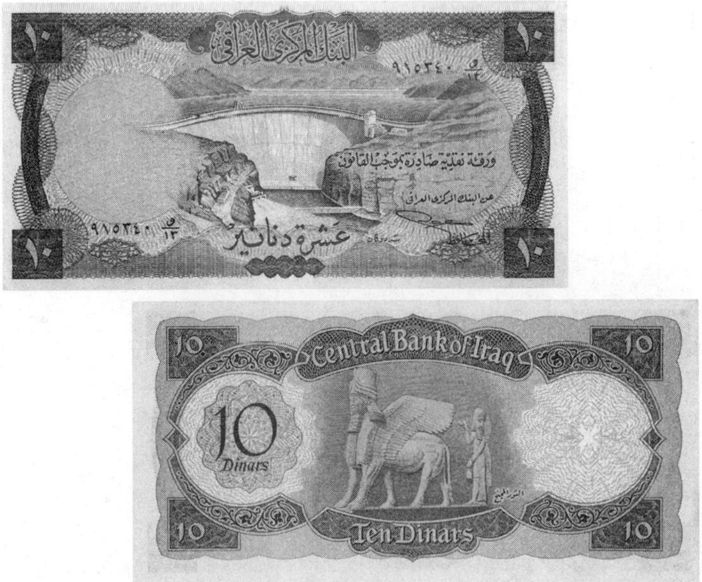

60 10 Dinars VF UNC

ND (1971). Purple, blue and brown on multicolor underprint. Dockdan dam at center. Signature 17. Back: Winged statues from the palace complex of Sargon II at Khorsabad at center, *10 Dinars* at left Watermark: Falcon's head. 15.00 45.00

1973 ND; 1978 Issue

61 1/4 Dinar

	VF	UNC
ND (1973). Green and black on multicolor underprint. Harbor at center. Signature 17, 18. Back: Palm trees at center, *Quarter Dinar* at bottom right. Watermark: Falcon's head.	1.50	5.00

62 1/2 Dinar

	VF	UNC
ND (1973). Brown on multicolor underprint. Cement factory at center. Signature 17, 18. Back: *Half Dinar* below Minaret of the Great Mosque at Samarra at center. Watermark: Falcon's head.	4.00	20.00

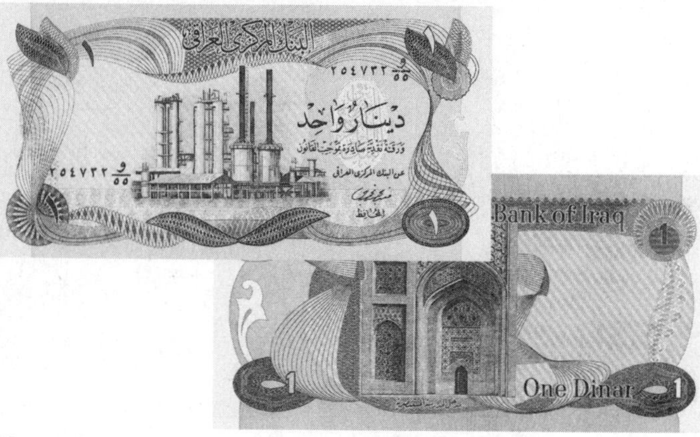

63 1 Dinar

ND (1973). Dark blue and aqua on multicolor underprint. Oil refinery at center. Signature 17, 18. Back: Entry to the al-Mustansiriyah School at center, *One Dinar* at bottom right. Watermark: Falcon's head.

	VF	UNC
a. 1 line of Arabic caption (factory name) below.	4.50	32.50
b. Without Arabic caption below factory.	3.00	12.00

64 5 Dinars

	VF	UNC
ND (1973). Deep lilac on multicolor underprint. Parliament building. Signature 17, 18. Back: Hammurabi (left) in conversation with sun god Shamash at center *5 Dinars* at bottom. Watermark: Falcon's head.	3.00	10.00

65 10 Dinars

	VF	UNC
ND (1973). Purple and red-brown on blue and multicolor underprint. Dockdan dam at right. Signature 17, 18. Back: Winged statues from the palace complex of Sargon II at Khorsabad at center, *Ten Dinars* at bot Watermark: Falcon's head.	5.00	15.00

66 25 Dinars

1978; 1980. Green and brown on multicolor underprint. Three Arabian horses at center, date below signature at lower right. Back: Abbasid Palace. Watermark: Falcon's head. 182x88mm.

	VF	UNC
a. 1978/AH1398. Signature 19.	10.00	30.00
b. 1980/AH1400. Signature 21.	7.50	22.50
s. Specimen.	—	—

1979-86 Issue

67 1/4 Dinar

1979/AH1399. Green and multicolor. Palm trees at center. Signature 20. Back: Building. Watermark: Arabian horse's head.

	VF	UNC
a. Issued note.	.50	1.50
s. Specimen.	—	—

68 1/2 Dinar

1980/AH1400; 1985/AH1405. Brown and multicolor. Astrolabe at right. Signature 21, 22. Back: Minaret of Samarra. Watermark: Arabian horse's head.

	VF	UNC
a. Issued note.	.50	1.50
s. Specimen.	—	—

69 1 Dinar

1979/AH1399; 1980/AH1400; 1984/AH1405. Olive-green and deep blue on multicolor underprint. Coin design at center. Signature 21. Back: Mustansiriyah School in Baghdad. Watermark: Arabian horse's head. UV: fibers fluoresce blue, Arabic 1s green.

	VF	UNC
a. Issued note.	.50	1.50
s. Specimen.	—	—

70 5 Dinars

1980/AH1400; 1981/AH1401; 1982/AH1402. Brown-violet and deep blue on multicolor underprint. Gali-Ali Beg waterfall at center. Signature 21. Back: Al-Ukhether castle at center. Watermark: Arabian horse's head.

	VF	UNC
a. Issued note.	1.50	4.00
s. Specimen.	—	450.

71 10 Dinars

1980/AH1400; 1981/AH1401; 1982/AH1402. Purple on blue, violet and multicolor underprint. Al-Hassan ibn al-Haitham (scientist) at right. Signature 21. Back: Hadba minaret in Mosul. Watermark: Arabian horse's head.

	VF	UNC
a. Issued note.	1.50	5.00
s. Specimen. Red overprint in Arabic.	—	450.

72 25 Dinars

	VF	UNC
1981/AH1401; 1982/AH1402. Green and brown. Three Arabian horses at center, date below. Signature 21. Back: Abbasid Palace. Watermark: Arabian horse's head. Reduced size. 175x80mm.	1.00	2.00

73 25 Dinars

1986. Brown, green and black on blue and multicolor underprint. Charging horsemen at center, Saddam Hussein at right. Signature 22. Back: City gate at left, Martyr's monument at center. Watermark: Saddam Hussein. UV: Arabic 2s fluoresce yellow.

	VF	UNC
a. Issued note.	1.50	4.50
s. Specimen. Red overprint in Arabic.	—	750.

1990 Emergency Gulf War Issue

#74-76 Iraq printing. Many color shade varieties exist because of poor printing quality.

74 25 Dinars VF UNC

1990/AH1411. Green and gray. Three Arabian horses at center, date below signature at lower right. Date below horses. Signature 23. Back: Abbasid Palace. Lithograph, without watermark.

	VF	UNC
a. Green underprint with pink highlights and brown ink.	.50	1.00
b. Green underprint without pink highlights and black ink.	.50	1.00
c. Green and pink underprint. with pink highlights and brown ink.	.50	1.00

75 50 Dinars VF UNC

1991/AH1411. Brown and blue-green on peach and multicolor underprint. Saddam Hussein at right. Signature 23. Back: Minaret of the Great Mosque at Samarra at center right. Lithograph. .50 2.00

76 100 Dinars VF UNC

1991/AH1411. Dark blue-green on lilac and multicolor underprint. Saddam Hussein at right. Signature 23. Back: Victory Arch Monument of crossed swords at center. 15.00 40.00

1992-93 Emergency Issue

#77-79 dull lithograph printing. With faint indelible ink wmk.

77 1/4 Dinar VF UNC

1993/AH1413. Green on multicolor underprint. Palm trees at center. Signature 24. Back: Building. Printer: Chinese. — .50

78 1/2 Dinar VF UNC

1993/AH1413. Brown on multicolor underprint. Astrolabe at right. Signature 24. Back: Minaret of Samarra. Printer: Chinese.

	VF	UNC
a. Dark brown underprint.	—	.50
b. Light lilac underprint.	—	.50

79 1 Dinar VF UNC

1992/AH1412. Green and blue-black on multicolor underprint. Coin design at center. Signature 24. Back: Mustansiriyah School in Baghdad. Printer: Chinese. — .50

80 5 Dinars VF UNC

1992/AH1412. Dull red-brown on pale orange, lilac and multicolor underprint. Color shade varieties. Temple at center. Saddam Hussein at right. Signature 24. Back: Hammurabi in conversation with the sun god Shamash at left. Tomb of the unknown soldier in center. Printer: Chinese. UV: threads fluoresce blue and orange.

	VF	UNC
a. With border around embossed text at center.	—	4.00
b. Without border around embossed text at center.	—	4.00
c. As b. without embossed text at center.	—	1.00

81 **10 Dinars** — VF: — UNC: 2.50

1992/AH1412. Purplish black, blue-green and multicolor. Saddam Hussein at right. Signature 24. Back: Statue of winged beast from the palace complex of Sargon II at Khorsabad at left. Printer: Chinese. UV: threads fluoresce yellow and blue, Arabic 10 yellow.

1994-95 Issue

83 **50 Dinars** — VF: — UNC: 1.50

1994/AH1414. Brown and pale green on multicolor underprint. Ancient statuette, monument at left center. Saddam Hussein at right. Signature 24. Back: "Aljahad Project" double deck Saddam bridge at center.

84 **100 Dinars** — VF UNC

1994/AH1414. Dark blue on light blue and pale ochre underprint. Al-Ukhether castle at center. Saddam Hussein at right. Signature 24. Back: Baghdad clock at center. Watermark: Printed Falcon's head.

- a1. First diacritical mark in the text of the denomination is above the first letter (from the right). Printed on white paper which fluoresces. — VF: — UNC: 1.00
- a2. As a. but printed on dark paper which does not fluoresce under UV light. — VF: — UNC: 1.00
- b. First diacritical mark in the text of the denomination is below the second letter (from the right). — VF: — UNC: 1.00

85 **250 Dinars** — VF UNC

1995/AH1415. Lavender on blue and multicolor underprint. Hydroelectric dam at left center. Saddam Hussein at right. Signature 25. Back: Friese from the Liberty Monument across back. Shade varieties exist.

- a1. First word of the text for the denomination has its second letters as a long 'a.' Printed on white paper which fluoresces. — VF: — UNC: 1.25
- a2. As a. but printed on dark paper which does not fluoresce under UV light. — VF: — UNC: 1.25
- b. First word of the text for the denomination has its second last letters as a long 'i', also with different diacritical marks. — VF: — UNC: 1.25

2001-02 Issue

86 **25 Dinars** — VF: — UNC: 1.50

2001/AH1422. Brown on light green underprint. Saddam Hussein at right. Signature 25. UV: fibers fluoresce blue and yellow.

87 **100 Dinars** — VF: — UNC: 3.00

2002/AH1422. Blue on blue and yellow underprint. Saddam Hussein at right. Signature 25. Back: Shenashils of old Baghdad. UV: fibers fluoresce blue and yellow

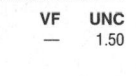

88 **250 Dinars** — VF: — UNC: 1.50

2002/AH1422. Purple on rose and blue underprint. Saddam Hussein at right. Signature 25. Back: Dome of the Rock in Jerusalem. UV: fibers fluoresce green, red and blue, security strip orange.

89 **10,000 Dinars** — VF: — UNC: 7.00

2002/AH1423. Tomb of unknown soldier in center, Saddam Hussein at right. Signature 25. Back: Al-Mustansiriyah University in Baghdad and Arabic astrolobe.

Democratic Republic

Central Bank of Iraq

2003-04 Issue

90 50 Dinars — VF / UNC

2003/AH1424. Purple on multicolor underprint. Grain silo at Basrah. Signature 26. Back: Date palms. Printer: TDLR. — FV / 1.00

91 250 Dinars — VF / UNC

2003/AH1424. Light and dark blue on multicolor underprint. Astrolobe. Signature 26. Back: Spiral Minaret in Samarra. Printer: TDLR. 130x66mm. — FV / 1.50

92 500 Dinars — VF / UNC

2004/AH1425. Green and blue on multicolor underprint. Ducan Dam at center. Signature 27. Back: Winged bull statue. Printer: TDLR. 142x66mm. — FV / 2.00

93 1000 Dinars — VF / UNC

2003/AH1424. Light and dark brown. Medieval dinar coin. Signature 26. Back: Al-Mustansiriyah University in Baghdad. Printer: TDLR. 142x66mm. — FV / 2.50

94 5000 Dinars — VF / UNC

2003/AH1424-. Dark blue on multicolor underprint. Gali Ali Beg and waterfall. Back: Al-Ukhether fortress. Printer: TDLR. UV: solid rectangle with Arabic 5000 fluoresces yellow. 158x79mm.

	VF	UNC
a. 2003/AH1424. Signature 26.	FV	14.00
b. 2006/AH1427. Signature 27.	FV	10.00
c. 2010/AH1431.	FV	10.00

95 10,000 Dinars — VF / UNC

2003/AH1424-. Green on multicolor underprint. Abu Ali Hasan Ibn al-Haitham (known as Alhazen), physicist and mathematician. Back: Hadba Minaret at the Great Nurid Mosque in Mosul. Printer: TDLR. 170x78mm.

	VF	UNC
a. 2003/AH1424. Signature 26.	FV	20.00
b. 2004/AH1425. Signature 27.	FV	17.00
c. 2006/AH1427. Signature 27.	FV	15.00
d. 2010/AH1431.	FV	15.00

96 25,000 Dinars — VF / UNC

2003/AH1424-. Red, purple and tan on multicolor underprint. Kurdish farmer holding sheaf of wheat, tractor in background. Back: Ancient Babylonian King Hammurabi. Printer: TDLR.

	VF	UNC
a. 2003/AH1424. Signature 26.	FV	35.00
b. 2004/AH1425. Signature 27.	FV	30.00
c. 2006/AH1427. Signature 27.	FV	27.50
d1. 2010/AH1431.	FV	27.50

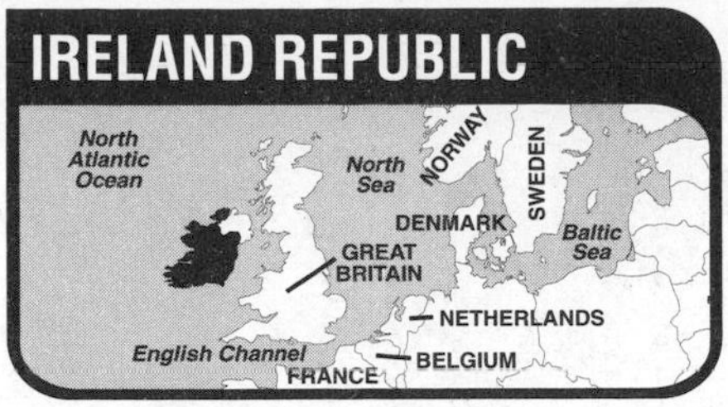

The Republic of Ireland, occupying five-sixths of the island of Ireland located in the Atlantic Ocean west of Great Britain, has an area of 70,280 sq. km. and a population of 4.16 million. Capital: Dublin.

Celtic tribes arrived on the island between 600-150 B.C. Invasions by Norsemen that began in the late 8th century were finally ended when King Brian Boru defeated the Danes in 1014. English invasions began in the 12th century and set off more than seven centuries of Anglo-Irish struggle marked by fierce rebellions and harsh repressions. A failed 1916 Easter Monday Rebellion touched off several years of guerrilla warfare that in 1921 resulted in independence from the UK for 26 southern counties; six northern (Ulster) counties remained part of the UK. In 1949, Ireland withdrew from the British Commonwealth; it joined the European Community in 1973.

Additional information on bank notes of Northern Ireland can be found in *Paper Money of Ireland* by Bob Blake and Jonathan Callaway, published by Pam West.

RULERS:

British to 1921

MONETARY SYSTEM:

1 Shilling = 12 Pence
1 Pound = 20 Shillings to 1971
1 Pound = 100 Pence, 1971-2001
1 Euro = 100 Cent, 2002-

REPUBLIC

BANC CEANNAIS NA hÉIREANN

CENTRAL BANK OF IRELAND

1961-63 ISSUE

#63-69 Replacement notes: From 1974-1976 single letter prefix plus 6-digit serial number for £1-£20. For £1 and £5 dated 1975 a "00" was used in front of a prefix letter.

63	10 Shillings	VF	UNC
	3.1.1962-6.6.1968. Orange on light green and lilac underprint. Portrait of Lady Hazel Lavery at left, denomination at bottom center. Signature M. O'Muimhneacháin and T. K. Whitaker. Back: Representation of river gods at center. 78x138mm.		
	a. Issued note.	30.00	100.
	s. Specimen.	—	350.

64	1 Pound	VF	UNC
	1962-76. Green on pale gold underprint. Portrait of Lady Hazel Lavery at left, denomination at bottom center. Back: Representation of river gods at center. 84x151mm.		
	a. Signature M. O'Muimhneacháin and T. K. Whitaker. 16.3.1962-8.10.1968.	25.00	85.00
	b. Signature T. K. Whitaker and C. H. Murray. 1.3.1969-17.9.1970.	22.50	75.00
	c. Signature like b, but metallic security thread at left center 8.7.1971-21.4.1975.	20.00	60.00
	d. Signature C. H. Murray and M. O'Murchu. 30.9.1976.	20.00	60.00
	r1. Replacement note. As c. 17.5.1974. Serial # prefix: *S.*	35.00	95.00
	r2. Replacement note. As c. 21.4.1975. Serial # prefix: *OOA.*	35.00	130.
	r3. Replacement note. As d. 30.9.1976. Serial # prefix: *OOA.*	35.00	130.
	s. Specimen.	—	—

65	5 Pounds	VF	UNC
	1961-75. Dark brown on light gold and orange underprint. Portrait of Lady Hazel Lavery at left, denomination at bottom center. Back: Representation of river gods at center. 92x165mm.		
	a. Signature M. O'Muimhneacháin and T. K. Whitaker. 15.8.1961-12.8.1968.	50.00	400.
	b. Signature T. K. Whitaker and C. H. Murray. 12.5.1969; 27.2.1970.	50.00	350.
	c. Signature like b., but metallic security thread at left center 18.1.1971-5.9.1975.	50.00	300.
	r1. Replacement note. As c. 10.1.1975. Serial # prefix: *R.*	150.	600.
	r2. Replacement note. As c. 5.9.1975. Serial # prefix: *OOK.*	90.00	450.
	s. As a. Specimen. Red overprint: *SPECIMEN* and TDLR oval on both sides. Punch hole cancelled.	—	750.

66	10 Pounds	VF	UNC
	1962-76. Blue on multicolor underprint. Lady Hazel Lavery in Irish national costume with chin resting on her hand and leaning on an Irish harp. Back: Representation of river gods at center. 108x191mm.		
	a. Signature M. O'Muimhneacháin and T. K. Whitaker. 2.5.1962-16.7.1968.	60.00	485.
	b. Signature T. K. Whitaker and C. H. Murray. 5.5.1969; 9.3.1970.	60.00	425.
	c. Signature like b, but metallic security thread at left center 19.5.1971-10.2.1975.	60.00	385.
	d. Signature C. H. Murray and M. O'Murchu. 2.12.1976.	55.00	350.
	r1. Replacement note. As c. 10.2.1975. Serial # prefix: *T.*	100.	600.
	r2. Replacement note. As d. 2.12.1976. Serial # prefix: *T.*	100.	600.

67	20 Pounds	VF	UNC
	1961-76. Red on multicolor underprint. Lady Hazel Lavery in Irish national costume with chin resting on her hand and leaning on an Irish harp. Back: Representation of river gods at center. 203x114mm.		
	a. Signature M. O'Muimhneacháin and T. K. Whitaker. 1.6.1961-15.6.1965.	200.	850.
	b. Signature T. K. Whitaker and C. H. Murray. 3.3.1969-6.1.1975.	190.	750.
	c. Signature C. H. Murray and M. O'Murchu. 24.3.1976.	190.	650.
	r. Replacement note. As c. 34.3.1976. Serial # prefix: *V.*	600.	2000.

68	50 Pounds	VF	UNC
	1962-77. Purple on multicolor underprint. Lady Hazel Lavery in Irish national costume with chin resting on her hand and leaning on an Irish harp. Back: Representation of river gods at center. 203x114mm.		
	a. Signature M. O'Muimhneacháin and T. K. Whitaker. 1.2.1962-6.9.1968.	850.	2300.
	b. Signature T. K. Whitaker and C. H. Murray. 4.11.1970-16.4.1975.	750.	2100.
	c. Signature C. H. Murray and M. O'Murchu. 4.4.1977.	675.	1900.

69	100 Pounds	VF	UNC
	1963-77. Green on multicolor underprint. Lady Hazel Lavery in Irish national costume with chin resting on her hand and leaning on an Irish harp. Back: Representation of river gods at center. 114x203mm.		
	a. Signature M. O'Muimhneacháin and T. K. Whitaker. 16.1.1963-9.9.1968.	800.	2200.
	b. Signature T. K. Whitaker and C. H. Murray. 26.10.1970; 3.3.1972; 26.2.1973; 10.4.1975.	700.	2000.
	c. Signature C. H. Murray and M. O'Murchu. 4.4.1977.	650.	1850.

1976-82 Issue

#70-74 replacement notes: Serial # prefixes *AAA; BBB;* etc.

70	1 Pound	VF	UNC
	1977-89. Dark olive-green and green on multicolor underprint. Queen Medb at right. Back: Old writing. Watermark: Lady Lavery. 148x78mm.		
	a. Signature C. H. Murray and M. O'Murchu. 10.6.1977-29.11.1977.	12.00	35.00
	b. Signature C. H. Murray and T. F. O'Cofaigh. 30.8.1978-30.10.1981.	10.00	30.00
	c. Signature T. F. O'Cofaigh and M. F. Doyle. 30.6.1982-24.4.1987.	9.00	25.00
	d. Signature M. F. Doyle and S. P. Cromien. 23.3.1988-17.7.1989.	8.00	20.00
	r1. Replacement note. As a. Serial # prefix: *BBB.*	25.00	100.
	r2. Replacement note. As b. Serial # prefix: *BBB; DDD; GGG.*	25.00	100.
	r3. Replacement note. As c. Serial # prefix: *BBB; GGG.*	25.00	100.
	r4. Replacement note. As d. Serial # prefix: *BBB.*	20.00	80.00
	s. Specimen. As a, c.	—	550.

71	5 Pounds	VF	UNC
	1976-93. Brown and red-violet on multicolor underprint. John Scotus Eriugena at right. Back: Old writing. 156x82mm.		
	a. Signature T. K. Whitaker and C. H. Murray. 26.2.1976.	35.00	100.
	b. Signature C. H. Murray and M. O'Murchu. 18.5.1976-17.10.1977.	30.00	90.00
	c. Signature C. H. Murray and T. F. O'Cofaigh. 25.4.1979-29.10.1981.	25.00	65.00
	d. Signature T. F. O'Cofaigh and M. F. Doyle. 1982; 17.10.1983-22.4.1987.	22.50	60.00
	e. Signature M. F. Doyle and S. P. Cromien. 12.8.1988-7.5.1993.	20.00	55.00
	r1. Replacement note. As a. Serial # prefix: *AAA.*	100.	250.
	r2. Replacement note. As b. Serial # prefix: *AAA.*	70.00	100.
	r3. Replacement note. As c. Serial # prefix: *AAA.*	70.00	200.
	r4. Replacement note. As d. Serial # prefix: *AAA.*	70.00	200.
	r5. Replacement note. As e. Serial # prefix: *AAA.*	100.	250.
	r6. Replacement note. As e. Serial # prefix: *FFF.*	20.00	170.
	s. Specimen. As b, d.	—	650.

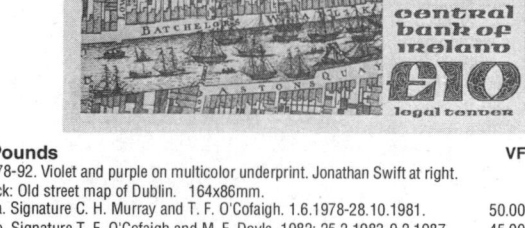

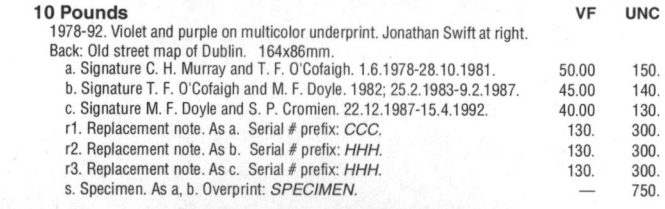

72	10 Pounds	VF	UNC
	1978-92. Violet and purple on multicolor underprint. Jonathan Swift at right. Back: Old street map of Dublin. 164x86mm.		
	a. Signature C. H. Murray and T. F. O'Cofaigh. 1.6.1978-28.10.1981.	50.00	150.
	b. Signature T. F. O'Cofaigh and M. F. Doyle. 1982; 25.2.1983-9.2.1987.	45.00	140.
	c. Signature M. F. Doyle and S. P. Cromien. 22.12.1987-15.4.1992.	40.00	130.
	r1. Replacement note. As a. Serial # prefix: *CCC.*	130.	300.
	r2. Replacement note. As b. Serial # prefix: *HHH.*	130.	300.
	r3. Replacement note. As c. Serial # prefix: *HHH.*	130.	300.
	s. Specimen. As a, b. Overprint: *SPECIMEN.*	—	750.

73 20 Pounds	VF	UNC
1980-92. Blue on multicolor underprint. William Butler Yeats at right, Abbey Theatre symbol at center. Back: Map. 172x90mm.		
a. Signature C. H. Murray and T. F. O'Cofaigh. 7.1.1980-28.10.1981.	90.00	225.
b. Signature T. F. O'Cofaigh and M. F. Doyle. 11.7.1983-28.8.1986.	80.00	200.
c. Signature M. F. Doyle and S. P. Cromien. 12.8.1987-14.2.1992.	75.00	185.
r1. Replacement note. As a. Serial # prefix: *EEE.*	300.	600.
r2. Replacement note. As b. Serial # prefix: *EEE.*	300.	600.
r3. Replacement note. As c. Serial # prefix: *EEE.*	300.	600.
r4. Replacement note. As c. Serial # prefix: *LLL.*	450.	800.
s. Specimen. As b.	—	850.

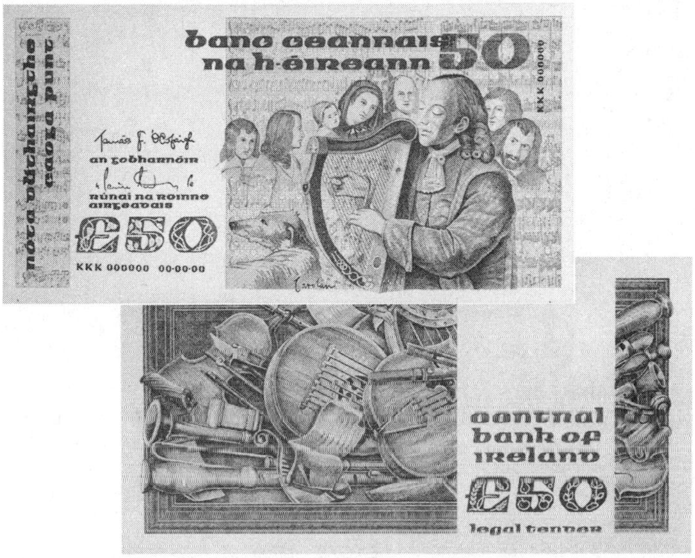

74 50 Pounds	VF	UNC
1982; 1991. Red and brown on multicolor underprint. Turlough O'Carolan playing harp in front of group. Back: Musical instruments. 180x94mm.		
a. Signature T. F. O'Cofaigh and M. F. Doyle. 1.11.1982.	200.	550.
b. Signature M. F. Doyle and S. P. Cromien. 5.11.1991.	185.	500.
r1. Replacement note. As a. Serial # prefix: *KKK.*	800.	2600.
r2. Replacement note. As b. Serial # prefix: *KKK.*	450.	1300.
s. Specimen. As a.		950.

1992-96 Issue

#75-78 Replacement notes: Serial # prefixes *BBB; CCC,* etc.

75 5 Pounds	VF	UNC
1994-99. Dark brown, reddish brown, and grayish purple on multicolor underprint. Mater Misericordiae Hospital at bottom left center, Sister Catherine McAuley at right. Back: School children at center. Watermark: Lady Lavery and value. 120x64mm.		
a. Signature M. F. Doyle and S. P. Cromien. 15.3.1994-28.4.1994.	FV	47.50
b. Signature M. O'Conaill and P. H. Mullarkey. 21.12.1994-15.10.1999.	FV	40.00
r1. Replacement note. As a. Serial # prefix: *HHH.*	10.00	80.00
r2. Replacement note. As b. Serial # prefix: *HHH.*	18.00	80.00
r3. Replacement note. As b. Serial # prefix: *MMM.*	25.00	100.

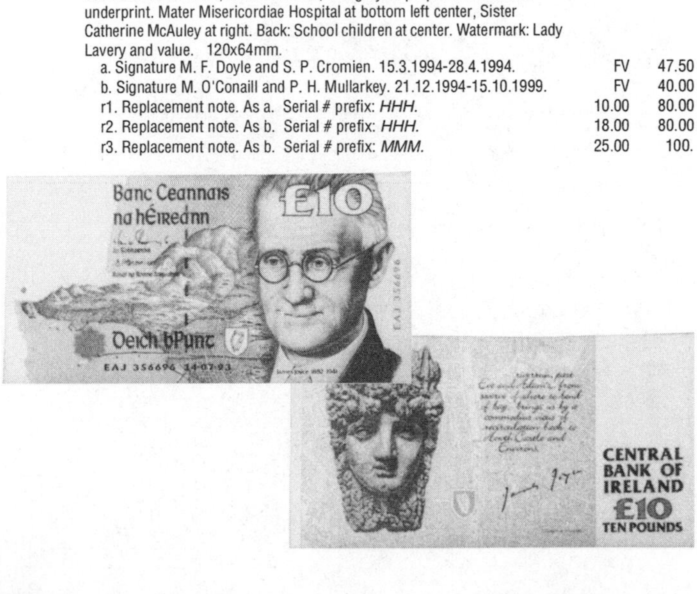

76 10 Pounds	VF	UNC
1993-99. Dark green and brown on multicolor underprint. Aerial view of Dublin at center, James Joyce at right. Back: Sculpted head representing Liffey River at left, map in underprint. Watermark: Lady Lavery and value. 128x68mm.		
a. Signature M. F. Doyle and S. P. Cromien. 14.7.1993-27.4.1994.	FV	80.00
b. Signature M. O'Conaill and P. H. Mullarkey. 13.3.1995-2.7.1999.	FV	75.00
r1. Replacement note. As a. Serial # prefix JJJ.	35.00	180.
r2. Replacement note. As b. Serial # prefix JJJ.	35.00	200.
r3. Replacement note. As b. Serial # prefix NNN.	35.00	200.

77 20 Pounds	VF	UNC
1992-99. Violet, brown and dark grayish blue on multicolor underprint. Derrynane Abbey at left center, Daniel O'Connell at right. Back: Writings and Four Courts building, Dublin. Watermark: Lady Lavery and value. 136x72mm.		
a. Signature M. F. Doyle and S. P. Cromien. 10.9.1992-29.4.1994.	FV	140.
b. Signature M. O'Conaill and P. H. Mullarkey. 14.6.1995-9.12.1999.	FV	125.
r1. Replacement note. 10.9.1992. As a. Serial # prefix: *BBB.* (Date exists only as a replacement).	400.	800.
r2. Replacement note. As a. (other dates). Serial # prefix: *BBB.*	50.00	260.
r3. Replacement note. As a. Serial # prefix: *FFF.*	50.00	200.
r4. Replacement note. As a. Serial # prefix: *CCC.*	100.	350.
r5. Replacement note. As b. Serial # prefix *PPP.*	90.00	350.

78 50 Pounds	VF	UNC
1995-2001. Dark blue and violet on multicolor underprint. Douglas Hyde at right, Áras an Uachtaráin building in background at center. Back: Dark gray and deep olive-green on multicolor underprint. Uilinn Piper at left, crest of *Conradh na Gaeilge* at upper center right. Watermark: Lady Lavery and value. 144x76mm.		
a. Signature M. O'Conaill and P. H. Mullarkey. 6.10.1995; 14.2.1996; 19.3.1999.	FV	325.
b. Signature M. O'Conaill and J. A. Hurley. 8.3.2001.	FV	300.
r1. Replacement note. As a. Serial # prefix: *EEE.*	250.	700.
r2. Replacement note. As b. Serial # prefix: *RRR.*	150.	550.

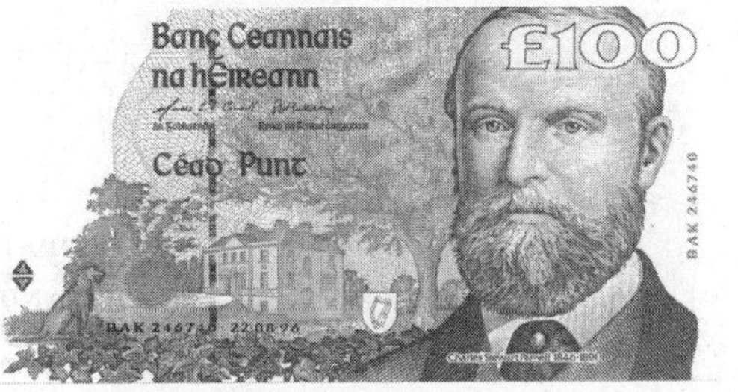

79 100 Pounds	VF	UNC
22.8.1996. Lilac brown, light orange-brown and slate. Charles Stewart Parnell at right, Avondale House and gardens in Rathdrum at lower left center, Irish Wolfhound at lower left. Signature M. O'Conaill and P. H. Mullarkey. Back: Parts of the Parnell monument in Dublin. 152x80mm.		
a. Issued note.	230.	800.
r1. Replacement note. As a. Serial # prefix: *KKK.*	400.	1200.

ISLE OF MAN

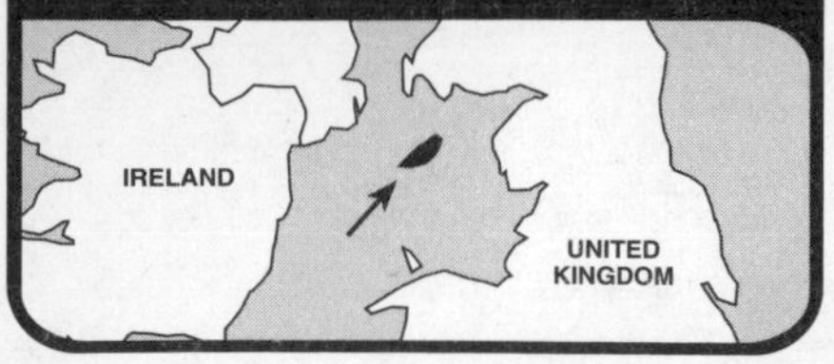

The Isle of Man, a dependency of the British Crown located in the Irish Sea equidistant from Ireland, Scotland and England, has an area of 572 sq. km. and a population of 76,220. Capital: Douglas. Agriculture, dairy farming, fishing and tourism are the chief industries.

Part of the Norwegian Kingdom of the Hebrides until the 13th century when it was ceded to Scotland, the isle came under the British crown in 1765. Current concerns include reviving the almost extinct Manx Gaelic language. Isle of Man is a British crown dependency but is not part of the UK. However, the UK Government remains constitutionally responsible for its defense and international representation. The Sovereign of the United Kingdom (currently Queen Elizabeth II) holds the title Lord of Man. The Isle of Man is ruled by its own legislative council and the House of Keys, one of the oldest legislative assemblies in the world. Acts of Parliament passed in London do not affect the island unless it is specifically mentioned.

United Kingdom bank notes and coinage circulate concurrently with Isle of Man money as legal tender.

RULERS:
British

MONETARY SYSTEM:
1 Pound = 20 Shillings to 1971
1 Pound = 100 Pence, 1971-

BRITISH ADMINISTRATION

LLOYDS BANK LIMITED

1955 ISSUE

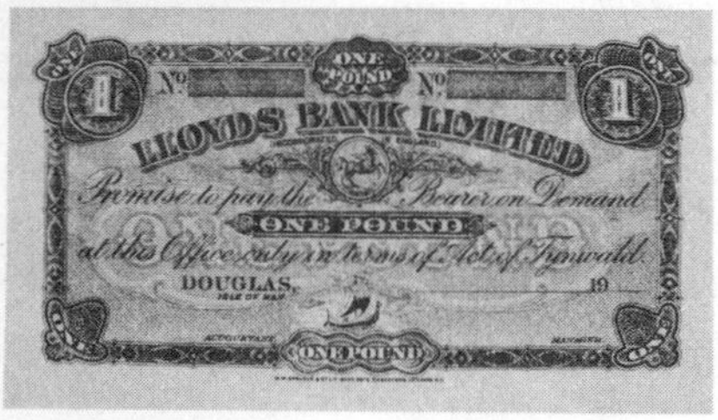

		Fine	XF
13	**1 Pound** 21.1.1955-14.3.1961. Black on green underprint. Bank arms at upper center. Signature varieties. Back: Bank title enlarged.		
	a. Issued note.	350.	750.
	r. Unsigned remainder. ND.	—	200.

WESTMINSTER BANK LIMITED

1955 ISSUE

		Fine	XF
23A	**1 Pound** 1955-61. Black on light yellow underprint. Crowned triskele supported by lion left, unicorn right at upper center. Text: *INCORPORATED IN ENGLAND* added below bank name. Signature varieties. Printer: W&S.		
	a. 23.11.1955.	200.	500.
	b. 4.4.1956-10.3.1961.	100.	225.

ISLE OF MAN GOVERNMENT

1961 ND ISSUE

		VF	UNC
24	**10 Shillings** ND (1961). Red on multicolor underprint. Triskele arms at lower center, young portrait of Queen Elizabeth II at right. Back: Old sailing boat. Watermark: Triskele arms. Printer: BWC.		
	a. Signature 1.	25.00	85.00
	b. Signature 2.	20.00	75.00
	s1. Signature 1. Specimen. 00000 serial #. (150 issued).	—	250.
	s2. Signature 2. Specimen.	—	260.

		VF	UNC
25	**1 Pound** ND (1961). Purple on multicolor underprint. Triskele arms at lower center, young portrait of Queen Elizabeth II at right. Back: Tynwald Hill. Watermark: Triskele arms. Printer: BWC.		
	a. Signature 1. Without serial # prefix, or Serial # prefix *B*.	40.00	180.
	b. Signature 2.	30.00	135.
	s1. Signature 1. Specimen. 00000 serial #. (150 issued).	—	280.
	s2. Signature 2. Specimen.	—	200.

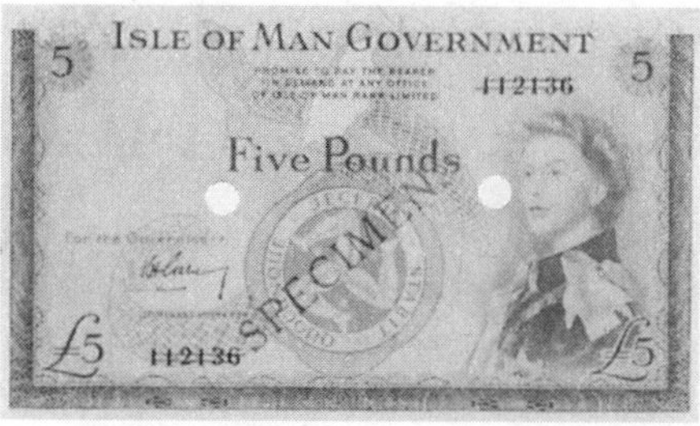

		VF	UNC
26	**5 Pounds** ND (1961). Green and blue on multicolor underprint. Triskele arms at lower center, young portrait of Queen Elizabeth II at right. Back: Castle Rushen. Watermark: Triskele arms. Printer: BWC.		
	a. Signature 1.	200.	1500.
	b. Signature 2.	185.	1350.
	s1. Specimen with normal serial #.	—	500.
	s2. Signature 1. Specimen with normal serial # blocked out, punch hole cancelled. (50 issued).	—	400.
	s3. Signature 1. Specimen. 000000 serial #. (150 issued).	—	350.
	s4. Signature 2. Specimen.	—	400.

1969 ND ISSUE

27	50 New Pence	VF	UNC
	ND (1969). Blue on multicolor underprint. Triskele arms at lower center, young portrait of Queen Elizabeth II at right. Signature 2. Back: Old sailing boat. Watermark: Triskele arms. Printer: BWC. 139 x 66mm.		
	a. Issued note.	10.00	45.00
	s. Specimen.	—	300.

1972 ND Issue

28	50 New Pence	VF	UNC
	ND (1972). Blue on multicolor underprint. Triskele arms at center, mature portrait of Queen Elizabeth II at right. Signature title: *LIEUTENANT GOVERNOR*. Back: Old sailing boat. Watermark: Triskele arms. Printer: BWC. 126 x 62mm.		
	a. Signature 2.	20.00	60.00
	b. Signature 3.	12.50	35.00
	c. Signature 4.	12.50	30.00
	s1. As a. Specimen. Punched hole cancelled.	—	220.
	s2. As b, c. Specimen.	—	220.

29	1 Pound	VF	UNC
	ND (1972). Purple on multicolor underprint. Triskele arms at center, mature portrait of Queen Elizabeth II at right. Signature title: *LIEUTENANT GOVERNOR*. Back: Tynwald Hill. Watermark: Triskele arms. Printer: BWC.		
	a. Signature 2.	25.00	110.
	b. Signature 3. Series D.	150.	550.
	c. Signature 3. Series E.	25.00	100.
	d. Signature 4.	7.50	50.00
	s1. As a. Specimen. Punched hole cancelled.	—	240.
	s2. As b, c. Specimen.	—	240.

30	5 Pounds		
	ND (1972). Blue-black and violet on multicolor underprint. Triskele arms at center, mature portrait of Queen Elizabeth II at right. Signature title: *LIEUTENANT GOVERNOR*. Back: Gray-green. Castle Rushen. Watermark: Triskele arms. Printer: BWC.		
	a. Signature 2.	75.00	600.
	b. Signature 3.	40.00	300.
	s. As a, b. Specimen. Punched hole cancelled.	—	340.

31	10 Pounds	VF	UNC
	ND (1972). Brown and dark green on multicolor underprint. Triskele arms at center, mature portrait of Queen Elizabeth II at right. Signature title: *LIEUTENANT GOVERNOR*. Back: Brown and orange. Peel Castle ca.1830 at center. Watermark: Triskele arms. Printer: BWC.		
	a. Signature 2.	600.	2000.
	b. Signature 3.	150.	550.
	s. As a, b. Specimen, punched hole cancelled.	—	700.

1979 Commemorative Issue

#32, Millennium Year 1979

32	20 Pounds	VF	UNC
	1979. Red-orange, orange and dark brown on multicolor underprint. Triskele at center. Queen Elizabeth II at right. Island outline at upper right. Commemorative text at lower right of triskele. Back: Laxey wheel ca. 1854, crowd of people with hills in background. Printer: BWC.	150.	450.

1979 ND Issue

#33s-38s were mounted on a board for bank display.

33	50 New Pence	VF	UNC
	ND. Blue on multicolor underprint. Queen Elizabeth II at right, arms at center. Signature title: *TREASURER OF THE ISLE OF MAN*. Signature 5. Back: Old sailing boat. Watermark: Triskele arms. Printer: BWC.		
	a. Issued note.	FV	15.00
	s. Specimen. Normal serial #, punched hole cancelled.	—	185.

34	1 Pound		
	ND. Purple on multicolor underprint. Queen Elizabeth II at right, arms at center. Signature title: *TREASURER OF THE ISLE OF MAN*. Signature 5. Back: Tynwald Hill. Watermark: Triskele arms. Printer: BWC.		
	a. Issued note.	FV	20.00
	s. Specimen. Normal serial #, punched hole cancelled.	—	175.

35	5 Pounds	VF	UNC
	ND. Blue-black and violet on multicolor underprint. Queen Elizabeth II at right, arms at center. Signature title: *TREASURER OF THE ISLE OF MAN*. Back: Castle Rushen. Watermark: Triskele arms. Printer: BWC.		
	a. Signature 5. Series B-C.	50.00	175.
	b. Signature 5. Series D. Large 'D' with serifs.	75.00	300.

35A	5 Pounds		
	ND. Blue-black and violet on multicolor underprint. Queen Elizabeth II at right, arms at center. Signature title: *TREASURER OF THE ISLE OF MAN*. Modified guilloche. Series D. Narrow 'D' without serifs. Back: Castle Rushen. Watermark: Triskele arms. Printer: BWC.		
	a. Issued note.	50.00	200.
	s. Specimen. Normal serial #, punched hole cancelled.	—	275.

36 10 Pounds

ND. Brown and dark green on multicolor underprint. Queen Elizabeth II at right, arms at center. Signature title: *TREASURER OF THE ISLE OF MAN.* Signature 5. Back: Brown and orange. Peel Castle ca.1830 at center. Watermark: Triskele arms. Printer: BWC.

	VF	UNC
a. Without prefix.	90.00	400.
b. Prefix A.	100.	425.
c. Prefix B. (10,000 printed).	600.	2000.
s1. As a. Specimen. Without prefix.	—	900.
s2. Specimen. Prefix A, normal serial #, punched hole cancelled.	—	400.

37 20 Pounds

ND (1979). Red-orange, orange and dark brown on multicolor underprint. Queen Elizabeth II at right, arms at center. Signature title: *TREASURER OF THE ISLE OF MAN.* Without commemorative text. Back: Laxey wheel ca. 1854, crowd of people with hills in background. Watermark: Triskele arms. Printer: BWC.

	VF	UNC
a. Issued note.	125.	500.
s. Specimen. Normal serial #, punched hole cancelled.	—	510.

1983 ND Issue

38 1 Pound

ND (1983). Green on multicolor underprint. Triskele arms at lower center, young portrait of Queen Elizabeth II at right. Back: Tynwald Hill. Watermark: Triskele arms. Printer: BWC. Printed on Bradvek, a plastic.

	VF	UNC
a. Issued note.	5.00	45.00
s. Specimen.	—	220.

39 50 Pounds

ND (1983). Blue gray, deep green and olive-green on multicolor underprint. Back: Douglas Bay.

	VF	UNC
a. Issued note.	100.	180.
s. Specimen. Normal serial #, punched hole cancelled.	—	700.

1983 ND Reduced Size Issue

40 1 Pound

ND. Purple on multicolor underprint. Queen Elizabeth II at right, arms at center. Back: Tynwald Hill. Watermark: Triskele. Printer: TDLR. 128x65mm.

	VF	UNC
a. Signature 5.	4.00	15.00
b. Signature 6.	FV	5.00
c. Signature 7.	FV	5.00
r1. As a. Replacement note.	150.	—
r2. As b. Replacement note.	10.00	45.00
s. As a. Specimen.	—	575.

41 5 Pounds

ND. Greenish blue and lilac-brown on multicolor underprint. Queen Elizabeth II at right, arms at center. Back: Gray-green. Castle Rushen. Watermark: Triskele. Printer: TDLR. 135x70mm.

	VF	UNC
a. Signature 5.	20.00	85.00
b. Signature 6.	FV	20.00
r. As b. Replacement note.	20.00	70.00

42 10 Pounds

	VF	UNC
ND. Brown and green on multicolor underprint. Queen Elizabeth II at right, arms at center. Signature 6. Back: Brown, orange and multicolor. Peel Castle ca.1830 at center. Watermark: Triskele. Printer: TDLR. 142x75mm.	FV	55.00

43 20 Pounds

ND. Brown and red-orange on multicolor underprint. Queen Elizabeth II at right, arms at center. Back: Laxey wheel ca. 1854, crowd of people with hills in background. Watermark: Triskele. Printer: TDLR. 150x80mm.

	VF	UNC
a. Signature 5.	125.	450.
b. Signature 6. Without prefix, prefix B, C.	FV	90.00
r. As b. Replacement note.	50.00	120.

1998; 2000 ND Issue

44 10 Pounds

ND (1998). Brown and green on multicolor underprint. Queen Elizabeth II at right, arms at center. Back: Peel Castle ca.1830 at center. Watermark: Triskele. Printer: TDLR. 142x75mm.

	VF	UNC
a. Signature 6.	FV	37.50
b. Signature 7.	FV	22.50
r. Replacement note.	50.00	90.00

45 20 Pounds

ND (2000). Brown and red-orange on multicolor underprint. Elizabeth II at right, arms at center. Signature 6. Without prefix, prefix B, C. Back: Laxey wheel (ca. 1854), crowd of people with hills in background. Watermark: Triskele. Printer: TDLR. 150x80mm.

	VF	UNC
a. Signatrue 6, Cashen.	FV	70.00
b. Signature 7, Shimmin.	FV	60.00
s. Specimen. Serial # *D000000.* Punch hole cancelled.	—	200.

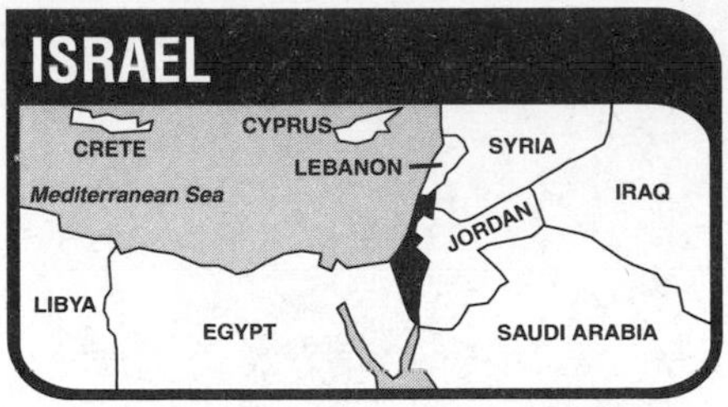

The State of Israel, at the eastern end of the Mediterranean Sea, bounded by Lebanon on the north, Syria on the northeast, Jordan on the east, and Egypt on the southwest, has an area of 20,770 sq. km. and a population of 7.11 million. Capital: Jerusalem. Diamonds, chemicals, citrus, textiles, and minerals are exported, local tourism to religious sites.

Following World War II, the British withdrew from their mandate of Palestine, and the UN partitioned the area into Arab and Jewish states, an arrangement rejected by the Arabs. Subsequently, the Israelis defeated the Arabs in a series of wars without ending the deep tensions between the two sides. The territories Israel occupied since the 1967 war are not included in the Israel country profile, unless otherwise noted. On 25 April 1982, Israel withdrew from the Sinai pursuant to the 1979 Israel-Egypt Peace Treaty. In keeping with the framework established at the Madrid Conference in October 1991, bilateral negotiations were conducted between Israel and Palestinian representatives and Syria to achieve a permanent settlement. Israel and Palestinian officials signed on 13 September 1993 a Declaration of Principles (also known as the "Oslo Accords") guiding an interim period of Palestinian self-rule.

MONETARY SYSTEM:

1 Lira = 1000 Prutot, 1948-1960
1 Lira = 100 Agorot, 1958-1980
1 Sheqel = 10 "old" Lirot, 1980-85
1 Sheqel = 100 New Agorot, 1980-1985
1 New Sheqel = 1000 "old" Sheqalim, 1985-
1 New Sheqel = 100 Agorot, 1985-

STATE OF ISRAEL

BANK OF ISRAEL

1958-60 / 5718-20 ISSUE

29	1/2 Lira	VF	UNC
	1958/5718. Green on green and peach underprint. Woman soldier with basket full of oranges at left. Back: Tombs of the Sanhedrin at right. Watermark: Woman soldier. Printer: JEZ (without imprint). UV: fibers fluoresce blue.		
	a. Issued note.	1.50	5.00
	s. Specimen.	—	275.

30	1 Lira	VF	UNC
	1958/5718. Blue on light blue and peach underprint. Fisherman with net and anchor at left. Back: Synagogue mosaic at right. Watermark: Fisherman. Printer: JEZ (without imprint). UV: fibers fluoresce blue.		
	a. Paper with security thread at left. Black serial #.	1.25	4.00
	b. Red serial #.	1.25	4.00
	c. Paper with security thread and morse tape, brown serial #.	1.00	3.00
	s. Specimen.	—	275.

31	5 Lirot	VF	UNC
	1958/5718. Brown on multicolor underprint. Worker with hammer in front of factory at left. Back: Seal of Shema at right. Watermark: Worker with hammer. Printer: TDLR (without imprint). UV: fibers fluoresce yellow.		
	a. Issued note.	2.00	5.00
	s. Specimen.	—	500.

32	10 Lirot	VF	UNC
	1958/5718. Lilac and purple on multicolor underprint. Scientist with microscope and test tube at left. Back: Dead Sea scroll and vases at right. Watermark: Scientist. Printer: TDLR (without imprint).		
	a. Paper with security thread. Black serial #.	2.00	12.00
	b. Paper with security thread and morse tape. Red serial #.	2.00	15.00
	c. Paper with security thread and morse tape. Blue serial #.	2.00	15.00
	d. Paper with security thread and morse tape. Brown serial #.	1.50	6.00
	s. Specimen.	—	500.

33	50 Lirot	VF	UNC
	1960/5720. Brown and multicolor. Boy and girl at left. Back: Mosaic of menorah at right. Watermark: Boy and girl. Printer: JEZ (without imprint).		
	a. Paper with security thread. Black serial #.	10.00	45.00
	b. Paper with security thread. Red serial #.	10.00	45.00
	c. Paper with security thread and morse tape. Blue serial #.	6.00	45.00
	d. Paper with security thread and morse tape. Green serial #.	6.00	30.00
	e. Paper with security thread and morse tape. Brown serial #.	5.00	30.00
	s. Specimen.	—	600.

1968 / 5728 Issue

34	5 Lirot	VF	UNC
	1968/5728. Gray-green and blue on multicolor underprint. Albert Einstein at right. Back: Atomic reactor at Nahal Sorek. Watermark: Albert Einstein. Printer: JEZ (without imprint).		
	a. Black serial #.	3.00	9.00
	b. Red serial #.	3.00	9.00
	s. Specimen.	—	225.

35	10 Lirot	VF	UNC
	1968/5728. Brown, purple and multicolor. Chaim Nahman Bialik at right. Back: Bialik's house in Tel Aviv. Watermark: Chaim Nahman Bialik. Printer: JEZ (without imprint). UV: fluoresce blue.		
	a. Black serial #.	1.00	5.00
	b. Green serial #.	1.00	5.00
	c. Blue serial #.	1.00	5.00
	s. Specimen.	—	225.

36	50 Lirot	VF	UNC
	1968/5728. Light and dark brown and green on multicolor underprint. President Chaim Weizmann at right. Back: Knesset building in Jerusalem. Watermark: President Chaim Weizmann. Printer: JEZ (without imprint).		
	a. Black serial #.	2.00	7.00
	b. Blue serial #.	2.00	7.00
	s. Specimen.	—	225.

37	100 Lirot	VF	UNC
	1968/5728. Blue and light green on multicolor underprint. Dr. Theodor Herzl at right. Back: Menorah and symbols of the twelve tribes of Israel at left center. Watermark: Dr. Theodor Herzl. Printer: JEZ (without imprint).		
	a. Watermark: Profile. Black serial #. 3.5mm.	10.00	30.00
	b. Watermark: 3/4 profile rright. Red serial #.	10.00	45.00
	c. Watermark: Profile. Black serial #. 2.8mm. Without series letter.	10.00	25.00
	d. Watermark: Profile. Brown serial #.	10.00	35.00
	s. Specimen.	—	225.

1973-75 / 5733-35 Issue

38	5 Lirot	VF	UNC
	1973/5733. Light and dark brown. Henrietta Szold at right. Marks for the blind. Back: Lion's Gate. Barely discernible bar code strips at lower left and upper right. Watermark: Henrietta Szold. Printer: JEZ (without imprint). UV: back barcodes fluoresce orange.	.50	1.50

39	10 Lirot	VF	UNC
	1973/5733. Purple on lilac underprint. Sir Moses Montefiore at right. Marks for the blind. Back: Jaffa Gate. Barely discernible bar code strips at lower left and upper right. Watermark: Sir Moses Montefiore. Printer: JEZ (without imprint). UV: back barcodes fluoresce orange.		
	a. Issued note.	.50	1.50
	s. Specimen.	—	—

40 50 Lirot

	VF	UNC
1973/5733. Green on olive-green underprint. Chaim Weizmann at right. Marks for the blind. Back: Sichem Gate. Barely discernible bar code strips at lower left and upper right. Watermark: Chaim Weizmann. Printer: JEZ (without imprint).	1.00	5.00

41 100 Lirot

	VF	UNC
1973/5733. Blue on blue and brown underprint. Dr. Theodor Herzl at right. Back: Zion Gate. Barely discernible bar code strips at lower left and upper right. Watermark: Dr. Theodor Herzl. Printer: JEZ (without imprint).	1.50	7.00

42 500 Lirot

	VF	UNC
1975/5735. Black on tan and brown underprint. David Ben-Gurion at right. Marks for the blind. Back: Golden Gate. Barely discernible bar code strips at lower left and upper right. Watermark: David Ben-Gurion. Printer: JEZ (without imprint).	10.00	45.00

1978-84 / 5738-44 Issue

Sheqel system

43 1 Sheqel

	VF	UNC
1978/5738 (1980). Purple on lilac underprint. Sir Moses Montefiore at right. Marks for the blind. Back: Jaffa Gate. Barely discernible bar code strips at lower left and upper right. Watermark: Sir Moses Montefiore. Printer: JEZ (without imprint). UV: back upper and lower barcodes fluoresce orange.		
a. Issued note.	.50	1.50
s. Specimen.	—	—

44 5 Sheqalim

	VF	UNC
1978/5738 (1980). Green on olive-green underprint. Chaim Weizmann at right. Marks for the blind. Back: Sichem Gate. Barely discernible bar code strips at lower left and upper right. Watermark: Chaim Weizmann. Printer: JEZ (without imprint). UV: back barcodes fluoresce orange.	.75	3.00

45 10 Sheqalim

	VF	UNC
1978/5738 (1980). Blue on blue and brown underprint. Dr. Theodor Herzl at right. Back: Zion Gate. Barely discernible bar code strips at lower left and upper right. Watermark: Dr. Theodor Herzl. Printer: JEZ (without imprint).	1.50	5.00

46 50 Sheqalim

	VF	UNC
1978/5738 (1980). Black on tan and brown underprint. David Ben-Gurion at right. Marks for the blind. Back: Golden Gate. Barely discernible bar code strips at lower left and upper right. Watermark: David Ben-Gurion. Printer: JEZ (without imprint). UV: back serial #s fluoresce orange.		
a. Without small bars below serial # or barely discernible bar code strips on back.	.50	2.00
b. Without small bars below serial #, but with bar code strips on back.	4.00	30.00
c. 2 green bars below serial # on back.	60.00	250.
d. 4 black bars below serial # on back.	35.00	200.
e. As a. 12-subject sheet.	—	20.00

47 **100 Sheqalim** | VF | UNC

1979/5739. Red-brown on light tan underprint. Ze'ev Jabotinsky at right. Marks for the blind. Back: Herod's Gate. Watermark: Ze'ev Jabotinsky. Printer: JEZ (without imprint).

	VF	UNC
a. Without bars below serial # on back.	1.50	10.00
b. 2 bars below serial # on back.	30.00	125.

48 **500 Sheqalim** | VF | UNC

1982/5742. Red on multicolor underprint. Farm workers at center, Baron Edmond de Rothschild at right. Marks for the blind. Back: Vine leaves. Watermark: Baron Edmond de Rothschild. Printer: JEZ (without imprint). | 1.50 | 6.00

49 **1000 Sheqalim** | VF | UNC

1983/5743. Green on multicolor underprint. Rabbi Moses Maimonides at right. Marks for the blind. Back: View of Tiberias at left. Watermark: Rabbi Moses Maimonides. Printer: JEZ (without imprint).

	VF	UNC
a. Error in first letter *he* of second word at right. in vertical text (right to left), partly completed letter resembling 7.	7.50	25.00
b. Corrected letter resembling *17*.	5.00	20.00
c. As a. Uncut sheet of 3 (3,610 sheets).	—	45.00
d. As b. Uncut sheet of 3 (3.365 sheets).	—	35.00

50 **5000 Sheqalim** | VF | UNC

1984/5744. Blue on multicolor underprint. City view at center, Levi Eshkol at right. Marks for the blind. Back: Water pipe and modern design. Watermark: Levi Eshkol. Printer: JEZ (without imprint).

	VF	UNC
a. Issued note.	7.50	45.00
b. Uncut sheet of 3 (2,755 sheets).	—	55.00

51 **10,000 Sheqalim** | VF | UNC

1984/5744. Brown, black, orange and dark green on multicolor underprint. Stylized tree at center, Golda Meir at right. Marks for the blind. Back: Gathering in front of Moscow synagogue. Watermark: Golda Meir. Printer: JEZ (without imprint).

	VF	UNC
a. Issued note.	10.00	30.00
b. Uncut sheet of 3 (2,720 sheets).	—	75.00

SIGNATURE VARIETIES

5	Mandelbaum, 1986	6	Shapira and Mandelbaum, 1985
7	Lorincz and Bruno, 1987-91	8	Lorincz and Frankel, 1992
9			

1985-92 / 5745-52 Issue

51A **1 New Sheqel** | VF | UNC

1986/5746. Green on multicolor underprint. Rabbi Moses Maimonides at right. Marks for the blind. Signature 5. Back: View of Tiberias at left. Watermark: Rabbi Moses Maimonides. Printer: JEZ (without imprint). 138x76mm.

	VF	UNC
a. Issued note.	.50	2.00
b. Uncut sheet of 3 (2,017 sheets).	—	7.00
c. Uncut sheet of 12 (1,416 sheets).	—	35.00
d. Uncut sheet of 18 (1.503 sheets).	—	50.00

52 5 New Sheqalim

1985/5745; 1987/5747. Blue on multicolor underprint. City view at center, Levi Eshkol at right. Marks for the blind. Back: Water pipe and modern design. Watermark: Levi Eshkol. Printer: JEZ (without imprint). 138x76mm.

	VF	UNC
a. Signature 6. 1985/5745.	3.00	15.00
b. Signature 7. 1987/5747.	2.50	18.00
c. As a. Uncut sheet of 3 (1,630 sheets).	—	40.00

53 10 New Sheqalim

1985/5745; 1987/5747; 1992/5752. Brown, black, orange and dark green on multicolor underprint. Stylized tree at center, Golda Meir at right. Marks for the blind. Back: Gathering in front of Moscow synagogue. Watermark: Golda Meir. Printer: JEZ (without imprint). 138x76mm.

	VF	UNC
a. Signature 6. 1985/5745.	6.00	35.00
b. Signature 7. 1987/5747.	4.00	30.00
c. Signature 8. 1992/5752.	2.00	20.00
d. As a. Uncut sheet of 3 (1,571 sheets)	—	40.00

54 20 New Sheqalim

1987/5747; 1993/5753. Dark gray on multicolor underprint. Moshe Sharett standing holding flag at center, his bust at right. Marks for the blind. Back: Herzlya High School at center. Watermark: Moshe Sharett. Printer: JEZ (without imprint). 138x76mm.

	VF	UNC
a. Without sm. double circle With dot in watermark. area face and back. signature 7. 1987/5747.	FV	45.00
b. With sm. double circle With dot in watermark. area face and back. signature 7. 1987/5747.	FV	20.00
c. Signature 8. 1993/5753.	FV	18.00

55 50 New Sheqalim

1985/5745-1992/5752. Purple on multicolor underprint. Shmuel Yosef Agnon at right. Marks for the blind. Back: Various buildings and book titles. Watermark: Shmuel Yosef Agnon. Printer: JEZ (without imprint). 138x76mm.

	VF	UNC
a. Signature 6. 1985/5745.	FV	90.00
b. Signature 7. Slight color variations. 1988/5748.	FV	90.00
c. Signature 8. 1992/5752.	FV	50.00

56 100 New Sheqalim

1986/5746; 1989/5749; 1995/5755. Brown on multicolor underprint. Itzhak Ben-Zvi at right. Marks for the blind. Back: Stylized village of Peki'in and carob tree. Watermark: Itzhak Ben-Zvi. Printer: JEZ (without imprint). 138x76mm.

	VF	UNC
a. Signature 5. Plain security thread and plain white paper. 1986/5746.	FV	95.00
b. Signature 6. With security thread inscribed: *Bank Israel*, paper with colored threads. 1989/5749.	FV	95.00
c. Signature 8. 1995/5755.	FV	85.00

57 200 New Sheqalim

1991/5751; 1994/5754. Deep red, purple and blue-green on multicolor underprint. Zalman Shazar at right. Back: School girl writing at center. Watermark: Zalman Shazar. 138x76mm.

	VF	UNC
a. Signature 7. 1991/5751.	FV	135.
b. Signature 8. 1994/5754.	FV	120.

1998 Commemorative Issue

#58, 50th Anniversary - State of Israel

58 **50 New Sheqalim** — VF — UNC

1998/5758. Purple on multicolor underprint. Shmuel Yosef Agnon at right. Marks for the blind. OVI *50* at upper left, 5-digit serial number below. Signature 8. Back: Various buildings and book titles. Watermark: Shmuel Yosef Agnon. Printer: JEZ (without imprint). 138x76mm.

	VF	UNC
a. Issued note.	FV	45.00
b. Sheetlet of three in folder. (10,001 sets)	—	100.

1998 Dated 1999 Issue

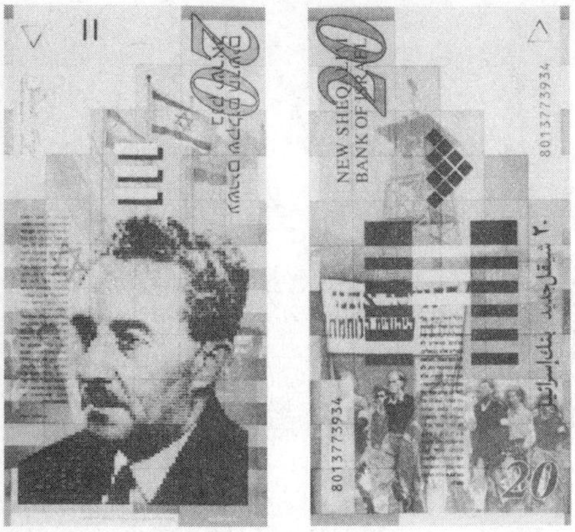

59 **20 New Sheqalim** — VF — UNC

1998; 2001. Dark green on multicolor underprint. Moshe Sharett at bottom, flags in background. Vertical format. Back: Scenes of his life and work. 71x138mm.

	VF	UNC
a. 1998 (1999).	FV	20.00
b. 2001 (2003). Signatures of Klein, Lorincz.	FV	18.00

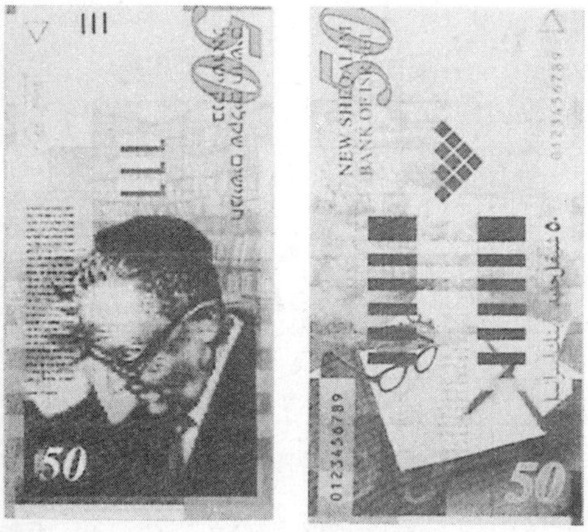

60 **50 New Sheqalim** — VF — UNC

1998; 2001; 2007. Purple on multicolor underprint. Shmuel Yosef Agnon at bottom, library shelves in background. Vertical format. Back: Western "wailing" Wall and Dome of the Rock. Book titles. 71x138mm.

	VF	UNC
a. 1998.	FV	40.00
b. 2001 (2003). Signatures of Klein, Lorincz.	FV	28.00
c. 5767/2007. Signatures of Fischer, Fogel.	FV	28.00

61 **100 New Sheqalim** — VF — UNC

1998; 2002; 2007. Dark brown on multicolor underprint. Itzhak Ben-Zvi at bottom. Vertical format. Back: Scenes of his life and work. 71x138mm.

	VF	UNC
a. 1998.	FV	50.00
b. 2002 (2003). Signatures of Klein, Lorincz.	FV	50.00
c. 5767/2007. Signatures of Fischer, Fogel.	FV	50.00

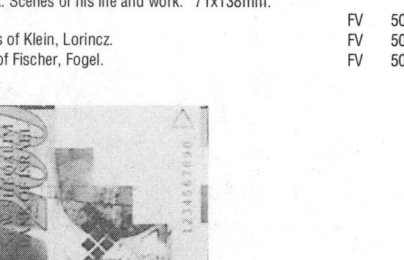

62 **200 New Sheqalim** — VF — UNC

1999, 2002; 2006; 2010. Red and red-orange on multicolor underprint. Zalman Shazar at bottom, classroom in background. Vertical format. Back: Scenes of his life and work. 71x138mm.

	VF	UNC
a. 1999.	FV	100.
b. 5761/2002 (2003). Signatures of Klein, Lorincz.	FV	90.00
c. 5766/2006. Signatures of Fischer, Fogel.	FV	90.00
d. 5770/2010.	FV	75.00

2008 Commemorative Issue

63 **20 New Sheqalim** — VF — UNC

Dark green on multicolor underprint. Moshe Sharett at bottom, flags in background. Commemorative inscription in red honoring the 60th Anniversary of the State of Israel. Back: Scenes of his life and work. Vertical format. Polymer Plastic. 71x138mm. — FV — 25.00

2008 Polymer Plastic Issue

64 **20 New Sheqalim**	VF	UNC
2008. Dark green on multicolor underprint. Moshe Sharett at bottom, flags in background. Back: Scenes of his life and work. Vertical format. Polymer plastic. 71x138mm.	FV	18.00

Collector Series

Bank of Israel

1990 Issue

		Mkt.	Value
CS1	**(1990). 1-50 New Sheqalim** 1985-87. #51Aa-55a with matching serial #. Issued in special packaging. (2,000).		95.00

1991 Issue

		Mkt.	Value
CS2	**(1991). 100, 200 New Sheqalim** 1985-86. #56a and 57a with matching serial # issued in special packaging. (2,000).		150.

The Italian Republic, a 700-mile-long peninsula extending into the heart of the Mediterranean Sea, has an area of 301,230 sq. km. and a population of 58.14 million. Captal: Rome. The economy centers about agriculture, manufacturing, forestry and fishing. Machinery, textiles, clothing and motor vehicles are exported.

Italy became a nation-state in 1861 when the regional states of the peninsula, along with Sardinia and Sicily, were united under King Victor Emmanuel II. An era of parliamentary government came to a close in the early 1920s when Benito Mussolini established a Fascist dictatorship. His alliance with Nazi Germany led to Italy's defeat in World War II. A democratic republic replaced the monarchy in 1946 and economic revival followed. Italy was a charter member of NATO and the European Economic Community (EEC). It has been at the forefront of European economic and political unification, joining the Economic and Monetary Union in 1999. Persistent problems include illegal immigration, organized crime, corruption, high unemployment, sluggish economic growth, and the low incomes and technical standards of southern Italy compared with the prosperous north.

MONETARY SYSTEM:

1 Lira = 100 Centesimi, to 2001
1 Euro = 100 Cents, 2001-

DECREES:

There are many different dates found on the following notes of the Banca d'Italia. These include ART. DELLA LEGGE (law date) and the more important DECRETO MINISTERIALE (D. M. date). The earliest D.M. date is usually found on the back of the note while later D.M. dates are found grouped together. The actual latest date (of issue) is referred to in the following listings.

FACE SEAL VARIETIES:

Type B
Facing head of Medusa

Type C
Winged lion of St. Mark of Venice above 3 shields of Genoa, Pisa and Amalfi

Republic

Repubblica Italiana - Biglietto di Stato

1966 Issue

		VF	UNC
93	**500 Lire** 1966-75. Dark gray on blue and multicolor underprint. Eagle with snake at left, Arethusa at right. Three signature varieties.		
	a. 20.6.1966; 20.10.1967; 23.2.1970.	5.00	40.00
	b. 23.4.1975.	120.	550.

Decreto Ministeriale 14.2.1974

		VF	UNC
94	**500 Lire** 14.2.1974; 2.4.1979. Grayish purple on blue and multicolor underprint. Mercury at right. Three signature varieties. Watermark: Star in wreath.	3.00	6.00

Decreto Ministeriale 5.6.1976

		VF	UNC
95	**500 Lire** 20.12.1976. Grayish purple on blue and multicolor underprint. Mercury at right. Three signature varieties. Watermark: Star in wreath.	1.50	3.50

BANCA D'ITALIA

BANK OF ITALY

1962 ISSUE

Decreto Ministeriale 12.4. 1962; Decreto Ministeriale 28.6.1962.

96	1000 Lire	VF	UNC
	1962-68. Blue on red and light brown underprint. G. Verdi at right. Watermark: Laureate head. Seal: Type B.		
	a. Signature Carli and Ripa. 14.7.1962.	20.00	130.
	b. Signature Carli and Ripa. 15.7.1963 14.1.1964.	40.00	225.
	c. Signature Carli and Ripa. 25.7.1964	70.00	275.
	d. Signature Carli and Febbraio. 10.8.1965; 20.5.1966.	25.00	120.
	e. Signature Carli and Pacini. 4.1.1968.	35.00	350.

97	10,000 Lire	VF	UNC
	1962-73. Brown, purple, orange and red-brown with dark brown text on multicolor underprint. Michaelangelo at right. Seal: Type B. Back: Piazza del Campidoglio in Rome. Watermark: Roman head.		
	a. Signature Carli and Ripa. 3.7.1962.	20.00	90.00
	b. Signature Carli and Febbraio. 14.1.1964; 27.7.1964.	45.00	185.
	c. Signature Carli and Febbraio. 20.5.1966.	20.00	90.00
	d. Signature Carli and Pacini. 4.1.1968.	40.00	150.
	e. Signature Carli and Lombardo. 8.6.1970.	25.00	100.
	f. Signature Carli and Barbarito. 15.2.1973; 27.11.1973.	25.00	100.

1967 ISSUE

Decreto Ministeriale 27.6.1967.

99	50,000 Lire	VF	UNC
	1967-74. Brownish black, dark brown and reddish brown with black text on multicolor underprint. Leonardo da Vinci at right. Seal: Type B. Back: City view at center. Watermark: Bust of Madonna.		
	a. Signature Carli and Febbraio. 3.7.1967; 4.12.1967.	300.	1700.
	b. Signature Carli and Lombardo. 8.6.1970.	200.	1250.
	c. Signature Carli and Barbarito. 15.5.1972; 4.2.1974.	180.	1150.

100	100,000 Lire	VF	UNC
	1967-74. Brownish black, brown and deep olive-green on multicolor underprint. A. Manzoni at right. Seal: Type B. Back: Mountain lake scene at center. Watermark: Archaic female bust.		
	a. Signature Carli and Febbraio. 3.7.1967.	400.	2250.
	b. Signature Carli and Lombardo. 8.6.1970.	300.	1250.
	c. Signature Carli and Barbarito. 15.5.1972; 6.2.1974.	325.	1350.

1964 ISSUE

Decreto Ministeriale 20.8.1964.

98	5000 Lire	VF	UNC
	1964-70. Green on pink underprint. Columbus at right. Seal: Type B. Back: Ship at left center.		
	a. Signature Carli and Ripa. 3.9.1964.	70.00	375.
	b. Signature Carli and Pacini. 4.1.1968.	70.00	375.
	c. Signature Carli and Lombardo. 20.1.1970.	70.00	375.

1969; 1971 ISSUE

Decreto Ministeriale 26.2.1969; Decreto Ministeriale 15.5.1971.

101	1000 Lire	VF	UNC
	1969-81. Black and brown on light blue and lilac underprint. Harp at left center, G. Verdi at right. Seal: Type B. Back: Milan's La Scala opera house at left center. Watermark: Vertical row of laureate heads. Paper with security thread.		
	a. Signature Carli and Lombardo. 25.3.1969.	2.00	10.00
	b. Signature Carli and Lombardo. 11.3.1971.	2.50	15.00
	c. Signature Carli and Barbarito. 15.2.1973.	3.00	15.00
	d. Signature Carli and Barbarito. 5.8.1975.	2.50	12.00
	e. Signature Baffi and Stevani. 10.1.1977.	2.50	12.00
	f. Signature Baffi and Stevani. 10.5.1979.	6.00	30.00
	g. Signature Ciampi and Stevani. 20.2.1980; 6.9.1980.	5.00	25.00
	h. Signature Ciampi and Stevani. 30.5.1981.	3.00	15.00

102 **5000 Lire** | VF | UNC

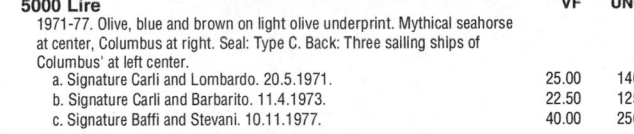

1971-77. Olive, blue and brown on light olive underprint. Mythical seahorse at center, Columbus at right. Seal: Type C. Back: Three sailing ships of Columbus' at left center.

		VF	UNC
a.	Signature Carli and Lombardo. 20.5.1971.	25.00	140.
b.	Signature Carli and Barbarito. 11.4.1973.	22.50	125.
c.	Signature Baffi and Stevani. 10.11.1977.	40.00	250.

1973; 1974 Issue

Decreto Ministeriale 10.9.1973; Decreto Ministeriale 20.12.1974.

103 **2000 Lire** | VF | UNC

1973; 1976; 1983. Brown and green on light tan and olive underprint. Galileo at center, ornate arms at left, buildings and leaning tower of Pisa at right. Seal: Type C. Back: Signs of the Zodiac. Watermark: Man's head.

		VF	UNC
a.	Signature Carli and Barbarito. 8.10.1973.	5.00	32.50
b.	Signature Baffi and Stevani. 22.10.1976.	5.00	32.50
c.	Signature Ciampi and Stevani. 24.10.1983.	2.50	15.00

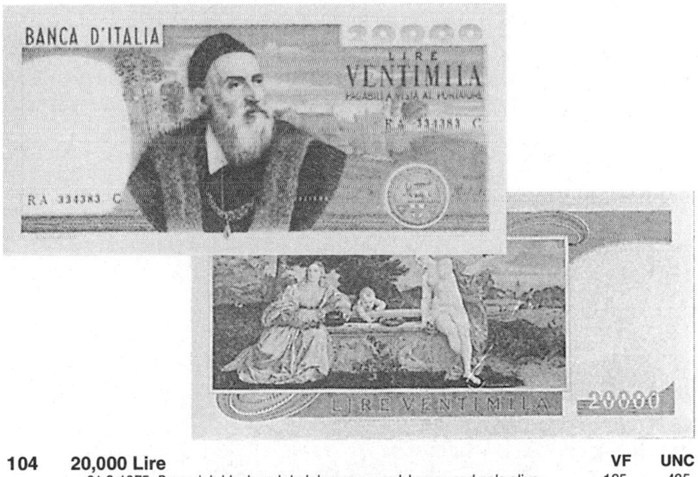

104 **20,000 Lire** | VF | UNC

21.2.1975. Brownish black and dark brown on red-brown and pale olive-green underprint. Titian at center. Seal: Type C. Signature Carli and Barbarito. Back: Titian's painting *Amor Sacro e Amor Profano* at left center. Watermark: Woman's head. | 125. | 425.

1976-79 Issue

Decreto Ministeriale 2.3.1979; Decreto Ministeriale 25.8.1976; Decreto Ministeriale 20.6.1977; Decreto Ministeriale 16.6.1978.

105 **5000 Lire** | VF | UNC

1979-83. Brown and green. Man at left. Seal: Type C. Back: Building and statuary at center right. Watermark: Man with cap.

		VF	UNC
a.	Signature Baffi and Stevani. 9.3.1979.	5.00	30.00
b.	Signature Ciampi and Stevani. 1.7.1980; 3.11.1982.	5.00	15.00
c.	Signature Ciampi and Stevani. 19.10.1983.	12.50	70.00

106 **10,000 Lire** | VF | UNC

1976-84. Black and multicolor. Man at left. Seal: Type C. Back: Column at right. Watermark: Man.

		VF	UNC
a.	Signature Baffi and Stevani. 30.10.1976; 29.12.1978.	10.00	40.00
b.	Signature Ciampi and Stevani. 6.9.1980; 3.11.1982.	10.00	40.00
c.	Signature Ciampi and Stevani. 8.3.1984.	25.00	110.

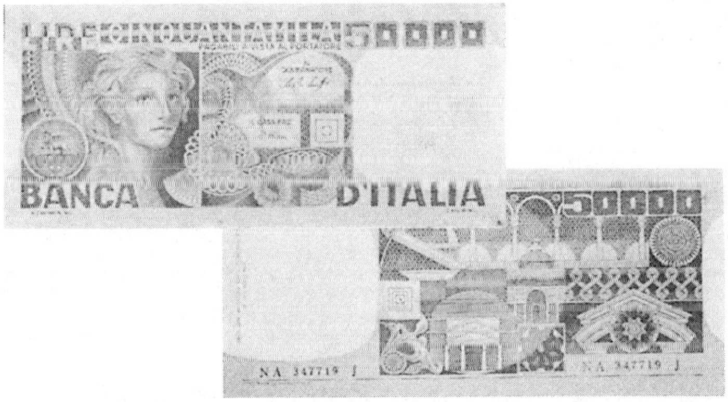

107 **50,000 Lire** | VF | UNC

1977-82. Blue, red and green. Young women and lion of St. Mark at left. Seal: Type C. Back: Modern design of arches.

		VF	UNC
a.	Signature Baffi and Stevani. 20.6.1977; 23.10.1978.	40.00	140.
b.	Signature Baffi and Stevani. 12.6.1978.	120.	425.
c.	Signature Ciampi and Stevani. 11.4.1980.	40.00	140.
d.	Signature Ciampi and Stevani. 2.11.1982.	50.00	385.

108 **100,000 Lire** | VF | UNC

D.1978. Red-violet and black on multicolor underprint. Woman's bust at left. Seal: Type C. Back: Modern building design at right. Watermark: Woman's bust.

		VF	UNC
a.	Signature Baffi and Stevani. 20.6.1978.	65.00	240.
b.	Signature Ciampi and Stevani. 1.7.1980.	65.00	240.
c.	Signature Ciampi and Stevani. 10.5.1982.	75.00	325.

1982; 1983 ISSUE

Decreto Ministeriale 6.1.1982; Decreto Ministeriale 1.9.1983.

		VF	UNC
109	**1000 Lire**		
	D.1982. Dark green and tan. Marco Polo at right. Seal: Type C. Back: Façade of the Doge's Palace in Venice at bottom of vertical format. Watermark: Marco Polo. Printer: ODBI. UV: fibers fluoresce green. 113x61mm.		
	a. Signature Ciampi and Stevani. 6.1.1982.	FV	6.00
	b. Signature Ciampi and Speziali. 6.1.1982.	FV	6.00

		VF	UNC
110	**100,000 Lire**		
	D.1983. Dark brown and brown on green and olive-green underprint. Couple at center, Caravaggio at right. Seal: Type C. Back: Fruit basket at left, castle at upper center. Watermark: Caravaggio. 157x70mm.		
	a. Signature Ciampi and Stevani. 1.9.1983.	FV	200.
	b. Signature Ciampi and Speziali. 1.9.1983.	FV	180.

1984; 1985 ISSUE

Decreto Ministeriale 4.1.1985; Decreto Ministeriale 3.9.1984; Decreto Ministeriale 6.2.1984.

		VF	UNC
111	**5000 Lire**		
	D.1985. Olive-green and blue on multicolor underprint. Coliseum at center, V. Bellini at right. Seal: Type C. Back: Scene from opera *Norma* at left center. Watermark: V. Bellini. 126x70mm.		
	a. Signature Ciampi and Stevani. 4.1.1985.	FV	40.00
	b. Signature Ciampi and Speziali. 4.1.1985.	FV	20.00
	c. Signature Fazio and Amici. 4.1.1985.	FV	15.00

		VF	UNC
112	**10,000 Lire**		
	D.1984. Dark blue on multicolor underprint. Lab instrument at center, A. Volta at right. Seal: Type C. Back: Mausoleum at left center. Watermark: A. Volta. 133x70mm.		
	a. Signature Ciampi and Stevani. 3.9.1984.	FV	45.00
	b. Signature Ciampi and Speziali. 3.9.1984.	FV	35.00
	c. Signature Fazio and Speziali. 3.9.1984.	FV	25.00
	d. Signature Fazio and Amici. 3.9.1984.	FV	20.00

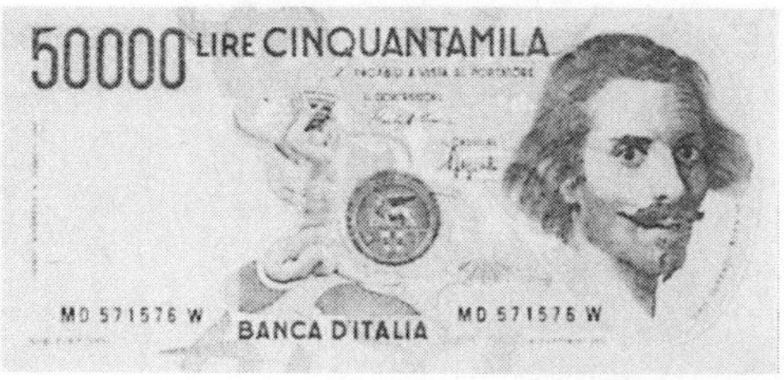

		VF	UNC
113	**50,000 Lire**		
	D.1984. Red-violet and multicolor. Figurine at center, G.L. Bernini at right. Seal: Type C. Back: Equestrian statue at left center. Watermark: G.L. Bernini. 149x70mm.		
	a. Signature Ciampi and Stevani. 6.2.1984; 5.12.1984; 28.10.1985; 1.12.1986.	FV	150.
	b. Signature Ciampi and Speziali. 25.1.1990.	FV	120.

1990-94 ISSUE

Decreto Ministeriale 3.10.1990; Decreto Ministeriale 27.5.1992; Decreto Ministeriale 6.5.1994.

		VF	UNC
114	**1000 Lire**		
	D.1990. Red-violet and multicolor. M. Montessori at right. Seal: Type C. Back: Teacher and student at left center. Watermark: M. Montessori. UV: fibers fluoresce yellow. 113x61mm.		
	a. Signature Ciampi and Speziali.	FV	5.00
	b. Signature Fazio and Speziali.	FV	5.00
	c. Signature Fazio and Amici.	FV	4.00

		VF	UNC
115	**2000 Lire**	FV	8.00
	D.1990. Dark brown on multicolor underprint. Arms at left center, G. Marconi at right. Seal: Type C. Signature Ciampi and Speziali. Back: Marconi's yacht *Elettra* at upper left center, radio towers at left, early radio set at center. Watermark: G. Marconi. 119x61mm.		

116 50,000 Lire | VF | UNC

D.1992. 27.5.1992. Violet and dull green on multicolor underprint. Figurine at center, G. L. Bernini at right. Seal: Type C. Back: Equestrian statue at left center. Watermark: G. L. Bernini. 149x70mm.

	VF	UNC
a. Signature Ciampi and Speziali.	FV	100.
b. Signature Fazio and Speziali.	FV	90.00
c. Signature Fazio and Amici.	FV	80.00

117 100,000 Lire | VF | UNC

D.1994. Dark brown, reddish brown and pale green on multicolor underprint. Couple at center, Caravaggio at right. Seal: Type C. Back: Fruit basket at left, castle at upper center. Watermark: Caravaggio. 157x70mm.

	VF	UNC
a. Signature Fazio and Speziali. 6.5.1994.	FV	185.
b. Signature Fazio and Amici.	FV	170.

1997 Issue

Decreto Ministeriale 6.5.1997.

118 500,000 Lire | VF | UNC

D.1997. Deep purple, dark blue and bright green on multicolor underprint. Raphaël at right, painting of *Triumph of Galatée* at center. Seal: Type C. Signature Fazio and Amici. Back: *The School of Athens* at left center. 163x78mm. | FV | 650.

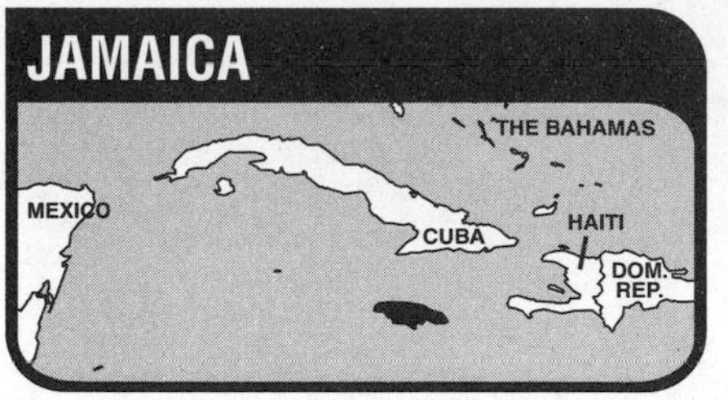

Jamaica, a member of the British Commonwealth situated in the Caribbean Sea 90 miles south of Cuba, has an area of 10,991 sq. km. and a population of 2.8 million. Capital: Kingston. The economy is founded chiefly on mining, tourism and agriculture. Alumina, bauxite, sugar, rum and molasses are exported.

The island - discovered by Christopher Columbus in 1494 - was settled by the Spanish early in the 16th century. The native Taino Indians, who had inhabited Jamaica for centuries, were gradually exterminated and replaced by African slaves. England seized the island in 1655 and established a plantation economy d on sugar, cocoa, and coffee. The abolition of slavery in 1834 freed a quarter million slaves, many of whom became small farmers. Jamaica gradually obtained increasing independence from Britain, and in 1958 it joined other British Caribbean colonies in forming the Federation of the West Indies. Jamaica gained full independence when it withdrew from the Federation in 1962. Deteriorating economic conditions during the 1970s led to recurrent violence as rival gangs affiliated with the major political parties evolved into powerful organized crime networks involved in international drug smuggling and money laundering. Violent crime, drug trafficking, and poverty pose significant challenges to the government today. Nonetheless, many rural and resort areas remain relatively safe and contribute substantially to the economy.

Jamaica is a member of the Commonwealth of Nations. Elizabeth II is the Head of State, as Queen of Jamaica.

A decimal standard currency system was adopted on Sept. 8, 1969.

RULERS:

British

MONETARY SYSTEM:

1 Shilling = 12 Pence
1 Pound = 20 Shillings to 1969
1 Dollar = 100 Cents, 1969-

SIGNATURE VARIETIES			
1	Stanley W. Payton, 1960-64	2	Richard T. P. Hall Acting Governor, 1964-66
3	Richard T. P. Hall Governor, 1966-67	4	G. Arthur Brown, 1967-77
5	Herbert Samuel Walker, 1977-81	6	Dr. Owen C. Jefferson, Acting Governor, 1981-83
7	Horace G. Barber, 1983-86	8	Headley A. Brown, 1986-89
9	Dr. Owen C. Jefferson Acting Governor, 1989-90	10	G. A. Brown, 1990-93
11	R. Rainsford, 1993	12	J. Bussieres, 1994-96
13	D.M. Lat. Ibeaudiere		

British Administration

Bank of Jamaica

Law 1960

1961 ND Issue

Pound System.

			VF	UNC
49	**5 Shillings**	*L.1960.* (1961). Red on multicolor underprint. Queen Elizabeth II at left. Latin motto below arms. Signature 1. Back: River rapids. Printer: TDLR. 145x68mm.	25.00	150.
50	**10 Shillings**	*L.1960.* (1961). Purple on multicolor underprint. Queen Elizabeth II at left. Latin motto below arms. Signature 1. Back: Men with bananas. Printer: TDLR. 145x68mm.	50.00	375.

			VF	UNC
51	**1 Pound**	*L.1960.* (1961). Green on multicolor underprint. Queen Elizabeth II at left. Latin motto below arms. Signature 1. Back: Harvesting. Printer: TDLR. 145x68mm.	50.00	325.

1964 ND Issue

			VF	UNC
51A	**5 Shillings**	*L.1960.* (1964). Red on multicolor underprint. Queen Elizabeth II at left. English motto below arms. Signature 1. Back: River rapids. Printer: TDLR. 145x68mm.		
		a. Signature 1. Gothic serial #.	15.00	100.
		b. Signature 1. Roman numeral serial #.	25.00	135.
		c. Signature 2.	15.00	120.
		d. Signature 4.	10.00	95.00
		e. Specimen. As b.	—	—

			VF	UNC
51B	**10 Shillings**	*L.1960.* (1964). Purple on multicolor underprint. Queen Elizabeth II at left. English motto below arms. Signature 1. Back: Men with bananas. Printer: TDLR. 145x68mm.		
		a. Signature 1. Gothic serial #.	12.50	200.
		b. Signature 1. Roman numeral serial #.	15.00	225.
		c. Signature 2.	15.00	250.
		d. Signature 3.	17.50	275.
		e. Signature 4.	12.00	165.

			VF	UNC
51C	**1 Pound**	*L.1960.* (1964). Green on multicolor underprint. Queen Elizabeth II at left. English motto below arms. Signature 1. Back: Harvesting. Printer: TDLR. 145x68mm.		
		a. Signature 1. Gothic serial #.	25.00	285.
		b. Signature 1. Roman numeral serial #.	35.00	325.
		c. Signature 2.	20.00	250.
		d. Signature 3.	35.00	325.
		e. Signature 4.	25.00	250.
		s. Specimen. As c.	—	—

			VF	UNC
52	**5 Pounds**	*L.1960.* Blue on multicolor underprint. Queen Elizabeth II at left. English motto below arms. Back: Storage plant at center, woman with fruit basket at right. Printer: TDLR. 145x68mm.		
		a. Signature 1. Gothic serial #.	450.	2000.
		b. Signature 1. Roman numeral serial #.	550.	2500.
		c. Signature 3.	500.	2350.
		d. Signature 4.	400.	2000.

Law 1960

1970 ND Issue

Dollar System. Replacement notes: Serial # prefix *ZZ*.

			VF	UNC
53	**50 Cents**	*L.1960* (1970). Red on multicolor underprint. Marcus Garvey at left, arms in underprint at center. Signature 4. Back: National shrine at right. Watermark: Pineapple. Printer: TDLR. 145x68mm.		
		a. Issued note.	2.00	8.00
		s. Specimen.	—	—
54	**1 Dollar**	*L.1960* (1970). Purple on multicolor underprint. Sir Alexander Bustamante at left, arms at bottom center right. Signature 4. Back: Tropical harbor at right. Watermark: Pineapple. Printer: TDLR. 145x68mm.	2.00	8.00

55 **2 Dollars** VF UNC

L.1960 (1970). Dark green and red-brown on multicolor underprint. Paul Bogle, arms at left, Red-billed streamer trail at center. Signature 4. Back: Group of people. Watermark: Pineapple. Printer: TDLR. 145x68mm.

a. Issued note. 4.00 15.00

s. Specimen. — —

56 **5 Dollars** VF UNC

L.1960 (1970). Dark brown, green and blue-gray on multicolor underprint. Norman Manley at left, arms at bottom center. Signature 4. Back: Old Parliament at center right. Watermark: Pineapple. Printer: TDLR. 145x68mm. 10.00 55.00

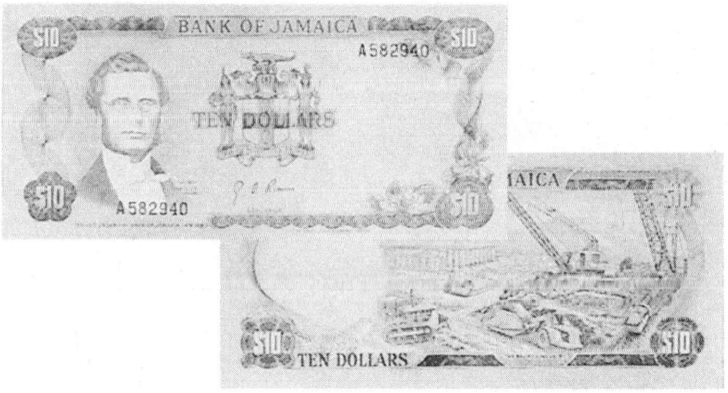

57 **10 Dollars** VF UNC

L.1960 (1970). Blue-black, brown and black on multicolor underprint. George William Gordon at left, arms in underprint at center. Signature 4. Back: Bauxite mining scene at center right. Watermark: Pineapple. Printer: TDLR. 145x68mm. 30.00 175.

1973 FAO Commemorative Issue

#58, 25th Anniversary Declaration of Human Rights 1948-73

58 **2 Dollars** VF UNC

1973. Dark green and red-brown on multicolor underprint. Paul Bogle, arms at left, Red-billed streamer trail at center. Signature 4. *Universal Declaration of Human Rights/1948 - 10 December - 1973. Serial number double prefix FA-O.* Back: Group of people. Toward Food Education Employment for All/Articles 23-26 added. Watermark: Pineapple. Printer: TDLR. 145x68mm. 3.00 15.00

1976; 1977 ND Issue

#59-63 Replacement notes: Serial # prefix *ZY* or *ZZ*.

59 **1 Dollar** VF UNC

L.1960 (1976). Purple on multicolor underprint. Sir Alexander Bustamante at left, arms at bottom center right. Signature 4. Back: Tropical harbor at right. Watermark: Pineapple. Printer: TDLR. 145x68mm.

a. Signature 4. 1.50 7.50

b. Signature 5. 1.00 6.50

60 **2 Dollars** VF UNC

L.1960 (1976). Dark green on multicolor underprint. Paul Bogle, arms at left, Red billed streamer trail at center. Signature 4. Back: Group of people. Watermark: Pineapple. Printer: TDLR. 145x68mm.

a. Signature 4. 2.00 12.50

b. Signature 5. 1.50 10.00

61 **5 Dollars** VF UNC

L.1960 (1976). Dark brown, green and blue-green on multicolor underprint. Norman Manley at left, arms at bottom center. Signature 4. Back: Old Parliament at center right. Watermark: Pineapple. Printer: TDLR. 145x68mm.

a. Signature 4. 5.00 32.50

b. Signature 5. 3.50 20.00

62 **10 Dollars**

L.1960 (1976). Blue-black and black on multicolor underprint. George William Gordon at left, arms in underprint at center. Signature 4. Back: Bauxite mining scene at center right. Watermark: Pineapple. Printer: TDLR. 145x68mm. 20.00 175.

63 **20 Dollars** VF UNC

L.1960 (1976). Maroon on multicolor underprint. Noel Nethersole at left, flag in underprint at center, arms below. Signature 4. Back: Bank of Jamaica building. Watermark: Pineapple. Printer: TDLR. 145x68mm. 35.00 200.

1978-84 Issue

Replacement notes: Serial # prefix *ZY* or *ZZ*.

		VF	UNC
64	**1 Dollar**		
	ND (1982-86). Purple on multicolor underprint. Sir Alexander Bustamante at left, arms at bottom center right. Signature 4. Back: Tropical harbor at right. Watermark: Pineapple. Printer: TDLR. 145x68mm.		
	a. Signature 6.	.50	2.50
	b. Signature 7.	.25	1.50
65	**2 Dollars**		
	ND (1982-86). Dark green and red-brown on multicolor underprint. Paul Bogle, arms at left, Red-billed streamer trail at center. Signature 4. Back: Group of people. Watermark: Pineapple. Printer: TDLR. 145x68mm.		
	a. Signature 6.	1.50	7.50
	b. Signature 7.	1.00	6.00
66	**5 Dollars**		
	ND (1984). Dark brown, green and blue-gray on multicolor underprint. Norman Manley at left, arms at bottom center. Signature 7. Back: Old Parliament at center right. Watermark: Pineapple. Printer: TDLR. 145x68mm.	2.00	10.00

		VF	UNC
67	**10 Dollars**		
	1978-81. Bluish purple on multicolor underprint. George William Gordon at left, arms in underprint at center. Signature 4. Back: Bauxite mining scene at center right. Watermark: Pineapple. Printer: TDLR. 145x68mm.		
	a. Signature 5. 1.10.1978; 1.10.1979.	2.50	25.00
	b. Signature 9. 1.12.1981.	1.00	7.50

		VF	UNC
68	**20 Dollars**		
	1978-83. Red and purple on multicolor underprint. Noel Nethersole at left, flag in underprint at center, arms below. Signature 4. Back: Bank of Jamaica building. Watermark: Pineapple. Printer: TDLR. 145x68mm.		
	a. Signature 5. 1.10.1978; 1.10.1979; 1.10.1981.	5.00	40.00
	b. Signature 6. 1.12.1981.	3.00	30.00
	c. Signature 7. 1.12.1983.	2.50	25.00

1985 Reduced Size Issue

#68A-72 note size: 144 x 68mm. Replacement notes: Serial # prefix *ZY* or *ZZ*.

		VF	UNC
68A	**1 Dollar**		
	1985-90. Purple on multicolor underprint. Sir Alexander Bustamante at left, arms at bottom center right. Signature 4. Back: Tropical harbor at right. Watermark: Pineapple. Printer: TDLR. UV: rays around sailfish, value 1 in broken box all fluoresce orange.		
	a. Signature 7. 1.1.1985.	FV	4.00
	b. Signature 8. 1.3.1986; 1.2.1987; 1.9.1987.	FV	2.25
	c. Signature 9. 1.7.1989.	FV	2.00
	d. Signature 10. 1.1.1990.	FV	1.00

		VF	UNC
69	**2 Dollars**		
	1985-93. Dark green and red-brown on multicolor underprint. Paul Bogle, arms at left, Red-billed streamer trail at center. Signature 4. Horizontal sorting bar at right. Back: Group of people. Watermark: Pineapple. Printer: TDLR. UV: Hummingbirds and value $2 in broken box fluoresce yellow. 145x68mm.		
	a. Signature 7. 1.1.1985.	FV	3.00
	b. Signature 8. 1.3.1986; 1.2.1987; 1.9.1987.	FV	2.25
	c. Signature 9. 1.7.1989.	FV	2.00
	d. Signature 10. 1.1.1990; 29.5.1992.	FV	1.25
	e. Signature 11. 1.2.1993.	FV	1.25

		VF	UNC
70	**5 Dollars**		
	1985-92. Dark brown, green and blue-gray on multicolor underprint. Norman Manley at left, arms at bottom center. Two horizontal blue-green sorting bars at left and right. Signature 7. Back: Old Parliament at center right. Watermark: Pineapple. Printer: TDLR. 145x68mm.		
	a. Signature 7. 1.1.1985.	FV	5.00
	b. Signature 8. 1.9.1987.	FV	3.50
	c. Signature 9. 1.5.1989.	FV	3.00
	d. Signature 10. 1.7.1991; 1.8.1992.	FV	1.75

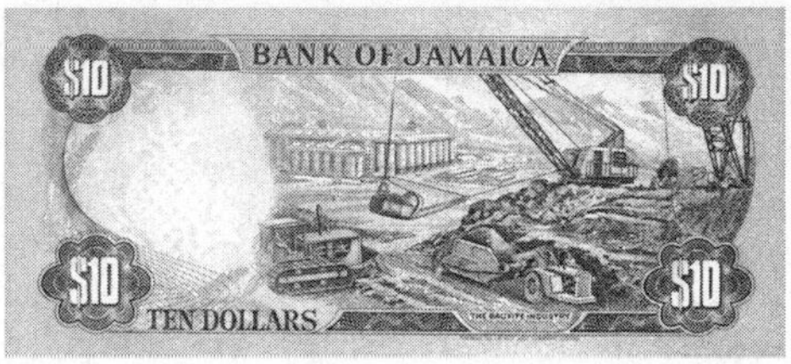

71 10 Dollars VF UNC

1985-94. Bluish purple on multicolor underprint. George William Gordon at left, arms in underprint at center. Three horizontal sorting bars at left and right. Signature 4. Back: Bauxite mining scene at center right. Watermark: Pineapple. Printer: TDLR. 145x68mm.

	VF	UNC
a. Signature 7. 1.1.1985.	FV	7.50
b. Signature 8. 1.9.1987.	FV	6.00
c. Signature 9. 1.8.1989.	FV	3.00
d. Signature 10. 1.5.1991; 1.8.1992.	FV	1.50
e. Signature 12. 1.3.1994.	FV	1.50

72 20 Dollars VF UNC

1985-99. Red-orange, purple and black on multicolor underprint. Noel Nethersole at left, flag in underprint at center, arms below. Circular electronic sorting mark at left. Signature 4. Back: Bank of Jamaica building. Watermark: Pineapple. Printer: TDLR. 145x68mm.

	VF	UNC
a. Signature 7. 1.1.1985.	FV	10.00
b. Signature 8. 1.3.1986; 1.2.1987; 1.9.1987.	FV	8.00
c. Signature 9. 1.9.1989.	FV	7.00
d. Signature 10. 1.10.1991.	FV	4.60
e. Signature 12. 1.2.1995.	FV	3.50
f. Signature 13. 24.5.1996.	FV	3.00
g. Signature 13. 15.2.1999.	FV	3.00

1986-91 Issue

#73-75 Replacement notes: Serial # prefix *ZZ*; *ZY*.

73 50 Dollars VF UNC

1988-99. Brown, purple and red-violet on multicolor underprint. Sam Sharpe at left. Back: Doctor's Cave Beach, Mointego Bay. Watermark: Pineapple. Printer: TDLR. UV: parrots and value $50 in broken box fluoresce yellow. 145x68mm.

	VF	UNC
a. Signature 8. 1.8.1988.	FV	12.00
b. Signature 11. 1.2.1993.	FV	7.50
c. Signature 12. 1.2.1995.	FV	5.00
d. Signature 13. 24.5.1996.	FV	4.50
e. Signature 13. 12.1.1998.	FV	4.50
f. Signature 13. 15.2.1999.	FV	4.50

74 100 Dollars VF UNC

1.12.1986; 1.9.1987. Black and purple on multicolor underprint. Sir Donald Sangster at left. Signature 8. Back: Dunn's River Falls, St. Ann, at right. Watermark: Pineapple. Printer: TDLR. 145x68mm. — VF 7.00, UNC 35.00

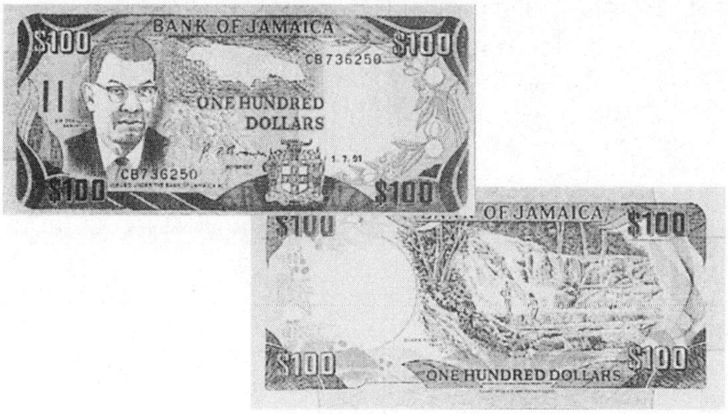

75 100 Dollars VF UNC

1991-93. Black and purple on lilac underprint. Sir Donald Sangster at left. Signature 8. Two circles at right, each with vertical orange bar. Back: Dunn's River Falls, St. Ann, at right. More silver waves added to both *$100* and across bottom. Watermark: Pineapple. Printer: TDLR. 145x68mm.

	VF	UNC
a. Signature 10. 1.7.1991.	FV	12.50
b. 1.6.1992.	FV	10.00
c. Signature 11. 1.2.1993.	FV	10.00

1994 Issue

#76-78 Replacement notes: Serial # prefix *ZY* or *ZZ*.

76 100 Dollars VF UNC

1994-2002. Black and purple on lilac underprint. Sir Donald Sangster at left. Signature 8. Two circles at right, each with vertical orange bar. Ascending size serial number and segmented foil over security thread. Back: Dunn's River Falls, St. Ann, at right. More silver waves added to both *$100* and across bottom. Watermark: Pineapple. Printer: TDLR. 145x68mm.

	VF	UNC
a. Signature 12. 1.3.1994.	FV	8.50
b. Signature 13. 24.5.1996; 12.1.1998; 12.2.1998; 15.2.1999.	FV	7.50
c. 15.3.2000. watermark: swallow-tailed hummingbird. Improved security thread.	FV	7.00

77 500 Dollars VF UNC

1994-99. Purple, violet and brown on multicolor underprint. Nanny of the Maroons at left. Back: Historical map of the islands above Port Royal architecture at center right. Watermark: Pineapple. Printer: TDLR. 145x68mm.

	VF	UNC
a. Signature 12. 1.5.1994.	FV	25.00
b. Signature 13. 24.5.1996; 12.2.1998; 15.2.1999.	FV	25.00

2000 Issue

78 **1000 Dollars** VF UNC
2000-01. Dark blue, green and purple on multicolor underprint. Michael Manley at left. Signature 13. Back: Jamaica House. Printer: TDLR. (without imprint). 145x68mm.

	VF	UNC
a. 15.2.2000.	FV	45.00
b. 15.10.2000.	FV	45.00
c. 15.1.2001.	FV	45.00

2001; 2002 Issue

79 **50 Dollars** VF UNC
2000-04. Multicolor. Sam Sharpe at left. Signature 13. Back: Doctor's Cave Beach, Mointego Bay. Watermark: Swallow-tailed Hummingbird. Printer: TDLR. UV: parrot, $50 and security strip all fluoresce green. 145x68mm.

	VF	UNC
a. 15.3.2000.	FV	4.00
b. 15.1.2001.	FV	4.00
c. 15.1.2002.	FV	4.00
d. 15.1.2003.	FV	4.00
e. 15.1.2004.	FV	4.00

80 **100 Dollars** VF UNC
2001-04. Black and purple on lilac underprint. 145x68mm.

	VF	UNC
a. 15.1.2001.	FV	7.00
b. 15.1.2002.	FV	7.00
c. 15.1.2003.	FV	7.00
d. 15.1.2004.	FV	7.00

81 **500 Dollars**
15.1.2002. Purple, violet and brown on multicolor underprint. Nanny of the Maroons at left. Back: Historical map of the islands above Port Royal architecture at center right. Watermark: Swallow-Tailed Hummingbird. Printer: TDLR. 145x68mm. FV 22.50

82 **1000 Dollars**
15.1.2002. Dark blue, green and purple on multicolor underprint. Michael Manley at left. Signature 13. Back: Jamaica House. Printer: (T)DLR. 145x68mm. FV 40.00

2003 Issue

83 **50 Dollars** VF UNC
2005-. Multicolor. Sam Sharpe at left. Back: Doctor's Cave Beach, Mointego Bay. Watermark: Sam Sharpe and value Printer: TDLR. 145x68mm.

	VF	UNC
a. 15.1.2005.	FV	2.50
b. 15.1.2007.	FV	2.50
c. 15.1.2008. Cornerstone watermarks.	FV	2.00
d. 15.1.2009.	FV	2.00
e. 15.1.2010.	FV	2.00

84 **100 Dollars** VF UNC
2003-. Black and purple on lilac and multicolor underprint. Donald Sagster at left. Back: Dunn's River Falls, St. Ann, at right. Watermark: Donald Sagster and value. Printer: TDLR. 145x68mm.

	VF	UNC
a. 15.1.2005.	FV	3.00
b. 15.1.2006.	FV	3.00
c. 15.1.2007.	FV	3.00
d. 15.1.2009.	FV	2.50
e. 15.1.2010. (two signature varieties.	FV	2.50
f. 15.1.2011.	FV	2.50

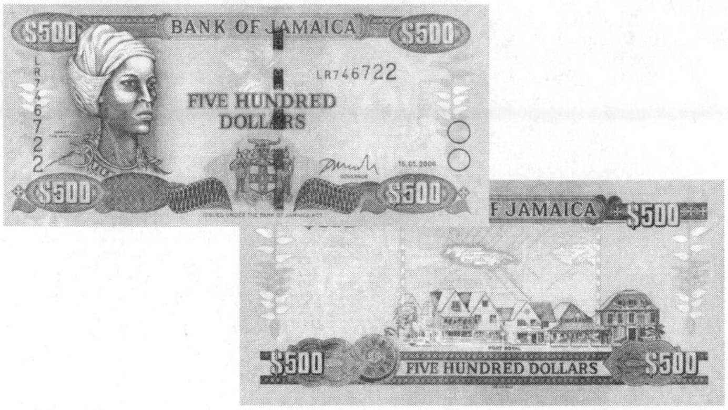

85 **500 Dollars** VF UNC
2003-. Purple, violet and brown on multicolor underprint. Nanny of the Maroons at left. Back: Historical map of the islands above Port Royal architecture at center right. Watermark: Nanny of the Narrons and value. Printer: TDLR. 145x68mm.

	VF	UNC
a. 15.1.2003.	FV	12.50
b. 15.1.2004.	FV	12.50
c. 15.1.2005.	FV	12.50
d. 15.1.2006.	FV	10.00
e. 15.1.2007.	FV	10.00
f. 15.1.2008. Cornerstone watermarks added.	FV	10.00
g. 15.1.2009.	FV	10.00
h. 15.1.2011.	FV	10.00

86 **1000 Dollars** VF UNC
2003-. Dark blue, green and purple on multicolor underprint. Michael Manley at left. Back: Jamaica House at center right. Watermark: Michael Manley and value. Printer: TDLR. 145x68mm.

	VF	UNC
a. 15.1.2003.	FV	22.50
b. 15.1.2004.	FV	20.00
c. 15.1.2005.	FV	20.00
d. 15.1.2006.	FV	20.00
e. 15.1.2007.	FV	17.50
f. 15.1.2008.	FV	17.50
g. 15.1.2009.	FV	17.50
h. 15.1.2010.	FV	17.50
i. 15.1.2011.	FV	17.50

87 **5000 Dollars** | VF | UNC

15.1.2009; 15.1.2010. Multicolor. High. Lawson Shearer at left. Back: Highway 2000 and frangipani blossoms. Printer: TDLR. 145x68mm.

	VF	UNC
a. 15.1.2009.	FV	80.00
b. 15.1.2010.	FV	80.00

2010 Commemorative Issue

88 **50 Dollars** | VF | UNC

1.1.2010. Multicolored. Samuel Sharpe at left. Back: Bank of Jamaca building at center. Overprint: Oval 1960-2010 Anniversary at right. Printer: DLR. 145x68mm. | FV | 15.00

2012 Issue

89 **50 Dollars** | VF | UNC

6.8.2012. Multicolor. Samuel Sharpe at left, 50th Anniversary overprint at right. Back: Group of youngsters. Printer: DLR. | FV | 2.50

90 **100 Dollars** | VF | UNC

6.8.2012. Multicolor. Sir Donald Sangster at left, 50th Anniversary overprint at right. Back: Group of youngsters. Printer: DLR. | FV | 3.00

91 **500 Dollars** | VF | UNC

6.8.2012. Multicolor. Nanny of the Maroons at left, 50th Anniversary overprint at right. Back: Group of youngsters. Printer: DLR. | FV | 12.50

92 **1000 Dollars** | VF | UNC

6.8.2012. Multicolor. Michael Manley at left, 50th Anniversary overprint at right. Back: Group of youngsters. Printer: DLR. | FV | 20.00

93 **5000 Dollars** | VF | UNC

6.8.2012. Multicolor. Hugh Shearer at left, 50th Anniversary overprint at right. Back: Group of youngsters. Printer: DLR. | FV | 80.00

Collector Series

Bank of Jamaica

1976 Issue

CS1 **1976 1-10 Dollars** | Mkt. Value

#54-57 with matching red star prefix serial # and *SERIES 1976.* (5000 sets issued). | 20.00

1977 Issue

CS2 **1977 1-10 Dollars** | Mkt. Value

#59a-61a, 62 with matching red star prefix serial # and *SERIES 1977.* (7500 sets issued). | 15.00

1978 Issue

CS3 **1978 1-10 Dollars** | Mkt. Value

#54-57 in double set. One is like #CS1-2 with *SERIES 1978* and the other with additional overprint: *Twenty-fifth Anniversary of the Coronation June 2, 1953* and *SERIES 1978* at right. All with matching red star prefix serial #. (6250 sets issued). | 30.00

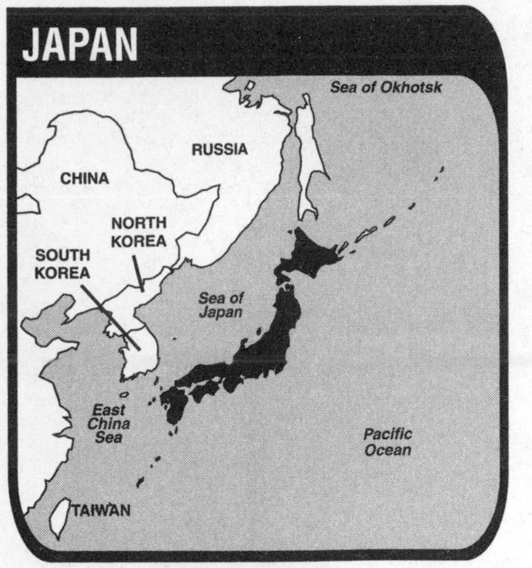

Japan, a constitutional monarchy situated off the east coast of Asia, has an area of 377,835 sq. km. and a population of 127.29 million. Capital: Tokyo. Japan, one of the three major industrial nations of the free world, exports machinery, motor vehicles, textiles and chemicals.

In 1603, a Tokugawa shogunate (military dictatorship) ushered in a long period of isolation from foreign influence in order to secure its power. For more than two centuries this policy enabled Japan to enjoy stability and a flowering of its indigenous culture. Following the Treaty of Kanagawa with the US in 1854, Japan opened its ports and began to intensively modernize and industrialize. During the late 19th and early 20th centuries, Japan became a regional power that was able to defeat the forces of both China and Russia. It occupied Korea, Formosa (Taiwan), and southern Sakhalin Island. In 1931-32 Japan occupied Manchuria, and in 1937 it launched a full-scale invasion of China. Japan attacked US forces in 1941 - triggering America's entry into World War II - and soon occupied much of East and Southeast Asia. After its defeat in World War II, Japan recovered to become an economic power and a staunch ally of the US. While the emperor retains his throne as a symbol of national unity, elected politicians - with heavy input from bureaucrats and business executives - wield actual decisionmaking power. The economy experienced a major slowdown starting in the 1990s following three decades of unprecedented growth, but Japan still remains a major economic power, both in Asia and globally.

See also Burma, China (Japanese military issues, Central Reserve Bank, Federal Reserve Bank, Hua Hsing Commercial Bank, Mengchiang Bank, Chanan Bank, Chi Tung Bank and Manchukuo), Hong Kong, Indochina, Malaya, Netherlands Indies, Oceania, the Philippines, Korea and Taiwan.

RULERS:

Hirohito (Showa), 1926-1989
Akihito (Heisei), 1989-

MONETARY SYSTEM:

1 Yen = 100 Sen, 1870-

REPLACEMENT NOTES:

#49, 50, 51, 57, 89, notes w/first digit 9 are replacements. #62-75, H prefix, #67b, B prefix but no suffix letter.

CONSTITUTIONAL MONARCHY

BANK OF JAPAN

日 本 銀 行 券
Nip-pon Gin-ko Ken

1963-69 ND ISSUE

			VF	UNC
95	500 Yen	ND (1969). Blue on multicolor underprint. Tomomi Iwakura at right. Back: Steel blue. Mt. Fuji at left center. Watermark: 5-petaled flowers. 160x72mm.		
		a. Single letter serial # prefix.	10.00	30.00
		b. Double letter serial # prefix.	FV	12.00
		s. As b. Specimen.	—	—

			VF	UNC
96	1000 Yen	ND (1963). Dark green and brown on multicolor underprint. Hirobumi Ito at right. Back: Brown. Bank of Japan at center. Watermark: Hirobumi Ito. 164x76mm.		
		a. Single letter serial # prefix. Black serial #.	25.00	80.00
		b. As a., but with double letter serial # prefix.	FV	25.00
		c. Single letter serial # prefix. Blue serial #.	15.00	40.00
		d. As c., but with double letter serial # prefix.	FV	22.00
		s. As b. Specimen.	—	—

1984 ND ISSUE

#97s-99s were released in a special booklet by Printing Bureau, Ministry of Finance.

			VF	UNC
97	1000 Yen	ND (1984-93). Blue on multicolor underprint. Soseki Natsume at right. Back: Two Manchurian cranes. Watermark: Soseki Natsume. 150x76mm.		
		a. Single letter serial # prefix. Black serial #. (1984).	15.00	35.00
		b. As a., but with double letter serial # prefix.	FV	22.00
		c. Single letter serial # prefix. Blue serial #. (1990).	FV	25.00
		d. As c., but with double letter serial # prefix.	FV	22.00
		s. As b. Specimen. Perforated *mihon*.	—	1500.

			VF	UNC
98	5000 Yen	ND (1984-93). Purple on multicolor underprint. Inazo Nitobe at right. Back: Lake and Mt. Fuji at center. Watermark: Inazo Nitobe. 155x76mm.		
		a. Single letter serial # prefix. Black serial #.	75.00	110.
		b. As a., but with double letter serial # prefix.	FV	95.00
		s. As b. Specimen. Perforated *mihon*.	—	1500.

99 10,000 Yen

ND (1984-93). Light brown on multicolor underprint. Yukichi Fukuzawa at right. Back: Pheasant at left and right. Watermark: Yukichi Fukuzawa. 160x76mm.

	VF	UNC
a. Single letter serial # prefix.	145.	220.
b. As a., but with double letter serial # prefix.	FV	170.
s. As b. Specimen. Perforated *mihon*.	—	1500.

1993 ND Issue

Due to a government reorganization, the Okurasho (Finance Ministry) was renamed Zaimusho (Ministry of Finance). The imprint on the notes (made at the Finance Ministry Pinting Bureau) was changed accordingly in 2001. In 2003 the imprint was changed again, to National Printing Bureau.

Printer a. 8 characters starting *O*. 大藏省印刷局製造

Printer b. 8 characters starting *Zai*. 財務省印刷局製造

Printer c. 7 characters. 國立印刷局製造

100 1000 Yen

ND (1993-). Blue on multicolor underprint. Soseki Natsume at right. Back: Two Manchurian cranes. Watermark: Soseki Natsume. Microprinting added to upper and lower right corner. 150x76mm.

	VF	UNC
a. Single letter serial # prefix. Brown serial #. Printer a. (1993).	FV	25.00
b. As a. Double letter serial # prefix.	FV	20.00
c. Single letter serial # prefix. Green serial #. Printer a (2000).	FV	25.00
d. As c. Double letter serial # prefix.	FV	20.00
e. As d. Double letter serial #. Printer b. (2001).	FV	22.00
f. As d, printer c. (2003).	FV	22.00

101 5000 Yen

ND (1993-). Violet on multicolor underprint. Inazo Nitobe at right. Back: Lake and Mt. Fuji at center. Watermark: Inazo Nitobe. Microprinting added to upper and lower right corner. 155x76mm.

	VF	UNC
a. Single letter serial # prefix. Brown serial # Printer a. (1993).	75.00	110.
b. As a., but with double letter serial # prefix.	FV	90.00
c. As b. Printer b. (2001).	FV	95.00
d. As b. Printer c. (2003).	FV	95.00

102 10,000 Yen

ND (1993-). Light brown on multicolor underprint. Yukichi Fukuzawa at right. Back: Pheasant at left and right. Watermark: Yukichi Fukuzawa. Microprinting added to upper and lower right corner. 160x76mm.

	VF	UNC
a. Single letter serial # prefix. Brown serial # (1993).	145.	215.
b. As a., but with double letter serial # prefix.	FV	165.
c. As b. printer b. (2001).	FV	170.
d. As b. Printer c. (2003).	FV	170.

2000 Commemorative Issue

#103, G-8 Economic Summit in Okinawa

103 2000 Yen

ND (2000). Slate, green and brown on multicolor underprint. Shureimon Gate in Naha, Okinawa at right. Back: Scene from *Genji Monogatari* (Tale of Genji). Watermark: Shureimon Gate 154x76mm.

	VF	UNC
a. Single letter serial # prefix.	FV	38.00
b. Double letter serial # prefix.	FV	38.00

2004 ND Issue

#104-106 include enhanced security features and bars added to portrait watermark. The iridescent ink feature (introduced at #103) is observed by holding the note at a shallow angle to incident light. The iridescent ink glistens like pink mother of pearl from the surface of the ends of the face of the note; it is otherwise virtually invisible and impossible to copy using available copying technologies.

104 1000 Yen

ND (2004). Blue on multicolor underprint. Hideo Noguchi (bacteriologist) at right. Back: Mt. Fuji. Watermark: Hideo Noguchi and bar. Enhanced security features. 150x76mm.

	VF	UNC
a. Single letter serial # prefix. Black serial #.	FV	25.00
b. Double letter serial # prefix.	FV	20.00
c. Brown serial #.	FV	18.00

105	5000 Yen	VF	UNC
	ND (2004). Violet on multicolor underprint. Ichiyo Higuchi (novelist) at right. Back: Irises (painting by Korin Ogata). Watermark: Ichiyo Higuchi and 2 bars. Enhanced security features. 155x76mm.		
	a. Single letter serial # prefix.	70.00	100.
	b. Double letter serial # prefix.	FV	90.00

106	10,000 Yen	VF	UNC
	ND (2004). Brown on multicolor underprint. Yukichi Fukuzawa (educator, futurist) at right. Back: Phoenix from Byohdoh-in Temple. Watermark: Yukichi Fukuzawa and 3 bars. Enhanced security features. 160x76mm.		
	a. Single letter serial # prefix. Black serial #.	135.	210.
	b. Double letter serial # prefix.	FV	170.
	c. Brown serial #.	FV	155.

JERSEY

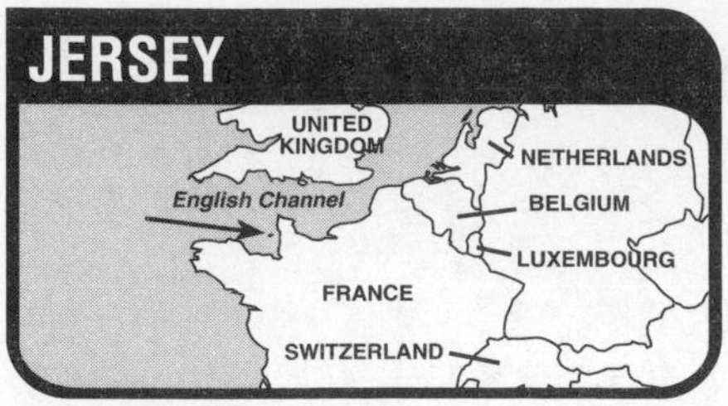

The Bailiwick of Jersey, a British Crown dependency located in the English Channel 12 miles (19 km.) west of Normandy, France, has an area of 45 sq. mi. (117 sq. km.) and a population of 90,000. Capital: St. Helier. The economy is d on agriculture and cattle breeding - the importation of cattle is prohibited to protect the purity of the island's world-famous strain of milk cows.

Jersey and the other Channel Islands represent the last remnants of the medieval Dukedom of Normandy that held sway in both France and England. These islands were the only British soil occupied by German troops in World War II. Jersey is a British crown dependency but is not part of the UK. However, the UK Government is constitutionally responsible for its defense and international representation.

RULERS:
British

MONETARY SYSTEM:
1 Shilling = 12 Pence
1 Pound = 20 Shillings to 1971
1 Pound = 100 Pence, 1971-

SIGNATURE VARIETIES			
1	 F. N. Padgham, 1963-72	2	 J. Clennett, 1972-83
3	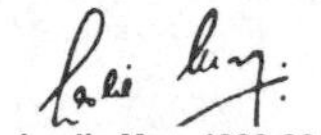 Leslie May, 1983-93	4	 Baird, 1993-
5	 Ian Black		

British Administration

States of Jersey, Treasury

1963 ND Issue

#7-10 Replacement notes: Serial # prefix *Z*.

7	10 Shillings	VF	UNC
	ND (1963). Brown on multicolor underprint. Queen Elizabeth II at right looking left, wearing cape. Signature 3. Back: St. Ouen's Manor. Watermark: Jersey cow's head. Printer: TDLR.		
	a. Issued note.	30.00	75.00
	s. Specimen.	—	250.

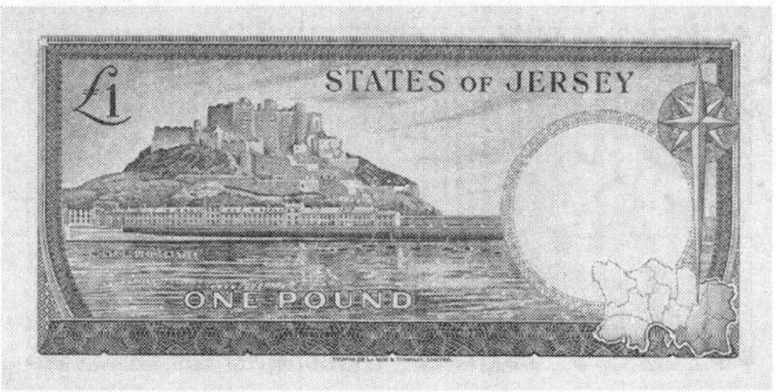

8	1 Pound	VF	UNC
	ND (1963). Green on multicolor underprint. Queen Elizabeth II at right looking left, wearing cape. Two signature varieties. Back: Mont Orgueil Castle. Watermark: Jersey cow's head. Printer: TDLR.		
	a. Signature 1.	50.00	135.
	b. Signature 2.	35.00	90.00
	c. Without signature.	200.	500.
	s1. As a. Specimen. Black or red overprint. Serial # prefix A-E.	—	250.
	s2. As b. Specimen. Red overprint. Serial # prefix F-K.	—	100.

9	5 Pounds	VF	UNC
	ND (1963). Dark red on multicolor underprint. Queen Elizabeth II at right looking left, wearing cape. Signature 3. Back: St. Aubin's Fort. Watermark: Jersey cow's head. Printer: TDLR.		
	a. Signature 1.	175.	500.
	b. Signature 2.	50.00	135.
	r. As b. Replacement note.	—	250.
	s1. As a. Specimen. Black or red overprint	—	125.
	s2. As b. Specimen. Red overprint.	—	100.

10	10 Pounds	VF	UNC
	ND (1972). Purple on multicolor underprint. Queen Elizabeth II at right looking left, wearing cape. Signature 3. Back: St. Ouen's Manor. Watermark: Jersey cow's head. Printer: TDLR.		
	a. Signature 2.	70.00	185.
	r. As a. Replacement note.	85.00	250.
	s. Specimen. Red overprint.	—	225.

1976 ND Issue

#11-14 Replacement notes: Serial # prefixes *ZB; ZC.*

11	1 Pound	VF	UNC
	ND (1976-88). Blue on multicolor underprint. Queen Elizabeth II at center right looking left, wearing tiara. Back: Battle of Jersey scene. Watermark: Jersey cow's head. Printer: TDLR.		
	a. Signature 2.	6.00	17.50
	b. Signature 3.	4.00	12.00
	r. As a. Replacement note.	10.00	30.00
	s. As a. Specimen.	—	17.50

12	5 Pounds	VF	UNC
	ND (1976-88). Brown on multicolor underprint. Queen Elizabeth II at center right looking left, wearing tiara. Back: Elizabeth Castle, sailing ships in foreground. Watermark: Jersey cow's head. Printer: TDLR.		
	a. Signature 2.	25.00	75.00
	b. Signature 3.	20.00	50.00
	r. As a. Replacement note.	45.00	120.
	s. As a, b. Specimen.	—	45.00

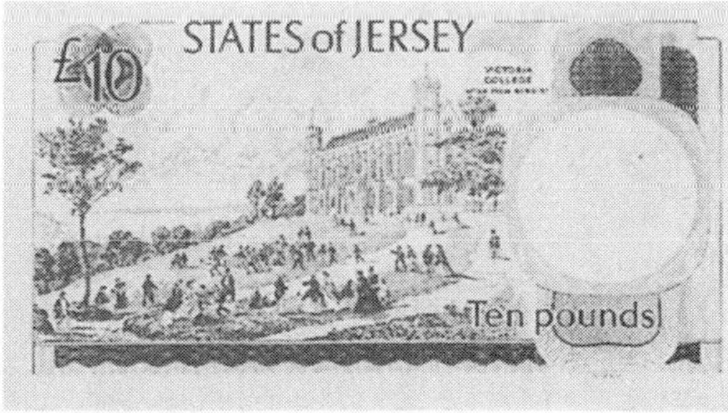

13	10 Pounds	VF	UNC
	ND (1976-88). Green on multicolor underprint. Queen Elizabeth II at center right looking left, wearing tiara. Back: Victoria College. Watermark: Jersey cow's head. Printer: TDLR.		
	a. Signature 2.	50.00	120.
	b. Signature 3.	45.00	100.
	r. As b. Replacement note.	75.00	180.
	s. As a, b. Specimen.	—	85.00

14 **20 Pounds** | VF | UNC

ND (1976-88). Red-brown on multicolor underprint. Queen Elizabeth II at center right looking left, wearing tiara. Back: Sailing ship, Gorey Castle. Watermark: Jersey cow's head. Printer: TDLR.

	VF	UNC
a. Signature 2.	90.00	225.
b. Signature 3.	90.00	225.
r. As b. Replacement note.	140.	350.
s. As a, b. Specimen.	—	150.

1989 ND Issue

#15-19 Replacement notes: Serial # prefix *CZ*.

15 **1 Pound** | VF | UNC

ND (1989). Dark green and violet on multicolor underprint. Birds at left corner, arms at center, mature Queen Elizabeth II at right, facing, wearing cape. Treecreepers at lower left. Signature 3. Back: Church at left center. Watermark: Jersey cow's head. UV: value 1 in box fluoresces orange. Back center light orange. 128x65mm.

	VF	UNC
a. Issued note.	5.00	12.00
s. Specimen.	—	9.00

16 **5 Pounds** | VF | UNC

ND (1989). Rose on multicolor underprint. Birds at left corner, arms at center, mature Queen Elizabeth II at right, facing, wearing cape. Whitethroat at lower left. Signature 3. Back: La Corbiere lighthouse. Watermark: Jersey cow's head. . 135x70mm.

	VF	UNC
a. Issued note.	14.00	32.50
r. Replacement note.	20.00	50.00
s. Specimen.	—	20.00

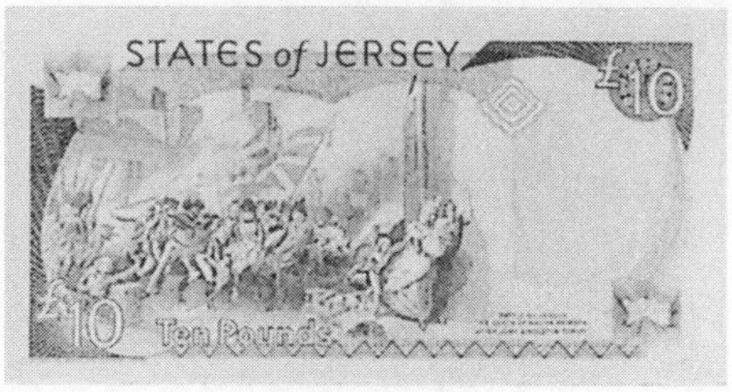

17 **10 Pounds** | VF | UNC

ND (1989). Orange-brown on multicolor underprint. Birds at left corner, arms at center, mature Queen Elizabeth II at right, facing, wearing cape. Oyster catchers at lower left. Signature 3. Back: Battle of Jersey. Watermark: Jersey cow's head. 142x75mm.

	VF	UNC
a. Issued note.	27.50	65.00
s. Specimen.	—	50.00

18 **20 Pounds** | VF | UNC

ND (1989). Blue on multicolor underprint. Birds at left corner, arms at center, mature Queen Elizabeth II at right, facing, wearing cape. Brent goose at lower left. Signature 3. Back: St. Ouen's Manor. Watermark: Jersey cow's head. 150x80mm.

	VF	UNC
a. Issued note.	55.00	125.
r. Replacement note.	70.00	160.
s. Specimen.	—	100.

19 **50 Pounds** | VF | UNC

ND (1989). Dark gray on multicolor underprint. Birds at left corner, arms at center, mature Queen Elizabeth II at right, facing, wearing cape. Fulmers at lower left. Signature 3. Back: Government House. Watermark: Jersey cow's head. 156x86mm.

	VF	UNC
a. Issued note.	FV	300.
s. Specimen.	—	225.

1993 ND Issue

20 **1 Pound** | VF | UNC

ND (1993). Dark green on multicolor underprint. Birds at left corner, arms at center, mature Queen Elizabeth II at right, facing, wearing cape. Treecreepers at lower left. Signature 3. Solid color denomination at upper right. Back: Church at left center. Watermark: Jersey cow's head. 128x65mm.

	VF	UNC
a. Signature 4.	FV	6.00
s. Specimen.	—	20.00

21 **5 Pounds** — VF | UNC

ND (1993). Rose on multicolor underprint. Birds at left corner, arms at center, mature Queen Elizabeth II at right, facing, wearing cape. Whitethroat at lower left. Signature 3. Solid color denomination at upper right. Back: La Corbiere lighthouse. Watermark: Jersey cow's head. 135x70mm.

	VF	UNC
a. Signature 4.	FV	25.00
s. Specimen.	—	20.00

22 **10 Pounds**

ND (1993). Orange-brown on multicolor underprint. Birds at left corner, arms at center, mature Queen Elizabeth II at right, facing, wearing cape. Oyster catchers at lower left. Solid color denomination at upper right. Back: Battle of Jersey. Watermark: Jersey cow's head. 142x75mm.

	VF	UNC
a. Signature 4.	FV	45.00
s. Specimen.	—	35.00

23 **20 Pounds** — VF | UNC

ND (1993). Blue on multicolor underprint. Birds at left corner, arms at center, mature Queen Elizabeth II at right, facing, wearing cape. Brent goose at lower left. Signature 3. Solid color denomination at upper right. Back: St. Ouen's Manor. Watermark: Jersey cow's head. 150x80mm.

	VF	UNC
a. Signature 4.	FV	85.00
r. Replacement note.	FV	100.
s. Specimen.	—	70.00

24 **50 Pounds**

ND (1993). Dark gray on multicolor underprint. Birds at left corner, arms at center, mature Queen Elizabeth II at right, facing, wearing cape. Fulmers at lower left. Signature 3. Solid color denomination at upper right. Back: Government House. Watermark: Jersey cow's head. 156x86mm.

	VF	UNC
a. Signature 4	FV	200.
s. Specimen.	—	175.

1995 Commemorative Issue

#25, 50th Anniversary Liberation of Jersey

25 **1 Pound** — VF | UNC

9.5.1995. Dark green and purple on multicolor underprint. Face like #20 with island outline at upper right, with text: *50th Anniversary...* at left in watermark area. Serial number prefix: *LJ*. Signature 4. Back: Face and back of German occupation 1 Pound #6. Watermark: Jersey cow's head. Printer: TDLR. 128x65mm.

	VF	UNC
a. Issued note.	FV	14.00
s. Specimen.	—	25.00

2000 ND Issue

26 **1 Pound** — VF | UNC

ND (2000). Dark green on multicolor underprint. Birds at left corner, arms at center, mature Queen Elizabeth II at right, facing, wearing cape. Treecreepers at lower left. Solid color denomination at upper right. Signature: Ian Black. Back: Church at left center. Watermark: Jersey cow's head. 128x65mm.

	VF	UNC
a. Two letter serial # prefix.	FV	5.00
b. Three letter serial # prefix.	FV	5.00
s. Specimen. Red overprint: *SPECIMEN* on both sides.	—	12.50

27 **5 Pounds**

ND (2000). Rose on multicolor underprint. Birds at left corner, arms at center, mature Queen Elizabeth II at right, facing, wearing cape. Whitethroat at lower left. Solid color denomination at upper right. Signature: Ian Black. Back: La Corbiere lighthouse. Watermark: Jersey cow's head. 135x70mm.

	VF	UNC
a. Issued note.	FV	20.00
s. Specimen.	—	17.50

28 **10 Pounds** — VF | UNC

ND (2000). Orange-brown on multicolor underprint. Birds at left corner, arms at center, mature Queen Elizabeth II at right, facing, wearing cape. Oyster catchers at lower left. Signature: Ian Black. Back: Battle of Jersey. Watermark: Jersey cow's head. 142x75mm.

	VF	UNC
a. Issued note.	FV	37.50
s. Specimen.	—	35.00

29 **20 Pounds**

ND (2000). Blue on multicolor underprint. Birds at left corner, arms at center, mature Queen Elizabeth II at right, facing, wearing cape. Brent goose at lower left. Solid color denomination at upper right. Signature: Ian Black. Back: St. Ouen's Manor. Watermark: Jersey cow's head. 150x80mm.

	VF	UNC
a. Issued note.	FV	70.00
s. Specimen.	—	65.00

30 **50 Pounds**

ND (2000). Dark gray on multicolor underprint. Birds at left corner, arms at center, mature Queen Elizabeth II at right, facing, wearing cape. Fulmers at lower left. Solid color denomination at upper right. Signature: Ian Black. Back: Government House. Watermark: Jersey cow's head. 156x86mm.

	VF	UNC
a. Issued note.	FV	185.
r. Replacement note.	—	300.
s. Specimen.	—	175.

2004 Commemorative Issue

800th Anniversary of the special relationship between Jersey and the British Crown.

31 **1 Pound** — VF | UNC

2004. Dark green and purple on multicolor underprint. Queen Elizabeth II at right. Back: Mount Orgueil Castle. 128x65mm.

	VF	UNC
a. Issued note.	FV	9.00
s. Specimen.	—	25.00

2010 ND Issue

32 1 Pound VF UNC

ND (2010). Green on multicolor underprint. Queen Elizabeth II facing at right, Monument to Freedom in Liberation Square at center. Back: La Hougue Bei Neolithic burial mount, Le Hocq in St. Clement. Watermark: Jersey cow head. Printer: (T)DLR. 130x65mm.

	VF	UNC
a. Issued note.	FV	7.50
s. Specimen.	—	50.00

33 5 Pounds

ND (2010). Blue on multicolor underprint. Queen Elizabeth II facing at right, Le Rat Cottage in St. Lawrence at center. Back: Archirondel Tower at left, Les Augres Manor at center. Watermark: Jersey cow head. Printer: (T)DLR. 135x70mm.

	VF	UNC
a. Issued note.	FV	15.00
s. Specimen.	—	50.00

34 10 Pounds

ND (2010). Redish-brown on multicolor underprint. Queen Elizabeth II facing at right, Hermitage of Elizabeth Castle in St. Aubin's Bay at center. Back: Seymour Tower in Groville Bay at left, Lalique glass sculptures in St. Matthew's Church in St. Lawrence at center. Watermark: Jersey cow head. Printer: (T)DLR. 145x75mm.

	VF	UNC
a. Issued note.	FV	30.00
s. Specimen.	—	50.00

35 20 Pounds

ND (2010). Violet on multicolor underprint. Queen Elizabeth II facing at right, The States (Parliament building) at center. Back: La Rocco Tower in St. Jean at left, interior of States chamber at center. Watermark: Jersey cow head. Printer: (T)DLR. 150x80mm.

	VF	UNC
a. Issued note.	FV	70.00
s. Specimen.	—	100.

36 50 Pounds VF UNC

ND (2010). Red on multicolor underprint. Queen Elizabeth II facing at right, Mont Orgueil Castle at center. Back: Ouaisne Tower at left, houses on La Marmotiere island in Les Ecrehous at center. Watermark: Jersey cow head. Printer: (T)DLR. 155x85mm.

	VF	UNC
a. Issued note.	FV	175.
s. Specimen.	—	200.

2012 Commemorative Issue

37 100 Pounds VF UNC

2012. Violet on multicolor underprint. Queen Elizabeth II bust facing at right. Back: Violet and blue. Royal Mace of Jersey at left, flag at lower right. Vertical format.

	VF	UNC
a. Issued note.	FV	250.
s. Specimen.	—	350.

Collector Series

States of Jersey, Treasury

1978 Issue

		Mkt. Value
CS1	**ND (1978) 1-20 Pounds** #11a-14a with overprint: *SPECIMEN* and Maltese cross prefix serial #.	75.00

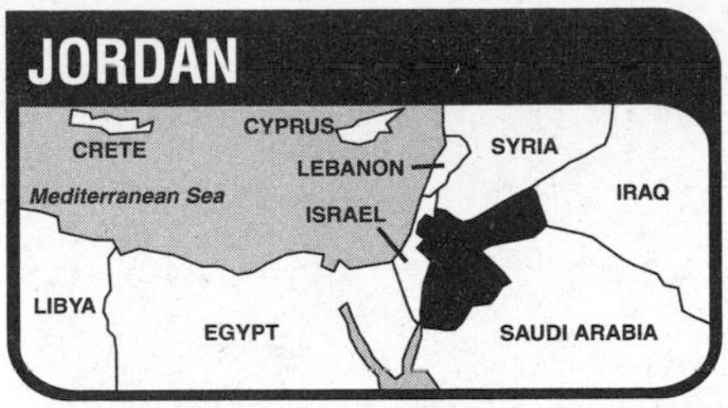

The Hashemite Kingdom of Jordan, a constitutional monarchy in southwest Asia, has an area of 37,738 sq. mi. (97,740 sq. km.) and a population of 5.46 million. Capital: Amman. Agriculture and tourism comprise Jordan's economic . Chief exports are phosphates, tomatoes and oranges.

Following World War I and the dissolution of the Ottoman Empire, the UK received a mandate to govern much of the Middle East. Britain separated out a semi-autonomous region of Transjordan from Palestine in the early 1920s, and the area gained its independence in 1946; it adopted the name of Jordan in 1950. The country's long-time ruler was King Hussen (1953-99). A pragmatic leader, he successfully navigated competing pressures from the major powers (US, USSR, and UK), various Arab states, Israel, and a large internal Palestinian population. Jordan lost the West Bank to Israel in the 1967 war and barely managed to defeat Palestinian rebels who threatened to overthrow the monarchy in 1970. Hussen in 1988 permanently relinquished Jordanian claims to the West Bank. In 1989, he reinstituted parliamentary elections and initiated a gradual political liberalization; political parties were legalized in 1992. In 1994, he signed a peace treaty with Israel. King Abdullah II, the son of King Hussein, assumed the throne following his father's death in February 1999. Since then, he has consolidated his power and undertaken an aggressive economic reform program. Jordan acceded to the World Trade Organization in 2000, and began to participate in the European Free Trade Association in 2001. In 2003, Jordan staunchly supported the Coalition ouster of Saddam in Iraq and following the outbreak of insurgent violence in Iraq, absorbed hundreds of thousands of displaced Iraqis, most of whom remain in the country. Municipal elections were held in July 2007 under a system in which 20% of seats in all municipal councils were reserved by quota for women. Parliamentary elections were held in November 2007 and saw independent pro-government candidates win the vast majority of seats. In November 2007, King Abdullah instructed his new prime minister to focus on socioeconomic reform, developing a healthcare and housing network for civilians and military personnel, and improving the educational system.

RULERS:

Abdullah I, 1946-1951
Hussein I, 1952-1999
Abdullah II, 1999-

MONETARY SYSTEM:

1 Dinar = 10 Dirhams
1 Dirham = 10 Piastres = 10 Qirsh
1 Piastre = 1 Qirsh = 10 Fils

REPLACEMENT NOTES:

#9-27, jj prefix (YY).

SIGNATURE VARIETIES

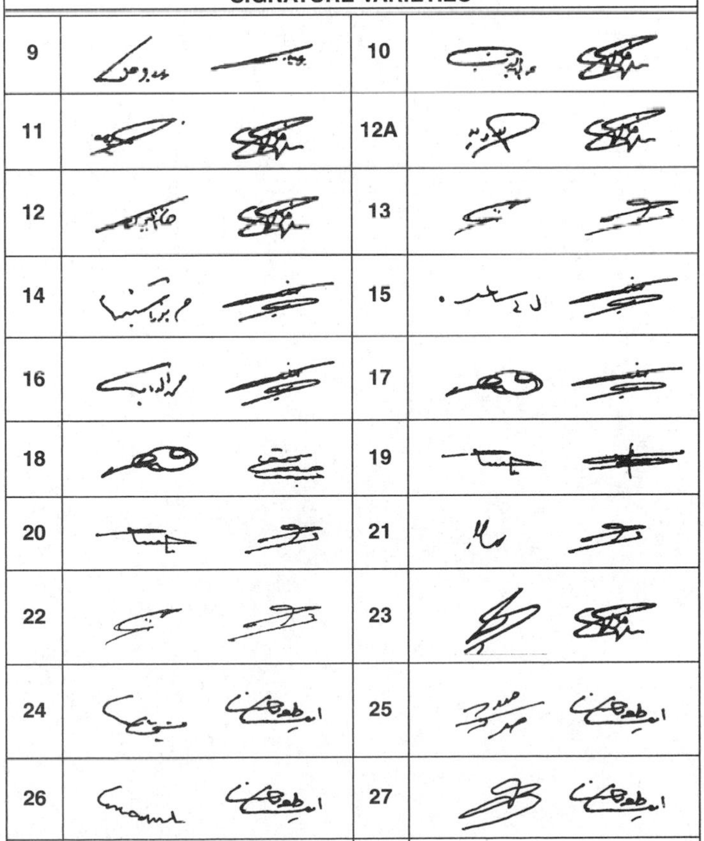

9
10
11
12A
12
13
14
15
16
17
18
19
20
21
22
23
24
25
26
27
28

Kingdom

Central Bank of Jordan

First Issue - Law 1959

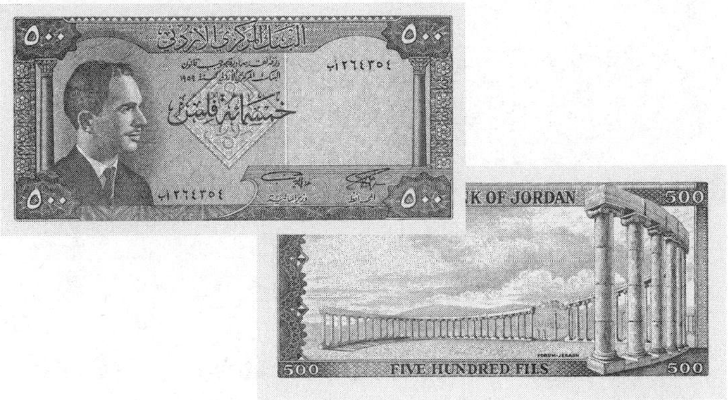

		VF	UNC
9	**500 Fils**		
	L.1959. (1965). Brown on multicolor underprint. King Hussein at left with law date 1959 (in Arabic *1909.*) Signature 10. Back: Jerash Forum. *FIVE HUNDRED FILS* at bottom margin. 140x70mm.		
	a. Issued note.	60.00	250.
	s. Specimen.	—	500.

		VF	UNC
10	**1 Dinar**		
	L.1959. (1965). Green on multicolor underprint. King Hussein at left with law date 1959 (in Arabic *1909.*) Signature 10. Back: Dome of the Rock at center with columns at right. 150x75mm.		
	a. Issued note.	25.00	200.
	s. Specimen.	—	500.

		VF	UNC
11	**5 Dinars**		
	L.1959. (1965). Red-brown on multicolor underprint. Hussein at left with law date 1959 (in Arabic *1909.*) Back: Al-Hazne, Treasury of Pharaoh at Petra at center right. 164x82mm.		
	a. Signature 10.	45.00	200.
	b. Signature 11.	45.00	200.
	c. Signature 12.	45.00	200.
	s. Specimen. Signature 10, 11, 12.	—	500.

12 **10 Dinars**

L.1959. (1965). Blue-gray on multicolor underprint. King Hussein at left with law date 1959 (in Arabic *1909.*) Back: Baptismal site on River Jordan. 175x88mm.

	VF	UNC
a. Signature 10.	95.00	275.
b. Signature 11.	95.00	275.
c. Signature 12.	95.00	275.
s. As a, b, c. Specimen. Red overprint: *SPECIMEN* on both sides. Punch hole cancelled.	—	750.

Second Issue - Law 1959

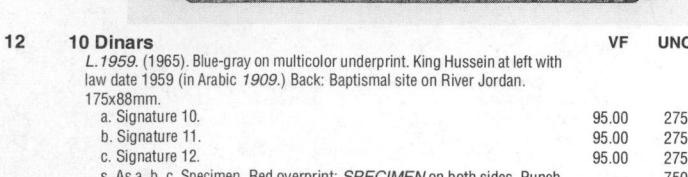

13 **1/2 Dinar**

ND. Brown on multicolor underprint. King Hussein at left. Back: Jerash Forum.*HALF DINAR* at bottom margin. Watermark: King Hussein wearing kuffiyeh. 140x70mm.

	VF	UNC
a. Signature 12.	10.00	40.00
b. Signature 12A.	10.00	40.00
c. Signature 14.	10.00	25.00
s. As a, b, c. Specimen. Black overprint: *SPECIMEN* on both sides.	—	500.

14 **1 Dinar**

ND. Green on multicolor underprint. King Hussein at left. Back: Dome of the Rock at center with columns at right. Watermark: King Hussein wearing kuffiyeh. 150x75mm.

	VF	UNC
a. Signature 13.	20.00	70.00
b. Signature 14.	15.00	50.00
s. Specimen. Signature 13, 14.	—	500.

15 **5 Dinars**

ND. Red-brown on multicolor underprint. King Hussein at left. Back: Al-Hazne, Treasury of Pharaoh at Petra at center right. Watermark: King Hussein wearing kuffiyeh. 164x82mm.

	VF	UNC
a. Signature 12.	25.00	80.00
b. Signature 15.	25.00	70.00
s. Specimen. Signature 12, 13.	—	700.

16 **10 Dinars**

ND. Blue-gray on multicolor underprint. King Hussein at left. Back: Baptismal site on River Jordan. Watermark: King Hussein wearing kuffiyeh. 175x88mm.

	VF	UNC
a. Signature 12.	70.00	200.
b. Signature 12A.	65.00	190.
c. Signature 13.	100.	275.
d. Signature 14.	90.00	250.
e. Signature 15.	40.00	160.
s. Specimen. Signature 12, 12A, 13, 14, 15.	—	850.
x. Forgery. Signature 13.	—	50.00

Third Issue

17 **1/2 Dinar**

ND (1975-92). Brown on multicolor underprint. King Hussein at left. Back: Jerash at right. Watermark: King Hussein wearing kuffiyeh. 136x67mm.

	VF	UNC
a. Signature 15. Serial # prefix starts with arabic 'I.'	4.00	10.00
b. Signature 15. Serial # prefix starts with arabic 'u.'	9.00	20.00
c. Signature 16.	5.00	11.00
d. Signature 17.	5.00	11.00
e. Signature 18.	4.00	8.00
s1. As a. Specimen. Signature 15.	—	200.
s2. As b. Specimen. Signature 15.	—	200.
s3. Specimen. Signature 16.	—	200.
s4. Specimen. Signature 17.	—	200.
s5. Specimen. Signature 18.	—	200.

18 1 Dinar

ND (1975-92). Dark green on multicolor underprint. King Hussein at left. Back: Dome of the Rock in Jerusalem, behind columns at right. Watermark: King Hussein wearing kuffiyeh. 144x71mm.

	VF	UNC
a. Text above doorway on back. Signature 15.	10.00	27.00
b. Without text above doorway on back. Signature 15.	9.00	20.00
c. Text above doorway on back. Signature 16.	8.00	18.00
d. Signature 17.	5.00	12.00
e. Signature 18.	5.00	12.00
f. Signature 19.	4.00	10.00
s1. Specimen. As a. Signature 15.	—	250.
s2. Specimen. As b. Signature 16.	—	250.
s3. Specimen. Signature 16.	—	250.
s4. Specimen. Signature 17.	—	250.
s5. Specimen. Signature 18.	—	250.
s6. Specimen. Signature 19.	—	250.

19 5 Dinars

ND (1975-92). Red on multicolor underprint. King Hussein at left. Back: Al-Hazne, Treasury of the Pharaoh at Petra at right. Watermark: King Hussein wearing kuffiyeh. 152x76mm.

	VF	UNC
a. Signature 15.	10.00	60.00
b. Signature 16.	10.00	55.00
c. Signature 18.	10.00	55.00
d. Signature 19.	10.00	50.00
s1. Specimen. Signature 15.	—	300.
s2. Specimen. Signature 16.	—	300.
s3. Specimen. Signature 18.	—	300.
s4. Specimen. Signature 19.	—	300.

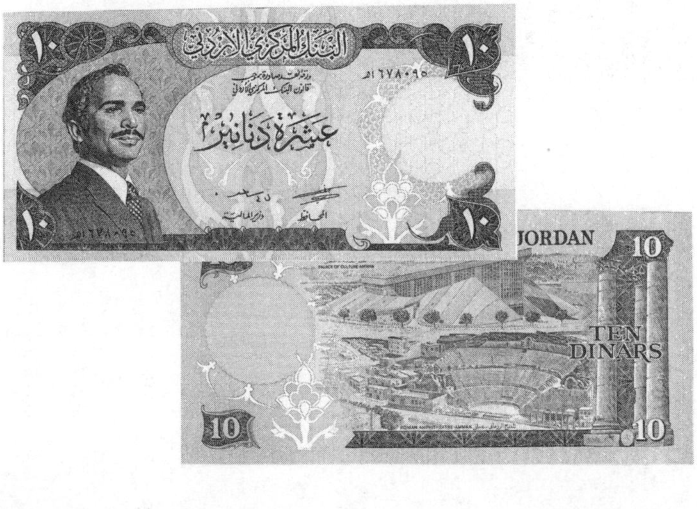

20 10 Dinars

ND (1975-92). Blue on multicolor underprint. King Hussein at left. Back: Cultural palace above and Roman amphitheater at center right. Watermark: King Hussein wearing kuffiyeh. 160x80mm.

	VF	UNC
a. Signature 15.	25.00	120.
b. Signature 16.	22.00	100.
c. Signature 18.	22.00	92.00
d. Signature 19.	22.00	74.00
s1. Specimen. As a. Signature 15.	—	275.
s2. Specimen. As b. Signature 16.	—	300.
s3. Specimen. As c. Signature 18.	—	300.
s4. Specimen. As d. Signature 19.	—	300.

21 20 Dinars

1977-1988. Deep brown on multicolor underprint. King Hussein at left. Back: Electric power station of Zerga. Watermark: King Hussein wearing kuffiyeh. 168x84mm.

	VF	UNC
a. Signature 16. 1977; 1981.	50.00	125.
b. Signature 17. 1985.	50.00	115.
c. Signature 18. 1987; 1988.	45.00	105.
s1. Specimen. Signature 16. 1977.	—	375.
s2. Specimen. Signature 16. 1981.	—	375.
s3. Specimen. Signature 17. 1985.	—	375.
s4. Specimen. Signature 18. 1987.	—	375.
s5. Specimen. Signature 18. 1988.	—	375.
x. Forgery. 1985.	—	50.00

22 20 Dinars

1977-85. Blue on multicolor underprint. King Hussein at left. Back: Electric power station of Zerga. Watermark: King Hussein wearing kuffiyeh. 168x84mm.

	VF	UNC
a. Signature 16. 1977 (1991).	70.00	140.
b. Signature 15. 1982 (1991).	60.00	125.
c. Signature 17. 1985 (1992).	60.00	110.
s1. Specimen. Signature 16. 1977 (1991).	—	2500.
s2. Specimen. Signature 15. 1982.	—	2500.
s3. Specimen. Signature 17. 1985 (1992).	—	2500.

FOURTH ISSUE (1992-93)

23 **1/2 Dinar** VF UNC

AH1412/1992; AH1413/1993. Lilac-brown and dark brown on multicolor underprint. King Hussein wearing kuffiyeh at center right. Signature 19. Back: Qusayr Amra fortress at right. Watermark: King Hussein wearing kuffiyeh. 131x62mm.

	VF	UNC
a. AH1412/1992.	FV	8.00
b. AH1413/1993.	FV	6.00
s1. As a. Specimen.	—	75.00
s2. As b. Specimen.	—	50.00

24 **1 Dinar** VF UNC

AH1412/1992; AH1413/1993. Green on olive and multicolor underprint. King Hussein wearing kuffiyeh at center right. Signature 19. Back: Ruins of Jerash at center right. Watermark: King Hussein wearing kuffiyeh. 137x66mm.

	VF	UNC
a. AH1412/1992.	FV	9.00
b. AH1413/1993.	FV	8.00
s1. As a. Specimen.	—	85.00
s2. As b. Specimen.	—	60.00

25 **5 Dinars** VF UNC

AH1412/1992; AH1413/1993. Red and violet-brown on multicolor underprint. King Hussein wearing kuffiyeh at center right. Signature 19. Back: Treasury of Petra. Watermark: King Hussein wearing kuffiyeh. 143x70mm.

	VF	UNC
a. AH1412/1992.	FV	55.00
b. AH1413/1993.	FV	40.00
s1. As a. Specimen.	—	100.
s2. As b. Specimen.	—	70.00

26 **10 Dinars** VF UNC

AH1412/1992. Blue, gray-violet and green on multicolor underprint. King Hussein wearing kuffiyeh at center right. Signature 19. Back: Al-Rabadh Castle ruins. Watermark: King Hussein wearing kuffiyeh. 149x74mm.

	VF	UNC
a. Issued note.	FV	70.00
s. Specimen.	—	125.

27 **20 Dinars** VF UNC

AH1412/1992. Dark brown, green and red-brown on multicolor underprint. King Hussein wearing kuffiyeh at center right. Signature 19. Back: Dome of the Rock at left center. Watermark: King Hussein wearing kuffiyeh. 155x78mm.

	VF	UNC
a. Issued note.	FV	125.
s. Specimen.	—	150.

Fifth Issue (1995-2002)

28 **1/2 Dinar** VF UNC

AH1415/1995; AH1417/1997. Lilac-brown and dark brown on multicolor underprint. King Hussein wearing kuffiyeh at center right. Signature 19. Back: Qusayr Amra fortress at right.Title: *THE HASHEMITE KINGDOM OF JORDAN.* Watermark: King Hussein wearing kuffiyeh. 131x62mm.

	VF	UNC
a. AH1415/1995. Signature 19.	FV	6.00
b. AH1417/1997. Signature 21.	FV	4.50
s1. As a. Specimen.	—	50.00
s2. As b. Specimen.	—	35.00

29 **1 Dinar** VF UNC

AH1415/1995-AH1423/2002. Green and olive on multicolor underprint. King Hussein wearing kuffiyeh at center right. Back: Ruins of Jerash at center right. Title: *THE HASHEMITE KINGDOM OF JORDAN.* Watermark: King Hussein wearing kuffiyeh. 137x66mm.

	VF	UNC
a. AH1415/1995. Signature 19.	FV	9.00
b. AH1416/1996. Signature 21.	FV	8.00
c. AH1422/2001. Signature 24.	FV	7.00
d. AH1423/2002. Signature 24.	FV	6.50
s1. As a. Specimen.	—	70.00
s2. As b. Specimen.	—	85.00

30 5 Dinars

AH1415 / 1995-AH1423 / 2001. Red-violet, purple and orange on multicolor underprint. King Hussein wearing kuffiyeh at center right. Signature 19. Back: Treasury of Petra. Title: *THE HASHEMITE KINGDOM OF JORDAN.* Watermark: King Hussein wearing kuffiyeh. 143x70mm.

	VF	UNC
a. AH1415/1995. Signature 19.	FV	35.00
b. AH1417/1997. Signature 22.	FV	28.00
s1. As a. Specimen.	—	125.
s2. As b. Specimen.	—	100.

31 10 Dinars

AH1416/1996; AH1422/2001. Purple, dark blue and black on multicolor underprint. King Hussein wearing kuffiyeh at center right. Signature 19. Back: Castle ruins. *AJLOUN CASTLE.* Title: *THE HASHEMITE KINGDOM OF JORDAN.* Watermark: King Hussein wearing kuffiyeh. 149x74mm.

	VF	UNC
a. AH1416/1996. Signature 20.	FV	55.00
b. AH1422/2001. Signature 24.	FV	45.00
s1. As a. Specimen.	—	150.
s2. As b. Specimen.	—	150.

32 20 Dinars

AH1415/1995; AH1422/2001. Dark brown, green and red-brown on multicolor underprint. King Hussein wearing kuffiyeh at center right. Signature 19. Back: Dome of the Rock at left center. Title: *THE HASHEMITE KINGDOM OF JORDAN.* Watermark: King Hussein wearing kuffiyeh. 155x78mm.

	VF	UNC
a. AH1415/1995. Signature 19.	FV	90.00
b. AH1422/2001. Signature 24.	FV	65.00
s1. As a. Specimen.	—	185.
s2. As b. Specimen.	—	200.

32A 50 Dinars

1994. Portrait of King Hussein waring kuffiyeh at center right within arch frame. Back: King Abdullah I at left, Raghadan Palace at right center. 149x74mm.

	VF	UNC
a. Unissued specimen. Red color.	—	10,000.
b. Unissued specimen. Orange color.	—	10,000.

32B 50 Dinars

1995. Portrait of King Hussein wearing kuffiyeh at right. no arch frame. Segmented security thread. Back: King Abdullah I at left, Raghadan Palace at right center. 149x74mm.

	VF	UNC
a. Unissued specimen. Green color.	—	10,000.
b. Unissued specimen. Blue color.	—	10,000.

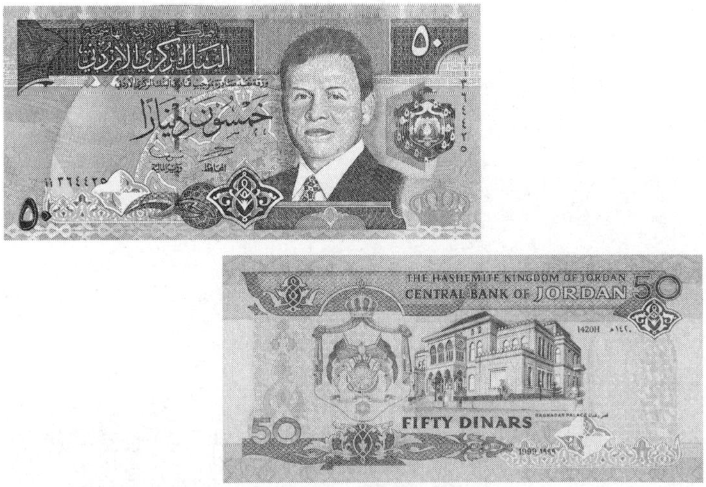

33 50 Dinars

AH1420/1999. Light green, blue, red and brown on multicolor underprint. King Abdullah II at right wearing business suit. Segmented security thread. Signature 23. Back: Raghadan Palace at right center. Coat of Arms at left. 149x74mm.

	VF	UNC
a. Issued note.	FV	150.
s. Specimen.	—	1250.

Sixth Issue (2002-)

34 **1 Dinar** — VF / UNC

AH1423/2002-. Green, gold and brown on multicolor underprint. Sherif Hussein ibn Ali at right. Silver coins. Back: Great Arab Revolt scene. Watermark: Sherif Hussein ibn Ali. Printer: (T)DLR. 133x74mm.

	VF	UNC
a. AH1423/2002. Signature 24.	FV	5.00
b. AH1426/2005. Signature 26.	FV	5.00
c. AH1427/2006. Signature 27.	FV	4.50
d. AH1429/2008. Signature 28.	FV	4.50
e. AH1430/2009. Signature 29.	FV	4.50
f. AH1432/2011. Signature 30.	FV	4.50
s. As a, b, c, d, e, f. Specimen.	—	250.

35 **5 Dinars** — VF / UNC

AH1423/2002-. Orange, brown and gold on multicolor underprint. King Abdullah I at right, calvary at center. Back: Ma'an Palace. Watermark: King Abdullah I. Printer: (T)DLR. 137x74mm.

	VF	UNC
a. AH1423/2002. Signature 24.	FV	18.00
b. AH1427/2006. Signature 27.	FV	15.00
c. AH1429/2008. Signature 28.	FV	15.00
d. AH1431/2010. Signature 30.	FV	15.00
e. AH1433/2012. Signature 31.	FV	15.00
s. As a, b, c, d, e. Specimen.	—	275.

36 **10 Dinars** — VF / UNC

AH1423/2002-. Blue, green and red on multicolor underprint. King Talal ibn Abdullah at right. First Parliament at center. Back: Camels at Petra. Watermark: King Talal ibn Abdullah. Printer: (T)DLR. 141x74mm.

	VF	UNC
a. AH1423/2002. Signature 24. Foil on vertical serial #.	FV	38.00
b. AH1425/2004. Signature 25. Foil to left of vertical serial #.	FV	32.00
c. AH1428/2007. Signature 27.	FV	32.00
d. AH1433/2012. Signature 31.	FV	32.00
s. As a, b, c, d. Specimen.	—	300.

37 **20 Dinars** — VF / UNC

AH1423/2002-. Blue-green and grey on multicolor underprint. King Hussein at right. Back: Dome of the Rock in Jerusalem. Watermark: King Hussein. Printer: (T)DLR. 145x74mm.

	VF	UNC
a. AH1423/2002. Signature 24.	FV	68.00
b. AH1427/2006. Signature 27.	FV	62.00
c. AH1430/2009. Signature 28.	FV	70.00
s. As a, b, c. Specimen.	—	325.

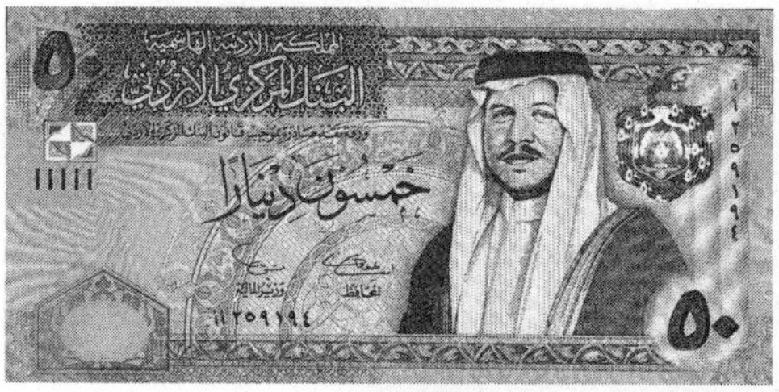
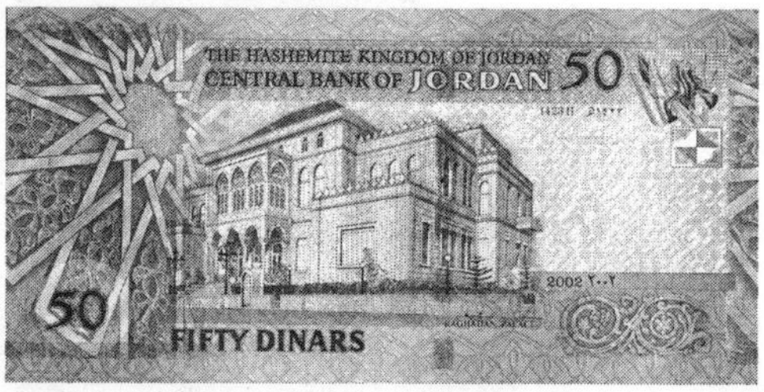

38 **50 Dinars** — VF / UNC

AH1423/2002; AH1425/2004; AH1427/2006; AH1428/2007; AH1430/2009. Light green, blue, red and brown on multicolor underprint. King Abdullah II at right. Back: Raghadan Palace. Watermark: Portrait of King Abdullah II. Printer: (T)DLR. 149x74mm.

	VF	UNC
a. AH1423/2002. Signature 24.	FV	140.
b. AH1425/2004. Signature 25.	FV	120.
c. AH1427/2006. Signature 27.	FV	120.
d. AH1428/2007. Signature 27.	FV	120.
e. AH1430/2009. Signature 28.	FV	120.
s. As a, b, c, d, e. Specimen.	—	325.

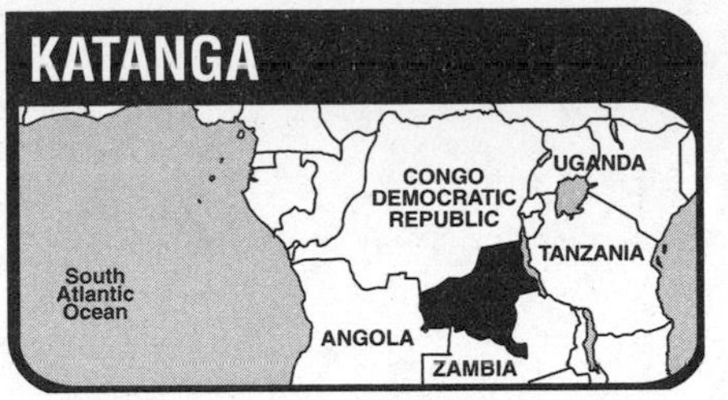

Katanga, the southern province of the former Zaïre extends northeast to Lake Tanganyika, east and south to Zambia, and west to Angola. It was inhabited by Luba and Bantu peoples, and was one of Africa's richest mining areas.

In 1960, Katanga, under the leadership of provincial president Moise Tshombe and supported by foreign mining interests, seceded from newly independent Republic of the Congo. A period of political confusion and bloody fighting involving Congolese, Belgian and United Nations forces ensued. At the end of the rebellion in 1962, Katanga was reintegrated into the republic, and is known as the Shaba region.

For additional history, see Zaïre.

MONETARY SYSTEM:

1 Franc = 100 Centimes

INDEPENDENT

GOVERNMENT KATANGA

1961 ND PROVISIONAL ISSUE

#1-4 with red overprint: *GOUVERNEMENT KATANGA* **on face and back of Banque D'Emission du Rwanda et du Burundi notes.**

		Fine	XF
1	**5 Francs** ND (1961 - old date 15.5.1961). Overprint: Red. *GOUVERNMENT KATANGA* on face and back of Banque D'Emission du Rwanda et du Burundi notes. Overprint on Rwanda & Burundi #1. Rare.	—	—
2	**10 Francs** ND (1961 - old date 15.9.1960; 5.10.1960). Overprint: Red. *GOUVERNMENT KATANGA* on face and back of Banque D'Emission du Rwanda et du Burundi notes. Overprint on Rwanda & Burundi #2. Rare.	—	—

		Fine	XF
3	**20 Francs** ND (1961 - old date/15.9.1960; 5.10.1960). Overprint: Red. *GOUVERNMENT KATANGA* on face and back of Banque D'Emission du Rwanda et du Burundi notes. Overprint on Rwanda & Burundi #3. Rare.	—	—

		Fine	XF
4	**50 Francs** ND (1961 - old date 1.10.1960). Overprint: Red. *GOUVERNMENT KATANGA* on face and back of Banque D'Emission du Rwanda et du Burundi notes. Overprint on Rwanda & Burundi #4. Rare.	—	—

BANQUE NATIONALE DU KATANGA

1960 ISSUE

		VF	UNC
5	**10 Francs** 1.12.1960; 15.12.1960. Lilac and yellow. Moise Tshombe at right. Signature 1. Back: Building at left.		
	a. Issued note.	135.	300.
	r. Remainder, without serial #.	—	185.
	s. Specimen.	—	200.

		VF	UNC
5A	**10 Francs** 1.12.1960. Green, brown and red. Moise Tshombe at left, reservoir at center, flag at right. Back: Foundry at center. Printer: W&S. (not issued)		
	r. Remainder without date or serial #. Rare.	—	—
	s. Specimen. Rare.	—	—

		VF	UNC
6	**20 Francs** 1960. Blue-green and brown. Moise Tshombe at right. Signature 1. Back: Building at left.		
	a. 21.11.1960.	100.	300.
	b. 1.12.1960.	225.	550.
	r. Remainder, without serial #.	—	275.
	s. Specimen.	—	300.

6A 20 Francs

	VF	UNC
1.12.1960. Multicolor. Aerial view at center. Moise Tshombe at left, flag at right. Back: Miners at center. Printer: W&S. (Not issued). Specimen. Rare.	—	—

7 50 Francs

10.11.1960. Red-brown and blue. Moise Tshombe at right. Signature 1. Back: Building at left.

	VF	UNC
a. Issued note.	100.	400.
r. Remainder, without serial #.	—	325.
s. Specimen.	—	375.

8 100 Francs

31.10.1960. Brown, green and yellow. Moise Tshombe at right. Signature 1. Back: Building at left.

	VF	UNC
a. Issued note.	200.	500.
r. Remainder, without serial #.	—	400.
s. Specimen.	—	425.

9 500 Francs

31.10.1960. Green, violet and olive. Moise Tshombe at right. Signature 1. Back: Building at left.

	VF	UNC
a. Issued note.	400.	1200.
r. Remainder, without serial #.	—	700.
s. Specimen.	—	400.

10 1000 Francs

31.10.1960. Blue and brown. Moise Tshombe at right. Signature 1. Back: Building at left.

	VF	UNC
a. Issued note.	500.	1500.
r. Remainder, without serial #.	—	700.
s. Specimen.	—	800.

1962 Issue

12 100 Francs

1962-63. Dark green and brown on multicolor underprint. Woman carrying ears of corn at right. Signature 2, 3. Back: Wheel of masks and spears. Watermark: Elephant.

	VF	UNC
a. 18.5.1962, 15.8.1962; 15.9.1962.	150.	400.
b. 15.1.1963.	235.	575.
s. Specimen.	—	350.

13 500 Francs

17.4.1962. Purple and multicolor. Man with fire at right. Signature 2, 3. Back: Wheel of masks and spears. Watermark: Elephant.

	VF	UNC
a. Issued note.	250.	800.
s. Specimen.	—	600.

14 1000 Francs

26.2.1962. Dark blue, red and brown on multicolor underprint. Woman carrying child on back while picking cotton at right. Ornate wheel at left. Signature 2, 3. Back: Wheel of masks and spears. Watermark: Elephant.

	VF	UNC
a. Issued note.	300.	850.
s. Specimen.	—	500.

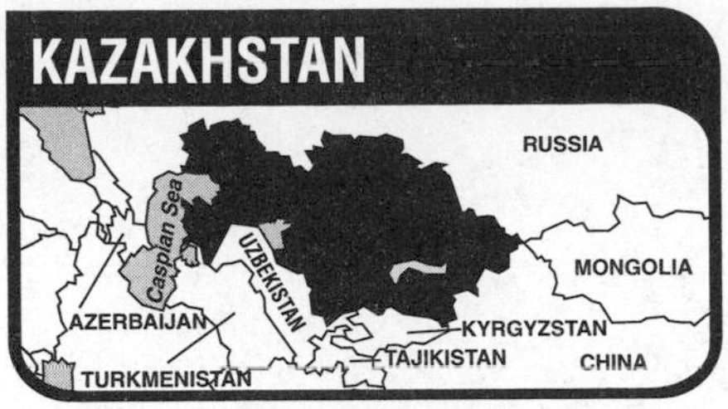

The Republic of Kazakhstan is bordered to the west by the Caspian Sea and Russia, to the north by Russia, in the east by the Peoples Republic of China and in the south by Uzbekistan and Kyrgyzstan. It has an area of 1,049,155 sq. mi. (2,717,300 sq. km.) and a population of 16.93 million. Capital: Astana. The country is rich in mineral resources including coal, tungsten, copper, lead, zinc and manganese with huge oil and natural gas reserves. Agriculture is important also non-ferrous metallurgy, heavy engineering and chemical industries are leaders in its economy.

Native Kazakhs, a mix of Turkic and Mongol nomadic tribes who migrated into the region in the 13th century, were rarely united as a single nation. The area was conquered by Russia in the 18th century, and Kazakhstan became a Soviet Republic in 1936. During the 1950s and 1960s agricultural "Virgin Lands" program, Soviet citizens were encouraged to help cultivate Kazakhstan's northern pastures. This influx of immigrants (mostly Russians, but also some other deported nationalities) skewed the ethnic mixture and enabled non-Kazakhs to outnumber natives. Independence in 1991 caused many of these newcomers to emigrate. Kazakhstan's economy is larger than those of all the other Central Asian states combined, largely due to the country's vast natural resources and a recent history of political stability. Current issues include: developing a cohesive national identity; expanding the development of the country's vast energy resources and exporting them to world markets; achieving a sustainable economic growth; diversifying the economy outside the oil, gas, and mining sectors; enhancing Kazakhstan's competitiveness; and strengthening relations with neighboring states and other foreign powers.

MONETARY SYSTEM:

1 Tengé = 100 Tyin = 500 Rubles (Russian), 1993 -

Republic

КАЗАКСТАН УЛТТЫК БАНКI

Kazakhstan National Bank

1993-98 Issue

1 — 1 Tyin — VF — UNC

1993. Red, blue and purple on yellow and multicolor underprint. Ornate denomination in circle at right. Serial number at left. Back: Circular arms at left. Three watermark varieties. Two serial # positions.

	VF	UNC
a. Watermark: large diamond lattice pattern. Low serial # position.	.50	1.00
b. Watermark: large diamond lattice pattern. Upper serial # position.	.50	1.00
c. Watermark: small snowflake pattern. Low serial # position.	.50	1.00
d. Watermark: small snowflake pattern. Upper serial # position.	.50	1.00
e. No watermark. Low serial # position.	.50	1.00

2 — 2 Tyin — VF — UNC

1993. Blue-violet on light blue and multicolor underprint. Ornate denomination in circle at right. Serial number at left. Back: Circular arms at left. Three watermark varieties. Two serial # positions.

	VF	UNC
a. Watermark: large diamond pattern. Low serial # position.	.50	1.00
b. Watermark: large diamond pattern. Upper serial # position.	.50	1.00
c. Watermark: small snowflake pattern. Low serial # position.	.50	1.00
d. Watermark: small snowflake pattern. Upper serial # position.	.50	1.00
e. Without watermark. Low serial # position.	.50	1.00

3 — 5 Tyin — VF — UNC

1993. Violet on light blue and multicolor underprint. Ornate denomination in circle at right. Serial number at left. Back: Circular arms at left.

	VF	UNC
a. Watermark: small snowflake pattern. Low serial # position.	.50	1.00
b. Watermark: small snowflake pattern. Upper serial # position.	.50	1.00

4 — 10 Tyin — VF — UNC

1993. Deep red on pink and multicolor underprint. Ornate denomination in circle at right. Serial number at left. Back: Circular arms at left.

	VF	UNC
a. Watermark: small snowflake pattern. Low serial # position.	.50	1.50
b. Watermark: small snowflake pattern. Upper serial # position.	.50	1.50

5 — 20 Tyin — VF — UNC

1993. Black and blue-gray on yellow and multicolor underprint. Ornate denomination in circle at right. Serial number at left. Back: Circular arms at left.

	VF	UNC
a. Watermark: small snowflake pattern. Low serial # position.	.50	1.50
b. Watermark: small snowflake pattern. Upper serial # position.	.50	1.50

6 — 50 Tyin — VF — UNC

1993. Dark brown and black on multicolor underprint. Ornate denomination in circle at right. Serial number at left. Back: Circular arms at left. Watermark: Design.

	VF	UNC
a. Watermark: small snowflake pattern. Low serial # position.	.50	3.00
b. Watermark: small snowflake pattern. Upper serial # position.	.50	3.00

7 — 1 Tengé — VF — UNC

1993. Dark blue on multicolor underprint. Al-Farabi at center right. Back: Light blue on multicolor underprint. Architectural drawings of mosque at left center, arms at upper right. Watermark: Symmetrical design repeated.

	VF	UNC
a. Issued note.	1.00	3.00
s. Specimen.	—	100.

8 — 3 Tengé — VF — UNC

1993. Dark green on multicolor underprint. Suinbai at center right. Back: Mountains, forest, and river at left center. Arms at upper center right. Watermark: Symmetrical design repeated.

	VF	UNC
a. Issued note.	1.00	4.00
s. Specimen.	—	100.

9	5 Tengé	VF	UNC
	1993. Dark brown-violet on multicolor underprint. Kurmangazy at center right. Back: Cemetery at left center, arms at upper center right. Watermark: Symmetrical design repeated.		
	a. Issued note.	1.00	4.00
	s. Specimen.	—	100.

10	10 Tengé	VF	UNC
	1993. Dark green on multicolor underprint. Shoqan Valikhanov at center right. Back: Mountains, forest, and lake at left center, arms at upper center right. Watermark: Shoqan Valikhanov.		
	a. Issued note.	1.00	6.00
	s. Specimen.	—	100.

11	20 Tengé	VF	UNC
	1993. Brown on multicolor underprint. Abai Kunanbrev at center right. Back: Equestrian hunter at left center, arms at upper center right. Watermark: Abai Kunanbrev.		
	a. Issued note.	2.00	10.00
	s. Specimen.	—	100.

12	50 Tengé	VF	UNC
	1993. Red-brown and deep violet on multicolor underprint. Abilkhair Khan at center right. Back: Native artwork at left center, arms at upper center right. Watermark: Abilkhair Khan.		
	a. Issued note.	3.00	12.00
	s. Specimen.	—	125.

13	100 Tengé	VF	UNC
	1993. Purple and dark blue on multicolor underprint. Abylai Khan at center right. Back: Domed building at left center, arms at upper center right. Watermark: Abylai Khan.		
	a. 1993. Silver colored OVD ink.	3.00	18.00
	b. 2004. Golden colored OVD ink.	2.00	15.00
	s. Specimen.	—	125.

14	200 Tengé	VF	UNC
	1993. Red and brown on multicolor underprint. Al-Farabi at right. Back: Blue on multicolor underprint. Domes of building at left, arms at upper center right. Watermark: Al-Farabi.		
	a. Issued note.	FV	20.00
	s. Specimen.	—	135.

15	500 Tengé	VF	UNC
	1994. Blue-black and violet on multicolor underprint. Al-Farabi at right. Back: Ancient building, arms at upper center right. Watermark: Al-Farabi.		
	a. Issued note.	FV	27.50
	s. Specimen.	—	150.

16	1000 Tengé	VF	UNC
	1994. Deep green, red and orange on multicolor underprint. Al-Farabi at right. Back: Ancient building. Watermark: Al-Farabi.		
	a. Issued note.	FV	40.00
	s. Specimen.	—	150.

17 **2000 Tengé** — **VF** / **UNC**

1996. Dark brown and green on multicolor underprint. Al-Farabi at right. Back: Gate. Watermark: Al-Farabi. — 25.00 / 80.00

18 **5000 Tengé** — **VF** / **UNC**

1998. Light brown on multicolor underprint. Al Farabi at center. Back: Mausoleum. — 35.00 / 100.

1999-2001 Issue

		VF	UNC
20	**200 Tengé**		
	1999. Brown and tan on multicolor underprint. Al-Farabi at right. Back: Domes of building at left, arms at upper center right. Watermark: Al-Farabi.		
	a. Security device at lower right with white linear design within.	FV	12.00
	b. Security device at lower right solid.	FV	12.00

		VF	UNC
21	**500 Tengé**		
	1999. Dark blue and violet on multicolor underprint. Al-Farabi at right. Back: Ancient building, arms at upper center right. Watermark: Al-Farabi.		
	a. Security device at lower right. with white linear designature	FV	20.00
	b. Security device at lower right. solid.	FV	20.00

22 **1000 Tengé** — **VF** / **UNC**

2000. Dark green, red and slate blue on multicolor underprint. Al-Farabi at right. Back: Ancient building. Watermark: Al-Farabi. — FV / 40.00

23 **2000 Tengé** — **VF** / **UNC**

2000. Green, brown and purple on multicolor underprint. Al-Farabi at right. Back: Mausoleum of Khodka Akhemd Yassavi. Watermark: Al-Farabi. — FV / 60.00

24 **5000 Tengé** — **VF** / **UNC**

2001. Light brown and red on multicolor underprint. Al Farabi at center. Back: Mausoleum. — FV / 90.00

25 **10,000 Tengé** — **VF** / **UNC**

2003. Blue and dark brown on multicolor underprint. Back: Snow leopard with mountains in background. — FV / 170.

2001 Commemorative Issue

		VF	UNC
26	**5000 Tengé** 2001. Light brown and red on multicolor underprint. Blue overprint at top of watermark area on face of number 18.	FV	80.00

2004 Issue

		VF	UNC
27	**500 Tengé** 1999 (2004). Dark blue and blue on violet and multicolor underprint. Al-Farabi at right. Additional security features at right. Back: Mausoleum of Khodka Akhmed Yassavi. Watermark: Al-Farabi.	FV	10.00

2006 Issue

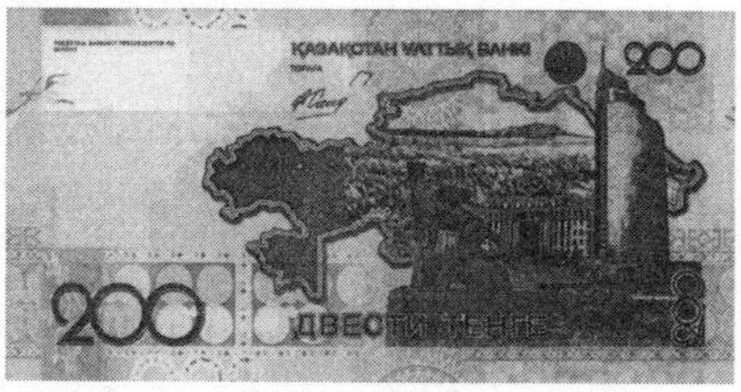

		VF	UNC
28	**200 Tengé** 2006. Multicolor. Hand at left, tower. Back: Map, birds in flight. 126x64mm.	FV	4.00

		VF	UNC
29	**500 Tengé** 2006. Blue and multicolor. Hand at left, tower. Back: Map, birds in flight. 130x67mm.	FV	8.00

		VF	UNC
30	**1000 Tengé** 2006. Yellow and multicolor. Hand at left, tower. Back: Map and mountains. 134x69mm.	FV	16.00

		VF	UNC
31	**2000 Tengé** 2006. Green and multicolor. Hand at left, tower. Back: Map and mountain lake. 138x72mm.		
	a. Error spelling in bank name.	FV	30.00
	b. Corrected spelling of bank name.	FV	35.00

		VF	UNC
32	**5000 Tengé** 2006. Reddish brown and multicolor. Hand at left, tower. Back: Map and statue. 144x76mm.		
	a. Error spelling of bank name.	FV	50.00
	b. Corrected spelling of bank name.	FV	45.00

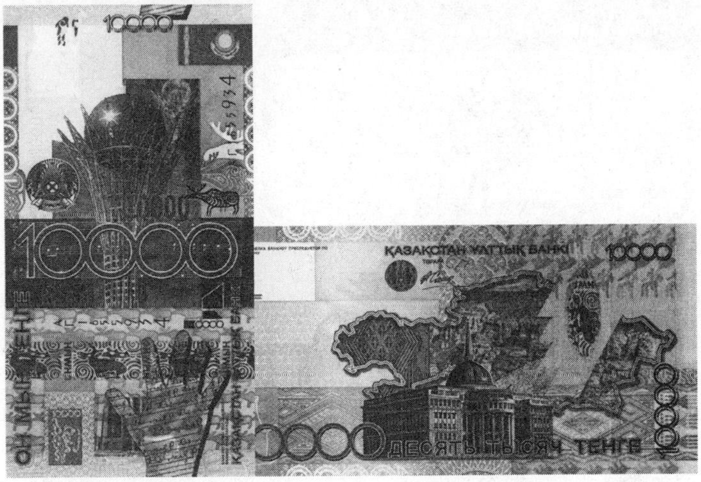

33	**10,000 Tengé**	**VF**	**UNC**
	2006. Multicolor. Hand at left, tower. Back: Map and building. 149x74mm.	FV	90.00

2008 Commemorative Issue

34	**5000 Tengé**	**VF**	**UNC**
	8.7.2008. Red and brown on multicolor underprint. Hand at left, tower. Eagle in device at top left. Back: Map, statue and Kazakhstan hotel in Almaty. Watermark: Snow leopard and value. Printer: TDLR. 144x76mm.		
	a. Issued note.	FV	75.00
	s. Specimen.	FV	150.

2010 Commemorative Issue

35	**1000 Tengé**	**VF**	**UNC**
	2010. Blue, green and red on multicolor underprint. Value at left within ornate design. Back: Domed building at center. 134x69mm.	FV	20.00

36	**2000 Tengé**	**VF**	**UNC**
	2010. Green on multicolor underprint. Hand at botom, tower. Back: Mountain and Ski Jumper.	FV	35.00

2011 OIC Commememorative Issue

37	**1000 Tengé**	**VF**	**UNC**
	2011. 134x69mm.	FV	16.00

38	**5000 Tengé**	**VF**	**UNC**
	2011. 144x76mm.	FV	45.00

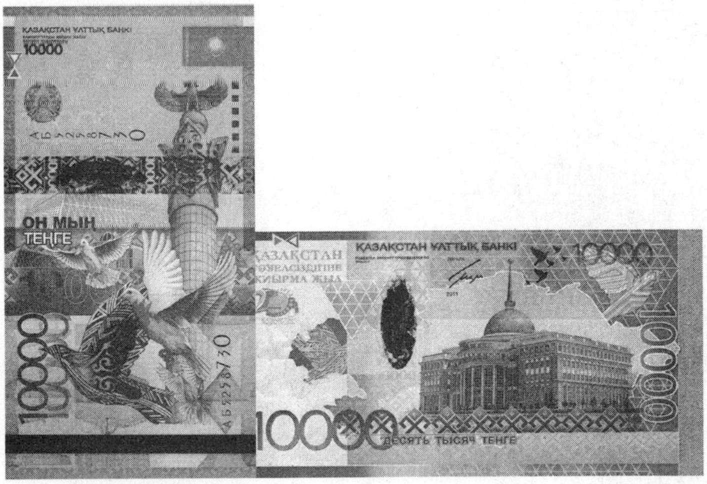

39	**10,000 Tengé**	**VF**	**UNC**
	2011. 149x79mm.	FV	90.00

2011 Commemorative Issue

40	**10,000 Tengé**	**VF**	**UNC**
	2011. Blue and multicolor.	FV	90.00

2011-12 Issue

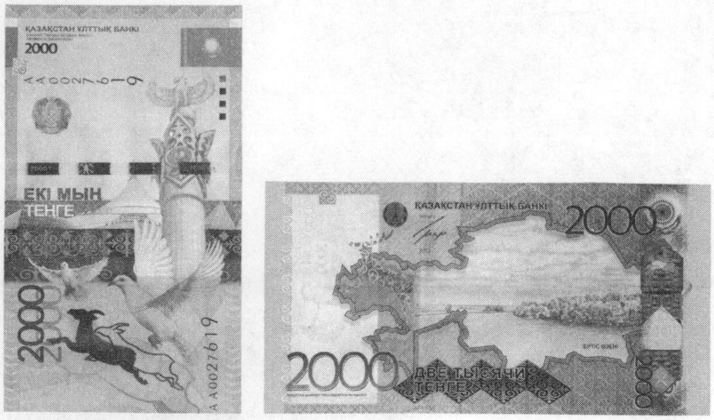

41 **2000 Tengé** — VF: FV — UNC: 35.00

2012. Dark and light green on multicolor underprint. Monument at right and flying doves at bottom center. Back: Kazakhstan map and Irtysh River image. 139x73mm.

42 **5000 Tengé** — VF: FV — UNC: 45.00

2011. Orange and multicolor.

43 **10,000 Tengé** — VF: FV — UNC: 125.

2012. Blue and multicolor.

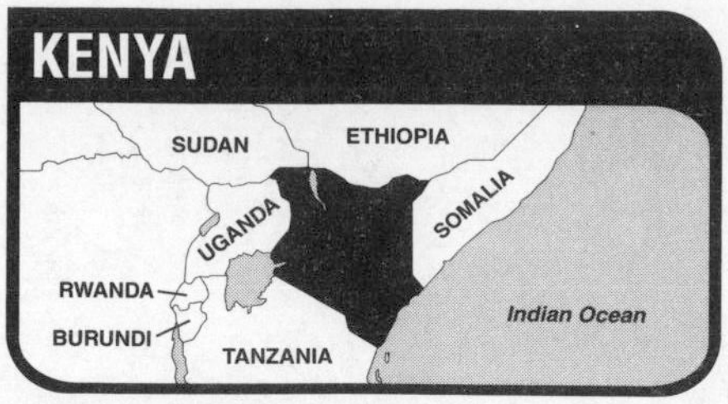

The Republic of Kenya, located on the east coast of Central Africa, has an area of 224,961 sq. mi. (582,646 sq. km.) and a population of 30.34 million. Capital: Nairobi. The predominantly agricultural country exports coffee, tea and petroleum products.

Founding president and liberation struggle icon Jomo Kenyatta led Kenya from independence in 1963 until his death in 1978, when President Daniel Toroitich arap Moi took power in a constitutional succession. The country was a de facto one-party state from 1969 until 1982 when the ruling Kenya African National Union (KANU) made itself the sole legal party in Kenya. Moi acceded to internal and external pressure for political liberalization in late 1991. The ethnically fractured opposition failed to dislodge KANU from power in elections in 1992 and 1997, which were marred by violence and fraud, but were viewed as having generally reflected the will of the Kenyan people. President Moi stepped down in December 2002 following fair and peaceful elections. Mwai Kibaki, running as the candidate of the multiethnic, united opposition group, the National Rainbow Coalition (NARC), defeated KANU candidate Uhuru Kenyatta and assumed the presidency following a campaign centered on an anticorruption platform. Kibaki's NARC coalition splintered in 2005 over the constitutional review process. Government defectors joined with KANU to form a new opposition coalition, the Orange Democratic Movement, which defeated the government's draft constitution in a popular referendum in November 2005. Kibaki's reelection in December 2007 brought charges of vote rigging from ODM candidate Raila Odinga and unleashed two months of violence in which as many as 1,500 people died. UN-sponsored talks in late February produced a powersharing accord bringing Odinga into the government in the restored position of prime minister.

Notes of the East African Currency Board were in use during the first years.

RULERS:

British to 1964

MONETARY SYSTEM:

1 Shilling (Shilingi) = 100 Cents

SIGNATURE VARIETIES		
	GOVERNOR	MEMBER
1	 Dr. Leon Barawski	 Gevau
2	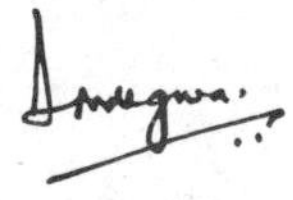 Duncan Ndegwa	 Gevau
3	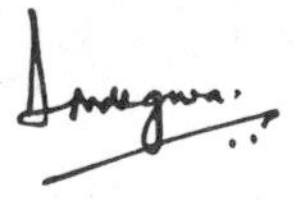 Duncan Ndegwa	
4	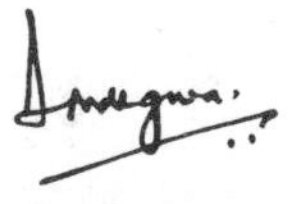 Duncan Ndegwa	 Iganga
5	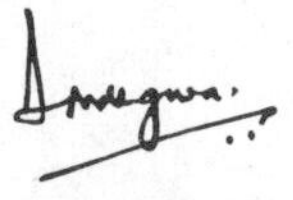 Duncan Ndegwa	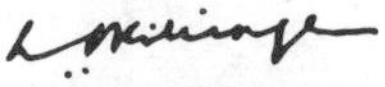 L. Mutenge
6	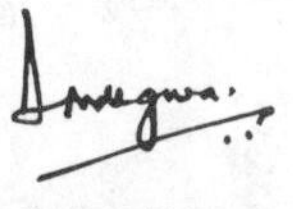 Duncan Ndegwa	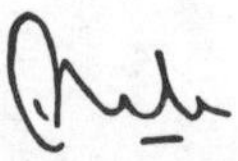 Harry Mule
7	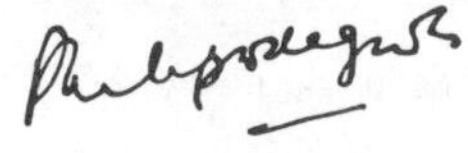 Philip Ndegwa	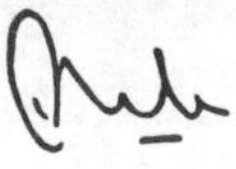 Harry Mule

SIGNATURE VARIETIES		
8	Philip Ndegwa	Subiudyo
9a	Eric Kotut	Subiudyo
9b	Eric Kotut	Subiudyo
10a	Eric Kotut	
10b	Eric Kotut	
11	Micah D. Cheserem	
12	Micah D. Cheserem	B.K. Kipkulei
13	Micah D. Cheserem	B.K. Kipkulei
14	Micah D. Cheserem	S.S. Lesima
15	Micah D. Cheserem	Emengich
16	Micah D. Cheserem	
17	Nahashon Nyagah	
18	Micah D. Cheserem	
19		

REPUBLIC

BANKI KUU YA KENYA

CENTRAL BANK OF KENYA

1966 ISSUE

		VF	UNC
1	**5 Shillings**		
	1966-68. Brown on multicolor underprint. Mzee Jomo Kenyatta at left, arms at center in underprint. Back: Woman picking coffee beans at right. Watermark: Lion's head. Values in Arabic numerals and letters.		
	a. 1.7.1966.	20.00	95.00
	b. 1.7.1967.	17.50	90.00
	c. 1.7.1968.	17.50	95.00
	s. As a. Specimen, punched hole cancelled.	—	150.

		VF	UNC
2	**10 Shillings**		
	1966-68. Green on multicolor underprint. Mzee Jomo Kenyatta at left, arms at center in underprint. Back: Tea pickers in field. Watermark: Lion's head. Values in Arabic numerals and letters.		
	a. 1.7.1966.	25.00	95.00
	b. 1.7.1967.	27.50	140.
	c. 1.7.1968.	20.00	120.
	s. As a. Specimen, punched hole cancelled.	—	200.

		VF	UNC
3	**20 Shillings**		
	1966-68. Blue on multicolor underprint. Mzee Jomo Kenyatta at left, arms at center in underprint. Back: Plants and train with sisal. Watermark: Lion's head. Values in Arabic numerals and letters.		
	a. 1.7.1966.	50.00	250.
	b. 1.7.1967.	60.00	275.
	c. 1.7.1968.	50.00	250.
	s. As a. Specimen, punched hole cancelled.	—	300.

4 **50 Shillings** VF UNC

1966-68. Dark brown on multicolor underprint. Mzee Jomo Kenyatta at left, arms at center in underprint. Back: Cotton picking below Mt. Kenya. Watermark: Lion's head. Values in Arabic numerals and letters.

	VF	UNC
a. 1.7.1966.	300.	950.
b. 1.7.1967.	400.	1500.
c. 1.7.1968.	350.	1450.
s. As a. Specimen, punched hole cancelled.	—	1250.

5 **100 Shillings** VF UNC

1966; 1968. Purple on multicolor underprint. Mzee Jomo Kenyatta at left, arms at center in underprint. Back: Workers at pineapple plantation. Watermark: Lion's head. Values in Arabic numerals and letters.

	VF	UNC
a. 1.7.1966.	55.00	525.
b. 1.7.1968.	60.00	575.
s. As a. Specimen, punched hole cancelled.	—	750.

1969 Issue

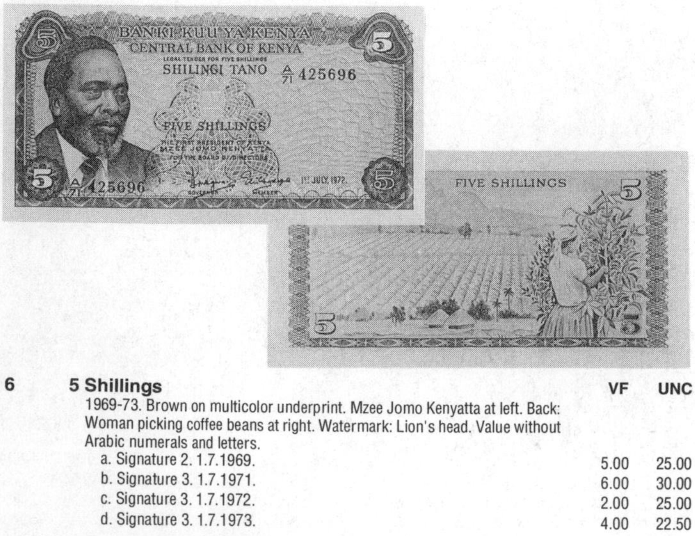

6 **5 Shillings** VF UNC

1969-73. Brown on multicolor underprint. Mzee Jomo Kenyatta at left. Back: Woman picking coffee beans at right. Watermark: Lion's head. Value without Arabic numerals and letters.

	VF	UNC
a. Signature 2. 1.7.1969.	5.00	25.00
b. Signature 3. 1.7.1971.	6.00	30.00
c. Signature 3. 1.7.1972.	2.00	25.00
d. Signature 3. 1.7.1973.	4.00	22.50

7 **10 Shillings** VF UNC

1969-74. Green on multicolor underprint. Mzee Jomo Kenyatta at left. Back: Tea pickers in field. Watermark: Lion's head. Value without Arabic numerals and letters.

	VF	UNC
a. Signature 2. 1.7.1969.	8.00	60.00
b. Signature 3. 1.7.1971.	6.00	50.00
c. Signature 3. 1.7.1972.	7.00	55.00
d. Signature 3. 1.7.1973.	7.00	55.00
e. Signature 3. 1.7.1974.	7.00	57.50

8 **20 Shillings** VF UNC

1969-73. Blue on multicolor underprint. Mzee Jomo Kenyatta at left. Back: Plants and train with sisal. Watermark: Lion's head. Value without Arabic numerals and letters.

	VF	UNC
a. Signature 2. 1.7.1969.	20.00	160.
b. Signature 3. 1.7.1971.	40.00	275.
c. Signature 3. 1.7.1972.	25.00	180.
d. Signature 3. 1.7.1973.	30.00	200.

9 **50 Shillings**

1969; 1971. Dark brown on multicolor underprint. Mzee Jomo Kenyatta at left. Back: Cotton picking below Mt. Kenya. Watermark: Lion's head. Value without Arabic numerals and letters.

	VF	UNC
a. Signature 2. 1.7.1969.	175.	750.
b. Signature 3. 1.7.1971.	65.00	200.

10 **100 Shillings** VF UNC

1969-73. Purple on multicolor underprint. Mzee Jomo Kenyatta at left. Back: Workers at pineapple plantation. Watermark: Lion's head. Value without Arabic numerals and letters.

	VF	UNC
a. Signature 2. 1.7.1969.	100.	500.
b. Signature 3. 1.7.1971.	40.00	350.
c. Signature 3. 1.7.1972.	40.00	350.
d. Signature 3. 1.7.1973.	75.00	375.

1974 Issue

11 5 Shillings

1974-77. Brown-orange on multicolor underprint. Mzee Jomo Kenyatta at left. Back: Woman picking coffee beans at right. Watermark: Lion's head. Values in latent images at bottom left.

	VF	UNC
a. Signature 3. 12.12.1974.	2.00	15.00
b. Signature 4. 1.1.1975.	2.00	15.00
c. Signature 4. 1.7.1976.	3.00	20.00
d. Signature 5. 1.7.1977.	2.00	15.00

12 10 Shillings

1975-77. Dark green and dark brown on multicolor underprint. Mzee Jomo Kenyatta at left. Back: Green. Cattle at center right. Watermark: Lion's head. Values in latent images at bottom left.

	VF	UNC
a. Signature 4. 1.1.1975.	3.00	15.00
b. Signature 4. 1.7.1976.	6.00	30.00
c. Signature 5. 1.7.1977.	4.00	17.50

13 20 Shillings

1974-77. Dark blue on multicolor underprint. Mzee Jomo Kenyatta at left. Back: Lions. Watermark: Lion's head. Values in latent images at bottom left.

	VF	UNC
a. Signature 3. 12.12.1974.	15.00	60.00
b. Signature 4. 1.1.1975.	7.50	35.00
c. Signature 4. 1.7.1976.	12.50	65.00
d. Signature 5. 1.7.1977.	9.00	45.00

14 100 Shillings

1974-77. Purple on light green and multicolor underprint. Mzee Jomo Kenyatta at left. Back: Kenyatta statue and tower. Watermark: Lion's head. 153 x 79mm. Values in latent images at bottom left.

	VF	UNC
a. Signature 3. 12.12.1974.	35.00	150.
b. Signature 4. 1.1.1975.	17.50	125.
c. Signature 4. 1.7.1976.	25.00	140.
d. Signature 5. 1.7.1977.	30.00	200.

1978 Issue

Note: #15-18 were withdrawn soon after Kenyatta's death. However, a shortage of currency resulted in a reissue during Dec. 1993 - Jan. 1994 of mostly circulated notes.

15 5 Shillings — VF 1.50, UNC 3.00

1.7.1978. Brown-orange on multicolor underprint. Mzee Jomo Kenyatta at left with English value only in third line. Signature 5. Back: Woman picking coffee beans at right. Watermark: Lion's head.

16 10 Shillings — VF 1.00, UNC 5.00

1.7.1978. Dark green and dark brown on multicolor underprint. Mzee Jomo Kenyatta at left with English value only in third line. Signature 5. Back: Cattle at center right. Watermark: Lion's head.

17	20 Shillings	VF	UNC
	1.7.1978. Blue-black and blue on multicolor underprint. Mzee Jomo Kenyatta at left with English value only in third line. Signature 5. Back: Lions. Watermark: Lion's head.	2.75	7.50

18	100 Shillings	VF	UNC
	1.7.1978. Purple, dark brown and dark blue on multicolor underprint. Mzee Jomo Kenyatta at left with English value only in third line. Signature 5. Different colors in guilloches. Back: Kenyatta statue and tower. Watermark: Lion's head. 157x81mm.	7.50	20.00

1980-81 Issue

19	5 Shillings	VF	UNC
	1981-84. Orange-brown on multicolor underprint. Arms at center. President Daniel Toroitich Arap Moi at right. Back: Three rams with giraffes and mountain in background. Watermark: Lion's head.		
	a. Signature 6. 1.1.1981.	1.00	6.00
	b. Signature 6. 1.1.1982.	1.00	5.00
	c. Signature 7. 1.7.1984.	1.50	7.00

20	10 Shillings	VF	UNC
	1981-88. Green, blue and brown on multicolor underprint. Arms at center. President Daniel Toroitich Arap Moi at right. Back: Two cows at left, two school children drinking milk at center. Watermark: Lion's head. UV: bottom front fluoresces yellow and orange.		
	a. Signature 6. 1.1.1981.	1.50	8.00
	b. Signature 6. 1.1.1982.	1.25	7.00
	c. Signature 7. 1.7.1984.	1.75	9.00
	d. Signature 7. 1.7.1985.	2.00	10.00
	e. Signature 7. 14.9.1986.	1.50	8.00
	f. Signature 8. 1.7.1987.	1.25	8.00
	g. Signature 9a. 1.7.1988.	1.25	7.00

21	20 Shillings	VF	UNC
	1981-87. Blue on multicolor underprint. Arms at center. President Daniel Toroitich Arap Moi at right. Back: Four women reading newspaper at center. Watermark: Lion's head.		
	a. Signature 6. 1.1.1981.	1.75	14.00
	b. Signature 6. 1.1.1982.	1.50	10.00
	c. Signature 7. 1.7.1984.	1.50	12.00
	d. Signature 7. 1.7.1985.	2.00	16.00
	e. Signature 7. 14.9.1986.	2.25	17.50
	f. Signature 8. 1.7.1987.	1.75	14.00

22	50 Shillings	VF	UNC
	1980-88. Dark red and multicolor. Arms at center. President Daniel Toroitich Arap Moi at right. Back: Olive. Jet aircraft flying over Jomo Kenyatta airport. Watermark: Lion's head.		
	a. Signature 4. 1.6.1980.	3.00	12.50
	b. Signature 7. 1.7.1985.	3.50	17.50
	c. Signature 7. 14.9.1986.	3.50	18.00
	d. Signature 8. 1.7.1987.	5.00	20.00
	e. Signature 9a. 1.7.1988.	5.00	20.00

23 100 Shillings

1980-88. Purple and multicolor. Arms at center. President Daniel Toroitich Arap Moi at right. Back: Kenyatta statue, tower and mountains. Watermark: Lion's head.

	VF	UNC
a. Signature 4. 1.6.1980.	5.00	25.00
b. Signature 6. 1.6.1981.	6.00	35.00
c. Signature 7. 1.7.1984.	5.00	30.00
d. Signature 7. 14.9.1986.	6.50	40.00
e. Signature 8. 1.7.1987.	7.00	50.00
f. Signature 9a. 1.7.1988.	4.00	22.00

23A 200 Shillings

1986-88. Dark brown on multicolor underprint. Arms at center. President Daniel Toroitich Arap Moi at right. Triangle in lower left border. No silvering on value at upper right. Back: Fountain at center. Watermark: Lion's head.

	VF	UNC
a. Signature 7. 14.9.1986.	10.00	55.00
b. Signature 8. 1.7.1987.	25.00	225.
c. Signature 9a. 1.7.1988.	50.00	325.

1986-90 Issue

#24-30 Replacement notes: Serial # prefix *ZZ*.

24 10 Shillings

1989-94. Dark green, dark blue and brown on multicolor underprint. President Daniel Toroitich Arap Moi at right center, arms at left center. Vertical seial number at left. Back: University at left center. Watermark: Lion's head. UV: vertical serial # fluoresces orange, lower left, upper right, middle devices yellow, Back middle design yellow.

	VF	UNC
a. Signature 9a. 14.10.1989	FV	3.00
b. Signature 9a. 1.7.1990.	FV	2.50
c. Signature 9a. 1.7.1991.	FV	1.75
d. Signature 10a. 2.1.1992. Small date font. Printer: H&S.	1.00	4.50
e. Signature 10a. 1.7.1993. Large date font.	1.00	4.50
f. Signature 11. 1.1.1994.	1.00	6.00

25 20 Shillings

1988-92. Dark blue and multicolor. President Daniel Toroitich Arap Moi at right center, arms at left center. Vertical seial number at left. Back: Moi International Sports Complex. Watermark: Lion's head.

	VF	UNC
a. Signature 9b. 12.12.1988.	5.00	22.50
b. Signature 9b. 1.7.1989.	1.00	5.00
c. Signature 9b. 1.7.1990.	1.00	3.50
d. Signature 9b. 1.7.1991.	2.00	6.00
e. Signature 10a. 2.1.1992. Large date font.	2.00	6.00
s. Specimen.	—	—

26 50 Shillings

1990; 1992. Red-brown on multicolor underprint. President Daniel Toroitich Arap Moi at right center, arms at left center. Vertical seial number at left. Back: Green. Modern buildings at left, flag at right. Watermark: Lion's head.

	VF	UNC
a. Signature 9b. 10.10.1990.	4.00	16.00
b. Signature 10b. 1.7.1992.	3.00	14.00
s. Specimen. As b.	—	—

27 100 Shillings

1989-95. Purple, dark green and red on multicolor underprint. President Daniel Toroitich Arap Moi at right center, arms at left center. Vertical seial number at left. Back: Monument to 25th Anniversary of Independence with Mt. Kenya. Watermark: Lion's head.

	VF	UNC
a. Signature 9a. 14.10.1989.	3.00	12.50
b. Signature 9a. 1.7.1990.	3.00	12.50
c. Signature 9a. 1.7.1991.	2.00	10.00
d. Signature 10a. 2.1.1992. Small date font. Printer: H&S.	3.00	12.50
e. Signature 10a. 1.7.1992. Large date font.	4.00	15.00
f. Signature 11. 1.1.1994.	3.00	15.00
g. Signature 12. 1.1.1995.	4.00	17.50

29 200 Shillings

1989-94. President Daniel Toroitich Arap Moi at right center, arms at left center. Rose replaces colored triangle to right of *200* at lower left. Additional silver diamond design under 200 at upper right Back: Fountain at center. Watermark: Lion's head.

	VF	UNC
a. Signature 9a. 14.10.1989.	4.50	27.50
b. Signature 9a. 1.7.1990.	4.50	25.00
c. Signature 10a. 2.1.1992. Small date font. Printer: H&S.	5.00	37.50
d. Signature 10a. 1.7.1992. Large date font.	4.00	25.00
e. Signature 11. 14.9.1993.	3.50	22.50
f. Signature 11. 1.1.1994.	4.00	25.00

30 500 Shillings

1988-95. Black, deep green and red on multicolor underprint. President Daniel Toroitich Arap Moi at right center, arms at left center. Vertical seial number at left. Roses at left. Back: Parliament building, Mt. Kenya. Watermark: Lion's head.

	VF	UNC
a. Signature 9b. 14.10.1988.	50.00	250.
b. Signature 9b. 1.7.1989.	25.00	100.
c. Signature 9b. 1.7.1990.	15.00	55.00
d. Signature 10a. 2.1.1992. Small date font. Printer: H&S.	20.00	75.00
e. Signature 10a. 1.7.1992. Large date font.	15.00	55.00
f. Signature 11. 14.9.1993.	17.50	65.00
g. Signature 12. 1.1.1995.	17.50	70.00

1993 Issue

31 20 Shillings

1993-94. Dark blue and multicolor. President Daniel Toroitich Arap Moi at center right. Roses added to left border, vertical red serial number. Back: Moi International Sports Complex. Male runner and other artistic enhancements added.

	VF	UNC
a. Signature 11. 14.9.1993.	2.00	5.00
b. Signature 11. 1.1.1994.	2.00	6.00

1994-95 Issue

32 20 Shillings

1.7.1995. Dark blue, brown and blue-green on multicolor underprint. President Daniel Toroitich Arap Moi at left center, arms at upper center right. Ascending size serial number. Signature 13. Back: Baton at left, Moi Int'l Sports Complex at left center, runner at center right. Watermark: Lion head facing.

VF	UNC
FV	3.00

33 500 Shillings

1.7.1995. Black, green and red on multicolor underprint. President Daniel Toroitich Arap Moi at left center, arms at upper center right. Ascending size serial number. Back: Parliament building at left center. Watermark: Lion head facing.

VF	UNC
7.50	25.00

34 1000 Shillings

1994-95. Brown on multicolor underprint. President Daniel Toroitich Arap Moi at left center, arms at upper center right. Ascending size serial number. Back: Water buffalo, elephants and egret. Watermark: Lion head facing.

	VF	UNC
a. 12.12.1994.	FV	50.00
b. 1.7.1995.	FV	50.00

1996-97 Issue

35 20 Shillings

1996-2001. Dark blue on multicolor underprint. President Daniel Toroitich Arap Moi at left center, arms at upper center right. Ascending size serial number. Back: Baton at left, Moi Int'l Sports Complex at left center, runner at center right. Watermark: Lion head facing. Segmented foil over security thread.

	VF	UNC
a1. 1.1.1996. Dark blue signature.	FV	3.00
a2. 1.1.1996. Black signatrue.	FV	5.00
b. 1.7.1997.	FV	5.00
c. 1.7.1998.	FV	7.00

36 50 Shillings

1996-2002. Brown-violet and blue-black on multicolor underprint. President Daniel Toroitich Arap Moi at left center, arms at upper center right. Ascending size serial number. Back: Dromedary caravan. Segmented foil over security thread. 138x72mm.

	VF	UNC
a1. 1.1.1996. Brown signatures.	FV	5.00
a2. 1.1.1996. Black signatures.	FV	8.50
b. 1.7.1997.	FV	7.00
c. 1.7.1998.	FV	4.00
d. 1.7.1999.	FV	5.00
e. 1.7.2000.	FV	3.00
f. 1.7.2001.	FV	15.00
g. 1.7.2002.	FV	2.50

37 100 Shillings

1996-2002. Purple, red and deep green on multicolor underprint. President Daniel Toroitich Arap Moi at left center, arms at upper center right. Ascending size serial number. Back: People by Monument to 25th Anniversary of Independence at center, branch of fruit at left. Segmented foil over security thread. 142x74mm.

	VF	UNC
a. 1.7.1996.	FV	6.00
b. 1.7.1997.	FV	12.00
c. 1.7.1998.	FV	5.00
d. 1.7.1999.	FV	7.50
e. 1.7.2000.	FV	4.00
f. 1.7.2001.	FV	8.00
g. 1.7.2002.	FV	4.00
h. 1.9.2002.	FV	5.00

38 200 Shillings

1996-2002. Dark brown, blue-gray and dark green on multicolor underprint. President Daniel Toroitich Arap Moi at left center, arms at upper center right. Ascending size serial number. Back: Unity monument at center, women harvesting at left. Segmented foil over security thread. 144x76mm.

	VF	UNC
a. 1.7.1996.	FV	16.00
b. 1.7.1997.	FV	12.50
c. 1.7.1998.	FV	16.00
d. 1.7.1999.	FV	16.00
e. 1.7.2000.	FV	16.00
f. 1.7.2001.	FV	8.00
g. 1.9.2002.	FV	7.00

39 500 Shillings

1997-2002. Black, green and red on multicolor underprint. President Daniel Toroitich Arap Moi at left center, arms at upper center right. Ascending size serial number. Back: Parliament building at left center. Watermark: Lion head facing. Segmented foil over security thread. 148x78mm.

	VF	UNC
a. 1.7.1997.	7.50	28.00
b. 1.7.1999.	FV	26.00
c. 1.7.2000.	FV	24.00
d. 1.7.2001.	FV	18.00

40 1000 Shillings

1997-2002. Brown-violet and olive-green on multicolor underprint. President Daniel Toroitich Arap Moi at left center, arms at upper center right. Ascending size serial number. Back: Water buffalo, elephants and egret. Watermark: Lion head facing. Segmented foil over security thread. 150x80mm.

	VF	UNC
a. 1.7.1997.	FV	60.00
b. 1.7.1999.	FV	45.00
c. 1.7.2000.	FV	35.00
d. 1.7.2001.	FV	40.00
e. 1.7.2002.	FV	35.00

2003-04 Issue

#41-45 2003 dates have thin security thread, 2004 onwards have a thick thread.

41 50 Shillings

2003-06. Brown-violet and blue-black on multicolor underprint. President Kenyatta at left center, arms at upper center right. Ascending size serial number. Back: Dromedary caravan. With enhanced security features. 138x72mm.

	VF	UNC
a. 1.4.2003. Narrow segmented security foil.	FV	2.50
b. 2.2.2004. Wide segmented security foil.	FV	2.50
c. 2.8.2004.	FV	2.50
s. Specimen.	—	—

42 **100 Shillings** — VF UNC

2004-06. Purple, orange and green on multicolor underprint. President Kenyatta at left center, arms at upper center right. Ascending size serial number. Back: Nyayo monument. With enhanced security features. 142x74mm.

	VF	UNC
a. 2.2.2004. Wide segmented security foil.	FV	3.50
b. 2.8.2004.	FV	3.50

43 **200 Shillings**

2004-06. Brown, blue and light green on multicolor underprint. President Kenyatta at left center, without commemorative text. Back: Cotton pickers. With enhanced security features. 144x76mm.

	VF	UNC
a. 2.2.2004. Wide segmented security foil.	FV	6.50
b. 2.8.2004.	FV	6.50
c. 1.6.2005.	FV	6.50
d. 1.4.2006.	FV	6.50

44 **500 Shillings** — VF UNC

2003-06. Black and green on multicolor underprint. President Kenyatta at left center, arms at upper center right. Ascending size serial number. Back: National Assembly building. With enhanced security features. 148x78mm.

	VF	UNC
a. 1.4.2003. Narrow segmented security foil.	FV	16.00
b. 2.2.2004. Wide segmented security foil.	FV	16.00

45 **1000 Shillings** — VF UNC

2003-06. Brown, lilac and light olive on multicolor underprint. President Kenyatta at left center, arms at upper center right. Ascending size serial number. Back: Elephants and other animals. With enhanced security features. 150x80mm.

	VF	UNC
a. 1.4.2003. Narrow segmented security foil.	FV	32.50
b. 2.2.2004. Wide segmented security foil.	FV	32.50
c. 2.8.2004. Value added to watermark.	FV	32.50

2003 Commemorative Issue

40th Anniversary of Independence.

46 **200 Shillings** — VF UNC

12.12.2003. Brown, blue and light green on multicolor underprint. Jomo Kenyatta at left center, commemorative text in watermark area at left. Back: Cotton pickers. 144x76mm. — FV 8.00

2005 Issue

47 **50 Shillings** — VF UNC

2005-. Brown-violet and blue-black on multicolor underprint. President Jomo Kenyatta at left center. Back: Dromedary caravan. Watermark: Value and Cornerstone stripes added Printer: DLR. 138x72mm.

	VF	UNC
a. 1.6.2005.	FV	2.50
b. 1.4.2006.	FV	2.50
c. 3.3.2008.	FV	2.50
d. 17.6.2009.	FV	2.50
e. 16.7.2010.	FV	2.50

48 **100 Shillings** — VF UNC

2005-. Purple, orange and green on multicolor underprint. President Jomo Kenyatta at left center. Back: Nyayo monument. Watermark: Value and Cornerstone stripes added Printer: DLR. 142x74mm.

	VF	UNC
a. 1.6.2005.	FV	3.50
b. 1.4.2006.	FV	3.50
c. 3.3.2008.	FV	3.50
d. 17.6.2009.	FV	3.50
e. 16.7.2010.	FV	3.50

49 **200 Shillings** | VF | UNC

2005-. Brown, blue and light green on multicolor underprint. President Jomo Kanyatta at left center. Back: Cotton pickers. Watermark: Value and Cornerstone stripes added Printer: DLR.

	VF	UNC
a. 1.6.2005.	FV	6.50
b. 1.4.2006.	FV	6.50
c. 3.3.2008.	FV	6.50
d. 17.6.2009.	FV	6.50
e. 16.7.2010.	FV	6.50

50 **500 Shillings** | VF | UNC

2004-. Black and green on multicolor underprint. President Jomo Kenyatta at left center. Back: National Assembly building at left center. Watermark: Value and Cornerstone stripes added Printer: DLR.

	VF	UNC
a. 2.8.2004.	FV	16.00
b. 1.6.2005.	FV	16.00
c. 1.4.2006.	FV	16.00
d. 3.3.2008.	FV	16.00
e. 17.6.2009.	FV	16.00
f. 16.7.2010.	FV	16.00

51 **1000 Shillings** | VF | UNC

2005-. Brown, lilac and ligth olive on multicolor underprint. President Jomo Kenyatta at left center. Back: Elephants and other animals Watermark: Value and Cornerstone stripes added Printer: DLR. 150x80mm.

	VF	UNC
a. 1.6.2005.	FV	32.50
b. 1.4.2006.	FV	32.50
c. 3.3.2008.	FV	30.00
d. 17.6.2009.	FV	30.00
e. 16.7.2010.	FV	25.00

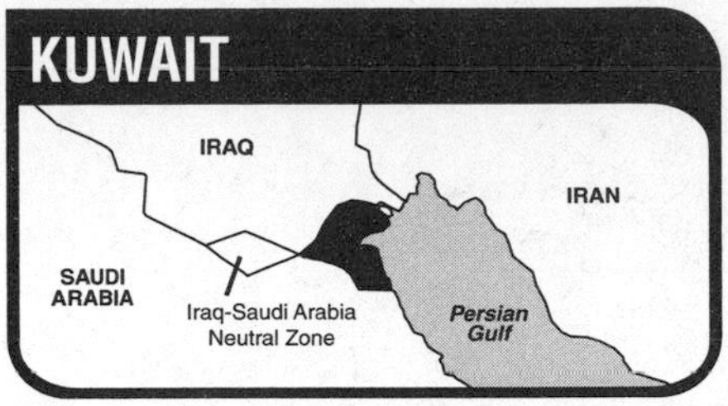

The State of Kuwait, a constitutional monarchy located on the Arabian Peninsula at the northwestern corner of the Persian Gulf, has an area of 6,880 sq. mi. (17,818 sq. km.) and a population of 1.97 million. Capital: Kuwait. Petroleum, the basis of the economy, provides 95 per cent of the exports.

Britain oversaw foreign relations and defense for the ruling Kuwaiti Al-Sabah dynasty from 1899 until independence in 1961. Kuwait was attacked and overrun by Iraq on 2 August 1990. Following several weeks of aerial bombardment, a US-led, UN coalition began a ground assault on 23 February 1991 that liberated Kuwait in four days. Kuwait spent more than $5 billion to repair oil infrastructure damaged during 1990-91. The Al-Sabah family has ruled since returning to power in 1991 and reestablished an elected legislature that in recent years has become increasingly assertive.

RULERS:

British to 1961
Abdullah, 1961-1965
Sabah Ibn Salim Al Sabah, 1965-1977
Jabir Ibn Ahmad Al Sabah, 1977-2006
Sabah Al Ahmad Al Sabah, 2006-

MONETARY SYSTEM:

1 Dinar = 1000 Fils

SIGNATURE VARIETIES

1	Amir Sheikh Jaber al-Ahmed				
	BANK GOVERNOR	FINANCE MINISTER		BANK GOVERNOR	FINANCE MINISTER
2	Hamza Abbas	A. R. al-Atiquel	3	Hamza Abbas	A. L. al-Hamad
4	A. al-Tammar	A. K. al-Sabah	5	A. al-Tammar	J. M. al-Kharafi
6	S. A. al-Sabah	N. A. al-Rodhan	7	S. A. al-Sabah	A. K. al-Sabah
8	S. A. al-Sabah	N. A. al-Rodhan	9	S. A. al-Sabah	A. S. al-Sabah
10	S. A. al-Sabah	A. A. al-Sabah	11	S. A. al-Sabah	Y. H. Al-Ibrahim
12	S. A. al-Sabah	M.A. Al Nouri	13	S. A. al-Sabah	B.Y. Al Houmaithy
14	S. A. al-Sabah				

STATE

KUWAIT CURRENCY BOARD

LAW OF 1960, 1961 ND ISSUE

1 **1/4 Dinar** VF UNC

L.1960 (1961). Brown on multicolor underprint. Amir Shaikh Abdullah at right. Signature 1. Back: Aerial view, Port of Kuwait at center. Watermark: Amir Shaikh Abdullah. 25.00 75.00

2 **1/2 Dinar** VF UNC

L.1960 (1961). Purple on multicolor underprint. Amir Shaikh Abdullah at right. Signature 1. Back: School at center. Watermark: Amir Shaikh Abdullah. 35.00 125.

3 **1 Dinar** VF UNC

L.1960 (1961). Red-brown on multicolor underprint. Amir Shaikh Abdullah at right. Signature 1. Back: Cement plant at center. Watermark: Amir Shaikh Abdullah. 50.00 175.

4 **5 Dinars** VF UNC

L.1960 (1961). Blue on multicolor underprint. Amir Shaikh Abdullah at right. Signature 1. Back: Street scene. Watermark: Amir Shaikh Abdullah. 250. 800.

5 **10 Dinars** VF UNC

L.1960 (1961). Green on multicolor underprint. Amir Shaikh Abdullah at right. Signature 1. Back: Dhow. Watermark: Amir Shaikh Abdullah. 200. 750.

Central Bank of Kuwait

Law #32 of 1968, First ND Issue

6 **1/4 Dinar** VF UNC

L.1968. Brown on multicolor underprint. Amir Shaikh Abdullah at right. Signature 2. Back: Aerial view, Port of Kuwait at center. Watermark: Amir Shaikh Abdullah.

	VF	UNC
a. Black signature	10.00	30.00
b. Brown signature	10.00	30.00
s. As a. Specimen.	—	250.

7 **1/2 Dinar** VF UNC

L.1968. Purple on multicolor underprint. Amir Shaikh Abdullah at right. Signature 2. Back: School at center. Watermark: Amir Shaikh Abdullah.

	VF	UNC
a. Black signature	10.00	40.00
b. Purple signature	10.00	40.00
s. As a. Specimen.	—	250.

8 **1 Dinar** VF UNC

L.1968. Red-brown and blue on multicolor underprint. Amir Shaikh Abdullah at right. Signature 2. Back: Oil refinery. Watermark: Amir Shaikh Abdullah.

	VF	UNC
a. Issued note.	9.00	45.00
s. Specimen.	—	350.

9	**5 Dinars**	VF	UNC
	L.1968. Blue and aqua on multicolor underprint. Amir Shaikh Abdullah at right. Signature 2. Back: View of Kuwait. Watermark: Amir Shaikh Abdullah.		
	a. Issued note.	75.00	175.
	s. Specimen.	—	350.

10	**10 Dinars**	VF	UNC
	L.1968. Green and brown on multicolor underprint. Amir Shaikh Abdullah at right. Signature 2. Back: Dhow. Watermark: Amir Shaikh Abdullah.		
	a. Issued note.	70.00	175.
	s. Specimen.	—	475.

Law #32 of 1968, Second ND Issue

11	**1/4 Dinar**	VF	UNC
	L.1968 (1980-91). Brown and purple on multicolor underprint. Oil rig at left. Arms at right. Black serial number. Back: Oil refinery. Watermark: Dhow.		
	a. Overall ornate underprint. Signature 2.	4.00	12.00
	b. Signature 3.	3.00	10.00
	c. Signature 4.	3.00	8.00
	d. Clear margins at top and bottom. Signature 6.	1.50	8.00
	s. Specimen.	—	80.00

12	**1/2 Dinar**	VF	UNC
	L.1968 (1980). Purple on multicolor underprint. Kuwait Towers at left. Arms at right. Black serial number. Back: Harbor scene. Watermark: Dhow.		
	a. Overall ornate underprint. Signature 2.	4.00	14.00
	b. Signature 3.	3.00	12.00
	c. Signature 4.	3.00	10.00
	d. Clear margins at top and bottom. Signature 6.	3.00	8.00
	s. Specimen.	—	80.00

13	**1 Dinar**	VF	UNC
	L.1968 (1980-91). Red-violet and purple on multicolor underprint. Telecommunications Center in Kuwait City at left. Arms at right. Black serial number. Back: Old fortress. Watermark: Dhow.		
	a. Overall ornate underprint. Signature 2.	7.00	25.00
	b. Signature 3.	4.00	20.00
	c. Signature 4.	3.50	14.00
	d. Clear margins at top and bottom. Signature 6.	3.00	8.00
	s. As a. Specimen.	—	100.

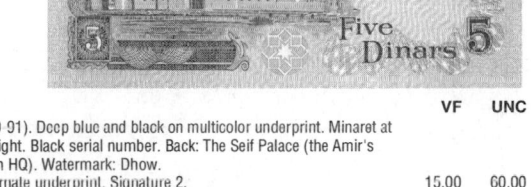

14	**5 Dinars**	VF	UNC
	L.1968 (1980-91). Deep blue and black on multicolor underprint. Minaret at left. Arms at right. Black serial number. Back: The Seif Palace (the Amir's Administration HQ). Watermark: Dhow.		
	a. Overall ornate underprint. Signature 2.	15.00	60.00
	b. Signature 4.	10.00	40.00
	c. Clear margins at top and bottom. Signature 6.	7.50	30.00
	s. Specimen.	—	—

15	**10 Dinars**	VF	UNC
	L.1968 (1980-91). Green on multicolor underprint. Falcon at left. Arms at right. Black serial number. Back: Sailing boat. Watermark: Dhow.		
	a. Overall ornate underprint. Signature 2.	20.00	80.00
	b. Signature 3.	12.50	50.00
	c. Signature 4.	12.50	40.00
	d. Clear margins at top and bottom. Signature 6.	12.50	40.00

16 **20 Dinars** VF UNC

L.1968 (1986-91). Brown and olive-green on multicolor underprint. Façade of Kuwait Stock Exchange at left. Arms at right. Black serial number. Back: The Justice Center of Kuwait at left center. Watermark: Eagle's head.

	VF	UNC
a. Signature 5.	80.00	200.
b. Signature 6.	12.00	50.00
s. Specimen.	—	—

Law #32 of 1968, 1992 ND Post Liberation Issue

Note: After the 1991 Gulf War, Kuwait declared all previous note issues worthless.

17 **1/4 Dinar** VF UNC

L.1968 (1992). Violet and black on silver and multicolor underprint. Oil rig at left. Arms at right. Red serial number at top right. Signature 7. Back: Brown on multicolor underprint. Oil refinery. Watermark: Dhow. FV 4.00

18 **1/2 Dinar** VF UNC

L.1968 (1992). Deep blue, blue-green and deep violet on silver and multicolor underprint. Kuwait Towers at left. Arms at right. Red serial number at top right. Signature 7. Back: Harbor scene. Watermark: Dhow. FV 7.00

19 **1 Dinar** VF UNC

L.1968 (1992). Deep olive-green, green and deep blue on silver and multicolor underprint. Telecommunications Center in Kuwait City at left. Arms at right. Red serial number at top right. Signature 7. Back: Old fortress. Watermark: Dhow. FV 10.00

20 **5 Dinars** VF UNC

L.1968 (1992). Olive-brown, green and pink on multicolor underprint. Minaret at left. Arms at right. Red serial number at top right. Signature 7. Back: The Seif Palace (the Amir's Administration HQ). Watermark: Dhow. FV 55.00

21 **10 Dinars** VF UNC

L.1968 (1992). Orange-red, olive-brown on multicolor underprint. Falcon at left. Arms at right. Red serial number at top right. Back: Sailing boat. Watermark: Dhow.

	VF	UNC
a. Signature 7.	FV	100.
b. Signature 8.	60.00	130.

22 **20 Dinars** VF UNC

L.1968 (1992). Violet-brown on multicolor underprint. Façade of Kuwait Stock Exchange at left. Arms at right. Red serial number at top right. Back: The Justice Center of Kuwait at left center. Watermark: Eagle's head.

	VF	UNC
a. Signature 7.	FV	140.
b. Signature 8.	70.00	200.

Law #32 of 1968, 1994 ND Issue

#23-27 Signature 8, were withdrawn in early 1995 because of the word *Allah* being present.

23 1/4 Dinar

L.1968 (1994). Brown, grayish purple and deep orange on multicolor underprint. Ship at bottom center right, arms at left, segmented silver vertical thread at center right. Outline of falcon's head at lower right near value. Back: Girls playing game. Watermark: Falcon's head. 110x67mm.

	VF	UNC
a. Signature 8.	FV	5.50
b. Signature 10.	FV	5.50
c. Signature 11.	FV	5.00
d. Signature 12.	FV	4.50
e. Signature 13.	FV	4.50
f. Signature 14.	FV	4.50
s. Specimen. Red overprint in Arabic.	—	100.

24 1/2 Dinar

L.1968 (1994). Brown and dark grayish green on multicolor underprint. Souk shops at lower right. Arms at left , segmented silver vertical thread at center right. Outline of falcon's head at upper left near value. Back: Boys playing game. Watermark: Falcon's head. 120x67mm.

	VF	UNC
a. Signature 8.	FV	10.00
b. Signature 10.	FV	10.00
c. Signature 11.	FV	9.00
d. Signature 12.	FV	8.00
e. Signature 13.	FV	8.00
f. Signature 14.	FV	8.00
s. Specimen. Red overprint in Arabic.	—	150.

25 1 Dinar

L.1968 (1994). Deep brown, purple and dark gray on blue and multicolor underprint. Kuwait Tower at center right. Arms at left, segmented silver vertical thread at center right. Outline of falcon's head at upper left near value. Back: Aerial view of harbor docks. Watermark: Falcon's head. 130x67mm.

	VF	UNC
a. Signature 8.	FV	15.00
b. Signature 10.	FV	15.00
c. Signature 11.	FV	13.00
d. Signature 12.	FV	12.00
e. Signature 13.	FV	12.00
f. Signature 14.	FV	12.00
s. Specimen. Red overprint in Arabic.	—	250.

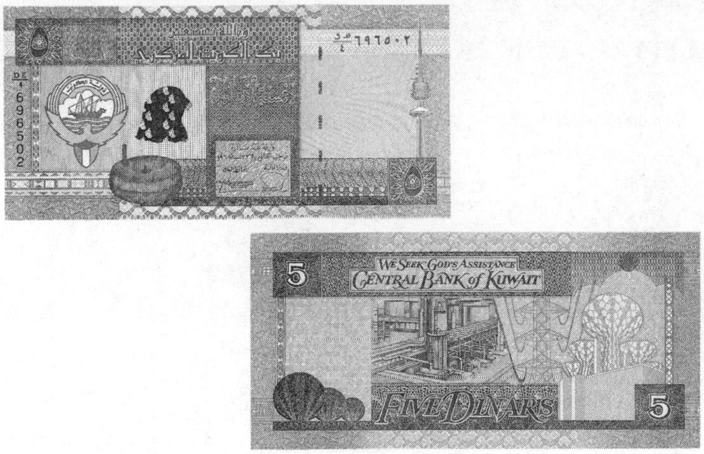

26 5 Dinars

L.1968 (1994). Dark red and grayish green on multicolor underprint. Liberation Tower at right. Arms at left, segmented silver vertical thread at center right. Silver foiling of falcon's head at left center. Signature 8, 9, 11, 12, 13. Back: Oil refinery at center. Watermark: Falcon's head. 140x67mm.

	VF	UNC
a. Signature 8.	FV	55.00
b. Signature 10.	FV	55.00
c. Signature 11.	FV	50.00
d. Signature 12.	FV	45.00
e. Signature 13.	FV	45.00
f. Signature 14.	FV	45.00
s. Specimen. Red overprint in Arabic.	—	250.

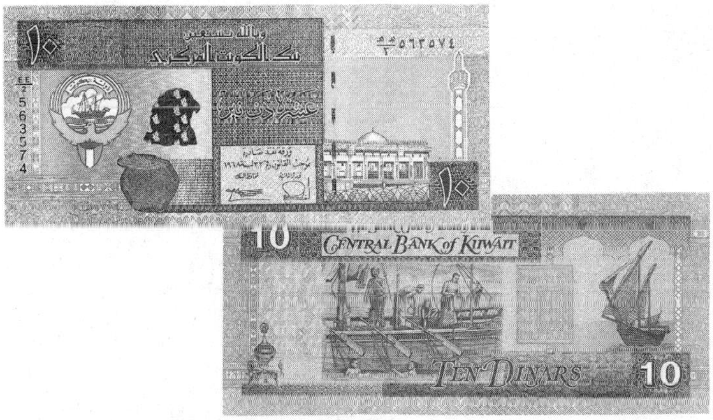

27 10 Dinars

L.1968 (1994). Purple, dark blue and dark brown on multicolor underprint. Mosque at lower right. Arms at left, segmented silver vertical thread at center right. Silver foiling of falcon's head at left center. Signature 8, 10, 11, 13, 14. Back: Pearl fisherman at left center, dhow at right. Watermark: Falcon's head. 150x67mm.

	VF	UNC
a. Issued note.	FV	90.00
s. Specimen. Red overprint in Arabic.	—	500.

28 20 Dinars

L.1968 (1994). Dark olive-green, orange and olive-brown on multicolor underprint. Fortress at lower right. Arms at left. segmented silver vertical thread at center right. Silver foiling of falcon's head at left center. Signature 8, 9, 10, 11, 12, 13. Back: Central Bank at bottom left center, old city gate. Watermark: Falcon's head. 160x67mm.

	VF	UNC
a. Issued note.	FV	130.
s. Specimen. Red overprint in Arabic.	—	750.

Collector Series

Central Bank of Kuwait

1993 Issue

#CS1 Issued in a special folder for "Second Anniversary of Liberation of Kuwait."

		Mkt.	Value
CS1	**1 Dinar** 26.2.1993. Orange-red, violet-blue and blue. Back: Text: *THIS IS NOT LEGAL TENDER.* Polymer plastic with silver foil window.		20.00

2001 Issue

#CS2 issued in a special folder for "10th Anniversary of the Liberation of the State of Kuwait."

		Mkt.	Value
CS2	**1 Dinar** 26.2.2001. Light blue and lilac. Arms at right. Back: Military man holding flag, town view. Text: *NOT A LEGAL TENDER...* at lower left. Polymer plastic with silver foil window.		17.50

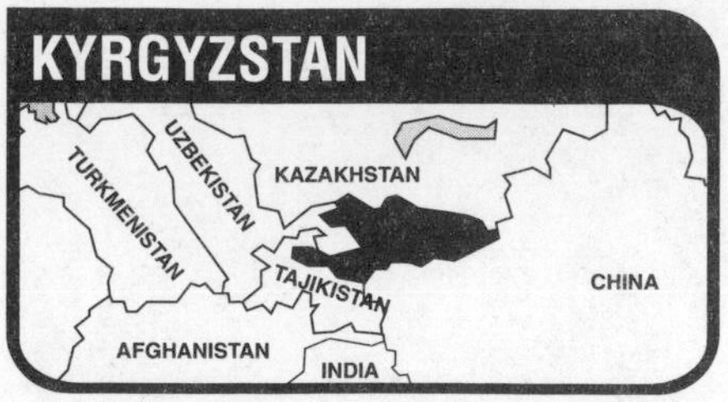

The Republic of Kyrgyzstan, an independent state since Aug. 31, 1991, is a member of the UN and of the C.I.S. It was the last state of the Union Republics to declare its sovereignty. Capital: Bishkek (formerly Frunze). Population of 4.54 million.

A Central Asian country of incredible natural beauty and proud nomadic traditions, most of Kyrgyzstan was formally annexed to Russia in 1876. The Kyrgyz staged a major revolt against the Tsarist Empire in 1916 in which almost one-sixth of the Kyrgyz population was killed. Kyrgyzstan became a Soviet republic in 1936 and achieved independence in 1991 when the USSR dissolved. Nationwide demonstrations in the spring of 2005 resulted in the ouster of President Askar Akaev, who had run the country since 1990. Subsequent presidential elections in July 2005 were won overwhelmingly by former prime minister Kurmanbek BAKIEV. The political opposition organized demonstrations in Bishkek in April, May, and November 2006 resulting in the adoption of a new constitution that transferred some of the president's powers to parliament and the government. In December 2006, the Kyrgyzstani parliament voted to adopt new amendments, restoring some of the presidential powers lost in the November 2006 constitutional change. By late-September 2007, both previous versions of the constitution were declared illegal, and the country reverted to the Akaev-era 2003 constitution, which was subsequently modified in a flawed referendum initiated by Bakiev. The president then dissolved parliament, called for early elections, and gained control of the new parliament through his newly-created political party, Ak Jol, in December 2007 elections. Current concerns include: privatization of state-owned enterprises, negative trends in democracy and political freedoms, reduction of corruption, improving interethnic relations, electricity generation, rising food prices, and combating terrorism.

Republic

КЫРГЫЗ РЕСПУБЛИКАСЫ

Kyrgyz Republic

1993 ND Issue

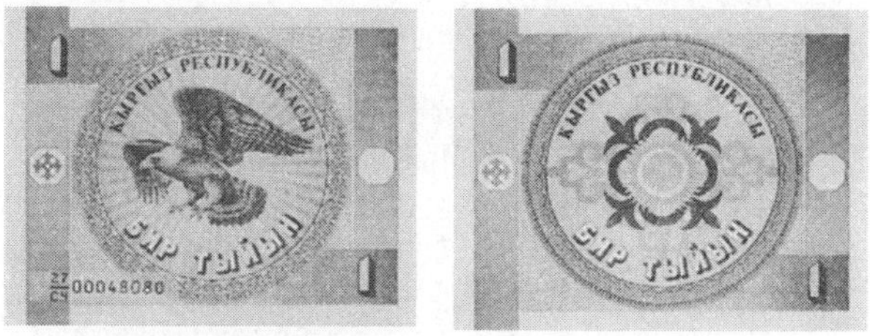

		VF	UNC
1	**1 Tyiyn** ND (1993). Dark brown on pink and brown-orange underprint. Bald eagle at center. Back: Ornate design at center.		
	a. Watermark: Stylized eagle.	.30	1.00
	b. Watermark: pattern	.30	1.00

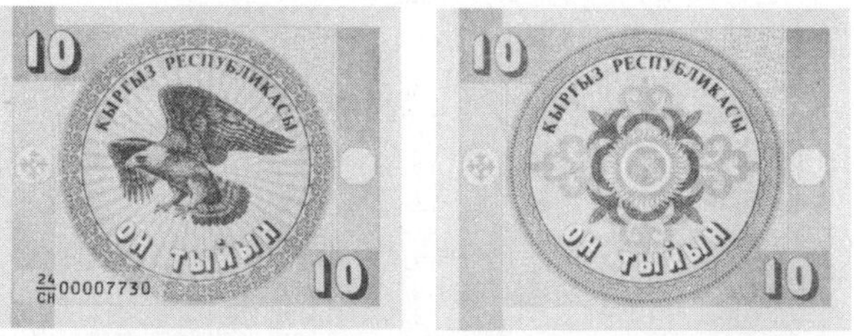

		VF	UNC
2	**10 Tyiyn** ND (1993). Brown on pale green and brown-orange underprint. Bald eagle at center. Back: Ornate design at center.		
	a. Watermark: stylized eage.	.40	1.00
	b. Watermark: pattern.	.40	1.00

		VF	UNC
3	**50 Tyiyn** ND (1993). Gray on blue and brown-orange underprint. Bald eagle at center. Back: Ornate design at center.		
	a. Watermark: stylized eagle.	.50	3.00
	b. Watermark: pattern.	.50	3.00

КЫРГЫЗСТАН БАНКЫ

KYRGYZSTAN BANK

1993; 1994 ND ISSUE

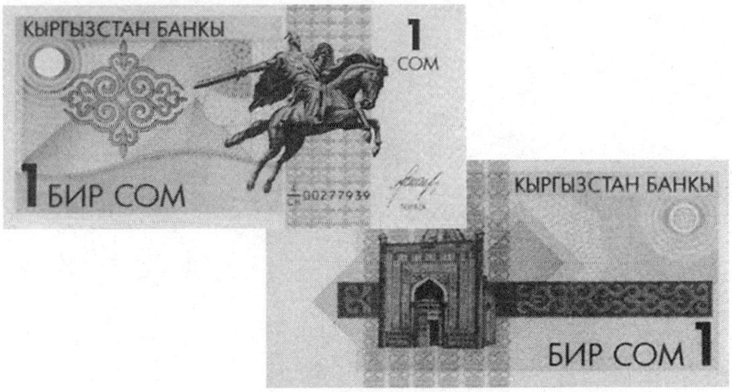

		VF	UNC
4	**1 Som** ND (1993). Red on multicolor underprint. Equestrian statue of Manas the Noble at center right. Back: Manas Mausoleum at left center. Watermark: Eagle in repeating pattern.	1.00	3.00

		VF	UNC
5	**5 Som** ND (1993). Deep grayish green on multicolor underprint. Equestrian statue of Manas the Noble at center right. Back: Manas Mausoleum at left center. Watermark: Eagle in repeating pattern. 140x70mm.	2.00	5.00

		VF	UNC
6	**20 Som** ND (1993). Purple on multicolor underprint. Equestrian statue of Manas the Noble at center right. Back: Manas Mausoleum at left center. Watermark: Eagle in repeating pattern. 140x70mm.	3.00	20.00

КЫРГЫЗ БАНКЫ

KYRGYZ BANK

1994 ND ISSUE

Replacement notes: Serial # prefix *ZZ*.

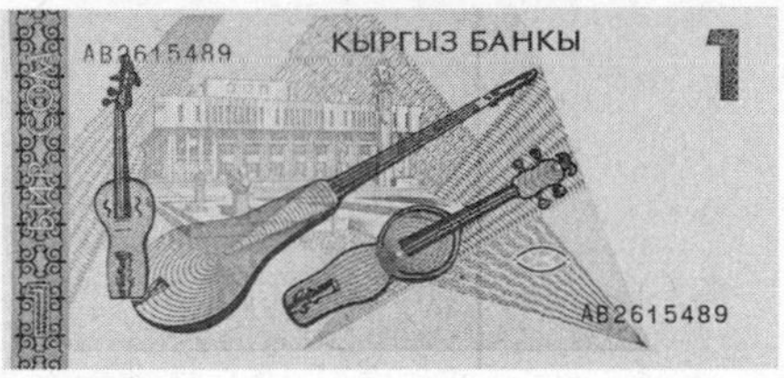

		VF	UNC
7	**1 Som** ND (1994). Brown on yellow and multicolor underprint. A. Maldybayev at right. Back: String musical instruments, Bishkek's Philharmonic Society and Manas Architectural Ensemble at left. Watermark: A. Maldybayev.		
	a. Issued note.	1.00	2.00
	r. Replacement note. Serial # prefix ZZ.	1.00	4.00

		VF	UNC
8	**5 Som** ND (1994). Dark blue on yellow and multicolor underprint. B. Beishenaliyeva at right. Back: National Opera Theatre at left center. Watermark: B. Beishenaliyeva. 135x65mm.		
	a. Issued note.	2.00	6.00
	r. Replacement note. Serial # prefix ZZ.	2.00	12.00

		VF	UNC
9	**10 Som** ND (1994). Green and brown on multicolor underprint. Kassim at right. Back: Mountains. Watermark: Kassim. 135x65mm.		
	a. Issued note.	2.00	10.00
	r. Replacement note. Serial # prefix ZZ.	2.00	17.50

		VF	UNC
10	**20 Som** ND (1994). Red-orange on multicolor underprint. T. Moldo at right. Back: Manas Mausoleum. Watermark: T. Moldo. 135x65mm.		
	a1. Issued note.	2.00	6.00
	r. Replacement note. Serial # prefix ZZ.	2.00	12.50

11 **50 Som** — VF UNC

ND (1994). Reddish brown on multicolor underprint. Czarina Kurmanjan Datka at right. Back: Uzgen Architectural Ensemble, mausoleum and minaret. Watermark: Czarina Kurmanjan Datka. 135x65mm.

	VF	UNC
a. Issued note.	5.00	15.00
r. Replacement note. Serial # prefix ZZ.	5.00	25.00

12 **100 Som** — VF UNC

ND (1994). Dark brown on multicolor underprint. Toktogul at right. Back: Hydroelectric dam at left center. Watermark: Toktogul.

	VF	UNC
a. Issued note.	5.00	25.00
r. Replacement note. Serial # prefix ZZ.	5.00	40.00

1997 Issue

Replacement notes: Serial # prefix *BZ*.

13 **5 Som** — VF UNC

1997. Dark blue and violet on multicolor underprint. B. Beishenaliyeva at right. Back: National Opera Theatre at left center. Watermark: B. Beishenaliyeva. 135x65mm.

	VF	UNC
a. Issued note.	FV	3.00
r. Replacement note. Serial # prefix BZ.	FV	6.00

14 **10 Som** — VF UNC

1997. Dark green, purple and red on multicolor underprint. Kassim at right. Back: Mountains Watermark: Kassim. 135x65mm.

	VF	UNC
a. Issued note.	FV	5.00
r. Replacement note. Serial # prefix BZ.	FV	10.00

2000 ND Issue

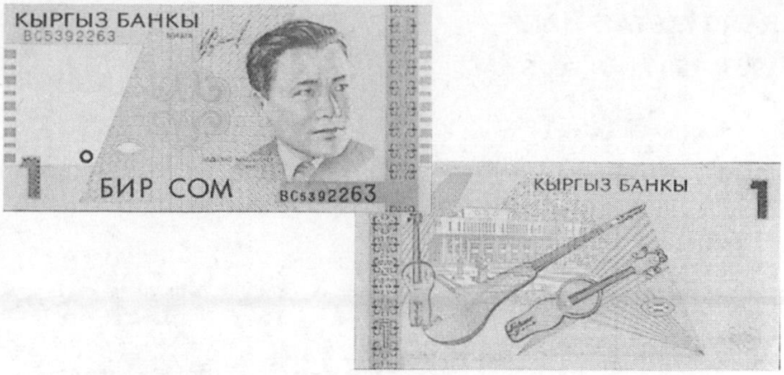

15 **1 Som** — VF UNC

1999. Brown and tan on multicolor underprint. Abdilas Maldibayeff at left. Back: Musical instruments.

	VF	UNC
a. Issued note.	FV	2.00
r. Replacement note. Serial # prefix BZ.	FV	5.00

16 **200 Som** — VF UNC

	VF	UNC
2000. Brown and tan on multicolor underprint. Alikul Osmonov at right. Back: Poetry verse and lake scene.	3.00	10.00

17 **500 Som** — VF UNC

	VF	UNC
2000. Rose, brown and olive on multicolor underprint. Sayakbai Karalaiev at right. Back: Karalaiev seated, in background horseman chasing an eagle. 160x76mm.	5.00	20.00

18 **1000 Som** — VF UNC

	VF	UNC
2000. Olive, slate, brown and multicolor. Jusul Balasagbin at right. Back: Gate, tree and mountains. 165x78mm.	6.00	30.00

2002 ND Issue

		VF	UNC
19	**20 Som** 2002. Dark brown and orange on multicolor underprint. Togolok Moldo at right. Back: Manas Mausoleum. Watermark: Togolok Moldo. 135x78mm.	1.00	5.00

		VF	UNC
20	**50 Som** 2002. Brown and blue on multicolor underprint. Czarina Krumanjan-Datka at right. Back: Uzgen Architectural ensemble: mausoleum and minaret. Watermark: Czarina Krumanjan-Datka. 145x70mm.	2.00	10.00

		VF	UNC
21	**100 Som** 2002. Green, pink and blue on multicolor underprint. Toktogul at right. Back: Khan Tenyiri Mountains at left center. Watermark: Toktogu. 150x72mm.	1.00	12.50

		VF	UNC
22	**200 Som** 2004. Brown and tan on multicolor underprint. Alikul Osmonov at right. Back: Poetry verse and lake scene. Watermark: Alikul Osmonov. 155x74mm.	4.00	8.00

		VF	UNC
23	**500 Som** 2005. Purple. 160x76mm.		
	a. Issued note.	FV	20.00
	s. Specimen. Overprint: *MINTA*.	—	—

2009 ND Issue

		VF	UNC
24	**20 Som** 2009. Red and multicolor. Togolok Moldo at left. Back: Tash-Rabat at center. Watermark. Togolok Moldo. Printer: FC-O.		
	a. Issued note.	FV	2.50
	r. Replacement note. Serial # prefix ZZ.	FV	5.00
	s. Specimen.	—	50.00
25	**50 Som** 2009. Orange and multicolor. Czarina Kurmanjan Datka at left. Back: 11th century complex, Uzgen. Watermark: Kurmanjan Datka. Printer: FC-O. 126x61mm.		
	a. Issued note.	FV	4.00
	s. Specimen.	—	50.00
26	**100 Som** 2009. Blue and multicolor. Toktogul Satylganov at left. Back: Toktogul hydroelectric power station. Watermark: Toktogul Satylganov. Printer: FC-O. 132x63mm.		
	a. Issued note.	FV	7.50
	s. Specimen.	FV	50.00
27	**200 Som** 2010. Printer: DLR. 138x66mm.		
	a. Issued note.	FV	12.50
	s. Specimen.	FV	50.00
28	**500 Som** 2010. Printer: DLR. 144x68mm.		
	a. Issued note.	FV	22.50
	s. Specimen.	—	100.
29	**1000 Som** 2010. Printer: DLR. 150x71mm.		
	a. Issued note.	FV	46.00
	s. Specimen.	—	100.
30	**5000 Som** 2010. Green and multicolor. Suimenkul Chokmorov at left. Back: Ala-too cinima in Bishkek. Watermark: Sayakbai Karalaev. Printer: FC-O. 156x73mm.		
	a. Issued note.	FV	220.
	s. Specimen.	—	225.

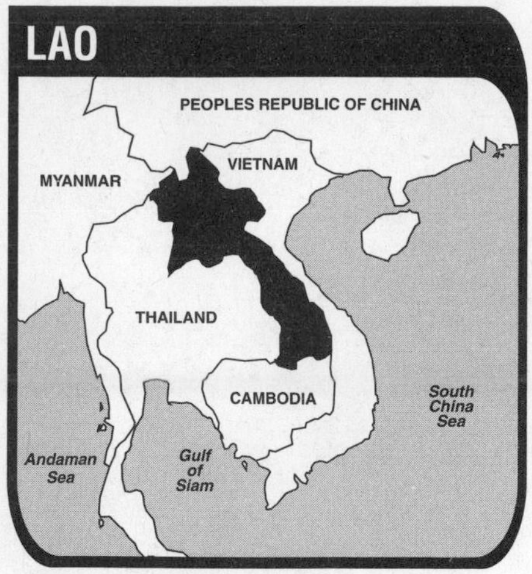

The Lao People's Democratic Republic is located on the Indo-Chinese Peninsula between the Socialist Republic of Viet Nam and the Kingdom of Thailand, has an area of 91,429 sq. mi. (236,800 sq. km.) and a population of 5.69 million. Captial: Vientiane. Agriculture employs 95 percent of the people. Tin, lumber and coffee are exported.

Modern-day Lao has its roots in the ancient Lao Kingdom of Lan Xang, established in the 14th Century under King Fa Ngum. For 300 years Lan Xang had influence reaching into present-day Cambodia and Thailand, as well as over all of what is now Lao. After centuries of gradual decline, Lao came under the domination of Siam (Thailand) and Viet Nam from the late 18th century until the late 19th century when it became part of French Indochina.

The Kingdome of Laos became fully independent of the French in 1955, and war soon ensued with the communist Pathet Lao. In 1975, the communist Pathet Lao took control of the government ending a six-century-old monarchy and instituting a strict socialist regime closely aligned to Viet Nam. A gradual return to private enterprise and the liberalization of foreign investment laws began in 1986. Lao became a member of ASEAN in 1997.

RULERS:

Sisavang Vong, 1949-1959
Savang Vatthana, 1959-1975

MONETARY SYSTEM:

1 Piastre = 100 Cents to 1955
1 Kip = 100 At, 1955-1975
1 (new) Kip = 100 Att, 1975-

SIGNATURE VARIETIES

	ຜູ້ອຳນວຍການ LE GOUVERNEUR	ຜູ້ກວດກາຜູ້ນຶ່ງ UN CENSEUR
1	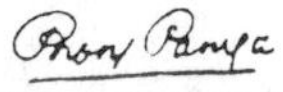	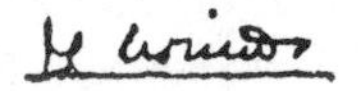
2	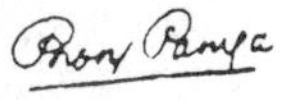	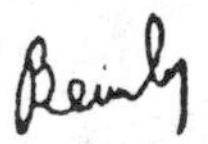
3	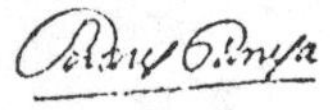	
4		
5		
6		

KINGDOM OF LAOS

BANQUE NATIONALE DU LAOS

1962-63 ND ISSUE

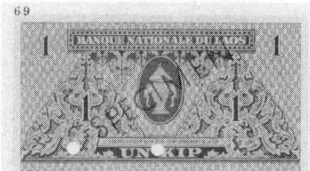

8	1 Kip	VF	UNC
	ND (1962). Brown on pink and bue underprint. Stylized figure at left. Back: Tricephalic elephant arms at center.		
	a. Signature 3; 4.	.20	.50
	s. Specimen. Signature 3.	—	40.00
	ct. Color trial. Blue. Signature 3.	—	—

9	5 Kip	VF	UNC
	ND (1962). Green on multicolor underprint. S. Vong at right. Back: Temple at left, man on elephant at center Watermark: Tricephalic elephant arms.		
	a. Signature 2.	17.50	50.00
	b. Signature 5.	.50	1.25
	s. As a. Specimen.	—	50.00
	ct. Color trial. Brown or Brown and blue.	—	—

10	10 Kip	VF	UNC
	ND (1962). Blue on yellow and green underprint. Woman at left. (like back of French Indochina #102). Back: Stylized sunburst on back (like face of #102). Watermark: Elephant's head.		
	a. Signature 1.	100.	200.
	b. Signature 5.	.50	1.75
	s1. As a. Specimen. Overprint: *SPECIMEN.*	—	100.
	s2. As b. Specimen. TDLR oval overprint.	—	100.

11	20 Kip	VF	UNC
	ND (1963). Brown on tan and blue underprint. King Savang Vatthana at left. Temple or pagoda at center. Back: Pagoda at center. Watermark: Tricephalic elephant arms.		
	a. Signature 5.	.40	2.00
	b. Signature 6.	.30	1.50
	r. Replacement notes: Serial # prefix *S9* (=Z9 in English).	—	—
	s1. As a. Specimen. Overprint: *SANS VALEUR.*	—	40.00
	s2. As a. Specimen. Overprint: TDLR oval.	—	40.00

12	50 Kip	VF	UNC
	ND (1963). Purple on brown and blue underprint. King Savang Vatthana at left. Pagoda at center. Back: Purple. Building at right. Watermark: Tricephalic elephant arms.		
	a. Signature 5; 6.	.25	2.00
	r. Replacement notes: Serial # prefix *S9* (=Z9 in English).	—	—
	s1. Signature 5. Specimen. Overprint: *SANS VALEUR.*	—	40.00
	s2. Signature 5. Specimen. Overprint: TDLR oval.	—	40.00

13	200 Kip	VF	UNC
	ND (1963). Blue on green and gold underprint. King Savang Vatthana at left Temple of That Luang at center. Back: Waterfalls. Watermark: Tricephalic elephant arms.		
	a. Signature 4.	1.00	6.00
	b. Signature 6.	.50	3.00
	r. Replacement notes: Serial # prefix *S9* (=Z9 in English).	—	—
	s1. As a. Specimen. Overprint: *SANS VALEUR.*	—	50.00
	s2. As a. Specimen. Overprint: TDLR oval.	—	60.00

14	1000 Kip	VF	UNC
	ND (1963). Brown on blue and gold underprint. King Savang Vatthana at left. Temple at center. Back: Three long canoes. Watermark: Tricephalic elephant arms.		
	a. Signature 5.	1.00	6.00
	b. Signature 6.	.75	4.00
	r. Replacement notes: Serial # prefix *S9* (=Z9 in English).	—	—
	s1. As a. Specimen. Overprint: *SANS VALEUR.*	—	60.00
	s2. As a. Specimen. Overprint: TDLR oval.	—	60.00

1974; 1975 ND Issue

15	10 Kip	VF	UNC
	ND (1974). Blue on multicolor underprint. King Savang Vatthana at center right. Signature 6. Back: Blue and brown. Ox cart.		
	a. Normal serial #. (Not issued).	—	10.00
	s. Specimen. Overprint: *SANS VALEUR.*	—	600.
	ct. Color trial. Red.	—	—

16	100 Kip	VF	UNC
	ND (1974). Brown on blue, green and pink underprint. King Savang Vatthana at left. Pagoda at center. Signature 6. Back: Ox cart. Watermark: Tricephalic elephant arms.		
	a. Issued note.	.50	3.00
	r. Replacement note. Serial # prefix (9).	—	—
	s. Specimen. Overprint: *SANS VALEUR.*	—	50.00

17	500 Kip	VF	UNC
	ND (1974). Red on multicolor underprint. King Savang Vatthana at left. Pagoda at center. Signature 6. Back: Hydroelectric dam. Watermark: Tricephalic elephant arms.		
	a. Issued note.	.75	4.00
	r. Replacement note. Serial # prefix (9).	—	—
	s. Specimen. Overprint: *SANS VALEUR.*	—	75.00

18	1000 Kip	VF	UNC
	ND. Black on multicolor underprint. King Savang Vatthana at left. Back: Elephant. Watermark: Tricephalic elephant arms.		
	a. Normal serial #. (Not issued.)	—	15.00
	s. Specimen. Overprint: *SANS VALEUR.*	—	900.

19 **5000 Kip**

ND (1975). Blue-gray on multicolor underprint. King Savang Vatthana at left. Pagoda at center. Back: Musicians with instruments. Watermark: Tricephalic elephant arms.

	VF	UNC
a. Issued note.	2.25	9.00
s. Specimen. Overprint: *SANS VALEUR.*	—	75.00

State of Lao

Pathet Lao Government

ND Issue

#19A-24 printed in Peoples Republic of China and circulated in areas under control of the Pathet Lao insurgents. These same notes became the accepted legal tender for the entire country in 1975.

19A **1 Kip**

ND. Green and blue on yellow and pink underprint. Threshing grain at center. Back: Medical clinic scene.

	VF	UNC
a. Issued note.	—	10.00
s. Specimen.	—	150.

20 **10 Kip**

ND. Red on light blue and gold underprint. Medical examination scene. Back: Fighters in the brush.

	VF	UNC
a. Watermark: Temples.	.15	2.00
b. Watermark: 5-pointed stars.	.15	1.00
s. As b. Specimen. Overprint in Lao.	—	50.00

21 **20 Kip**

ND. Brown on light pink and olive-brown underprint. Rice distribution. Back: Forge workers.

	VF	UNC
a. Watermark: Temples.	.20	3.00
b. Watermark: 5-pointed stars.	.20	2.00
s. As b. Specimen. Overprint in Lao.	—	50.00

22 **50 Kip**

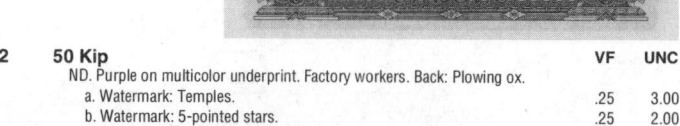

ND. Purple on multicolor underprint. Factory workers. Back: Plowing ox.

	VF	UNC
a. Watermark: Temples.	.25	3.00
b. Watermark: 5-pointed stars.	.25	2.00
s. As b. Specimen. Overprint in Lao.	—	50.00

23 **100 Kip**

ND. Blue on multicolor underprint. Long boats on lake. Back: Scene in textile store. Watermark: Temples.

	VF	UNC
a. Issued note.	3.00	6.00
s. Specimen. Overprint in Lao.	—	50.00

23A **200 Kip**

ND. Green on multicolor underprint. Road and trail convoys. Back: Factory scene. Watermark: Temples

	VF	UNC
a. Issued note.	4.00	12.00
s. Specimen. Overprint in Lao.	—	50.00
x. Lithograph counterfeit (1974) on plain paper, without serial #. Ho Chi Minh at right on back.	500.	800.

24 **500 Kip** — VF — UNC

ND. Brown on multicolor underprint. Armsed field workers in farm scene. Back: Soldiers shooting down planes. Watermark: Temples.

	VF	UNC
a. Issued note.	5.00	15.00
s. Specimen. Overprint in Lao.	—	50.00

Lao Peoples Democratic Republic

Government

1979 Provisional Issue

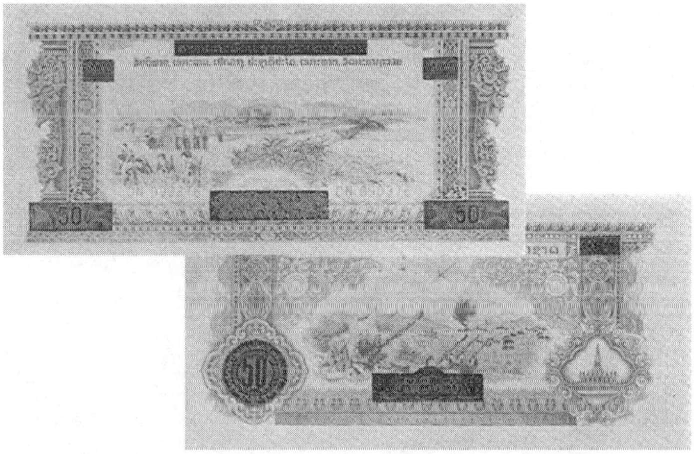

24A **50 Kip on 500 Kip** — VF — UNC

	VF	UNC
ND. New legends and denomination overprint on #24. (Not issued).	400.	800.

Bank of the Lao PDR

1979 ND; 1988 Issue

25 **1 Kip** — VF — UNC

ND (1979). Blue-gray on multicolor underprint. Militia unit at left, arms at upper right. Back: Schoolroom scene at left. Watermark: Stars, hammer and sickles.

	VF	UNC
a. Issued note.	.35	1.00
s. Specimen. Overprint in Lao.	—	15.00

26 **5 Kip** — VF — UNC

ND (1979). Green on multicolor underprint. Shoppers at a store, arms at upper right. Back: Logging elephants at left. Watermark: Stars, hammer and sickles.

	VF	UNC
a. Issued note.	.35	1.00
r. Replacement note. Block letters CA.	4.00	7.50
s. Specimen. Red overprint in Lao on face and English on back.	—	25.00

27 **10 Kip** — VF — UNC

ND (1979). Dark brown on multicolor underprint. Lumber mill at left, arms at upper right. Back: Medical scenes at left. Watermark: Stars, hammer and sickles.

	VF	UNC
a. Issued note.	.15	1.00
r. Replacement note. Block letters DA.	4.00	7.50
s. Specimen. Overprint in Lao.	—	15.00

28 **20 Kip** — VF — UNC

ND (1979). Brown and red-brown on underprint. Arms at left, tank with troop column at center. Back: Brown and maroon. Textile mill at center. Watermark: Stars, hammer and sickles.

	VF	UNC
a. Issued note.	.20	1.00
r. Replacement note. Block letters FA.	4.00	7.50
s. Specimen. Red overprint in Lao on face and in English on back.	—	25.00

29 **50 Kip** — VF — UNC

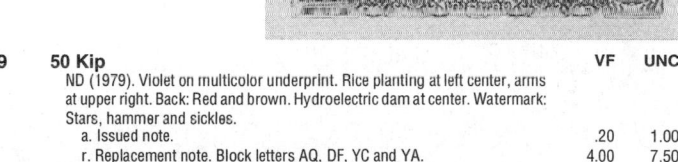

ND (1979). Violet on multicolor underprint. Rice planting at left center, arms at upper right. Back: Red and brown. Hydroelectric dam at center. Watermark: Stars, hammer and sickles.

	VF	UNC
a. Issued note.	.20	1.00
r. Replacement note. Block letters AQ, DF, YC and YA.	4.00	7.50
s. Specimen. Red overprint in Lao on face and in English on back.	—	25.00

30 **100 Kip** — VF — UNC

ND (1979). Deep blue-green and deep blue on multicolor underprint. Grain harvesting at left, arms at upper right. Back: Bridge, storage tanks, and soldier. Watermark: Stars, hammer and sickles.

	VF	UNC
a. Issued note.	.75	2.00
r. Replacement note. Block letters: *TT, XA, YM, ZB.*	4.00	7.50
s. Specimen. Red overprint in Lao on face and English on back.	—	30.00

31 500 Kip

1988. Dark brown, purple and deep blue on multicolor underprint. Modern irrigation systems at center, arms above. Back: Harvesting fruit at center. Watermark: Stars, hammer and sickles.

	VF	UNC
a. Issued note.	1.50	3.00
r. Replacement note. Block letters: *DD, WW, XC.*	4.00	7.50
s. Specimen. Red overprint in Lao on face, English on back.	—	35.00

1998-2003 Issue

32 1000 Kip

1992-96. Dark green, deep purple and green on multicolor underprint. Three women at left, temple at center right, arms at upper right. Underprint in sweeping arc. Back: Cattle at center. Watermark: Star. 152x68mm.

	VF	UNC
a. 1992. Without security thread. Red serial #.	1.00	6.00
b. 1994. With security thread.	1.00	3.50
c. 1995. With security thread.	1.00	3.50
d. 1996. With security thread.	1.00	3.50
r. Replacement note. Block letters: *VA, VB and ZK.*	4.00	7.50
s. As a (overprint in Lao); a, b (overprint in English). Specimen.	—	27.50

32A 1000 Kip

1998; 2003. Dark green, deep purple and green on multicolor underprint. Three women at left, temple at center right, arms at upper right. Underprint design as three lobes. Back: Cattle at center. Watermark: Star. 152x68mm.

	VF	UNC
a. 1998.	1.00	3.50
b. 2003.	1.00	3.50
r1. Replacement note. 1998. Block DD.	4.00	7.50
r2. Replacement note. 2003. Block EE, II and KK.	4.00	7.50
s. Specimen. As a. Overprint: *SPECIMEN.*	—	15.00

32B 1000 Kip

2008. Dark green. Three women.

a. Issued note. Recalled.	2.00	4.00
r. Replacement note. Recalled.	4.00	7.50

33 2000 Kip

1997; 2003. Blue-black and purple on multicolor underprint. Kaysone Phomvihane at left, arms at upper right. Temple in underprint at center right. Back: Hydroelectric complex at center. 152x68mm.

	VF	UNC
a. 1997.	1.00	3.50
b. 2003.	1.00	3.50
r1. Replacement note. As a. Block AA, QI.	4.00	7.50
r2. Replacement note. As b. Block EE, PP and QI.	4.00	7.50
s. Specimen. As a. Red overprint: *SPECIMEN* on both sides.	—	25.00

34 5000 Kip

1997; 2003. Dark brown and purple on multicolor underprint. Kaysone Phomvihane at left, arms at upper right. Temple in underprint at center right. Back: Cement factory at center. Watermark: Temple. 152x68mm.

	VF	UNC
a. 1997.	FV	4.50
b. 2003.	FV	4.50
r1. Replacement note. As a. Block LH.	4.00	7.50
r2. Replacement note. As b. Block DD, NN.	4.00	7.50
s. Specimen. As a. Red overprint: *SPECIMEN* on both sides.	—	35.00

35 10,000 Kip

2002; 2003; 2008. Slate blue and brown on multicolor underprint. Kaysone Phomuihane at left, temple at center. Bridge over Mekong river at center. Brown and green serial number. Back: Blue and green. Road at center. 152x68mm.

	VF	UNC
a. 2002.	FV	5.00
b. 2003.	FV	5.00
c. 2008.	FV	5.00
r1. Replacement note. As a. Block AD.	4.00	7.50
r2. Replacement note. As b. Block CC.	4.00	7.50
r3. Replacement note. As c. Block FF, HH.	4.00	7.50
s. Specimen. As a.	—	20.00

36 20,000 Kip

2002; 2003; 2008. Red-brown on multicolor underprint. Brown and green serial number. Back: Theun-Hinboune Hydroelectric complex at center. 152x68mm.

	VF	UNC
a. 2002.	4.00	10.00
b. 2003.	4.00	10.00
c. 2008.	4.00	10.00
r1. Replacement note. Block BY.	6.00	12.50
r2. Replacement note. Block DD, EE.	6.00	12.50
r3. Replacement note. Block GE.	6.00	12.50
s. Specimen. As a.	—	20.00

37 **50,000 Kip** — VF / UNC

2004. Brown and orange and rose on multicolor underprint. Kaysonne Phomvihane at center. Back: Theun-Hinboune hydroelectric complex at center. 156x70mm.

	VF	UNC
a. Issued note.	8.00	15.00
r. Replacement note. Block AH.	12.50	20.00
s. Specimen. Perforated: *SPECIMEN.*	—	60.00

	VF	UNC
38 **50,000 Kip** 2004. Purple on red, blue and multicolor underprint. Kaysone Phomvihane at left. Back: Building at left center. 156x70mm.	FV	20.00

2008 Issue

39 **1000 Kip** — VF / UNC

2008. Blue on green underprint. Three women at left center. Back: Grazing cattle and power lines in distance. Watermark: Coat of arms 144x66mm.

	VF	UNC
a. Issued note.	FV	1.50
s. Specimen.	—	—

2010 Issue

	VF	UNC
40 **100,000 Kip** 2010. Dark blue, yellow and orange on multicolor underprint. Chao Zaysettha at center. Back: Building 159x68mm.	FV	45.00

2011 Issue

	VF	UNC
41 **2000 Kip** 2011. Slate blue on multicolor underprint. Kaysonne Phomvihane at left center. Back: Cement factory. 141x65mm.	FV	7.50

	VF	UNC
42 **100,000 Kip** 2011. Dark green on multicolor underprint. Kaysonne Phomvihane at left center. Back: Building and statue. 152x68mm.	FV	45.00

The Republic of Latvia, the central Baltic state in east Europe, has an area of 24,595 sq. mi. (43,601 sq. km.) and a population of 2.4 million. Capital: Riga. Livestock raising and manufacturing are the chief industries. Butter, bacon, fertilizers and telephone equipment are exported.

The name "Latvia" originates from the ancient Latgalians, one of four eastern Baltic tribes that formed the ethnic core of the Latvian people (ca. 8th-12th centuries A.D.). The region subsequently came under the control of Germans, Poles, Swedes, and finally, Russians. A Latvian republic emerged following World War I, but it was annexed by the USSR in 1940 - an action never recognized by the US and many other countries. Latvia reestablished its independence in 1991 following the breakup of the Soviet Union. Although the last Russian troops left in 1994, the status of the Russian minority (some 30% of the population) remains of concern to Moscow. Latvia joined both NATO and the EU in the spring of 2004.

MONETARY SYSTEM:

1 Rublis = 100 Kapeikas, 1919-22
1 Lats = 100 Santimu, 1923-40; 1992
1 Lats = 200 Rublu, 1993
1 Rublis = 1 Russian Ruble, 1992

Republic

Government

1992 Issue

			VF	UNC
35	**1 Rublis**	1992. Violet on yellow and ochre underprint. Back: Violet-brown on light green and yellow underprint. Watermark: Symmetrical design. UV: fibers flouresce blue.	.50	1.00

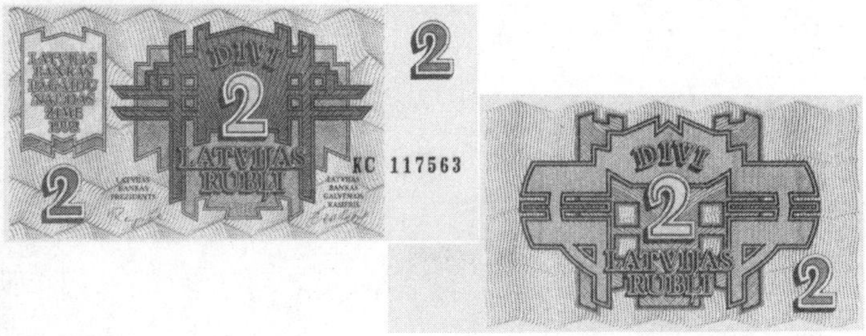

			VF	UNC
36	**2 Rubli**	1992. Purple on brown-orange and yellow underprint. Watermark: Symmetrical design.	.50	2.00

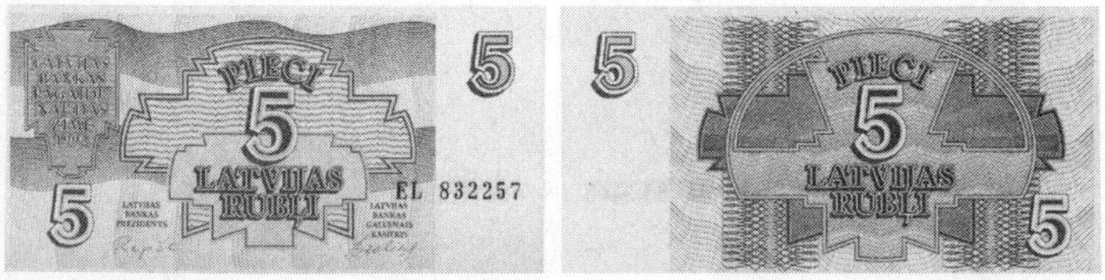

			VF	UNC
37	**5 Rubli**	1992. Deep blue on light blue and light yellow-orange underprint. Back: Blue-black on blue and light blue underprint. Watermark: Symmetrical design.	2.00	5.00

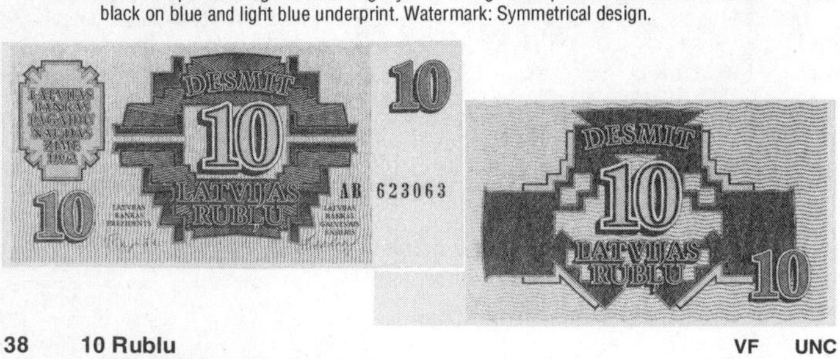

			VF	UNC
38	**10 Rublu**	1992. Purple on red-orange and pale orange underprint. Watermark: Symmetrical design.	1.00	4.00

			VF	UNC
39	**20 Rublu**	1992. Violet on lilac and pink underprint. Watermark: Symmetrical design.	2.00	6.00

			VF	UNC
40	**50 Rublu**	1992. Gray-green on light blue and pink underprint. Watermark: Symmetrical design.	3.00	10.00

			VF	UNC
41	**200 Rublu**	1992. Greenish black on yellow and blue-green underprint. Back: Greenish black on light blue and pink underprint.	8.00	18.00

			VF	UNC
42	**500 Rublu**	1992. Violet-brown on gray and dull orange underprint.	10.00	30.00

Latvijas Bankas Naudas Zime

1992 Dated 1993-1998 Issue

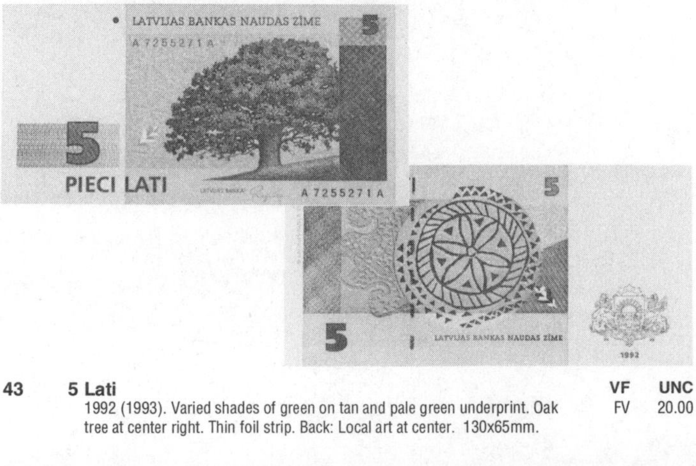

			VF	UNC
43	**5 Lati**	1992 (1993). Varied shades of green on tan and pale green underprint. Oak tree at center right. Thin foil strip. Back: Local art at center. 130x65mm.	FV	20.00

44 **10 Latu** VF UNC
1992 (1993). Violet and purple on multicolor underprint. Panoramic view of Daugava River at center. Back: Traditional bow broach at center. 130x65mm. FV 30.00

45 **20 Latu** VF UNC
1992 (1993). Brown and dark brown on multicolor underprint. Rural homestead at right. Back: Traditional ornamented woven linen at left center. 130x65mm. FV 60.00

46 **50 Latu** VF UNC
1992 (1994). Deep blue on multicolor underprint. Sailing ship at right. Back: Two crossed keys and a cross on back (Historical seal of Riga) superimposed on medieval fortification. 130x65mm. FV 120.

47 **100 Latu** VF UNC
1992 (1994). Red and dark brown on multicolor underprint. Krisjanis Barons at right. Back: Lielvarde belt ornaments. 130x65mm. FV 260.

48 **500 Latu** VF UNC
1992 (1998). Purple on multicolor underprint. Young woman in national costume at right. Back: Small ornamental brass crowns. 130x65mm. FV 1200.

1996-2001 Issue

49 **5 Lati** VF UNC
1996; 2001. Varied shades of green on tan and pale green underprint. Oak tree at center. Back: Local art at center. 130x65mm.
- a. 1996. Wide security strip. FV 14.00
- b. 2001. FV 14.00

50 **10 Latu**
2000. Violet and purple on multicolor underprint. Panoramic view of Daugava River at center. Back: Traditional bow broach at center. Engraving and color modifications. 130x65mm. FV 25.00

51 **20 Latu** VF UNC
2004. Brown and dark brown on multicolor underprint. Rural homestead at right. Back: Traditional ornamented woven linen at left center. 130x65mm.
- a. 2004. FV 48.00

52 **100 Latu**
2006. Brown and red on multicolor underprint.
- a. 2006. FV 275.

2006-09 Issue

53 **5 Lati** VF UNC
2006-07; 2009. Green and tan on pale green underprint. Oak tree at center right. Back: Local art at center. 130x65mm.
- a. 2006. FV 17.50
- b. 2007. FV 17.50
- c. 2009. FV 17.50

54 **10 Latu**
2008. Violet and purple on multicolor underprint. Panoramic view of Daugava River at center. Back: Traditional bow broach at center. FV 30.00

55 **20 Latu**
2007; 2009. Brown and dark brown on multicolor underprint. Rural homestead at center right. Back: Traditional ornamented woven linen at left center.
- a. 2007. FV 55.00
- b. 2009. FV 55.00

56 **50 Latu**
2010. Expected new issue. — —

57 **100 Latu** VF UNC
2007. Brown and red on multicolor underprint. Krisjanis Barons at right center. Back: Leilvarde belt ornaments at left center.
- a. Issued note. FV 260.
- s. Specimen. — 200.

58 **500 Latu**
2008. Purple on multicolor underprint. Young woman in national costume at center right. Back: Small ornamental brass crowns. FV 1000.

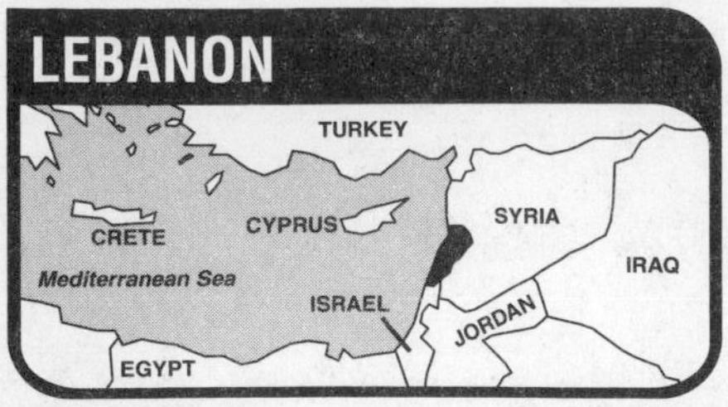

The Republic of Lebanon, situated on the eastern shore of the Mediterranean Sea between Syria and Israel, has an area of 4,015 sq. mi. (10,400 sq. km.) and a population of 3.29 million. Capital: Beirut. The economy is d on agriculture, trade and tourism. Fruit, other foodstuffs and textiles are exported.

Following the capture of Syria from the Ottoman Empire by Anglo-French forces in 1918, France received a mandate over this territory and separated out the region of Lebanon in 1920. France granted this area independence in 1943. A lengthy civil war (1975-1990) devastated the country, but Lebanon has since made progress toward rebuilding its political institutions. Under the Ta'if Accord - the blueprint for national reconciliation - the Lebanese established a more equitable political system, particularly by giving Muslims a greater voice in the political process while institutionalizing sectarian divisions in the government. Since the end of the war, Lebanon has conducted several successful elections. Most militias have been disbanded, and the Lebanese Armed Forces (LAF) have extended authority over about two-thirds of the country. Hizballah, a radical Shia organization listed by the US State Department as a Foreign Terrorist Organization, retains its weapons. During Lebanon's civil war, the Arab League legitimized in the Ta'if Accord Syria's troop deployment, numbering about 16,000 d mainly east of Beirut and in the Bekaa Valley. Israel's withdrawal from southern Lebanon in May 2000 and the passage in October 2004 of UNSCR 1559 - a resolution calling for Syria to withdraw from Lebanon and end its interference in Lebanese affairs - encouraged some Lebanese groups to demand that Syria withdraw its forces as well. The assassination of former Prime Minister Rafiq Hariri and 22 others in February 2005 led to massive demonstrations in Beirut against the Syrian presence ("the Cedar Revolution"), and Syria withdrew the remainder of its military forces in April 2005. In May-June 2005, Lebanon held its first legislative elections since the end of the civil war free of foreign interference, handing a majority to the bloc led by Saad HARIRI, the slain prime minister's son. Lebanon continues to be plagued by violence - Hizballah kidnapped two Israeli soldiers in July 2006 leading to a 34-day conflict with Israel. The LAF in May-September 2007 battled Sunni extremist group Fatah al-Islam in the Nahr al-Barid Palestinian refugee camp; and the country has witnessed a string of politically motivated assassinations since the death of Rafiq Hariri. Lebanese politicians in November 2007 were unable to agree on a successor to Emile Lahud when he stepped down as president, creating a political vacuum until the election of Army Commander Michel Sulaymanin May 2008 and the formation of a new unity government in July 2008.

RULERS

French to 1943

MONETARY SYSTEM

1 Livre (Pound) = 100 Piastres

République Libanaise

Banque de Syrie et du Liban

1952; 1956 Issue

55	1 Livre	VF	UNC
	1.1.1952-1.1.1964. Crusader Castle at Saida (Sidon) at left. Signature varieties. Back: Columns of Baalbek. Printer: TDLR.		
	a. Without security strip.	10.00	60.00
	b. With security strip.	10.00	60.00
	s1. Specimen. Oval TDLR stamp, punch hole cancelled.	—	30.00
	s2. Specimen. Perforated: *SPECIMEN* and large double lined X inked on face.	—	150.

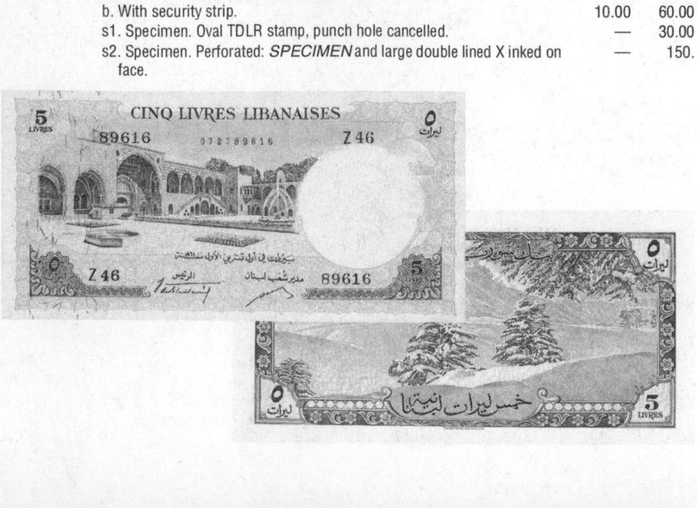

56	5 Livres	VF	UNC
	1.1.1952-1.1.1964. Blue on multicolor underprint. Courtyard of the Palais de Beit-ed-Din. Signature varieties. Back: Snowy mountains with trees. Printer: TDLR.		
	a. Without security strip.	45.00	160.
	b. With security strip.	45.00	160.
	s1. Specimen. Oval TDLR stamp, punch hole cancelled.	—	40.00
	s2. Specimen. Perforated: *SPECIMEN* and large double lined X inked on face.	—	250.

57	10 Livres	VF	UNC
	1.1.1956; 1.1.1961; 1.1.1963. Green on multicolor underprint. Ruins of Temple of Bacchus temple at Baalbek. Signature varieties. Back: Shoreline with city in hills. Printer: TDLR.		
	a. Issued note.	60.00	230.
	s1. Specimen. Oval TDLR stamp, punch hole cancelled.	—	100.
	s2. Specimen. Perforated: *SPECIMEN* and large double lined X inked on face.	—	500.

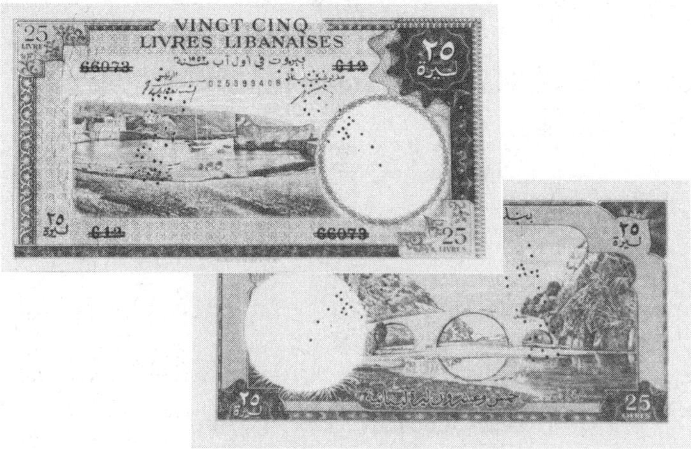

58	25 Livres	VF	UNC
	1.1.1952; 1.1.1953. Blue-gray on multicolor underprint. Harbor town. Signature varieties. Back: Stone arch bridge at center right. Watermark: Lion's head. Printer: TDLR.		
	a. Issued note.	210.	900.
	s1. Specimen. Oval TDLR stamp, punch hole cancelled.	—	1000.
	s2. Specimen. Perforated: *SPECIMEN* and large double lined X inked on face.	—	1250.

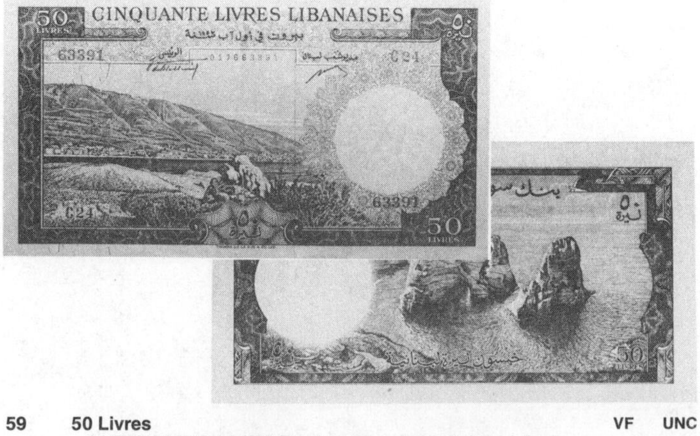

59	50 Livres	VF	UNC
	1.1.1952; 1.1.1953; 1.1.1964. Deep brown on multicolor underprint. Coast landscape. Signature varieties. Back: Large rock formations in water. Watermark: Lion's head. Printer: TDLR.		
	a. Issued note.	200.	900.
	s1. Specimen. Oval TDLR stamp, punch hole cancelled.	—	1000.
	s2. Specimen. Perforated: *SPECIMEN* and large double lined X inked on face.	—	1250.

60 100 Livres

1.1.1952; 1.1.1953; 1.1.1958; 1.1.1963. Blue on multicolor underprint. View of Beirut and harbor. Signature varieties. Back: Cedar tree at center. Watermark: Cedar tree. Printer: TDLR.

	VF	UNC
a. Issued note.	50.00	250.
s1. Specimen. Oval TDLR stamp, punch hole cancelled.	—	1000.
s2. Specimen. Perforated: *SPECIMEN* and large double lined X inked on face.	—	1250.

Republic

Banque du Liban

1964; 1978 Issue

61 1 Livre

1964-80. Brown or light blue underprint. Columns of Baalbek. Back: Jeita Cavern. Watermark: Two eagles. Printer: TDLR.

	VF	UNC
a. 1964; 1968.	6.00	30.00
b. 1971; 1972; 1973; 1974.	6.00	30.00
c. 1978; 1980.	3.00	4.50

62 5 Livres

1964-86. Green on blue and light yellow underprint. Buildings. Back: Bridge over Kalb at center right. Watermark: Ancient galley. Printer: TDLR. UV: Arabic 5 fluoresce yellow, fibers blue.

	VF	UNC
a. 1964.	8.00	40.00
b. 1967; 1968.	5.00	25.00
c. 1972; 1974; 1.2.1978; 1.4.1978.	3.00	10.00
d. 1986.	1.50	2.00

63 10 Livres

1964-86. Purple on multicolor underprint. Ruins of Anjar. Back: Large rocks in water near Beirut. Watermark: Man's head. Printer: TDLR.

	VF	UNC
a. 1964.	10.00	50.00
b. 1967; 1968.	8.00	35.00
c. 1971; 1972; 1973; 1974.	4.00	20.00
d. 1.2.1978.	8.00	25.00
e. 1.4.1978.	4.00	16.00
f. 1986.	1.50	2.50

64 25 Livres

1964-83. Brown on gold underprint. Crusader Castle at Saida (Sidon). Back: Ruins on rocks. Watermark: Lion's head. Printer: TDLR.

	VF	UNC
a. 1964; 1967; 1968.	20.00	90.00
b. 1972; 1973; 1974; 1978.	13.00	55.00
c. 1983.	2.00	3.50

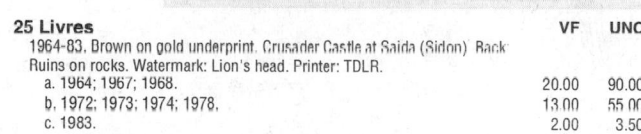

65 50 Livres

1964-88. Dark gray, purple and dark olive-green on multicolor underprint. Ruins of Temple of Bacchus at Baalbek. Back: Building. Watermark: Cedar tree. Printer: TDLR.

	VF	UNC
a. 1964; 1967; 1968.	22.00	95.00
b. 1972; 1973; 1974; 1978.	18.00	60.00
c. Guilloche added above temple ruins with 10-petaled rosette at left in underprint. Clear watermark area on back. 1983; 1985.	2.00	4.00
d. Without control # above ruins on face. 1988.	1.50	4.00

66	**100 Livres**	VF	UNC
	1964-88. Blue on light pink and light blue underprint. Palais Beit-ed-din with inner courtyard. Back: Snowy cedars on Lebanon mountains. Watermark: Bearded male elder. Printer: TDLR.		
	a. 1964; 1967; 1968.	35.00	120.
	b. 1972; 1973; 1974; 1977; 1978; 1980.	20.00	80.00
	c. Guilloche added under bank name on face and back. Clearer watermark area on back. 1983; 1985.	2.00	5.00
	d. Without control # at upper center 1988.	2.00	4.50

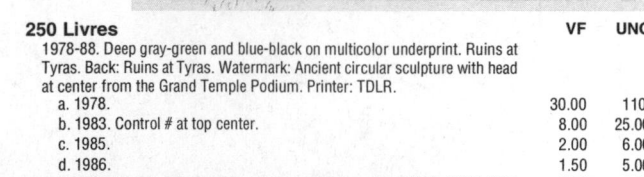

67	**250 Livres**	VF	UNC
	1978-88. Deep gray-green and blue-black on multicolor underprint. Ruins at Tyras. Back: Ruins at Tyras. Watermark: Ancient circular sculpture with head at center from the Grand Temple Podium. Printer: TDLR.		
	a. 1978.	30.00	110.
	b. 1983. Control # at top center.	8.00	25.00
	c. 1985.	2.00	6.00
	d. 1986.	1.50	5.00
	e. Without control # above signature at archway on face. 1986; 1987; 1988.	1.00	4.50

1988; 1993 Issue

Law of 1988.

68	**500 Livres**	VF	UNC
	1988. Brown and olive-green on multicolor underprint. Beirut city view at center. Back: Brown on multicolor underprint. Ruins at left center. Watermark: Lion's head. Printer: TDLR.	1.50	3.50

69	**1000 Livres**	VF	UNC
	1988; 1990-92. Dark blue, blue-black and green on multicolor underprint. Map at right. Back: Ruins at center, modern building at center right. Watermark: Cedar tree. Printer: TDLR. 157x67mm.		
	a. 1988.	FV	4.00
	b. 1990; 1991.	FV	3.00
	c. 1992.	FV	3.00

70	**10,000 Livres**	VF	UNC
	1993. Purple and olive-brown on multicolor underprint. Ancient ruins at Tyros at center. Back: City ruins with five archaic statues. Watermark: Ancient circular sculpture with head at center from the Grand Temple Podium.	15.00	40.00

1994 Issue

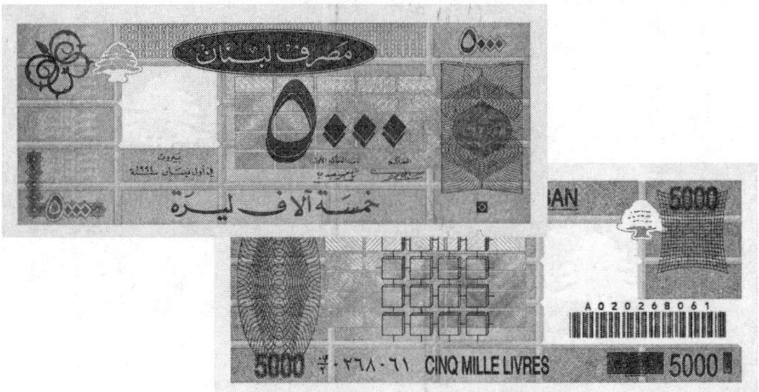

71	**5000 Livres**	VF	UNC
	1994; 1995. Dark purple and red on pink and multicolor underprint. Arabic serial number and matching bar code number. Ornate block designs as underprint. Back: Geometric designs. Watermark: Cedar tree. Printer: BABN.		
	a. 1994.	12.00	24.00
	b. 1995.	10.00	22.00

72	**20,000 Livres**	VF	UNC
	1994; 1995. Red-brown and orange on yellow and multicolor underprint. Arabic serial number and matching bar code number. Ornate block designs as underprint. Back: Geometric designs with large *LIBAN* left center Watermark: Cedar tree. Printer: BABN. 150x80mm.	25.00	55.00

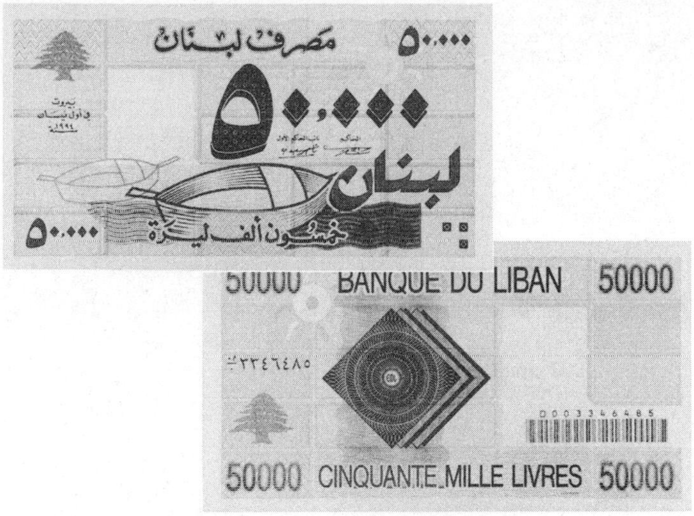

73	50,000 Livres	VF	UNC
	1994; 1995. Blue-black and brown-violet on multicolor underprint. Cedar tree at upper left, artistic boats at lower left center. Arabic serial number and matching bar code number. Back: Large diamond with BDL at left center, cedar tree at lower left. Watermark: Cedar tree. Printer: BABN. Ornate block designs as underprint. 155x85mm.	55.00	120.

74	100,000 Livres	VF	UNC
	1994; 1995. Dark blue-green and dark green on multicolor underprint. Cedar tree at lower right. Arabic serial number and matching bar code number. Back: Artistic bunch of grapes and grain stalks at left center. Watermark: Cedar tree. Printer: BABN. 160x90mm.	85.00	170.

1998-99 Issue

75	5000 Livres	VF	UNC
	1999. Dark purple and red on multicolor underprint. Arabic serial number and matching bar code number. Back: Geometric designs. Watermark: Cedar tree. Printer: BABN. Like #71 but smaller size. 140x70mm.	FV	18.00

76	10,000 Livres	VF	UNC
	1998. Orange and green on yellow and multicolor underprint. Back: Patriotic Monument, stylized landscape. Iridescent planchets in paper. 145x73mm.	FV	24.00

77	50,000 Livres	VF	UNC
	1999. Blue-black and brown-violet on multicolor underprint. Cedar tree at upper left, artistic boats at lower left center. Arabic serial # and matching bar code number. Enhanced security features and holographic foil strip at left. Back: Large diamond with BDL at left center, cedar tree at lower left. Watermark: Cedar tree. Printer: BABN. 155x85mm.	FV	95.00

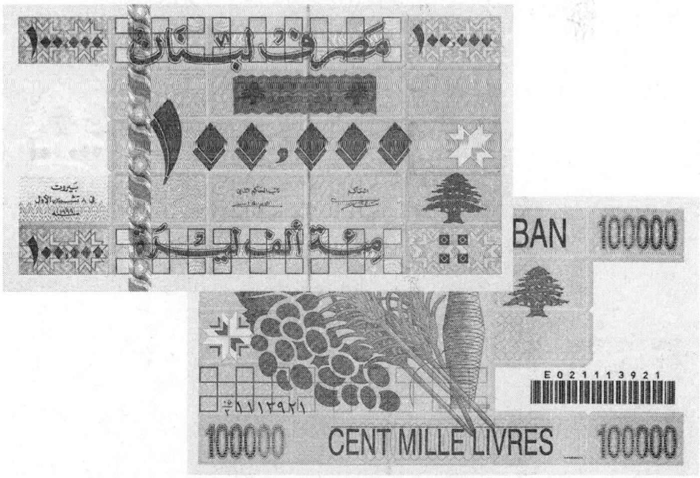

78	100,000 Livres	VF	UNC
	1999. Dark blue-green and dark green on multicolor underprint. Cedar tree at lower right. Arabic serial # and matching bar code number. Enhanced security features. Back: Artistic bunch of grapes and grain stalks at left center. 160x90mm.	FV	140.

2001 Issue

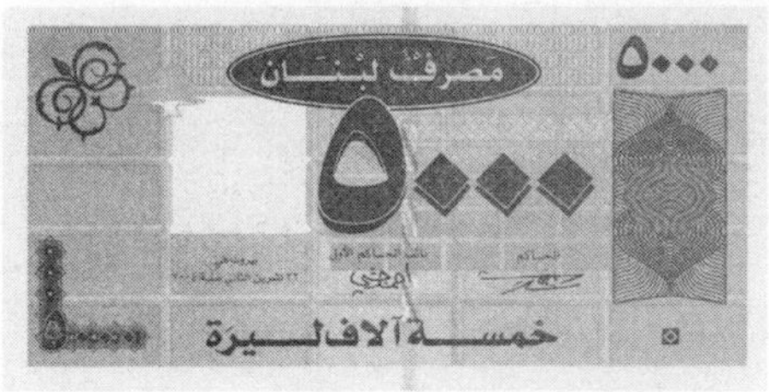

79 **5000 Livres** — VF / UNC
2001. Dark purple and red on multicolor underprint. Printer: BABN. Wide security thread. 140x70mm. — FV / 12.00

81 **20,000 Livres** — VF / UNC
2001. Red-brown and orange on multicolor underprint. Printer: BABN. Wide security thread. 150x80mm. — FV / 60.00

82 **50,000 Livres** — VF / UNC
2001. Blue-black and brown-violet on multicolor underprint. Printer: G&D. Wide security thread. 155x85mm. — FV / 95.00

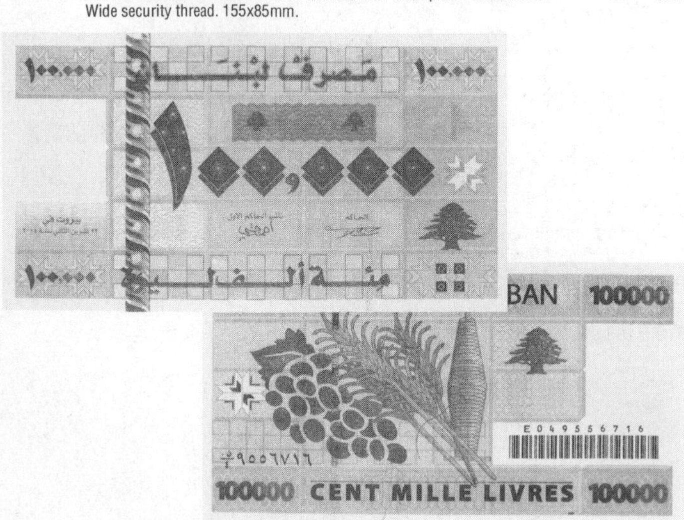

83 **100,000 Livres** — VF / UNC
2001. Dark blue-green and dark green on multicolor underprint. Printer: BABN. 160x90mm. — FV / 130.

2004 Issue

84 **1000 Livres** — VF / UNC
2004; 2008. Green. Alphabet development in arc. Back: Numeral development. 116x60mm.
a. 2004 (2006). — FV / 3.00
b. 2008. — FV / 2.00

85 **5000 Livres** — VF / UNC
2004; 2008. Dark purple and red on multicolor underprint. 120x62mm.
a. 2004. — FV / 10.00
b. 2008. — FV / 7.50

86 **10,000 Livres** — VF / UNC
2004; 2008. Orange and green on yellow and multicolor underprint. 128x66mm.
a. 2004. — FV / 18.00
b. 2008. — FV / 14.00

No.	Denomination / Description	VF	UNC
87	**20,000 Livres** 2004. Red-brown and orange on multicolor underprint. 131x72mm.	FV	42.00
88	**50,000 Livres** 2004. Blue-black and brown-violet on multicolor underprint. 140x77mm.	FV	85.00
89	**100,000 Livres** 2004. Dark blue-green and dark green on multicolor underprint. 147x82mm.	FV	120.

2011 Issue

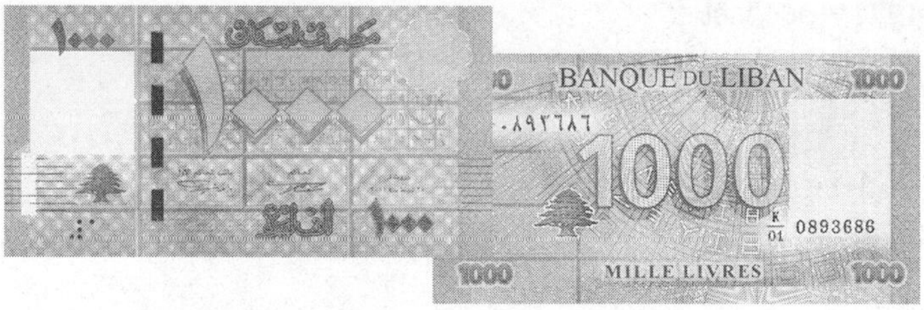

			VF	UNC
90	**1000 Livres**	2011. Green and tan. Value in Arabic at center. Wide segmented security thread. Back: Value. Printer: Goznak (without imprint). 115x60mm.	FV	2.00
91	**5000 Livres**	2012. Pink, purple, orange and green. Cedar tree, geometric block desing. Arabic value. Back: Geometric block design, cedar tree. Watermark: Cedar tree and value Printer: Goznak (without imprint). 120x62mm.	FV	7.50
92	**10,000 Livres**	2012. Yellow, orange and green. Cedar tree, geometric block design. Value in Arabic. Back: Geometric block design, statue by Renato Marino Mazzacurati of three lebanese nationalists in Martyr's Square, Beirut. Watermark: Cedar tree and value. Printer: OT. 127x66mm.	FV	17.50

			VF	UNC
93	**20,000 Livres**	6.17.2012. Value in Arabic. Back: Value. 131x72mm.	FV	35.00

			VF	UNC
94	**50,000 Livres**	2011. Violet, green, blue and multicolor. Value in Arabic. Back: Blue and violet. Diamond shaped square at left center, value in corners. Printer: Goznak (without imprint). 140x77mm.	FV	70.00

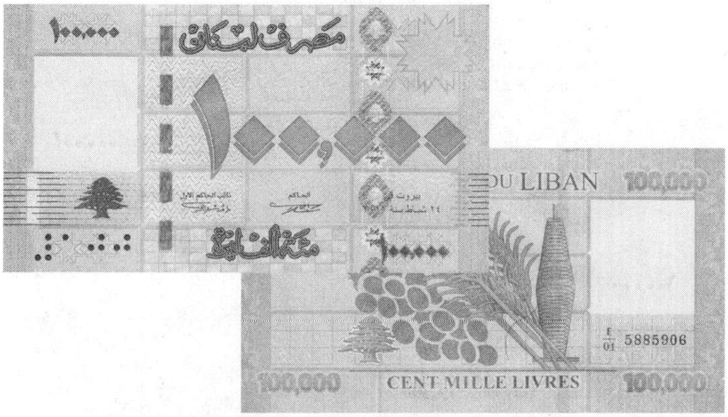

			VF	UNC
95	**100,000 Livres**	2011; 2012. Green, light blue, yellow and multicolor. Value in Arabic. Wide security thread. Back: Green. Grapes, grain and thread at center, value in corners. Printer: Goznak (without imprint). 147x82mm.		
		a. 2011.	FV	135.
		b. 2012.	FV	135.

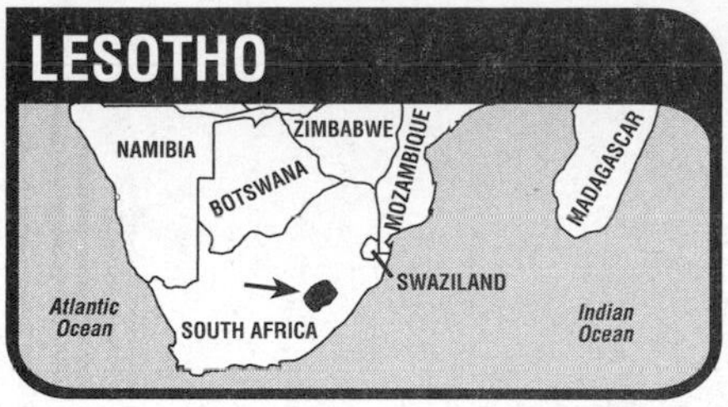

The Kingdom of Lesotho, a constitutional monarchy located within the east-central part of the Republic of South Africa, has an area of 11,716 sq. mi. (30,355 sq. km.) and a population of 2.29 million. Capital: Maseru. The economy is d on subsistence agriculture and livestock raising. Wool, mohair, water through Katse Dam, and cattle are exported.

Basutoland was renamed the Kingdom of Lesotho upon independence from the UK in 1966. The Basuto National Party ruled for the first two decades. King Moshoeshoe was exiled in 1990, but returned to Lesotho in 1992 and was reinstated in 1995. Constitutional government was restored in 1993 after seven years of military rule. In 1998, violent protests and a military mutiny following a contentious election prompted a brief but bloody intervention by South African and Botswanan military forces under the aegis of the Southern African Development Community. Subsequent constitutional reforms restored relative political stability. Peaceful parliamentary elections were held in 2002, but the National Assembly elections of February 2007 were hotly contested and aggrieved parties continue to periodically demonstrate their distrust of the results.

RULERS:

King Motlotlehi Moshoeshoe II, 1966-1996
King Letsi III, 1997-

MONETARY SYSTEM:

1 Loti = 100 Lisente

Kingdom

Lesotho Monetary Authority

1979 Issue

#1-3A Dating: Partial date given in the 2 numbers of the serial # prefix for #1-8.

			VF	UNC
1	**2 Maloti**	(19)79. Dark brown on multicolor underprint. Arms at center, military bust of King Moshoeshoe II at right. Signature 1. Back: Building and Lesotho flag at left. Watermark: Basotho hat.		
		a. Blue and brown underprint at right of King	4.50	24.00
		s. Specimen. Serial # prefix R/79.	—	135.

			VF	UNC
2	**5 Maloti**	(19)79. Deep blue on multicolor underprint. Arms at center, military bust of King Moshoeshoe II at right. Signature 1. Back: Craftsmen weaving at left center. Watermark: Basotho hat.		
		a. Issued note.	12.50	37.00
		s. Specimen. Serial # prefix J/79.	—	135.

3 **10 Maloti** VF UNC

(19)79. Red and purple on multicolor underprint. Arms at center, military bust of King Moshoeshoe II at right. Signature 1. Back: Basotho horseman in maize field at center. Watermark: Basotho hat.

	VF	UNC
a. Issued note.	30.00	145.
s. Specimen. Serial # prefix C/79.	—	135.

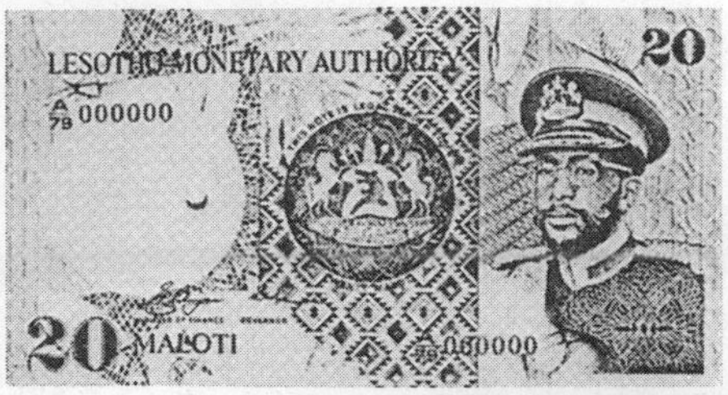

3A **20 Maloti** VF UNC

(19)79. Arms at center, military bust of King Moshoeshoe II at right. Signature 1. Back: Herdsmen with cattle at left center. Watermark: Basotho hat. Specimen (Not issued.) — —

SIGNATURE VARIETIES

	MINISTER OF FINANCE	GOVERNOR
1	E. R. Sekhonyana	E. K. Molemohi
2A	K. Rakhetla	S. Schoenbeg 08.11.1982-08.11.1985
2B	K. Rakhetla	S. Schoenbeg 08.11.1982-08.11.1985
2C	K. Rakhetla	S. Schoenbeg 08.11.1982-08.11.1985
1985-1988	K. Rakhetla	Mr. E. L. Karlsson 09.11.1985-30.6.1988
3	E. R. Sekhonyana	Dr. A. M. Maruping 01.07.1988-15.05.1998
4	E. L. Thoahlane	Dr. A. M. Maruping 01.07.1988-15.05.1998
5	Dr. L. V. Ketso	Dr. A. M. Maruping 01.07.1988-15.05.1998
6	Dr. L. V. Ketso	S. M. Swaray 9.9.1998

Central Bank of Lesotho

1981; 1984 Issue

#4-8 Partial year date given as the denominator of the serial # prefix.

4 **2 Maloti** VF UNC

(19)81; 84. Dark brown on multicolor underprint. Arms at center, military bust of King Moshoeshoe II at right. Signature 1. Back: Building and Lesotho flag at left. Watermark: Basotho hat.

	VF	UNC
a. Signature 1 (19)81.	4.00	15.00
b. Signature 2A (19)84.	3.00	12.50
s1. Specimen. Serial # prefix A/81.	—	135.
s2. Specimen. Serial # prefix D/84.	—	135.

5 **5 Maloti** VF UNC

(19)81 Deep blue on multicolor underprint. Arms at center, military bust of King Moshoeshoe II at right. Signature 1. Back: Waterfalls at center. Watermark: Basotho hat.

	VF	UNC
a. Issued note.	5.00	22.00
s. Specimen. Serial # prefix A/81.	—	135.

6 **10 Maloti** VF UNC

(19)81. Red and purple on multicolor underprint. Arms at center, military bust of King Moshoeshoe II at right. Signature 1. Back: Basotho horseman in maize field at center. Watermark: Basotho hat.

	VF	UNC
a. Signature 1 (19)81.	15.00	55.00
b. Signature 2A (19)81 (1984).	5.00	22.50
s1. Specimen. Serial # prefix A/81.	—	135.
s2. Specimen. Serial # prefix C/81.	—	135.

7 20 Maloti

(19)81; 84. Dark green and olive-green on multicolor underprint. Arms at center, military bust of King Moshoeshoe II at right. Back: Mosotho herdsboy with cattle at left center. Watermark: Basotho hat.

	VF	UNC
a. Signature 1 (19)81.	30.00	110.
b. Signature 2A (19)84.	12.50	50.00
s1. Specimen. Serial # prefix A/81.	—	135.
s2. Specimen. Serial # prefix A/84.	—	135.

8 50 Maloti

(19)81. Purple and deep blue on multicolor underprint. Arms at center, military bust of King Moshoeshoe II at right. Signature 1. Back: "Qiloane" mountain at left. Watermark: Basotho hat.

	VF	UNC
a. Issued note.	80.00	375.
s. Specimen. Serial # prefix A/81.	—	175.

1989 Issue

9 2 Maloti

1989. Dark brown on multicolor underprint. Arms at center, civilian bust of King Moshoeshoe II at right. Signature 3. Back: Building and Lesotho flag at left. Watermark: King Moshoeshoe II.

	VF	UNC
a. Issued note.	1.25	2.75
s. Specimen. Serial # prefix G.	—	115.

10 5 Maloti

1989. Deep blue on multicolor underprint. Arms at center, civilian bust of King Moshoeshoe II at right. Signature 3. Back: Waterfalls at center. Watermark: King Moshoeshoe II.

	VF	UNC
a. Issued note.	2.00	7.50
s. Specimen. Serial # prefix C.	—	115.

11 10 Maloti

1990. Red and purple on multicolor underprint. Arms at center, civilian bust of King Moshoeshoe II at right. Signature 3. Back: Basotho horseman in maize field at center. Watermark: King Moshoeshoe II.

	VF	UNC
a. Issued note.	3.50	12.50
s. Specimen. Serial # prefix R.	—	115.

12 20 Maloti

1990. Dark green and blue-black on multicolor underprint. Arms at center, civilian bust of King Moshoeshoe II at right. Signature 3. Back: Mosotho herdsboy with cattle at left center. Watermark: King Moshoeshoe II.

	VF	UNC
a. 1990.	10.00	40.00
b. 1993.	100.	400.
s1. As a. Specimen. Serial # prefix F.	—	115.
s2. As b. Specimen. Serial # prefix J.		160.

13 50 Maloti

1989. Purple and deep blue on multicolor underprint. Arms at center, civilian bust of King Moshoeshoe II at right. Signature 3. Back: Sheep by shed and home at center right. Watermark: King Moshoeshoe II.

	VF	UNC
a. Issued note.	30.00	135.
s. Specimen. Serial # prefix A.	—	115.

1992 Issue

14 50 Maloti

1992. Purple, dark olive-green and dark blue on multicolor underprint. Seated King Moshoeshoe I at right. Signature 4. Back: *Qiloane* mountain at left center.

	VF	UNC
a. Issued note.	20.00	90.00
s1. As a. 1992. Specimen. Serial # prefix A.	—	110.
s2. As a. 1993. Specimen. Serial # prefix B.	—	160.

1994-2000 Issue

15	10 Maloti	VF	UNC
	2000-. Red and purple on multicolor underprint. Seated King Moshoeshoe I at left, arms at center. Back: Traditionally dressed Masotho on horseback, maize crops and mountain. Watermark: Arms. Printer: TDLR. 128x70mm.		
	a. Signature 6. 2000.	FV	4.50
	b. Signature 7. 2003.	FV	3.50
	c. Signature 7. 2005.	FV	3.50
	d. Signature 7. 2006.	FV	3.50
	e. 2007.	FV	3.50
	f. 2009.	FV	3.50
	s. Specimen. Serial # prefix A.	—	100.

16	20 Maloti	VF	UNC
	1994-. Deep olive-green and blue-black on multicolor underprint. Seated King Moshoeshoe I at left, arms at center. Back: Mosotho herdsboy with cattle near huts at center right. Watermark: Arms. Printer: TDLR. 135x70mm.		
	a. Signature 5. 1994.	6.00	20.00
	b. Signature 6. 1999.	FV	9.00
	c. Signature 6. 2001.	FV	6.50
	d. Signature 7. 2005	FV	6.50
	e. Signature 7. 2006.	FV	6.50
	f. Signature 8. 2007. Thin security foil.	FV	6.50
	g. 2009.	FV	6.50
	s1. As a. Specimen. Serial # prefix A.	—	100.
	s2. As b. Specimen. Serial # prefix F.	—	100.

17	50 Maloti	VF	UNC
	1994-. Purple, olive-green and dark blue on multicolor underprint. Seated King Moshoeshoe I at left, arms at center. Back: Herdsman on horseback with pack mule at center, *Qiloane* mountain at right. Watermark: Arms. Printer: TDLR. 138x70mm.		
	a. Signature 5. 1994.	12.50	50.00
	b. Signature 5. 1997.	—	30.00
	c. Signature 6. 1999.	FV	20.00
	d. Signature 6. 2001.	FV	17.00
	e. 2009.	FV	17.00
	s1. As a. Specimen. Serial # prefix A.	—	100.
	s2. As b. Specimen. Serial # prefix C.	—	100.
	s3. As c. Specimen. Serial # prefix F.	—	100.

18	100 Maloti		
	1994. Dark olive-green, orange and brown on multicolor underprint. Seated King Moshoeshoe I at left, arms at center. Back: Sheep by shed and home at center right. Watermark: Arms. Printer: BABN. 141x70mm.		
	a. Signature 5.	20.00	65.00
	s. Specimen. Serial # prefix AA.	—	100.

19	100 Maloti	VF	UNC
	1999-. Dark olive-green, orange and brown on multicolor underprint. Seated King Moshoeshoe I at left, arms at center. Back: Sheep by shed and home at center right. Watermark: Arms. Printer: TDLR. 141x70mm.		
	a. Signature 6. 1999.	15.00	55.00
	b. Signature 6. 2001.	FV	45.00
	c. Signature 7. 2006. Thin security foil.	FV	45.00
	d. Signature 8. 2007.	FV	45.00
	e. 2009.	FV	45.00
	s. As a. Specimen. Serial # prefix A.	—	100.

20	200 Maloti	VF	UNC
	1994; 2001. Dark brown, brown and orange on multicolor underprint. Seated King Moshoeshoe I at left, arms at center. Kinegram strip vertically at right. Back: Herdsman with sheep. Watermark: Arms. Printer: TDLR. 144x70mm.		
	a. Signature 5. 1994.	FV	80.00
	b. Signature 6. 2001.	FV	100.
	s. As a. Specimen. Serial # prefix A.	—	100.

2010 Issue

21	10 Maloti	VF	UNC
	2010. Red and lilac on multicolor underprint. Portraits of Kings Moshoeshoe II, Letsie III and Morena Moshoeshoe I. Back: Flowers.	FV	3.50
22	20 Maloti		
	2010. Blue and light blue on multicolor underprint. Portraits of Kings Moshoeshoe II, Letsie III and Morena Moshoeshoe I. Back: Small houses.	FV	6.50
23	50 Maloti		
	2010. Brown and purple on multicolor underprint. Portraits of Kings Moshoeshoe II, Letsie III and Morena Moshoeshoe I. Back: Horsemen.	FV	17.00
24	100 Maloti		
	2010. Green on multicolor underprint. Portraits of Kings Moshoeshoe II, Letsie III and Morena Moshoeshoe I. Back: Goats.	FV	45.00

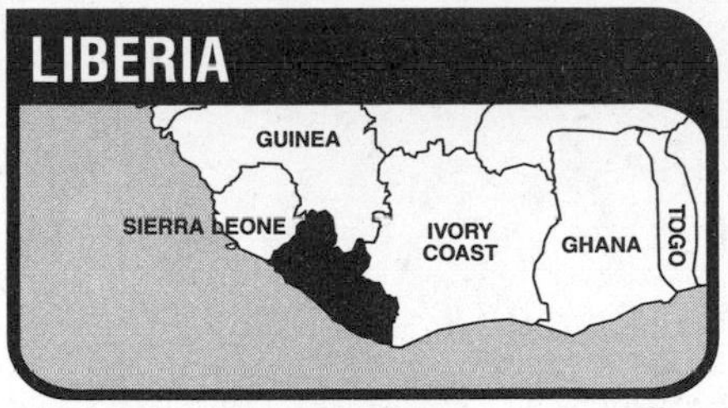

The Republic of Liberia, located on the southern side of the west African bulge between Sierra Leone and the Ivory Coast, has an area of 38,250 sq. mi. (111,369 sq. km.) and a population of 3.26 million. Capital: Monrovia. The major industries are agriculture, mining and lumbering. Iron ore, diamonds, rubber, coffee and cocoa are exported.

Settlement of freed slaves from the US in what is today Liberia began in 1822; by 1847, the Americo-Liberians were able to establish a republic. William Tubman, president from 1944-71, did much to promote foreign investment and to bridge the economic, social, and political gaps between the descendents of the original settlers and the inhabitants of the interior. In 1980, a military coup led by Samuel Doe ushered in a decade of authoritarian rule. In December 1989, Charles Taylor launched a rebellion against Doe's regime that led to a prolonged civil war in which Doe himself was killed. A period of relative peace in 1997 allowed for elections that brought Taylor to power, but major fighting resumed in 2000. An August 2003 peace agreement ended the war and prompted the resignation of former president Charles Taylor, who faces war crimes charges in The Hague related to his involvement in Sierra Leone's civil war. After two years of rule by a transitional government, democratic elections in late 2005 brought President Ellen Johnson Sirleaf to power. The UN Mission in Liberia (UNMIL) maintains a strong presence throughout the country, but the security situation is still fragile and the process of rebuilding the social and economic structure of this war-torn country will take many years.

MONETARY SYSTEM:

1 Dollar = 100 Cents

REPLACEMENT NOTES:

#19, 20: ZZ prefix.

Note: Certain listings encompassing issues circulated by various bank and regional authorities are contained in Volume 1.

REPUBLIC

NATIONAL BANK OF LIBERIA

1989 ISSUE

#19 replacement note: Serial # prefix *ZZ*.

19 5 Dollars VF 2.50 UNC 7.00

12.4.1989. Black and deep green on multicolor underprint. Latent image star at left, portrait J. J. Roberts at center, tapping trees at right. Back: Deep green on multicolor underprint. National Bank building at center. Printer: TDLR. 157x67mm.

1991 ISSUE

#20 replacement note: Serial # prefix *ZZ*.

20 5 Dollars VF 2.00 UNC 6.00

6.4.1991. Black and deep green on multicolor underprint. Latent image star at left, arms at center, tapping trees at right. Back: Deep green on multicolor underprint. National Bank building. Printer: TDLR. 157x67mm.

CENTRAL BANK OF LIBERIA

1999 ISSUE

21 5 Dollars VF FV UNC 2.50

1999. Red and brown on yellow underprint. Edward J. Roye at center. 2 signature varieties. Back: Female farmer harvesting rice, arms at left. *REPUBLIC OF LIBERIA* at top. Date for establishment of Central Bank shown as 1974. 157x67mm.

22 10 Dollars VF FV UNC 3.50

1999. Purple and black on multicolor underprint. Joseph Jenkins Roberts at center. Back: Worker tapping rubber, *REPUBLIC OF LIBERIA*. at top. 157x67mm.

23 20 Dollars

1999; 2002; 2003. Brown, black and olive on multicolor underprint. William V. S. Tubman, Sr. at center. Back: Market, *REPUBLIC OF LIBERIA*. at top. 157x67mm.

	VF	UNC
a. 1999.	FV	3.00
b. 2002.	FV	2.50
c. 2003.	FV	2.50

24 50 Dollars VF FV UNC 7.50

1999. Purple; red and blue on multicolor underprint. Samuel Kayon Doe at center. Back: Palm nut harvesting. Watermark: Arms. 157x67mm.

25 **100 Dollars**

1999. Green, brown and black on multicolor underprint. William R. Tolbert, Jr. at center. Back: Market woman and child. Watermark: Arms. 157x67mm.

	VF	UNC
	FV	15.00

2003 Issue

26 **5 Dollars**

2003-. Red and brown on yellow underprint. 2 signature varieties. Back: *CENTRAL BANK OF LIBERIA* at top. Printer: FC-O 157x67mm.

	VF	UNC
a. 2003.	FV	2.00
b. 2004.	FV	2.00
c. 2006.	FV	1.50
d. 2008.	FV	1.50

27 **10 Dollars**

2003-. Purple and black on multicolor underprint. 2 signature varieties. Back: *CENTRAL BANK OF LIBERIA* at top. . 157x67mm.

	VF	UNC
a. 2003.	FV	3.50
b. 2004.	FV	3.50
c. 2006.	FV	3.50
d. 2008.	FV	3.50
e. 2009.	FV	3.50
f. 2011.	FV	3.50

28 **20 Dollars**

2003-. Brown, black and olive on multicolor underprint. 2 signature varieties. Back: *CENTRAL BANK OF LIBERIA* at top. 157x67mm.

	VF	UNC
a. 2003.	FV	2.50
b. 2004.	FV	2.50
c. 2006.	FV	2.00
d. 2008.	FV	2.00
e. 2009.	FV	2.00
f. 2011.	FV	2.00

29 **50 Dollars**

2003-. Purple, red and blue on multicolor underprint. 2 signatures. Back: *CENTRAL BANK OF LIBERIA* at top. 157x67mm.

	VF	UNC
a. 2003.	FV	4.50
b. 2004.	FV	4.00
c. 2008.	FV	3.00
d. 2009.	FV	3.00
e. 2011.	FV	3.00

30 **100 Dollars**

2003-. Green, brown and black on multicolor underprint. 2 signature varieties. Back: *CENTRAL BANK OF LIBERIA* at top. 157x67mm.

	VF	UNC
a. 2003.	FV	6.00
b. 2004.	FV	6.00
c. 2006.	FV	5.50
d. 2008.	FV	5.00
e. 2009.	FV	5.00

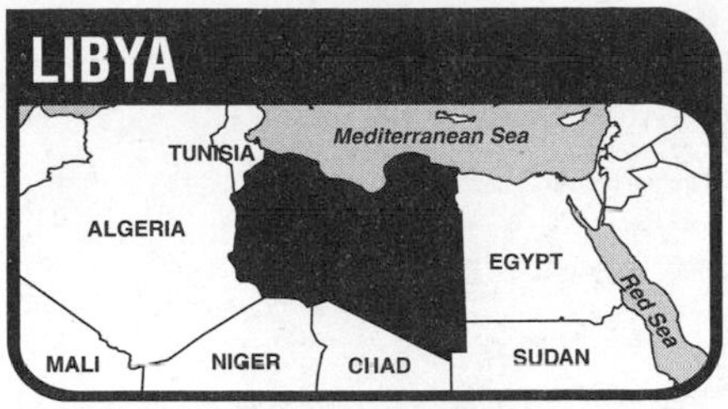

The Socialist People's Libyan Arab Jamahiriya, located on the north central coast of Africa between Tunisia and Egypt, has an area of 679,359 sq. mi. (1,759,540 sq. km.) and a population of 6.39 million. Capital: Tripoli. Crude oil, which accounts for 90 percent of the export earnings, is the mainstay of the economy.

The Italians supplanted the Ottoman Turks in the area around Tripoli in 1911 and did not relinquish their hold until 1943 when defeated in World War II. Libya then passed to UN administration and achieved independence in 1951. Following a 1969 military coup, Col. Muammar Abu Minyar al-Qadhafi began to espouse his own political system, the Third Universal Theory. The system is a combination of socialism and Islam derived in part from tribal practices and is supposed to be implemented by the Libyan people themselves in a unique form of "direct democracy." Qadhafi has always seen himself as a revolutionary and visionary leader. He used oil funds during the 1970s and 1980s to promote his ideology outside Libya, supporting subversives and terrorists abroad to hasten the end of Marxism and capitalism. In addition, beginning in 1973, he engaged in military operations in northern Chad's Aozou Strip - to gain access to minerals and to use as a of influence in Chadian politics - but was forced to retreat in 1987. UN sanctions in 1992 isolated Qadhafi politically following the downing of Pan AM Flight 103 over Lockerbie, Scotland. During the 1990s, Qadhafi began to rebuild his relationships with Europe. UN sanctions were suspended in April 1999 and finally lifted in September 2003 after Libya accepted responsibility for the Lockerbie bombing. In December 2003, Libya announced that it had agreed to reveal and end its programs to develop weapons of mass destruction and to renounce terrorism. Qadhafi has made significant strides in normalizing relations with Western nations since then. He has received various Western European leaders as well as many working-level and commercial delegations, and made his first trip to Western Europe in 15 years when he traveled to Brussels in April 2004. The US rescinded Libya's designation as a state sponsor of terrorism in June 2006. In January 2008, Libya assumed a nonpermanent seat on the United Nations Security Council for the 2008/09 term. In August 2008, the US and Libya signed a bilateral comprehensive claims settlement agreement to compensate claimants in both countries who allege injury or death at the hands of the other country, including the Lockerbie bombing, the LaBelle disco bombing, and the UTA 772 bombing. In October 2008, the US Government received $1.5 billion pursuant to the agreement to distribute to US national claimants, and as a result effectively normalized its bilateral relationship with Libya. The two countries then exchanged ambassadors for the first time since 1973 in January 2009.

RULERS:

Idris I, 1951-1969

MONETARY SYSTEM:

1 Piastre = 10 Milliemes
1 Pound = 100 Piastres = 1000 Milliemes, 1951-1971
1 Dinar = 1000 Dirhams, 1971-

CONSTITUTIONAL MONARCHY

BANK OF LIBYA

LAW OF 5.2.1963 - FIRST ISSUE

Pound System.

		VF	UNC
23	**1/4 Pound** *L.1963/AH1382.* Red on multicolor underprint. Crowned arms at left. Watermark: Arms.		
	a. Issued note.	20.00	150.
	s. Specimen.	—	—
24	**1/2 Pound** *L.1963/AH1382.* Purple on multicolor underprint. Crowned arms at left. Watermark: Arms.	37.50	250.
25	**1 Pound** *L.1963/AH1382.* Blue on multicolor underprint. Crowned arms at left. Watermark: Arms.	65.00	475.

		VF	UNC
26	**5 Pounds** *L.1963/AH1382.* Green on multicolor underprint. Crowned arms at left. Watermark: Arms.	250.	—

		VF	UNC
27	**10 Pounds** *L.1963/AH1382.* Brown on multicolor underprint. Crowned arms at left. Watermark: Arms.	350.	—

LAW OF 5.2.1963 - SECOND ISSUE

#28-32 Reduced size notes.

		VF	UNC
28	**1/4 Pound** *L.1963/AH1382.* Red on multicolor underprint. Crowned arms at left. Watermark: Arms.	25.00	175.
29	**1/2 Pound** *L.1963/AH1832.* Purple on multicolor underprint. Crowned arms at left. Watermark: Arms.	35.00	325.
30	**1 Pound** *L.1963/AH1382.* Blue on multicolor underprint. Crowned arms at left. Watermark: Arms.	50.00	425.

			VF	UNC
31	**5 Pounds**	*L.1963/AH1382.* Green on multicolor underprint. Crowned arms at left. Watermark: Arms.	150.	700.

			VF	UNC
32	**10 Pounds**	*L.1963/AH1382.* Brown on multicolor underprint. Crowned arms at left. Watermark: Arms.	250.	1650.

Socialist Peoples Republic

SIGNATURE VARIETIES			
1		2	
3		4	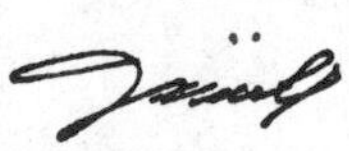
5	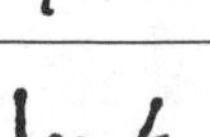	6	
7	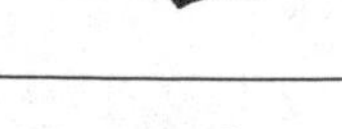	8	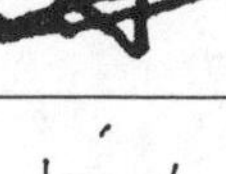
9	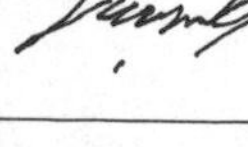	10	

Central Bank of Libya

1971 Issue - Series 1

Dinar System.

The series is indicated by the digit placed before the serial number prefix fraction.

			VF	UNC
33	**1/4 Dinar**	ND. Orange-brown on multicolor underprint. Arms at left, Arabic inscription at bottom of watermark area at lower right. Signature 1. Back: Doorway. Watermark: Arms (Heraldic eagle).		
		a. Without inscription (1971).	20.00	150.
		b. With inscription (1972).	10.00	35.00
		s. Specimen. Red overprint in Arabic.	—	100.

			VF	UNC
34	**1/2 Dinar**	ND. Purple on multicolor underprint. Arms at left, Arabic inscription at bottom of watermark area at lower right. Signature 1. Back: Oil refinery. Watermark: Arms (Heraldic eagle).		
		a. Without inscription (1971).	35.00	225.
		b. With inscription (1972).	15.00	60.00
		s. Specimen. Red overprint in Arabic.	—	250.

			VF	UNC
35	**1 Dinar**	ND. Blue on multicolor underprint. Gate and minatet at left, Arabic inscription at botto9m of watermark area at lower right. Signature 1.. Back: Hilltop fortress. Watermark: Arms (Heraldic eagle).		
		a. Without inscription (1971).	45.00	425.
		b. With inscription (1972).	25.00	100.
		s. Specimen. Red overprint in Arabic.	—	500.

36	5 Dinars	VF	UNC
	ND. Olive on multicolor underprint. Arms at left, Arabic inscription at bottom of watermark area at lower right. Signature 1. Back: Fortress at center. Watermark: Arms (Heraldic eagle).		
	a. Without inscription (1971).	75.00	600.
	b. With inscription (1972).	15.00	125.
	s. Specimen. Red overprint in Arabic.	—	750.

37	10 Dinars	VF	UNC
	ND. Blue-gray on multcolor underprint. Omar El Mukhtar at left, without Arabic inscription. Signature 1. Back: Three horsemen at center. Watermark: Arms (Heraldic eagle).		
	a. Without inscription (1971).	100.	750.
	b. With inscription (1972).	12.50	50.00
	s. Specimen. Red overprint in Arabic.	—	1000.

1980-81 Issue - Series 2

42A	1/4 Dinar	VF	UNC
	ND (1981). Green on multicolor underprint. Ruins at left. Back: Fortress and palms at center right. Watermark: Heraldic falcon.		
	a. Signature 1.	1.75	6.00
	b. Signature 2.	1.50	4.50

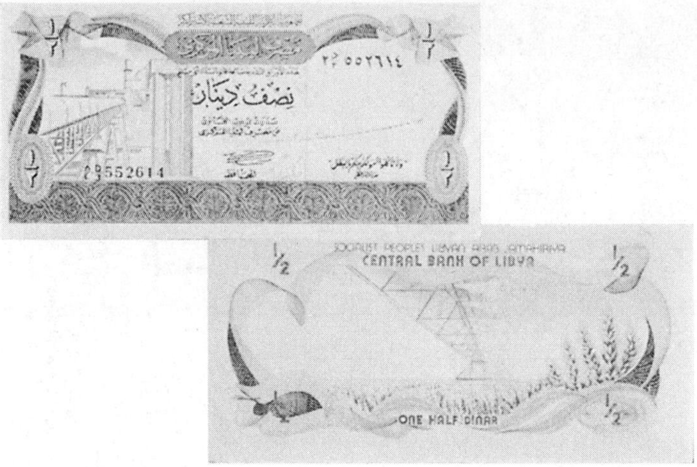

43	1/2 Dinar	VF	UNC
	ND (1981). Green on multicolor underprint. Petroleum refinery at left. Back: Irrigation system above wheat field. Watermark: Heraldic falcon.		
	a. Signature 1.	3.00	7.50
	b. Signature 2.	2.25	6.00

44	1 Dinar	VF	UNC
	ND (1981). Green on multicolor underprint. Mosque at left. Back: Interior of mosque at center right. Watermark: Heraldic falcon.		
	a. Signature 1.	4.00	11.50
	b. Signature 2.	3.00	10.00

45	5 Dinars	VF	UNC
	ND (1980). Green on multicolor underprint. Camels at left. Back: Crowd around monument at center right. Watermark: Heraldic falcon.		
	a. Signature 1.	12.00	50.00
	b. Signature 2.	10.00	40.00

46 **10 Dinars**

ND (1980). Green on multicolor underprint. Omar El Mukhtar at left. Back: Large crowd below hilltop fortress at center. Watermark: Heraldic falcon.

	VF	UNC
a. Signature 1.	22.00	85.00
b. Signature 2.	20.00	60.00

1984 Issue - Series 3

47 **1/4 Dinar**

ND (1984). Green and brown on multicolor underprint. Ruins at left. Signature 2. Back: Fortress and palms at center right. Watermark: Heraldic falcon.

VF	UNC
2.50	10.00

48 **1/2 Dinar**

ND (1984). Green and purple on multicolor underprint. Petroleum refinery at left. Signature 2. Back: Irrigation system above wheat field. Watermark: Heraldic falcon.

VF	UNC
2.50	10.00

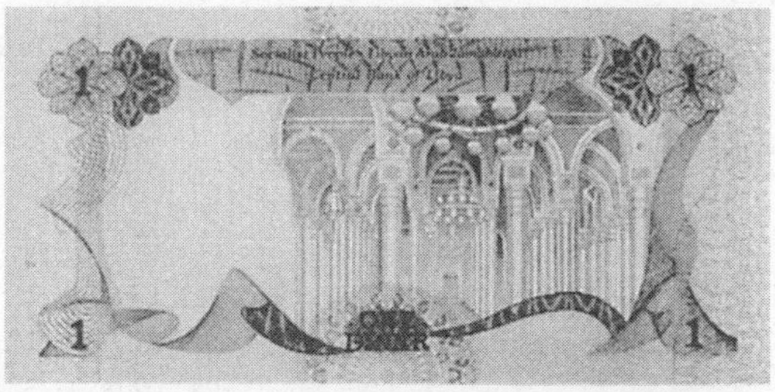

49 **1 Dinar**

ND (1984). Green and dark blue on multicolor underprint. Mosque at left. Signature 2. Back: Interior of mosque at center right. Watermark: Heraldic falcon.

VF	UNC
4.00	15.00

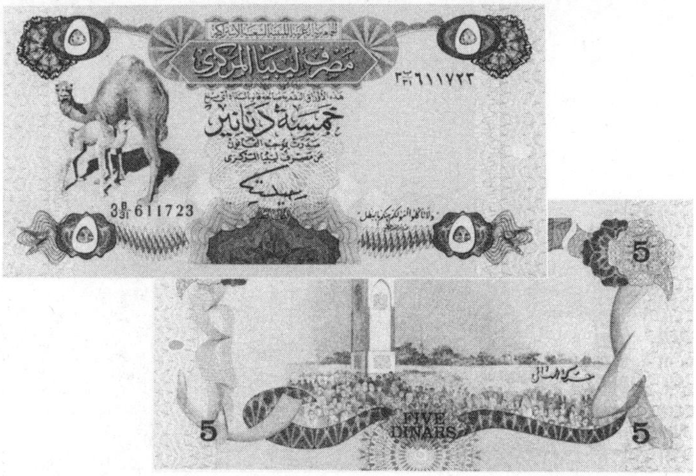

50 **5 Dinars**

ND (1984). Dark olive-green and light green on multicolor underprint. Camels at left. Signature 2. Back: Crowd around monument at center right. Watermark: Heraldic falcon.

VF	UNC
12.50	50.00

51 **10 Dinars**

ND (1984). Dark green and blue-green on multicolor underprint. Omar El Mukhtar at left. Signature 2. Back: Large crowd below hilltop fortress at center. Watermark: Heeraldic falcon.

VF	UNC
15.00	60.00

1988-90 Issue - Series 4

52 1/4 Dinar — VF UNC

ND (ca.1990). Green, blue and black on multicolor underprint. Ruins at center. Signature 3. Back: Brown. English text at top, fortress with palm trees at left center. Watermark: Heraldic falcon. — 1.00 4.00

53 1/2 Dinar — VF UNC

ND (ca.1990). Deep purple and aqua on multicolor underprint. Oil refinery at left center. Signature 3. Back: Purple. English text at top, irrigation system at left center. Watermark: Heraldic falcon. — 1.75 7.50

54 1 Dinar — VF UNC

ND (1988). Blue and green on multicolor underprint. Muammar Qaddafi at left center. Signature 3. Back: Temple at lower center right. Watermark: Heraldic falcon. — 2.50 10.00

55 5 Dinars

ND (ca.1991). Brown and violet on multicolor underprint. Camel at center. Signature 3. Back: Crowd and monument. English text at top. Watermark: Heraldic falcon. — 8.00 35.00

56 10 Dinars

ND (1989). Green on multicolor underprint. Omar el-Mukhtar at left. Signature 3. Back: Arabic text; large crowd before hilltop fortress at center. Octagonal frame without underprint at upper right. Watermark: Heraldic falcon. — 15.00 60.00

1991-93 Issue - Series 4

57 1/4 Dinar

ND (ca.1991). Green, blue and black on multicolor underprint, more pink in underprint. Ruins at center. Back: Arabic text at top, fortress with palm trees at left center. Watermark: Heraldic falcon. 142x71mm.

	VF	UNC
a. Signature 3.	1.00	5.00
b. Signature 4.	1.00	4.00
c. Signature 5.	.75	3.00

58 1/2 Dinar

ND (ca. 1991). Deep purple and blue on multicolor underprint. Oil refinery at left center. Back: All Arabic text, irrigation system at left center. Watermark: Heraldic falcon. More color in underprint at upper corners. 152x76mm.

	VF	UNC
a. Signature 3.	1.50	6.00
b. Signature 4.	1.00	5.00
c. Signature 5.	1.00	4.00

59 1 Dinar

ND (1993). Blue and green on multicolor underprint. Muammar Qaddafi at left center. Back: Temple at lower center right. Watermark: Heraldic falcon. Modified green and pink underprint. 162x81mm.

	VF	UNC
a. Signature 4.	2.00	7.50
b. Signature 5.	1.50	6.00

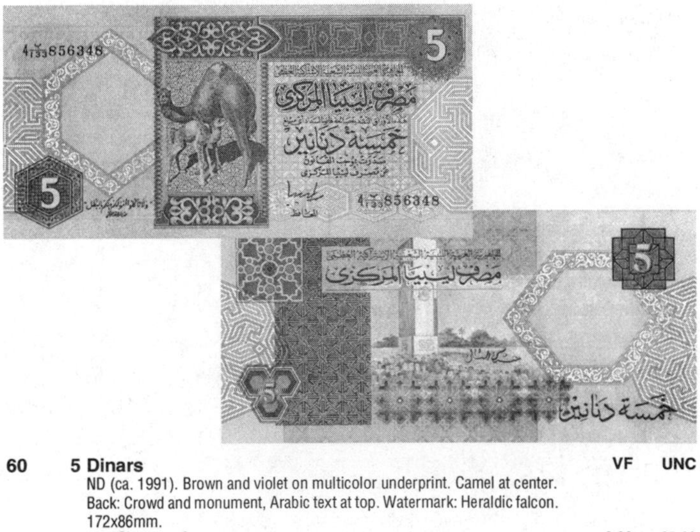

60 5 Dinars

ND (ca. 1991). Brown and violet on multicolor underprint. Camel at center. Back: Crowd and monument, Arabic text at top. Watermark: Heraldic falcon. 172x86mm.

	VF	UNC
a. Signature 3.	8.00	35.00
b. Signature 4.	7.00	30.00
c. Signature 5.	6.00	25.00

61 **10 Dinars** VF UNC

ND (1991). Green on multicolor underprint. Omar el-Mukhtar at left. Back: Large crowd before hilltop fortress at center, octagonal frame with underprint at upper right. 182x91mm.

	VF	UNC
a. Signature 4.	10.00	45.00
b. Signature 5.	10.00	45.00

2002 Issue - Series 5

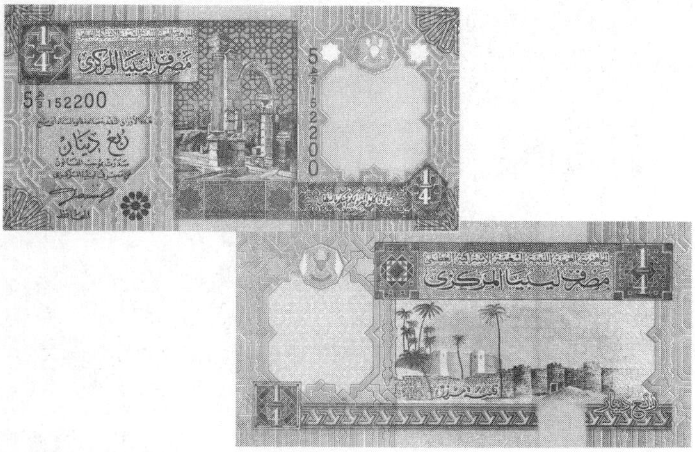

62 **1/4 Dinar** VF UNC

	VF	UNC
ND (2002). Ochre on multicolor underprint. Ruins at center.Signature 4. Back: Walled compound. 142x71mm.	.75	2.50

63 **1/2 Dinar** VF UNC

	VF	UNC
ND (2002). Dark blue on blue and multicolor underprint. Oil refinery at center. Signature 4. Back: Irrigation system. 152x76mm.	1.00	4.00

64 **1 Dinar**

ND (2002). Blue and green on multicolor underprint. Muammar Qaddafi at center. Back: Mosque. 162x81mm.

	VF	UNC
a. Signature 4.	1.50	6.00
b. Signature 5.	1.50	6.00

65 **5 Dinars** VF UNC

ND (2002). Green and yellow on multicolor underprint. Camels at center. Back: Monument and crowd. 172x86mm.

	VF	UNC
a. Signature 4.	FV	22.50
b. Signature 5.	FV	22.50

66 **10 Dinars**

	VF	UNC
ND (2002). Green and dark green on multicolor underprint. Omar el-Mukhtar at center left. Signature 4. Back: Fortress and crowd. 182x91mm.	FV	30.00

67 **20 Dinars** VF UNC

ND (2002). Green, blue and brown on multicolor underprint. Map with water tunnels at center. Signature 6. Series 1. Back: Muammar Qaddafi with OAU members at center, map of Africa at right. 9.9.1999 meeting date. 166x83mm.

	VF	UNC
a. Signatrue 6.	FV	45.00
b. Signature 7.	FV	40.00

2004 Issue - Series 6

#68-70 are reduced in size.

68 **1 Dinar** VF UNC

ND (2004). Purple and blue on multicolor underprint. Muammar Qaddafi at center. Back: Mosque. 142x71mm.

	VF	UNC
a. Signature 6.	FV	7.50
b. Signatrue 7.	FV	6.00

69 **5 Dinars** | VF | UNC

ND (2004). Black and violet on multicolor underprint. Camels at center. Back: Monument and crowd. 149x75mm.

	VF	UNC
a. Signature 6.	FV	15.00
b. Signature 7.	FV	12.50

70 **10 Dinars** | VF | UNC

ND (2004). Multicolor. Omar el-Mukhtar at center. Back: Fortress and crowd. 157x79mm.

	VF	UNC
a. Signature 6.	FV	26.00
b. Signature 7.	FV	22.50

2008 Issue - Series 7

71 **1 Dinar** | VF | UNC

ND (2009). Blue and multicolor. Muammar Qaddafi. Back: Mosque. Watermark: Qaddafi and 1 140x70mm. | FV | 5.00

72 **5 Dinars** | VF | UNC

2011. Red and multicolor. Two camels at right. Back: Monument. Watermark: Camels and 5 150x75mm. | FV | 11.50

73 **10 Dinars** | VF | UNC

2.17.2011. Green and multicolor. Omar el-Mukhtar at right. Back: Fortress and crowd. Watermark: Omar el-Mukhtar and 10 Bank name on back in Upper and Lower case English letters. 156x78mm. | FV | 20.00

74 **20 Dinars**

ND (2009). Purple and tan on multicolor underprint. Map of Northern Africa. Back: Organization of African Unity leaders. 166x81mm. | FV | 30.00

75 **50 Dinars**

ND (2008). Brown and tan on multicolor underprint. Muammar Qaddafi at right. Back: Building. | 15.00 | 65.00

Post Revolutionary

Central Bank of Libya

2012-13 Issue

76 **1 Dinar** | VF | UNC

ND (2013). Purple, violet and multicolor. Citizens with flags in celebration at lower right. Cornerstone devices. Back: Lybian flag and flock of doves. Watermark: Omar al-Mukhtar and value. Printer: DLR. 130x65mm. | FV | 6.00

77 **5 Dinars**

ND (2013). Expected new issue. | — | —

78 **10 Dinars**

ND (2012). Name of the bank on back in upper case English letters. | FV | 20.00

79 **20 Dinars** | VF | UNC

2012. Red and orange on multicolor underprint. School in Ghadames. Back: Al-Ateeq mosque in Oujlah. Watermark: Omar al-Mukhtar. 148x74mm. | FV | 35.00

80 **50 Dinars**

ND (2013). Green on multicolor underprint. 1922 Italian lighthouse in Benghazi. SPARK patch with crescent moon and star, cornerstone devices. Back: Rock arch in Tadrart Acacus. Watermark: Omar el-Mukhtar and value. Printer: TDLR. 155x77mm. | FV | 95.00

The Republic of Lithuania southernmost of the Baltic states in east Europe, has an area of 26,173 sq. mi. (65,301 sq. km.) and a population of 3.69 million. Capital: Vilnius. The economy is d on livestock raising and manufacturing. Hogs, cattle, hides and electric motors are exported.

Lithuanian lands were united under Mlinfaugas in 1236; over the next century, through alliances and conquest, Lithuania extended its territory to include most of present-day Belarus and Ukraine. By the end of the 14th century Lithuania was the largest state in Europe. An alliance with Poland in 1386 led the two countries into a union through the person of a common ruler. In 1569, Lithuania and Poland formally united into a single dual state, the Polish-Lithuanian Commonwealth. This entity survived until 1795, when its remnants were partitioned by surrounding countries. Lithuania regained its independence following World War I but was annexed by the USSR in 1940 - an action never recognized by the US and many other countries. On 11 March 1990, Lithuania became the first of the Soviet republics to declare its independence, but Moscow did not recognize this proclamation until September of 1991 (following the abortive coup in Moscow). The last Russian troops withdrew in 1993. Lithuania subsequently restructured its economy for integration into Western European institutions; it joined both NATO and the EU in the spring of 2004.

MONETARY SYSTEM:

1 Litas = 100 Centu

Republic

Lietuvos Bankas

Bank of Lithuania

1991 Issue

Talonas System.

29 0.10 Talonas — VF UNC

1991. Brown on green and gold underprint. Plants. Back: Arms at center in gray. Watermark: Design.

	VF	UNC
a. Without 3 lines of black text at center.	1.00	3.00
b. With 3 lines of black text at center.	1.00	2.00
x. Error. As b. but with text: *PAGAL ISTATYMA* repeated.	5.00	10.00

30 0.20 Talonas

	VF	UNC
1991. Lilac on green and gold underprint. Plants, three lines of black text at center. Back: Arms at center in gray. Watermark: Design.	1.00	4.00

31 0.50 Talonas

1991. Blue-green on green and gold underprint. Plants. Back: Arms at center in gray. Watermark: Design.

	VF	UNC
a. Without 3 lines of black text at center.	1.00	2.00
b. With 3 lines of black text at center.	1.00	4.00
x1. As b. but first word of text: *VALSTYBINIS.* (error).	—	3.00
x2. As x1 but with inverted text. (contemporary counterfeit).	—	—

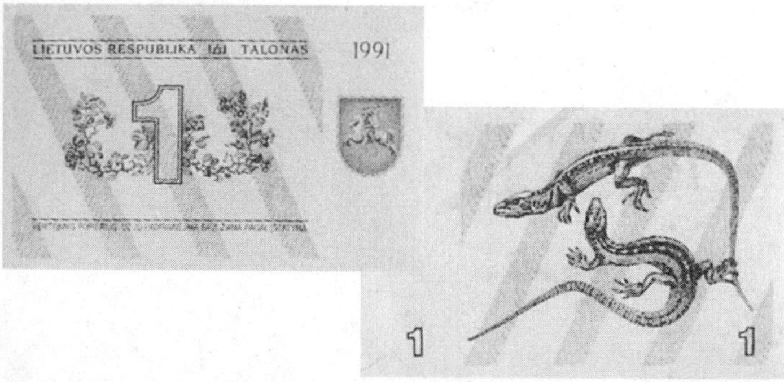

32 1 (Talonas) — VF UNC

1991. Brown on yellow-gold underprint. Value with cranberry branch at center, arms in gray at right. Counterfeiting clause at bottom. Back: Two lizards. Watermark: Large squarish diamond with symbol of the republic throughout paper.

	VF	UNC
a. Without counterfeit text at bottom.	1.50	3.00
b. With counterfeit text at bottom.	1.50	3.00

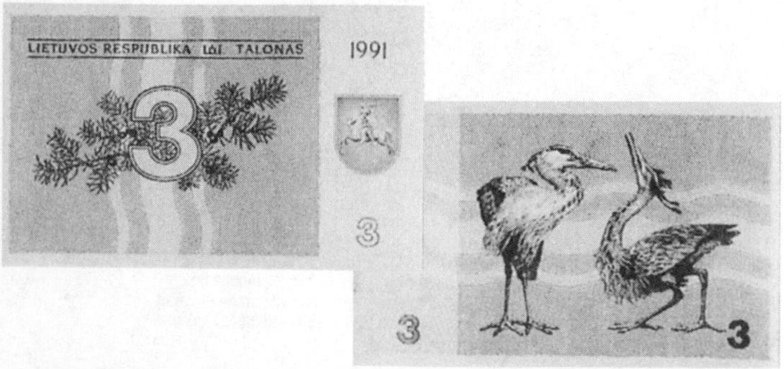

33 3 (Talonas) — VF UNC

1991. Dark green and gray on blue-green, ochre and brown underprint Value with Juniper branch at center, arms in gray at right. Back: Two Grey Herons. Watermark: Large squarish diamond with symbol of the republic throughout paper.

	VF	UNC
a. Without counterfeit text at bottom.	3.00	5.00
b. With counterfeit text at bottom.	2.00	5.00

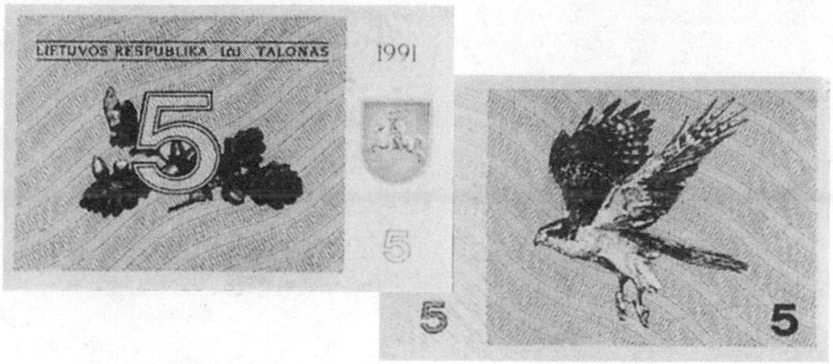

34 5 (Talonas) — VF UNC

1991. Dark purple and gray on blue and gray underprint. Value with oak tree branch at center, arms in gray at right. Back: Osprey at center. Watermark: Large squarish diamond with symbol of the republic throughout paper.

	VF	UNC
a. Without counterfeit text at bottom.	5.00	15.00
b. With counterfeit text at bottom.	3.00	5.00

35 10 (Talonas) — VF UNC

1991. Brown on pinkish underprint. Value with walnut tree branch at center, arms in gray at right. Counterfeiting clause at bottom. Back: Two martens. Watermark: Large squarish diamond with symbol of the republic throughout paper.

	VF	UNC
a. Without counterfeit text at bottom.	10.00	30.00
b. With counterfeit text at bottom.	5.00	10.00

36 25 (Talonas) — VF UNC

1991. Purplish gray on blue and orange underprint. Value with pine tree branch at center, arms in gray at right. Counterfeiting clause at bottom. Back: Lynx. Watermark: Large squarish diamond with symbol of the republic throughout paper.

	VF	UNC
a. Without counterfeit text at bottom.	15.00	40.00
b. With counterfeit text at bottom.	5.00	10.00

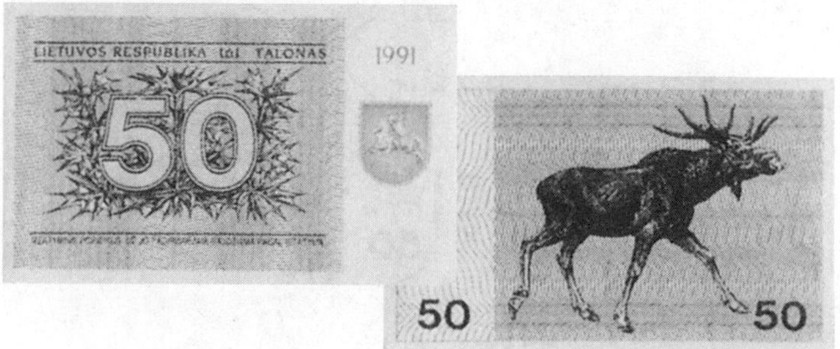

37 50 (Talonas) — VF UNC

1991. Green and orange on orange underprint. Value with seashore plant at center, arms in gray at right. Counterfeiting clause at bottom. Back: Moose. Watermark: Large squarish diamond with symbol of the republic throughout paper.

	VF	UNC
a. Without counterfeit text at bottom.	10.00	30.00
b. With counterfeit text at bottom.	5.00	10.00

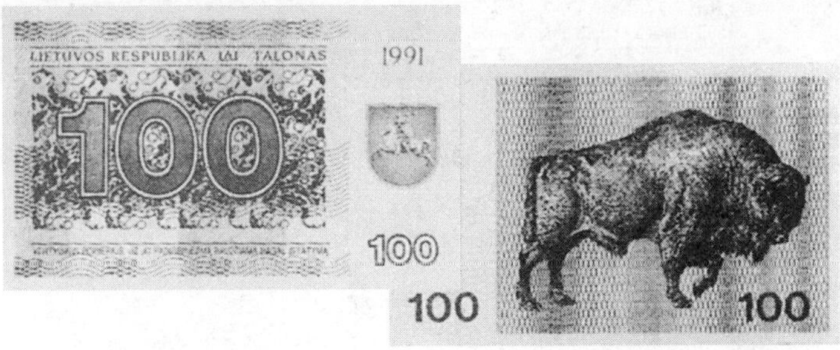

38 **100 (Talonas)** — VF | UNC

1991. Green and brown on brown underprint. Value and dandelions at center, arms in gray at right. Counterfeiting clause at bottom. Back: European bison. Watermark: Large squarish diamond with symbol of the republic throughout paper.

	VF	UNC
a. Without counterfeit text at bottom.	15.00	40.00
b. With counterfeit text at bottom.	5.00	10.00
s. Specimen. Red overprint: *PAVYZDYS*.	—	100.

1992 Issue

#39-44 Smaller size

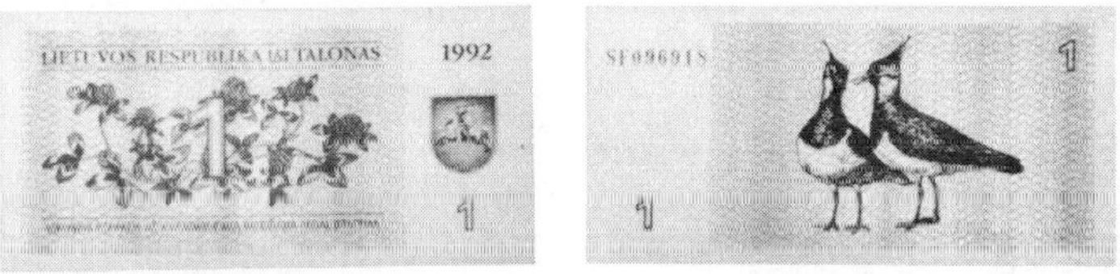

		VF	UNC
39	**1 (Talonas)** 1992. Brown on orange and ochre underprint. Value on plant at center, dark brown shield of arms at right. Back: Two Eurasian lapwings. Watermark: Large squarish diamond with symbol of the republic throughout paper.	1.00	3.00

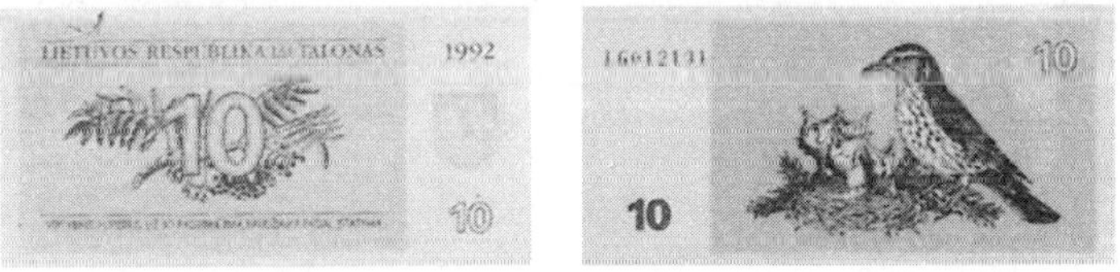

		VF	UNC
40	**10 (Talonas)** 1992. Brown on tan and ochre underprint. Value on plant at center, gray shield of arms at right. Back: Nest of mistle thrush. Watermark: Large squarish diamond with symbol of the republic throughout paper.	6.00	15.00

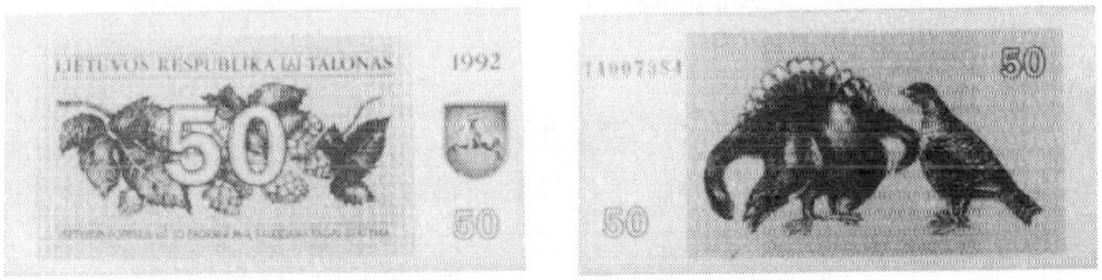

		VF	UNC
41	**50 (Talonas)** 1992. Dark grayish green on light green and gray underprint. Value on plant at center, dark gray-green shield of arms at right. Back: Two black grouse. Watermark: Large squarish diamond with symbol of the republic throughout paper.	15.00	40.00

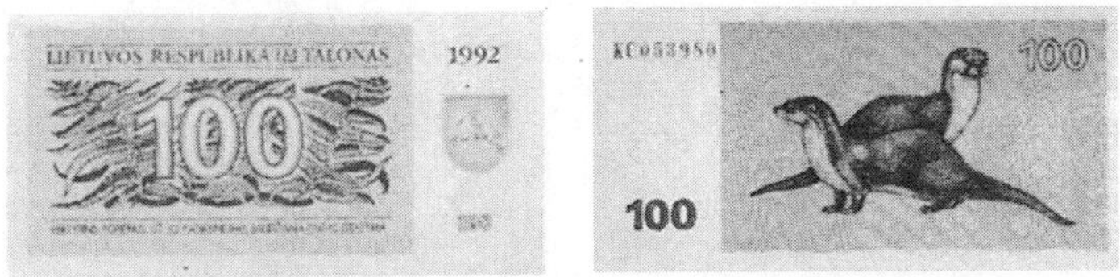

		VF	UNC
42	**100 (Talonas)** 1992. Grayish purple on blue and red-orange underprint. Value on plant at center, gray. shield of arms at right. Back: Two otters. Watermark: Large squarish diamond with symbol of the republic throughout paper.	8.00	16.00

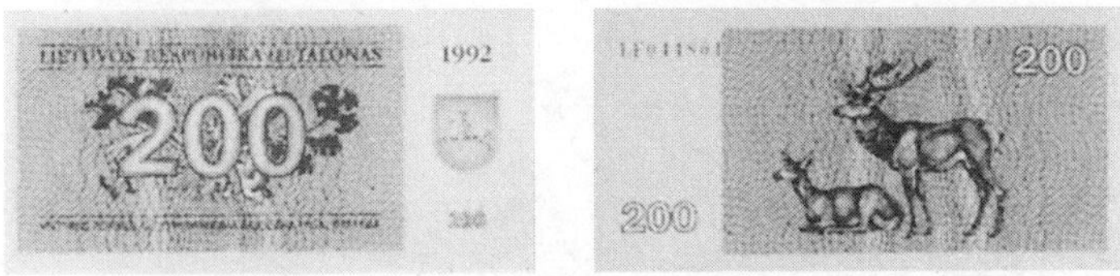

43 **200 (Talonas)** — VF | UNC

1992. Dark brown on red and brown underprint. Value on plant at center, gray shield of arms at right. Back: Two Red deer. Watermark: Large squarish diamond with symbol of the republic throughout paper.

	VF	UNC
a. Issued note.	8.00	16.00
x. Error. Without gray shield at right.	—	—

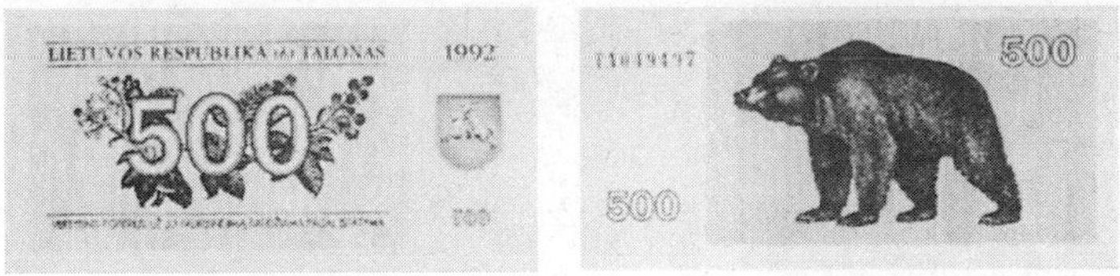

		VF	UNC
44	**500 (Talonas)** 1992. Brown-violet on blue underprint. Value on plant at center, brown shield of arms at right. Back: Bear. Watermark: Large squarish diamond with symbol of the republic throughout paper.	3.00	6.00

1993 Issue

		VF	UNC
45	**200 Talonu** 1993. Brown and red on blue underprint. Value with branches at center, brown arms at left. Back: Two Red Deer. Watermark: Circle with design inside, repeated.	2.00	5.00

		VF	UNC
46	**500 Talonu** 1993. Brown on blue and brown underprint. Value with branches at center, brown arms at left. Back: Two wolves. Watermark: Circle with design inside, repeated.	2.00	4.00

1991 Dated Issue (1993)

47 **10 Litu** — VF | UNC

1991 (1993). Brownish black and brown on tan underprint. Aviators Steponas Darius and Stasys Girėnas at center. Back: Monoplane *Lituanica* at upper center, arms "Vytis" at upper right. Watermark: Arms "Vytis". Printer: USBNC (without imprint). 135x65mm.

	VF	UNC
a. *GIRENAS* name without accent dot on E (error).	10.00	25.00
b. *GIRĖNAS* name with accent dot on E.	10.00	30.00
x. Quadrupled engraved face printing. Error.	—	300.

		VF	UNC
48	**20 Litu** 1991 (1993). Dark brown and green on violet and tan underprint. Jonas Maironis at right. Back: Liberty at left, Museum of History in Kaunas at center, arms "Vytis" at upper right. Watermark: Arms "Vytis". Printer: USBNC (without imprint). 135x65mm.	15.00	40.00

49	50 Litu	VF	UNC
	1991 (1993). Yellowish black and brown on ochre and tan underprint. Jonas Basanavicius at right. Back: Cathedral at Vilnius at left, arms "Vytis" at upper right. Watermark: Arms "Vytis". Printer: USBNC (without imprint). 135x65mm.		
	a. VALDYBOS with regular L.	30.00	80.00
	b. VALDYBOS with heel on L (error).	35.00	80.00

50	100 Litu	VF	UNC
	1991 (1993); 1994. Deep green, blue and brown on multicolor underprint. Arms "Vytis" at center, Simonas Daukantas at right. Back: Brown and green. Aerial view of University of Vinius at left center. 135x65mm.		
	a. 1991. One signature.	70.00	180.
	b. 1994. Two signatures (Not issued.)	—	—
51	**500 Litu**		
	1991. Arms "Vytis" at center, Vincas Kudirka at right. Back: Liberty bell. (Not issued). 135x65mm.	—	—
52	**1000 Litu**		
	1991. Arms "Vytis" at center, Mykolas Ciurlionis at right. Back: Two Kings. (Not issued). 135x65mm.		
	a. Unissued note.	—	—
	s. Specimen. Overprint: *SPECIMEN* and serial #0000000.	—	2100.

1993; 1994 Issue

53	1 Litas	VF	UNC
	1994. Black and dark brown on orange and multicolor underprint. Julija Zemaite at right. Back: Shield with "Vytis" at center, old church at left. Watermark: Arms "Vytis." Printer: TDLR (without imprint). UV: value 1 in box fluoresce yellow, right design yellow, fibers red and green. 135x65mm.		
	a. Issued note.	2.00	5.00
	b. Uncut sheet of 40.	—	150.
	r. Replacement note, ZZ serial # prefix.	3.00	14.00

54	2 Litai	VF	UNC
	1993. Black and dark green on pale green and multicolor underprint. Samogitian Bishop Motiejus Valancius at center right. Back: Shield with "Vytis" at center. Trakai castle at left. Watermark: Arms "Vytis." Printer: TDLR (without imprint). 135x65mm.		
	a. Issued note.	5.00	10.00
	b. Uncut sheet of 40.	—	250.
	r. Replacement note, ZZ serial # prefix.	5.00	20.00

55	5 Litai	VF	UNC
	1993. Purple, violet and dark blue-green on multicolor underprint. Jonas Jablonskis at center right. Back: Shield with "Vytis" at center. Mother and daughter at spinning wheel at left center. Watermark: Arms "Vytis." Printer: TDLR (without imprint). 135x65mm.		
	a. Issued note.	10.00	25.00
	b. Uncut sheet of 40.	—	450.
	r. Replacement note, ZZ serial # prefix.	10.00	30.00

56	10 Litu	VF	UNC
	1993. Dark blue, dark green, and brown-violet on multicolor underprint. Aviators Steponas Darius and Stasys Girénas at right. Back: Shield with "Vytis" at center, monoplane "Lituanica" at upper center. Watermark: Arms "Vytis." Printer: TDLR (without imprint). 135x65mm.		
	a. Issued note.	10.00	25.00
	r. Replacement note, *(letter) as serial # prefix.	15.00	30.00

57	20 Litu	VF	UNC
	1993. Dark brown, purple and deep blue-green on multicolor underprint. Jonas Maironis at right. Back: Shield with "Vytis" at center. Liberty at left, Museum of History in Kaunas at center. Watermark: Arms "Vytis." Printer: TDLR (without imprint). 135x65mm.		
	a. Issued note.	15.00	35.00
	r. Replacement note, *(letter) as serial # prefix.	20.00	40.00

58 50 Litu
1993. Dark brown, red-brown and blue-black on multicolor underprint. Jonas Basanavicius at right. Back: Shield with "Vytis" at center, Cathedral at Vilnius at left. Watermark: Arms "Vytis." Printer: TDLR (without imprint). 135x65mm.

	VF	UNC
a. Issued note.	30.00	70.00
r. Replacement note, * (letter) as serial # prefix.	40.00	80.00

1997-2000 Issue

59 10 Litu
1997. Dark blue, dark green and brown-violet on multicolor underprint. Aviators Steponas Darius and Stasys Girėnas at right. One signature. Back: Shield with "Vytis" at center, monoplane *Lituanica* at upper center. Watermark: Arms "Vytis". Printer: G&D (without imprint). 135x65mm.

VF	UNC
10.00	20.00

60 20 Litu
1997. Dark brown, purple and deep green on multicolor underprint. Jonas Maironis at right, one signature. Back: Shield with "Vytis" at center. Liberty at left. Museum of History in Kaunas at center. Watermark: Jonas Maironis. Printer: G&D (without imprint). 135x65mm.

VF	UNC
10.00	30.00

61 50 Litu
1998. Brown and green on ochre and multicolor underprint. Jonas Basanavicius at right. Back: Vilnius Cathedral, belfry and Gediminas hill. Printer: G&D (without imprint). 135x65mm.

VF	UNC
30.00	70.00

62 100 Litu
2000. Dark green and green on multicolor underprint. Simonas Daukantas at right. Back: Vilnius's Old Town view. Printer: OFZ. 135x62mm.

VF	UNC
FV	130.

63 200 Litu
1997. Dark blue on blue and multicolor underprint. Vilius Vydúnas at right, "Vytis" at lower left center. Back: Lighthouse at left. Printer: G&D. 135x65mm.

VF	UNC
FV	260.

64 500 Litu
2000. Brown and rose on multicolor underprint. Vincas Kudirka at right. Back: Bell of Freedom of Lithuania against landscape view. Printer: G&D. 135x65mm.

VF	UNC
FV	650.

2001-03 Issue

#65-67 Replacement notes *AZ* serial # prefix.

65 10 Litu
2001. Violet and blue on multicolor underprint. Aviators Steponas Darius and Stasys Girėnas at right. One signature. Security features and an airplane hologram at lower left. Back: Shield with "Vytis" at center, monoplane *Lituanica* at upper center. Watermark: "Vytis." Printer: OFZ. 135x65mm.

VF	UNC
FV	15.00

66 20 Litu
2001. Dark brown on multicolor underprint. Jonas Maironis at right, additional security features. Back: Book and quill hologram at lower left. Watermark: Jonas Maironis. Printer: OFZ. 135x65mm.

VF	UNC
FV	30.00

#	Description	VF	UNC
67	**50 Litu** 2003. Brown and green on ochre and multicolor underprint. Jonas Basanavicius at right, added security features. Back: Vilnius Cathedral, belfry and Gediminas hill. Watermark: Jonas Basanavicius. Printer: OFZ. 135x65mm.	FV	65.00

2007 Issue

#	Description	VF	UNC
68	**10 Litu** 2007. Slate Blue and blue, green on multicolor underprint. Aviators Steponas Darius and Stasys Girėnas at right. Back: Blue on multicolor underprint. Monoplane *Lituabica* above clouds, maps of North America and Europe. Watermark: Vytis Printer: G&D. 135x65mm.	FV	10.00

#	Description	VF	UNC
69	**20 Litu** 2007. Brown and lilac on multicolor underprint. Jonas Maironis at right. Back: Lilac and blue. Liberty statue, Museum of History in Kaunas at center. Watermark: Jonas Maironis Printer: G&D. 135x65mm.	FV	15.00

#	Description	VF	UNC
70	**100 Litu** 2007. Brown adn green on multicolor underprint. Simonas Daukantas at right. Back: Green and tan. Vilnius's old town view. Watermark: Simonas Daukantas Printer: G&D. 135x65mm.	FV	80.00

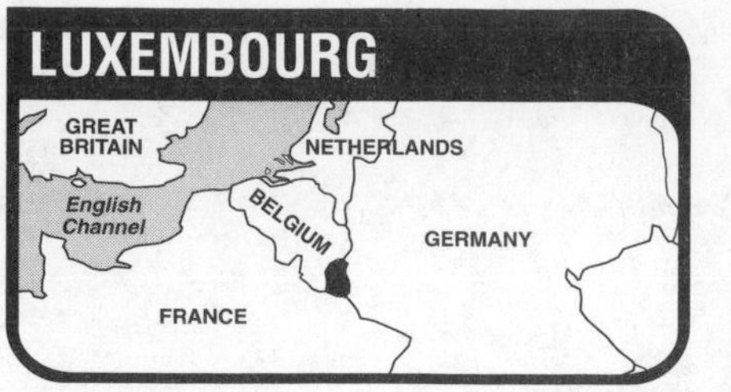

The Grand Duchy of Luxembourg is located in western Europe between Belgium, Germany and France. It has an area of 998 sq. mi. (2,586 sq. km.) and a population of 430,000. Capital: Luxembourg. The economy is d on steel - Luxembourg's per capita production of 16 tons is the highest in the world.

Founded in 963, Luxembourg became a grand duchy in 1815 and an independent state under the Netherlands. It lost more than half of its territory to Belgium in 1839, but gained a larger measure of autonomy. Full independence was attained in 1867. Overrun by Germany in both World Wars, it ended its neutrality in 1948 when it entered into the Benelux Customs Union and when it joined NATO the following year. In 1957, Luxembourg became one of the six founding countries of the European Economic Community (later the European Union), and in 1999 it joined the euro currency area

RULERS:

William III (Netherlands), 1849-90 (represented by brother Henry)
Adolphe, 1890-1905
William IV, 1905-12
Marie Adelaide, 1912-19
Charlotte, 1919-64
Jean, 1964-

MONETARY SYSTEM:

1 Thaler = 30 Groschen
1 Mark = 100 Pfennig = 1 Franc (Franken) 25 Centimes
1 Franc = 100 Centimes, to 2001
1 Euro = 100 Cents, 2001-

Grand Duchy

Banque Internationale a Luxembourg

International Bank in Luxembourg

1968 Issue

#	Description	VF	UNC
14	**100 Francs** 1.5.1968. Green-blue and blue on multicolor underprint. Tower at left, portrait Grand Duke Jean at right. Back: Steelworks and dam. Watermark: *BIL*. Printer: F-CO.		
	a. Issued note.	4.00	15.00
	s. Specimen.	—	65.00

1981 Issue

#	Description	VF	UNC
14A	**100 Francs** 8.3.1981. Brown and tan on multicolor underprint. Bridge to Luxembourg City at left, Grand Duke Jean at right, Prince Henry of the Netherlands in the background. Back: Purple on multicolor underprint. Two stylized female figures swirling around watermark area. Watermark: *BIL*.	3.50	12.50

Grand Duché de Luxembourg

1961; 1963 Issue

		VF	UNC
51	**50 Francs**		
	6.2.1991. Brown on multicolor underprint. Portrait of Grand Duchess Charlotte at right. Back: Landscape with combine harvester. Watermark: Grand Duchess Charlotte.		
	a. Issued note.	4.00	10.00
	s. Specimen, punched hole cancelled.	—	45.00
52	**100 Francs**		
	18.9.1963. Dark red on multicolor underprint. Portrait of Grand Duchess Charlotte at right. Back: Hydroelectric dam. Watermark: Grand Duchess Charlotte.		
	a. Issued note.	10.00	30.00
	s. Specimen, punched hole cancelled.	—	65.00

		VF	UNC
52A	**500 Francs**		
	ND. Portrait of Grand Duchess Charlotte at right. Back: Ducal Palace. Watermark: Grand Duchess Charlotte. Specimen only.	—	2400.

		VF	UNC
52B	**1000 Francs**		
	ND. Portrait of Grand Duchess Charlotte at right. Back: Crowned and mantled arms at center. Watermark: Grand Duchess Charlotte. Specimen only.	—	3000.

1966-72 Issue

		VF	UNC
53	**10 Francs**		
	20.3.1967. Green on mujlticolor underprint. Grand Duke Jean at left center. Back: Grand Duchess Charlotte Bridge in city.		
	a. Issued note.	2.25	5.00
	s. Specimen, punched hole cancelled.	—	75.00

		VF	UNC
54	**20 Francs**		
	7.3.1966. Blue on multicolor underprint. Grand Duke Jean at left center. Back: Moselle River with dam and lock.		
	a. Issued note.	2.25	5.00
	s. Specimen, punched hole cancelled.	—	250.

		VF	UNC
55	**50 Francs**		
	25.8.1972. Dark brown on multicolor underprint. Grand Duke Jean at left center, guilloche underprint at left. Back: Factory. .		
	a. Signature title: *LE MINISTRE DES FINANCES.*	4.00	8.50
	b. Signature title: *LE MINISTRE D'ÉTAT.*	3.50	7.00
	s. As a. Specimen, punched hole cancelled.	—	175.

56 **100 Francs** — VF — UNC

15.7.1970. Red on multicolor underprint. Grand Duke Jean at left center Back: View of Adolphe Bridge.

	VF	UNC
a. Issued note.	4.00	12.50
s. Specimen, punched hole cancelled.	—	50.00

1980 Issue

57 **100 Francs** — VF — UNC

14.8.1980. Brownish red on multicolor underprint. Grand Duke Jean at center right, building at left. Signature varieties. Back: Gold and red. City of Luxembourg scene.

	VF	UNC
a. Issued note.	4.50	7.50
s. Specimen.	—	140.

SIGNATURE VARIETIES MINISTRE DU TRESOR			
1	J. Poos	2	J. Santer

Institut Monetaire Luxembourgeois

1985-93 ND Issue

58 **100 Francs** — VF — UNC

ND (1986). Red on multicolor underprint. Grand Duke Jean at center right, building at left. Back: Gold and red. City of Luxembourg scene. Watermark: Grand Duke Jean. 142x76mm.

	VF	UNC
a. Without © symbol. Signature 1. Series A-K.	FV	6.50
b. With © symbol. Signature 2. Series L-.	FV	4.50

59 **1000 Francs** — VF — UNC

ND (1985). Brown on multicolor underprint. Grand Duke Jean at center right. Castle of Vianden at left. Back: Building sketches at center right. Watermark: Grand Duke Jean. 153x76mm.

	VF	UNC
a. Issued note.	FV	65.00
s. Specimen.	—	300.

60 **5000 Francs**

ND(1993); 1996. Green, orange and olive-green on brown and multicolor underprint. Grand Duke Jean at center right. Chateau de Clevaux at left. Two signature varieties. Back: 17th century map, European Center at Luxembourg-Kirchberg at center right on back. Watermark: Grand Duke Jean. 160x76mm.

	VF	UNC
a. Serial # prefix A. ND.	200.	325.
b. Serial # Prefix B. 10.1996.	FV	235.

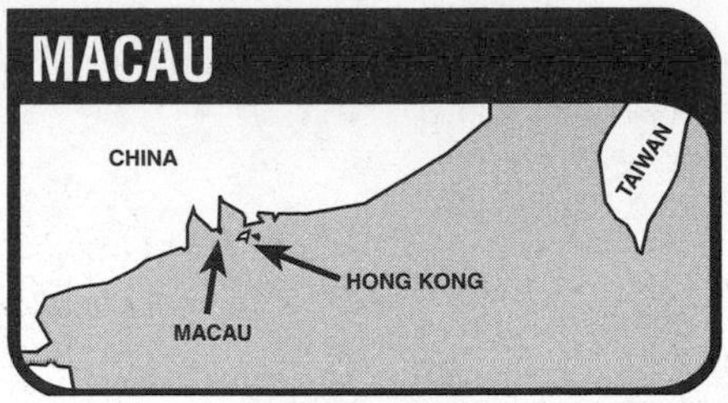

The Macau R.A.E.M., a former Portuguese overseas province located in the South China Sea 35 miles (56 km.) southwest of Hong Kong, consists of the peninsula and the islands of Taipa and Coloane. It has an area of 14 sq. mi. (21.45 sq. km.) and a population of 415,850. Capital: Macau. The economy is d on tourism, gambling, commerce and gold trading - Macau is one of the few entirely free markets for gold in the world. Cement, textiles, vegetable oils and metal products are exported.

Established by the Portuguese in 1557, Macau is the oldest European settlement in the Far East. Pursuant to an agreement signed by China and Portugal on 13 April 1987, Macau became the Macau R.A.E.M. of the People's Republic of China on 20 December 1999. In this agreement, China promised that, under its "one country, two systems" formula, China's socialist economic system would not be practiced in Macau, and that Macau would enjoy a high degree of autonomy in all matters except foreign and defense affairs for the next 50 years.

RULERS:

Portuguese from 1849-1999

MONETARY SYSTEM:

1 Dollar = 100 Cents
1 Pataca = 100 Avos

Portuguese Administration

Banco Nacional Ultramarino

行銀理滙外海國洋西大

Ta Hsi Yang Kuo Hai Wai Hui Li Yin Hang

1963-68 Issue

		VF	UNC
49	**5 Patacas**		
	21.3.1968. Brown on multicolor underprint. Portrait of Bishop D. Belchior Carneiro at lower right. Bank seal with sailing ship at left. Signature varieties. Back: Woman and sailing ships at center. Watermark: Bishop D. Belchior Carneiro. Printer: BWC.		
	a. Issued note.	50.00	175.
	s. Specimen.	—	165.

		VF	UNC
50	**10 Patacas**		
	8.4.1963. Deep blue-violet on multicolor underprint. Portrait of Bishop D. Belchior Carneiro at lower right. Bank seal with sailing ship at left. Signature varieties. Back: Woman and sailing ships at center. Watermark: Bishop D. Belchior Carneiro. Printer: BWC.		
	a. Issued note.	30.00	135.
	s. Specimen.	—	185.

		VF	UNC
51	**100 Patacas**		
	18.1966. Brown on multicolor underprint. Portrait M. de Arriaga Brum da Silveira at right. Back: Arms at left, flag atop archway at center. Printer: TDLR.		
	a. Issued note.	600.	1500.
	s. Specimen.	—	1000.

		VF	UNC
52	**500 Patacas**		
	8.4.1963. Green on multicolor underprint. Portrait of Bishop D. Belchior Carneiro at lower right. Bank seal with sailing ship at left. Back: Woman and sailing ships at center. Watermark: Bishop D. Belchior Carneiro. Printer: BWC.		
	a. Issued note.	300.	1600.
	s. Specimen.	—	750.

1973 Issue

		VF	UNC
53	**100 Patacas**		
	13.12.1973. Deep blue-violet on multicolor underprint. Ruins of S. Paulo Cathedral at right. Signature titles: *GOVERNADOR* and *ADMINISTRADOR* above signs. Back: Junk at left, bank seal with sailing ship at center. Watermark: S. Paulo Cathedral.		
	a. Issued note.	200.	950.
	s. Specimen.	—	550.

1976-79 Issue

54	5 Patacas	VF	UNC
	18.11.1976. Brown on multicolor underprint. Portrait of Bishop D. Belchior Carneiro at lower right. Bank seal with sailing ship at left, with text: *CONSELHO DE GESTAO* at center. Signature varieties. Back: Woman and sailing ships at center. Watermark: Bishop D. Belchior Carneiro. Printer: BWC.		
	a. Issued note.	23.00	125.
	s. Specimen.	—	200.

55	10 Patacas	VF	UNC
	7.12.1977. Deep blue-violet on multicolor underprint. Portrait of Bishop D. Belchior Carneiro at lower right. Bank seal with sailing ship at left, with text: *CONSELHO DE GESTAO* at center. Back: Woman and sailing ships at center. Watermark: Bishop D. Belchior Carneiro. Printer: BWC.		
	a. Issued note.	25.00	130.
	s. Specimen.	—	180.

56	50 Patacas	VF	UNC
	1.9.1976. Greenish-gray on multicolor underprint. Portrait L. de Camoes at right, with text: *CONSELHO DE GESTAO* at center. Back: Bank seal with sailing ship at left, woman and sailing ships at center.		
	a. Issued note.	250.	900.
	s. Specimen.	—	320.

57	100 Patacas	VF	UNC
	8.6.1979. Blue on multicolor underprint. Ruins of S. Paulo Cathedral at right, with text: *CONSELHO DE GESTAO* at center. Signature title: *PRESIDENTE* at left signature. Back: Junk at left, bank seal with sailing ship at center. Watermark: Ruins of S. Paulo Cathedral.		
	a. Issued note.	160.	650.
	s. Specimen.	—	465.

57A	500 Patacas	VF	UNC
	24.4.1979. Green on multicolor underprint. Portrait of Bishop D. Belchior Carneiro at lower right. Bank seal with sailing ship at left. Back: Woman and sailing ships at center. Watermark: Portrait of Bishop D. Belchior Carneiro. Printer: BWC.		
	a. Issued note.	300.	1300.
	s. Specimen. 2 different signature varieties at right hand side.	—	515.

1981; 1988 Issue

58	5 Patacas	VF	UNC
	8.8.1981. Green on multicolor underprint. Temple at right. Back: Bank seal with sailing ship at left, 19th century harbor scene.		
	a. With signature title: *PRESIDENTE* at left.	13.00	70.00
	b. With signature title: *VICE-PRESIDENTE* at left.	13.00	70.00
	c. Without signature title: *PRESIDENTE* at left.	13.00	70.00
	s. As b. Specimen.	—	160.

59	10 Patacas	VF	UNC
	1981; 1984. Brown on multicolor underprint. Lighthouse with flag at right. Back: Bank seal with sailing ship at left, 19th century harbor scene.		
	a. With signature title: *PRESIDENTE* at left. 2 decrees at upper left. 8.8.1981.	20.00	125.
	b. As a. Without signature title at left. 8.8.1981.	16.00	100.
	c. Signature title as a. 3 decrees at upper left. 12.5.1984.	16.00	90.00
	d. With signature title: *VICE-PRESIDENTE* at left. 12.5.1984.	16.00	90.00
	e. Without signature title under signature at left. 3 signature varieties. 12.5.1984.	16.00	90.00
	s1. As a. Specimen.	—	205.
	s2. As d. Specimen.	—	205.

60	50 Patacas	VF	UNC
	8.8.1981. Purple on multicolor underprint. Portrait of L. de Camoes at right. Back: Bank seal with sailing ship at left, 19th century harbor scene. Watermark: L. de Camoes.		
	a. With signature title: *PRESIDENTE* at left.	50.00	200.
	b. Without signature title: *PRESIDENTE* at left.	30.00	160.
	s1. As a. Specimen.	—	250.
	s2. As b. Specimen.	—	250.

61	100 Patacas	VF	UNC
	1981; 1984. Blue and purple on multicolor underprint. Portrait of C. Pessanha at right. Back: Bank seal with sailing ship at left, 19th century harbor scene. Watermark: C. Pessanha.		
	a. With signature title: *PRESIDENTE* at left. 8.8.1981; 12.5.1984.	70.00	250.
	b. Without signature title: *PRESIDENTE* at left. 8.8.1981; 12.5.1984.	30.00	170.
	s1. As a. Specimen. 8.8.1981; 12.5.1984.	—	290.
	s2. As b. Specimen. 2 signature varieties. 8.8.1981.	—	290.

62	500 Patacas	VF	UNC
	1981; 1984. Olive-green on multicolor underprint. Portrait V. de Morais at right. Back: Bank seal with sailing ship at left, 19th century harbor scene.		
	a. 8.8.1981; 12.5.1984. Signature title: *PRESIDENTE* at left.	110.	530.
	a1. 8.8.1981. Signature title: *VICE-PRESIDENTE.*	110.	530.
	b. 8.8.1981; 12.5.1984. Signature title: *ADMINISTRADOR* at left.	110.	500.
	s1. As a. Specimen.	—	380.
	s2. As b. Specimen.	—	380.
	s3. Specimen. 12.5.1984. Signature title: *VICE-PRESIDENTE* at left.	—	720.

63	1000 Patacas	VF	UNC
	1988. Brown and yellow-orange on multicolor underprint. Stylized dragon at right. Back: Modern view of bridge to Macau.		
	a. Issued note.	170.	645.
	s. Specimen.	—	610.

1988 Commemorative Issue

#64, 35th Anniversary Grand Prix

64	10 Patacas	VF	UNC
	11.26-27.1988 (- old date 1984). Black overprint at left on face of #59c. Back: Black overprint at center. Overprint: Front, black logo; Back: GRAND PRIX MACAU and checkerboard wheel. Issued in a small folder. 140x69mm.	15.00	75.00

1990-96 Issue

65	10 Patacas	VF	UNC
	8.7.1991. Brown and olive-green on multicolor underprint. Building at right. Back: Bank seal with sailing ship at left, bridge and city view. Watermark: Junk. 140x69mm.		
	a. Issued note.	6.00	30.00
	s. Specimen.	—	200.

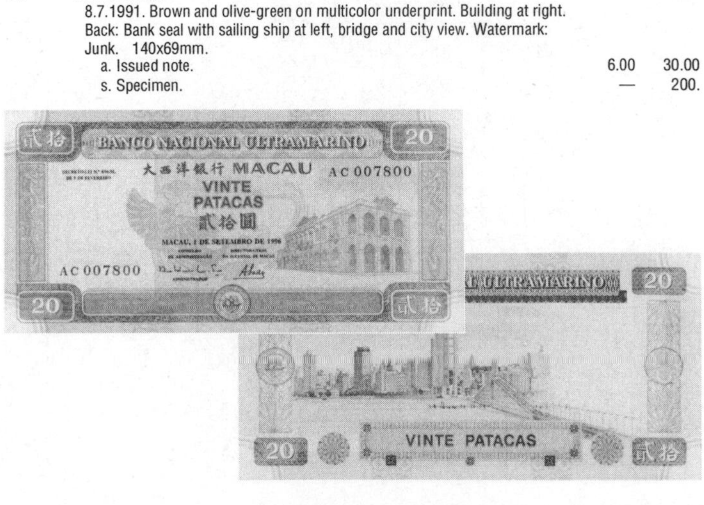

66	20 Patacas	VF	UNC
	1.9.1996. Lilac and purple on light green and multicolor underprint. B.N.U. building at right, facing dragons in border at left and right. Back: Bank seal with sailing ship at left, bridge and city view. Watermark: Junk. 143x71mm.		
	a. Issued note.	6.00	40.00
	s. As a. Specimen.	—	300.

67	50 Patacas	VF	UNC
	13.7.1992. Olive-brown on multicolor underprint. Holiday marcher with dragon costume at center right, man at right. Back: Bank seal with sailing ship at left, bridge and city view. Watermark: Junk. 149x75mm.		
	a. Issued note.	15.00	80.00
	s. As a. Specimen.	—	350.

68	100 Patacas	VF	UNC
	13.7.1992. Black on multicolor underprint. Early painting of Settlement at center, junk at right. Back: Bank seal with sailing ship at left, bridge and city view. Watermark: Junk. 154x76mm.		
	a. Issued note.	FV	150.
	s. As a. Specimen.	—	500.

69	500 Patacas	VF	UNC
	3.9.1990. Olive-green on multicolor underprint. Building at right. Two signature varieties. Back: Bank seal with sailing ship at left, bridge and city view. Watermark: Junk. 160x80mm.		
	a. Issued note.	FV	400.
	s1. Specimen. Signature as a. Serial # AA00000.	—	700.
	s2. Specimen. Signature different. Serial # AW00000.	—	700.

70	1000 Patacas	VF	UNC
	8.7.1991. Brown and yellow-orange on multicolor underprint. Stylized dragon at right. Two signature varieties. Back: Bank seal with sailing ship at left, bridge and city view. Watermark: Junk. 164x82mm.		
	a. 8.7.1991. Signature title at left: *ADMINISTRATOR.* Serial # prefix AP.	FV	625.
	b. 8.7.1991. Signature title at left: *PRESIDENTE.* Serial # prefix AQ.	FV	640.
	s. As b. Specimen but different signature. Serial # AF00000.	—	800.

1999 Issue

All notes issued since 20 December 1999 are issued under Macau as a Special Administrative Region in China.

71	20 Patacas	VF	UNC
	20.12.1999. Lilac and purple on light green and multicolor underprint. B.N.U. building at right, facing dragons in border at left and right. Back: Bank seal with sailing ship at left, bridge and city view. Watermark: Junk.		
	a. Issued note.	FV	25.00
	b. Uncut sheet of 12. Serial # prefix *JJ* or *KK*.	—	255.
	s. As a. Specimen.	—	150.

72	50 Patacas	VF	UNC
	Olive-brown on multicolor underprint. Holiday marcher with dragon costume at center right, man at right. Back: Bank seal with sailing ship at left, bridge and city view. Watermark: Junk.		
	a. Issued note.	FV	52.50
	b. Uncut sheet of 12. Serial # prefix: *CC*.	—	450.
	s. As a. Specimen.	—	200.

1999 Issue

73 100 Patacas VF UNC

20.12.1999. Black on multicolor underprint. Early painting of Settlement at center, junk at right. Back: Bank seal with sailing ship at left, bridge and city view. Watermark: Junk.

	VF	UNC
a. Issued note.	FV	75.00
s. Specimen.	—	250.

74 500 Patacas VF UNC

20.12.1999. Olive-green on multicolor underprint. Building at right. Two signature varieties. Back: Bank seal with sailing ship at left, bridge and city view. Watermark: Junk.

	VF	UNC
a. Issued note.	FV	270.
s. Specimen.	—	450.

75 1000 Patacas VF UNC

20.12.1999. Brown and yellow-orange on multicolor underprint. Stylized dragon at right. Back: Bank seal with sailing ship at left, bridge and city view. Watermark: Junk.

	VF	UNC
a. Signature title: *PRESIDENTE.*	FV	450.
b. Signature title: *ADMINISTRADOR.*	FV	440.
s. Specimen. As a.	—	500.

2001 Issue

76 10 Patacas VF UNC

8.1.2001. Dark red and orange with multicolor underprint. Building at right. Back: Bank seal with sailing ship at left, bridge and city view. Watermark: Junk.

	VF	UNC
a. Signature title: *PRESIDENTE.*	FV	19.00
b. Signature title: *ADMINISTRATOR*	FV	17.00
c. Uncut sheet of 4. Archive use only.	—	—
d. Uncut sheet of 40.	—	350.
s. As a. Specimen.	—	200.

2003 Issue

77 10 Patacas VF UNC

8.6.2003. Dark red and orange on multicolor underprint. Building at right. Back: Bank seal with sailing ship at left, bridge and city view. Watermark: Junk. FV 25.00

78 100 Patacas VF UNC

8.6.2003. Black on multicolor underprint. Early painting of Settlement at center, junk at right. Back: Bank seal with sailing ship at left, bridge and city view. Watermark: Junk. FV 65.00

79 500 Patacas VF UNC

8.6.2003. Olive-green on multicolor underprint. Building at right. Back: Bank seal with sailing ship at left, bridge and city view. Watermark: Junk. FV 265.

2005 Issue

80	10 Patacas	VF	UNC
	8.8.2005 (2006). Orange and rose. Goddess A-ma at left. Back: B.N.U. headquarters building at left.	FV	11.00

81	20 Patacas	VF	UNC
	8.8.2005 (2006). Blue and grey. Macau International Airport runway and terminal. Back: B.N.U. headquarters building at left.	FV	20.00

81B	50 Patacas	VF	UNC
	8.8.2009. Brown on yellow underprint. Bridge. Back: B.N.U. headquarters building.	FV	35.00

82	100 Patacas	VF	UNC
	8.8.2005 (2006). Purple and blue. *Largo do Senado* at right. Back: B.N.U. headquarters building at left.	FV	57.50

83	500 Patacas	VF	UNC
	8.8.2005 (2006). Green and aqua. *Torre de Macau* at left. Back: B.N.U. headquarters building at left.	FV	195.

Banco da China

Chung Kuo Yin Hang

1995; 1996 Issue

90	10 Patacas	VF	UNC
	16.10.1995. Dark brown and deep green on multicolor underprint. Farel de Guia lighthouse at right. Back: Bank of China - Macau building at left, lotus blossom at lower center. Watermark: Lotus blossom(s). 140x69mm.	FV	27.50

91	20 Patacas	VF	UNC
	1.9.1996. Purple and violet on multicolor underprint. Ama Temple at right. Back: Bank of China - Macau building at left, lotus blossom at lower center. Watermark: Lotus blossom(s). 143x72mm.		
	a. Issued note.	FV	45.00
	r. Replacement note. Serial # prefix *CZ*.	FV	70.00

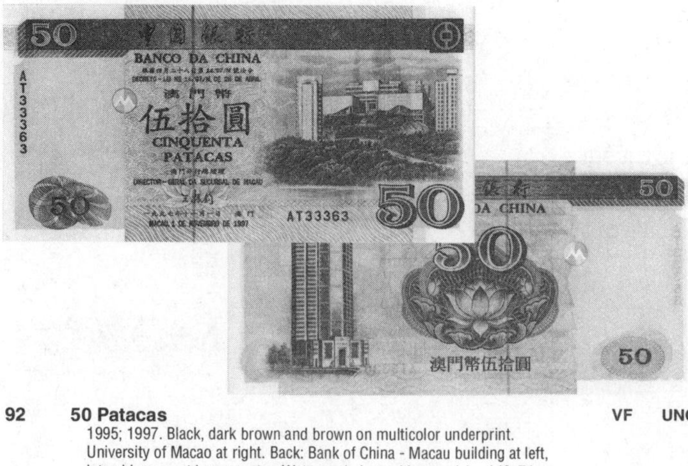

92	50 Patacas	VF	UNC
	1995; 1997. Black, dark brown and brown on multicolor underprint. University of Macao at right. Back: Bank of China - Macau building at left, lotus blossom at lower center. Watermark: Lotus blossom(s). 149x74mm.		
	a. 16.10.1995.	FV	85.00
	b. 1.11.1997.	FV	75.00

93 **100 Patacas**

16.10.1995. Black, brown and purple on multicolor underprint. New terminal of Port Exterior at right. Back: Bank of China - Macau building at left, lotus blossom at lower center. Watermark: Lotus blossom(s). 152x76mm.

VF	UNC
FV	120.

94 **500 Patacas**

16.10.1995. Dark green and dark blue on multicolor underprint. Ponte de Amizade bridge at right. Back: Bank of China - Macau building at left, lotus blossom at lower center. Watermark: Lotus blossom(s). 158x80mm.

VF	UNC
FV	450.

95 **1000 Patacas**

16.10.1995. Brown, orange and red on multicolor underprint. Aerial view of Praia Oeste at right. Back: Bank of China - Macau building at left, lotus blossom at lower center. Watermark: Lotus blossom(s). 164x82mm.

VF	UNC
FV	750.

1999 Issue

All notes issued since 20 December 1999 are issued under Macau as a Special Administrative Region in China.

96 **20 Patacas**

20.12.1999. Purple and violet on multicolor underprint. Ama Temple at right. Back: Bank of China - Macau building at left, lotus blossom at lower center. Watermark: Lotus blossom(s).

VF	UNC
FV	30.00

97 **50 Patacas**

20.12.1999. Black, dark brown and brown on multicolor underprint. University of Macao at right. Back: Bank of China - Macau building at left, lotus blossom at lower center. Watermark: Lotus blossom(s).

VF	UNC
FV	60.00

98 **100 Patacas**

1999; 2002. Black, brown and purple on multicolor underprint. New terminal of Port Exterior at right. Back: Bank of China - Macau building at left, lotus blossom at lower center. Watermark: Lotus blossom(s).

	VF	UNC
a. 20.12.1999.	FV	110.
b. 2.2.2002.	FV	100.

99 **500 Patacas**

1999; 2002. Dark green and dark blue on multicolor underprint. Ponte de Amizade bridge at right. Back: Bank of China - Macau building at left, lotus blossom at lower center. Watermark: Lotus blossom(s).

	VF	UNC
a. 20.12.1999.	FV	340.
b. 2.2.2002.	FV	300.

100 **1000 Patacas** VF UNC

20.12.1999. Brown, orange and red on multicolor underprint. Aerial view of Praia Oeste at right. Back: Bank of China - Macau building at left, lotus blossom at lower center. Watermark: Lotus blossom(s). FV 550.

2001 Issue

101 **10 Patacas** VF UNC

2001; 2002. Red and orange on multicolor underprint. Farel de Guia lighthouse at right. Back: Bank of China - Macau building at left, lotus blossom at lower center. Watermark: Lotus blossom(s).

	VF	UNC
a. 8.1.2001.	FV	22.50
b. 2.2.2002.	FV	20.00
c. Uncut sheet of 30. 8.1.2001.	—	300.

Special Administrative Region

Banco da China

Chung Kuo Yin Hang

1995; 1996 Issue

104 **100 Patacas** VF UNC

8.12.2003 (2005). Black, brown and purple on multicolor underprint. New terminal of Port Exterior at right. Back: Bank of China - Macau building at left, lotus blossom at lower center. Watermark: Lotus blossom(s). FV 110.

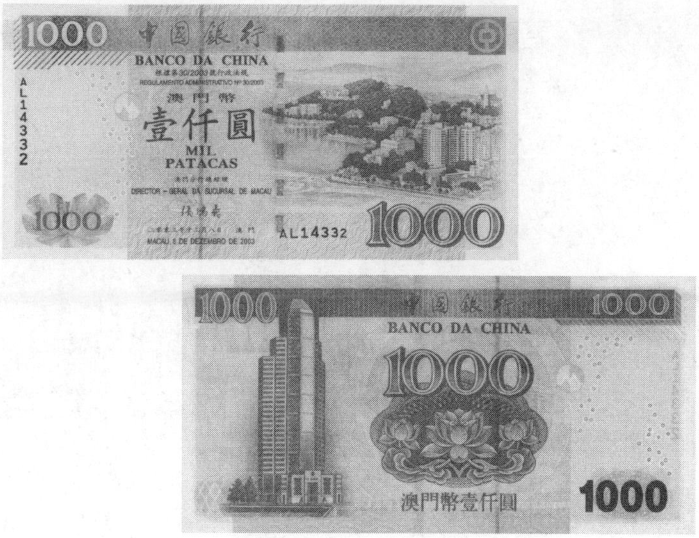

106 **1000 Patacas** VF UNC

8.12.2003 (2005). Brown, orange and red on multicolor underprint. Aerial view of Praia Oeste at right. Back: Bank of China - Macau building at left, lotus blossom at lower center. Watermark: Lotus blossom(s). FV 520.

107 **20 Patacas** VF UNC

3.5.2008. Lilac and blue on multicolor underprint. Bank of China Headquarters, calassical Greek column, Bejing olympic logo in red. Back: Bejing Olympic stadium *the Bird's Nest* at left. Watermark: Stadium and value.

	VF	UNC
a. Issued note	FV	85.00
b. In original folder with matching serial # Hong Kong note.	—	175.

2008 Issue

108 **10 Patacas** VF UNC

8.8.2008. Rose on yellow underprint. A-Ma Miu temple of Barra at right center. Back: Bank of China - Macau building at left center. 140x69mm. FV 10.00

109 **20 Patacas** — VF | UNC

8.8.2008. Purple. São Paulo Cathedral ruins. Back: Bank of China - Macau building at left center. 143x72mm. — FV | 17.50

No.	Denomination / Description	VF	UNC
110	**50 Patacas** 8.8.2008. Purple. Dom Pedro V theatre at center right. Back: Bank of China - Macau building at left center. 149x75mm.	FV	35.00
111	**100 Patacas** 8.8.2008. Light blue on green underprint. Lighthouse at right center. Back: Bank of China - Macau building at left center. 152x76mm.	FV	55.00
112	**500 Patacas** 8.8.2008. Green on blue underprint. Mandarin House at right center. Back: Bank of China - Macau building at left center. 158x80mm.	FV	195.
113	**1000 Patacas** 8.8.2008. Yellow orange on multicolor underprint. Senate's palace at right. Back: Bank of China - Macau building at left center. 163x81mm.	FV	340.

Collector Series

Banco Nacional Ultramarino

1999 Issue

No.	Denomination / Description	Mkt. Value
CS1	**20-1000 Patacas** One each of #71-74 in a special folder. Matching serial #.	930.

Banco Da China and Banco Nacional Ultramarino

2001 Issue

No.	Denomination / Description	Mkt. Value
CS2	**10 Pataca Sheetlets of 4** One mini-sheet from each bank in a special folder.	230.

The Republic of Macedonia is land-locked, and is bordered in the north by Yugoslavia, to the east by Bulgaria, in the south by Greece and to the west by Albania. It has an area of 9,923 sq. mi. (25,713 sq. km.) and its population at the 1991 census was 2.23 million. of which the predominating ethnic groups were Macedonians. The capital is Skopje.

Macedonia gained its independence peacefully from Yugoslavia in 1991, but Greece's objection to the new state's use of what it considered a Hellenic name and symbols delayed international recognition, which occurred under the provisional designation of "the Former Yugoslav Republic of Macedonia." In 1995, Greece lifted a 20-month trade embargo and the two countries agreed to normalize relations. The United States began referring to Macedonia by its constitutional name, Republic of Macedonia, in 2004 and negotiations continue between Greece and Macedonia to resolve the name issue. Some ethnic Albanians, angered by perceived political and economic inequities, launched an insurgency in 2001 that eventually won the support of the majority of Macedonia's Albanian population and led to the internationally-brokered Framework Agreement, which ended the fighting by establishing a set of new laws enhancing the rights of minorities. Fully implementating the Framework Agreement and stimulating economic growth and development continue to be challenges for Macedonia, although progress has been made on both fronts over the past several years.

MONETARY SYSTEM:

1 DHNAR **(Denar) = 100** DHNI **(Deni)**

Republic

НАРОДНА БАНКА НА МАКЕДОНИЈА

National Bank of Macedonia

1992 Issue

1 **10 (Denar)** — VF | UNC

1992. Pale blue on lilac underprint. Farmers harvesting at left. Back: Ilenden monument in Krushevo at left. Watermark: Design.

		VF	UNC
a.	Issued note.	.20	.75
s.	Specimen. Red overprint ПРИМЕРОК.	—	—

2 **25 (Denar)** — VF | UNC

1992. Red on lilac underprint. Farmers harvesting at left. Back: Ilenden monument in Krushevo at left. Watermark: Design.

		VF	UNC
a.	Issued note.	.20	1.00
s.	Specimen.	—	—

3	50 (Denar)	VF	UNC
	1992. Brown on ochre underprint. Farmers harvesting at left. Back: Ilenden monument in Krushevo at left. Watermark: Design.		
	a. Issued note.	.20	1.00
	s. Specimen.	—	—

4	100 (Denar)	VF	UNC
	1992. Blue-gray on light blue underprint. Farmers harvesting at left. Back: Ilenden monument in Krushevo at left. Watermark: Design.		
	a. Issued note.	.20	1.00
	s. Specimen.	—	—

5	500 (Denar)	VF	UNC
	1992. Bright green on ochre underprint. Farmers harvesting at left. Back: Ilenden monument in Krushevo at left. Watermark: Design.		
	a. Issued note.	.20	1.25
	s. Specimen.	—	—

6	1000 (Denar)	VF	UNC
	1992. Dull blue-violet on pink underprint. Farmers harvesting at left. Back: Ilenden monument in Krushevo at left. Watermark: Design.		
	a. Issued note.	.75	1.75
	s. Specimen.	—	—

7	5000 (Denar)	VF	UNC
	1992. Deep brown and dull red on multicolor underprint. Woman at desk top computer at center. Back: Ilenden monument at left. Watermark: Design.		
	a. Issued note.	1.50	6.00
	s. Specimen.	—	—

8	10,000 (Denar)	VF	UNC
	1992. Blue-black on pink and gray underprint. Buildings at center right. Back: Musicians at left of Ilenden monument at center right. Watermark: Design.		
	a. Issued note.	2.50	8.50
	s. Specimen.	—	—

НАРОДНА БАНКА НА РЕПУБЛИКА МАКЕДОНИЈА

National Bank of the Republic of Macedonia

1993 Issue

Currency Reform

1 "New" Denar = 100 "Old" Denars

9	10 Denari	VF	UNC
	1993. Light blue on multicolor underprint. Houses on mountainside in Krushevo at center right. Back: Ilenden monument at left center Watermark: Ilenden monument.		
	a. Issued note.	FV	1.50
	s. Specimen.	—	15.00

		VF	UNC
10	**20 Denari**		
	1993. Wine-red on multicolor underprint. 16th century Tower in Skopje in vertical format. Back: Turkish bath in Skopje at left center. Watermark: Ilenden monument.		
	a. Issued note.	FV	2.50
	s. Specimen.	—	15.00

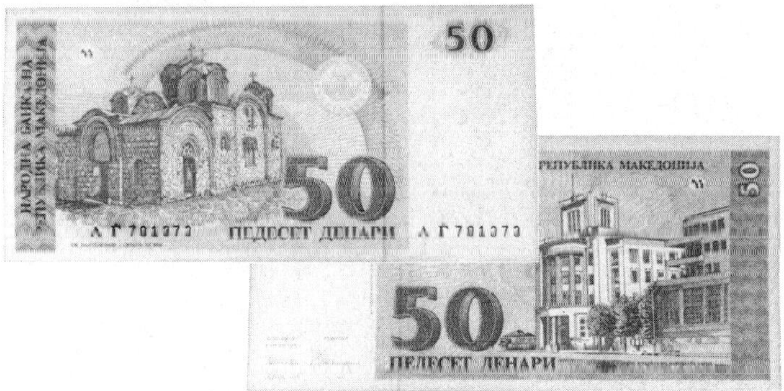

		VF	UNC
11	**50 Denari**		
	1993. Light red on multicolor underprint. National Bank building in Skopje at right. Back: 12th century Orthodox Church of St. Pantileimon at left. Watermark: Ilenden monument.		
	a. Issued note.	FV	4.00
	s. Specimen.	—	15.00

		VF	UNC
12	**100 Denari**		
	1993. Brown on multicolor underprint. Bovev Palace, National Museum in Ohrid at right. Back: 11th century Monastery of St. Sophia in Ohrid at left. Watermark: Ilenden monument.		
	a. Issued note.	FV	8.00
	s. Specimen.	—	15.00

		VF	UNC
13	**500 Denari**		
	1993. Greenish on multicolor underprint. Ohrid castle ruins at upper center. Back: 12th century Orthodox church of St. John in Ohrid at left. Watermark: 12th century Orthodox church of St. John in Ohrid.		
	a. Issued note.	FV	35.00
	s. Specimen.	—	15.00

1996 Issue

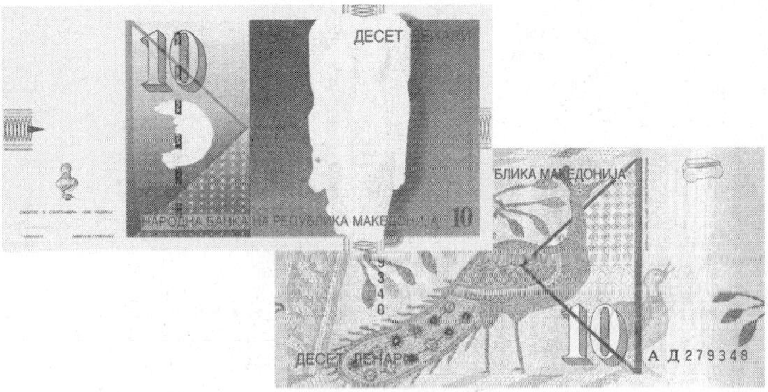

		VF	UNC
14	**10 Denari**		
	8.9.1996-12.2011. Deep olive-green with black text on multicolor underprint. Statue torso of Goddess Isida at right. Back: Blue-green, deep olive-green with black text on multicolor underprint. Mosaic of branch over peacock and duck. Watermark: Statue torso of Goddess Isida. UV: fibers fluoresce yellow, blue and green. 140x70mm.		
	a. 8.9.1996. Two signatrues at bottom left.	FV	1.75
	b. 8.1997.	FV	1.50
	c. 1.2001. One signature at bottom left.	FV	1.50
	d. 1.2003.	FV	1.50
	e. 1.2005. New signature.	FV	1.50
	f. 1.2006.	FV	1.00
	g. 1.2007.	FV	1.00
	h. 1.2008.	FV	1.00
	i. 12.2011.	FV	1.00

		VF	UNC
15	**50 Denari**		
	8.9.1996-1.2007. Brown with black text on multicolor underprint. Byzantine copper follis of Anastasia at center right. Back: Archangel Gabriel at left center. Watermark: Byzantine copper follis of Anastasia. UV: fibers fluoresce yellow, blue and green. 143x70mm.		
	a. 8.9.1996. Two signatures at bottom left.	FV	3.00
	b. 8.1997.	FV	3.00
	c. 1.2001. One signature at bottom left.	FV	3.00
	d. 1.2003.	FV	3.00
	e. 1.2007. New signature.	FV	3.00
	s. Specimen.	—	20.00

16 100 Denari VF UNC

8.9.1996-2009. Brown with purple text on multicolor underprint. Large baroque wooden ceiling rosette in Debar town house at center right. Back: J. Harevin's engraving of Skopje "seen" through town house window frame at left center. Watermark: Large baroque wooden ceiling rosette. 146x70mm.

	VF	UNC
a. 8.9.1996. Two signatures at bottom left.	FV	5.00
b. 8.1997.	Unc	5.00
c. 1.2000.	FV	5.00
d. 1.2002. One signature at bottom left.	Unc	5.00
e. 5.2004.		
f. 1.2005. New Signature.		
g. 1.2007.		
h. 9.2008.		
i. 1.2009.		
s. Specimen.	—	25.00

17 500 Denari VF UNC

8.9.1996. Black and violet on multicolor underprint. 6th century golden death mask, Trebenista, Ohrid at right. Back: Violet poppy flower and plant at left center. Watermark: 6th century golden death mask, Trebenista, Ohrid. 149x70mm.

	VF	UNC
a. Issued note.	FV	22.50
s. Specimen.	—	25.00

18 1000 Denari VF UNC

8.9.1996. Brown and orange on multicolor underprint. 14th century icon of Madonna Episkepsis and Christ Child, church of St. Vrach-Mali, Ohrid at center right. Back: Partial view of the St. Sophia church in Ohrid at left center. Watermark: Madonna. 152x70mm.

	VF	UNC
a. Issued note.	FV	40.00
s. Specimen.	—	30.00

19 5000 Denari VF UNC

8.9.1996. Black and violet on olive-green and multicolor underprint. 6th century bronze figurine of Tetovo Maenad VI (horizontally) at center right. Back: 6th century mosaic of Cerberus the Dog tied to a fig tree, representing the watcher of Heaven (horizontally) at left center. Watermark: 6th century bronze figurine of Tetovo Maenad VI (horizontally). 155x70mm.

	VF	UNC
a. Issued note.	FV	175.
s. Specimen.	—	60.00

2000 Commemorative Issue

20 100 Denari VF UNC

1.2000. Brown with purple text on multicolor underprint. Large baroque wooden ceiling rosette in Debar town house at center right, *2000* added at left. Back: J. Harevin's engraving of Skopje "seen" through town house window frame at left center. Watermark: Large baroque wooden ceiling rosette. 146x70mm. — VF 35.00, UNC 80.00

2003 Issue

21 500 Denari VF UNC

1.2003; 1.2008; 1.2009. Black and violet on multicolor underprint. 6th century golden death mask, Trebenista, Ohrid at right. Gold foil at center. Back: Violet poppy flower and plant at left center. Watermark: Golden death mask. 149x70mm.

	VF	UNC
a. 1.2003. One signature at bottom left.	FV	22.50
b. 1.2008. New Signature.	FV	22.50
c. 1.2009.	FV	22.50
s. Specimen.	FV	25.00

22 1000 Denari VF UNC

1.2003; 1.2008; 1.2009. Brown and orange on multicolor underprint. 14th century icon of Madonna Episkepsis and Christ Child, church of St. Vrach-Mali, Ohrid at center right. Hologram on center top. Back: Partial view of the St. Sophia church in Ohrid at left center. Watermark: Madonna. 152x70mm.

	VF	UNC
a. 1.2003. One signature at bottom left.	FV	40.00
b. 1.2008. New Signature.	FV	40.00
c. 1.2009.	FV	40.00
s. Specimen.	—	25.00

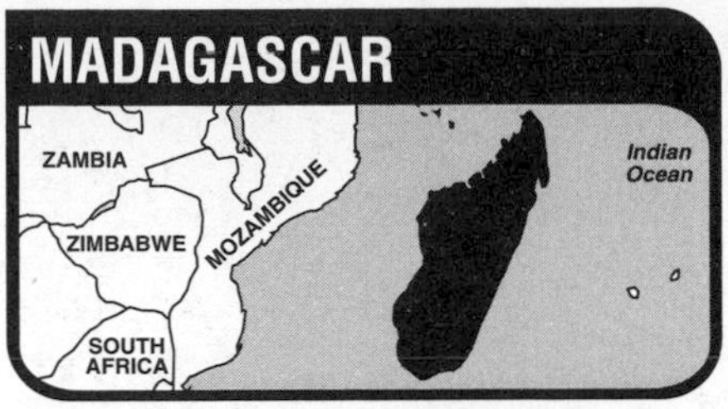

The Democratic Republic of Madagascar, an independent member of the French Community located in the Indian Ocean 250 miles (402 km.) off the southeast coast of Africa, has an area of 226,658 sq. mi. (587,041 sq. km.) and a population of 17.39 million. Capital: Antananarivo. The economy is primarily agricultural; large bauxite deposits are presently being developed. Coffee, vanilla, graphite and rice are exported.

Formerly an independent kingdom, Madagascar became a French colony in 1896 but regained independence in 1960. During 1992-93, free presidential and National Assembly elections were held ending 17 years of single-party rule. In 1997, in the second presidential race, Didier Ratsiraka, the leader during the 1970s and 1980s, was returned to the presidency. The 2001 presidential election was contested between the followers of Didier Ratsiraka and Marc Ravalomanana, nearly causing secession of half of the country. In April 2002, the High Constitutional Court announced Ravalomanana the winner. Ravalomanana is now in his second term following a landslide victory in the generally free and fair presidential elections of 2006.

MONETARY SYSTEM:

1 French Franc = 100 Centimes to 1945
1 CFA Franc = 1.70 French Francs, 1945-1948
1 CFA Franc = 2 French Francs, 1948-1959
1 CFA Franc = 0.02 French Franc, 1959-1961
5 Malagasy Francs (F.M.G.) = 1 Ariary, 1961-2003
1 Ariary = 5 Francs, 2003-

MALAGASY

INSTITUT D'EMISSION MALGACHE

1961 ND PROVISIONAL ISSUE

#51-55 new bank name and new Ariary denominations overprint on previous issue of Banque de Madagascar et des Comores.

		VF	UNC
51	**50 Francs = 10 Ariary** ND (1961). Multicolor. Woman with hat at center right. Back: Man at center. Overprint: On #45. Watermark: Woman's head.		
	a. Signature title: *LE CONTROLEUR GENERAL.*	17.50	70.00
	b. Signature title: *LE DIRECTEUR GENERAL ADJOINT.*	20.00	75.00
52	**100 Francs = 20 Ariary** ND (1961). Multicolor. Woman at center right, palace of the Queen of Tananariva in background. Back: Woman, boats and animals. Overprint: On #46b. Watermark: Woman's head.	30.00	110.

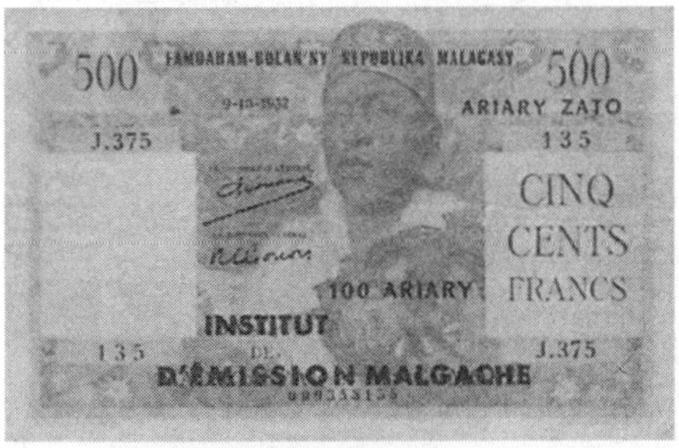

		VF	UNC
53	**500 Francs = 100 Ariary** ND (1961 - old date 9.10.1952). Multicolor. Man with fruit at center. Overprint: On #47. Watermark: Woman's head.	90.00	400.
54	**1000 Francs = 200 Ariary** ND (1961 - old date 9.10.1952). Multicolor. Man and woman at left center. Back: Ox cart at center right. Overprint: On #48. Watermark: Woman's head.	175.	500.
55	**5000 Francs = 1000 Ariary** ND (1961). Multicolor. Gallieni at upper left, woman at right. Back: Woman and baby. Overprint: On #49. Watermark: Woman's head.	325.	800.

1963 ND REGULAR ISSUE

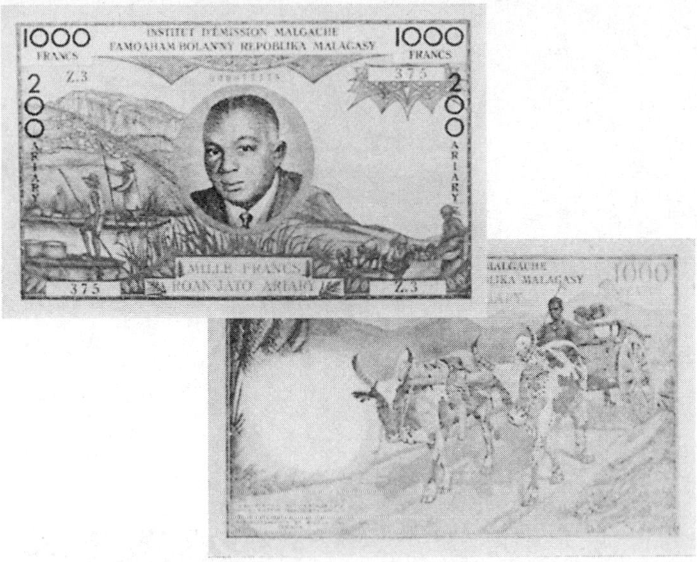

		VF	UNC
56	**1000 Francs = 200 Ariary** ND (1963). Multicolor. Portrait President P. Tsiranana, people in canoes at left. Back: Ox cart at center right. Watermark: Woman's head.		
	a. Without signature and title.	375.	800.
	b. With signature and title.	250.	700.

1966 ND ISSUE

		VF	UNC
57	**100 Francs = 20 Ariary** ND (1966). Multicolor. Three women spinning. Two signature varieties. Back: Trees. Watermark: Woman's head.		
	a. Issued note.	10.00	30.00
	s. Specimen.	—	25.00

		VF	UNC
58	**500 Francs = 100 Ariary** ND (1966). Multicolor. Woman at left, landscape in background. Two signature varieties. Back: River scene. Watermark: Woman's head.		
	a. Issued note.	45.00	185.
	s. Specimen.	—	35.00

		VF	UNC
59	**1000 Francs = 200 Ariary** ND (1966). Multicolor. Woman and man at left. Back: Ox cart at center right. Watermark: Woman's head. 150x80mm.		
	a. Issued note.	65.00	250.
	s. Specimen.	—	35.00

60 **5000 Francs = 1000 Ariary** — VF / UNC
ND (1966). Portrait President P. Tsiranana at left, workers in rice field at right. Back: Woman and boy. Watermark: Woman's head.
a. Issued note. — 45.00 / 200.
s. Specimen. — — / 45.00

1969 ND Issue

61 **50 Francs = 10 Ariary** — VF / UNC
ND (1969). Multicolor. Woman with hat at center right, like #51 but different signature title. Back: Man at center. Watermark: Woman's head. — 7.50 / 25.00

Madagascar Democratic Republic

Banky Foiben'ny Repoblika Malagasy

Banque Centrale de la République Malgache

1974 ND Issue

#62-66 replacement notes: Serial # prefix *Z/*.

62 **50 Francs = 10 Ariary** — VF / UNC
ND (1974-75). Purple on multicolor underprint. Young man at center right. Signature 1. Back: Fruit stand under umbrella at left center. Watermark: Zebu's head.
a. Issued note. — 4.00 / 12.50
s. Specimen. — — / 25.00

63 **100 Francs = 20 Ariary**
ND. Brown on multicolor underprint. Old man at right. Signature 1. Back: Rice planting. Watermark: Zebu's head.
a. Issued note. — 3.00 / 10.00
s. Specimen. — — / 25.00

64 **500 Francs = 100 Ariary** — VF / UNC
ND. Green on multicolor underprint. Butterfly at left, young woman at center right holding ornate bag on head. Signature 1. Back: Dancers at center. Watermark: Zebu's head.
a. Issued note. — 6.00 / 30.00
s. Specimen. — — / 25.00

65 **1000 Francs = 200 Ariary** — VF / UNC
ND. Bue on multicolor underprint. Ring-tailed Lemurs at left, man in straw hat at right. Signature 1. Back: Trees and designs. Watermark: Zebu's head.
a. Issued note. — 8.00 / 45.00
s. Specimen. — — / 25.00

66 **5000 Francs = 1000 Ariary** — VF / UNC
ND. Red and violet on multicolor underprint. Oxen at left, young woman at center right. Back: Violet and orange. Tropical plants and African carving at center. Watermark: Zebu's head.
a. Issued note. — 30.00 / 80.00
s. Specimen. — — / 25.00

Banky Foiben'i Madagasikara

1983 ND Issue

#67-70 Replacement notes: Serial # prefix *Z/*.

67	**500 Francs = 100 Ariary**	VF	UNC
	ND (1983-87). Brown and red on multicolor underprint. Boy with fish in net at center. Back: Aerial view of port at right. Watermark: Zebu's head.		
	a. Signature 1.	1.50	5.00
	b. Signature 2.	2.50	10.00

68	**1000 Francs = 200 Ariary**	VF	UNC
	ND (1983-87). Violet and brown on multicolor underprint. Man with hat playing flute at center. Back: Fruits and vegetables at right. Watermark: Zebu's head.		
	a. Signature 1.	2.00	7.50
	b. Signature 2.	2.50	10.00

69	**5000 Francs = 1000 Ariary**	VF	UNC
	ND (1983-87). Blue on multicolor underprint. Woman and child at center. Back: Book at upper center, school at center right, monument at lower right. Watermark: Zebu's head.		
	a. Signature 1.	10.00	35.00
	b. Signature 2.	12.50	50.00

70	**10,000 Francs = 2000 Ariary**	VF	UNC
	ND (1983-87). Green on multicolor underprint. Young girl with sheaf at center. Back: Harvesting rice at center right. Watermark: Zebu's head.		
	a. Signature 1.	20.00	65.00
	b. Signature 2.	25.00	85.00

1988 ND Issue

#71-74 Replacement notes: Serial # prefix *ZZ*.

71	**500 Francs = 100 Ariary**	VF	UNC
	ND (1988-93). Brown and red on multicolor modified underprint Boy with fish in net at center, vertical serial number at right. Signature varieties. Back: Aerial view of port at right. Watermark: Zebu's head.		
	a. Signature 2.	1.50	5.00
	b. Signature 3.	1.50	5.00

72	**1000 Francs = 200 Ariary**	VF	UNC
	ND (1988-93). Violet and brown on multicolor modified underprint. Man with hat playing flute at center, vertical serial number at right. Back: Fruits and vegetables at right. Watermark: Zebu's head.		
	a. Signature 2.	2.00	7.50
	b. Signature 3.	2.00	7.50
72A	**2500 Francs = 500 Ariary**		
	ND (1993). Red, green, blue and black on multicolor underprint. Older woman at center, vertical serial number at right. Back: Grey heron, tortoise, Verreaux's Sifaka and butterfly in foliage on vertical format. Watermark: Zebu's head.		
	a. Signature 3.	.75	2.50
	b. Signature 5.	.75	2.50

73	**5000 Francs = 1000 Ariary**	VF	UNC
	ND (1988-94). Blue on multicolor modified underprint. Woman and child at center, vertical serial number at right. Back: Book at upper center, school at center right, monument at lower right. Watermark: Zebu's head.		
	a. Signature 2.	4.00	15.00
	b. Signature 3.	4.00	15.00

74 **10,000 Francs = 2000 Ariary**

ND (1988-94). Green on multicolor modified underprint. Young girl with sheaf at center, vertical serial number at right. Back: Harvesting rice at center right. Watermark: Zebu's head.

	VF	UNC
a. Signature 2.	10.00	30.00
b. Signature 3.	10.00	30.00

74A **25,000 Francs = 5000 Ariary**

	VF	UNC
ND (1993). Olive-green and green on multicolor underprint. Old man at center, island outline at left. Signature 3. Back: Scene of traditional bullfighting at right. Watermark: Zebu's head.	5.00	17.50

1994-95 ND Issue

75 **500 Francs = 100 Ariary**

ND (1994). Dark brown and dark green on multicolor underprint. Girl at center right, village in underprint at upper center. Back: Herdsmen with Zebus, village in upper background at left center. Watermark: Zebu's head. UV: value 500 fluoresces yellow, security strip blue.

	VF	UNC
a. Signature 4.	.50	1.75
b. Signature 5.	.50	1.75

76 **1000 Francs = 200 Ariary**

ND (1994). Dark brown and dark blue on multicolor underprint. Young man at center right, boats in background. Back: Young woman with basket of shellfish at center, fisherman with net at left center. Watermark: Zebu's head. UV: value 1000 fluoresces yellow, security strip blue.

	VF	UNC
a. Signature 4.	.50	1.50
b. Signature 5.	.50	1.00

78 **5000 Francs = 1000 Ariary**

ND (1995). Dark brown and purple on lilac and multicolor underprint. Young male head at right, ox cart, cane cutters at center. Back: Ringtailed Lemur, Diademed Sifaka, Red-ruffed Lemur and birds - Madagascar pigmy kingfisher, Madagascar fody and helmet vanga, plus seashells. Watermark: Zebu's head.

	VF	UNC
a. Signature 4.	1.25	6.00
b. Signature 5.	1.25	6.00

79 **10,000 Francs = 2000 Ariary**

ND (1995). Dark brown on tan and multicolor underprint. Old man at right, statuette, local artifacts at center. Back: Artisans at work. Watermark: Zebu's head.

	VF	UNC
a. Signature 4.	2.50	10.00
b. Signature 5.	2.50	10.00

1998 ND Issue

81 **2500 Francs = 500 Ariary** | VF .75 | UNC 3.50
ND (1998). Multicolor. Woman at right, village in background. Signature 5. Back: Woman weaving at left center.

82 **25,000 Francs = 5000 Ariary** | VF 3.00 | UNC 25.00
ND (1998). Multicolor. Mother with child at center right, fruit trees in background. Signature 5. Back: Woman harvesting at center.

2003 Issue

83 **2000 Ariary** | VF FV | UNC 10.00
ND (2003). Green on multicolor underprint. Baobabs trees at left. Signature 5. Back: Terrace farming. 120x60mm.

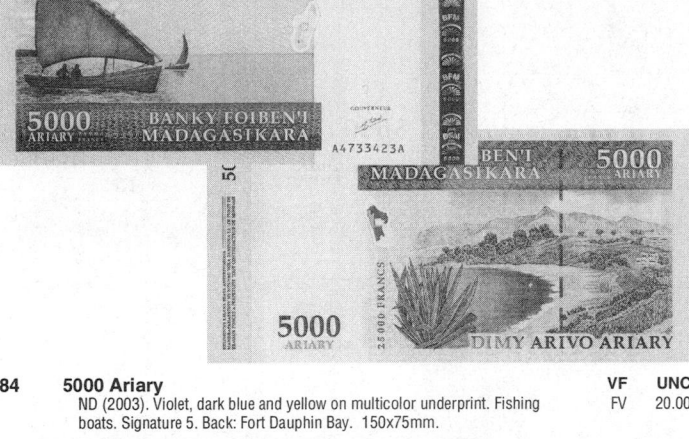

84 **5000 Ariary** | VF FV | UNC 20.00
ND (2003). Violet, dark blue and yellow on multicolor underprint. Fishing boats. Signature 5. Back: Fort Dauphin Bay. 150x75mm.

85 **10,000 Ariary** | VF FV | UNC 35.00
ND (2003). Green on multicolor underprint. Palais d'Argent at left. Signature 5. Back: Green, blue, yellow and brown. Road construction. 156x78mm.

2004-06 Issue

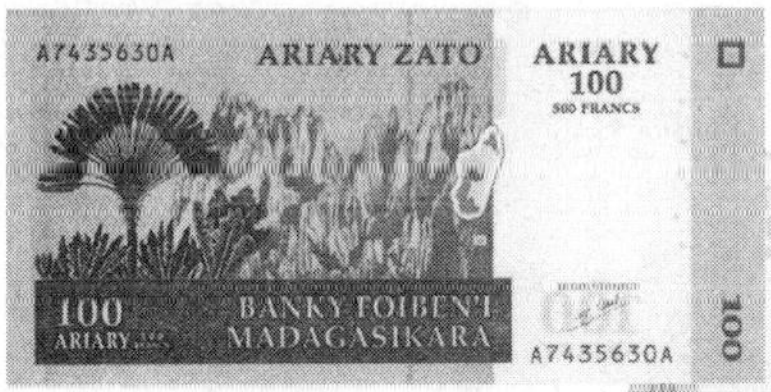

86 **100 Ariary** | VF | UNC
2004. Blue and tan on multicolor underprint. Ravinala and Tsingi plants. Back: Sugarloaf mountain at Antsiranana Bay. 120x60mm.
a. Signature 5. | FV | 1.00
b. Signature 6. | FV | 1.00

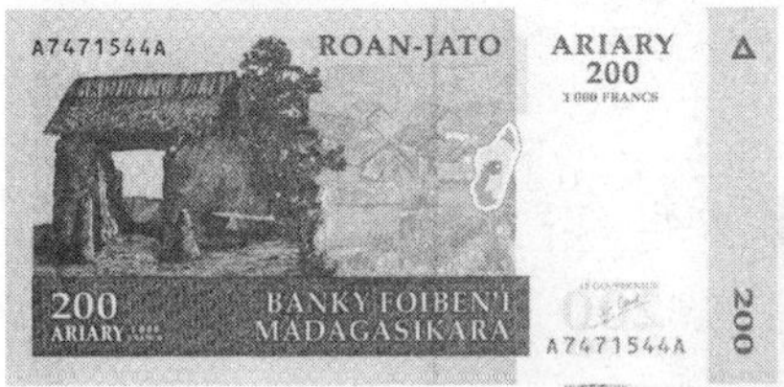

87 **200 Ariary** | VF | UNC
2004. Green and tan on multicolor underprint. Village entrance. Back: "Aloalo" (wooden monuments). 126x63mm.
a. Signature 5. | FV | 1.50
b. Signature 6. | FV | 1.50

#	Description	VF	UNC
88	**500 Ariary** 2004. Tan on blue underprint. Man weaving basket at left. Back: Zebu cattle. 132x66mm.	VF	UNC
	a. Signature 5.	FV	3.00
	b. Signature 6.	FV	3.00

#	Description	VF	UNC
89	**1000 Ariary** 2004. Purple on multicolor underprint. Lemur on tree branch at left. Back: Cactus and sisal plants. 138x69mm.	VF	UNC
	a. Signature 5.	FV	3.50
	b. Signature 6.	FV	3.50

#	Description	VF	UNC
90	**2000 Ariary** 2006, 2009. Green on multicolor underprint. Baobabs trees at right. Signature 6. Omron rings. Back: Terrace farming. 144x72mm.	VF	UNC
	a. 2006. With Francs equivalent.	FV	7.00
	b. 2009. Without Francs equivalent.	FV	7.00
91	**5000 Ariary** 2006, 2009. Dark blue, violet and yellow on multicolor underprint. Fishing boats at left. Signature 5. Omron rings. Back: Fort Dauphin Bay. 150x75mm.		
	a. 2006. With Francs equivalent.	FV	12.50
	b. 2009. Without Francs equivalent.	FV	12.50
92	**10,000 Ariary** 2006; 2009. Green on multicolor underprint. Palais d'Argent at left. Signature 5. Omron rings. Back: Road construction. 156x78mm.		
	a. 2006. With Francs equivalent.	FV	25.00
	b. 2009. Without Francs equivalent.	FV	25.00

2007 Commemorative Issue

#	Description	VF	UNC
93	**2000 Ariary** 2007. Multicolor. Signature 6. Overprint: 2007-2012 Madagascar Action Plan. 144x72mm.	VF	UNC
	a. Issued note.	FV	9.00
	s. Specimen. Red overprint.	—	50.00
94	**5000 Ariary** ND. (2008). Multicolor. Sailing ship. Signature 6. Back: Beach. Overprint: Madagascar Action Plan 2007-2012 150x75mm.		
	a. Issued note.	FV	35.00
	s. Specimen. Red overprint.	—	50.00

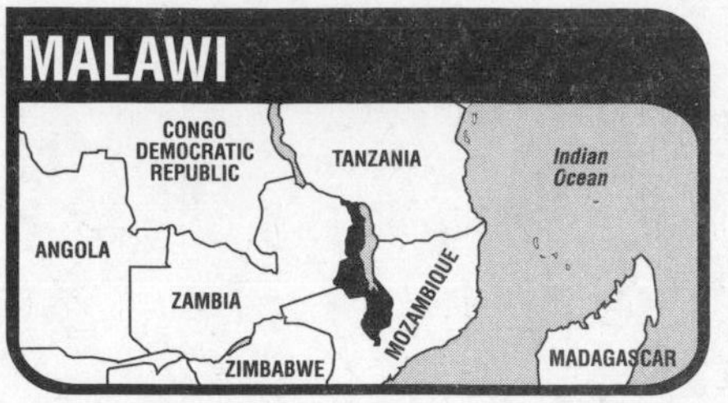

The Republic of Malawi (formerly Nyasaland), located in southeastern Africa to the west of Lake Malawi (Nyasa), has an area of 45,747 sq. mi. (118,484 sq. km.) and a population of 10.98 million. Capital: Lilongwe. The economy is predominantly agricultural. Tobacco, tea, peanuts and cotton are exported. Established in 1891, the British protectorate of Nyasaland became the independent nation of Malawi in 1964. After three decades of one-party rule under President Hastings Kamuzu Banda the country held multiparty elections in 1994, under a provisional constitution that came into full effect the following year. Current President Bingu wa Mitharika, elected in May 2004 after a failed attempt by the previous president to amend the constitution to permit another term, struggled to assert his authority against his predecessor and subsequently started his own party, the Democratic Progressive Party (DPP) in 2005. As president, Mutharika has overseen substantial economic improvement but because of political deadlock in the legislature, his minority party has been unable to pass significant legislation, and anti-corruption measures have stalled. Population growth, increasing pressure on agricultural lands, corruption, and the spread of HIV/AIDS pose major problems for Malawi.

RULERS:
British to 1964

MONETARY SYSTEM:
1 Pound = 20 Shillings to 1971
1 Kwacha = 100 Tambala 1971-

REPLACEMENT NOTES:
#13-17, ZZ prefix. #18-22, V/1, W/1, X/1, Y/1, Z/1 prefix by denomination.
#23-27, ZZ prefix.

Republic

Reserve Bank of Malawi

1964 Reserve Bank Act; First Issue

#	Description	VF	UNC
1	**5 Shillings** *L.1964*. Blue-gray on multicolor underprint. Portrait of Dr. Hastings Kamuzu Banda at left, fishermen in boat on Lake Malawi at center. Signature title: *GOVERNOR* only. Back: Arms with bird. Watermark: Rooster.	17.50	100.

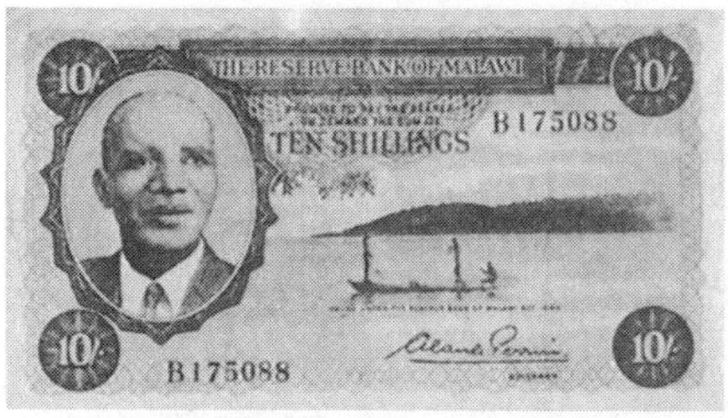

#	Description	VF	UNC
2	**10 Shillings** *L.1964*. Brown on multicolor underprint. Portrait of Dr. Hastings Kamuzu Banda at left, fishermen in boat on Lake Malawi at center. Signature title: *GOVERNOR* only. Back: Workers in tobacco field. Watermark: Rooster.	60.00	250.
3	**1 Pound** *L.1964*. Green on multicolor underprint. Portrait of Dr. Hastings Kamuzu Banda at left, fishermen in boat on Lake Malawi at center. Signature title: *GOVERNOR* only. Back: Workers picking cotton at center right. Watermark: Rooster.	85.00	350.

#	Description	VF	UNC
4	**5 Pounds** *L.1964*. Blue and brown on multicolor underprint. Portrait of Dr. Hastings Kamuzu Banda at left, fishermen in boat on Lake Malawi at center. Signature title: *GOVERNOR* only. Back: Tea pickers below Mt. Mulanje. Watermark: Rooster.	300.	1500.

1964 Reserve Bank Act; Second Issue

1A **5 Shillings** — VF — UNC
L.1964. Blue-gray on multicolor underprint. Portrait of Dr. Hastings Kamuzu Banda at left, fishermen in boat on Lake Malawi at center. Signature titles: *GOVERNOR* and *GENERAL MANAGER*. Back: Arms with bird. Watermark: Rooster.
- a. Issued note. — 15.00 — 85.00
- s. Specimen. — — — —

2A **10 Shillings** — VF — UNC
L.1964. Brown on multicolor underprint. Portrait of Dr. Hastings Kamuzu Banda at left, fishermen in boat on Lake Malawi at center. Signature titles: *GOVERNOR* and *GENERAL MANAGER*. Back: Workers in tobacco field. Watermark: Rooster.
- a. Issued note. — 20.00 — 120.
- s. Specimen. — — — —

3A **1 Pound** — VF — UNC
L.1964. Green on multicolor underprint. Portrait of Dr. Hastings Kamuzu Banda at left, fishermen in boat on Lake Malawi at center. Signature titles: *GOVERNOR* and *GENERAL MANAGER*. Back: Worders picking cotton at center right. Watermark: Rooster.
- a. Issued note. — 40.00 — 225.
- s. Specimen. — — — —

1964 Reserve Bank Act; 1971 Issue

Kwacha System

5 **50 Tambala** — VF — UNC
L.1964 (1971). Blue-gray on multicolor underprint. Portrait of Dr. Hastings Kamuzu Banda at left, fishermen in boat on Lake Malawi at center. Signature titles: *GOVERNOR* and *GENERAL MANAGER*. Back: Independence Arch in Blantyre at right.
- a. Issued note. — 50.00 — 325.
- s. Specimen. — — — —

6 **1 Kwacha**
L.1964 (1971). Brown on multicolor underprint. Portrait of Dr. Hastings Kamuzu Banda at left, fishermen in boat on Lake Malawi at center. Signature titles: *GOVERNOR* and *GENERAL MANAGER*. Back: Workers in tobacco field. Watermark: Rooster.
- a. Issued note. — 50.00 — 350.
- s. Specimen. — — — —

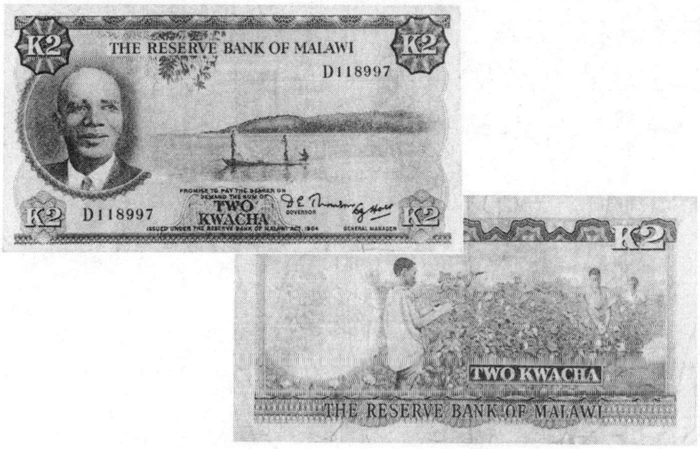

7 **2 Kwacha** — VF — UNC
L.1964 (1971). Green on multicolor underprint. Portrait of Dr. Hastings Kamuzu Banda at left, fishermen in boat on Lake Malawi at center. Signature titles: *GOVERNOR* and *GENERAL MANAGER*. Back: Workers picking cotton at center right. Watermark: Rooster.
- a. Issued note. — 50.00 — 300.
- s. Specimen. — — — —

8 **10 Kwacha** — VF — UNC
L.1964 (1971). Blue and brown on multicolor underprint. Portrait of Dr. Hastings Kamuzu Banda at left, fishermen in boat on Lake Malawi at center. Signature titles: *GOVERNOR* and *GENERAL MANAGER*. Back: Tea pickers below Mount Mulanje.
- a. Issued note. — 175. — 1200.
- s. Specimen. — — — —

1973-74 Issue

9 50 Tambala

L.1964 (ND); 1974-75. Blue-gray on multicolor underprint. Portrait Dr. Hastings Kamuzu Banda as Prime Minister at right, fishermen in boat on Lake Malawi and palm tree at center. Back: Sugar cane harvesting. Watermark: Rooster.

	VF	UNC
a. ND (1973).	30.00	200.
b. 30.6.1974.	15.00	100.
c. 31.1.1975.	5.00	40.00
s. As a. Specimen.	—	—
ct. Color trial. Purple on multicolor underprint.	—	275.

10 1 Kwacha

L.1964 (ND); 1974-75. Red-brown on multicolor underprint. Portrait Dr. Hastings Kamuzu Banda as Prime Minister at right, fishermen in boat on Lake Malawi and palm tree at center. Back: Plantation worker, hill in background. Watermark: Rooster.

	VF	UNC
a. ND (1973).	20.00	135.
b. 30.6.1974.	15.00	85.00
c. 31.1.1975.	7.00	75.00
ct. Color trial. Orange on multicolor underprint.	—	250.

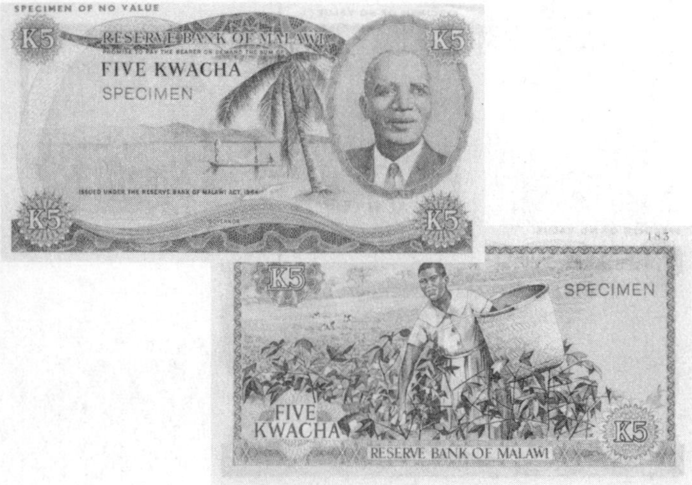

11 5 Kwacha

L.1964 (ND); 1974-75. Red-orange on multicolor underprint. Portrait Dr. Hastings Kamuzu Banda as Prime Minister at right, fishermen in boat on Lake Malawi and palm tree at center. Back: Worker with basket at center, *K5* at upper left. Watermark: Rooster.

	VF	UNC
a. ND (1973).	55.00	350.
b. 31.1.1975.	40.00	300.
ct. Color trial. Green on multicolor underprint.	—	550.

12 10 Kwacha

L.1964 (ND); 1974-75. Blue and brown on multicolor underprint. Portrait Dr. Hastings Kamuzu Banda as Prime Minister at right, fishermen in boat on Lake Malawi and palm tree at center. Back: Plantation workers with mountains in background. Watermark: Rooster.

	VF	UNC
a. ND (1973).	65.00	500.
b. 30.6.1974.	75.00	550.
c. 31.1.1975.	45.00	425.

1976; 1983 Issue

13 50 Tambala

1976-84. Blue-gray on multicolor underprint. Portrait of Dr. Hastings Kamuzu Banda as President at right. Signature varieties. Back: Cotton harvest. Watermark: Rooster.

	VF	UNC
a. 31.1.1976.	3.00	25.00
b. 1.7.1978.	4.50	30.00
c. 1.1.1981.	5.00	40.00
d. 1.5.1982.	2.50	15.00
e. 1.1.1983.	5.00	35.00
f. 1.11.1984.	7.50	60.00
s. As. a. Specimen.	—	35.00

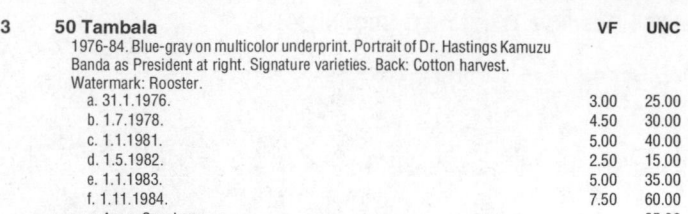

14 1 Kwacha

1976-84. Red-brown on multicolor underprint. Portrait of Dr. Hastings Kamuzu Banda as President at right. Signature varieties. Back: Workers harvesting, mountains in background. Watermark: Rooster.

	VF	UNC
a. 31.1.1976.	3.00	22.50
b. 1.7.1978.	3.00	25.00
c. 30.6.1979.	20.00	150.
d. 1.1.1981.	2.00	20.00
e. 1.5.1982.	2.75	20.00
f. 1.1.1983.	3.00	25.00
g. 1.4.1984.	1.50	12.50
h. 1.11.1984.	2.00	15.00
s. Specimen. 31.1.1976.	—	40.00

15 5 Kwacha

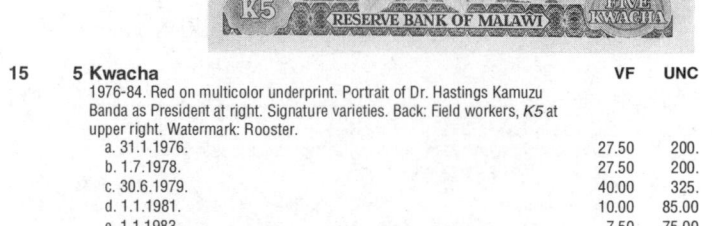

1976-84. Red on multicolor underprint. Portrait of Dr. Hastings Kamuzu Banda as President at right. Signature varieties. Back: Field workers, *K5* at upper right. Watermark: Rooster.

	VF	UNC
a. 31.1.1976.	27.50	200.
b. 1.7.1978.	27.50	200.
c. 30.6.1979.	40.00	325.
d. 1.1.1981.	10.00	85.00
e. 1.1.1983.	7.50	75.00
f. 1.11.1984.	20.00	250.
s. Specimen. 31.1.1976.	—	50.00

16 10 Kwacha — VF / UNC

1976-85. Deep blue and brown on multicolor underprint. Portrait of Dr. Hastings Kamuzu Banda as President at right. Signature varieties. Back: Capital building at Lilongwe. Watermark: Rooster.

	VF	UNC
a. 31.1.1976.	37.50	450.
b. 1.7.1978.	37.50	450.
c. 30.6.1979.	55.00	550.
d. 1.1.1981.	35.00	400.
e. 1.1.1983.	35.00	400.
f. 1.4.1984.	35.00	400.
g. 1.11.1984.	45.00	525.
h. 1.8.1985.	50.00	500.
s. Specimen. 31.1.1976.	—	45.00

17 20 Kwacha — VF / UNC

1983; 1984. Green, brown-violet on multicolor underprint. Portrait of Dr. Hastings Kamuzu Banda as President at right. Signature varieties. Back: Green. Reserve Bank in Lilongwe at center. Watermark: Rooster.

	VF	UNC
a. 1.7.1983.	15.00	125.
b. 1.11.1984.	35.00	325.
s. Specimen.	—	240.

1986 Issue

18 50 Tambala — VF 2.00 / UNC 12.50

1.3.1986. Black and dark brown on multicolor underprint. Portrait of President Dr. Hastings Kamuzu Banda at right. Back: Picking corn. Watermark: Rooster.

19 1 Kwacha — VF / UNC

1986; 1988. Red-brown on multicolor underprint. Portrait of President Dr. Hastings Kamuzu Banda at right. Back: Cultivating tobacco. Watermark: Rooster.

	VF	UNC
a. 1.3.1986.	2.50	15.00
b. 1.4.1988.	1.50	10.00

20 5 Kwacha — VF / UNC

1986; 1988. Red-orange on multicolor underprint. Portrait of President Dr. Hastings Kamuzu Banda at right. Back: University of Malawi at Zomba. Watermark: Rooster.

	VF	UNC
a. 1.3.1986.	7.00	40.00
b. 1.4.1988.	5.00	30.00

21 10 Kwacha — VF / UNC

1986; 1988. Deep blue and brown on multicolor underprint. Portrait of President Dr. Hastings Kamuzu Banda at right. Back: Lilongwe, capital city. Watermark: Rooster.

	VF	UNC
a. 1.3.1986.	15.00	95.00
b. 1.4.1988.	10.00	50.00

		VF	UNC
22	**20 Kwacha** 1986; 1988. Deep green on multicolor underprint. Portrait of President Dr. Hastings Kamuzu Banda at right. Back: Kamuzu International Airport . Watermark: Rooster.		
	a. 1.3.1986.	35.00	285.
	b. 1.4.1988.	20.00	160.

1989 Act; 1990; 1993 Issue

		VF	UNC
23	**1 Kwacha** 1990; 1992. Red-brown on multicolor underprint. Portrait of Dr. Hastings Kamuzu Banda as President at right, palm tree, man in dugout canoe and rayed silver circle at center. Ascending size serial number at left and lower right. Back: Cultivating tobacco. Watermark: Rooster. UV: fibers fluoresce yellow, four 1s yellow.		
	a. 1.12.1990.	FV	5.00
	b. 1.5.1992.	FV	2.00

		VF	UNC
24	**5 Kwacha** 1990; 1994. Red-orange and olive-green on multicolor underprint. Portrait of Dr. Hastings Kamuzu Banda as President at right, palm tree, man in dugout canoe and rayed silver circle at center. Ascending size serial number at left and lower right. Back: University of Malawi at left center. Watermark: Rooster.		
	a. 1.12.1990.	FV	6.50
	b. 1.1.1994.	FV	4.50

		VF	UNC
25	**10 Kwacha** 1990-94. Blue-gray, blue-violet and dark brown on multicolor underprint. Portrait of Dr. Hastings Kamuzu Banda as President at right, palm tree, man in dugout canoe and rayed silver circle at center. Ascending size serial number at left and lower right. Back: Lilongwe City municipal building at left center. Watermark: Rooster.		
	a. 1.12.1990.	FV	12.50
	b. 1.9.1992.	FV	6.00
	c. Smaller signature as b. 1.1.1994.	FV	4.00
	s. As b. Specimen.	—	135.

		VF	UNC
26	**20 Kwacha** 1.9.1990. Green, orange and blue on multicolor underprint. Portrait of Dr. Hastings Kamuzu Banda as President at right, palm tree, man in dugout canoe and rayed silver circle at center. Ascending size serial number at left and lower right. Back: Kamuzu International Airport at left center. Watermark: Rooster.	10.00	60.00

		VF	UNC
27	**20 Kwacha** 1.7.1993. Green, orange and blue on multicolor underprint. Portrait of Dr. Hastings Kamuzu Banda as President at right, palm tree, man in dugout canoe and rayed silver circle at center. Ascending size serial number at left and lower right. Back: Like #26 but with larger airplane. Watermark: Rooster.	FV	10.00

		VF	UNC
28	**50 Kwacha** 1990; 1994. Pale purple, violet and blue on multicolor underprint. Portrait of Dr. Hastings Kamuzu Banda as President at right, palm tree, man in dugout canoe and rayed silver circle at center. Ascending size serial number at left and lower right. Back: Independence Arch at Blantyre at center. Watermark: Rooster.		
	a. 1.6.1990.	12.50	55.00
	b. 1.1.1994.	5.00	35.00

		VF	UNC
29	**100 Kwacha** 1993; 1994. Blue, green and dark brown on multicolor underprint. Portrait of Dr. Hastings Kamuzu Banda as President at right, palm tree, man in dugout canoe and rayed silver circle at center. Ascending size serial number at left and lower right. Back: Trucks hauling maize to storage facility at center.		
	a. 1.4.1993.	30.00	75.00
	b. 1.1.1994.	10.00	50.00

1995 Issue

30 **5 Kwacha** VF UNC
1.6.1995. Red and orange-brown on multicolor underprint. President Muluzi at right, sunrise above fisherman in boat on Lake Malawi at center, Spoonbill at upper left, silver segmented sunburst at lower left. Back: Zebras at left. Watermark: Fish. FV 1.75

31 **10 Kwacha** VF UNC
1.6.1995. Black, dark blue and dark brown on multicolor underprint. President Muluzi at right, sunrise above fisherman in boat on Lake Malawi at center, Crowned Crane at upper left, silver segmented sunburst at lower left. Back: Capital Hill, Lilongwe at left center. Watermark: Fish. FV 4.00

32 **20 Kwacha** VF UNC
1.6.1995. Deep green and dark brown on multicolor underprint. President Muluzi at right, sunrise above fisherman in boat on Lake Malawi at center, Lesser Striped Swallow at upper left, silver segmented sunburst at lower left. Back: Harvesting tea leaves at left center. Watermark: Fish. FV 7.50

33 **50 Kwacha** VF UNC
1.6.1995. Purple and violet on multicolor underprint. President Muluzi at right, sunrise above fisherman in boat on Lake Malawi at center, Pink-backed Pelican at upper left, silver segmented sunburst at lower left. Back: Independence Arch in Blantyre at left center. Watermark: Fish. FV 12.00

34 **100 Kwacha** VF UNC
1.6.1995. Purple and deep ultramarine on multicolor underprint. President Muluzi at right, sunrise above fisherman in boat on Lake Malawi at center, Sacred Ibis at upper left, silver segmented sunburst at lower left. Back: Trucks hauling maize to storage facility at left center. Watermark: Fish. FV 25.00

35 **200 Kwacha** VF UNC
1.6.1995. Brown-violet and blue-green and silver on multicolor underprint. President Muluzi at right, sunrise above fisherman in boat on Lake Malawi at center, African Fish Eagle at upper left, silver segmented sunburst at lower left. Back: Elephants. Watermark: Fish. 10.00 45.00

1989 Act; 1997 Issue

36 **5 Kwacha** VF UNC
1997; 2004-05. Deep olive-green, green and olive-brown on multicolor underprint. J. Chilembwe at right, sunrise, fishermen at center, bank stylized logo at lower left. Back: Villagers mashing grain at left, bank seal at top center right. Watermark: J. Chilembwe. UV: fibers fluoresce blue, green and red. Security strip rainbow.

a. 1.7.1997.	FV	1.25
b. 1.3.2004.	FV	.50
c. 1.12.2005.	FV	.50

37 **10 Kwacha** VF UNC
1.7.1997. Dark brown and brown-violet on multicolor underprint. J. Chilembwe at right, sunrise, fishermen at center, bank stylized logo at lower left. Back: Children in "bush" school at left center, bank seal at top center right. Watermark: J. Chilembwe. FV 1.50

38 **20 Kwacha** VF UNC
1.7.1997. Blackish purple, purple and violet on multicolor underprint. J. Chilembwe at right, sunrise, fishermen at center, bank stylized logo at lower left. Back: Workers harvesting tea leaves, mountains in background at left , bank seal at top center right. Watermark: J. Chilembwe. 138x70mm.

	VF	UNC
a. Even height serial #s.	FV	3.50
b. Ascending size serial #.	FV	3.25

39 **50 Kwacha** VF UNC
1.7.1997. Dark green, deep blue and aqua on multicolor underprint. J. Chilembwe at right, sunrise, fishermen at center, bank stylized logo at lower left. Back: Independence arch in Blantyre at left center, bank seal at top center right. Watermark: J. Chilembwe. 144x72mm. FV 5.00

40 **100 Kwacha** VF UNC
1.7.1997. Purple, red and violet on multicolor underprint. J. Chilembwe at right, circular kinegram bank seal at right, sunrise, fishermen at center, bank stylized logo at lower left. Back: Capital Hill Lilongwe at left center. Watermark: J. Chilembwe. 150x75mm. FV 12.50

41 **200 Kwacha** VF UNC
1.7.1997. Dark gray, dull blue and deep blue-green on multicolor underprint. J. Chilembwe at right, oval kinegram bank seal at right, sunrise, fishermen at center, bank stylized logo at lower left. Back: Reserve Bank building in Lilongwe at left center. Watermark: J. Chilembwe. 156x78mm. FV 17.50

2001-03 Issue

43 **10 Kwacha** VF UNC
2003. Dark brown and brown-violet on multicolor underprint. J. Chilembwe at right. Ascending size serial number. Back: Children in "bush" school at left center. UV: fibers fluoresce red, blue and green, Chilembwe's face yellow in a box, security strip rainbow.

	VF	UNC
a. 1.1.2003.	FV	1.50
b. 1.10.2003.	FV	1.50

44 **20 Kwacha** VF UNC
2001-07. Black and purple on multicolor underprint. J. Chilembwe at right. Ascending size serial number. 138x70mm.

	VF	UNC
a. 1.10.2001.	FV	3.00
b. 1.4.2004.	FV	2.00

45 **50 Kwacha** VF UNC
2001-03. Dark green, deep blue and aqua on multicolor underprint. J. Chilembwe at right. Ascending size serial number. 144x72mm.
a. 1.10.2001. FV 4.00
b. 1.1.2003. FV 2.75

46 **100 Kwacha** VF UNC
2001-03. Dark purple and red on red and multicolor underprint. J. Chilembwe at right. Ascending size serial number. 150x75mm.
a. 1.10.2001. FV 10.00
b. 1.1.2003. FV 5.00
c. 1.10.2003. FV 4.00

47 **200 Kwacha**
2001-03. Multicolor. J. Chilembwe at right, oval kinegram bank seal at right, sunrise, fishermen at center, bank stylized logo at lower left. Ascending size serial number. Back: Reserve Bank building in Lilongwe at left center. 156x78mm.
a. 1.7.2001. FV 15.00
b. 1.10.2003. FV 9.00

48 **500 Kwacha** VF UNC
2001. Multicolor. J. Chilembwe at right. Holographic square at left center. Ascending size serial number. 163x81mm.
a. 1.12.2001. FV 30.00

48A **500 Kwacha** VF UNC
2003. Multicolor. J. Chilembwe at right. Holographic strip at right. 163x81mm.
a. 1.6.2003. FV 17.50

2004 Commemorative Issue

#49, 40th Anniversary of Independence.

49 **50 Kwacha** VF UNC
6.7.2004. Blue on yellow-orange underprint. Back: Modern buildings. 144x72mm. FV 5.00

2004 Regular Issue

50 **5 Kwacha** VF UNC
1.6.2004. FV 1.00

51 **10 Kwacha**
2004-. Black and purple on multicolor underprint. J. Chilembwe at right.
a. 1.6.2004. FV 1.50
b. 31.10.2006. FV 1.50

52 **20 Kwacha**
2004-. Black purple, purple and violet on multicolor underprint. J. Chilembwe at right. 138x70mm.
a. 1.6.2004. FV 1.00
b. 31.10.2005. FV 1.00
c. 31.10.2006. FV 1.00
d. 31.10.2007. FV .75
e. 31.10.2009. FV .75

53 **50 Kwacha** VF UNC
2005-. Dark green, deep blue and aqua on multicolor underprint. J. Chilrmbwe at right. 144x72mm.
a. 31.10.2005. FV 1.50
b. 31.10.2006. FV 1.50
c. 31.10.2007. FV 1.00
d. 31.10.2009. FV 1.00
e. 30.6.2011. FV 1.00

54 100 Kwacha VF UNC

2005-. Purple, red and violet on multicolor underprint. J. Chilembwe at right. 150x75mm.

	VF	UNC
a. 31.10.2005.	FV	3.00
b. 31.10.2006.	FV	3.00
c. 31.10.2007.	FV	2.50
d. 31.10.2009.	FV	2.50
e. 30.6.2011.	FV	2.50

55 200 Kwacha

2004-. Dark gray, dull blue and deep blue-green on multicolor underprint. J. Chilembwe at right. 156x78mm.

	VF	UNC
a. 1.6.2004.	FV	9.00
b. 31.10.2007.	FV	9.00

56 500 Kwacha VF UNC

2005-. J. Chilembwe at right. 163x81mm.

	VF	UNC
a. 1.11.2005.	FV	15.00
b. 31.10.2007.	FV	9.50
c. 31.1.2011.	FV	9.00

2012 Issue

57 20 Kwacha VF UNC FV 1.00

1.1.2012. Purple and orange on multicolor underprint. Fishermen in boat, Reserve Bank building, Inkosi ya Makhosi M'mbelwa II. Back: Domadi Teachers Training College building and tree Watermark: Inkosi ya Makhosi M'mbelwa II. 128x64mm.

58 50 Kwacha VF UNC FV 2.00

1.1.2012. Light blue, orange and green on multicolor underprint. Fishermen in boat, Reserve Bank building, Inkosi Ya Mokhosi Gomani II. Back: Elephants, tree and safari vehicle in Kasungu National Park. Watermark: Inkosi Ya Mokhosi Gomani II. 128x64mm.

59 100 Kwacha VF UNC FV 3.00

1.1.2012. Red-brown and orange on multicolor underprint. Fishermen in boat, Reserve Bank building, James Federick Sangala. Back: College of Medicine in Blantyre. Watermark: James Federick Sangala. 128x64mm.

60 200 Kwacha VF UNC FV 5.00

1.1.2012. Blue, violet and orange on multicolor underprint. Fishermen in boat, Reserve Bank building, Rose Lomathinda Chibambo. Back: New Parliament building in Lilongwe. Watermark: Rose Lomathinda Chibambo. 132x66mm.

61 500 Kwacha VF UNC FV 6.00

1.1.2012. Brown, orange and light blue on multicolor underprint. Fishermen in boat, Reserve Bank building, Rev. John Chilembwe. Back: Mulunguzi dam in Zomba. Watermark: John Chilembwe 132x66mm.

62 1000 Kwacha VF UNC FV 12.50

1.1.2012. Green and orange on multicolor underprint. Fishermen in boat, Reserve Bank building, Dr. Hastings Kamuzu Banda. Back: Mzuzu maize silos, stalk of maize (corn), silhouette of 2 people mashing maize into flower with poles Watermark: Hastings Kamuzu Banda. 132x66mm.

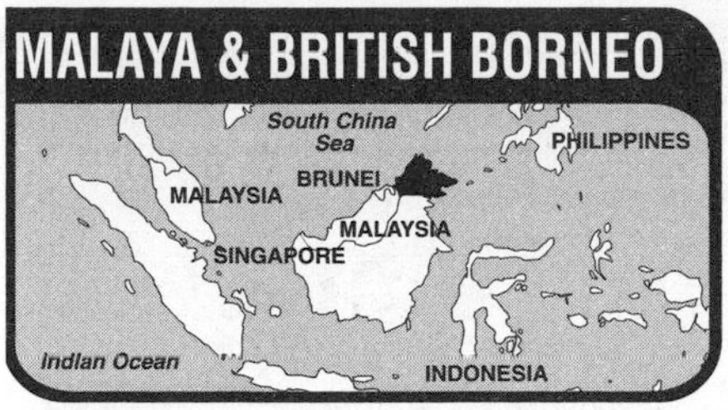

Malaya and British Borneo, a Currency Commission named the Board of Commissioners of Currency, Malaya and British North Borneo, was initiated on Jan. 1, 1952, for the purpose of providing a common currency for use in Johore, Kelantan, Kedah, Perlis, Trengganu, Negri Sembilan, Pahang, Perak, Salangor, Penang, Malacca, Singapore, North Borneo, Sarawak and Brunei.

For later issues see Brunei, Malaysia and Singapore.

RULERS:
British

MONETARY SYSTEM:
1 Dollar = 100 Cents

British Administration

Board of Commissioners of Currency

1959-61 Issue

8 — 1 Dollar (VF / UNC)
1.3.1959. Blue on multicolor underprint. Sailing boat at left. Back: Men with boat and arms of five states. Watermark: Tiger's head. Printer: W&S.

	VF	UNC
a. Issued note.	50.00	250.
s. Specimen.	—	—

8A — 1 Dollar (VF / UNC)
1.3.1959. Blue on multicolor underprint. Sailing boat at left. Back: Men with boat and arms of five states. Watermark: Tiger's head. Printer: TDLR. — 50.00 / 150.

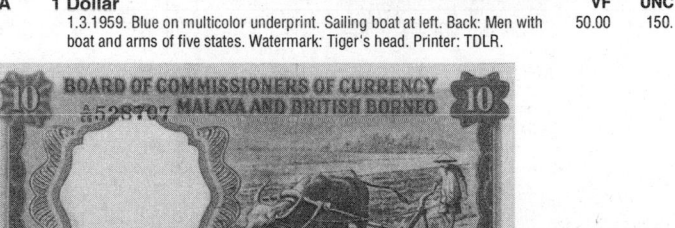

9 — 10 Dollars (VF / UNC)
1.3.1961. Red and dark brown on multicolor underprint. Farmer plowing with ox at right. Watermark: Tiger's head. Printer: TDLR.

	VF	UNC
a. Small serial #. Series A.	125.	550.
b. Large serial #. Series A.	225.	800.
c. Large serial #. Series B.	400.	1500.
s. As a. Specimen.	—	—

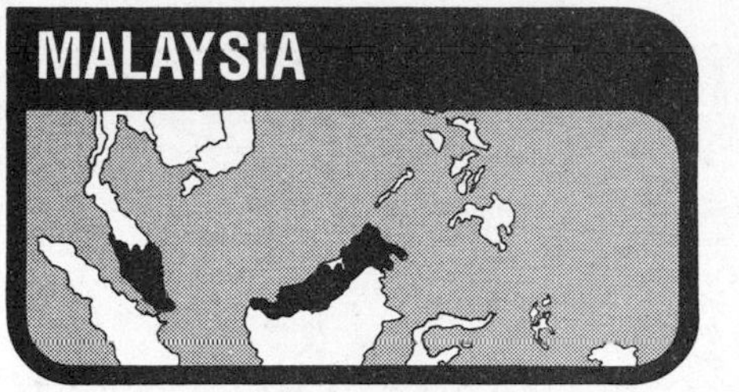

Malaysia, an independent federation of southeast Asia consisting of 11 states of West Malaysia on the Malay Peninsula and two states of East Malaysia on the island of Borneo, has an area of 127,316 sq. mi. (329,747 sq. km.) and a population of 22.3 million. Capital: Kuala Lumpur. The federation came into being on Sept. 16, 1963. Rubber, timber, tin, iron ore and bauxite are exported.

During the late 18th and 19th centuries, Great Britain established colonies and protectorates in the area of current Malaysia; these were occupied by Japan from 1942 to 1945. In 1948, the British-ruled territories on the Malay Peninsula formed the Federation of Malaya, which became independent in 1957. Malaysia was formed in 1963 when the former British colonies of Singapore and the East Malaysian states of Sabah and Sarawak on the northern coast of Borneo joined the Federation. The first several years of the country's history were marred by a Communist insurgency, Indonesian confrontation with Malaysia, Philippine claims to Sabah, and Singapore's secession from the Federation in 1965. During the 22-year term of Prime Minister Mahathir bin Mohamad (1981-2003), Malaysia was successful in diversifying its economy from dependence on exports of raw materials to expansion in manufacturing, services, and tourism.

MONETARY SYSTEM:
1 Ringgit (Dollar) = 100 Sen

DEMONETIZED NOTES:
All 500 and 1000 Ringgitt notes ceased to be legal tender on July 1, 1999.

Federation

Bank Negara Malaysia

1967 ND Issue

1 — 1 Ringgit (VF / UNC)
ND (1967-72). Blue on multicolor underprint. T. A. Rahman at right. Old spelling of *DI-PERLAKUKAN*. Signature Ismail Md. Ali with title: GABENOR. Back: Arms Watermark: Arms Printer: BWC

	VF	UNC
a. Solid security thread.	3.00	25.00

2 — 5 Ringgit (VF / UNC)
ND (1967-72). Green on multicolor underprint. T. A. Rahman at right. Old spelling of *DI-PERLAKUKAN*. Signature Ismail Md. Ali with title: *GABENOR*. Back: Arms. Watermark: Tiger's head. Printer: BWC.

	VF	UNC
a. Solid security thread.	12.00	60.00

3 — 10 Ringgit
ND (1967-72). Red-orange on multicolor underprint. T. A. Rahman at right. Old spelling of *DI-PERLAKUKAN*. Signature Ismail Md. Ali with title: *GABENOR (SA-PULOH)*. Back: Arms. Watermark: Tiger's head. Printer: TDLR.

	VF	UNC
a. Solid security thread.	17.50	80.00

4 — 50 Ringgit
ND (1967-72). Blue and greenish gray on multicolor underprint. T. A. Rahman at right. Old spelling of *DI-PERLAKUKAN*. Signature Ismail Md. Ali with title: *GABENOR(LIMA PULOH)*. Back: Arms. Watermark: Tiger's head. Printer: TDLR.

	VF	UNC
a. Solid security thread.	70.00	350.

5 **100 Ringgit** VF UNC
ND (1967-72). Purple and brown on multicolor underprint. T. A. Rahman at right. Old spelling of *DI-PERLAKUKAN.* Signature Ismail Md. Ali with title: *GABENOR (SA-RATUS).* Back: Arms. Watermark: Tiger's head. Printer: TDLR.
a. Solid security thread. 330. 850.

6 **1000 Ringgit**
ND (1967-72). Brown-violet on multicolor underprint. T. A. Rahman at right. Old spelling of *DI-PERLAKUKAN.* Signature Ismail Md. Ali with title: *GABENOR (SA-RIBU).* Back: Arms. Watermark: Tiger's head. Printer: BWC. 3500. 6500.

1972; 1976 ND Issue

7 **1 Ringgit** VF UNC
ND (1972-76). Blue on multicolor underprint. T. A. Rahman at right. New spelling of *DIPERLAKUKAN.* Signature Ismail Md. Ali with title: *GABENUR.* Back: Arms. Watermark: Tiger's head. Printer: BWC. 2.50 12.50

8 **5 Ringgit** VF UNC
ND (1976). Green on multicolor underprint. T. A. Rahman at right. New spelling of *DIPERLAKUKAN.* Signature Ismail Md. Ali with title: *GABENUR.* Back: Arms. Watermark: Tiger's head. Printer: BWC. .
a. Issued note. 7.50 37.50
s. Specimen. — —

9 **10 Ringgit** VF UNC
ND (1972-76). Red-orange and brown on multicolor underprint. T. A. Rahman at right. New spelling of *DIPERLAKUKAN.* Signature Ismail Md. Ali with title: *GABENUR(SEPULUH).* Back: Arms. Watermark: Tiger's head. Printer: TDLR.
a. Solid security thread. 15.00 75.00
s. Specimen. — —

10 **50 Ringgit** VF UNC
ND (1972-76). Blue and greenish gray on multicolor underprint. T. A. Rahman at right. New spelling of *DIPERLAKUKAN.* Signature Ismail Md. Ali with title: *GABENUR(LIMA PULUH).* Back: Arms. Watermark: Tiger's head. Printer: TDLR.
a. Solid security thread. 100. 300.

11 **100 Ringgit**
ND (1972-76). Purple and brown on multicolor underprint. T. A. Rahman at right. New spelling of *DIPERLAKUKAN.* Signature Ismail Md. Ali with title: *GABENUR(SERATUS).* Back: Arms. Watermark: Tiger's head. Printer: TDLR. 250. 800.

12 **1000 Ringgit**
ND (1972-76). Brown-violet on multicolor underprint. T. A. Rahman at right. New spelling of *DIPERLAKUKAN.* Signature Ismail Md. Ali with title: *GABENUR(SERIBU).* Back: Arms. Watermark: Tiger's head. Printer: BWC. 1000. 4000.

1976; 1981 ND Issues

13 **1 Ringgit** VF UNC
ND (1976-81). Blue on multicolor underprint. T. A. Rahman at right. Signature title: *GABENUR.* Back: Arms, different guilloche with latent image numeral at lower left. Watermark: Tiger's head. Printer: BWC.
a. Signature Ismail Md. Ali. (1976). 1.00 10.50
b. Signature Abdul Aziz Taha. (1981). 1.00 12.50
s. Specimen. — —

14 **5 Ringgit**
ND (1976-81). Green on multicolor underprint. T. A. Rahman at right. Signature title: *GABENUR.* Back: Arms, different guilloche with latent image numeral at lower left. Watermark: Tiger's head. Printer: BWC.
a. Signature Ismail Md. Ali. (1976). 8.00 38.00
b. Signature Abdul Aziz Taha. (1981). 8.00 38.00
s. Specimen. — —

15 **10 Ringgit**
ND (1976-81). Red-orange and brown on multicolor underprint. T. A. Rahman at right. Signature Ismail Md. Ali with title: *GABENUR(SEPULUH).* Back: Arms, different guilloche with latent image numeral at lower left. Watermark: Tiger's head. Printer: BWC. 15.00 50.00

15A **10 Ringgit** VF UNC
ND (1976-81). T. A. Rahman at right. Signature Abdul Aziz Taha. *(SEPULUH).* Back: Arms, different guilloche with latent image numeral at lower left. Watermark: Tiger's head. Printer: TDLR.
a. Issued note. 15.00 50.00
s. Specimen. — —

16 **50 Ringgit** | VF | UNC
ND (1976). Blue and greenish gray on multicolor underprint. T. A. Rahman at right. Signature Ismail Md. Ali. *(LIMA PULUH)*. Back: Arms, different guilloche with latent image numeral at lower left. Watermark: Tiger's head. Printer: BWC. | 100. | 260.

16A **50 Ringgit**
ND (1981). Blue and greenish gray on multicolor underprint. T.A. Rahman at right. Signature Abdul Aziz Taha. Printer: TDLR. | 100. | 350.

17 **100 Ringgit**
ND (1976). Purple and brown on multicolor underprint. T. A. Rahman at right. Signature title: *GABENUR (SERATUS)*. Back: Arms. Watermark: Tiger's head. Printer: BWC.
a. Signature Ismail Md. Ali. (1976). | 100. | 300.

17A **100 Ringgit**
ND (1981). Purple and brown on multicolor underprint. T.A. Rahman at right. Signature Abdul Aziz Taha. Printer: TDLR. | 300. | 800.

18 **1000 Ringgit** | VF | UNC
ND (1976-81). Purple and green on multicolor underprint. T. A. Rahman at right. Signature Ismail Md. Ali with title: *GABENUR (SERIBU)*. Back: Arms, Parliament building in Kuala Lumpur. Watermark: Tiger's head. Printer: BWC. | 700. | 3000.

1981-83 ND Issues

#19-26 Replacement notes: Serial # prefixes *BA; WA; UZ; ZZ.*

19 **1 Ringgit** | VF | UNC
ND (1982-84). Dark blue and brown on pink and multicolor underprint. T. A. Rahman at right. Signature Abdul Aziz Taha. Back: National Monument Kuala Lumpurate at center. Watermark: T. A. Rahman. Printer: BWC. | 2.00 | 10.00

19A **1 Ringgit**
ND (1981-83). Dark blue and brown on pink and multicolor underprint. T. A. Rahman at right. Signature Abdul Aziz Taha. Back: National Monument Kuala Lumpurate at center. Watermark: T. A. Rahman. Printer: TDLR. | 4.00 | 20.00

20 **5 Ringgit**
ND (1983-84). Dark green and blue on multicolor underprint. T. A. Rahman at right. Signature Abdul Aziz Taha. Back: King's Palace at Kuala Lumpur. Watermark: T. A. Rahman. Printer: TDLR. | 8.00 | 25.00

21 **10 Ringgit** | VF | UNC
ND (1983-84). Red and brown on multicolor underprint. T. A. Rahman at right. Signature Abdul Aziz Taha. Back: Railway station at Kuala Lumpur. Watermark: T. A. Rahman. Printer: TDLR. | 15.00 | 42.50

22 **20 Ringgit** | VF | UNC
ND (1982-84). Deep brown and dark blue on multicolor underprint. T. A. Rahman at right. Signature Abdul Aziz Taha. Back: Bank Negara Malaysia building in Kuala Lumpur. Watermark. T. A. Rahman. Printer. BWC. | 15.00 | 60.00

23 **50 Ringgit** | VF | UNC
ND (1983-84). Black and blue-gray on multicolor underprint. T. A. Rahman at right. Signature Abdul Aziz Taha. Back: National Museum at Kuala Lumpur. Watermark: T. A. Rahman. Printer: TDLR. | 60.00 | 120.

24 **100 Ringgit** | VF | UNC
ND (1983-84). Red-brown and violet on multicolor underprint. T. A. Rahman at right. Signature Abdul Aziz Taha. Back: National Mosque in Kuala Lumpur. Watermark: T. A. Rahman. Printer: TDLR. | 80.00 | 160.

25 **500 Ringgit** — VF / UNC
ND (1982-84). Dark red and purple on multicolor underprint. T. A. Rahman at right. Signature Abdul Aziz Taha. Back: High Court building in Kuala Lumpur. Watermark: T. A. Rahman. Printer: BWC. — 400. / 800.

26 **1000 Ringgit** — VF / UNC
ND (1983-84). Gray-green on multicolor underprint. T. A. Rahman at right. Signature Abdul Aziz Taha. Back: Parliament building in Kuala Lumpur. Watermark: T. A. Rahman. Printer: TDLR. — 700. / 1400.

1986-95 ND Issues

#27-31, 32, 33 and 34 Replacement notes: Serial # prefixes *BA; WA; UZ or ZZ.*

27 **1 Ringgit** — VF / UNC
ND (1986; 1989). Dark blue and purple on multicolor underprint. T. A. Rahman at right. Signature Datuk Jaafar Hussein. Vertical serial number. Back: National Monument Kuala Lumpurate at center. Watermark: T. A. Rahman. Printer: TDLR.

	VF	UNC
a. Solid security thread (1986).	FV	5.00
b. Segmented foil over security thread (1989).	FV	5.00

28 **5 Ringgit** — VF / UNC
ND (1986-91). Dark green and green on multicolor underprint. T. A. Rahman at right. Signature Datuk Jaafar Hussein. Vertical serial number. Back: King's Palace at Kuala Lumpur. Watermark: T. A. Rahman. Printer: TDLR.

	VF	UNC
a. Solid security thread (1986).	FV	35.00
b. Segmented foil over security thread (1989).	FV	15.00
c. Flagpole without crossbar at top of back (1991).	FV	12.50

29 **10 Ringgit** — VF / UNC
ND (1989). Red-orange and brown on multicolor underprint. T. A. Rahman at right. Signature Datuk Jaafar Hussein. Vertical serial number. Segmented foil over security thread. Back: Railway station at Kuala Lumpur. Watermark: T. A. Rahman. Printer: TDLR. — FV / 18.00

29A **10 Ringgit**
ND (1989). Brown, red-orange and violet on multicolor underprint. T. A. Rahman at right. Signature Datuk Jaafar Hussein. Vertical serial number. Segmented foil over security thread. Back: Railway station at Kuala Lumpur. Watermark: T. A. Rahman. Printer: BABN. — FV / 17.50

30 **20 Ringgit** — VF / UNC
ND (1989). Deep brown and olive on multicolor underprint. T. A. Rahman at right. Signature Datuk Jaafar Hussein. Vertical serial number. Back: Bank Negara Malaysia building in Kuala Lumpur. Watermark: T. A. Rahman. Printer: TDLR. — FV / 30.00

31 **50 Ringgit** — VF / UNC
ND (1987). Blue and black on multicolor underprint. T. A. Rahman at right. Signature Jafar Hussein. Vertical serial number. Segmented foil over security thread. Back: National Museum at Kuala Lumpur. Watermark: T. A. Rahman. Printer: TDLR. — FV / 60.00

31A **50 Ringgit**
ND (1991-92). Blue and black on multicolor underprint. T. A. Rahman at right. Signature Datuk Jafar Hussein. Vertical serial number. Segmented foil over security thread. Back: National Museum at Kuala Lumpur. Watermark: T. A. Rahman. Printer: BABN. — FV / 70.00

31B **50 Ringgit**
ND (1995). Blue and black on multicolor underprint. T. A. Rahman at right. Signature Ahmad M. Don. Vertical serial number. Segmented foil over security thread. Back: National Museum at Kuala Lumpur. Watermark: T. A. Rahman. Printer: F-CO. — FV / 70.00

31C **50 Ringgit**
ND (1995). Blue and black on multicolor underprint. T. A. Rahman at right. Signature Ahmad M. Don. Vertical serial number. Segmented foil over security thread. Back: National Museum at Kuala Lumpur. Watermark: T. A. Rahman. Printer: TDLR. — FV / 65.00

31D **50 Ringgit**
ND (1997). Blue and black on multicolor underprint. T. A. Rahman at right. Signature Ahmad M. Don. Vertical serial number. Segmented foil over security thread. Back: National Museum at Kuala Lumpur. Watermark: T. A. Rahman. Printer: BABN. — FV / 55.00

32 100 Ringgit — VF | UNC
ND (1989). Purple on multicolor underprint. T. A. Rahman at right. Signature Datuk Jaafar Hussein. Vertical serial number. Segmented foil over security thread. Back: National Mosque in Kuala Lumpur. Watermark: T. A. Rahman. Printer: TDLR. — FV | 120.

32A 100 Ringgit
ND (1992). Purple on multicolor underprint. T. A. Rahman at right. Signature Jafar Hussein. Vertical serial number. Segmented foil over security thread. Back: National Mosque in Kuala Lumpur. Watermark: T. A. Rahman. Printer: USBNC. — FV | 180.

32B 100 Ringgit
ND (1995). Purple on multicolor underprint. T. A. Rahman at right. Signature Ahmad M. Don. Vertical serial number. Segmented foil over security thread. Back: National Mosque in Kuala Lumpur. Watermark: T. A. Rahman. Printer: TDLR. — FV | 100.

32C 100 Ringgit
ND (1988). Purple on multicolor underprint. T. A. Rahman at right. Signature Ahmad M. Don. Vertical serial number. Segmented foil over security thread. Back: National Mosque in Kuala Lumpur. Watermark: T. A. Rahman. Printer: H&S. — FV | 90.00

33 500 Ringgit
ND (1989). Red and brown on yellow and multicolor underprint T. A. Rahman at right. Signature Datuk Jaafar Hussein. Vertical serial number. Segmented foil over security thread. Back: High Court building in Kuala Lumpur. Watermark: T. A. Rahman. Printer: TDLR. — 325. | 1000.

33A 500 Ringgit
ND (1989). Red and brown on yellow and multicolor underprint. T. A. Rahman at right. Signature Datuk Jaafar Hussein. Vertical serial number. Segmented foil over security thread. Back: High Court building in Kuala Lumpur. Watermark: T. A. Rahman. Printer: H&S. — 350. | 1100.

34 1000 Ringgit — VF | UNC
ND (1987). Blue, green and purple on multicolor underprint. T. A. Rahman at right. Signature Jafar Hussein. Vertical serial number. Segmented foil over security thread. Back: Parliament building in Kuala Lumpur. Watermark: T. A. Rahman. Printer: TDLR. — 550. | 1200.

34A 1000 Ringgit
ND (1995). Blue, green and purple on multicolor underprint. T. A. Rahman at right. Signature Ahmad M. Don. Vertical serial number. Segmented foil over security thread. Back: Parliament building in Kuala Lumpur. Watermark: T. A. Rahman. Printer: G&D. — 550. | 1200.

1995 ND Issues

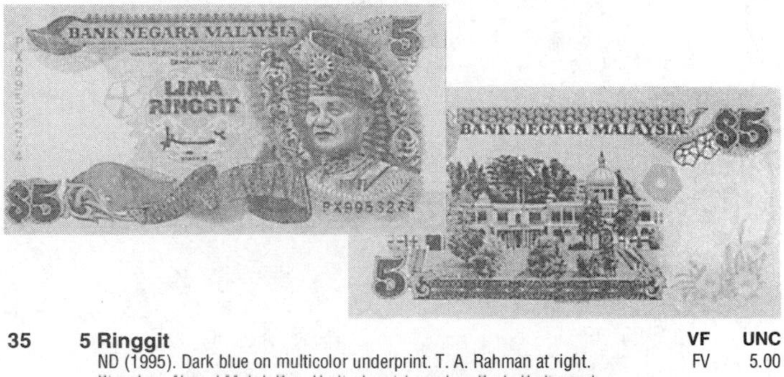

35 5 Ringgit — VF | UNC
ND (1995). Dark blue on multicolor underprint. T. A. Rahman at right. Signature Ahmed Mohd. Don. Vertical serial number. Back: Parliament building in Kuala Lumpur. Watermark: T. A. Rahman. Printer: TDLR. — FV | 5.00

35A 5 Ringgit — VF | UNC
ND (1998). Dark green. T. A. Rahman at right. Signature Ahmed Mohd. Don. Vertical serial number. Segmented security thread. Back: Parliament building in Kuala Lumpur. Watermark: T. A. Rahman. Printer: CBN. — FV | 5.00

36 10 Ringgit — VF | UNC
ND (1995). Dark brown, red-orange and violet on multicolor underprint. T. A. Rahman at right. Signature Datuk Jaafar Hussein. Vertical serial number. Segmented foil over security thread. Back: Railway station in Kuala Lumpur. Watermark: T. A. Rahman. Printer: F-CO. — FV | 10.00

38 10 Ringgit — VF | UNC
ND (1995). Dark brown, red-orange and violet on multicolor underprint. T. A. Rahman at right. Signature Ahmed Mohd. Don. Vertical serial number. Segmented foil over security thread. Back: Railway station in Kuala Lumpur. Watermark: T. A. Rahman. Printer: G&D. — FV | 8.00

1996-2000 ND Issue

39 1 Ringgit — VF | UNC
ND (1998-). Blue and multicolor. T. A. Rahman at right. Ascending size serial number. Back: Flora and mountain landscape with lake. Watermark: T. A. Rahman. Printer: TDLR. 120x65mm.

	VF	UNC
a. Unissued note. Signature Ali Abu Hassen, horizontal.	—	450.
b. Issued note. Signature Zeti Akhtar Aziz, horizontal.	FV	1.00
s. Specimen. Overprinted: *SPECIMEN* in red.	—	200.

40 2 Ringgit — VF | UNC
ND (1996-99). Purple and red-violet on multicolor underprint. T. A. Rahman at right. Ascending size serial number. Back: Modern tower at left, communications satellite at upper center. Watermark: T. A. Rahman. Printer: NBM (without imprint). 130x65mm.

	VF	UNC
a. Signature Ahmad M. Don vertical at left. Long arabic text on back.	FV	3.00
b. Signature Ali Abu Hassan vertical at left. Long Arabic text on back.	FV	2.50
c. Signature Ali Abu Hassan horizontal at lower center. Short Arabic text on back.	FV	2.00
s. As a. Specimen. Overprint in red.	—	200.

41 5 Ringgit — VF — UNC

ND (1999; 2001). Green on multicolor underprint. T. A. Rahman at right. Ascending size serial number. Short Arabic text on back. Back: Modern buildings. Watermark: T. A. Rahman. 135x65mm.

	VF	UNC
a. ND (1999). Signature Ali Abu Hassan. Printer: TDLR.	FV	3.50
b. ND (2001). Signature Zeti Akhtar Aziz. Printer: CBNC.	FV	3.50
s. As a. Specimen. Overprinted: *SPECIMEN* in red.	—	250.

42 10 Ringgit — VF — UNC

ND (1997-). Red on multicolor underprint. T. A. Rahman at right. Ascending size serial number. Back: Modern passenger train at left, passenger jet airplane, freighter ship at center. Watermark: T. A. Rahman. 140x65mm.

	VF	UNC
a. ND (1997). Signature Ahmad M. Don vertical at left. Long arabic text on back. Printer: TDLR.	FV	7.50
b. ND (1999). Signature Ali Abu Hassan vertical at left. Long Arabic text on back. Printer: BABN.	FV	7.50
c. ND (1999). Signature Ali Abu Hassan at center. Short Arabic text on back. Printer: TDLR.	FV	6.00
d. ND (2001). Signature Zeti Akhtar Aziz. Short Arabic text on back. Printer: TDLR.	FV	6.00
s. As a. Specimen. Overprint in red.	—	250.

43 50 Ringgit — VF — UNC

ND (1998-). Dark green and green on multicolor underprint. T. A. Rahman at right. Ascending size serial number. Back: Offshore oil platform at left. Watermark: T. A. Rahman. 145x69mm.

	VF	UNC
a. ND (1998). Signature Ahmad M. Don vertical at left. Long Arabic text on back. Printer: G&D.	FV	35.00
b. ND (1999). Signature Ali Abu Hassan vertical at left. Long Arabic text on back. Printer: G&D.	FV	35.00
c. ND (1999). Signature Ali Abu Hassan at center. Short Arabic text on back. Printer: TDLR.	FV	25.00
d. ND (2001). Signature Zeti Akhtar Aziz. Short Arabic text on back. Printer: TDLR.	FV	25.00

44 100 Ringgit — VF — UNC

ND (1998-). Purple and brown on multicolor underprint. T. A. Rahman at right. Ascending size serial number. Back: Automobile production themes. Watermark: T. A. Rahman. 150x69mm.

	VF	UNC
a. ND (1998). Signature Ahmad M. Don vertical at left. Long Arabic text on back. Printer: TDLR.	FV	55.00
b. ND (1999). Signature Ali Abu Hassan vertical at left. Long Arabic text on back. Printer: G&D.	FV	60.00
c. ND (1999). Signature Ali Abu Hassan at center. Short Arabic text on back. Printer: G&D.	FV	50.00
d. ND (2001). Signature Zeti Akhtar Aziz. Short Arabic text on back. PrinterL G&D.	FV	50.00

1998 Commemorative Issue

#45, XVI Commonwealth Games, Kuala Lumpur, 1998.

45 50 Ringgit — VF — UNC

(19)98. Black and purple on multicolor underprint. T. A. Rahman at right, Petronas Towers at center, multimedia corridor in underprint at right. Serial number prefix: *KL/98*. Back: Utama Bukit Jalil Stadium at center, games logo at left. Polymer plastic. 145x69mm. — FV — 45.00

2004 ND First Issue

46 10 Ringgit — VF — UNC

ND (2004). Red and orange on multicolor underprint. T. A. Rahman at right. Wide holographic strip at far right. Back: Train, ship and jet plane. Printer: G&D. 140x65mm. — FV — 8.00

2004 ND Polymer Issue

47 **5 Ringgit** — VF: FV — UNC: 3.00

ND (2004). Green on multicolor underprint. T.A. Rahman at right. Back: Petronas Towers at center. Polymer plastic. 135x65mm.

2007 Commemorative Issue

49 **50 Ringgit** — VF: FV — UNC: 30.00

2007. Blue, green and multicolor underprint. T. A. Rahman at right, wide holographic strip at far right. Flower at lower center. Gold bands at both ends. Back: Malaysia's first Prime Minister declaring Independence. Logo and commemorative dates. Issued in a folder. 145x69mm.

2009 Issue

50 **50 Ringgit** — VF: FV — UNC: 30.00

ND (2009). Green-blue on multicolor underprint. Tuanku Abdul Rahman at right. Back: Malaysia's first Prime Minister declairing independence at right. Printer: G&D. 145x69mm.

2012 Issue

51 **1 Ringgit** — VF: FV — UNC: 1.00

2012. Blue and multicolor. Tuanku Abdul Rahman at right, flower at lower center. Back: *Wau bulan*, a moon kite. Polymer plastic.

52 **5 Ringgit** — VF: FV — UNC: 2.00

2012. Green and multicolor. Tuanku Abdul Rahman at right, flower at lower center. Back: Pair of Rhinocerus hornbills. Polymer plastic.

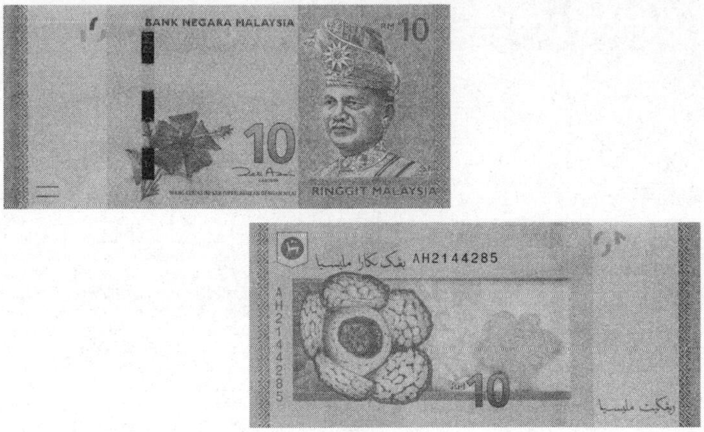

53 **10 Ringgit** — VF: FV — UNC: 6.50

2012. Red and multicolor. Tuanku Abdul Rahman at right, flower at lower center. Segmented security thread. Back: Rafflesia

54 **20 Ringgit** — VF: FV — UNC: 12.50

2012. Orange and multicolor. Tuanku Abdul Rahman at right, flower at lower center. Segmented security thread. Back: Hawksbill and Leatherback turtle.

55 **100 Ringgit** — VF: FV — UNC: 50.00

2012. Purple, brown and multicolor. Tuanku Abdul Rahman at right, flower at lower center. Segmented security thread. Back: Mount Kinabalu and rock formations of Gunung Api Valley

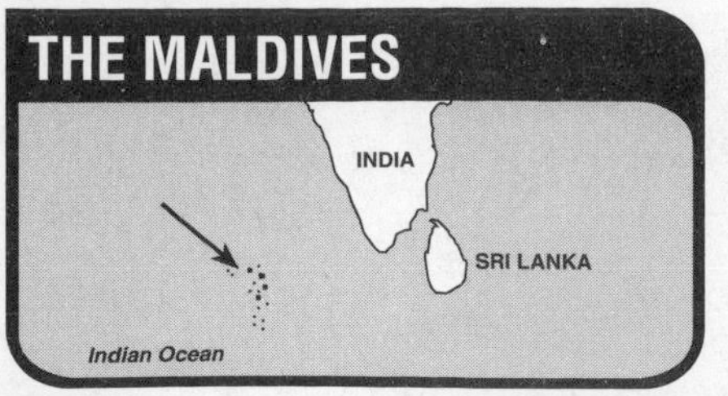

The Republic of Maldives, an archipelago of about 2,000 coral islets in the northern Indian Ocean 417 miles (671 km.) southwest of Ceylon, has an area of 115 sq. mi. (298 sq. km.) and a population of 302,000. Capital: Malé. Fishing employs 95 percent of the work force. Dried fish, copra and coir yarn are exported.

The Maldives was long a sultanate, first under Dutch and then under British protection. It became a republic in 1968, three years after independence. President Maumoon Abdul Gayoom dominated the islands' political scene for 30 years, elected to six successive terms by single-party referendums. Following riots in the capital Male in August 2004, the president and his government pledged to embark upon democratic reforms including a more representative political system and expanded political freedoms. Progress was sluggish, however, and many promised reforms were slow to be realized. Nonetheless, political parties were legalized in 2005. In June 2008, a constituent assembly - termed the "Special Majlis" - finalized a new constitution, which was ratified by the president in August. The first-ever presidential elections under a multi-candidate, multi-party system were held in October 2008. Gayoom was defeated in a runoff poll by Mohamed Nasheed, a political activist who had been jailed several years earlier by the former regime. Challenges facing the new president include strengthening democracy and combating poverty and drug abuse.

RULERS:

British to 1965

MONETARY SYSTEM:

1 Rufiyaa (Rupee) = 100 Lari

REPUBLIC

MALDIVIAN STATE, GOVERNMENT TREASURER

1951; 1960; 1980 ISSUE

		VF	UNC
6	**50 Rupees**		
	1951-80. Blue on multicolor underprint. Palm tree and dhow at left, dhow at right. Back: Royal Embarkation Gate at Malé at center.		
	a. 1951/AH1371.	150.	400.
	b. 4.6.1960/AH1379.	20.00	90.00
	c. Lithographed 1.8.1980/AH17.7.1400.	25.00	100.
	s. As c. Specimen.	—	175.

		VF	UNC
7	**100 Rupees**		
	1951; 1960. Green on multicolor underprint. Palm tree and dhow at left, dhow at right. Back: Brown, violet and multicolor. Park and building complex at center.		
	a. 1951/AH1371.	175.	500.
	b. 4.6.1960/AH1379.	50.00	200.

MALDIVES MONETARY AUTHORITY

1983 ISSUE

		VF	UNC
9	**2 Rufiyaa**		
	7.10.1983/AH1404. Dark olive-green on multicolor underprint. Dhow at right. Back: Shoreline village. Watermark: Arms. Printer: BWC. 150x70mm.		
	a. Issued note.	FV	4.00
	s. Specimen.	—	30.00

		VF	UNC
10	**5 Rufiyaa**		
	7.10.1983/AH1404. Deep purple on green and multicolor underprint. Dhow at right. Back: Fishing boats at center. Watermark: Arms. Printer: BWC. 150x70mm.		
	a. Issued note.	FV	4.00
	s. Specimen.	—	30.00

		VF	UNC
11	**10 Rufiyaa**		
	7.10.1983/AH1404. Brown on green and multicolor underprint. Dhow at right. Back: Villagers working at center. Watermark: Arms. Printer: BWC. 150x70mm.		
	a. Issued note.	FV	4.00
	s. Specimen.	—	30.00

12 **20 Rufiyaa** VF UNC

1983; 1987. Red-violet on multicolor underprint. Dhow at right. Back: Fishing boats at dockside in Malé Harbour. Watermark: Arms. Printer: BWC. 150x70mm.

	VF	UNC
a. 7.10.1983/AH1404. Imprint at bottom center on back.	FV	7.00
b. 25.8.1987/AH1408. Without imprint at bottom center on back.	FV	5.50
s. Specimen. As a.	—	30.00

13 **50 Rufiyaa** VF UNC

1983; 1987. Blue-violet on multicolor underprint. Dhow at right. Back: Village market in Malé at center. Watermark: Arms. Printer: BWC. 150x70mm.

	VF	UNC
a. 7.10.1983/AH1404. Imprint at bottom center on back.	FV	25.00
b. 25.8.1987/AH1408. Without imprint at bottom center on back.	FV	17.50
s. Specimen.	—	30.00

14 **100 Rufiyaa** VF UNC

1983; 1987. Dark green and brown on multicolor underprint. Dhow at right. Back: Tomb of Medhuziyaaraiy at center. Watermark: Arms. Printer: BWC. 150x70mm.

	VF	UNC
a. 7.10.1983/AH1404. Imprint at bottom center on back.	FV	35.00
b. 25.8.1987/AH1408. Without imprint at bottom center on back.	FV	27.50
s. Specimen.		30.00

1990 Issue

		VF	UNC
15	**2 Rufiyaa** 26.7.1990/AH1411. Dark olive-green on multicolor underprint. Dhow at right. Back: Shoreline village. Watermark: Arms. Printer: TDLR. 150x70mm.	FV	2.50
16	**5 Rufiyaa** 26.7.1990/AH1411. Deep purple on multicolor underprint. Dhow at right. Back: Fishing boats at center. Watermark: Arms. Printer: TDLR. 150x70mm.	FV	3.00

		VF	UNC
17	**500 Rufiyaa** 26.7.1990/AH1411. Orange and green on multicolor underprint. Back: Grand Friday Mosque and Islamic Center. Watermark: Arms. Printer: TDLR. 150x70mm.	FV	120.

1995-98 Issue

18 **5 Rufiyaa** VF UNC

1988; 2000; 2006; 2011. Deep purple, dark blue and violet on multicolor underprint. Design to edge of paper. Dhow at right. Ascending size serial numbers at left and lower right. Back: Fishing boats at center. Watermark: Arms. Printer: TDLR. 150x70mm.

	VF	UNC
a. 27.4.1998/AH1419.	FV	2.00
b. 2000/AH1421.	FV	2.00
c. 2006/AH1427.	FV	2.00
d. 2011/AH1432.	FV	2.00

19 **10 Rufiyaa** VF UNC

1998; 2006. Dark brown, green and orange on multicolor underprint. Design to edge of paper. Dhow at right. Ascending size serial numbers at left and lower right. Back: Vilagers working at center. Watermark: Arms. 150x70mm.

	VF	UNC
a. 25.10.1998/AH1419. Series C. DLR imprint.	FV	3.00
b. 25.10.1998/AH1419. Series D. Without imprint.	FV	3.00
c. 2006/AH1427.	FV	3.00

#	Denomination	VF	UNC
20	**20 Rufiyaa** 2000/AH1421; 2008/AH1430. Red-violet and green on multicolor underprint. Dhow at right. Ascending size serial numbers at left and lower right. Back: Fishing boats at dockside in Malé Harbor. Watermark: Arms. Design into borders. 150x70mm.		
	a. 2000/AH1421. Series B. With DLR imprint	FV	5.00
	b. 2000/AH1421 Series C. Without imprint.	FV	5.00
	c. 2008/AH1430.	FV	3.50

#	Denomination	VF	UNC
21	**50 Rufiyaa** 2000/AH1421; 2008/AH1430. Blue-violet and light green on multicolor underprint. Dhow at right. Ascending size serial numbers at left and lower right. Back: Village market in Malé at center. Watermark: Arms. Printer: TDLR. Design into borders. 150x70mm.		
	a. 2000/AH1421.	FV	12.50
	b. 2008/AH1430.	FV	12.50
22	**100 Rufiyaa** 1995; 2000. Dark green and brown on multicolor underprint. Dhow at right. Back: Tomb of Medhuziyaaraiy at center. Watermark: Arms. 150x70mm.		
	a. 29.7.1995/AH1416. Series D. Printer BWC, without imprint.	FV	25.00
	b. 2000/AH1421. Series G. Enhanced UV features.	FV	22.50

#	Denomination	VF	UNC
23	**500 Rufiyaa** 1996; 2000. Orange and green on multicolor underprint. Dhow at right. Back: Grand Friday Mosque and Islamic Center. Watermark: Arms. Printer: TDLR. 150x70mm.		
	a. 1.5.1996/AH1416.	FV	90.00
	b. 2000/AH1421. Wide segmented security thread.	FV	90.00

#	Denomination	VF	UNC
24	**500 Rufiyaa** 2006/AH1426. Red, orange and green on multicolor underprint. Dhow at right. Back: Grand Friday Mosque and Islamic Center. Watermark: Arms Printer: TDLR. 150x70mm.	FV	90.00

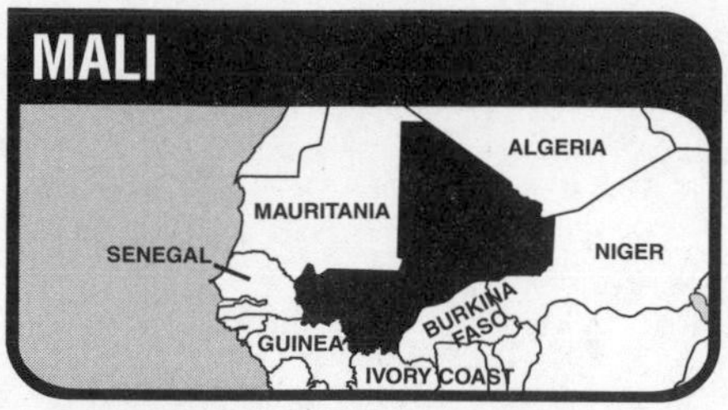

The Republic of Mali, a landlocked country in the interior of West Africa southwest of Algeria, has an area of 478,764 sq. mi. (1,240,000 sq. km.) and a population of 12.56 million. Capital: Bamako. Livestock, fish, cotton and peanuts are exported. The Sudanese Republic and Senegal became independent of France in 1960 as the Mali Federation. When Senegal withdrew after only a few months, what formerly made up the Sudanese Republic was renamed Mali. Rule by dictatorship was brought to a close in 1991 by a military coup - led by the current president Amadou Toure - enabling Mali's emergence as one of the strongest democracies on the continent. President Alpha Konare won Mali's first democratic presidential election in 1992 and was reelected in 1997. In keeping with Mali's two-term constitutional limit, Konare stepped down in 2002 and was succeeded by Amadou Toure, who was subsequently elected to a second term in 2007. The elections were widely judged to be free and fair

Mali seceded from the African Financial Community in 1962, then rejoined in 1984. Issues specially marked with letter *D* for Mali were made by the Banque des Etats de l'Afrique de l'Ouest. See also French West Africa, and West African States.

MONETARY SYSTEM:

1 Franc = 100 Centimes

SIGNATURE VARIETIES

1	Ministre Des Finances		Gouverneur de La Banque
2	Ministre d'Etat	Ministre Des Finances	Gouverneur de La Banque
3	Le Président du Council d' Administration		Le Directeur Genéral
4	Le Président du Council d' Administration		Le Directeur Genéral
5	Le Président du Council d' Administration		Le Directeur Genéral
6	Le Président du Council d' Administration		Le Directeur Genéral
7	Le Président du Council d' Administration		Le Directeur Genéral
8	Le Président du Council d' Administration		Le Directeur Genéral
9	Le Président du Council d' Administration		Le Directeur Genéral

Republic

Banque de la République du Mali

First 1960 (1962) Issue

Note: Post-dated to Day of Independence.

		VF	UNC
1	**50 Francs** 22.9.1960. Purple on multicolor underprint. President Modibo Keita at left. Signature 1. Back: Village.	100.	350.

		VF	UNC
2	**100 Francs** 22.9.1960. Brown on yellow underprint. President Modibo Keita at left. Signature 1. Back: Cattle.	90.00	325.

		VF	UNC
3	**500 Francs** 22.9.1960. Red on light blue and orange underprint. President Modibo Keita at left. Signature 1. Back: Woman and tent.	500.	1300.

		VF	UNC
4	**1000 Francs** 22.9.1960. Blue on light green and orange underprint. President Modibo Keita at left. Signature 1. Farmers with oxen at lower right. Back: Blue. Man and huts.	180.	600.
5	**5000 Francs** 22.9.1960. Green on multicolor underprint. President Modibo Keita at left. Signature 1. Farmers with oxen at lower right. Two farmers plowing with oxen at right. Back: Market scene and building.	450.	—

Second 1960 (1967) Issue

Note: Post-dated to Day of Independence.

		VF	UNC
6	**50 Francs** 22.9.1960 (1967). Purple on blue and light green underprint. Modibo Keita at right, dam at lower left. Signature 2. Back: Purple. Woman and village. Printer: TDLR.		
	a. Issued note.	100.	350.
	s. Specimen. Red overprint: *SPECIMEN* and TDLR logo on both sides.	—	1250.

		VF	UNC
7	**100 Francs** 22.9.1960 (1967). Brown on green and lilac underprint. Modibo Keita at right, tractors at lower left. Signature 2. Back: Brown. Old man at right, canoes at center, city view behind. Printer: TDLR.		
	a. Issued note.	90.00	325.
	s. Specimen. Red overprint: *SPECIMEN* and TDLR logo on both sides.	—	1250.

8	500 Francs	VF	UNC
	22.9.1960 (1967). Green on yellow, blue and red underprint. Modibo Keita at right, building at lower left. Signature 2. Back: Longhorn cattle. Printer: TDLR.		
	a. Issued note.	235.	750.
	s. Specimen. Red overprint: *SPECIMEN* and TDLR logo on both sides.	—	1250.

9	1000 Francs	VF	UNC
	22.9.1960 (1967). Blue on lilac and brown underprint. Modibo Keita at right, bank at lower left. Signature 2. Back: Blue. People and Djenne mosque. Printer: TDLR.		
	a. Issued note.	550.	1400.
	s. Specimen. Red overprint: *SPECIMEN* and TDLR logo on both sides.	—	1250.

10	5000 Francs	VF	UNC
	22.9.1960 (1967). Dark red on green underprint. Modibo Keita at right, farmers at center. Signature 2. Back: Market scene and buildings. Printer: TDLR.		
	a. Issued note.	450.	1200.
	s. Specimen. Red overprint: *SPECIMEN* and TDLR logo on both sides.	—	1250.

Banque Centrale du Mali

1970-73 ND Issues

11	100 Francs	VF	UNC
	ND (1972-73). Brown and multicolor. Woman at left, hotel at right. Signature 4. Back: Woman at left, boats docking at center.	70.00	275.

12	500 Francs	VF	UNC
	ND (1973-84). Brown and multicolor. Soldier at left, tractors at right. Back: Man and camels. Watermark: Man's head.		
	a. Signature 4.	35.00	120.
	b. Signature 5.	25.00	80.00
	c. Signature 6.	20.00	70.00
	d. Signature 7.	20.00	70.00
	e. Signature 8.	20.00	70.00
	f. Signature 9.	75.00	250.

13	1000 Francs	VF	UNC
	ND (1970-84). Brownish black, purple and multicolor. Building at left, older man at right. Back: Carvings at left, mountain village at center. Watermark: Man's head.		
	a. Signature 4.	27.50	90.00
	b. Signature 5.	27.50	90.00
	c. Signature 6.	25.00	80.00
	d. Signature 7.	25.00	80.00
	e. Signature 8.	25.00	80.00

14 5000 Francs

ND (1972-84). Blue, brown and multicolor. Cattle at lower left, man with turban at right. Back: Woman and flowers at left center, woman at textile machinery at right. Watermark: Man's head.

	VF	UNC
a. Signature 4.	200.	700.
b. Signature 5.	185.	650.
c. Signature 6.	185.	650.
d. Signature 7.	185.	650.
e. Signature 8.	175.	600.

15 10,000 Francs

ND (1970-84). Multicolor. Man with fez at left, factory at lower right. Back: Weaver at left, young woman with coin headband at right. Watermark: Man's head.

	VF	UNC
a. Signature 3.	275.	900.
b. Signature 4.	235.	800.
c. Signature 5.	250.	850.
d. Signature 6.	235.	800.
e. Signature 7.	235.	800.
f. Signature 8.	235.	800.
g. Signature 9.	250.	850.

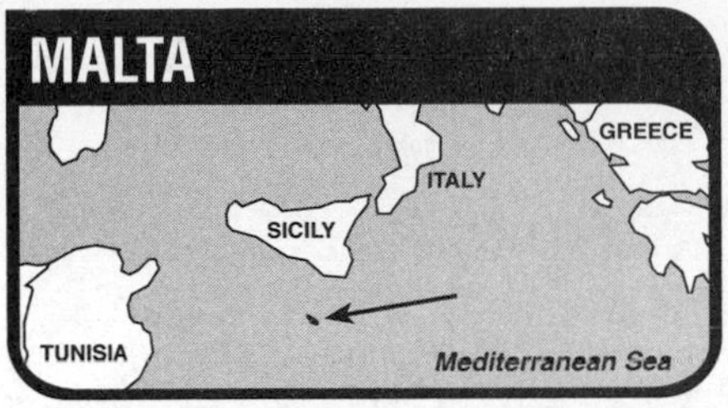

The Republic of Malta, an independent parliamentary democracy within the British Commonwealth, is situated in the Mediterranean Sea between Sicily and North Africa. With the islands of Gozo and Comino, Malta has an area of 122 sq. mi. (316 sq. km.) and a population of 379,000. Capital: Valletta. With the islands of Gozo (Ghawdex), Comino, Cominetto and Filfla, Malta has no proven mineral resources, an agriculture insufficient to its needs and a small but expanding, manufacturing facility. Clothing, textile yarns and fabrics, and knitted wear are exported.

Great Britain formally acquired possession of Malta in 1814. The island staunchly supported the UK through both World Wars and remained in the Commonwealth when it became independent in 1964. A decade later Malta became a republic. Since about the mid-1980s, the island has transformed itself into a freight transshipment point, a financial center, and a tourist destination. Malta became an EU member in May 2004 and began to use the euro as currency in 2008.

RULERS:

British to 1974

MONETARY SYSTEM:

1 Shilling = 12 Pence
1 Pound = 20 Shillings to 1971
1 Lira = 100 Centesimi, 1972-2007
1 Euro = 100 Cents, 2008-

REPUBLIC

GOVERNMENT OF MALTA

1949 ORDINANCE; 1963 ND ISSUE

25 10 Shillings

L.1949 (1963). Green and blue on multicolor underprint. Queen Elizabeth II at right, cross at center. Signature R. Soler. Back: Mgarr Harbor, Gozo. Printer: BWC.

	VF	UNC
a. Issued note.	175.	475.
s. Specimen.	—	600.
ct. Color trial. Red on multicolor underprint.	—	650.

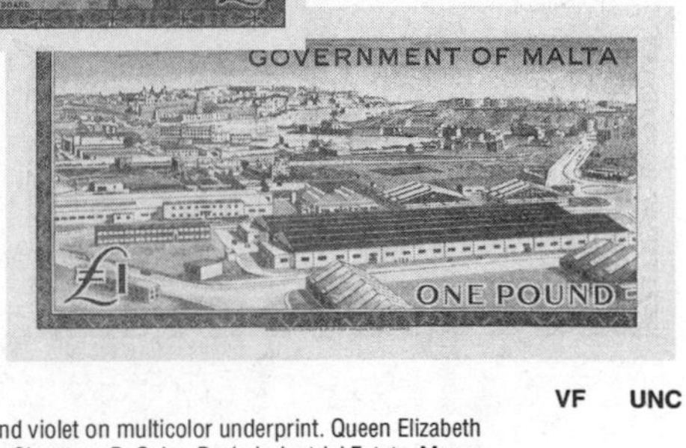

26 1 Pound

L.1949 (1963). Brown and violet on multicolor underprint. Queen Elizabeth II at right, cross at center. Signature R. Soler. Back: Industrial Estate, Marsa. Printer: BWC.

	VF	UNC
a. Issued note.	115.	350.
s. Specimen.	—	500.
ct. Color trial. Blue on multicolor underprint.	—	600.

27 5 Pounds

L.1949 (1961). Blue on multicolor underprint. Queen Elizabeth II at right, cross at center. Back: Grand Harbor. Printer: BWC.

	VF	UNC
a. Signature D. A. Shepherd (1961).	375.	1600.
b. Signature R. Soler (1963).	600.	2000.
s. As a. Specimen, punch hole cancelled.	—	850.
ct. Color trial. Brown and violet on multicolor underprint.	—	1000.

Central Bank of Malta

1967 Central Bank Act; 1968-69 ND Issue

28 10 Shillings

L.1967 (1968). Red on multicolor underprint. Similar to #25. Signature P.L. Hogg. Printer: BWC

	VF	UNC
a. Issued note.	100.	225.
s. Specimen.	—	400.
ct. Color trial. Dark olive on multicolor underprint.	—	500.

29 1 Pound

L.1967 (1969). Olive-green on multicolor underprint. Similar to #26. Signature P.L. Hogg. Printer: BWC

	VF	UNC
a. Issued note.	125.	300.
s. Specimen.	—	400.
ct. Color trial. Blue on multicolor underprint.	—	500.

30 5 Pounds

L.1967 (1968). Brown and violet on multicolor underprint. Similar to #27. Signature P.L. Hogg. Printer: BWC

	VF	UNC
a. Issued note.	175.	450.
s. Specimen.	—	700.
ct. Color trial. Red on multicolor underprint.	—	800.

Bank Centrali ta' Malta

1967 Central Bank Act; 1973 ND Issue

#31-33 Replacement notes: Serial # prefix *X/1*, *Y/1* or *Z/1* (by denomintation).

31 1 Lira

L.1967 (1973). Green on multicolor underprint. Arms at right, map at center, War Memorial at left. Back: PrehistoricTemple in Tarxien at left, old capital city of Medina at center. Watermark: Allegorical head of Malta. Printer: TDLR.

	VF	UNC
a. Signature J. Sammut and A. Camilleri.	25.00	60.00
b. Signature H. de Gabriele and J. Laspina.	25.00	60.00
c. Signature H. de Gabriele and A. Camilleri.	25.00	60.00
d. Signature J. Laspina and J. Sammut.	25.00	60.00
e. Signature A. Camilleri and J. Laspina.	25.00	60.00
f. Signature J. Sammut and H. de Gabriele.	25.00	60.00
s. Specimen.	—	200.

32 5 Liri

L.1967 (1973). Blue on multicolor underprint. Arms at right, map at center, Neptune at left. Back: Marina at left, boats at center right. Watermark: Allegorical head of Malta. Printer: TDLR.

	VF	UNC
a. Signature H. de Gabriele and J. Laspina.	60.00	130.
b. Signature H. de Gabriele and A. Camilleri.	60.00	130.
c. Signature J. Laspina and J. Sammut.	60.00	130.
d. Signature A. Camilleri and J. Laspina.	60.00	130.
e. Signature J. Sammut and H. de Gabriele.	60.00	130.
f. Signature J. Sammut and A. Camilleri.	60.00	130.
s. Specimen.	—	300.

33 10 Liri

L.1967 (1973). Brown on multicolor underprint. Arms at right, map at center, Neptune at left. Back: View of Grand Harbour and boats. Watermark: Allegorical head of Malta. Printer: TDLR.

	VF	UNC
a. Signature H. de Gabriele and A. Camilleri.	90.00	300.
b. Signature J. Laspina and J. Sammut.	90.00	300.
c. Signature A. Camilleri and J. Laspina.	90.00	300.
d. Signature J. Sammut and H. de Gabriele.	90.00	300.
e. Signature L. Spiteri with title: *DEPUTAT GOVERNATUR.*	90.00	225.
s. Specimen.	—	400.

1979 ND Issue

Central Bank Act, 1967

#34-36 Replacement notes: Serial prefix *X/2, Y/2* or *Z/2* (by denomination).

34 1 Lira

L.1967 (1979). Brown on multicolor underprint. Map at upper left, arms at upper right. Watch tower "Gardjola" at center. Back: New University at left center. Watermark: Allegorical head of Malta. Printer: TDLR.

	VF	UNC
a. Without dot.	25.00	50.00
b. With 1 dot added for blind at upper right.	25.00	50.00
s. Specimen. Red overprint: *SPECIMEN.*	—	60.00

35 5 Liri

L.1967 (1979). Purple and violet on multicolor underprint. Map at upper left, arms at upper right. Statue of "Culture" at center. Back: Aerial view of Marsa Industrial Estate at left center. Watermark: Allegorical head of Malta. Printer: TDLR.

	VF	UNC
a. Without 2 dots.	25.00	75.00
b. With 2 dots added for blind at upper right.	90.00	180.
s. Specimen. Red overprint: *SPECIMEN.*	—	130.

36 10 Liri

L.1967 (1979). Gray and pink on multicolor underprint. Map at upper left, arms at upper right.Statue of "Justice" at center. Back: Aerial view of Malta drydocks at left center. Watermark: Allegorical head of Malta. Printer: TDLR.

	VF	UNC
a. Without 3 dots.	50.00	125.
b. With 3 dots added for blind at upper right.	60.00	150.
s. Specimen. Red overprint: *SPECIMEN.*	—	300.

1986 ND Issue

#37-40 Replacement notes: Serial # prefix *W/2, X/2, Y/2* or *Z/2* (by denomination).

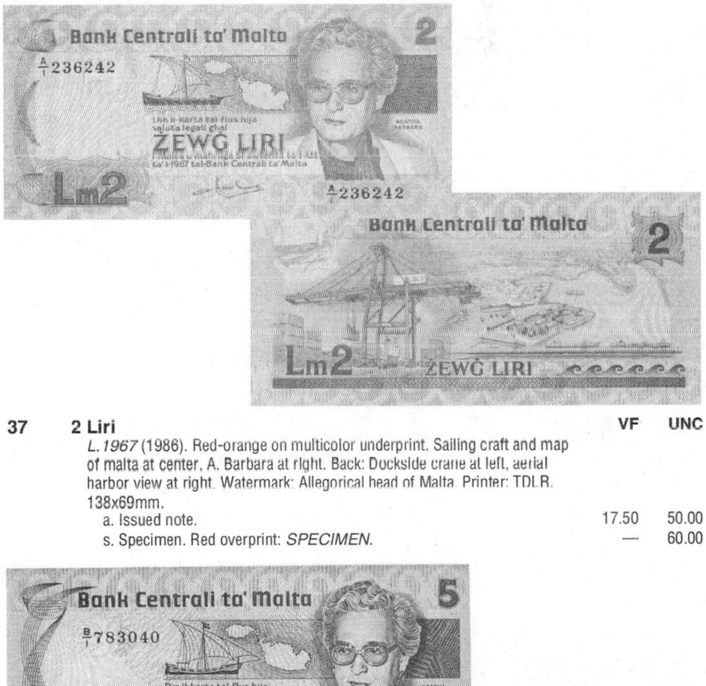

37 2 Liri

L.1967 (1986). Red-orange on multicolor underprint. Sailing craft and map of malta at center, A. Barbara at right. Back: Dockside crane at left, aerial harbor view at right. Watermark: Allegorical head of Malta. Printer: TDLR. 138x69mm.

	VF	UNC
a. Issued note.	17.50	50.00
s. Specimen. Red overprint: *SPECIMEN.*	—	60.00

38 5 Liri

L.1967 (1986). Gray-green and blue on multicolor underprint, with two black horizontal accounting bars at lower rig Sailing craft and map of malta at center, A. Barbara at right. Back: Sailboats in harbor and repairing of fishing nets. Watermark: Allegorical head of Malta. Printer: TDLR. 145x69mm.

	VF	UNC
a. Issued note.	30.00	85.00
s. Specimen. Red overprint: *SPECIMEN.*	—	130.

39 **10 Liri** VF UNC

L.1967 (1986). Olive and dark green on multicolor underprint, with three dark green horizontal accounting bars at l Sailing craft and map of malta at center, A. Barbara at right. Back: Shipbuilding. Watermark: Allegorical head of Malta. Printer: TDLR. 152x73mm.

	VF	UNC
a. Issued note.	55.00	165.
s. Specimen. Red overprint: *SPECIMEN.*	—	300.

40 **20 Lira** VF UNC

L.1967 (1986). Brown and red-brown on multicolor underprint, with four brown horizontal accounting bars at lower ri Sailing craft and map of malta at center, A. Barbara at right. Back: Statue and government building at center. Watermark: Allegorical head of Malta. Printer: TDLR. 179x76mm.

	VF	UNC
a. Issued note.	125.	300.
s. Specimen. Red overprint: *SPECIMEN.*	—	400.

1989 ND Issue

#41-44 Replacement notes: Serial # prefix *W/2, X/2, Y/2* or *Z/2* (by denomination).

41 **2 Liri** VF UNC

L.1967 (1989). Purple on multicolor underprint. Doves at left, Malta standing with rudder at center. Back: Buildings in Malta and Gozo. Watermark: Turreted head of Malta. Printer: TDLR. 138x69mm.

	VF	UNC
a. Issued note.	15.00	35.00
s. Specimen. Red overprint: *SPECIMEN.*	—	60.00

42 **5 Liri**

L.1967 (1989). Blue on multicolor underprint. Doves at left, Malta standing with rudder at center. Back: Historical tower. Watermark: Turreted head of Malta. Printer: TDLR. 145x69mm.

	VF	UNC
a. Issued note.	20.00	60.00
s. Specimen. Red overprint: *SPECIMEN.*	—	130.

43 **10 Liri**

L.1967 (1989). Green on multicolor underprint. Doves at left, Malta standing with rudder at center. Back: Wounded people being brought into National Assembly. Watermark: Turreted head of Malta. Printer: TDLR. 159x73mm.

	VF	UNC
a. Issued note.	40.00	115.
s. Specimen. Red overprint: *SPECIMEN.*	—	300.

44 **20 Lira**

L.1967 (1989). Brown on multicolor underprint. Doves at left, Malta standing with rudder at center. Back: Prime Minister Dr. G. B. Olivier. Watermark: Turreted head of Malta. Printer: TDLR. 179x76mm.

	VF	UNC
a. Issued note.	85.00	220.
s. Specimen. Red overprint: *SPECIMEN.*	—	400.

1994 ND Issue

45 **2 Liri** VF UNC

L.1967 (1994). Purple on multicolor underprint. Doves at left, Malta standing with rudder at center. Segmented foil over security threads and ascending size serial numbers at upper left. Back: Buildings in Malta and Gozo. Watermark: Turreted head of Malta. Printer: TDLR. 138x69mm.

	VF	UNC
a. Signature Anthony P. Galdes.	FV	40.00
b. Signature Francis J. Vasallo.	FV	40.00
c. Signature Emanuel Ellul.	FV	40.00
d. Signature Michael P. Bonello.	FV	40.00
s. Specimen. Red overprint: *SPECIMEN.*	—	60.00

46 **5 Liri** VF UNC

L.1967 (1994). Blue on multicolor underprint. Doves at left, Malta standing with rudder at center. Segmented foil over security threads and ascending size serial numbers at upper left. Back: Historical tower. Watermark: Turreted head of Malta. Printer: TDLR. 145x69mm.

	VF	UNC
a. Signature Anthony P. Galdes.	FV	85.00
b. Signature Francis J. Vassallo.	FV	80.00
c. Signature Emanuel Ellul.	FV	75.00
d. Signature Michael P. Bonello.	FV	70.00
s. Specimen. Red overprint: *SPECIMEN.*	—	130.

47 **10 Liri** VF UNC

L.1967 (1994). Green on multicolor underprint. Doves at left, Malta standing with rudder at center. Segmented foil over security threads and ascending size serial numbers at upper left. Back: Wounded people being brought into National Assembly. Watermark: Turreted head of Malta. Printer: TDLR. 159x73mm.

	VF	UNC
a. Signature Anthony P. Galdes.	FV	110.
b. Signature Emanuel Ellul.	FV	90.00
c. Signature Michael P. Bonello.	FV	70.00
s. Specimen. Red overprint: *SPECIMEN.*	—	300.

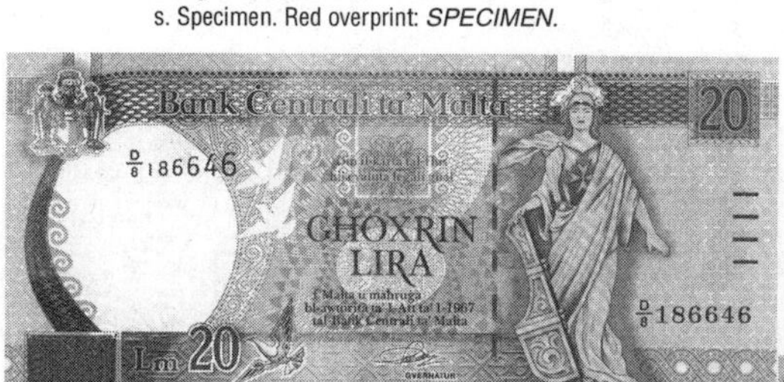

48 **20 Lira** VF UNC

L.1967 (1994). Brown on multicolor underprint. Doves at left, Malta standing with rudder at center. Segmented foil over security threads and ascending size serial numbers at upper left. Signature; Anthony P. Galdes. Back: Prime Minister Dr. G. B. Olivier. Watermark: Turreted head of Malta. Printer: TDLR. 159x76mm.

	VF	UNC
a. Issued note.	FV	180.
s. Specimen. Red overprint: *SPECIMEN.*	—	400.

2000 Issue

#49-51 Millennium Commemorative issue.

49 **2 Liri** — VF | UNC

2000 *(L. 1967.)* Purple on multicolor underprint. Doves at left, Malta standing with rudder at center. Segmented foil over security threads and ascending size serial numbers at upper left. Map and clock hologram on watermark area. Back: Buildings in Malta and Gozo. Watermark: Turreted head of Malta. Printer: TDLR. 138x69mm. — FV | 50.00

50 **5 Liri** — VF | UNC

2000 *(L. 1967.)* Blue on multicolor underprint. Doves at left, Malta standing with rudder at center. Segmented foil over security threads and ascending size serial numbers at upper left. Map and clock hologram on watermark area. Back: Historical tower. Watermark: Turreted head of Malta. Printer: TDLR. 145x69mm. — FV | 100.

51 **10 Liri** — VF | UNC

2000 *(L. 1967.)* Green on multicolor underprint. Doves at left, Malta standing with rudder at center. Segmented foil over security threads and ascending size serial numbers at upper left. Map and clock hologram on watermark area. Back: Wounded people being brought into National Assembly. Watermark: Turreted head of Malta. Printer: TDLR. 152x73mm. — FV | 150.

Collector Series

Bank Centrali ta' Malta

1979 Issue

CS1 **ND (1979) 1-10 Liri** — Mkt. Value

#34a-36a with overprint: *SPECIMEN* and Maltese cross prefix serial #. — 180.

2000 Issue

CS2 **ND (2000) 2-5-10 Liri** — Mkt. Value

#49-51 in individual folders titled: *Special Millennium Issue.* Hologram on watermark area: *1999 Towards a New Millennium 2000.* 25,000 sets issued. — 300.

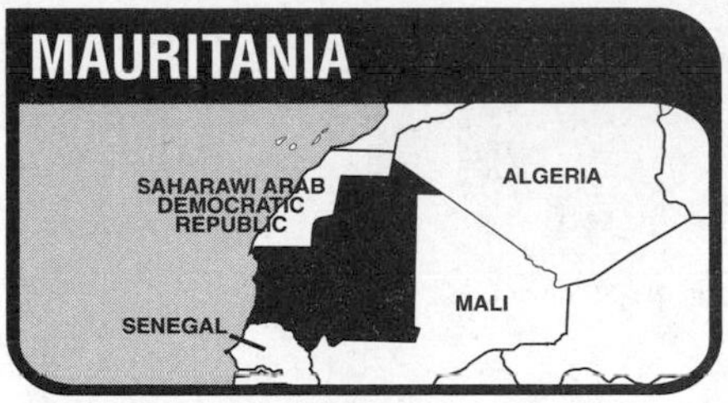

The Islamic Republic of Mauritania, located in northwest Africa bounded by Spanish Sahara, Mali, Algeria, Senegal and the Atlantic Ocean, has an area of 397,955 sq. mi. (1,030,700 sq. km.) and a population of 2.58 million. Capital: Nouakchott. The economy centers on herding, agriculture, fishing and mining. Iron ore, copper concentrates and fish products are exported.

Independent from France in 1960, Mauritania annexed the southern third of the former Spanish Sahara (now Western Sahara) in 1976, but relinquished it after three years of raids by the Polisario guerrilla front seeking independence for the territory. Maaouya Ould Sid Ahmed Taya seized power in a coup in 1984 and ruled Mauritania with a heavy hand for over two decades. A series of presidential elections that he held were widely seen as flawed. A bloodless coup in August 2005 deposed President TAYA and ushered in a military council that oversaw a transition to democratic rule. Independent candidate Sidi Ould Cheikh Abadallahi was inaugurated in April 2007 as Mauritania's first freely and fairly elected president. His term ended prematurely in August 2008 when a military junta deposed him and ushered in a military council government. Meanwhile, the country continues to experience ethnic tensions among its black population (Afro-Mauritanians) and White and Black Moor (Arab-Berber) communities.

On June 28, 1973, in a move designed to emphasize its non-alignment with France, Mauritania converted its currency from the old French-supported CFA franc unit to a new unit called the Ouguiya.

MONETARY SYSTEM:

1 Ouguiya = 5 Khoum
100 Ouguiya = 500 CFA Francs, 1973-

Note: Issues specially marked with letter *E* for Mauritania were issued by the Banque Centrale des Etats de l'Afrique de l'Ouest. These issues were used before Mauritania seceded from the French Community of the West African States in 1973. For those listings see West African States.

Republic

Banque Centrale de Mauritanie

1973 Issue

1 **100 Ouguiya** — VF | UNC

20.6.1973. Blue on multicolor underprint. Mauritanian girl at center. Back: Men loading boat. Printer: Algerian.

	VF	UNC
a. Issued note.	25.00	85.00
s. Specimen.	—	50.00

2 **200 Ouguiya** — VF | UNC

20.6.1973. Brown on multicolor underprint. Bedouin woman at left, tents in background. Back: Camels and huts. Printer: Algerian.

	VF	UNC
a. Issued note.	45.00	150.
s. Specimen.	—	75.00

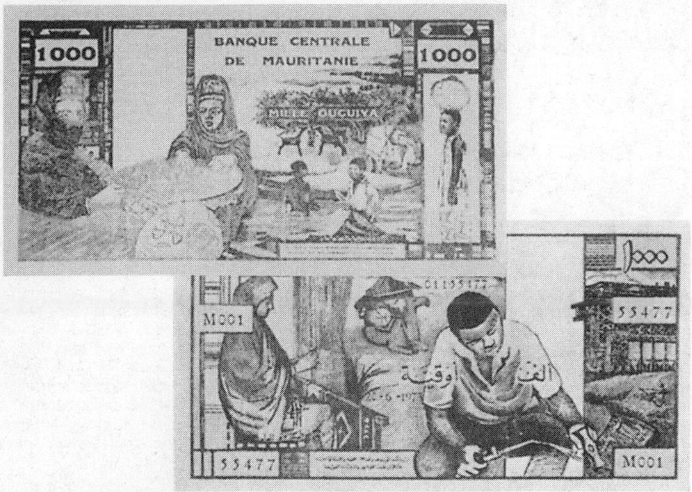

3 **1000 Ouguiya**

20.6.1973. Green and multicolor. Woman weaving on loom at left, metal worker at right center. Back: Local musicians and scenes. Printer: Algerian.

	VF	UNC
a. Issued note.	100.	400.
s. Specimen.	—	250.

1975, 1977, 1981 Unissued Notes

3A **100 Ouguiya**

28.11.1975. Blue and purple on multicolor underprint. Man facing at left, two women at lower center preparing tea service. Back: Bearded man standing with large fish at center, fishing boats in background. Printer: TDLR. Unissued Specimen. Rare. 145x70mm.

	VF	UNC
	—	—

3B **200 Ouguiya**

6.29.1977. Violet on multicolor underprint. Man with goatee, camel, woman. Printer: TDLR.

	VF	UNC
	—	—

3C **1000 Ouguiya**

26.6.1977. Multicolor. Female at left. Back: Mine shaft. Printer: TDLR. Unissued Specimen. Rare.

	VF	UNC
	—	—

3D **1000 Ouguiya**

28.11.1981. Red and orange on multicolor underprint. Bearded man at left. Back: Camel and palm tree at right center, mine at center, men working field at right center. Printer: G&D.

	VF	UNC
	—	—

1974; 1979 Issue

4 **100 Ouguiya**

1974-2002. Purple, violet and brown on multicolor underprint. Back: Musical instruments at left, cow and tower at right. Watermark: Old man with beard. Printer: G&D (without imprint).

	VF	UNC
a. 28.11.1974. Narrow black security thread. Two signature varieties.	10.00	25.00
b. 28.11.1983.	15.00	40.00
c. 28.11.1985.	7.50	20.00
d. 28.11.1989. Wide green security thread.	5.00	12.50
e. 28.11.1992.	4.00	10.00
f. 28.11.1993.	3.00	10.00
g. 28.11.1995.	2.50	10.00
h. 28.11.1996.	2.00	8.00
i. 28.11.1999.	2.00	8.00
j. 28.11.2001.	2.00	8.00
k. 28.11.2002	2.00	8.00
s. As a. Specimen.	—	35.00

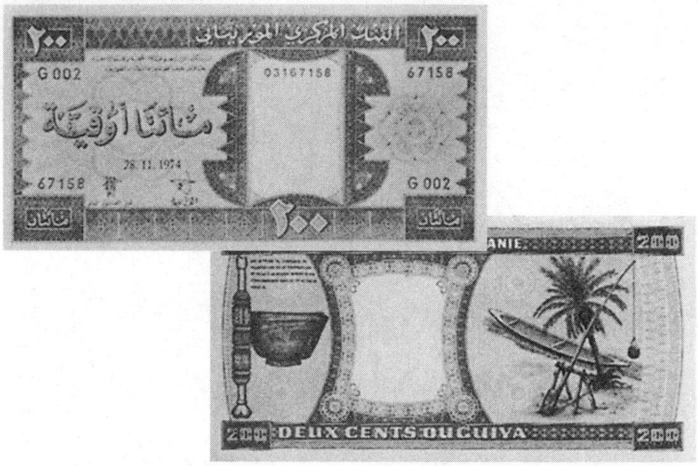

5 **200 Ouguiya**

1974-2002. Brown, dark olive-green and brown-orange on multicolor underprint. Back: Bowl and rod at left, dugout canoe and palm tree at right. Watermark: Old man with beard. Printer: G&D (without imprint).

	VF	UNC
a. 28.11.1974. Thin security thread. Two signature varieties.	15.00	30.00
b. 28.11.1985.	10.00	25.00
c. 28.11.1989. Thick security thread.	6.00	22.50
d. 28.11.1992.	5.00	20.00
e. 28.11.1993.	5.00	15.00
f. 28.11.1995.	4.00	10.00
g. 28.11.1996.	4.00	10.00
h. 28.11.1999.	3.00	10.00
i. 28.11.2001.	3.00	10.00
j. 28.11.2002.	3.00	10.00
s. As a. Specimen.	—	55.00

6 **500 Ouguiya**

1979-1996. Green, brown and dark green on multicolor underprint. Back: Brown, green and black. Field workers at left, mine entrance complex at right. Watermark: Old man with beard. Printer: G&D (without imprint).

	VF	UNC
a. 28.11.1979. Thin security thread.	40.00	90.00
b. 28.11.1983.	40.00	100.
c. 28.11.1985.	15.00	35.00
d. 28.11.1989. Thick security thread.	12.00	40.00
e. 28.11.1991.	10.00	40.00
f. 28.11.1992.	8.00	30.00
g. 28.11.1993.	8.00	25.00
h. 28.11.1995.	8.00	25.00
i. 28.11.1996.	8.00	25.00
s. As a. Specimen.	—	100.

#	Description	VF	UNC
7	**1000 Ouguiya** 1974-1996. Blue, violet and blue-black on multicolor underprint. Back: Bowl of fish at left, camel, hut and tower at right. Watermark: Old man with beard. Printer: G&D (without imprint).		
	a. 28.11.1974. Thin security thread. Two signature varieties.	40.00	85.00
	b. 28.11.1985.	30.00	75.00
	c. 28.11.1989. Thick security thread.	25.00	50.00
	d. 28.10.1991.	20.00	45.00
	e. 28.11.1992.	15.00	45.00
	f. 28.11.1993.	15.00	35.00
	g. 28.11.1995.	15.00	35.00
	h. 28.11.1996.	12.50	30.00
	s. As a. Specimen.	—	150.

1999 Issue

#	Description	VF	UNC
8	**500 Ouguiya** 28.11.1999; 28.11.2001; 28.11.2002. Green, brown and dark green on multicolor underprint. Signature varieties. Back: Brown, green and black. Field workers at left, mine entrance complex at right. Watermark: Old man with beard. Similar to #6 but hologram image added to right center.		
	a. 28.11.1999.	7.50	25.00
	b. 28.11.2001.	7.50	20.00
	c. 28.11.2002.	7.50	20.00

#	Description	VF	UNC
9	**1000 Ouguiya** 28.11.1999; 28.11.2001; 28.11.2002. Blue on tan underprint. Signature varieties. Back: Bowl of fish at left, camel, hut and tower at right. Watermark: Old man with beard. Similar to #7 but with hologram value added at right center.		
	a. 28.11.1999.	10.00	30.00
	b. 28.11.2001.	10.00	30.00
	c. 28.11.2002.	10.00	30.00

2004 Issue

#10-14 Replacement notes: Second letter of serial # prefix: *Z.*

#	Description	VF	UNC
10	**100 Ouguiya** 28.11.2004; 28.11.2006; 11.28.2011. Green and purple on multicolor underprint. Geometric design at right. Back: Musical instruments at left, cow feeding before tower at center. Printer: G&D (without imprint). 130x65mm.		
	a. 28.11.2004.	FV	4.00
	b. 28.11.2006.	FV	3.00

#	Description	VF	UNC
11	**200 Ouguiya** 28.11.2004; 28.11.2006. Brown and blue on multicolor underprint. Geometric pattern at right. Back: Bowl at left, canoe at center. Printer: G&D (without imprint). 136x68mm.		
	a. 28.11.2004.	FV	6.00
	b. 28.11.2006.	FV	4.00
12	**500 Ouguiya** 28.11.2004; 28.11.2006. Green and brown on multicolor underprint. Geometric patern at right. Back: Men harvesting at left, factory at center. Printer: G&D (without imprint). 142x71mm.		
	a. 28.11.2004.	FV	10.00
	b. 28.11.2006.	FV	8.00

#	Description	VF	UNC
13	**1000 Ouguiya** 28.11.2004; 28.11.2006. Multicolor. Printer: G&D (without imprint). 148x74mm.		
	a. 28.11.2004.	FV	15.00
	b. 28.11.2006.	FV	12.50

14	**2000 Ouguiya**	VF	UNC
	28.11.2004; 28.11.2006. Multicolor. Printer: G&D (without imprint). 154x78mm.		
	a. 28.11.2004.	FV	25.00
	b. 28.11.2006.	FV	22.50

15	**5000 Ouguiya**	VF	UNC
	28.11.2009. Olive green on multicolor underprint. Ibn Abbas Mosque in Nouakchott at center. Back: Diesel locomotive at center. Watermark: Bearded man. Printer: G&D. 150x70mm.		
	a. Issued note.	FV	50.00
	r. Replacement note. Second letter in serial # prefix: *Z*.	FV	75.00
	s. Specimen. Red overprint.	—	75.00

2011 Issue

16	**100 Ouguiya**	VF	UNC
	28.11.2011. Green and purple on multicolor underprint. Watermark: Bearded male head and 100 130x65mm.	FV	2.50
17	**200 Ouguiya**		
	28.11.2011. Expected new issue.	—	—
18	**500 Ouguiya**		
	28.11.2011. Expected new issue.	—	—
19	**1000 Ouguiya**		
	28.11.2011. Expected new issue.	—	—

20	**2000 Ouguiya**	VF	UNC
	28.11.2011. Blue on multicolor underprint. Watermark: Bearded male head and 2000. 146x70mm.	FV	30.00

21	**5000 Ouguiya**	VF	UNC
	28.11.2011. Olive and multicolor. Mosque. Back: Airport tower at left, desiel locomotive at left center.	FV	50.00

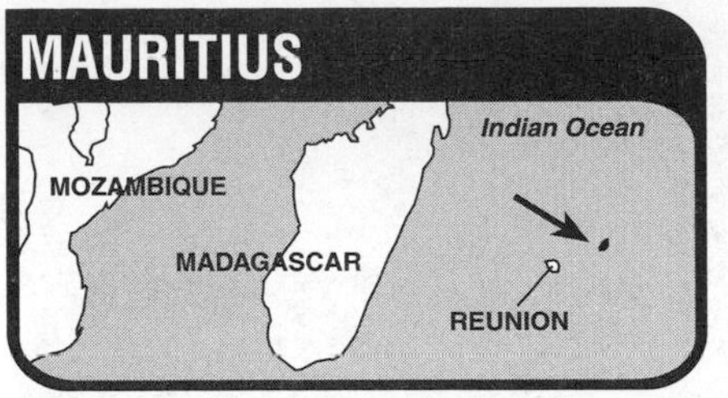

The island of Mauritius, a member of the British Commonwealth located in the Indian Ocean 500 miles (805 km.) east of Madagascar, has an area of 790 sq. mi. (2,045 sq. km.) and a population of 1.18 million. Capital: Port Louis. Sugar provides 90 percent of the export revenue.

Although known to Arab and Malay sailors as early as the 10th century, Mauritius was first explored by the Portuguese in the 16th century and subsequently settled by the Dutch - who named it in honor of Prince Maurits van Nassau - in the 17th century. The French assumed control in 1715, developing the island into an important naval overseeing Indian Ocean trade, and establishing a plantation economy of sugar cane. The British captured the island in 1810, during the Napoleonic Wars. Mauritius remained a strategically important British naval , and later an air station, playing an important role during World War II for anti-submarine and convoy operations, as well as the collection of signals intelligence. Independence from the UK was attained in 1968. A stable democracy with regular free elections and a positive human rights record, the country has attracted considerable foreign investment and has earned one of Africa's highest per capita incomes. Recent poor weather, declining sugar prices, and declining textile and apparel production, have slowed economic growth, leading to some protests over standards of living in the Creole community.

NOTE: Certain listings encompassing issues circulated by various bank and regional authorities are contained in Volume 1.

SIGNATURE VARIETIES

	GOVERNOR	MANAGING DIRECTOR
1	Mr. A. Beejadhur 1.7.1967-31.12.1972	Mr. D. G. H. Cook 1.7.1967-27.7.1968
2	Mr. A. Beejadhur 1.7.1967-31.12.1972	Mr. D. C. Keys 28.7.1968-27.21920
3	Mr. A. Beejadhur 1.7.1967-31.12.1972	Mr. G. Bunwaree 20.2.1970-01.12.1972
4	Mr. G. Bunwaree 1.1.1973-9.6.1982	Sir I. Ramphul 1.1.1973-9.6.1982
5	Sir I. Ramphul 10.6.1982-31.3.1996	Mr. R. Tacouri 10.6.1982-28.2.1997
6	Mr. D. Maraye 1.4.1996-30.11.1998	Mr. B. Gujadhur 1.3.1997-1.12.1998
7	Mr. R. Basant Roi 1.12.1998-	Mr. B. R. Gujadhur 17.12.1998-

British Administration

Bank of Mauritius

1967 ND Issue

#30-33 Replacement notes: Serial # prefix *Z/#*.

		VF	UNC
30	**5 Rupees** ND (1967). Blue on multicolor underprint. Queen Elizabeth II at right. Back: Sailboat. Watermark: Dodo bird. Printer: TDLR.		
	a. Signature 1.	12.00	45.00
	b. Signature 3.	15.00	70.00
	c. Signature 4.	4.00	15.00
	s. As a. Specimen.	—	—

		VF	UNC
31	**10 Rupees** ND (1967). Red on multicolor underprint. Queen Elizabeth II at right. Back: Government building. Watermark: Dodo bird. Printer: TDLR.		
	a. Signature 1.	15.00	60.00
	b. Signature 2.	25.00	100.
	c. Signature 4.	3.50	12.50

		VF	UNC
32	**25 Rupees** ND (1967). Green on multicolor underprint. Queen Elizabeth II at right. Back: Ox cart. Watermark: Dodo bird. Printer: TDLR.		
	a. Signature 1.	25.00	110.
	b. Signature 4.	20.00	90.00

33 **50 Rupees** VF UNC

ND (1967). Purple on multicolor underprint. Queen Elizabeth II at right. Back: Ships docked at Port Louis harbor. Watermark: Dodo bird. Printer: TDLR.

	VF	UNC
a. Signature 1.	65.00	250.
b. Signature 2.	75.00	300.
c. Signature 4.	30.00	120.

1985-91 ND Issue

#34-41 replacement notes: Serial # prefix *Z/#*.

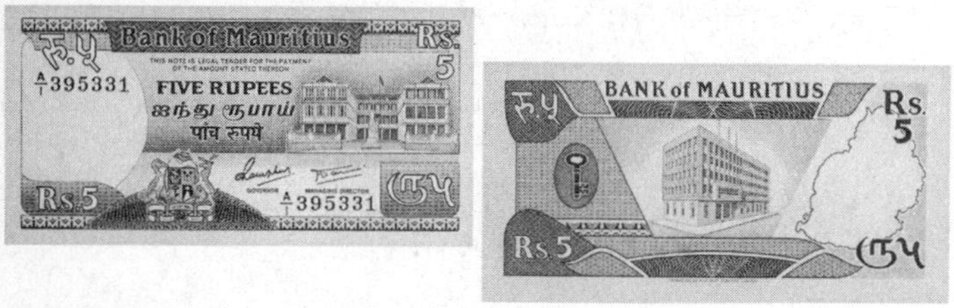

34 **5 Rupees** VF UNC

ND (1985). Dark brown. Arms at lower left center, building with flag at right. Signature 5. Back: Bank, outline of Mauritius map at right. Watermark: Dodo bird. Printer: TDLR. 1.50 5.00

35 **10 Rupees** VF UNC

ND (1985). Green on multicolor underprint. Arms at lower left center, building with flag at center right. Signature 5. Back: Bridge, outline of Mauritius map at right. Watermark: Dodo bird. Printer: TDLR.

	VF	UNC
a. Orange UV latent printing. Dark green printing.	2.00	8.00
b. Dark green printing. Green UV latent printing.	2.00	7.00

36 **20 Rupees** VF UNC

ND. Bluish purple, blue-green, blue and orange on multicolor underprint. Lady Jugnauth at left, arms at center, building with flag at lower right. Signature 5. Back: Satellite dishes at center, outline of Mauritius map at right. Watermark: Dodo bird. Printer: TDLR. 2.50 9.00

37 **50 Rupees** VF UNC

ND (1986). Dark blue on multicolor underprint. Arms at lower center, building with flag at right. Signature 5. Back: Two deer, butterfly and Mauritius Kestrel. Watermark: Dodo bird. Printer: BWC (without imprint).

	VF	UNC
a. Printer's imprint on back.	4.00	15.00
b. Without printer's imprint on back.	4.00	15.00

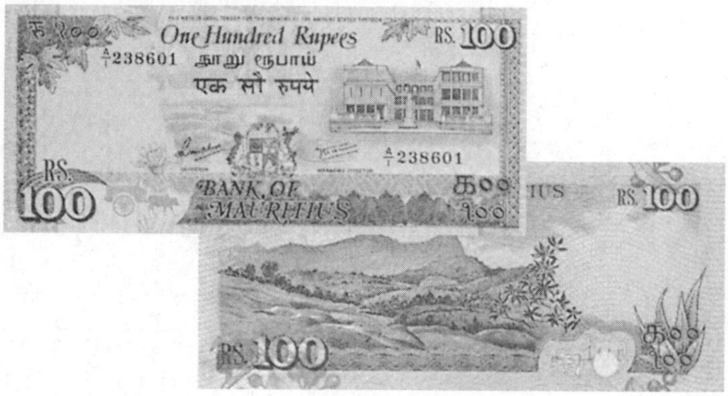

38 **100 Rupees** VF UNC

ND (1986). Red on multicolor underprint. Arms at lower center, building with flag at right. Signature 5. Back: Landscape. Watermark: Dodo bird. Printer: BWC (without imprint). 7.50 25.00

39 **200 Rupees** VF UNC

ND (1985). Blue on multicolor underprint. Sir Seewoosagur Ramgoolam at left. Signature 5. Back: Large home (Le Réduit). Printer: TDLR.

	VF	UNC
a. Orange UV latent printing.	18.00	50.00
b. Green UV latent printing.	15.00	40.00

40 500 Rupees VF UNC

ND (1988). Brown and orange on multicolor underprint. Building with flag at center, arms below, Sir A. Jugnaurh (Prime Minister) at right. Signature 5. Back: Sugar cane field workers loading wagon with mountains in background. Watermark: Dodo bird. Printer: TDLR (without imprint).

	VF	UNC
a. Orange UV latent printing.	40.00	110.
b. Green UV latent printing.	35.00	100.

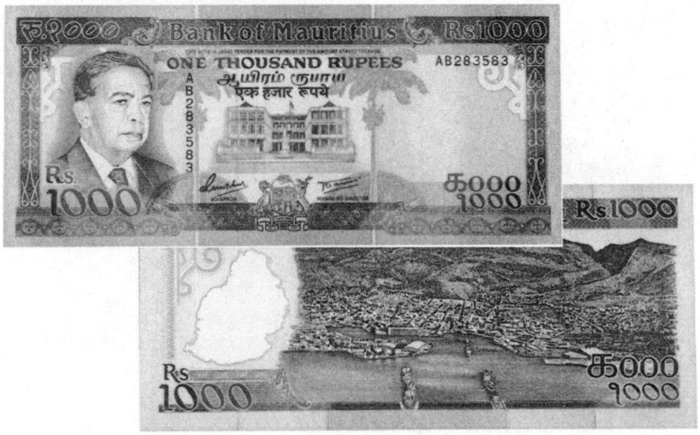

41 1000 Rupees VF UNC

ND (1991). Blue and red on multicolor underprint. Sir V. Ringadoo at left, palm trees and building with flag at center. Signature 5. Back: Port Louis harbor. Watermark: Dodo bird. Printer: TDLR. — 65.00 180.

1998 Issue

#42-48 raised much public controversy when the values were printed in the order of English/ Sanskrit/ Tamil instead of the usual order of English/ Tamil/ Sanskrit. The note were withdrawn and replaced with #49-55.

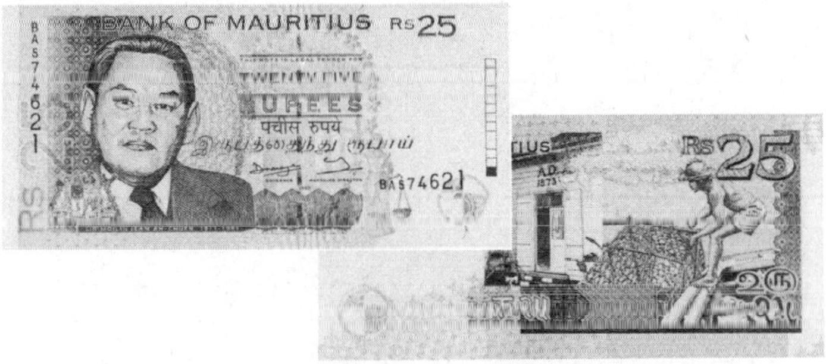

42 25 Rupees VF UNC

1998. Black, violet and brown on multicolor underprint. Sir M. J. Ah-chuen at left, arms at lower left, building façades at center, standing Justice with scales at lower right in underprint. Ascending size serial number. Back: Building façade at center, worker at right. Watermark: Dodo bird's head. UV: value 25 in box fluoresces yellow, left design faint yellow. — FV 7.00

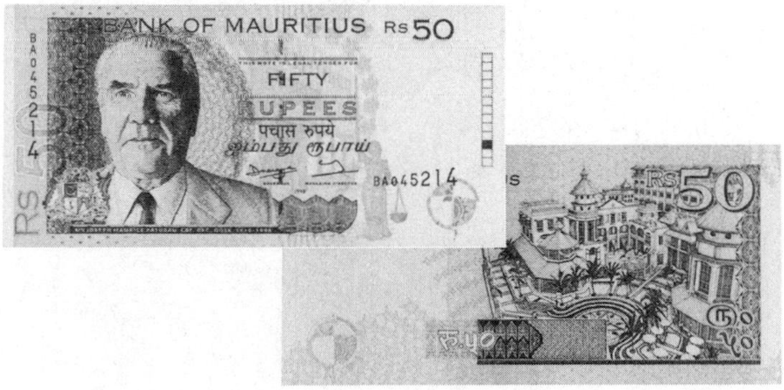

43 50 Rupees VF UNC

1998. Black, purple and deep blue on multicolor underprint. J. M. Paturau at left, arms at lower left, building façades at center, standing Justice with scales at lower right in underprint. Ascending size serial number. Back: Building complex at center right. Watermark: Dodo bird's head. — FV 12.00

44 100 Rupees VF UNC

1998. Black, blue and deep blue-green on multicolor underprint. R. Seeneevassen at left, arms at lower left, building façades at center, standing Justice with scales at lower right in underprint. Ascending size serial number. Back: Building at left. Watermark: Dodo bird's head. — FV 20.00

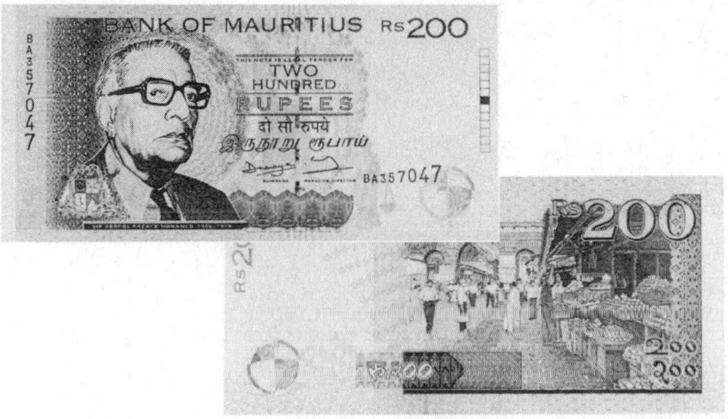

45 200 Rupees VF UNC

1998. Black, deep green and violet on multicolor underprint. Sir A. R. Mohamed at left, arms at lower left, building façades at center, standing Justice with scales at lower right in underprint. Ascending size serial number. Back: Market street scene at right. Watermark: Dodo bird's head. — FV 32.50

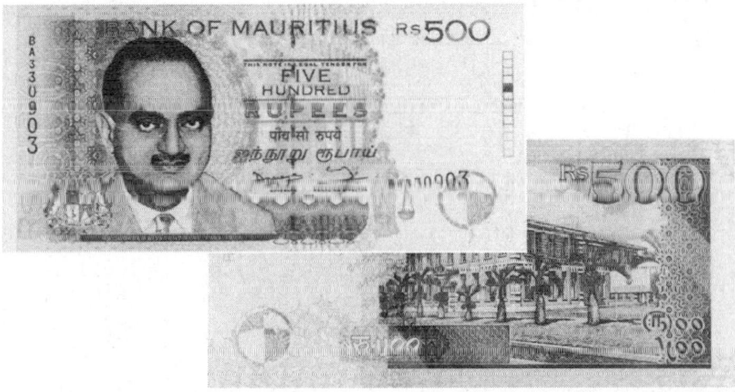

46 500 Rupees VF UNC

1998. Black, brown and orange on multicolor underprint. S. Bissoondoyal at left., arms at lower left, building façades at center, standing Justice with scales at lower right in underprint. Ascending size serial number. Back: University of Mauritius at center right. Watermark: Dodo bird's head. — FV 60.00

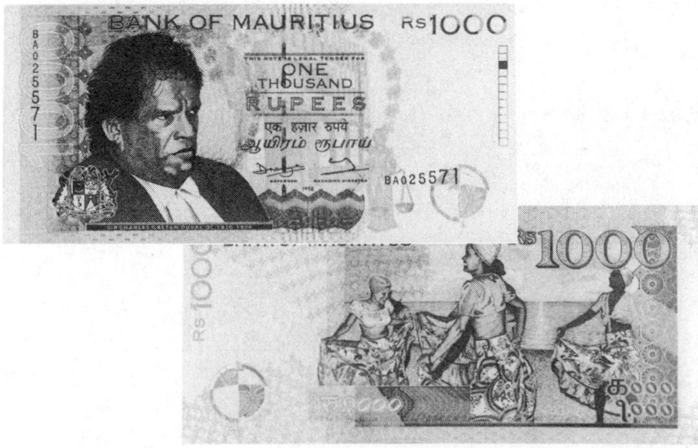

47 1000 Rupees VF UNC

1998. Black and blue on multicolor underprint. Sir Charles G. Duval at left., arms at lower left, building façades at center, standing Justice with scales at lower right in underprint. Ascending size serial number. Back: Women dancing at center right. Watermark: Dodo bird's head. — FV 110.

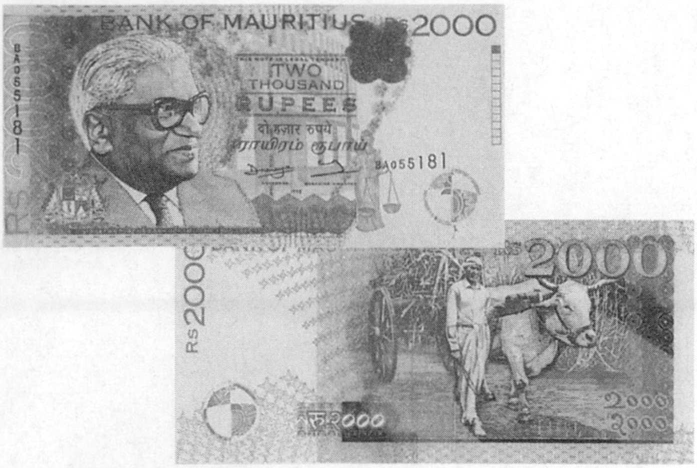

48 **2000 Rupees** | VF | UNC
1998. Rose, orange, black, yellow-brown on multicolor underprint. Seewoosagur Ramgoolam at left., arms at lower left, building façades at center, standing Justice with scales at lower right. Ascending size serial number. Back: Ox cart. Watermark: Dodo bird's head. | FV | 200.

1999 Issue

#49-55 language text correctly ordered as: English/ Tamil/ Sanskrit.

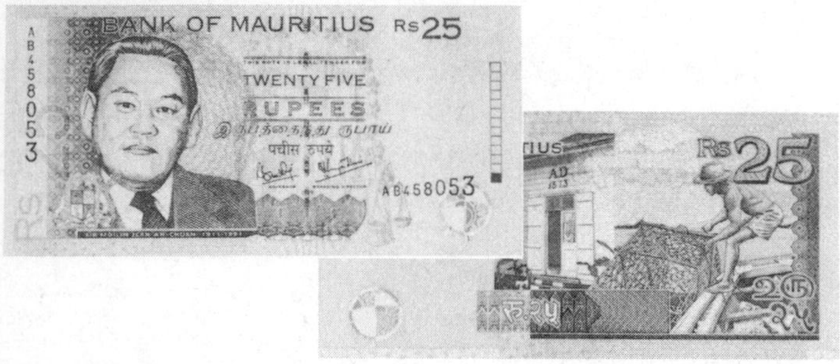

49 **25 Rupees** | VF | UNC
1999; 2003; 2006. Black, violet and brown on multicolor underprint. Sir M. J. Ah-chuen at left, arms at lower left, building facades at center, standing Justice with scales at lower right in underprint. Ascending size serial number. Signature 7. Back: Building facade at center, worker at right. Watermark: Dodo bird's head. UV: 25 in box fluoresces yellow. 135x67mm.

	VF	UNC
a. 1999.	FV	3.00
b. 2003.	FV	2.50
c. 2006.	FV	2.25

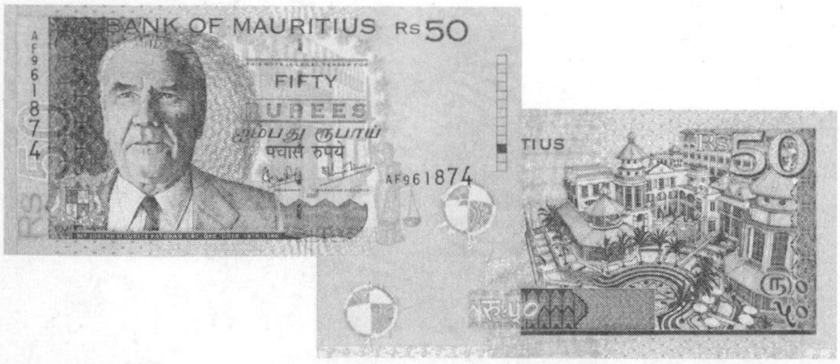

50 **50 Rupees** | VF | UNC
1999; 2001; 2003; 2006; 2009. Black, purple and deep blue on multicolor underprint. J. M. Paturau at left, arms at lower left, building facades at center, standing Justice with scales at lower right in underprint. Ascending size serial number. Signature 7. Back: Building complex at center right. Watermark: Dodo bird's head. 140x68mm.

	VF	UNC
a. 1999.	FV	6.00
b. 2001.	FV	4.50
c. 2003.	FV	4.00
d. 2006.	FV	3.25
e. 2009.	FV	3.25

51 **100 Rupees** | VF | UNC
1999; 2001. Black, blue and deep blue-green on multicolor underprint. R. Seeneevassen at left, arms at lower left, building façades at center, standing Justice with scales at lower right in underprint. Ascending size serial number. Signature 7. Back: Building at left. Watermark: Dodo bird's head. 145x70mm.

	VF	UNC
a. 1999.	FV	12.00
b. 2001.	FV	10.00

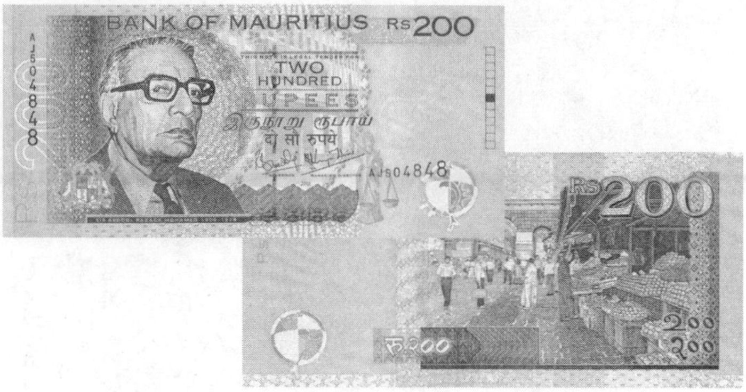

52 **200 Rupees** | VF | UNC
1999; 2001. Black, deep green and violet on multicolro underprint. Sir A. R. Mohamed at left, arms at lower left, building façades at center, standing Justice with scales at lower right in underprint. Ascending size serial number. Signature 7. Back: Market street scene at right. Watermark: Dodo bird's head. 150x72mm.

	VF	UNC
a. 1999.	FV	20.00
b. 2001.	FV	17.50

53 **500 Rupees** | VF | UNC
1999. Black, brown and orangeon multicolor underprint. S. Bissoondoyal at left, arms at lower left, building façades at center, standing Justice with scales at lower right in underprint. Ascending size serial number. Signature 7. Back: University of Mauritius at center right. Watermark: Dodo bird's head. 1999. 155x75mm. | FV | 45.00

54 **1000 Rupees** | VF | UNC
1999. Slate black, light blue and red underprint. Sir Charles Duval at left. Signature 7. Back: Light blue and red. Building at center. 160x76mm.

	VF	UNC
a. 1999.	FV	75.00
b. 2001.	FV	75.00

		VF	UNC
55	**2000 Rupees** 1999. Rose, orange, black, yellow-brown on multicolor underprint. Seewoosagur Ramgoolam at left., arms at lower left, building façades at center, standing Justice with scales at lower right in underprint. Ascending size serial number. Signature 7. Back: Ox cart. Watermark: Dodo bird's head. 165x79mm.	FV	140.

2001 Issue

		VF	UNC
56	**100 Rupees** 2001; 2007; 2009. Black, blue and deep blue-green on multicolor underprint. R. Seeneevassen at left, arms at lower left, building façades at center, standing Justice with scales at lower right in underprint. Ascending size serial number. Signature 7. Back: Building at left. Watermark: Dodo bird's head. Similar to #51 but iridescent strip added. 145x70mm.		
	a. 2001.	FV	6.00
	b. 2007.	FV	5.00
	c. 2009.	FV	5.00

		VF	UNC
57	**200 Rupees** 2001; 2007. Black, deep green and violet on multicolor underprint. Sir A. R. Mohamed at left, arms at lower left, building façades at center, standing Justice with scales at lower right in underprint. Ascending size serial number. Signature 7. Back: Market street scene at right. Watermark: Dodo bird's head. Similar to #52 but iridescent strip added. 150x72mm.		
	a. 2001.	FV	15.00
	b. 2007.	FV	15.00

		VF	UNC
58	**500 Rupees** 2001; 2003. Green and brown on multicolor underprint. Bust at left. Back: Building. 155x75mm.		
	a. 2001.	FV	37.50
	b. 2003.	FV	37.50

		VF	UNC
59	**1000 Rupees** 2003; 2004; 2006; 2007. Slate black, light blue and red munticolor underprint. Sir Charles Duval at left. Back: Light blue and red. Building at center. 160x76mm.		
	a. 2003. 2 Signatures.	FV	65.00
	b. 2004.	FV	65.00
	c. 2006.	FV	62.50
	d. 2007. 3 Signatures.	FV	60.00
60	**2000 Rupees** 2003. Rose, orange, black, yellow brown on multicolor underprint. Seewoosagur Ramgoolam at left. Back: Ox cart. 165x79mm.	FV	125.

2010 Enhanced Issue

		VF	UNC
61	**200 Rupees** 2010. Black, deep green and violet on multicolor underprint. Sir A.R. Mohamed at left. Building façades at center. Hologram at top right. Back: Market street scene at right.	FV	15.00
62	**500 Rupees** 2010. Green and brown on multicolor underprint. S. Bissoondoyal at left. Building façades at center. Hologram at top right. Back: University of Mauritus at center right.	FV	37.50
63	**1000 Rupees** 2010. Slate black, light blue and red on multicolor underprint. Sir Charles Duval at left. Building façades at center. Hologram at top right. Back: Building at center.	FV	60.00

2013 Issue

		VF	UNC
64	**25 Rupees** 2013. Violet and brown on multicolor underprint. Coat of arms. Milin Jean ah-Chuen. Building façades at center. Back: Dodo bird, buildign façade, Rodrigues Island map. Polymer plastic.	FV	3.50
65	**50 Rupees** 2013. Blue on multicolor underprint. Coat of arms, Joseph Maurice Paturau. Building façades at center. Back: Dodo bird, Le Caudan waterfront buildings. Printer: OT. Polymer plastic.	FV	5.00

Collector Series

Bank of Mauritius

1978 ND Issue

		Mkt.	Value
CS1	**ND (1978) 5-50 Rupees** #30c, 31c, 32b, 33c with overprint.: *SPECIMEN* and Maltese cross prefix serial #.		80.00

The United States of Mexico, located immediately south of the United States, has an area of 1,222,612 sq. mi. (1,967,183 sq. km.) and a population of 98.88 million. Capital: Mexico City. The economy is based on agriculture, manufacturing and mining. Cotton, sugar, coffee and shrimp are exported.

Mexico was the site of highly advanced Indian civilizations 1,500 years before conquistador Hernando Cortes conquered the wealthy Aztec empire of Montezuma, 1519-1521, and founded a Spanish colony which lasted for nearly 300 years. During the Spanish period, Mexico, then called New Spain, stretched from Guatemala to the present states of Wyoming and California, its present northern boundary having been established by the secession of Texas (1836) and the war of 1846-1848 with the United States.

Independence from Spain was declared by Father Miguel Hidalgo on Sept. 16, 1810, Mexican Independence Day, and was achieved by General Agustin de Iturbide in 1821. Iturbide became emperor in 1822 but was deposed when a republic was established a year later. For more than half a century following the birth of the republic, the political scene of Mexico was characterized by turmoil which saw two emperors (including the unfortunate Maximilian), several dictators and an average of one new government every nine months passing swiftly from obscurity to oblivion. The land, social, economic and labor reforms promulgated by the Reform Constitution of Feb. 5, 1917 established the basis for a sustained economic development and participative democracy that have made Mexico one of the most politically stable countries of modern Latin America.

Estados Unidos Méxicanos

United States of Mexico

Banco de México

1945-51 Issue

49 50 Pesos

1948-72. Engraved. Blue on multicolor underprint. Portrait I.de Allende at left. Middle signature title: *INTERVENTOR DE LA COM. NAC. BANCARIA.* Signature varieties. Back: Blue. Independence Monument at center. Printer: ABNC.

	VF	UNC
a. 22.12.1948. Black series letters. Series: BA-BD.	6.00	15.00
b. 23.11.1949. Series: BU-BX.	6.00	15.00
c. 26.7.1950. Series: BY-CF.	5.00	15.00
d. 27.12.1950. Series: CS-DH.	5.00	15.00
e. 19.1.1953. Series: DK-DV.	4.00	15.00
f. 10.2.1954. Series: DW-EE.	4.00	15.00
g. 8.9.1954. Series: EF-FF.	4.00	15.00
h. 11.1.1956. Series: FK-FV.	4.00	15.00
i. 19.6.1957. Series: FW-GP.	4.00	15.00
j. 20.8.1958. Series: HC-HR.	4.00	15.00
k. 18.3.1959. 2 red series letters. Series: HS-IP.	4.00	15.00
l. 20.5.1959. Series: IQ-JN.	4.00	15.00
m. 25.1.1961. Series: JO-LB.	3.00	8.00
n. 8.11.1961. Series: LC-AID.	3.00	8.00
o. 24.4.1963. Series: AIE-BAP.	3.00	6.00
p. 17.2.1965. Series: BAQ-BCD.	2.50	6.00
q. 10.5.1967. Series: BCY-BEN.	2.50	6.00
r. 19.11.1969. Series: BGK-BIC.	2.50	4.00
s. 22.7.1970. Series: BIG-BKN.	2.50	4.00
t. 27.6.1972. Series: BLI-BMG.	2.50	3.00
u. 29.12.1972. Series: BMO-BRB.	2.00	3.00
v. Specimen, punch hole cancelled.	—	135.

50 100 Pesos

17.1.1945. Printed. Brown on multicolor underprint. Portrait M. Hidalgo at left, series letters above serial #. Middle signature title: *INTERVENTOR DEL GOBIERNO.* Signature varieties. Back: Olive-green. Coin with national coat-of-arms at center. Series: S-Z. Printer: ABNC.

	VF	UNC
a. Issued note.	15.00	70.00
s. Specimen, punch hole cancelled.	—	200.

51 500 Pesos

1948-78. Black on multicolor underprint. Like #43 but without *No.* above serial #. Middle signature title: *INTERVENTOR DE LA COM. NAC. BANCARIA.* Signature varieties. Back: Green. Palace of Mining at center. Printer: ABNC.

	VF	UNC
a. 22.12.1948. Series: BA.	40.00	125.
b. 27.12.1950. Series: CS; CT.	12.00	30.00
c. 3.12.1951. Series: DI; DJ.	12.00	30.00
d. 19.1.1953. Series: DK-DN.	12.00	30.00
e. 31.8.1955. Series: FG-FJ.	12.00	30.00
f. 11.1.1956. Series: FK-FL.	12.00	30.00
g. 19.6.1957. Series: FW-GB.	12.00	30.00
h. 20.8.1958. Series: HC-HH.	12.00	30.00
i. 18.3.1959. Series: HS-HX.	12.00	30.00
j. 20.5.1959. Series: IQ-IV.	12.00	30.00
k. 25.1.1961. Series: JO-JT.	8.00	25.00
l. 8.11.1961. Series: LC-MP.	7.00	20.00
m. 17.2.1965. Series: BAQ-BCN.	12.00	25.00
n. 24.3.1971. Series: BKO-BKT.	5.00	12.50
o. 27.6.1972. Series: BLI-BLM.	5.00	12.50
p. 29.12.1972. Series: BNG-BNP.	5.00	12.50
q. 18.7.1973. Series: BUY-BWB.	5.00	12.50
r. 2.8.1974. Series: BXV-BZI.	3.50	10.00
s. 18.2.1977. Series: BZJ-CCK.	3.50	10.00
t. 18.1.1978. Series: CCL-CDY.	3.50	8.50

52 1000 Pesos

1948-77. Black on multicolor underprint. Cuauhtemoc at left. Middle signature title: *IN-TERVENTOR DE LA COM. NAC. BANCARIA.* Signature varieties. Back: Brown. Chichen itza pyramid at center. Printer: ABNC.

	VF	UNC
a. 22.12.1948. Series: BA.	15.00	60.00
b. 23.11.1949. Series: BU.	15.00	60.00
c. 27.12.1950. Series: CS.	15.00	60.00
d. 3.12.1951. Series: DI; DJ.	15.00	60.00
e. 19.1.1953. Series: DK; DL.	15.00	60.00
f. 31.8.1955. Series: FG; FH.	15.00	60.00
g. 11.1.1956. Series: FK; FL.	15.00	60.00
h. 19.6.1957. Series: FW-FZ.	15.00	60.00
i. 20.8.1958. Series: HC-HE.	15.00	60.00
j. 18.3.1959. Series: HS-HU.	15.00	60.00
k. 20.5.1959. Series: IQ-IS.	15.00	60.00
l. 25.1.1961. Series: JO-JQ.	15.00	60.00
m. 8.11.1961. Series: LC-LV.	10.00	20.00
n. 17.2.1965. Series: BAQ-BCN.	8.00	15.00
o. 24.3.1971. Series: BKO-BKT.	6.00	10.00
p. 27.6.1972. Series: BLI-BLM.	6.00	10.00
q. 29.12.1972. Series: BNG-BNK.	3.00	5.00
r. 18.7.1973. Series: BUY-BWB.	6.00	10.00
s. 2.8.1974. Series: BXV-BYY.	5.00	8.00
t. 18.2.1977. Series: BZJ-CBQ.	5.00	8.00
x. Error: *EERIE HD* rather than SERIE at left.	45.00	85.00

1950; 1951 Issue

53 10 Pesos

1951; 1953. Black on multicolor underprint. Portrait E. Ruiz de Velazquez at right. Like #47 but without *No.* above serial #. Signature varieties. Printer: ABNC.

	VF	UNC
a. 3.12.1951. Series: DI, DJ.	2.00	5.00
b. 19.1.1953. Series: DK, DL.	2.00	5.00

1950 Issue

54 20 Pesos

1950-70. Black on multicolor underprint. Portrait J. Ortiz de Dominguez at left. Like number 48 but without *No.* above serial #. Signature varieties. Back: Olive-green. Federal Palace courtyard at center. Printer: ABNC.

	VF	UNC
a. 27.12.1950. Black series letters. Series: CS; CT.	3.00	15.00
b. 19.1.1953. Series: dark	3.00	15.00
c. 10.2.1954. Red series letters. Series: DW.	2.00	10.00
d. 11.1.1956. Series: FK.	2.00	10.00
e. 10.6.1957. Series: FW.	2.00	10.00
f. 20.8.1958. Series: HC, HD.	2.00	10.00
g. 18.3.1959. Series: HS, HT.	2.00	10.00
h. 20.5.1959. Series: IQ, IR.	2.00	10.00
i. 25.1.1961. Series: JO, JP.	1.50	10.00
j. 8.11.1961. Series: LC-LG.	1.50	10.00
k. 24.4.1963. Series: AIE-AIH.	1.50	5.00
l. 17.2.1965. Series: BAQ-BAV.	1.50	5.00
m. 10.5.1967. Series: BCY-BDB.	1.50	5.00
n. 27.8.1969. Series: BGA; BGB.	1.50	5.00
o. 18.3.1970. Series: BID-BIF.	1.50	5.00
p. 22.7.1970. Series: BIG-BIK.	1.50	5.00
s. Specimen, punch hole cancelled.	Unc	135.

55 100 Pesos

1950-61. Engraved. Brown on multicolor underprint. Portrait M. Hidalgo at left, series letters above serial #. Middle signature title: *INTERVENTOR DE LA COM. NAC. BANCARIA*. Signature varieties. Back: Olive-green. Coin with national seal at center. Printer: ABNC.

	VF	UNC
a. 27.12.1950. Black series letters. Series: CS-CZ.	8.00	30.00
b. 19.1.1953. Series: DK-DP.	7.00	25.00
c. 10.2.1954. Series: DW-DZ.	7.00	25.00
d. 8.9.1954. Series: EI-ET.	7.00	25.00
e. 11.1.1956. Series: FK-FV.	7.00	25.00
f. 19.6.1957. Series: FW-GH.	7.00	25.00
g. 20.8.1958. Series: HC-HR.	7.00	25.00
h. 18.3.1959. Series: HS-IH.	7.00	25.00
i. 20.5.1959. Series: IQ-JF.	7.00	25.00
j. 25.1.1961. Series: JO-KL.	7.00	25.00

1954 Issue

58 10 Pesos

1954-67. Black on multicolor underprint. Portrait E. Ruiz de Velazquez at right. Like #53 but with text: *MEXICO D.F.* above series letters. Signature varieties. Back: Brown. Road to Guanajuato at center. Printer: ABNC.

	VF	UNC
a. 10.2.1954. Series: DW, DX.	1.50	5.00
b. 8.9.1954. Series: EI-EN.	1.50	5.00
c. 19.6.1957. Series: FW, FX.	1.50	5.00
d. 24.7.1957. Series: GQ.	1.50	5.00
e. 20.8.1958. Series: HC-HF.	1.50	6.00
f. 18.3.1959. Series: HS-HU.	1.00	5.00
g. 20.5.1959. Series: IQ-IS.	1.00	4.00
h. 25.1.1961. Series: JO-JT.	1.00	4.00
i. 8.11.1961. Series: LC-LV.	1.00	4.00
j. 24.4.1963. Series: AIE-AIT.	1.00	3.00
k. 17.2.1965. Series: BAQ-BAX.	1.00	3.00
l. 10.5.1967. Series: BCY-BDA.	1.00	3.00
s. Specimen, punch hole cancelled.	Unc	150.

1957; 1961 Issue

59 1 Peso

1957-70. Black on multicolor underprint. Aztec calendar stone at center. Like #56 but with text: *MEXICO D.F.* added above date at lower left. Back: Red. Independence monument at center. Printer: ABNC.

	VF	UNC
a. 19.6.1957. Series: FW-GF.	1.00	4.50
b. Deleted.	—	—
c. 4.12.1957. Series: GS-HB.	1.00	4.50
d. 20.8.1958. Series: HC-HL.	.75	2.50
e. 18.3.1959. Series: HS-IB.	.50	2.50
f. 20.5.1959. Series: IQ-IZ.	.50	2.50
g. 25.1.1961. Series: JO-KC.	.25	2.00
h. 8.11.1961. Series: LC; LD.	.50	2.00
i. 9.6.1965. Series: BCO-BCX.	.25	2.00
j. 10.5.1967. Series: BCY-BED.	.25	1.00
k. 27.8.1969. Series: BGA-BGJ.	.25	1.00
l. 22.7.1970. Series: BIG-BIP.	.20	1.00
s. Specimen.	—	—

60 5 Pesos

1957-70. Black on multicolor underprint. Portrait gypsy at center. Like #57 but with Text: *MEXICO D.F.* before date. Back: Gray. Independence Monument at center. Printer: ABNC.

	VF	UNC
a. 19.6.1957. Series: FW, FX.	2.00	7.00
b. 24.7.1957. Series: GQ, GR.	2.00	7.00
c. 20.8.1958. Series: HC-HJ.	1.50	6.00
d. 18.3.1959. Series: HS-HV.	1.50	6.00
e. 20.5.1959. Series: IQ-IT.	1.50	6.00
f. 25.1.1961. Series: JO-JV.	.50	4.00
g. 8.11.1961. Series: LC-MP.	.50	3.00
h. 24.4.1963. Series: AIE-AJJ.	.50	2.50
i. 27.8.1969. Series BGJ.	.50	2.50
j. 19.11.1969. Series: BGK-BGT.	.50	2.50
k. 22.7.1970. Series: BIG-BII.	.50	2.50

61 100 Pesos

1961-73. Brown on multicolor underprint. Portrait M. Hodalgo at left. Like #55 but series letters below serial #. Back: Coin with national seal at center. Printer: ABNC.

	VF	UNC
a. 8.11.1961. Red series letters. Series: LE-ZZ; AAA-AEG.	5.00	12.50
b. 24.4.1963. Series: AIK-AUG.	5.00	12.50
c. 17.2.1965. Series: BAQ-BCD.	3.00	8.00
d. 10.5.1967. Series: BCY-BFZ.	3.00	8.00
e. 22.7.1970. Series: BIO-BJK.	3.00	8.00
f. 24.3.1971. Series: BKP-BLH.	3.00	8.00
g. 27.6.1972. Series: BLI-BNF.	3.00	8.00
h. 29.12.1972. Series: BNG-BUX.	1.50	5.00
i. 18.7.1973. Series: BUY-BXU.	1.50	5.00

1969-74 Issue

62 5 Pesos VF UNC

1969-72. Black on multicolor underprint. J. Ortiz de Dominguez at right, bank titie with S. A. 3 signatures and signature varieties. Back: Yucca plant, aqueduct, village of Queretaro and national arms. Printer: BdM.

		VF	UNC
a.	3.12.1969.	.50	3.00
b.	27.10.1971.	.25	2.00
c.	27.6.1972.	.25	1.50

63 10 Pesos VF UNC

1969-77. Dark green on multicolor underprint. Bell at left, M. Hidalgo y Castilla at right, bank titie with S. A. 3 signatures and signature varieties. Back: National arms and Dolores Cathedral. Printer: BdM.

		VF	UNC
a.	16.9.1969. (This is Mexican Independence Day).	.50	5.00
b.	3.12.1969.	.25	1.50
c.	22.7.1970.	.25	1.50
d.	3.2.1971.	.25	1.25
e.	29.12.1972.	.25	1.25
f.	18.7.1973.	.20	1.25
g.	16.10.1974.	.20	1.00
h.	15.5.1975.	.20	.75
i.	18.2.1977.	.20	.75
s.	Specimen.	—	—

64 20 Pesos VF UNC

1972-77. Red and black on multicolor underprint. J. Morelos y Pavon at right with building in background, bank titie with S. A. 3 signatures and signature varieties. Back: Pyramid of Quetzalcoatl. Printer: BdM.

		VF	UNC
a.	29.12.1972.	.50	3.00
b.	18.7.1973.	.30	2.25
c.	8.7.1976.	.20	2.00
d.	8.7.1977.	.20	1.50

65 50 Pesos VF UNC

1973-78. Blue on multicolor underprint. Government palace at left, Benito Juárez at right, bank titie with S. A. 3 signatures and signature varieties. red and black series letters and serial number. Back: Temple and Zapotec figural urn. Printer: BdM.

		VF	UNC
a.	18.7.1973.	1.00	4.00
b.	8.7.1976.	.50	3.00
c.	5.7.1978.	.50	3.00

66 100 Pesos VF UNC

1974; 1978. Purple on multicolor underprint. V. Carranza at left, *La Trinchera* painting at center, bank titie with S. A. 3 signatures and signature varieties. red and black series letters and serial number. Back: Stone figure. Printer: BdM.

		VF	UNC
a.	30.5.1974.	1.00	3.00
b.	5.7.1978.	1.00	3.00
s.	Specimen.	—	—

1978-80 Issue

67 50 Pesos VF UNC

1978; 1979. Blue on multicolor underprint. Government palace at left, Benito Juárez at right, bank titile with S. A. Red series letters and black serial number. 3 signatures. Back: Temple and Zapotec figural urn. Printer: BdM.

		VF	UNC
a.	5.7.1978.	.75	2.00
b.	17.5.1979.	.40	1.50

68 100 Pesos

1978-79. Purple on multicolor underprint. V. Carranza at left, *La Trinchera* painting at center, bank titile with S. A. Red series letters and a black serial number. 3 signatures. Back: Stone figure. Printer: BdM. UV: fibers fluoresce green. Back left design green.

		VF	UNC
a.	5.7.1978.	.40	1.50
b.	17.5.1979. Engraved and litho back. Series before LL.	.40	1.00
c.	17.5.1979. Litho back. Series LM and later.	.40	1.00

69 500 Pesos — VF | UNC

29.6.1979. Black on dark olive-green on multicolor underprint. F. I. Madero at left, bank titile with S. A. 3 signatures. Back: Aztec calendar stone. Pink. Watermark: F. I. Madero. Printer: BdM. — 3.00 | 11.00

70 1000 Pesos — VF | UNC

1978-79. Dark brown and brown on multicolor underprint. J. de Asbaje at right, bank titile with S. A. 3 signatures. Back: Santo Domingo plaza at left center. Light tan. Watermark: J. de Asbaje. Printer: BdM.

	VF	UNC
a. 5.7.1978.	4.50	20.00
b. 17.5.1979.	4.00	12.50
c. 29.6.1979.	3.00	10.00

71 5000 Pesos — VF | UNC

25.3.1980. Red on multicolor underprint. Cadets at left center, bank titile with S. A. 3 signatures. Back: Chapultepec castle. Light blue. Watermark: Cadet. Printer: BdM. — 15.00 | 45.00

72 10,000 Pesos

18.1.1978. Purple on multicolor underprint. Portrait M. Romero at left. Series CCL-CES. Back: Green. National Palace at center. Printer: ABNC. — 20.00 | 75.00

1981 Issue

73 50 Pesos — VF | UNC

27.1.1981. Blue on multicolor underprint. Government palace at left, Benito Juárez at right, bank titile with S. A. Red series letters and black serial number. 4 signatures and signature varieties. Back: Temple and Zapotec figural urn. Printer: BdM. — .25 | 1.00

74 100 Pesos — VF | UNC

1981-82. Purple on multicolor underprint. V. Carranza at left, *La Trinchera* painting at center, bank titile with S. A. Red series letters and a black serial number. 4 signatures and signature varieties. Back: Stone figure. Printer: BdM. UV: fibers fluoresce green and blue.

	VF	UNC
a. 27.1.1981.	.30	1.50
b. 3.9.1981.	.30	1.50
c. 25.3.1982.	.20	.75

75 500 Pesos — VF | UNC

1981-82. Green on multicolor underprint. F. I. Madero at left, bank titile with S. A. 4 signatures and signature varieties, narrow serial number style. Back. Aztec calendar stone. Watermark: F. I. Madero. Printer: BdM.

	VF	UNC
a. 27.1.1981.	1.25	4.50
b. 25.3.1982.	1.25	4.50

76 1000 Pesos — VF | UNC

1981-82. Dark brown and brown on multicolor underprint. J. de Asbaje at right, bank titile with S. A. 4 signatures and signature varieties, narrow serial number style. Back: Santo Domingo plaza at left center. Watermark: J. de Asbaje. Printer: BdM.

	VF	UNC
a. Engraved buildings on back. 27.1.1981. Black or red serial #.	2.00	10.00
b. Litho buildings on back. 27.1.1981.	2.00	10.00
c. 3.9.1981.	2.00	9.00
d. 25.3.1982.	1.50	7.00

77 5000 Pesos

1981; 1982. Red and black on multicolor underprint. Cadets at left center, bank titile with S. A. 4 signatures and signature varieties, narrower serial number. Back: Chapultepec castle. Light blue. Watermark: Cadet. Printer: BdM.

	VF	UNC
a. 27.1.1981.	6.00	30.00
b. 25.3.1982.	6.00	30.00

78 10,000 Pesos — VF | UNC

1981-82. Blue-black, brown and deep blue-green on multicolor underprint. Power plant at center, General Lazaro Cardenas at right, bank titile with S. A. 4 signatures and signature varieties. Back: Dark green, red and blue. Coyolxauhqui stone carving at center. Light green. Watermark: General Lazaro Cardenas. Printer: BdM.

	VF	UNC
a. 8.12.1981.	25.00	55.00
b. 25.3.1982.	15.00	50.00
c. Red and blue serial #. 30.9.1982.	15.00	50.00
d. Green and red serial #. 30.9.1982.	15.00	50.00
e. Green and blue serial #. 30.9.1982. Series CJ.	15.00	50.00

1983-84 Issues

79 500 Pesos VF UNC

1983; 1984. Green on multicolor underprint. F. I. Madero at left, bank titile without S. A., narrow serial number style. 4 signatures. Like #75, but with threads. Design over watermark area, no watermark.. Back: Aztec calendar stone. White. Printer: BdM. UV: fibers fluoresce blue and green.

	VF	UNC
a. 14.3.1983.	1.00	4.00
b. 7.8.1984.	.75	2.50

80 1000 Pesos VF UNC

1983; 1984. Dark brown and brown on multicolor underprint. J. de Asbaje at right, bank titile without S. A. 4 signatures and signature varieties, narrow serial number style. Back: Santo Domingo plaza at left center. Watermark: J. de Asbaje. Printer: BdM.

	VF	UNC
a. 13.5.1983.	2.00	5.00
b. 7.8.1984.	2.00	5.00

81 1000 Pesos

30.10.1984. Dark brown and brown on multicolor underprint. J. de Asbaje at right, bank titile without S. A. 4 signatures and signature varieties, narrow serial number style. Back: Santo Domingo plaza at left center. Watermark: J. de Asbaje. Printer: BdM. Similar to #80 but radiant quill pen printed over watermark area at left. .75 3.00

82 2000 Pesos VF UNC

1983-84. Black, dark green and brown on multicolor underprint. J. Sierra at left center, University building at right. 4 signatures. Back: 19th century courtyard. Printer: BdM.

	VF	UNC
a. 26.7.1983.	3.00	10.00
b. 7.8.1984.	1.25	5.00
c. 30.10.1984.	1.25	5.00

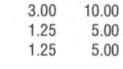

83 5000 Pesos VF UNC

1983. Red and black on multicolor underprint. Cadets at left center, bank titile without S. A. 4 signatures and signature varieties, narrower serial number. Back: Chapultepec castle. Watermark: Cadet. Printer: BdM.

	VF	UNC
a. 13.5.1983.	3.50	12.50
b. 26.7.1983.	3.00	9.00
c. 5.12.1983. Series FB; FC.	10.00	25.00

84 10,000 Pesos

1983. Blue-black, brown and deep blue-green on multicolor underprint. Power plant at center, General Lazaro Cardenas at right, bank titile without S. A. 4 signatures and signature varieties. Back: Coyolxauhqui stone carving at center. Watermark: General Lazaro Cardenas Printer: BdM.

	VF	UNC
a. Serial # upper left on face and lower left on back. 13.5.1983.	4.50	15.00
b. Serial # upper right and lower left on back. Red and dark blue serial #. 26.7.1983.	4.50	15.00
c. Green and blue serial #. 26.7.1983.	4.50	15.00
d. Purple and blue serial #. 26.7.1983.	4.50	17.50
e. 5.12.1983.	5.00	20.00

1985 Issues

85 1000 Pesos VF UNC

19.7.1985. Dark brown and brown on multicolor underprint. J. de Asbaje at right, bank titile without S. A. 3 signatures and signature varieties, narrow serial number style. Back: Santo Domingo plaza at left center. Watermark: J. de Asbaje. Printer: BdM. .75 2.50

86 2000 Pesos VF UNC

1985-89. Black, dark green and brown on multicolor underprint. J. Sierra at left center, University building at right. 3 signatures. Back: 19th century courtyard. Printer: BdM. UV: fibers fluoresce red, security strip green.

	VF	UNC
a. With *SANTANA* at lower left 2 date positions. 19.7.1985.	1.25	4.00
b. As a. 24.2.1987.	1.25	3.00
c. Without *SANTANA*. 28.3.1989.	1.00	2.25

87 5000 Pesos — VF | UNC

19.7.1985. Red on multicolor underprint. Cadets at left center, bank titile without S. A. 4 signatures and signature varieties, narrower serial number. Back: Chapultepec castle. Blue tint. Watermark: Cadet. Printer: BdM. — 2.25 | 7.50

88 5000 Pesos — VF | UNC

1985-89. Purple and brown-orange on multicolor underprint. Cadets at left center, bank titile without S. A. 3 signatures and signature varieties, narrower serial number. Without watermark, design continued over watermark area. Back: Chapultepec castle. Light tan. Printer: BdM.

	VF	UNC
a. With *SANTANA* vertically at lower left 19.7.1985.	2.00	6.00
b. As a. 24.2.1987.	1.75	5.00
c. Without *SANTANA*. 28.3.1989.	1.50	3.00

89 10,000 Pesos — VF | UNC

1985; 1987. Blue-black, brown and deep blue-green on multicolor underprint. Power plant at center, General Lazaro Cardenas at right, bank titile without S. A. 3 signatures and signature varieties. Back: Coyolxauhqui stone carving at center. Printer: BdM.

	VF	UNC
a. Purple and blue serial #. 19.7.1985.	5.00	12.50
b. Green and blue serial #. 19.7.1985.	5.00	12.50
c. Red and blue serial #. 19.7.1985; 24.2.1987.	5.00	12.50
d. Green and blue serial #. 24.7.1987.	5.00	12.50

90 10,000 Pesos

1987-91. Deep blue-black on brown and blue-green underprint. Power plant at center, General Lazaro Cardenas at right, bank titile without S. A. 3 signatures and signature varieties. Back: Coyolxauhqui stone carving at center. Light tan. Printer: BdM. Similar to #89 but watermark area filled in.

	VF	UNC
a. With *SANTANA*. at lower left under refinery designature 24.2.1987.	3.00	10.00
b. Without *SANTANA*. 1.2.1988.	2.50	7.00
c. 28.3.1989.	2.50	6.00
d. 16.5.1991.	2.00	6.00

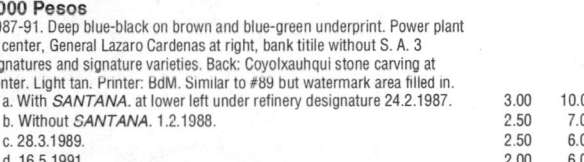

91 20,000 Pesos — VF | UNC

1985-87. Deep blue on blue and multicolor underprint. Fortress above coastal cliffs at center, Don A. Quintana Roo at right. 3 signature titles, S. A. remoned from bank title. Back: Artwork. Watermark: Don A. Quintana Roo. Printer: BdM.

	VF	UNC
a. 19.7.1985.	7.00	22.50
b. 24.2.1987.	6.50	17.50
c. 27.8.1987.	6.50	17.50

92 20,000 Pesos — VF | UNC

1988; 1989. Blue-black on blue and pink underprint. Fortress above coastal cliffs at center, Don A. Quintana Roo at right. 3 signatures, S. A. removed from bank titile. Back: Artwork. Printer: BdM. Similar to #91 but design continued over watermark area.

	VF	UNC
a. 1.2.1988.	5.00	15.00
b. 28.3.1989.	5.00	12.50

93 50,000 Pesos — VF | UNC

1986-90. Purple on multicolor underprint. Aztec symbols at center, Cuauhtémoc at right. 3 signatures, S.A. removed from bank title. Back: Aztec and Spaniard fighting at left center. Pink. Watermark: Cuauhtémoc. Printer: BdM.

	VF	UNC
a. 12.5.1986; 24.2.1987; 27.8.1987; 1.2.1988.	17.50	60.00
b. 28.3.1989; 10.1.1990; 20.12.1990.	15.00	45.00

94 100,000 Pesos — VF | UNC

1988; 1991. Blue-black and maroon on multicolor underprint. P. E. Calles at left, Banco de Mexico at center. 3 signatures, S.A. removed from bank title. Back: Desert Mule Deer, cactus, lake and mountain at center right. Watermark: P. E. Calles. Printer: BdM.

	VF	UNC
a. 4.1.1988.	27.50	85.00
b. 2.9.1991.	27.50	85.00

1992 First Issue

Nuevos Pesos System

1000 "old" Pesos = 1 Nuevo Peso

95 10 Nuevos Pesos — VF | UNC

31.7.1992. Blue-black, brown and deep blue-green on multicolor underprint. Power plant at center, General Lazaro Cardenas at right, bank titile without S. A. 3 signatures and signature varieties. Series A-Y. Back: Coyolxauhqui stone carving at center. Printer: BdM. — FV | 7.50

96 20 Nuevos Pesos — VF | UNC

31.7.1992. Deep blue on blue and multicolor underprint. Fortress above coastal cliffs at center, Don A. Quintana Roo at right. 3 signatures and signature varieties, S. A. removed from bank titile. Series A-Q. Back: Artwork. Printer: Bdm. — FV | 12.50

97 50 Nuevos Pesos — VF | UNC

31.7.1992. Purple on multicolor underprint. Aztec symbols at center, Cuauhtémoc at right. 3 signatures and signature titiles, S.A. removed from bank title. Series A-P. Back: Aztec and Spaniard fighting at left center. Printer: BdM. — FV | 27.50

98 100 Nuevos Pesos — VF | UNC

31.7.1992. Blue-black and maroon on multicolor underprint. P. E. Calles at left, Banco de Mexico at center. 3 signatures and signature titles, S.A. removed from bank title. Series A-Q. Back: Desert Mule Deer, cactus, lake and mountain at center right. Printer: BdM. — FV | 40.00

1992 (1994) Second Issue

99 10 Nuevos Pesos — VF | UNC

10.12.1992. (1994). Deep blue-green and gold on multicolor underprint. E. Zapata at right, hands holding corn at center. Series A-T. Back: Machinery at lower left, statue of Zapata on horseback near peasant at center right, building in background. Printer: BdM. — FV | 4.00

100 20 Nuevos Pesos — VF | UNC

10.12.1992 (1994). Purple and dark blue on multicolor underprint. B. Juárez at right, eagle on cactus with snake (arms) at center. Back: Monument, statues "Hemiciclo a Juárez." Printer: BdM. — FV | 6.50

101 50 Nuevos Pesos — VF | UNC

10.12.1992 (1994). Red-violet and black on multicolor underprint. J. M. Morelos at right, crossed cannons on outlined bow and arrow below his flag at left center. Series A-AF. Back: Butterflies at left, boat fishermen at center. Printer: BdM. — FV | 15.00

102 100 Nuevos Pesos — VF | UNC

10.12.1992 (1994). Red and brown on multicolor underprint. Nezahualcóyotl at right, Aztec figure at center. Series A-V. Back: Xochipilli statue. Watermark: Nezahualcóyotl. Printer: BdM. — FV | 25.00

103 200 Nuevos Pesos — VF | UNC

10.12.1992 (1994). Dark olive-green, dark brown and olive-brown on multicolor underprint. J. de Asbaje at right, open book and quill pen at center. Series A-E. Back: Temple de San Jerónimo. Watermark: J. de Asbaje. Printer: BdM. — FV | 45.00

104 500 Nuevos Pesos

10.12.1992 (1994). Red-brown, deep purple and dark brown-violet on multicolor underprint. I. Zaragoza at center right, Battle of Puebla at left center. Series A-C. Back: Cathedral at Puebla at center. Watermark: I. Zaragoza. Printer: BdM.

	VF	UNC
	FV	110.

1994; 1995 (1996) Issue

105 10 Pesos

1994 (1996); 1996. Deep blue-green and gold on multicolor underprint. E. Zapata at right, hands holding corn at center. *EL* omitted from bank titile. 2 signatures. Series A-. Back: Machinery at lower left, statue of Zapata on horseback near peasant at center right, building in background. Printer: BdM.

	VF	UNC
a. 6.5.1994.	FV	3.00
b. 10.5.1996.	FV	3.00

106 20 Pesos

1994 (1996); 1996; 1998-99. Purple and dark blue on multicolor underprint. B. Juárez at right, eagle on cactus with snake (arms) at center. *El* omitted from bank title. 2 signatures. Series A-. Back: Monument, statues *Hemiciclo a Juárez.* Printer: BdM. 120x66mm.

	VF	UNC
a. 6.5.1994.	FV	6.00
b. 10.5.1996.	FV	5.50
c. 3.17.1998.	FV	5.50
d. 23.4.1999.	FV	5.50

107 50 Pesos

1994 (1996); 1998-99. Red-violet and black on multicolor underprint. J. M. Morelos at right, crossed cannons on outlined bow and arrow below his flag at left center. *El* omitted from bank title. 2 signatures. Series A-. Back: Butterflies at left, boat fishermen at center. Printer: BdM. 127x65mm.

	VF	UNC
a. 6.5.1994.	FV	15.00
b. 10.5.1996.	FV	10.00
c. 17.3.1998.	FV	10.00
d. 23.4.1999.	FV	10.00

108 100 Pesos

1994 (1996); 1996; 1998-99. Red and brown-orange on multicolor underprint. Nezahualcóyotl at right, Aztec figure at center. *El* omitted from bank title. Series A-BS. 2 signatures. Series A-. Back: Xochipilli statue. Printer: BdM. 155x66mm.

	VF	UNC
a. 6.5.1994.	FV	22.50
b. 10.5.1996.	FV	22.50
c. 17.03.1998. Series AX-BG.	FV	22.50
d. 23.4.1999. Series BC-BS.	FV	22.50

109 200 Pesos

1995 (1996); 1996; 1998-99. Dark olive-green, dark brown and olive-brown on multicolor underprint. J. de Asbaje at right, open book and quill pen at center. *El* omitted from bank title. Series A-E. 2 signatures. Series A-. Back: Temple de San Jerónimo. Watermark: J. de Asbaje. Printer: BdM. 155x66mm.

	VF	UNC
a. 7.2.1995.	FV	45.00
b. 10.5.1996.	FV	37.50
c. 17.3.1998.	FV	37.50
d. 23.4.1999.	FV	37.50

110 500 Pesos

1995 (1996); 1996. Red-brown, deep purple and dark brown-violet on multicolor underprint. I. Zaragoza at center right, Battle of Puebla at left center. *El* omitted from bank title. Series A-C. 2 signatures. Back: Cathedral at Puebla at center. Watermark: I. Zaragoza. Printer: BdM. 155x66mm.

	VF	UNC
a. 7.2.1995.	FV	95.00
b. 10.5.1996.	FV	95.00
c. 17.3.1998.	FV	95.00
d. 23.4.1999.	FV	95.00

2000 Commemorative Issue

#111-115, 75th Anniversary Banco de Mexico. Commemorative text immediately below bank name.

111 20 Pesos — VF / UNC
25.8.2000. Purple and dark blue on multicolor underprint. B. Juárez at right, eagle on cactus with snake (arms) at center. Commemorative text immediately below bank name. Back: Monument, statues *Hemiciclo a Juárez*. Printer: BdM. 120x66mm. — 3.50 / 9.50

112 50 Pesos — VF / UNC
25.8.2000. Red-violet and black on multicolor underprint. J. M. Morelos at right, crossed cannons on outlined bow and arrow below his flag at left center. Commemorative text immediately below bank name. Back: Butterflies at left, boat fishermen at center. Printer: BdM. 127x65mm. — 9.00 / 17.50

113 100 Pesos
25.8.2000. Red and brown-orange on multicolor underprint. Nezahualcóyotl at right, Aztec figure at center. Commemorative text immediately below bank name. Back: Xochipilli statue. Printer: BdM. 155x66mm. — 15.00 / 35.00

114 200 Pesos — VF / UNC
25.8.2000. Dark olive-green, dark brown and olive-brown on multicolor underprint. J. de Asbaje at right, open book and quill pen at center. Commemorative text immediately below bank name. Back: Temple de San Jerónimo. Watermark: J. de Asbaje. Printer: BdM. 155x66mm. — 30.00 / 70.00

115 500 Pesos — VF / UNC
25.8.2000. Red-brown, deep purple and dark brown-violet on multicolor underprint. I. Zaragoza at center right, Battle of Puebla at left center. Commemorative text immediately below bank name. Back: Cathedral at Puebla at center. Watermark: I. Zaragoza. Printer: BdM. 155x66mm. — 65.00 / 150.

2000-01 Issue

116 20 Pesos — VF / UNC
2001; 2002; 2003; 2005. Blue and multicolor underprint. B. Juárez at right, eagle on cactus with snake (arms) at center. 2 signatures. Back: Monument, statues "Hemiciclo a Juárez." Printer: NPA and BdM. Polymer plastic. 120x66mm.

		VF	UNC
a.	17.5.2001. Series A-F. Two electronic sorting bars at upper left.	FV	5.50
b.	17.5.2001. Series G-T. Three electronic sorting bars at upper left.	FV	4.50
c.	26.3.2002. Two electronic sorting bars. Series U.	FV	4.50
d.	23.5.2003. Two electronic sorting bars. Series V-.	FV	4.50
e.	9.11.2005.	FV	4.50

117 50 Pesos — VF / UNC
2000 (2001); 2002-03. Red-violet and black on multicolor underprint. J. M. Morelos at right, crossed cannons on outlined bow and arrow below his flag at left center. 2 signatures. Back: Butterflies at left, boat fishermen at center. Vertical iridescent strip at left. Additional enhanced security features. 127x65mm.

		VF	UNC
a.	18.10.2000.	FV	10.00
b.	26.3.2002.	FV	10.00
c.	21.11.2003.	FV	10.00

118 100 Pesos — VF / UNC
2000-05; 2007-08. Red and brown-orange on multicolor underprint. Nezahualcóyotl at right, Aztec figure at center. 2 signatures. Back: Xochipilli statue. Vertical iridescent strip at left. Additional enhanced security features. 155x66mm.

		VF	UNC
a.	18.10.2000.	FV	15.00
b.	26.3.2002.	FV	15.00
c.	23.5.2003.	FV	15.00
d.	21.11.2003.	FV	15.00
e.	31.5.2004.	FV	12.50
f.	5.11.2004.	FV	12.50
g.	31.5.2005. Series DM.	FV	12.50
h.	7.9.2005.	FV	12.50
i.	19.6.2006. Series DT.	FV	12.50
j.	20.11.2007. Series DY.	FV	12.50
k.	28.4.2008.	FV	12.50
l.	28.4.2008. Series DZ.	FV	12.50
m.	28.4.2008. Series EA.	FV	12.50
n.	28.4.2008. Series EB.	FV	12.50

119 200 Pesos VF UNC

2000-07. Dark olive-green, dark brown and olive-brown on multicolor underprint. J. de Asbaje at right, open book and quill pen at center. Series A-E. 2 signatures. Back: Temple de San JerÛnimo. Watermark: J. de Asbaje. Vertical iridescent strip at left. Additional enhanced security features. 155x66mm.

a. 18.10.2000.	FV	27.50
b. 23.3.2002.	FV	27.50
c. 3.6.2004. Blind markings added at top right.	FV	25.00
d. 23.5.2006.	FV	25.00
e. 19.6.2006.	FV	22.50
f. 14.5.2007. Series DM, DN.	FV	22.50

120 500 Pesos

2000; 2005-06; 2008. Red-brown, deep purple and dark brown-violet on multicolor underprint. I. Zaragoza at center right, Battle of Puebla at left center. Series A-C. 2 signatures. Back: Cathedral at Puebla at center. Watermark: Zaragoza. Vertical iridescent strip at left. Additional enhanced security features. 155x66mm.

a. 18.10.2000.	FV	65.00
b. 7.9.2005.	FV	60.00
c. 19.6.2006.	FV	60.00
d. 28.10.2008. Series AW.	FV	55.00

121 1000 Pesos VF UNC

26.3.2002. Multicolor. Miguel Hidalgo at right, eagle on cactus with snake (arms) at center. 2 signatures. Back: Monument, statues *Hemiciclo a Juárez*. 155x66mm.

a. Issued note.	FV	150.
s. Specimen. Overprinted: *ESPECIMEN*.	—	750.

2004-06 Polymer & Paper Issue

122 20 Pesos VF UNC

2006-10. Blue. Benito Juarez at right center, book and scales at center. Back: View of Cocijo. Polymer plastic. 122x66mm.

a. 29.3.2006.	FV	4.00
b. 19.6.2006.	FV	4.00
c. 22.11.2006. Series C.	FV	4.00
d. 14.5.2007. Series E.	FV	4.00
e. 3.5.2010.	FV	4.00

123 50 Pesos VF UNC

2004-. Lilac, red and violet. Jose Maria Morelos at right center. Back: Morelia Aqueduct. Polymer plastic. 127x65mm.

a. 5.11.2004.	FV	7.50
b. 7.9.2005.	FV	7.50
c. 19.6.2006.	FV	7.50
d. 22.11.2006.	FV	7.50
e. 28.4.2008. Series J.	FV	7.50
f. 28.10.2008. Series K.	FV	7.50
g. 23.4.2009.	FV	7.50
h. 3.5.2010. Series Q.	FV	6.00
i. 3.5.2010. Series R; S.	FV	6.00
j. 24.6.2011. Series T; U.	FV	6.00
k. 10.1.2012. Series V.	FV	6.00
l. 12.6.2012.	FV	6.00

124 100 Pesos VF UNC

2008-10. Red and yellow on multicolor underprint. Ear of corn at left, Nezahualcóyotl at right. Back: Temple and central square of Tenochtitlán. Watermark: Nezahualcóyotl and 100. 148x66mm.

a. 28.10.2008. Series A.	FV	18.00
b. 23.4.2009. Series E.	FV	18.00
c. 5.10.2009.	FV	15.00
d. 3.5.2010.	FV	15.00
e. 4.11.2010. Series M.	FV	12.50

125 200 Pesos

15.2.2007-. Green and brown on multicolor underprint. Juana de Asbaje at right center. Back: Hacienda de Panoayán. Watermark: Asbaje and 200. 141x66mm.

a. 15.2.2007. Serie A, B.	FV	25.00
b. 14.5.2007. Serie C, D, E, F.	FV	25.00
c. 20.11.2007. Serie G, H.	FV	25.00
d. 5.10.2009.	FV	25.00

126 500 Pesos VF UNC

8.3.2010; 4.11.2010. Brown on tan underprint. Diego Rivera at center. Back: Two of Rivera's paintings at center. Watermark: Rivera and 500. Printer: BdM. 148x66mm.

a. 8.3.2010.	FV	70.00
b. 8.3.2010. Three signature varieties.	FV	70.00
s. Specimen.	—	100.

127 1000 Pesos

2006. Violet and brown on multicolor underprint. Miguel Hidalgo at right center. Back: Universidad de Guanajato.

a. 8.5.2006. Series A.	FV	150.
b. 28.11.2006.	FV	150.

2010 Independence and Revolution Commemorative Issues

		Mkt.	Value
128	**100 Pesos** 2007. Brown and multicolor. Steam Locomotive at center. Back: Revolutionary crowd at center. 134x66mm.		
	a. Series A/A-A/E. Error in microprinted text: *SUFRAGIO ELECTIVO.*	FV	10.00
	b. Corrected microprinted text: *SUFRAGIO EFECTIVO.*	FV	15.00

		Mkt.	Value
129	**200 Pesos** 15.9.2008. Brown on green underprint. Miguel Hidalgo with standard at lower center. Back: Statue of the Angel of Independence. Watermark: Angel of Independence and 200. 141x66mm.		FV

MOLDOVA

The area of Moldova is bordered in the north, east, and south by the Ukraine and on the west by Romania.

The historical Romanian principality of Moldova was established in the 14th century. It fell under Turkish suzerainty in the 16th century. From 1812 to 1918, Russians occupied the eastern portion of Moldova which they named Bessarabia. In March 1918, the Bessarabian legislature voted in favor of reunification with Romania.

Part of Romania during the interwar period, Moldova was incorporated into the Soviet Union at the close of World War II. Although independent from the USSR since 1991, Russian forces have remained on Moldovan territory east of the Dniester River supporting the Slavic majority population, mostly Ukrainians and Russians, who have proclaimed a "Transnistria" republic. One of the poorest nations in Europe, Moldova became the first former Soviet state to elect a Communist as its president in 2001.

MONETARY SYSTEM:

3 Ducati = 100 Lei
100 Rubles = 1000 Cupon, 1992
1 Leu = 1000 Cupon, 1993-

Republic

Minister of Finance

Ruble Control Coupons, March 1992 Issue

		VF	UNC
A11	**20 Rubles** Martie 1992.		
	a. Full sheet.	1.00	5.00
	b. One coupon.	FV	.15
A12	**50 Rubles** Martie 1992.		
	a. Full sheet.	1.00	5.00
	b. One coupon.	—	.15
A13	**75 Rubles** Martie 1992.		
	a. Full sheet.	1.00	5.00
	b. One coupon.	—	.15
A14	**100 Rubles** Martie 1992.		
	a. Full sheet.	1.00	5.00
	b. One coupon.	—	.15

Ruble Control Coupons, April 1992 Issues

		VF	UNC
A15	**20 Rubles** April 1992. Brown.		
	a. Full sheet.	1.00	5.00
	b. One coupon.	—	.15
A16	**20 Rubles** April 1992. Violet.		
	a. Full sheet.	1.00	5.00
	b. One coupon.	—	.15
A17	**50 Rubles** April 1992. Brown.		
	a. Full sheet.	1.00	5.00
	b. One coupon.	—	.15
A18	**50 Rubles** April 1992. Violet.		
	a. Full sheet.	1.00	5.00
	b. One coupon.	—	.15
A19	**75 Rubles** April 1992. Brown.		
	a. Full sheet.	1.00	5.00
	b. One coupon.	—	.15
A20	**75 Rubles** April 1992. Violet.		
	a. Full sheet.	1.00	5.00
	b. One coupon.	—	.15

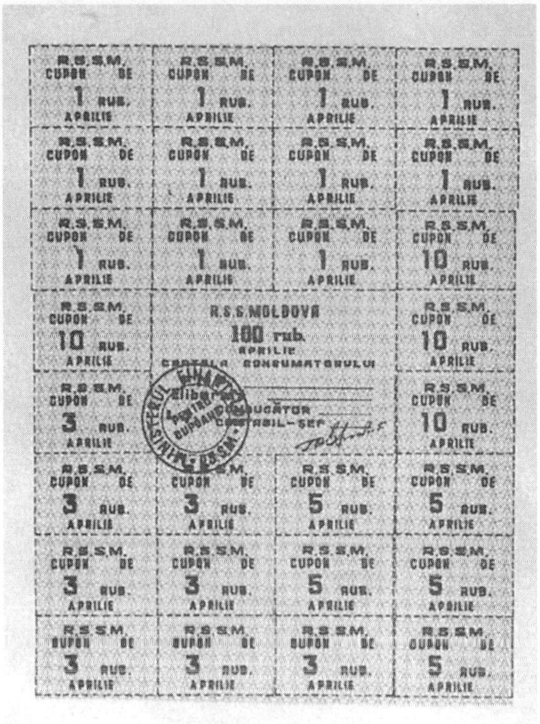

A21	**100 Rubles** 1992. Brown.	**VF**	**UNC**
	a. Full sheet.	1.00	5.00
	b. Coupon.	—	.10
A22	**100 Rubles** April 1992. Violet.		
	a. Full sheet.	1.00	5.00
	b. One coupon.	—	.15

Banca Nationala a Moldovei

1992; 1993 "Cupon" Issue

1	**50 Cupon** 1992. Gray-green on gray underprint. Arms at left. Back: Castle at right. Watermark: Design (varies).	**VF** 2.00	**UNC** 6.00

2	**200 Cupon** 1992. Purple on gray underprint. Arms at left. Back: Purple on lilac underprint. Castle at right. Watermark: Design (varies).	**VF** 4.00	**UNC** 8.00

3	**1000 Cupon** 1993. Brown on pale blue-green and ochre underprint. Bank monogram at upper left, arms at left. Back: Castle at right. Watermark: Design (varies).	**VF** 5.00	**UNC** 10.00

4	**5000 Cupon** 1993. Pale brown-violet on orange and pale olive-green underprint. Bank monogram at upper left, arms at left. Back: Pale brown-violet on pale brown-orange underprint. Castle at right. Watermark: Design (varies).	**VF** 7.00	**UNC** 15.00

1992 (1993) Issue

5	**1 Leu** 1992 (1993). Brown and dark olive-green on ochre underprint. King Stefan at left, arms at upper center right. Signature L. Talmaci. Back: Soroca Fortress at center right. Printer: Romanian.	**VF** 3.00	**UNC** 6.00

6	**5 Lei** 1992 (1993). Purple on light blue and ochre underprint. King Stefan at left, arms at upper center right. Signature L. Talmaci. Back: Soroca Fortress at center right. Watermark: Design.	**VF** 5.00	**UNC** 10.00

7	**10 Lei** 1992 (1993). Red brown and olive-green on pale orange underprint. King Stefan at left, arms at upper center right. Signature L. Talmaci. Back: Soroca Fortress at center right. Watermark: Design. Printer: Romanian.	**VF** 4.00	**UNC** 15.00

1992; 1994 Issue

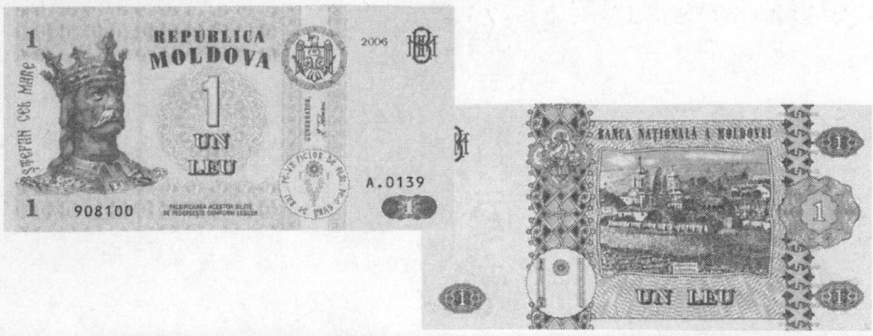

8 1 Leu

1994-2010. Brown on ochre, pale yellow-green and multicolor underprint. King Stefan at left, arms at upper center right. Bank monogram at upper right corner. Back: Monastery at Capriana at center right. Watermark: King Stefan. Printer: BdF.

	VF	UNC
a. 1994.	.50	2.50
b. 1995.	.50	2.50
c. 1998.	.50	2.50
d. 1999.	.50	2.50
e. 2002.	.50	2.50
f. 2005.	.50	2.00
g. 2006.	.50	1.50
h. 2010.	.50	1.50

9 5 Lei

1994-. Blue-green on lilac and pale aqua underprint. King Stefan at left, arms at upper center right. Bank monogram at upper right corner. Back: Basilica of St. Dumitru in Orhei at center right. Watermark: King Stefan. Printer: BdF. 114x58mm.

	VF	UNC
a. 1994.	1.00	3.50
b. 1995.	1.00	3.00
c. 1999.	1.00	3.00
d. 2005.	1.00	2.50
e. 2006.	1.00	2.50
f. 2009.	FV	2.00
g. 2013.	FV	2.00

10 10 Lei

1994-. Red-brown on pale blue and gold underprint. King Stefan at left, arms at upper center right. Bank monogram at upper right corner. Back: Monastery at Hîrjauca at center right. Watermark: King Stefan. 120x61mm.

	VF	UNC
a. 1994.	FV	5.00
b. 1995.	FV	5.00
c. 1998.	FV	8.00
d. 2005.	FV	4.50
e. 2006.	FV	4.00
f. 2009.	FV	3.00
g. 2013. Signature Dorin Dragutanu.	FV	3.00

13 20 Lei

1992-. Blue-green on light green, aqua and ochre underprint. King Stefan at left, arms at upper center right. Bank monogram at upper right corner. Back: Soroca Fortress at center right. Watermark: King Stefan. 121x61mm.

	VF	UNC
a. 1992.	FV	8.00
b. 1995.	FV	15.00
c. 1997.	FV	8.00
d. 1999.	FV	8.00
e. 2002.	FV	8.00
f. 2004.	FV	7.00
g. 2005.	FV	7.00
h. 2006.	FV	6.00
i. 2010.	FV	5.00
j. 2013.	FV	4.50

14 50 Lei

1992-. Red-violet on lilac and multicolor underprint. King Stefan at left, arms at upper center right. Bank monogram at upper right corner. Back: Monastery at Hîrbovet at center right. Watermark: King Stefan. 121x61mm.

	VF	UNC
a. 1992.	FV	12.00
b. 2002.	FV	10.00
c. 2005.	FV	10.00
d. 2006.	FV	10.00
e. 2008. Caption on back corrected.	FV	8.00
f. 2013. Signature Dorin Dragutanu.	FV	7.50

1992 (1995) Issue

15 100 Lei

1992 (1995); 2008; 2013. Brown on multicolor underprint. King Stefan at left, arms at upper center right. Back: Thighina Fortress. Watermark: King Stefan. 121x61mm.

	VF	UNC
a. 1992.	10.00	25.00
b. 2008. Caption on back corrected: CETATEA TIGHINA.	FV	20.00
c. 2013. Signature Dorin Dragutanu.	FV	15.00

16 200 Lei

1992 (1995); 2007; 2008; 2013. Purple on multicolor underprint. King Stefan at left, arms at upper center right. Back: Chisinau City Hall. Watermark: King Stefan. 133x66mm.

	VF	UNC
a. 1992	FV	45.00
b. 2007.	FV	35.00
c. 2008.	FV	30.00
d. 2013.	FV	30.00

1992 (1999) Issue

17 500 Lei VF UNC
1992 (1999). Slate black, orange and green on multicolor underprint. Back: Chisinau Cathedral. 133x66mm. 60.00 100.

18 1000 Lei VF UNC
1992 (2003). Blue and purple on multicolor underprint. King Stefan at left. 133x66mm. 100. 180.

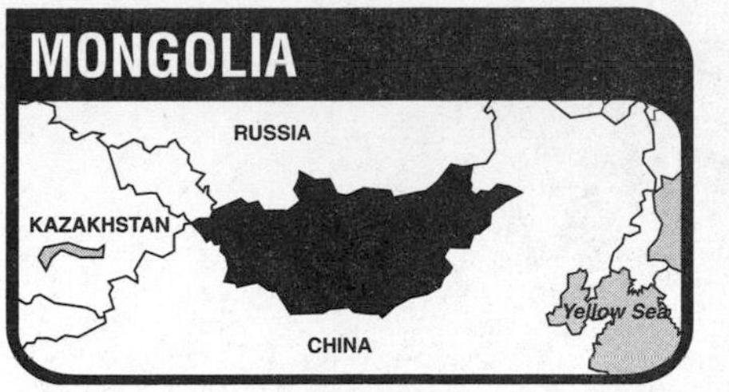

The State of Mongolia, a landlocked country in central Asia between Russia and the Peoples Republic of China, has an area of 604,247 sq. mi. (1,565,000 sq. km.) and a population of 2.74 million. Capital: Ulan Bator. Animal herds and flocks are the chief economic asset. Wool, cattle, butter, meat and hides are exported.

The Mongols gained fame in the 13th century when under Chinggis Khan they established a huge Eurasian empire through conquest. After his death the empire was divided into several powerful Mongol states, but these broke apart in the 14th century. The Mongols eventually retired to their original steppe homelands and in the late 17th century came under Chinese rule. Mongolia won its independence in 1921 with Soviet backing and a Communist regime was installed in 1924. The modern country of Mongolia, however, represents only part of the Mongols' historical homeland; more Mongols live in the Inner Mongolia Autonomous Region in the People's Republic of China than in Mongolia. Following a peaceful democratic revolution, the ex-Communist Mongolian People's Revolutionary Party (MPRP) won elections in 1990 and 1992, but was defeated by the Democratic Union Coalition (DUC) in the 1996 parliamentary election. The MPRP won an overwhelming majority in the 2000 parliamentary election, but the party lost seats in the 2004 election and shared power with democratic coalition parties from 2004-2008. The MPRP regained a solid majority in the 2008 parliamentary elections; the prime minister and a majority of cabinet members are currently MPRP members.

RULERS:

Chinese to 1921

MONETARY SYSTEM:

1 Tugrik (Tukhrik) = 100 Mongo

State

УЛСЫН БАНК

State Bank

1966 Issue

			VF	UNC
35	**1 Tugrik**	1966. Brown on pale green and yellow underprint. Socialist arms at upper left. Back: Multicolor. Watermark: Circles forming a 6-petaled flower-like pattern.		
		a. Issued note.	.40	.75
		s. Specimen.	—	15.00
36	**3 Tugrik**	1966. Dark green on light green and pink underprint. Socialist arms at upper left, portrait of Sukhe-Bataar at right. Back: Multicolor. Watermark: Circles forming a 6-petaled flower-like pattern.		
		a. Issued note.	.50	1.00
		s. Specimen.	—	15.00
37	**5 Tugrik**	1966. Dark blue on light blue and pale green underprint. Socialist arms at upper left, portrait of Sukhe-Bataar at right. Back: Multicolor. Watermark: Circles forming a 6-petaled flower-like pattern.		
		a. Issued note.	.50	1.00
		s. Specimen.	—	15.00
38	**10 Tugrik**	1966. Red on pale red and blue underprint. Socialist arms at upper left, portrait of Sukhe-Bataar at right. Back: Multicolor. Watermark: Circles forming a 6-petaled flower-like pattern.		
		a. Issued note.	.75	1.25
		s. Specimen.	—	15.00
39	**25 Tugrik**	1966. Brown-violet on pale green underprint. Socialist arms at upper left, portrait of Sukhe-Bataar at right. Back: Multicolor. Watermark: Circles forming a 6-petaled flower-like pattern.		
		a. Issued note.	1.00	1.50
		s. Specimen.	—	15.00
40	**50 Tugrik**	1966. Dark green on light green and gold underprint. Socialist arms at upper left, portrait of Sukhe-Bataar at right. Back: Multicolor. Government Building at Ulan-Bator. Watermark: Circles forming a 6-petaled flower-like pattern.		
		a. Issued note.	2.50	3.00
		s. Specimen.	—	15.00

41 **100 Tugrik** VF UNC
1966. Dark brown on ochre and blue-green underprint. Socialist arms at upper left, portrait of Sukhe-Bataar at right. Back: Multicolor. Government Building at Ulan-Bator. Watermark: Circles forming a 6-petaled flower-like pattern.

	VF	UNC
a. Issued note.	4.00	7.50
s. Specimen.	—	15.00

1981-83 Issue

Replacement notes: Serial # prefix ЯА.

42 **1 Tugrik** VF .25 UNC 1.00
1983. Brown on pale green and yellow underprint. Socialist arms at upper left. Back: Multicolor. Watermark: Circles forming a 6-petaled flower-like pattern.

43 **3 Tugrik** VF .25 UNC 1.25
1983. Dark green on light green and pink underprint. Socialist arms at upper left, portrait of Sukhe-Bataar at right. Back: Multicolor. Watermark: Circles forming a 6-petaled flower-like pattern.

44 **5 Tugrik** VF .25 UNC 1.75
1981. Blue on light blue and pale green underprint. Socialist arms at upper left, portrait of Sukhe-Bataar at right. Back: Multicolor. Watermark: Circles forming a 6-petaled flower-like pattern.

45 **10 Tugrik** VF .25 UNC 2.00
1981. Red on pale red and blue underprint. Socialist arms at upper left, portrait of Sukhe-Bataar at right. Back: Multicolor. Watermark: Circles forming a 6-petaled flower-like pattern.

46 **20 Tugrik** VF .35 UNC 2.25
1981. Yellow-green on light green and brown underprint. Sukhe-Bataar at center, arms at left. Back: Power station at Ulan-Bator at center right.

47 **50 Tugrik** VF 1.00 UNC 5.00
1981. Dark green on light green and gold underprint. Socialist arms at upper left, portrait of Sukhe-Bataar at right. Back: Multicolor. Government Building at Ulan-Bator. Watermark: Circles forming a 6-petaled flower-like pattern.

48 **100 Tugrik** VF .10 UNC 9.00
1981. Dark brown on ochre and blue-green underprint. Socialist arms at upper left, portrait of Sukhe-Bataar at right. Back: Multicolor. Government Building at Ulan-Bator. Watermark: Circles forming a 6-petaled flower-like pattern.

МОНГОЛ БАНК

Mongol Bank

1993 ND; 1994-95 Issue

#41-51Replacement notes: Serial # prefix *ZZ*.

49 **10 Mongo** VF .10 UNC .75
ND (1993). Red-violet on pale red-orange underprint. "Soemba" arms at upper center, two archers at lower center. Back: Two archers at lower center.

50 **20 Mongo** VF .15 UNC .75
ND (1993). Brown on ochre and yellow-brown underprint. "Soemba" arms at upper center, two athletes at lower center. Back: Two athletes at lower center.

51 **50 Mongo** VF .50 UNC .75
ND (1993). Greenish-black on blue and pale green underprint. "Soemba" arms at upper center, two horsemen at lower center. Back: Two horsemen at lower center.

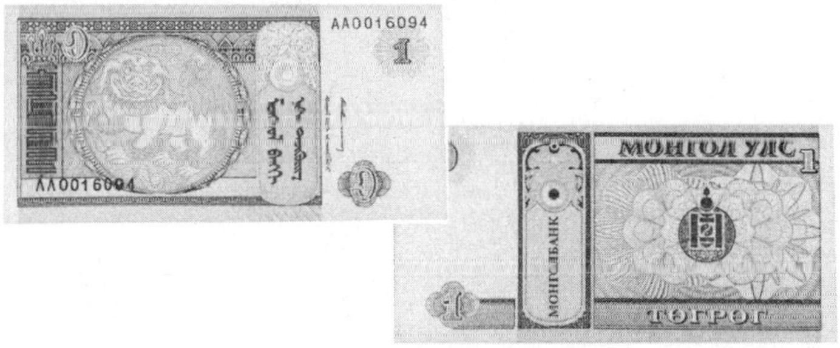

52 **1 Tugrik** VF .15 UNC 1.00
ND (1993). Dull olive-green and brown-orange on ochre underprint. Chinze at left. Back: "Soemba" arms at center right. Watermark: Genghis Khan. UV: left design as a square with Mongolian 1 fluoresces yellow, upper serial # orange. Back central design orange.

53 **5 Tugrik** VF .25 UNC 1.25
ND (1993). Deep orange, ochre and brown on multicolor underprint. Youthful portrait Sukhe-Bataar at left, "Soemba" arms at center. Back: Horses grazing in mountainous landscape at center right. Watermark: Genghis Khan. UV: left design as a square with Mongolian 5 fluoresces yellow, upper serial # orange. Back portions of scene yellow.

54 **10 Tugrik** VF .25 UNC 1.25
ND (1993). Green, blue and light green on multicolor underprint. Youthful portrait Sukhe-Bataar at left, "Soemba" arms at center. Back: Horses grazing in mountainous landscape at center right. Watermark: Genghis Khan. UV: left design as a square with Mongolian 10 fluoresces green, upper serial # orange. Back central design green.

55 **20 Tugrik** VF .25 UNC 1.25
ND (1993). Violet, orange and red on multicolor underprint. Youthful portrait Sukhe-Bataar at left, "Soemba" arms at center. Back: Horses grazing in mountainous landscape at center right. Watermark: Genghis Khan. UV: left design as a square with Mongolian 20 fluoresces green, upper serial # orange. Back central design green.

56 **50 Tugrik** VF .25 UNC 1.50
ND (1993). Dark brown on multicolor underprint. Youthful portrait Sukhe-Bataar at left, "Soemba" arms at center. Back: Horses grazing in mountainous landscape at center right. Watermark: Genghis Khan.

57 **100 Tugrik** VF .50 UNC 2.00
ND (1993); 1994. Purple, brown and dark blue on multicolor underprint. Youthful portrait Sukhe-Bataar at left, "Soemba" arms at center. Back: Horses grazing in mountainous landscape at center right. Watermark: Genghis Khan.

58 **500 Tugrik** VF 1.00 UNC 5.00
ND (1993); 1997. Dark green, brown and yellow-green on multicolor underprint. Genghis Khan at left, "Soemba" arms at center. Back: Ox drawn yurte, village at center right. Watermark: Genghis Khan. 145x70mm.

59	**1000 Tugrik**	VF	UNC
	ND (1993); 1997-98. Blue-gray, brown and blue on multicolor underprint. Genghis Khan at left, "Soemba" arms at center. Back: Ox drawn yurte, village at center right. Watermark: Genghis Khan. 150x72mm.		
	a. ND (1993).	5.00	10.00
	b. 1997.	5.00	10.00
	c. 1998.	5.00	10.00

60	**5000 Tugrik**	VF	UNC
	1994. Purple, violet and red on multicolor underprint. Genghis Khan at left, "Soemba" arms at center. Back: Building with fountain. Watermark: Genghis Khan. 150x72mm.	7.50	17.50
61	**10,000 Tugrik**		
	1995. Black, dark olive-green and orange on multicolor underprint. Genghis Khan at left, "Soemba" arms at center. Back: Ox drawn yurte, village at center right. Building complex, tree, people. Watermark: Genghis Khan. 150x72mm.	16.00	35.00

2000; 2003 Issue

61A	**1 Tugrik**	VF	UNC
	2008. Dull olive-green and brown-orange on ochre underprint. Chinze at left center. Back: "Soemba" arms at center right. 115x57mm.	.15	1.00

61B	**5 Tugrik**	Mkt.	Value
	2008. Deep orange, ochre and brown on multicolor underprint. Youthful portrait of Sukhe-Bataar at left, "Soemba" arms at center. Back: Horses grazing in mountainous landscape at center right. 120x60mm.		—

62	**10 Tugrik**	VF	UNC
	2000-. Dark green and multicolor. Youthful portrait Sukhe-Bataar at left, "Soemba" arms at center. 128x60mm.		
	a. 2000.	FV	.50
	b. 2002.	FV	.50
	c. 2005.	FV	.50
	d. 2007.	FV	.50
	e. 2009.	FV	.50
	f. 2011.	FV	.50

63	**20 Tugrik**	VF	UNC
	2000-. Red on rose, green and orange underprint. Youthful portrait Sukhe-Bataar at left, "Soemba" arms at center. . 150x72mm.		
	a. 2000.	FV	.75
	b. 2002.	FV	.75
	c. 2005.	FV	.75
	d. 2007.	FV	.75
	e. 2009.	FV	.75
	f. 2011.	FV	.75

64	**50 Tugrik**	VF	UNC
	2000; 2008. Brown-gold. Sukhe-Bataar at left. Segmented security thread. Microprinting, UV ink and embossed *50* below arms.		
	a. 2000.	FV	1.25
	b. 2008.	FV	1.25

		VF	UNC
65	**100 Tugrik** 2000; 2008. Multicolor. Youthful portrait Sukhe-Bataar at left, "Soemba" arms at center.		
	a. 2000.	FV	2.00
	b. 2008.	FV	2.00
65A	**500 Tugrik** 2000. Dark green, brown and yellow-green on multicolor underprint. Genghis Khan at left. Back: Ox drawn yurte, village at center right. 145x70mm.	FV	5.00

		VF	UNC
66	**500 Tugrik** 2003; 20072011. Blue and brown on multicolor underprint. Genghis Khan at left. Back: Ox drawn yurte, village at center right. Wide security thread added to #65A. 145x70mm.		
	a. 2003.	FV	5.00
	b. 2007.	FV	5.00
	c. 2011.	FV	5.00

		VF	UNC
67	**1000 Tugrik** 2003; 2007; 2011. Blue and brown on multicolor underprint. Genghis Khan at left. Back: Ox drawn yurtle, village at upper left. 145x70mm.		
	a. 2003.	FV	10.00
	b. 2007.	FV	10.00
	c. 2011.	FV	10.00

		VF	UNC
68	**5000 Tugrik** 2003; 2013. Purple and orange on multicolor underprint. Genghis Khan at left. Back: Building with fountain. 150x72mm.		
	a. 2003.	FV	17.50
	b. 2013. Signature Naidansuren Zoljargal.	FV	12.50

		VF	UNC
69	**10,000 Tugrik** 2002; 2009. Dark green and orange on multicolor underprint. Genghis Khan at left. Back: Large old building, tree and groups of people. 150x72mm.		
	a. 2002.	FV	35.00
	b. 2009.	FV	35.00
70	**20,000 Tugrik** 2006. Green on purple, yellow and multicolor underprint. Genghis Khan at left. Back: Pennants. 150x72mm.		
	a. 2006.	FV	60.00

		VF	UNC
71	**20,000 Tugrik** 2009. Green on purple, yellow and multicolor underprint. Genghis Khan at left, transparent window at bottom. Back: Nine white banners. Watermark: Khan and letters. Printer: G&D. 150x72mm.	FV	60.00

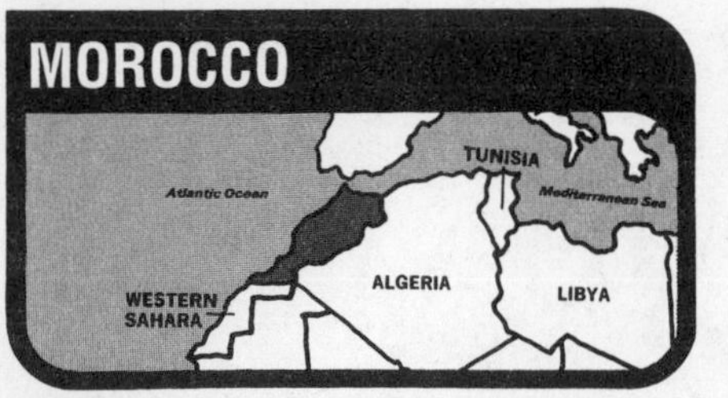

The Kingdom of Morocco, situated on the northwest corner of Africa south of Spain, has an area of 172,413 sq. mi. (712,550 sq. km.) and a population of 28.98 million. Capital: Rabat. The economy is essentially agricultural. Phosphates, fresh and preserved vegetables, canned fish and raw material are exported.

In 788, about a century after the Arab conquest of North Africa, successive Moorish dynasties began to rule in Morocco. In the 16th century, the Sa'adi monarchy, particularly under Ahmad Al-Mansur (1578-1603), repelled foreign invaders and inaugurated a golden age. In 1860, Spain occupied northern Morocco and ushered in a half century of trade rivalry among European powers that saw Morocco's sovereignty steadily erode; in 1912, the French imposed a protectorate over the country. A protracted independence struggle with France ended successfully in 1956. The internationalized city of Tangier and most Spanish possessions were turned over to the new country that same year. Morocco virtually annexed Western Sahara during the late 1970s, but final resolution on the status of the territory remains unresolved. Gradual political reforms in the 1990s resulted in the establishment of a bicameral legislature, which first met in 1997. The country has made improvements in human rights under King Mohammed VI and its press is moderately free. Despite the continuing reforms, ultimate authority remains in the hands of the monarch.

RULERS:

Muhammad V, AH1346-1380/1927-1961AD
Hassan II, AH1380-1420 /1961-1999AD
Muhammad VI, AH1420- /1999- AD

MONETARY SYSTEM:

1 Franc = 100 Centimes
1 Dirham = 100 Francs, 1921-1974
1 Dirham = 100 Centimes = 100 Santimat, 1974-
1 Riffan = 1 French Gold Franc = 10 British Pence

SIGNATURE VARIETIES

	GOVERNMENT COMISSONER	GOVERNOR
1	Mohamed Tahiri, 1960	M'hamed Zeghari
2	Ahmed Ben Nani, 1963-65	M'Hamed Zeghari
3		Driss Slaovi
4	Mohamed Lemniai, 1966	Driss Slaovi
5	Abdelaziz El Alami, 1967	Driss Slaovi
6	Abdelkrim Lazrek, 1968	M'hamed Zeghari
7	Abdelkrim Lazrek, 1969	Prince Moulay Hassan Ben Mehdi El Alaovi
8	Mohamed El Mdaghri, 1970	Prince Moulay Hassan Ben Mehdi El Alaovi
9	Hassan Lukash, 1985-89	Ahmed Ben Nani
10	Hassan Lukash	Mohamed Es Sakat
11	Abdul el Fatah ben Mansour	Mohamed Es Sakat

SIGNATURE VARIETIES

12	Noureddin Omary	Mohamed Es Sakat

KINGDOM

BANQUE DU MAROC

1960 (ND); 1965 ISSUE

53	5 Dirhams	VF	UNC
	ND (1960); 1965-69. Brown and multicolor. King Muhammad V wearing a fez at right. Back: Harvesting at left, man holding sheaf at right. Watermark: Lion's head. Printer: Banque de France.		
	a. Signature 1. ND (1960).	25.00	100.
	b. Signature 2. ND (1963).	20.00	90.00
	c. Signature 3. 1965/AH1384.	15.00	65.00
	d. Signature 4. 1966/AH1386.	15.00	65.00
	e. Signature 6. 1968/AH1387.	15.00	60.00
	f. Signature 7. 1969/AH1389.	15.00	60.00

54	10 Dirhams	VF	UNC
	ND (1960); 1965-69. Brown and multicolor. King Muhammad V wearing fez at left, Hassan Tower in Rabat at center. Back: Orange picking. Watermark: Lion's head. Printer: Banque de France.		
	a. Signature 1. ND (1960).	20.00	75.00
	b. Signature 2. ND (1963).	20.00	75.00
	c. Signature 3. 1965/AH1384.	15.00	65.00
	d. Signature 6. 1968/AH1387.	15.00	60.00
	e. Signature 7. 1969/AH1389.	15.00	60.00

55	50 Dirhams	VF	UNC
	1965-69. Brown and multicolor. King Hassan II at right. Back: Miners at work. Watermark: Lion's head. Printer: Banque de France.		
	a. Signature 3. 1965/AH1385.	120.	500.
	b. Signature 5. 1966/AH1386.	100.	400.
	c. Signature 6. 1968/AH1387.	100.	400.
	d. Signature 7. 1969/AH1389.	100.	400.

1970 Issue

56	5 Dirhams	VF	UNC
	1970/AH1390. Purple on light blue and multicolor underprint. King Hassan II at left, castle at center. Signature 8. Back: Industrial processing. Watermark: King Hassan II. Printer: TDLR. Replacement notes: Serial # prefix *Z*.		
	a. Issued note.	2.50	10.00
	s. Specimen.	—	32.50

57	10 Dirhams	VF	UNC
	1970; 1985. Brown on light green and multicolor underprint. King Hassan II at left, villa at center. Back: Processing oranges. Watermark: King Hassan II. Printer: TDLR. Replacement notes: Serial # prefix *Y*.		
	a. Signature 8. 1970/AH1390.	2.50	10.00
	b. Signature 9. 1985/AH1405.	2.50	10.00
	s. As a. Specimen.	—	35.00

58	50 Dirhams	VF	UNC
	1970; 1985. Green and brown on multicolor underprint. King Hassan II at left, city at center. Back: Dam. Watermark: King Hassan II. Printer: TDLR. Replacement notes: Serial # prefix *X*.		
	a. Signature 8. 1970/AH1390.	10.00	30.00
	b. Signature 9. 1985/AH1405.	8.00	30.00
	s. As b. Specimen.	—	50.00

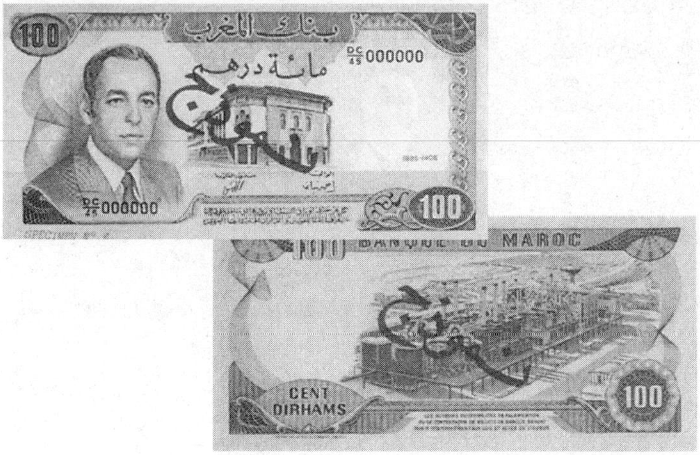

59	100 Dirhams	VF	UNC
	1970; 1985. Brown and blue on light green and multicolor underprint. King Hassan II at left, building at center. Back: Oil refinery. Watermark: King Hassan II. Printer: TDLR. Replacement notes: Serial # prefix *W*.		
	a. Signature 8. 1970/AH1390.	15.00	60.00
	b. Signature 9. 1985/AH1405.	15.00	60.00
	s. As b. Specimen.	—	70.00

Bank al-Maghrib

1987 Issue

60	10 Dirhams	VF	UNC
	1987/AH1407. Red-brown and red on multicolor underprint. King Hassan II facing at right. Back: Musical instrument and pillar at left center. Watermark: King Hassan II. 142x70mm.		
	a. Signature 9.	3.00	12.50
	b. Signature 10.	2.50	10.00

61	50 Dirhams	VF	UNC
	1987/AH1407. Green on multicolor underprint. King Hassan II facing at right. Back: Mounted militia charging, flowers at center. Watermark: King Hassan II. 148x70mm.		
	a. Signature 9.	12.00	50.00
	b. Signature 10.	10.00	40.00
62	**100 Dirhams**		
	1987/AH1407. Brown on multicolor underprint. King Hassan II facing at right. Back: Demonstration. Watermark: King Hassan II. . 153x75mm.		
	a. Signature 9.	15.00	65.00
	b. Signature 10.	FV	50.00

1987 (1991) Issue

63	10 Dirhams	VF	UNC
	1987/AH407 (ca.1991). Brown-violet and purple on multicolor underprint. Older bust of King Hassan II at right facing half left. Back: Like #60, but different colors of underprint. Watermark: King Hassan II facing. 142x70mm.		
	a. Signature 10.	FV	7.50
	b. Signature 11.	FV	6.00

64	50 Dirhams	VF	UNC
	1987/AH1407 (ca.1991). Green on multicolor underprint. Older bust of King Hassan II at right facing half left. Back: Mounted militia charging, flowers at center. Watermark: King Hassan II facing. 148x70mm.		
	a. Signature 10.	FV	30.00
	b. Signature 11.	FV	25.00
	c. Signature 12.	FV	20.00
	d. Signature 13.	FV	20.00
	e. Signature 16.	FV	20.00

65	100 Dirhams	VF	UNC
	1987/AH1407 (ca.1991). Brown and blue on multicolor underprint. Older bust of King Hassan II at right facing half left. Back: Demonstration. Watermark: King Hassan II facing. 153x75mm.		
	a. Signature 10.	FV	45.00
	b. Signature 11.	FV	40.00
	c. Signature 12.	FV	35.00
	d. Signature 13.	FV	35.00
	e. Signature 16.	FV	30.00

66	200 Dirhams	VF	UNC
	1987/AH1407 (ca.1991). Blue-violet and blue on multicolor underprint. Older bust of King Hassan II at right facing half left. Mausoleum of King Muhammad V at center. Back: Sailboat, shell and coral. Watermark: King Hassan II facing. 158x75mm.		
	a. Signature 10.	FV	75.00
	b. Signature 11.	FV	65.00
	c. Signature 12.	FV	60.00
	d. Signature 13.	FV	55.00
	e. Signature 16.	FV	50.00

1996 Issue

67	20 Dirhams	VF	UNC
	1996. Multicolor. King Hassan II at left, Great Mosque of Casablanca at center. Back: Fountain. 130x68mm.		
	a. Signature 12.	FV	7.50
	b. Signature 13.	FV	6.00
	c. Signature 14.	FV	6.00
	d. Signature 15.	FV	6.00
	e. Signature 16.	FV	6.00

2002 (2004-) Issue

68	20 Dirhams	VF	UNC
	2005/AH1426. Black and purple on multicolor underprint. Mohammed VI at left, city gate at center. Signature 16. Back: Ancient seaside city. 140x70mm.	FV	5.00

69	50 Dirhams	VF	UNC
	2002/AH1423. Green on multicolor underprint. Mohammed VI at left, dam at center. Signature 16. Back: Old building in ksour and wheat. 148x70mm.		
	a. With dash between dates.	FV	12.50
	b. Without dash between dates.	FV	12.50

70 **100 Dirhams** — VF / UNC

2002/AH1423. Brown on multicolor underprint. Mohammed VI, Hassan II and Mohammed V at right, building at center. Signature 16. Back: People marching with flags. 150x78mm. — FV / 20.00

71 **200 Dirhams** — VF / UNC

2002/AH1423. Dark blue, blue and multicolor underprint. Mohammed VI and Hassan II at left, buildign at center. Signature 16. Back: Window of the Theological School at the Hassan II Mosque. 158x78mm. — FV / 35.00

2009 Commemorative Issue

72 **50 Dirhams** — VF / UNC

AH1430/2009. Green on multicolor underprint. Kings Mohammed VI, Hassan II and Mohammed V at left center. Holographic stripe with three portraits. Back: Bank al-Maghrib building in Rabat. Watermark: Mohammed VI and 50. Printer: TK. 147x70mm. — FV / 15.00

2012 Commemorative Issue

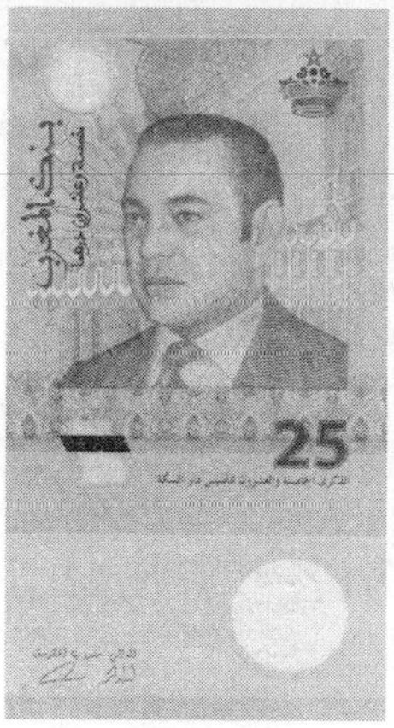

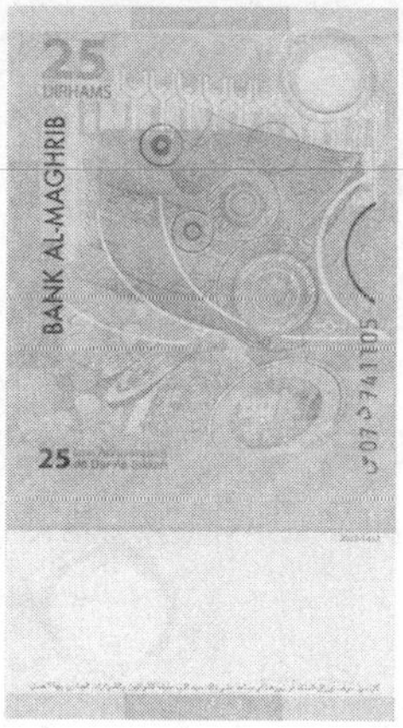

73 **25 Dirhams** — VF / UNC

2012. Red and multicolor Mohammed VI facing left. Vertical format. 25th Anniversary of Dar As Sikkah. 145x70mm. — FV / 7.50

2012-14 Issue

No.	Denomination / Description	VF	UNC
74	**20 Dirhams** Expected new issue.	—	—
75	**50 Dirhams** Expected new issue.	—	—
76	**100 Dirhams** 2012. Brown, pink and beige. Archway, coat mof arms, King Mohammed VI. SPARK crown and star. Back: Camels with riders, touareg tent, desert tema. Watermark: Mohammed VI and 100. 145x70mm.	FV	30.00
77	**200 Dirhams** 2012. Blue and dark violet. King Mohammed VI at right. Royal crown at upper right Back: Tangier harbor at left, lighthouse at center. Watermark: Mohammed VI and 200. 151x70mm.	FV	45.00

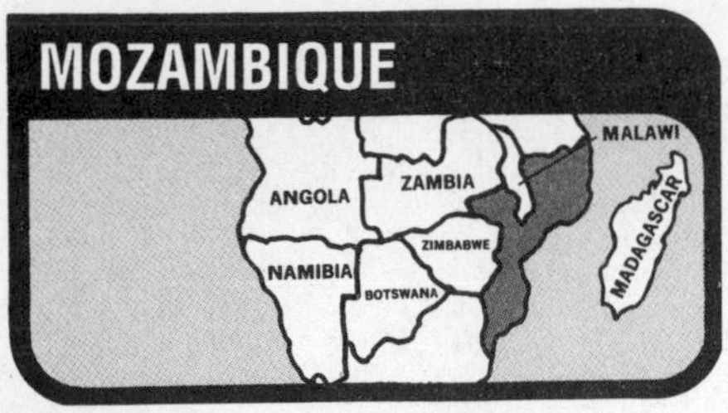

The People's Republic of Mozambique, a former overseas province of Portugal stretching for 1,430 miles (2,301 km.) along the southeast coast of Africa, has an area of 309,494 sq. mi. (783,030 sq. km.) and a population of 19.56 million. Capital: Maputo. Agriculture is the chief industry. Cashew nuts, cotton, sugar, copra and tea are exported.

Almost five centuries as a Portuguese colony came to a close with independence in 1975. Large-scale emigration by whites, economic dependence on South Africa, a severe drought, and a prolonged civil war hindered the country's development until the mid 1990's. The ruling Front for the Liberation of Mozambique (FRELIMO) party formally abandoned Marxism in 1989, and a new constitution the following year provided for multiparty elections and a free market economy. A UN-negotiated peace agreement between FRELIMO and rebel Mozambique National Resistance (RENAMO) forces ended the fighting in 1992. In December 2004, Mozambique underwent a delicate transition as Joaquim Chissano stepped down after 18 years in office. His elected successor, Armando Emilio Guebuza, promised to continue the sound economic policies that have encouraged foreign investment. Mozambique has seen very strong economic growth since the end of the civil war largely due to post-conflict reconstruction.

RULERS:

Portuguese to 1975

MONETARY SYSTEM:

1 Escudo = 100 Centavos, 1911-1975
1 Escudo = 1 Metica = 100 Centimos, 1975-

REPLACEMENT NOTES:

#116, 117, 119: Z prefix.
#125-133, ZA, ZB, ZC prefix.
#134-137, AW, BW, CY, DZ prefix by denomination.

Portuguese Administration

Banco Nacional Ultramarino

Moçambique Branch

1961; 1967 Issue

109	100 Escudos	VF	UNC
	27.3.1961. Green on multicolor underprint. Portrait A. de Ornelas at right, arms at upper center. Back: Bank steamship seal at left. Printer: BWC without imprint.		
	a. Watermark: Arms.	4.00	17.50
	b. Without watermark.	3.00	10.00
	s. As a. Specimen.	—	140.

110	500 Escudos	VF	UNC
	22.3.1967. Purple on multicolor underprint. Portrait C. Xavier at right, arms at upper center. Printer: BWC without imprint.		
	a. Issued note.	20.00	75.00
	s. Specimen.	—	150.

1970 Issue

111	50 Escudos	VF	UNC
	27.10.1970. Black on multicolor underprint. J. de Azevedo Coutinho at left center, arms at upper center right. Signature varieties. Back: Green. Bank steamship seal at left. Watermark: Arms.	3.00	15.00

First 1972 Issue

112	1000 Escudos	VF	UNC
	16.5.1972. Black-blue on multicolor underprint. King Afonso V at right, arms at upper center. 3 signature varieties. Back: Allegorical woman with ships at left on back, bank steamship seal at upper center. Watermark: King Afonso V.		
	a. Serial number without prefix. 2.5mm tall.	22.50	125.
	b. Serial number with three letter prefix. 3mm tall.	22.50	125.

Second 1972 Issue

113	100 Escudos	VF	UNC
	23.5.1972. Blue on multicolor underprint. G. Coutinho and S. Cabral at left center. Back: Surveyor at center. Watermark: G. Coutinho.	7.50	50.00

114 500 Escudos | VF | UNC

23.5.1972. Purple on multicolor underprint. G. Coutinho at left. Back: Cabral and airplane. Watermark: G. Coutinho. | 15.00 | 85.00

115 1000 Escudos | VF | UNC

23.5.1972. Green on multicolor underprint. G. Coutinho at left center. Back: Two men in cockpit of airplane at left center. | 25.00 | 120.

Peoples Republic

Banco de Moçambique

1976 ND Provisional Issue

116 50 Escudos | VF | UNC

ND (1976 - old date 27.10.1970). Black on multicolor underprint. J. de Azevedo Coutinho at left center, arms at upper center right. Signature varieties. Overprint. Back: Bank steamship seal at left. Overprint: New bank name in black. | 1.00 | 2.00

117 100 Escudos | VF | UNC

ND (1976 - old date 27.3.1961). Green on multicolor underprint. Portrait A. de Ornelas at right, arms at upper center. Overprint. Back: Bank steamship seal at left. Overprint: New bank name in black.

- a. Issued note. | 1.00 | 3.00
- s. Specimen. | — | 100.

118 500 Escudos | VF | UNC

ND (1976 - old date 22.3.1967). Purple on multicolor underprint. Portrait C. Xavier at right, arms at upper center. Overprint. Overprint. New bank name in black.

- a. Issued note. | 1.00 | 5.00
- s. Specimen. | — | 115.

119 1000 Escudos | VF | UNC

ND (1976 - old date 23.5.1972). Green on multicolor underprint. G. Coutinho at left center. Overprint. Back: Two men in cockpit of airplane at left center. Overprint: New bank name in black. | 1.00 | 6.00

1976 Issue

 # 120-124 These appear to be unadopted designs.

			VF	UNC
120	5 Meticas	25.6.1976. Brown and multicolor. President S. Machel at left center. Back: Kudu. Printer: TDLR. Specimen, punch hole cancelled.	—	—
121	10 Meticas	25.6.1976. Blue on multicolor. President S. Machel at left center. Back: Lions. Printer: TDLR. Specimen, punch hole cancelled.	—	—
122	20 Meticas	25.6.1976. Red and multicolor. President S. Machel at left center. Back: Giraffes. Printer: TDLR. Specimen, punch hole cancelled.	—	—
123	50 Meticas	25.6.1976. Purple and multicolor. President S. Machel at left center. Back: Cape buffalo. Printer: TDLR. Specimen, punch hole cancelled.	—	—

		VF	UNC
124	**100 Meticas** 25.6.1976. Green and multicolor. President S. Machel at left center. Back: Elephants. Printer: TDLR. Specimen, punch hole cancelled.	—	—

República Popular de Moçambique

1980 Issue

		VF	UNC
125	**50 Meticais** 16.6.1980. Dark brown and brown on multicolor underprint. Soldiers at left, flag ceremony at right, arms at center. Large size serial number. Back: Soldiers in training.	.50	2.00

		VF	UNC
126	**100 Meticais** 16.6.1980; 16.6.1983. Green on multicolor underprint. Soldiers at flagpole at left, E. Mondlane at right, arms at center. Large size serial number. Back: Public ceremony.	.75	3.00

		VF	UNC
127	**500 Meticais** 16.6.1980. Deep blue-violet and dark blue-green on multicolor underprint. Government assembly at left, chanting crowd at right, arms at center. Large size serial number. Back: Chemists and school scene.	1.00	5.00

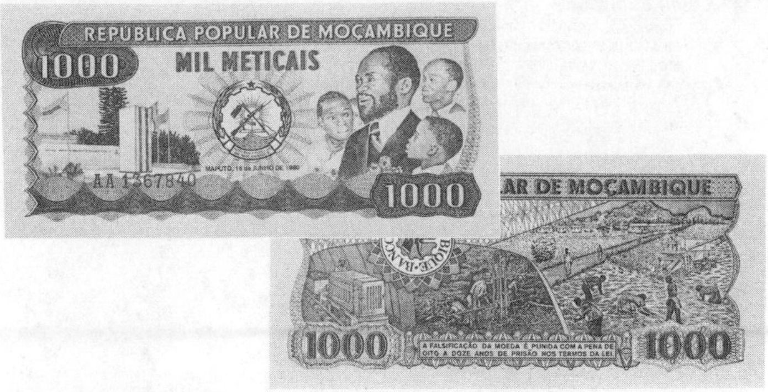

		VF	UNC
128	**1000 Meticais** 16.6.1980. Deep red on multicolor underprint. President S. Machel with three young boys at right, revolutionary monument at left, arms at center. Large size serial number. Back: Mining and harvesting scenes.	1.75	8.50

1983-88 Issue

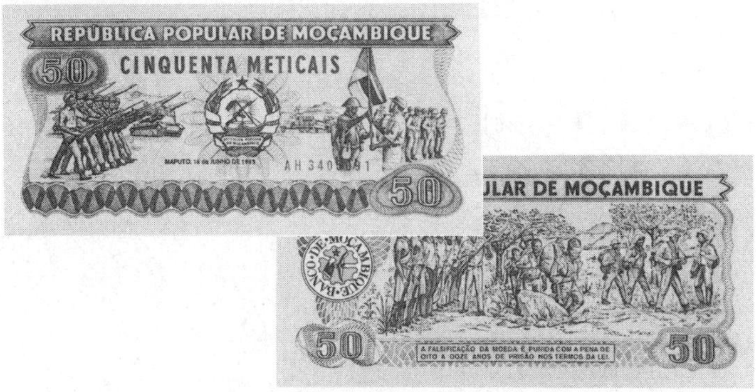

		VF	UNC
129	**50 Meticais** 16.6.1983; 16.6.1986. Dark brown and brown on multicolor underprint. Soldiers at left, flag ceremony at right, modified arms at center. Smaller size serial number. Back: Soldiers in training.		
	a. 16.6.1983.	.25	1.50
	b. 16.6.1986.	.25	1.50

		VF	UNC
130	**100 Meticais** 16.6.1983; 16.6.1986; 16.6.1989. Green on multicolor underprint. Soldiers at left, flag ceremony at right, E. Mondlane at right, modified arms at center. Smaller size serial number. Back: Public ceremony.		
	a. 16.6.1983.	.50	2.00
	b. 16.6.1986.	.50	2.00
	c. 16.6.1989.	.50	2.00

131 500 Meticais VF UNC

16.6.1983; 16.6.1986; 16.6.1989. Deep blue-violet and dark blue-green on multicolor underprint. Government assembly at left, chanting crowd at right, modified arms at center. Smaller size serial number. Back: Chemists and school scene.

	VF	UNC
a. 16.6.1983.	1.00	3.00
b. 16.6.1986.	1.00	3.00
c. 16.6.1989.	1.00	3.00

132 1000 Meticais VF UNC

16.6.1983; 16.6.1986; 16.6.1989. Deep red on multicolor underprint. President S. Machel with three young boys at right, revolutionary monument at left, modified arms at center. Smaller size serial number. Back: Mining and harvesting scene.

	VF	UNC
a. 16.6.1983.	1.50	6.00
b. 16.6.1986.	2.00	7.50
c. 16.6.1989.	1.00	3.00

133 5000 Meticais VF UNC

3.2.1988; 3.2.1989. Purple, brown and violet on multicolor underprint. Carved statues at left, painting at right. Back: Dancers and musicians.

	VF	UNC
a. 3.2.1988.	1.75	5.00
b. 3.2.1989.	1.75	5.00

1991-93 Issue

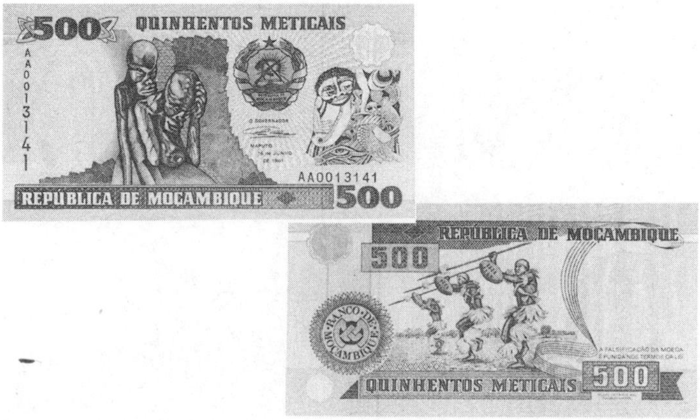

134 500 Meticais VF UNC

16.6.1991. Brown and blue on multicolor underprint. Native carving of couple in grief at left center, native art at right, arms at upper center right printed on silver or gold underlay. Back: Dancing warriors at center, bank seal at lower left. Watermark: J. Chissano. Printer: TDLR. 1.00 2.00

135 1000 Meticais VF UNC

16.6.1991. Brown and red on multicolor underprint. E. Mondlane at left center, military flag raising ceremony at right, arms at upper center right printed on silver or gold underlay. Back: Monument at left center, bank seal at lower left. Watermark: J. Chissano. Printer: TDLR. 1.00 3.00

136 5000 Meticais VF UNC

16.6.1991. Purple, violet and orange-brown on multicolor underprint. S. Machel at left center, monument to the Socialist vanguard at right, arms at upper center right printed on silver or gold underlay. Back: Foundry workers at center, bank seal at lower left. Watermark: J. Chissano. Printer: TDLR. 1.00 3.00

137 10,000 Meticais VF UNC

16.6.1991. Blue-green, brown and orange on multicolor underprint. J. Chissano at left center, high tension electrical towers at right, with farm tractor in field and high-rise city view in background at right, arms at upper center right printed on silver or gold und Back: Plowing with oxen at center, bank seal at lower left. Watermark: J. Chissano. Printer: TDLR. 150x69mm. 1.00 4.00

138	**50,000 Meticais**	VF	UNC
	16.6.1993 (1994). Dark brown, red-brown on multicolor underprint. Bank of Mozambique building at left center, arms at upper right. Back: Cabora Bassa hydroelectric dam. Watermark: Bank monogram. 157x69mm.	2.00	8.00

139	**100,000 Meticais**	VF	UNC
	16.6.1993 (1994). Red, brown-orange and olive-brown on multicolor underprint. Bank of Mozambique building at left center, arms at upper right. Back: Cabora Bassa hydroelectric dam. Watermark: Bank monogram. 135x69mm.	2.00	14.00

1999 Issue

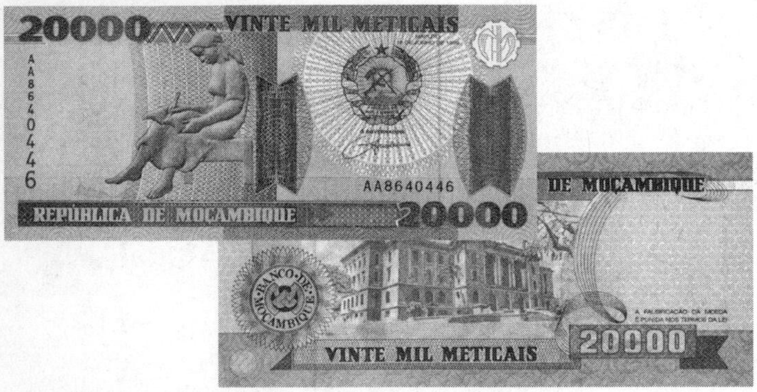

140	**20,000 Meticais**	VF	UNC
	16.6.1999. Green on multicolor underprint. Young woman seated writing at center. Back: Maputo city hall. 153x69mm.	1.00	4.00

2004 Issue

141	**200,000 Meticais**	VF	UNC
	16.6.2003 (2004). Dark blue and aqua on multicolor underprint. Banco de Moçambique building at center. Back: Dancing warriors. 154x65mm.	FV	25.00

142	**500,000 Meticais**	VF	UNC
	16.6.2003 (2004). Purple, tan and multicolor. Banco de Moçambique building at center. Holographic seal at right. Serial numbers in green and black. Back: Steelworkers. 157x65mm.	FV	55.00

Banco de Moçambique

2006 Issue

143	**20 Meticais**	VF	UNC
	16.6.2006. Purple on multicolor underprint. Samora Moises Machel at left center. Back: Rhinoceros at left center. 141x65mm.		
	a. Issued note.	FV	2.50
	s. Specimen. Red overprint: *ESPECIMEN.*	—	100.
144	**50 Meticais**		
	16.6.2006 Brown and tan on multicolor underprint. Samora Moises Machel at left center. Back: Impalas at left center. 144x65mm.		
	a. Issued note.	FV	5.00
	s. Specimen. Red overprint: *ESPECIMEN.*	—	100.

145	**100 Meticais**	VF	UNC
	16.6.2006 Brown and orange on multicolor underprint. Samora Moises Machel at left center. Back: Giraffes at left center. 147x65mm.		
	a. Issued note.	FV	10.00
	s. Specimen. Red overprint: *ESPECIMEN.*	—	100.

146	**200 Meticais**	VF	UNC
	16.6.2006. Dark blue and green on multicolor underprint. Samora Moises Machel at left center. Back: Lions at left center. 150x65mm.		
	a. Issued note.	FV	15.00
	s. Specimen. Red overprint: *ESPECIMEN.*	—	100.

147	**500 Meticais**	VF	UNC
	16.6.2006. Red-brown and lilac on multicolor underprint. Samora Moises Machel at left center. Back: Buffaloes at left center. 153x65mm.		
	a. Issued note.	FV	20.00
	s. Specimen. Red overprint: *ESPECIMEN.*	—	100.

148 **1000 Meticais** | VF | UNC

16.6.2006. Dark green and green on multicolor underprint. Samora Moises Machel at left center. Back: Elephants at left center. 156x65mm.

a. Issued note.	FV	50.00
s. Specimen. Red overprint: *ESPECIMEN.*	—	100.

2011 Issue

		VF	UNC
149	**20 Meticas** 1.10.2011. Violet. Samora Moises Machel at left center. Back: Rhinoceros. Polymer plastic.	FV	2.50

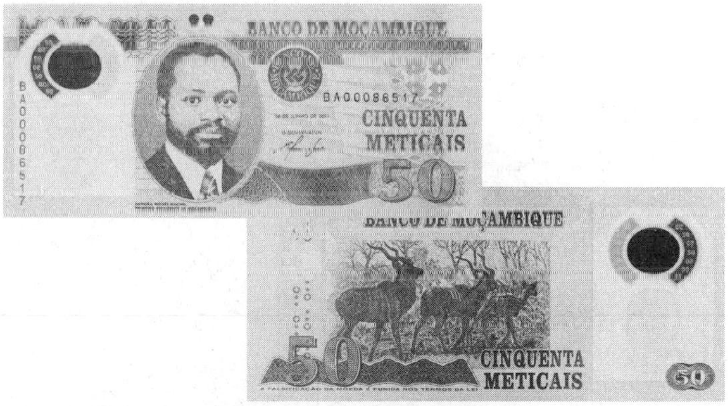

		VF	UNC
150	**50 Meticais** 1.10.2011. Brown and multicolor. Samora Moises Machel at left center. Back: Impalas Polymer plastic.	FV	5.00

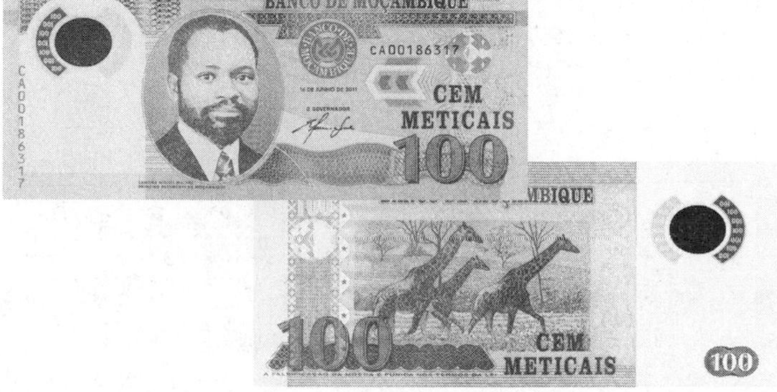

		VF	UNC
151	**100 Meticais** 1.10.2011. Red, brown and multicolor. Samora Moises Machel at left center. Back: Giraffes Polymer plastic.	FV	10.00

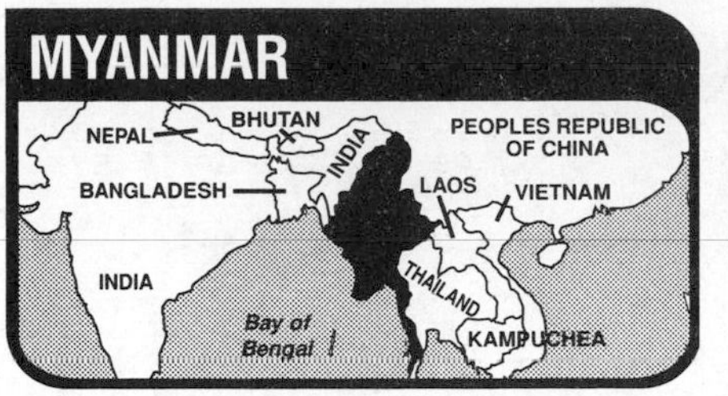

The Socialist Republic of the Union of Myanmar (formally called Burma), a country of Southeast Asia fronting on the Bay of Bengal and the Andaman Sea, has an area of 261,789 sq. mi. (676,552 sq. km.) and a population of 49.34 million. Capital: Rangoon. Myanmar is an agricultural country heavily dependent on its leading product (rice) which embodies two-thirds of the cultivated area and accounts for 40 percent of the value of exports. Petroleum, lead, tin, silver, zinc, nickel, cobalt and precious stones are exported.

Britain conquered Burma over a period of 62 years (1824-1886) and incorporated it into its Indian Empire. Burma was administered as a province of India until 1937 when it became a separate, self-governing colony; independence from the Commonwealth was attained in 1948. Gen. Ne Win dominated the government from 1962 to 1988, first as military ruler, then as self-appointed president, and later as political kingpin. In September 1988, the military deposed Ne Win and established a new ruling junta. Despite multiparty legislative elections in 1990 that resulted in the main opposition party - the National League for Democracy (NLD) - winning a landslide victory, the junta refused to hand over power. NLD leader and Nobel Peace Prize recipient Aung San Suu Kyi, who was under house arrest from 1989 to 1995 and 2000 to 2002, was imprisoned in May 2003 and subsequently transferred to house arrest. After the ruling junta in August 2007 unexpectedly increased fuel prices, tens of thousands of Burmese marched in protest, led by prodemocracy activists and Buddhist monks. In late September 2007, the government brutally suppressed the protests, killing at least 13 people and arresting thousands for participating in the demonstrations. Since then, the regime has continued to raid homes and monasteries and arrest persons suspected of participating in the pro-democracy protests. The junta appointed Labor Minister Aung Kyi in October 2007 as liaison to Aung San Suu Kyi, who remains under house arrest and virtually incommunicado with her party and supporters. Burma in early May 2008 was struck by Cyclone Nargis which official estimates claimed left over 80,000 dead and 50,000 injured. Despite this tragedy, the junta proceeded with its May constitutional referendum, the first vote in Burma since 1990, setting the stage for the 2010 parliamentary elections.The country name in English was changed to Union of Myanmar in 1989.

RULERS:

British to 1948
Japanese, 1942-1945

MONETARY SYSTEM:

1 Rupee (Kyat) = 10 Mu = 16 Annas (Pe) to 1942, 1945-1952
1 Rupee = 100 Cents, 1942-1943
1 Kyat = 100 Pyas, 1943-1945, 1952-

Republic

Central Bank of Myanmar

1990 ND Issue

		VF	UNC
67	**1 Kyat** ND (1990). Pale brown and orange on multicolor underprint. General Aung San at left. Back: Dragon carving at left. Watermark: General Aung San. UV: fibers fluoresce blue.	FV	.30

1991-98 ND Issue

		VF	UNC
68	**50 Pyas** ND (1994). Dull purple and dull brown on gray and tan underprint. Musical string instrument at center. Printer: B/CM.	FV	.30

69 1 Kyat VF UNC

ND (1996). Gray, blue and purple on multicolor underprint. Chinze at right. Printer: B/CM. FV .30

70 5 Kyats VF UNC

ND (1996). Dark brown and blue-green on multicolor underprint. Chinze at left center. Back: Ball game scene. UV: fibers fluoresce blue.

a. Watermark: Chinze. (1996). FV .75

b. Watermark: Chinze bust over value. (1997). FV .50

71 10 Kyats VF UNC

ND (1996). Deep purple and violet on multicolor underprint. Chinze at right center. Back: Elaborate barge.

a. Watermark: Chinze. (1996). FV 1.00

b. Watermark: Chinze bust over value. (1997). FV .50

72 20 Kyats VF UNC

ND (1994). Deep olive-green, brown and blue-green on multicolor underprint. Watermark: Chinze bust over value. FV 1.00

73 50 Kyats VF UNC

ND (1994-). Red-brown, tan and dark brown on multicolor underprint. Chinze at right. Back: Coppersmith at left center. Watermark: Chinze.

a. Watermark: Chinze. (1994). FV 3.00

b. Watermark: Chinze bust over value. (1997). FV 2.00

74 100 Kyats VF UNC

ND (1994). Blue-violet, blue-green and dark brown on multicolor underprint. Chinze at left. Back: Workers restoring temple and grounds at center right.

a. Security thread in negative script. Watermark: Chinze. FV 4.00

b. Security thread in positive script. Watermark: Chinze above value. FV 3.00

75 200 Kyats VF UNC

ND (ca.1991; 1998). Dark blue and green on multicolor underprint. Chinze at right. Back: Elephant pulling log at center right. Watermark: Chinze head. 167x80mm.

a. Security thread in negative script. Watermark: Chinze. FV 8.00

b. Security thread in positive script. Watermark: Chinze above value. FV 6.00

			VF	UNC
76	**500 Kyats**	ND (1994). Brown, purple and brown-orange on multicolor underprint. Chinze at left. Back: Workers restoring medieval statue, craftsman and water hauler at center right. 167x80mm.		
		a. Security thread in negative script. Watermark: Chinze.	FV	14.00
		b. Security thread in positive script. Watermark: Chinze above value.	FV	10.00

			VF	UNC
77	**1000 Kyats**	ND (1998). Deep green and purple on multicolor underprint. Chinze at right. Back: Central Bank building at left center. 177x70mm.		
		a. Security thread in negative script. Watermark: Chinze.	FV	15.00
		b. Security thread in positive script. Watermark: Chinze above value.	FV	15.00

2004 ND Reduced Size Issue

			VF	UNC
78	**200 Kyats**	ND (2004). Greenish blue on multicolor underprint. Chinze at right center. Back: Elephant pulling log at center. 150x70mm.	FV	6.00
79	**500 Kyats**	ND (2004). Brown, purple-brown and ochre on multicolor underprint. Chinze at left. Back: Workers restoring medieval statue, craftsman and water hauler at right center. 150x70mm.	FV	6.00

			VF	UNC
80	**1000 Kyats**	ND (2004). Green, purple-brown on multicolor underprint. Chinze at right center. Back: Central Bank building at left center. 150x70mm.	FV	7.50

			VF	UNC
81	**5000 Kyats**	ND (2009). Purple on multicolor underprint. Elephant at center. Back: Building complex. Printer: Security Printing Wazi CBM. 150x70mm.	FV	10.00

			VF	UNC
82	**10000 Kyats**	2012. Blue and multicolor. 150x70mm.	FV	15.00

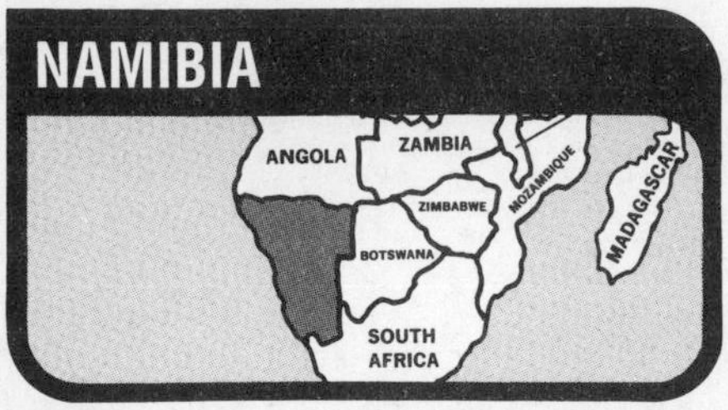

The Republic of Namibia, once the German colonial territory of German South West Africa, is situated on the Atlantic coast of southern Africa, bounded on the north by Angola, on the east by Botswana, and on the south by South Africa. It has an area of 318,261 sq. mi. (824,290 sq. km.) and a population of 1.73 million. Capital: Windhoek. Diamonds, copper, lead, zinc and cattle are exported.

South Africa occupied the German colony of South-West Africa during World War I and administered it as a mandate until after World War II, when it annexed the territory. In 1966 the Marxist South-West Africa People's Organization (SWAPO) guerrilla group launched a war of independence for the area that became Namibia, but it was not until 1988 that South Africa agreed to end its administration in accordance with a UN peace plan for the entire region. Namibia has been governed by SWAPO since the country won independence in 1990. Hifikepunye Pohamba was elected president in November 2004 in a landslide victory replacing Sam Nujoma who led the country during its first 14 years of self rule.

MONETARY SYSTEM:

1 Namibia Dollar = 1 South African Rand
1 Namibia Dollar = 100 Cents

Note: For earlier issues see German South West Africa. For notes of the 3 commercial banks that circulated until 1963 see South West Africa listings in Volume I.

Note: For notes of the 3 commercial banks circulating until 1963, see Southwest Africa listings in Vol. II.

SIGNATURE VARIETIES

Mr. Erik L. KarlssonDr. Jaafar B. Ahmad
Mr. T. Alwendo

REPUBLIC

NAMIBIA RESERVE BANK

1990 ISSUE

#A1-E1 Unadopted designs.

		VF	UNC
A1	**2 Kalahar** ND. Red on multicolor underprint. Zebra head at left. Back: Plant at center, rock formation at right. Printer: BWC. Unissued specimen.	—	—

		VF	UNC
B1	**5 Kalahar** ND. Red and purple on multicolor underprint. Oryx head at left. Back: Blue. Road graders at center. Printer: BWC. Unissued specimen.	—	—

		VF	UNC
C1	**10 Kalahar** ND. Red and purple on multicolor underprint. Oryx head at left. Back: Commercial fishing boat at center. Printer: BWC. Unissued specimen.	—	—

		VF	UNC
D1	**20 Kalahar** ND. Purple on multicolor underprint. Lion head in round frame at left, watermark circle at right. Back: Sheep herd, herdsman on horseback. Printer: BWC. Unissued specimen.	—	—

		VF	UNC
E1	**20 Kalahar** ND. Purple on multicolor underprint. Lion head at left, flag at center. Back: Sheep heerd on back, walking herdsman. Printer: BWC. Unissued specimen.	—	—

SIGNATURE VARIETIES	
	Dr. W. L. Benard 16 July 1990-31 August 1991
1	Erik L. Karlsson Mr. Erik L. Karlsson Acting: 1 Semtember 1991-24 November 1992 25 November 1992-31 December 1993
2	Jaafar B Ahmad Dr. Jaafar B. Ahmad 1 January 1994-31 December 1996
3	Kalweendo Mr. Tom K. Alweendo 1 January 1997-

Bank of Namibia

1993 ND Issue

#1-3 Replacement notes: Serial # prefix *X; Y; Z* for #1, 2 and 3 respectively.

1 10 Namibia Dollars — VF / UNC

ND (1993). Blue-black on multicolor underprint. Captain H. Wittbooi at left center, arms at upper left. Back: Springbok at right. Watermark: Captain H. Wittbooi. Printer: Tumba Bruk A.B. (without imprint). 129x70mm.

	VF	UNC
a. Signature 1.	2.00	8.25
s. Specimen. Serial # prefix *S*.	—	150.

2 50 Namibia Dollars — VF / UNC

ND (1993). Blue-green and dark brown on multicolor underprint. Captain H. Wittbooi at left center, arms at upper center. Back: Kudu at right. Watermark: Captain H. Wittbooi. Printer: Tumba Bruk A.B. (without imprint). 140x70mm.

	VF	UNC
a. Signature 1.	11.00	38.50
s. Specimen. Serial # prefix *U*.		150.

3 100 Namibia Dollars — VF / UNC

ND (1993). Red, brown and red-brown on multicolor underprint. Captain H. Wittbooi at left center, arms at upper center right. Back: Oryx a right. Watermark: Captain H. Wittbooi. Printer: Tumba Bruk A.B. (without imprint). 146x70mm.

	VF	UNC
a. Signature 1.	20.00	70.00
s. Specimen. Serial # prefix *S*.	—	150.

1996-2001 ND Issue

#4-8 Replacement notes: Serial # prefix *X; V; Y; Z; W* respectively for #4-8.

4 10 Namibia Dollars — VF / UNC

ND (2001). Blue on multicolor underprint. Captain H. Wittbooi at left center, arms at upper left. Segmented foil over security thread and ascending size serial number. Back: Springbok at right. Watermark: Captain H. Wittbooi. Printer: F-CO. 129x70mm.

	VF	UNC
a. Signature 3. 7-digit serial #.	FV	3.75
b. 8-digit serial #. Prefix A.	FV	3.75
c. 8-digit serial #. Prefix B. No UV 10 at right.	FV	3.50
s. Specimen. Serial # prefix *A*.	—	120.

5 20 Namibia Dollars — VF / UNC

ND (1996). Orange and violet on multicolor underprint. Captain H. Wittbooi at left center, arms at upper left. Segmented foil over security thread. Ascending size serial number. Back: Red hartebeest at right. Watermark: Captain H. Wittbooi. Printer: TDLR. 133x70mm.

	VF	UNC
a. Signature 2. 7-digit serial #.	FV	15.00

6 20 Namibia Dollars

ND (2002). Orange and violet on multicolor underprint. Captain H. Wittbooi at left center, arms at upper left. Segmented foil over security thread and ascending size serial number. Back: Red hartebeest at right. Watermark: Captain H. Wittbooi. Printer: SABN. 133x70mm.

	VF	UNC
a. Signature 3. 8-digit serial #.	FV	6.75
b. 8-digit serial #. Prefix H, J.	FV	6.50
s. Specimen. Serial # prefix *J*.	—	120.

7 50 Namibia Dollars — VF / UNC

ND (1999). Blue-green and dark brown on multicolor underprint. Captain H. Wittbooi at left center, arms at upper left. Segmented foil over security thread and ascending size serial number. Back: Kudu at right. Watermark: Captain H. Wittbooi. Printer: TDLR. 140x70mm.

	VF	UNC
a. Signature 3. 7-digit serial #.	FV	23.00
s. Specimen. Serial # prefix *P*.	—	130.

8 50 Namibia Dollars

ND (2003). Blue green and dark brown on multicolor underprint. Captain H. Wittbooi at left center, arms at upper left. Segmented foil over security thread and ascending size serial number. Back: Kudu at right. Watermark: Captain H. Wittbooi. Printer: SABN. 140x70mm.

	VF	UNC
a. Signature 3. 8-digit serial #.	FV	17.00
s. Specimen. Serial # prefix *N*.	—	120.

9 100 Namibia Dollars — VF / UNC

ND (1999). Red, brown and red-brown on multicolor underprint. Captain H. Wittbooi at left center, arms at upper center right. Back: Oryx at right. Printer: TDLR. 146x70mm.

	VF	UNC
a. Signature 3. 7-digit serial #.	FV	47.50
c. Signature 3. 7-digit serial #. Prefix TT.	30.00	100.
s. Specimen. Serial # prefix *T*.	—	130.

9A 100 Namibia Dollars

ND (2003). Red, brown and red-brown on multicolor underprint. Captain H. Wittbooi at left center. 8-digit serial number. Back: Oryz at right. Printer: SABN. 146x70mm. — FV 30.00

10	200 Namibia Dollars	VF	UNC
	ND (1996). Purple and violet on multicolor underprint. Captain H. Wittbooi at left center. Arms at upper center. Back: Roan antelope at right. Printer: TDLR. 152x70mm.		
	a. Signature 2.	FV	80.00
	b. Signature 3.	FV	80.00
	s. Specimen. Serial # prefix *U*.	—	130.

2012 Issue

11	10 Namibia Dollars	VF	UNC
	2012-. Blue and green on multicolor underprint. Bust at left. Signature Ipumbu Shiimi. 129x70mm.		
	a. 2012. Diamond shape OVI device at top center.	FV	3.75
	b. 2013. Diamond shape OVI device at side.	FV	3.75

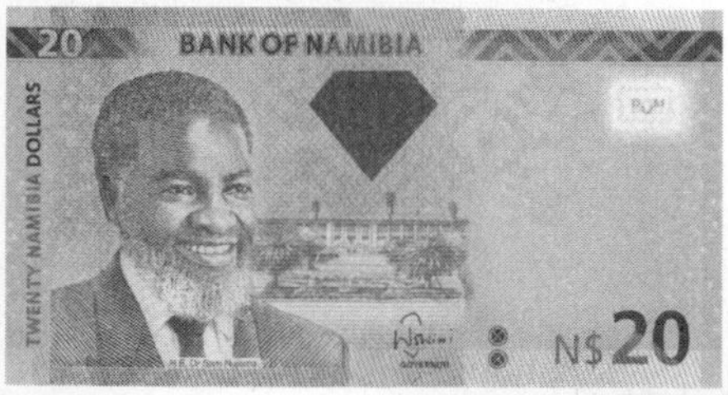

12	20 Namibia Dollars	VF	UNC
	2012-. Brown and orange on multicolor underprint. Bust at left. Signature Ipumbu Shiimi. 137x70mm.		
	a. 2012. Diamond shape OVI device at top center.	FV	6.50
	b. 2013. Diamond shape OVI device at side.	FV	6.50

13	50 Namibia Dollars	VF	UNC
	2012. Green on multicolor underprint. 140x70mm.	FV	17.00

14	100 Namibia Dollars	VF	UNC
	2012. Purple on multicolor underprint. 147x70mm.	FV	30.00

15	200 Namibia Dollars	VF	UNC
	2012. Violet on multicolor underprint. 152x70mm.	FV	80.00

Collector Series

Bank of Namibia

1993 ND Issue

CS1	10, 50, 100 Dollars	Mkt. Value
	ND (1993). #1-3 with matched serial # mounted in a special plexiglass frame.	225.

1996; 1999 ND Issue

CS2	20, 50, 100, 200 Dollars	Mkt. Value
	ND (1996; 1999). #5, 7, 9, 10 with matched serial #.	330.

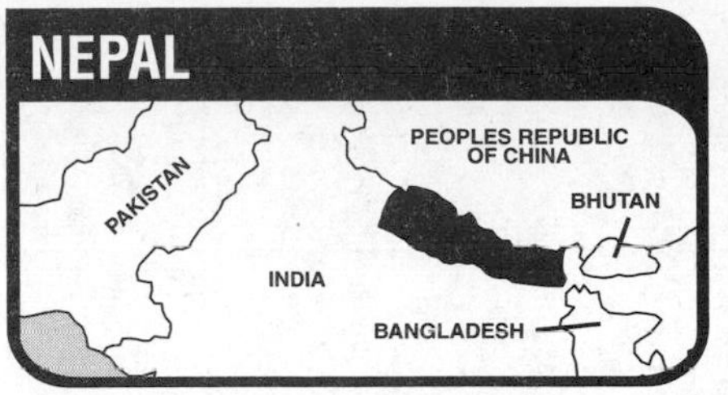

The Kingdom of Nepal, the world's only Hindu kingdom, is a landlocked country located in central Asia along the southern slopes of the Himalayan Mountains. It has an area of 56,136 sq. mi. (140,797 sq. km.) and a population of 24.35 million. Capital: Káthmandu. Nepal has substantial deposits of coal, copper, iron and cobalt but they are largely unexploited. Agriculture is the principal economic activity. Livestock, rice, timber and jute are exported.

In 1951, the Nepalese monarch ended the century-old system of rule by hereditary premiers and instituted a cabinet system of government. Reforms in 1990 established a multiparty democracy within the framework of a constitutional monarchy. An insurgency led by Maoist extremists broke out in 1996. The ensuing nine-year civil war between insurgents and government forces witnessed the dissolution of the cabinet and parliament and assumption of absolute power by the king. Several weeks of mass protests in April 2006 were followed by several months of peace negotiations between the Maoists and government officials, and culminated in a November 2006 peace accord and the promulgation of an interim constitution. The newly formed interim parliament declared Nepal a democratic federal republic at its first meeting in May 2008, the king vacated the throne in mid-June 2008, and parliament elected the country's first president the following month.

RULERS:

Mahendra Vira Vikrama Shahi Deva, 1955-1972
Birendra Bir Bikram Shahi Deva, 1972-2001
Ginendra, 2001-

MONETARY SYSTEM:

1 Mohru = 100 Paisa to 1961
1 Rupee = 100 Paisa, 1961-

SIGNATURE VARIETIES

1	Janak Raj	2	Bharat Raj
3	Narendra Raj	4	Himalaya Shamsher (J.B. Rama)
5	Lekshmi Nath Gautam	6	Pradhumna Lal (Rajbhandari)
7	Bekh Bahadur Thapa	8	Yadav Prasad Pant
9	Kul Shekhar Sharma	10	Kalyan Dikram Adhikary
11	Ganesh Bahadur Thapa	12	Harishankar Trfipathi
13	Satyendra Pyara Shrestha	14	Dipendra Purush Dhakal
15	Dr. Tilak Rawal	16	Bijay Nath Bhattaraí

Kingdom

Central Bank of Nepal

1961; 1965 ND Issue

		VF	UNC
12	**1 Rupee** ND (1965). Lilac and olive-green. Coin at left, temple at center. Signature 8. Back: Lilac and green. Arms at center, coin at right. Watermark: Plumed crown.	2.00	7.00

		VF	UNC
13	**5 Rupees** ND (1961). Purple and aqua. Portrait of King Mahendra Vira Vikrama at upper left, Stupa at center. Signature 5; 7; 8. Back: Himalayas. Watermark: Plumed crown.	3.00	12.00

		VF	UNC
14	**10 Rupees** ND (1961). Dark brown and red. Portrait of King Mahendra Vira Vikrama at upper left, temple at center. Signature 5; 6; 7; 8. Back: Arms at center. Watermark: Plumed crown.	3.00	15.00

		VF	UNC
15	**100 Rupees** ND (1961). Green and brown. Portrait of King Mahendra Vira Vikrama at upper left. Temple at Lalitpor at center. Signature 5; 6; 7; 8. Back: Indian rhinoceros at center. Watermark: Plumed crown.	10.00	35.00

1972 ND Issue

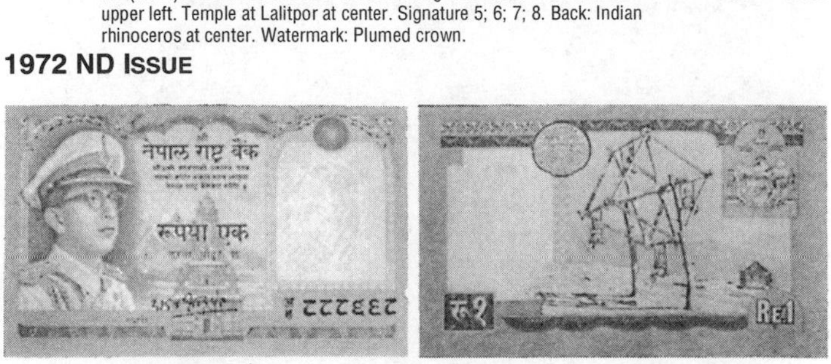

		VF	UNC
16	**1 Rupee** ND (1972). Light brown on blue underprint. King Mahendra Vira Vikrama wearing military uniform with white cap at left. Signature 8. Back: Brown and purple. Lashing pioneering project rotary swing at center right, arms at upper right. Watermark: Plumed crown.	2.00	6.00

No.	Denomination	VF	UNC
17	**5 Rupees** ND (1972). Light green on lilac underprint. King Mahendra Vira Vikrama wearing military uniform with white cap at left. Signature 8. Back: Green and blue. Terraced hillside with himalayas in background. Watermark: Plumed crown.	3.00	8.00

No.	Denomination	VF	UNC
18	**10 Rupees** ND (1972). Light brown on dull olive-green and light blue underprint. King Mahendra Vira Vikrama wearing military uniform with white cap at left. Signature 8. Back: Green and brown. Singha Dunbar at Kathmandu at center. Watermark: Plumed crown.	2.00	5.00

No.	Denomination	VF	UNC
19	**100 Rupees** ND (1972). Green on lilac underprint. King Mahendra Vira Vikrama wearing military uniform with white cap at left, Himalayas at center. Signature 8. Back: Ornate building, temple and arms at right. Watermark: Plumed crown.	7.00	30.00
20	**500 Rupees** ND (1972). Brown and violey. King Mahendra Vira Vikrama wearing military uniform with white cap at left. Signature 8. Back: Two tigers. Watermark: Plumed crown.	75.00	200.

No.	Denomination	VF	UNC
21	**1000 Rupees** ND (1972). Blue and multicolor. King Mahendra Vira Vikrama wearing military uniform with white cap at left, Great Stupa at Bodhnath. Signature 8. Back: House and mountains. Watermark: Plumed crown.	60.00	175.

1974 ND Issue

No.	Denomination	VF	UNC
22	**1 Rupee** ND (1974). Blue on purple and gold underprint. King Birendra Bir Bikram in military uniform with dark cap at left, temple at center. Signature 9; 10; 11; 12. Back: Blue and brown. Two musk deer at center, arms at upper right. Watermark: Plumed crown.	1.00	2.00

No.	Denomination	VF	UNC
23	**5 Rupees** ND (1974). Red, brown and green. King Birendra Bir Bikram in military uniform with dark cap at left, temple at center. signature 9; 10; 11. Back: Red and brown. Two yaks at center. Watermark: Plumed crown.		
	a. Issued note.	6.00	12.00
	s. Specimen.	—	100.
	ct. Color trial. Green and purple face, back blue.	—	165.

No.	Denomination	VF	UNC
24	**10 Rupees** ND (1974). Dark and light brown on multicolor underprint. King Birendra Bir Bikram in military uniform with dark cap at left, Vishnu on Garnda at center. signature 9; 10; 11. Back: Brown and green. Buck Antelope at center, arms at right. Watermark: Plumed crown.		
	a. Issued note.	2.00	5.00
	s. Specimen.	—	100.
	ct. Color trial. Green and purple on multicolor underprint.	—	165.

No.	Denomination	VF	UNC
25	**50 Rupees** ND (1974). Purple on green and multicolor underprint. King Birendra Bir Bikram in military uniform with dark cap at left, building at center. Signature 9. Back: Blue and brown. Himalayan Tahr standing facing right at center, arms at right. Watermark: Plumed crown.		
	a. Issued note.	5.00	10.00
	s. Specimen.	—	135.

26	100 Rupees	VF	UNC
	ND (1974). Green and purple on multicolor underprint. King Birendra Bir Bikram in military uniform with dark cap at left, mountains at center, temple at right. Signature 9. Back: Green. Indian Rhinoceros walking left, "eye" at upper left corner, arms at upper right. Watermark: Plumed crown.	7.00	20.00

27	500 Rupees	VF	UNC
	ND (1974). Brown on multicolor underprint. King Birendra Bir Bikram in military uniform with dark cap at left, monastery at center. Signature 9; 10. Back: Brown and gold. Two tigers at center right, arms at upper right. Watermark: Plumed crown.	75.00	200.

28	1000 Rupees	VF	UNC
	ND (1974). Blue on multicolor underprint. King Birendra Bir Bikram in military uniform with dark cap at left, temple and Great Stupa at center. Back: Elephant at center, arms at upper right on back. Watermark: Plumed crown.		
	a. Issued note.	80.00	225.
	s. Specimen.	—	—

1981-87 ND Issue

29	2 Rupees	VF	UNC
	ND (1981-). Green on light blue and lilac underprint. King Birendra Bir Bikram wearing plumed crown at left, temple at center. Back: Multicolored. Leopard at center. Watermark: Plumed crown.		
	a. Line from king's lower lip extending downward. Serial # 24mm long. Signature 10.	.50	2.00
	b. No line from king's lower lip. Signature 10; 11; 13.	.50	1.00
	c. As b. Serial # 20mm long. Signature 12.	.50	1.00

30	5 Rupees	VF	UNC
	ND (1987-). Brown on red and multicolor underprint. King Birendra Bir Bikram wearing plumed crown at left, temple at center. Back: Red and brown. Two yaks at center right. Watermark: Plumed crown.		
	a. Serial # 24mm long. Signature 11; 12; 13.	.50	2.00
	b. Serial # 20mm long. Signature 12.	.50	2.00

31	10 Rupees	VF	UNC
	ND (1985-87). Dark brown and orange on lilac and multicolor underprint. King Birendra Bir Bikram wearing plumed crown at left, Vishnu on Garnda at center. Back: Antelopes at center, arms at right. Watermark: Plumed crown.		
	a. Serial # 24mm long. Signature 11; 12.	1.00	3.00
	b. Segmented foil over security thread. Signature 13, 14.	1.00	2.00

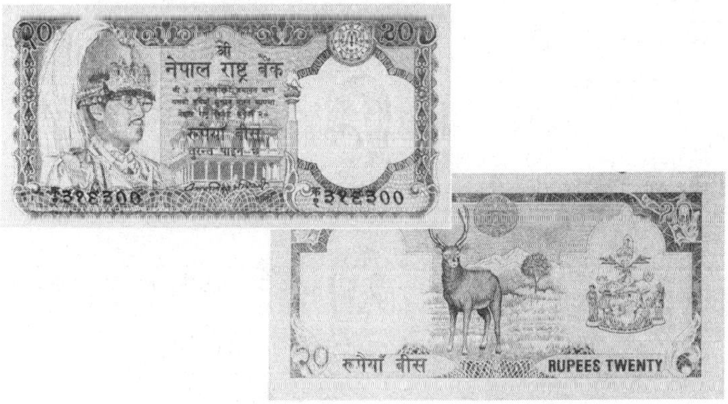

32	20 Rupees	VF	UNC
	ND (1982-87). Orange on multicolor underprint. King Birendra Bir Bikram wearing plumed crown at left, Janakpur Temple at center. Signature 10; 11. Serial # 24mm long. Back: Orange and multicolor. Sambar Deer at center, arms at right. Watermark: Plumed crown.		
	a. Issued note.	1.00	5.00
	s. Specimen.	—	135.

33	50 Rupees	VF	UNC
	ND (1983-). Blue on multicolor underprint. King Birendra Bir Bikram wearing plumed crown at left, Palace at center. Back: Himalayan Tahr at center, arms at right. Watermark: Plumed crown.		
	a. With title at right. Serial # 24mm long. Signature 10. (1983).	1.00	7.00
	b. With title at center. Serial # 20mm long. Signature 11; 12.	1.00	5.00
	c. Segmented foil over security thread. Signature 13, 14.	1.00	5.00

34 100 Rupees — VF | UNC

ND (1981-). Green on pale lilac and multicolor underprint. King Birendra Bir Bikram wearing plumed crown at left, temple at right. Back: Rhinoceros walking left, arms at upper right, without "eye" at upper left. Watermark: Plumed crown. UV: value 100 in box, serial #, signatures fluoresce green.

	VF	UNC
a. Line from king's lower lip extending downward. With security thread. Serial # 24mm long. signature 10.	2.00	8.00
b. No line from king's lower lip. Serial # at lower left. Signature 10.	2.00	8.00
c. Serial # 20mm long. Signature 11.	2.00	7.00
d. As b. Segmented foil over security thread. Signature 12.	2.00	7.00
e. Serial # 20mm long. Signature 13.	1.00	6.00
f. Serial # 24mm long. Signature 13.	1.00	6.00

35 500 Rupees — VF | UNC

ND (1981-). Brown and blue-violet on multicolor underprint. King Birendra Bir Bikram wearing plumed crown at left, temple at center. Back: Brown and gold on blue underprint. Two tigers at center right, arms at upper right. Watermark: Plumed crown. .

	VF	UNC
a. Line from King's lip extending downwards. Serial # 24mm long. Signature 10.	5.00	45.00
b. Serial # 20mm long. Signature 11.	3.00	25.00
c. Segmented foil over security thread. Signature 12.	3.00	20.00
d. Signature 13. (1996).	3.00	20.00

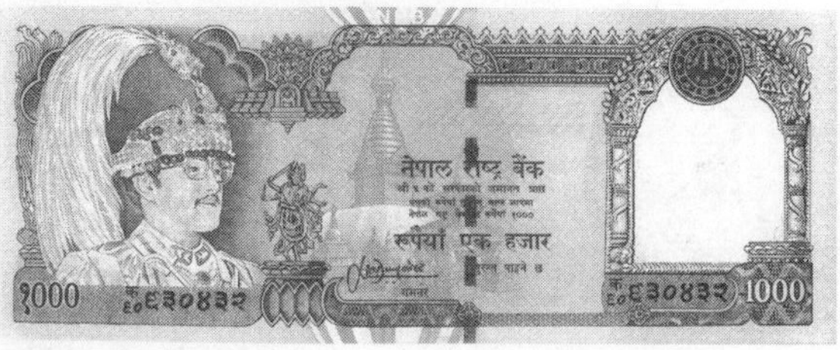

36 1000 Rupees — VF | UNC

ND (1981-). Red-brown and gray on multicolor underprint. King Birendra Bir Bikram wearing plumed crown at left, Stupa and temple on face. Back: Elephant at center, arms at upper right. Watermark: Plumed crown.

	VF	UNC
a. Line from King's lip extending downwards. Serial # 24mm long. Signature 10.	10.00	85.00
b. Serial # 20mm long. Signature 11.	5.00	45.00
c. Segmented foil over security thread. Signature 12.	5.00	45.00
d. Signature 13. (1996).	5.00	45.00

1988-96 ND Issue

37 1 Rupee — VF | UNC

ND (1991-). Purple and dull blue on multicolor underprint. King Birendra Bir Bikram wearing plumed crown at left. Signature 12; 13. Back: Two musk deer at center, arms at upper right. Watermark: Crown. — FV | .40

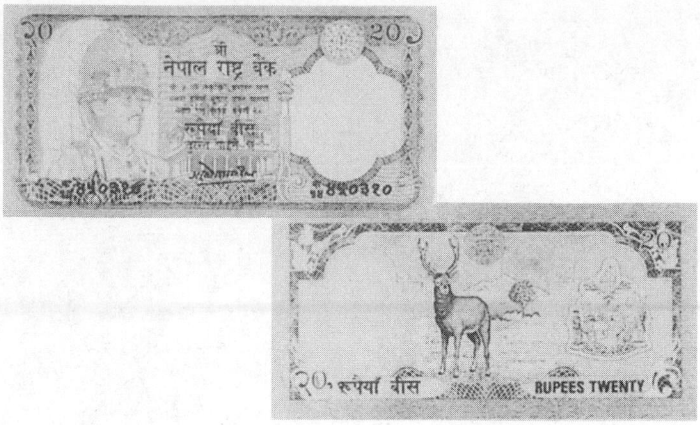

38 20 Rupees — VF | UNC

ND (1988-). Orange on multicolor underprint. King Birendra Bir Bikram wearing plumed crown at left. Janakpur Temple at center. Multicolor border. Back: Orange and multicolor. Sambar Deer at center, arms at right. Multicolor border. Watermark: Crown.

	VF	UNC
a. Serial # 24mm long. Signature 11; 12.	1.00	3.00
b. Segmented foil over security thread. Serial # 20mm long. Signature 13.	1.00	3.00
s. As a. Specimen.	—	115.

1997 ND Commemorative Issue

#41 and 42, Silver Jubilee of Accession, 1972-1997

41 25 Rupees — VF | UNC

ND (1997). Black and dark brown on multicolor underprint. King Birenda Bir Bikram wearing plumed crown at left, Royal palace at center right. Back: Dull green and orange. Pillars with chinze at left, steer at center, arms at right. Watermark: Plumed crown. 140x70mm. — 1.00 | 4.00

42 250 Rupees — VF | UNC

ND (1997). Dark gray and blue-gray on multicolor underprint. King Birenda Bir Bikram wearing plumed crown at left, House of Representatives in underprint at center, royal palace at center right. Back: Blue and orange on green underprint. Pillars with chinze at left, steer at center, arms at right. Watermark: Plumed crown. — 4.00 | 25.00

2000 ND Issue

43 500 Rupees — VF | UNC

ND (2000). Brown, blue-violet and silver on multicolor underprint. Large portrait of King Birendra Bir Bikram wearing plumed crown at left, temple at center. Back: Brown and gold. Two tigers at center right, arms at upper right. Watermark: Plumed crown. — 3.00 | 20.00

44 **1000 Rupees** | VF 5.00 | UNC 40.00

ND (2000). Blue, brown and silver on multicolor underprint. Large portrait of King Birendra Bir Bikram wearing plumed crown at left, Stupa and temple on face. Back: Elephant at center, arms at upper right.

2002 ND Commemorative Issue

Accession to the throne of King Gyanendra Bir Bikram

45 **10 Rupees** | VF FV | UNC 2.00

ND (30.9.2002). Multicolor. King Gyanendra Bir Bikram wearing plumed crown at left. Commemorative text in horse-shoe shaped window: *This is issued on the occasion of King Gyanendra Bir Bikram Shah Dev's accession to the thron* Back: Two antelopes at center. Printer: NPA. 133x70mm.

2002 ND Issue

46 **5 Rupees** | VF FV | UNC 3.00

ND (2002). Red and brown on multicolor underprint. Darkly engraved portrait of King Gyanendra Bir Bikram at left. Signature Tilak Rawal. Back: Two yaks at center. UV: value 5 in box fluoresce green.

47 **20 Rupees** | VF | UNC

ND (2002). Portrait King Gyanendra Bir Bikram at right. Signature Tilak Rawal. Back: Deer at center. 138x70mm.

		VF	UNC
a.	Center title looks like 3 characters. Short signature 15.	FV	4.00
b.	Center title looks like 4 characters. Long signature 15.	FV	4.00

48 **50 Rupees** | VF | UNC

ND (2002). Black and blue on multicolor underprint. Portrait King Gyanendra Bir Bikram at right, building at center. Signature Tilak Rawal. Back: Himalayan Tahr at center. 142x70mm.

		VF	UNC
a.	Hat in black.	FV	5.00
b.	Hat in blue.	FV	5.00

49 **100 Rupees** | VF FV | UNC 8.00

ND (2002). Green, light purple and blue on multicolor underprint. Portrait King Gyanendra Bir Bikram at right. Signature Tilak Rawal. Back: Rhinocerous walking left at center. 145x70mm.

50 **500 Rupees** | VF FV | UNC 25.00

ND (2002). Black and orange on multicolor underprint. Portrait King Gyanendra Bir Bikram at right, building at center. Signature Tilak Rawal. Back: Two tigers at center. 158x70mm.

51 **1000 Rupees** | VF FV | UNC 40.00

ND (2002). Black and red on multicolor underprint. Portrait King Gyanendra Bir Bikram at right, temple at center. Signature Tilak Rawal. Back: Elephant at center. 172x70mm.

2005 Commemorative Issue

		VF	UNC
52	**50 Rupees** 2005 Green, yellow and red-orange. King Gyanendra Bir Bikram at left. Nepal Rastra Bank building at left center. Back: Two quail, mountains in background. 142x70mm.	FV	5.00

2005 Issue

		VF	UNC
53	**5 Rupees** 2005 Red brown on multicolor underprint. King Gyanendra Bir Bikram at left. Back: Two Oxen at center. 119x69mm.		
	a. Signature 15.	FV	3.00
	b. Top line center text with three characters. Signature 16.	FV	3.00
	c. Top line center text with four characters.	FV	3.00

		VF	UNC
54	**10 Rupees** ND (2005). Brown, light blue and green on munticolor underprint. King Gyanendra Bir Bikram at left. Back: Two antelopes at center. Polymer plastic. 133x70mm.	FV	3.00
55	**20 Rupees** ND (2005). Orange on multicolor underprint. King Gyanendra Bir Bikram at left center. Signature 16. Back: Stag at center. 138x70mm.	FV	4.00
56	**50 Rupees** ND (2005). Blue and green on multicolor underprint. King Gyanendra Bir Bikram at right. Back: Himalayan Thar at center. 142x70mm.	FV	5.00
57	**100 Rupees** ND (2005). Brown and green on multicolor underprint. King Gyanendra Bir Bikram at right. Signature 16. Back: Rhinocerous walking left at center. 145x70mm.	FV	4.00

Federal Democratic Republic

Central Bank of Nepal

2008 Issue

		VF	UNC
60	**5 Rupees** 2008. Red and multicolor. Mt. Everest at left, temple at center. Back: Yaks at center. Watermark: Rhododendron. Expected new issue. 119x69mm.	—	—

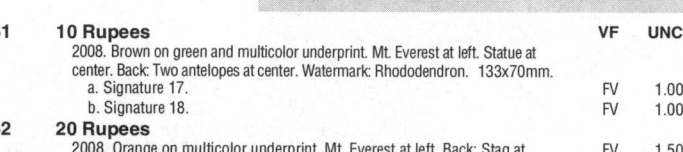

		VF	UNC
61	**10 Rupees** 2008. Brown on green and multicolor underprint. Mt. Everest at left. Statue at center. Back: Two antelopes at center. Watermark: Rhododendron. 133x70mm.		
	a. Signature 17.	FV	1.00
	b. Signature 18.	FV	1.00
62	**20 Rupees** 2008. Orange on multicolor underprint. Mt. Everest at left. Back: Stag at center. Watermark: Rhododendron. 138x70mm.	FV	1.50

		VF	UNC
63	**50 Rupees** 2008. Purple, green and blue on multicolor underprint. Mr. Everest at left, Rama-Janaki temple of Janakpur at center. Back: Himalayan Tahr at center, mountains.. Watermark: Rhododendron. 142x70mm.	FV	2.50

		VF	UNC
64	**100 Rupees** 2008. Green on multicolor underprint. Mt. Everest at left. Back: Rhinocerous at center. Watermark: Rhododendron. 140x70mm.		
	a. Signature 15.	FV	3.00
	b. Signatrue 16.	FV	3.00

#	Denomination / Description	VF	UNC
65	**500 Rupees** 2008. Brown and blue-violet on multicolor underprint. Mt. Everest at left center. Red rhododedrum covers watermark area. Back: Two tigers at center. Watermark: Gyanendra Bir Bikram. 160x70mm.	FV	10.00
66	**500 Rupees** ND (2009). Brown and violet on multicolor underprint. Mt. Everest at left Mt. Amadablam and Thyangboche monastery at center. Wide windowed security thread. Back: Two tigers at center drinking. 160x70mm.	FV	20.00
67	**1000 Rupees** 2008. Blue and brown on multicolor underprint. Mt. Everest at left. Red rhododendron in watermark area. Back: Elephant at center. Watermark: King Gyanendra Bir Bikram.		
	a. Signature 16.	100.	200.
	b. Signature 17.	FV	30.00
	s. Specimen.	—	100.
68	**1000 Rupees** ND (2010). Blue and brown on multicolor underprint. Mt. Everest at left, Swayambhunath stupa at center. Signature 16. Back: Elephant at center. Watermark: Rhododendron. 172x70mm.	120.	200.

2012 Issue

#	Denomination / Description	VF	UNC
69	**5 Rupees** 2012 (2013). Lilac, brown and green. Mt. Everest, temple of taleju, obverse of coin. Back: Bank logo, two yaks grazing, Mt. Everest. Watermark: Rhododendron Printer: TDLR. 120x70mm.	FV	.75
70	**10 Rupees** 2012 (2013). Brown, green and lilac. Mt. Everest, Garud Narayan of Changu Narayan temple, obverse of coin. Back: Three black bucks grazing. Watermark: Rhododendron Printer: TDLR. 100x70mm.	FV	1.00
71	**20 Rupees** 2012 (2013). Orange and brown. Mt. Everest, temple of Krishna of Patan, Garuda atop pillar, obverse of coin. Back: Swamp deer, trees, mountain. Watermark: Rhododendron Printer: TDLR. 138x70mm.	FV	1.25
72	**50 Rupees** 2012 (2013). Purple, green and blue. Mt. Everest, Rama-Janaki temple of Janakpur, obverse of coin. Back: Male thar, mountains, bank logo. Watermark: Rhododendron Printer: TDLR. 142x70mm.	FV	2.00
73	**100 Rupees** 2012 (2013). Green and lilac. Mt. Everest, Mayadevi inside silver metallic oval. Map of Nepal, Ashoka pillar, wood carvings from temple of Tremple of Taleju in Kathmandu, clouds, obverse of coin. Back: One-horned rhinoceros in grassy plain, bank logo. Watermark: Rhododendron Printer: TDLR. 146x70mm.	FV	3.25
74	**500 Rupees** 2012 (2013). Brown and violet. Mt. Everest, Indra, Mt. Amadablam and Thyangboche monastery, wood carvings, clouds. Back: Two tigers drinking melted snow. Watermark: Rhododendron Printer: TDLR. 160x70mm.	FV	15.00
75	**1000 Rupees** 2012 (2013). Watermark: Rhododendron Printer: TDLR. Expected new issue.	—	—

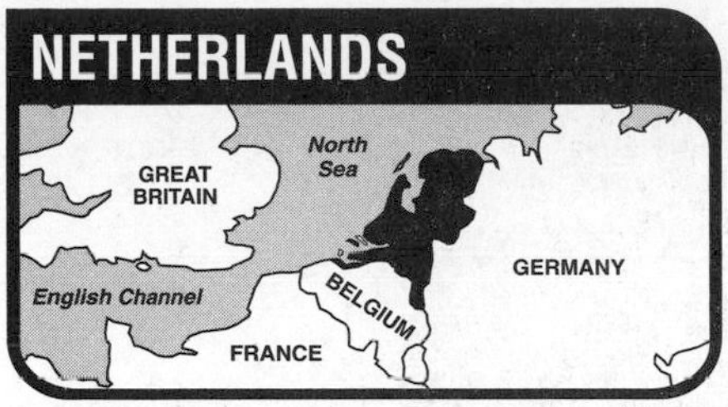

The Kingdom of the Netherlands, a country of western Europe fronting on the North Sea and bordered by Belgium and Germany, has an area of 15,770 sq. mi. (40,844 sq. km.) and a population of 15.87 million. Capital: Amsterdam, but the seat of government is at The Hague. The economy is d on dairy farming and a variety of industrial activities. Chemicals, yarns and fabrics, and meat products are exported.

The Dutch United Provinces declared their independence from Spain in 1579; during the 17th century, they became a leading seafaring and commercial power, with settlements and colonies around the world. After a 20-year French occupation, a Kingdom of the Netherlands was formed in 1815. In 1830 Belgium seceded and formed a separate kingdom. The Netherlands remained neutral in World War I, but suffered invasion and occupation by Germany in World War II. A modern, industrialized nation, the Netherlands is also a large exporter of agricultural products. The country was a founding member of NATO and the EEC (now the EU), and participated in the introduction of the euro in 1999.

RULERS:

Juliana, 1948-1980
Beatrix, 1981-

MONETARY SYSTEM:

1 Gulden = 20 Stuivers
1 Gulden = 100 Cents, to 2001
1 Rijksdaalder = 2 1/2 Gulden
1 Euro = 100 Cents, 2002-

REPLACEMENT NOTES:

#37-60, 72-74, 77-79, 81-82, 84-89, JEZ-printed notes only, serial numbers starting with "1" instead of normal "0".

Koninkrijk - Kingdom

De Nederlandsche Bank

Netherlands Bank

1966-72 Issue

#	Denomination / Description	VF	UNC
90	**5 Gulden** 26.4.1966. Green on multicolor underprint. Joost van den Vondel at right. Back: Modern design of Amsterdam Play-house. Watermark: Inkwell, quill pen and scroll. 136x76mm.		
	a. Serial # at upper left and lower right. Gray paper with clear watermark.	FV	40.00
	b. Serial # at upper left and lower right. White paper with vague watermark. Series XA/XM.	50.00	200.
	c. Serial # at upper left and center right in smaller type. (Experimental issue; circulated initally in the province of Utrecht.) Series 6AA.	125.	750.

		VF	UNC
91	**10 Gulden**	VF	UNC
	25.4.1968. Dark blue on violet and multicolor underprint. Stylized self-portrait of Frans Hals at right. Back: Modern design. Watermark: Cornucopia. UV: fibers fluoresce yellow. 136x76mm.		
	a. *O* in "bullseye" at upper left on back.	30.00	100.
	b. Plain "bullseye" at upper left on back.	FV	25.00

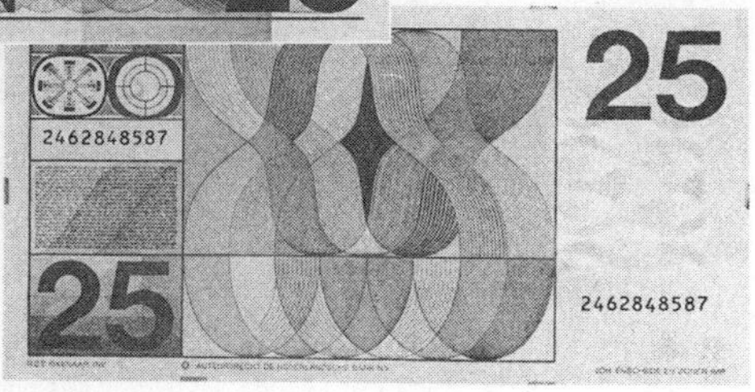

		VF	UNC
92	**25 Gulden**	VF	UNC
	10.2.1971. Red on orange and pink underprint. Jan Pietersz Sweelinck at right. Back: Modern design. Watermark: Rectangular wave design. 148x76mm.		
	a. Issued note. 10 digit serial #.	FV	80.00
	b. Issued note. 11 digit serial #.	FV	90.00
	s. Specimen.	—	950.

		VF	UNC
93	**100 Gulden**	VF	UNC
	14.5.1970. Dark brown on multicolor underprint. Michiel Adriaensz de Ruyter at right. Back: Compass-card or rhumbcard design at center. 154x76mm.		
	a. Issued note.	FV	300.
	s. Specimen.	—	1100.

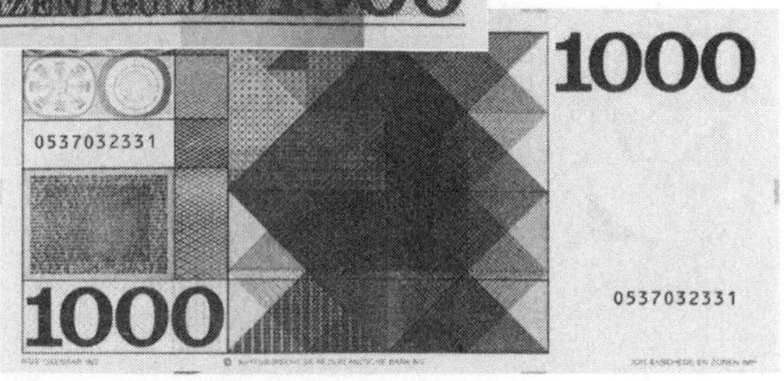

		VF	UNC
94	**1000 Gulden**	VF	UNC
	30.3.1972. Black and dark green on multicolor underprint. Baruch d' Espinoza at right. Back: Graphic design. Watermark: Pyramid in bowl on slab. 160x76mm.		
	a. Issued note.	FV	1000.
	s. Specimen.	—	1400.

1973 Issue

		VF	UNC
95	**5 Gulden**	VF	UNC
	28.3.1973. Dark green on green and multicolor underprint. Joost van den Vondel at right. Back: Graphic design. Watermark: Inkwell, quill pen and scroll. 136x76mm.		
	a. Issued note.	FV	20.00
	s. Specimen.	—	1300.

1977-85 Issue

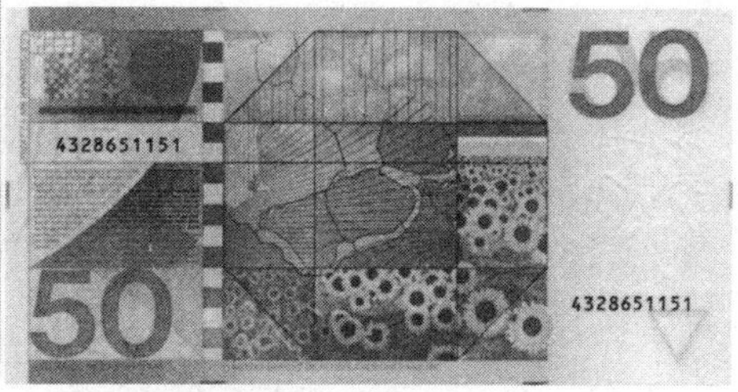

		VF	UNC
96	**50 Gulden**	VF	UNC
	4.1.1982. Orange and yellow on multicolor underprint. Sunflower with bee at lower center. Vertical format. Back: Map and field of sun flowers. Watermark: Bee. 148x76mm.	FV	80.00

		VF	UNC
97	**100 Gulden**	VF	UNC
	28.7.1977 (1981). Dark brown on multicolor underprint. Snipe at right. Back: Head of Great Snipe. Watermark: Head of Great Snipe. 154x76mm.		
	a. Issued note.	FV	175.
	s. Specimen.	—	1200.

98	250 Gulden	VF	UNC
	25.7.1985 (1986). Violet on multicolor underprint. Lighthouse. Vertical format. Back: Lighthouse and map. Watermark: Rabbit and *VHP*. 160x76mm.		
	a. Issued note.	FV	300.
	s. Specimen.	—	1700.

1989-97 Issue

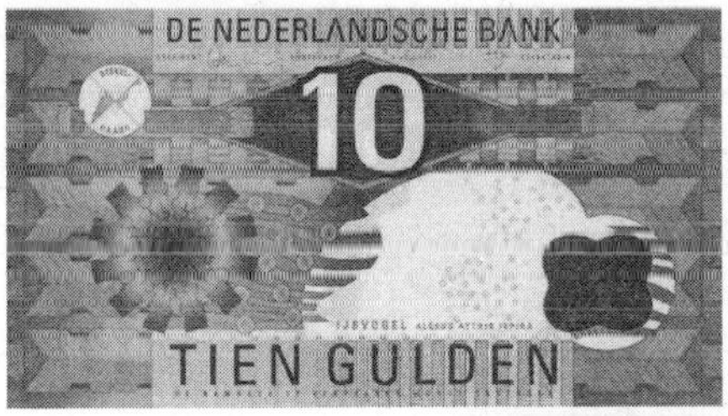

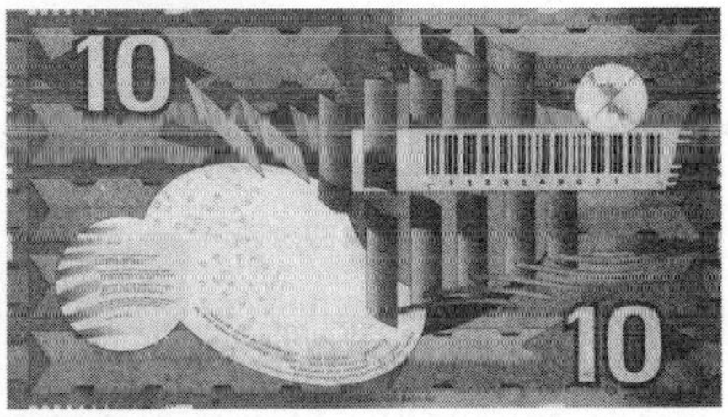

99	10 Gulden	VF	UNC
	1.7.1997. Purple and blue-violet on multicolor underprint. Value and geometric designs. Back: Value and geometric designs. Watermark: Bird. 136x76mm.	FV	20.00

100	25 Gulden	VF	UNC
	5.4.1999. Red on multicolor underprint. Value and geometric designs. Back: Value and geometric designs. Watermark: Robin. 141x76mm.	FV	50.00

101	100 Gulden	VF	UNC
	9.1.1992 (7.9.1993). Dark and light brown, gray and gold on multicolor underprint. Value and geometric designs. Back: Value and geometric designs. Watermark: Little owl. 154x76mm.	FV	125.

102	1000 Gulden	VF	UNC
	2.0.1994 (1990). Dark gray and green. Geometric designs. Back: Geometric designs. Watermark: Lapwing's head. 166x76mm.	FV	1100.

The Netherlands Antilles, part of the Netherlands realm, comprise two groups of islands in the West Indies: Bonaire and Curaçao near the Venezuelan coast; St. Eustatius, Saba, and the southern part of St. Maarten (St. Martin) southeast of Puerto Rico. The island group has an area of 385 sq. mi. (961 sq. km.) and a population of 210,000. Capital: Willemstad. Chief industries are the refining of crude oil, and tourism. Petroleum products and phosphates are exported.

Once the center of the Caribbean slave trade, the island of Curaçao was hard hit by the abolition of slavery in 1863. Its prosperity (and that of neighboring Aruba) was restored in the early 20th century with the construction of oil refineries to service the newly discovered Venezuelan oil fields. The island of St. Martin is shared with France; its southern portion is named Sint Maarten and is part of the Netherlands Antilles; its northern portion, called Saint Martin, is an overseas collectivity of France.On Dec. 15, 1954, the Netherlands Antilles were given complete domestic autonomy and granted equality within the Kingdom with Surinam and the Netherlands. The island of Aruba gained independence in 1986.

In October 2010 Curaçao and Saint Marten became autonomous entities of the Netherlands with the guilder being a valid currency until 31.12.2011. The islands of Bonaire, Saba and St. Eustatius became direct dependentcies of the Netherlands and will use the US dollar starting 1.1.2011.

RULERS:
Dutch

MONETARY SYSTEM:
1 Gulden = 100 Cents

DUTCH ADMINISTRATION

NEDERLANDSE ANTILLEN

1955 MUNTBILJET NOTE ISSUE

		VF	UNC
A1	**2 1/2 Gulden**		
	1955; 1964. Blue. Ship in dry dock at center. Back: Crowned supported arms at center. Printer: ABNC.		
	a. 1955.	70.00	330.
	b. 1964.	55.00	280.
	s. As a or b. Specimen.	—	340.

1962 ISSUE

		VF	UNC
1	**5 Gulden**		
	2.1.1962. Blue on multicolor underprint. View of Curaçao at center, woman seated with scroll and flag in oval at left. Back: Crowned arms at center right. Watermark: *NA* monogram. Printer: JEZ.		
	a. Issued note.	35.00	165.
	s. Specimen.	—	115.

		VF	UNC
2	**10 Gulden**		
	2.1.1962. Green on multicolor underprint. High-rise building (Aruba) at center, woman seated with scroll and flag in oval at left. Back: Crowned arms at center right. Watermark: *NA* monogram. Printer: JEZ.		
	a. Issued note.	45.00	230.
	s. Specimen.	—	130.

		VF	UNC
3	**25 Gulden**		
	2.1.1962. Black-gray on multicolor underprint. View of Bonaire at center, woman seated with scroll and flag in oval at left. Back: Crowned arms at center right. Watermark: *NA* monogram. Printer: JEZ.		
	a. Issued note.	60.00	310.
	s. Specimen.	—	160.

		VF	UNC
4	**50 Gulden**		
	2.1.1962. Brown on multicolor underprint. City by the seaside (St. Maarten) at center, woman seated with scroll and flag in oval at left. Back: Crowned arms at center right. Watermark: *NA* monogram. Printer: JEZ.		
	a. Issued note.	125.	500.
	s. Specimen.	—	190.

		VF	UNC
5	**100 Gulden**		
	2.1.1962. Violet on multicolor underprint. Monument (St. Eustatius) at center, woman seated with scroll and flag in oval at left. Back: Crowned arms at center right. Watermark: *NA* monogram. Printer: JEZ.		
	a. Issued note.	210.	700.
	s. Specimen.	—	230.

6	**250 Gulden**	VF	UNC
	2.1.1962. Olive-green on multicolor underprint. Boats on the beach (Saba) at center, woman seated with scroll and flag in oval at left. Back: Crowned arms at center right. Watermark: *NA* monogram. Printer: JEZ.		
	a. Issued note.	900.	—
	s. Specimen.	—	300.

7	**500 Gulden**	VF	UNC
	2.1.1962. Red on multicolor underprint. Oil refinery (Curaçao) at center, woman seated with scroll and flag in oval at left. Back: Crowned arms at center right. Watermark: *NA* monogram. Printer: JEZ.		
	a. Issued note.	450.	1200.
	s. Specimen.	—	550.

1967 Issue

8	**5 Gulden**	VF	UNC
	1967; 1972. Dark blue and green on multicolor underprint. View of Curaçao at center, monument *Steunend op eigen Kracht...*at left. Back: Crowned arms at center. Watermark: *NA* monogram. Printer: JEZ.		
	a. 28.8.1967.	25.00	130.
	b. 1.6.1972.	20.00	100.
	s. As a. Specimen.	—	240.

9	**10 Gulden**	VF	UNC
	1967; 1972. Green on multicolor underprint. View of Aruba at center, monument *Steunend op eigen Kracht...*at left. Back: Crowned arms at center. Watermark: *NA* monogram. Printer: JEZ.		
	a. 28.8.1967.	25.00	140.
	b. 1.6.1972.	20.00	110.
	s. As a. Specimen.	—	240.

10	**25 Gulden**	VF	UNC
	1967; 1972. Black-gray on multicolor underprint. View of Bonaire at center, monument *Steunend op eigen Kracht...*at left. Back: Crowned arms at center. Watermark: *NA* monogram. Printer: JEZ.		
	a. 28.8.1967.	50.00	260.
	b. 1.6.1972.	37.50	205.
	s. As a. Specimen.	—	240.

11	**50 Gulden**	VF	UNC
	1967; 1972. Brown on multicolor underprint. Beach (St. Maarten) at center, monument *Steunend op eigen Kracht...*at left. Back: Crowned arms at center. Watermark: *NA* monogram. Printer: JEZ.		
	a. 28.8.1967.	85.00	380.
	b. 1.6.1972.	65.00	300.
	s. As a. Specimen.	—	240.

12	**100 Gulden**	VF	UNC
	1967; 1972. Violet on multicolor underprint. Boats and fishermen on the beach (St. Eustatius) at center, monument *Steunend op eigen Kracht...*at left. Back: Crowned arms at center. Watermark: *NA* monogram. Printer: JEZ.		
	a. 28.8.1967.	110.	550.
	b. 1.6.1972.	100.	490.
	s. As a. Specimen.	—	240.

		VF	UNC
13	**250 Gulden**		
	28.8.1967. Olive-green on multicolor underprint. Mountains (Saba) at center, monument *Steunend op eigen Kracht*...at left. Back: Crowned arms at center. Watermark: *NA* monogram. Printer: JEZ.		
	a. Issued note.	170.	675.
	s. Specimen.	—	470.

1979; 1980 Issue

		VF	UNC
15	**5 Gulden**		
	1980; 1984. Purplish blue on multicolor underprint. View of Curaçao at center, monument *Steunend op eigen Kracht*...at left. Back: Crowned arms at center. Watermark: *NA* monogram. Printer: JEZ.		
	a. 23.12.1980.	17.50	85.00
	b. 1.6.1984.	FV	45.00

		VF	UNC
16	**10 Gulden**		
	1979; 1984. Green and blue-green on multicolor underprint. View of Aruba at center, monument *Steunend op eigen Kracht*...at left. Back: Crowned arms at center. Watermark: *NA* monogram. Printer: JEZ.		
	a. 14.7.1979.	23.00	125.
	b. 1.6.1984.	14.00	75.00
17	**25 Gulden**		
	14.7.1979. Blue and blue-green on multicolor underprint. View of Bonaire at center, monument *Steunend op eigen Kracht*...at left. Back: Crowned arms at center. Watermark: *NA* monogram. Printer: JEZ.	65.00	300.

		VF	UNC
18	**50 Gulden**		
	23.12.1980. Red on multicolor underprint. Beach (St. Maarten) at center, monument *Steunend op eigen Kracht*...at left. Back: Crowned arms at center. Watermark: *NA* monogram. Printer: JEZ.	90.00	430.
19	**100 Gulden**		
	14.7.1979. Red-brown and violet on multicolor underprint. Boats and fishermen on the beach (St. Eustatius) at center, monument *Steunend op eigen Kracht*...at left. Back: Crowned arms at center. Watermark: *NA* monogram. Printer: JEZ.		
	a. 14.7.1979.	140.	670.
	b. 9.12.1981.	FV	425.

1970 Muntbiljet Issue

		VF	UNC
20	**1 Gulden**		
	8.9.1970. Red on orange underprint. Aerial view of harbor at left center. Back: Crowned arms at right. Printer: JEZ.		
	a. Issued note.	FV	10.00
	s. Specimen. Black overprint: *SPECIMEN* on both sides.	—	225.

		VF	UNC
21	**2 1/2 Gulden**		
	8.9.1970. Blue on light blue underprint. Jetliner at left center. Back: Crowned arms at right. Printer: JEZ.		
	a. Issued note.	FV	17.50
	s. Specimen. Red overprint: *SPECIMEN* on both sides.	—	225.

1986 Bank Issue

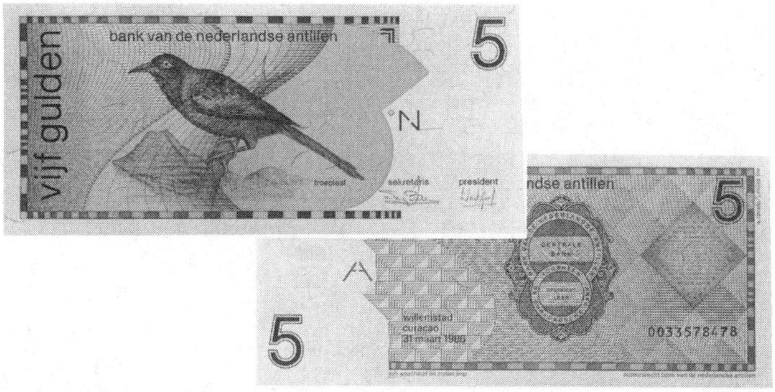

		VF	UNC
22	**5 Gulden**		
	1986; 1990; 1994. Dark blue on multicolor underprint. Troupial at center. Back: Shield-like bank logo. Watermark: Shield-like bank logo. Printer: JEZ. 147x60mm.		
	a. Signature titles: *SEKRETARIS; PRESIDENT*. 31.3.1986.	FV	70.00
	b. Signature titles: *DIRECTEUR SEKRETARIS; PRESIDENT*. 1.1.1990.	FV	60.00
	c. 1.5.1994.	FV	55.00
	s. As a. Specimen.	—	220.

		VF	UNC
23	**10 Gulden**	VF	UNC

1986; 1990; 1994. Dark green on multicolor underprint. Purple-throated carib at left center. Back: Shield-like bank logo. Watermark: Shield-like bank logo. Printer: JEZ. 147x66mm.

	VF	UNC
a. 31.3.1986. Signature titles as 22a.	FV	100.
b. 1.1.1990. Signature titles as 22b.	FV	85.00
c. 1.5.1994.	FV	75.00
s. As a. Specimen.	—	220.

24 25 Gulden VF UNC

1986; 1990; 1994. Red on multicolor underprint. Flamingo at left center. Back: Shield-like bank logo. Watermark: Shield-like bank logo. Printer: JEZ. 147x66mm.

	VF	UNC
a. 31.3.1986. Signature titles as 22a.	FV	220.
b. 1.1.1990. Signature titles as 22b.	FV	175.
c. 1.5.1994.	FV	150.
s. As a. Specimen.	—	250.

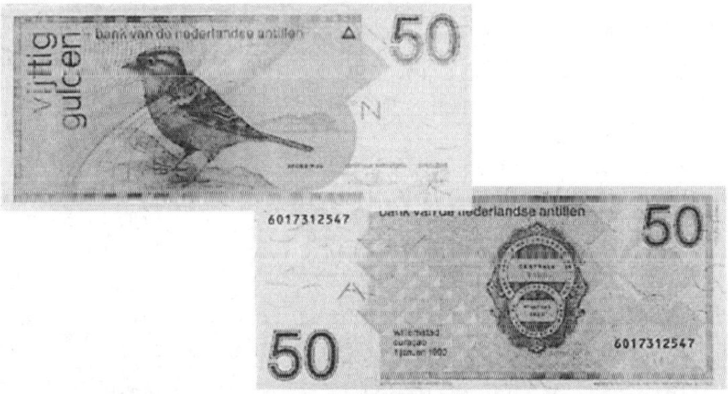

25 50 Gulden VF UNC

1986; 1990; 1994. Brown and orange on multicolor underprint. Rufous-collared sparrow at left center. Back: Shield-like bank logo. Watermark: Shield-like bank logo. Printer: JEZ. 147x66mm.

	VF	UNC
a. 31.3.1986. Signature titles as 22a.	FV	280.
b. 1.1.1990. Signature titles as 22b.	FV	230.
c. 1.5.1994.	FV	210.
s. As a. Specimen.	—	280.

26 100 Gulden VF UNC

1986; 1990; 1994. Brown on multicolor underprint. Bananaquit at left center. Back: Shield-like bank logo. Watermark: Shield-like bank logo. Printer: JEZ. 147x66mm.

	VF	UNC
a. 31.3.1986. Signature titles as 22a.	FV	400.
b. 1.1.1990. Signature titles as 22b.	FV	360.
c. 1.5.1994.	FV	320.
s. As a. Specimen.	—	390.

27 250 Gulden VF UNC

31.3.1986. Purple and red-violet on multicolor underprint. Caribbean mockingbird at left center. Back: Shield-like bank logo. Watermark: Shield-like bank logo. Printer: JEZ. 147x66mm.

	VF	UNC
a. Issued note.	FV	760.
s. Specimen.	—	520.

1998-2012 Issue

28 10 Gulden VF UNC

1998-. Dark and light green on multicolor underprint. Purple-throated carib at left center with gold foil at lower right. Additional enhanced security devices include surface overlays. 2 signature varieties. Back: Shield-like bank logo. Additional enhanced security devices include small sparkling dots at top and bottom. Watermark: Shield-like bank logo. 147x66mm.

	VF	UNC
a. 1.1.1998.	FV	60.00
b. 1.12.2001.	FV	55.00
c. 1.12.2003.	FV	45.00
d. 1.1.2006.	FV	37.50
e. 1.6.2011.	FV	30.00
f. 1.6.2012.	FV	29.00

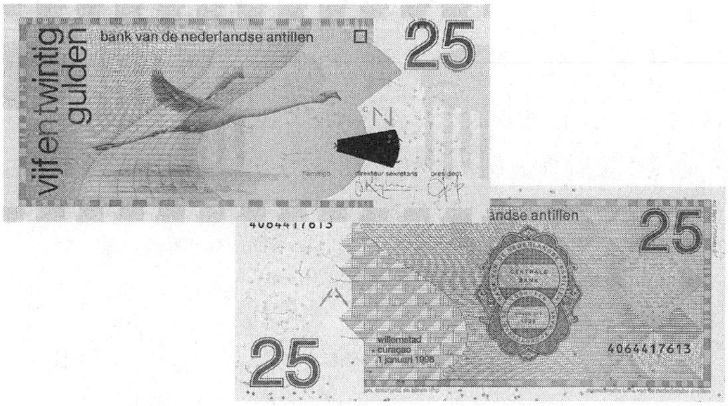

29 25 Gulden VF UNC

1998-. Red on multicolor underprint. Flamingo at left center with gold foil at lower right. Additional enhanced security devices include surface overlays. 2 signature varieties. Back: Shield-like bank logo. Additional enhanced security devices include small sparkling dots at top and Watermark: Shield-like bank logo. 147x66mm.

	VF	UNC
a. 1.1.1998.	FV	135.
b. 1.12.2001.	FV	105.
c. 1.12.2003.	FV	85.00
d. 1.1.2006.	FV	65.00
e. 1.1.2008.	FV	57.50
f. 1.6.2011.	FV	50.00
g. 1.6.2012.	FV	48.00

		VF	UNC
30	**50 Gulden** 1998-. Brown-ornage on multicolor underprint. Rufous-collared sparrow at left center with gold foil at lower right. Additional enhanced security devices include surface overlays. 2 signature varieties. Back: Shield-like bank logo. Additional enhanced security devices include small sparkling dots at top and Watermark: Shield-like bank logo. 147x66mm.		
	a. 1.1.1998.	FV	190.
	b. 1.12.2001.	FV	150.
	c. 1.12.2003.	FV	130.
	d. 1.1.2006.	FV	120.
	e. 1.6.2011.	FV	110.
	f. 1.6.2012.	FV	105.

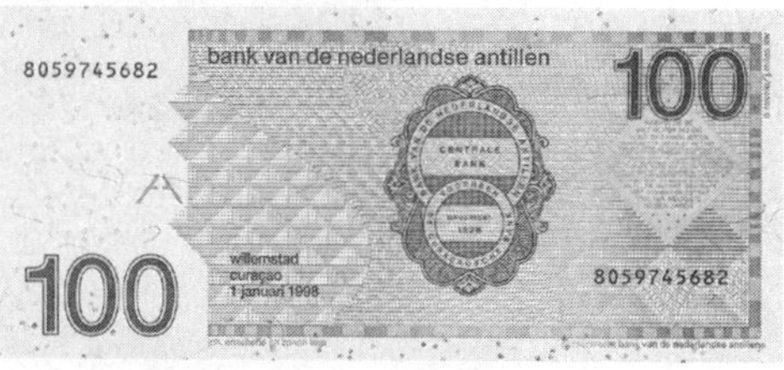

		VF	UNC
31	**100 Gulden** 1998-. Brown on multicolor underprint. Bananaquit at left center with gold foil at lower right. Additional enhanced security devices include surface overlays. 2 signature varieties. Back: Shield-like bank logo. Additional enhanced security devices include small sparkling dots at top and Watermark: Shield-like bank logo. 147x66mm.		
	a. 1.1.1998.	FV	280.
	b. 1.12.2001.	FV	220.
	c. 1.12.2003.	FV	200.
	d. 1.1.2006.	FV	190.
	e. 1.1.2008.	FV	180.
	f. 1.6.2012.	FV	170.

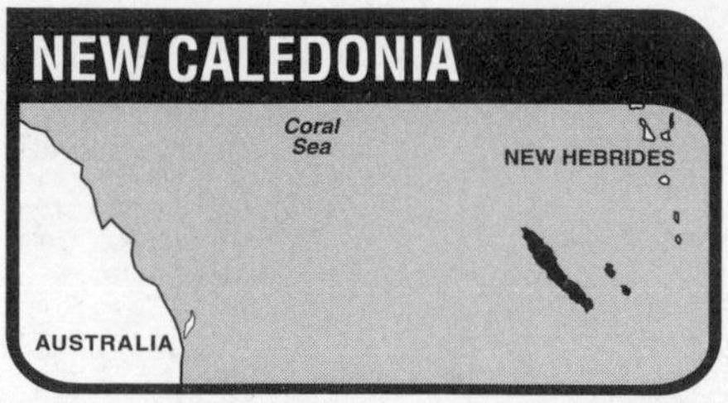

The French Overseas Territory of New Caledonia, a group of about 25 islands in the South Pacific, is situated about 750 miles (1,207 km.) east of Australia. The territory, which includes the dependencies of Ile des Pins, Loyalty Islands, Ile Huon, Isles Belep, Isles Chesterfield, and Ile Walpole, has a total land area of 6,530 sq. mi. (19,058 sq. km.) and a population of 152,000. Capital: Noumea. The islands are rich in minerals; New Caledonia has the world's largest known deposit of nickel. Nickel, nickel castings, coffee and copra are exported.

Settled by both Britain and France during the first half of the 19th century, the island was made a French possession in 1853. It served as a penal colony for four decades after 1864. Agitation for independence during the 1980s and early 1990s ended in the 1998 Noumea Accord, which over a period of 15 to 20 years will transfer an increasing amount of governing responsibility from France to New Caledonia. The agreement also commits France to conduct as many as three referenda between 2013 and 2018, to decide whether New Caledonia should assume full sovereignty and independence.

RULERS:
French

MONETARY SYSTEM:
1 Franc = 100 Centimes

SIGNATURE VARIETIES		
	DIRECTEUR GÉNÉRAL	**PRÉSIDENT DU CONSEIL DE SURVEILLANCE**
1	André Postel-Vinay, 1967-1972	Bernard Clappier, 1966-1972
2	Claude Panouillot, 1972-1973	André De Lattre, 1973
3	Claude Panouillot, 1974-1978	Marcel Theron, 1974-1979
4	Yves Roland-Billecart, 1979-1984	Gabriel Lefort, 1980-1984
5	Yves Roland-Billecart, 1985-1973	Jacques Waitzenegger, 1985-

French Administration

Institut d'Emission d'Outre-Mer

Nouméa

1969 ND Issue

		VF	UNC
59	**100 Francs** ND (1969). Brown on multicolor underprint. Girl wearing wreath and playing guitar at right. Without overprint: *RÉPUBLIQUE FRANÇAISE* at lower center. Signature 1. Back: Girl at left, harbor scene at center. Intaglio.	70.00	225.

		VF	UNC
60	**500 Francs**		
	ND (1969-92). Blue, brown and multicolor. Dugout canoe with sail at center, fisherman at right. *RÉPUBLIQUE FRANÇAISE* at lower left. Back: Man at left, rock formation at left center, native art at right.		
	a. Signature 1.	55.00	125.
	b. Signature 2.	45.00	110.
	c. Signature 3.	40.00	100.
	d. Signature 4.	40.00	100.
	e. Signature 5.	40.00	100.
61	**1000 Francs**		
	ND (1969). Orange, brown and multicolor. Hut under palm tree at left, girl at right. Without overprint: *RÉPUBLIQUE FRANÇAISE* at lower left. Signature 1. Back: Building, Kagu bird at left, deer near hut at right.	120.	285.

1971 ND Issue

		VF	UNC
63	**100 Francs**		
	ND (1971; 1973). Brown on multicolor underprint. Girl wearing wreath and playing guitar at right, overprint at lower center. Signature 1. Back: Girl at left, harbor scene at center.		
	a. Intaglio. Signature 1 (1971).	65.00	150.
	b. Lithographed. Series beginning #H2, from #51,000. Signature 1 (1973).	55.00	135.
	c. As b. Signature 2 (1975).	35.00	85.00
	d. As b. Signature 3 (1977).	20.00	60.00
	s. As a. Specimen.	—	—
64	**1000 Francs**		
	ND (1971; 1983). Orange, brown and multicolor. Hut under palm tree at left, girl at right. Signature 1. *RÉPUBLIQUE FRANÇAISE* at lower left. Back: Building, Kagu bird at left, deer near hut at right.		
	a. Signature 1 (1971).	90.00	200.
	b. Signature 4 (1983).	55.00	125.

		VF	UNC
65	**5000 Francs**		
	ND (1971-84). Multicolor. Bougainville at left, sailing ships at center, *RÉPUBLIQUE FRANÇAISE* at top center. Back: Admiral Febvrier-Despointes at right, sailboat at center right.		
	a. Signature 1 (1971).	165.	350.
	b. Signature 2 (1975).	150.	325.
	c. Signature 4 (1982-84).	140.	300.
	s. As a. Specimen.	—	400.

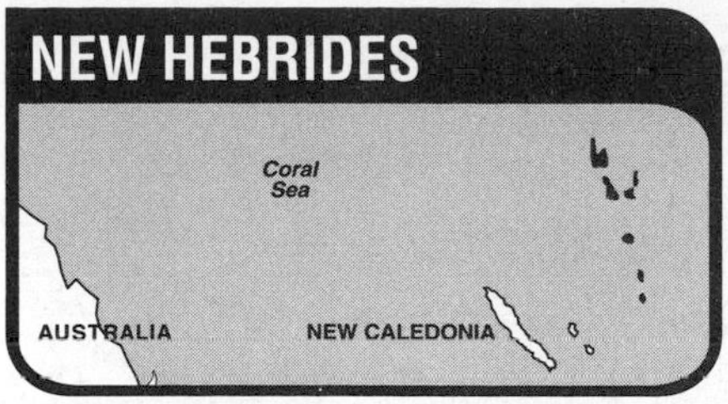

New Hebrides Condominium, a group of islands located in the South Pacific 500 miles (800 km.) west of Fiji, were under the joint sovereignty of Great Britain and France. The islands have an area of 5,700 sq. mi. (14,763 sq. km.) and a population of mainly Melanesians of mixed blood. Capital: Port-Vila. The volcanic and coral islands, while malarial and subject to frequent earthquakes, are extremely fertile, and produce copra, coffee, tropical fruits and timber for export.

The New Hebrides were discovered by Portuguese navigator Pedro de Quiros in 1606, visited by French explorer Bougainville in 1768, and named by British navigator Capt. James Cook in 1774. Ships of all nations converged on the islands to trade for sandalwood, prompting France and Britain to relinquish their individual claims and declare the islands a neutral zone in 1878. The New Hebrides were placed under the control of a mixed Anglo-French commission of naval officers during the native uprisings of 1887, and established as a condominium under the joint sovereignty of France and Great Britain in 1906.

RULERS:

British and French to 1980

MONETARY SYSTEM:

1 Franc = 100 Centimes

SIGNATURE VARIETIES		
	DIRECTEUR GÉNÉRAL	PRÉSIDENT DU CONSEIL DE SURVEILLANCE
1	André Postel-Vinay, 1967-1972	Bernard Clappier, 1966-1972
2	Claude Panouillot, 1972-1973	André De Lattre, 1973
3	Claude Panouillot, 1974-1978	Marcel Theron, 1974-1979
4	Yves Roland-Billecart, 1979-1984	Gabriel Lefort, 1980-1984
5	Yves Roland-Billecart, 1985-1973	Jacques Waitzenegger, 1985-

British and French Administration

Institut d'Emission d'Outre-Mer, Nouvelles Hébrides

1965; 1967 ND Issue

		VF	UNC
16	**100 Francs**		
	Multicolor. Printer: TDLR.	120.	275.

			VF	UNC
17	**1000 Francs**	ND (1967-71). Red. Hut under palm tree at left, girl at right. Signature 1. *NOUVELLES HÉBRIDES*. Back: Building, Kagu bird at left, deer near hut at right, overprint in capital letters at upper center.	160.	400.

1970 ND Issue

			VF	UNC
18	**100 Francs**	ND (1970; 1972; 1977). Multicolor. Like #16, but red and blue underprint. *Nouvelles Hébrides* in script. Back: *Nouvelles Hébrides* in script.		
		a. Intaglio plates. Signature 1. (1970).	75.00	175.
		b. Lithographed series beginning E1, from no. 51,000. Signature 1. (1972).	70.00	160.
		c. As b. Signature 2. (1975).	40.00	135.
		d. As b. Signature 3. (1977).	35.00	80.00

			VF	UNC
19	**500 Francs**	ND (1970-80). Blue, brown and multicolor. Dugout canoe with sail at center, fisherman at right. Back: Man at left, rock formation at left center, native art at right.		
		a. Signature 1. (1970).	75.00	175.
		b. Signature 3. (1979).	60.00	135.
		c. Signature 4. (1980).	40.00	100.

			VF	UNC
20	**1000 Francs**	ND (1970-80). Orange, brown and multicolor. Hut under palm tree at left, girl at right. *Nouvelles Hébrides* in script. Back: Building , Kagu bird at left, deer near hut at right. *Nouvelles Hébrides* in script.		
		a. Signature 1. (1970).	95.00	225.
		b. Signature 2. (1975).	80.00	185.
		c. Signature 3. (1980).	65.00	150.

NEW ZEALAND

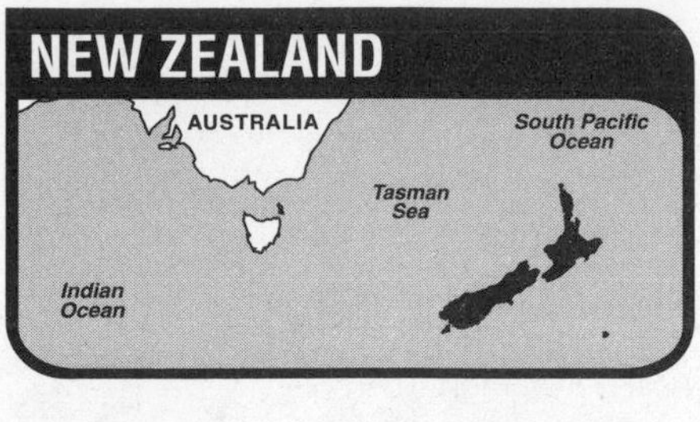

New Zealand, a parliamentary state located in the southwestern Pacific 1,250 miles (2,011 km.) east of Australia, has an area of 103,736 sq. mi. (269,056 sq. km.) and a population of 4.3 million. Capital: Wellington. Wool, meat, dairy products and some manufactured items are exported.

The Polynesian Maori reached New Zealand in about A.D. 800. In 1840, their chieftains entered into a compact with Britain, the Treaty of Waitangi, in which they ceded sovereignty to Queen Victoria while retaining territorial rights. In that same year, the British began the first organized colonial settlement. A series of land wars between 1843 and 1872 ended with the defeat of the native peoples. The British colony of New Zealand became an independent dominion in 1907 and supported the UK militarily in both World Wars. New Zealand's full participation in a number of defense alliances lapsed by the 1980s. In recent years, the government has sought to address longstanding Maori grievances.

RULERS:
British

MONETARY SYSTEM:
1 Shilling = 12 Pence
1 Pound = 20 Shillings (also 2 Dollars) to 1967
1 Dollar = 100 Cents, 1967-

British Administration

Reserve Bank of New Zealand

1940 ND Issue

			VF	UNC
158	**10 Shillings**	ND (1940-67). Brown on multicolor underprint. Arms at upper center. Portrait of Capt. James Cook at lower right. Signature title: *CHIEF CASHIER*. Back: Kiwi at left, Waitangi Treaty signing scene at center. Watermark: Maori chief. Printer: TDLR.		
		a. Signature T. P. Hanna. (1940-55).	80.00	600.
		b. Signature G. Wilson. (1955-56).	150.	1000.
		c. Signature R. N. Fleming. Without security thread. (1956-60).	60.00	500.
		d. As c. With security thread. (1960-67).	20.00	100.

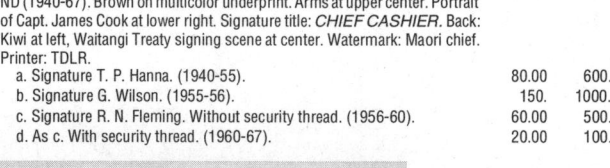

159	**1 Pound**	VF	UNC
	ND (1940-67). Purple on multicolor underprint. Arms at upper center. Portrait of Capt. James Cook at lower right. Signature title: *CHIEF CASHIER.* Back: Sailing ship on sea at left. Watermark: Maori chief. Printer: TDLR.		
	a. Signature T. P. Hanna. (1940-55).	80.00	500.
	b. Signature G. Wilson. (1955-56).	80.00	600.
	c. Signature R. N. Fleming. Without security thread. (1956-60).	40.00	300.
	d. As c. With security thread. (1960-67).	12.50	70.00

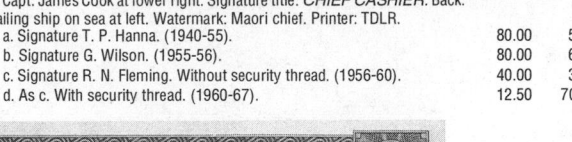

160	**5 Pounds**	VF	UNC
	ND (1940-67). Blue on multicolor underprint. Crowned arms at upper center. Portrait of Capt. James Cook at lower right. Signature title: *CHIEF CASHIER.* Back: Lake Pukaki and Mt. Cook. Watermark: Maori chief. Printer: TDLR.		
	a. Signature T. P. Hanna. (1940-55).	100.	700.
	b. Signature G. Wilson. (1955-56).	100.	750.
	c. Signature R. N. Fleming. Without security thread. (1956-60).	70.00	500.
	d. As c. With security thread. (1960-67).	40.00	150.
	s. As a. Specimen. Black overprint of TDLR oval.	—	750.

161	**10 Pounds**	VF	UNC
	ND (1940-67). Green on multicolor underprint. Crowned arms, sailing ship at left. Portrait of Capt. James Cook at lower right. Signature title: *CHIEF CASHIER.* Back: Flock of sheep at left center. Watermark: Maori chief. Printer: TDLR.		
	a. Signature T. P. Hanna. (1940-55).	300.	1500.
	b. Signature G. Wilson. (1955-56).	400.	1600.
	c. Signature R. N. Fleming. (1956-60).	200.	1500.
	d. As c. With security thread. (1960-67).	150.	500.

162	**50 Pounds**	VF	UNC
	ND (1940-67). Red on multicolor underprint. Crowned arms, sailing ship at left. Portrait of Capt. James Cook at lower right. Signature title: *CHIEF CASHIER.* Back: Dairy farm and Mt. Egmont. Printer: TDLR.		
	a. Signature T. P. Hanna. (1940-55).	4000.	12,000.
	b. Signature G. Wilson. (1955-56).	4000.	10,000.
	c. Signature R. N. Fleming. (1956-67).	2000.	5000.

1967 ND Issue

#163b-168b replacement notes: Special serial # prefix and * suffix.

163	**1 Dollar**	VF	UNC
	ND (1967-81). Brown on multicolor underprint. Queen Elizabeth II at right. Back: Pied fantail at center and plants. Watermark: Capt. James Cook. Printer: TDLR.		
	a. Signature R. N. Fleming. (1967-68).	20.00	50.00
	b. Signature D. L. Wilks. (1968-75).	10.00	25.00
	c. Signature R. L. Knight. (1975-77).	10.00	20.00
	d. Signature H. R. Hardie. (1977-81).	10.00	20.00
	s. Specimen.	—	—

164	**2 Dollars**		
	ND (1967-81). Purple on multicolor underprint. Queen Elizabeth II at right. Back: Riffleman at center and plants. Watermark: Capt. James Cook. Printer: TDLR.		
	a. Signature R. N. Fleming. (1967-68).	15.00	50.00
	b. Signature D. L. Wilks. (1968-75).	15.00	40.00
	c. Signature R. L. Knight. (1975-77).	10.00	30.00
	d. Signature H. R. Hardie. (1977-81).	10.00	25.00
	s. Specimen.	—	—

165	**5 Dollars**	VF	UNC
	ND (1967-81). Orange on multicolor underprint. Queen Elizabeth II at right. Back: Tui at center and plants. Watermark: Capt. James Cook. Printer: TDLR.		
	a. Signature R. N. Fleming. (1967-68).	20.00	85.00
	b. Signature D. L. Wilks. (1968-75).	40.00	275.
	c. Signature R. L. Knight. (1975-77).	20.00	65.00
	d. Signature H. R. Hardie. (1977-81).	20.00	60.00
	s. Specimen.	—	—

166 10 Dollars

ND (1967-81). Blue on multicolor underprint. Queen Elizabeth II at right. Back: Kea at center and plants. Watermark: Capt. James Cook. Printer: TDLR.

	VF	UNC
a. Signature R. N. Fleming. (1967-68).	35.00	150.
b. Signature D. L. Wilks. (1968-75.)	30.00	200.
c. Signature R. L. Knight. (1975-77).	30.00	200.
d. Signature H. R. Hardie. (1977-81).	20.00	100.
s. Specimen.	—	—

167 20 Dollars

ND (1967-81). Green on multicolor underprint. Queen Elizabeth II at right. Back: New Zealand pigeon at center and plants. Watermark: Capt. James Cook. Printer: TDLR.

	VF	UNC
a. Signature R. N. Fleming. (1967-68).	70.00	200.
b. Signature D. L. Wilks. (1968-75).	80.00	400.
c. Signature R. L. Knight. (1975-77).	70.00	300.
d. Signature H. R. Hardie. (1977-81).	40.00	120.
s. Specimen.	—	—

168 100 Dollars

ND (1967-77). Red on multicolor underprint. Queen Elizabeth II at right. Back: Takahe at center and plants. Watermark: Capt. James Cook. Printer: TDLR.

a. Signature R. N. Fleming. (1967-68).	300.	1600.
b. Signature R. L. Knight. (1975-77).	300.	800.
s. Specimen.	—	—

1981-92 ND Issue

#169a, 170a, 171a, 171b, 172a, 172b and 173a replacement note: Special serial # prefix and * suffix.

169 1 Dollar

ND (1981-92). Dark brown on multicolor underprint Mature portrait of Queen Elizabeth II. Back: Pied fantail at center and plants. Watermark: Capt. James Cook. Printer: BWC. UV: central design fluoresce orange, security striop blue. Back left and value 1 orange.

	VF	UNC
a. Signature H. R. Hardie with title: *CHIEF CASHIER.* (1981-85).	4.00	8.00
b. Signature S. T. Russell with title: *GOVERNOR.* (1985-89).	4.00	7.00
c. Signature D. T. Brash. (1989-92).	3.00	6.00

170 2 Dollars

ND (1981-92). Purple on multicolor underprint. Mature portrait of Queen Elizabeth II. Back: Riffleman at center and plants. Watermark: Capt. James Cook. Printer: BWC.

	VF	UNC
a. Signature H. R. Hardie with title: *CHIEF CASHIER.* (1981-85).	6.00	10.00
b. Signature S. T. Russell with title: *GOVERNOR.* (1985-89).	5.00	10.00
c. Signature D. T. Brash. (1989-92).	4.00	8.00

171 5 Dollars

ND (1981-92). Orange on multicolor underprint. Mature portrait of Queen Elizabeth II. Back: Tui at center and plants. Watermark: Capt. James Cook. Printer: BWC.

	VF	UNC
a. Signature H. R. Hardie with title: *CHIEF CASHIER.* (1981-85).	20.00	40.00
b. Signature S. T. Russell with title: *GOVERNOR.* (1985-89).	15.00	30.00
c. Signature D. T. Brash. (1989-92).	12.00	20.00

172 10 Dollars

ND (1981-92). Blue on multicolor underprint. Mature portrait of Queen Elizabeth II. Back: Kea at center and plants. Watermark: Capt. James Cook. Printer: BWC.

	VF	UNC
a. Signature H. R. Hardie with title: *CHIEF CASHIER.* (1981-85).	25.00	50.00
b. Signature S. T. Russell with title: *GOVERNOR.* (1985-89).	20.00	40.00
c. Signature D. T. Brash. (1989-92).	20.00	40.00
s. As b. Specimen. Overprinted: *SPECIMEN* and TDLR oval.	—	750.

173 20 Dollars

ND (1981-92). Green on multicolor underprint. Mature portrait of Queen Elizabeth II. Back: New Zealand pigeon at center and plants. Watermark: Capt. James Cook. Printer: BWC.

	VF	UNC
a. Signature H. R. Hardie with title: *CHIEF CASHIER.* (1981-85).	45.00	120.
b. Signature S. T. Russell with title: *GOVERNOR.* (1985-89).	40.00	70.00
c. Signature D. T. Brash. (1989-92).	40.00	70.00

174 **50 Dollars** | VF | UNC

ND (1983-92). Yellow-orange on multicolor underprint. Mature portrait of Queen Elizabeth II. Back: Morepork Owl at center and plants. Watermark: Capt. James Cook. Printer: BWC.

	VF	UNC
a. Signature H. R. Hardie, with title: *CHIEF CASHIER.* (1981-85).	100.	220.
b. Signature D. T. Brash, with title: *GOVERNOR.* (1989-92).	70.00	140.

175 **100 Dollars** | VF | UNC

ND (1981-89). Red on multicolor underprint. Mature portrait of Queen Elizabeth II. Back: Takahe at center and plants. Watermark: Capt. James Cook. Printer: BWC.

	VF	UNC
a. Signature H. R. Hardie with title: *CHIEF CASHIER.* (1981-85).	150.	350.
b. Signature S. T. Russell with title: *GOVERNOR.* (1985-89).	150.	300.

1990 Commemorative Issue

#176, 150th Anniversary - Treaty of Waitangi, 1840-1990

176 **10 Dollars** | VF | UNC

1990. Blue-violet and pale blue on multicolor underprint. Mature portrait of Queen Elizabeth II with addition of 1990 Commission logo, the White Heron (in red and white with date 1990) at right of Queen. Serial # prefix *BBB; CCC; DDD.* Back: Special inscription and scene of treaty signing. Watermark: Capt. James Cook. Printer: BWC. | 15.00 | 25.00

1992-97 ND Issue

#177-181 Replacement notes: Serial # prefix *ZZ*.

177 **5 Dollars** | VF | UNC

ND (1992-97). Brown and brown-orange on multicolor underprint. Mt. Everest at left, Sir Edmund Hillary at center. Signature D.T. Brash. Back: Brown and blue. Flora with Yellow-eyed Penguin at center. Watermark: Queen Elizabeth II. Printer: TDLR. UV: value 5 in box fluoresce green. Back central design yellow. 135x66mm.

	VF	UNC
a. Issued note.	15.00	40.00
b. Uncut block of 4 in special folder.	—	60.00
c. Uncut block of 8 in special folder.	—	250.

178 **10 Dollars** | VF | UNC

ND (1992-97). Blue and purple on multicolor underprint. Camellia flowers at left, K. Sheppard at center right. Signature D.T. Brash. Back: Pair of green ducks at center right. Watermark: Queen Elizabeth II. Printer: TDLR. 140x68mm.

	VF	UNC
a. Green ducks.	25.00	50.00
b. Blue ducks.	FV	20.00
c. Uncut pair in special folder.	—	40.00
d. Uncut block of 4 in special folder.	—	70.00

179 **20 Dollars** | VF | UNC

ND (1992). Green on multicolor underprint. Queen Elizabeth II at right, government building at left in underprint. Signature D.T. Brash. Back: Pale green and blue. New Zealand falcons at center. Watermark: Queen Elizabeth II. Printer: TDLR. 145x70mm.

	VF	UNC
a. Blue background.	27.50	60.00
b. Green background.	25.00	45.00
c. Uncut block of 4 in special folder.	—	120.

180 **50 Dollars**

ND (1992). Purple, violet and deep blue on multicolor underprint. Sir A. Ngata at right, Maori meeting house at left in underprint. Signature D.T. Brash. Back: Kokako at right. Watermark: Queen Elizabeth II. Printer: TDLR. 150x72mm.

	VF	UNC
a. Issued note.	55.00	80.00
b. Uncut block of 4 in special folder.	—	300.

181 **100 Dollars** | VF | UNC

ND (1992). Violet-brown and red on multicolor underprint. Lord Rutherford of Nelson at center, Nobel prize medal in underprint at left. Signature D.T. Brash. Back: Yellowhead on tree trunk at center right, moth at lower left. Watermark: Queen Elizabeth II. Printer: TDLR. 155x74mm.

	VF	UNC
a. Issued note.	140.	250.
b. Uncut block of 4 in special folder.	—	500.
s. Specimen.	—	—

1994 ND Issue

#182 and 183 replacement notes: Serial # prefix *ZZ*.

		VF	UNC
182	**10 Dollars** ND (1994). Blue and purple on multicolor underprint. Camellia flowers at left, K. Sheppard at center right. Signature D.T. Brash. Back: Bright blue at center behind Whio ducks. Watermark: Queen Elizabeth II. Printer: TDLR. 140x68mm.	12.50	20.00
183	**20 Dollars** ND (1994). Green on multicolor underprint. Queen Elizabeth II at right, government building at left in underprint. Signature D.T. Brash. Back: Bright green at center behind Karearea falcon. Watermark: Queen Elizabeth II. Printer: TDLR. 145x70mm.	25.00	45.00

1996 Commemorative Issue

#184, 70th Birthday - Queen Elizabeth II

		VF	UNC
184	**20 Dollars** ND (1996). Green on multicolor underprint. Commemorative overprint on number 183. Serial # prefix *ER*. 145x70mm.	75.00	215.

1999 Issue

Note: See Collector Series for special sets.

		VF	UNC
185	**5 Dollars** (19)99; (20)04; (20)05 (20)06. Brown and brown-orange on multicolor underprint. Mt. Everest at left, Sir Edmund Hillary at center. Signature D.T. Brash. Back: Flora with Yellow-eyed Penguin at center. Watermark: Queen Elizabeth II. Printer: NPA (without imprint). Polymer plastic. 135x66mm.		
	a. Signature Donald T. Brash.	FV	15.00
	b. Signature Alan Bollard.	FV	9.00

		VF	UNC
186	**10 Dollars** (19)99; (20)03; (20)04; (20)05; (20)06 (20)07. Blue and multicolor. Camellia flowers at left, K. Sheppard at center right. Signature D.T. Brash. Back: Pair of blue ducks at center right. Watermark: Queen Elizabeth II. Printer: NPA (without imprint). Polymer plastic. 140x68mm.		
	a. Signature Donald T. Brash.	FV	15.00
	b. Signature Alan Bollard.	FV	15.00

		VF	UNC
187	**20 Dollars** (19)99; (20)02; (20)04; (20)05. Gray and multicolor. Queen Elizabeth II at right, government building at left in underprint. Signature D.T. Brash. Back: New Zealand falcons at center. Watermark: Queen Elizabeth II. Printer: NPA (without imprint). Polymer plastic. 145x70mm.		
	a. Signature Donald T. Brush.	FV	40.00
	b. Signature Alan Bollard.	FV	27.50

		VF	UNC
188	**50 Dollars** (19)99; (20)04; (20)05; (20)07. Purple and multicolor. Sir A. Ngata at right, Maori meeting house at left in underprint. Signature D.T. Brash. Back: Kokako at right. Watermark: Queen Elizabeth II. Printer: NPA (without imprint). Polymer plastic. 150x72mm.		
	a. Signature Donald T. Brash.	FV	100.
	b. Signatrue Alan Bollard.	FV	80.00

		VF	UNC
189	**100 Dollars** (19)99; (20)05. Brownish red and multicolor. Lord Rutherford of Nelson at center, Nobel prize medal in underprint at left. Signature D.T. Brash. Back: Yellowhead on tree trunk at center right, moth at lower left. Watermark: Queen Elizabeth II. Printer: NPA (without imprint). Polymer plastic. 155x74mm.		
	a. Signature Donald T. Brush.	FV	150.
	b. Signature Alan Bollard.	FV	140.

2000 Commemorative Issue

#190, Millennium Commemorative.

190 10 Dollars

2000. Blue, orange and multicolor. Earth, map of New Zealand at left, ceremonial boat at center. Back: Five sport activities. Printer: NPA (without imprint). Polymer plastic. 140x68mm.

	VF	UNC
a. Black serial #. Serial # prefix *AA; AB.*	FV	25.00
b. Red serial #. Serial # prefix *NZ.*	FV	25.00

Collector Series

Reserve Bank of New Zealand

1990 ND Commemorative Issue

CS176 10 Dollars

1990 With special serial number prefix.

	Mkt. Value
a. Serial # prefix *CWB* (for Country Wide Bank).	9.00
b. Serial # prefix *FTC* (for Farmers Trading Co.).	9.00
c. Serial # prefix *MBL* (for Mobil Oil Co.).	9.00
d. Serial # prefix *RNZ* (for Radio New Zealand).	9.00
e. Serial # prefix *RXX* (for Rank Xerox Co.).	9.00
f. Serial # prefix *TNZ* (for Toyota New Zealand).	9.00

1992 Issue

CS180 50 Dollars

	Mkt. Value
ND (1993). Red serial number.	65.00

1993 ND Issue

CS183 20 Dollars

As #183.

	Mkt. Value
a. Uncut pair. with serial # prefix: *TRBNZA* on back in folder.	—
b. In folder with $20 phone card. 2500 sets.	40.00

1999 Issue

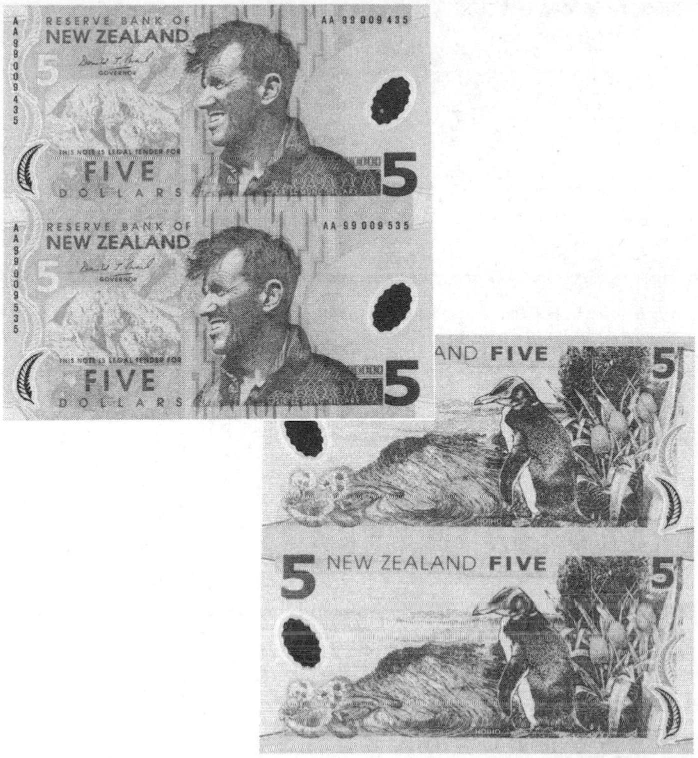

CS185 5 Dollars

As #185. Serial # prefix: *AA.*

	Mkt. Value
a. Uncut pair.	20.00
b. Uncut sheet of 40 notes. 150 sheets.	150.

CS186 10 Dollars

As #186. Serial # prefix: *AA.*

	Mkt. Value
a. Uncut pair. 2,000 pairs.	25.00
b. Uncut sheet of 40 notes. 150 sheets.	300.

CS187 20 Dollars

As #187. Serial # prefix: *AA.*

	Mkt. Value
a. Uncut pair. 4,000 pairs.	50.00
b. Uncut sheet of 40. 150 sheets.	600.

CS188 50 Dollars

Expected new issue.

CS189 100 Dollars

As #189. Serial # prefix: *AA.*

	Mkt. Value
a. Uncut pair. 1,000 pairs.	150.
b. Uncut sheet of 28. 100 sheets.	1800.

1999 Commemorative Issue

#CS190, Millennium Commemorative

CS190 10 Dollars

As #190 but with bank overprint in red under 10 on face. Red serial #.

	Mkt. Value
a. Single note in folder with serial # prefix: *NZ.*	12.50
b. Uncut pair in folder with serial # prefix: *NZ.*	25.00
c. Uncut sheet of 20 with serial # prefix: *NZ.*	225.

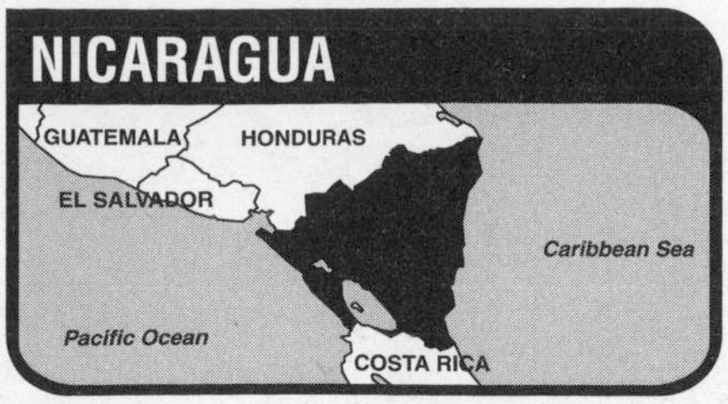

The Republic of Nicaragua, situated in Central America between Honduras and Costa Rica, has an area of 50,193 sq. mi (130,000 sq. km.) and a population of 4.69 million. Capital: Managua. Agriculture, mining (gold and silver) and hardwood logging are the principal industries. Cotton, meat, coffee, tobacco and sugar are exported.

The Pacific coast of Nicaragua was settled as a Spanish colony from Panama in the early 16th century. Independence from Spain was declared in 1821 and the country became an independent republic in 1838. Britain occupied the Caribbean Coast in the first half of the 19th century, but gradually ceded control of the region in subsequent decades. Violent opposition to governmental manipulation and corruption spread to all classes by 1978 and resulted in a short-lived civil war that brought the Marxist Sandinista guerrillas to power in 1979. Nicaraguan aid to leftist rebels in El Salvador caused the US to sponsor anti-Sandinista contra guerrillas through much of the 1980s. Free elections in 1990, 1996, and 2001, saw the Sandinistas defeated, but voting in 2006 announced the return of former Sandinista President Daniel Ortega Saavedra. Nicaragua's infrastructure and economy - hard hit by the earlier civil war and by Hurricane Mitch in 1998 - are slowly being rebuilt.

MONETARY SYSTEM:

1 Peso = 100 Centavos to 1912
1 Córdoba = 100 Centavos, 1912-1987
1 New Córdoba = 1000 Old Córdobas, 1988-90
1 Córdoba Oro = 100 Centavos, 1990-

REPLACEMENT NOTES:

1985-dated issues printed by TDLR, ZA; ZB prefix.

Republic

Banco Central de Nicaragua

Decreto 26.4.1962

107 1 Córdoba VF UNC
D.1962. Blue on multicolor underprint. Banco Central at upper center. Back: Portrait of F. Hernandez Córdoba at center. Printer: ABNC. 1.00 7.50

108 5 Córdobas VF UNC
D.1962. Green on multicolor underprint. C. Nicarao at upper center. Back: Portrait of F. Hernandez Córdoba at center. Printer: ABNC.
a. Issued note. 3.00 15.00
s. Specimen. — 125.

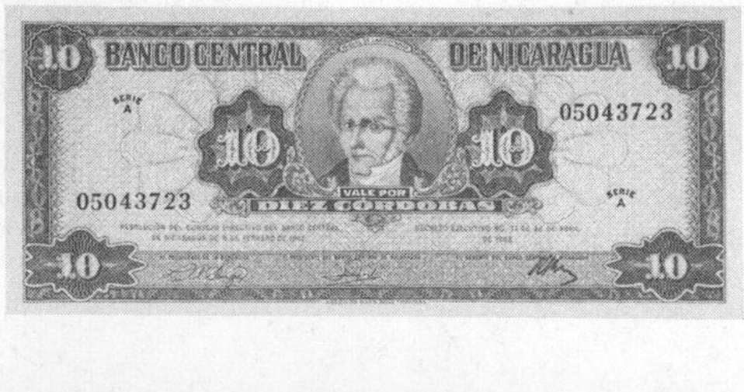

109 10 Córdobas VF UNC
D.1962. Red on multicolor underprint. Portrait of M. de Larreynaga at upper center. Back: Portrait of F. Hernandez Córdoba at center. Printer: ABNC.
a. Issued note. 5.00 22.50
s. Specimen. — —

110 20 Córdobas VF UNC
D.1962. Orange-brown on multicolor underprint. Portrait of T. Martinez at upper center. Back: Portrait of F. Hernandez Córdoba at center. Printer: ABNC. 10.00 45.00

111 50 Córdobas VF UNC
D.1962. Purple on multicolor underprint. Portrait of M. Jerez at upper center. Back: Portrait of F. Hernandez Córdoba at center. Printer: ABNC. 25.00 85.00

112 100 Córdobas VF UNC
D.1962. Red-brown on multicolor underprint. Portrait of J. D. Estrada at upper center. Back: Portrait of F. Hernandez Córdoba at center. Printer: ABNC. 12.50 60.00

113 500 Córdobas
D.1962. Black on multicolor underprint. Portrait of R. Dario at upper center. Back: Portrait of F. Hernandez Córdoba at center. Printer: ABNC.
a. Issued note. 175. 425.
s. Specimen. — 500.

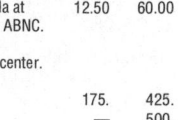

114 1000 Córdobas — VF / UNC

D.1962. Brown on multicolor underprint. Portrait of A. Somoza at upper center. Back: Portrait of F. Hernandez Córdoba at center. Printer: ABNC.

	VF	UNC
a. Issued note.	200.	550.
s. Specimen.	—	500.

DECRETO 25.5.1968

115 1 Córdoba — VF / UNC

D.1968. Blue on multicolor underprint. Banco Central at upper center. Series B. Back: Portrait of F. Hernandez Córdoba. Printer: TDLR.

	VF	UNC
a. With 3 signatures.	1.00	6.00
b. Pres. A. Somoza hand signed at left.	—	—

116 5 Córdobas — VF / UNC

D.1968. Green on multicolor underprint. C. Nicarao at upper center. Series B. Back: Portrait of F. Hernandez Córdoba. Printer: TDLR.

	VF	UNC
a. Issued note.	3.00	15.00
s. Specimen. Without right hand signature. Overprint: *MUESTRA SIN VALOR* twice.	—	—

117 10 Córdobas — VF / UNC

D.1968. Red on multicolor underprint. Portrait of M. de Larreynaga at upper center. Series B. Back: Portrait of F. Hernandez Córdoba. Printer: TDLR.

	VF	UNC
a. Issued note.	4.00	22.50
s. Specimen. Without right hand signature. Overprint: *MUESTRA SIN VALOR* twice.	—	—

118 20 Córdobas

D.1968. Orange-brown on multicolor underprint. Portrait of T. Martinez at upper center. Series B. Back: Portrait of F. Hernandez Córdoba. Printer: TDLR.

	VF	UNC
a. With 3 signatures.	5.00	30.00
b. Without right hand signature.	—	—
s. Specimen. Without right hand signature. Overprint: *MUESTRA SIN VALOR* twice.	—	—

119 50 Córdobas

D.1968. Purple on multicolor underprint. Portrait of M. Jerez at upper center. Series B. Back: Portrait of F. Hernandez Córdoba. Printer: TDLR.

	VF	UNC
a. With 3 signatures.	12.50	50.00
b. Without right hand signature.	—	—

120 100 Córdobas

D.1968. Red-brown on multicolor underprint. Portrait of J. D. Estrada at upper center. Series B. Back: Portrait of F. Hernandez Córdoba. Printer: TDLR.

	VF	UNC
a. With 3 signatures.	17.50	75.00
b. Without right hand signature.	—	—

DECRETO 27.4.1972

121 2 Córdobas — VF / UNC

D.1972. Olive-green on multicolor underprint. Banco Central at right. Series C. Back: Furrows at left. Printer: TDLR.

	VF	UNC
a. 3 signatures.	1.00	6.00
b. 2 signatures (without right hand signature).	—	400.
s. As a. Specimen.	—	35.00

122 5 Córdobas — VF 1.50 / UNC 10.00

D.1972. Dark green on multicolor underprint. C. Nicarao standing at right with bow. Series C. Back: Fruitseller at left. Printer: TDLR.

123 10 Córdobas — VF 3.00 / UNC 12.50

D.1972. Red on multicolor underprint. A. Castro standing at right atop rocks. Series C. Back: Hacienda at left Printer: TDLR.

124 20 Córdobas — VF 4.00 / UNC 17.50

D.1972. Orange-brown on multicolor underprint. R. Herrera igniting cannon at right. Series C. Back: Signing ceremony of abrogation of Chamorro-Bryan Treaty of 1912, Somoza at center. Printer: TDLR.

125 50 Córdobas — VF: 30.00 — UNC: 85.00

D.1972. Purple on multicolor underprint. M. Jerez at right. Series C. Back: Cows at left. Printer: TDLR.

126 100 Córdobas — VF: 2.50 — UNC: 10.00

D.1972. Violet on multicolor underprint. J. Dolores Estrada at right. Series C. Back: National flower at left. Printer: TDLR.

127 500 Córdobas — VF: 35.00 — UNC: 115.

D.1972. Black on multicolor underprint. R. Darío at right. Series C. Back: National Theater at left. Printer: TDLR.

128 1000 Córdobas — VF — UNC

D.1972. Brown on multicolor underprint. A. Somoza G. at right. Series C. Back: View of Managua at left. Printer: TDLR.

- a. 3 signatures. — VF: 40.00 — UNC: 135.
- b. 2 signatures (without right hand signature). — VF: — — UNC: 90.00

DECRETO 20.2.1978

129 20 Córdobas — VF: 1.50 — UNC: 7.50

D.1978. Orange-brown on multicolor underprint. R. Herrera igniting cannon at right. Series D. Back: Signing ceremony of abrogation of Chamorro-Bryan Treaty of 1912, Somoza at center. Printer: TDLR.

130 50 Córdobas — VF: 2.50 — UNC: 9.00

D.1978. Purple on multicolor underprint. M. Jerez at right. Series D. Back: Cows at left. Printer: TDLR.

DECRETO 16.8.1979

Series E, first issue.

131 50 Córdobas — VF: 1.50 — UNC: 5.00

D.1979. Purple on multicolor underprint. Comdt. C. F. Amador at right. Series E. Back: Liberation of 19.7.1979. Printer: TDLR. With square outer frame. Engraved.

132 100 Córdobas — VF: 1.50 — UNC: 5.00

D.1979. Dark brown on multicolor underprint. J. Dolores Estrada at right. Series E. Back: National flower at left. Printer: TDLR. With square outer frame. Engraved.

133 **500 Córdobas** | VF 2.50 | UNC 7.00
D.1979. Deep blue on multicolor underprint. R. Dario at right. Series E. Back: National Theater at left. Printer: TDLR. With square outer frame. Engraved.

1979 ND Second Issue

Series E, second issue.

134 **10 Córdobas** | VF .75 | UNC 4.00
D.1979. Red on multicolor underprint. A. Castro standing atop rocks at right. Series E. Back: Miners. Watermark: Sandino. Printer: TDLR. Underprint to paper edge. Lithographed.

135 **20 Córdobas** | VF 1.00 | UNC 5.00
D.1979. Orange-brown on multicolor underprint. Comdt. G. P. Ordoñez at right. Series E. Back: Marching troops. Watermark: Sandino. Printer: TDLR. Underprint to paper edge. Lithographed.

136 **50 Córdobas** | VF 1.00 | UNC 7.50
D.1979. Purple on multicolor underprint. Comdt. C. F. Amador at right. Series E. Back: Liberation of 19.7.1979. Watermark: Sandino. Printer: TDLR. Underprint to paper edge. Lithographed.

137 **100 Córdobas** | VF 1.00 | UNC 10.00
D.1979. Brown on multicolor underprint. J. D. Estrada at right. Series E. Signature varieties. Back: Flower. Watermark: Sandino. Printer: TDLR. Underprint to paper edge. Lithographed.

138 **500 Córdobas** | VF 2.50 | UNC 17.50
D.1979. Deep olive-green on multicolor underprint. R. Darío at right. Series E. Signature varieties. Back: Teatro Popular at left. Watermark: Sandino. Printer: TDLR. Underprint to paper edge. Engraved.

139 **1000 Córdobas** | VF 15.00 | UNC 45.00
D.1979. Blue-gray on multicolor underprint. General A. C. Sandino at right. Series E. Signature varieties. Back: Hut (Sandino's birthplace). Watermark: Sandino. Printer: TDLR. Underprint to paper edge. Engraved.

Resolution of 6.8.1984

140 **50 Córdobas** | VF .50 | UNC 2.00
L.1984 (1985). Purple on multicolor underprint. Comdt. C. F. Amador at right. Series F. Back: Liberation of 19.7.1979. Watermark: Sandino. Printer: TDLR.

141 **100 Córdobas** | VF 1.00 | UNC 3.00
L.1984 (1985). Brown on multicolor underprint. J. D. Estrada at right. Series F. Signature varieties. Back: Flower. Watermark: Sandino. Printer: TDLR.

142 **500 Córdobas** — VF | UNC

L.1984 (1985). Deep olive-green on multicolor underprint. R. Dario at right. Series F. Back: Teatro Popular at left. Watermark: Sandino. Printer: TDLR. 156x67mm. — 1.00 | 5.00

143 **1000 Córdobas**

L.1984 (1985). Blue-gray on multicolor underprint. General A. C. Sandino at right. Series F. Back: Hut (Sandino's birthplace). Watermark: Sandino. Printer: TDLR. — 2.00 | 9.00

Resolution of 11.6.1985

Replacement notes: Serial # prefix *ZA; ZB.*

144 **500 Córdobas** — VF | UNC

L.1985 (1987). Deep olive-green on multicolor underprint. R. Dario at right. Series G. Back: Teatro Popular at left. Watermark: Sandino. Printer: TDLR. Lithographed. 156x67mm. — 1.00 | 5.00

145 **1000 Córdobas** — VF | UNC

L.1985 (1987). Dark gray on multicolor underprint. General A. C. sandino at right. Series G. Back: Hut (Sandino's birthplace). Watermark: Sandino. Printer: TDLR.

a. Engraved. — 1.00 | 5.00

b. Lithographed. — .50 | 3.50

146 **5000 Córdobas** — VF | UNC

L.1985 (1987). Brown, orange and black on multicolor underprint. Map at upper center, General B. Zeledon at right. Series G. Back: National Assembly building. Watermark: Sandino. Printer: TDLR. — 1.00 | 7.50

A.P.E. del 26 Oct.

1987 ND Provisional Issue

147 **20,000 Córdobas on 20 Córdobas** — VF | UNC

D.1987 (1987). Orange-brown on multicolor underprint. Comdt. G. P. OrdoÒez at right. Overprint on unissued 20 Cordobas Series F. Back: Marching troops. Overprint: Black new denomination on face and back. Watermark: Sandino. Printer: TDLR. — .75 | 5.00

148 **50,000 Córdobas on 50 Córdobas** — VF | UNC

D.1987 (1987). Purple on multicolor underprint. Comdt C. F. Amador at right. Back: Liberation of 19.7.1979. Overprint: Black new denomination on face and back. Watermark: Sandino. Printer: TDLR. — .75 | 7.50

149 **100,000 Córdobas on 500 Córdobas** — VF | UNC

D.1987 (1987). Deep olive-green on multicolor underprint. R. Dario at right. Back: Teatro Popular at left. Overprint: Black new denomination on face and back. Watermark: Sandino. Printer: TDLR. Lithographed. — .75 | 10.00

150 **500,000 Córdobas on 1000 Córdobas** — VF | UNC

D.1987 (1987). Dark gray on multicolor underprint. General A. C. Sandino at right. Back: Hut (Sandino's birthplace). Overprint: Black new denomination on face and back. Watermark: Sandino. Printer: TDLR. Lithographed. (Not issued). — 2.50 | 12.50

1985 (1988) Issue

#151-156 Replacement notes: Serial # prefix *ZA; ZB*.

151 10 Córdobas — VF | UNC

1985 (1988). Green and olive on multicolor underprint. Comdt. C. F. Amador at right. Back: Troop formation marching at left. Watermark: Sandino. — 1.00 | 3.50

152 20 Córdobas — VF | UNC

1985 (1988). Blue-black and blue on multicolor underprint. Comdt. G. P. Ordoñez at right. Back: Demonstration for agrarian reform at left. Watermark: Sandino. — 1.00 | 5.00

153 50 Córdobas — VF | UNC

1985 (1988). Brown and dark red on multicolor underprint. General J. D. Estrada at right. Back: Medical clinic scene at left. Watermark: Sandino. — 1.25 | 7.50

154 100 Córdobas — VF | UNC

1985 (1988). Deep blue, blue and gray on multicolor underprint. R. Lopez Perez at right. Back: State council building at left. Watermark: Sandino. — 1.25 | 10.00

155 500 Córdobas — VF | UNC

1985 (1988). Purple, blue and brown on multicolor underprint. R. Dario at right. Back: Classroom with students at left. Watermark: Sandino. UV: fibers fluoresce blue. — 1.25 | 15.00

156 1000 Córdobas — VF | UNC

1985 (1988). Brown on multicolor underprint. General A. C. Sandino at right. Back: Liberation of 19.7.1979. Watermark: Sandino.

- a. Engraved with watermark. Serial # prefix FA. — 1.25 | 20.00
- b. Lithographed without watermark. Serial # prefix FC. — .75 | 4.00

1988-89 ND Provisional Issue

157 5000 Córdobas — VF | UNC

ND (1988). Brown, orange and black on multicolor underprint. Map at upper center, Gen. Zeledon at right with black overprint elements. Overprint: signature and title: *PRIMER VICE PRESIDENTE BANCO CENTRAL DE NICARAGUA* at left, two lines of text at lower c Back: National Assembly building. Overprint: Black guilloche at left and right on back. — .50 | 2.50

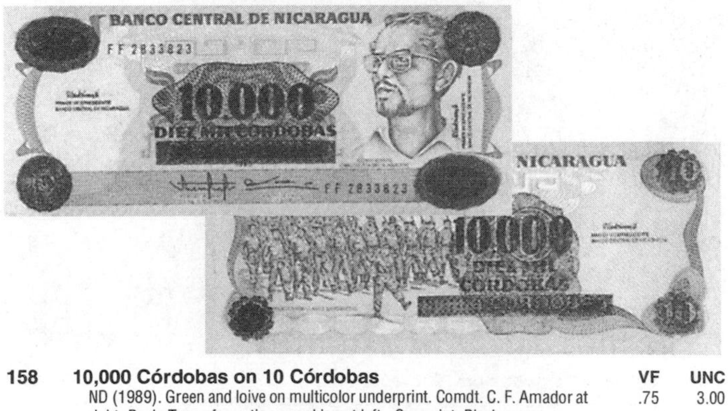

158 10,000 Córdobas on 10 Córdobas — VF | UNC

ND (1989). Green and loive on multicolor underprint. Comdt. C. F. Amador at right. Back: Troop formation marching at left. Overprint: Black new denomination on face and back of earlier notes. Watermark: Sandino. — .75 | 3.00

159 **100,000 Córdobas on 100 Córdobas** | VF 1.25 | UNC 6.00

ND (1989). Deep blue, blue and gray on multicolor underprint. R. Lopez Perez at right. Back: State council building at left. Overprint: Black new denomination on face and back of earlier notes. Watermark: Sandino.

1989 ND Emergency Issue

160 **20,000 Córdobas** | VF 1.00 | UNC 4.50

ND (1989). Black on blue, yellow and multicolor underprint. Comdt. Cleto Ordoñez at right, grid map of Nicaragua at center. Back: Church of San Francisco Granada at left, grid map of Nicaragua at center. Watermark: Sandino.

161 **50,000 Córdobas** | VF 1.00 | UNC 4.00

ND (1989). Brown on purple, orange and multicolor underprint. General J. D. Estrada at right, grid map of Nicaragua at center. Back: Hacienda San Jacinto at left, grid map of Nicaragua at center. Watermark: Sandino.

1990 ND Provisional Issue

162 **200,000 Córdobas on 1000 Córdobas** | VF .40 | UNC 1.75

ND (1990). Brown on multicolor underprint. General A. C. Sandino at right. Serial number prefix FC. Back: Liberation of 19.7.1979. Overprint: Black new denomination on face and back of earlier notes. Lithographed without watermark.

163 **500,000 Córdobas on 20 Córdobas** | VF 1.00 | UNC 3.50

ND (1990). Blue-black and blue on multicolor underprint. Comdt. G. P. Ordoñez at right. Back: Demonstration for agrarian reform at left. Overprint: Black new denomination on face and back of earlier notes.

164 **1 Million Córdobas on 1000 Córdobas** | VF 1.00 | UNC 3.50

ND (1990). Brown on multicolor underprint. General A. C. Sandino at right. Serial number prefix FC. Back: Liberation of 19.7.1979. Overprint: Black new denomination on face and back of earlier notes. Lithographed without watermark.

1990 ND Emergency Issue

165 **5 Million Córdobas** | VF .50 | UNC 2.00

ND (1990). Purple and orange on red and multicolor underprint. Comdt. Cleto Ordoñez at right, grid map of Nicaragua at center. Back: Church of San Francisco Granada at left, grid map of Nicaragua at center. Watermark: Sandino head, repeated.

166 **10 Million Córdobas** | VF .75 | UNC 2.50

ND (1990). Purple and lilac on blue and multicolor underprint. General J. D. Estrada at right, grid map of Nicaragua at center. Back: Hacienda San Jacinto at left, grid map of Nicaragua at center. Watermark: Sandino head, repeated.

1990; 1991-92 ND Issues

#173-177, 2 sign. varieties.

167 **1 Centavo** | VF .05 | UNC .15

ND (1991). Purple on pale green and multicolor underprint. F. H. Córdoba at right. 2 signature varieties. Back: Arms at left, flower at right. Printer: Harrison. UV: fibers and value 1 fluoresce yellow.

168 5 Centavos — VF | UNC

ND (1991). Red-violet on pale green and multicolor underprint. F. H. Córdoba at right. 2 signature varieties. Back: Arms at left, flower at right. Printer: Harrison. UV: fibers and value 5 fluoresce yellow.

	VF	UNC
a. Issued note.	.05	.20
s. Specimen.	—	100.

169 10 Centavos — VF | UNC

ND (1991). Olive-green on light green and multicolor underprint. F. H. Córdoba at right. 2 signature varieties. Back: Arms at left, flower at right. Printer: Harrison. UV: fibers and value 10 fluoresce yellow.

	VF	UNC
a. Issued note.	.10	.25
b. Specimen.	—	100.

170 25 Centavos — VF | UNC

ND (1991). Blue on pale green and multicolor underprint. F. H. Córdoba at right. 2 signature varieties. Back: Arms at left, flower at right. Printer: Harrison. UV: fibers and value 25 fluoresce yellow.

	VF	UNC
a. Issued note.	—	.25
s. Specimen.	—	100.

171 1/2 Córdoba — VF FV | UNC .50

ND (1991). Brown and green on multicolor underprint. F. H. de Córdoba at left, plant at right. Back: Green. Arms at center. Printer: CBNC. UV: right design and value 1/2 fluoresce green. Back center design and legends green. 156x67mm.

172 1/2 Córdoba — VF FV | UNC .50

ND (1992). F. H. de Córdoba at left, plant at right. Back: Green. Arms at left, national flower at right. Printer: CBNC. UV: right design and valyue 1/2 fluoresce green; fibers red, yellow and green. Back background legend green. 156x67mm.

173 1 Córdoba — VF FV | UNC 1.00

1990. Blue on purple and multicolor underprint. Sunrise over field of maize at left, F. H. Córdoba at right. 2 signature varieties. Back: Green and multicolor. Arms at center. Printer: TDLR. UV: left and right designs fluoresce yellow. Maize and sun yellow and green, Serial # and series green. Back corners green. 156x67mm.

174 5 Córdobas — VF FV | UNC 2.00

ND (1991). Red-violet and deep olive-green on multicolor underprint. Indian Chief Diriangén at left, sorghum plants at right. 2 signature varieties. Back: Green. R. Herrera firing cannon at British warship. Printer: CBNC. 156x67mm.

175 10 Córdobas — VF FV | UNC 3.50

1990. Green on blue and multicolor underprint. Sunrise over rice field at left, M. de Larreynaga at right. 2 signature varieties. Back: Dark green and multicolor. Arms at center. Printer: TDLR. 156x67mm.

176 20 Córdobas VF UNC
ND (1990). Pale red-orange and dark brown on multicolor underprint. Sandino at left, coffee plant at right. Two signature varieties. Back: Green. E. Mongalo at left, fire in the Mesón de Rivas (1854) at center. Printer: CBNC. 156x67mm. FV 6.00

177 50 Córdobas VF UNC
ND (1991). Purple and violet on multicolor underprint. Dr. P. J. Chamorro at left, banana plants at right. Series A: three signatures; Series B. 2 signature varieties. Back: Green. Toppling of Somoza's statue and scene at polling place. Printer: CBNC. 156x67mm. FV 12.50

178 100 Córdobas VF UNC
1990. Blue and red on multicolor underprint. Sunrise over cotton field at left, R. Darío at right. Three signatures. Series A. Back: Green and multicolor. Arms at center. Printer: TDLR. 156x67mm. FV 25.00

178A 500 Córdobas VF UNC
1991. Brown and red on multicolor underprint. Estrada at right, cattle and sunrise at left. Back: Arms at center. Printer: H&S. 156x67mm.
a. Issued note. FV 50.00
s. Specimen. — 175.

178B 1000 Córdobas VF UNC
1991. Purple and brown on multicolor underprint. Coffee plants at left, peace demonstration at right. Back: Arms at center Printer: H&S. 156x67mm.
a. Issued note. FV 90.00
s. Specimen. — 200.

1992-96 Issue

179 1 Córdoba VF UNC
1995. Blue on purple and multicolor underprint. Sunrise over field of maize at left, F. H. Córdoba at right. 2 signature varieties. Series B. Back: Arms at center. Printer: BABN. 156x67mm. FV 1.00

180 5 Córdobas VF UNC
1995. Red, deep olive-green and brown on multicolor underprint. Indian Chief Diriangén at left, sorghum plants at right. 2 signature varieties. Back: R. Herrera firing cannon at British warship. Printer: F-CO. 156x67mm. FV 1.75

181 10 Córdobas
1996. Green on blue and mlticolor underprint. Sunrise over rice field at left, M. de Larreynaga at right. 2 signature varieties. Back: Arms at center. Printer: G&D. 156x67mm. FV 3.00

182 20 Córdobas VF UNC
1995. Pale red-orange and dark brown on multicolor underprint. Sandino at left, coffee plant at right. 2 signature varieties. Back: E. Mongalo at left, fire in the Mesón de Rivas (1854) at center. Printer: F-CO. 156x67mm. FV 5.00

183 50 Córdobas VF UNC
1995. Purple and brown on multicolor underprint. Dr. P. J. Chamorro at left, banana plants at right. Series A. 3 signatures; Series B. 2 signatures. Back: Arms at center. Printer: F-CO. 156x67mm. FV 10.00

184 100 Córdobas VF UNC
1992. Blue and red multicolor underprint. Sunrise over cotton field at left, R. Darío at right. 2 signatures. Series B. Back: Arms at center. 156x67mm. FV 22.50

1997 Issue

		VF	UNC
185	**20 Córdobas** 1997. Orange-brown, green and multicolor. J. Santos Zelaya at right. Series C. Back: Arms at center. Printer: TDLR. 156x67mm.	FV	6.00

		VF	UNC
187	**100 Córdobas** 1997. Blue and red on multicolor underprint. Sunrise over cotton field at left, R. Darío at right. 2 signatures. Series C. Back: Arms at center. Printer: TDLR. 156x67mm.	FV	17.50

1999 Issue

		VF	UNC
188	**10 Córdobas** 1999. Green on blue and multicolor underprint. Sunrise over rice field at left, M. de Larreynaga at right. Series D. Back: Arms at center. Printer: F-CO. 156x67mm.	FV	2.50
189	**20 Córdobas** 1999. Pale red-orange and dark brown on multicolor underprint. Sandino at left, coffee plant at right. Two signature varieties. Back: E. Mongalo at left, fire in the Mesón de Rivas (1854) at center. Printer: F-CO. 156x67mm.	FV	5.00

		VF	UNC
189A	**50 Córdobas** 2001. Purple and brown on multicolor underprint. Dr. P. J. Chamorro at right. Back: Arms at center. Printer: G&D. Denomination added to watermark. Windowed security thread. 156x67mm.		
	a. Issued note.	FV	7.50
	s1. Specimen. Red overprint: *SPECIMEN* on both sides.	—	80.00
	s2. Specimen. Red overprint: *SPECIMEN* on face and *ESPECIMEN* on back.	—	150.

		VF	UNC
190	**100 Córdobas** 1999. Blue and red on multicolor underprint. Sunrise over cotton field at left, R. Darío at right. Two signatures. Series C. Back: Arms at center. With windowed security thread. 156x67mm.	FV	15.00

2002 Issue

		VF	UNC
191	**10 Córdobas** 2002. Green on blue and multicolor underprint. Miguel de Larreynaga at right. Back: Isletas de Granada at left, arms at center. 156x67mm.	FV	3.00

		VF	UNC
192	**20 Córdobas** 2002. Pale red-orange and dark brown on multicolor underprint. José Santos Zelaya at right. Back: Playa del Caribe at left, arms at center. 156x67mm.	FV	5.00

		VF	UNC
193	**50 Córdobas** 2002. Purple and brown on multicolor underprint. Pedro Joaquin Chamorro at right. Back: Castillo de la Inmaculada Concepcion at left, arms at center. 156x67mm.	FV	10.00

194 **100 Córdobas** | VF | UNC
2002. Blue and red on multicolor underprint. Rubén Darío at right. Back: Teatro Nacional Rubén Darío at left, arms at center. 156x67mm. | FV | 15.00

195 **500 Córdobas** | VF | UNC
2002. Brown and red on multicolor underprint. José Dolores Estrada at right. Back: Hacienda San Jacinto at left, arms at center. 156x67mm. | FV | 50.00

2006 Issue

196 **10 Córdobas** | VF | UNC
10.3.2006. Green on multicolor underprint. Miguel de Larreynaga at right. Back: Isletas de Granada. 156x67mm. | FV | 2.00

197 **20 Córdobas** | VF | UNC
10.3.2006. Orange and brown on light green underprint. José Santos Zelaya at right. Back: Rlaya del Caribe. Denomination added to watermark. 156x67mm. | FV | 4.00

198 **50 Córdobas** | VF | UNC
10.3.2006. Purple on yellow underprint. Pedro Joaquin Chamorro at right. Back: Castillo des la Inmaculada Conception. Denomination added to watermark. 156x67mm. | FV | 9.00

199 **100 Córdobas** | VF | UNC
10.3.2006. Blue on light blue underprint. Rubén Dario at right. Back: Teatro Nacional Rubén Dario. Golden security ink band added. 156x67mm. | FV | 15.00

200 **500 Córdobas**
10.3.2006. Rose and brown on multicolor underprint. José Dolores Estrada at right, wide security foil at right. Back: Hacienda San Jacinto. 156x67mm. | FV | 70.00

2007 Polymer Issue

201 **10 Córdobas** | VF | UNC
L. 12.9.2007 (2012). Green and light blue on multicolor underprint. Castillo Inmaculada Concepción in San Juan at right center. Back: Hacienda San Jacinto in Managua. Polymer plastic. 131x67mm. | FV | 2.00

202 **20 Córdobas** | VF | UNC
L. 12.9.2007 (2012) Brown, green and multicolor Costa Caribe (native hut) at center. Back: *Palo de Mayo,* group of women dancing. 136x67mm. | FV | 4.00

203 **50 Córdobas** | VF | UNC
L. 12.9.2007 (2012). Black and purple on multicolor underprint. Four vases in a bowl. Back: Cañon de Somoto. Watermark: Pottery and 50. 140x67mm. | FV | 9.00

204 **100 Córdobas** | VF | UNC
L. 12.9.2007 (2012). Blue, green and multicolor. Monumento a Rubén Darío at center. Back: Cathedral de León at center. 146x67mm. | FV | 15.00

205 **200 Córdobas** | VF | UNC
L. 12.9.2007 (2012). Olive, brown and multicolor. Bailes Folklóricos at center. Back: Guardabarranco bird. Ometepe island. Polymer plastic. 151x67mm. | FV | 30.00

206 **500 Córdobas** | VF | UNC
L. 12.9.2007 (2012). Red and orange on multicolor underprint. House where Sandino was born. Back: Line art and statues at center. Watermark: Sandino and 500. 156x67mm. | FV | 70.00

2011 Commemorative Issue

207 **50 Córdobas** | VF | UNC
1.1.2011. Black and purple on multicolor underprint. Central Bank building. Back: Canon de Somoto. | FV | 9.00

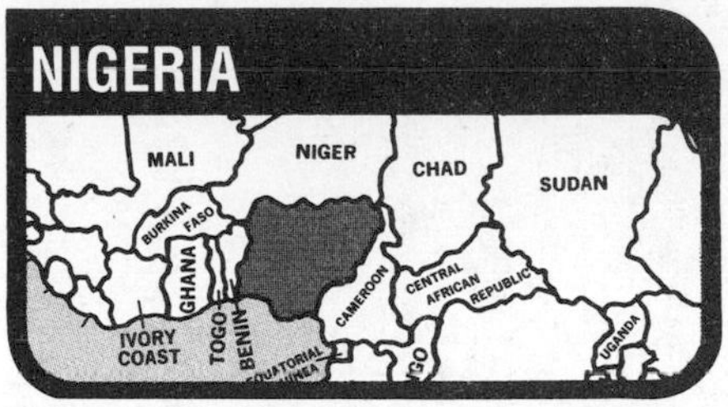

The Federal Republic of Nigeria, situated on the Atlantic coast of Africa between Benin and Cameroon, has an area of 356,667 sq. mi. (923,768 sq. km.) and a population of 128.79 million. Capital: Abuja. The economy is d on petroleum and agriculture. Crude oil, cocoa, tobacco and tin are exported.

British influence and control over what would become Nigeria and Africa's most populous country grew through the 19th century. A series of constitutions after World War II granted Nigeria greater autonomy; independence came in 1960. Following nearly 16 years of military rule, a new constitution was adopted in 1999, and a peaceful transition to civilian government was completed. The government continues to face the daunting task of reforming a petroleum-d economy, whose revenues have been squandered through corruption and mismanagement, and institutionalizing democracy. In addition, Nigeria continues to experience longstanding ethnic and religious tensions. Although both the 2003 and 2007 presidential elections were marred by significant irregularities and violence, Nigeria is currently experiencing its longest period of civilian rule since independence. The general elections of April 2007 marked the first civilian-to-civilian transfer of power in the country's history.

RULERS:
British to 1963

MONETARY SYSTEM:
1 Shilling = 12 Pence
1 Pound = 20 Shillings to 1973
1 Naira (10 Shillings) = 100 Kobo, 1973-

SIGNATURE VARIETIES					
	GOVERNOR	CHIEF OF BANKING OPERATIONS		GOVERNOR	CHIEF OF BANKING OPERATIONS
1			2		
3			4		DIRECTOR OF DOMESTIC OPERATIONS
5			6		
	GOVERNOR	DIRECTOR OF CURRENCY OPERATIONS			DIRECTOR OF CURRENCY OPERATIONS
7			8		
9			10		
11			12		
13			14		

Federal Republic of Nigeria

Central Bank of Nigeria

1967 ND Issue

Pound System

6 **5 Shillings** | VF | UNC
ND (1967). Lilac and blue. Bank building at left. Back: Lilac. Log cutting. Watermark: Lion's head. | 20.00 | 140.

7 **10 Shillings**
ND (1967). Green and brown. Bank building at left. Back: Green. Stacking grain sacks. Watermark: Lion's head. | 35.00 | 200.

		VF	UNC
8	**1 Pound** ND (1967). Red and dark brown. Bank building at left. Back: Red. Man beating cluster from date palm at right. Watermark: Lion's head.	2.00	8.00
9	**5 Pounds** ND (1967). Blue-gray and blue-green on multicolor underprint. Bank building at left. Back: Blue-gray. Food preparation. Watermark: Lion's head.	30.00	350.

1968 ND Issue

		VF	UNC
10	**5 Shillings** ND (1968). Green and orange on multicolor underprint. Bank building at left. Back: Green. Log cutting. Watermark: Lion's head.		
	a. Right signature title: *GENERAL MANAGER.*	15.00	150.
	b. Right signature title: *CHIEF OF BANKING OPERATIONS.*	25.00	200.
	s. As a. Specimen.	—	25.00
11	**10 Shillings** ND (1968). Blue and black on multicolor underprint. Bank building at left. Back: Blue. Stacking grain sacks. Watermark: Lion's head.		
	a. Right signature title: *GENERAL MANAGER.*	25.00	200.
	b. Right signature title: *CHIEF OF BANKING OPERATIONS.*	35.00	325.
	s. As a. Specimen.	—	25.00

		VF	UNC
12	**1 Pound** ND (1968). Olive-brown and purple on multicolor underprint. Bank building at left. Back: Olive-brown. Man beating cluster from date palm at right. Watermark: Lion's head.		
	a. Right signature title: *GENERAL MANAGER.*	25.00	200.
	b. Right signature title: *CHIEF OF BANKING OPERATIONS.*	35.00	325.
	s. As a. Specimen.	—	25.00

		VF	UNC
13	**5 Pounds** ND (1968). Red-brown and blue on multicolor underprint. Bank building at left. Back: Red-brown. Food preparation. Watermark: Lion's head.		
	a. Right signature title: *GENERAL MANAGER.*	75.00	500.
	b. Right signature title: *CHIEF OF BANKING OPERATIONS.*	100.	550.
	s. As a. Specimen.	—	60.00

1973; 1977 ND Issue

 # 14-17 Naira System. Replacement notes: Serial # prefix DZ/.

		VF	UNC
14	**50 Kobo** ND (1973-78). Blue and purple on multicolor underprint. Bank building at left center. Back: Brown. Logging at right. Watermark: Heraldic eagle.		
	a. Signature 1.	4.00	8.00
	b. Signature 2.	5.00	35.00
	c. Signature 3.	2.00	15.00
	d. Signature 4.	2.00	15.00
	e. Signature 5.	2.00	15.00
	f. Signature 6.	1.75	10.00
	g. Signature 7.	FV	1.50
	h. Signature 8.	FV	1.50
	j. Signature 9.	FV	1.50

		VF	UNC
15	**1 Naira** ND (1973-78). Red and brown on multicolor underprint. Bank building at left center. Back: Red. Stacking grain sacks. Watermark: Heraldic eagle.		
	a. Signature 1.	5.00	12.50
	b. Signature 2.	4.00	12.50
	c. Signature 3.	4.00	12.50
	d. Signature 4.	17.50	50.00

16 — 5 Naira

ND (1973-78). Blue-gray and olive-green on multicolor underprint. Bank building at left center. Back: Blue-gray. Man beating cluster from date palm at right. Watermark: Heraldic eagle.

	VF	UNC
a. Signature 1.	15.00	70.00
b. Signature 2.	10.00	50.00
c. Signature 3.	60.00	275.
d. Signature 4.	75.00	325.

17 — 10 Naira

ND (1973-78). Carmine and dark blue on multicolor underprint. Bank building at left center. Back: Carmin. Dam at center. Watermark: Heraldic eagle.

	VF	UNC
a. Signature 1.	35.00	110.
b. Signature 2.	22.50	85.00
c. Signature 3.	125.	400.
d. Signature 4.	150.	475.

18 — 20 Naira

ND (1977-84). Yellow-green and black on red and multicolor underprint. General M. Muhammed at left. Back: Arms at center right.

	VF	UNC
a. Signature 2.	100.	325.
b. Signature 3.	60.00	200.
c. Signature 4.	20.00	65.00
d. Signature 5.	15.00	45.00
e. Signature 6.	10.00	35.00

1979 ND Issue

19 — 1 Naira

ND (1979-84). Red on orange and multicolor underprint. H. Macaulay at left. Signature titles: *GOVERNOR* and *DIRECTOR OF DOMESTIC OPERATIONS*. Back: Mask at center right. Watermark: Heraldic eagle.

	VF	UNC
a. Signature 4.	2.00	7.50
b. Signature 5.	1.00	5.00
c. Signature 6.	.75	3.00

20 — 5 Naira

ND (1979-84). Green on multicolor underprint. Sir AbubakarTafawa Balewa Alaji at left. Signature titles: *GOVERNOR* and *DIRECTOR OF DOMESTIC OPERATIONS*. Back: Dancers at center right. Watermark: Heraldic eagle.

	VF	UNC
a. Signature 4.	5.00	15.00
b. Signature 5.	4.00	12.50
c. Signature 6.	3.00	10.00

21 — 10 Naira

ND (1979-84). Brown, purple and violet on multicolor underprint. A. Ikoku at left. Signature titles: *GOVERNOR* and *DIRECTOR OF DOMESTIC OPERATIONS*. Back: Two women with bowls on heads at center right. Watermark: Heraldic eagle.

	VF	UNC
a. Signature 4.	12.00	30.00
b. Signature 5.	8.00	25.00
c. Signature 6.	20.00	—

1984; 1991 ND Issue

23 — 1 Naira

ND (1984-). Red, violet and green. H. Macaulay at left. Signature titles: *GOVERNOR* and *DIRECTOR OF DOMESTIC OPERATIONS*. Back: Olive and light violet. Mask at center right. Watermark: Heraldic eagle. Reduced size.

	VF	UNC
a. Signature title at right: *DIRECTOR OF DOMESTIC OPERATIONS*. Signature 6.	1.00	3.00
b. Signature title at right: *DIRECTOR OF CURRENCY OPERATIONS*. Signature 7.	FV	2.50
c. Titles as b. Signature 8.	FV	2.50
d. Titles as b. Signature 9.	FV	2.50

24 **5 Naira**

ND (1984-); 2001-5. Purple and brown-violet on multicolor underprint. Sir Abubakar Tafawa Balewa alhaji at left. Back: Dancers at center right. Watermark: Heraldic eagle. Reduced size. UV: fibers fluoresce red and blue; security strip red; value 5, serial #s yellow.

	VF	UNC
a. Signature title at right: *DIRECTOR OF DOMESTIC OPERATIONS.* Signature 6.	2.00	6.50
b. Signature title at right: *DIRECTOR OF CURRENCY OPERATIONS.* Signature 7.	1.00	4.00
c. Titles as b. Signature 8.	FV	2.00
d. Titles as b. Signature 9.	FV	2.00
e. Titles as b. Signature 10.	FV	1.75
f. Titles as b. Signature 11.	FV	1.75
g. 2001; 2002. Signature 11.	FV	1.75
h. 2004; 2005. Signature 12.	FV	1.75
i. 2005. Signature 13.	FV	1.75
j. 2005. Signature 14.	FV	1.75

25 **10 Naira**

ND (1984-); 2001-2005. Red-violet and orange on multicolor underprint. A. Ikoku at left. Back: Red. Two women with bowls on heads at center right. Watermark: Heraldic eagle. Reduced size.

	VF	UNC
a. Signature title at right: *DIRECTOR OF DOMESTIC OPERATIONS.* Signature 6.	2.50	9.00
b. Signature title at right: *DIRECTOR OF CURRENCY OPERATIONS.* Signature 7.	2.50	6.00
c. Titles as b. Signature 8.	FV	3.25
d. Titles as b. Signature 9.	FV	3.00
e. Titles as b. Signature 10.	FV	3.00
f. 2001; 2002; 2003.Titles as b. Signature 11.	FV	3.00
g. 2003; 2004; 2005. Signature 12.	FV	3.00
h. 2005. Signature 13.	FV	3.00
i. 2005. Signature 14.	FV	3.00

26 **20 Naira**

ND (1984-); 2001-05. Dark blue-green, dark green and green on multicolor underprint. General M. Muhammed at left. Back: Arms at center right. Watermark: Heraldic eagle. UV: value 20 and serial #s fluoresce yellow; fibers blue.

	VF	UNC
a. ND (1984). Signature title at right: *DIRECTOR OF DOMESTIC OPERATIONS.* Signature 6.	5.00	20.00
b. ND. Signature title at right: *DIRECTOR OF CURRENCY OPERATIONS.* Signature 7.	FV	6.00
c. ND. Titles as b. Signature 8.	FV	4.00
d. ND. Titles as b. Signature 9.	FV	4.00
e. ND. *Serie* in big letters.Titles as b. Signature 10.	FV	3.00
f. ND. *Serie* in small letters. Titles as b. Signature 10.	FV	3.00
g. 2001; 2002; 2003. Signature 11.	FV	3.00
h. 2003; 2004. Signature 12.	FV	3.00
i. 2005. Signature 13.	FV	3.00
j. 2005. Signature 14.	FV	3.00

27 **50 Naira**

ND (1991-); 2001-2005. Dark blue, black and gray on multicolor underprint. Four busts reflecting varied citizenry at left center. Back: Three farmers in field at center right, arms at lower right. Watermark: Heraldic eagle.

	VF	UNC
a. ND (1991). Signature 8.	3.50	12.50
b. ND. Signature 9.	FV	7.50
c. ND. Signature 10.	FV	6.50
d. 2001. Signature 11.	FV	6.50
e. 2004. Signature 12.	FV	6.50
f. 2005. Signature 14.	FV	6.50

1999-2001 ND Issue

28 **100 Naira**

1999-. Brown and red on multicolor underprint. Chief Obafemi Awolowo at left. Back: Zuma rock.

	VF	UNC
a. 1999. Back with *Abuja Province* identification by rock. Signature 11.	FV	4.00
b. 1999. Back modified without identification. Signature 11.	FV	3.50
c. 2001. Signature 11.	FV	3.50
d. 2004. Signature 12.	FV	3.00
e. 2005. Signature 13.	FV	3.00
f. 2005. Signature 14.	FV	3.00
g. 2006.	FV	2.50
h. 2007.	FV	2.50
i. 2009.	FV	2.50
j. 2010.	FV	2.50
k. 2011.	FV	2.50
l. 2012. Two signature varieties.	FV	2.50

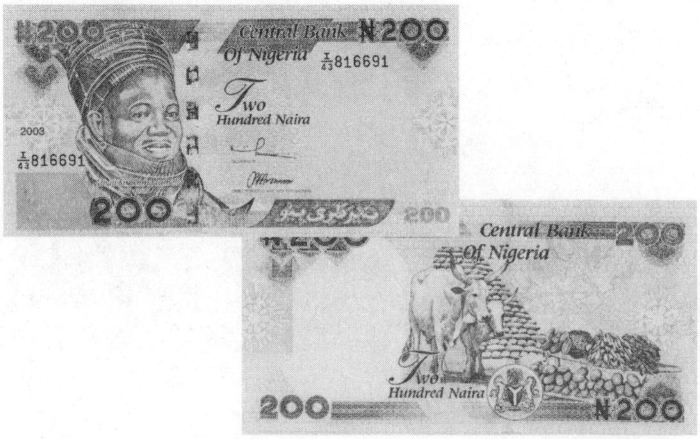

29 200 Naira

2000-. Brown, dark blue and green on multicolor underprint. Sir Ahmadu Bello at left. Back: Two cows and agricultural products. Watermark: Sir Ahmadu Bello. 151x78mm.

	VF	UNC
a. 2000; 2001; 2002. Signature 11.	FV	4.00
b. 2003. Signature 12.	FV	3.50
c. 2004; 2005. *Serie* in big letters. Signature 13.	FV	3.50
d. 2005. *Serie* in small letters. Signature 13.	FV	3.50
e. 2006. Signature 14.	FV	3.50
f. 2007.	FV	3.00
g. 2008.	FV	3.00
h. 2009.	FV	3.00
i. 2010.	FV	3.00
j. 2011.	FV	3.00
k. 2012. Signature 16.	FV	3.00
l. 2012. Signature 17.	FV	3.00

30 500 Naira

2001-. Purple and olive-green on rose and multicolor underprint. Dr. Nnamdi Azikiwe at left. Wide segmented security thread at left center. Back: Oil platform at center right. Watermark: Dr. Nnamdi Azikiwe. 151x78mm.

	VF	UNC
a. 2001; 2002. Signature 11.	FV	7.50
b. 2004. Signature 12.	FV	6.50
c. 2005. Signature 12.	FV	6.50
d. 2005. Signature 13.	FV	6.50
e. 2005. Signature 14.	FV	6.50
f. 2006. Signature 14.	FV	6.50
g. 2007.	FV	6.50
h. 2009.	FV	6.00
i. 2010.	FV	6.00
j. 2011.	FV	6.00

2005-06 Issue

31 2 Naira

	VF	UNC
2006.	FV	1.50

32 5 Naira

2006; 2009. Brown and orange. Alhaji Sir Abubakar Tafawa Salewa at left. Back: Drum players

	VF	UNC
a. 2006.	FV	1.50
b. 2009.	FV	1.50

33 10 Naira

2006-. Red-brown and orange. Aslvan Ikoku at left. Back: Two women carrying baskets on their heads. Polymer plastic.

	VF	UNC
a. 2006.	FV	1.50
b. 2007.	FV	1.25
c. 2008.	FV	1.25
d. 2009. Signatures Chukwuma Soludo and Benjamin Onyido.	FV	1.25
e. 2009. Signatures Lamido Aminu Sanusi and Benjamin Onyido.	FV	1.25
f. 2010. Signatures Lamido Aminu Sanusi and Muhammad Nda.	FV	1.25
g. 2010. Signatures Lamido Aminu Sanusi and Benjamin Onyido.	FV	1.25

34 20 Naira

2006-. Dark green and green. General Murtalla R. Muhammed Back: Potter. Polymer plastic. 121x72mm.

	VF	UNC
a. 2006.	FV	2.00
b. 2007. 7-Digit serial #. Printer: G&D.	FV	1.50
c. 2007. 6-Digit serial #. Printer: Nigeria Security Printing. Matte or Glossy finish.	FV	1.50
d. 2008.	FV	1.00
e. 2009.	FV	1.00
f. 2010.	FV	1.00
g. 2011.	FV	1.00

35 50 Naira

2006-. Slate blue and blue. Four portraits. Signature 14. Back: Fishermen. 121x72mm.

	VF	UNC
a. 2006. Signature 14.	FV	2.50
b. 2007. 7-digit serial #.	FV	2.00
c. 2008. 6-digit serial #.	FV	2.00
d. 2009.	FV	2.00

36 1000 Naira

2005-. Brown, lilac and multicolor underprint. Alhaji Aliyu Mai-Bornu and Dr. Clement Isong at left center. Signature 14. Back: Central Bank building. 151x78mm.

	VF	UNC
a. 2005.	FV	12.50
b. 2006.	FV	10.00
c. 2007.	FV	10.00
d. 2010.	FV	10.00
e. 2012.	FV	10.00

2010 Commemorative Issue

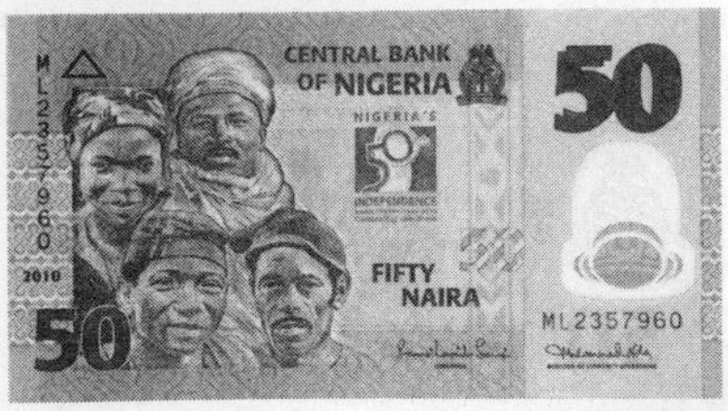

37 **50 Naira** — VF | UNC
2010. Slate blue and blue on multicolor underprint. Four portraits. Back: Fishermen. Overprint: Green square commemorative logo at center. 130x72mm. — FV | 5.00

2009 Polymer Issue

38 **5 Naira** — VF | UNC
2009. Mauve on multicolor underprint. Alhaji Dir Abubakar Tafawa Balewa at left. Back: Four Nkpokiti dancers with drums. 130x72mm. — FV | 1.00

39 **10 Naira** — VF | UNC
2009-. Red on multicolor underprint. Alvan Ikoku at left. Back: Two females carrying bowls on their heads. Watermark: Coat-of-arms and CBN 130x72mm.

	VF	UNC
a. 2009.	FV	2.50
b. 2010.	FV	2.50
c. 2011.	FV	2.50

40 **50 Naira** — VF | UNC
2009-. Blue on multicolor underprint. Four portraits at left. Back: Three fishermen and two fish. Watermark: Coat-of-arms and CBN 130x72mm.

	VF	UNC
a. 2009.	FV	5.00
b. 2011.	FV	5.00

The Democratic Peoples Republic of Korea, situated in in northeastern Asia on the northern half of the Korean peninsula between the Peoples Republic of China and the Republic of Korea, has an area of 46,540 sq. mi. (120,538 sq. km.) and a population of 23.26 million. Capital: Pyongyang. The economy is d on heavy d on heavy industry and agriculture. Metals, minerals and farm produce are exported.

Japan replaced China as the predominant foreign influence in Korea in 1895 and annexed the peninsular country in 1910. Defeat in World War II brought an end to Japanese rule. U.S. troops entered Korea from the south and Soviet forces entered from the north. The Cairo conference (1943) had established that Korea should be "free and independent." The Potsdam conference (1945) set the 38th parallel as the line dividing the occupation forces of the United States and Russia. When Russia refused to permit a U.N. commission designated to supervise reunification elections to enter North Korea, an election was held in South Korea which established the Republic of Korea on Aug. 15, 1948. North Korea held an unsupervised election on Aug. 25, 1948, and on the following day proclaimed the establishment of the Democratic Peoples Republic of Korea.

MONETARY SYSTEM:
1 Won = 100 Chon

Democratic Peoples Republic

Korean Central Bank

1959 Issue

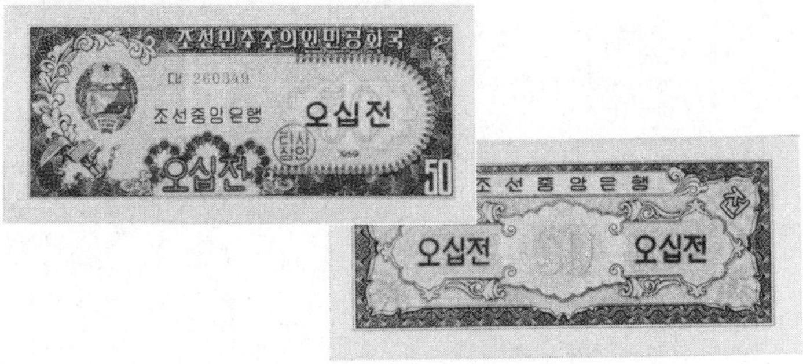

12 **50 Chon** — VF | UNC
1959. Blue on multicolor underprint. Arms at upper left. With watermark. — 2.50 | 8.00

13 **1 Won** — VF | UNC
1959. Red-brown on multicolor underprint. Fishing boat at center. Arms at upper left. With watermark. — 1.75 | 6.00

14 **5 Won** — VF | UNC
1959. Green on multicolor underprint. Large building at center. Arms at upper left. With watermark. — 2.00 | 7.00

15	10 Won	VF	UNC
	1959. Red on multicolor underprint. Fortress gateway at center right. Arms at upper left. Back: Woman picking fruit. With watermark.	2.25	8.00

16	50 Won	VF	UNC
	1959. Purple on multicolor underprint. Bridge and city at center. Arms at upper left. Back: Woman with wheat. With watermark.	3.50	10.00

17	100 Won	VF	UNC
	1959. Green on multicolor underprint. Steam freight train in factory area at center. Arms at upper left. Back: River with cliffs. With watermark.	4.50	15.00

1978 Issue

Note: Circulation of varieties #18-21:

a. For general circulation.

b. For Socialist visitors.

c. For non-Socialist visitors.

d. Replaced a for general circulation.

e. Use not known.

18	1 Won	VF	UNC
	1978. Olive-green on multicolor underprint. Two adults and two children at center, arms at upper left. Back: Purple and multicolor. Soldier at left, woman with flowers at center, woman at right.		
	a. Red and black serial #. No seal on back.	.75	2.50
	b. Black serial #. Green seal at left. on back.	.25	1.25
	c. Red serial #. Red seal at left. on back.	.25	1.25
	d. Red serial #. Large numeral *1* in red guilloche on back.	.25	1.25
	e. Black serial #. Large numeral *1* in blue guilloche on back.	.25	1.25
	s. Specimen.	—	—

19	5 Won	VF	UNC
	1978. Blue-gray on multicolor underprint. Worker with book and gear, and woman with wheat at center, arms at upper left. Back: Mount gumgang.		
	a. Red and black serial #. No seal on back.	.50	1.50
	b. Black serial #. Green seal at left. on back.	.50	1.50
	c. Red serial #. Red seal at left. on back.	.50	1.50
	d. Red serial #. Large numeral *5* in red guilloche on back.	.50	1.50
	e. Black serial #. Large numeral *5* in blue guilloche on back.	.50	1.50
	s. Specimen.	—	—

20	10 Won	VF	UNC
	1978 Brown on multicolor underprint. Winged equestrian statue "Chonllima" at center, arms at upper left. Back: Waterfront factory.		
	a. Red and black serial #. No seal on back.	.50	2.50
	b. Black serial #. Green seal at upper right on back.	.50	2.00
	c. Red serial #. Red seal at upper right on back.	.50	2.00
	d. Red serial #. Large numeral *10* in red guilloche on back.	.50	2.00
	e. Black serial #. Large numeral *10* in blue guilloche on back.	.50	2.00
	s. Specimen.	—	—

21 50 Won

1978. Olive-green on multicolor underprint. Soldier with man holding torch, woman with wheat, man with book at center, arms at upper left. Back: Lake scene.

	VF	UNC
a. Red and black serial #. No seal on back.	.50	3.00
b. Black serial #. Green seal at lower right on back.	.50	2.50
c. Red serial #. Red seal at lower right on back.	.50	2.50
d. Red serial #. Large numeral *50* in red guilloche on back.	.50	2.50
e. Black serial #. Large numeral *50* in blue guilloche on back.	.50	2.50
s. Specimen.	—	—

22 100 Won

1978. Brown on lilac and multicolor underprint. Kim Il Sung at center right, arms at upper left. Red and black serial number. Back: House with trees. No seal.

	VF	UNC
a. Issued note.	1.00	5.00
s. Specimen. Overprint in red on face.	—	200.

1988 "Capitalist Visitor" Issue

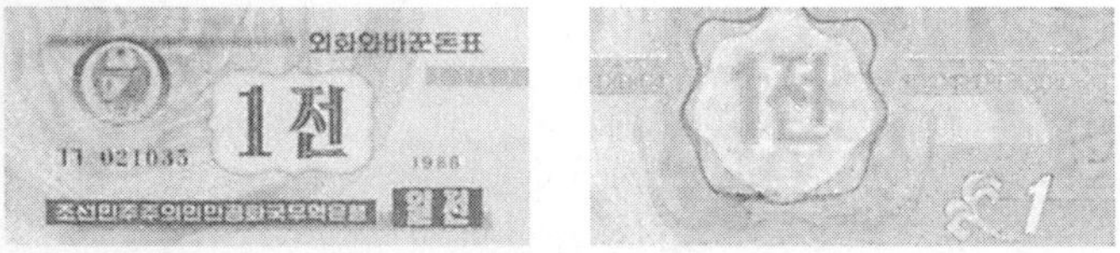

23 1 Chon

	VF	UNC
1988. Blue on purple underprint. Arms at upper left, red serial number. Back: Value.	.20	.40

24 5 Chon

	VF	UNC
1988. Blue on pink underprint. Arms at upper left, red serial number. Back: Value.	.75	1.00

25 10 Chon

	VF	UNC
1988. Blue and black on green-yellow underprint. Arms at upper left, red serial number. Back: Value.	.40	1.00

26 50 Chon

	VF	UNC
1988. Blue on yellow underprint. Arms at upper left, red serial number. Back: Value.	.50	1.00

27 1 Won

	VF	UNC
1988. Dark green on blue and pink underprint. Winged equestrian statue "Chonllima" at center, arms at upper right. Red serial number.	.75	2.50

28 5 Won

	VF	UNC
1988. Dark green on blue and pink underprint. Winged equestrian statue "Chonllima" at center, arms at upper right. Red serial number.	1.50	7.50

29 10 Won

	VF	UNC
1988. Dark green on blue and pink underprint. Winged equestrian statue "Chonllima" at center, arms at upper right. Red serial number.	3.00	12.50

30 50 Won

	VF	UNC
1988. Dark green on blue and pink underprint. Winged equestrian statue "Chonllima" at center, arms at upper right. Red serial number.	8.00	40.00

1988 "Socialist Visitor" Issue

31 1 Chon

	VF	UNC
1988. Red-brown on pink and blue underprint. Arms at upper right. Black serial number. Back: Value.	FV	1.25

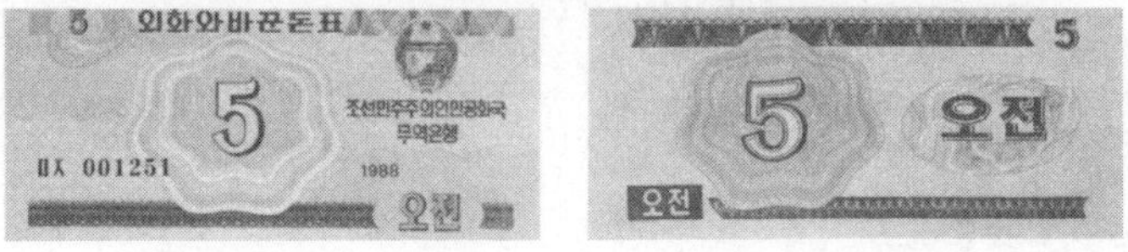

32 5 Chon

	VF	UNC
1988. Purple on pink and blue underprint. Arms at upper right. Black serial number. Back: Value.	FV	1.75

33 **10 Chon** VF UNC
1988. Olive-green on pink and blue underprint. Arms at upper right. Black serial number. Back: Value. FV 2.50

34 **50 Chon** VF UNC
1988. Brown-violet on pink and blue underprint. Arms at upper right. Black serial number. Back: Value. FV 3.00

35 **1 Won** VF UNC
1988. Red on blue and ochre underprint. Temple at center, olive sprig on globe at right, arms at upper right. Black serial number. Back: Olive sprig on globe, value. FV 3.50

36 **5 Won** VF UNC
1988. Red on blue and ochre underprint. Temple at center, olive sprig on globe at right, arms at upper right. Black serial number. Back: Olive sprig on globe, value. FV 12.50

37 **10 Won** VF UNC
1988. Red on blue and ochre underprint. Temple at center, olive sprig on globe at right, arms at upper right. Black serial number. Back: Olive sprig on globe, value. 3.50 15.00

38 **50 Won** VF UNC
1988. Red on blue and ochre underprint. Temple at center, olive sprig on globe at right, rms at upper right. Black serial number. Back: Olive sprig on globe, value. 15.00 60.00

1992; 1998 Issue

39 **1 Won** VF UNC
1992; 1998. Grayish olive-green and olive-brown on multicolor underprint. Young woman with flower basket at center right, arms at upper left. Back: Mount Gumgang. Watermark: Winged equestrian statue "Chonllima".
a. Issued note. 1.00 2.00
s. 1992. Specimen. Red overprint at left face. — 15.00

40 **5 Won**
1992; 1998. Blue-black and deep purple on multicolor underprint. Students at center right with modern building and factory in background, arms at upper left. Back: Palace. Watermark: Winged equestrian statue "Chonllima".
a. Issued note. 1.00 3.00
s. 1998. Specimen. Red overprint at left face. — 12.50

41 **10 Won** VF UNC
1992; 1998. Deep brown and red brown on multicolor underprint. Factory worker, winged equestrian statue "Chonllima" at center, factories in background at right, arms at upper left. Back: Flood gates. Watermark: Winged equestrian statue "Chonllima".
a. Issued note. 1.00 4.00
s. 1992. Specimen. Red overprint at right face. — 15.00

42 **50 Won** VF UNC
1992; 1998. Deep brown and deep olive-brown on multicolor underprint. Monument to five year plan at left, young professionals at center right, arms at upper right. Back: Landscape of pine trees and mountains. Watermark: Monument to five year plan.
a. Issued note. 2.00 5.00
s. 1992. Specimen. Red overprint at left face. — 15.00

43	100 Won	VF	UNC
	1992; 1998. Deep brown and brown-violet on multicolor underprint. Arms at lower left center, Kim Il Sung at right. Back: Rural home at center. Watermark: Arched gateway.		
	a. Issued note.	3.00	7.50
	s. Specimen. Red overprint at left face.	—	35.00

44	500 Won	VF	UNC
	1998. Slate gray on light blue and purple underprint. Assembly Hall. Back: Red and black. Suspension bridge.		
	a. Issued note.	5.00	12.50
	s1. Specimen. Red overprint at left center. Regular serial #s.	—	50.00
	s2. Specimen. Serial # as 000000.	—	50.00

2002 Issue

45	1000 Won	VF	UNC
	2002, 2006. Dark green on multicolor underprint. Arms at lower left center, Kim Il Sung at right. Back: Slate blue on multicolor underprint. Rural home at center. Watermark: Arched gateway.		
	a. 2002.	5.00	10.00
	b. 2006.	5.00	10.00
	s1. Specimen. Red overprint at upper left. Regular serial #.	—	40.00
	s2. Specimen. Serial # as 000000.	—	40.00

46	5000 Won	VF	UNC
	2002. Purple on multicolor underprint. Arms at lower left center, Kim Il Sung at right. Back: Rural home at center.		
	a. Orange *5000* in upper left measures 19x9mm.	10.00	30.00
	b. Orange *5000* in upper left measures 20x10.	10.00	30.00
	s1. Specimen. Red overprint at upper left. Regular serial #.	—	50.00
	s2. Specimen. Serial # as 000000.	—	50.00
	s3. Specimen. Uncut sheet of 20 notes, regular serial #.	—	275.

2002 Commemorative Issue

47	500 Won	VF	UNC
	2002.	FV	17.50

2005 Issue

48	200 Won	VF	UNC
	2005 Green on multicolor underprint. Flower. Back: Large 200.		
	a. Issued note.	FV	12.50
	s. Specimen. Red overprint at left face.	—	22.50

2007 Commemorative Overprint Issue

No.	Denomination / Description	VF	UNC
49	**1 Won** (2007). Grayish olive-green and olive brown on multicolor underprint. As #39. Overprint: Kim Il Sung 95th Birthday	FV	1.00
50	**5 Won** (2007). Blue-black and deep purple on multicolor underprint. As #40. Overprint: Kim Il Sung 95th Birthday	FV	2.00
51	**10 Won** (2007). Deep brown and red-brown on multicolor underprint. As #41. Overprint: Kim Il Sung 95th Birthday	FV	3.00
52	**50 Won** (2007). Deep brown and deep olive-brown on multicolor underprint. As #42. Overprint: Kim Il Sung 95th Birthday		
	a. Issued note.	FV	5.00
	s. Specimen.	—	50.00
53	**100 Won** (2007). Deep brown and brown-violet on multicolor underprint. As #43. Overprint: Kim Il Sung 95th Birthday	FV	7.50
54	**200 Won** (2007). Green on multicolor underprint. As #48. Overprint: Kim Il Sung 95th Birthday	FV	12.50
55	**500 Won** (2007). Slate gray on light blue and purple underprint. As #44. Overprint: Kim Il Sung 95th Birthday	FV	15.00
56	**1000 Won** (2007). Dark green on multicolor underprint. As #45. Overprint: Kim Il Sung 95th Birthday	FV	20.00
56A	**5000 Won** (2007). Purple on multicolor underprint As #46. Overprint: Kim Ii Sung 95th Birthday.	FV	50.00

2002 (2009) Issue

No.	Denomination / Description	VF	UNC
57	**1 Won** 2002 (2009).	FV	.25
58	**5 Won** 2002 (2009). Slate black on multicolor underprint. Man with glasses, boy with cap at right center. Back: Dam. Watermark: Flowers. 145x65mm.	FV	.25
59	**10 Won** 2002 (2009). Blue, green and purple on multicolor underprint. Pilot, sailor and solder at right center. Back: Military statue group. 145x65mm.	FV	.25
60	**50 Won** 2002 (2009). Purple on multicolor underprint. Man in suit, man in overalls, female at right center. Back: Party Foundation Monument in Pyongyang 145x65mm.	FV	.25
61	**100 Won** 2002 (2009). Green on multicolor underprint. Seibold magnolia at center. Back: Value at center. 145x65mm.	FV	7.50
62	**200 Won** 2002 (2009). Violet and lilac on multicolor underprint. Equestrian statue at center. Back: Value at center. 145x65mm.	FV	12.50
63	**500 Won** 2002 (2009). Gray and purple on multicolor underprint. Arch of Triumph. Back: Value at center. 145x65mm.	FV	12.50

64 **1000 Won** — VF / UNC

2002 (2009). Red on lilac underprint. Birthplace of Kim Jong Suk in Hoeryong. Back: Birch tree forest along Lake Samji. 145x65mm.

	VF	UNC
a. Issued note.	FV	12.50
s. Specimen. Red overprint.	—	75.00

65 **2000 Won** — VF / UNC

2002 (2009). Gray and blue on multicolor underprint. Cabin birthplace of Kim Hong Il and Jong Il peak. Back: Forest and Baekdu Mountains. 145x65mm.

	VF	UNC
a. Issued note.	FV	20.00
s. Specimen. Red overprint.	—	75.00

66 **5000 Won** — VF / UNC

2002 (2009). Brown on pink underprint. Kim Il Sung at right center with Seibold's magnolia wreath at right. Back: Birthplace of Kim Il Sung in Mangyongdae. 145x65mm.

	VF	UNC
a. Issued note.	FV	50.00
s. Specimen. Red overprint.	—	75.00

Collector Series

Korean Central Bank

1978 Issue

CS1 **1978 1-100 Won.** — Mkt. Value

Red overprint Korean characters for specimen on #18a-21a, 22 (with all zero serial #). — 60.00

1992 Issue

CS2 **1992 1-100 Won.** — Mkt. Value

Red, rectangular overprint Korean characters for specimen on #39-43. (39, 42 and 43 with all zero serial #, 40-41 with normal serial #). — 50.00

2000 Issue

#CS3-CS8 ovpt. in Korean or English: *The 55th Anniversary of Foundation of the Workers' Party of Korea 10th.10.Juche 89 (2000).*

			Mkt. Value
CS3	**1 Won**	Overprint: *The 55th Anniversary of Foundation of the Worders' Party of korea 10th. 10. juche 89 (2000).* Black overprint in English on face of #18e.	3.00
CS4	**5 Won**	Overprint: *The 55th Anniversary of Foundation of the Worders' Party of korea 10th. 10. juche 89 (2000).* Red overprint in Korean on face of #19d.	3.00
CS5	**10 Won**	Overprint: *The 55th Anniversary of Foundation of the Worders' Party of korea 10th. 10. juche 89 (2000).* Black overprint in English on face of #20e.	3.00
CS6	**50 Won**	Overprint: *The 55th Anniversary of Foundation of the Worders' Party of korea 10th. 10. juche 89 (2000).* Red overprint in Korean on face of #21b.	3.00
CS7	**50 Won**	Overprint: *The 55th Anniversary of Foundation of the Worders' Party of korea 10th. 10. juche 89 (2000).* Red overprint in English on face of #21b.	3.00
CS8	**50 Won**	Overprint: *The 55th Anniversary of Foundation of the Worders' Party of korea 10th. 10. juche 89 (2000).* Black overprint in English on face of #21b.	3.00

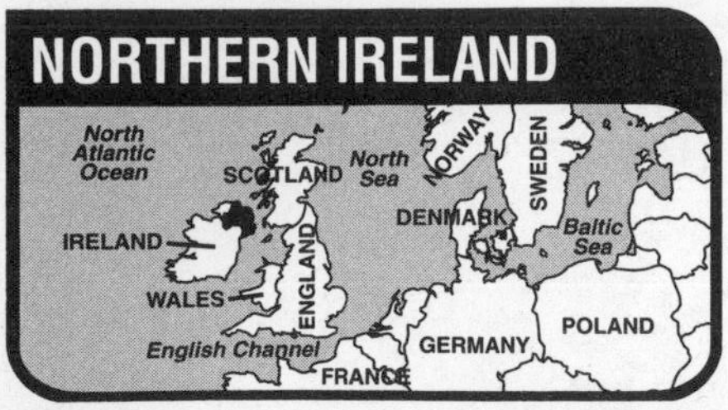

From 1800 to 1921 Ireland was an integral part of the United Kingdom. The Anglo-Irish treaty of 1921 established the Irish Free State of 26 counties within the Commonwealth of Nations and recognized the partition of Ireland. The six predominantly Protestant counties of northeast Ulster chose to remain a part of the United Kingdom with a limited self-government.

Up to 1928 banknotes issued by six of the nine joint stock commercial banks were circulating in the whole of Ireland. After the establishment of the Irish Free State, the commercial notes were issued for circulation only in Northern Ireland, with the Consolidated Banknotes being issued by the eight commercial banks operating in the Irish Free State.

Additional information on bank notes of Northern Ireland can be found in *Paper Money of Ireland* by Bob Blake and Jonathan Callaway, published by Pam West.

RULERS:
British

MONETARY SYSTEM:
1 Shilling = 12 Pence
1 Pound = 20 Shillings to 1971
1 Pound = 100 New Pence, 1971-

British Administration

Allied Irish Banks Ltd.

1982 Issue

#1-5 designs similar to Provincial Bank of Ireland Ltd. (#247-251) except for bank title and signature.

		VF	UNC
1	**1 Pound**		
	1.1.1982; 1.7.1983; 1.12.1984. Green on multicolor underprint. Young girl at right. Back: Sailing ship *Girona* at center. Printer: TDLR.		
	a. 1.1.1982.	15.00	45.00
	b. 1.7.1983.	15.00	45.00
	c. 1.12.1984.	15.00	45.00

		VF	UNC
2	**5 Pounds**		
	1.1.1982; 1.7.1983. Blue and purple on multicolor underprint. Young woman at right. Back: Dunluce Castle at center. Printer: TDLR.		
	a. 1.1.1982.	35.00	95.00
	b. 1.7.1983.	35.00	95.00

		VF	UNC
3	**10 Pounds**		
	1.1.1982; 1.12.1984. Brown and gray-green on multicolor underprint. Young man at right. Back: Wreck of the *Girona* at center. Printer: TDLR.		
	a. 1.1.1982.	50.00	160.
	b. 1.12.1984.	50.00	160.

		VF	UNC
4	**20 Pounds**		
	1.1.1982; 1.7.1983; 1.12.1984. Purple and green. Elderly woman at right. Back: Chimney at Lacada Point at center. Printer: TDLR.		
	a. 1.1.1982.	75.00	325.
	b. 1.7.1983.	75.00	325.
	c. 1.12.1984.	75.00	325.
5	**100 Pounds**		
	1.1.1982. Black, olive and green. Elderly man at right. Back: The *Armada* at center. Printer: TDLR.	400.	850.

Allied Irish Banks Public Limited Company

1987-88 Issue

#6-9 like #2-5 except for bank title and signatrue.

		VF	UNC
6	**5 Pounds**		
	1.1.1987; 1.1.1990. Blue and purple on multicolor underprint. Young woman at right. Back: Dunluce castle at center. Printer: TDLR.		
	a. 1.1.1987.	30.00	75.00
	b. 1.1.1990.	30.00	75.00

		VF	UNC
7	**10 Pounds**		
	1.6.1988; 1.1.1990; 18.5.1993. Brown and gray-green on multicolor underprint. Young man at right. Back: Wreck of the *Girona* at center. Printer: TDLR.		
	a. 1.6.1988.	45.00	110.
	b. 1.1.1990.	45.00	110.
	c. 18.5.1993.	40.00	90.00

8 20 Pounds VF UNC
1.1.1987; 1.4.1987; 1.1.1990. Purple and green. Elderly woman at right. Back: Chimney at Lacada Point at center. Printer: TDLR.
a. 1.1.1987. 70.00 180.
b. 1.4.1987. 65.00 140.
c. 1.1.1990. 65.00 140.

9 100 Pounds VF UNC
1.12.1988. Black, olive and green. Elderly man at right. Back: The *Armada* at center. Printer: TDLR. 350. 700.

Bank of Ireland

Belfast

1967 ND Issue

56 1 Pound VF UNC
ND (1967). Black on green and lilac underprint. Mercury at left, woman with harp at right. Signature W. E. Guthrie. Signature title as *Agent*. Back: Airplane, bank building and boat. 151x72mm. 20.00 70.00

57 5 Pounds
ND (1967-68). Brown-violet. Mercury at left, woman with harp at right. Signature title as *Agent*. Back: Airplane, bank building and boat.
a. Signature W. E. Guthrie. (1967). 200. 700.
b. Signature H. H. M. Chestnutt. (1968). 200. 700.

58 10 Pounds
ND (1967). Brown and yellow. Mercury at left, woman with harp at right. Signature W. E. Guthrie. Signature title as *Agent*. Back: Airplane, bank building and boat. 400. 1100.

1971-74 ND Issues

#61-63 replacement notes: Serial # prefix *Z*.

61 1 Pound VF UNC
ND (1972-77). Black on light green and lilac underprint. Mercury at left, woman with harp at right. Back: Airplane, bank building and boat. Like # 56 but smaller size. 134x66mm.
a. Signature H. H. M. Chestnutt. (1972). 30.00 60.00
b. Signature A. S. J. O'Neill. (1977). 25.00 45.00

62 5 Pounds VF UNC
ND (1971-77). Blue on light green and lilac underprint. Mercury at left, woman with harp at right. Back: Airplane, bank building and boat. 146x78mm.
a. Signature H. H. M. Chestnutt. (1971). 90.00 160.
b. Signature A. S. J. O'Neill. (1977). 75.00 150.

63 10 Pounds
ND (1971-77). Brown on light green and pale orange underprint. Mercury at left, woman with harp at right. Back: Airplane, bank building and boat.
a. Signature H. H. M. Chestnutt. (1971). 300. 600.
b. Signature A. S. J. O'Neill. (1977). 200. 375.
s. Specimen. As a. — —

64 100 Pounds
ND (1974-78). Red on multicolor underprint. Mercury at left, woman with harp at right. Back: Airplane, bank building and boat.
a. Signature H. H. M. Chestnutt. (1974). 950. 1400.
b. Signature A. S. J. O'Neill. (1978). 600. 950.

1980s ND Issue

65 1 Pound VF UNC
ND. Black on light green and lilac underprint. Mercury at left, woman with harp at right. *STERLING* added below value. Signature A. S. J. O'Neill. Back: Airplane, bank building and boat. Watermark: Bank name repeated.
a. Issued note. 12.50 20.00
r. Replacement note. — —

66 5 Pounds
ND. Blue on light green and lilac underprint. Mercury at left, woman with harp at right. £ signs added in corners. *STERLING* added below value. Back: Airplane, bank building and boat.
a. Signature A. S. J. O'Neill. 65.00 120.
b. Signature D. F. Harrison. 45.00 80.00

67 10 Pounds VF UNC
ND (1984). Dark brown on light green and pale orange underprint. Mercury at left, woman with harp at right. *STERLING* added below value. Back: Airplane, bank building and boat.
a. Signature A. S. J. O'Neill. 120. 190.
b. Signature D. F. Harrison. 100. 140.

67A 20 Pounds
ND. Dark olive-green on multicolor underprint. Mercury at left, woman with harp at right. *STERLING* added below value. Back: Airplane, bank building and boat.
a. Signature A. S. J. O'Neill. 180. 275.
b. Signature D. F. Harrison. 170. 225.

68 100 Pounds
ND. Red on multicolor underprint. Mercury at left, woman with harp at right. £ sign at upper right and lower left corners. *Sterling* added at lower center. Back: Airplane, bank building and boat.
a. Signature A. S. J. O'Neill. 525. 750.
b. Signature D. F. Harrison. 400. 650.

1983 Commemorative Issue

#69, Bank of Ireland Bicentenary, 1783-1983

69 20 Pounds — VF / UNC
1983. Dark olive-green on multicolor underprint. Like number 67A but commemorative text below bank title. Signature A. S. J. O'Neill. Back: Airplane, bank building and boat. — 600. / 1200.

1990-95 Issue

70 5 Pounds
28.8.1990; 18.1.1992; 1.7.1994. Blue and purple on multicolor underprint. Bank seal (Hibernia seated) at left, six county shields at upper center. Signature D. F. Harrison. Back: Queen's University in Belfast. Watermark: Medusa head.

	VF	UNC
a. 28.8.1990.	22.50	40.00
b. 18.1.1992.	22.50	40.00
c. 1.7.1994.	22.50	40.00
s. Specimen.	—	150.

71 10 Pounds
14.5.1991; 24.5.1992. Purple and maroon on multicolor underprint. Bank seal (Hibernia seated) at left, six county shields at upper center. Signature D. F. Harrison. Back: Queen's University in Belfast. Watermark: Medusa head.

	VF	UNC
a. 14.5.1991.	35.00	65.00
b. 24.5.1992.	35.00	65.00
s. Specimen.	—	190.

72 20 Pounds
9.5.1991; 1.5.1993. Green and brown on multicolor underprint. Bank seal (Hibernia seated) at left, six county shields at upper center. Signature D. F. Harrison. Back: Queen's University in Belfast. Watermark: Medusa head.

	VF	UNC
a. 9.5.1991.	80.00	130.
b. 1.5.1993.	80.00	130.
s. Specimen.	—	250.

73 100 Pounds
28.8.1992. Red on multicolor underprint. Bank seal (Hibernia seated) at left, six county shields at upper center. Signature D. F. Harrison. Back: Queen's University in Belfast. Watermark: Medusa head.

	VF	UNC
a. Issued note.	275.	600.
s. Specimen.	—	400.

1995; 1998 Issue

74 5 Pounds
1.7.1997; 4.8.1998; 5.9.2000. Blue and purple on multicolor underprint. Bank seal (Hibernia seated) at left, six county shields at upper center. Signature D. F. Harrison. Ascending size seial number at lower right. Back: Queen's University in Belfast. Watermark: Medusa head.

	VF	UNC
a. 1.7.1997.	15.00	30.00
b. 4.8.1998.	15.00	30.00
c. 5.9.2000.	15.00	30.00
s. Specimen. 1.3.2003.	—	—

75 10 Pounds
1.7.1995; 1.7.1998; 5.9.2000. Purple and maroon on multicolor underprint. Bank seal (Hibernia seated) at left, six county shields at upper center. Signature D. F. Harrison. Ascending size serial number at lower right. Back: Queen's University in Belfast. Watermark: Medusa head.

	VF	UNC
a. 1.7.1995.	27.50	45.00
b. 1.7.1998.	27.50	45.00
c. 5.9.2000.	27.50	45.00
s. Specimen. 1.7.1995.	—	400.

		VF	UNC
76	**20 Pounds**		
	1.7.1995; 1.1.1999; 5.9.2000. Green and brown on multicolor underprint. Bank seal (Hibernia seated) at left, six county shields at upper center. Signature D. F. Harrison. Ascending size serial number at lower right. Back: Queen's University in Belfast. Watermark: Medusa head.		
	a. 1.7.1995.	55.00	85.00
	b. 1.1.1999.	55.00	85.00
	c. 5.9.2000.	55.00	85.00
	s. Specimen. 5.9.2000.	—	—
77	**50 Pounds**		
	1.7.1995; 1.9.1999. Brown, olive and multicolor. Bank seal (Hibernia seated) at left, six county shields at upper center. Signature D. F. Harrison. Ascending size serial number at lower right. Back: Queen's University in Belfast. Watermark: Medusa head.		
	a. 1.7.1995.	140.	190.
	b. 1.9.1999.	140.	190.
	s. Specimen. 1.7.1995.	—	—
78	**100 Pounds**		
	1.7.1995. Red on multicolor underprint. Bank seal (Hibernia seated) at left, six county shields at upper center. Signature D. F. Harrison. Ascending size serial number at lower right. Back: Queen's University in Belfast. Watermark: Medusa head.		
	a. Issued note.	225.	480.
	s. Specimen. 1.7.1995.	—	—

2003 Issue

		VF	UNC
79	**5 Pounds**		
	1.3.2003. Blue and violet on multicolor underprint. Back: Queen's University in Belfast.		
	a. 1.3.2003. Signature Sowden.	FV	25.00

		VF	UNC
80	**20 Pounds**		
	1.1.2003; 1.5.2005; 22.2.2007. Multicolor. Signature D. McGowan.		
	a. 1.1.2003.	FV	65.00
	b. 1.5.2005.	FV	65.00
	c. 22.2.2007.	FV	65.00

		VF	UNC
81	**50 Pounds**		
	5.4.2004. Multicolor. Signature R. Keenan.	FV	160.

		VF	UNC
82	**100 Pounds**		
	1.3.2005. Multicolor. Signature D. McGowan.	FV	275.

2008 Issue

		VF	UNC
83	**5 Pounds**		
	20.4.2008. Bank seal (Hibernia seated) at left. Signature D. McGowan. Back: Old Bushmills distillery.		
	a. Issued note.	FV	20.00
	r. Replacement note. Serial # prefix ZZ.	—	—

		VF	UNC
84	**10 Pounds**		
	20.4.2008. Signature S. Kirkpatrick. Back: Old Bushmills distillery.		
	a. Issued note.	FV	45.00
	r. Replacement note. Serial # prefix: ZZ.	—	—
85	**20 Pounds**		
	20.4.2008. Bank seal (Hibernia seated) at left. Signature S. Kirkpatrick. Back: Old Bushmills distillery.		
	a. Issued note.	FV	85.00
	r. Replacement note. Serial # prefix ZZ.	—	—

2013 Issue

		VF	UNC
86	**5 Pounds**		
	1.1.2013. Blue on multicolor underprint. Bank seal (Hibernia seated) at left.. Signature Stephen Matchett. Back: Old Bushmills distillery.	FV	15.00
87	**10 Pounds**		
	1.1.2013. Brown-red on multicolor underprint. Bank seal (Hibernia seated) at left. Signature Stephen Matchett. Back: Old Bushmills distillery.	FV	30.00
88	**20 Pounds**		
	1.1.2013. Green on multicolor underprint. Bank seal (Hibernia seated) at left. Signature Stephen Matchett. Back: Old Bushmills distillery.	FV	60.00
89	**50 Pounds**		
	1.1.2013. Violet on multicolor underprint. Bank seal (Hibernia seated) at left. Signatrue: Stephen Matchett Back: Old Bushmills distillery.	FV	150.

Belfast Banking Company Limited

1922-23 Issue

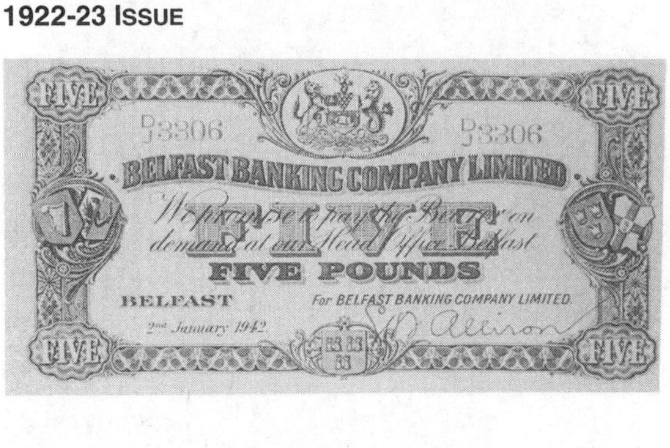

127 5 Pounds

1923-66. Black on red underprint. Arms at top center with payable text...*at our Head Office, Belfast.*

	VF	UNC
a. Black serial #. 3.1.1923; 3.5.1923; 7.9.1927.	350.	850.
b. Red serial #. 8.3.1928-2.10.1942.	60.00	200.
c. Red serial #. 6.1.1966.	50.00	140.
p. Proof.	—	300.

128 10 Pounds

1923-65. Black on green underprint. Arms at top center with payable text...*at our Head Office, Belfast.*

	VF	UNC
a. Black serial #. 3.1.1923.	625.	—
b. Green serial #. 9.1.1929-1.1.1943.	275.	625.
c. Green serial #. 3.12.1963; 5.6.1965.	70.00	170.
p. Proof.	—	300.

129 20 Pounds

1923-65. Black on purple underprint. Arms at top center with payable text...*at our Head Office, Belfast.*

	VF	UNC
a. Black serial #. 3.1.1923.	900.	1825.
b. Mauve serial #. 9.11.1939; 10.8.1940.	500.	1200.
c. Black serial #. 3.2.1943.	500.	1200.
d. Black serial #. 5.6.1965.	550.	1400.
p. Proof.	—	600.

130 50 Pounds

1923-63. Black on orange underprint. Arms at top center with payable text...*at our Head Office, Belfast.*

	VF	UNC
a. Black serial #. 3.1.1923; 3.5.1923.	1200.	2100.
b. Yellow serial #. 9.11.1939; 10.8.1940.	550.	1400.
c. Black serial #. 3.2.1943.	500.	1400.
d. Black serial #. 3.12.1963.	700.	1750.
p. Proof.	—	600.

131 100 Pounds

1923-68. Black on red underprint. Arms at top or upper center with payable text...*at our Head Office, Belfast.*

	VF	UNC
a. 3.1.1923; 3.5.1923.	1000.	2000.
b. 9.11.1939; 3.2.1943.	700.	1700.
c. 3.12.1963.	700.	1700.
d. 8.5.1968.	700.	1700.
p. Proof.	—	600.

First Trust Bank

1994 Issue

132 10 Pounds

10.1.1994; 1.3.1996. Dark brown and purple. Five shields at bottom center. Young man at right. Signature title: *GROUP MANAGING DIRECTOR.* Back: Sailing ship Girona at center. Watermark: Young woman. Printer: TDLR.

	VF	UNC
a. 10.1.1994.	50.00	80.00
b. 1.3.1996.	60.00	110.
s1. As a. Specimen.	—	260.
s2. As b. Specimen.	—	300.

133 20 Pounds

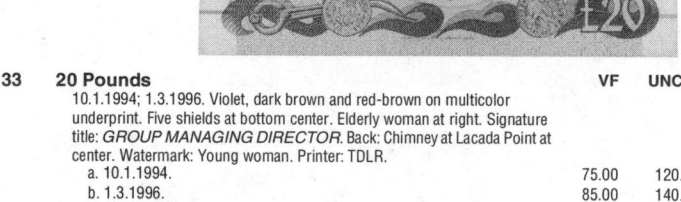

10.1.1994; 1.3.1996. Violet, dark brown and red-brown on multicolor underprint. Five shields at bottom center. Elderly woman at right. Signature title: *GROUP MANAGING DIRECTOR.* Back: Chimney at Lacada Point at center. Watermark: Young woman. Printer: TDLR.

	VF	UNC
a. 10.1.1994.	75.00	120.
b. 1.3.1996.	85.00	140.
s1. As a. Specimen.	—	450.
s2. As b. Specimen.	—	500.

134 50 Pounds

10.1.1994. Black, dark olive-green and blue on multicolor underprint. Five shields at bottom center. Elderly man at right. Signature title: *GROUP MANAGING DIRECTOR.* Back: Cherubs holding Armada medallion at center. Watermark: Young woman. Printer: TDLR.

	VF	UNC
a. Issued note.	160.	300.
s. Specimen.	—	500.

#	Denomination / Description	VF	UNC
135	**100 Pounds** 10.1.1994; 1.3.1996. Black and olive-brown on multicolor underprint. Five shields at bottom center. Elderly couple at right. Signature title: *GROUP MANAGING DIRECTOR*. Back: The *Armada* at center. Watermark: Young woman. Printer: TDLR.		
	a. 10.1.1994.	275.	500.
	b. 1.3.1996.	275.	600.
	s1. As a. Specimen.	—	500.
	s2. As b. Specimen.	—	700.

1998 Issue

#	Denomination / Description	VF	UNC
136	**10 Pounds** 1.1.1998. Dark brown and purple. Five shields at bottom center. Young man at right. Signature title: *GROUP MANAGING DIRECTOR*. Scalloped gold seal over value at upper right. Back: Sailing ship Girona at center. Watermark: Young woman. Printer: TDLR.		
	a. Signature Dennis Licence.	25.00	50.00
	b. Signature John Kilty.	FV	30.00
	r. Replacement note. Serial # prefix: ZZ.	—	—
	s. Specimen.	—	300.
137	**20 Pounds** 1998; 1.5.2007. Violet, dark brown and red-brown on multicolor underprint. Five shields at bottom center. Elderly woman at right. Signature title: *GROUP MANAGING DIRECTOR*. Windowed security thread and gold seal at upper right. Back: Chimney at Lacada Point at center. Watermark: Young woman. Printer: TDLR.		
	a. 1.1.1998.	55.00	90.00
	b. 1.5.2007.	55.00	90.00
	s1. Specimen. 1.1.1998. With gold seal and windowed security thread.	—	400.
	s2. Specimen. 1.3.1996. Without gold seal, with windowed security thread.	—	400.
138	**50 Pounds** 1998; 2009. Black, dark olive-green and blue on multicolor underprint. Five shields at bottom center. Elderly man at right. Signature title: *GROUP MANAGING DIRECTOR*. Windowed security thread and silver seal at upper right. Back: Cherubs holding Armada medallion at center. Watermark: Young woman. Printer: TDLR.		
	a. 1.1.1998. Signature Dennis Licence.	110.	175.
	b. 1.6.2009. Signature Terry McDaid.	FV	150.
	s. Specimen.	—	440.

#	Denomination / Description	VF	UNC
139	**100 Pounds** 1998. Black and olive-brown on multicolor underprint. Five shields at bottom center. Elderly couple at right. Windowed security thread and gold seal at upper right. Signature Dennis Licence. Back: The *Armada* at center. Watermark: Young woman. Printer: TDLR. 163x90mm.		
	a. Signature title: *GROUP MANAGING DIRECTOR*.	250.	350.
	b. Signature title: *MANAGING DIRECTOR FIRST TRUST BANK*.	250.	350.
	s. Specimen.	—	475.

Northern Bank Limited

1929 Regular Issue

#	Denomination / Description	VF	UNC
178	**1 Pound** 1929-68. Black. Blue guilloche. Sailing ship, plow and man at grindstone at upper center.		
	a. Red serial #. 6.5.1929; 1.7.1929; 1.8.1929.	85.00	175.
	b. Black prefix letters and serial #. 1.1.1940.	45.00	70.00
	c. 1.10.1968.	40.00	85.00
	p. Proof. 1.9.1940.	—	350.

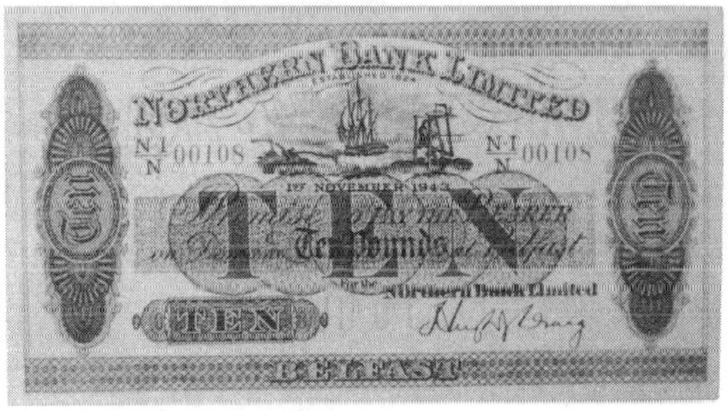

#	Denomination / Description	VF	UNC
181	**10 Pounds** 1930-68. Black on red underprint. Sailing ship, plow and man at grindstone at upper center.		
	a. Red serial #. 1.1.1930-1.1.1940.	125.	350.
	b. Black serial #. 1.8.1940, 1.9.1940.	85.00	175.
	c. Red serial #. 1.1.1942-1.11.1943.	50.00	140.
	d. Imprint on back below central signature 1.10.1968.	50.00	240.
	p. Proof.	—	175.
	s. Specimen.	—	250.

1968 Issue

#	Denomination / Description	VF	UNC
184	**5 Pounds** 1.10.1968. Black on green underprint.	70.00	200.
185	**50 Pounds** 1.10.1968. Black on dark blue underprint. Back: *NBLD* monogram.		
	a. Issued note.	500.	160.
	s. Specimen.	—	1200.
186	**100 Pounds** 1.10.1968. Black on dark blue underprint. Back: *NBLD* monogram.		
	a. Issued note.	900.	1400.
	s. Specimen.	—	1400.

1970 Issue

#	Denomination / Description	VF	UNC
187	**1 Pound** 1970-82. Green on pink underprint. Cows at left, shipyard at bottom center, loom at right. Back: Stylized arms at center. Printer: BWC.		
	a. Signature Wilson.	27.50	50.00
	b. Signature Gabbey.	25.00	50.00
	c. Signatrue Ervin.	22.50	40.00

188 5 Pounds

1.7.1970-1.4.1982. Light blue. Cows at left, shipyard at bottom center, loom at right. Back: Stylized arms at center.

	VF	UNC
a. Signature Wilson.	90.00	200.
b. Signature Gabbey.	90.00	180.
c. Signature Newland.	60.00	100.
d. Signature Ervin.	50.00	80.00
e. Signature Roberts.	60.00	100.

189 10 Pounds

1970-88. Brown. Cows at left, shipyard at bottom center, loom at right. Back: Stylized arms at center.

	VF	UNC
a. Signature Wilson.	90.00	400.
b. Signature Gabbey.	200.	375.
c. Signature Newland.	150.	300.
d. Signature Ervin.	120.	225.
e. Signature Roberts.	100.	190.
f. Signature Torrens.	90.00	150.

190 20 Pounds

1.7.1970; 1.3.1981; 2.3.1987; 15.6.1988. Purple. Cows at left, shipyard at bottom center, loom at right. Back: Stylized arms at center.

	VF	UNC
a. Signature Wilson.	300.	600.
b. Signature Ervin.	225.	400.
c. Signature Roberts.	200.	375.
d. Signature Torrens.	130.	200.

191 50 Pounds

1.7.1970; 1.3.1981. Orange. Cows at left, shipyard at bottom center, loom at right. Back: Stylized arms at center.

	VF	UNC
a. Signature Wilson.	450.	850.
b. Signature Newland.	450.	700.
c. Signature Ervin.	275.	600.

192 100 Pounds

1.7.1970; 1.10.1971; 1.1.1975; 1.7.1976; 1.1.1980. Red. Cows at left, shipyard at bottom center, loom at right. Back: Stylized arms at center.

	VF	UNC
a. Signature Wilson.	500.	1400.
b. Signature Gabbey.	450.	1300.
c. Signature Newland.	375.	750.
d. Signature Ervin.	375.	800.

1988-90 Issue

193 5 Pounds

24.8.1988; 24.8.1989; 24.8.1990. Blue and multicolor. Station above trolley car at center, W. A. Traill at right. Back: Dish antenna at left, stylized *N* at center and computer. Printer: TDLR.

	VF	UNC
a. 24.8.1988; 24.8.1989.	22.50	50.00
b. 24.8.1990.	20.00	40.00
s. Specimen. 24.8.1988.	—	300.

194 10 Pounds

24.8.1988; 14.5.1991; 24.8.1993. Red and brown on multicolor underprint. Early automobile above bicyclist at center, J. B. Dunlop at right. Back: Dish antenna at left, stylized *N* at center and computer. Printer: TDLR.

	VF	UNC
a. 24.8.1988; 24.8.1990.	100.	160.
b. 14.5.1991; 24.8.1993.	80.00	160.
c. 30.8.1996.	50.00	100.
r. 24.8.1990. Replacement note.	40.00	140.
s. Specimen. 24.8.1988.	—	400.

195 20 Pounds

24.8.1988; 24.8.1989; 24.8.1990; 9.5.1991; 30.3.1992; 8.24.1993. Purple-brown, red and multicolor. Airplane at center, H. G. Ferguson at right, tractor at bottom right. Back: Dish antenna at left, stylized *N* at center and computer. Printer: TDLR.

	VF	UNC
a. 24.8.1988.	140.	225.
b. 24.8.1989; 24.8.1990; 9.5.1991; 30.3.1992; 8.24.1993.	110.	200.
c. 30.8.1996.	90.00	150.
s. Specimen.	—	400.

196 50 Pounds

1.11.1990. Bluish green, black and multicolor. Tea dryer, centrifugal machine at center, Sir S. Davidson at right. Back: Dish antenna at left, stylized *N* at center and computer. Printer: TDLR.

	VF	UNC
a. Issued note.	180.	275.
s. Specimen. 1.11.1990.	—	450.

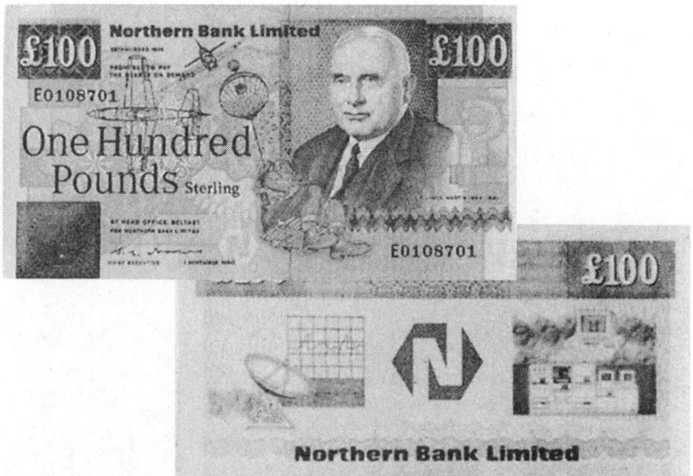

197 100 Pounds

1.11.1990. Lilac, black, blue and multicolor. Airplanes and ejection seat at center, Sir J. Martin at right. Back: Dish antenna at left, stylized *N* at center and computer. Printer: TDLR.

	VF	UNC
a. Issued note.	375.	500.
s. Specimen. 1.11.1990.	—	450.

1997; 1999 Issue

			VF	UNC
198	**10 Pounds** 24.2.1997. Dark brown and violet on multicolor underprint. J. B. Dunlop at right, bicycle at lower left. Back: City Hall in Belfast at center, buildings and architectural drawings in underprint. Watermark: J. B. Dunlop.			
		a. 24.2.1997. Signature Savage.	32.50	60.00
		b. 8.10.1999. Signature Price.	27.50	60.00
		s. Specimen. As a.	—	400.
199	**20 Pounds** 24.2.1997; 8.10.1999. Purple and dark brown on multicolor underprint. H. Ferguson at right, farm tractor at lower left. Back: City Hall in Belfast at center, buildings and architectural drawings in underprint. Watermark: H. Ferguson.			
		a. 24.2.1997. Signature Savage.	50.00	80.00
		b. 8.10.1999. Signature Price.	55.00	80.00
		s. As a or b. Specimen.	—	420.

			VF	UNC
200	**50 Pounds** 8.10.1999. Olive brown on multicolor underprint. Sir Samuel Davidson at right. Back: City Hall in Belfast at center, buildings and architectural drawings in underprint.			
		a. Issued note.	160.	225.
		s. Specimen.	—	500.

			VF	UNC
201	**100 Pounds** 8.10.1999. Brown olive on multicolor underprint. Sir James Martin at right. Martin Baker ejection seat at left. Back: City Hall in Belfast at center, buildings and architectural drawings in underprint.			
		a. Issued note.	250.	400.
		s. Specimen.	—	550.

1999 Commemorative Issue

#202, 175 Years of Banking, 1824-1999

			VF	UNC
202	**20 Pounds** 1.9.1999. Purple and dark brown on multicolor underprint. H. Ferguson at right, farm tractor at lower left. Commemorative text and gold rectangle at upper left center. Back: City Hall in Belfast at center, buildings and architectural drawings in underprint. Watermark: H. Ferguson.			
		a. Issued note.	65.00	100.
		s. Specimen.	—	400.

2000 Commemorative Issue

#203, Millennium and Y2K Commemoratives

			VF	UNC
203	**5 Pounds** 1999; 2000. Blue, red and multicolor. Ovals, globe pattern. Back: Space shuttle, electronics. Polymer plastic.			
		a. 8.10.1999. Serial # prefix MM.	12.50	25.00
		b. 1.1.2000. Serial # prefix Y2K.	17.50	32.50
		s. As a. Specimen.	—	600.

2004 Issue

		VF	UNC
205	**10 Pounds** 29.4.2004. Green and blue on multicolor underprint. J. B. Dunlop at right, bicycle at lower left. Signature Price. Back: Pediment of City Hall, Belfast at center, buildings and architectural drawings in underprint. Watermark: J. B. Dunlop.	37.50	80.00

2005 Issue

206	10 Pounds	VF	UNC
	19.1.2005. Green and blue on multicolor underprint. J. B. Dunlop at right, bicycle at lower left. Signature Price. Back: Pediment of City Hall, Belfast at center, buildings and architectural drawings in underprint. Watermark: J. B. Dunlop.		
	a. Issued note.	FV	30.00
	s. Specimen.	—	400.

207	20 Pounds	VF	UNC
	19.1.2005; 6.11.2006. Blue and rose on multicolor underprint. H. Ferguson at right, farm tractor at lower left. Signature Price. Back: Pediment of City Hall, Belfast at center, buildings and architectural drawings in underprint. Watermark: H. Ferguson.		
	a. 19.1.2005.	FV	65.00
	b. 6.11.2006. Signature D. Price.	FV	65.00
	r. Replacement note. Serial # prefix: YY.	—	—
	s. Specimen.	—	400.

208	50 Pounds	VF	UNC
	19.1.2005. Viloet on multicolor underprint. Sir Samuel Davidson at right. Signature Price. Back: Pediment of City Hall, Belfast at center, buildings and architectural drawings in underprint. Watermark: Sir Samuel Davidson.		
	a. Issued note.	FV	160.
	s. Specimen.	—	400.

209	100 Pounds	VF	UNC
	19.1.2005. Rose and blue on multicolor underprint. Sir James Martin at right. Signature Price. Back: Pediment of City Hall, Belfast at center, buildings and architectural drawings in underprint. Watermark: Sir James Martin.		
	a. Issued note.	FV	275.
	s. Specimen.	—	400.

Provincial Bank of Ireland Limited

Belfast

1948; 1951 Issue

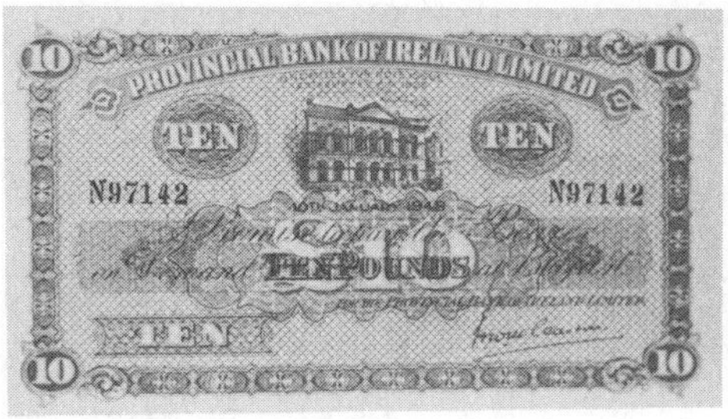

240	10 Pounds	VF	UNC
	10.1.1948. Green on red underprint and green and pink mesh.		
	a. Signature Clarke.	280.	775.
	p. Proof. 1946; 1948.	—	300.

1954 Issue

241	1 Pound	VF	UNC
	1.10.1954. Green. 148x84mm.	280.	525.

1965 Issue

243	1 Pound	VF	UNC
	1.12.1965. Green. Cameo portrait of archaic woman at upper center. Back: Bank building at center. Printer: TDLR.	300.	500.
244	5 Pounds		
	6.12.1965. Brown. Cameo Portrait of archaic woman at upper center. Back: Bank building at center. Printer: TDLR.	200.	300.

1968 Issue

245	1 Pound	VF	UNC
	1.1.1968-1.1.1972. Green. Cameo portrait of archaic woman at upper center. Back: Bank building at center. Printer: TDLR. 150x71mm.	60.00	110.
246	5 Pounds		
	5.1.1968; 5.1.1970; 5.1.1972. Brown. Cameo portrait of archaic woman at upper center. Back: Bank building at center. Printer: TDLR. 139x84mm.	50.00	90.00

1977; 1981 Issue

		VF	UNC
247	**1 Pound**		
	1977; 1979. Green on multicolor underprint. Young girl at right. Back: Sailing ship *Girona* at center.		
	a. Signature J. G. McClay. 1.1.1977.	25.00	45.00
	b. Signature F. H. Hollway. 1.1.1979.	25.00	37.50
	r. As b. Replacement note.	—	180.

		VF	UNC
248	**5 Pounds**		
	1977; 1979. Blue and purple on multicolor underprint. Young woman at right. Back: Dunluce Castle at center.		
	a. Signature J. G. McClay. 1.1.1977.	52.50	125.
	b. Signature F. H. Hollway. 1.1.1979.	42.50	100.
249	**10 Pounds**		
	1977; 1979. Brown and gray-green on multicolor underprint. Young man at right. Back: Wreck of the *Girona* at center.		
	a. Signature J. G. McClay. 1.1.1977.	100.	175.
	b. Signature F. H. Hollway. 1.1.1979.	90.00	150.
250	**20 Pounds**		
	1.3.1981. Purple and green. Elderly woman at right. Back: Chimney at Lacada Point at center.	150.	350.
251	**100 Pounds**		
	1.3.1981. Black, olive and green. Elderly man at right. Back: The *Armada* at center.	450.	950.

Ulster Bank Limited

1966-70 Issue

		VF	UNC
321	**1 Pound**		
	4.10.1966. Blue-black on multicolor underprint. Rural and urban views of Belfast at lower left and right. Port with bridge at lower center. Signature: Jno. J. A. Leitch. Back: Arms at center. Printer: BWC. 151x72mm.		
	a. Issued note.	35.00	65.00
	s. Specimen.	—	400.

		VF	UNC
322	**5 Pounds**		
	4.10.1966. Brown on multicolor underprint. Rural and urban views of Belfast at lower left and right. Port with bridge at lower center. Signature: Jno. J. A. Leitch. Back: Arms at center. Printer: BWC. 140x85mm.		
	a. Issued note.	90.00	350.
	s. Specimen, punch hole cancelled.	—	600.

		VF	UNC
323	**10 Pounds**		
	4.10.1966. Green on multicolor underprint. Rural and urban views of Belfast at lower left and right. Port with bridge at lower center. Signature: Jno. J. A. Leitch. Back: Arms at center. Printer: BWC. 151x93mm.		
	a. Issued note.	120.	400.
	s. Specimen, punch hole cancelled.	—	750.

		VF	UNC
324	**20 Pounds**		
	1.7.1970. Lilac on multicolor underprint. Rural and urban views of Belfast at lower left and right. Port with bridge at lower center. Signature: Jno. J. A. Leitch. Back: Arms at center. Printer: BWC. 161x90mm.		
	a. Issued note. Rare.	—	4000.
	s. Specimen. Punch hole cancelled.	—	900.

1971-82 Issue

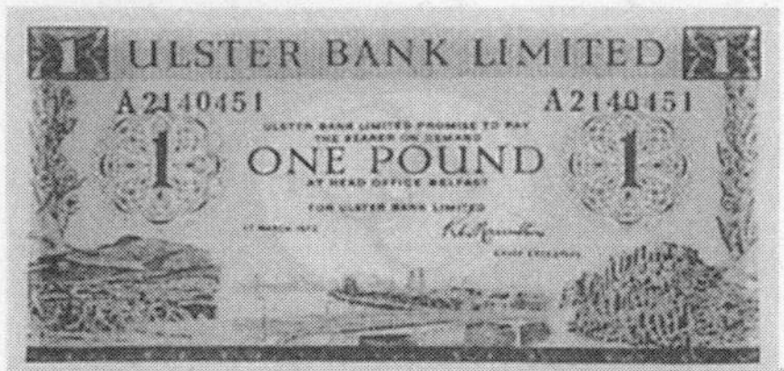

		VF	UNC
331	**5 Pounds**		
	1.12.1989; 1.1.1992; 4.1.1993. Brown on multicolor underprint. Rural and urban views of Belfast at lower left and right. Port with bridge at lower center. Signature: D. Went. Back: Arms at center. Printer: TDLR. Smaller size notes.		
	a. 1.12.1989	22.50	50.00
	b. 1.1.1992; 4.1.1993.	20.00	40.00
	s. Specimen. 4.1.1993	—	300.

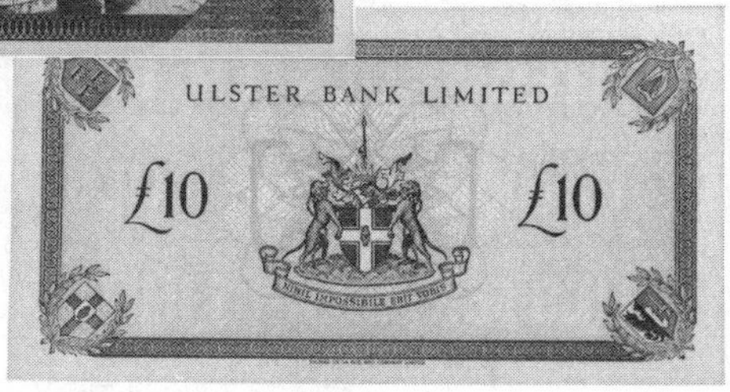

		VF	UNC
325	**1 Pound**		
	1971-76. Blue-black on multicolor underprint. Rural and urban views of Belfast at lower left and right. Port with bridge at lower center. Back: Arms at center. Watermark: Bank name repeated. Printer: BWC. 135x67mm.		
	a. Signature A. E. G. Brain. 15.2.1971.	22.50	60.00
	b. Signature R. W. Hamilton. 1.3.1973; 1.3.1976.	12.50	30.00
	s. As a. Specimen.	—	100.
326	**5 Pounds**		
	1971-86. Brown on multicolor underprint. Rural and urban views of Belfast at lower left and right. Port with bridge at lower center. Back: Arms at center. Printer: BWC. 146x78mm.		
	a. Signature A. E. G. Brain. 15.2.1971.	125.	300.
	b. Signature R. W. Hamilton. 1.3.1973; 1.3.1976.	45.00	130.
	c. Signature V. Chambers. 1.10.1982; 1.10.1983; 1.9.1986; 1.2.1988.	30.00	65.00

		VF	UNC
332	**10 Pounds**		
	1.12.1990. Green on multicolor underprint. Rural and urban views of Belfast at lower left and right. Port with bridge at lower center. Signature: D. Went. Back: Arms at center. Printer: TDLR. Smaller size notes.		
	a. Issued note.	35.00	85.00
	s. Specimen.	—	375.
333	**20 Pounds**		
	1.11.1990. Violet on multicolor underprint. Rural and urban views of Belfast at lower left and right. Port with bridge at lower center. Signature: D. Went. Back: Arms at center. Printer: TDLR. Smaller size notes.		
	a. Issued note.	75.00	160.
	s. Specimen.	—	450.
334	**100 Pounds**		
	1.12.1990. Red on multicolor underprint. Rural and urban views of Belfast at lower left and right. Port with bridge at lower center. Signature: D. Went. Back: Arms at center. Printer: TDLR. Smaller size notes.		
	a. Issued note.	400.	750.
	s. Specimen.	—	700.

		VF	UNC
327	**10 Pounds**		
	1971-89. Green on multicolor underprint. Rural and urban views of Belfast at lower left and right. Port with bridge at lower center. Back: Arms at center. Printer: BWC. 151x86mm.		
	a. Signature A. E. G. Brain. 15.2.1971.	200.	350.
	b. Signature R. W. Hamilton. 1.3.1973; 1.3.1976; 2.6.1980.	80.00	160.
	c. Signature V. Chambers. 1.10.1982; 1.10.1983; 1.2.1988.	75.00	140.
	d. Signature D. Went. 1.12.1989.	60.00	120.
328	**20 Pounds**		
	1976-83. Violet on multicolor underprint. Rural and urban views of Belfast at lower left and right. Port with bridge at lower center. Back: Arms at center. Printer: BWC.		
	a. Signature A. E. G. Brain. 15.2.1971.	1300.	2000.
	b. Signature R. W. Hamilton. 1.3.1976.	150.	250.
	c. Signature V. Chambers. 1.10.1982; 1.10.1983; 1.2.1988.	140.	200.
329	**50 Pounds**		
	1.10.1982. Brown on multicolor underprint. Rural and urban views of Belfast at lower left and right. Port with bridge at lower center. Signature: V. Chambers. Back: Arms at center. Printer: BWC.		
	a. Issued note.	275.	450.
	s. Specimen.	—	550.
330	**100 Pounds**		
	1973; 1982. Red on multicolor underprint. Rural and urban views of Belfast at lower left and right. Port with bridge at lower center. Back: Arms at center. Printer: BWC.		
	a. Signature R. W. Hamilton. 1.3.1973; 1.3.1977.	400.	700.
	b. Signature Chambers. 1.10.1982.	400.	700.
	s. Specimen.	—	650.

1996; 1998 Issue

		VF	UNC
335	**5 Pounds**		
	2.1.1998; 1.7.1998; 1.1.2001. Brown on multicolor underprint. Rural and urban views of Belfast at lower left and right. Port with bridge at lower center below signature at center right, date at left. Ascending size serial numbers. Signature Wilson. Back: Arms at center. Printer: TDLR.		
	a. 2.1.1998.	12.50	27.50
	b. 1.7.1998.	12.50	27.50
	c. 1.1.2001.	10.00	17.50

1989-90 Issue

Note: The Bank of Ireland sold to collectors matched serial # sets of £5-10-20 notes as well as 100 sets of replacement serial # prefix *Z*.

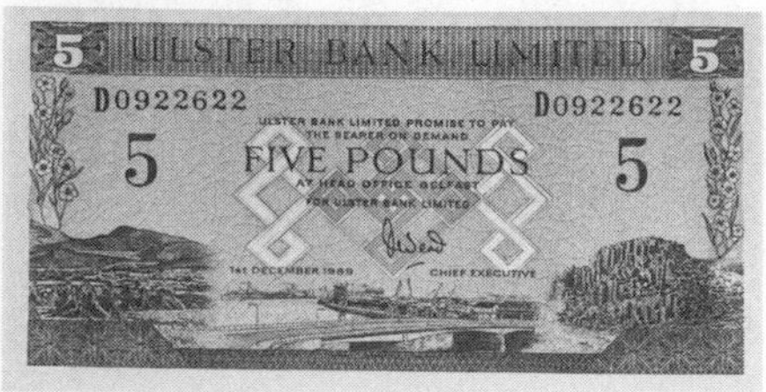

336 10 Pounds VF UNC

1.1.1997' 1.7.1999. Blue and green on multicolor underprint. Rural and urban views of Belfast at lower left and right. Port with bridge at lower center below signature at center right, date at left. Ascending size serial numbers. Back: Arms at center. Printer: TDLR.

	VF	UNC
a. 1.1.1997. Signature Kells.	22.50	40.00
b. 1.7.1999. Signature Wilson.	20.00	32.50
s. Specimen. As a.	—	400.

337 20 Pounds VF UNC

1.1.1996; 1.7.1999; 1.7.2002; 6.1.2004; 1.1.2007. Purple and violet on multicolor underprint. Rural and urban views of Belfast at lower left and right. Port with bridge at lower center below signature at center right, date at left. Ascending size serial numbers. Back: Arms at center. Printer: TDLR.

	VF	UNC
a. 1.1.1996. Signature Kells.	75.00	150.
b. 1.7.1999. Signature Wilson.	47.50	80.00
c. 1.7.2002. Signature Wilson.	42.50	70.00
d. 6.1.2004. Signature McCarthy.	FV	65.00
e. 1.1.2007.	FV	65.00

338 50 Pounds VF UNC

1.1.1997. Brown on multicolor underprint. Rural and urban views of Belfast at lower left and right. Port with bridge at lower center below signature at center right, date at left. Signature: V. Chambers. Ascending size serial numbers. Back: Arms at center. Printer: TDLR. — VF 120. UNC 220.

2006 Commemorative Issue

339 5 Pounds VF UNC

25.11.2006. Brown on multicolro underprint. Rural and urban views of Belfast at lower left and right. Back: George Best. — VF FV UNC 20.00

2007 Issue

340 5 Pounds VF UNC

1.7.2007. Violet and brown on multicolor underprint. Rural and urban vews of Belfast at left and right. Port with bridge at lower center. — VF — UNC 17.50

341 10 Pounds

1.1.2007; 1.1.2008; 1.1.2012. Blue and green on multicolor underprint. Rural and urban views of Belfast at lower left and right.

	VF	UNC
a. 1.1.2007; 1.1.2008. Signature L. McCarthy.	FV	30.00
b. 1.1.2012. Signature J. Brown.	FV	30.00
r. Replacement note. Serial # prefix Z.	—	—

342 20 Pounds

1.1.2007; 1.1.2010; 3.1.2012. Purple and violet on multicolor underprint. Rural and urban views of Belfast at lower left and right.

	VF	UNC
a. 1.1.2007; 1.1.2010. Signature L. McCarthy.	FV	60.00
b. 3.1.2012. Signature J. Brown.	FV	60.00

Collector Series

Bank of Ireland

1978 ND Issue

CS1 ND (1978). 1, 5, 10, 100 Pounds — Mkt. Value 85.00

#61b-64b overprint: *SPECIMEN* and Maltese cross prefix serial #.

Provincial Bank of Ireland Limited

1978 Issue

CS2 1978 1, 5, 10 Pounds — Mkt. Value 60.00

#247a-249a dated 1.1.1977. Overprint: *SPECIMEN* and Maltese cross prefix serial #.

Bank of Ireland

1995 ND Issue

CS3 ND (1995). 5, 10, 100 Pounds — Mkt. Value 300.

#62b-64b overprint: *SPECIMEN.*

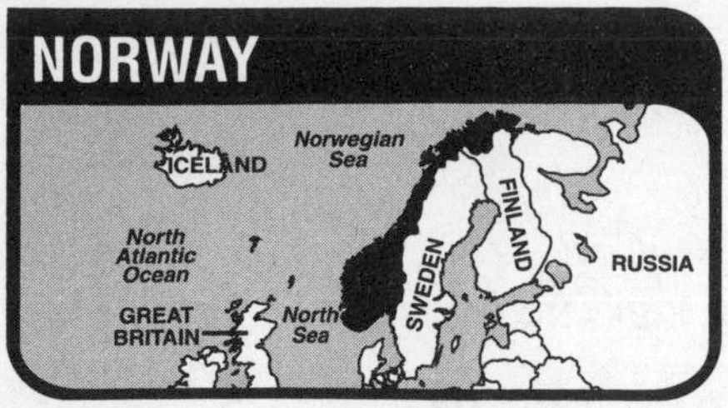

The Kingdom of Norway, a constitutional monarchy located in northwestern Europe, has an area of 150,000 sq. mi. (388,500 sq. km.) including the island territories of Spitzbergen (Svalbard) and Jan Mayen, and a population of 4.46 million. Capital: Oslo. The diversified economic of Norway includes shipping, fishing, forestry, agriculture and manufacturing. Nonferrous metals, paper and paperboard, paper pulp, iron, steel and oil are exported.

Two centuries of Viking raids into Europe tapered off following the adoption of Christianity by King Olav Tryggvason in 994. Conversion of the Norwegian kingdom occurred over the next several decades. In 1397, Norway was absorbed into a union with Denmark that lasted more than four centuries. In 1814, Norwegians resisted the cession of their country to Sweden and adopted a new constitution. Sweden then invaded Norway but agreed to let Norway keep its constitution in return for accepting the union under a Swedish king. Rising nationalism throughout the 19th century led to a 1905 referendum granting Norway independence. Although Norway remained neutral in World War I, it suffered heavy losses to its shipping. Norway proclaimed its neutrality at the outset of World War II, but was nonetheless occupied for five years by Nazi Germany (1940-45). In 1949, neutrality was abandoned and Norway became a member of NATO. Discovery of oil and gas in adjacent waters in the late 1960s boosted Norway's economic fortunes. The current focus is on containing spending on the extensive welfare system and planning for the time when petroleum reserves are depleted. In referenda held in 1972 and 1994, Norway rejected joining the EU.

RULERS:

Olav V, 1957-1991
Harald V, 1991-

MONETARY SYSTEM:

1 Speciedaler = 96 Skilling to 1816
1 Speciedaler = 120 Skilling, 1816-1873
1 Krone = 100 Øre, 1873-

KINGDOM

NORGES BANK - POST WW II

1948-55 ISSUE

#30-33 Replacement notes: Serial # prefix *Z.*

		VF	UNC
30	**5 Kroner** 1955-63. Blue on gray and multicolor underprint. Portrait Fridtjof Nansen at left. Back: Fishing scene. Watermark: Value repeated.		
	a. Signature Brofoss - Thorp. 1955-56. Prefix A-D.	40.00	100.
	b. Signature Brofoss - Thorp. 1957. Prefix D.	40.00	100.
	c. Signature Brofoss - Thorp. 1957. Prefix E.	17.50	65.00
	d. Signature Brofoss - Thorp. 1957. Prefix F.	40.00	100.
	e. Signature Brofoss - Ottesen. 1959. Prefix F.	17.50	65.00
	f. Signature Brofoss - Ottesen. 1959. Prefix G.	40.00	105.
	g. Signature Brofoss - Ottesen. 1960-63. Prefix G-L.	17.50	65.00
	s1. As a. Specimen. 1955. Overprint: *SPECIMEN.* Punch hole cancelled.	150.	300.
	s2. Specimen. Perforated.	—	750.

		VF	UNC
31	**10 Kroner** 1954-73. Yellow-brown on gray underprint. Portrait Christian Michelsen at left. Back: Mercury with ships. Watermark: Value repeated.		
	a. Signature Jahn - Thorp. 1954. Prefix A-D.	8.50	45.00
	b1. Signature Brofoss - Thorp. 1954-55. Prefix D-G.	8.00	40.00
	b2. Signature Brofoss - Thorp. 1955. Prefix H.	375.	825.
	b3. Signature Brofoss - Thorp. 1956. Prefix H-I.	8.00	40.00
	b4. Signature Brofoss - Thorp. 1957. Prefix I.	40.00	115.
	b5. Signature Brofoss - Thorp. 1957-58. Prefix J-M.	8.00	40.00
	b6. Signature Brofoss - Thorp. 1958. Prefix N.	35.00	105.
	c. Signature Brofoss - Ottesen. 1959-65. Prefix N-E.	4.50	25.00
	d. Signature Brofoss - Petersen. 1965-69. Prefix F-V.	3.00	12.50
	e. Signature Brofoss - Odegaard. 1970. Prefix W-Ø.	2.00	10.00
	f. Signature Wold - Odegaard. 1971-73. Prefix Å-R.	1.75	7.50
	p. Face or back proof. Uniface. Blue.	—	500.
	s. As a, d, f. Specimen. Punch hole cancelled.	150.	750.

		VF	UNC
32	**50 Kroner** 1950-65. Dark green. Portrait Bjørnstjerne Björnson at upper left. Crowned arms at upper center. Back: Harvesting. Watermark: Bjørnstjerne Björnson.		
	a1. Signature Jahn - Thorp. 1950-52. Prefix A.	55.00	200.
	a2. Signature Jahn - Thorp. 1952. Prefix B.	120.	550.
	a3. Signature Jan - Thorp. 1953-54. Prefix B.	55.00	200.
	b1. Signature Brofoss - Thorp. 1954. Prefix B.	150.	650.
	b2. Signature Brofoss - Thorp. 1955-58. Prefix B; C.	50.00	170.
	b3. Signature Brofoss - Thorp. 1958. Prefix D.	95.00	350.
	c. Signature Brofoss - Ottesen. 1959-65. Prefix D-F.	35.00	130.
	s. As a. 1951. Specimen. Punch hole cancelled.	—	—

33 **100 Kroner**

1949-62. Red. Portrait Henrik Wergeland at upper left. Crowned arms at upper center. Back: Logging. Watermark: Henrik Wergeland.

	VF	UNC
a1. Signature Jahn - Thorp. 1949-52. Prefix A.	50.00	175.
a2. Signature Jahn - Thorp. 1952. Prefix C.	1250.	—
a3. Signature Jahn - Thorp. 1953-54. Prefix C.	50.00	175.
b. Signature Brofoss - Thorp. 1954-58. Prefix D-G.	50.00	175.
c. Signature Brofoss - Ottesen. 1959-62. Prefix G-I.	40.00	140.
s. As a. 1950. Specimen. Punch hole cancelled.	—	200.

34 **500 Kroner**

1948-76. Dark green. Portrait Niels Henrik Abel at upper left. Crowned supported arms at upper center. Prefix A. Back: Factory workers. Watermark: Niels Henrik Abel.

	VF	UNC
a. Signature Jahn - Thorp. 1948; 1951.	350.	1000.
b1. Signature Brofoss - Thorp. 1954; 1956.	350.	1000.
b2. Signature Brofoss - Thorp. 1958.	200.	675.
c. Signature Brofoss - Ottesen. 1960-64.	160.	550.
d. Signature Brofoss - Petersen. 1966-69.	140.	400.
e. Signature Brofoss - Odegaard. 1970.	130.	325.
f. Signature Wold - Odegaard. 1971-76.	120.	275.
s. As a. Specimen. 1948. Punch hole cancelled.	600.	850.

35 **1000 Kroner**

1949-74. Red-brown. Portrait H. Ibsen at left. Crowned supported arms at upper center. Prefix A. Back: Old man and child. Watermark: Portrait H. Ibsen.

	VF	UNC
a. Signature Jahn - Thorp. 1949; 1951; 1953.	425.	800.
b. Signature Brofoss - Thorp. 1955; 1958.	290.	600.
c. Signature Brofoss - Ottesen. 1961; 1962.	225.	500.
d. Signature Brofoss - Petersen. 1965-70.	210.	400.
e. Signature Brofoss - Odegaard. 1971-74	200.	325.
s. As a. Specimen. Punch hole cancelled.	600.	850.

1962-78 Issue

36 **10 Kroner**

1972-84. Dark blue on multicolor underprint. Fridtjof Nansen at left, arms at center. Back: Fisherman and cargo ship at right. Watermark: Value *10* repeated.

	VF	UNC
a. 1972. Replacement note. Prefix Q.	50.00	100.
b. Signature Wold and Odegaard. 1973-76.	4.00	11.00
c. Signature Wold and Sagård. 1977-79; 1981-84.	2.00	6.50
s. As a. Specimen.	500.	900.

37 **50 Kroner**

1966-83. Green on multicolor underprint. Bjørnstjerne Bjõrnson at left, arms at left center. Back: Old church at right. Watermark: Bjørnstjerne Bjõrnson.

	VF	UNC
a. Signature Brofoss and Petersen. 1966-67; 1969. Prefix A-C.	25.00	80.00
b. Signature Wold and Odegaard. 1971-73. Prefix C-E.	17.50	60.00
c. As b. with security thread. 1974-75. Prefix F-G.	15.00	40.00
d. Signature Wold and Sagård. 1976-83. Prefix H-R.	12.50	35.00
s. As a. Specimen.	450.	750.

38 **100 Kroner**

1962-77. Red-violet on multicolor underprint. H. Wergeland at left, arms at left center. Back: Establishment of Constitution in 1814 at right. Watermark: H. Wergeland.

	VF	UNC
a. Signature Brofoss and Óttesen. 1962-65. Prefix A-D.	20.00	80.00
b. Signature Brofoss and Petersen. 1965-69. Prefix D-L.	17.50	80.00
c. Signature Brofoss and Petersen. 1969. Prefix M.	90.00	350.
d. Signature Brofoss and Ødegaard. 1970. Prefix M-P.	17.50	55.00
e. Signature Wold and Ødegaard. 1971-72. Prefix P-T.	17.50	50.00
f. Signature Wold and Ødegaard. 1972. Prefix U.	45.00	180.
g. Signature Wold and Ødegaard. 1973-76. Prefix U-C.	17.50	45.00
h. Signature Wold and Sagård. 1977. Prefix D-K.	FV	40.00
s. As a. Specimen.	450.	800.

39 **500 Kroner**

1978-85. Green on brown underprint. Niels Henrik Abel at left, arms at left center. Back: University of Oslo at right. Watermark: Niels Henrik Abel.

	VF	UNC
a. Signature Wold and Sagård. 1978; 1982.	100.	200.
b. Signature Skånland and Sagård. 1985.	100.	200.
s. As a. Specimen.	1000.	1900.

40 **1000 Kroner**

1975-87. Brown and violet on multicolor underprint. Henrik Ibsen at left, arms at left center. Back: Scenery. Watermark: Henrik Ibsen.

	VF	UNC
a. Signature Wold and Odegaard. 1975. Prefix A.	200.	275.
b. Signature Wold and Sagård. 1978; 1980; 1982-85. Prefix A-C.	160.	250.
c. Signature Skånland and Sagård. 1985-87. Prefix C-E.	140.	225.
s. As a. Specimen.	800.	1400.

1977 Issue

41 **100 Kroner**

1977-82. Purple on pink and multicolor underprint. Cahilla Collett at left, date at top left center. Signature Wold and Sagård. Back: Filigree design. .

	VF	UNC
a. Brown serial #. 1977.	17.50	55.00
b. Black serial #. 1979; 1980.	17.50	45.00
c. 1981; 1982.	17.50	45.00
s. As a. Specimen.	800.	1400.

1983-91 Issue

42 **50 Kroner**

1984-95. Green on multicolor underprint. Aasmund Olavsson Vinje at left. Back: Stone carving with soldier slaying dragon. Watermark: 50 repeated within diagonal bars.

	VF	UNC
a. Signature Wold and Sagård. 1984.	15.00	30.00
b. Signature Skånland and Sagård. 1985.	9.00	22.50
c. Signature Skånland and Sagård. 1986.	12.00	25.00
d. Signature Skånland and Sagård. 1987.	9.00	22.50
e. Signature Skånland and Johansen. 1989-90; 1993.	9.00	17.50
f. Signature Moland and Johansen. 1995.	FV	15.00
s. As a. Specimen.	800.	1400.

43 **100 Kroner**

1983-94. Red-violet on pink and multicolor underprint. Similar to number 41 but smaller print area, and date at lower right. Back: Filigree design. Watermark: Cahilla Collett.

	VF	UNC
a. Signature Wold and Sagård. 1983.	17.50	40.00
b. As a. but large date. 1984.	17.50	40.00
c. Signature Skånland and Sagård. 1985-87.	17.50	35.00
d. Signature Skånland and Johansen. 1988-93.	15.00	27.50
e. Signature Moland and Johansen. 1994.	FV	27.50

44 **500 Kroner** VF UNC

1991; 1994; 1996; 1997. Blue-violet on multicolor underprint. Edvard Grieg at left. Back: Floral mosaic at center. Watermark: Grieg repeated vertically.

a. Signature Skånland and Johansen. 1991.	FV	140.
b. Signature Moland and Johansen. 1994.	FV	120.
c. Signature Storvik and Johansen. 1996; 1997.	FV	120.

45 **1000 Kroner** VF UNC

1989; 1990. Purple and dark blue on multicolor underprint. C. M. Falsen at left. Back: 1668 royal seal.

a. Signature Skånland and Johansen. 1989; 1990.	FV	275.
b. Signature Storvik and Johansen. 1998.	FV	225.

1994-96 Issue

46 **50 Kroner** VF UNC

1996-. Dark green on pale green and multicolor underprint. P. C. Asbjörnsen at right. Back: Water lilies and dragonfly. Watermark: P. C. Asbjörnsen repeated vertically.

a. Signature Storvik and Johansen. 1996; 1998.	FV	17.50
b. Signature Gjedrem and Johansen. 1999; 2000; 2003.	FV	15.00
c. Signature Gjedrem and Eklund. 2003; 2005.	FV	15.00
d. Signature Olsen and Eklund. 2011.	FV	15.00

47 **100 Kroner** VF UNC

1995; 1997-99. Deep brown-violet and red-violet on multicolor underprint. Kirsten Flagstad at right. Signature: K. Storvik and S. Johansen. Back: Theatre layout. Watermark: Kirsten Flagstad repeated vertically.

a. Signature Storvik and Johansen. 1995; 1997; 1998. 10-digit serial # upper left and lower right on face. Date on back.	FV	30.00
b. Signature Gjedrem and Johansen. 1999. 10-digit serial # upper left, 8-digit # lower right on face, where last four digits are the date.	FV	27.50

48 **200 Kroner** VF UNC

1994; 1998; 1999; 2000. Blue-black and dark blue on multicolor underprint. Kristian Birkeland at right. Back: Map of the North Pole; North America and Northern Europe at left center. Watermark: Kristian Birkeland repeated vertically.

a. Signature Moland and Johansen. 1994.	FV	50.00
b. Signature Storvik and Johansen. 1998.	FV	45.00
c. Signature Gjedrem and Johansen. 1999; 2000.	FV	42.50

1999-2002 Issue

49 **100 Kroner** VF UNC

2003-04; 2006-07. Deep brown-violet and red-violet on multicolor underprint. Kirsten Flagstad at right. Wide holographic strip at right. Signature: Gjdren and Eklund. Back: Theatre layout. Watermark: Kirsten Flagstad repeated vertically.

a. 2003.	FV	27.50
b. 2004.	FV	27.50
c. 2006.	FV	27.50
d. 2007.	FV	27.50

50	**200 Kroner**	VF	UNC
	2002-. Blue-black and dark blue on multicolor underprint. Kristian Birkeland at right, wide holographic strip at right. Back: Map of the North Pole; North America and Northern Europe at left center. Watermark: Birkeland repeated vertically.		
	a. 2002. Signature Gjedrem and Johansen.	FV	45.00
	b. 2003. Signature Gjedrem and Eklund.	FV	42.50
	c. 2004.	FV	42.50
	d. 2006.	FV	42.50
	e. 2009.	FV	42.50

51	**500 Kroner**	VF	UNC
	1999-. Brown on tan and multicolor underprint. Sigrid Undste and wide holographic strip at right. Signature: Gjedrem and Johansen. Back: Wreath of wheat and roses.		
	a. 1999.	FV	125.
	b. 2000.	FV	125.
	c. 2002.	FV	125.
	d. 2005.	FV	125.

52	**1000 Kroner**	VF	UNC
	2001; 2004. Lilac, blue, yellow and multicolor. Edvard Munch at right, wide holographic strip at right edge, part of his painting *Melancholy* at left center. Signature: Gjedrem and Johansen. Back: Munch's great work *The Sun*.		
	a. 2001.	FV	275.
	b. 2004.	FV	275.

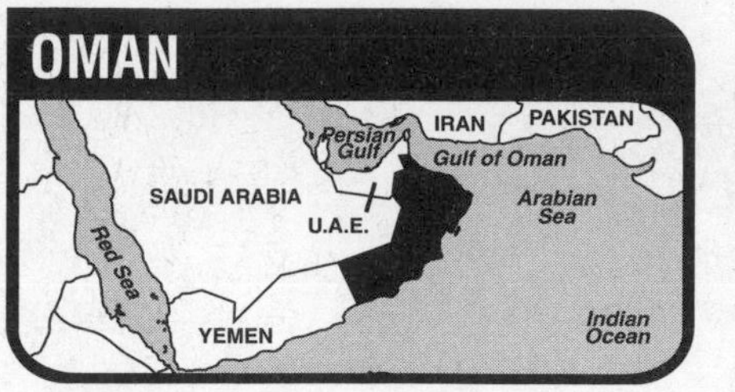

The Sultanate of Oman (formerly Muscat and Oman), an independent monarchy located in the southeastern part of the Arabian Peninsula, has an area of 82,030 sq. mi. (212,457 sq. km.) and a population of 2.72 million. Capital: Muscat. The economy is d on agriculture, herding and petroleum. Petroleum products, dates, fish and hides are exported.

The inhabitants of the area of Oman have long prospered on Indian Ocean trade. In the late 18th century, a newly established sultanate in Muscat signed the first in a series of friendship treaties with Britain. Over time, Oman's dependence on British political and military advisors increased, but it never became a British colony. In 1970, Qaboos bin Said al-Said overthrew the restrictive rule of his father; he has ruled as sultan ever since. His extensive modernization program has opened the country to the outside world while preserving the longstanding close ties with the UK. Oman's moderate, independent foreign policy has sought to maintain good relations with all Middle Eastern countries.

RULERS:

Sa'id bin Taimur, AH1351-1390/1932-1970 AD
Qaboos bin Sa'id, AH1390-1419/1970-1999AD

MONETARY SYSTEM:

1 Rial Omani = 1000 Baiza (Baisa)
1 Rial Saidi = 1000 Baiza (Baisa)

Muscat and Oman

Sultanate of Muscat and Oman

1970 ND Issue

1	**100 Baiza**	VF	UNC
	ND (1970). Brown on blue-green and multicolor underprint. Arms at right. Watermark: Arms.		
	a. Issued note.	15.00	40.00
	s. Specimen.	—	150.
	ct. Color trial in violet.	—	200.

2	**1/4 Rial Saidi**	VF	UNC
	ND (1970). Blue and brown on multicolor underprint. Arms at right. Back: Jalali Fortress. Watermark: Arms.		
	a. Issued note.	18.00	40.00
	s. Specimen.	—	150.
	ct. Color trial in green.	—	200.

3	1/2 Rial Saidi	VF	UNC
	ND (1970). Green and purple on multicolor underprint. Arms at right. Back: Sumail Fortress. Watermark: Arms.		
	a. Issued note.	30.00	85.00
	s. Specimen.	—	180.
	ct. Color trial in purple.	—	250.

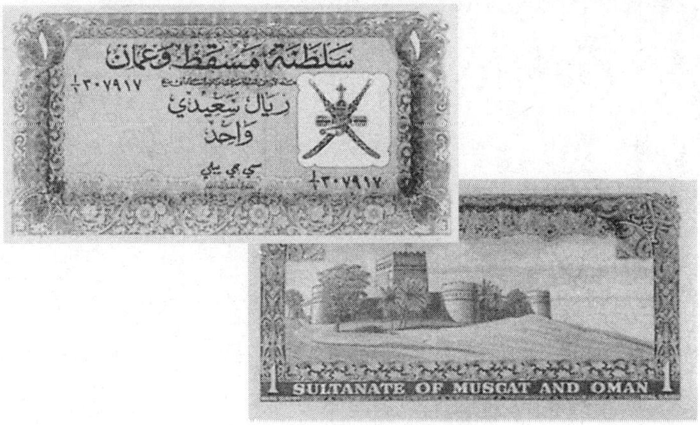

4	1 Rial Saidi	VF	UNC
	ND (1970). Red and olive-green on multicolor underprint. Arms at right. Back: Sohar Fort. Watermark: Arms.		
	a. Issued note.	45.00	120.
	s. Specimen.	—	225.
	ct. Color trial in blue.	—	300.

5	5 Rials Saidi	VF	UNC
	ND (1970). Purple and blue on multicolor underprint. Arms at right. Back. Nizwa Fort. Watermark: Arms.		
	a. Issued note.	125.	350.
	s. Specimen.	—	400
	ct. Color trial in red.	—	500.

6	10 Rials Saidi	VF	UNC
	ND (1970). Dark brown and blue on multicolor underprint. Arms at right. Back: Mirani Fort. Watermark: Arms.		
	a. Issued note.	225.	650.
	s. Specimen.	—	700.
	ct. Color trial in blue-green.	—	800.

Oman

Oman Currency Board

1973 ND Issue

7	100 Baiza	VF	UNC
	ND (1973). Brown on blue-green and multicolor underprint. Arms at right. Watermark: Arms.		
	a. Issued note.	7.50	20.00
	s. Specimen.	—	125.
	ct. Color trial. Violet-brown on multicolor underprint.	—	150.

8	1/4 Rial Omani	VF	UNC
	ND (1973). Blue and brown on multicolor underprint. Arms at right. Back: Jalali Fortress. Watermark: Arms.		
	a. Issued note.	10.00	30.00
	s. Specimen.	—	125.
	ct. Color trial. Green on multicolor underprint.	—	150.

9	1/2 Rial Omani	VF	UNC
	ND (1973). Green and purple on multicolor underprint. Arms at right. Back: Sumail Fortress. Watermark: Arms.		
	a. Issued note.	20.00	50.00
	s. Specimen.	—	150.
	ct. Color trial. Black and purple on multicolor underprint.	—	200.

10 **1 Rial Omani** | VF | UNC
ND (1973). Red and olive-green on multicolor underprint. Arms at right. Back: Sohar Fort. Watermark: Arms.

	VF	UNC
a. Issued note.	35.00	95.00
s. Specimen.	—	200.
ct. Color trial. Blue on multicolor underprint.	—	250.

11 **5 Rials Omani**
ND (1973). Purple and blue on multicolor underprint. Arms at right. Back: Nizwa Fort. Watermark: Arms.

	VF	UNC
a. Issued note.	100.	285.
s. Specimen.	—	350.
ct. Color trial. Red and blue on multicolor underprint.	—	425.

12 **10 Rials Omani**
ND (1973). Dark brown and blue on multicolor underprint. Arms at right. Back: Mirani Fort. Watermark: Arms.

	VF	UNC
a. Issued note.	200.	550.
s. Specimen.	—	600.
ct. Color trial in blue-green.	—	700.

Central Bank of Oman

1977; 1985 ND Issue

13 **100 Baisa**
ND (1977). Light brown on multicolor underprint. Arms at right. Back: Port of Qaboos.

	VF	UNC
a. Issued note.	3.00	8.00
s. Specimen.	—	120.

14 **200 Baisa**

	VF	UNC
ND (1985). Purple on multicolor underprint. Arms at right. Back: Rustaq Fortress. Watermark: Arms.	4.50	10.00

15 **1/4 Rial**
ND (1977). Blue and brown on multicolor underprint. Arms at right. Back: Jalali Fortress. Watermark: Arms.

	VF	UNC
a. Issued note.	7.50	18.00
s. Specimen.	—	120.

16 **1/2 Rial**
ND (1977). Green and purple on multicolor underprint. Arms at right. Back: Sumail fortress. Watermark: Arms.

	VF	UNC
a. Issued note.	15.00	35.00
s. Specimen.	—	135.

17 **1 Rial**
ND (1977). Red and brown on multicolor underprint. Arms at right. Back: Rustaq Fortress. Watermark: Arms.

	VF	UNC
a. Issued note.	25.00	55.00
s. Specimen.	—	150.

18 **5 Rials** — VF — UNC

ND (1977). Lilac and blue on multicolor underprint. Arms at right. Back: Jalali Fortress. Watermark: Arms.

	VF	UNC
a. Issued note.	60.00	125.
s. Specimen.	—	225.

19 **10 Rials** — VF — UNC

ND (1977). Brown and blue on multicolor underprint. Arms at right. Back: Sumail Fortress. Watermark: Arms.

	VF	UNC
a. Issued note.	100.	200.
s. Specimen.	—	275.

20 **20 Rials** — VF — UNC

ND (1977). Gray-blue and orange on multicolor underprint. Sultan Qaboos bin Sa'id at right. Back: Central Bank at left center. Watermark: Arms.

	VF	UNC
a. Issued note.	190.	400.
s. Specimen.	—	350.

21 **50 Rials** — VF — UNC

ND. Olive-brown, blue and dark brown on multicolor underprint. Sultan at right. Back: Jabreen Fort at left center.

	VF	UNC
a. Issued note.	400.	850.
s. Specimen.	—	700.

1985-90 Issue

22 **100 Baisa** — VF — UNC

AH1408-1414/1987-1994AD. Light brown on multicolor underprint. Sultan Qaboos bin Sa'id at right. Back: Port of Qaboos. Watermark: Sultan Qaboos bin Sa'id. UV: center design elements fluoresce yellow.

	VF	UNC
a. 1987/AH1408.	3.50	8.00
b. 1989/AH1409.	3.00	7.00
c. 1992/AH1413.	15.00	35.00
d. 1994/AH1414.	2.50	6.00

23 **200 Baisa** — VF — UNC

AH1407-1414/1987-1994AD. Purple on multicolor underprint. Sultan Qaboos bin Sa'id at right. Back: Rustaq Fort. Watermark: Sultan Qaboos bin Sa'id.

	VF	UNC
a. 1987/AH1407.	6.00	14.00
b. 1993/AH1413.	5.00	11.00
c. 1994/AH1414.	4.00	9.00

24 **1/4 Rial** — VF — UNC

1989/AH1409. Blue, brown and red on multicolor underprint. Sultan Qaboos bin Sa'id at right. Back: Modern fishing industry. Watermark: Sultan Qaboos bin Sa'id. — 7.50 — 18.00

25	1/2 Rial	VF	UNC
	1987/AH1408. Green on multicolor underprint. Sultan Qaboos bin Sa'id at right. Back: Aerial view of Sultan Qaboos University. Watermark: Sultan Qaboos bin Sa'id.	10.00	22.50

26	1 Rial	VF	UNC
	AH1407-1414/1987-1994AD. Red, black and olive-brown on multicolor underprint. Sultan Qaboos bin Sa'id at right. Back: Sohar Fort at left. Watermark: Sultan Qaboos bin Sa'id.		
	a. 1987/AH1407.	16.00	37.50
	b. 1989/AH1409.	15.00	35.00
	c. 1994/AH1414.	14.00	30.00

27	5 Rials	VF	UNC
	1990/AH1411. Dark rose, brown-violet and multicolor underprint. Sultan Qaboos bin Sa'id at right. Back: Fort Nizwa. Watermark: Sultan Qaboos bin Sa'id.	55.00	120.

28	10 Rials	VF	UNC
	AH1408/1987AD; AH1413/1993AD. Dark brown, red-brown and blue on multicolor underprint. Sultan Qaboos bin Sa'id at right. Back: Fort Mirani at left center. Watermark: Sultan Qaboos bin Sa'id.		
	a. 1987/AH1408.	90.00	190.
	b. 1993/AH1413.	85.00	180.

29	20 Rials	VF	UNC
	AH1407/1987AD; AH1414/1994AD. Brown, dark olive-brown and blue-gray on multicolor underprint. Sultan Qaboos bin Sa'id at right. Back: Central Bank at left center. Watermark: Sultan Qaboos bin Sa'id.		
	a. 1987/AH1408.	140.	300.
	b. 1994/AH1414.	135.	285.

30	50 Rials	VF	UNC
	AH1405/1985AD; AH1413/1992AD. Olive-brown, blue and dark brown on multicolor underprint. Sultan Qaboos bin Sa'id at right. Back: Jabreen Fort at left center, *Jabreen Fort*added at lower right. Watermark: Sultan Qaboos bin Sa'id.		
	a. 1985/AH1405.	450.	1000.
	b. 1992/AH1413.	300.	650.
	s. As a. Specimen.	—	750.

1995 Issue

31 **100 Baisa** | VF FV | UNC 1.00

1995/AH1416. Deep olive-green, dark green-blue and purple on multicolor underprint. Sultan Qaboos bin Sa'id at right, Faslajs irrigation system at center, arms at upper left. Back: Verreaux's eagle and white oryx at center. Watermark: Sultan Qaboos bin Sa'id. 122x64mm.

32 **200 Baisa** | VF FV | UNC 4.00

1995/AH1416. Black, deep blue and green on multicolor underprint. Sultan Qaboos bin Sa'id at right, Seeb & Salalah Airports at left center, arms at upper left. Back: Raysut Port and Marine Science & Fisheries Center at lower left, aerial view of Sultan Qaboos port at center. Watermark: Sultan Qaboos bin Sa'id. 128x64mm.

33 **1/2 Rial** | VF FV | UNC 3.00

1995/AH1416. Dark brown and gray on multicolor underprint. Sultan Qaboos bin Sa'id at right, Bahla Castle at center, arms at upper left. Back: Nakhl Fort and Al-Hazm castle at lower left, Nakhl Fort at center. Watermark: Sultan Qaboos bin Sa'id. 135x64mm.

34 **1 Rial** | VF FV | UNC 10.00

1995/AH1416. Deep purple, purple and blue-green on multicolor underprint. Sultan Qaboos bin Sa'id at right, Sultan Qaboos Sports Complex, Burj al-Sahwa, road overpass at center, arms at upper left. Back: Omani Khanjar, traditional silver bracelets and ornaments with shipbuilding in background underprint. Watermark: Sultan Qaboos bin Sa'id. 145x76mm.

35 **5 Rials** | VF | UNC

1995/AH1416. Red on pale blue and multicolor underprint. Sultan Qaboos bin Sa'id at right, Sultan Qaboos University building with clock tower at center, arms at upper left. Back: Nizwa city view at left center. Watermark: Sultan Qaboos bin Sa'id. 152x76mm.

a. Without reflective pattern of Khanjars (State Emblem) on back. 30.00 65.00

b. With reflective pattern of Khanjars on back. 22.00 52.00

36 **10 Rials** | VF 35.00 | UNC 80.00

1995/AH1416. Dark brown on pale blue and multicolor underprint. Sultan Qaboos bin Sa'id at right, al Nahdha in Salalah Tower, Jabreen coconut palm and frankincense tree at center, arms at upper left. Back: Mutrah Fort and Corniche at left center. Watermark: Sultan Qaboos bin Sa'id. 159x27mm.

37 **20 Rials** | VF 70.00 | UNC 150.

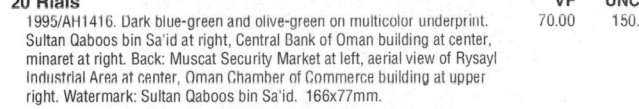

1995/AH1416. Dark blue-green and olive-green on multicolor underprint. Sultan Qaboos bin Sa'id at right, Central Bank of Oman building at center, minaret at right. Back: Muscat Security Market at left, aerial view of Rysayl Industrial Area at center, Oman Chamber of Commerce building at upper right. Watermark: Sultan Qaboos bin Sa'id. 166x77mm.

38 **50 Rials** | VF FV | UNC 350.

1995/AH1416. Purple and violet on multicolor underprint. Sultan Qaboos bin Sa'id at right, Ministry of Finance and Economy building at center, Mirani Fort at right, arms at upper left. Back: Cabinet building at left, Ministry of Commerce and Industry building at center right. Watermark: Sultan Qaboos bin Sa'id. 174x77mm.

2000 Issue

		VF	UNC
39	**5 Rials** 2000/AH1420. Red on multicolor underprint. Sultan Qaboos bin Sa'id at right, Sultan Qaboos University building with clock tower at center, arms at upper left. Holographic strip at right. Back: Nizwa city view at left center. Watermark: Sultan Qaboos bin Sa'id. 152x76mm.	FV	27.50

		VF	UNC
40	**10 Rials** 2000/1420AH. Brown on multicolor underprint. Sultan Qaboos bin Sa'id at right, al-Nahdha in Salalah Tower, Jabreen coconut palm and frankincense tree at center, arms at upper left. Holographic strip at right. Back: Mutrah Fort and Corniche at left center. Watermark: Sultan Qaboos bin Sa'id. 159x77mm.	FV	50.00

		VF	UNC
41	**20 Rials** 2000/1420AH. Green on multicolor underprint. Sultan Qaboos bin Sa'id at right, Central Bank of Oman building at center, minaret at right. Holographic strip at right. Back: Muscat Security Market at left, aerial view of Rysayl Industrial Area at center, Oman Chamber of Commerce building at upper right. Watermark: Sultan Qaboos bin Sa'id. 166x77mm.	FV	100.

		VF	UNC
42	**50 Rials** 2000/1420AH. Purple on multicolor underprint. Sultan Qaboos bin Sa'id at right, Ministry of Finance and Economy building at center, Mirani Fort at right, arms at upper left. Holographic strip at right. Back: Cabinet building at left, Ministry of Commerce and Industry building at center right. Watermark: Sultan Qaboosbin Sa'id. 174x77mm.	FV	225.

2005 Commemorative Issue

		VF	UNC
43	**1 Rial** 2005/AH1426. Red. Sultan Qaboos at right Back: Sailing ship at left. 145x76mm.		
	a. Issued note.	FV	10.00
	s. Specimen	—	75.00

2010 Commemorative Issue

		VF	UNC
44	**5 Rials** 2010. Multicolor. 153x76mm.	FV	27.50

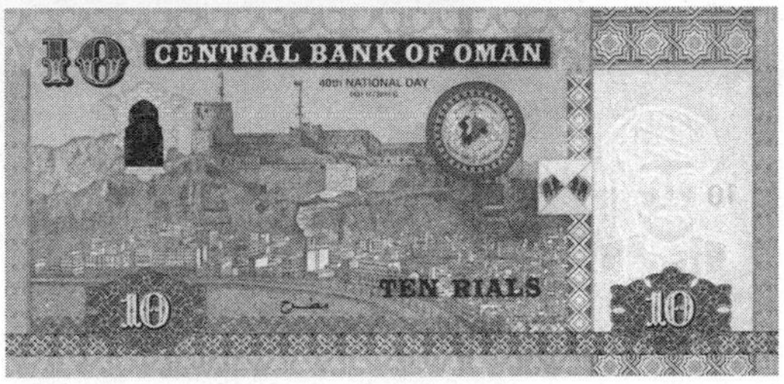

45	**10 Rials**	**VF**	**UNC**
	2010. Multicolor. 160x76mm.	FV	50.00

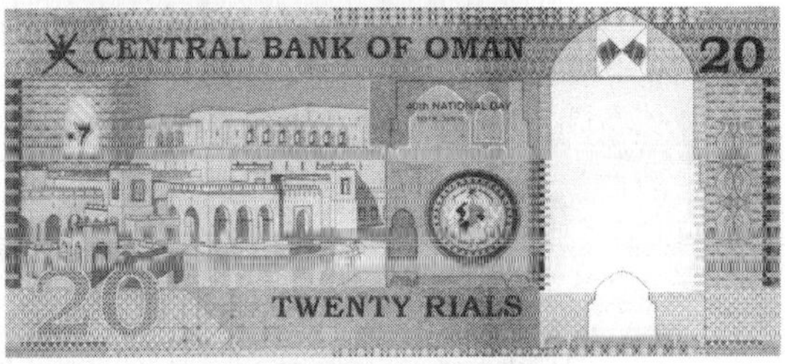

46	**20 Rials**	**VF**	**UNC**
	2010. Blue, olive and multicolor. Sultan Qaboos at right center, mosque at lower left. Back: Palace. 166x77mm.	FV	130.

47	**50 Rials**	**VF**	**UNC**
	2010. Multicolor. 174x76mm.	FV	225.

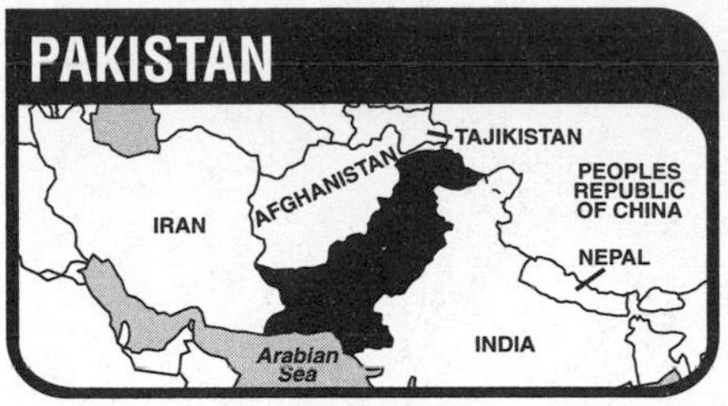

The Islamic Republic of Pakistan, located on the Indian subcontinent between India and Afghanistan, has an area of 310,404 sq. mi. (803,943 sq. m.) and a population of 170 million. Capital: Islamabad. Pakistan is mainly an agricultural land. Yarn, cotton, rice and leather are exported.

The Indus Valley civilization, one of the oldest in the world and dating back at least 5,000 years, spread over much of what is presently Pakistan. During the second millennium B.C., remnants of this culture fused with the migrating Indo-Aryan peoples. The area underwent successive invasions in subsequent centuries from the Persians, Greeks, Scythians, Arabs (who brought Islam), Afghans, and Turks. The Mughal Empire flourished in the 16th and 17th centuries; the British came to dominate the region in the 18th century. The separation in 1947 of British India into the Muslim state of Pakistan (with West and East sections) and largely Hindu India was never satisfactorily resolved, and India and Pakistan fought two wars - in 1947-48 and 1965 - over the disputed Kashmir territory. A third war between these countries in 1971 - in which India capitalized on Islamabad's marginalization of Bengalis in Pakistani politics - resulted in East Pakistan becoming the separate nation of Bangladesh. In response to Indian nuclear weapons testing, Pakistan conducted its own tests in 1998. The dispute over the state of Kashmir is ongoing, but discussions and confidence-building measures have led to decreased tensions since 2002. Mounting public dissatisfaction with President Musharraf, coupled with the assassination of the prominent and popular political leader, Benazir Bhutto, in late 2007, and Musharraf's resignation in August 2008, led to the September presidential election of Asif Zardari, Bhutto's widower. Pakistani government and military leaders are struggling to control Islamist militants, many of whom are located in the tribal areas adjacent to the border with Afghanistan. The November 2008 Mumbai attacks again inflamed Indo-Pakistan relations. The Pakistani Government is also faced with a deteriorating economy as foreign exchange reserves decline, the currency depreciates, and the current account deficit widens.

MONETARY SYSTEM:

1 Rupee = 16 Annas to 1961
1 Rupee = 100 Paisa (Pice), 1961-

REPLACEMENT NOTES:

#24, 24A, 24B, 1/X or 2/X prefix. #25-33, X as first of double prefix letters.

REPUBLIC

GOVERNMENT OF PAKISTAN

1951-73 ND ISSUES

8	**1 Rupee**	**VF**	**UNC**
	ND (1951). Blue on multicolor underprint. Crescent moon and star at right. 2 signature varieties. Back: Violet. Archway at left center.	100.	150.

9	**1 Rupee**	**VF**	**UNC**
	ND (1953-63). Blue on multicolor underprint. Crescent moon and star at right. Like #8 but larger size serial #. 6 signature varieties. Back: Blue. Archway at left center.	7.00	12.00

9A	**1 Rupee**	**VF**	**UNC**
	ND (1964). Blue on multicolor underprint. Crescent moon and star at right. Like #8 but different font for serial #. 3 signature varieties. Back: Violet. Archway at left center.	4.00	7.00

10 **1 Rupee** VF UNC

ND (1973). Brown on multicolor underprint. Crescent moon and star at right. Like #8 but larger size serial #. 6 signature varieties. Back: Archway at left center.

	VF	UNC
a. Signature 1. *Aftab Qazi.*	1.50	3.50
b. Signature 2. *Abdul Rauf.*	1.50	3.00

State Bank of Pakistan

City Overprint Varieties

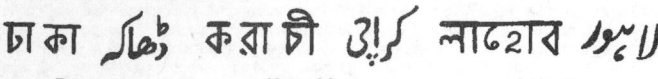

ঢাকা ڈھاکہ করাচী کراچی লাহোর لاہور

Dacca Karachi Lahore

Some notes exist w/Urdu and some w/Bengali ovpt. denoting city of issue, Dacca, Karachi or Lahore. These are much scarcer than the regular issues. Sign. varieties.

1957-66 ND Issue

15 **5 Rupees** VF UNC

	VF	UNC
ND (1966). Purple on light blue and maroon underprint. Portrait of Mohammed Ali Jinnah at center. Three signature varieties. Back: Terraces. Watermark: Portrait of Mohammed Ali Jinnah.	3.50	6.00

16 **10 Rupees** VF UNC

ND (1970). Brown on multicolor underprint. Portrait of Mohammed Ali Jinnah at left. Back: Gardens. Watermark: Mohammed Ali Jinnah.

	VF	UNC
a. Latin signature	7.50	15.00
b. Urdu & Bengali signature	6.00	12.50

17 **50 Rupees** VF UNC

ND (1964). Blue-green on peach underprint. Portrait of Mohammed Ali Jinnah at center. Back: Green. Sailing ships. Watermark: Mohammed Ali Jinnah.

	VF	UNC
a. Latin signature 2 signature varieties.	6.00	10.00
b. 1 Urdu and 1 Bengali signature of the same signatory.	6.00	10.00

18 **100 Rupees**

ND (1957). Green on violet and peach underprint. Portrait of Mohammed Ali Jinnah at center. Back: Badshahi Mosque in Lahore. Watermark: Mohammed Ali Jinnah.

	VF	UNC
a. Without overprint. 2 signature varieties.	6.00	10.00
b. Overprint: *Dhaka.* 2 signature varieties.	6.00	12.00
c. Overprint: *Karachi.* 2 signature varieties.	6.00	10.00
d. Overprint: *Lahore.* 2 signature varieties.	6.00	10.00

19 **500 Rupees** VF UNC

ND (1964). Red on gold and light green underprint. Portrait of Mohammed Ali Jinnah at center. Back: State Bank of Pakistan building. Watermark: Mohammed Ali Jinnah.

	VF	UNC
a. overprint: *Dhaka.*	25.00	45.00
b. overprint: *Karachi.* 2 signature varieties.	20.00	30.00
c. overprint: *Lahore.*	20.00	30.00

1973 ND Issue

20 **5 Rupees** VF UNC

ND (1972-78). Orange-brown on pale blue and dull green underprint. Mohammed Ali Jinnah at center. Three signature varieties. Back: Terraces. Watermark: Mohammed Ali Jinnah.

	VF	UNC
a. Serial # prefix of single or double letters.	5.00	8.00
b. Serial # prefix fractional with double letters over numerals.	5.00	8.00

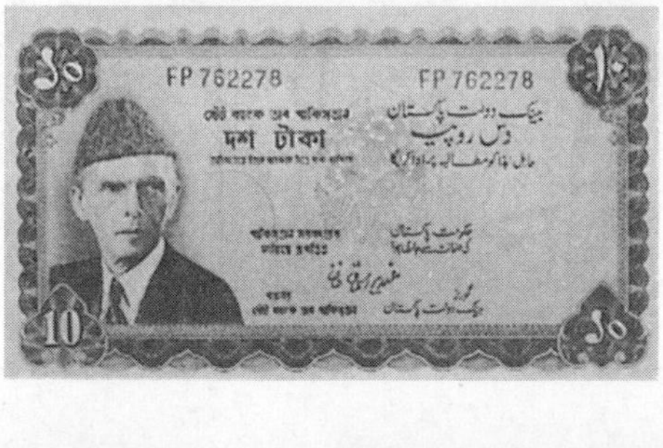

21	10 Rupees	VF	UNC
	ND (1972-75). Green on multicolor underprint. Mohammed Ali Jinnah at left. Two signature varieties. Back: Shalimar Gardens, Lahore. Watermark: Mohammed Ali Jinnah.		
	a. Sans-serif font for serial #.	5.00	10.00
	b. Serif font for serial #. Printer: TDLR (without imprint.)	10.00	20.00
	c. Serial # prefix with two **.	40.00	100.

22	50 Rupees	VF	UNC
	ND (1972-78). Blue on multicolor underprint. Mohammed Ali Jinnah at center. Three signature varieties. Back: Sailing ships. Watermark: Mohammed Ali Jinnah.	12.50	25.00

23	100 Rupees	VF	UNC
	ND (1973-78). Dark blue on multicolor underprint. Mohammed Ali Jinnah at left. Two signature varieties. Back: Badshahi Mosque, Lahore. Watermark: Mohammed Ali Jinnah.	20.00	55.00

SIGNATURE VARIETIES

1	Abdur Rauf Shaikh	2	Aftab Ahmad Khan
3	Habibullah Baig	4	Izharul-Haq
5	Saeed Ahmad Qureshi	6	R. A. Akhund
7	Qazi Alimullah	8	Khalid Javed

SIGNATURE VARIETIES

9	Javed Talat	10	Mian Tayeb Hasan
11	Moeen Afzal	12	Mohammad Younus Khan
13			

Government of Pakistan

1975 ND Issue

24	1 Rupee	VF	UNC
	ND (1974). Blue on light green and lilac underprint. Arms at right. Lower border on face is 14mm high and includes text in four languages. Signature 1. Back: Minar-i-Pakistan monument at left. Watermark: Arms.	10.00	35.00
24A	1 Rupee		
	ND (1975-81). Blue on light green and lilac underprint. Arms at right. Signature 1-3. New broader panel is 22mm. high and without four-language text along bottom. Back: Minar-i-Pakistan monument at left. Watermark: Arms.	2.00	3.50

1981-83 ND Issue

رزقِ حلال عینِ عبادت ہے

URDU TEXT LINE A

حصولِ رزقِ حلال عبادت ہے

URDU TEXT LINE B

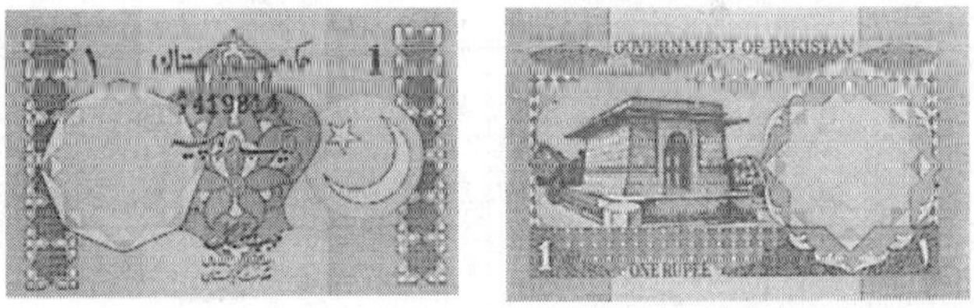

25	1 Rupee	VF	UNC
	ND (1981-82). Dull brown on multicolor underprint. Arms at right. Signature 3. Serial number at upper center. Back: Tomb of Allama Mohammed Iqbal, no Urdu text line at bottom.	2.00	3.50

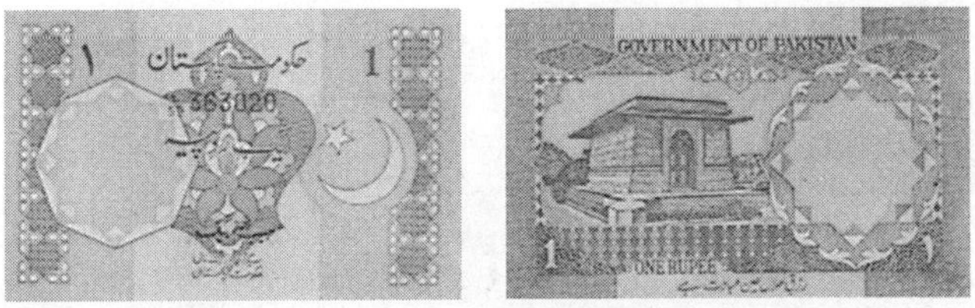

26	1 Rupee	VF	UNC
	ND (1982). Dull brown on multicolor underprint. Arms at right. Back: Tomb of Allama Mohammed Iqbal. Urdu text line A at bottom. Watermark: Arms.		
	a. Serial # at upper center. Signature 3.	2.00	3.00
	b. Serial # at lower right. Signature 3.	2.00	3.00

27	1 Rupee	VF	UNC
	ND (1983-). Dull brown on multicolor underprint. Arms at right. Back: Tomb of Allama Mohammed Iqbal. Urdu text line B at bottom. Watermark: Arms.		
	a. Serial # at upper center. Signature 3.	1.00	2.00
	b. Serial # at lower right. Signature 3.	.50	1.00

	VF	UNC
c. As a. Signature 4.	1.00	2.00
d. As b. Signature 4.	.50	1.00
e. As a. Signature 5.	1.00	2.00
f. As b. Signature 5.	.50	1.00
g. As a. Signature 6.	1.00	2.00
h. As b. Signature 6.	.50	1.00
i. As a. Signature 7.	1.00	2.00
j. As b. Signature 7.	.50	1.00
k. As b. Signature 8.	.50	1.00
l. As b. Signature 9.	.50	1.00
m. As b. Signature 10.	.50	1.00
n. As b. Signature 11.	.50	1.00
o. As b. Signature 12.	.50	1.00

GOVERNORS OF THE BANK

1	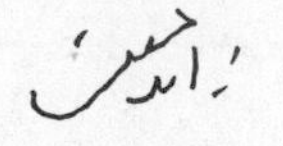	2	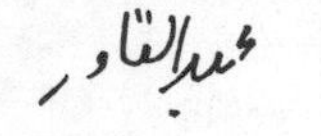
3	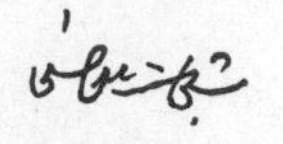	4	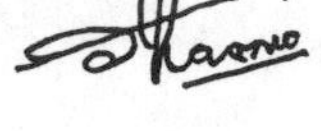
5	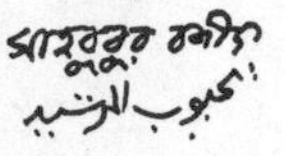	6	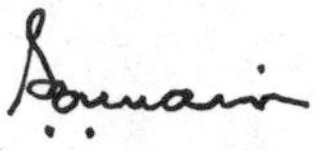
7	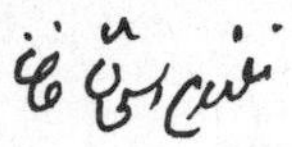	8	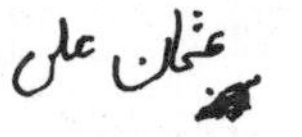
9	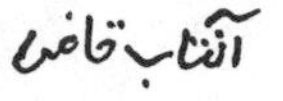	10	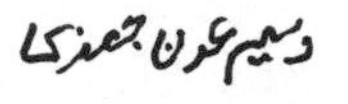
11	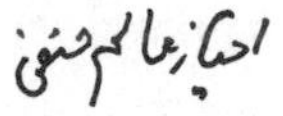	12	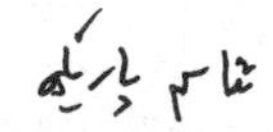
13		14	
15	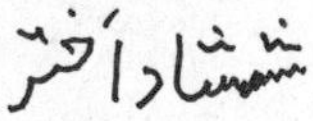	16	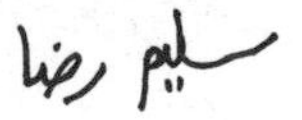

State Bank of Pakistan

1976-77 ND Issue

		VF	UNC
28	**5 Rupees** ND (1976-84). Dark brown on tan and pink underprint. Mohammed Ali Jinnah at right. Two signature varieties. Serial number varieties. Back: Khajak railroad tunnel. No Urdu text line beneath upper title. Watermark: Mohammed Ali Jinnah.	2.50	4.00

		VF	UNC
29	**10 Rupees** ND (1976-84). Pale olive-green on multicolor underprint. Mohammed Ali Jinnah at right. Two signature varieties. Serial number varieties. Back: View of Moenjodaro. No Urdu text line beneath upper title. Watermark: Mohammed Ali Jinnah.	2.50	4.00
30	**50 Rupees** ND (1977-84). Purple on multicolor underprint. Mohammed Ali Jinnah at right. Two signature varieties. Serial number varieties. Back: Main gate of Lahore fort. No Urdu text line beneath upper title. Watermark: Mohammed Ali Jinnah.	5.00	12.50

		VF	UNC
31	**100 Rupees** ND (1976-84). Red and orange on multicolor underprint. Mohammed Ali Jinnah at right. Two signature varieties. Serial number varieties. Back: Islamic College, Peshawar. No Urdu text line beneath upper title. Watermark: Mohammed Ali Jinnah.	12.50	25.00

1981-82 ND Issue

#32 Not assigned.

		VF	UNC
33	**5 Rupees** ND (1981-82). Dark brown on tan and pink underprint. Mohammed Ali Jinnah at right. Back: Khajak railroad tunnel. Urdu text line A beneath upper title. Watermark: Mohammed Ali Jinnah.	2.50	5.00
34	**10 Rupees** ND (1981-82). Pale olive-green on multicolor underprint. Mohammed Ali Jinnah at right. Back: View of Moenjodaro. Urdu text line A beneath upper title. Watermark: Mohammed Ali Jinnah.	2.50	5.00

		VF	UNC
35	**50 Rupees** ND (1981-82). Purple on multicolor underprint. Mohammed Ali Jinnah at right. Back: Main gate of Lahore fort. Urdu text line A beneath upper title. Watermark: Mohammed Ali Jinnah.	7.50	12.50

36 100 Rupees VF UNC
ND (1981-82). Red and orange on multicolor underprint. Mohammed Ali Jinnah at right. Back: Islamic College, Peshawar. Urdu text line A beneath upper title. Watermark: Mohammed Ali Jinnah. 12.50 25.00

1983-88 ND Issue

37 2 Rupees VF UNC
ND (1985-99). Pale purple on multicolor underprint. Shade varieties exist. Arms at right. Five signature varieties. Back: Badshahi mosque. Urdu text line B beneath upper title. Watermark: Arms. 2.00 4.00

38 5 Rupees VF UNC
ND (1983-84). Dark brown on tan and pink underprint. Mohammed Ali Jinnah at right. Six signature varieties. Back: Khajak railroad tunnel. Urdu text line B beneath upper title. Watermark: Mohammed Ali Jinnah. FV 1.00

39 10 Rupees VF UNC
ND (1983-84). Pale olive-green on multicolor underprint. Mohammed Ali Jinnah at right. Six signature varieties. Back: View of Moenjodaro. Urdu text line B beneath upper title. Watermark: Mohammed Ali Jinnah. 141x73mm. FV 1.50

40 50 Rupees VF UNC
ND (1986-). Purple on multicolor underprint. Mohammed Ali Jinnah at right. Six signatue varieties. Back: Main gate of Lahore fort. Urdu text line B beneath upper title. Watermark: Mohammed Ali Jinnah. 154x73mm. FV 6.00

41 100 Rupees
ND (1986-). Red and orange on multicolor underprint. Mohammed Ali Jinnah at right. Six signature varieties. Back: Islamic College, Peshawar. Urdu text line B beneath upper title. Watermark: Mohammed Ali Jinnah. 165x73mm. FV 7.50

42 500 Rupees VF UNC
ND (1986-). Deep blue-green and olive-green on multicolor underprint. Mohammed Ali Jinnah at right. Six signature varieties. Back: State Bank of Pakistan building at center. Watermark: Mohammed Ali Jinnah. 175x73mm. FV 30.00

43 1000 Rupees VF UNC
ND (1988-). Deep purple and blue-black on multicolor underprint. Mohammed Ali Jinnah at right. Four signature varieties. Back: Tomb of Jahangir. Watermark: Mohammed Ali Jinnah. 175x73mm. FV 50.00

1997 Commemorative Issue

#44, Golden Jubilee of Independence, 1947-1997

44 5 Rupees VF UNC
1997. Dull violet on light green and pale orange-brown underprint. Star-burst with text and dates at left, Mohammed Ali Jinnah at right. Back: Tomb of Shah Ruke-e-Alam at left center, bank seal at upper right. Watermark: Mohammed Ali Jinnah. 3.50 5.00

2005 Reduced Size Issue

45 10 Rupees

2006-. Light olive green. Muhammad Ali Jinnah at right center. Back: Khyber Pass, Peshawar. 114x65mm.

	VF	UNC
a. 2006.	FV	1.50
b. 2007.	FV	1.50
c. 2008.	FV	1.50
d. 2009.	FV	1.50

46 20 Rupees

2005; 2006, 2007. Brown and tan. Muhammad Ali Jinnah at right center. Back: View of Mohen jo Daro complex, Larkana. 123x65mm.

	VF	UNC
a. 2005.	FV	6.00
b. 2006.	FV	6.00
c. 2007. Slight change to face/back registration device at top left.	FV	6.00

47 50 Rupees

2007; 2008. Muhammad Ali Jinnah at right center.

	VF	UNC
a. 2007.	FV	7.00
b. 2008.	FV	7.00

48 100 Rupees

2006; 2007. Rose red. Muhammad Ali Jinnah at right center. Back: Quaid-e-Azam residence. 149x64mm.

	VF	UNC
a. 2006.	FV	7.50
b. 2007.	FV	7.50
c. 2009.	FV	7.50

49 500 Rupees

2006-. Green and olive on multicolor underprint. Muhammad Ali Jinnah at right center. Back: Badshahi Mosque, Lahore. 146x65mm.

	VF	UNC
a. 2006.	FV	30.00
b. 2007.	FV	30.00
c. 2008.	FV	10.00
d. 2010.	FV	10.00
e. 2011.	FV	10.00

50 1000 Rupees

2006-. Dark blue and light blue on multicolor underprint. Muhammad Ali Jinnah at right center. Back: Islamia College, Peshawar. 154x64mm.

	VF	UNC
a. 2006.	FV	25.00
b. 2007.	FV	25.00
c. 2008.	FV	20.00
d. 2009.	FV	20.00
e. 2010.	FV	20.00
f. 2011.	FV	20.00
g. 2012.	FV	20.00

51 5000 Rupees

2006-. Brown and tan on multicolor underprint. Muhammad Ali Jinnah at right center. Back: Faisalo Mosque, Islamabad. 164x65mm.

	VF	UNC
a. 2006.	FV	120.
b. 2007.	FV	115.
c. 2008.	FV	115.
d. 2009.	FV	110.
e. 2012.	FV	110.

2008 Issue

52 5 Rupees

2008. Olive green on multicolor underprint. Muhammad Ali Jinnah. Back: View of port. 115x65mm.

	VF	UNC
	FV	3.00

53 5 Rupees

2008-. Brown on light blue and olive underprint. Muhammad Ali Jinnah at right center. Back: Gwadar Sea Port at center. 115x65mm.

	VF	UNC
a. 2008.	FV	1.00
b. 2009.	FV	1.00
c. 2010.	FV	1.00
s. As a. Specimen.	—	50.00

54 10 Rupees

2008-. Olive green on violet background. Muhammad Ali Jinnah. Back: View of port.

	VF	UNC
a. 2008.	FV	1.00
b. 2009.	FV	1.00
c. 2010.	FV	1.00
d. 2011.	FV	1.00

55 20 Rupees

2008-. Orange and red. Muhammad Ali Jinnah. Back: Mohen Jo Daro, Larkana

	VF	UNC
a. 2008.	FV	3.00
b. 2009.	FV	2.00
c. 2010.	FV	2.00
d. 2011.	FV	2.00

56 50 Rupees

2008-. Purple and blue. Muhammad Ali Jinnah. Back: Mountains.

	VF	UNC
a. 2008.	FV	7.00
b. 2010.	FV	7.00
c. 2011.	FV	7.00

57 **100 Rupees** | VF | UNC
2008-. Purple and blue. Muhammad Ali Jinnah. Back: Mountains.

	VF	UNC
a. 2008.	FV	5.00
b. 2010.	FV	4.00
c. 2011.	FV	4.00

REGIONAL

STATE BANK OF PAKISTAN

1950 ND HAJ PILGRIM ISSUE

R3 **10 Rupees**
ND. Green on multicolor underprint. Portrait of Mohammed Ali Jinnah at left. Two signature varieties. Back: Shalimar Gardens. Watermark: Portrait of Mohammed Ali Jinnah. Like #16 but with overprint.

R4 **10 Rupees** — VF 20.00, UNC 35.00
ND. Purple on multicolor underprint. Portrait of Mohammed Ali Jinnah at left. Back: Shalimar Gardens. Like #16 and #21 but with overprint.

R5 **100 Rupees** — VF 150., UNC 350.
ND. Brown on multicolor underprint. Mohammed Ali Jinnah at left. Back: Badshahi Mosque, Lahore. Like #23; black overprint.

1970 ND HAJ PILGRIM ISSUE

Haj Pilgrim notes were discontinued in 1994 and notes on hand were destroyed.

R6 **10 Rupees** — VF 20.00, UNC 35.00
ND (1978). Blue-black on multicolor underprint. Portrait of Mohammed Ali Jinnah at right. Back: View of Moenjodaro. Urdu text line A beneath upper title. Watermark: Portrait of Mohammed Ali Jinnah. Like #34; black overprint.

R7 **100 Rupees** — VF 20.00, UNC 35.00
ND (1975-78). Gold on multicolor underprint. Portrait of Mohammed Ali Jinnah at right. Two signature varieties. Back: Islamic College, Peshawar. No Urdu text line beneath upper title. Like #31; dark brown overprint.

Papua New Guinea, an independent member of the British Commonwealth, occupies the eastern half of the island of New Guinea. It lies north of Australia near the equator and borders on West Irian. The country, which includes nearby Bismarck Archipelago, Buka and Bougainville, has an area of 462,820 sq. km. and a population of 5.93 million. Capital: Port Moresby. The economy is agricultural, and exports include copra, rubber, cocoa, coffee, tea, gold and copper.

The eastern half of the island of New Guinea - second largest in the world - was divided between Germany (north) and the UK (south) in 1885. The latter area was transferred to Australia in 1902, which occupied the northern portion during World War I and continued to administer the combined areas until independence in 1975. A nine-year secessionist revolt on the island of Bougainville ended in 1997 after claiming some 20,000 lives.

RULERS:
British

MONETARY SYSTEM:
1 Kina = 100 Toea, 1975-
1 Shilling = 12 Pence
1 Crown = 5 Shillings
1 Pound = 4 Crowns

SIGNATURE VARIETIES	
1	
2	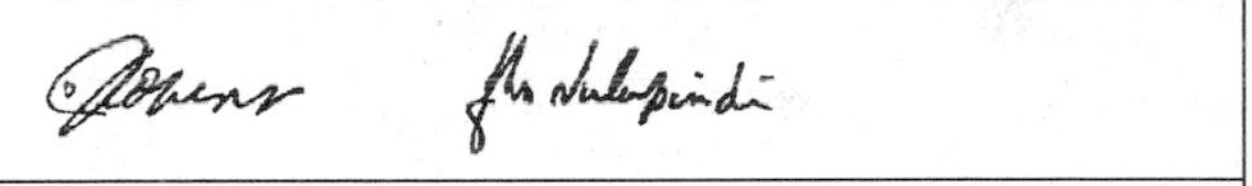
3	
4	
5	
6	
7	
8	
9	
10	

British Administration

Bank of Papua New Guinea

1975 Issue

			VF	UNC
1	**2 Kina**	ND (1975). Black on light green and multicolor underprint. Stylized Bird of Paradise at left center. Signature 1. Back: Artifacts. Watermark: Bird of Paradise.		
		a. Issued note.	6.00	17.50
		s1. Specimen. Overprint: *SPECIMEN.* Serial # all zeros.	—	35.00
		s2. Specimen. Serial # all zeros, without overprint.	—	250.

			VF	UNC
2	**5 Kina**	ND (1975). Violet and purple on multicolor underprint. Stylized Bird of Paradise at left center. Signature 1. Back: Mask at center right. Watermark: Bird of Paradise.		
		a. Issued note.	8.50	27.50
		s1. Specimen. Overprint: *SPECIMEN.* Serial # all zeros.	—	75.00
		s2. Specimen. Sperial # all zeros, without overprint.	—	250.

			VF	UNC
3	**10 Kina**	ND (1975). Dark blue-green and purple on multicolor underprint. Stylized Bird of Paradise at left center. Signature 1. Back: Bowl, ring and other artifacts. Watermark: Bird of Paradise.		
		a. Issued note.	20.00	60.00
		s1. Specimen. Overprint: *SPECIMEN.* Serial # all zeros.	—	125.
		s2. Specimen. Serial # all zeros, without overprint.	—	250.

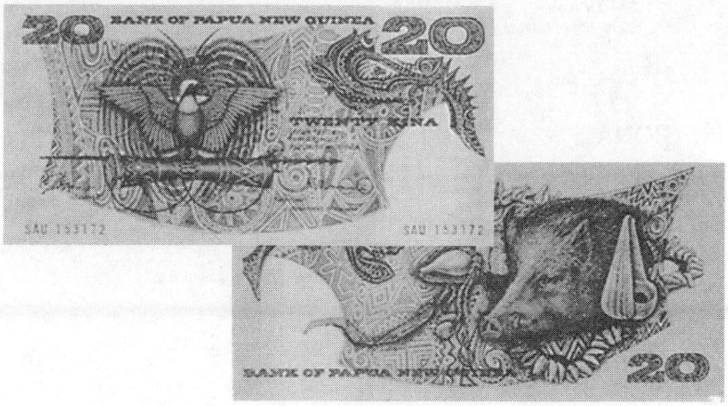

			VF	UNC
4	**20 Kina**	ND (1977). Dark brown and deep red on multicolor underprint. Stylized Bird of Paradise at left center. Signature 1. Back: Boar's head. Watermark: Bird of Paradise.		
		a. Issued note.	25.00	80.00
		s1. Specimen. Overprint: *SPECIMEN.* Serial # all zeros.	—	150.
		s2. Specimen. Serial # all zeros, without overprint.	—	180.

1981-85 Issues

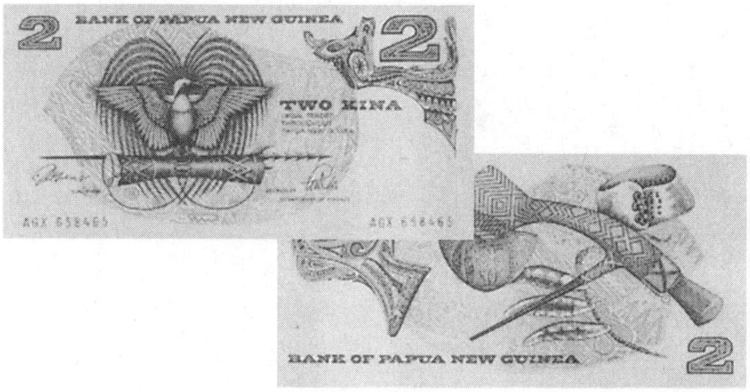

			VF	UNC
5	**2 Kina**	ND (1981). Black and dark green on light green and multicolor underprint. Stylized Bird of Paradise at left center. Signature 1. White strip 16mm wide at right. Back: Artifacts. Watermark: Bird of Paradise.		
		a. Signature 1.	FV	10.00
		b. Signature 2.	7.50	30.00
		c. Signature 3.	FV	7.50
6	**5 Kina**	ND (1981). Violet and purple on multicolor underprint. Stylized Bird of Paradise. White strip 22mm wide at right. Back: Mask at center. Watermark: Bird of Paradise.		
		a. Signature 1.	6.50	30.00
		b. Signature 2.	7.00	32.50
7	**10 Kina**	ND (1985). Dark blue, purple and green on multicolor underprint. Stylized Bird of Paradise at left center. White strip 18mm wide at right. Signature 1. Back: Bowl, ring and other artifacts. Watermark: Bird of Paradise.	10.00	50.00

			VF	UNC
9	**10 Kina**	ND (1988). Dark blue, dark green and brown-violet on multicolor underprint. Stylized Bird of Paradise at left center, design elements in underprint aerial view of Parliament House. Back: Bowl, ring and other artifacts. Watermark: Bird of Paradise. Ornate corner designs omitted on both sides.		
		a. Signature 2.	15.00	85.00
		b. Signature 3.	FV	25.00
		c. Signature 5.	FV	22.50
		d. Signature 7.	FV	22.50
		e. Signature 8.	FV	22.50
		s. As a. Specimen. Overprint: *SPECIMEN.*	—	150.

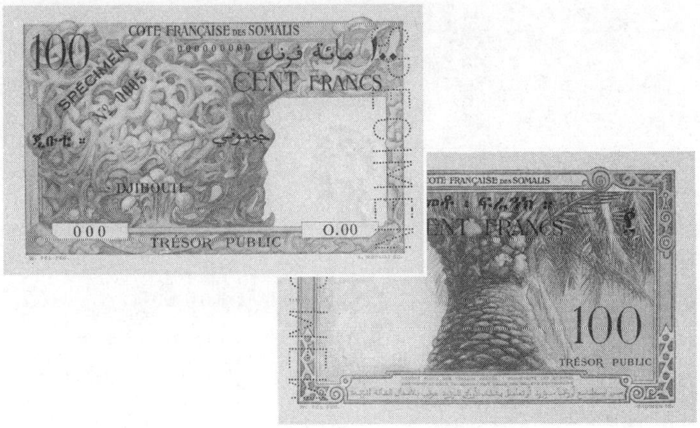

10	20 Kina	VF	UNC
	ND. Dark brown and deep red on multicolor underprint. Stylized Bird of Paradise, similar to # 4 but different design elements in underprint. Back: Boar's head,similar to number 4 but different design elements in underprint. Watermark: Bird of Paradise.		
	a. Signature 3.	FV	50.00
	b. Signature 6.	FV	40.00
	c. Signature 8.	FV	30.00
	d. Signature 10. Signature title: *SECRETARY DEPARTMENT OF FINANCE.*	FV	35.00
	e. (20)02. Signature 10.	FV	35.00

11	50 Kina	VF	UNC
	ND (1989). Brown, red, blue and multicolor underprint. National Parliament building at center. Signature 3. Back: Foreign Affairs Minister M. Somare at left center, ceremonial masks at right. Watermark: Central Bank logo.		
	a. Issued note.	FV	75.00
	s. Specimen. Overprint: *SPECIMEN.*	—	150.

1991 Commemorative Issue

#12, 9th South Pacific Games 1991

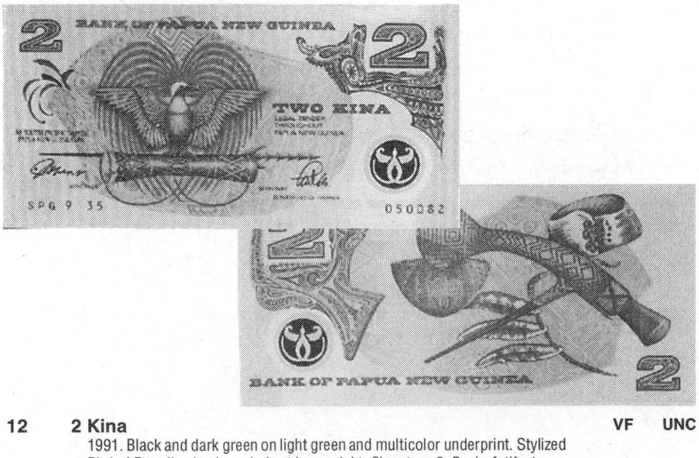

12	2 Kina	VF	UNC
	1991. Black and dark green on light green and multicolor underprint. Stylized Bird of Paradise in clear circle at lower right. Signature 3. Back: Artifacts. Printer: NPA (without imprint). Polymer plastic. UV: serial # and logo fluoresce yellow.		
	a. Issued note.	FV	6.50
	s. Specimen. Overprint: *SPECIMEN.*	—	100.

1992; 1993 ND Regular Issues

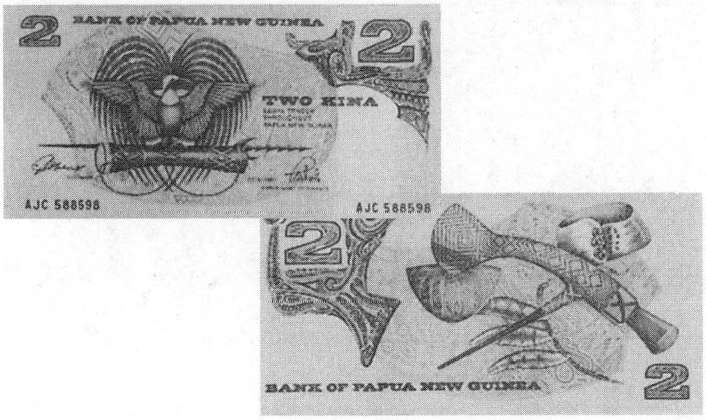

12A	2 Kina	VF	UNC
	ND (1992). Black and dark green on light green and multicolor underprint. Stylized Bird of Paradise at left center. Signature 3. Back: Artifacts. Watermark: Bird of Paradise. Like #5 but most design elements much lighter. Serial # darker and heavier type face.	FV	6.00

13	5 Kina	VF	UNC
	ND (1992). Violet and purple on multicolor underprint. Stylized Bird of Paradise at left center. Back: Mask at center right. Watermark: Bird of Paradise. Like #6 but most design elements much lighter. Serial # darker, heavier type face.		
	a. Signature 3. Signature title: *SECRETARY DEPARTMENT OF FINANCE.*	FV	15.00
	b. Signature 7.	FV	15.00
	c. Signature 9. Signature title: *SECRETARY DEPARTMENT OF TREASURY.*	FV	7.50
	d. Signature 10.	FV	5.00
	e. (20)02. Signature 10.	FV	5.00
	f. (20)05. Serial # prefix: *STK.* Signature 11.	FV	7.50

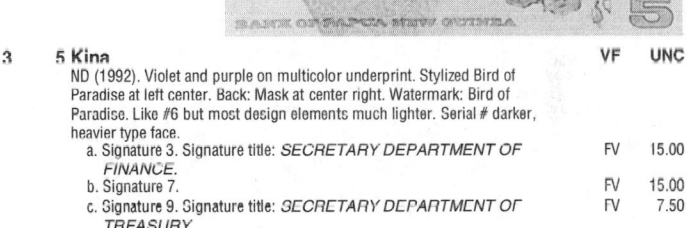

14	5 Kina	VF	UNC
	ND (1993). Violet and purple on multicolor underprint. Stylized Bird of Paradise at left center, with segmented security thread and new signature title: *Secretary for Finance and Planning.* Back: Mask at center right. Watermark: Bird of Paradise.		
	a. Signature 4.	FV	20.00
	b. Signature 5.	FV	20.00
	s. Specimen. Overprint: *SPECIMEN.*	—	125.

1995 ND Commemorative Issue

#15, 20th Anniversary of Independence

15	**2 Kina** ND (1995). Black and dark green on light green and multicolor underprint. Similar to number 12 but with ornate *20 ANNIVERSARY* logo at left, *PNG 20* at lower left. Signature 5. Back: Artifacts. Printer: NPA (without imprint). Polymer plastic.	VF FV	UNC 7.50

1996 ND Regular Issue

16	**2 Kina** ND (1996). Black and dark green on light green and multicolor underprint. Stylized Bird of Paradise at left center. Back: Artifacts. Polymer plastic.	VF	UNC
	a. Signature 5.	FV	5.50
	b. Signature 7.	FV	5.50
	c. Signature 10. Signature title: *SECRETARY DEPARTMENT OF FINANCE.*	FV	5.00
	d. (20)02. Signature 10.	FV	5.00
	s. As b. Specimen. Serial # all zeros, without overprint.	—	100.

1998 Commemorative Issue

#17, Bank's 25th Anniversary

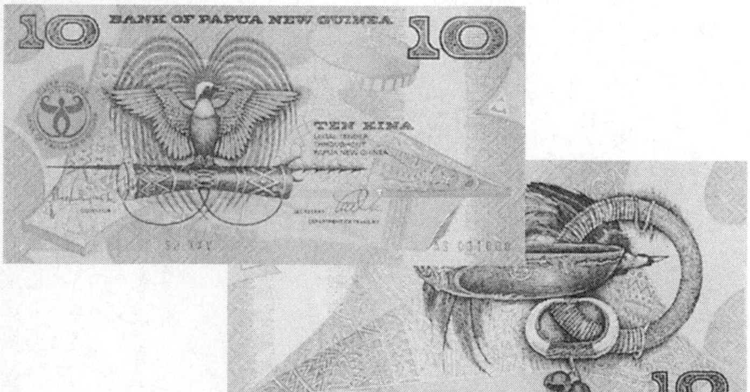

17	**10 Kina** 1998. Dark blue, dark green and brown-violet on multicolor underprint. Stylized Bird of Paradise at left center, design elements representing a modern building. Signature 8. Silver Jubilee foil with arms and commemorative dates *1973-1998* at left, and *SJ XXV* Back: Bowl, ring and other artifacts at lower left center.	VF	UNC
	a. Issued note.	FV	20.00
	s1. Specimen. Overprint: SPECIMEN.	—	150.
	s2. Specimen. Serial # all zeros, without overprint.	—	150.

1999 Issue

18	**50 Kina** 1999; 2002. Black and red on orange, yellow and multicolor underprint. Similar to #11 but with ornate window design. Printer: NPA (without imprint). Polymer plastic.	VF	UNC
	a. Signature 9.	FV	70.00
	b. Signature 10.	FV	65.00
	s. Specimen. Serial # all zeros, without overprint.	—	150.

2000 Commemorative Issue

19	**5 Kina** 2000; 2002. Violet and purple on multicolor underprint. Similar to #14 but with *YEAR 2000* at lower left center in dull gold and serial # prefix: *PNG20.* Signature 9. Back: Mask at center right.	VF FV	UNC 11.00

2000 Second Commemorative Issue

#20 Currency Silver Jubilee

20	**5 Kina** 2000. Similar to #19 but with silver imprint at lower center right and red inscription overprint at lower center: *PNG1942000 (19 4 2000 date).* Signature 10. Back: Mask at center right.	VF	UNC
	a. Issued note.	FV	10.00
	s. Specimen. Overprint: *SPECIMEN.*	—	150.

2000 Third Commemorative Issue

#21-25, 25th Anniversary, of Papua New Guinea.

21	**2 Kina** (20)00. Black and dark green on light green and multicolor underprint. Stylized Bird of Paradise at left center. Signature 10. 25th Anniversary logo at left. Back: Artifacts. Watermark: Bird of Paradise. Polymer plastic.	VF FV	UNC 5.00

22 **5 Kina** VF UNC
ND (2000). Violet and purple on multicolor underprint. Stylized Bird of Paradise at left center. Signature 10. 25th Anniversary logo at left. Back: Mask at center right. Watermark: Bird of Paradise.
a. Issued note. FV 10.00
s. Specimen. Overprint: *SPECIMEN.*

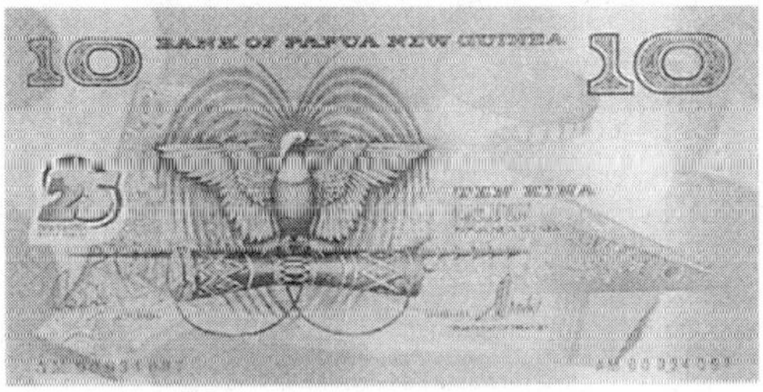

23 **10 Kina** VF UNC
(20)00. Dark blue, dark green and brown-violet on multicolor underprint. Stylized Bird of Paradise at left center, aerial view of Parliament House. Signature 10. 25th Anniversary logo at left. Back: Bowl, ring and other artifacts. Watermark: Bird of Paradise. Polymer plastic.
a. Issued note. FV 18.50
s. Specimen. Overprint: SPECIMEN. — 150.

24 **20 Kina** VF UNC
(20)02. Orange-red and brown on multicolor underprint. Stylized Bird of Paradise, similar to #4 but different design elements in underprint. Signature 10. 25th Anniversary logo at left. Back: Boar's head at right. Watermark: Bird of Paradise. FV 35.00

25 **50 Kina** VF UNC
(20)00. National Parliament building at center. Signature 10. 25th Anniversary logo at upper left center. Back: Foreign Affairs Minister M. Somare at left center, ceremonial masks at right. Polymer plastic. FV 65.00

2000 Issue

26 **10 Kina** VF UNC
July, 2000; (20)02. Stylized Bird of Paradise at left center, aerial view of Parliament House. Signature 10. Back: Bowl, ring and other artifacts. Watermark: Bird of Paradise. Polymer plastic.
a. July, 2000. FV 20.00
b. (20)02. Signature 10. FV 20.00

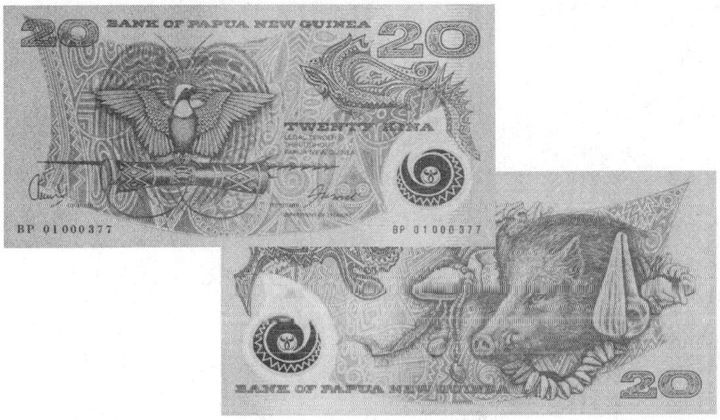

26a **20 Kina** VF UNC
(20)01. Bird of Paradise at left and Parliament building at center. Polymer plastic. FV 35.00

2004 Commemorative Issue

#27, 30th Anniversary of the Bank.

27 **20 Kina** VF UNC
2004. Polymer plastic. 150x75mm. FV 35.00

2005-08; ND Issue

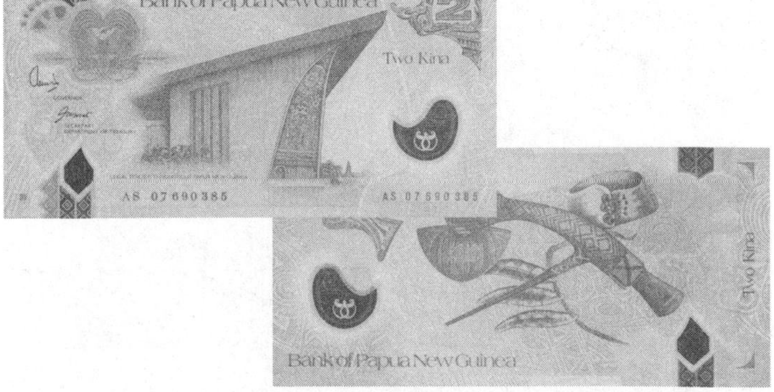

28 **2 Kina** VF UNC
(20)07. Light and dark green. Bird of Paradise at left and Parliament building at center. Polymer plastic. 140x70mm.
a. Issued note. FV 5.00
s. Specimen. Red overprint: *SPECIMEN.* — 250.

		VF	UNC
29	**5 Kina** (20)08. Violet, purple and tan. Bird of Paradise at left and Parliament building at center. Polymer plastic. 140x70mm.	FV	10.00

		VF	UNC
30	**10 Kina** (20)08. Blue and tan. Bird of Paradise at left and Parliament building at center. Polymer plastic. 145x73mm.	FV	18.50
31	**20 Kina** (20)07. Bird of Paradise at left and Parliament building at center. Polymer plastic. 150x75mm.		
	a. Issued note.	FV	35.00
	s. Specimen. Overprint: *SPECIMEN.*	—	125.
32	**50 Kina** (20)08; (20)12. Black, orange and multicolor Bird of Paradise at left, Parliament building at center. Back: M. Somare at center, headdresses and masks at right. Polymer plastic. 150x75mm.		
	a. (20)08.	FV	50.00
	b. (20)09.	FV	50.00
	s. Specimen. Overprint: *SPECIMEN.*	—	150.

		VF	UNC
33	**100 Kina** (20)05; (20)07. Bird of Paradise at left and Parliament building at center. Polymer plastic. 150x75mm.		
	a. (20)05.	FV	120.
	b. (20)07.	FV	120.
	s. Specimen. Overprint: *SPECIMEN.*	FV	225.

2007 Commemorative Issue

		VF	UNC
34	**5 Kina** 2007. Violet on multicolor underprint. Bird of Paradise. XIII South Pacific Games logo at left end. 148x73mm.	FV	8.00

2008 Commemorative Issue

		VF	UNC
35	**2 Kina** (20)08. Green on multicolor underprint. Parliament house in center. Overprint: BPNG logo and *35 YEARS 1973-2008.* at lower left. Polymer plastic. 140x70mm.	FV	3.00
36	**20 Kina** (20)08. Orange-red and brown on multicolor underprint. Parliament house at center. Back: Boar's head. Overprint: BPNG logo and *35 YEARS 1973-2008.* at lower left. Printer: TDLR.		
	a. Issued note.	FV	17.50
	s. Specimen.	—	100.
37	**100 Kina** (20)08. Green and brown on multicolor underprint. Parliament house at center. Back: Palm tree, fishing boat, mining truck. Overprint: BPNG logo and *35 YEARS 1973-2008.* at lower left. Printer: TDLR. Paper. 150x75mm.		
	a. Issued note.	FV	110.
	s. Specimen.	—	150.

2010 Commemorative Issue

		VF	UNC
38	**2 Kina** (20)10. Green. National Parliament building at center.35th Anniversary of independence logo at top center. Printer: NPA. Polymer plastic. 140x70mm.	FV	4.00
39	**5 Kina** (20)10. Violet. National Parliament building at center.35th Anniversary of independence logo at top center. Printer: NPA. Polymer plastic. 148x73mm.	FV	6.50
40	**10 Kina** (20)10. Blue. National Parliament building at center.35th Anniversary of independence logo at top center. Printer: NPA. Polymer plastic. 150x75mm.	FV	10.00
41	**20 Kina** (20)10. Red-brown. National Parliament building at center.35th Anniversary of independence logo at top center. Printer: NPA. Polymer plastic. 150x75mm.	FV	15.00
42	**50 Kina** (20)10. Orange. National Parliament building at center.35th Anniversary of independence logo at top center. Back: Prime Minister Michael Somare at center. Printer: NPA. Polymer plastic. 150x75mm.	FV	40.00
43	**100 Kina** (20)10. Green and gold. National Parliament building at center.35th Anniversary of independence logo at top center. Back: Ship, plane, oil rig, dump truck, communications tower. Printer: NPA. Polymer plastic. 150x75mm.	FV	75.00

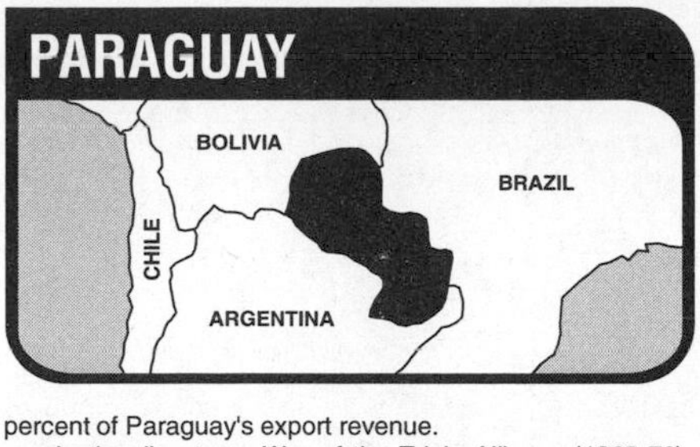

The Republic of Paraguay, a landlocked country in the heart of South America surrounded by Argentina, Bolivia and Brazil, has an area of 157,042 sq. mi. (406,752 sq. km.) and a population of 5.5 million, 95 percent of whom are of mixed Spanish and Indian descent. Capital: Asunción. The country is predominantly agrarian, with no important mineral deposits or oil reserves. Meat, timber, oilseeds, tobacco and cotton account for 70 percent of Paraguay's export revenue.

In the disastrous War of the Triple Alliance (1865-70) - between Paraguay and Argentina, Brazil, and Uruguay - Paraguay lost two-thirds of all adult males and much of its territory. It stagnated economically for the next half century. In the Chaco War of 1932-35, Paraguay won large, economically important areas from Bolivia. The 35-year military dictatorship of Alfredo Stroessner ended in 1989, and, despite a marked increase in political infighting in recent years, Paraguay has held relatively free and regular presidential elections since then.

MONETARY SYSTEM:

1 Peso = 100 Centavos to 1870
1 Peso = 8 Reales to 1872
1 Peso = 100 Centésimos to 1870
1 Peso = 100 Centavos (Centésimos) to 1944
1 Guaraní = 100 Céntimos, 1944-

Republic

Banco Central del Paraguay

Decreto Ley de No. 18 del 25 de Marzo de 1952

(from Aug.1963)

#192-201 Replacement notes: Serial # prefix *Z*.

		VF	UNC
192	**1 Guaraní** *L.1952.* Green on multicolor underprint. Soldier at right, arms at left. Black serial # at lower left and lower right. Back: Banco Central. Printer: TDLR. 157x67mm.	1.00	4.00

		VF	UNC
193	**1 Guaraní** *L.1952.* Green on multicolor underprint. Soldier at right, arms at left. Two signature varieties. Back: Palacio Legislativo. Printer: TDLR. 157x67mm.		
	a. Black serial # at lower left and lower right.	.25	1.75
	b. Black serial # at upper left and lower right.	.25	1.25
	s. As a. Specimen.	—	25.00

		VF	UNC
194	**5 Guaraníes** *L.1952.* Blue on multicolor underprint. Girl holding jug at right, arms at left. Black serial # at lower left and lower right. Back: Hotel Guarani. Printer: TDLR. 157x67mm.	1.50	6.00

		VF	UNC
195	**5 Guaraníes** *L.1952.* Black on multicolor underprint. Girl holding jug at right, arms at left. Black serial number at lower left and lower right. Two signature varieties. Back: Hotel Guarani. Printer: TDLR. UV: value fluoresce yellow. 157x67mm.		
	a. Red serial # at lower left and lower right.	.25	1.50
	b. Red serial # at upper left and lower right.	.25	1.25
	s. As a. Specimen.	—	25.00

		VF	UNC
196	**10 Guaraníes** *L.1952.* Deep red on multicolor underprint. General Eugenio A. Garay at right, arms at left. Two signature varieties. Back: International bridge. Printer: TDLR. 157x67mm.		
	a. Black serial # at lower left and lower right.	.40	2.25
	b. Black serial # at upper left and lower right.	.40	2.00
	s. As a. Specimen. Overprint: *SPECIMEN* in black.	—	35.00

		VF	UNC
197	**50 Guaraníes** *L.1952.* Brown on multicolor underprint. Mariscal José F. Estigarribia at right, arms at left. Two signature varieties. Back: Country road. Printer: TDLR. 157x67mm.		
	a. Black serial # at lower left and lower right.	1.75	7.00
	b. Black serial # at upper left and lower right.	.75	4.00
	s. As a. Specimen.	—	25.00

198 **100 Guaraníes** VF UNC
L.1952. Green on multicolor underprint. General José E. Diaz at right, arms at left. Black serial number at lower left and lower right. Back: Ruins of Humaita. Printer: TDLR. 157x67mm.

	VF	UNC
a. Issued note.	3.00	15.00
s. Specimen.	—	25.00

199 **100 Guaraníes** VF UNC
L.1952. Orange on multicolor underprint. General José E. Diaz at right, arms at left. Black serial number at lower left and lower right. Two signature varieties (small size signature). Back: Ruins of Humaita. Printer: TDLR. 157x67mm.

	VF	UNC
a. Black serial # at lower left and lower right.	2.50	7.00
b. Black serial # at upper left and lower right.	1.00	3.00

200 **500 Guaraníes** VF UNC
L.1952. Blue-gray on multicolor underprint. General Bernardino Caballero at right, arms at left. Two signature varieties. Back: Federal merchant ship. Printer: TDLR. 157x67mm.

	VF	UNC
a. Black serial # at lower left and lower right.	4.00	10.00
b. Black serial # at upper left and lower right.	2.00	6.00
s. As a. Specimen.	—	25.00

201 **1000 Guaraníes** VF UNC
L.1952. Purple on multicolor underprint. Mariscal Francisco Solano Lopez right, arms at left. Two signature varieties. Back: National shrine. Printer: TDLR. 157x67mm.

	VF	UNC
a. Black serial # at lower left and lower right.	7.50	20.00
b. Black serial # at upper left and lower right.	6.00	15.00
s. As a. Specimen.	—	25.00

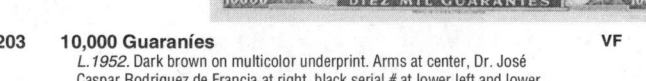

202 **5000 Guaraníes** VF UNC
L.1952. Red-orange on multicolor underprint. Arms at center, Don Carlos Antonio López at right. Two signature varieties. Back: López Palace. Printer: TDLR. 157x67mm.

	VF	UNC
a. Black serial # at lower left and lower right.	25.00	60.00
b. Black serial # at upper left and lower right.	75.00	45.00
s. As a. Specimen. Red overprint:*SPECIMEN* on both sides.	—	70.00

203 **10,000 Guaraníes** VF UNC
L.1952. Dark brown on multicolor underprint. Arms at center, Dr. José Caspar Rodriguez de Francia at right, black serial # at lower left and lower right. Back: Historical scene from 14.5.1811. Printer: TDLR. 157x67mm.

	VF	UNC
a. Issued note.	40.00	100.
s. Specimen.	—	25.00

204 **10,000 Guaraníes** VF UNC
L.1952. Dark brown on multicolor underprint. Like number 203 but *CASPAR* changed to *GASPAR* below Francia. Two signature varieties. Back: Historical scene from 14.5.1811. Printer: TDLR. 157x67mm.

	VF	UNC
a. Black serial # at lower left and lower right.	40.00	100.
b. Black serial # at upper left and lower right.	30.00	75.00

1982; 1990 ND Issue

#205-210 replacement notes: Serial # prefix *Z*.

205	**100 Guaraníes**	VF	UNC
	L.1952 (1982). Green on multicolor underprint. General José E. Diaz at right, arms at left. Black serial number at lower left and lower right. Four signature varieties (small size signature). Back: Ruins of Humaita, value stated as: *SA GUARANI*. Printer: TDLR. 157x67mm.	.25	1.25

206	**500 Guaraníes**	VF	UNC
	L.1952. Blue-gray on multicolor underprint. General Bernardino Caballero at right, arms at left. Six signature varieties. Back: Federal merchant ship, value stated as: *PO SA GUARANI*. Printer: TDLR. 157x67mm.	FV	1.75

207	**1000 Guaraníes**	VF	UNC
	L.1952 (1982). Purple on multicolor underprint. Mariscal Francisco Solano Lopez right, arms at left. Six signature varieties. Back: National shrine, value stated as: *SU GUARANI*. Printer: TDLR. 157x67mm.	FV	2.00

208	**5000 Guaraníes**	VF	UNC
	L.1952 (1982). Red-orange on multicolor underprint. Arms at center, Don Carlos Antonio López at right. Six signature varieties. Back: López Palace, value stated as: *PO SU GUARANI*. Printer: TDLR. 157x67mm.	FV	7.50

209	**10,000 Guaraníes**	VF	UNC
	L.1952 (1982). Dark brown on multicolor underprint. Arms at center, Dr. José Caspar Rodriguez de Francia at right, black serial # at lower left and lower right. Five signature varieties. Back: Historical scene from 14.5.1811, value stated as: *PA SU GUARANI*. Printer: TDLR. 157x67mm.	FV	10.00

210	**50,000 Guaraníes**	VF	UNC
	L.1952 (1990). Deep purple and light blue on multicolor underprint. Soldier at right, outline map of Paraguay at center. Plain security thread. Three signature varieties. Back: Purple and olive-green on multicolor underprint. House of Independence at center. Watermark: Bust of soldier. Printer: TDLR. 157x67mm.	FV	45.00

1994 ND Issue

211	**50,000 Guaraníes**	VF	UNC
	L.1952 (1994). Purple and light blue on multicolor underprint. Soldier at right, outline map of Paraguay at center. Segmented foil over plain security thread. Three signature varieties. Series A. Back: House of Independence at center. Watermark: Bust of soldier. Printer: TDLR. 157x67mm.	FV	40.00

1995 ND Issue

212	**500 Guaraníes**	VF	UNC
	L.1952 (1995). Blue-gray on multicolor underprint. General Bernardino Caballero at right, arms at left. Two signature varieties. Back: Federal merchant ship, value stated as: *PO SA GUARANI*. Printer: F-CO. 157x67mm.	FV	1.25

213	**1000 Guaraníes**	VF	UNC
	L.1952 (1995). Purple on multicolor underprint. Mariscal Francisco Solano Lopez right, arms at left. Six signature varieties. Back: National shrine, value stated as: *SU GUARANI*. Printer: F-CO. 157x67mm.	FV	2.00

Ley 489 del 29 de Junio de 1995; 1997-98 Issue

214 1000 Guaraníes VF UNC

1998; 2001; 2003. Purple on multicolor underprint. Mariscal Francisco Solano Lopez right, arms at left. Series B. Back: National shrine, value stated as: *SU GUARANI.* 157x67mm.

	VF	UNC
a. 1998. Printer: Ciccone Calcografica S.A.	FV	2.00
b. 2001. Printer: De La Rue.	FV	2.00
c. 2003. Printer: F-CO.	FV	2.00

215 5000 Guaraníes VF UNC

1997. Red-orange on multicolor underprint. Arms at center, Don Carlos Antonio López at right. Two signature varieties. Series B. Silver foil over security thread. Back: López Palace, value stated as: *PO SU GUARANI.* Printer: TDLR. 157x67mm. FV 5.00

216 10,000 Guaraníes VF UNC

1998; 2003. Brown. Arms at center, Dr. José Caspar Rodriguez De Francia at right, black serial # at lower left and lower right. Series B. Back: Historical scene from 14.5.1811, value stated as: *PA SU GUARANI.* Printer: Ciccone Calcografica, S.A. 157x67mm.

	VF	UNC
a. 1998. Lower left corner has *10000.*	FV	7.50
b. 2003. Lower left corner has: Triangles.	FV	7.50

217 50,000 Guaraníes VF UNC

1997. Purple and light blue on multicolor underprint. Soldier at right, outline map of Paraguay at center. Segmented foil over plain security thread. Three signature varieties. Series B. Back: House of Independence at center. Printer: TDLR. 157x67mm. FV 35.00

218 50,000 Guaraníes VF UNC

1998. Purple and light blue on multicolor underprint. Like # 217 but with staircase metallic impression at lower left corner. Series B. Back: House of Independence at center. Printer: (T)DLR. 157x67mm. FV 27.50

219 100,000 Guaraníes VF UNC

1998. Green, yellow-brown and multicolor. San Rogue González de Santa Cruz at right. Series A. Back: *Represa de Itaipu,* Itaipu Hydroelectric Dam. Printer: TDLR. 157x67mm. FV 45.00

2000 Issue

220 5000 Guaraníes VF UNC

2000; 2003. Red-orange on multicolor underprint. Arms at center, Don Carlos Antonio López at right. Two signature varieties. Series C. Silver foil over security thread. Back: López Palace, value stated as: *PO SU GUARANI.* Printer: Ciccone Calcografica S.A. 157x67mm.

	VF	UNC
a. 2000. Lower left corner: small diamond.	FV	4.00
b. 2003. Lower left corner: large diamond.	FV	4.00

2002 Commemorative Issue

50th Anniversary of the Banco Cenral del Paraguay

221 1000 Guaraníes — VF | UNC

2002. Purple on multicolor underprint. Mariscal Francisco Solano Lopez right, arms at left, anniversary text below date. Series B. Back: National shrine, value stated as: *SU GUARANI*. Printer: F-CO. 157x67mm. — FV | 2.00

2004 Issue

222 1000 Guaraníes — VF | UNC

2004; 2005. Purple on multicolor underprint. Mariscal Francisco Solano Lopez right, arms at left, without anniversary text below date. Six signature varieties. Series B. Back: National shrine, value stated as: *SU GUARANI*. Printer: DLR. 157x67mm.

- a. 2004. 1 MIL at upper left and right corners on face. Series C. — FV | 2.00
- b. 2005. Series D. — FV | 2.00

223 5000 Guaraníes — VF | UNC

2005; 2008; 2010. Red-orange on multicolor underprint. 5 MIL at upper left and right corner on face. Printer: (T)DLR. 157x67mm.

- a. 2005. Series D. — FV | 4.00
- b. 2008. Series E. Segmented security thread. — FV | 4.00
- c. 2010. Series F. — FV | 4.00

224 10,000 Guaraníes — VF | UNC

2004; 2005; 2008. Brown on multicolor underprint. 10 MIL at upper left corner on face. Printer: (T)DLR. 157x67mm.

- a. 2004. Series C. — FV | 6.00
- b. 2005. Series D. — FV | 6.00
- c. 2008. Series E. Segmented security thread. — FV | 6.00

225 20,000 Guaraníes — VF | UNC

2005. La Mujer Paraguaya at right. 20 MIL at upper left corner. Series A. Back: Banco Central building at center. 20 MIL at upper left and right. Printer: G&D. 157x67mm. — FV | 10.00

2005 Issue

225A 50,000 Guaraníes — VF | UNC

2005. Purple and light blue on multicolor underprint. Soldier at right. Series C. Back: House of Independence at center. 157x67mm. — FV | 27.50

226 100,000 Guaraníes — VF | UNC

2004. Purple on multicolor underprint. Francisco Solano Lopez at right. 100 MIL at upper left and right corners. Holographic silver florette, lion face-to-back registery device. Series B. Back: Church of the Assuncion at center. 100 MIL at lower right. Printer: (T)DLR. 157x67mm. — FV | 40.00

227 100,000 Guaraníes

2005. Brown holographic florette. Series C. Printer: F-CO. 157x67mm. — FV | 40.00

2007 Issue

228	2000 Guaraníes	VF	UNC
	2008-. Purple on multicolor underprint. Adela and Celsa Speratti at right. Back: Parade with flags. Polymer plastic. 157x67mm.		
	a. 2008. Printer: Oberthur Technologies.	FV	2.00
	b. 2009. Printer: G&D.	FV	2.00
	c. 2011. Printer: CBNC.	FV	2.00
	s. Specimen. Red overprint *MUESTRA SIN VALOR.*	—	75.00

230	20,000 Guaraníes	VF	UNC
	2007; 2009. Blue and green on multicolor. Paraguayan woman holding vase at right. Back: Modern Bank building at center. Printer: G&D. 157x67mm.		
	a. 2007.	FV	10.00
	b. 2009.	FV	10.00

231	50,000 Guaraníes	VF	UNC
	2005. Blue, green and orange on multicolor underprint. Map of Paraguay at center, Paraguayan soldier at right. Back: *Casa de la Independencia* at center. Printer: F-CO. Thin segmented security strip. 250,000 notes were stollen during shipment and thus the bank cancelled their release. 157x67mm.	—	100.

232	50,000 Guaraníes	VF	UNC
	2008-. Purple, green and light brown on multicolor underprint. Agustín Pio Barros at center. Series E. Back: Guitar. Printer: G&D. Wide segmented security strip. 157x67mm.		
	a. 2008.	FV	22.50
	b. 2009.	FV	20.00
	c. 2011.	FV	20.00
	s. Specimen. Red overprint: *MUESTRA SIN VALOR.*	—	100.

233	100,000 Guaraníes	VF	UNC
	2007-11. Printer: Oberthur Technologies. 157x67mm.		
	a. 2007.	FV	40.00
	b. 2008.	FV	40.00
	c. 2011.	FV	35.00
	s. Specimen.	—	125.

2011 Polymer Issue

234	5000 Guaraníes	VF	UNC
	2011 (2013). Red-orange. Printer: CBNC (without imprint).	FV	5.00

Collector Series

Banco Central del Paraguay

1979 Issue

CS1	100-10,000 Guaraníes	Mkt.	Value
	L.1972 (1979). 199b-202b, 204b overprint: *SPECIMEN* and with serial # prefix Maltese cross.		25.00

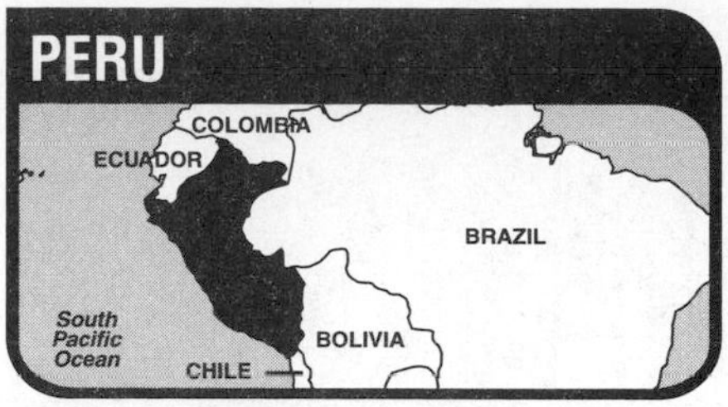

The Republic of Perú, located on the Pacific coast of South America, has an area of 496,222 sq. mi. (1,285,216 sq. km.) and a population of 25.66 million. Capital: Lima. The diversified economy includes mining, fishing and agriculture. Fish meal, copper, sugar, zinc and iron ore are exported.

Ancient Peru was the seat of several prominent Andean civilizations, most notably that of the Incas whose empire was captured by the Spanish conquistadors in 1533. Peruvian independence was declared in 1821, and remaining Spanish forces defeated in 1824. After a dozen years of military rule, Peru returned to democratic leadership in 1980, but experienced economic problems and the growth of a violent insurgency. President Alberto Fujimori's election in 1990 ushered in a decade that saw a dramatic turnaround in the economy and significant progress in curtailing guerrilla activity. Nevertheless, the president's increasing reliance on authoritarian measures and an economic slump in the late 1990s generated mounting dissatisfaction with his regime, which led to his ouster in 2000. A caretaker government oversaw new elections in the spring of 2001, which ushered in Alejandro Toledo Manrique as the new head of government - Peru's first democratically elected president of Native American ethnicity. The presidential election of 2006 saw the return of Alan Garcia Perez who, after a disappointing presidential term from 1985 to 1990, returned to the presidency with promises to improve social conditions and maintain fiscal responsibility.

MONETARY SYSTEM:

1 Sol = 1 Sol de Oro = 100 Centavos, 1879-1985
1 Libra = 10 Soles
1 Inti = 1000 Soles de Oro, 1986-1991
1 Nuevo Sol = 100 Centimes = 1 Million Intis, 1991-
1 Sol = 100 Centavos (10 Dineros)

República del Perú

Banco Central de Reserva del Peru

Ley 10535, 1956 Issue

76 5 Soles — VF | UNC

22.3.1956; 18.3.1960. Green on patterned light blue underprint. Seated Liberty holding shield and staff at center. Like #70. Signature varieties. Back: Arms at center. Printer: TDLR. — 1.50 | 5.00

77 10 Soles — VF | UNC

9.7.1956. Orange on multicolor underprint. Seated Liberty holding shield and staff at center. Similar to #71. Signature varieties. Back: Arms at center. Printer: G&D. — 6.00 | 20.00

78 50 Soles — VF | UNC

22.3.1956; 24.10.1957; 13.5.1959. Dark blue on lilac underprint. Seated Liberty holding shield and staff at center. Serial # at upper left and right. Like #72. Signature varieties. Back: Arms at center. Printer: TDLR.

	VF	UNC
a. Issued note.	4.50	17.50
s. Specimen.	—	—

79 100 Soles — VF | UNC

1956-61. Black on light blue underprint. Seated Liberty holding shield and staff at center. Like #73 but different guilloche. Signature varieties. Back: Black. Arms at center. Printer: TDLR.

	VF	UNC
a. *LIMA* at lower left. 22.3.1956; 24.10.1957.	12.00	30.00
b. *LIMA* at lower right. 13.5.1959.	12.00	30.00
c. As b. Series and serial # at lower left and upper right. 1.2.1961.	12.00	30.00
s. As a. Specimen.	—	—

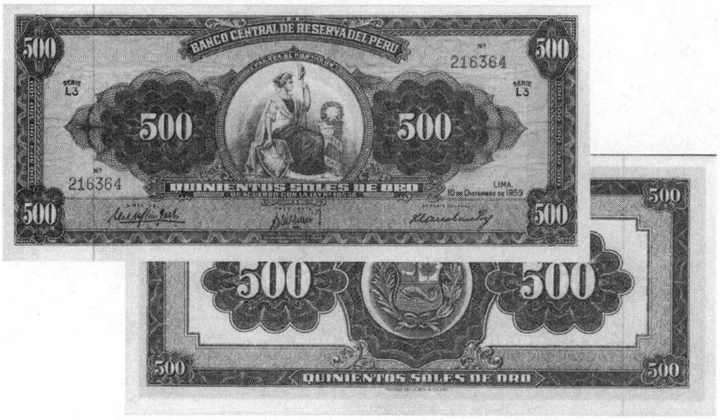

80 500 Soles — VF | UNC

1956-61. Brown on light brown and lilac underprint. Seated Liberty holding shield and staff at center. Similar to #74. Signature varieties. Back: Brown. Arms at center. Printer: TDLR.

	VF	UNC
a. Series and serial # at upper corners. 22.3.1956; 24.10.1957.	25.00	75.00
b. Series and serial # at lower left and upper right. 10.12.1959; 16.6.1961.	25.00	75.00
s. As b. Specimen.	—	—

1958 Issue

81 5 Soles — VF | UNC

21.8.1958. Green. Seated Liberty holding shield and staff at center. Back: Arms at center. Like #70 but different guilloche. Printer: W&S. — 4.00 | 7.50

82 10 Soles — VF | UNC

21.8.1958. Orange on multicolor underprint. Seated Liberty holding shield and staff at center. Similar to #71. Back: Orange. Arms at center. Printer: W&S. — 4.00 | 15.00

1960 Issue

82A 10 Soles — VF | UNC

8.7.1960; 1.2.1961. Orange on multicolor underprint. Liberty seated holding shield and staff at center. Serial # and series at lower left and upper right. Printer: TDLR. — 1.50 | 6.00

Republic

Banco Central de Reserva del Perú

Ley 13958, 1962; 1964 Issue

83 **5 Soles de Oro** | VF | UNC
9.2.1962; 20.9.1963; 18.6.1965; 18.11.1966; 23.2.1968. Green on multicolor underprint. Liberty seated holding shield and staff at center. Serial number at lower left and upper right. Series J. Back: Arms at center. Printer: TDLR.

	VF	UNC
a. Issued note.	1.00	4.00
s. Specimen.	—	25.00

84 **10 Soles de Oro**
8.6.1962; 20.9.1963; 20.5.1966; 25.5.1967; 23.2.1968. Orange on multicolor underprint. Liberty seated holding shield and staff at center. Series I. Back: Arms at center. Printer: TDLR.

	VF	UNC
a. Issued note.	1.50	4.00
s. Specimen.	—	25.00

85 **50 Soles de Oro**
9.2.1962; 20.9.1963; 23.2.1968. Blue on multicolor underprint. Liberty seated holding shield and staff at center. Serial number at lower left and upper right. Series H. Back: Arms at center. Printer: TDLR.

	VF	UNC
a. Issued note.	3.50	12.50
s. Specimen.	—	25.00

86 **100 Soles de Oro**
13.3.1964; 23.2.1968. Black on light blue and multicolor underprint. Liberty seated holding shield and staff at center. Series G. Back: Arms at center. Printer: TDLR.

	VF	UNC
a. Issued note.	6.00	20.00
s. Specimen.	—	25.00

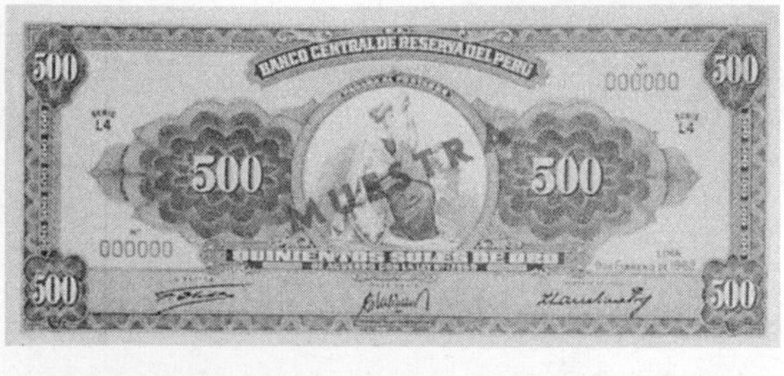

87 **500 Soles de Oro**
9.2.1962; 20.9.1963; 20.5.1966; 23.2.1968. Brown on light brown and multicolor underprint. Liberty seated holding shield and staff at center. Series L. Back: Arms at center. Printer: TDLR.

	VF	UNC
a. Issued note.	10.00	40.00
s. Specimen.	—	25.00

1962; 1965 Issue

88 **10 Soles de Oro** | VF 2.00 | UNC 7.50
26.2.1965. Red-orange on light green and multicolor underprint. Liberty seated holding shield and staff at center. Series C. *Pagar· al Portador* added under bank name at top center. Back: Arms at center. Printer: ABNC.

89 **50 Soles de Oro**
20.8.1965. Blue on multicolor underprint. Liberty seated holding shield and staff at center. Series B. *Pagar· al Portador* added under bank name at top center. Back: Arms at center. Printer: ABNC.

	VF	UNC
a. Issued note.	5.00	20.00
s. Specimen.	—	100.

90 **100 Soles de Oro** — VF / UNC
12.9.1962; 20.8.1965. Black on light blue and multicolor underprint. Liberty seated holding shield and staff at center. Series A. *Pagar- al Portador* added under bank name at top center. Back: Arms at center. Printer: ABNC.

	VF	UNC
a. Issued note.	6.50	22.50
s. Specimen.	—	100.

91 **500 Soles de Oro** — VF / UNC
26.2.1965. Brown on multicolor underprint. Liberty seated holding shield and staff at center. Series P. *Pagar- al Portado* added under bank name at top center. Back: Arms at center. Printer: ABNC. — 25.00 / 70.00

Ley 13 958 1968 Issue

#92-98 Replacement notes: Serial # *Z999 . . .*

92 **5 Soles de Oro** — VF / UNC
23.2.1968. Green on multicolor underprint. Artifacts at left, Inca Pachacútec at right, arms at center. 3 signatures. Series J. Back: *Fortaleza de Sacsahuaman.* Printer: TDLR.

	VF	UNC
a. Issued note.	.75	3.00
s. Specimen.	—	25.00

93 **10 Soles de Oro** — VF / UNC
23.2.1968. Red-orange on multicolor underprint. Building at left, Garcilaso Inca de la Vega at right, arms at center. 3 signatures. Series I. Back: Lake Titicaca, boats. Printer: TDLR.

	VF	UNC
a. Issued note.	.50	2.00
s. Specimen.	—	25.00

94 **50 Soles de Oro** — VF / UNC
23.2.1968. Blue-gray on multicolor underprint. Workers at left, Tupac Amaru II at right, arms at center. 3 signatures. Series H. Back: Scene of historic town of Tinta. Printer: TDLR.

	VF	UNC
a. Issued note.	1.00	5.00
s. Specimen.	—	25.00

95 **100 Soles de Oro** — VF / UNC
23.2.1968. Black on multicolor underprint. Dock workers at left, *Hipolito Unanue* at right, arms at center. 3 signatures. Series G. Back: Church, site of first National Congress. Printer: TDLR.

	VF	UNC
a. Issued note.	1.50	6.50
s. Specimen.	—	25.00

96 **200 Soles de Oro** — VF / UNC
23.2.1968. Purple on multicolor underprint. Fishermen at left, Ramon Castilla at right, arms at center. 3 signatures. Series Q. Back: Frigate *Amazonas* at center. Printer: TDLR.

	VF	UNC
a. Issued note.	3.50	12.50
s. Specimen.	—	25.00

97 **500 Soles de Oro** — VF / UNC
23.2.1968. Brown on multicolor underprint., tan near center. Builders at left, Nicolas de Pierola at right, arms at center. 3 signatures. Series L. Back: National mint. Printer: TDLR.

	VF	UNC
a. Issued note.	3.00	20.00
s. Specimen.	—	25.00

98 **1000 Soles de Oro**
23.2.1968. Violet on multicolor underprint. Miguel Grau at left, Francisco Bolognesi (misspelled *BOLOGÑESI*) at right, arms at center. 3 signatures. Series R. Back: Scene of Machu Picchu. Printer: TDLR.

	VF	UNC
a. Issued note.	12.50	30.00
s. Specimen.	—	25.00

1969 Issue

#99-105 Replacement notes: Serial # *Z999 . . .*

99 **5 Soles de Oro** VF UNC
1969-74. Green on multicolor underprint. Like #92 but text changed to: *De Acuerdo Con Su Ley Organica.* 2 signatures. Series J. Back: *Fortaleza de Sacsahuaman.* Printer: TDLR.

	VF	UNC
a. 20.6.1969.	.25	2.50
b. 16.10.1970; 9.9.1971; 4.5.1972.	.25	2.00
c. 24.5.1973; 16.5.1974; 15.8.1974.	.25	1.25

100 **10 Soles de Oro**
1969-74. Red-orange on multicolor underprint. Like #93 but text changed to: *De Acuerdo Con Su Ley Organica.* 2 signatures. Series I. Back: Lake Titicaca, boats. Printer: TDLR.

	VF	UNC
a. 20.6.1969.	.25	2.00
b. 16.10.1970; 9.9.1971.	.25	1.50
c. 4.5.1972; 24.5.1973; 16.5.1974.	.25	1.50

101 **50 Soles de Oro**
1969-74. Blue-gray on multicolor underprint. Like #94 but text changed to: *De Acuerdo Con Su Ley Organica.* 2 signatures. Series H. Back: Scene of historic town of Tinta. Printer: TDLR.

	VF	UNC
a. 20.6.1969.	.50	5.00
b. 16.10.1970; 9.9.1971; 4.5.1972.	.50	4.00
c. 24.5.1973; 16.5.1974; 15.8.1974.	.50	2.50

102 **100 Soles de Oro**
1969-74. Black on multicolor underprint. Like #95 but text changed to: *De Acuerdo Con Su Ley Organica.* 2 signatures. Series G. Back: Church, site of first National Congress. Printer: TDLR.

	VF	UNC
a. 20.6.1969.	1.00	5.00
b. 16.10.1970; 9.9.1971; 4.5.1972.	.50	3.50
c. 24.5.1973; 16.5.1974; 15.8.1974.	.50	3.00

103 **200 Soles de Oro**
1969-74. Purple on multicolor underprint. Like #96 but text changed to: *De Acuerdo Con Su Ley Organica.* 2 signatures. Series Q. Back: Frigate *Amazonas* at center. Printer: TDLR.

	VF	UNC
a. 20.6.1969.	3.00	10.00
b. 24.5.1973; 16.5.1974; 15.8.1974.	2.00	9.00

104 **500 Soles de Oro** VF UNC
1969-74. Brown on multicolor underprint. Like #97 but text changed to: *De Acuerdo Con Su Ley Organica.* 2 signatures. Series L. Back: National mint. Printer: TDLR.

	VF	UNC
a. 20.6.1969.	5.00	20.00
b. 16.10.1970; 9.9.1971; 4.5.1972; 24.5.1973.	4.00	15.00
c. 16.5.1974; 15.8.1974.	2.50	10.00

105 **1000 Soles de Oro** VF UNC
1969-73. Violet on multicolor underprint. Like #98 but *BOLOGNESI* correctly spelled at right and text changed to: *De Acuerdo Con Su Ley Organica.* 2 signatures. Series R. Back: Scene of Macchu Picchu. Printer: TDLR.

	VF	UNC
a. 20.6.1969; 16.10.1970.	7.50	30.00
b. 9.9.1971; 4.5.1972; 24.5.1973.	5.00	25.00

1975 Issue

#106-111 Replacement notes: Serial # *Z999 . . .*

		VF	UNC
106	**10 Soles de Oro** 2.10.1975. Red-orange on multicolor underprint. Building at left, Garcilaso Inca de la Vega at right, arms at center. 3 signatures. Series I. Back: Lake Titicaca, boats. Printer: TDLR.	.25	1.50

		VF	UNC
107	**50 Soles de Oro** 2.10.1975. Blue-gray on multicolor underprint. Workers at left, Tupac Amaru II at right, arms at center. 3 signatures. Series H. Back: Scene of historic town of Tinta. Printer: TDLR.	.25	1.50
108	**100 Soles de Oro** 2.10.1975. Black on multicolor underprint. Dock workers at left, *Hipolito Unanue* at right, arms at center. 3 signatures. Series G. Back: Church, site of first National Congress. Printer: TDLR.	.50	2.50

		VF	UNC
110	**500 Soles de Oro** 2.10.1975. Brown on multicolor underprint, pale green underprint near center. Builders at left, Nicolas de Pierola at right, arms at center. 3 signatures. Series L. Back: National mint. Printer: TDLR.	3.00	15.00

		VF	UNC
111	**1000 Soles de Oro** 2.10.1975. Miguel Grau at left, Francisco Bolognesi, name spelled correctly at right, arms at center. 3 signatures. Series R. Back: Scene of Macchu Picchu. Printer: TDLR.	5.00	27.50

1976-77 Issues

#112 and 113 Replacement notes: Serial # *Z999....*

		VF	UNC
112	**10 Soles de Oro** 17.11.1976. Red-orange on multicolor underprint. Like #106 but without *Pagará al Portador* at top and without security thread. 3 signatures. Series I. Back: Lake Titicaca. Printer: TDLR.	.25	1.50
113	**50 Soles de Oro** 15.12.1977. Blue-gray on multicolor underprint. Like #107 but without *Pagará al Portador* at top and without security thread. 3 signatures. Series H. Back: Scene of historic town of Tinta. Printer: TDLR.	.25	1.25
114	**100 Soles de Oro** 22.7.1976. Green, brown and multicolor. Arms at left, Tupac Amaru II at right. Back: Machu Picchu. Printer: IPS-Roma.	.25	1.25

115 500 Soles de Oro | VF .25 | UNC 1.50

22.7.1976. Green, blue and yellow. Arms at center, Jose Quiñones at right. Back: Logging scene. Printer: IPS-Roma.

116 1000 Soles de Oro | VF 2.00 | UNC 7.50

22.7.1976. Black, green, brown and multicolor. Arms at center, Miguel Grau at right. Back: Fishermen. Printer: BDDK.

117 5000 Soles de Oro | VF | UNC

1976-85. Brown and maroon on multicolor underprint. Arms at center, Colonel Bolognesi at right. Back: Two miners in mine at left. Watermark: Colonel Bolognesi. Printer: BDDK.

	VF	UNC
a. 22.7.1976.	2.50	10.00
b. 5.11.1981.	.50	2.50
c. 21.6.1985.	.25	1.50

1979 Issue

#118-120 Replacement notes: Serial # prefix *Y* and suffix letter *A*.

118 1000 Soles de Oro | VF 1.00 | UNC 3.00

1.2.1979; 3.5.1979. Black, green and multicolor. Admiral Grau at right, arms at center, denominations below coat of arms. Back: Fishermen and boats at left. Watermark: Admiral Grau. Printer: TDLR.

119 5000 Soles de Oro | VF 1.50 | UNC 7.50

1.2.1979. Brown-violet and multicolor. Colonel Bolognese at right, arms at center, denominations below coat of arms. *CINCO MIL* added at bottom. Back: Miners. Watermark: Colonel Bolognese. Printer: TDLR.

120 10,000 Soles de Oro | VF 3.00 | UNC 15.00

1.2.1979; 5.11.1981. Black, blue-violet and purple on multicolor underprint. Garcilaso Inca de la Vega, arms at center, denominations below coat of arms. Back: Indian digging at left, woman with flowers at center. Watermark: Garcilaso Inca de la Vega. Printer: TDLR.

1981 Issue

#121 *Deleted.* **See #125B.**

#122-125 Replacement notes: Serial # prefix *Y*, suffix *A*.

122 1000 Soles de Oro | VF | UNC

5.11.1981. Black, green and multicolor. Similar to #118 but slightly modified guilloche in underprint at center. Back: Fishermen and boats. Watermark: Admiral Grau. Printer: ABNC.

	VF	UNC
a. Issued note.	.30	1.50
s. Specimen.	—	75.00

123 5000 Soles de Oro | VF | UNC

5.11.1981. Black and red-brown on multicolor underprint. Similar to #119 but denomination is above signatures at center. Back: Miners. Watermark: Colonel Bolognesi. Printer: ABNC. | 1.00 | 5.00

124 10,000 Soles de Oro | VF | UNC

5.11.1981. Black, blue-violet and purple on multicolor underprint. Similar to #120 but slight variations on borders. Back: Indian digging at left, woman with flowers at center. Watermark: Garcilaso Inca de la Vega. Printer: ABNC. | 2.00 | 7.00

125 50,000 Soles de Oro | VF | UNC

5.11.1981; 2.11.1984. Black and orange on multicolor underprint. Arms at center, Nicolas de Pierola at right. Back: Drilling rig at left on back, helicopter approaching. Watermark: Nicolas de Pierola. Printer: ABNC.

	VF	UNC
a. Issued note.	3.00	12.50
s. Specimen.	—	125.

1982; 1985 Issue

Replacement notes: Serial # prefix *Y*, suffix *A* and *ZZ* respectively.

125A 500 Soles de Oro | VF | UNC

18.3.1982 Green, blue and yellow. Arms at center, Jose Quiñones at right. Back: Logging scene. Printer: (T)DLR. | .50 | 3.00

125B 50,000 Soles de Oro

23.8.1985. Black, orange and multicolor. Arms at center, Nicolas de Pierola at right. Back: Drilling rig at left on back, helicopter approaching. Watermark: Nicolas de Pierola. Printer: TDLR. | 2.25 | 6.50

1985 Provisional Issue

126 100,000 Soles de Oro | VF | UNC

23.8.1985. Black, green and multicolor. Admiral Grau at right, arms at center. Back: Fishermen and boats. Overprint: Bank name and new denomination in red on face and back. Watermark: Admiral Grau. Printer: ABNC. | 150. | 375.

127 500,000 Soles de Oro

23.8.1985. Black and red-brown on multicolor underprint. Colonel Bolognesi at right, arms at center. Back: Miners. Overprint: Bank name and new denomination in red on face and back. Watermark: Colonel Bolognesi. Printer: ABNC. | — | —

1985-91 Issues

During the period from around 1984 and extending beyond 1990, Perú suffered from a hyperinflation that saw the Sol depreciate in value dramatically and drastically. A sudden need for new Inti banknotes caused the government to approach a number of different security printers in order to satisfy the demand for new notes.

#128-150 involve 7 different printers: BdM, BDDK, CdM-B, FNMT, G&D, IPS-Roma and TDLR. Listings proceed by denomination and in chronological order. Replacement notes:

BdM - Serial # prefix *Y; Z.*
BDDK - Serial # prefix *Y.*
FNMT - Serial # prefix *Y.*
IPS-Roma - Serial # prefix Y; Z.
TDLR - Serial # prefix Y; Z.

128 10 Intis | VF | UNC

3.4.1985; 17.1.1986. Black, dark blue and purple on multicolor underprint. Ricardo Palma at right, arms at center. Back: Aqua and purple. Indian farmer digging at left and another picking cotton at center. Watermark: Ricardo Palma. Printer: TDLR. | .20 | .50

129 10 Intis | VF | UNC

26.6.1987. Black, dark blue and purple on multicolor underprint. Ricardo Palma at right, arms at center. Back: Aqua and purple. Indian farmer digging at left and atother picking cotton at center. Watermark: Ricardo Palma. Printer: IPS-Roma. UV: fibers fluoresce yellow and blue. | .15 | .75

130 **50 Intis** — VF | UNC

3.4.1985. Black, orange and green on multicolor underprint. Nicolas de Pierola at right. Back: Drilling rig at left on back, helicopter approaching. Watermark: Nicolas de Pierola. Printer: TDLR. — .50 | 2.00

131 **50 Intis**

1986; 1987 Black, orange and green on multicolor underprint. Nicolas de Pierola at right, arms at center. Back: Drilling rig at left, hilicopter approaching. Watermark: Nicolas de Pierola. Printer: CdM-Brazil. UV: fibers fluoresce green and orange.

		VF	UNC
a.	6.3.1986.	.25	1.50
b.	26.6.1987.	.25	1.25

132 **100 Intis** — VF | UNC

1985; 1986. Black and dark brown on multicolor underprint. Ramon Castilla at right, arms at center. Back: Women workers by cotton spinning frame at left center. Watermark: Ramon Castilla. Printer: CdM-Brazil.

		VF	UNC
a.	1.2.1985, 1.3.1985.	2.00	12.00
b.	6.3.1986. With additional pink and light green vertical underprint at right.	.75	3.50

133 **100 Intis** — VF | UNC

26.6.1987. Black and dark brown on multicolor underprint. Ramon Castilla at right, arms at center with additional pink and light green vertical underprint at right. Back: Women workers by cotton spinning frame at left center. Watermark: Ramon Castilla. Printer: BDDK. UV: fibers fluoresce yellow and blue, security strip yellow. — .10 | .35

134 **500 Intis** — VF | UNC

1985; 1987. Deep brown-violet and olive-brown on multicolor underprint. Jose Cabriel Condorcanqui Tupac Amaru II at right, arms at center. Back: Mountains and climber at center. Watermark: Jose Cabriel Condorcanqui Tupac Amaru II. Printer: BDDK. UV: fibers and security thread fluoresce yellow and blue.

		VF	UNC
a.	1.3.1985.	.30	3.00
b.	26.6.1987.	.20	.50

135 **500 Intis** — VF | UNC

6.3.1986 Deep brown-violet and olive-brown on multicolor underprint. Jose Cabriel Condorcanqui Tupac Amaru II at right, arms at center. Ornate red-orange vertical strip at left end of design with added security thread underneath. Back: Mountains and climber at center. Watermark: Jose Gabriel Condorcanqui Tupac Amaru II. Printer: FNMT. — 3.50 | 12.50

136 **1000 Intis** — VF | UNC

1986-88. Deep green, olive-brown and red on multicolor underprint. Mariscal Andres Avelino Caceres at right, arms at center. Back: Ruins of Chan Chan. Watermark: Mariscal Andres Avelino Caceres. Printer: TDLR. UV: fibers fluoresce green adn blue; signatures green; security strip yellow.

		VF	UNC
a.	6.3.1986.	.50	2.00
b.	26.6.1987; 28.6.1988.	.25	1.50

137 **5000 Intis** — VF | UNC

28.6.1988. Prurple, deep brown and red-orange on multicolor underprint. Admiral Miguel Grau at right, arms at center. Back: Fishermen repairing nets. Watermark: Admiral Miguel Grau. Printer: G&D. UV: security strip fluoresces red, blue and yellow; fibers yellow and blue, center design yellow. — .20 | 1.00

138 **5000 Intis**

28.6.1988. Purple, deep brown and red-orange on multicolor underprint. Admiral Miguel Grau at right, arms at center. Back: Fishermen repairing nets. Watermark: Admiral Miguel Grau. Printer: IPS-Roma. . — 1.00 | 3.50

139 **5000 Intis**

9.9.1988. Purple, deep brown and red-orange on multicolor underprint. Admiral Miguel Grau at right, arms at center. Back: Fishermen repairing nets. Printer: TDLR. — 1.00 | 4.50

140 10,000 Intis
VF .20 UNC 1.00
28.6.1988. Aqua, blue and orange on light green and multicolor underprint. Cesar Vallejo at right, arms at center. Black and red increasing size serial # (anti-counterfeiting device). Back: Santiago de Chuco street scene. Watermark: Cesar Vallejo. Printer: IPS-Roma. UV: fibers fluoresce blue and green; value yellow; security strip multicolor; some notes have vertical serial # red and signatures green.

141 10,000 Intis
VF .75 UNC 3.00
28.6.1988. Dark blue and orange on light green and multicolor underprint. Like # 140 but with broken silver security thread. Cesar Vallejo at right, arms at center. Black and red increasing size serial # (anti-counterfeiting device). Back: Santiago de chuco street scene. Watermark: Cesar Vallejo. Printer: TDLR.

142 50,000 Intis
VF 1.00 UNC 4.00
28.6.1988. Red, violet and dark blue on multicolor underprint. Victor Raul Haya de la Torre at right, arms at center. Back: Chamber of National Congress. Watermark: Victor Raul Haya de la Torre. Printer: IPS-Roma.

143 50,000 Intis
VF 1.50 UNC 5.00
28.6.1988. Red, violet and dark blue on multicolor underprint. Like #142 but with segmented foil security thread. Victor Raul Haya de la Torre at right, arms at center. Back: Chamber of National Congress. Watermark: Victor Raul Haya de la Torre. Printer: TDLR.

144 100,000 Intis
VF .75 UNC 2.25
21.11.1988. Brown and black on multicolor underprint. Francisco Bolognesi at right, arms at center. Back: Local boats in Lake Titicaca. Watermark: Francisco Bolognesi. Printer: TDLR.

144A 100,000 Intis
VF .75 UNC 2.50
21.12.1988. Brown and black on multicolor underprint. Francisco Bolognesi at right, arms at center. Segmented foil over security thread. Back: Local boats in Lake Titicaca. Watermark: Francisco Bolognesi. Printer: TDLR.

145 100,000 Intis
VF .75 UNC 3.00
21.12.1989. Brown and black on multicolor underprint. Francisco Bolognesi at right, arms at center, black security thread at right of arms. Back: Local boats in Lake Titicaca. Printer: BdeM.

146 500,000 Intis
VF 1.00 UNC 6.50
21.11.1988. Blue and blue-violet on multicolor underprint. Ricardo Palma at right, arms at center. Back: Church of *La Caridád* (charity), site of first National Congress. Watermark: Ricardo Palma's printed image. Printer: TDLR.

146A 500,000 Intis
VF 1.75 UNC 7.50
21.12.1988. Blue and blue-violet on multicolor underprint. Ricardo Palma at right, arms at center. Segmented foil over security thread. Back: Indian farmer digging at left and another picking cotton at center. Watermark: Ricardo Palma. Printer: TDLR.

147 500,000 Intis
VF 1.25 UNC 5.50
21.12.1989. Blue and blue-violet on multicolor underprint. Ricardo Palma at right, arms at center, black security thread at right. Back: Indian farmer digging at left and another picking cotton at center. Watermark: Picardo Palma. Printer: BdeM.

148 1,000,000 Intis — VF | UNC
5.1.1990. Red-brown, green and multicolor. Hipolito Unanue at right, arms at center. Back: Medical college at San Fernando at left center. Watermark: Hipolito Unanue. Printer: TDLR. — 1.00 | 5.00

149 5,000,000 Intis — VF | UNC
5.1.1990. Brown, red and multicolor. Antonio Raimondi at right, arms at center. Back: Indian comforting Raimundi. Watermark: Antonio Raimondi. Printer: BdeM. — 7.50 | 20.00

150 5,000,000 Intis — VF | UNC
16.1.1991. Brown, red and multicolor. Antonio Raimondi at right, arms at center, plants printed on watermark area at left. Back: Old building at right. Watermark: Antonio Raimondi. Printer: IPS-Roma. — 2.00 | 7.50

1991; 1992 Issues

MONETARY REFORM:

1 Nuevo Sol = 1 Million Intis

151 10 Nuevos Soles — VF | UNC
1.2.1991. Dark green and blue-green on multicolor underprint. WW II era fighter plane as monument at upper center, José Abelardo Quiñones at right, arms at upper right. Back: Biplane inverted (signifying pilot's death) at left center. Watermark: José Abelardo Quiñones. Printer: TDLR. 140x65mm. — FV | 9.50

151A 10 Nuevos Soles — VF | UNC
10.9.1992. Dark green and blue-green on multicolor underprint. WW II era fighter plane as monument at upper center, José Abelardo Quiñones at right, arms at upper right. Back: Biplane inverted (signifying pilot's death) at left center. Watermark: José Abelardo Quiñones. Printer: IPS-Roma. 140x65mm. — FV | 9.50

152 20 Nuevos Soles — VF | UNC
1.2.1991. Black, brown and orange on multicolor underprint. Patio of San Marcos University at center, Raul Porras B. at right, arms at upper right. Back: Palace of TorreTagle at left center. Watermark: Raul Porras B. Printer: TDLR. 140x65mm. — FV | 22.50

153 20 Nuevos Soles
25.6.1992. Black, brown and orange on multicolor underprint. Patio of San Marcos University at center, Raul Porras B. at right, arms at upper right. Back: Palace of TorreTagle at left center. Watermark: Raul Porras B. Printer: IPS-Roma. 140x65mm. — FV | 17.50

154 50 Nuevos Soles — VF | UNC
1.2.1991; 25.6.1992. Red-brown, blue-violet and black on multicolor underprint. Building at center, Abraham Valdelomar at right, arms at upper right. Back: Laguna de Huacachina at left center. Watermark: Abraham Valdelomar. Printer: IPS-Roma. 140x65mm. — FV | 40.00

155 100 Nuevos Soles — VF | UNC
1.2.1991; 25.6.1992; 10.9.1992. Black, blue-black, red-violet and deep green on multicolor underprint. Arch monument at center, Jorge Basadre (Grohmann) at right. Back: National Library at left center. Watermark: Jorge Basadre (Grohmann). Printer: IPS-Roma. 140x65mm.
a. Name as: *Jorge Basadre*. 1.2.1991. — FV | 75.00
b. Name as: *Jorge Basadre Grohmann*. 10.9.1992. — FV | 70.00

1994; 1995 Issue

#156-161 similar to #151-155 but w/clear wmk. area.

156 **10 Nuevos Soles** — VF | UNC

16.6.1994. Dark green and blue-green on multicolor underprint. WW II era fighter plane as monument at upper center, José Abelardo Quiñones at right, arms at upper right. Back: Biplane inverted (signifying pilot's death) at left center. Printer: TDLR. 140x65mm. — FV | 7.50

157 **10 Nuevos Soles** — VF | UNC

20.4.1995. Dark green and blue-green on multicolor underprint. WW II era fighter plane as monument at upper center, José Abelardo Quiñones at right, arms at upper right. Back: Biplane inverted (signifying pilot's death) at left center. Printer: G&D. 140x65mm. — FV | 7.00

158 **20 Nuevos Soles** — VF | UNC

16.6.1994. Black, brown and orange on multicolor underprint. Patio of San Marcos University at center, Raul Porras B. at right, arms at upper right. Back: Palace of Torre Tagle at left center. Printer: TDLR. 140x65mm. — FV | 15.00

159 **20 Nuevos Soles**

20.4.1995. Black, brown and orange on multicolor underprint. Patio of San Marcos University at center, Raul Porras B. at right, arms at upper right. Back: Palace of Torre Tagle at left center. Printer: TDLR. 140x65mm. — FV | 14.00

160 **50 Nuevos Soles** — VF | UNC

16.6.1994; 20.4.1995. Brown, deep blue and black on multicolor underprint. Building at center, Abraham Valdelomar at right, arms at upper right. Back: Laguna de Huacachina at left center. Printer: IPS-Roma. 140x65mm. — FV | 37.50

161 **100 Nuevos Soles** — VF | UNC

20.4.1995. Black, blue-black, red-violet and deep green on multicolor underprint. Like #155b. Arch monument at center, Jorge Basadre (Grohmann) at right, arms at upper right. Back: National Library at left center. Printer: IPS-Roma. 140x65mm. — FV | 65.00

162 **200 Nuevos Soles** — VF | UNC

20.4.1995. Red, brown-violet and dark blue on multicolor underprint. Isabel Flores de Oliva, St. Rose of Lima at right, well in underprint at center. Back: Convent of Santo Domingo at left. Watermark: Isabel Flores de Oliva, St. Rose of Lima. Printer: IPS-Roma. 140x65mm.

- a. Issued note. — FV | 120.
- s. Specimne. — — | 150.

1996 Issue

163 **10 Nuevos Soles** — VF | UNC

24.4.1996. Dark green and blue-green on multicolor underprint. WW II era fighter plane as monument at upper center, José Abelardo Quiñones at right, arms at upper right. Back: Biplane inverted (signifying pilot's death) at left center. Printer: IPS-Roma. 140x65mm. — FV | 10.00

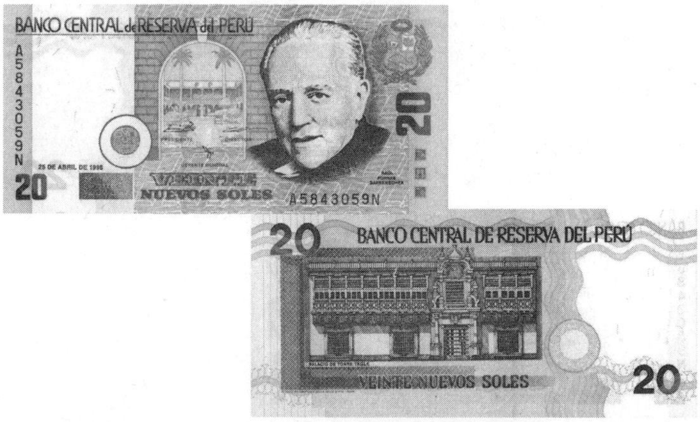

164 **20 Nuevos Soles** — VF | UNC

25.4.1996; 11.6.1997. Black, brown and orange on multicolor underprint. Patio of San Marcos University at center, Raul Porras B. at right, arms at upper right. Back: Palace of Torre Tagle at left center. Printer: IPS-Roma. 140x65mm. — FV | 15.00

165 **100 Nuevos Soles**

25.4.1996. Black, blue-black, red-violet and deep green on multicolor underprint. Like #155b. Arch monument at cetnr, Jorge Basadre (Grohmann) at right, arms at upper right. Back: National Library at left. Printer: IPS-Roma. 140x65mm. — FV | 65.00

1997 Issue

166 **10 Nuevos Soles** — VF | UNC

11.6.1997; 6.8.1998; 20.5.1999. Dark green and blue-green on multicolor underprint. WW II era fighter plane as monument at upper center, José Abelardo Quiñones at right, arms at upper right. Back: Biplane inverted (signifying pilot's death) at left center. Printer: BABN. 140x65mm. — FV | 9.00

167 **20 Nuevos Soles**

11.6.1997; 6.8.1998. Black, brown and orange on multicolor underprint. Patio of San Marcos University at center, Raul Porras B. at right, arms at upper right. Back: Palace of TorreTagle at left center. Printer: BABN. 140x65mm.

- a. 11.6.1997. — FV | 15.00
- b. 6.8.1998. — FV | 15.00

		VF	UNC
168	**50 Nuevos Soles** 11.6.1997. Red-brown, blue-violet and black on multicolor underprint. Building at center, Abraham Valdelomar at right, arms at upper right. Back: Laguna de Huacachina at left center. Printer: IPS-Roma. 140x65mm.	FV	37.50

1998 Issue

		VF	UNC
169	**50 Nuevos Soles** 6.8.1998. Red-brown, blue-violet and black on multicolor underprint. Building at center. Abraham Valdelomar at right, arms at upper right. Back: Laguna de Huacachina. Printer: BABN. 140x65mm.	FV	37.50

1999 Issue

		VF	UNC
170	**20 Nuevos Soles** 20.5.1999. Black, blue-black, red-violet and deep green on multicolor underprint. Patio of San Marcos University at center. Raúl Porras Barrenechea at right, arms at upper right. Back: Palace of Torre Tagle at left center. Printer: FNMT. 140x65mm.	FV	15.00

		VF	UNC
171	**50 Nuevos Soles** 20.5.1999. Red-brown, blue-violet and black on multicolor underprint. Building at center. Abraham Valdelomar at right, arms at upper right. Back: Laguna de Huacachina. Printer: (T)DLR. 140x65mm.	FV	37.50
172	**100 Nuevos Soles** 20.5.1999. Black, blue-black, red-violet and green on multicolor underprint. Arch monument at center, Jorge Basadre Grohmann at right, arms at upper center. Back: National Library. Printer: BABN. 140x65mm.	FV	65.00

2000 Series

		VF	UNC
173	**20 Nuevos Soles** 20.5.1999; 12.10.2000. Black, brown and orange on multicolor underprint. Patio of San Marcos University at center. Raúl Porras Barrenechea at right. Back: Palace of Torre Tagle at left center. Printer: BABN. 140x65mm.		
	a. 20.5.1999.	FV	15.00
	b. 12.10.2000.	FV	12.50

2001; 2004 Issue

		VF	UNC
174	**10 Nuevos Soles** 1.3.2001. Dark green and blue-green on multicolor underprint. WW II era fighter plane as monument at upper center. José Abelardo Quiñones at right, arms at upper center. Back: Biplane inverted (signifying pilot's death). Printer: F-CO. 140x65mm.	FV	9.00
175	**10 Nuevos Soles** 27.9.2001. Dark green and blue-green on multicolor underprint. WW II era fighter plane as monument at upper center. José Abelardo Quiñones at right, arms at upper center. Back: Biplane inverted (signifying pilot's death). Printer: (T)DLR. 140x65mm.	FV	9.00

		VF	UNC
176	**20 Nuevos Soles** 2001; 2004; 2006. Black, brown and orange on multicolor underprint. Patio of San Marcos University at center. Raúl Porras Barrenechea at right, arms at upper right. Back: Palace of Torre Tagle at left center. Printer: F-CO. 140x65mm.		
	a. 27.9.2001.	FV	15.00
	b. 28.10.2004.	FV	15.00
	c. 25.12.2006.	FV	15.00

		VF	UNC
177	**50 Nuevos Soles** 27.9.2001. Red-brown, blue-violet and black on multicolor underprint. Building at center. Abraham Valdelomar at right, arms at upper center. Back: Laguna de Huacachina. Printer: JEZ. 140x65mm.	FV	37.50

		VF	UNC
178	**100 Nuevos Soles** 2001; 2004. Black, blue-black, red-violet and green on multicolor underprint. Arch monument at center, Jorge Basadre Grohmann at right, arms at upper right. Back: National Library. Printer: F-CO. 140x65mm.		
	a. 27.9.2001.	FV	65.00
	b. 28.10.2004.	FV	65.00

2005 Issue

		VF	UNC
179	**10 Nuevos Soles** 11.8.2005; 21.12.2006. Dark green and blue-green on multicolor underprint. WW II era fighter plane as monument at upper center, José Abelardo Quiñones at right, arms at upper right. Back: Biplane inverted (signifying pilot's death). Printer: F-CO. Without colored planchettes as on #174. 140x65mm.		
	a. 11.8.2005.	FV	7.50
	b. 21.12.2006.	FV	6.50

		VF	UNC
180	**50 Nuevos Soles** 21.12.2006. Red brown, blue violet and black on multicolor underprint. Building at center. Abraham Valdelomar at right, arms at upper right. Back: Laguna de Huacachina. Printer: BDDK. 140x65mm.	FV	37.50
181	**100 Nuevos Soles** 21.12.2006. Black, blue-black, red-violet and green on multicolor underprint. Arch monument at center, Jorge Basadre Grohmann at right, arms at upper right. Back: National Library. Printer: G&D. 140x65mm.	FV	65.00

2009 Issue

		VF	UNC
182	**10 Nuevos Soles** 13.8.2009. Green, orange, brown and multicolor underprint. José Abelardo Quiñones Gonzales at right. Back: Inca site of Machu Picchu mountian top ruins at left. 140x65mm.	FV	10.00
183	**20 Nuevos Soles** 13.8.2009. Brown, orane, green, red and multicolor underprint. Raúl Porras Barrenechea at right. Back: Chan Chan archaeological complex at left. 140x65mm.	FV	15.00

		VF	UNC
184	**50 Nuevos Soles** 13.8.2009. Rose and green on multicolor underprint. Abraham Valdelomar at right. Back: Templo Nuevo at left. Watermark: Valdelomar and 50. 140x65mm.	FV	37.50

		VF	UNC
185	**100 Nuevos Soles** 13.8.2009. Blue on multicolor underprint. Jorge Basadre Grohman at right. Back: Gran Pajatén. Watermark: Grohmann and 100. 140x65mm.	FV	65.00

		VF	UNC
186	**200 Nuevos Soles** 13.8.2009. Black and rose on multicolor underprint. St. Rose of Lima at right. Back: Ciudad Sagrada de Caral at left. Watermark: St. Rose and 200. 140x65mm.	FV	120.

Banco de Credito del Perú / Banco Central de Reserva del Perú

1985 Emergency Check Issue

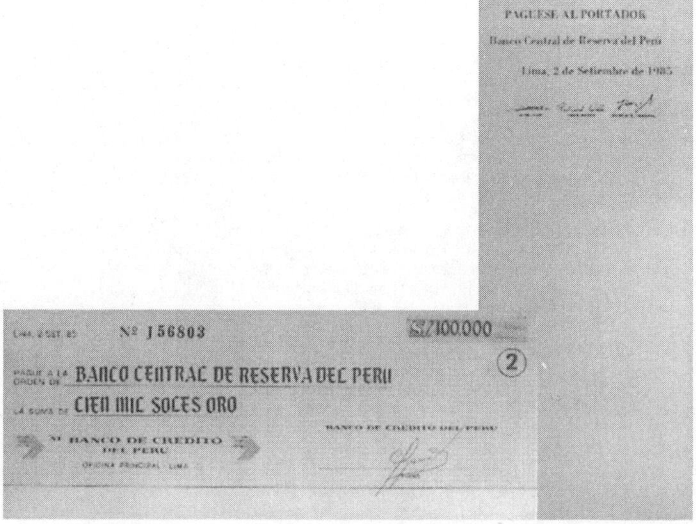

		VF	UNC
R2	**100,000 Soles** 2.9.1985. Black text on light blue text underprint. Two signature varieties.	150.	—

Banco de la Nación / Banco Central de Reserva del Perú

1985 Cheques Circulares de Gerencia Issue

#R6-R8 bank monogram at upper l.

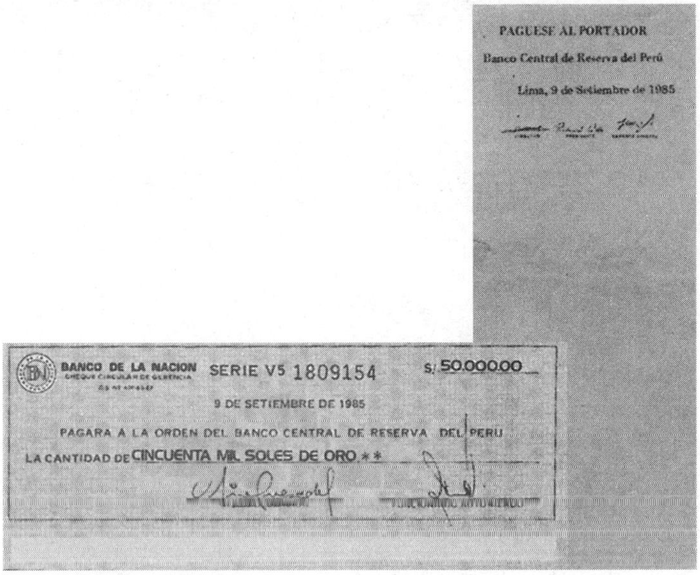

		VF	UNC
R6	**50,000 Soles** 9.9.1985; 16.9.1985. Black text on tan underprint. Bank at center, bank monogram at upper left.	125.	—
R7	**100,000 Soles** 2.9.1985. Black text on light blue underprint. Bank at center, bank monogram at upper left.	125.	—
R8	**200,000 Soles** 2.9.1985. Black text on pink underprint. Bank at center, bank monogram at upper left.	125.	—

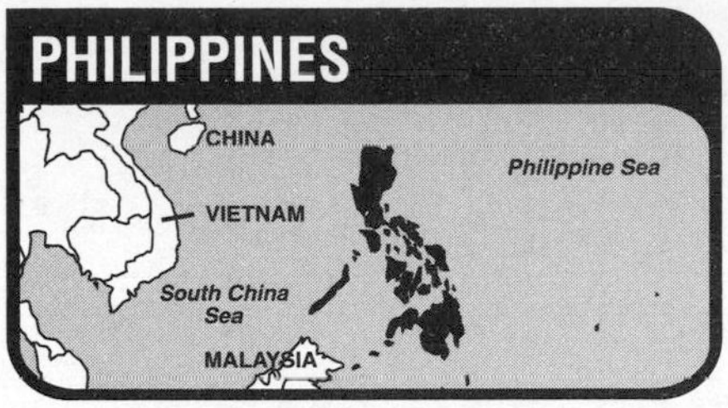

The Republic of the Philippines, an archipelago in the western Pacific 500 miles (805 km.) from the southeast coast of Asia, has an area of 115,830 sq. mi. (300,000 sq. km.) and a population of 75.04 million. Capital: Manila. The economy of the 7,000-island group is d on agriculture, forestry and fishing. Timber, coconut products, sugar and hemp are exported.

The Philippine Islands became a Spanish colony during the 16th century; they were ceded to the US in 1898 following the Spanish-American War. In 1935 the Philippines became a self-governing commonwealth. Manuel Quezon was elected president and was tasked with preparing the country for independence after a 10-year transition. In 1942 the islands fell under Japanese occupation during World War II, and US forces and Filipinos fought together during 1944-45 to regain control. On 4 July 1946 the Republic of the Philippines attained its independence. The 20-year rule of Ferdinand Marcos ended in 1986, when a "people power" movement in Manila ("EDSA 1") forced him into exile and installed Corazon Aquino as president. Her presidency was hampered by several coup attempts, which prevented a return to full political stability and economic development. Fidel Ramos was elected president in 1992 and his administration was marked by greater stability and progress on economic reforms. In 1992, the US closed its last military s on the islands. Joseph Estrada was elected president in 1998, but was succeeded by his vice-president, Gloria Macapagal-Arroyo, in January 2001 after Estrada's stormy impeachment trial on corruption charges broke down and another "people power" movement ("EDSA 2") demanded his resignation. Macapagal-Arroyo was elected to a six-year term as president in May 2004. The Philippine Government faces threats from three terrorist groups on the US Government's Foreign Terrorist Organization list, but in 2006 and 2007 scored some major successes in capturing or killing key wanted terrorists. Decades of Muslim insurgency in the southern Philippines have led to a peace accord with one group and on-again/off-again peace talks with another.

RULERS:

Spanish to 1898
United States, 1898-1946

MONETARY SYSTEM:

1 Peso = 100 Centavos to 1967
1 Piso = 100 Sentimos, 1967-

Type1

Type 2

Type3

Type 4

Type 5

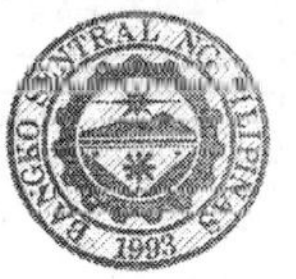

SIGNATURE VARIETIES		
1	E. Quirino	M. Cuaderno
2	R. Magsaysay	M. Cuaderno
3	C. Garcia	M. Cuaderno
4	C. Garcia	A. Castillo
5	D. Macapagal	A. Castillo
6	F. Marcos	A. Castillo
7	F. Marcos	A. Calalang

SIGNATURE VARIETIES		
8	F, Marcos	G. Licaros
9	F. Marcos	J. Laya
10	F. Marcos	J. Fernandez
11	C. Aquino	J. Fernandez
12	C. Aquino	J. Cuisia
13	M. Ramos	J. Cuisia
14	M. Ramos	G.C. Singson
15	J. E. Estrada	G. C. Singson
16	J.E. Estrada	R. B. Buenaventura
17	G. Macapagal-Arroyo	R. B. Buenaventura

REPUBLIC

CENTRAL BANK OF THE PHILIPPINES

1949 ND "ENGLISH" ISSUES

		VF	UNC
125	**5 Centavos**		
	ND (1949). Red on tan underprint. Central Bank Seal Type 1 at left. Signature 1. Back: Red. Printer: SBNC.		
	a. Issued note.	.50	2.75
	s. Specimen. Punch hole cancelled.	—	200.
	ct. Color trial. Black on green underprint.	—	150.

		VF	UNC
126	**5 Centavos**		
	ND. Red on tan underprint. Central Bank Seal Type 1 at left. Signature 2. Like #125. Back: Red. Printer: W&S.		
	a. Issued note.	.25	2.50
	p. Proof.	—	250.
	s. Specimen.	—	300.
127	**10 Centavos**		
	ND. Brownish purple on tan underprint. Central Bank Seal Type 1 at left. Signature 1. Back: Brownish purple. Printer: SBNC.		
	a. Issued note.	.50	1.75
	r. Remainder without serial #.	75.00	125.
	s. Specimen.	—	250.

		VF	UNC
128	**10 Centavos**		
	ND. Brownish purple on tan underprint. Central Bank Seal Type 1 at left. Signature 2. LIke #127. Back: Brownish purple. Printer: W&S.		
	a. Issued note.	.50	1.25
	s. Specimen.	—	400.
129	**20 Centavos**		
	ND. Green on light green underprint. Central Bank Seal Type 1 at left. Signature 1. Back: Green. Printer: SBNC.		
	a. Issued note.	1.00	4.50
	r. Remainder without serial #.	75.00	125.
	s. Specimen.	—	300.

		VF	UNC
130	**20 Centavos**		
	ND. Green on light green underprint. Back: Green. Printer: TDLR.		
	a. Signature 2.	.50	2.00
	b. Signature 3.	.50	1.50
	s1. Specimen. Pin perforated.	—	500.
	s2. Specimen. Red overprint.	—	500.

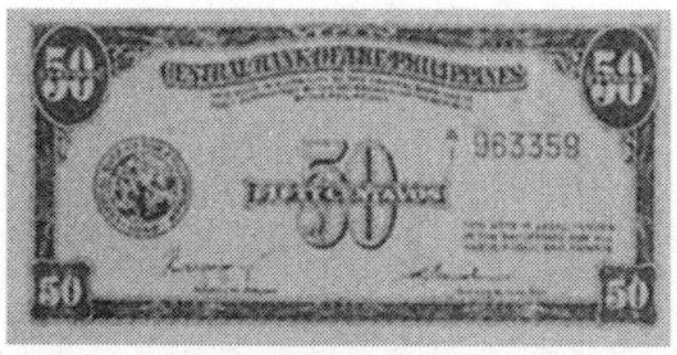

		VF	UNC
131	**50 Centavos**		
	ND. Blue on light blue underprint. Signature 2. Back: Blue. Printer: TDLR.		
	a. Issued note.	.50	3.75
	p. Proof.	—	250.
	s. Specimen.	—	150.
	ct. Color trial. Brown on tan underprint.	—	150.

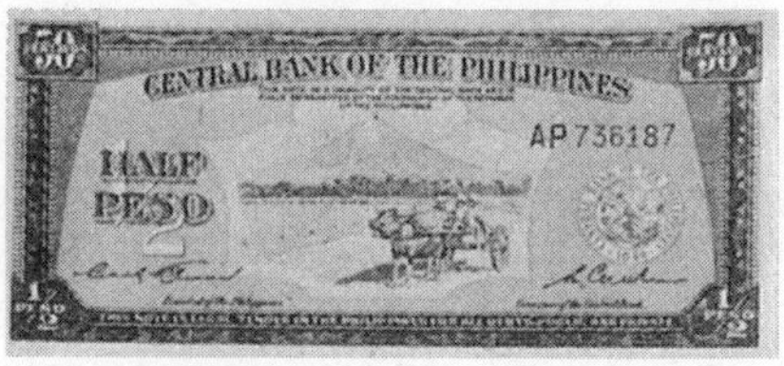

		VF	UNC
132	**1/2 Peso**		
	ND. Green on yellow and blue underprint. Ox-cart with Mt. Mayon in background at center. Large Central Bank Seal Type 1 at lower right. Signature 2. Back: Green. Printer: TDLR.		
	a. Issued note.	2.50	15.00
	s. Specimen.	—	550.

133 1 Peso

ND. Black on light gold and blue underprint. Portrait of A. Mabini at left. Large Central Bank Seal Type 1 at lower right. Back: Black. Barasoain Church at center. Printer: TDLR.

	VF	UNC
a. Signature 1. *GENUINE* in very light tan letters just beneath top heading on face.	30.00	110.
b. Signature 1. Without *GENUINE* on face.	2.00	12.50
c. Signature 2.	2.50	15.00
d. Signature 3.	2.00	12.00
e. Signature 4.	1.25	8.00
f. Signature 5.	1.00	3.00
g. Signature 6.	.50	2.00
h. Signature 7.	1.00	2.00
s1. Signature as a. Specimen.	—	200.
s2. Signature as b. Specimen. (De La Rue).	—	200.
s3. Signature as c. Specimen. (De La Rue).	—	200.
s4. Signature as d. Specimen. (De La Rue).	—	200.
s5. Signature as e. Specimen. (De La Rue).	—	200.
s6. Signature as f. Specimen.	—	45.00
s7. Signature as f. Specimen. (De La Rue).	—	250.
s8. Signature as g. Specimen.	—	55.00
s9. Signature as g. Specimen. (De La Rue).	—	250.
10. Signature as h. Specimen.	—	30.00
11. Signature as h. Specimen. (De La Rue).	—	250.

134 2 Pesos

ND. Black on blue and gold underprint. Portrait of J. Rizal at left. Large Central Bank Seal Type 1 at lower right. Back: Blue. Landing of Magellan in the Philippines. Printer: TDLR.

	VF	UNC
a. Signature 1.	7.50	15.00
b. Signature 2.	2.00	5.00
c. Signature 4.	2.50	10.00
d. Signature 5.	.50	2.00
p. Signature as b. Proof.	—	125.
s1. Signature as a. Specimen. (De La Rue) Cancelled.	—	250.
s2. Signature as b. Specimen.	—	60.00
s3. Signature as b. Specimen. (De La Rue).	—	250.
s4. Signature as c. Specimen. (De La Rue).	—	250.
s5. Signature as d. Specimen.	—	60.00

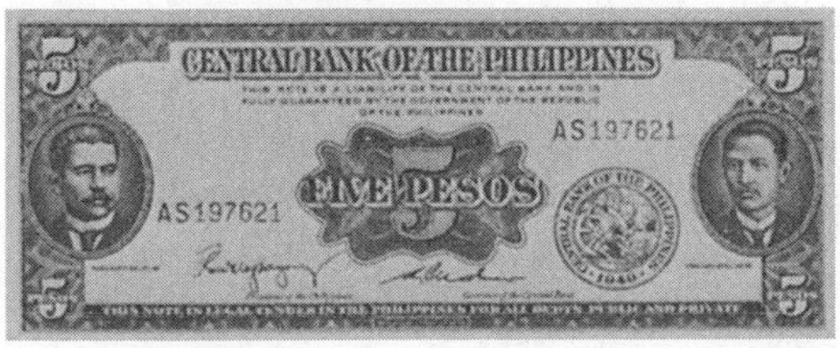

135 5 Pesos

ND. Black on yellow and gold underprint. Portrait of M. H. del Pilar at left, Lopez Jaena at right. Large Central Bank Seal Type 1 at lower right. Back: Gold. Newspaper *La Solidaridad*. Printer: TDLR.

	VF	UNC
a. Signature 1.	7.50	40.00
b. Signature 2.	3.50	10.00
c. Signature 3.	7.50	40.00
d. Signature 4.	3.00	10.00
e. Signature 5.	.50	2.50

	VF	UNC
f. Signature 8.	.50	2.00
p. Proof.	—	150.
s1. Signature as a. Specimen. (De La Rue).	—	250.
s2. Signature as b. Specimen. (De La Rue).	—	250.
s3. Signature as d. Specimen. (De La Rue).	—	250.
s4. Signature as e. Specimen.	—	85.00
s5. Signature as e. Specimen. (De La Rue).	—	200.
s6. Signature as f. Specimen. Red overprint *SPCEIMEN* on each side.	—	25.00

136 10 Pesos

ND. Black on tan and light red underprint. Fathers Burgos, Gomez and Zamora at left. Large Central Bank Seal Type 1 at lower right. Back: Brown. Monument. Printer: TDLR.

	VF	UNC
a. Signature 1.	500.	5775.
b. Signature 2.	5.00	25.00
c. Signature 3.	5.00	25.00
d. Signature 4.	5.00	30.00
e. Signature 5.	1.00	2.50
f. Signature 8.	1.00	2.50
s1. Signature as b. Specimen.	—	70.00
s2. Signature as c. Specimen.	—	70.00
s3. Signature as c. Specimen. (De La Rue).	—	250.
s4. Signature as d. Specimen.	—	75.00
s5. Signature as d. Specimen. (De La Rue).	—	250.
s6. Signature as e. Specimen.	—	50.00
s7. Signature as e. Specimen. (De La Rue).	—	200.
s8. Signature as f. Specimen.	—	35.00

137 20 Pesos

ND. Black on yellow underprint. Portrait of A. Bonifacio at left, E. Jacinto at right. Large Central Bank Seal Type 1 at lower right. Back: Brownish orange. Flag and monument. Printer: TDLR.

	VF	UNC
a. Signature 1.	375.	1000.
b. Signature 2.	20.00	50.00
c. Signature 4.	10.00	20.00
d. Signature 5.	1.50	3.25
e. Signature 8.	1.00	2.50
p. Signature as d. Proof.	—	150.
s1. Signature as a. Specimen.	—	175.
s2. Signature as c. Specimen. (De La Rue).	—	200.
s3. Signature as d. Specimen.	—	90.00
s4. Signature as d. Specimen (De La Rue).	—	175.
s5. Signature as e. Specimen. Red overprint: *SPECIMEN* on both sides.	—	20.00

138 50 Pesos

ND. Black on pink and light tan underprint. Portrait of A. Luna at left. Large Central Bank Seal Type 1 at lower right. Back: Red. Scene of blood compact of Sikatuna and Legaspi. Printer: TDLR.

	VF	UNC
a. Signature 1.	500.	—
b. Signature 2.	50.00	125.
c. Signature 3.	12.50	30.00
d. Signature 5.	1.50	7.50
p. Signature as d. Proof.	—	185.
s1. Signature as a. Specimen. (De La Rue).	—	500.
s2. Signature as b. Specimen. (De La Rue).	—	300.
s3. Signature as d. Specimen.	—	60.00
s4. Signature as d. Specimen. (De La Rue).	—	500.

139 100 Pesos | VF | UNC
ND. Black on gold underprint. Portrait of T. Sora at left. Large Central Bank Seal Type 1 at lower right. Signature 1. Back: Yellow. Regimental flags. Printer: TDLR. 160x66mm.

a. Issued note.	6.00	12.50
s. Specimen.	—	550.
ct. Color trial. Green on tan and light blue underprint.	—	550.

140 200 Pesos | VF | UNC
ND. Green on pink and light blue underprint. Portrait of President Manuel Quezon at left. Large Central Bank Seal Type 1 at lower right. Signature 1. Back: Green. Legislative building. Printer: TDLR. 160x66mm.

a. Issued note.	7.50	20.00
s. Specimen (De La Rue).	—	350.

141 500 Pesos | VF | UNC
ND. Black on purple and light tan underprint. Portrait of President Manuel Roxas at left. Large Central Bank Seal Type 1 at lower right. Signature 1. Back: Purple. Central Bank. Printer: TDLR.

a. Issued note.	50.00	90.00
s. Specimen. (De La Rue).	—	750.
ct. Brown on light green and tan underprint.	—	1300.

Bangko Sentral ng Pilipinas

1969 ND "Pilipino" Issue

#142-147 Replacement notes: Serial # prefix "+".

142 1 Piso | VF | UNC
ND (1969). Blue and black on multicolor underprint. J. Rizal at left, heading at top in double outline. Central Bank Seal Type 2. Back: Scene of Aguinaldo's Independence Declaration of June 12, 1898. 160x66mm.

a. Signature 7.	.50	2.00
b. Signature 8.	.50	1.00
s1. Signature as a. Specimen.	—	40.00
s2. Signature as a. Specimen. (De La Rue).	—	45.00
s3. Signature as b. Specimen. Red overprint: *SPECIMEN* on face.	—	40.00

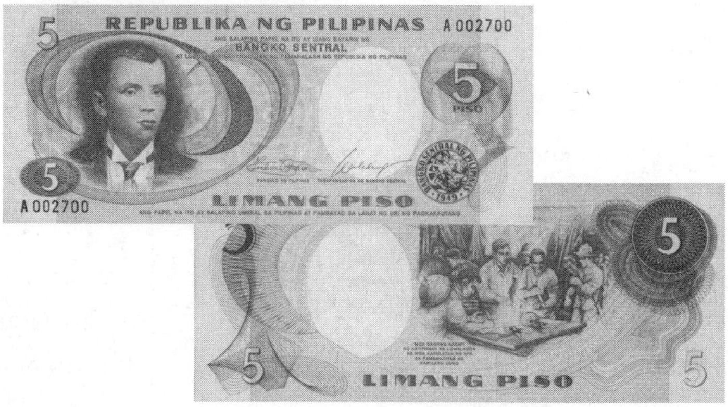

143 5 Piso | VF | UNC
ND (1969). Green and brown on multicolor underprint. A. Bonifacio at left in brown, heading at top in double outline. Central Bank Seal Type 3. Back: Scene of the Katipunan organization. Watermark: A. Bonifacio. Printer: G&D (without imprint). 160x66mm.

a. Signature 7.	1.50	2.00
b. Signature 8.	1.00	2.00
s1. Signature as a. Specimen.	—	125.
s2. Signature as b. Specimen.	—	15.00

144 10 Piso | VF | UNC
ND (1969). Brown on multicolor underprint. A. Mabini at left, heading at top in double outline. Central Bank Seal Type 3. Back: Barasoain Church. Watermark: A. Mabini. Printer: G&D (without imprint). 160x66mm.

a. Signature 7.	1.50	4.00
b. Signature 8.	1.50	4.00
s1. Signature as a. Specimen.	—	65.00
s2. Signature as b. Specimen.	—	20.00

145 20 Piso | VF | UNC
ND (1969). Orange and brown on multicolor underprint. M. L. Quezon at left in brown, heading at top in double outline. Central Bank Seal Type 3. Back: Malakanyang Palace. Watermark: M. L. Quezon. Printer: G&D (without imprint). 160x66mm.

a. Signature 7.	2.00	6.00
b. Signature 8.	2.00	6.00
s1. Signature as a. Specimen.	—	100.
s2. Signature as b. Specimen. Red overprint: *SPECIMEN* on face.	—	50.00

146 50 Piso VF UNC

ND (1969). Red on multicolor underprint. S. Osmeña at left, heading at top in double outline. Central Bank Seal Type 2. Back: Legislative Building. Watermark: S. Osmeña. 160x66mm.

	VF	UNC
a. Signature 7.	4.00	9.00
b. Signature 8.	3.00	9.00
s1. Signature as a. Specimen. (De La Rue).	—	225.
s2. Signature as b. Specimen.	—	30.00
s3. Signature as b. Specimen. (De La Rue).	—	225.

147 100 Piso VF UNC

ND (1969). Purple on multicolor underprint. M. Roxas at left, heading at top in double outline. Central Bank Seal Type 2. Back: Old Central Bank. Watermark: M. Roxas. 160x66mm.

	VF	UNC
a. Signature 7.	7.50	22.00
b. Signature 8.	7.50	22.00
p. Signature as a. Proof.	—	475.
s1. Signature as a. Specimen.	—	50.00
s2. Signature as a. Specimen. (De La Rue).	—	175.
s3. Signature as b. Specimen.	—	50.00
s4. Signature as b. Specimen. (De La Rue).	—	200.

1970's ND First Issue

#148-151 Replacement notes: Serial # prefix "+".

148 5 Piso VF UNC

ND. Green on multicolor underprint. A. Bonifacio at left in green. Central Bank Seal Type 2. Heading at top in single outline, left and right ends completely filled in. Signature 8. Back: Scene of the Katipunan organization. Watermark: A. Bonifacio. Printer: G&D (without imprint). 160x66mm.

	VF	UNC
a. Issued note.	.75	3.00
s. Specimen.	—	20.00

149 10 Piso

ND. Brown on multicolor underprint. A. Mabini at left. Central Bank Seal Type 2. Heading at top in single outline, left and right ends completely filled in without white paper showing at sides. Signature 8. Back: Barasoain Church, without white paper showing at sides. Watermark: A. Mabini at left. Printer: G&D (without imprint). 160x66mm.

	VF	UNC
a. Issued note.	3.00	10.00
s. Specimen.	—	40.00

150 20 Piso VF UNC

ND. Orange and blue on multicolor underprint. M. L. Quezon at left in orange. Central Bank Seal Type 2. Heading at top in single outline, left and right ends completely filled in. Signature 8. Back: Malakanyang Palace. Watermark: M. L. Quezon. Printer: G&D (without imprint). 160x66mm.

	VF	UNC
a. Issued note.	1.00	4.00
s. Specimen.	—	75.00

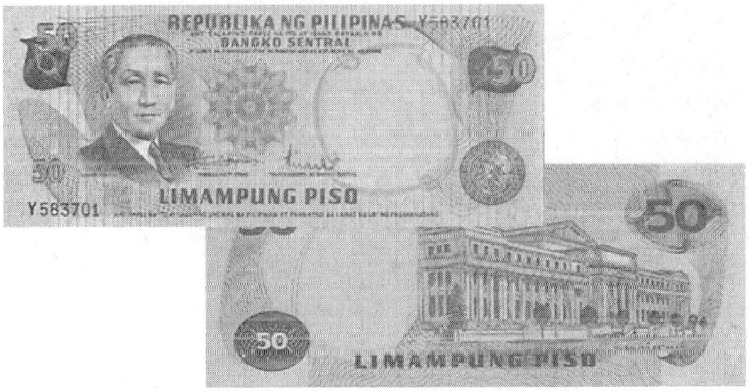

151 50 Piso VF UNC

ND. Red on multicolor underprint. Similar to #146. Seal under denomination instead of over, signature closer, *LIMAMPUNG PISO* in one line, and other modifications. Central Bank Seal Type 2. Heading at top in single outline, left Back: Legislative building. Watermark: S. Osmeña. 160x66mm.

	VF	UNC
a. Issued note.	4.00	10.00
s. Specimen.	—	70.00

1970's ND Second Issue

#152-158 Central Bank Seal Type 2. Ovpt: *ANG BAGONG LIPUNAN* (New Society) on wmk. area, 1974-85. Replacement notes: Serial # prefix "+".

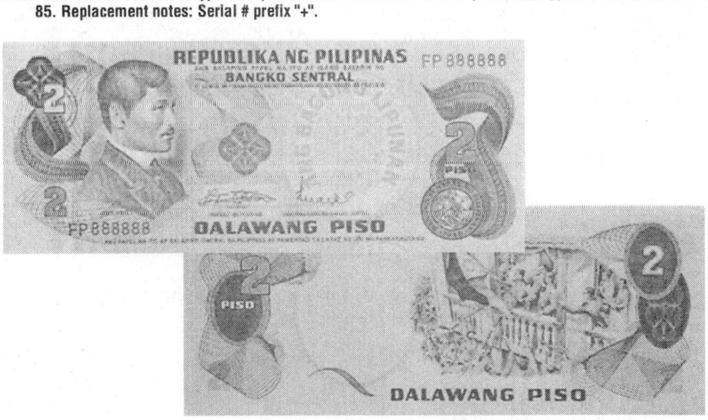

152 2 Piso VF UNC

ND. Blue on multicolor underprint. J. Rizal at left. Central Bank Seal Type 2. Signature 8. Back: Scene of Aguinaldo's Independence Declaration of June 12, 1898. Overprint: *ANG BAGONG LIPUNAN* (New Society) on watermark area, 1974-85. Watermark: J. Rizal. UV: legend in curve over Rizal portrait fluoresce orange. 160x66mm.

	VF	UNC
a. Issued note.	.50	1.50
s1. Specimen.	—	12.00
s2. Specimen. (De La Rue).	—	225.

153 5 Piso

ND. Green on multicolor underprint. A. Bonifacio in green at left. Central Bank Seal Type 2. Signature 8. Back: Scene of the Katipunan organization. Overprint: *ANG BAGONG LIPUNAN* (New Society) on watermark area, 1974-85. Watermark: A. Bonifacio. Printer: G&D (without imprint). 160x66mm.

	VF	UNC
a. Dark overprint.	1.00	5.00
b. Light overprint.	1.00	4.00
s1. Specimen.	—	15.00
s2. Specimen. (De La Rue).	—	225.

154 10 Piso

ND. Brown on multicolor underprint. A. Mabini at left. Heading at top in single outline, left and right ends completely filled in without white paper showing at sides.Central Bank Seal Type 2. Signature 8. Back: Barasoain Church, without white paper showing at sides. Overprint: *ANG BAGONG LIPUNAN* (New Society) on watermark area, 1974-85. Watermark: A. Mabini at left. Printer: G&D (without imprint). 160x66mm.

	VF	UNC
a. Issued note.	1.00	3.50
s1. Specimen.	—	25.00
s2. Specimen. (De La Rue).	—	225.

155 20 Piso

ND. Orange on multicolor underprint. M. L. Quezon at left in orange. Heading at top in single outline, left and right ends completely filled in. Central Bank Seal Type 2. Signature 8. Back: Malakanyang Palace. Overprint: *ANG BAGONG LIPUNAN* (New Society) on watermark area, 1974-85. Watermark: M. L. Quezon. Printer: G&D (without imprint). 160x66mm.

	VF	UNC
a. Issued note.	1.50	3.00
s1. Specimen.	—	35.00
s2. Specimen. (De La Rue).	—	250.

156 50 Piso

ND. Red on multicolor underprint. Similar to #146. Seal under denomination, signature closer, *LIMAMPUNG PISO* in one line, and other modifications. Heading at top in single outline, left and right. Central B Back: Legislative building. Overprint: *ANG BAGONG LIPUNAN* (New Society) on watermark area, 1974-85. Watermark: S. Osmeña. Printer: G&D (without imprint). 160x66mm.

	VF	UNC
a. Brown signature title.	4.00	8.00
b. Red signature title.	7.50	17.50
s1. Signature as b. Specimen.	—	35.00
s2. Signature as. b. Specimen. (De La Rue).	—	250.

157 100 Piso

ND. Purple on multicolor underprint. M. Roxas at left, heading at top in double outline. Central Bank Seal Type 2 in purple at left. Back: Old Central Bank. Overprint: *ANG BAGONG LIPUNAN* (New Society) on watermark area, 1974-85. Printer: G&D (without imprint). 160x66mm.

	VF	UNC
a. Signature 7.	15.00	30.00
b. Signature 8.	10.00	20.00
s1. Signature as a. Specimen.	—	200.
s2. Signature as b. Specimen.	—	50.00

158 100 Piso

ND. Purple on multicolor underprint. M. Roxas at left, heading at top solid letters, denomintaion near upper right. Green Central Bank Seal Type 2 at lower right. Signature 8. Back: Old Central Bank, denomination at bottom. Overprint: *ANG BAGONG LIPUNAN* (New Society) on watermark area, 1974-85. Watermark: M. Roxas. Printer: G&D (without imprint). 160x66mm.

	VF	UNC
a. Issued note.	25.00	50.00
s. Specimen.	—	175.

1978 ND Issue

#159-167 Replacement notes: Serial # prefix "+".

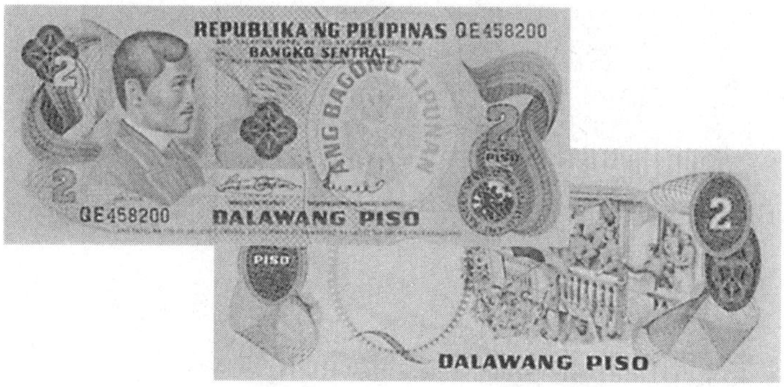

159 2 Piso

ND. Blue on multicolor underprint. J. Rizal at left. Signature 8. Central Bank Seal Type 4. Back: Scene of Aguinaldo's Independence Declaration of June 12, 1898. Overprint: *ANG BAGONG LIPUNAN* (New Society) on watermark area, 1974-85. Watermark: J. Rizal. UV: legend in curve over Rizal portrait fluoresce orange. 160x66mm.

	VF	UNC
a. Signature 8.	.30	2.00
b. Signature 9. Black serial #.	.50	3.50
c. Signature 9. Red serial #. Single and double letter serial # prefix varieties.	.30	1.00
d. Signature as b. Uncut sheet of 4.	—	15.00
s1. Signature as a. Specimen.	—	15.00
s2. Signature as b. Specimen.	—	15.00

160 5 Piso

ND. Green on multicolor underprint. A. Bonifacio in green at left. Signature 8. Central Bank Seal Type 4. Back: Scene of the Katipunan organization. Overprint: *ANG BAGONG LIPUNAN* (New Society) on watermark area, 1974-85. Watermark: A. Bonifacio. Printer: G&D (without imprint). UV: legend in curve over Bonifacio portrait fluoresce orange. 160x66mm.

	VF	UNC
a. Signature 8.	.50	2.50
b. Signature 9. Black serial #.	1.00	4.25
c. Signature 9. Red serial #.	.40	1.50
d. Signature 10.	.40	2.00
e. Signature as b. Uncut sheet of 4.	—	30.00
f. Signature as d. Uncut sheet of 4.	—	30.00
s1. Signature as a. Specimen.	—	15.00
s2. Signature as b. Specimen.	—	20.00

161 10 Piso

ND. Brown on multicolor underprint. A. Mabini at left. Heading at top in single outline, left and right ends completely filled in without white paper showing at sides. Signature 8. Central Bank Seal Type 4. Back: Barasoain Church, without white paper showing at sides. Overprint: *ANG BAGONG LIPUNAN* (New Society) on watermark area, 1974-85. Printer: G&D (without imprint). 160x66mm.

	VF	UNC
a. Signature 8.	.75	2.00
b. Signature 9.	1.00	4.50
c. Signature 10. Black serial #.	.60	2.00
d. Signature 10. Red serial #.	1.00	8.00
e. Signature as b. Uncut sheet of 4.	—	35.00
f. Signature as c. Uncut sheet of 4.	—	35.00
s1. Signature as a. Specimen.	—	15.00
s2. Signature as b. Specimen.	—	15.00

162 20 Piso

ND. Orange and blue on multicolor underprint. M. L. Quezon at left in orange. Heading at top in single outline, left and right ends completely filled in. Signature 8. Central Bank Seal Type 4. Back: Malakanyang Palace. Overprint: *ANG BAGONG LIPUNAN* (New Society) on watermark area, 1974-85. Watermark: M. L. Quezon. Printer: G&D (without imprint). 160x66mm.

	VF	UNC
a. Signature 8.	1.00	3.50
b. Signature 9.	1.00	5.00
c. Signature 10.	1.00	3.00
d. Signature as b. Uncut sheet of 4.	—	40.00
e. Signature as d. Uncut sheet of 4.	—	40.00
s1. Signature as a. Specimen.	—	20.00
s2. Signature as b. Specimen.	—	30.00

163 50 Piso

ND. Red on multicolor underprint. Like #156. Central Bank Seal Type 4. Back: Legislative building. Overprint: *ANG BAGONG LIPUNAN* (New Society) on watermark area, 1974-85. Watermark: S. Osmeña. Printer: G&D (without imprint). 160x66mm.

	VF	UNC
a. Signature 8.	2.00	5.00
b. Signature 9.	2.00	5.00
c. Signature 10.	1.50	5.00
s1. Signature as a. Specimen.	—	35.00
s2. Signature as b. Specimen.	—	35.00

164 100 Piso

ND. Purple and deep olive-green on multicolor underprint. M. Roxas at left, heading at top solid letters, denomintaion near upper right. Green Central Bank Seal Type 4 at lower right. Signature 8. Back: New Central Bank complex with ships behind. Overprint: *ANG BAGONG LIPUNAN* (New Society) on watermark area, 1974-85. 160x66mm.

	VF	UNC
a. Signature 8.	10.00	27.50
b. Signature 9.	4.00	8.00
c. Signature 10. Black serial #.	3.00	6.00
s1. Signature as a. Specimen.	—	35.00
s2. Signature as b. Specimen.	—	40.00

1978 Commemorative Issue

#165, Centennial - Birth of Pres. Osmeña, 1978

		VF	UNC
165	**50 Piso** 1978. Red on multicolor underprint. Black circular commemorative overprint at left on #163a. Central Bank Seal Type 4. Back: Legislative building. Watermark: S. Osmeña. 160x66mm.	4.00	10.00

1981 Commemorative Issues

#166, Papal Visit of John Paul II, 1981

166 2 Piso

1981. Blue on multicolor underprint. Black commemorative overprint at center right on #159b. Central Bank Seal Type 4. Back: Scene of Aguinaldo's Independence Declaration of June 12,1898. 160x66mm.

	VF	UNC
a. Regular prefix letters before serial #.	.50	2.25
b. Special prefix letters *JP* and all zero numbers (presentation).	—	100.

167 10 Piso

1981. Brown on multicolor underprint. Black commemorative overprint at center right on #161b. Central Bank Seal Type 4. Back: Barasoain Church, without white paper showing at sides. 160x66mm.

	VF	UNC
a. Regular prefix letters before serial #. Wide and narrow collar varieties.	.50	2.25
b. Special prefix letters *FM* and all zero numbers (presentation).	—	35.00
s. As a. Specimen. Wide or narrow collar.	—	50.00

1985-91 ND Issue

#168-173 replacement notes: Serial # prefix "+".

168 5 Piso

ND (1985-94. Deep green and brown on multicolor underprint. Aguinaldo at left center, plaque with cannon at right. Back: Aguinaldo's Independence Declaration of June 12, 1898. Watermark: Aguinaldo. 160x66mm.

	VF	UNC
a. Signature 10. Black serial #.	FV	2.00
b. Signature 11. Black serial #.	FV	1.25
c. Signature as b. Red serial # (1990).	FV	1.25
d. Signature 12. Red serial #.	FV	1.00
e. Signature 13. Red serial #.	FV	1.00
f. Signature as b. Uncut sheet of 4.	—	30.00
g. Signature as d. Uncut sheet of 4.	—	30.00
h. Signature as e. Uncut sheet of 4.	—	15.00
s1. Signature as b. Specimen.	—	15.00
s2. Signature as c. Specimen.	—	15.00
s3. Signature as d. Specimen.	—	20.00

169 10 Piso

ND (1985-94). Dark brown, brown and blue-gray on multicolor underprint. Mabini at left center, handwritten scroll at right. Back: Barasoain church. Watermark: Mabin. UV: legend in curve over Mabini portrait fluoresce orange. 160x66mm.

	VF	UNC
a. Signature 10.	.50	3.00
b. Signature 11.	FV	1.50
c. Signature 12. Black serial #.	FV	2.50
d. Signature as c. Red serial #.	.50	5.00
e. Signature 13.	—	2.00
f. Signature as b. Uncut sheet of 4.	—	25.00
g. Signature as b. Uncut sheet of 32.	—	100.
s. Signature as b. Specimen.	—	25.00

170 20 Piso

ND (1986-94). Orange and blue on multicolor underprint. President M. Quezon at left center, arms at right. Back: Malakanyang Palace. Watermark: President M. Quezon. 160x66mm.

	VF	UNC
a. Signature 10. Black serial #.	1.50	9.00
b. Signature 11. Black serial #.	FV	3.00
c. Signature 12. Black serial #.	1.00	5.00
d. Signature as c. Red serial #. Not confirmed.	—	—
e. Signature 13. Red serial #.	1.00	5.00
f. Signature as e. Black serial #.	FV	4.00
g. Signature as b. Uncut sheet of 4.	—	45.00
s. Signature as b. Specimen.	—	35.00

171 50 Piso

ND (1987-94). Red and purple on multicolor underprint. President Sergio Osmeña at left center, gavel at right. Back: Legislative building. Watermark: Sergio Osmeña. 160x66mm.

	VF	UNC
a. Signature 11. Black serial #.	1.00	6.00
b. Signature 12. Black serial #.	FV	5.00
c. Signature 13. Black serial #.	FV	4.00
s1. Signature as a. Specimen.	—	75.00
s2. Signature as b. Specimen.	—	60.00
s3. Signature as b. Uncut sheet of 4. Specimen.	—	30.00
s4. Signature as c. Specimen.	—	35.00

172 100 Piso

ND (1987-94). Purple on multicolor underprint. President M. Roxas at left center, USA and Philippine flags at right. Back: New Central Bank complex at left center with old building facade above. Watermark: M. Roxas. 160x66mm.

	VF	UNC
a. Signature 11. Black serial #.	FV	7.50
b. Signature 11. Red serial #.	FV	35.00
c. Signature 12. Black serial #.	FV	12.50
d. Signature as b. Red serial #.	FV	12.50
e. Signature 13. Red serial #.	FV	7.50
f. Signature as d. Blue serial #.	FV	7.50
s1. Signature as a. Specimen.	—	120.
s2. Signature as b. Specimen.	—	100.
s3. Signature as c. Specimen.	—	50.00
s4. Signature as d. Specimen.	—	50.00
s5. Signature as d. Specimen. Uncut sheet of 4.	—	25.00
s6. Signature as b. Specimen. Uncut sheet of 4.	—	75.00
s7. Signature as b. Specimen. Uncut sheet of 32.	—	200.
s8. Signature as e. Specimen. Blue serial #.	—	75.00
cr. Replacement note. Sign. as a. Red serial #. Rare.	—	—

173 500 Piso

ND (1987-94). Black and brown on multicolor underprint. Aquino at left center, flag in underprint at center, typewriter at lower right. Back: Various scenes and gatherings of Aquino's career. Watermark: Aquino. 160x66mm.

	VF	UNC
a. Signature 11.	FV	40.00
b. Signature 12.	FV	50.00
c. Signature 13.	FV	30.00
s1. Signature as a. Specimen.	—	80.00
s2. Signature as b. Specimen.	—	55.00
s3. Signature as b. Specimen. Uncut sheet of 4.	—	75.00

174 1000 Pioo

ND (1991-94). Dark blue and blue-black on multicolor underprint. J. A. Santos, J. L. Escoda and V. Lim at left center, flaming torch at right. Back: Banawe rice terraces at left, to center, local carving and hut at center right. Watermark: J. A. Santos, J. L. Escoda and V. Lim. 160x66mm.

	VF	UNC
a. Signature 12.	FV	85.00
b. Signature 13.	FV	60.00

1986-91 Commemorative Issues

Commemorative overprints not listed were produced privately in the Philippines.

#175, Visit of President Aquino to the United States

175 5 Piso

1986. Deep green and brown on multicolor underprint. Aguinaldo at left center, plaque with cannon at right, with commemorative text, seal and visit dates in watermark area. Prefix letters CA. Signature 11. Back: Aguinaldo's Independence Declaration of June 12, 1898. Watermark: Aguinaldo. 160x66mm.

	VF	UNC
a. Serial #1-20,000 in special folder.	FV	12.50
b. Serial # above 20,000.	FV	1.25
c. Uncut sheet of 4.	—	30.00

176 5 Piso

18.10.1987. Deep green and brown on multicolor underprint. Aguinaldo at left center, plaque with cannon at right, commemorative design, text and date in watermark area. Signature 11. Back: Aguinaldo's Independence Declaration of June 12, 1898. Watermark: Aguinaldo. 160x66mm.

	VF	UNC
a. Issued note.	FV	1.50
b. Uncut sheet of 8 in special folder.	—	20.00

177 5 Piso

1989. Deep green and brown on multicolor underprint. Aguinaldo at left center, plaque with cannon at right, red commemorative design, text and date in watermark area. Signature 11. Back: Aguinaldo's Independence Declaration of June 12, 1898. 160x66mm.

	VF	UNC
a. Issued note.	FV	1.25
b. Uncut sheet of 8 in special folder.	—	20.00

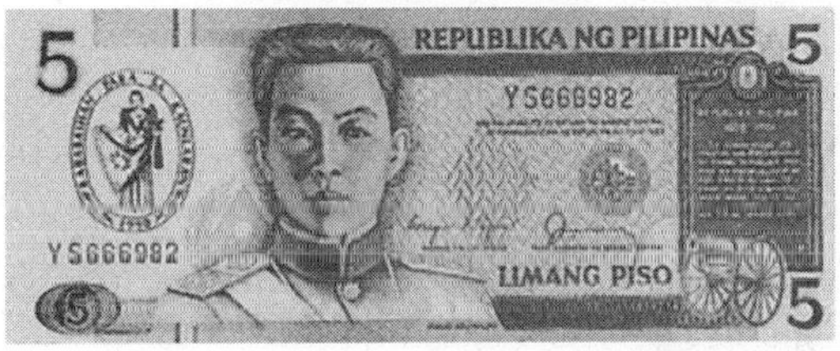

178 5 Piso

1990. Deep green and brown on multicolor underprint. Aguinaldo at left center, plaque with cannon at right, black commemorative design, text and date in watermark area. Signature 11. Back: Aguinaldo's Independence Declaration of June 12, 1898. 160x66mm.

	VF	UNC
a. Black serial #.	FV	1.25
b. Red serial #.	FV	4.00

179 5 Piso — VF: FV; UNC: 1.25

1991. Deep green and brown on multicolor underprint. Aguinaldo at left center, plaque with cannon at right, black commemorative design and date in watermark area. Signature 12. Red serial #. Back: Aguinaldo's Independence Declaration of June 12, 1898. 160x66mm.

1995 ND; 1998-99 Issue

180 5 Piso — VF: FV; UNC: 1.00

ND (1995). Deep green and rown on multicolor underprint. Aguinaldo at left center, plaque with cannon at right. Cental Bank Seal Type 5. Signature 14. Back: Aguinaldo's Independence Declaration of June 12, 1898. Watermark: Aguinaldo. 160x66mm.

181 10 Piso VF UNC

ND (1995-97). Dark brown and blue-gray on multicolor underprint. Mabini at left center, handwritten scroll at right. Cental Bank Seal Type 5. Signature 14. Back: Barasoain church. Watermark: Mabini. 160x66mm.

	VF	UNC
a. Red serial #.	FV	1.50
b. Signature as a. Black serial #.	FV	2.50

182 20 Piso VF UNC

ND (1997); 1998-. Orange and blue on multicolor underprint. President M. Quezon at left center, arms at right. Cental Bank Seal Type 5. Back: Malakanyang Palace. Watermark: M. Quezon. 160x66mm.

	VF	UNC
a. Signature 14. Red serial #. ND.	FV	2.00
b. Signature 14. Black serial #.	FV	2.00
c. Signature 15. Black serial #. 1998; 1999.	FV	3.00
d. Signature 15. Blue serial #. 1999.	FV	6.50
e. Signature 16. Blue serial #. 1999, 2000.	FV	15.00
f. Signature 16. Blue serial #. 2001.	FV	6.00
g. Signature 17. Blue serial #. 2001.	FV	4.00
h. Signature 17. Black serial #. 2001; 2002; 2003; 2004, 2005.	FV	3.50
i. Signature 18. Black serial #. 2005; 2006; 2007; 2008; 2008A; 2009; 2010.	FV	4.00
j. Signature 19. 2010; 2011.	FV	4.00
s1. As a. Specimen.	—	50.00
s2. Uncut sheet of 4. Specimen.	—	100.

183 50 Piso VF UNC

ND; 1998-2001. Red and purple on multicolor underprint. President Sergio Osmeña at left center, gavel at right. Cental Bank Seal Type 5. Back: Legislative building. Watermark: Sergio Osmeña. 160x66mm.

	VF	UNC
a. Signature 14. ND (1995).	FV	4.00
b. Signature as a. Red serial #. 1998.	FV	6.00
c. Signature 16. Red serial #. 1999; 2000; 2001.	FV	4.00
d. Signature 16. Black serial #. 2001.	FV	8.00
s. Specimen.	—	—

184 100 Piso VF UNC

ND; 1998-. Purple on multicolor underprint. President M. Roxas at left center, USA and Philippine flags at right. Cental Bank Seal Type 5. Back: New Central Bank complex at left center with old building facade above. Watermark: M. Roxas. 160x66mm.

	VF	UNC
a. Signature 14. ND.	FV	10.00
b. Signature as a. 1998.	FV	8.00
c. Signature 15. Red serial #. 1998.	FV	5.00
d. Signature as c. Black serial #. 1998; 1999.	FV	6.00
e. Signature 16. 1999; 2000.	FV	6.00
f. Signature 16. 2001.	FV	12.50
s. Signature as a. Specimen.	—	30.00

185 500 Piso VF UNC

ND; 1998-2001. Black on multicolor underprint. Aquino at left center, flag in underprint at center, typewriter at lower right. Cental Bank Seal Type 5. Back: Various scenes and gatherings of Aquino's career. Watermark: Aquino. 160x66mm.

	VF	UNC
a. Signature 14. ND; 1998.	FV	30.00
b. Signature 15. 1998; 1999.	FV	25.00
c. Signature 16; 1999; 2000; 2001.	FV	40.00
s. As a. Specimen.	—	50.00

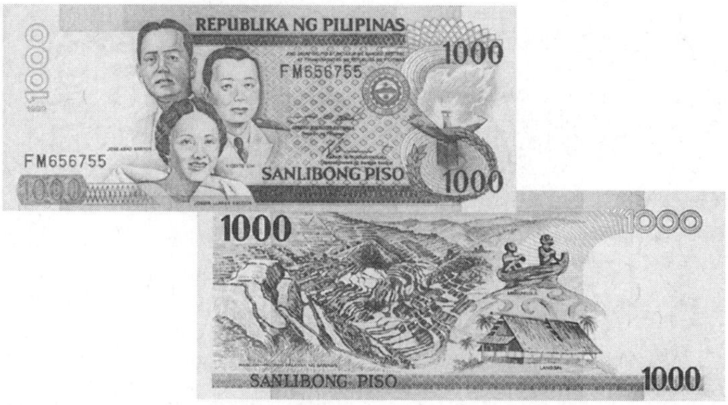

186 1000 Piso VF UNC

ND; 1998-2001. Dark blue on multicolor underprint. J. A. Santos, J. L. Escoda and V. Lim at left center, flaming torch at right. Cental Bank Seal Type 5. Back: Banawe rice terraces at left, to center, local carving and hut at center right. Watermark: J. A. Santos, J. L Escoda and V. Lim. 160x66mm.

	VF	UNC
a. Signature 14. ND; 1998.	FV	45.00
b. Signature 15. 1998; 1999.	FV	45.00
c. Signature 16. 1999; 2000.	FV	45.00
d. Signature 17. 2001. Red serial #.	FV	85.00
s1. Signature as a. Specimen.	—	85.00
s2. Signature as c. Specimen. 1999.	—	50.00

1997 Issue

187 10 Piso VF UNC

1997-. Dark brown and blue-gray on multicolor underprint. A. Mabini and A. Bonifacio at left center; flag, book, declaration and quill pen at right. Back: Barasoain church at left, blood *Pacto de Sangre* meeting at lower right. 160x66mm.

	VF	UNC
a. Signature 14. Single figure watermark. 1997.	FV	2.00
b. Signature 14. Single figure watermark. 1998.	FV	1.50
c. Signature 14. Double figures as watermark. Black serial #. 1998.	FV	3.00
d. Signature 14. Double figures as watermark. Red serial #. 1998.	5.00	20.00
e. Signature 15. Red serial #. 1999.	FV	2.50
f. Signature 16. Red serial #. 1999; 2000; 2001.	FV	3.00
g. Signature 16. Red serial #.	FV	7.00
h. Signature 17. Red serial #. 2001.	FV	2.00
i. Signature 17. Black serial #. 2001.	FV	2.00

1998 Commemorative Issue

#188-190, Centennial of First Republic, 1898-1998

		VF	UNC
188	**100 Piso** ND (1997); 1998. Purple on multicolor underprint. Like #184 but with centennial design and inscription in rectangular frame at left in watermark area. Signature 14. Back: New Central Bank complex at left center with old building facade above. 160x66mm.		
	a. Without date at upper left. (1997).	FV	6.00
	b. 1998 under value at left.	FV	12.00
189	**2000 Piso** 1998; 2001. Multicolor. President J. E. Estrada taking his oath of office on June 30, 1998 in the Barasoain Church at center. Back: Re-enactment of the declaration of Philippine Independence at the Aguinaldo Shrine in Kawit, Cavit Watermark: Estrada and Ramos. 160x66mm.		
	a. 1998. Signature 15. Issued in folder. 216x133mm.	—	135.
	b. 2001. Signature 15. Limited release.	—	200.
190	**100,000 Piso** 1998. Green, yellow and brown. President F. V. Ramos being greated by crowd, Bank seal at right. Signature 14. Back: President Ramos greeting crowd from inside enclosed porch. Only 1,000 pieces issued.	—	3500.

1999 Commemorative Issue

#191, 50th Anniversary Bangko Sentral

		VF	UNC
191	**50 Piso** ND: 1999. Red and purple on multicolor underprint. Overprint on #183. Iridescent denomination strip at left center and metallic segmented security strip at center right. Back: Legislative building. 160x66mm.		
	a. Without date at upper left. Signature 14.	FV	3.50
	b. 1999 at upper left. Signature 15.	FV	7.50

2001-02 Issue

#195-196 like #185-186 but w/iridescent denomination strip at l. ctr. and metallic segmented security strip at ctr. r.

		VF	UNC
193	**50 Piso** 2001-. Red and purple on multicolor underprint. President Sergio Osmeña at left center, gavel at right. Cental Bank Seal Type 5 with date 1993 at right. Back: National Museum.		
	a. 2001; 2002; 2003; 2004. Signature 17.	FV	3.50
	b. 2005; 2006; 2007; 2008; 2009. Signature 18. Black serial #.	FV	5.00
	c. 2010. Signature 19. Black serial #.	FV	4.00
	d. 2011; 2012.	FV	5.00

		VF	UNC
194	**100 Piso** 2001-. Purple on multicolor underprint. Like #184. Black serial number. Back: New Central Bank complex at left center with old building facade above. 160x65mm.		
	a. 2001; 2002; 2003; 2004. Signature 16, 17.	FV	6.50
	b. 2005; 2006; 2007; 2008 (wide and narrow date); 2009; 2010; 2010A. Signature 18.	FV	6.00
	c. 2005. Signature 18. Signature spelled Arrovo.	FV	8.25
	d. 2010A. Signature 19.	FV	7.50
	e. 2011.	FV	5.00
	f. 2012.	FV	5.00

		VF	UNC
195	**200 Piso** 2002-. Green and purple on multicolor underprint. Diosdado Macapagal at left, Aguinaldo shrine at lower right. Back: Scene of swearing in of Gloria Macapagal-Arroyo. 160x66mm.		
	a. 2002; 2003; 2004. Signature 17.	FV	10.00
	b. 2007. Signature 18.	FV	10.00
	c. 2010. Signature 19.	FV	12.50

		VF	UNC
196	**500 Piso** 2001-. Black on multicolor underprint. Like #185 but with iridescent denomination strip at left center and metallic segmented security strip at center right. Back: Various scenes and gatherings of Aquino's career. 160x66mm.		
	a. 2001; 2002; 2003; 2004; 2005. Signature 17.	FV	20.00
	b. 2005; 2007; 2008. Signature 18. Black serial #.	FV	20.00
	c. 2010. Signature 19.	FV	18.00
	d. 2011.	FV	18.00

		VF	UNC
197	**1000 Piso** 2001-. Dark blue on multicolor underprint. Like #186 but with iridescent denomination strip at left center and metallic segmented security strip at center right. Back: Banawe rice terraces at left, to center, local carving and hut at center right. 160x66mm.		
	a. 2001; 2002; 2003; 2004. Signature 17.	FV	35.00
	b. 2005; 2006; 2008; 2009, 2010. Signatrue 18.	FV	35.00
	c. 2007. Signature 18. (limited printing).	40.00	100.
	d. 2010, 2011. Signature 19.	FV	30.00

2008 Commemorative Overpritnts

198	**50 Piso**	**VF**	**UNC**
	2008 Red and purple on multicolor underprint. Overprint: National Museum.	FV	5.00

199	**100 Piso**	**VF**	**UNC**
	2008. Purple on multicolor. Overprint: University of the Philippines Centennial. 160x66mm.	FV	7.50

2009 Commemorative Issue

200	**20 Piso**	**VF**	**UNC**
	2009. Orange and blue on multicolor underprint. Signature 18. Overprint: 60th Anniversary of Central Banking. 160x66mm.	FV	3.50

201	**50 Piso**	**VF**	**UNC**
	2009. Red and purple on multicolor underprint. Signature 18. Overprint: 60th Anniversary of Central Banking. 160x66mm.	FV	6.00

202	**100 Piso**	**VF**	**UNC**
	2009. Purple on multicolor underprint. Signature 18. Overprint: 60th Anniversary of Central Banking. 160x66mm.	FV	10.00

203	**200 Piso**	**VF**	**UNC**
	2009. Green adn purple on multicolor underprint. Signature 18. Overprint: 60th Anniversary of Central Banking. 160x66mm.		
	a. Issued note.	FV	20.00
	s. Specimen. Red overprint *SPECIMEN* on each side.	—	50.00

204	**500 Piso**	**VF**	**UNC**
	2009. Black on multicolor underprint. Signature 18. Overprint: 60th Anniversary of Central Banking. 160x66mm.	FV	30.00

205	**1000 Piso**	**VF**	**UNC**
	2009. Dark blue on multicolor underprint. Signature 18. Overprint: 60th Anniversary of Central Banking. 160x66mm.	FV	40.00

2010 Issue

206	**20 Piso**	**VF**	**UNC**
	2010. Orange on multicolor underprint. Manuel Luis Quezón at left center. Presidential palace at lower center. Back: Map, palm civet, Banaue rice terraces. Watermark: Quezón and 20. 160x66mm.		
	a. 2010; 2012; 2013. Signature 19.	FV	3.50

207	**50 Piso**	**VF**	**UNC**
	2010. Red on multicolor underprint. Sergio Osmeña at left center, MacArthur's Leyte landing of 1944, National Assembly interior. Back: Map, maliputo fish, Taal lake. Watermark: Osmeña and 50. 160x66mm.		
	a. 2010; 2012. Signature 19.	FV	7.00

208 **100 Piso** — VF | UNC

2010. Purple on multicolor underprint. Manuel Acuña Rozas at left center, Central Bank building at left. Back: Map, white shark, Mayon Volcano in Legazpi City. Watermark: Roxas and 100. 160x66mm.

a. 2010. Signature 19. — FV | 10.00

209 **200 Piso** — VF | UNC

2010. Green on multicolor underprint. Diosdado Macapagal at left center, Aguinaldo Shrine at left, Malolos City Catholic Church. Back: Map, tarsier, Bohol Chocolate Hills. Watermark: Macapagal and 200. 160x66mm.

a. 2010. Signature 19. — FV | 15.00

210 **500 Piso** — VF | UNC

2010. Yellow on multicolor underprint. Corazon and Benigno Aquino at left center. Back: Map, blue-naped parrot, Puerto Princesa Subterranean River Park. Watermark: Aquinos and 500. 160x66mm.

a. 2010. Signature 19. — FV | 25.00

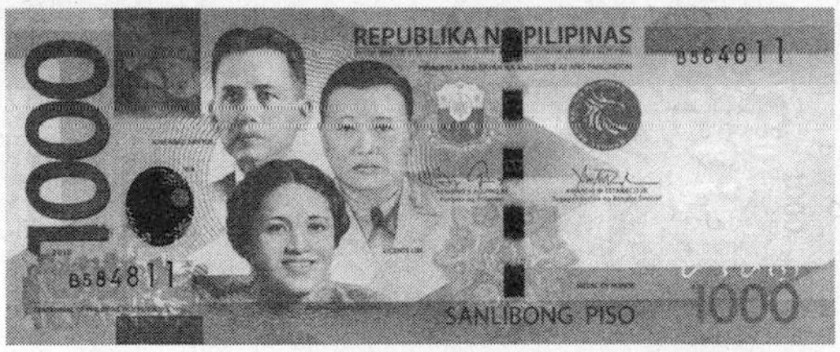

211 **1000 Piso** — VF | UNC

2010. Blue on multicolor underprint. José Santos, Josefa Escoda and Vicente Lim. Back: Map, South sea pearl in shell, turtle, Tubbataha Reefs Natural Park. Watermark: Santos, Escoda, Lim and 1000. 166x60mm.

a. 2010. Signature 19. — FV | 40.00

2011-13 Commemorative Issues

No.	Denomination / Description	VF	UNC
212	**100 Piso** 2011 (2012). Overprint: De La Salle University 1911-2011. Overprint on #194.	FV	8.00
213	**100 Piso** 2012. Overprint: Manila Hotel Overprint on #194.	FV	8.00
214	**100 Piso** 2012. Overprint: Grand Mason Lodge Overprint on #194.		
	a. Issued note.	FV	8.00
	b. Uncut sheet of 4 in folder.	—	30.00
215	**50 Piso** 2013. Overprint: Philippine Deposit Insurance Corporation. Overprint on #193.	FV	4.00
216	**50 Piso** 2013. Overprint: Trinity University, 1963-2013 Overprint on #193.	FV	4.00
217	**50 Piso** 2012 (2013). Overprint: St. Pedro Calungsod Canonization. Overprint on #193.	FV	5.00
218	**100 Piso** 2013. Overprint: Wastong Pananalapi Tungo Sa Kaunlaran 1993-2013. Overprint on #194.	FV	8.00

Collector Series

Bangko Sentral ng Pilipinas

1978 ND Issue

CS1 **1978 ND 2-100 Piso** — Mkt. Value

#159a-164a overprint: *SPECIMEN* and with serial # prefix Maltese cross. — 45.00

The Republic of Poland, formerly the Polish Peoples Republic, located in central Europe, has an area of 120,725 sq. mi. (312,677 sq. km.) and a population of 38.73 million. Capital: Warsaw. The economy is essentially agricultural, but industrial activity provides the products for foreign trade. Machinery, coal, coke, iron, steel and transport equipment are exported.

Poland is an ancient nation that was conceived near the middle of the 10th century. Its golden age occurred in the 16th century. During the following century, the strengthening of the gentry and internal disorders weakened the nation. In a series of agreements between 1772 and 1795, Russia, Prussia, and Austria partitioned Poland amongst themselves. Poland regained its independence in 1918 only to be overrun by Germany and the Soviet Union in World War II. It became a Soviet satellite state following the war, but its government was comparatively tolerant and progressive. Labor turmoil in 1980 led to the formation of the independent trade union "Solidarity" that over time became a political force and by 1990 had swept parliamentary elections and the presidency. A "shock therapy" program during the early 1990s enabled the country to transform its economy into one of the most robust in Central Europe, but Poland still faces the lingering challenges of high unemployment, underdeveloped and dilapidated infrastructure, and a poor rural underclass. Solidarity suffered a major defeat in the 2001 parliamentary elections when it failed to elect a single deputy to the lower house of Parliament, and the new leaders of the Solidarity Trade Union subsequently pledged to reduce the Trade Union's political role. Poland joined NATO in 1999 and the European Union in 2004. With its transformation to a democratic, market-oriented country largely completed, Poland is an increasingly active member of Euro-Atlantic organizations.

RULERS:

Stanislaw Augustus, 1764-1795
Fryderyk August I, King of Saxony, as Grand Duke, 1807-1814
Alexander I, Czar of Russia, as King, 1815-1825
Nikolaj (Mikolay) I, Czar of Russia, as King, 1825-1855

MONETARY SYSTEM:

1 Marka = 100 Fenigow to 1919
1 Zloty = 100 Groszy, 1919-

PEOPLES REPUBLIC

NARODOWY BANK POLSKI

POLISH NATIONAL BANK

1962; 1965 ISSUE

			VF	UNC
140A	**20 Zlotych**	2.1.1965. Multicolor. Man at right, arms at upper left center. (Not issued).	—	—

			VF	UNC
141	**1000 Zlotych**	1962; 1965. Orange, red and green on multicolor underprint. Copernicus at center right, arms at upper right. Back: Zodiac signs in ornate sphere at left. Watermark: Copernicus. 150x74mm.		
		a. 29.10.1965. Series S.	5.00	20.00
		b. 29.10.1965. Series X.	25.00	120.
		s1. Specimen overprint: *WZOR*. 24.5.1962. (Not issued).	—	200.
		s2. Specimen overprint: *WZOR* with regular serial #. 29.10.1965.	—	30.00

1974-76 ISSUE

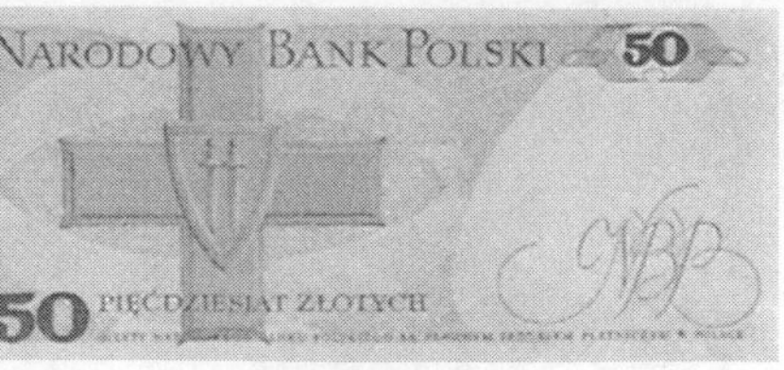

			VF	UNC
142	**50 Zlotych**	1975-88. Olive-green on multicolor underprint. K. Swierczewski at center, eagle arms at lower right. Signature varieties. Back: Order of Grunwald at left. Watermark: Eagle arms. 138x63mm.		
		a. 9.5.1975.	1.50	10.00
		b. 1.6.1979; 1.6.1982.	.30	2.75
		c. 1.6.1986; 1.12.1988.	.20	.75
		s1. Specimen overprint: *WZOR*. 1975; 1986; 1988.	—	8.00
		s2. Specimen overprint: *WZOR*. 1979.	—	7.00
		s3. Specimen overprint: *WZOR*. 1982.	—	10.00

			VF	UNC
143	**100 Zlotych**	1975-88. Brown on lilac and multicolor underprint. L. Warynski at right, eagle arms at lower center. Signature varieties. Back: Old paper at left. Watermark: Eagle arms. 138x63mm.		
		a. 15.1.1975.	4.00	25.00
		b. 17.5.1976.	2.00	8.00
		c. 1.6.1979.	.75	3.00
		d. 1.6.1982.	.20	2.00
		e. 1.6.1986; 1.5.1988.	—	.50
		s1. Specimen overprint: *WZOR*. 1975; 1982.	—	8.00
		s2. Specimen overprint: *WZOR*. 1976.	—	7.00
		s3. Specimen overprint: *WZOR*. 1979.	—	10.00

			VF	UNC
144	**200 Zlotych**	1976-88. Purple on orange and multicolor underprint. J. Dabrowski at right, eagle arms at lower center. Signature varieties. Back: Standing woman at wall. Watermark: Eagle arms. 138x63mm.		
		a. 25.5.1976.	4.00	20.00
		b. 1.6.1979; 1.6.1982.	.30	4.50
		c. 1.6.1986; 1.12.1988.	.25	1.00
		s1. Specimen overprint: *WZOR*. 1976; 1986.	—	8.00
		s2. Specimen overprint: *WZOR*. 1979.	—	7.00
		s3. Specimen overprint: *WZOR*. 1982.	—	10.00

145	**500 Zlotych**	VF	UNC
	1974-82. Brown on tan and multicolor underprint. T. Kosciuszko at right, eagle arms at lower center. Signature varieties. Back: Arms and flag at left center. Watermark: Eagle arms. . 138x63mm.		
	a. 16.12.1974.	7.00	30.00
	b. 15.6.1976.	3.00	10.00
	c. 1.6.1979.	.75	7.00
	d. 1.6.1982.	.25	1.00
	s1. Specimen overprint: *WZOR.* 1974; 1976.	—	8.00
	s2. Specimen overprint: *WZOR.* 1979.	—	7.00
	s3. Specimen overprint: *WZOR.* 1982.	—	10.00

146	**1000 Zlotych**	VF	UNC
	1975-82. Blue on olive-green and multicolor underprint. Copernicus at right, eagle arms at lower center. Signature varieties. Back: Atomic symbols. Watermark: Eagle arms. 138x63mm.		
	a. 2.7.1975.	4.00	35.00
	b. 1.6.1979.	1.25	10.00
	c. 1.6.1982.	.50	1.50
	s1. Specimen overprint: *WZOR.* 1975; 1982.	—	10.00
	s2. Specimen overprint: *WZOR.* 1979.	—	7.00

Polska Rzeczpospolita Ludowa

Polish Peoples Republic

Narodowy Bank Polski

Polish National Bank

1977 Issue

147	**2000 Zlotych**	VF	UNC
	1977-82. Dark brown on multicolor underprint. Mieszko I at right, arms at lower center. Back: B. Chrobry. Watermark: Arms. 63x138mm.		
	a. 1.5.1977.	1.00	5.00
	b. 1.6.1979.	1.75	13.50
	c. 1.6.1982.	.50	1.00
	s1. Specimen overprint: *WZOR.* 1977.	—	10.00
	s2. Specimen overprint: *WZOR.* 1979.	—	7.00
	s3. Specimen overprint: *WZOR.* 1982.	—	15.00

1982 Issue

148	**10 Zlotych**	VF	UNC
	1.6.1982. Blue and green on multicolor underprint. J. Bem at left center, arms at lower right. Back: Large value. Watermark: Arms. 138x63mm.		
	a. Issued note.	.25	1.50
	s. Specimen overprint: *WZOR.*	—	10.00

149	**20 Zlotych**	VF	UNC
	1.6.1982. Brown and purple on multicolor underprint. R. Traugutt at left center, arms at lower right. Back: Large value. Watermark: Arms. 138x63mm.		
	a. Issued note.	.25	.75
	s. Specimen overprint: *WZOR.*	—	10.00

150	**5000 Zlotych**	VF	UNC
	1982-88. Dark green, purple and black on multicolor underprint. F. Chopin at right, arms at lower center. Back: *Polonaise* music score at center. Watermark: Arms.		
	a. 1.6.1982.	1.00	4.00
	b. 1.6.1986.	2.00	7.00
	c. 1.12.1988.	FV	2.50
	s. Specimen overprint: *WZOR.*	—	12.50

1987-90 Issue

151	**10,000 Zlotych**	VF	UNC
	1.2.1987; 1.12.1988. Dark blue and red on green and multicolor underprint. S. Wyspianski at left center, arms at lower right. Back: Trees and city scene. Watermark: Arms.		
	a. 1.2.1987.	2.25	10.00
	b. 1.12.1988.	.50	3.00
	s. Specimen overprint: *WZOR.*	—	10.00

152 20,000 Zlotych

1.2.1989. Dark brown on tan and gold underprint. M. Curie at right, arms atlower center. Back: Scientific instrument. Watermark: Arms.

	VF	UNC
a. Issued note.	1.25	4.00
s. Specimen overprint: *WZOR.*	—	10.00

153 50,000 Zlotych

1.2.1989. Dark brown and greenish black on multicolor underprint. S. Staszic at left center, arms at lower right. Back: S. Staszic at left center. Watermark: Arms.

	VF	UNC
a. Issued note.	5.00	10.00
s. Specimen overprint: *WZOR.*	—	10.00

154 100,000 Zlotych

1.2.1990. Black and grayish blue on multicolor underprint. S. Moniuszko at right, arms at lower center. Back: Warsaw Theatre at left. Watermark: Arms.

	VF	UNC
a. Issued note.	5.00	12.50
s. Specimen overprint: *WZOR.*	—	10.00

155 200,000 Zlotych

1.2.1989. Dark purple on red, tan and multicolor underprint. Coin of Sigismund III at lower center, arms at right. Back: Purple on brown underprint. Warsaw shield at left, view of Warsaw. Watermark: Geometric design repeated.

	VF	UNC
a. Issued note.	10.00	30.00
s. Specimen overprint: *WZOR.*	—	15.00

Rzeczpospolita Polska

Republic of Poland

Narodowy Bank Polski

Polish National Bank

1990-92 Issue

156 500,000 Zlotych

20.4.1990. Dark blue-green and black on multicolor underprint. H. Sienkiewicz at left center, arms at lower right. Back: Shield with three books, also four flags.

	VF	UNC
a. Issued note.	25.00	65.00
s. Specimen overprint: *WZOR.*	—	37.50

157 1,000,000 Zlotych

15.2.1991. Brown-violet, purple and red on multicolor underprint. W. Reymont at right, arms. Back: Tree with rural landscape in background. Watermark: Arms.

	VF	UNC
a. Issued note.	50.00	150.
s. Specimen overprint: *WZOR.*	—	70.00

158 2,000,000 Zlotych

14.8.1992. Black and deep brown-violet on multicolor underprint. I. Paderewski at left center, arms at lower right. Back: Imperial eagle at left. Watermark: Arms.

	VF	UNC
a. Issued note, misspelling *KONSTYTUCYJY* on back. Series A.	—	250.
b. As a, but corrected spelling *KONSTYTUCYJNY* on back. Series B.	90.00	200.
s. Specimen overprint: *WZOR.*	—	100.

1993 Issue

159 50,000 Zlotych

16.11.1993. Dark blue-green and brown on multicolor underprint. S. Staszic at left center, arms at lower right with color in watermark area. Back: S. Staszic at left center. Watermark: Eagle's head.

	VF	UNC
a. Issued note.	3.00	7.00
s. Specimen overprint: *WZOR.*	—	8.50

160 100,000 Zlotych

16.11.1993. Black and grayish blue on multicolor underprint. S. Moniuszko at right, arms at lower center with color in watermark area. Back: Scientific instrument. Watermark: Eagle's head.

	VF	UNC
a. Issued note.	5.00	10.00
s. Specimen overprint: *WZOR.*	—	10.00

161 500,000 Zlotych

16.11.1993. Dark blue-green and black on multicolor underprint. H. Sienkiewicz at left center, eagle with crown at lower right with color in watermark area. Back: Shield with three books, also four flags. Watermark: Eagle's head.

	VF	UNC
a. Issued note.	20.00	30.00
s. Specimen overprint: *WZOR*.	—	37.50

162 1,000,000 Zlotych

16.11.1993. Brown violet, purple and red on multicolor underprint. W. reymont at right, eagle with crown with color in watermark area. Back: Tree with rural landscape in background. Watermark: Eagle's head.

	VF	UNC
a. Issued note.	45.00	100.
s. Specimen overprint: *WZOR*.	—	70.00

163 2,000,000 Zlotych

16.11.1993. Black and deep brown on multicolor underprint. I. Paderewski at left center, eagle with crown at lower right with color in watermark area. Back: Staszic Palace in Warsaw. Watermark: Eagle's head.

	VF	UNC
a. Issued note.	95.00	200.
s. Specimen overprint: *WZOR*.	—	100.

1990 (1996) "Cancelled" Issue

Currency Reform

1 "new" Zloty = 10,000 "old" Zlotych

#164-172 arms at l. and as wmk. These notes were printed in Germany (w/o imprint). Before their release, it was decided a more sophisticated issue of notes should be prepared and these notes were later overprinted: *NIEOBIEGOWY* (non-negotiable) in red and released to the collecting community. Specimens are also known.

164 1 Zloty

1.3.1990. Blue-gray and brown on multicolor underprint. Building in Gdynia at right, arms at left. Back: Sailing ship at left. Watermark: Arms.

	VF	UNC
a. Cancelled note.	—	3.00
s. Specimen overprint: *WZOR*.	—	25.00

165 2 Zlote

1.3.1990. Dark brown and brown on multicolor underprint. Mining conveyor tower at Katowice at right, arms at left. Back: Battle of Upper Silesia (1921) monument at left. Watermark: Arms.

	VF	UNC
a. Cancelled note.	—	3.00
s. Specimen overprint: *WZOR*.	—	25.00

166 5 Zlotych

1.3.1990 Deep green on multicolor underprint. Building in Zamosc at right, arms at left. Back: Order of Grunwald at left. Watermark: Arms.

	VF	UNC
a. Cancelled note.	—	3.00
s. Specimen overprint: *WZOR*.	—	25.00

167 10 Zlotych

1.3.1990. Red and purple on multicolor underprint. Building in Warsaw at right, arms at left. Back: Statue of Warszawa at left. Watermark: Arms.

	VF	UNC
a. Cancelled note.	—	3.00
s. Specimen overprint: *WZOR*.	—	25.00

168 20 Zlotych

1.3.1990. Brownish black and deep violet on multicolor underprint. Grain storage facility in Gdansk at right, arms at left. Back: Male statue at left. Watermark: Arms.

	VF	UNC
a. Cancelled note.	—	3.00
s. Specimen overprint: *WZOR*.	—	25.00

169 50 Zlotych

1.3.1990. Purple on lilac and multicolor underprint. Church in Wroclaw at right, arms at left. Back: Medallion at left. Watermark: Arms.

	VF	UNC
a. Cancelled note.	—	3.00
s. Specimen overprint: *WZOR*.	—	35.00

170 100 Zlotych VF UNC

1.3.1990. Dark brown and black on orange and multicolor underprint. Building in Poznan at right, arms at left. Back: Medieval seal at left. Watermark: Arms.

	VF	UNC
a. Cancelled note.	—	3.00
s. Specimen overprint: *WZOR*.	—	35.00

171 200 Zlotych VF UNC

1.3.1990. Black and deep purple on multicolor underprint. Buildings in Krakow at right, arms at left. Back: Medieval coin at left. Watermark: Arms.

	VF	UNC
a. Cancelled note.	—	3.00
s. Specimen overprint: *WZOR*.	—	25.00

172 500 Zlotych VF UNC

1.3.1990. Black on green and multicolor underprint. Church in Gniezno at right, arms at left. Back: Medieval seal at left. Watermark: Arms.

	VF	UNC
a. Cancelled note.	—	3.00
s. Specimen overprint: *WZOR*.	—	25.00

1994 (1995) Regular Issue

#173-177 Replacement notes: Serial # prefix *ZA*.

173 10 Zlotych VF UNC

25.3.1994 (1995). Dark brown, brown and olive-green on multicolor underprint. Prince Mieszko I at center right, arms at upper left center. Back: Medieval denar of Mieszko I at left center. UV: value in box and circle under eagle fluoresce yellow; serial # orange. 120x60mm.

	VF	UNC
a. Issued note.	FV	6.50
r. Replacement.	FV	17.00
s. Specimen overprint: *WZOR*.	—	7.50

174 20 Zlotych VF UNC

25.3.1994 (1995). Purple and deep blue on multicolor underprint. King Boleslaw I Chrobry at center right, arms at upper left center. Back: Medieval denar of Boleslaw II at left center. UV: value in box fluoresce yellow; serial # orange. 126x63mm.

	VF	UNC
a. Issued note.	FV	10.00
r. Replacement.	FV	27.00
s. Specimen overprint: *WZOR*.	—	12.50

175 50 Zlotych VF UNC

25.3.1994 (1995). Blue-violet and deep blue and green on multicolor underprint. King Kazimierz III Wielki at center right, arms at upper left center. Back: Eagle from seal, orb and sceptre at left center, town views of Cracow and Kazimierz. 132x66mm.

	VF	UNC
a. Issued note.	FV	22.50
r. Replacement.	FV	50.00
s. Specimen overprint.: *WZOR*.	—	35.00

176 100 Zlotych VF UNC

25.3.1994 (1995). Olive-green on multicolor underprint. Wladyslaw II Jagiello at center right. Back: Arms and Teutonic Knights' castle in Malbork. 138x69mm.

	VF	UNC
a. Issued note.	FV	45.00
r. Replacement.	FV	100.
s. Specimen overprint: *WZOR*.	—	65.00

177 200 Zlotych VF UNC

25.3.1994. Brown on multicolor underprint. King Zygmunt I the old at center right. Back: Arms and eagle in hexagon from the Zygmunt's chapel in the Wawel Cathedral and Wawel's court. 144x72mm.

	VF	UNC
a. Issued note.	FV	85.00
r. Replacement.	FV	170.
s. Specimen overprint: *WZOR.*	—	100.

2006 Commemorative Issue

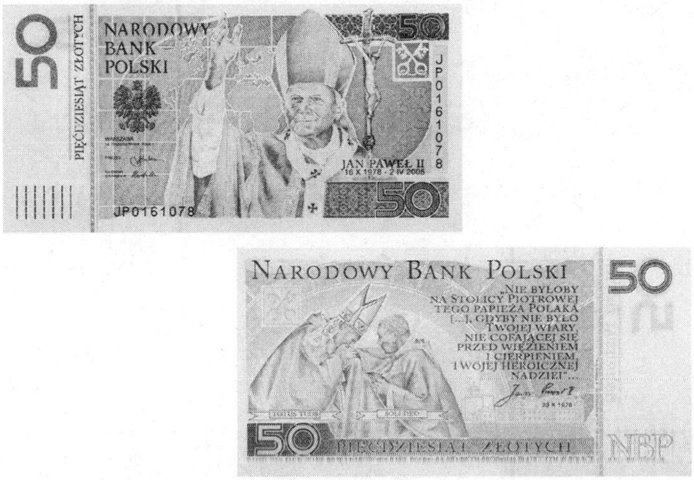

178 50 Zlotych VF UNC

16.10.2006. Light blue and yellow. Pope John Paul II at right center, hand raised in blessing. World map as background. Pope John Paul II seated at left, kissing hand of kneeling Cardinal Stefan Wyszynski at right. Back: Text from letter to Poles, and rendering of Jasna Góra Monastery. 144x72mm. — 65.00

2008 Commemorative Issue

179 10 Zlotych VF UNC

4.6.2008. Olive, tan and rose on multicolor underprint. Jozef Pilsudski at right, Belweder Palace at center. Back: Eagle and monument of four soldiers. 90th Anniversary of the Restoration of Independence. 80,000 notes printed. 138x69mm. FV 25.00

2009 Commemorative Issue

180 20 Zlotych VF UNC

23.9.2009. Brown and tan on yellow underprint. Juliusz Slowacki at right, his house in Krzemieniec at center. Back: Sigismund III column at Warsaw's castle square at left, fragment of the poem *Uspokojenie* at right. Printer: PSPW FV 10.00

2010 Commemorative Issue

181 20 Zlotych VF UNC

29.3.2009. Brown and tan on yellow underprint. Frédéric Chopin profile at center, home in Zelazowa Wola and score of the *Mazurka in B-flat major, Op 7 #1*. Back: Score fraglment of *Etude in F-minor, Op 10 #9. Willow tree landscape.* Printer: PSPW. Released in special folder. 120,000 pieces issued. FV 10.00

2011 Commemorative Issue

182 20 Zlotych VF UNC

20.4.2011. Brown on multicolor underprint. M. Curie at left. Back: Nobel prize medal at right. 138x69mm. FV 10.00

Collector Series

Narodowy Bank Polski

ND (1948; 1965) Issue

CS1 Collector Set Mkt. Value

Deep red overprint: *WZOR* on 1948-dated 20, 50, 100, 500 Zlotych #137, 138, 139 and on 1965-dated 1000 Zlotych #141a. All with normal serial #. 75.00

1967 Issue

CS2 Collector Set Mkt. Value

Red overprint: *WYSTAWA PIENIEDZY RADZIECKICH - LISTOPAD 1967* and *50 LAT WIELKIEGO PAZDZIERNIKA.* with *NBP* monogram at corners on faces of 1937 Russian 1, 3, 5, 10 Chervonetz #202-205. Made for the 50th anniversary of the Socialist revolution of 1917. Released by the National Bank of Poland in a special booklet. 50.00

1974 Issue

CS3 Collector Set Mkt. Value

Reprints of 1944 Russian issue from 50 Groszy-500 Zlotych #104b-119b. Indicated as reprints of 1974 but without other overprint. Made for the 30th anniversary of the Polish Peoples Republic. 20.00

1978 Issue

CS4 Collector Set Mkt. Value

Dark blue-black overprint: *150 LAT BANKU POLSKIEGO 1828-1978* on faces of 1948-dated 20, 100 Zlotych #137, 139a. Made for 150th anniversary of Polish banknotes. Issued in a folder. 25.00

1979 Issues

CS5 Collector Set Mkt. Value

Reprints of 1944 Soviet issue as #C3, but dated 1979 and with red overprint on face: *XXXV - LECIE PRL 1944-1979.* Made for the 35th anniversary of the Polish Peoples Republic. 25.00

CS6 Collector Set

Reprint of 1919-dated 100 Marek with red overprint on face: *60-LECIE POLSKIEGO BANKNOTU PO ODZY SANIU NIEPODLEGLOSCI 1919-1979.* Made for 60th anniversary of modern Polish bank notes. Released by National Bank of Poland in a folder. 15.00

CS7 Collector Set

Red overprint: *WYSTAWA WSPOLCZESNE MONETY I BANKNOTY POLSKIE I OBCE NBP 1979* on 1948 dated 2 Zlote #134. Issued in a small leatherette folder by the National Bank of Poland for a numismatic exposition. 10.00

1979-92 Issue

CS8 Collector Set Mkt. Value

#142-157a, 148a with red overprint: *WZOR* on face; all zero serial # and additional black specimen # with star suffix. Red overprint: *SPECIMEN* on back. 300.

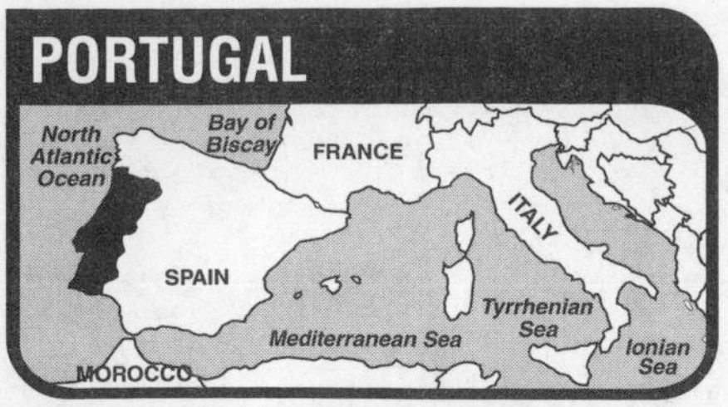

The Portuguese Republic, located in the western part of the Iberian Peninsula in southwestern Europe, has an area of 35,553 sq. mi. (91,905 sq. km.) and a population of 9.79 million. Capital: Lisbon. Portugal's economy is d on agriculture and a small but expanding industrial sector. Textiles, machinery, chemicals, wine and cork are exported.

Following its heyday as a global maritime power during the 15th and 16th centuries, Portugal lost much of its wealth and status with the destruction of Lisbon in a 1755 earthquake, occupation during the Napoleonic Wars, and the independence of its wealthiest colony of Brazil in 1822. A 1910 revolution deposed the monarchy; for most of the next six decades, repressive governments ran the country. In 1974, a left-wing military coup installed broad democratic reforms. The following year, Portugal granted independence to all of its African colonies. Portugal is a founding member of NATO and entered the EC (now the EU) in 1986.

MONETARY SYSTEM:

1 Escudo = 100 Centavos, 1910-2001
1 Euro = 100 Cents, 2002- Note: Prata = Silver, Ouro = Gold.

Republic

Banco de Portugal

1960; 1961 Issue

163 **20 Escudos** | VF | UNC

26.7.1960. Dark green and purple on multicolor underprint. Portrait of Dom Antonio Luiz de Menezes at right. Chapa 6A. 8 signature varieties. Back: Purple and multicolor. Bank seal at left. Watermark: Portrait of Dom Antonio Luiz de Menezes. Printer: BWC (without imprint).

	VF	UNC
a. Issued note.	25.00	80.00
ct. Color trial. Blue and brown on multicolor underprint.	—	500.

164 **50 Escudos** | VF | UNC

24.6.1960. Blue on multicolor underprint. Arms at upper center, Fontes Pereira de Mello at right. Chapa 7A. 8 signature varieties. Back: Dark green and multicolor. Bank seal at upper left, statue *The Thinker* at left. Watermark: Fontes Pereira de Mello. Printer: TDLR (without imprint). | 90.00 | 250.

165 **100 Escudos** | VF | UNC

19.12.1961. Deep violet and purple on orange, green and multicolor underprint. Pedro Nunes at right, arms at upper center. Ch. 6A. 7 signature varieties. Back: Fountain and arches at left, bank seal at center. Watermark: Pedro Nunes. Printer: BWC (without imprint).

	VF	UNC
a. Issued note.	70.00	200.
ct. Color trial. Deep green and purple on multicolor underprint.	—	650.

166 **1000 Escudos** | VF | UNC

30.5.1961. Purple on multicolor underprint. Queen Filipa de Lancastre at right. Ch. 8A. 8 signature varieties. Back: Blue. Watermark: Queen Filipa de Lancastre. Printer: BWC (without imprint). | 225. | 600.

1964-66 Issue

167 **20 Escudos** | VF | UNC

26.5.1964. Olive-green and purple on multicolor underprint. Santo Antonio of Padua at right. Ch. 7. 7 signature varieties. Back: Church of Santo Antonio de Lisboa at left. Watermark: Santo Antonio of Padua.

	VF	UNC
a. Olive-brown underprint at left and right.	6.00	20.00
b. Green underprint at left and right.	4.50	15.00
ct. Color trial. Blue and purple on multicolor underprint.	—	275.

168 50 Escudos | VF | UNC
28.2.1964. Dark brown on multicolor underprint. Queen Isabella at right. Ch. 8. 15 signature varieties. Back: Old city Conimbria. Watermark: Queen Isabella. | 4.00 | 14.00

169 100 Escudos | VF | UNC
1965; 1978. Blue on light tan and multicolor underprint. Camilo Castello Branco at right. Ch. 7. Back: City of Porto in 19th century at left. Watermark: Camilo Castello Branco.
- a. 22 signature varieties. 30.11.1965. | 7.00 | 20.00
- b. 6 signature varieties. 20.9.1978. | 8.00 | 25.00

170 500 Escudos | VF | UNC
1966; 1979. Brown on multicolor underprint. Old map at center, João II at right. Ch. 10. Back: Compass-card or Rhumb-card and double statue. Watermark: João II. Printer: JEZ (without imprint).
- a. 7 signature varieties. 25.1.1966. | 47.50 | 110.
- b. 9 signature varieties. 6.9.1979. | 42.50 | 95.00

171 1000 Escudos | VF | UNC
2.4.1965. Gray-blue on red-brown and multicolor underprint. Pillar at left, arms at upper center, Dom Diniz at right. Ch. 9. 7 signature varieties. Back: Scene of founding of University of Lisbon in 1290. Watermark: Dom Diniz. Printer: JEZ (without imprint). | 2000. | 5000.

1967 Issue

172 1000 Escudos | VF | UNC
19.5.1967. Blue, dark brown and violet on multicolor underprint. Queen Maria II at right. Ch. 10. 24 signature varieties. Back: Her medallion portrait at left, Banco de Portugal in 1846 building at lower right. Watermark: Queen Maria II. Printer: JEZ (without imprint).
- a. Signature titles: *O GOVERNADOR* and *O ADMINISTRADOR.* | 50.00 | 125.
- b. Signature titles: *O VICE-GOVERNADOR* and *O ADMINISTRADOR.* | 50.00 | 125.

1968; 1971 Issue

173 20 Escudos | VF | UNC
27.7.1971. Green (shades) on multicolor underprint. Garcia de Orta at right. Ch. 8. 15 signature varieties. Back: 16th century market in Goa. Watermark: Garcia de Orta. | 2.25 | 8.00

174 50 Escudos | VF | UNC
1968; 1980. Dark brown on multicolor underprint. Arms at left, Infante Dona Maria at right. Ch. 9. Back: Sintra in 1507. Watermark: Infante Dona Maria.
- a. 7 signature varieties. 28.5.1968. | 5.00 | 18.00
- b. 9 signature varieties. 1.2.1980. | 4.50 | 16.00

175 1000 Escudos | VF | UNC
1968-82. Blue and black on multicolor underprint. Dom Pedro V at right. Ch. 11. Back: Conjoined busts at left, ceremonial opening of the first railway at bottom center and right. Watermark: Dom Pedro V. Printer: Printer: BWC (without imprint).
- a. 24 signature varieties. 28.5.1968. | 30.00 | 70.00
- b. 8 signature varieties. 16.9.1980. | 20.00 | 50.00
- c. 9 signature varieties. 3.12.1981. | 20.00 | 50.00
- d. 9 signature varieties. 21.9.1982. | 85.00 | 175.
- e. 11 signature varieties. 26.10.1982. | 20.00 | 50.00
- ct. Color trial. Purple and green. | — | 450.

1978; 1979 Issue

176	20 Escudos	VF	UNC
	1978. Green (shades) on multicolor underprint. Admiral Gago Coutinho at right. Ch. 9. Large or small size numerals in serial number. Back: Airplane. Watermark: Admiral Gago Coutinho.		
	a. 6 signature varieties. 13.9.1978.	2.50	9.00
	b. 6 signature varieties. 4.10.1978.	2.25	8.00

177	500 Escudos	VF	UNC
	4.10.1979 (1982). Brown on multicolor underprint. Old street layout of part of Braga at center, Francisco Sanches at right. Ch. 11. 9 signature varieties. Back: 17th century street scene in Braga. Watermark: Francisco Sanches. Printer: JEZ (without imprint).		
	a. Issued note.	17.50	40.00
	s. Specimen. Overprinted: <ESPCECIMEN. on both sides.	—	750.

1980-89 Issues

178	100 Escudos	VF	UNC
	1980-85. Dark blue on multicolor underprint. Manuel M. B. du Bocage seated at right. Ch. 8. Back: Early 19th century scene of Rossio Square in Lisbon. Watermark: Manuel M. B. du Bocage.		
	a. 8 signature varieties. Darker underprint through center 2.9.1980.	7.00	30.00
	b. 8 signature varieties. Light underprint through center 24.2.1981.	5.00	20.00
	c. 7 signature varieties. 31.1.1984.	3.50	16.00
	d. 6 signature varieties. 12.3.1985.	3.50	15.00
	e. 6 signature varieties. 4.6.1985.	3.25	14.00
	s. Specimen.	—	195.
	ct. Color trial. Blue and green on multicolor underprint.	—	250.

179	100 Escudos	VF	UNC
	1986-88. Blue (shades) on multicolor underprint. Fernando Antonio Nogueira Pessoa at center right. Ch. 9. Back: Rosebud. Watermark: Fernando Antonio Nogueira Pessoa.		
	a. 5 signature varieties. 16.10.1986.	3.75	16.00
	b. 8 signature varieties. 12.2.1987.	5.00	20.00
	c. Prefix letters *FIL*. 12.2.1987.	—	200.
	d. 8 signature varieties. 3.12.1987.	3.75	16.00
	e. 6 signature varieties. 26.5.1988.	3.25	12.00
	f. 6 signature varieties. 24.11.1988.	3.25	12.00
	s. As a. Specimen. Overprinted: *ESPECIMEN* on both sides.	—	150.

180	500 Escudos	VF	UNC
	1987-94. Brown and multicolor. José Xavier Mouzinho da Silveira at center right, arms at upper left. Ch. 12. Back: Sheaf. Watermark: José Xavier Mouzinho da Silveira.		
	a. 8 signature varieties. 20.11.1987.	17.50	40.00
	b. 6 signature varieties. 4.8.1988.	20.00	45.00
	c. 6 signature varieties. 4.10.1989.	15.00	35.00
	d. 5 signature varieties. 13.2.1992.	15.00	35.00
	e. 7 signature varieties. 18.3.1993.	15.00	35.00
	f. 6 signature varieties. 4.11.1993.	15.00	35.00
	g. 5 signature varieties. 29.9.1994.	17.50	40.00
	s. As a. Specimen.	—	250.

181	1000 Escudos	VF	UNC
	1983-94. Purple and dark brown on multicolor underprint. Teofilo Braga at center right. Ch. 12. Back: Museum artifacts. Watermark: Teofilo Braga.		
	a. 9 signature varieties. 2.8.1983.	22.50	50.00
	b. 5 signature varieties. 12.6.1986.	25.00	60.00
	c. 8 signature varieties. 26.2.1987.	25.00	60.00
	d. 8 signature varieties. 3.9.1987.	25.00	60.00
	e. 6 signature varieties. 22.12.1988.	25.00	60.00
	f. 6 signature varieties. 9.11.1989.	25.00	60.00
	g. 5 signature varieties. 26.7.1990.	22.50	50.00
	h. 5 signature varieties. 20.12.1990.	20.00	45.00
	i. 5 signature varieties. 6.2.1992.	25.00	55.00
	j. 6 signature varieties. 17.6.1993.	20.00	45.00
	k. 6 signature varieties. 3.3.1994.	20.00	45.00
	s. As a. Specimen.	—	400.

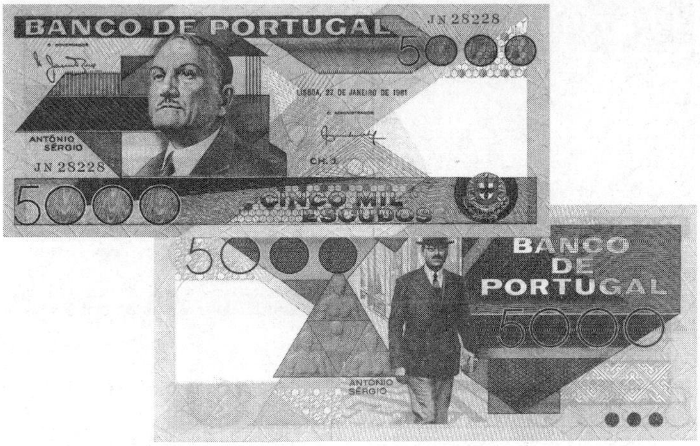

182 5000 Escudos

1980-86. Brown and multicolor. Antonio Sergio de Sousa at left center. Ch. 1. Back: Antonio Sergio de Sousa walking at center. Watermark: Antonio Sergio de Sousa. Printer: TDLR (without imprint).

	VF	UNC
a. 8 signature varieties. 10.9.1980.	90.00	200.
b. 8 signature varieties. 27.1.1981.	85.00	190.
c. 10 signature varieties. 24.5.1983.	80.00	180.
d. 6 signature varieties. 4.6.1985.	110.	240.
e. 6 signature varieties. 7.1.1986.	90.00	200.
s. Specimen.	—	500.

183 5000 Escudos

1987. Olive-green and brown on multicolor underprint. Antero de Quental at center right. Ch. 2. Back: Six hands with rope and chain at center. Watermark: Antero de Quental.

	VF	UNC
a. 8 signature varieties. 12.2.1987.	60.00	140.
b. 8 signature varieties. 3.12.1987.	60.00	140.
s. As a. Specimen.	—	400.

184 5000 Escudos

1988-93. Olive-green and brown on multicolor underprint. Antero de Quental at center right. Ch. 2A. Back: Six hands with rope and chain at center. Watermark: Antero de Quental.

	VF	UNC
a. 6 signature varieties. 28.10.1988.	60.00	140.
b. 6 signature varieties. 6.7.1989.	65.00	150.
c. 6 signature varieties. 19.10.1989.	55.00	130.
d. 5 signature varieties. 31.10.1991.	60.00	140.
e. 7 signature varieties. 18.3.1993.	60.00	140.
f. 7 signature varieties. 2.9.1993.	60.00	140.

185 10,000 Escudos

1989-91. Orange, light brown and yellow. Dr. Antonio Gaetano de Abreu Preire Egas Moniz by human brain at center. Ch. 1. Back: Nobel Prize medal, snakes, tree at center. Watermark: Dr. Antonio Gaetano de Abreu Preire Egas Moniz.

	VF	UNC
a. 6 signature varieties. 12.1.1989.	130.	300.
b. 6 signature varieties. 14.12.1989.	120.	260.
c. 5 signature varieties. 16.5.1991.	120.	260.
s. As a. Specimen.	—	500.

1991 Issue

186 2000 Escudos

1991-93. Dark brown and blue on multicolor underprint. Bartholomeu Dias at left, astrolabe at center. Ch. 1. Back: Sailing ship at center, arms at right. Watermark: Bartholomeu Dias. .

	VF	UNC
a. 5 signature varieties. 23.5.1991.	35.00	85.00
b. 5 signature varieties. 29.8.1991.	50.00	125.
c. 6 signature varieties. 16.7.1992.	30.00	70.00
d. 6 signature varieties. 21.10.1993.	45.00	100.
s. As a. Specimen.	—	400.

1995-97 Issue

Note: #187-191, Quincentenary of Portuguese Discoveries Series

187 500 Escudos

1997; 2000. Violet and brown on multicolor underprint. João de Barros at right, crowned shields on global view at upper center, angels below at left and right in underprint. Ch. 13. Back: Allegory of the Portuguese Discoveries at left center, illustrations from the *Grammer* at left in underprint. Watermark: João de Barros. 125x68mm.

	VF	UNC
a. 6 signature varieties. 17.4.1997.	FV	18.00
b. 6 signature varieties. 11.9.1997.	FV	15.00
c. 7.11.2000.	FV	14.00
s. As a. Specimen.	—	200.

188	1000 Escudos	VF	UNC
	1996; 1998; 2000. Purple and brown on multicolor underprint. Pedro Alvares Cabral wearing helmet at right, Brazilian arms at center. Ch. 13. Back: Old sailing ship at center, birds and animals of Brazilian jungle in underprint. Watermark: Pedro Alvares Cabral. 132x68mm.		
	a. 6 signature varieties. 18.4.1996.	FV	32.50
	b. 6 signature varieties. 31.10.1996.	FV	30.00
	c. 6 signature varieties. 12.3.1998; 21.5.1998.	FV	25.00
	d. 7.11.2000.	FV	22.50
	s. As a. Specimen.	—	250.

189	2000 Escudos	VF	UNC
	1995-97. Blue-violet and deep blue-green on multicolor underprint. Bartholomeu Dias at right, cruzado coin of Dom João II at upper center, sailing instrument below. Ch. 2. Back: Old sailing ship at center right, compass, map at left center. Watermark: Bartholomeu Dias. 140x68mm.		
	a. 5 signature varieties. 21.9.1995.	FV	60.00
	b. 6 signature varieties. 1.2.1996.	FV	55.00
	c. 31.7.1997; 11.9.1997.	FV	50.00
	d. 7.11.2000.	FV	55.00
	s. As a. Specimen.	—	300.

190	5000 Escudos	VF	UNC
	1995-98. Deep olive-green and brown-violet on underprint. Vasco da Gama at right, medallion at upper center. Ch. 3. Back: Old sailing ship at center right, da Gama with authorities in Calcutta at left. Watermark: Vasco da Gama. 147x75mm.		
	a. 5 signature varieties. 5.1.1995.	FV	130.
	b. 6 signature varieties. 12.9.1996.	FV	120.
	c. 6 signature varieties. 20.2.1997.	FV	120.
	d. 6 signature varieties. 11.9.1997.	FV	110.
	e. 2.7.1998.	FV	110.
	s. As a. Specimen.	—	400.

191	10,000 Escudos	VF	UNC
	1996-98. Violet and dark brown on multicolor underprint. Infante Dom Henrique at right, arms at center. Ch. 2. 6 signature varieties. Back: Old sailing ship at center. Watermark: Infante Dom Henrique. 153x75mm.		
	a. 2.5.1996.	FV	200.
	b. 10.7.1997.	FV	190.
	c. 12.2.1998; 12.7.1998.	FV	190.
	s. As a. Specimen.	—	500.

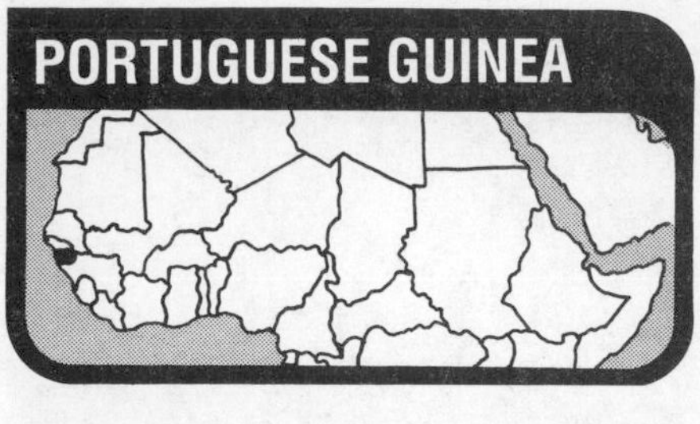

Portuguese Guinea (now Guinea-Bissau), a former Portuguese province off the west coast of Africa bounded on the north by Senegal and on the east and southeast by Guinea, had an area of 13,948 sq. mi. (36,125 sq. km.). Capital: Bissau. The province exported peanuts, timber and beeswax.

Portuguese Guinea was discovered by Portuguese navigator Nuno Tristao in 1446. Trading rights in the area were granted to Cape Verde islanders but few prominent posts were established before 1851, and they were principally coastal installations. The chief export of this colony's early period was slaves for South America, a practice that adversely affected trade with the native people and retarded subjection of the interior. Territorial disputes with France delayed final demarcation of the colony's frontiers until 1905.

The African Party for the Independence of Guinea-Bissau was founded in 1956, and several years later began a guerrilla warfare that grew in effectiveness until 1974, when the rebels controlled most of the colony. Portugal's costly overseas wars in her African territories resulted in a military coup in Portugal in April 1974, that appreciably brightened the prospects for freedom for Guinea-Bissau. In August, 1974, the Lisbon government signed an agreement granting independence to Portuguese Guinea effective Sept. 10, 1974. The new republic took the name of Guinea-Bissau.

RULERS:

Portuguese to 1974

MONETARY SYSTEM:

1 Mil Reis = 1000 Reis to 1910
1 Escudo = 100 Centavos, 1910-1975

STEAMSHIP SEALS

Type I
LOANDA

Type II
LISBOA

Type III
C,C,A

C,C,A = Colonias, Commercio, Agricultura.

Portuguese Administration

Banco Nacional Ultramarino, Guiné

Decretos - Leis 39221 E 44891; 1964 Issue

40	50 Escudos	VF	UNC
	30.6.1964. Dark green on lilac and multicolor underprint. Texeira Pinto at left, bank ship seal at right. Back: Woman sitting, ships through the ages in background at center.		
	a. Issued note.	125.	350.
	s. Specimen, punch hole cancelled.	—	250.

41	100 Escudos	VF	UNC
	30.6.1964. Blue-green on multicolor underprint. Texeira Pinto at left, bank ship seal at right. Back: Woman sitting, ships through the ages in background at center.		
	a. Issued note.	175.	450.
	s. Specimen, punch hole cancelled.	—	325.

42	500 Escudos	VF	UNC
	30.6.1964. Brown on multicolor underprint. Texeira Pinto at left, bank ship seal at right. Back: Woman sitting, ships through the ages in background at center.		
	a. Issued note.	350.	850.
	s. Specimen, punch hole cancelled.	—	500.

43	1000 Escudos	VF	UNC
	30.6.1964. Red-orange on multicolor underprint. Portrait of H. Barreto at right, bank ship seal at upper center. Back: Woman standing, ships through the ages in background at left center. Printer: BWC.		
	a. Issued note.	275.	650.
	s. Specimen.	—	375.
	ct. Color trial. Brown on multicolor underprint.	—	350.

Decretos - Leis 39221 E 44891; 1971 Issue

44	50 Escudos	VF	UNC
	17.12.1971. Olive-green on multicolor underprint. Portuguese arms at upper center, N. Tristao at right. Back: Woman standing, ships through the ages in background at left center, bank ship seal at lower left. Watermark: N. Tristao.		
	a. Issued note.	35.00	80.00
	s. Specimen.	—	175.
	ct. Color trial. Green on multicolor underprint.	—	195.

45	100 Escudos	VF	UNC
	17.12.1971. Blue on multicolor undderprint. Portuguese arms at upper center, portrait of N.Tristaoat right. Back: Woman standing, ships through the ages in background at left center, bank ship seal at lower left. Watermark: N. Tristao.		
	a. Issued note.	37.50	90.00
	s. Specimen.	—	200.
	ct. Color trial. Olive on multicolor underprint.	—	195.

46	500 Escudos	VF	UNC
	27.7.1971. Purple on multicolor underprint. Portuguese arms at upper center, portrait H. Barreto at right. Back: Woman standing, ships through the ages in background at left center, bank ship seal at lower left.		
	a. Issued note.	225.	600.
	ct. Color trial. Brown on multicolor underprint.	—	450.

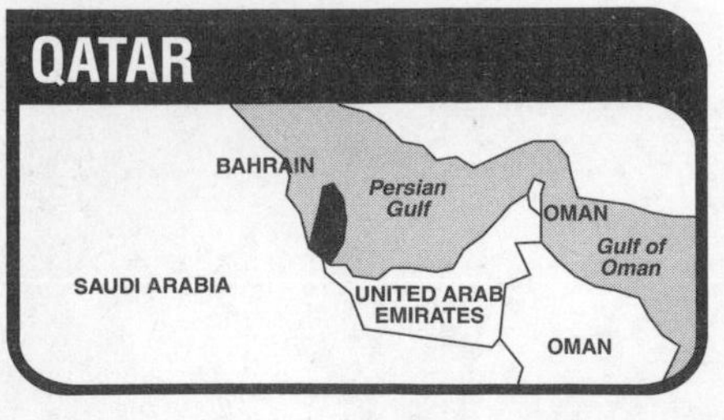

The State of Qatar, an emirate in the Persian Gulf between Bahrain and the United Arab Emirates, has an an area 4,247 sq. mi. (11,437 sq. km.) and a population of 700,000. Capital: Doha.

Ruled by the al-Thani family since the mid-1800s, Qatar transformed itself from a poor British protectorate noted mainly for pearling into an independent state with significant oil and natural gas revenues. During the late 1980s and early 1990s, the Qatari economy was crippled by a continuous siphoning off of petroleum revenues by the Amir, who had ruled the country since 1972. His son, the current Amir Hamad bin Khalifa al-Thani, overthrew him in a bloodless coup in 1995. In 2001, Qatar resolved its longstanding border disputes with both Bahrain and Saudi Arabia. As of 2007, oil and natural gas revenues had enabled Qatar to attain the highest per capita income in the world.

Also see Qatar and Dubai.

MONETARY SYSTEM:

1 Riyal = 100 Dirhem

EMIRATE

QATAR MONETARY AGENCY

1973 ND ISSUE

1 1 Riyal — VF UNC

ND (1973). Red on lilac and multicolor underprint. Arms in circle at right. Back: Port of Doha at left. Watermark: Falcon's head.

	VF	UNC
a. Issued note.	12.00	60.00
s. Specimen.	—	200.

2 5 Riyals — VF UNC

ND (1973). Dark brown on lilac and multicolor underprint. Arms in circle at right. Back: National Museum at left. Watermark: Falcon's head.

	VF	UNC
a. Issued note.	30.00	120.
s. Specimen.	—	300.

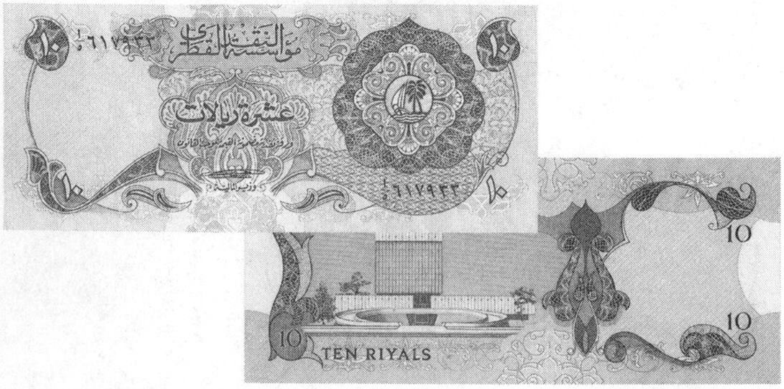

3 10 Riyals — VF UNC

ND (1973). Green on multicolor underprint. Arms in circle at right. Back: Qatar Monetary Agency building at left. Watermark: Falcon's head.

	VF	UNC
a. Issued note.	40.00	170.
s. Specimen.	—	400.

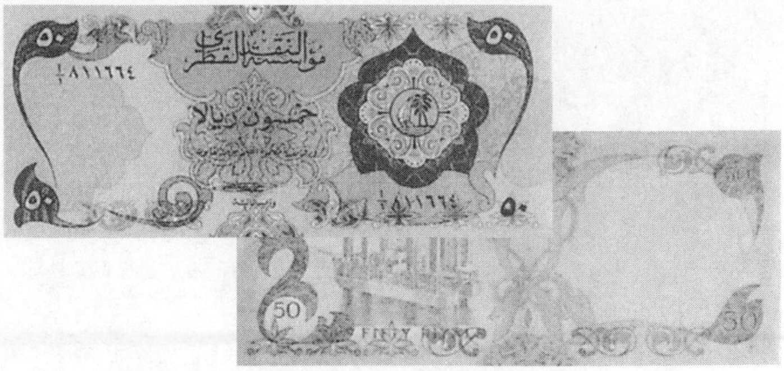

4 50 Riyals — VF UNC

ND (1976). Blue on multicolor underprint. Arms in circle at right. Back: Offshore oil drilling platform at left. Watermark: Falcon's head.

	VF	UNC
a. Issued note.	400.	1400.
s. Specimen.	—	1000.

5 100 Riyals — VF UNC

ND (1973). Olive-green and orange-brown on multicolor underprint. Arms in circle at right. Back: Ministry of Finance building at left. Watermark: Falcon's head.

	VF	UNC
a. Issued note.	220.	850.
s. Specimen.	—	1500.

6 500 Riyals — VF UNC

ND (1973). Blue-green on multicolor underprint. Arms in circle at right. Back: Mosque of the Sheikhs and minaret at left. Watermark: Falcon's head.

	VF	UNC
a. Issued note.	850.	2700.
s. Specimen.	—	2000.

1980's ND ISSUE

		VF	UNC
7	**1 Riyal** ND. Brown on multicolor underprint. Arms at right. Back: City street scene in Doha at left center. Watermark: Falcon's head.	6.00	12.00

8 **5 Riyals** VF UNC

ND. Dark red and purple on multicolor underprint. Arms at right. Back: Red-brown, green and brown. Sheep and plants at left center. Watermark: Falcon's head.

	VF	UNC
a. Watermark: Hawk, nostril visible, and top bill overlaps bottom.	7.00	15.00
b. Watermark: Hawk, without nostril, beak even.	7.00	12.00

9 **10 Riyals** VF UNC

ND. Green on blue and multicolor underprint. Arms at right. Back: National Museum at left center. Watermark: Falcon's head. 12.00 30.00

10 **50 Riyals** VF UNC

ND (1989). Blue on multicolor underprint. Arms at right. Back: Furnace at a steel factory. Watermark: Falcon's head. 45.00 100.

11 **100 Riyals** VF UNC

ND. Green on multicolor underprint. Arms at right. Back: Qatar Monetary Agency building at left center. Watermark: Falcon's head. 85.00 140.

12 **500 Riyals** VF UNC

ND. Blue and green on multicolor underprint. Arms at right. Back: Offshore oil drilling platform on vertical format. Watermark: Falcon's head.

	VF	UNC
a. Issued note.	365.	650.
s. Specimen.	—	1500.

1985 ND Issue

13 **1 Riyal** VF UNC

ND (1985). Brown on multicolor underprint. Arms at right. Back: Purple. Boat beached at left, Ministry of Finance, Emir's Palace in background at center. Watermark: Falcon's head. 134x66mm.

	VF	UNC
a. Watermark: Hawk, nostril visible, and top bill overlaps bottom.	FV	0.00
b. Watermark: Hawk, without nostril, beak even.	FV	5.00

Qatar Central Bank

1996 ND Issue

14 **1 Riyal** VF UNC

ND (1996). Brown on multicolor underprint. Arms at right. 2 signatures. Back: Boat beached at left, Ministry of Finance, Emir's Palace in background at center. Watermark: Falcon's head. 134x66mm.

	VF	UNC
a. Security thread reads: *QATAR MONETARY AGENCY.*	FV	5.00
b. Security thread reads: *QATAR CENTRAL BANK.*	FV	4.00

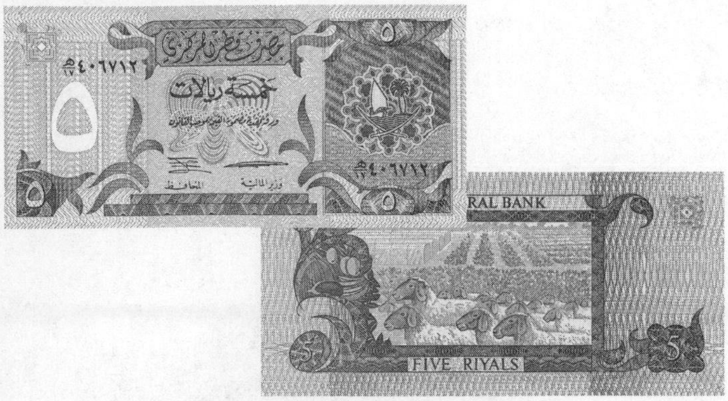

15 **5 Riyals** VF UNC

ND (1996). Red and purple on multicolor underprint. Arms at right. 2 signatures. Back: Red-brown, green and brown. Sheep and plants at left center. Watermark: Falcon's head. 140x67mm.

	VF	UNC
a. Security thread reads: *QATAR MONETARY AGENCY.*	FV	14.00
b. Security thread reads: *QATAR CENTRAL BANK.*	FV	10.00

16 **10 Riyals** VF UNC

ND (1996). Green and blue on multicolor underprint. Arms at right. 2 signatures. Back: National Museum at left center. Watermark: Falcon's head. 145x69mm.

	VF	UNC
a. Security thread reads: *QATAR MONETARY AGENCY.*	FV	20.00
b. Security thread reads: *QATAR CENTRAL BANK.*	FV	12.00

		VF	UNC
17	**50 Riyals** ND (1996). Blue on multicolor underprint. Arms at right. 2 signatures. Back: Furnace at a steel factory. Watermark: Falcon's head. 152x70mm.	FV	60.00

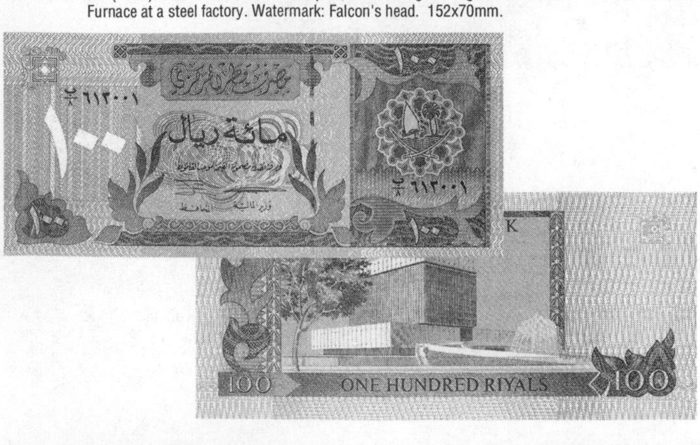

		VF	UNC
18	**100 Riyals** ND (1996). Green on multicolor underprint. Arms at right. 2 signatures. Back: Qatat Monetary Agency building at left center. Watermark: Falcon's head. 152x72mm.	FV	100.

		VF	UNC
19	**500 Riyals** ND (1996). Blue on multicolor underprint. Arms at right. 2 signatures. Silver foil emblem at upper left. Back: Offshore oil drilling platform. Watermark: Falcon's head. 165x74mm.	FV	475.

2003 ND Issue

		VF	UNC
20	**1 Riyal** ND (2003). Purple and blue on multicolor underprint. Back: Three native birds - Crested Lark, Eurasian Bee Eater and lesser Sand Plover at left. Watermark: Falcon's head. UV: fibers fluoresce yellow and blue; left serial # orange; central design elements yellow. 134x66mm.	FV	2.00

		VF	UNC
21	**5 Riyals** ND (2003). Light and dark green on multicolor underprint. Back: National Museum and native animals at left. Watermark: Falcon's head. 140x67mm.	FV	6.00

No.	Description	VF	UNC
22	**10 Riyals** ND (2003). Orange-brown and tan on multicolor underprint. Back: Traditional Dhow and sand dunes Khor Al-Udeid at left. Watermark: Falcon's head. 146x69mm.	FV	11.00

No.	Description	VF	UNC
23	**50 Riyals** ND (2003). Rose on multicolor underprint. Back: Qatar Central Bank building and Oyster and Pearl Monument at left. Watermark: Falcon's head. 152x70mm.	FV	62.50

No.	Description	VF	UNC
24	**100 Riyals** ND (2003). Green on multicolor underprint. Back: Mosque of the Sheikhs and Al-Shaqab Institute at left. Watermark: Falcon's head. 158x72mm.	FV	95.00

No.	Description	VF	UNC
25	**500 Riyals** ND (2003). Light and dark blue on multicolor underprint. Back: Royal Palace, Al-Wajbah Fort and Falcon's head at left. Watermark: Falcon's head. 164x74mm.	FV	425.

2007 ND Issue

No.	Description	VF	UNC
26	**100 Riyals** ND (2007). Green on multicolor underprint. Solid security thread at left and windowed foil thread with QCB 100 repeatedly cut out. Foil over clear window at center. 158x72mm.	FV	50.00

No.	Description	VF	UNC
27	**500 Riyals** ND (2007). Light and dark blue on multicolor underprint. Solid security thread at left and windowed foil thread with QCB 500 repeatedly cut out. Clear window at center. 164x74mm.	FV	225.

2008 ND Issue

No.	Description	VF	UNC
28	**1 Riyal** ND (2008). Purple and blue on multicolro underprint. Tactile markings for visually impaired added at center left edge.	FV	2.00

		VF	UNC
29	**5 Riyals** ND (2008). Light and dark green on multicolor underprint. Tactile markings for visually impaired added at center left edge.	FV	6.00

		VF	UNC
30	**10 Riyals** ND (2008). Orange-brown and tan on multicolor underprint. Tactile markings for visually impaired added at center left edge.	FV	11.00

		VF	UNC
31	**50 Riyals** ND (2008). Rose on multicolor underprint. Tactile markings for visually imparred added at center left edge. Back: Qatar Central Bank building and Oyster and Pearl Monument at left.	FV	35.00

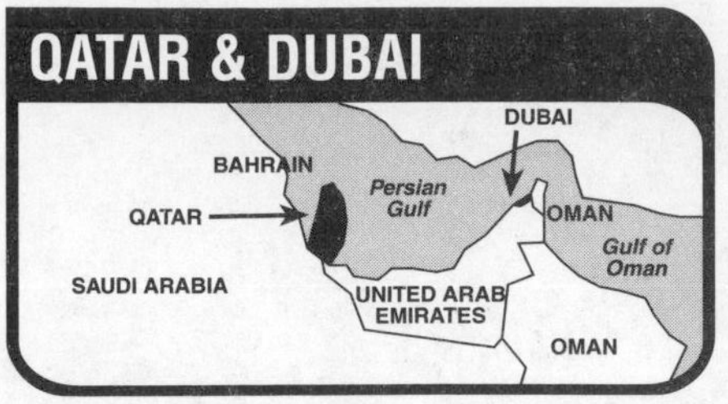

The State of Qatar, which occupies the Qatar Peninsula jutting into the Persian Gulf from eastern Saudi Arabia, has an area of 4,247 sq. mi. (11,000 sq. km.) and a population of 382,000. Capital: Doha. The traditional occupations of pearling, fishing and herding have been replaced in economics by petroleum-related industries. Crude oil, petroleum products, and tomatoes are exported.

Dubai is one of the seven sheikhdoms comprising the United Arab Emirates (formerly Trucial States) located along the southern shore of the Persian Gulf. It has a population of about 60,000. Qatar, which initiated protective treaty relations with Great Britain in 1820, achieved independence on Sept. 3, 1971, upon withdrawal of the British military presence from the Persian Gulf, and replaced its special treaty arrangement with Britain with a treaty of general friendship. Dubai attended independence on Dec. 1, 1971, upon termination of Britain's protective treaty with the trucial sheikhdoms, and on Dec. 2, 1971, entered into the union of the United Arab Emirates.

Despite the fact that the sultanate of Qatar and the sheikhdom of Dubai were merged under a monetary union, the two territories were governed independently from each other. Qatar now uses its own currency while Dubai uses the United Arab Emirates currency and coins.

The Department of Reunion, an overseas department of France located in the Indian Ocean 400 miles (640 km.) east of Madagascar, has an area of 969 sq. mi. (2,510 sq. km.) and a population of 556,000. Capital: Saint-Denis. The island's volcanic soil is extremely fertile. Sugar, vanilla, coffee and rum are exported. Although first visited by Portuguese navigators in the 16th century, Reunion was uninhabited when claimed for France by Capt. Goubert in 1638. It was first colonized as Isle de Burbon by the French in 1662 as a layover station for ships rounding the Cape of Good Hope to India. It was renamed Reunion in 1793. The island remained in French possession except for the period of 1810-15, when it was occupied by the British. Reunion became an overseas department of France in 1946, and in 1958 voted to continue that status within the new French Union. Baque du France notes were introduced 1.1.1973.

MONETARY SYSTEM:

1 Riyal = 100 Dirhem

Sultanate and Sheikhdom

Qatar and Dubai Currency Board

1960s ND Issue

			VF	UNC
1	**1 Riyal**		VF	UNC
	ND. Dark green on multicolor underprint. Dhow, derrick and palm tree at left. Watermark: Falcon's head.			
		a. Issued note.	150.	450.
		s. Specimen, punch hole cancelled.	—	500.
2	**5 Riyals**			
	ND. Purple on multicolor underprint. Dhow, derrick and palm tree at left. Watermark: Falcon's head.			
		a. Issued note.	1000.	2750.
		s. Specimen, punch hole cancelled.	—	1000.

			VF	UNC
3	**10 Riyals**		VF	UNC
	ND. Gray-blue on multicolor underprint. Dhow, derrick and palm tree at left. Watermark: Falcon's head.			
		a. Issued note.	500.	2500.
		s. Specimen, punch hole cancelled.	—	1250.

4	**25 Riyals**	**VF**	**UNC**
	ND. Blue on multicolor underprint. Dhow, derrick and palm tree at left. Watermark: Falcon's head.		
	a. Issued note.	6000.	13,000.
	s. Specimen, punch hole cancelled.	—	5500.
5	**50 Riyals**		
	ND. Red on multicolor underprint. Dhow, derrick and palm tree at left. Watermark: Falcon's head.		
	a. Issued note.	4500.	11,000.
	s. Specimen, punch hole cancelled.	—	6500.

6	**100 Riyals**	**VF**	**UNC**
	ND. Olive on multicolor underprint. Dhow, derrick and palm tree at left. Watermark: Falcon's head.		
	a. Issued note.	2500.	6500.
	s. Specimen, punch hole cancelled.	—	4000.

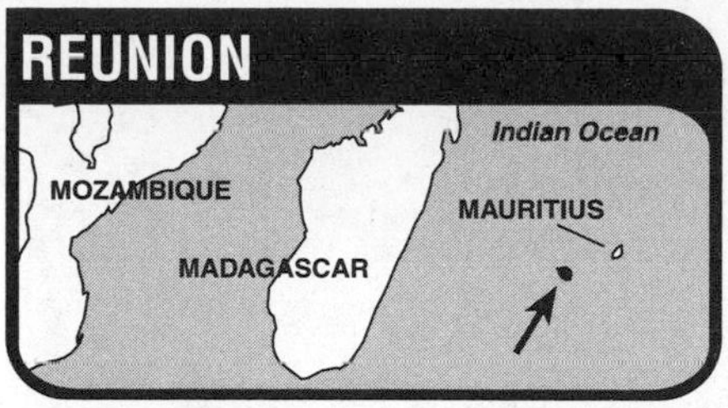

The Department of Reunion, an overseas department of France located in the Indian Ocean 400 miles (640 km.) east of Madagascar, has an area of 969 sq. mi. (2,510 sq. km.) and a population of 556,000. Capital: Saint-Denis. The island's volcanic soil is extremely fertile. Sugar, vanilla, coffee and rum are exported.

Although first visited by Portuguese navigators in the 16th century, Reunion was uninhabited when claimed for France by Capt. Goubert in 1638. It was first colonized as Isle de Bourbon by the French in 1662 as a layover station for ships rounding the Cape of Good Hope to India. It was renamed Reunion in 1793. The island remained in French possession except for the period of 1810-15, when it was occupied by the British. Reunion became an overseas department of France in 1946, and in 1958 voted to continue that status within the new French Union. Banque de France notes were introduced 1.1.1973.

MONETARY SYSTEM:

1 Franc = 100 Centimes
1 Nouveau Franc = 50 Old Francs, 1960

French Administration

Institut d'Emission des Départements d'Outre-Mer, République Française

Department de la Réunion

1964; 1965 ND Issue

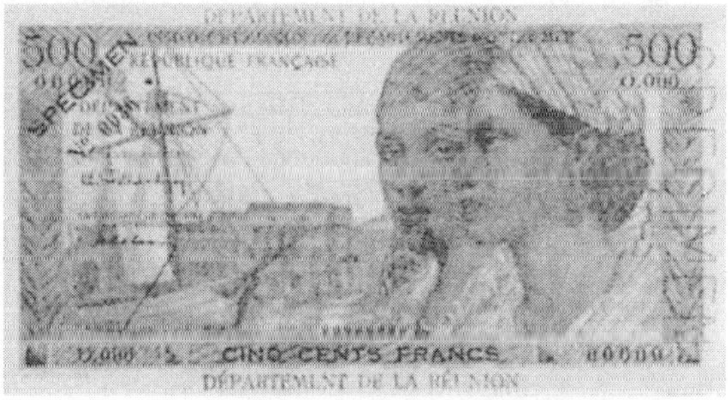

51	**500 Francs**	**VF**	**UNC**
	ND (1964). Multicolor. Two girls at right, sailboat at left. Back: Farmers with ox-carts.		
	a. Signature A. Postel-Vinay and P. Calvet.	325.	900.
	b. Signature A. Postel-Vinay and B. Clappier.	275.	800.
	s. As a. Specimen. Overprint and perforated: *SPECIMEN.*	—	450.

52 1000 Francs VF UNC

ND (1964). Multicolor. Two women (symbol of the *"Union Française"*) at right. Signature A. Postel-Vinay and P. Calvet. Back: Two men in canoe at left, female at right.

	VF	UNC
a. Issued note.	350.	1000.
s. Specimen.	—	600.

53 5000 Francs VF UNC

ND (1965). Brown on multicolor underprint. General Schoelcher at center right. Signature A. Postel-Vinay and P. Calvet.

	VF	UNC
a. Issued note.	600.	1500.
s. Specimen.	—	900.

1967 ND Provisional Issue

54 10 Nouveaux Francs on 500 Francs VF UNC

ND (1967-71). Multicolor. Two girls at right, sailboat at left with overprint. Back: Farmers with ox-carts.

	VF	UNC
a. Signature A. Postel-Vinay and P. Calvet. (1967).	175.	650.
b. Signature A. Postel-Vinay and B. Clappier. (1971).	140.	500.
s. Specimen.	FV	700.

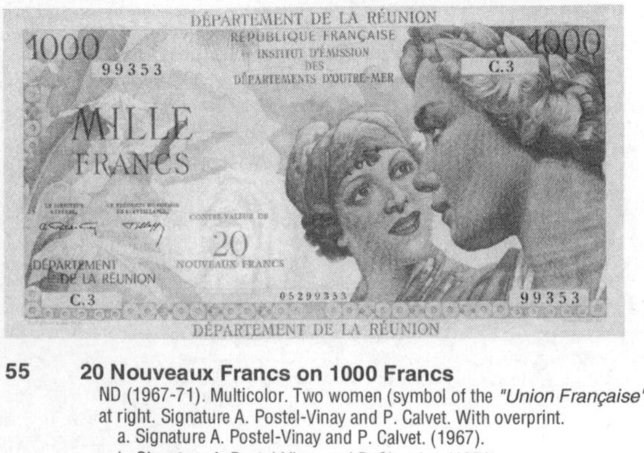

55 20 Nouveaux Francs on 1000 Francs VF UNC

ND (1967-71). Multicolor. Two women (symbol of the *"Union Française"*) at right. Signature A. Postel-Vinay and P. Calvet. With overprint.

	VF	UNC
a. Signature A. Postel-Vinay and P. Calvet. (1967).	200.	750.
b. Signature A. Postel-Vinay and B. Clappier. (1971).	160.	600.
s. Specimen.	—	900.

56 100 Nouveaux Francs on 5000 Francs VF UNC

ND (1967-71). Multicolor. General Schoelcher at center right. Signature A. Postel-Vinay and P. Calvet. With overprint.

	VF	UNC
a. Signature A. Postel-Vinay and P. Calvet. (1967).	450.	1250.
b. Signature A. Postel-Vinay and B. Clappier. (1971).	375.	1000.
s. Specimen.	—	1500.

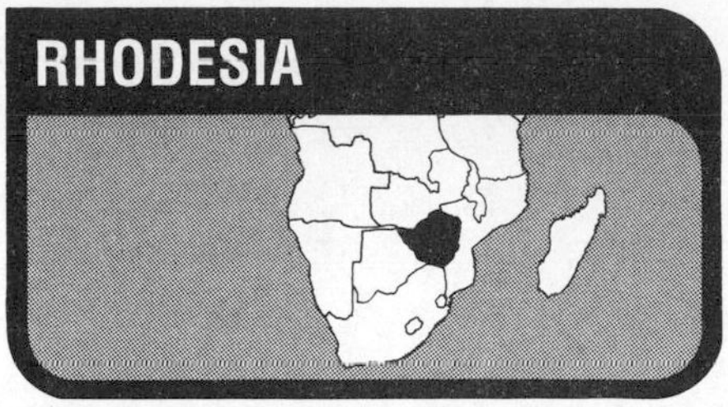

The "Republic of" Rhodesia (never recognized by the British government and was referred to as Southern Rhodesia, now Zimbabwe) located in the east-central part of southern Africa, has an area of 150,804 sq. mi. (390,580 sq. km.) and a population of 9.9 million. Capital: Harare. The economy is d on agriculture and mining. Tobacco, sugar, asbestos, copper and chrome ore and coal are exported.

The Rhodesian area, the habitat of paleolithic man, contains extensive evidence of earlier civilizations, notably the world-famous ruins of Zimbabwe, a gold-trading center that flourished about the 14th or 15th century AD. The Portuguese of the 16th century were the first Europeans to attempt to develop south-central Africa, but it remained for Cecil Rhodes and the British South Africa Co. to open the hinterlands. Rhodes obtained a concession for mineral rights from local chiefs in 1888 and administered his African empire (named Southern Rhodesia in 1895) through the British South Africa Co. until 1923, when the British government annexed the area after the white settlers voted for existence as a separate entity, rather than for incorporation into the Union of South Africa.

From Sept. of 1953 through 1963 Southern Rhodesia was joined with the British protectorates of Northern Rhodesia and Nyasaland into a multiracial federation. When the federation was dissolved at the end of 1963, Northern Rhodesia and Nyasaland became the independent states of Zambia and Malawi.

Britain was prepared to grant independence to Southern Rhodesia but declined to do so when the politically dominant white Rhodesians refused to give assurances of representative government. In November 1965, the white minority government of Southern Rhodesia unilaterally declared Southern Rhodesia an independent dominion. The United Nations and the British Parliament both proclaimed this unilateral declaration of independence null and void. Following a conference in London in December 1979, the opposition government conceded and it was agreed that the British government should resume control. In 1970, the government proclaimed a republic, but this too received no recognition. In 1970, the government purported to change the name of the Colony to Zimbabwe Rhodesia, but again this was never recognized. A British governor soon returned to Southern Rhodesia. One of his first acts was to affirm the nullification of the purported declaration of independence. On April 18, 1980, pursuant to an act of the British Parliament, the colony of Southern Rhodesia became independent within the commonwealth as the Republic of Zimbabwe.

RULERS:

British to 1970 (1980)

MONETARY SYSTEM:

1 Shilling = 12 Pence
1 Pound = 20 Shillings to 1970
1 Dollar = 100 Cents, 1970-80

REPLACEMENT NOTES:

#30-33 later dates, W/1, X/1, Y/1 and Z/1, respectively.

SIGNATURE VARIETIES

	Governor	Term of Office
1	 N.H.B. Bruce	1964 - 1974
2	 Dr. D.C. Krogh	1974 - 1982

British Administration

Reserve Bank of Rhodesia

1964 Issue

Pound System

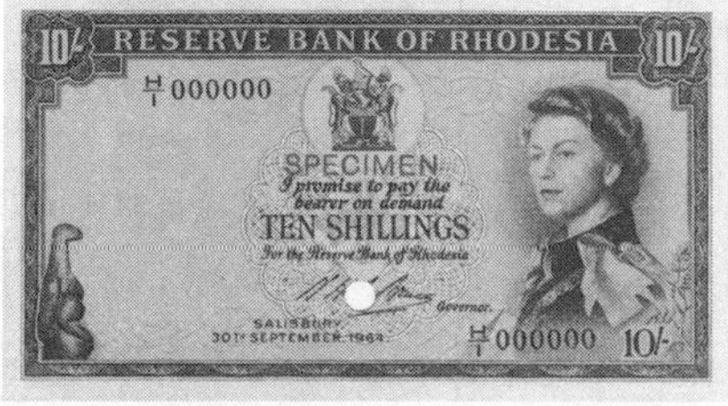

		VF	UNC
24	**10 Shillings**		
	30.9.1964-16.11.1964. Blue on multicolor underprint. Blue portrait of Queen Elizabeth II at right, arms at upper center, black serial number. Signature 1. Back: Tobacco field at left center. Watermark: C. Rhodes. Printer: BWC.		
	a. Issued note.	250.	850.
	ct. Color trial. Brown on multicolor underprint.	—	1100.

		VF	UNC
25	**1 Pound**		
	3.9.1964-16.11.1964. Red on multicolor underprint. Red portrait of Queen Elizabeth II at right, arms at upper center, black serial number. Signature 1. Back: Victoria Falls at left center. Watermark: C. Rhodes. Printer: BWC.		
	a. Issued note.	225.	750.
	ct. Color trial. Green on multicolor underprint.	—	900.

		VF	UNC
26	**5 Pounds**		
	10.11.1964; 12.11.1964; 16.11.1964. Blue-green on multicolor underprint. Blue portrait of Queen Elizabeth II at right, arms at upper center, black serial number. Sable antelope at lower left. Signature 1. Back: Zimbabwe ruins at left center. Watermark: C. Rhodes. Printer: BWC.		
	a. Issued note.	275.	900.
	ct. Color trial. Light blue on multicolor underprint.	—	1250.

1966 Issue

		VF	UNC
27	**10 Shillings**		
	1.6.1966; 10.9.1968. Blue on multicolor underprint. Black portrait of Queen Elizabeth II at right, arms at upper center, Red serial number. Signature 1. Lithographed. Back: Tobacco field at left center. Watermark: C. Rhodes. Printer: Rhodesian (without imprint).		
	a. 1.6.1966.	120.	425.
	b. 10.9.1968.	100.	325.
	s. Specimen.	—	—

		VF	UNC
28	**1 Pound**		
	15.6.1966-14.10.1968. Pale red on multicolor underprint. Brown portrait of Queen Elizabeth II at right, arms at upper center, red serial number. Signature 1. Lithographed. Back: Victoria Falls at left center. Watermark: C. Rhodes. Printer: Rhodesian (without imprint).		
	a. 15.6.1966.	150.	550.
	b. 18.8.1967.	125.	500.
	c. 1.9.1967.	100.	450.
	d. 14.10.1968.	80.00	400.
	s. Specimen.	—	900.

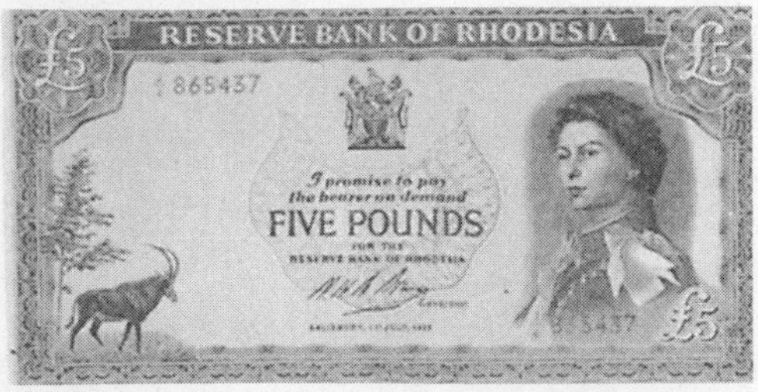

29	5 Pounds	VF	UNC
	1.7.1966. Blue-green on multicolor underprint. Purple portrait of Queen Elizabeth II at right, arms at upper center, red serial number. Sable antelope at lower left. Various dates and signature varieties. Lithographed. Back: Zimbabwe ruins at left center. Watermark: C. Rhodes. Printer: Rhodesian (without imprint).		
	a. 1.7.1966.	285.	1000.
	s. Specimen.	—	—

Republic

Reserve Bank of Rhodesia

1970-75 Issue

Dollar System

#30-33 Replacement notes: Serial # prefixes *W/1, X/1, Y/1, Z/1* respectively.

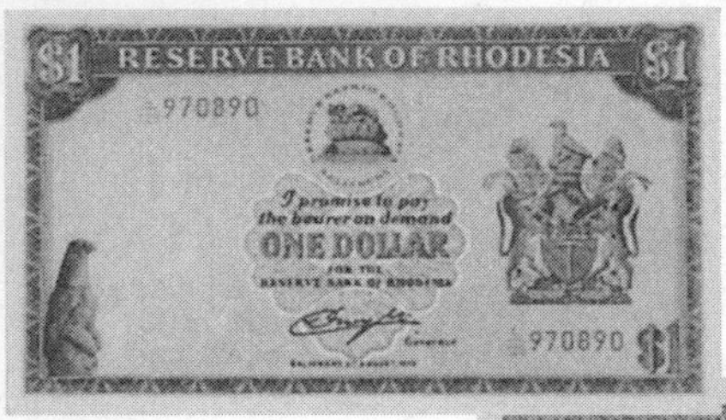

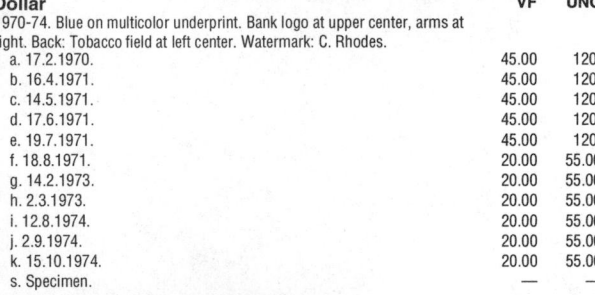

30	1 Dollar	VF	UNC
	1970-74. Blue on multicolor underprint. Bank logo at upper center, arms at right. Back: Tobacco field at left center. Watermark: C. Rhodes.		
	a. 17.2.1970.	45.00	120.
	b. 16.4.1971.	45.00	120.
	c. 14.5.1971.	45.00	120.
	d. 17.6.1971.	45.00	120.
	e. 19.7.1971.	45.00	120.
	f. 18.8.1971.	20.00	55.00
	g. 14.2.1973.	20.00	55.00
	h. 2.3.1973.	20.00	55.00
	i. 12.8.1974.	20.00	55.00
	j. 2.9.1974.	20.00	55.00
	k. 15.10.1974.	20.00	55.00
	s. Specimen.	—	—

31	2 Dollars	VF	UNC
	1970-75. Red on multicolor underprint. Bank logo at upper center, arms at right. Back: Victoria Falls at left center. Watermark: C. Rhodes.		
	a. 17.2.1970.	35.00	100.
	b. 15.8.1970.	35.00	100.
	c. 8.9.1970.	35.00	100.
	d. 10.11.1970.	35.00	100.
	e. 12.11.1971.	35.00	100.
	f. 4.1.1972.	35.00	100.
	g. 29.6.1973.	32.50	90.00
	h. 10.1.1974.	32.50	90.00
	i. 20.1.1975.	32.50	90.00
	j. 4.3.1975.	32.50	90.00
	k. 7.4.1975.	32.50	90.00
	s. As b, d. Specimen.	—	—

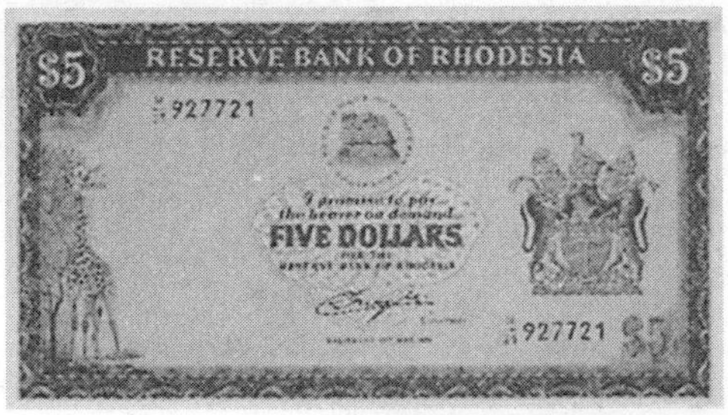

32	5 Dollars	VF	UNC
	16.10.1972. Brown on multicolor underprint. Bank logo at upper center, arms at right. Giraffe at lower left. Back: Two lions. Watermark: C. Rhodes.		
	a. 16.10.1972.	37.50	110.
	s. Specimen.	—	—

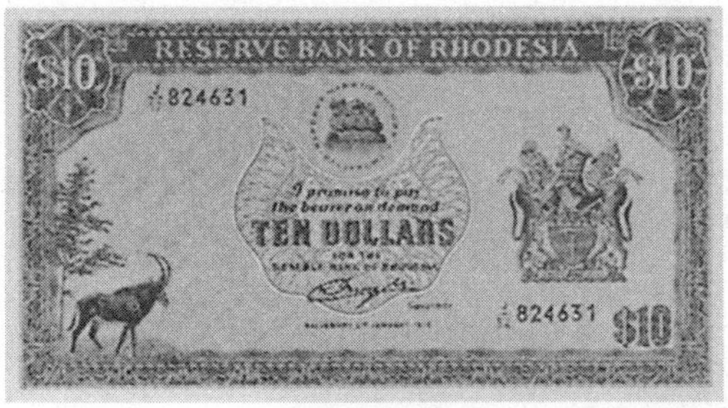

33	10 Dollars	VF	UNC
	1970-75. Black on blue-green and multicolor underprint. Bank logo at upper center, arms at right. Sable antelope at lower left. Back: Zimbabwe ruins at left center. Watermark: C. Rhodes.		
	a. 17.2.1970.	110.	300.
	b. 25.1.1971.	110.	300.
	c. 24.2.1971.	110.	300.
	d. 8.5.1972.	110.	300.
	e. 20.11.1973.	50.00	140.
	f. 15.12.1973.	50.00	140.
	g. 15.9.1975.	50.00	140.
	h. 19.11.1975.	50.00	140.
	i. 3.12.1975.	50.00	140.
	s. Specimen.	—	—

1976-79 Issue

		VF	UNC
34	**1 Dollar**		
	1976-78. Watermark: C. Rhodes.		
	a. 1.3.1976.	20.00	55.00
	b. 1.11.1976.	20.00	55.00
	c. 18.4.1978.	20.00	55.00
35	**2 Dollars**		
	1976-79. Watermark: C. Rhodes.		
	a. 1.3.1976.	32.50	90.00
	b. 15.4.1977.	32.50	90.00
	c. 5.8.1977.	32.50	90.00
	d. 10.4.1979.	200.	500.
36	**5 Dollars**		
	1976-78. Watermark: C. Rhodes.		
	a. 1.3.1976.	35.00	100.
	b. 20.10.1978.	35.00	100.
37	**10 Dollars**		
	1976. Watermark: C. Rhodes.		
	a. 1.3.1976.	50.00	140.

1979 Issue

		VF	UNC
38	**1 Dollar**		
	1.8.1979. Signature 2. Watermark: Zimbabwe bird.		
	a. 1.8.1979.	16.00	45.00
39	**2 Dollars**		
	10.4.1979; 24.5.1979. Signature 2. Watermark: Zimbabwe bird.		
	a. 10.4.1979.	25.00	70.00
	b. 24.5.1979.	25.00	70.00
40	**5 Dollars**		
	15.5.1979. Signature 2. Watermark: Zimbabwe bird.		
	a. 15.5.1979.	32.50	90.00
41	**10 Dollars**		
	2.1.1979. Signature 2. Watermark: Zimbabwe bird.		
	a. 2.1.1979.	45.00	125.

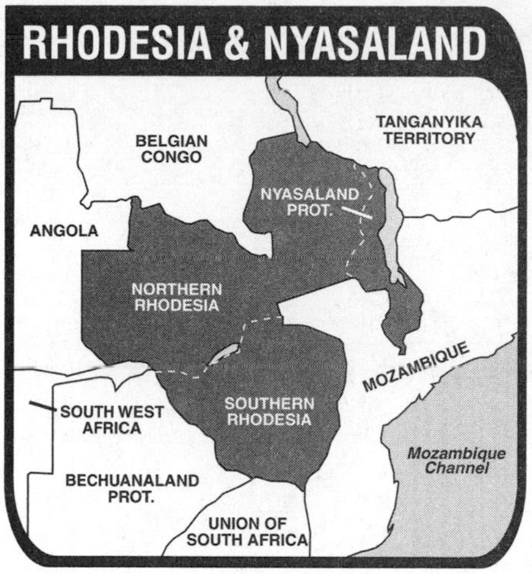

Rhodesia and Nyasaland (now the Republics of Malawi, Zambia and Zimbabwe) was located in the east-central part of southern Africa, had an area of 487,133 sq. mi. (1,261,678 sq. km.). Capital: Salisbury. The area was the habitat of paleolithic man, contains extensive evidence of earlier civilizations, notably the world-famous ruins of Zimbabwe, a gold-trading center that flourished about the 14th or 15th century AD. The Portuguese of the 16th century were the first Europeans to attempt to develop south-central Africa, but it remained for Cecil Rhodes and the British South Africa Co. to open the hinterlands. Rhodes obtained a concession for mineral rights from local chiefs in 1888 and administered his African empire (named Southern Rhodesia in 1895) through the British South Africa Co. until 1923, when the British government annexed the area after the white settlers voted for existence as a separate entity, rather than for incorporation into the Union of South Africa. From Sept. of 1953 through 1963 Southern Rhodesia was joined with the British protectorates of Northern Rhodesia and Nyasaland into a multiracial federation. When the federation was dissolved at the end of 1963, Northern Rhodesia and Nyasaland became the independent states of Zambia and Malawi.

RULERS:

British to 1963

MONETARY SYSTEM:

1 Shilling = 12 Pence
1 Pound = 20 Shillings to 1963

British Administration

Bank of Rhodesia and Nyasaland

1956 Issue

		VF	UNC
20	**10 Shillings**		
	1956-61. Reddish brown on multicolor underprint. Fish eagle at lower left. Portrait of Queen Elizabeth II at right. Back: River scene. Watermark: Cecil Rhodes. Printer: BWC.		
	a. Signature A. P. Grafftey-Smith. 3.4.1956-17.6.1960.	550.	2300.
	b. Signature B. C. J. Richards. 30.12.1960-1.2.1961.	600.	2400.
	s. As a. Specimen punch hole cancelled. 3.4.1956.	—	1600.
	ct. Color trial. Green on pink underprint.	—	2150.

		VF	UNC
21	**1 Pound**		
	1956-61. Green on multicolor underprint. Leopard at lower left. Portrait of Queen Elizabeth II at right. Back: Zimbabwe ruins at center. Watermark: Cecil Rhodes. Printer: BWC.		
	a. Signature A. P. Grafftey-Smith. 3.4.1956-17.6.1960.	575.	2400.
	b. Signature B. C. J. Richards. 28.11.1960-1.2.1961.	625.	2500.
	s. As a. Specimen punch hole cancelled. 2.5.1956.	—	1750.
	ct. Color trial. Blue on orange underprint.	—	2250.

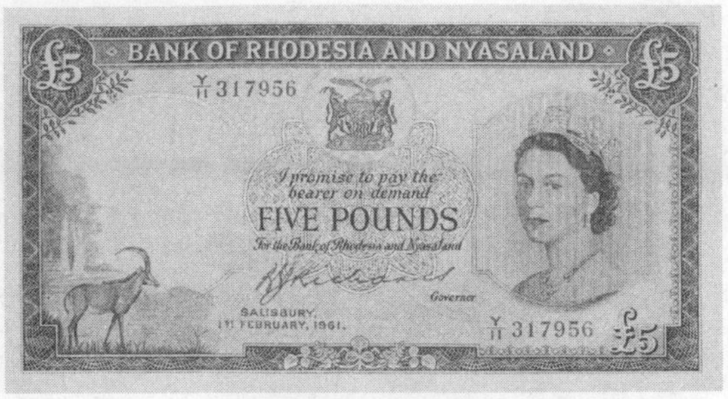

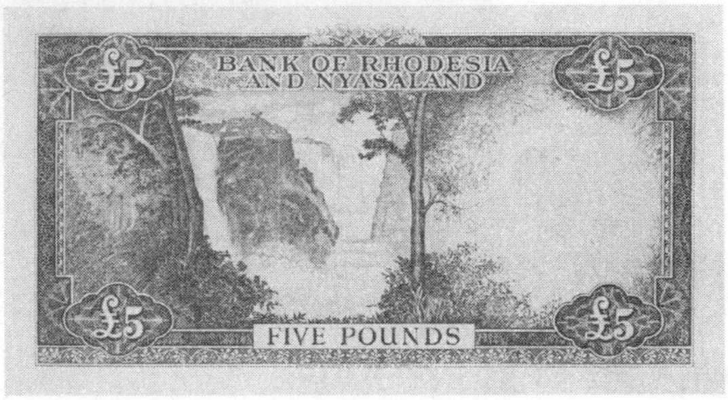

		VF	UNC
22	**5 Pounds**		
	1956-61. Blue on multicolor underprint. Sable antelope at lower left. Portrait of Queen Elizabeth II at right. Back: Victoria Falls. Watermark: Cecil Rhodes. Printer: BWC.		
	a. Signature A. P. Grafftey-Smith. 3.4.1956-17.6.1960.	1200.	3600.
	b. Signature B. C. J. Richards. 23.1.1961-3.2.1961.	1300.	4000.
	s. As a. Specimen punch hole cancelled. 3.4.1956.	—	2500.
	ct. Color trial. Red-brown on blue underprint.	—	3000.

		VF	UNC
23	**10 Pounds**		
	1956-61. Brown on multicolor underprint. Portrait of Queen Elizabeth II at right. Back: Gray-green. Elephants at center. Watermark: Cecil Rhodes. Printer: BWC.		
	a. Signature A. P. Grafftey-Smith. 3.4.1956-17.6.1960.	3000.	—
	b. Signature B. C. J. Richards. 1.2.1961; 3.1.1961.	3500.	—
	s. As a. Specimen punch hole cancelled. 3.4.1956.	—	4500.
	ct. Color trial. Green on multicolor underprint.	—	5000.

ROMANIA

Romania, located in southeast Europe, has an area of 91,699 sq. mi. (237,500 sq. km.) and a population of 22.5 million. Capital: Bucharest. Machinery, foodstuffs, raw minerals and petroleum products are exported.

The principalities of Wallachia and Moldavia - for centuries under the suzerainty of the Turkish Ottoman Empire - secured their autonomy in 1856; they united in 1859 and a few years later adopted the new name of Romania. The country gained recognition of its independence in 1878. It joined the Allied Powers in World War I and acquired new territories - most notably Transylvania - following the conflict. In 1940, Romania allied with the Axis powers and participated in the 1941 German invasion of the USSR. Three years later, overrun by the Soviets, Romania signed an armistice. The post-war Soviet occupation led to the formation of a Communist "people's republic" in 1947 and the abdication of the king. The decades-long rule of dictator Nicolae Ceausescu, who took power in 1965, and his Securitate police state became increasingly oppressive and draconian through the 1980s. Ceausescu was overthrown and executed in late 1989. Former Communists dominated the government until 1996 when they were swept from power. Romania joined NATO in 2004 and the EU in 2007.

MONETARY SYSTEM:

10,000 "old" Lei = 1 "new" Leu, 1.7.2005
1 Leu = 100 Bani

SOCIALIST REPUBLIC

BANCA NATIONALA A REPUBLICII SOCIALISTE ROMÂNIA

1966 ISSUE

		VF	UNC
91	**1 Leu**		
	1966. Olive-brown and tan. Arms at center. Back: Value at center. Watermark: Rhombuses.		
	a. Issued note.	2.00	5.00
	s. Specimen.	—	12.50

		VF	UNC
92	**3 Lei**		
	1966. Blue on orange and multicolor underprint. Arms at center. Back: Value at center. Watermark: Rhombuses.		
	a. Issued note.	5.00	85.00
	s. Specimen.	—	12.50

		VF	UNC
93	**5 Lei**		
	1966. Brown and dark blue on multicolor underprint. Arms at center. Back: Cargo ships at dockside. Watermark: Rhombuses.		
	a. Issued note.	1.50	4.50
	s. Specimen.	—	12.50

94 10 Lei — VF — UNC

1966. Purple on multicolor underprint. Arms at center. Back: Harvest scene. Watermark: Rhombuses.

	VF	UNC
a. Issued note.	2.50	6.00
s. Specimen.	—	12.50

95 25 Lei — VF — UNC

1966. Dark green on multicolor underprint. Portrait of Tudor Vladimirescu at left. Arms at center right. Back: Large refinery. Watermark: Rhombuses.

	VF	UNC
a. Issued note.	3.00	7.50
s. Specimen.	—	17.50

96 50 Lei — VF — UNC

1966. Dark green on multicolor underprint. Portrait of Alexandru Ioan Cuza at left. Arms at center right. Back: Culture Palace in Iasi at center right. Watermark: Rhombuses.

	VF	UNC
a. Issued note.	5.00	15.00
s. Specimen.	—	17.50

97 100 Lei — VF — UNC

1966. Dark blue and purple on multicolor underprint. Portrait of Nicolae Balcescu at left. Arms at center right. Back: The Athenaeum in Bucharest at center right. Watermark: Rhombuses.

	VF	UNC
a. Issued note.	3.00	12.00
s. Specimen.	—	20.00

Republic

Banca Nationala a României

1991 Issue

98 500 Lei — VF — UNC

1991. Dark brown on multicolor underprint. Constantin Brâncusi at right. Signature Isarescu. Back: Brâncusi seated with statue at left center. Watermark: Constantin Brâncusi.

	VF	UNC
a. Jan. 1991.	8.00	23.00
b. April 1991.	3.00	10.00
x. As b, with *APRILIED* (error). Requires confirmation.	—	—

1991-94 Issue

100 200 Lei — VF — UNC

Dec. 1992. Dull deep brown and brown-violet on multicolor underprint. Square-topped shield at left center, steamboat *Tudor Vladimirescu* above grey heron and Sulina Lighthouse in underprint at center, Grigore Antipa at right. Back: Herons, fish, and net on outline of Danube Delta at left center. Watermark: Bank monogram repeated.

	VF	UNC
a. Issued note.	1.00	4.00
s. Specimen.	—	50.00

101 500 Lei — VF — UNC

Dec. 1992. Dull deep green, reddish brown and violet on multicolor underprint. Square topped shield at left center, sculptures at center, Constantin Brâncusi at right. Back: Sculptures at left center. Watermark: C. Brâncusi.

	VF	UNC
a. Watermark: C. Brâncusi facing as #98.	4.00	12.50
b. Watermark: C. Brâncusi right.	1.25	3.50

101A 1000 Lei — VF / UNC

Sept. 1991. Red-brown, blue-green and brown-orange on multicolor underprint. Circular shield at left center, sails of sailing ships at lower center, Mihai Eminescu at right. Signature: Isarescu and Florescu. Back: Putna monastery at left center. Watermark: Mihai Eminescu.

- a. Issued note. — 4.50 / 17.50
- s. Specimen. Serial # prefix as: A.001 or A001. — — / 50.00

102 1000 Lei

May 1993. Dull deep green, reddish brown and violet on multicolor underprint. Square topped shield at left center, sculptures at center, Constantin Brâncusi at right. Back: Sculptures at left center. Watermark: Bust right. — 2.00 / 5.00

103 5000 Lei — VF / UNC

March 1992. Pale purple on multicolor underprint. Round seal at left center, church at center, Avram Iancu at right. Back: Church at left, the gate of Alba Iulia stronghold at left center, seal at center right. Watermark: Avram Iancu.

- a. Issued note. — 5.00 / 20.00
- s. Specimen. — — / 50.00

104 5000 Lei — VF / UNC

May 1993. Pale purple on multicolor underprint. Square-topped shield at left center, church at center, Avram Iancu at right. Back: Church at left, the gate of Alba Iulia stronghold at left center, seal at center right. Watermark: Avram Iancu.

- a. Issued note. — 2.00 / 7.50
- s. Specimen. — — / 50.00

105 10,000 Lei — VF / UNC

Feb. 1994. Dull violet and reddish brown on multicolor underprint. Nicolae Iorga at right, snake god Glycon at center. Back: Statue of Fortuna at left, historical Museum in Bucharest at center, The Thinking Man of Hamangia at Watermark: Nicolae Iorga.

- a. Issued note. — 3.00 / 12.50
- s. Specimen. — — / 50.00

1996-2000 Paper Issue

106 1000 Lei — VF / UNC

1998. Blue-violet, dark green and olive-brown on multicolor underprint. Mihai Eminescu at right, lily flower and quill pen at center. Arms at top left, bank monogram at top right. Back: Lime and blue flowers at left center, ruins of ancient fort of Histria at center, bank monogram at t Watermark: Mihai Eminescu. UV: security strip fluoresces blue. Back value 1000 in box yellow. — 1.00 / 2.50

107 5000 Lei — VF / UNC

1998. Violet, dark brown and brown-orange on multicolor underprint. Lucian Blaga at right, daffodil at center. Arms at top left, bank monogram at upper center right. Back: Vine leaf at left center, roadside crucifix at center, bank monogram at top right. Watermark: Lucian Blaga.

- a. Issued note. BNR watermark vertical only. — 1.50 / 3.75
- b. Issueed note. BNR watermark vertical and partially horizontal. — — / 15.00
- s. Specimen. — — / 50.00

108 10,000 Lei — VF / UNC

1999. Green-yellow and blue on multicolor underprint. Nicolae Iorga at right, gentian flower at center. Arms at top left, bank monogram at upper center right. Back: The church of Curtea de Arges monastery at center, Wallachian arms of Prince Brancoveanu at left. Watermark: Nicolae Iorga.

- a. Issued note. BNR watermark vertical only. — 2.25 / 7.50
- b. Issued note. BNR watermark vertical and partially horizontal. — — / 15.00
- s. Specimen. — — / 50.00

109 50,000 Lei VF UNC

1996. Purple and red-violet on lilac and multicolor underprint. George Enescu at right, floral ornament, musical notes at center, arms at upper left. Bank monogram at upper center right. Back: Sphinx of Carpathian mountains at left center, musical chord from *Oedip King* above, bank monogram at top right. Watermark: George Enescu.

	VF	UNC
a. Issued note.	5.00	25.00
s. Specimen.	—	50.00

109A 50,000 Lei VF UNC

2000. Purple and red-violet on lilac and multicolor underprint. Like #109 but violin shaped bronze area near portrait, and changed underprint design. Back. Sphinx of Carpathian mountains at left center, musical chord from *Oedip King* above, bank mon Watermark: George Enescu.

	VF	UNC
a. Issued note.	3.00	12.00
s. Specimen.	—	50.00

110 100,000 Lei VF 6.00 UNC 24.00

1998. Dull red on olive-green and multicolor underprint. Nicolae Grigorescu at right, mallow flowers and artist's brush at center. Arms at top left, bank monogram at upper center right. Back: Peasant girl with ewe at left, cottage at center, bank monogram at top right. Watermark: Nicolae Grigorescu.

1999 Commemorative Issue

#111, Total Solar Eclipse, August 11, 1999

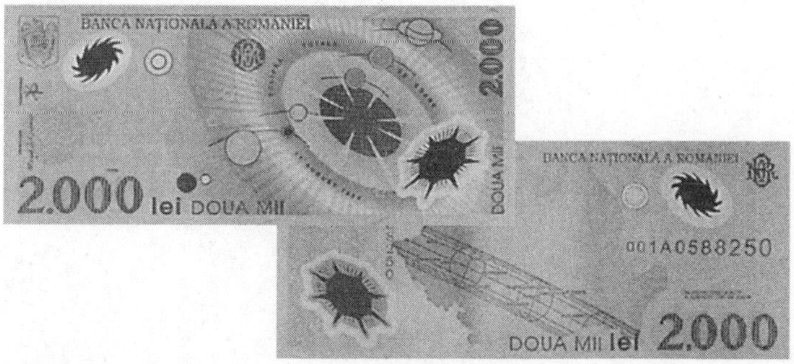

111 2000 Lei VF UNC

1999. Blue on multicolor underprint. Imaginative reproduction of the Solar System at right, with mention of the ecilpse. Back: The map of Romania having the colors of the national flag, (blue, yellow, red) marking the route of the solar eclipse where it was total at center. Polymer plastic. UV: value in box fluoresce green, vertical serial # blue, horizontal serial # red with blue frame. The clear window is a latent hologram, shine a lazer pointer thru it and view a solar eclipse on a sheet of paper or a wall.

	VF	UNC
a. Issued note.	.75	3.00
b. Serial # prefix 001A in folder. (One million pieces.)	—	12.00
s. As a. Specimen.	—	50.00

2000-01 Polymer Issue

112 10,000 Lei VF UNC

2000. Green and blue on multicolor underprint. Nicolae Igora at right, gentian flower at center. Signature Ghizari; Nitu. Back: The church of Curtea de Arges monastery at center. Wallachian arms of Prince Brancoveanu at left. Watermark: George Enescu. Polymer plastic. UV: value 10000 fluoresce yellow.

	VF	UNC
a. Issued note.	1.00	5.00
b. Uncut sheet of 4 (5000 sheets).	—	17.50
s. Specimen.	—	50.00

113 50,000 Lei VF UNC

2001. Purple and red-violet on lilac and multicolor underprint. George Enescu at right, floral ornament, musical notes at center, arms at upper left. Bank monogram at upper center right. Back: Rumanian Athenaeum and piano at left center. Watermark: George Enescu. Polymer plastic.

	VF	UNC
a. Issued note.	3.50	9.00
b. Uncut sheet of 4 (500 sheets).	—	60.00
s. Specimen.	—	50.00

114 100,000 Lei VF UNC

2001. Dull red on olive-green and multicolor underprint. Nicolae Grigorescu at right, mallow flowers and artist's brush at center. Arms at top left, bank monogram at upper center right. Signature Isarescu; Nitu. Back: Peasant girl with ewe at left, cottage at center, bank monogram at top right. Watermark: Nicolae Grigorescu. Polymer plastic.

	VF	UNC
a. Issued note.	6.00	10.00
s. Specimen.	—	50.00

115 500,000 Lei VF UNC

2000. Brown on yellow and multicolor underprint. Aurel Vlaicu at right, edelweiss flower at center. Back: Imperial Eagle head at center, *Vlaicu II* plane and *Gnome* engine sketch at left center. Polymer plastic.

	VF	UNC
a. Issued note.	30.00	45.00
b. Uncut sheet of 4 (2000 sheets).	—	150.
s. Issued note.	—	100.

116 1,000,000 Lei VF UNC

2003. Blue, green, violet and yellow. Luca Caragiale at right. Back: Statue and building.

	VF	UNC
a. Issued note.	50.00	80.00
s. Specimen.	—	100.

2005 Revaluation Issue

117 1 Leu VF UNC

1.7.2005; (20)11; (20)12. Green and blue on multicolor underprint. Nicolae Iorga at right, gentain flower at center. Back: Church of Curtea de Arges monastery at center. 120x62mm.

	VF	UNC
a. 1.7.2005.	FV	1.25
b. (20)11.	FV	1.25
c. (20)12.	FV	1.25
d. (20)13.	FV	1.25

118 5 Lei VF UNC

1.7.2005; (20)11. Violet and purple on blue and multicolor underprint. George Enescu at right. Back: Romanian Athenaeum and piano. Polymer plastic. 127x67mm.

	VF	UNC
a. 1.7.2005.	FV	3.75
b. (20)11.	FV	3.75

119 10 Lei VF UNC

1.7.2005; 1.12.2008; (20)11; (20)12. Blue and yellow on rose and multicolor underprint. Nicolae Grigorescu at right, paintbrush and flower at center. Artist palate in window. Back: Female with canister on shoulder, house at center. Polymer plastic. 133x72mm.

	VF	UNC
a. 1.7.2005.	FV	7.00
b. 1.12.2008.	FV	6.00
c. (20)11.	FV	5.00
d. (20)12.	FV	5.00

120 50 Lei VF UNC

1.7.2005. Yellow, light green, light blue and orange. Aurel Vlaicu at right. Back: Eagle and airplane. Polymer plastic. 140x77mm. FV 30.00

121 100 Lei VF UNC
1.7.2005. Blue, green, violet and yellow. Luca Caragiale at right. Back: Old national Theatre in Bucharest, statue of Caragiale at left. Polymer plastic. 147x82mm. FV 55.00

122 200 Lei VF UNC
1.12.2006; (20)09. Brown, tan and multicolor. Lucian Blaga at right. Back: Neolithic statues. Polymer plastic. 150x82mm.
a. 1.12.2006. FV 105.
b. (20)09. FV 105.

123 500 Lei VF UNC
1.7.2005 Blue, violet, green and multicolor. Mihai Eminescu at right. Back: Lasi University Library and page from Timpul. Polymer plastic. 153x82mm. FV 250.

RUSSIA

Russia, (formerly the central power of the Union of Soviet Socialist Republics and now of the Commonwealth of Independent States) occupying the northern part of Asia and the far eastern part of Europe, has an area of 17,075,200 sq. km. and a population of 140.7 million. Capital: Moscow. Exports include machinery, iron and steel, oil, timber and nonferrous metals.

Founded in the 12th century, the Principality of Muscovy, was able to emerge from over 200 years of Mongol domination (13th-15th centuries) and to gradually conquer and absorb surrounding principalities. In the early 17th century, a new Romanov Dynasty continued this policy of expansion across Siberia to the Pacific. Under Peter I (ruled 1682-1725), hegemony was extended to the Baltic Sea and the country was renamed the Russian Empire. During the 19th century, more territorial acquisitions were made in Europe and Asia. Defeat in the Russo-Japanese War of 1904-05 contributed to the Revolution of 1905, which resulted in the formation of a parliament and other reforms. Repeated devastating defeats of the Russian army in World War I led to widespread rioting in the major cities of the Russian Empire and to the overthrow in 1917 of the imperial household. The Communists under Vladimir Lenin seized power soon after and formed the USSR. The brutal rule of Iosif STALIN (1928-53) strengthened Communist rule and Russian dominance of the Soviet Union at a cost of tens of millions of lives. The Soviet economy and society stagnated in the following decades until General Secretary Mikhail Gorbachev (1985-91) introduced glasnost (openness) and perestroika (restructuring) in an attempt to modernize Communism, but his initiatives inadvertently released forces that by December 1991 splintered the USSR into Russia and 14 other independent republics. Since then, Russia has shifted its post-Soviet democratic ambitions in favor of a centralized semi-authoritarian state whose legitimacy is buttressed, in part, by carefully managed national elections, former President Putin's genuine popularity, and the prudent management of Russia's windfall energy wealth. Russia has severely disabled a Chechen rebel movement, although violence still occurs throughout the North Caucasus.

RULERS:

Catherine II (the Great), 1762-1796
Paul I, 1796-1801
Alexander I, 1801-1825
Nicholas I, 1825-1855
Alexander II, 1855-1881
Alexander III, 1881-1894
Nicholas II, 1894-1917

MONETARY SYSTEM:

1 Ruble = 100 Kopeks, until 1997
1 Chervonetz = 10 Gold Rubles
1 Ruble = 1000 "old" Rubles, 1998- (Some other areas where notes are listed in this volume had local currencies.)

А	а	А	а	A	С	с	С	с	S
Б	б	Б	б	B	Т	т	Т	т	T
В	в	В	в	V	У	у	У	у	U
Г	г	Г	г	G	Ф	ф	Ф	ф	F
Д	д	Д	д	D	Х	х	Х	х	Kh
Е	е	Е	е	ye	Ц	ц	Ц	ц	C
Ё	ё	Ё	ё	yo	Ч	ч	Ч	ч	ch
Ж	ж	Ж	ж	zh	Ш	ш	Ш	ш	sh
З	з	З	з	Z	Щ	щ	Щ	щ	shch
И	и	И	и	I	Ъ*)	ъ*)	—	ъ	'
Й	й	Й	й	J	Ы	ы	—	ы	
К	к	К	к	K	Ь**)	ь**)	—	ь	'
Л	л	Л	л	L	Э		Э	—	E
М	м	М	м	M	Ю	ю	Ю	ю	yu
Н	н	Н	н	N	Я	я	Я	я	ya
О	о	О	о	O	І	і	І	і	I
П	п	П	п	P	Ѣ	ѣ	Ѣ	ѣ	ye
Р	р	Р	р	R					

*) "hard", and **) "soft" signs; both soundless. I and Ѣ were dropped in 1918.

U.S.S.R. - Union of Soviet Socialist Republics

ГОСУДАРСТВЕННЫЙ КАЗНАЧЕЙСКИЙ БИЛЕТ

State Treasury Note

1961 Issue

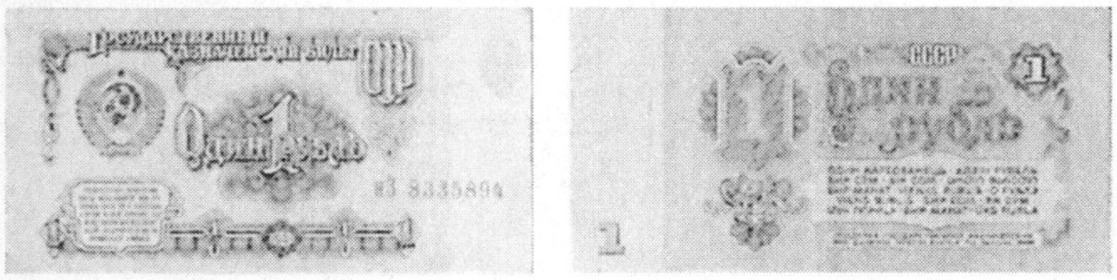

222 1 Ruble VF UNC

1961. Brown on pale green underprint. Arms at upper left. Back: Red on multicolor underprint. Watermark: Stars. 104x54mm.

	VF	UNC
a. Issued note.	.50	2.00
s. Specimen.	—	150.

223 3 Rubles

1961. Dark green on multicolor underprint. View of Kremlin at center. Arms at upper left. Back: Light blue on green and multicolor underprint. Watermark: Stars. 113x53mm.

	VF	UNC
a. Issued note.	1.00	3.00
s. Specimen.	—	150.

224 5 Rubles

1961. Blue on peach underprint. Kremlin Spasski tower at left. Arms at upper left. Back: Blue on multicolor underprint. Watermark: Stars.

	VF	UNC
a. Issued note.	2.00	5.00
s. Specimen.	—	150.

БИЛЕТ ГОСУДАРСТВЕННОГО БАНКА С.С.С.Р.

State Bank Note U.S.S.R.

1961 Issue

233 10 Rubles

1961. Red-brown on pale gold underprint. Arms at upper left, portrait of V. I. Lenin at right. Watermark: Stars. 121x62mm.

	VF	UNC
a. Issued note.	1.00	3.00
s. Specimen.	—	150.

234 25 Rubles

1961. Purple on pale light green underprint. Portrait of V. I. Lenin at upper left, arms at upper center. Watermark: Stars.

	VF	UNC
a. Lilac tinted paper. 124 x 61mm.	15.00	30.00
b. White paper. 121 x 62mm.	2.00	4.00
s. Specimen.	—	150.

235 50 Rubles

1961. Dark green and green on green and pink underprint. Portrait of V. I. Lenin at upper left, arms at upper center. Back: Kremlin at upper center. 140x70mm.

	VF	UNC
a. Issued note.	7.00	18.00
s. Specimen.	—	150.

236 100 Rubles

1961. Brown on light blue underprint. Portrait of V. I. Lenin at upper left, arms at upper center. Back: Kremlin tower at center with date. Watermark: V. I. Lenin. 140x70mm.

	VF	UNC
a. Issued note.	7.00	15.00
s. Specimen.	—	150.

1991 Issue

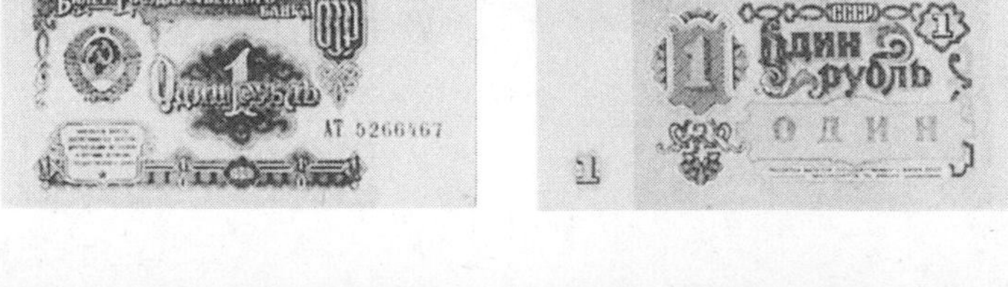

237	1 Ruble	VF	UNC
	1991. Dark green and red-brown on tan underprint. Arms at upper left. Back: Red on multicolor underprint. Watermark: Star in circle repeated. 104x54mm.		
	a. Issued note.	.50	2.00
	s. Specimen.	—	150.

238	3 Rubles	VF	UNC
	1991. Green on blue and multicolor underprint. View of Kremlin at center. Arms at upper left. Back: Light blue on green and multicolor underprint. Watermark: Star in circle repeated. 113x57mm.		
	a. Issued note.	.50	3.00
	s. Specimen.	—	150.

239	5 Rubles	VF	UNC
	1991. Blue-gray on light blue, pale green and pink underprint. Kremlin Spasski tower at left. Arms at upper left. Back. Blue on multicolor underprint. Watermark: Star in circle repeated. 113x57mm.		
	a. Issued note.	.50	2.00
	s. Specimen.	—	150.

240	10 Rubles	VF	UNC
	1991. Red-brown and green on multicolor underprint. Arms at upper left, portrait of V. I. Lenin at right. Watermark: Stars. 124x62mm.		
	a. Issued note.	1.00	3.00
	s. Specimen.	—	150.

241	50 Rubles	VF	UNC
	1991. Dark brown, green and red on multicolor underprint. Portrait of V. I. Lenin at upper left, arms at upper center. Back: Kremlin at upper center. Watermark: V. I. Lenin. 145x70mm.		
	a. Issued note.	2.00	12.00
	s. Specimen.	—	150.

242	100 Rubles	VF	UNC
	1991. Deep red-brown and blue on multicolor underprint. Portrait of V. I. Lenin at upper left, arms at upper center. Date at right. Back: Kremlin tower at center with date. Watermark: V. I. Lenin. 145x70mm.		
	a. Issued note.	2.00	15.00
	s. Specimen.	—	150.

243	100 Rubles	VF	UNC
	1991. Deep red-brown and blue on multicolor underprint. Portrait of V. I. Lenin at upper left, arms at upper center. Pink and green guilloche at right in watermark area. Date at right. Back: Kremlin tower at center with date. Blue guilloche added at upper left. Watermark: Stars.		
	a. Issued note.	2.00	10.00
	s. Specimen.	—	150.

244	200 Rubles	VF	UNC
	1991. Green and brown on multicolor underprint. Portrait of V. I. Lenin at upper left, arms at upper center. Back: View of Kremlin. Watermark: V. I. Lenin. 145x70mm.		
	a. Issued note.	10.00	40.00
	s. Specimen.	—	150.

245 **500 Rubles** VF UNC
1991. Red and green on multicolor underprint. Portrait of V. I. Lenin at upper left, arms at upper center. Back: View of Kremlin. Watermark: V. I. Lenin. 145x70mm.

	VF	UNC
a. Issued note.	20.00	55.00
s. Specimen.	—	150.

246 **1000 Rubles** VF UNC
1991. Brown and blue on green and multicolor underprint. Portrait of V. I. Lenin at upper left, arms at upper center. Back: View of Kremlin. Watermark: V. I. Lenin. 145x70mm.

	VF	UNC
a. Issued note.	20.00	60.00
s. Specimen.	—	150.

Russian Federation

РОССИЙСКАЯ ФЕДЕРАЦИЯ

Russian Federation

1992 Issue

247 **50 Rubles** VF UNC
1992. Brown and gray on green and multicolor underprint. Portrait of V. I. Lenin at upper left, arms at upper center. Back: Kremlin at upper center. Watermark: Star in circle repeated.

	VF	UNC
a. Issued note.	2.00	4.00
s. Specimen.	—	150.

248 **200 Rubles** VF UNC
1992. Green and brown on multicolor underprint. Portrait of V. I. Lenin at upper left, arms at upper center. Back: View of Kremlin with guilloche in watermark area. Watermark: Star in circle repeated.

	VF	UNC
a. Issued note.	2.00	5.00
s. Specimen.	—	150.

249 **500 Rubles** VF UNC
1992. Red, violet and dark green on multicolor underprint. Portrait of V. I. Lenin at upper left, arms at upper center. Back: View of Kremlin with guilloche in watermark area. Watermark: Stars.

	VF	UNC
a. Issued note.	2.00	6.00
s. Specimen.	—	150.

250 **1000 Rubles** VF UNC
1992. Dark brown and deep green on multicolor underprint. Portrait of V. I. Lenin at upper left, arms at upper center. Back: View of Kremlin with guilloche in watermark area. Watermark: Stars.

	VF	UNC
a. Issued note.	2.00	5.00
s. Specimen.	—	150.

1992 Government Privatization Check Issue

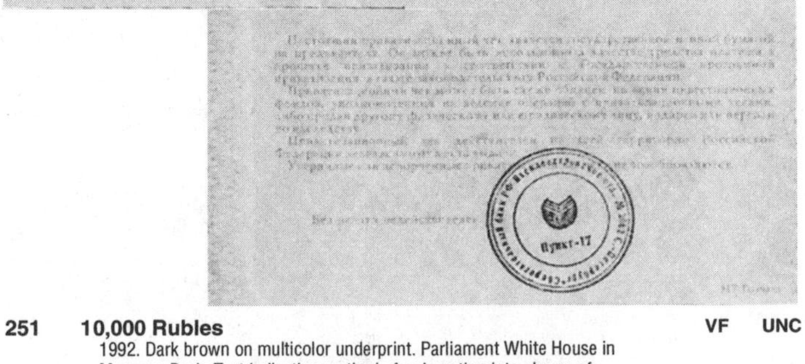

251 **10,000 Rubles** VF UNC
1992. Dark brown on multicolor underprint. Parliament White House in Moscow. Back: Text indicating method of redemption into shares of government-owned property. Handstamp from bank added at bottom. Valid until Dec. 31, 1993.

	VF	UNC
a. Issued note.	20.00	50.00
s. Specimen.	—	150.

БАНК РОССИИ

Bank of Russia

1992 Issue

252	**5000 Rubles**	**VF**	**UNC**
	1992. Blue and maroon on multicolor underprint. St. Basil's Cathedral at left. Signature Georgui Matiukhin. Back: Kremlin. Watermark: Stars. 145x79mm.		
	a. Issued note.	1.00	4.00
	s. Specimen.	—	150.

253	**10,000 Rubles**	**VF**	**UNC**
	1992. Brown, black and red on multicolor underprint. Kremlin with new tricolor flag at left center. Back: Kremlin towers at center right. Watermark: Kremlin with new tricolor flag. 145x79mm.		
	a. Issued note.	1.00	4.00
	s. Specimen.	—	150.

1993 Issue

254	**100 Rubles**	**VF**	**UNC**
	1993. Blue-black on pink and light blue underprint. Tricolor flag over stylized Kremlin at left, monogram at upper right. Back: Kremlin, Spasski Tower at center right. Watermark: Stars within wavy lines repeated. 130x53mm.	.50	2.00

255	**200 Rubles**	**VF**	**UNC**
	1993. Brown on pink and multicolor underprint. Tricolor flag over stylized Kremlin at left, monogram at upper right. Back: Kremlin gate at center. Watermark: Stars within wavy lines repeated. UV: fibers fluoresce yellow and red. 130x53mm.	.50	3.00

256	**500 Rubles**	**VF**	**UNC**
	1993. Green, blue and purple on multicolor underprint. Tricolor flag over stylized Kremlin at left, monogram at upper right. Back: Kremlin at left center. Watermark: Stars within wavy lines repeated. 130x53mm.	1.00	2.00

257	**1000 Rubles**	**VF**	**UNC**
	1993. Green, olive-green and brown on multicolor underprint. Tricolor flag over stylized Kremlin at left, monogram at upper right. Back: Kremlin at center. Watermark: Stars. 151x68mm.	1.00	8.00

258	**5000 Rubles**	**VF**	**UNC**
	1993; 1993/94. Blue, brown and violet on multicolor underprint. Tricolor flag over house of Government in the Kremlin at left, monogram at upper center. Back: Kremlin at center. Watermark: Flag over House of Goverment. 152x68mm.		
	a. 1993.	5.00	25.00
	b. 1993//94.	5.00	20.00

259	**10,000 Rubles**	**VF**	**UNC**
	1993; 1993//94. Violet, greenish blue, brownish purple and multicolor. Tricolor flag over house of Goverment in the Kremlin at left, monogram at upper right. Back: Kremlin at center right. Watermark: Flag over house of Goverment. 152x68mm.		
	a. 1993.	10.00	30.00
	b. 1993//94.	12.00	35.00

260 **50,000 Rubles** | VF | UNC

1993; 1993//94. Olive-green, black and reddish brown on multicolor underprint. Tricolor flag over house of Government in the Kremlin at left, monogram at upper right. Back: Kremlin at center right. Watermark: Flag over house of Goverment. 152x68mm.

	VF	UNC
a. 1993.	15.00	120.
b. 1993//94.	15.00	100.

1995 Issue

261 **1000 Rubles** | VF | UNC

1995. Dark brown and brown on multicolor underprint. Seaport of Vladivostok at left center, memorial column at center right. Back: Entrance to Vladivostok Bay at center. Watermark: *1000* and memorial column. | 1.00 | 6.00

262 **5000 Rubles** | VF | UNC

1995. Deep blue-green and dark olive-green on multicolor underprint. Monument of the Russian Millennium in Novgorod at left center. Cathedral of St. Sophia at center. Back: Old towered city wall of Novgorod at upper left center. Watermark: Cathedral of St. Sophia. 137x60mm. | 2.00 | 15.00

263 **10,000 Rubles** | VF | UNC

1995. Dark brown and dark gray on multicolor underprint. Arch bridge over Yenisei River in Krasnoyarsk at left center, steeple at center right. Back: Hydroelectric dam at Krasnoyarsk at center. Watermark: Steeple. 150x65mm. | 3.00 | 20.00

264 **50,000 Rubles** | VF | UNC

1995. Dark brown, grayish purple and black on multicolor underprint. Personification of river Neva on foot of Rostral Column, Peter and Paul Fortress in St. Petersburg. Back: Rostral Column and Naval Museum at upper left center. Watermark: Building with steeple. 150x65mm. | 10.00 | 50.00

265 **100,000 Rubles** | VF | UNC

1995. Purple and brown on multicolor underprint. Apollo and chariot freize on Bolshoi (Great) Theatre in Moscow at center. Back: Bolshoi Theatre. Watermark: Building over value. 150x65mm. | 20.00 | 70.00

266 **500,000 Rubles** | VF | UNC

1995 (1997). Brown-violet on multicolor underprint. Statue of Peter the Great, sailing ship dockside in port of Arkhangelsk at center. Back: Monastery in Solovetsky Island. 150x65mm. | 100. | 250.

1997 (1998) "New Ruble" Issue

1 Ruble = 1000 "old" Rubles

267 **5 Rubles** | VF | UNC

1997 (1998). Deep blue-green and dark olive-green on multicolor underprint. Monument of the Russian Millennium in Novgorod at left center. Cathedral of St. Sophia at center. Back: Old towered city wall in Novgorod at upper left center. Watermark: Cathedral of St. Sophia. 138x60mm. | FV | 3.00

268 10 Rubles VF UNC

1997 (1998); 2001; 2004. Dark brown and dark gray on multicolor underprint. Arch bridge over Yenisei River in Krasnoyarsk at left center, steeple at center right. Back: Hydroelectric dam in Krasnoyarsk at center. Watermark: Steeple. UV: fibers fluoresce red and yellow. 150x65mm.

	VF	UNC
a. 1997.	FV	6.00
b. 2001. Date vertically in very small text to left of bridge.	FV	5.00
c. 2004.	FV	2.00

269 50 Rubles VF UNC

1997 (1998); 2001; 2004. Dark brown, grayish purple and black on multicolor underprint. Personification of river Neva on foot of Rostral Column, Peter and Paul Fortress in St. Petersburg. Back: Rostral Column and Naval Museum at upper left center. Watermark: Building with steeple. 150x65mm.

	VF	UNC
a. 1997.	FV	12.50
b. 2001. Date vertically in very small text to left of bridge.	FV	8.00
c. 2004. Segmented security thread right center on back.	FV	5.00

270 100 Rubles VF UNC

1997 (1998); 2001; 2004. Violet and brown on multicolor underprint. Apollo and chariot freize on Bolshoi (Great) Theatre in Moscow at center. Back: Bolshoi Theatre. Watermark: Building over value. UV: fibers fluoresce red and yellow. 150x65mm.

	VF	UNC
a. 1997.	FV	20.00
b. 2001. Date vertically in very small text to left of bridge.	FV	15.00
c. 2004. Segmented security thread right center on back.	FV	10.00

271 500 Rubles VF UNC

1997 (1998); 2001; 2004; 2010. Brown-violet on multicolor underprint. Statue of Peter the Great, sailing ship dockside in port of Arkhangelsk at center. Back: Monastery in Solovetsky Island. 150x65mm.

	VF	UNC
a. 1997.	FV	50.00
b. 2001. Date vertically in very small text to left of bridge.	FV	40.00
c. 2004. Segmented security thread right center on back.	FV	35.00
d. 2010.	FV	35.00

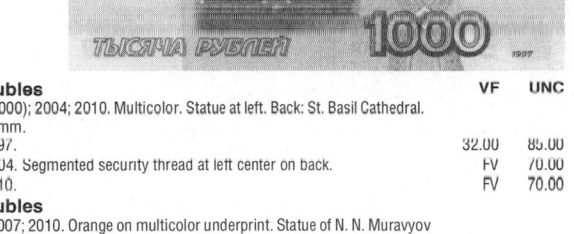

272 1000 Rubles VF UNC

1997 (2000); 2004; 2010. Multicolor. Statue at left. Back: St. Basil Cathedral. 157x69mm.

	VF	UNC
a. 1997.	32.00	85.00
b. 2004. Segmented security thread at left center on back.	FV	70.00
c. 2010.	FV	70.00

273 5000 Rubles

2006; 2007; 2010. Orange on multicolor underprint. Statue of N. N. Muravyov at center. Back: Khavarkovsk city view at center. 157x69mm.

	VF	UNC
a. 2006.	FV	220.
b. 2007.	FV	220.
c. 2010.	FV	220.

2014 Sochi Olympics Commemorative

274 100 Rubles VF UNC

	VF	UNC
2013. Vertical format.	FV	12.50

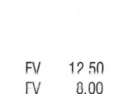

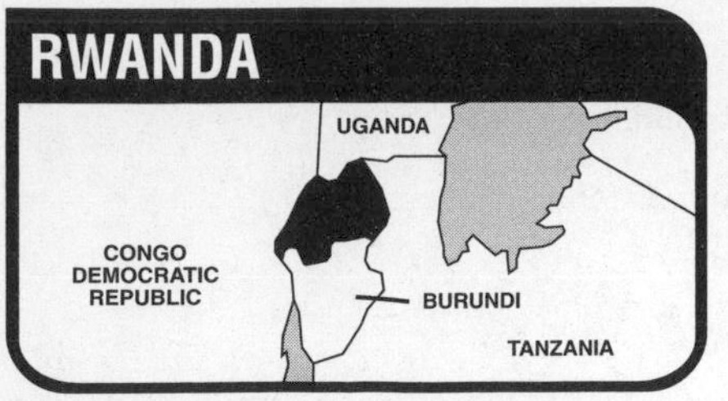

The Republic of Rwanda, located in central Africa between the Republic of the Congo and Tanzania, has an area of 26,338 sq. km. and a population of 10.186 million. Capital: Kigali. The economy is d on agriculture and mining. Coffee and tin are exported.

In 1959, three years before independence from Belgium, the majority ethnic group, the Hutus, overthrew the ruling Tutsi king. Over the next several years, thousands of Tutsis were killed, and some 150,000 driven into exile in neighboring countries. The children of these exiles later formed a rebel group, the Rwandan Patriotic Front (RPF), and began a civil war in 1990. The war, along with several political and economic upheavals, exacerbated ethnic tensions, culminating in April 1994 in the genocide of roughly 800,000 Tutsis and moderate Hutus. The Tutsi rebels defeated the Hutu regime and ended the killing in July 1994, but approximately 2 million Hutu refugees - many fearing Tutsi retribution - fled to neighboring Burundi, Tanzania, Uganda, and Zaire. Since then, most of the refugees have returned to Rwanda, but several thousand remained in the neighboring Democratic Republic of the Congo (DRC; the former Zaire) and formed an extremist insurgency bent on retaking Rwanda, much as the RPF tried in 1990. Despite substantial international assistance and political reforms - including Rwanda's first local elections in March 1999 and its first post-genocide presidential and legislative elections in August and September 2003 - the country continues to struggle to boost investment and agricultural output, and ethnic reconciliation is complicated by the real and perceived Tutsi political dominance. Kigali's increasing centralization and intolerance of dissent, the nagging Hutu extremist insurgency across the border, and Rwandan involvement in two wars in recent years in the neighboring DRC continue to hinder Rwanda's efforts to escape its bloody legacy.

Also see Belgian Congo, Rwanda-Burundi.

MONETARY SYSTEM:

1 Franc (Amafranga, Amafaranga) = 100 Centimes

REPLACEMENT NOTES:

#6e, 17:ZZ prefix. #12, VV prefix. Others probably exist.

REPUBLIC

BANQUE NATIONALE DU RWANDA

BANKI NASIYONALI Y'U RWANDA

1962 PROVISIONAL ISSUE

#	Denomination / Description	Fine	XF
1	**20 Francs** ND (1962 -old date 5.10.1960). Green on tan and pink underprint. Maroon or black stamped overprint on Rwanda-Burundi # 3. Signature title: *LE GOUVERNEUR.* Overprint: *BANQUE NATIONALE DU RWANDA.*	175.	—

#	Denomination / Description	Fine	XF
2	**50 Francs** ND (1962 -old dates 15.9.1960; 1.10.1960). Red on multicolor underprint. Maroon stamped overprint on Rwanda-Burundi # 4. Signature title: *LE GOUVERNEUR.* Overprint: *BANQUE NATIONALE DU RWANDA.*	350.	—

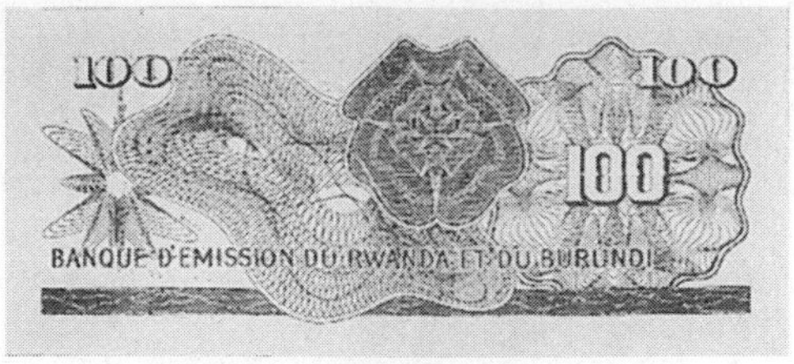

#	Denomination / Description	Fine	XF
3	**100 Francs** ND (1962 -old dates 15.9.1960; 1.10.1960; 31.7.1962). Blue on light green and tan underprint. Stamped overprint on Rwanda-Burundi # 5. Signature title: *LE GOUVERNEUR.* Overprint: *BANQUE NATIONALE DU RWANDA.*		
	a. Black overprint.	250.	2000.
	b. Purple overprint.	250.	2000.
4	**500 Francs** ND (1962 -old dates 15.9.1960; 15.9.1961). Lilac-brown on multicolor underprint. Embossed overprint and blind embossed facsimile signature on Rwanda-Burundi # 6. Signature title: *LE GOUVERNEUR.* Overprint: *BANQUE NATIONALE DU RWANDA.*	1250.	5000.
5	**1000 Francs** ND (1962 -old dates 15.5.1961; 1.7.1962). Green on multicolor underprint. Embossed overprint and blind facsimile signature on Rwanda-Burundi # 7. Signature title: *LE GOUVERNEUR.* Overprint: *BANQUE NATIONALE DU RWANDA.*	1000.	4000.

1964 ISSUE

#6-10 Replacement notes: Serial # prefix *ZZ*.

#	Denomination / Description	VF	UNC
6	**20 Francs** 1964-76. Brown on multicolor underprint. Flag of Rwanda at left. Various date and signature title varieties. Back: Four young boys at left center with pipeline in background at center.		
	a. Signature titles: *VICE-GOUVERNEUR* and *GOUVERNEUR,* with security thread. 1.7.1964; 31.3.1966; 15.3.1969; 1.9.1969.	15.00	40.00
	b. Signature titles: *VICE GOUVERNEUR* and *ADMINISTRATEUR,* with security thread. 1.7.1965.	12.50	25.00
	c. Signature titles: *GOUVERNEUR* and *ADMINISTRATEUR,* with security thread. 1.7.1971.	3.00	7.50
	d. Signature titles: *ADMINISTRATEUR* and *ADMINISTRATEUR,* with security thread. 30.10.1974.	1.50	22.50
	e. Signature titles: *ADMINISTRATEUR* and *GOUVERNEUR,* without security thread. 1.1.1976.	.75	5.25
	s1. As a. Specimen. 1.7.1964; 1.7.1965; 31.3.1966; 15.3.1969.	Unc	42.00
	s2. As b. Specimen. 1.7.1965.	Unc	50.00
	s3. As c. Specimen. 1.7.1971.	Unc	15.00
	s4. As d. Specimen. 30.10.1974.	Unc	15.00

#	Denomination / Description	VF	UNC
7	**50 Francs** 1964-76. Blue on green underprint. Map of Rwanda at left center. Various date and signature title varieties. Back: Miner at left with miners digging at center.		
	a. Signature titles: *VICE-GOUVERNEUR* and *GOUVERNEUR,* with security thread. 1.7.1964; 31.1.1966; 1.9.1969.	20.00	65.00
	b. Signature titles: *ADMINISTRATEUR* and *GOUVERNEUR,* with security thread. 1.7.1971; 30.10.1974.	2.00	25.00
	c. Signature titles: *ADMINISTRATEUR* and *GOUVERNEUR,* without security thread. 1.1.1976.	1.00	9.00
	s1. As a. Specimen. 1.7.1964; 31.1.1966; 1.9.1969.	—	25.00
	s2. As b. Specimen. 1.7.1971; 30.10.1974.	—	25.00

8 **100 Francs** — VF / UNC

1964-76. Purple on multicolor underprint. Map of Rwanda at left. Various date and signature title varieties. Back: Woman with basket on head at left, banana trees at center.

	VF	UNC
a. Signature titles: *VICE-GOUVERNEUR* and *GOUVERNEUR,* with security thread. 1.7.1964; 31.3.1966; 31.10.1969.	12.50	50.00
b. Signature titles: *VICE-GOUVERNEUR* and *ADMINISTRATEUR,* with security thread. 1.7.1965.	8.00	20.00
c. Signature titles: *ADMINISTRATEUR* and *GOUVERNEUR,* with security thread. 1.7.1971; 30.10.1974.	3.50	10.00
d. Signature titles: *ADMINISTRATEUR* and *GOUVERNEUR,* without security thread. 1.1.1976.	1.50	15.00
s1. As a. Specimen. 1.7.1964; 1.7.1965; 31.3.1966; 31.10.1969. Red overprint: *SPECIMEN* on both sides.	—	50.00
s2. As c. Specimen. 1.7.1971; 30.10.1974. Black overprint: *SPECIMEN.* on both sides.	—	25.00

9 **500 Francs** — VF / UNC

1964-76. Dark green and multicolor. Arms of Rwanda at left. Various date and signature title varieties. Back: Man with basket on head at left, rows of plants in background.

	VF	UNC
a. Signature titles: *VICE-GOUVERNEUR* and *GOUVERNEUR.* 1.7.1964; 31.3.1966; 31.10.1969.	12.50	50.00
b. Signature titles: *ADMINISTRATEUR* and *GOUVERNEUR.* 1.7.1971; 30.10.1974; 1.1.1976.	10.00	40.00
s1. As a. Specimen. 1.7.1964; 31.3.1966; 31.10.1969. Black overprint: *SPECIMEN* on both sides.	—	30.00
s2. As b. Specimen. 1.7.1971; 30.10.1974	—	30.00

10 **1000 Francs** — VF / UNC

1964-76. Red and multicolor. Arms of Rwanda at left. Various date and signature title varieties. Back: Man and terraced hills at center.

	VF	UNC
a. Signature titles: *VICE-GOUVERNEUR* and *GOUVERNEUR.* 1.7.1964; 31.3.1966; 15.3.1969.	35.00	200.
b. Signature titles: *ADMINISTRATEUR* and *GOUVERNEUR.* 1.7.1971; 30.10.1974.	20.00	45.00
c. Printed signature titles like b. 1.1.1976.	15.00	85.00
s1. As a. Specimen. 1.7.1964; 31.3.1966; 15.3.1969. Black overprint: *SPECIMEN* on both sides.	—	45.00
s2. As b. Specimen. 1.7.1971.	—	45.00

1974 Issue

11 **500 Francs** — VF / UNC

19.4.1974. Green and multicolor. General Habyarimana at left. Back: Man with basket on head at left, rows of plants in background.

	VF	UNC
a. Issued note.	10.00	20.00
s. Specimen.	—	45.00

1978 Issue

12 **100 Francs** — VF / UNC

1.1.1978. Gray on light blue and multicolor underprint. Zebras. Back: Woman carrying child at left, mountains in background at center right.

	VF	UNC
a. Issued note.	4.00	15.00
s. Specimen.	—	12.50

13 **500 Francs** — VF / UNC

1.1.1978. Brown, orange and multicolor. Impalas. Back: Eight drummers at left, strip mining at right.

	VF	UNC
a. Watermark: Impala's head.	10.00	25.00
b. Without watermark.	60.00	150.
s. As a. Specimen.	—	20.00

14 **1000 Francs** — VF — UNC

1.1.1978. Green and multicolor. Boys picking tea leaves at left. Back: Tribal dancer at right. Watermark: Impala's head.

	VF	UNC
a. Issued note.	15.00	50.00
s. Specimen.	—	25.00

15 **5000 Francs** — VF — UNC

1.1.1978. Green, blue and multicolor. Female with basket on her head at left, field workers at center. Back: Lake and mountains. Watermark: Impala's head.

	VF	UNC
a. Issued note.	65.00	150.
s. Specimen.	—	100.

1981 Issue

16 **500 Francs** — VF — UNC

1.7.1981. Brown and multicolor. Arms at left, three Impalas at right. Back: Men working in field at left. Watermark: Crowned crane's head.

	VF	UNC
a. Issued note.	10.00	52.00
s. Specimen.	—	20.00

17 **1000 Francs** — VF — UNC

1.7.1981. Green, brown and multicolor. Two Watusi warriors at right. Back: Two Eastern Gorillas at left, canoe in lake at right. Watermark: Crowned crane's head.

	VF	UNC
a. Issued note.	12.00	55.00
s. Specimen. Black overprint: *SPECIMEN* on both sides.	—	45.00

1982 Issue

18 **100 Francs** — VF — UNC

1.8.1982. Black on lilac and multicolor underprint. Zebras at center and right. Back: Purple and multicolor. Woman carrying baby at left, view of mountains at center. Watermark: Impala's head. — 1.50 — 9.50

1988-89 Issue

19 **100 Francs** — VF — UNC

24.4.1989. Black on lilac and multicolor underprint. Zebras at center and right. Signature titles: *2E VICE-GOUVERNEUR* and *GOUVERNEUR*. Back: Woman carrying baby at left, view of mountains at center. New spelling *AMAFARANGA*.

	VF	UNC
a. Issued note.	1.25	4.00
s. Specimen. Overprint: *SPECIMEN* on both sides.	—	25.00

21 **1000 Francs** — VF — UNC

1.1.1988; 24.4.1989. Green, brown and multicolor. Two Watusi warriors at right. Signature titles: *2E VICE-GOUVERNEUR* and *GOUVERNEUR*. Back: Two Eastern Gorillas at left, canoe in lake at right. New spelling *AMAFARANGA*.

	VF	UNC
a. Issued note.	2.50	5.00
s. Specimen. Black overprint: *SPECIMEN* on both sides.	—	55.00

22 **5000 Francs** VF UNC

1.1.1988; 24.4.1989. Green, blue and multicolor. Female with basket on her head at left, field workers at center. Signature titles: *2E VICE-GOUVERNEUR* and *GOUVERNEUR*. Back: Lake and mountains. New spelling *AMAFARANGA*.

	VF	UNC
a. Issued note.	3.00	6.00
s. Specimen. Overprint: *SPECIMEN* on both sides.	—	25.00

1994 Issue

23 **500 Francs** VF UNC

1.12.1994. Blue-black, black and dark blue-green on multicolor underprint. Mountainous landscape at center right. Back: Female Waterbuck at left center. Watermark: Impala's head. Printer: G&D (without imprint).

	VF	UNC
a. Issued note.	FV	17.00
s. Specimen. Black overprint: *SPECIMEN* on both sides.	—	25.00

24 **1000 Francs** VF UNC

1.12.1994. Purple, red-brown and dark brown on multicolor underprint. Mountainous landscape at center right. Back: Vegetation at left, African Buffalo at center. Watermark: Impala's head. Printer: G&D (without imprint).

	VF	UNC
a. Issued note.	FV	27.00
s. Specimen. Black overprint: *SPECIMEN* on both sides.	—	25.00

25 **5000 Francs** VF UNC

1.12.1994. Dark brown, violet and purple on multicolor underprint. Mountainous landscape at center right. Back: Reclining lion at left center. Watermark: Impala's head. Printer: G&D (without imprint).

	VF	UNC
a1. Issued note.	FV	32.00
s. Specimen. Black overprint: *SPECIMEN* on both sides.	—	35.00

1998 Issue

26 **500 Francs** VF UNC

1.12.1998. Blue and green on multicolor underprint. Mountain gorillas at right. Back: National Museum of Butare and schoolchildren.

	VF	UNC
a. Issued note.	FV	6.00
s. Specimen. Red overprint: *SPECIMEN* on both sides.	—	40.00

27 **1000 Francs** VF UNC

1.12.1998. Blue and brown on multicolor underprint. Volcano range at right. Back: Tea plantation and cattle.

	VF	UNC
a. Issued note.	FV	5.50
s. Specimen. Red overprint: *SPECIMEN* on both sides.	—	40.00

28	5000 Francs	VF	UNC
	1.12.1998. Black, red and green on multicolor underprint. *Intore* dancers at right. Back: National Bank building.		
	a. Issued note.	FV	15.00
	s. Specimen. Red overprint: *SPECIMEN* on both sides.	—	50.00

2003-04 Issue

29	100 Francs	VF	UNC
	1.5.2003; 1.9.2003. Green, brown and blue on yellow underprint. Oxen and farmer plowing at center. Back: Mountain and lake. UV: fibers fluoesce yellow and blue; design elements yellow and orange. 129x65mm.		
	a. 1.5.2003. Bank name in English.	FV	4.00
	b. 1.9.2003. Bank name in English and French.	FV	2.50
	s. As a or b. Specimen. Red overprint.	—	25.00

30	500 Francs	VF	UNC
	1.7.2004. Green on tan and blue underprint. 136x72mm.		
	a. 1.7.2004.	FV	6.00

31	1000 Francs	VF	UNC
	1.7.2004. Blue on tan underprint. Doggett's Guenon. 141x72mm.		
	a. 1.7.2004.	FV	12.00

33	5000 Francs	VF	UNC
	1.4.2004. Purple on tan and multicolor underprint. Baskets. Back: Gorilla. 145x72mm.		
	a. 1.4.2004.	FV	45.00

Banki Nkuru Y'u Rwanda

2007-2009 Issue

34	500 Francs	VF	UNC
	1.2.2008.	FV	3.50
35	1000 Francs		
	1.2.2008.	FV	7.00

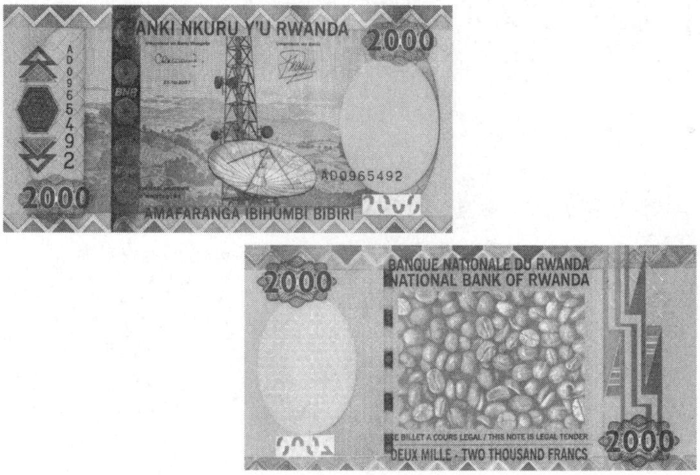

36	2000 Francs	VF	UNC
	31.10.2007.	FV	12.00

37	5000 Francs	VF	UNC
	1.2.2009.	FV	22.00

2013 Issue

38	500 Francs	VF	UNC
	1.1.2013. Blue-gray on multicolor underprint. Three cows. Back: Students in computer class. Watermark: Coat of arms 135x72mm.	FV	3.00

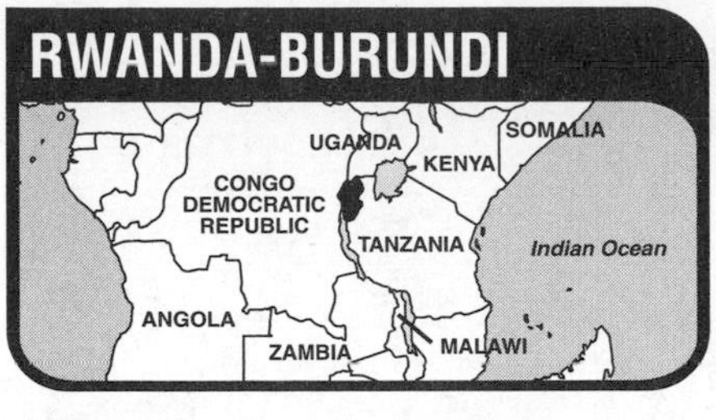

Rwanda-Burundi, a Belgian League of Nations mandate and United Nations trust territory comprising the provinces of Rwanda and Burundi of the former colony of German East Africa, was located in central Africa between the present Republic of the Congo, Uganda and mainland Tanzania. The mandate-trust territory had an area of 20,916 sq. mi. (54,272 sq. km.).

For specific statistics and history of Rwanda and Burundi see individual entries.

When Rwanda and Burundi were formed into a mandate for administration by Belgium, their names were changed to Ruanda and Urundi and they were organized as an integral part of the Belgian Congo, during which time they used a common banknote issue with the Belgian Congo. After the Belgian Congo acquired independence as the Republic of the Congo, the provinces of Ruanda and Urundi reverted to their former names of Rwanda and Burundi and issued notes with both names on them. In 1962, both Rwanda and Burundi became separate independent states.

Also see Belgian Congo, Burundi and Rwanda.

MONETARY SYSTEM:

1 Franc = 100 Centimes

Mandate - Trust Territory

Banque d'Emission du Rwanda et du Burundi

1960 Issue

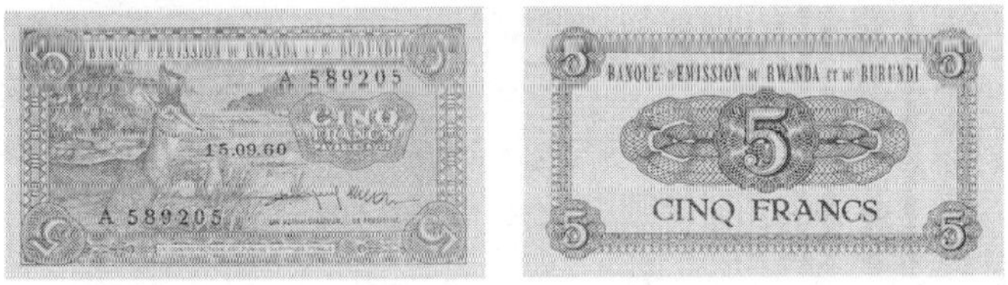

		VF	UNC
1	**5 Francs**		
	1960-63. Light brown on green underprint. Impala at left. Signature varieties.		
	a. 15.9.1960; 15.5.1961.	125.	450.
	b. 15.4.1963.	120.	450.

		Fine	XF
2	**10 Francs**		
	15.9.1960; 5.10.1960. Dull gray on pale blue and pale orange underprint. Hippopotamus at left. Signature varieties. Printer: TDLR.		
	a. Issued note.	250.	550.
	s. Specimen.	Unc	450.

		Fine	XF
3	**20 Francs**		
	15.9.1960; 5.10.1960. Green on tan and pink underprint. Crocodile at right. Signature varieties. Printer: TDLR.		
	a. Issued note.	220.	525.
	s. Specimen.	Unc	600.

		Fine	XF
4	**50 Francs**		
	15.9.1960; 1.10.1960. Red on multicolor underprint. Lioness at center right. Signature varieties.		
	a. Issued note.	375.	900.
	s. Specimen.	Unc	500.
	ct. Color trial. Green on multicolor underprint.	Unc	750.

		Fine	XF
5	**100 Francs**		
	15.9.1960; 1.10.1960; 31.7.1962. Blue on light green and tan underprint. Zebu at left. Signature varieties.		
	a. Issued note.	300.	1400.
	s. Specimen.	Unc	650.
	ct. Color trial. Brown on multicolor underprint.	Unc	700.

		Fine	XF
6	**500 Francs**		
	15.9.1960; 15.5.1961; 15.9.1961. Lilac-brown on multicolor underprint. Black Rhinoceros at center right. Signature varieties.		
	a. Issued note.	850.	3000.
	s. Specimen.	Unc	1500.

		Fine	XF
7	**1000 Francs**		
	15.9.1960; 15.5.1961; 31.7.1962. Green on multicolor underprint. Zebra at right. Signature varieties.		
	a. Issued note.	1100.	2500.
	s. Specimen.	Unc	1500.
	ct. Color trial. Purple on multicolor underprint.	Unc	2000.

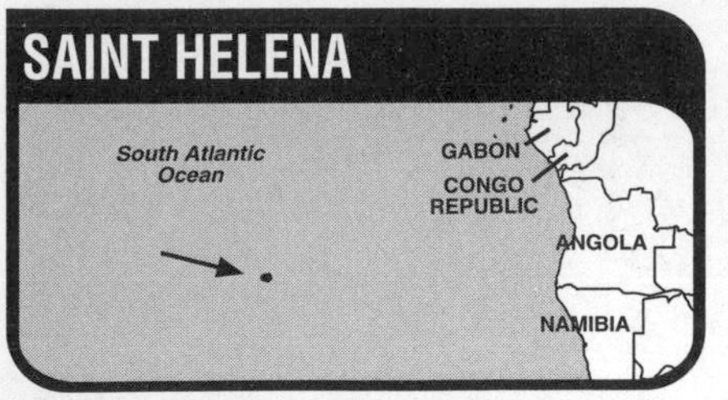

The British Overseas Territory of St. Helena, is located about 1,150 miles (1,850 km.) from the west coast of Africa, has an area of 413 sq. km. and a population of 7,600. Capital: Jamestown. Flax, lace and rope are produced for export. Ascension and Tristan da Cunha are dependencies of St. Helena.

Saint Helena was uninhabited when first discovered by the Portuguese in 1502, it was garrisoned by the British during the 17th century. It acquired fame as the place of Napoleon Bonaparte's exile, from 1815 until his death in 1821, but its importance as a port of call declined after the opening of the Suez Canal in 1869. During the Anglo-Boer War in South Africa, several thousand Boer prisoners were confined on the island between 1900 and 1903. St. Helena banknotes are also used on the islands of Assencion and Tristan de Cunia.

RULERS:

British

MONETARY SYSTEM:

1 Pound = 20 Shillings to 1971
1 Pound = 100 New Pence, 1971-

SIGNATURE VARIETIES	
1	
2	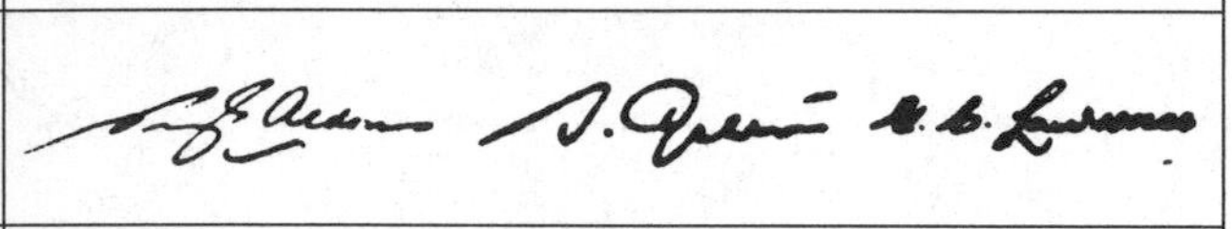
3	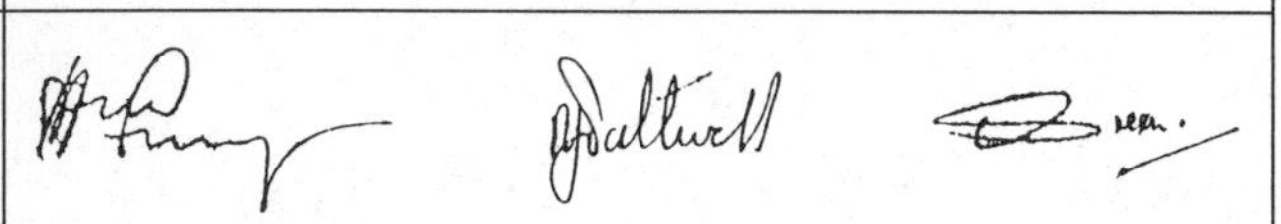
4	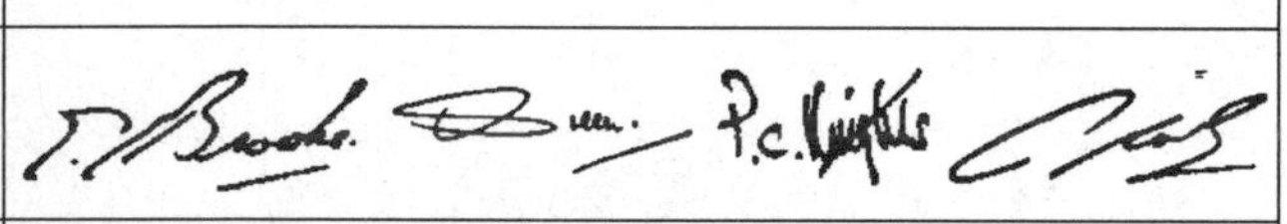
5	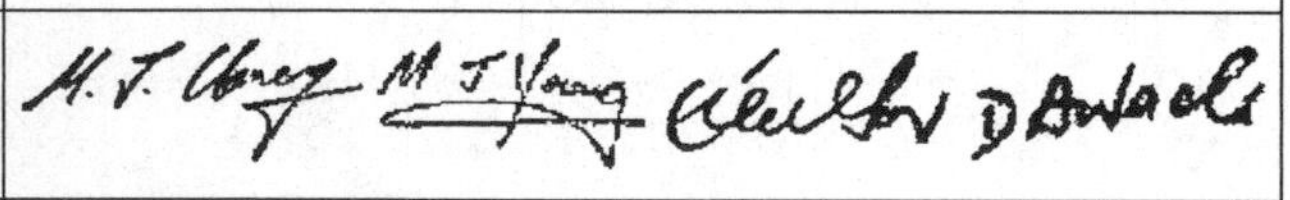
6	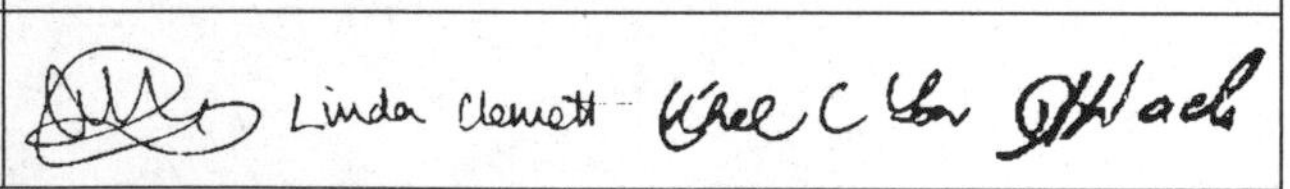

British Administration

Government of St. Helena

1976; 1979 ND Issue

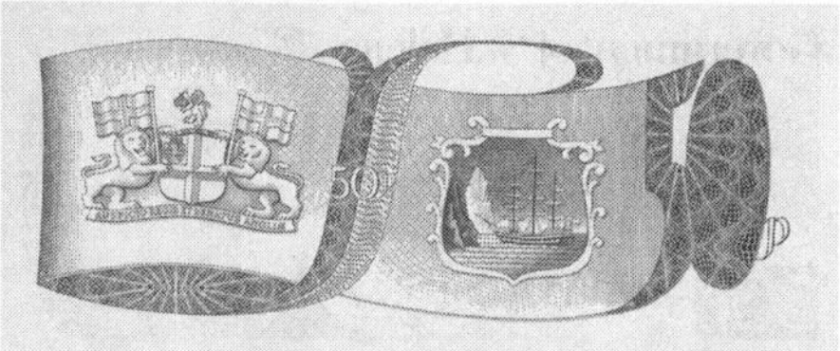

			VF	UNC
5	**50 Pence** ND (1979). Purple on pink and pale yellow-green underprint. Views of the island at left, Queen Elizabeth II at right. Signature 2. Back: Royal arms with motto at left, shield with ship at right. Correctly spelled *ANGLIAE* in motto 140x60mm.			
	a. Issued note.		11.00	60.00
	s. Specimen.		—	140.

		VF	UNC
6	**1 Pound** ND (1976). Deep olive-green on pale orange and ochre underprint. Views of the island at left, Queen Elizabeth II at right. Back: Royal arms with motto at left, shield with ship at right. Incorrect spelling *ANGLAE* in motto. 153x67mm.		
	a. Issued note.	20.00	110.
	s. Specimen.	—	170.

		VF	UNC
7	**5 Pounds** ND (1976). Blue on light brown underprint. Views of the island at left, Queen Elizabeth II at right. Back: Royal arms with motto at left, shield with ship at right. 153x72mm.		
	a. Incorrect spelling *ANGLAE* in motto. Signature 1. (1976).	25.00	170.
	b. Corrected spelling *ANGLIAE* in motto. Signature 2. (1981).	18.00	100.
	s. As a. Specimen.	—	270.

		VF	UNC
8	**10 Pounds** ND (1979). Pale red on multicolor underprint. Views of the island at left, Queen Elizabeth II at right. Back: Arms, correctly spelled *ANGLIAE* in motto. 159x80mm.		
	a. Signature 2. (1979).	40.00	230.
	b. Signature 3. (1985).	FV	110.
	c. As a. Uncut sheet of 3.	—	500.
	r. Remainder without signature or serial #.	—	320.
	s. As a. Specimen.	—	300.

1981; 1986 ND Issue

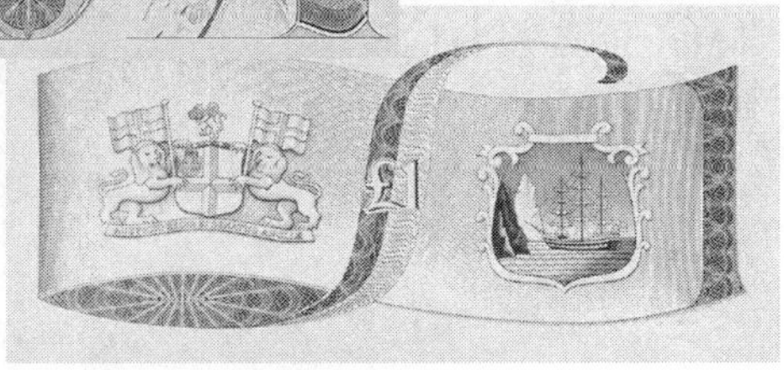

9 1 Pound

ND (1981). Deep olive-green on pale orange and ochre underprint. Queen Elizabeth II at right. Signature 2. Back: Royal arms with motto at left, corrected spelling *ANGLIAE* in motto. Reduced size. 147x66mm.

	VF	UNC
a. Issued note.	5.00	32.50
s. Specimen.	—	160.

10 20 Pounds

ND (1986). Dark brown on multicolor underprint. Harbor view at left center, Queen Elizabeth II at right. Four signatures in block form. Signature 4. Back: Light green. Arms at center. 164x85mm.

	VF	UNC
a. Issued note.	FV	165.
s. Specimen.	—	275.

1998 ND Issue

11 5 Pounds

ND (1998). Blue on light brown underprint. Views of the island at left, Queen Elizabeth II at right. Four signatures in block form. Signature 5. Back: Royal arms with motto at left, shield with ship at right. 135x71mm.

	VF	UNC
a. Issued note.	FV	50.00
s. Specimen.	—	190.

2004 Issue

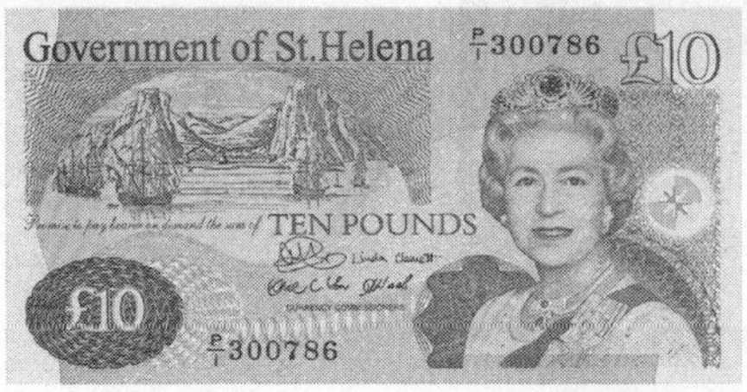

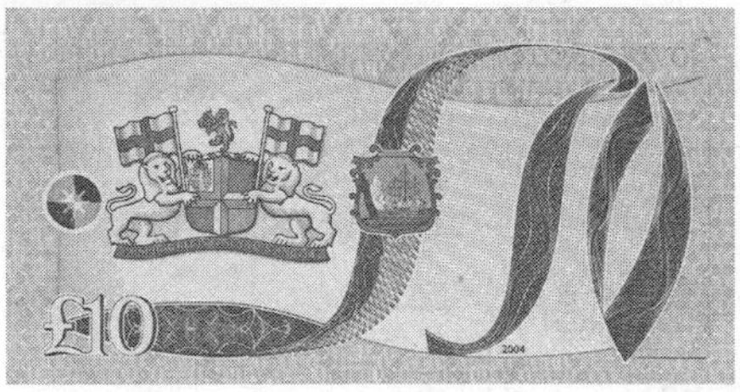

12 10 Pounds

2004. Rose on multicolor underprint. Historic harbor view at left. Queen Elizabeth II at right. Signature 6, four signatures in block form. Back: Arms at left, large 10 at right, year date. 135x71mm.

	VF	UNC
a. Issued note.	FV	90.00
s. Specimen (300 issued). Red overprint: *SPECIMEN* on both sides.	—	220.

13 20 Pounds

2004. Brown on multicolor underprint. Modern harbor view. Queen Elizabeth II at right. Signature 6, four signatures in block form. Back: Arms at left, large 20 at right, year date. 135x71mm.

	VF	UNC
a. Issued note.	FV	150.
s. Specimen (300 issued). Red overprint: *SPECIMEN* on both sides.	—	290.

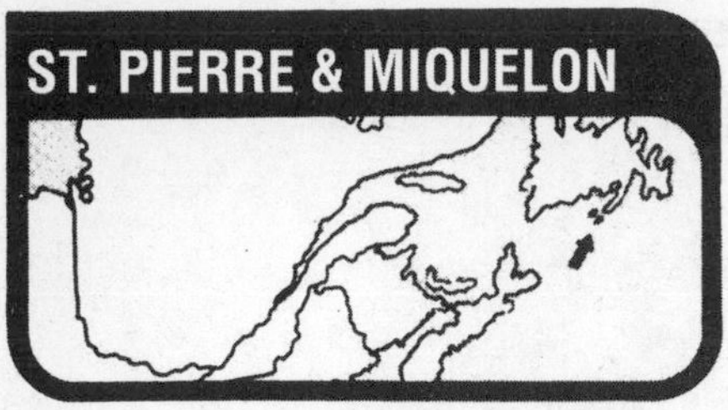

The Territorial Collectivity of St. Pierre and Miquelon, a French overseas territory located 10 miles (16 km.) off the south coast of Newfoundland, has an area of 242 sq. km. and a population of 7,045. Capital: St. Pierre. The economy of the barren archipelago is d on cod fishing and fur farming Fish and fish products, and mink and silver fox pelts are exported.

The islands, occupied by the French in 1604, were captured by the British in 1702 and held until 1763 when they were returned to the possession of France and employed as a fishing station. They passed between France and England on six more occasions between 1778 and 1814 when they were awarded permanently to France by the Treaty of Paris. The rugged, soil-poor granite islands, which will support only evergreen shrubs, are all that remain to France of her extensive colonies in North America. In 1958 St. Pierre and Miquelon voted in favor of the new constitution of the Fifth Republic of France, thereby choosing to remain within the French Community.

Notes of the Banque de France circulated 1937-1942; afterwards notes of the Caisse Centrale de la France Libre and the Caisse Centrale de la France d'Outre-Mer were in use.

RULERS:

French

MONETARY SYSTEM:

1 Franc = 100 Centimes
5 Francs 40 Centimes = 1 Canada Dollar
1 Nouveau Franc = 100 "old" Francs, 1960-

French Administration

Caisse Centrale de la France d'Outre-Mer

Saint-Pierre-et-Miquelon

1960 ND Provisional Issue

#30-35 overprint: *SAINT-PIERRE-ET-MIQUELON* and new denomination.

30	1 Nouveau Franc on 50 Francs	VF	UNC
	ND (1960). Multicolor. Overprint on Reunion number 25. Overprint: *SAINT-PIERRE-ET-MIQUELON* and new denomination.		
	a. Special series *A.1-Y.1* with 3 digit serial # and 5 digit control #.	40.00	200.
	b. Normal series with 5 digit serial # and 9 digit control #.	20.00	75.00
	s. As a, b. Specimen.	—	—

1961; 1964 ND Provisional Issue

31	1 Nouveau Franc on 50 Francs	VF	UNC
	ND (1961). Multicolor. B. d'Esnambuc at left, ship at right. Back: Woman. Overprint: *SAINT-PIERRE-ET-MIQUELON* and new denomination.	200.	650.

32	2 Nouveaux Francs on 100 Francs	VF	UNC
	ND (1963). Multicolor. La Bourdonnais at left, two women at right. Back: Woman looking at mountains. Overprint: *SAINT-PIERRE-ET-MIQUELON* and new denomination.	25.00	90.00

32A	2 Nouveaux Francs on 100 Francs	VF	UNC
	ND (1963). Multicolor. La Bourdonnais at left, two women at right. Woman looking at mountains on back.	45.00	100.

33	10 Nouveaux Francs on 500 Francs	VF	UNC
	ND (1964). Multicolor. Buildings and sailboat at left, two women at right. Back: Ox-carts with wood and plants. Overprint: *SAINT-PIERRE-ET-MIQUELON* and new denomination.		
	a. Issued note.	175.	425.
	s. Specimen. Overprinted and perforated: *SPECIMEN.*	—	1250.

34	20 Nouveaux Francs on 1000 Francs	VF	UNC
	ND (1964). Multicolor. Two women at right. Back: Women at right, two men in small boat. Overprint: *SAINT-PIERRE-ET-MIQUELON* and new denomination.		
	a. Issued note.	225.	700.
	s. Specimen. Overprinted and perforated: *SPECIMEN.*	—	1250.
35	**100 Nouveaux Francs on 5000 Francs**		
	ND (1961). Multicolor. General Schoelcher at center right. Back: Family. Overprint: *SAINT-PIERRE-ET-MIQUELON* and new denomination.		
	a. Issued note.	450.	2000.
	s. Specimen.	—	—

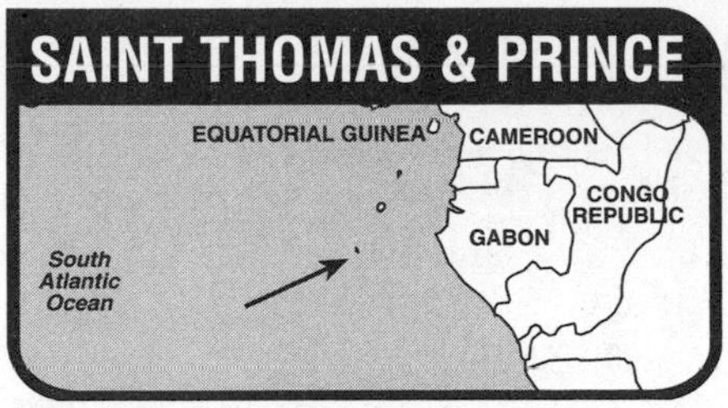

The Democratic Republic of Sao Tomé and Príncipe (formerly the Portuguese overseas province of St. Thomas and Prince Islands) is located in the Gulf of Guinea 150 miles (241 km.) off the West African coast. It has an area of 372 sq. mi. (960 sq. km.) and a population of 149,000. Capital: São Tomé. The economy of the islands is d on cocoa, copra and coffee.

Discovered and claimed by Portugal in the late 15th century, the islands' sugar-d economy gave way to coffee and cocoa in the 19th century - all grown with plantation slave labor, a form of which lingered into the 20th century. While independence was achieved in 1975, democratic reforms were not instituted until the late 1980s. The country held its first free elections in 1991, but frequent internal wrangling between the various political parties precipitated repeated changes in leadership and two failed coup attempts in 1995 and 2003. The recent discovery of oil in the Gulf of Guinea promises to attract increased attention to the small island nation.

RULERS:

Portuguese to 1975

MONETARY SYSTEM:

1 Mil Reis = 1000 Reis to 1914
1 Escudo = 100 Centavos, 1911-1976
1 Dobra = 100 Centimos, 1977-

STEAMSHIP SEALS

Type I LOANDA — Type II LISBOA — Type III C,C,A

C,C,A = Colonias, Commercio, Agricultura.

Portuguese Administration

Banco Nacional Ultramarino

S. Tomé e Príncipe

1956-64 Issue

		VF	UNC
40	**1000 Escudos** 11.5.1964. Green on multicolor underprint. J. de Santarem at right, bank arms at upper center. Back: Woman, sailing ships at left center, arms at upper right.		
	a. Issued note.	95.00	250.
	s. Specimen, punch hole cancelled.	—	150.
	ct. Color trial. Purple on multicolor underprint.	—	300.

1974 Circulating Bearer Check Issue

		VF	UNC
41	**100 Escudos** 31.3.1974.	—	—
42	**500 Escudos** 28.4.1974.	—	—
43	**500 Escudos** 31.12.1974.	85.00	160.
43A	**1000 Escudos** 23.12.1974; 31.12.1974 Red.	85.00	160.

Democratic Republic

Banco Nacional de S. Tomé e Príncipe

1976 Provisional Issue

		VF	UNC
44	**20 Escudos** 1.6.1976 (- old date 20.11.1958). Brown on multicolor underprint. Bank seal at left, Portuguese arms at lower center, King D. Afonso V at right. Overprint on #36. Overprint: New bank name in red on both sides of Banco Nacional Ultramarino notes. Printer: BWC.		
	a. Issued note.	10.00	25.00
	s. Specimen.	—	—

		VF	UNC
45	**50 Escudos** 1.6.1976 (- old date 20.11.1958). Brown-violet on multicolor underprint. Bank seal at left, Portuguese arms at lower center, King D. Afonso V at right.Overprint on #37. Overprint: New bank name in red on both sides of Banco Nacional Ultramarino notes. Printer: BWC.	10.00	30.00

		VF	UNC
46	**100 Escudos** 1.6.1976 (- old date 20.11.1958). Purple on multicolor underprint. Bank seal at left, Portuguese arms at lower center, King D. Afonso V at right. Overprint on #38. Overprint: New bank name in red on both sides of Banco Nacional Ultramarino notes. Printer: BWC.		
	a. Issued note.	15.00	45.00
	s. Specimen.	—	—

		VF	UNC
47	**500 Escudos**		
	1.6.1976 (- old date 18.4.1956). Blue on multicolor underprint. Overprint on #39. Overprint: New bank name in red on both sides of Banco Nacional Ultramarino notes.		
	a. Issued note.	40.00	150.
	s. Specimen.	—	—
48	**1000 Escudos**		
	1.6.1976 (- old date 11.5.1964). Green on multicolor underprint. Overprint on #40. Overprint: New bank name in red on both sides of Banco Nacional Ultramarino notes.	40.00	120.

1976 Circulating Bearer Check Issue

		VF	UNC
50	**500 Escudos**		
	21.6.1976. Black on pink and light aqua underprint. 167x75mm.		
	a. Issued note.	27.50	85.00
	ct. Uniface. Signatures mauve and blue, or blue and blue.	—	—
51	**1000 Escudos**		
	21.6.1976. 167x75mm.	35.00	100.

Decreto-Lei No. 50/76; 1977 Issue

		VF	UNC
52	**50 Dobras**		
	12.7.1977. Red and multicolor. African grey parrot at center in underprint. Rei Amador at right, arms at lower left. Signature titles: *O MINISTRO DA COORDENACÃO ECONOMICA* and *O GOVERNADOR*. Back: Scene with two fishermen in boats. Watermark: Rei Amador. Printer: BWC.		
	a. Issued note.	3.00	8.00
	s. Specimen.	—	125.

		VF	UNC
53	**100 Dobras**		
	12.7.1977. Green and multicolor. Flower at center in underprint. Rei Amador at right, arms at lower left. Signature titles: *O MINISTRO DA COORDENACÃO ECONOMICA* and *O GOVERNADOR*. Back: Group of people preparing food. Watermark: Rei Amador. Printer: BWC.		
	a. Issued note.	4.00	10.00
	s. Specimen.	—	125.

		VF	UNC
54	**500 Dobras**		
	12.7.1977. Purple and multicolor. Sea Turtle at center in underprint. Rei Amador at right, arms at lower left. Signature titles: *O MINISTRO DA COORDENACÃO ECONOMICA* and *O GOVERNADOR*. Back: Waterfall. Watermark: Rei Amador. Printer: BWC.		
	a. Issued note.	10.00	25.00
	s. Specimen.	—	150.

		VF	UNC
55	**1000 Dobras**		
	12.7.1977. Blue and multicolor. Bananas at center in underprint. Rei Amador at right, arms at lower left. Signature titles: *O MINISTRO DA COORDENACÃO ECONOMICA* and *O GOVERNADOR*. Back: Fruit gatherer. Watermark: Rei Amador. Printer: BWC.		
	a. Issued note.	35.00	90.00
	s. Specimen.	—	200.

Decreto-Lei No. 6/82; 1982 Issue

		VF	UNC
56	**50 Dobras**		
	30.9.1982. Red and multicolor. African grey parrot at center in underprint. Rei Amador at right, arms at lower left. Signature titles: *O MINISTRO DO PLANO* and *O GOVERNADOR*. Back: Scene with two fishermen in boats. Watermark: Rei Amador. Printer: BWC.	2.50	6.50
57	**100 Dobras**		
	30.9.1982. Green and multicolor. Flower at center in underprint. Rei Amador at right, arms at lower left. Signature titles: *O MINISTRO DO PLANO* and *O GOVERNADOR*. Back: Group of people preparing food. Watermark: Rei Amador. Printer: BWC.	3.50	9.00
58	**500 Dobras**		
	30.9.1982. Purple and multicolor. Sea Turtle at center in underprint. Rei Amador at right, arms at lower left. Signature titles: *O MINISTRO DO PLANO* and *O GOVERNADOR*. Back: Waterfall. Watermark: Rei Amador. Printer: BWC.	9.00	22.50

		VF	UNC
59	**1000 Dobras** 30.9.1982. Blue and multicolor. Bananas at center in underprint. Rei Amador at right, arms at lower left. Signature titles: *O MINISTRO DO PLANO* and *O GOVERNADOR*. Back: Fruit gatherer. Watermark: Rei Amador. Printer: BWC,	12.00	32.50

Decreto-Lei No. 1/88; 1989 Issue

		VF	UNC
60	**100 Dobras** 4.1.1989. Green and multicolor. Flower at center in underprint. Rei Amador at right, arms at lower left. Signature title at left: *O MINISTRO DA ECONOMIA E FINANÇAS*. Back: Group of people preparing food. Watermark: Rei Amador. Printer: TDLR.	2.50	6.00

		VF	UNC
61	**500 Dobras** 4.1.1989. Violet, red, orange and tan on multicolor underprint. Sea Turtle at center in underprint. Rei Amador at right, arms at lower left. Signature title at left: *O MINISTRO DA ECONOMIA E FINANÇAS*. Back: Waterfall. Watermark: Rei Amador. Printer: TDLR.	4.00	9.00
62	**1000 Dobras** 4.1.1989. Blue, green and multicolor underprint. Bananas at center in underprint. Rei Amador at right, arms at left. Signature title at left: *O MINISTRO DA ECONOMIA E FINANÇAS*. Back: Fruit gatherer. Watermark: Rei Amador. Printer: TDLR.	7.00	17.50

Banco Central de S.Tomé e Príncipe

Decreto Lei No. 29/93; 1993 Issue

#63 and 64 like #61 and 62. Ascending size serial #. Printer: TDLR.

		VF	UNC
63	**500 Dobras** 26.8.1993. Violet, red, orange and tan on blue and multicolor underprint. Sea Turtle at center in underprint. Rei Amador at right, blue arms at lower left. Green ascending size serial number at right. Signature title at left: *O MINISTRO DA ECONOMIA E FINANÇAS*. Back: Waterfall. Watermark: Rei Amador. Printer: TDLR. UV: arms over turtle fluoresce yellow.	1.00	4.00

		VF	UNC
64	**1000 Dobras** 26.8.1993. Purple and deep blue and blue-green on multicolor underprint. Bananas at center in underprint. Rei Amador at right, arms at left. Red serial number at right. Signature title at left: *O MINISTRO DA ECONOMIA E FINANÇAS*. Back: Fruit gatherer. Watermark: Rei Amador. Printer: TDLR.	2.00	10.00

Decreto Lei No. 42/96; 1996 Issue

#65-68 Replacement notes: Serial # prefix ZZ.

		VF	UNC
65	**5000 Dobras** 22.10.1996; 26.8.2004; 26.8.2006. Purple, lilac and olive-green on multicolor underprint. Papa Figo bird (Principe Glossy Starling) at left center, Rei Amador at right, arms at upper center right. Back: Esplanade, modern building at left center. Watermark: Rei Amador. Printer: TDLR. 129x67mm.		
	a. 22.10.1996. One security thread.	FV	10.00
	b. 26.8.2004. Two security threads.	FV	8.00
	c. 26.8.2006.	FV	8.00
	s. Specimen.	—	75.00

		VF	UNC
66	**10,000 Dobras** 22.10.1996; 26.8.2004; 26.8.2006. Dark green, blue-violet and tan on multicolor underprint. Emerald Cuckoo at left center, Rei Amador at right, arms at upper center right. Back: Bridge over river at left center. Watermark: Rei Amador. Printer: TDLR. 136x67mm.		
	a. 22.10.1996. One security thread.	FV	17.50
	b. 26.8.2004. Two security threads.	FV	15.00
	c. 26.8.2006.	FV	15.00
	s. Specimen.	—	75.00

67 **20,000 Dobras** | VF | UNC
22.10.1996; 26.8.2004; 26.8.2006; 10.12.2010. Red, olive-brown and blue-black on multicolor underprint. Sao Tome Oriole at left center, Rei Amador at right, arms at upper center right. Back: Beach scene at left center. Watermark: Rei Amador. Printer: TDLR. 143x67mm.

	VF	UNC
a. 22.10.1996. One security thread.	FV	25.00
b. 26.8.2004. Two security threads.	FV	22.50
c. 26.8.2006.	FV	22.50
d. 10.12.2010.	FV	22.50
s. Specimen.	—	75.00

68 **50,000 Dobras** | VF | UNC
22.10.1996; 26.8.2004; 26.8.2006; 10.12.2010. Brown, purple and red on multicolor underprint. Black-winged Kingfisher at left center, Rei Amador at right, arms at upper center right. Back: Central Bank building at left center. Watermark: Rei Amador. Printer: TDLR. 150x67mm.

	VF	UNC
a. 22.10.1996. One security thread.	FV	50.00
b. 26.8.2004. Two security threads.	FV	50.00
c. 26.8.2006.	FV	50.00
d. 10.12.2010.	FV	50.00
s. Specimen overprint: *ESPECIME*, 0's in serial #.	—	75.00

69 **100,000 Dobras** | VF | UNC
2.6.2005; 10.12.2010. Green on multicolor underprint. Francisco José Tenreiro at right, bird at center. Back: Auto de Floripes. 150x67mm.

	VF	UNC
a. 2.6.2005.	FV	100.
b. 10.12.2010.	FV	100.

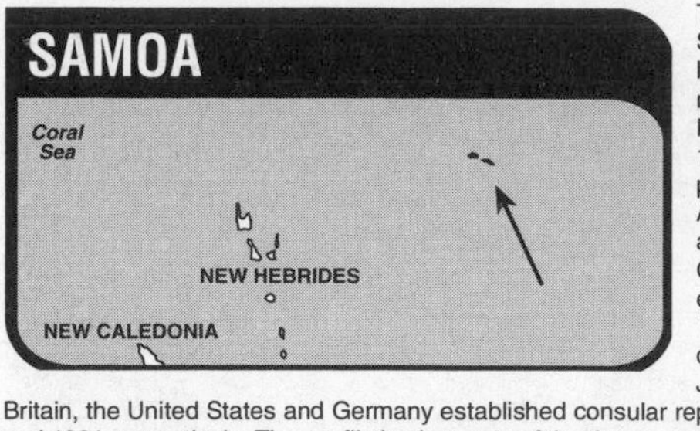

The Independent State of Western Samoa (formerly German Samoa), located in the Pacific Ocean 1,600 miles (2,574 km.) northeast of New Zealand, has an area of 1,097 sq. mi. (2,860 sq. km.) and a population of 157,000. Capital: Apia. The economy is d on agriculture, fishing and tourism. Copra, cocoa and bananas are exported.

The Samoan group of islands was discovered by Dutch navigator Jacob Roggeveen in 1772. Great Britain, the United States and Germany established consular representation at Apia in 1847, 1853 and 1861 respectively. The conflicting interests of the three powers produced the Berlin agreement of 1889 which declared Samoa neutral and had the effect of establishing a tripartite protectorate over the islands. A further agreement, 1899, recognized the rights of the United States in those islands east of 171 deg. west longitude (American Samoa) and of Germany in the other islands (Western Samoa). New Zealand occupied Western Samoa at the start of World War I and administered it as a League of Nations mandate and U.N. trusteeship until Jan. 1, 1962, when it became an independent state.

Western Samoa is a member of the Commonwealth of Nations. The Chief Executive is Chief of State. The prime minister is the Head of Government. The present Head of State, Malietoa Tanumafili II, holds his position for life. Future Heads of State will be elected by the Legislature Assembly for five-year terms.

RULERS:

British, 1914-1962
Malietoa Tanumafili II, 1962-2007

MONETARY SYSTEM:

1 Shilling = 12 Pence
1 Pound = 20 Shillings to 1967
1 Tala = 100 Sene, 1967-

Faletupe Tutotonu O Samoa

Central Bank of Samoa

1985 ND Issue

25 **2 Tala** | VF | UNC
ND (1985). Deep blue-violet on multicolor underprint. Woodcarver at right, national flag at left center. Back: Arms at lower center right, national flag at left center, hut with palms on small island at left cen Watermark: M. Tanumafili II. | FV | 4.00

26 **5 Tala**
ND (1985). Red on multicolor underprint. Child writing at right, national flag at left center. Back: Small port city at left center, arms at lower center, national flag at center right. Watermark: M. Tanumafili II. | FV | 6.50

27 **10 Tala**
ND (1985). Dark brown and purple on multicolor underprint. Man picking bananas at right, national flag at left center. Back: Shoreline landscape, arms at lower center, national flag at center right. Watermark: M. Tanumafili II.

	VF	UNC
a. Issued note.	FV	10.00
s. Specimen.	—	45.00

28 **20 Tala**
ND (1985). Brown and orange-brown on multicolor underprint. Fishermen with net at right, national flag at left center. Back: Arms at lower center, national flag at center right, round building at left. Watermark: M. Tanumafili II.

	VF	UNC
a. Issued note.	FV	20.00
s. Specimen. Red overprint: *SPECIMEN* on both sides.	—	50.00

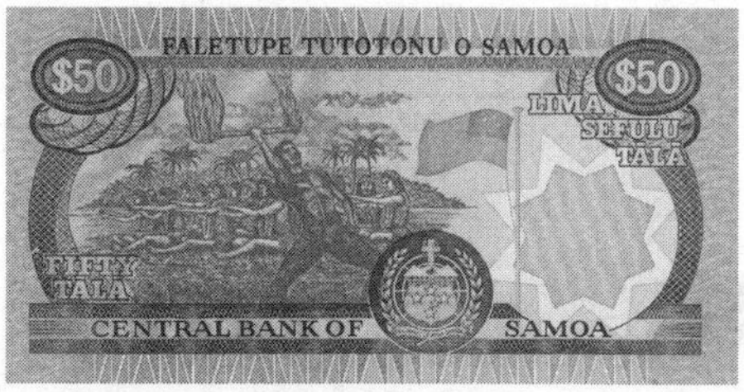

29 **50 Tala** | VF | UNC
ND (ca.1990). Green on multicolor underprint. Former home of Robert Louis Stevenson, current residence of Head of State at center, M. Tanumafili II at right. Back: Man performing traditional knife dance. Watermark: M. Tanumafili II. | FV | 40.00

		VF	UNC
30	**100 Tala** ND (ca.1990). Violet and light brown on multicolor underprint. Flag and Parliament building at center, M. Tanumafili II at right. Back: Harvest scene. Watermark: M. Tanumafili II.		
	a. Issued note.	FV	65.00
	s. Specimen.	—	—

1990 Commemorative Issue

#31, Golden Jubilee of Service of the Head of State, Susuga Malietoa Tanumafili II, 1990

		VF	UNC
31	**2 Tala** ND (1990). Brown, blue and purple on multicolor underprint. Samoan village at center, M. Tanumafili II at right. Clear area at lower right containing a Bava bowl visible from both sides. Back: Family scene at center, arms at upper right. Printer: NPA (without imprint). Polymer plastic. UV: serial # fluoresces orange. 140x72mm.		
	a. Text on face partly engraved. Serial # prefix *AAA*.	FV	6.50
	b. Printing as a. Uncut sheet of 4 subjects. Serial # prefix *AAB*.	—	25.00
	c. Face completely lithographed, deeper blue, purple and dull brown. Serial # prefix *AAC*.	FV	3.50
	d. Serial # prefix: *AAD*.	FV	3.50
	e. Serial # prefix: *AAE-AAK*.	FV	3.50

2002-2008 ND Issue

		VF	UNC
32	**2 Tala** ND (2003). Brown, blue and purple on multicolor underprint. Woodcarver at right, islands at center. Back: Hut and palm tree. Expected new issue. 140x72mm.	—	—

		VF	UNC
33	**5 Tala** ND (2002). Red on multicolor underprint. Child writing at right, national flag at left center. Back: Small port city at left center, arms at lower center, national flag at center right. Watermark: M. Tanumafili II. 140x72mm.		
	a. Signature title: *MINISTER OF FINANCE*.	FV	6.50
	b. Signature titles: *MINISTER OF FINANCE* and *Governor*.	FV	6.50

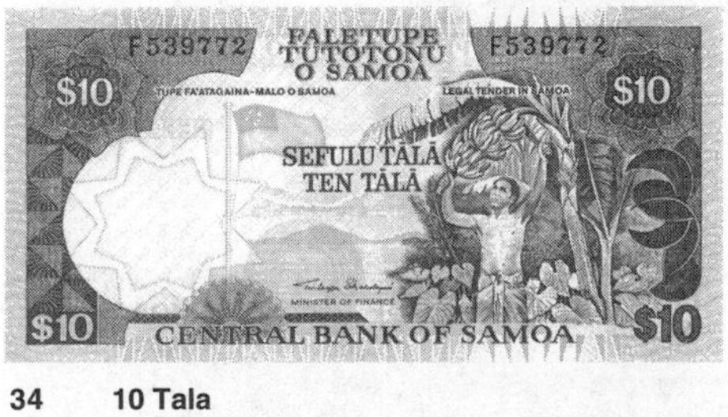

		VF	UNC
34	**10 Tala** ND (2002). Dark brown and purple on multicolor underprint. Man picking bananas at right, national flag at left center. Back: Shoreline landscape, arms at lower center, national flag at center right. Watermark: M. Tanumafili II. 140x72mm.		
	a. Signatrue title: *MINISTER OF FINANCE*.	FV	10.00
	b. Signature titles: *MINISTER OF FINANCE* and *GOVERNOR*.	Unc	10.00

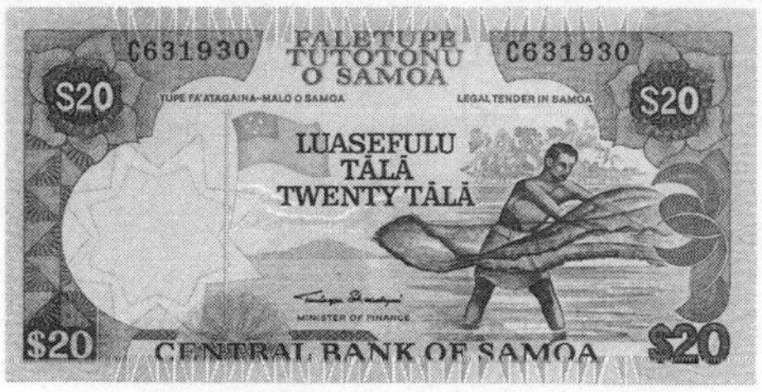

		VF	UNC
35	**20 Tala** ND (2002). Brown and orange-brown on multicolor underprint. Fishermen with net at right, national flag at left center. Back: Arms at lower center, national flag at center right, round building at left. Watermark: M. Tanumafili II. 140x72mm.		
	a. Signature title: *MINISTER OF FINANCE*.	FV	20.00
	b. Signature titles: *MINISTER OF FINANCE* and *GOVERNOR*.	FV	20.00
36	**50 Tala** ND (2006). Green on multicolor underprint. Malietoa Tanumafili II at right, National Museum at center. Back: Man performing traditional knife dance. Signature titles: *MINISTER OF FINANCE* and *GOVERNOR*. 140x72mm.	FV	40.00
37	**100 Tala** ND (2006). Olive and brown on multicolor underprint. Malietoa Tanumafili at right, flag and Fono House (Parliament) at center. Back: Harvest scene. Signature titles: *MINISTER OF FINANCE* and *GOVERNOR*. 140x72mm.	FV	65.00

2008 Issue

		VF	UNC
38	**5 Tala** 2008. Rose and purple on multicolor underprint. Beach scene at center. Back: Home of Robert Louis Stevenson. 140x70mm.		
	a. Issued note.	FV	6.00
	r. Replacement note. Serial # prefix: *ZZ*.	FV	10.00
	s. Specimen. Red overprint: *SPECIMEN* on both sides.	—	50.00

		VF	UNC
39	**10 Tala** 2008. Blue and green on multicolor underprint. Championship rugby team at center. Back: Group of children. 140x70mm.		
	a. Issued note.	FV	10.00
	r. Replacement note. Serial # prefix: *ZZ*.	FV	17.50
	s. Specimen. Red overprint: *SPECIMEN* on both sides.	—	50.00

40 **20 Tala** | VF | UNC
2008. Brown, yellow and orange on multicolor underprint. Waterfall. Back: Bird. 140x70mm.

	VF	UNC
a. Issued note.	FV	20.00
r. Replacement note. Serial # prefix: *ZZ*.	FV	30.00
s. Specimen. Red overprint: *SPECIMEN* on both sides.	—	50.00

41 **50 Tala** | VF | UNC
2008. Purple, blue and multicolor. Government building at center. Back: Central Bank building. 140x70mm.

	VF	UNC
a. Issued note.	FV	40.00
r. Replacement note. Serial # prefix: *ZZ*.	FV	60.00
s. Specimen. Red overprint: *SPECIMEN* on both sides.	—	100.

42 **100 Tala** | VF | UNC
2008. Dark green and light green on multicolor underprint. Malietoa Tanumfili II at center. Back: Church. 140x70mm.

	VF	UNC
a. Issued note.	FV	65.00
r. Replacement note. Serial # prefix: *ZZ*.	FV	100.
s. Specimen. Red overprint: *SPECIMEN* on both sides.	—	125.

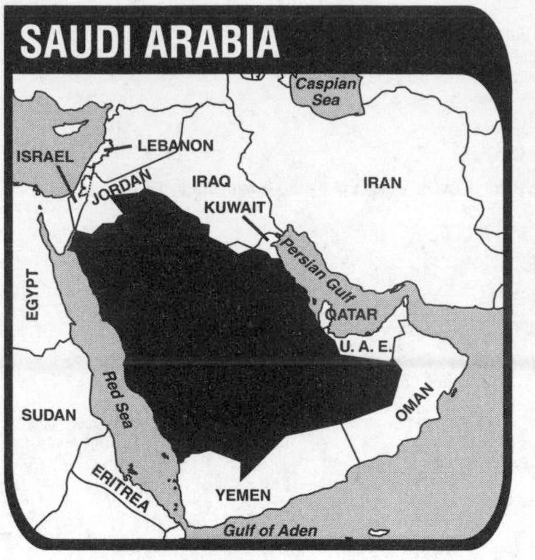

The Kingdom of Saudi Arabia, an independent and absolute hereditary monarchy comprising the former sultanate of Nejd, the old kingdom of Hejaz, Asir and el Hasa, occupies four-fifths of the Arabian peninsula. The kingdom has an area of 2,149,690 sq. km. and a population of 28.15 million. Capital: Riyadh. The economy is d on oil, which provides 85 percent of Saudi Arabia's revenue.

Saudi Arabia is the birthplace of Islam and home to Islam's two holiest shrines in Mecca and Medina. The king's official title is the Custodian of the Two Holy Mosques. The modern Saudi state was founded in 1932 by Abd al-Aziz bin Abd al-Rahman al Saud (Ibn Saud) after a 30-year campaign to unify most of the Arabian Peninsula. A male descendent of Ibn Saud, his son Abdallah bin Abd al-Aziz, rules the country today as required by the country's 1992 Basic Law. Following Iraq's invasion of Kuwait in 1990, Saudi Arabia accepted the Kuwaiti royal family and 400,000 refugees while allowing Western and Arab troops to deploy on its soil for the liberation of Kuwait the following year. The continuing presence of foreign troops on Saudi soil after the liberation of Kuwait became a source of tension between the royal family and the public until all operational US troops left the country in 2003. Major terrorist attacks in May and November 2003 spurred a strong on-going campaign against domestic terrorism and extremism. King Abdallah has continued the cautious reform program begun when he was crown prince. To promote increased political participation, the government held elections nationwide from February through April 2005 for half the members of 179 municipal councils. In December 2005, King Abdallah completed the process by appointing the remaining members of the advisory municipal councils. The country remains a leading producer of oil and natural gas and holds more than 20% of the world's proven oil reserves. The government continues to pursue economic reform and diversification, particularly since Saudi Arabia's accession to the WTO in December 2005, and promotes foreign investment in the kingdom. A burgeoning population, aquifer depletion, and an economy largely dependent on petroleum output and prices are all ongoing governmental concerns.

RULERS:

Sa'ud Ibn Abdul Aziz, AH1373-1383/1953-1964AD
Faisal, AH1383-1395/1964-1975AD
Khaled, AH1395-1402/1975-1982AD
Fahd, AH1402-/1982AD-

MONETARY SYSTEM:

1 Riyal = 20 Ghirsh

REPLACEMENT NOTES:

#1-4, serial number starting with an Arabic zero.

KINGDOM

SAUDI ARABIAN MONETARY AGENCY

LAW OF 1.7. AH1379; 1961 ND ISSUE

6 **1 Riyal** | VF | UNC
L. AH1379 (1961). Brown on light blue and green underprint. Hill of Light at center. Signature 1. Back: Violet-brown and green. Arms (palm tree and crossed swords). Watermark: Arms (palm tree and crossed swords). Embedded security thread. | 25.00 | 85.00

7	5 Riyals	VF	UNC
	L. AH1379 (1961). Blue and green on multicolor underprint. Fortress at center. Back: Arms (palm tree and crossed swords). Watermark: Arms (palm tree and crossed swords). Embedded security thread.		
	a. Signature #1.	80.00	350.
	b. Signature #2.	150.	500.

8	10 Riyals	VF	UNC
	L. AH1379 (1961). Green on pink and multicolor underprint. Dhows in Jedda harbor. Back: Arms (palm tree and crossed swords). Watermark: Arms (palm tree and crossed swords). Embedded security thread.		
	a. Signature #1.	150.	500.
	b. Signature #2.	200.	750.

9	50 Riyals	VF	UNC
	L. AH1379 (1961). Violet and olive-green on multicolor underprint. Derrick at center right. Back: Arms (palm tree and crossed swords). Watermark: Arms (palm tree and crossed swords). Embedded security thread.		
	a. Signature #1.	300.	1250.
	b. Signature #2.	350.	1400.

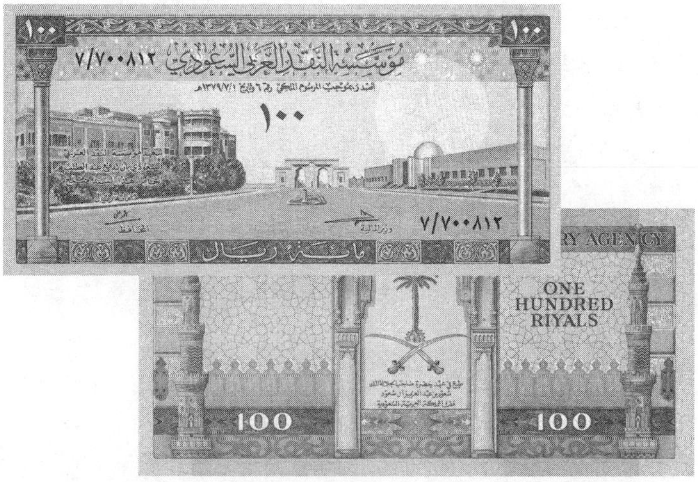

10	100 Riyals	VF	UNC
	L. AH1379 (1961). Red on multicolor underprint. Building at left, archway in background at center, building at right. Back: Arms (palm tree and crossed swords). Watermark: Arms (palm tree and crossed swords). Embedded security thread.		
	a. Signature #1.	1250.	3000.
	b. Signature #2.	1100.	2750.

Law of 1.7. AH1379; 1968 ND Issue

11	1 Riyal	VF	UNC
	L. AH1379 (1968). Purple on multicolor underprint. Goverment building at center right. Back: Saudi arms. Watermark: Arms. Embedded security thread.		
	a. Signature #2.	5.00	30.00
	b. Signature #3.	6.00	35.00
	s. As a. Specimen.	—	—

12	5 Riyals	VF	UNC
	L. AH1379 (1968). Green on multicolor underprint. Airport. Back: Oil loading on ships at dockside. Watermark: Arms. Embedded security thread.		
	a. Signature #2.	20.00	75.00
	b. Signature #3.	75.00	300.

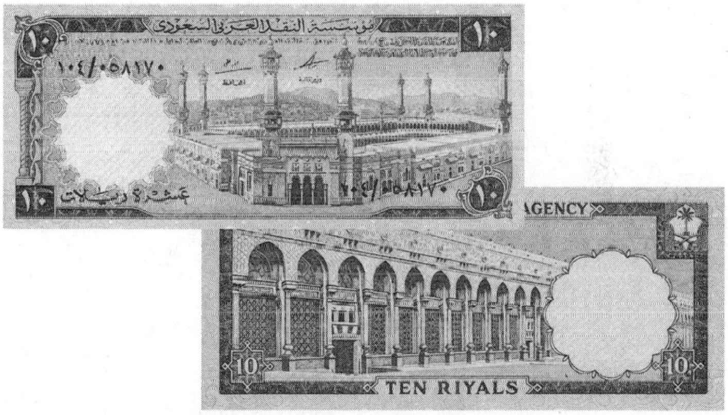

13	10 Riyals	VF	UNC
	L. AH1379 (1968). Gray-blue on multicolor underprint. Mosque. Signature 2. Back: Al-Masa Wall with arches. Watermark: Arms. Embedded security thread.	20.00	75.00

14	50 Riyals	VF	UNC
	L. AH1379 (1968). Brown on multicolor underprint. Courtyard of mosque at right. Back: Saudi arms at left, row of palms at center. Watermark: Arms. Embedded security thread.		
	a. Signature #2.	95.00	340.
	b. Signature #3.	85.00	310.

15 **100 Riyals** | VF | UNC

L. AH1379 (1966). Red on multicolor underprint. Government Building at center right. Back: Derricks at left center. Watermark: Arms. Embedded security thread.

	VF	UNC
a. Signature #2.	110.	400.
b. Signature #3.	90.00	350.

LAW OF 1.7. AH1379; 1976; 1977 ND ISSUE

16 **1 Riyal** | VF 1.00 | UNC 6.00

L. AH1379 (1977). Red-brown on multicolor underprint. Portrait of King Faisal at right, Hill of Light at center. Signature 4. Back: Airport at left center. Watermark: King Faisal.

Incorrect

Correct

17 **5 Riyals** | VF | UNC

L. AH1379 (1977). Green and brown on multicolor underprint. Portrait of King Faisal at right, Irrigation canal at center. Signature 4. Back: Dam at left center. Watermark: King Faisal.

	VF	UNC
a. Incorrect Khamsa (five) in lower center panel of text.	8.00	30.00
b. Correct Khamsa (five) in lower center panel of text.	4.00	20.00

18 **10 Riyals** | VF 6.00 | UNC 30.00

L. AH1379 (1977). Lilac and brown on multicolor underprint. Portrait of King Faisal at right, oil drilling platform at center. Signature 4. Back: Oil refinery. Watermark: King Faisal.

19 **50 Riyals** | VF 32.50 | UNC 95.00

L. AH1379 (1976). Green, purple and brown on multicolor underprint. Portrait of King Faisal at right, Arches of mosque at center. Signature 4. Back: Courtyard of mosque at left center. Watermark: King Faisal.

20 **100 Riyals** | VF 48.50 | UNC 150.

L. AH1379 (1976). Blue and turquoise on multicolor underprint. Mosque at center, King 'Abd al-'Aziz Ibn Saud at right. Back: Long building with arches.

LAW OF 1.7. AH1379; 1983; 1984 ND ISSUE

#21-26 wmk: Kg. Fahd.

Lower l. serial # fluoresces gold under UV light. Non-visible portr. of King fluoresces yellow under UV light.

#21-24 upper l. panel also exists w/unnecessary upper accent mark in "Monetary." at ctr. r. in text.

21 **1 Riyal** | VF | UNC

L. AH1379 (1984). Dark brown on multicolor underprint. 7th century gold dinar at left, portrait King Fahd at center right. Two signature varieties. Back: Flowers and landscape. Watermark: King Faud. UV: fibers fluoresce yellow, lower serial # orange, King's face yellow. 134x62mm.

	VF	UNC
a. Incorrect text. Signature 5 with acting in title.	1.00	4.00
b. Correct "Monetary" text. Signature 5 with acting in title.	FV	3.00
c. As b. but without acting in title.	FV	2.00
d. Signature 6.	FV	2.00

Incorrect

Correct

#	Note	VF	UNC
22	**5 Riyals** *L. AH1379* (1983). Purple, brown, and blue-green on multicolor underprint. Dhows at left, portrait King Fahd at center right. Back: Oil refinery at center right. Watermark: King Faud. 145x66mm.		
	a. Incorrect text. Signature 5 with acting in title.	2.50	10.00
	b. Correct "Monetary" text. Signature 5 with acting in title.	FV	8.00
	c. Like b, but without acting in title.	FV	5.00
	d. Signature 6.	FV	4.50

#	Note	VF	UNC
23	**10 Riyals** *L. AH1379* (1983). Black, brown and purple on multicolor underprint. Fortress at left, portrait King Fahd at center right. Back: Palm trees at center right. Watermark: King Faud. 150x68mm.		
	a. Incorrect text. Signature 5 with acting in title.	FV	18.00
	b. Correct "Monetary" text. Signature 5 with acting in title.	FV	13.00
	c. As b. without acting in title.	FV	10.00
	d. Signature 6.	FV	9.00
	s. Specimen. Red overprint in Arabic on face and English on back.	—	1250.

#	Note	VF	UNC
24	**50 Riyals** *L. AH1379* (1983). Dark green and dark brown on multicolor underprint. Dome of the Rock in Jerusalem at left, portrait King Fahd at center right. Back: Al-Aqsa Mosque at center. Watermark: King Faud. 155x70mm.		
	a. Incorrect text. Signature 5 with acting in title.	FV	60.00
	b. Correct "Monetary" text. Signature 5 with acting in title.	FV	52.00
	c. Signature 6.	FV	42.00
	s. As b. Specimen. Red overprint in English on both sides. Punch hole cancelled.	—	2000.

#	Note	VF	UNC
25	**100 Riyals** *L. AH1379* (1984). Brown-violet and olive-green on multicolor underprint. Mosque at left, portrait King Fahd at center right. Saudi arms in blind embossed latent image area at left center. Back: Mosque at center. Watermark: King Faud. 160x72mm.		
	a. Signature 5 with acting in title.	FV	85.00
	b. Signature 5 without acting in title.	FV	70.00
	c. Signature 6.	FV	70.00
	s. Specimen. Red overprint in Arabic on face and English on back.	—	2000.

Incorrect

Correct

#	Note	VF	UNC
26	**500 Riyals** *L. AH1379* (1983). Purple and green on multicolor underprint. Ka'aba at left, portrait King 'Abd al-'Aziz Ibn Saud at center right. Saudi arms in blind embossed latent image area at left center. Back: Courtyard of Great Mosque at center. Watermark: King Faud. 163x73mm.		
	a. Incorrect "Five Hundred Riyals" in lower center panel of text. Signature 5 with acting in title.	150.	420.
	b. Correct "Five Hundred Riyals" in lower center panel of text. Signature 5 with acting in title.	FV	350.
	c. As b. without acting in title.	FV	275.
	d. Signature 6.	FV	275.
	s. As a. Specimen. Red overprint in Arabic on face and English on back.	—	2000.

2000 Commemorative Issue

#27 and 28, Centennial of Kingdom

#	Note	VF	UNC
27	**20 Riyals** AH1419, 1999. Brown, red, gray and blue on multicolor underprint. Abdul Aziz at left center. Signature 6. Back: Annur Mouuntain at center, commemorative logo and text at left. Watermark: Abdul Aziz. 152x69mm.	FV	15.00

#	Note	VF	UNC
28	**200 Riyals** 2000. Red, brown, gray and green on multicolor underprint. Abdul Aziz at left center. Signature 6. Back: Al Mussmack Palace at lower right and its gate. Commemorative logo and text at right. Watermark: Abdul Aziz. 163x73mm.	FV	130.

2003 Issue

29	**100 Riyals**	VF	UNC
	2003. Brown, violet and multicolor. Hologram added at upper center. Back: Mosque at center. 160x72mm.	FV	68.50

30	**500 Riyals**	VF	UNC
	2003. Purple, green and peach on multicolor underprint. King 'Abd al-'Aziz Ibn Saud at right, Ka'aba at left. Back: Couryard of Great Mosque at center. 166x74mm.	FV	255.

2007 Issue

31	**1 Riyal**	VF	UNC
	2007; 2009; 2012. Black, green and peach on multicolor underprint. King Abdullah at right, coin at center. Back: Saudi Arabian Monetary Authority building. 133x63mm.		
	a. 2007.	FV	1.25
	b. 2009.	FV	1.25
	c. 2012.	FV	1.25
	s. Specimen.	—	75.00

32	**5 Riyals**	VF	UNC
	AH1428 2007. Violet, blue and multicolor. King 'Abd al-'Aziz ibn Saud at right, Ras Tanura refinery at center. Back: Oil tanker at pier in the port of Jubayl. 145x66mm.		
	a. Issued note.	FV	5.00
	s. Specimen.	—	75.00

33	**10 Riyals**	VF	UNC
	2007. Black and brown on multicolor underprint. King Abdullah at right, palace at center. Back: King Abdullah Historical Center in Riyadh. 150x68mm.		
	a. Issued note.	FV	8.00
	s. Specimen.	—	100.
34	**20 Riyals**		
	2007. Expected new issue. 152x69mm.	—	—

35	**50 Riyals**	VF	UNC
	2007. Black, green and yellow on multicolor underprint. King Abdullah at right, Dome of the Rock at center. Back: Mosque. 155x70mm.		
	a. Issued note.	FV	35.00
	s. Specimen.	—	150.

36	**100 Riyals**	VF	UNC
	2007. Violet and light blue on multicolor underprint. King Abdullah at right, Green Dome Mosque in Medina at center. Back: Mosque. 160x72mm.		
	a. Issued note.	FV	55.00
	s. Specimen	—	200.
37	**200 Riyals**		
	2007. Expected new issue. 163x73mm.	—	—
38	**500 Riyals**		
	2007. Black and blue on multicolor underprint. King Abdullah at right, Ka'aba at center. Back: Great Mosque in Mecca. 166x74mm.		
	a. Issued note.	FV	250.
	s. Specimen.	—	400.

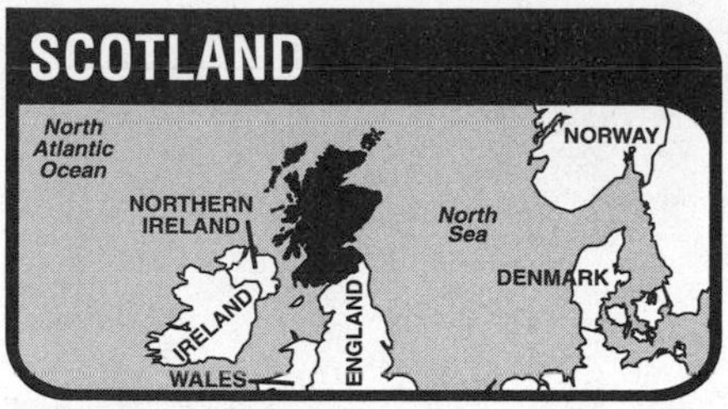

Scotland, a part of the United Kingdom of Great Britain and Northern Ireland, consists of the northern part of the island of Great Britain. It has an area of 30,414 sq. mi. (78,772 sq. km.). Capital: Edinburgh. Principal industries are agriculture, fishing, manufacturing and ship-building.

In the 5th century, Scotland consisted of four kingdoms; that of the Picts, the Scots, Strathclyde, and Northumbria. The Scottish kingdom was united by Malcolm II (1005-34), but its ruler was forced to payo homage to the English crown in 1174. Scotland won independence under Robert Bruce at Bannockburn in 1314 and was ruled by the house of Stuart from 1371 to 1688. The personal union of the kingdoms of England and Scotland was achieved in 1603 by the accession of King James VI of Scotland as James I of England. Scotland was united with England by Parliamentary act in 1707.

RULERS:

British

MONETARY SYSTEM:

1 Pound = 20 Shillings to 1971
1 Pound = 100 New Pence, 1971-1981
1 Pound = 100 Pence, 1982-
1 Pound = 20 Shillings to 1971

REPLACEMENT NOTES:

#111, Z/1, Z/2 or Z/3 prefix; #112 ZA or ZB prefix; #113 ZB prefix.

British Administration

Bank of Scotland

1935; 1938 Issue

		VF	UNC
91	**1 Pound** 1937-43. Yellow-brown, dark brown and gray-blue. Arms of the bank at left. Back: Bank building.		
	a. Signature Lord Elphinstone and A. W. M. Beveridge. 15.1.1935-15.9.1937.	90.00	280.
	b. Signature Lord Elphinstone and J. Macfarlane. 5.1.1939-7.5.1941.	80.00	260.
	c. Signature Lord Elphinstone and J. B. Crawford. 2.6.1942; 16.10.1943.	80.00	240.
	s. As c. Specimen.	—	225.
92	**5 Pounds** 1935-44. Yellow-brown, dark brown and gray-blue. Thistle motif at left. Back: Bank building.		
	a. Signature Lord Elphinstone and A. W. M. Beveridge. 17.1.1935-17.3.1938.	300.	975.
	b. Signature Lord Elphinstone and J. Macfarlane. Black value panels. 24.4.1939-16.10.1941.	300.	975.
	c. Signature Lord Elphinstone and J. B. Crawford. 5.6.1942-26.9.1944.	250.	850.
	s. As c. Specimen.	—	350.
93	**10 Pounds** 1938-63. Scottish arms in panel at left, medallion of Goddess of fortune below arms at right. Back: Bank building.		
	a. Signature Lord Elphinstone and A. W. M. Beveridge. 24.1.1935; 28.6.1938.	1200.	2500.
	b. Signature Lord Elphinstone and J. B. Crawford. 16.7.1942; 15.10.1942.	1100.	2250.
	c. Signature Lord Bilsland and Sir Wm. Watson. 26.9.1963; 27.9.1963.	700.	1600.
94	**20 Pounds** 1935-65. Scottish arms in panel at left, medallion of Goddess of fortune below arms at right. Back: Bank building.		
	a. Signature Lord Elphinstone and A. W. M. Beveridge. 11.1.1935-22.7.1938.	500.	1400.
	b. Signature Lord Elphinstone and J. Macfarlane. 16.5.1939; 12.7.1939.	550.	1600.
	c. Signature Lord Elphinstone and J. B. Crawford. 5.6.1942-11.8.1952.	425.	1200.
	d. Signature Lord Elphinstone and Sir Wm. Watson. 5.12.1952; 14.4.1953.	500.	1400.
	e. Signature Sir J. Craig and Sir Wm. Watson. 6.4.1955-12.6.1956	350.	1000.
	f. Signature Lord Bilsland and Sir Wm. Watson. 21.3.1958-3.10.1963.	300.	900.

		VF	UNC
95	**100 Pounds** 1935-62. Scottish arms in panel at left, medallion of Goddess of fortune below arms at right. Back: Bank building.		
	a. Signature Lord Elphinstone and A. W. M. Beveridge. 8.1.1935-12.8.1937.	2000.	5000.
	b. Signature Lord Elphinstone and J. Macfarlane. 2.4.1940; 15.7.1940.	1750.	4200.
	c. Signature Lord Elphinestone and J. B. Crawford. 10.6.1942; 14.12.1951.	1500.	3800.
	d. Signature John Craig and Sir Wm. Watson. 14.9.1956-3.12.1956.	1500.	3500.
	e. Signature Lord Bilsland and Sir Wm. Watson. 24.3.1959-30.11.1962	1500.	3500.

1961 Issue

		VF	UNC
102	**1 Pound** 1961-65. Light brown and pale blue. Medallion at center, date below. Back: Ship at center.		
	a. Imprint ends: *LD.* Signature Lord Bilsland and Sir Wm. Watson. 10.5.1961-13.2.1964.	25.00	80.00
	b. Imprint ends: *LTD.* Signature Lord Bilsland and Sir Wm. Watson. 4.5.1965; 11.5.1965.	20.00	70.00
	c. Magnetic ink encoded experimental note. Four short parallel lines overprinted at right and left borders. (1903-64).	—	400.
103	**5 Pounds** 14.9.1961-22.9.1961. Light brown and pale blue. Medallion at center, date below. Signature Lord Bilsland and Sir Wm. Watson. Back: Arms at left, ship at right. Reduced size.	70.00	250.

1961; 1966 Issue

		VF	UNC
105	**1 Pound** 1966; 1967. Light brown and pale blue. Similar to #102 but *EDINBURGH* and date at right. Signature Lord Polwarth and J. Letham with titles: *GOVERNOR* and *TREASURER & GENERAL MANAGER.* Two watermark varieties. Back: Ship at center.		
	a. Without electronic sorting marks on back. 1.6.1966.	18.50	65.00
	b. With electronic sorting marks on back. 3.3.1967.	17.50	60.00
	s. As b. Specimen.	—	250.

106 5 Pounds

1961-67. Blue and light brown. Medallion of fortune at center, numerals of value filled in at base. Back: Arms at left, ship at right.

	VF	UNC
a. Signature Lord Bilsland and Sir Wm. Watson with titles: *GOVERNOR* and *TREASURER*. 25.9.1961-12.1.1965.	50.00	180.
b. Signature Lord Polwarth and Sir Wm. Watson. 7.3.1966-8.3.1966.	55.00	200.
c. Lighter shades of printing. Signature Lord Polwarth and J. Letham with titles: *GOVERNOR* and *TREASURER & GENERAL MANAGER*. 1.2.1967; 2.2.1967.	50.00	180.
d. Signature titles as b. with electronic sorting marks on back. 1.11.1967.	60.00	200.
s. As c. Specimen.	—	300.

1968; 1969 Issue

109 1 Pound

1968; 1969. Ochre on blue and multicolor underprint. Arms at center flanked by two women. Back: Arms at upper left, shield at upper center, sailing ship at upper right.

	VF	UNC
a. *EDINBURGH* 19mm in length. 17.7.1968.	20.00	80.00
b. *EDINBURGH* 24mm in length. 18.8.1969.	20.00	80.00
s. As b. Specimen.	—	400.

110 5 Pounds

1968-69. Green on multicolor underprint. Arms at center flanked by two women. Back: Arms at upper left, shield at upper center, sailing ship at upper right.

	VF	UNC
a. *EDINBURGH* 19mm in length. 1.11.1968; 4.11.1968.	80.00	250.
b. *EDINBURGH* 24mm in length. 8.12.1969; 9.12.1969.	80.00	250.

110A 20 Pounds

	VF	UNC
5.5.1969. Scottish arms in panel at left, medallion of Goddess of Fortune below arms at center right. Signature: Lord Polwarth and J. Letham. With security thread. Watermark: Thistle.	175.	425.

1970-74 Issue

#111-113 Replacement notes: #111 - Serial # prefix *Z/1*, *Z/2* or *Z/3*; #112 - Serial # prefix *ZA* or *ZB*; #113 - Serial # prefix *ZB*.

111 1 Pound

1970-88. Green on multicolor underprint. Arms at center flanked by two women, Sir W. Scott at right. Back: Sailing ship at left, arms at upper center, medallion of Pallas seated at right.

	VF	UNC
a. Signature Lord Polwarth and T. W. Walker. 10.8.1970; 31.8.1971.	17.50	55.00
b. Signature Lord Clydesmuir and T. W. Walker. 1.11.1972; 30.8.1973.	17.50	55.00
c. Signature Lord Clydesmuir and A. M. Russell. 28.10.1974-3.10.1978.	6.00	22.50
d. Signature Lord Clydesmuir and D. B. Pattullo. 15.10.1979; 4.11.1980.	6.00	15.00
e. Signature T. N. Risk and D. B. Pattullo. 30.7.1981.	8.00	18.00
f. Without sorting marks on back. Signature like e. 7.10.1983; 9.11.1984; 12.12.1985; 18.11.1986.	5.00	16.00
g. Signature T. N. Risk and L. P. Burt. 19.8.1988.	4.00	12.50
s. As a (1970); c (1974). Specimen.	—	225.

112 5 Pounds

1970-88. Blue on multicolor underprint. Arms at center flanked by two women, Sir W. Scott at right. Back: Sailing ship at let, arms at upper center, medallion of Pallas seated at right.

	VF	UNC
a. Signature Lord Polwarth and T. W. Walker. 10.8.1970; 2.9.1971.	60.00	175.
b. Signature Lord Clydesmuir and T. W. Walker. 4.12.1972; 5.9.1973.	40.00	125.
c. Signature Lord Clydesmuir and A. M. Russell. 4.11.1974; 1.12.1975; 21.11.1977; 19.10.1978.	35.00	105.
d. Signature Lord Clydesmuir and D. B. Pattullo. 28.9.1979; 28.11.1980.	30.00	90.00
e. Signature T. N. Risk and D. B. Pattullo. 27.7.1981; 25.6.1982.	25.00	85.00
f. Without encoding marks. 13.10.1983; 3.12.1985; 29.2.1988.	25.00	60.00
s. As a (1970); c (1974). Specimen.	—	225.

113 10 Pounds

1974-90. Brown on multicolor underprint. Arms at center flanked by two women, Sir W. Scott at right. Back: Medallions of sailing ship at lower left, Pallas seated at upper left center, arms at right.

	VF	UNC
a. Signature Lord Clydesmuir and A. M. Russell. 1.5.1974-10.10.1979.	50.00	190.
b. Signature Lord Clydesmuir and D. B. Pattullo. 5.2.1981.	50.00	175.
c. Signature T. N. Risk and D. B. Pattullo. 22.7.1981; 16.6.1982; 14.10.1983; 17.9.1984; 8.1.1986; 20.10.1986; 6.8.1987.	35.00	70.00
d. Signature T. N. Risk and P. Burt. 1.9.1989; 31.10.1990.	35.00	70.00
cr. As c. Replacement.	60.00	200.

114 20 Pounds

1970-87. Purple on multicolor underprint. Arms at center flanked by two women, Sir W. Scott at right. Back: Arms at upper left, above sailing ship with medallion of Pallas seated below, head office building at center.

	VF	UNC
a. Signature Lord Polwarth and T. W. Walker. 1.10.1970.	175.	500.
b. Signature Lord Clydesmuir and T. W. Walker. 3.1.1973.	150.	450.
c. Signature Lord Clydesmuir and A. M. Russell. 8.11.1974; 14.1.1977.	120.	425.
d. Signature Lord Clydesmuir and D. B. Pattullo. 16.7.1979; 2.2.1981.	125.	325.
e. Signature T. N. Risk and D. B. Pattullo. 4.8.1981-15.12.1987.	85.00	300.
s. As a. Specimen. 1.10.1970.	—	475.

115 100 Pounds

1971-86. Red on multicolor underprint. Arms at center flanked by two women, Sir W. Scott at right. Back: Arms at upper left, medallions of sailing ship at lower left, Pallas seated at lower right, head office building at center.

	VF	UNC
a. Signature Lord Polwarth and T. W. Walker. 6.12.1971.	625.	1500.
b. Signature Lord Clydesmuir and T. W. Walker. 6.9.1973.	600.	1400.
c. Signature Lord Clydesmuir and A. M. Russell. 11.10.1978.	550.	1200.
d. Signature Lord Clydesmuir and D. B. Pattullo. 26.1.1981.	525.	1100.
e. Signature T. N. Risk and D. B. Pattullo. 11.6.1982; 26.11.1986.	450.	900.
s. As a. Specimen.	—	600.

1990-92 Sterling Issue

116 5 Pounds

1990-94. Blue on multicolor underprint. Arms at center flanked by two women, Sir W. Scott at right. *STERLING* added below value. Back: Sailing ship at left, arms at upper center, medallion of Pallas seated at right. 135x70mm.

	VF	UNC
a. Signature T. N. Risk and P. Burt. 20.6.1990.	17.50	40.00
b. Signature D. B. Pattullo and P. Burt. 6.11.1991; 18.1.1993; 7.1.1994.	17.50	40.00

117 10 Pounds

7.5.1992; 9.3.1993; 13.4.1994. Deep brown on multicolor underprint. Arms at center flanked by two women, Sir W. Scott at right. *STERLING* added below value. Signature D. B. Pattullo and P. Burt. Back: Medallions of sailing ship at lower left, Pallas seated at upper left center, arms at right. 142x75mm.

	VF	UNC
a. Issued note.	25.00	70.00
r. Replacement.	30.00	90.00

118 20 Pounds

	VF	UNC
1.7.1991; 3.2.1992; 12.1.1993. Purple on multicolor underprint. Arms at center flanked by two women, Sir W. Scott at right. *STERLING* added below value. Signature D. B. Pattullo and P. Burt. Back: Arms at upper left, above sailing ship with medallion of Pallas seated below, head office building at center. 148x81mm.	50.00	100.

118A 100 Pounds

14.2.1990; 22.1.1992; 2.12.1992; 9.2.1994. Red on multicolor underprint. *STERLING* added below value. Similar to #115.

	VF	UNC
a. 14.2.1990. Signature T.N. Risk and Peter Burt.	350.	750.
b. 22.1.1992; 2.12.1992; 9.2.1994. Signature D.B. Pattullo and Peter Burt.	325.	700.
s. Specimen.	—	600.

1995 Commemorative Issue

#119-122, Tercentenary - Bank of Scotland

119 5 Pounds

1995-2006. Dark blue and purple on multicolor underprint. Sir Walter Scott at left, bank arms at center. Back: Bank head office building at lower left, medallion of Pallas seated, arms and medallion of sailing ship at right. Watermark: Sir Walter Scott. Printer: TDLR (without imprint). 135x70mm.

	VF	UNC
a. Signature D. Bruce Pattullo and Peter A. Burt. 4.1.1995. Signature titles as: *GOVERNOR* and *TREASURER & CHIEF GENERAL MANAGER.*	FV	40.00
b. Signature D. Bruce Pattullo and Gavin Masterton. 13.9.1996.	FV	35.00
c. Signature Alistair Grant and Gavin Masterton. 5.8.1998.	FV	20.00
d. Signature Peter Burt and George Mitchell. 25.6.2002. Signature titles as: *GOVERNOR* and *TREASURER & MANAGING DIRECTOR.*	FV	18.50
e. Signature Dennis Stevenson and Colin Matthew. 1.1.2006.	FV	18.50

120 10 Pounds VF UNC

1995-2006. Dark brown and deep olive-green on multicolor underprint. Sir Walter Scott at left, bank arms at center. Back: Workers by distilling equipment at center. Bank head office building at lower left, medallion of Pallas seated, arms and medallion of sailing ships at right. Watermark: Sir Walter Scott. Printer: TDLR (without imprint). 142x72mm.

	VF	UNC
a. Signature D. Bruce Pattullo and Peter A. Burt. 1.2.1995. Signature titles as: *GOVERNOR and TREASURER & CHIEF GENERAL MANAGER.*	FV	50.00
b. Signature Bruce Pattullo and Gavin Masterton. 5.8.1997.	FV	45.00
c. Signature Alistair Grant and Gavin Masterton. 18.8.1998.	FV	40.00
d. Signature John Shaw and George Mitchell. 18.6.2001. Signature titles as: *GOVERNOR and TREASURER & MANAGING DIRECTOR.*	FV	40.00
e. Signature George Mitchell. 26.11.2003; 24.9.2004. Signature title as: *GOVERNOR.*	FV	37.50
f. Signature Lord Stevenson adn Colin Matthew. 1.1.2006. Signature titles as: *GOVERNOR* and *TREASURER.*	FV	35.00

121 20 Pounds VF UNC

1995-2004. Violet and brown on multicolor underprint. Sir Walter Scott at left, bank arms at center. Back: Woman researcher at laboratory station at center. Bank head office building at lower left, medallion of Pallas seated, arms and medallion of sailing ships at right. Watermark: Sir Walter Scott. Printer: TDLR (without imprint). 150x80mm.

	VF	UNC
a. Signature D. Bruce Pattullo and Peter A. Burt. 1.5.1995. Signature titles as: *GOVERNOR* and *TREASURER & CHIEF GENERAL MANAGER.*	50.00	100.
b. Signature Bruce Pattullo and Gavin Masterton. 25.10.1996; 1.4.1998.	FV	90.00
c. Signature Alistair Grant and Gavin Masterton. 22.3.1999. Signature titles as: *GOVERNOR* and *TREASURER & MANAGING DIRECTOR.*	FV	85.00
d. Signature John Shaw and George Mitchell. 18.6.2001.	FV	75.00
e. Signature George Mitchell. 26.11.2003; 24.9.2004. Signature title as: *GOVERNOR.*	FV	70.00

122 50 Pounds VF UNC

1995-2006. Dark green and olive-brown on multicolor underprint. Sir W. Scott at left, bank arms at center. Back: Music director and violinists at center. Bank head office building at lower left, medallion of Pallas seated, arms and medallion of sailing ships at right. Watermark: Sir W. Scott. Printer: TDLR (without imprint). 155x85mm.

	VF	UNC
a. Signature D. Bruce Pattullo and Peter A. Burt. 1.5.1995. Signature titles as: *GOVERNOR* and *TREASURER & MANAGING DIRECTOR.*	110.	250.
b. Signature Alistair Grant and Gavin Masterton. 15.4.1999. Signature titles as: *GOVERNOR* and *TREASURER & MANAGING DIRECTOR.*	FV	200.
c. Signature George Mitchell. 29.1.2003. Signature title as *GOVERNOR.*	FV	170.
d. Signature Dennis Stevenson and Colin Matthew. 1.1.2006.	FV	160.

123 100 Pounds VF UNC

1995-2006. Red-violet and red-orange on multicolor underprint. Sir Walter Scott at left, bank arms at center. Back: Golf outing at center. Bank head office building at lower left, medallion of Pallas seated, arms and medallion of sailing ships at right. Watermark: Sir Walter Scott. Printer: TDLR (without imprint). 164x90mm.

	VF	UNC
a. Signature D. Bruce Pattullo and Peter A. Burt. 17.7.1995. Signature titles as: *GOVERNOR* and *TREASURER & CHIEF GENERAL MANAGER.*	300.	700.
b. Signature D. Bruce Pattullo and Gavin Masterton. 18.8.1997.	250.	500.
c. Signature Alistair Grant and Gavin Masterton. 19.5.1999. Signature titles as: *GOVERNOR* and *TREASURER & MANAGING DIRECTOR.*	FV	400.
d. Signature George Mitchell. 26.11.2003. Signature title as: *GOVERNOR.*	FV	375.
e. Signature Dennis Stevenson and Colin Matthew. 1.1.2006.	FV	350.

2007 Issue

124 5 Pounds VF UNC

2007-. Dark blue on multicolor underprint. Sir Walter Scott at center. Back: Statue and Brig o'Doon in South Ayrshire. Watermark: Sir Walter Scott. Printer: TDLR (without imprint). 135x70mm.

	VF	UNC
a. Signature Lord Stevenson and Colin Matthew. 17.9.2007. Signature titles as: *GOVERNOR* and *TREASURER.*	FV	17.50
s. Specimen.	—	125.

125 10 Pounds

2007-. Dark brown and deep olive green on multicolor underprint. Sir Walter Scott at center. Back: Glenfinnan Viaduct, West Highlands. Watermark: Sir Walter Scott. Printer: TDLR (without imprint). 142x75mm.

	VF	UNC
a. Signature Lord Stevenson and Colin Matthew. 17.9.2007. Signature titles as: *GOVERNOR* and *TREASURER.*	FV	35.00
s. Specimen.	—	125.

126 20 Pounds

2007-. Violet on multicolor underprint. Sir Walter Scott at center. Back: Firth of Forth rail and road bridges as seen from South Queensferry. Watermark: Sir Walter Scott. Printer: TDLR (without imprint). 150x80mm.

	VF	UNC
a. Signature Lord Stevenson and Colin Matthew. 17.9.2007. Signature titles as: *GOVERNOR* and *TREASURER.*	FV	70.00
s. Specimen.	—	150.

127 50 Pounds

2007-. Dark green on multicolor underprint. Sir Walter Scott at center. Back: Falkirk Wheel. Watermark: Sir Walter Scott. Printer: TDLR (without imprint). 155x85mm.

	VF	UNC
a. Signature Lord Stevenson and Colin Matthew. 17.9.2007. Signature titles as: *GOVERNOR* and *TREASURER.*	FV	150.
s. Specimen.	—	200.

128 100 Pounds

2007-. Red-violet and orange on multicolor underprint. Sir Walter Scott at center. Back: Kessock Bridge, Inverness. Watermark: Sir Walter Scott. Printer: TDLR (without imprint). 164x90mm.

	VF	UNC
a. Signature Lord Stevenson and Colin Matthew. 17.9.2007. Signature titles as: *GOVERNOR* and *TREASURER.*	FV	300.
s. Specimen.	—	400.

British Linen Bank

1961; 1962 Issue

162	**1 Pound**	VF	UNC
	30.9.1961. Blue and red. Sideview of seated Britannia in emblem at left, arms at upper right. Back: Blue. Printer: TDLR.	30.00	85.00
163	**5 Pounds**		
	2.1.1961; 3.2.1961. Blue and red. Sideview of seated Britannia in emblem at left, arms at upper right. Back: Blue. Printer: TDLR.	125.	325.
164	**20 Pounds**		
	14.2.1962, 3.3.1962, 4.4.1962. Blue and red. Sideview of seated Britannia in emblem at left, arms at upper right. Back: Blue. Printer: TDLR.	275.	800.
165	**100 Pounds**		
	9.5.1962; 1.6.1962. Blue and red. Sideview of seated Britannia in emblem at left, arms at upper right. Back: Blue. Printer: TDLR.	550.	1850.

1962 Issue

166	**1 Pound**	VF	UNC
	1962-67. Blue and red. Sideview of seated Britannia in emblem at left, arms at upper right. Back: Blue. Printer: TDLR. 155x85mm.		
	a. Signature A. P. Anderson. 31.3.1962.	27.50	75.00
	b. Test note with lines for electronic sorting on back. 31.3.1962.	—	350.
	c. Signature T. W. Walker. 1.7.1963-13.6.1967.	20.00	60.00
	s. As a, c. Specimen.	—	250.
167	**5 Pounds**		
	21.9.1962-18.8.1964. Blue and red. Sir Walter Scott at right, sideview of seated Britannia in emblem at left, arms at upper right. Back: Blue. Printer: TDLR. 140x85mm.		
	a. Signature A. P. Anderson. 21.9.1962; 20.10.1962; 16.6.1962.	30.00	100.
	b. Signature T. W. Walker. 16.6.1964; 17.7.1964; 18.8.1964.	30.00	100.
	c. As b. Test note with lines for electronic sorting. 17.7.1964.	150.	400.

1967 Issue

168	**1 Pound**	VF	UNC
	13.6.1967. Blue on multicolor underprint. Sideview of seated Britannia in emblem at left, arms at upper right. Back: Blue. Similar to number 166 but modified design and with lines for electronic sorting. Printer: TDLR.	20.00	60.00

1968 Issue

169	**1 Pound**	VF	UNC
	1968-70. Blue on multicolor underprint. Sir W. Scott at right, sideview of seated Britannia in emblem at left, supported arms at top center. Back: Blue. Printer: TDLR.		
	a. 29.2.1968; 5.11.1969.	20.00	60.00
	b. 20.7.1970.	40.00	120.
170	**5 Pounds**		
	22.3.1968; 23.4.1968; 24.5.1968. Blue and red. Sideview of seated Britannia in emblem at left, arms at upper right. Back: Blue. Printer: TDLR. Similar to #167, but reduced size and many plate changes. 146x78mm.	40.00	120.

Clydesdale and North of Scotland Bank Ltd.

1950-51 Issue

191	**1 Pound**	VF	UNC
	1950-60. Blue, red and orange. Ships at dockside at left, landscape (sheaves) at right. Back: River scene with trees.		
	a. 1.11.1950-1.11.1956.	45.00	150.
	b. 1.5.1958-1.11.1960.	40.00	125.
	s. As a. Specimen.	—	250.

192	**5 Pounds**	VF	UNC
	2.5.1951-1.3.1960. Purple. King's College at Aberdeen at lower left, Glasgow Cathedral at lower right.		
	a. Signature J. J. Campbell.	90.00	300.
	b. Signature R. D. Fairbairn.	90.00	300.
	s. As a. Specimen. TDLR oval overprint.	—	500.

		VF	UNC
193	**20 Pounds**		
	2.5.1951-1.8.1962. Green on multicolor underprint. King's College at Aberdeen at lower left, Glasgow Cathedral at lower right. 180x97mm.		
	a. Signature J. J. Campbell.	160.	550.
	b. Signature R. D. Fairbairn.	150.	500.
194	**100 Pounds**		
	2.5.1951. Blue. King's College at Aberdeen at lower left, Glasgow Cathedral at lower right. Signature J. J. Campbell. 180x97mm.	1200.	3000.

1961 Issue

		VF	UNC
195	**1 Pound**		
	1.3.1961; 2.5.1962; 1.2.1963. Green on multicolor underprint. Arms at right. Back: Ship and tug at center.		
	a. Issued note.	35.00	100.
	s. Specimen.	—	160.

		VF	UNC
196	**5 Pounds**		
	20.9.1961; 1.6.1962; 1.2.1963. Dark blue on multicolor underprint. Arms at right. Back: King's College at Aberdeen.	75.00	200.

Clydesdale Bank Limited

1963-64 Issue

		VF	UNC
197	**1 Pound**		
	2.9.1963-3.4.1967. Green on multicolor underprint. Arms at right. Back: Ship and tug at center.	25.00	80.00
198	**5 Pounds**		
	2.9.1963-1.9.1969. Blue and violet. Arms at right. Back: King's College at Aberdeen.	60.00	200.

		VF	UNC
199	**10 Pounds**		
	20.4.1964; 1.12.1967. Brown on multicolor underprint. Arms at right. Back: University of Glasgow.	200.	700.

		VF	UNC
200	**20 Pounds**		
	19.11.1964; 1.12.1967. Carmine on multicolor underprint. Arms at right. Back: George Square in Glasgow.	200.	650.

		VF	UNC
201	**100 Pounds**		
	1.2.1965; 29.4.1965; 1.2.1968. Violet on multicolor underprint. Back: Multiple arch bridge across river at center.	600.	1750.

1967 Issue

		VF	UNC
202	**1 Pound**		
	3.4.1967; 1.10.1968; 1.9.1969. Green on multicolor underprint. Arms at right. Back: Like number 197 but lines for electronic sorting.	20.00	80.00

203 5 Pounds — VF / UNC
1.5.1967; 1.11.1968; 1.9.1969. Blue and violet on multicolor underprint. Arms at right. Back: Like number 198 but lines for electronic sorting. — 60.00 / 200.

1971-81 Issue

204 1 Pound

1971-81. Dark olive-green on multicolor underprint. Robert the Bruce at left. Back: Scene of Battle of Bannockburn, 1314. Watermark: Old sailing ships.

	VF	UNC
a. Signature R. D. Fairbairn, with title: *GENERAL MANAGER.* 1.3.1971.	12.00	50.00
b. Signature A. R. Macmillan, with title: *GENERAL MANAGER.* 1.5.1972; 1.8.1973.	12.00	55.00
c. Signature A. R. Macmillan, with title: *CHIEF GENERAL MANAGER.* 1.3.1974-27.2.1981.	10.00	35.00
s. As c. Specimen.	—	—

205 5 Pounds

1971-80. Grayish lilac on multicolor underprint. Robert Burns at left. Back: Harvest Mouse and rose from Burns' poems. Watermark: Old sailing ships.

	VF	UNC
a. Signature R. D. Fairbairn, with title: *GENERAL MANAGER.* 1.3.1971.	65.00	200.
b. Signature A. R. Macmillan, with title: *GENERAL MANAGER.* 1.5.1972; 1.8.1973.	65.00	200.
c. Signature A. R. Macmillan, with title: *CHIEF GENERAL MANAGER.* 1.3.1974; 6.1.1975; 2.2.1976; 31.1.1979; 1.2.1980.	45.00	120.
s. As c. Specimen.	—	—

207 10 Pounds

1972-81. Brown and pale purple on multicolor underprint. David Livingstone at left. Back: Dromedary Camel and African scene. Watermark: Old sailing ships.

	VF	UNC
a. Signature A. R. MacMillan, with title: *GENERAL MANAGER.* 1.3.1972; 1.8.1973.	150.	500.
b. Signature A. R. MacMillan, with title: *CHIEF GENERAL MANAGER.* 1.3.1974-27.2.1981.	130.	450.

208 20 Pounds

1972-81. Lilac on multicolor underprint. Lord Kelvin at left. Back: Kelvin's lecture room at Glasgow University. Watermark: Old sailing ships.

	VF	UNC
a. Signature A. R. MacMillan, with title: *GENERAL MANAGER.* 1.3.1972.	175.	500.
b. Signature A. R. MacMillan, with title: *CHIEF GENERAL MANAGER.* 2.2.1976; 27.2.1981.	165.	450.

209 50 Pounds

	VF	UNC
1.9.1981. Olive on multicolor underprint. A. smith at left. Back: Sailing ships, blacksmith implements and farm. Watermark: Old sailing ships.	275.	650.

210 100 Pounds

1972; 1975; 1976. Red on multicolor underprint. Lord Kelvin at left. Back: Kelvin's lecture room at Glasgow University. Watermark: Old sailing ships.

	VF	UNC
a. Signature A. R. MacMillan, with title: *GENERAL MANAGER.* 1.3.1972.	600.	1400.
b. Signature A. R. MacMillan, with title: *CHIEF GENERAL MANAGER.* 6.1.1975, 2.2.1976.	500.	1250.

Clydesdale Bank PLC

1982-89 "Sterling" Issues

211 1 Pound

1982-88. Dark olive-green on multicolor underprint. Robert the Bruce at left. Back: Scene of Battle of Bannockburn, 1314. Watermark: Old sailing ship repeated vertically.

	VF	UNC
a. With sorting marks. Signature A. R. Macmillan. 29.3.1982.	8.00	25.00
b. Like a. signature A. R. Cole Hamilton. 5.1.1983.	8.00	25.00
c. Without sorting marks. Signature A. R. Cole Hamilton. 8.4.1985; 25.11.1985.	6.00	22.50
d. Signature title: *CHIEF EXECUTIVE.* 18.9.1987; 9.11.1988.	5.00	17.50

212 5 Pounds

1982-89. Blue on multicolor underprint. Robert Burns at left. Back: Harvest Mouse and rose from Burns' poems. Watermark: Old sailing ship repeated vertically.

	VF	UNC
a. Signature A. R. Macmillan. 29.3.1982.	40.00	125.
b. Signature A. R. Cole Hamilton. 5.1.1983.	35.00	110.
c. Without sorting marks. Signature A. R. Cole Hamilton. 18.9.1986.	35.00	100.
d. Signature title: *CHIEF EXECUTIVE.* 18.9.1987; 2.8.1988; 28.6.1989.	25.00	70.00
s. As d. Specimen.	—	200.

213 **10 Pounds** — VF UNC

1982-87. Brown and pale purple on multicolor underprint. David Livingstone at left. Back: Dromedary Camel and African scene. Watermark: Old sailing ship repeated vertically.

	VF	UNC
a. Signature A. R. Macmillan. 29.3.1982; 5.1.1983.	80.00	325.
b. Signature A. R. Cole Hamilton. 8.4.1985; 18.9.1986.	75.00	300.
c. Signature title: *CHIEF EXECUTIVE.* 18.9.1987.	75.00	275.
s. As d. Specimen.	—	—

214 **10 Pounds** — VF UNC

	VF	UNC
7.5.1988; 3.9.1989; 1.3.1990; 9.11.1990. Dark brown on multicolor underprint. D. Livingstone in front of map at left. Back: Blantyre (Livingstone's birthplace). Watermark: Old sailing ship repeated vertically.	45.00	120.

215 **20 Pounds** — VF UNC

1982-90. Lilac on multicolor underprint. Lord Kelvin at left. Back: Kelvin's lecture room at Glasgow University. Watermark: Old sailing ship repeated vertically.

	VF	UNC
a. Signature A. R. Macmillan. 29.3.1982.	150.	450.
b. Signature A. R. Cole Hamilton. 5.1.1983; 8.4.1985.	140.	425.
c. Signature title: *CHIEF EXECUTIVE.* 18.9.1987; 2.8.1990.	150.	450.

217 **100 Pounds** — VF UNC

1985; 1991. Red on multicolor underprint. Lord Kelvin at left. Back: Kelvin's lecture room at Glasgow University. Watermark: Old sailing ship repeated vertically. 163x90mm.

	VF	UNC
a. Signature title: *CHIEF GENERAL MANAGER.* 8.4.1985.	550.	1150.
b. Signature title: *CHIEF EXECUTIVE.* 9.11.1991.	500.	1050.

1989-96 "Sterling" Issue

218 **5 Pounds** — VF UNC

1990-. Black and gray on multicolor underprint. Robert Burns at left. Back: Harvest Mouse and rose from Burns' poems. Watermark: Old sailing ship repeated vertically. 135x70mm.

	VF	UNC
a. Signature A. R. Cole Hamilton. 2.4.1990.	17.50	35.00
b. Signature F. Cicutto. 1.9.1994.	15.00	30.00
c. Signature F. Goodwin. 21.7.1996; 1.12.1997.	FV	25.00
d. Signature G. Savage. 19.6.2002. Larger size date and title.	FV	22.50

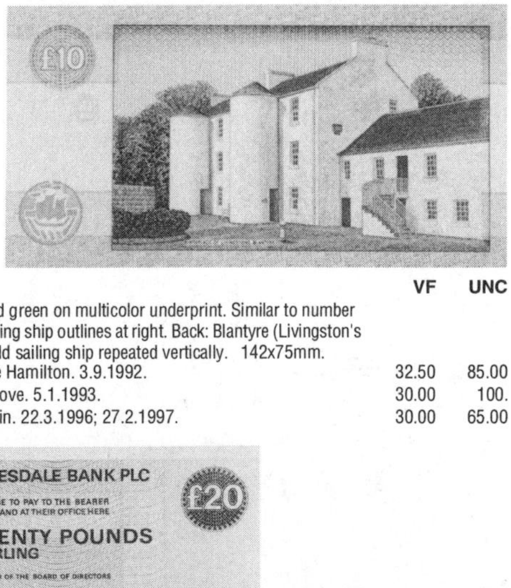

219 **10 Pounds** — VF UNC

1992-97. Deep brown and green on multicolor underprint. Similar to number 214 but with modified sailing ship outlines at right. Back: Blantyre (Livingston's birthplace) Watermark: Old sailing ship repeated vertically. 142x75mm.

	VF	UNC
a. Signature A. R. Cole Hamilton. 3.9.1992.	32.50	85.00
b. Signature Charles Love. 5.1.1993.	30.00	100.
c. Signature F. Goodwin. 22.3.1996; 27.2.1997.	30.00	65.00

220 **20 Pounds** — VF UNC

1990-93. Violet, purple, brown and brown-orange on multicolor underprint. Robert the Bruce at left. Back: His equestrian statue, Monymusk reliquary, Stirling Castle and Wallace Monument. Watermark: Old sailing ship repeated vertically. 148x80mm.

	VF	UNC
a. Signature A. R. Cole Hamilton. 30.11.1990; 2.8.1991; 3.9.1992.	70.00	175.
b. Signature Charles Love. 5.1.1993.	75.00	180.

221 20 Pounds

1994; 1996. Purple, dark brown and deep orange on multicolor underprint. Robert the Bruce at left. Back: His equestrian statue, Monymusk reliquary, Stirling Castle and Wallace Monument. Watermark: Old sailing ship repeated vertically. Ascending size serial number at upper left. Reduced size.

	VF	UNC
a. Signature F. Cicutto. 1.9.1994.	60.00	120.
b. Signature F. Goodwin. 2.12.1996.	55.00	100.

222 50 Pounds

	VF	UNC
3.9.1989; 20.4.1992. Olive-green on multicolor underprint. A. Smith at left Signature A. R. Cole Hamilton. Back: Sailing ships, blacksmith implements and farm. Watermark: Old sailing ships.	250.	700.

223 100 Pounds

	VF	UNC
2.10.1996. Olive-green on multicolor underprint. Lord Kelvin at left. signature F. Goodwin. Vertical serial number at right. Back: Glasgow University.	250.	400.

1996 Commemorative Issue

#224, Poetry of Robert Burns

224 5 Pounds

21.7.1996. Black and gray on multicolor underprint. Robert Burns at left, lines of poetry. Back: Harvest Mouse and rose from Burns' poems. Watermark: Sailing ship. 135x70mm.

	VF	UNC
a. "A man's a man for a'that - Then let us..."	12.50	25.00
b. "Tam O'Shanter - Now, wha this..."	12.50	25.00
c. "Ae Fond Kiss - But to see..."	12.50	25.00
d. "Scots wha hae - By oppressions woes..."	12.50	25.00

1996 Regular Issue

225 50 Pounds

1996; 2003; 2005. Olive-green on multicolor underprint. A. Smith at left. Back: Sailing ships, blacksmith implements and farm. Watermark: Sailing ships. 157x85mm.

	VF	UNC
a. 22.3.1996. Signature F. Goodwin.	150.	250.
b. 25.4.2003. Signature Ross Pinney as *Chief Operating Officer.*	FV	200.
c. 9.1.2006. Signature David Thorburn.	FV	200.

1997 Commemorative Issues

#226, Work of Mary Slessor

226 10 Pounds

1997-. Dark brown and brown on multicolor underprint. Mary Slessor at left. Back: Map of Calabar in Nigeria in wreath at center, sailing ship at upper left, Slessor seated below and with children at right. Watermark: Mary Slessor. 142x75mm.

	VF	UNC
a. Signature F. Goodwin. 1.5.1997.	25.00	55.00
b. Signature J. Wright. 5.11.1998; 20.10.1999.	25.00	42.50
c. Signature S. Targett. 28.1.2003.	25.00	40.00
d. Signature Ross Pimney. 25.4.2003.	FV	35.00
e. Signature David Thorburn as *Chief Operating Officer.* 21.11.2004.	FV	32.50
f. Signature David Thorburn, larger CB bank emblem. 14.3.2006; 16.4.2007.	FV	32.50

227 20 Pounds

	VF	UNC
30.9.1997. Purple, dark brown and deep orange on multicolor underprint. Robert the Bruce at left. Signature F. Goodwin. Back: Edinburgh International Conference Centre at lower right, Clydesdale Bank plaza and Edinburgh Castle 150x80mm.	55.00	100.

1997 Regular Issue

228 20 Pounds

1.11.1997-. Purple, dark brown and deep orange on multicolor underprint. Like number 221 but square design replaces *£20* at lower left, segmented foil over security thread, bank logo added to value panel at lower center right. 150x80mm.

	VF	UNC
a. Signature Fred Goodwin. 1.11.1997.	FV	100.
b. Signature John Wright. 12.10.1999.	FV	70.00
c. Signature Grahm Savage. 19.6.2002.	FV	90.00
d. Signature Steve Targett. 26.1.2003; 26.4.2003.	FV	75.00
e. Signature Ross Pinney. 25.4.2003.	FV	62.50
f. Signature David Thorburn as *Chief Operating Officer.* 21.11.2004.	FV	62.50
g. Signature David Thorburn, larger CB emblem. 24.6.2006.	FV	62.50

1999 Commemorative Issue

#229, Glasgow as UK City of Architecture and Design

			VF	UNC
229	20 Pounds	9.4.1999. Purple, brown and multicolor. Alex "Greek" Thompson at left. Special text at lower right. Back: Holmwood House. Special text at lower right. 150x80mm.	FV	95.00

2000 Commemorative Issues

#229A and 229B, special text: *COMMEMORATING THE YEAR 2000.*

			VF	UNC
229A	10 Pounds	1.1.2000. Brown and green on multicolor underprint. Mary Slessor at left, commemorative text added at right. Back: Map of Calabar in Nigeria in wreath at center, sailing ship at upper left, Slessor seated below and with children at right. Watermark: Mary Slessor. Special text: *COMMEMORATING THE YEAR 2000.* 142x75mm.	25.00	55.00
229B	20 Pounds	1.1.2000. Purple, dark brown and deep orange on multicolor underprint. Like #221 but square design replaces £*20* at lower left, segmented foil over security thread, bank logo added to value panel at lower center right. Back: Similar to #228 but commemorative text added at right. Special text: *COMMEMORATING THE YEAR 2000.* 150x80mm.	50.00	100.

2001 Commemorative Issues

			VF	UNC
229C	50 Pounds	6.1.2001. Olive-green on multicolor underprint. Like #225 but with commemorative emblem and text at right. 155x85mm.	FV	200.

			VF	UNC
229D	100 Pounds	6.1.2001. Purple, red and violet on multicolor underprint. Like #223 but with commemorative emblem and text at right. 164x90mm.	FV	375.

2005 Commemorative Issues

			VF	UNC
229E	10 Pounds	2005. Dark brown and brown on multicolor underprint. Mary Slessor at left. Serial #prefix *CG*. Back: Commonwealth Games. Athletics - Montage of sports events. Watermark: Mary Slessor. 142x75mm.	FV	68.00

			VF	UNC
229F	20 Pounds	2005. Like #221 but square design replaces £*20* at lower left, segmented foil over security thread, bank logo added to value panel at lower center right. Signature David Thorburn. Back: Clysesdale Bank Exchange in Glasgow. 150x80mm.	FV	70.00

2006 Commemorative Issue

			VF	UNC
229G	20 Pounds	25.3.2006 Like #228 but with addition of "700th Anniversary 1306 / 2006" and shield. Serial # prefix *RB*. Back: Bruce on horseback right. Overprint: on back: 700th Anniversary of the enthronment of Robert the Bruce as King of Scotts 150x80mm.	FV	70.00

2006 Issue

			VF	UNC
229H	20 Pounds	24.6.2006. Back: Like #221 150x80mm.	FV	50.00

2009 Issue

			VF	UNC
229I	5 Pounds	2009. Black and blue on multicolor underprint. Sir Alexander Fleming at right center, microscope at right. Back: St. Kilda. 135x70mm.	FV	15.00
229J	10 Pounds	2009. Brown and tan on multicolor underprint. Robert Burns at right center. Back: Old and new views of Edinburgh. 142x75mm.	FV	22.50
229K	20 Pounds	2009. Purple and brown on multicolor underprint. Robert the Bruce at right center. Back: New Lanark. 150x80mm.	FV	50.00
229L	50 Pounds	2009. Olive and green on multicolor underprint. Elsie Inglis at right center. Back: Antonine Wall. 155x85mm.	FV	100.
229M	100 Pounds	2009. Rose on multicolor underprint. Charmes Rennie Mackintosh at right center. Back: Neart of Neolithic Orkney. 164x90mm.	FV	200.

National Commercial Bank of Scotland Limited

1961 Issue

		VF	UNC
269	**1 Pound** 1.11.1961-4.1.1966. Green on multicolor underprint. Forth Railway bridge. Back: Arms at center. Printer: BWC. Reduced size. 151x72mm.		
	a. Issued note.	20.00	60.00
	s. Specimen.	—	200.

		VF	UNC
270	**5 Pounds** 3.1.1961. Green on multicolor underprint. Arms at bottom center right. Back: Forth Railway bridge. Printer: W&S. Reduced size. 159x90mm.	90.00	325.

1963-67 Issue

		VF	UNC
271	**1 Pound** 4.1.1967. Green on multicolor underprint. Forth Railway bridge. Back: Arms at center, electronic sorting lines. Printer: BWC. 152x72mm.		
	a. Issue note.	25.00	80.00
	s. Specimen.	—	—

		VF	UNC
272	**5 Pounds** 2.1.1963; 1.8.1963; 1.10.1964; 4.1.1966; 1.8.1966. Blue on multicolor underprint. Arms at lower center. Back: Landscape with Edinburgh Castle, National Gallery Printer: BWC. 142x85mm.		
	a. Issued note.	45.00	120.
	s. Specimen.	—	260.
273	**10 Pounds** 18.8.1966. Brown on multicolor underprint. Arms at lower center. Back: Forth Railway bridge. Printer: BWC. 151x94mm.	350.	1100.

1967; 1968 Issue

		VF	UNC
274	**1 Pound** 4.1.1968. Green on multicolor underprint. Forth Railway Bridge and road bridge. Back: Arms at center, electronic sorting lines. Printer: BWC. 136x67mm.		
	a. Issued note.	17.50	70.00
	s. Specimen.	—	160.

		VF	UNC
275	**5 Pounds** 4.1.1968. Blue, red and green on multicolor underprint. Arms at lower center. Back: Landscape with Edinburgh Castle, National Gallery; electronic sorting marks. Printer: BWC.		
	a. Issued note.	50.00	160.
	s. Specimen.	—	225.
275A	**20 Pounds** 1.6.1967. Red on multicolor underprint. Arms at lower right. Back: Bridge. Printer: TDLR.		
	a. Issued note.	4000.	6000.
	s. Specimen.	—	600.
275B	**100 Pounds** 1.6.1967. Purple on multicolor underprint. Arms at lower right. Back: Bridge. Printer: TDLR. Specimen.	—	1500.

Royal Bank of Scotland

1875; 1887 Issue

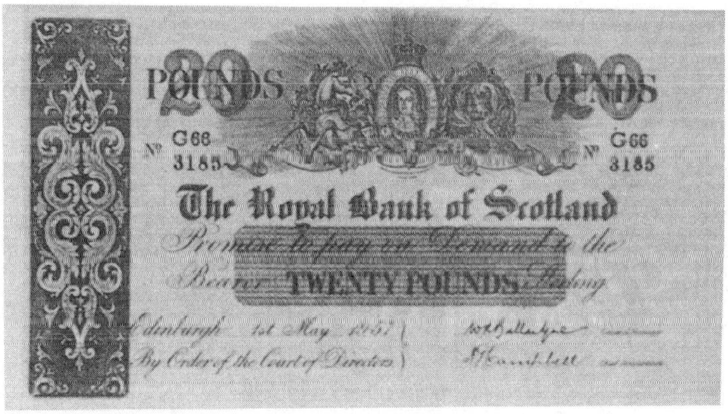

		Fine	XF
319	**20 Pounds** 1877-1969. Blue and brown. Uniface.		
	a. Plate C. 1877-1911.	950.	2850.
	b. Plate D. Yellow underprint. Imprint: W. & A. K. Johnston 1931-47.	600.	1400.
	c. Plates E; F; G; H. Underprint without red. Imprint: W. & A. K. Johnston & G. W. Bacon Ltd. Both signatures printed 1947-66.	325.	700.
320	**100 Pounds** 1877-1969. Blue and red. Uniface.		
	a. Plate C. 1877-1918.	4500.	—
	b. Plates D; E. Yellow underprint. 1918-60.	1250.	3000.
	c. Plates F; G. Imprint: W. & A. K. Johnston & G. W. Bacon Ltd. Both signatures printed. 1960-66.	1000.	2750.

1952 Issue

	VF	UNC
323 5 Pounds		
1952-63. Blue and red on yellow underprint. Like number 317 but reduced size. Uniface.		
a. 2 signatures. Imprint: W. & A.K. Johnston Ltd. 2.1.1952-1.7.1953.	125.	325.
b. 3 signatures. Imprint: W. & A. K. Johnston & G. W. Bacon Ltd. 1.7.1953-1.2.1954.	150.	400.
c. 2 signatures. Imprint: W. & A. K. Johnston & G. W. Bacon. 1.4.1955-3.1.1963.	100.	250.

1955 Issue

	VF	UNC
324 1 Pound		
1955-64. Dark blue on yellow and brown underprint. Signature W. R. Ballantyne with title: *General Manager.* 152x85mm.		
a. Without engraver's name on back. 1.4.1955-1.11.1955.	40.00	125.
b. With engraver's name W. H. Egan upside down and in very small letters below the right hand bank building on back. 1.2.1956-1.7.1964.	30.00	80.00
s. As a. Specimen.	—	—

1964 Issue

	VF	UNC
325 1 Pound		
1964-67. Black and brown on yellow underprint. Like number 324, but 150 x 71mm.		
a. Signature W. R. Ballantyne. 1.8.1964-1.6.1965.	32.50	85.00
b. Signature G. P. Robertson. 2.8.1965-1.11.1967.	25.00	75.00
s. As a. Specimen.	—	250.

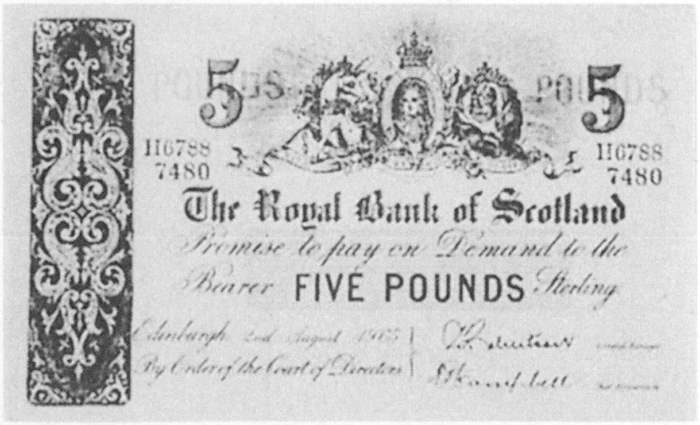

	VF	UNC
326 5 Pounds		
1964-65. Dark blue, orange-brown and yellow. Like number 323, but 140 x 85mm. Uniface.		
a. 2.11.1964. Signature W. R. Ballantyne & A. G. Campbell.	100.	250.
b. 2.8.1965. Signature G. P. Robertson & A. G. Campbell.	100.	250.
s1. As a. Specimen.	—	600.
s2. As b. Specimen.	—	275.

1966; 1967 Issue

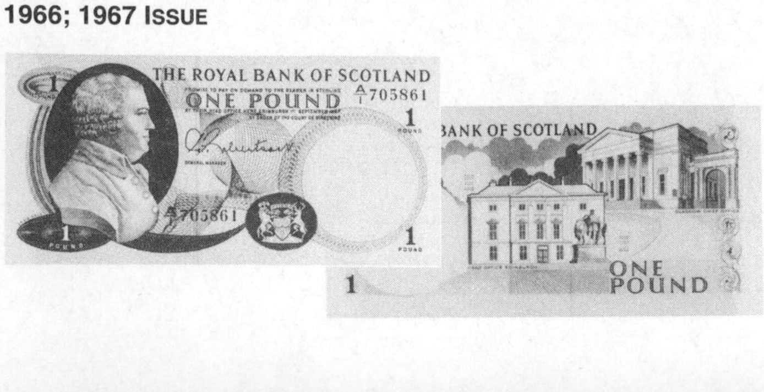

	VF	UNC
327 1 Pound		
1.9.1967. Green on multicolor underprint. Portrait of D. Dale at left, bank arms at lower right. Back: Bank head office building at center and upper right. Watermark: D. Dale.		
a. Issued note.	25.00	70.00
s. Specimen.	—	260.

	VF	UNC
328 5 Pounds		
1.11.1966; 1.3.1967. Blue on multicolor underprint. Portrait of D. Dale at left, bank arms at lower right. Back: Bank head office building at center and upper right. Watermark: D. Dale.	75.00	200.

Royal Bank of Scotland Limited

1969 Issue

	VF	UNC
329 1 Pound		
19.3.1969. Green on multicolor underprint. Forth Road Bridge at left center, old Forth Railway bridge in background. Signature G. P. Robertson and J. B. Burke. Back: Arms at center right. Watermark: D. Dale. Printer: BWC.		
a. Issued note.	25.00	60.00
s. Specimen.	—	180.

	VF	UNC
330 5 Pounds		
19.3.1969. Blue on multicolor underprint. Arms at left. Signature G. P. Robertson and J. B. Burke. Back: Edinburgh Castle. Watermark: D. Dale. Printer: BWC.	75.00	200.

			VF	UNC
331	**10 Pounds**	19.3.1969. Brown on mjulticolor underprint. Arms at center. Signature G. P. Robertson and J. B. Burke. Back: Tay road bridge. Watermark: D. Dale. Printer: BWC.	125.	450.
332	**20 Pounds**	19.3.1969. Purple on multicolor underprint. Signature G. P. Robertson and J. B. Burke. Back: Forth Road Bridge. Watermark: D. Dale. Printer: BWC.	150.	550.

			VF	UNC
333	**100 Pounds**	19.3.1969. Red on multicolor underprint. Signature G. P. Robertson and J. B. Burke. Back: Forth Road Bridge. Watermark: D. Dale. Printer: BWC.		
		a. Issued note.	700.	1800.
		s. Specimen.	—	—

1970 Issue

			VF	UNC
334	**1 Pound**	15.7.1970. Green on multicolor underprint. Forth Road Bridge at left center, old Forth Railway bridge in background. Signature; J. B. Burke. Back: Arms at center right. Printer: BWC.		
		a. Issued note.	15.00	55.00
		s. Specimen.	—	—

			VF	UNC
335	**5 Pounds**	15.7.1970. Blue on multicolor underprint. Arms at left. Signature; J. B. Burke. Back: Edinburgh Castle. Printer: BWC.	65.00	175.

1972 Issue

			VF	UNC
336	**1 Pound**	5.1.1972-1.5.1981. Dark green on multicolor underprint. Arms at right. Back: Edinburgh Castle at left center. Watermark: A. Smith. Printer: BWC.		
		a. Issued note.	9.00	32.50
		s. Specimen.	—	250.

			VF	UNC
337	**5 Pounds**	5.1.1972; 2.4.1973; 1.5.1975; 3.5.1976; 1.5.1979; 1.5.1980; 1.5.1981. Blue on multicolor underprint. Arms at right. Back: Culzean Castle at left center. Watermark: A. Smith. Printer: BWC.		
		a. Issued note.	35.00	100.
		s. Specimen.	—	260.

			VF	UNC
338	**10 Pounds**	5.1.1972; 1.3.1974; 15.12.1975; 2.5.1978; 10.1.1981. Brown on multicolor underprint. Arms at right. Back: Glamis Castle at left center. Watermark: A. Smith. Printer: BWC.		
		a. Issued note.	75.00	225.
		s. Specimen.	—	380.
339	**20 Pounds**	5.1.1972; 1.5.1981. Purple on multicolor underprint. Arms at right. Back: Brodick Castle. Watermark: A. Smith. Printer: BWC.	150.	350.

			VF	UNC
340	**100 Pounds**	5.1.1972; 1.5.1979; 1.5.1981. Red on multicolor underprint. Arms at right. Back: Balmoral Castle. Watermark: A. Smith. Printer: BWC.		
		a. Issued note.	550.	1400.
		s. Specimen.	—	800.

Royal Bank of Scotland PLC

1982-86 Issues

#341. Replacement note: Serial # prefix *Y/1*.

			VF	UNC
341	**1 Pound**	1982-85. Dark green on multicolor underprint. Arms at right. Signature C. Winter. Back: Edinburgh Castle at left center. Watermark: A. Smith. Printer: BWC.		
		a. With sorting marks. 3.5.1982.	20.00	60.00
		b. Without sorting marks. 1.10.1983; 4.1.1984; 3.1.1985.	10.00	30.00

341A 1 Pound | VF | UNC

1986. Dark green on multicolor underprint. Arms at right. Signature C. Winter. Back: Edinburgh Castle at left center. Watermark: A. Smith. Printer: TDLR.

	VF	UNC
a. Signature C. Winter. 1.5.1986.	10.00	30.00
b. Signature R. M. Maiden. 17.12.1986.	10.00	35.00

342 5 Pounds | VF | UNC

1982-86. Blue on multicolor underprint. Arms at right. Signature title varies. Back: Culzean Castle at left center. Watermark: A. Smith. Printer: BWC.

	VF	UNC
a. Signature C. M. Winter. With electronic sorting marks. 3.5.1982; 5.1.1983.	40.00	130.
b. Without sorting marks. 4.1.1984.	40.00	125.
c. Signature C. M. Winter title larger size. 3.1.1985.	40.00	130.
d. Signature R. M. Maiden. 17.12.1986.	40.00	120.

343 10 Pounds

1982-86. Brown on multicolor underprint. Arms at right. Signature titile varies. Back: Glamis Castle at left center. Watermark: A. Smith. Printer: BWC.

	VF	UNC
a. Signature C. M. Winter. 3.5.1982; 4.1.1984; 3.1.1985.	65.00	200.
b. Signature R. M. Maiden. 17.12.1986.	65.00	190.

		VF	UNC
344	**20 Pounds** 3.5.1982; 3.1.1985. Purple on multicolor underprint. Arms at right. Signature title varies. Back: Brodick Castle. Watermark: A. Smith. Printer: BWC.	125.	325.
345	**100 Pounds** 3.5.1982; 3.1.1985. Red on multicolor underprint. Arms at right. Signature title varies. Back: Balmoral Castle. Watermark: A. Smith. Printer: BWC.	400.	1000.

1987 Issue

346 1 Pound

25.3.1987. Dark green and green on multicolor underprint. Lord Ilay at right. Back: Edinburgh Castle at left center. Watermark: Lord Ilay. Printer: TDLR.

	VF	UNC
a. Issued note	5.00	15.00
r. Replacement note. Serial # prefix: *Z/1*.	15.00	50.00

347 5 Pounds

25.3.1987; 22.6.1988. Black and blue-black on multicolor underprint. Lord Ilay at right. Back: Culzean Castle at left center. Watermark: Lord Ilay. Printer: TDLR.

	VF	UNC
a. Issued note.	17.50	35.00
r. Replacement note. Serial # prefix: *Z/1*.	20.00	100.

348 10 Pounds

25.3.1987; 24.2.1988; 22.2.1989; 24.1.1990. Deep brown and brown on multicolor underprint. Lord Ilay at right. Signature right. M. Maiden. Back: Glamis Castle at left center. Watermark: Lord Ilay. Printer: TDLR.

	VF	UNC
a. Issued note	40.00	90.00
r. Replacement note. Serial # prefix: *Z/1*.	40.00	200.

		VF	UNC
349	**20 Pounds** 25.3.1987; 24.1.1990. Black and purple on multicolor underprint. Lord Ilay at right. Signature right. M. Maiden. Back: Brodick Castle at left center. Watermark: Lord Ilay. Printer: TDLR.	70.00	175.

350 100 Pounds — VF / UNC

1987-. Red on multicolor underprint. Lord Ilay at right. Back: Balmoral Castle at left center. Watermark: Lord Ilay. Printer: TDLR. 170x96mm.

- a. Signature R. M. Maiden, with title: *MANAGING DIRECTOR.* 25.3.1987; 24.1.1990. — 300. / 700.
- b. Signature G. R. Mathewson, with title: *CHIEF EXECUTIVE.* 28.1.1992; 23.3.1994; 24.1.1996; 26.3.1997; 30.9.1998. — 260. / 600.
- c. Signature G. R. Matthewson, with title: *GROUP CHIEF EXECUTIVE.* 30.3.1999. — FV / 600.
- d. Signature Fred Goodwin. 27.6.2000. — FV / 350.

1988-92 Issue

#351-355 similar to #346-350, but reduced size. Replacement notes: Serial # prefix: *Z/1*.

351 1 Pound — VF / UNC

1988-. Dark green and green on multicolor underprint. Lord Ilay at right. Back: Edinburgh Castle. Watermark: Lord Ilay. Printer: TDLR. UV: left part of castle and central design fluoresce yellow. 128x65mm.

- a. Signature R. M. Maiden with title: *MANAGING DIRECTOR.* 13.12.1988; 26.7.1989; 19.12.1990. — 4.00 / 11.00
- b. Signature C. Winter with title: *CHIEF EXECUTIVE.* 24.7.1991. — 3.00 / 8.00
- c. Signature G. R. Mathewson with title: *CHIEF EXECUTIVE.* 24.3.1992; 24.2.1993; 24.2.1994; 24.1.1996; 1.10.1997. — 3.00 / 7.00
- d. Signature G. R. Mathewson, with title: *GROUP CHIEF EXECUTIVE.* 30.3.1999. — FV / 6.00
- e. Signature Fred Goodwin. 27.6.2000; 1.10.2001. — FV / 5.00

352 5 Pounds — VF / UNC

1988-. Black and blue-black on multicolor underprint. Lord Ilay at right. Back: Culzean Castle at left center. Watermark: Lord Ilay. Printer: TDLR. 135x70mm.

- a. Signature R. M. Maiden, with title: *MANAGING DIRECTOR.* 13.12.1988; 24.1.1990. — 17.50 / 45.00
- b. Signature G. R. Mathewson. with title: *CHIEF EXECUTITIVE.* 23.3.1994; 24.1.1996; 26.3.1997; 29.4.1998. — 12.00 / 30.00
- c. Signature G. R. Matthewson, with title: *GROUP CHIEF EXECUTIVE.* 30.3.1999. — 15.00 / 35.00
- d. Signature Fred Goodwin. 27.6.2000; 20.1.2005. — FV / 17.50

353 10 Pounds — VF / UNC

1992-. Deep brown and brown on multicolor underprint. Lord Ilay at right. Signature right, M. Maiden. Back: Glamis Castle at left center. Watermark: Lord Ilay. Printer: TDLR. 142x75mm.

- a. Signature G. R. Mathewson, with title: *CHIEF EXECUTIVE.* 28.1.1992; 7.5.1992; 24.2.1993; 23.3.1994. — FV / 40.00
- b. Signature Fred Goodwin, with title: *GROUP CHIEF EXECUTIVE.* 27.6.2000; 1.10.2001; 19.9.2006. — FV / 35.00

354 20 Pounds — VF / UNC

1991-. Black and purple on multicolor underprint. Lord Ilay at right. Signature right, M. Maiden. Back: Brodick Castle at left center. Watermark: Lord Ilay. Printer: TDLR. 150x81mm.

- a. Signature C. Winter with title: *CHIEF EXECUTIVE.* 27.3.1991. — 45.00 / 120.
- b. Signature G. R. Mathewson. 28.1.1992; 24.2.1993; 26.3.1997; 29.4.1998. — 45.00 / 105.
- c. Signature G. R. Mathewson, with title: *GROUP CHIEF EXECUTIVE.* 30.3.1999. — 45.00 / 110.
- d. Signature Fred Goodwin. 27.6.2000; 19.9.2006. — FV / 70.00

1992 Commemorative Issue

#356, European Summit at Edinburgh, Dec. 1992

356 1 Pound — VF / UNC

8.12.1992. Dark green and green on multicolor underprint. Like number 351c but with additional blue-violet overprint containing commemorative inscription at left. Serial # prefix: EC. 128x65mm.

- a. Issued note. — FV / 7.00
- s. Specimen. — — / 180.

1994 Regular Issue

#357, Replacement note: Serial # prefix *Y/1*.

357 1 Pound — VF / UNC

23.3.1994. Dark green and green on multicolor underprint. Lord Ilay at right. Back: Edinburgh Castle at left center. Printer: BABN. 128x65mm. — 20.00 / 60.00

1994 Commemorative Issue

#358, Centennial - Death of Robert Louis Stevenson

		VF	UNC
358	**1 Pound** 3.12.1994. Dark green and green on multicolor underprint. Commemorative overprint in watermark area on #351c. Serial number prefix: RLS. Back: Portrait R. L. Stevenson and images of his life and works. 128x65mm.		
	a. Issued note.	3.00	7.50
	s. Specimen.	—	180.

1997 Commemorative Issue

#359, 150th Anniversary - Birth of Alexander Graham Bell, 1847-1997

		VF	UNC
359	**1 Pound** 3.3.1997. Dark green and green on multicolor underprint. Overprint telephone, text and OVD on watermark area of face like #351c. Serial number prefix: AGB. Back: Portrait Alexander Graham Bell and images of his life and work. UV: Back central design fluoresces yellow and green. 128x65mm.	FV	6.50

1999 Commemorative Issue

#360, Opening of the Scottish Parliament

		VF	UNC
360	**1 Pound** 12.5.1999. Dark green on multicolor underprint. Overprint Scottish Parliament text at left on watermark area of face like #351c. Serial number prefix: SP. Back: Scottish Parliament building. UV: central design fluoresces yellow. 128x65mm.	FV	6.00

2000 Commemorative Issue

#361, Birth centennial of the Queen Mother

		VF	UNC
361	**20 Pounds** 4.8.2000. Black and purple on multicolor underprint. Gold crown with inscription beneath at left. Serial number prefix: QETQM. Back: Queen Mother. 150x80mm.	FV	70.00
361A	**100 Pounds** 4.8.2000. Black and purple on multicolor underprint. Special presentation item for the Queen Mother.Unique	—	—

2002 Commemorative Issue

#362, Queen's Golden Jubilee. Printer: TDLR.

		VF	UNC
362	**5 Pounds** 6.2.2002. Black and dark blue on multicolor underprint. Gold crown overprint at left. Back: Dark and light blue. 1952 and 2002 portraits of Queen Elizabeth II. Printer: TDLR. 135x70mm.	FV	25.00

2004 Commemorative Issue

#363 250th Anniversary of St. Andrews Royal & Ancient Golf Club.

		VF	UNC
363	**5 Pounds** 14.5.2004. Black and blue-black on multicolor underprint. Similar to number 352 but shield and 1754 at left. Serial number prefix: *R&A*. Back: Tom Morris and images of St. Andrews. 135x70mm.	FV	30.00

2005 Commemorative Issues

500th Anniversary, College of Surgeons.

364 **5 Pounds** | VF | UNC
1.7.2005. Commemorative overprint at left. Serial number prefix RCS. 135x70mm. | FV | 17.50

365 **5 Pounds** | VF | UNC
14.7.2005. Commemorative overprint at left. Serial number prefix JWN. Back: Jack Nicklaus. 135x70mm. | FV | 19.00

366 **50 Pounds**
14.9.2005. Serial number prefix RBS. Back: New Bank headquarters at Gogarburn. 155x85mm. | FV | 200.

2005 Regular Issue

367 **50 Pounds** | VF | UNC
14.9.2005. Back: Inverness Castle. 155x85mm. | FV | 150.

2012 Commemorative Issue

368 **10 Pounds** | VF | UNC
2012. Deep brown and tan on multicolor underprint. Lord Ilay at right. Back: Violet, brown, yellow and green Four portraits of Queen Elizabeth II, crowned text at right. 142x76mm. | FV | 60.00

Collector Series

Clydesdale Bank Plc

1996 Issue

CS1 **1996 5 Pounds** | Mkt. | Value
Matched serial # (prefix R/B 0 - R/B 3) set #224a-224d. | | 90.00

Serbia, a former inland Balkan kingdom (now a federated republic with Montenegro) has an area of 34,116 sq. mi. (88,361 sq. km.) Capital: Belgrade.

The Kingdom of Serbs, Croats, and Slovenes was formed in 1918; its name was changed to Yugoslavia in 1929. Various paramilitary bands resisted Nazi Germany's occupation and division of Yugoslavia from 1941 to 1945, but fought each other and ethnic opponents as much as the invaders. The military and political movement headed by Josip Tito (Partisans) took full control of Yugoslavia when German and Croatian separatist forces were defeated in 1945. Although Communist, Tito's government and his successors (he died in 1980) managed to steer their own path between the Warsaw Pact nations and the West for the next four and a half decades. In 1989, Slobodan Milosevic became president of the Serbian Republic and his ultranationalist calls for Serbian domination led to the violent breakup of Yugoslavia along ethnic lines. In 1991, Croatia, Slovenia, and Macedonia declared independence, followed by Bosnia in 1992. The remaining republics of Serbia and Montenegro declared a new Federal Republic of Yugoslavia in April 1992 and under Milosevic's leadership, Serbia led various military campaigns to unite ethnic Serbs in neighboring republics into a "Greater Serbia." These actions led to Yugoslavia being ousted from the UN in 1992, but Serbia continued its - ultimately unsuccessful - campaign until signing the Dayton Peace Accords in 1995. Milosevic kept tight control over Serbia and eventually became president of the FRY in 1997. In 1998, an ethnic Albanian insurgency in the formerly autonomous Serbian province of Kosovo provoked a Serbian counterinsurgency campaign that resulted in massacres and massive expulsions of ethnic Albanians living in Kosovo. The Milosevic government's rejection of a proposed international settlement led to NATO's bombing of Serbia in the spring of 1999 and to the eventual withdrawal of Serbian military and police forces from Kosovo in June 1999. UNSC Resolution 1244 in June 1999 authorized the stationing of a NATO-led force (KFOR) in Kosovo to provide a safe and secure environment for the region's ethnic communities, created a UN interim Administration Mission in Kosovo (UNMIK) to foster self-governing institutions, and reserved the issue of Kosovo's final status for an unspecified date in the future. In 2001, UNMIK promulgated a constitutional framework that allowed Kosovo to establish institutions of self-government and led to Kosovo's first parliamentary election. FRY elections in September 2000 led to the ouster of Milosevic and installed Vojislav Kostunica as president. A broad coalition of democratic reformist parties known as DOS (the Democratic Opposition of Serbia) was subsequently elected to parliament in December 2000 and took control of the government. DOS arrested Milosevic in 2001 and allowed for him to be tried in The Hague for crimes against humanity. (Milosevic died in March 2006 before the completion of his trial.) In 2001, the country's suspension from the UN was lifted. In 2003, the FRY became Serbia and Montenegro, a loose federation of the two republics with a federal level parliament. Widespread violence predominantly targeting ethnic Serbs in Kosovo in March 2004 caused the international community to open negotiations on the future status of Kosovo in January 2006. In May 2006, Montenegro invoked its right to secede from the federation and - following a successful referendum - it declared itself an independent nation on 3 June 2006. Two days later, Serbia declared that it was the successor state to the union of Serbia and Montenegro. A new Serbian constitution was approved in October 2006 and adopted the following month. After 15 months of inconclusive negotiations mediated by the UN and four months of further inconclusive negotiations mediated by the US, EU, and Russia, on 17 February 2008, the UNMIK-administered province of Kosovo declared itself independent of Serbia.

MONETARY SYSTEM:

1 Dinar = 100 Para

Federation of Serbia and Montenegro

Narodna Banka Srbija

National Bank of Serbia

2003 Issue

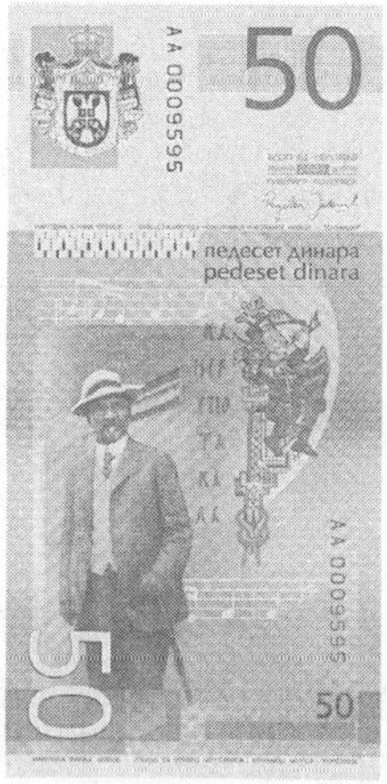

40 **50 Dinara** | VF | UNC
2005. Purple and tan on multicolor underprint. Stevan Stojanovic Mokranjac at left center, violin, keyboard and music score at center. Back: Mokranjac standing, scores and linear art from Gospel of Miroslav illuminated manuscript. 139x66mm.

		VF	UNC
a.	Issued note.	FV	2.00
s.	Specimen.	—	—

41 **100 Dinara** VF UNC

2003; 2004. Light and dark blue on multicolor underprint. NikolaTesla at left. Back: Detail from theTesla electromagnetic induction engine at center, Tesla at left on vertical format. 143x68mm.

	VF	UNC
a. 2003.	FV	4.00
b. 2004.	FV	4.00
s. Specimen.	—	—

44 **1000 Dinara** VF UNC

2003; 2005. Red on multicolor underprint. Dorde Vajfert at left. Back: Vajfert seated, details of National Bank's interior on vertical format. 151x72mm.

	VF	UNC
a. Signature Mladjan Dinkic.	FV	35.00
b. Signature Kori Udovicki.	FV	30.00
s. Specimen.	—	—

42 **200 Dinara** VF UNC

2005. Black and blue on tan underprint. Nadezda Petrovic at left center, Petrovic sculpture and Gracanica monastery at center. Back: Petrovic photo as WWI nurse, Gracanica monastery and painting detail on vertical format. 147x70mm.

	VF	UNC
a. Issued note.	FV	8.50
s. Specimen.	—	—

45 **5000 Dinara** VF UNC

2003. Green on multicolor underprint. Slibodan Jovanovic at left. Back: Jovanovic and Parliament building views on vertical format. 151x76mm.

	VF	UNC
a. Signature Mladjan Dinkic	FV	150.
b. Signature Kori Udovicki. Expected new issue.	—	—
s. Specimen.	—	—

43 **500 Dinara** VF UNC

2004. Blue and green on multicolor underprint. 147x69mm.

	VF	UNC
a. Issued note.	FV	17.50
s. Specimen.	—	—

2006 Issue

46 **10 Dinara** VF UNC

2006. Black and tan on multicolor underprint. Vuk Stefanovic Karadzic at left. Back: First Slavic Congress, Prague, 1848. 131x62mm.

	VF	UNC
a. 2006.	FV	.75
s. Specimen.	—	15.00

47 **20 Dinara** VF UNC
2006. Green on multicolor underprint. Petar II Petrovic Njegos at left. Back: Mausoleum Statue. 135x64mm.
- a. 2006. FV .75
- s. Specimen. FV 15.00

48 **50 Dinara** VF UNC
2006. Violet and tan on multicolor underprint. Stevan Stojanovic Mokranjac at left. Back: Photograph of Mokranjac. 139x66mm.
- a. 2006. FV 2.00
- s. Specimen. — 25.00

49 **100 Dinara** VF UNC
2006. Light and dark blue on multicolor underprint. Nikola Tesla at left. Back: Details from Tesla's electromagnetic induction machine. 143x68mm.
- a. 2006. FV 4.00
- s. Specimen. — 25.00

50 **200 Dinara** VF UNC
2006. Brown and purple on multicolor underprint. Nadezda Petrovic at left. Back: Gracanica Monastery. 147x70mm.
- a. 2006. FV 8.00
- s. Specimen. — 25.00

51 **500 Dinara**
2006; 2007. Olive and green on multicolor underprint. Jovan Cvijic at left. Back: Cvijic and ethnographic motifs. 147x70mm.
- a. 2006. FV 17.50
- b. 2007. FV 17.50
- s. Specimen. — 50.00

52 **1000 Dinara**
2006. Rose on multicolor underprint. Dorde Vajfert at left. 151x72mm.
- a. 2006. FV 35.00
- s. Specimen. — 100.

53 **5000 Dinara** VF UNC
2010. Green and lilac on multicolor underprint. Slobodan Javanovic at left, female sculpture at center. Back: Interior of Parliament, Jovanovic wearing hat and coat. 155x76mm.
- a. 2010. FV 150.

2011 Issue

54 **10 Dinara** VF UNC
2011, 2013. Brown and tan on multicolor underprint. Vuk Stefanovic Karadzic at left. Back: First Slavic Congress, Prague, 1848. Vertical format. 131x62mm.
- a. 2011. FV .75
- b. 2013. FV .75
- s. Specimen. Red overprint. — 50.00

		VF	UNC
55	**20 Dinara**		
	2011; 2013. Green on multicolor underprint. Petar II Petrovic Njegos at left. Back: Mausoleum Statue.		
	a. 2011.	FV	1.00
	b. 2013.	FV	1.00
	s. Specimen. Red overprint.	—	50.00
56	**50 Dinara**		
	2011. Violet and tan on multicolor underprint. Stevan Stojanovic Mokranjac at left. Back: Photograph of Mokranjac.		
	a. Issued note.	FV	2.00
	s. Specimen. Red overprint.	—	50.00

		VF	UNC
57	**100 Dinara**		
	2012; 2013.		
	a. 2012.	FV	5.00
	b. 2013.	FV	5.00
58	**200 Dinara**		
	2011; 2013. Brown and purple on multicolor underprint. Nadezda Petrovic at left. Back: Gracanica Monastery		
	a. 2011.	FV	8.00
	b. 2013.	FV	8.00
	s. Specimen. Red overprint.	—	50.00

		VF	UNC
59	**500 Dinara**		
	2011; 2012. 147x69mm.		
	a. 2011.	FV	17.50
	b. 2012.	FV	17.50

		VF	UNC
60	**1000 Dinara**		
	2011.	FV	35.00

		VF	UNC
61	**2000 Dinara**		
	2011; 2012. 155x74mm.		
	a. 2011.	FV	75.00
	b. 2012.	FV	70.00
62	**5000 Dinara**		
	2011.	FV	150.

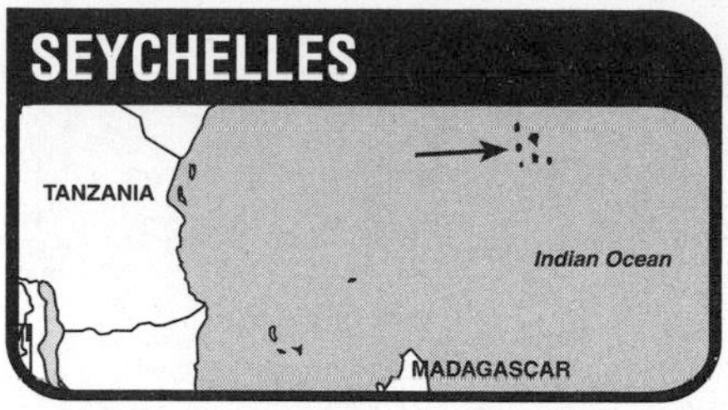

The Republic of Seychelles, an archipelago of 85 granite and coral islands situated in the Indian Ocean 600 miles (965 km.) northeast of Madagascar, has an area of 156 sq. mi. (455 sq. km.) and a population of 82,400. Among these islands are the Aldabra Islands, the Farquhar Group, and Ile Desroches, which the United Kingdom ceded to the Seychelles upon its independence. Capital: Victoria, on Mahe. The economy is d on fishing, a plantation system of agriculture and tourism. Copra, cinnamon and vanilla are exported.

A lengthy struggle between France and Great Britain for the islands ended in 1814, when they were ceded to the latter. Independence came in 1976. Socialist rule was brought to a close with a new constitution and free elections in 1993. President France-Albert Rene, who had served since 1977, was re-elected in 2001, but stepped down in 2004. Vice President James Michel took over the presidency and in July 2006 was elected to a new five-year term.

RULERS:

British to 1976

MONETARY SYSTEM:

1 Rupee = 100 Cents

British Administration

Government of Seychelles

1954 Issue

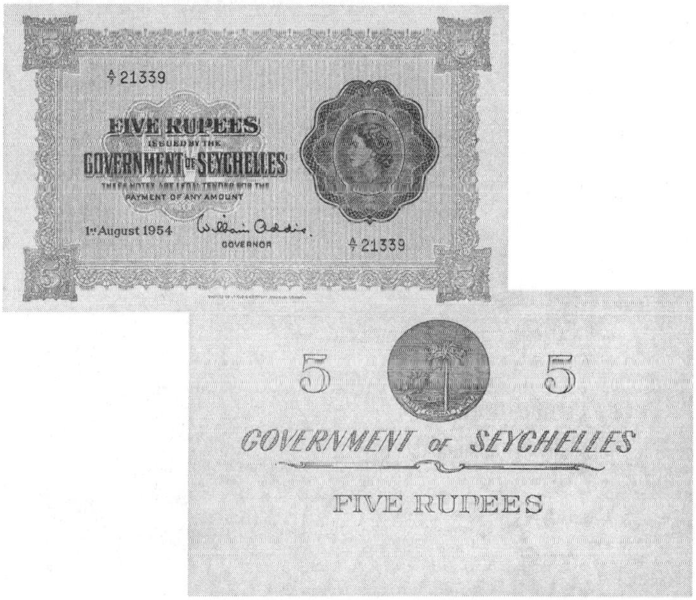

11	**5 Rupees**	VF	UNC
	1954; 1960. Lilac and green. Portrait Queen Elizabeth II in profile at right. Signature varieties. Back: Denomination. Printer: TDLR. 160x98mm.		
	a. 1.8.1954.	65.00	425.
	b. 1.8.1960.	60.00	350.

12	**10 Rupees**	VF	UNC
	1954-67. Green and red. Portrait Queen Elizabeth II in profile at right. Signature varieties. Back: Denomination. Printer: TDLR. 157x98mm.		
	a. 1.8.1954.	150.	1400.
	b. 1.8.1960.	125.	1300.
	c. 1.5.1963.	125.	1250.
	d. 1.1.1967.	100.	1250.

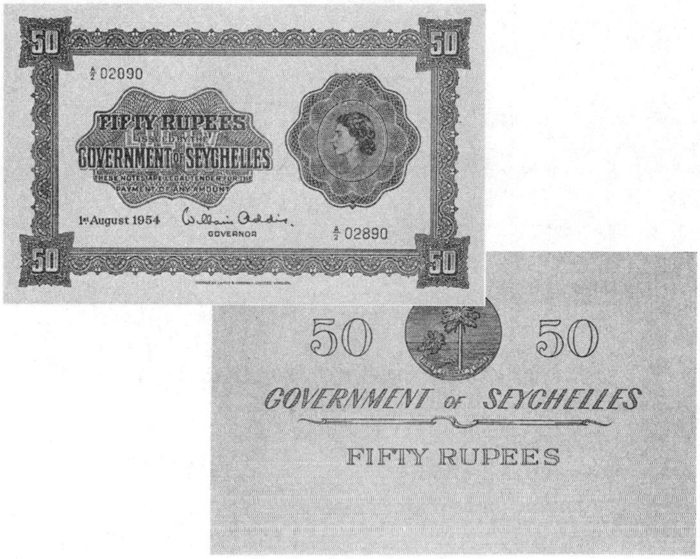

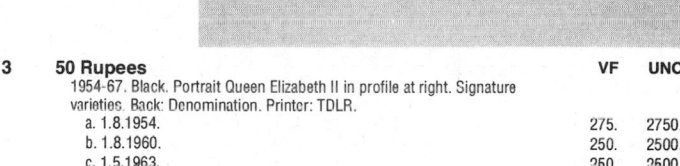

13	**50 Rupees**	VF	UNC
	1954-67. Black. Portrait Queen Elizabeth II in profile at right. Signature varieties. Back: Denomination. Printer: TDLR.		
	a. 1.8.1954.	275.	2750.
	b. 1.8.1960.	250.	2500.
	c. 1.5.1963.	250.	2500.
	d. 1.1.1967.	350.	2250.

1968 Issue

14	**5 Rupees**	VF	UNC
	1.1.1968. Dark brown on multicolor underprint. Queen Elizabeth II at right. Various signature varieties. Back: Seychelles black parrot at left. Watermark: Black parrot's head.		
	a. Issued note.	45.00	150.
	s. Specimen.	—	—
	ct. Color trial. Blue-green on multicolor underprint.	—	575.

		VF	UNC
15	**10 Rupees**		
	1968; 1974. Light blue on multicolor underprint. Queen Elizabeth II at right. Various signature varieties. Back: Sea tortoise at left center. Letters *SCUM* discernible beneath tortoise's rear flipper at left Watermark: Black parrot's head.		
	a. 1.1.1968.	125.	525.
	b. 1.1.1974.	100.	400.
	s. As a. Specimen.	—	—

		VF	UNC
16	**20 Rupees**		
	1968-74. Purple on multicolor underprint. Queen Elizabeth II at right. Various signature varieties. Back: Bridled tern at left center. Watermark: Black parrot's head.		
	a. 1.1.1968.	185.	800.
	b. 1.1.1971.	160.	675.
	c. 1.1.1974.	140.	625.
	s. As c. Specimen.	—	—

		VF	UNC
17	**50 Rupees**		
	1968-73. Olive on multicolor underprint. Queen Elizabeth II at right. Various signature varieties. Back: Sailing ship at left. Word *SEX* discernible in trees at right. Watermark: Black parrot's head.		
	a. 1.1.1968.	425.	1650.
	b. 1.1.1969.	550.	2250.
	c. 1.10.1970.	450.	1750.
	d. 1.1.1972.	225.	900.
	e. 1.8.1973.	250.	1000.
	s. As d. Specimen.	—	—
	ct. Color trial. Green on multicolor underprint.	—	2350.

		VF	UNC
18	**100 Rupees**		
	1968-75. Red on multicolor underprint. Queen Elizabeth II at right. Various signature varieties. Back: Land turtles at left center. Watermark: Black parrot's head.		
	a. 1.1.1968.	1400.	5000.
	b. 1.1.1969.	2000.	7000.
	c. 1.1.1972.	1250.	4500.
	d. 1.8.1973.	1200.	4000.
	e. 1.6.1975.	1200.	4000.
	s. Specimen.	—	—
	ct. Color trial. Blue on multicolor underprint.	—	6000.

Republic

Republic of Seychelles

1976; 1977 ND Issue

		VF	UNC
19	**10 Rupees**		
	ND (1976). Dark blue and blue on multicolor underprint. President J. R. Mancham at right, seashell at lower left. Back: Hut with boats and cliffs. Watermark: Black parrot's head.		
	a. Issued note.	5.00	17.50
	s. Specimen.	—	175.

		VF	UNC
20	**20 Rupees**		
	ND (1977). Purple on multicolor underprint. President J. R. Mancham at right, Sea Tortoise at lower left. Back: Sailboat at left center. Watermark: Black parrot's head.		
	a. Issued note.	10.00	30.00
	s. Specimen.	—	125.

		VF	UNC
21	**50 Rupees**		
	ND (1977). Olive on multicolor underprint. President J. R. Mancham at right, fish at lower left. Back: Fishermen at left center. Watermark: Black parrot's head. .		
	a. Issued note.	25.00	80.00
	s. Specimen.	—	165.

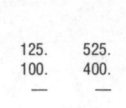

22 **100 Rupees** | VF | UNC
ND (1977). Red and multicolor. President J. R. Mancham at right, Fairy Terns at lower left. Back: Dock area and islands. Watermark: Black parrot's head.

	VF	UNC
a. Issued note.	40.00	150.
s. Specimen.	—	235.

Seychelles Monetary Authority

1979 ND Issue

23 **10 Rupees** | VF | UNC
ND (1979). Blue, green and light red on multicolor underprint. Red-footed booby at center. Back: Girl picking flowers in vertical format. Watermark: Black parrot's head.

	VF	UNC
a. Issued note.	4.00	15.00
s. Specimen.	—	125.

24 **25 Rupees** | VF | UNC
ND (1979). Brown, purple and gold on multicolor underprint. Coconuts at center. Back: Man and basket in vertical format. Watermark: Black parrot's head.

	VF	UNC
a. Issued note.	10.00	25.00
s. Specimen.	—	125.

25 **50 Rupees** | VF | UNC
ND (1979). Olive-green, brown and lilac on multicolor underprint. Turtle at center. Back: Buildings and palm trees in vertical format. Watermark: Black parrot's head.

	VF	UNC
a. Issued note.	20.00	55.00
s. Specimen.	—	150.

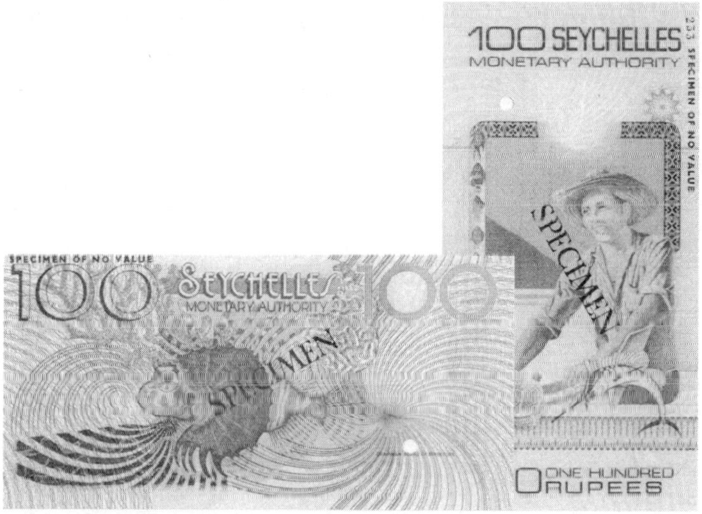

26 **100 Rupees** | VF | UNC
ND (1979). Red and light blue on multicolor underprint. Tropical fish at center. Back: Man with tools, swordfish in vertical format. Watermark: Black parrot's head.

	VF	UNC
a. Issued note.	40.00	120.
s. Specimen.	—	250.

1980 ND Issue

		VF	UNC
27	**100 Rupees**		
	ND (1980). Brown and light blue on multicolor underprint. Tropical fish at center. Back: Man with tools, swordfish in vertical format. Watermark: Black parrot's head.		
	a. Issued note.	35.00	90.00
	s. Specimen, punch hole cancelled.	—	175.

Central Bank of Seychelles

1983 ND Issue

		VF	UNC
28	**10 Rupees**		
	ND (1983). Blue, green and light red on multicolor underprint. Red-footed booby at center, new bank name and signature title. Back: Girl picking flowers in vettical format. Watermark: Black parrot's head.		
	a. Issued note.	FV	7.00
	s. Specimen.	—	125.

		VF	UNC
29	**25 Rupees**		
	ND (1983). Brown, purple and gold on multicolor underprint. Coconuts at center, new bank name and signature title. Back: Man and basket in vertical format. Watermark: Black parrot's head.		
	a. Issued note.	FV	17.00
	s. Specimen.	—	125.

		VF	UNC
30	**50 Rupees**		
	ND (1983). Olive-green, brown and lilac on multicolor underprint. Turtle at center, new bank name and signature title. Back: Buildings and palm trees in vertical format. Watermark: Black parrot's head.		
	a. Issued note.	FV	35.00
	s. Specimen.	—	150.

		VF	UNC
31	**100 Rupees**		
	ND (1983). Brown and light blue on multicolor underprint. Tropical fish at center, new bank name and signature title. Back: Man with tools, swordfish in vertical format. Watermark: Black parrot's head.		
	a. Issued note.	FV	65.00
	s. Specimen.	—	175.

Labank Santral Sesel

Central Bank of Seychelles

1989 ND Issue

		VF	UNC
32	**10 Rupees**	VF	UNC
	ND (1989). Blue-black and deep blue-green on multicolor underprint. Boy Scouts at lower left, image of man with flags and broken chain at right, bank at center, flying fish at left and center right. Back: Local people dancing to drummer at center. Watermark: Black parrot's head.	FV	7.00

		VF	UNC
33	**25 Rupees**	VF	UNC
	ND (1989). Purple on multicolor underprint. Two men with coconuts at lower left, boy near palms at upper right, bank at center, flying fish at left and center right. Back: Primitive ox-drawn farm equipment. Watermark: Black parrot's head.	FV	16.00

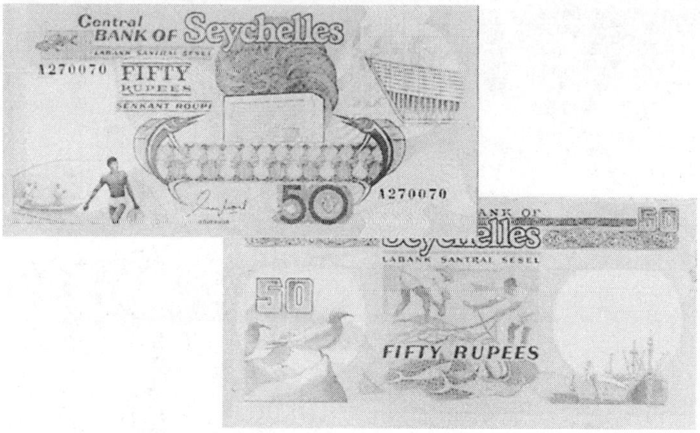

34 **50 Rupees** — VF | UNC
ND (1989). Dark green and brown on multicolor underprint. Two men in boat, Seychelles man at lower left, prow of boat in geometric outline at upper right, bank at center, flying fish at left and center right. Back: Lesser noddy at lower left, fishermen with nets at center, modern cargo ships at right. Watermark: Black parrot's head. — FV | 30.00

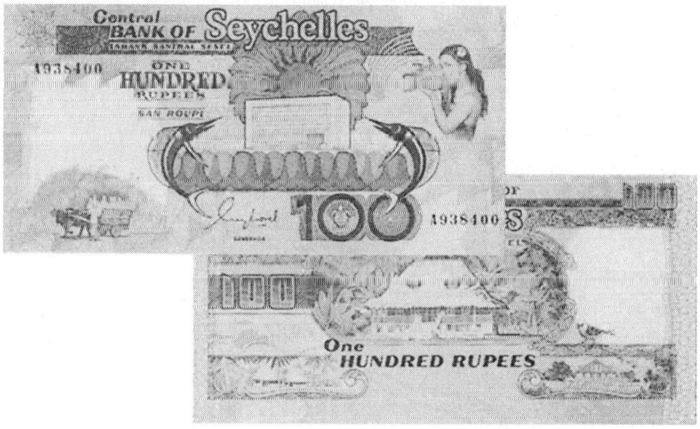

35 **100 Rupees** — VF | UNC
ND (1989). Red and brown on multicolor underprint. Men in ox cart at lower left, girl with shell at upper right, bank at center, flying fish at left and center right. Back: Building at center. Watermark: Black parrot's head. — FV | 55.00

1998 ND Issue

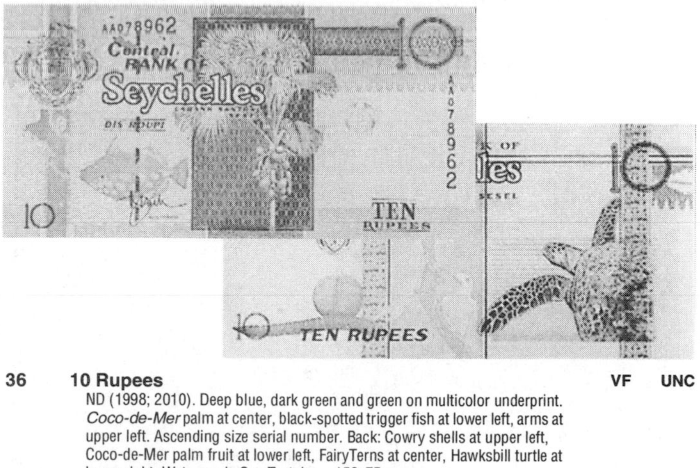

36 **10 Rupees** — VF | UNC
ND (1998; 2010). Deep blue, dark green and green on multicolor underprint. *Coco-de-Mer* palm at center, black-spotted trigger fish at lower left, arms at upper left. Ascending size serial number. Back: Cowry shells at upper left, Coco-de-Mer palm fruit at lower left, FairyTerns at center, Hawksbill turtle at lower right. Watermark: Sea Tortoise. 150x75mm.

	VF	UNC
a. Signature 1.	FV	5.00
b. Signature 2.	FV	5.00

37 **25 Rupees** — VF | UNC
ND (1998). Purple, violet and blue-violet on multicolor underprint. *Wrights gardenia* flower at center, Lion fish at lower left, arms at upper left. Ascending size serial number. Back: Cowry shells at upper left, Bi-Centennary monument at lower left, coconut crab at center, Seychelles blue Pigeon at right. Watermark: Sea Tortoise. 150x75mm. — FV | 14.00

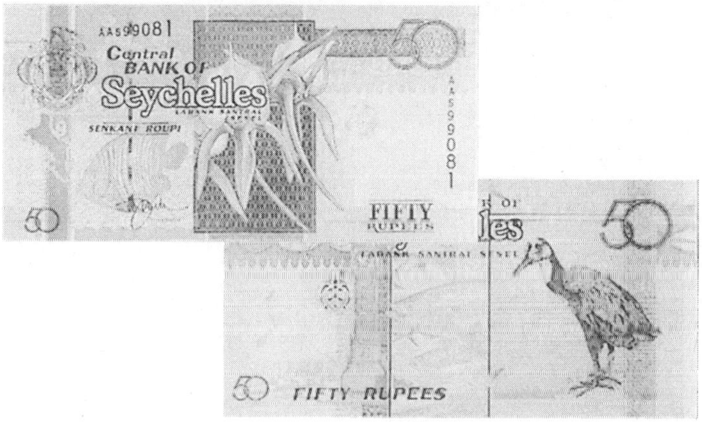

38 **50 Rupees** — VF | UNC
ND (1990). Dark green, deep olive-green and brown on multicolor underprint. *Paille en Que* orchids at center, Angel fish at lower left, arms at upper left. Ascending size serial number. Back: Cowry shells at upper left. Clock tower, autos at lower left, Yellow fin tuna at center, Flightless white throated rail or tiomitio at right. Watermark: Sea Tortoise. 150x75mm. — FV | 30.00

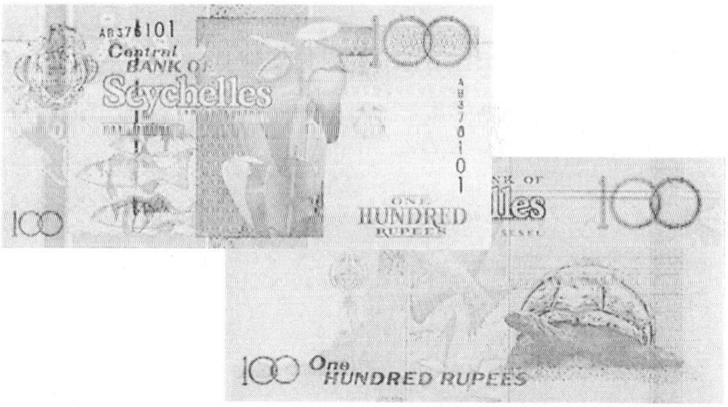

39 **100 Rupees** — VF | UNC
ND (1998). Red, brown-orange and violet on multicolor underprint. Pitcher plant at center, Vielle Babone Cecile fish at lower left, arms at upper left. Ascending size serial number. Back: Cowry shells at upper left, shoreline at lower left, Bridled terns at center, giant land tortoise at lower right. Watermark: Sea Tortoise. 150x75mm. — FV | 47.50

2001 ND Issue

39A **50 Rupees** — VF | UNC
ND (2004). Silver foil impression of sailfish added at top right. — FV | 30.00

40 **100 Rupees** — VF | UNC
ND (2001). Red, brown-orange and violet on multicolor underprint. Pitcher plant at center, Vielle Babone Cecile fish at lower left. Gold foil impression of sailfish at top right. Signature varieties. Back: Cowry shells at top left, shoreline at lower left, Bridled terns at center, giant land tortoise at lower right. 150x75mm. — FV | 45.00

41 **500 Rupees** | VF FV | UNC 150.

ND (2005). Brown and red orange on tan and multicolor underprint. *Coco de Mer* fish. Gold foin sailrish at top right. Back: Owl at right. 150x75mm.

2011 ND Issue

42 **50 Rupees** | VF FV | UNC 25.00

ND (2011). Dark green and lavender on multicolor underprint. Paile en Que orchids at center, angel fish at lower left. Back: Yellowfin tuna at center, flightless bird at right.

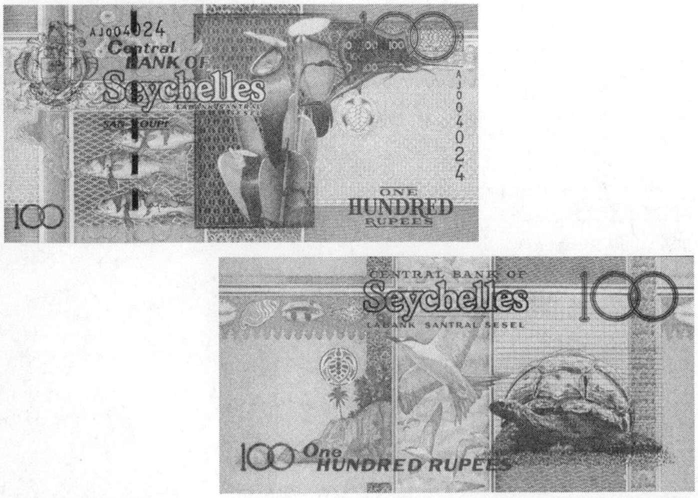

43 **100 Rupees** | VF FV | UNC 47.50

ND (2011). Rose on multicolor underprint. Pitcher plant at center, Vielle Babone Cecile fish at lower left. Back: Brided terns at center, giant land tortoise at right.

44 **500 Rupees** | VF FV | UNC 150.

ND (2011). Brown and red orange on multicolor underprint. Coco de Mer at center, foil sailfish at top right. Back: Owl at right.

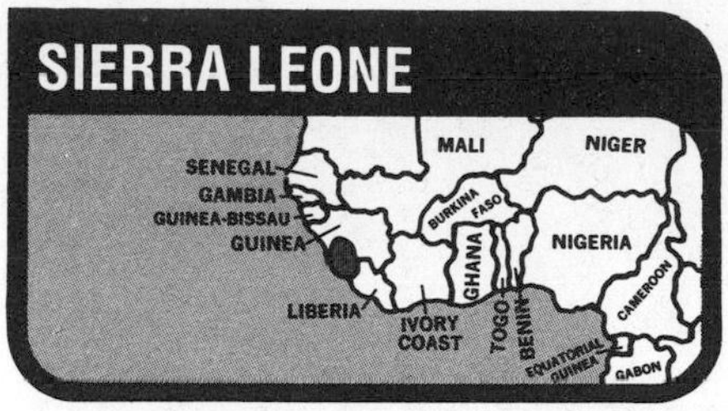

The Republic of Sierra Leone, a British Commonwealth nation located in western Africa between Guinea and Liberia, has an area of 71,740 sq. km. and a population of 6.29 million. Capital: Freetown. The economy is predominantly agricultural but mining contributes significantly to export revenues. Diamonds, iron ore, palm kernels, cocoa and coffee are exported.

Democracy is slowly being reestablished after the civil war from 1991 to 2002 that resulted in tens of thousands of deaths and the displacement of more than 2 million people (about one-third of the population). The military, which took over full responsibility for security following the departure of UN peacekeepers at the end of 2005, is increasingly developing as a guarantor of the country's stability. The armed forces remained on the sideline during the 2007 presidential election, but still look to the UN Integrated Office in Sierra Leone (UNIOSIL) - a civilian UN mission - to support efforts to consolidate peace. The new government's priorities include furthering development, creating jobs, and stamping out endemic corruption.

RULERS:

British to 1971

MONETARY SYSTEM:

1 Leone = 100 Cents
1 Pound = 20 Shillings

REPUBLIC

BANK OF SIERRA LEONE

1964 ND ISSUE

1 — 1 Leone

ND (1964-70). Green on multicolor underprint. 300-Year old cottonwood tree and court building at left. Signature varieties. Back: Diamond mining at the city of Hangha. Watermark: Lion's head. Printer: TDLR.

	VF	UNC
a. ND (1964). Prefix A/1-A/6.	12.50	65.00
b. ND (1969). Prefix A/7-A/8.	18.50	85.00
c. ND (1970). Prefix A/9-A/12.	7.50	45.00
s. As a. Specimen.	—	—

2 — 2 Leones

ND (1964-70). Red on multicolor underprint. 300-Year old cottonwood tree and court building at left. Signature varieties. Back: Village scene. Watermark: Lion's head. Printer: TDLR.

	VF	UNC
a. ND (1964). Prefix B/1-B/21.	15.00	60.00
b. ND (1967). Prefix B/22-B/25.	17.50	85.00
c. ND (1969). Prefix B/26-B/30.	17.50	85.00
d. ND (1970). Prefix B/31-B/41.	15.00	70.00
s. As a. Specimen.	—	—

3 — 5 Leones

ND (1964). Purple on multicolor underprint. 300-Year old cottonwood tree and court building at left. Signature varieties. Prefix C/1. Back: Dockside at Freetown at center right with boats in harbor. Watermark: Lion's head. Printer: TDLR.

	VF	UNC
a. Issued note.	75.00	450.
s. Specimen.	—	—

1974-80 ISSUE

#4-8 Replacement notes: Serial # prefix *Z/1*.

4 — 50 Cents

ND, 1979-84. Dark brown on multicolor underprint. President S. Stevens at left, arms at upper left, flowers in underprint at right. Back: Central Bank building at center. Printer: TDLR. .

	VF	UNC
a. ND (1972). Prefix D/1-D/2.	2.00	6.00
b. ND (1974). Prefix D/3-D/5.	1.50	4.00
c. Prefix D/6-D/8. 1.7.1979.	1.00	3.00
d. Prefix D/9; D/10. 1.7.1981.	.50	1.50
e. 4.8.1984.	.25	.75
s. As a. Specimen, without prefix.	—	—

5 — 1 Leone

1974-84. Olive-green and dark green on multicolor underprint. President S. Stevens at left. Back: Central Bank building at center right, arms at upper right. Watermark: Lion's head. Printer: TDLR.

	VF	UNC
a. Prefix A/1-A/7. 19.4.1974.	2.25	7.50
b. Prefix A/8-A/12. 1.1.1978.	4.00	10.00
c. Prefix A/13-A/17. 1.3.1980.	1.00	4.00
d. Prefix A/18-A/26. 1.7.1981.	.50	2.00
e. 4.8.1984.	.50	1.00

6 — 2 Leones

1974-85. Red, deep red-orange and dark brown on multicolor underprint. President S. Stevens at left. Back: Central Bank building at center right, arms at upper right. Watermark: Lion's head. Printer: TDLR.

	VF	UNC
a. Prefix B/1-B/20. 19.4.1974.	3.50	10.00
b. Prefix B/21-B/22. 1.1.1978.	15.00	65.00
c. Prefix B/23-B/27. 1.7.1978.	4.00	12.50
d. Prefix B/28-B/31. 1.7.1979.	2.00	7.50
e. Prefix B/32-B/37. 1.5.1980.	2.00	7.00
f. 1.7.1983.	.75	3.00
g. 4.8.1984.	.45	1.25
h. 4.8.1985.	.45	1.25

7 — 5 Leones

1975-85. Purple and blue-black on multicolor underprint. President S. Stevens at left, plant leaves at center. Back: Parliament building at center right, arms at upper right. Watermark: Lion's head. Printer: TDLR.

	VF	UNC
a. Prefix C/1. 4.8.1975.	10.00	35.00
b. Prefix C/2. 1.7.1978.	7.00	25.00
c. Prefix C/3. 1.3.1980.	4.00	12.50
d. Prefix C/4-C/6. 1.7.1981.	3.00	7.50
e. 19.4.1984.	1.00	3.50
f. 4.8.1984.	1.00	3.50
g. 4.8.1985.	1.00	3.25

8 — 10 Leones

1981; 1984. Blue-gray, black and blue-green on multicolor underprint. President S. Stevens at left. Back: Dredging operation at center right, arms at upper right. Watermark: Lion's head. Printer: TDLR.

	VF	UNC
a. Prefix E/1-E/4. 1.7.1981.	4.00	12.50
b. 19.4.1984.	1.00	3.00
c. 4.8.1984.	1.00	3.00

1980 Commemorative Issue

#9-13, Commemorating The Organisation of African Unity Conference in Freetown

Note: #9-13 were prepared in special booklets (1800 sets).

9 — 50 Cents

	VF	UNC
1.7.1980. Dark brown on multicolor underprint. President S. Stevens at left, arms at upper left, flowers in underprint at right. Back: Central Bank building at center. Overprint: Red overprint in four lines at upper left center. Printer: TDLR.	4.00	15.00

10 — 1 Leone

	VF	UNC
1.7.1980. Olive-green and dark green on multicolor underprint. President S. Stevens at left, date below overprint. Back: Central Bank building at center right, arms at upper right. Overprint: Red overprint in circle around watermark area at right. Printer: TDLR.	5.00	15.00

11 — 2 Leones

	VF	UNC
1.7.1980. Red, deep red-orange and dark brown on multicolor underprint. President S. Stevens at left, date below overprint. Back: Central Bank building at center right, arms at upper right. Overprint: Red overprint in circle around watermark area at right. Printer: TDLR.	7.50	20.00

12 — 5 Leones

	VF	UNC
1.7.1980. Purple and blue-black on multicolor underprint. President S. Stevens at left, plant leaves at center, date below overprint. Back: Parliament building at center, arms at upper right Overprint: Red overprint in circle around watermark area at right. Printer: TDLR.	7.50	22.50

		VF	UNC
13	**10 Leones** 1.7.1980. Blue-gray, black and blue-green on multicolor underprint. President S. Stevens at left, date below overprint. Back: Dredging operation at center right, arms at upper right. Overprint: Red overprint in circle around watermark area at right. Printer: TDLR.	10.00	30.00

1982 Issue

		VF	UNC
14	**20 Leones** 1982; 1984. Brown, red and green on multicolor underprint. Tree at center, President S. Stevens at right. Back: Two youths pan mining (gold or diamonds). Watermark: Lion's head. Printer: BWC. UV: Bank name, value and crest fluoresce orange. 160x74mm.		
	a. 24.8.1982.	2.50	10.00
	b. 24.8.1984.	1.00	4.00
	s. As a, b. Specimen.	—	100.

1988-93 Issue

#15-21 Replacement notes: Serial # prefix ***Z/1.***

		VF	UNC
15	**10 Leones** 27.4.1988. Dark green and purple on multicolor underprint. President Dr. Joseph Saidu Momoh at right, arms at upper center. Back: Steer at left, farmer harvesting at center. Watermark: Lion's head. 160x74mm.	.50	2.00

		VF	UNC
16	**20 Leones** 27.4.1988. Brown, red and green on multicolor underprint. President Dr. Joseph Saidu Momoh at right, arms at upper center. Back: Two youths pan mining (gold or diamonds). Watermark: Lion's head. 160x74mm.	.75	2.50

		VF	UNC
17	**50 Leones** 1988-89. Purple, blue and black on multicolor underprint. President Dr. Joseph Saidu Momoh at right, sports stadium at center, arms at upper center. Back: Dancers at left center. Watermark: Lion's head. 160x74mm.		
	a. Without imprint. 27.4.1988.	1.50	3.00
	b. Printer: TDLR. 27.4.1989.	.75	2.00

		VF	UNC
18	**100 Leones** 1988-90. Blue and black on multicolor underprint. President Dr. Joseph Saidu Momoh at right, building and ship at left center, arms at upper center. Back: Local designs at left and right, Central Bank building at left center. Watermark: Lion's head. 160x74mm.		
	a. Without imprint. 27.4.1988.	1.00	5.00
	b. Printer: TDLR. 27.4.1989.	.75	2.00
	c. 26.9.1990.	FV	2.00

		VF	UNC
19	**500 Leones** 27.4.1991. Red-brown and dark green on multicolor underprint. President Dr. Joseph Saidu Momoh at right, arms at upper center, modern building below arms at left center. Back: Two fishing boats at left center, artistic carp at right. Watermark: Lion's head. 160x74mm.	1.00	3.75

20	1000 Leones	VF	UNC
	1993-98. Black, red and yellow on multicolor underprint. Bai Bureh at right, carving at lower center, arms at upper center. Back: Dish antenna at left center. Watermark: Lion's head. Printer: TDLR. 160x74mm.		
	a. 4.8.1993.	1.50	5.00
	b. 27.4.1996.	1.50	5.00
	c. 27.4.1997.	1.50	5.00
	d. 27.4.1998.	1.50	5.00

21	5000 Leones	VF	UNC
	1993-98. Blue and violet on multicolor underprint. Sengbe Pieh at right, building at lower center, arms at upper center. Back: Dam at left center. Watermark: Lion's head. Printer: TDLR. 160x74mm.		
	a. 4.8.1993.	6.00	22.50
	b. 27.4.1996.	6.00	22.50
	c. 27.4.1997.	6.00	22.50
	d. 15.7.1998.	6.00	22.50

1995-2000 Issues

#22 Not assigned.

23	500 Leones	VF	UNC
	27.4.1995 (1996); 15.7.1998; 1.3.2003. Blue-green, brown and green on multicolor underprint. K. Londo at right, arms at upper center, spearhead at left, building at lower center. Back: Fishing boats at left center, artistic carp at right. Watermark: Lion's head. Printer: TDLR. 160x74mm.		
	a. 27.4.1995 (1996).	FV	3.00
	b. 15.7.1998.	FV	3.00
	c. 1.3.2003.	FV	3.00

24	1000 Leones	VF	UNC
	1.2.2002; 1.3.2003; 4.8.2006. Brown and red on multicolor underprint. Bai Bureh at left. Back: Antenna. 160x74mm.		
	a. 1.2.2002.	FV	5.00
	b. 1.3.2003.	FV	5.00
	c. 4.8.2006.	FV	5.00

25	2000 Leones	VF	UNC
	1.1.2000. Brown and blue on multicolor underprint. I. T. A. Wallace-Johnson at right, cargo ship and storage shed at center. Back: Modern building at left center. Printer: TDLR. 160x74mm.	FV	9.00

2002-2004 Issue

26	2000 Leones	VF	UNC
	1.2.2002; 1.3.2003; 4.8.2006. Brown and blue on multicolor underprint. I. T. A. Wallace-Johnson at righ, cargo ship and storage shed at center. Back: Modern building at left center. Printer: TDLR. Metallic printing. 160x74mm.		
	a. 1.2.2002.	FV	9.00
	b. 1.3.2003.	FV	9.00
	c. 4.8.2006.	FV	9.00

#	Denomination / Description	VF	UNC
27	**5000 Leones**	VF	UNC
	1.2.2002; 1.3.2003; 4.8.2006. Blue and violet on multicolor underprint. Serge Pieh at right. Back: Dam. 160x74mm.		
	a. 1.2.2002.	FV	22.50
	b. 1.3.2003.	FV	22.50
	c. 4.8.2006.	FV	22.50
28	**5000 Leones**		
	1.2.2002; 1.3.2003; 4.8.2006. Blue and violet on multicolor underprint. Serge Pieh at right. Back: Dam. 160x74mm.		
	a. 1.2.2002.	FV	22.50
	b. 1.3.2003.	FV	22.50
	c. 4.8.2006.	FV	22.50

#	Denomination / Description	VF	UNC
29	**10,000 Leones**	VF	UNC
	4.8.2004; 4.8.2007. Blue, green and multicolor. Dove at center, flag at right center. Back: Tree at center. 160x74mm.		
	a. 4.8.2004.	FV	7.50
	b. 4.8.2007.	FV	6.00

2010 Issue

#	Denomination / Description	VF	UNC
30	**1000 Leones**	VF	UNC
	27.4.2010. Brown and red on multicolor underprint. Bai Bureh at right. Back: Antenna. Printer: TDLR. 160x74mm.	FV	5.00

#	Denomination / Description	VF	UNC
31	**2000 Leones**	VF	UNC
	27.4.2010. Brown and blue on multicolor underprint. I.T.A. Wallace-Johnson at right. Back: Modern building at center. Printer: TDLR. 160x74mm.	FV	9.00

#	Denomination / Description	VF	UNC
32	**5000 Leones**	VF	UNC
	27.4.2010. Blue and violet on multicolor underprint. Serge Pieh at right. Back: Dam. Printer: TDLR. 160x74mm.	FV	22.50

#	Denomination / Description	VF	UNC
33	**10,000 Leones**	VF	UNC
	27.4.2010. Blue and green on multicolor underprint. Dove and Flag at center. Back: Tree. Printer: TDLR. 160x74mm.	FV	40.00

Collector Series

Bank of Sierra Leone

1972 ND Issue

#CS1, First Anniversary of Republic, 1972

#	Issue / Description	Mkt.	Value
CS1	**ND (19.4.1972) - 50 Cents**	Mkt.	Value
	#4 laminated in plastic with two 50 cent coins in special maroon case.		10.00

1979 ND Issue

#	Issue / Description	Mkt.	Value
CS2	**ND (1979) 50 Cents - 5 Leones**	Mkt.	Value
	#4, 5b-7b with overprint: *SPECIMEN* and serial # prefix Maltese cross.		20.00

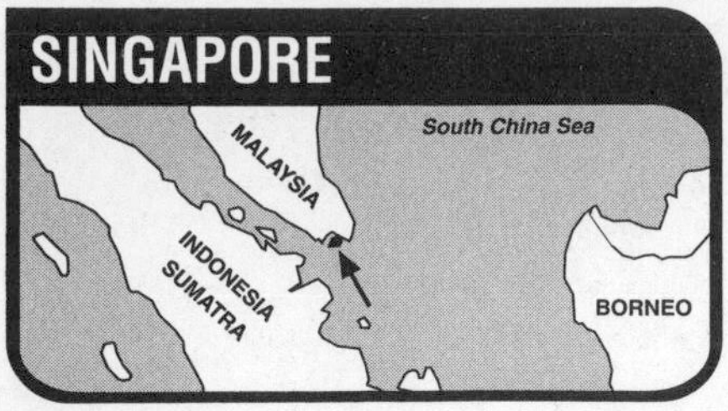

The Republic of Singapore, a British Commonwealth nation situated at the southern tip of the Malayan peninsula, has an area of 712 sq. km. and a population of 5.1 million. Capital: Singapore. The economy is d on electronics production, petrochemicals, pharmaceuticals and shipbuilding/repairs. It is a world financial, business E-commerce, oil refining and air services center, besides having the busiest port in terms of shipping tonnage and containers handled.

Singapore was founded as a British trading colony in 1819. It joined the Malaysian Federation in 1963 but separated two years later and became independent. Singapore subsequently became one of the world's most prosperous countries with strong international trading links (its port is one of the world's busiest in terms of tonnage handled) and with per capita GDP equal to that of the leading nations of Western Europe.

MONETARY SYSTEM:

1 Dollar = 100 Cents

SIGNATURE SEAL VARIETIES	
 Type I: Dragon, seal script, lion	 Type II: Seal script w/symbol

REPUBLIC

BOARD OF COMMISSIONERS OF CURRENCY

1967-73 ND ISSUE

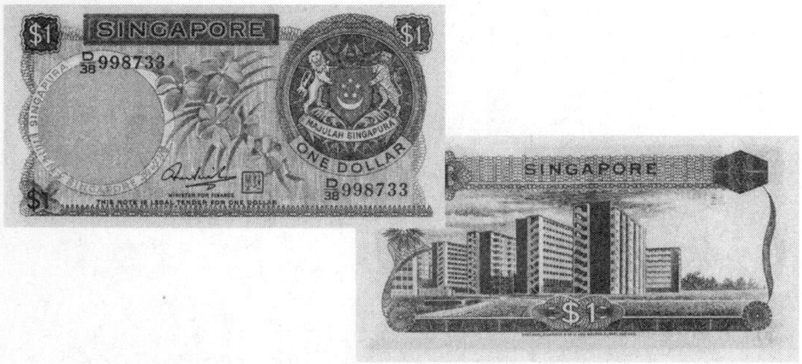

1 **1 Dollar** — VF / UNC

ND (1967-72). Blue on multicolor underprint. Light red flowers (Janet Kaneali Orchid) at center, arms at right. Back: Apartment buildings. Watermark: Lion's head. Printer: BWC. UV: left design, leaves, watermark area legend fluoresce yellow.

	VF	UNC
a. Without red seal. Signature Lim Kim San (1967).	7.50	25.00
b. Red signature seal Type I at center. Signature Dr. Goh Keng Swee (1970).	17.50	50.00
c. Without red seal. Signature Hon Sui Sen (1971).	8.00	35.00
d. Red signature seal Type II at center. Signature Hon Sui Sen (1972).	5.00	20.00

2 **5 Dollars** — VF / UNC

ND (1967-73). Light orange flowers (T. M. A. Orchid) at center, arms at upper right. Back: Busy scene on the Singapore River. Watermark: Lion's head. Printer: BWC.

	VF	UNC
a. Without red seal. Signature Lim Kim San (1967).	35.00	125.
b. Red signature seal Type I at center. Signature Dr. Goh Keng Swee (1970).	225.	1200.
c. Without red seal. Signature Hon Sui Sen (1972).	60.00	220.
d. Red signature seal Type II at center. Signature Hon Sui Sen (1973).	25.00	110.

3 **10 Dollars** — VF / UNC

ND (1967-73). Red on multicolor underprint. Lilac flowers (Dendrobium Marjorie Orchid) at center, arms at lower right. Back: Four hands clasping wrists over map of Singapore at left center. Watermark: Lion's head. Printer: TDLR.

	VF	UNC
a. Without red seal. Signature Lim Kim San (1967).	40.00	130.
b. Red signature seal Type I at center. Signature Dr. Goh Keng Swee (1970).	55.00	180.
c. Without red seal. Signature Hon Sui Sen (1972).	45.00	170.
d. Red signature seal Type II at center. Signature Hon Sui Sen (1973).	25.00	100.
s. As d. Specimen.	—	300.

4 **25 Dollars** — VF / UNC

ND (1972). Dark brown on multicolor underprint. Yellow flowers (Renanthopsis Aurora Orchid) at center, arms at upper right. Back: Supreme Court building. Watermark: Lion's head. Printer: TDLR. — 75.00 / 200.

5 **50 Dollars** — VF / UNC

ND (1967-73). Blue on multicolor underprint. Violet flowers (Vanda Rothschildiana Orchid) at center, arms at lower right. Back: Singapore seafront and Clifford Pier. Watermark: Lion's head. Printer: TDLR.

	VF	UNC
a. Without red seal. Signature Lim Kim San (1967).	125.	300.
b. Red signature seal Type I at center. Signature Dr. Goh Keng Swee (1970).	225.	600.
c. Without red seal. Signature Hon Sui Se Sen (1972).	85.00	275.
d. Red signature seal Type II at center. Signature Hon Sui Sen (1973).	75.00	250.
s. As d. Specimen.	—	530.

6 **100 Dollars** — VF | UNC

ND (1967-73). Blue and violet on multicolor underprint. Red flowers (Cattleya Orchid) at center, arms at right. Back: Sailing vessels along Singapore waterfront. Watermark: Lion's head. Printer: BWC.

	VF	UNC
a. Without red seal. Signature Lim Kim San (1967).	150.	500.
b. Red signature seal Type I at center. Signature Dr. Goh Keng Swee (1970).	750.	2500.
c. Without red seal. Signature Hon Sui Sen (1972).	175.	500.
d. Red signature seal Type II at center. Signature Hon Sui Sen (1973).	100.	300.
s. Specimen.	—	700.

7 **500 Dollars** — VF 700. UNC 1500.

ND (1972). Dark green, lilac on multicolor underprint. Pink flowers (Dendrobium Shangri-la) at center. Back: Government offices at St. Andrew's road. Watermark: Lion's head. Printer: TDLR.

8 **1000 Dollars**

ND (1967-75). Purple on multicolored underprint. Lilac-brown colored flowers (Dendrobium Kimiyo Kondo) at center, arms at right. Back: Victoria Theatre and Empress Palace. Watermark: Lion's head. Printer: TDLR.

	VF	UNC
a. Without red seal. Signature Lim Kim San (1967).	1200.	2200.
b. Red signature seal Type I at center. Signature Dr. Goh Keng Swee (1970).	1500.	3000.
c. Without red seal. Signature Hon Sui Sen (1973).	1300.	2500.
d. Red signature seal Type II at center. Signature Hon Sui Sen (1975).	900.	2000.

8A **10,000 Dollars** — VF 8000. UNC 17,000.

ND (1973). Green on multicolor underprint. Orchids (Aranda Majulah) at center, arms at at right. Signature Hon Sui Sen. Back: The Istana (Presidential residence) at left center. Watermark: Lion's head. Printer: TDLR.

1976-80 ND Issue

9 **1 Dollar** — VF FV UNC 7.00

ND (1976). Blue-black on multicolor underprint. Black-naped tern at left, city skyline along bottom, arms at upper right. Back: National Day parade passing large building at center right. Watermark: Lion's head. Printer: BWC.

10 **5 Dollars** — VF FV UNC 20.00

ND (1976). Green and brown on multicolor underprint. Red-whiskered bulbul at left, city skyline along bottom, arms at upper right. Back: Ariel tram cars and view of harbor. Watermark: Lion's head. Printer: BWC.

11 **10 Dollars**

ND (1979). Red and dark blue on multicolor underprint. White collared kingfisher at left, city skyline along bottom, arms at upper right. Back: Garden City with high rise public housing in background. Watermark: Lion's head. Printer: TDLR.

	VF	UNC
a. With security thread (1979).	20.00	90.00
b. With segmented foil over security thread (1980).	15.00	50.00

12 **20 Dollars** — VF 40.00 UNC 75.00

ND (1979). Brown, yellow and blue on multicolor underprint. Yellow-breasted Sunbird at left, city skyline along bottom, arms at upper right. Back: Brown. Dancer at left, Concorde over Changi International airport center right. Watermark: Lion's head. Printer: BWC.

13	50 Dollars	VF	UNC
	ND (1976). Dark blue on multicolor underprint. White-rumped shama at left, city skyline along bottom, arms at upper right. Back: School band on parade. Watermark: Lion's head. Printer: TDLR.		
	a. With security thread.	40.00	150.
	b. With segmented foil over security thread.	35.00	125.

14	100 Dollars	VF	UNC
	ND (1977). Blue on multicolor underprint. Blue-throated bee eater at left, city skyline along bottom, arms at upper right. Back: Various ethnic dancers. Watermark: Lion's head. Printer: BWC.	100.	300.

15	500 Dollars	VF	UNC
	ND (1977). Green and multicolor. Black-naped oriole at left, city skyline along bottom, arms at upper right. Back: Green. View of island and oil refinery at center. Watermark: Lion's head. Printer: TDLR.		
	a. Issued note.	500.	1000.
	s. Specimen.	—	—

16	1000 Dollars	VF	UNC
	ND (1978). Violet and brown on multicolor underprint. Brahminy Kite bird at left, city skyline along bottom, arms at upper right. Back: Container ship terminal. Watermark: Lion's head. Printer: TDLR.	1000.	2000.

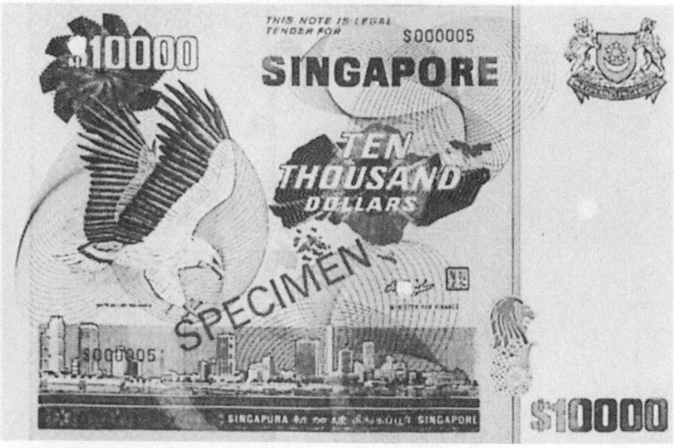

17	10,000 Dollars	VF	UNC
	ND (1980). Green on multicolor underprint. White-bellied Sea Eagle at left, city skyline along bottom, arms at upper right. Back: 19th century Singapore River scene above, modern view below on back. Watermark: Lion's head. Printer: TDLR.		
	a. Issued note.	10,000.	18,000.
	s. Specimen, punched hole cancelled.	—	1500.

1984-89 ND Issue

#18-25 Replacement notes: Serial # prefix *Z/1, Z/2,* etc.

18	1 Dollar	VF	UNC
	ND (1987). Deep blue and green. Sailing ship *Sha Chuan* at left. Chinese Crasse and carp at lower right, arms at upper left. Back: Orchids and satellite tracking station at center. Watermark: Lion's head. Printer: TDLR. UV: Chop fluoresce orange. 160x74mm.		
	a. Signature Goh Keng Swee.	FV	5.00
	b. Signature Hu Tsu Tau.	FV	4.00
19	**5 Dollars**		
	ND (1989). Green and red-violet on multicolor underprint. Chinese lion with ball and Commerson's Anchovy at right, arms at upper left. Back: *Twkow* boats at left, View of the PSA container terminal at right. Watermark: Lion's head. Printer: TDLR.	FV	10.00

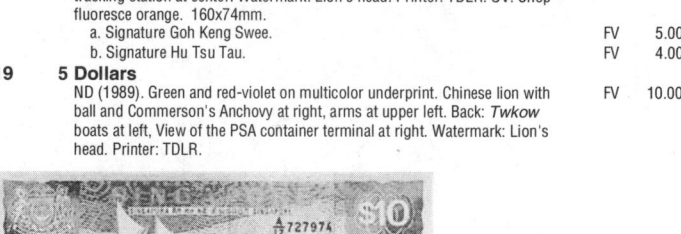

20	10 Dollars	VF	UNC
	ND (1988). Red-orange and violet on multicolor underprint. Trader vessel *Palari* at left, Phoenix and round scad at lower right, arms at upper left. Back: Stylized map at center, public housing at right. Watermark: Lion's head. Printer: TDLR.	FV	15.00

22	50 Dollars	VF	UNC
	ND (1987). Blue on multicolor underprint. Coastal vessel *Perak* at left. Mountain ducks and six-banded grouper at lower right, two raised areas in circles at lower right, arms at upper left. Back: Benjamin Sheares Bridge and city view. Watermark: Lion's head. Printer: TDLR.		
	a. With security thread.	FV	100.
	b. With segmented foil over security thread.	FV	95.00

23	100 Dollars	VF	UNC
	ND (1985; 1995). Dark brown, violet and orange-brown on multicolor underprint. Passenger liner *Chusan* at left center, slender shad and three raised areas in circles at lower right, arms at upper left. Back: Airplane above with Changi air terminal at center right. Watermark: Lion's head. Printer: TDLR.		
	a. With security thread. Signature Dr. Goh Keng Swee. (1985).	FV	175.
	b. With segmented foil over "Cleartext" security thread with $100 *SINGAPORE* in four languages. (1995)	FV	160.
	c. As b. signature Hu Tsu Tau.	FV	150.

24	500 Dollars	VF	UNC
	ND (1988). Green on multicolor underprint. Cargo vessel *Neptune Sardonyx* at left, arms at upper left. Back: Members of the three Armed Forces and the Civil Defence Force with outline map of Singapore. Watermark: Lion's head. Printer: TDLR.	FV	800.

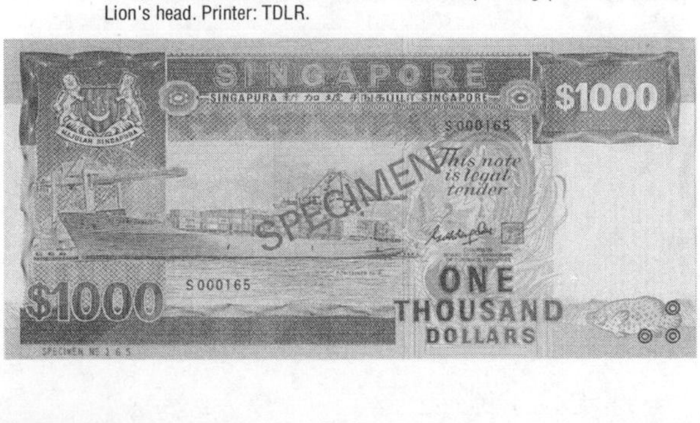

25	1000 Dollars	VF	UNC
	ND (1984). Purple and red on multicolor underprint. Container ship *Neptune Garnet* at left center, Phoenix and Polka-dot grouper at lower right, arms at upper left. Back: Shipyard. Watermark: Lion's head. Printer: TDLR.		
	a. Signature Dr. Goh Keng Swee.	FV	1500.
	b. Signature Dr. Hu Tsu Tau.	FV	1400.
	s. As a. Specimen.	—	—

26	10,000 Dollars	VF	UNC
	ND (1987). Red and purple on multicolor underprint. General bulk carrier *Neptune Canopus* at left, Chinese dragon at center right. Back: 1987 National Day parade.	8500.	12,000.

1990 ND Issue

#27 and 28. Replacement notes: Serial prefix *ZZ*.

27	2 Dollars	VF	UNC
	ND (ca.1990). Orange and red on yellow-green underprint. Arms at upper left, *Tongkang* boat and two smaller boats at center. Back: Chingay procession. Watermark: Lion's head. Printer: TDLR.	FV	7.00

28	2 Dollars	VF	UNC
	ND (1992). Deep purple and brown-violet on multicolor underprint. Arms at upper left, *Tongkang* boat and two smaller boats at center. Ascending size serial number. Back: Chingay procession. Printer: TDLR. UV: Chop fluoresce orange.	FV	6.00

1992 Commemorative Issues

#29, 25th Anniversary - Board of Commissioners of Currency

		VF	UNC
29	**2 Dollars** ND(1992). Deep purple and brown-violet on multicolor underprint. Overprint on #28. (5000). Overprint: *25 YEARS OF CURRENCY 1967-1992...*		
	a. Issued note.	—	400.
	x. Without overprint text: *COMMISSONERS* (error).	—	50.00

		VF	UNC
30	**50 Dollars** 9.8.1990. Red and purple on multicolor underprint. Silver hologram of Yusof bin Ishak at center. Old harbor scene at left, modern buildings at right. Back: First parliament at left, group of people below flag and arms at right. Polymer plastic. 300,000 pieces printed.	FV	125.
31	**50 Dollars** ND (1990). Red and purple on multicolor underprint. Silver hologram of Yusof bin Ishak at center. Old harbor scene at left, modern buildings at right, without date. Back: First parliament at left, group of people below flag and arms at right, without date. 4.817 million pieces printed.	FV	100.

1994 ND Commemorative Issue

#31A, 25th Anniversary - Board of Commissioners of Currency

		VF	UNC
31A	**2 Dollars** ND (1994). Deepm purple and brown-violet on multicolor underprint. *Tongkang* boat and twl smaller boats at center. Overprint: Red logo of the Board at left beneath arms.	—	125.

1994 Regular Issue

		VF	UNC
32	**50 Dollars** ND (1994). Deep blue-black and red on multicolor underprint. Coastal vessel *Perak* at left. Mountain ducks and six-banded grouper at lower right, two raised areas in circles at lower right, arms at upper left, with segmented foil over security thread. Back: Benjamin Sheares Bridge and city view. Printer: TDLR.	FV	90.00

1996 Commemorative Issue

#33, 25th Anniversary of Monetary Authority, 1971-1996

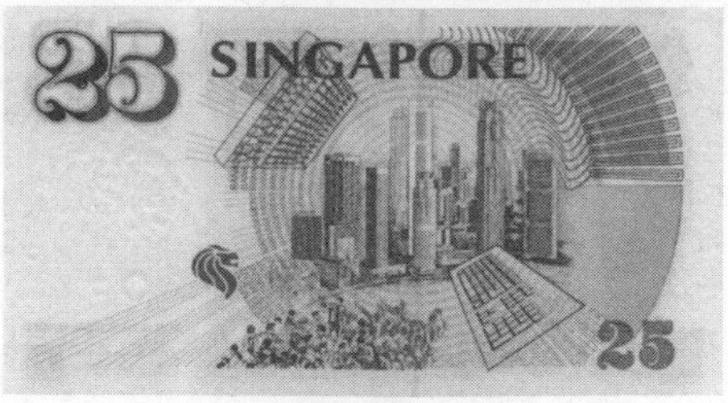

		VF	UNC
33	**25 Dollars** 1.1.1996. Red-brown and green on multicolor underprint. Arms at upper left, Monetary Authority building at center. Optical variable device at left center in addition to many other security features. Signature Hu Tsu Tau. Back: Financial sector skyline. Watermark: Lion's head.	FV	100.

1997 ND Regular Issue

		VF	UNC
34	**2 Dollars** ND (1997). Deep purple and brown-violet on multicolor underprint. Arms at upper left, *Tongkang* boat and two smaller boats at center. Ascending size serial number. Back: Chingay procession. Watermark: Lion's head. Printer: H&S.	FV	6.00

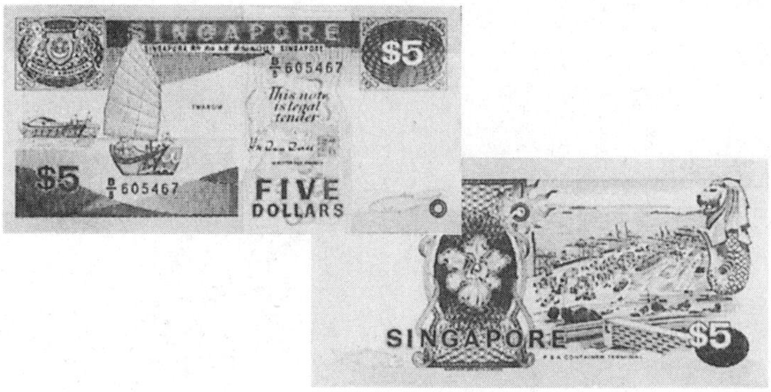

		VF	UNC
35	**5 Dollars** ND (1997). Green and red-violet on multicolor underprint. Chinese lion with ball and Commerson's Anchovy at right, arms at upper left. Back: *Twkow* boats at left, View of the PSA container terminal at right. Watermark: Lion's head. Printer: H&S.	FV	10.00
36	**50 Dollars** ND (1997). Slate gray and red on multicolor underprint. Like #32. Segmented foil over "Cleartext" security thread with $50 *SINGAPORE* in four languages. Back: Benjamin Sheares Bridge and city view. Watermark: Lion's head.	FV	90.00

1998 ND Issue

		VF	UNC
37	**2 Dollars** ND(1998). Deep purple and brown-violet on multicolor underprint. Arms at upper left, *Tongkang* boat and two smaller boats at center. Ascending size serial number. Back: Chingay procession. Watermark: Lion's head. Printer: BABN. 126x63mm.	FV	6.00

1999 ND Issue

38 2 Dollars — VF | UNC

ND (1999). Purple, brown and multicolor underprint. President Encik Yusof bin Ishak at right. Back: Education - Victoria Bridge School, Raffles Institue, College of Medicine views with children. Watermark: Encik Yusof bin Ishak. UV: value in box and vertical serial # fluoresce yellow. 126x63mm. — FV | 5.00

39 5 Dollars — VF | UNC

ND (1999). Green, red and multicolor. President Encik Yusof bin Ishak at right. Back: Garden City - trees and flowers, skyline in background. Watermark: Encik Yusof bin Ishak. 133x66mm. — FV | 9.00

40 10 Dollars — VF | UNC

ND (1999). Red, brown and multicolor. President Encik Yusof bin Ishak at right. Back: Sports - swimming, tennis, soccer, sailing, running. Watermark: Encik Yusof bin Ishak. . 141x69mm. — FV | 18.00

41 50 Dollars — VF | UNC

ND (1999). Slate blue and multicolor. President Encik Yusof bin Ishak at right. Back: Arts - music, graphics. Watermark: Encik Yusof bin Ishak. 156x74mm.

- a. Signature as illustration. — 55.00 | 85.00
- b. Signature Lee Hsieh Loong. — 75.00 | 125.

42 100 Dollars — VF | UNC

ND (1999). Orange, brown and multicolor. President Encik Yusof bin Ishak at right. Back: Youth - Members of the Singapore Red Cross, St. John's Ambulance Brigade, National Police Cadet Corp Watermark: Encik Yusof bin Ishak. 162x77mm. — FV | 140.

43 1000 Dollars — VF | UNC

ND (1999). Purple, lilac and multicolor. President Encik Yusof bin Ishak at right. Back: Parliament House at left, Istana (Presidential residence) at center, Supreme Court at right. Watermark: Encik Yusof bin Ishak. 170x83mm. — FV | 1300.

44 10,000 Dollars — VF | UNC

ND (1999). Light brown and multicolor. President Encik Yusof bin Ishak at right. Back: Technology - computer chip research lab. Watermark: Encik Yusof bin Ishak. 180x90mm.

- a. Issued note. — FV | 12,000.
- s. Specimen. — — | 1000.

2000 Issue

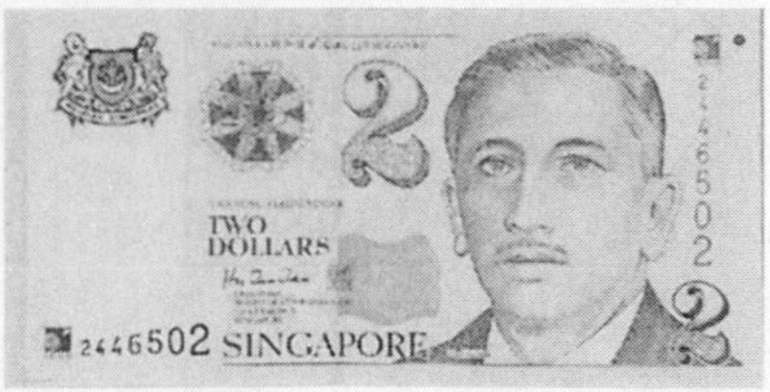

45 **2 Dollars** — VF | UNC
2000. Purple, brown and multicolor. President Encik Yusof bin Ishak at right. #38 with 2000 overprint in red at upper right and lower left. Watermark: Encik Yusof bin Ishak. 126x63mm. — 4.00 | 6.00

Monetary Authority of Singapore

2005 Issue

45A **2 Dollars** — VF | UNC
NS (2005). — FV | 4.00

46 **2 Dollars** — VF | UNC
ND (2005). Purple, brown and multicolor underprint. President Encik Yusof bin Ishak at right. Back: Education - Victoria Bridge School, Raffles Institue, College of Medicine views with children. Polymer plastic. 126x63mm. — FV | 4.00

47 **5 Dollars**
ND (2005). Green, red and multicolor. President Encik Yusof bin Ishak at right. Back: Garden City - trees and flowers, skyline in background. Watermark: Encik Yusof bin Ishak. 133x66mm. — FV | 7.00

48 **10 Dollars** — VF | UNC
ND (2005). Red, brown and multicolor. President Encik Yusof bin Ishak at right. Back: Sports - swimming, tennis, soccer, sailing, running. Polymer plastic. 141x69mm.
- a. ND (2005). No diamonds under the word SPORTS on lower left back. — FV | 14.00
- b. ND (2013). Two diamonds under the word SPORTS on lower left back. — FV | 14.00

49 **50 Dollars** — VF | UNC
ND (2008). Slate blue and multicolor. President Encik Yusof bin Ishak at right. Back: Arts - music graphics Watermark: Encik Yusof bin Ishak 156x74mm. — FV | 75.00

50 **100 Dollars**
Expected new issue. 170x83mm. — — | —

51 **1000 Dollars**
ND (2009). Purple on multicolor underprint. Yusof bin Ishak at right. Back: Government buildigns: Parliament House, Istana and the Old Supreme Court Building. Watermark: Ishak and braille codes 170x83mm. — FV | 1200.

52 **10,000 Dollars**
Expected new issue. — — | —

2007 Singapore-Brunei Commemorative Issue

53 **20 Dollars** — VF | UNC
6.2007. Brown, yellow and multicolor underprint. President Yusof bin Ishak at right. Back: 40th Anniversary of Currency Interchangeability with Buruni. Polymer plastic. 141x69mm. — FV | 25.00

2004 MAS Commemorative Issue

54 **10 Dollars** — VF | UNC
ND (2004). Purple, brown and multicolor. President Encik Yusof bin Ishak at right. Overprint: Red. Watermark: Encik Yusof bin Ishak. 141x69mm. — FV | 40.00

55 **50 Dollars**
ND (2004). Slate blue and multicolor. President Encik Yusof bin Ishak at right. Back: Arts - Music and Graphics. Overprint: Red. 156x74mm. — FV | 60.00

Collector Series

Singapore

1989 ND Issues

CS1 **ND (1989). 1 Dollar - 100 Dollars** — Mkt. Value
#1a-3a, 5a and 6a overprint: *SPECIMEN.* (77 sets). — 2500.

CS2 **ND (1989). 1 Dollar - 100 Dollars**
#1c-3c, 5c and 6c overprint: *SPECIMEN.* (89 sets). — 3500.

CS3 **ND (1989). 1 Dollar - 100 Dollars**
#1d-3d, 4, 5d and 6d overprint: *SPECIMEN.* (82 sets). — 4000.

CS4 **ND (1989). 1-100 Dollars**
#9-11, 13 and 14 overprint: *SPECIMEN.* (311 sets). — 1200.

2000 Issue

CS5 **2 Dollars** — Mkt. Value
Twin sets of albums, each with 3 Two Dollar notes that bear identical serial #s for the last 6 digits. Albums titled: *The Twin Collection of the Millennium Dragon Circa 2000 Singapore.* — 20.00

Slovakia as a republic has an area of 18,923 sq. mi. (49,011 sq. km.) and a population of 5.37 million. Capital: Bratislava. Textiles, steel, and wood products are exported.

The dissolution of the Austro-Hungarian Empire at the close of World War I allowed the Slovaks to join the closely related Czechs to form Czechoslovakia. Following the chaos of World War II, Czechoslovakia became a Communist nation within Soviet-dominated Eastern Europe. Soviet influence collapsed in 1989 and Czechoslovakia once more became free. The Slovaks and the Czechs agreed to separate peacefully on 1 January 1993. Slovakia joined both NATO and the EU in the spring of 2004 and the Eurozone on 1 January 2009.

MONETARY SYSTEM:
1 Korun = 100 Halierov, 1945-2008
1 Euro = 100 Euro Cent, 2009-

REPUBLIC

SLOVENSKA REPUBLIKA

REPUBLIC OF SLOVAKIA

1993 ND PROVISIONAL ISSUE

#15-19 Czechoslovakian issue w/affixed adhesive stamps w/*SLOVENSKA / arms / REPUBLIKA.*

		VF	UNC
15	**20 Korun** ND (1993- old date 1988). Black and light blue adhesive stamp on Czechoslovakia number 95.	2.50	5.50

		VF	UNC
16	**50 Korun** ND (1993- old date 1987). Black and yellow adhesive stamp on Czechoslovakia number 96. Serial number prefixes: *F* and *I*.	3.50	25.00

		VF	UNC
17	**100 Korun** ND (1993- old date 1961). Black and orange adhesive stamp on Czechoslovakia # 91. Series G37-.		
	a. Stamp on Czechoslovakia #91a.	25.00	150.
	b. Stamp on Czechoslovakia #91b.	5.00	22.50
	c. Stamp on Czechoslovakia #91c.	4.00	20.00
18	**500 Korun** ND (1993- old date 1973). Adhesive stamp on Czechoslovakia number 93. Serial number prefixes: *Z*, *V* and *W*.	25.00	65.00
19	**1000 Korun** ND (1993- old date 1985). Adhesive stamp on Czechoslovakia number 98.	45.00	110.

NÁRODNÁ BANKA SLOVENSKA

SLOVAK NATIONAL BANK

1993 ISSUE

		VF	UNC
20	**20 Korun** 1993-2006. Black and green on multicolor underprint. Prince Pribina at right. Signature varieties. Back: Nitra Castle at left, shield of arms at lower center right. Watermark: Prince Pribina. 128x65mm.		
	a. Pale green underprint. 1.9.1993. Serial # prefix B. Printer BABN.	FV	5.00
	b. As a. but with green underprint at right. Security thread closer to center. 1.6.1995. Serial # prefix B. Printer: BABN.	FV	6.00
	c. 31.10.1997. Serial # prefix B, J. Printer: BABN.	FV	2.50
	d. 1.7.1999. Serial # prefix B, J. Printer; BABN.	FV	2.00
	e. 31.8.2001. Serial # prefix J, S. Printer: BABN.	FV	2.50
	f. 8.9.2004. Serial # prefix S. Printer: BAT Ottawa.	FV	2.50
	g. 20.10.2006. Serial # prefix S, V. Printer: PWPW Warszawa.	FV	2.50
	h. As a. Serial # prefix A. Uncut sheet of 60 (6000 sheets).	—	120.
	r1. Replacement note. As a. Serial # prefix A.	FV	5.00
	r2. Replacement note. As b. Serial # prefix A.	5.00	13.00
	r3. Replacement note. As c. Serial # prefix A.	10.00	25.00
	r4. Replacement note. As d. Serial # prefix A.	5.00	13.00
	r5. Replacement note. As e. Serial # prefix A.	5.00	13.00
	r6. Replacement note. As f. Serial # prefix A.	5.00	13.00
	r7. Replacement note. As g. Serial # prefix A.	5.00	13.00

		VF	UNC
21	**50 Korun** 1993-2005. Black, blue and aqua on multicolor underprint. St. Cyril and St. Method at right, Signature varieties. Back: Medieval church at Drazovce and first 7 letters of Slavic alphabet, shield of arms at lower center right. Watermark: St. Cyril and St. Method. Printer: BABN. 134x68mm.		
	a. 1.8.1993. Serial # prefix A, C. 7 or 8 digit serial #.	FV	10.00
	b. Security thread closer to center. 1.6.1995. Serial # prefix A, C.	FV	20.00
	c. 1.7.1999. Serial # prefix A, C.	FV	12.00
	d. 2.5.2002. Serial # prefix A, C, K.	FV	8.00
	e. 16.11.2005. Serial # prefix K.	FV	5.00
	f. As a. Serial # prefix A. Uncut sheet of 45 (4000 sheets).	—	220.
	r1. Replacement note. As a. Serial # A.	FV	10.00
	r2. Replacement note. As b. Serial # A.	20.00	50.00
	r3. Replacement note. As c. Serial # prefix A.	10.00	40.00
	r4. Replacement note. As d. Serial # prefix A.	10.00	40.00
	r5. Replacement note. As e. Serial # prefix A.	4.00	20.00

22	100 Korun	VF	UNC
	1.9.1993. Red and black on orange and multicolor underprint. Madonna (by master woodcarver Pavol) from the altar of the Birth in St. Jacob's Church in Levoca at right. Signature varieties. Back: Levoca town view, shield of arms at lower center right. Watermark: Madonna. Printer: TDLR. 140x71mm.		
	a. Serial # prefix D.	FV	18.00
	b. Serial # prefix A. Uncut sheet of 35 (4000 sheets).	—	300.
	r. Replacement note. Serial # prefix A.	FV	18.00

23	500 Korun	VF	UNC
	1.10.1993. Dark gray and brown on multicolor underprint. Ludovit Stúr at right. Signature varieties. Back: Bratislava Castle and St. Michael's Church at left, shield of arms at lower center right. Watermark: Ludovit Stúr. Printer: TDLR. 152x77mm.		
	a. Serial # prefix F.	FV	150.
	b. Serial # prefix A. Uncut sheet of 28 (2500 sheets).	—	1050.
	r. Replacement note. Serial # prefix A.	FV	100.
	s. Specimen. Perforated: *SPECIMEN.*	—	—

24	1000 Korun	VF	UNC
	1993; 1995; 1997. Dark gray and purple on red-violet and multicolor underprint. Andrej Hlinka at right. Signature varieties. Back: Madonna of the Church of Liptovké Sliace near Ruzomberok and Church of St. Andrew in Ruzomberok at left center. Watermark: Andrej Hlinka. Printer: TDLR. 158x80mm.		
	a. 1.10.1993. Serial # prefix G.	FV	200.
	b. Security thread closer to center 1.6.1995. Serial # prefix G.	FV	120.
	c. 1.7.1997. Serial # prefix G.	FV	90.00
	d. As a. Serial # prefix A. Uncut sheet of 28 (1500 sheets).	—	2100.
	r1. Replacement note. As a. Serial # prefix A.	70.00	175.
	r2. Replacement note. As b. Serial # prefix A.	100.	250.
	r3. Replacement note. As c. Serial # prefix A.	100.	250.
	s. Specimen. Perforated: *SPECIMEN.*	—	—

1995; 1996 Issue

25	100 Korun	VF	UNC
	1996-2001. Red and black on orangte and multicolor underprint. Madonna (by master woodcarver Pavol) from the altar of the Birth in St. Jacob's Church in Levoca at right. Signature varieties. Back: Levoca town view, shield of arms at lower center right, red-orange replaces dull orange in corners. Watermark: Madonna. Printer: TDLR. 140x71mm.		
	a. Printer as: *TDLR.* 1.7.1996. Serial # prefix D.	FV	18.00
	b. Serial # prefix: *D, L.* 1.10.1997.	FV	18.00
	c. Printer as: *DLR.* 1.7.1999. Serial # prefix L.	FV	9.00
	d. 10.10.2001. Serial # prefix L, U.	FV	8.00
	r1. Replacement note. As a. Serial # prefix A.	10.00	30.00
	r2. Replacement note. As b. Serial # prefix A.	10.00	30.00
	r3. Replacement note. As c. Serial # prefix A.	15.00	40.00
	r4. Replacement note. As d. Serial # prefix A.	10.00	30.00
	s. Specimen. Perforated: *SPECIMEN.*	—	—

26	200 Korun	VF	UNC
	1.8.1995. Dark gray and blue-green on multicolor underprint. Anton Bernolák at right. Back: Trnava town view at left center, shield of arms at lower center. Watermark: Anton Bernolák. Printer: G&D. 146x74mm.		
	a. Issued note. Serial # prefix E.	FV	45.00
	r. Replacement note. Serial # prefix A.	20.00	50.00
	s. Specimen. Perforated: *SPECIMEN.*	—	—

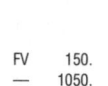

27	500 Korun	VF	UNC
	31.10.1996. Like #23 but blue underprint at left center and in corners. Ludovit Stúr at right. Signature varieties. Back: Blue underprint in upper left center and in corners, dark brown at center. Bratislava Castle and St. Michael's Church at left, shield of arms at lower center. Watermark: Ludovit Stúr. Printer: TDLR. 152x77mm.		
	a. Issued note. Serial # prefix F.	FV	55.00
	r. Replacement note. Serial # prefix A.	80.00	200.
	s. Specimen. Perforated: *SPECIMEN.*	—	—

29 5000 Korun VF UNC

3.4.1995. Brown-violet and pale yellow-brown on multicolor underprint. Milan Rastislav Stefánik at right, sun and moon at center. Back: Stefánik's grave at Bradlo Hill, part of *Ursa Major* constellation, and a pasque flower at left center. Watermark: Milan Rastislav Stefánik. Printer: G&D. 164x82mm.

	VF	UNC
a. Issued note. Serial # prefix H.	FV	420.
r. Replacement note. Serial # prefix A.	270.	380.
s. Specimen. Perforated: *SPECIMEN*.	—	—

1999-2000 Issue

30 200 Korun VF UNC

31.3.1999. Dark gray and blue-green on multicolor underprint. Anton Bernolák at right, but with optical variable ink and champagne dots in watermark area. Back: Trnava town view at left center, shield of arms at lower center. Watermark: Anton Bernolák. Printer: G&D. 146x74mm.

	VF	UNC
a. Issued note. Serial # prefix E.	FV	20.00
r. Replacement note. Serial # prefix A.	40.00	100.

31 500 Korun VF UNC

20.10.2000. Dark gray and brown on multicolor underprint. Ludovit Stúr at right, optical variable device and champagne dots in watermark area. Signature varieties. Back: Bratislava Castle and St. Michael's Church at left, shield of arms at lower center. Watermark: Ludovit Stúr. Printer: TDLR. 152x77mm.

	VF	UNC
a. Issued note. Serial # prefix F.	FV	55.00
r. Replacement note. Serial # prefix A.	80.00	100.

32 1000 Korun VF UNC

1.10.1999. Dark gray and purple on red-violet and multicolor underprint. Andrej Hlinka at right, optical variable device and champagne dots in watermark area. Signature varieties. Back: Madonna of the Church of Liptovké Sliace near Ruzomberok and Church of St. Andrew in Ruzomberok at left center. Watermark: Andrej Hlinka. Printer: TDLR. 158x80mm.

	VF	UNC
a. Issued note. Serial # prefix G, P.	FV	65.00
r. Replacement note. Serial # prefix A.	80.00	200.

33 5000 Korun VF UNC

11.5.1999. Orange-brown and olive on multicolor underprint. Milan Rastislav Stefánik at right, sun and moon at center. Optical variable device and champagne dots in watermark area and Kinegram at left center. Back: Stefánik's grave at Bradlo Hill, part of *Ursa Major* constellation, and a pasque flower at left center. Printer: G&D. 164x82mm.

	VF	UNC
a. Issued note. Serial # prefix H.	FV	330.
r. Replacement note. Serial # prefix A.	260.	330.

2000 Commemorative Issue

Previously Series A notes were available only as uncut sheets. These overprints caused problems with bank counting machines and were not in circulation for an extended period of time.

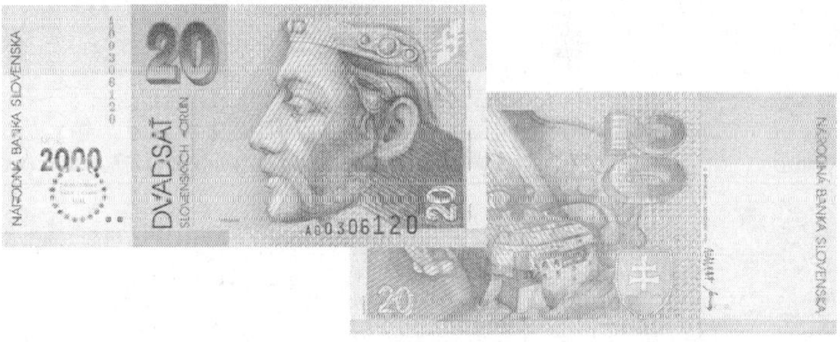

34 20 Korun VF UNC

1.9.1993. Black and green on multicolor underprint. Overprint: Silver legend and circle of stars. 330,000 pieces. 128x65mm. FV 4.25

35 50 Korun VF UNC

1.8.1993. Black, blue and aqua on multicolor underprint. Overprint: Silver legend and circle of stars. 168,750 pieces. 134x68mm. FV 9.00

36 100 Korun VF UNC

1.9.1993. Red and black on orange and multicolor underprint. Overprint: Silver legend and circle of stars. 133,000 pieces. 140x71mm. FV 16.00

37	**200 Korun**	VF	UNC
	1.8.1995. Dark gray and blue green on multicolor underprint. Overprint: Silver legend and circle of stars. 108,000 pieces. 146x74mm.	FV	32.50

38	**500 Korun**	VF	UNC
	1.10.1993. Dark gray and brown on multicolor underprint. Overprint: Silver legend and circle of stars. 67,200 pieces. 152x77mm.	FV	60.00

39	**1000 Korun**	VF	UNC
	1.10.1993. Dark gray and purple on red-violet and multicolor underprint. Overprint: Silver legend and circle of stars 40,600 pieces. 158x80mm.	FV	110.

40	**5000 Korun**	VF	UNC
	3.4.1995. Orange-brown and olive on multicolor underprint. Overprint: Gold legend and circle of stars. 10,800 pieces. 164x82mm.	FV	400.

2002 Issue

41	**200 Korun**	VF	UNC
	30.8.2002. Dark gray and blue-green on multicolor underprint. Anton Bernolák at right, but with optical variable ink in watermark area and additional security features. Serial # prefix E. Back: Trnava town view at left center, shield of arms at lower center. Watermark: Anton Bernolák. Printer: F-CO. 146x74mm.		
	a. Issued note. Serial # prefix E.	FV	17.50
	r. Replacement note. Serial # prefix A.	20.00	50.00

42	**1000 Korun**	VF	UNC
	10.6.2002. Dark gray and purple on red-violet and multicolor underprint. Andrej Hlinka at right, optical variable device in watermark area; additional security features added. Signature varieties. Back: Madonna of the Church of Liptovké Sliace near Ruzomberok and Church of St. Andrew in Ruzomberok a Watermark: Andrej Hlinka. Printer: (T)DLR. 158x80mm.		
	a. Issued note. Serial # prefix P.	FV	85.00
	r. Replacement note. Serial # prefix A.	80.00	200.

43	**5000 Korun**	VF	UNC
	17.11.2003. Orange-brown and olive on multicolor underprint. Milan Rastislav Stefánik at right, sun and moon at center. Optical variable device in watermark area and Kinegram at left center, also additional security features. Back: Stefánik's grave at Bradlo Hill, part of *Ursa Major* constellation, and a pasque flower. Watermark: Milan Rastislav Stefánik. Printer: DeBS, Wein. 164x82mm.		
	a. Issued note. Serial # prefix H.	FV	330.
	r. Replacement note. Serial # prefix A.	250.	300.

2004-2006 Issue

No.	Denomination / Description	VF	UNC
44	**100 Korun**		
	5.11.2004. Red and black on orange and multicolor underprint. Madonna (by master woodcarver Pavol) from the altar of the Birth in St. Jacob's Church in Levoca at right. Back: Levoca town view, shield of arms at lower center right. Watermark: Madonna. Printer: PWPW, Warszawa. 140x71mm.		
	a. Issued note. Serial # prefix U.	FV	7.00
	r. Replacement note. Serial # prefix A.	6.00	13.00
45	**200 Korun**		
	1.6.2006. Dark gray and blue-green on multicolor underprint. Anton Bernolák at right. Back: Trnava town view at left center, shield of arms at lower center. Watermark: Anton Bernolák. Printer: F-CO. 146x74mm.		
	a. Issued note. Serial # prefix E.	FV	15.00
	r. Replacement note. Serial # prefix A.	120.	300.
46	**500 Korun**		
	10.7.2006. Dark gray and brown on multicolor underprint. Ludovit Stúr at right. Back: Bratislava Castle and St. Michael's Chruch at left, shield of arms at lower center. Watermark: Ludovit Stúr. Printer: TDLR. 152x77mm.		
	a. Issued note. Serial # prefix F.	FV	40.00
	r. Replacement note. Serial # prefix A.	160.	400.
47	**1000 Korun**		
	25.8.2005; 1.8.2007. Dark gray and purple on red-violet and multicolor underprint. Andrej Hinka at right. Back: Madonna of the Church of Liptovké Sliace near Ruzomberok and Church of St. Andrew in Ruzomberok a Watermark: Andrej Hinka. Printer: TDLR. 158x80mm.		
	a. 25.8.2005. Serial # prefix P.	FV	62.50
	b. 1.8.2007. Serial # prefix W.	FV	62.50
	ar. As a. Replacement note. Serial # prefix A.	80.00	200.
	br. As b. Replacement note. Serial # prefix A.	70.00	175.

The Republic of Slovenia is bounded in the north by Austria, northeast by Hungary, southeast by Croatia and to the west by Italy. It has an area of 20,251 sq. km. and a population of 2.01 million. Capital: Ljubljana. The economy is d on electricity, minerals, forestry, agriculture and fishing. Small industries are being developed during privatization.

The Slovene lands were part of the Austro-Hungarian Empire until the latter's dissolution at the end of World War I. In 1918, the Slovenes joined the Serbs and Croats in forming a new multinational state, which was named Yugoslavia in 1929. After World War II, Slovenia became a republic of the renewed Yugoslavia, which though Communist, distanced itself from Moscow's rule. Dissatisfied with the exercise of power by the majority Serbs, the Slovenes succeeded in establishing their independence in 1991 after a short 10-day war. Historical ties to Western Europe, a strong economy, and a stable democracy have assisted in Slovenia's transformation to a modern state. Slovenia acceded to both NATO and the EU in the spring of 2004.

MONETARY SYSTEM:

1 (Tolar) = 1 Yugoslavian Dinar
1 Tolar = 100 Stotinas

REPLACEMENT NOTES:

#11-19, ZA prefix.

Republic

Banka Slovenije

1989 Issue

No.	Denomination / Description	VF	UNC
A1	**1 Lipa**		
	29.11.1989 (1990). Green. Plants at left, Dr. France Preseren at right. Back: Slovenian Parliament.		
	a. Issued note.	8.00	20.00
	s. Specimen.	—	20.00

Republika Slovenija

1990-92 Issue

Note: About 500 sets of Specimens #1s-10s were released to the general collecting public. Specimens exist with normal serial #'s and with 0's as serial #'s. Zero serial #'s are valued up to $20.00 each.

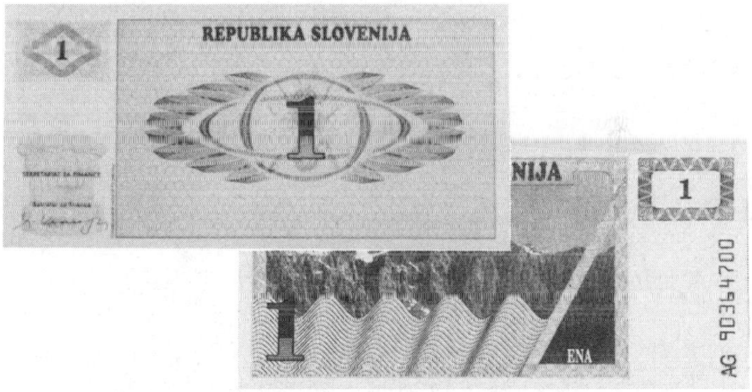

No.	Denomination / Description	VF	UNC
1	**1 (Tolar)**		
	(19)90. Dark olive-green on light gray and light olive-green underprint. Pedimented beehive at lower left, denomination numeral in guilloche over a representation of the dance of the Catrniolan bee on an underprint of honeycomb at center right. Back: Mountain ridge of Triglav at left center. Watermark: Symmetrical designs repeated. UV: fibers fluoresce yellow.		
	a. Issued note.	.10	.30
	s1. Specimen overprint: *VZOREC.*	—	4.00
	s2. Specimen overprint *SPECIMEN.*	—	4.00
1A	**.50 (Tolar)**		
	(19)90. Dark olive-green on light gray and light olive-green underprint. Pedimented beehive at lower left, denomination numeral in guilloche over a representation of the dance of the Catrniolan bee on an underprint of honeycomb at center right. Back: Mountain ridge of Triglav at left center. Watermark: Symmetrical designs repeated.	—	50.00
2	**2 (Tolarjev)**		
	(19)90. Brown on tan and ochre underprint. Pedimented beehive at lower left, denomination numeral in guilloche over a representation of the dance of the Catrniolan bee on an underprint of honeycomb at center right. Back: Mountain ridge of Triglav at left center. Watermark: Symmetrical designs repeated.		
	a. Issued note.	.10	.40
	s1. Specimen overprint: *VZOREC.*	—	4.00
	s2. Specimen overprint: *SPECIMEN.*	—	4.00
3	**5 (Tolarjev)**		
	(19)90. Maroon on pale maroon and pink underprint. Pedimented beehive at lower left, denomination numeral in guilloche over a representation of the dance of the Catrniolan bee on an underprint of honeycomb at center right. Back: Mountain ridge of Triglav at left center. Watermark: Symmetrical designs repeated.		
	a. Issued note.	.15	.50
	s1. Specimen overprint: *VZOREC.*	—	4.00
	s2. Specimen overprint: *SPECIMEN.*	—	4.00

4 10 (Tolarjev)

(19)90. Dark blue-green and grayish purple on light blue-green underprint. Pedimented beehive at lower left, denomination numeral in guilloche over a representation of the dance of the Catrniolan bee on an underprint of honeycomb at center right. Back: Mountain ridge of Triglav at left center. Watermark: Symmetrical designs repeated.

	VF	UNC
a. Issued note.	FV	3.00
s1. Specimen overprint: *VZOREC.*	—	4.00
s2. Specimen overprint: *SPECIMEN.*	—	4.00

5 50 (Tolarjev)

(19)90. Dark gray on tan and light gray underprint. Pedimented beehive at lower left, denomination numeral in guilloche over a representation of the dance of the Catrniolan bee on an underprint of honeycomb at center right. Back: Mountain ridge of Triglav at left center. Watermark: Symmetrical designs repeated.

	VF	UNC
a. Issued note.	FV	5.00
s1. Specimen overprint: *VZOREC.*	—	3.50
s2. Specimen overprint: *SPECIMEN.*	—	4.00

6 100 (Tolarjev)

(19)90. Reddish brown and violet on orange and light violet underprint. Pedimented beehive at lower left, denomination numeral in guilloche over a representation of the dance of the Catrniolan bee on an underprint of honeycomb at center right. Back: Mountain ridge of Triglav at left center. Watermark: Symmetrical designs repeated.

	VF	UNC
a. Issued note.	FV	8.00
s1. Specimen overprint: *VZOREC.*	—	3.50
s2. Specimen overprint: *SPECIMEN.*	—	4.00

7 200 (Tolarjev)

(19)90. Greenish black and dark brown on light gray and light green underprint. Pedimented beehive at lower left, denomination numeral in guilloche over a representation of the dance of the Catrniolan bee on an underprint of honeycomb at center right. Back: Mountain ridge of Triglav at left center. Watermark: Symmetrical designs repeated.

	VF	UNC
a. Issued note.	FV	25.00
s. Specimen overprint: *SPECIMEN.*	—	4.00

8 500 (Tolarjev)

(19)90; (19)92. Deep lilac and red on pink and pale blue underprint. Pedimented beehive at lower left, denomination numeral in guilloche over a representation of the dance of the Catrniolan bee on an underprint of honeycomb at center right. Back: Mountain ridge of Triglav at left center. Watermark: Symmetrical designs repeated.

	VF	UNC
a. 1990.	FV	25.00
b. 1992.	FV	40.00
s1. Specimen overprint: *VZOREC.*	—	3.50
s2. Specimen overprint: *SPECIMEN.*	—	4.00

9 1000 (Tolarjev)

(19)91; (19)92. Dark blue-gray and gray on light gray and pale blue underprint. Pedimented beehive at lower left, denomination numeral in guilloche over a representation of the dance of the Catrniolan bee on an underprint of honeycomb at center right. Back: Mountain ridge of Triglav at left center. Watermark: Symmetrical designs repeated.

	VF	UNC
a. 1991.	FV	35.00
b. 1992.	FV	45.00
s1. Specimen overprint: *VZOREC..* Watermark: Column pedestal.	—	7.50
s2. Specimen overprint: *SPECIMEN.* Watermark: Column pedestal.	—	7.50
s3. Specimen overprint: *SPECIMEN.* Watermark: Snowflake (error).	—	150.

9A 2000 (Tolarjev)

(19)91. Multicolor. Pedimented beehive at lower left, denomination numeral in guilloche over a representation of the dance of the Catrniolan bee on an underprint of honeycomb at center right. Back: Mountain ridge of Triglav at left center. Watermark: Symmetrical designs repeated. (Not issued).

VF	UNC
—	60.00

10 5000 (Tolarjev)

(19)92. Purple and lilac on pink underprint. Pedimented beehive at lower left, denomination numeral in guilloche over a representation of the dance of the Catrniolan bee on an underprint of honeycomb at center right. Back: Mountain ridge of Triglav at left center. Watermark: Symmetrical designs repeated.

	VF	UNC
a. Issued note.	FV	130.
s1. Specimen overprint: *VZOREC.*	—	20.00
s2. Specimen overprint: *SPECIMEN.*	—	10.00

BANKA SLOVENIJE

1992-93 ISSUE

#11-20 replacement notes: Serial # prefix *AZ* and possibly others.

11 10 Tolarjev — VF UNC

15.1.1992. Black, brown-violet and brown-orange on multicolor underprint. P. Trubar at right, quill pen at left center. Back: Ursuline church in Ljubljana at center. Watermark: P. Trubar. UV: fibers and box over feather fluoresce yellow; back value 10 yellow; serial # orange.

	VF	UNC
a. Issued note.	FV	.50
s. Specimen overprint: *SPECIMEN* and *VZOREC.*	—	8.50

12 20 Tolarjev — VF UNC

15.1.1992. Brownish black, deep brown and brown-orange on multicolor underprint. J. Vajkard Valvasor at right, compass at left. Back: Topographical outlines at left center, cherub arms at right.

	VF	UNC
a. Issued note.	FV	.75
s. Specimen overprint: *SPECIMEN* and *VZOREC.*	—	10.00

13 50 Tolarjev — VF UNC

15.1.1992. Black, purple and brown-orange on multicolor underprint. J. Vega at right, geometric design and calculations at left center. Back: Academy at upper left, planets and geometric design at center. Watermark: J. Vega.

	VF	UNC
a. Issued note.	FV	1.50
s. Specimen overprint: *SPECIMEN* and *VZOREC.*	—	12.50

14 100 Tolarjev — VF UNC

15.1.1992. Black, blue-black and brown-orange on multicolor underprint. R. Jakopic at right. Back: Outline of the Jakopicev Pavilion at center right. Watermark: R. Jakopic.

	VF	UNC
a. Issued note.	FV	2.75
s. Specimen overprint: *SPECIMEN* and *VZOREC.*	—	15.00

15 200 Tolarjev — VF UNC

1992; 1997; 2001; 2004. Black, violet-brown and brown-orange on multicolor underprint. I. Gallus at right, musical façade at left. Back: Drawing of Slovenia's Philharmonic building at upper left, five lines of medieval music at upper center. Watermark: I. Gallus.

	VF	UNC
a. 15.1.1992.	FV	20.00
b. 8.10.1997.	FV	3.25
c. 15.1.2001.	FV	3.00
d. 15.1.2004.	FV	3.00
s. Specimen overprint: *SPECIMEN* and *VZOREC.*	—	17.50

16 500 Tolarjev — VF UNC

1992, 2001, 2005. Black, red and brown-orange on multicolor underprint. J. Plecnik at right. Back: Drawing of the National and University Library of Ljubljana at left center. Watermark: J. Plecnik.

	VF	UNC
a. 15.1.1992.	FV	9.00
b. 15.1.2001.	FV	8.00
c. 15.1.2005.	FV	8.00
s. Specimen overprint: *SPECIMEN* and *VZOREC.*	—	20.00

17 1000 Tolarjev — VF UNC

15.1.1992. Brownish black, deep green and brown-orange on multicolor underprint. F. Preseren at right. Back: The poem *Drinking Toast* at center. Watermark: F. Preseren.

	VF	UNC
a. Issued note.	FV	22.50
s. Specimen overprint: *SPECIMEN* and *VZOREC.*	—	25.00

18 **1000 Tolarjev** VF UNC

1.6.1993. Black, deep blue-green and brown-orange on multicolor underprint. F. Preseren at right. Like #17 but modified portrait and other changes including color. Back: The poem *Drinking Toast* at center. Watermark: F. Preseren.

a. Without *1000* in UV ink on back.	FV	15.00
b. With *1000* in UV ink on back.	FV	15.00
s. Specimen overprint: *SPECIMEN* and *VZOREC.*	—	25.00

19 **5000 Tolarjev** VF UNC

1.6.1993. Brownish black, dark brown and brown-orange on multicolor underprint. I. Kobilika at right. Back: National Gallery in Ljubljana at upper left. Watermark: I. Kobilika.

a. Issued note.	FV	80.00
s. Specimen overprint: *SPECIMEN* and *VZOREC.*	—	30.00

20 **10,000 Tolarjev** VF UNC

28.6.1994. Black, purple and brown-orange on multicolor underprint. I. Cankar at right. Back: Chrysanthemum blossom at left. Watermark: I. Cankar.

a. Issued note.	FV	110.
s. Specimen overprint: *SPECIMEN* and *VZOREC.*	—	35.00

1997 Issue

21 **5000 Tolarjev** VF UNC

8.10.1997. Brownish black, dark brown and brown-orange on multicolor underprint. I. Kobilika at right. Like #19 but with scalloped kinegram. Back: National Gallery in Ljubljana at upper left. Watermark: I. Kobilika.

a. Kinegram 5000 vertical.	FV	50.00
b. Kinegram 5000 horizontal.	FV	50.00
s. Specimen overprint: *SPECIMEN* and *VZOREC.*	—	25.00

2000 Issue

22 **1000 Tolarjev** VF UNC

15.1.2000. Black, green and yellow. F. Preseren at left. Like #17 with modified portrait and other changes. Back: The poem *Drinking Toast* at center. Watermark: F. Preseren.

a. Issued note.	FV	10.00
s. Specimen overprint: *SPECIMEN* and *VZOREC.*	—	—

23 **5000 Tolarjev** VF UNC

15.1.2000. Black, green, red and orange. I. Kobilika at right. Similar to #21a. Back: National Gallery in Ljubljana at upper left. Watermark: I. Kobilika.

a. Issued note.	FV	45.00
s. Specimen overprint: *SPECIMEN* and *VZOREC.*	—	—

24	**10,000 Tolarjev** 15.1.2000. Brown-black, purple and red. I. Cankar at right, holographic band at right edge. Back: Chrysanthemum blossom at left. Watermark: I. Cankar.	**VF**	**UNC**
	a. Issued note.	FV	80.00
	s. Specimen overprint: *SPECIMEN* and *VZOREC*.	—	—

2000 Commemorative Issue

#25-27, 10th Anniversary of Bank Slovenije

25	**100 Tolarjev** 2001. Black, blue-black and brown-orange on multicolor underprint. R. Jakopic at right. Back: Outline of the Jakopicev Pavilion at center right. Overprint: Special spiral logo text at left. Watermark: R. Jakopic. 10,000 pieces.	**VF** FV	**UNC** 3.00
26	**1000 Tolarjev** 2001. Black, green and yellow. F. Preseren at right. Back: The poem *Drinking Toast* at center. Overprint: Special spiral logo text at left. Watermark: F. Preseren. 5,000 pieces.	FV	10.00

27	**10,000 Tolarjev** 2001. Brown'black, purple and red. I. Cankar at right, holographic band at right edge. Back: Chrysanthemum blossom at left. Overprint: Special spiral logo text at left. Watermark: I. Cankar. 1,000 pieces.	**VF** FV	**UNC** 80.00

2004 Commemorative Issue

#28-30 EU entry on May 1, 2004.

28	**100 Tolarjev** 2003. Black and blue on multicolor underprint. R. Jakopic at right. Back: Outline of the Jakopicev Pavilion at center right. Overprint: 2004 (stars). Watermark: R. Jakopic. 10,000 pieces.	**VF** FV	**UNC** 7.50

29	**1000 Tolarjev** 2003. Black, green and yellow. F. Preseren at right. Back: The poem *Drinking Toast* at center. Overprint: 2004 (stars). Watermark: F. Preseren. 5,000 pieces.	**VF** FV	**UNC** 25.00

30	**10,000 Tolarjev** 2003. Brown, black, purple and red. I. Cankar at right, holographic band at right edge. Back: Chrysanthemum blossom at left. Overprint: 2004 (stars). Watermark: I. Cankar. 1,000 pieces.	**VF** FV	**UNC** 125.

2003 Issue

31	**100 Tolarjev** 15.1.2003. Black and blue on multicolor underprint. R. Jakopic at right. Watermark: R. Jakopic. .	**VF**	**UNC**
	a. Issued note.	FV	3.50
	s. Specimen overprint: *SPECIMEN* and *VZOREC*.	—	—
31A	**200 Tolarjev** 15.1.2004. Black and rose on multicolor underprint. I Gallus at right. Back: Drawing of Slovenia's Philharmonic building at upper left, five lines of medieval music at upper center. Watermark: I. Gallus.	FV	5.00
31B	**500 Tolarjev** 15.1.2004. Blak and pink on multicolor underprint. J. Plecnik at right. Back: Drawing of the National and University Library of Ljubljana at left center. Watermark: J. Plecnik.	FV	10.00

32 **1000 Tolarjev** — VF — UNC

2003-05. Black and green on multicolor underprint. F. Preseren at right. Back: The poem *Drinking Toast* at center. Watermark: F. Preseren.

	VF	UNC
a. 15.1.2003.	FV	12.00
b. 15.1.2004.	FV	12.00
c. 15.1.2005.	FV	12.00
s. Specimen overprint: *SPECIMEN* and *VZOREC*.	—	—

33 **5000 Tolarjev** — VF — UNC

15.1.2002; 15.1.2004. Black, green, red and orange. I. Kobilika at right. Similar to #21a. Back: National Gallery in Ljubljana at upper left. Watermark: I. Kobilika.

	VF	UNC
a. 15.1.2002.	FV	50.00
b. 15.1.2004.	FV	50.00
s. Specimen.	—	—

34 **10,000 Tolarjev** — VF — UNC

15.1.2003; 15.1.2004. Black and purple on multicolor underprint. I. Cankar at right, holographic band at right edge. Back: Chrysanthemum blossom at left, Iridescent ink added onto it. Watermark: I. Cankar.

	VF	UNC
a. 15.1.2003.	FV	95.00
b. 15.1.2004.	FV	95.00
s. Specimen overprint: *SPECIMEN* and *VZOREC*.	—	—

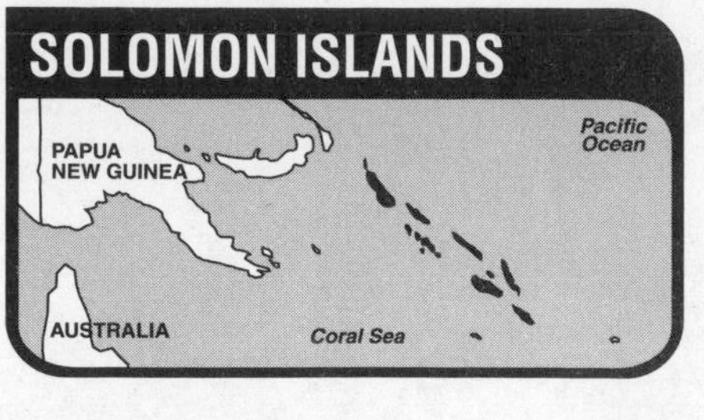

The Solomon Islands, located in the Southwest Pacific east of Papua New Guinea, has an area of 28,450 sq. km. and a population of 581,300. Capital: Honiara. The most important islands of the Solomon chain are Guadalcanal (scene of some of the fiercest fighting of World War II), Malaitia, New Georgia, Florida, Vella Lavella, Choiseul, Rendova, San Cristobal, the Lord Howe group, the Santa Cruz islands, and the Duff group. Copra is the only important cash crop but it is hoped that timber will become an economic factor.

The UK established a protectorate over the Solomon Islands in the 1890s. Some of the bitterest fighting of World War II occurred on this archipelago. Self-government was achieved in 1976 and independence two years later. Ethnic violence, government malfeasance, and endemic crime have undermined stability and civil society. In June 2003, then Prime Minister Sir Allan Kemakeza sought the assistance of Australia in reestablishing law and order; the following month, an Australian-led multinational force arrived to restore peace and disarm ethnic militias. The Regional Assistance Mission to the Solomon Islands (RAMSI) has generally been effective in restoring law and order and rebuilding government institutions.

RULERS:

British

MONETARY SYSTEM:

1 Shilling = 12 Pence
1 Pound = 20 Shillings to 1966
1 Dollar = 100 Cents, 1966-

SIGNATURE VARIETIES

	CHAIRMAN	MEMBER		GOVERNOR	DIRECTOR
1			4		
2			5		
3			6		
	GOVERNOR	SEC. OF FINANCE		GOVERNOR	SEC. OF FINANCE
7		George Kiriau	8	Rick N. Houenipwela	

British Administration

Solomon Islands Monetary Authority

1977; 1981 ND Issue

Replacement notes: Serial # prefix: *Z/1.*

5 **2 Dollars** — VF — UNC

ND (1977). Dark green on pink and pale green underprint. Queen Elizabeth II at right. Signature 1. Back: Fishermen. Watermark: Falcon. Printer: TDLR (without imprint). 139x70mm.

	VF	UNC
a. Issued note.	2.00	10.00
s. Specimen.	—	30.00

6 **5 Dollars** — VF / UNC
ND (1977). Dark blue on multicolor underprint. Queen Elizabeth II at right. Back: Long boats and hut. Watermark: Falcon. Printer: TDLR (without imprint). 144x72mm.

	VF	UNC
a. Signature 1.	5.00	27.50
b. Signature 2.	6.00	30.00
s. As a. Specimen.	—	30.00

7 **10 Dollars** — VF / UNC
ND (1977). Purple and violet on multicolor underprint. Queen Elizabeth II at right. Back: Weaver. Watermark: Falcon. Printer: TDLR (without imprint). 147x74mm.

	VF	UNC
a. Signature 1.	7.50	35.00
b. Signature 2.	8.00	40.00
s. As a. Specimen.	—	30.00

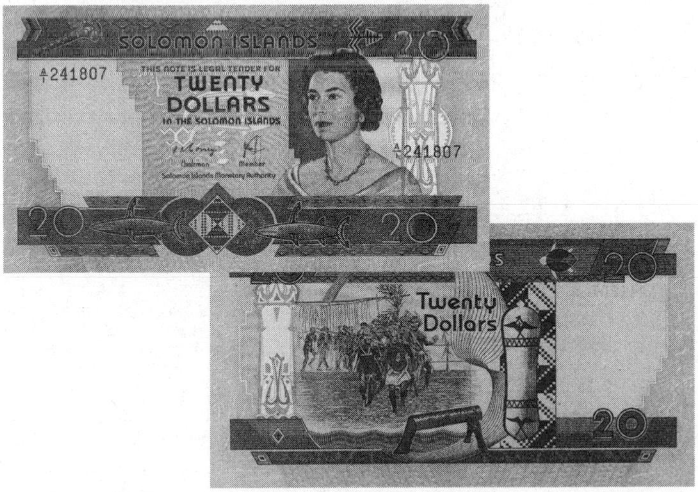

8 **20 Dollars** — VF 20.00, UNC 65.00
ND (1981). Brown and deep orange on multicolor underprint. Queen Elizabeth II at right. Signature 3. Back: Line of people. Watermark: Falcon. Printer: TDLR (without imprint). 153x77mm.

Central Bank of Solomon Islands

1984 ND Issue

#11 and 12. Replacement notes: Serial # prefix *Z/1*.

11 **10 Dollars** — VF 7.50, UNC 30.00
ND (1984). Purple and violet on multicolor underprint. Queen Elizabeth II at right, new bank name. Signature 4. Back: Weaver. Watermark: Falcon. 147x74mm.

12 **20 Dollars** — VF 15.00, UNC 55.00
ND (1984). Brown and dark orange on multicolor underprint. Queen Elizabeth II at right, new bank name. Signature 4. Back: Line of people. Watermark: Falcon. 154x77mm.

1986 ND Issue

#13-17 Replacement notes: Serial # prefix *Y/1*.

13 **2 Dollars** — VF / UNC
ND (1986). Green on multicolor underprint. Arms at right. Signature 5. Back: Fishermen. Watermark: Falcon. UV: central design fluoresces yellow. 139x70mm.

	VF	UNC
a. Issued note.	FV	2.25
s. Specimen.	—	25.00

14 **5 Dollars** — VF / UNC
ND (1986). Dark blue, deep purple and violet on multicolor underprint. Arms at right. Signature 5. Back: Long boats and hut. Watermark: Falcon. 144x72mm.

	VF	UNC
a. Issued note.	FV	5.00
s. Specimen.	—	25.00

		VF	UNC
15	**10 Dollars**	VF	UNC
	ND (1986). Purple and violet on multicolor underprint. Arms at right. Signature 5. Back: Weaver. Watermark: Falcon. 147x74mm.		
	a. Issued note.	FV	10.00
	s. Specimen.	—	10.00

		VF	UNC
16	**20 Dollars**	VF	UNC
	ND (1986). Brown and deep orange on multicolor underprint. Arms at right. Signature 5. Back: Line of people. Watermark: Falcon. 153x77mm.		
	a. Issued note.	FV	20.00
	s. Specimen.	—	25.00

		VF	UNC
17	**50 Dollars**	VF	UNC
	ND (1986). Blue-green and purple on multicolor underprint. Arms at right. Signature 5. Back: Butterflies and reptiles. Watermark: Falcon. 160x80mm.		
	a. Issued note.	FV	45.00
	s. Specimen.	—	30.00

1996; 1997 ND Issue

#18-22. Replacement notes: Serial # prefix *X/1*.

		VF	UNC
18	**2 Dollars**	VF	UNC
	ND (1997). Greenish black and olive-green on multicolor underprint. Queen Elizabeth II at right, security thread. Ascending size serial number. Back: Fishermen. Printing in watermark area. Watermark: Falcon.	FV	2.00

		VF	UNC
19	**5 Dollars**	VF	UNC
	ND (1997). Dark blue, deep purple and violet on multicolor underprint. Queen Elizabeth II at right, security thread. Ascending size serial number. Back: Long boats and hut. Printing in watermark area. Watermark: Falcon. 144x72mm.	FV	4.00

		VF	UNC
20	**10 Dollars**	VF	UNC
	ND (1996). Purple and red-violet on multicolor underprint. Queen Elizabeth II at right, security thread. Ascending size serial number. Back: Weaver. Printing in watermark area. Watermark: Falcon. 147x74mm.	FV	7.00

		VF	UNC
21	**20 Dollars**	VF	UNC
	ND (1996). Brown and brown-orange on multicolor underprint. Queen Elizabeth II at right, security thread. Ascending size serial number. Back: Line of people. Printing in watermark area. Watermark: Falcon. 154x77mm.	FV	12.50

22 **50 Dollars** — VF / UNC
ND (1996). Green, Blue-gray and purple on multicolor underprint. Queen Elizabeth II at right, security thread. Ascending size serial number. Back: Butterflies and reptiles. Printing in watermark area. Watermark: Falcon. 160x80mm. — FV / 30.00

2001 Commemorative Issue

#23, 25th Anniversary Central Bank of Solomon Islands

23 **2 Dollars** — VF / UNC
(20)01. Dark and light green on multicolor underprint. Queen Elizabeth II at right; with ornate window design. Silver imprint *CBSI Silver Jubilee.* Back: Fishermen, silver imprint; *COMMEMORATING CBSI SILVER JUBILEE.* Polymer plastic. 139x70mm. — FV / 2.50

2001 ND Issue

24 **50 Dollars** — VF / UNC
ND (2001). Green, blue-gray and purple on multicolor underprint. Similar to #22 but flag added at left center, segmented silver security strip at center right, and vertical serial # at right. Smaller size in width. 160x72mm. — FV / 30.00

2004-2006 ND Issue

25 **2 Dollars** — VF / UNC
ND (2004). Green. Signature varieties. Polymer plastic. 139x70mm. — FV / 2.50

26 **5 Dollars** — VF / UNC
ND (2006). Blue. Signature varieties. Back: Long boats and hut. 144x72mm. — FV / 4.00

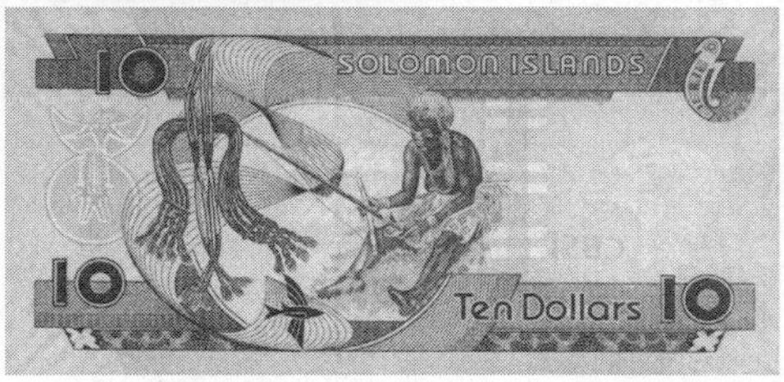

27 **10 Dollars** — VF / UNC
ND (2006). Purple. Signature varieties. Back: Shell money manufacturing. 147x74mm. — FV / 7.50

28 **20 Dollars** — VF / UNC
ND (2006). Brown. Back: Dancers. 154x72mm. — FV / 15.00

29 **50 Dollars**
ND (2004). Green. Back: Butterflies and reptiles. 160x72mm. — FV / 30.00

30 **100 Dollars**
ND (2006). Brown on tan and multicolor underprint. Signature varieties. Back: Coconut harvest. 160x72mm. — FV / 75.00

Collector Series

Solomon Islands Monetary Authority

1979 ND Issue

CS1 **ND (1979) 2-10 Dollars** — Mkt. Value
#5, 6b, 7b with overprint: *SPECIMEN* and serial # prefix Maltese cross. — 25.00

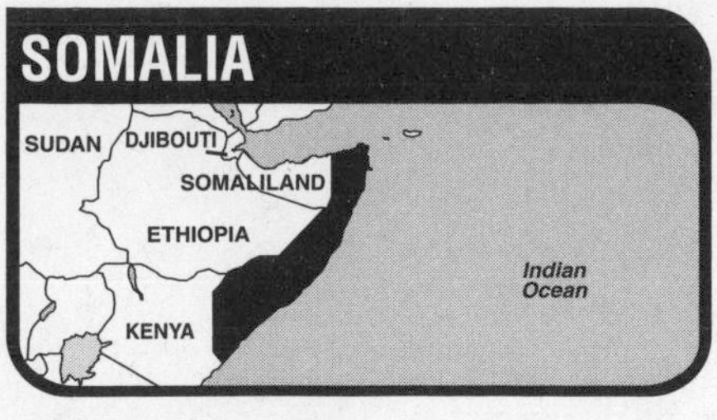

Somalia, the Somali Democratic Republic, comprising the former Italian Somaliland, is located on the coast of the eastern projection of the African continent commonly referred to as the *Horn*. It has an area of 178,201 sq. mi. (461,657 sq. km.) and a population of 11.53 million. Capitol Mogadishu. The economy is pastoral and agricultural. Livestock, bananas and hides are exported. The area of the British Somaliland Protectorate was known to the Egyptians at least 1,500 years B.C., and was occupied by the Arabs and Portuguese before British sea captains obtained trading and anchorage rights in 1827. The land of sandy clay and sporadic rainfall acquired a strategic importance with the opening of the Suez Canal in 1869. After negotiating treaties with the tribes, Britain declared the area a protectorate in 1888. Italy acquired Italian Somaliland in 1895 by purchase from the sultan of Zanzibar. Britain occupied Italian Somaliland in 1941 and administered it until April 1, 1950, when it was returned to Italy as a U.N. trusteeship. The British Somaliland protectorate became independent on June 26, 1960. Five days later it joined with Italian Somaliland to form the Somali Republic. The country was under a revolutionary military regime installed Oct. 21, 1969. After 11 years of civil war rebel forces fought their way into the capital. A. M. Muhammad became president in Aug. 1991 but interfactional fighting continued. A UN-sponsored truce was signed in March 1992 and a peace plan and pact was signed Jan. 15, 1993. The northern Somali National Movements (SNM) declared a secession of the northwestern Somaliland Republic on May 17, 1991 which is not recognized by the Somali Democratic Republic.

MONETARY SYSTEM:

1 Scellino = 1 Shilling = 100 Centesimi
1 Shilin = 1 Shilling = 100 Centi

Republic

Banca Nazionale Somala

1962 Issue

1 **5 Scellini = 5 Shillings** VF UNC
1962. Red on green and orange underprint. Antelope at left. Signature title: *IL PRESIDENTE* at left. Back: Orange-brown. Dhow at center. Watermark: Leopard's head. Printer: OCV.

	VF	UNC
a. Issued note.	35.00	200.
s. Specimen.	—	110.

2 **10 Scellini = 10 Shillings** VF UNC
1962. Green oon red-brown and green underprint. Flower at left. Signature title: *IL PRESIDENTE* at left. Back: Brown and green. River scene at center right. Watermark: Leopard's head. Printer: OCV.

	VF	UNC
a. Issued note.	55.00	325.
s. Specimen.	—	185.

3 **20 Scellini = 20 Shillings** VF UNC
1962. Brown on blue and gold underprint. Banana plant at left.Signature title: *IL PRESIDENTE* at left. Back: Brown and blue. Bank building at center right. Watermark: Leopard's head. Printer: OCV.

	VF	UNC
a. Issued note.	75.00	600.
s. Specimen.	—	750.

4 **100 Scellini = 100 Shillings** VF UNC
1962. Blue on green and orange underprint. Artcraft at left.Signature title: *IL PRESIDENTE* at left. Back: Blue and red. Building. Watermark: Leopard's head. Printer: OCV.

	VF	UNC
a. Issued note.	125.	750.
s. Specimen.	—	400.

1966 Issue

5 **5 Scellini = 5 Shillings** VF UNC
1966. Red on green and orange underprint. Antelope at left, different guilloche in underprint. Signature title: *IL PRESIDENTE* at left. Back: Orange-brown with blue underprint. Dhow at center. Watermark: Leopard's head. Printer: OCV (without imprint).

	VF	UNC
a. Issued note.	30.00	175.
s. Specimen perforated: *ANNULLATO*.	—	100.

6 **10 Scellini = 10 Shillings**
1966. Green on red-brown and green underprint. Flower at left, different guilloche in underprint. Signature title: *IL PRESIDENTE* at left. Back: Green with light tan underprint. River scene at center right. Watermark: Leopard's head. Printer: OCV (without imprint).

	VF	UNC
a. Issued note.	50.00	325.
s. Specimen perforated: *ANNULLATO*.	—	225.

7 **20 Scellini = 20 Shillings** VF UNC
1966. Brown on pink, blue and green underprint. Banana plant at left. Signature title: *IL PRESIDENTE* at left. Back: Brown and blue. Brown bank building at center right. Watermark: Leopard's head. Printer: OCV (without imprint).
- a. Issued note. 65.00 450.
- s. Specimen perforated: *ANNULLATO.* — 325.

8 **100 Scellini = 100 Shillings**
1966. Blue on green, purple and tan underprint. Artcraft at left.Signature title: *IL PRESIDENTE* at left. Back: Blue and red. Building. Watermark: Leopard's head. Printer: OCV (without imprint).
- a. Issued note. 120. 600.
- s. Specimen perforated: *ANNULLATO.* — 435.

1968 Issue

9 **5 Scellini = 5 Shillings** VF UNC
1968. Red on green and orange underprint. Antelope at left, different guilloche in underprint. Signature titile: *IL GOVERNATORE* at left. Back: Orange-brown with blue underprint. Dhow at center. Watermark: Leopard's head. Printer: OCV (without imprint). 40.00 250.

10 **10 Scellini = 10 Shillings**
1968. Green on red-brown and green underprint Flower at left, different guilloche in underprint. Signature titile: *IL GOVERNATORE* at left. Back: Green with light tan underprint. River scene at center right. Watermark: Leopard's head. Printer: OCV (without imprint). . 55.00 450.

11 **20 Scellini = 20 Shillings**
1968. Brown on blue and gold underprint. Banana plant at left. Signature titile: *IL GOVERNATORE* at left. Back: Brown and blue. Brown bank building. Watermark: Leopard's head. Printer: OCV (without imprint). 85.00 575.

12 **100 Scellini = 100 Shillings**
1968. Blue on green and orange underprint. Artcraft at left. Signature titile: *IL GOVERNATORE* at left. Back: Blue and red. Building. Watermark: Leopard's head. Printer: OCV (without imprint). 125. 850.

Democratic Republic

Banca Nazionale Somala

1971 Issue

13 **5 Scellini = 5 Shillings** VF UNC
1971. Purple-brown on blue, green and gold underprint. Artcraft at left. Signature title: *IL GOVERNATORE* and *IL CASSIERE* at right. Back: Blue and red. Building. Watermark: Leopard's head. Printer: OCV (without imprint).
- a. Issued note. 25.00 200.
- s. Specimen. — 110.

14 **10 Scellini = 10 Shillings** VF UNC
1971. Green on red-brown and green underprint. Flower at left, different guilloche in underprint. Signature title: *IL GOVERNATORE* and *IL CASSIERE* at right. Back: Green with light tan underprint. River scene at center right. Watermark: Leopard's head. Printer: OCV (without imprint).
- a. Issued note. 30.00 325.
- s. Specimen. — 175.

15 **20 Scellini = 20 Shillings** VF UNC
1971. Brown on blue and gold underprint. Banana plant at left. Signature title: *IL GOVERNATORE* and *IL CASSIERE* at right. Back: Brown and blue. Brown bank building at center right. Watermark: Leopard's head. Printer: OCV (without imprint).
- a. Issued note. 70.00 500.
- s. Specimen. — 275.

16 **100 Scellini = 100 Shillings** VF UNC
1971. Blue on green and orange underprint. Artcraft at left. Signature title: *IL GOVERNATORE* and *IL CASSIERE* at right. Back: Blue and red. Building. Watermark: Leopard's head. Printer: OCV (without imprint).
- a. Issued note. 85.00 650.
- s. Specimen. — 375.

Bankiga Qaranka Soomaaliyeed

Somali National Bank

Law of 11.12.1974

17 **5 Shilin = 5 Shillings** VF UNC
1975. Purple on gold and multicolor underprint. Gnus and zebras at bottom center, arms at left. Back: Banana harvesting at center right. Watermark: Sayyid Mohammed Aabdullah Hassan.
- a. Issued note. 12.50 50.00
- s. Specimen. — —

18 **10 Shilin = 10 Shillings** VF UNC
1975. Dark green on pink and multicolor underprint. Minaret at left center, arms at left. Back: Shipbuilders at work at center right. Watermark: Sayyid Mohammed Aabdullah Hassan. 15.00 60.00

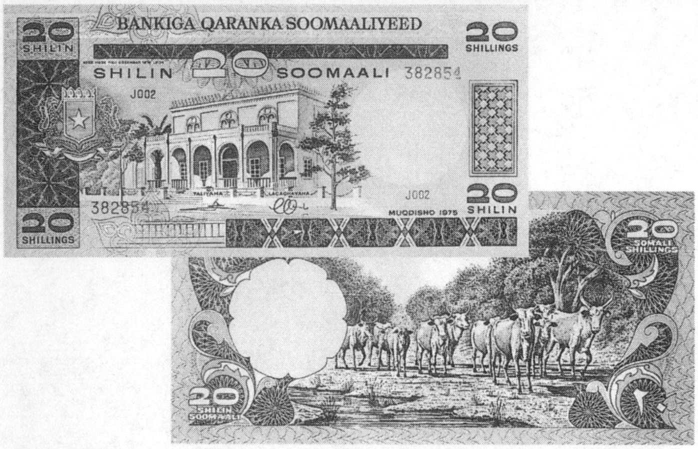

19 **20 Shilin = 20 Shillings** VF UNC
1975. Brown on multicolor underprint. Bank building at center, arms at left. Back: Cattle. Watermark: Sayyid Mohammed Aabdullah Hassan. 15.00 125.

20 **100 Shilin = 100 Shillings** VF UNC
1975. Blue on gold and multicolor underprint. Womam with baby, rifle and farm tools at left center, Dagathur Monument at center right, arms at left. Back: Workers in factory. Watermark: Sayyid Mohammed Aabdullah Hassan. 35.00 160.

Bankiga Dhexe ee Soomaaliya

Central Bank of Somalia

Law of 6.12.1977

20A **5 Shilin = 5 Shillings** VF UNC
1978. Purple on gold and multicolor underprint. Gnus and zebras at bottom center, arms at left. Black series and serial number. Back: Banana harvesting at center right. Watermark: Sayyid Mohammed Aabdullah Hassan.

	VF	UNC
a. Issued note.	25.00	85.00
s. Specimen.	—	25.00

21 **5 Shilin = 5 Shillings** VF UNC
1978. Purple on gold and multicolor underprint. Cape Buffalo herd at bottom left center, arms at left. Black series and serial number. Back: Banana harvesting at center right. Watermark: Sayyid Mohammed Aabdullah Hassan. 10.00 42.50

22 **10 Shilin = 10 Shillings**
1978. Dark green on pink and multicolor underprint. Minaret at left center, arms at left. Black series and serial number. Back: Shipbuilders at work at center right. Watermark: Sayyid Mohammed Aabdullah Hassan.

	VF	UNC
a. Issued note.	8.00	45.00
s. Specimen.	—	25.00

23 **20 Shilin = 20 Shillings** VF UNC
1978. Brown on multicolor underprint. Bank building at center, arms at left. Black series and serial number. Back: Cattle. Watermark: Sayyid Mohammed Aabdullah Hassan.

	VF	UNC
a. Issued note.	15.00	85.00
s. Specimen.	—	40.00

24 **100 Shilin = 100 Shillings** VF UNC
1978. Blue on gold and multicolor underprint. Woman with baby, rifle and farm tools at left center, Dagathur Monument at center right, arms at left. Black series and serial number. Back: Workers in factory. Watermark: Sayyid Mohammed Aabdullah Hassan.

	VF	UNC
a. Issued note.	22.50	130.
s. Specimen.	—	25.00

Law of 5.4.1980

#26-28. Replacement ntoes: Serial # prefix *Z001*.

#25 not assigned.

26 **10 Shilin = 10 Shillings** — VF 8.00, UNC 27.50

1980. Dark green on pink and multicolor underprint. Minaret at left center, arms at left. Red series and serial number. Back: Shipbuilders at work at center right. Watermark: Sayyid Mohammed Aabdullah Hassan.

27 **20 Shilin = 20 Shillings** — VF 9.00, UNC 55.00

1980. Brown on multicolor underprint. Bank building at center, arms at left. Red series and serial number. Back: Cattle. Watermark: Sayyid Mohammed Aabdullah Hassan.

28 **100 Shilin = 100 Shillings** — VF 17.50, UNC 85.00

1980. Blue on gold and multicolor underprint. Woman with baby, rifle and farm tools at left center, Dagathur Monument at center right, arms at left. Red series and serial number. Back: Workers in factory. Watermark: Sayyid Mohammed Aabdullah Hassan.

Law of 9.12.1981

#29-30 Replacement notes: Serial # prefix *ZZ001*.

29 **20 Shilin = 20 Shillings** — VF 17.50, UNC 55.00

1981. Brown on multicolor underprint. Bank building at center, arms at left. Red series and serial number. Back: Cattle. Watermark: Sayyid Mohammed Aabdullah Hassan.

30 **100 Shilin = 100 Shillings** — VF 15.00, UNC 50.00

1981. Blue on gold and multicolor underprint. Woman with baby, rifle and farm tools at left center, Dagathur Monument at center right, arms at left. Red series and serial number. Back: Workers in factory. Watermark: Sayyid Mohammed Aabdullah Hassan.

Law of 30.12.1982; 1983 Issue

#31-35 Replacement notes: Serial # prefix *Z001*.

31 **5 Shilin = 5 Shillings**

1983-87. Brown-violet. Cape Buffalo herd at left center, arms at top left center, star near lower center. Back: Harvesting bananas. Reduced size.

	VF	UNC
a. 1983.	3.00	7.00
b. 1986.	3.00	6.00
c. 1987.	3.00	5.00

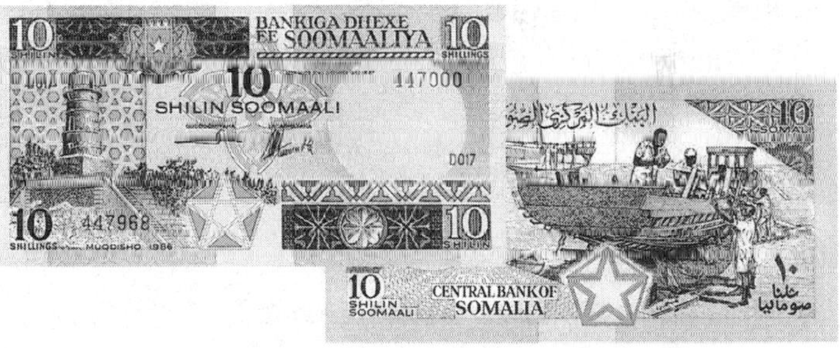

32 **10 Shilin = 10 Shillings**

1983-87. Green and multicolor. Lighthouse at left, arms at top left center, star at lower center. Back: Shipbuilders at center right. Watermark: Sayyid Mohammed Aabdullah Hassan. Reduced size.

	VF	UNC
a. 1983.	3.00	8.00
b. 1986.	3.00	7.00
c. 1987.	2.50	5.00

33 **20 Shilin = 20 Shillings**

1983-89. Brown and multicolor. Bank at left, arms at top left center, star at lower center. Back: Cattle. Watermark: Sayyid Mohammed Aabdullah Hassan. Reduced size.

	VF	UNC
a. 1983.	5.00	15.00
b. 1986.	4.00	12.50
c. 1987.	3.00	10.00
d. 1989.	3.00	6.00

34	50 Shilin = 50 Shillings	VF	UNC
	1983-89. Red-brown and multicolor underprint. Walled city at left and center, arms at top left center, star near lower center. Back: Watering animals at center right. Watermark: Sayyid Mohammed Aabdullah Hassan. Reduced size.		
	a. 1983.	3.00	12.00
	b. 1986; 1987. 2 signature varieties for 1987.	2.00	8.00
	c. 1988.	2.00	5.00
	d. 1989.	2.00	4.00

35	100 Shilin = 100 Shillings	VF	UNC
	1983-89. Blue-black, dark blue and dark green on multicolor underprint. Woman with baby, rifle and farm tools at left center, Dagathur Monument at center right, arms at top left center, star at lower center. Back: Workers in factory. Watermark: Sayyid Mohammed Aabdullah Hassan. Reduced size.		
	a. 1983.	5.00	12.00
	b. 1986; 1987. Two signature varieties for 1987.	2.00	10.00
	c. 1988.	2.00	7.00
	d. 1989.	2.00	4.00

Law of 1.1.1989

36	500 Shilin = 500 Shillings	VF	UNC
	1989; 1990; 1996. Green and aqua on multicolor underprint. Fishermen mending net at left center, arms at top left center. Two signature varieties. Back: Mosque at left center. Watermark: Sayyid Mohammed Aabdullah Hassan.		
	a. 1989.	2.00	9.00
	b. 1990.	2.00	8.00
	c. 1996.	2.00	8.00

Law of 1.1.1990; 1990 Issue

37	1000 Shilin = 1000 Shillings	VF	UNC
	1990; 1996. Violet and orange on multicolor underprint. Women seated weaving baskets at left center; arms above at top left center. Back: City view at bottom, Port of Mogadishu at upper center right. Watermark: Sayyid Mohammed Aabdullah Hassan. UV: value 1000 fluoresce yellow; serial # orange. Back design elements yellow.		
	a. 1990.	2.00	5.00
	b. 1996.	2.00	7.00

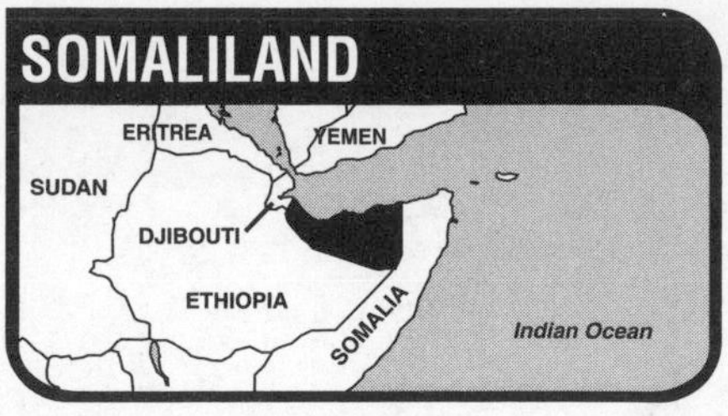

The Somaliland Republic, comprising the former British Somaliland Protectorate, is located on the coast of the northeastern projection of the African continent commonly referred to as the "Horn" on the southwestern end of the Gulf of Aden.

Bordered by Eritrea to the west, Ethiopia to west and south and Somalia to the east, it has an area of 68,000* sq. mi. (176,000* sq. km). Capital: Hargeysa. It is mostly arid and mounainous except for the gulf shoreline.

The Protectorate of British Somaliland was established in 1888 and from 1905 the territory was administered by a commissioner under the British Colonial Office. Italian Somaliland was administered as a colony from 1893 to 1941, when the territory was occupied by British forces. In 1950 the United Nations allowed Italy to resume control of Italian Somaliland under a trusteeship. In 1960 British and Italian Somaliland were united as Somalia, an independent republic outside the Commonwealth.

Civil War erupted in the late 1970's and continued until the capital of Somalia was taken in 1990. The United Nations provided aid and peacekeepers. A UN sponsored truce was signed in March 1992 and a peace plan and pact was signed Jan. 15, 1993. The northern Somali National Movement (SMN) declared a secession of the Somaliland Republic on May 17, 1991 which is not recognized by the Somali Democratic Republic.

The currency issued by the East African Currency Board was used in British Somaliland from 1945 to 1961. Somali currency was then used until 1995.

MONETARY SYSTEM:

1 Somaliland Shilling = 1 Shilin

SIGNATURE VARIETIES					
	Guddoomiyaha	Lacaghayaha		Lacaghayaha	Guddoomiyaha
1			4		

Republic

Baanka Somaliland

1994 Issue

1	5 Shillings = 5 Shilin	VF	UNC
	1994. Bright green, olive-green and red-brown on multicolor underprint. Greater Kudu at right, building at center. Back: Trader with camels.		
	a. Issued note.	FV	1.00
	s. Specimen.	—	100.

2	10 Shillings = 10 Shilin	VF	UNC
	1994-96. Violet, purple and red-brown on multicolor underprint. Greater Kudu at right, building at center. Back: Trader with camels.		
	a. 1994.	FV	1.25
	b. 1996.	FV	1.00
	s. Specimen.	—	100.

		VF	UNC
3	**20 Shillings = 20 Shilin**		
	1994-96. Brown and red-brown on multicolor underprint. Greater Kudu at right, building at center. Back: Trader with camels.		
	a. 1994.	FV	2.25
	b. 1996.	FV	2.00
	s. Specimen.	—	110.

		VF	UNC
4	**50 Shillings = 50 Shilin**		
	1994-96. Blue-violet, blue-gray and red-brown on multicolor underprint. Greater Kudu at right, building at center. Back: Trader with camels.		
	a. 1994.	FV	4.00
	b. 1996.	FV	3.50
	s. Specimen.	—	110.

		VF	UNC
5	**100 Shillings = 100 Shilin**		
	1994-. Brownish black and red-violet on multicolor underprint. Building at center. Back: Ship dockside in background, herdsmen w/sheep at front center. 135x61mm.		
	a. 1994.	FV	6.50
	b. 1996.	FV	5.00
	c. 1999. Signature 3.	FV	5.00
	d. 2002.	FV	5.00
	s. Specimen. As a, b.	—	110.

		VF	UNC
6	**500 Shillings = 500 Shilin**		
	1994-. Purple, blue-black and blue-green on multicolor underprint. Building at center. Back: Ship dockside in background, herdsmen w/sheep at front center. 145x66mm.		
	a. 1994.	FV	15.00
	b. 1996.	FV	10.00
	c. 1999.	FV	10.00
	d. 2002.	FV	10.00
	e. 2005.	FV	10.00
	f. 2006.	FV	10.00
	g. 2008.	FV	10.00
	h. 2011.	FV	10.00
	s. Specimen. As a, b.	—	125.

1996 Issue

		VF	UNC
7	**50 Shillings = 50 Shilin**		
	1996; 1999; 2002. Blue-violet, blue-gray and violet on multicolor underprint. Greater Kudu at right, building at center. Back: Trader with camels. Increased size. 130x58mm.		
	a. Signature 1.	FV	.75
	b. Signature 2.	FV	.75
	c. Signature 3. 1999.	FV	.50
	d. 2002.	FV	.50
	s. Specimen.	—	125.

1996 "Bronze" Commemorative Issue

#8-13, 5th Anniversary of Independence

		VF	UNC
8	**5 Shillings = 5 Shilin**		
	18.5.1996 (- old date 1994). Bright green, olive-green and red-brown on multicolor underprint. Overprint on #1. Back: Traders with camels. Overprint: Bronze on face: *5th Anniversary of Independence 18 May 1996 - Sanad Gurada 5ee Gobanimadda 18 May 1996.*	FV	1.75

		VF	UNC
9	**10 Shillings = 10 Shilin**		
	18.5.1996 (- old date 1994). Violet, purple and red-brown on multicolor underprint. Overprint on #2a. Back: Traders with camels. Overprint: Bronze on face: *5th Anniversary of Independence 18 May 1996 - Sanad Gurada 5ee Gobanimadda 18 May 1996.*	FV	2.00

		VF	UNC
10	**20 Shillings = 20 Shilin**		
	18.5.1996 (- old date 1994). Brown and red-brown on multicolor underprint. Overprint on #3a. Back: Traders with camels. Overprint: Bronze on face: *5th Anniversary of Independence 18 May 1996 - Sanad Gurada 5ee Gobanimadda 18 May 1996.*	FV	3.00

		VF	UNC
11	**50 Shillings = 50 Shilin**		
	18.5.1996. Overprint: Bronze on face: *5th Anniversary of Independence 18 May 1996 - Sanad Gurada 5ee Gobanimadda 18 May 1996.*		
	a. Overprint on #4a. (- old date 1994).	FV	4.25
	b. Overprint on #4b. 1996.	FV	3.00

11A 50 Shillings = 50 Shilin | VF FV | UNC 3.50

18.5.1996. Blue-violet, blue-gray and violet on multicolor underprint. Bronze overprint on #7a. Back: Traders with camels. Overprint: Bronze on face: *5th Anniversary of Independence 18 May 1996 - Sanad Gurada 5ee Gobanimadda 18 May 1996.*

12 100 Shillings = 100 Shilin | VF FV | UNC 7.50

18.5.1996 (- old date 1994). Brownish black and red-violet on multicolor underprint. Overprint on #5a. Back: Ship dockside in background, herdsmen with sheep at front center. Overprint: Bronze on face: *5th Anniversary of Independence 18 May 1996 - Sanad Gurada 5ee Gobanimadda 18 May 1996.*

13 500 Shillings = 500 Shilin | VF FV | UNC 25.00

18.5.1996 (- old date 1994). Purple, blue-black and blue-green on multicolor underprint. Overprint on #6a. Back: Ship dockside in background, herdsmen with sheep at front center. Overprint: Bronze on face: *5th Anniversary of Independence 18 May 1996 - Sanad Gurada 5ee Gobanimadda 18 May 1996.*

1996 "Silver" Commemorative Issue

#14-19, 5th Anniversary of Independence

14 5 Shillings = 5 Shilin | VF FV | UNC 1.75

18.5.1996 (- old date 1994). Bright green, olive-green and red-brown on multicolor underprint. Overprint on #1. Back: Traders with camels. Overprint: Silver on face: *Sanad Gurada 5ee Gobanimadda 18 May 1996.*

15 10 Shillings = 10 Shilin | VF FV | UNC 2.00

18.5.1996 (- old date 1994). Violet, purple and red-brown on multicolor underprint. Overprint on #2a. Back: Traders with camels. Overprint: Silver on face: *Sanad Gurada 5ee Gobanimadda 18 May 1996.*

16 20 Shillings = 20 Shilin | VF FV | UNC 3.00

18.5.1996 (- old date 1994). Brown and red-brown on multicolor underprint. Overprint on #3a. Back: Traders with camels. Overprint: Silver on face: *Sanad Gurada 5ee Gobanimadda 18 May 1996.*

17 50 Shillings = 50 Shilin | VF | UNC

18.5.1996. Overprint: Silver on face: *Sanad Gurada 5ee Gobanimadda 18 May 1996.*

	VF	UNC
a. overprint on #4a. (- old date 1994).	FV	4.25
b. overprint on #4b. 1996.	FV	3.00

17A 50 Shillings = 50 Shilin | VF FV | UNC 3.50

1996. Blue-violet, blue-gray and violet on multicolor underprint. Overprint on number 7b. Back: Ship dockside in background, herdsmen with sheep at front center.

18 100 Shillings = 100 Shilin | VF FV | UNC 7.50

18.5.1996 (- old date 1994). Brownesh black and red-violet on multicolor underprint. Overprint on #5a. Back: Ship dockside in background, herdsmen with sheep at front center. Overprint: Silver on face: *Sanad Gurada 5ee Gobanimadda 18 May 1996.*

19 500 Shillings = 500 Shilin | VF FV | UNC 25.00

18.5.1996 (- old date 1994). Purple, blue-black and blue-green on multicolor underprint. Overprint on #6a. Back: Ship dockside in background, herdsmen with sheep at front center. Overprint: Silver on face: *Sanad Gurada 5ee Gobanimadda 18 May 1996.*

2011 Issue

		VF	UNC
20	**1000 Shillings** 2011. Purple on multicolor underprint. 145x66mm.	FV	35.00

		VF	UNC
21	**5000 Shillings** 2011. Green on multicolor underprint. 145x66mm.	FV	60.00

Collector Series

Baanka Somaliland

2006 Issue

		VF	UNC
CS1	**1000 Shillings** 2006 Purple on tan and purple underprint. Young girl at right, lion at left. Back: Lion standing at center, camel at right. 159x76mm.		
	a. Issued note	—	5.00
	b. Uncut sheet, 3 notes.	—	10.00
	r. Replacement note. Serial # prefix *AX*.	—	7.50
	s. Specimen. Red overprint: *SPECIMEN* on both sides.	—	30.00

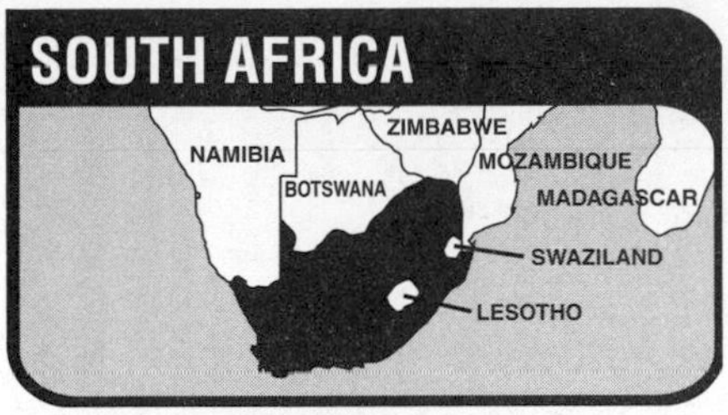

The Republic of South Africa, located at the southern tip of Africa, has an area, including the enclave of Walvis Bay, of 1,219,912 sq. km. and a population of 48.78 million. Capital: Administrative, Pretoria; Legislative, Cape Town; Judicial, Bloemfontein. Manufacturing, mining and agriculture are the principal industries. Exports include wool, diamonds, gold and metallic ores.

Dutch traders landed at the southern tip of modern day South Africa in 1652 and established a stopover point on the spice route between the Netherlands and the East, founding the city of Cape Town. After the British seized the Cape of Good Hope area in 1806, many of the Dutch settlers (the Boers) trekked north to found their own republics. The discovery of diamonds (1867) and gold (1886) spurred wealth and immigration and intensified the subjugation of the native inhabitants. The Boers resisted British encroachments but were defeated in the Boer War (1899-1902); however, the British and the Afrikaners, as the Boers became known, ruled together under the Union of South Africa. In 1948, the National Party was voted into power and instituted a policy of apartheid - the separate development of the races. The first multi-racial elections in 1994 brought an end to apartheid and ushered in black majority rule under the African National Congress (ANC). ANC infighting, which has grown in recent years, came to a head in September 2008 after President Thabo Mneki resigned. Kgalema Motlanthe, the party's General-Secretary, succeeded as interim president until general elections scheduled for 2009.

South African currency carries inscriptions in both Afrikaans and English.

RULERS:

British to 1961

MONETARY SYSTEM:

1 Shilling = 12 Pence
1 Shilling = 12 Pence
1 Pound = 20 Shillings to 1961
1 Pound = 20 Shillings to 1961
1 Rand = 100 Cents (= 10 Shillings), 1961-

SIGNATURE VARIETIES			
3	M. H. de Kock, 1.7.1945-30.6.1962	4	G. Rissik, 1.7.1962-30.6.1967
5	T. W. de Jongh, 1.7.196731.12.1980	6	G. P. C. de Kock, 1.1.1981-7.8.1989
7	C. L. Stals, 8.8.1989-7.8.1999	8	T. T. Mboweni, 8.8.1999-

Republic of South Africa

South African Reserve Bank

Suid-Afrikaanse Reserwebank

1961 ND Issue

#102-105 replacement notes: Serial # prefix *Z/1; Y/1; X/1; W/1* respectively.

		VF	UNC
102	**1 Rand** ND (1961-65). Rust brown on multicolor underprint. Portrait of Jan van Riebeeck at left, first line of bank name and value in English. Watermark: Jan van Riebeeck. 135x77mm.		
	a. Signature 3. (1961).	22.50	65.00
	b. Signature 4. (1962-65).	11.00	28.00
	s. As a. Specimen.	—	550.

103 1 Rand VF UNC

ND (1961-65). Rust brown on multicolor underprint. Portrait of Jan van Riebeeck at left, first line of bank name and value in Afrikaans. Watermark: Jan van Riebeeck. 137x78mm.

	VF	UNC
a. Signature 3. (1961).	22.50	65.00
b. Signature 4. (1962-65).	11.00	27.50

104 2 Rand VF UNC

ND (1961-65). Blue on multicolor underprint. Portrait of Jan van Riebeeck at left, first line of bank name and value in English. Watermark: Jan van Riebeeck. 150x85mm.

	VF	UNC
a. Signature 3. (1961).	12.50	36.00
b. Signature 4. (1962-65).	6.50	20.00

105 2 Rand VF UNC

ND (1961-65). Blue on multicolor underprint. Portrait of Jan van Riebeeck at left, first line of bank name and value in Afrikaans. Watermark: Jan van Riebeeck. 150x85mm.

	VF	UNC
a. Signature 3. (1961).	12.50	36.00
b. Signature 4. (1962-65).	6.50	20.00
s. As a. Specimen.	—	550.

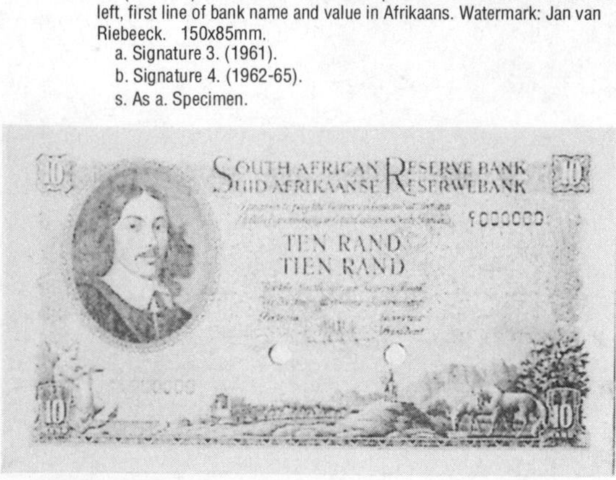

106 10 Rand VF UNC

ND (1961-65). Green and brown on multicolor underprint. Portrait of Jan van Riebeeck at left, first line of bank name and value in English. Back: Sailing ship. Watermark: Jan van Riebeeck. 170x97mm.

	VF	UNC
a. Signature 3. (1961).	25.00	65.00
b. Signature 4. (1962-65).	17.50	37.50
s. Specimen. Punch hole cancel.	—	—

107 10 Rand VF UNC

ND (1961-65). Green and brown on multicolor underprint. Portrait of Jan van Riebeeck at left, first line of bank name and value in Afrikaans. Watermark: Jan van Riebeeck. 170x97mm.

	VF	UNC
a. Signature 3. (1961).	25.00	65.00
b. Signature 4. (1962-65).	17.50	37.50
s. Specimen.	—	550.

108 20 Rand VF UNC

ND (1961). Brown-violet. Portrait of Jan van Riebeeck at left, first line of bank name and value in English. Signature 3. Back: Machinery. Watermark: Jan van Riebeeck.

	VF	UNC
a. Issued note.	50.00	160.
s. Specimen.	—	550.

108A 20 Rand — VF | UNC

ND (1962-65). Brown-violet. Portrait of Jan van Riebeeck at left, first line of bank name in Afrikaans. Signature 4. Watermark: Jan van Riebeeck. — 50.00 | 160.

1966 ND Issue

#109-114 Replacement notes: Serial # prefix Z/1; Y/1; X/1; W/1 respectively.

109 1 Rand

ND (1966-72). Dark reddish brown on multicolor underprint. Jan van Riebeeck at left, first lines of bank name and value in English. Back: Rams in field. Watermark: Springbok. 126x64mm.

	VF	UNC
a. Signature 4. (1966).	2.50	13.50
b. Signature 5. (1967).	1.50	8.00
s1. As a. Specimen.	—	35.00
s2. As b. Specimen.	—	35.00

110 1 Rand

ND (1966-72). Dark reddish brown on multicolor underprint. Jan van Riebeeck at left,first lines of bank name and value in Afrikaans. Back: Rams in field. Watermark: Springbok. 126x64mm.

	VF	UNC
a. Signature 4. (1966).	2.50	13.50
b. Signature 5. (1967).	1.50	8.00
s1. As a. Specimen.	—	35.00
s2. As b. Specimen.	—	35.00

111 5 Rand

ND (1966-76). Purple on multicolor underprint. Jan van Riebeeck at left, covered wagons on trail at right corner, first lines of bank name and value in English. Back: Ore mine with train. 133x70mm.

	VF	UNC
a. Signature 4. Watermark: Springbok (1966).	15.00	90.00
b. Signature 5. Watermark: Springbok (1967-74).	6.00	17.50
c. Signature 5. Watermark: J. van Riebeeck (1975).	6.50	20.00
s1. As a. Specimen.	—	35.00
s2. As b. Specimen.	—	35.00

112 5 Rand

ND (1966-76). Purple on multicolor underprint. Jan van Riebeeck at left, first lines of bank name and value in Afrikaans. Back: Ore mine with train.

	VF	UNC
a. Signature 4. Watermark: Springbok (1966).	15.00	90.00
b. Signature 5. Watermark: Springbok (1967-74).	6.00	17.50
c. Signature 5. Watermark: J. van Riebeeck (1975).	6.50	20.00
s1. As a. Specimen.	—	35.00
s2. As b. Specimen.	—	

113 10 Rand

ND (1966-76). Dark green and brown on multicolor underprint. Jan van Riebeeck at left, Capital building at center, first lives of bank name and value in English. Back: Old sailing ships. 140x76mm.

	VF	UNC
a. Signature 4. Watermark: Springbok (1966).	10.00	35.00
b. Signature 5. Watermark: Springbok (1967-74).	5.00	16.50
c. Signature 5. Watermark: J. van Riebeeck (1975).	5.00	16.50
s1. As a. Specimen.	—	50.00
s2. As b. Specimen.	—	50.00

114 10 Rand

ND (1966-76). Dark green and brown on multicolor underprint. Jan van Riebeeck at left, Capital building at center, first lines of bank name and value in Afrikaans. Back: Old sailing ships. 140x76mm.

	VF	UNC
a. Signature 4. Watermark: Springbok (1966).	10.00	35.00
b. Signature 5. Watermark: Springbok (1967-74).	5.00	16.50
c. Signature 5. Watermark: J. van Riebeeck (1975).	5.00	16.50
s1. As a. Specimen.	—	50.00
s2. As b. Specimen.	—	50.00

1973-84 ND Issue

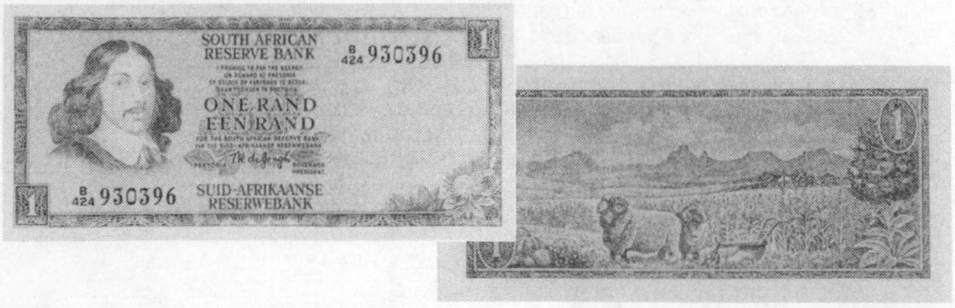

115 1 Rand

ND (1973-75). Dark reddish brown on multicolor underprint. Jan van Riebeeck at left, first lines of bank name and value in English. Signature 5. Back: Rams in field. 120x57mm.

	VF	UNC
a. Watermark: Springbok (1973).	1.75	5.00
b. Watermark: J. van Riebeeck (1975).	2.00	6.00

116 1 Rand

ND (1973-75). Dark reddish brown on multicolor underprint. Jan van Riebeeck at left,first lines of bank name and value in Afrikaans. Signature 5. Back: Rams in field. Watermark: Springbok. 120x57mm.

	VF	UNC
a. Watermark: Springbok (1973).	1.75	5.00
b. Watermark: J. van Riebeeck (1975).	2.00	6.00

117 2 Rand

ND (1974-76). Blue on multicolor underprint. Jan van Riebeek at left, first lines of bank name and value in Afrikaans. Signature 5. Back: Hydroelectric dam. 127x62mm.

	VF	UNC
a. Watermark: Springbok (1974).	3.00	15.00
b. Watermark: J. van Riebeeck (1976).	4.50	16.00

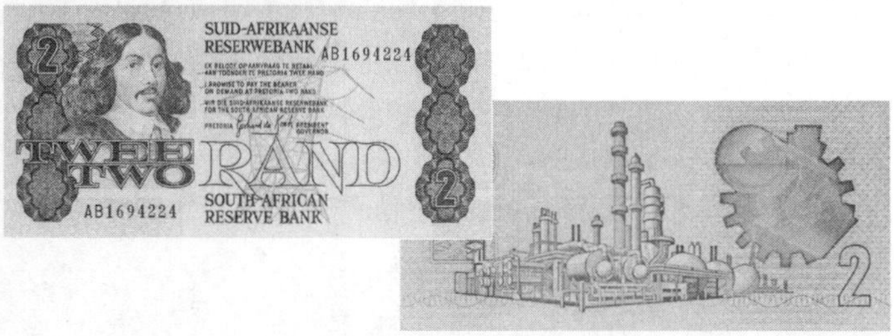

118 2 Rand

ND (1978-90). Blue on multicolor underprint. Jan van Riebeek at left, electrical tower at center. Back: Refinery at left center. Watermark: Jan van Riebeek. 120x57mm.

	VF	UNC
a. Signature 5. (1978-81).	1.00	6.50
b. Signature 6. Fractional numbering system. Without security thread (1981).	3.00	20.00
c. As b. With security thread. (1981-83).	1.00	4.50
d. As c. Alpha-numeric system. (1983-90).	.50	3.50
e. Signature 7. (1990).	2.00	6.50

119 5 Rand

ND (1978-94). Purple on multicolor underprint. Jan van Riebeek at left, first lines of bank name and value in English, diamond at center. Back: Grain storage at left center. Watermark: Jan van Riebeek. 127x63mm.

	VF	UNC
a. Signature 5. (1978-81).	2.50	13.50
b. Signature 6. Fractional numbering system. Without security thread (1981).	40.00	165.
c. As b. With security thread. (1981-89).	1.50	14.00
d. As c. Alpha-numeric system. (1989-90).	2.50	12.00
e. Signature 7. (1990-94).	2.50	12.50

120 10 Rand

ND (1978-93). Green on multicolor underprint. Jan van Riebeek at left, flower at center. Back: Bull and ram at left center. Watermark: Jan van Riebeek. 134x70mm.

	VF	UNC
a. Signature 5. (1978-81).	4.50	17.00
b. Signature 6. Fractional numbering system. Without security thread (1981).	12.50	55.00
c. As b. With security thread. (1982-85).	3.25	16.50
d. As c. Alpha-numeric system. (1985-90).	3.00	20.00
e. Signature 7. (1990-93).	2.00	12.50

121 20 Rand

ND (1984-93). Brown on multicolor underprint. Jan van Riebeek at left, building in underprint at center. Back: Three sailing ships at left center with arms at right. Watermark: Jan van Riebeek. 144x77mm.

	VF	UNC
a. Signature 5. (1978-81).	7.00	27.50
b. Signature 6. Fractional numbering system. Without security thread (1981).	22.50	80.00
c. As b. With security thread. (1982-85).	5.00	25.00
d. As c. Alpha-numeric system. (1985-90).	10.00	50.00
e. Signature 7. (1990-93).	6.00	16.50

122 50 Rand

ND (1984-90). Red on multicolor underprint. Jan van Riebeek at left, lion in underprint at center. Back: Local animals at lower left, mountains at center, plants at right. Watermark: Jan van Riebeek. 147x83mm.

	VF	UNC
a. Signature 6. (1984).	15.00	40.00
b. Signature 7. (1990).	22.50	50.00

1992-94 Issue

123 10 Rand

ND (1993; 1999). Dark green and dark blue on brown and multicolor underprint. White rhinoceros at center, large white rhino at right. Back: Ram's head over sheep at left. Watermark: White rhinoceros. 128x70mm.

		VF	UNC
a.	Signature 7. (1993).	FV	10.00
b.	Signature 8. (1999).	2.50	4.50

124 20 Rand

ND (1993; 1999). Deep brown and red-brown on multicolor underprint. Elephants at center, large elephant head at right. Back: Open pit mining at left center. Watermark: Elephant head. 134x70mm.

		VF	UNC
a.	Signature 7 (1993).	FV	10.00
b.	Signature 8 (1999).	FV	7.50

125 50 Rand

ND (1992; 1999). Maroon, brown and deep blue-green on multicolor underprint. Lions with cub drinking water at center, male lion head at right. Back: Sasol oil refinery at lower left center. Watermark: Male lion head. 140x70mm.

		VF	UNC
a.	Signature 7 (1992). Reddish lion drinking water (serial # prefix lower than AL).	25.00	85.00
b.	Signature 7. (1992). Brownish blue lion drinking water. (serial # prefix greater than AL).	FV	25.00
c.	Signature 8 (1999).	FV	17.50
x.	Like a. Watermark on wrong side. Serial # prefix: *BP*.	22.50	50.00

126 100 Rand

ND (1994; 1999). Blue-violet and dark gray on multicolor underprint. Cape buffalo at center and large water buffalo head at right. Back: Zebras along bottom from left to center. Watermark: Water buffalo head. 146x70mm.

		VF	UNC
a.	Signature 7 (1994).	FV	72.50
b.	Signature 8 (1999).	FV	30.00

127 200 Rand

ND (1994; 1999). Orange on multicolor underprint. Leopard at center, large leopard's head at right. Back: Dish antenna at upper left, modern bridge at lower left. 152x70mm.

		VF	UNC
a.	Signature 7 (1994).	FV	85.00
b.	Signature 8 (1999).	FV	60.00

2005 Issue

128 10 Rand

2005. Green on multicolor underprint. White rhinoceros at center, large white rhino head at right, coat of arms at top left, various geometric shapes at lower portion. Back: Ram's head over sheep at left. Watermark: Rhino head. 128x70mm.

		VF	UNC
a.	Signature: Tito Mboweni.	FV	4.00
b.	Signature: Gill Marcus.	FV	3.50

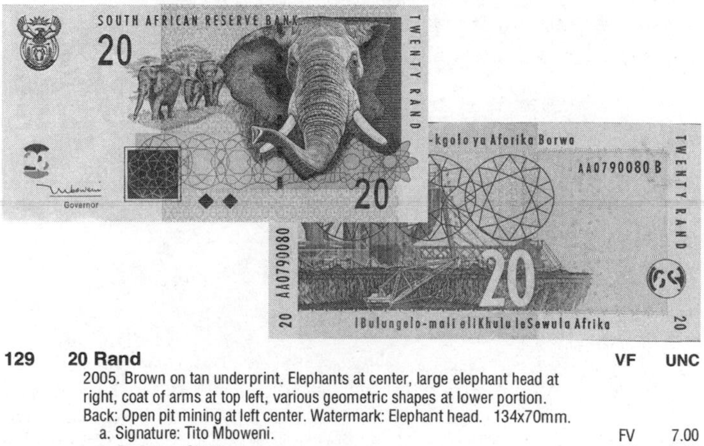

129 20 Rand

2005. Brown on tan underprint. Elephants at center, large elephant head at right, coat of arms at top left, various geometric shapes at lower portion. Back: Open pit mining at left center. Watermark: Elephant head. 134x70mm.

		VF	UNC
a.	Signature: Tito Mboweni.	FV	7.00
b.	Signature: Gill Marcus.	FV	5.00

130 50 Rand — VF | UNC

2005. Red on multicolor underprint. Lions with cub drinking water at center, male lion head at right, coat of arms at top left, various geometric shapes at lower portion. Back: Sasol oil refinery at lower left center. Watermark: Male lion head. 140x70mm.

- a. Signature: Tito Mboweni. — FV | 13.00
- b. Signature: Gill Marcus. — FV | 12.50

131 100 Rand — VF | UNC

2005. Blue on multicolor underprint. Cape buffalo at center and large water buffalo head at right, coat of arms at top left, various geometric shapes at lower portion. Back: Zebras along bottom from left to center. Watermark: Water buffalo head. 146x70mm.

- a. Signature: Tito Mboweni. — FV | 27.50
- b. Signature: Gill Marcus. — FV | 22.50

132 200 Rand — VF | UNC

2005. Brown on green and multicolor underprint. Leopard at center, large leopard's head at right, coat of arms at top left, various geometric shapes at lower portion. Back: Dish antenna at upper left, modern bridge at lower left. 152x70mm. — FV | 60.00

2012 Issue

133 10 Rand — VF | UNC

ND (2012). Green and multicolor. Nelson Mandela at right. Back: Rhinoceros head at center. 128x70mm. — FV | 3.50

134 20 Rand — VF | UNC

ND (2012). Brown, tan and multicolor. Nelson Mandela at right. Back: Elephant head at center. 134x70mm. — FV | 5.00

135 50 Rand — VF | UNC

ND (2012). Red and multicolor. Nelson Mandela at right. Back: Lion head at center. 140x70mm. — FV | 12.50

136 100 Rand — VF | UNC

ND (2012). Blue and multicolor. Nelson Mandela at right. Back: Cape buffalo head at center. 146x70mm. — FV | 22.50

137 200 Rand — VF | UNC

ND (2012). Brown, green and multicolor. Nelson Mandela at right. Back: Leopard head at center. 152x70mm. — FV | 60.00

The Republic of Korea, situated in northeastern Asia on the southern half of the Korean peninsula between North Korea and the Korean Strait, has an area of 38,025 sq. mi. (98,484 sq. km.) and a population of 44.61 million. Capital: Seoul. The economy is d on agriculture and textiles. Clothing, plywood and textile products are exported.

Japan replaced China as the predominant foreign influence in Korea in 1895 and annexed the peninsular country in 1910. Defeat in World War II brought an end to Japanese rule. U.S. troops entered Korea from the south and Soviet forces entered from the north. The Cairo Conference (1943) had established that Korea should be "free and independent." The Potsdam Conference (1945) set the 38th parallel as the line dividing the occupation forces of the United States and Russia. When Russia refused to permit a U.N. commission designated to supervise reunification elections to enter North Korea, an election was held in South Korea on May 10, 1948. By its determination, the Republic of Korea was inaugurated on Aug. 15, 1948.

Note: For Bank of Chosen notes issued in South Korea under the Allied occupation during the post WWII period 1945 to 1948 refer to Korea listings.

MONETARY SYSTEM:

1 Won (Hwan) = 100 Chon
1 new Won = 10 old Hwan, 1962-

REPLACEMENT NOTES:

#3: H prefix. #13-15: D prefix and no suffix letter.
#30-32, 34, 36-37, sm. crosslet design in front of serial #. #35, 38, 38A, 39, 43-49: notes w/first digit 9 in serial number.

DATING:

The modern notes of Korea are dated according to the founding of the first Korean dynasty, that of the house of Tangun, in 2333 BC.

REPUBLIC

BANK OF KOREA

1958-60 ISSUE

			VF	UNC
23	**50 Hwan** 4291 (1958). Green-blue on olive-green underprint. Archway at left. Back: Green. Statue at center, medieval tortoise warship at right.		60.00	350.

			VF	UNC
24	**500 Hwan** 4291 (1958); 4292 (1959). Dark green. Portrait Syngman Rhee at right. Back: Brownish purple.		40.00	350.

			VF	UNC
25	**1000 Hwan** 4293 (1960); 4294 (1961); 1962. Black on olive underprint. King Sejong the Great at right. Back: Blue-green and light brown. Flaming torch at center.			
		a. 4293 (1960).	10.00	100.
		b. 4294 (1961).	6.00	60.00
		c. 1962.	7.00	65.00

1961-62 ISSUE

			VF	UNC
26	**100 Hwan** 1962. Green on orange and multicolor underprint. Woman reading to child at right. Back: Archway at left, date at bottom right margin.		60.00	325.

			VF	UNC
27	**500 Hwan** 4294 (1961). Blue-green on multicolor underprint. King Sejong the Great at right. Back: Green. Building at right. Eight-character imprint.		80.00	475.

1962 ND ISSUES

Won System

			VF	UNC
28	**10 Jeon** 1962. Deep blue on pale blue and pink underprint.			
		a. Issued note.	.10	.40
		s. Specimen.	—	50.00

			VF	UNC
29	**50 Jeon** 1962. Black on pale green and ochre underprint. Back: Brown.			
		a. Issued note.	.10	.50
		s. Specimen.	—	50.00

30	1 Won	VF	UNC
	ND (1962). Violet on brown underprint.		
	a. Issued note.	.10	1.00
	s. Specimen.	—	100.

31	5 Won	VF	UNC
	ND (1962). Black on gray-green underprint.		
	a. Issued note.	10.00	90.00
	s. Specimen.	—	150.

32	10 Won	VF	UNC
	ND (1962). Brown on green underprint.		
	a. Issued note.	2.00	10.00
	s. Specimen.	—	200.

33	10 Won	VF	UNC
	1962-65; ND. Brown on lilac and green underprint. Tower at left. Back: Medieval tortoise warship at center, date at lower left.		
	a. 1962.	8.00	50.00
	b. 1963.	8.50	52.50
	c. 1964.	4.50	27.50
	d. 1965.	3.00	20.00
	e. ND.	.50	3.00

34	50 Won	VF	UNC
	ND (1962). Red-brown on blue and lilac underprint. Rock in the sea at left. Back: Torch at center.		
	a. Issued note.	15.00	95.00
	s. Specimen.	—	—

35	100 Won	VF	UNC
	1962-69. Green on olive underprint. Archway at left. Underprint: *100 Won* at center. Back: Pagoda and date.		
	a. 1962.	17.50	110.
	b. 1963.	12.50	80.00
	c. 1964.	12.50	75.00
	d. 1965.	12.50	75.00
	e. 1969.	15.00	90.00

36	100 Won	VF	UNC
	ND (1962). Green on blue and gold underprint. Archway at left. Five-petaled blossom at center in underprint. Back: Torch at center.		
	a. Issued note.	12.50	80.00
	s. Specimen.	—	—

37	500 Won	VF	UNC
	ND (1962). Blue on lilac and green underprint. Pagoda portal at left. Back: Torch at center.		
	a. Issued note.	22.50	135.
	s. Specimen.	—	—

1965; 1966 ND Issue

38	100 Won	VF	UNC
	ND (1965). Dark green and blue on multicolor underprint. Bank name and denomination in red. King Sejong the Great at right. Back: Building.		
	a. Issued note.	1.75	5.50
	s. Specimen.	—	—

38A **100 Won** VF UNC
ND (1965). Dark blue-green. Bank name and denomination in brown, King Sejong the Great at right. Back: Building. 2.25 10.00

39 **500 Won** VF UNC
ND (1966). Black on multicolor underprint. City gate at left. Back: Medieval turtle warships.
a. Issued note. 1.50 9.00
s. Specimen. — —

1969-73 ND Issue

40 **50 Won** VF UNC
ND (1969). Black on green and brown underprint. Pavilion at left. Back: Blue. Torch at center.
a. Issued note. 1.00 4.00
s. Specimen. — —

41 **5000 Won**
ND (1972). Brown on green and multicolor underprint. Yi I at right. Back: Large building. Watermark: Yi I. 12.50 40.00

42 **10,000 Won** VF UNC
ND (1973). Dark brown on multicolor underprint. King Sejong the Great at left center. Back: Buildings and pavilion. Watermark: Woman with headdress. 25.00 60.00

1973-79 ND Issue

43 **500 Won** VF UNC
ND (1973). Blue and green on multicolor underprint. Admiral Yi Sun-shin at left, medieval turtle warship at center. Back: Building with steps. 1.00 3.50

44 **1000 Won** VF UNC
ND (1975). Purple on multicolor underprint. Yi Hwang at right. Back: Toansowon Academy at center. Watermark: Flowers. UV: threads fluoresce green. 2.00 5.00

45 **5000 Won** VF UNC
ND (1977). Brown on multicolor underprint. Yi I at right. Back: Ojukon, birthplace of Yi I. Watermark: Yi I. 8.50 20.00

46 **10,000 Won** VF UNC
ND (1979). Black and dark green on multicolor underprint. Water clock at left, King Sejong at right. Back: Kyonghoeru Pavilion at center. Watermark: King Sejong. 20.00 40.00

1983 ND Issue

47 **1000 Won** | VF FV | UNC 4.00

ND (1983). Purple on multicolor underprint. Yi Hwang at right. One raised colored dot for visually impaired at lower left. Back: Buildings of Tosansowon Academy. Watermark: Yi Hwang. UV: threads fluoresce green, central design in shades of green. 151x76mm.

48 **5000 Won** | VF FV | UNC 12.00

ND (1983). Brown on multicolor underprint. Yi I at right. Two raised colored dots for visually impaired at lower left. Back: Ojukon, birthplace of Yi I. Watermark: Yi I. UV: threads fluoresce green, central design shades of green. 156x76mm.

49 **10,000 Won** | VF FV | UNC 22.50

ND (1983). Dark green on multicolor underprint. Water clock at left, King Sejong at right.Three raised colored dots in green for visually impaired at lower left. Back: Kyonghoeru Pavilion at center. Watermark: King Sejong. 161x76mm.

50 **10,000 Won** | VF FV | UNC 20.00

ND (1994). Dark green on multicolor underprint. Like number 49, but with circular dark green lines over watermark area at left, microprinting added under water tower, segmented silver security thread at left center. Back: Kyonghoeru Pavilion at center. Watermark: King Sejong. UV: threads fluoresce green. 161x76mm.

2000-2002 Issue

51 **5000 Won** | VF FV | UNC 9.00

2002. Brown and orange on multicolor underprint. Scholar Yi I at right. Back: Ojukon, the house where Yi I was born. 156x76mm.

52 **10,000 Won**

2000. Dark green on multicolor underprint. Water clock at left, King Sejong at right. Three raised dots in variable ink at lower left. Back: Kyonghoeru Pavilion at center. (c) 2000 in Korean at lower left on face, in English at lower right. 161x76mm.

	VF	UNC
a. Issued note.	FV	20.00
s. Specimen. Red overprint.	—	750.

2004 Bank Check Issue

		VF	UNC
52A	**100,000 Won** 6.2004.	FV	7.50
53	**1,000,000 Won** 6.2004.	FV	20.00

2006; 2007 Issue

54 **1000 Won**

ND (2007). Purple and blue on multicolor underprint. Yi Hwang at right, Myeongnyundang at center. 136x68mm.

	VF	UNC
a. Issued note.	FV	4.00
s. Specimen.	—	75.00

55 5000 Won VF UNC

ND (2006). Brown, rose and green on multicolor underprint. Scholar Yi I at right and the house where he was born at center. Hologram at left center. Back: Tree branch and flowers at left. UV: Security strip fluoresces yellow, threads yellow and blue. 142x68mm.

	VF	UNC
a. Issued note.	FV	5.00
s. Specimen.	—	75.00

56 10,000 Won VF UNC

ND (2007). Dark Green on light green and multicolor underprint. King Sejong at right. Hologram at left center. Back: Astrolabe. 148x68mm.

	VF	UNC
a. Issued note.	FV	10.00
s. Specimen.	—	75.00

57 50,000 Won

ND (2009). Brown and yellow on multicolor underprint. Shin Saim-dang at at right. Back: Painting of Bamboo and Apricot trees. Watermark: Shin and 5 within pentagon. 154x68mm. FV 80.00

SOUTH SUDAN

Egypt attempted to colonize the region of southern Sudan by establishing the province of Equatoria in the 1870s. Islamic Mahdist revolutionaries overran the region in 1885, but in 1898 a British force was able to overthrow the Mahdist regime. An Anglo-Egyptian Sudan was established the following year with Equatoria being the southernmost of its eight provinces. The isolated region was largely left to itself over the following decades, but Christian missionaries converted much of the population and facilitated the spread of English. When Sudan gained its independence in 1956, it was with the understanding that the southerners would be able to participate fully in the political system. When the Arab Khartoum government reneged on its promises, a mutiny began that led to two prolonged periods of conflict (1955-1972 and 1983-2005) in which perhaps 2.5 million people died - mostly civilians - due to starvation and drought. Ongoing peace talks finally resulted in a Comprehensive Peace Agreement, signed in January 2005. As part of this agreement the south was granted a six-year period of autonomy to be followed by a referendum on final status. The result of this referendum, held in January 2011, was a vote of 98% in favor of secession. Independence was attained on 9 July 2011.

REPUBLIC

BANK OF SOUTH SUDAN

(NO BRANCH)

2011 ISSUE

1 5 Piasters VF UNC

ND (2011). Dr. John Garang de Mabior at right. Printer: TLDR (without imprint). 5.00 20.00

2 10 Piasters VF UNC

ND (2011). Dr. John Garang de Mabior at right. Printer: TLDR (without imprint). 5.00 20.00

3 25 Piasters VF UNC

ND (2011). Dr. John Garang de Mabior at right. Printer: TLDR (without imprint). 5.00 20.00

5 1 Pound

ND (2011). Brown and green on multicolor underprint. Dr. John Garang de Mabior at left. Back: Giraffe heard at right. Printer: TDLR (without imprint). 1.00 4.00

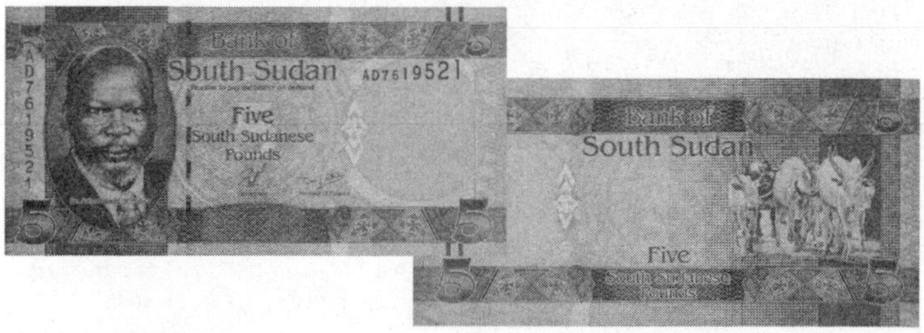

No.	Denomination / Description	VF	UNC
6	**5 Pounds** ND (2011). Brown and rose on multicolor underprint. Dr. John Garang de Mabior at left. Back: Water buffalo pair ar right. Printer: TLDR (without imprint). 120x60mm.	2.00	8.00
7	**10 Pounds** ND (2011). Brown and aqua on multicolor underprint. Dr. John Garang de Mabior at left. Back: Water buffalo pair at right. Printer: TDLR (without imprint). 120x60mm.	4.00	15.00
8	**25 Pounds** ND (2011). Brown and tan on multicolor underprint. Dr. John Garang de Mabior at left. Back: Ibex pair at right. Printer: TDLR (without imprint). 120x60mm.	8.00	25.00
9	**50 Pounds** ND (2011). Brown and purple on multicolor underprint. Dr. John Garang de Mabior at left. Back: Elephant line at right. Printer: TDLR (without imprint).	12.00	45.00
10	**100 Pounds** ND (2011). Brown and blue on multicolor underprint. Dr. John Garang de Mabior at left. Back: Lion lying on ground at right. Printer: TDLR (without imprint).	20.00	90.00

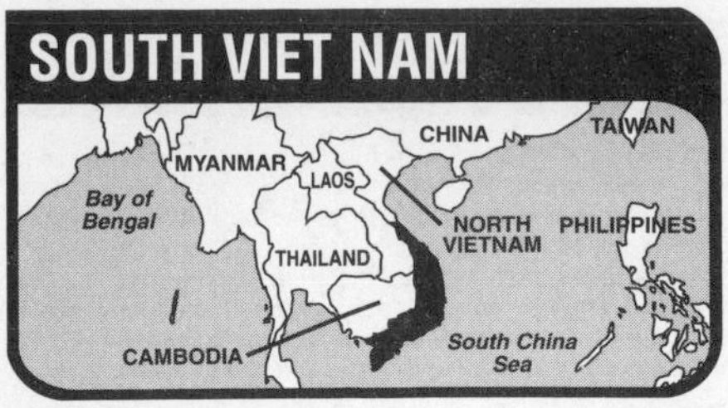

South Viet Nam (the former Republic of Viet Nam), located in Southeast Asia, bounded by North Viet Nam on the north (the former Democratic Republic of Viet Nam), Laos and Cambodia on the west, and the South China Sea on the east and south, had an area of 66,280 sq. mi. (171,665 sq. km.) and a population of 20 million. Capital: Saigon. The economy of the area was predominantly agricultural.

South Viet Nam, the direct successor to the French-dominated regime (also known as the State of Viet Nam), was created after the first Indochina War (between the French and the Viet-Minh) by the Geneva agreement of 1954 which divided Viet Nam at the 17th parallel of latitude.

The elections which would have reunified North and South Viet Nam in 1956 never took place, and the North restarted their war for unification of the country in 1959. In 1975, North Vietnamese forces overran the South reuniting the country under communist rule.

There followed a short period of co-existence of the two Vietnamese states, but the South was now governed by the North through the Peoples Revolutionary Government (PRG). On July 2, 1976, South and North Viet Nam joined to form the Socialist Republic of Viet Nam.

See also Viet Nam.

MONETARY SYSTEM

1 Dông = 100 Xu

Viet Nam - Republic

Ngân-Hàng Quô'c-Gia Viêt-Nam

National Bank of Viet Nam

1962 ND Issue

5	10 Dông	VF	UNC
	ND (1962). Red. Young farm couple at left. Back: Ornate arch. Printer: SBNC. Shade varieties.		
	a. Issued note.	2.00	8.00
	p. Proof. Uniface face and back pair.	—	450.
	s. Specimen. Overprint: *GIAY MAU.*	—	300.

6	20 Dông	VF	UNC
	ND (1962). Brown. Ox cart at left. Back: Woman digging. Printer: SBNC.		
	a. Issued note.	6.00	35.00
	p. Proof. Uniface face and back pair.	—	450.
	s. Specimen. Overprint: *GIAY MAU.*	—	350.
	x. Counterfeit.	—	—

6A	500 Dông	VF	UNC
	ND (1962). Green-blue on gold and pinkish underprint. Dragon at left, palace-like building at left center. Back: Farmer with two water buffalos at right. Watermark: Ngo Dinh Diem.		
	a. Issued note.	200.	700.
	s1. Specimen. Overprint: *GIAY MAU.*	—	1000.
	s2. Specimen. TDLR oval.	—	1000.

1964; 1966 ND Issues

15	1 Dông	VF	UNC
	ND (1964). Light and dark brown on orange and light blue underprint. Back: Red-brown. Farm tractor at right. Watermark: Plant.		
	a. Issued note.	3.00	5.00
	s1. Specimen. *GIAY MAU.*	—	1200.
	s2. Specimen. TDLR oval.	—	1200.

16	20 Dông	VF	UNC
	ND (1964). Green on multicolor underprint. Back: Stylized fish at center. Watermark: Dragon's head.		
	a. Issued note.	.75	9.00
	s. Specimen. *GIAY MAU.*	—	300.

17	50 Dông	VF	UNC
	ND (1966). Purple on multicolor underprint. Leaf tendrils at right		
	a. Issued note.	5.00	25.00
	s. Specimen. *GIAY MAU.*	—	300.

18 100 Dông	VF	UNC
ND (1966). Light and dark brown on light blue underprint. Building with domed roof at right. Back: Power plant, water reservoir and dam. Watermark: Plant.		
a. Issued note.	5.00	35.00
s1. Specimen. Red overprint *GIAY MAU.*	—	300.
s2. Specimen. Black overprint	—	300.

19 100 Dông	VF	UNC
ND (1966). Red on multicolor underprint. Le Van Duyet in national costume at left. Back: Building and ornate gateway at center right.		
a. Watermark: Demon's head.	10.00	40.00
b. Watermark: Le Van Duyet's head.	3.00	15.00
s1. As a. Specimen. TDLR oval.	—	500.
s2. As b. Specimen.	—	500.

20 200 Dông	VF	UNC
ND (1966). Dark brown on multicolor underprint. Nguyen-Hue, warrior, at left. Back: Warrior on horseback leading soldiers.		
a. Watermark: Demon's head.	10.00	45.00
b. Watermark: Nguyen Hue's head.	3.00	25.00
s1. As a. Specimen.	—	500.
s2. As b. Specimen.	—	500.

22 500 Dông		
ND (1964). Brown on multicolor underprint. Museum in Saigon at center. Back: Stylized creatures at center. Watermark: Demon's head.		
a. Issued note.	12.50	50.00
s1. Specimen.	—	300.
s2. Specimen. TDLR oval.	—	600.

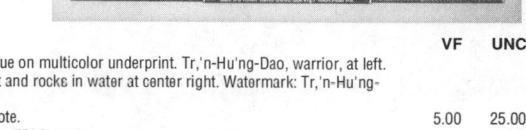

23 500 Dông	VF	UNC
ND (1966). Blue on multicolor underprint. Tr,'n-Hu'ng-Dao, warrior, at left. Back: Sailboat and rocks in water at center right. Watermark: Tr,'n-Hu'ng-Dao, warrior.		
a. Issued note.	5.00	25.00
s. Specimen. TDLR oval.	—	500.
x. Counterfeit. Series S; U; X.	—	15.00

1969-71 ND Issue

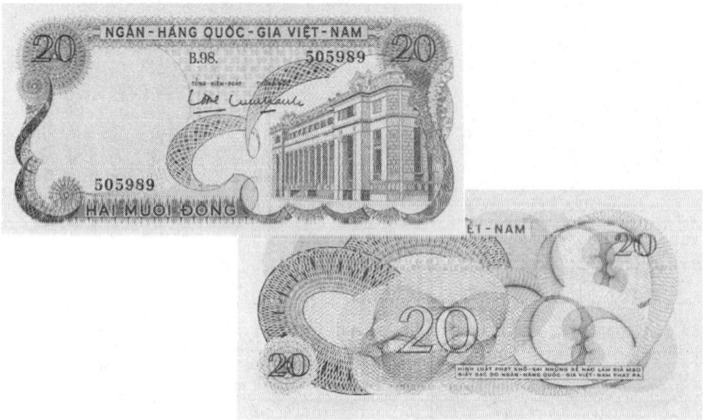

24 20 Dông	VF	UNC
ND (1969). Red on multicolor underprint. Bank building at right. Back: Lathework. Watermark: Tr,'n-Hu'ng-Dao, warrior.		
a. Issued note.	.50	5.00
s. Specimen. *GIAY MAU.*	—	175.

25 50 Dông	VF	UNC
ND (1969). Blue-green on multicolor underprint. Bank building at right. Back: Lathework. Watermark: Tr,'n-Hu'ng-Dao, warrior.		
a. Issued note.	.50	5.00
s. Specimen. *GIAY MAU.*	—	175.

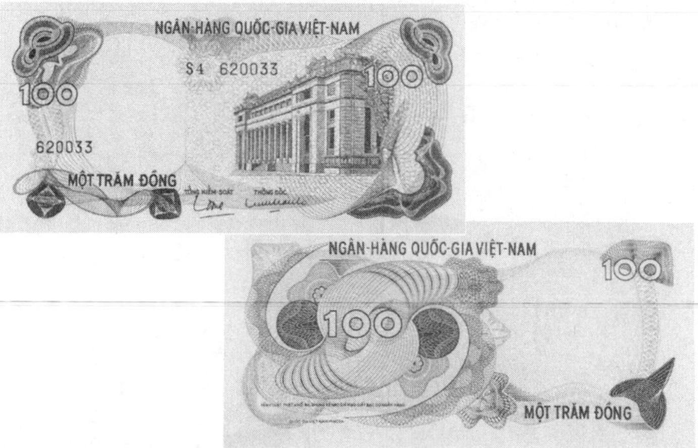

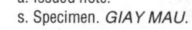

26 100 Dông	VF	UNC
ND (1970). Dark green on multicolor underprint. Bank building at right. Back: Lathework. Watermark: Tr,'n-Hu'ng-Dao, warrior.		
a. Issued note.	.75	5.00
s. Specimen. *GIAY MAU.*	Unc	175.

27 **200 Dông** VF UNC

ND (1970). Purple on multicolor underprint. Bank building at right. Back: Lathework. Watermark: Tr,'n-Hu'ng-Dao, warrior.

	VF	UNC
a. Issued note.	1.25	25.00
s. Specimen. Overprint: *GIAY MAU.*	—	300.

28 **500 Dông** VF UNC

ND (1970). Orange and dark brown on multicolor underprint. Bank building at right. Back: Orange and pale olive-green on multicolor underprint. Lathework. Watermark: Tr,'n-Hu'ng-Dao, warrior.

	VF	UNC
a. Issued note.	.75	5.00
s. Specimen. Overprint: *GIAY MAU.*	—	200.

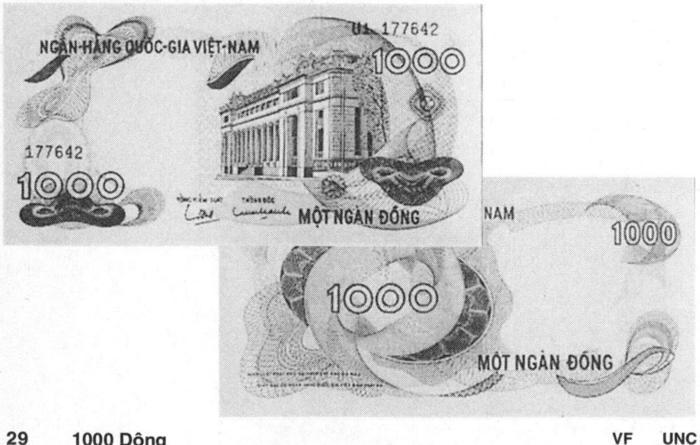

29 **1000 Dông** VF UNC

ND (1971). Turquoise on multicolor underprint. Bank building at right. Back: Lathework. Watermark: Tr,'n-Hu'ng-Dao, warrior.

	VF	UNC
a. Issued note.	5.00	15.00
s. Specimen. *GIAY MAU.*	—	250.

1972; 1975 ND Issue

30 **50 Dông** VF UNC

ND (1972). Blue-gray on multicolor underprint. Palace of Independence at right. Back: Three horses at left center. Watermark: Young woman's head in profile.

	VF	UNC
a. Issued note.	.50	4.00
s. Specimen.	—	400.
ct. Color trial. Purple Palace on face.	—	—

31 **100 Dông** VF UNC

ND (1972). Green on multicolor underprint. Palace of Independence at right. Back: Farmer with two water buffalo at left center. Watermark: Young woman's head in profile.

	VF	UNC
a. Issued note.	.75	5.00
s. Specimen.	—	400.

32 **200 Dông** VF UNC

ND (1972). Wine red on multicolor underprint. Palace of Independence at right. Back: Three deer at left center. Watermark: Young woman's head in profile.

	VF	UNC
a. Issued note.	2.50	15.00
s. Specimen. TDLR oval.	—	500.

		VF	UNC
33	**500 Dông**		
	ND (1972). Orange and olive-brown on multicolor underprint. Palace of Independence at right. Back: Tiger at left center. Watermark: Young woman's head in profile.		
	a. Issued note.	1.25	6.00
	s. Specimen.	—	500.

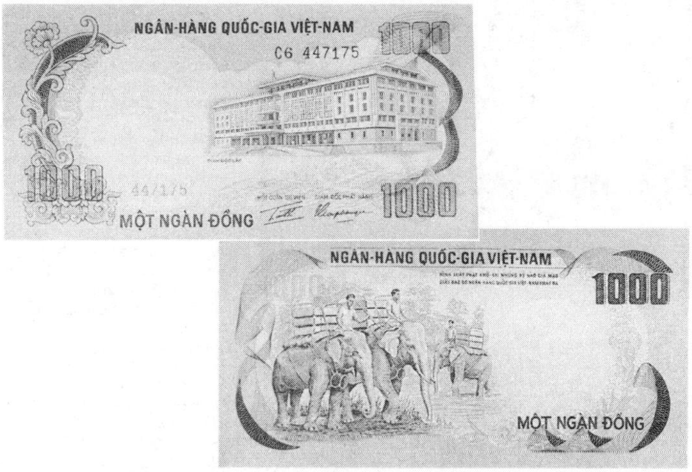

		VF	UNC
34	**1000 Dông**		
	ND (1972). Blue on multicolor underprint. Palace of Independence at right. Back: Three elephants carrying loads at left center. Watermark: Young woman's head in profile. .		
	a. Issued note.	1.25	5.00
	s. Specimen.	—	500.

		VF	UNC
34A	**1000 Dông**		
	ND (1975). Green and multicolor. Stylized fish at left, Truong Cong Dinh at right. Back: Dinh's tomb at upper left, stylized fish at right. Specimen. (Not issued).	—	5000.
35	**5000 Dông**		
	ND (1975). Brown, blue and multicolor. Palace of Independence at right. Back: Leopard at left center. Watermark: Young woman's head in profile. Printer: TDLR. (Not issued).		
	a. Normal serial #.	80.00	500.
	s. Specimen. Overprint: *GAIY MAU.*	—	700.

		VF	UNC
36	**10,000 Dông**		
	ND (1975). Violet and multicolor. Palace of Independence at right. Back: Water buffalo at left center. Watermark: Young woman's head in profile. Printer: TDLR. (Not issued).		
	a. Normal serial #.	80.00	500.
	s. Specimen. Overprint: *GIAY MAU.*	—	700.

Ngân Hàng Viêt Nam

1966 Dated (1975) Transitional Issue

#37-44 were printed in the People's Republic of China for use in South Viet Name after liberation by the National Liberation Front. The Republic of Viet Name notes were converted to these notes before there was another conversion to unite the currency for the entire country.

		VF	UNC
37	**10 Xu**		
	1966 (1975). Brown on multicolor underprint. Drying salt at center. Back: Unloading boats.		
	a. Issued note.	1.25	3.00
	s. Specimen.	—	15.00

		VF	UNC
38	**20 Xu**		
	1966 (1975). Blue on multicolor underprint. Workers on rubber plantation at center. Back: Soldiers greeting farmers with oxen.		
	a. Issued note.	1.25	3.00
	s. Specimen.	—	15.00

		VF	UNC
39	**50 Xu**		
	1966 (1975). Brownish purple on multicolor underprint. Harvesting cane at center. Back: Women weaving rugs.		
	a. Issued note.	2.50	8.00
	s. Specimen.	—	20.00

		VF	UNC
40	**1 Dông**		
	1966 (1975). Red-orange on multicolor underprint. Boats on canal at center. Back: Workers in field.		
	a. Issued note.	3.00	10.00
	s. Specimen.	—	20.00

		VF	UNC
41	**2 Dông**		
	1966 (1975). Blue and green on multicolor underprint. Houseboats under a bridge at center. Back: Soldiers and workers.		
	a. Issued note.	5.00	15.00
	s. Specimen.	—	20.00

42 **5 Dông** VF UNC

1966 (1975). Purple on multicolor underprint. Four women in textile factory at center. Back: Armed soldiers with downed helicopters. .

	VF	UNC
a. Issued note.	6.00	20.00
s. Specimen.	—	25.00

43 **10 Dông** VF UNC

1966 (1975). Red on multicolor underprint. Three women and train at center. Back: Soldiers and people with flag. 148x75mm.

	VF	UNC
a. Issued note.	20.00	40.00
s. Specimen. Overprint: *GIAY MAU* in black on both sides.	—	40.00

44 **50 Dông** VF UNC

1966 (1975). Green and blue on multicolor underprint. Workers in factory at center. Back: Combine harvester.

	VF	UNC
a. Issued note.	75.00	200.
s. Specimen.	—	50.00

The Spanish State, forming the greater part of the Iberian Peninsula of southwest Europe, has an area of 504,782 sq. km. and a population of 40.5 million. Capital: Madrid. The economy is d on agriculture, industry and tourism. Machinery, fruit, vegetables and chemicals are exported.

Spain's powerful world empire of the 16th and 17th centuries ultimately yielded command of the seas to England. Subsequent failure to embrace the mercantile and industrial revolutions caused the country to fall behind Britain, France, and Germany in economic and political power. Spain remained neutral in World Wars I and II but suffered through a devastating civil war (1936-39). A peaceful transition to democracy following the death of dictator Francisco Franco in 1975, and rapid economic modernization (Spain joined the EU in 1986) gave Spain a dynamic and rapidly growing economy and made it a global champion of freedom and human rights. The government continues to battle the Basque Fatherland and Liberty (ETA) terrorist organization, but its major focus for the immediate future will be on measures to reverse the severe economic recession that started in mid-2008.

RULERS:

Francisco Franco, regent, 1937-1975
Juan Carlos I, 1975-

MONETARY SYSTEM:

1 Peseta = 100 Centimos 1874-2001
1 Euro = 100 Cents, 2002-

REPLACEMENT NOTES:

#150 and later, *9A, 9B, 9C* type prefix.

REPUBLIC

BANCO DE ESPAÑA

1965 (1970; 1971) ISSUE

150 **100 Pesetas** VF UNC

19.11.1965 (1970). Brown on multicolor underprint. Gustavo Adolfo Bécquer at center right, couple near fountain at lower left. Back: Woman with parasol at center, Cathedral of Sevilla at left. Watermark: Woman's head. Printer: FNMT. 7.50 20.00

151 **1000 Pesetas** — VF 40.00 — UNC 140.
19.11.1965 (1971). Green on multicolor underprint. San Isidoro at left. Back: Imaginary figure with basilica behind. Watermark: San Isidoro. Printer: FNMT.

1970-71 Issue

152 **100 Pesetas**
17.11.1970 (1974). Brown on pale orange and multicolor underprint. Manuel de Falla at right. Back: The summer residence of the Moorish kings in Granada at left center. Watermark: Manuel de Falla. Printer: FNMT.

	VF	UNC
a. Issued note.	4.00	15.00
s. Specimen.	—	—

153 **500 Pesetas**
23.7.1971 (1973). Blue-gray and black on multicolor underprint. Jacinto Verdaguer at right. Back: View of Mt. Canigó with village of Vignolas d'Oris. Watermark: Jacinto Verdaguer. Printer: FNMT.

	VF	UNC
a. Issued note.	22.50	50.00
s. Specimen.	—	—

1974 Commemorative Issue

#154, Centennial of the Banco de España's becoming the sole issuing bank, 1874-1974

154 **1000 Pesetas** — VF 40.00 — UNC 100.
17.9.1971 (1974). Green and black on multicolor underprint. José Echegaray at right. Back: Bank of Spain in Madrid and commemorative legend. Watermark: José Echegaray. Printer: FNMT.

1976 Issue

155 **5000 Pesetas** — VF 80.00 — UNC 275.
6.2.1976 (1978). Purple and brown on multicolor underprint. King Carlos III at right. Back: Museum of Prado in Madrid at left center. Watermark: King Carlos III.

1982-87 Issue

156 **200 Pesetas** — VF 12.00 — UNC 30.00
16.9.1980 (1984). Brown and orange on multicolor underprint. Leopoldo Garcí de las Alas, known as *Clarín* at right, cross at lower center. Back: Tree at left, cross at center. Watermark: Leopoldo Garcí de las Alas. Printer: FNMT.

157 **500 Pesetas** — VF 14.00 — UNC 35.00
23.10.1979 (1983). Dark blue and black on multicolor underprint. Rosalia de Castro at right. Back: Villa at left center. Watermark: Rosalia de Castro. Printer: FNMT.

		VF	UNC
158	**1000 Pesetas** 23.10.1979 (1982). Gray-blue and green on multicolor underprint. Tree at center, Benito Pérez Galdos at right. Back: Rock formations, mountains and map of Canary Islands. Watermark: Benito Pérez Galdos. Printer: FNMT. 138x76mm.	22.50	55.00
159	**2000 Pesetas** 22.7.1980 (1983). Deep red and orange on multicolor underprint. Rose at center, Juan Ramón Jiménez at right. Back: Villa de la Rosa at left center. Watermark: Juan Ramón Jiménez. Printer: FNMT. 147x79mm.	35.00	85.00

		VF	UNC
160	**5000 Pesetas** 23.10.1979 (1982). Brown and purple on multicolor underprint. Fleur-de-lis at center, King Juan Carlos I at right. Back: Royal Palace in Madrid at left center. Watermark: Juan Carlos I. Printer: FNMT. 156x85mm.	80.00	180.

		VF	UNC
161	**10,000 Pesetas** 24.9.1985 (1987). Gray-black on multicolor underprint. Arms at center, King Juan Carlos I at rigfht. Back: Blue-gray on multicolor underprint. Felipe, Prince of Asturias at left, view of the Escorial at center. Watermark: Juan Carlos I. Printer: FNMT. 165x85mm.	120.	250.

1992 Issue

		VF	UNC
162	**2000 Pesetas** 24.4.1992. Red-violet and orange on multicolor underprint. José Celistino Mutis observing flower at right. Two serial numbers. Back: Royal Botanical Garden and title page of Mutis' work on vertical format. Watermark: José Celistino Mutis. 147x79mm.	27.50	65.00

1992 (1996) Issue

Issued for the 500th Centennial Anniversary of the Discovery of America by Spain.

		VF	UNC
163	**1000 Pesetas** 12.10.1992 (1996). Dark green, purple and red-brown on multicolor underprint. Hernán Cortes at right, with blurred *BANCO DE ESPAÑA* at right margin. Back: Francisco Pizarro on vertical format. Watermark: Francisco Pizarro. 130x65mm.	15.00	37.50

		VF	UNC
164	**2000 Pesetas** 24.4.1992 (1996). Red-violet and orange on multicolor underprint. Modified portrait of José Celistino Mutis observing flower at right, with blurred *BANCO DE ESPAÑA* at right margin. One serial number. Back: Royal Botanical Garden and title page of Mutis' work on vertical format. Watermark: José Celistino Mutis. 138x68mm.	25.00	60.00

		VF	UNC
165	**5000 Pesetas** 12.10.1992 (1996). Violet-brown, brown and red-brown on multicolor underprint. Christopher Columbus at right, with blurred *BANCO DE ESPAÑA* at right margin. Back: Astrolabe at lower center on vertical format. Watermark: Christopher Columbus. 146x71mm.	55.00	135.

		VF	UNC
166	**10,000 Pesetas** 12.10.1992 (1996). Slate blue on multicolor underprint. King Juan Carlos I at right, *Casa de América* in Madrid at lower center, with blurred *BANCO DE ESPAÑA* at right margin. Back: A. de Ulloa y de Jorge Juan above astronomical navigation diagram on vertical format. Watermark: Juan Carlos I. 154x74mm.	110.	225.

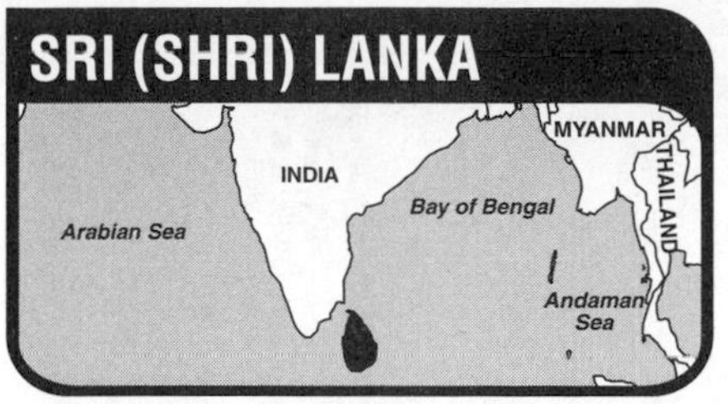

The Democratic Socialist Republic of Sri Lanka is situated in the Indian Ocean 18 miles (29 km.) southeast of India, has an area of 65,610 sq. km. and a population of 21.13 million. Capital: Colombo. The economy is chiefly agricultural. Tea, coconut products and rubber are exported.

The first Sinhalese arrived in Sri Lanka late in the 6th century B.C. probably from northern India. Buddhism was introduced in about the mid-third century B.C., and a great civilization developed at the cities of Anuradhapura (kingdom from circa 200 B.C. to circa A.D. 1000) and Polonnaruwa (from about 1070 to 1200). In the 14th century, a south Indian dynasty established a Tamil kingdom in northern Sri Lanka. The coastal areas of the island were controlled by the Portuguese in the 16th century and by the Dutch in the 17th century. The island was ceded to the British in 1796, became a crown colony in 1802, and was united under British rule by 1815. As Ceylon, it became independent in 1948; its name was changed to Sri Lanka in 1972. Tensions between the Sinhalese majority and Tamil separatists erupted into war in 1983. Tens of thousands have died in the ethnic conflict that continues to fester. After two decades of fighting, the government and Liberation Tigers of Tamil Eelam (LTTE) formalized a cease-fire in February 2002 with Norway brokering peace negotiations. Violence between the LTTE and government forces intensified in 2006 and the government regained control of the Eastern Province in 2007. In January 2008, the government officially withdrew from the ceasefire, and has begun engaging the LTTE in the northern portion of the country.

See also Ceylon for earlier listings.

RULERS:

British, 1796-1972

MONETARY SYSTEM:

1 Rupee = 100 Cents, ca. 1830-

REPUBLIC

CENTRAL BANK OF CEYLON

1977 ISSUE

		VF	UNC
81	**50 Rupees** 26.8.1977. Purple and green on multicolor underprint. Sri Lanka arms at right. Signature: Ronnie de Mel and Herbert Tennekoon. Serial # prefix: *N*. Back: Terraced hillside. Watermark: Lion with sword. Printer: BWC. 151x79mm.	15.00	50.00

		VF	UNC
82	**100 Rupees** 26.8.1977. Purple and brown on multicolor underprint. Sri Lanka arms at right. Signature: Ronnie de Mel and Herbert Tennekoon. Serial # prefix: *W*. Back: Shrine at left center. Watermark: Lion with sword. Printer: BWC. 162x86mm.		
	a. Issued note.	20.00	95.00
	s. Specimen.	—	150.

1979 ISSUE

#83-88 Replacement notes: Serial # prefix *Z/1*.

		VF	UNC
83	**2 Rupees** 26.3.1979. Red on multicolor underprint. Fish at right. Signatures: Ronnie de Mel and Warnasena Rasaputram. Serial # prefix: *A*. Back: Butterfly and lizard. Vertical format. Watermark: Lion with sword. 108x60mm.		
	a. Issued note.	1.25	6.00
	s. Specimen.	—	100.

		VF	UNC
84	**5 Rupees** 26.3.1979. Gray on multicolor underprint. Butterfly and lizard at right. Signatures: Ronnie de Mel and Warnasena Rasaputram. Serial # prefix: *F*. Back: Flying squirrel and White-faced Starling. Vertical format. Watermark: Lion with sword. 117x64mm.		
	a. Issued note.	4.00	15.00
	s. Specimen.	—	100.

		VF	UNC
85	**10 Rupees** 26.3.1979. Green, brown and black on multicolor underprint. Sri Lanka Grey Hornbill in tree at center. Signatures: Ronnie de Mel and Warnasena Rasaputram. Serial # prefix: *H*. Back: Flowers and Yellow-eared Bulbul. Vertical format. Watermark: Lion with sword. 127x67mm.		
	a. Issued note.	7.50	30.00
	s. Specimen.	—	125.

86 20 Rupees VF UNC

26.3.1979. Brown and green on multicolor underprint. Ceylon Wood Pigeon at center, monkey at right. Signatures: Ronnie de Mel and Warnasena Rasaputram. Serial # prefix: *K*. Back: Bird, tree and animals. Vertical format. Watermark: Lion with sword. 137x70mm.

	VF	UNC
a. Issued note.	10.00	40.00
s. Specimen.	—	150.

87 50 Rupees VF UNC

26.3.1979. Blue and brown on multicolor underprint. Butterfly at center, Red-faced Malcoha at right. Signatures: Ronnie de Mel and Warnasena Rasaputram. Serial # prefix: *T*. Back: Lizard and Ceylon Spurfowl. Vertical format. Watermark: Lion with sword. 146x73mm.

	VF	UNC
a. Issued note.	25.00	100.
s. Specimen.	—	220.

88 100 Rupees VF UNC

26.3.1979. Gold, green and black on multicolor underprint. Snakes and tree at center, Sri Lanka Myna at right.Signatures: Ronnie de Mel and Warnasena Rasaputram. Serial # prefix: *Z*. Back: Yellow-fronted Barbet in tree, butterfly below. Vertical format. Watermark: Lion with sword. 156x76mm.

	VF	UNC
a. Issued note.	30.00	150.
s. Specimen.	—	325.

1981 Issue

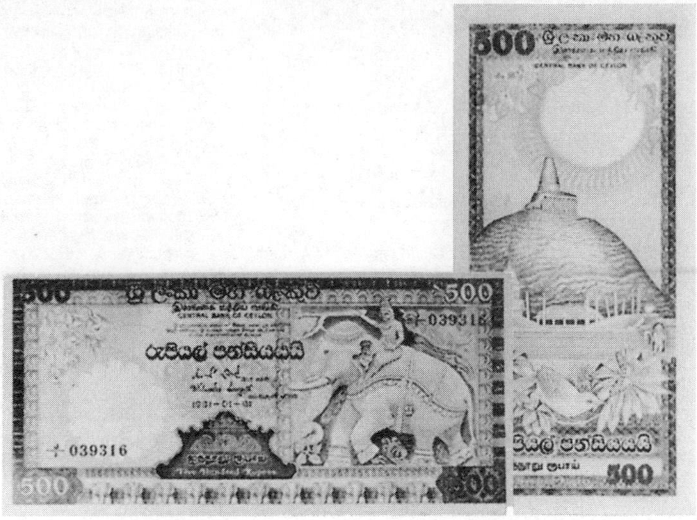

89 500 Rupees VF UNC

1981; 1985. Brown and purple on multicolor underprint. Elephant with rider at right. Signatures: Ronnie de Mel and Warnasena Rasaputram. Serial # prefix: *J*. Back: Abhayagiri Stupa, Anuradhapura temple on hill in vertical format. Watermark: Lion with sword. 165x79mm.

	VF	UNC
a. 1.1.1981.	30.00	150.
b. 1.1.1985.	50.00	200.

90 1000 Rupees VF UNC

1.1.1981. Green on multicolor underprint. Dam at right. Signatures: Ronnie de Mel and Warnasena Rasaputram. Serial # prefix: *P*. Back: Peacock and mountains in vertical format. Watermark: Lion with sword. 75x250mm.

	VF	UNC
a. Issued note.	75.00	250.
s. Specimen.	—	—

1982 Issue

91	5 Rupees	VF	UNC
	1.1.1982. Light red on multicolor underprint. Ruins at right. Signatures: Ronnie de Mel and Warnasena Rasaputram. Serial # prefix: *A*. Back: Stone carving of deity and child in vertical format. Watermark: Lion with sword. Printer: BWC. 119x64mm.		
	a. Issued note.	.75	5.00
	s. Specimen.	—	100.

92	10 Rupees	VF	UNC
	1982; 1985. Olive-green on multicolor underprint. Temple of the Tooth in Kandy at right.Signatures: Ronnie de Mel and Warnasena Rasaputram. Serial # prefix: *D*. Back: Shrine in vertical format. Watermark: Lion with sword. Printer: BWC. 127x67mm.		
	a. 1.1.1982.	1.00	7.50
	b. 1.1.1985.	1.00	6.00
	s. Specimen.	—	100.

93	20 Rupees	VF	UNC
	1982; 1985. Purple and red on multicolor underprint. Moonstone at right. Signatures: Ronnie de Mel and Warnasena Rasaputram. Serial # prefix: *F*. Back: Dagoba Shrine in vertical format. Watermark: Lion with sword. Printer: BWC. 137x70mm.		
	a. 1.1.1982.	2.00	12.50
	b. 1.1.1985.	2.00	11.00
	s. Specimen.	—	110.

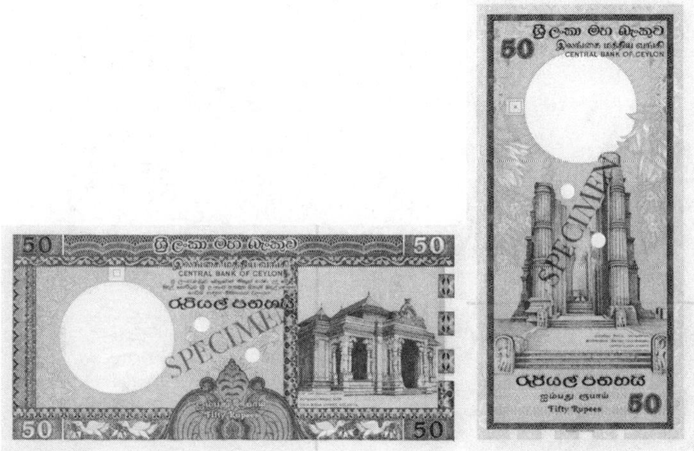

94	50 Rupees	VF	UNC
	1.1.1982. Dark blue and dark brown on multicolor underprint. Building in Kelaniya at right. Signatures: Ronnie de Mel and Warnasena Rasaputram. Serial # prefix: *H*. Back: Ruins of temple at Polonnaruwa at center in vertical format. Watermark: Lion with sword. Printer: BWC. 146x73mm.		
	a. Issued note.	4.00	20.00
	s. Specimen.	—	125.

95	100 Rupees	VF	UNC
	1.1.1982. Orange and brown on multicolor underprint. Stone carving of lion at lower right. .Signatures: Ronnie de Mel and Warnasena Rasaputram. Serial # prefix: *S*. Back: Parliament building in vertical format. Watermark: Lion with sword. Printer: BWC. 146x76mm.		
	a. Issued note.	5.00	37.50
	s. Specimen.	—	160.

Srí Lanká Maha Bänkuva

Central Bank of Sri Lanka

1987-89 Issue

#96-100 similar to #89 and 92-95 but with bank name changed in English from *Ceylon* to *Sri Lanka*. Printer: BWC.

96	10 Rupees	VF	UNC
	1987-90. Green on multicolor underprint. Temple of the Tooth in Kandy at right. Serial # prefix: *F*. Back: Shrine in vertical format. Watermark: Lion with sword. Printer: BWC. UV: value 10 and lion with sword fluoresce yellow. Back leaves yellow. 127x67mm.		
	a. Signature: Ronnie de Mel and warnasena Rasaputram. 1.1.1987.	.75	4.00
	b. Signature: M. H. M. Nainamarikkar & H. N. S. Karunatellake. 21.11.1988.	.75	4.00
	c. Signature: D. B. Wijethunga & H. N.S. Karunatillake. 21.2.1989.	.75	4.00
	d. As c. Dot after second signature. 21.2.1989.	.75	4.00
	e. Signature: D. B. Wijethunga and H. N. S. Karunatillake. 5.4.1990.	.75	4.00
	r. Replacement note. Serial # prefix: *R/1*.	—	9.00

97 20 Rupees VF UNC

1988-90. Purple and red on multicolor underprint. Moonstone at right. Serial # prefix: *E.* Back: Dagoba Shrine in vertical format. Watermark: Lion with sword. Printer: BWC. 137x70mm.

	VF	UNC
a. Signature: M. H. M. Nainamarikkar and H. N. S. Karunatillake. 21.11.1988.	4.00	25.00
b. Signature: D. B. Wijethunga and H. N. S. Karunatillake. 21.2.1989	1.00	6.00
c. Signature: D. B. Wijethunga and H. N. S. Karunatillake. 5.4.1990.	1.00	6.00
r. Replacement note. Serial # prefix: *R/3.*	—	11.00

98 50 Rupees VF UNC

1988-90. Blue and brown on multicolor underprint. Building in Kelaniya at right. Serial # prefix *D.* Back: Ruins of temple at Polonnaruwa at center in vertical format. Watermark: Lion with sword. Printer: BWC. 146x73mm.

	VF	UNC
a. Signature: M. H. M. Nainamarikkar and H. N. S. Karunatillake. 21.11.1988.	2.00	12.50
b. Signature: D. B. Wijethunga and H. N. S. Karunatillake. 21.2.1989.	2.00	12.50
c. As b. 5.4.1990.	2.00	12.50

99 100 Rupees

1987-90. Orange and brown on multicolor underprint. Stone carving of lion at lower right. Serial # prefix: *C.* Back: Parliament building in vertical format. Watermark: Lion with sword. Printer: BWC. 146x73mm.

	VF	UNC
a. Signature: Ronnie de Mel and Warnasena Rasaputram. 1.1.1987.	2.00	20.00
b. Signature: M. H. M. Nainamarikkar and Warnasena Rasaputram. 1.2.1988.	3.00	20.00
c. Signature: D. B. Wijethunga & H. N. S. Karunatillake. 21.2.1989.	3.00	20.00
d. As c. 5.4.1990.	3.00	20.00

100 500 Rupees

1987-90. Brown and purple on multicolor underprint. Similar to #89 but with larger watermark area, vertical silver segmented security strip, bird and borders deeper red brown. Serial # prefix: *B.* Back: Hill and temple in purple in vertical format. Watermark: Lion with sword. Printer: BWC. 165x79mm.

	VF	UNC
a. Signature: Ronnie de Mel and Warnasena Rasaputram. 1.1.1987.	14.00	75.00
b. Signature: M. H. M. Nainamarikkar & H. N. S. Karunatellake. 21.11.1988.	14.00	75.00
c. Signature: D. B. Wijetunga & H. N. S. Karunatillake. 21.2.1989.	14.00	75.00
d. As c. 5.4.1990.	14.00	75.00
r. Replacement note: Serial # prefix: *R/7.*	—	80.00

101 1000 Rupees VF UNC

1987-90. Deep green and purple on multicolor underprint. Victoria Dam at right. Serial # prefix: *A.* Back: Peacock and University of Ruhuna in vertical format. Watermark: Lion with sword. Printer: BWC. 175x83mm.

	VF	UNC
a. Signature: Ronnie de Mel and Warnasena Rasaputram. 1.1.1987.	25.00	35.00
b. Signature: D. B. Wijethunga and H. N. S. Karunatillake. 21.2.1989.	25.00	100.
c. As b. 5.4.1990.	25.00	100.

1991 Issue

#102-107 Replacement notes: Serial # prefix *Z/1.*

102 10 Rupees VF UNC

1991-94. Deep brown and green on multicolor underprint. Sinhalese Chinze at right. Serial # prefix: *M.* Back: Painted stork at top left, Presidential Secretariat building in Colombo, flowers in lower foreground Watermark: Lion with sword. Printer: TDLR. UV: value 10 in box fluoresce yellow. 122x61mm.

	VF	UNC
a. Signature: D. B. Wijethunga and H. N. S. Karunatillake. 1.1.1991.	.50	2.00
b. Signature: D. B. Wijethunga and H. B. Disanayaka. 1.7.1992.	.50	2.00
c. Signature: C. B. Kumaratunga and H. B. Disanayaka. 19.8.1994.	.50	2.00
r. Replacement note: Serial # prefix: *Z/1.*	—	7.00

No.	Description	VF	UNC
103	**20 Rupees**		
	1991-94. Purple and red on multicolor underprint. Native bird mask at right. Serial # prefix: *L*. Back: Two youths fishing, sea shells in vertical format. Watermark: Lion with sword. Printer: TDLR. 129x64mm.		
	a. Signatures: D. B. Wijethunga & H. N. S. Karunatillake. 1.1.1991.	.75	3.50
	b. Signatures: D. B. Wijethunga & H. B. Disanayaka. 1.7.1992.	.75	3.50
	c. Signatures: C. B. Kumaratunga and H. B. Disanayaka. 19.8.1994.	5.00	20.00
	r. Replacement note: Serial # prefix: *Z/2*.	—	8.00

No.	Description	VF	UNC
104	**50 Rupees**		
	1991-94. Brown-violet, deep blue and blue-green on multicolor underprint. Male dancer with local headdress at right. Serial # prefix: *K*. Back: Butterflies above temple ruins, with shield and ornamental sword hilt in lower foreground in vertical format. Watermark: Lion with sword. Printer: TDLR. 136x68mm.		
	a. Signature: D. B. Wijethunga and H. N. S. Karunatillake. 1.1.1991.	1.00	6.00
	b. Signatures: D. B. Wijethunga and H. B. Disanayaka. 1.7.1992.	1.00	6.00
	c. Signatures: C. B. Kumaratunga and H. B. Disanayaka. 19.8.1994.	1.00	6.00
	r. Replacement note: Serial # prefix: *Z/3*.	—	11.00

No.	Description	VF	UNC
105	**100 Rupees**		
	1991-92. Orange and dark brown on multicolor underprint. Decorative urn at right. Serial # prefix: *J*. Back: Tea leaf pickers, two Rose-ringed Parakeets at bottom in vertical format. Watermark: Lion with sword. Printer: TDLR. 143x72mm.		
	a. Signature: D. B. Wijethunga and H. N. S. Karunatillake. Without dot on value in Tamil at left. 1.1.1991.	20.00	100.
	b. As a. With dot on value in Tamil at left. 1.1.1991.	4.00	15.00
	c. Signatures: D. B. Wijethunga and H. B. Disanayaha. 1.7.1992.	4.00	15.00
	r. Replacement note: Serial # prefix: *Z/4*.	—	20.00
105A	**100 Rupees**		
	1.7.1992. Orange and dark brown on multicolor underprint. Decorative urn at right. Signatures: D. B. Wijethunga and H. B. Disanayaka. Serial # prefix: *J*. Back: Orange on multicolor underprint. Tea leaf pickers, two Rose-ringed Parakeets at bottom in vertical format. Watermark: Chinze. 3x8.5mm.	3.00	10.00

No.	Description	VF	UNC
106	**500 Rupees**		
	1991-92. Dark brown, purple and brown-orange on multicolor underprint. Musicians at right, dancer at left center. Serial # prefix: *H*. Back: Stork-billed Kingfisher above temple and orchids in vertical format. Watermark: Lion with sword. Printer: TDLR. 150x75mm.		
	a. Signatures: D. B. Wijethunga and H. N. S. Karunatillake. 1.1.1991.	10.00	45.00
	b. Signatures: D. B. Wijethunga and H. B. Disanayaka. 1.7.1992.	15.00	60.00
	r. Replacement note. Serial # prefix: *Z/5*.	—	65.00

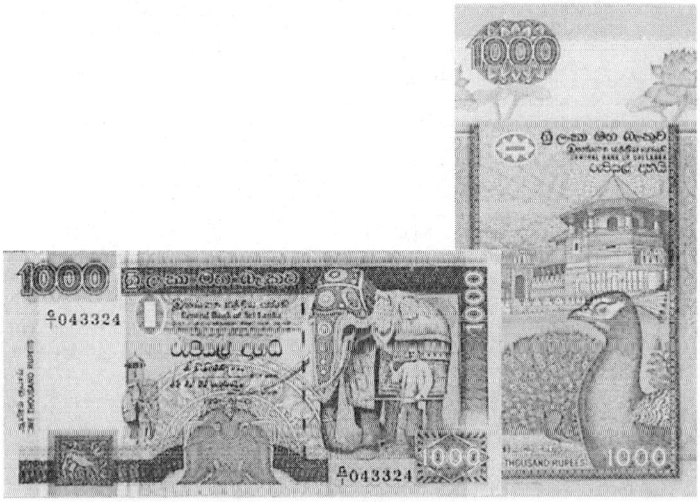

No.	Description	VF	UNC
107	**1000 Rupees**		
	1991-92. Brown, dark green and purple on multicolor underprint. Chinze at lower left, two-headed bird at bottom center, elephant with trainer at right. Serial # prefix: *G*. Back: Peacocks on palace lawn; lotus flowers above and Octagon Temple of the Tooth in Kandy in vertical format. Watermark: Lion with sword. Printer: TDLR. 157x79mm.		
	a. Signatures: D. B. Wijethunga and H. N. S. Karunatillake. 1.1.1991.	15.00	65.00
	b. Signatures: D. B. Wijethunga and H. B. Disanayaka. 1.7.1992.	20.00	65.00
	r. Replacement note: Serial # prefix: *Z/6*.	—	70.00

1995 Issue

#108-113 backs have a vertical format. Enhanced latent image security feature at lower ctr. on face. Printer: TDLR.

No.	Description	VF	UNC
108	**10 Rupees**		
	15.11.1995. Deep brown and green on multicolor underprint. Sinhalese Chinze at right. Enhanced latent image security feature at lower center. Signatures: C. B. Kumaratunga and A. S. Jayawardena. Serial # prefix: *M*. Back: Painted stork at top left, Presidential Secretariat building in Colombo, flowers in lower foreground Watermark: Lion with sword. Printer: TDLR. UV: value 10 in box fluoresce yellow. Back: bird's beak and flowers yellow. 122x61mm.		
	a. Issued note.	FV	2.00
	r. Replacement note: Serial # prefix: *Z/1*.	—	6.00
109	**20 Rupees**		
	15.11.1995. Purple and red on multicolor underprint. Native bird mask at right. Enhanced latent image security feature at lower center. Signatures: CX. B. Kumaratunga and A. S. Jayawardena. Serial # prefix: *L*. Back: Two youths fishing, sea shells in vertical format. Watermark: Lion with sword. Printer: TDLR. 129x64mm.		
	a. Issued note.	FV	2.00
	r. Replacement note. Serial # prefix: *Z/3*.	—	6.00

		VF	UNC
110	**50 Rupees** 15.11.1995. Brown-violet, deep blue and blue-green on multicolor underprint. Male dancer with local headdress at right.Enhanced latent image security feature at lower center. Signatures: C. B. Kumaratunga and A. S. Jayawardena. Serial # prefix: *K*. Back: Butterflies above temple ruins, with shield and ornamental sword hilt in lower foreground in vertical format. Watermark: Lion with sword. Printer: TDLR. 136x68mm.		
	a. Issued note.	FV	4.00
	r. Replacement note. Serial # prefix: *Z/3*.	—	9.00

		VF	UNC
111	**100 Rupees** 15.11.1995. Dark brown and orange on multicolor underprint. Decorative urn at right. Enhanced latent image security feature at lower center. Signatures C. B. Kumaratunga and A. S. Jayawardena. Serial # prefix: *J*. Back: Tea leaf pickers, two Rose-ringed Parakeets at bottom in vertical format. Watermark: Lion with sword. Printer: TDLR. 143x72mm.		
	a. Issued note.	FV	10.00
	r. Replacement note. Serial # prefix: *Z/4*.	—	15.00
112	**500 Rupees** 15.11.1995. Dark brown, purple and brown-orange on multicolor underprint. Musicians at right, dancer at left center. Enhanced latent image security feature at lower center. Signatrues: C. B. Kumaratunga and A. S. Jayawardena. Serial # prefix: *H*. Back: Stork-billed Kingfisher above temple and orchids in vertical format. Watermark: Lion with sword. Printer: TDLR. . 150x75mm.		
	a. Issued note.	FV	35.00
	r. Replacement note. Serial # prefix: *Z/5*.	—	40.00
113	**1000 Rupees** 15.11.1995. Brown, dark green and purple on multicolor underprint. Chinze at lower left, two-headed bird at bottomcenter, elephant with traineer at right. Enhanced latent image security feature at lower center. Signatures: C. B. Kumaratunga and A. S. Jayawardena. Ser Back: Peacocks on palace lawn; lotus flowers above and Octagon Temple of the Tooth in Kandy in vertical format. Watermark: Lion with sword. Printer: TDLR. 157x79mm.		
	a. Issued note.	FV	50.00
	r. Replacement note: Serial # prefix: *Z/6*.	—	55.00

1998 Commemorative Issue

#114, 50th Anniversary of Independence, 1948-1998

		VF	UNC
114	**200 Rupees** 4.2.1998. Greenish black on blue, orange and multicolor underprint. Temple at upper center right above a collage of modern scenes across bottom. Signatures: C. B. Kumaratunga and A. S. Jayawardena. Back: Palace at upper left center above collage of medieval scenes of British landing across bottom right. Polymer plastic. 146x74mm.		
	a. Red serial # in folder.	FV	20.00
	b. Black serial #.	FV	10.00

2001 Issue

		VF	UNC
115	**10 Rupees** 2001-06. Deep brown and green on multicolor underprint. Sinhalese Chinze at right. Enhanced latent image security feature at lower center. Back: Painted stork at top left, Presidential Secretariat building in Colombo, flowers in lower foreground Watermark: Lion with sword. Printer: TDLR. UV: value 10 in box and central design fluoresce yellow. Back flowers and bird beak yellow. 122x61mm.		
	a. Signatures: K. N. Choksy and A. S. Jayawardena. 12.12.2001.	FV	2.00
	b. Signatures: Sarath Amunugama and A. S. Jayawardena. 10.4.2004.	FV	1.00
	c. Signatures: Sarath Amunugama and Sunil Mendis. 1.7.2004.	FV	1.00
	d. Signatures: Mahinda Rajapaksa and Sunil Mendis. 19.11.2005.	FV	1.00
	e. Signatures: Mahinda Rahapaksa and Ajith Nivard Cabral. 3.7.2006.	FV	1.00

		VF	UNC
116	**20 Rupees** 2001; 2004; 2005; 2006. Purple and red on multicolor underprint. Native bird mask at right. Enhanced latent image security feature at lower center. Serial # prefix: *L*. Back: Two youths fishing, sea shells on vertical format. Watermark: Lion with sword. Printer: TDLR. UV: value 20 in box fluoresce yellow. Back fish and design elements orange. 130x65mm.		
	a. Signatures: K. N. Choksy and A. S. Jayawardena. 12.12.2001.	FV	2.50
	b. Signatures: Sarath Amunugama and A. S. Jayawardena. 10.4.2004.	FV	1.00
	c. Signatures: Sarath Amunugama and Sunil Mendis. 1.7.2004.	FV	1.00
	d. Signatures: Mahinda Rajapaksa and Sunil Mendis. 19.11.2005.	FV	1.00
	e. Signatures: Mahinda Rajapaksa and Ajith Nivard Cabral. 7.3.2006.	FV	1.00
	r. Replacement note. Serial # prefix: *Z/2*.	—	—

117	50 Rupees	VF	UNC
	2001-06. Brown-violet, deep blue and blue-green on multicolor underprint. Male dancer with local headdress at right. Enhanced latent image security feature at lower center. Serial # prefix: *K*. Back: Butterflies above temple ruins, with shield and ornamental sword hilt in lower foreground on vertical format. Watermark: Lion with sword. Printer: TDLR. 136x68mm.		
	a. Signatures: K. N. Choksy and A. S. Jayawardena. 12.12.2001.	FV	3.00
	b. Signatures: Sarath Amunugama and A. S. Jayawardena. 10.4.2004.	FV	2.00
	c. Signatures: Sarath Amunugama and Sunil Mendis. 1.7.2004.	FV	2.00
	d. Signatures: Mahinda Rajapaksa and Sunil Mendis. 19.11.2005.	FV	2.00
	e. Signatures: Mahinda Rajapaksa and Ajith Nivard Cabral. 3.7.2006.	FV	2.00
	r. Replacement note. Serial # prefix: *Z/3*.	—	—

118	100 Rupees	VF	UNC
	2001; 2004; 2005. Dark brown and orange on multicolor underprint. Decorative urn at right. Enhanced latent image security feature at lower center. Serial # prefix: *J*. Back: Tea leaf pickers, two Rose-ringed Parakeets at bottom on vertical format. Watermark: Lion with sword. Printer: TDLR. UV: value 100 in box fluoresce yellow. Back portions of flowerand upper design yellow. 144x72mm.		
	a. Signatures: K. N. Choksy and A. S. Jayawardena. 12.12.2001.	FV	5.00
	b. Signatures: Sarath Amunugama and A. S. Jayawardena. 1.7.2004.	FV	4.00
	c. Signatures: Mahinda Rajapaksa and Sunil Mendis. 19.11.2005.	FV	4.00
	r. Replacement note. Serial # prefix: *Z/4*.	—	—

119	500 Rupees	VF	UNC
	2001; 2004; 2005. Dark brown, purple and brown-orange on multicolor underprint. Musicians at right, dancer at left center. Enhanced latent image security feature at lower center. Serial # prefix: *H*. Back: Stork-billed Kingfisher above temple and orchids on vertical format. Watermark: Lion with sword. Printer: TDLR. 150x75mm.		
	a. Signatures: K. N. Choksy and A. S. Jayawardena. 12.12.2001.	FV	17.50
	b. Signatures: Sarath Amunugama and A. S. Jayawardena. 10.4.2004.	FV	15.00
	c. Signatures: Sarath Amunugama and Sunil Mendis. 1.7.2004.	FV	15.00
	d. Signatures: Mahinda Rajapaksa and Sunil Mendis. 19.11.2005.	FV	14.00
	r. Replacement note. Serial # prefix: *Z/5*.	—	—

120	1000 Rupees	VF	UNC
	2001; 2004, 2006. Brown, dark green and purple on multicolor underprint. Chinze at lower left, two-headed bird at bottomcenter, elephant with traineer at right. Enhanced latent image security feature at lower center. Serial # prefix: *G*. Back: Peacocks on palace lawn; lotus flowers above and Octagon Temple of the Tooth in Kandy on vertical format. Watermark: Lion with sword. Printer: TDLR. 156x78mm.		
	a. Signatures: K. N. Choksy and A. S. Jayawardena. 12.12.2001.	FV	22.50
	b. Signatures: Sarath Amunugama and A. S. Jayawardena. 10.4.2004.	FV	20.00
	c. Signatures: Sarath Amunugama and Sunil Mendis. 1.7.2004.	FV	20.00
	d. Signatures: Mahinda Rajapaksa and Ajith Nivard Cabral. 7.3.2006.	FV	20.00
	r. Replacement note: Serial # prefix: *Z/6*.	—	—

121	2000 Rupees	VF	UNC
	2.11.2005; 7.3.2006. Green on orange and yellow on multicolor underprint. Sirigiya mountain top, elephants and forest. Serial # prefix: *P*. Back: Maiden of Sirigiya Frescoe. Vertical format. Watermark: Lion with sword. Printer: TDLR 164x82mm.		
	a. Signature Sarath Amunugama and Sunil Mendis. 2.11.2005.	FV	35.00
	b. Signatures: Mahinda Rajapaksa and Ajith Nivard Cabral. 7.3.2006.	FV	30.00
	r. Replacement note: Serial # prefix: *Z/7*.	—	—

2009 Commemorative Issue

122	1000 Rupees	VF	UNC
	20.5.2009. Light blue and multicolor. President Mahinda Rajapaksa with arms raised at right. Signatures: Mahinda Rajapaksa and Ajith Nivard Cabral. Serial # prefix *Q*. Back: Security forces raising flag. Watermark: Lion with sword. 156x82mm.		
	a. Issued note.	FV	15.00
	b. Low serial # in a commemorative folder.	—	20.00
	r. Replacement note: Serial # prefix: *X/1*.	12.00	50.00

2010 Issue

123 20 Rupees | VF | UNC

1.1.2010. Maroon and multicolor Port of Colombo at center, owl at right. Signatures: Mahinda Rajapaksa and Ajith Nivard Cabral. Serial # prefix: *W*. Back: Ves Netuma dancer and Geta Bera drummer. Vertical format. Watermark: Owl and 20. Printer: DLR. 128x67mm.

	VF	UNC
a. Issued note.	FV	.50
b. Low serial # in a commemorative folder.	—	2.00
r. Replacement note: Serial # prefix: *Z/2*.	—	4.00

124 50 Rupees | VF | UNC

1.1.2010. Blue and multicolor Manampitlya bridges at center, dull blue flycatcher at right. Signatures: Mahinda Rajapaksa and Ajith Nivard Cabral. Serial # prefix: *V*. Back: Yakbera drummer and Vadiga Patuna dancer. Vertical format. Watermark: Flycatcher bird and 50. Printer: DLR. 133x67mm.

	VF	UNC
a. Issued note.	FV	2.00
b. Low serial # in commemorative folder.	—	2.50
r. Replacement note: Serial # prefix: *Z/3*.	—	6.00

125 100 Rupees | VF | UNC

1.1.2010. Orange and yellow. Norochocholai Power plant at center, orange billed babbler at right. Signature Mahinda Rajapaksa and Ajith Nivard Cabral. Serial # prefix: *U*. Back: Bharatanatyam dancer and Mridirangam drummer. Vertical format. Watermark: Babbler and 100. Printer: DLR. 138x67mm.

	VF	UNC
a. Issued note.	FV	1.50
b. Low serial # in commemorative folder.	—	3.00
c. Uncut sheet of 40 notes. Serial # prefix: *CB/60*.	—	125.
r. Replacement note: Serial # prefix: *Z/4*.	—	5.00

126 500 Rupees | VF | UNC

1.1.2010. Purple and green. World Trade Center, Bank of Ceylon building at center, parakeet at right. Signatures: Mahinda Rajapaksa and Ajith Nivard Cabral. Serial # prefix: *T*. Back: Thelma dancer and Yak Bera drummer. Vertical format. Watermark: Parakeet and 500. 143x67mm.

	VF	UNC
a. Issued note.	FV	5.50
b. Low serial # in commemorative folder.	—	8.00
r. Replacement note. Serial # prefix: Z/5.	—	11.00

127 1000 Rupees | VF | UNC

1.1.2010. Green and multicolor. Ramboda tunnel at center, parrot at right. Signature: Mahinda Rajapaksa and Ajith Nivard Cabral. Serial # prefix: *S*. Back: Malpadaya dancer and Dawul Bera drummer. Vertical format. Watermark: Parrot and 1000. 148x67mm.

	VF	UNC
a. Issued note.	FV	11.00
b. Low serial # in a commemorative folder.	—	13.50
r. Replacement note: Serial # prefix: *Z/6*.	—	16.00

128 5000 Rupees VF UNC

1.1.2010. Tan and golden multicolor. Weheragala dam at center, yellow eastern bulbyl at right. Signature: Mahinda Rajapaksa and Ajith Nivard Cabral. Serial # prefix: *R*. Back: Nagaraksha dancer and Guruluraksha dancer. Vertical format. Watermark: Bulbul bird and 5000. 153x67mm.

	VF	UNC
a. Issued note.	FV	55.00
b. Low serial # in a commemorative folder.	—	60.00
r. Replacement note: Serial # prefix: *Z/8*.	—	65.00

2013 Commemorative Issue

129 500 Rupees VF UNC

15.11.2013. Purple and green World Trade Center, Bank of Ceylon building at center, parakeet at right. Signatures Mahinda Rajapaksa and Ajith Nivard Cabral. Serial # prefix V. Overprint: CHOGM logo at lower left. Watermark: Parakeet and 500 143x67mm.

	VF	UNC
a. Issued note.	FV	7.50
b. Low serial # in commemorative folder.	—	10.00

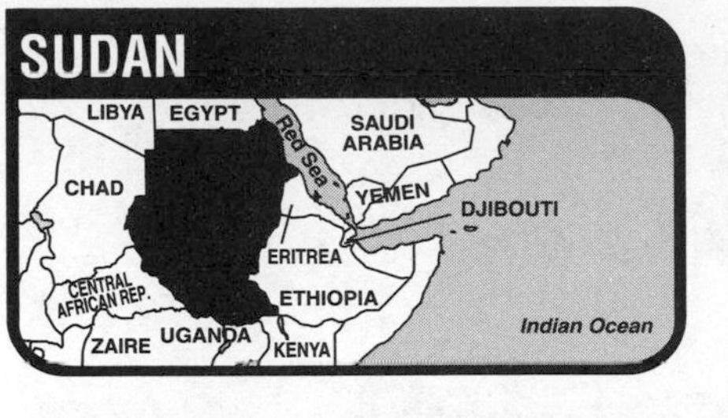

The Democratic Republic of the Sudan, was located in northeast Africa on the Red Sea between Egypt and Ethiopia, it had an area of 2,505,810 sq. km. and a population of 40.22 million. Capital: Khartoum. Agriculture and livestock raising are the chief occupations. Cotton, gum arabic and peanuts are exported. Military regimes favoring Islamic-oriented governments have dominated national politics since independence from the UK in 1956. Sudan was embroiled in two prolonged civil wars during most of the remainder of the 20th century. These conflicts were rooted in northern economic, political, and social domination of largely non-Muslim, non-Arab southern Sudanese. The first civil war ended in 1972 but broke out again in 1983. The second war and famine-related effects resulted in more than four million people displaced and, according to rebel estimates, more than two million deaths over a period of two decades. Peace talks gained momentum in 2002-04 with the signing of several accords. The final North/South Comprehensive Peace Agreement (CPA), signed in January 2005, granted the southern rebels autonomy for six years. After which, a referendum for independence is scheduled to be held. A separate conflict, which broke out in the western region of Darfur in 2003, has displaced nearly two million people and caused an estimated 200,000 to 400,000 deaths. The UN took command of the Darfur peacekeeping operation from the African Union on 31 December 2007. As of early 2009, peacekeeping troops were struggling to stabilize the situation, which has become increasingly regional in scope, and has brought instability to eastern Chad, and Sudanese incursions into the Central African Republic. Sudan also has faced large refugee influxes from neighboring countries, primarily Ethiopia and Chad. Armed conflict, poor transport infrastructure, and lack of government support have chronically obstructed the provision of humanitarian assistance to affected populations. After an election, the country voted to split, forming North Sudan and South Sudan in 2011.

MONETARY SYSTEM:

1 Ghirsh (Piastre) = 10 Millim (Milliemes)
1 Sudanese Pound = 100 Piastres to 1992
1 Dinar = 10 Old Sudanese Pounds, 1992

Republic

Bank of Sudan

1961-64 Issue

6 25 Piastres VF UNC

1964-68. Red on multicolor underprint. Soldiers in formation at left, date and signature varieties. Back: Arms (desert camel rider).

	VF	UNC
a. 6.3.1964; 20.1.1966.	25.00	225.
b. 25.1.1967.	22.50	200.
c. Without Arabic text *al-Khartoum*. 7.2.1968.	25.00	225.

7 50 Piastres VF UNC

1964-68. Green on multicolor underprint. Elephants at left, date and signature varieties. Back: Arms (desert camel rider).

	VF	UNC
a. 6.3.1964.	150.	950.
b. 25.1.1967.	130.	900.
c. Without Arabic text *al-Khartoum*. 7.2.1968.	135.	950.

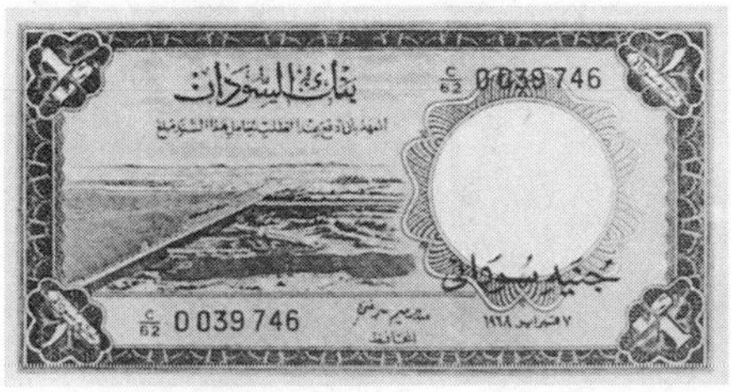

8 1 Pound VF UNC

1961-68. Blue on yellow and multicolor underprint. Dam at left, date and signature varieties. Back: Arms (desert camel rider).

	VF	UNC
a. 8.4.1961.	35.00	325.
b. 2.3.1965.	35.00	325.
c. 20.1.1966.	25.00	300.
d. 25.1.1967.	25.00	300.
e. Without Arabic text *al-Khartoum*. 7.2.1968.	30.00	320.

9 5 Pounds

1962-68. Lilac-brown on multicolor underprint. Dhow at left, date and signature varieties. Back: Arms (desert camel rider).

	VF	UNC
a. 1.7.1962.	150.	1350.
b. 2.3.1965.	150.	1200.
c. 20.1.1966.	140.	1100.
d. 25.1.1967.	140.	1100.
e. Without Arabic text *al-Khartoum*. 7.2.1968.	150.	1200.

10 10 Pounds

1964-68. Gray-black on multicolor underprint. Bank of Sudan building at left, date and signature varieties. Back: Arms (desert camel rider).

	VF	UNC
a. 6.3.1964.	85.00	900.
b. 20.1.1966.	100.	1000.
c. 25.1.1967.	135.	1200.
d. Without Arabic text *al-Khartoum*. 7.2.1968.	150.	1250.

1970 Issue

11 25 Piastres

1970-80. Red on multicolor underprint. Bank of Sudan at left. Various date and signature varieties. Back: Textile industry. Printer: TDLR.

	VF	UNC
a. Jan. 1970; Jan. 1971; Jan. 1972.	15.00	75.00
b. 1.4.1973-28.5.1978.	3.50	15.00
c. 2.1.1980.	1.50	10.00

12 50 Piastres

1970-80. Green on multicolor underprint. Bank of Sudan at left. Various date and signature varieties. Back: University of Khartoum. Printer: TDLR.

	VF	UNC
a. Jan. 1970; Jan. 1971; Jan. 1972.	25.00	90.00
b. 1.4.1973-28.5.1978.	4.00	18.00
c. 2.1.1980.	5.00	20.00

13 1 Pound

1970-80. Blue on multicolor underprint. Bank of Sudan at left. Various date and signature varieties. Back: Ancient temple. Printer: TDLR.

	VF	UNC
a. Watermark: Rhinoceros head. Jan. 1970.	20.00	100.
b. Watermark: Arms (secretary bird). Jan. 1971-28.5.1978.	3.00	32.50
c. 2.1.1980.	4.00	35.00

14 5 Pounds

1970-80. Brown on lilac on multicolor underprint. Bank of Sudan at left. Various date and signature varieties. Back: Domestic and wild animals. Printer: TDLR.

	VF	UNC
a. Watermark: Rhinoceros head. Jan. 1970.	50.00	325.
b. Watermark: Arms. Jan. 1971-28.5.1978.	37.50	275.
c. 2.1.1980.	37.50	275.

15 10 Pounds

1970-80. Purple and green on multicolor underprint. Bank of Sudan at left. Various date and signature varieties. Back: Transportation elements (ship, plane, etc.). Printer: TDLR.

	VF	UNC
a. Watermark: Rhinoceros head. Jan. 1970.	50.00	275.
b. Watermark: Arms. Jan. 1971-28.5.1978.	20.00	90.00
c. 2.1.1980.	15.00	40.00

1981 Issue

16 25 Piastres

	VF	UNC
1.1.1981. Brown on multicolor underprint. President J. Nimeiri wearing national headdress at left, arms at center. Back: Kosti bridge.	1.00	2.50
s. Specimen. Red overprint in Arabic.	—	100.

17 50 Piastres — VF | UNC

1.1.1981. Purple on brown underprint. President J. Nimeiri wearing national headdress at left, arms at center. Back: Bank of Sudan.

	VF	UNC
a. Issued note.	1.50	6.00
s. Specimen. Red overprint in Arabic.	—	150.

18 1 Pound — VF | UNC

1.1.1981. Blue on multicolor underprint. President J. Nimeiri wearing national headdress at left, arms at center. Back: People's Assembly. Watermark: Arms.

	VF	UNC
a. Issued note.	4.00	20.00
s. Specimen. Red overprint in Arabic.	—	150.

	VF	UNC
19 5 Pounds 1.1.1981. Green and brown on multicolor underprint. President J. Nimeiri wearing national headdress at left, arms at center. Back: Green. Islamic Centre Mosque in Khartoum. Watermark: Arms.	6.00	40.00

20 10 Pounds — VF | UNC

1.1.1981. Blue and brown on multicolor underprint. President J. Nimeiri wearing national headdress at left, arms at center. Back: Kenana sugar factory. Watermark: Arms.

	VF	UNC
a. Issued note.	20.00	90.00
s. Specimen. Red overprint in Arabic.	—	150.

21 20 Pounds

1.1.1981. Green on multicolor underprint. President J. Nimeiri wearing national headdress at left, arms at center; without commemorative text. Back: Unity Monument at left, People's Palace at center right. Watermark: Arms.

	VF	UNC
a. Issued note.	35.00	150.
s. Specimen. Red overprint in Arabic.	—	150.

1981 Commemorative Issue

#22, 25th Anniversary of Independence

	VF	UNC
22 20 Pounds 1.1.1981. Green on multicolor underprint. President J. Nimeiri with native headdress at left, map at center, commemorative legend in circle at right around watermark, monument at right. Back: Unity Monument at left, People's Palace at center right.	22.50	90.00

1983-84 Issue

23 25 Piastres — VF | UNC

1.1.1983. Red-orange on pale yellow underprint. President J. Nimeiri wearing national headdress at left, arms at center. Back: Kosti bridge. Watermark: Arms.

	VF	UNC
a. Issued note.	.50	1.50
s. Specimen. Red overprint in Arabic.	—	150.

	VF	UNC
24 50 Piastres 1.1.1983. Purple on brown underprint. President J. Nimeiri wearing national headdress at left, arms at center. Back: Bank of Sudan. Watermark: Arms.	1.25	2.00
25 1 Pound 1.1.1983. Blue on multicolor underprint. President J. Nimeiri wearing national headdress at left, arms at center. Back: People's Assembly, building is blue. Watermark: Arms.	2.00	4.50

26 5 Pounds — VF | UNC

1.1.1983. Green. President J. Nimeiri wearing national headdress at left, arms at center. Back: Islamic Centre Mosque in Khartoum at right. Watermark: Arms.

	VF	UNC
a. Issued note.	4.00	17.50
s. Specimen. Red overprint in Arabic.	—	150.

27 10 Pounds

1.1.1983. Purple and red-brown on multicolor underprint. President J. Nimeiri wearing national headdress at left, arms at center. Back: Kenana sugar factory. Watermark: Arms.

	VF	UNC
a. Issued note.	10.00	50.00
s. Specimen. Red overprint in Arabic.	—	200.

	VF	UNC
28 20 Pounds 1.1.1983. Green on multicolor underprint. President J. Nimeiri with native headdress at left, map at center, without commemorative legend in circle at right around watermark, monument at right. Back: Unity Monument at left, People's Palace at center right. Watermark: Arms.	12.50	75.00

29 50 Pounds — VF | UNC

25.5.1984. Brown-orange, blue and olive-brown on multicolor underprint. President Nimeiri at left. Back: Blue on multicolor underprint. Sailing ship at center, modern oil tanker at right. Watermark: Arms.

	VF	UNC
a. Issued note.	20.00	90.00
s. Specimen. Red overprint in Arabic.	—	200.

Law of 30.6.1985/AH1405

Replacement notes: Serial # prefix *Z/1; Z/11; Z/21; Z/31; Z/41; Z/51; Z/61; Z/71.*

30 25 Piastres VF .40 UNC 1.50
L.1985. Purple on multicolor underprint. Camels at left, outline map of Sudan at center. Signature title with 2 lines of Arabic text (Acting Governor). Back: Bank of Sudan at center right. Watermark: Arms.

31 50 Piastres VF .50 UNC 2.50
L.1985. Red on lilac and peach underprint. Lyre and drum at left, peanut plant at right, outline map of Sudan at center. Signature title with 2 lines of Arabic text (Acting Governor). Back: Bank of Sudan at center right. Watermark: Arms.

32 1 Pound VF .75 UNC 3.00
L.1985. Green and blue on multicolor underprint. Cotton boll at left, outline map of Sudan at center. Signature title with 2 lines of Arabic text (Acting Governor). Back: Blue on multicolor underprint. Bank of Sudan at center right. Watermark: Arms.

33 5 Pounds VF 5.00 UNC 30.00
L.1985. Olive and brown on multicolor underprint. Cattle at left, outline map of Sudan at center. Signature title with 2 lines of Arabic text (Acting Governor). Back: Bank of Sudan at center right. Watermark: Arms.

34 10 Pounds VF 10.00 UNC 50.00
L.1985. Brown on multicolor underprint. City gateway at left, outline map of Sudan at center. Signature title with 2 lines of Arabic text (Acting Governor). Back: Bank of Sudan at center right. Watermark: Arms.

35 20 Pounds VF 45.00 UNC 250.
L.1985. Green and purple on multicolor underprint. Feluka at left, outline map of Sudan at center. Signature title with 2 lines of Arabic text (Acting Governor). Back: Bank of Sudan at center right. Watermark: Arms.

36 50 Pounds VF 37.50 UNC 225.
L.1985. Brown, purple and red-orange on multicolor underprint. Columns along pool below National Museum at left, spear at right, outline map of Sudan at center. Signature title with 2 lines of Arabic text (Acting Governor). Back: Red. Bank of Sudan at center right. Watermark: Arms.

1987-90 Issue

37 25 Piastres VF .20 UNC 1.00
1987. Purple on multicolor underprint. Camels at left, outline map of Sudan at center. Signature title in 1 lines of Arabic text (Governor). Back: Bank of Sudan at center right. Watermark: Arms. UV: Arabic 25 and 25 in box fluoresce yellow.

38 50 Piastres VF .25 UNC 1.00
1987. Red on lilac and peach underprint. Lyre and drum at left, peanut plant at right, outline map of Sudan at center. Signature title in 1 lines of Arabic text (Governor). Back: Bank of Sudan at center right. Watermark: Arms.

39 1 Pound — VF .50 — UNC 1.50

1987. Green and blue on multicolor underprint. Cotton boll at left, outline map of Sudan at center. Signature title in 1 lines of Arabic text (Governor). Back: Blue on multicolor underprint. Bank of Sudan at center right. Watermark: Arms. UV: Arabic value 1 and in a box fluoresce yellow.

40 5 Pounds

1987-90. Olive and brown on multicolor underprint. Cattle at left, outline map of Sudan at center. Signature title in 1 lines of Arabic text (Governor). Back: Bank of Sudan at center right. Watermark: Arms.

	VF	UNC
a. 1987.	1.00	8.50
b. 1989.	1.50	7.50
c. 1990.	2.00	17.50

41 10 Pounds

1987-90. Brown on multicolor underprint. City gateway at left, outline map of Sudan at center. Signature title in 1 lines of Arabic text (Governor). Back: Bank of Sudan at center right. Watermark: Arms.

	VF	UNC
a. 1987.	2.00	25.00
b. 1989.	3.00	30.00
c. 1990.	3.00	25.00

42 20 Pounds

1987-90. Green and purple on multicolor underprint. Feluka at left, outline map of Sudan at center. Signature title in 1 lines of Arabic text (Governor). Back: Bank of Sudan at center right. Watermark: Arms.

	VF	UNC
a. 1987.	5.00	25.00
b. 1989.	4.00	20.00
c. 1990.	6.00	27.50

43 50 Pounds

1987; 1989; 1990. Brown, purple and red-orange on multicolor underprint. Columns along pool below national Museum at left, spear at right, outline map of Sudan at center. Signature title in 1 lines of Arabic text (Governor). Back: Red. Bank of Sudan at center right. Watermark: Arms.

	VF	UNC
a. 1987	4.00	20.00
b. 1989.	3.50	15.00
c. 1990.	3.50	17.50

44 100 Pounds

1988-90. Brown, purple and deep green on multicolor underprint. Shield, University of Khartoum building at left, open book at lower right. Back: Bank of Sudan and shiny coin design. Watermark: Arms.

	VF	UNC
a. 1988.	3.00	20.00
b. 1989.	1.50	5.00
c. 1990.	1.50	5.00

1991 Issue

45 5 Pounds — VF .50 — UNC 1.75

1991/AH1411. Red, orange and violet on multicolor underprint. Cattle at left, outline map of Sudan at center. Signature title in 1 lines of Arabic text (Governor). Back: Red-orange on multicolor underprint. Bank of Sudan at center right. Watermark: Arms.

46 **10 Pounds** | VF | UNC
1991/AH1411. Black and deep green on multicolor underprint. City gateway at left, outline map of Sudan at center. Signature title in 1 lines of Arabic text (Governor). Back: Black on multicolor underprint. Bank of Sudan at center right. Watermark: Arms. | .75 | 2.00

47 **20 Pounds** | VF | UNC
1991/AH1411. Purple and violet on multicolor underprint. Feluka at left, outline map of Sudan at center. Signature title in 1 lines of Arabic text (Governor). Back: Violet on multicolor underprint. Bank of Sudan at center right. Watermark: Arms. | .75 | 2.50

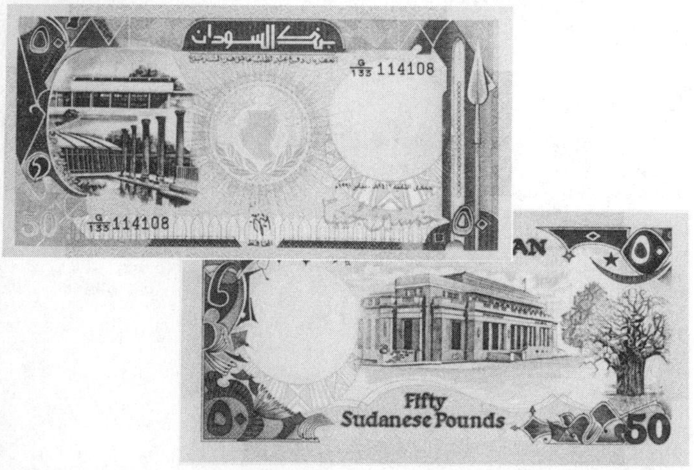

48 **50 Pounds** | VF | UNC
1991/AH1411. Yellow-orange, brownish black and dark brown on multicolor underprint. Columns along pool below national Museum at left, spear at right, outline map of Sudan at center. Signature title in 1 lines of Arabic text (Governor). Back: Dark brown on multicolor underprint. Bank of Sudan at center right. Watermark: Arms. | 1.00 | 3.50

49 **100 Pounds** | VF | UNC
1991/AH1411. Ultramarine and blue-green on multicolor underprint. Ultramarine shield at left, light blue-green map image at center, University of Khartoum building at left, open book at lower right. Back: Shiny light green coin design at right on back (partially engraved), Bank of Sudan at center right. Watermark: Arms. | 5.00 | 30.00

50 **100 Pounds** | VF | UNC
1991/AH1411; 1992/AH1412. Similar to number 49 but colors rearranged. Blue-green shield at left, darker details on building and ultramarine map image at center. Back: Bank of Sudan at center right, pink coin design at right. (litho). Watermark: Arms.

	VF	UNC
a. 1991/AH1411.	1.50	5.00
b. 1992/AH1412.	1.00	4.00

1992-98 Issue

Note: First issues w/fractional serial # prefix (Type I) replaced w/local printings w/double letter serial # prefix (Type II).

51 **5 Dinars** | VF | UNC
1993/AH1413. Dark brown and red-orange on multicolor underprint. People's Palace at lower right. Serial # Type II. Replacement note: *GZ*. Back: Plants including sunflowers at center. Watermark: Domed building with tower.

	VF	UNC
a. Issued note.	1.50	2.50
s. Specimen.	—	85.00

52	**10 Dinars**	VF	UNC
	1993/AH1413. Deep red and dark brown on multicolor underprint. People's Palace at lower right. Serial # Type II. Replacement note: *HZ*. Back: Domed building with tower at left center. Watermark: Domed building with tower.		
	a. Issued note.	1.00	4.00
	s. Specimen.	—	85.00

53	**25 Dinars**	VF	UNC
	1992/AH1412. Brownish black and green on multicolor underprint. People's Palace at lower right. Back: Circular design at left. Watermark: Domed building with tower.		
	a. With artist's name *DOSOUGI* at lower right. Serial # Type I.	3.00	10.00
	b. Without artist's name. Serial # Type I. Replacement note: *IZ*.	2.00	6.00
	c. As b. Serial # Type II.	1.00	3.00
	s. Specimen.	—	50.00

54	**50 Dinars**	VF	UNC
	1992/AH1412. Dark blue-green, black and purple on multicolor underprint. People's Palace at lower right. Watermark: Domed building with tower.		
	a. With artist's name *DOSOUGI* at lower right below palace. Serial # Type I.	5.00	20.00
	b. Without artist's name. 2 signature varieties. Serial # Type I.	1.50	5.00
	c. As b. Serial # Type II. Replacement note: *JZ*.	1.50	6.00
	d. As c. Segmented security thread. 7 or 8 digit serial #.	1.50	4.00
	s. Specimen.	—	50.00

55	**100 Dinars**	VF	UNC
	1994/AH1414. Black and deep brown-violet on multicolor underprint. People's Palace at center or lower right, double doorway at center. Serial # Type I. Replacement note: *KZ*. Back: Building at left center. Watermark: Domed building with tower.		
	a. Issued note.	3.00	10.00
	s. Specimen.	—	50.00

56	**100 Dinars**	VF	UNC
	1994/AH1414. Black and deep brown-violet on multicolor underprint. Like number 55 but with segmented foil over security thread. 7 or 8 digit serial #. Serial # Type II. Replacement note: *LZ*. Back: Building at left center. Watermark: Domed building with tower.		
	a. Issued note.	1.50	4.00
	s. Specimen.	—	50.00

57	**200 Dinars**	VF	UNC
	1998/AH1419. Green and black on multicolor underprint. Peoples Palace at right, crop line art at center. Back: Building at upper center, line art at lower center.		
	a. 7 digit serial #. Embedded security thread.	2.00	6.50
	b. 8 digit serial #. Segmented security thread.	2.00	5.50

58	**500 Dinars**	VF	UNC
	1998/AH1419. Red, black and green on multicolor underprint. Serial number Type II.. Back: Oil well and building.		
	a. 7 digit serial #. Embedded security thread.	2.50	7.50
	b. 8 digit serial #. Segmented security thread.	2.50	7.50
	s. Specimen.	—	50.00

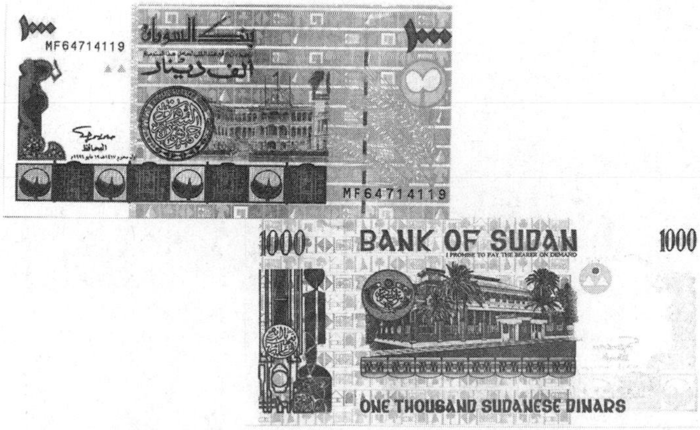

59	**1000 Dinars**	VF	UNC
	1996/AH1416. Green, yellow-brown and purple. Seal at left center, building in background at center. Serial # Type II. Replacement note: *MZ*. Back: Building.		
	a. 8 digit serial #. Signature 11.	4.00	15.00
	b. 7 digit serial #. Signature 12.	FV	15.00
	c. 8 digit serial #. Signature 12.	FV	15.00
	s. Specimen.	—	50.00
60	**10,000 Dinars**		
	1996. Brown and multicolor. Presidential Palace in Khartoum at center, leaf and front at right. Back: Building at center. Watermark: Domed building. Unissued specimen. 140x65mm.	—	1000.

2002-03 Issue

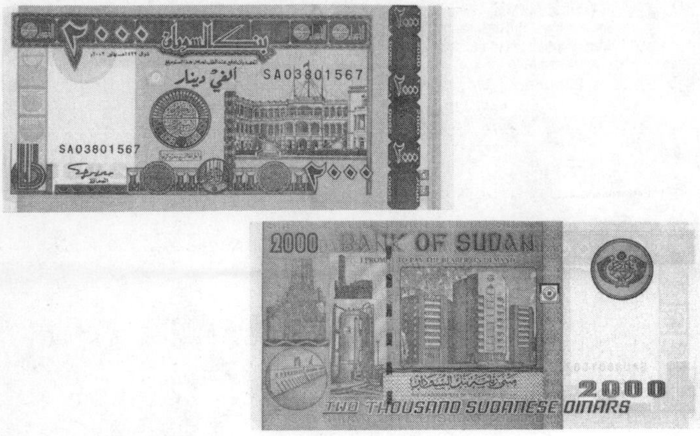

62 2000 Dinars VF UNC
2002/AH1422. Tan, blue, maroon and black on multicolor underprint. Back: Dam, oil rig and Bank of Sudan building.
a. Issued note. 7.00 32.50
s. Specimen. — 50.00

63 5000 Dinars VF UNC
2002. Orange and multicolor. Foil at left.
a. Issued note. FV 50.00
s. Specimen. — 50.00

Central Bank of Sudan

2006 Issue

64 1 Pound VF UNC
9.7.2006. Brown and yellow on multicolor underprint. Dove and modern buildings at right center. Back: Two doves. 139x64mm.
a. Issued note. FV 4.00
s. Specimen. — 50.00

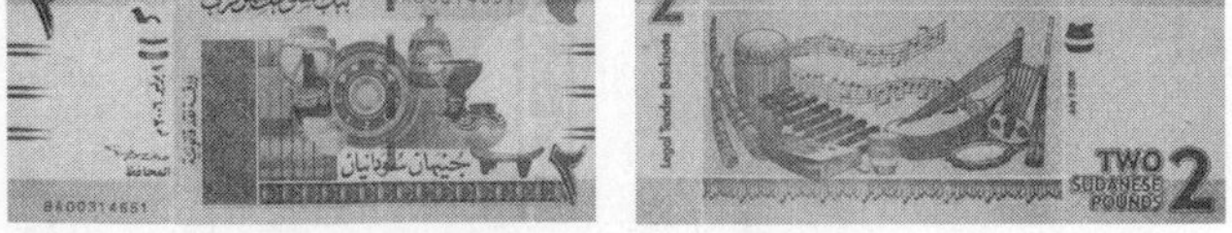

65 2 Pounds VF UNC
9.7.2006. Blue on multicolor underprint. Objects at right center. Back: Musical instruments. 144x64mm.
a. 9.7.2006. FV 7.00
s. Specimen. — 50.00

66 5 Pounds
9.7.2006. Rose and brown on multicolor underprint. Building at right center. Back: Dam. 150x69mm.
a. Issued note. FV 10.00
s. Specimen. — 50.00

67 10 Pounds
9.7.2006. Purple on multicolor underprint. Tree, ox and cart at right center. Back: Building. 155x69mm.
a. Issued note. FV 17.50
s. Specimen. — 50.00

68 20 Pounds VF UNC
9.7.2006. Rose, brown and yellow on multicolor underprint. Machine and oil rig at right center. Back: Factories, antenna and fruits. 160x75mm.
a. Issued note. FV 30.00
s. Specimen. — 50.00

69 50 Pounds
9.7.2006. Greenish yellow, brown and multicolor. Rhinoceros, elephant, gnu, zebras, giraffe adn primate at right center. Back: Cattle and camels. 165x74mm.
a. Issued note. FV 55.00
s. Specimen. — 75.00

2011 Issue

71 2 Pounds VF UNC
6.2011. Red-brown and ochre. 139x64mm. FV 2.50

72 5 Pounds VF UNC
6.2011. 144x64mm.
a. Segmented foil security thread on back. FV 5.00
b. Segmented foil security thread on face. FV 5.00

73 10 Pounds VF UNC
6.2011. Green, blue and multicolor. Tree at center, camel at right Back: Building at center. 155x69mm. FV 10.00

74 **20 Pounds** VF UNC

6.2011. Tan, blue and multicolor. Costal city and oil rig. Back: Ancient ruins. 160x75mm.

	VF	UNC
a. Segmented foil security thread on back.	FV	18.00
b. Segmented foil security thread on face.	FV	18.00

75 **50 Pounds** VF UNC

6.2011. Blue, brown and multicolor. Heard of animals at center. Back: Camels at top, animals at lower center. 165x74mm.

	VF	UNC
a. Segmented foil security thread on back.	FV	40.00
b. Segmented foil security thread on face.	FV	40.00

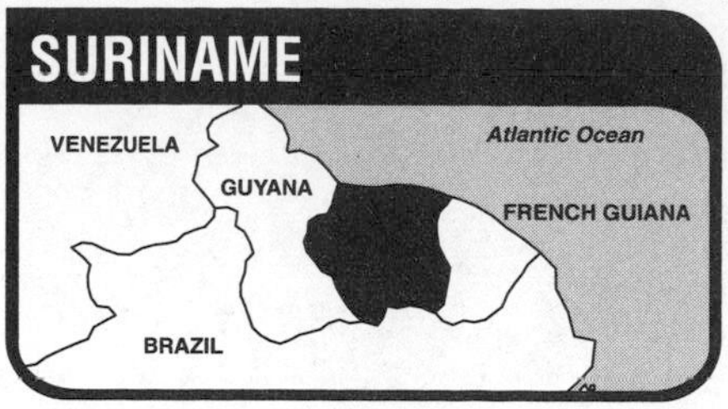

The Republic of Surinam, formerly known as Dutch Guiana, located on the north central coast of South America between Guyana and French Guiana, has an area of 163,270 sq. km. and a population of 476,000. Capital: Paramaribo. The country is rich in minerals and forests, and self-sufficient in rice, the staple food crop. The mining, processing and exporting of bauxite is the principal economic activity.

First explored by the Spaniards in the 16th century and then settled by the English in the mid-17th century, Suriname became a Dutch colony in 1667. With the abolition of slavery in 1863, workers were brought in from India and Java. Independence from the Netherlands was granted in 1975. Five years later the civilian government was replaced by a military regime that soon declared a socialist republic. It continued to exert control through a succession of nominally civilian administrations until 1987, when international pressure finally forced a democratic election. In 1990, the military overthrew the civilian leadership, but a democratically elected government - a four-party New Front coalition - returned to power in 1991 and has ruled since; the coalition expanded to eight parties in 2005.

RULERS:

Dutch to 1975

MONETARY SYSTEM:

1 Gulden = 1 Florin = 100 Cents, to 2004
1 Dollar = 1000 "old" Gulden, 2004-

Dutch Administration

Muntbiljet

Law 8.4.1960

Replacement notes: 6-digit serial number beginning with "1".

116 **1 Gulden** VF UNC

1961-86. Dark green with black text on pale olive-green and brown underprint. Building with tower and flag at left. Signature varieties. Back: Brown and green. Printer: JEZ.

	VF	UNC
a. Signature title: *De Minister van Financien* with printed signature but without name. 1.8.1961-1.4.1969.	2.00	10.00
b. Signature in facsimile with printed name below. 1.4.1971.	2.00	7.00
c. Similar to b., but printed name of signer at right. 1.11.1974.	2.00	5.50
d. Like c. without printed name at right. 1.11.1974.	2.00	5.50
e. Similar to a., but shorter text, and signature title centered. 1.11.1974; 25.6.1979.	1.50	7.00
f. Similar to d., but signature title: *De Minister van Financien en Planning.* 1.9.1982.	.50	2.50
g. 2.1.1984.	.50	2.25
h. 1.12.1984.	.50	2.25
i. 1.10.1986.	.50	2.00

117 **2 1/2 Gulden** VF UNC

1961; 1967. Red-brown. Girl wearing hat at left. Signature varieties. Back: Red-brown and brown. Printer: JEZ.

	VF	UNC
a. 2.1.1961.	3.00	12.50
b. 2.7.1967.	2.25	7.50

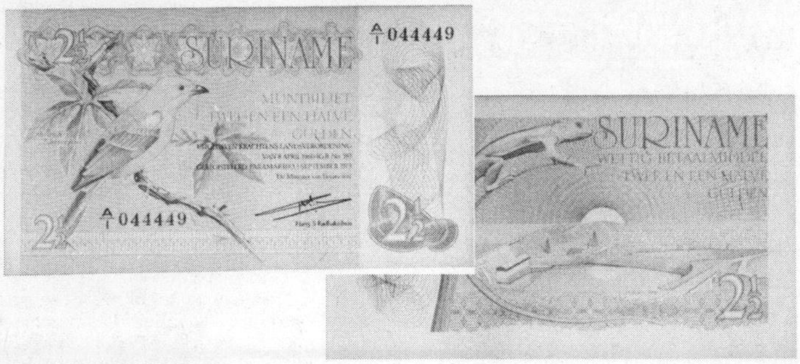

118 **2 1/2 Gulden** VF UNC

1973; 1978. Red-brown, light blue and multicolor. Blue-gray Tanager on branch at left. Three lines of text above signature title at center. Back: Lizard and Afobaka Dam. Printer: BWC.

	VF	UNC
a. Signature title: *De Minister van Financien.* Printed name below Signature 1.9.1973.	2.25	9.00
b. Without printed name below signature 1.8.1978.	.75	4.50
s1. As a. Specimen.	—	—
s2. As b. Specimen.	—	—

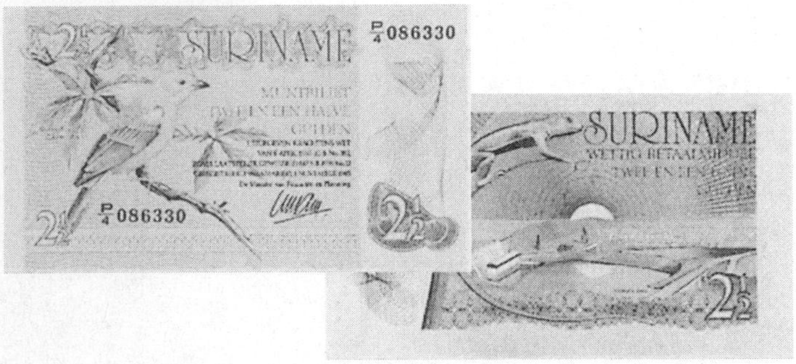

119 **2 1/2 Gulden** VF UNC

1.11.1985. Red-brown, light blue and multicolor. Blue-gray Tanager on branch at left. four lines of text above signature with signature title: *De Minister van Financien en Planning* . Back: Lizard and Afobaka Dam. Printer: BWC. UV: fibers fluoresce yellow. Back design green and yellow.

	VF	UNC
a. Issued note.	.75	3.50
s. Specimen.	—	

Centrale Bank van Suriname

1963 Issue

120 **5 Gulden** VF UNC

1.9.1963. Blue on multicolor underprint. Two serial number varieties. Back: Different arms than 1957 issue. Watermark: Toucan's head. Printer: JEZ.

	VF	UNC
a. Serial # first three digits smaller than last three digits.	.25	.75
b. Serial # digits of equal height.	.25	.75

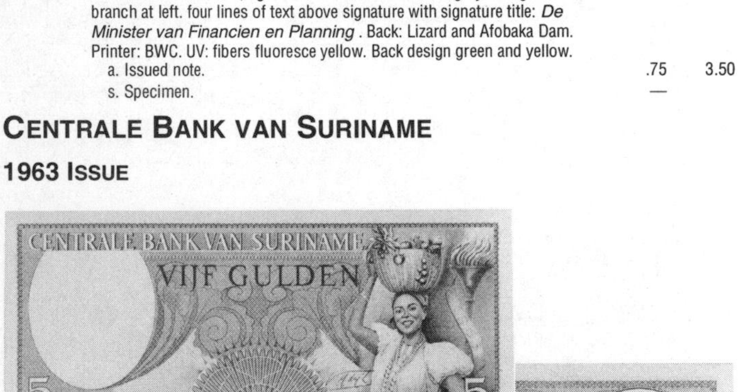

121 **10 Gulden** VF UNC

1.9.1963. Orange on multicolor underprint. Back: Different arms than 1957 issue. Watermark: Toucan's head. Printer: JEZ.

	VF	UNC
a. Serial # first three digits smaller than last three digits.	.25	1.00
b. Serial # digits of equal height.	.25	1.00

122 **25 Gulden** VF UNC

1.9.1963. Green on multicolor underprint. Back: Different arms than 1957 issue. Watermark: Toucan's head. Printer: JEZ. 3.00 10.00

123 **100 Gulden** VF UNC

1.9.1963. Purple on multicolor underprint. Back: Different arms than 1957 issue. Watermark: Toucan's head. Printer: JEZ. 5.00 12.50

124 **1000 Gulden** VF UNC

1.9.1963. Brown on multicolor underprint. Back: Different arms than 1957 issue. Watermark: Toucan's head. Printer: JEZ. 5.00 12.50

Republic

Centrale Bank van Suriname

1982 Issue

		VF	UNC
125	**5 Gulden** 1.4.1982. Blue on multicolor underprint. Soldiers and woman at right. Back: Building with flag. Watermark: Toucan's head. Printer: JEZ.	.50	1.00
126	**10 Gulden** 1.4.1982. Red on multicolor underprint. Soldiers and woman at right. Back: Building with flag. Watermark: Toucan's head. Printer: JEZ.	.40	1.25

127 25 Gulden

	VF	UNC
1982; 1985. Green on multicolor underprint. Soldiers and woman at right. Back: Building with flag. Watermark: Toucan's head. Printer: JEZ.		
a. 1.4.1982.	2.50	5.00
b. 1.11.1985.	.25	.75

128 100 Gulden

	VF	UNC
1982; 1985. Purple on multicolor underprint. Soldiers and woman at right. Back: Building with flag. Watermark: Toucan's head. Printer: JEZ.		
a. 1.4.1982.	10.00	20.00
b. 1.11.1985.	1.25	3.50

129 500 Gulden

	VF	UNC
1.4.1982. Brown on multicolor underprint. Soldiers and woman at right. Back: Building with flag on back. Watermark: Toucan's head. Printer: JEZ.	1.00	7.50

1986-88 Issue

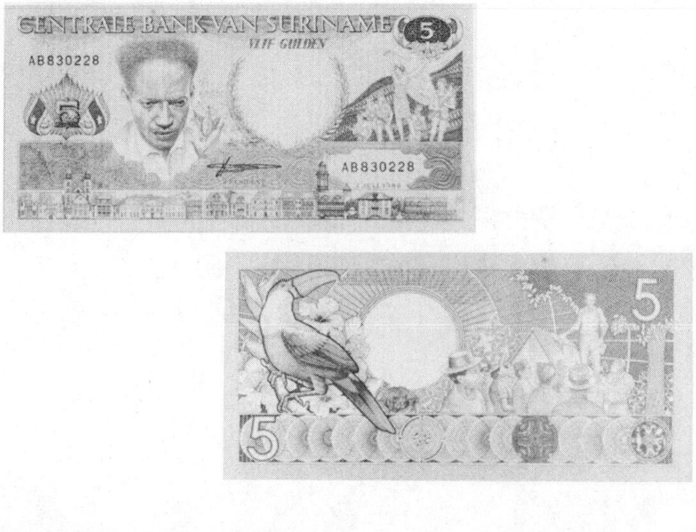

130 5 Gulden

	VF	UNC
1986; 1988. Blue on multicolor underprint. Anton DeKom at left, militia at right, row of buildings across bottom. Back: Toucan at left, speaker with people at right. Watermark: Toucan. Printer: TDLR.		
a. 1.7.1986.	.75	3.00
b. 9.1.1988.	FV	2.00

131 10 Gulden

	VF	UNC
1986; 1988. Orange and red on multicolor underprint. Anton DeKom at left, militia at right, row of buildings across bottom. Back: Toucan at left, speaker with people at right. Watermark: Toucan. Printer: TDLR.		
a. 1.7.1986.	1.25	4.00
b. 9.1.1988.	FV	2.00

132 25 Gulden

	VF	UNC
1986; 1988. Green on multicolor underprint. Anton DeKom at left, militia at right, row of buildings across bottom. Back: Toucan at left, speaker with people at right. Watermark: Toucan. Printer: TDLR.		
a. 1.7.1986.	2.00	8.00
b. 9.1.1988.	FV	3.50

133 100 Gulden

	VF	UNC
1986; 1988. Purple on multicolor underprint. Anton DeKom at left, militia at right, row of buildings across bottom. Two serial number varieties. Back: Toucan at left, speaker with people at right. Watermark: Toucan. Printer: TDLR.		
a. 1.7.1986.	7.50	20.00
b. 9.1.1988.	FV	2.50

134 250 Gulden — VF | UNC

9.1.1988. Blue-gray on multicolor underprint. Anton DeKom at left, militia at right, row of buildings across bottom. Back: Toucan at left, speaker with people at right. Watermark: Toucan. Printer: TDLR. — 2.00 | 8.00

135 500 Gulden — VF | UNC

1.7.1986; 9.1.1988. Brown and orange on multicolor underprint. Anton DeKom at left, militia at right, row of buildings across bottom. Back: Toucan at left, speaker with people at right. Watermark: Toucan. Printer: TDLR.

		VF	UNC
a.	1.7.1986.	15.00	50.00
b.	9.1.1988.	3.50	12.50

1991-97 Issue

136 5 Gulden — VF | UNC

1991; 1995-96; 1998. Deep blue and green on multicolor underprint. Central Bank building, Paramaribo at center, log trucks at upper left. Back: Arms at upper right, logging at center right. Watermark: Toucan. Printer: TDLR. UV: fibers fluoresce blue; CBVS in box yellow; serial # orange. Back top central design yellow.

		VF	UNC
a.	9.7.1991.	FV	1.50
b.	1.6.1995; 1.12.1996; 10.2.1998.	FV	.25

137 10 Gulden — VF | UNC

1991; 1995; 1998. Red and dark green on multicolor underprint. Central Bank building, Paramaribo at center, bananas at upper left. Back: Arms at upper right, banana harvesting at center right. Watermark: Toucan. Printer: TDLR.

		VF	UNC
a.	9.7.1991.	FV	3.00
b.	1.6.1995; 1.12.1996; 10.2.1998.	FV	.25

138 25 Gulden — VF | UNC

1991; 1995; 1996; 1998. Green and brown-orange on multicolor underprint. Central Bank building, Paramaribo at center, Track participants at upper left. Back: Arms at upper right, Competition swimmer (Olympian Anthony Neste) in butterfly Watermark: Toucan. Printer: TDLR.

		VF	UNC
a.	9.7.1991.	FV	4.00
b.	1.6.1995.	FV	3.50
c.	1.12.1996.	FV	2.50
d.	10.2.1998.	FV	2.50

139 100 Gulden — VF | UNC

9.7.1991; 10.2.1998. Violet and purple on multicolor underprint. Central Bank building, Paramaribo at center, factory at upper left. Back: Arms at upper right, strip mining at cetner right. Watermark: Toucan. Printer: TDLR.

		VF	UNC
a.	9.7.1991.	FV	6.50
b.	10.2.1998.	FV	6.50

140 500 Gulden — VF | UNC

9.7.1991. Brown and red-orange on multicolor underprint. Central Bank building, Paramaribo at center, crude oil pump at upper left. Back: Arms at upper right, drilling for crude oil at center right.. Watermark: Toucan. Printer: TDLR. — FV | 10.00

141 1000 Gulden — VF | UNC

1993; 1995. Black and red on multicolor underprint. Central Bank building, Paramaribo at center, combine at upper left. Back: Arms at upper right, combining grain at center right. Watermark: Toucan. Printer: TDLR.

		VF	UNC
a.	1.7.1993.	FV	10.00
b.	1.3.1995.	FV	5.00

142 2000 Gulden — VF | UNC

1.6.1995. Purple and green on multicolor underprint. Central Bank building, Paramaribo at center. Back: Arms at upper right, logging at center right. Watermark: Toucan. Printer: TDLR. — FV | 10.00

143 5000 Gulden — VF | UNC

5.10.1997; 1.2.1999. Purple on multicolor underprint. Central Bank building, Paramaribo at center. Back: Long Billed Gnatwren, banana bunches. Watermark: Toucan. Printer: TDLR.

a. 5.10.1997. — FV | 20.00

b. 1.2.1999. — FV | 20.00

144 10,000 Gulden — VF | UNC

5.10.1997. Green, red and multicolor. Central Bank building, silver segmented security thread. Back: Bird, industrial complex. Watermark: Toucan. Printer: TDLR. — FV | 37.50

145 10,000 Gulden

5.10.1997. Green, red and multicolor. Central Bank building, Purple segmented security thread. Back: More red used on buildings at center and arms at left center on back than with #144. — FV | 37.50

2000 Issue

146 5 Gulden — VF | UNC

1.1.2000. Blue and multicolor. Red-necked Woodpecker at left center, arms at upper center. Ascending size serial number. Back: Flower. Printer: TDLR. UV: value 5 in box, butterflies, batwings, trees fluoresce green. — FV | 1.50

147 10 Gulden — VF | UNC

1.1.2000. Green, purple, brown on multicolor underprint. Black-throated mango at left center, arms at upper center. Ascending size serial number. Back: Flower. Printer: TDLR. UV: value 10 in box, right of bird fluoresce yellow; beetle wings, trees orange. — FV | 2.00

148 25 Gulden — VF | UNC

1.1.2000. Blue and black on multicolor underprint. Red-billed Toucan at left center, arms at upper center. Ascending size serial number. Back: Flower. Printer: TDLR. UV: value 25 in box, mantis wings, trees fluoresce yellow. — FV | 3.00

149 100 Gulden — VF | UNC

1.1.2000. Rose on multicolor underprint. Long-tailed Hermit at left center, arms at upper center. Ascending size serial number. Back: Flower. Printer: TDLR. UV: value 100 in box, chameleon, trees fluoresce yellow. — FV | 4.00

150 500 Gulden — VF | UNC

1.1.2000. Orange and green on multicolor underprint. Guianan Cock-of-the-Rock at left center, arms at upper center. Ascending size serial number. Back: Flower. Printer: TDLR. — FV | 6.00

151 **1000 Gulden** — VF: FV, UNC: 8.00
1.1.2000. Green and red on multicolor underprint. Royal Flycatcher at left center, arms at upper center. Ascending size serial number. Back: Flower. Printer: TDLR.

152 **5000 Gulden** — VF: FV, UNC: 15.00
1.1.2000. Green, yellow, blue and orange on multicolor underprint. Sun Parakeet at left center, arms at upper center. Ascending size serial number. Back: Flowers. Printer: TDLR.

153 **10,000 Gulden** — VF: FV, UNC: 22.50
1.1.2000. Brown, black and red on multicolor underprint. Ornate Hawk-eagle at left center, arms at upper center. Ascending size serial number. Back: Flower. Printer: TDLR.

154 **25,000 Gulden** — VF: FV, UNC: 45.00
1.1.2000. Brown and green on multicolor underprint. Specktacled Owl at left center, arms at upper center. Ascending size serial number. Back: Flower and long leaves. Printer: TDLR.

155 **1 Dollar** — VF: FV, UNC: 1.00
1.1.2004. Green. Central Bank building at left. Back: Value. 168x73mm.

156 **2 1/2 Dollars** — VF: FV, UNC: 2.00
1.1.2004. Violet blue and red-brown. Central Bank building at left. Back: Value. 168x73mm.

2004 Issue

157 **5 Dollars** — VF / UNC
1.1.2004; 1.5.2009. Orange and brown on multicolor underprint. Central Bank building at center. Back: Gran - Rio Suia. 140x70mm.
- a. 1.1.2004. — VF: FV, UNC: 2.00
- b. 1.5.2009. — VF: FV, UNC: 2.00

158 **10 Dollars** — VF: FV, UNC: 2.50
1.1.2004. Olive green on multicolor underprint. Central Bank building at center. Back: Surinam river. 140x70mm.

159 **20 Dollars** VF UNC

1.1.2004; 1.5.2009. Slate black and lilac on multicolor underprint. Central Bank building at center. Back: Volzberg mountain. 140x70mm.

	VF	UNC
a. 1.1.2004.	FV	10.00
b. 1.5.2009.	FV	10.00

160 **50 Dollars** VF UNC

1.1.2004. Olive and lilac on multicolor underprint. Central Bank building at center. Back: Kasi Kasima rock formation. 140x70mm. FV 20.00

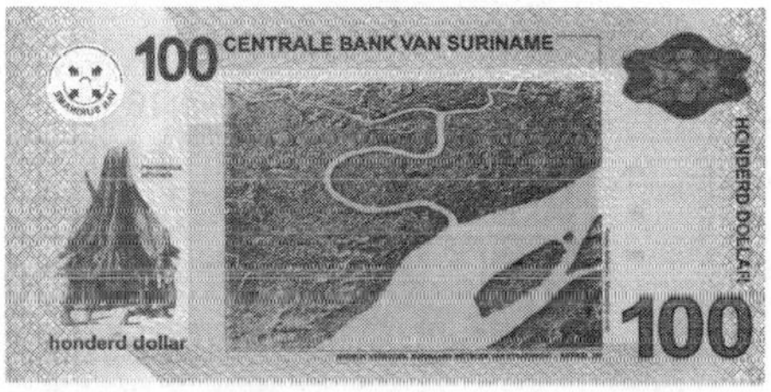

161 **100 Dollars** VF UNC

1.1.2004. 140x70mm. FV 40.00

2010 Issue

162 **5 Dollars** VF UNC

1.9.2010. Rose and brown on multicolor underprint. Central Bank building at center. Wide security strip at right. Back: Gran - Rio Suia. FV 2.00

163 **10 Dollars** VF UNC

1.9.2010. Green and yellow on multicolor underprint. Central Bank building at center. Wide security strip at right. Back: Surinam river. FV 2.50

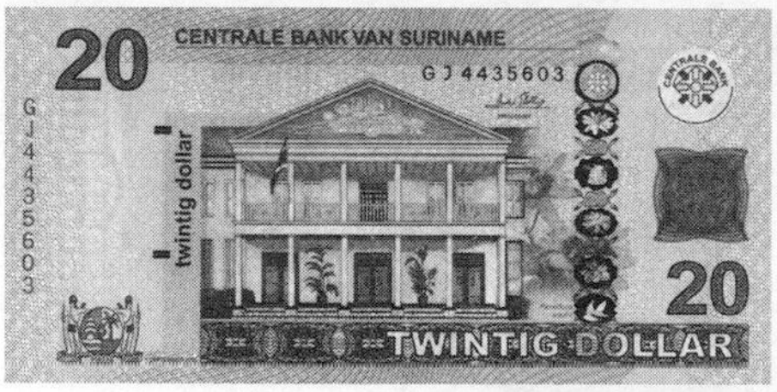

164 **20 Dollars** VF UNC

1.9.2010. Slate black and lilac on multicolor underprint. Central Bank building at center. Wide security strip at right. Back: Colzberg mountain. FV 10.00

165 **50 Dollars** VF UNC

1.9.2010. Slate black and lilac on multicolor underprint. Central Bank building at center. Wide security strip at right. Back: Kasi Kasima rock formation. FV 20.00

166 **100 Dollars** VF UNC

1.9.2010. Slate black and lilac on multicolor underprint. Central Bank building at center. Wide security strip at right. Back: River. FV 40.00

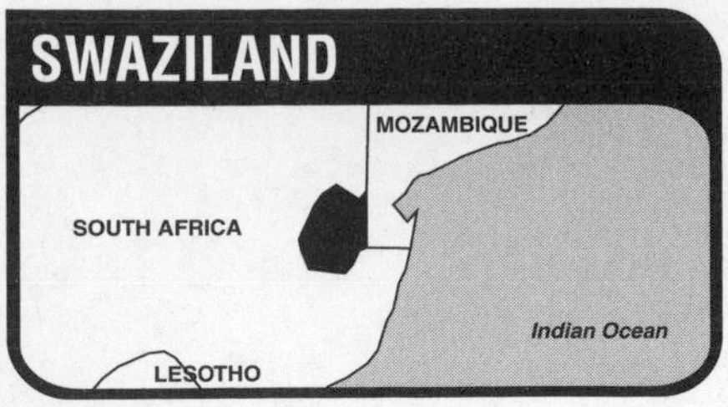

The Kingdom of Swaziland, located in southeastern Africa, has an area of 6,704 sq. mi. (17,360 sq. km.) and a population of 984,000. Capital: Mbabane (administrative); Lobamba (legislative). The diversified economy includes mining, agriculture and light industry. Asbestos, iron ore, wood pulp and sugar are exported.

Autonomy for the Swazis of southern Africa was guaranteed by the British in the late 19th century; independence was granted in 1968. Student and labor unrest during the 1990s pressured King Mswati III, the world's last absolute monarch, to grudgingly allow political reform and greater democracy, although he has backslid on these promises in recent years. A constitution came into effect in 2006, but political parties remain banned. The African United Democratic Party tried unsuccessfully to register as an official political party in mid 2006. Talks over the constitution broke down between the government and progressive groups in 2007. Swaziland recently surpassed Botswana as the country with the world's highest known HIV/AIDS prevalence rate.

RULERS:

British to 1968
Sobhuza II, 1968-82
Queen Ntombi, as regent, 1982-86
King Mswati III, 1986-

MONETARY SYSTEM:

1 Lilangeni = 100 Cents
(plural: Emalangeni)

SIGNATURE VARIETIES

	MINISTER FOR FINANCE	GOVERNOR
1	R. P. Stephens 1.6.1972 - 11.1.1979	E. A. Z. Mayisela 1.4.1974 - 31.10.1976
	J. L. F. Simelane 12.1.1979 - 20.11.1983	Deputy Governor H. B. B. Oliver 1.11.1976 - 30.6.1978 Acting Governor: A. D. Ockenden 1.6.1978 - 30.6.1981
2	J. L. F. Simelane 12.1.1979 - 20.11.1983	H. B. B. Oliver 1.7.1981 - 30.6.1992
3	Dr. S. S. Nxumalo 21.11.1983 - 8.6.1984	H. B. B. Oliver 1.7.1981 - 30.6.1992
4	B. S. Dlamini 27.8.1984 - 5.11.1993	H. B. B. Oliver 1.7.1981 - 30.6.1992
5	B. S. Dlamini 27.8.1984 - 5.11.1993	J. Nxumalo 1.7.1992 - 30.6.1997
6	I. S. Shabangu 10.11.1993 - 3.3.1995	J. Nxumalo 1.7.1992 - 30.6.1997
7A	Dr. D. von Wissell 3.3.1995 - 12.11.1996	J. Nxumalo 1.7.1992 - 30.6.1997
	MINISTER FOR FINANCE	GOVERNOR
7B	Dr. D. von Wissell 3.3.1995 - 12.11.1996	J. Nxumalo 1.7.1992 - 30.6.1997

SIGNATURE VARIETIES

8	T. Masuku 12.11.1996 - 19.11.1998	J. Nxumalo 1.7.1992 - 30.6.1997
9A	T. Masuku 12.11.1996 - 19.11.1998	M. G. Dlamini 1.7.1997 →
9B	T. Masuku 12.11.1996 - 19.11.1998	M. G. Dlamini 1.7.1997 →
	J. Charmichael 20.11.1998 - 14.2.2001	M. G. Dlamini 21.7.1997 →
10A	Majozi V. Sithole 15.2.2001 →	M. G. Dlamini 1.7.1997 →
10B	Majozi V. Sithole 15.2.2001 →	M. G. Dlamini 1.7.1997 →
11	Majozi V. Sithole	M. G. Dlamini

KINGDOM

MONETARY AUTHORITY OF SWAZILAND

1974-78 ND ISSUE

Replacement notes: Serial # prefix *Z*.

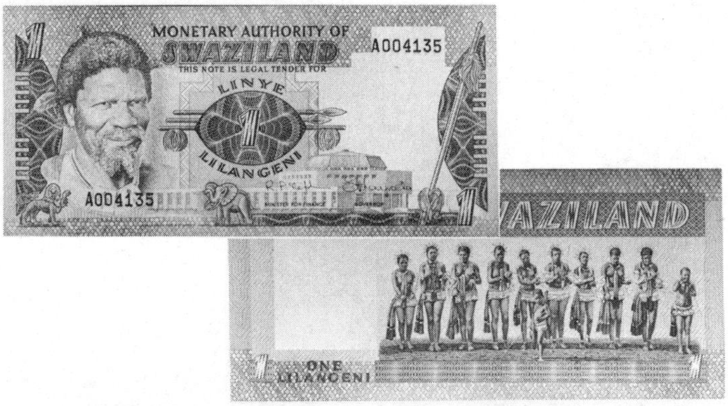

		VF	UNC
1	**1 Lilangeni** ND (1974). Red-brown on multicolor underprint. King Sobhuza II at left, Parliament House at bottom center right. Signature 1. Back: Princesses taking part in the *Ncwala* (kingship ceremony). Watermark: Shield and spears. Printer: TDLR.		
	a. Issued note.	.75	6.00
	s. Specimen. Serial # prefix *A; G*. Red overprint: *SPECIMEN* on both sides.	—	65.00

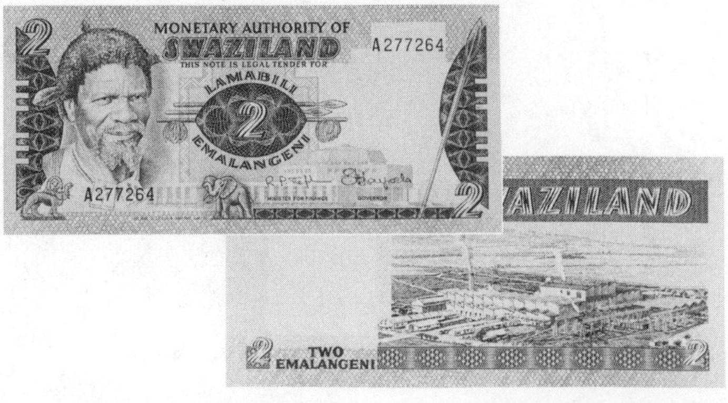

2 **2 Emalangeni** VF UNC

ND (1974). Dark brown on pink and multicolor underprint. King Sobhuza II at left, Parliament House at bottom center right. Signature 1. Back: Sugar mill. Watermark: Shield and spears. Printer: TDLR.

	VF	UNC
a. Issued note.	1.75	12.00
s. Specimen. Serial # prefix *A; C.* Red overprint: *SPECIMEN* on both sides.	—	65.00

3 **5 Emalangeni** VF UNC

ND (1974). Dark green on yellow-green and multicolor underprint. King Sobhuza II at left, Parliament House at bottom center right. Signature 1. Back: Mantenga Fallls and landscape. Watermark: Shield and spears. Printer: TDLR.

	VF	UNC
a. Issued note.	5.00	37.50
s. Specimen. Serial # prefix *A; D.* Red overprint: *SPECIMEN* on both sides.	—	65.00

4 **10 Emalangeni** VF UNC

ND (1974). Blue-black on blue and multicolor underprint. King Sobhuza II at left, Parliament House at bottom center right. Signature 1. Back: Asbestos mine. Watermark: Shield and spears. Printer: TDLR.

	VF	UNC
a. Issued note.	10.00	80.00
s. Specimen. Serial # prefix *A; B.*	—	65.00

5 **20 Emalangeni** VF UNC

ND (1978). Purple and green on multicolor underprint. King Sobhuza II at left, Parliament House at bottom center right. Signature 1. Back: Agricultural products and cows. Watermark: Shield and spears. Printer: TDLR.

	VF	UNC
a. Issued note.	35.00	185.
s. Specimen. Serial # prefix *A.*	—	65.00

Central Bank of Swaziland

1981 Commemorative Issue

#6 and 7, Diamond Jubilee of King Sobhuza II

6 **10 Emalangeni** VF UNC

1981. Blue-black on blue and multicolor underprint. Black commemorative text on watermark area. Signature 2. Back: Asbestos mine. Watermark: Shield and spears. Printer: TDLR.

	VF	UNC
a. Issued note.	85.00	300.
s. Specimen. Serial # prefix *K.*	—	185.

7 **20 Emalangeni** VF UNC

1981. Purple and green on multicolor underprint. King Sobhuza II at left, Parliament House at bottom center right. Black commemorative text on watermark area. Signature 2. New issuer's name at top. Back: Agricultural products and cows. Watermark: Shield and spears. Printer: TDLR.

	VF	UNC
a. Issued note.	100.	335.
s. Specimen. Serial # prefix *C.*	—	185.

1982; 1983 ND Issue

Replacement notes: Serial # prefix *Z*.

8 **2 Emalangeni** VF UNC

ND (1983-86). Dark brown on pink and multicolor underprint. King Sobhuza II at left, Parliament House at bottom center right. Signature 2. New issuer's name at top. Back: Sugar mill. Watermark: Shield and spears. Printer: TDLR.

	VF	UNC
a. Signature 2. (1983).	3.75	22.50
b. Signature 4. (1984).	1.50	6.00
s1. As a. Specimen. Serial # prefix *F.* Red overprint: *SPECIMEN* on both sides.	—	65.00
s2. As b. Specimen. Serial # prefix *G, J.* Red overprint: *SPECIMEN* on each side.	—	65.00

9	5 Emalangeni	VF	UNC
	ND (1982-86). Dark green on yellow-green and multicolor underprint. King Sobhuza II at left, Parliament House at bottom center right. Signature 1. New issuer's name at top. Back: Mantenga Falls and landscape. Watermark: Shield and spears. Printer: TDLR.		
	a. Signature 2. (1982).	5.00	37.50
	b. Signature 4. (1984).	2.00	11.00
	s1. As a. Specimen. Serial # prefix *D; E.* Red overprint: *SPECIMEN* on each side.	—	65.00
	s2. As b. Specimen. Serial # prefix *F.* Red overprint: *SPECIMEN* on both sides.	—	65.00

10	10 Emalangeni	VF	UNC
	ND (1982-86). Blue-black on blue and multicolor underprint. King Sobhuza II at left, without commemorative inscription. Back: Asbestos mine. Watermark: Shield and spears. Printer: TDLR.		
	a. Signature 2. (1982).	25.00	135.
	b. Signature 3. (1984).	22.50	120.
	c. Signature 4. (1985).	4.00	16.50
	s1. As a. Specimen. Serial # prefix *Q.*	—	65.00
	s2. As b. Specimen. Serial # prefix *U.*	—	65.00
	s3. As c. Specimen. Serial # prefix *W.*	—	65.00

11	20 Emalangeni	VF	UNC
	ND (1984-86). Purple and green on multicolor underprint. King Sobhuza II at left, Parliament House at bottom center right. Signature 2. New issuer's name at top. Without commemorative inscription. Back: Agricultural products and cows. Watermark: Shield and spears. Printer: TDLR.		
	a. Signature 3. (1984).	45.00	200.
	b. Signature 4. (1985).	8.00	38.50
	s1. As a. Specimen. Serial # prefix *E.*	—	65.00
	s2. As b. Specimen. Serial # prefix *F.*	—	65.00

1986 ND Issue

12	20 Emalangeni	VF	UNC
	ND (1986). Purple and green on multicolor underprint. King Mswati III at left, Parliament House at bottom center right. Signature 4. New issuer's name at top. Without commemorative inscription. Back: Agricultural products and cows. Watermark: Shield and spears. Printer: TDLR.		
	a. Issued note.	6.50	30.00
	s. Specimen. Serial # prefix *A.*	—	110.

1986; 1987 ND Issues

Replacement notes: Serial # prefix *Z*.

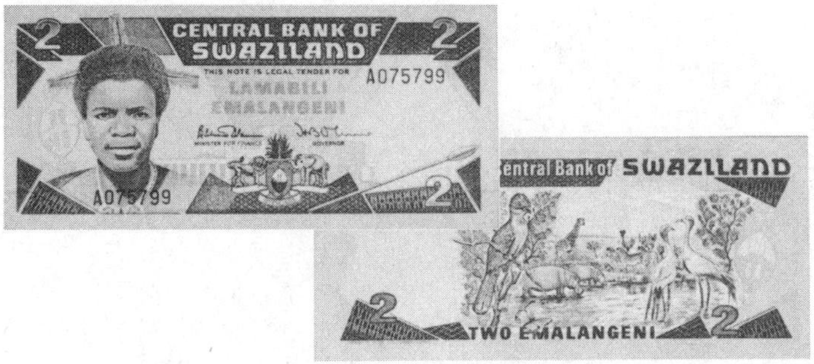

13	2 Emalangeni	VF	UNC
	ND (1987). Dark brown and orange on multicolor underprint. Facing portrait of young King Mswati III at left, arms at lower center. Signature 4. Back: Grey lourie, blue crane, hippos and other wildlife. Watermark: Shield and spears. Printer: TDLR.		
	a. Issued note.	1.50	7.00
	s. Specimen. Serial # prefix *A.*	—	110.

14	5 Emalangeni	VF	UNC
	ND (1987). Dark green, dark brown and bright green on multicolor underprint. Facing portrait of young King Mswati III at left, arms at lower center. Signature 4. Back: Warriors. Watermark: Shield and spears. Printer: TDLR.		
	a. Issued note.	2.50	12.50
	s. Specimen. Serial # prefix *A.*	—	110.

#	Note	VF	UNC
15	**10 Emalangeni**	VF	UNC
	ND (1986). Dark blue and black on multicolor underprint. Facing portrait of young King Mswati III at left, arms at lower center. Signature 4. Back: Hydroelectric plant at Luphohlo and bird. Watermark: Shield and spears. Printer: TDLR. 144x66mm.		
	a. Issued note.	3.50	20.00
	s. Specimen. Serial # prefix *A; F.*	—	110.
16	**20 Emalangeni**		
	ND (1986). Violet, brown and purple on multicolor underprint. Facing portrait of young King Mswati III at left, arms at lower center. Signature 4. Back: Cattle and truck. Watermark: Shield and spears. Printer: TDLR. 150x69mm.		
	a. Issued note.	32.50	160.
	s. Specimen. Serial # prefix *A.*	—	110.

1989 Commemorative Issue

#17, 21st Birthday of King Mswati III

#	Note	VF	UNC
17	**20 Emalangeni**	VF	UNC
	19.4.1989. Violet, brown and purple on multicolor underprint. Like number 16, with silver commemorative text and dates overprint on watermark area. Signature 4. Back: Cattle and truck. Watermark: Shield and spears. Printer: TDLR.		
	a. Issued note.	7.50	27.50
	s. Specimen. Serial # prefix *A.*	—	100.

1990; 1992 ND Issue

Replacement notes: Serial # prefix *Z*.

#	Note	VF	UNC
18	**2 Emalangeni**	VF	UNC
	ND (1992-95). Dark brown on multicolor underprint. Older portrait of King Mswati III at left facing half right, arms at lower center. Signature 4. Back: Grey lourie, blue crane, hippos and other wildlife. Watermark: Shield and spears. Printer: TDLR.		
	a. Signature 4. (1992).	1.50	5.00
	b. Signature 6. (1994).	4.00	15.00
	s1. As a. Specimen. Serial # prefix *M.*	—	100.
	s2. As b. Specimen. Serial # prefix *S.*	—	100.

#	Note	VF	UNC
19	**5 Emalangeni**	VF	UNC
	ND (1990-95). Dark green, dark brown and bright green on multicolor underprint. Older portrait of King Mswati III at left facing half right, arms at lower center. Signature 4. Back: Warriiors. Watermark: Shield and spears. Printer: TDLR.		
	a. Signature 4. (1990).	2.50	8.50
	b. Signature 6. (1994).	7.50	37.50
	s1. As a. Specimen. Serial # prefix *D.*	—	100.
	s2. As b. Specimen. Serial # prefix *J.*	—	90.00

#	Note	VF	UNC
20	**10 Emalangeni**	VF	UNC
	ND (1990-95). Dark blue and black on multicolor underprint. Older portrait of King Mswati III at left facing half right, arms at lower center. Signature 4. Back: Hydroelectric plant at Luphohlo and bird. Watermark: Shield and spears. Printer: TDLR. 146x67mm.		
	a. Signature 4. (1990).	4.50	22.50
	b. Signature 5. (1992).	5.00	25.00
	s1. As a. Specimen. Serial # prefix *J.*	—	100.
	s2. As b. Specimen. Serial # prefix *N.*	—	100.

#	Note	VF	UNC
21	**20 Emalangeni**	VF	UNC
	ND (1990-95). Violet, brown and purple on multicolor underprint. Older portrait of King Mswati III at left facing half right, arms at lower center. Signature 4. Back: Cattle and truck. Watermark: Shield and spears. Printer: TDLR. 150x69mm.		
	a. Signature 4. (1990).	9.00	37.50
	b. Signature 5. (1992).	8.00	35.00
	s1. As a. Specimen. Serial # prefix *D.*	—	100.
	s2. As b. Specimen. Serial # prefix *G.*	—	100.

#	Note	VF	UNC
22	**50 Emalangeni**	VF	UNC
	ND (1990-95). Dull red-brown, orange and dark green on multicolor underprint. King Mswati III at left. Back: Central Bank seal at left center, head office building at right. Watermark: Shield and spears. Printer: TDLR. 157x72mm.		
	a. Signature 4. (1990).	20.00	80.00
	b. Signature 6. (1995).	60.00	240.
	s1. As a. Specimen. Serial # prefix *A.*	—	90.00
	s2. As b. Specimen. Serial # prefix *C.*	—	85.00

1995 ND; 1995-98 Issue

		VF	UNC
23	**5 Emalangeni**		
	ND (1995). Dark green, dark brown and bright green on multicolor underprint. Older portrait of King Mswati III at left facing half right, arms at lower center. Ascending size serial number. Signature 7a. Segmented foil over security thread. Back: Warriors in dark brown. Printer: H&S. UV: right of King's face, value 5 and vertical bars fluoresce yellow.		
	a. Issued note.	2.00	7.00
	s. Specimen. Serial # prefix *AA*.	—	85.00

		VF	UNC
24	**10 Emalangeni**		
	ND (1995); 1997; 1998. Dark blue and black on multicolor underprint. Older portrait of King Mswati III at left facing half right, arms at lower center. Signature 4. Segmented foil over security thread. Back: Hydroelectric plant at Luphohlo and bird. Printer: F-CO. 148x67mm.		
	a. Signature 7a. ND.	13.00	32.50
	b. Signature 8. 8.4.1997.	4.50	18.50
	c. Signature 9a. 1.4.1998.	1.75	5.00
	s1. As a. Specimen. Serial # prefix *AA*.	—	85.00
	s2. As b. Specimen. Serial # prefix *AG*.	—	85.00
	s3. As c. Specimen. Serial # prefix *AK, AL, AN*.	—	85.00

		VF	UNC
25	**20 Emalangeni**		
	ND (1995); 1997; 1998. Violet, brown and purple on multicolor underprint. Facing portrait of young King Mswati III at left, arms at lower center. Signature 4. Segmented foil over security thread. Back: Cattle and truck. Printer: F-CO. 150x69mm.		
	a. Signature 7a. ND.	5.00	22.50
	b. Signature 8. 8.4.1997.	8.25	32.50
	c. Signature 9a. 1.4.1998.	FV	8.50
	s1. As a. Specimen. Serial # prefix *AA*.	—	85.00
	s2. As b. Specimen. Serial # prefix *AF; AG*.	—	85.00
	s3. As c. Specimen. Serial # prefix *AK, AL*.	—	85.00

		VF	UNC
26	**50 Emalangeni**		
	1995; 1998. Dull red-brown and dark green on multicolor underprint King Mswati III at left. OVD strip at right with C B of S repeated. Back: Central Bank seal at let center, head office building at right. Printer: G&D. 152x70mm.		
	a. Signature 7b. 1.4.1995.	12.00	50.00
	b. Signature 9b. 1.4.1998.	FV	24.00
	s1. As a. Specimen. Serial # prefix *AA*.	—	85.00
	s2. As b. Specimen. Serial # prefix *AA*.	—	85.00

		VF	UNC
27	**100 Emalangeni**		
	6.9.1996. Dark brown on multicolor underprint. King Mswati III at left. OVD strip at right with C B of S repeated. Signature 7b. Back: Central Bank seal at upper left center, rock formation at center. Printer: G&D. 156x70mm.		
	a. Issued note.	FV	40.00
	s. Specimen. Serial # prefix *AA*.	—	85.00

1998 Commemorative Issue

#28, 30th Anniversary of Independence

		VF	UNC
28	**200 Emalangeni**		
	6.9.1998. Dark green and green on multicolor underprint. King Mswati III at left, OVD strip at right with C B of S repeated. Commemorative text vertically at left and right. Signature 9b. Back: Swazi villagers by thatched circular domed and fenced huts at center. Printer: G&D. 161x70mm.		
	a. Issued note.	FV	65.00
	s. Specimen. Serial # prefix *AA*.	—	85.00

2001 Issue

29 10 Emalangeni — VF | UNC

1.4.2001; 1.4.2004; 1.4.2006. Dark blue and black on multicolor underprint. Older portrait of King Mswati III at left facing half right, arms at lower center. Signature 10. Segmented foil over security thread. Back: Hydroelectric plant at Luphohlo and bird. Motto; *GOD IS OUR SOURCE* added. Printer: F-CO. 148x67mm.

	VF	UNC
a. 1.4.2001. Signature 10a.	FV	3.75
b. 1.4.2004. Signature 11.	FV	3.75
c. 1.4.2006. Signature 11.	FV	3.75
s. Specimen.	—	80.00

30 20 Emalangeni — VF | UNC

2001; 2004; 2006. Violet, brown and purple on multicolor underprint. Facing portrait of young King Mswati III at left, arms at lower center. Signature 10. Segmented foil over security thread. Back: Rice, corn, cotton, pineapple, cattle, lumber on truck. Motto; *GOD IS OUR SOURCE* added. Printer: F-CO. 150x70mm.

	VF	UNC
a. 1.4.2001. Signature 10a.	FV	6.50
b. 1.4.2004. Signature 11.	FV	6.50
c. 1.4.2006.	FV	6.50
s. Specimen.	—	80.00

31 50 Emalangeni — VF | UNC

1.4.2001. Dull red-brown and dark green on multicolor underprint. King Mswati III at left. OVD strip at right with C B of S repeated. Signature 10. Back: Central Bank seal at left center, hed office building at right. Motto; *GOD IS OUR SOURCE* adde Printer: G&D. 152x70mm.

	VF	UNC
a. Signature 10b.	FV	12.50
b. Signature 11.	FV	10.00
s. Specimen.	—	80.00

32 100 Emalangeni — VF | UNC

1.4.2001. Dark brown on multicolor underprint. King Mswati III at left. OVD strip at right with C B of S repeated. Signature 10. Back: Central Bank seal at upper left center, rock formation at center.Motto; *GOD IS OUR SOURCE* add Printer: G&D. 156x70mm.

	VF	UNC
a. 1.4.2001. Signature 10b.	FV	17.50
b. Signature 11.	FV	15.00
s. Specimen.	—	80.00

2004 Commemorative Issue

33 100 Emalangeni — VF | UNC

2004. Dark brown on multicolor underprint. King Mswati III at left, commemorative overprint in center. OVD strip at right with C B of S repeated. Signature 11. Back: Central Bank seal at upper left center, rock formation at center.Motto; *GOD IS OUR SOURCE* add 156x70mm. — FV | 17.50

2008 Commemorative Issue

34 100 Emalangeni — VF | UNC

19.4.2008. Dark brown on multicolor underprint. King Mswati III facing at left. Signature 11. Back: Rock formation at center. Overprint: *The King's 40th Birthday.* in red at center. 157x70mm. — FV | 17.50

35 200 Emalangeni

19.4.2008. Green and multicolor. King Mswati III facing at left. Back: Parliament House in Lobamba at center. Overprint: *The King's 40th Birthday.* in red at center. Watermark: Shield and spears. Printer: G&D. 160x70mm. — FV | 35.00

2010 Issue

			VF	UNC
36	**10 Emalangeni**	6.9.2010. Blue on multicolor underprint. King Mswati III at left. Back: Nine princesses taking part in the Ncwala (kingship ceremony). Watermark: Mswati and 10. Printer: G&D. 148x70mm.		
		a. Issued note.	FV	3.00
		s. Specimen. Red overprint.	—	75.00
37	**20 Emalangeni**	6.9.2010. Purple on multicolor underprint. King Mswati III at left. Back: Flower, corn, pineapple, steer, refinery. Watermark: Mswati and 20. Printer: G&D. 151x70mm.		
		a. Issued note.	FV	6.00
		s. Specimen. Red overprint.	—	80.00

			VF	UNC
38	**50 Emalangeni**	6.9.2010. Violet on multicolor underprint. King Mswati III at left. Back: Central Bank building at center. Watermark: Mswati and 50. Printer: G&D. 154x70mm.		
		a. Issued note.	FV	15.00
		s. Specimen. Red overprint.	—	100.
39	**100 Emalangeni**	6.9.2010. Brown on multicolor underprint. King Mswati III at left. Back: Elephant, rhinoceros, lion, flowers, bird. Watermark: Mswati and 100. Printer: G&D. 157x70mm.		
		a. Issued note.	FV	30.00
		s. Specimen. Red overprint.	—	100.

			VF	UNC
40	**200 Emalangeni**	6.9.2010. Green on multicolor underprint. King Mswati III at left. Back: Straw huts, goats, warrior, rock formation. Watermark: Mswati and 200. Printer: G&D. 160x70mm.		
		a. Issued note.	FV	60.00
		s. Specimen. Red overprint.	—	125.

Collector Series

Monetary Authority of Swaziland

1974 Issue

			Mkt.	Value
CS1	**ND (1974). 1-20 Emalangeni**	#1-5 with overprint: *SPECIMEN* and serial # prefix Maltese cross.		80.00

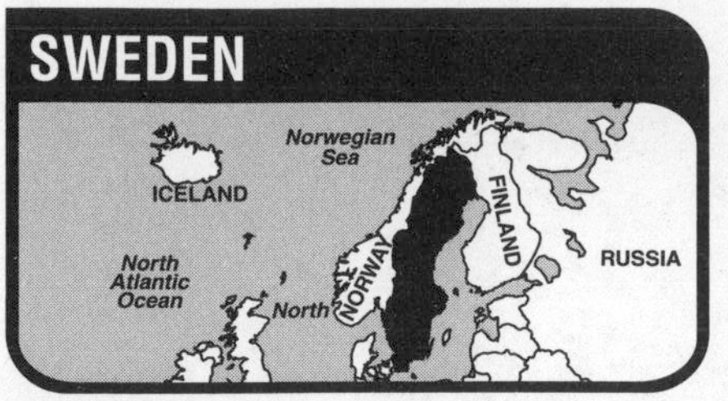

The Kingdom of Sweden, a limited constitutional monarchy located in northern Europe between Norway and Finland, has an area of 449,964 sq. km. and a population of 9.04 million. Capital: Stockholm. Mining, lumbering and a specialized machine industry dominate the economy. Machinery, paper, iron and steel, motor vehicles and wood pulp are exported.

A military power during the 17th century, Sweden has not participated in any war in almost two centuries. An armed neutrality was preserved in both World Wars. Sweden's long-successful economic formula of a capitalist system interlarded with substantial welfare elements was challenged in the 1990s by high unemployment and in 2000-02 by the global economic downturn, but fiscal discipline over the past several years has allowed the country to weather economic vagaries. Sweden joined the EU in 1995, but the public rejected the introduction of the euro in a 2003 referendum.

RULERS:

Gustaf VI Adolf, 1950-1973
Carl XVI Gustaf, 1973-

MONETARY SYSTEM:

1 Krona = 100 Öre

REPLACEMENT NOTES:

Issues since 1956 with asterisk following serial number. Asterisk following the serial number for note issued since 1956.

Kingdom

Sveriges Riksbank

1952-55 Issue

			VF	UNC
42	**5 Kronor**	1954-61. Dark brown on red and blue underprint. Portrait King Gustaf VI Adolf at right center. Back: Svea standing with shield at left center. Beige with red safety fibers. Watermark: Gustaf VI Adolf.		
		a. 1954.	3.00	6.00
		b. 1955.	3.00	5.00
		c. 1956.	3.00	5.00
		d. 1959.	3.00	7.50
		e. 1960.	3.00	5.50
		f. 1961.	3.00	4.00
		r1. Replacement note: Serial # suffix with star. 1956.	30.00	120.
		r2. Replacement note: Serial # suffix with star. 1959.	20.00	80.00
		r3. Replacement note: Serial # suffix with star. 1960. Rare.	—	—
		r4. Replacement note: Serial # suffix with star. 1961	20.00	80.00

			VF	UNC
43	**10 Kronor**	1953-62. Gray-blue on multicolor underprint. Portrait King Gustav Vasa at left. Blue date and serial #. Like #40. Back: Arms at center. Watermark: Gustav Vasa.		
		a. 1953.	2.50	6.00
		b. 1954.	2.50	5.50
		c. 1955.	2.50	5.50
		d. 1956.	2.50	5.00
		e. 1957.	2.50	5.00
		f. 1958.	2.50	5.00
		g. 1959.	2.50	5.00
		h. 1960.	2.00	10.00
		i. 1962.	2.00	6.00
		r1. Replacement note: Serial # suffix with star. 1956.	40.00	150.
		r2. Replacement note: Serial # suffix with star. 1957.	25.00	100.
		r3. Replacement note: Serial # suffix with star. 1958.	25.00	100.
		r4. Replacement note: Serial # suffix with star. 1959.	25.00	100.
		r5. Replacement note: Serial # suffix with star. 1960.	40.00	150.
		r6. Replacement note: Serial # prefix with star. 1962.	25.00	100.

46 1000 Kronor

1952-73. Brown and multicolor. Svea standing. Back: King Gustaf V. Watermark: Gustaf V.

	VF	UNC
a. Blue and red safety fibers. 1952.	200.	600.
b. 1957.	200.	600.
c. 1962.	150.	500.
d. 1965.	150.	450.
e. With security thread. 1971.	150.	450.
f. 1973.	150.	400.

1958; 1959 Issue

47 50 Kronor

1959-62. Seated Svea at lower right. Second signature at left. Small date and serial number. Back: King Gustaf Vasa at center. Beige.

	VF	UNC
a. 1959.	25.00	60.00
b. 1960.	25.00	60.00
c. 1961.	100.	200.
d. 1962.	25.00	60.00
r1. Replacement note: Serial # suffix with star. 1959.	100.	200.
r2. Replacement note: Serial # suffix with star. 1960. Rare.	—	—
r3. Replacement note: Serial # suffix with star. 1961.	200.	400.
r4. Replacement note: Serial # suffix with star. 1962.	75.00	150.

48 100 Kronor

1959-63. Seated Svea at lower right. Second signature at left. Small date and serial number. Back: King Gustaf Vasa at center.

	VF	UNC
a. 1959.	30.00	100.
b. 1960.	25.00	80.00
c. 1961.	25.00	80.00
d. 1962.	20.00	60.00
e. 1963.	20.00	60.00
r1. Replacement note: Serial # suffix with star. 1959. Rare.	—	—
r2. Replacement note: Serial # suffix with star. 1960.	100.	200.
r3. Replacement note: Serial # suffix with star. 1961.	100.	200.
r4. Replacement note: Serial # suffix with star. 1962.	100.	200.
r5. Replacement note: Serial # suffix with star. 1963. Rare.	—	—

49 10,000 Kronor

	VF	UNC
1958. Green and multicolor. King Gustaf VI Adolf at right. Back: Svea standing with shield at center. Watermark: Gustaf VI Adolf.	3000.	5000.

1962 Issue

50 5 Kronor

1962-63. Dark brown on red and blue underprint. Portrait King Gustaf VI Adolf at center. With security thread. Back: Svea standing with shield. Beige. Watermark: Esaias Tegnér (repeated).

	VF	UNC
a. 1962.	2.00	6.00
b. 1963.	2.00	4.00
r1. Replacement note: Serial # suffix with star. 1962.	15.00	40.00
r2. Replacement note: Serial # suffix with star. 1963.	—	12.00

1963-76 Issue

#51-55 replacement notes: Serial # suffix star.

51 5 Kronor

1965-81. Purple, green and orange. King Gustav Vasa at right. Back: Blue and reddish brown. Abstract design of rooster crowing at left. Beige. Watermark: Square with *5* repeated.

	VF	UNC
a. With year in dark red letter press. 1965-69.	2.00	5.00
b. With year in deep red offset. 1970.	2.00	3.00
c. As a. 1972-74; 1976-77.	2.00	3.00
d. With year in pale red offset. 1977-79; 1981.	2.00	3.00
r1. Replacement note. Serial # suffix with star. 1965-67.	25.00	50.00
r2. Replacement note. Serial # suffix with star. 1972.	100.	200.
r3. Replacement note. Serial # suffix with star. 1974.	5.00	10.00
r4. Replacement note. Serial # suffix with star. 1979.	40.00	75.00

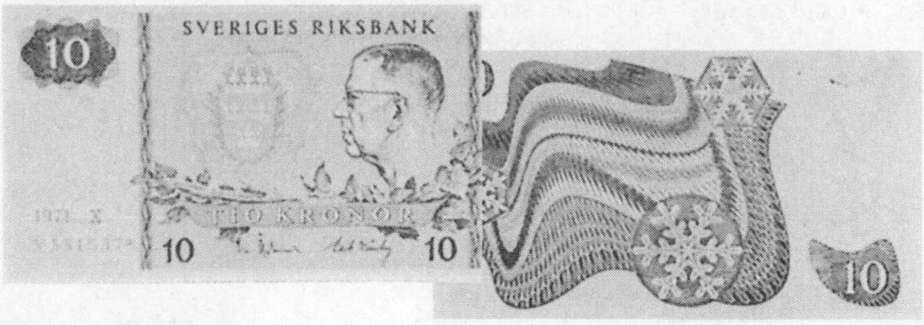

52 10 Kronor

1963-90. Dark green, with red and blue guilloche at center. King Gustaf VI Adolf at right, arms at center. Back: Northern lights and snowflakes at left center. Pale blue. Watermark: August Strindberg (repeated).

	VF	UNC
a. With year in dark red letter press. 1963.	3.00	6.00
b. As a. 1966; 1968.	2.00	5.00
c. As a. 1971; 1972; 1975.	2.00	4.00
d. With year in pale red offset. Engraved signature. 1976-77; 1979; 1983; 1985.	2.00	4.00
e. As d. but with signature printed by offset. 1980-81; 1983-84; 1987-90.	1.00	3.00
r1. Replacement note. Serial # suffix with star. 1963; 1966; 1968; 1971; 1972; 1975.	6.00	12.00
r2. Replacement note. Serial # suffix with star. 1976; 1979; 1983.	5.00	10.00
r3. Replacement note. Serial # suffix with star. 1980.	5.00	10.00
r4. Replacement note. Serial # suffix with star. 1984.	25.00	50.00

55 1000 Kronor

1976-88. Red-brown on green and violet underprint. King Carl XIV Johan at right. Back: Bessemer steel process. Watermark: Jacob Berzelius.

	VF	UNC
a. 1976-78.	200.	400.
b. 1980; 1981; 1983-86; 1988.	200.	300.
r1. Replacement note. Serial # suffix with star. 1976-1978; 1981.	250.	450.
r2. Replacement note. Serial # suffix with star. 1983; 1985.	250.	350.

53 50 Kronor

1965-90. Blue on green and brown underprint. King Gustaf III at right. Back: Carl von Linné (Linnaeus) at center. Beige. Watermark: Anna Maria Lenngren (repeated).

	VF	UNC
a. Small watermark. 1965; 1967; 1970.	10.00	30.00
b. Large watermark with year in dark red letter press. 1974; 1976.	10.00	25.00
c. Large watermark as b. with year in red-brown offset. 1978; 1979; 1981.	10.00	20.00
d. As c. Black serial #. 1982; 1984; 1986; 1989; 1990.	10.00	20.00
r1. Replacement note. Serial # suffix with star. 1965; 1967; 1970.	25.00	50.00
r2. Replacement note. Serial # suffix with star. 1974; 1976.	15.00	30.00
r3. Replacement note. Serial # suffix with star. 1979; 1981.	12.00	25.00
r4. Replacement note. Serial # suffix with star. 1989.	35.00	70.00

1968 Commemorative Issue

#56, 300th Anniversary Sveriges Riksbank, 1668-1968

56 10 Kronor

1968. Deep blue on multicolor underprint. Svea standing with ornaments at right. Back: Violet-brown. Old Riksbank building at left center. Watermark: Charles XI crowned monogram.

	VF	UNC
a. Issued note.	3.00	8.00
b. In printed banquet program folder with bank name, date and seal.	—	50.00

1985-89 Regular Issues

#57-65 the last digit of the year is first digit of the serial #. All notes have 2 sign. but only the right one is mentioned. Replacement notes: Serial # suffix star.

54 100 Kronor

1965-85. Red-brown, blue and gray. King Gustav II Adolf at right. Back: Figure head at left, Admiral ship *Vasa* of 1628 in center. Light blue paper. Watermark: Axel Oxenstierna (repeated).

	VF	UNC
a. Small watermark. 22mm. 1965; 1968; 1970.	20.00	40.00
b. Large watermark. 27mm. with year in dark blue letter press. 1971; 1972; 1974; 1976.	20.00	30.00
c. Large watermark. as b. with year in blue-green offset. 1978; 1980-83; 1985.	20.00	27.50
r1. Replacement note. Serial # suffix with star. 1965; 1968; 1970.	30.00	60.00
r2. Replacement note. Serial # suffix with star. 1971; 1974; 1976.	20.00	40.00
r3. Replacement note. Serial # suffix with star. 1972.	200.	350.
r4. Replacement note. Serial # suffix with star. 1978; 1980; 1981.	20.00	40.00

57 100 Kronor

(198)6-(200)0. Blue-green and brown-violet on multicolor underprint. Carl von Linné (Linnaeus) at right, building in background. Plants at left center. Back: Bee pollinating flowers at center. Watermark: Carl von Linné. 140x72mm.

	VF	UNC
a. Watermark: Large portrait. Signature Bengt Dennis. (198)6; 7; 8; (199)2.	FV	30.00
b. Watermark: Small portrait repeated vertically. Signature Urban Bäckström. (199)6; 8; 9; (200)0.	FV	25.00
r1. Replacement note. Serial # suffix with star. (198)6; 8.	20.00	35.00
r2. Replacement note. Serial # suffix with star. (199)6.	40.00	75.00

58	500 Kronor	VF	UNC
	(198)5-(198)6. Gray-blue and red-brown. King Carl XI at right. Back: Christopher Polhem seated at left center. Watermark: King Carl XI. 150x82mm.		
	a. (198)5.	FV	150.
	b. (198)6.	FV	170.
	r. Replacement note. Serial # suffix with star. (198)5.	175.	300.

59	500 Kronor	VF	UNC
	(198)9-(200)0. Red and multicolor underprint. King Carl XI at right; without white margin. Back: Christopher Polhem seated at left center. Watermark: Carl XI. 150x82mm.		
	a. Signature Bengt Dennis. (198)9; (199)1; 2.	FV	120.
	b. Signature Urban Bäckström. (199)4; 5; 7; 8; 9; (200)0.	FV	120.
	r. Replacement note. Serial # suffix with star. (198)9; (199)4; 9; (200)0.	150.	200.

60	1000 Kronor	VF	UNC
	(198)9-(199)2. Brownish black on multicolor underprint. King Gustav Vasa at right. Back: Medieval harvest and threshing scene at left center. Watermark: Gustav Vasa. 160x82mm.		
	a. Issued note.	FV	220.
	r. Replacement note. Serial # suffix with star. (198)9; (199)1.	200.	300.

1991; 1996 Issue

61	20 Kronor	VF	UNC
	(199)1-(199)5. Dark blue on multicolor underprint. Horse-drawn carriage at lower center, Selma Lagerlöf at right. Back: Story scene with boy riding a snow goose in flight at left center. Watermark: Selma Lagerlöf. 130x72mm.		
	a. Signature Bengt Dennis. (199)1; 2.	FV	12.00
	b. Signature Urban Bäckström. (199)4; 5.	FV	10.00
	r. Replacement note. Serial # suffix with star. (199)1.	15.00	25.00

62	50 Kronor	VF	UNC
	(199)6-(200)3. Deep olive-brown on multicolor underprint. Jenny Lind at center, music lines at left, stage at right. Back: Violin, treble clef with line of notes, abstract musical design. Watermark: Jenny Lind (repeated). 120x77mm.		
	a. Signature Urban Bäckström. (199)6; 7; 9; (200)0; 2.	FV	17.00
	b. Signature Lars Heikensten. (200)3.	FV	14.00
	r. Replacement note. Serial # suffix with star. (199)6.	40.00	75.00

1997 Issue

63	20 Kronor	VF	UNC
	(199)7-(200)0. Purple on multicolor underprint. Horse-drawn carriage at lower center, Selma Lagerlöf at right. Back: Story scene with boy riding a snow goose in flight at left center. Watermark: Selma Lagerlöf. 120x67mm.		
	a. Signature Urban Bäckström. (199)7; 8; 9; (200)1; 2.	FV	6.00
	b. Signature Lars Heikensten. (200)3; 5.	FV	5.00
	c. Signature Stefan Ingves. (200)6.	FV	5.00
	d. (200)8.	FV	5.00
	r. Replacement note. Serial # suffix with star. (199)7.	30.00	50.00

2001-06 Issue

64	50 Kronor	VF	UNC
	(200)4; (200)8. Deep olive-brown on multicolor underprint. Jenny Lind at right center, music lines at center, stage at right. Wide Foil hologram at left. Back: Violin, treble clef with line of notes, abstract musical design. Watermark: Jenny Lind. 120x77mm.		
	a. Signature Lars Heikensten.(200)4.	FV	12.50
	b. Signature Stefan Ingves. (200)8.	FV	12.00

			VF	UNC
65	**100 Kronor**			
	(200)1-(20)10. Blue-green and brown-violet on multicolor underprint. Carl von Linné (Linnaeus) at right, building in background. Plants at left center. Foil hologram. Back: Bee pollinating flowers at center. Watermark: Carl von Linné. 140x72mm.			
	a. Signature Urban Bäckström. (200)1; 2.		FV	27.00
	b. Signature Lars Heikensten. (200)3.		FV	22.50
	c. Signature Stefan Ingves. (200)6; 8; 9; (201)0.		FV	22.50

			VF	UNC
66	**500 Kronor**			
	(200)1-(200)9. Red on multicolor underprint. King Carl XI at right; without white margin. Foil hologram. Back: Christopher Polhem seated at left center. Watermark: Carl XI. 150x82mm.			
	a. Signature Urban Bäckström. (200)1; 2.		FV	110.
	b. Signature Lars Heikensten. (200)3.		FV	100.
	c. Signature Stefan Ingves. (200)7.		FV	100.

			VF	UNC
67	**1000 Kronor**		VF	UNC
	(200)5. Brown, black on multicolor underprint. Gustav Vasa at right. Wide foil hologram. Back: Harvest and threshing scene from *History of the Nordic Peoples* by Olaus Magnus. Watermark: Gustav Vasa (200)5. 160x82mm.		FV	200.

2005 Commemorative Issue

#66 250th anniversary of the Tumba Paper Mill.

			VF	UNC
68	**100 Kronor**			
	2005. Green on multicolor underprint. Seated Svea. Back: Paper production and old map. Issued in a folder.		—	50.00

The Swiss Confederation, located in central Europe north of Italy and south of Germany, has an area of 15,941 sq. mi. (41,290 sq. km.) and a population of 7.41 million. Capital: Berne. The economy centers about a well developed manufacturing industry, however the most important economic factor is services (banks and insurance).

Switzerland, the habitat of lake dwellers in prehistoric times, was peopled by the Celtic Helvetians when Julius Caesar made it a part of the Roman Empire in 58 BC. After the decline of Rome, Switzerland was invaded by Teutonic tribes who established small temporal holdings which, in the Middle Ages, became a federation of fiefs of the Holy Roman Empire. As a nation, Switzerland originated in 1291 when the districts of Nidwalden, Schwyz and Uri united to defeat Austria and attain independence as the Swiss Confederation. After acquiring new cantons in the 14th century, Switzerland was made independent from the Holy Roman Empire by the 1648 Treaty of Westphalia. The revolutionary armies of Napoleonic France occupied Switzerland and set up the Helvetian Republic, 1798-1803. After the fall of Napoleon, the Congress of Vienna, 1815, recognized the independence of Switzerland and guaranteed its neutrality. The Swiss Constitutions of 1848, 1874, and 1999 established a union modeled upon that of the United States.

MONETARY SYSTEM:

1 Franc (Franken) = 10 Batzen = 100 Centimes (Rappen)
Plural: Francs, Franchi or Franken.

SIGNATURE VARIETIES

	PRESIDENT, BANK COUNCIL	DIRECTOR	CASHIER
39	Dr. Brenno Galli 1959-78	Dr. Walter Schwegler	Otto Kunz 1954-66
40	Dr. Brenno Galli	Dr. Riccardo Motta 1955-66	Otto Kunz
41	Dr. Brenno Galli	Dr. Max Iklé 1956-68	Otto Kunz
42	Dr. Brenno Galli 1959-78	Dr. Edwin Stopper 1966-74	Rudolf Aebersold 1954-66
43	Dr. Brenno Galli	Alexandre Hay 1966-75	Rudolf Aebersold
44	Dr. Brenno Galli	Max Iklé	Rudolf Aebersold
45	Dr. Brenno Galli	Dr. Fritz Leutwiler 1968-84	Rudolf Aebersold
46	Dr. Brenno Galli	Dr. Leo Schürmann 1974-80	Rudolf Aebersold
47	Dr. Brenno Galli	Dr. Pierre Languetin 1976-88	Rudolf Aebersold

NOTE: From #180 onward w/o the Chief Cashier's signature.

	PRESIDENT, BANK COUNCIL	DIRECTOR
48	Dr. Brenno Galli	Dr. Leo Schürmann
49	Dr. Brenno Galli	Alexandre Hay
50	Dr. Brenno Galli	Dr. Fritz Leutwiler
51	Dr. Brenno Galli	Dr. Pierre Languetin
52	Dr. Edmund Wyss, 1978-86	Dr. Leo Schürmann
53	Dr. Edmund Wyss	Dr. Pierre Languetin
54	Dr. Edmund Wyss	Dr. Fritz Leutwiler
55	Dr. Edmund Wyss	Dr. Markus Lusser, 1981-96
56	Dr. Edmund Wyss	Dr. Hans Meyer, 1985-2000
57	Dr. Francois Schaller, 1986-89	Dr. Markus Lusser
58	Dr. Francois Schaller	Dr. Pierre Languetin
59	Dr. Francois Schaller	Dr. Hans Meyer
60	Dr. Francois Schaller	Jean Zwahlen (18mm), 1988-96
61	Peter Gerber, 1989-93	Dr. Markus Lusser
62	Peter Gerber	Jean Zwahlen (18mm)
63	Peter Gerber	Jean Zwahlen (15mm)
64	Peter Gerber	Dr. Hans Meyer
65	Dr. Jakob Schönenberger, 1993-99	Dr. Markus Lusser
66	Dr. Jakob Schönenberger	Dr. Hans Meyer
67	Dr. Jakob Schönenberger	Jean Zwahlen (12mm)
68	Dr. Jakob Schönenberger	Dr. Jean-Pierre Roth, 1996-
69	Dr. Jakob Schönenberger	Dr. Bruno Gehrig, 1996-2003
70	Eduard Belser, 1999-2002	Dr. Hans Meyer
71	Eduard Belser	Dr. Jean-Pierre Roth
72	Eduard Belser	Dr. Bruno Gehrig
73	Eduard Belser	Dr. Niklaus Blattner, 2001-
74	Dr. Hansueli Raggenbass, 2002-	Dr. Jean-Pierre Roth
75	Dr. Hansueli Raggenbass	Dr. Bruno Gehrig
76	Dr. Hansueli Raggenbass	Dr. Niklaus Blattner
77	Dr. Hansueli Raggenbass	Dr. Philipp Hildebrand, 2003

Confederation

Schweizerische Nationalbank

Swiss National Bank

1954-61 Issue

45 10 Franken

1955-77. Purple on red-brown underprint. Gottfried Keller at right. Back: Carnation flower at left center. Printer: OFZ.

	VF	UNC
a. 25.8.1955. (34, 36, 37).	10.00	50.00
b. 20.10.1955 (34, 36, 37).	10.00	50.00
c. 29.11.1956 (34, 37, 38).	10.00	45.00
c. 29.11.1956 (34, 37, 38).	10.00	45.00
d. 18.12.1958 (34, 37, 38).	30.00	125.
e. 23.12.1959 (34, 37, 38).	3.50	30.00
f. 22.12.1960 (39, 40, 41).	3.50	30.00
g. 26.10.1961 (39, 40, 41).	3.50	20.00
h. 28.3.1963 (39, 40, 41).	3.50	20.00
i. 2.4.1964 (39, 40, 41).	3.50	20.00
j. 21.1.1965 (39, 40, 41).	3.50	20.00
k. 23.12.1965 (39, 40, 41).	3.50	20.00
l. 1.1.1967 (42, 43, 44).	15.00	40.00
m. 30.6.1967 (42, 43, 44).	3.50	15.00
n. 15.5.1968 (42, 43, 45).	3.50	15.00
o. 15.1.1969 (42, 43, 45).	3.50	15.00
p. 5.1.1970 (42, 43, 45).	3.50	15.00
q. 10.2.1971 (42, 43, 45).	3.50	15.00
r. 24.1.1972 (42, 43, 45).	3.50	15.00
s. 7.3.1973 (42, 43, 45).	3.50	14.00
s1. As a. Specimen.	—	75.00
t. 7.2.1974 (42, 43, 45).	3.50	14.00
u. 6.1.1977 (45, 46, 47).	3.00	14.00

46 20 Franken

1954-76. Blue on multicolor underprint. General Guillaume-Henri Dufour at right. Back: Silver thistle at left center. Printer: OFZ.

	VF	UNC
a. 1.7.1954 (34, 35, 36).	22.50	120.
b. 7.7.1955 (34, 36, 37).	22.50	120.
c. 20.10.1955 (34, 36, 37).	22.50	120.
d. 5.7.1956 (34, 37, 38).	22.50	120.
e. 4.10.1957 (34, 37, 38).	25.00	110.
f. 18.12.1958 (34, 37, 38).	40.00	150.
g. 23.12.1959 (39, 40, 41).	8.00	30.00
h. 22.12.1960 (39, 40, 41).	8.00	30.00
i. 26.10.1961 (39, 40, 41).	8.00	30.00
j. 28.3.1963 (39, 40, 41).	8.00	30.00
k. 2.4.1964 (39, 40, 41).	8.00	30.00
l. 21.1.1965 (39, 40, 41).	8.00	30.00
m. 23.12.1965 (39, 40, 41).	8.00	30.00
n. 1.1.1967 (42, 43, 44).	10.00	30.00
o. 30.6.1967 (42, 43, 44).	8.00	30.00
p. 15.5.1968 (42, 43, 45).	8.00	25.00
q. 15.1.1969 (42, 43, 45).	8.00	25.00
r. 5.1.1970 (42, 43, 45).	8.00	25.00
s. 10.2.1971 (42, 43, 45).	8.00	25.00
s1. As a. Specimen.	—	75.00
t. 24.1.1972 (42, 43, 45).	8.00	25.00
u. 7.3.1973 (42, 43, 45).	8.00	22.50
v. 7.2.1974 (42, 43, 45).	8.00	22.50
w. 9.4.1976 (45, 46, 47).	7.50	22.50

47 50 Franken

1955-58. Green and red-brown on yellow-green underprint. Girl at upper right. Back: Apple harvesting scene (symbolizing fertility). Printer: W&S.

	VF	UNC
a. 7.7.1955 (34, 36, 37).	42.50	175.
b. 4.10.1957 (34, 37, 38).	37.50	175.
c. 18.12.1958 (34, 37, 38).	500.	800.

48 50 Franken

1961-74. Green and red on multicolor underprint. Girl at upper right. Like #47. Back: Apple harvesting scene (symbolizing fertility).

	VF	UNC
a. 4.5.1961 (39, 40, 41).	60.00	200.
b. 21.12.1961 (39, 40,41).	30.00	90.00
c. 28.3.1963 (39, 40, 41).	85.00	220.
d. 2.4.1964 (39, 40, 41).	90.00	250.
e. 21.1.1965 (39, 40, 41).	30.00	90.00
f. 23.12.1965 (39, 40, 41).	30.00	90.00
g. 30.6.1967 (42, 43, 44).	30.00	90.00
h. 15.5.1968 (42, 43, 45).	30.00	90.00
i. 15.1.1969 (42, 43, 45).	30.00	75.00
j. 5.1.1970 (42, 43, 45).	30.00	75.00
k. 10.2.1971 (42, 43, 45).	30.00	75.00
l. 24.1.1972 (42, 43, 45).	30.00	75.00
m. 7.3.1973 (42, 43, 45).	30.00	75.00
n. 7.2.1974 (42, 43, 45).	30.00	75.00
s. As a. Specimen.	—	75.00

49 **100 Franken**

1956-73. Dark blue and brown-olive on multicolor underprint. Boy's head at upper right with lamb. Back: St. Martin cutting his cape (to share) at center right. Printer: TDLR.

	VF	UNC
a. 25.10.1956 (34, 37, 38).	57.50	350.
b. 4.10.1957 (34, 37, 38).	55.00	350.
c. 18.12.1958 (34, 37, 38).	60.00	500.
d. 21.12.1961 (39, 40, 41);	30.00	200.
e. 28.3.1963 (39, 40, 41).	30.00	200.
f. 2.4.1964 (39, 40, 41).	30.00	200.
g. 21.1.1965 (39, 40, 41).	32.50	200.
h. 23.12.1965 (39, 40, 41).	35.00	200.
i. 1.1.1967 (42, 43, 44).	35.00	200.
j. 30.6.1967 (42, 43, 44).	27.50	200.
k. 15.1.1969 (42, 43, 45).	25.00	200.
l. 5.1.1970 (42, 43, 45).	35.00	175.
m. 10.2.1971 (42, 43, 45).	25.00	175.
n. 24.1.1972 (42, 43, 45).	25.00	175.
o. 7.3.1973 (42, 43, 45).	25.00	175.
p. As o. Specimen.	—	150.

50 **500 Franken**

1957-58. Red-brown and olive on multicolor underprint. Woman looking in mirror at right. Back: Elders with four girls bathing at center right (Fountain of Youth). Printer: W&S.

	VF	UNC
a. 31.1.1957 (34, 37, 38).	400.	1200.
b. 4.10.1957 (34, 37, 38).	350.	1200.
c. 18.12.1958 (34, 37, 38).	500.	1400.
s. Specimen. Red overprint: *SPECIMEN* and punch hole cancelled.	—	1000.

51 **500 Franken**

1961-74. Brown-orange and olive on multicolor underprint. Woman looking in mirror at right. Like #50. Back: Elders with four girls bathing at center right (Fountain of Youth).

	VF	UNC
a. 21.12.1961 (39, 40, 41).	275.	1000.
b. 28.3.1963 (39, 40, 41).	240.	1000.
c. 2.4.1964 (39, 40, 41).	250.	1000.
d. 21.1.1965 (39, 40, 41).	250.	1000.
e. 1.1.1967 (42, 43, 44).	250.	1000.
f. 15.5.1968 (42, 43, 45).	250.	1000.
g. 15.1.1969 (42, 43, 45).	250.	1000.
h. 5.1.1970 (42, 43, 45).	235.	950.
i. 10.2.1971 (42, 43, 45).	235.	950.
j. 24.1.1972 (42, 43, 45).	225.	950.
k. 7.3.1973 (42, 43, 45).	200.	900.
l. 7.2.1974 (42, 43, 45).	200.	900.
s. As a. Specimen.	—	750.

52 **1000 Franken**

1954-74. Red-violet and turquoise on green and light violet underprint. Female head at upper right. Back: Allegorical scene *Dance Macabre.* Printer: TDLR.

	VF	UNC
a. 30.9.1954 (34, 35, 36).	500.	2500.
b. 4.10.1957 (34, 37, 38).	425.	2000.
c. 18.12.1958 (34, 37, 38).	1200.	2500.
d. 22.12.1960 (39, 40, 41).	350.	1800.
e. 21.12.1961 (39, 40, 41).	350.	1700.

	VF	UNC
f. 28.3.1963 (39, 40, 41).	350.	1600.
g. 21.1.1965 (39, 40, 41).	350.	1500.
h. 1.1.1967 (42, 43, 44).	350.	1500.
i. 5.1.1970 (42, 43, 45).	350.	1500.
j. 10.2.1971 (42, 43, 45).	350.	1400.
k. 24.1.1972 (42, 43, 45).	300.	1400.
l. 1.10.1973 (42, 43, 45).	280.	11,400.
m. 7.2.1974 (42, 43, 45).	260.	1300.
s. As a. Specimen.	—	1250.

1976-79 Issue; 6th Series

#53-59 series of notes printed in 4 languages - the traditional German, French and Italian plus Romansch; (Rhaeto - Romanic), the language of the mountainous areas of Graubünden Canton. Wmk. as portr. The first 2 numerals before the serial # prefix letter are date (year) indicators. Printer: OFZ.

Note: Sign. varieties listed after date.

53 10 Franken

(19)79-92. Orange-brown and multicolor. Leonhard Euler at right. Back: Water turbine, light rays through lenses and Solar System in vertical format. Watermark: Leonhard Euler. Printer: OFZ. 137x66mm.

	VF	UNC
a. 1979 (52, 53, 54).	FV	35.00
b. 1980 (52, 53, 54).	FV	40.00
c. 1981 (53, 54, 55).	FV	40.00
d. 1982 (53, 54, 55).	FV	35.00
e. 1983 (53, 54, 55).	FV	35.00
f. 1986 (53, 55, 56).	FV	30.00
g. 1987 (57, 58, 59).	FV	30.00
h. 1990 (61, 63, 64).	FV	30.00
i. 1990 (62).	FV	200.
j. 1991 (61, 63, 64).	FV	30.00
k. 1992 (61, 62, 64).	FV	35.00

54 20 Franken

1978 (52, 53, 54). Light blue on multicolor underprint. Horace-Bénédict de Saussure at right, hygrometer at left. Underprint on face ends 2mm before the margin, only plain blue underprint visible within the 2mm. Back: Fossel and early mountain expedition team hiking in the Alps. Watermark: Horace-Bénédict de Saussure. Printer: OHZ. 148x70mm. — FV 55.00

55 20 Franken

(19)78-92. Blue and multicolor. Horace-Bénédict de Saussure at right, hygrometer at left. Similar to #54, but underprint at upper margin on face goes to the margin. Back: Fossel and early mountain expedition team hiking in the Alps on vertical format. Watermark: Horace-Bénédict de Saussure. Printer: OHZ. 148x70mm.

	VF	UNC
a. 1978 (52, 53, 54).	FV	110.
b. 1980 (52, 53, 54).	FV	65.00
c. 1981 (53, 54, 55).	FV	80.00
d. 1982 (53, 54, 55).	FV	55.00
e. 1983 (53, 54, 55).	FV	55.00
f. 1986 (57, 58, 59).	FV	55.00
g. 1987 (57, 58, 59).	FV	55.00
h. 1989 (61, 62, 64).	FV	50.00
i. 1990 (61, 63, 64).	FV	45.00
j. 1992 (61, 63, 64).	FV	50.00
s. Perforated: *SPECIMEN.*	—	1650.

56 50 Franken

(19)78-88. Green and multicolor. Konrad Gessner at right. Back: Eagle owl, *Primula auricu-la* plant and stars on vertical format. Watermark: Konrad Gessner. Printer: OHZ. 159x74mm.

	VF	UNC
a. 1978 (48, 50, 51).	FV	120.
b. 1979 (52, 53, 54).	FV	145.
c. 1980 (52, 53, 54).	FV	120.
d. 1981 (53, 54, 55).	FV	120.
e. 1983 (53, 54, 55).	FV	135.
f. 1985 (53, 55, 56).	FV	165.
g. 1987 (57, 58, 59).	FV	100.
h. 1988 (57, 59, 60).	FV	95.00
s. Perforated: *SPECIMEN.*	—	1950.

57 100 Franken

(19)75-93. Blue and multicolor. Francesco Borromini at right. Back: Baroque architectural drawing and view of S. Ivo alla Sapienza on vertical format. Watermark: Francesco Borromini. Printer: OHZ. 170x78mm.

	VF	UNC
a. 1975 (48, 49, 50).	FV	220.
b. 1977 (48, 50, 51).	FV	280.
c. 1980 (52, 53, 54).	FV	220.
d. 1981 (53, 54, 55).	FV	190.
e. 1982 (53, 54, 55).	FV	190.
f. 1983 (53, 54, 55).	FV	240.
g. 1984 (53, 54, 55).	FV	280.
h. 1986 (57, 58, 59).	FV	220.
i. 1988 (57, 59, 60).	FV	190.
j. 1989 (57, 59, 60).	FV	190.
k. 1991 (61, 63, 64).	FV	180.
l. 1992 (61, 63, 64).	FV	180.
m. 1993 (61, 63, 64).	FV	180.
s. Perforated: *SPECIMEN.*	—	2200.

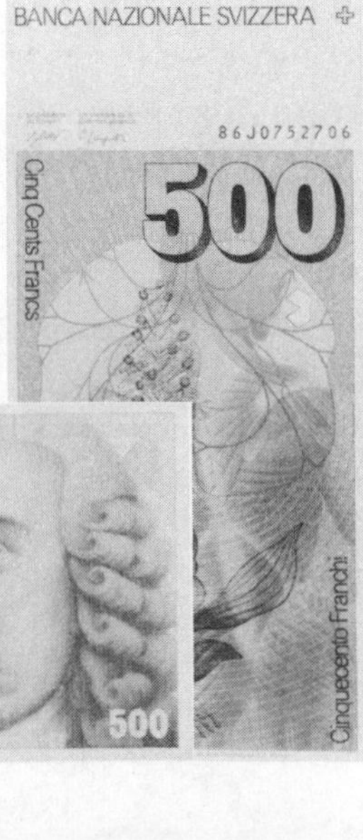

58 500 Franken

(19)76-92. Brown and multicolor. Albrecht von Haller at right, mountains (Gemmi Pass) at left. Back: Anatomical muscles of the back, schematic blood circulation and a purple orchid flower on vertical format. Watermark: Albrecht von Haller. Printer: OHZ. 181x82mm.

	VF	UNC
a. 1976 (48, 50, 51).	FV	1050.
b. 1986 (57, 58, 59).	FV	1200.
c. 1992 (61, 63, 64).	FV	1050.
s. Perforated: *SPECIMEN.*	—	2750.

59 1000 Franken

(19)77-93. Purple on multicolor underprint. Auguste Forel at right, diagrams through a brain and a nerve cell at left. Back: Ants and ant hill schematic on vertical format. Watermark: Auguste Forel. Printer: OFZ. 192x96mm.

	VF	UNC
a. 1977 (48, 50, 51).	FV	1950.
b. 1980 (52, 53, 54).	FV	2050.
c. 1984 (53, 54, 55).	FV	2050.
d. 1987 (57, 58, 59).	FV	2150.
e. 1988 (57, 59, 60).	FV	1750.
f. 1993 (61, 63, 64).	FV	1700.
s. Perforated: *SPECIMEN.*	—	3000.

1983-85 Reserve Issue

		VF	UNC
60	**10 Franken** 1983. Orange-brown and multicolor. Leonhard Euler at right. Back: Polyhedron in center, calculations, table for calculation of numbers and solar system diagram.	—	—
61	**20 Franken** 1985. Blue on multicolor underprint. Horace-Bénédict de Saussure at right, crystal in center. Back: Hair hygrometer, mountains and mountain team hiking.	—	—
62	**50 Franken** 1985. Olive-green and multicolor. Konrad Gessner at right. Back: Cherry tree branch, eagle, animals.	—	—
63	**100 Franken** 1985. Violet-blue and multicolor. Francesco Borromini at right, architectural motif at center. Back: Drawing and tower of S. Ivo.	—	—
64	**500 Franken** 1985. Brown and multicolor. Albrecht von Haller at right, hexagonal structure of a cell in center. Back: Anatomy plate and X-ray of a human thorax.	—	—
65	**1000 Franken** 1985. Violet and multicolor. Louis Agassiz at right, structure of the surface of a shellfish. Back: Perch in three parts: head, skeleton and fossil, fishscales and ammonite.	—	—

1994-98 Issue; 8th Series

#66-71 vertical format, reduced size. First two numerals before serial # prefix letter indicates the year of printing. Many sophisticated security features added.

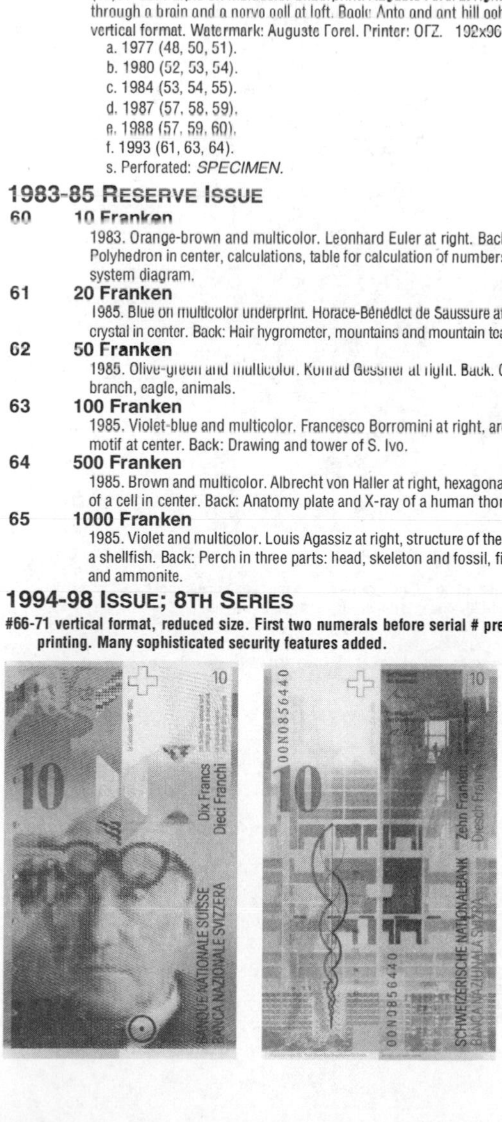

66 10 Franken

(19)95; (19)96. Brown-orange, dark brown and blue on multicolor underprint. Architect Le Corbusier (Charles Édouard Jeanneret-Gris) at upper left and bottom center. Vertical format. Back: "Modular" measuring system and buildings in Chandigarh designed by Le Corbusier. Vertical format. Watermark: Le Corbusier. 74x126mm.

	VF	UNC
a. 1995. (65, 66, 67).	FV	20.00
b. 1996. (65, 66, 67).	FV	23.00

67 10 Franken

2000; 2006; 2008. Brown-orange, dark brown and blue on multicolor underprint. Architect Le Corbusier (Charles Édouard Jeanneret-Gris) at upper left and bottom center. Vertical format. Back: "Modular" measuring system and buildings in Chandigarh designed by Le Corbusier. Vertical format. Watermark: Le Corbusier. Like #66 but with microperforation '10' added. 74x126mm.

	VF	UNC
a. 2000. (70, 71, 72).	FV	28.00
b. 2006. (74, 75, 76).	FV	25.00
c. 2008. (74, 77, 78).	FV	15.00
d. 2010. (77, 78, 79).	FV	15.00

68 20 Franken

(19)94; (19)95. Red-violet and green on multicolor underprint. Composer Arthur Honegger at upper left and bottom center. Vertical format. Back: Trumpet valves at top, steam locomotive wheel at center, musical score and piano keys at bottom. Vertical format. Watermark: Arthur Honegger. 74x137mm.

	VF	UNC
a. 1994. (65, 66, 67).	FV	31.00
b. 1995. (65, 66, 67).	FV	35.00

69 20 Franken

(20)00-. Red-violet and green on multicolor underprint. Composer Arthur Honegger at upper left and bottom center. Vertical format. Back: Trumpet valves at top, steam locomotive wheel at center, musical score and piano keys at bottom. Ver Watermark: Arthur Honegger. Like #68 but with microperforation '20' added. 74x137mm.

	VF	UNC
a. 2000. (71, 72, 73).	FV	40.00
b. 2003. (74, 75, 76).	FV	40.00
c. 2004. (74, 76, 77).	FV	40.00
d. 2005. (74, 76, 77).	FV	32.00
e. 2008. (74, 77, 78).	FV	28.00

		VF	UNC
70	**50 Franken** (19)94 (1995). Deep olive-green and purple on multicolor underprint. Artist Sophie Taeuber-Arp at upper left, bottom. Vertical format. Back: Examples of her abstract art works. Signatures (65, 66, 67). Vertical format. Watermark: Sophie Taeuber-Arp. 74x148mm.	FV	85.00
71	**50 Franken** 2002 (2003)-. Deep olive-green and purple on multicolor underprint. Artist Sophie Taeuber-Arp at upper left, bottom. Vertical format. Back: Examples of her abstract works. Ver Watermark: Sophie Taeuber-Arp. Like #70 but with microperforation '50' added. 74x148mm.		
	a. 2002 (71, 72, 73).	FV	85.00
	b. 2004 (85, 76, 77).	FV	85.00
	c. 2006. (74, 76, 77).	FV	72.00
	d. 2010. (77, 78, 79).	FV	65.00

		VF	UNC
73	**200 Franken** (19)96; (20)00; (20)06. Brown and purple on multicolor underprint. Author Charles-Ferdinand Ramuz at upper left and bottom center. Vertical format. Back: Diablerets massif at top, Lavaux area by Lake Geneva repeated at center to bottom with partial manuscript overlay. Vertical format. Watermark: Charles-Ferdinand Ramuz. 74x170mm.		
	a. 1996 (66, 68, 69).	FV	280.
	b. 2002 (71, 72, 73).	FV	300.
	c. 2006. (74, 76, 77).	FV	250.

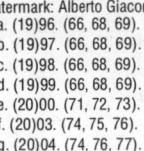

		VF	UNC
72	**100 Franken** (19)96-. Dark blue, purple and brown-orange on multicolor underprint. Alberto Giacometti (artist) at upper left and bottom. Vertical format. Back: Bronze bust *Lotar II* at top, sculpture *Homme Qui Marche I* repeated at center, time-space relationship scheme at lower center. Vertical format. Watermark: Alberto Giacometti. 74x159mm.		
	a. (19)96. (66, 68, 69).	FV	165.
	b. (19)97. (66, 68, 69).	FV	165.
	c. (19)98. (66, 68, 69).	FV	165.
	d. (19)99. (66, 68, 69).	FV	165.
	e. (20)00. (71, 72, 73).	FV	150.
	f. (20)03. (74, 75, 76).	FV	165.
	g. (20)04. (74, 76, 77).	FV	140.
	h. (20)07. (74, 76, 77).	FV	125.

		VF	UNC
74	**1000 Franken** (19)96 (1998); (19)99; (20)06. Purple and violet on multicolor underprint. Jacob Burckhardt (art historian) at upper left and bottom. Vertical format. Back: Window and the Pergamon Altar at top, the Rotunda of the Pantheon in Rome and a section of the fa<c,ade of Palazzo Strossi in Florence at center, overlapped by Burkhardt's view of history scheme. Vert Watermark: Jacob Burckhardt. 74x181mm.		
	a. 1996 (1998). (66; 67, 68).	FV	1250.
	b. 1999. (66, 68, 69).	FV	1200.
	c. 2006. (74, 76, 77).	FV	1200.

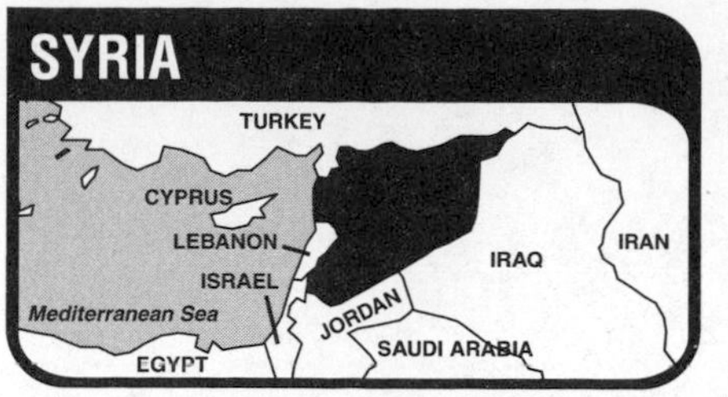

The Syrian Arab Republic, located in the Near East at the eastern end of the Mediterranean Sea, has an area of 185,180 sq. km. and a population of 19.75 million. Capital: Damascus. Agriculture and animal breeding are the chief industries. Cotton, crude oil and livestock are exported.

Following the breakup of the Ottoman Empire during World War I, France administered Syria until its independence in 1946. The country lacked political stability, however, and experienced a series of military coups during its first decades. Syria united with Egypt in February 1958 to form the United Arab Republic. In September 1961, the two entities separated, and the Syrian Arab Republic was reestablished. In November 1970, Hafiz al-Asad, a member of the Socialist Ba'th Party and the minority Alawite sect, seized power in a bloodless coup and brought political stability to the country. In the 1967 Arab-Israeli War, Syria lost the Golan Heights to Israel. During the 1990s, Syria and Israel held occasional peace talks over its return. Following the death of President al-Asad, his son, Bashar al-Asad, was approved as president by popular referendum in July 2000. Syrian troops - stationed in Lebanon since 1976 in an ostensible peacekeeping role - were withdrawn in April 2005. During the July-August 2006 conflict between Israel and Hizballah, Syria placed its military forces on alert but did not intervene directly on behalf of its ally Hizballah.

MONETARY SYSTEM:

1 Pound (Livre) = 100 Piastres

Republic

Banque Centrale de Syrie

Central Bank of Syria

1958 Issue

86 1 Pound — VF | UNC

1958/AH1377. Brown on multicolor underprint. Worker at right. Back: Water wheel of Hama. Bank name in English. Watermark: Arabian horse's head. Printer: Pakistan Security Printing Corp. Ltd.

	VF	UNC
a. Issued note.	7.50	30.00
s. Specimen.	—	35.00

87 5 Pounds

1958/AH1377. Green on multicolor underprint. Worker at right. Similar to #86. Back: Citadel of Aleppo. Bank name in English. Watermark: Arabian horse's head. Printer: Pakistan Security Printing Corp. Ltd.

	VF	UNC
a. Issued note.	20.00	100.
s. Specimen.	—	50.00

88 10 Pounds — VF | UNC

1958/AH1377. Purple on multicolor underprint. Worker at right. Similar to #86. Back: Courtyard of Omayad Mosque. Bank name in English. Watermark: Arabian horse's head. Printer: Pakistan Security Printing Corp. Ltd.

	VF	UNC
a. Issued note.	30.00	135.
s. Specimen.	—	100.

89 25 Pounds

1958/AH1377. Blue on multicolor underprint. Girl with basket at right. Back: Interior view of Azem Palace in Damascus. Bank name in English. Watermark: Arabian horse's head. Printer: JEZ.

	VF	UNC
a. Issued note.	35.00	150.
s. Specimen.	—	150.

90 50 Pounds — VF | UNC

1958/AH1377. Red and brown on multicolor underprint. Girl with basket at right. Similar to #89. Back: Mosque of Sultan Selim. Bank name in English. Watermark: Arabian horse's head. Printer: JEZ.

	VF	UNC
a. Issued note.	40.00	175.
s. Specimen.	—	175.

91 100 Pounds

1958;1962. Olive-green on multicolor underprint. Girl with basket at right. Similar to #89. Back: Old ruins of Palmyra. Bank name in English. Watermark: Arabian horse's head. Printer: JEZ.

	VF	UNC
a. 1958.	70.00	250.
b. 1962.	60.00	210.
s. Specimen.	—	200.

92 500 Pounds — VF | UNC

1958/AH1377. Brown and purple on multicolor underprint. Motifs from ruins of Kingdom of Ugarit, head at right. Back: Ancient religious wheel and cuneiform clay tablet. Bank name in English. Watermark: Arabian horse's head. Printer: JEZ.

	VF	UNC
a. Issued note.	160.	410.
s. Specimen.	—	400.

1963-66 Issue

93 1 Pound — VF | UNC

1963-82/AH1383-1402. Brown on multicolor underprint. Worker at right. Back: Water wheel of Hama. Bank name in English. Watermark: Arabian horse's head.

	VF	UNC
a. Without security thread. 1963/AH1383.	4.00	20.00
b. 1967/AH1387.	4.00	16.00
c. 1973/AH1393.	3.00	10.00
d. Security thread with *Central Bank of Syria* in small letters. 1978/AH1398.	2.00	8.00
e. 1982/AH1402.	1.00	4.00
s. As a. Specimen.	—	85.00

94 5 Pounds — VF | UNC

1963-73/AH1383-93. Green on multicolor underprint. Worker at right. Back: Citadel of Aleppo on back. Bank name in English. Watermark: Arabian horse's head.

	VF	UNC
a. 1963/AH1383.	18.00	75.00
b. 1967/AH1387.	12.00	60.00
c. 1970.	10.00	55.00
d. 1973/AH1393.	8.00	50.00

95 10 Pounds

1965-73/AH138x-93. Purple on multicolor underprint. Worker at right. Back: Courtyard of Omayad Mosque. Bank name in English. Watermark: Arabian horse's head.

	VF	UNC
a. 1965.	15.00	85.00
b. 1968.	12.00	65.00
c. 1973/AH1393.	8.00	55.00

96 25 Pounds

1966-73/AH1386-93. Blue and brown on multicolor underprint. Worker at the loom at left. Back: Bosra theater at center right. Watermark: Arabian horse's head.

	VF	UNC
a. 1966/AH1386.	32.00	220.
b. 1970.	30.00	160.
c. 1973/AH1393.	25.00	140.

97 50 Pounds

1966-73/AH1386-93. Brown and olive-green on multicolor underprint. Arab driving combine at left. Back: Fortress. Watermark: Arabian horse's head.

	VF	UNC
a. 1966/AH1386; 1970.	55.00	250.
b. 1973/AH1393.	45.00	145.

98 100 Pounds

1966-74/AH1386-139x. Green and blue on multicolor underprint. Port installation at left. Back: Purple. Dam at center. Watermark: Arabian horse's head.

	VF	UNC
a. 1966/AH1386.	55.00	165.
b. 1968.	70.00	200.
c. 1971/AH1391.	45.00	130.
d. 1974.	35.00	100.

1976-77 Issue

99 1 Pound

1977/AH1397. Orange and brown on multicolor underprint. Omayyad Mosque at center, craftsman at right. Back: Red-brown. Combine at center. Watermark: Arabian horse's head.

	VF	UNC
a. Issued note.	4.00	16.00
s. Specimen.	—	—

100 5 Pounds

1977-91/AH1397-1412. Dark green on multicolor underprint. Bosra theater and statue of female warrior at right. Back: Cotton picking and spinning frame. Watermark: Arabian horse's head.

	VF	UNC
a. Security thread. 1977/AH1397.	4.00	12.00
b. Security thread. With *Central Bank of Syria* in small letters. 1978/AH1398.	FV	4.00
c. 1982/AH1402.	FV	3.00
d. 1988/AH1408.	FV	2.00
e. 1991/AH1412.	FV	1.50
s. As a. Specimen.	—	—

101 10 Pounds

1977-91/AH1397-1412. Purple and violet on multicolor underprint. Al-Azem Palace in Damascus at center, dancing woman at right. Back: Water treatment plant. Watermark: Arabian horse's head. UV: Arabic 10, horse head, central design, fibers all fluoresce yellow.

	VF	UNC
a. Like #100a. 1977/AH1397.	6.00	16.00
b. Like #100b. 1978/AH1398.	FV	5.00
c. 1982/AH1402.	FV	3.00
d. 1988/AH1408.	FV	2.00
e. 1991/AH1412.	FV	1.50

102 25 Pounds

1977-91/AH1397-1412. Dark blue and dark green on multicolor underprint. Krak des Chevaliers castle at center, Saladdin at right. Back: Central Bank building. Watermark: Arabian horse's head.

	VF	UNC
a. Like #100a. 1977/AH1397.	12.00	32.00
b. Like #100b. 1978/AH1398.	3.00	15.00
c. 1982/AH1402.	2.50	10.00
d. 1988/AH1408.	1.00	6.00
e. 1991/AH1412.	FV	4.00

103 50 Pounds

1977-91/AH1397-1412. Brown, black and green on multicolor underprint. Dam at center, ancient statue at right. Back: Citadel of Aleppo. Watermark: Arabian horse's head. 155x75mm.

	VF	UNC
a. Like #100a. 1977/AH1397.	12.00	42.00
b. Like #100b. 1978/AH1398.	5.00	21.00
c. 1982/AH1402.	4.00	16.00
d. 1988/AH1408.	3.00	8.00
e. 1991/AH1412.	2.00	6.00

104 100 Pounds

1977-90/AH1397-1411. Dark blue, dark green and dark brown on multicolor underprint. Ancient Palmyra ruins at center, Queen Zenobia bust at right. Back: Grain silos at Lattakia. Watermark: Arabian horse's head. 167x80mm.

	VF	UNC
a. Like #100a. 1977/AH1397.	21.00	65.00
b. Like #100b. 1978/AH1398.	12.00	40.00
c. 1982/AH1402.	4.00	20.00
d. 1990/AH1411.	3.00	10.00

105 500 Pounds

1976-90/AH1396-1411. Dark violet-brown and brown on multicolor underprint. Motifs from ruins of Kingdom of Ugarit, head at right. Back: Ancient religious wheel and cuneiform clay tablet. Bank name in English. Watermark: Arabian horse's head. 180x85mm.

	VF	UNC
a. 1976/AH1396.	25.00	75.00
b. 1979.	45.00	200.
c. 1982/AH1402.	25.00	80.00
d. 1986.	20.00	75.00
e. 1990/AH1411.	15.00	50.00
f. 1992/AH1413.	15.00	40.00

1997-98 Issue

107 50 Pounds VF UNC

1998/AH1419. Dark and light brown, green and lilac on multicolor underprint. Aleppo Citadel at center, water wheel of Hama at right. Back: Al-Assad library, Abbyssian stadium and students. Watermark: Arabian horse's head. UV: value 50SP in rectangle and horse head fluoresce yellow; fibers fluoresce yellow, red and blue. 150x75mm. — FV 4.50

108 100 Pounds VF UNC

1998/AH1419. Light blue, red-brown and purple on multicolor underprint. Bosra theater at center, ancient bust of Philip at right. Back: Hajaz railway locomotive; Damascus station and road. Watermark: Arabian horse's head. 166x80mm. — FV 6.50

109 200 Pounds VF UNC

1997/AH1418. Red-orange, purple and light brown on multicolor underprint. Monument to the Unknown soldier at center, Islamic coin at lower center right, Statue of Saladdin at right. Back: Cotton weaving and energy plant. Watermark: Arabian horse's head. 160x75mm. — FV 11.00

110 500 Pounds

1998/AH1419 (2000). Gray and bluish-green on multicolor underprint. Queen Zenobia at right, Palmyra theater at center. Back: Eufrate dam, irrigation and agricultural products. 165x75mm.

	VF	UNC
a. Without map of Syria on back.	FV	30.00
b. Map of Syria added to back.	FV	25.00

111	1000 Pounds	VF	UNC
	1997/AH1418. Green, blue and light brown on multicolor underprint. Omayyad Mosque main entrance at center, Islamic dinar coin and clay tablet at lower center, H. Assad at right. Back: Oil industry workers at left, harvesting machinery and fishing boat. Watermark: H. Assad. 170x75mm.		
	a. Without map of Syria on back.	FV	48.00
	b. With map of Syria on back.	FV	40.00

2009 Issue

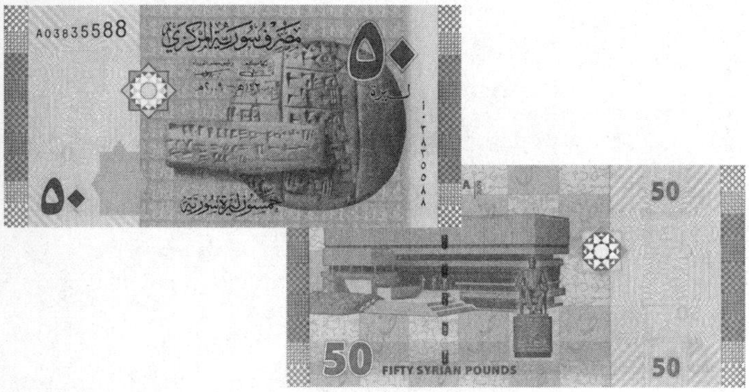

112	50 Pounds	VF	UNC
	2009. Blue and ton on multicolor underprint. Clay tablets from Ebla. Back: Hafiz al Assad Library in Damascus. Watermark: Horse head and 50. 135x65mm.	FV	3.00

113	100 Pounds	VF	UNC
	2009. Red and tan on multicolor underprint. Ancient Roman theater and archway of Bosra gate. Back: Umayyad Mosque in Damascus safe; Central Bank building, coin. Watermark: Horse head and 100 141x65mm.	FV	6.00

114	200 Pounds	VF	UNC
	2009. Tan and green on multicolor underprint. Norias (waterwheels) of Hama. Back: Bel Temple ceiling in Palmyra. Watermark: Horse head and 200. 146x65mm.	FV	8.00

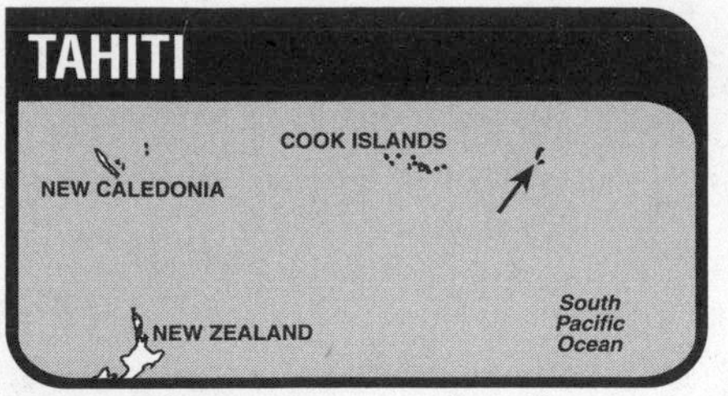

Tahiti, the largest island of the central South Pacific French overseas territory of French Polynesia, has an area of 402 sq. mi. (1,042 sq. km.) and a population of 79,024. Papeete on the northwest coast is the capital and administrative center of French Polynesia. Copra, sugar cane, vanilla and coffee are exported. Tourism is an important industry.

Capt. Samuel Wallis of the British Navy discovered Tahiti in 1768 and named it King George III Island. Louis-Antoine de Bougainville arrived the following year and claimed it for France. Subsequent English visits were by James Cook in 1769 and William Bligh in the HMS "Bounty" in 1788.

Members of the Protestant London Missionary Society established the first European settlement in 1797, and with the aid of the local Pomare family gained control of the entire island and established a "missionary kingdom" with a scriptural code of law. Nevertheless, Tahiti was subsequently declared a French protectorate (1842) and a colony (1880), and since 1958 is part of the overseas territory of French Polynesia.

RULERS:

French

MONETARY SYSTEM:

1 Franc = 100 Centimes

<AFrame <BRect 0.0 0.0 3.5 3.75><TextLine <TLOrigin 1.5 0.75><TLAlignment Center><String "003.75'>>>

SIGNATURE VARIETIES		
	DIRECTEUR GÉNÉRAL	PREÉSIDENT DU CONSEIL DE SURVEILLANCE
1	André Postel-Vinay, 1967-1972	Bernard Clappier, 1966-1972
2	Claude Panouillot, 1972-1973	André de Lattre, 1973
3	Claude Panouillot, 1974-1978	Marcel Theron, 1974-1979
4	Yves Roland-Billecart, 1979-1984	Gabriel Lefort, 1980-1984
5	Yves Roland-Billecart, 1985-	Jacques Waitzenegger, 1985-

French Administration

Banque de l'Indochine

Papeete

1939-40 ND Issue

14	100 Francs	Fine	XF
	ND (1939-65). Brown and multicolor. Woman wearing wreath and holding small figure of Athena at center. Back: Angkor statue.		
	a. Signature M. Borduge and P. Baudouin with titles: *LE PRÉSIDENT* and *LE ADMINISTRATEUR DIRECTEUR GÉNÉRAL.*	85.00	300.
	b. Signature titles: *LE PRÉSIDENT* and *LE ADMINISTRATEUR DIRECTEUR GÉNÉRAL.*	75.00	250.
	c. Signature titles: *LE PRÉSIDENT* and *LE VICE-PRÉSIDENT DIRECTEUR GÉNÉRAL.*	60.00	225.
	d. Signature titles: *LE PRÉSIDENT* and *LE DIRECTEUR GÉNÉRAL.*	50.00	200.

1951 ND Issue

21	20 Francs	VF	UNC
	ND (1951-63). Multicolor. Youth at left, flute player at right. Back: Fruit at left, woman at right. Watermark: Man with hat.		
	a. Signature titles: *LE PRÉSIDENT* and *LE DIRECTEUR GAL.* (1951).	50.00	125.
	b. Signature titles: *LE PRÉSIDENT* and *LE VICE-PRÉSIDENT DIRECTEUR GÉNÉRAL* (1954-1958).	30.00	75.00
	c. Signature titles: *LE PRÉSIDENT* and *LE DIRECTEUR GÉNÉRAL.* (1963).	20.00	50.00
	s. As b, c. Specimen. Pin hole perforated *SPECIMEN.*	—	250.

Institut d'Emission d'Outre-Mer

1969-71 ND Issues

23	100 Francs	VF	UNC
	ND (1969). Brown and multicolor. Girl wearing wreath holding guitar at right, without *REPUBLIQUE FRANCAISE* near bottom center. Signature 1. Back: Girl at left, town scene at center. Printed from engraved copper plates.	10.00	75.00

24	100 Francs	VF	UNC
	ND. (1971; 1973). Multicolor. Girl wearing wreath holding guitar at right, with overprint *REPUBLIQUE FRANCAISE* near bottom center. Signature 1. Back: Girl at left, town scene at center.		
	a. Printed from engraved copper plates. (1971).	25.00	65.00
	b. Offset printing. (1973).	20.00	55.00

25	500 Francs	VF	UNC
	ND (1970-85). Blue and multicolor. Harbor view with boat in background at center, fisherman at lower right. Back: Man at left, objects at right.		
	a. Signature 1. (1970).	40.00	95.00
	b1. Signature 3. (1977).	32.50	80.00
	b2. Signature 3A.	35.00	85.00
	c. Signature 4. (1983).	27.50	70.00
	d. Signature 5. (1985).	20.00	55.00

26	1000 Francs	VF	UNC
	ND (1969). Dark brown on red and multicolor underprint. Hut under palms at left, girl at right. Without *REPUBLIQUE FRANCAISE* overprint at bottom center. Signature 1. Back: Kagu, deer, buildings, native carvings. Watermark: Marianne.	90.00	225.

27 **1000 Francs** — **VF** **UNC**

ND (1971-85). Dark brown on multicolor underprint. Hut under palms at left, girl at right. With overprint *REPUBLIQUE FRANCAISE* overprint at bottom center. Signature 1. Back: Kagu, deer, buildings, native carvings. Watermark: Marianne.

	VF	UNC
a. Signature 1. (1971).	55.00	125.
b. Signature 3. (1977).	45.00	100.
c. Signature 4. (1983).	40.00	100.
d. Signature 5. (1985).	35.00	90.00

28 **5000 Francs** — **VF** **UNC**

ND (1971-85). Brown with black text on olive-green and multicolor underprint. Bougainville at left, sailing ships at center. Back: Admiral Febvrier-Despointes at right, sailboat at center right.

	VF	UNC
a. Signature 1. (1971).	120.	250.
b. Signature 2. (1975).	100.	225.
c. Signature 4. (1982; 1984).	95.00	190.
d. Signature 5. (1985).	85.00	165.

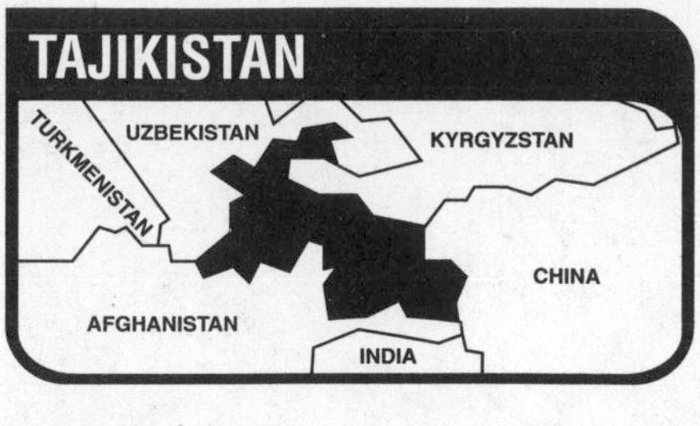

The Republic of Tajikistan, was formed from those regions of Bukhara and Turkestan where the population consisted mainly of Tajiks. It is bordered in the north and west by Uzbekistan and Kyrgyzstan, in the east by China and in the south by Afghanistan. It has an area of 143,100 sq. km. and a population of 7.21 million. It includes 2 provinces of Khudzand and Khatlon together with the Gorno-Badakhshan Autonomous Region. Capital: Dushanbe.

The Tajik people came under Russian rule in the 1860s and 1870s, but Russia's hold on Central Asia weakened following the Revolution of 1917. Bolshevik control of the area was fiercely contested and not fully reestablished until 1925. Much of present-day Sughd province was transferred from the Uzbekistan SSR to newly formed Tajikistan SSR in 1929. Ethnic Uzbeks form a substantial minority in Sughd province. Tajikistan became independent in 1991 following the breakup of the Soviet Union, and it is now in the process of strengthening its democracy and transitioning to a free market economy after its 1992-97 civil war. There have been no major security incidents in recent years, although the country remains the poorest in the former Soviet sphere. Attention by the international community in the wake of the war in Afghanistan has brought increased economic development and security assistance, which could create jobs and increase stability in the long term. Tajikistan is in the early stages of seeking World Trade Organization membership and has joined NATO's Partnership for Peace.

MONETARY SYSTEM:

1 Ruble = 100 Tanga, to 2000
1 Somoni = 1,000 Rubles
1 Somoni = 100 Diram

REPUBLIC

БОНКИ МИЛЛИИ ЧУМХУРИИ ТОЧИКИСТОН

NATIONAL BANK OF THE REPUBLIC OF TAJIKISTAN

1994 ISSUE

1 **1 Ruble** — **VF** **UNC**

1994. Brown on multicolor underprint. Arms at upper left. Back: *Majlisi Olii* (Parliament). Watermark: Multiple stars. Printer: Goznak (without imprint).

	VF	UNC
a. Issued note.	.50	1.00
s. Specimen.	—	—

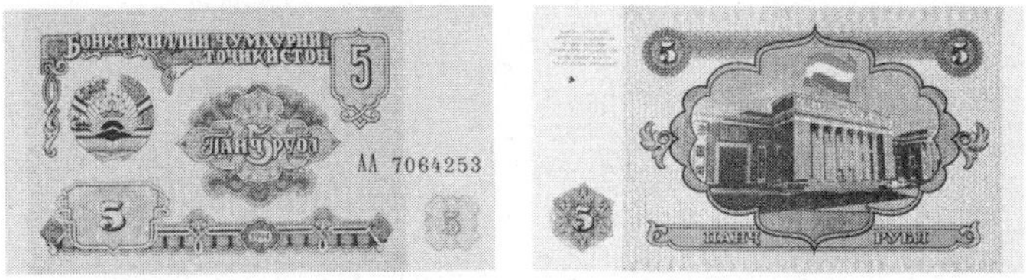

2 **5 Rubles** — **VF** **UNC**

1994. Deep blue on multicolor underprint. Arms at upper left. Back: *Majlisi Olii* (Parliament). Watermark: Multiple stars. Printer: Goznak (without imprint).

	VF	UNC
a. Issued note.	.50	2.00
s. Specimen.	—	—

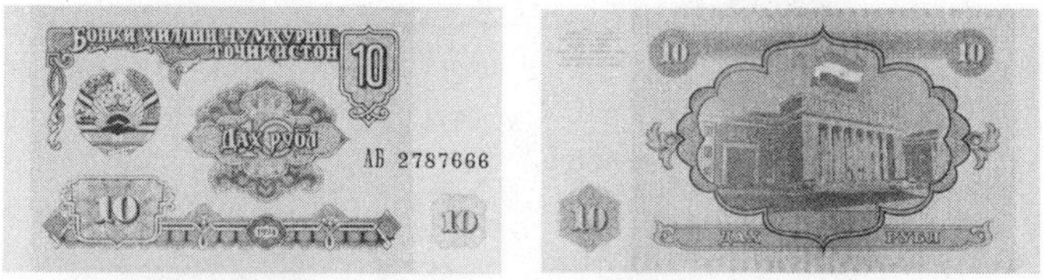

3 **10 Rubles** — **VF** **UNC**

1994. Deep red on multicolor underprint. Arms at upper left. Back: *Majlisi Olii* (Parliament). Watermark: Multiple stars. Printer: Goznak (without imprint).

	VF	UNC
a. Issued note.	1.00	3.00
s. Specimen.	—	—

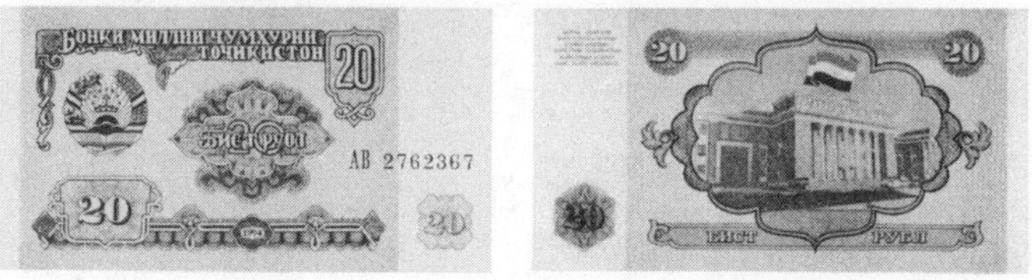

		VF	UNC
4	**20 Rubles**		
	1994. Purple on multicolor underprint. Arms at upper left. Back: *Majlisi Olii* (Parliament). Watermark: Multiple stars. Printer: Goznak (without imprint).		
	a. Issued note.	1.00	3.00
	s. Specimen.	—	—

		VF	UNC
5	**50 Rubles**		
	1994. Dark olive-green on multicolor underprint. Arms at upper left. Back: *Majlisi Olii* (Parliament). Watermark: Multiple stars. Printer: Goznak (without imprint).		
	a. Issued note.	1.00	4.00
	s. Specimen.	—	—

		VF	UNC
6	**100 Rubles**		
	1994. Blue-black and brown on multicolor underprint. Arms at left. Back: *Majlisi Olii* (Parliament). Watermark: Multiple stars. Printer: Goznak (without imprint).		
	a. Issued note.	1.00	5.00
	s. Specimen. Red overprint: *SPECIMEN* on both sides.	—	27.50

		VF	UNC
7	**200 Rubles**		
	1994. Deep olive-green and pale violet on multicolor underprint. Arms at left. Back: *Majlisi Olii* (Parliament). Watermark: Multiple stars. Printer: Goznak (without imprint).		
	a. Issued note.	1.00	6.00
	s. Specimen.	—	—

		VF	UNC
8	**500 Rubles**		
	1994. Brown-violet on multicolor underprint. Arms at upper left. Back: *Majlisi Olii* (Parliament). Watermark: Multiple stars. Printer: Goznak (without imprint).		
	a. Issued note.	2.00	8.00
	s. Specimen. Red overprint: *SPECIMEN* on both sides.	—	30.00

		VF	UNC
9	**1000 Rubles**		
	1994 (1999). Brown and purple on multicolor underprint.		
	a. Issued note.	.50	5.00
	s. Specimen. Black overprint: *HAMYHA* on both sides.	—	35.00

		VF	UNC
9A	**5000 Rubles**		
	1994. Dark green and blue on multicolor underprint. Coat of Arms at left. Back: Parliament building with flag. (Not issued).	—	50.00

		VF	UNC
9B	**10,000 Rubles**		
	1994. Pink and brown on multicolor underprint. Coat of Arms at center. Back: Parliament building with flag.		
	a. Unissued note.	—	50.00
	s. Specimen.		

БОНКИ МИЛЛИИ ТОЧИКИСТОН

NATIONAL BANK OF TAJIKISTAN

1999 ISSUE

		VF	UNC
10	**1 Diram**		
	1999 (2000). Brown on tan and red underprint. Sadriddin Ayni Theatre and Opera house at center. Back: Pamir mountains. Watermark: Two mountains over rectangle. Printer: German. 110x60mm.		
	a. Issued note.	FV	2.00
	s. Specimen. Red overprint: *SPECIMEN* on both sides.	—	10.00
11	**5 Diram**		
	1999 (2000). Blue on tan underprint. Arbob Culture Palace at center. Back: Shrine of Mirzo Tursunzoda. Watermark: Two mountains over rectangle. Printer: German. 110x60mm.		
	a. Issued note.	FV	2.00
	s. Specimen. Red overprint: *SPECIMEN* on both sides.	—	10.00
12	**20 Diram**		
	1999 (2000). Green on tan underprint. *Majlisi Olii*, Meeting Hall of the National Bank. Back: Road pass in the mountains. Watermark: Two mountains over rectangle. Printer: German. 110x60mm.		
	a. Issued note.	FV	3.00
	s. Specimen. Red overprint: *SPECIMEN* on both sides.	—	10.00

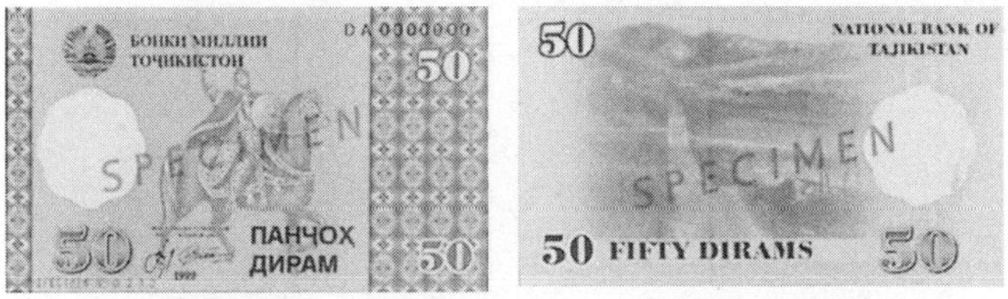

		VF	UNC
13	**50 Diram**		
	1999 (2000). Purple on tan underprint. Statue of Ismoili Somoni at center. Back: Road in a valley. Watermark: Two mountains over rectangle. Printer: German. 100x60mm.		
	a. Nominal value and bank name reflect UV.	FV	4.00
	b. Nominal value and bank name does not reflect UV.	FV	4.00
	s. Specimen. Red overprint: *SPECIMEN* on both sides.	—	10.00

14	1 Somoni	VF	UNC
	1999 (2000). Green and blue on multicolor underprint. Mirzo Tursunzoda (poet) at right. Globe at center is green and orange. Back: National Bank of Tajikistan building. Watermark: Mirzo Tursunzoda. 141x65mm.		
	a. Globe green-yellow and glows under UV light.	FV	4.00
	b. Globe green-yellow and does not glow UV. Series AK.	FV	4.00
	r. Replacement note. Series AZ.	—	—
	s. Specimen. Red overprint: *SPECIMEN* on both sides.	—	40.00

14A	1 Somoni	VF	UNC
	1999 (2010). Green and blue on multicolor underprint. Mirzo Tursunzoda at right. Globe at center is green. Back: National Bank building at center. Watermark: Tursunzoda. 141x65mm.	FV	4.00

15	5 Somoni	VF	UNC
	1999 (2000). Blue and green on multicolor underprint. Sadriddin Ayni at right. Back: Tomb of Abuabdullo Rudaki in Panjakent. Watermark: Sadriddin Ayni. 144x65mm.		
	a. Gray table on face, right number is not UV reflective. Back middle element is UV reflective.	FV	8.00
	b. Blue table on face, right number is not UV reflective. Series BG.	FV	8.00
	c. Blue table on face. Right number is UV reflective. Series BK.	FV	8.00
	r. Replacement note. Series BZ.	—	—
	s. Specimen. Red overprint: *SPECIMEN* on both sides.	—	40.00

16	10 Somoni	VF	UNC
	1999 (2000). Purple and orange-red. Mir Saiid Alii Hamadoni at right. Back: Tomb of Mir Said Alii Hamadoni in Kulob Watermark: Mir Saiid Alii Hamadoni. 147x65mm.		
	a. Back middle element glows under UV light.	FV	15.00
	b. Back middle does not glow under UV light. Series CG.	FV	15.00
	r. Replacement note. Series CZ.	—	—
	s. Specimen. Red overprint: *SPECIMEN* on both sides.	—	40.00

17	20 Somoni	VF	UNC
	1999 (2000). Brown and blue on multicolor underprint. Abuali Ibn Sino at right. Holographic strip at right. Back: Hissar fortress near Dushanbe. Watermark: Abuali Ibn Sino. 150x65mm.		
	a. Bowl on face glows under UV light.	FV	20.00
	b. Bowl on face does not glow under UV light.	FV	20.00
	r. Replacement note. Series DZ.	—	—
	s. Specimen. Red overprint: *SPECIMEN* on both sides.	—	40.00

18	50 Somoni	VF	UNC
	1999 (2000). Dark blue and black on multicolor underprint. Bobojon Gafurov at right. Holographic strip at right. Back: *Choikhanai Sina*, a tea house in Dushanbe. Watermark: Bobojon Gafurov. 153x65mm.		
	a. Issued note. Serial # not on kinegram foil.	FV	25.00
	r. Replacement note. Series EZ.	—	—
	s. Specimen. Red overprint: *SPECIMEN* on both sides.	—	40.00

19	100 Somoni	VF	UNC
	1999 (2000). Brown and blue on multicolor underprint. Ismoili Somoni at right. Holographic strip at right. Back: Presidential Palace in Dushanbe. Watermark: Ismoili Somoni. 156x65mm.		
	a. Issued note. Serial # not on kinegram foil.	FV	85.00
	r. Replacement note. Series FZ.	—	—
	s. Specimen. Red overprint: *SPECIMEN* on both sides.	—	50.00

2010 Commemorative Issue

20	3 Somoni	VF	UNC
	2010. Violet on multicolor underprint. Shirinsho Shotemur at right. Back: Majlisi Oli (parliament) building at center. 142x65mm.	FV	1.25

		VF	UNC
21	**200 Somoni** 2010. Brown and yellow on multicolor underprint. Nusratullo Makhsum at right. Back: National Library in Dushanbe. Watermark: Makhsum. 159x65mm.	FV	90.00

		VF	UNC
22	**500 Somoni** 2010. Purple and gray on multicolor underprint. Abuabdullo Rudaki at right. Back: Palace of Nations in Dushanbe. Watermark: Rudaki. 162x65mm.	FV	300.

1999 (2013 Enhanced) Issue

		VF	UNC
23	**5 Somoni** 1999 (2013). Blue on multicolor underprint. Sadriddin Ayni at right, blue central design. Series BN. Wide security foil at right. Back: Tomb of Abuabdullo Rudaki in Panjakent. 144x65mm.	FV	3.00

		VF	UNC
24	**10 Somoni** 1999 (2013). Purple and orange-red on multicolor underprint. Mir Saiid Alii Hamadoni at right. Series CM. Wide foil strip at right. Back: Tomb of Mir Said Alii Hamadoni in Kulob. 147x65mm.	FV	5.00
25	**20 Somoni** 1999 (2013).	FV	10.00
26	**50 Somoni** 1999 (2013).	FV	20.00
27	**100 Somoni** 1999 (2013).	FV	40.00

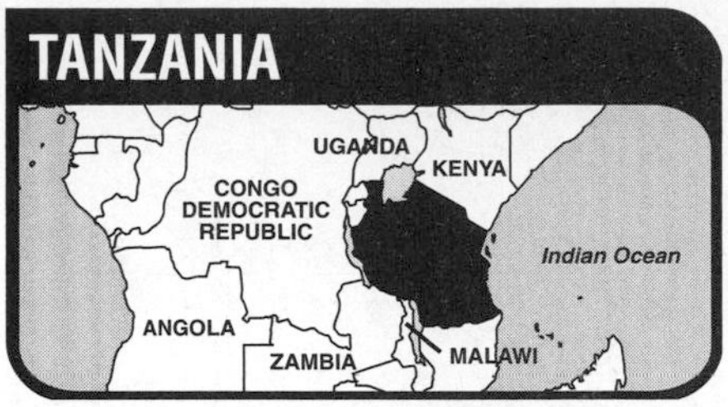

The United Republic of Tanzania, located on the east coast of Africa between Kenya and Mozambique, consists of Tanganyika and the islands of Zanzibar and Pemba. It has an area of 945,090 sq. km. and a population of 40.21 million. Capital: Dodoma. The chief exports are cotton, coffee, diamonds, sisal, cloves, petroleum products and cashew nuts.

Shortly after achieving independence from Britain in the early 1960s, Tanganyika and Zanzibar merged to form the nation of Tanzania in 1964. One-party rule came to an end in 1995 with the first democratic elections held in the country since the 1970s. Zanzibar's semi-autonomous status and popular opposition have led to two contentious elections since 1995, which the ruling party won despite international observers' claims of voting irregularities.

MONETARY SYSTEM:

1 Shilingi (Shilling) = 100 Senti

SIGNATURE VARIETIES

1	MINISTER FOR FINANCE	GOVERNOR	2	MINISTER FOR FINANCE	GOVERNOR
3			4		
5			6	WAZIRI WA FEDHA	GAVANA
7	WAZIRI WA FEDHA	GAVANA	7A		
8			9		
10			11		
12			13		
14					

Republic

Bank of Tanzania

1966 ND Issue

Note: Signature 3-5 with English titles on #2 and 3, changed to Swahili titles for later issues. #1-5 Replacement notes: Serial # prefix *ZZ; ZY*.

1 5 Shillings
ND (1966). Brown on multicolor underprint. Arms at center, President J. Nyerere at right. Signature 1. Back: Mountain view. Watermark: Giraffe's head.

	VF	UNC
a. Issued note.	3.00	12.50
s. Specimen.	—	25.00

2 10 Shillings
ND (1966). Green on multicolor underprint. Arms at center, President J. Nyerere at right. Back: Sisal drying. Watermark: Giraffe's head.

	VF	UNC
a. Signature 1.	3.00	9.00
b. Signature 2.	4.00	10.00
c. Signature 3.	30.00	225.
d. Signature 4.	2.00	7.50
e. Signature 5.	2.00	6.00
s. As a. Specimen.	—	25.00

3 20 Shillings
ND (1966). Blue on multicolor underprint. Arms at center, President J. Nyerere at right. Back: Work buildings. Watermark: Giraffe's head.

	VF	UNC
a. Signature 1.	5.00	12.50
b. Signature 2.	5.00	12.50
c. Signature 3.	7.00	20.00
d. Signature 4.	5.00	15.00
e. Signature 5.	3.00	9.00
s. As a. Specimen.	—	25.00

4 100 Shillings
ND (1966). Red on multicolor underprint. Arms at center, President J. Nyerere at right. Signature 1. Back: Masai herdsman with animals. Watermark: Giraffe's head.

	VF	UNC
a. Issued note.	60.00	375.
s. Specimen.	—	85.00

5 100 Shillings
ND (1966). Red on multicolor underprint. Arms at center, President J. Nyerere at right. Back: Various animals. Watermark: Giraffe's head.

	VF	UNC
a. Signature 1.	50.00	350.
b. Signature 3.	40.00	275.

Benki Kuu Ya Tanzania

1977-78 ND Issue

#6-8 Replacement notes: Serial # prefix *ZZ; ZY.*

Note: For #6-8, sign. are shown in chronological order of appearance. It seems sign. 3 was used again following several later combinations.

6 10 Shilingi
ND (1978). Green on multicolor underprint. Arms at top center, President J. Nyerere at right. Back: Monument and mountain at center. Watermark: Giraffe's head.

	VF	UNC
a. Signature 5.	1.50	7.50
b. Signature 6.	1.25	4.50
c. Signature 3. Signature titles: *WAZIRI WA FEDHA* and *GAVANA*.	.75	3.00

7 20 Shilingi
ND (1978). Blue on multicolor underprint. Arms at top center, President J. Nyerere at right. Back: Cotton knitting machine. Watermark: Giraffe's head.

	VF	UNC
a. Signature 5.	2.25	10.00
b. Signature 6.	2.25	7.00
c. Signature 3. Signature titles: *WAZIRI WA FEDHA* and *GAVANA*.	2.25	6.00

8	**100 Shilingi**	VF	UNC
	ND (1977). Purple on multicolor underprint. Arms at top center, President J. Nyerere at right. Back: Teacher and students at left, farmers at center. Watermark: Giraffe's head.		
	a. Signature 4.	6.00	40.00
	b. Signature 5.	5.00	35.00
	c. Signature 6.	4.00	27.50
	d. Signature 3. Signature titles: *WAZIRI WA FEDHA* and *GAVANA.*	4.50	20.00

1985 ND Issue

#9-11 Replacement notes: Serial # prefix *ZZ; ZY*.

9	**20 Shilingi**	VF	UNC
	ND (1985). Purple, brown on multicolor underprint. Arms at center, torch at left, portrait of an older President J. Nyerere at right. Signature 3. Back: Tire factory scene, islands of Mafia, Pemba and Zanzibar are omitted from map. Watermark: Giraffe's head.	.50	2.50

10	**50 Shilingi**	VF	UNC
	ND (1985). Red-orange, light brown on multicolor underprint. Arms at center, torch at left, portrait of an older President J. Nyerere at right. Signature 3. Back: Brick making, islands of Mafia, Pemba and Zanzibar are omitted from map. Watermark: Giraffe's head. UV: value 50 in box fluoresce orange. Back torch and wreath yellow.	1.50	5.00

11	**100 Shilingi**	VF	UNC
	ND (1985). Blue, purple on multicolor underprint. Arms at center, torch at left, portrait of an older President J. Nyerere at right. Signature 3. Back: Graduation procession, islands of Mafia, Pemba and Zanzibar are omitted from map. Watermark: Giraffe's head.	3.00	12.00

1986 ND Issue

#12-14 Replacement notes: Serial # prefix *ZZ; ZY*.

12	**20 Shilingi**	VF	UNC
	ND (1986). Purple, brown on multicolor underprint. Arms at center, torch at left, portrait of an older President J. Nyerere at right. Signature 3. Signature titles: WAZIRI WA FEDHA and *GAVANA.* Back: Tire factory scene, islands of Mafia, Pemba and Zanzibar are included in map.	.50	2.00

13	**50 Shilingi**	VF	UNC
	ND (1986). Red-orange, light brown on multicolor underprint. Arms at center, torch at left, portrait of an older President J. Nyerere at right. Signature 3. Signature titles: *WAZIRI WA FEDHA* and *GAVANA.* Back: Brick making, islands of Mafia, Pemba and Zanzibar are included in map.	1.00	3.50

14	**100 Shilingi**	VF	UNC
	ND (1986). Blue, purple on multicolor underprint. Arms at center, torch at left, portrait of an older President J. Nyerere at right. Signature 3. Back: Graduation procession, islands of Mafia, Pemba and Zanzibar are included in map.		
	a. Signature 3 with titles: *WAZIRI WA FEDHA* and *GAVANA.*	1.50	7.50
	b. Signature 8.	1.00	5.00

1986-90 ND Issue

#15-18 Replacement notes: Serial # prefix *ZZ; ZY*.

15	**20 Shilingi**	VF	UNC
	ND (1987). Purple, red-brown on multicolor underprint. Arms at center, President Mwinyi at right. Signature 3 but with titles: *WAZIRI WA FEDHA* and *GAVANA.* Back: Tire factory scene, islands of Mafia, Pemba and Zanzibar are included in map. Watermark: Giraffe's head.	.25	2.00

16	**50 Shilingi**	VF	UNC
	ND (1986). Red-orange, light brown on multicolor underprint. Arms at center, President Mwinyi at right. Back: Brick making, islands of Mafia, Pemba and Zanzibar are included in map. Watermark: Giraffe's head.		
	a. Signature 3 but with titles: *WAZIRI WA FEDHA* and *GAVANA.*	1.00	4.00
	b. Signature 7.	.75	3.00
	c. Signature 7B.	1.25	8.00

18 **200 Shilingi**

ND (1986). Black, orange and ochre on multicolor underprint. Arms at center, President Mwinyi at right. Back: Two fishermen. Watermark: Giraffe's head.

	VF	UNC
a. Signature 3 but with titles: *WAZIRI WA FEDHA* and *GAVANA.*	2.00	9.00
b. Signature 7.	4.00	20.00

1989-92 ND Issue

#19-22 Replacement notes: Serial # prefix *ZZ; ZY*.

19 **50 Shilingi**

	VF	UNC
ND (1992). Red-orange and light brown on multicolor underprint. Arms at center, modified portrait of President Mwinyi at right. Signature 8. Back: Brick making, islands of Mafia, Pemba and Zanzibar are included in map. Watermark: Giraffe's head.	.50	1.75

20 **200 Shilingi**

	VF	UNC
ND (1992). Black, orange and ochre on multicolor underprint. Arms at center, modified portrait of President Mwinyi at right. Signature 7, 8. Back: Two fishermen. Watermark: Giraffe's head.	1.50	6.00

21 **500 Shilingi**

ND (1989). Dark blue on multicolor underprint. Arms at center, modified portrait of President Mwinyi at right. Zebra at lower left. Back: Harvesting. Watermark: Giraffe's head.

	VF	UNC
a. Signature 3 but with titles: *WAZIRI WA FEDHA* and *GAVANA.*	10.00	40.00
b. Signature 7.	5.00	25.00
c. Signature 8.	3.00	17.50

22 **1000 Shilingi**

	VF	UNC
ND (1990). Green and brown on multicolor underprint. Arms at center, modified portrait of President Mwinyi at right. Elephants at lower left. Signature 8. Back: Kiwira Coal Mine at left center, door to the Peoples Bank of Zanzibar at lower right. Watermark: Giraffe's head.	5.00	35.00

1993; 1995 ND Issue

#23, 25-27 Reduced size. Replacement notes: Serial # prefix *ZZ; ZY*.

23 **50 Shilingi**

	VF	UNC
ND (1993). Red-orange and brown on multicolor underprint. Arms at center, President Mwinyi at right. Wildebeest grazing at left. Signature 9. Back: Men making bricks. Watermark: Giraffe's head.	FV	1.00

24 **100 Shilingi**

	VF	UNC
ND (1993). Blue and aqua on multicolor underprint. Kudu at left, arms at center, J. Nyerere at right. Signature 9. Back: Graduation procession.	FV	2.00

25 200 Shilingi VF UNC

ND (1993). Black and orange on multicolor underprint. Arms at center, President Mwinyi at right. Leopards at left. Back: Two fishermen. Watermark: Giraffe's head.

- a. Signature 9. FV 3.50
- b. Signature 11. FV 3.00

26 500 Shilingi VF UNC

ND (1993). Purple, blue-green and violet on multicolor underprint. Arms at center, President Mwinyi at right. Zebra at lower left. Back: Harvesting. Watermark: Giraffe's head. Back similar to #21 with arms at lower right.

- a. Signature 9. FV 9.00
- b. Signature 10. FV 5.00
- c. Signature 11. FV 5.00

27 1000 Shilingi VF UNC

ND (1993). Dark green, brown and orange-brown on multicolor underprint. Arms at center, President Mwinyi at right. Elephants at lower left. Back: Kiwira Coal Mine at left center, door to the Peoples Bank of Zanzibar at lower right. Watermark: Giraffe's head.

- a. Signature 9. FV 15.00
- b. Signature 10. FV 10.00
- c. Signature 11. FV 7.50

28 5000 Shilingi VF UNC

ND (1995). Brown on multicolor underprint. Arms at center, President Mwinyi at right. Rhinoceros at lower left. Signature 10. Back: Giraffes with Mt. Kilimanjaro in background. FV 40.00

29 10,000 Shilingi VF UNC

ND (1995). Multicolor. Lion at lower left. Signature 10. Back: Bank of Tanzania Head Office building at left center, Zanzibar House of Wonder at lower right. FV 50.00

1997 ND Issue

30 500 Shilingi VF UNC

ND (1997). Blue-black and dark green on multicolor underprint. Zebra at lower left. Arms at upper center, giraffe's head at right. Signature 12. Back: Woman harvesting cloves at left center. Watermark: Giraffe's head. FV 2.50

31 1000 Shilingi VF UNC

ND (1997). Deep olive-green, red-orange and dark brown on multicolor underprint. Elephants at lower left. Arms at upper center, giraffe's head at right. Signature 12. Back: Industrial buildings at left center, door to the Peoples Bank of Zanzibar at lower right. Watermark: Giraffe's head. FV 5.00

32 5000 Shilingi VF UNC

ND (1997). Dark brown and purple on multicolor underprint. Rhinoceros at lower left. Arms at upper center, giraffe's head at right. Signature 12. Back: Giraffes with Mt. Kilimanjaro in background. Watermark: Giraffe's head. Segmented foil over security thread. FV 17.50

33 **10,000 Shilingi** | **VF** | **UNC**
ND (1997). Blue-black and dark gray on multicolor underprint. Lion at lower left. Arms at upper center, giraffe's head at right. Vertical foil strip at right. Signature 12. Back: Bank of Tanzania Head Office building at left center, Zanzibar House of Wonder at lower right. Watermark: Giraffe's head. | FV | 35.00

2000 ND Issue

34 **1000 Shilingi** | **VF** | **UNC**
ND (2000). Brown and green on multicolor underprint. Elephants at lower left, Julius Nyerere at right. Signature 13. Back: Industrial buildings at left center, door to the Peoples Bank of Zanzibar at lower right. Watermark: Giraffe's head. | FV | 5.00

2003 ND Issue

35 **500 Shilingi** | **VF** | **UNC**
ND (2003). Green and blue on multicolor underprint. Cape Buffalo at center right. Signature 14. Back: Hospital at center, boats in background. Printer: G&D. 130x63mm. | FV | 1.50

36 **1000 Shilingi** | **VF** | **UNC**
ND (2003). Blue and slate blue on multicolor underprint. Julius Nyerere at center right. Signature 14. Back: Palace. Printer: G&D. 135x66mm.
a. ND (2003). Button on Nyerere's jacket on right side of split. | FV | 3.50
b. ND (2006). Button on Nyerere's jacket on left side of spilt. | FV | 3.00

37 **2000 Shilingi** | **VF** | **UNC**
ND (2003); 2009. Brown, tan and green on multicolor underprint. Lion and Mt. Kilimanjaro at center. Back: Fort. Printer: G&D. 140x69mm.
a. ND (2003). Signature 14. | FV | 6.00
b. ND (2009). Signature 15. | FV | 4.00

38 **5000 Shilingi** | **VF** | **UNC**
ND (2003). Purple on multicolor underprint. Black Rhinoceros at center left. Signature 14. Back: Mining and House of Wonder. Printer: G&D. 145x72mm. | FV | 14.00

39 **10,000 Shilingi** | **VF** | **UNC**
ND (2003). Rose and green on multicolor underprint. Elephant at center left. Signature 14. Back: Central Bank building. Printer: G&D. 150x75mm. | FV | 28.00

2010 ND Issue

40 **500 Shilingi** | **VF** | **UNC**
ND (2010). Green on multicolor underprint. Sheikh Abeid Amani Karume at center. Back: Central Hall at Dar es Salaam University. Printer: TDLR. 120x60mm. | FV | 1.50

41	1000 Shilingi	VF	UNC
	ND (2010). Blue on multicolor underprint. Julius Kambarage Nyerere at center. Back: Coffee plant and State House (Ikulu) building. Printer: TDLR. 124x65mm.	FV	1.25

42	2000 Shilingi	VF	UNC
	ND (2010). Tan and brown on multicolor underprint. Lion head at center. Back: Omani Arab fort (Ngome Kongwe) at left. Printer: TDLR. 130x66mm.	FV	2.25

43	5000 Shilingi	VF	UNC
	ND (2010). Purple on multicolor underprint. Black Rhinoceros head at center. Back: Mining machinery, diamonds. Printer: TDLR. 135x67mm.	FV	7.50

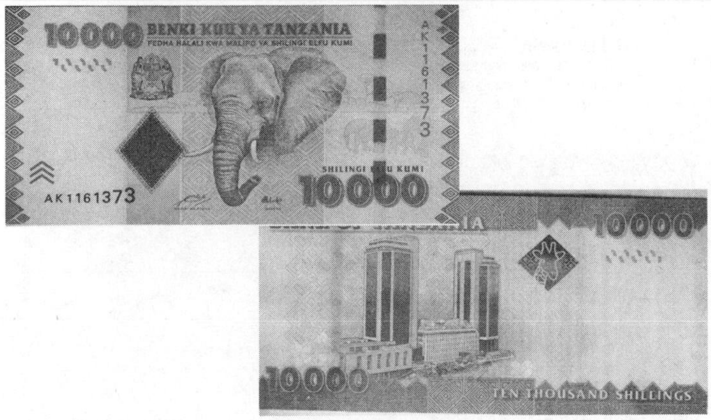

44	10,000 Shilingi	VF	UNC
	ND (2010). Red and yellow on multicolor underprint. Elephant head at center. Back: Bank of Tanzania building at center. Printer: TDLR. 140x68mm.	FV	13.00

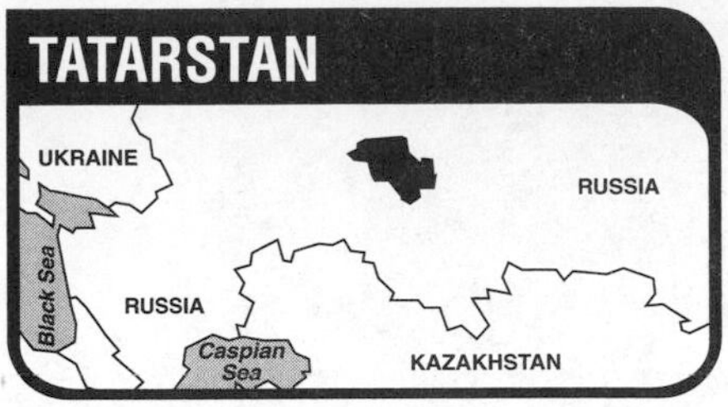

Tatarstan, an autonomous republic in the Russian Federation, is situated between the middle of the Volga River and its tributary Kama, extends east to the Ural mountains, covering 26,500 sq. mi. (68,000 sq. km.) and as of the 1970 census has a population of 3,743,600. Captial: Kazan. Tatarstan's economy combines its ancient traditions in the craftsmanship of wood, leather, cloth and ceramics with modern engineering, chemical, and food industries.

Colonized by the Bulgars in the 5th century, the territory of the Volga-Kama Bulgar State was inhabited by Turks. In the 13th century, Ghengis Khan conquered the area and established control until the 15th century when residual Mongol influence left Tatarstan as the Tatar Khanate, seat of the Kazar (Tatar) Khans. In 1552, under Ivan IV (the Terrible), Russia conquered, absorbed and controlled Tatarstan until the dissolution of the U.S.S.R.

Constituted as an autonomous republic on May 27, 1990, and as a sovereign state equal with Russia in April, 1992, Tatarstan, signed a treaty in February, 1994, defining it as a state united with the Commonwealth of Independent States.

MONETARY SYSTEM:

1 Ruble = 100 Kopeks

ТАТАРСКАЯ С.С.Р.

REPUBLIC OF TATARSTAN

TREASURY

1992 ND КУРОН - RUBLE CONTROL COUPON ISSUES

#1-3 red and green stripes w/black ТАТАРСКАЯ repeated on back.

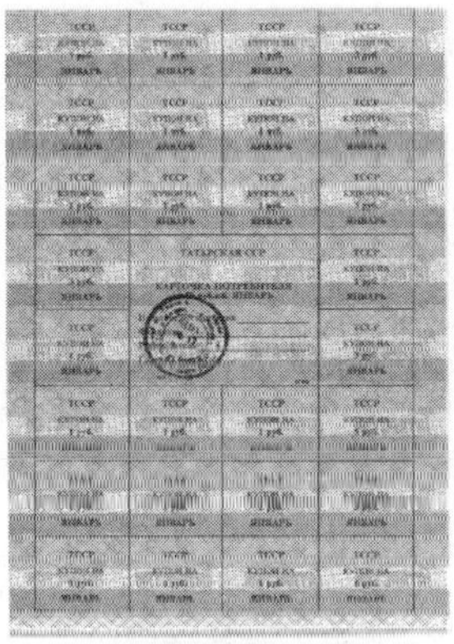

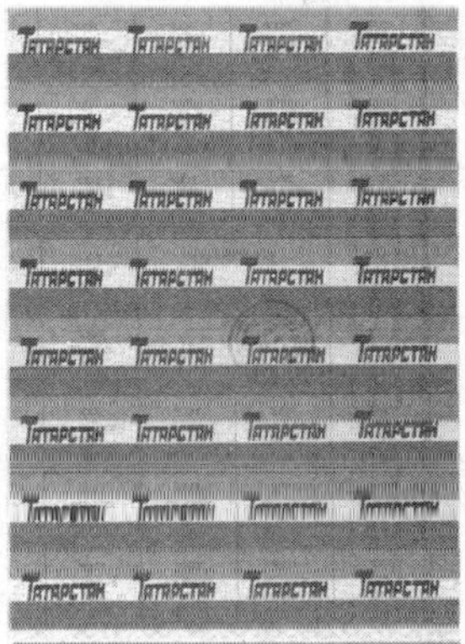

1	50 Rubles	VF	UNC
	ND (1992). Black text on green underprint. With month: S{chn6. **(January).**		
	a. Issued full sheet.	10.00	15.00
	b. Remainder full sheet.	6.00	10.00
	c. Coupon.	.20	.50

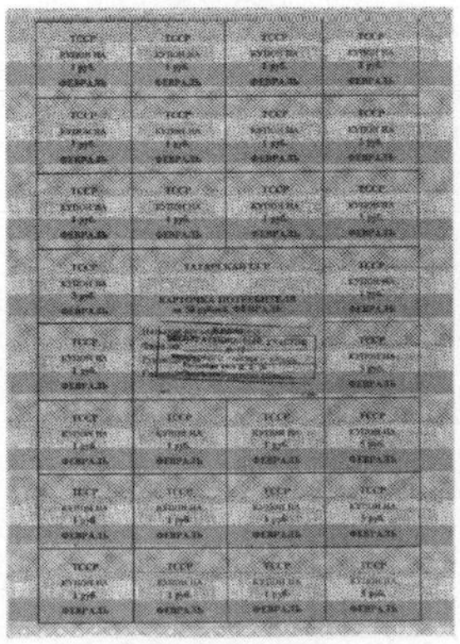

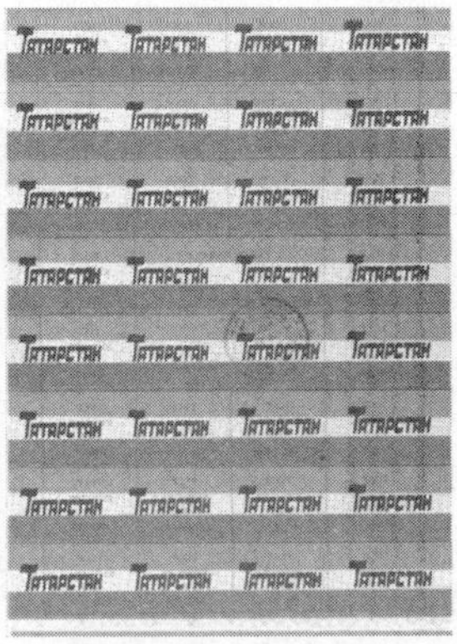

2	50 Rubles	VF	UNC
	ND (1992). Black text on pink underprint. With month: L3ti9. **(February).**		
	a. Issued full sheet.	7.50	15.00
	b. Remainder full sheet.	5.00	9.00
	c. Coupon.	.20	.50

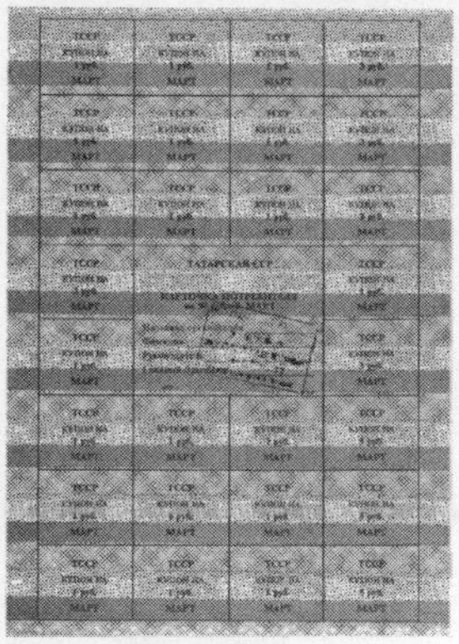

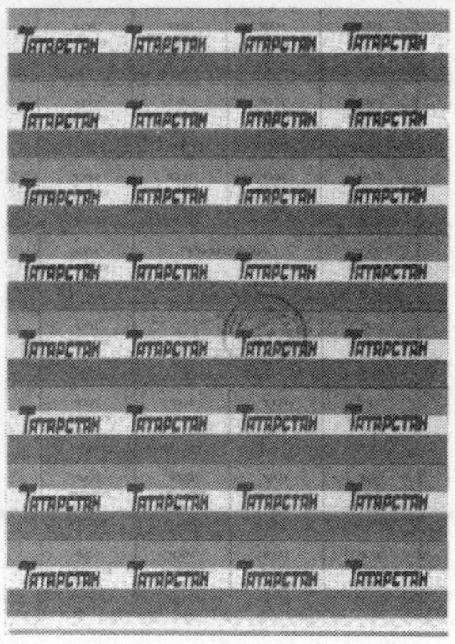

3 **50 Rubles**

ND (1992). Black text on blue underprint. With month: bhrhzh6. **(March).**

	VF	UNC
a. Issued full sheet.	7.50	15.00
b. Remainder full sheet.	4.00	8.00
c. Coupon.	.20	.50

Government

1993 Privatization Check Issue

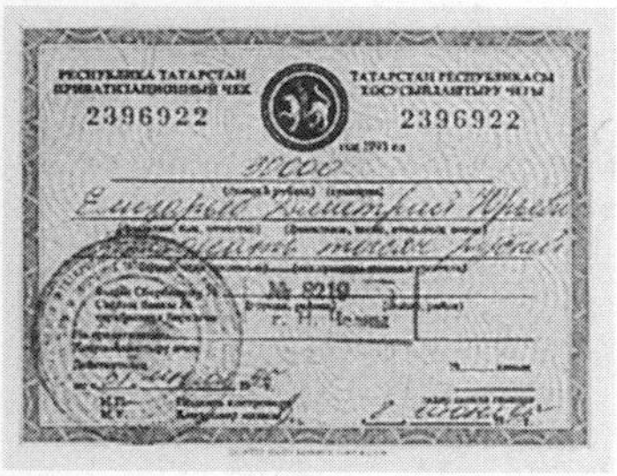

4A **30,000 Rubles**

1993. Black text on green underprint. Arms with number. Back: Black text on white. Printer: USBN.

	VF	UNC
a. Issued note. With registration and without privatization book.	25.00	40.00
b. Issued note. With registration and with privatization book.	40.00	80.00
c. Not issued. All with coupons and without registration.	—	50.00

4B **40,000 Rubles**

1993. Black text on green. Arms with number. Back: Black text on white. Printer: USBN.

	VF	UNC
a. Issued note. With registration and without privatization book.	17.50	30.00
b. Issued note. With registration and with privatization book.	30.00	50.00
c. Not issued. All with coupons and without registration.	—	50.00

4C **60,000 Rubles**

1993. Black text on green underprint. Arms with number. Back: Black text on white. Printer: USBN (without imprint).

	VF	UNC
a. Issued note. With registration and without privatization book.	20.00	35.00
b. Issued note. With registration and with privatization book.	35.00	60.00
c. Not issued. All with coupons and without registration.	—	50.00

4D **80,000 Rubles**

1993. Black text on green. Arms with number. Back: Black text on white. Printer: USBN.

	VF	UNC
a. Issued note. With registration and without privatization book.	25.00	40.00
b. Issued note. With registration and with privatization book.	40.00	75.00
c. Not issued. All with coupons and without registration.	—	50.00

4E **90,000 Rubles**

1993. Black text on green. Arms with number. Back: Black text on white. Printer: USBN.

	VF	UNC
a. Issued note. With registration and without privatization book.	30.00	50.00
b. Issued note. With registration and with privatization book.	40.00	80.00
c. Not issued. All with coupons and without registration.	—	50.00

4F **100,000 Rubles**

1993. Black text on green. Arms with number. Back: Black text on white. Printer: USBN.

	VF	UNC
a. Issued note. With registration and without privatization book.	35.00	60.00
b. Issued note. With registration and with privatization book.	45.00	85.00
c. Not issued. All with coupons and without registration.	—	—

1991; 1993 ND First Currency Check Issue

5 **(100 Rubles)**

ND (1991-92). Blue-gray. State flag inside circle at left, stylized image of old castle Suumbeky in Kazan (ca. 16th century) in ornate frame at right. Watermark: Lozenges. Uniface. 138x66mm.

	VF	UNC
a. Gray underprint.	3.00	15.00
b. Red underprint.	10.00	25.00
c. Yellow underprint.	12.50	25.00
d. Orange underprint.	12.50	25.00

6 **(100 Rubles)**

ND (1993). Red and pink. Red and green arms at left, stylized image of old castle Suumbeky in ornate frame at right. Watermark: Lozenges. Uniface. 138x66mm.

	VF	UNC
a. Gray underprint.	10.00	22.00
b. Violet on pink underprint.	10.00	22.00
c. dark blue on pale blue underprint.	10.00	22.00
d. Brown underprint.	10.00	22.00
e. Olive-green underprint.	10.00	22.00

1994 ND Second Currency Check Issue

7 **(200 Rubles)**

ND (1994). Medical emblem inside oval at right, stylized image of old castle Suumbeky in Kazan (ca. 16th century) at left. Watermark: Lozenges. Uniface. 138x66mm.

	VF	UNC
a. Blue-black and pale blue on multicolor underprint.	10.00	20.00
b. Deep olive-green and green on tan and pale green underprint.	10.00	20.00

1993-95 ND Third Currency Check Issue

		VF	UNC
8	**(500 Rubles)** ND (1993). Red-brown on multicolor underprint. Arms at top center, Kazan Kremlin (ca. 16th century) at lower left. Arabic *TATAR* at right. Back: Olive-green. Woman feeding geese. Watermark: Mosaic. 105x53mm.	10.00	20.00

		VF	UNC
9	**(500 Rubles)** ND (1993). Green on multicolor underprint. Arms at top center, Kazan Kremlin (ca. 16th century) at lower left. Arabic *TATAR* at right. Back: Olive-green. Horses galloping at center. Watermark: Mosaic. 150x53mm.	10.00	20.00

		VF	UNC
10	**(1000 Rubles)** ND (1994). Pink on multicolor underprint. Arms at top center, Kazan Kremlin (ca. 16th century) at lower left. Arabic *TATAR* at right. Back: Gulls flying over raging waves. Watermark: Mosaic. 105x53mm.	10.00	20.00
11	**(1000 Rubles)** ND (1995). Blue on multicolor underprint. Arms at top center, Kazan Kremlin (ca. 16th century) at lower left. Arabic *TATAR* at right. Back: Deer at watering hole. Watermark: Mosaic. 105x53mm.	10.00	20.00

1996 ND Fourth Currency Check Issue

		VF	UNC
12	**(50 Shamil = 5000 Rubles)** ND (1996). Kazan Kremlin (ca. 16th century) with English and Russian text "Tatarstan" in frame below. Back: Women from national epic. Watermark: Light lines. 135x65mm.		
	a. dark blue on pale blue-gray underprint.	15.00	30.00
	b. Deep green on pale green underprint.	10.00	20.00

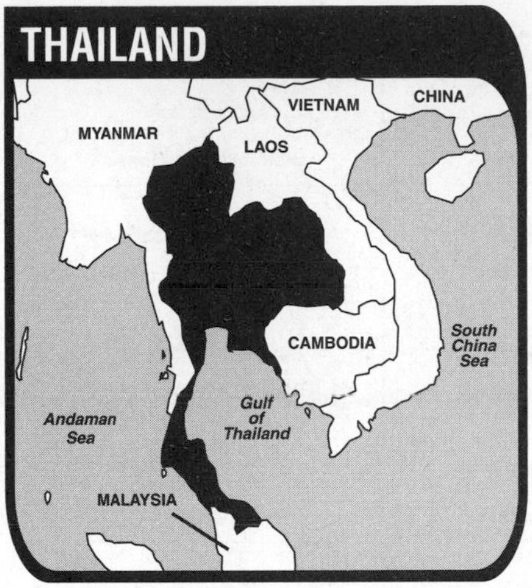

The Kingdom of Thailand, a constitutional monarchy located in the center of mainland southeast Asia between Burma and Lao, has an area of 514,000 sq. km. and a population of 65.49 million. Capital: Bangkok. The economy is d on agriculture and mining. Rubber, rice, teakwood, tin and tungsten are exported.

A unified Thai kingdom was established in the mid-14th century. Known as Siam until 1939, Thailand is the only Southeast Asian country never to have been taken over by a European power. A bloodless revolution in 1932 led to a constitutional monarchy. In alliance with Japan during World War II, Thailand became a US treaty ally following the conflict. A military coup in September 2006 ousted then Prime Minister Thaksin Chinnawat. The interim government held elections in December 2007 that saw the pro-Thaksin People's Power Party (PPP) emerge at the head of a coalition government. The anti-Thaksin People's Alliance for Democracy (PAD) in May 2008 began street demonstrations against the new government, eventually occupying the prime minister's office in August. Clashes in October 2008 between PAD protesters blocking parliament and police resulted in the death of at least two people. The PAD occupied Bangkok's international airports briefly, ending their protests in early December 2008 following a court ruling that dissolved the ruling PPP and two other coalition parties for election violations. The Democrat Party then formed a new coalition government with the support of some of Thaksin's former political allies, and Abhist Wetchachiwa became prime minister. Since January 2004, thousands have been killed as separatists in Thailand's southern ethnic Malay-Muslim provinces increased the violence associated with their cause.

RULERS:

Rama IX (Bhumiphol Adulyadej), 1946-

MONETARY SYSTEM:

1 Baht (Tical) = 100 Satang
1 Tamlung = 4 Baht

REPLACEMENT NOTES:

#63-67, notes w/o suffix letter.

SIGNATURE VARIETIES

	MINISTER OF FINANCE	GOVERNOR OF THE BANK OF THAILAND
34		
35		
36		
37		
38		
39	Chote Kvnakasem - no error -	Chote Kvnakasem
40		Puey Ungpakorn
41	S. Vinichchaikul	Puey Ungpakorn
42	S. Vinichchaikul	Bisudhi Nimmanhaemin
43	Boonma Wongesesawan	Bisudhi Nimmanhaemin

SIGNATURE VARIETIES		
44	Sommai Hoontrakul	Bisudhi Nimmanhaemin
45	Sawet Piempongsarn	Bisudhi Nimmanhaemin
46	Boonchu Rojanasathien	Bisudhi Nimmanhaemin
47	Boonchu Rojanasathien	Sanoh Unakul
48	Sawet Piempongsarn	Sanoh Unakul
49	Suphat Suthatham	Sanoh Unakul
50	Gen. K. Chomanan	Sanoh Unakul
51	Gen. K. Chomanan	Nukul Prachuabmoh
52	Amnuey Virawan	Nukul Prachuabmoh
53	Sommai Hoontrakul	Nukul Prachuabmoh
54	Sommai Hoontrakul	Kamchorn Sathirakul
55	Suthee Singsaneh	Kamchorn Sathirakul
56	Pramual Sabhavasu	Kamchorn Sathirakul
57	Pramual Sabhavasu	Chavalit Thanachanan
57a	Virabongsa Ramangkul	Chavalit Thanachanan
58	Virabongsa Ramangkul	Vigit Supinit
59	Banharn Silpa-acha	Vigit Supinit
60	Suthee Singsaneh	Vigit Supinit

SIGNATURE VARIETIES		
61	Phanas Simasathien	Vigit Supinit
62	Pedro Malan, 1999-	Vigit Supinit
63		
64	Surakiart Satirathai	Vigit Supinit
65	Bhodi Joonanond	Vigit Supinit
66	Bhodi Joonanond	Rerngchai Marakanond
67	Amnuey Virawan	Rerngchai Marakanond
68	Thanon Pithaya	Rerngchai Marakanond
69	Thanon Pithaya	Chaiwat Viboonswat
70	Kosit Pampiernras	Chaiwat Viboonswat
71	Tharin Nimahaemin	Chaiwat Viboonswat
72	Tharin Nimahaemin	Jatumongkol Sonakul
73	Somkid Chatusripitak	Jatumongkol Sonakul
74	Somkid Chatusripitak	Preeyadhorn Dhevakul
75	Suchart Chaovisit	Preeyadhorn Dhevakul
76		Preeyadhorn Dhevakul
77		
78		

Kingdom

Government of Thailand

1953-56 ND Issue

74	1 Baht	VF	UNC
	ND (1955). Blue on multicolor underprint. Portrait of King in Field Marshal's uniform with collar insignia and three decorations. Black serial number. Printer: TDLR.		
	a. Watermark: Constitution. Red and blue security threads. Signature 34.	1.00	4.00
	b. Watermark: Constitution. Metal security strip. Signature 34; 35 (Large size).	1.00	3.50
	c. Watermark: King profile. Small letters in 2-line text on back. Signature 35.	.75	3.00
	d. Watermark: King profile. Larger letters in 2-line text on back. Signature 36; 37; 38; 39; 40; 4l.	.75	2.50
	s. As a; d. Specimen.	—	250.

75	5 Baht	VF	UNC
	ND (1956). Purple on multicolor underprint. Portrait of King in Field Marshal's uniform with collar insignia and three decorations. Black serial number. Printer: TDLR.		
	a. Watermark: Constitution. Red and blue security threads. Signature 34.	15.00	50.00
	b. Watermark: Constitution. Metal security strip. Signature 34; 35 (Large size).	2.50	10.00
	c. Watermark: King profile. Small letters in 2-line text on back. Signature 35; 36.	2.50	10.00
	d. Watermark: King profile. Larger letters in 2-line text on back. Signature 38; 39; 40; 41	1.50	4.50
	s. As a. Specimen	—	250.

76	10 Baht	VF	UNC
	ND (1953). Brown on multicolor underprint. Portrait of King in Field Marshal's uniform with collar insignia and three decorations. Black serial number. Printer: TDLR.		
	a. Watermark: Constitution. Red and blue security threads. Signature 34.	2.50	8.00
	b. Watermark: Constitution. Metal security strip. Signature 34; 35 (Large size).	2.50	8.00
	c. Watermark: King profile. Small letters in 2-line text on back. Signature 35; 36; 37; 38; 39.	4.00	12.00
	d. Watermark: King profile. Larger letters in 2-line text on back. Signature 39; 40; 41; 44.	1.00	4.00
	s. As a. Specimen.	—	250.

77	20 Baht	VF	UNC
	ND (1953). Olive-green on multicolor underprint. Portrait of King in Field Marshal's uniform with collar insignia and three decorations. Black serial number. Printer: TDLR.		
	a. Watermark: Constitution. Red and blue security threads. Signature 34.	4.00	15.00
	b. Watermark: Constitution. Metal security strip. Signature 34; 35 (Large size).	8.00	20.00
	c. Watermark: King profile. Small letters in 2-line text on back. Signature 35; 37; 38.	6.00	15.00
	d. Watermark: King profile. Larger letters in 2-line text on back. Signature 38; 39; 40; 41; 44.	2.00	6.00
	s. As a. Specimen.	—	250.

78	100 Baht	VF	UNC
	ND (1955). Red on multicolor underprint. Portrait of King in Field Marshal's uniform with collar insignia and three decorations. Black serial number. Printer: TDLR.		
	a. Watermark: Constitution. Red and blue security threads. Signature 34.	20.00	60.00
	b. Watermark: Constitution. Metal security strip. Signature 34; 35; 37; 38.	12.50	30.00
	c. Watermark: King profile. Small letters in 2-line text on back. Signature 38.	10.00	35.00
	d. Watermark: King profile. Larger letters in 2-line text on back. Signature 38-41.	6.00	15.00
	s. As a; c. Specimen.	—	250.

Bank of Thailand

1968 Issue; Series 10

79 100 Baht — VF | UNC

ND (1968). Red, blue and multicolor. Rama IX in uniform at right. Signature 41; 42. Back: Royal barge. Watermark: Rama IX in uniform. Printer: TDLR.

- a. Issued note. — 6.50 | 13.00
- s. Specimen. — — | —

1969 Commemorative Issue

Reportedly 6,000 or 7,000 sets issued.

<AFrame <BRect 0.0 0.0 3.5 0.50>> #80 and 81 text at bottom: *opening of the Thai Banknote Printing Works 24 June 2512* **(1969).**

80 5 Baht — VF | UNC

24.6.1969. Purple and multicolor. King Rama IX wearing traditional robes at right. Signature of Finance Minister above, Governor of the Bank of Thailand below at center. Serial number prefix 00A. Signature 41. Back: Aphonphimok Prasat Pavilion. Watermark: King Rama IX. Printer: Thai Banknote Printing Works — — | 150.

81 10 Baht — VF | UNC

24.6.1969. Brown on multicolor underprint. King Rama IX wearing traditional robes at right. Signature of Finance Minister above, Governor of the Bank of Thailand below at center. Serial number prefix 00A. Signature 41. Back: Wat Benchamabophitr temple. Watermark: King Rama IX. Printer: Thai Banknote Printing Works — — | 175.

1969-75 ND Issue; Series 11

#82-86 replacement notes: Serial # prefix *S-(W).*

82 5 Baht — VF | UNC

ND (1969). Purple and multicolor underprint. Like #80 but without commemorative line at bottom. Signature 41; 42. Back: Aphonphimok Prasat Pavilion. Watermark: King Rama IX. Printer: Thai Banknote Printing Works.

- a. Issued note. — .50 | 2.00
- s. Specimen. — — | —

83 10 Baht — VF | UNC

ND (1969-78). Brown and multicolor. Like #81 but without commemorative line at bottom. Signature 41; 42; 43; 44; 45; 46; 47; 48; 49; 50; 51; 52; 53. Back: Wat Benchamabophitr temple. Watermark: King Rama IX. Printer: Thai Banknote Printing Works.

- a. Issued note. — .50 | 2.00
- s. Specimen. — — | —

84 20 Baht — VF | UNC

ND (1971-81). Dark green, olive-green and multicolor. King Rama IX wearing traditional robes at right. Signature of Finance Minister above, Governor of the Bank of Thailand below at center. Signature 41; 42; 43; 44; 45; 46; 47; 48; 49; 50; 51; 52; 53. Back: Royal barge at left center. Watermark: King Rama IX. Printer: Thai Banknote Printing Works.

- a. Issued note. — 1.00 | 4.00
- s. Specimen. — — | —

85 100 Baht — VF | UNC

ND (1969-78). Red-brown and multicolor. King Rama IX wearing traditional robes at right. Signature of Finance Minister above, Governor of the Bank of Thailand below at center. Back: Emerald Buddha section of Grand Palace. Watermark: King Rama IX. Printer: Thai Banknote Printing Works.

- a. Without black Thai overprint on face. Signature 42; 43; 44; 45; 46; 47; 48; 49. — 4.00 | 8.00
- b. Black Thai overprint line just below upper signature for change of title. Signature 43. — 10.00 | 20.00
- s. As a. Specimen. — — | 40.00

86 500 Baht — VF | UNC

ND (1975-88). Purple and multicolor. King Rama IX wearing traditional robes at right. Signature of Finance Minister above, Governor of the Bank of Thailand below at center. Signature 47; 49; 50; 51; 52; 53; 54; 55. Back: Pra Prang Sam Yod Lopburi (three towers). Watermark: King Rama IX. Printer: Thai Banknote Printing Works.

- a. Issued note. — 10.00 | 20.00
- s. Specimen. — — | —

1978-81 ND Issue; Series 12

#87-89 Kg. Rama IX wearing dk. Field Marshal's uniform at r. and as wmk. Sign. of Finance Minister (upper) and Governor of the Bank of Thailand (lower) at ctr. Replacement notes: Serial # prefix *S-(W)*.

		VF	UNC
87	**10 Baht** BE2523 (1980). Dark brown on multicolor underprint. King Rama IX wearing dark Field Marshal's uniform at right. Signature of Finance Minister above, Governor of the Bank of Thailand below at center. Signature 52; 53; 54; 55; 56; 57; 58; 59; 60; 61; 63 Back: Mounted statue of King Chulalongkorn. Watermark: King Rama IX.	.50	1.25

		VF	UNC
88	**20 Baht** BE2524 (1981). Dark green on multicolor underprint. King Rama IX wearing dark Field Marshal's uniform at right. Signature of Finance Minister above, Governor of the Bank of Thailand below at center. Signature 53-61; 63; 64; 66; 67; 72-74. Back: King Taksin's statue at Chantaburi with three armed men. Watermark: King Rama IX. 139x72mm.	.75	2.00

		VF	UNC
89	**100 Baht** ND (1978). Violet, red and orange on multicolor underprint. King Rama IX wearing dark Field Marshal's uniform at right. Signature of Finance Minister above, Governor of the Bank of Thailand below at center. Signature 49-63. Back: King Narasuan the Great atop elephant. Watermark: King Rama IX.	2.00	5.00

1985-92 ND Issue; Series 13

#90-92 replacement notes: Serial # prefix *S-(W)*.

		VF	UNC
90	**50 Baht** ND (1985-96). Dark blue and purple on multicolor underprint. King Rama IX facing at right, wearing traditional robe. Back: Palace at left, statue of King Rama VII at center, his arms and signature at upper left. Watermark: King Rama IX.		
	a. King with pointed eartips. Signature 54.	2.00	6.00
	b. Darker blue color obscuring pointed eartips. Signature 54; 60; 63.	1.50	3.00

		VF	UNC
91	**500 Baht** ND (1988-96). Purple and violet on multicolor underprint. King Rama IX at right in Field Marshal's uniform. Signature 55-61; 63. Back: Statue at center right, palace in background in underprint at left center. Watermark: King Rama IX.	8.50	20.00

		VF	UNC
92	**1000 Baht** BE2535 (1992). Gray, brown, orange and multicolor. King Rama IX at center right. Signature 62-64; 66-67; 69; 71-72. Back: King Rama IX and Queen Sirikit greeting children at left center in underprint, viewing map at center right. Watermark: King Rama IX.	17.50	35.00

1987 Commemorative Issue

#93, King's 60th Birthday

93 **60 Baht** | VF | UNC
BE2530 (5.12.1987). Dark brown on multicolor underprint. King Rama IX seated on throne at center, Victory crown at left, Royal regalia at right. Signature 55. Back: Royal family seated with subjects. UV: fibers and security strip fluoresce blue.

	VF	UNC
a. Issued note.	—	4.00
s. Specimen in blue folder.	—	100.

1992 Commemorative Issue

#94 and 95, 90th Birthday of Princess Mother

94 **50 Baht** | VF | UNC
ND (1992). Blue on multicolor underprint. King Rama IX facing at right, wearing traditional robe over Field Marshall's uniform. Two lines of text added under watermark. Signature 57. Back: Palace at left, statue of King Rama VII at center, his arms and signature at upper left. Watermark: Princess Mother's portrait. | FV | 3.00

95 **500 Baht** | VF | UNC
ND (1992). Purple and multicolor. King Rama IX facing at right, wearing dark Field Marshall's uniform. Two lines of text added under watermark. Signature 57. Back: Palace at left, statue of King Rama VII at center, his arms and signature at upper left. Watermark: Princess Mother's portrait. | FV | 20.00

96 **1000 Baht** | VF | UNC
ND (1992). Black, deep olive-green and yellow-brown on multicolor underprint. King Rama IX facing at right. Three lines of commemorative text added under watermark. Signature 61. Back: King Rama IX and Queen Sirikit greeting children at left center in underprint, viewing map at center Watermark: Queen Sirikit's portrait. 166x80mm. | FV | 32.50

1994 ND Issue

97 **100 Baht** | VF | UNC
BE2537 (1994). Violet, red and brown-orange on multicolor underprint. King Rama IX at right. Signature 63-65; 67-75. Back: Statue of King Rama V and Rama VI with children; Royal initial emblem in center. 150x72mm. | FV | 4.00

1995 Commemorative Issue

Text at lower margin:
<AFrame <BRect 0.0 0.0 3.5 0.30>> #98, 120th Anniversary Ministry of Finance

98 **10 Baht** | VF | UNC
ND (1995). Dark brown on multicolor underprint. King Rama IX wearing dark Field Marshal's uniform at right. Signature of Finance Minister above, Governor of the Bank of Thailand below at center. Commemorative text in lower margin. Signature 63. Back: Mounted statue of King Chulalongkorn. Watermark: King Rama IX. | — | 2.00

1996 Commemorative Issue

#99 and 101, 50th Anniversary of Reign

99 50 Baht — VF | UNC

ND (1996). Purple on light blue and multicolor underprint. King Rama IX wearing Field Marshal's uniform at right and as a shadow design in clear area at left, royal seal of kingdom at upper right. Signature 66, 67. Back: Palace at left, statue of King Rama VII at center, his arms and signature at upper left. Printer: NPA (without imprint). Polymer plastic. — FV | 4.00

100 500 Baht — VF | UNC

ND (1996). Purple and red violet on multicolor underprint. King Rama IX at right with Crowned Royal seal with *50* at center right, arms above dancers at right replacing crowned radiant Chakra at left center. Signature 64. Back: Temple of the Emerald Buddha at left, King Rama I and Rama II at left center. — FV | 20.00

101 500 Baht — VF | UNC

ND (1996). Multicolor. King Rama IX seated in royal attire at center right, hologram of King at upper right. Signature 64; 66. Back: King holding map at center, waterfalls at left, farmers in terraced landscape at right. Printer: NPA (without imprint). Polymer plastic.

a. Issued note. — — | 60.00

s. Specimen. Red overprint. Issued in folder. — — | 300.

1996-97 ND Regular Issue

102 50 Baht — VF | UNC

BE2540. (1997). Black on light blue and multicolor underprint. King Rama IX in Field Marshal's uniform at center right, arms at upper left. Signature 67, 71; 72; 74. Back: King Rama VI seated at table at center right, royal arms at upper left center, medieval ship's prow at lower right. Printer: NPA (without imprint). Polymer plastic. 144x72mm.

a. Issued note. — FV | 2.00

s. Specimen. — — | 400.

103 500 Baht — VF | UNC

BE2539 (1996). Purple and red-violet on multicolor underprint. King Rama IX at right in Field Marshall's uniform. Arms at upper left, radiant crowned Chakra seal on platform at left center. Signature 64; 66; 67; 69; 72. Back: Temple of the Emerald Buddha at left, King Rama I and Rama II at left center. Watermark: King Rama IX. 156x71mm. — FV | 20.00

1999 Commemorative Issue

#104, 72nd Birthday of King

104 1000 Baht — VF | UNC

BE2542. 1999. Brown, orange and yellow on multicolor underprint. King Rama IX at right center in Field Marshall's uniform. Green seal has scroll below. Signature 72. Back: King with camera at right, Pa Sak Jolasid Dam at left. 162x72mm. — FV | 32.50

2000 Commemorative Issue

#105, 106 Golden Wedding Anniversary

105 50 Baht VF UNC
ND (2000). Brown and tan on multicolor underprint. Conjoined profiles of King Rama IX and Queen Sirikit. Signature 72. Back: Views of their family life. Issued in special folder. 126x205mm. — 60.00

106 500,000 Baht
ND (2000). Brown and tan on multicolor underprint. Conjoined profiles of King Rama IX and Queen Sirikit. Signature 72. Back: Views of their family life. (1998 pieces printed). — 31,000.

2000-01 ND Issue

107 500 Baht VF UNC
ND (2001). Blue and rose on multicolor underprint. King Rama IX at right in Field Marshall's unfirom. Signature 74; 75; 76; 78. Back: Statue and palace. 156x72mm. FV 22.50

108 1000 Baht VF UNC
ND (2000). Brown, orange and yellow on multicolor underprint. King Rama IX at right center in Field Marshall's unform. Center green seal set on an octagonal base. Signature 72; 73; 74; 75; 76; 78. Back: King with camera at right, Pa Sak Jolasid Dam at left. 162x72mm. FV 45.00

2002 ND Issue

109 20 Baht VF UNC
ND (2003). Green on green and tan multicolor underprint. King Rama IX wearing Field Marshal's uniform at center right. Signature 74; 75; 76; 77; 78. Back: Procession with King in military uniform and new bridge. FV 1.50

2002 Commemorative Issue

110 100 Baht VF UNC
ND (2002). Brown and slate blue on green and multicolor underprint. Kings Rama V and Rama IX at right. Signature 74; 75. Back: Slate blue on green underprint. Facsimile print of #12a. — 7.00

2004 Commemorative Issue

#111, Queen's 72nd Birthday. Issued in a folder.

111 100 Baht VF UNC
2004. Multicolor. King Rama IX standing and Queen Sirikit seated. Signature 72.. Signature 74. Back: Queen standing, views of her life. — 10.00

2004 Second Commemorative Issue

111A 50 Baht VF UNC
ND (2004). Slate black on light blue and multicolor underprint. King Rama IX wearing uniform. Red overprint above emblem at left center, and line of text below portrait Back: King Rama IV seated. Printer: NPW. 144x72mm. FV 25.00

118 100 Baht
ND (2010). Red and orange on multicolor underprint. King Rama IX wearing uniform. Back: King Rama IX and Queen Sirikit at center. Rama IX seated at right wearing crown. Printer: NPW. FV 5.00

2004 Issue

112 50 Baht VF UNC

ND (2004). Slate black on light blue and multicolor. King Rama IX in Field Marshal's uniform at center right, arms at upper left. Signature 74; 75; 76. Back: King Rama VI seated at table at center right, telescope and globe at center left, royal arms at upp Printer: NPA (without imprint). Like #102 but paper. 144x72mm. FV 2.00

113 100 Baht VF UNC

ND (2004). Violet, red and brown orange on multicolor underprint. King Rama IX at right. Back: Statue of King Rama V and Rama VI with children. Royal emblem at center. Holographic strip at left. Like #97. 150x80mm. FV 3.50

2005 Issue

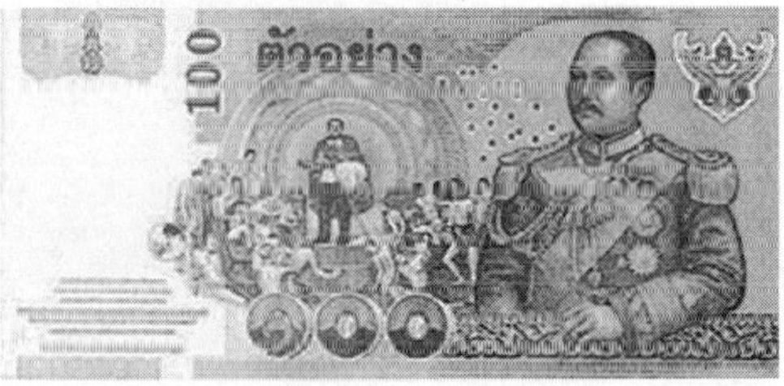

114 100 Baht VF UNC

21.10.2005. Violet on multicolor underprint. King Rama IX at right center in Field Marshall uniform. Back: King Chulalongkom in navy uniform and in scene ready to abolish slavery. 150x73mm. Unc 3.50

115 1000 Baht VF UNC

ND (2005). Brown, orange and yellow on multicolor underprint. King Rama IX at rigth center in Field Marshal uniform. Wide security foil at left. Back: King with camera at right, Pa Sak Jolasid Dam at left. Like #108. FV 35.00

2006 Commemorative Issue

116 60 Baht VF UNC

9.6.2006. Red and orange. King Rama IX seated on royal throne at left. Back: King visiting his people, Khun Dan Prakan Chon Dam in Nakon Nayok province in background. 162x81mm. FV 8.00

2007 Commemorative Issue

117 16 Baht VF UNC

2007. Blue, purple, brown on multicolor underprint. Three early notes of 1, 5 and 10 Bhat. Back: Golden yellow and brown. Full design forming a montage of important events in king's life

	VF	UNC
a. Issued note in commemorative folder.	—	25.00
b. Issued note without folder.	—	10.00
s. Specimen.	—	100.

Collector Series

1991 Commemorative Issue

#CS1, World Bank Group / International Monetary Fund Annual Meetings

CS1 1991 10, 20, 50, 100, 500 Baht Mkt. Value

#87-91 with overprint: 1991 World Bank Group/IMF Annual Meetings in English and Thai. Specimen. (Issued in blue hanging folder). 600.

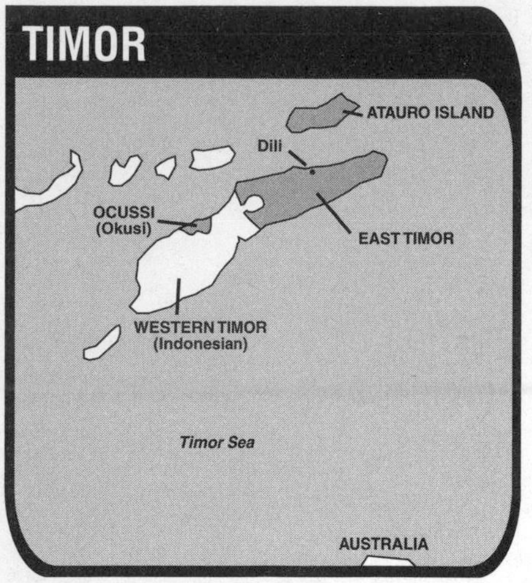

Timor, is an island between the Savu and Timor Seas, has an area, including the former colony of Portuguese Timor, of 11,883 sq. mi. (30,775 sq. km.) and a population of 1.5 million. Western Timor is administered as part of Nusa Tenggara Timur (East Nusa Tenggara) province. Capital: Kupang. The eastern half of the island, the former Portuguese colony, forms a single province, Timor Timur (East Timor). Originally the Portuguese colony also included the area around Ocussi-Ambeno and the small island of Atauro (Pulau Kambing) located north of Dili. Capital: Dili. Timor exports sandalwood, coffee, tea, hides, rubber and copra.

Portuguese traders reached Timor about 1520, and moved to the north and east when the Dutch established themselves in Kupang, a sheltered bay at the southwestern tip, in 1613. Treaties effective in 1860 and 1914 established the boundaries between the two colonies. Japan occupied the entire island during World War II. The former Dutch colony in the western part of the island became part of Indonesia in 1950.

At the end of Nov., 1975, the Portuguese Province of Timor attained independence as the People's Democratic Republic of East Timur. In Dec., 1975 or early in 1976 the government of the People's Democratic Republic was seized by a guerilla faction sympathetic to the Indonesian territorial claim to East Timur which ousted the constitutional government and replaced it with the Provisional Government of East Timur. On July 17, 1976, the Provisional Government enacted a law which dissolved the free republic and made East Timur the 24th province of Indonesia.

In 1999 a revolution suceeded, and it is once again an independent country. Note: For later issues see Indonesia.

MONETARY SYSTEM:

1 Pataca = 100 Avos to 1958
1 Escudo = 100 Centavos, 1958-1975

SIGNATURE VARIETIES

1		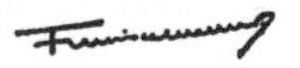
2	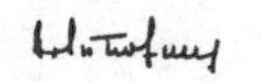	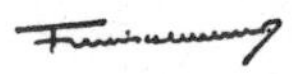
3	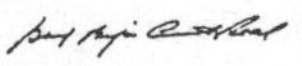	
4	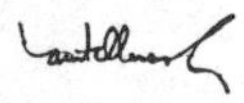	
5	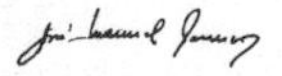	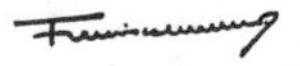
6	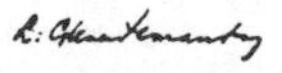	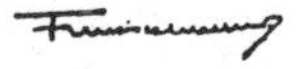
7		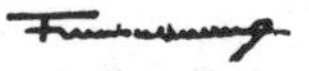
8	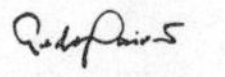	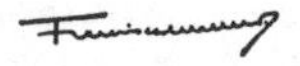

Portuguese Administration

Banco Nacional Ultramarino

Decretos - Lei 39221e 44891; 1963-68 Issue

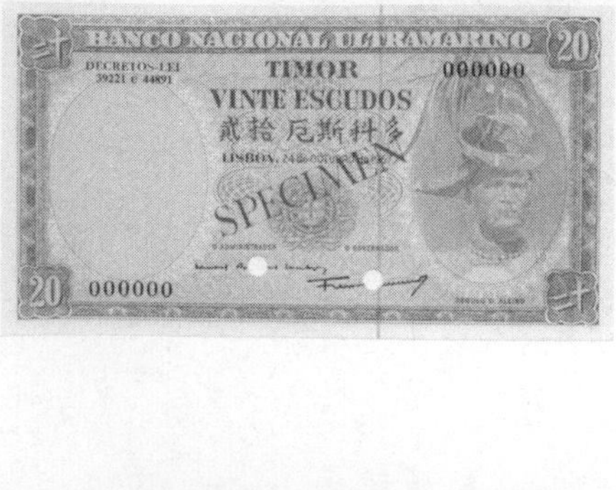

26	20 Escudos	VF	UNC
	24.10.1967. Olive-brown on multicolor underprint. Portrait of R. D. Aleixo at right. Signature 3; 8. Back: Bank ship seal at left, crowned arms at center. Printer: BWC.		
	a. Issued note.	2.50	7.50
	s. Specimen.	—	—

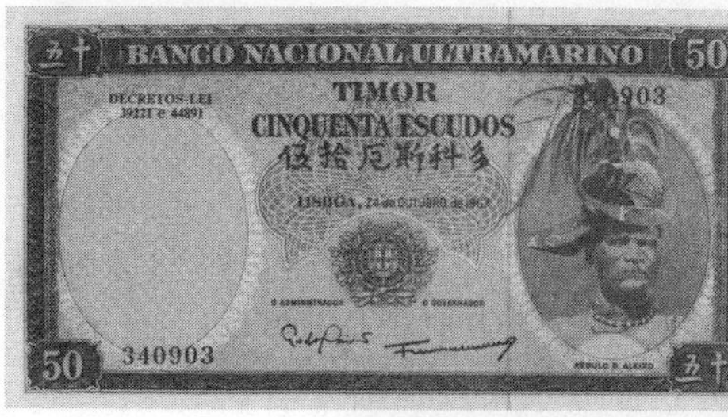

27	50 Escudos	VF	UNC
	24.10.1967. Blue on multicolor underprint. Portrait of R. D. Aleixo at right. Signature 2; 4; 5; 6; 8. Back: Bank ship seal at left, crowned arms at center. Printer: BWC.		
	a. Issued note.	4.00	12.50
	s. Specimen.	—	160.

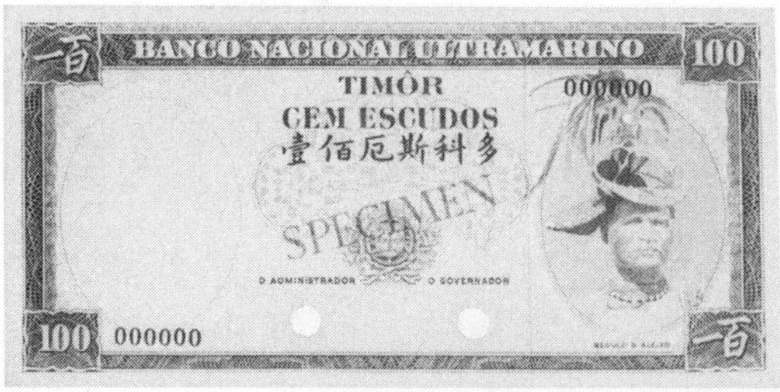

28	100 Escudos	VF	UNC
	25.4.1963. Brown on multicolor underprint. Portrait of R. D. Aleixo at right. Signature 1-3; 8. Back: Bank ship seal at left, crowned arms at center. Printer: BWC.		
	a. Issued note.	4.50	15.00
	s. Specimen. Punched hole cancelled.	—	160.

29	500 Escudos	VF	UNC
	25.4.1963. Dark brown on multicolor underprint. Portrait of R. D. Aleixo at right. Signature 1-3; 8; 9. Back: Bank ship seal at left, crowned arms at center. Printer: BWC.		
	a. Issued note.	10.00	30.00
	s. Specimen.	—	175.

30	1000 Escudos	VF	UNC
	21.3.1968. Green on multicolor underprint. Portrait of R. D. Aleixo at right. Signature 2; 8. Back: Bank ship seal at left, crowned arms at center. Printer: BWC.		
	a. Issued note.	20.00	55.00
	s. Specimen.	—	185.

1969 ND Provisional Issue

		VF	UNC
31	**20 Escudos**	—	—
	ND. Green on multicolor underprint. Régulo Jose Nunes at left. Back: Bank seal at center, local huts on pilings at right. Specimen.		
32	**500 Escudos**	350.	750.
	ND (1969 - old date 22.3.1967). Brown and violet on multicolor underprint. Overprint: *PAGAVEL EM TIMOR* on Mozambique #110. Back: Overprint: *PAGAVEL EM TIMOR* on Mozambique #110.		

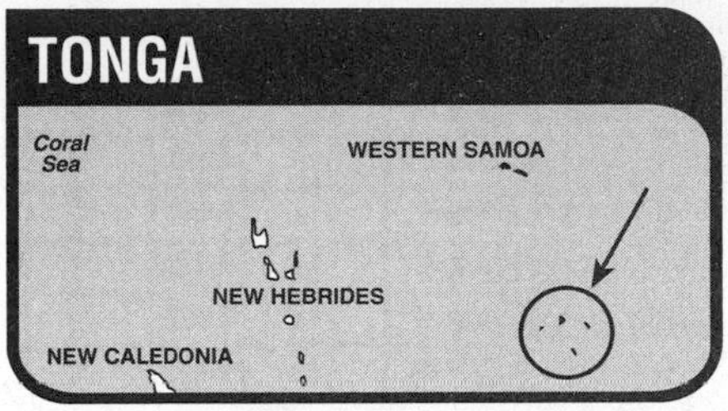

The Kingdom of Tonga (or Friendly Islands), a member of the British Commonwealth, is an archipelago situated in the southern Pacific Ocean south of Western Samoa and east of Fiji comprising 150 islands. Tonga has an area of 748 sq. km. and a population of 119,000. Capital: Nuku'alofa. Primarily agricultural, the kingdom exports bananas and copra.

Tonga - unique among Pacific nations - never completely lost its indigenous governance. The archipelagos of "The Friendly Islands" were united into a Polynesian kingdom in 1845. Tonga became a constitutional monarchy in 1875 and a British protectorate in 1900; it withdrew from the protectorate and joined the Commonwealth of Nations in 1970. Tonga remains the only monarchy in the Pacific.

RULERS:

Queen Salote III, 1918-1965
King Taufa'ahau IV, 1967-2005
King Taufa'ahau V, 2005-2012
King Tupoutoía Lavaka Ata, 2012-

MONETARY SYSTEM:

1 Shilling = 12 Pence
1 Pound = 20 Shillings to 1967
1 Pa'anga = 100 Seniti, 1967-

REPLACEMENT NOTES:

#18-24, Z/1 prefix.

Kingdom

Government of Tonga

1939-42 Issue

9	4 Shillings	VF	UNC
	1941-66. Brown on multicolor underprint. *FOUR SHILLINGS* at left and right. Arms at center. Printer: TDLR.		
	a. 1.12.1941-8.9.1947. 3 signatures.	125.	450.
	b. 7.2.1949; 15.2.1951; 20.7.1951; 6.9.1954.	100.	375.
	c. 19.9.1955-30.11.1959.	25.00	150.
	d. 24.10.1960-27.9.1966.	25.00	85.00
	e. 3.11.1966. 2 signatures.	20.00	50.00

10	10 Shillings	VF	UNC
	1939-66. Green on multicolor underprint. *TEN SHILLINGS* at left and right. Arms at center. Printer: TDLR.		
	a. 3.5.1940; 17.10.1941-28.11.1944. 3 signatures.	250.	—
	b. 9.7.1949-1955.	150.	450.
	c. 2.5.1956; 22.7.1957; 10.12.1958; 13.10.1959.	35.00	300.
	d. 24.10.1960; 28.11.1962; 29.7.1964; 22.6.1965.	30.00	125.
	e. 3.11.1966. 2 signatures.	22.50	65.00
	s. Specimen. As b, d. Perforated: *CANCELLED.*	—	300.

11	1 Pound	VF	UNC
	1940-66. Red on multicolor underprint. *ONE POUND* at left and right. Arms at center. Printer: TDLR.		
	a. 3.5.1940-7.11.1944. 3 signatures.	275.	—
	b. 15.6.1951; 11.9.1951; 19.9.1955.	175.	550.
	c. 2.5.1956; 10.12.1958; 30.11.1959; 12.12.1961.	70.00	425.
	d. 28.11.1962; 30.10.1964; 2.11.1965; 3.11.1966.	40.00	150.
	e. 2.12.1966. 2 signatures.	15.00	100.
	s. Specimen. Perforated: *CACNELLED.*	—	500.

12	5 Pounds	VF	UNC
	1942-66. Dark blue on multicolor underprint. *FIVE POUNDS* at left and right. Arms at center. Printer: TDLR.		
	a. 11.3.1942-1945. 3 signatures.	2000.	—
	b. 15.6.1951; 5.7.1955; 11.9.1956; 26.6.1958.	1500.	—
	c. 30.11.1959; 2.11.1965.	500.	1000.
	d. 2.12.1966. 2 signatures.	60.00	150.

Pule' Anga 'o Tonga

Government of Tonga

1967 Issue

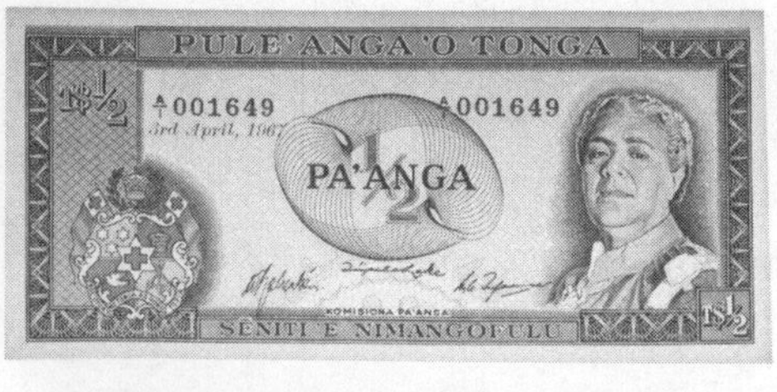

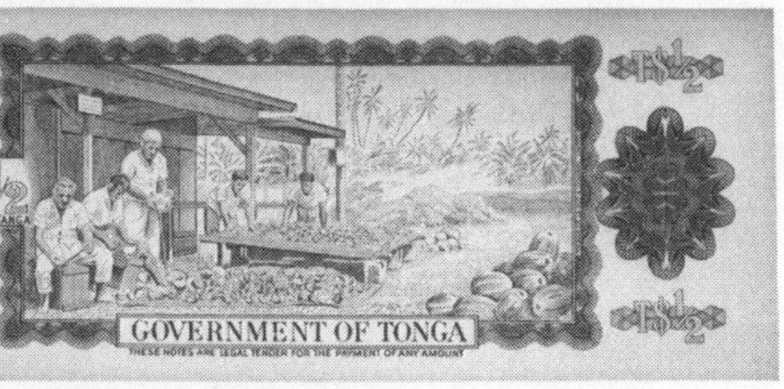

13	1/2 Pa'anga	VF	UNC
	1967-73. Dark brown on pink underprint. Arms at lower left. Queen Salote III at right. Various date and signature varieties. Back: Brown and blue. Coconut workers at left.		
	a. 3.4.1967.	20.00	100.
	b. 19.5.1969; 27.10.1969.	35.00	125.
	c. 10.3.1970; 16.6.1970.	32.50	125.
	d. 4.2.1971; 14.4.1971; 24.7.1972.	35.00	150.
	e. 13.6.1973; 2.8.1973. 2 signatures.	50.00	250.
	s. ND. Specimen.	—	70.00

14	1 Pa'anga	VF	UNC
	1967; 1970-71. Olive-green on multicolor underprint. Arms at lower left. Queen Salote III at right. Various date and signature varieties. Back: Olive and blue. River scene, palm trees.		
	a. 3.4.1967.	20.00	125.
	b. 12.4.1967; 2.10.1967; 8.12.1967.	40.00	150.
	c. 10.3.1970; 16.6.1970.	45.00	165.
	d. 4.2.1971; 19.10.1971.	60.00	235.
	s. ND. Specimen.	—	70.00

15	2 Pa'anga	VF	UNC
	1967-73. Red on multicolor underprint. Arms at lower left. Queen Salote III at right. Various date and signature varieties. Back: Red and brown. Women making Tapa cloth.		
	a. 3.4.1967.	35.00	200.
	b. 2.10.1967; 8.12.1967.	50.00	250.
	c. 19.5.1969; 10.3.1970; 19.10.1971.	60.00	250.
	d. 24.7.1972; 10.11.1972; 2.8.1973.	60.00	300.
	e. 12.11.1973. 2 signatures.	100.	500.
	s. ND. Specimen.	—	70.00
16	5 Pa'anga		
	1967; 1973. Purple on multicolor underprint. Arms at lower left. Queen Salote III at right. Various date and signature varieties. Back: Purple and olive-green. Ha'amonga stone gateway.		
	a. 3.4.1967.	80.00	350.
	b. 13.6.1973.	100.	550.
	c. 4.9.1973; 6.12.1973. 2 signatures.	150.	600.
	s. ND. Specimen.	—	100.
17	10 Pa'anga		
	1967; 1973. Dark blue on multicolor underprint. Arms at lower left. Queen Salote III at right. Various date and signature varieties. Back: Blue and purple. Royal Palace.		
	a. 3.4.1967.	125.	600.
	b. 2.10.1967; 8.12.1967.	200.	775.
	c. 13.6.1973; 16.7.1973.	250.	1200.
	s. ND. Specimen.	—	150.

1974; 1985 Issue

#18-22 Replacement notes: Serial # prefix *Z/1*.

18	1/2 Pa'anga	VF	UNC
	1974-83. Dark brown on pink underprint. Arms at lower left. King Taufa'ahau at right. Signature varieties. Back: Brown and blue. Coconut workers at left.		
	a. 2 signatures. 2.10.1974; 19.6.1975.	6.00	17.50
	b. 3 signatures. 12.1.1977; 17.5.1977; 10.9.1979.	4.00	15.00
	c. As b. 28.11.1979; 27.8.1980; 31.7.1981; 17.8.1982; 29.7.1983.	3.00	12.00
	s. As a. Specimen.	—	—

19	1 Pa'anga	VF	UNC
	1974-89. Olive-green on multicolor underprint. Arms at lower left. King Taufa'ahau at right. Signature varieties. Back: Olive and blue. River scene, palm trees.		
	a. 6.12.1973.	25.00	100.
	b. 2 signatures. 31.7.1974; 19.6.1975; 21.8.1975; 5.8.1976; 21.1.1981; 18.5.1983.	3.50	12.50
	c. 3 signatures. 5.8.1976-11.6.1980; 31.7.1981-28.10.1982; 27.7.1983-30.6.1989.	2.00	7.50
	s. As a. Specimen.	—	—

20	2 Pa'anga	VF	UNC
	1974-89. Red on multicolor underprint. Arms at lower left. King Taufa'ahau at right. Signature varieties. Back: Red and brown. Women making Tapa cloth.		
	a. 2 signatures. 2.10.1974; 19.6.1975; 21.8.1975; 21.1.1981.	3.50	15.00
	b. 3 signatures. 12.1.1977-27.8.1980;	4.00	17.50
	c. 3 signatures. 31.7.1981-30.6.1989.	2.75	12.00
	s. As a. Specimen.	—	—

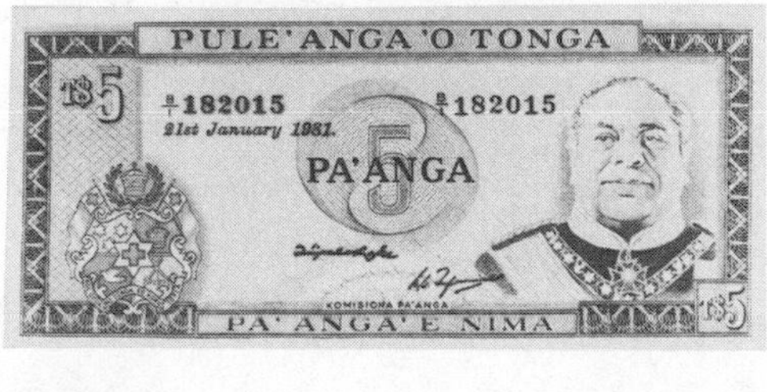

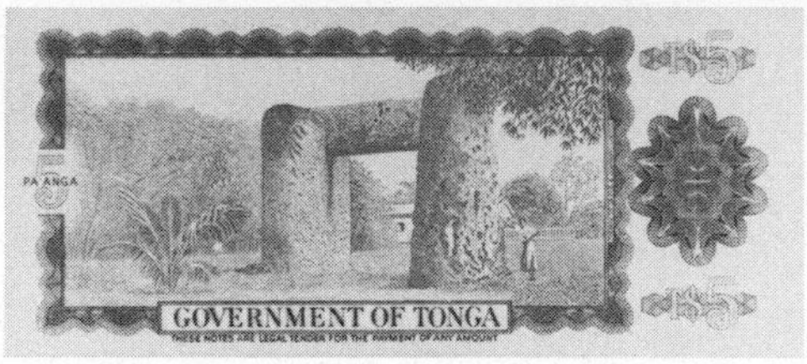

21	5 Pa'anga	VF	UNC
	1974-89. Purple on multicolor underprint. Arms at lower left. King Taufa'ahau at right. Signature varieties. Back: Purple and olive-green. Ha'amonga stone gateway.		
	a. 2 signatures. 3.9.1974; 2.10.1974; 19.6.1975; 21.1.1981.	7.50	37.50
	b. 3 signatures. 21.12.1976-28.11.1980.	6.50	27.50
	c. 3 signatures. 27.5.1981-30.6.1989.	5.00	20.00
	s. As a. Specimen.	—	—

22	10 Pa'anga		
	1974-89. Dark blue on multicolor underprint. Arms at lower left. King Taufa'ahau at right. Signature varieties. Back: Blue and purple. Royal Palace.		
	a. 2 signatures. 3.9.1974; 31.7.1974; 3.9.1974; 19.6.1975; 21.1.1981.	12.00	65.00
	b. 3 signatures. 12.12.1976-28.11.1980.	10.00	50.00
	c. 3 signatures. 27.5.1981-30.6.1989.	7.50	35.00
	s. As a. Specimen.	—	—

23	20 Pa'anga		
	1985-89. Orange on green and multicolor underprint. King in new design at center right, arms at right. Back: Tonga Development Bank. Watermark: King in new design.		
	a. 4.7.1985.	35.00	150.
	b. 18.7.1985; 3.10.1985; 8.1.1986; 27.2.1987; 28.9.1987.	27.50	55.00
	c. 20.5.1988; 14.12.1988; 23.1.1989; 30.6.1989.	25.00	50.00

Kingdom of Tonga

1988 Issue

24	50 Pa'anga	VF	UNC
	1988-89. Brown and green on multicolor underprint. King in new design at center right, arms at right. Back: Vava'u Harbor. Watermark: Portrait of King in new design.		
	a. 4.7.1988.	65.00	225.
	b. 14.12.1988; 30.6.1989.	55.00	100.

National Reserve Bank of Tonga

1992 ND Issue

25	1 Pa'anga	VF	UNC
	ND (1992-95). Olive-green on multicolor underprint. Arms at lower left. King Taufa'ahau at right. Two signatures with Tongan titles beneath. Back: Olive and blue. River scene, palm trees.	FV	3.50

		VF	UNC
26	**2 Pa'anga** ND (1992-95). Red on multicolor underprint. Arms at lower left. King Taufa'ahau at right. Two signatures with Tongan titles beneath. Back: Red and brown. Women making Tapa cloth.	FV	6.00

		VF	UNC
27	**5 Pa'anga** ND (1992-95). Purple on multicolor underprint. Arms at lower left. King Taufa'ahau at right. Two signatures with Tongan titles beneath. Back: Purple and olive-green. Ha'amonga stone gateway.	FV	15.00
28	**10 Pa'anga** ND (1992-95). Dark blue on multicolor underprint. Arms at lower left. King Taufa'ahau at right. Two signatures with Tongan titles beneath. Back: Blue and purple. Royal Palace.	FV	30.00
29	**20 Pa'anga** ND (1992-95). Orange and green on multicolor underprint. King in new design at center right, arms at right. Two signatures with Tongan titles beneath. Back: Tonga Development Bank. Watermark: Portrait of King.	FV	45.00

1989 Commemorative Issue

#30, Inauguration of National Reserve Bank of Tonga

		VF	UNC
30	**20 Pa'anga** 1.7.1989. Orange on green and multicolor underprint. King in new design at center right, arms at right, commemorative text in circle on watermark area. Back: Vava'u Harbour, commemorative text in circle on watermark area. Watermark: King in new design.	20.00	65.00

1995 ND Issue

		VF	UNC
31	**1 Pa'anga** ND (1995). Olive-green and green on multicolor underprint. King Taufa'ahau at upper center right, arms at right. Signature varieties. Back: River scene, palm trees. Watermark: King Taufa'ahau. Printer: TDLR. UV: value 1 in box fluorese yellow. 150x70mm.		
	a. Signature N-D.	2.00	6.00
	b. Signature U-F.	FV	3.00
	c. Signature U-U.	FV	3.00

		VF	UNC
32	**2 Pa'anga** ND (1995). Red and reddish-brown on multicolor underprint. King Taufa'ahau at upper center right, arms at right. Signature varieties. Back: Women making Tapa cloth. Watermark: King Taufa'ahau. Printer: TDLR. 150x70mm.		
	a. Signature N-D.	3.00	7.50
	b. Signature U-F.	FV	4.50

		VF	UNC
33	**5 Pa'anga** ND (1995). Purple and violet on multicolor underprint. King Taufa'ahau at upper center right, arms at right. Signature varieties. Back: Ha'amonga stone gateway. Watermark: King Taufa'ahau. Printer: TDLR. 150x70mm.		
	a. Signature N-F. Series A.	FV	10.00
	b. Signature U-U. Series B.	FV	8.00
	c. Series C.	FV	8.00

		VF	UNC
34	**10 Pa'anga** ND (1995). Dark blue on multicolor underprint. King Taufa'ahau at upper center right, arms at right. Signature varieties. Back: Royal Palace. Watermark: King Taufa'ahau. Printer: TDLR. 150x70mm.		
	a. Signature N-D.	20.00	35.00
	b. Signature U-F.	FV	22.50
	c. Signature U-U.	FV	17.50

		VF	UNC
35	**20 Pa'anga** ND. Orange and multicolor. King in new design at center right, arms at right. Two signatures with Tongan titles beneath. Back: Tonga Development Bank. Watermark: Portrait of King in new design. 150x70mm.		
	a. Signature N-D.	40.00	35.00
	b. Signature N-F.	FV	40.00
	c. Signature U-U.	FV	30.00
	d. Signature U-F.	FV	30.00

36 **50 Pa'anga** — VF: FV — UNC: 85.00
ND. Brown and green on multicolor underprint. King in new design at center right. Signature U-U. Back: View of the harbor. 150x70mm.

2008 Issue

37 **1 Pa'anga** — VF: FV — UNC: 2.50
ND (2008). Green on multicolor underprint. King Tupou V at right. Back: Whale.

38 **2 Pa'anga** — VF: FV — UNC: 5.00
ND (2008). Red and reddish brown on multicolor underprint. King Tupou V at right. Back: Education and sports.

39 **5 Pa'anga** — VF: FV — UNC: 8.50
ND (2008). Purple and violet on multicolor underprint. King Tupou V at right. Back: Langi (large ceremonial tomb).

40 **10 Pa'anga** — VF: FV — UNC: 15.00
ND (2008). Blue and olive green on multicolor underprint. King Tupou V at right. Back: Royal tomb.

41 **20 Pa'anga** — VF: FV — UNC: 27.50
ND (2008). Brown and light olive green on multicolor underprint. King Tupou V at right. Back: National Reserve Bank of Tonga building.

42 **50 Pa'anga** — VF: FV — UNC: 70.00
ND (2008). Green and tan on multicolor underprint. King Tupou V at right. Back: Palace.

43 **100 Pa'anga** — VF: FV — UNC: 135.
ND (2008). Maroon and red on multicolor underprint. King Tupou V at right. Back: Vava'u harbor.

Collector Series

Government of Tonga

1978 Issue

CS1 **1978 1-10 Pa'anga** — Mkt. Value: 70.00
#19b-22b overprint: *SPECIMEN* and prefix serial # Maltese cross.

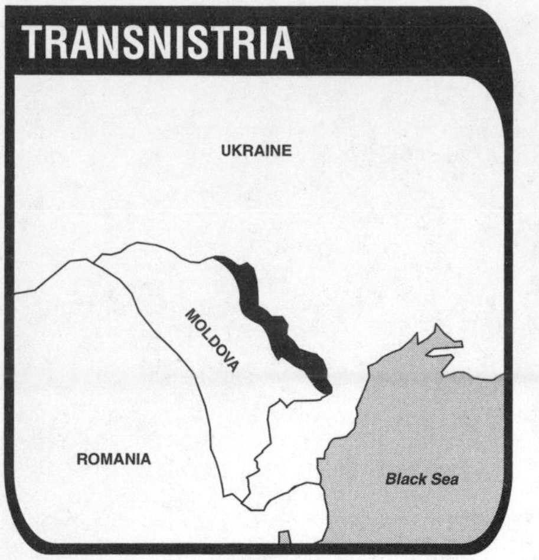

The Transnistria Moldavian Republic was formed in 1990, even before the separation of Moldavia from Russia. It has an area of 11,544 sq. mi. (29,900 sq. km). and a population of 700,000. Capital: Tiraspol.

The area was conquered from the Turks in the last half of the 18th Century, and in 1792 the capital city of Tiraspol was founded. After 1812, the area called Bessarabia (present Moldova and part of the Ukraine) became part of the Russian Empire. During the Russian Revolution, in 1918, the area was taken by Romanian troops, and in 1924 the Moldavian Autonomous SSR was formed on the left bank of the Dniester River. A Romanian occupation area between the Dniester and Bug Rivers called *Transnistria* was established in October 1941. Its center was the port of Odessa. A special issue of notes for use in Transnistria was made by the Romanian government. In 1944 the Russians recaptured Transnistria.

Once the Moldavian SSR declared independence in August 1991. Transnistria did not want to be a part of Moldavia. In 1992, Moldova tried to solve the issue militarily.

Transnistria has a president, parliament, army and police forces, but as yet is lacking international recognition.

MONETARY SYSTEM:

1 Ruble = 1,000 old Rubles (August 1994)
1 Ruble = 1,000,000 old Rubles (January 2001)

REPUBLIC

GOVERNMENT

1994 ND PROVISIONAL ISSUES

#1-15 issued 24.1.1994, invalidated on 1.12.1994.

The Bank purchased used Russian notes and placed stickers on them. Most collectors feel that "uncirculated" notes currently available were made after 1994.

		VF	UNC
1	**10 Rublei** ND (1994- old date 1961). Green on pink tint adhesive stamp on Russia #233.	2.00	4.00

		VF	UNC
2	**10 Rublei** ND (1994- old date 1991). Green on pink tint adhesive stamp on Russia # 240.	2.00	4.00

		VF	UNC
3	**25 Rublei** ND (1994- old date 1961). Red-violet on buff tint adhesive stamp on Russia # 234.	2.00	5.00

		VF	UNC
4	**50 Rublei** ND (1994- old date 1991). Red on pale green tint adhesive stamp on Russia #241.	6.00	12.00
5	**50 Rublei** ND (1994- old date 1992). Red on pale green tint adhesive stamp on Russia #247.	3.00	8.00

		VF	UNC
6	**100 Rublei** ND (1994- old date 1991). Black on pale blue tint adhesive stamp on Russia #242.	6.00	12.00
7	**100 Rublei** ND (1994- old date 1991). Black on pale blue tint adhesive stamp on Russia #243.	3.00	8.00

		VF	UNC
8	**200 Rublei** ND (1994- old date 1991). Green on yellow tint adhesive stamp on Russia # 244.	10.00	30.00

		VF	UNC
9	**200 Rublei** ND (1994- old date 1992). Green on yellow tint adhesive stamp on Russia #248.	3.00	6.00

#	Denomination	VF	UNC
10	**500 Rublei** ND (1994- old date 1991). Blue adhesive stamp on Russia #245.	20.00	40.00
11	**500 Rublei** ND (1994- old date 1992). Blue adhesive stamp on Russia # 249.	2.00	7.00

#	Denomination	VF	UNC
12	**1000 Rublei** ND (1994- old date 1991). Violet on yellow tint adhesive stamp on Russia #246.	20.00	50.00
13	**1000 Rublei** ND (1994- old date 1992). Violet on yellow tint adhesive stamp on Russia #250.	3.00	8.00
14	**5000 Rublei** ND (1994- old date 1992). Dark brown on pale blue-gray tint adhesive stamp on Russia #252.	2.00	6.00

#	Denomination	VF	UNC
14A	**5000 Rublei** ND (1994 -old date 1961). Adhesive stamp on Russia 5 Rubles #224.	2.00	4.00

#	Denomination	VF	UNC
14B	**5000 Rublei** ND (1994 -old date 1991). Adhesive stamp on Russia 5 Rubles # 239.	2.00	5.00
15	**10,000 Rublei** ND (1994- old date 1992). Purple on yellow tint adhesive stamp on Russia #253.	2.00	5.00

БАНКА НИСТРЯНЭ

BANKA NISTRIANA

1993; 1994 КУПОН KUPON ISSUE

#16-18 Note: Postal adhesive stamps have been seen affixed to #16-18 to imitate revalidated notes.

#	Denomination	VF	UNC
16	**1 Ruble** 1994. Dark green on multicolor underprint. Alexander Vassilievitch Suvurov at right. Back: Parliament building at center. Watermark: Block design. UV: fibers fluoresce yellow and red.	.50	1.00
17	**5 Rublei** 1994. Blue on multicolor underprint. Alexander Vassilievitch Suvurov at right. Back: Parliament building at center. Watermark: Block design. UV: fibers fluoresce yellow and red.	.50	1.00
18	**10 Rublei** 1994. Red-violet on multicolor underprint. Alexander Vassilievitch Suvurov at right. Back: Parliament building at center. Watermark: Block design. UV: fibers fluoresce yellow and red.	.50	1.00

#	Denomination	VF	UNC
19	**50 Rublei** 1993 (1994). Green on multicolor underprint. Equestrian statue of Alexander Vassilievitch Suvurov at right. Back: Parliament building at center. Watermark: Block design.	1.00	2.00
20	**100 Rublei** 1993 (1994). Dark brown on multicolor underprint. Equestrian statue of Alexander Vassilievitch Suvurov at right. Back: Parliament building at center. Watermark: Block design.	1.00	2.00
21	**200 Rublei** 1993 (1994). Red-violet on multicolor underprint. Equestrian statue of Alexander Vassilievitch Suvurov at right. Back: Parliament building at center. Watermark: Block design.	1.00	4.00
22	**500 Rublei** 1993 (1994). Blue on multicolor underprint. Equestrian statue of Alexander Vassilievitch Suvurov at right. Back: Parliament building at center. Watermark: Block design.	2.00	5.00
23	**1000 Rublei** 1993 (1994). Purple and red-violet on multicolor underprint. Equestrian statue of Alexander Vassilievitch Suvurov at right. Back: Parliament building at center. Watermark: Block design.	2.00	5.00
24	**5000 Rublei** 1993 (1995). Black on deep olive-green and multicolor underprint. Equestrian statue of Alexander Vassilievitch Suvurov at right. Back: Parliament building at center. Watermark: Block design.	2.00	6.00

1994 (1995) ISSUE

1 Ruble = 1000 "Old" Rublei

#	Denomination	VF	UNC
26	**1000 Rublei = 100,000 Rublei** 1994 (1995). Blue-violet and purple. Alexander Vassilievitch Suvurov at right. Back: Parliament building. Printer: German.	3.00	7.00

1995; ND (1996) PROVISIONAL ISSUE

#	Denomination	VF	UNC
27	**50,000 Rublei on 5 Rublei** ND (1996 - old date 1994). Blue on multicolor underprint. Alexander Vassilievitch Suvurov at right. Hologram with *50,000* at upper left. Back: Parliament building at center.	2.00	4.00

28 **50,000 Rublei = 500,000 Rublei** — VF / UNC
1995 (1996). Brown-violet and brown on multicolor underprint. Bogdan Khmelnitsky at right. Signature Vyacheslav Zagryatsky. Back: Drama and comedy theatre. Printer: German.

	VF	UNC
a. Issued note.	8.00	15.00
s. Specimen. Red overprint.	—	40.00

1996 ND Provisional Issue

29 **10,000 Rublei on 1 Ruble** — VF 1.00, UNC 2.00
ND (1996 - old date 1994). Dark green on multicolor underprint. General Alexander Vassilievitch Suvurov at right, with overprint. Back: Parliament building at center, with overprint.

29A **10,000 Rublei on 1 Ruble** — VF 1.00, UNC 2.00
1998. Green and tan on multicolor underprint. General Alexander Vassilievitch Suvurov at right, with overprint. Back: Parliament building at center.

30 **50,000 Rublei on 5 Rublei** — VF 1.00, UNC 3.00
ND (1996 - old date 1994). Blue on multicolor underprint. General Alexander Vassilievitch Suvurov at right, with overprint. Back: Parliament building at center with overprint.

31 **100,000 Rublei on 10 Rublei** — VF 1.00, UNC 3.00
ND (1996 - old date 1994). Red-violet on multicolor underprint. General Alexander Vassilievitch Suvurov at right, with overprint. Back: Parliament building at center with overprint.

1997; 1999 Issue

33 **500,000 Rublei** — VF 3.00, UNC 5.00
1997. Purple and violet on multicolor underprint. Equestrian statue of Alexander Vassilievitch Suvurov at right. Back: Parliament building at center. Watermark: Block design.

2000 Issue

34 **1 Ruble** — VF / UNC
2000. Orange-brown on multicolor underprint. General Alexander Vassilievitch Suvurov at left. Back: Kitskansky Bridgehead Memorial complex. 129x56mm.

	VF	UNC
a. Issued note.	.50	1.00
s. Specimen.	—	—

35 **5 Rublei** — VF / UNC
2000. Blue on multicolor underprint. General Alexander Vassilievitch Suvurov at left. Back: *Kvint* destillery administrative building. 129x56mm.

	VF	UNC
a. Issued note.	1.00	3.00
s. Specimen. ОБРАЗЕЦ.	—	—

36 **10 Rublei** — VF / UNC
2000. Brown on multicolor underprint. General Alexander Vassilievitch Suvurov at left. Back: Novo Nyametsky Monastery in Kitzkansk. 129x56mm.

	VF	UNC
a. Issued note.	FV	5.00
s. Specimen.	—	—

37 **25 Rublei** — VF / UNC
2000. Rose on multicolor underprint. General Alexander Vassilievitch Suvurov at left. Back: Bendery fortress and a Russian soldiers' Memorial. 129x56mm.

	VF	UNC
a. Issued note.	FV	10.00
s. Specimen.	—	—

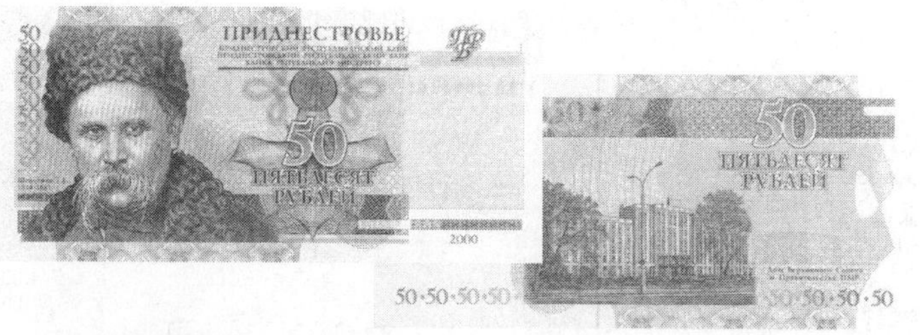

38 **50 Rublei** — VF / UNC
2000. Deep green on multicolor underprint. Taras Shevchenko (poet) at left. Back: Transnistria Parliament building. 129x60mm.

	VF	UNC
a. Issued note.	FV	15.00
s. Specimen.	—	—

39 100 Rublei VF UNC
2000. Purple on multicolor underprint. Prince Dimitrie Cantemir at left. Back: The Christmas Church. 129x60mm.
- a. Issued note. FV 30.00
- s. Specimen. — —

40 200 Rublei VF UNC
2004. Brown. Bust at left. Back: 1757 Battle scene. 135x64mm.
- a. Incorrect spelling of bank name in Ukrainian. Series AA. FV 60.00
- b. Correct spelling of bank name in Ukrainian. From Series AB. FV 40.00
- c. Modikatsiya 2012. FV 40.00

41 500 Rublei VF UNC
2004. Green. Catherine II at left. Back: Fort. 140x68mm.
- a. Incorrect spelling of bank name in Ukrainian. Series AA. FV 150.
- b. Correct spelling of bank name in Ukrainian. Series AB. FV 75.00
- c. Modikatsiya 2012. FV 75.00

2007 Issue

42 1 Ruble VF UNC
2007. Orange-brown on multicolor underprint. General Alexander Vassilievitch Suvurov at left. Secureaty band. Back: Kitskansky Bridgehead memorial complex. 129x56mm.
- a. 2007. FV 1.00
- b. Modikatsiya 2012. FV 1.00

43 5 Rublei VF UNC
2007. Blue on multicolor underprint. General Alexander Vassilievitch Suvurov at left. Secureaty band. Back: *Kvint* destiliery administrative building. 129x56mm.
- a. 2007. FV 2.00
- b. Modikatsiya 2012. FV 2.00

44 10 Rublei VF UNC
2007. Brown on multicolor underprint. General Alexander Vassilievitch Suvurov at left. Secureaty band. Back: Novo Nyametssky Monastery in Kitzkansk. 129x56mm.
- a. 2007. FV 3.50
- b. Modikatsiya 2012. FV 3.50

45 25 Rublei VF UNC
2007. Rose on multicolor underprint. General Alexander Vassilievitch Suvurov at left. Secureaty band. Back: Bendery Fortress and a Russian soldier's memorial. 129x56mm.
- a. 2007. FV 6.00
- b. Modikatsiya 2012. FV 6.00

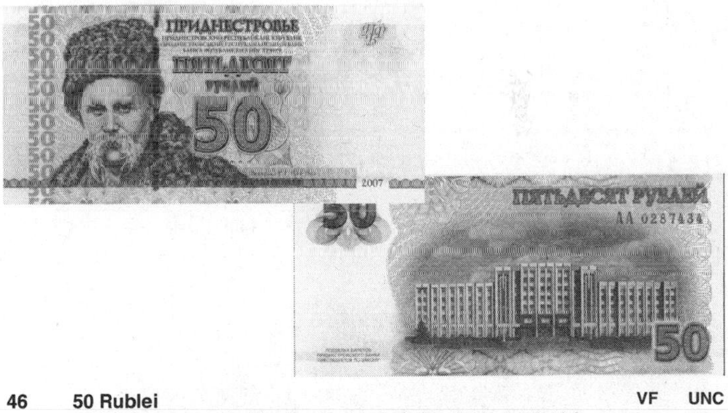

46 50 Rublei VF UNC
2007. Deep green on multicolor underprint.. Taras Shevchenko (poet) at left. Security band. Back: Transnistria Parliament building. 129x56mm.
- a. 2007. FV 12.50
- b. Modikatsiya 2012. FV 14.00

47 100 Rublei VF UNC
2007. Purple on multicolor underprint. Prince Dimitrie Cantemir at left. Security foil. Back: The Christmas Church. 129x56mm.
- a. 2007. FV 25.00
- b. Modikatsiya 2012. FV 22.50

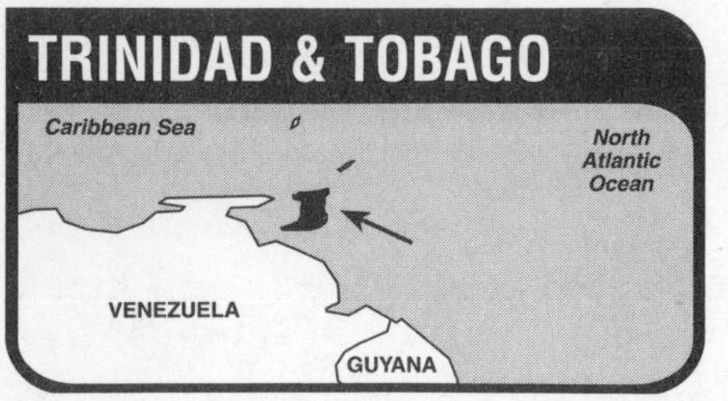

The Republic of Trinidad and Tobago, a member of the British Commonwealth situated 11 km. off the coast of Venezuela, has an area of 5,128 sq. km. and a population of 1.23 million. Capital: Port-of-Spain. The Island of Trinidad contains the world's largest natural asphalt bog. Birds of Paradise live on little Tobago, the only place outside of their native New Guinea where they can be found in a wild state. Petroleum and petroleum products are the mainstay of the economy. Petroleum products, crude oil and sugar are exported.

First colonized by the Spanish, the islands came under British control in the early 19th century. The islands' sugar industry was hurt by the emancipation of the slaves in 1834. Manpower was replaced with the importation of contract laborers from India between 1845 and 1917, which boosted sugar production as well as the cocoa industry. The discovery of oil on Trinidad in 1910 added another important export. Independence was attained in 1962. The country is one of the most prosperous in the Caribbean thanks largely to petroleum and natural gas production and processing. Tourism, mostly in Tobago, is targeted for expansion and is growing.

Notes of the British Caribbean Territories circulated between 1950-1964.

RULERS:

British to 1976

MONETARY SYSTEM:

1 Dollar = 100 Cents
5 Dollars = 1 Pound 10 Pence

SIGNATURE VARIETIES			
1	J.F. Pierce	2	A.N. McLeod
3	J.E.Bruce	4	Linn OHB
5	W. Demas	6	N. Hareward
7		8	

REPUBLIC

CENTRAL BANK OF TRINIDAD AND TOBAGO

1964 CENTRAL BANK ACT

		VF	UNC
26	**1 Dollar** *L.1964.* Red on multicolor underprint. Arms at left, portrait of Queen Elizabeth II at center. Back: Central Bank building at center right. Oil rig in water at upper right. Watermark: Bird of Paradise. 156x66mm.		
	a. Signature 1.	8.00	55.00
	b. Signature 2. Serial # single letter or fractional letters prefix.	10.00	75.00
	c. Signature 3.	7.00	45.00
	s. As a, c. Specimen.	—	200.
	ct. Color trial. As a, c. Purple on multicolor underprint.	—	300.

		VF	UNC
27	**5 Dollars** *L.1964.* Green on multicolor underprint. Arms at left, portrait of Queen Elizabeth II at center. Back: Central Bank building at center right. Crane loading sugar cane at upper right. Watermark: Bird of Paradise. 156x66mm.		
	a. Signature 1.	125.	500.
	b. Signature 2.	75.00	375.
	c. Signature 3.	35.00	150.
	s. As a, c. Specimen.	—	300.
	ct. Color trial, As a, c. Brown on multicolor underprint.	—	450.

		VF	UNC
28	**10 Dollars** *L.1964.* Dark brown on multicolor underprint. Arms at left, portrait of Queen Elizabeth II at center. Back: Central Bank building at center right. Factory at upper right. Watermark: Bird of Paradise. 156x66mm.		
	a. Signature 1.	300.	1350.
	b. Signature 2.	265.	1150.
	c. Signature 3.	150.	600.
	s. As a, c. Specimen.	—	350.
	ct. Color trial. As a, c. Olive-green on multicolor underprint.	—	600.

		VF	UNC
29	**20 Dollars** *L.1964.* Purple on multicolor underprint. Arms at left, portrait of Queen Elizabeth II at center. Back: Central Bank building at center right. Cocoa pods at upper right. Watermark: Bird of Paradise. 156x66mm.		
	a. Signature 1.	275.	1250.
	b. Signature 2.	250.	1100.
	c. Signature 3.	140.	550.
	s. As a, c. Specimen.	—	400.
	ct. Color trial. As a, c. Red on multicolor underprint.	—	750.

1977 ND ISSUE

#30-35 authorization date 1964. Replacement notes: Serial # prefix *XX*.

		VF	UNC
30	**1 Dollar**		
	L.1964 (1977). Red on multicolor underprint. Arms at center, two scarlet Ibis at left. Back: Central bank building at center right. Oil rig in water at upper right. Watermark: Bird of Paradise. 156x66mm.		
	a. Signature 3.	.50	2.50
	b. Signature 4.	1.00	4.00
	s. As a. Specimen.	—	150.

		VF	UNC
31	**5 Dollars**		
	L.1964 (1977). Dark green on multicolor underprint. Arms at center, branches and leaves at left. Back: Central Bank building at center right. Crane loading sugar cane at upper right. Watermark: Bird of Paradise. 156x66mm.		
	a. Signature 3.	1.00	6.00
	b. Signature 4.	4.00	20.00
	s. As a. Specimen.	—	—

		VF	UNC
32	**10 Dollars**		
	L.1964 (1977). Dark brown on multicolor underprint. Arms at center. Piping guan on branch at left. Signature 3. Back: Central Bank building at center right. Factory at upper right. Watermark: Bird of Paradise. 156x66mm.		
	a. Issued note.	2.50	12.50
	s. Specimen.		

		VF	UNC
33	**20 Dollars**		
	L.1964 (1977). Purple on multicolor underprint. Arms at center, flowers at left. Signature 3. Back: Central Bank building at center right, cocoa pods at upper right. Watermark: Bird of Paradise. 156x66mm.		
	a. Issued note.	5.00	25.00
	s. Specimen, punch hole cancelled.	—	—

		VF	UNC
34	**50 Dollars**		
	L.1964 (1977). Dark brown on multicolor underprint. Arms at center, long-billed starthroat at left. Signature 3. Back: Central Bank building at center right, net fishing at upper right. Watermark: Bird of Paradise. 156x66mm.		
	a. 1963 (error date in authorization).	75.00	350.
	b. 1964 (corrected authorization date).	175.	900.
	s. As b. Specimen.	—	—

		VF	UNC
35	**100 Dollars**		
	L.1964 (1977). Deep blue on multicolor underprint. Arms at center, branch with leaves and berries at left. Back: Central Bank building at center right. Huts and palm trees at upper right. Watermark: Bird of Paradise. 156x66mm.		
	a. Signature 3.	30.00	125.
	b. Signature 4.	35.00	150.
	s. As a. Specimen.	—	—

Central Bank Act Chap. 79.02; 1985 ND Issue

#36-40 Replacement notes: Serial # prefix *XX*.

		VF	UNC
36	**1 Dollar**		
	ND (1985). Red-orange and purple on multicolor underprint. Arms at center, scarlet Ibis at left. Back: Twin towered modern bank building at center, oil refinery at right. Watermark: Bird of Paradise. UV: Back two vertical stripes at left fluoresce blue. 156x66mm.		
	a. Signature 4.	FV	1.50
	b. Signature 5.	FV	1.50
	c. Signature 6.	FV	1.00
	d. Signature 7.	FV	1.00
	s. Specimen.	—	150.

		VF	UNC
37	**5 Dollars**		
	ND (1985). Dark green and blue on multicolor underprint. Arms at center, blue crowned motmot at left. Back: Twin towered modern bank building at center, woman at roadside produce stand at right. Watermark: Bird of Paradise. 156x66mm.		
	a. Signature 4.	FV	5.00
	b. Signature 5.	FV	3.00
	c. Signature 6.	FV	2.00
	d. Signature 7.	FV	2.00
	s. Specimen.	—	150.

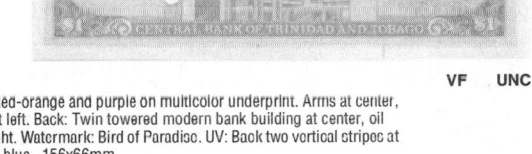

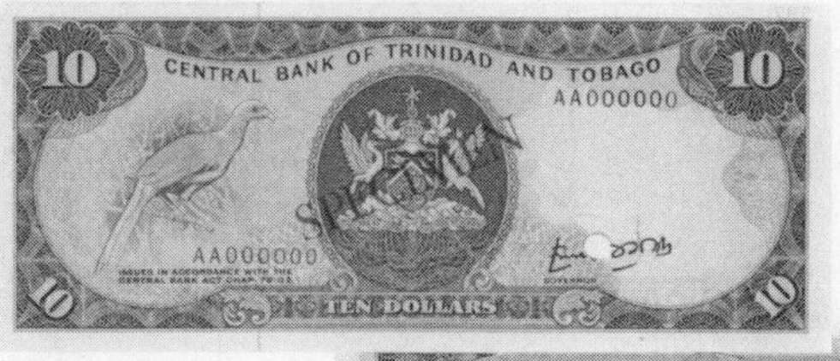

38 **10 Dollars** VF UNC

ND (1985). Dark green and brown on multicolor underprint. Arms at center, piping guan on branch at left. Back: Twin towered modern bank building at center, cargo ship dockside at right. Watermark: Bird of Paradise. 156x66mm.

	VF	UNC
a. Signature 4.	FV	7.50
b. Signature 5.	FV	6.00
c. Signature 6.	FV	4.00
d. Signature 7.	FV	4.00
s. Specimen.	—	175.

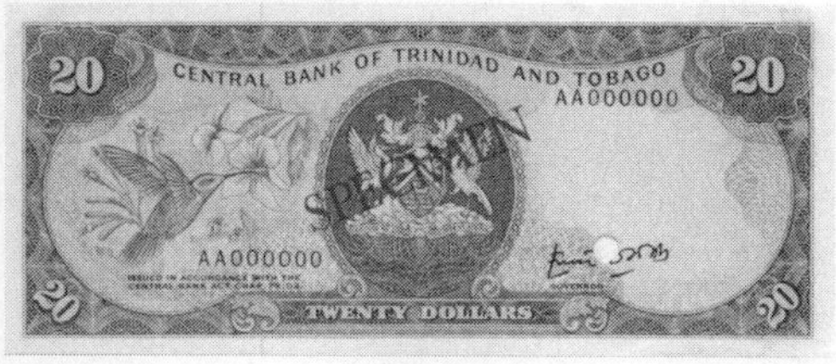

39 **20 Dollars** VF UNC

ND (1985). Purple and green on multicolor underprint. Arms at center, white-tailed Saberwing in flowers at left. Back: Twin towered modern bank building at center, steel drums at right. Watermark: Bird of Paradise. 156x66mm.

	VF	UNC
a. Signature 4.	FV	12.50
b. Signature 5.	FV	7.50
c. Signature 6.	FV	6.00
d. Signature 7.	FV	6.00
s. Specimen.	—	175.

40 **100 Dollars** VF UNC

ND (1985). Deep blue on multicolor underprint. Arms at center, Greater Bird of Paradise at left. Back: Twin towered modern bank building at center, oil rig at right. Watermark: Bird of Paradise. 156x66mm.

	VF	UNC
a. Signature 4.	FV	50.00
b. Signature 5.	FV	37.50
c. Signature 6.	FV	30.00
d. Signature 7.	FV	30.00
s. Specimen.	—	225.

2002 Issue

41 **1 Dollar** VF UNC

2002. Red on multicolor underprint. Arms at center, scarlet Ibis at left. Segmented security foil. Back: Twin towered modern bank building at center, oil refinery at right. Watermark: Bird of Paradise. 156x66mm.

	VF	UNC
a. Signature 7.	FV	1.00
b. Signature 8.	FV	1.00

42 **5 Dollars** VF UNC

2002. Green and blue on multicolor underprint. Arms at center, blue crowned motmot at left. Segmented security foil. Back: Twin towered modern bank building at center, woman at roadside produce stand at right. Watermark: Bird of Paradise. 156x66mm.

	VF	UNC
a. Signature 7.	FV	2.00
b. Signature 8.	FV	2.00

43 **10 Dollars** VF UNC

2002. Dark green on multicolor underprint. Arms at center, piping guan on branch at left. Segmented security foil. Back: Twin towered modern bank building at center, cargo ship dockside at right. Watermark: Bird of Paradise. 156x66mm.

	VF	UNC
a. Signature 7.	FV	4.00
b. Signature 8.	FV	4.00

44 **20 Dollars** | VF | UNC
2002. Purple on multicolor underprint. Arms at center, white-tailed Saberwing in flowers at left. Segmented security foil. Back: Twin towered modern bank building at center, Steel drums at right. Watermark: Bird of Paradise. 156x66mm.

	VF	UNC
a. Signature 7.	FV	6.00
b. Signature 8.	FV	6.00

45 **100 Dollars** | VF | UNC
2002. Deep blue on multicolor underprint. Arms at center, Greater Bird of Paradise at left. Segmented security foil. Back: Twin towered modern bank building at center, oil rig at right. Watermark: Bird of Paradise. 145x66mm.

	VF	UNC
a. Signature 7.	FV	30.00
b. Signature 8.	FV	30.00

2006 Issue

0 **1 Dollar** | VF | UNC
ND (2009). Red on multicolor underprint. Arms at center, scarlet Ibis at left. Back: Twin towered bank building at center, refinery at right. Watermark: Bird of Paradise. Printer: TDLR (without imprint). | FV | 1.00

46 **1 Dollar**
2006. Red on multicolor underprint. Arms at center, scarlet ibis at left. Back: Twin towered bank building at center, oil refinery at right. Watermark: Bird of Paradise. Printer: TDLR (without imprint). | FV | 1.00

47 **5 Dollars** | VF | UNC
2006. Green and blue on multicolor underprint. Arms at center, blue crowned motmot at left. Back: Twin towered bank building at center, women at roadside produce stand at right. Watermark: Bird of Paradise. Printer: TDLR (without imprint). | FV | 2.00

48 **10 Dollars**
2006. Dark green on multicolor underprint. Arms at center, piping guan at left. Back: Twin towered bank building at center, cargo ship dockside at right. Watermark: Bird of Paradise. Printer: TDLR (without imprint). | FV | 4.00

49 **20 Dollars**
ND (2009). Purple on multicolor underprint. Arms at center, white-tailed Saberwing at left. Back: Twin towered bank building at center, Steel drum at right. Watermark: Bird of Paradise. Printer: TDLR (without imprint). | FV | 6.00

50 **50 Dollars** | VF | UNC
2006. Green on multicolor 152x70mm. | FV | 17.50

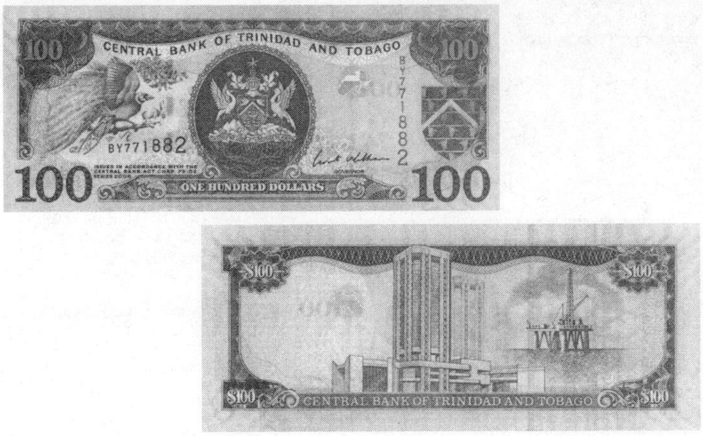

51 **100 Dollars** | VF | UNC
2006. Deep blue on multicolor underprint. Arms at center, Greater Bird of Paradise at left. Wreath around face-to-back register. Blue serial #. Back: Twin towered modern bank building at center, oil rig at right. Watermark: Bird of Paradise and value. 156x66mm. | FV | 30.00

2009 Commemorative Issue

52 **100 Dollars** | VF | UNC
ND (2009). Deep blue on multicolor underprint. Arms at center, Great Bird of Paradise at left. Back: Twin towered bank building at center, oil rig at right. Overprint: 60th Anniversary of Commonwealth. Watermark: Bird of Paradise. Printer: TDLR (without imprint). | FV | 35.00

2012 Commemorative Issue

53 **50 Dollars** | VF | UNC
2012. Green on multicolor underprint. 152x70mm. | FV | 35.00

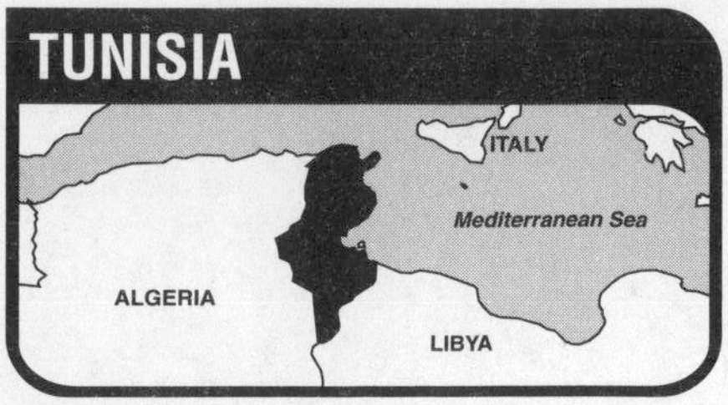

The Republic of Tunisia, located on the northern coast of Africa between Algeria and Libya, has an area of 163,610 sq. km. and a population of 10.38 million. Capital: Tunis. Agriculture is the backbone of the economy. Crude oil, phosphates, olive oil, and wine are exported.

Rivalry between French and Italian interests in Tunisia culminated in a French invasion in 1881 and the creation of a protectorate. Agitation for independence in the decades following World War I was finally successful in getting the French to recognize Tunisia as an independent state in 1956. The country's first president, Habib Bourguiba, established a strict one-party state. He dominated the country for 31 years, repressing Islamic fundamentalism and establishing rights for women unmatched by any other Arab nation. In November 1987, Bourguiba was removed from office and replaced by Zine el Abidine Ben Ali in a bloodless coup. Ben Ali served well into his fifth consecutive five-year term but was overthrown as part of the *Arab Spring* events of 2011. Elections are expected soon.

RULERS:

French, 1881-1956

MONETARY SYSTEM:

1 Franc = 100 Centimes to 1960

1 Dinar = 1000 Millimes, 1960-

REPLACEMENT NOTES:

#61-89 with second prefix letter *R* added after regular letter.

REPUBLIC

BANQUE CENTRALE DE TUNISIE

1962 ISSUE

		VF	UNC
61	**5 Dinars** 20.3.1962. Blue on multicolor underprint. Habib Bourguiba at right, bridge at left. Back: Archways. Watermark: Arms. Printer: TDLR.	75.00	425.

1965-69 ISSUE

		VF	UNC
62	**1/2 Dinar** 1.6.1965. Blue on multicolor underprint. Habib Bourguiba at left, mosque at right. Back: Mosaic from Monastir. Watermark: Habib Bourguiba. Printer: TDLR.		
	a. Issued note.	25.00	150.
	s. Specimen.	—	100.

		VF	UNC
63	**1 Dinar** 1.6.1965. Blue on purple and multicolor underprint. Habib Bourguiba at right. Factory at left. Back: Mosaic. Watermark: Habib Bourguiba. Printer: TDLR.		
	a. Issued note.	25.00	125.
	s. Specimen.	—	100.

		VF	UNC
64	**5 Dinars** 1.6.1965. Lilac-brown and green on multicolor underprint. Habib Bourguiba at right. Sadiki College at left. Back: Mosaic with woman in sprays at left, Roman arch in Sbeitla at center, Sunface at lower right. Watermark: Habib Bourguiba.		
	a. Issued note.	35.00	150.
	s. Specimen.	—	100.

		VF	UNC
65	**10 Dinars** 1.6.1969. Multicolor. Habib Bourguiba at right, refinery at left. Back: Palm trees in field. Watermark: Habib Bourguiba.		
	a. Issued note.	25.00	100.
	s. Specimen.	—	100.

1972 ISSUE

		VF	UNC
66	**1/2 Dinar** 3.8.1972. Brown on multicolor underprint. Habib Bourguiba at right. City with river at left. Back: View of Tunis. Watermark: Habib Bourguiba. Printer: (T)DLR.		
	a. Issued note.	2.50	12.50
	s. Specimen.	—	40.00

67 1 Dinar VF UNC

3.8.1972. Purple on multicolor underprint. Habib Bourguiba at right. Old fortin Sousse at left. Back: Minaret at left, girl at center. Watermark: Habib Bourguiba. Printer: (T)DLR.

	VF	UNC
a. Issued note.	6.00	25.00
s. Specimen.	—	40.00

68 5 Dinars VF UNC

3.8.1972. Green on multicolor underprint. Habib Bourguiba at right. Modern building at left. Back: Amphitheater at El-Djem. Watermark: Habib Bourguiba. Printer: (T)DLR.

	VF	UNC
a. Issued note.	15.00	50.00
s. Specimen.	—	40.00

1973 Issue

69 1/2 Dinar VF UNC

15.10.1973. Green on multicolor underprint. Habib Bourguiba at left center. Man with camel and trees at left. Back: Landscape with sheep and assorted produce. Watermark: Habib Bourguiba.

	VF	UNC
a. Issued note.	2.50	7.50
r. Replacement note. Serial # prefix: *AR/1*.	4.00	12.50

70 1 Dinar VF UNC

15.10.1973. Blue and green on multicolor underprint. Habib Bourguiba at left center, building at right. Back: Industrial scenes. Watermark: Habib Bourguiba. 4.00 12.50

71 5 Dinars VF UNC

15.10.1973. Dark brown on multicolor underprint. Habib Bourguiba at left center. City view at left. Back: Montage of old and new. Watermark: Habib Bourguiba. 10.00 40.00

72 10 Dinars VF UNC

15.10.1973. Purple and brown on multicolor underprint. Habib Bourguiba at left center. Refinery in background at center. Back: Montage with students, column, train and drummers. Watermark: Habib Bourguiba. 17.50 70.00

1980 Issue

74 1 Dinar VF UNC

15.10.1980. Red-brown and brown on red and multicolor underprint. Habib Bourguiba at right. Amphitheater at center. Back: Village of Korbous in the "Cap Bon". Watermark: Habib Bourguiba. 2.00 7.50

75 5 Dinars VF UNC

15.10.1980. Brown, red-brown and olive-green on multicolor underprint. Habib Bourguiba at right. Buildings at center. Back: Ruins and hills at left. Watermark: Habib Bourguiba. 7.50 35.00

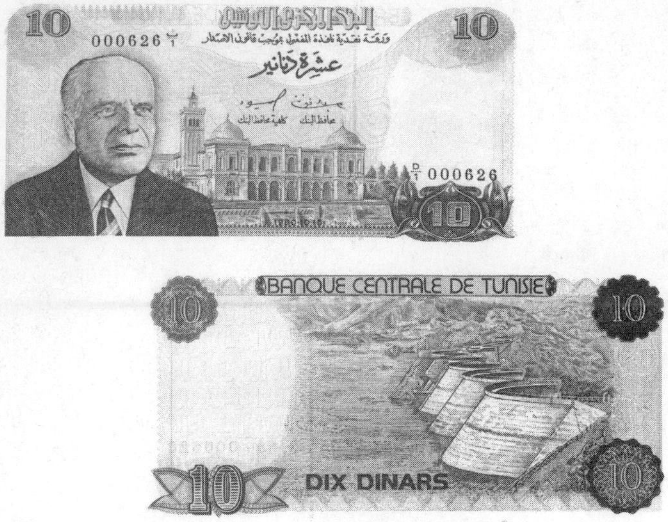

76 **10 Dinars** VF UNC

15.10.1980. Blue-green on bistre and multicolor underprint. Habib Bourguiba at left, building at center. Back: Reservoir at center. Watermark: Habib Bourguiba. 20.00 85.00

77 **20 Dinars** VF UNC

15.10.1980. Dark blue-green and brown on multicolor underprint. Habib Bourguiba at right. Amphitheater at center. Back: Harbor of Sousse. Watermark: Habib Bourguiba. 25.00 90.00

1983 Issue

79 **5 Dinars** VF UNC

3.11.1983. Red-brown and purple on lilac underprint. Habib Bourguiba at left, desert scene at bottom center. Back: Hydroelectric dam at center right. Watermark: Habib Bourguiba. 7.50 20.00

80 **10 Dinars** VF UNC

3.11.1983. Blue and lilac on multicolor underprint. Workers at lower left center, Habib Bourguiba at center, offshore oil rig at right. Back: Modern building at center, old city gateways at right. Watermark: Habib Bourguiba. 12.50 40.00

81 **20 Dinars** VF UNC

3.11.1983. Light blue and dark blue on green and multicolor underprint. Habib Bourguiba at left, building at bottom center. Back: Building at lower left, aerial view of harbor at right. Watermark: Habib Bourguiba. 22.50 70.00

1986 Issue

#82 and 83 Held in reserve.

84 **10 Dinars** VF UNC

20.3.1986. Yellow-brown on green underprint. Habib Bourguiba at left center, agricultural scene at bottom center. Back: Offshore oil rig at left center. Watermark: Habib Bourguiba. 170x84mm. 10.00 35.00

1992-97 Dated Issues

#86-89 replacement notes: *R* **in denominator of lserial # at the lower right or lower left.**

No.	Denomination / Description	VF	UNC
86	**5 Dinars** 7.11.1993. Green, olive-brown and black. Head of Hannibal at left center, Carthage harbor fortress at right. Back: Nov. 7, 1987 collage at left center. Watermark: Head of Hannibal. 130x70mm.	FV	15.00

No.	Denomination / Description	VF	UNC
87	**10 Dinars** 7.11.1994. Purple, blue-green and red-brown on multicolor underprint. Ibn Khaldoun at center. Back: Open book of 7 Novembre 1987 at left center. Watermark: Ibn Khaldoun. 145x73mm.	FV	25.00

No.	Denomination / Description	VF	UNC
87A	**10 Dinars** 7.11.1994 (2005). Brown on multicolor underprint. Ibn Khaldoun at center. Back: Open book of '7 Novembre 1987' at left center. Watermark: Ibn Khaldoun. 145x73mm.	FV	20.00

No.	Denomination / Description	VF	UNC
88	**20 Dinars** 7.11.1992. Deep purple, blue-black and red-brown on multicolor underprint. Kheoreddome ET-Tounsi on horseback at left center, buildings in background. Back: Montage of city view; a "7" with 1987 date over flag on stylized dove at center. Watermark: Head of Kheireddine ET-Tounsi. 153x76mm.	FV	30.00

No.	Denomination / Description	VF	UNC
89	**30 Dinars** 7.11.1997. Green and yellow on multicolor underprint. Abou EL Kacem Chebbi at right. Back: Schoolgirls, sheep and weaver. Watermark: Abou EL Kacem Chebbi. 161x79mm.	FV	45.00

2005 Issue

No.	Denomination / Description	VF	UNC
90	**10 Dinars** 7.11.2005. Blue on multicolor underprint. Mosque. Elissa, Queen of Carthage. 146x73mm.	FV	15.00

2008 Commemorative Issue

No.	Denomination / Description	VF	UNC
91	**50 Dinars** 7.11.2008. Green and violet on multicolor underprint. Ibn. Rashiq al Qirwani, Cité de la Culture in Tunis in background. Back: New bridge over Rades Harbor, the former Zin El Abridine Ben Ali airport in Enfidha. Watermark: Ibn Rachiq and 50. 167x80mm.		
	a. Issued note.	FV	60.00
	s. Specimen.	—	100.

2008 Issue

No.	Denomination / Description	VF	UNC
92	**5 Dinars** 2008. Green on multicolor underprint. Hannibar head right, Carthage harbor fortress at right. Back: Nov. 7, 1987 collage at left center. Watermark: Hannibal and 5. Printer: TDLR (without imprint). Omron rings added. 130x70mm.	FV	6.50

2011 Issue

93 20 Dinars VF UNC
2011. Red and blue on multicolor underprint. K. Et-tounsi on horseback at left center, building in backgorund. Back: Mosque. 153x76mm. FV 20.00

94 50 Dinars VF UNC
20.3.2011. Blue and green on multicolor underprint. Rashiq al Qirwani at left center, building in backgorund. Back: City square. 168x81mm. FV 45.00

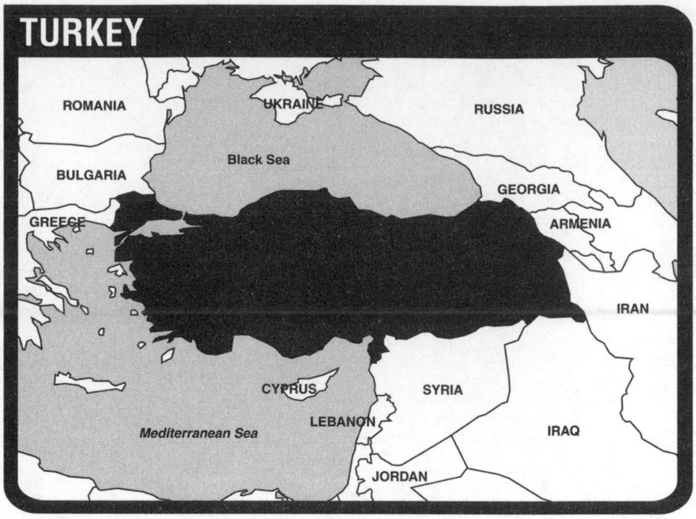

The Republic of Turkey, a parliamentary democracy of the Near East located partially in Europe and partially in Asia between the Black and the Mediterranean seas, has an area of 301,382 sq. mi. (780,580 sq. km.) and a population of 65.73 million. Capital: Ankara. Turkey exports cotton, hazelnuts and tobacco, and enjoys a virtual monopoly in meerschaum.

Modern Turkey was founded in 1923 from the Anatolian remnants of the defeated Ottoman Empire by national hero Mustafa Kemal, who was later honored with the title Ataturk or "Father of the Turks." Under his authoritarian leadership, the country adopted wide-ranging social, legal, and political reforms. After a period of one-party rule, an experiment with multi-party politics led to the 1950 election victory of the opposition Democratic Party and the peaceful transfer of power. Since then, Turkish political parties have multiplied, but democracy has been fractured by periods of instability and intermittent military coups (1960, 1971, 1980), which in each case eventually resulted in a return of political power to civilians. In 1997, the military again helped engineer the ouster - popularly dubbed a "post-modern coup" - of the then Islamic-oriented government. Turkey intervened militarily on Cyprus in 1974 to prevent a Greek takeover of the island and has since acted as patron state to the "Turkish Republic of Northern Cyprus," which only Turkey recognizes. A separatist insurgency begun in 1984 by the Kurdistan Workers' Party (PKK) - now known as the People's Congress of Kurdistan or Kongra-Gel (KGK) - has dominated the Turkish military's attention and claimed more than 30,000 lives. After the capture of the group's leader in 1999, the insurgents largely withdrew from Turkey mainly to northern Iraq. In 2004, KGK announced an end to its ceasefire and attacks attributed to the KGK increased. Turkey joined the UN in 1945 and in 1952 it became a member of NATO; it holds a non-permanent seat on the UN Security Council from 2009-2010. In 1964, Turkey became an associate member of the European Community. Over the past decade, it has undertaken many reforms to strengthen its democracy and economy; it began accession membership talks with the European Union in 2005.

MONETARY SYSTEM:

1 Lira (Livre, Pound) = 100 Piastres

Republic

Türkiye Cümhuriyet Merkez Bankasi

Central Bank of Turkey

Law 11 Haziran 1930; 1961-65 ND Issue

173 5 Lira VF UNC
L.1930 (25.10.1961). Blue with orange, blue and multicolor guilloche. Portrait of President Kemal Atatürk at right. Back: Blue. Three women with baskets of hazelnuts at center. Watermark: Kemal Atatürk. Printer: DBM-A (without imprint).

	VF	UNC
a. Issue note.	10.00	60.00
s. Specimen.	—	200.

174 5 Lira | VF | UNC

L.1930 (4.1.1965). Blue-green. Portrait of President Kemal Atatürk at right. Back: Blue-gray. Three women with baskets of hazelnuts at center. Watermark: Kemal Atatürk. Printer: DBM-A (without imprint).

	VF	UNC
a. Issued note.	8.00	60.00
s. Specimen.	—	200.

175 50 Lira | VF | UNC

L.1930 (1.6.1964). Brown on multicolor underprint. Portrait of President Kemal Atatürk at right. Three signatures. Back: Soldier holding rifle figure from the Victory statue at Ulus Square in Ankara at center. Watermark: Kemal Atatürk. Printer: DBM-A (without imprint).

	VF	UNC
a. Issued note.	20.00	75.00
s. Specimen.	—	250.

176 100 Lira | VF | UNC

L.1930 (15.3.1962). Olive on orange and multicolor guilloche. Portrait of President Kemal Atatürk at right. Back: Youth Park with bridge in Ankara. Watermark: Kemal Atatürk. Printer: DBM-A (without imprint).

	VF	UNC
a. Issued note.	50.00	125.
s. Specimen.	—	350.

177 100 Lira | VF | UNC

L.1930 (1.10.1964). Olive on blue, lilac and multicolor guilloche. Portrait of President Kemal Atatürk at right. Different signature. Back: Youth Park with bridge in Ankara. Watermark: Kemal Atatürk. Printer: DBM-A (without imprint).

	VF	UNC
a. Issued note.	50.00	125.
s. Specimen.	—	350.

178 500 Lira | VF | UNC

L.1930 (1.12.1962). Purple and brown on multicolor underprint. Portrait of President Kemal Atatürk at right. Back: Sultan Ahmet Mosque, the Obelisc and the Hippodrome in Istanbul. Watermark: Kemal Atatürk. Printer: DBM-A (without imprint).

	VF	UNC
a. Issued note.	150.	400.
s. Specimen.	—	500.

Law 11 Haziran 1930; 1966-69 ND Issue

		VF	UNC
179	**5 Lira** *L.1930* (8.1.1968). Grayish purple on multicolor underprint. President Kemal Atatürk at right. Three signatures. Back: Manavgat waterfall in Antalya at left center. Watermark: Kemal Atatürk. Printer: DBM-A (without imprint).	1.00	4.00

		VF	UNC
180	**10 Lira** *L.1930* (4.7.1966). Green on multicolor underprint. President Kemel Atatürk at right. Three signatures. Back: Bosporus Tower in Istanbul at center. Watermark: Kemel Atatürk. Printer: DBM-A (without imprint).	3.00	9.00

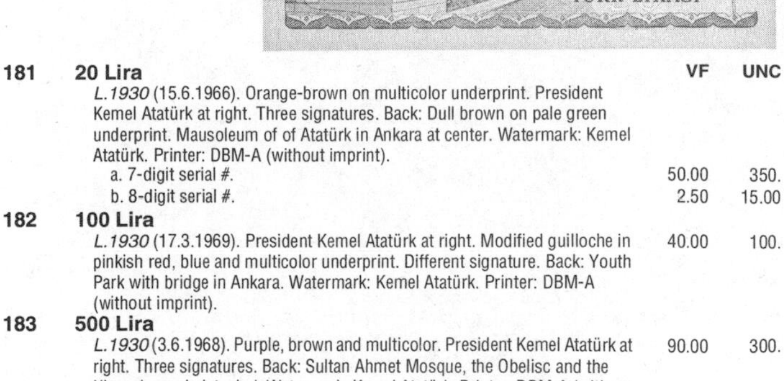

181 20 Lira | VF | UNC

L.1930 (15.6.1966). Orange-brown on multicolor underprint. President Kemel Atatürk at right. Three signatures. Back: Dull brown on pale green underprint. Mausoleum of of Atatürk in Ankara at center. Watermark: Kemel Atatürk. Printer: DBM-A (without imprint).

	VF	UNC
a. 7-digit serial #.	50.00	350.
b. 8-digit serial #.	2.50	15.00

		VF	UNC
182	**100 Lira** *L.1930* (17.3.1969). President Kemel Atatürk at right. Modified guilloche in pinkish red, blue and multicolor underprint. Different signature. Back: Youth Park with bridge in Ankara. Watermark: Kemel Atatürk. Printer: DBM-A (without imprint).	40.00	100.
183	**500 Lira** *L.1930* (3.6.1968). Purple, brown and multicolor. President Kemel Atatürk at right. Three signatures. Back: Sultan Ahmet Mosque, the Obelisc and the Hippodrome in Istanbul. Watermark: Kemel Atatürk. Printer: DBM-A (without imprint).	90.00	300.

Law Ocak 14 (Jan. 26), 1970; 1971-82 ND Issues

#185, 188, 190 and 191 replacement notes: Serial # prefix *Z91-Z95*.

185 **5 Lira** — VF | UNC

L.1970 (1976). Grayish purple on multicolor underprint. President Kemel Atatürk at right. Two signatures. Back: Manavgat waterfall in Antalya at left center. Watermark: Kemel Atatürk. Printer: DBM-A (without imprint). — .50 | 2.00

186 **10 Lira** — VF | UNC

L.1970 (1975). Green on multicolor underprint. President Kemel Atatürk at right. Two signatures. Back: Maiden's Tower on the Bosphorus in Istanbul at center. Watermark: Kemel Atatürk. Printer: DBM-A (without imprint). — 1.50 | 5.00

187 **20 Lira** — VF | UNC

L.1970 (1974). Orange-brown on multicolor underprint. President Kamel Atatürk at right. Two signatures. Back: Mausoleum of of Atatürk in Ankara at center. Watermark: Kamel Atatürk. Printer: DBM-A (without imprint).

a. Black signature. 2 varieties. — 1.00 | 5.00

b. Brown signature. — .50 | 1.00

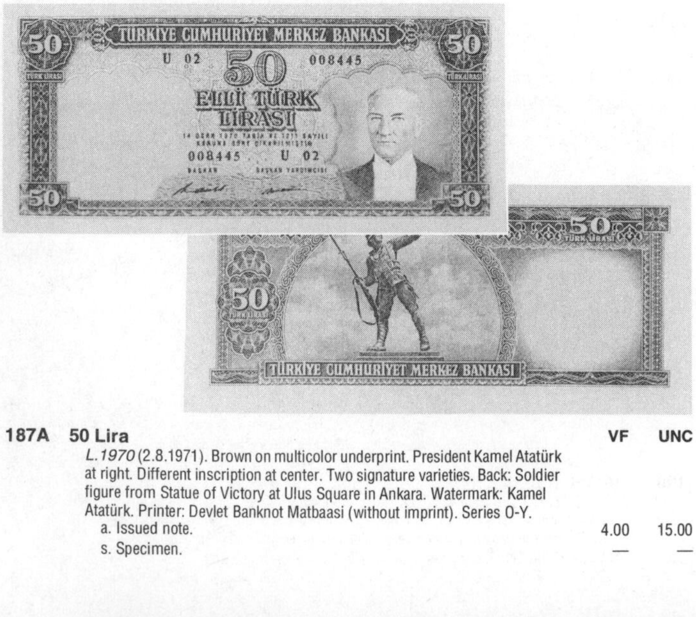

187A **50 Lira** — VF | UNC

L.1970 (2.8.1971). Brown on multicolor underprint. President Kamel Atatürk at right. Different inscription at center. Two signature varieties. Back: Soldier figure from Statue of Victory at Ulus Square in Ankara. Watermark: Kamel Atatürk. Printer: Devlet Banknot Matbaasi (without imprint). Series O-Y.

a. Issued note. — 4.00 | 15.00

s. Specimen. — — | —

188 **50 Lira** — VF | UNC

L.1970 (1976). Dark brown on multicolor underprint. President Kamel Atatürk at right. Two signature varieties. Back: Marble Fountain in Topkapi Palace in Istanbul. Watermark: Kamel Atatürk. — .50 | 2.00

189 **100 Lira** — VF | UNC

L.1970 (15.5.1972). Blue-green on multicolor underprint. President Kamel Atatürk at right. Three signature varieties. Back: Brown. Mt. Ararat at center. Watermark: Kamel Atatürk.

a. Issued note. — 1.00 | 3.00

s. Specimen. — — | —

190 **500 Lira** — VF | UNC

L.1970 (1.9.1971). Dark blue and dark green on multicolor underprint. President Kamel Atatürk at right. Two signature varieties. Back: Main Gate of Istanbul University. Watermark: Kamel Atatürk. — 10.00 | 25.00

191 **1000 Lira** — VF | UNC

L.1970. Deep purple and brown-violet on multicolor underprint. President Kamel Atatürk at right. Three signature varieties. Back: Bosphorus River with boat and suspension bridge. Watermark: Kamel Atatürk. — 6.00 | 20.00

Law Ocak 14 (Jan. 26), 1970; 1984-97 ND Issues

Some sign. varieties.

			VF	UNC
192	**10 Lira**	*L.1970* (1979). Dull gray-green on multicolor underprint. President Kamel Atatürk at right. Young boy and girl in medallion in underprint at center. Back: Children presenting flowers to Atatürk. Watermark: Kamel Atatürk. UV: security thread fluoresces blue.	.20	.50
193	**10 Lira**	*L.1970* (1982). Black on multicolor underprint. President Kemel Atatürk at right. Back: Children presenting flowers to Atatürk. Watermark: Kemel Atatürk. UV: security thread fluoresces blue, serial # yellow.		
		a. Back is dark olive green. (1979).	.20	.50
		b. Back is black. (1982).	.20	.50

			VF	UNC
194	**100 Lira**	*L.1970* (1984). Violet and brown on multicolor underprint. President Kamel Atatürk at right. Back: Fort of Ankara, Mehmet Akif Ersoy, his home and document. Watermark: Kamel Atatürk.		
		a. Watermark: Head small, bust facing right, dotted security thread.	.30	1.25
		b. Watermark: Head large, bust facing 3/4 right.	.25	1.00

			VF	UNC
195	**500 Lira**	*L.1970* (1983). Blue on multicolor underprint. President Kamel Atatürk at right. Two signature varieties. Back: Clock Tower in Izmir at left center. Watermark: Varieties.	.50	1.50

			VF	UNC
196	**1000 Lira**	*L.1970* (1986). Purple and blue on multicolor underprint. President Kamel Atatürk at right. Two signature varieties. One dot for visually impaired at lower left. Back: Istanbul coastline at left, Fathi Sultan Mehmet at center right. Watermark: Kamel Atatürk. UV: fibers fluoresce blue and red; security thread red.	.75	1.75

			VF	UNC
196A	**5000 Lira**	*L.1970* (1981). Dark brown and olive-green on multicolor underprint. Portrait of President K. Atat¸rk at right. Back: Mevlana Museum in Konya and figure of Mevlana at right. Watermark: Portrait of K. Atat¸rk.	12.00	35.00

			VF	UNC
197	**5000 Lira**	*L.1970* (1985). Dark brown, red-brown and blue on multicolor underprint. President Kamel Atatürk at right. Two signature varieties. Back: Seated Mevlana at left center, Mevlana Museum at center. Watermark: Kamel Atatürk.	3.00	10.00

			VF	UNC
198	**5000 Lira**	*L.1970* (1990). Deep brown and deep green on multicolor underprint. President Kamel Atatürk at right. Back: Afsin-Elbistan thermal power plant at left center. Watermark: Kamel Atatürk. UV: fibers fluoresce blue and red.	1.25	4.00

			VF	UNC
199	**10,000 Lira**	*L.1970* (1982). Purple and deep green on multicolor underprint. President Kamel Atatürk at right. Three dots for visally impaired at lower left. Back: Dark green and multicolor. Selimiye Mosque in Edirne, Mimar Sinan (architect) at center. Watermark: Kamel Atatürk. UV: fibers fluoresce blue and red.	1.75	10.00

200 **10,000 Lira** — VF UNC

L.1970 (1989). Purple and deep green on multicolor underprint. President Kamel Atatürk at right. Three dots for visally impaired at lower left. Back: Pale green. Selimiye Mosque in Edirne, Mimar Sinan (architect) at center. Watermark: Kamel Atatürk. UV: fibers fluoresce blue and red. — 1.00 5.00

201 **20,000 Lira** — VF UNC

L.1970 (1988). Red-brown and purple on multicolor underprint. President Kamel Atatürk at right. Back: New Central Bank building in Ankara at left center. Watermark: Kamel Atatürk UV: fibers fluoresce blue and red; serial # yellow. — FV 9.00

202 **20,000 Lira**

L.1970 (1995). President Kamel Atatürk at right. Lighter underprint at center. Red signature. Series G-. Back: Lithographed back in lighter shade. New Central Bank building in Ankara at left center. Watermark: Kamel Atatürk. — FV 2.75

203 **50,000 Lira** — VF UNC

L.1970 (1989). Blue-green and dark green on multicolor underprint. President Kamel Atatürk at right. Back: National Parliament House in Ankara at left center. Watermark: Kamel Atatürk.

a. Issued note. — FV 7.50

b. Issued note. Serial # prefix *H01-H03*. — 200. 650.

204 **50,000 Lira**

L.1970 (1995). Blue-green and dark green on multicolor underprint. President Kamel Atatürk at right. Series K-. Back: National Parliament House in Ankara at left center. Value in gray. Watermark: Kamel Atatürk — FV 2.50

205 **100,000 Lira** — VF UNC

L.1970 (1991). Reddish brown, dark brown and dark green on multicolor underprint. President Kamel Atatürk facing at center right. Equestrian statue of Atatürk at lower left center. Security device at upper right. Signature varieties. Back: Children presenting flowers to Atatürk at left center. Watermark: Kamel Atatürk. — FV 10.00

206 **100,000 Lira**

L.1970 (1997). Multicolor. President Kamel Atatürk facing at center right. Without security device at upper right. Signature varieties. Back: Lithographed; lighter brown color. Children presenting flowers to Atatürk at left center. Watermark: Kamel Atatürk. — FV 4.00

207 **250,000 Lira** — VF UNC

L.1970 (1992). Blue-gray, dark green and violet on multicolor underprint. President Kamel Atatürk facing at center right. Triangular security device at upper right. Signature varieties. Back: Kizilkale Fortress at Alunya at center. Watermark: Kamel Atatürk — FV 10.00

208 **500,000 Lira** — VF UNC

L.1970 (1993). Purple, blue-black and violet on multicolor underprint. President Kamel Atatürk facing at center right. Square security device at upper right. Signature varieties. Back: Aerial view of Canakkale Martyrs Monument. Watermark: Kamel Atatürk UV: fibers fluoresce blue, red and pink. — FV 15.00

209 **1,000,000 Lira** — VF UNC

L.1970 (1995). Claret red and blue-gray on multicolor underprint. President Kamel Atatürk facing at center right. Signature varieties. Back: Atatürk dam in Sanliurfa. Watermark: Kamel Atatürk. — FV 20.00

210 **5,000,000 Lira** — VF UNC

L.1970 Ocak (January) 1997 (at bottom left). Dark brown and red-brown on multicolor underprint. President Kamel Atatürk facing at center right. Gold oval seal with AH1329 date at right. Signature varieties. Back: Anitkabir complex (mausoleum of Ataturk) in Ankara at left center. Watermark: Kamel Atatürk. — FV 25.00

Law Ocak 14 (Jan. 26), 1970; 1998-2002 ND Issue

211 **250,000 Lira** VF UNC
L.1970 (1998). Blue-gray and violet on multicolor underprint. President Kamel Atatürk facing at center right. Triangular security device at upper right printed in solid ink. Signature varieties. Back: Blue lithograph. Kizilkale Fortress at Alunya at center. Watermark: Kamel Atatürk FV 3.00

212 **500,000 Lira** VF UNC
L.1970 (1998). Purple, blue-black and violet on multicolor underprint. President Kamel Atatürk facing at center right. Without square security device at upper right. Signature varieties. Back: Pale purple. Aerial view of Canakkale Martyrs Monument. Watermark: Kamel Atatürk Lithograph. FV 4.50

213 **1,000,000 Lira** VF UNC
L.1970 (2002). Claret red and blue-gray on multicolor underprint. President Kamel Atatürk facing at center right. Signature varieties. Back: Pale color, Lithograph. Sanliurfa-Adiyaman dam in Sanliurfa. Watermark: Kamel Atatürk FV 8.00

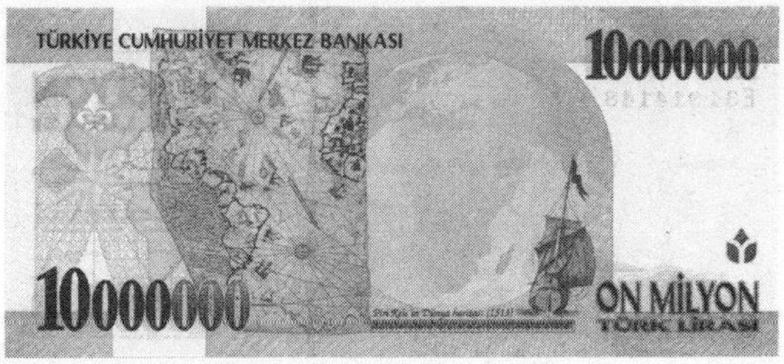

214 **10,000,000 Lira** VF UNC
L.1970 (1999). Red and purple on multicolor underprint. President Kamel Atatürk at left center. Square security device in gold at right. Back: World map of 1513 by Piri Reis. FV 35.00

215 **20,000,000 Lira** VF UNC
L.1970 (2000). Green and red. Kamel Atatürk at center globe and olive branch behind. Back: Efes ancient city. FV 45.00

2005 New Lira Issue

#216-221 Atatürk at ctr. or r. and as wmk.

Monetary reform: 100,000 "old" lira = 1 "new" lira

216 **1 New Lira** VF UNC
2005. Claret red and blue. President Kamel Atatürk at center or right. Back: Atatürk Dam in Sanliurfa-Adiyaman. Watermark: Kamel Atatürk. 156x76mm. FV 3.00

217 **5 New Lira** VF UNC
2005. Greenish brown. President Kamel Atatürk at center or right. Back: Mausolem of Atatürk. Watermark: Kamel Atatürk. 162x76mm. FV 11.00

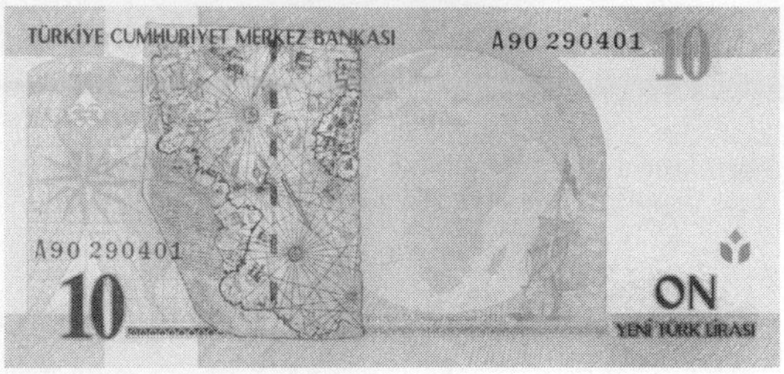

218 **10 New Lira** — VF: FV — UNC: 20.00

2005. Greenish brown. President Kamel Atatürk at center or right. Back: World map of 1513 by Piri Reis. Watermark: Kamel Atatürk. 162x76mm.

219 **20 New Lira** — VF: FV — UNC: 40.00

2005. Green. President Kamel Atatürk at center or right. Back: Ancient city of Ephesus. Watermark: Kamel Atatürk. 162x76mm.

220 **50 New Lira** — VF: FV — UNC: 75.00

2005. Orange. President Kamel Atatürk at center or right. Back: Goreme National Park, Capadoccia. Watermark: Kamel Atatürk. 152x81mm.

221 **100 New Lira** — VF: FV — UNC: 135.

2005. Blue. President Kamel Atatürk at center or right. Back: Ishak Pasha Palace, Dogu Bayazit. Watermark: Kamel Atatürk. 152x81mm.

Law Ocak 14 (Jan. 26), 1970; 2009 ND Issue

222 **5 Lira** — VF: FV — UNC: 4.50

ND (2009). Brown and yellow on multicolor underprint. Kamel Atatürk at right. Back: Aydin Sayili, historical scientist, at left. 130x64mm.

223 **10 Lira** — VF: FV — UNC: 9.00

ND (2009). Rose on multicolor underprint. Kamel Atatürk at right. Back: Cahit Arf, mathematician, at right. 136x64mm.

224 **20 Lira** — VF: FV — UNC: 16.00

ND (2009). Green and brown on multicolor underprint. Kamel Atatürk at right. Back: Kemaleddin, architect, at right. 142x68mm.

225 **50 Lira** | VF | UNC
ND (2009). Light brown and green on multicolor underprint. Kamel Atatürk at right. Back: Fatma Aliye, writer, at right. 148x68mm. | FV | 37.50

226 **100 Lira** | VF | UNC
ND (2009). Light blue and rose on multicolor underprint. Kamel Atatürk at right. Back: Itri, composer, at right. 154x72mm. | FV | 70.00

227 **200 Lira** | VF | UNC
ND (2009). Purple and light blue on multicolor underprint. Kamel Atatürk at right. Back: Yunus Emre, writer, at right. 160x72mm. | FV | 145.

The Turkmenistan Republic covers the territory of the Trans-Caspian Region of Turkestan, the Charjiui Vilayet of Bukhara and the part of Khiva located on the right bank of the Oxus. Bordered on the north by the Autonomous Kara-Kalpak Republic (a constituent of Uzbekistan), by Iran and Afghanistan on the south, by the Uzbek Republic on the east and the Caspian Sea on the west. It has an area of 488,100 sq. km. and a population of 5.18 million. Capital: Ashgabat (formerly Poltoratsk). Main occupation is agricultural products including cotton and maize. It is rich in minerals, oil, coal, sulphur and salt,and is also famous for it's carpets, Turkoman horses and Karakul sheep.

Eastern Turkmenistan for centuries formed part of the Persian province of Khurasan; in medieval times Merv (today known as Mary) was one of the great cities of the Islamic world and an important stop on the Silk Road. Annexed by Russia between 1865 and 1885, Turkmenistan became a Soviet republic in 1924. It achieved independence upon the dissolution of the USSR in 1991. Extensive hydrocarbon/natural gas reserves could prove a boon to this underdeveloped country if extraction and delivery projects were to be expanded. The Turkmenistan Government is actively seeking to develop alternative petroleum transportation routes to break Russia's pipeline monopoly. President for Life Saparmurat Nyyazow died in December 2006, and Turkmenistan held its first multi-candidate presidential electoral process in February 2007. Gurbanguly Berdimuhamedow, a vice premier under Nyyazow, emerged as the country's new president.

Republic

Türkmenistanyñ Merkezi Döwlet Banky

Central Bank of Turkmenistan

1993 ND; 1995-98 Issue

#1-9 Replacement notes: Serial # prefix *ZZ*.

1 **1 Manat** | VF | UNC
ND (1993). Brown and tan on orange and multicolor underprint. Ylymlar Academy at center, native craft at right. Signature Khudaiberdy Orazov. Back: Arms at left, Temple at center. Watermark: Rearing Arabian horse. | .50 | 1.00

2 **5 Manat**
ND (1993). Blue and green on multicolor underprint. Building at center. Signature Khudaiberdy Orazov. Back: Arms at left, building at center. Watermark: Rearing Arabian horse. UV: value 5 in blx fluoresce yellow; right serial # orange. | 1.00 | 2.00

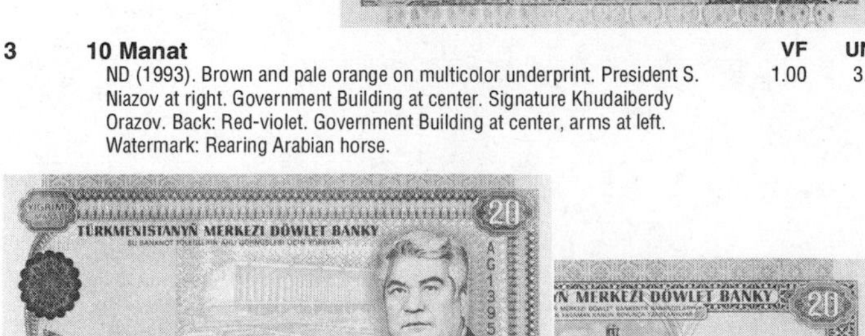

3 **10 Manat** | VF | UNC
ND (1993). Brown and pale orange on multicolor underprint. President S. Niazov at right. Government Building at center. Signature Khudaiberdy Orazov. Back: Red-violet. Government Building at center, arms at left. Watermark: Rearing Arabian horse. | 1.00 | 3.00

4	20 Manat	VF	UNC
	ND (1993); 1995. Blue-gray and blue on multicolor underprint. President S. Niazov at right. National library at center. Signature Khudaiberdy Orazov. Back: Large Building at center, arms at left. Watermark: Rearing Arabian horse.		
	a. ND (1993).	3.00	6.00
	b. 1995.	1.00	3.00

5	50 Manat	VF	UNC
	ND (1993); 1995. Brown and green on multicolor underprint. President S. Niazov at right. Monument at center. Signature Khudaiberdy Orazov. Back: Mosque ruins, arms at left. Watermark: Rearing Arabian horse.		
	a. ND (1993).	5.00	10.00
	b. 1995.	2.00	4.00

6	100 Manat	VF	UNC
	ND (1993); 1995. Dark blue and dark gray on multicolor underprint. President S. Niazov at right. Presidential Palace at center. Signature Khudaiberdy Orazov. Back: Sultan Sanjaryn mausoleum, arms at left. Watermark: Rearing Arabian horse.		
	a. ND (1993).	7.00	15.00
	b. 1995.	2.00	5.00
7	500 Manat		
	ND (1993); 1995. Violet, dark brown and orange on multicolor underprint. President S. Niazov at right. National theatre at center. Signature Khudaiberdy Orazov. Back: Hanymyn mausoleum, arms at left. Watermark: Rearing Arabian horse.		
	a. ND (1993).	10.00	24.00
	b. 1995.	4.00	10.00
8	1000 Manat		
	1995. Green on multicolor underprint. President S. Niazov at right. Building at center. Signature Khudaiberdy Orazov. Back: Arms at center. Watermark: Rearing Arabian horse.	5.00	12.00
9	5000 Manat		
	1996. Violet, purple and red on multicolor underprint. President S. Niazov at right. Building at center. Signature Khudaiberdy Orazov. Back: Arms. Watermark: Rearing Arabian horse.	6.00	14.00
10	10,000 Manat		
	1996. Dark brown on multicolor underprint. President S. Niazov at right. Presidential palace at center. Back: Arms. 156x78mm.	5.00	15.00

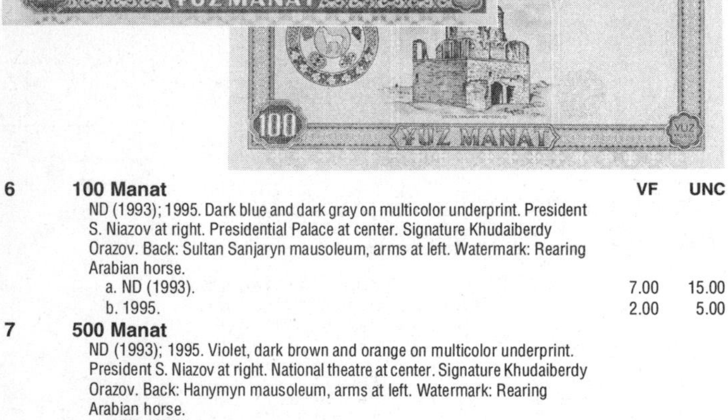

11	10,000 Manat	VF	UNC
	1998. Light blue, light brown, and red on multicolor underprint. President S. Niazov at right. Palace of Turkmenbashy. Back: Light blue, violet, and purple on multicolor underprint. Mosque of Saparmurat at center. 156x78mm.	5.00	15.00

1999-2005 Issues

12	5000 Manat	VF	UNC
	1999; 2000. Violet, purple and red on multicolor underprint. President S. Niazov at right. Building at center. Signature Khudaiberdy Orazov. Back: Arms. Watermark: Rearing Arabian horse. 156x78mm.		
	a. 1999. Signature Khudaiberdy Orazov.	4.00	12.00
	b. 2000. Signature S. Kandymov.	4.00	12.00

13	10,000 Manat	VF	UNC
	1999. Light blue and light brown on multicolor underprint. President Niyazov with medals at right. Palace of Turkmenbashy at center. Signature Khudaiberdy Orazov. Back: Mosque of Saparmurat at center. 156x78mm.	3.00	10.00

14	10,000 Manat	VF	UNC
	2000. Light blue and light brown on multicolor underprint. President Niyazov with medals at right. Palace of Turkmenbashy at center. Stars and crescent at upper left. Signature S. Kandymov. Back: Circular design at upper right. 156x78mm.	FV	15.00

15 **10,000 Manat** | VF | UNC
2003. Light blue and light brown on multicolor underprint. President Niyazov with medals at right. Palace of Turkmenbashy at center. Stars and crescent at upper left. Signature S. Kandymov. Back: Circular design at upper right. Arms at upper left. 156x78mm. | FV | 15.00

16 **10,000 Manat** | VF | UNC
2005. Black and green on multicolor underprint. President Niyazov at center. Back: Monument. 156x78mm. | FV | 15.00

2005 Issue

17 **50 Manat** | VF | UNC
2005. Slate black on multicolor underprint. President Niyazov at center. Back: Horse standing left, racetrack stands in background. 156x78mm. | FV | 1.00

18 **100 Manat** | VF | UNC
2005. Rose on multicolor underprint President Niyazov at center. Back: Building at left. 156x78mm. | FV | 3.00

19 **500 Manat** | VF | UNC
2005. Purple on brown and multicolor underprint. President Niyazov at center. Back: Traditional jewelry designs at left. 156x78mm. | FV | 5.00

20 **1000 Manat** | VF | UNC
2005. Blue on multicolor underprint. President Niyazov at center. Back: Palace of Turkmenbasy at left. 156x78mm. | FV | 7.50

21 **5000 Manat** | VF | UNC
2005. Blue. President Niyazov at center. 156x78mm. | FV | 10.00

2009 Issue

22 **1 Manat** | VF | UNC
2009. Slate black and green on tan and multicolor underprint. Togrul Beg Türkmen Back: Beyik Sparmyrat Türkmenbasynyn 120x60mm.
a. 2009. | FV | 2.00

23 5 Manat VF UNC

2009. Brown and green on multicolor underprint. Soltan Sanjar Türkmen at right. Back: Bitaraplyk Binasy. Printer: TDLR (without imprint). 126x63mm.

a. 2009. FV 7.00

24 10 Manat VF UNC

2009. Rose and carmine on multicolor underprint. Magtymguy Pyragy at right. Back: Turkmenistan National Bank building. Printer: TDLR (without imprint). 132x66mm.

a. 2009. FV 12.00

25 20 Manat VF UNC

2009. Purple on multicolor underprint. Gorogly Beg Türkmen at right. Back: Ruhyyet Palace. Printer: TDLR (without imprint). 138x69mm.

a. 2009. FV 22.50

26 50 Manat VF UNC

2009. Green on multicolor underprint. Gorkut Ata Türkmen at right. Back: National Assembly building. Printer: TDLR (without imprint). FV 45.00

27 100 Manat VF UNC

2009. Violet and blue on multicolor underprint. Oguz Han Türkmen at right. Back: Presidential Palace. Printer: TDLR (without imprint). FV 90.00

28 500 Manat

2009. Blue on multicolor underprint. President Sasparmyrat Nijjazow at right center. Back: Kipchak mosque. Printer: TDLR (without imprint). Not issued. — 70.00

2012 Issue

No.	Denomination	VF	UNC
29	**1 Manat** 2012.	FV	2.00
30	**5 Manat** 2012.	FV	7.00
31	**10 Manat** 2012.	FV	12.00
32	**20 Manat** 2012.	FV	22.00

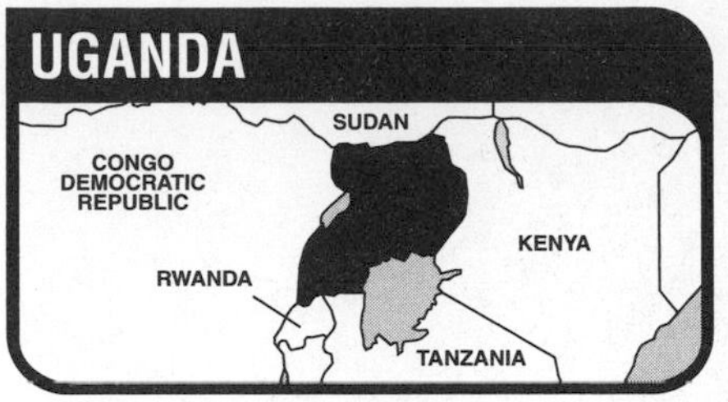

The Republic of Uganda, a former British protectorate located astride the equator in east-central Africa, has an area of 236,040 sq. km. and a population of 31.37 million. Capital: Kampala. Agriculture, including livestock, is the basis of the economy; there is some mining of copper, tin, gold and lead. Coffee, cotton, copper and tea are exported.

The colonial boundaries created by Britain to delimit Uganda grouped together a wide range of ethnic groups with different political systems and cultures. These differences prevented the establishment of a working political community after independence was achieved in 1962. The dictatorial regime of Idi Amin (1971-79) was responsible for the deaths of some 300,000 opponents; guerrilla war and human rights abuses under Milton Obote (1980-85) claimed at least another 100,000 lives. The rule of Yoweri Museveni since 1986 has brought relative stability and economic growth to Uganda. During the 1990s, the government promulgated non-party presidential and legislative elections.

Notes of East African Currency Board circulated before Bank of Uganda notes were available.

Also see East Africa.

MONETARY SYSTEM:

1 Shilling = 100 Cents

Caution: Several years ago the Bank of Uganda sold quantities of demonetized notes, most of which were made available for only $1.00 per note. Condition of notes thus sold is not reported. A listing of some pieces NOT available from the bank includes #4, 6a, 7a, 8a and b, 9a and b, 13a, 14a, 21, 23, and 24a and b.

REPUBLIC

BANK OF UGANDA

1966 ND ISSUE

#1-5 Replacement notes: Serial # prefix *Z/1* (5/ and 10/); *Y/1; X/1; W/1* respectively.

		VF	UNC
1	**5 Shillings** ND (1966). Dark blue on multicolor underprint. Arms at right. Signature titles: *GOVERNOR* and *SECRETARY*. Back: River and waterfall. Watermark: Hand.		
	a. Issued note.	1.50	5.00
	s. Specimen.	—	25.00
	ct. Color trial.	—	75.00
2	**10 Shillings** ND (1966). Brown on multicolor underprint. Arms at center. Signature titles: *GOVERNOR* and *SECRETARY*. Back: Workers picking cotton. Watermark: Hand.		
	a. Issued note.	2.50	5.00
	s. Specimen.	—	25.00
	ct. Color trial.	—	125.

		VF	UNC
3	**20 Shillings** ND (1966). Purple on multicolor underprint. Arms at upper left. Signature titles: *GOVERNOR* and *SECRETARY*. Back: Marabou stork, Green Monkey, Lion, Elephants, Zebra and Impala. Watermark: Hand.		
	a. Issued note.	2.00	6.00
	s. Specimen.	—	25.00
	ct. Color trial.	—	250.

		VF	UNC
4	**100 Shillings** ND (1966). Green on multicolor underprint. Crowned crane at left, without *FOR BANK OF UGANDA* just below value at center. Signature titles: *GOVERNOR* and *SECRETARY*. Back: Building at right. Watermark: Hand.		
	a. Issued note.	75.00	750.
	s. Specimen.	—	125.
	ct. Color trial.	—	500.

		VF	UNC
5	**100 Shillings** ND (1966). Green on multicolor underprint. Crowned crane at left, wih text: *FOR BANK OF UGANDA* just below value at center. Signature titles: *GOVERNOR* and *SECRETARY*. Back: Building at right. Watermark: Hand.		
	a. Issued note.	1.50	6.00
	s. Specimen.	—	25.00

1973-77 ND ISSUE

#5A-9 Replacement notes: Serial # prefix *Z/1* (5/ and 10/); *Y/1; X/1; W/1* respectively.

		VF	UNC
5A	**5 Shillings** ND (1977). Blue on multicolor underprint. President Idi Amin at left, arms at lower right. Back: Woman picking coffee beans. Watermark: Crested crane.	.50	2.50

		VF	UNC
6	**10 Shillings**		
	ND (1973). Brown on multicolor underprint. President Idi Amin at left, arms at lower right. Back: Elephants, antelope and hippopotamus. Watermark: Crested crane.		
	a. Signature titles: *GOVERNOR* and *DIRECTOR*.	40.00	285.
	b. Signature titles: *GOVERNOR* and *SECRETARY*. Signature 1.	2.50	12.50
	c. Signature titles as b. Signature 2.	1.00	6.00
	s. As a. Specimen.	—	80.00

		VF	UNC
7	**20 Shillings**		
	ND (1973). Purple and brown on multicolor underprint. President Idi Amin at left, arms at lower right. Back: Large building. Watermark: Crested crane.		
	a. Signature titles: *GOVERNOR* and *DIRECTOR*.	50.00	300.
	b. Signature titles: *GOVERNOR* and *SECRETARY*. Signature 1.	10.00	75.00
	c. Signature titles as b. Signature 2.	2.00	7.50
	s. As a. Specimen.	—	90.00

		VF	UNC
8	**50 Shillings**		
	ND (1973). Blue (shade) on multicolor underprint. President Idi Amin at left, arms at lower right. Back: Hydroelectric dam. Watermark: Crested crane.		
	a. Signature titles: *GOVERNOR* and *DIRECTOR*.	40.00	275.
	b. Signature titles: *GOVERNOR* and *SECRETARY*. Signature 1.	8.00	85.00
	c. Signature titles as b. Signature 2.	2.00	7.00
	s. As a. Specimen.	—	135.

		VF	UNC
9	**100 Shillings**		
	ND (1973). Green (shades) on multicolor underprint. President Idi Amin at left, arms at lower right. Back: Scene of lake and hills. Watermark: Crested crane.		
	a. Signature titles: *GOVERNOR* and *DIRECTOR*.	30.00	150.
	b. Signature titles: *GOVERNOR* and *SECRETARY*. Signature 1.	12.50	85.00
	c. Signature titles as b. Signature 2.	2.00	8.50
	s. As a. Specimen.	—	110.

1979 Issue

#10-14 Replacement notes: Serial # prefix *Z/1* (5/ and 10/); *Y/1*; *X/1*; *W/1* respectively.

		VF	UNC
10	**5 Shillings**		
	ND (1979). Blue on multicolor underprint. Bank of Uganda at left. Signature titles: *GOVERNOR* and *DIRECTOR*. Back: Woman picking coffee beans. Watermark: Crested crane's head.	.20	1.00

		VF	UNC
11	**10 Shillings**		
	ND (1979). Brown on multicolor underprint. Bank of Uganda at left. Signature titles: *GOVERNOR* and *DIRECTOR*. Back: Elephants, antelope and hippopotamus. Watermark: Crested crane's head.		
	a. Light printing on bank.	1.50	5.00
	b. Dark printing on bank.	.50	2.00

		VF	UNC
12	**20 Shillings**		
	ND (1979). Purple and brown on multicolor underprint. Bank of Uganda at left. Signature titles: *GOVERNOR* and *DIRECTOR*. Back: Large building. Watermark: Crested crane's head.		
	a. Light printing on bank.	2.00	7.50
	b. Dark printing on bank.	.50	2.50

		VF	UNC
13	**50 Shillings**		
	ND (1979). Dark blue and purple on multicolor underprint. Bank of Uganda at left. Signature titles: *GOVERNOR* and *DIRECTOR*. Back: Hydroelectric dam. Watermark: Crested crane's head.		
	a. Light printing on bank.	17.50	100.
	b. Dark printing on bank.	1.00	4.50

		VF	UNC
14	**100 Shillings**		
	ND (1979). Green (shades) on multicolor underprint. Bank of Uganda at left. Signature titles: *GOVERNOR* and *DIRECTOR*. Back: Scene of lake and hills. Watermark: Crested crane's head.		
	a. Light printing on bank.	3.00	12.00
	b. Dark printing on bank.	2.50	8.50

1982 Issue

#15-19 Replacement notes: Serial # prefix *Z/1* (5/ and 10/); *Y/1*; *X/1*; *W/1* respectively.

		VF	UNC
15	**5 Shillings**		
	ND (1982). Olive green on multicolor underprint. Arms at left. Signature titles: *GOVERNOR* and *SECRETARY*. Back: Woman picking coffee beans. Watermark: Crested crane's head.	.25	1.50

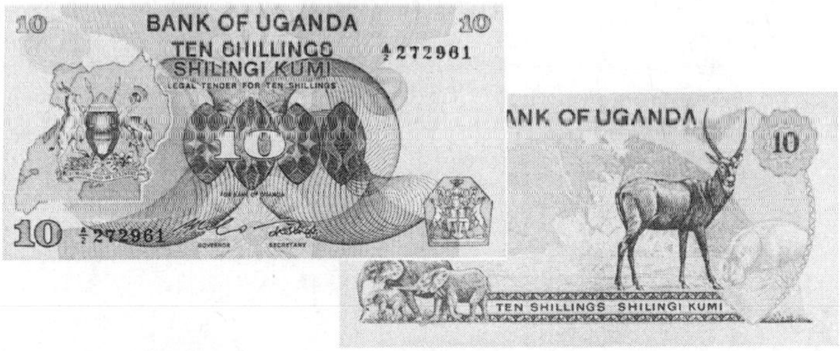

		VF	UNC
16	**10 Shillings**		
	ND (1982). Purple on multicolor underprint. Arms at left. Signature titles: *GOVERNOR* and *SECRETARY*. Back: Elephants, antelope and hippopotamus. Watermark: Crested crane's head.	.50	3.00

		VF	UNC
17	**20 Shillings**		
	ND (1982). Green, dark red and multicolor. Arms at left. Signature titles: *GOVERNOR* and *SECRETARY*. Back: Large building. Watermark: Crested crane's head.	2.00	7.00

		VF	UNC
18	**50 Shillings**		
	ND (1982). Brown, orange and multicolor. Arms at left. Signature titles: *GOVERNOR* and *SECRETARY*. Back: Hydroelectric dam. Watermark: Crested crane's head.		
	a. Signature titles: *GOVERNOR* and *SECRETARY*.	.75	4.00
	b. Signature titles: *GOVERNOR* and *DEPUTY GOVERNOR*.	1.00	10.00

		VF	UNC
19	**100 Shillings**		
	ND (1982). Red-violet, orange and multicolor. Arms at left. Signature titles: *GOVERNOR* and *SECRETARY*. Back: Scene of lake and hills. Watermark: Crested crane's head.		
	a. Signature titles: *GOVERNOR* and *SECRETARY*.	1.00	4.50
	b. Signature titles: *GOVERNOR* and *DEPUTY GOVERNOR*. Small or large prefix letter and # before serial #.	1.50	7.50

1983-85 Issue

#20-23 Replacement notes: Serial # prefix *X/1*, *W/1*, *U/1*, *T/1*, *S/1* respectively.

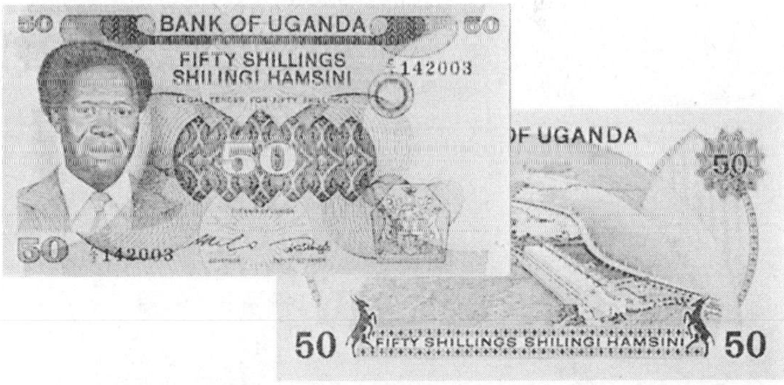

		VF	UNC
20	**50 Shillings**		
	ND (1985). Brown and orange on multicolor underprint. President Milton Obote at left. Signature titles: *GOVERNOR* and *DEPUTY GOVERNOR*. Back: Hydroelectric dam. Watermark: Hand.	1.00	4.50

21	**100 Shillings**	VF	UNC
	ND (1985). Red-violet and orange on multicolor underprint. President Milton Obote at left. Signature titles: *GOVERNOR* and *DEPUTY GOVERNOR.* Back: Scene of lake and hills. Watermark: Hand.	4.00	22.50

22	**500 Shillings**	VF	UNC
	ND (1983). Blue, purple and multicolor. President Milton Obote at left. Signature titles: *GOVERNOR* and *DEPUTY GOVERNOR.* Serial number prefix varieties as #19b. Back: Cattle and harvesting. Watermark: Hand.		
	a. Issued note.	1.00	5.00
	s. Specimen.	—	10.00

23	**1000 Shillings**	VF	UNC
	ND (1983). Red and multicolor. President Milton Obote at left. Signature titles: *GOVERNOR* and *DEPUTY GOVERNOR.* Serial number prefix varieties as #19b. Back: Building. Watermark: Hand.		
	a. Issued note.	4.00	22.50
	s. Specimen.	—	12.50

24	**5000 Shillings**	VF	UNC
	1985-86. Purple and multicolor. Arms at left. Back: Building with clock tower at center right.		
	a. Watermark: Hand. 1985.	6.00	30.00
	b. Watermark: Crested crane. 1986.	1.50	5.00

1985-86 Issue

#25 and 26 Replacement notes: Serial # prefix *U/1; T/1* respectively.

25	**500 Shillings**	VF	UNC
	1986. Blue, purple and multicolor. Arms at left. Back: Cattle and harvesting. Watermark: Crested crane's head.	.75	3.00

26	**1000 Shillings**	VF	UNC
	1986. Red and multicolor. Arms at left. Back: Building. Watermark: Crested crane's head.	1.00	4.50

1987 Issue

#27-34 Replacement notes: Serial # prefix *ZZ.*

27	**5 Shillings**	VF	UNC
	1987. Brown on multicolor underprint. Arms at right and upper left. Map at center. Back: Crowned crane, hippo, elephant and waterbuck. Printer: TDLR. UV: value 5 in box fluoresces orange. Back design elements green.	.30	2.00

28	**10 Shillings**	VF	UNC
	1987. Green on multicolor underprint. Arms at right and upper left. Map at center. Back: Two antelope grazing, two men fishing in canoe at center. Printer: TDLR. UV: value 10 fluoresces orange. back design elements green.	.30	2.50

			VF	UNC
29	**20 Shillings**	1987-88. Purple, blue-black and violet on multicolor underprint. Arms at upper left, map at center. Back: Modern buildings at center right. Watermark: Crested crane's head. Printer: TDLR.		
		a. Imprint on back. 1987.	.50	2.50
		b. Without imprint. 1988.	.25	1.50

			VF	UNC
30	**50 Shillings**	1987-98. Red, orange and dark brown on multicolor underprint. Arms at upper left, map at center. Back: Parliament building at center right. Watermark: Crested crane's head. Printer: TDLR. UV: value 50 fluoresce yellow. Back design elements yellow.		
		a. Imprint on back. 1987.	.50	2.50
		b. Without imprint. 1988; 1989.	.50	2.00
		c. 1994; 1996; 1997; 1998.	.25	1.00

			VF	UNC
31	**100 Shillings**	1987-98. Deep blue-violet, black and aqua on multicolor underprint. Arms at upper left, map at center. Back: High Court building with clock tower at center right. Watermark: Crested crane's head. Printer: TDLR.		
		a. Signature titles: *GOVERNOR* and *SECRETARY, TREASURY.* Imprint on back. 1987.	1.00	4.50
		b. As a. but without imprint on back. 1988.	.75	2.00
		c. As b. but with signature titles: *GOVERNOR* and *SECRETARY.* 1994; 1996; 1997; 1998.	.25	1.50

			VF	UNC
32	**200 Shillings**	1987-98. Brown, orange and olive-brown on multicolor underprint. Arms at upper left, map at center. Back: Worker in textile factory at center right. Watermark: Crested crane's head. Printer: TDLR.		
		a. 1987.	.50	4.00
		b. 1991; 1994; 1996; 1998.	.50	2.50

1991 Issue

			VF	UNC
33	**500 Shillings**	1991. Dark brown and deep purple on multicolor underprint. Elephant at left, arms at upper center and lower right. Back: Uganda Independence Monument at left, municipal building with clock tower at center. Watermark: Crested crane's head.		
		a. Signature titles: *GOVERNOR* and *SECRETARY, TREASURY.*	1.00	4.00
		b. Signature titles: *GOVERNOR* and *SECRETARY.*	1.00	4.50
		s. As a. Specimen.	—	25.00

			VF	UNC
34	**1000 Shillings**	1991. Black, deep brown-violet and dark green on multicolor underprint. Farmers at left, arms at upper center and lower right. Back: Grain storage facility at center. Watermark: Crested crane's head.		
		a. Signature titles: *GOVERNOR* and *SECRETARY, TREASURY.*	2.50	5.00
		b. Signature titles: *GOVERNOR* and *SECRETARY.*	1.25	4.00

1993-95 Issue

#35-38 Replacement notes: Serial # prefix *ZZ*.

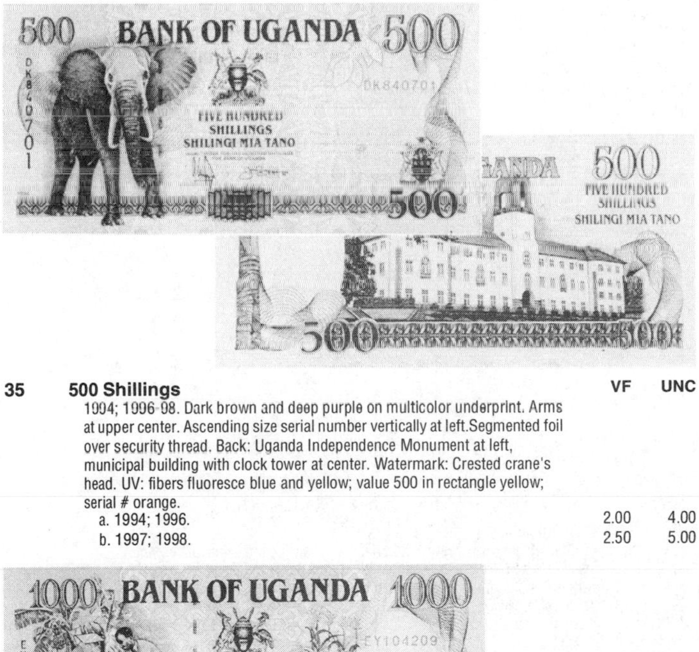

			VF	UNC
35	**500 Shillings**	1994; 1996-98. Dark brown and deep purple on multicolor underprint. Arms at upper center. Ascending size serial number vertically at left. Segmented foil over security thread. Back: Uganda Independence Monument at left, municipal building with clock tower at center. Watermark: Crested crane's head. UV: fibers fluoresce blue and yellow; value 500 in rectangle yellow; serial # orange.		
		a. 1994; 1996.	2.00	4.00
		b. 1997; 1998.	2.50	5.00

			VF	UNC
36	**1000 Shillings**	1994; 1996; 1998; 1999. Black, deep brown-violet and dark green on multicolor underprint. Arms at upper center. Ascending size serial number vertically at left. Back: Grain storage facility at center. Watermark: Crested crane's head. Segmented foil over security thread. 152x74mm.	1.25	3.50

37	5000 Shillings	VF	UNC
	1993; 1998. Red-violet, deep purple and dark green on multicolor underprint. Arms at upper center. Lake Bunyonyi, terraces at left. Ascending size serial number vertically at left. Back: Railroad cars being loaded onto Kaawa Ferry at center, plant at lower right. Watermark: Crested crane's head. 152x74mm.		
	a. 1993.	5.00	12.50
	b. 1998.	FV	12.00

38	10,000 Shillings	VF	UNC
	1995; 1998. Green and red on multicolor underprint. Arms at upper center. Musical instruments at left. Ascending size serial number vertically at left. Back: Owen Falls dam, kudu. Watermark: Crested crane's head. 152x74mm.		
	a. 1995.	10.00	25.00
	b. 1998.	FV	22.50

1999-2002 Issue

39	1000 Shillings	VF	UNC
	2000; 2003. Black, deep brown-violet and dark green on multicolor underprint. Arms at upper center in brown and green. Numerals of value at lower right all in dark brown. Ascending size serial number vertically at left. Back: Grain storage facility at center. Watermark: Crested crane's head. 152x74mm.		
	a. 2000.	FV	3.00
	b. 2003.	FV	3.00

39A	1000 Shillings	VF	UNC
	2001. Black, deep brown-violet and dark green on multicolor underprint. Arms at upper center in brown and green. Numerals of value at lower right all in dark brown. Ascending size serial number vertically at left. Different security devices. Back: Grain storage facility at center. Different security devices. Watermark: Crested crane's head.	FV	3.00

40	5000 Shillings	VF	UNC
	2000; 2002. Red-violet, deep purple and dark green on multicolor underprint. Arms at upper center. Lake Bunyonyi, terraces at left. Ascending size serial number vertically at left. Silver leaf overlay at upper left center and security V symbol at lower right. Back: Railroad cars being loaded onto Kaawa Ferry at center, plant at lower right. Watermark: Crested crane's head. 152x74mm.	FV	10.00

40A	5000 Shillings	VF	UNC
	2002. Red-violet, deep purple and dark green on multicolor underprint. Like #40 but different devices added. Back: Railroad cars being loaded onto Kaawa Ferry at center, plant at lower right. Watermark: Crested crane's head. 152x74mm.	FV	10.00

41	10,000 Shillings	VF	UNC
	2001; 2003; 2004. Red, green, brown and multicolor. Arms at upper center. Musical instruments at left. Ascending size serial number vertically at left. Changes in security devices. Back: Owen Falls dam, kudu. Changes in security devices. Watermark: Crested crane's head. 157x76mm.		
	a. 2001.	FV	17.50
	b. 2003.	FV	17.50
	c. 2004.	FV	17.50

42	20,000 Shillings	VF	UNC
	1999; 2002. Green on multicolor underprint. Crested crane at left, arms at upper center. Silver vertical OVD strip with repeated value at right. Two signature varieties. Back: Modern building. Watermark: Arms. 160x78mm.	FV	30.00

2003-04 Issue

43	1000 Shillings	VF	UNC
	2005; 2008; 2009. Black, deep brown-violet and dark green on multicolor underprint. Farmer at left. Silver OVD strip at right. Back: Grain storage facility at center. 152x74mm.		
	a. 2005.	FV	3.00
	a. 2008.	FV	3.00
	c. 2009.	FV	3.00

44	5000 Shillings	VF	UNC
	2004; 2005; 2008; 2009. Red-violet, deep purple and dark green on multicolor underprint. Lake Bunyonyi , terraces at left. Arms at upper center. Back: Railroad cars being loaded onto Kaawa Ferry at center. 152x74mm.		
	a. 2004.	FV	7.50
	b. 2005.	FV	7.50
	c. 2008.	FV	7.50
	d. 2009.	FV	7.50

45	10,000 Shillings	VF	UNC
	2005; 2008; 2009. Red, green, brown and multicolor. Musical instruments at left. Back: Owen Falls Dam at center, kudu at right. 157x76mm.		
	a. 2005.	FV	12.50
	b. 2008.	FV	12.50
	c. 2009.	FV	12.50

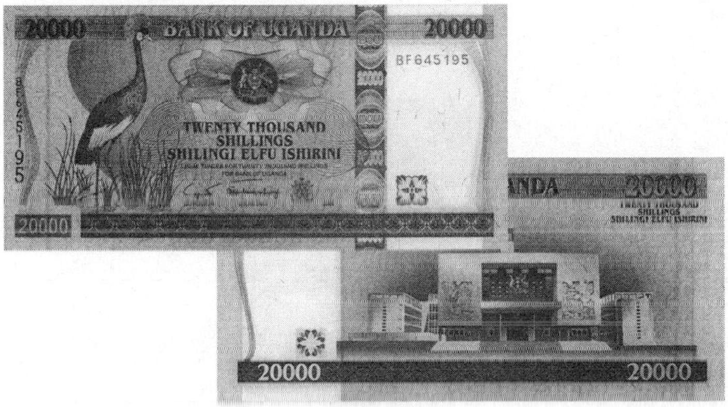

46	20,000 Shillings	VF	UNC
	2004; 2005; 2008; 2009. Multicolor. Crested crane at left, arms at upper center. Silver vertical OVD strip with repeated value at right. Two signature varieties. Different security devices. Back: Modern building. Different security devices. Watermark: Arms. 160x78mm.		
	a. 2004.	FV	20.00
	b. 2005.	FV	20.00
	c. 2008.	FV	20.00
	d. 2009.	FV	20.00

47	50,000 Shillings	VF	UNC
	2003; 2007; 2008. Brown. Monument at left. Back: Cotton harvest. 164x80mm.		
	a. 2003.	FV	45.00
	b. 2007.	FV	45.00
	c. 2008.	FV	45.00

2007 Commemorative Issue

		VF	UNC
48	**10,000 Shillings** 23-25.11.2007. Orange, brown, green and multicolor CHOGM logo at left center. Back: Own Falls dam and gorillas. For the Commonwealth Heads of Goverment Meeting. 157x76mm.	FV	15.00

2010 Issue

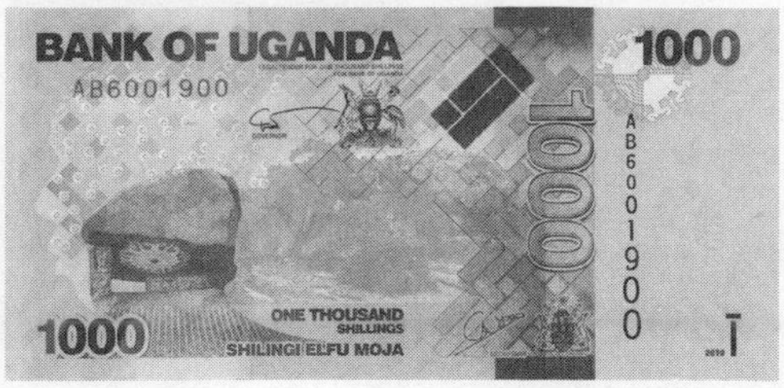

		VF	UNC
49	**1000 Shillings** 2010 Brown and orange on multicolor underprint.	FV	3.00

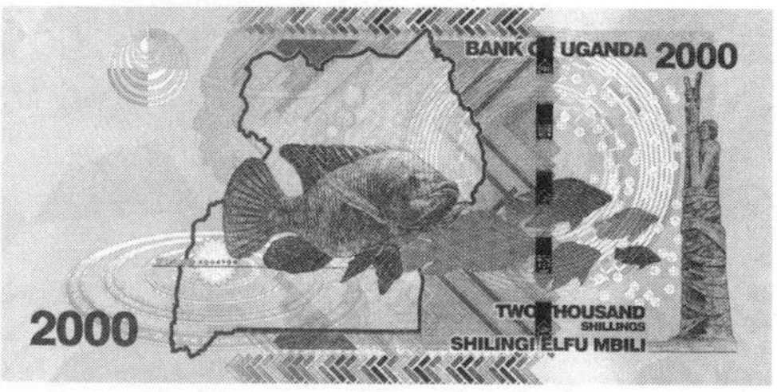

		VF	UNC
50	**2000 Shillings** 2010 Blue on multicolor underprint.	FV	5.00

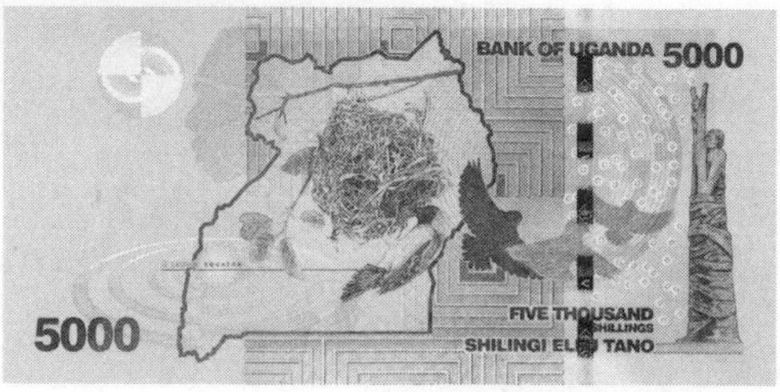

		VF	UNC
51	**5000 Shillings** 2010 Green on multicolor underprint.	FV	7.50

		VF	UNC
52	**10,000 Shillings** 2010; 2011. Purple on multicolor underprint.		
	a. 2010.	FV	12.50
	b. 2011.	FV	12.50

		VF	UNC
53	**20,000 Shillings** 2010 Rose on multicolor underprint.	FV	20.00

		VF	UNC
54	**50,000 Shillings** 2010 Yellow and ochre on multicolor underprint.	FV	45.00

Ukraine is bordered by Russia to the east, Russia and Belarus to the north, Poland, Slovakia and Hungary to the west, Romania and Moldova to the southwest and in the south by the Black Sea and the Sea of Azov. It has an area of 603,700 sq. km. and a population of 45.99 million. Capital: Kyiv (Kiev). Coal, grain, vegetables and heavy industrial machinery are major exports.

The territory of Ukraine has been inhabited for over 30,000 years. As the result of its location, Ukraine has served as the gateway to Europe for millennia and its early history has been recorded by Arabic, Greek, Roman, as well as Ukrainian historians.

Ukraine was the center of the first eastern Slavic state, Kyivan Rus, which during the 10th and 11th centuries was the largest and most powerful state in Europe. Weakened by internecine quarrels and Mongol invasions, Kyivan Rus was incorporated into the Grand Duchy of Lithuania and eventually into the Polish-Lithuanian Commonwealth. The cultural and religious legacy of Kyivan Rus laid the foundation for Ukrainian nationalism through subsequent centuries. A new Ukrainian state, the Cossack Hetmanate, was established during the mid-17th century after an uprising against the Poles. Despite continuous Muscovite pressure, the Hetmanate managed to remain autonomous for well over 100 years. During the latter part of the 18th century, most Ukrainian ethnographic territory was absorbed by the Russian Empire. Following the collapse of czarist Russia in 1917, Ukraine was able to bring about a short-lived period of independence (1917-20), but was reconquered and forced to endure a brutal Soviet rule that engineered two artificial famines (1921-22 and 1932-33) in which over 8 million died. In World War II, German and Soviet armies were responsible for some 7 to 8 million more deaths. Although final independence for Ukraine was achieved in 1991 with the dissolution of the USSR, democracy remained elusive as the legacy of state control and endemic corruption stalled efforts at economic reform, privatization, and civil liberties. A peaceful mass protest "Orange Revolution" in the closing months of 2004 forced the authorities to overturn a rigged presidential election and to allow a new internationally monitored vote that swept into power a reformist slate under Viktor Yushchenko. Subsequent internal squabbles in the Yushchenko camp allowed his rival Viktor Yanukovych to stage a comeback in parliamentary elections and become prime minister in August of 2006. An early legislative election, brought on by a political crisis in the spring of 2007, saw Yuliya Tymoshenko, as head of an "Orange" coalition, installed as a new prime minister in December 2007.

MONETARY SYSTEM:

1 Karbovanets (Karbovantsiv) = 2 Hryven
1917-1920 = 200 Shahiv
1 Karvovanets (Karbovantsiv) = 1 Russian Ruble, 1991-96
1 Hryvnia (Hryvni, Hryven) = 100,000 Karbovantsiv, 1996-

УКРАЇНСЬКА Р.С.Р.

TREASURY

1990-92 КУПОН RUBLE CONTROL COUPON ISSUE

#68-72 are Consumer cards (coupons) were not legal tender on their own but were required to be used in conjunction with U.S.S.R. rubles and only then could they perform the function of money within the Ukraine. Tense cards were issued once a month, with the month preprinted. Various authorization handstamps are used in central registry square. Uniface.

68 20 Karbovantsiv

1990-92. Sheet of 28 coupons and registry.

	VF	UNC
a. 1990. November. Листопад.	—	4.00
b. 1990. December. Грудень.	—	4.00
c. 1991. January. Січень.	—	4.00
d. 1991. February. Лютий.		4.00
e. 1991. March. Березень.	—	4.00
f. 1991. April. Квітень.	—	4.00
g. 1991. May. Травень.	—	4.00
h. 1991. June. Червень.	—	4.00
i. 1991. July. Липень.	—	4.00
j. 1991. August. Серпень.	—	4.00
k. 1991. September. Вересень.	—	4.00
l. 1991. October. Жовтень.	—	4.00
m. 1991. November. Листопад.	—	4.00
n. 1991. December. Грудень.	—	4.00
o. 1992. January. Січень.	—	4.00

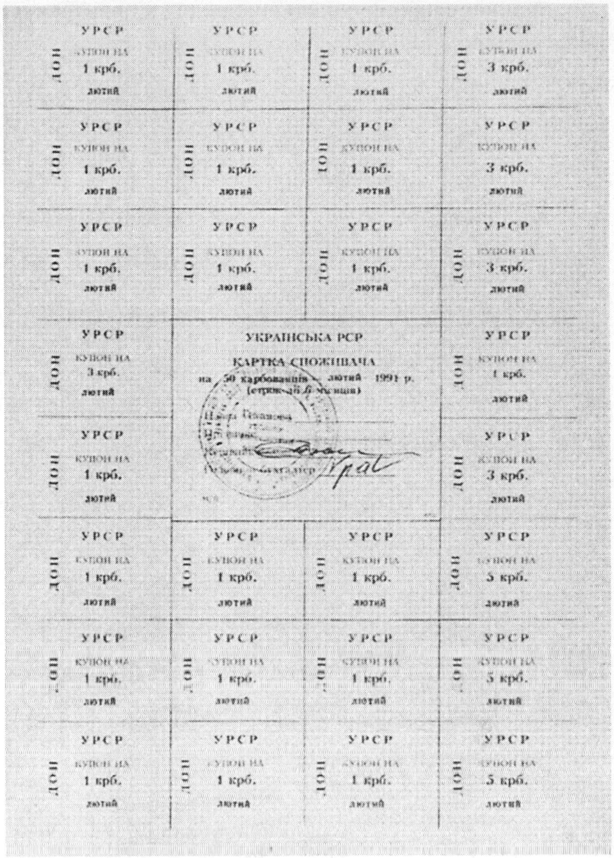

69 50 Karbovantsiv

1990-92. Sheet of 28 coupons and registery.

	VF	UNC
a. 1990. November. Листопад.	—	4.00
b. 1990. December. Грудень.	—	4.00
c. 1991. January. Січень.	—	4.00
d. 1991. February. Лютий.	—	4.00
e. 1991. March. Березень.	—	4.00
f. 1991. April. Квітень.	—	4.00
g. 1991. May. Травень.	—	4.00
h. 1991. June. Червень.	—	4.00
i. 1991. July. Липень.	—	4.00
j. 1991. August. Серпень.	—	4.00
k. 1991. September. Вересень.	—	4.00
l. 1991. October. Жовтень.	—	4.00
m. 1991. November. Листопад.	—	4.00
n. 1991. December. Грудень.	—	4.00
o. 1992. January. Січень.		4.00

70 75 Karbovantsiv

1990-92. Sheet of 28 coupons and registery.

	VF	UNC
a. 1990. November. Листопад.	—	4.00
b. 1990. December. Грудень.	—	4.00
c. 1991. January. Січень.	—	4.00
d. 1991. February. Лютий.	—	4.00
e. 1991. March. Березень.	—	4.00
f. 1991. April. Квітень.	—	4.00
g. 1991. May. Травень.	—	4.00
h. 1991. June. Червень.	—	4.00
i. 1991. July. Липень.	—	4.00
j. 1991. August. Серпень.	—	4.00
k. 1991. Sptember. Вересень.	—	4.00
l. 1991. October. Жовтень.	—	4.00
m. 1991. November. Листопад.	—	4.00
n. 1991. December. Грудень.	—	4.00
o. 1991. January. Січень.	—	4.00

71 100 Karbovantsiv

1990-92. Sheet of 28 coupons plus registery.

	VF	UNC
a. 1990. November. Листопад.	—	4.00
b. 1990. December. Грудень.	—	4.00
c. 1991. January. Січень.	—	4.00
d. 1991. February. Лютий.	—	4.00
e. 1991. March. Березень.	—	4.00
f. 1991. April. Квітень.	—	4.00
g. 1991. May. Травень.	—	4.00
h. 1991. June. Червень.	—	4.00
i. 1991. July. Липень.	—	4.00
j. 1991. August. Серпень.	—	4.00
k. 1991. September. Вересень.	—	4.00
l. 1991. October. Жовтень.	—	4.00
m. 1991. November. Листопад.	—	4.00
n. 1991. December. Грудень.	—	4.00
o. 1992. January. Січень.	—	4.00

72	200 Karbovantsiv	VF	UNC
	1990-92. Sheet of 28 coupons and registry.		
	a. 1990. November. Листопад.	—	4.00
	b. 1990. December. Грудень.	—	4.00
	c. 1991. January. Січень.	—	4.00
	d. 1991. February. Лютий.	—	4.00
	e. 1991. March. Березень.	—	4.00
	f. 1991. April. Квітень.	—	4.00
	g. 1991. May. Травень.	—	4.00
	h. 1991. June. Червень.	—	4.00
	i. 1991. July. Липень.	—	4.00
	j. 1991. August. Серпень.	—	4.00
	k. 1991. September. Вересень.	—	4.00
	l. 1991. October. Жовтень.	—	4.00
	m. 1991. November. Листопад.	—	4.00
	n. 1991. December. Грудень.	—	4.00
	o. 1992. January. Січень.	—	4.00

НАЦІОНАЛЬНИЙ БАНК УКРАЇНИ

UKRAINIAN NATIONAL BANK

1991 КУПОН CONTROL COUPON ISSUE

Karbovanets System

Originally issued at par and temporarily to be used jointly with Russian rubles in commodity purchases as a means of currency control (similar to Ruble Control Coupons above). They soon became more popular while the ruble slowly depreciated in exchange value. This did not last very long and the karbovanets has since suffered a higher inflation rate than the Russian ruble.

81	1 Karbovanets	VF	UNC
	1991. Dull brown and pale orange on yellow underprint. Lybid, Viking sister of the founding brothers at left. All notes without serial number. Back: Cathedral of St. Sophia in Kiev at left center. Watermark: Paper. Printer: ISPB (France). 1 KRB printed sideways with fluorescent ink at left.		
	a. Issued note.	.50	1.00
	s1. Specimen. Perforated *SPECIMEN.*	—	200.
	s2. Specimen. Overprint *SPECIMEN.*	—	200.

82	3 Karbovantsi	VF	UNC
	1991. Greenish gray and pale orange on yellow underprint. Lybid, Viking sister of the founding brothers at left. All notes without serial number. Back: Cathedral of St. Sophia in Kiev at left center. Watermark: Paper. Printer: ISPB (France). 3 KRB printed sideways with fluorescent ink at left.		
	a. Issued note.	1.00	2.00
	b. Issued note with imprint *3 Kpe* at left.	1.00	2.00
	s1. Specimen. Perforated *SPECIMEN.*	—	200.
	s2. Specimen. Overprint *SPECIMEN.*	—	200.

83	5 Karbovantsiv	VF	UNC
	1991. Dull blue-violet and pale orange on yellow underprint. Lybid, Viking sister of the founding brothers at left. All notes without serial number. Back: Cathedral of St. Sophia in Kiev at left center. Watermark: Paper. Printer: ISPB (France). 5 KRB printed sideways with fluorescent ink at left.		
	a. Issued note.	1.00	2.00
	s1. Specimen. Perforated *SPECIMEN.*	—	200.
	s2. Specimen. Overprint *SPECIMEN.*	—	200.
	x. Error. No printing on face.	—	10.00

84	10 Karbovantsiv	VF	UNC
	1991. Pink and pale orange on yellow underprint. Lybid, Viking sister of the founding brothers at left. All notes without serial number. Back: Cathedral of St. Sophia in Kiev at left center. Watermark: Paper. Printer: ISPB (France). 10 KRB printed sideways with fluorescent ink at left.		
	a. Issued note.	1.00	2.00
	s1. Specimen. Perforated *SPECIMEN.*	—	200.
	s2. Specimen. Overprint *SPECIMEN.*	—	200.

85	25 Karbovantsiv	VF	UNC
	1991. Purple and pale orange on yellow underprint. Lybid, Viking sister of the founding brothers at left. All notes without serial number. Back: Cathedral of St. Sophia in Kiev at left center. Watermark: Paper. Printer: ISPB (France). 25 KRB printed sideways with fluorescent ink at left.		
	a. Issued note.	2.00	5.00
	s1. Specimen. Perforated *SPECIMEN.*	—	200.
	s2. Specimen. Overprint *SPECIMEN.*	—	200.

86	50 Karbovantsiv	VF	UNC
	1991. Blue-green and pale orange on yellow underprint. Lybid, Viking sister of the founding brothers at left. All notes without serial number. Back: Cathedral of St. Sophia in Kiev at left center. Watermark: Paper. Printer: ISPB (France). 50 KRB printed sideways with fluorescent ink at left.		
	a. Issued note.	1.00	3.00
	b. Issued note with *50 Kps* at left.	.70	1.00
	s1. As a. Specimen. Perforated *SPECIMEN.*	—	200.
	s2. As a. Specimen. Overprint *SPECIMEN.*	—	200.

87	100 Karbovantsiv	VF	UNC
	1991. Brown-violet and pale orange on yellow underprint. Lybid, Viking sister of the founding brothers at left. All notes without serial number. Back: Cathedral of St. Sophia in Kiev at left center. Watermark: Paper. Printer: ISPB (France). 100 KRB printed sideways with fluorescent ink at left.		
	a. Issued note.	3.00	7.00
	s1. Specimen. Perforated *SPECIMEN.*	—	200.
	s2. Specimen. Overprint *SPECIMEN.*	—	200.
87A	250 Karbovantsiv		
	1991. Blue and red. Proof perforated: *SPECIMEN.* Unissued. Eight color varieties.	—	500.
87B	500 Karbovantsiv		
	1991. Proof perforated *SPECIMEN.* Unissued. Eight color varieties.	—	500.

1992 ISSUE

#88-91 Replacement notes: Serial # prefix *.../99* in denominator.

88	100 Karbovantsiv	VF	UNC
	1992. Orange on lilac and ochre underprint. Founding Viking brothers Kyi, Shchek and Khoryv with sister Libyd in bow of boat at left. All notes with serial number. Back: Cathedral of St. Sophia in Kiev at left center. Watermark: Paper. Printer: TDLR (without imprint).		
	a. Issued note.	1.00	4.00
	r. Replacement note.	3.00	6.00
	s. Specimen.	—	10.00

89 200 Karbovantsiv VF UNC

1992. Dull brown and silver on lilac and ochre underprint. Founding Viking brothers Kyi, Shchek and Khoryv with sister Libyd in bow of boat at left. All notes with serial number. Back: Cathedral of St. Sophia in Kiev at left center. Watermark: Paper. Printer: TDLR (without imprint).

	VF	UNC
a. Issued note.	2.00	6.00
r. Replacement note.	2.50	7.00
s. Specimen.	—	10.00

90 500 Karbovantsiv VF UNC

1992. Blue-green and silver on lilac and ochre underprint. Founding Viking brothers Kyi, Shchek and Khoryv with sister Libyd in bow of boat at left. All notes with serial number. Back: Cathedral of St. Sophia in Kiev at left center. Watermark: Paper. Printer: TDLR (without imprint).

	VF	UNC
a. Issued note.	1.00	5.00
r. Replacement note.	3.00	7.00
s. Specimen.	—	25.00

91 1000 Karbovantsiv VF UNC

1992. Red-violet and light green on lilac and ochre underprint. Founding Viking brothers Kyi, Shchek and Khoryv with sister Libyd in bow of boat at left. All notes with serial number. Back: Cathedral of St. Sophia in Kiev at left center. Watermark: Paper. Printer: TDLR (without imprint).

	VF	UNC
a. Issued note.	.75	2.00
r. Replacement note.	2.50	6.00
s. Specimen.	—	25.00

Government

Treasury

1992 СЕРТИФІКАТ - Compensation Certificate Issue

#91A and 91B The exact use of these notes has come into question.

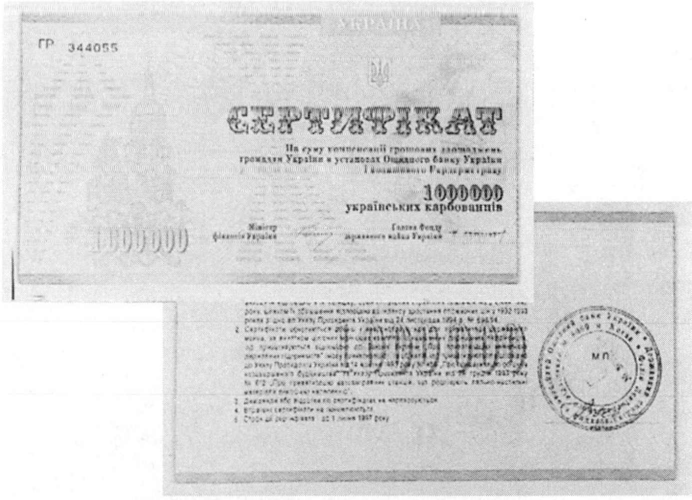

91A 1,000,000 Karbovantsiv VF UNC

1992. Dull blue-green, orange and gray on pale orange and pale green underprint. Church at left, small arms at upper right. Back: Text. 2.00 7.00

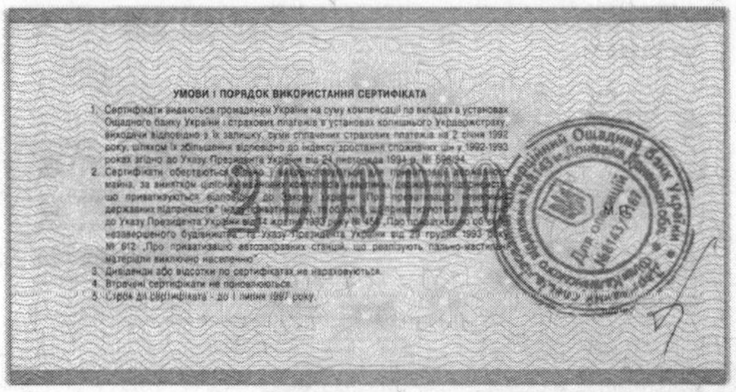

91B 2,000,000 Karbovantsiv VF UNC

1992. Green, orange and pink with black text on light blue, pink and multicolor underprint. Church at left, small arms at upper right. Back: Text. 6.00 10.00

НАЦІОНАЛЬНИЙ БАНК УКРАЇНИ

Ukrainian National Bank

1993 Issue

#92 and 93 Replacement notes: Serial # prefix *001/92-001/99; 001/99* for notes dated 1993.

92 2000 Karbovantsiv VF UNC

1993. Blue and olive-green on aqua and gold underprint. Founding Viking brothers Kyi, Shchek and Khoryv with sister Libyd in bow of boat at left. All notes with serial number.Trident shield added at left. Back: Cathedral of St.Sophia in Kiev at left center.Trident shield added at right. Watermark: Paper. Printer: TDLR (without imprint).

	VF	UNC
a. Issued note.	2.00	5.00
s. Specimen.	—	10.00

93 5000 Karbovantsiv VF UNC

1993; 1995. Red-orange and olive-brown on pale blue and ochre underprint. Founding Viking brothers Kyi, Shchek and Khoryv with sister Libyd in bow of boat at left. All notes with serial number.Trident shield added at left. Back: Cathedral of St.Sophia in Kiev at left center.Trident shield added at right. Watermark: Paper. Printer: TDLR (without imprint).

	VF	UNC
a. 1993.	1.00	3.00
b. 1995.	2.50	5.00
r. Replacement note. 1993.	3.00	6.00
s1. Specimen. 1993.	—	25.00
s2. Specimen. 1995.	—	25.00

94 10,000 Karbovantsiv VF UNC

1993-96. Apple green and tan on pale blue and ochre underprint. Statue of St. Volodymyr standing with long cross at left. Trident shield at left. Back: Building facade at left, trident shield at right. Watermark: Ornamental shield repeated vertically.

	VF	UNC
a. 1993.	1.00	2.00
b. 1995.	.50	1.00
c. 1996. Watermark: Zig-zag of 4 bars. (parquet-paper).	1.00	2.00
s1. Specimen. 1993.	—	25.00
s2. Specimen. 1995.	—	25.00
s3. Specimen. 1996.	—	25.00

95 20,000 Karbovantsiv
1993-96. Lilac and tan on blue and yellow underprint. Statue of St. Volodymyr standing with long cross at left. Trident shield at left. Back: Building façade at left, trident shield at right. Watermark: Ornamental shield repeated vertically.

	VF	UNC
a. 1993.	1.00	4.00
b. 1994.	1.00	4.00
c. 1995.	1.00	3.00
d. 1996. Watermark: Zig-zag of 4 bars. (parquet-paper).	1.00	3.00
s1. Specimen. 1993.	—	25.00
s2. Specimen. 1994.	—	25.00
s3. Specimen. 1995.	—	25.00
s4. Specimen. 1996.	—	25.00

96 50,000 Karbovantsiv
1993-95. Dull orange and blue on multicolor underprint. Statue of St. Volodymyr standing with long cross at left. Trident shield at left. Back: Building façade at left, trident shield at right. Watermark: Ornamental shield repeated vertically.

	VF	UNC
a. 1993.	2.00	6.00
b. 1994.	1.00	4.00
c. 1995.	1.00	4.00
s1. Specimen. 1993.	—	25.00
s2. Specimen. 1994.	—	25.00
s3. Specimen. 1995.	—	25.00

97 100,000 Karbovantsiv
1993; 1994. Gray-green and ochre on multicolor underprint. Statue of St. Volodymyr standing with long cross at left. Trident shield at left. Back: Building façade at left, trident shield at right. Watermark: Trident shield repeated.

	VF	UNC
a. Prefix fraction before serial #. 1993.	4.00	10.00
b. Prefix letters with serial #. 1994.	2.00	6.00
s1. Specimen. 1993.	—	30.00
s2. Specimen. 1994.	—	17.50

98 200,000 Karbovantsiv
1994. Dull red-brown and light blue on aqua and gray underprint. Statue of St. Volodymyr standing with long cross at right. Back: Multicolor. Opera house at left center. Watermark: Trident shield repeated.

	VF	UNC
a. Prefix fraction before serial #. 1994.	5.00	15.00
b. Prefix letters with serial #. 1994.	5.00	10.00
s1. Specimen. 1994. Serial # prefix as a fraction.	—	30.00
s2. Specimen. 1994. Serial # prefix as letter.	—	17.50

99 500,000 Karbovantsiv
1994. Light blue and lilac on yellow and gray underprint. Statue of St. Volodymyr standing with long cross at right. Back: Opera house at left center. Watermark: Trident shield repeated.

	VF	UNC
a. Issued note.	10.00	20.00
s. Specimen.	—	30.00

1995 Issue

100 1,000,000 Karbovantsiv
1995. Dark brown on pale orange, light blue and multicolor underprint. Statue of T. G. Shevchenko at right, arms at lower left. Back: Kiev State University at left center, arms at lower right.

	VF	UNC
a. Issued note.	15.00	30.00
s. Specimen.	—	30.00

1995 Privatization Certificate Issue

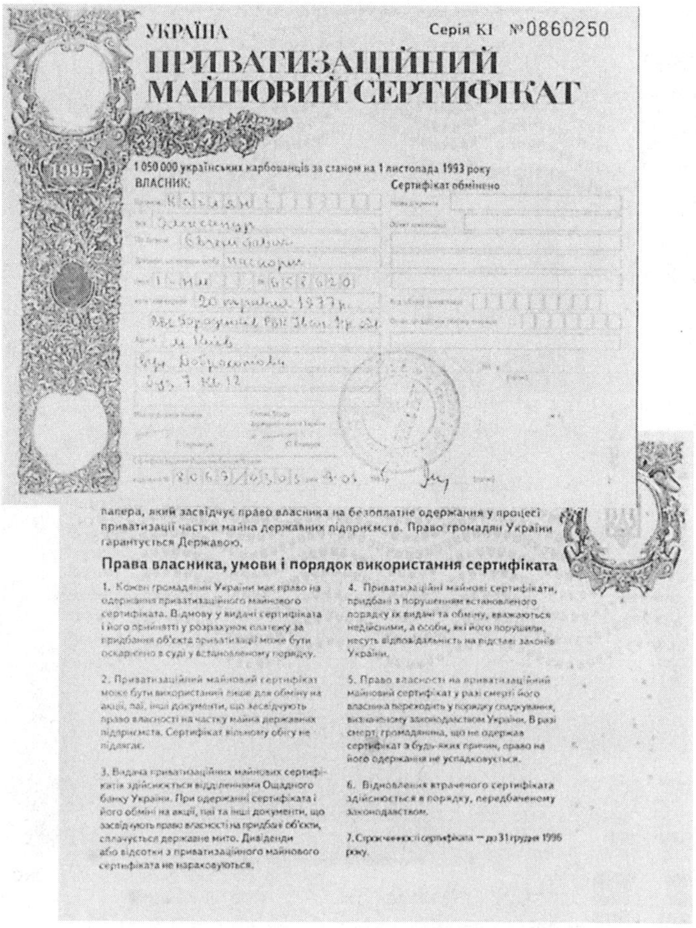

101 1,050,000 Karbovantsiv
1995. Dark gray on light gray and ochre underprint. Arms at upper left. Back: Text.

VF	UNC
15.00	35.00

1992 (1996) Regular Issue

#103-107 wmk: Trident repeated. Printer: CBNC (w/o imprint). Replacement notes: First digit of serial # is *9*.

103	1 Hryvnia	VF	UNC
	1992 (1996). Olive-brown on multicolor underprint. Ruins of Kherson at center. Back: St. Volodymr at center.		
	a. Signature 1.	1.00	2.00
	b. Signature 3.	1.00	2.00
	s. As a or b. Specimen.	—	25.00

104	2 Hryvni	VF	UNC
	1992 (1996). Brown on multicolor underprint. Cathedral of St. Sophia at center. Back: Prince Yaroslav at center.		
	a. Signature 1.	FV	3.00
	b. Signature 2.	FV	5.00
	c. Signature 3.	FV	3.00
	s. As a, b, c. Specimen.	—	25.00

105	5 Hryven	VF	UNC
	1992 (1996). Blue-gray on multicolor underprint. Illinska Church in Subotiv at center. Back: B. Khmelnytsky at center.		
	a. Signature 1.	FV	4.00
	b. Signature 2.	FV	6.00
	c. Signature 3.	FV	3.00
	s. As a, b, c. Specimen.	—	25.00

106	10 Hryven	VF	UNC
	1992 (1996). Purple on multicolor underprint. Kyiv-Pecherska Monastery at center. Back: I. Mazepa at center.		
	a. Signature 1.	FV	9.00
	b. Signature 3.	FV	9.00
	s. As a, b. Specimen.	—	50.00

107	20 Hryven	VF	UNC
	1992 (1996). Brown on multicolor underprint. Lviv Opera House at center. Back: Ivan Franko at center.		
	a. Signature 1.	5.00	25.00
	b. Signature 3.	5.00	25.00
	s. As a, b. Specimen.	—	50.00

107A	50 Hryven	VF	UNC
	1992. Back: Man at center. Printer: CBNC. (Not issued).	—	—

107B	100 Hryven	VF	UNC
	1992. Back: Man at center. Printer: CBNC. (Not issued).	—	—

1994-98 ND and Dated Issue

108	1 Hryvnia	VF	UNC
	1994; 1995. Grayish brown and green on multicolor underprint. St. Volodymyr at center right. Signature 3. Back: City of Khersonnes at center. Watermark: St. Volodymyr. 133x66mm.		
	a. 1994 (1996).	FV	1.00
	b. 1995 (1997).	FV	1.00
	s. Specimen. 1994; 1995.	—	35.00

109 2 Hryvni VF UNC

1995; 2001. Multicolor. Prince Yaroslav at center right. Back: Cathedral of St. Sophia in Kyiv. Watermark: Prince Yaroslav. 133x66mm.

	VF	UNC
a. 1995 (1997).	FV	2.00
b. 2001.	FV	2.00
s. Specimen. 1995; 2001.	—	30.00

110 5 Hryven VF UNC

1994; 1997; 2001. Multicolor. Bohdan Khmelnytsky at center right. Back: Illinska Church in Subotiv at center. Printer: TDLR (without imprint). 133x66mm.

	VF	UNC
a. 1994 (1997).	FV	4.00
b. 1997 (1998).	FV	4.00
c. 2001.	FV	4.00
s. Specimen. 1994; 1997; 2001.	—	30.00

111 10 Hryven VF UNC

1994; 2000. Multicolor. L. Mazepa at center right. Back: Kyiv-Pecherska Monastery at center. Watermark: L. Mazepa. 133x66mm.

	VF	UNC
a. 1994 (1997). Series in "Arial" font. Printer: TDLR.	FV	6.00
b. 1994 (1997). Series in "Times Roman" font. Ukrainian printer.	FV	6.00
c. 2000. Ukrainian printer.	FV	6.00
s. As b, c. Specimen.	—	40.00

112 20 Hryven VF UNC

1995; 2000. Multicolor. Ivan Franko at right. Back: Opera House in Lviv. Watermark: Ivan Franko. 133x66mm.

	VF	UNC
a. 1995. With segmented security thread.	FV	12.00
b. 2000.	FV	12.00
s. As a, b. Specimen.	—	30.00

113 50 Hryven VF UNC

ND (1996). Purple and dark blue-gray on multicolor underprint. M. Hrushevsky at right. Back: Parliament building at center. Watermark: M. Hrushevsky. 133x66mm.

	VF	UNC
a. Signature 1.	FV	30.00
b. Signature 3.	FV	30.00
s. As a, b. Specimen.	—	150.
x. Watermark. T. Shevchenko (error). Rare.	—	200.

114 100 Hryven VF UNC

ND (1996). Brown and dark green on multicolor underprint. T. Shevchenko at right. Back: Cathedral of St. Sophia in Kyiv at center, statue of St. Volodymyr standing at left. Watermark: T. Shevchenko. 133x66mm.

	VF	UNC
a. Signature 1.	FV	45.00
b. Signature 3.	FV	45.00
s. As a, b. Specimen.	—	175.
x. Watermark: M. Hrushevsky (error).	—	200.

115 200 Hryven VF UNC

ND (2001). Black and blue on multicolor underprint. Lesia Ukrainka (L. P. Kosach) at right. Signature 1. Back: Castle gate. Watermark: Lesia Ukrainka (L. P. Kosach). 133x66mm.

	VF	UNC
a. Issued note.	FV	80.00
s. Specimen.	—	200.

2003-07 Issue

116 1 Hryvnia VF UNC

2004; 2005. Green and blue on multicolor underprint. Prince Volodymyr at right. Back: Volodymyr's burg in Kyiv. Watermark: Prince Volodymyr 118x63mm.

	VF	UNC
a. 2004.	FV	1.00
b. 2005.	FV	1.00
s. Specimen.	—	50.00

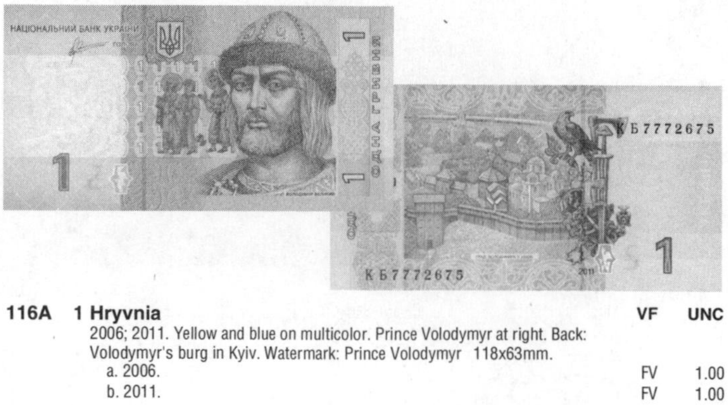

116A 1 Hryvnia VF UNC

2006; 2011. Yellow and blue on multicolor. Prince Volodymyr at right. Back: Volodymyr's burg in Kyiv. Watermark: Prince Volodymyr 118x63mm.

	VF	UNC
a. 2006.	FV	1.00
b. 2011.	FV	1.00

117	2 Hryven	VF	UNC
	2004; 2005; 2011. Brown on multicolor underprint. Yaroslav the Wise at right. Back: Cathedral of St. Sophia in Kyiv. Watermark: Yaroslav the Wise. 118x63mm.		
	a. 2004.	FV	2.00
	b. 2005.	FV	2.00
	c. 2011.	FV	2.00
	s. Specimen.	—	50.00

118	5 Hryven	VF	UNC
	2004; 2005; 2011; 2013. Blue on multicolor underprint. Bohdan Khmelnytsky at center. Back: Iliynska Church in Subotiv. Watermark: Bohdan Khmelnytsky 118x63mm.		
	a. 2004.	FV	4.00
	b. 2005.	FV	4.00
	c. 2011.	FV	4.00
	d. 2013.	FV	4.00
	s. Specimen.	—	50.00

119	10 Hryven	VF	UNC
	2004; 2005. Black, red and multicolor. Ivan Mazepa at right. Back: Pecherska Monastery in Kyiv at center. Watermark: Ivan Mazepa 123x65mm.		
	a. 2004.	FV	6.00
	b. 2005.	FV	6.00
	s. Specimen.	—	75.00

119A	10 Hryven	VF	UNC
	2006; 2011; 2013. Gray on multicolor. Ivan Mazepa at right. Back: Pecherska Monastery in Kyiv at center. Watermark: Ivan Mazepa. 123x65mm.		
	a. 2006.	FV	6.00
	b. 2011.	FV	6.00
	c. 2013.	FV	6.00

120	20 Hryven	VF	UNC
	2003; 2005; 2011. Slate black and green on multicolor underprint. Ivan Franko at right. Back: Opera House in Lviv. Watermark: Ivan Franko. 133x69mm.		
	a. 2003.	FV	12.00
	b. 2005.	FV	12.00
	c. 2011.	FV	12.00
	s. Specimen.	—	75.00

121	50 Hryven	VF	UNC
	2004; 2005; 2011; 2013. Brown and lilac on multicolor underprint. Mikhaylo Hrushevsky at right. Back: Parliament building at cetner. Watermark: Mikhaylo Hrushevsky. 136x72mm.		
	a. 2004.	FV	17.50
	b. 2005.	FV	15.00
	c. 2011.	FV	15.00
	d. 2013.	FV	15.00
	s. Specimen.	—	50.00

122	100 Hryven	VF	UNC
	2005; 2011. Green and burgundy on multicolor underprint. Taras Shevchenko at right. Back: Shevchenko playing instrument. Watermark: Taras Shevchenko. 142x75mm.		
	a. 2005.	FV	40.00
	b. 2011.	FV	40.00
	s. Specimen.	—	50.00

123	200 Hryven	VF	UNC
	2007; 2011; 2013. Purple and rose on multicolor underprint. Lesia Ukrainka at right. Back: Kutsk Castle Gate Tower at right. Watermark: Lesia Ukrainka. 148x74mm.		
	a. 2007.	FV	50.00
	b. 2011.	FV	50.00
	c. 2013.	FV	50.00
	s. Specimen.	—	75.00

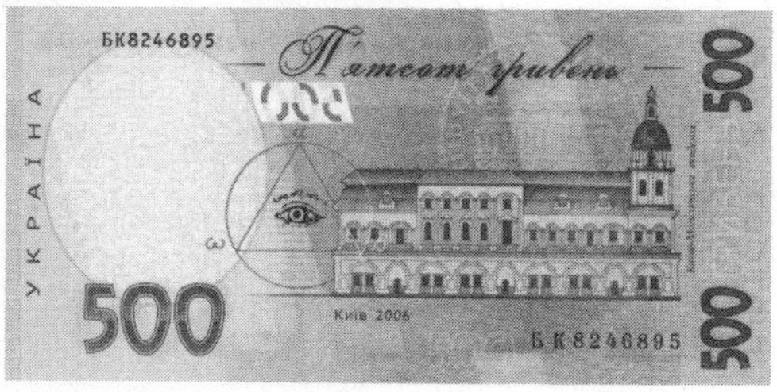

124	500 Hryven	VF	UNC
	2006; 2011. Brown, tan and green on multicolor underprint. Grigori Skovoroda at right. Back: Kyiv Mohyla Academy at center. Watermark: Grigori Skovoroda. 154x75mm.		
	a. 2006.	FV	110.
	b. 2011.	FV	110.
	s. Specimen.	—	125.

2011 Commemorative Issue

125	50 Hryven	VF	UNC
	2011. HBY hologram. 20th Anniversary of Bank. 1000 pieces issued in folder.	—	350.

Collector Series

НАЦІОНАЛЬНИЙ БАНК УКРАЇНИ

Ukrainian National Bank

1996 Issue

CS1	1 Hryvnia	Mkt.	Value
	#103 and 2 Karbovantsiv 1996 Independence coins in a folder.		—

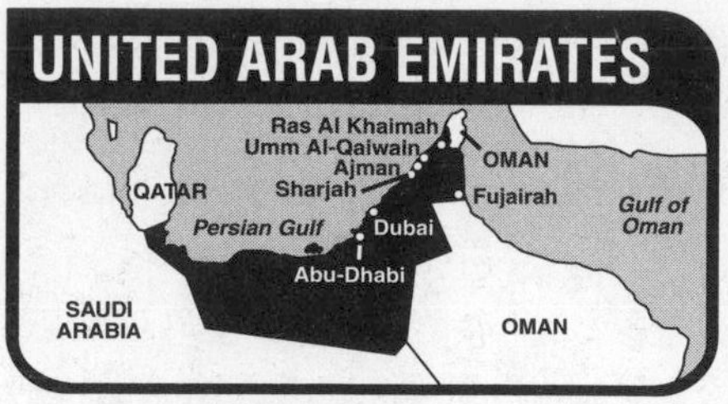

The seven United Arab Emirates (formerly known as the Trucial Sheikhdoms or States), located along the southern shore of the Persian Gulf, are comprised of the Sheikhdoms of Abu Dhabi, Dubai, Sharjah, Ajman, Umm al Qaiwain, Ras al-Khaimah and Fujairah. They have a combined area of 83,600 sq. km. and a population of 4.62 million. Capital: Abu Dhabi. Since the oil strikes of 1958-60, the economy has centered on petroleum.

The Trucial States of the Persian Gulf coast granted the UK control of their defense and foreign affairs in 19th century treaties. In 1971, six of these states - Abu Zaby, 'Ajman, Al Fujayrah, Ash Shariqah, Dubayy, and Umm al Qaywayn - merged to form the United Arab Emirates (UAE). They were joined in 1972 by Ra's al Khaymah. The UAE's per capita GDP is on par with those of leading West European nations. Its generosity with oil revenues and its moderate foreign policy stance have allowed the UAE to play a vital role in the affairs of the region.

MONETARY SYSTEM:

1 Dirham = 1000 Fils

Sheikhdoms

United Arab Emirates Currency Board

1973; 1976 ND Issue

1	1 Dirham	VF	UNC
	ND (1973). Green on multicolor underprint. Dhow, camel caravan, palm tree and oil derrick at left. Back: Police station at center right. Watermark: Arabian horse's head. Printer: (T)DLR.		
	a. Issued note.	12.00	60.00
	s. Specimen.	—	75.00

2	5 Dirhams	VF	UNC
	ND (1973). Purple on multicolor underprint. Dhow, camel caravan, palm tree and oil derrick at left. Back: Fortress Fujairah at center right. Watermark: Arabian horse's head. Printer: (T)DLR.		
	a. Issued note.	25.00	90.00
	s. Specimen.	—	75.00

3	10 Dirhams	VF	UNC
	ND (1973). Gray-blue on multicolor underprint. Dhow, camel caravan, palm tree and oil derrick at left. Back: Aerial view of Umm al-Qaiwan at center right. Watermark: Arabian horse's head. Printer: (T)DLR.		
	a. Issued note.	16.00	90.00
	s. Specimen.	—	100.

4 50 Dirhams

ND (1973). Red on multicolor underprint. Dhow, camel caravan, palm tree and oil derrick at left. Back: Sheikh's Palace of Ajman at center right. Watermark: Arabian horse's head. Printer: (T)DLR.

	VF	UNC
a. Issued note.	85.00	450.
s. Specimen.	—	225.

5 100 Dirhams

ND (1973). Olive-green on multicolor underprint. Dhow, camel caravan, palm tree and oil derrick at left. Back: Ras al-Khaimah city at center right. Watermark: Arabian horse's head. Printer: (T)DLR.

	VF	UNC
a. Issued note.	80.00	450.
s. Specimen.	—	325.

6 1000 Dirhams

ND (1976). Blue on multicolor underprint. Dhow, camel caravan, palm tree and oil derrick at left. Back: Fortress at center right. Watermark: Arabian horse's head. Printer: (T)DLR.

	VF	UNC
a. Issued note.	850.	3000.
s. Specimen.	—	1000.

United Arab Emirates Central Bank

1982; 1983 ND Issue

7 5 Dirhams

ND (1982). Brown on multicolor underprint. Sharjah Market at right. Arms at upper center. Back: Seacoast cove with tower. Sparrowhawk at left. Watermark: Sparrowhawk's head. UV: value 5, eagle and shield fluoresce orange.

	VF	UNC
a. Issued note.	5.00	16.00
s. Specimen.	—	50.00

8 10 Dirhams

ND (1982). Green on multicolor underprint. Arab dagger at right. Arms at upper center. Back: Ideal farm with trees at left center. Sparrowhawk at left. Watermark: Sparrowhawk's head.

	VF	UNC
a. Issued note.	7.00	30.00
s. Specimen.	—	50.00

9 50 Dirhams

ND (1982). Purple, dark brown and olive on multicolor underprint. Oryx at right, arms at upper center. Back: Al Jahilie Fort at left center. Sparrowhawk at left. Watermark: Sparrowhawk's head.

	VF	UNC
a. Issued note.	50.00	120.
s. Specimen.	—	95.00

10 100 Dirhams

ND (1982). Red, violet and black on multicolor underprint. Al Fahidie Fort at right, arms at upper center. Back: Dubai Trade center at left center. Sparrowhawk at left. Watermark: Sparrowhawk's head.

	VF	UNC
a. Issued note.	70.00	130.
s. Specimen.	—	100.

11 500 Dirhams VF UNC

ND (1983). Dark blue, purple and brown on multicolor underprint. Sparrowhawk at right, arms at upper center. Back: Mosque in Dubai at left center. Sparrowhawk at left. Watermark: Sparrowhawk's head.

a. Issued note. 275. 650.

s. Specimen. — 350.

1989-96 Issues

12 5 Dirhams VF UNC

1993/AH1414-1995/AH1416. Dark brown, red-orange and violet on multicolor underprint. Sharjah market at right. Condensed Arabic text in titles, modified designs and slight color variations. Large value outline type in watermark area. Silver arms at upper center. Arabic serial number in Back: Seacoast cove with tower. Sparrowhawk at left. Watermark: Sparrowhawk's head.

a. 1993/AH1414. 6.00 13.00

b. 1995/AH1416. FV 7.50

13 10 Dirhams VF UNC

1993/AH1414-199/AH1416. Green and pale olive-green on multicolor underprint. Arab dagger at right. Condensed Arabic text in titles, modified designs and slight color variations. Large value outline type in watermark area. Silver arms at upper center. Arabic serial number in re Back: Ideal farm with trees at left. Sparrowhawk at left. Watermark: Sparrowhawk's head.

a. 1993/AH1414. 10.00 20.00

b. 1995/AH1416. 7.00 15.00

14 50 Dirhams VF UNC

1995/AH1415-1996/AH1417. Purple, black and violet on multicolor underprint. Oryx at right. Condensed Arabic text in titles, modified designs and slight color variations. Large value outline type in watermark area. Silver arms at upper center. Arabic serial number in red at le Back: Al Jahilie Fort at left center. Sparrowhawk at left. Watermark: Sparrowhawk's head. With segmented foil over security thread.

a. 1995/AH1415. 20.00 85.00

b. 1996/AH1417. 20.00 75.00

15 100 Dirhams VF UNC

1993/AH1414-1995/AH1416. Red, red-violet and black on multicolor underprint. Al Fahidie Fort at right. Condensed Arabic text in titles, modified designs and slight color variations. Large value outline type in watermark area. Silver arms at upper center. Arabic serial number i Back: Dubai Trade center at left center. Sparrowhawk at left. Watermark: Sparrowhawk's head. With segmented foil over security thread.

a. 1993/AH1414. FV 100.

b. 1995/AH1416. FV 90.00

16 200 Dirhams VF UNC

1989/AH 1410. Brown, green and multicolor. Sharia Court building and Zayed Sports City. Back: Central Bank building at left center. With segmented foil over security thread. 90.00 240.

17 500 Dirhams

1993/AH1414. Dark blue, black, purple and silver on multicolor underprint. Sparrowhawk at right. Back: Mosque in Dubai at left center. Sparrowhawk at left. Watermark: Sparrowhawk's head. With segmented foil over security thread. 300. 825.

18 500 Dirhams

1996/AH1416. Dark blue, black, purple and silver on multicolor underprint. Sparrowhawk at right. Kinegram added at lower left. Back: Mosque in Dubai at left center. Sparrowhawk at left. Watermark: Sparrowhawk's head. 250. 650.

1997-2000 Issue

19 5 Dirhams VF UNC

2000/AH1420-. Brown and orange. Similar to #12 but with color and minor design variations. Watermark area shaded. Back: Seacoast cove with tower. Sparrowhawk at left. Watermark: Sparrowhawk's head. . 143x60mm.

a. 2000/AH1420. FV 8.00

b. 2001/AH1422. FV 7.00

c. 2004/AH1425. FV 7.00

d. 2007/AH1428. FV 7.00

e. 2009/AH1430. FV 7.00

		VF	UNC
20	**10 Dirhams**		
	1998/AH1419-. Green and pale olive-green on multicolor underprint. Arab dagger at right. Condensed Arabic text in titles, modified designs and slight color variations. Large value outline type in watermark area. Silver arms at upper center. Arabic serial number in re Back: Ideal farm with trees at left. Sparrowhawk at left. Watermark: Sparrowhawk's head. 145x62mm.		
	a. 1998/AH1419.	FV	12.00
	b. 2001/AH1422.	FV	10.00
	c. 2004/AH1425.	FV	10.00
	d. 2007/AH1428.	FV	9.00
	e. 2009/AH1430.	FV	8.00

		VF	UNC
21	**20 Dirhams**		
	1997/AH1418-. Green, blue and multicolor. Dubai Creek Golf and Yacht Club at right. Watermark area shaded. Back: Dhow. Sparrowhawk at left. Watermark: Sparrowhawk's head. 150x63mm.		
	a. 1997/AH1418.	FV	25.00
	b. 2000/AH1420.	FV	20.00
	c. 2008/AH1428.	FV	16.00
	s. As a. Specimen. Perforated: *SPECIMEN.*	—	350.

		VF	UNC
22	**50 Dirhams**		
	1998/AH1419. Purple, black and violet on multicolor underprint. Oryx at right. Condensed Arabic text in titles, modified designs and slight color variations. Large value outline type in watermark area. Silver arms at upper center. Arabic serial number in red at le Back: Al Jahilie Fort at left center. Sparrowhawk at left. Watermark: Sparrowhawk's head. 150x63mm.	FV	50.00

		VF	UNC
23	**100 Dirhams**		
	1998/AH1419. Red, red-violet and black on multicolor underprint. Al Fahidie Fort at right. Condensed Arabic text in titles, modified designs and slight color variations. Silver arms at upper center. Arabic serial number in red at left, electronic sorting style in b Back: Dubai Trade center at left center. Sparrowhawk at left. Watermark: Sparrowhawk's head. 155x66mm.	FV	85.00

		VF	UNC
24	**500 Dirhams**		
	1998-. Dark blue, black, purple and silver on multicolor underprint. Sparrowhawk at right. Kinegram added at lower left. Wide silver foil at right, silver seal at left. Watermark area shaded. Back: Mosque in Dubai at left center. Sparrowhawk at left. Watermark: Sparrowhawk's head. 160x68mm.		
	a. 1998/AH1419.	FV	350.
	b. 2000/AH1420.	FV	320.
	c. 2004/AH1425.	FV	300.

		VF	UNC
25	**1000 Dirhams**		
	1998-2000. Brown, green and multicolor. Palace corner tower at right. Holographic strip vertically at right. Watermark area shaded. Back: City view. Sparrowhawk at left. Watermark: Sparrowhawk's head. 163x70mm.		
	a. 1998/AH1419.	FV	850.
	b. 2000/AH1420.	FV	700.

2003-04 Issue

		VF	UNC
26	**5 Dirhams**		
	2004; 2007; 2009; 2013. Brown and orange on multicolor underprint. Dallah (coffee pot) added to watermark area. 143x60mm.		
	a. 2004/AH1425.	FV	5.00
	b. 2007/AH1428.	FV	5.00
	c. 2009/AH1430.	FV	5.00
	d. 2013/AH1434. Left serial # vertical.	FV	5.00

27 10 Dirhams

2004; 2007; 2009. Green and pale-olive-green on multicolor underprint. Arab dagger at right. 145x62mm.

	VF	UNC
a. 2004/AH1425.	FV	8.00
b. 2007/AH1428.	FV	8.00
c. 2007/AH1430.	FV	8.00

28 20 Dirhams

2007; 2009; 2013. Green, blue and multicolor. Dubai Creek Golf and Yacht Club at right. 150x63mm.

	VF	UNC
a. 2007/AH1428.	FV	16.00
b. 2009/AH1430.	FV	16.00
c. 2013/AH1434.	FV	14.00

29 50 Dirhams

2004-. Purple, black and violet on multicolor underprint. Oryx at right. Condensed Arabic text in titles, modified designs and slight color variations. Large value outline type in watermark area. Silver arms at upper center. Arabic serial number in red at le Back: Al Jahilie Fort at left center. Watermark: Sparrowhawk's head. 150x63mm.

	VF	UNC
a. 2004/AH1425.	FV	45.00
b. 2006/AH1427.	FV	40.00
c. 2008/AH1429.	FV	35.00
d. 2011/AH1432.	FV	35.00

30 100 Dirhams

2003; 2004; 2006. Red, red-violet and black on multicolor underprint. Similar to #23 but with silver overprint of tower at upper right. Dallah (coffee pot) added to watermark area. Back: Dubai Trade center at left center. Watermark: Sparrowhawk's head. 155x66mm.

	VF	UNC
a. 2003/AH1424.	FV	60.00
b. 2004/AH1425.	FV	55.00
c. 2006/AH1427.	FV	50.00

31 200 Dirhams

2004/AH1425-. Brown and black on yellow and multicolor underprint. Sharia Court building and Zayed Sports City at right. Back: U.A.E. Central Bank building at center, falcon at left end. 157x67mm.

	VF	UNC
a. 2004/AH1425.	FV	225.
b. 2008/AH1429.	FV	240.

32 500 Dirhams

2006/AH1427-. Dark blue, black, purple and silver on multicolor underprint. Al Hosn palace in Abu Dhabi at right. Back: Abu Dhabi cornice. Security foil strip with denomination. 160x68mm.

	VF	UNC
a. 2006/AH1427.	FV	280.
b. 2008/AH1429.	FV	240.
c. 2011/AH1432.	FV	225.

33 1000 Dirhams

2006/AH1427-. Brown, green and multicolor. Al Hosn palace in Abu Dhabi. Back: Abu Dhabi cornice. Security foil strip with alternating arms and denomination in Arabic. 163x70mm.

	VF	UNC
a. 2006/AH1427.	FV	500.
b. 2008/AH1429. Slighly modified arms on face.	FV	475.
c. 2012/AH1433.	FV	475.

UNITED STATES OF AMERICA

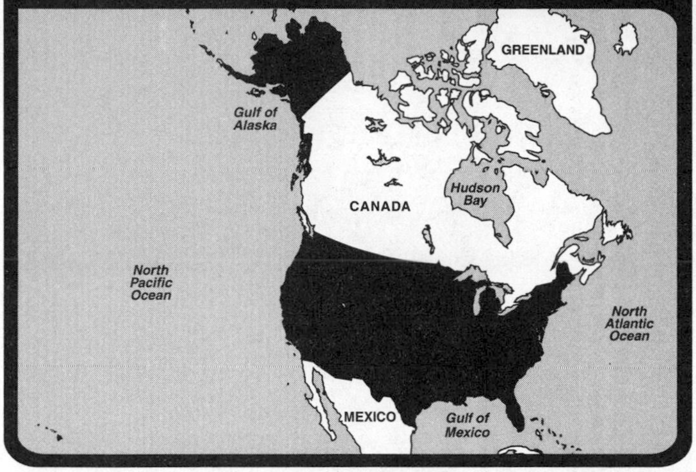

The area of the North American continent currently controlled by the United States of America was originally inhabited by numerous groups of Indian tribes. Some of these groups settled in particular areas, creating permanent settlements, while others were nomadic, traveling great distances and living off the land.

English explorers John and Sebastian Cabot reached Nova Scotia in what is today Canada in 1497; in 1534 the French gained a foothold with the explorations of Jacques Cartier. In 1541 the Spanish explorer Coronado traversed the south central portion of the country in what was to become the states of New Mexico, Texas, Nebraska and Oklahoma. In 1542 another Spaniard, Juan Cabrillo navigated north from Mexico along the Pacific coastline to California. The Spanish set up the first permanent settlement of Europeans in North America at St. Augustine, Florida in 1565. In 1607 the English settled in Jamestown, Virginia, and in 1620 at Plymouth, Massachusetts. This was followed closely by Dutch settlements in Albany and New York in 1624, and in 1638 the Swedes arrived in Delaware. From their foothold in Canada, French explorers pushed inland through the Great Lakes. Jean Nicolet explored what was to become Wisconsin in 1634, and in 1673 explorers Marquette and Joliet reached Iowa. In the 1650s the Dutch won the Swedish lands, and in 1664 the English gained control of the Dutch lands, thus giving the English control all along the Atlantic Coast. The resulting thirteen British colonies; New Hampshire, Vermont, Massachusetts, Rhode Island, Connecticut, New York, Pennsylvania, Delaware, Maryland, Virginia, North Carolina, South Carolina and Georgia formed the nucleus of what would become the United States of America.

From this point on tensions grew between the English, who could not expand westward from their settlements along the Atlantic Coast, and the French who had settled inland into the Ohio river valley. This dispute ended in 1763 after a war with the French loosing control of lands east of the Mississippi river. Manufacturing, textiles and other industry was developing at this time, and by 1775 about one-seventh of the world's production of raw iron came from the colonies. From 1771-1783 the war for American Independence was fought by the colonists against the English, and settled by the Peace of Paris in 1783. Americans gained control of lands south of the St. Lawrence and Great Lakes, and east of the Mississippi, with the exception of Florida which would remain under Spanish control until 1821. At the close of the war, the population was about 3 million, many of whom lived on self-sufficient family farms. Fishing, lumbering and the production of grains for export were becoming major economic endeavors. The newly independent states formed a loose confederation, but in 1787 approved the Constitution of the United States which is the framework for the goverment today. In 1789 it's first president, George Washington was elected, and the capitol was set up in New York City. In 1800 the capitol was moved to a planned city, Washington, D.C. where it remains.

Westward expansion was an inevitability as population grew. French territory west of the Mississippi, stretching to the northern Pacific was purchased in 1804 under the presidency of Thomas Jefferson, who then sent out Lewis and Clark on expedition of discovery. Spain granted independence to Mexico in 1821, which included lands which would become the states of California, New Mexico, Arizona and Texas. From 1836-1845 Texas was an independent republic, not joining the United States until 1845. Upon losing a war with the United States, Mexico ceded California (including most of Arizonia and New Mexico) to the United States in 1848. Gold was discovered in California that year, and western migration took off on overland wagon trains or around-the-horn sail and steam ships. Hawaii came under U.S. protection in 1851. As the country developed in the 19th century, the northern states increased in commerce and industry while the southern states developed a vast agricultural through the use of slave labor. Northern political and social threats to slavery lead twelve southern states to secede from the Union in 1860 forming the Confederate States of America. The ensuing Civil War lasted until 1865, at which time slavery was abolished and the States reunited.

In 1867 Alaska was purchased from Russia. The transcontinental railroad was completed in 1869. The central region of the country west of the Mississippi River and east of the Rocky Mountains was the last to be developed, beginning after the Civil War, with the establishment of cattle ranches and farms. Between 1870 and 1891 the nomadic Native American population clashed with settlers and federal troops. By 1891 the Native Americans were confined to reservations.

At the close of the 19th century the United States embarked on a colonial mission of its own, with advances into Cuba, Puerto Rico, Panama, Nicaragua and the Philippines. This resulted in the Spanish-American War which was quickly decided, ending Spanish colonial dominance, and signaling the rise of the United States as a world power. Slow to enter both World Wars of the 20th century, it was a major contributor to the conclusion of both, making it one of the major nations of the 20th century.

MONETARY SYSTEM:

1 Dollar = 100 Cents

SIGNATURE VARIETIES

SERIES	TREASURER	SECRETARY
1963	Kathryn O'Hay Granahan	C. Douglas Dillon
1963A	Kathryn O'Hay Granahan	Henry H. Fowler
1963B	Kathryn O'Hay Granahan	Joseph W. Barr
1969	Dorothy Andrews Elston	David M. Kennedy
1969A	Dorothy Andrews Kabis	David M. Kennedy
1969B	Dorothy Andrews Kabis	John B. Connally
1969C	Romana Acosta Banuelos	John B. Connally
1969D	Romana Acosta Banuelos	George P. Schultz
1974	Francine I. Neff	William E. Simon
1977	Azie Taylor Morton	W. Michael Blumenthal
1977A	Azie Taylor Morton	J. William Miller
1981	Angela M. Buchanan	Donald T. Regan
1981A	Katherine Davalos Ortega	Donald T. Regan
1985	Katherine Davalos Ortega	John A. Baker III
1988	Katherine Davalos Ortega	Nicholas F. Brady
1988A-1990	Catalina Vasquez Villalpando	Nicholas F. Brady
1993	Mary Ellen Withrow	Lloyd Bentson
1995, 1996	Mary Ellen Withrow	Robert E. Rubin
1999	Mary Ellen Withrow	Lawrence Summers
2001	Rosario Marin	Paul H. O'Neill
2003, 2004	Rosario Marin	John Snow

REPLACEMENT NOTES:

All issues since about 1916 have a star either before or after the serial number, depending on type of note.

REPUBLIC

UNITED STATES NOTES - SMALL SIZE

SERIES OF 1963

Replacement Notes: Serial # suffix is an *.

		VF	UNC
382	**2 Dollars**		
	1963. Thomas Jefferson at center. Red Treasury seal. Back: Monticello.		
	a. 1963.	FV	12.00
	b. 1963A.	FV	15.00

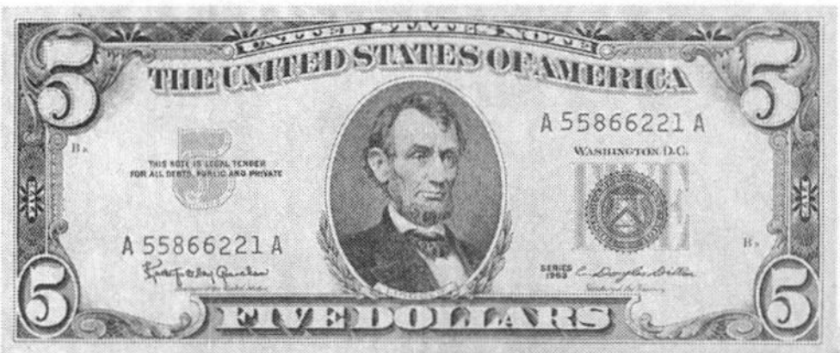

		VF	UNC
383	**5 Dollars**		
	1963. Abraham Lincoln at center. Red Treasury seal. Back: Lincoln Memorial.	9.00	20.00

Series of 1966

384	100 Dollars	VF	UNC
	1966 Benjamin Franklin at center. Back: Independence Hall.		
	a. 1966.	125.	550.
	b. 1966A.	250.	1250.

Federal Reserve Notes - Small Size

1963 Series

443	1 Dollar	VF	UNC
	1963. George Washington at center. Back: Great Seal flanking ONE.		
	a. 1963. (A-L).	FV	4.00
	b. 1963A. (A-L).	FV	4.00
	c. 1963B. (B; E; G; J; L).	FV	5.00

444	5 Dollars	VF	UNC
	1963. Abraham Lincoln at center. Back: Lincoln Memorial.		
	a. 1963. (A-D; F-H; J-L).	FV	20.00
	b. 1963A. (A-L).	FV	15.00

445	10 Dollars	VF	UNC
	1963. Alexander Hamilton at center. Back: Treasury Building.		
	a. 1963. (A-H; J-L).	FV	50.00
	b. 1963A. (A-L).	FV	37.50

446	20 Dollars	VF	UNC
	1963. Andrew Jackson at center. Back: White House.		
	a. 1963. (A-B; D-H; J-L).	FV	75.00
	b. 1963A. (A-L).	FV	60.00
447	50 Dollars		
	1963A. (A-L). Ulysses Grant at center. Back: Unites States Capital Building.	FV	150.

448	100 Dollars	VF	UNC
	1963A. (A-L). Benjamin Franklin at center. Back: Independence Hall.	FV	275.

1969 Series

449	1 Dollar	VF	UNC
	1969 George Washington at center. Back: Great Seal flanking ONE.		
	a. 1969. (A-L).	FV	4.00
	b. 1969A. (A-L).	FV	4.00
	c. 1969B. (A-L).	FV	4.00
	d. 1969C. (B; D-L).	FV	5.00
	e. 1969D. (A-L).	FV	5.00

450	5 Dollars	VF	UNC
	1969. Abraham Lincoln at center. Back: Lincoln Memorial.		
	a. 1969. (A-L).	FV	15.00
	b. 1969A. (A-L).	FV	20.00
	c. 1969B. (A-L).	FV	50.00
	d. 1969C. (A-L).	FV	20.00

		VF	UNC
451	**10 Dollars**		
	1969. Alexander Hamilton at center. Back: Treasury Building.		
	a. 1969. (A-L).	FV	35.00
	b. 1969A. (A-L).	FV	35.00
	c. 1969B. (A-L).	FV	100.
	d. 1969C. (A-L).	FV	40.00

		VF	UNC
452	**20 Dollars**		
	1969. Andrew Jackson at center. Back: White House.		
	a. 1969. (A-L).	FV	60.00
	b. 1969A. (A-L).	FV	75.00
	c. 1969B. (B; D-L).	FV	150.
	d. 1969C. (A-L).	FV	50.00

		VF	UNC
453	**50 Dollars**		
	1969. Ulysses Grant at center. Back: United States Capital Building.		
	a. 1969. (A-L).	FV	200.
	b. 1969A. (A-L).	FV	200.
	c. 1969B. (A-B; E-G; K).	FV	120.
	d. 1969C. (A-L).	FV	150.

		VF	UNC
454	**100 Dollars**		
	1969. Benjamin Franklin at center. Back: Independence Hall.		
	a. 1969. (A-L).	FV	225.
	b. 1969A. (A-L).	FV	225.
	c. 1969C. (A-L).	FV	225.

1974 Series

		VF	UNC
455	**1 Dollar**		
	1974. (A-L). George Washington at center. Back: Great Seal flanking ONE.	FV	4.00
456	**5 Dollars**		
	1974. (A-L). Abraham Lincoln at center. Back: Lincoln Memorial.	FV	15.00

		VF	UNC
457	**10 Dollars**		
	1974. (A-L). Alexander Hamilton at center. Back: Treasury Building.	FV	35.00
458	**20 Dollars**		
	1974. (A-L). Andrew Jackson at center. Back: White House.	FV	60.00

		VF	UNC
459	**50 Dollars**		
	1974. (A-L). Ulysses Grant at center. Back: United States Capital Building.	FV	200.
460	**100 Dollars**		
	1974. (A-L). Benjamin Franklin at center. Back: Independence Hall.	FV	200.

1976 Series

#461, U.S. Bicentennial - Trumbull's painting *Signing of the Declaration of Independence*

		VF	UNC
461	**2 Dollars**		
	1976. (A-L). Thomas Jefferson at center. Back: Signing of the Declaration of Independence.	FV	10.00

1977 Series

		VF	UNC
462	**1 Dollar**		
	1977. George Washington at center. Back: Great Seal flanking ONE.		
	a. 1977. (A-L).	FV	4.00
	b. 1977A. (A-L).	FV	4.00

		VF	UNC
463	**5 Dollars**		
	1977. Abraham Lincoln at center. Back: Lincoln Memorial.		
	a. 1977. (A-L).	FV	10.00
	b. 1977A. (A-L).	FV	18.00
464	**10 Dollars**		
	1977. Alexander Hamilton at center. Back: Treasury Building.		
	a. 1977. (A-L).	FV	40.00
	b. 1977A. (A-L).	FV	35.00

		VF	UNC
465	**20 Dollars**		
	1977. (A-L). Andrew Jackson at center. Back: White House.	FV	60.00

466 **50 Dollars** VF UNC
1977. (A-L). Ulysses Grant at center. Back: United States Capital Building. FV 175.

467 **100 Dollars** VF UNC
1977. (A-L). Benjamin Franklin at center. Back: Independence Hall. FV 225.

1981 Series

Note: Since Oct. 1981 the Bureau of Engraving and Printing has made available to collectors uncut sheets of 4, 16, and 32 notes of the $1.00 and $2.00 denominations.

		VF	UNC
468	**1 Dollar**		
	1981. George Washington at center. Back: Great Seal flanking ONE.		
	a. 1981. (A-L).	FV	4.00
	b. 1981A. (A-L).	FV	4.00
469	**5 Dollars**		
	1981. Abraham Lincoln at center. Back: Lincoln Memorial.		
	a. 1981. (A-L).	FV	20.00
	b. 1981A. (A-L).	FV	20.00
470	**10 Dollars**		
	1981. Alexander Hamilton at center. Back: Treasury Building.		
	a. 1981. (A-L).	FV	40.00
	b. 1981A. (A-L).	FV	40.00

		VF	UNC
471	**20 Dollars**		
	1981. Andrew Jackson at center. Back: White House.		
	a. 1981. (A-L).	FV	75.00
	b. 1981A. (A-L).	FV	60.00

		VF	UNC
472	**50 Dollars**		
	1981. Ulysses Grant at center. Back: United States Capital Building.		
	a. 1981. (A-L).	FV	200.
	b. 1981A. (A-L).	FV	225.
473	**100 Dollars**		
	1981. Benjamin Franklin at center. Back: Independence Hall.		
	a. 1981. (A-L).	FV	275.
	b. 1981A. (A-L).	FV	275.

1985 Series

474 **1 Dollar** VF UNC
1985. (A-L). George Washington at center. Back: Great Seal flanking ONE. FV 4.00

		VF	UNC
475	**5 Dollars**		
	1985. (A-L). Abraham Lincoln at center. Back: Lincoln Memorial.	FV	15.00
476	**10 Dollars**		
	1985. (A-L). Alexander Hamilton at center. Back: Treasury Building.	FV	35.00
477	**20 Dollars**		
	1985. (A-L). Andrew Jackson at center. Back: White House.	FV	50.00
478	**50 Dollars**		
	1985. (A-L). Ulysses Grant at center. Back: United States Capital Building.	FV	120.

479 **100 Dollars** VF UNC
1985. (A-L). Benjamin Franklin at center. Back: Independence Hall. FV 175.

1988 Series

		VF	UNC
480	**1 Dollar**		
	1988. George Washington at center. Back: Great Seal flanking ONE.		
	a. 1988. (A-L).	FV	4.00
	b. 1988A. (A-L).	FV	4.00
	c. 1988A Web Press. (A-C; E-G).	8.00	40.00
481	**5 Dollars**		
	1988. Abraham Lincoln at center. Back: Lincoln Memorial.		
	a. 1988. (A-L).	FV	15.00
	b. 1988A. (A-L).	FV	15.00

482 **10 Dollars** VF UNC
1988A (A-L). Alexander Hamilton at center. Back: Treasury Building. FV 35.00

483 20 Dollars VF UNC
1988A (A-L). Andrew Jackson at center. Back: White House. FV 50.00

484 50 Dollars VF UNC
1988 (A-L). Ulysses Grant at center. Back: United States Capital Building. FV 150.

485 100 Dollars VF UNC
1988 (A-L). Benjamin Franklin at center. Back: Independence Hall. FV 200.

1990 Series

#486-489 w/additional row of micro-printing: ***THE UNITED STATES OF AMERICA*** **repeated around portr. Filament w/value and** ***U.S.A.*** **repeated inversely at l.**

486 10 Dollars VF UNC
1990. (A-L). Alexander Hamilton at center. Back: Treasury Building. FV 20.00

487 20 Dollars VF UNC
1990. (A-L). Andrew Jackson at center. Back: White House. FV 30.00

488 50 Dollars
1990. (A-L). Ulysses Grant at center. Back: United States Capital Building. FV 100.

489 100 Dollars
1990. (A-L). Benjamin Franklin at center. Back: Independence Hall. FV 150.

1993 Series

490 1 Dollar VF UNC
1993. George Washington at center. Back: Great Seal flanking ONE.
a. 1993. (A-G; L). FV 2.00
b. 1993. Web Press. (G-I; K; L). 4.00 15.00

491 5 Dollars
1993 (A-C; E-L). Abraham Lincoln at center. Back: Lincoln Memorial. FV 15.00

492 10 Dollars VF UNC
1993 (A-D, F-H, J, L). Alexander Hamilton at center. Back: Treasury Building. FV 20.00

493 20 Dollars
1993. (A-L). Andrew Jackson at center. Back: White House. FV 40.00

494 50 Dollars VF UNC
1993 (A, B, D, E, G, H, J, K). Ulysses Grant at center. Back: Unites States Capital Building. FV 135.

495 100 Dollars VF UNC
1993. (A-L). Benjamin Franklin at center. Back: Independence Hall. FV 150.

1995 Series

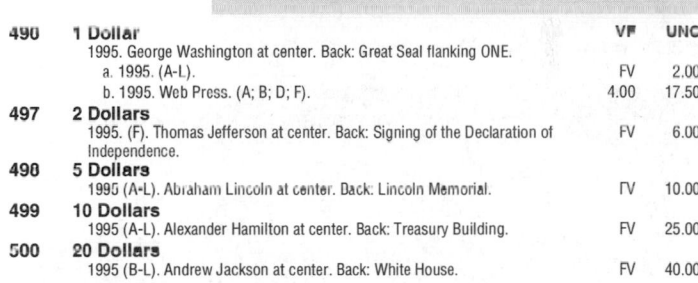

496 1 Dollar VF UNC
1995. George Washington at center. Back: Great Seal flanking ONE.
a. 1995. (A-L). FV 2.00
b. 1995. Web Press. (A; B; D; F). 4.00 17.50

497 2 Dollars
1995. (F). Thomas Jefferson at center. Back: Signing of the Declaration of Independence. FV 6.00

498 5 Dollars
1995 (A-L). Abraham Lincoln at center. Back: Lincoln Memorial. FV 10.00

499 10 Dollars
1995 (A-L). Alexander Hamilton at center. Back: Treasury Building. FV 25.00

500 20 Dollars
1995 (B-L). Andrew Jackson at center. Back: White House. FV 40.00

1996 Series

#501-503 redesigned and enlarged portr. on face at l. ctr. and as wmk. Green value at lower r. Security thread at l. Backs similar to #493-495.

501 20 Dollars VF UNC
1996. (A1-L12). Andrew Jackson at left center. Green value at lower right. Security thread at left. Back: White House. Watermark: Andrew Jackson. FV 30.00

502 **50 Dollars** | VF FV | UNC 60.00

1996 (A1-L12). Ulysses Grant at left center. Green value at lower right. Security thread at left. Back: United States Capital Building. Watermark: Ulysses Grant.

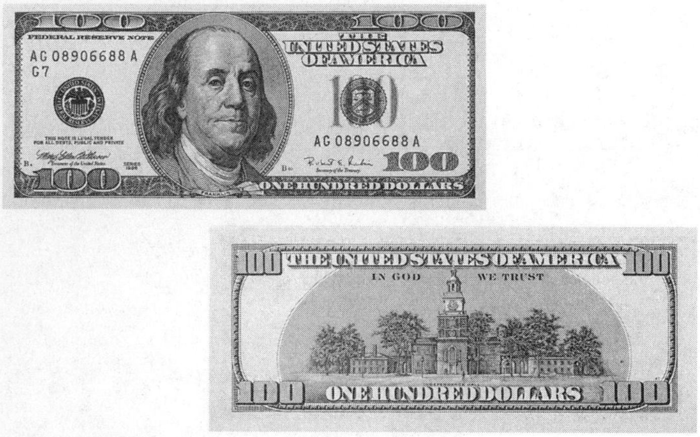

503 **100 Dollars** | VF FV | UNC 115.

1996 (A1-L12). Benjamin Franklin at left center. Green value at lower right. Security thread at left. Back: Independence Hall. Watermark: Benjamin Franklin.

1999 Series

#505-507 redesigned and enlarged portr. on face at l. ctr. and as wmk.

504 **1 Dollar** | VF FV | UNC 2.00

1999 (A-L). Black. George Washington at left center. Back: Great Seal flanking ONE.

505 **5 Dollars** | VF FV | UNC 10.00

1999 (A1-L12). Abraham Lincoln at left center. Back: Lincoln Memorial. Watermark: Abraham Lincoln.

506 **10 Dollars** | VF FV | UNC 15.00

1999 (A1-L12). Alexander Hamilton at left center. Redesigned and enlarged portrait at left center. Back: Treasury Building. Watermark: Alexander Hamilton.

507 **20 Dollars** | VF FV | UNC 30.00

1999 (A1-L12). Andrew Jackson at left center. Back: White House. Watermark: Andrew Jackson.

508 **100 Dollars** | VF FV | UNC 115.

1999(A1-L12). Benjamin Franklin at center. Back: Independence Hall.

2001 Series

509 **1 Dollar** | VF FV | UNC 2.00

2001 (A-L). George Washington at center. Back: Great Seal flanking ONE.

510 **5 Dollars** | VF FV | UNC 10.00

2001 (A1-L12). Abraham Lincoln at center. Back: Lincoln Memorial. Watermark: Abraham Lincoln.

511 **10 Dollars** | VF FV | UNC 20.00

2001 (A1-L12). Alexander Hamilton at center. Back: Treasury Building. Watermark: Alexander Hamilton.

512 20 Dollars — VF | UNC
2001 (A1-L12). Andrew Jackson at center. Back: White House. Watermark: Andrew Jackson. — FV | 30.00

513 50 Dollars — VF | UNC
2001 (A1-L12). Ulysses Grant at center. Back: United States Capital Building. Watermark: Ulysses Grant. — FV | 60.00

514 100 Dollars — VF | UNC
2001 (A1-L12). Benjamin Franklin at center. Back: Independence Hall. Watermark: Benjamin Franklin. — FV | 115.

2003 Series

515 1 Dollar — VF | UNC
2003. George Washington at center. Back: Great Seal flanking ONE.

	VF	UNC
a. 2003 (A-L).	FV	2.00
b. 2003A (A-L).	FV	2.00

516 2 Dollars — VF | UNC
2003. Thomas Jefferson at center. Back: Signing of the Declaration of Independence.

	VF	UNC
a. 2003. (A-L).	FV	7.50
b. 2003A. (A-L).	FV	7.50

517 5 Dollars
2003. Abraham Lincoln at center. Back: Lincoln Memorial. Watermark: Abraham Lincoln.

	VF	UNC
a. 2003. (A1-L12).	FV	10.00
b. 2003A. (A1-L12).	FV	10.00

518 10 Dollars
2003 (A1-L12). Alexander Hamilton at center. Back: Treasury Building. Watermark: Alexander Hamilton. — FV | 17.50

519 100 Dollars — VF | UNC
2003. Benjamin Franklin at center. Back: Indepence Hall. Watermark: Benjamin Franklin.

	VF	UNC
a. 2003. (A1-L12).	FV	120.
b. 2003A. (A1-L12).	FV	120.

2004 Series

#519-520 redesigned face and back, color underprint.

520 10 Dollars — VF | UNC
2004A (A1-L12). Black on beige underprint. Alexander Hamilton at left center. Back: Treasury Building. Watermark: Alexander Hamilton. — FV | 15.00

521 20 Dollars — VF | UNC
2004. Black on light green, blue and tan underprint. Andrew Jackson at left center. Back: Green. White House. Watermark: Andrew Jackson.

	VF	UNC
a. 2004 (A1-L12).	FV	27.50
b. 2004A (A1-A12).	FV	27.50

522 50 Dollars — VF | UNC
2004. Black on multicolor underprint. Ulysses Grant at center. Back: Green United States Capital Building. Watermark: Ulysses Grant.

	VF	UNC
a. 2004 (A1-L12).	FV	60.00
b. 2004A (A1-A12).	FV	60.00

2006 Series

523 1 Dollar VF UNC

2006. Black. George Washington at center. Back: Green. Great Seal flanking ONE.

a. 2006 (A-L). FV 2.00

b. 2006A (A-E, F-H, K-L). FV 2.00

523A 5 Dollars

2006. Black. Abraham Lincoln at center. Back: Lincoln Memorial. Watermark: Abraham Lincoln FV 10.00

524 5 Dollars VF UNC

2006. Black on blue underprint. Abraham Lincoln at left center. Back: Lincoln Memorial. Watermark: Large 5. FV 7.50

525 10 Dollars VF UNC

2006. Black on beige underprint. Alexander Hamilton at left center. Back: Treasury Building. Watermark: Alexander Hamilton. FV 15.00

526 20 Dollars VF UNC

2006. Black on light green underprint. Andrew Jackson at left center. Back: Green. White House. Watermark: Andrew Jackson. FV 27.50

527 50 Dollars VF UNC

2006. Black on red and blue underprint. Ulysses Grant at left center. Back: Green. United States Capital Building. Watermark: Ulysses Grant. FV 60.00

528 100 Dollars VF UNC

2006. Black. Benjamin Franklin at center. Back: Green. Independence Hall. Watermark: Benjamin Franklin. FV 120.

2006A Colorized Series

529 100 Dollars Mkt. Value

2006A. Black and multicolor. Benjamin Franklin at left center. Back: Independence Hall. Watermark: Benjamin Franklin —

2009 Series

530 1 Dollar VF UNC

2009. Black. George Washington at center. Back: Great Seal flanking ONE. FV 2.00

531 5 Dollars

2009. Black on blue underprint. Abraham Lincoln at left center. Back: Lincoln Memorial. Watermark: Large 5. FV 10.00

532 10 Dollars

2009. Black on beige underprint. Alexander Hamilton at left center. Back: Treasury Building. Watermark: Alexander Hamilton. FV 15.00

533 20 Dollars

2009. Black on light green underprint. Andrew Jackson at left center. Back: White House. Watermark: Andrew Jackson. FV 27.50

534 50 Dollars

2009. Black on red and blue underprint. Ulysses Grant at left center. Back: United States Capital Building. Watermark: Ulysses Grant. FV 60.00

535 100 Dollars

2009. Black. Benjamin Franklin at left center. Back: Independence Hall. Watermark: Benjamin Franklin. FV 125.

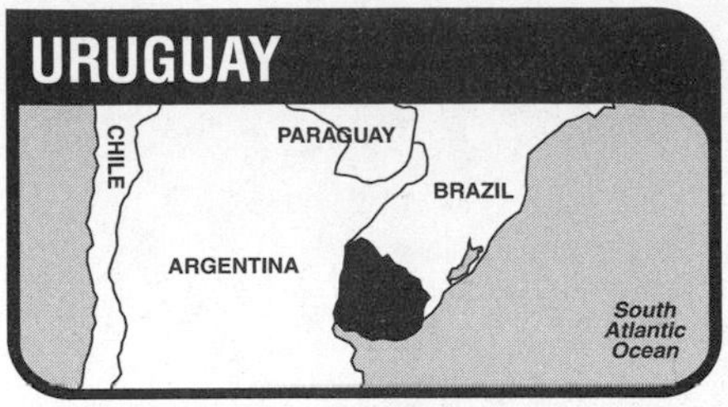

The Oriental Republic of Uruguay (so called because of its location on the east bank of the Uruguay River) is situated on the Atlantic coast of South America between Argentina and Brazil. This most advanced of South American countries has an area of 176,220 sq. km. and a population of 3.48 million. Capital: Montevideo. Uruguay's chief economic asset is its rich, rolling grassy plains. Meat, wool, hides and skins are exported.

Montevideo, founded by the Spanish in 1726 as a military stronghold, soon took advantage of its natural harbor to become an important commercial center. Claimed by Argentina but annexed by Brazil in 1821, Uruguay declared its independence four years later and secured its freedom in 1828 after a three-year struggle. The administrations of President Jose Battle in the early 20th century established widespread political, social, and economic reforms that established a statist tradition. A violent Marxist urban guerrilla movement named the Tupamaros, launched in the late 1960s, led Uruguay's president to cede control of the government to the military in 1973. By year end, the rebels had been crushed, but the military continued to expand its hold over the government. Civilian rule was not restored until 1985. In 2004, the left-of-center Frente Amplio Coalition won national elections that effectively ended 170 years of political control previously held by the Colorado and Blanco parties. Uruguay's political and labor conditions are among the freest on the continent.

MONETARY SYSTEM:

1 Peso = 100 Centésimos, 1860-1975
1 Nuevo Peso = 1000 Old Pesos, 1975-1993
1 Peso Uruguayo = 1000 Nuevos Pesos, 1993-

Office Titles:

1 - Gerente General, Secretario General, Presidente
2 - Co-Gerente General, Secretario General, Presidente
3 - p.Gerente General, Secretario General, Presidente
4 - Gerente General, Secretario General, Vicepresidente
5 - Gerente General, Secretario General, 2o Vicepresidente
6 - p.Gerente General, Secretario General, Vicepresidente
7 - Secretario General, Presidente

REPUBLIC

BANCO CENTRAL DEL URUGUAY

1967 ND PROVISIONAL ISSUE

#42-45 Banco Central was organized in 1967 and used notes of previous issuing authority with Banco Central signature title overprint.

42	10 Pesos	VF	UNC
	L.1939 (1967). Purple on multicolor underprint. J. G. Artigas at lower center, arms at upper left. Series D. Signature title 1. Back: Farmer with 3-team ox-cart. Printer: TDLR.		
	a. Bank name below title: *Banco Central de la República.*	3.00	10.00
	b. Bank name below title: *Banco Central del Uruguay.*	2.50	7.50

42A	50 Pesos	VF	UNC
	L.1939 (1967). Blue and brown on multicolor underprint. Warrior wearing helmet at right, arms at upper left. Series D. Back: Group of people with flag. Printer: TDLR.		
	a. Bank name below all 3 signatures. Signature title: 1.	3.00	7.50
	b. Bank name below 2 signatures at right. Signature title: 3.	3.00	10.00

43	100 Pesos	VF	UNC
	L.1939 (1967). Red and brown. "Constitution" at right, arms at center. Series D. Back: People in town square. Printer: TDLR.		
	a. Bank name below 3 signature *Banco Central del Uruguay.* Signature title: 1, 3; *PRESIDENTE* at right.	3.50	12.00
	b. Bank name below 2 signature at l.: *Banco Central del Uruguay.* Signature title: 4; 6 *VICE PRESIDENTE* at right.	3.50	12.00
	c. Bank name below 2 signature at right. Signature title: 3.	3.50	12.00

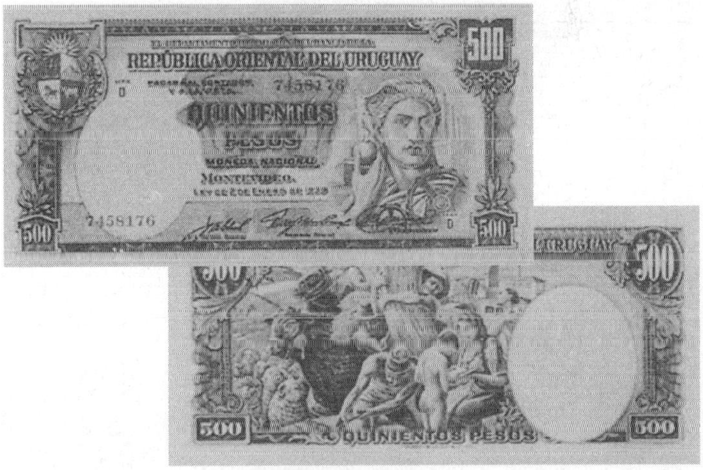

44	500 Pesos	VF	UNC
	L.1939. Green and blue. "Industry" at right, arms at upper left. Series D. Back: People with symbols of agriculture. Printer: TDLR.		
	a. Signature Like #42a.	6.00	17.50
	b. Signature like #42b.	6.00	17.50

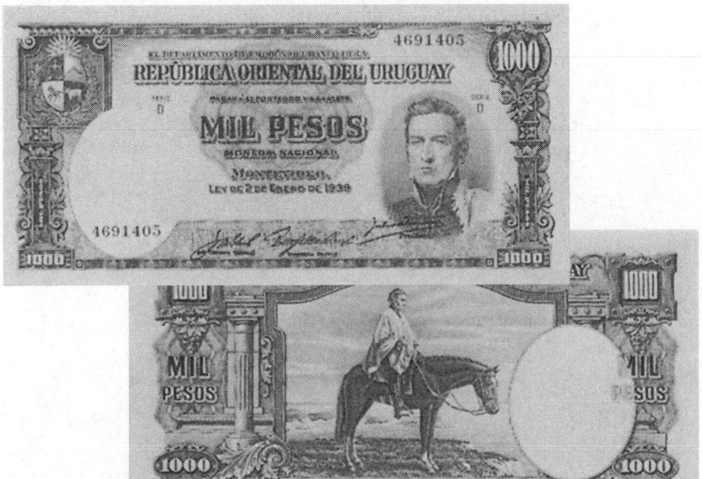

45	1000 Pesos	VF	UNC
	L.1939. Purple and black on pale yellow underprint. Jose Gervasio Artigas at right, arms at upper left. Series D. Signature like # 42a. Back: Man on horseback at center. Printer: TDLR.	8.00	25.00

1967 ND Issue

#46-51 Jose Gervasio Artigas at ctr.

46	50 Pesos	VF	UNC
	ND (1967). Deep blue on light green and lilac underprint. Arms at left. Jose Gervasio Artigas at center. Signature titles: 1; 2; 4. Series A. Back: Group of 33 men with flag. Printer: TDLR. UV: rays around Artigas head fluoresce green.		
	a. Issued note.	.25	1.75
	s. Specimen.	—	55.00

47	100 Pesos	VF	UNC
	ND (1967). Red on lilac and light gold underprint. Arms at left. Jose Gervasio Artigas at center. Signature titles: 1; 2; 3. Back: Man presiding at independence meeting. Printer: TDLR.		
	a. Issued note.	.25	1.75
	s. Specimen.	—	55.00

48	500 Pesos	VF	UNC
	ND (1967). Green and blue on orange and light green underprint. Jose Gervasio Artigas at center. Signature titles: 1; 2. Back: Dam. Watermark: Arms. Printer: TDLR.		
	a. Issued note.	1.25	7.00
	s. Specimen.	—	55.00

49	1000 Pesos	VF	UNC
	ND (1967). Purple and black on blue and yellow underprint. Jose Gervasio Artigas at center. Signature titles: 1; 2; 3; 4. Back: Large building. Watermark: Arms. Printer: TDLR.		
	a. Issued note.	1.25	6.00
	s. Specimen.	—	60.00

50	5000 Pesos	VF	UNC
	ND (1967). Brown and blue-green on lilac and light blue underprint. Jose Gervasio Artigas at center. Signature title varieties. Back: Bank. Watermark: Arms. Printer: TDLR.		
	a. Series A; B. Signature titles: 1, 4, 5, 6.	5.00	25.00
	b. Series C. Signature title: 2.	1.00	4.50
	s. Specimen.	—	60.00

51	10,000 Pesos	VF	UNC
	ND (1967). Dark green and black on yellow and light orange underprint. Jose Gervasio Artigas at center. Signature title varieties. Back: Building. Watermark: Arms. Printer: TDLR.		
	a. Series A. Signature title: 1.	12.50	35.00
	b. Series A. Signature title: 6.	15.00	40.00
	c. Series B. Signature titles: 2, 3, 4.	12.50	30.00
	s. Specimen.	—	65.00

1974 ND Issue

#52 replacement notes: Serial # prefix *R*.

52	1000 Pesos	VF	UNC
	ND (1974). Violet and dark green on multicolor underprint. Arms at upper left center, Artigas at right. Signature title: 2. Back: Building. Watermark: Artigas. Printer: CdeM-A.	1.00	3.00

53	10,000 Pesos	VF	UNC
	ND (1974). Orange on multicolor underprint. Arms at upper left center, J. G. Artigas at right. Signature varieties. Back: Palace Esteze at left center. Watermark: Artigas. Printer: TDLR.		
	a. Series A. Signature titles: 2.	3.00	10.00
	b. Series B. Signature titles: 2.	2.50	7.00
	c. Series C. Signature titles: 1.	2.00	6.00

1975 ND Provisional Issue

#54-58 new value ovpt. in black on wmk. area on face only.

54	0.50 Nuevo Peso on 500 Pesos	VF	UNC
	ND (1975). Green and blue on orange and light green underprint. Jose Gervasio Artigas at center with overprint. Signature titles: 1. Back: Dam. Overprint: Value in black on watermark area on face only. Watermark: Arms. Printer: TDLR.	.25	1.50

55	1 Nuevo Peso on 1000 Pesos	VF	UNC
	ND (1975). Purple and black on blue and yellow underprint. Jose Gervasio Artigas at center with overprint. Signature titles: 1. Back: Large building. Overprint: Value in black on watermark area on face only. Watermark: Arms. Printer: TDLR.	1.00	3.50

56	1 Nuevo Peso on 1000 Pesos	VF	UNC
	ND (1975). Violet and dark green on multicolor underprint. Arms at upper left center, Artigas at right with overprint. Signature title: 2. Back: Building. Overprint: Value in black on watermark area on face only. Watermark: Artigas. Printer: CdeM-A.	1.00	4.00

57	5 Nuevos Pesos on 5000 Pesos	VF	UNC
	ND (1975). Brown on multicolor underprint. J. G. Artigas at right, arms at left center, overprint new value at left. Signature titles: 2. Back: Old Banco de la República. Overprint: Value in black on watermark area on face only. Printer: CdM-A.	1.25	5.00

58	10 Nuevos Pesos on 10,000 Pesos	VF	UNC
	ND (1975). Orange on multicolor underprint. Arms at upper left center, J. G. Artigas at right with overprint. Series C. Signature titles: 1. Back: Palace Esteze at left center. Overprint: Value in black on watermark area on face only. Watermark: J. G. Artigas. Printer: TDLR.	4.00	15.00

Ley No. 14.316; 1975 ND Issue

59	50 Nuevos Pesos	VF	UNC
	ND (1975). Deep blue on multicolor underprint. Arms near center, J. G. Artigas at right. Series A.Three signatures. Signature titles: 1. Back: Old Government palace. Watermark: J. G. Artigas. Printer: TDLR.	5.00	9.00

60	100 Nuevos Pesos	VF	UNC
	ND (1975). Olive-green on multicolor underprint. Arms near center, J. G. Artigas at right. Series A.Three signatures. Signature titles: 1. Back: Old Government palace. Watermark: J. G. Artigas. Printer: TDLR.		
	a. Issued note.	6.00	15.00
	s. Specimen.	—	—

Ley No. 14.316; 1978-88 ND Issues

#61-64A Replacement notes: 8 digit serial # starting w/*9*.

61 50 Nuevos Pesos VF UNC

ND (1978-87). Deep blue on multicolor underprint. Arms near center, J. G. Artigas at right, without text: *PAGARA....A LA VISTA* at center. Series A.Three signatures. Back: Old Government palace. Watermark: J. G. Artigas. Printer: TDLR.

	VF	UNC
a. 2 Signatures. Series B (1978). Signature titles: 7.	1.50	6.00
b. 3 Signatures. Series C (1980). Signature titles: 1.	1.00	5.00
c. 2 Signatures. Series D (1981). Signature titles: 7.	.75	3.00
d. 3 Signatures. Series E (1987). Signature titles: 1.	.50	2.00

61A 50 Nuevos Pesos VF UNC

ND (1988-89). Arms near center, J. G. Artigas at right, portrait of Artigas in watermark area, without text *PAGARA....A LA VISTA* at center. Series F (1988); Series G (1989). Three signatures. Signature titl Back: Old Government palace. Watermark: J. G. Artigas. Printer: TDLR. .20 .75

62 100 Nuevos Pesos VF UNC

ND (1978-86). Olive-green on multicolor underprint. Arms near center, J. G. Artigas at right, without text: *PAGARA....A LA VISTA* at center. Series A.Three signatures. Back: Old Government palace. Watermark: J. G. Artigas. Printer: TDLR.

	VF	UNC
a. 2 Signature. Series B (1978). Signature titles: 7.	2.50	7.50
b. 3 Signature. Series C (1980); Series D (1981). Signature titles: 1.	.50	3.00
c. Series E (1985); Series F (1986). Signature titles: 1.	.25	1.00
s. Specimen. As c. Series E. Black overprint: *MUESTRA SIN VALOR* on both sides.	—	75.00

62A 100 Nuevos Pesos VF UNC

ND (1987). Olive-green on multicolor underprint. Arms near center, J. G. Artigas at right, without text: *PAGARA....A LA VISTA* at center. Portrait of Artigas printed in watermark area. Series G (1987). Three signatures. Signature titles: 1. Back: Old Government palace. Watermark: J. G. Artigas. Printer: TDLR. .50 2.00

63 500 Nuevos Pesos VF UNC

ND (1978-85). Red on multicolor underprint. Arms near center, J. G. Artigas at right, without text: *PAGARA....A LA VISTA* at center. Series A.Three signatures. Signature titles: 1. Back: Old Government palace. Watermark: J. G. Artigas. Printer: TDLR.

	VF	UNC
a. 2 Signature. Series A (1978). Signature titles: 7.	4.00	12.50
b. 3 Signature. Series B (1978); Series C (1985). Signature titles: 1.	.75	3.50
s. Specimen. As b. Series C. Black overprint: *MUESTRA SIN VALOR* on both sides.	—	75.00

63A 500 Nuevos Pesos VF UNC

ND (1991). Red on multicolor underprint. Arms near center, J. G. Artigas at right, without text: *PAGARA....A LA VISTA* at center. Portrait of Artigas printed in watermark area. Series D (1991). Three signatures. Signature titles: 1. Back: Old Government palace. Printer: TDLR. .50 1.50

64 1000 Nuevos Pesos VF UNC

ND(1978-81). Purple on multicolor underprint. Arms near center, J. G. Artigas at right, without text: *PAGARA....A LA VISTA* at center. Series A.Three signatures. Back: Old Government palace. Watermark: J. G. Artigas. Printer: TDLR.

	VF	UNC
a. 2 Signature. Series A (1978). Signature titles: 7.	4.50	12.50
b. 3 Signature. Series B (1981). Signature titles: 1.	1.50	5.00

64A	1000 Nuevos Pesos	VF	UNC
	ND (1991-92). Purple on multicolor underprint. Arms near center, J. G. Artigas at right, without text: *PAGARA....A LA VISTA* at center. Portrait of Artigas printed in watermark area. Series A. Three signatures. Back: Old Government palace. Printer: TDLR.		
	a. Series C (1991). Signature titles: 1.	1.00	3.50
	b. Series D (1992). Signature titles: 1.	.50	2.50

65	5000 Nuevos Pesos	VF	UNC
	ND (1983). Deep brown, orange-brown and blue on multicolor underprint. Arms at top left center, Brig. General Juan Antonio Lavalleja at right. Series A; B; C. Signature titles: 1. Back: Multicolor. 1830 scene of pledging allegiance at center. Printer: TDLR.		
	a. Issued note.	1.50	5.00
	s. Specimen. Black overprint. *MUESTRA SIN VALOR* on both sides.	—	75.00

Ley No. 14.316; 1986; 1987 ND Issue

#66 replacement notes. Series A-R.

66	200 Nuevos Pesos	VF	UNC
	1986. Dark and light green on brown and multicolor underprint. Quill and scroll at left, arms at center, J. E. Rodo at right. Series A. Signature titles: 1 Back: Rodo Monument at center, statuary at left and center. Watermark: J. G. Artigas. Printer: C. Ciccone S.A.		
	a. Isused note.	.25	1.50
	s. Specimen. Red overprint: *SIN VALOR* on face.	—	75.00

67	10,000 Nuevos Pesos	VF	UNC
	ND (1987). Purple, dark blue, dark olive-green and violet on multicolor underprint. Plaza of Democracy with flag at left center. Signature titles: 1. Back: 19 departmental arms. Printer: ABNC.		
	a. Overprint gold gilt bars on description and law designation. Series A.	25.00	75.00
	b. No overprint bars on new inscription at left, *DECRETO-LEY NO. 14.316* at upper right. Series B; C.	2.00	7.50
	s1. Note as printed but without gold bar overprint. Series A. Specimen.	—	1250.
	s2. Note as printed, with gold bar overprint. Specimen. Red overprint: *MUESTRA SIN VALOR* on face. Punch hole cancelled.	—	1250.
	s3. Specimen. As b. Series B. Red overprint: *MUESTRA SIN VALOR* on face, punch hole cancelled.	—	250.

1989-92 Issue

67A	1000 Nuevos Pesos	VF	UNC
	1989. Brown and orange on multicolor underprint. Pedro Figari at right. Back: Allegory of Music. Overprint: *NO EMITIDO*. Specimen. (Not issued.)	—	35.00

68	2000 Nuevos Pesos	VF	UNC
	1989. Dark brown and orange on multicolor underprint. Arms at upper left. Latent image with letters B/CU at upper right. J. M. Blanes at center right. Series A. Signature titles: 1. Back: Altar of the Homeland (allegory of the Republic). Watermark: J.G. Artigas. Printer: TDLR. UV: value 2000 in box fluoresces orange, BCU yellow; vertical serial # orange. Back right design yellow.		
	a. Issued note.	.50	2.00
	b. Specimen. Black overprint: *NUESTRA SIN VALOR* on both sides.	—	75.00

68A	5000 Nuevos Pesos	VF	UNC
	1989. Brown and orange on multicolor underprint. Pedro Figari at right. Arms at upper left, latent image at upper right with letters B/CU. Signature titles: 1. Back: *Baile Antiguo* (old dance). Overprint: *NO EMITIDO*. Watermark: J.G. Artigas. Printer: TDLR. Specimen. (Not issued.)	—	35.00

68B	10,000 Nuevos Pesos	VF	UNC
	1989. Brown and orange on multicolor underprint. Arms at upper left. Latent image at upper right with letters B/CU. Alfredo Vasquez Acevedo at right. Signature titles: 1. Back: University of the Republic. Overprint: *NO EMITIDO*. Watermark: J. G. Artigas. Printer: TDLR. Specimen. (Not issued.)	—	35.00

69	20,000 Nuevos Pesos	VF	UNC
	1989; 1991. Dark green and violet on multicolor underprint. Arms at upper left. Latent image (silver oval) at upper right with letters B/CU. Dr. J. Zorrilla de San Martin at center right. Series A. Signature titles: 1. Back: Manuscript and allegory of the legend of the homeland (Victory with wings). Watermark: J.G. Artigas. Printer: TDLR.		
	a. 1989.	3.50	8.00
	b. 1991.	3.50	8.00
	s. Specimen. As a. Black overprint: *NUESTRA SIN VALOR* on both sides.	—	100.

70	50,000 Nuevos Pesos	VF	UNC
	1989; 1991. Black, violet and red on multicolor underprint. Arms at upper left. Latent image (silver oval) at upper right with letters B/CU. José Pedro Varela at center right. Series A. Signature titles: 1. Back: Varela Monument at left. Watermark: J. G. Artigas. Printer: TDLR.		
	a. 1989.	7.50	17.50
	b. 1991.	7.50	17.50
	s. Specimen. As a, b. Black overprint: *MUESTRA SIN VALOR* on both sides.	—	100.

71	100,000 Nuevos Pesos	VF	UNC
	1991. Purple and dark brown on multicolor underprint. Arms at upper left. Latent image (silver oval) at upper right with letters B/CU. Eduardo Fabini at right center. Series A. Signature titles: 1. Back: Musical allegory. Watermark: J. G. Artigas. Printer: TDLR.		
	a. Issued note.	15.00	32.50
	s. Specimen. Black overprint: *MUESTRA SIN VALOR* on both sides.	—	125.

72	200,000 Nuevos Pesos	VF	UNC
	1992. Dark brown and violet and orange on multicolor underprint. Arms at upper left. Latent image (silver oval) at upper right with letters B/CU. Pedro Figari at center right. Series A. Signature titles: 1. Back: Old dance at left. Watermark: J. G. Artigas. Printer: TDLR.		
	a. Issued note.	27.50	65.00
	s. Specimen. Black overprint: *MUESTRA SIN VALOR* on both sides.	—	150.
73	**500,000 Nuevos Pesos**		
	1992. Blue-gray, violet and pale red on multicolor underprint. Arms at upper left. Latent image (silver oval) at upper right with letters B/CU. Alfredo Vaquez Acevedo at center right. Series A. Signature titles: 1. Back: University of Montevideo at left. Watermark: J. G. Artigas. Printer: TDLR.		
	a. Issued note.	65.00	125.
	s. Specimen. Black overprint: *MUESTRA SIN VALOR* on both sides.	—	150.

1994-97 Issue

1 Peso Uruguayo = 1000 Nuevos Pesos, 1993-

73A	5 Pesos Uruguayos	VF	UNC
	ND (1997). Dark brown, red-brown and blue on multicolor underprint. Arms at top left center, Brig. General Juan Antonio Lavalleja at right. Series A. Signature titles: 1. Back: 1830 scene of pledging allegiance at center. Printer: TDLR.		
	a. Issued note.	FV	2.00
	s. Specimen. Red overprint: *MUESTRA SIN VALOR* on both sides.	—	75.00

73B	10 Pesos Uruguayos	VF	UNC
	ND (1995). Purple, dark blue, dark olive-green and violet on multicolor underprint. Plaza of Democracy with flag at left center. Signature titles: 1. Back: 19 departmental arms. Printer: G&D.		
	a. With Decreto-Ley No.14.316 (error). Series A.	FV	4.00
	b. Without Ley. Series B.	FV	3.50
	s. Specimen. As a. Red overprint: *MUESTRA SIN VALOR* on each side.	—	75.00

74 20 Pesos Uruguayos VF UNC

1994; 1997. Dark green and violet on multicolor underprint. Arms at upper left. Latent image (silver oval) at upper right with letters B/CU. Dr. J. Zorrilla de San Martin at center right. Signature titles: 1. Back: Manuscript and allegory of the legend of the homeland (Victory with wings). Watermark: J. G. Artigas. Printer: TDLR.

	VF	UNC
a. 1994. Series A.	FV	4.50
b. 1997. Series B.	FV	4.50
s. Specimen. As a. Pin hole cancelled.	—	75.00

75 50 Pesos Uruguayos VF UNC

1994; 2000. Black, red and violet on multicolor underprint. Arms at upper left. Latent image (silver oval) at upper right with letters B/CU. José Pedro Varela at center right. Series A, B. Signature titles: 1. Back: Varela Monument at left. Watermark: J. G. Artigas. Printer: TDLR.

	VF	UNC
a. 1994.	FV	10.00
b. 2000.	FV	10.00
s. Specimen. As a. Pin hole cancelled.	—	100.

76 100 Pesos Uruguayos VF UNC

1994; 1997; 2000. Purple and dark brown on multicolor underprint. Arms at upper left. Latent image (silver oval) at upper right with letters B/CU. Eduardo Fabini at right center. Series A; B; C. Signature titles: 1. Back: Musical allegory. Watermark: J. G. Artigas. Printer: TDLR.

	VF	UNC
a. 1994.	FV	17.50
b. 1997.	FV	17.50
c. 2000.	FV	17.50
s. Specimen. As a. Pin hole cancelled.	—	100.

77 200 Pesos Uruguayos VF UNC

1995; 2000. Dark brown-violet on multicolor underprint. Arms at upper left. Latent image (silver oval) at upper right with letters B/CU. Pedro Figari at center right. Series A; B. Signature titles: 1. Back: Old dance at left. Watermark: J. G. Artigas. Printer: TDLR.

	VF	UNC
a. 1995.	FV	35.00
b. 2000.	FV	35.00
s. Specimen. As a. Pin hole cancelled.	—	150.

78 500 Pesos Uruguayos VF UNC

1994. Blue-gray, violet and pale red on multicolor underprint. Arms at upper left. Latent image (silver oval) at upper right with letters B/CU. Alfredo Vaquez Acevedo at center right. Series A. Signature titles: 1. Back: University of Montevideo at left. Watermark: J. G. Artigas. Printer: TDLR.

	VF	UNC
a. Issued note.	FV	75.00
s. Specimen. Pin hole cancelled.	—	175.

79 1000 Pesos Uruguayos VF UNC

1995, 2004. Brown and olive-green on multicolor underprint. Arms at upper right. Latent image at upper right with letters B/CU. Juana de Ibarbourou at right. Signature titles: 1. Back: Palm tree in Ibarbourou Square at left, books. Watermark: J. G. Artigas. Printer: TDLR

	VF	UNC
a. 1995. Series A. Imprint as TDLR.	FV	140.
b. 2004. Series B. Imprint as DLR.	FV	140.
s. Specimen. As a. Pin hole cancelled.	—	175.

1998 Issue

80 5 Pesos Uruguayos VF UNC

1998. Brown and orange-brown on blue and multicolor underprint. Joaquín Torres Garcia at right center. Series A. Signature titles: 1. Back: Garcia's painting at left. Printer: (T)DLR.

	VF	UNC
a. Issued note.	FV	2.00
s. Specimen. Red overprint: *MUESTRA SIN VALOR* one both sides.	—	75.00

81 10 Pesos Uruguayos VF UNC

1998. Slate black and light rose on multicolor underprint. Eduardo Acevedo Vásquez at right. Series A. Signature titles: 1. Back: Agronomy building at left. Printer: (T)DLR.

	VF	UNC
a. Issued note.	FV	3.00
s. Specimen. Red overprint: *MUESTRA SIN VALOR* on both sides.	—	75.00

1999 Issue

82	500 Pesos Uruguayos	VF	UNC
	1999. Blue on multicolor underprint. Arms at upper left. Latent image (silver oval) at upper right with letters B/CU. Alfredo Vaquez Acevedo at center right. Series B. Signature titles: 1. Back: University of Montevideo at left. Watermark: J. G. Artigas. Printer: FC-O.	FV	75.00

2000 Issue

83	20 Pesos Uruguayos	VF	UNC
	2000; 2003. Dark green and violet on multicolor underprint. Arms at upper left. Latent image (silver oval) at upper right with letters B/CU. Dr. J. Zorrilla de San Martin at center right. Series C. Signature titles: 1. Back: Manuscript and allegory of the legend of the homeland (Victory with wings). Watermark: J. G. Artigas. Printer: TDLR.		
	a. 2000.	FV	4.50
	b. 2003.	FV	4.50
83A	20 Pesos Uruguayos		
	2003. Dark green and violet on multicolor underprint. Dr. J. Zorrille de San Martin at center right. Arms at upper left. Latent image (silver oval) at upper right with letters B/CU. Series D. Signature titles: 1. Back: Manuscript and allegory of the legend of the homelaqnd (Victory with wings). Watermark: J. G. Artigas. Printer: F-CO.	FV	4.50

84	50 Pesos Uruguayos	VF	UNC
	2003. Black, red and violet on multicolor underprint. Arms at upper left. Latent image (silver oval) at upper right with letters B/CU. José Pedro Varela at center right. Series C. Signature titles: 1. Back: Varela Monument at left. Watermark: J. G. Artigas. Printer: F-CO.	FV	10.00

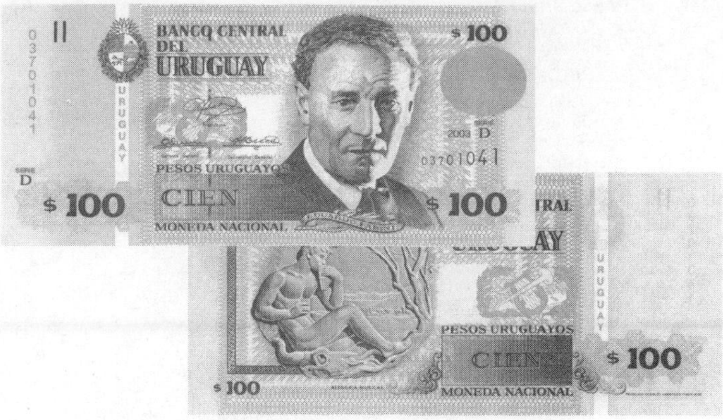

85	100 Pesos Uruguayos	VF	UNC
	2003. Purple and dark brown on multicolor underprint. Arms at upper left. Latent image (silver oval) at upper right with letters B/CU. Eduardo Fabini at right center. Series D. Signature titles: 1. Back: Musical allegory. Watermark: J. G. Artigas. Printer: F-CO.	FV	35.00

2003-2011 Issue

86	20 Pesos Uruguayos	VF	UNC
	2008; 2011. Green on multicolor underprint. Dr. Juan Zorrilla de San Martin at right center. Back: Allegory of the homeland at left. Printer: TDLR. 159x74mm.		
	a. 2008. Series E.	FV	3.50
	b. 2011. Series F.	FV	3.50

87	50 Pesos Uruguayos	VF	UNC
	2008; 2011. Black and rose on multicolor underprint. Jose Pedro Varela at right. Printer: F-CO. 159x74mm.		
	a. 2008. Series D.	FV	7.50
	b. 2011. Series E.	FV	7.50

88	100 Pesos Uruguayos	VF	UNC
	2008; 2011. Pruple on multicolor underprint. Eduardo Fabani at left center. Back: Musical muse seated under tree. Printer: TDLR. 159x74mm.		
	a. 2008. Series E.	FV	15.00
	b. 2011. Series F.	FV	15.00

		VF	UNC
89	**200 Pesos Uruguayos** 2006; 2009. Brown and orange on multicolor underprint. Pedro Figari. Signatrue titles: 1. Watermark: Figari and value. Printer: F-CO. 159x74mm.		
	a. 2006. Series C.	FV	30.00
	b. 2009. Series D.	FV	30.00
90	**500 Pesos Uruguayos** 2006. Alfredo Vaquez Acevedo. Similar to #82. Series C. Signatrue titles: 1. Watermark: Alfredo Acevedo and value. Printer: F-CO. 159x74mm.	FV	60.00

		VF	UNC
91	**1000 Pesos Uruguayos** 2004; 2006; 2008; 2011. Brown and green on multicolor underprint. Juana de Ibarbourou at right. Printer: F-CO. 159x74mm.		
	a. 2004. Series B.	FV	100.
	b. 2006.	FV	100.
	c. 2008. Series C.	FV	100.
	d. 2011. Series D.	FV	100.

		VF	UNC
92	**2000 Pesos Uruguayos** 2003. Gray and light olive-green. Dámaso Antonio Larrañaga at right. Series A. Signature titles: 1. Back: National Library. 159x74mm.		
	a. Issued note.	FV	250.
	s. Specimen. Red overprint: *MUESTRA SIN VALOR* on both sides.	—	300.

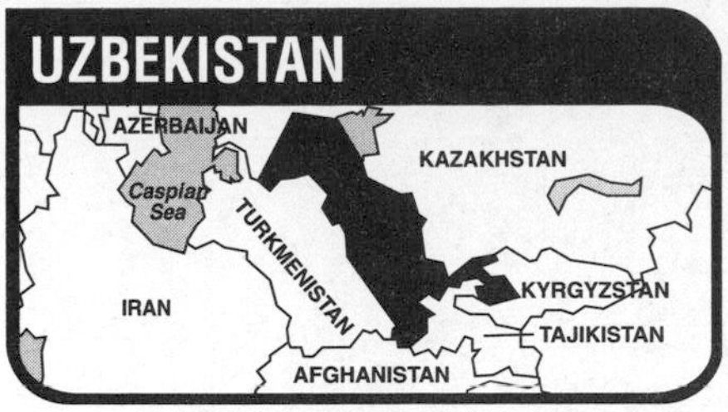

The Republic of Uzbekistan (formerly the Uzbek S.S.R.), is bordered on the north by Kazakhstan, to the east by Kirghizia and Tajikistan, on the south by Afghanistan and on the west by Turkmenistan. The republic is comprised of the regions of Andizhan, Bukhara, Dzhizak, Ferghana, Kashkadar, Khorezm (Khiva), Namangan, Navoi, Samarkand, Surkhan-Darya, Syr-Darya, Tashkent and the Karakalpak Autonomous Republic. It has an area of 447,400 sq. km. and a population of 27.34 million. Capital: Tashkent. Crude oil, natural gas, coal, copper and gold deposits make up the chief resources, while intensive farming, d on artificial irrigation, provides an abundance of cotton.

Russia conquered Uzbekistan in the late 19th century. Stiff resistance to the Red Army after World War I was eventually suppressed and a socialist republic set up in 1924. During the Soviet era, intensive production of "white gold" (cotton) and grain led to overuse of agrochemicals and the depletion of water supplies, which have left the land poisoned and the Aral Sea and certain rivers half dry. Independent since 1991, the country seeks to gradually lessen its dependence on agriculture while developing its mineral and petroleum reserves. Current concerns include terrorism by Islamic militants, economic stagnation, and the curtailment of human rights and democratization.

Monetary System:

1 THN_GA (Tenga) = 20 KOP_HK$ (Kopeks)
5 THN_GOV$ (Tengov) = 1 RCBP((Ruble)
1 Sum (Ruble) = 100 Kopeks, 1991
1 Sum = 1,000 Sum Coupon, 1994
1 S)M (Sum) = 100 TI(IN (Tiyin)

REPUBLIC

GOVERNMENT

КУПОНГА КАРТОЧКА - 1993 RUBLE CONTROL COUPONS

		VF	UNC
43	**10 and 25 Coupons** ND (1993). Black on pale blue underprint. Uniface.		
	a. Full sheet of 35 coupons with 2 registries.	—	5.00
	b. Top half sheet of 10 coupons with registry.	—	5.00
	c. Bottom half sheet of 25 coupons with registry.	—	5.00
	d. Coupon.	—	.10
44	**10 and 25 Coupons** ND (1993). Black on orange underprint. Uniface.		
	a. Full sheet of 35 coupons with 2 registries.	—	3.00
	b. Top half sheet of 10 coupons with registry.	—	2.00
	c. Bottom half sheet of 25 coupons with registry.	—	2.00
	d. Coupon.	—	.10
45	**10 and 25 Coupons** ND (1993). Black on pink underprint. Uniface.		
	a. Full sheet of 35 coupons with 2 registries.	—	7.00
	b. Top half sheet of 10 coupons with registry.	—	5.00
	c. Bottom half sheet of 25 coupons with registry.	—	5.00
	d. Coupon.	—	.10
46	**50 Coupons** ND (1993). Black on pale ochre underprint. Uniface.		
	a. Full sheet of 28 coupons with registry.	—	5.00
	b. Coupon.	—	.10
47	**100 Coupons** ND (1993). Black on violet underprint. Uniface.		
	a. Full sheet of 100 coupons with registry.	—	5.00
	b. Coupon.	—	.10

48 100 Coupons VF UNC

ND (1993). Black on tan underprint. Uniface.

a. Full sheet of 100 coupons with registry.	—	5.00
b. Coupon.	—	.10

49 100 Coupons

ND (1993). Black on light blue underprint. Uniface.

a. Full sheet of 100 coupons with registry.	—	5.00
b. Coupon.	—	.10

50 150 Coupons

ND (1993). Red on pale gray underprint. Uniface.

a. Full sheet of 150 coupons with registry.	—	5.00
b. Coupon.	—	.10

51 200 Coupons

ND (1993). Black on pink underprint. Uniface.

a. Full sheet of 200 coupons with registry.	—	5.00
b. Coupon.	—	.10

52 200 Coupons

ND (1993). Black on tan underprint. Uniface.

a. Full sheet of 200 coupons with registry.	—	.10
b. Coupon.	—	.10

58 2000 Coupons VF UNC

ND (1993). Blue on pink underprint. Uniface.

a. Full sheet of 28 coupons with registry.	—	8.00
b. Coupon.	—	.10

УЗБЕКИСТОН ДАВЛАТ БАНКИ

Bank of Uzbekistan

1992 (1993) Issue

61 1 Sum VF UNC

1992 (1993). Blue-gray on light blue and gold underprint. Arms at left. Back: Gray. Mosque at center. Watermark: Flower pattern repeated. Printer: H&S (without imprint).

a. Issued note.	1.00	2.00
s. Specimen.	—	25.00

62 3 Sum VF UNC

1992 (1993). Green on light blue and gold underprint. Arms at left. Back: Light green. Mosque at center. Watermark: Flower pattern repeated. Printer: H&S (without imprint).

a. Issued note.	1.00	2.50
s. Specimen.	—	25.00

63 5 Sum

1992 (1993). Purple on light blue and gold underprint. Arms at left. Back: Lilac. Mosque at center. Watermark: Flower pattern repeated. Printer: H&S (without imprint).

a. Issued note.	1.00	3.00
s. Specimen.	—	25.00

64 10 Sum

1992 (1993). Red on light blue and gold underprint. Arms at left. Back: Mosque at center. Watermark: Flower pattern repeated. Printer: H&S (without imprint).

a. Issued note.	1.00	3.50
s. Specimen.	—	25.00

65 25 Sum

1992 (1993). Blue-green on light blue and gold underprint. Arms at left. Back: Green. Mosque at center. Watermark: Flower pattern repeated. Printer: H&S (without imprint).

a. Issued note.	1.50	4.50
s. Specimen.	—	25.00

66 50 Sum VF UNC

1992 (1993). Rose on light blue and gold underprint. Arms at left. Back: Mosque at center. Watermark: Large detailed cotton flower. Printer: H&S (without imprint).

a. Issued note.	2.00	6.00
s. Specimen.	—	25.00

67 100 Sum — VF — UNC

1992 (1993). Dark brown on light blue and gold underprint. Arms at left. Back: Blue. Mosque at center. Watermark: Large detailed cotton flower. Printer: H&S (without imprint).

	VF	UNC
a. Issued note.	2.50	7.50
s. Specimen.	—	25.00

68 200 Sum

1992 (1993). Violet on light blue and gold underprint. Arms at left. Back: Mosque at center. Watermark: Large detailed cotton flower. Printer: H&S (without imprint).

	VF	UNC
a. Issued note.	4.50	10.00
s. Specimen.	—	25.00

69 500 Sum

1992 (1993). Orange on light blue and gold underprint. Arms at left. Back: Light tan. Mosque at center. Watermark: Large detailed cotton flower. Printer: H&S (without imprint).

	VF	UNC
a. Larger and italicized serial #. 8 digits	6.00	15.00
b. Smaller and regular serial #. 7 digits.	6.00	15.00
s. Specimen.	—	25.00

70 1000 Sum

1992 (1993). Brown on lilac and pale green underprint. Arms at left. Back: Mosque at center. Watermark: Large detailed cotton flower. Printer: H&S (without imprint).

	VF	UNC
a. Low and wide serial #.	7.00	18.00
b. High and narrow serial #.	7.00	18.00
s. Specimen.	—	30.00

71 5000 Sum — VF — UNC

1992 (1993). Blue-gray on lilac and pale green underprint. Arms at left. Back: Mosque at center. Watermark: Large detailed cotton flower. Printer: H&S (without imprint).

	VF	UNC
a. 3mm high serial #.	10.00	25.00
b. 4mm high serial #.	10.00	25.00
s. Specimen.	10.00	25.00

72 10,000 Sum

1992 (1993). Red-orange on lilac and pale green underprint. Arms at left. Back: Mosque at center. Printer: H&S (without imprint).

	VF	UNC
a. 4mm high serial #. Watermark simple outline of cotton flower.	10.00	25.00
b. 4mm high serial #. Watermark: detailed cotton flower.	10.00	25.00
c. 3mm high serial #. Watermark: detailed cotton flower.	10.00	25.00
s. Specimen.	—	30.00

ЎЗБЕКИСТОН РЕСПУБЛИКАСИ МАРКАЗИЙ БАНКИ

Central Bank of Uzbekistan Republic

1994; 1997 Issue

#73-80 Replacement notes: serial # prefix *ZZ*.

73 1 Sum — VF — UNC

1994. Dark green on multicolor underprint. Arms at left. Back: Building, fountain at center right. Watermark: Design.

	VF	UNC
a. Issued note.	FV	2.00
r. Replacement note. Serial # prefix: ZZ.	—	—

74 3 Sum — VF — UNC

1994. Violet and red-violet on multicolor underprint. Arms at left. Back: Mosque of Çaçma Ayub Mazar in Bukhara. Watermark: Design.

	VF	UNC
a. Issued note.	FV	3.00
r. Replacement note. Serial # prefix: ZZ.	—	—

75 5 Sum — VF — UNC

1994. Dark blue and red-violet on multicolor underprint. Arms at upper center. Back: Ali Shir Nawai Monument in Tashkent at center right. Watermark: Arms.

	VF	UNC
a. Issued note.	FV	4.00
r. Replacement note. Serial # prefix: ZZ.	—	—

76 10 Sum — VF — UNC

1994. Purple and blue-gray on multicolor underprint. Arms at upper center. Back: Tomb of Tamerlane in Samarakand at center right. Watermark: Arms.

	VF	UNC
a. Issued note.	FV	5.00
r. Replacement note. Serial # prefix: ZZ.		

77 25 Sum — VF — UNC

1994. Dark blue and brown on multicolor underprint. Arms at upper center. Back: Mausoleum Kazi Zadé Rumi in the necropolis Shakhi-Zinda in Samarkand at center right. Watermark: Arms.

	VF	UNC
a. Issued note.	FV	6.00
r. Replacement note. Serial # prefix: ZZ.	—	—

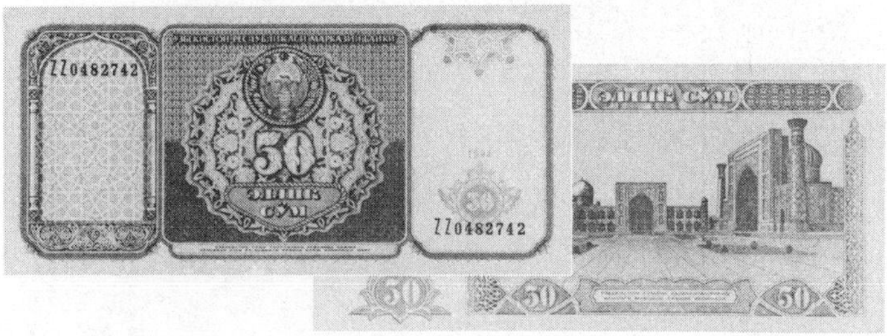

78 50 Sum — VF — UNC

1994. Dark brown, olive-brown and dull brown-orange on multicolor underprint. Arms at upper center. Back: Esplanade in Reghistan and the two Medersas in Samarkand at center right. Watermark: Arms.

	VF	UNC
a. Issued note.	FV	6.00
r. Replacement note. Serial # prefix: ZZ.	—	—

79	**100 Sum**	**VF**	**UNC**
	1994. Purple and blue on multicolor underprint. Stylized facing peacocks at left. Arms at upper center. Back: *Drubja Narodov* palace in Tashkent at center right. Watermark: Arms.		
	a. Issued note.	FV	7.00
	r. Replacement note. Serial # prefix: ZZ.	—	—

80	**200 Sum**	**VF**	**UNC**
	1997. Dark blue, black, deep purple on green and multicolor underprint. Arms at left. Back: Sunface over mythological tiger at center. Watermark: Arms.	FV	7.00

81	**500 Sum**	**VF**	**UNC**
	1999. Red, blue and green on multicolor underprint. Arms at left. Back: Equestrian statue at center right. Watermark: Arms.	FV	7.00

82	**1000 Sum**	**VF**	**UNC**
	2001. Brown & purple. Arms at left. Back: Amir Temur Museum. Watermark: Arms.	FV	7.00
83	**5000 Sum**		
	2013. Green, blue and brown. Coat of arms. Back: Oliy Majlis parliament building in Tashkent. Watermark: Coat of arms and 5000. 144x77mm.	FV	9.00

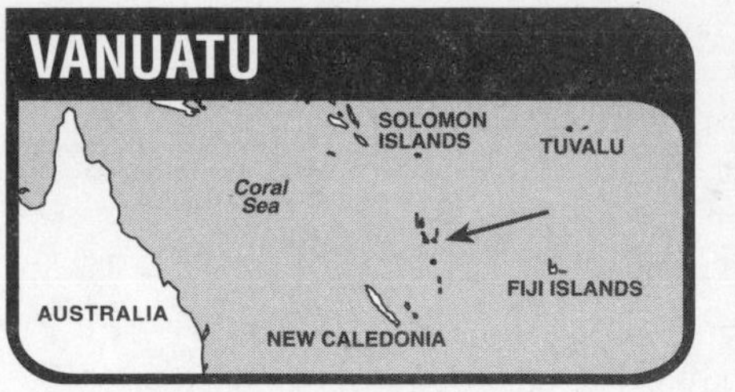

Vanuatu (formerly the New Hebrides Condominium), a group of islands located in the South Pacific 800 km. west of Fiji, were under the joint sovereignty of Great Britain and France. The islands have an area of 12,200 sq. km. and a population of 215,450. Capital: Vila. The volcanic and coral islands, while malarial and subject to frequent earthquakes, are extremely fertile, and produce copra, coffee, tropical fruits and timber for export.

Multiple waves of colonizers, each speaking a distinct language, migrated to the New Hebrides in the millennia preceding European exploration in the 18th century. This settlement pattern accounts for the complex linguistic diversity found on the archipelago to this day. The British and French, who settled the New Hebrides in the 19th century, agreed in 1906 to an Anglo-French Condominium, which administered the islands until independence in 1980, when the new name of Vanuatu was adopted.

RULERS:

British and French to 1982

MONETARY SYSTEM:

100 Vatu = 100 Francs

SIGNATURE VARIETIES

1	President	General Manager	2	Governor	Minister of Finance
3	President	General Manager	4	Governor	Minister of Finance

Independent

Banque Centrale de Vanuatu

Central Bank of Vanuatu / Central Bank Blong Vanuatu

1982; 1989 ND Issue

1	**100 Vatu**	**VF**	**UNC**
	ND (1982). Dark green on multicolor underprint. Arms with Melanesian chief standing with spear at center right. Signature 1. Back: Cattle among palm trees at left center. Watermark: Melanesian male head. Printer: BWC.		
	a. Issued note.	2.50	15.00
	s. Specimen.	—	160.

2	500 Vatu	VF	UNC
	ND (1982). Light red on multicolor underprint. Arms with Melanesian chief standing with spear at center right. Signature 1. Back: Three carvings at left, two men beating upright hollow log drums at left center. Watermark: Melanesian male head. Printer: BWC. 140x70mm.		
	a. Issued note.	5.00	20.00
	s. Specimen.	—	180.

3	1000 Vatu	VF	UNC
	ND (1982). Black on light orange, green and multicolor underprint. Arms with Melanesian chief standing with spear at center. Signature 1. Back: Three carvings at lower left, three men in outrigger sailboat at center. Watermark: Melanesian male head. Printer: BWC. 150x75mm.		
	a. Issued note.	12.50	35.00
	s. Specimen.	—	225.
4	5000 Vatu		
	ND (1989). Brown and lilac on multicolor underprint. Arms with Melanesian chief standing with spear at center right. Signature 2. Back: Man watching another *Gol* diving from log tower at center. Watermark: Melanesian male head. Printer: BWC. 160x79mm.	50.00	95.00

Banque de Reserve de Vanuatu

Reserve Bank of Vanuatu / Reserve Bank Blong Vanuatu

1993 ND Issue

5	500 Vatu	VF	UNC
	ND (1993). Light red on multicolor underprint. Arms with Melanesian chief standing with spear at center right, new bank name. Signature 3. Back: Three carvings at left, two men beating upright hollow log drums at left center. Watermark: Melanesian male head. Printer: BWC. 140x70mm.	FV	12.50

6	1000 Vatu	VF	UNC
	ND (1993). Black on light orange, green and multicolor underprint. Arms with Melanesian chief standing with spear at center right, new bank name. Signature 3. Back: Three carvings at lower left, three men in outrigger sailboat at center. Watermark: Melanesian male head. Printer: BWC. 150x75mm.	FV	22.50
7	5000 Vatu		
	ND. Arms with Melanesian chief standing with spear at center right, new bank name. Signature 3. Back: Man watching another *Gol* diving from log tower at center. Watermark: Melanesian male head. Printer: BWC. 160x79mm.	FV	100.

1995 ND Issue

8	200 Vatu	VF	UNC
	ND (1995). Purple and violet on multicolor underprint. Arms with Melanesian chief standing with spear at center right. Signature varieties. Back: Statue of family life, "Traditional parliament in session" and flag. Watermark: Melanesian male head. Printer: TDLR. 135x68mm.		
	a. Imprint at left end as TDLR.	FV	7.50
	b. Imprint at left end as DLR.	FV	7.50

1995 Commemorative Issue

#9, 15th Anniversary of Independence

9	200 Vatu	VF	UNC
	ND (1995). Purple and violet on multicolor underprint. Commemorative text overprint in watermark area at left on #8. 135x68mm.	FV	7.50

2002 ND Issue

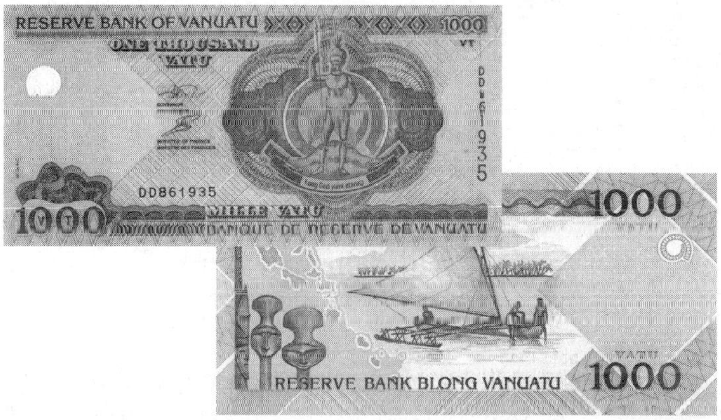

10	1000 Vatu	VF	UNC
	ND (2002). Black and green on orange underprint. Arms with Melanesian chief standing with spear at center right. Back: Outrigger sailboat. Printer: (T)DLR. 150x75mm.		
	a. Signature 3.	FV	25.00
	b. Signature 5.	FV	25.00

2006 Commemorative Issue

11	1000 Vatu	VF	UNC
	2006. Black and green on orange underprint. Signature 5. Overprint: 25th Anniversary of the Reserve Bank, on #10b. 150x75mm.	FV	22.50

2006; 2010 Regular Issue

12	5000 Vatu	VF	UNC
	2006. Red on yellow and multicolor underprint. Arms with Melanesian chielf standing with spear at center right. Signature 5. Back: "Goi" diver.	FV	100.

13	10,000 Vatu	VF	UNC
	ND (2010). Blue and multicolor Arms - Man holding spear, at right center. Back: Building and telecommunications theme Printer: NPA. 155x65mm.	FV	175.

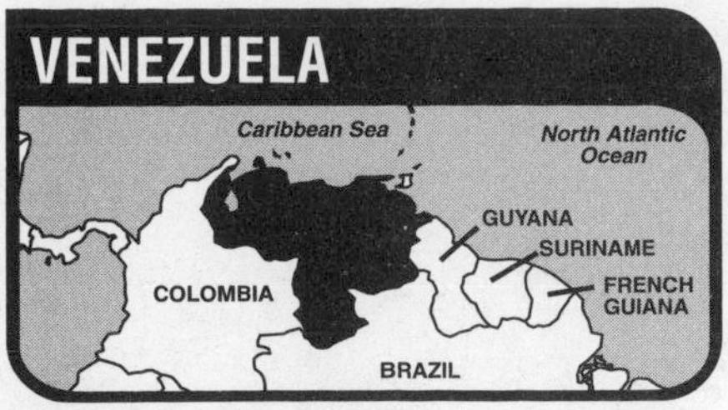

The Republic of Venezuela, located on the northern coast of South America between Colombia and Guyana, has an area of 912,050 sq. km. and a population of 26.41 million. Capital: Caracas. Petroleum and mining provide 90 percent of Venezuela's exports although they employ less than 2 percent of the work force. Coffee, grown on 60,000 plantations, is the chief crop.

Venezuela was one of three countries that emerged from the collapse of Gran Colombia in 1830 (the others being Ecuador and New Granada, which became Colombia). For most of the first half of the 20th century, Venezuela was ruled by generally benevolent military strongmen, who promoted the oil industry and allowed for some social reforms. Democratically elected governments have held sway since 1959. Hugo Chavez, president since 1999, seeks to implement his "21st Century Socialism," which purports to alleviate social ills while at the same time attacking globalization and undermining regional stability. Current concerns include: a weakening of democratic institutions, political polarization, a politicized military, drug-related violence along the Colombian border, increasing internal drug consumption, overdependence on the petroleum industry with its price fluctuations, and irresponsible mining operations that are endangering the rain forest and indigenous peoples.

Republic

Banco Central de Venezuela

1940-45 Issues

#	Description	VF	UNC
31	**10 Bolívares**	VF	UNC
	19.7.1945-11.3.1960. Purple on multicolor underprint. Portrait Simon Bolívar at left, Antonio Jose de Sucre at right. Back: Arms at right. Printer: ABNC.		
	a. 19.7.1945-17.5.1951.	40.00	125.
	b. 31.7.1952. Serial # prefix F-G.	50.00	100.
	c. 23.7.1953-17.4.1958.	30.00	60.00
	d. 18.6.1959-11.3.1960.	20.00	45.00
	s. As a. Specimen. Without signature. Punched hole cancelled.	—	250.
32	**20 Bolívares**		
	15.2.1941-18.6.1959. Dark green on multicolor underprint. Portrait Simon Bolívar at right. Back: Arms at left. Printer: ABNC.		
	a. 15.2.1941-17.1.1952.	60.00	125.
	b. 21.8.1952. Serial # prefix G-H.	50.00	100.
	c. 23.7.1953-18.6.1959.	30.00	75.00
	s. As a. Specimen. Without signature. Punched hole cancelled.	—	125.
33	**50 Bolívares**		
	12.12.1940-11.3.1960. Black on multicolor underprint. Portrait Simon Bolívar at left. Back: Orange. Arms at right. Printer: ABNC.		
	a. 12.12.1940-17.1.1952.	100.	250.
	b. 23.7.1953. Serial # prefix C.	125.	225.
	c. 22.4.1954-11.3.1960.	65.00	125.
	s. As a. Specimen. Without signature. Punched hole cancelled.	—	175.
35	**500 Bolívares**		
	10.12.1940-21.12.1940. Blue on multicolor underprint. Portrait Simon Bolívar at right. Back: Arms at left. Printer: ABNC.		
	a. Issued note.	1000.	—
	s. Specimen.	—	2000.
36	**500 Bolívares**		
	21.1.1943-29.11.1946. Red on multicolor underprint. Portrait Simon Bolívar at right. Like #35. Back: Arms at left. Printer: ABNC.		
	a. Issued note.	1000.	—
	s. As a or ND. Specimen.	—	1250.

1947 Issue

#	Description	VF	UNC
37	**500 Bolívares**	VF	UNC
	1947-71. Orange on multicolor underprint. Portrait Simon Bolívar at right. Like #35. Back: Arms at left. Printer: ABNC.		
	a. 14.8.1947-21.8.1952.	250.	—
	b. 23.7.1953-29.5.1958.	125.	300.
	c. 11.3.1960-17.8.1971.	80.00	200.
	s. As b or ND. Specimen. Without signature. Punched hole cancelled.	—	500.

1952-53 Issue

#	Description	VF	UNC
38	**10 Bolívares**	VF	UNC
	31.7.1952. Purple on multicolor underprint. Portrait Simon Bolívar at left, Antonio Jose de Sucre at right. Similar to #31. Series E, F. 7 digit serial #. Back: Arms at right. Monument at center. Printer: TDLR.	125.	350.
39	**20 Bolívares**		
	21.8.1952. Dark green on multicolor underprint. Portrait Simon Bolívar at right, bank name in 1 line. Series G. 7 digit serial #. Similar to #43. Back: Arms at left. Monument at center. Printer: TDLR.	175.	450.

#	Description	VF	UNC
40	**50 Bolívares**	VF	UNC
	26.2.1953; 23.7.1953. Simon Bolívar at left, *CINCUENTA BOLÍVARES* at right. Series C. 7 digit serial #. Back: Arms at right. Monument at center. Printer: TDLR.	135.	450.
41	**100 Bolívares**		
	23.7.1953. Portrait Simon Bolívar at right. Series C, D. 7 digit serial #. Back: Arms at left. Monument at center. Printer: TDLR.	125.	425.

1960-61 Issue

#	Description	VF	UNC
42	**10 Bolívares**	VF	UNC
	6.6.1961. Purple on multicolor underprint. Portrait Simon Bolívar at left. Antonio Jose de Sucre at right. Similar to #31. Series E-J. 7 digit serial #. Back: Arms at right, monument to Battle of Carabobo at center. Like #38. Printer: TDLR.		
	a. Issued note.	15.00	35.00
	s. Specimen with black overprint: *SPECIMEN*. Serial # prefix *E*.	—	12.50

#	Description	VF	UNC
43	**20 Bolívares**	VF	UNC
	1960-66. Dark green on multicolor underprint. Portrait Simon Bolívar at right, bank name in 1 line. 7 digit serial #. Similar to #32. Back: Arms at left, monument at center. Printer: TDLR.		
	a. 11.3.1960. Serial # prefix *U-X*.	20.00	50.00
	b. 6.6.1961. Serial # prefix *X-Z*.	15.00	40.00
	c. 7.5.1963. Serial # prefix *A-B*.	—	40.00
	d. 2.6.1964. Serial # prefix *C-D*.	15.00	40.00
	e. 10.5.1966. Serial # preifx *E-G*.	15.00	40.00
	s1. Specimen with red overprint: *SPECIMEN*. Paper with colored planchettes. Serial # prefix *X*.	—	15.00
	s2. Specimen with red overprint: *ESPECIMEN SIN VALOR*. Paper with security thread. Punched hole cancelled.	—	15.00
	s3. Specimen with black overprint: *SPECIMEN*. Serial # prefix *U*.	—	15.00

#	Description	VF	UNC
44	**50 Bolívares**	VF	UNC
	6.6.1961; 7.5.1963. Black on multicolor underprint. Modified portrait of Simon Bolívar at left, value *CINCUENTA BOLIVARES* at right. 7 digit serial #. Serial # prefix *H-J; J-K*. Back: Orange. Monument at center, arms at right. Printer: TDLR.		
	a. Issued note.	50.00	125.
	s. Specimen with red overprint: *SPECIMEN SIN VALOR*. Punched hole cancelled.	—	17.50

1963-67 Issue

45 10 Bolívares

1963-70. Purple on multicolor underprint. Similar to #42 but much different portrait of Antonio Jose de Sucre at right. 7-digit serial number. Back: Monument to Battle of Carabobo. Printer: TDLR.

	VF	UNC
a. 7.5.1963. Serial # prefix *K-N.*	2.50	15.00
b. 2.6.1964. Serial # prefix *P-T.*	2.50	12.50
c. 10.5.1966. Serial # prefix *T-V; X-Z.*	2.50	12.50
d. 8.8.1967. Serial # prefix *A-D.*	2.50	10.00
e. 5.3.1968. Serial # prefix *G-H; J-K.*	2.50	10.00
f. 19.11.1968. Serial # prefix *E-F.*	2.50	7.50
g. 27.1.1970. Serial # prefix *L-N; P-U.*	2.50	7.50
s. Specimen with red overprint: *ESPECIMEN SIN VALOR.* ND. Punched hole cancelled.	—	30.00

46 20 Bolívares

1967-74. Green on orange and blue underprint. Portrait Simon Bolívar at right, bank name in three lines. Back: Arms without circle at left, Monument to Battle of Carabobo. Watermark: Simon Bolívar. Printer: TDLR.

	VF	UNC
a. 8.8.1967. Serial # prefix *H-J.*	4.00	20.00
b. 5.3.1968. Serial # prefix *L-M.*	3.50	17.50
c. 30.9.1969. Serial # prefix *K.*	3.50	17.50
d. 27.1.1970. Serial # prefix *N; P-R.*	3.00	15.00
e. 29.1.1974. Serial # prefix *Y-Z* (7 digits); *A-C* (7 or 8 digits).	3.00	15.00
s1. Specimen with red overprint: *ESPECIMEN SIN VALOR.* ND. Punched hole cancelled.	—	15.00
s2. Specimen with red overprint as S1. 27.1.1970.	—	15.00

47 50 Bolívares

1964-72. Black on orange and green underprint. Portrait Simon Bolívar at left. *CINCUENTA BOLÍVARES* above *50* at center. Back: Orange. Monument to Battle of Carabobo at center, arms at right. Printer: TDLR.

	VF	UNC
a. 2.6.1964. Serial # prefix *K-L.*	6.00	40.00
b. 27.7.1965. Serial # preifx *L-M.*	6.00	30.00
c. 10.5.1966. Serial # prefix *M-N.*	6.00	30.00
d. 8.8.1967. Serial # prefix *P.*	6.00	30.00
e. 18.3.1969. Serial # prefix *P-Q.*	6.00	30.00
f. 7.4.1970. Serial # prefix *Q-S.*	6.00	30.00
g. 22.2.1972. Serial # prefix *T-U.*	6.00	30.00
s. Specimen with red overprint: *ESPECIMEN SIN VALOR.* ND.	—	37.50

48 100 Bolívares

1963-73. Brown on multicolor underprint. Portrait Simon Bolívar at right. Back: Monument to Battle of Carabobo, arms at left. Watermark: Simon Bolívar. Printer: TDLR.

	VF	UNC
a. 7.5.1963. Serial # prefix *M-N.*	5.00	40.00
b. 2.6.1964. Serial # prefix *P-Q.*	5.00	40.00
c. 27.7.1965. Serial # prefix *Q.*	5.00	40.00
d. 10.5.1966. Serial # prefix Q-R.	5.00	40.00
e. 8.8.1967. Serial # prefix *S-T.*	5.00	40.00
f. 18.3.1969. Serial # prefix *U-V.*	5.00	40.00
g. 26.5.1970. Serial # prefix *X-Y.*	5.00	40.00
h. 17.8.1971. Serial # prefix *Z; A-B.*	5.00	40.00
i. 24.10.1972. Serial # prefix *C-D.*	5.00	40.00
j. 6.2.1973. Serial # prefix *E-F.*	5.00	40.00
s1. Specimen with red overprint: *ESPECIMEN SIN VALOR.* ND.	—	20.00
s2. Specimen with red overprint: *SPECIMEN* and TDLR oval stampings. ND. Punched hole cancelled.	—	95.00

1966 Commemorative Issue

#49, 400th Anniversary Founding of Caracas 1567-1967

49 5 Bolívares

	VF	UNC
10.5.1966. Blue on green and yellow underprint. Scene of the founding and commemorative text at center and left, portrait Simon Bolívar at right. Serial number prefix *A-D.* Back: Blue. City arms at left, early map (1578) of the city at center, national arms at right. Printer: ABNC.	3.00	22.50

1968-71 Issue

50 5 Bolívares

1968-74. Red on multicolor underprint. Simon Bolívar at left, Francisco de Miranda at right. Back: Arms at left, National Pantheon at center. Printer: TDLR.

	VF	UNC
a. 24.9.1968. Serial # prefix *E; F.*	2.25	12.50
b. 29.4.1969. Serial # prefix *H-J.*	2.00	12.00
c. 30.9.1969. Serial # prefix *G; H.*	2.00	12.00
d. 27.1.1970. Serial # prefix *J-M.*	1.50	9.00
e. 22.6.1971. Serial # prefix *M-P.*	1.50	7.50
f. 11.4.1972. Serial # prefix *P; R.*	1.50	7.50
g. 13.3.1973. Serial # prefix *S; T.*	1.00	6.00
h. 29.1.1974. Serial # prefix *U-Z* (7 digits); *A-E* (7 or 8 digits).	1.00	5.50
r. Remainder without date, signature or serial #.	—	8.00
s. Specimen.	—	10.00

51 10 Bolívares

1971-79. Purple on green and lilac underprint. Similar to #42 but much different portrait of Antonio Jose de Sucre at right. 7-digit serial number. Back: Monument to Battle of Carabobo. Printer: ABNC.

	VF	UNC
a. 22.6.1971. dark blue serial # with prefix *U-A*.	2.50	12.50
b. 11.4.1972. Serial # prefix *A-H*.	2.00	10.00
c. 13.3.1973. Serial # prefix *H-R*.	1.50	9.00
d. 29.1.1974. Serial # prefix *R-Z; A-H*.	1.50	9.00
e. 27.1.1976. Serial # prefix *J-Y*.	1.50	8.00
f. 7.6.1977. Serial # prefix *Y-C*.	1.50	7.00
g. 18.9.1979. Black serial # with prefix *C; D*.	1.50	7.50
s1. Specimen with red overprint: *MUESTRA*. Punch hole cancelled. 11.4.1972.	—	125.
s2. Specimen with red overprint: *MUESTRA,* twice on each side. Punch hole cancelled. 27.1.1976.	—	125.
s3. Specimen with red overprint: *MUESTRA*. Punch hole cancelled. 7.6.1977.	—	125.
s4. Specimen with red overprint: *MUESTRA*. Punch hole cancelled. 18.9.1979.	—	125.

52 20 Bolívares

1971; 1972. Dark green on multicolor underprint. Portrait Simon Bolívar at right, bank name in three lines. Back: Arms without circle at left, Monument to Battle of Carabobo. Watermark: Simon Bolívar. Printer: ABNC.

	VF	UNC
a. 22.6.1971. Serial # prefix *S-T*.	2.00	12.50
b. 11.4.1972. Serial # prefix *U-V; X-Y*.	2.00	12.50
s. Specimen with red overprint: *MUESTRA*. Punched hole cancelled. 11.4.1972.	—	125.

1971-74 Issue

53 20 Bolívares

1974-79. Dark green on multicolor underprint. Jose Antonio Paez at right. 7 or 8 digit serial number. Back: Arms at left, monument to Battle of Carabobo at center. Watermark: Jose Antonio Paez. Printer: ABNC.

	VF	UNC
a. 23.4.1974. Serial # prefix *A-H; J*.	1.50	9.00
b. 7.6.1977. Serial # prefix *J-N; P-T*.	1.50	8.00
c. 18.9.1979. Serial # prefix *T-V; X-Z; A-D*. 7 or 8-digit serial #.	1.50	9.00
s1. Specimen with red overprint: *ESPECIMEN SIN VALOR*. 23.4.1974.	—	150.
s2. Specimen with red overprint: *MUESTRA*. Punched hole cancelled. 7.6.1977.	—	150.
s3. Specimen with red overprint: *MUESTRA*. Punched hole cancelled. 18.9.1979.	—	150.

54 50 Bolívares

1972-77. Purple, orange and multicolor. Academic building at center, Andres Bello at right. Back: Orange. Arms at left, bank at center. Watermark: Andres Bello. Printer: TDLR.

	VF	UNC
a. 21.11.1972. Serial # prefix *A-B*.	4.00	15.00
b. 29.1.1974. Serial # prefix *B-D*.	4.00	14.50
c. 27.1.1976. Serial # prefix *D-F*.	4.00	15.00
d. 7.6.1977. Serial # prefix *F-H; J-N*.	3.00	12.50
s. Specimen with red overprint: *ESPECIMEN SIN VALOR*. 21.11.1972.	—	17.50

55 100 Bolívares

1972-81. Dark brown and brown-violet on multicolor underprint. Simon Bolívar at right. Back: National Capitol at left, arms at right. Watermark: Simon Bolívar. Printer: BDDK.

	VF	UNC
a. Red serial #. 21.11.1972. Serial # prefix *A-D*.	12.50	65.00
b. Watermark: Bolívar. 5.3.1974. Serial # prefix *D-H; J*.	10.00	45.00
c. Blue serial #. *B-C* added to watermark. 27.1.1976.	5.00	27.50
d. 23.11.1976. Serial # prefix *Q-V; X-Z; A* (8 digit serial #.)	5.00	27.50
e. 12.12.1978. Serial # prefix *A-H; J-M*.	5.00	25.00
f. 18.9.1979. Serial # prefix *N; P-V; X-Z; A-F*.	5.00	25.00
g. 1.9.1981. Serial # prefix *F-H; J-N; P-R*.	4.50	20.00
s1. Specimen with red overprint: *ESPECIMEN SIN VALOR*. 21.11.1972.	—	100.
s2. Specimen. 27.1.1976.	—	100.

56 500 Bolívares

1971-72. Brown and blue on multicolor underprint. Simon Bolívar at left, horsemen with rifles riding at center. Serial number prefix A. Back: Brown. Dam at center, arms at right. Watermark: Simon Bolívar. Printer: TDLR.

	VF	UNC
a. 9.11.1971.	15.00	50.00
b. 11.1.1972.	8.50	45.00
s. Specimen with red overprint: *ESPECIMEN SIN VALOR*. ND.	—	22.50

1980 Issue

57	10 Bolívares	VF	UNC
	29.1.1980. Purple on multicolor underprint. Antonio Jose de Sucre at right. Serial number prefix *A*. 7 or 8 digit serial number. Back: Arms at left, officers on horseback at center right. Printer: ABNC.		
	a. Issued note.	1.00	3.00
	p. Uniface Proofs, face and back. 29.1.1980.	—	150.
	s. Specimen with red overprint: *MUESTRA*, once on face, twice on back. Punch hole cancelled.	—	200.

1980-81 Commemorative Issues

#58, Bicentennial Birth of Andres Bello, 1781-1981

58	50 Bolívares	VF	UNC
	27.1.1981. Dark brown and green on multicolor underprint. Andres Bello at right. Serial number prefix *A*. Back: Arms at left, scene showing Bello teaching young Bolívar. Watermark: Andres Bello. Printer: TDLR.		
	a. Issued note.	3.00	12.50
	s. Specimen.	—	—

59	100 Bolívares	VF	UNC
	29.1.1980. Red, purple and black on multicolor underprint. Simon Bolívar at right, his tomb at center right. Serial number prefix *A*. Back: Arms at left, scene of hand to hand combat aboard ship. Watermark: Simon Bolívar. Printer: TDLR.		
	a. Issued note.	5.00	27.50
	s. Specimen with red overprint: *ESPECIMEN SIN VALOR*.	—	15.00

1981-88 Issues

60	10 Bolívares	VF	UNC
	6.10.1981. Purple on light blue and multicolor underprint. Similar to #57 but underprint is different, and there are many significant plate changes. Back: Arms at left, officers on horseback at center right. Printer: CdM-B (without imprint). 157x69mm.		
	a. 7 or 8 digit serial #. Serial # prefix: *B-D*.	.50	4.50
	s. Specimen. Red overprint: *MUESTRA* on both sides.	—	40.00

61	10 Bolívares	VF	UNC
	1986-95. Purple on light green and lilac underprint. Like #51, but *CARACAS* removed from upper center beneath bank title. Back: Monument to Battle of Carabobo. Printer: ABNC (without imprint). UV: fibers fluoresce red and green. value 10 and central design elements orange. Back: central design elements, bank name and 10 orange.		
	a. 18.3.1986. Serial # prefix: *D-F*.	FV	2.50
	b. 31.5.1990. Serial # prefix: *G-H, J-L*.	FV	1.50
	c. 8.12.1992. Serial # prefix: *L-N, P*.	FV	1.00
	d. 5.6.1995. Serial # prefix: *P-U*.	FV	1.00
	s. Specimen. Overprint: *MUESTRA SIN VALOR*.	—	—

62	10 Bolívares	VF	UNC
	3.11.1988. Purple on ochre underprint. Like #45, but *CARACAS* removed from upper center beneath bank title. Serial number prefix *F-G*. Printer: TDLR (without imprint).	FV	1.50

63	20 Bolívares	VF	UNC
	1981-95. Dark green on multicolor underprint. Similar to #53 but *CARACAS* deleted under bank title. Title 82mm, horizontal central design in left center guilloche. Back: Arms at left, monument to Battle of Carabobo at center. Watermark: Jose Antonio Paez. Printer: TDLR (without imprint). UV: fibers fluoresce yellow; value 20 green; central design elements orange. Back: bank name and 20 orange.		
	a. 6.10.1981. Serial # prefix: *D-H, J*.	FV	5.00
	b. 7.9.1989; 31.3.1990. Serial # prefix: *X-Z, A-H, J, Y*.	FV	3.50
	c. 31.5.1990. Serial # prefix: *X*.	FV	2.50
	d. 8.12.1992. Short design in guilloche. Serial # prefix: *D-H, J-N, P-Z, A*.	FV	2.00
	e. 5.6.1995. Serial # prefix: *A-E*.	FV	1.00
	f. 10.2.1998. Serial # prefix: *E-F*.	FV	1.00
	s. Specimen. As a. Red overprint: *ESPECIMEN SIN VALOR*. on both sides.	—	35.00

64 **20 Bolívares** — VF: FV, UNC: 3.00

25.9.1984. Dark green on multicolor underprint. Like #63, but title 84mm and without central design in left center guilloche, also other minor plate differences. Latent image *BCV* in guilloches easily seen. Serial # prefix *J* (8 Watermark: Jose Antonio Paez. Printer: CdM-B (without imprint).

64A **20 Bolívares** — VF: FV, UNC: 2.50

7.7.1987. Dark green on multicolor underprint. Similar to #53 but *CARACAS* deleted under bank title. Title 82mm, horizontal central design in left center guilloche. Serial number prefix *T-X*. 7 or 8 digit serial number. Back: Arms at left, monument to Battle of Carabobo at center. Watermark: Jose Antonio Paez. Printer: ABNC (without imprint).

65 **50 Bolívares**

1985-98. Purple, black and orange on multicolor underprint. Like #54, but *CARACAS* removed under bank name. Back: Orange. Arms at left, bank at center. Watermark: Andres Bello.

	VF	UNC
a. 10.12.1985. Serial # prefix: *N, P-S*. Printer BDDK (without imprint).	FV	4.00
b. 3.11.1988. Serial # prefix: *S-V, X-Z, A*.	FV	4.00
c. 31.5.1990. Serial # prefix: *A-H, J-K*.	FV	3.00
d. 8.12.1992. Serial # prefix: *K, L-N, P-V, X-Z*. 7 or 8 digit serial #. Printer TDLR.	FV	2.50
e. 5.6.1995. Serial # prefix: *Q-U*. Printer BDDK (without imprint).	FV	2.00
f. 5.2.1998. Serial # prefix: *U-V*.	FV	1.50
g. 13.10.1998. Serial # prefix: *V-Z*.	FV	1.50
s. Specimen. 10.12.1985. Serial # prefix *N*.	—	20.00

66 **100 Bolívares**

1987-98. Dark brown and brown-violet on multicolor underprint. Simon Bolívar at right. Back: National Capitol at left, arms at right. Watermark: Simon Bolívar. Printer: BDDK (without imprint).

	VF	UNC
a. 3.2.1987. Serial # prefix: *R-V, X-Z, A-H, J-K*.	FV	5.00
b. 16.3.1989. Serial # prefix: *K-N, P-V, X-Z, A-G*.	FV	3.50
c. 31.5.1990. Serial # prefix: *G-H, J-N, P-V, X-Y*.	FV	3.50
d. 12.5.1992. Serial # prefix: *Y-Z, A-E*.	FV	2.00
e. 8.12.1992. Serial # prefix: *E-H, K-N*.	FV	2.00
f. 5.2.1998. Serial # prefix: *E-G*.	FV	2.00
g. 13.10.1998.	FV	2.00

67 **500 Bolívares**

1981-98. Purple and black on multicolor underprint. Simon Bolívar at right. Back: Green and multicolor. Arms at left, orchids at center. Watermark: Simon Bolívar. Printer: BDDK (without imprint). UV: fibers fluoresce yellow.

	VF	UNC
a. 25.9.1981. Serial # prefix: *A*.	5.00	30.00
b. 3.2.1987. Serial # prefix: *B-C*.	FV	15.00
c. 16.3.1989. Serial # prefix: *C-F*.	FV	15.00
d. 31.5.1990. Serial # prefix: *F-H, J-N, P-V, X-Z, A-C*.	FV	5.00
e. 5.6.1995. Serial # prefix: *C-H, J-N, P-Q*.	FV	5.00
f. 5.2.1998. Serial # prefix: *Q-Z*.	FV	2.50

1989 Issue

#68 and 69 replacement notes: Serial # prefix *X XX* and *W*.

68 **1 Bolívar** — VF: FV, UNC: .25

5.10.1989. Purple on blue and green underprint. Large *1* at left, coin with Simon Bolívar at right. Serial number prefix: *A-D; X*. Back: Arms at left, rosette at right. Printer: BDDK (without imprint). UV: fibers fluoresce green.

69 **2 Bolívares** — VF: FV, UNC: .50

5.10.1989. Blue and brownish gray on light blue underprint. Coin head of Simon Bolívar at right. Serial number prefix: *AA-AH, AJ-AM, AW-AZ, BA, BJ, BL, BN, BP, BU-BW, XX*. Back: Large *2* at left, arms at right. Printer: USBNC (without imprint). UV: value 2 and DES fluoresce yellow.

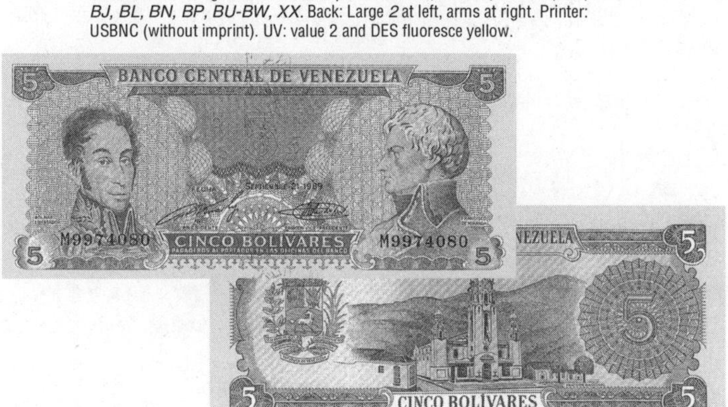

			VF	UNC
70	**5 Bolívares** 21.9.1989. Red on multicolor underprint. Like #50, but *CARACAS* removed from upper center beneath bank title. Lithographed. Back: Like #50, but *CARACAS* removed from upper center beneath bank title. Printer: TDLR (without imprint). UV: fibers fluoresce red and green; serial # and signatures green.			
	a. 7 digit serial #. Serial # prefix: *F-Z (no I or O.)*		FV	1.00
	b. 8 digit serial #. Serial # prefix: *A-E, J, W.*		FV	.50

1989 Commemorative Issue

#71, Bicentennial Birth of General Rafael Urdaneta, 1789-1989

		VF	UNC
71	**20 Bolívares** 20.10.1987 (1989). Deep green and black on multicolor underprint. General Rafael Urdaneta at right. Serial number prefix *A C*. Back: Battle of Lake Maracaibo at left center. Watermark: Rafael Urdaneta.	FV	2.00

1990-94 Issue

		VF	UNC
72	**50 Bolívares** 31.5.1990. Purple, black and orange on multicolor underprint. Similar to #65 but modified plate design, ornaments in "50's". Serial number prefix *A-H; J-K.* Back: Deeper orange. Arms at left, bank at center. Watermark: Andres Bello. Printer: BDDK (without imprint).	FV	2.50

		VF	UNC
73	**1000 Bolívares** 1991-92. Red-violet on multicolor underprint. Part of independence text at far left, Simon Bolívar at left. Back: Signing of the Declaration of Independence at center right, arms at upper right. Watermark: Simon Bolívar. Without imprint.		
	a. Dot instead of accent above *i* (error) in *Bolívares* on face and back. 8.8.1991. Serial # prefix: *A*.	10.00	45.00
	b. Accent above *í* in *Bolívares* on face and back. 30.7.1992. Serial # prefix: *A*.	FV	25.00
	c. As b. 8.12.1992. Serial # prefix: *A* (8-digits); *B* (8 or 9-digits).	FV	4.00
	s1. As a. Specimen.	—	40.00
	s2. As b. Specimen.	—	40.00

		VF	UNC
74	**2000 Bolívares** 1994; 1995. Dark green and black on multicolor underprint. Antonio Jose de Sucre at right. Value at lower left in green. Back: Scene of Battle of Ayacucho at left center, arms at upper right. Watermark: Antonio Jose de Sucre.		
	a. 12.5.1994. Serial # prefix: *A*.	FV	7.50
	b. Serial # prefix: *A-B*. 21.12.1995. Large serial #.	FV	6.00

		VF	UNC
75	**5000 Bolívares** 1994; 1996. Dark brown and brown-violet on multicolor underprint. Simon Bolívar at right. Back: Gathering at palace for Declaration of Independence at center, arms at upper right. Watermark: Simon Bolívar.		
	a. 12.5.1994. Serial # prefix *A*.	FV	15.00
	b. 14.3.1996. Serial # prefix *A-B*.	FV	15.00

1994 Issue

		VF	UNC
76	**1000 Bolívares** 1994-98. Red-violet on multicolor underprint. Part of independence text at far left, Simon Bolívar at left, green OVD *1000* at lower right. Back: Signing of the Declaration of Independence at center right, arms at upper right. Watermark: Simon Bolívar.		
	a. 17.3.1994. Serial # prefix: *C-E*. (8 or 9-digits).	FV	3.00
	b. 5.6.1995. Serial # prefix: *E-H, J, W*. (9 digits).	FV	3.00
	c. 5.2.1998. Serial # prefix: *J-M, Z*. (8 or 9 digits).	FV	2.50
	d. 6.8.1998. Serial # prefix: *M-Q, Z*. (8 or 9 digits)	FV	2.50
	e. 10.9.1998.	FV	2.50

1997 Issue

77 2000 Bolívares VF UNC

1997; 1998. Dark green, brown and black on multicolor underprint. Antonio Jose de Sucre at right, with *2000* at lower left in black. Back: Scene of Battle of Ayacucho at left center, arms at upper right. Watermark: Antonio Jose de Sucre.

	VF	UNC
a. 16.6.1997. Serial # prefix *B-C.*	FV	9.00
b. 10.2.1998 Serial # prefix *C-D.*	FV	9.00
c. 6.8.1998. Serial # prefix: D-F.	FV	9.00

78 5000 Bolívares VF UNC

1997-98. Brown and red-brown on multicolor underprint. Simon Bolívar at left center. Back: Gathering at palace for Declaration of Independence at center, arms at upper right.

	VF	UNC
a. 16.6.1997. Serial # prefix: *B-C.*	FV	17.50
b. 10.2.1998. Serial # prefix: *C-D.*	FV	15.00
c. 6.8.1998. Serial # prefix: *D-F.*	FV	15.00

1998 Issue

Replacement notes are indicated by a *Z* serial # prefix for all notes dated 1998 but for the 5.6.1998 1000 Bolívares which uses a *W*.

79 1000 Bolívares VF UNC

10.9.1998. Violet and multicolor underprint. Simon Bolívar at right. Serial number prefix; *A.* Back: Panteon Nacional at right center. FV 2.50

80 2000 Bolívares VF UNC

29.10.1998. Olive green and gray. Andrea Bello at right. Serial number prefix; *A.* Back: Pico Bolívar mountain range at right center. FV 5.00

81 10,000 Bolívares VF UNC

10.2.1998. Black, red and olive-brown on multicolor underprint. Simon Bolívar at right. Serial number prefix: *Z, A-B.* Back: Teresa Carreño Theatre at left center, arms at top center right. Watermark: Simon Bolívar. FV 27.50

82 20,000 Bolívares VF UNC

24.8.1998. Green on multicolor underprint. Simon Rodriguez at right. Serial number prefix: *Z, A-B.* Back: Arms at left, parrot at left center, Angel Falls at center right. FV 45.00

83 50,000 Bolívares VF UNC

24.8.1998. Orange and multicolor. Dr. Jose Maria Vargas at center. Serial number prefix; *A.* Back: Central University at center, araguaney flower at left. Printer: CMV. FV 50.00

Republica Bolivariana de Venezuela

Banco Central de Venezuela

2000-01 Issue

84 5000 Bolívares VF UNC

2000-04. Blue and multicolor. Francisco de Miranda at right. Back: Electric power dam at Guri at center. Watermark: Francisco de Miranda. Printer: CMV.

	VF	UNC
a. 25.5.2000.	FV	7.50
b. 13.8.2002.	FV	7.50
c. 25.4.2004.	FV	7.50

85 10,000 Bolívares VF UNC

2000-06. Black on brown and multicolor underprint. Antonio J. Sucre at center right. Serial number prefix; *A*. Back: Supreme Court building at center. Printer: CMV.

	VF	UNC
a. 25.8.2001.	FV	20.00
b. 16.8.2001.	FV	20.00
c. 13.8.2002.	FV	20.00
d. 25.4.2004.	FV	20.00
e. 25.4.2006.	FV	20.00

86 20,000 Bolívares VF UNC

2001-06. Green on multicolor underprint. Simon Rodriguez at right. Back: Arms at left, parrot at left center, Angel Falls at center right. Printer: CMV.

	VF	UNC
a. 16.8.2001.	FV	30.00
b. 25.4.2004.	FV	30.00
c. 25.4.2006.	FV	30.00

87 50,000 Bolívares

2002-06. Orange and multicolor. Dr. Jose Maria Vargas at center. Serial # prefix: *A*. Back: Central University at center, araguaney flower at left. Printer: CMV.

	VF	UNC
a. 2002.	FV	45.00
b. 29.9.2005.	FV	45.00
c. 25.4.2006.	FV	45.00

2007 Issue

88 2 Bolívares VF UNC

20.3.2007; 24.5.2007. Dark blue and light brown on multicolor underprint. Francisco de Miranda. Back: Two porpose. Printer: CMV 69x157mm.

	VF	UNC
a. 20.3.2007.	FV	2.00
b. 24.5.2007.	FV	2.00

89 5 Bolívares VF UNC

2007; 2008. Brown and orange on multicolor underprint. Negro Primero. Back: Two armadillos. Printer: CMV 69x157mm.

	VF	UNC
a. 20.3.2007.	FV	4.00
b. 19.12.2008.	FV	4.00

90 10 Bolívares VF UNC

20.3.2007; 3.9.2009; 3.2.2011. Red-brown and tan on multicolor underprint. Cacique Guaicaipuro. Back: Harpy eagle. Printer: CMV 69x157mm.

	VF	UNC
a. 20.3.2007.	FV	6.00
b. 3.9.2009.	FV	6.00
c. 3.2.2011.	FV	6.00

		VF	UNC
91	**20 Bolívares** 2007-. Purple, green and lilac on multicolor underprint. Luisa Cáceres de Arismendi. Back: Two sea turtles. Printer: CMV 69x157mm.		
	a. 20.3.2007.	FV	10.00
	b. 24.5.2007.	FV	10.00
	c. 3.9.2009.	FV	10.00
	d. 3.2.2011.	FV	10.00
92	**50 Bolívares** 20.3.2007; 3.9.2009; 3.2.2011. Green and yellow on multicolor underprint. Simon Rodrigues. Back: Bear. Printer: CMV 69x157mm.		
	a. 20.3.2007.	FV	25.00
	b. 3.9.2009.	FV	22.50
	c. 3.2.2011.	FV	20.00
93	**100 Bolívares** 20.3.2007; 19.12.2008; 3.9.2009; 3.2.2011. Brown and tan on multicolor underprint. Simon Bolívar. Back: Two birds. Printer: CMV 69x157mm.		
	a. 20.3.2007.	FV	50.00
	b. 19.12.2008.	FV	50.00
	c. 3.9.2009.	FV	50.00
	d. 3.2.2011.	FV	50.00

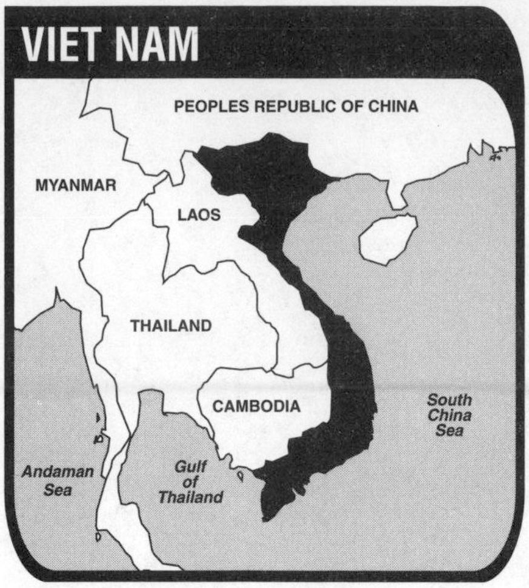

The Socialist Republic of Viet Nam, located in Southeast Asia west of the South China Sea, has an area of 329,560 sq. km. and a population of 86.12 million. Capital: Hanoi. Agricultural products, saltwater fish, shellfish, coal, mineral ores and electronic products are exported.

The conquest of Viet Nam by France began in 1858 and was completed by 1884. It became part of French Indochina in 1887. Viet Nam declared independence after World War II, but France continued to rule until its 1954 defeat by communist forces under Ho Chi Minh. Under the Geneva Accords of 1954, Viet Nam was divided into the communist North and anti-communist South. The US and its allies' sent economic and military aid to South Viet Nam and the Soviety Union and its allies sent their aid to the North. The US and its allies were withdrawn following a cease-fire agreement in 1973. Two years later, North Vietnamese forces overran the South reuniting the country under Communist rule. Despite the return of peace, for over a decade the country experienced limited economic growth because of the communist leadership policies. However, since the enactment of Viet Nam's *doi moi* (renovation) policy in 1986, Vietnamese authorities have committed to increased economic liberalization and enacted structural reforms needed to modernize the economy and to produce more competitive, export-driven industries, which greatly reduced inflation and greatly increased economic growth.

MONETARY SYSTEM:

1 Dong = 100 Xu = 100 Su to 1975
1 New Dong = 500 Old Dong, 1975-76
Replacement Notes: #5-7, 11-14, star instead of series prefix of letter and number.
Note: HCM = Ho Chi Minh

Democratic Republic

Ngân Hàng Nhà Nu'ó'c Viêt Nam

State Bank of Viet Nam

1964 ND; 1972; 1975 Issue

		VF	UNC
74A	**20 Dông** 1969. Oleve on dark green underprint. HCM at left. Coat of arms at right. Back: Tractor. (Not issued).	—	400.
75	**2 Xu** ND (1964). Purple on green underprint. Arms at center.		
	a. Issued note.	15.00	75.00
	s. Specimen.	—	200.

		VF	UNC
76	**5 Xu** 1975 (date in light brown above *VIET* at lower left center). Purple on brown underprint. Arms at upper right.		
	a. Watermark: 15mm stars.	3.00	10.00
	b. Watermark: 30mm radiant star.	3.00	10.00
	s1. Specimen. Without watermark.	—	15.00
	s2. Specimen. As a. Red overprint: *MAU BAC.NI>*	—	20.00

		VF	UNC
77	**1 Hao** 1972. Violet on multicolor underprint. Arms at center. Back: Woman feeding pigs. 103x57mm.		
	a. Watermark: 15mm stars. Series KG-?.	3.00	10.00
	b. Watermark: 32mm encircled stars. Series MK-?.	3.00	10.00
	c. Without watermark. Series ML.	3.00	10.00
	s1. Specimen. Without watermark.	—	15.00
	s2. Specimen. As a. Red overprint: *MAU BAC.NI>*	—	20.00
77A	**1 Hao** 1972. Violet on multicolor underprint. Arms at center. Back: Woman feeding pigs. Reduced size. Specimen. 96x48mm.	Unc	20.00
78	**2 Hao** 1975. Brownish gray on green and peach underprint. Arms at center. Back: Two men spraying rice field.		
	a. Issued note.	3.00	10.00
	s. Specimen.	—	15.00

Socialist Republic

The country was united under the name of Socialist Republic of Viet Nam on July 2, 1976 after the Democratic Republic of (North) Viet Nam and the southern Peoples Revolutionary Government with assistance from China, Eastern Europe and the Soviet Union, won their long war against the Republic of (South) Viet Nam.

Ngân Hàng Nhà Nu'ó'c Việt Nam

State Bank of Viet Nam

1976 Dated Issue

Northern 1958 and Southern 1966-dated notes were exchanged in 1978 for 1976-dated notes to unify the currency of North and South Viet Nam. All of the old northern and southern Xu and Hao notes continued as legal tender, but the old Dong notes were overstamped with *Da Thu*, **marked with an *X*, and/or destroyed.**

			VF	UNC
79	**5 Hao**			
	1976. Purple on multicolor underprint. Back: Coconut palms and river scene.			
		a. Issued note.	1.00	3.00
		s. Specimen. Reported not confirmed.	—	—

			VF	UNC
80	**1 Dông**			
	1976. Brown on multicolor underprint. Arms at center. Back: Factory.			
		a. Issued note.	1.00	3.00
		s. Specimen.	—	30.00

			VF	UNC
81	**5 Dông**			
	1976. Blue-gray and green on pink underprint. Back: Green on yellow underprint. Two women with fish in foreground, boats in harbor in background.			
		a. Watermark: Flower. Block letter at left, six digit serial # at right.	1.00	4.00
		b. Block letter and seven digit serial # together. Without watermark.	1.00	3.00
		s. Specimen. As b. Red overprint: *SPECIMEN* on face.	—	25.00

			VF	UNC
82	**10 Dông**			
	1976. Purple and brown on multicolor underprint. Back: Elephants logging at center.			
		a. Issued note.	1.00	5.00
		s. Specimen.	—	30.00

			VF	UNC
83	**20 Dông**			
	1976. Blue on pink and green underprint. HCM at right, arms at left. Back: Tractors and dam.			
		a. Issued note.	2.00	10.00
		s. Specimen.	—	30.00
84	**50 Dông**			
	1976. Red-brown on pink and green underprint. HCM at right, arms at left. 2 serial number varieties. Back: Hong Gay open pit mining scene.			
		a. Large block letters and serial #.	1.25	7.00
		b. Small block letters and serial #.	1.25	7.00
		s. Specimen.	—	25.00

Socialist Republic of Viet Nam

Ngân Hàng Nhà Nu'ó'c Việt Nam

State Bank of Viet Nam

1980; 1981 Issue

			VF	UNC
85	**2 Dông**			
	1980 (1981). Brown on multicolor underprint. Arms at center. Back: River scene.			
		a. Issued note.	.75	2.00
		s. Specimen. Red overprint: *SPECIMEN* on face.	—	30.00

			VF	UNC
86	**10 Dông**			
	1980 (1981). Brown on multicolor underprint. Arms at right. Back: House and trees.			
		a. Issued note.	.75	4.00
		s1. Specimen. Serial # of zeroes.	—	50.00
		s2. Specimen. Serial # of 1's.	—	15.00

87	**30 Dông**	VF	UNC
	1981 (1982). Purple, brown and multicolor. Arms at left center, HCM at right. Large and small serial number varieties. Back: Harbor scene.		
	a. Small block letters and serial #.	1.50	8.00
	b. Large block letters and serial #.	15.00	30.00
	s1. Specimen overprint: *SPECIMEN.* Small block letters and serial #.	30.00	60.00
	s2. Specimen overprint: *GIAY MÂU.* Large Block letters and serial #.	—	40.00

88	**100 Dông**	VF	UNC
	1980 (1981). Brown, dark blue and multicolor. Portrait HCM at right, arms at center. Large or small digits in serial number. Back: Blue, purple and brown. Boats and rock formations in sea cove. Watermark: HCM.		
	a. Small block letters and serial #.	1.00	8.00
	b. Large block letters and serial #.	2.00	10.00
	s. Specimen.	—	40.00

1985 Issue

89	**5 Hao**	VF	UNC
	1985. Red-violet on light blue underprint. Tower of Ha Noi at left center, arms at right. Back: Large 5 at center.		
	a. Issued note.	2.00	4.00
	s. Specimen. Red overprint: *SPECIMEN* on face.	—	20.00

90	**1 Dông**	VF	UNC
	1985. Blue-green on multicolor underprint. Tower of Ha Noi at left center, arms at right. Back: Sampans along rocky coastline. UV: fibers fluoresce blue.		
	a. Issued note.	.50	2.00
	s. Specimen. Red overprint: *SPECIMEN* on face. Serial # prefix AA, AE.	—	25.00

91	**2 Dông**	VF	UNC
	1985. Purple on multicolor underprint. Tower of Ha Noi at left center, arms at right. Back: Sampans anchored along coastline.		
	a. Issued note.	.75	2.00
	s. Specimen. Red overprint: *SPECIMEN* on face.	—	20.00

92	**5 Dông**	VF	UNC
	1985. Green on multicolor underprint. Tower of Ha Noi at left center, arms at right. Back: Sampans anchored in river.		
	a. Issued note.	.50	2.00
	s. Specimen. Red overprint: *SPECIMEN* on face.	—	20.00

93	**10 Dông**	VF	UNC
	1985. Brown-violet on multicolor underprint. Tower of Ha Noi at left center, arms at right. Back: Island in the Lake Hoan Kiem in Hanoi		
	a. Issued note.	.75	3.00
	s. Specimen. Red overprint: *SPECIMEN* on face.	—	20.00

94	**20 Dông**	VF	UNC
	1985 (1986). Brown, dark purple and multicolor. HCM at right, arms at center right. Back: One pillar pagoda in Hanoi.		
	a. Issued note.	.75	2.00
	s. Specimen. Red overprint: *SPECIMEN* on face. Serial # prefix AD, AH.	—	30.00

95	**30 Dông**	VF	UNC
	1985 (1986). Blue and multicolor. HCM at right, arms at left. Back: Large building with clock tower at center.		
	a. Issued note.	1.25	5.00
	s. Specimen. Red overprint: *SPECIMEN* on face.	—	27.50

96 50 Dông VF UNC

1985. Green, brown and multicolor. HCM at right, arms at left center. Back: Thac Ba hydro power plant and reservoir (Hoang Lien Son Province).

	VF	UNC
a. Issued note.	1.50	7.00
s. Specimen.	—	25.00

97 50 Dông VF UNC

1985 (1987). Blue-gray on orange and multicolor underprint. HCM at right, arms at center. Back: Thang Loing bridge crossing the Red River (north of Ha Noi) at center.

	VF	UNC
a. Issued note.	.75	3.00
s. Specimen.	—	15.00

98 100 Dông VF UNC

1985. Brown, green, yellow and multicolor. HCM at right, arms at left center. Back: Planting rice. Watermark: HCM.

	VF	UNC
a. Issued note.	2.50	15.00
s. Specimen.	—	30.00

99 500 Dông VF UNC

1985. Red on blue and multicolor underprint. HCM at right, arms at upper center. Back: Bim Son Cement plant (Thanh Hoa Province) at left center. Watermark: HCM.

	VF	UNC
a. Issued note.	3.00	12.50
s. Specimen.	—	40.00

1987; 1988 Issue

100 200 Dông VF UNC

1987. Red-brown and tan on multicolor underprint. HCM at right, arms at left center. Back: Field workers at left and tractor at center right. UV: fibers fluoresce red and blue; serial # red. 131x62mm.

	VF	UNC
a. Small sans serif serial # digits.	.50	1.00
b. Large sans serif serial # digits.	3.00	5.00
c. Small serif serial # digits.	.50	1.00
s. Specimen. Green overprint: *SPECIMEN* on face.	—	20.00

101 500 Dông VF UNC

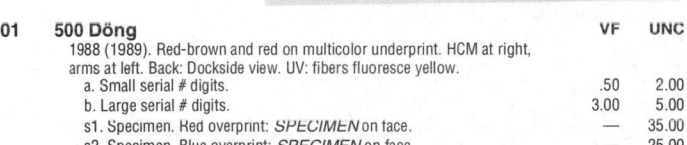

1988 (1989). Red-brown and red on multicolor underprint. HCM at right, arms at left. Back: Dockside view. UV: fibers fluoresce yellow.

	VF	UNC
a. Small serial # digits.	.50	2.00
b. Large serial # digits.	3.00	5.00
s1. Specimen. Red overprint: *SPECIMEN* on face.	—	35.00
s2. Specimen. Blue overprint: *SPECIMEN* on face.	—	25.00

102 1000 Dông VF UNC

1987 (1988). Dark brown and deep olive-green on multicolor underprint. HCM at right, arms at left center. Back: Open pit mining equipment at left center. Watermark: HCM.

	VF	UNC
a. Issued note.	3.00	20.00
s. Specimen. Red overprint: *SPECIMEN* on each side.	—	27.50

103 2000 Dông

1987 (1988). Dark and light brown on green and multicolor underprint. HCM at right, arms at left center. Back: Dark purple. Pha Lai thermo power plant (Hai Hung Province) at left center. Watermark: HCM.

	VF	UNC
a. Issued note.	4.00	40.00
s. Specimen. Red overprint: *SPECIMEN* on each side.	—	30.00

104 5000 Dông

1987 (1989). Deep blue, purple, brown and green on multicolor underprint. HCM at right, arms at left center. Back: Offshore oil rigs at left center. Watermark: HCM.

	VF	UNC
a. Issued note.	2.00	10.00
s. Specimen. Red overprint: *SPECIMEN* on each side.	—	32.50

1988-91 Issue

105 100 Dông

1991 (1992). Light brown on multicolor underprint. Arms at left. Back: Temple and pagoda at left center.

	VF	UNC
a. Small serif serial # digits. Serif or sans serif.	.50	1.00
b. Large sans serif serial # digits.	3.00	5.00
s1. Specimen. Red overprint: *TIEN MÂU* on face.	—	32.50
s2. Specimen. Red overprint: *SPECIMEN.*	—	40.00

106 1000 Dông

1988 (1989). Purple on gold and multicolor underprint. HCM at right, arms at left center. Back: Elephant logging at center. UV: fibers fluoresce red and blue.

	VF	UNC
a. Small serif serial # digits.	.25	1.50
b. Large sans serif serial # digits.	3.00	5.00
s. Specimen. Red overprint: *SPECIMEN* on face.	—	45.00

107 2000 Dông

1988 (1989). Brownish purple on lilac and multicolor underprint. HCM at right, arms at left. Back: Women workers in textile factory. UV: fibers fluoresce yellow and blue. 135x65mm.

	VF	UNC
a. Small serif serial # digits.	.50	2.00
b. Large sans serif serial # digits.	3.00	5.00
s1. Specimen. Red overprint: *TIÊ MÂU* on face and *SPECIMEN* on back.	—	20.00
s2. Specimen. Red overprint: *SPECIMEN* on face and *TIÊ MÂU* on back.	—	35.00

108 5000 Dông

1991 (1993). Dark blue on multicolor underprint. HCM at right, arms at left. Back: Electric lines. UV: fibers fluoresce blue. 134x64mm.

	VF	UNC
a. Issued note.	.75	3.00
s. Specimen. Red overprint: *SPECIMEN* on face.	—	45.00

109 10,000 Dông

1990 (1992). Red and red-violet on multicolor underprint. HCM at right, arms at center. Back: Junks along coastline at center. Watermark: HCM. 140x68mm.

	VF	UNC
a. Issued note.	1.50	20.00
s. Specimen. Red overprint: *SPECIMEN* on each side.	—	32.50

110 20,000 Dông

1991 (1993). Blue-green on multicolor underprint. HCM at right, arms at center. Back: Packing factory. Watermark: HCM. 140x68mm.

	VF	UNC
a. Issued note.	1.25	8.00
s. Specimen. Red overprint: *SPECIMEN* on each side.	—	35.00

111 **50,000 Dông** — **VF** / **UNC**

1990 (1993). Dark olive-green and black on multicolor underprint. HCM at right, arms at upper left center, date at lower right. Back: Dockside view. Watermark: HCM.

	VF	UNC
a. Issued note.	3.50	25.00
s. Specimen. Red overprint: *SPECIMEN* on each side.	—	32.50

1992 Bank Cheque Issue

#112-114A Negotiable Bank Cheques/Certificates with expiration dates used for high value merchandise and large transactions. Specimens are valued a 2x the Unc. price.

112 **100,000 Dông** — **VF** / **UNC**

1992-94.

	VF	UNC
a. Issued note.	600.	1000.
s. Specimen.	—	1000.

113 **500,000 Dông** — **VF** / **UNC**

1992-2000.

	VF	UNC
a. Issued note	300.	450.
s. Specimen.	—	400.

114 **1,000,000 Dông** — **VF** / **UNC**

1992-2001.

	VF	UNC
a. Issued note.	300.	450.
s. Specimen.	—	400.

114A **5,000,000 Dông**

1992-2001.

	VF	UNC
a. Issued note.	300.	450.
s. Specimen.	—	400.

1993; 1994 Issue

115 **10,000 Dông** — **VF** / **UNC**

1993. Red and red-violet on multicolor underprint. HCM at right, arms at center, optical registry device at lower left, modified underprint color around arms. Back: Brown -violet on multicolor underprint. Junks along coastline at center. Watermark: HCM. 140x68mm.

	VF	UNC
a. Issued note.	FV	4.00
s. Specimen. Black overprint: *SPECIMEN* on face.	—	45.00

116 **50,000 Dông** — **VF** / **UNC**

1994. Dark olive-green and black on multicolor underprint. HCM at right with date below, arms at upper left center. Back: Dockside view. Watermark: HCM. 140x68mm.

	VF	UNC
a. Issued note.	FV	8.00
s. Specimen. Red overprint: *SPECIMEN* on face.	—	45.00

117 **100,000 Dông** — **VF** / **UNC**

1994 (2000). Brown and light green on multicolor underprint. HCM at right. Back: HCM's house. 145x71mm.

	VF	UNC
a. Issued note.	FV	20.00
s. Specimen. Red overprint: *SPECIMEN* on face.	—	45.00

2001 Commemorative Issue

#118, 50th Anniversary National Bank of Viet Nam

Released in a special folder and envelope. Face value is minimal.

118 50 Dông

2001. Rose on multicolor underprint. HCM at right center. Back: Bank building. Polymer plastic. Released in a special folder and envelope. Face value is minimal.

	VF	UNC
a. Issued note.	—	30.00

2003 Issue

#118A-9-121 HCM at r. Printed originally at NPA, later printings done at the National banknote Printing Plant (NBPP) in Viet Nam.

119 10,000 Dông

(20)06-. Brown, green and yellow on multicolor underprint. HCM at right. Back: Sea platform. Polymer plaster. 132x59mm.

	VF	UNC
a. (20)06.	FV	2.00
b. (20)07.	FV	1.50
c. (20)08.	FV	1.00
d. (20)09.	FV	1.00
e. (20)10.	FV	1.00
f. (20)11.	FV	1.00
s. Specimen.	—	25.00

120 20,000 Dông

(20)06-. Purple and blue on multicolor underprint. HCM at right. Back: Palace. Polymer plastic. 136x65mm.

	VF	UNC
a. (20)06.	FV	4.00
b. (20)07.	FV	3.50
c. (20)08.	FV	3.00
d. (20)09.	FV	3.00
e. (20)12.	FV	3.00
s. Specimen.	—	35.00

121 50,000 Dông

(20)03-. Rose on multicolor underprint. HCM at right. Back: Buildings in Hua. Polymer plastic. 139x65mm.

	VF	UNC
a. (20)03.	FV	7.00
b. (20)04.	FV	6.50
c. (20)05.	FV	6.00
d. (20)06.	FV	5.50
e. (20)07.	FV	5.00
f. (20)08.	FV	5.00
g. (20)09.	FV	5.00
h. (20)11.	FV	5.00
i. (20)12.	FV	5.00
s. Specimen.	—	45.00

122 100,000 Dông

(20)04-. Green on multicolor underprint. HCM at right. Back: Van Mieu Quoc Tu Giam (National University). Ploymer plastic. 144x65mm.

	VF	UNC
a. (20)04.	FV	12.00
b. (20)05.	FV	11.00
c. (20)06.	FV	10.00
d. (20)07.	FV	9.50
e. (20)08.	FV	9.00
f. (20)09.	FV	9.00
g. (20)11.	FV	9.00
s. Specimen.	—	55.00

123 200,000 Dông

(20)06-. Rose on yellow and multicolor underprint. HCM at right. Back: Lake with rock formations. Polymer plastic. 148x64mm.

	VF	UNC
a. (20)06.	FV	25.00
b. (20)07.	FV	24.00
c. (20)08.	FV	23.00
d. (20)09.	FV	22.00
e. (20)11.	FV	22.00
s. Specimen.	—	65.00

124 500,000 Dông

(20)03-. Blue and green on multicolor underprint. HCM at right. Back: HCM's birthplace in Kim Lien, Nghean Province. Polymer plastic. 151x65mm.

	VF	UNC
a. (20)03.	FV	70.00
b. (20)04.	FV	69.00
c. (20)05.	FV	68.00
d. (20)06.	FV	67.00
e. (20)08.	FV	65.00
f. (20)11.	FV	65.00
s. Specimen.	—	70.00

WEST AFRICAN STATES

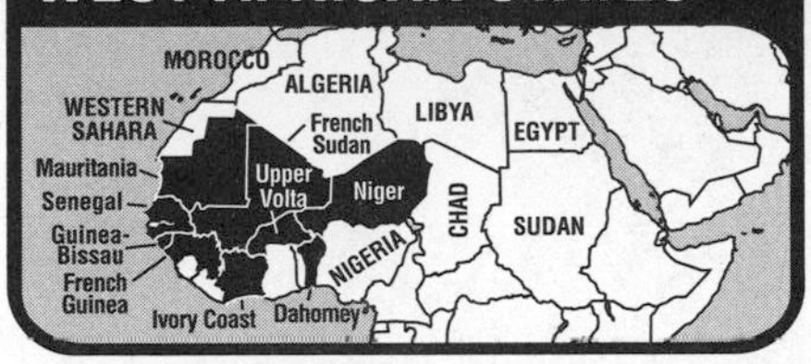

The West African States, a former federation of eight French colonial territories on the northwest coast of Africa, had an area of 1,813,079 sq. mi. (4,742,495 sq. km.) and a population of about 60 million. Capital: Dakar. The constituent territories were Mauritania, Senegal, Dahomey, French Sudan, Ivory Coast, Upper Volta, Niger and French Guinea.

The members of the federation were overseas territories within the French Union until Sept. of 1958 when all but French Guinea approved the constitution of the Fifth French Republic, thereby electing to become autonomous members of the new French Community. French Guinea voted to become the fully independent Republic of Guinea. The other seven attained independence in 1960. The French West Africa territories were provided with a common currency, a practice which was continued as the monetary union of the West African States which provides a common currency to the autonomous republics of Dahomey (now Benin), Mali, Senegal, Upper Volta (now Burkina Faso) Ivory Coast, Togo, Niger, and Guinea-Bissau.

MONETARY SYSTEM:

1 Franc = 100 Centimes

DATING:

The year of issue on the current notes appear in the first 2 digits of the serial number, i.e. (19)91, (19)92, etc.

SIGNATURE VARIETIES

	LE PRÉSIDENT	LE DIRECTEUR GÉNÉRAL	DATE
1			Various dates - 1959 20.3.1961
2			20.3.1961
3			20.12.1964
4			2.3.1965, ND
5			ND
6			ND
7			ND
8			ND
9			ND
	LE PRÉSIDENT DU CONSEIL DES MINISTRES	LE GOUVERNEUR	DATE
10			ND
11			ND (1977); 1977
12			ND (1978); 1978; 1979

SIGNATURE VARIETIES

13			ND (1980); 1980
14			ND (1977); 1977; 1988; 1989
15			ND (1981); 1981; 1982
16			ND (1983); 1983
17			1981; 1983; 1984
18			ND (1984); 1984
19			1984; 1985
20			1986; 1987
21			1989
22			1991
23			1992
24			1992
25			1993
26			1994
27			1994; 1995
28			1996; 1997
29			1999
30			2000; 2001
31			2002; 2003
32			2003

Banque Centrale des Etats de l'Afrique de l'Ouest

A for Cote d'Ivoire (Ivory Coast)

1959-65; ND Issue

101A 100 Francs

1961-65; ND. Dark brown, orange and multicolor. Design like #201B.

	VF	UNC
a. Engraved. Signature 1. 20.3.1961.	18.00	65.00
b. Signature 2. 20.3.1961.	18.00	65.00
c. Litho. Signature 2. 20.3.1961.	18.00	65.00
d. Signature 3. 2.12.1964.	18.00	65.00
e. Signature 4. 2.3.1965.	18.00	65.00
f. Signature 4. ND.	15.00	40.00
g. Signature 5. ND.	15.00	50.00

102A 500 Francs

1959-64; ND. Brown, green and multicolor. Field workers at left, mask carving at right. Back: Woman at left, farmer on tractor at right. Watermark: Woman's head.

	VF	UNC
a. Engraved. Signature 1. 15.4.1959.	55.00	—
b. Signature 1. 20.3.1961.	30.00	90.00
c. Signature 2. 20.3.1961.	45.00	—
d. Signature 3. 2.12.1964.	55.00	—
e. Signature 5. ND.	35.00	90.00
f. Signature 6. ND.	25.00	75.00
g. Litho. Signature 6. ND.	30.00	90.00
h. Signature 7. ND.	30.00	90.00
i. Signature 8. ND.	50.00	—
j. Signature 9. ND.	18.00	50.00
k. Signature 10. ND.	15.00	40.00
l. Signature 11. ND.	12.00	35.00
m. Signature 12. ND.	18.00	55.00

103A 1000 Francs

1959-65; ND. Brown, blue and multicolor. Man and woman at center. Back: Man with rope suspension bridge in background and pineapples. Watermark: Man's head.

	VF	UNC
a. Engraved. Signature 1. 17.9.1959.	—	—
b. Signature 1. 20.3.1961.	30.00	90.00
c. Signature 2. 20.3.1961.	25.00	75.00
d. Signature 4. 2.3.1965.	80.00	—
e. Signature 5. ND.	20.00	60.00
f. Signature 6. ND.	20.00	60.00
g. Litho. Signature 6. ND.	20.00	60.00
h. Signature 7. ND.	22.00	65.00
i. Signature 8. ND.	22.00	75.00
j. Signature 9. ND.	20.00	60.00
k. Signature 10. ND.	15.00	40.00
l. Signature 11. ND.	15.00	40.00
m. Signature 12. ND.	15.00	40.00
n. Signature 13. ND.	15.00	40.00

104A 5000 Francs

1961-65; ND. Blue, brown and multicolor. Bearded man at left, building at center. Back: Woman, corn grinders and huts.

	VF	UNC
a. Signature 1. 20.3.1961.	125.	—
b. Signature 2. 20.3.1961.	75.00	—
c. Signature 3. 2.12.1964.	100.	—
d. Signature 4. 2.3.1965.	125.	—
e. Signature 6. ND.	75.00	225.
f. Signature 7. ND.	90.00	—
g. Signature 8. ND.	125.	—
h. Signature 9. ND.	55.00	200.
i. Signature 10. ND.	55.00	200.
j. Signature 11. ND.	55.00	200.

1977-81; ND Issue

#105A-109A smaller size notes.

105A 500 Francs

1979-80. Lilac, light olive-green and multicolor. Artwork at left, long horn animals at center, man wearing hat at right. Back: Cultivated palm at left, aerial view at center, mask at right. Watermark: Woman in profile.

	VF	UNC
a. Signature 12. 1979.	12.00	30.00
b. Signature 13. 1980.	12.00	30.00

106A 500 Francs

1981-90. Pale olive-green and multicolor. Artwork at left, long horn animals at center, man wearing hat at right. Back: Cultivated palm at left, aerial view at center, mask at right. Watermark: Woman in profile.

	VF	UNC
a. Signature 14. 1988.	3.00	8.00
b. Signature 15. 1981. (BF).	15.00	35.00
c. Signature 15. 1981. (F-CO).	3.00	10.00
d. Signature 15. 1982. (BF).	20.00	50.00
e. Signature 17. 1981. (F-CO).	20.00	50.00
f. Signature 17. 1983.	3.00	10.00
g. Signature 18. 1984.	3.00	9.00
h. Signature 19. 1984.	3.00	9.00
i. Signature 19. 1985.	3.00	9.00
j. Signature 20. 1986.	3.00	8.00
k. Signature 20. 1987.	3.00	8.00
l. Signature 21 (reversed order). 1989.	3.00	8.00
m. Signature 22. 1990.	3.00	8.00

107A 1000 Francs

1981-90. Brown on multicolor underprint. Artwork at left, open pit mine at center, woman at right. Back: Wood carver with finished works. Watermark: Woman.

	VF	UNC
a. Signature 14. 1988.	4.00	10.00
b. Signature 15. 1981.	4.00	15.00
c. Signature 17. 1981.	5.00	15.00
d. Signature 18. 1984.	5.00	12.00
e. Signature 19. 1984.	10.00	30.00
f. Signature 19. 1985.	4.00	12.00
g. Signature 20. 1986.	4.00	10.00
h. Signature 20. 1987.	4.00	10.00
i. Signature 21. 1989.	4.00	10.00
j. Signature 22. 1990.	4.00	10.00

108A 5000 Francs

1977-91. Black and red on multicolor underprint. Woman at left, fish and boats on shore at center, carving at right. Back: Carvings, fishing boats and mask.

	VF	UNC
a. Signature 11. 1977.	25.00	65.00
b. Signature 12. 1978.	25.00	65.00
c. Signature 12. 1979.	35.00	90.00
d. Signature 13. 1980.	35.00	90.00
e. Signature 14. 1977.	35.00	—
f. Signature 14. 1988.	10.00	35.00
g. Signature 14. 1989.	10.00	35.00
h. Signature 15. 1981.	20.00	50.00
i. Signature 15. 1982.	20.00	50.00
j. Signature 16. 1983.	—	—
k. Signature 17. 1983.	—	—
l. Signature 18. 1984.	22.00	55.00
m. Signature 19. 1984.	20.00	50.00
n. Signature 19. 1985.	20.00	50.00
o. Signature 20. 1986.	35.00	—
p. Signature 20. 1987.	10.00	35.00
q. Signature 21. 1990.	10.00	35.00
r. Signature 22. 1991.	10.00	35.00

109A 10,000 Francs

ND (1977-92). Red-brown on multicolor underprint. Two men seated operating primitive spinning apparatus, woman with headwear at right. Back: Figurine and girl at left, modern textile spinning machine at center. Watermark: Woman with headwear.

	VF	UNC
a. Signature 11. ND.	35.00	100.
b. Signature 12. ND.	90.00	—
c. Signature 13. ND.	35.00	100.
d. Signature 14. ND.	20.00	90.00
e. Signature 15. ND.	20.00	70.00
f. Signature 18. ND.	35.00	
g. Signature 19. ND.	40.00	110.
h. Signature 20. ND.	35.00	
i. Signature 21. ND.	20.00	60.00
j. Signature 22. ND.	20.00	60.00
k. Signature 23. ND.	25.00	—

1991-92 Issue

#113A and 114A were first issued on 19.9.1994.

110A 500 Francs

(19)91-(20)02. Dark brown and dark green on multicolor underprint. Man at right, flood control dam at center. Back: Farmer riding spray rig behind garden tractor at center, native art at left. Watermark: Man.

	VF	UNC
a. Signature 22. (19)91.	3.00	8.00
b. Signature 23. (19)92.	3.00	8.00
c. Signature 25. (19)93.	3.00	7.00
d. Signature 26. (19)94.	3.00	7.00
e. Signature 27. (19)95.	3.00	7.00
f. Signature 28. (19)96.	3.00	7.00
g. Signature 28. (19)97. 10-digit serial #.	3.00	7.00
h. Signature 28. (19)97. 11-digit serial #.	5.00	10.00
i. Signature 28. (19)98.	3.00	7.00
j. Signature 28. (19)99.	3.00	6.00
k. Signature 29. (19)99.	9.00	—
l. Signature 30. (20)01.	3.00	6.00
m. Signature 31. (20)02.	3.00	6.00

111A 1000 Francs

(19)91-(20)03. Dark brown-violet on tan, yellow and multicolor underprint. Workmen hauling peanuts to storage at center, woman's head at right. Back: Twin statues and mask at left, two women with baskets, elevated riverside storage bins in background at center. Watermark: Woman's head.

	VF	UNC
a. Signature 22. (19)91.	5.00	10.00
b. Signature 23. (19)92.	5.00	10.00
c. Signature 25. (19)93.	5.00	10.00
d. Signature 26. (19)94.	4.00	9.00
e. Signature 27. (19)95.	4.00	9.00
f. Signature 28. (19)96.	4.00	9.00
g. Signature 28. (19)97.	4.00	9.00
h. Signature 28. (19)98.	3.00	8.00
i. Signature 29. (19)99.	3.00	8.00
j. Signature 30. (20)01.	3.00	8.00
k. Signature 31. (20)02.	3.00	8.00
l. Signature 31. (20)03.	3.00	8.00

112A 2500 Francs

(19)92-(19)94. Deep purple and dark brown on lilac and multicolor underprint. Dam at center, young woman's head at right. Back: Statue at left, harvesting and spraying of fruit at left center. Watermark: Young woman's head.

	VF	UNC
a. Signature 23. (19)92.	7.00	20.00
b. Signature 25. (19)93.	6.00	15.00
c. Signature 27. (19)94.	6.00	15.00

113A 5000 Francs

(19)92-(20)03. Dark brown and deep blue on multicolor underprint. Woman wearing headdress adorned with cowrie shells at right, smelting plant at center. Back: Women with children and various pottery at left center. Watermark: Woman wearing headdress adorned with cowrie shells.

	VF	UNC
a. Signature 23. (19)92.	9.00	25.00
b. Signature 25. (19)93.	9.00	25.00
c. Signature 27. (19)94.	8.00	20.00
d. Signature 27. (19)95.	8.00	20.00
e. Signature 28. (19)96.	8.00	20.00
f. Signature 28. (19)97.	8.00	20.00
g. Signature 28. (19)98.	8.00	20.00
h. Signature 29. (19)98.	8.00	20.00
i. Signature 29. (19)99.	8.00	20.00
j. Signature 30. (20)00.	20.00	—
k. Signature 30. (20)01.	8.00	20.00
l. Signature 31. (20)02.	8.00	20.00
m. Signature 31. (20)03.	8.00	20.00

114A 10,000 Francs

(19)92-(20)01. Dark brown on multicolor underprint. Headman with scepter at right, skyscraper at center. Back: Native art at left, woman crossing vine bridge over river at center. Watermark: Headman with scepter.

	VF	UNC
a. Signature 25. (19)92.	15.00	45.00
b. Signature 27. (19)94.	15.00	45.00
c. Signature 27. (19)95.	15.00	45.00
d. Signature 28. (19)96.	15.00	45.00
e. Signature 28. (19)97.	15.00	45.00
f. Signature 28. (19)98.	25.00	—
g. Signature 29. (19)98.	15.00	45.00
h. Signature 29. (19)99.	15.00	45.00
i. Signature 30. (20)00.	25.00	—
j. Signature 30. (20)01.	15.00	45.00

2003 Issue

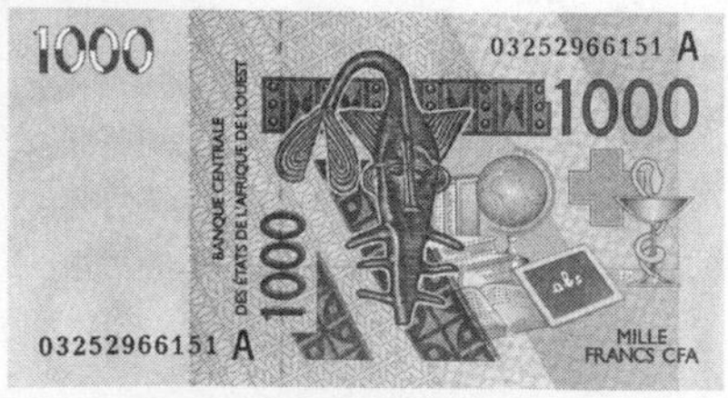

115A 1000 Francs

(20)03-. Red-brown on red and multicolor underprint. 125x65mm.

	VF	UNC
a. Signature 32. (20)03.	FV	6.00
b. Signature 32. (20)04.	FV	6.00

116A 2000 Francs

(20)03-. Blue on light blue and multicolor underprint. 130x66mm.

	VF	UNC
a. Signature 32. (20)03.	FV	10.00
b. Signature 32. (20)04.	FV	8.00

117A 5000 Francs

(20)03-. Multicolor. 141x74mm.

	VF	UNC
a. Signature 32. (20)03.	FV	20.00
b. Signature 32. (20)04.	FV	17.50
c. Signature 33. (20)05.	FV	17.50

118A 10,000 Francs

(20)03-. Multicolor. 145x74mm.

	VF	UNC
a. Signature 32. (20)03.	FV	40.00
b. Signature 32. (20)04.	FV	35.00

B for Benin (Dahomey)

1959-65; ND Issue

201B 100 Francs

1961-65; ND. Dark brown, orange and multicolor. Like #101A.

	VF	UNC
a. Engraved. Signature 1. 20.3.1961.	40.00	120.
b. Signature 2. 20.3.1961.	35.00	100.
c. Litho. Signature 2. 20.3.1961.	35.00	100.
d. Signature 3. 2.12.1964.	65.00	—
e. Signature 4. 2.3.1965.	20.00	65.00
f. Signature 4. ND.	15.00	45.00

202B 500 Francs

1961-64; ND. Brown, green and multicolor. Field workers at left, mask carving at right. Back: Woman at left, farmer on tractor at right. Watermark: Woman's head.

	VF	UNC
a. Signature 1. 20.3.1961.	—	—
b. Engraved signature 2. 20.3.1961.	—	—
d. Signature 3. 2.12.1964.	—	—
e. Signature 4. 2.3.1965.	—	—
f. Signature 5. ND.	70.00	—
g. Signature 6. ND.	30.00	85.00
h. Litho. Signature 7. ND.	35.00	100.
i. Signature 8. ND.	70.00	—
j. Signature 9. ND.	30.00	85.00
k. Signature 10. ND.	20.00	60.00
l. Signature 11. ND.	15.00	50.00

203D 1000 Francs

1961-65; ND. Brown, blue and multicolor. Man and woman at center. Back: Man with rope suspension bridge in background and pineapples. Watermark: Man's head.

	VF	UNC
a. Engraved. Signature 1. 17.9.1959.	—	—
b. Signature 1. 20.3.1961.	—	—
c. Signature 2. 20.3.1961.	90.00	—
d. Signature 4. 2.3.1965.	60.00	—
g. Signature 6. ND.	35.00	—
h. Litho. Signature 6. ND.	35.00	75.00
i. Signature 7. ND.	60.00	150.
j. Signature 8. ND.	35.00	100.
k. Signature 9. ND.	35.00	—
l. Signature 10. ND.	20.00	60.00
m. Signature 11. ND.	15.00	50.00
n. Signature 12. ND.	20.00	60.00

204B 5000 Francs

1961; ND. Blue, brown and multicolor. Bearded man at left, building at center. Back: Woman, corn grinders and huts.

	VF	UNC
a. Signature 1. 20.3.1961.	150.	—
b. Signature 2. 20.3.1961.	150.	—
h. Signature 6. ND.	75.00	250.
j. Signature 7. ND.	75.00	250.
k. Signature 9. ND.	50.00	—
l. Signature 10. ND.	50.00	—

1977-81; ND ISSUE

#205B-209B smaller size notes.

205B 500 Francs

1979-80. Lilac, light olive-green and multicolor. Artwork at left, long horn animbals at center, man wearing hat at right. Back: Cultivated palm at left, aerial view at center, mask at right.

	VF	UNC
a. Signature 12. 1979.	65.00	—
b. Signature 13. 1980.	12.00	30.00

206B 500 Francs

1981-90. Pale olive-green and multicolor. Artwork at left, long horn animals at center, man wearing hat at right. Back: Cultivated palm at left, aerial view at center, mask at right. Watermark: Woman in profile.

	VF	UNC
a. Signature 14. 1988.	15.00	—
b. Signature 15. 1981. (BF).	7.00	20.00
c. Signature 15. 1981. (F-CO).	3.00	12.00
d. Signature 15. 1982. (BF).	20.00	50.00
e. Signature 17. 1981. (F-CO).	—	—
f. Signature 17. 1983. (BF).	—	—
g. Signature 18. 1984.	5.00	15.00
h. Signature 19. 1984.	5.00	15.00
i. Signature 19. 1985.	7.00	20.00
j. Signature 20. 1986.	3.00	12.00
k. Signature 20. 1987.	15.00	—
l. Signature 21. 1989.	3.00	10.00
m. Signature 22. 1990.	3.00	10.00

207B 1000 Francs

1981-90. Brown on multicolor underprint. Artwork at left, open pit mine at center, woman at right. Back: Wood carver with finished works. Watermark: Woman.

	VF	UNC
a. Signature 14. 1988.	5.00	15.00
b. Signature 15. 1981.	7.00	20.00
c. Signature 18. 1984.	5.00	15.00
d. Signature 19. 1984.	40.00	—
e. Signature 19. 1985.	5.00	15.00
f. Signature 20. 1986.	5.00	15.00
g. Signature 20. 1987.	5.00	15.00
h. Signature 21. 1989.	7.00	20.00
i. Signature 22. 1990.	5.00	15.00

208B 5000 Francs

1977-92. Black and red on multicolor underprint. Woman at left, fish and boats on shore at center, carving at right. Back: Carvings, fishing boats and mask.

	VF	UNC
a. Signature 12. 1979.	55.00	—
b. Signature 14. 1977.	35.00	90.00
c. Signature 14. 1988.	75.00	—
d. Signature 14. 1989.	10.00	40.00
e. Signature 15. 1981.	25.00	65.00
f. Signature 15. 1982.	25.00	60.00
g. Signature 17. 1983.	75.00	—
h. Signature 18. 1984.	75.00	—
i. Signature 19. 1985.	75.00	—
j. Signature 20. 1986.	75.00	—
k. Signature 20. 1987.	20.00	55.00
l. Signature 21. 1990.	10.00	40.00
m. Signature 22. 1991.	15.00	55.00
n. Signature 22. 1992.	10.00	40.00
o. Signature 23. 1992.	10.00	40.00
p. Signature 24. 1992.	40.00	—

209B 10,000 Francs

ND (1977-92). Red-brown on multicolor underprint. Two men seated operating primitive spinning apparatus, woman with headwear at right. Back: Figurine and girl at left, modern textile spinning machine at center. Watermark: Woman with headwear.

	VF	UNC
a. Signature 11. ND.	75.00	—
b. Signature 12. ND.	75.00	175.
c. Signature 14. ND.	35.00	90.00
d. Signature 15. ND.	90.00	—
e. Signature 16. ND.	100.	—
f. Signature 18. ND.	75.00	—
g. Signature 19. ND.	35.00	110.
h. Signature 20. ND.	65.00	—
i. Signature 21. ND.	20.00	60.00
j. Signature 22. ND.	20.00	60.00
k. Signature 23. ND.	20.00	65.00

1991-92 Issue

210B 500 Francs

(19)91-(20)02. Dark brown and dark green on multicolor underprint. Man at right, flood control dam at center. Back: Farmer riding spray rig behind garden tractor at center, native art at left. Watermark: Man.

	VF	UNC
a. Signature 22. (19)91.	3.00	8.00
b. Signature 22. (19)92.	30.00	—
c. Signature 23. (19)92.	25.00	—
d. Signature 25. (19)93.	25.00	—
e. Signature 26. (19)94.	3.00	8.00
f. Signature 27. (19)95.	3.00	7.00
g. Signature 28. (19)96.	3.00	7.00
h. Signature 28. (19)97. 10-digit serial #.	—	—
i. Signature 28. (19)97. 11-digit serial #.	3.00	7.00
j. Signature 28. (19)98.	3.00	7.00
k. Signature 29. (19)99.	3.00	6.00
l. Signature 30. (20)00.	3.00	6.00
m. Signature 30. (20)01.	3.00	6.00
n. Signature 31. (20)02.	3.00	6.00

211B 1000 Francs

(19)91-(20)02. Dark brown-violet on tan, yellow and multicolor underprint. Workmen hauling peanuts to storage at center, woman's head at right. Back: Twin statues and mask at left, two women with baskets, elevated riverside storage bins in background at center. Watermark: Woman's head.

	VF	UNC
a. Signature 22. (19)91.	5.00	12.00
b. Signature 22. (19)92.	40.00	—
c. Signature 23. (19)92.	30.00	—
d. Signature 25. (19)93.	30.00	—
e. Signature 26. (19)94.	5.00	10.00
f. Signature 27. (19)95.	5.00	10.00
g. Signature 28. (19)96.	5.00	10.00
h. Signature 28. (19)97.	4.00	9.00
i. Signature 28. (19)98.	4.00	9.00
j. Signature 29. (19)99.	4.00	9.00
k. Signature 30. (20)00.	15.00	—
l. Signature 30. (20)01.	4.00	8.00
m. Signature 31. (20)02.	4.00	8.00
n. Signature 31. (20)03.	9.00	—

212B 2500 Francs

(19)92-(19)94. Deep purple and dark brown on lilac and multicolor underprint. Dam at center, young woman's head at right. Back: Statue at left, harvesting and spraying of fruit at left center. Watermark: Young woman's head.

	VF	UNC
a. Signature 23. (19)92.	8.00	20.00
b. Signature 25. (19)93.	8.00	25.00
c. Signature 27. (19)94.	8.00	25.00

213B 5000 Francs

(19)92-(20)02. Dark brown and deep blue on multicolor underprint. Woman wearing headdress adorned with cowrie shells at right, smelting plant at center. Back: Women with children and various pottery at left center. Watermark: Woman wearing headdress adorned with cowrie shells.

	VF	UNC
a. Signature 23. (19)92.	15.00	45.00
b. Signature 25. (19)93.	10.00	35.00
c. Signature 27. (19)94.	9.00	30.00
d. Signature 27. (19)95.	9.00	30.00
e. Signature 28. (19)96.	9.00	25.00
f. Signature 28. (19)97.	9.00	25.00
g. Signature 28 (19)98.	10.00	30.00
h. Signature 29. (19)98.	9.00	25.00
i. Signature 29. (19)99.	9.00	25.00
j. Signature 30. (20)00.	10.00	35.00
k. Signature 30. (20)01.	10.00	35.00
l. Signature 31. (20)02.	9.00	25.00
m. Signature 31. (20)03.	9.00	25.00

214B 10,000 Francs

(19)92-(20)01. Dark brown on multicolor underprint. Headman with scepter at right, skyscraper at center. Back: Native art at left, woman crossing vine bridge over river at center. Watermark: Headman with scepter.

	VF	UNC
a. Signature 25. (19)92.	15.00	50.00
b. Signature 27. (19)94.	15.00	50.00
c. Signature 27. (19)95.	15.00	45.00
d. Signature 28. (19)96.	25.00	—
e. Signature 28. (19)97.	15.00	45.00
f. Signature 28. (19)98.	25.00	—
g. Signature 29. (19)98.	15.00	45.00
h. Signature 29. (19)99.	25.00	—
i. Signature 30. (20)00.	15.00	45.00
j. Signature 30. (20)01.	25.00	—

2003 Issue

215B 1000 Francs

(20)03-. Red-brown on red and multicolor underprint. 125x65mm.

	VF	UNC
a. Signature 32. (20)03.	FV	6.00
b. Signature 32. (20)04.	FV	6.00
c. Signature 33. (20)05.	FV	6.00

216B 2000 Francs

(20)03-. Blue on light blue and multicolor underprint. 130x66mm.

	VF	UNC
a. Signature 32. (20)03.	FV	10.00
b. Signature 32. (20)04.	FV	10.00
c. Signature 33. (20)05.	FV	10.00

217B 5000 Francs

(20)03-. Multicolor. 141x74mm.

	VF	UNC
a. Signature 32. (20)03.	FV	20.00
b. Signature 32. (20)04.	FV	17.50
c. Signature 33. (20)05.	FV	17.50

218B 10,000 Francs

(20)03-. Multicolor. 145x74mm.

	VF	UNC
a. Signature 32. (20)03.	FV	40.00
b. Signature 32. (20)04.	FV	35.00
c. Signature 33. (20)05.	FV	35.00

C for Burkina Faso (Upper Volta)

1961; ND Issue

301C 100 Francs

1961-65; ND. Dark brown, orange and multicolor. Like #101A.

	VF	UNC
a. Engraved. signature 1. 20.3.1961.	45.00	140.
b. Signature 2. 20.3.1961.	35.00	120.
c. Litho. Signature 2. 20.3.1961.	35.00	120.
d. Signature 3. 2.12.1964.	20.00	75.00
e. Signature 4. 2.3.1965.	20.00	75.00
f. Signature 4. ND.	15.00	55.00

302C 500 Francs

1961-65; ND. Brown, green and multicolor. field workers at left, mask carving at right. Back: Woman at left, farmer on tractor at right. Watermark: Woman's head.

	VF	UNC
a. Signature 1. 15.4.1959.	110.	—
b. Signature 1. 20.3.1961.	110.	—
c. Engraved. Signature 2. 20.3.1961.	75.00	—
d. Signature 4. 20.3.1961.	65.00	—
e. Signature 4. 2.3.1965.	90.00	—
f. Signature 5. ND.	75.00	—
g. Signature 6. ND.	45.00	—
h. Litho. Signature 6. ND.	35.00	—
i. Signature 7. ND.	45.00	—
k. Signature 8. ND.	45.00	100.
l. Signature 9. ND.	35.00	80.00
m. Signature 11. ND.	15.00	45.00
n. Signature 12. ND.	15.00	50.00

303C 1000 Francs

1961; ND. Brown, blue and multicolor. Mand and woman at center. Back: Man with rope suspension bridge in background and pineapples. Watermark: Man's head.

	VF	UNC
a. Engraved. Signature 1. 17.9.1959.	175.	—
b. Signature 1. 20.3.1961.	—	—
d. Signature 2. 20.3.1961.	100.	—
e. Signature 4. 2.3.1965.	100.	—
f. Signature 5. ND.	120.	—
g. Signature 6. ND.	40.00	110.
h. Litho. Signature 6. ND.	40.00	110.
i. Signature 7. ND.	45.00	120.
j. Signature 8. ND.	55.00	150.
k. Signature 9. ND.	35.00	
l. Signature 10. ND.	15.00	65.00
m. Signature 11. ND	12.00	45.00
n. Signature 12. ND.	15.00	55.00
o. Signature 13. ND.	15.00	55.00

304C 5000 Francs

1961; ND. Blue, brown and multicolor. Bearded man at left, building at center. Back: Woman, corn grinders and huts.

	VF	UNC
a. Signature 1. 20.3.1961.	100.	—
b. Signature 2. 20.3.1961.	—	—
d. Signature 4. 2.3.1965.	150.	—
h. Signature 6. ND.	75.00	250.
i. Signature 7. ND.	75.00	250.
k. Signature 9. ND.	60.00	225.
l. Signature 11. ND.	55.00	200.

1977-81; ND Issues

#305C-309C smaller size notes.

305C 500 Francs

1979-80. Lilac, light olie-green and multicolor. Artwork at left, long horn animals at center, man wearing hat at right. Back: Cultivated palm at left, aerial view at center, mask at right. Watermark: Woman in profile.

	VF	UNC
a. Signature 12. 1979.	13.00	35.00
b. Signature 13. 1980.	12.00	30.00

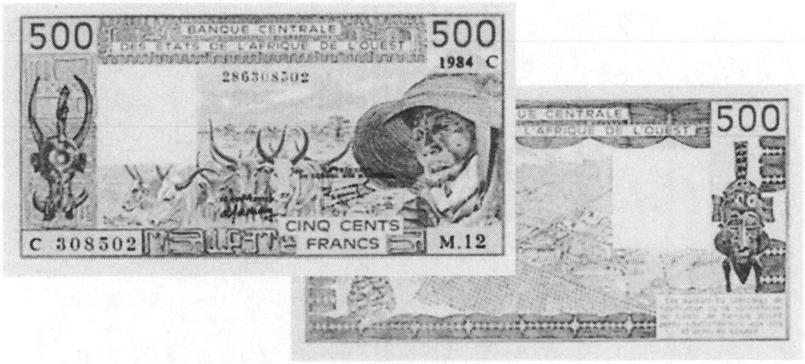

306C 500 Francs

1981-90. Pale olive-green and multicolor. Artwork at left, long horn animals at center, man wearing hat at right. Back: Cultivated palm at left, aerial view at center, mask at right. Watermark: Woman in profile.

	VF	UNC
a. Signature 14. 1988.	3.00	10.00
b. Signature 15. 1981. (BF).	3.00	12.00
c. Signature 15. 1981. (F-CO).	3.00	12.00
d. Signature 15. 1982. (BF).	3.00	12.00
e. Signature 17. 1981. (F-CO).	3.00	12.00
f. Signature 17. 1983. (BF).	9.00	—
g. Signature 18. 1984.	3.00	12.00
h. Signature 19. 1984.	3.00	10.00
i. Signature 19. 1985.	3.00	10.00
j. Signature 20. 1986.	3.00	10.00
k. Signature 20. 1987.	3.00	10.00
l. Signature 21. 1989.	3.00	10.00
m. Signature 22. 1990.	3.00	10.00

307C 1000 Francs

1981-90. Brown on multicolor underprint. Artwork at left, open pit mine at center, woman at right. Back: Wood carver with finished works. Watermark: Woman.

	VF	UNC
a. Signature 14. 1988.	5.00	15.00
b. Signature 15. 1981.	7.00	20.00
c. Signature 17. 1981.	9.00	—
d. Signature 18. 1984.	9.00	—
e. Signature 19. 1984.	10.00	—
f. Signature 19. 1985.	9.00	25.00
g. Signature 20. 1986.	5.00	15.00
h. Signature 20. 1987.	5.00	15.00
i. Signature 21. 1989.	10.00	—
j. Signature 22. 1990.	5.00	15.00

308C 5000 Francs

1977-92. Black and red on multicolor underprint. Woman at left, fish and boats on shore at center, carving at right. Back: Carvings, fishing boats and mask.

	VF	UNC
a. Signature 12. 1978.	35.00	85.00
b. Signature 12. 1979.	35.00	85.00
c. Signature 14. 1977.	35.00	85.00
d. Signature 14. 1988.	10.00	40.00
e. Signature 14. 1989.	10.00	40.00
f. Signature 15. 1981.	15.00	60.00
g. Signature 15. 1982.	15.00	65.00
h. Signature 17. 1983.	15.00	65.00
i. Signature 18. 1984.	15.00	65.00
k. Signature 19. 1985.	15.00	65.00
l. Signature 20. 1986.	20.00	80.00
m. Signature 20. 1987.	18.00	75.00
n. Signature 21. 1990.	10.00	40.00
o. Signature 22. 1991.	10.00	40.00
p. Signature 22. 1992.	10.00	40.00
q. Signature 23. 1992.	10.00	40.00
r. Signature 24. 1992.	15.00	—

309C 10,000 Francs

ND (1977-92). Red-brown on multicolor underprint. Two men seated operating primitive spinning appartaus, woman with headwear at right. Back: Figurine and girl at left, modern textile spinning machine at center. Watermark: Woman with headwear.

	VF	UNC
a. Signature 11. ND.	[illegible]	200.
b. Signature 12. ND.	50.00	110.
c. Signature 13. ND.	50.00	110.
d. Signature 14. ND.	—	—
e. Signature 15. ND.	65.00	—
f. Signature 20. ND.	35.00	80.00
g. Signature 21. ND.	20.00	55.00
h. Signature 22. ND.	20.00	55.00
i. Signature 23. ND.	20.00	55.00

1991 Issue

310C 500 Francs

(19)91-(20)02. Dark brown and dark green on multicolr underprint. Man at right, flood control dam at center. Back: Farmer riding spray rig behind garden tractor at center, native art at left. Watermark: Man.

	VF	UNC
a. Signature 22. (19)91.	3.00	8.00
b. Signature 23. (19)92.	7.00	20.00
c. Signature 25. (19)93.	3.00	8.00
d. Signature 26. (19)94.	3.00	8.00
e. Signature 27. (19)95.	3.00	7.00
f. Signature 28. (19)96.	3.00	7.00
g. Signature 28. (19)97. 10-digit serial #.	3.00	7.00
h. Signature 28. (19)97. 11-digit serial #.	3.00	7.00
i. Signature 28. (19)98.	3.00	7.00
j. Signature 29. (19)99.	3.00	7.00
k. Signature 30. (20)00.	3.00	6.00
l. Signature 30. (20)01.	3.00	6.00
m. Signature 31. (20)02.	3.00	6.00

311C 1000 Francs

(19)91-(20)02. Dark brown-violet on tan, yellow and multicolor underprint. Workmen hauling peanuts to storage at center, woman's head at right. Back: Twin statues and mask at left, two women with baskets, elevated riverside storage bins in background at center. Watermark: Woman's head.

	VF	UNC
a. Signature 22. (19)91.	5.00	12.00
b. Signature 22. (19)92.	40.00	—
c. Signature 23. (19)92.	30.00	—
d. Signature 25. (19)93.	5.00	10.00
e. Signature 26. (19)94.	5.00	10.00
f. Signature 27. (19)95.	5.00	10.00
g. Signature 28. (19)96.	4.00	9.00
h. Signature 28. (19)97.	4.00	9.00
i. Signature 28. (19)98.	4.00	9.00
j. Signature 29. (19)99.	4.00	9.00
k. Signature 30. (20)00.	4.00	8.00
l. Signature 30. (20)01.	4.00	8.00
m. Signature 31. (20)02.	4.00	8.00
n. Signature 31. (20)03.	4.00	8.00

312C 2500 Francs

(19)92-(19)94. Deep purple and dark brown on lilac and multicolor underprint. Dam at center, young woman's head at right. Back: Statue at left, harvesting and spraying of fruit at left center. Watermark: Young woman's head.

	VF	UNC
a. Signature 23. (19)92.	8.00	20.00
b. Signature 25. (19)93.	8.00	20.00
c. Signature 27. (19)94.	8.00	20.00

313C 5000 Francs

(19)92-(20)02. Dark brown and deep blue on multicolor underprint. Woman wearing headdress adorned with cowrie shells at right, smelting plant at center. Back: Women with children and various pottery at left center. Watermark: Woman wearing headdress adorned with cowrie shells.

	VF	UNC
a. Signature 23. (19)92.	9.00	30.00
b. Signature 25. (19)93.	9.00	25.00
c. Signature 27. (19)94.	9.00	25.00
d. Signature 27. (19)95.	8.00	20.00
e. Signature 28. (19)96.	8.00	20.00
f. Signature 28. (19)97.	8.00	20.00
g. Signature 28. (19)98.	8.00	20.00
h. Signature 29. (19)98.	8.00	20.00
i. Signature 29. (19)99.	7.00	20.00
j. Signature 30. (20)00.	30.00	—
k. Signature 30. (20)01.	7.00	20.00
l. Signature 31. (20)02.	7.00	20.00
m. Signature 31. (20)03.	7.00	20.00

314C 10,000 Francs

(19)92-(20)01. Dark brown on multicolor underprint. Headman with scepter at right, skyscraper at center. Back: Native art at left, woman crossing vine bridgte over river at center. Watermark: Headman with scepter.

	VF	UNC
a. Signature 25. (19)92.	25.00	—
b. Signature 27. (19)94.	15.00	50.00
c. Signature 27. (19)95.	15.00	45.00
d. Signature 28. (19)96.	15.00	45.00
e. Signature 28. (19)97.	15.00	45.00
f. Signature 28. (19)98.	15.00	45.00
g. Signature 29. (19)98.	15.00	45.00
h. Signature 29. (19)99.	15.00	40.00
i. Signature 30. (20)00.	15.00	40.00
j. Signature 30. (20)01.	15.00	40.00

2003 Issue

315C 1000 Francs

(20)03-. Red-brown on red and multicolor underprint. 125x65mm.

	VF	UNC
a. Signature 32. (20)03.	FV	6.00
b. Signature 32. (20)04.	FV	6.00

316C 2000 Francs

(20)03-. Blue on light blue and multicolor underprint. 130x66mm.

	VF	UNC
a. Signature 32. (20)03.	FV	10.00
b. Signature 32. (20)04.	FV	10.00
c. Signature 33. (20)05.	FV	10.00

317C 5000 Francs

(20)03-. Multicolor. 141x74mm.

	VF	UNC
a. Signature 32. (20)03.	FV	20.00
b. Signature 32. (20)04.	FV	17.50

318C 10,000 Francs

(20)03-. Multicolor. 145x74mm.

	VF	UNC
a. Signature 32. (20)03.	FV	40.00
b. Signature 32. (20)04.	FV	35.00
c. Signature 33. (20)05.	FV	35.00

D for Mali

1959-61; ND Issue

		Fine	XF
401D	**100 Francs**		
	20.3.1961. Dark brown, orange and multicolor. Signature left. Like #101A.	200.	400.
402D	**500 Francs**		
	1959; 1961. Brown, green and multicolor. Field workers at left, mask carving at right. Like #102A. Back: Woman at left, farmer on tractor at right. Watermark: Woman's head.		
	a. Signature 1. 15.4.1959.	600.	—
	b. Signature 1. 20.3.1961.	—	—
403D	**1000 Francs**		
	1959; 1961. Brown, blue and multicolor. Man and woman at center. Like #103A. Back: Man with rope suspension bridge in background and pineapples. Watermark: Man's head.		
	a. Signature 1. 17.9.1959.	400.	1000.
	b. Signature 1. 20.3.1961.	400.	1000.
404D	**5000 Francs**		
	20.3.1961. Blue, brown and multicolor. Bearded man at left, building at center. Signature left. Back: Woman, corn grinders and huts. .	500.	1300.

1981; ND Issue

#405D-408D smaller size notes.

405D 500 Francs

1981-90. Pale olive-green and multicolor. Artwork at left, long horn animals at center, man wearing hat at right. Back: Cultivated palm at left, aerial view at center, mask at right. Watermark: Woman in profile.

	VF	UNC
a. Signature 14. 1988.	3.00	9.00
b. Signature 15. 1981. (BF).	3.00	10.00
c. Signature 17. 1981. (F-CO).	3.00	11.00
e. Signature 19. 1985.	4.00	15.00
f. Signature 20. 1986.	3.00	10.00
g. Signature 20. 1987.	3.00	10.00
h. Signature 21. 1989.	3.00	9.00
i. Signature 22. 1990.	3.00	9.00

406D 1000 Francs

1981-90. Brown on multicolor underprint. Artwork at left, open pit mine at center, woman at right. Back: Wood carver with finished works. Watermark: Woman.

	VF	UNC
a. Signature 14. 1988.	5.00	12.00
b. Signature 15. 1981.	5.00	12.00
c. Signature 17. 1981.	6.00	15.00
f. Signature 19. 1985.	6.00	15.00
g. Signature 20. 1986	6.00	15.00
h. Signature 20. 1987.	6.00	15.00
i. Signature 21. 1989.	5.00	12.00
j. Signature 22. 1990.	20.00	—

407D 5000 Francs

1981-92. Black and red on multicolor underprint. Woman at left, fish and boats on shore at center, carving at right. Back: Carvings, fishing boats and mask.

	VF	UNC
a. Signature 14. 1988.	15.00	60.00
b. Signature 14. 1989.	40.00	—
c. Signature 15. 1981.	15.00	55.00
d. Signature 17. 1984.	15.00	55.00
e. Signature 18. 1984.	35.00	80.00
f. Signature 19. 1985.	15.00	55.00
g. Signature 20. 1986.	15.00	55.00
h. Signature 20. 1987.	15.00	55.00
i. Signature 21. 1990.	15.00	55.00
j. Signature 22. 1991.	10.00	45.00
k. Signature 23. 1992.	15.00	55.00
l. Signature 24. 1992.	35.00	—

408D 10,000 Francs

ND (1981-92). Red-brown on multicolor underprint. Two men seated operating primitive spinning apparatus, woman with headwear at right. Back: Figurine and girl at left, modern textile spinning machine at center. Watermark: Woman with headwear.

	VF	UNC
a. Signature 14. ND.	60.00	—
b. Signature 15. ND.	35.00	85.00
c. Signature 18. ND.	55.00	120.
d. Signature 19. ND.	—	—
e. Signature 20. ND.	30.00	75.00
f. Signature 21. ND.	20.00	55.00
g. Signature 22. ND.	20.00	55.00

1991-92 Issue

410D 500 Francs

(19)91-(20)02. Dark brown and dark green on multicolor underprint. Man at right, flood control dam at center. Back: Farmer riding spray rig behind garden tractor at center, native art at left. Watermark: Man.

	VF	UNC
a. Signature 22. (19)91.	3.00	10.00
b. Signature 23. (19)92.	7.00	20.00
c. Signature 25. (19)93.	3.00	8.00
d. Signature 26. (19)94.	3.00	8.00
e. Signature 27. (19)95.	3.00	7.00
f. Signature 28. (19)96.	3.00	7.00
g. Signature 28. (19)97. 10-digit serial #.	3.00	7.00
h. Signature 28. (19)97. 11-digit serial #.	3.00	7.00
i. Signature 28. (19)98.	3.00	7.00
j. Signature 29. (19)99.	3.00	7.00
k. Signature 30. (20)00.	3.00	6.00
l. Signature 30. (20)01.	3.00	6.00
m. Signature 31. (20)02.	3.00	10.00
n. Signature 31. (20)03.	3.00	6.00

411D 1000 Francs

(19)91-(20)02. Dark brown-violet on tan, yellow and multicolor underprint. Workmen hauling peanuts to storage at center, woman's head at right. Back: Twin statues and mask at left, two women with baskets, elevated riverside storage bins in background at center. Watermark: Woman's head.

	VF	UNC
a. Signature 22. (19)91.	5.00	12.00
b. Signature 23. (19)92.	30.00	—
c. Signature 25. (19)93.	5.00	10.00
d. Signature 26. (19)94.	5.00	10.00
e. Signature 27. (19)95.	5.00	10.00
f. Signature 28. (19)96.	4.00	9.00
g. Signature 28. (19)97.	4.00	9.00
h. Signature 28. (19)98.	4.00	9.00
i. Signature 29. (19)99.	4.00	9.00
j. Signature 30. (20)00.	4.00	8.00
k. Signature 30. (20)01.	4.00	8.00
l. Signature 31. (20)02.	4.00	8.00
m. Signature 31. (20)03.	4.00	8.00

412D 2500 Francs

(19)92-(19)94. Deep purple and dark brown on lilac and multicolor underprint. Dam at center, young woman's head at right. Back: Statue at left, harvesting and spraying of fruit at left center. Watermark: Young woman's head.

	VF	UNC
a. Signature 23. (19)92.	8.00	20.00
b. Signature 25. (19)93.	20.00	—
c. Signature 27. (19)94.	8.00	20.00

413D 5000 Francs

(19)92-(20)02. Dark brown and deep blue on multicolor underprint. Woman wearing headdress adorned with cowrie shells at right, smelting plant at center. Back: Women with children and various pottery at left center. Watermark: Woman wearing headdress adorned with cowrie shells.

	VF	UNC
a. Signature 23. (19)92.	9.00	30.00
b. Signature 27. (19)94.	9.00	25.00
c. Signature 27. (19)95.	15.00	35.00
d. Signature 28. (19)96.	8.00	20.00
e. Signature 28. (19)97.	8.00	20.00
f. Signature 28. (19)98.	8.00	20.00
g. Signature 29. (19)98.	15.00	35.00
h. Signature 29. (19)99.	8.00	20.00
i. Signature 30. (20)00.	35.00	—
j. Signature 30. (20)01.	15.00	35.00
k. Signature 31. (20)02.	8.00	20.00
l. Signature 32. (20)03.	8.00	20.00

414D 10,000 Francs

(19)92-(20)02. Dark brown on multicolor underprint. Headman with scepter at right, skyscraper at center. Back: Native art at left, woman crossing vine bridge over river at center. Watermark: Headman with scepter.

	VF	UNC
a. Signature 25. (19)92.	25.00	—
b. Signature 27. (19)94.	35.00	—
c. Signature 27. (19)95.	15.00	45.00
d. Signature 28. (19)96.	15.00	45.00
e. Signature 28. (19)97.	15.00	45.00
f. Signature 28. (19)98.	15.00	45.00
g. Signature 29. (19)98.	15.00	45.00
h. Signature 29. (19)99.	15.00	45.00
i. Signature 30. (20)00.	35.00	—
j. Signature 30. (20)01.	15.00	45.00

2003 Issue

415D 1000 Francs

(20)03-. Red on light red and multicolor underprint. . 125x65mm.

	VF	UNC
a. Signature 32. (20)03.	FV	6.00
b. Signature 32. (20)04.	FV	6.00
c. Signature 33. (20)05.	FV	6.00

416D 2000 Francs

(20)03-. Red-brown on red and multicolor underprint. 130x65mm.

	VF	UNC
a. Signature 32. (20)03.	FV	10.00
b. Signature 32. (20)04.	FV	10.00

417D 5000 Francs

(20)03-. Multicolor. 141x74mm.

	VF	UNC
a. Signature 32. (20)03.	FV	25.00
b. Signature 32. (20)04.	FV	17.50
c. Signature 33. (20)05.	FV	17.50
d. Signature 34. (20)06.	FV	17.50

418D 10,000 Francs

(20)03-. Multicolor. 145x74mm.

	VF	UNC
a. Signature 32. (20)03.	FV	40.00
b. Signature 32. (20)04.	FV	35.00
c. Signature 33. (20)05.	FV	35.00
e. Signature 35. (20)07.	FV	32.50
f. Signature 36. (20)08.	FV	32.50

E for Mauritania

1959-64; ND Issue

501E 100 Francs

1961-65. Dark brown, orange and multicolor. Like #101A.

	Fine	XF
b. Engraved. Signature 1. 20.3.1961.	100.	300.
c. Litho. Signature 3. 2.12.1964.	100.	300.
e. Signature 4. 2.3.1965.	90.00	275.
f. Signature 4. ND.	90.00	275.

502E 500 Francs

1959-64; ND. Brown, green and multicolor. Field workers at left, mask carving at right. Like #102A. Back: Woman at left, farmer on tractor at right. Watermark: Woman's head.

	VF	UNC
a. Engraved. Signature 1. 15.4.1959.	—	—
b. Signature 1. 20.3.1961.	200.	—
c. Signature 2. 20.3.1961.	175.	—
e. Signature 4. 2.3.1965.	200.	—
f. Signature 5. ND.	175.	650.
g. Signature 6. ND.	175.	600.
h. Litho. Signature 6. ND.	200.	—
i. Signature 7. ND.	175.	600.

503E 1000 Francs

1961-65. Brown, blue and multicolor. Man and woman at center. Back: Man with rope suspension bridge in background and pineapples. Watermark: Man's head.

	VF	UNC
a. Engraved. Signature 1. 17.9.1959.	—	—
b. Signature 1. 20.3.1961.	175.	600.
e. Signature 4. 2.3.1965.	175.	600.
g. Signature 6. ND.	175.	600.
h. Litho. Signature 6. ND.	175.	600.

504E 5000 Francs

1961-65; ND. Blue, brown and multicolor. Bearded man at left, building at center. Back: Woman, corn grinders and huts.

	VF	UNC
a. Signature 1. 20.3.1961.	350.	—
b. Signature 2. 20.3.1961.	275.	—
c. Signature 4. 2.3.1965.	275.	900.
d. Signature 6. ND.	275.	900.
e. Signature 7. ND.	275.	—

H for Niger

1959-65; ND Issue

601H 100 Francs

1961-65; ND. Dark brown, orange and multicolor. Like #101A.

	VF	UNC
a. Engraved. Signature 1. 20.3.1961.	50.00	—
b. Signature 2. 20.3.1961.	65.00	—
c. Litho. Signature 2. 20.3.1961.	50.00	—
d. Signature 3. 2.12.1964.	—	—
e. Signature 4. 2.3.1965.	35.00	100.
f. Signature 4. ND.	35.00	100.

602H 500 Francs

1959-65; ND. Brown, green and multicolor. Field workers at left, mask carving at right. Like #102A. Back: Woman at left, farmer on tractor at right. Watermark: Woman's head.

	VF	UNC
a. Engraved. Signature 1. 15.4.1959.	—	—
c. Signature 2. 20.3.1961.	125.	—
d. Signature 3. 2.12.1964.	75.00	200.
e. Signature 4. 2.3.1965.	75.00	200.
f. Signature 5. ND.	125.	—
g. Signature 6. ND.	40.00	120.
h. Litho. Signature 6. ND.	40.00	120.
i. Signature 7. ND.	65.00	150.
j. Signature 8. ND.	40.00	120.
k. Signature 9. ND.	30.00	90.00
l. Signature 10. ND.	—	—
m. Signature 11. ND.	25.00	75.00

603H 1000 Francs

1959-65; ND. Brown, blue and multicolor. Man and woman at center. Like #103A. Back: Man with rope suspension bridge in background and pineapples. Watermark: Man's head.

	VF	UNC
a. Engraved. Signature 1. 17.9.1959.	100.	—
b. Signature 1. 20.3.1961.	100.	—
c. Signature 2. 20.3.1961.	—	—
e. Signature 4. 2.3.1965.	100.	250.
f. Signature 5. ND.	100.	250.
g. Signature 6. ND.	80.00	—
h. Litho. Signature 6. ND.	80.00	200.
i. Signature 7. ND.	80.00	200.
j. Signature 8. ND.	100.	—
k. Signature 9. ND	40.00	120.
l. Signature 10. ND.	40.00	120.
m. Signature 11. ND.	30.00	90.00
n. Signature 12. ND.	40.00	120.
o. Signature 13. ND.	50.00	150.

604H 5000 Francs

1961; 1965; ND. Blue, brown and multicolor. Bearded man at left, building at center. Back: Woman, corn grinders and huts.

	VF	UNC
a. Signature 1. 20.3.1961.	—	—
b. Signature 2. 20.3.1961.	200.	—
d. Signature 4. 2.3.1965.	200.	—
e. Signature 6. ND.	200.	—
i. Signature 7. ND.	200.	—
k. Signature 9. ND.	150.	350.
l. Signature 10. ND.	200.	—
m. Signature 11. ND.	150.	350.

1977-81; ND Issue

#605H-608H smaller size notes.

605H 500 Francs

1979-80. Lilac, light olive-green and multicolor. Artwork at left, long horn animals at center, man wearing hat at right. Back: Cultivated palm at left, aerial view at center, mask at right. Watermark: Woman in profile.

	VF	UNC
a. Signature 12. 1979.	20.00	50.00
b. Signature 13. 1980.	12.00	30.00

606H 500 Francs

1981-90. Pale olive-green and multicolor. Artwork at left, long horn animals at center, man wearing hat at right. Back: Cultivated palm at left, aerial view at center, mask at right. Watermark: Woman in profile.

	VF	UNC
a. Signature 14. 1988.	3.00	10.00
b. Signature 15. 1981. (BF).	20.00	5.00
c. Signature 15. 1981. (F-CO).	4.00	12.00
d. Signature 15. 1982. (BF).	—	—
e. Signature 17. 1981. (F-CO).	4.00	12.00
f. Signature 18. 1984.	50.00	—
g. Signature 19. 1984.	—	—
h. Signature 19. 1985.	—	—
i. Signature 20. 1986.	3.00	10.00
j. Signature 20. 1987.	3.00	10.00
k. Signature 21. 1989.	3.00	9.00
l. Signature 22. 1990.	3.00	9.00

607H 1000 Francs

1981-90. Brown on multicolor underprint. Artwork at left, open pit mine at center, woman at right. Back: Wood carver with finished works. Watermark: Woman.

	VF	UNC
a. Signature 14. 1988.	5.00	12.00
b. Signature 15. 1981.	6.00	20.00
c. Signature 17. 1981.	—	—
d. Signature 18. 1984.	20.00	—
e. Signature 19. 1984.	25.00	—
f. Signature 19. 1985.	6.00	20.00
g. Signature 20. 1986.	5.00	12.00
h. Signature 20. 1987.	5.00	12.00
i. Signature 21. 1989.	5.00	12.00
j. Signature 22. 1990.	5.00	12.00

608H 5000 Francs

1977-90. Black and red on multicolor underprint. Woman at left, fish and boats on shore at center, carving at right. Back: Carvings, fishing boats and mask.

	VF	UNC
a. Signature 12. 1978.	40.00	100.
b. Signature 12. 1979.	40.00	100.
c. Signature 13. 1980.	50.00	120.
d. Signature 14. 1977.	40.00	100.
e. Signature 14. 1989.	20.00	50.00
f. Signature 15. 1981.	25.00	60.00
g. Signature 15. 1982.	25.00	60.00
h. Signature 17. 1983.	25.00	60.00
i. Signature 18. 1984.	40.00	100.
j. Signature 19. 1985.	30.00	70.00
k. Signature 20. 1986.	25.00	60.00
l. Signature 20. 1987.	20.00	50.00
m. Signature 21. 1990.	20.00	50.00
n. Signature 27. 1995.	20.00	50.00

609H 10,000 Francs

ND (1977). Red-brown on multicolor underprint. Two men seated operating primitive spinning apparatus, woman with headwear at right. Back: Figurine and girl at left, modern textile spinning machine at center. Watermark: Woman with headwear.

	VF	UNC
a. Signature 11. ND.	75.00	200.
b. Signature 12. ND.	—	—
c. Signature 13. ND.	—	—
d. Signature 14. ND.	35.00	100.
e. Signature 15. ND.	40.00	110.
f. Signature 18. ND.	55.00	140.
g. Signature 19. ND.	—	—
h. Signature 20. ND.	35.00	90.00
i. Signature 21. ND.	30.00	75.00
j. Signature 22. ND.	30.00	75.00

1991-92 Issue

610H 500 Francs

(19)91-(20)02. Dark brown and dark green on multicolor underprint. Man at right, flood control dam at center. Back: Farmer riding spray rig behind garden tractor at center, native art at left. Watermark: Man.

	VF	UNC
a. Signature 22. (19)91.	3.00	8.00
b. Signature 23. (19)92.	25.00	—
c. Signature 25. (19)93.	3.00	8.00
d. Signature 26. (19)94.	3.00	8.00
e. Signature 27. (19)95.	3.00	7.00
f. Signature 28. (19)96.	3.00	7.00
g. Signature 28. (19)97. 10-digit serial #.	3.00	7.00
h. Signature 28. (19)97. 11-digit serial #.	3.00	7.00
i. Signature 28. (19)98.	3.00	7.00
j. Signature 29. (19)99.	5.00	10.00
k. Signature 30 (20)00.	3.00	7.00
l. Signature 30. (20)01.	—	—
m. Signature 31. (20)02.	3.00	7.00

611H 1000 Francs

(19)91-(20)02. Dark brown-violet on tan, yellow and multicolor underprint. Workmen hauling peanuts to storage at center, woman's head at right. Back: Twin statues and mask at left, two women with baskets, elevated riverside storage bins in background at center. Watermark: Woman's head.

	VF	UNC
a. Signature 22. (19)91.	5.00	12.00
b. Signature 23. (19)92.	5.00	12.00
c. Signature 25. (19)93.	5.00	12.00
d. Signature 26. (19)94.	30.00	—
e. Signature 27. (19)95.	5.00	10.00
f. Signature 28. (19)96.	5.00	10.00
g. Signature 28. (19)97.	4.00	8.00
h. Signature 28. (19)98.	30.00	—
i. Signature 29. (19)99.	4.00	8.00
j. Signature 30. (20)00.	4.00	8.00
k. Signature 30. (20)02.	4.00	8.00
l. Signature 31. (20)03.	4.00	8.00

612H 2500 Francs

(19)92-(19)94. Deep purple and dark brown on lilac and multicolor underprint. Dam at center, young woman's head at right. Back: Statue at left, harvesting and spraying of fruit at left center. Watermark: Young woman's head.

	VF	UNC
a. Signature 23. (19)92.	9.00	25.00
b. Signature 25. (19)93.	9.00	25.00
c. Signature 27. (19)94.	9.00	25.00

613H 5000 Francs

(19)92-(20)02. Dark brown and deep blue on multicolor underprint. Woman wearing headdress adorned with cowrie shells at right, smelting plant at center. Back: Women with children and various pottery at left center. Watermark: Woman wearing headdress adorned with cowrie shells.

	VF	UNC
a. Signature 23. (19)92.	9.00	30.00
b. Signature 27. (19)94.	9.00	25.00
c. Signature 27. (19)95.	9.00	25.00
d. Signature 28. (19)96.	9.00	25.00
e. Signature 28. (19)97.	8.00	20.00
f. Signature 28. (19)98.	40.00	—
g. Signature 29. (19)98.	8.00	20.00
h. Signature 29. (19)99.	8.00	20.00
i. Signature 30. (20)00.	40.00	—
j. Signature 30. (20)01.	40.00	—
k. Signature 31. (20)02.	8.00	20.00
l. Signature 31. (20)03.	8.00	20.00

614H 10,000 Francs

(19)92-(20)01. Dark brown on multicolor underprint. Headman with scepter at right, skyscraper at center. Back: Native art at left, woman crossing vine bridge over river at center. Watermark: Headman with scepter.

	VF	UNC
a. Signature 25. (19)92.	20.00	50.00
b. Signature 27. (19)94.	15.00	45.00
c. Signature 27. (19)95.	15.00	45.00
d. Signature 28. (19)96.	15.00	45.00
e. Signature 28. (19)97.	15.00	45.00
f. Signature 28. (19)98.	25.00	—
g. Signature 29. (19)98.	—	—
h. Signature 29. (19)99.	15.00	45.00
i. Signature 30. (20)00.	—	—
j. Signature 30. (20)01.	15.00	45.00

2003 Issue

615H 1000 Francs

(20)03-. Red-brown on red and multicolor underprint. 125x65mm.

	VF	UNC
a. Signature 32. (20)03.	FV	6.00
b. Signature 32. (20)04.	FV	6.00

616H 2000 Francs

(20)03-. Blue on light blue and multicolor underprint. 130x66mm.

	VF	UNC
a. Signature 32. (20)03.	FV	10.00
b. Signature 32. (20)04.	FV	10.00

617H 5000 Francs

(20)03-. Multicolor. 141x74mm.

	VF	UNC
a. Signature 32. (20)03.	FV	20.00
b. Signature 32. (20)04.	FV	17.50
c. Signature 33. (20)05.	FV	17.50

618H 10,000 Francs

(20)03-. Multicolor. 145x74mm.

	VF	UNC
a. Signature 32. (20)03.	FV	40.00
b. Signature 32. (20)04.	FV	35.00

K for Senegal

1959-65; ND Issue

701K 100 Francs

1961-65; ND. Dark brown, orange and multicolor. Like #101A.

	VF	UNC
a. Engraved. Signature 1. 20.3.1961.	45.00	—
b. Signature 2. 20.3.1961.	25.00	70.00
c. Litho. Signature 2. 20.3.1961.	25.00	70.00
d. Signature 3. 2.12.1964.	30.00	—
e. Signature 4. 2.3.1965.	20.00	65.00
f. Signature 4. ND.	15.00	45.00
g. Signature 5. ND.	45.00	—

702K 500 Francs

1959-65; ND. Brown, green and multicolor. Field workers at left, mask carving at right. Like #102A. Back: Woman at left, farmer on tractor at right. Watermark: Woman's head.

	VF	UNC
a. Engraved. Signature 1. 15.4.1959.	—	—
b. Signature 1. 20.3.1961.	45.00	120.
c. Signature 2. 20.3.1961.	45.00	120.
d. Signature 3. 2.12.1964.	45.00	120.
e. Signature 4. 2.3.1965.	40.00	100.
f. Signature 5. ND.	45.00	120.
g. Signature 6. ND.	25.00	85.00
h. Litho. Signature 6. ND.	25.00	85.00
i. Signature 7. ND.	40.00	—
j. Signature 8. ND.	40.00	100.
k. Signature 9. ND.	20.00	60.00
l. Signature 10. ND.	20.00	60.00
m. Signature 11. ND.	15.00	45.00
n. Signature 12. ND.	15.00	45.00

703K 1000 Francs

1959-65; ND. Brown, blue and multicolor. Man and woman at center. Like #103A. Back: Man with rope suspension bridge in background and pineapples. Watermark: Man's head.

	VF	UNC
a. Engraved. Signature 1. 17.9.1959.	65.00	—
b. Signature 1. 20.3.1961.	65.00	—
c. Signature 2. 20.3.1961.	50.00	—
e. Signature 4. 2.3.1965.	50.00	—
f. Signature 5. ND.	90.00	—
g. Signature 6. ND.	75.00	120.
h. Litho. Signature 6. ND.	25.00	60.00
i. Signature 7. ND.	30.00	75.00

	VF	UNC
j. Signature 8. ND.	35.00	—
k. Signature 9. ND.	15.00	50.00
l. Signature 10. ND.	15.00	50.00
m. Signature 11. ND.	15.00	50.00
n. Signature 12. ND.	15.00	50.00
o. Signature 13. ND.	15.00	50.00

704K 5000 Francs

1961-65; ND. Blue, brown and multicolor. Bearded man at left, building at center. Back: Woman, corn grinders and huts.

	VF	UNC
b. Signature 1. 20.3.1961.	—	—
c. Signature 2. 20.3.1961.	90.00	—
d. Signature 3. 2.12.1964.	90.00	—
e. Signature 4. 2.3.1965.	75.00	—
h. Signature 6. ND.	55.00	—
i. Signature 7. ND.	75.00	—
j. Signature 8. ND.	—	—
k. Signature 9. ND.	75.00	—
l. Signature 10. ND.	75.00	—
m. Signature 11. ND.	55.00	200.

1977-81; ND Issue

#705K-709K smaller size notes.

705K 500 Francs

1979-80. Lilac, light olive-green and multicolor. Artwork at left, long horn animals at center, man wearing hat at right. Back: Cultivated palm at left, aerial view at center, mask at right. Watermark: Woman in profile.

	VF	UNC
a. Signature 12. 1979.	12.00	35.00
b. Signature 13. 1980.	12.00	30.00

706K 500 Francs

1981-90. Pale olive-green and multicolor. Artwork at left, long horn animals at center, man wearing hat at right. Back: Cultivated palm at left, aerial view at center, mask at right. Watermark: Woman in profile.

	VF	UNC
a. Signature 14. 1988.	3.00	9.00
b. Signature 15. 1981 (BF).	15.00	35.00
c. Signature 15. 1981. (F-CO).	3.00	10.00
d. Signature 15. 1982. (BF).	4.00	12.00
e. Signature 17. 1981. (F-CO).	3.00	10.00
f. Signature 17. 1983. (BF).	4.00	12.00
g. Signature 18. 1984.	3.00	10.00
h. Signature 19. 1985.	3.00	10.00
i. Signature 20. 1986.	3.00	9.00
j. Signature 20. 1987.	3.00	9.00
k. Signature 21. (reversed order). 1989.	3.00	9.00
l. Signature 22. 1990.	3.00	9.00

707K 1000 Francs

1981-90. Brown on multicolor underprint. Artwork at left, open pit mine at center, woman at right. Back: Wood carver with finished works. Watermark: Woman.

	VF	UNC
a. Signature 14. 1988.	4.00	10.00
b. Signature 15. 1981.	4.00	14.00
c. Signature 17. 1981.	4.00	14.00
d. Signature 18. 1984.	4.00	14.00
e. Signature 19. 1984.	30.00	—
f. Signature 19. 1985.	4.00	12.00
g. Signature 20. 1986.	4.00	12.00
h. Signature 20. 1987.	4.00	12.00
i. Signature 21. 1989.	4.00	10.00
j. Signature 22. 1990.	4.00	10.00

708K 5000 Francs

1977-92. Black and red on multicolor underprint. Woman at left, fish and boats on shore at center, carving at right. Back: Carvings, fishing boats and mask.

	VF	UNC
a. Signature 12. 1978.	25.00	70.00
b. Signature 12. 1979.	35.00	100.
c. Signature 13. 1980.	45.00	110.
d. Signature 14. 1977.	25.00	70.00
e. Signature 14. 1989.	15.00	50.00
f. Signature 15. 1982.	45.00	110.
g. Signature 16. 1983.	55.00	130.
h. Signature 17. 1983.	25.00	65.00
i. Signature 18. 1984.	25.00	65.00
j. Signature 19. 1985.	60.00	—
k. Signature 20. 1986.	50.00	—
l. Signature 20. 1987.	15.00	40.00
m. Signature 21. 1990.	15.00	40.00
n. Signature 22. 1991.	15.00	40.00
o. Signature 22. 1992.	15.00	40.00
p. Signature 23. 1992.	15.00	40.00
q. Signature 24. 1992.	15.00	40.00

709K 10,000 Francs

ND. (1977-92). Red-brown on multicolor underprint. Two men seated operating primitive spinning apparatus, woman with headwear at right. Back: Figurine and girl at left, modern textile spinning machine at center. Watermark: Woman with headwear.

	VF	UNC
a. Signature 11. ND.	40.00	100.
b. Signature 12. ND.	40.00	100.
c. Signature 13. ND.	45.00	110.
d. Signature 14. ND.	25.00	60.00
e. Signature 15. ND.	25.00	70.00
f. Signature 16. ND.	55.00	130.
h. Signature 18. ND.	30.00	85.00
i. Signature 19. ND.	40.00	—
j. Signature 20. ND.	25.00	65.00
k. Signature 21. ND.	20.00	60.00
l. Signature 22. ND.	20.00	60.00
m. Signature 23. ND.	20.00	60.00

1991-92 Issue

710K 500 Francs

(19)91-(20)02. Dark brown and dark green on multicolor underprint. Man at right, flood control dam at center. Back: Farmer riding spray rig behind garden tractor aat center, native art at left. Watermark: Man.

	VF	UNC
a. Signature 22. (19)91.	3.00	8.00
b. Signature 23. (19)92.	3.00	8.00
c. Signature 25. (19)93.	3.00	8.00
d. Signature 26. (19)94.	3.00	7.00
e. Signature 27. (19)95.	3.00	7.00
f. Signature 28. (19)96.	3.00	7.00
g. Signature 28. (19)97. 10-digit serial #.	3.00	7.00
h. Signature 28. (19)97. 11-digit serial #.	3.00	7.00
i. Signature 28. (19)98.	3.00	7.00
j. Signature 29. (19)99.	3.00	6.00
k. Signature 30. (20)00.	3.00	6.00
l. Signature 30. (20)01.	3.00	6.00
m. Signature 31. (20)02.	3.00	6.00

711K 1000 Francs

(19)91-(20)02. Dark brown-violet on tan, yellow and multicolor underprint. Workmen hauling peanuts to storage at center, woman's head at right. Back: Twin statues and mask at left, two women with baskets, elevated riverside storage bins in background at center. Watermark: Woman's head.

	VF	UNC
a. Signature 22. (19)91.	5.00	12.00
b. Signature 23. (19)92.	5.00	12.00
c. Signature 25. (19)93.	4.00	10.00
d. Signature 26. (19)94.	4.00	10.00
e. Signature 27. (19)95.	4.00	10.00
f. Signature 28. (19)96.	3.00	9.00
g. Signature 28. (19)97.	3.00	9.00
h. Signature 28. (19)98.	3.00	9.00
i. Signature 29. (19)99.	3.00	8.00
j. Signature 30. (20)00.	3.00	8.00
k. Signature 30. (20)01.	3.00	8.00
l. Signature 31. (20)02.	3.00	8.00
m. Signature 31. (20)03.	7.00	—

712K 2500 Francs

(19)92-(19)94. Deep purple and dark brown on lilac and multicolor underprint. Dam at center, young woman's head at right. Back: Statue at left, harvesting and spraying of fruit at left center. Watermark: Young woman's head.

	VF	UNC
a. Signature 23. (19)92.	8.00	20.00
b. Signature 25. (19)93.	8.00	20.00
c. Signature 27. (19)94.	8.00	20.00

713K 5000 Francs

(19)92-(20)02. Dark brown and deep blue on multicolor underprint. Woman wearing headdress adorned with cowrie shells at right, smelting plant at center. Back: Women with children and various pottery at left center. Watermark: Woman wearing headdress adorned with cowrie shells.

	VF	UNC
a. Signature 23. (19)92.	9.00	30.00
b. Signature 25. (19)93.	9.00	30.00
c. Signature 27. (19)94.	9.00	25.00
d. Signature 27. (19)95.	9.00	25.00
e. Signature 28. (19)96.	—	—
f. Signature 28. (19)97.	9.00	25.00

	VF	UNC
g. Signature 28. (19)98.	9.00	25.00
h. Signature 29. (19)98.	9.00	25.00
i. Signature 29. (19)99.	9.00	25.00
j. Signature 30. (20)00.	8.00	20.00
k. Signature 30. (20)01.	8.00	20.00
l. Signature 31. (20)02.	9.00	25.00
m. Signature 31. (20)03.	8.00	20.00

714K 10,000 Francs

(19)92-(20)01. Dark brown on multicolor underprint. Headman with scepter at right, skyscraper at center. Back: Native art at left, woman crossing vine bridge over river at center. Watermark: Headman with scepter.

	VF	UNC
a. Signature 25. (19)92.	15.00	50.00
b. Signature 27. (19)94.	15.00	45.00
c. Signature 27. (19)95.	15.00	45.00
d. Signature 28. (19)96.	15.00	45.00
e. Signature 28. (19)97.	15.00	45.00
f. Signature 28. (19)98.	15.00	45.00
g. Signature 29. (19)98.	15.00	45.00
h. Signature 29. (19)99.	15.00	45.00
i. Signature 30. (20)00.	—	—
j. Signature 30. (20)01.	15.00	45.00

2003 Issue

715K 1000 Francs

(20)03-. Red-brown on red and multicolor underprint. 125x65mm.

	VF	UNC
a. Signature 32. (20)03.	FV	6.00
b. Signature 32. (20)04.	FV	6.00
e. Signature 36. (20)07.	FV	5.00

716K 2000 Francs

(20)03-. Blue on light blue and multicolor underprint. 130x66mm.

	VF	UNC
a. Signature 32. (20)03.	FV	10.00
b. Signature 32. (20)04.	FV	10.00
e. Signature 36. (20)07.	FV	9.00

717K 5000 Francs

(20)03-. Multicolor. 141x74mm.

	VF	UNC
a. Signature 32. (20)03.	FV	20.00
b. Signature 32. (20)04.	FV	17.50
e. Signature 36. (20)07.	FV	17.50

718K 10,000 Francs

(20)03-. Multicolor. 145x74mm.

	VF	UNC
a. Signature 32. (20)03.	FV	40.00
b. Signature 32. (20)04.	FV	35.00
d. Signature 34. (20)06.	FV	32.50
e. Signature 36. (20)07.	FV	32.50

T for Togo

1959-65; ND Issue

801T 100 Francs

1961-65; ND. Dark brown, orange and multicolor. Like #101A.

	VF	UNC
a. Engraved. Signature 1. 20.3.1961.	35.00	100.
b. Signature 2. 20.3.1961.	25.00	70.00
c. Litho. Signature 2. 20.3.1961.	25.00	70.00
d. Signature 3. 2.12.1964.	30.00	85.00
e. Signature 4. 2.3.1965.	20.00	60.00
f. Signature 4. ND.	15.00	45.00
g. Signature 5. ND.	35.00	100.

802T 500 Francs

1959-61; ND. Brown, green and multicolor. Field workers at left, mask carving at right. Like #102A. Back: Woman at left, farmer on tractor at right. Watermark: Woman's head.

	VF	UNC
a. Engraved. Signature 1. 15.4.1959.	75.00	—
b. Signature 1. 20.3.1961.	75.00	—
c. Signature 2. 20.3.1961.	75.00	—
f. Signature 5. ND.	85.00	—
g. Signature 6. ND.	30.00	80.00
i. Litho. Signature 7. ND.	60.00	130.
j. Signature 8. ND.	50.00	—
k. Signature 9. ND.	20.00	60.00
l. Signature 10. ND.	—	—
m. Signature 11. ND.	10.00	35.00

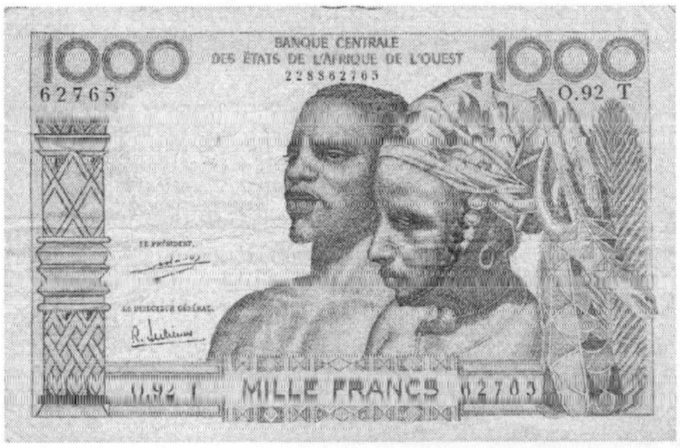

803T 1000 Francs

1959-65; ND. Brown, blue and multicolor. Man and woman at center. Like #103A. Back: Man with rope suspension bridge in background and pineapples. Watermark: Man's head.

	VF	UNC
a. Engraved. Signature 1. 17.9.1959.	—	—
b. Signature 1. 20.3.1961.	60.00	—
c. Signature 2. 20.3.1961.	75.00	—
e. Signature 4. 2.3.1965.	60.00	—
f. Signature 5. ND.	30.00	80.00
g. Signature 6. ND.	70.00	—
h. Litho. Signature 6. ND.	80.00	—
i. Signature 7. ND.	30.00	80.00
j. Signature 8. ND.	90.00	—
k. Signature 9. ND.	20.00	55.00
l. Signature 10. ND.	15.00	45.00
m. Signature 11. ND.	12.00	40.00
n. Signature 12. ND.	12.00	40.00
o. Signature 13. ND.	15.00	45.00

804T 5000 Francs — VF / UNC

1961; ND. Blue, brown and multicolor. Bearded man at left, building at center. Back: Woman, corn grinders and huts.

	VF	UNC
b. Signature 1. 20.3.1961.	125.	300.
h. Signature 6. ND.	75.00	250.
i. Signature 7. ND.	125.	—
j. Signature 8. ND.	125.	—
k. Signature 9. ND.	65.00	200.
m. Signature 11. ND.	50.00	175.

1977-81; ND Issue

#805T-809T smaller size notes.

805T 500 Francs — VF / UNC

1979. Lilac, light olive-green and multicolor. Artwork at left, long horn animals at center, man wearing hat at right. Back: Cultivated palm at left, aerial view at center, mask at right. Watermark: Woman in profile. Signature 12. — 12.00 / 30.00

806T 500 Francs

1981-90. Pale olive-green and multicolor. Artwork at left, long horn animals at center, man wearing hat at right. Back: Cultivated palm at left, aerial view at center, mask at right. Watermark: Woman in profile.

	VF	UNC
a. Signature 14. 1988.	15.00	—
b. Signature 15. 1981. (BF).	4.00	12.00
c. Signature 15. 1981. (F-CO).	4.00	12.00
d. Signature 15. 1982. (BF).	12.00	30.00
e. Signature 17. 1981. (F-CO).	12.00	30.00
f. Signature 18. 1984.	15.00	40.00
g. Signature 19. 1984.	4.00	12.00
h. Signature 19. 1985.	3.00	9.00
i. Signature 20. 1986.	3.00	9.00
j. Signature 20. 1987.	3.00	9.00
k. Signature 21. 1989.	3.00	9.00
l. Signature 22. 1990.	3.00	9.00

807T 1000 Francs

1981-90. Brown on multicolor underprint. Artwork at left, open pit mine at center, woman at right. Back: Wood carver with finished works. Watermark: Woman.

	VF	UNC
a. Signature 14. 1988.	4.00	12.00
b. Signature 15. 1981.	5.00	15.00
c. Signature 17. 1981.	7.00	—
d. Signature 18. 1984.	4.00	12.00
e. Signature 19. 1984.	15.00	—
f. Signature 19. 1985.	4.00	12.00
g. Signature 20. 1986.	—	—
h. Signature 20. 1987.	4.00	10.00
i. Signature 21. 1989.	4.00	10.00
j. Signature 22. 1990.	4.00	10.00

808T 5000 Francs

1977-92. Black and red on multicolor underprint. Woman at left, fish and boats on shore at center, carving at right. Back: Carvings, fishing boats and mask.

	VF	UNC
a. Signature 12. 1978.	35.00	100.
b. Signature 12. 1979.	35.00	100.
c. Signature 14. 1977.	35.00	95.00
d. Signature 14. 1989.	10.00	40.00
e. Signature 15. 1981.	50.00	120.
f. Signature 15. 1982.	50.00	120.
g. Signature 17. 1983.	—	—
h. Signature 18. 1984.	30.00	75.00
i. Signature 20. 1987.	10.00	40.00
j. Signature 21. 1990.	10.00	40.00
k. Signature 22. 1991.	—	—
l. Signature 22. 1992.	10.00	40.00
m. Signature 23. 1992.	10.00	40.00
n. Signature 24. 1992.	20.00	50.00

809T 10,000 Francs

ND. (1977-92). Red-brown on multicolor underprint. Two men seatedoperating primitive spinning apparatus, woman with headwear at right. Back: Figurine and girl at left, modern textile spinning machine at center. Watermark: Woman with headwear.

	VF	UNC
a. Signature 11. ND.	40.00	110.
b. Signature 12. ND.	—	—
c. Signature 13. ND.	—	—
d. Signature 14. ND.	65.00	—
e. Signature 15. ND.	30.00	80.00
f. Signature 16. ND.	55.00	125.
h. Signature 18. ND.	30.00	80.00
k. Signature 22. ND.	25.00	65.00
l. Signature 23. ND.	25.00	65.00

1991-92 Issue

810T 500 Francs

(19)91-(20)02. Dark brown and dark green on multicolor underprint. Man at right, flood control dam at center. Back: Farmer riding spray rig behind garden tractor at center, native art at left. Watermark: Man.

	VF	UNC
a. Signature 22. (19)91.	3.00	8.00
b. Signature 23. (19)92.	—	—
c. Signature 25. (19)93.	3.00	8.00
d. Signature 26. (19)94.	3.00	7.00
e. Signature 27. (19)95.	3.00	7.00
f. Signature 28. (19)96.	3.00	7.00
g. Signature 28. (19)97. 10-digit serial #.	3.00	7.00
h. Signature 28. (19)97. 11-digit serial #.	3.00	7.00
i. Signature 28. (19)98.	3.00	7.00
j. Signature 29. (19)99.	3.00	7.00
k. Signature 30. (20)00.	3.00	6.00
l. Signature 30. (20)01.	3.00	6.00
m. Signature 31. (20)02.	3.00	6.00

811T 1000 Francs

(19)91-(20)02. Dark brown-violet on tan, yellow and multicolor underprint. Workmen hauling peanuts to storage at center, woman's head at right. Back: Twin statues and mask at left, two women with baskets, elevated riverside storage bins in background at center. Watermark: Woman's head.

	VF	UNC
a. Signature 22. (19)91.	5.00	12.00
b. Signature 23. (19)92.	12.00	—
c. Signature 25. (19)93.	5.00	10.00
d. Signature 26. (19)94.	5.00	10.00
e. Signature 27. (19)95.	4.00	9.00
f. Signature 28. (19)96.	4.00	9.00
g. Signature 28. (19)97.	4.00	9.00

	VF	UNC
h. Signature 28. (19)98.	4.00	9.00
i. Signature 29. (19)99.	4.00	8.00
j. Signature 30. (20)00.	4.00	8.00
k. Signature 30. (20)01.	4.00	8.00
l. Signature 31. (20)02.	4.00	8.00
m. Signature 31. (20)03.	4.00	8.00

812T 2500 Francs

(19)92-(19)94. Deep purple and dark brown on lilac and multicolor underprint. Dam at center, young woman's head at right. Back: Statue at left, harvesting and spraying of fruit at left center. Watermark: Young woman's head.

	VF	UNC
a. Signature 23. (19)92.	8.00	20.00
b. Signature 25. (19)93.	8.00	20.00
c. Signature 27. (19)94.	8.00	20.00

813T 5000 Francs

(19)92-(20)02. Dark brown and deep blue on multicolor underprint. Woman wearing headdress adorned with cowrie shells at right, smelting plant at center. Back: Women with children and various pottery at left center. Watermark: Woman wearing headdress adorned with cowrie shells.

	VF	UNC
a. Signature 23. (19)92.	9.00	30.00
b. Signature 25. (19)93.	9.00	30.00
c. Signature 27. (19)94.	9.00	25.00
d. Signature 27. (19)95.	9.00	25.00
e. Signature 28. (19)97.	—	—
f. Signature 28. (19)98.	—	—
g. Signature 29. (19)98.	9.00	25.00
h. Signature 29. (19)99.	9.00	25.00
i. Signature 30. (20)00.	9.00	25.00
j. Signature 30. (20)01.	8.00	20.00
k. Signature 31. (20)02.	8.00	20.00
l. Signature 31. (20)03.	—	—

814T 10,000 Francs

(19)92-(20)01. Dark brown on multicolor underprint. Headman with scepter at right, skyscraper at center. Back: Native art at left, woman crossing vine bridge over river at center. Watermark: Headman with scepter.

	VF	UNC
a. Signature 25. (19)92.	15.00	50.00
b. Signature 27. (19)94.	15.00	45.00
c. Signature 27. (19)95.	15.00	45.00
d. Signature 28. (19)96.	15.00	45.00
e. Signature 28. (19)97.	15.00	45.00
f. Signature 28. (19)98.	—	
g. Signature 29. (19)98.	15.00	45.00
h. Signature 29. (19)99.	15.00	45.00
i. Signature 30. (20)00.	15.00	45.00
j. Signature 30. (20)01.	15.00	45.00

2003 Issue

815T 1000 Francs

(20)03-. Red-brown on red and multicolor underprint. .

	VF	UNC
a. Signature 32. (20)03.	FV	6.00
b. Signature 32. (20)04.	FV	6.00

816T 2000 Francs

(20)03-. Blue on light blue and multicolor underprint.

	VF	UNC
a. Signature 32. (20)03.	FV	10.00
b. Signature 32. (20)04.	FV	10.00

817T 5000 Francs

(20)03-. Multicolor.

	VF	UNC
a. Signature 32. (20)03.	FV	20.00
b. Signature 32. (20)04.	FV	17.50

818T 10,000 Francs

(20)03-. Multicolor.

	VF	UNC
a. Signature 32. (20)03.	FV	40.00
b. Signature 32. (20)04.	FV	35.00

S for Guinea-Bissau

1997 Issue

910S 500 Francs

(19)97-(19)99. Dark brown and dark green on multicolor underprint. Man at right, flood control dam at center. Back: Farmer riding spray rig behind garden tractor at center, native art at left. Watermark: Man.

	VF	UNC
a. Signature 28. (19)97. 10-digit.	3.00	7.00
b. Signature 28. (19)97. 11-digit.	9.00	20.00
c. Signature 28. (19)98.	3.00	7.00
d. Signature 29. (19)99.	10.00	30.00
e. Signature 30. (20)00.	—	—
g. Signature 31. (20)02.	10.00	30.00

911S 1000 Francs

(19)97-(19)99. Dark brown-violet on tan, yellow and multicolor underprint. Workmen hauling peanuts to storage at center, woman's head at right. Back: Twin statues and mask at left, two women with baskets, elevated riverside storage bins in background at center. Watermark: Woman's head.

	VF	UNC
a. Signature 28. (19)07.	4.00	10.00
b. Signature 28. (19)98.	4.00	10.00
c. Signature 29. (19)99.	4.00	10.00
e. Signature 30. (20)01.	—	—
f. Signature 31. (20)02.	4.00	10.00

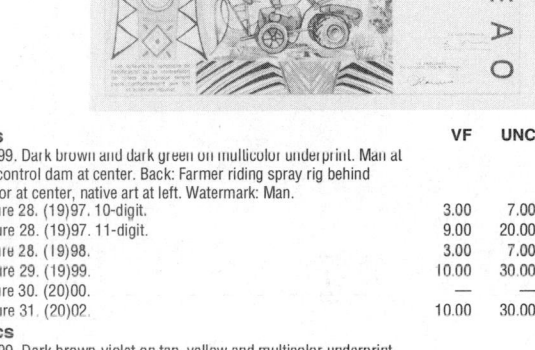

913S 5000 Francs

(19)97-(20)00. Dark brown and deep blue on multicolor underprint. Woman wearing headdress adorned with caowrie shells at right, smelting plant at center. Back: Women with children and various pottery at left center. Watermark: Woman wearing headdress adorned with cowrie shells.

	VF	UNC
a. Signature 28. (19)97.	9.00	30.00
b. Signature 28. (19)98.	9.00	30.00
c. Signature 29. (19)98.	—	—
d. Signature 29. (19)99.	9.00	30.00
e. Signature 30. (20)00.	25.00	45.00
g. Signature 31. (20)02.	8.00	25.00
h. Signature 31. (20)03.	—	—

914S 10,000 Francs

(19)97-(19)98. Dark brown on multicolor underprint. Headman with scepter at right, skyscraper at center. Back: Native art at left, woman crossing vine bridge over river at center. Watermark: Headman with scepter.

	VF	UNC
a. Signature 28. (19)97.	15.00	50.00
b. Signature 28. (19)98.	—	—
c. Signature 29. (19)98.	30.00	65.00
d. Signature 29. (19)99.	—	—
e. Signature 30. (20)00.	—	—

2003 Issue

		VF	UNC
915S	**1000 Francs**		
	(20)03-. Red-brown on red and multicolor underprint. 125x65mm.		
	a. Signature 32. (20)03.	FV	6.00
	b. Signature 32. (20)04.	FV	6.00
916S	**2000 Francs**		
	(20)03-. Blue on light blue and multicolor underprint. 130x66mm.		
	a. Signature 32. (20)03.	FV	10.00
	b. Signature 32. (20)04.	FV	10.00
917S	**5000 Francs**		
	(20)03-. Multicolor. 141x74mm.		
	a. Signature 32. (20)03.	FV	20.00
	b. Signature 32. (20)04.	FV	17.50
918S	**10,000 Francs**		
	(20)03-. Multicolor. 145x74mm.		
	a. Signature 32. (20)03.	FV	40.00
	b. Signature 32. (20)04.	FV	35.00

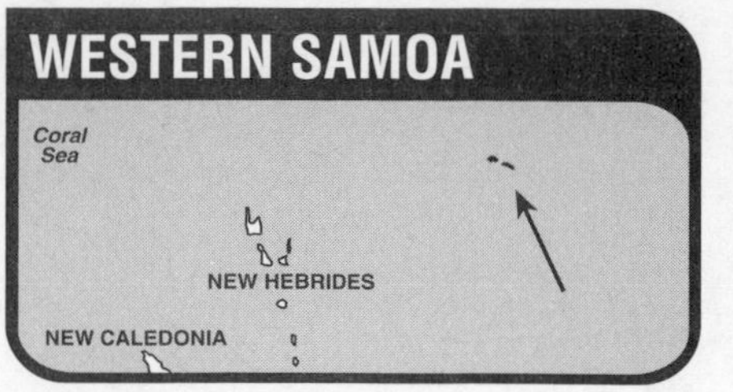

The Independent State of Western Samoa (formerly German Samoa), located in the Pacific Ocean 1,600 miles (2,574 km.) northeast of New Zealand, has an area of 1,097 sq. mi. (2,860 sq. km.) and a population of 157,000. Capital: Apia. The economy is d on agriculture, fishing and tourism. Copra, cocoa and bananas are exported.

The Samoan group of islands was discovered by Dutch navigator Jacob Roggeveen in 1772. Great Britain, the United States and Germany established consular representation at Apia in 1847, 1853 and 1861 respectively. The conflicting interests of the three powers produced the Berlin agreement of 1889 which declared Samoa neutral and had the effect of establishing a tripartite protectorate over the islands. A further agreement, 1899, recognized the rights of the United States in those islands east of 171 deg. west longitude (American Samoa) and of Germany in the other islands (Western Samoa). New Zealand occupied Western Samoa at the start of World War I and administered it as a League of Nations mandate and U.N. trusteeship until Jan. 1, 1962, when it became an independent state.

Western Samoa is a member of the Commonwealth of Nations. The Chief Executive is Chief of State. The prime minister is the Head of Government. The present Head of State, Malietoa Tanumafili II, holds his position for life. Future Heads of State will be elected by the Legislature Assembly for five-year terms.

RULERS:

British, 1914-1962
Malietoa Tanumafili II, 1962-2007

MONETARY SYSTEM:

1 Shilling = 12 Pence
1 Pound = 20 Shillings to 1967
1 Tala = 100 Sene, 1967-

New Zealand Administration

Territory of Western Samoa

1920-22 Treasury Note Issue

By Authority of New Zealand Government

Note: Some of these hand stamped dated notes may appear to be ND, probably through error or that the date has faded, been washed out or worn off.

		VF	UNC
7	**10 Shillings**		
	1922-59. Black on brown and green underprint. Palm trees along beach at center. Signature varieties. Printer: BWC.		
	a. 3.3.1922.	—	—
	b. Signature title: *MINISTER OF EXTERNAL AFFAIRS FOR NEW ZEALAND* at left. 13.4.1938-21.11.1949.	175.	650.
	c. Signature title: *MINISTER OF ISLAND TERRITORIES FOR NEW ZEALAND* at left. 24.5.1951-27.5.1958; 29.10.1959.	250.	750.
	d. Signature title: *HIGH COMMISSIONER* at left. 20.3.1957-22.12.1959.	150.	600.
8A	**1 Pound**		
	1948-61. Purple on multicolor underprint. Hut, palm trees at center. Like #8 but *STERLING* omitted from center. Signature varieties. Printer: BWC.		
	a. Signature title: *MINISTER OF ISLAND TERRITORIES FOR NEW ZEALAND* at left. 6.8.1948-7.8.1958.	450.	—
	b. Signature title: *HIGH COMMISSIONER* at left. 20.4.1959; 10.12.1959; 1.5.1961.	250.	1600.

Bank of Western Samoa

1960-61 Provisional Issue

#10-12 red overprint: *Bank of Western Samoa / Legal Tender in Western Samoa by virtue of the Bank of Western Samoa Ordinance 1959* **on older notes.**

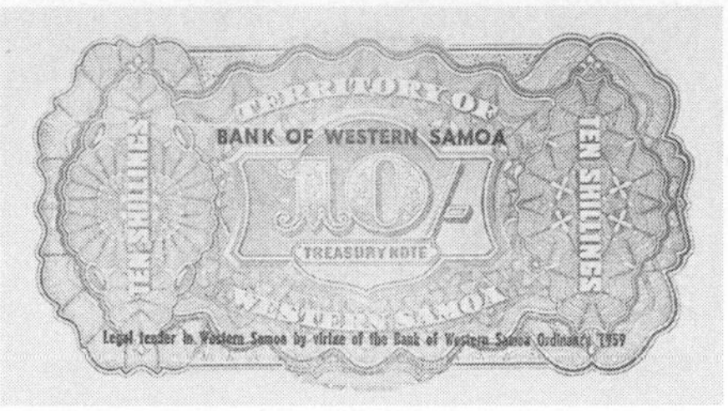

		VF	UNC
10	**10 Shillings**		
	1960-61; ND. Black on brown and green underprint. Palm trees along beach at center. Signature varieties. Overprint: Red on #7.		
	a. Signature title: *HIGH COMMISSIONER* blocked out at lower left, with *MINISTER OF FINANCE* below. 8.12.1960; 1.5.1961.	150.	550.
	b. ND. signature title: *MINISTER OF FINANCE* in plate without overprint., at lower left	150.	550.
11	**1 Pound**		
	1960-61. Purple on multicolor underprint. Hut, palm trees at center. *STERLING* directly appears close beneath spelled out denomination at center. Signature varieties. Overprint: Red on #8.		
	a. Signature title: *HIGH COMMISSIONER* blocked out at lower left, with *MINISTER OF FINANCE* below. 8.11.1960; 1.5.1961.	500.	1500.
	b. Signature title: *MINISTER OF FINANCE* in plate without overprint., at lower left 1.5.1961.	400.	1450.
12	**5 Pounds**		
	1.5.1961. Purple on multicolor underprint. Boat at lower center. *STERLING* omitted from center. Signature varieties. Overprint: Red on #9A.	2000.	7500.

STATE

FALE TUPE O SAMOA I SISIFO

BANK OF WESTERN SAMOA

1963 ND ISSUE

		VF	UNC
13	**10 Shillings**		
	ND (1963). Dark green on multicolor underprint. Arms at left, boat at right. Back: Hut and two palms at center.		
	a. Issued note.	10.00	65.00
	s. Specimen.	—	50.00

		VF	UNC
14	**1 Pound**		
	ND (1963). Blue on multicolor underprint. Palms and rising sun at left and right, arms at center. Back: Small Building and lagoon at center. 159x83mm.		
	a. Issued note.	20.00	100.
	s. Specimen.	—	50.00

		VF	UNC
15	**5 Pounds**		
	ND (1963). Brown on multicolor underprint. Rava bowl at left, red and blue flag over arms at right. Back: Shoreline with trees, sea and islands. 166x89mm.		
	a. Issued note.	50.00	200.
	s. Specimen.	—	200.

1967 ND ISSUE

Tala System.

SIGNATURE VARIETIES			
1	MANAGER	2	MANAGER
3	MANAGER	4	SENIOR MANAGER

		VF	UNC
16	**1 Tala**		
	ND (1967). Dark green on multicolor underprint. Arms at left, boat at right. Signature varieties. Back: Hut and two palms at center. Watermark: BWS repeated.		
	a. Signature 1.	8.00	55.00
	b. Signature 2.	7.00	45.00
	c. Signature 3.	7.00	35.00
	d. Signature 4.	8.00	40.00
	s. Signature as a, b, d. Specimen.	—	40.00
17	**2 Tala**		
	ND (1967). Blue on multicolor underprint. Palms and rising sun at left and right, arms at center. Signature varieties. Watermark: BWS repeated. 144x77mm.		
	a. Signature 1.	7.50	45.00
	b. Signature 3.	5.00	40.00
	c. Signature 4.	8.00	50.00
	s. Signature as a, c. Specimen.	—	50.00

18 **10 Tala** VF UNC
ND (1967). Brown on multicolor underprint. Tava bowl at left, red and blue flag over arms at right. Back: Shoreline with trees, sea and islands. Watermark: BWS repeated. 150x76mm.

	VF	UNC
a. Signature 1.	75.00	300.
b. Signature 2.	90.00	350.
c. Signature 3.	30.00	150.
d. Signature 4.	35.00	165.
s. Signature as a, b, d. Specimen.	—	60.00

Komiti Faatino o Tupe a Samoa I Sisifo

Monetary Board of Western Samoa

1980-84 ND Issue

19 **1 Tala** VF UNC
ND (1980). Dark green on multicolor underprint. Two weavers at right, national flag at left center. Back: Two fishermen in canoe at left center, arms at lower center, national flag at center right. Watermark: M. Tanumafili II. 2.00 10.00

20 **2 Tala** VF UNC
ND (1980). Deep blue-violet on multicolor underprint. Woodcarver at right, national flag at left center. Back: Hut with palms on small island at left center, arms at lower center, national flag at center right. Watermark: M. Tanumafili II. 3.00 15.00

21 **5 Tala** VF UNC
ND (1980). Red on multicolor underprint. Child writing at right, national flag at left center. Back: Small port city at left center, arms at lower center, national flag at center right. Watermark: M. Tanumafili II. 7.00 27.50

22 **10 Tala** VF UNC
ND (1980). Dark brown and purple on multicolor underprint. Man picking bananas at right, national flag at left center. Back: Shoreline landscape, arms at lower center, national flag at center right. Watermark: M. Tanumafili II. 50.00 150.

23 **20 Tala**
ND (1984). Brown and orange-brown on multicolor underprint. Fishermen with net at right, national flag at left center. Back: Arms at lower center, national flag at center right, round building at left. Watermark: M. Tanumafili II. 90.00 350.

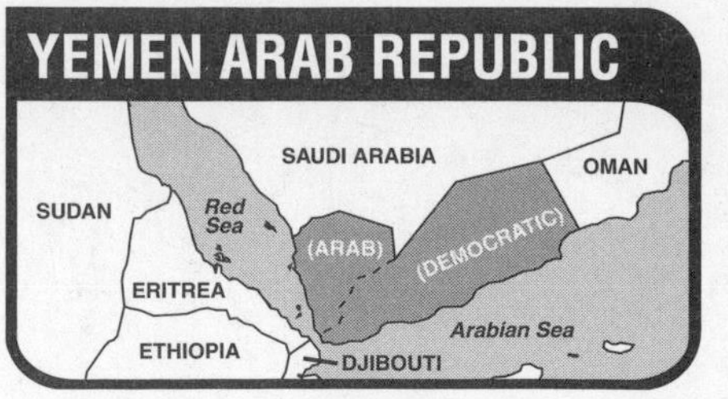

The Yemen Arab Republic, located in the southwestern corner of the Arabian Peninsula, has an area of 75,290 sq. mi. (195,000 sq. km.) and a population of 18.12 million. Capital: San'a. The industries of Yemen, one of the world's poorest countries, are agriculture and local handicrafts. Qat (a mildly narcotic leaf), coffee, cotton and rock salt are exported.

One of the oldest centers of civilization in the Near East, Yemen was once part of the Minaean Kingdom and of the ancient Kingdom of Sheba, after which it was captured successively by Egyptians, Ethiopians and Romans. It was converted to the Moslem religion in 628 AD and administered as a caliphate until 1538, when it came under Turkish occupation which was maintained until 1918 when autonomy was achieved through revolution.

On Feb. 1, 1958, Egypt and Syria formed the United Arab Republic. Yemen joined on March 8 in an association known as the United Arab States. Syria withdrew from the United Arab Republic on Sept. 29, 1961, and on Dec. 26 Egypt dissolved its ties with Yemen in the United Arab States.

Provoked by the harsh rule of Imam Mohammed al-Badr, last ruler of the Kingdom of Mutawwakkilite, the National Liberation Front seized control of the government on Sept. 27, 1962. Badr fled to Saudi Arabia.

An agreement for a constitution for a unified state was reached in Dec. 1989 uniting the Yemen Arab Republic with the People's Democratic Republic of Yemen into the Republic of Yemen on May 22, 1990. Both currencies circulated for a number of years, but the PDR dinar lost legal tender status on June 11, 1996.

RULERS:

Imam Ahmad, AH1367-1382/1948-1962AD
Imam al-Badr, AH1382-1388/1962-1968AD

MONETARY SYSTEM:

1 Rial = 40 Buqshas
1 Rial = 100 Fils (from April 1, 1995).

SIGNATURE VARIETIES

1	Minister of the Treasury Abdul Ghani Ali, 1964	2	Minister of the Treasury and Economy Abdul Ghani Ali, 1967
3	Minister of the Treasury Ahmad al-Ruhumi, 1966 (actually inverted)	4	Minister of the Treasury Ahmad Abdu Said, 1968
5	Governor & Chairman, CBY Abdul Aziz Abdul Ghani, 1971-85	6	Governor & Chairman, CBY Abdulla Mohamed al-Sanabani, 1978-85
7	Governor & Chairman, CBY Abdulla Mohamed al-Sanabani, 1978-85	8	Governor, CBY Muhammad Ahmad Gunaid, 1985-94
9	Governor, CBY Aluwi Salih al-Salami, 1994	10	Governor, CBY Ahmed Abdul Rahman al-Samani, 1997-

Arab Republic

Yemen Currency Board

1964 ND Issue

1	**1 Rial**	VF	UNC
	ND (1964; 1967). Green on multicolor underprint. Arms at left. Back: Houses in Sana'a with minaret at center. Watermark: Arms.		
	a. Signature 1. (1964).	20.00	110.
	b. Signature 2. (1967).	25.00	135.
	s. As a. Specimen.	—	225.

2	**5 Rials**	VF	UNC
	ND (1964; 1967). Red on multicolor underprint. Arms at left. Back: Lion of Timna sculpture at right. Watermark: Arms.		
	a. Signature 1. (1964).	65.00	275.
	b. Signature 2. (1967).	75.00	300.
	s. As a. Specimen.	—	300.

3	**10 Rials**	VF	UNC
	ND (1964; 1967). Blue-green on multicolor underprint. Arms at left. Back: Dam at right. Watermark: Arms.		
	a. Signature 1. (1964).	90.00	375.
	b. Signature 2. (1967).	90.00	375.
	s. As a. Specimen.	—	300.

1966-71 ND Issue

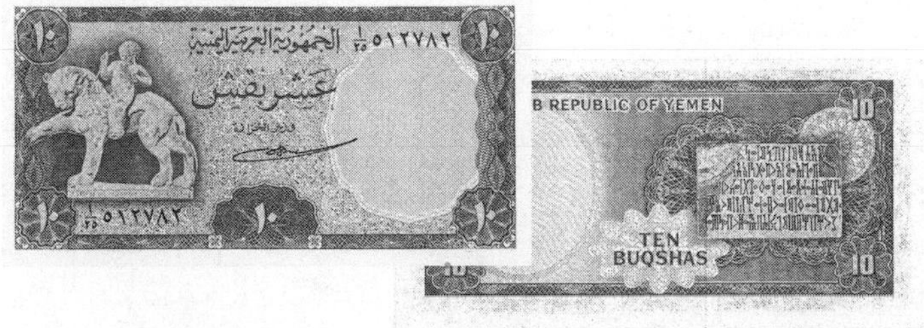

4	**10 Buqshas**	VF	UNC
	ND (1966). Brown on multicolor underprint. Lion of Timna sculpture at left. Signature 3. Back: Ancient dedication stone from a temple at Ma'rib at right. Watermark: Arms.	4.00	25.00

5	**20 Buqshas**	VF	UNC
	ND (1966). Green on multicolor underprint. Tall alabaster head at left. Signature 3. Back: Olive-green. Ruins of the Bara'an temple at right. Watermark: Arms.	5.00	35.00

6	**1 Rial**	VF	UNC
	ND (1969). Green on multicolor underprint. Alabaster head at left. Signature 4. Back: Houses in Sana'a with minaret at center. Watermark: Arms.		
	a. Issued note.	15.00	75.00
	s. Specimen.	—	175.

7	**5 Rials**	VF	UNC
	ND (1969). Red on multicolor underprint. Bronze lion's head sculpture at left. Signature 4. Back: Lion of Timna sculpture at right. Watermark: Arms.		
	a. Issued note.	35.00	180.
	s. Specimen.	—	250.

8	**10 Rials**	VF	UNC
	ND (1969). Blue-green on multicolor underprint. Shadhili Mosque at left. Signature 4. Back: Dam at right. Watermark: Arms.		
	a. Issued note.	20.00	130.
	s. Specimen.	—	250.

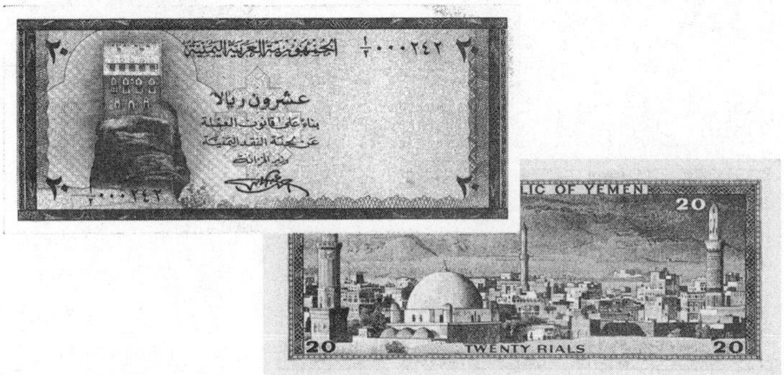

9	**20 Rials**	VF	UNC
	ND (1971). Purple and blue-green on multicolor underprint. Palace on the rock at Wadi Dahr. Signature 4. Back: Purple and gold. City view of Sana'a. Watermark: Arms.		
	a. Issued note.	25.00	160.
	s. Specimen.	—	—

10 50 Rials — VF | UNC

ND (1971). Dark olive-green on multicolor underprint. Crossed *jambiyas* (daggers) at left. Signature 4. Back: Coffee branch and tree, mountains in background at center right. Watermark: Arms. — 20.00 | 140.

Central Bank of Yemen

1973-77 ND Issues

11 1 Rial

ND (1973). Green on multicolor underprint. Al Baqiliyah Mosque at left. Back: Coffee plants with mountains in background at center. Watermark: Arms.

	VF	UNC
a. Signature 5.	.50	2.50
b. Signature 7.	2.50	10.00
s. Specimen.	—	—
ct. Color trial.	—	—

12 5 Rials

ND (1973). Red on multicolor underprint. Buildings in Wadi Du'an at left. Signature 5. Back: Beit al Midie on high rock hill at center. Watermark: Arms.

	VF	UNC
a. Issued note.	5.00	17.50
s. Specimen.	—	—

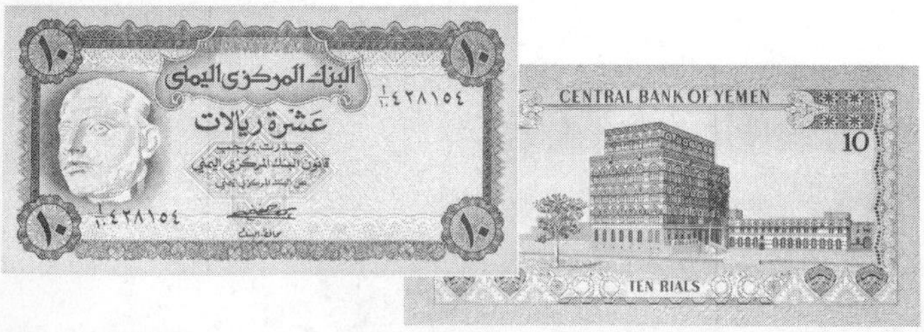

13 10 Rials

ND (1973). Blue-green on multicolor underprint. Bronze head of King Dhamer Ali at left. Back: Republican Palace in Sana'a at center. Watermark: Arms.

	VF	UNC
a. Signature 5.	5.00	20.00
b. Signature 7.	4.00	16.00
s. Specimen.	—	—
ct. Color trial.	—	—

14 20 Rials

ND (1973). Purple on multicolor underprint. Marble sculpture of seated figure with grapes at left. Signature 5. Back: Purple and brown. Terraced slopes along mountain at center right. Watermark: Arms. 145x75mm.

	VF	UNC
a. Issued note.	7.50	25.00
ct. Color trial.	—	—

15 50 Rials

ND (1973). Dark olive-green on multicolor underprint. Bronze statue of Ma'adkarib at left. Back: Bab al Yemen (main gate of Sana'a). Watermark: Arms. 150x75mm.

	VF	UNC
a. Signature 5.	5.00	20.00
b. Signature 7.	3.00	10.00
s. Specimen.	—	—

16 100 Rials

ND (1976). Red-violet on multicolor underprint. Marble sculpture of cherub and griffin at left. Signature 5. Back: View of Ta'izz. Watermark: Arms. 150x75mm.

	VF	UNC
a. Issued note.	20.00	75.00
s. Specimen.	—	—

1979-85 ND Issues

16B 1 Rial — VF | UNC

ND (1983). Darker green on multicolor underprint. Al Baqiliyah Mosque at left. Smaller serial number. Signature 7. Back: Coffee plants with mountains in background at center. Clearer underprint design over watermark area Watermark: Arms. The rays in all four guilloches are much more pronounced in this note than in P#11, a note with which is is often confused. — .50 | 1.25

17	5 Rials	VF	UNC
	ND (1981). Red on orange and multicolor underprint. Dhahr al Dahab at left. Back: Fortress Qal'at al Qahira overlooking Ta'izz at center right. Watermark: Arms.		
	a. Signature 5. (1981).	1.00	5.00
	b. Signature 7. (1983).	.75	5.00
	c. Signature 8. (1991).	.40	2.00

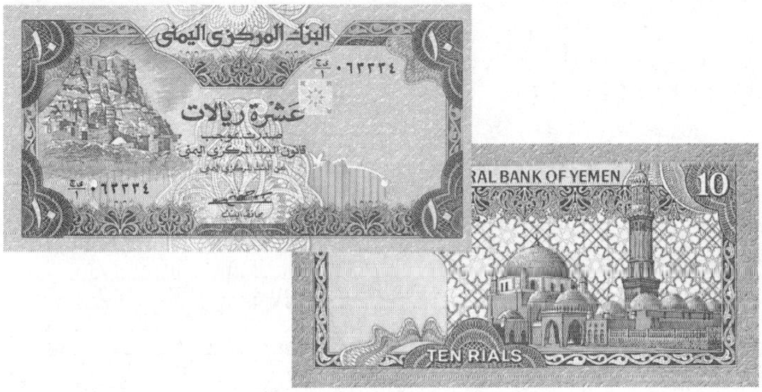

18	10 Rials	VF	UNC
	ND (1981). Blue on green and multicolor underprint. Village of Thulla at left. Back: Al Baqiliyah Mosque. Watermark: Arms.		
	a. Signature 5. (1981).	3.00	15.00
	b. Signature 7. (1983).	2.50	10.00

19	20 Rials	VF	UNC
	ND (1985). Purple on multicolor underprint. Marble sculpture of seated figure with grapes at left. Signature 5. Back: View of San'a. Watermark: Arms. 145x75mm.		
	a. Bank title on tan underprint. on back. Signature 7. (1983). 4mm serial #.	7.50	25.00
	b. As a. Signature 8. 3mm serial #.	5.00	20.00
	c. Bank title on light brown underprint of vertical lines on back. Signature 8.	2.00	10.00
	s. Specimen.	—	—

21	100 Rials	VF	UNC
	ND (1979). Red-violet on multicolor underprint. Al Ashrafiya Mosque and Ta'izz city view at left. Signature 6. Back: View of San'a with mountains. Watermark: Arms. 150x75mm.	5.00	25.00

21A	100 Rials	VF	UNC
	ND (1984). Red-violet on multicolor underprint. Marble sculpture of cherub and griffin at left. Signature 7. Back: Central Bank of Yemen building at center right. Watermark: Arms. 150x75mm.		
	a. Issued note.	2.50	10.00
	s. Specimen.	—	—

1990-97 ND Issues

23	10 Rials	VF	UNC
	ND (1990-). Blue and black on multicolor underprint. Al Baqilyah Mosque at left. Signature 8. Back: Blue and brown. Ma'rib Dam at center right, *10* at upper corners. Watermark: Arms.		
	a. Watermark: Arms have flags with a star at the center.	FV	3.00
	b. Watermark: Arms have flags without star at center.	FV	3.00

24	10 Rials	VF	UNC
	ND (ca.1992). lue and black on multicolor underprint. Al Baqilyah Mosque at left. Signature 8. *10* at upper left and lower right. Back: Blue and brown. Ma'rib Dam at center right, *10* at upper corners with Arabic text: *Sadd Marib* near lowe Watermark: Arms.	FV	3.00

25	20 Rials	VF	UNC
	ND (1995). Dark brown on multicolor underprint. Arch ends straight border across upper center Marble sculpture of cupid with grapes at left. Signature 8. Back: Coastal view of Aden, dhow. Watermark: Arms. 145x75mm.	FV	4.00

26 20 Rials VF UNC

ND (1990). Dark brown on multicolor underprint. Arch ends straight border across upper center Marble sculpture of cupid with grapes at left. Signature 8. Back: Different city view of San'a without minarets or dhow at center right. Watermark: Arms. 145x75mm.

	VF	UNC
a. Without shading around title of the bank.	3.00	10.00
b. With shading around title of the bank.	2.00	3.00

27 50 Rials VF UNC

ND (1993). Black and deep olive-brown on multicolor underprint. Bronze statue of Ma'adkarib at left. Signature 8. Back: Shibam city view at center right. Without Arabic title at lower left. Watermark: Arms. 150x75mm. FV 4.50

27A 50 Rials

ND (199?). Black and deep olive-brown on multicolor underprint. Bronze statue of Ma'adkarib at left. Signature 8, 9. Back: Shibam city view at center right with Arabic title *Shibam Hadramaut* at lower left. Watermark: Arms. 150x75mm. FV 4.00

28 100 Rials VF UNC

ND (1993). Violet, purple and black on multicolor underprint. Ancient culvert in Aden at left. Signature 8, 9. Back: City view of Sana'a. Watermark: Arms. 150x75mm. FV 3.00

29 200 Rials VF UNC

ND (1996). Deep blue-green on multicolor underprint. Alabaster sculpture of a man at left. Signature 9. Back: Harbor view of Mukalla at center right. Watermark: Arms. 155x75mm. FV 8.00

30 500 Rials VF UNC

ND (1997). Blue-violet and red-brown on multicolor underprint. Central Bank of Yemen building at left. Signature 9. Back: Bara'an temple ruins in brown at right. Watermark: Arms. 155x80mm. FV 16.00

1998-2001 ND Issues

31 500 Rials VF UNC

AH1422/2001. Light blue and gray on beige and multicolor underprint. Palace on the Rock at left. Holographic strip with arms repeated at left. Signature 10. Back: Al Muhdar mosque in Tarim, Hadramaut at center. Watermark: Arms. 155x80mm. FV 11.00

32 1000 Rials VF UNC

ND (1998). Pink and dark green on multicolor underprint. Sultan's palace in Seiyun, Hadramaut at center. Holographic strip with arms repeated at left. Signature 10. Back: Bab al-Yemen and old city of Sana'a. 157x85mm. FV 30.00

2004 Issue

		VF	UNC
33	**1000 Rials** 2004/AH1424; 2006/AH1426. Brown and dark green on multicolor underprint. Sultan's palace in Seiym at left. Color changes and date on front at lower right. Back: Bab al Yemen (main gate of Sana'a). Watermark: Arms. 155x85mm.		
	a. 2004/AH1424.	FV	25.00
	b. 2006/AH1426.	FV	25.00

2007 Issue

		VF	UNC
34	**500 Rials** 2007. Light blue and grey on beige and multicolor underprint. Palace on the Rock at left. Holographic strip at left with irregular edge. Back: Al Muhdar Mosque in Tarim Hadramaut at center. Arms. 155x80mm.	FV	12.00

2009 Issue

		VF	UNC
35	**250 Rials** 2009/AH1430. Tan on blue and multicolor underprint. Al Saleh Mosque in Sana'a at center. Back: Mukalla Khor waterway. 155x75mm.	FV	6.00

		VF	UNC
36	**1000 Rials** 2009/AH1430. Green on multicolor underprint. Castle of Sayoun. Back: View of old Sana'a.	FV	20.00

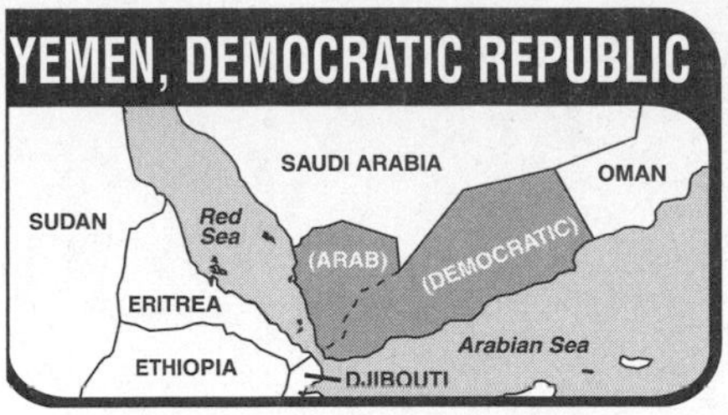

The People's Democratic Republic of Yemen, (formerly the Peoples Republic of Southern Yemen) was located on the southern coast of the Arabian Peninsula. It had an area of 128,560 sq. mi. (332,968 sq. km.). Capital: Aden. It consisted of the port city of Aden, 17 states of the former South Arabian Federation, 3 small sheikhdoms, 3 large sultanates, Quaiti, Kathiri and Mahri, which made up the Eastern Aden Protectorate, and Socotra, the largest island in the Arabian Sea. The port of Aden is the area's most valuable natural resource. Cotton, fish, coffee and hides are exported.

Between 1200 BC and the 6th century AD, what is now the People's Democratic Republic of Yemen was part of the Minaean kingdom. In subsequent years it was controlled by Persians, Egyptians and Turks. Aden, one of the cities mentioned in the Bible, had been a port for trade between the East and West for 2,000 years. British rule began in 1839 when the British East India Co. seized control to put an end to the piracy threatening trade with India. To protect their foothold in Aden, the British found it necessary to extend their control into the area known historically as the Hadramaut, and to sign protection treaties with the sheikhs of the hinterland. Eventually, 15 of the 16 Western Protectorate states, the Wahidi state of the Eastern Protectorate, and Aden Colony joined to form the Federation of South Arabia. In 1959, Britain agreed to prepare South Arabia for full independence, which was achieved on Nov. 30, 1967, at which time South Arabia, including Aden, changed its name to the People's Republic of Southern Yemen. On Dec. 1, 1970, following the overthrowing of the new government by the National Liberation Front, Southern Yemen changed its name to the People's Democratic Republic of Yemen. On May 22, 1990 the People's Democratic Republic merged with the Yemen Arab Republic into a unified Republic of Yemen. The YDR currency ceased to circulate on June 11, 1996.

MONETARY SYSTEM:

1 Dinar = 1000 Fils

Federated State

SIGNATURE VARIETIES			
1		2	
3		4	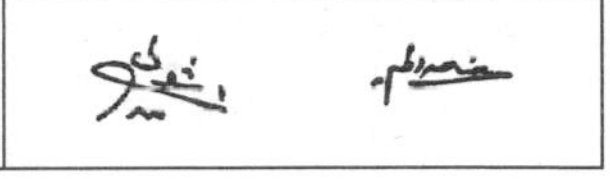

South Arabian Currency Authority

1965 ND Issue

		VF	UNC
1	**250 Fils** ND (1965). Brown on multicolor underprint. Aden harbor, dhow at center. Back: Date palm at center. Watermark: Camel's head. Printer: TDLR.		
	a. Signature 1.	7.50	35.00
	b. Signature 2.	5.00	20.00
	s. As a. Specimen.	—	35.00

2 **500 Fils** — VF | UNC

ND (1965). Green on multicolor underprint. Aden harbor, dhow at center. Back: Date palm at center, heads of wheat at lower left. Watermark: Camel's head. Printer: TDLR.

	VF	UNC
a. Signature 1.	20.00	85.00
b. Signature 2.	6.00	30.00
s. As a. Specimen.	—	50.00

3 **1 Dinar** — VF | UNC

ND (1965). Dark blue on multicolor underprint. Aden harbor, dhow at center. Back: Date palm at center, branch of a cotton plant at left. Watermark: Camel's head. Printer: TDLR.

	VF	UNC
a. Signature 1.	25.00	150.
b. Signature 2.	20.00	60.00
s. As a. Specimen.	—	75.00

4 **5 Dinars** — VF | UNC

ND (1965). Red on multicolor underprint. Aden harbor, dhow at center. Back: Date palm at center, cotton plant branch and millet flanking. Watermark: Camel's head. Printer: TDLR.

	VF	UNC
a. Signature 1.	100.	500.
b. Signature 2.	20.00	95.00
s. As a. Specimen.	—	100.

5 **10 Dinars** — VF | UNC

ND (1967). Deep olive-green on multicolor underprint. Aden harbor, dhow at center. Signature 2. Back: Date palm at center, cotton branch, corn cobs and heads of wheat. Watermark: Camel's head. Printer: TDLR. — 90.00 | 400.

Peoples Democratic Republic

Bank of Yemen

1984 ND Issue

6 **500 Fils** — VF | UNC

ND (1984). Green on multicolor underprint. Aden harbor, dhow at center. Without English. Back: Date palm at center, heads of wheat at lower left. New bank name. Capital *ADEN* added to botto Watermark: Camel's head. — 5.00 | 20.00

7 **1 Dinar** — VF | UNC

ND (1984). Dark blue on multicolor underprint. Aden harbor, dhow at center. Without English. Back: Date palm at center, branch of cotton plant at left. New bank name. Capital *ADEN* added to bot Watermark: Camel's head. — 8.00 | 32.00

8 **5 Dinars** — VF | UNC

ND (1984). Red on multicolor underprint. Aden harbor, dhow at center. Without English. Back: Date palm at center, cotton plant branch and millet flanking. New bank name. Capital *ADEN* add Watermark: Camel's head.

	VF	UNC
a. Signature 3.	20.00	75.00
b. Signature 4.	15.00	52.00

9 **10 Dinars** — VF | UNC

ND (1984). Deep olive-green on multicolor underprint. Aden harbor, dhow at center. Without English. Back: Date palm at center, cotton branch, corn cobs and heads of wheat. New bank name. Capital *ADEN* Watermark: Camel's head.

	VF	UNC
a. Signature 3.	27.00	110.
b. Signature 4.	22.00	80.00

The Federal Republic of Yugoslavia is a Balkan country located on the east shore of the Adriatic Sea bordering Bosnia-Herzegovina and Croatia to the west, Hungary and Romania to the north, Bulgaria to the east, and Albania and Macedonia to the south. It has an area of 39,449 sq. mi. (102,173 sq. km.) and a population of 10.5 million. Capital: Belgrade. The chief industries are agriculture, mining, manufacturing and tourism. Machinery, nonferrous metals, meat and fabrics are exported.

The first South-Slavian State - Yugoslavia - was proclaimed on Dec. 1, 1918, after the union of the Kingdom of Serbia, Montenegro and the South Slav territories of Austria-Hungary; it then changed its official name from the Kingdom of the Serbs, Croats, and Slovenes to the Kingdom of Yugoslavia on Oct. 3, 1929. The Royal government of Yugoslavia attempted to remain neutral in World War II but, yielding to German pressure, aligned itself with the Axis powers in March of 1941; a few days later it was overthrown by a military-led coup and its neutrality reasserted. The Nazis occupied the country on April 17, and throughout the remaining years were resisted by a number of guerrilla armies, notably that of Marshal Josip Broz known as Tito. After the defeat of the Axis powers, a leftist coalition headed by Tito abolished the monarchy and, on Jan. 31, 1946, established a "People's Republic". Tito's rival General Draza Mihajlovic, who led the Chetniks against the Germans and Tito's forces, was arrested on March 13, 1946 and executed the following day after having been convicted by a partisan court.

The Federal Republic of Yugoslavia was composed of six autonomous republics: Serbia, Croatia, Slovenia, Bosnia-Herzegovina, Macedonia and Montenegro with two autonomous provinces within Serbia: Kosovo-Metohija and Vojvodina. The collapse of the Socialist Federal Republic of Yugoslavia during 1991-92 has resulted in the autonomous republics of Croatia, Slovenia, Bosnia-Herzegovina and Macedonia declaring their respective independence.

The Federal Republic of Yugoslavia was proclaimed in 1992; it consists of the former Republics of Serbia and Montenegro.

MONETARY SYSTEM:

1 Dinar = 100 Para
1 Dinar = 100 *Old* Dinara, 1965
1 Dinar = 10,000 *Old* Dinara, 1990-91
1 Dinar = 10 *Old* Dinara, 1992
1 Dinar = 1 Million *Old* Dinara, 1.10.1993
1 Dinar = 1 Milliard *Old* Dinara, 1.1.1994
1 Novi Dinar = 1 German Mark = 12,000,000 Dinara, 24.1.1994

SIGNATURE VARIETIES

	VICE GOVERNOR	GOVERNOR
5	Isak Sion	Nikola Maljanich
6	Borivoje Jelich	Nikola Maljanich
7	Branislav Colanovich	Nikola Maljanich
8	Branislav Colanovich	Ivo Perishin
9	Joshko Shtrukelj	Branislav Colanovich
10	Ilija Marjanovich	Ksente Bogoev
11	Miodrag Veljkovich	Radovan Makich

SIGNATURE VARIETIES

12	Dr. Slobodan Stanojevich	Radovan Makich
13	Dr. Slobodan Stanojevich	Dushan Vlatkovitch
14	Mitja Gaspari	Dushan Vlatkovitch
15		Dushan Vlatkovitch
16		Vuk Ognjanovich
17		Borivoje Atanockovich
18		
19	Bozidar Gazivoda	
20	Bozidar Gazivoda	Dragoslav Avramovich

SOCIALIST FEDERAL REPUBLIC

НАРОДНА БАНКА ЈУГОСЛАВИЈЕ

NARODNA BANKA JUGOSLAVIJE

NATIONAL BANK OF YUGOSLAVIA

1963 ISSUE

#73-76 Replacement notes: Serial # prefix *ZA*.

73 100 Dinara VF UNC

1.5.1963. Dark red on multicolor underprint. Woman wearing national costume at left. Signature 5. Back: View of Dubrovnik at center.

	VF	UNC
a. Issued note.	.25	3.00
s. Specimen.	—	40.00

74 500 Dinara VF UNC

1.5.1963. Dark green on multicolor underprint. Farm woman with sickle at left. Signature 5. Back: Two combine harvesters at center.

	VF	UNC
a. Issued note.	1.00	5.00
s. Specimen.	—	50.00

		VF	UNC
75	**1000 Dinara** 1.5.1963. Dark brown on multicolor underprint. Male steelworker at left. Signature 5. Back: Factory complex at center.		
	a. Issued note.	1.00	4.00
	s. Specimen.	—	50.00
76	**5000 Dinara** 1.5.1963. Dark blue on multicolor underprint. Relief of Mestrovic at left. Signature 5. Back: Parliament building in Belgrade at center.		
	a. Issued note.	30.00	150.
	p. Proof. Without serial #.	125.	200.
	s. Specimen.	—	80.00

1965 Issue

#77-80 Replacement notes: Serial # prefix *ZA*.

		VF	UNC
77	**5 Dinara** 1.8.1965. Dark green on multicolor underprint. Farm woman with sickle at left. Signature 6. Back: Two combine harvesters at center. UV: fibers fluoresce red and yellow. Design elements around value 5 green. 134x64mm.		
	a. Small numerals in serial number.	3.00	25.00
	b. Large numerals in serial number.	1.50	15.00
	s. Specimen.	—	40.00
78	**10 Dinara** 1.8.1965. Dark brown on multicolor underprint. Male steelworker at left. Signature 6. Back: Factory complex at center. 143x66mm.		
	a. Small numerals in serial number.	1.50	15.00
	b. Large numerals in serial number.	5.00	25.00
	s. Specimen.	—	40.00
79	**50 Dinara** 1.8.1965. Dark blue on multicolor underprint. Relief of Mestrovic at left. Signature 6. Back: Parliament building in Belgrade at center. 151x72mm.		
	a. Small numerals in serial number.	5.00	40.00
	b. Large numerals in serial number.	5.00	50.00
	s. Specimen.	—	40.00

		VF	UNC
80	**100 Dinara** 1.8.1965. Red on multicolor underprint. Equestrian statue "Peace" of Augustincic in garden of United Nations, New York at left. Signature 6.		
	a. Small numerals in serial number.	5.00	30.00
	b. Large numerals in serial number, without security thread.	2.00	10.00
	c. Large numerals in serial number, with security thread. 7 digit serial #.	.75	5.00
	s. Specimen.	—	40.00

1968-70 Issue

#81-84 Replacement notes: Serial # prefix *ZA*.

		VF	UNC
81	**5 Dinara** 1.5.1968. Dark green on multicolor underprint. Farm woman with sickle at left. Signature 7, 8 Back: Large numerals of value at left center. 123x59mm.		
	a. Small numerals in serial number.	.20	1.00
	b. Large numerals in serial number.	.20	1.00
	s. Specimen.	—	30.00

		VF	UNC
82	**10 Dinara** 1.5.1968. Dark brown on multicolor underprint. Male steelworker at left. Signature 7, 8. Back: Large numerals of value at left center. UV: fibers fluoresce yellow; security strip green. Design elements orange. 131x63mm.		
	a. Small numerals in serial number.	1.00	20.00
	b. Large numerals in serial number, without security thread.	3.00	25.00
	c. Large numerals in serial number, with security thread.	1.00	5.00
	s. Specimen.	—	30.00

		VF	UNC
83	**50 Dinara** 1.5.1968. Dark blue on multicolor underprint. Relief of Mestrovic at left. Signature 7, 8. Back: Large numerals of value at left center. 139x66mm.		
	a. Small numerals in serial number.	1.50	20.00
	b. Large numerals in serial number, without security thread.	.50	4.00
	c. Large numerals in serial number, with security thread.	.25	1.00
	s. Specimen.	—	45.00
84	**500 Dinara** 1.8.1970. Dark olive-green on multicolor underprint. Statue of Nicola Tesla seated with open book at left. Signature 7, 8. Back: Large numerals of value at left center.		
	a. Without security thread. Signature 8.	.50	2.50
	b. With security thread.	1.50	6.00

1974 Issue

#85 and 86 Replacement notes: Serial # prefix *ZA*.

		VF	UNC
85	**20 Dinara** 19.12.1974. Purple on multicolor underprint. Ship dockside at left. Two prefix letters plus 6 or 7-digit serial number. Signature 9.	.25	1.50
86	**1000 Dinara** 19.12.1974. Blue-black on multicolor underprint. Woman with fruit at left. Signature 9.	1.00	4.50

1978 Issue

#87-92 Replacement notes: Serial # prefix *ZA; ZB; ZC.*

87	**10 Dinara**	VF	UNC
	1978; 1981. Dark brown on multicolor underprint. Male steelworker at left. Long, 2-line signature title at left. Back: Large numerals of value at left center.		
	a. Signature 10. 12.8.1978.	.20	.75
	b. Signature 11. 4.11.1981.	.20	.75
88	**20 Dinara**		
	1978; 1981. Purple on multicolor underprint. Ship dockside at left. Two prefix letters plus 6 or 7-digit serial number. Long 2-line signature title at left.		
	a. Signature 10. 12.8.1978.	.15	.75
	b. Signature 11. 4.11.1981.	.25	2.00
89	**50 Dinara**		
	1978; 1981. Dark blue on multicolor underprint. Relief of Mestrovic at left. Large 2-line signature title at left. Back: Large numerals of value at left center. UV: fibers fluoresce yellow, security strip blue.		
	a. Signature 10. 12.8.1978.	.20	1.00
	b. Signature 11. 4.11.1981.	.20	1.00

90	**100 Dinara**	VF	UNC
	1978; 1981; 1986. Red on multicolor underprint. Equestrian statue "Peace" of Augustincic in garden of United Nations, New York at left. Long 2-line signature title at left. UV: fibers fluoresce yellow; serial # and design elements red.		
	a. Signature 10. 12.8.1978.	.25	1.25
	b. Signature 11. 4.11.1981.	.25	1.25
	c. Signature 13. 16.5.1986.	.20	1.00

91	**500 Dinara**	VF	UNC
	1978; 1981; 1986. Dark olive-green on multicolor underprint. Statue of Nicola Tesla seated with open book at left. Long 2-line signature title at left. Back: Large numerals of value at left center.		
	a. Signature 10. 12.8.1978.	.50	2.00
	b. Signature 11. 4.11.1981.	.50	1.00
	c. Signature 13. 16.5.1986.	.50	2.00

92	**1000 Dinara**	VF	UNC
	1978; 1981. Blue-black on multicolor underprint. Woman with fruit at left. Long 2-line signature title at left.		
	a. Signature 10 with title at right: *GUVERNE* in Latin without final letter *R* (engraving error). Series AF. 12.8.1978.	1.00	7.50
	b. As a. Series AR.	3.00	15.00
	c. Corrected signature title.	.50	3.00
	d. Signature 11. 4.11.1981.	.25	1.00

1985-89 Issue

93	**5000 Dinara**	VF	UNC
	1.5.1985. Deep blue on multicolor underprint. Josip Broz Tito at left, arms at center. Signature 12. Back: Jajce in Bosnia at center. Watermark: Josip Broz Tito.		
	a. Corrected year of Tito's death - *1980.*	.50	3.50
	x. Error: Tito's death date as *1930* instead of *1980.*	10.00	65.00

95	**20,000 Dinara**	VF	UNC
	1.5.1987. Brown on multicolor underprint. Miner at left, arms at center. Signature 13. Back: Mining equipment at center. Watermark: Miner.	.25	1.50

96	**50,000 Dinara**	VF	UNC
	1.5.1988. Green and blue on multicolor underprint. Girl at left, arms at center. Signature 13. Back: City of Dubrovnik at center. Watermark: Girl.	1.00	3.50

97 **100,000 Dinara** — VF .75 — UNC 3.50
1.5.1989. Violet and red on multicolor underprint. Young girl at left, arms at center. Signature 14. Back: Abstract design with letters and numbers at center right. Watermark: Young girl.

98 **500,000 Dinara**
Aug. 1989. Deep purple and blue on lilac underprint. Arms at left, Partisan monument "Kozara" at right. Signature 14. Back: Partisan monument "Sutjeska" at center.

	VF	UNC
a. Issued note.	1.50	7.00
s. Specimen.	—	50.00

99 **1,000,000 Dinara** — VF 1.50 — UNC 10.00
1.11.1989. Light olive-green on orange and gold underprint. Young woman at left, arms at center. Signature 14. Back: Stylized stalk of wheat. Watermark: Young woman. UV: fibers fluoresce yellow.

100 **2,000,000 Dinara**
Aug. 1989. Pale olive-green and brown on light orange underprint. Arms at left, Partisan monument "Kozara" at right. Signature 14. Back: Partisan "V3" monument at Kragujevac at center.

	VF	UNC
a. Issued note.	12.50	65.00
s. Specimen.	—	50.00

1990 First Issue

#101 and 102 Replacement notes: Serial # prefix *ZA*.

101 **50 Dinara**
1.1.1990. Deep purple and blue on lilac underprint. Arms at left, Partisan monument "Kozara" at right. Signature 14. Back: Partisan monument "Sutjeska" at center.

	VF	UNC
a. Issued note.	3.00	25.00
s. Specimen.	—	50.00

101A **100 Dinara** — VF 400. — UNC 700.
ND (1990). Black and dark olive-green on pink and yellow-green underprint. Marshal Tito at right, flags in underprint at center, arms at upper left. Back: Partisan monument "Sutjeska" at center. (Not issued). Like #98. 7-digit serial #. Proof designed in 1979 and re-considered for issue in 1990.

102 **200 Dinara**
1.1.1990. Pale olive-green and brown on light orange underprint. Arms at left, Partisan monument "Kozara" at right. Signature 14. Back: Partisan "V3" monument at Kragujevac at center.

	VF	UNC
a. Issued note.	4.00	25.00
s. Specimen.	—	50.00

1990 Second Issue

#103-107 Replacement notes: Serial # prefix *ZA*.

103 **10 Dinara** — VF .20 — UNC 1.50
1.9.1990. Violet and red on multicolor underprint. Young girl at left, arms at center. Signature 14. Back: Abstract design with letters and numbers at center right. Watermark: Young girl.

104 **50 Dinara** — VF .25 — UNC 1.50
1.6.1990. Purple. Young boy at left. Signature 14. Back: Roses at center right. Watermark: Young boy. UV: fibers fluoresce yellow.

105 100 Dinara | VF | UNC
1.3.1990. Light olive-green on orange and gold underprint. Young woman at left, arms at center. Signature 14. Back: Stylized stalk of wheat. Watermark: Young woman. UV: fibers fluoresce yellow. | .50 | 7.00

106 500 Dinara | VF | UNC
1.3.1990. Blue and purple. Young man at left. Arms at center. Signature 14. Back: Mountain scene. Watermark: Young man. UV: fibers fluoresce yellow. | .50 | 7.00

106A 500 Dinara | VF | UNC
Brown and orange. Young man at left. Arms at center. Signature 14. Back: Mountain scene. Watermark: Young man. (Not issued). | — | 225.

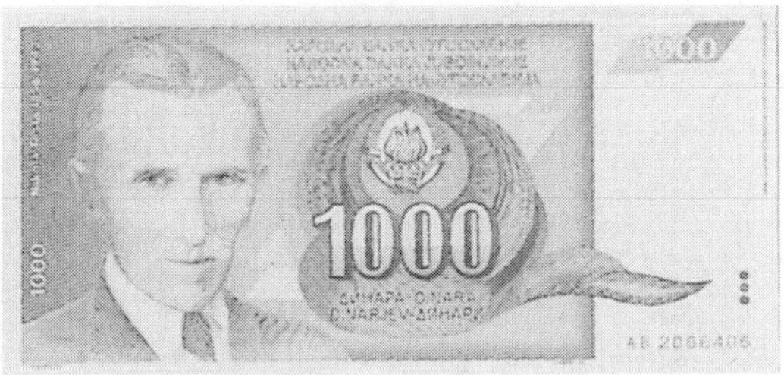

107 1000 Dinara | VF | UNC
26.11.1990. Brown and orange. Nicola Tesla at left. Arms at center. Signature 14. Back: High frequency transformer. Watermark: Nicola Tesla. UV: fibers fluoresce yellow. | 1.00 | 12.50

1991 Issue

#107A-111 Replacement notes: Serial # prefix *ZA*.

107A 10 Dinara | VF | UNC
1991. Purple, black and lilac. Young girl at left, arms at center. Signature 15. Back: Abstract design with letters and numbers at center right. Watermark: Young girl. (Not issued). | — | 175.

107B 50 Dinara | VF | UNC
1991. Orange and red. Young boy at left. Signature 15. Back: Roses at center right. Watermark: Young boy. (Not issued). UV: fibers fluoresce yellow. | — | 175.

108 100 Dinara | VF | UNC
1991. Black and olive-brown on yellow underprint. Young woman at left, arms at center. Signature 15. Back: Stylized stalk of wheat. Watermark: Young woman. UV: fibers fluoresce yellow. | .50 | 1.50

109 500 Dinara | VF | UNC
1991. Brown, dark brown and orange on tan underprint. Young man at left. Arms at center. Signature 15. Back: Mountain scene. Watermark: Young man. UV: fibers fluoresce yellow. | .50 | 2.50

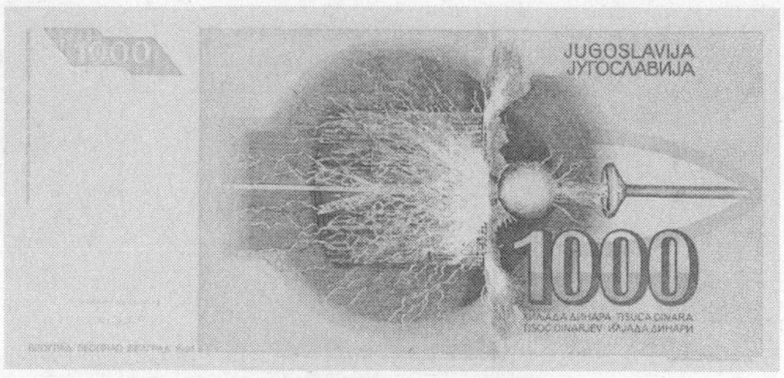

110 **1000 Dinara** | VF .50 | UNC 7.00
1991. Blue and purple. Nicola Tesla at left. Arms at center. Signature 15. Back: High frequency transformer. Watermark: Nicola Tesla. UV: fibers fluoresce yellow. 165x80mm.

111 **5000 Dinara** | VF 1.50 | UNC 7.50
1991. Purple, red-orange and blue-gray on gray underprint. Ivo Andric at left. Arms at center. Signature 15. Back: Multiple arch stone bridge on the Drina River at Visegrad at center. Watermark: Ivo Andric.

1992 Issue

#112-117 National Bank monogram arms at ctr. Replacement notes: Serial # prefix *ZA*.

112 **100 Dinara** | VF .40 | UNC 1.00
1992. Pale blue and purple. Young woman at left. National Bank monogram at center. Signature 15. Back: Stylized stalk of wheat. Watermark: Young woman. UV: fibers fluoresce yellow.

113 **500 Dinara** | VF .50 | UNC 4.00
1992. Pale purple and lilac. Young man at left. National Bank monogram at center. Signature 15. Back: Mountain scene. Watermark: Youn man.

114 **1000 Dinara** | VF .50 | UNC 7.50
1992. Red, orange and purple on lilac underprint. Nicola Tesla at left. National Bank monogram at center. Signature 15. Back: High frequency transformer. Watermark: Nicola Tesla.

115 **5000 Dinara** | VF 1.50 | UNC 6.00
1992. Deep blue-green, purple and deep olive-brown on gray underprint. Ivo Andric at left. National Bank monogram at center. Signature 15. Back: Multiple arch stone bridge on the Drina River at Visegrad at center. Watermark: Ivo Andric.

116 **10,000 Dinara**
1992. Varied shades of brown and salmon on tan underprint. Young girl at left. National Bank monogram at center. Signature 16. Back: Abstract design with letters and numbers at center right. Watermark: Young girl.
- a. With dot after date. | .20 | 2.00
- b. Without dot after date. | .20 | 2.00

117 **50,000 Dinara** | VF .75 | UNC 4.50
1992. Purple, olive-green and deep blue-green. Young boy at left. National Bank monogram at center. Signature 16. Back: Roses at center right. Watermark: Young boy.

1993 Issue

#118-127 replacement notes: Serial # prefix *ZA*.

118 **100,000 Dinara** | VF .50 | UNC 3.50
1993. Olive-green on orange and gold underprint. Young woman at left. National Bank monogram at center. Signature 16. Back: Sunflowers at center right.

119 **500,000 Dinara** | VF 2.50 | UNC 20.00
1993. Blue-violet and orange on multicolor underprint. Young man at left. National Bank monogram at center. Signature 16. Back: Koponik Sky Center.

120 **1,000,000 Dinara** | VF 4.00 | UNC 20.00
1993. Purple on blue, orange and multicolor underprint. Young boy at left. National Bank monogram at center. Signature 16. Back: Iris flowers at center right.

121 **5,000,000 Dinara** | VF .50 | UNC 3.00
1993. Violet, lilac, turquoise and multicolor. Nicola Tesla at left. National Bank monogram at center. Signature 16. Back: Vertical rendition of high frequency transformer at center, hydroelectric dam at right.

122 10,000,000 Dinara VF UNC
1993. Slate blue, light and dark brown. Ivo Andric at left. National Bank monogram at center. Signature 16. Back: National library at center right. .50 3.00

123 50,000,000 Dinara
1993. Black and orange. Young girl at left. National Bank monogram at center. Signature 16. Back: Belgrade University. .75 5.00

124 100,000,000 Dinara VF UNC
1993. Grayish purple and blue. Young man at left. National Bank monogram at center. Signature 17. Back: Academy of Science at center right. .50 3.00

125 500,000,000 Dinara
1993. Black and lilac. Young woman at left. National Bank monogram at center. Signature 17. Back: Department of Agriculture building. 1.00 6.00

126 1,000,000,000 Dinara VF UNC
1993. Red and purple on orange and blue-gray underprint. Young girl at left. National Bank monogram at center. Signature 17. Back: Parliament building (National Assembly) at center. UV: fibers fluoresce yellow. 2.50 12.50

127 10,000,000,000 Dinara VF UNC
1993. Black, purple and red. Nicola Tesla at left. National Bank monogram at center. Signature 17. Back: High frequency transformer. Watermark: Nicola Tesla. 1.50 10.00

1993 Reform Issue

#128-137 replacement notes: Serial # prefix *ZA*.

128 5000 Dinara VF UNC
1993. Pale reddish brown, pale olive-green and orange. Nicola Tesla at left. National Bank monogram at center. Signature 17. Back: Tesla Museum at center right. UV: fibers fluoresce yellow. 1.00 6.00

129 10,000 Dinara VF UNC
1993. Gray and green on orange and olive-green underprint. Vuk. Stefanovic Karadzic at left. National Bank monogram at center.Signature 17. Back: Orthodox church, house. .75 5.00

130 50,000 Dinara VF UNC
1993. Dark blue on pink and aqua underprint. Petar II Petrovic Niegos Prince-Bishop of Montenegro, at left. National Bank monogram at center. Signature 17. Back: Monastery in Cetinje at right. .50 2.00

131 500,000 Dinara VF UNC
1993. Dark green on blue-green and yellow-orange underprint. Dositej Obradovic at left. Signature 18. Back: Monastery Hopovo at center right. .50 2.00

132 5,000,000 Dinara VF UNC
1993. Dark brown on orange, blue-green and pale olive-brown underprint. Karadjordj Petrovich, Prince of Serbia, at left. Signature 18. Back: Orthodox church at center right. .50 2.00

133 50,000,000 Dinara VF UNC
1993. Red and purple on orange and lilac underprint. Michajlo Pupin at left. Signature 18. Back: Telephone Exchange building at center right. .25 2.00

134 500,000,000 Dinara | VF | UNC
1993. Purple on aqua, brown-orange and dull pink underprint. Jovan Cvijich at left. Signature 18. Back: University at center right. | .50 | 3.00

135 5,000,000,000 Dinara | VF | UNC
1993. Olive-brown on light green, ochre and orange underprint. Djura Jaksich at left. Signature 18. Back: Monastery in Vrazcevsnitza at center right.
a. Issued note. | .50 | 3.00
s. Specimen with red overprint. | — | 60.00

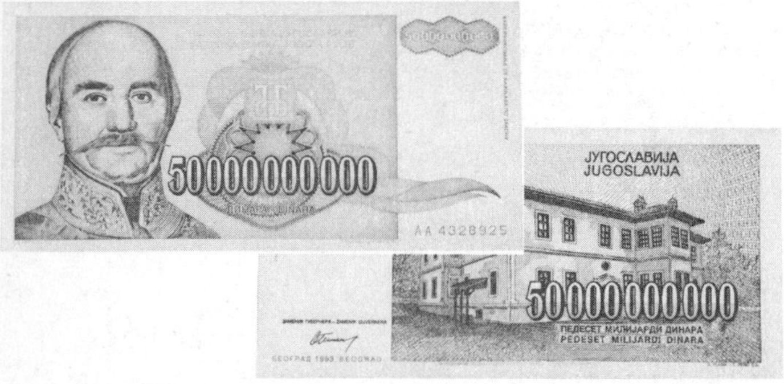

136 50,000,000,000 Dinara | VF | UNC
1993. Dark brown on blue-violet, orange, red-violet and gray underprint. Serbian Prince Milan Obrenovich at left. Signature 18. Back: Villa of Obrenovich at center right. | .75 | 5.00

137 500,000,000,000 Dinara | VF | UNC
1993. Red-violet on orange, pale blue-gray and olive-brown underprint. Poet J. Zmaj at left. Signature 18. Back: National Library at center right.
a. Issued note. | 1.50 | 10.00
s. Specimen with red overprint. | — | 70.00

1994 Issue

138 10 Dinara | VF | UNC
1994. Chocolate brown on brown and gray-green underprint. Joseph Panchic at left. Signature 18. Back: Aqua. Mountain view, pine trees at center right. Watermark: Design.
a. Issued note. Without serial #. | .50 | 1.00
b. Issued note. Privately added serial #, serial # prefix *AR*. | — | —
s. Specimen with red overprint: *SPECIMEN* once on face. Serial #AA 0000000. | — | 65.00

139 100 Dinara | VF | UNC
1994. Grayish purple on pink and pale blue underprint. Nicola Tesla at left. National Bank monogram arms at center. Signature 18. Back: Tesla Museum at center right. Watermark: Design.
a. Issued note. Without serial #. | .25 | 1.00
s. Specimen with red overprint *SPECIMEN* once on face. Serial # AA 0000000. | — | 65.00

140 1000 Dinara | VF | UNC
1994. Dark olive-gray on red-orange, olive-brown and lilac underprint. Petar II Petrovic Niegos, Prince-Bishop of Montenegro, at left. Signature 18. Back: Monastery in Cetinje at right. Watermark: Design.
a. Issued note. | .50 | 2.00
s. Specimen with red overprint. | — | 40.00

141 5000 Dinara | VF | UNC
1994. Dark blue on lilac, orange and aqua underprint. Dositej Obradovic at left. Signature 18. Back: Monastery Hopovo at center right. Watermark: Design.
a. Issued note. | .50 | 2.00
s. Specimen with red overprint. | — | 40.00

142 50,000 Dinara | VF | UNC
1994. Dull red and lilac on orange underprint. Karadjordj Petrovich, Prince of Serbia, at left. Signature 18. Back: Orthodox church at center right. Watermark: Design.
a. Issued note. | .75 | 3.00
s. Specimen with red overprint | Unc | 40.00

142A 100,000 Dinara

1994. Red-brown on ochre and pale olive-green underprint. Michajlo Pupin at left. Signature 18. Back: Telephone Exchange building. Watermark: Design. (Not issued).

	VF	UNC
	—	350.

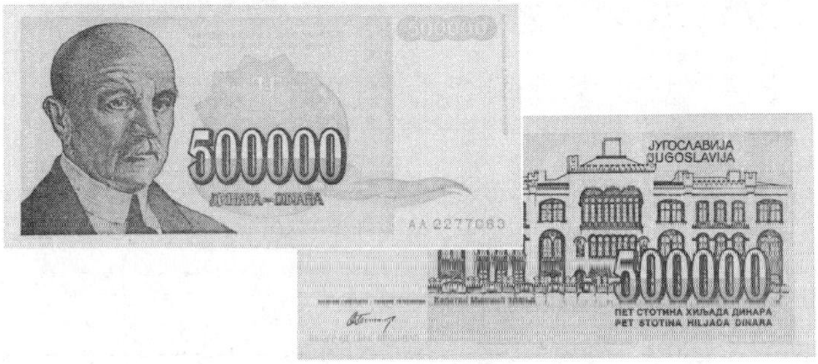

143 500,000 Dinara

1994. Dull olive-green and orange on yellow underprint. Jovan Cvijich at left. Signature 18. Back: University at center right. Watermark: Design.

	VF	UNC
a. Issued note.	.40	1.50
s. Specimen with red overprint.		40.00

1994 Provisional Issue

144 10,000,000 Dinara

1994 (-old date 1993). Slate blue, light and dark brown. Ivo Andric at left. National Bank monogram at center. Signature 18. Back: National Library at center right with signature title. Overprint: Red: *1994* on face and back of #122 with silver overprint.

	VF	UNC
a. Issued note.	1.00	5.00
s. Specimen with red overprint.	—	50.00

1994 Reform Issues

Note: #145-147 withdrawn from circulation on 1.1.1995.

145 1 Novi Dinar

1.1.1994. Blue-gray and brown on pale olive-green and tan underprint. Joseph Panchic at left. National Bank monogram at center. Signature 19. Back: Mountain view, pine trees at center right. Watermark: Diamond grid.

	VF	UNC
	1.00	4.00

146 5 Novih Dinara

1.1.1994. Red-brown and pink on ochre and pale orange underprint. Nicola Tesla at left. National Bank monogram at center. Signature 19. Back: Tesla Museum at center right. Watermark: Diamond grid.

	VF	UNC
	2.50	15.00

147 10 Novih Dinara

1.1.1994. Purple and pink on aqua and olive-green underprint. Petar II Petrovic Niegos Prince-Bishop of Montenegro, at left. National Bank monogram at center. Signature 19. Back: Monastery in Cetinje at right. Watermark: Diamond grid.

	VF	UNC
	2.50	15.00

1994; 1996 Issue

#148-152 Replacement notes: Serial # prefix *ЗА*.

148 5 Novih Dinara

3.3.1994. Black, deep purple and violet. NicolaTesla at left. Arms with double headed eagle at upper center. Signature 20. Back: Tesla Museum at center right. Watermark: Symmetrical design repeated. 131x62mm.

	VF	UNC
	.25	2.00

149 10 Novih Dinara

3.3.1994. Purple, violet and brown. Petar II Petrovic Niegos Prince-Bishop of Montenegro, at left. Arms with double-headed eagle at upper center. Signature 20. Back: Monastery in Cetinje at right. Watermark: Symmetrical design repeated. 135x64mm.

	VF	UNC
	1.00	4.00

150 20 Novih Dinara

3.3.1994. Dark green, brown-orange and brown. D. Jaksich at left. Arms with double-headed eagle at upper center. Signature 20. Back: Monastery in Vrazcevcnitza at center right. Watermark: Symmetrical design repeated. 139x66mm.

	VF	UNC
	2.00	6.00

151 50 Novih Dinara — VF 3.00 — UNC 14.00

June 1996. Black and blue. Serbian Prince Milan Obrenovich at left. Arms with double-headed eagle at upper center. Signature 19. Back: Villa of Obrenovich at center right. Watermark: Symmetrical design repeated. 143x68mm.

152 100 Novih Dinara — VF 2.50 — UNC 25.00

Oct. 1996. Black on olive-brown and grayish green underprint. Dositej Obradovic at left. Arms with double-headed eagle at upper center. Signature 19. Back: Monastery Hopovo at center right. Watermark: Symmetrical design repeated. 148x70mm.

152A 200 Dinara — VF — — UNC —

1999. Blak and dark green on multicolor underprint. Stevân St. Mokianjac bust at left. Back: Piano. Not issued.

2000-01 Issue

153 10 Dinara

2000. Brown on ochre-yellow and green underprint. Vuk Stefanovich Karadzic at left. Back: Karadzic and alphabet. Arms at upper left. Watermark: Portrait. Vertical back. 131x62mm.

	VF	UNC
a. Signature Dusan Vlatkovic (not issued).	—	150.
b. Signature Mladjan Dinkich.	FV	1.25
s. Specimen.	—	40.00

154 20 Dinara

2000 (2001). Green and black on tan underprint. Petar II Petrovic Njegos, Prince-Bishop of Montenegro at left. Back: Statue from Njegos' mausoleum, mosaic and mountains. Arms at upper left. Watermark: Portrait. Vertical back. 135x64mm.

	VF	UNC
a. Issued note.	.50	2.00
s. Specimen.	—	40.00

155 50 Dinara

2000. Light and dark violet on tan underprint. Stevan Stojanovic Mokranjac at left, piano keyboard at lower center. Back: Full-length photo and musical bars. Arms at upper left. Watermark: Portrait. Vertical back. 139x66mm.

	VF	UNC
a. Issued note.	FV	4.00
s. Specimen.	—	40.00

156 100 Dinara

2000. Blue on green and tan underprint. Nikola Tesla at left, motor at lower center. Back: Tesla photo, schematic of electro-magnetic induction engine, dove. Arms at upper left. Watermark: Portrait. Vertical back. 143x68mm.

	VF	UNC
a. Issued note.	FV	6.00
s. Specimen.	—	40.00

157 200 Dinara

2001. Black and blue on tan underprint. Nadezda Petrovic at left. Back: Figure of the artist and Gracanica monastery. Arms at upper left. Watermark: Portrait. Vertical back. 147x70mm.

	VF	UNC
a. Issued note.	FV	14.00
s. Specimen.	—	40.00

158 1000 Dinara

2001. Red on blue and tan underprint. Djordje Vajfert at left. Back: Vajfert portrait and Central Bank interior. 151x72mm.

	VF	UNC
a. Issued note.	FV	40.00
s. Specimen.	—	80.00

		VF	UNC
159	**5000 Dinara**		
	2002. Green, violet and gray on multicolor underprint. Slobodan Jovanovic (Serbian historian, 1869-1958) at left. Back: Jovanovic in front of the Federal Assembly. 159x76mm.		
	a. Issued note.	FV	175.
	s. Specimen.	—	200.

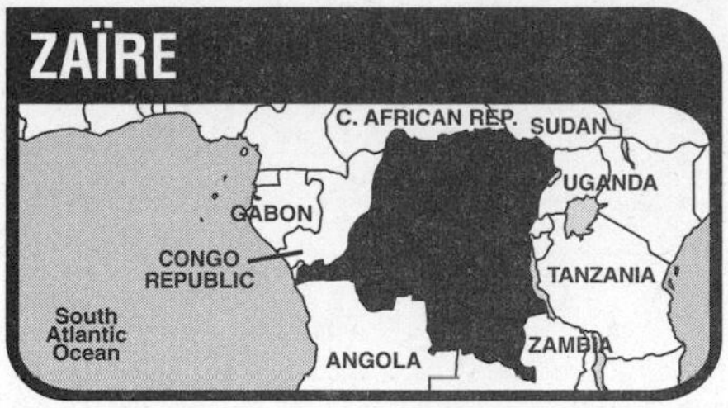

The Republic of Zaïre (formerly the Congo Democratic Republic) located in the south-central part of Africa, has an area of 905,568 sq. mi. (2,345,409 sq. km.) and a population of 43.81 million. Capital: Kinshasa. The mineral-rich country produces copper, tin, diamonds, gold, zinc, cobalt and uranium.

In ancient times the territory comprising Zaïre was occupied by Negrito peoples (Pygmies) pushed into the mountains by Bantu and Nilotic invaders. The interior was first explored by the American correspondent Henry Stanley, who was subsequently commissioned by King Leopold II of Belgium to conclude development treaties with the local chiefs. The Berlin conference of 1885 awarded the area to Leopold, who administered and exploited it as his private property until it was annexed to Belgium in 1908. Following the eruption of bloody independence riots in 1959, Belgium granted the Belgian Congo independence as the Republic of the Congo on June 30, 1960. The Belgian Congo attained independence with the distinction of being the most ill-prepared country to ever undertake self-government. Without a single doctor, lawyer or engineer, with no organized unit capable of maintaining law and order, independence disintegrated into an orgy of anarchy. Provinces seceded. Intertribal warfare erupted. Belgian troops intervened to protect Belgian citizens from retributive massacre. By 1961, four groups were fighting for political dominance. The most serious threat to the viability of the country was posed by the secession of mineral-rich Katanga province on July 11, 1960.

After two and one-half years of sporadic warfare with a U.N. military force, Katanga's leaders capitulated, Jan. 14, 1963 and the rebellious province was partioned into three provinces. The nation officially changed its name to Zaïre on Oct. 27, 1971. In May 1997, the dictator was overthrown after a three-year rebellion. The country changed its name to the Democratic Republic of the Congo.

See also Rwanda, Rwanda-Burundi or Congo Democratic Republic.

MONETARY SYSTEM.

1 Franc = 100 Centimes to 1967
1 Zaïre = 100 Makuta, 1967-1993
1 Nouveau Zaïre = 100 N Makuta = 3 million "old" Zaïres, 1993-1998

Banque du Zaïre

	GOVERNOR		GOVERNOR
3	J. Sambwa Mbagui	4	Bofossa W. Amba
5	EmonyJ	6	Sambwa Mbagui
7	Pay Pay wa Syakassighe	8	Nyembo Shabanga
9	B. Mushaba	10	Ndiang Kabul
11	L. O. Djamboleka		

REPUBLIC

BANQUE DU ZAÏRE

1971-80 ISSUES

#16-25 Replacement notes: Serial # suffix *Z*.

16 50 Makuta

1973-78. Red, dark brown and multicolor. Mobutu at left, leopard at lower right facing right. Various date and signature varieties. Back: Man and structure in water. Watermark: Mobutu. Printer: G&D. Intaglio.

	VF	UNC
a. Red guilloche at left center on back. Signature 3. 30.6.1973; 4.10.1974; 4.10.1975.	6.00	30.00
b. Red and purple guilloche at left center on back. Signature 3. 24.6.1976; 24.6.1977.	7.00	35.00
c. Guilloche as b. Signature 4. 20.5.1978.	5.00	24.00
s. Specimen. As a. Red overprint: *SPECIMEN* on both sides.	—	75.00

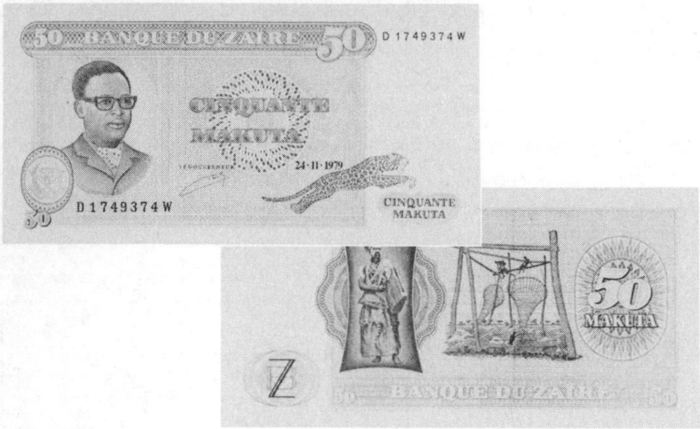

17 50 Makuta

1979; 1980. Like #16 but slight color differences. Mobutu at left, leopard at lower right facing right. Various date and signature varieties. Back: Man and structure in water. Intaglio. Watermark: Mobutu. Printer: G&D. Lithographed.

	VF	UNC
a. Signature 5. 24.11.1979.	1.25	7.00
b. Signature 3. 14.10.1980.	1.25	6.00
s. Specimen.	—	75.00

18 1 Zaïre

1972-77. Brown and multicolor. Mobutu at left, leopard at lower right facing right. Various date and signature varieties. Back: Factory, pyramid, flora and elephant tusks at center right. Watermark: Mobutu. Printer: G&D. Intaglio.

	VF	UNC
a. Signature 3 with title: *LE GOUVERNEUR* placed below line. 15.3.1972; 27.10.1974; 20.5.1975; 27.10.1975; 27.10.1976.	2.25	14.00
b. Signature 4 with title: *LE GOUVERNEUR* placed above line. 27.10.1977.	2.00	10.00
s. Specimen. As a. Red overprint: *SPECIMEN* on both sides.	—	75.00

19 1 Zaïre

1979-81. Like number 18 but slight color differences. Mobutu at left, leopard at lower right facing right. Various date and signature varieties. Back: Factory, pyramid, flora and elephant tusks at center right. Watermark: Mobutu. Printer: G&D. Lithographed.

	VF	UNC
a. Signature 5. 22.10.1979.	1.25	5.25
b. Signature 3. 27.10.1980; 20.5.1981.	1.00	4.50
s. Specimen.	—	75.00

20 5 Zaïres

24.11.1972. Green, black, brown and multicolor. Mobutu at left, leopard at lower right facing right. Various date and signature varieties. Signature 3. Back: Carving at left, hydroelectric dam at center right. Watermark: Mobutu. Printer: G&D. Like Congo #14.

	VF	UNC
a. Issued note.	50.00	200.
p. Proof. Uniface face and back pasted together. Back ovprinted *UNGÜLTIG* in gray.	—	—
s. Specimen. Red overprint: *SPECIMEN* on both sides.	—	250.

21 5 Zaïres

1974-77. Green, black, brown and multicolor. Mobutu with cap at left, leopard at lower right facing right. Various date and signature varieties. Back: Carving at left, hydroelectric dam at center right. Watermark: Mobutu. Printer: G&D.

	VF	UNC
a. Signature 3. 30.11.1974; 30.6.1975; 24.11.1975; 24.11.1976.	7.50	30.00
b. Signature 4. 24.11.1977.	3.00	14.00
s. As a. Specimen.	—	75.00

22 5 Zaïres

1979; 1980. Blue, brown, violet and multicolor. Mobutu at left, leopard at lower right facing right. Various date and signature varieties. Back: Carving at left, hydroelectric dam at center right. Watermark: Mobutu. Printer: G&D.

	VF	UNC
a. Signature 5. 20.5.1979.	2.00	9.50
b. Signature 3. 27.10.1980.	3.00	17.50
s. Specimen. As a. Red overprint: *SPECIMEN* on both sides.	—	65.00

23 10 Zaïres

1972-77. Dark brown and blue on multicolor underprint. Mobutu at left, leopard at lower right facing right. Various date and signature varieties. Back: Similar to Congo number 15 but arms with hand holding torch at left center. Watermark: Mobutu. Printer: G&D.

	VF	UNC
a. Signature 3. 30.6.1972; 22.6.1974; 30.6.1975; 30.6.1976; 27.10.1976.	12.00	65.00
b. Signature 4. 27.10.1977.	3.00	15.00
s. As a. Specimen without serial #.	—	85.00

24 10 Zaïres

1979; 1981. Green, brown and multicolor. Mobutu at left, leopard at lower right facing right. Various date and signature varieties. Back: Similar to Congo number 15 but arms with hand holding torch at left center. Watermark: Mobutu. Printer: G&D.

	VF	UNC
a. Signature 5. 24.6.1979.	4.00	17.50
b. Signature 3. 4.1.1981.	3.00	15.00
s. Specimen. As a. Red overprint: *SPECIMEN* on both sides.	—	85.00

25 50 Zaïres

1980. Red, violet, brown and multicolor. Mobutu at left, leopard at lower right facing right. Various date and signature varieties. Back: Arms at left center. Watermark: Mobutu. Printer: G&D.

	VF	UNC
a. Signature 5. 4.2.1980.	12.50	47.50
b. Signature 3. 24.11.1980.	20.00	70.00
s. Specimen. 4.2.1980.	—	100.

1982-85 Issues

#26-31 replacement notes: Serial # suffix *Z*.

26 5 Zaïres

17.11.1982. Blue, black and multicolor. Mobutu in civilian dress at center right, leopard at lower left facing left. Signature 6. Back: Hydroelectric dam at center right. Watermark: Mobutu. Printer: G&D.

	VF	UNC
a. Issued note.	1.00	5.00
s. Specimen.	—	85.00

26A 5 Zaïres

	VF	UNC
24.11.1985. Blue, black and multicolor. Mobutu in civilian dress at center right, leopard at lower left facing left. Signature 7. Back: Hydroelectric dam at center right. Watermark: Mobutu. Printer: HdMZ.	.50	1.75

27 10 Zaïres

27.10.1982. Green, black and multicolor. Mobutu in civilian dress at center right, leopard at lower left facing left. Signature 6. Back: Arms with hand holding torch. Watermark: Mobutu. Printer: G&D.

	VF	UNC
a. Issued note.	1.00	5.50
s. Specimen. Red overprint: *SPECIMEN* on both sides.	—	50.00

27A 10 Zaïres

	VF	UNC
27.10.1985. Green, black and multicolor. Mobutu in civilian dress at center right, leopard at lower left facing left. Signature 7. Back: Arms with hand holding torch. Watermark: Mobutu. Printer: HdMZ.	.50	1.75

28 50 Zaïres

1982; 1985. Purple, blue and multicolor. Mobutu in civilian dress at center right, leopard at lower left facing left. Back: Blue and multicolor. Men fishing with stick nets at center. Watermark: Mobutu. Printer: G&D.

	VF	UNC
a. Signature 6. 24.11.1982.	2.50	15.00
b. Signature 7. 24.6.1985.	1.50	9.00
s. Specimen.	—	50.00

29 100 Zaïres

1983; 1985. Dark brown, orange and multicolor. Mobutu in civilian dress at center right, leopard at lower left facing left. Back: Bank of Zaïre at center right. Watermark: Mobutu. Printer: G&D.

	VF	UNC
a. Signature 6. 30.6.1983.	3.00	16.50
b. Signature 7. 30.6.1985.	1.00	7.50
s. Specimen. As a. Red overprint: *SPECIMEN* on both sides.	—	50.00

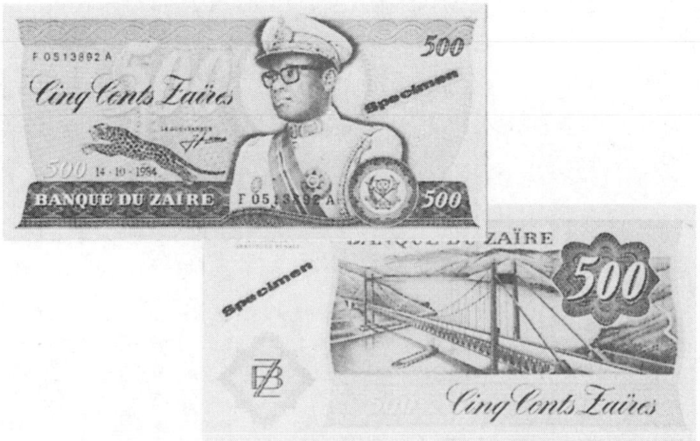

30 500 Zaïres

1984; 1985. Gray, purple and multicolor. Mobutu in military dress at center right, leopard at lower left facing left, arms at lower right. Back: Suspension bridge over river at center right. Watermark: Mobutu. Printer: G&D.

	VF	UNC
a. Signature 6. 14.10.1984.	15.00	70.00
b. Signature 7. 14.10.1985.	6.00	30.00
s. Specimen. As b. Red overprint: *SPECIMEN* on both sides.	35.00	100.

31 **1000 Zaïres** VF UNC
24.11.1985. Blue-black and green on multicolor underprint. Mobutu in military dress at center right, leopard at lower left facing left, arms at lower right. Signature 7. Back: Civic building, water fountain at center right. Watermark: Mobutu. Printer: G&D.

	VF	UNC
a. Issued note.	6.00	15.00
s. Specimen. Red overprint: *SPECIMEN* on both sides.	65.00	110.

1988-92 Issues

#32-46 Replacement notes: serial # suffix *Z*.

32 **50 Zaïres** VF UNC
30.6.1988. Green and multicolor. Mobutu in military dress at right, leopard at lower left center facing left, arms at lower right. Signature 7. Back: Blue and multicolor. Men fishing with stick nets at left. Watermark: Mobutu. Printer: HdMZ.

	VF	UNC
a. Issued note.	.50	1.50
s. Specimen. Red overprint: *SPECIMEN* on both sides.	—	45.00

33 **100 Zaïres** VF UNC
14.10.1988. Blue and multicolor. Mobutu in military dress at right, leopard at lower left center facing left, arms at lower right. Signature 7. Back: Bank of Zaïre at left center. Watermark: Mobutu. Printer: HdMZ.

	VF	UNC
a. Issued note.	.75	3.00
s. Specimen. Red overprint: *SPECIMEN* on both sides.	30.00	50.00

34 **500 Zaïres** VF UNC
24.6.1989. Brown, orange and multicolor. Mobutu in military dress at right, leopard at lower left center facing left, arms at lower right. Signature 7. Back: Suspension bridge over river at left center. Watermark: Mobutu. Printer: HdMZ.

	VF	UNC
a. Issued note.	1.25	6.00
s. Specimen. Red overprint: *SPECIMEN* on both sides.	40.00	65.00

35 **1000 Zaïres** VF UNC
24.11.1989. Purple, brown and multicolor. Mobutu in military dress at right, leopard at lower left center facing left, arms at lower right. Signature 7. Back: Civic building, fountain at left center. Watermark: Mobutu. Printer: HdMZ.

	VF	UNC
a. Issued note.	4.00	21.00
s. Specimen. Red overprint: *SPECIMEN* on both sides.	35.00	60.00

36 **2000 Zaïres** VF UNC
1.10.1991. Purple and peach on multicolor underprint. Mobutu in military dress at right, leopard at lower left center facing left, arms at lower right. Signature 8. Back: Men fishing with stick nets at left, carved figure at center right. Watermark: Mobutu. Printer: HdMZ. (Smaller size than #35.)

	VF	UNC
a. Issued note.	.75	2.50
s. Specimen. Red overprint: *SPECIMEN* on both sides.	30.00	50.00

37 **5000 Zaïres** VF UNC
20.5.1988. Blue, green and multicolor. Mobutu in military dress at right, leopard at lower left center facing left, arms at lower right. Signature 7. Back: Factory at left, elephant tusks and plants at center. Watermark: Mobutu. Printer: G&D.

	VF	UNC
a. Brown central diamond to right of Mobutu's ear.	30.00	150.
b. Green central diamond to right of Mobutu's ear.	1.25	6.00
s1. Specimen. As a. Red overprint: *SPECIMEN* on both sides.	—	40.00
s2. Specimen. As b. Red overprint: *SPECIMEN* on both sides.	—	40.00

38 **10,000 Zaïres** VF UNC
24.11.1989. Purple, brown-orange and red on multicolor underprint. Mobutu in military dress at right, leopard at lower left center facing left, arms at lower right. Signature 7. Back: Government Building complex at left center. Watermark: Mobutu. Printer: G&D.

	VF	UNC
a. Issued note.	1.25	5.50
s. Specimen. Red overprint: *SPECIMEN* on both sides.	30.00	50.00

39 **20,000 Zaïres** | VF | UNC

1.7.1991. Black on multicolor underprint. Mobutu in military dress at right, leopard at lower left center facing left, arms at lower right. Signature 8. Back: Bank of Zaïre at left, other buildings across center. Watermark: Mobutu. Printer: HdMZ.

	VF	UNC
a. Issued note.	.50	3.50
s. Specimen. Red overprint: *SPECIMEN* on both sides.	40.00	60.00

40 **50,000 Zaïres** | VF | UNC

24.4.1991. Wine and blue-black on multicolor underprint. Mobutu in military dress at right, leopard at lower left center facing left, arms at lower right. Signature 7. Back: Family of Western Gorillas. Watermark: Mobutu. Printer: G&D. Replacement notes: Serial # prefix Z.

	VF	UNC
a. Issued note.	2.50	8.00
s. Specimen.	60.00	70.00

41 **100,000 Zaïres** | VF | UNC

4.1.1992. Black and deep olive-green on multicolor underprint. Mobutu in military dress at right, leopard at lower left center facing left, arms at lower right. Signature 8. Back: Domed building at left center. Watermark: Mobutu. Printer: G&D.

	VF	UNC
a. Issued note.	1.25	6.00
s. Specimen. Red overprint: *SPECIMEN* on both sides.	30.00	50.00

42 **200,000 Zaïres** | VF | UNC

1.3.1992. Deep purple and deep blue on multicolor underprint. Mobutu in military dress at right, leopard at lower left center facing left, arms at lower right. Signature 8. Back: Civic building and fountain at left center. Watermark: Mobutu. Printer: HdMZ.

	VF	UNC
a. Issued note.	1.00	5.50
s. Specimen. Red overprint: *SPECIMEN* on both sides.	30.00	50.00

43 **500,000 Zaïres** | VF | UNC

15.3.1992. Brown and orange on multicolor underprint. Mobutu in military dress at right, leopard at lower left center facing left, arms at lower right. Signature 8. Back: Hydroelectric dam at left center. Watermark: Mobutu. Printer: G&D.

	VF	UNC
a. Issued note.	1.50	7.75
s. Specimen. Red overprint: *SPECIMEN* on both sides.	40.00	60.00

44 **1,000,000 Zaïres** | VF | UNC

31.7.1992. Red-violet and deep red on multicolor underprint. Mobutu in military dress at right, leopard at lower left center facing left, arms at lower right. Signature 8. Back: Suspension bridge at left center. Watermark: Mobutu. Printer: G&D.

	VF	UNC
a. Issued note.	3.00	12.00
s. Specimen. Red overprint: *SPECIMEN* on both sides.	—	60.00

45 **1,000,000 Zaïres**

1993. Red-violet and deep red on multicolor underprint. Mobutu in military dress at right, leopard at lower left center facing left, arms at lower right. Back: Suspension bridge at left center. Watermark: Mobutu. Printer: HdMZ.

	VF	UNC
a. Signature 8. 15.3.1993.	2.50	13.00
b. Signature 9. 17.5.1993; 30.6.1993.	1.25	7.00
s. Specimen. As a, b. Red overprint: *SPECIMEN* on both sides.	50.00	80.00

46 **5,000,000 Zaïres** VF UNC

1.10.1992. Deep brown and brown on multicolor underprint. Mobutu in military dress at right, leopard at lower left center facing left, arms at lower right. Signature 8. Back: Factory, pyramids at center, flora and elephant tusks at left. Watermark: Mobutu. Printer: H&S.

	VF	UNC
a. Issued note.	2.00	8.25
s. Specimen. Red overprint: *SPECIMEN* on both sides.	40.00	75.00

1993 Issue

#47-58 Replacement notes: serial # suffix *Z*.

47 **1 Nouveau Likuta** VF UNC

24.6.1993. Light brown on pink and multicolor underprint. Mobutu in military dress at right, arms at lower right, leopard at lower left. Signature 9. Back: Independence Monument at left. Printer: G&D. UV: fibers fluoresce yellow, red and blue.

	VF	UNC
a. Issued note.	.20	.75
s. Specimen. Red overprint: *SPECIMEN* on both sides.	—	15.00

48 **5 Nouveaux Makuta** VF UNC

24.6.1993. Black on pale violet and blue-green underprint. Mobutu in military dress at right, arms at lower right, leopard at lower left. Signature 9. Back: Independence Monument at left. Printer: G&D.

	VF	UNC
a. Issued note.	.20	1.00
s. Specimen. Red overprint: *SPECIMEN* on both sides.	—	25.00

49 **10 Nouveaux Makuta** VF UNC

24.6.1993. Green on multicolor underprint. Mobutu in military dress at right, arms at lower right, leopard at lower left. Signature 9. Back: Factory, pyramids at center, flora and elephant tusks at left. Watermark: Mobutu. Printer: HdMZ (CdM-A). .50 1.75

51 **50 Nouveaux Makuta** VF UNC

24.6.1993. Brown-orange on light green and multicolor underprint. Mobutu in military dress at right, arms at lower right, leopard at lower left. Signature 9. Back: Chieftain at left, men fishing with stick nets at center. Watermark: Mobutu. Printer: HdMZ (CdM-A). .30 1.25

52 **1 Nouveau Zaïre** VF UNC

24.6.1993. Violet and purple on multicolor underprint. Mobutu in military dress at right, arms at lower right, leopard at lower left. Signature 9. Back: Banque du Zaïre at left center. Watermark: Mobutu. Printer: G&D.

	VF	UNC
a. Issued note.	.30	1.75
s. Specimen. Red overprint: *SPECIMEN* on both sides.	—	30.00

53 **5 Nouveaux Zaïres** VF UNC

24.6.1993. Brown on multicolor underprint. Mobutu in military dress at right, arms at lower right, leopard at lower left. Signature Back: Domed building at left center. Watermark: Mobutu. Printer: G&D.

	VF	UNC
a. Signature 9.	.50	1.75
b. Signature 10.	1.50	4.00
s. Specimen. Red overprint: *SPECIMEN* on both sides.	—	40.00

54 **10 Nouveaux Zaïres** VF UNC

24.6.1993. Dark gray and dark blue-green on multicolor underprint. Mobutu in military dress at right, arms at lower right, leopard at lower left. Signature 9. Back: Civic building, water fountain at center right. Watermark: Mobutu. Printer: G&D.

	VF	UNC
a. Issued note.	.75	3.00
s. Specimen. Red overprint: *SPECIMEN* on both sides.	—	40.00

55 **10 Nouveaux Zaïres**

24.6.1993. Dark gray and dark blue-green on multicolor underprint. Mobutu in military dress at right, arms at lower right, leopard at lower left. Signature 9. Back: Civic building, water fountain at center right. Watermark: Mobutu. Printer: HdMZ (CdM-A). .50 1.75

56 **20 Nouveaux Zaïres** VF UNC

24.6.1993. Brown and blue on pale green and lilac underprint. Mobutu in military dress at right, arms at lower right, leopard at lower left. Signature 9. Back: Civic building and water fountain at left center. Watermark: Mobutu. Printer: HdMZ (CdM-A). .75 3.50

57 50 Nouveaux Zaïres — VF | UNC

24.6.1993. Brown and deep red on multicolor underprint. Mobutu in military dress at right, arms at lower right, leopard at lower left. Signature 9. Back: Hydroelectric dam at left center. Watermark: Mobutu. Printer: HdMZ (CdM-A). — .75 | 4.00

58 100 Nouveaux Zaïres — VF | UNC

1993-94. Grayish purple and blue-violet on aqua and ochre underprint. Mobutu in military dress at right, arms at lower right, leopard at lower left. Back: Suspension bridge at left center. Watermark: Mobutu. Printer: G&D.

- a. Signature 9. 24.6.1993. — 1.00 | 4.75
- b. Signature 10. 15.2.1994. — 1.25 | 5.50
- s. Specimen. As a. Red overprint: *SPECIMEN* on both sides. — — | 50.00

58A 100 Nouveaux Zaïres

1993. Grayish purple and blue-violet on aqua and ochre underprint. Mobutu in military dress at right, arms at lower right, leopard at lower left. Back: Suspension bridge at left center. Watermark: Mobutu. Printer: HdMZ. — 1.00 | 4.75

1994-96 Issues

#59-77 Replacement notes: serial # suffix *Z*.

59 50 Nouveaux Zaïres — VF | UNC

15.2.1994. Dull red-violet and red on multicolor underprint. Mobutu in military dress at right, arms at lower right, leopard at lower left center. Signature 10. Back: Hydroelectric dam at left center. Watermark: Mobutu. Printer: HdMZ.

- a. Issued note. — 2.00 | 8.25
- s. Specimen. Red overprint: *SPECIMEN* on both sides. — — | 40.00

60 100 Nouveaux Zaïres — VF | UNC

15.2.1994. Grayish purple and blue-violet on aqua and ochre underprint. Mobutu in military dress at right, arms at lower right, leopard at lower left center. Signature 10. Back: Suspension bridge at left center. Watermark: Mobutu. Printer: HdMZ. — 1.00 | 4.75

61 200 Nouveaux Zaïres

15.2.1994. Deep olive-brown on orange and multicolor underprint. Mobutu in military dress at right, arms at lower right, leopard at lower left center. Signature 10. Back: Men fishing with stick nets at left center. Watermark: Mobutu. Printer: HdMZ.

- a. Issued note. — .25 | 3.00
- s. Specimen. Red overprint: *SPECIMEN* on both sides. — — | 61.00

62 200 Nouveaux Zaïres — VF | UNC

15.2.1994. Deep olive-brown on orange and multicolor underprint. Mobutu in military dress at right, arms at lower right, leopard at lower left center. Back: Men fishing with stick nets at left center. Watermark: Mobutu. Printer: G&D.

- a. Issued note. — .50 | 3.00
- s. Specimen. Red overprint: *SPECIMEN* on both sides. — — | 40.00

63 500 Nouveaux Zaïres

15.2.1994. Gray and deep olive-green on multicolor underprint. Mobutu in military dress at right, arms at lower right, leopard at lower left center. Back: Banque du Zaïre at left center. Watermark: Mobutu. Printer: HdMZ.

- a. Issued note. — .50 | 1.75
- s. Specimen. Red overprint: *SPECIMEN* on both sides. — — | 40.00

64 500 Nouveaux Zaïres — VF | UNC

15.2.1994. Gray and deep olive-green on multicolor underprint. Mobutu in military dress at right, arms at lower right, leopard at lower left center. Back: Banque du Zaïre at left center. Watermark: Mobutu. Printer: G&D.

- a. Issued note. — .50 | 4.00
- s. Specimen. Red overprint: *SPECIMEN* on both sides. — — | 45.00

64A 500 Nouveaux Zaïres

15.2.1994. Gray and deep olivegreen on multicolor underprint. Mobutu in military dress at right, arms at lower right, leopard at lower left center. Serial number prefix *X*. Back: Banque du Zaïre at left center. Watermark: Mobutu. Printer: Printed in Argentina. — 1.00 | 4.75

65 500 Nouveaux Zaïres — VF | UNC

30.1.1995. Blue on multicolor underprint. Mobutu in military dress at right, arms at lower right, leopard at lower left center. Signature 11. Back: Large value. Watermark: Mobutu.

- a. Issued note. — .50 | 1.75
- s. Specimen. Red overprint: *SPECIMEN* on both sides. — — | 45.00

66 1000 Nouveaux Zaïres — VF | UNC

30.1.1995. Olive-green and olive-gray on multicolor underprint. Mobutu in military dress at right, arms at lower right, leopard at lower left center. Back: Large value. Watermark: Mobutu. Printer: G&D.

- a. Issued note. — 1.00 | 4.75
- s. Specimen. Red overprint: *SPECIMEN* on both sides. — — | 50.00

67 1000 Nouveaux Zaïres

30.1.1995. Olive-green and loive-gray on multicolor underprint. Mobutu in military dress at right, arms at lower right, leopard at lower left center. Back: Large value. Watermark: Mobutu. Printer: HdMZ. — .75 | 4.00

68 5000 Nouveaux Zaïres VF UNC
30.1.1995. Brown-violet and red-violet on multicolor underprint. Mobutu in military dress at right, arms at lower right, leopard at lower left center. Signature 11. Watermark: Mobutu. Printer: G&D.
a. Issued note. 2.00 9.50
s. Specimen. Red overprint: *SPECIMEN* on both sides. — 50.00

69 5000 Nouveaux Zaïres
30.1.1995. Brown-violet and red-violet on multicolor underprint. Mobutu in military dress at right, arms at lower right, leopard at lower left center. Signature 11. Watermark: Mobutu. Printer: HdMZ. 1.25 7.00

70 10,000 Nouveaux Zaïres VF UNC
30.1.1995. Blue-violet on multicolor underprint. Mobutu in military dress at right, arms at lower right, leopard at lower left center, OVD vertical band at left. Signature 11. Watermark: Mobutu. Printer: G&D.
a. Issued note. 1.50 7.50
s. Specimen. Red overprint: *SPECIMEN* on both sides. — 50.00

71 10,000 Nouveaux Zaïres
30.1.1995. Blue-violet on multicolor underprint. Mobutu in military dress at right, arms at lower right, leopard at lower left center, OVD vertical band at left. Signature 11. Watermark: Mobutu. Printer: HdMZ. 1.25 6.00

72 20,000 Nouveaux Zaïres VF UNC
30.1.1996. Brown on multicolor underprint. Mobutu in military dress at right, arms at lower right, leopard at lower left center,OVD vertical band at left. Signature 11. Watermark: Mobutu. Printer: G&D.
a. Issued note. 1.50 7.00
s. Specimen. Red overprint: *SPECIMEN* on both sides. — 40.00

73 20,000 Nouveaux Zaïres
30.1.1996. Brown on multicolor underprint. Mobutu in military dress at right, arms at lower right, leopard at lower left center, OVD vertical band at left. Signature 11. Watermark: Mobutu. Printer: HdMZ. 1.50 7.00

74 50,000 Nouveaux Zaïres
30.1.1996. Violet and pale blue on multicolor underprint. Mobutu in military dress at right, arms at lower right, leopard at lower left center, OVD vertical band at left. Signature 11. Watermark: Mobutu. Printer: G&D.
a. Issued note. 3.00 12.00
s. Specimen. — 40.00

75 50,000 Nouveaux Zaïres
30.1.1996. Violet and pale blue on multicolor underprint. Mobutu in military dress at right, arms at lower right, leopard at lower left center, OVD vertical band at left. Signature 11. Watermark: Mobutu. Printer: HdMZ. 3.00 12.00

76 100,000 Nouveaux Zaïres
30.6.1996. Dull orange on green and multicolor underprint. Mobutu in military dress at right, arms at lower right, leopard at lower left center, OVD vertical band at left. Signature 11. Watermark: Mobutu. Printer: G&D.
a. Issued note. 2.00 9.50
s. Specimen. Red overprint: *SPECIMEN* on both sides. — 55.00

77 100,000 Nouveaux Zaïres
30.6.1996. Dull orange on green and multicolor underprint. Mobutu in military dress at right, arms at lower right, leopard at lower left center, OVD vertical band at left. Signature 11. Watermark: Mobutu. Printer: HdMZ. 2.00 9.50

77A 100,000 Nouveaux Zaïres VF UNC
30.6.1996. Gray and blue-green on multicolor underprint. Mobutu in military dress at right, arms at lower right, leopard at lower left center. Watermark: Mobutu. Printer: HdMZ.
a. Issued note. 4.50 20.00
s. Specimen. Red overprint: *SPECIMEN* on both sides. — 60.00

78 500,000 Nouveaux Zaïres VF UNC
25.10.1996. Green and yellow-green on multicolor underprint. Mobutu at right. Signature 11. Back: Map of Zaïre, family in canoe. Watermark: Mobutu. Printer: G&D.
a. Issued note. 3.00 12.00
s. Specimen. Red overprint: *SPECIMEN* on both sides. — 65.00

79 1,000,000 Nouveaux Zaïres
25.10.1996. Light violet and red on multicolor underprint. Mobutu at right, diamonds at lower left center. Signature 11. Back: Map of Zaïre, mining facility. Watermark: Mobutu. Printer: G&D.
a. Issued note. 4.00 17.50
s. Specimen. Red overprint: *SPECIMEN* on both sides. — 55.00

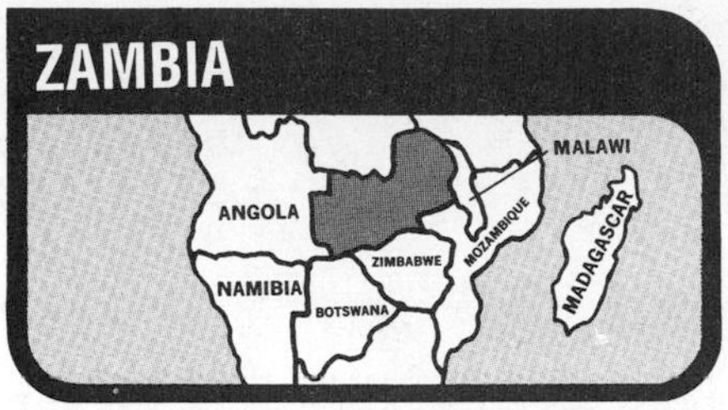

The Republic of Zambia is a landlocked country in south-central Africa, has an area of 752,614 sq. km. and a population of 11.67 million. Capital: Lusaka. The economy is d principally on copper, of which Zambia is the world's third largest producer. Copper, zinc, lead, cobalt and tobacco are exported.

The territory of Northern Rhodesia was administered by the [British] South Africa Company from 1891 until it was taken over by the UK in 1923. During the 1920s and 1930s, advances in mining spurred development and immigration. The name was changed to Zambia upon independence in 1964. In the 1980s and 1990s, declining copper prices and a prolonged drought hurt the economy. Elections in 1991 brought an end to one-party rule, but the subsequent vote in 1996 saw blatant harassment of opposition parties. The election in 2001 was marked by administrative problems with three parties filing a legal petition challenging the election of ruling party candidate Levy Mwanawasa. The new president launched an anticorruption investigation in 2002 to probe high-level corruption during the previous administration. In 2006-07, this task force successfully prosecuted four cases, including a landmark civil case in the UK in which former President Chiluba and numerous others were found liable for USD 41 million. Mwanawasa was reelected in 2006 in an election that was deemed free and fair. Upon his abrupt death in August 2008, he was succeeded by his Vice-president Rupiah Banda, who subsequently won a special presidential election in October 2008.

Also see Rhodesia and Malawi.

RULERS:

British to 1964

SIGNATURE VARIETIES

1	R. C. Hallet, 1964-67	2	Dr. J. B. Zulu, 1967-70
3	V. S. Musakanya, 1970-72	4	B. R. Kuwani, 1972-76, 1982-84
5	L. J. Mwananshiku, 1976-81	6	D. A. R. Phiri, 1984-8
7	Dr. L. S. Chivuno, 1986-88	8	F. Nkhoma, 1988-9
9	J. A. Bussiere, 1991- (ca.1993)	10	D. Mulaisho, 1993-95
11	Dr. J. Mwanza, 1995-2002	12	K. Fundanga 2002 -

Republic

Bank of Zambia

1963 ND Issue

		VF	UNC
A1	**1 Pound** 1963. Blue on lilac underprint. Fisherman with net and boat at center, portrait Queen Elizabeth II at right. Back: Purple. Ross's Turaco at left center. Printer: H&S (Not issued).	—	4500.

1964 ND Issue

		VF	UNC
1	**10 Shillings** ND (1964). Brown on multicolor underprint. Chaplins Barbet bird at right, arms at upper center. Signature 1. Back: Farmers plowing with tractor and oxen. Watermark: Wildebeest's head. Printer: TDLR.		
	a. Issued note.	150.	400.
	s. Specimen.	—	300.

		VF	UNC
2	**1 Pound** ND (1964). Green on multicolor underprint. Black-cheeked Lovebird at right, arms at upper center. Signature 1. Back: Mining tower and conveyors at left center. Watermark: Wildebeest's head. Printer: TDLR.		
	a. Issued note.	200.	900.
	s. Specimen.	—	300.

		VF	UNC
3	**5 Pounds** ND (1964). Blue on multicolor underprint. Wildebeest at right, arms at upper center. Signature 1. Back: Victoria Falls of Zambezi at left center. Watermark: Wildebeest's head. Printer: TDLR.		
	a. Issued note.	450.	2500.
	s. Specimen.	—	400.

1968 ND Issue

#4-8 Replacement notes: Serial # prefix *1/Z; 1/Y; 1/X; 1/W; 1/V* respectively.

		VF	UNC
4	**50 Ngwee** ND (1968). Red-violet on multicolor underprint. President K. Kaunda at right, arms at left. Dot between letter and value. Signature 2. Back: Two antelope. Printer: TDLR.		
	a. Issued note.	27.50	80.00
	s. Specimen.	—	75.00

		VF	UNC
5	**1 Kwacha** ND (1968). Dark brown on multicolor underprint. President K. Kaunda at right, arms at upper center. Dot between letter and value. Signature 2. Back: Farmers plowing with tractor and oxen. Watermark: Kaunda. Printer: TDLR.		
	a. Issued note.	40.00	95.00
	s. Specimen.	—	80.00

#	Denomination	VF	UNC
6	**2 Kwacha**		
	ND (1968). Green on multicolor underprint. President K. Kaunda at right, arms at upper center. Dot between letter and value. Signature 2. Back: Mining tower and conveyors at left center. Watermark: Kaunda. Printer: TDLR.		
	a. Issued note.	50.00	150.
	s. Specimen.	—	120.
7	**10 Kwacha**		
	ND (1968). Blue on multicolor underprint. President K. Kaunda at right, arms at upper center. Dot between letter and value. Signature 2. Back: Waterfall at center. Watermark: Kaunda. Printer: TDLR.		
	a. Issued note.	125.	850.
	s. Specimen.	—	175.
8	**20 Kwacha**		
	ND (1968). Purple on multicolor underprint. President K. Kaunda at right, arms at upper center. Dot between letter and value. Signature 2. Back: National Assembly. Watermark: Kaunda. Printer: TDLR.		
	a. Issued note.	200.	950.
	s. Specimen.	—	225.

1969 ND Issue

#9-13 Replacement notes: Serial # prefix *1/Z; 1/Y; 1/X; 1/W; 1/V* respectively.

#	Denomination	VF	UNC
9	**50 Ngwee**		
	ND (1969). Red-violet on multicolor underprint. President K. Kaunda at right, arms at left, without dot between letter and value. Back: Two antelope. Watermark: K. Kaunda. Printer: TDLR.		
	a. Signature 3.	20.00	75.00
	b. Signature 4.	10.00	45.00
	s. As c. Specimen.	—	50.00

#	Denomination	VF	UNC
10	**1 Kwacha**		
	ND (1969). Dark brown on multicolor underprint. President K. Kaunda at right, arms at upper center, without dot between letter and value. Back: Farmers plowing with oxen. Watermark: K. Kaunda. Printer: TDLR.		
	a. Signature 2.	20.00	75.00
	b. Signature 3.	9.00	45.00
	s. Specimen.	—	50.00
11	**2 Kwacha**		
	ND (1969). Green on multicolor underprint. President K. Kaunda at right, arms at upper center, without dot between letter and value. Back: Mining tower and conveyors at left center. Watermark: K. Kaunda. Printer: TDLR.		
	a. Signature 2.	40.00	200.
	b. Signature 3.	30.00	200.
	c. Signature 4.	22.50	160.
	s. As s. Specimen.	—	90.00

#	Denomination	VF	UNC
12	**10 Kwacha**		
	ND (1969). Blue on multicolor underprint. President K. Kaunda at right, arms at upper center, without dot between letter and value. Back: Waterfall at center. Watermark: K. Kaunda. Printer: TDLR.		
	a. Signature 2.	75.00	350.
	b. Signature 3.	125.	700.
	c. Signature 4.	60.00	300.
	s. Specimen.	—	100.

#	Denomination	VF	UNC
13	**20 Kwacha**		
	ND (1969). Purple on multicolor underprint. President K. Kaunda at right, arms at upper center, without dot between letter and value. Back: National Assembly. Watermark: K. Kaunda. Printer: TDLR.		
	a. Signature 2.	100.	600.
	b. Signature 3.	150.	800.
	c. Signature 4.	25.00	75.00
	s. Specimen.	—	125.

1973 ND Issue

#14 and 15 Replacement notes: Serial # prefix *1/Z; 1/U* respectively.

#	Denomination	VF	UNC
14	**50 Ngwee**		
	ND (1973). Black on lilac and multicolor underprint. President K. Kaunda at right, arms at upper center. Signature 4. Back: Miners. Watermark: K. Kaunda. Printer: TDLR.		
	a. Issued note.	5.00	12.50
	s. Specimen.	—	40.00

#	Denomination	VF	UNC
15	**5 Kwacha**		
	ND (1973). Red-violet on multicolor underprint. President K. Kaunda at right, arms at upper center. Signature 4. Back: Children by school. Watermark: K. Kaunda.		
	a. Issued note.	150.	450.
	s. Specimen.	—	200.

1973 ND Commemorative Issue

#16, Birth of the Second Republic, December 13, 1972

		VF	UNC
16	**1 Kwacha** ND (1973). Red-orange and brown on multicolor underprint. President K. Kaunda at right. Signature 4. Back: Document signing, commemorative text and crowd. Watermark: K. Kaunda. Printer: TDLR.		
	a. Issued note.	12.50	45.00
	s. Specimen.	—	40.00

1974 ND Issue

#17 and 18 Replacement notes: Serial # prefix *1/W; 1/V* respectively.

		VF	UNC
17	**10 Kwacha** ND (1974). Blue on multicolor underprint. President K. Kaunda at right, arms at upper center. Signature 4. Back: Waterfalls at left center. Watermark: K. Kaunda. Printer: BWC.		
	a. Issued note.	100.	350.
	s. Specimen.	—	175.
18	**20 Kwacha** ND (1974). Purple and red on multicolor underprint. President K. Kaunda at right, arms at upper center. Signature 4. Back: National Assembly. Watermark: K. Kaunda. Printer: BWC.		
	a. Issued note.	65.00	260.
	s. Specimen.	—	220.

1974-76 ND Issue

#19-22A Replacement notes: Serial # prefix *1/Y, 1/X; 1/U; 1/W* respectively.

		VF	UNC
19	**1 Kwacha** ND (1976). Brown on multicolor underprint. Older President K. Kaunda at right, earlier frame design, arms at upper center. Signature 5. Back: Farmers plowing with tractor and oxen. Watermark: K. Kaunda. Printer: TDLR.		
	a. Issued note.	6.00	12.50
	s. Specimen.	—	30.00
20	**2 Kwacha** ND (1974). Green on multicolor underprint. Older President K. Kaunda at right, earlier frame design, arms at upper center. Signature 4. Back: Mining tower and conveyors at left center. Watermark: K. Kaunda. Printer: TDLR.		
	a. Issued note.	7.00	22.50
	s. Specimen.	—	30.00
21	**5 Kwacha** ND (1976). Brown and violet on multicolor underprint. Older President K. Kaunda at right, earlier frame design, arms at upper center. Signature 5. Back: Document signing, commemorative text and crowd. Watermark: K. Kaunda. Printer: TDLR.		
	a. Issued note.	10.00	35.00
	s. Specimen.	—	55.00
22	**10 Kwacha** ND (1976). Blue on multicolor underprint. Older President K. Kaunda at right, earlier frame design, arms at upper center. Signature 5. Back: Waterfalls at left center. Watermark: K. Kaunda. Printer: TDLR.		
	a. Issued note.	20.00	50.00
	s. Specimen.	—	75.00

		VF	UNC
22A	**20 Kwacha** ND. Purple, red and multicolor. Older President K. Kaunda at right, earlier frame design, arms at upper center. Back: National Assembly. Watermark: K. Kaunda. Printer: TDLR. (Not issued.)	—	—

1980; 1986 ND Issue

#23-28 Replacement notes: Serial # prefix *Z/1*.

		VF	UNC
23	**1 Kwacha** ND (1980-88). Dark brown on multicolor underprint. President K. Kaunda at right, African fish eagle at left center. Back: Workers picking cotton at left center. Watermark: K. Kaunda. Printer: TDLR.		
	a. Signature 5.	2.00	8.00
	b. Signature 7.	2.00	5.00
	s. Specimen.	—	40.00

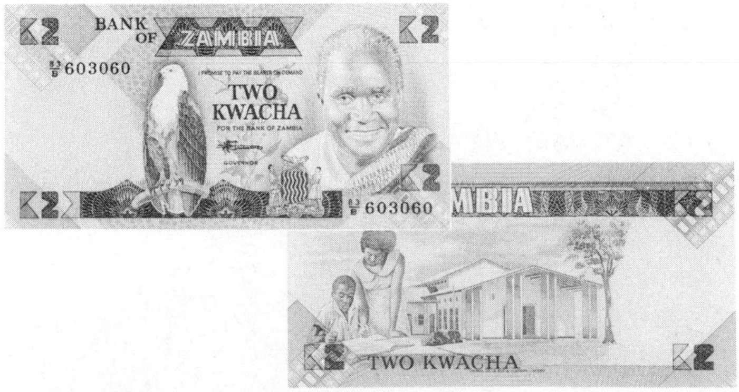

		VF	UNC
24	**2 Kwacha** ND (1980-88). Olive-green on multicolor underprint. President K. Kaunda at right, African fish eagle at left center. Back: Teacher with student at left, school building at center. Watermark: K. Kaunda. Printer: TDLR.		
	a. Signature 5.	4.00	10.00
	b. Signature 6.	3.00	8.00
	c. Signature 7.	2.00	7.00
	s. Specimen.	—	40.00

25 5 Kwacha

ND (1980-88). Brown on multicolor underprint. President K. Kaunda at right, African fish eagle at left center. Back: Hydroelectric dam at left center. Watermark: K. Kaunda. Printer: TDLR.

	VF	UNC
a. Signature 5.	2.00	10.00
b. Signature 4.	10.00	45.00
c. Signature 6.	4.00	8.00
d. Signature 7.	2.00	5.00
s. Specimen.	—	40.00

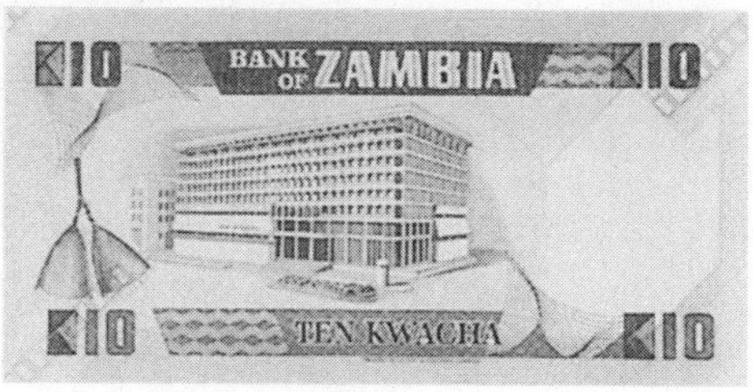

26 10 Kwacha

ND (1980-88). Blue, green and black on multicolor underprint. President K. Kaunda at right, African fish eagle at left center. Back: Bank at left center. Watermark: K. Kaunda. Printer: TDLR.

	VF	UNC
a. Signature 5.	10.00	45.00
b. Signature 4 in black.	18.00	125.
c. Signature 4 in blue.	15.00	100.
d. Signature 6.	6.00	14.00
e. Signature 7.	3.00	6.00
s. Specimen. As a, d. Red overprint: *SPECIMEN* on both sides.	—	40.00

27 20 Kwacha

ND (1980-88). Green and olive-brown on multicolor underprint. President K. Kaunda at right, African fish eagle at left center. Back: Woman with basket on head at center right. Watermark: K. Kaunda. Printer: TDLR.

	VF	UNC
a. Signature 5.	15.00	60.00
b. Signature 4 in black.	20.00	150.
c. Signature 4 in dark green.	15.00	100.
d. Signature 6.	8.00	17.50
e. Signature 7.	4.00	9.00
s. Specimen. As a. Red overprint: *SPECIMEN* on both sides.	—	60.00

28 50 Kwacha

ND (1986-88). Purple, violet and multicolor. President K. Kaunda at right, African fish eagle at left center. Signature 7. Back: "Chainbreaker" statue at left, modern building at left center. Watermark: K. Kaunda. Printer: TDLR. UV: value 50 fluoresce orange.

	VF	UNC
a. Issued note.	2.00	8.00
s. Specimen. Red overprint: *SPECIMEN* on both sides.	—	60.00

1989 ND Issue

29 2 Kwacha

ND (1989). Olive-brown on multicolor underprint. President K. Kaunda at right, fish eagle at lower left, butterfly over arms at center. Signature 8. Back: Rhinoceros head at lower left facing left, cornfield at center, tool at right, "Chainbreaker" statue at left. Watermark: K. Kaunda.

	VF	UNC
a. Issued note.	1.50	5.00
s. Specimen.	—	40.00

30 5 Kwacha

ND (1989). Brown and red-orange on multicolor underprint. President K. Kaunda at right, fish eagle at lower left, butterfly over arms at center. Signature 8. Back: Brown. "Chainbreaker" statue at left, lion cub head facing at lower left, building at center, jar at right. Watermark: K. Kaunda. UV: value 5 fluoresce yellow.

	VF	UNC
a. Issued note.	2.00	7.00
s. Specimen.	—	40.00

31 10 Kwacha

ND (1989-91). Black, dark blue and red-violet on multicolor underprint. President K. Kaunda at right, fish eagle at lower left, butterfly over arms at center. Signature Back: Dark blue. "Chainbreaker" statue at left, giraffe head at lower left, facing left, building at center, carving at right. Watermark: K. Kaunda. UV: value 10 fluoresce yellow.

	VF	UNC
a. Signature 8.	3.00	8.00
b. Signature 9.	1.00	4.50
s. Specimen.	—	40.00

32 20 Kwacha

ND (1989-91). Dark olive-green, brown and blue on multicolor underprint. President K. Kaunda at right, fish eagle at lower left, butterfly over arms at center. Signature 8. Back: Dark green. "Chainbreaker" statue at left, Dama gazelle head at lower left, facing 3/4 left, building at center, carving at right. Watermark: K. Kaunda. UV: value 20 fluoresce yellow.

	VF	UNC
a. Signature 8.	5.00	10.00
b. Signature 9.	4.00	8.00
s. Specimen.	—	60.00

33 50 Kwacha | VF | UNC

ND (1989-91). Red-violet and purple on multicolor underprint. President K. Kaunda at right, fish eagle at lower left, butterfly over arms at center. Signature Back: Zebra head at lower left, facing left, manufacturing at center, carving of woman's bust at right, "Chainbreaker" statue at left. Watermark: K. Kaunda.

	VF	UNC
a. Signature 8.	10.00	30.00
b. Signature 9.	5.00	15.00
s. Specimen.	—	60.00

1991 ND Issue

34 100 Kwacha | VF | UNC

ND (1991). Purple, red and blue on multicolor underprint. Older President K. Kaunda at right, gish eagle at left, palm trees at center. Back: Victoria Falls of Zambezi with rainbow through center. Watermark: K. Kaunda.

	VF	UNC
a. Issued note.	6.00	12.00
s. Specimen.	—	50.00

35 500 Kwacha

ND (1991). Brown on multicolor underprint. Older President K. Kaunda at right, fish eagle at left, tree over arms at center. Signature 9. Back: Elephant at left, workers picking cotton at center. Watermark: K. Kaunda.

	VF	UNC
a. Issued note.	10.00	25.00
s. Specimen.	Unc	60.00

1992; 1996 ND Issue

#36-42 Replacement notes: Serial # prefix *1/X.*

36 20 Kwacha | VF | UNC

1992. Green on multicolor underprint. Fish eagle at right, seal of arms with date at lower left. Back: Fig tree at center, Kudu at left, 3/4 facing left, State House at Lusaka at center, "Chainbreaker" statue at right center. Watermark: Fish eagle's head. Printer: TDLR. UV: value 20 in blox fluoresce yellow; vertical serial # orange. Back design elements orange.

	VF	UNC
a. Signature 10.	.50	3.00
b. Signature 11.	.50	2.50
s. Specimen. As a. Red overprint: *SPECIMEN* on both sides.	—	65.00

37 50 Kwacha | VF | UNC

1992; 2001; 2003; 2006-08. Red on multicolor underprint. Fish eagle at right, seal of arms with date at lower left, sausage tree at center, zebra at left. Back: Copper refining at Nkana Mine at center, "Chainbreaker" statue at center right. Watermark: Fish eagle's head. Printer: TDLR. UV: value 50 in square fluoresces yellow.

	VF	UNC
a. 1992. Signature 10.	.60	3.25
b. 1992. Signature 11.	.60	3.00
c. 2001. Signature 11.	.50	2.75
d. 2003. Signature 12.	.50	2.50
e. 2006. Signature 12.	FV	1.25
f. 2007. Signature 12.	FV	1.00
g. 2008. Signature 12.	FV	.75
h. 2009. Signature. 12.	FV	.75
s. Specimen. As a. Red overprint: *SPECIMEN* on both sides.	—	65.00

38 100 Kwacha | VF | UNC

1992; 2001; 2003; 2005; 2006. Deep purple on multicolor underprint. Fish eagle at right, palm tree at center, seal of arms with date at lower left. Serial # varieties. Back: Water buffalo head facing at left, Victoria falls at center, "Chainbreaker" statue at center right. Watermark: Fish eagle's head. Printer: TDLR.

	VF	UNC
a. 1992. Signature 10.	.60	3.00
b. 1992. Signature 11.	.60	3.00
c. 2001. Signature 11.	FV	2.50
d. 2003. Signature 12.	FV	2.00
e. 2005. Signature 12.	FV	2.00
f. 2006. Signatrue 12.	FV	2.25
g. 2008. Signature 12.	FV	1.00
h. 2009. Signature 12.	FV	1.00
i. 2010. Signature 12.	FV	1.00
s. Specimen. As a. Red overprint: *SPECIMEN* on both sides.	—	65.00

39 500 Kwacha | VF | UNC

1992; 2001; 2003. Brown on multicolor underprint. Fish eagle at right, seal of arms with date at lower left, Baobab tree. Back: Elephant head at left, workers picking cotton at center, "Chainbreaker" statue at center right. Watermark: Fish eagle's head. Printer: TDLR.

	VF	UNC
a. 1992. Signature 10.	1.75	6.00
b. 1992. Signature 11.	1.00	5.00
c. 2001. Signature 11.	FV	3.00
d. 2003. Signature 12.	FV	3.00
s. Specimen. As a. Red overprint: *SPECIMEN* on both sides.	—	65.00

40 1000 Kwacha

1992 (1996); 2001; 2003. Red-violet, deep orange and dark olive-green on multicolor underprint. Fish eagle at right, seal of arms with date at lower left, Jacaranda tree. Back: Aardvark at left, sorghum farmer on tractor at center, "Chainbreaker" statue at center right. Watermark: Fish eagle's head. Printer: TDLR.

	VF	UNC
a. 1992 (1996). Signature 11.	1.25	5.50
b. 2001. Signature 11.	.75	4.50
c. 2003. Signature 12.	FV	3.00
s. Specimen. As a. Red overprint: *SPECIMEN* on both sides.	—	50.00

41 5000 Kwacha

1992 (1996); 2001. Purple, dark brown and deep red on multicolor underprint. Fish eagle at right, Murera / Acacia / Mopani tree at center, seal of arms with date at lower left. Back: Lion facing at left, root cassava plant at center, "Chainbreaker" statue at center right. Watermark: Fish eagle's head. Printer: TDLR. Large zero's in denomination.

	VF	UNC
a. 1992 (1996). Signature 11.	2.50	10.00
b. 2001. Signature 11.	1.75	5.50
s. Specimen. As a. Red overprint: *SPECIMEN* on both sides.	—	50.00

42 10,000 Kwacha

1992 (1996); 2001; 2003. Aqua, brown-violet and yellow-brown on multicolor underprint. Fish eagle at right, Musuku tree at center, seal of arms with date at lower left. Back: Porcupine at left, harvesting rice paddy at center, "Chainbreaker" statue at center right. Watermark: Fish eagle's head facing left. Printer: TDLR.

	VF	UNC
a. 1992 (1996). Signature 11.	5.00	17.50
b. 2001. Signature 11.	3.00	12.00
c. 2003. Signature 12.	3.00	20.00
s. Specimen. As a. Red overprint: *SPECIMEN* on both sides.	—	75.00

2003 Issue

43 500 Kwacha

2003-11. Multicolor. Fish eagle at right, Baobab tree at center. Back: Elephant's head at left, workers picking cotton at center, "Chainbreaker" statue at center right. Watermark: Fish eagle's head. Polymer plastic. 145x70mm.

	VF	UNC
a. 2003. Serial # wears off.	—	15.00
b. 2003. Second printing.	FV	1.00
c. 2004. Signature 12.	FV	1.00
d. 2005. Signature 12.	FV	1.00
e. 2006. Signature 12.	FV	1.00
f. 2008. Signature 12. Altered security features.	FV	.75
g. 2009. Signature 12.	FV	.75
h. 2011. Signature 12.	FV	.75
s. Specimen.	—	40.00

44 1000 Kwacha

2003-12. Multicolor. Fish eagle at left, tree at center. Back: Aardvark at left, sorghum farmer on tractor at center, "Chainbreaker" statue at center right. Polymer plastic. UV: value 500 in box and design elements fluoresce yellow; vertical serial # orange. 145x70mm.

	VF	UNC
a. 2003. Serial # wears off.	—	20.00
b. 2003. Second Printing.	FV	3.00
c. 2004. Signature 12.	FV	3.00
d. 2005. Signature 12.	FV	3.00
e. 2006. Signature 12.	FV	3.00
f. 2008. Signature 12.	FV	1.50
g. 2009. Signature 12.	FV	1.50
h. 2011. Signature 12.	FV	1.50
i. 2012. Signature 12.	FV	1.50
s. Specimen.	—	40.00

45 5000 Kwacha

2003-12. Multicolor. Fish eagle at right, Murera / Acacia / Mopani tree at center, seal of arms with date at lower left. Back: Lion at left center, root cassava plant at center, "Chainbreaker" statue at center right. Small zero's in denomination. 145x70mm.

	VF	UNC
a. 2003. Signature 12.	FV	4.50
b. 2005. Signature 12.	FV	3.00
c. 2006. Signature 12.	FV	2.00
d. 2008. Signature 12.	FV	1.75
e. 2009. Signature 12.	FV	1.75
f. 2010. Signature 12.	FV	1.75
g. 2011. Signature 12.	FV	1.75
h. 2012. Signature 12.	FV	1.75
s. Specimen.	—	40.00

46 10,000 Kwacha

2003-12. Aqua, brown-violet and yellow-brown on multicolor underprint. Fish eagle at right, Musuku tree at center, seal of arms with date at lower left. Foil fish eagle head at lower left. Back: Porcupine at left, harvesting rice paddy at center, "Chainbreaker" statue at center right. Watermark: Fish eagle's head. Printer: TDLR. 145x70mm.

	VF	UNC
a. 2003. Date as denominator. Foil fish eagle head points right.	FV	6.00
b. 2005. Signature 12.	FV	6.00
c. 2006. Signature 12.	FV	6.00
d. 2007. Signature 12.	FV	5.00
e. 2008. Signature 12. Altered security features.	FV	4.00
f. 2009. Signature 12.	FV	4.00
g. 2011. Signature 12.	FV	4.00
h. 2012. Signature 12.	FV	4.00
s. Specimen.	—	40.00

47 20,000 Kwacha — VF | UNC

2003-12. Multicolor. Fish eagle at right, Murea / Acacia / Mopani tree at center. seal of arms with date at lower left. Back: Lion head at left. Root cassava plant at center, "Chainbreaker" statue at center right. Watermark: Fish eagle's head. 145x70mm.

	VF	UNC
a. 2003. Signature 12.	FV	10.00
b. 2005. Signature 12.	FV	10.00
c. 2006. Signature 12.	FV	10.00
d. 2008. Signature 12.	FV	8.00
e. 2009. Signature 12.	FV	8.00
f. 2010. Signature 12.	FV	8.00
g. 2011. Signature 12.	FV	8.00
h. 2012. Signature 12.	FV	8.00
s. Specimen.	—	50.00

48 50,000 Kwacha

2003-12. Multicolor. Fish eagle at right, tree at center. Back: Leopard at left, Bank of Zambia building at center, "Chainbreaker" statue at right center. 145x70mm.

	VF	UNC
a. 2003. Signature 12.	FV	25.00
b. 2006. Signature 12.	FV	25.00
c. 2007. Signature 12.	FV	22.00
d. 2008. Signature 12.	FV	20.00
e. 2009. Signature 12.	FV	15.00
f. 2010. Signature 12.	FV	15.00
g. 2011. Signature 12.	FV	15.00
h. 2012. Signature 12.	FV	15.00
s. Specimen.	—	60.00

2012 Issue

49 2 Kwacha — VF FV | UNC 1.50

2012. Gray and multicolor. Fish eagle at right. Baobab tree at center. Back: Roan antelope; two women and Freedom statue. Watermark: Fish eagle and value. Printer: G&D. 140x70mm.

50 5 Kwacha — VF FV | UNC 2.00

2012. Purple and multicolor. Fish eagle at right. Baobab tree at center. Back: Lion head at left, plant and Freedom statue. Watermark: Fish eagle and 5. Printer: G&D. 140x70mm.

51 10 Kwacha — VF FV | UNC 4.00

2012. Blue and multicolor. Fish eagle at right. Baobab tree at center. Back: Porcupine, harvest scene and Freedom Statue. Watermark: Fish eagle and 10. Printer: G&D. 145x70mm.

52 20 Kwacha — VF FV | UNC 8.00

2012. Brown and multicolor. Fish eagle at right. Baobab tree at center. Back: Black lechwe antelope, men working pneumatic drill in mine. Watermark: Fish eagle and 20. 145x70mm.

53 50 Kwacha — VF FV | UNC 20.00

2012. Blue and multicolor. Fish eagle at right. Baobab tree at center. Back: Leopard and Bank of Zambia building. Watermark: Fish eagle and 50 Printer: G&D. 145x70mm.

54 100 Kwacha — VF FV | UNC 40.00

2012. Olive green and multicolor. Fish eagle at right. Baobab tree at center. Back: Buffalo, National Assembly building and Freedom Statue. Watermark: Fish eagle and 100. Printer: G&D. 145x70mm.

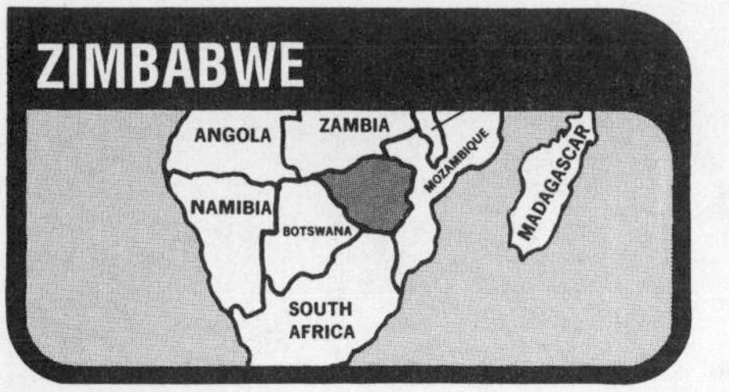

The Republic of Zimbabweis located in the east-central part of southern Africa, has an area of 390,580 sq. km. and a population of 11.35 million. Capital: Harare (formerly Salisbury). The economy is d on agriculture and mining. Tobacco, sugar, asbestos, copper and chrome ore and coal are exported.

The UK annexed Southern Rhodesia from the [British] South Africa Company in 1923. A 1961 constitution was formulated that favored whites in power. In 1965 the government unilaterally declared its independence, but the UK did not recognize the act and demanded more complete voting rights for the black African majority in the country (then called Rhodesia). UN sanctions and a guerrilla uprising finally led to free elections in 1979 and independence (as Zimbabwe) in 1980. Robert Mugabe, the nation's first prime minister, has been the country's only ruler (as president since 1987) and has dominated the country's political system since independence. His chaotic land redistribution campaign, which began in 2000, caused an exodus of white farmers, crippled the economy, and ushered in widespread shortages of basic commodities. Ignoring international condemnation, Mugabe rigged the 2002 presidential election to ensure his reelection. The ruling ZANU-PF party used fraud and intimidation to win a two-thirds majority in the March 2005 parliamentary election, allowing it to amend the constitution at will and recreate the Senate, which had been abolished in the late 1980s. In April 2005, Harare embarked on Operation Restore Order, ostensibly an urban rationalization program, which resulted in the destruction of the homes or businesses of 700,000 mostly poor supporters of the opposition. President Mugabe in June 2007 instituted price controls on all basic commodities causing panic buying and leaving store shelves empty for months. General elections held in March 2008 contained irregularities but still amounted to a censure of the ZANU-PF-led government with significant gains in opposition seats in parliament. MDC opposition leader Morgan Tsvangirai won the presidential polls, and may have won an out right majority, but official results posted by the Zimbabwe Electoral Committee did not reflect this. In the lead up to a run-off election in late June 2008, considerable violence enacted against opposition party members led to the withdrawal of Tsvangirai from the ballot. Extensive evidence of vote tampering and ballot-box stuffing resulted in international condemnation of the process. A power sharing agreement has been negoated allowing Mugabe to remain as president and creating the new position of prime minister for Tsvangirai.

For earlier issues see Rhodesia.

MONETARY SYSTEM:

1 Dollar = 100 Cents

SIGNATURE/TITLE VARIETIES

	GOVERNOR		GOVERNOR
1	Dr. D. C. Krogh	2	K. Moyana
3	L. Tsumba	4	Dr. D. C. Krogh
5	Dr. K. J. Moyana	6	Dr. L. L. Tsumba
7	C. Chikaura	8	Dr. G. Gono
	FINANCE DIRECTOR		**OPERATIONS DIRECTOR**
A	Priscilla P. Mutembwa		Stephen J. Newton-Howes

ZIMBABWEAN BIRD WATERMARK VARIETIES

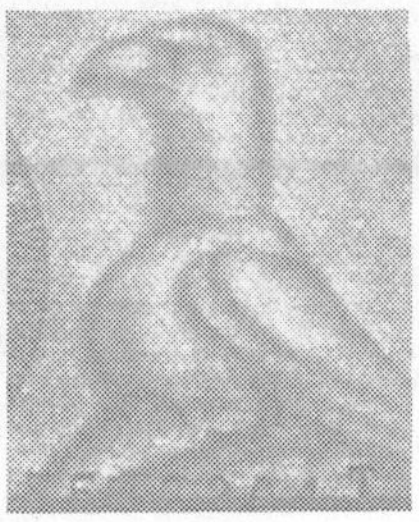

Type A
Profile short neck

Type B
3/4 view medium neck

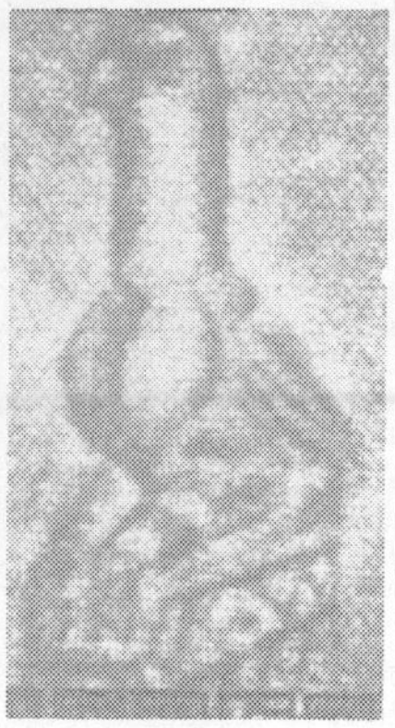

Type C
3/4 view long neck

Republic

Reserve Bank of Zimbabwe

1980 Issue

#1-4 Replacement notes: Serial # prefix: *AW; BW; CW; DW* **respectively.**

		VF	UNC
1	**2 Dollars**		
	1980 (1981); 1983; 1994. Blue and multicolor. Water buffalo at left. Chiremba balancing rock formation. Epworth (Harare) at center right. Signature varieties. Back: Tigerfish at center, Kariba Dam and reservoir at right. Watermark: Zimbabwe bird.		
	a. Signature 1. Salisbury. 1980.	2.25	10.00
	b. Signature 2. Harare. 1983.	1.25	5.00
	c. Signature 3. Watermark: Type A. 1994.	.75	3.75
	d. Signature 3. Watermark: Type B. 1994.	22.50	95.00

		VF	UNC
2	**5 Dollars**		
	1980 (1981); 1982-83; 1994. Green and multicolor. Zebra at left. Chiremba balancing rock formation. Epworth (Harare) at center right. Signature varieties. Back: Village scene with two workers. Watermark: Zimbabwe bird.		
	a. Signature 1. Salisbury. 1980.	5.50	24.00
	b. Signature 1. Harare. 1982.	5.00	22.50
	c. Signature 2. 1983.	1.50	6.00
	d. Signature 3. 1994. Watermark: Type A.	2.75	11.00
	e. Signature 3. 1994. Watermark: Type B.	12.50	50.00

3 **10 Dollars**

1980 (1981); 1982-83; 1994. Red and multicolor. Sable antelope at left. Chiremba balancing rock formation. Epworth (Harare) at center right. Signature varieties. Back: View of Harare and Freedom Flame monument. Watermark: Zimbabwe bird.

	VF	UNC
a. Signature 1. Salisbury. 1980.	10.00	50.00
b. Signature 1. Salisbury. 1982 (error).	35.00	125.
c. Signature 1. Harare. 1982.	25.00	120.
d. Signature 2. 1983.	2.75	11.00
e. Signature 3. 1994.	1.50	6.50

4 **20 Dollars**

1980 (1982); 1982-83; 1994. Blue, black and dark green on multicolor underprint. Giraffe at left. Chiremba balancing rock formation. Epworth (Harare) at center right. Signature varieties. Back: Elephant and Victoria Falls. Watermark: Zimbabwe bird.

	VF	UNC
a. Signature 1. Salisbury. 1980.	17.50	70.00
b. Signature 1. Harare. 1982.	75.00	300.
c. Signature 2. 1983.	5.00	15.00
d. Signature 3. 1994.	3.50	14.00

1994; 1997; 2001 Issues

5 **5 Dollars**

1997. Brown, red-orange and purple on multicolor underprint. Chiremba balancing rock formation. Epworth (Harare) at center right. Signature 3. Back: Terraced hills at center right. Watermark: Zimbabwe bird. Type C. UV: fibers fluoresce blue and red; vertical serial # and central design elements orange. Back 5s and design elements orange.

	VF	UNC
a. Light brown back (litho).	.75	3.00
b. Darker brown back (intaglio).	.20	1.00
r. Replacement. Serial number prefix AB.	—	—

6 **10 Dollars**

1997. Red-brown, deep green and blue-black on multicolor underprint. Chiremba balancing rock formation. Epworth (Harare) at center right. Signature 3. Back: Chilolo Cliffs at center right. Watermark: Zimbabwe bird. Type C. UV: fibers fluoresce yellow and blue; vertical serial # orange.

	VF	UNC
a. Issued note.	FV	2.00
r. Replacement note. Serial number prefix AC.	—	—

7 **20 Dollars**

1997. Deep blue, purple and gray-green on multicolor underprint. Chiremba balancing rock formation. Epworth (Harare) at right. Back: Victoria Falls at center right.

	VF	UNC
a. Issued note.	FV	2.50
r. Replacement note. Serial number prefix AD.	—	—

8 **50 Dollars**

1994. Dark brown, olive-brown and red-orange on multicolor underprint. Chiremba balancing rock formation. Epworth (Harare) at right. Back: Great Zimbabwe ruins.

	VF	UNC
a. Issued note.	FV	3.00
r. Replacement note. Serial # prefix AE.	—	—

9 **100 Dollars**

1995. Brownish black and purple on multicolor underprint. Chiremba balancing rock formation. Epworth (Harare) at right. Back: Aerial view of Kariba Dam and reservoir at center right.

	VF	UNC
a. Issued note.	FV	3.00
r. Replacement note. Serial # prefix AF.	—	—

10 **500 Dollars**

2001. Dark brown and red on multicolor underprint. Chiremba balancing rock formation. Epworth (Harare) at right. Hologram silver foil at left. Back: Hwange power station. Watermark: Zimbabwe bird and *500*.

	VF	UNC
	FV	5.00

11 **500 Dollars** VF UNC
2001; 2004. Dark brown on tan and multicolor underprint. Chiremba balancing rock formation. Epworth (Harare) at right. Without foil at left. Back: Hwange power station. Watermark: Zimbabwe bird and *500*.
- a. 2001. FV 5.00
- b. 2004. Signature: Gideon Gono. FV 5.00

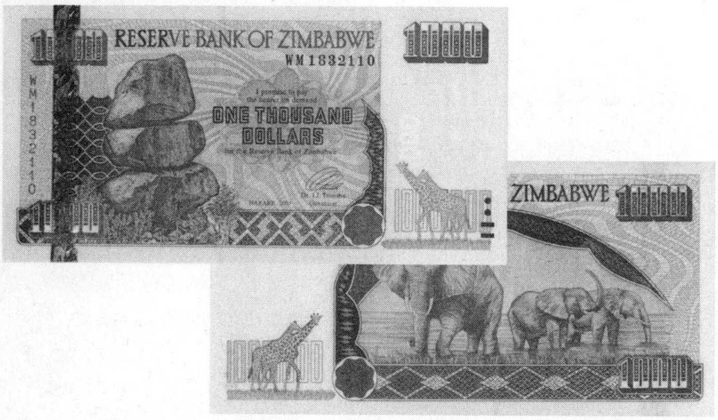

12 **1000 Dollars** VF UNC
2003. Brown, purple and green on multicolor underprint. Chiremba balancing rock formation at left. Back: Elephants.
- a. Large digits in serial number. FV 3.00
- b. Small digits in serial number. FV 6.00

2003 Emergency Cargill Bearer Checks

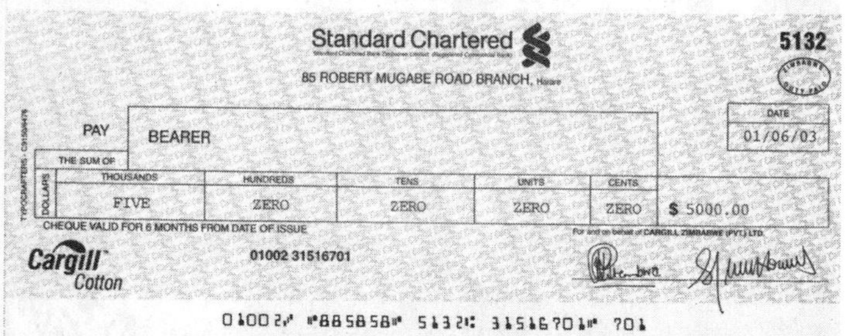
Standard Chartered
85 ROBERT MUGABE ROAD BRANCH, Harare
5132
PAY BEARER
DATE 01/06/03
THE SUM OF
THOUSANDS	HUNDREDS	TENS	UNITS	CENTS
FIVE	ZERO	ZERO	ZERO	ZERO

$ 5000.00
CHEQUE VALID FOR 6 MONTHS FROM DATE OF ISSUE
For and on behalf of CARGILL ZIMBABWE (PVT) LTD.
Cargill Cotton
01002 31516701

13 **5000 Dollars** VF UNC
2003. Pink and green underprint. Reseve Bank of Zimbabwe logo. Signature 4. Back: Wave pattern. Watermark: Cotton plant. Printer: Typocrafters.
- a. 1.6.2003. Green. 35.00 150.
- b. 1.9.2003. Blue. 45.00 175.

14 **10,000 Dollars**
2003. Blue. Reserve Bank of Zimbabwe logo. Signature 4. Back: Pink and green underprint. Wave pattern. Watermark: Cotton plant. Printer: Typocrafters.
- a. 1.5.2003. 45.00 175.
- b. 1.9.2003. 55.00 200.

2003 Emergency Travellers' Checks

15 **1000 Dollars** VF UNC
2003. Gray. Reserve Bank of Zimbabwe logo. Signature 4. Back: Pink and green underprint. Wave pattern. Watermark: Zimbabwe bird. Type 1. 2.50 4.00

16 **5000 Dollars**
2003. Red. Reserve Bank of Zimbabwe logo. Signature 4. Back: Pink and green underprint. Wave pattern. Watermark: Zimbabwe bird. Type 1. 3.00 10.00

17 **10,000 Dollars**
2003. Light blue. Reserve Bank of Zimbabwe logo. Signature 4. Back: Pink and green underprint. Wave pattern. Watermark: Zimbabwe bird. Type 1. 2.50 5.00

18 **20,000 Dollars**
2003. Olive green. Reserve Bank of Zimbabwe logo. Signature 4. Back: Pink and green underprint. Wave pattern. Watermark: Zimbabwe bird. Type 1. 2.50 5.00

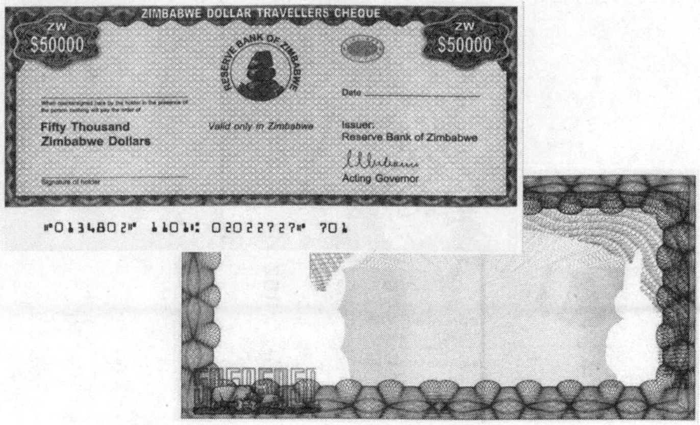

19 **50,000 Dollars** VF UNC
2003. Dark blue. Reserve Bank of Zimbabwe logo. Watermark: Zimbabwe bird. Type 3. 2.50 7.50

20 **100,000 Dollars**
2003. Brown. Reserve Bank of Zimbabwe logo. Watermark: Zimbabwe bird. Type 3. 2.50 7.50

2003 Emergency Bearer Checks

21 **5000 Dollars** VF UNC
2003. Blue. Reserve Bank of Zimbabwe logo. Watermark: Zimbabwe bird. Type 3.
- a. Signature 4. Redemption date: 31.1.2004. No RZB in watermark. Serial # prefix: A. 7.50 35.00
- b. Signature 4. Redemption date: 30.6.2004. No RBZ in watermark. Serial # prefix: B-C. 5.00 25.00
- c. Signature 5. Redemption date: 31.12.2004. With RZB in watermark. Serial # prefix: AA. 5.00 20.00
- d. Signature 5. Redemption date: 31.12.2004. *GOVERNOR / DR. G. GONO.* 5.00 10.00

22 **10,000 Dollars**
2003. Red.
- a. Signature 4. Redemption date: 31.1.2004. Without RZB in watermark. Serial # prefix: E. 10.00 80.00
- b. Signature 4. Redemption date: 30.6.2004. Without RZB in watermark. Serial # prefix: F-G. 5.00 60.00
- c. Signature 5. Redemption date: 31.12.2004. With RZB in watermark. Serial # prefix: BA. 5.00 50.00
- d. Signature 5. Redemption date: 31.12.2004. With RZB in watermark. *GOVERNOR / DR. G. GONO.* 5.00 20.00

23 **20,000 Dollars** VF UNC
2003. Brown.
- a. Signature 4. Redemption date: 31.1.2004. Without RZB in watermark. Serial # prefix: J. 12.50 115.
- b. Signature 4. Redemption date: 30.6.2004. Without RZB in watermark. Serial # prefix: K-L. 6.25 85.00
- c. Signature 5. Redemption date: 31.12.2004. Without RZB in watermark. Serial # prefix: AA. 30.00 125.
- d. Signature 5. Redemption date: 31.12.2004. *GOVERNOR* with RZB in watermark. Serial # prefix AA. 7.50 60.00
- e. Signature 5. Redemption date: 31.12.2004. *GOVERNOR / DR. G. GONO.* with RZB in watermark. — 35.00

2004 Emergency Cargill Bearer Checks

No.		VF	UNC
24	**10,000 Dollars** 1.4.2004. Blue.	20.00	75.00
25	**20,000 Dollars** 1.4.2004. Green.	35.00	125.
26	**50,000 Dollars** 1.4.2004. Orange.	65.00	200.
27	**100,000 Dollars** 1.4.2004. Red.	85.00	250.

2005-06 Emergency Bearer Checks

No.		VF	UNC
28	**50,000 Dollars** 1.10.2005. Serial # prefix AA-AB.	10.00	20.00
29	**50,000 Dollars** 1.2.2006. Serial # prefiex CA-CK. Printer: G&D.	10.00	20.00

No.		VF	UNC
30	**50,000 Dollars** 1.2.2006. Violet on green and red underprint. Back: Waterfall. Redemption date of 31.12.2006. 147x74mm.	3.00	7.50
31	**100,000 Dollars** 1.10.2005. Serial # prefix: AA-AC.	15.00	35.00
32	**100,000 Dollars** 1.6.2006. Green on light green and red underpint. Back: Waterfalls. 147x74mm.	3.50	10.00

2006-08 Emergency Bearer Checks, Second Dollar (ZWN)

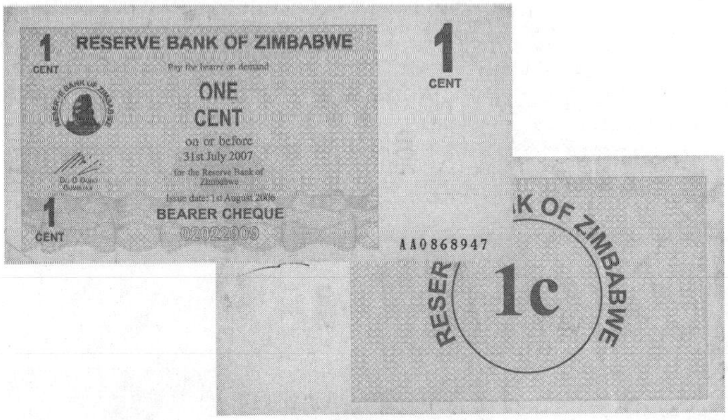

No.		VF	UNC
33	**1 Cent** 1.8.2006. Rose. Back: Large value in circle. 153x78mm.	.25	1.00
34	**5 Cents** 1.8.2006. Green. Back: Large value in circle. 153x78mm.	.25	1.00
35	**10 Cents** 1.8.2006. Brown. Back: Large value in circle. 153x78mm.	.25	1.00
36	**50 Cents** 1.8.2006. Black. Back: Large value in circle. 153x78mm.	.35	1.25
37	**1 Dollar** 1.8.2006. Blue on light blue and rose underprint. Back: Two women mashing grain. 148x75mm.	.20	.75
38	**5 Dollars** 1.8.2006. Green on brown underprint. Back: Torch in city park. 147x75mm.	.20	.75
39	**10 Dollars** 1.8.2006. Rose. Back: Two women mashing grain. 148x74mm.	.30	.80
40	**20 Dollars** 1.8.2006. Brown on light orange and green underprint. Back: Waterfalls. 146x75mm.	.25	.75
41	**50 Dollars** 1.8.2006. Violet on light tan underpint. Back: Waterfalls. 147x75mm.	.35	.80

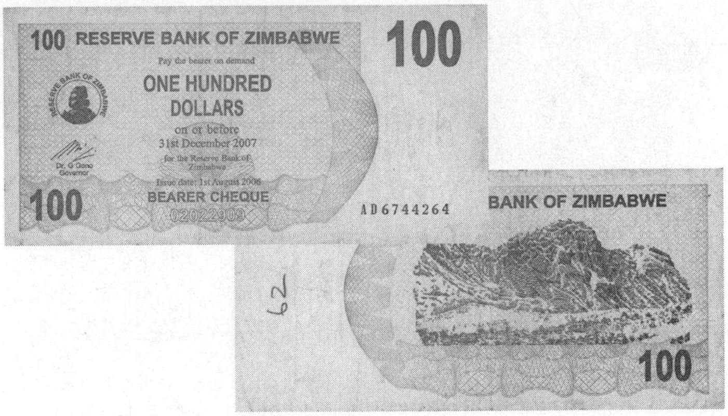

No.		VF	UNC
42	**100 Dollars** 1.8.2006. Green on light blue underprint. Back: Mountain. 147x75mm.	.35	.80
43	**500 Dollars** 1.8.2006. Brown on light green, blue and rose underprint. Back: Tiger fish at center, Kariba Dam at right. 148x75mm.	.30	.75
44	**1000 Dollars** 1.8.2006. Brown on light grey, rose and green underprint. Back: Mountain. 148x75mm.	.30	.75
45	**5000 Dollars** 1.2.2007. Blue on light blue, green and rose underprint. Back: Kariba Dam. 147x75mm.	.60	1.50

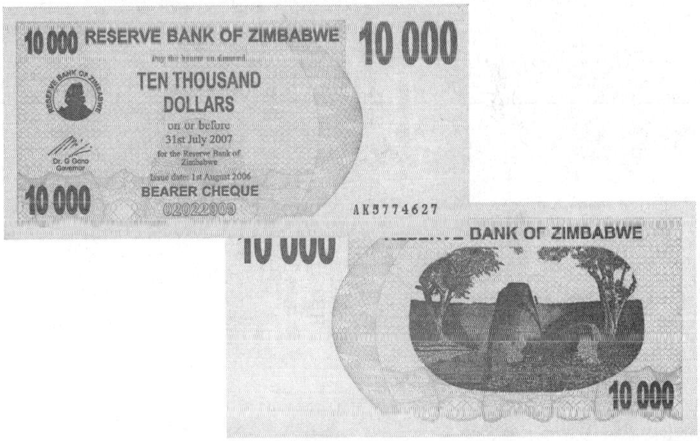

No.		VF	UNC
46	**10,000 Dollars** 1.8.2006. Violet on light blue and green underprint. Back: Great Zimbabwe ruins. 147x75mm.		
	a. Without space in value: 10000. Serial # prefix: AA.	15.00	100.
	b. With space in value: 10 000.	1.00	3.00
47	**50,000 Dollars** 1.3.2007. Orange. Back: Elephant at waterfall at right.	.70	2.00
48	**100,000 Dollars** 1.8.2006. Blue-green. Back: Great Zimbabwe ruins at right.		
	a. Without space in value 100000. Serial # prefix: AA.	15.00	100.
	b. With space in value 100 000.	.90	2.75
49	**200,000 Dollars** 1.7.2007. Red brown and multicolor. Back: Power plant and cooling towers	.80	2.50
50	**250,000 Dollars** 20.12.2007. Black and multicolor. Back: Great Zimbabwe ruins at right.	1.00	3.00

No.		VF	UNC
51	**500,000 Dollars** 1.7.2007. Olive and green on multicolor. Back: Three elephants at right.	.45	1.50

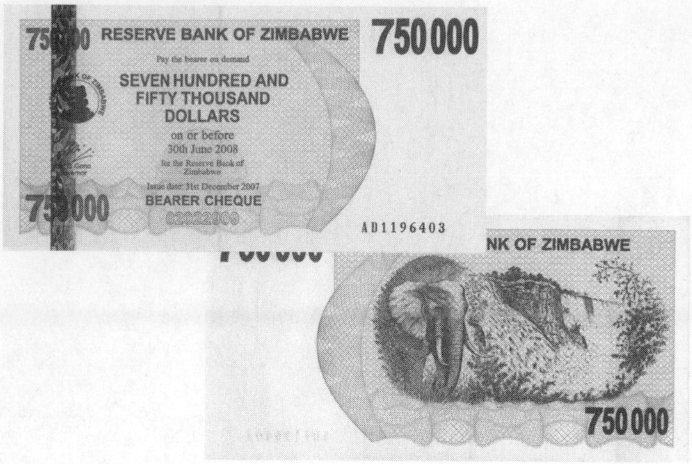

		VF	UNC
52	**750,000 Dollars**		
	31.12.2007. Purple. Back: Elephant at waterfall at right.	.50	1.75
53	**1 Million Dollars**		
	1.1.2008. Brown and orange. Back: Two women mashing grain.	.75	2.25
54	**5 MillionDollars**		
	1.1.2008. Blue. Back: Mountain range.	2.75	7.00
55	**10 Million Dollars**		
	1.1.2008. Red and green. Back: Tiger fish at center, Kariba Dam at right.		
	a. Series A.	1.75	4.00
	b. Series D.	.65	2.00
56	**25 Million Dollars**		
	2.4.2008. Green.	1.00	3.00
57	**50 Million Dollars**		
	2.4.2008. Purple and violet. Back: Three elephants at right.	1.20	3.50
58	**100 Million Dollars**		
	2.5.2008. Green on multicolor underprint. Back: Two women mashing grain.	1.20	3.50
59	**250 Million Dollars**		
	2.5.2008. Blue on multicolor underprint. Back: Elephant at waterfall.	1.25	4.00

		VF	UNC
60	**500 Million Dollars**		
	2.5.2008. Rose on multicolor underprint. Back: Tiger fish at center, Kariba Dam at right.	.80	2.50

2008 Special Agro Checks

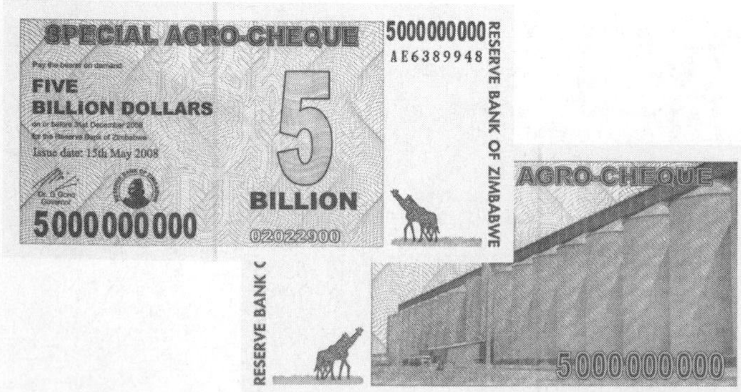

		VF	UNC
61	**5 Billion Dollars**		
	15.5.2008. Violet.	1.00	3.00
62	**25 Billion Dollars**		
	15.5.2008. Green.	1.50	4.50
63	**50 Billion Dollars**		
	15.5.2008. Brown.	1.75	5.50

		VF	UNC
64	**100 Billion Dollars**		
	1.7.2008. Blue.	2.00	6.50

2007-08 Issue, Third Dollar (ZWR)

		VF	UNC
65	**1 Dollar**		
	1.8.2008. Purple and black. Chiremba balanced rock formation. Back: Waterfall and water buffalo. 153x76mm.	.30	1.00
66	**5 Dollars**		
	1.8.2008. Brown on green underprint. Chiremba balanced rock formation. Back: Dam and elephant.	.40	1.25

		VF	UNC
67	**10 Dollars**		
	1.8.2008. Dark green on light green underprint. Chiremba balanced rock formation. Back: Tractor in field, cilos.	.50	1.75

		VF	UNC
68	**20 Dollars**		
	1.8.2008. Burgundy on violet underprint. Chiremba balanced rock formation. Back: Mine tower and earth pile, Miner with jack hammer.	.60	2.25
69	**100 Dollars**		
	1.8.2008. Blue and black on light blue underprint. Chiremba balanced rock formation. Back: Palm trees and ancient fortification.	1.00	3.00

70 **500 Dollars** — VF / UNC
1.8.2008. Violet on blue underprint. Chiremba balanced rock formation. Back: Cow milking parlor and cattle. 152x77mm. — .80 / 3.00

71 **1000 Dollars**
1.8.2008. Red-brown on tan and light green underprint. Chiremba balanced rock formation. Back: Buildings. 155x79mm. — .80 / 3.00

72 **10,000 Dollars** — VF / UNC
29.9.2008. Brown on violet underprint. Chiremba balanced rock formation. Back: Harvester and tractor. 153x76mm. — 1.25 / 5.00

73 **20,000 Dollars**
29.9.2008. Brown on green underprint. Chiremba balanced rock formation. Back: Victoria Falls and Kariba Dam. 153x76mm.
a. Plain paper. — 1.25 / 5.00
b. Lined (laid) paper. — 1.25 / 5.00

74 **50,000 Dollars**
13.10.2008. Green on pink and yellow underprint. Chiremba balanced rock formation. Back: Tractor in fields and miner with jackhammer. 153x76mm.
a. Plain paper. — 1.00 / 4.00
b. Lined (laid) paper. — 1.00 / 4.00

75 **100,000 Dollars** — VF / UNC
5.11.2008. Dark blue on light blue underprint. Chiremba balanced rock formation. Back: Water buffalo and elephant. 153x76mm. — 1.25 / 5.00

76 **500,000 Dollars** — VF / UNC
5.11.2008. Dark green light green underprint. Chiremba balanced rock formation. Back: Palm trees and dairy cow milking parlor. 148x74mm.
a. Plain paper. — 1.50 / 6.00
b. Lined (laid) paper. — 1.50 / 6.00

77 **1 Million Dollars**
5.11.2008. Blue on light green underprint. Chiremba balanced rock formation. Back: Great Zimbabwe ruins and cattle. 153x73mm. — .75 / 3.00

78 **10 Million Dollars** — VF / UNC
3.12.2008. Blue and tan. Chiremba balanced rock formation. Back: Parliament and Great Zimbabwe ruins. 148x74mm. — 1.25 / 5.00

79 **50 Million Dollars**
3.12.2008. Green on blue underprint. Chiremba balanced rock formation. Back: Water buffalo and Great Zimbabew ruins. — 1.00 / 3.50

80 **100 Million Dollars** — VF / UNC
3.12.2008. Red on light green underprint. Chiremba balanced rock formation. Back: Grain pile and cilos. 147x74mm. — 1.00 / 3.50

81 **200 Million Dollars** — VF / UNC
5.12.2008. Brown on light green underprint. Chiremba balanced rock formation. Back: Parliament and Hero's monument. 148x74mm. — 1.00 / 3.50

82 **500 Million Dollars**
12.12.2008. Purple on light blue and green underprint. Chiremba balanced rock formation. Back: Cows in milking parlor and miner with jackhammer. 148x74mm. — 1.10 / 4.00

83 **1 Billion Dollars** — VF / UNC
19.12.2008. Green on light green underprint. Chiremba balanced rock formation. Back: Palm trees and elephant. — 1.25 / 4.50

84 **5 Billion Dollars** — VF / UNC
19.12.2008. Brown on light blue underprint. Chiremba balanced rock formation. Back: Tractor in fields, dairy cow milking parlor. — 1.25 / 5.00

85 **10 Billion Dollars** VF UNC
19.12.2008. Blue on tan and light green underprint. Chiremba balanced rock formation. Back: Dam, miner with jack hammer. 1.20 4.50

86 **20 Billion Dollars** VF UNC
2008. Green on light orange underprint. Chiremba balanced rock formation. Back: Great Zimbabwe ruins and palm trees. .80 3.00

87 **50 Billion Dollars**
2008. Light red-brown on light green underprint. Chiremba balanced rock formation. Back: Great Zimbabwe ruins and modern building tower. 1.00 4.00

88 **10 Trillion Dollars** VF UNC
2008. Green on light green underprint. Chiremba balanced rock formation. Back: Modern building tower and Great Zimbabew ruins. 2.25 7.00

89 **20 Trillion Dollars** VF UNC
2008. Red-brown on light blue underprint. Chiremba balanced rock formation. Back: Miner with jack hammer, cilos 5.75 15.00

90 **50 Trillion Dollars** VF UNC
2008. Black and green. Chiremba balanced rock formation. Back: Karba Dam and elephant. 1.50 5.00

91 **100 Trillion Dollars** VF UNC
2008. Light blue on tan underprint. Chiremba balanced rock formation. Back: Victoria Falls and water buffalo. .75 10.00

2009 Issue, Fourth Dollar (ZWL)

92 **1 Dollar** VF UNC
2.2.2009. Blue on light blue underprint. Chiremba balanved rock formation. Back: Two women mashing grain. .35 1.25

93 **5 Dollars**
2.2.2009. Green on tan underprint. Chiremba balanced rock formation. Back: Tiger fish at center, Kariba Dam at right. .40 1.50

94 **10 Dollars**
2.2.2009. Rose on tan underprint. Chiremba balanced rock formation. Back: Great Zimbabwe ruins. .50 2.00

95 **20 Dollars**
2.2.2009. Rose on light red underprint. Chiremba balanced rock formation. Back: Power plant and cooling towers. 1.00 3.00

96 **50 Dollars**
2.2.2009. Violet on light blue underprint. Chiremba balanced rock formation. Back: Power plant and cooling towers. 1.50 4.00

97 **100 Dollars**
2.2.2009. Brown on tan underprint. Chiremba balanced rock formation. Back: Torch and skyline. 1.75 5.00

98 **500 Dollars**
2009. Green on lime underprint. Chiremba balanced rock formation. Back: Three elephants. 3.50 10.00

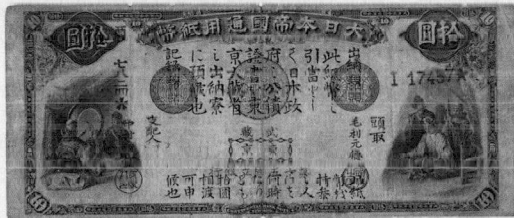

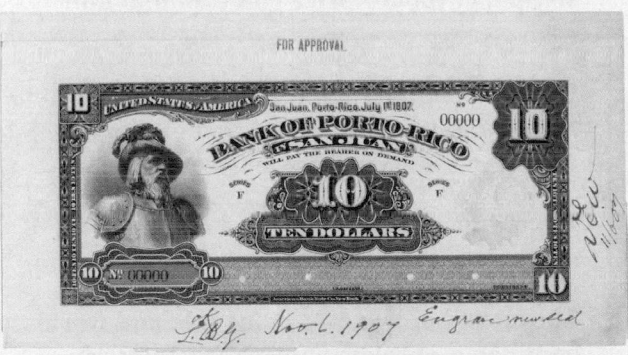

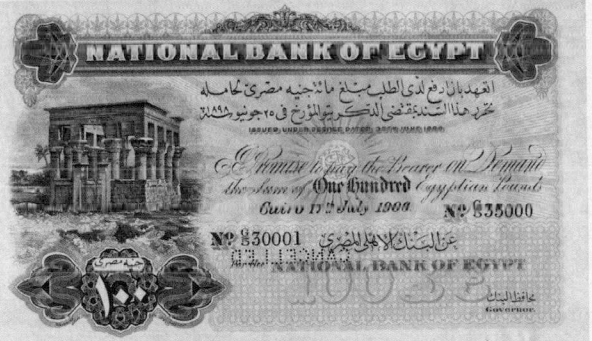

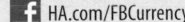

SOME BANKNOTES APPEAR PERFECT

We have all seen banknotes which look perfect at first sight but which disappoint us on closer inspection. They may be pressed, cleaned or repaired or have other defects which are not easy to spot on a scan. With an ICG graded note you don't have to worry about those hard-to-see imperfections. Our grades and the ICG asterisk (*) tell the full story so you are never again disappointed

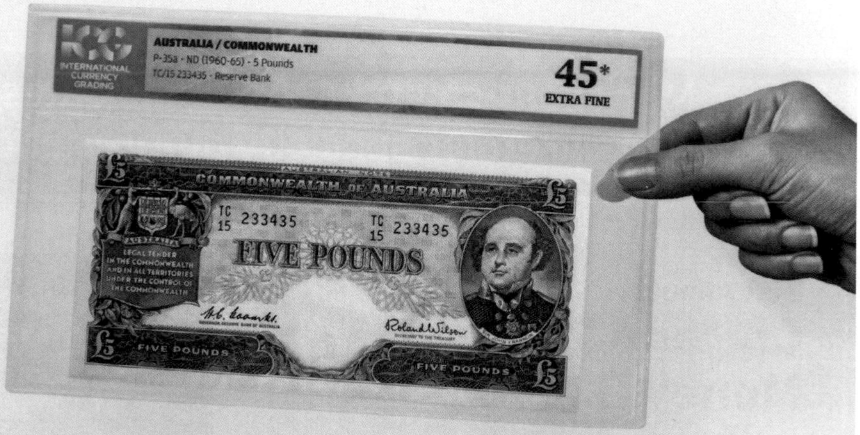

OTHERS ARE REALLY REALLY PERFECT

Then, let's admit it: Some banknotes are REALLY perfect. Banknotes with zero folds, bends, pinholes, marks or other blemishes. When an ICG grader comes across one of these perfect notes, he can only do one thing: give it a "Perfect UNC - 70" grade. Well, that and admire its beauty

If you love paper money, you will love our grading.

ICG

INTERNATIONAL CURRENCY GRADING

Your guiding light in banknote grading

www.icgrading.com

NEW AUCTION CONSIGN SERVICE

ICG ONE-STOP SHOP GRADE YOUR NOTES, LIST THEM ON EBAY OR SUBMIT THEM TO THE BEST FLOOR AUCTIONS IN ONE STEP

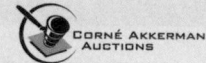

Corné Akkermans Auctions | Lyn Knight Currency Auctions | SPINK